P9-EDG-678

Handbook of

North American Indians

Handbook of North American Indians

WILLIAM C. STURTEVANT

General Editor

VOLUME 11

Great Basin

WARREN L. D'AZEVEDO

Volume Editor

SMITHSONIAN INSTITUTION

WASHINGTON

1986

Copyright © 1986 by Smithsonian Institution
All rights reserved.

For sale by the Superintendent of Documents,
U.S. Government Printing Office, Washington, D.C. 20402.

Library of Congress Cataloging in Publication Data

Handbook of North American Indians.

    Bibliography.
    Includes index.
    CONTENTS:

                v. 11 Great Basin.

    1. Indians of North America.
I. Sturtevant, William C.

E77.H25   970'.004'97   77–17162

Great Basin Volume Planning Committee

Warren L. d'Azevedo, Volume Editor

William C. Sturtevant, General Editor

Catherine S. Fowler, Associate Volume Editor

Jesse D. Jennings, Coordinator for Prehistory Chapters

Don D. Fowler

William H. Jacobsen, Jr.

Contents

This map is a diagrammatic guide to the coverage of this volume; it is not an authoritative depiction of territories for several reasons. Sharp boundaries have been drawn and no area is unassigned. The groups mapped are in some cases arbitrarily defined, subdivisions are not indicated, no joint or disputed occupations are shown, and different kinds of land use are not distinguished. Since the map depicts the situation at the earliest periods for which evidence is available, the ranges mapped for different groups often refer to different periods, and there may have been intervening movements, extinctions, and changes in range. Not shown are groups that came into separate existence later than the map period for their areas. The simplified ranges shown are a generalization of the situation in the 19th century, with those of the Washoe, Northern Paiute, and Ute more for the first part of the century and the rest slightly later. For more specific information see the maps and text in the appropriate chapters.

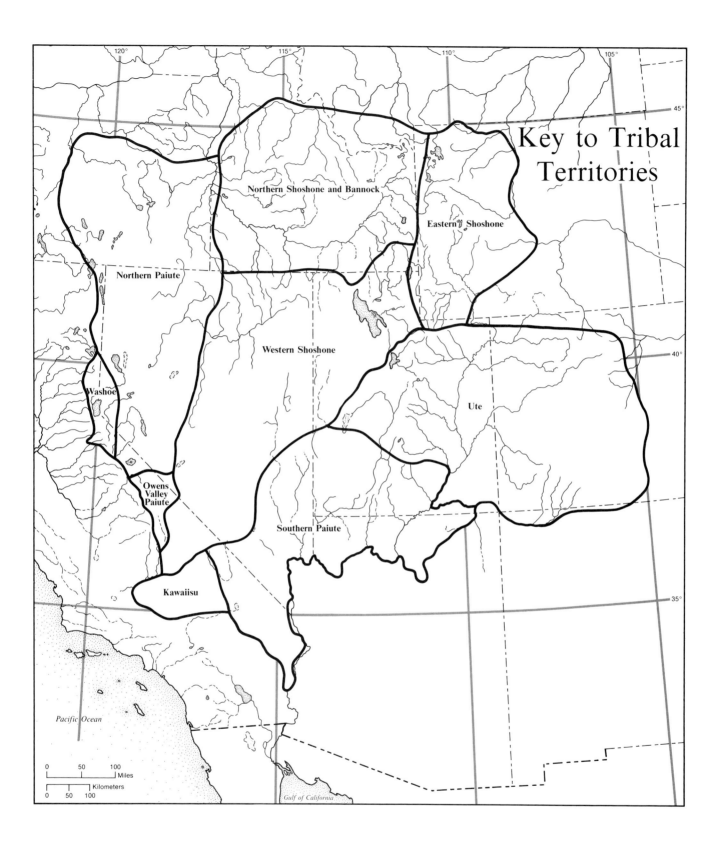

Key to Tribal
Territories

Northern Shoshone and Bannock

Eastern Shoshone

Northern Paiute

Western Shoshone

Ute

Washoe

Owens
Valley
Paiute

Southern Paiute

Kawaiisu

Pacific Ocean

Gulf of California

0   50   100
|___|____| Miles

|___|____| Kilometers
0   50   100

Technical Alphabet

Consonants

		bilabial	labiodental	dental	alveolar	alveopalatal	velar	back velar	glottal
stop	vl	p		t	t		k	q	ʔ
	vd	b		d	d		g	ġ	
affricate	vl			θ̂	c	č			
	vd			δ̂	ʒ	ǯ			
fricative	vl	φ	f	θ	s	š	x	x̣	h
	vd	β	v	δ	z	ž	γ	γ̇	
nasal	vl	M		N			Ŋ		
	vd	m		n			ŋ	ŋ̇	
lateral	vl				ł				
	vd				l				
semivowel	vl	W				Y			
	vd	w				y			

vl = voiceless; vd = voiced

Other symbols include: λ (voiced lateral affricate), ƛ (voiceless lateral affricate), ʕ (voiced pharyngeal fricative), ḥ (voiceless pharyngeal fricative), r (medial flap, trill, or retroflex approximant). Where in contrast, r is a flap and R is a continuant.

Vowels

	front	central	back
high	i (ü)	ɨ	u (ɨ)
	ɪ		ʊ
mid	e (ö)	ə	o
	ε		ɔ
		ʌ	
low	æ	a	a

Unparenthesized vowels are unrounded if front or central, and rounded if back; ü and ö are rounded; ɨ is unrounded. The special symbols for lax vowels (ɪ, ʊ, ε, ɔ) are generally used only where it is necessary to differentiate between tense and lax high or mid vowels. ɨ and a are used for both central and back vowels, as the two values seldom contrast in a given language.

Modifications indicated for consonants are: glottalization (ṭ, ḳ, etc.), retroflexion (ṭ, ç, ʒ̣), palatalization (tʸ, kʸ, nʸ, lʸ), labialization (kʷ), aspiration (tʰ), length (t·). For vowels: length (a·), three-mora length (a:), nasalization (ą), voicelessness (A). The commonest prosodic markings are, for stress: á (primary) and à (secondary), and for pitch: á (high), à (low), â (falling), and ǎ (rising); however, the details of prosodic systems and the uses of accents differ widely from language to language.

Words in Great Basin Indian languages cited in italics in this volume are written in phonemic transcription. That is, the letters and symbols are used in specific values defined for them by the structure of the sound system of the particular language. However, as far as possible, these phonemic transcriptions use letters and symbols in generally consistent values, as specified by the standard technical alphabet of the *Handbook*. Deviations from these standard values as well as specific details of the phonology of each language (or references to where they may be found) are given in an orthographic footnote in each tribal chapter. Some special conventions for transcription are used in "Numic Languages." For the transcription of Indian words in languages from outside the Great Basin, see the orthographic information in the appropriate other volumes of the *Handbook*.

No italicized Indian word is broken at a line end except when a hyphen would be present anyway as part of the word. Words in italicized phonemic transcription are never capitalized, except that the Navajo practical orthography follows the English rules of capitalization. Pronunciations or phonetic values given in the standard technical alphabet without regard to phonemic analysis are put in roman in brackets rather than in italics. The glosses, or conventionalized translations, of Indian words are enclosed in single quotation marks.

Indian words recorded by nonspecialists or before the phonemic systems of their languages had been analyzed are often not written accurately enough to allow respelling in phonemic transcription. Where phonemic retranscription has been possible the citation of source has been modified by the label "phonemicized" or "from." A few words that could not be phonemicized have been "normalized"—rewritten by mechanical substitution of the symbols of the standard technical alphabet. Others have been rationalized by eliminating redundant or potentially misleading diacritics and substituting nontechnical symbols. Words that do not use the standard alphabet occasionally contain some letters used according to the values of other technical alphabets or traditional orthographies. The most common of these are c and sh for the *Handbook*'s š; b, в, and v for β; g for γ; ts, tz, and dz for c; tc, tsh, and tj for č; dj for ǯ; p' and ph for pʰ (and similarly with some other consonants); hl for ł; j for ž, ǯ, or y; ' for ʔ; ' for h (or nondistinctive aspiration); oñ or oⁿ for ǫ (and with other vowels, for nasalization); ar for a and er for ə; u, ü, or ö for ɨ; and x or j for š, x, or h, and z for c (in early Spanish sources). All nonphonemic transcriptions give only incomplete, and sometimes imprecise, approximations of the correct pronunciation.

Nontechnical Equivalents

Correct pronunciation, as with any foreign language, requires extensive training and practice, but simplified (incorrect) pronunciations may be obtained by ignoring the diacritics and reading the vowels as in Italian or Spanish and the consonants as in English. For a closer approximation to the pronunciation or to rewrite into a nontechnical transcription the substitutions indicated in the following table may be made.

technical	nontechnical	technical	nontechnical	technical	nontechnical
æ	ae	M	mh	Y	yh
β	bh	N	nh	ž	zh
c	ts	ŋ	ng	ʒ	dz
č	ch	$N̦$	ngh	ǯ	j
δ	dh	ɔ	o	ʔ	'
δ̂	ddh	θ	th	k̓, ṗ, ṭ, etc.	k', p', t', etc.
ε	e	θ̂	tth	a·, e·, k·, s·, etc.	aa, ee, kk, ss, etc.
γ	gh	φ	ph	ą, ę, etc.	an, en, etc.
ł	lh	š	sh	kʸ, tʸ, etc.	ky, ty, etc.
λ	dl	W	wh	kʷ	kw
λ̣	tlh	x	kh		

English Pronunciations

The English pronunciations of the names of tribes and a few other words are indicated parenthetically in a dictionary-style orthography in which most letters have their usual English pronunciation. Special symbols are listed below, with sample words to be pronounced as in nonregional United States English. Approximate phonetic values are given in parentheses in the standard technical alphabet.

ŋ: thing (ŋ)
θ: thin (θ)
ð: this (δ)
zh: vision (ž)
ă: bat (æ)

ä: father (a)
ā: bait (ey)
e: bet (ε)
ē: beat (iy)

ə: about, gallop (ə)
ĭ: bit (ɪ)
ī: bite (ay)
ô: bought (ɔ)

ō: boat (ow)
o͞o: book (ʊ)
o͞o: boot (uw)
u: but (ʌ)

'(primary stress), ˌ(secondary stress): elevator ('elə,vātər) (éləvèytər)

Conventions for Illustrations

Map Symbol

●   Native settlement

○   Abandoned settlement

■   Non-native or mixed settlement

□   Abandoned settlement

   Mountain range, peak

   Desert

   Intermittent lake

   Sink, dry lake

   River or stream

   Intermittent stream

Ute   Tribe

Uncompahgre   Tribal subdivision

Carson City   Settlement, site

Great Salt L.   Geographical feature

Toned areas on tribal maps represent estimated core territory.

Credits and Captions

Credit lines give the source of the illustrations or the collections where the artifacts shown are located. The numbers that follow are the catalog or inventory numbers of that repository. When the photographer mentioned in the caption is the source of the print reproduced, no credit line appears. "After" means that the *Handbook* illustrators have redrawn, rearranged, or abstracted the illustration from the one in the cited source. All maps and drawings not otherwise credited are by the *Handbook* illustrators. Measurements in captions are to the nearest millimeter if available; "about" indicates an estimate or a measurement converted from inches to centimeters. The following abbreviations are used in credit lines:

Amer.	American	Histl.	Historical
Anthr.	Anthropology, Anthropological	Ind.	Indian
		Inst.	Institute
Arch.	Archives	Instn.	Institution
Arch(a)eol	Arch(a)ecology, Arch(a)ecological	Lib.	Library
		Mus.	Museum
Assoc.	Association	NAA	National Anthropological
Co.	County		Archives
Coll.	Collection(s)	Nat.	Natural
Dept.	Department	Natl.	National
Div.	Division	opp.	opposite
Ethnol.	Ethnology, Ethnological	pl(s).	plate(s)
fol.	folio	Prov.	Provincial
Ft.	Fort	Soc.	Society
Hist.	History	U.	University

Metric Equivalents

10 mm = 1 cm	10 cm = 3.937 in.	1 km = .62 mi.	1 in. = 2.54 cm	25 ft. = 7.62 m
100 cm = 1 m	1 m = 39.37 in.	5 km = 3.1 mi.	1 ft. = 30.48 cm	1 mi. = 1.60 km
1,000 m = 1 km	10 m = 32.81 ft.	10 km = 6.2 mi.	1 yd. = 91.44 cm	5 mi. = 8.02 km

centimeters / inches (actual size)

meters / feet

degrees C / degrees F

Preface

This is the seventh volume to be published of a 20-volume set planned to give an encyclopedic summary of what is known about the prehistory, history, and cultures of the aboriginal peoples of North America north of the urban civilizations of central Mexico. Volumes 5–10 and 12–15 treat the other major culture areas of the continent.

Some topics relevant to the Great Basin area are excluded from this volume because they are more appropriately discussed on a continent-wide basis. Readers should refer to volume 1, Introduction, for general descriptions of anthropological and historical methods and sources and for summaries for the whole continent of certain topics regarding social and political organization, religion, and the performing arts. Volume 2 contains detailed accounts of the different kinds of Indian and Eskimo communities in the twentieth century, especially since 1950, and describes their relations with one another and with the surrounding non-Indian societies and nations. Volume 3 gives the environmental and biological backgrounds within which Native American societies developed, summarizes the early and late human biology or physical anthropology of Indians and Eskimos, and surveys the earliest prehistoric cultures. (Therefore the Paleo-Indian or Early Man period in the Great Basin receives major treatment in volume 3 rather than in this volume.) Volume 4 contains details on the history of the relations between Whites and Native American societies. Volume 16 is a continent-wide survey of technology and the visual arts—of material cultures broadly defined. Volume 17 surveys the Native languages of North America, their characteristics and historical relationships. Volumes 18 and 19 are a biographical dictionary; included in the listing are many Great Basin Indians. Volume 20 contains an index to the whole, which will serve to locate materials on Great Basin Indians in other volumes as well as in this one; it also includes a list of errata found in all preceding volumes.

Preliminary discussions on the feasibility of the *Handbook* and alternatives for producing it began in 1965 in what was then the Smithsonian's Office of Anthropology. (A history of the early development of the whole *Handbook* and a listing of the entire editorial staff will be found in volume 1.) As the *Handbook* was originally conceived, the Great Basin and Plateau areas were to be treated together; the General Editor's preliminary mapping for the coverage of the various *Handbook* volumes showed one large region labeled "Great Basin–Plateau." The decision to differentiate the two areas more sharply, made in 1968, was based on the advice of consultants with a continental comparative perspective. George Peter Murdock and Harold E. Driver especially urged that a boundary be drawn. As "Introduction," this volume, makes clear, recognition of the Great Basin as a distinct culture area has become well-established in Americanist anthropology. Following a planning meeting for the *Handbook* as a whole that was held in Chicago in November 1970, separate editors were appointed for the Great Basin and the Plateau. However, it still seemed then that a single volume would suffice to cover the available knowledge of the two areas at a level of detail comparable to that of the other areas of North America (except the two volumes for Southwest). Accordingly, a joint meeting to plan the detailed contents of such a volume was held in Reno, Nevada, March 19–20, 1971, which was attended by the separate editors and planning committees for the two areas, and the General Editor. That meeting resulted in the decision to treat the two areas in separate volumes.

During the March 1971 planning meeting a tentative table of contents for this volume was drawn up, and qualified specialists on each topic were listed as potential authors. As published, the volume contains 36 chapters essentially as first planned and nine chapters on topics not envisioned in 1971; three proposed chapters were dropped. About half the 50 authors are those selected in 1971 for their topics, the rest being additional co-authors, authors on new topics, or replacement authors for people who were unable to accept invitations or later found that they could not meet their commitments to write. A major loss to the volume was the death of Julian H. Steward in 1972; he had agreed to contribute an important chapter on patterns of economic and social adaptation and had corresponded with the Volume Editor about the organization of the volume.

At the time they were invited, the Volume Editor sent contributors instructions that gave brief chapter descriptions. Those for the chapters on prehistory were prepared by Jesse D. Jennings. Authors were also sent a "Guide for Contributors" prepared by the General Editor describing the general aims and methods of the *Handbook* and the editorial conventions. One convention has been to avoid the present tense, where possible, in historical and cultural descriptions. Thus a statement in the past tense, with a recent date or approximate date, may also hold true for the time of writing. As they were received, the manuscripts were reviewed by the Volume Editor, the General Editor, and usually one or more referees—frequently including a member of the Planning Committee, and often authors of other chapters. Suggestions for changes and additions often resulted. The published versions frequently reflect more editorial intervention than is customary for academic writings, since the encyclopedic aims and format of the *Handbook* made it necessary to attempt to eliminate duplication, avoid gaps in coverage, prevent contradictions, impose some standardization of organization and terminology, and keep within strict constraints on length. Where the evidence seemed so scanty or obscure as to allow different authorities to come to differing conclusions, authors have been permitted to elaborate their own views although the editors have endeavored to draw attention to alternative interpretations in other chapters.

The first draft manuscript submitted was received in the General Editor's office on December 7, 1971, and others followed over the next couple of years. The publication schedule for the whole *Handbook* was then revised, and editorial attention turned to the six volumes that were published first. In March 1983 intensive work to complete the *Great Basin* volume began. At that time, all authors of manuscripts then on hand were asked to revise and bring them up to date, and several new assignments were made. Major changes resulted. Thus, the contents of this volume generally reflect the state of knowledge in the mid-1980s rather than in the early 1970s. The first editorial acceptance of an author's manuscript was on September 9, 1983, and the last on May 14, 1985. Edited manuscripts were sent from the Washington office to authors for their final approval between June 28, 1984, and May 17, 1985. These dates for all chapters are given in the list of Contributors. Late dates may reflect late invitations as well as late submissions.

Linguistic Editing

As far as possible, all cited words in Indian languages were referred to consultants with expert knowledge of the respective languages and rewritten by them in the appropriate technical orthography. The consultants and the spelling systems are identified in the orthographic footnotes, drafted by the Linguistic Editor, Ives Goddard.

Statements about the genetic relationships of the Numic languages and Washoe have also been checked with linguist consultants, to ensure conformity with recent findings and terminology in comparative linguistics and to avoid conflicting statements within the *Handbook*. In general, only the less remote genetic relationships are mentioned in the individual chapters. The chapters "Numic Languages" and "Washoe Language" discuss the wider relationships of these languages.

The Linguistic Editor served as coordinator and editor of these efforts by linguist consultants. A special debt is owed to these consultants, who provided advice and assistance without compensation and, in many cases, took time from their own research in order to check words with native speakers. The Linguistic Editor is especially grateful to Wick R. Miller, Sven Liljeblad, and William H. Jacobsen, Jr.

In the case of words that could not be respelled in a technical orthography, an attempt has been made to rationalize the transcriptions used in earlier anthropological writings in order to eliminate phonetic symbols that are obsolete and diacritics that might convey a false impression of phonetic accuracy.

Synonymies

Toward the end of ethnological chapters is a section called Synonymy. This describes the various names that have been applied to the groups and subgroups treated in that chapter, giving the principal variant spellings used in English and sometimes in Spanish, self-designations, and often the names applied to the groups in neighboring Indian languages. For the major group names, an attempt has been made to cite the earliest attestations in English.

Many synonymies have been expanded or reworked by the Linguistic Editor, who has added names and analyses from the literature and as provided by linguist consultants. Where a synonymy is wholly or substantially the work of the Linguistic Editor, a footnote specifying authorship is given.

These sections should assist in the identification of groups mentioned in the earlier historical and anthropological literature. They should also be examined for evidence on changes in the identifications and affiliations of groups, as seen by their own members as well as by neighbors and by outside observers.

Radiocarbon Dates

Authors were instructed to convert radiocarbon dates into dates in the Christian calendar. Such conversions have often been made from the dates as originally published, without taking account of changes that may be required by developing research on revisions of the half-life of carbon 14, long-term changes in the amount of carbon 14 in the atmosphere, and other factors that may require modifications of absolute dates based on radiocarbon determinations. Another type of conversion of radiocarbon dates was imposed in the chapter "Prehistoric Environments."

Binomials

The scientific names of animal and plant genera and species, printed in italics, have been checked by the General Editor to ensure that they reflect modern usage by biological taxonomists. Especially the plant names (but also most of the animal names) submitted in the chapter "Subsistence" were taken as standard. Binomials in other chapters have been brought into agreement with those in that chapter, or, if they do not appear there, have been checked against the sources for taxonomic usage cited on p. 97, or revised in consultation with curators in the appropriate departments of the National Museum of Natural History, Smithsonian Institution. There was in 1985 no complete source for the botanical nomenclature of the Great Basin. When the whole flora has been revised (when Cronquist et al. 1972, 1977 reaches completion), some differences from the interpretations followed here can be expected.

Bibliography

All references cited by contributors have been unified in a single list at the end of the volume. Citations within the text by author, date, and often page, identify the works in this unified list. Wherever possible the *Handbook* Bibliographer, Lorraine H. Jacoby, has resolved conflicts between citations of different editions, corrected inaccuracies and omissions, and checked direct quotations against the originals. The bibliographic information has been verified by examination of the original work or from standard reliable library catalogs (especially the National Union Catalog and the published catalog of the Harvard Peabody Museum Library). The unified bibliography lists all and only the sources cited in the text of the volume, except personal communications. In the text "personal communications" to an author are distinguished from personal "communications to editors." The sections headed Sources at the ends of most chapters provide general guidance to the most important sources of information on the topics covered.

Illustrations

Illustrations were the primary focus of the responsibility of Associate Volume Editor Catherine S. Fowler, who was formally named to this position by d'Azevedo in 1984. Although authors submitted suggestions for illustrations much original material was provided by editorial staff members from research they conducted in museums and other repositories, in the published literature, and from correspondence. Research on photographs, drawings, and paintings was the responsibility of the Illustrations Researcher Joanna Cohan Scherer. Research on artifacts was the responsibility of the Artifact Researcher Ernest S. Lohse. All uncredited drawings are by Jo Ann Moore and Brigid Sullivan.

Many individuals, including professional photographers, have generously provided photographs free or at cost. Victor Krantz of the Smithsonian Photographic Laboratory photographed the artifacts illustrated from the Smithsonian collections, and most of those illustrated from the collections of the American Museum of Natural History and the Museum of the American Indian, New York, and the Peabody Museum of Harvard University.

All maps were drawn by the Cartographer, Judith Crawley Wojcik, who redrew some submitted by authors and compiled many new ones using information from the chapter manuscripts and from other sources. The base maps for all are authoritative standard ones, especially sheet maps produced by the U.S. Geological Survey. When possible, the hydrography has been reconstructed as of the date depicted by each map, except that only modern hydrography is shown on maps in the prehistory section. The Cartographic Services of R.R. Donnelley and Sons Company provided many base maps and devoted meticulous care to converting the map artwork into final film.

Layout and design of the illustrations have been the responsibility of the Scientific Illustrator, Jo Ann Moore. Captions for illustrations were usually composed by Fowler, Scherer, Lohse, and Moore, and for the maps by Wojcik. However, all illustrations, including maps and drawings, and all captions, have been approved by the General Editor, the Volume Editor, the Associate Volume Editor, and the authors of the chapters in which they appear, and authors and editors frequently have participated actively in the selection process and in the improvement of captions.

The List of Illustrations was compiled by Frances Galindo.

Acknowledgements

Beyond the members of the Planning Committee and those persons whose special contributions are identified in appropriate sections of the text, important aid in reviewing manuscripts was also received from C. Melvin Aikens, Betty Anderson, Beverly Crum, Steven Crum, Fred Eggan, Gordon L. Grosscup, Patrick Hogan, Joseph G. Jorgensen, Sven S. Liljeblad, Karen M. Nissen, Elmer Rusco, and Imre Sutton. Special thanks are due to Catherine S. Fowler, who contributed extensively to a number of chapters in addition to those of which she is listed as an author and provided valuable editorial assistance during the final two years of volume preparation. Jesse D. Jennings contributed substantial editing of most of the prehistory chapters. Don D. Fowler and William H. Jacobsen, Jr., were generous advisors on archeological and linguistic matters, respectively. We are indebted to individuals on the staffs of many museums and other repositories for much time and effort spent in their collections locating photographs and artifacts and providing documentation on them. Special help in this regard was received from: Anibal Rodriguez (American Museum of Natural History, New York); Howard Piepenbrink (Bureau of Indian Affairs, Washington, for up-to-date maps of reservations); David Epley and Anna Kelly (Eastern California Museum, Independence); Phyllis Rabineau (Field Museum of Natural History, Chicago); Robert Blesse, Lenore Kosso, and Tim Gorelangton (Getchell Library, University of Nevada Reno); Frank Norick and Richard Keeling (Lowie Museum of Anthropology, University of California, Berkeley); James G.E. Smith, Natasha Bonilla, and Sanda Alexandride (Museum of the American Indian, Heye Foundation, New York); Steve Kane (*Native Nevadan*, Reno-Sparks Colony); Nancy Peterson Walter (Natural History Museum of Los Angeles County); Donald R. Tuohy and Amy Dansie (Nevada State Museum, Carson City); Ian Brown and Victoria Swedlow (Peabody Museum, Harvard University); Clayton B. Sampson (Reno-Sparks Colony); Ruth Kirk (Seattle, Washington); Bonnie C.W.W. Teton (Shoshone-Bannock Tribes, Fort Hall Reservation); A. Brian Wallace and Jo Ann Nevers (Washoe Tribe).

Ives Goddard was of particular assistance on matters of historical and geographical accuracy as well as on decisions made by the General Editor regarding organization, consistency, and other editorial procedures. The help of many other individuals is acknowledged in footnotes, in credit lines, and as communications to editors.

During the first few years of this project, the *Handbook* editorial staff in Washington worked on materials for all volumes of the series. Since 1983, when intensive preparation of this volume began, especially important contributions were provided by: the Editorial Assistant, Nikki L. Lanza (until 1984) and Paula Cardwell (1984–); the Production Manager and Manuscript Editor, Diane Della-Loggia; the Bibliographer, Lorraine H. Jacoby; the Researcher, Cesare Marino; the Scientific Illustrator, Jo Ann Moore, the Cartographer, Judith Crawley Wojcik; the Graphic Arts Technicians, William Dreher and Veronica Freeman; the Illustrations Researcher, Joanna Cohan Scherer; the Assistant Illustrations Researcher, Frances Galindo; the Artifact Researcher, Ernest S. Lohse; the Administrative Assistant, Melvina Jackson; and the Secretaries, Nancy Mottershaw, Justine Ickes, and Tujuanna L. Evans. Lottie Katz served as the volunteer assistant for the Bibliographer. Helen Ingersoll Sanders was a volunteer research assistant to the Linguistic Editor from June to August 1983. Betsy Eisendrath compiled the index.

Valuable administrative supervision was provided until November 1983 by James F. Mello, then Associate Director, National Museum of Natural History, Smithsonian Institution, and from November 1983 to January 1985 by Douglas H. Ubelaker, then Chairman, Department of Anthropology, Smithsonian Institution. From November 1982 through October 1983 Colin I. Busby was Managing Editor. Beginning in January 1985 Ives Goddard served as Managing Editor in addition to his other *Handbook* responsibilities.

Acknowledgement is due to the Department of Anthropology, Smithsonian Institution (and to its other curatorial staff) for releasing Sturtevant and Goddard from part of their curatorial and research responsibilities so that they could devote time to editing the *Handbook*.

Preparation and publication of this volume have been supported by federal appropriations made to the Smithsonian Institution, in part through its Bicentennial Programs.

The Volume Editor, Warren L. d'Azevedo, acknowledges the skillful research and editorial assistance of Judy Ann Knokey (1982–1983) and Jane M. Pilotte (1984–1985). Generous secretarial assistance was provided to him by Alma Smith during the initial period of volume preparation (1971–1972) and by Lynn Herman in the final stages. Grateful acknowledgement is made to Richard O. Davies, Vice-President for Academic Affairs, and Paul Page, Dean of the College of Arts and Science at the University of Nevada Reno for special funding and released time from teaching during 1984, which enabled Warren d'Azevedo to devote much of his time to editing this volume.

October 17, 1985   William C. Sturtevant

                                          Warren L. d'Azevedo

Introduction

WARREN L. D'AZEVEDO

The Great Basin region, which provides the geographic and cultural domain of this volume, comprises about 400,000 square miles of western North America between the Sierra Nevada and the Rocky Mountains (fig. 1). It includes all of Nevada and Utah, most of western Colorado, and portions of southern Oregon, Idaho, and Wyoming, as well as of eastern California, and northern Arizona and New Mexico. Though encompassing almost one-tenth of the conterminous United States, it was the last major frontier of North America to be explored and settled by Euro-American intruders.

Historical Perspective

The first reports to give some glimpse of the land and its people were made in the late eighteenth century by Spanish explorers seeking routes between their possessions on the southern fringes of the Great Basin and in California. British and American trappers penetrated the northern periphery early in the nineteenth century providing sketchy but important information about the country and the peoples they encountered along the route that became the Oregon Trail. But the vast interior of the Great Basin remained the legendary "Mysterious Land" or "Unknown Land" of early maps until the first parties of trappers, explorers, and immigrants attempted to traverse the region in search of furs and a direct overland route. Some, such as Jedediah Strong Smith in 1827, Peter Skene Ogden in 1829, Joseph Walker in 1833, and John Bidwell in 1841, actually succeeded in crossing the deserts and mountain ranges to the central Sierra Nevada and California. Bancroft (1890:39–45) noted that the first passage was made by Smith from California across what is now northern Nevada to the Great Salt Lake, the reverse of the "usual direction of marching empire."

It was not until after the widely heralded explorations of John C. Frémont that the American public in the East became convinced that the difficult passage could be made safely. It had been part of the lore of this unknown area that a great river, often referred to as the Buenaventura, emerged in the Rocky Mountains and flowed westward over the deserts to empty in San Francisco Bay. Frémont was among those who held doggedly to the view that he would find this river and

make an easy descent to California. On his second expedition in 1844 he was led at last to the conclusion that the legendary waterway did not exist, and he noted on the map of the expedition that the area between the Wasatch Mountains and the Sierra Nevada was "surrounded by lofty mountains: contents almost unknown, but believed to be filled with rivers and lakes which have no connection with the sea." Having affirmed that this enormous and largely uncharted territory was one of interior drainage, he gave it the name "great basin" (Frémont 1845:map).

After 1845, an increasing number of immigrant parties began to follow the Humboldt or Overland Trail, across the central Great Basin to California rather than taking either the Oregon or Old Spanish Trails, even though it continued to be known as a perilous route. Because of the remoteness and the apparent inaccessibility of much of the region, the Mormons ventured into it in 1847 choosing the valley of the Great Salt Lake as a place of refuge from religious persecution, thus becoming its first White settlers. They dreamed of building a new society, remote from the "Americats" to the north and east and from the distant Mexican claimants to the territory in the south and west, where

Fig. 1. Land forms of the Great Basin.

the deserts would bloom with their labors and the Indians would join in defense of the land. Within a year they had proclaimed the state of Deseret, which included all of the region now known as the Great Basin, as well as other areas in the Southwest and southern California acquired by the United States in the Treaty of Guadalupe Hidalgo.

The discovery of gold in California in 1849 was followed by a rush of thousands of new immigrants across the corridors of the Great Basin to the Pacific Coast. During the following decade, thousands more were attracted to the Comstock mines of western Nevada, many of whom remained to settle as ranchers and townspeople. The tide of immigration transformed the region into new territories and states with networks of American enterprise and settlement. A transcontinental railroad was joined by the driving of a golden spike at Ogden, Utah, in 1869.

Sequel To Conquest

In many areas the original character of the country was altered drastically. Grasslands along the rivers were destroyed by livestock grazing, springs in arid sections were fenced by ranchers, some timbered areas were all but denuded by the needs of mines and towns, and large game became scarce. The conquest of the new territory was complete, but the impact upon the way of life of the native people, who had at first cautiously welcomed the intruders and later attempted sporadic resistance, was devastating. Starvation and diseases brought by Whites decimated large numbers. Those that survived were forced onto reservations containing lands least desirable to the new settlers, and their access to the wide range of resources that had sustained traditional economy and society was denied them. Others became dependents and laborers on ranches and on the fringes of White communities. So desperate was their condition that White observers in the latter part of the nineteenth century predicted their imminent extinction, and some even welcomed the possibility as a solution to "the Indian problem."

Because the destruction of the native habitat and way of life began early in the nineteenth century and continued with increasing catastrophic effects after the 1850s, most early immigrants and settlers met a landscape and a native people already transformed by alien exploitation. What they saw laid the basis for White lore and perception of the land and native peoples for a century to come. Written reports had prepared them for what seemed to be the endless vistas of desolation contrasted with the bustling spirit of enterprise in widely spaced frontier settlements. The Indians were generally viewed with contempt, as improvident and a nuisance, except on those occasions when reports of "wars," "raids,"

and "massacres" swept through the west raising exaggerated fears of massive uprisings. To the White immigrants of the 1850s and 1860s who had gained a grudging respect for the mounted warriors of the eastern and northern plains, the small scattered groups of Western Shoshone, Northern and Southern Paiute, and Washoe beyond the Wasatch Mountains were perceived as the most wretched of the earth, a people depicted as roaming the land on foot to scratch out a meager survival on roots, seeds, and small animals. Concern for their condition, or interest in their history and traditional way of life, was all but nonexistent except for a rare Indian Agent or enlightened settler who attempted to plead their case.

These attitudes reflected a familiar pattern of American conquest of the continent in which those who put up the most formidable resistance to domination became romanticized in historical lore and were rewarded by gifts and treaties, while the generally peaceable and helpless were despised and ignored. All but a few of the remnant groups in the Great Basin and California in this period (referred to derogatively as Diggers) fared badly in this process and suffered the full brunt of American expansion into the West within two or three explosive decades of the mid-nineteenth century.

Perhaps the most eloquent expression of chauvinism in this regard was written by Mark Twain (Samuel L. Clemens), who had come by stagecoach across the Great Basin in 1861. As an ambitious young man seeking his fortune in Virginia City, the country of the Mormons had whetted his appetite for satire; but the westward ordeal over the Salt Lake Desert and the descent into the country of the Gosiute Western Shoshone apparently exceeded the limit of his tolerance.

> It was along in this wild country somewhere, and far from any habitation of white men, except the stage-stations, that we came across the wretchedest type of mankind I have ever seen, up to this writing. I refer to the Goshoot Indians. From what we could see and all we could learn, they are very considerably inferior to even the despised Digger Indians of California; inferior to all races of savages on our continent; inferior to even the Terra del Fuegans; inferior to the Hottentots, and actually inferior in some respects to the Kytches of Africa. Indeed, I have been obliged to look the bulky volumes of Wood's *Uncivilized Races of Men* clear through in order to find a savage tribe degraded enough to take rank with the Goshoots. I find but one people fairly open to that shameful verdict. It is the Bosjesmans (Bushmen) of South Africa . . . . The Bushmen and our Goshoots are manifestly descended from the self-same gorilla, or kangaroo or Norway rat, whichever animal-Adam the Darwinians trace them to (Twain 1872:146–147).

This diatribe, the full extent of which appears as a chapter in Twain's *Roughing It*, is described by a Nevada historian as "a classic every Nevadan loves. He reads it more often than he does the Bible" (Mack 1947:49–50). It stands as probably the most malicious characterization of a conquered people in the history of White contact with Native Americans. It is, also, quite possibly the first instance in which the Great Basin Indians were employed for world-wide comparison of levels of civilization. For Native Americans, it will remain as only one of a plethora of reminders of the character of the social period through which they have survived as a people.

Mark Twain in the 1860s was a voice of the arrogant optimism of frontier America and its nineteenth-century assurance of unlimited resources, progress, and domination. His reaction to the Indian peoples he encountered in the Great Basin reflected both popular and scientific attitudes of the time concerning the human condition. The relegation of the Gosiute to the lowest level of human society was consistent with nineteenth-century notions of the ranking of races and cultures on a scale of worthiness in which Western civilization exemplified a superior and ultimate stage of development. These attitudes served to rationalize the domination of White intruders over a people who already had been brought to a state of degradation by decades of aggressive contact. Their helpless condition was viewed as a universal and timeless expression of their nature. When they fought back in desperate efforts to defend the remnants of their lands, or when they were forced to plunder for food because their former resources had been depleted by the invaders, this too was taken as evidence of their unrelenting savagery.

In this context, the continuity of subsequent generations of Native Americans in the Great Basin is a tribute to their tenacity as a people whose predecessors had successfully adapted to life in the region for thousands of years. Moreover, as Steward (1955:57–58) pointed out, it may have been the very inhospitableness of large reaches of the Great Basin, in the view of Whites, that allowed many small mobile groups to retain a semblance of their traditional way of life for a few additional decades and that spared the majority the worse fate of near extinction experienced by the Indians of California. The major factor, however, was clearly the remarkable resilience of an ancient lifeway that had prepared the native inhabitants of the Great Basin for utilization of highly effective strategies of survival in a demanding environment. The patterns of subsistence activity and social organization were well adapted to the requirements of mobility, flexible alternatives, and the detailed ecological knowledge necessary for the collecting of a wide range of resources over large expanses of terrain. Small groups moved freely in traditionally recognized domains, sharing relatively abundant resources with other groups and maintaining networks of cooperative alliance through intermarriage. The major focus of concern was the precarious balance of the fragile environment itself, which in periods of climatic and ecological change might bring scarcity and even starvation. Thus respect for the land and its living things

was a fundamental tenet of the religious and ceremonial life of the people, one which continues to function as a major value among their descendants.

With the advent of White conquest of the region, this way of life was subverted. In areas of most intensive foreign exploitation the drastic changes took place within a decade or two of first contact. Yet despite the increasing pressure of transformation and domination after 1870, during which the former inhabitants of this huge province were relegated to the status of supplicants or dependents, the ancient patterns of survival sustained them in the process of accommodating to the new situation. Indian men soon became some of the most skilled and sought-after ranch hands throughout the region and worked as laborers in the burgeoning construction projects of the opening west. Many were engaged as woodcutters or used their skills as hunters and fishermen for trade in the White settlements. The women were employed as laundresses and cooks in most of the homes and ranches of the area, and some of the children began to be sent to special Indian schools as the federal government slowly responded to the need for improvement of their ability to cope with the new world into which they had been introduced.

For most of the people, however, destitution remained extreme and they were forced to eke out a precarious existence on the few reservations and on the fringes of White settlements. Many lived in camps around the refuse dumps of towns where they scavenged for materials to make their shelters or for cast-off food and clothing. They were not welcome in the towns except as laborers or customers and were expected to return to their own camps by nightfall. Local customs of discrimination and segregation were severe and all the rights of citizenship or legal recourse were denied them. Disease and periodic starvation ravaged their communities during subsequent decades and intensified White perception of the hopelessness of their plight. These conditions, grim as they were, nevertheless served to maintain a sense of common identity and shared destiny in the dislocated Indian communities. Out of necessity, and where possible, they supplemented their diet with the game and plants that were still available. The old knowledge of medicinal herbs and minerals continued to be relied upon for therapeutic treatment. Major seasonal events of the past, such as the harvesting of pine nuts or fish runs, brought hundreds of people together for festivals and related activities giving continuity to important elements of the cultural heritage. Though much of the technology of aboriginal life quickly fell into disuse, traditions remained vigorous in the languages, the lore, the kinship patterns, and family life of the people. A world view distinct from that of the surrounding White society linked the past to the present and spared them the alternatives of cultural obliteration or extinction. They survived as a people through an era

3

of American history that brought destruction and even annihilation to many of their kind elsewhere.

Population estimates indicate that the number of Great Basin Indians in 1873 was about 21,500 ("Population," table 1, this vol.; see also Kroeber 1939:134–142 for a similar estimate based on Mooney's early contact figures). The figures for 1930 show that there had been a steady decline to about 12,000 persons. This occurred during the period of White frontier occupation and establishment of Indian reservations. But from the 1930s to 1970 the Native American population increased to about 19,500 and, over the next 10 years, made an unprecedented leap to about 29,000, exceeding the estimates for early contact. There can be little doubt that this remarkable population recovery is in large part attributable to improvement of economic, educational, and health conditions instituted by the federal government, and the rapid positive response of local Indian groups to long awaited opportunities. This was the era of "tribal reorganization," of numerous cases involving land and other rights filed with the Indian Claims Commission, and the revival of a strong Indian identity. The 1970s, in particular, witnessed the awakening of new leadership, vigorous development programs, and a spirit of involvement on the part of youth. Throughout the Great Basin, Native Americans are participating in local, state, and national affairs to a degree not possible before, and their contributions to the larger American society are receiving a belated recognition. In retrospect, the continued existence of culturally identifiable and developing communities of descendants of the ancient inhabitants of the Great Basin through the turbulent nineteenth century and into the late twentieth century is testimony to the viability of a culture and the perserverance of its people. It is to those people and their culture that the present volume is dedicated.

Volume Organization

This volume constitutes the first attempt to present a concise resume of what is known about the environment, culture history, and way of life of the indigenous inhabitants of the Great Basin. Knowledge of the region and its peoples accumulated slowly in the nineteenth century, and, with a few notable exceptions, systematic investigation by archeologists and ethnographers did not begin until well into the twentieth century.

By the 1970s, archeological and linguistic investigation in the Great Basin had reached the point where generalization and synthesis were becoming possible; yet scarcely a half-dozen ethnologists continued to focus their attention on Great Basin cultural materials, and the status of knowledge about large sections of the area had not advanced substantially beyond what had been learned during the early part of the century. In this context, Steward's (1938) monumental survey was for decades the prime resource of information about the distribution and cultural characteristics of the widely scattered indigenous populations of the region. However, it was not a comprehensive ethnographic account, though it was generally reputed to be such, and constituted the principal basis for cultural evolutionist classifications in which the "Shoshoneans" are made representative of the most minimal level of human society (Thomas 1981a:22). The ethnographic coverage was limited to an environmentally oriented analysis of subsistence, kinship systems, and political organization of Northern and Western Shoshone groups (also Owens Valley Paiute), but mainly with reference to the Western Shoshone in the central Basin. The Northern Paiute, Ute, and Southern Paiute are but briefly mentioned, and there is little indication that Steward recognized the existence of important variations, such as the many lakeside and riverine adaptations. Owens Valley is discussed as a special case. This imbalance is reflected in the model of Great Basin social organization and environmental adaptation that was employed by a generation of prehistorians and ethnologists working in the region. Nevertheless, as the first major attempt at ethnographic synthesis of the region, it provided an integrative perspective and theoretical orientation that stimulated and shaped the course of Great Basin research (cf. C. S. Fowler 1977:19, 21–25). The data from Steward's early fieldwork are also indispensable; their importance and range are attested by extensive references throughout the literature and in the chapters of this volume.

Though few might wish to take issue with Baumhoff's (1958:4) observation that "Steward's work alone would have been sufficient to change the Great Basin from an ethnographic no-man's land into one of the better known areas of the world," it also should be pointed out that the remarkably rich and detailed early investigations of Robert Lowie, Omer Stewart, Demitri Shimkin, Isabel Kelly, Sven Liljeblad, and Willard Park, among others, have created a wealth of ethnographic data the potential of which has yet to be fully explored. In archeology, Jesse Jennings, Robert Heizer, and Luther Cressman were carrying out the seminal research that was to revolutionize conceptions of Great Basin prehistory from a "no-man's land" into 10,000 years or more of successful human occupation.

Critical assessment of Steward's contribution emerged in the 1970s and 1980s as new research revealed a diversity of ecological adaptation and cultural forms that were not addressed in the models derived from his Great Basin work (for example, C.S. Fowler 1977, 1982; Madsen 1982:210–212; Thomas 1982a:162–167, 1983b:60–62). It is no longer possible to define the region in terms of a generalized "Basin Shoshonean" type either in prehistory or in the historical ethnographic period, for it has proved to be a larger and more complex area than was previously envisioned.

Despite the history of differing views and approaches, the Great Basin has emerged as a distinct natural and cultural area of study. This has taken place despite a relatively sparse archeological and ethnographic record that perpetuated the notion that the region offered meager potentialities for continued anthropological research and that its aboriginal cultures represented essentially hinterland extensions of adjacent areas (cf. Kroeber 1939:49–53). Moreover, the conventional image of the region as a barren wasteland of deserts and steppes inhabited by a thinly scattered population living on a level of bare subsistence was underscored by studies that portrayed the inhabitants as having "acquired most of their hunting and gathering techniques from other peoples" and whose cultures were especially notable for "quantitative simplicity" (Steward 1955:101–102). The relative paucity of ethnographic work after the 1940s indicates that researchers tended to seek out areas of greater social complexity, historical depth, and concentration of investigation. A similar lag is evident in the development of the archeological record. Before the 1950s, investigation of Great Basin prehistoric cultures was dominated by the view that they were peripheral to those of the Plains, the Southwest, and California. It was not until the appearance of radiometric techniques of dating that the great antiquity and possible priority of Great Basin cultural materials began to be confirmed (Fowler and Jennings 1982). Consequently, there has been a rapid increase in archeological investigation and theoretical work, particularly in the 1970s and 1980s, which offers promise of important synthesis. This development has not been accompanied by an equivalent growth in ethnographic studies, a problem that has made prehistorians "dependent upon the baseline data of the 1930s and 1940s for their analogies" (C.S. Fowler 1977:30). Moreover, as Thomas (1981a:22) points out, the tendency to use the Great Basin Numic society described by Steward as "typical" has been misleading "because it avoids consideration of the internal variability that exists in their society."

Despite the phenomenal increase in archeological work the most significant data is concentrated in a few sites where intensive stratigraphic investigation has been carried out and that have provided the evidence for prehistoric sequences. In some subareas, such as those of the southern Great Basin, the record is still so slight that prehistoric cultural conditions and chronologies must be extrapolated from widely scattered finds. The correlation of prehistoric materials and sequences for the entire Great Basin, though advancing rapidly, is limited not only by the enormous size of the region but also by the tendency of archeologists to focus their interests exclusively on a particular locale. There is a widely recognized need for more systematic work throughout the region as well as for new theoretical perspectives (Madsen and O'Connell 1982:6–7). The task of the authors of chapters in the prehistory section was to prepare a cogent summary of the most reliable archeological data available for a subarea or special feature of the Great Basin about which they have expert knowledge. Discussion of the history of ideas or various theoretical approaches is kept to a minimum in order to allow the fullest use of the space allocated for presentation of substantive data and bibliographic referencing.

The authors of the ethnographic summaries were confronted with similar if not greater difficulties. It must be emphasized here that the lines drawn on the diagrammatic areal map on page ix are merely intended to indicate the commonly distinguished subareas of the Great Basin addressed by authors of the ethnographic chapters and are based upon early historic distributions. It would have been unfeasible to attempt to deal with each of the multiplicity of small groups of the region as discrete entities in separate cultural summaries. Though there may be some justification for such a procedure, literally hundreds of such groups have been identified and variously named in the historic record. Many no longer exist as identifiable units, and the impact of vast changes during the nineteenth and twentieth centuries has dispersed or reassembled others in different locations. Peoples such as the Northern Paiute, the Northern and Eastern Shoshone, and the Ute and Southern Paiute, while sharing similar cultural characteristics with the Western Shoshone, are speakers of three widespread branches of the Numic languages whose ecological setting and historical interrelations have produced notable subregional variations.

Great Basin people have been highly mobile throughout prehistory and in historic times and have engaged in extensive interrelations through marriage, trade, and joint use of lands. There have been no firm boundaries, but only recognized ranges of traditional occupation and overlapping use. The maps accompanying each of the chapters represent the actual situation more realistically than does the "Key to Tribal Territories" on page ix. In each summary chapter, the authors have given attention to the fluid nature of social organization, spatial distribution, and the external relations of groups. Taken together, they provide a mosaic of the characteristic cultural variants of the Great Basin region revealing the integrative stratum of common features and interconnected social relations that serve to define a relatively distinctive cultural area.

The ethnographic chapters constitute the first effort to compile a comprehensive summary of Great Basin cultures. For many of the larger subareas the available information is extremely limited for some sections; and no previous surveys have been published excepting those of the schematic Cultural Element Distribution projects (Driver 1937; Ray 1942; Steward 1941, 1943a; O.C.

Stewart 1941, 1942), Lowie (1909, 1924) on the Northern Shoshone, Steward's (1938) study of Western Shoshone sociopolitical groups, O.C. Stewart's (1939) work on Northern Paiute bands, and Kelly (1964) on the Southern Paiute. Few ethnological monographs exist on any of the groups and these are devoted to specific peoples in widely separated locations—for example, Kelly (1932) for the Surprise Valley Northern Paiute; Laird (1976) for the Chemehuevi; Steward (1933b) for the Owens Valley Paiute; Barrett (1917), Lowie (1939), Downs (1966), and Price (1980) for the Washoe; Lowie (1909) and Murphy and Murphy (1960) for the Northern Shoshone; Malouf (1940b) for the Gosiute; B.G. Madsen (1958) for the Bannock; Smith (1974) for the Northern Ute. Detailed ethnohistorical studies also are sparse, though it is through early reports and documents that knowledge of many of the groups is to be gained (for example, Euler 1966; Steward and Wheeler-Voegelin 1974; Johnson 1975).

The efforts presented here should help stimulate further ethnological investigation as well as work with the enormous untapped resources of archives and museum collections. There is also a pressing need for studies of sociocultural change and the response of Native American peoples to the acculturative situation (such as Lee 1967; Shimkin and Reid 1970). No major published studies exist on either the history or societal formations of twentieth-century reservations and the many other rural and urban communities, though a number of theses and dissertations (Lang 1954; Mordy 1966; Houghton 1968, 1973; Brink 1969; Lynch 1971; S.J. Crum 1983; Roth 1976; Knack 1975) have shown the importance of this topic. Chapters in the history section of this volume also indicate the potentialities for continued research in these fields, while those in the introductory and special topics sections suggest a wide range of other subjects for future work.

The Great Basin Region

The Great Basin is an area of distinctive cultural distributions and natural environment, yet it has been delineated in various ways, reflecting the approaches of different disciplines as well as differing substantive arguments. Despite the growth of knowledge about specific aspects and subareas, the general designation of the region as a geographic entity has been vague and often arbitrary. Kroeber (1939:49) commented that "California has generally been reckoned a distinct area ever since American culture began to be classified geographically; but the Great Basin has been bandied about." In a similar vein, Steward (1940:445) wrote: "It is unfortunate that the term Basin is rapidly becoming fixed in the literature, for both the natural and cultural areas extended far beyond this physiographic province." The

problem of designation had been noted by Barrett (1917:5) in attempting to establish a standard ethnographic usage:

> The term Plateau culture area has been hitherto applied to this region, but in view of the fact that the term is, from a standpoint of physiography, a misnomer, and that the term Great Basin, is generally accepted as the name for this physiographic division of the continent, it seems best to adopt it for anthropology as well. Especially is this advisable since the name is so perfectly descriptive of this region and since the cultural limits of the inhabitants so closely approximate the limits of the Great Basin area when considered from a physiographic standpoint.

The problem remains to the extent that archeologists, ethnographers, and others seldom define the Great Basin as a general region, taking for granted that the criteria that they apply are commonly shared and understood.

Natural Provinces

As Fenneman (1931:326) points out, "the term 'Great Basin' is often used in a hydrographic sense but its more general use is physiographic." This can lead to some confusion unless the differentiation is clearly made. The hydrographic basin (fig. 2), often referred to as "the Great Basin proper," is the area of interior drainage of rivers and streams into remnant Pleistocene lakes or playas. As the most striking geological feature of the larger provinces, it has come to characterize the whole region.

The physiographic Great Basin, however, includes marginal areas such as the upper Pit River, Goose Lake and the eastern Klamath Lake area, southern portions of the Snake River Plain, and extreme southern Nevada, where drainage is to the sea (cf. Fenneman 1931:326–327; Kroeber 1939:51, map 7; Morrison 1965:266; C.B. Hunt 1967:309–311). Despite slightly varying renditions in maps and descriptions, the physiographic Great Basin is essentially defined by a distinctive topography characteristic of a larger Basin and Range Province of which it makes up about one-half (fig. 2). The province includes not only the Great Basin but also physiographically similar portions of southern California, northern and western Arizona, northern New Mexico, and northern Mexico. It contains roughly parallel mountain ranges and long desert basins, both trending north and south. The climate is generally arid to semiarid and dependent upon moisture from the Pacific, which is largely caught or deflected by the rain shadow of the many transverse ranges.

The Basin and Range Province is, in turn, part of a more extensive physiographic division of western North America known as the Intermontane Plateaus division, which extends from Alaska into Mexico. This includes the Columbia Plateaus and the Colorado Plateaus, as well as the Basin and Range Province, which is its largest section (C.B. Hunt 1967:3–9). It comprises an enormous expanse of the North American high altitude regions between the Rocky Mountains and the Coast, Cascade, Sierra Nevada, and Sierra Madre mountain systems on the western periphery of the continent. For this reason, it was known in the earlier literature as the "Plateau area," which accounts for the term "Basin-Plateau" often applied to the Great Basin region itself (Lowie 1923:145; Steward 1938:xi; Kroeber 1920:169, 1939:49, 188–191, 196). However, the physiographic features that define the various divisions, provinces, and sections are not in reality sharply bounded but in many instances grade into one another (Fenneman 1931:328; C.B. Hunt 1967:3–6, 309). This accounts for the somewhat different versions of these entities depicted in the maps and writings of geologists, geographers, and ethnographers.

In addition to the hydrographic and physiographic provinces of the Great Basin region, a relatively distinctive biotic province also may be delineated where characteristic plant and animal communities (biomes) exist in response to local climates and other natural conditions (fig. 2). Descriptions of these distributions are usually based on vegetation because, as D.E. Brown (1982:9, 13) points out, "though animal constituents are an important factor as well, it is the vegetative structures that provide readily observable and measurable manifestation of ecosystems." The term floristic province for such an area involves the identification of a reasonably distinctive plant geography. The Great Basin floristic province is mapped and described by Gleason and Cronquist (1964:fig. 15.1, 372–388) and by Cronquist et al. (1972:78–159).

About one-fourth of the Great Basin floristic region, as here defined, lies outside of the hydrographic Great Basin. . . . Most of this area with external drainage lies along the northern part of the Region. The Owyhee Desert and Snake River Plains sections drain into the Snake River and the very northwestern tip of the Lake Section drains into the Deschutes River via southern Crooked River tributaries. Another externally drained area in the south-central part drains into the Colorado River via the Virgin River drainate. . . . This division includes most of the physiographer's Great Basin Section of the Basin and Range Province . . . plus a part of the Columbia Plateau Province on the north (Cronquist et al. 1972:80).

Therefore, the Great Basin floristic province not only extends beyond the limits of the hydrographic area of interior drainage but also exceeds the physiographic province defined by geologists. Though sagebrush and piñon-juniper woodland is the most typical vegetation, the flora is more diverse than is often recognized and occupies a wide variety of econiches "ranging from alpine to subtropic, and from desert to humid" (Cronquist et al. 1972:77). This fact has important implications for the range of faunal species, as well as for the distribution of aboriginal human populations ("Historical Environments," "Subsistence," this vol.).

Cultural Provinces

The close relation between natural vegetation and cultural distribution was noted by Kroeber (1939:13–14, 206 ff.), a correspondence that has largely determined the boundaries of the inclusive Great Basin region as defined here. This region constitutes the "culture area" covered in this volume. In all but a few marginal instances it reflects real historical and sociocultural re-

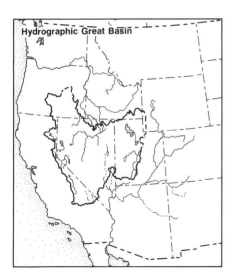

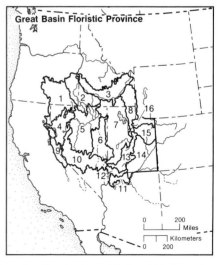

Fig. 2. Great Basin natural provinces: left, the hydrographic Great Basin (after Morrison 1965); center, the physiographic Great Basin, part of the Basin and Range Province, which together with the Columbia and Colorado plateaus constitutes the Intermontane Plateaus division (after Fenneman 1946); right, Intermountain Region floristic sections (after Cronquist et al. 1972:79): 1, Lake; 2, Owyhee Desert; 3, Snake River Plains; 4, Lahontan Basin; 5, Central Great Basin; 6, Calcareous Mountains; 7, Bonneville Basin; 8, Wasatch Mountains; 9, Reno; 10, Tonopah; 11, Grand Canyon Plateaus; 12, Dixie Corridor; 13, Utah Plateaus; 14, Canyon Lands; 15, Uinta Basin; 16, Uinta Mountains.

lationships. However, as Kroeber (1939:1–2) pointed out, "The concept of a culture area is a means to an end. The end may be the understanding of cultural processes as such, or of the historic events of culture." In this sense, and despite its controversial career, the term "cultural area" is a reasonably appropriate designation with reference to the inclusive Great Basin region.

The designation of a Great Basin culture area is based upon a synthesis of prehistoric and historic cultural and linguistic features characteristic of the human populations native to the region. Excepting for the Hokan-speaking Washoe, the cultural boundaries of the region are coterminous with those of peoples who speak languages of one of the three widespread branches of Numic, a division of the Uto-Aztecan language family. Several linguistic traits are found among all languages in the Great Basin, including Washoe, leading Sherzer (1976a:160–161) to conclude that the region is not only a uniform linguistic area created by language spread and intergroup communication but also an instance where linguistic area and culture area largely coincide. This view must be somewhat qualified (W. Bright 1976:232; "Washoe Language," this vol.); nevertheless, the coincidence of a language and culture area in the Great Basin remains strong and relatively unusual.

The archeological subareas defined in this volume ("Prehistory: Introduction, " fig. 1, this vol.) only roughly approximate the historic culture area. This is partly because they are based on the clustering of sites in a number of prehistoric ecological zones where research has been concentrated. A few major sites have provided the predominant resources for reconstructing prehistoric sequences, changing habitation patterns, and the development of material culture in specific areas, while large sections of the region remain unstudied or are known only through cursory surveys. Moreover, little is known of the actual connections between prehistoric cultures and the languages and cultures of historic peoples. There is some evidence to indicate that the Numic-speaking people did not spread into the region until after about A.D. 1000 and that they absorbed or replaced earlier occupants, though the Washoe may have been in their present location for a much greater period ("Numic Languages," "Washoe Language," this vol.).

The question of continuity between cultures of great antiquity and those of historic times remains unresolved and a matter of disagreement among archeologists; for example, Grosscup (1960, 1963) posited a hiatus between the ancient Lovelock culture in the western Great Basin and the historic peoples of the area, whereas Heizer and Napton (1970:1–86) saw continuity and a direct connection. A similar problem obtains in the eastern Great Basin where an extensive and unique horticultural pattern developed during a brief period between about A.D. 500 and 1400. Regional variants of these cultures, referred to as Fremont, existed north of the Colorado River in western Colorado, Utah, and eastern Nevada, characterized not only by horticulture but also by housing of adobe or masonry, distinctive pottery and basketry types, and other features unique in the region. It was once believed that this complex represented a peripheral extension of the Anasazi area of the Southwest, but archeologists now generally agree that the Fremont shows a clear continuity with the Archaic tradition of the Great Basin, though indicating some influences from either the Southwest or the Plains (Aikens 1978a:153–156).

The record of Great Basin prehistory is known to extend back 10,000 years or more involving variants of a lifeway termed the Western Archaic, which in its earliest stages was characteristic of the entire West from the Columbia Plateau to the Southwest and from the western Plains to California. Within this common ancient tradition somewhat different yet related regional traditions developed over thousands of years in response to environmental and demographic conditions. In the Great Basin the ancient way of life was maintained with relatively fewer changes into historic times. Though there was considerable local variation of settlement and subsistence pattern and many influences from surrounding regions, the prehistoric Great Basin has presented a basic cultural unity through time (Spencer and Jennings 1977:188–190; Aikens 1978a:131–133).

The ethnographic culture area of the Great Basin region in some sections extends beyond the limits of the physiographic province to include parts of the Snake and Salmon river drainages, the Wyoming Basin, the far Western Plains, and the Colorado Plateau known to have been occupied by peoples identified with Great Basin cultures and languages from early historic times. The region, defined in this way, is both an ethnographic and historical entity involving processes of internal diversification, external interaction, and change. Sections of the region are culturally distinguishable not only in terms of specific environmental adaptation but also because of long contact and interchange with peoples of surrounding regions as well as epochal historic events. Among these events were the far-reaching effects of European contact and the acquisition of horses. The Southern Ute and Eastern Shoshone had obtained horses late in the seventeenth century, and by the early eighteenth century most of the Ute and the Northern and Eastern Shoshone and Bannock not only had horses but also had become deeply influenced by the equestrian cultures of the Plains. This phenomenon led early observers to divide the peoples of the region in terms of horse-using and non–horse-using groups, holding the former to be in a more advanced stage of development. It also, in part, led Wissler (1914, 1917) to assign most of the Great Basin region to a Plains culture area and the remainder to his Plateau, California, and Southwestern culture areas. This classification was dismissed by Kroeber (1939:49, 82) who objected that it "dissolves the Basin away" and that "the inclusion of all the easterly Basin tribes in the Plains area has validity for the last century or so, but would misrepresent earlier conditions." He also noted that "no one seems ever to have doubted the close internal cultural unity of the Shoshonean Basin tribes," and adds a comment characteristic of all earlier views of Great Basin groups: "It is the meagreness of their culture on levels above that of mere subsistence which has made it difficult to specify their affinities." Nevertheless, it was the nonhorse groups of the region who represented the basic Great Basin sociocultural patterns in historic times, patterns that had a wider prehistoric and early historic distribution than was generally recognized, as well as a rich diversity and complexity that clearly emerges in the chapters of this volume.

The changing conceptions of the Great Basin as a culture area are aptly illustrated by a progression of attempts to map the ethnographic relations of the region (fig. 3). Mason (1896:646, 650–651, 1907:427–430), though providing no maps, was among the first to distinguish a Great Basin area ("Interior Basin") in a classification of 12 North American culture areas or "ethnic environments." He noted what he perceived to be a close correspondence between the linguistic map that had been prepared by John Wesley Powell and the geographic distributions posed by C. Hart Merriam, concluding that the natural conditions in North America were "diversified enough to bring into prominence arts adapted to each culture area and obtrusively different from those of other areas" (Mason 1896:646). This pioneering work laid the basis for area classification schemes in which the covariations of cultural and environmental features became a predominant focus of interest (Kroeber 1931:250; Vayda and Rappaport 1968:480–481).

Wissler's (1914:449–454, 466–467, pl.xxxiii) attempt to construct culture area divisions suffered from a misconstrual of the historical situation and, consequently, obliterated the Great Basin as a distinct area (fig. 3a). Later Wissler (1917:8, 16–17) presented a diagrammatic map based upon the distribution of the use of acorns and other seeds in which central and southern California and most of the central Great Basin are included in an "Area of Wild Seeds" (fig. 3b). These depictions were significantly altered by Kroeber, who at first suggested a "California-Great Basin" area of general culture (1920:167–169) (fig. 3c), and later (1923:786–788) posited an "Intermediate" area among six basic "areas of native culture" in North America. This "Intermediate" area comprised a "California subarea" and a larger "Intermountain subarea" that included most of the Great Basin culture area as well as the Columbia and Fraser plateaus (fig. 3d). Kroeber (1931:251) states that his own map is based on Wissler "and differs chiefly in attempting to follow natural boundaries instead of representing the areas diagrammatically." But a glance at the renditions provided by each would indicate that Kroeber had already acquired a more sophisticated command of the physiographic and cultural provinces. Wissler (1926:214) noted that Kroeber's map closely paralleled the floristic and climatic distributions indicated on a map prepared by the Ecological Society of America, showing "a consistent relation between the generalized culture areas on the one hand and environmental areas on the other."

The first maps to show the detailed and accurate placement of groups and distribution of languages were those of Steward (1937b, 1938) based primarily on his own fieldwork and informed to some extent by the work of Lowie (1909, 1924) with the Northern Shoshone and Kelly (1932, 1964) with the Surprise Valley Northern Paiute and the Southern Paiute. Though the 1937 map is entitled "Distribution of Shoshonean groups in the Great Basin," and partial linguistic boundaries are shown for the Northern Paiute, Shoshone, Ute, and Southern Paiute roughly corresponding to what later would be defined as the three branches of Numic, the detailed emphasis is on the Shoshone groups, which are assigned to bounded and named districts (figs. 3e, 4). The Northern Paiute area is bounded by the Sierra Nevada on the west, but no limit is given in the north, and the general area is devoid of groups excepting for a bounded section denoting Surprise Valley.

It was Kroeber (1939:map 6) who was the first to delineate a Great Basin culture area, as such, in a revised version of his earlier "Intermediate and Intermountain Areas" (compare fig. 3d and 3f). In figure 3f the Great Basin is clearly designated and includes a much larger area than that allocated in his initial "California-Basin" version of 1920 (fig. 3c). Moreover, four subareas are identified that, with one or two exceptions, define the extent of the cultural region as generally accepted by later scholars (cf. Driver and Massey 1957; Murdock 1960: opp. page 107; C.S. Fowler 1970:map 4; O.C. Stewart 1966:map 4, 1982:map 2). Kroeber's inclusion of the most northeasterly Klamath-Modoc and Achumawi-Atsugewi groups (as well as the eastern Maidu) did have a good basis, for the physiography of their habitats and their cultures reveal affinities with the Great Basin. Of the Achumawi, Atsugewi, and Maidu, though acknowledging their marginality, Kroeber (1939:52) declares: "I reckon them here with the Great Basin in order to draw attention to their status, and to break down the tradition, to which I have myself contributed, that because they live in the state of California they are to be assumed as Californian culturally." Early planning for the *Handbook* showed that there was still disagreement over the culture area assignment of these groups. Negotiations resulted in the

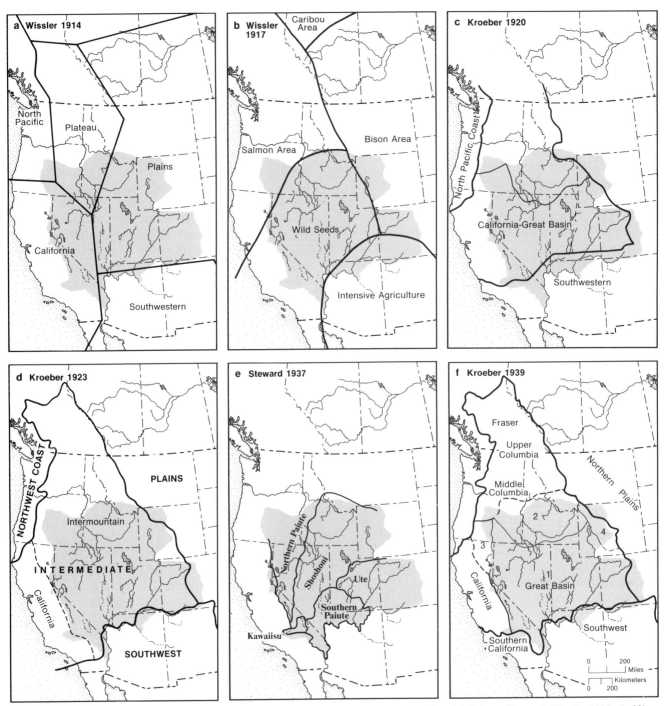

Fig. 3. Anthropologists' interpretations of the Great Basin and adjacent culture areas: a, "Material Culture Centers" (Wissler 1914:pl. 33); b, "Food Areas" (Wissler 1917:8); c, "The relation of California to the adjacent major culture areas" (Kroeber 1920:167); d, "Areas of native culture" (Kroeber 1923:fig.41); e, "Distribution of Shoshonean groups in the Great Basin" (Steward 1937b:fig.1); f, Intermediate and Intermountain "Culture areas" with Great Basin subareas indicated: 1, "The cultural Basin area proper"; 2, "The Bannock and Shoshone of the Snake-Salmon drainage"; 3, "The non-Shoshonean tribes of the Klamath Lakes and Pit River"; 4, "The eastern border tribes recently influenced by those of the Plains, especially the Wind River Shoshone across the Rockies" (Kroeber 1939: map 6, 55). The Great Basin as interpreted in this volume is shown in tone.

placement of the Atsugewi-Achumawi in California, and the Klamath and Modoc in the Plateau, with recognition that these were relatively arbitrary decisions.

Instances such as this demonstrate the tentativeness of mapped boundaries for culture areas where the actual situation involves intergrading through processes of cultural exchange and population mobility. The entire periphery of the Great Basin region is in this sense unbounded, and schematic depictions of its limits are based on variable criteria and often arbitrary judgments. O.C.

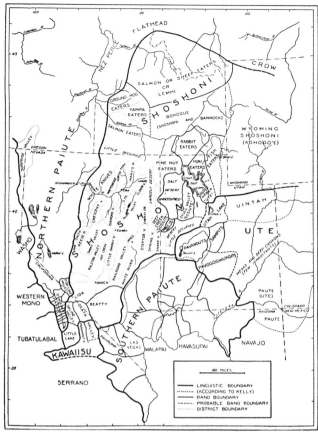

Fig. 4. Steward's (1937b) "Distribution of Shoshonean groups in the Great Basin."

Stewart's (1966) compilation of the maps assembled during Indian Claims Commission litigation reveals the cumulative complexity of previous efforts to show the territorial placement or range of historically known peoples in the region. Nevertheless, the general outline of a cultural province as established for this volume is based upon well-considered justifications for the inclusion or omission of groups and, with few exceptions, reflects collective views of the participating scholars.

The case of the Washoe is clear. Though their range extended westward over the crest of the Sierra Nevada, and many of their cultural traits are shared with California peoples, their major habitat and relations were along the eastern slope of the mountains in close proximity to the Northern Paiute. Because of their Hokan language and their location straddling state boundaries, they frequently were dealt with as a part of the California culture area, but their position as a Great Basin people has been generally acknowledged (Barrett 1917:5–8; Kroeber 1925:569). In California, speakers of the Mono language in the Western branch of Numic are divided into two sections by the Sierra Nevada; they differ in dialect and cultural affinities. The Owens Valley Paiute ("Eastern Mono") are the larger group and are culturally and linguistically related to the Northern Paiute, while the mountain or western groups (Mon-

ache) are mainly oriented to neighbors in the California foothills and valleys. The Owens Valley Paiute are treated separately in this volume because of their relatively high degree of sociopolitical integration, their sedentary village pattern, and their unique irrigation practices.

At the southwestern extremity of the Great Basin culture area the Panamint-speaking Western Shoshone people in and around Death Valley establish the limit of distribution of the Central Numic languages. Their western neighbors, the Tubatulabal, speak a distinct language distantly related to Numic but are culturally associated with peoples of the westerly California foothills and valleys. The Panamint Shoshone, however, are clearly connected with Great Basin cultures such as those of the Owens Valley Paiute, the Southern Paiute, and other Western Shoshone (Kroeber 1925:589–592; Steward 1938:70–93). The small section inhabited by the Kawaiisu presents something of an anomaly. Their language is distinct enough to be considered separate from the large Southern Numic division to the east that includes related peoples such as the Southern Paiute and Ute. Culturally, however, their affinities appear to be with California, though their early connections with the Chemehuevi have been noted (Kroeber 1925:601–602). Few identifiable Kawaiisu people remained in the mid-twentieth century, and these were scattered throughout southern California. Description of their former range and culture is included here because of their linguistic and early historic connections with Great Basin peoples.

The well-defined Southern Paiute bands along the Colorado River constitute a firm boundary between speakers of the Southern Numic languages and the Yuman and Hopi-speaking peoples of the Southwest. South of the San Juan River, the Navajo began to expand into their territory in the nineteenth century. Though there were many influences across the river divides, including the adoption of some horticultural practices, the Southern Paiute maintained an essentially Great Basin pattern of subsistence and general culture. Along with the Ute peoples to the east, they are speakers of the Ute language, the most extensively distributed language of the Southern Numic branch of the Uto-Aztecan family. The separation between the Southern Paiute and Ute peoples is, therefore, not linguistic but cultural. As O.C. Stewart (1982:17–19) points out, the major distinction between them was brought about by historic events and cultural changes in the eighteenth and nineteenth centuries. The Ute, particularly those east of the Colorado and Green rivers, were among the first groups to adopt the horse and were instrumental in the spread of equestrian practices from the Spanish settlements and to the north. In this process they were able to hunt buffalo on the western Plains and soon acquired many new elements of culture that led early anthropologists to classify them ethnologically in the Plains culture area (Wissler

1917:222–223). However, the western groups retained their central Great Basin cultural orientation.

The Eastern Shoshone ranged over most of the Wyoming Basin along the upper reaches of the Green, Sweetwater, and Big Horn rivers east of the Central Rocky Mountains. However, since earliest historic times, they also ranged far out into the Northern Plains, and, like the Ute, were among the first peoples to adopt the horse and to transmit elements of Plains culture to the northern Great Basin (Kroeber 1939:82–206). A segment of these peoples known as the Comanche split off in the eighteenth century and slowly moved into their present location in the southern Plains in search of buffalo (Shimkin 1980:198–206). Together with the Northern and Western Shoshone, the Eastern Shoshone and Comanche are speakers of Central Numic languages. For historical and cultural reasons, the Eastern Shoshone have been included in this volume of the series, while the Comanche are placed in the Plains volume.

The Eastern and Northern Shoshone (and Bannock) are closely linked in late prehistory as well as in the historic period, and their combined ranges have been referred to as a "Northeastern subarea" of the Great Basin (Butler 1981:245–247). In this area, several physiographic provinces come together: the Basin and Range, the Columbia Plateau and Snake River Plain, the Middle Rocky Mountains, and the Wyoming Basin. The Northern Shoshone inhabited the area of the Snake and Salmon river drainages from earliest historic times, and their culture, like that of the Eastern Shoshone and the Utes, was deeply influenced by the Plains, especially after their acquisition of the horse. Despite these influences their language and early basic cultural patterns were those of the other Shoshone of the Great Basin region. Moreover, their general range of habitation and land use was in a section of the southern Columbia Plateau where the sagebrush and juniper plant cover was similar to that of the Great Basin floristic province. Except for their partial reliance on salmon, their subsistence practices were essentially like those of their Shoshone and Northern Paiute neighbors.

The Northern Paiute of Oregon, speakers of a Western Numic language, also represent a Great Basin people whose range extends beyond the physiographic province and in the eighteenth century was even farther north (Ray et al. 1938; O.C. Stewart 1966:191–195, map 4). There was also a large area of joint use with the Northern Shoshone on the border of Oregon and Idaho that cannot be assigned to either people. In eastern Idaho, a small but often politically dominant minority of Northern Paiute people, known in the literature as the Bannock, have lived among the Northern Shoshone for hundreds of years (Liljeblad 1957:22–23, 81–91; O.C. Stewart 1966:190–191, 1970). They are speakers of a dialect of the Western Numic Northern Paiute language but are bilingual in Shoshone from which considerable linguistic borrowing has taken place ("Numic Languages," this vol.). They are treated here as a cultural subgroup of the Northern Shoshone.

It is apparent that a major criterion for the delineation of a Great Basin culture area is linguistic distribution in early historic times. With the exception of the Washoe, the picture presented is one of a wide fanlike extension of the three branches of Numic languages from the southwest corner of the region spreading out to the north and east. Around the entire periphery are the historic territories of peoples who speak quite different or very distantly related languages. However, the general cultural situation is not so easily bounded. All the peoples of the Great Basin share significant traits with contiguous groups in surrounding regions and have for centuries intermingled with them, establishing many areas of joint use of lands, intermarriage, and multilingualism. Moreover, evidence for long-distance trade reveals that Great Basin peoples were far from insular, maintaining extensive prehistoric and early historic connections with other regions ("Early Trade," this vol.). Any attempt to depict bounded limits for the culture area or its internal groupings must be perceived, therefore, as largely heuristic and requiring qualification in terms of historical events, mobility, and the record of self-identification of the groups involved. Much confusion can be avoided by the full recognition of the commonly acknowledged fact that linguistic, cultural, and environmental distributions, though significantly interdependent phenomena, are seldom spatially coterminous in any but a relative and general sense.

Conclusion

An effort has been made to define the Great Basin region as a comprehensive arena of research and to distinguish its component natural and cultural provinces. The diversity of interpretations and usages in this regard have been the source of some ambiguity and misunderstanding. Another source of confusion has been the complex history of nomenclature for the languages and ethnographic groups of the region. Therefore, such designations have been standardized throughout this volume in conformance with authoritative usage at the time of publication. The synonymies in the ethnographic chapters will provide the reader with detailed summaries of changing reference to each of the historic groups.

A final comment about nomenclature is reserved for those ostensibly immortal entities known as "bands," "tribes," and "nations." A considerable body of scholarship has been devoted to the analysis of concepts to which these terms should refer. It has produced important analytic distinctions in social theory that have helped to focus attention on specific aspects of group formation ("Kinship," this vol.). As an early proponent of a social evolutionary approach, Steward developed some of his major concepts while working with materials collected in the Great Basin. Steward (1970:147) believed "the concept of tribes among the Shoshoneans is an anthropologist's fiction," and he urged typological precision by the identification of groupings in terms defined by him as "family clusters," "proto-bands," "bands," or geographic "districts" (1937b:629, 1938:xi–xii, 263–264, 1939:262). The disagreements over interpretation of data incurred by these views figured significantly in the extensive proceedings of the Indian Claims Commission and remain matters of critical discussion among Great Basin anthropologists (C.S. Fowler 1982:132, 1982a).

Quite apart from the merits of contending viewpoints in anthropological discourse, normative patterns of usage are so deeply embedded in the general culture that few writers are inclined to explain their choices of given terms unless a particular problem of analysis requires it: bands, tribes, and nations continue to populate the literature and the political divisions of geographic space with little apparent regard for the disclaimers of anthropologists. The imposition of these terms and the alien concepts they represent began with the earliest records of European and American observation of Native American peoples, have become inextricably woven into official government parlance, and prevail in popular media and speech. A consequence of major import is that Native Americans themselves have adopted these designations in long-established reference to their societies, and it was largely on the basis of such legally validated categories that they have successfully justified demands for federal compensation for former lands. As Sturtevant (1983:13) comments, "it ill behooves anthropologists now to suggest that tribes do not exist." There are approximately 45 officially constituted reservations and colonies throughout the Great Basin region, most of which comprise, or are part of, units defined by the inhabitants and referred to by the general population as tribes, such as Walker River Tribe of Paiute and Shoshone, Yomba Shoshone Tribe of Western Shoshone, and, in some instances, as politically merged entities, such as Shoshone Paiute Tribes of the Duck Valley Reservation, or Confederated Tribes of the Goshute Reservation. A few units use the designation band either because of long-standing convention or to denote the close cultural relations of cooperating groups—Moapa Band of Paiute Indians of the Moapa River Reservation, or Te-Moak Bands of Western Shoshone Indians.

The term nation also appears in public statements and documents with reference to more inclusive categories of peoples considered by tradition to be culturally homogenous (The Washoe Nation, The Shoshone Na-

tion). In the 1960s and 1970s regional organizations such as the Inter-Tribal Council of Nevada and the United Ute Tribe were formed to improve intergroup communication and more effective negotiation with state and federal agencies. On a much larger scale, many rural and urban Native Americans of the region increasingly perceive themselves as sharers in a common ethnic heritage embracing all Indian peoples of the United States and even of the hemisphere. Concepts of local and pan-Indian nationalism have emerged rapidly as the population experiences a dramatic recovery and as recognition of common social and economic problems impels the scattered and fragmented communities to joint defense of remaining lands, of a culture, and of promised opportunity.

It is unlikely that these trends will be altered substantially by the specialized concepts of social science, for the acculturative process of past centuries has left an indelible mark. Archeologists and ethnologists have been preoccupied largely with the reconstruction of past cultures and the study of aboriginal lifeways, an emphasis also reflected in the contents of this volume. But the discourse appropriate to the detailed description and analysis of early cultures (from data selected from the writings of countless investigators and the recorded recollections of their myriad human subjects) may be singularly inappropriate in the context of the changing structures and orientations of the new societies of living peoples in the late twentieth century. Thus for some who read the chapters in this volume, the formal language and distilled style of presentation may produce the effect of peering through the large end of a telescope: all that once was large as life seems reduced to distant miniature. Native American readers may find the compact summaries of what White scholars know of their forebears strangely at variance with their own intimate perceptions of on-going community experience or with the vivid quality of the heritage passed down to them by elder relatives and friends. Some essential aspect of reality will appear to be absent.

Similar obstacles to intercultural consensus are common in the colonial situation where one people have been the object of subjugation by another and, as part of the same process, become the passive subjects of study. For 500 years the original inhabitants of this continent and their descendants have been the observed. Though they were and are the ultimate source of all knowledge about themselves, it is the curious alien investigator who has dominated the disciplines of scholarship through which this vast store of information has been selectively analyzed and published. The time has come when many more from the ranks of the observed are joining the observers. As this occurs, the character of understanding and communication is undergoing transformation along with the image of "the Indian."

This volume is offered as a contribution to the anthropology and history of a region and to the Native American people of the Great Basin who will be reassessing and extending the record of their heritage into the future. It is hoped that there is much here that will be useful to the task envisioned by a young Northern Paiute who later became the chairman of the Walker River Tribal Council. In a publication of the National Indian Youth Council, Melvin Thom (1965; also in Forbes 1967:272–276) gave eloquent expression to a view shared by the contributors to this volume:

> As this Nation, having moved upon the full span of this continent and beyond, and having become the strongest and most wealthy of all nations on earth, stands upon the threshold of a new great society—the native people of this land are compelled to ask and evaluate, "Where has the course of human events brought us? What does the future hold for Indian America?" . . . What has become of the multitude of tribes and Indian people whose homes have been set upon this land, not a few centuries but since time immemorial? . . . Being the first people of this land, but the last citizens of this Nation, American Indians have a perspective of America and the United States that is exclusively ours . . . . We cannot change the past, but we must know the past in order to contemplate a better future. Although it may be said of the past century that American Indians have not been the beneficiary of this Nation's strengths, but the victim of its weaknesses—we can direct our energies to the task and challenge that this expression shall bear no truth in the future.

History of Research

DON D. FOWLER

Reports containing anthropological information on Great Basin native peoples and cultures began with the advent of Euro-American exploring parties into the region in 1776. The journal (Bolton 1950) kept by Fray Silvestre Vélez de Escalante during the traverse he and Fray Francisco Atanasio Domínguez and their party made in that year provides the first substantial ethnographic information on several Great Basin groups in present-day western Colorado, central and southern Utah, and northern Arizona. In the same year Fray Francisco T.H. Garcés followed a route parallel to the lower Colorado River, thence across the Mojave Desert to the southern California missions. His diary (Coues 1900) contains some data on Chemehuevi groups he encountered. Subsequent early information is contained in diaries and journals of early fur trappers and explorers between 1805 and 1850 and in reports of federally sponsored parties of exploration (Cline 1963).

Reports of federal expeditions are a particularly important source of ethnographic and archeological information beginning with the Meriwether Lewis and William Clark expedition of 1803–1805 and continuing through the "great surveys"—the four geographical and geological surveys of the 1870s (Bartlett 1962; Goetzmann 1966), led by F.V. Hayden, Clarence King, John Wesley Powell, and Lt. George Wheeler (Schmeckebier 1904). The Lewis and Clark expedition set a pattern for federal exploring parties and nineteenth-century American anthropology generally. The party carried detailed linguistic and ethnographic instructions (Jackson 1962:17–18) based on anthropological questions developed by an American Philosophical Society committee chaired by Thomas Jefferson (Jefferson et al. 1799) and on a 276-word vocabulary list developed and widely circulated by Jefferson (1792) to collect linguistic materials for a general genetic classification of American Indian languages. Lewis and Clark's *Instructions* in turn were the basis for ethnographic inquiries developed by another American Philosophical Society committee for the Stephen Long expedition of 1819 (Du Ponceau et al. 1819). Subsequent sets of inquiries—in effect ethnographic field manuals—were produced by Lewis Cass (1823), Henry Rowe Schoolcraft (1847), and Lewis Henry Morgan (1861). These were combined and refined by Powell (1877, 1880) into a linguistic field manual widely used by the Bureau of American Ethnology (Fowler 1975).

Lewis and Clark's only contact with Great Basin Indians was with bands of Northern Shoshone near the headwaters of the Missouri River. Their descriptions provided the first systematic ethnographic information on the Northern Shoshone (Biddle 1962:221–263).

After 1850 and the beginning of Euro-American settlement in the Great Basin, the number of federal and private expeditions grew, and increasing attention was paid to Indians and archeological sites. Excepting Lewis and Clark, the history of systematic anthropological reportage begins about 1850. The remainder of this essay presents a review of that history. It is based on Great Basin anthropological literature and on previous summaries of anthropological research (Baumhoff 1958; C.S. Fowler 1970, 1982a; Fowler 1980; Fowler and Jennings 1982; Rohn 1973; E.R. Smith 1950; O.C. Stewart 1982; Wallace 1978).

The Great Basin Culture Area

The Great Basin culture area as defined in this volume is much larger than the hydrographic region of interior drainage first clearly defined by the explorer John C. Frémont (1845). The culture area encompasses a variety of physiographic and ecological provinces (Fowler and Koch 1982; McKenzie 1982; Rowlands et al. 1982). Elements of prehistoric Great Basin cultures occur throughout the Basin and Range core area of the Great Basin. They appear as well on the Snake River plain and adjacent uplands in Idaho, in the Bridger Basin in Wyoming, on the Colorado Plateau in western Colorado, eastern Utah, and northern Arizona, and in the central Rocky Mountains. Carriers of historically known Great Basin cultures occupied all these regions and in the eighteenth and nineteenth centuries ranged far to the east of the Rockies on the northern Great Plains.

American anthropologists began formulating various culture area schemes for North America around 1900. The criteria used in these schemata varied, but they were usually defined in terms of the distribution of material culture traits and subsistence practices vis-à-vis ecological regions.

The first major culture area scheme was proposed by Mason (1896) who delineated 18 "environments" or "culture areas" (he used both terms interchangeably) within the western hemisphere. Mason (1896:650–651) included an Interior Basin area comprising "most of Colorado, Utah, Nevada, eastern Oregon, Idaho, and a corner of Wyoming" characterized by "partial deserts among mountains with rich and wooded patches," within which a variety of foraging-oriented subsistence patterns and associated material culture traits were found. Mason (1907:428) reiterated his classification, using the term "ethnic environments" rather than culture areas. Holmes (1914:414–415) incorporated the Great Basin into a larger Plains and Rocky Mountains "area of culture characterization" in a delineation of prehistoric regions of North America. Clark Wissler (1914:449, 466–467) divided the Great Basin between his California and Plains areas, principally on the basis of material culture distributions. By 1917 Wissler had shifted his criteria and defined 6 food areas and 10 culture areas. Under this scheme the Great Basin and California were subsumed within a "Wild Seed" food area (Wissler 1917:11–12). Alfred L. Kroeber (1920) on cultural grounds also grouped California and the Great Basin into one "area of general culture." Similarly, Robert H. Lowie (1923:156), on the basis of nonmaterial culture trait distributions, lumped California and the Great Basin into a "single basic ultramontane culture area or stratum, marked off from the rest of the continent."

The modern and still generally accepted definition of North American culture areas was formulated by Kroeber in his classic *Cultural and Natural Areas of Native North America,* completed by 1931, but not published until 1939. Kroeber (1939:49–53) defined the Great Basin areally and culturally essentially as it is defined in this volume. The exceptions are the "non-Shoshonean [non–Numic speaking] tribes of the Klamath Lakes and Pit River" (Kroeber 1939:53), who are included respectively, in the *Plateau* and *California* volumes of the *Handbook.* Kroeber clearly recognized that the Great Basin culture area extended beyond the limits of the physiographic and ecologic boundaries of the Basin but that the cultures of the peoples outside those bounds derived from the "cultural Basin area proper."

Kroeber's scheme was followed in the main by Park et al. (1938) and Murdock and O'Leary (1975). Driver and Massey (1957:173–174, 179, 209, map 2) propose an extensive Desert culture area (also called a Wild Plant and Small Game area) that includes the Great Basin proper, the central Rocky Mountains, west Texas, and northern Mexico east of the Sierra Madre Occidental. Their criteria are principally those of ecological and subsistence bases rather than cultural.

Culture area schemes reflected several assumptions current in American anthropology between 1900 and 1940, particularly museum-based anthropology. These assumptions articulated what is often called the "American historical school," or the "historical particularist school" (Willey and Sabloff 1980:83–129). A major assumption was that cultures are made up of disparate, atomistic "traits." A trait might be a particular style of basketry; or the construction techniques or design elements on a basket might each constitute a separate trait. A trait might also be the bow and arrow or, again, particular bow forms; styles of arrowheads or the methods of fletching or nocking an arrow might each be regarded as a trait. In the nonmaterial realm a trait might be a particular form or system of kinship nomenclature or a "motif" or element within a folk tale or a legend. Behind the assumption of cultural traits lay two further assumptions. One was that cultural phenomena are patterned, that is, they occur in set ways, for example, a particular "type" of corner-notched arrowheads or a specific set of kin terms to designate relatives standing in specific genealogical relationships to a speaker. The second assumption was that a specific culture, for example, Western Shoshone culture, was comprised of an agglomeration of patterned "traits." Some traits were thought to be indigenously developed; others, to have been developed elsewhere and "diffused" to the Shoshone who then adopted them.

Given the foregoing assumptions, the task of the anthropologist or the archeologist was to trace the distributions of cultures and particularly of culture elements in space and time.

The history of a trait or a "trait complex" was thought to be known if its spatial and temporal distributions were known. Ethnologists and archeologists mapped the distributions of traits and complexes and observed that there was a general correlation between the occurrences of trait complexes and specific ecological areas. Lines were drawn and "culture areas" delineated. Since the cultural and ecological criteria varied among different students, the boundaries of culture areas varied.

Two other assumptions were made. One was that, in lieu of any certain means of establishing absolute chronologies, the wider the spatial distribution, the relatively older a trait or trait complex was considered. This is the so-called age-area hypothesis most clearly formulated by Wissler (1923). The second assumption, derived principally from linguistics, was that traits tended to diffuse from centers of invention toward peripheral areas, the center being the point of highest elaboration or complexity. Between 1900 and 1940 all these assumptions underlay and structured most of the ethnographic and archeological research programs and interpretations of prehistoric and historic Great Basin cultures, as they did elsewhere in North America.

Archeology

Reports of parties of exploration in the Great Basin between 1850 and 1880 contain scattered references to archeological remains, including village sites, petrographs, aboriginal salt mines, and artifact surface scatters (Bancroft 1875–1876,4:713–715; Beckwith 1855: 63; Carvalho 1858:207; Remy and Brenchley 1861,1:364–365; Stansbury 1852:182). In 1872 members of the U.S. Geographical Survey West of the 100th Meridian excavated "mounds" (apparently of the Sevier Fremont culture) near Provo, Utah, and described similar mounds near Beaver and Paragonah, Utah (Severance 1874; Severance and Yarrow 1879). In 1875, Edward Palmer, a collector employed jointly by the Smithsonian Institution and the Harvard University Peabody Museum, excavated Virgin branch Anasazi sites near Kanab and Santa Clara, Utah (Palmer 1876, 1878a). Pottery vessels from the Santa Clara sites were exhibited at the 1876 Philadelphia Centennial Exposition and partially described and illustrated by Holmes (1886:278–288); the entire remaining collection in the Smithsonian Institution is described by Fowler and Matley (1978). The site Palmer excavated near Kanab was in Johnson Canyon, probably the Bonanza Dune site (Aikens 1965:9–40). In 1876 Palmer excavated in Sevier Fremont culture "mounds" near Payson and Paragonah, Utah, and later at a variety of Virgin branch sites in Washington and Kane counties, Utah. Collections from these sites were deposited in the Peabody Museum (Putnam 1878:213). While at Payson, Palmer (1878b) was constrained to refute reports (Parry 1877a:28–29) that a nearby mound had yielded a six-foot, seven-inch skeleton holding a "hugh iron or steel weapon" and lying near a sealed stone box of "light, mouldy wheat" that, when planted, grew. Parry (1877:82) too, noted that the report was fraudulent.

Henry Montgomery (1894), a University of Utah biologist, excavated various "mounds" in central and western Utah in the late 1880s and early 1890s. His report summarizes Utah archeology as he interpreted it and relates the sites to a vague "Mexican Empire."

Byron Cummings, an assistant professor of Latin and Greek at the University of Utah, became fascinated with the archeology of the Four Corners and led numerous expeditions there between 1895 and 1914 (Cummings 1910, 1915). While his researches were not directly related to the Great Basin, he did found a Department of Archaeology at Utah (E.R. Smith 1950). In 1914 Cummings moved to the University of Arizona where he played a central role in the encouragement of research in Southwestern archeology.

In 1915, Neil M. Judd, a former student of Cummings, joined the staff of the U.S. National Museum of the Smithsonian Institution. Judd (1916, 1917a, 1919, 1926) initiated the first systematic archeological program in the Great Basin between 1915 and 1920. He recorded and excavated Sevier Fremont sites along the Wasatch Front, Fremont sites in eastern Utah, and Anasazi sites in southern Utah and northern Arizona.

In 1930 Julian H. Steward was hired by the University of Utah to develop an archeological research program in the state (Manners 1973:889; Murphy 1981:172; E.R. Smith 1950:23). Steward conducted several surveys including portions of southern Utah and in Glen Canyon (Steward 1941a) and carried out important excavations in several cave sites around the periphery of the Great Salt Lake (Steward 1937a). In 1933 Steward left Utah and returned to ethnographic research under the auspices of the University of California, Berkeley. In 1935 he joined the Bureau of American Ethnology of the Smithsonian Institution. His ethnographic studies were very influential.

Steward was succeeded at Utah from 1935 to 1937 by John P. Gillin, who excavated a number of Sevier Fremont sites (Gillin 1938, 1941). Between 1934 and 1941 Carling Malouf, Elmer R. Smith, and Charles E. Dibble, students and faculty members at Utah, conducted archeological research in southern Utah (E.R. Smith 1934), in the Deep Creek region along the Utah-Nevada border (Malouf 1940a, 1944), and in caves near the Great Salt Lake (E.R. Smith 1941). Other archeological work in Utah in the 1930s included numerous surveys made by Albert B. Reagan, an Indian Field Service employee in the Uintah Basin. Reagan authored over 50 short papers on the archeology of eastern Utah (for example, Reagan 1931, 1934, 1935) as well as on various Indian groups.

In 1948 the University of Utah established a separate anthropology department chaired by E. Adamson Hoebel. Jesse D. Jennings was hired, took charge of the nascent Museum of Anthropology, and established a statewide archeological survey (Gunnerson 1959) and a long-range program of archeological research (see Aikens 1970; Dalley 1976; Gunnerson 1957, 1960; Jennings 1957, 1966, 1978; Jennings, Schroedl, and Holmer 1980; Marwitt 1970; Taylor 1954). In 1973 the Antiquities Section of the Utah Historical Society, Salt Lake City, was established. The section initiated a second program of archeological survey and research throughout the state (Madsen and Lindsay 1977). An archeological research program also was established by Brigham Young University, Provo, Utah, in the early 1960s (Nielson 1978).

Archeological research in Nevada began in 1912 with the work of L.L. Loud (a guard at the University of California Museum of Anthropology), who salvaged artifacts uncovered by guano miners in Lovelock Cave near Lovelock, Nevada (Heizer 1970). In 1924 Mark R. Harrington (fig. 1) of the Heye Foundation conducted further excavations in Lovelock Cave (Loud and Harrington 1929) including the recovery of the famous duck decoys made of tule stalks ("Prehistory of the Western Area," fig. 11, this vol.). In 1925 Harrington, cosponsored by the Heye Foundation and the state of Nevada, began excavations at the Virgin branch Anasazi complex of Lost City in southern Nevada (Simpson 1965:10; Shutler 1961). Work continued there in

17

Southwest Mus., Los Angeles: 24,076.
Fig. 1. M.R. Harrington at the entrance to Gypsum Cave, near Las Vegas, Nev. Photographed 1930–1931.

subsequent years, as well as at Mesa House and Paiute Cave (Harrington, Hayden, and Schellbach 1930). In 1928 Harrington became affiliated with the Southwest Museum, Los Angeles, California. Through 1933–1935 Harrington was again at Lost City conducting archeological salvage operations of sites to be inundated by Lake Mead behind Hoover (then Boulder) Dam. In 1930–1931 Harrington (1933) excavated Gypsum Cave near Las Vegas, Nevada. He reported finding artifacts in association with, and under the dung of, an extinct Pleistocene ground sloth *Nothrotherium* sp. (now *Nothrotheriops*). He posited great antiquity for the "Gypsum culture" and was widely cited (for example, Roberts 1943). The association has subsequently been disproved (Heizer and Berger 1970). Harrington and his associate, Sessions M. Wheeler, conducted surveys and excavations in Meadow Valley Wash and Snake Valley, particularly at Etna Cave and Smith Creek Cave. In the latter, Harrington (1934a, 1936) reported an association of artifacts and Pleistocene horse bones; in the former, Wheeler (1942) reported an association of a "Yuma" projectile point and "Pleistocene age" horse dung. Both associations have since been disproved (Fowler 1973; Tuohy and Rendell 1980:195). Etna Cave did yield a number of the enigmatic split-twig figurines found in archaic levels in widely scattered sites in the Grand Canyon, southeastern California, southern Nevada, and central and eastern Utah (Euler and Olson 1965; Fowler 1973; Davis and Smith 1981; Schroedl 1977).

In 1933 an unworked obsidian flake was found in apparent association with Pleistocene faunal remains at Tule Springs, Nevada (G.G. Simpson 1933). Harrington's excavations there in 1934 and 1955-1956 seemingly demonstrated artifacts in association with Pleistocene fauna dated at more than 26,000 years B.C. (Harrington 1934; Harrington and Simpson 1961:75–76; Simpson 1965:17–18, 20). A large-scale excavation of the site in 1962–1963, directed by Richard Shutler, Jr., failed to

verify the early dates or to demonstrate clear association of artifacts and Pleistocene fauna (Wormington and Ellis 1967). The project did develop considerable data on southern Great Basin late Pleistocene and Holocene paleoenvironments. Harrington also directed excavations at various early Holocene pluvial lake sites in the Mojave Desert, California (Harrington 1948, 1957; Campbell et al. 1937).

In the mid-1930s Robert F. Heizer initiated archeological research at several rockshelter sites in the Humboldt Sink area of Nevada (Heizer 1951; Heizer and Krieger 1956; M. Heizer 1979). In 1948 Heizer (1949) established the University of California Archaeological Survey at Berkeley. He and his students conducted surveys and excavated several important sites throughout Nevada, including Wagon Jack Shelter (Heizer and Baumhoff 1961), Eastgate Shelter (Elsasser and Prince 1961), Lovelock Cave (fig. 2) (Grosscup 1960; Heizer and Napton 1970), Southfork Shelter (Heizer, Baumhoff, and Clewlow 1968), various sites in southeastern Nevada (Busby 1979), Surprise Valley, California (O'Connell 1975), and Lassen and Inyo counties, California (Riddell 1956, 1960).

In 1939 Sessions M. Wheeler was hired as an archeologist by the Nevada Parks Commission and in 1941 was appointed curator of the Nevada State Museum, Carson City. Wheeler conducted some survey and excavations during his tenure (Wheeler and Wheeler 1944). In 1958 Richard Shutler, Jr., reinstituted archeological research at the Nevada State Museum, a program subsequently carried on under the direction of Donald R. Tuohy. Research was undertaken at various cave sites (Shutler, Shutler, and Griffith 1960; Shutler and Shutler 1963; Tuohy and Rendell 1980; Tuohy 1984a; Hattori 1982) and at Tule Springs (Wormington and Ellis 1967). In 1964–1966 programs of archeological survey and excavation were established by the Reno and Las Vegas campuses and the Desert Research Institute of the University of Nevada (for example, Brooks 1976; Elston 1982; Fowler, Madsen, and Hattori 1973; Lyneis 1982; Pippin, Davis, and Budy 1979; Warren 1980).

Beginning in the early 1960s a number of archeologists with institutional affiliations outside Nevada initiated long-range programs in the central and western regions of the Great Basin. These included David Hurst Thomas, American Museum of Natural History, New York, who worked extensively in central Nevada (Thomas 1972, 1973, 1983, 1982a; Thomas and Bettinger 1976); Robert L. Bettinger, University of California, Davis, who worked in Owens Valley, eastern California (Bettinger 1976, 1977a, 1977, 1979); and Thomas N. Layton, San Jose State University, who worked in northwestern Nevada (Layton 1970, 1979; Layton and Thomas 1979). Others included William C. Clewlow, Jr., University of California, Los Angeles, and his associates who carried out an intensive program of pre-

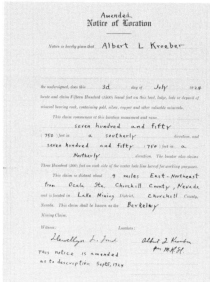

right, Mus. of the Amer. Ind., Heye Foundation, New York: P–21014–B.

Fig. 2. left, Robert Heizer with crew at Lovelock Cave, Churchill Co., Nevada. The cave was occupied from about 2500 B.C. to A.D. 1835. left to right: Albert Elsasser, David Clement, Heizer, Gary Encinas, Monica Ley, Suzanne DeAtley, Ethel Chang, Jennifer Scharetg, Mark Estis. Photograph by F.H. Stross, spring 1969. right, Mining claim for Lovelock Cave made out to Albert (sic) L. Kroeber by M.R. Harrington, archeologist in charge, Sept. 1924.

historic and historic archeology in Grass Valley, north of Austin, Nevada, in the early 1970s (Clewlow and Rusco 1972; Clewlow, Wells, and Ambro 1978); Emma Lou Davis, Great Basin Foundation, who began research in eastern and southeastern California in the early 1960s (Davis 1963, 1978); William W. Wallace (1962, 1978), also in southeastern California; and Alan Bryan and Ruth Gruhn, University of Alberta, who conducted excavations in the early 1970s in Smith Creek Canyon, eastern Nevada, in cooperation with the Nevada State Museum (Tuohy and Rendell 1980).

In southern Idaho archeological research began with a survey along the Snake River by Louis Schellbach (1930, 1967) of the Heye Foundation in 1929. In the late 1930s a museum was established at what became Idaho State University, Pocatello, and sporadic collections and excavations were undertaken (Gruhn 1961a; Swanson and Sneed 1971). Earl H. Swanson, Jr. (fig. 3), who became Museum Director in 1957, established a major research program in the Upper Snake River region (Butler 1978; Gruhn 1961; Swanson 1972). Other institutions conducting archeological research in Great Basin areas of Idaho include Boise State University (Pavesic, Plew, and Sprague 1979).

Archeological research in the Great Basin portion of Oregon began in 1932, when Luther S. Cressman (fig. 4), of the University of Oregon, initiated a survey of rock art (Cressman 1937). He and his students excavated a number of rockshelter sites, particularly in the Fort Rock Basin (Cressman 1936, 1943, 1956, 1977; Cressman et al. 1942; Bedwell 1973; see also Fagan 1974). In 1968 C. Melvin Aikens, University of Oregon,

began a variety of research projects in eastern Oregon, most notably the excavation of Dirty Shame Rockshelter (Aikens, Cole, and Stuckenrath 1977; Hanes 1977) and the Steens Mountain prehistory project (Aikens, Grayson, and Mehringer 1980). Other im-

Idaho State U. News Bureau, Pocatello.

Fig. 3. Earl H. Swanson, Jr. (left) and B. Robert Butler examining finds at Bison Rockshelter (site 10–CL–10), in Birch Creek Valley, Clark Co., Idaho. The shelter contains remains indicating continuous occupation for over 8,000 years. Photograph by Lloyd Furniss, July 1960.

portant archeological research in eastern Oregon includes that of Weide (1968, 1975) in Warner Valley.

In 1953 Jesse D. Jennings (fig. 5) and others established an annual Great Basin Archeological Conference to discuss archeological research in the region. Subsequently, the conference was broadened to the Great Basin Anthropological Conference, meeting biennially. From its inception the Conference provided a major forum for summarizing and assessing the state of the art in Great Basin research (d'Azevedo et al. 1966; Swanson 1968; Fowler 1972, 1977; Madsen and O'-Connell 1982).

In addition to the archeological researches discussed above, since about 1960 there have been numerous studies carried out under contracts as required by federal antiquities legislation.

Conceptual Frameworks

For many years Great Basin prehistoric cultures were regarded as peripheral to those in adjacent areas. Such "second class" status grew out of the assumptions of the early twentieth century museum-based American historicalist school. Given those assumptions, and in lieu of any certain means for establishing absolute chronologies, the Great Basin was viewed as peripheral to both the Southwest and California. In both those areas more elaborate (and therefore presumably earlier) trait complexes were found than in the Great Basin.

The theory of the Great Basin's status as peripheral to the Anasazi region of the Southwest was most cogently advanced by A.V. Kidder (1924:78–82) who des-

ignated all of Utah north and west of the San Juan River drainage as a "Northern Peripheral District" on the grounds that Puebloan house types, ceramics, and other classes of artifacts found therein were less elaborate than those in the Anasazi heartland.

A second related constraint to understanding Great Basin prehistory for nearly three decades was the Pecos classification, the well-known eight sequential states or periods, Basketmaker I–III, Pueblo I–V. As dendrochronology was, in 1927, not yet viable, the periods or stages (except the historic period Pueblo V) were of unknown duration. Basketmaker I was defined as "a postulated . . . stage, pre-agricultural, yet adumbrating later developments;" Basketmaker II as "the agricultural, atlatl-using, non-pottery-making state" (Kidder 1927:490). Since there were trait similarities between Great Basin and Southwest basketry, it was implicitly assumed that non-pottery-bearing sites or strata in the Great Basin in which Southwestern-like basketry occurred were coeval with Basketmaker sites in the Anasazi core region. After the development of dendrochronology and the dating of many Basketmaker II sites in the Southwest, the assumption of equivalent age between Anasazi Basketmaker and various Great Basin sites was continued.

These assumptions led Steward (1940) into a labyrinthine explanation of Great Basin prehistory. Arti-

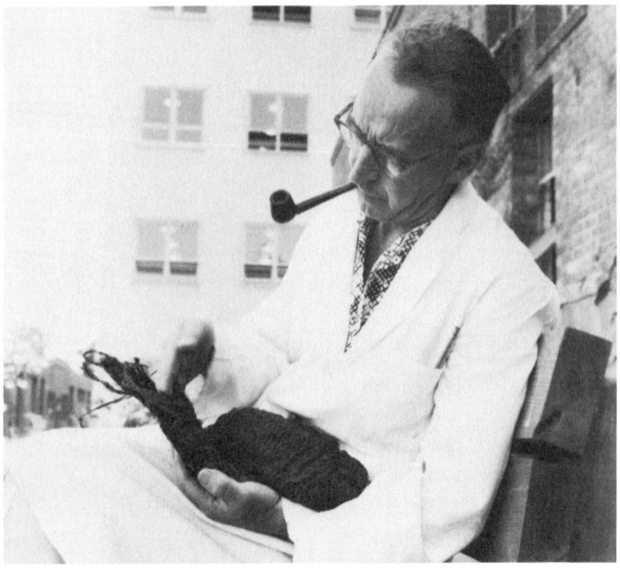

©Natl. Geographic Soc., Washington.

Fig. 4. Luther S. Cressman examining a prehistoric sandal of sagebrush bark, found in Ft. Rock Cave, Oreg., probably in 1937. Photograph by Paul Snides, early 1950s.

U. of Utah, Archeol. Center, Salt Lake City.

Fig. 5. Jesse D. Jennings at Hogup Cave, Utah. Photographed about 1967–1968.

20

facts, especially textiles, from several cave sites were thought to be Basketmaker II. Moreover, Basketmaker II in the Anasazi region was dated after A.D.1 (the dendrochronology record had been extended back to A.D.11; Judd 1940:419). Consequently Steward (1940:465–466) managed to explain away any great antiquity for the caves around the Great Salt Lake, those in Oregon (excavated by Cressman), and at Lovelock Cave, Nevada. He did, however, admit great antiquity for Gypsum Cave and the Lake Mojave complexes (Steward 1940:457). The assumptions of the age-area hypothesis seemingly ruled out an antiquity of more than 2,000 years for most Great Basin sites (see Roberts 1940:94–95 for a similar conclusion). This conclusion was held by many until the advent of radiometric dating radically changed interpretations.

Pre-Archaic Cultures

The existence of Pre-Archaic (Paleo-Indian, about 11,000 to 7,000 B.C.) traditions and possible "pre–projectile point" (before 11,000 B.C.) traditions has been demonstrated in several areas of the North American continent. In the Great Basin the existence of such traditions is enigmatic (Aikens 1978a:147, 1978:74–76; Tuohy 1974; Watters 1979). In the China Lake area of the Mojave Desert, remains of numerous fossils of late Pleistocene megafauna are found as surface deposits, as are a variety of lithic assemblages (Davis 1978). However, because the deposits are surface occurrences only, it cannot be judged whether the fauna and at least some of the lithic artifacts were contemporaneous. There are widely scattered surface finds of Clovis projectile points and other apparently early lithic assemblages, especially on fossil Pleistocene beach terraces throughout the Great Basin, but they cannot be dated except by analogy with typologically similar artifacts from adjacent culture areas.

The Desert Culture Concept

The advent of radiometric dating in the early 1950s had a revolutionary impact on archeology (Willey and Sabloff 1980:155–156). Cressman (1936, 1943; Cressman et al. 1942) had posited considerable antiquity for the caves he had excavated in the 1930s in Oregon, but his interpretations were widely discounted (Roberts 1940:94–95; Steward 1940:465–466). But carbon-14 dates of 8,000 B.C. or more from the lower levels of Danger Cave, Utah (fig. 6) (Jennings 1957:93), Fort Rock Cave, and other Oregon sites (Cressman 1951) clearly vitiated the notion that nonceramic Great Basin cultures were derivative from, or coterminous with, early Anasazi cultures. Rather, Jennings (1953, 1957; Jennings and Norbeck 1955) posited a much older tradition, beginning in Early Holocene times, and extending over nearly

U. of Utah, Archeol. Center, Salt Lake City: 42T013–138.

Fig. 6. Excavation at Danger Cave, Utah, with Jesse D. Jennings standing at right. Radiocarbon specimens from deposits here demonstrated an occupation of the Great Basin for 10 millennia—far longer than previously believed. Photograph by Sara Sue Price Rudy, 1951.

all the North American desert West. This tradition, initially called the Desert culture, was seen as an antecedent to, and forming a substratum of, Anasazi and other Puebloan cultures in the Southwest (Jennings 1957:280). The possibility of such an early, underlying culture had long been discussed (for example, Krieger 1928; Zingg 1939; Steward 1937a; Heizer and Krieger 1956), but it was not until radiometric dating demonstrated a 10 millennia time-depth that Jennings could articulate the Desert culture concept.

The Desert culture, later the Desert Archaic (Jennings 1964), provided a useful heuristic focal point for two decades of archeological research and discussion in the Great Basin (Jennings 1973; cf. Warren and Ranere 1968; Warren 1967; Swanson 1962). The Desert culture concept was explicitly based on analogy derived from Steward's (1938) ethnographic-ethnohistoric synthesis of data on central Great Basin Numic groups (C.S. Fowler 1977, 1982). Steward demonstrated an ethnographic pattern of low population density, kin-based band structure, and a simple but efficient technology supporting a hunting and gathering lifeway based on an annual cycle of exploitation of plant and animal resources. The archeological evidence, particularly from Danger Cave, indicated to Jennings (1957) that essentially the same lifeway had continued for 10 millennia, until historic times in some parts of the Great Basin, but had developed variant patterns in other parts. Ultimately, Jennings (1974:154–170) posited a Western Archaic culture—a regional variant of a continent-wide culture stage based on a hunting and gathering subsistence economy closely adapted to local resources.

The Fremont Concept

The "Northern Periphery" area included most of Utah, including the Fremont (Morss 1931) and Sevier Fremont (Judd 1919, 1926) archeological sites. Steward (1933, 1936) distinguished four vaguely defined subareas, including a "Western Periphery" area centering on southwest Utah tributaries of the Colorado River. Gladwin and Gladwin (1934) separated the Kayenta and Nevada branches of the San Juan Anasazi "stem," the Nevada branch being subdivided into Moapa and Parowan phases. Colton (1942) renamed the Nevada branch the Virgin branch, geographically equivalent to Steward's Western Periphery.

After 1950 as more sites were located and excavated, nomenclature problems continued. It was recognized (Wormington 1955, 1956:72–73) that the Virgin branch should be separated from the rest of the Northern Periphery Fremont. Jennings et al. (1956) designated the area east of the Wasatch Mountains as Fremont, the area to the west as Sevier Fremont, a usage followed by Taylor (1957) and Gunnerson (1969), and the Northern Periphery designation was abandoned (Jennings and Norbeck 1955:8; Ambler 1966:170; Aikens 1972:64). This cleared the way to study the cultures on their own terms and not simply as diluted or peripheral Anasazi cultures (Judd 1940:426–429); however, problems of chronology and areal extent continue (Berry 1980; Madsen 1979, 1980).

Genetic Models

The use of genetic models, or attempts to relate prehistoric peoples, languages, and cultures to one another and to historic ethnic groups, has a long history in Great Basin research. Lowie (1923) made the first modern attempt, followed by Krieger's (1928) speculations. The first comprehensive model was advanced by Robert Zingg (1939), who attempted to relate various archeological complexes to different Uto-Aztecan languages in western North America and Mexico. D.B. Shimkin (1940) focused more narrowly on Shoshone and Comanche origins and relationships within the Great Basin. Subsequent models on the scale of Zingg's included Romney (1957), W.W. Taylor (1961), and Hopkins (1965).

Genetic models relating specifically to the Great Basin have centered principally on the Sevier Fremont and Fremont cultures, their carriers, and relationships with antecedent and subsequent cultures and their carriers. Sevier Fremont and Fremont cultures appear some time after A.D. 500 and disappear by about A.D. 1200. Areas occupied by carriers of these cultures were occupied by historic Numic peoples. Archeological cultures related to Numic peoples are found mixed with Sevier Fremont cultural materials by A.D. 1000 and supersede them after A.D. 1400 (Fowler, Madsen, and Hattori 1973).

On linguistic grounds Lamb (1958) advanced the "Numic spread" hypothesis—that around A.D. 1000 Numic-speaking peoples began a rapid expansion across the Great Basin from somewhere in southeastern California. Lamb's hypothesis and elements of the larger-scale genetic models noted above have been examined on ethnobiological grounds by C.S. Fowler (1972a, 1972).

Various hypotheses have been advanced to account for the advent and disappearance of Sevier Fremont and Fremont peoples and cultures and their relationships with Numic peoples and cultures (Aikens 1966, 1967, 1972; Gunnerson 1960; Rudy 1953; Steward 1933a; Taylor 1957; Wormington 1955; Madsen 1979, 1980). Although a date of A.D. 1000 for the advent of the "Numic spread" may be too late, it is fairly clear that in late prehistoric times Numic-speaking peoples did spread rapidly across the Great Basin from southwest to northeast, either displacing or replacing Sevier Fremont and Fremont peoples. By A.D. 1500 some of the Central Numic groups began to turn south from Wyoming along the Rocky Mountains to emerge as the historic Plains Comanche; others remained on the northwestern Plains—the "Snakes" reported by explorers in the late eighteenth and early nineteenth centuries (Wright 1978). The fate of the Sevier Fremont and Fremont people remains uncertain.

Ethnography

The first written descriptions of Great Basin Indians were made in 1776 by Garcés (Coues 1900) in the lower Colorado River and Mojave Desert areas and by Domínguez and Escalante in Colorado, Utah, and northern Arizona. Garcés encountered a group of Chemehuevi and briefly described them, their clothing, and their weapons. Escalante's journal contains several passages describing Numic groups encountered by the party (Bolton 1950). Ute bands were met in western Colorado and the Uintah Basin, Timpanogots Utes near Utah Lake, Pahvant Utes south of Utah Lake, and various groups of Southern Paiute near present-day Cedar City, Utah, along the Virgin River, and in northern Arizona. These brief descriptions provide an ethnohistoric baseline for the several groups.

Lewis and Clark's descriptions of Northern Shoshone in 1805 (Biddle 1962:221–263) provide initial information on that group. Lewis and Clark provided detailed accounts of subsistence, dress, and territorial and political organization, but little information on social organization or religion (Ray and Lurie 1954). Lewis and Clark also collected numerous vocabularies from the Northern Shoshone and other tribes encountered on the expedition; there are conflicting accounts of what happened to these materials, which have dissapeared (Gallatin 1836:134; Jackson 1978, 2:465, 611, 636).

The vast potpourri of information on North American Indians collected through questionnaires between 1847 and 1849 by Henry Rowe Schoolcraft (1851–1857) includes scattered materials on Great Basin Indians, principally the Eastern Shoshone. Schoolcraft did confirm the close linguistic connection between Shoshone and Comanche. He also provided a general synthetic sketch of both horse-using and non–horse-using Shoshone, but his sources could not provide any real detail on either Southern Paiute or Northern Paiute, and very little on the Ute.

The several federally sponsored exploring expeditions and wagon road and railroad surveys that passed through the Great Basin after 1850 produced varying amounts of ethnographic and linguistic data. For example, Stansbury's (1852) report contains only scattered information, but the Gunnison-Beckwith report (Beckwith 1855) and Macomb's (1876) report of his 1859 survey all contain substantial amounts of ethnographic data. Some information on the Chemehuevi along the lower Colorado River was reported by Ives (1861). Additional ethnographic materials are contained in the annual reports and unpublished correspondence of the commissioner of Indian affairs and the Indian agents stationed at Great Basin reservations and colonies between the 1850s and 1900 (see C.S. Fowler 1970:293–359 for relevant bibliography).

The first person to devote extended periods of time to the study of Great Basin ethnography and linguistics was John Wesley Powell (figs. 7–8). Between 1868 and 1880, Powell collected substantial amounts of data on subsistence, technology, social organization, mythology, religion, and linguistics, with the aim of producing a general ethnography of Numic-speaking peoples (Fowler and Fowler 1969). He did not complete the project, and his extensive manuscript and material culture collections were not published until a century later (Fowler and Fowler 1971; Fowler and Matley 1979). Powell, with George W. Ingalls, did produce the first baseline survey of Great Basin Indian demography and political organization (Powell and Ingalls in ARCIA 1874; reprinted in Fowler and Fowler 1971:97–119).

Between 1866 and 1877, Edward Palmer collected miscellaneous ethnographic data on the Northern Ute and Southern Paiute in the course of his archeological and botanical collecting expeditions in southern and central Utah (Palmer 1876, 1878a; Bye 1972; Heizer 1954, 1962; Fowler and Matley 1978; McVaugh 1956). In 1875 Stephen Powers collected ethnographic and linguistic data on the Washoe and Northern Paiute in western Nevada during an expedition to gather Indian materials for the 1876 Centennial Exposition in Philadelphia (Powers 1877; Fowler and Fowler 1970; Park 1975). Also in the 1870s, members of the geological survey under F.V. Hayden made ethnographic observations on Great Basin peoples (for example, Barber 1876, 1877; Hoffman 1876, 1878; Loew 1876). The historian Hubert Howe Bancroft (1875–1876) compiled a variety

Smithsonian, NAA: 1621.
Fig. 7. John Wesley Powell and Jacob Hamblin meeting with Kaibab Southern Paiutes near Kanab, Utah. Hamblin accompanied Powell between 1870–1873, on the advice of Brigham Young, as guide and go-between with the Indians in southern Utah and northern Ariz. Photograph by John K. Hillers, Oct. 1872.

Smithsonian, NAA: 1540.

Fig. 8. John Wesley Powell "artfully" posed examining a mirror case with a Ute woman named Yan-mo, or Tau-ruv, from the Uintah Valley, Utah. Photograph by John K. Hillers, 1874.

of miscellaneous ethnographic and linguistic data, much of it inaccurate, on Great Basin Indians. A further, albeit somewhat romanticized, contribution to Northern Paiute ethnography was made by Sarah Winnemucca Hopkins (1883), the daughter of Winnemucca, the famed Northern Paiute leader.

An interesting indicator of changes in knowledge about Great Basin Indians throughout the nineteenth century is contained in the introduction to the compilation of information on "Indians Taxed and Not Taxed" undertaken by the 1890 census (U.S. Census Office. 11th Census 1894:1–45). The introduction reviews compilations of Indian tribal names and population estimates in the United States from the 1787 figures of Thomas Jefferson's (1964) *Notes on the State of Virginia* through the 1890 census. The volume (U.S. Census Office. 11th Census 1894:224–241, 381–395, 559–571, 595–601, 627–634) also contains data of variable accuracy on aboriginal cultures, reservation conditions, and the impacts of federal Indian policy on specific Great Basin groups. These data were collected by Indian agents and Census Office personnel.

In January 1892 James Mooney (1896), the Bureau of American Ethnology ethnographer, briefly visited Wovoka (Jack Wilson) (fig. 9), the Northern Paiute prophet of the 1890 Ghost Dance. Other ethnographic research included the botanist F.V. Coville's (1892) sketch of the Panamint Shoshone.

By 1900 anthropology was becoming an established university discipline. In that year, Alfred L. Kroeber, the first recipient of a doctoral degree in anthropology from Columbia University, did some brief ethnographic fieldwork among the Northern Ute (Kroeber 1901, 1908). In 1910 Kroeber joined the newly founded Department and Museum of Anthropology at the University of California, Berkeley. Between 1902 and 1917 as Kroeber compiled data for his massive *Handbook of the Indians of California* (Kroeber 1925) he visited groups within the western Great Basin culture area, especially the Washoe, Northern Paiute bands, and Kawaiisu (Kroeber 1907, 1917).

left, Smithsonian, NAA: 1659–a; right, Nev. State Mus., Carson City.

Fig. 9. left, seated, Jack Wilson, the Ghost Dance prophet, also known as Wovoka; standing, unidentified man, possibly Charley Sheep, Wilson's uncle, who guided the anthropologist James Mooney to Mason Valley where Wilson lived. The eagle feather at his right elbow and the wide brim hat in his hand were important parts of Wilson's spiritual paraphernalia (Mooney 1896:767–775). Photograph by James Mooney, Jan. 1892. right, Remains of Wilson's house, Mason Valley. Photograph by Robert H. Lowie, about 1912.

Another Columbia University student, Robert H. Lowie, on his first ethnographic field trip in 1906, briefly studied the Lemhi Northern Shoshone of Idaho (Lowie 1909). In later years Lowie "paid scouting visits to a good many Shoshonean [Numic] groups in Idaho, Wyoming, Utah and Nevada" (Lowie 1959:76, 1924, 1924a) collecting data incorporated into several major analytic studies, for example, Lowie (1919). In 1926 he worked for some weeks with the Washoe (Lowie 1939, 1963).

Other ethnographic work conducted in the first decade of the twentieth century includes that of biologist Ralph V. Chamberlin (1908, 1909, 1911, 1913), who collected materials on Ute and Gosiute ethnobiological nomenclature and toponyms. Edward S. Curtis (1907–1930,15) worked among the Northern Paiute and Washoe. C. Hart Merriam (fig. 10) conducted ethnographic, linguistic, and ethnobotanical research among several Great Basin groups sporadically between 1902 and 1936 (Merriam 1903–1935, 1955, 1966, 1979) but did not synthesize his materials.

The second decade saw only the work of Frances Densmore (1922) on Northern Ute music in 1914 and 1916, and that of Samuel Barrett (1917) among the Washoe and Pyramid Lake and Walker Lake Northern Paiute in 1915 (Fowler and Fowler 1981:187–193) during an expedition to collect museum specimens.

Grace Dangberg (1922, 1927) collected text materials on the Washoe. Scattered and brief ethnographic and ethnohistoric studies of various Ute and Gosiute groups were made between 1917 and 1935 by Albert B. Reagan (1917, 1937). A brief ethnographic and linguistic study of the Surprise Valley Northern Paiute was conducted in 1926 by Angulo and Freeland (1929).

In 1927 Julian H. Steward (fig. 11) initiated studies of various Great Basin groups with the Owens Valley Paiute (Steward 1933b, 1936b). In 1929, Isabel T. Kelly spent three months with the Surprise Valley Northern Paiute (Kelly 1932a, 1932, 1938). She worked a total of 11 months with several Southern Paiute groups in 1932–1934 (Kelly 1939, 1964).

The 1930s was a most active period for Great Basin ethnographic research. Stimulus was provided in part by the University of California Culture Element Distribution Survey of Western American Indian groups directed by Kroeber (1935). The thrust of the Survey was two-pronged. One was an attempt to fill in the ethnographic record, especially in California. The second was by means of long trait lists to determine the presence or absence of each trait for each band or tribe. Given the assumptions of the historical method about culture as an agglomeration of traits, it was thought that such data could be statistically manipulated. Such a "scientific" approach might elucidate aboriginal "internal history" (Kroeber 1935), that is, it was seen as a device to determine culture relationships, hence, "his-

U. of Calif. Berkeley, Bancroft Lib., C.H. Merriman Coll.:1978.8–X/23a/P4 no. 2.
Fig. 10. Dave Mauwee, Northern Paiute from Pyramid Lake, Nev., with C. Hart Merriam. Mauwee also worked with the anthropologists Omer C. Stewart (in 1941) and Willard Z. Park (in 1933–1940). Photographed in Sept. 1938.

U. of Ill., Urbana.
Fig. 11. Julian H. Steward at work. Photographed 1949–1952.

25

torical" connections between and among tribes. Some 279 filled-in lists from 254 western tribes or groups were collected (vol. 8:10), including several dozen from Great Basin groups. Perhaps more important than the lists were the extensive annotations published with them. For some Great Basin groups these lists provide the only ethnographic data of the time.

Surveys of Great Basin groups were conducted principally by Julian Steward (1937, 1941, 1943a) during a six-month field season in 1935, and four months in 1936, and by Omer Stewart (1941) during nine weeks in 1936 and 12 weeks in 1937–1938. Schedules for some Great Basin groups are also found in Driver (1937) and Drucker (1937, 1941). Both Steward and Stewart collected additional materials leading to their studies of sociopolitical organization and mythology (Steward 1938, 1943), Peyotism (fig. 12) (O.C. Stewart 1944, 1948, 1968), and band organization (O.C. Stewart 1966).

Demitri B. Shimkin, who worked with the Eastern Shoshone in 1937–1939, published papers on Shoshone ethnopsychology, ethnogeography, literary forms, and the Sun Dance (Shimkin 1939, 1947a, 1947, 1953). He returned to Wind River Reservation in 1966 and 1975.

Under the direction of Leslie Spier and Edward Sapir five Yale University students conducted ethnographic research in the Great Basin during the 1930s. Willard Z. Park (1933–1940, 1938) worked extensively among the Pyramid Lake and Walker Lake Northern Paiute, collecting materials on shamanism and general ethnography (fig. 13). Beatrice Blyth Whiting studied the Northern Paiute, especially sorcery, in Burns, Oregon, 1936–1938 (Blyth 1938; Whiting 1950). Maurice Zigmond worked with the Kawaiisu principally on ethno-

Catherine Fowler, Reno, Nev.
Fig. 13. Willard Z. Park at Pyramid Lake Reservation, Nev. Photograph by Susan Park, about 1934.

botany 1936–1940, and again in the late 1970s (Zigmond 1938, 1941, 1972, 1980, 1981). Edgar Siskin worked with the Washoe in 1937 and 1938, principally on Peyotism (Siskin 1941, 1983). Anne Cooke Smith (1937, 1940, 1974) studied Northern Ute material culture and mythology.

Other study during the 1930s included research among the Gosiute in 1938 and 1939 (Malouf 1940b; Malouf and Smith 1942), research with Shoshone groups (Hoebel 1935, 1938; Jack Harris 1940), and research with the Southern Ute (Opler 1940). An important ethnobiology project was conducted in 1935 and 1937–1941, under the auspices of the Works Progress Administration (Train, Henrichs, and Archer 1941).

In the 1940s, ethnographic research included Fred W. Voget's (1948, 1953) work with the Eastern Shoshone in 1948 and that of Åke Hultkrantz between 1948 and 1958 (Hultkrantz 1953, 1954, 1958, 1960, 1961, 1966, 1966–1967, 1968, 1976, 1981). Sven S. Liljeblad initiated his ethnographic and linguistic researches in 1940 (Liljeblad 1940–1983, 1959, 1972).

During the 1950s the Washoe were studied by several individuals. Ruth and Stanley Freed worked intermittently with them between 1952 and 1957 (Freed 1960, 1963; Freed and Freed 1963). In 1953, Warren d'Azevedo (1963) began long-term ethnographic and ethnohistoric work with the tribe. Philip Leis (1963) conducted research on witchcraft in 1954 and Norman Scotch and Freda Scotch (1963) studied epidemiology, nutrition, and diet in 1955. James Downs (1961, 1966) studied Washoe religion. John A. Price (1962, 1980) studied Washoe economic practices in 1961.

Ethnographic research among other Great Basin peoples was also continued in the 1950s. Margaret Wheat

Omer C. Stewart, Boulder, Colo.
Fig. 12. Omer C. Stewart with Peyote participants following a service of the Ute Mountain Ute, Towoac, Colo. seated: John Cuthair, Herbert Stacher, Alfred Lang; standing: Stewart, Charlie Lang, Edward Eytoo (or Tom Root, Jr.), Louis Wing. Photographed Jan. 1938.

26

(1959, 1967) began extended studies of Northern Paiute material culture and technology. Robert Euler (1966, 1967, 1972) worked with Southern Paiutes. Joseph G. Jorgensen (1960, 1964, 1972) began an extended study of Northern Ute culture, society, and history, and Gottfried Lang (1953, 1954) and Paul Hauck (1955) carried out studies in psychological anthropology of the Northern Ute. In the western Great Basin two archeologists conducted ethnographic research as part of ongoing regional archeological research projects—Emma Lou Davis (1965) with the Northern Paiute at Mono Lake, California, in 1959–1960, and Francis A. Riddell (1960a) with the Honey Lake Northern Paiute in 1951.

With the passage of the Indian Claims Commission Act of 1946, anthropologists were employed by the U.S. Justice Department or by attorneys for the plaintiff tribes to collect data relating to aboriginal tribal distributions and lands (O.C. Stewart 1966). Works relating to the Great Basin derived from these data include Steward (1974), Steward and Voegelin (1974), Murphy and Murphy (1960), and Manners (1974). Extensive files of unpublished ethnohistoric data relating to the claims cases for the Great Basin and elsewhere, collected by Omer C. Stewart, are deposited at the University of Colorado Library, Boulder.

The 1960s saw an expansion of ethnographic research. In 1961–1963, research on Southern Paiute ethnography and ethnohistory was conducted (Euler 1966, 1972; C.S. Fowler 1966) in conjunction with the Upper Colorado River Basin Archaeological Salvage Project of the University of Utah. Beginning in 1964, Catherine S. Fowler and others (C.S. Fowler 1972a, 1972, 1982a; Fowler and Leland 1967; C.S. Fowler and D. Fowler 1981; and Fowler and C.S. Fowler 1981) have conducted extended studies of comparative Numic ethnoscience, linguistics, ethnohistory, and material culture. In 1964 and 1965, Warren d'Azevedo directed field school projects on several western Nevada Indian reservations and colonies under National Science Foundation sponsorship. Several students connected with these projects continued research (for example, Handelman 1967a, 1967, 1968; Spring 1967, 1967a; Speth 1969; Hittman 1973; Houghton 1973; Lee 1967; Lynch 1971, 1978; Mordy 1966; Olofson 1979; Shimkin and Reid 1970). Archival materials from the field schools are on file at the Department of Anthropology, University of Nevada, Reno. Studies of culture change were also undertaken in the 1960s among the Chemehuevi (K.M. Stewart 1967) and Owens Valley Paiute (B.L. Roberts 1965).

Important ethnographic work since then includes Laird's (1976) work on the Chemehuevis. Lawton et al. (1976; see also Wilke and Lawton 1976:46–47) have reviewed ethnographic and ethnohistoric data relating to aboriginal irrigation practices in Owens Valley, California. In the 1970s there was a renewed interest in ethnobotany and foraging practices among Great Basin native peoples (C.S. Fowler 1982a; Couture 1978; Statham 1982). Great Basin Indians also began compiling tribal histories.

Language Studies

The collection of vocabulary lists in the nineteenth century was for the purpose of establishing genetic connections between languages, the aim being a comprehensive classification of all American Indian languages. Such a classification would, it was thought, provide answers to the longstanding and vexing question of Indian "origins" and clues to internal migrations once Indians reached the New World. The question of whether it was better to compare grammars or lexicons in establishing genetic relationships was answered variously throughout the nineteenth century (Haas 1969), but as a practical matter, lexical lists comprised the bulk of the collected data. This was because traders, explorers, missionaries, and soldiers in contact with Indians could reasonably elicit a list of "common" words but scarcely could be expected to provide accurate information on the intricacies of grammatical structure, even if they spoke the language well.

There was a potential problem of comparability of different word lists, since only if more or less standard lists were used was it possible to discover widespread cognates. But although lists varied somewhat, they all contained "common appelations," as Thomas Jefferson (1964:13) called them: words for basic kin terms, body parts, colors, animals, common utensils, the weather, and astronomical phenomena. Lists of words to be obtained were developed and some were printed and circulated (Jefferson 1792; Cass 1823; Gallatin 1826; Schoolcraft 1847; Gibbs 1863; Powell 1877). There were also many unpublished lists, such as Peter Stephen Du Ponceau's (1819) for the Stephen Long expedition (Fowler 1975).

The first published information on a Great Basin language was a 24-word Shoshone (presumably Eastern Shoshone) vocabulary collected from an Indian agent in 1819 by Thomas Say (1905), a member of the Stephen Long expedition, and appearing in 1823. In his pioneering classification of Indian languages, Albert Gallatin (1836) used the Say list to establish the "Shoshonee" language family, one of 28 language families he recognized north of Mexico.

The linguistic data collected by Horatio Hale in Oregon while on the U.S. Exploring Expedition under Charles Wilkes, 1838–1842 (Tyler 1968) included "Wihinasht," a Northern Paiute dialect (Hale 1846:569–629), and Northern Shoshone. Using Hale's data and other information accumulated after his 1836 classification, Gallatin (1848) produced a new classification. In this classification he included "Snakes," "Bonnorks" 27

(Bannock), and "Wihinasht," in his "Shoshonee" family, noting that "Cumanche" and "Eutaw" probably should be added. By 1853 there was sufficient lexical evidence available to include Comanche under "Shoshonee," and Schoolcraft (1851–1857,3:403) did so.

Between 1846 and 1860 the British philologist Robert G. Latham developed several classifications of New World languages. In his later efforts he grouped "Shoshoni," "Wihinast," "Cumanch" and "Utah with its dialects" under a "Paduca" family (Latham 1856:97, 102). The data collected by the Amiel Whipple expedition of 1853–1854 permitted William W. Turner (1856) to expand the "Shoshonee" stock to include both Numic and Takic languages—Shoshone, Northern Paiute, Ute, Southern Paiute, Comanche, Chemehuevi, and Gabrielino, Juaneño, Luiseño, and Cahuilla.

In 1859 the German philologist Johann Carl Eduard Buschmann (1859) produced a classification in which he established a "Sonoran stock" comprising two branches, one containing the Tarahumara, Cora, Cahita, and Tepehuan languages (now known to belong to four separate branches of Uto-Aztecan), the other branch including Numic, Takic, and Hopi (Lamb 1964:114–115). Buschmann did not include Aztec in this branch, as Powell (1891:140) erroneously asserted.

In Pimentel's (1874–1875) study of the languages of Mexico he postulated a Mexican-Opata group containing three families, one of which, the Comanche-Shoshone branch, included Numic, Takic, and Hopi, as well as Kiowa (Lamb 1964:116). Bancroft (1875–1876, 3:660–61) proposed a family of "Shoshones" that included Takic, Numic, and Hopi branches, but also Washoe (though with no Washoe data).

The George Wheeler survey collected several vocabularies in the Great Basin, the Southwest, and California in the 1870s. These data were analyzed by Albert S. Gatschet in several papers. In his final classification (Gatschet 1879) he renamed the Shoshonean stock the "Numa" stock and included Numic, Takic, and Hopi within it. He also recognized clearly that "Numa" languages were related to Aztec and Uto-Aztecan languages of northern Mexico (Gatschet 1879:409; Lamb 1964:118).

The Powell (1891) classification became standard for several years. It was a very conservative classification, establishing 58 separate language families north of Mexico. Within his Shoshonean family Powell included the Numic and Takic languages and Hopi. In the same year Daniel G. Brinton coined the term Uto-Aztecan in his linguistic classification for the New World. Under this stock he listed three branches, two of them being the two branches of Buschmann's (1859) Sonoran and the third being Nahuatl (Brinton 1891:118–119).

By 1900 the Numic languages had been recognized as forming a distinct branch or family within some larger Uto-Aztecan grouping, but the parameters of the larger grouping were uncertain and the relationships within it were not worked out in detail (Lamb 1964:120–121).

In 1907 Kroeber (1907a) presented a definitive classification of the four northern branches of Uto-Aztecan that stood until the late 1950s, setting up four "Shoshonean" groups: Plateau, Kern River, Southern California, and Pueblo; these branches are now designated Numic, Tubatulabal, Takic, and Hopi, respectively (Miller 1964:145, 1966:78; Lamb 1964:109–110). Kroeber divided Plateau Shoshonean into three subbranches: Mono-Paviotso, Shoshoni-Comanche, and Ute-Chemehuevi, now designated Western, Central, and Southern Numic, respectively (Miller 1966:78). The subsequent history of Numic linguistic classification is discussed in "Numic Languages," this volume.

In 1909 Edward Sapir and J. Alden Mason collected linguistic and mythological materials from the Uintah Ute (J.A. Mason 1910; Sapir 1910a). In 1910 Sapir worked with Tony Tillohash, a Kaibab Southern Paiute who was then a student at the Indian School in Carlisle, Pennsylvania. The results of his work are contained in various articles (Sapir 1910, 1910a, 1913, 1916) and in an extensive grammar, dictionary, and collection of texts (Sapir 1930–1931). Some ethnographic notes (Sapir 1910b) remain unpublished, although portions are quoted by Kelly (1964) and Fowler and Matley (1979).

Between 1910 and 1913 T.T. Waterman, from the University of California, Berkeley, collaborated with a physician, W.C. Marsden (1923), in analyzing Northern Paiute texts and vocabularies that Marsden had collected between 1890 and 1913. Marsden's materials were

Susan Shaw, Coronado, Calif.

Fig. 14. Carobeth Laird and her husband, George Laird, a Chemehuevi. Photographed about 1940.

deposited at Berkeley. In 1914, a Pyramid Lake Paiute, Gilbert Natches (fig. I), was brought to Berkeley to analyze Marsden's materials. Due to dialect differences he was unsuccessful, but he did learn to write his own dialect phonetically (Natches 1923). Waterman (1911) also pioneered in the use of the wax cylinder phonograph to record Northern Paiute "phonetic elements."

In 1918–1920 Carobeth Tucker Harrington (fig. 14), under the direction of John Peabody Harrington, of the Bureau of American Ethnology, collected texts, songs, and myths of the Chemehuevi, principally from George Laird, later her husband (Walsh 1976:43; Laird 1975, 1976). J.P. Harrington (1911a, 1911) had worked briefly with the Ute.

In 1958, James Goss initiated studies of Southern Numic linguistics (Goss 1961, 1967, 1968, 1972, 1972a), and after 1965 Wick Miller and his students developed an extensive program in the study of Central Numic languages (Miller 1966, 1972; Miller, Tanner, and Foley 1971).

Washoe is the only non-Numic language spoken within the Great Basin culture area. It is grouped with the Hokan languages spoken in western California (Jacobsen 1964, 1966). Some Whites thought Washoe was related, or similar to, the Numic languages, an opinion reiterated by the historian Bancroft (1875–1876, 1:469, 3:660–661).

The first Washoe vocabulary (17 words) was collected by Jules Remy (1860, 1:41). The second, some 200 items, was collected by C.R. Collins with the James H. Simpson Expedition in 1859. C.R. Collins (1876:467–468) was the first to point out that Washoe was linguistically distinct from the adjacent Numic languages. Albert S. Gatschet (1882:255) also thought the language distinct, basing his opinion on a vocabulary collected by Stephen Powers in 1875 (Fowler and Fowler 1970:117–122), as did Henry Wetherbee Henshaw, who collected a Washoe vocabulary in 1883 (Powell 1887:xxx). Both Gatschet and Henshaw worked on the Powell classification; hence their conclusion of Washoe's distinctiveness is reflected in the establishment of a separate Washoan family therein (Powell 1891:131).

Washoe was regarded as an isolated language family until 1917. Dixon and Kroeber (1913) had postulated the Hokan stock, comprising several California languages, and Edward Sapir (1917) proposed a possible relationship between Washoe and Hokan, a relationship supported by Dixon and Kroeber (1919:104–112). The subsequent history of Washoe linguistic studies is reviewed by Jacobsen (1964, 1966), who began linguistic research among the Washoe in 1955.

Summary

The foregoing discussion of ethnographic and linguistic studies in the Great Basin is illustrative, not exhaustive.

An evaluation of what has been learned about Great Basin aboriginal peoples over two centuries must take into account the changing situations of the people themselves during that time. Account must also be taken of the shifts in orientation of those collecting and analyzing ethnographic and linguistic information.

In 1776 when Garcés and Escalante and Domínguez made their journeys into the hydrographic Great Basin, some Indian groups were living in a strictly precontact manner. Others on the eastern edge of the Basin were already well established as horse users and were becoming increasingly oriented toward the Plains. By 1805, the Northern Shoshone described by Lewis and Clark were also horse-using and oriented toward the Plains-Mountains subsistence regime common to eastern Shoshone groups until the advent of reservations after 1872. Non–horse-using groups farther west and south were soon affected by the White fur trappers or slave raids by other Indians. Despite these impacts most non–horse-using Great Basin peoples were able to maintain traditional cultures until about 1840. With the advent of large-scale White emigration across the Basin in the 1840s and settlement after 1846, traditional lifeways began to shatter quickly (Gould, Fowler, and Fowler 1972).

By 1875 most Great Basin Indian peoples had been forced onto reservations or into dependent satellite "colonies" adjacent to White settlements.

Escalante and Lewis and Clark observed functioning Indian societies and cultures. By 1868–1873 when John Wesley Powell did the bulk of his ethnographic research in the Great Basin he could observe societies still functioning but starting to change rapidly under acculturative impacts (Fowler and Fowler 1971). He was the last anthropological observer in the Great Basin to see aboriginal lifeways in operation. Thereafter, data increasingly derived from "memory culture," not functioning culture. In 1872 Powell could (and did) observe the manufacture and use of aboriginal tools and implements. In 1910 the Southern Paiute Tony Tillohash could make only imperfect models of tools, as could Isabel Kelly's informants in the 1930s (Fowler and Fowler 1981).

Thus, the bulk of the ethnographic data collected on Great Basin Indians (and elsewhere in North America) was "memory culture." The orientation of the American historical school of anthropology between 1900 and 1940 necessarily was toward salvage ethnography—salvaging what social and cultural data remained and attempting to reconstruct the "ethnographic present," that is, aboriginal cultures as they were at the time of contact. The University of California Culture Element Distribution Survey was, in part, conceived of as a "last" salvage operation. It proved not to be so.

The single most influential study of Great Basin peoples, Julian Steward's (1938) work on aboriginal sociopolitical organization, combined culture element data (assumed to reflect aboriginal practices but probably in fact reflecting 80 years of varying degrees of acculturation) with ethnohistoric information. The resultant picture was one of atomistic social systems and a meager culture inventory developed in response to a sparse environment throughout the Great Basin culture area. Steward was describing only the Shoshone. But the impact of his work, especially after Jennings (1957) made the "Steward model" the basis for his archeological Desert culture concept, obfuscated the range and variety of early historic Great Basin social systems and cultural inventories. On the other hand, Steward's work also made Great Basin aboriginal sociopolitical systems a focal point for general anthropological discussions of the nature of social evolution, family, and kinship structure, a discussion ongoing in the 1980s (Eggan 1980; C.S. Fowler 1982a, 1982; Service 1962; Shimkin 1941; Shimkin and Reid 1970; Steward 1936a, 1938, 1955:101–121, 1970; O.C. Stewart 1959, 1980). Steward's (1938) second contribution was the formulation of the concept of cultural ecology, a concept that has had world-wide application in anthropological research (Murphy 1970, 1977, 1981).

Studies of culture process and ethnopsychology were initiated in the Great Basin in the 1930s in consonance with new theoretical interests in American anthropology. Shimkin's (1939, 1953) work on psychology and the Sun Dance are major examples, as are the works of W.Z. Park (1938), Siskin (1941, 1983), O.C. Stewart (1944, 1948) on Peyotism, and Whiting (1950) on Northern Paiute sorcery. After World War II interested continued in psychological and medical anthropology, reflected in the Great Basin in the studies by Lang (1953, 1954), Scotch and Scotch (1963), and Voget (1948, 1953) on the Sun Dance.

By the 1960s Great Basin anthropologists were turning their attention to studies of contemporary Indian communities and problems of acculturation (Brink 1969; Clemmer 1978; Collins 1971; Hittman 1973; Houghton 1973; Lynch 1971, 1978; Mordy 1966; Olofson 1979).

Studies of ethnobiology have a long history in the Great Basin, beginning with Edward Palmer (1871), F.V. Coville (1892), and R.V. Chamberlin (1908, 1909, 1911, 1913) and followed by Zigmond's (1941) work with the Kawaiisu, and Train, Hendrichs, and Archer's (1941) general study of medicinal plants. There has been a resurgence of interest in ethnobiology since the 1960s (Zigmond 1981; C.S. Fowler 1982a; Fowler and Leland 1967; Couture 1978; Statham 1982).

Prehistoric Environments

PETER J. MEHRINGER, JR.

Environments and cultures are closely woven in the fabric of archeological research through understandings originating in antiquity. Writings of the earliest civilizations demonstrate awareness that variations in nature have influenced the vitality of the human spirit, of beliefs, institutions, and technologies and have directed the course of empires (Butzer 1983; W.K. Simpson 1978:211). Archeologists recognize relationships among strength of the westerlies, course of the Gulf Stream and the Viking frontier, or the retreat of glaciers, expanding monsoons, and the Sahara Neolithic (Bryson and Murray 1977; H.H. Lamb 1982; Wendorf and Schild 1980). They likewise attribute cultural responses to expansion of the Great Basin's arid core (Aikens and Witherspoon 1984).

By the 1930s archeologists, such as Malcolm Rogers (Pourade 1966) and the Campbells (Campbell and Campbell 1937), and interdisciplinary teams had described unmistakable evidence for fluctuating Great Basin Holocene environments and for corresponding human responses. One team assembled in 1939 by the vertebrate paleontologist John C. Merriam (1941) included Luther S. Cressman (archeologist), Howel Williams (volcanologist), E.L. Packard and Chester Stock (paleontologists), Daniel Axelrod (paleobotanist), Henry P. Hansen (palynologist), and I.S. Allison, Ernst Antevs, J.P. Buwalda, and W.D. Smith (geologists). Radiocarbon dating in the 1950s proved Cressman's insistence on antiquity of man in the Great Basin. Hansen was the pioneering paleoecologist who broke trail in deciphering late Quaternary vegetational history in northwestern North America. Antevs carried a varved-dated, three-part Holocene climatic sequence (Anathermal-Altithermal-Medithermal) from Scandinavia and captivated western North American archeologists with notions of severe mid-Holocene (Altithermal) drought about 7,000 to 4,500 years ago (Antevs 1948, 1952, 1955; Aikens 1983). The Merriam team studied the archeological remains in wave-excavated caves along the shores of extinct Oregon lakes. Late Quaternary lake levels remain a subject of considerable importance to Great Basin archeologists (D.L. Weide 1974) as witnessed by their continued studies of pluvial Lake Mohave, California (Warren and Ore 1978).

In conjunction with M.R. Harrington's investigations in southern Nevada, Laudermilk and Munz (1934) studied plants from Gypsum Cave, Nevada, and paleontologists reported extinct fauna that later led to Shutler's (1967) revitalization of interdisciplinary studies there in the early 1960s, and to C.V. Hayne's (1967) report on the Quaternary geology of the Las Vegas Valley. P.V. Wells pioneered the study of plant remains of ancient woodrat middens (Wells and Jorgensen 1964). Biogeographers found that relict fish attested to former drainage connections (Hubbs and Miller 1948), and they brought pollen analysis to bear on archeological questions of the Southwest and Great Basin (Martin 1963).

Differences of opinion among geologists as important to archeology as Ernst Antevs, Kirk Bryan, and John T. Hack (Haury 1950:fig. 114) are a reminder that interpretations of climatic change and chronologies remain limited by both data and methods. For example, Jesse D. Jennings (1957:95–98) estimated the age and conditions of occupation at Danger Cave, Utah, correctly though contrary to the best advice of those geologists and archeologists who did not appreciate differing degrees of regional variability or a cultural scheme not clearly fulfilling the prophecy of Altithermal drought (Baumhoff and Heizer 1965:697). As illustrated at Gatecliff Shelter, Nevada (Thomas 1983a), cooperative ventures between archeologists and other scientists continue to produce rich results.

The Great Basin is a laboratory of unusual variety and potential for studying the dynamics of human responses to environmental changes. Although ecological shifts lasting millennia are clearly illustrated, it seems that Great Basin inhabitants reacted to variations resulting from sharp, punctuated events measured in decades or at most a few centuries. As anticipated (Mehringer 1977:134), some important resources such as piñon pine (*Pinus monophylla*) and mesquite (*Prosopis* spp.) (Steward 1933b:241, 1938:20, 80) are relatively recent arrivals in parts of the Great Basin. Their Holocene histories and vegetational changes in general must be considered in judging potential adaptations to climatic events. Volcanic activity, dune building, and vegetational changes all have elicited human responses; but overall, the extent of Great Basin lakes and marshes was most important to the numbers and distribution of people.

As the most intelligent and adaptable of all creatures, humans may not appear to qualify as a sensitive bio-

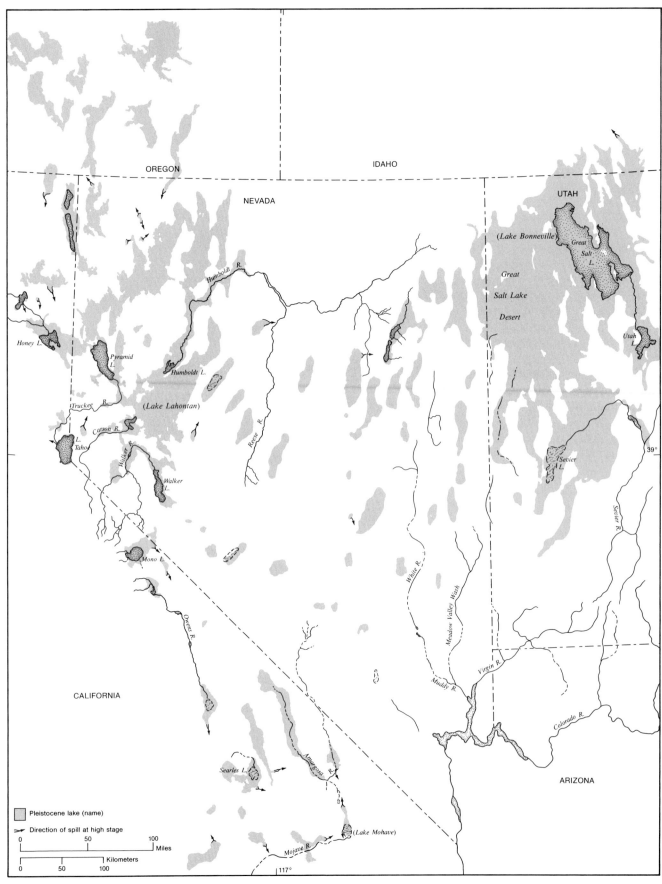

OREGON

IDAHO

NEVADA

UTAH

(Lake Bonneville)

*Great
Salt
L.*

*Great

Salt Lake

Desert*

Humboldt R.

Honey L.

*Pyramid
L.*

Humboldt L.

*Utah
L.*

Truckee R.

(Lake Lahontan)

Catson R.

Reese R.

*L.
Tahoe*

Walker R.

39°

*Walker
L.*

*Sevier
L.*

Sevier R.

Mono L.

White R.

Meadow Valley Wash

Owens R.

CALIFORNIA

Virgin R.

Muddy R.

Colorado R.

Searles L.

Amargosa R.

ARIZONA

Pleistocene lake (name)

Direction of spill at high stage

(Lake Mohave)

0   50   100
⊢⊣⊣⊣⊣⊣⊣⊣⊣⊣⊣
                    Miles

Mojave R.

0   50   100
⊢⊣⊣⊣⊣⊣⊣⊣⊣⊣⊣
      Kilometers

117°

after Snyder, Hardman, and Zdenek 1964; Mifflin and Wheat 1979.

32   Fig. 1. Great Basin pluvial lakes.

logical indicator species; but history has proved otherwise, and cultural remains also testify to the nature of past environments. Moreover, through use of fire (Barrett and Arno 1982; Bohrer 1983; Lewis 1973), diversion of water (Lawton et al. 1976), and as carriers of seeds and vegetative propagules, Great Basin peoples undoubtedly have modified local habitats to their liking and in ways yet to be understood.

Geological Evidence

Pleistocene Lakes

The most obvious indications of late Quaternary climatic changes in the Great Basin—strandlines, algal tufas, deltas, bars, and subsurface salts amd muds—attest to former deep lakes and rushing rivers (fig. 1). Early observations, descriptions, and interpretations of such features (Gale 1915; Gilbert 1890; Meinzer 1922; Russell 1885) reinforced notions of moist-cool conditions south of continental ice sheets. The history of these great lakes is important to understanding archeological remains in the Desert West where even relatively minor fluctuations of streams and marshes within their Holocene remnants determined changing patterns of human occupation.

The concept of global "pluvials," everywhere coeval with glaciation, has been abandoned in the face of evidence from Australia, India, and North Africa, where lowered water tables and deflation marked the last glacial period, and expanding lakes followed in the early Holocene (Haynes 1982; Maley 1977; Street and Grove 1979; Swain, Kutzbach, and Hastenrath 1983). Still, the apparent chronological correspondence between the waxing and waning of Great Basin lakes and continental glaciers (Clayton and Moran 1982:fig. 1; Mickelson et al. 1983:fig. 1–9; Porter, Pierce, and Hamilton 1983) implies a related cause in Pleistocene atmospheric circulation over western North America (Barry 1983) where shallow lakes both preceded and followed deeper ones lasting from about 22,000 to 10,000 B.C. (fig. 2). Although the use of "pluvial" implies increased rainfall, the nature of pluvial climates and their consequences remain a controversial subject of study and spirited speculation (Galloway 1983; Mifflin and Wheat 1979; Van Devender and Spaulding 1979; Wells 1979).

The fluctuations of Lakes Bonneville, Lahontan, Searles, and Mohave indicate current understanding of the history of Great Basin Pleistocene lakes. Figure 3 shows the interpretations of Donald R. Currey that include two stands at the Bonneville level. Scott et al. (1983) challenged long-held notions of a series of deep lakes through the past 100,000 years or so. Their modified history of the last two cycles of Lake Bonneville proposes a halting rise of more than 800 feet starting

U.S. Geological Survey, Denver.

Fig. 2. Mouth of Little Cottonwood Canyon, Utah, showing glacial moraines. Shorelines visible on these moraines (Madsen and Currey 1979:fig. 2) document the high stands of Lake Bonneville. View is east toward the Wasatch Mountains. The faulted terminal moraine of Bells Canyon is on the right. Photographed in 1964.

about 26,000 years ago. Water reached the Bonneville shoreline about 14,000 B.C. Overflow, catastrophic downcutting, and flooding northward through Red Rock Pass to the Snake River (Malde 1968) occurred within the next 1,000 to 2,000 years, and the lake fell nearly 350 feet to form the Provo strandline. The shrinking lake stood below the Provo level by 11,000 B.C. and by 9000 B.C. had fallen to the level of the present Great Salt Lake. The ages of the highest late stands of pluvial Lake Lahontan remain uncertain (Smith and Street-Perrott 1983:fig. 10–3). Benson (1978, 1981) placed this level from 11,600 to 9000 B.C. whereas J.O. Davis (1982:60, 63, 1983a:314), concluded that Lake Lahontan began a rapid fall of nearly 350 feet starting about 10,600 B.C. (figs. 4–5).

The classic stratigraphic succession at Searles Lake, with salts representing shallow lakes and muds representing deep lakes (Gale 1915), reveals a final late Wis-

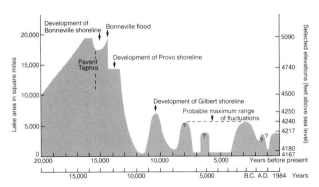

after Currey, Atwood, and Mabey 1984:fig. 4.

Fig. 3. Area of Pleistocene and Holocene lakes in the Bonneville Basin.

consin period of high water following a period of smaller lakes correlated with the preceding interstadial (G.I. Smith 1979; Smith et al. 1983). Searles Lake received drainage from the Sierra Nevada as far north as the present Mono Lake. When its basin was filled to overflowing by pluvial Lake Russell, water moved via Adobe Valley to the Owens River, Owens Lake, China Lake, and Searles Lake, which overflowed into Panamint Valley and finally to Death Valley.

Hooke (1972:2093) suspected that lakes in Death Valley fluctuated in phase with Searles Lake and, further, that Panamint Valley probably overflowed into Death Valley via Wingate Wash between 9000 and 8600 B.C. to produce a lake 300 feet deep. In contrast, R.S.U. Smith (1978) considered Panamint Valley lakes of this age to lie 800 feet below the spillway to Death Valley, and radiocarbon dates on deposits of a shallow cattail marsh give a minimum age of 10,000–10,500 years for the last major overflow of Lakes Searles and Panamint. (Davis, Brott, and Weide 1969:15; Mehringer 1967a:172, table 5; Peterson 1980).

Historically, Lake Mohave has been important in understanding human occupations during the waning phases of the last pluvial (Campbell and Campbell 1937; Warren 1967; Warren and Ore 1978). Geomorphic studies by Ore and Warren (1971:fig. 7) contributed the first chronological controls necessary to evaluate the contemporaneity of lake levels and man. Based on radiocarbon dates on tufa or the shells of freshwater mussels, they suggested four overflow stages from 12,600 to 6000 B.C. (D.L. Weide 1982:table 4).

Great Basin lakes have shown rapid water budget

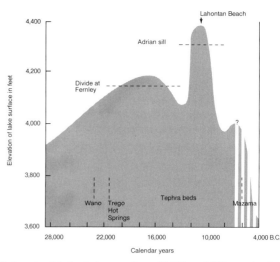

Fig. 5. Levels of Lake Lahontan from 28,000 to 4,000 B.C. As the lake rose past 4,150 feet, the Truckee and Carson rivers were united across the divide near Fernley, Nev.; as it rose past 4,290 feet, waters of the Walker River drainage joined those of the Carson and Truckee rivers across the Adrian Sill (J.O. Davis 1983a, personal communication 1984).

changes over the last 40,000 years. Most, if not all, were deepest sometime between 20,000 and 12,500 years ago and at or below historic levels at times between 7,000 and 4,000 years ago (Smith and Street-Perrott 1983:fig. 10–6). Agreement on details of the ages and magnitudes of fluctuations and their climatic causes varies. Over such a large area shifting atmospheric circulation patterns (Bryson, Baerreis, and Wendland 1970:55; Smith et al. 1979) might have varied through time as a result of geographic relationship to climatic boundaries (Mitchell 1976:fig. 5.1) as well as changing latitudinal patterns of seasonal precipitation and temperature (Houghton, Sakamoto, and Gifford 1975; P.A. Kay 1982:fig. 1; D.L. Weide 1982:fig. 4).

Holocene Lakes and Marshes

As the great Pleistocene lakes shrank, some isolated basins desiccated rapidly, but in others, streams from the Colorado Plateaus, the Sierra Nevada, and the Rocky and Cascade mountains sustained smaller lakes. For example, the Bear, Provo, and Sevier rivers supplied remnants of Lake Bonneville (Great Salt, Sevier, and Utah lakes). In the western Great Basin, the Owens River fed Owens Lake, the Carson and Walker rivers flowed to Carson Sink, and the Truckee River sustained Pyramid and Winnemucca lakes (Benson 1978:table 1; J.O. Davis 1982:table 1, figs. 4–6). Archeological remains from nearby caves and artifacts concentrated on strandlines long dry attest to a people who rapidly took up residence around the diminished lakes (Bedwell 1973; Cressman 1962; Davis 1978; Hattori 1982:fig. 7; Jennings 1957; Tuohy 1974, 1981; Warren 1967; Warren

Fig. 4. Pyramid Lake, Nev., where strandlines on the hills register the history of pluvial Lake Lahontan. The broad, white strandline in the right foreground and center of the picture marks the 3,873 foot stand of Pyramid Lake, the elevation at which flow from the Truckee River spills over into the Lake Winnemucca basin. Photograph by J.O. Davis, 1976.

and Ranere 1968). Their expedience in adapting to available resources is reflected in the variety of archeologists' conceptions (Desert Archaic and Western Pluvial Lakes traditions; San Dieguito, Hascomat, and Lake Mohave complexes). Holocene fluctuations of closed basin lakes are excellent gauges of the climatically controlled balance between inflow and evaporation (Harding 1965; Hardman and Venstrom 1941; Peck and Richardson 1966).

About 9000 to 8000 B.C., as Lake Bonneville shrank to within 50 feet or so of the present level of Great Salt Lake, Sevier Lake drained northward through the rebounding Old River Bed threshold to the now dry Great Salt Desert to form lakes apparently responsible for the distinctive Gilbert shorelines (fig. 3) (Currey and James 1982:34; Currey, Atwood, and Mabey 1984; Eardley 1962:18; Eardley, Gvosdetsky, and Marsell 1957:pls. 1–3). Because occupation of Stansbury Island near the southern shore of Great Salt Lake probably required a connection with the mainland to the south, a 5800 B.C.* date from Sandwich Shelter provides a minimum age for a water level below the connecting shoal at 4,206 feet, about five feet above the historic mean level (Marwitt, Fry, and Adovasio 1971). Currey (1980:78, personal communication 1984) speculated that giant desiccation polygons, visible beneath the Great Salt Lake, formed during one or more Holocene shallow water phases.

Pollen and stable isotope analyses of a core from Great Salt Lake, Utah, reveal a history of lake oscillations with relatively high levels soon after the fall of volcanic ash from Mount Mazama, and again about 2000 and 1000 B.C. Currey (1982:24) places a lake in the Great Salt Desert sometime between A.D. 1605 and 1840; a storm beach of oolitic sand was left at the lake edge near 4,218 feet. Morrison (1965:281) suggested several rises of Great Salt Lake within the past 4,000 years, with the maximum at 4,260 feet and equivalent to the Gilbert level. Van Horn (1979) also referred the Gilbert level (fig. 3) to a lake of the past 4,000 years, whereas Currey (1980:77, personal communication 1984) attributes the Eardley shoreline at about 4,220 feet to the post-Mazama ash deepwater period.

In addition to Danger Cave and Sandwich Shelter (Madsen 1980b:fig. 2), several sites along the Bear River and northeastern arm of Great Salt Lake (Aikens 1966, 1967a; Shields and Dalley 1978; Fry and Dalley 1979) provide further evidence for former lake levels, for they lie at an elevation of about 4,210 feet, a foot below the highest historic stand of 4,211.5 feet in 1873 (Arnow 1980:figs. 1, 6, 1983). The sites were flooded within

*In this chapter radiocarbon dates of the past 7,200 radiocarbon years have been converted to calendar dates following Klein et al. 1982: table 2. The midpoint of their "sigma = 20 yrs." column has been used, rounding to 100-year intervals.—Editors

historic times but must have been above the lake when occupied between A.D. 500 and 1300. Such evidence led Currey and James (1982:41) to conclude that since 1550 Great Salt Lake probably lay below 4,220 feet.

As Lake Bonneville receded, isostatic adjustment (Crittenden 1963:fig. 3) caused doming and tilting from the center of the basin that controlled water depth, direction of flow, and threshold elevation between Great Salt Lake, the Great Salt Desert, and the Sevier Desert. These in turn contributed directly to the distribution, extent, and type of marsh and salt flat habitats available for human use. Further, habitation sites and communication among aboriginal groups would have been influenced by the position and total area of salt water. In northwestern Utah, isostatic rebound has been as important archeologically as climatic change, especially in the early Holocene (Mehringer 1977); J.O. Davis (1982) suggests the same for parts of the Lake Lahontan Basin.

By 9200 B.C. Lake Lahontan had separated into three or four lakes as it dropped from a Pleistocene high level of about 4,380 feet to 4,000 feet. Water in Carson Sink may occasionally have approached the previous 4,000-foot level, but it must also have stood much lower than 3,940 feet when water from Humboldt Sink breached the Humboldt Bar eroding a channel to Carson Sink (J.O. Davis 1982:65). Early to mid-Holocene flow of the Walker River into the Carson River (G.Q. King 1978) complicates climatic interpretations of water depth within Carson Sink. About 5800 B.C. when volcanic ash from Mount Mazama fell on Carson Sink, water stood near 3,940 feet (J.O. Davis 1982).

Morrison (1964a:105, fig. 39) related lake history to archeological sites and speculated on the relationships among lake levels, climate, and aboriginal occupation. He described a dry period, characterized by deflation, and followed by five lake cycles since about 2600 B.C. (Morrison and Frye 1965:19). Although shallow lakes existed during this time, the number and ages of those described by Morrison conflict with other interpretations of radiocarbon and tephra dates (J.O. Davis 1982:67).

Walker, Eagle, and Pyramid lakes show similar trends with return of deeper water after 2600 B.C. (J.O. Davis 1982:67–68). Between 7000 and 3800 B.C. Walker Lake was shallow and at times perhaps dry (Benson 1978:fig. 6) because flow of the Walker River was diverted to Carson Sink. Walker Lake underwent at least one major recession between 2600 B.C. and the 1800s (Benson 1981:fig. 2). During this time the Walker River most probably followed its present course to Walker Lake. The 1500 to 300 B.C. period shows markedly higher water at Eagle Lake (Davis and Pippin 1979).

Pyramid Lake is fed by the Truckee River originating at Lake Tahoe in the Sierra Nevada (Hyne et al. 1972). From the middle 1800s until the 1905 diversion of the Truckee River, Pyramid Lake fluctuated between high water stands of about 3,880 and 3,860 feet. An archeological site exposed at 3,788 feet was radiocarbon dated at about 600 B.C. (Tuohy and Clark 1979) and illustrates the considerable magnitude of late Holocene changes in water budget.

When Pyramid Lake rises above 3,870 feet, the Truckee River may feed both Pyramid and Winnemucca lakes (Hattori 1982:fig. 10). The Winnemucca Lake Basin apparently contained a dry playa in 1844. By 1882 water stood 85 feet deep, and within three years a commercial fishery flourished; the playa was dry again by 1939. Because the Winnemucca Caves harbored abundant radiocarbon-dated artifacts, particularly baskets, along with the remains of fish, waterfowl, and marsh plants, Hattori (1982:fig. 16) proposed a sequence in which occupation of archeological sites indicated lakes or marshes in the Winnemucca Basin; at such times Pyramid Lake would have stood above 3,870 feet.

That the Truckee River was cut off from its source for at least several hundred years before 2900 B.C. is indicated by inundated shore features (Davis, Elston, and Townsend 1976) and the submerged stumps of coniferous trees. Some trees, represented by stumps with up to 100 annual rings, grew on the exposed bed of Lake Tahoe two feet below the present outflow sill. Others growing just below the rim displayed more than 150 annual rings (Harding 1965:137). Lake Tahoe rose again, killing the trees and spilling through its outlet to the Truckee River and Pyramid Lake. Droughts of the 1930s and 1960s briefly exposed some stumps. However, the well-preserved stumps suggest that previous exposure was unusual and brief.

In the southern Great Basin recent lakes are known from Searles and Death valleys; the postulated spilling of Owens Lake within the past 2,000 years presents special problems. A radiocarbon date of about 1800 B.C. on wood serves as a maximum age for its burial in the Overburden Mud of Searles Lake, which indicates a shallow lake or lakes following a period of desiccation suggested by the Upper Salt (G.I. Smith 1979). In Death Valley, shorelines and salt deposits record a 30-foot deep lake (Hunt et al. 1966:48; Hunt and Mabey 1966:82). A minimum age of about 2,000 years comes from overlying dunes lacking artifacts older than those characteristic of Death Valley III times (Hunt 1960:111). Although the salts in Owens Lake could have accumulated within the past 2,000 years, the implied overflow at that time (G.I. Smith 1976:99) was not recognized downstream in cores from Little Lake that span more than 5,000 years. There, shallow lakes replaced wet meadows and marsh about 1200 B.C. (Mehringer and Sheppard 1978).

The foregoing review illustrates that sometime after the fall of Mazama ash and before 3800 B.C. Great Basin lakes became shallower, but their levels varied considerably in response to climatic differences. Manifestations of a most important archeological period (for example, the Lovelock culture) resulted directly from rising lakes after 3100 B.C. (Elston 1982). Fishing and waterfowling paraphernalia and the actual remains of fish, fowl, and shellfish, and evidence of a diet including marsh plants (Loud and Harrington 1929; Heizer and Napton 1969; Wigand and Mehringer 1985) leave no doubt of human attraction to expanding marsh and lake resources. But even during periods of abundance in the Great Basin resources varied from time to time and from place to place, and the archeological record itself may be an accurate indicator of local environments. Changing intensity of occupation of Fort Rock Valley and Abert Lake, Oregon (Bedwell 1973:fig. 10; Pettigrew 1980), relative stability, as shown by the long record of salt-tolerant species from Danger Cave, and the brief but intense uses of Hidden Cave in the Carson Sink (Thomas 1985) and of the Winnemucca Caves show flexibility on a regional scale. Visits to particular sites may indicate nearby marshes for perhaps a few decades or less, piñon nuts since the mid-Holocene, or palatable playa-edge halophytes for 11,000 years.

To the south, some lakes resulted from geologic accident rather than climatic change. There, it is demonstrated by myth (Wilke and Lawton 1975) and archeological remains that opportunists responded quickly by emphasizing different subsistence practices. For example, the playa of Cronise Dry Lake in the Mojave Desert was flooded occasionally by exceptional storms or when the Mojave River was diverted from its usual course. Desert peoples, bearing Anasazi and Yuman pottery, visited the ephemeral lakes and left mussel-shell middens (Drover 1979; M.J. Rogers 1929). There are no cases to rival the rapidity and magnitude of lake fluctuations and corresponding human responses revealed by Philip J. Wilke's (1978) studies of Lake Cahuilla.

At its maximum, Lake Cahuilla was a body of fresh water over 100 miles long and 300 feet deep that periodically occupied the Salton Basin of southeastern California. It filled when water from the Colorado River flowed westward across its delta to the Salton Trough, rather than south to the Gulf of California. Three to five such lacustral cycles occurred between A.D. 500 and 1400 (Waters 1983:fig. 6; Wilke 1978:fig. 14). Songs of the Cahuilla Indians retell legends of lakes, abounding with fish and waterfowl, and the return of desert. One of these songs recounts how, when the water receded, Coyote went down from the mountain and planted mesquite beans on the dry lake bed (Wilke 1978:6).

Remains of plants and animals and contents of human coprolites indicate consumption of freshwater mussel, fish, waterfowl, cattail, and bulrush at lakeside dunes occupied throughout the year (Wilke 1978:87). Once the Colorado River regained its course to the Gulf of

California, Lake Cahuilla shrank in a single, continuous decline lasting 55 to 60 years. At one site initial annual progress of this decline is marked by U- or V-shaped fish weirs built on 15 levels each separated elevationally by about five feet (figs. 6–7), which approaches the present annual water loss by evaporation. The decline in construction of weirs accompanied increasing salinity and the demise of fish. As the lake dwindled the Cahuilla returned to the deserts and foothills, retelling stories of the grand lake—of mussels and mosquitos, fish and geese, and clouds of blackbirds in the cattails—and the way the Old Ones lived.

Human resilience in responding to fluctuating environments makes an understanding of the rate and degree of change (if any) in these environments essential to unlocking the secrets of the human past in the Great Basin. The cultural responses seen at Lake Cahuilla and Winnemucca Caves seem compatible with the scale of changing river flows and lake levels of the past century. Winnemucca Lake went from a barren playa in the time of Fremont to a lake rich in fish and waterfowl only to dry up again in the 1930s. As in prehistoric times, people came, claimed the lake's bounty and as quickly left when it diminished (Hattori 1982:36).

Figure 8 illustrates historic variation in the level of Great Salt Lake that may provide an analogue for the rate and degree of change over the past 9,000 years. The Malheur-Harney Lake of southeastern Oregon, dry in the 1930s, in 1984 covers ranches and roads that lie above its previous historic high level. If water were not diverted from cities and irrigated farms (Arnow 1980: fig. 8), the Great Salt Lake would stand in 1984 above any level of the last 150 years.

Despite regional variation of climate in the Great Basin, the declining river flows and water tables of the

Fig. 7. Remains of a fish weir, Lake Cahuilla, Calif. Most weirs had sides 6–10 feet long that extended onto the shore from openings 1–2 feet wide constructed in shallow water. Philip Wilke (personal communication 1984) postulates that razorback suckers (*Xyrauchen texanus*) entered the structures to spawn in quiet, shallow water and were netted as they attempted to flee through the apexes of the weirs. Photograph by Philip Wilke, 1978.

late 1920s and early 1930s (Matthai 1979:47) and the general increases since that time are also seen in the records from Abert, Bear, Goose, Pyramid, Sevier, Walker, and Warner lakes and the Bear, Blitzen, Mojave, Silvies, Truckee, and Virgin rivers. Perhaps the climatic variation from the 1850s to the 1980s is exactly the sort that would have resulted in evidence for corresponding cultural responses. Lakes and rivers of the Great Basin provide the most important link between human occupation and climatic fluctuations. Only volcanic activity in the western Great Basin came as close to guiding human economy.

Volcanic and Tectonic Activity

Volcanic ashes are important Pleistocene time-stratigraphic markers throughout the Great Basin (Bailey, Dalrymple, and Lanphere 1976; Currey 1982:27; Izett 1981; Izett et al. 1970:fig. 1; Sheppard and Gude 1968). A remarkable sequence at Summer Lake, southern Oregon, contains 54 tephra (volcanic ash) beds of late Quaternary age (J.O. Davis 1985a) in exposures of sediments of pluvial Lake Chewaucan (Allison 1982). Some of these tephra originated from Mount Mazama or Mount Saint Helens, and others are correlated with different volcanic ashes identified from sediments of pluvial Lake Lahontan (J.O. Davis 1985a).

Holocene volcanic flows and ashfalls are also common in western North America and are distinguishable by physical and chemical properties, mineral suites, regional and stratigraphic occurrence, and age (Kittleman 1979). Late glacial tephra from Glacier Peak, Washington (Beget 1982; Mehringer, Sheppard, and Foit 1984; Porter 1978), and mid-Holocene ashfalls from Mount Mazama (Williams 1942), the precursor of Crater Lake,

Fig. 6. Remains of fish weirs, in rows marking annual recession beaches of Lake Cahuilla, Calif. The decline in beach line elevation averages about 5 feet per year. Photograph by Philip Wilke, 1978.

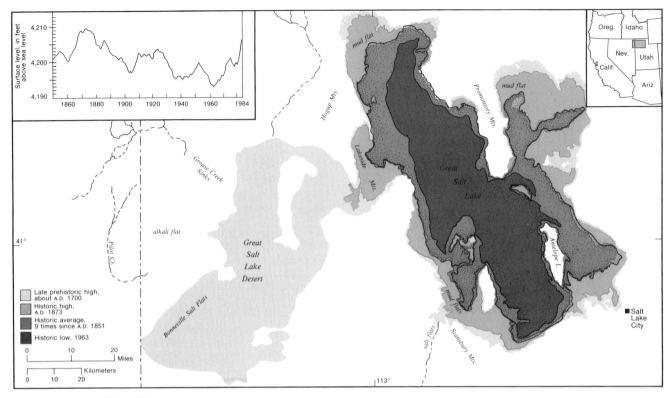

after Currey, Atwood, and Mabey 1984.

Fig. 8. Historic annual high levels of Great Salt Lake. The highest level (4,211.5 feet) occurred in 1873 and the lowest level (4,191.35 feet) in 1963. In 1984 the high level was just over 4,209 feet, shown on the map in black line.

Oregon (Bacon 1983), are well-known to American archeologists. The ages and stratigraphic relationships of other tephra will become important for precisely correlating Great Basin archeological sites with each other and with deposits (lake beds, peat bogs, soils, dunes, and alluvium) containing evidence of past environments.

Besides the eruptions at Sunset Craters, Arizona, about A.D. 1065 (Pilles 1979) and loosely dated volcanic events (Friedman and Obradovich 1981:41) at Salton Buttes, southeastern California (Robinson, Elders, and Muffler 1976), Holocene explosive eruptions and extrusions occurred in the Cascade Range and along the periphery of the Great Basin (Sarna-Wojcicki, Champion, and Davis 1983:figs. 5–1, 5–2). On May 18, 1980, Mount Saint Helens, Washington, erupted sending volcanic ash eastward across North America. Mount Saint Helens has been the most active Cascade volcano, producing over 19 tephra eruptions of varying magnitudes over the past 4,500 years (Shipley and Sarna-Wojcicki 1983). At least one lobe extended southeast to Nevada (J.O. Davis 1985a).

Several eruptions of Mount Mazama between 5900 and 5700 B.C. produced the most voluminous (at least 7 cubic miles) (Bacon 1983:91) and widespread tephra of Holocene age in the United States. The reported distribution of Mazama ash includes the northern Great Basin as far south as central Nevada and the central

Sierra Nevada, California, and east to northwestern Utah (Adam 1967; J.O. Davis 1978, 1982, 1983; Mehringer, Nash, and Fuller 1971). Volcanic areas in northern California sent tephra toward the Great Basin. Included are the Medicine Lake Highlands, active within the last 1,100 years (Heiken 1981); Lassen Peak, which last erupted in 1914–1917; and Mono-Inyo Craters. The Mono-Inyo Craters run south as a chain from Mono Lake along the east flank of the Sierra Nevada to the vicinity of Mammoth Lakes (fig. 9). Explosive volcanism has been common there for 40,000 years; at least 18 separate events are known since 600 B.C. Several eruptions and extrusions of rhyolite domes occurred during the past 400 years, the last in 1890 (Kilbourne, Chesterman, and Wood 1980:table 2, fig. 5; M.C. Hall 1983:fig. 2).

Mono-Inyo tephra layers of the last 1,500 years occur in northwestern Nevada and were found in association with cultural deposits at the Borealis site near Hawthorne (Pippin 1980), and in Hidden Cave and dunes near Fallon (J.O. Davis 1982, 1985). They are also known from Yosemite Valley to the east and from as far south as Kings Canyon National Park in the southwestern Sierra Nevada (Kilbourne, Chesterman, and Wood 1980; Sarna-Wojcicki, Champion, and Davis 1983).

Volcanism in the Black Rock Desert of western Utah is indicated by basalt flows, with and without strandlines (Condie and Barsky 1972:fig. 2; J.D. Hoover 1974),

Fig. 9. Mono Craters, Calif., view to the south toward the Inyo Craters and the snow-capped Sierra Nevada. Panum Crater, lower right, is about 0.5 miles in diameter. Its eruption about A.D. 1300 produced a distinctive tephra useful in dating paleoecological and archeological events. Photographed by John S. Shelton, 1982.

and by a 15,400-year-old tephra from Pavant Butte recognized in sediments of pluvial Lake Bonneville (Currey 1982). Here, volcanic activity continued through and after the last deep lake cycle. At Craters of the Moon, eastern Snake River Plain, Idaho, basaltic lava erupted in at least eight episodes during the past 15,000 years (Kuntz et al. 1980).

Just as Mono-Inyo tephras serve to correlate archeological sites in alluvium, caves, and dunes of the region, the Mazama ash bed allows correlation of environmental conditions over much of western North America. In northern Nevada it occurs near the base of dunes and below a characteristic soil. During a time of vegetational flux indicated by fossil pollen from mountain bogs and desert caves, ash fell into shallow lakes, into streams that were entrenched and others that were not, and onto aggrading colluvium of steep mountain slopes. From these observations J.O. Davis (1982:65–66) concluded that Mount Mazama erupted when effective moisture was declining and summer rain was increasing.

In the Steens Mountain area, southeastern Oregon, at least six volcanic ashes are known from the past 7,000 years; the two oldest are from Mount Mazama. As in northern Nevada, the Mazama ashes occur with archeological remains in cave fill and dunes at a time of changing vegetation. Sand began accumulating shortly before the eruption, and volcanic ash was deposited between distinctive soils. The six volcanic ashes precisely correlate pollen sequences from within and between lakes in shadscale desert, sagebrush-grass, and alpine grassland associations. They also allowed the exact matching of overlapping cores from a single lake

that, in turn, provided a Holocene paleomagnetic record for the northern Great Basin (Verosub and Mehringer 1984:fig. 1).

Tephra studies are important in reconstructing late Quaternary climates and their effects on natural processes and on human populations. But, as illustrated in archeological investigations of the Mono-Inyo Craters area, volcanic events may have also directed the course of human pursuits (Bettinger 1982:85). In the shadow of Mammoth Mountain, California, recurrent volcanism periodically created shortages leading to political and economic disruptions. According to M.C. Hall (1983) after 1800 B.C. an optimal climate for population growth coincided with minimal volcanic activity, and obsidian poured across the Sierra Nevada to central California in exchange for shell. Then, with recurrent eruptions following the explosion of South Coulee (Mono Craters, about A.D. 200; M.C. Hall 1983:fig. 2) and deteriorating climate, came shortages, declining population, and the resulting collapse of the trans-Sierra obsidian exchange system.

Although the immediate detrimental effects of volcanic eruptions and ashfalls are certain (Malde 1964; Thorarinsson 1979; Wilcox 1959), the longer-term ecological consequences are not easily determined (Blinman, Mehringer, and Sheppard 1979). However, because volcanic activity may trigger climatic change or result from climatic fluctuations (Sarna-Wojcicki, Champion, and Davis 1983:52), coincidence of climate change and volcanic activity deserves especial attention in the evaluation of human responses (Cressman 1977:53). The apparent drastic decline and continued small human populations from 5900 to 3800 B.C. in the Fort Rock Basin, Oregon (fig. 10), have fostered considerable speculation about mid-Holocene drought or the lingering effects of the eruption of Mount Mazama (Aikens 1982:148–151, fig. 2; Bedwell 1973; Grayson 1979). Nonetheless, short-term consequences of recurrent volcanic activity both at Mount Mazama and at Newberry Volcano are most likely involved. The Newberry caldera rim is visible from Fort Rock only 25 miles to the south; many of the more than 400 cinder cones and fissure vents are much closer (Chitwood, Jenson, and Groh 1977; Heiken, Fisher, and Peterson 1981; MacLeod et al. 1981).

Mount Mazama erupted several times in the 150 years or so before its climactic explosion (Mullineaux and Wilcox 1980) and must have created a certain dilemma for those living in its shadow and perhaps already adjusting to shrinking lakes and diminishing marshes. The final explosion was incomprehensible within the experience of the people; then came new rumblings, but this time from the nearby Newberry Volcano (Friedman 1977). After a spurt of activity from 5400 to 4800 B.C. eruptions slowed. The crunch of pumice beneath sandals and plumes of fine dust marked passage of adventuresome bands who occasionally found their way to Fort Rock. With improving 39

Oreg. Dept. of Transportation, Salem: 5199.
Fig. 10. Fort Rock, Oreg., a maar volcano with prominent wave-cut notches (inset) some 65 feet above the valley floor. The south rim of the tuff ring has been eroded and swept away by waves (Walker and Nolf 1981). Photographed in 1979.

climate ephemeral ponds again dotted the valley floors and people returned in large numbers. Newberry Volcano was relatively quiet until activity increased sharply again about A.D. 300 to 800 (fig. 11).

Holocene tectonic activity is concentrated in two north-south belts following the western and eastern bound-

Oreg. State Dept. of Geology and Mineral Industries, Portland.
Fig. 11. The Big Obsidian Flow of Newberry Volcano, near Bend, Oreg., seen from above Paulina Lake with Little Crater at the lower left. Many parasitic cones are visible on the south flank of the volcano beyond the outer caldera rim at the top of the picture. The Big Obsidian Flow is part of the youngest period of volcanism that also sent tephra to the east and produced local ash flows between 1,400 and 1,300 years ago. Photographed in 1960s.

40

aries of the Great Basin (Bucknam and Thenhaus 1983). From 1852 to 1977, 1,222 shocks had Nevada epicenters; 49 of these occurred from 1961 to 1977 (Askew and Algermissen 1983). Faults control the location and discharge of many Great Basin springs; thus, in more arid regions, their histories are pertinent to aboriginal demography.

Soon it may be possible to assess more precisely the prehistoric effects of earthquakes such as the Owens Valley disaster of 1872 (M.R. Hill 1972; Oakeshott, Greensfelder, and Kahle 1972) and the Mammoth Lakes tremors culminating in May 1980 (Savage and Clark 1982). An eruption such as Mount Mazama would influence, for example, resources (including new obsidian sources), settlement patterns, or a view of the earth and the heavens. If coincidence of climatic stress and recurrent volcanism wrought catastrophic cultural consequences, evidence for population adjustments on a grand scale should emerge from archeological investigations in western Nevada and adjacent areas to the north, south, and west. It is now obvious that the immediate and lasting effects of major eruptions and ash-falls locally have been far more important to humans than regional climatic change.

Wind Action

Dunes are conspicuous features found leeward of the remnants of virtually every Great Basin pluvial lake and river. Presence of important food plants is partly responsible for the occurrence of archeological remains in dunes. Also, being well-drained, dunes make ideal campsites. Because dunes act as sponges, rapidly absorbing occasional rain but releasing it slowly (Bowers 1982:202), mesquite (*Prosopis juliflora, P. pubescens*) and Indian ricegrass (*Oryzopsis hymenoides*)—both especially important resources in the Great Basin (Steward 1933b:244, 1938:18, 26, 28, 74, 96)—often owe their existence in harvestable numbers to semistable sand substrates. Dunes have produced extensive marshes by damming spring-fed drainages, thereby increasing local productivity and attracting waterfowl and mammals. Such marshes occur at Saratoga Springs (fig. 12), Death Valley (Wallace and Taylor 1959), and Ash Meadows, Amargosa Desert, Nevada.

The position of active dunes results from availability of source material, topography, vegetation cover, fossil dune patterns, and wind direction, velocity, and duration (McKee 1979; R.S.U. Smith 1982). Regardless of impressive recent wind action, former periods of more extensive activity as well as greater stability are evidenced by dune migration followed by deflation, stabilization, fine-grained eolian deposition, weathering, and dissection by streams (Ahlbrandt 1974; Allison 1966:table 5; Davis and Elston 1972; Hawley and Wilson 1965:49; Morrison 1964a:76, 84–85; Rusco and Davis

Fig. 12. The spring-fed marsh at Saratoga Springs, on the Amargosa River, Death Valley, Calif., formed by a dune dam. Desert pupfish (R.R. Miller 1950; R.S.U. Smith 1978) have been isolated there since the springs last flowed into the Amargosa River. Photograph by Peter J. Mehringer, 1966.

1982; Sharp 1966:1059; H.T.U. Smith 1967:6, 16). Recurrent eolian activity in the Amargosa Desert (Mehringer and Warren 1976) is radiocarbon dated from before 4100 to about 600 B.C. (with brief reduction in activity about 2300 B.C.), from A.D. 15 to A.D. 1000 and again after 1550 (fig. 13). A chronologically similar sequence occurs at Corn Creek Dunes, Las Vegas Valley, Nevada (Williams and Orlins 1963:fig. 1), where radiocarbon-dated hearths placed dune activity between 3800 and 2600 B.C. After a minor hiatus, accumulating sand was stabilized by a soil, which in turn was partially deflated and buried by younger dunes (Haynes 1967:60–65, fig. 18). Absence of pre–Death Valley III artifacts (Hunt 1960:112; Hunt and Mabey 1966:82) suggests a minimum age of about 2,000 years for formation of some existing dunes in Death Valley.

Skull Creek Dunes, Catlow Valley, southeastern Oregon, revealed distinctive volcanic ashes, conspicuous paleosols, and numerous artifacts, whose abundance was exaggerated by their accumulation as lag in blowouts. By 6000 B.C. eolian deposits overlying pluvial lake sediments had stabilized, weathered, and eroded. Windblown sand accumulated again shortly before 5900 B.C., and human presence is indicated by archeological middens below, through, and above volcanic ash from two eruptions of Mount Mazama. Although people used the dunes briefly thereafter, there is little evidence of their presence for the next 3,000 years. During this period another volcanic ash fell before stability and weathering produced a soil.

Catlow Valley dunes were on the march again by 1800 B.C. Between A.D. 500 and 1000 the most strongly developed Holocene soil sealed loose sand containing remains of ancient campsites. Another relatively minor period of dune building and subsequent stability preceded the current episode of blowing sand. Skull Creek Dunes, like those of the Humboldt River (Rusco and Davis 1982), Black Rock Desert, Nevada (Davis and Elston 1972), and Death Valley region, show distinct periods and intensities of activities and human use.

The pumice dunes of the Fort Rock Basin (Allison 1966) harbor remain as important as those of the Famous Fort Rock, Connley Hills, and Cougar Mountain caves. Studies there revealed living surfaces, concentrations of charcoal, lithic debitage, charred seeds, and bones of fish and fowl. These occupations are radiocarbon dated around 1800 B.C., a time when lakelets (Allison 1979) filled troughs between juniper-covered dunes. Other sites stratigraphically beneath these date to 6000 B.C. Through much of the Great Basin, dunes offer the best possibility for determining age and stratigraphic succession of archeological assemblages.

Sediments, Deposition, and Erosion

Estimates of the effect of climate on geomorphic rates and processes (erosion, deposition, and wind action)

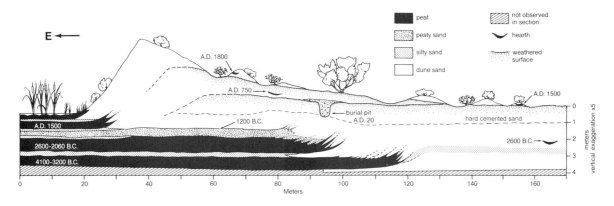

after Mehringer and Warren 1976:fig.6.

Fig. 13. Generalized stratigraphic section of dunes in Ash Meadows, Amargosa Desert, Nev., with positions and ages of hearths and a burial pit relative to marsh and dune deposits.

and their influence on aboriginal subsistence (K. Bryan 1941; Hack 1942), together with assumptions of synchronous and parallel regional climatic change (Antevs 1948, 1955:329), continue to influence archeological interpretations. Cut-fill sequences, so well dated in parts of the Plains and Southwest (Haynes 1968:figs. 2, 4), are more poorly known in the Great Basin except in the Las Vegas Valley. However, in river valleys and tributary streams throughout the Great Basin, casual observation reveals evidence for episodes of channel cutting and filling over the last 12,000 years (Rusco and Davis 1982).

The stage of channel erosion or aggradation along the Moapa and Virgin rivers and their tributaries was no doubt important to horticulture and settlement (Shutler 1961). Severe erosion, destruction of fertile floodplain, and lowered water tables would inhibit farming. Although the poorly drained valley of the Moapa River, choked with sediments, weeds, and mesquite thickets, seems an equally formidable deterrent to successful horticulture (but exceedingly productive for gatherers), it could have been cleared easily by repeated burning (S.C. Martin 1983). Along Meadow Valley Wash, near Caliente, Nevada (fig. 14), aggradation following extensive erosion is radiocarbon dated to A.D. 300 and 1400 (Madsen 1972).

Studies of Deer Creek Cave (G.M. Wilson 1963), Stuart Rockshelter (Howell 1960; Sabels 1960), and Rampart Cave (Martin, Sabels, and Shutler 1961) provide examples in which sediment size analysis, degree of weathering, organic and trace element content, and mode of deposition have contributed information on past environments. Swanson and Muto (1975) attributed relatively less rockfall in rockshelters of eastern Idaho (6000–4700 B.C.) and at Hogup Cave (6100–5000 B.C.) to the supposed aridity of these periods. Varying percentages of sand, silt, and clay from Rock Creek, an open site, have been used as an index of climatic history for correlation with cave sites (J.P. Green 1972:25, figs. 8, 9). At Hidden Cave, Nevada, the question of human use between obvious occupation levels was settled by a simple application of sediment size analysis. When people used the cave they mixed the fill. Therefore, sediment of occupation levels is poorly sorted throughout the cave, whereas sediment naturally deposited and undisturbed becomes finer away from the entrance (Wigand and Mehringer 1985:fig. 9.6).

In an exemplary study, investigators at Gatecliff Shelter described 56 geological strata from 35 feet of fill containing 16 cultural horizons. Mazama tephra and 47 radiocarbon dates provided ages for natural deposits and for human use since 4200 B.C. Geologists studied stratigraphic relationships, sediment texture and structure, mode and rate of deposition, and weathering (Davis et al. 1983). From these studies they constructed either an eight-part (J.O. Davis 1983:table 7) or four-part

Fig. 14. Modern arroyo and alluvial channel fill of Meadow Valley Wash, about 12 miles south of Caliente, Nev. This fill began to accumulate about 450 years ago following arroyo cutting that began after 1,700 years ago. Episodes of extensive arroyo cutting have lowered water tables and destroyed fertile floodplains. Photograph by Peter J. Mehringer, 1971.

(Melhorn and Trexler 1983:table 8) sequence of climatic variation since 5800 B.C. They recognized a particularly important soil-forming period about 2600 B.C. Remarkable differences in the deposits indicated variation in available sediment, stability of slopes, and intensity of rainfall. For example, basal strata consist of angular chert and limestone fragments derived from roof fall, and silt lenses and talus. This colluvial rubble contrasts with overlying sands and silts containing varying amounts of dispersed rubble. Differing sediment of the Gatecliff Shelter sequence apparently resulted from season, intensity, and amount of precipitation. Most important, variation in mid-Holocene climate was an inescapable conclusion of these studies; part of this variation seemingly included more summer precipitation.

Other geological features, events, and processes may prove important to understanding human life in the Great Basin by furnishing clues to regional climatic change, ecological conditions, or chronological relationships. In eastern Oregon, periglacial patterned ground of stone polygons and stripes marks the sites of abundant root crops, such as bitterroot and biscuit-root (Couture 1978). The chronology of alpine glaciation (Burke and Birkeland 1983; Porter, Pierce, and Hamilton 1983) and the history of temperature-sensitive upper tree line bristlecone pines could prove essential to understanding trade across the Sierra Nevada and the remains of mountain villages such as Alta Toquima (Thomas 1982). Although soils are sometimes used in correlation, and as indicators of past vegetation and climate (Ruhe 1983; Shroba and Birkeland 1983), assumptions of contemporaneity over great distances, time represented by weathering episodes, and responsible climatic parameters will require further study in the Great Basin. Yet, soil-forming periods characterize the Holocene and, at least locally, provide an independent means of correlation.

Biological Evidence

Plant Macrofossils

Until the 1970s, the history of vegetational fluctuations accompanying late Quaternary climatic change in the Great Basin was derived primarily from exceptionally well-preserved macrofossils from dry caves and rockshelters. Sloth dung and other debris of man and beast recovered from archeological cave excavations provided most of the data. Ground sloth (*Nothrotheriops shastensis*) dung from Rampart and Muav caves in the Grand Canyon, Arizona, and Gypsum Cave near Las Vegas, Nevada, contained plants still occurring in their vicinities; however, other species indicated significant vegetational changes between 40,000 and 11,000 years ago. The dominant species before 12,000 to 11,000 years ago now grow at considerably higher elevations (Laudermilk and Munz 1934:34, pl. 11; Long and Martin 1974; Martin, Sabels, and Shutler 1961:115; Mehringer 1967:figs. 4, 5; Phillips 1977).

Of the scores of studies of plant remains from Great Basin dry caves, Harper and Alder's (1970, 1972:fig. 3) investigations of Hogup and Danger caves, Utah, remain the most thorough. In addition to providing information on specific human uses of plants and confirming long dependence on playa-edge resources, they also used plant assemblages to reconstruct past vegetation and climate. Macrofossils that most clearly tell of human activities come from human coprolites in dry caves and dunes. From these the varieties and importance of foods (Kelso 1970; Wilke 1978), their preparation (Napton and Kelso 1969:26), and the season and region of their collection (Fry 1976; Heizer and Napton 1969; Wilke 1978) are discovered. Seeds from human coprolites, in conjunction with pollen, can further delimit the time of harvest and the likelihood of storage of certain foods (Wigand and Mehringer 1985).

Remains of the urine-coated dens and dung of woodrats are proving nearly as important. Ancient packrat or woodrat (*Neotoma* spp.) middens, from dry caves and shelters of the Mojave Desert, were found to contain the remains of woodland trees and shrubs thousands of years old (Wells and Jorgensen 1964). This discovery revolutionized the understanding of late Quaternary vegetation of North American deserts. At first, some suspected the woodrat midden fossils indicated only slight downward displacement of xeric woodlands (Wells and Berger 1967:1646), but Pleistocene-age middens containing the remains of bristlecone pine, limber pine, and white fir were then discovered on an isolated Mojave Desert mountain (Mehringer and Ferguson 1969).

Studies of radiocarbon-dated plant remains from woodrat middens of western North America (most initiated by Paul S. Martin and his students at the University of Arizona) continue to reveal the surprising late Quaternary histories of desert shrubs and forest trees and their climatic significance (Siegel 1983). Plant assemblages with abundant conifers remains, but without local modern counterparts, dominated Pleistocene woodrat middens from the eastern Grand Canyon (Cole 1982). Both single-needle piñon and giant sequoia were more widely distributed in the southwestern Sierra Nevada (Cole 1983). Spruce, limber pine, Douglas fir, and dwarf juniper all grew together in Canyon de Chelly, northeastern Arizona, and also well below their present lower elevational limits in southeastern Utah (Betancourt 1984; Betancourt and Davis 1984). The vegetation of the Chihuahuan and Sonoran deserts resulted from replacement of Pleistocene woodlands by individual species with varying requirements and migration rates. Only during the last 7,000 to 4,000 years have species finally come together at different times and in different places to produce assemblages characteristic of the Arizona deserts (Van Devender 1983). The post-pluvial northward movement, ascent, and subsequent adjustment of species as revealed by their occurrence in woodrat middens of the Great Basins is a tale not fully told but is essential to understanding the human story. The changing late Quaternary vegetation of Great Basin mountains is explored by Spaulding, Leopold, and Van Devender (1983), Thompson and Mead (1982), Thompson (1984), and Wells (1983).

Thompson and Mead (1982) described the pluvial-age occurrence of limber (*Pinus flexilis*) and bristlecone (*P. longaeva*) pines on southern and eastern Great Basin ranges, geographically distinct distributions of spruce (*Picea engelmannii*) to the north, and white fir (*Abies concolor*) and Douglas fir (*Pseudotsuga menziesii*) in the southeast. This discussion is continued by Wells (1983), who envisioned a subarctic landscape with dwarf and prostrate junipers (*Juniperus communis, J. horizontalis*) on the fringe of the north-central Great Basin. Subalpine forests of the central Great Basin were dominated by bristlecone pine (fig. 15) that extended downward nearly to the Bonneville lakeshore (Wells 1983:fig. 11) in association with dwarf juniper and occasionally Engelmann spruce. Limber pine, Douglas fir, and Rocky Mountain juniper (*Juniperus scopulorum*) occurred to the southeast (Wells 1983:table 3).

The northern perimeter of juniper-piñon woodlands extended across the southern Great Basin below 5,900 feet elevation in the northern Mojave Desert (Rowlands et al. 1982) at about 37° north latitude. Here full glacial, single-needle piñon pine (*Pinus monophylla*) extended downward toward the Las Vegas Valley to below 3,500 feet elevation on limestone outliers on the east flank of the Spring Range (Spaulding, Leopold, and Van Devender 1983:268). Utah junipers (*Juniperus osteosperma*) grew below 2,000 feet on limestone on the northwest side of the Spring Range (Mehringer and

Fig. 15. Bristlecone pine growing on Deep Springs dolomite at 10,800 feet in the White Mountains, Calif. The trees on the slope in the background show the upper tree line and are part of the Ancient Bristlecone Pine Forest within the Inyo National Forest. Before retreating in the path of Holocene warming, bristlecone pines were widespread at lower elevations. At present, they are isolated on the highest peaks of the larger Great Basin mountains. Photograph by E.B. Ferguson, 1962.

Warren 1976:125; Spaulding 1983). Woodlands of pygmy conifers and xerophytic shrubs dominated southward through the Mojave, Sonoran, and Chihuahuan deserts. When released from the chilling grip of glacial climates by 12,000 years ago, woodland species extended northward and upward into territory relinquished by pluvial lakes, cold steppe species, and subalpine or montane conifers. Some retreated to small mountains or favored ravines only to become locally extinct in isolation or to withstand repeated onslaughts by Holocene desert invaders well-suited to the new climatic regimes. By 6500 B.C. the woodland survivors of the southern Great Basin had all but withdrawn to areas they still occupy.

Although losing ground to woodland in the south, the more mesic conifers (Rocky Mountain juniper, white fir, Douglas fir, and ponderosa pine) reached the high mountains of the east-central Great Basin in the Holocene. While retreating from ice age positions on their southern flank, single-needle piñon pine and Utah juniper advanced along a broad northern front that saw piñon extend its range across Nevada south of the Humboldt River and about 400 miles north through western Utah to Idaho (Lanner 1983:tables 37–39; Tueller et al. 1979:fig. 2; Wells 1983:372; West et al. 1978). Some

researchers credit birds such as Clark's nutcracker, piñon jay, and bandtailed pigeon with late-glacial and Holocene dispersal of conifers, especially heavy wingless piñon seeds. Yet, human seed carriers have roamed the places of piñons for at least 11,500 years and can hardly be doubted as accidental distributors, if not intentional propagators, of foods so overwhelmingly desirable as the piñon and the mesquite. Mesquite is commonly represented in woodrat middens from southwestern Arizona after 9000–8000 B.C. (T.R. Van Devender, personal communication 1984). Although present in aboriginal hearths in the Amargosa Desert (Ash Meadows, southern Nevada), about 3700 B.C. (Mehringer and Warren 1976:138), it was absent from woodrat middens at 8000 B.C. (Spaulding 1983).

Radiocarbon-dated, charred seeds from Gatecliff Shelter confirm piñon pine's arrival in the Toquima Range, central Nevada, by about 4200 B.C. Nearby woodrat middens occurring in modern juniper-piñon communities date since 3800 B.C. These contain fossils of single-needle piñon and Utah juniper, whereas those dating 7600–7000 B.C. lack both piñon pine and Utah juniper but harbor mesic species such as willow, aspen, rose, and serviceberry (Thompson and Hattori 1983:table 32). Utah juniper and piñon seemingly appeared sometime between 7000 and 4200 B.C., and the sudden increase in percentage of juniper and then pine pollen in the fill of Gatecliff Shelter about 5000 B.C. may herald their advance (Thompson and Kautz 1983). Likewise, increasing pine pollen in the Ruby Marshes, northeastern Nevada, could signal expansion of piñon pine there about 2600 B.C. Piñon remains are known from ranges of the east-central Great Basin from shortly before 5000 B.C. and from the Ruby Mountains by 1200 B.C. (Thompson and Hattori 1983:table 36, fig. 64).

Fossil Pollen

Hansen (1947, 1947a) established the presence of significant postpluvial changes in pollen deposition of southeastern Oregon. He inferred pine forests during the waning phases of the last pluvial and suggested that composite pollen indicated drier and warmer conditions between 8,000 and 4,000 years ago. His studies were completed before the advent of radiocarbon dating, yet they illustrated the usefulness of pollen analysis for correlation and relative dating.

Pollen from pluvial lake deposits shows conifer importance prior to 12,000–10,000 years ago. At Searles Lake (Spaulding, Leopold, and Van Devender 1983:fig. 14–17) and Tule Springs (Mehringer 1967a) abundant pine and juniper pollen indicate woodland near the sites and expansion or increased density of conifers at higher elevations. Sagebrush (*Artemisia*) pollen is also more abundant than it has been during the last 10,000 years. To the north, in the pluvial Lake Bonneville Basin, spruce accompanies pine as an important tree (Martin and Mehringer 1965:fig. 2). In southeastern Oregon pollen spectra dating to 13,000 years ago demonstrate dominance of sagebrush and juniper indicating cold steppe that is in keeping with permafrost evidenced by patterned ground (Péwé 1983). Although subalpine and woodland trees grew at lower elevations during the last pluvial, the abundance of sagebrush pollen from Oregon and Idaho to southern Nevada and from the Sierra Nevada to the Wasatch Front highlights the ice-age importance of this genus.

Few pollen records from the Great Basin span the last 10,000 to 12,000 years, but those that do offer interesting glimpses into secrets of the past despite individual problems of interpretation, dating, ecological site sensitivity, and regional variation. At Tule Springs, Las Vegas Valley, Nevada, the major trend toward warmer and drier conditions after 10,600 B.C. is marked by a change from juniper-sagebrush to sagebrush-shadscale. By 5800 B.C. the vegetation was probably similar to the present flora at lower elevations in the Mojave Desert. Short-term reversals of this drying trend are dated about 8600–8000 B.C. and 6600–6000 B.C.; the record is incomplete after 5800 B.C..

Changing discharge at spring-fed salt marshes of the Great Basin (fig. 12) is reflected by their sedimentation pattern, fossil pollen, mollusks, and diatoms that furnish data on past salinity and water depth. Pollen records from salt marshes in the Death Valley area contain evidence for nearly total desiccation and deflation, as well as higher than present spring discharge. In both Panamint Valley and Ash Meadows, initiation of peat formation and accompanying dominance of sedge and cattail pollen and macrofossils is dated at about 2000 B.C. These deposits are eroded and weathered, probably as a result of significant desiccation (after 300 B.C.?). Another episode of marsh growth started about A.D. 1550.

Over the last 5,000 years nearly 40 feet of meadow, marsh, and lake deposits have filled the channel of the pluvial Owens River at Little Lake, California. These are rich in pollen and macrofossils that reveal fluctuating water levels. From 4300 to about 1200 B.C. meadow or marsh occupied the basin. With fluctuations, the water rose to form a shallow lake that has persisted for most of the time since then (Mehringer and Sheppard 1978).

Holocene pollen profiles are available from two localities in northeastern California—Osgood Swamp, near the south end of Lake Tahoe, and Adobe Valley, 15 miles southeast of Mono Lake. Osgood Swamp was formed within a terminal moraine; its deposits are dated by Mazama ash and radiocarbon. The pollen diagram was interpreted by Adam (1967) as indicating colder and drier conditions in the basal inorganic zone dominated by sagebrush and juniper. The most obvious

change is reflected in the transition to organic sediment and dominance of conifer pollen about 8000 B.C. Adam, primarily utilizing aquatic and bog-edge types as indicators of water depth, recognized a two-part postglacial climatic optimum with the later temperature maximum terminating about 1100 B.C. A 2,500-year sequence from nearby Ralston Ridge Bog included buried roots indicating dry conditions about A.D. 800 and 700 when trees invaded the normally wet depression (Šercelj and Adam 1975).

At Black Lake, Adobe Valley, California, Batchelder (1970) studied plant microfossils, fossil mollusks, and the geochemistry of Holocene sediments. Plant indicators of water depth and lake size suggested that organic sediments dating from about 9600 B.C. indicated conditions drier and somewhat colder than those of the present. A trend toward deeper water culminated about 6600–6000 B.C. Drier conditions prevailed 6000 to 3200 B.C. The most xeric interval, about 5900–5000 B.C., was followed by deeper water before 4100 B.C. After A.D. 15 temperature and moisture approached their modern values.

Several pollen records from the northeastern Great Basin indicate patterns of Holocene vegetation. At Snowbird Bog, Little Cottonwood Canyon, Wasatch Mountains near Salt Lake City, Utah, deposits dating from 10,400 B.C. are initially dominated by spruce, sagebrush, and other nonarboreal pollen, then birch and alder pollen increase (Madsen and Currey 1979:fig 4). Pine pollen remains relatively unimportant until about 6000 B.C. when both spruce and pine increase sharply, suggesting a change from cool-dry to warmer conditions. Two subsequent changes in pollen ratios are thought to correspond to stages of neoglaciation in the Rocky Mountains.

Pollen sequences from Swan Lake and the Raft River Mountains show equally impressive indications of late-glacial and mid-Holocene vegetational differences. Swan Lake, Idaho, occupies a shallow depression about 4.5 miles south of Red Rock Pass, the outlet of pluvial Lake Bonneville to the Snake River (Bright 1966). Basal deposits are radiocarbon dated at 10,000 B.C. For the next 2,000 years, pine with some spruce and fir accounted for 70 to 90 percent of total pollen. With minor fluctuations, the coniferous trees thinned or retreated to higher elevations as the climate warmed. About 8000 B.C. they were replaced by sagebrush steppe. The lowest values of arboreal pollen, indicating a semiarid climate, occurred between 6000 and 1200 B.C. Increased pine pollen values from about 1200 B.C. to A.D. 300 probably resulted from a return to more effective moisture and minor expansion or increasing density of pines.

Pollen from Curelom Cirque, Raft River Mountains, Utah (fig. 16), shows trends similar to those from Swan Lake. From about 10,000 to 8600 B.C. the vegetation is represented by large sagebrush pollen values, appar-

Fig. 16. Curelom Cirque, Raft River Mountains, Utah, which contains a meadow that harbors a 12,000-year record of pollen and macrofossils as well as Mazama ash (Mehringer, Nash, and Fuller 1971). Approximately 10,000 B.C. is the minimum date for withdrawal of the ice. At that time, and for another 1,000 years, sagebrush pollen dominated the sequence; then conifers, beginning with spruce, filled the higher elevations of these mountains. Sagebrush resumed dominance during the mid-Holocene. Photograph by Peter J. Mehringer, 1970.

ently reflecting cold, nearly treeless conditions. Coniferous trees—first spruce, then fir and pine—either moved upslope or immigrated from distant ice age regions. By about 8600 B.C. conifer pollen reached its highest percentages; shortly before the fall of Mazama ash these values decreased sharply as sagebrush pollen increased. A sudden resurgence of conifer pollen percentages, which might correlate with a similar event near the middle of Zone S3 at Swan Lake, follows the fall of Mazama ash by less than 1,000 years. As at Swan Lake, there are significant fluctuations recording increased effective moisture, indicated by a return to conifer dominance during the last 3,500 years or so. Pollen and macrofossil studies of Lake Cleveland, Albion Mountains, south-central Idaho, also revealed a basal zone of sagebrush pollen. However, by about 9000 B.C. Engelmann spruce and limber pine were present; subalpine fir (*Abies lasiocarpa*) followed within 1,000 years. Lodgepole pine (*Pinus contorta*) macrofossils replace those of limber pine shortly after the fall of Mazama ash (O. K. Davis 1981).

Analyses of cores from the Great Salt Lake, Hogup Cave, and nearby Crescent Spring indicate significant changes in regional vegetation during the past 4,000 years. Most important are two distinct trends toward increased sagebrush and conifer pollen relative to that of saltbush between about 2000 and 300 B.C. They may correlate with Zone S2 at Swan Lake.

Kelso (1970:fig. 2) illustrated the utility of pollen spectra for correlating cave strata and, with others, has suggested vegetational reconstructions based on pollen from Great Basin and Snake River Plain caves and rockshelters (Bright and Davis 1982; Byrne, Busby, and Heizer 1979; Dalley 1976; Sears and Roosma 1961; Thompson and Kautz 1983; Wigand and Mehringer 1985). The increase in grass pollen from Hogup Cave (Level 12) starting about A.D. 500 (Kelso 1970) is indicative of a vegetation producing pollen spectra unlike those of the preceding 7,000 years. The low relative frequency of Chenopodiaceae pollen about 6000 B.C. (Levels 1 and 2) may indicate more effective moisture and/or less area of suitable halophytic habitat. At Swallow Shelter, Goose Creek Mountains, northwestern Utah, increase in pine, juniper, and sagebrush pollen relative to that of saltbush and composite pollen suggests a change to more effective moisture about 1800 B.C. The relative increase in grass pollen starting about A.D. 15–500 parallels a similar event at Hogup Cave (Dalley 1976:172).

Byrne, Busby, and Heizer (1979) reported a three-part pollen sequence (pine-saltbush-pine) from Leonard Rockshelter, Nevada, indicating a drier interval (5000–2600 B.C.) marked by mid-Holocene desiccation of Humboldt Sink. They concluded that sedge and cattail pollen were wind-borne to the cave along with silts from shrinking lake margins. At Hidden Cave, Carson Sink, Nevada, pine and sagebrush pollen percentages declined between 13,000 and 8000 B.C., and sagebrush pollen values decreased further as saltbush pollen increased about 5800 B.C. Wigand and Mehringer (1985) attribute cattails and bulrushes—represented by both pollen and macrofossils of cave fill and human coprolites—to the expansion of lakes and marshes. The abundance of these remains in Hidden Cave (Thomas 1985) indicates that people exploited nearby marshes about 2300 to 2000 B.C., a time corresponding to occupation of Kramer Cave, Winnemucca Lake. The intensity of occupation of and abundance of marsh plant remains from these two sites leave little doubt of a climatic event leading to a short episode, less than 200 years (about 2100 B.C.) of greatly increased effective moisture in the northwestern Great Basin.

Steens Mountain, southeastern Oregon, is unusual in lacking a post-glacial montane coniferous forest zone, but it is ideal for study of changing steppe vegetation (McKenzie 1982:fig. 3.8). Fossil pollen, algae and macrofossils of cores from Wildhorse (8,400 feet) and Fish (7,380 feet) lakes in subalpine and sagebrush steppe, and from Diamond Pond (4,150 feet) in sagebrush-shadscale desert indicate that sagebrush steppe followed retreating glaciers (fig. 17) to 7,500 feet by 10,000 B.C. and that Wildhorse Cirque was ice-free by 7400 B.C., and subalpine steppe had become established around Wildhorse Lake by 7000 B.C. The records from all three lakes are precisely correlated by volcanic ashes and radiocarbon dates. Fossil pollen exhibits a three-part division of the Holocene climatic record with variations in the timing of specific events at each of the sites stud-

46

Fig. 17. The great glacier-carved, U-shaped valley of Kiger Gorge, Steens Mountain, Oreg. The high plateau of Steens Mountain rises to nearly 10,000 feet and was once covered by an ice sheet that extended below 7,000 feet on open, west-facing slopes. Glaciers followed canyons to the base of the mountain. Ice was wasting at its maximum positions before 11,000 B.C. when sediments began accumulating in the glacially scoured basin of Fish Lake. Photograph by Leonard Delano, 1963.

ied. These differences resulted from the varying effects of temperature and precipitation at different elevations.

Sagebrush pollen abundance in relation to grass pollen between 6800 and 3600 B.C. at Fish Lake indicates less effective moisture than before or since. This mid-Holocene period of sagebrush dominance began 1,500 years earlier than the temperature-controlled (Nelson and Tiernan 1983) upward expansion of sagebrush to Wildhorse Lake about 6000 B.C. and ended 1,300 years before grass again assumed dominance at Wildhorse Lake about 1800 B.C. The end of this later period of higher temperatures and reduced snowpack about 2000 B.C. is recorded in the Diamond Pond cores by marked expansion of juniper grassland into shadscale desert. The return to more mesic conditions is further supported by radiocarbon-dated macrofossils of western juniper (*Juniperus occidentalis*) from Holocene woodrat middens in lava tubes and caves of the Diamond Craters flow (fig. 18).

Slight warming and drying after A.D. 1 is punctuated by droughts with the most severe occurring about A.D. 1500. Relatively cooler and/or moister conditions since then are indicated in the records from all lakes studied. Increased sagebrush pollen values near the top of each core represent historic disturbance.

Fossil Animals

Records of organisms from algae to piñon pines, to bats (Durrant 1970) and birds (Grayson 1977), to parasitic

worms (Fry 1976) and vermin (B. C. Nelson 1972) can explain much about human conditions and potential human adaptations. But this information by itself is not nearly so interesting as the larger question of how these plants and animals came to be where they are in the Great Basin (Billings 1950, 1978; Hubbs, Miller, and Hubbs 1974; Harper et al. 1978; Young, Evans, and Tueller 1976). The Holocene distribution of bison, retreat of bristlecones, and the travel of piñons, with their obvious implications for human activities, are good examples. Late Quaternary distributions of plants and animals remain incompletely understood, and definitive answers must await firm evidence from the fossil record. However, knowledge and theoretical considerations of present distributions provide testable hypotheses and the necessary framework for reconstructing past environments. This has been especially apparent in ap-

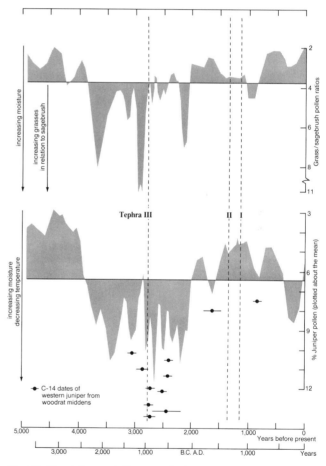

Fig. 18. Vegetation and climate at the lower sagebrush border, from Diamond Pond (Malheur Maar), Diamond Craters, Oreg. Increasing grass pollen in relation to sagebrush pollen would most likely result from conditions of more effective moisture. Larger juniper pollen percentages would indicate wetter and perhaps cooler conditions. The downward expansion of juniper into shadscale desert below the sagebrush border (the equivalent of at least 100 feet elevation), rather than increased abundance of juniper, is confirmed by juniper macrofossils in woodrat middens.

proaches to the study of fossil small mammals and their current ranges (J. H. Brown 1978; Grayson 1982). During the last pluvial some small mammals extended their ranges with changes in habitats. Subsequent contractions or expansions from these ranges are probably still occurring.

The distribution and abundance of small mammals, their changes through the late Quaternary, their usefulness as evironmental indicators, and their importance to people are reviewed by Grayson (1982:table 3, fig. 3). Pluvial-age small mammals (pikas, ground squirrels, voles, pocket gophers, marmots, pygmy cottontails, and martens) dispersed to mountain ranges, now isolated by desert, along Pleistocene avenues flanked by woodlands or across cold steppe. Perhaps more important, mountains were tied to adjacent valley lakes and marshes by riparian ribbons. Subsequent Holocene warming resulted in slow local extinctions of small mammals from isolated mountains or contractions from their low elevation and southern latitude ranges (Mehringer 1977:fig. 21). As with the fossil plants there appear to be critical times, at or after which the remains of certain small mammals are less commonly recovered. For example at Connley Cave, Fort Rock Basin, Oregon, pika remains are unknown from sediments postdating the fall of Mazama ash, and pygmy cottontails and jackrabbits were less abundant than before. Although with different timing, Grayson (1983) observed similar patterns in the Gatecliff Shelter faunal remains. Butler (1972) concluded that a climatically induced decrease in rodents from archeological sites on the Snake River Plain 7000–5800 B.C. was indicative of a decline in human carrying capacity, and Harper and Alder (1970:231–235, fig. 3, 1972:18–19) used faunal remains from Hogup and Danger caves in support of their fossil plant-based interpretations of climatic change.

Varying frequencies of bison, deer, mountain sheep, and antelope bones in archeological sites such as Hogup Cave (Aikens 1970:fig. 62) suggest Holocene changes in the abundance and distribution of these large mammals as well as changing human preference. However, the consequences of such changes must have been infinitesimal by comparison with the most important biological event of the late Quaternary—the sudden and massive extinction of the Pleistocene megafauna by 8600 B.C. (Meltzer and Mead 1983; Martin and Klein 1984). Modern bison, antelope, deer, and mountain sheep are but a small remnant of the large mammals that once existed. Their fossils attested to the long, and for a time successful, experiment in evolution and coexistence of autochthonous and immigrant species from Eurasia and South America. From Fossil Lake, Oregon (Allison 1966), to the Las Vegas Valley, Nevada (Mawby 1967), and from caves and lake beds between (Long and Martin 1974; Nelson and Madsen 1980) comes evidence for a fauna whose demise must have affected man, the

surviving fauna, and flora as well. All comparisons of present with pre-extinction biotic associations seem limited without consideration of the extinct megafauna.

Dendroclimatology

Studies of past tree growth and distribution provide the most precise evidence for both chronology and magnitude of climatic change. Opportunity for such study is unique, in its great age, to the Great Basin where living bristlecone pines (D.K. Bailey 1970) may be older than 4,000 years, and their wood survives many thousands of years past death of the trees (Ferguson 1968). Using both living and dead standing trees and wood remnants, Ferguson (1969, 1970, 1979; Ferguson and Graybill 1983) has established a continuous chronology back to 6700 B.C. and reported yet older wood. The long bristlecone pine chronology is of prime importance in understanding variation in radiocarbon production (Klein et al. 1982; Stuiver 1982). Though small, branches from ancient woodrat middens are thousands of years older and could provide a glimpse of the Pleistocene behavior of tree-ring series of bristlecone pine or other conifers. Very wide rings in the piñon pine branch from Clark Mountain, California, apparently indicate climatic conditions exceedingly conducive to piñon growth about 10,600 B.C. Such conditions were unlike any occurring in southern Nevada in recent times.

Analyses of climatic factors responsible for formation of wide or narrow rings together with the use of statistical models of tree response to environmental change are leading toward reconstruction of Great Basin climate of the past hundreds if not thousands of years (Fritts 1971, 1976, 1982; Fritts, Lofgren, and Gordon 1979), including perhaps a measure of the climatic effects of volcanic eruptions (LaMarche and Hirschboeck 1984). By comparing regional tree growth patterns with weather records, researchers have produced maps of temperature, precipitation, and pressure systems from the trees alone. The statistical relationships among ring widths or densities, and precipitation and temperature are then used to estimate climatic parameters from tree rings beyond the period of recorded weather (fig. 19). These may indicate similar trends in temperature or precipitation anomalies for the western United States or for only a portion of the Great Basin (Fritts 1982:fig. 5.26, 5.27). Thus, the influence of a particular short-term climatic change on resources and their users might vary across the Great Basin.

Dead bristlecone pines well above where any grow today (LaMarche 1973, 1974, 1978) as well as changes in the growth form of living trees (LaMarche and Mooney 1972:fig. 10) indicate tree line fluctuations during the last 6,000 years. Because minimum summer temperatures limit the elevations to which trees can survive, higher tree lines imply warmer growing seasons. Through

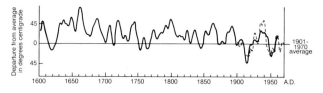

after Fritts 1982:fig.5.25.

Fig. 19. Reconstruction of temperatures in the Great Basin derived from tree rings, plotted as departures from the 1901–1970 averages. Dashed line indicates the filtered values of the corresponding instrumented record.

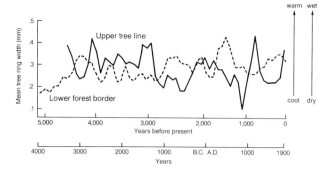

after LaMarche 1978:fig.4.

Fig. 20. Climatic fluctuation indicated by mean tree ring widths at 100-year intervals from upper tree line (temperature-sensitive) and lower forest border (drought-sensitive) sites in the White Mountains, Calif.

most of the past 6,000 years, the upper limit of trees in the White Mountains, California, has been higher than during the last few hundred years; from about 4300 to 1800 B.C. the tree line was 500 feet above its modern position (LaMarche 1973:fig. 3). Also, ring widths of bristlecone pines show significant variability. Wide rings near the upper tree line record warm summers, whereas wide rings in trees growing near the precipitation-controlled lower forest border register ample soil moisture during the growing season. Together, tree-ring widths from bristlecone pines living near both their upper and lower altitudinal limits provide estimates of relative temperature and precipitation for the White Mountains during the last 6,000 years (fig. 20).

Conclusions

During the last pluvial many basins, now dry and salt encrusted, were fed to overflowing by cool waters, joined by great fish-filled rivers, and tied by riparian ribbons of green. As glaciers carved beds in the snow-capped mountains, woodlands filled the treeless deserts. Herds of camels, horses, and mammoths grazed the steppes and fertile marshes. And then, from 10,600 to 8600 B.C., lakes shrank, rivers ceased to flow, and springs began to dry. Plants and animals started the long retreat northward and to higher elevations, or faced local extinction in isolation, and man witnessed the demise of the Pleistocene megafauna. By comparison, most subsequent environmental changes were minor.

A trend toward aridity prevailed for the next few thousand years. As lakes grew even smaller and spring discharge decreased due to the dwindling supply of pluvial-age ground water, both plants and animals continued to adjust their ranges, perhaps under the increasing influence of summer rainfall. With short-term reversals, the trend continued until about 6000 B.C., by which time conditions were clearly different from the preceding 5,000 years. Temperatures were rising as indicated by the upward advancing bristlecone pines and sagebrush that replaced montane forest trees or advanced into subalpine grassland. Lakes at lower elevation continued to shrink, perhaps as a result of reduced snow pack,

and marshes disappeared. Despite evidence for generally reduced effective moisture until about 3100 B.C. and higher temperatures until 2000 B.C. the mid-Holocene was a time of considerable and rapid climatic fluctuations. It was also a period of major adjustments in the ranges of plants as illustrated by the spread of piñon, no doubt aided by man.

About 7,000 years ago, when dunes were on the move, peoples of the northern Great Basin were unknowingly forewarned of a cataclysm by explosions preceding the climactic eruption of Mount Mazama. The collapse of Mount Mazama was followed by recurrent volcanism at Newberry Craters, and parts of eastern Oregon lay barren beneath shrouds of lava and pumice. With passing time the land recovered, rains returned with regularity, lakes and marshes again dotted basin floors, and volcanos were the subjects of myths. Snow-laden Pacific storms and longer winters occurred more frequently, and late summer monsoon rains lost influence in the north. The cooler or shorter summers pinched back bristlecone pines from their upper limits of the preceding several thousand years. Sagebrush retreated in the path of grass, woodland, and patches of snow that lasted through the summers; to the south and at lower elevations shadscale lost ground to sagebrush.

Studies of tree rings eventually will establish regional climatic patterns for the last 2,000 years. It is now possible to select periods likely to have seriously influenced human activities. For example, analyses of White Mountain bristlecones indicate that a warm-dry episode from the early 1100s to the early 1400s followed 100 years of warm-moist conditions and preceded cool-moist conditions lasting to the early 1600s (LaMarche 1974: fig. 6).

During the last 2,000 years, as during the preceding 10,000, there has been geological and biological instability of sufficient magnitude to affect the abundance of local resources. Changing lake levels and tree lines, renewed dune activity and stabilization, peat formation   *49* in desert salt marshes, arroyo cutting and filling, and significant tectonic and volcanic activity all continued through the past 1,000 years. Of special interest is the coincidence of grass, bison, and the Fremont culture of western Utah, the rise and fall of lakes in the Salton Trough and Winnemucca Basin, and the possible collapse of the trans-Sierra obsidian exchange system with deteriorating climate and recurrent eruptions of Mono-Inyo Craters.

The dynamic nature of Great Basin environments is apparent whether measured by geological or biological criteria, but most instability of the last 10,000 years is mirrored in the ecological variation encountered by Great Basin inhabitants within a single year; variability itself typifies the Great Basin. There were several periods when the cumulative effects of regional climatic change were sufficient to directly influence human populations; but locally, volcanic and tectonic activity or lakes resulting from geological accident have been even more important. In the western Great Basin, the coincidence of climatic stress and recurrent volcanism may have wrought catastrophic cultural consequences.

Historical Environments

KIMBALL T. HARPER

Topography and Climate

An alternation of high mountains and intervening valleys characterizes most of the Great Basin culture area. In the east and north, valleys become larger and the mountains more massive and lofty. Nevertheless, a mountain-valley theme prevails throughout this vast area. Rare indeed is the spot from which one cannot see mountains towering above the flatlands.

The environmental diversity associated with such topographic complexity profoundly influenced the ecology of native peoples of the region. Climate, vegetation, fauna, and culture all show intricate and generally predictable correlations with topography. Almost universally, temperature declines and precipitation increases with increasing elevation (Daubenmire 1979). Plant and animal distributions in the mountains of the region are strongly molded by the dual gradient of temperature and precipitation.

Although climate is a less obvious variable than topography or vegetation, both of the latter owe much of their character to climate. Low precipitation (fig. 1a) and severe evaporative stress (fig. 1b) combine to produce the sparsest vegetation in the southwestern quarter of the region. Cooler conditions in valleys of the remainder of the region give rise to a more dense (but still scant) plant cover. The regional distribution of cactus and succulent-leaved species such as yuccas is representative of many groups that are strongly influenced by the gradients of decreasing temperature and increasing available moisture that run from south to north across the region. The cacti and succulents have numerous species in the Southwest and decrease to few or none in the Plateau area.

Less arid and more complex climates characterize the mountains. The higher of these stand as humid islands above parched lowlands. Relatively dense vegetations develop in response to increased water supply. Many of the ranges accumulate sufficient moisture to support lakes and ponds and feed springs and streams. Nevertheless, mountains of the region often remain bold and angular. Too little moisture is available for rapid chemical weathering or for a profusion of vegetative growth that would obscure their stony skeletons.

It has long been known that variability of precipitation increases as the annual total declines (Trewartha and Horn 1980). Thus, the vast majority of the land not only receives little precipitation, but the meager supply that does fall varies widely from year to year. Consequently, the plant resource is both small and unpredictable. Hutchings and Stewart (1953) have shown that highly variable precipitation in the central Great Basin may result in an annual forage production that is six times larger in wet than dry years. This combination of low and unpredictable production is undoubtedly related to the fact that native peoples of the region were superb resource generalists (Jennings 1978). Few resources were present in sufficient quantity or with adequate reliability to invite cultural specialization and consequent dependence upon them. The native peoples thus verify the ecological dictum that species specializing on rare resources or resources that are temporally unreliable are unlikely to persist (Ricklefs 1979).

Along the drainage basin of the Colorado River in the central and southern portions of the region, erosion has carved immense canyons and laid bare large expanses of bedrock. Towering walls of richly colored rock dominate a labyrinth of meandering canyons and cliff slopes of breathtaking beauty (fig. 2). To the north, more stable landscapes have permitted deep-soiled plains to develop between the tributaries that eventually combine to produce the Green and Snake rivers. In that area, olive green mosaics of sagebrush (*Artemisia* spp.) and grasses (*Agropyron*, *Festuca*, and *Poa* spp. primarily) blanket the valleys and plains.

In the hydrologic Basin province, absence of external drainage to the sea has resulted in the development of over 150 more-or-less closed basins (Morrison 1965). In each, millions of years of erosion have stripped sediments and dissolved salts from the gray, block mountains and deposited them in the intervening basins. Alluvium and salts thus washed into the valleys are concentrically stratified around the valley bottoms. Lakes that developed in many of the basins during the Pleistocene were particularly influential in the stratifying process. As sediment-laden torrents lost speed, progressively smaller particles were dropped until only clays and salts remained to be deposited at the lake's center. From alluvial fan to playa of now extinct lakes, one finds a soil sequence dominated by progressively finer sized particles. The playa itself is clayey and usually so

51

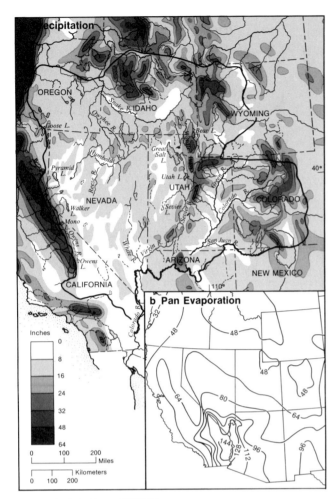

after U.S. Geological Survey 1970:97, 96.

Fig. 1. a, Mean annual precipitation and b, pan evaporation (both measured in inches) in the Great Basin area.

impregnated with soluble salts as to exclude most plants that could otherwise tolerate the environment.

Such a concentric arrangement of soil texture and salinity inevitably produces a continually changing spectrum of plant species and productivity from alluvial fan to playa floor. This biotic panorama is more related to geologic sorting of alluvium than to climatic change across the gradient.

Vegetation

Küchler's (1964) map of the potential natural vegetation in the United States illustrates the diversity of the vegetation of the region considered in this volume. It varies in the valleys from creosote (*Larrea tridentata*) dominated deserts of the Mojave (the so-called warm deserts) in southern Nevada and adjacent California to saltbush (*Atriplex* spp.) and sagebrush deserts (the cold deserts) of the Basin province, Colorado Plateau, and Snake River Plains. Both desert types are dominated by low, widely spaced shrubs. In total, deserts account for over 18 percent of the area.

Northward on much of the Snake River Plains and the flatlands of northern Wyoming, grasslands with open canopies of sagebrush were the dominant vegetation at the time of Euro-American settlement. Foothills across the Great Basin, on the edges of the Snake River Plains, and along the main backbone of the Rocky Mountains were apparently almost universally dominated by shrubby grasslands of variable composition (Cronquist et al. 1972). Sagebrush, sagebrush-grass, and grassland covered about 40 percent of the land area at time of contact with Europeans. The majority of that area is dominated by sagebrush-grass steppe. In early historic times, the steppes supported less brush and more grasses and broadleaved herbs than they did even a score of years

U.S. Dept. of the Interior, Bureau of Reclamation, Upper Colo. Region, Salt Lake City: top, P-557–420–8060; bottom, P-557–420–8064.

Fig. 2. The Colorado River drainage, a landscape of deeply eroded canyons flanked by rows of steps rising to overreaching ledges and pinnacles of caprock. top, North Wash, Henry Mountains in the background, near Hite, Utah, River Mile 167.7; bottom, junction of the Green River and the Colorado, River Mile 216.5. Photographed in March 1963, shortly after gates of the Glen Canyon Dam were closed and Lake Powell started to fill up.

after contact (Leopold 1950; Sauer 1950; O. C. Stewart 1955; Cottam 1961a; S. W. Barrett 1980). The rapid and dramatic change in valley and foothill vegetation is attributed to a sharp decrease in number and size of wildfires, many of which had been purposefully ignited by native peoples.

Mountains of the area show local variations in respect to vegetative cover but tend to support more-or-less distinct altitudinal zones of vegetation of contrasting appearance. In the southeastern and eastern parts of the region, for instance, lower slopes support sagebrush-grasslands while successively higher elevations support forests of juniper (*Juniperus osteosperma*) and piñon (*Pinus edulis*), followed by zones of scrub oak

(*Quercus gambelii*), ponderosa pine (*Pinus ponderosa*) forest, aspen (*Populus tremuloides*) forest, spruce (*Picea engelmannii*) and fir (*Abies lasiocarpa*) forest, and finally open herblands above timberline (fig. 3 top). In the northwestern portion of the region (central Nevada) vegetational zoning on mountain sides is far less complex (fig. 3 bottom). There lower slopes support a dry vegetation dominated by sagebrush. That zone quickly yields dominance to juniper and piñon (*P. monophylla*) woodland, and that, in turn, surrenders control to another sagebrush zone that supports considerably more perennial herbs (primarily grasses) than does the lower sagebrush zone. At yet higher elevations, scattered, open forests of conifers (*Abies concolor, Pseudotsuga*

Fig. 3. Characteristic altitudinal zones of vegetation. top, La Sal Mountains, southeastern Utah: 1, sagebrush-grass; 2, piñon-juniper (modified by a man-made grassland); 3, scrub oak; 4, ponderosa pine; 5, aspen; 6, spruce-fir; and 7, alpine herblands (too small and localized to show in the talus above tree line). bottom, Shell Creek Range, western Nevada: 1, sagebrush-grass; 2, piñon-juniper; 3, upper sagebrush-grass; 4, mountain conifer patches; and 5, subalpine herbs (distributed as localized patches on ridge crests). Photograph by Kimball T. Harper, top in 1975, bottom about 1978.

HISTORICAL ENVIRONMENTS

54

menziesii, Pinus ponderosa, P. flexilis, P. aristata, Picea engelmanniii depending on geographic location and elevation) characterize the slopes. On deep-soiled spots that are well watered, small aspen groves may occur. In this area, the occurrence of individual tree species on any given mountain range is highly unpredictable apparently due to the vagaries of dispersal and survival on these more humid sections of the arid region (Harper et al. 1978; Wells 1983). Above timberline, the terrain is rough and rocky, with shallow, poorly weathered soils; alpine herblands are uncommon and poorly developed.

Along the northern edge of the Great Basin and across the plains of the Snake River and Wyoming, vegetational zoning of mountain slopes is likely to commence with a brushy grassland community. That community is ultimately replaced on higher slopes by a zone of brushland of highly variable composition, for example, birchleaf mountain mahogany (*Cercocarpus montanus*), Rocky Mountain juniper (*Juniperus osteosperma*), serviceberry (*Amelanchier alnifolia*), maple (*Acer grandidentatum* or *A. gladbrum*), snowberry (*Symphoricarpos* spp.), ninebark (*Physocarpus malvaceus*), or chokecherry (*Prunus virginiana*). Closed forests of Douglas fir, ponderosa or lodgepole pine (*Pinus contorta*), aspen, or spruce and fir characterize developed soils on geologically stable sites at higher elevations. All forests combined and the adjacent brushy woodlands cover roughly 40 percent of the land area of the region. Perhaps half this vegetative cover is open and savannalike.

Above the spruce-fir zone in the east and north of the region, well developed herblands often appear. During the flowering season, the alpine herblands are frequently spectacularly beautiful. In aggregate, this type of vegetation and interspersed areas of barren rock account for about 2 percent of the area considered in this volume.

Small marshy spots exist around freshwater seeps and springs throughout the region, but in the hydrologic Basin province and Death Valley, numerous marshes of significant size occur in the basins of Pleistocene lakes. First-time visitors to these arid areas are almost universally surprised at the productivity and wondrous animal diversity of these expanses of rushes (*Scirpus* spp.), grasses (*Distichlis spicata, Phragmites australis, Puccinellia nuttalliana*), and succulent halophytes (*Allenrolfea occidentalis, Salicornia virginica* and relatives). Especially large expanses of such vegetation occur in the basins of the extinct lakes, Lahontan and Bonneville. Evidence indicates that such marshy environments have been more extensive at various times in the post-Pleistocene than they are now (Harper 1967; Harper and Alder 1970). Although only 0.2 percent of the region now supports marshlands, high and dependable productivity made these vegetation types some of the most important natural resources to native peoples (Jennings 1957; Heizer and Napton 1970a; Aikens 1970; Madsen 1982).

Depending on soil salinity and depth and duration of flooding, the vegetation of the marshes varies markedly. Vast areas that are moderately saline and never deeply or permanently flooded may support pure swards of saltgrass (*Distichlis spicata*). Highly saline soils that are seasonally irrigated by natural flooding may produce dense stands of alkali bulrush (*Scirpus paludosus*) or glasswort (*Salicornia rubra*). Sites that are permanently submerged with relatively fresh water may become dominated by cattails (*Typha latifolia*), hardstem bulrush (*Scirpus acutus*), or three-square bulrush (*Scirpus americanus*) depending upon water depth and salinity (Bolen 1964).

The more complex vegetational zoning in the southeastern and eastern portions of the region may have resulted in more technological complexity in local valley-mountain systems than was to be found in less vegetationally complex areas such as central or northwestern Nevada. Some evidence supports that expectation. In the Reese River valley of Nevada, Thomas (1971) concluded that native people alternated between piñon-juniper woodlands and the riparian zone along the river during the course of a year. In the Bonneville Basin, people apparently moved among at least four distinctly different ecosystems with marsh, riparian, montane, and piñon-juniper environments being exploited annually (Steward 1938).

Fauna

As might be expected, this arid region supports relatively few species of fishes, amphibians, and turtles, but the topographic and associated environmental diversity permits organisms able to cope with aridity such as

U.S. Dept. of the Interior, Bureau of Land Management, Nev. State Office, Reno: top left, 2032.2; top right, 2032.3; center left, 2032.1; center right, U. of Utah Archeol. Center, Salt Lake City; U.S. Dept. of the Interior, Bureau of Land Management, Calif. State Office, Sacramento: bottom left, 2/24; bottom right, 3/33.

Fig. 4. Semidesert and desert vegetation. top left, Humboldt Sink, western Nev., 1981; in wet years, such as 1983–1984, it is a lake; in dry years, such as 1981, it is a partial playa with salt-tolerant plants at its margin and stands of tule and cattail and sagebrush-grass on the foothills. top right, Valley floor, near Austin, Nev., Toiyabe Mountains in the background, 1962. Piñon, juniper, and sagebrush-grass are found here. center left, Diamond Valley near Eureka, Nev., 1963. Sagebrush-winterfat grows on the nearly level floor; piñon-juniper in the uplands. center right, Parunuweap Canyon, south fork of the Virgin River, southwestern Utah, 1962. bottom left, Joshua trees, bursage, and saltbush in the Lanfair Valley, Mojave Desert, Calif., 1980. bottom right, Sparse cover dominated by creosote bush in the Mojave Desert, Calif., Piute Range in the background, 1980.

56

lizards, snakes, and rodents to attain unusual species diversity for temperate North American (Harper 1968). Birds and hooved mammals are represented by about as many species here as in more mesic environments of similar latitudes elsewhere in North America. Martin (1961) has shown that the number of species of each of the major vertebrate groups declines steadily with increasing elevation. Clokey (1951) shows a similar trend for plants on a Nevada mountain. Thus most species are apparently excluded from the best-watered habitats—the upper slopes of mountains—by severe winters and short growing seasons.

Animal resources are so sparse in both creosote and shadscale deserts as to make these the least attractive portions of the region to native peoples. Small burrowing rodents such as kangaroo rats (*Dipodomys* spp.), kangaroo mice (*Microdipodops megacephalus*), pocket mice (*Perognathus parvus*), and antelope ground squirrel (*Ammospermophilus leucurus*) are among the more common residents of these deserts. Small birds of regular occurrence include the horned lark (*Eremophila alpestris*), vesper sparrow (*Pooecetes gramineus*), western king bird (*Tyrannus verticalis*), and loggerhead shrike (*Lanius ludovicianus gambeli*). In undrained valleys with a well-developed greasewood zone, black-tailed jackrabbits (*Lepus californicus*) may be abundant (Shelford 1963). Sparse but wide-ranging populations of predators such as kit fox (*Vulpes macrotis*), coyote (*Canis latrans*), and ferruginous hawk (*Buteo regalis*) occur throughout the deserts and would have competed vigorously with man for the meager animal resources. Less mobile and conspicuous small predators such as snakes, lizards, and certain arthropods were more abundant in the deserts than in any other of the major habitats.

Along the desert edges, sagebrush, sagebrush-grass, and juniper-piñon communities supported progressively more dense animal populations. In the sagebrush and sagebrush-grass communities, kangaroo rats are locally common while other, larger mammals that are infrequent in extreme deserts become abundant. For example, chipmunks (*Eutamias* spp.), woodrats (*Neotoma* spp.), ground squirrels, jackrabbits, and cottontails (*Sylvilagus* spp.) become important resources here. In addition the pronghorn antelope (*Antilocapra americana*) occurred throughout the region in sagebrush communities. Along the northern edge of the region, historic evidence (Roe 1951) and food bones from archeological sites indicate that bison (*Bison bison*) were locally common on at least the grassier portions of this zone. Where sagebrush communities cover the base of

U.S. Forest Service: 418859.
Fig. 6. Mule deer feeding at the mouth of Perry Canyon, Cache National Forest, near Willard, Utah, 1942.

high mountains, mule deer (*Odocoileus hemionus*) undoubtedly ventured into the sagebrush during winter (fig. 6). Sagehens (*Centrocercus urophasianus*) were likewise to be found in this zone, and during the nesting season, the mourning dove (*Zenaida macroura marginella*) would have been present in significant numbers. Coyote populations are known to have been high (especially in winter) in this zone (Shelford 1963).

A combination of characteristics including moderately high plant production and consequent larger animal populations, topographically sheltered habitats, protective plant cover, a relative abundance of springs, and moderate winters must have made the juniper-piñon zone a prime winter habitat for native peoples. Sizable resident populations of small game and wintering concentrations of big game probably attracted humans (Thomas 1983c) just as other large predators such as the mountain lion and the coyote are still seasonally attracted to this zone (Shelford 1963).

In the deep canyon country of the lower Colorado Plateau, most large mammals were rare. However, the desert race of the bighorn sheep (*Ovis canadensis*) thrived along the rough canyon edges (Irvine 1969). Small mammals of regular occurrence included woodrat, cottontail and jackrabbits, beaver (*Castor canadensis*), and deer mice (*Peromyscus maniculatus*).

During the fleeting summer seasons, the forested and alpine zones of the high mountains became pastureland for large, widely scattered populations of big game such as mountain races of the bighorn sheep, elk (*Cervus*

U.S. Forest Service: top, 417433, center right, 474952, bottom left, 482349, bottom right 447970; center left, Utah State Histl. Soc. Lib., Salt Lake City.
Fig. 5. Montane, subalpine, and riparian vegetation. top, Grand Canyon of the Snake River, Payette National Forest, Idaho, 1941. center left, Fish Springs marshland, view east from mouth of Barn Owl Cave, western Utah, 1982. center right, Aspen stand on Bunker Creek in the Panguitch Lake district of Dixie National Forest, Utah, 1953. bottom left, Lower reach of the Provo River, Uinta National Forest, near Provo, Utah, 1953. bottom right, Spruce-fir forest with aspen near Puffer Lake, Fishlake National Forest, central Utah, 1947.

canadensis), and mule deer. Trout (*Salmo* spp.) were abundant in lakes and streams, and numerous small mammals, such as pocket gophers (*Thomomys talpoides*), ground squirrels, red squirrels (*Tamiasciurus hudsonicus*), pikas (*Ochotona princeps*), snowshoe hare (*Lepus americanus*), porcupines (*Erethizon dorsatum*), marmots (*Marmota flaviventris*), and beavers are locally abundant. Blue grouse (*Dendragapus obscurus*) and ptarmigan (*Lagopus leucurus*) are but two of numerous nesting birds of these high elevations. Mountain lions (*Felis concolor*), coyotes, foxes, and hawks migrate into these high areas each summer to harvest a portion of the available bounty (Shelford 1963). Numerous small, open campsites and hunting blinds attest that prehistoric people also shared in the summer harvest at higher elevations (Spencer and Jennings 1965; Wylie 1971–1972, 2; Dalley 1976; Thomas 1983d).

Environment and Man

An intensive survey of archeological sites of the Raft River Mountains of northwestern Utah and the Goose Creek Mountains of northeastern Nevada provides some clues to the manner in which Indians utilized the environmental complex that varied from saline marshland to alpine herbland (Wylie 1971–1972). The sites ranged from large airy caves to small, open camps. Only 11 percent of the sites occurred on the deserts below 5,000 feet, while 7 percent appeared above 7,000 feet. The intervening elevations supported the remaining 82 percent of the sites. Wylie shows that the paucity of sites below 5,000 feet is not related to inadequate space since 27 percent of the area sampled fell in that zone. Land area above 7,000 feet accounted for 8 percent of the total; thus, total archeological sites were only slightly underrepresented there. When the size of the high elevation sites was considered, the intensity of human utilization of that zone appeared less intense than elsewhere, since only 2 percent of the large sites occurred above 7,000 feet. The 5,000 to 7,000 foot zone that appears to have supported the bulk of human activity is dominated by sagebrush, juniper-piñon, and mountain brush vegetation.

Another way of viewing human utilization of the environment is to tabulate the relative use made of the species in each habitat. Table 1 summarizes the results of such an analysis of the native plants of Nevada utilized by Indians for medicinal purposes (Train, Henrichs, and Archer 1941; Benson 1982). Using Tidestrom's (1925) flora of Utah and Nevada, 176 of those medicinal species have been assigned to broad vegetation zones. Where a plant was considered to occur in more than one zone, it was tallied in each zone of occurrence. Over half the plants considered occur in the sagebrush-grass zone. Mountain brush and juniper-piñon

Table 1. Distribution of 176 Native Medicinal Plants in Nevada

Vegetational zone	Percent of state area	Number of medicinal plants	Percent of medicinal plants
Alpine	0.1	1	0.6
Forest	2.7	41	23.3
Mountain brush	0.6	72	40.9
Piñon-juniper	18.8	81	46.0
Sagebrush-grass	47.1	99	56.3
Desert	30.4	48	27.3
Marsh	0.3	5	2.8

woodland zones each support over 40 percent of the species. Elevational zones above and below these three contiguous foothill vegetations contribute markedly fewer of the medicinal plants. These data support Wylie's (1971–1972, 2) dwelling-site analysis in showing that prehistoric Indians preferred the foothill zones.

It would thus seem that natives habitually avoided open desert whenever possible. Low productivity, general absence of protective cover, and intense heat and aridity offer plausible reasons for such avoidance. Likewise, the intensity of the utilization of high elevations appears to have been light, but Thomas (1982) shows that adaptation at high elevations might have been attractive. Severe winters and a seasonal near absence of game undoubtedly drove most people out for well over half of each year. Thus, rigorous environments above and below tended to concentrate prehistoric populations and many resource animals in the foothills where available forage and protective cover overlap a moderate winter climate.

Wherever they lived prehistoric peoples utilized a bewildering array of resources (Jennings 1978). Numerous animal species were harvested, of course, but an even longer list of plants was sought for food, medicine, and fiber. Not surprisingly, the majority of known food and fiber plants also occur within the mid-elevational zones previously described as centers of human activity on the basis of dwelling-place and medicinal plant criteria. Major root crops—camas (*Camassia quamash*), bitterroot (*Lewisia rediviva*), wild caraway (*Perideridia gairdneri*), wild onion (*Allium* spp.), sego lily (*Calochortus* spp.), yellow bells (*Fritillaria pudica*), and Indian potato (*Orogenia linearifolia*)—occur within this zone, especially in the north. Native salad plants include miner's lettuce (*Claytonia perfoliata*), sweet cicely (*Osmorhiza* spp.), violets (*Viola* spp.), and bracken fern (*Pteridium aquilinum*). Fruit and nut crops occurring in abundance in the riparian and foothill zones are chokecherry, currants (*Ribes* spp.), blue elderberry (*Sambucus caerulea*), oregon grape (*Berberis repens*), true wild grape (*Vitis arizonica*) (in the south only), wildrose (*Rosa* spp.), serviceberry, ground-cherry (*Physalis* spp.), silver buffaloberry (*Shepherdia argentea*), and oaks (*Quercus* spp.). Seeds were regularly collected from plants indigenous to this zone, such as native amaranths (*Amaranthus* spp.) and chenopods (*Chenopodium* spp.), which flourished on sites disturbed by natural erosion or deposition, pine nuts, sunflowers (*Helianthus annuus*) (especially profuse on burned areas), Rocky Mountain bee-plants or bee-weeds (*Cleome serrulata, C. lutea*), and a variety of grasses known to include ricegrass (*Oryzopsis hymenoides*), sand dropseed (*Sporobolus cryptandrus*), bluegrasses (*Poa* spp.), wildryes (*Elymus* spp.). Native fiber plants included several sagebrush species, cottonwood (*Populus fremontii*), juniper, cliffrose (*Cowania mexicana*), wild flax (*Linum perenne*), species of dogbane (*Apocynum* spp.) and milkweed (*Asclepius speciosa*).

It should be noted that the region has two species of piñon or nutpine. The two-needle piñon occurs in the southeastern corner of the area, while single-leaf piñon occurs across the Great Basin and onto portions of the southern edge of the Snake River Plains. Fossil evidence suggests that the single-leaf species did not occupy most of the Great Basin until about 4000 B.C. (Thompson and Hattori 1983; Wells 1983; Lanner 1983). Single-leaf piñon is characterized by larger cones and seeds than its two-needle relative. This size difference makes it more difficult to accumulate a supply of seeds from the two-needle species. Pine nuts seem to have played a less important role in the economy of Colorado Plateau peoples than they did among Basin province tribes (Jennings 1978). This apparent difference may be related in part to seed size characteristics.

Another aspect of the biology of piñon pine that was significant is the periodicity of the nut crop. H. D. Harrington (1967) comments that "the Indians expected a bumper crop every seven years." Spencer and Jennings (1965:276) note that the piñon "trees produce many cones irregularly, usually not more often than once in three or four years." Good nut years are irregular: no definite cycle exists.

Inasmuch as it takes 26 months for the cones to mature (Lanner 1981) it is to be expected that prediction of good crops would be difficult. The crop is dependent on two consecutive years of at least "adequate" climate and low populations of insect pests that feed on the developing seeds. Furthermore, depletion of energy reserves through production of a bumper crop would insure that copious crops could not be expected in consecutive years even though environmental conditions were otherwise ideal. But some cones are always produced. Local environmental differences among groves of a single valley system of any size should insure that complete synchrony of production (high or low) from grove-to-grove will never occur. This assures that any sizable area would not likely be totally devoid of nuts.

Consequently mobile peoples would be able to harvest some nuts every year, but probably no group could depend on pine nuts in adequate supply to be a major winter food every year.

Below the foothill zone, streambank and marsh communities must also have been resource magnets attracting humans. Both communities are of local distribution and limited area but are highly productive and diversified. All evidence indicates that both systems were of immense local importance to native peoples (Jennings 1957; Aikens 1970; Heizer and Napton 1970a; Thomas 1971; Madsen 1982).

Marshes especially must have been attractive (fig. 7). The animal components of that community are easily the most conspicuous and abundant of any of the region's ecosystems. In all other communities, animals tend to be secretive and are rarely seen by casual observers, but in the marshes, animals are more conspicuous than the plants that support them. A visit to one of the major marshes of the region in April is revealing. At any instant, the sky is likely to be full of raucous birds representing as many as 40 species with each individual intent on intimidating and expelling the intruder from the nesting ground. Such a conspicuous and noisy assemblage could hardly have failed to attract indigenous peoples accustomed to meager resources for a large part of their annual cycle.

That people did indeed harvest the bounteous and diverse crop of the region's marshes is evidenced by numerous eggshell and bone-strewn sites along the edges of the great Bear River marsh of northern Utah (Aikens 1967a) and coprolites containing waterfowl feathers and

U.S. Dept. of the Interior, Stillwater Wildlife Management Area, Fallon, Nev.
Fig. 7. Stillwater National Wildlife Refuge, near Fallon, Nev., Stillwater Range in the background. This aquatic vegetation is typical of the Humboldt-Carson Sink area in well-watered years. Although artificially augmented in the 1980s, this area has been a major breeding and nesting ground for waterfowl species for millennia. Photographed in 1952.

59

bird and fish bones at Lovelock Cave in western Nevada (Heizer and Napton 1969). The marshes and associated saline meadows appear also to have yielded an animal bonus in the form of mammals as diverse as muskrats (*Ondatra zibethica*) and rabbits. Plant resources too in the form of abundant fleshy rhizomes, greens, and seeds are known to have been regularly harvested from the marsh ecosystem and adjoining saltflat edges (Heizer and Napton 1970a; Shields and Dalley 1978; Harper and Alder 1970). In addition, tule reeds (*Scirpus acutus*) for mats and dogbane and milkweed fibers for superior cordage were gathered primarily in the marshes and along their moist margins (Jennings 1957; Harper and Alder 1970). In early spring and fall, the marshes must have been as benevolent a habitat as any in the region. Mosquitoes (*Culex* spp. and *Aedes* spp.) and other blood feeding insects would have made this environment unpleasant if not unbearable in the summer.

Fruits of gooseberries (*Ribes* spp.), serviceberries, strawberries (*Fragaria* spp.), raspberries (*Rubus* spp.), western wintergreen (*Gaultheria humifusa*), and blueberries (*Vaccinium* spp.) (generally stingy producers in the area) undoubtedly combined with available animal resources to entice some native peoples into the high elevation forests and meadows each summer. Other plant resources there might have included native water lily (*Nuphar polysepalum*) rhizomes and seeds, greens from marsh marigold (*Caltha leptosepala*) or edible valerian (*Valeriana edulis*) rootstocks. Cow parsnip (*Heracleum lanatum*) from these environments was also utilized in a variety of ways (H. D. Harrington 1967).

The hunting and gathering way of life that sustained the vast majority of the prehistoric people of this region was supplemented by agriculture among the Numic speakers that occupied the region's southern and southeastern sections in the 1770s (Dominguez 1976; Winter 1976; Jennings 1978). Localized and weak agricultural efforts appear to have persisted in particularly favorable portions of that area even after Euro-American settlement (Woodbury 1944, 1965). It seems apparent that only small fields in choice locations were farmed at the time of Euro-American settlement in the late nineteenth century (Berry 1972). Locations of archeological sites with abundant evidence of cultivated crops indicate that low alluvial terraces along perennial or intermittent drainage ways (where ground water was likely to be recharged with some frequency and where there were soils at the base of sloping exposures of "slickrock") were favored sites for fields (Woodbury 1965; Jennings 1966). In light of the fact that sandy soils permit more of the applied water to infiltrate deeply and release more of it to plants than do heavier textured soils (Black 1968), it is interesting that fields of prehistoric farmers generally occurred on sands (Jennings 1966).

Woodbury (1944) cited several early historical records of the use of irrigation by southern Utah Indians.

Such operations were reported to be uncommon and small. Archeological (Cutler 1966) and historical evidence (Woodbury 1950) indicates the crops grown in prehistoric and early historic times included corn (*Zea mays*), cucurbits (*Cucurbita mixta, C. pepo*), and beans (*Phaseolus vulgaris*). Prehistoric remains of cotton (*Gossypium* sp.) bolls and cotton seeds and fibers also occur in many sites on the lower Colorado Plateau (Cutler 1966). Weeds such as amaranths, chenopods, ground cherries, and bee-weeds that sprung up in the gardens were probably gratefully harvested along with the crop (Jennings 1966; Fry 1970). Jennings (1966) suggests that certain fleshy-fruited prickly pears (*Opuntia* spp.) and sunflowers were wild plants that were deliberately cultivated. The frequency of wolfberry (*Lycium pallidum*) around prehistoric dwellings on the lower Colorado Plateau seems to indicate that it too was cultivated by man (Yarnell 1965).

Environmental Change

Postcontact modifications of the natural environment occurred quickly after Euro-American settlement and often had undesirable effects on native peoples (Cottam 1961a; Harper 1968; Thomas 1971). Like indigenous man before him, European man was inseparably tied to sources of free water in this arid region. Even before Europeans settled, their trails paralleled waterways, and there is evidence that the trails alone had disrupted Northern Paiute cultural patterns in the Humboldt Valley of Nevada by 1862 (Malouf 1966; Ranere 1970). After settlement, permanent communities grew up at points where water and forage could be readily obtained for people and their livestock and where timber for fuel and construction was available without great effort. Such sites were often seasonal campsites of Indians also. Superior weaponry insured that European settlers would preempt such sites for themselves.

Once established at such sites, the settlers proceeded to "develop" the environment for their own purposes. Almost invariably such developments eliminated resources essential to the economy of the natives. Fertile bottomlands that were once the most productive in the area and supported large populations of small mammals and birds and big game at least seasonally were rapidly cleared and plowed or converted to permanent pastureland (Thomas 1971). Thus, many animal resources of the natives were eliminated as irreplaceable habitat was destroyed. Perhaps other species could have continued to survive in the new environments had they not been considered competitors for the settlers' crops. With trap, rifle, and poison, Europeans moved to reserve the produce of their fields for themselves.

The aquatic resources of small streams and associated marshes were likewise drastically altered by agricultural activities. In these arid lands, dependable crop production demanded irrigation. The required water could come only from nearby streams, and while such streams were not usually permanently diverted from their beds, diversions coincided with periods of minimal precipitation. At such times, even temporary diversions were sufficient to deplete drastically if not to eliminate fish and waterfowl populations and, often, even the riparian vegetation. In the process, resources essential for survival of indigenous peoples were reduced or destroyed.

Drier uplands surrounding streambank or meadow settlements were also rapidly modified. In this case, domestic herds, rather than Europeans, were responsible for the modifications (Young, Evans, and Tueller 1976). Inasmuch as the more productive lowlands were diverted to cultivation, forage for animals had to come from adjacent uplands. Danger of loss to predators or hungry native peoples required that flocks be herded and returned to settlements at night. Such a management program produced within a few years a halo of denuded or severely depleted range around each settlement that expanded outward with each succeeding year. In the process, indigenous peoples were pushed farther and farther into unproductive and harsh environments where the natural carrying capacity of the land was many times lower than along the stream courses. Loss of good production sites for wild seed crops through overgrazing by domestic livestock is known to have threatened some native peoples with starvation. In 1880, the Mormon scout, Jacob Hamblin, formally petitioned his friend John Wesley Powell, then special commissioner in the Indian Bureau, for "merchandise" for the relief of about 40 Indian families in the Kanab, Utah, area. Foothills that only a few years before produced "hundreds of acres of sunflowers which produced quantities of rich seed, the grass also that grew so luxuriantly" had been grazed out by livestock (cited in Fowler and Fowler 1971:22).

Analysis of food bone assemblages from prehistoric archeological sites throughout this region (Dalley 1970) suggests that settlement activities also seriously upset the ecology of big game animals. As shown in table 2, Fremont and Anazasi sites in Utah yield bones of a surprising number of big game species. The archeological deposits of some subregions are dominated by bones of species that no longer occur there or are now rare. Throughout Utah, the mule deer is now the most common big game animal (Durrant 1952), yet the major food bone of archeological sites near the Bear River marshes came from bison. Likewise, the bighorn sheep was the second most common hooved animal at sites in the Great Salt Lake Desert and along the edges of the complex of mountains running down the center of the state, but in the 1980s that species is exceedingly rare if not extinct in those areas.

This disparity between modern big game populations and those represented in the archeological record has occasioned considerable comment and speculation (Taylor 1957; Jennings 1957, 1966; Woodbury 1965; Dalley 1970). There does seem to be good evidence that mule deer were less abundant in prehistoric times (Leopold 1950; Durrant 1952; Julander 1962), but the data in table 2 demonstrate that mule deer was nevertheless the major big game animal (except bison in Bear River marshes) harvested in prehistoric times in Utah. They are prominent at all sites near mountains high enough to support large areas of range that remain succulent and inviting to them throughout most of the summer season. Bighorn sheep and pronghorn antelope were also consistently killed but were less often represented than deer. Bison and elk were important in the food bone collections at only a few sites.

The disappearance of bison from the area seems clearly related to the intrusions of Europeans. Historic references assembled by Roe (1951) indicate the bison had found their way across the Rockies from their preferred

Table 2. Relative Importance of Big Game Species in Preshistoric Sites in Utah

Subregion	Number of Sites	Bighorn Sheep	Bison	Elk	Mule Deer	Pronghorn
Fremont Culture						
Great Salt Lake Desert	3	1.7	0.3	0.0	1.3	1.0
Edge of Bear River marshes	3	0.0	3.0	1.0	1.7	0.3
Uintah Basin	2	0.5	0.0	1.0	2.5	1.5
Edges and foothills of						
Central Mountain System	6	2.0	0.6	0.3	2.4	0.6
Anazasi Culture						
Lower Colorado Plateau	5	2.0	0.3	0.3	2.3	0.0
Average Importance		1.2	0.8	0.5	2.0	1.1

SOURCE: Dalley 1970 and comparable data from Danger and Hogup caves.
NOTE: At each site, the 3 major big game species (as indicated by number of bones) were ranked in order of importance. Then by assigning the commonest animal in the bone remains at a site 3 points, the second commonest 2 points, and the third most abundant 1 point and averaging the values for each species at all sites in a subregion, an index of relative importance was obtained for each game animal. In event of a tie, each species was tallied in both groups.

HISTORICAL ENVIRONMENTS

habitat on the Great Plains only since about A.D. 1600. Butler (1971) has challenged that interpretation on the basis of skeleton material from archeological sites on the upper Snake River Plains of Idaho. The sites yield radiocarbon dates corresponding to the period from early postglacial to late prehistoric. Grayson (1982) documents a similar pattern of prehistoric occurrence in Nevada. Bison obviously entered the Intermontane region much earlier than Roe (1951) considered. In any event, herds were generally small, and distribution was spotty at time of first White contact. Roe (1951) considers that bison had largely been eliminated west of the Rockies by 1855. This early demise of bison appears related to the marginal nature of the habitat and the impact of the Oregon Trail, which cut through the heart of the best bison habitat. Heavy hunting pressure and competition from pioneer travelers' livestock for feed appear to have imposed a burden that the bison herds could not endure. Once eliminated, heavy pioneer traffic through the natural immigration corridors at South Pass in central Wyoming and along the Bear River into Idaho discouraged further colonization from the Plains.

There is good reason to believe that the pronghorn was also more abundant in presettlement times. This species, like the bison, prefers grassy environments and relatively gentle terrain, but it penetrated farther and persisted longer in desert areas than did the bison. It was most abundant on grassy portions of the sagebrush zone and lower foothills (Hayward, Beck, and Tanner 1958; Shelford 1963). These were among the first environments preempted by settlers for their grazing animals.

Research has also demonstrated that the pronghorn prefers broadleaved herbs (forbs) to grasses or shrubs when all are equally available. The studies of Smith and Beale (1980) indicate that abundance of succulent forbs in the diet may have both direct and indirect effects on reproductive success of the animal. Their studies and those of Harner and Harper (1973) demonstrate that forbs increase with precipitation. Since there was apparently more effective precipitation during Fremont times in the northern Great Basin (Harper and Alder 1970), one might logically expect more forbs in the vegetation and larger antelope herds at that time. The food bone assemblage at Hogup Cave during the Fremont period bears out that expectation (Harper and Alder 1970).

Settlement activities appear to have had an even more disastrous impact on bighorn sheep populations (Wilson 1968; Irvine 1969). Unlike the bison and pronghorn, bighorn sheep ranged from mountain top to low elevations. Throughout this range, it appears to have preferred broken terrain where scattered herbs and shrubs were available. With the introduction of domestic livestock, the species was exposed to competition for forage and at least two serious parasites previously unknown among the animals. Scabies ear mites have become widespread among bighorns on the lower Colorado Plateau (Wilson 1968). In more humid environments, lung worm became a deadly parasite. The joint effect of infestations of parasites to which they had little resistence and range depletion undoubtedly lowered the bighorn's reproductive success. In the 1950s uranium mining brought hundreds of men into the most remote portions of the desert bighorn's range. Poaching by miners is believed to have reduced populations to an all-time low (Irvine 1969).

Eventually domestic grazers and human activities associated with Euro-American settlement appear to have profoundly altered the population size of the mule deer, too. In this case, the alterations probably came too late to have much effect on the decline of Indian populations. The case is discussed here because it relates to the puzzling problems generated when prehistoric food bone assemblages are interpreted in the light of modern populations of big game species.

The explanation for the apparent dramatic increase in mule deer seems tied to settlement-related environmental changes. There is well-documented evidence that domestic grazers, through a preference for herbaceous forage, caused the shrub components of the sagebrush-grass communities of the Great Basin to increase rapidly until they came to dominate the vegetation (Leopold 1950; Julander 1962; Harper 1968). It also appears that the areal extent of fires, which had once favored herbs over shrubs, was greatly reduced by the construction of numerous trails, roads, and canals (which served as firebreaks) through the seasonally flammable foothills. Thus, the increase in shrubs was preserved by a network of unintentional firebreaks and regular removal by domestic grazers of the highly flammable herbaceous cover from interspaces between shrubs. The ascendance of shrubs on the traditional winter ranges of mule deer improved range quality for the deer. Herbs are often unavailable under the winter snow and are also known to provide low quality forage in their dormant state. In contrast, shrubs usually project above the snow and provide a palatable and well balanced diet in winter. Thus, shrubs increased the amount and quality of usable winter forage for mule deer. Deer numbers rose accordingly. A concomitant reduction of large predators such as cougar and coyote by settlers and management of the deer by "buck only" hunts appear also to have contributed to the mule deer population rise that peaked in the 1940s and began a decline that continued in the 1980s. In retrospect, it appears that the large mule deer herds of the first half of the twentieth century were an ecological accident spawned by many unintended side-effects of settlement.

Lumbering activities in the mountains appear not to have had important influences on the ecology of indigenous people. In contrast, cutting of piñon-juniper forests around Nevada mining districts had dire effects for Indians (Thomas 1971). The minor impacts associated with lumbering at higher elevations were probably related to the fact that until the 1950s, selective rather than clear-cutting was the common logging practice in the area. To be sure, old photographs clearly show that slopes around mining towns such as Alta, Utah, in the Wasatch Range were completely deforested, but such cases appear to have affected only relatively small portions of the total area of concern. Furthermore, heavily forested lands occur primarily in areas that prehistoric people seem to have used only briefly during the short summer (Wylie 1971–1972, 2). As a consequence, resources used by Indians would have been disrupted only locally by forest removal.

Reduction of acreage burned by wildfires was a consequence of settlement. This was partly a result of purposeful fire suppression and partly an unplanned consequence of settlement, but the result was the same in either event. Prior to Euro-American settlement, fires appear to have repeatedly swept all vegetations where cover was sufficient to carry a fire and conditions were seasonally dry (O.C. Stewart 1955). With control of fire, vast acreages underwent a natural succession in which fire-sensitive species (such as sagebrush, juniper, piñon, and montane conifers) gradually increased. Such alterations probably developed too slowly to have significantly affected many native peoples. Other factors probably disrupted their cultures long before plant succession could have proceeded far enough to have produced important changes in the natural vegetation. Nevertheless, much natural vegetation is now unquestionably quite different than it was prior to control of wildfire (Sauer 1950).

Just what role Indians played in the ecology of fire in former times is still unclear. It is known that Indians purposely burned certain communities to favor plants such as wild tobacco and seed crops (Steward 1941a). Jennings (1966) suggests that reedgrass marshes in the Glen Canyon area may have been burned during hunting activities. On the basis of a wide array of historical accounts, it seems clear that prehistoric people encouraged fires in both brushlands and forests of the Intermontane West to enhance the value of the land for their own needs (O. C. Stewart 1955).

It is well documented that Europeans and their grazing animals greatly accelerated processes of natural erosion (Cottam 1961; Young, Evans, and Tueller 1976). As in the case of fire, it is likely that such modifications came too late to have had much influence on indigenous populations. In contrast, direct removal by livestock of plants whose seeds were used by native people had immediate and severe impacts (Fowler and Fowler 1971).

Another impact of White settlers on regional ecosystems involved the introduction of alien plants and animals (Young, Evans, and Major 1972). The magnitude of that change can be partially appreciated in the fact that almost exactly 10 percent (325 species) of the uncultivated plants in Utah are alien to the area (Welsh et al. 1981). In many parts of the region, especially on the Snake River Plains of southern Idaho, one can stand at any one of scores of spots on unplowed rangeland and see primarily alien plants within the range of vision. The introduced taxa perform best where White impacts (grazing, vehicular traffic, plowing) are the greatest, but many of the alien plants occur regularly in undisturbed areas as well. Cheatgrass (*Bromus tectorum*), goatsbeard (*Tragopogon dubius*), houndstongue (*Cynoglossum officinale*), prickly lettuce (*Lactuca serriola*), and toadflax (*Linaria genistifolia*) are representative of aliens that are competitive in undisturbed vegetations. The invaders have undoubtedly permanently altered the natural cover of the region.

Alien plants have their counterparts in the animal assemblages of the region. Introduced mammals that live without the aid of man include the house mouse (*Mus musculus*), norway rat (*Rattus norvegicus*), nutria (*Myocastor coypus*), and the domestic cat (*Felis catus*). The nutria and cat are the most likely of the four to occur well apart from man. Birds have proven to be successful introductions in a variety of situations: English sparrows (*Passer domesticus*), ring-necked pheasant (*Phasianus colchicus*), and starlings (*Sturnus vulgaris*) rarely occur far from the buildings and fields of man. Chukar partridges (*Alectoris chukar*), on the other hand, range far beyond cultivated fields; there they apparently depend heavily on another alien, cheatgrass, for food (seeds).

Perhaps the most common fish on a weight basis in the region is the German carp (*Cyprinus carpio*), an introduced species. This species has become a serious competitor with desirable game fish in warmer waters everywhere in the area. It is such a vigorous herbivore in marshes that it often denudes the waterways, and the value of the habitat is seriously impaired for waterfowl.

Introduced species are often sufficiently common to make it difficult for the field archeologist to visualize what the resource spectrum at a site might have been like before the time of White settlement. In fact, Yarnell's (1965) work demonstrates that native agriculturalists also made plant introductions and compositional changes in vegetation important considerations even before the coming of Europeans.

Subsistence

CATHERINE S. FOWLER

The diverse flora and fauna of the Great Basin are associated in a complex set of ecological relationships. Thus, the effective distribution of any particular resource used for food, medicine, or manufacture by Great Basin peoples whether in the prehistoric, protohistoric, or postcontact periods is tied to a complex set of factors, many as yet poorly understood and documented. The effect of postcontact features, including the introduction of nonindigenous herbivores; exploitative strategies such as lumbering, farming, ranching, and mining; and the diversion and storage of water, make assessments that much more difficult. Yet, in spite of the difficulties, the need to understand something of the subsistence potential of this region and to compare that with the resulting foraging patterns is great. Through the years, field workers have given subsistence a central role in the theoretical discussions (Heizer and Napton 1970a; Jennings 1957; Madsen and O'Connell 1982; Steward 1938). It is for this reason that a separate section on Great Basin subsistence is provided. Specifically, the role of plants and animals in the diets of ethnographically known Great Basin groups, the degree to which certain species were manipulated for desired ends, and the general role that these resources played in the world view of peoples in this region are outlined and discussed.

Plants and Animals

Data on the utilization as food by Great Basin peoples of species of plants and animals have been provided by explorers (for example, Fremont 1887; Lewis and Clark in Biddle 1962; J. H. Simpson 1869), biologists (for example, Chamberlin 1909, 1911; Coville 1892; Merriam 1979; Palmer 1871, 1878; Bye 1972), and ethnographers (for example, Barrett 1916; C. S. Fowler 1972a; Kelly 1932, 1964; Lowie 1924; Steward 1933b, 1938; O. C. Stewart 1941; Zigmond 1941, 1981). Although far from complete, these data allow for some useful comparisons of species distributions and utilization. Tables 1–5 give comparative data on plants, mammals, birds, fish, and insects and reptiles commonly used for food by Great Basin peoples. Undoubtedly some of the species listed were utilized by groups other than those indicated; however, where specific documentation is lacking, attribution was avoided. The tables list family

and genus alphabetically; the organization does not represent phylogenetic relationships.

Plants

Data on plant utilization in the region are by far the richest, although they have been the subject of few specific works (for example, Chamberlin 1911; C. S. Fowler 1972a; Murphey 1959; Zigmond 1941, 1981). Table 1 summarizes by taxonomic family the species commonly used for food, the parts taken and, by general designation, the cultural groups involved. Note that certain plant families provided several species for utilization, whereas others provided only a limited array. In some cases, utilization is related proportionately to the number of genera and species available within a family in the region (for example, Asteraceae). In others, it is related to the production of an important edible structure by the plant species regardless of the number of taxa within its family in the region (for example, Caprifoliaceae). Although the data base is far from adequate to compare species utilization by tribe or more appropriately by subgroup, one can rather quickly see that utilization varied considerably. Natural plant distributions are obviously involved in some cases (such as the utilization of mesquite and agave in the southern "hot deserts," the use of piñon pine in the central Great Basin, the focus on biscuit-roots in the north). However, it is unlikely that such factors explain all the appreciable variation. Rather, it is clear from the data that Great Basin peoples exercised a certain degree of selectivity in harvesting their floral environments (see also Downs 1966a:43).

Given that different plant structures were the focus of harvesting, and also that plants from certain families and genera required more or less complicated processing to make them edible, several specific subsistence technologies were developed. Among them, for example, were the technological complexes for procuring and processing piñon seeds, acorns, mesquite beans, and the stems of agave. In addition, there were more generalized complexes for dealing with hard and soft shelled seeds, roots and corms, berries and leaves. Each complex can be defined in terms of some specific tool types as well as technological procedures.

• THE PIÑON COMPLEX The seeds of nut pines, including specifically the single-needled and double-needled piñons (*Pinus monophylla, P. edulis*), as well as to a lesser extent those of limber, sugar, and ponderosa pine (*P. flexilis, P. lambertiania, P. ponderosa*), were highly prized. Piñons were the focus of intensive activity by groups in the central core of the Great Basin (fig. 1), especially in years of abundance (occurring in 3–7 year cycles, according to Lanner 1981:78). Harvests began in late summer with the taking of green cones using long hooked and straight harvesting poles (fig. 2). Cones were transported to a central processing station in large conical baskets. The green cones were then pit roasted, causing their bracts to open and the seeds to be partially released. Cones collected after a frost did not require pit roasting, as under these circumstances the bracts of the cones open naturally, releasing most of the seeds. In either case, seeds were further extracted by beating the pile with sticks or by tapping each cone with a small handstone against a flat rock anvil. Once extracted, the seeds were given a preliminary parching in an open-twined fan-shaped tray to make the seed coats brittle. They were then shelled using a flat metate and, depending on the area, differing types of large hullers. The seed coats were removed by winnowing in a fan-shaped tray. A final parching in twined or circular coiled trays prepared the seeds for grinding.

Although the shelled seeds could be eaten raw or parched, most people preferred to eat them in the form of a mush or gruel. For this, the shelled and parched seeds were ground on the metate with a mano. The meal was then mixed with cold water in a mush basket by stirring with a looped stick. Although most groups preferred to eat the mush cold, others continued to process it by stone-boiling. In some areas, small baskets of mush were also set outside in freezing temperatures rendering a kind of "ice cream" much enjoyed by children.

Piñon seeds were cached in several ways: in the cones, usually after pit roasting if green; in the shells in the raw state; and in the shells after preliminary parching. Cones were buried in large open pits under piles of rocks, limbs, and pine needles (fig. 2). Raw or processed seeds were stored in grass- or bark-lined pits or in skin bags placed in pits. Seeds in whole cone caches (particularly of *Pinus edulis*) would keep four to five years if the caches were well constructed (Steward 1943a:271). This was an important factor given the cyclic or unpredictable nature of piñon yields.

So important were piñon resources that groves of trees were considered family property in several locations (Steward 1933b, 1938, 1941, 1943a; O.C. Stewart 1941, 1942).

Certain ceremonialism was associated with piñon harvesting. Several months before harvest time, prayers were offered to "fix" the crop. Round dances were held at the time of harvesting, and special prayers of thanksgiving were offered over the first seeds collected. The prayers ensured good harvests of other seeds and game for the remainder of the year. Piñon harvesting is still associated with ceremony in the 1980s, and it remains as one of the key features of Native identity.

• THE ACORN COMPLEX The acorn complex in the

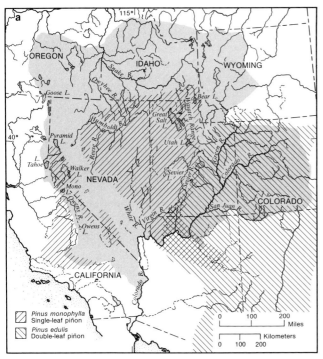
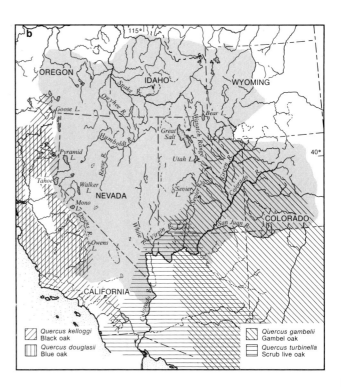

Fig. 1. Distribution of a, piñon and b, oaks in the Great Basin.

65

Great Basin is not so common or so characteristic as the piñon complex, for gatherable acorns occur only on the western, southern, and eastern fringes of the region (fig. 1). In the west, most of the species sought required the lengthy leaching process like that used in California, to which this technology is undoubtedly related. After the acorns were picked, they were transported to a central camp area for shelling. This was accomplished by cracking the shells one at a time using a small hand-stone on a flat stone anvil. The shells were discarded. The meats were rubbed vigorously to remove their inner skins, then ground, ordinarily in a bedrock mortar with a cylindrical pestle. Portable stone and wooden mortars may have also served this purpose in some areas.

Leaching took place on a sand and gravel bar near a stream. A basin was prepared in the clean sand and the pounded meal placed in it. Water was poured through the meal until all the bitterness (tannic acid) was removed. The packed meal was then carefully removed and the sand washed from it. Then it was mixed with water to form a mush that was stone-boiled. Different groups further prepared the acorn mush. The Washoe preferred to make acorn biscuit by placing small cupfuls of the hot mush into a cold water basin at streamside. The small dumplings were then served cold with meat. The Kawaiisu formed the mush into cakes that were later sun-dried (Zigmond 1981:57).

Acorn processing in the southern and eastern Great Basin, focused as it was on scrub oaks (*Quercus turbinella, Q. gambelii*), was simpler as no leaching was required. These acorns were pit roasted, shelled, ground into meal on the metate, and then made into a mush by stone-boiling. Acorns were stored in the shells in bags or in bark- or grass-lined pits, as in the western Great Basin. More elaborate storage techniques are reported only for the Kawaiisu, who built elevated acorn granaries similar to those of their California neighbors (Zigmond 1981:56).

• THE MESQUITE COMPLEX Mesquite (*Prosopis juliflora*) and screwbean (*P. pubescens*) are plants of the Mojave and Sonoran deserts and were thus known primarily to the Panamint and Death Valley Shoshone, the Chemehuevi, and Southern Paiute groups as far east as the edge of the Colorado Plateau. Pods of mesquite were taken in the spring when they were eaten raw as snacks. However, more elaborate processing attended the taking of mesquite and screwbean in late summer after the pods had dried. At that time, the collected pods were placed in large tree-stump mortars (fig. 3) or occasionally bedrock mortars and pounded to a fine powder with large cylindrical pestles. The meal was tightly packed into a conical burden basket and set out to dry. After a few days, the basket was inverted and the large cone of meal left to dry further. The cones were then stored in grass- or bark-lined pits in rock-shelters or caves. A cone was kept in the house and pieces removed and eaten or added to cooked agave and made into small cakes. These were suitable for the trail or for meals in camp (Stuart 1945).

Mesquite bean meal was a staple in the southern Great Basin. As with piñon, family ownership of mesquite groves was reported for various Southern Paiute groups (Kelly 1932–1933).

• THE AGAVE COMPLEX Like mesquite and screwbean, agaves (*Agave utahensis, A. deserti*) are primarily plants of the southern hot deserts in this region. However, *Agave utahensis* does occur at higher elevations, extending along the Grand Canyon through the territory of the Kaibab Southern Paiute. The agave complex, where it occurs in the Great Basin, is part of the larger complex of the Southwest and Mexico (Castetter, Bell, and Grove 1938).

Processing of agave began in the spring with collection of plants just as they were about to send up flower stalks. The plants were severed from their roots using a chisel-shaped wooden wedge or a special knife (fig. 4). The leaves were then trimmed to within one or two inches of the base with the knife and the agaves returned to a central location in a special pack frame. A large pit was dug and a fire built in it. After the fire died down, rocks were added to the pit and each family placed its agaves in a section of the pit. More rocks were added and a fire built on top. The pit was left unopened for 24 hours, during which time singing and dancing took place. Prohibitions were also in effect to insure good baking. After the pit was opened, the sweet, dark mass was removed by each family and cooled, pounded, and formed into large, flat cakes for drying and storage. Portions were also eaten fresh out of the pit. Agave was mixed with other types of meal or meats

top left, center, bottom, U. of Nev., Reno, Special Coll; top right, Catherine S. Fowler, Reno.
Fig. 2. Harvesting and preparing pinenuts. top left, Mabel Wright and Kathy Frazier, Northern Paiutes of Pyramid Lake Reservation, bring piñon cones within easy reach with a hooked harvesting pole. top right, Susie Dick, Washoe from Carson Valley, in front of a pinenut cache made of brush, piñon branches and needles, and rocks. She is removing pinenuts from the cones with a stick beater. Photograph by Grace Dangberg, 1917–1920. center left, Wuzzie George, Northern Paiute from Stillwater, winnowing pinenuts to remove those without nut meats as well as piñon needles and other debris. center right, Wuzzie George adding charcoal to winnowed pinenuts for a preliminary parching of the nut meats. bottom left, Cracking the shells on a stone metate (or wooden board) with a mano. Winnowing a second time removes the shells. A second parching with coals cooks the nut meats. bottom center, Grinding the cooked nut meats into meal on the metate using a mano. bottom right, Mixing the pinenut meal into a paste with water. More water is added to make a cold soup. All photographs except top right by Margaret M. Wheat, 1956.

SUBSISTENCE

a

b

c

top left, U. of Nev. Reno, Special Coll.; top right, Natl. Arch: 75-N-Uintah-Ouray-A-5; bottom left, Smithsonian, NAA: 85363; a, Amer. Mus. of Nat. Hist., New York: 50.2/3508; b, Mus. of the Amer. Ind., Heye Foundation, New York: 16/5391; c, Eastern Calif. Mus., Independence: A850.

Fig. 3. Collecting berries and seeds. top left, Pyramid Lake Northern Paiute woman removing sunflower seed in a close twined basketry tray. Photograph by Margaret M. Wheat, 1958. top right, Northern Ute woman removing buffalo berries from branches using a stick beater. Photographed about 1940s. bottom left, Northern Ute woman with baskets for gathering berries. The small twined basket in front is filled as she picks berries with both hands, then emptied into the large twined burden basket suspended from her shoulders. Photograph by Frances Densmore, Uintah Reservation, Utah, 1916. a, Basketry seedbeater in openwork twill twining made for Isabel Kelly by Kaputs of the Shivwits Southern Paiute Reservation, Utah, 1932. b, Northern Paiute openwork plain twined tray, used to winnow or parch large seeds. c, Panamint Shoshone wooden mortar. Commonly made from a mesquite or cottonwood trunk, this mortar was used by the women to pulverize mesquite pods. Collected in the Saline Valley, Calif., 1959. Height 32.0 cm, rest same scale.

68

FOWLER

and made into stew. According to Kelly (1932–1933), the spring harvesting and cooking of agave, especially by the Southern Paiute in southern Nevada, was under the direction of a woman specialist. She supervised the activities and also offered special prayers for the success of the roast. There are no data indicating that agave collecting areas were family-owned.

• SEEDS, ROOTS, BERRIES, LEAVES Various other forms of processing attended the collection of other plant products by Great Basin peoples. Several seed-yielding species, but particularly those where seed heads shatter on impact (such as *Mentzelia* spp., *Sporobolus* spp., *Elymus* spp.) were harvested using sticks or special basketry seed beaters (fig. 3). The seeds were deflected into the seed beater or into close-twined basketry trays or burden baskets. Other seeds that were best gathered by hand or other means posed separate problems of processing. For example, the seeds of both cattail (*Typha latifolia*) and Indian ricegrass (*Oryzopsis hymenoides*) had to be flash burned to remove unwanted chaff (C. S. Fowler 1976; Harrington 1933a). Some groups preferred to process hard-shelled seeds, such as Indian ricegrass and alkali bullrush (*Scirpus paludosus*) with specialized grinding tools, such as the flat surface of the metate and a flat stone muller. Cooking and storage requirements might also differ depending on species and locality.

Roots and corms of various species were taken everywhere in the region, using another favored Great Basin tool, the hardwood digging stick. Products from some species might be eaten raw, but often people preferred to process them by roasting them in the sand. A few, such as camas (*Camassia quamash*), edible valerian (*Valeriana edulis*), and swamp onion (*Allium validum*) required more elaborate pit roasting similar to that described for agave. Camas was cooked for three days in a specially constructed stone-lined pit. During this time activities were closely supervised. Camas technology in the northern Great Basin is related to that of several Plateau tribes from whom it probably derives (Downing and Furniss 1968).

Root harvesting took on more significance in the northern Great Basin than elsewhere in the region. This area, on the fringe of the root-abundant Columbia Plateau, was well supplied with various species of biscuit-roots (*Lomatium* spp.), yampa (*Perideridia* spp.), bitterroot (*Lewisia rediviva*), and camas. All were subject to intensive collecting activities in the spring of the year by the Northern Paiute, Bannock, and Northern Shoshone. In order to facilitate digging roots in the lithosols, digging sticks were curved and handled, as were those of the Plateau (Steward 1943a:363).

Berries and other fruits, which were commonly taken throughout the Great Basin region with various techniques and tools, were accorded varying importance among the groups. The Northern Shoshone and Ute manufactured berry-picking baskets, meant to be suspended on the chest from the picker's neck (fig. 3). Her hands would thus be freed for work. The Northern Paiute of western Nevada manufactured a large seed beater–shaped basketry sieve for seeding and pulping the fruits of buckberry (*Shepherdia argentia*) and wolfberry (*Lycium andersonii*). Several groups pulverized chokecherries (*Prunus virginiana*) on the metate and then formed small cakes of the pulp that were dried and stored. In most locations berries were sun-dried whole and stored in pits and bags.

Leaves and stalks taken as greens presented few specific problems to the harvesters unless they contained an undesirable agent or character. Chenopod (*Chenopodium* spp.) and amaranth leaves (*Amaranthus* spp.), as well as those of prince's plume (*Stanleya pinnata*) were always boiled at least twice to remove bitterness. The stalks of thistles (*Cirsium* spp.) were peeled of their prickly outer skins and only the inner pith was consumed. Yet other leafy plants could be eaten raw without processing (for example, *Glyptoplura marginata*). Leaves were rarely stored except for medicinal teas.

Table 1. Common Food Plants in the Great Basin

Agavaceae Agave family
  Agave utahensis Utah agave
    Apical meristem   Nev. and Utah Southern Paiute
  A. deserti
    Apical meristem   Chemehuevi
  Yucca baccata Datil yucca
    Fruits   Chemehuevi, Nev. and Utah Southern Paiute
  Y. baileyi
    Fruits   Utah Southern Paiute
  Y. brevifolia Joshua tree
    Seeds, fruits   Owens Valley Paiute, Panamint,
      Kawaiisu, Chemehuevi, Nev. Southern Paiute
  Y. schidigera Mohave yucca
    Stalks, flowers   Owens Valley Paiute

Table 1. Common Food Plants in the Great Basin
(*continued*)

  Y. utahensis Soaptree yucca
    Apical meristem   Utah Southern Paiute
  Y. whipplei caespitosa Whipple yucca
    Stalks, seeds, apical meristem   Kawaiisu

Alismaceae Water plantain family
  Sagittaria latifolia   Common arrowhead
    Fruit   Gosiute

Amaranthaceae Amaranth family
  Amaranthus sp. Amaranth
    Seeds   Gosiute
  A. albus Amaranth
    Seeds   Utah Southern Paiute

Table 1. Common Food Plants in the Great Basin
(*continued*)

    A. blitoides Amaranth
      Seeds Kawaiisu
    A. hydridus (introduced) Slim amaranth
      Seeds Western Shoshone
    A. hypochondriacus
      Seeds Western Shoshone, Utah Southern Paiute
    A. palmeri Palmer amaranth
      Seeds Utah, Nev. Southern Paiute
    A. powelli Powell amaranth
      Seeds, leaves Utah Southern Paiute
    A. retroflexus Redroot amaranth
      Seeds, leaves Kawaiisu, Utah Southern Paiute

Anacardiaceae Sumac family
    Rhus glabra Smooth sumac
      Fruits Nev. and Utah Southern Paiute, Northern Ute
    R. trilobata Skunkbush sumac
      Fruits Western Shoshone, Gosiute, Nev. and Utah
        Southern Paiute, Northern Ute

Apiaceae Parsley family
    Cymopterus globosus
      Roots Nev. Northern Paiute
    C. longpipes
      Leaves Gosiute, Northern Ute
    C. newberryi
      Roots Utah Southern Paiute
    C. purpurascens
      Seeds Gosiute

Table 1. Common Food Plants in the Great Basin
(*continued*)

    Heracleum lanatum Common cowparsnip
      Roots, leaves Northern Paiute
    Lomatium californicum California lomatium
      Leaves Kawaiisu
    L. canbyi Canby's desert parsley
      Root Northern Paiute
    L. cous Cous biscuitroot
      Roots Oreg. Northern Paiute, Western Shoshone,
        Northern Shoshone
    L. gormanii Gorman's lomatium
      Root Oreg. Northern Paiute
    L. grayi Gray's lomatium
      Roots Oreg. Northern Paiute
    L. leptocarpum Bicolor biscuitroot
      Root Northern Paiute
    L. macrocarpum Bigseed lomatium
      Root Northern Paiute
    L. nevadense Nevada desert parsley
      Root Northern Paiute, Panamint?
    L. nudicaule Barestem lomatium
      Stems, leaves Oreg. Northern Paiute
    L. triternatum Nineleaf lomatium
      Stems, leaves Oreg. Northern Paiute
    L. utriculatum Pomo-celery lomatium
      Leaves Kawaiisu
    L. watsonii Watson's desert parsley
      Root Oreg. Northern Paiute
    Perideridia bolanderi Yampa
      Root Washoe, Northern Paiute

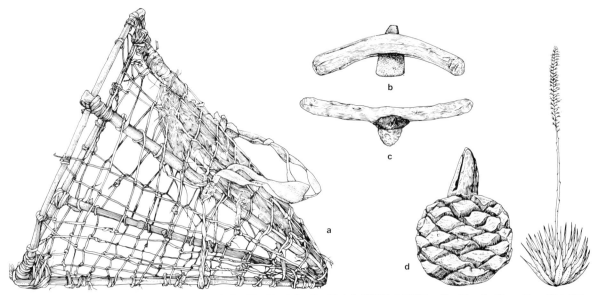

a, Amer. Mus. of Nat. Hist., New York: 50.2/3510; Mus. of the Amer. Indian, Heye Foundation, New York: b, 16/4059; d, 14/6962; c, U. of Nev. Las Vegas, Mus. of Nat. Hist.: 5–286–11.

Fig. 4. Agave processing. a, Model of a wrapped-stitch carrying frame used to transport agave. Made for Isabel T. Kelly on the Shivwits Southern Paiute Reservation, Utah. b, Metal-bladed knife collected on the Moapa Southern Paiute Reservation, Nev., 1929. c, Stone-bladed knife set in a mesquite handle, recovered in Las Vegas Wash and probably Southern Paiute. Similar knives were used to cut the apical meristem of the agave from its roots and to sever the leaves. d, Agave "heart" with the leaves removed, ready for cooking. Collected by M.R. Harrington on the Moapa Southern Paiute Reservation in 1925. Rim diameter of a 56 cm, others to same scale.

Table 1. Common Food Plants in the Great Basin
(*continued*)

P. gairdneri Yampa
  Root Northern Paiute, Western Shoshone, Gosiute, Northern Shoshone, Eastern Shoshone, Kawaiisu
P. oregona Oregon yampa
  Root Northern Paiute
Sium suave Hemlock water parsnip
  Root Washoe
Sphenosciadium capitellatum Woollyhead parsnip
  Owens Valley Paiute, Ore. Northern Paiute

Asteraceae
  Agoseris aurantiaca False dandelion
    Leaves Northern Ute
  A. retrorsa
    Leaves Kawaiisu
  Anisocoma acaulis
    Leaves Panamint, Nev. Southern Paiute
  Artemisia arbuscula Black sagebrush
    Seeds Western Shoshone
  A. biennis Biennial wormwood
    Seeds Gosiute
  A. carruthii Carruth sagebrush
    Seeds Utah Southern Paiute
  A. dracunculus Tarragon
    Seeds Gosiute
  A. ludoviciana
    Seeds Utah Southern Paiute
  A. michauxiana Michaux sagebrush
    Seeds Gosiute
  A. tridentata Big sagebrush
    Seeds Owens Valley Paiute, Nev. Northern Paiute, Western Shoshone, Gosiute, Northern Shoshone, Southern Paiute
  Balsamorhiza hirsuta Hairy balsamroot
    Root, seed Nev. Northern Paiute
  B. hookeri Hooker balsamroot
    Seeds Ore. Northern Paiute, Gosiute, Eastern Shoshone
  B. sagittata Arrowlead balsamroot
    Seeds, roots, young leaves Washoe, Northern Paiute, Western Shoshone, Gosiute, Eastern Shoshone, Utah Southern Paiute, Northern Ute
  Chaetadelpha wheeleri
    Leaves Nev. Northern Paiute
  Cirsium sp. Thistle
    Stems Nev. Northern Paiute, Panamint, Western Shoshone, Gosiute, Northern Shoshone, Utah Southern Paiute
  C. acaulescens
    Stems Ore. Northern Paiute
  C. brevistylum
    Stems Nev. Northern Paiute
  C. californicum California thistle
    Stems Kawaiisu
  C. eatoni
    Stems Gosiute
  C. foliosum Elk thistle
    Stems, root Western Shoshone, Northern Shoshone

Table 1. Common Food Plants in the Great Basin
(*continued*)

  C. mohavense
    Stems Western Shoshone
  C. occidentale
    Stems Kawaiisu
  C. parryi
    Stems Eastern Shoshone, Kawaiisu
  C. undulatum Wayleaf thistle
    Stems Gosiute, Eastern Shoshone
  C. utahense
    Stems Western Shoshone
  Coreopsis bigllovii
    Leaves Panamint
  Crepis runcinata Hawksbeard
    Leaves Gosiute
  Glyptopleura marginata
    Leaves Nev. Northern Paiute
  Haplopappus macronema Whitestem goldenweed
    Seeds Owens Valley Paiute, Panamint
  Helianthella uniflora Oneflower helianthella
    Seeds Utah Southern Paiute
  Helianthus sp. Sunflower
    Seeds Owens Valley Paiute, Bannock, Western Shoshone, Gosiute, Northern Shoshone, Eastern Shoshone, Nev. Southern Paiute
  H. annuus Sunflower
    Seeds Washoe, Owens Valley Paiute, Northern Paiute, Panamint, Western Shoshone, Gosiute, Northern Shoshone, Eastern Shoshone, Kawaiisu, Utah Southern Paiute
  H. bolanderi
    Seeds Owens Valley Paiute
  H. petiolaris Prairie sunflower
    Seeds Nev. Northern Paiute, Western Shoshone, Eastern Shoshone, Utah Southern Paiute
  Lactuca ludoviciana Lettuce
    Leaves Western Shoshone, Gosiute
  Lygodesmia spinosa Thorn skeletonweed
    Seeds Ore. Northern Paiute
  Microceris sp.
    Seeds Ore. Northern Paiute
  Viguiera multiflora Showy gondeneye
    Seeds Utah Southern Paiute
  Wyethia amplexicaulis Mulesear wyethia
    Seeds Ore. Northern Paiute, Western Shoshone, Gosiute
  W. mollis Wooly wyethia
    Seeds Washoe, Northern Paiute, Western Shoshone, Northern Shoshone
  W. ovata
    Seeds Owens Valley Paiute

Berberidaceae Barberry family
  Berberis fremontii Fremont barberry
    Fruits Utah Southern Paiute

Betulaceae Birch family
  Corylus cornuta California hazelnut
    Nuts Washoe, Ore. Northern Paiute

Table 1.   Common Food Plants in the Great Basin
(*continued*)

Boraginaceae   Borage family
  Amsinckia tessellata   Fiddleneck
    Leaves   Panamint, Kawaiisu
  Lappula occidentalis   Stickseed
    Seeds   Western Shoshone

Brassicaceae   Mustard family
  Arabis holboelli   Rock cress
    Seeds   Utah Southern Paiute
  Caulanthus coulteri   Wild cabbage
    Leaves   Kawaiisu
  C. crassicaulis   Thickstem wild cabbage
    Leaves   Panamint, Kawaiisu, Northern Ute
  Descurainia pinnata var. *filipes*   Tansy mustard
    Seeds   Washoe, Owens Valley Paiute, Northern
      Paiute, Panamint, Kawaiisu, Nev. and Utah
      Southern Paiute
  D. richardsonii
    Seeds   Washoe, Panamint
  D. sophia (introduced)   Flaxweed, tansy mustard
    Seeds   Owens Valley Paiute, Northern Paiute,
      Panamint, Kawaiisu, Nev. and Utah Southern Paiute
  Draba nemorosa   Woods draba
    Seeds   Northern Ute
  Lepidium sp.   Pepperweed
    Seeds   Owens Valley Paiute, Oreg. Northern Paiute?
  L. densiflorum
    Seeds   Panamint
  L. fremontii   Desert pepperweed
    Seeds   Utah Southern Paiute
  L. lasiocarpum
    Seeds   Kawaiisu, Utah Southern Paiute
  Rorippa curvisiliqua   Yellow cress
    Seeds, leaves   Washoe, Owens Valley Paiute, Ore.
      Northern Paiute, Kawaiisu, Utah Southern Paiute
  Sisymbrium altissimum   Tumble mustard
    Oreg. Northern Paiute
  S. sophia
    Seeds   Oreg. Northern Paiute, Utah Southern Paiute
  Stanleya pinnata   Desert prince's plume
    Leaves, stems, seeds   Nev. Northern Paiute,
      Panamint, Western Shoshone, Kawaiisu,
      Chemehuevi, Nev. and Utah Southern Paiute

Cactaceae   Cactus family
  Echinocactus lecontei   Echinocactus
    Stems, seeds   Utah Southern Paiute
  E. mohavensis   Echinocactus
    Fruits   Utah Southern Paiute
  E. polycephalus   Cottontop echinocactus
    Seeds   Utah Southern Paiute
  Echinocereus engelmanni
    Fruits   Panamint, Utah Southern Paiute
  Mammillaria sp.   Mammilaria
    Inner stem   Gosiute
  M. tetrancistra
    Inner stem   Utah Southern Paiute

Table 1.   Common Food Plants in the Great Basin
(*continued*)

  Neolloydia johnsoni
    Stem   Utah Southern Paiute
  Opuntia sp.   Prickly pear
    Stems, fruits   Owens Valley Paiute, Nev. Northern
      Paiute, Western Shoshone, Gosiute, Chemehuevi,
      Nev. and Utah Southern Paiute, Northern Ute
  O. basilaris   Beavertail prickly pear
    Buds, blossoms, stems, fruits   Washoe, Panamint,
      Kawaiisu
  O. polyacantha   Prickly pear
    Stems, buds   Nev. Northern Paiute, Gosiute, Utah
      Southern Paiute
  O. whipplei   Whipple cholla
    Buds, fruit   Utah Southern Paiute

Capparidaceae   Caper family
  Cleome lutea   Yellow bee plant
    Seeds   Owens Valley Paiute
  C. serrulata   Bee plant
    Leaves   Gosiute, Eastern Shoshone
  Isomeris arborea
    Flowers   Kawaiisu

Caprifoliaceae   Honeysuckle family
  Sambucus caerulea
    Fruits   Washoe, Owens Valley Paiute, Nev. and Oreg.
      Northern Paiute, Panamint, Gosiute, Kawaiisu
  S. mexicana
    Fruits   Owens Valley Paiute
  S. racemosa ssp. *pubens* var. *melanocarpa*
    Fruits   Washoe, Nev. Northern Paiute, Utah Southern
      Paiute
  S. racemosa sp.p. *pubens* var. *microbotrys*   Elderberry
    Fruits   Nev. Northern Paiute, Western Shoshone,
      Gosiute, Eastern Shoshone

Chenopodiaceae   Chenopod family
  Allenrolfea occidentalis   Iodine bush
    Seeds   Northern Paiute, Gosiute, Utah Southern
      Paiute
  Atriplex argentea
    Seeds   Owens Valley Paiute, Northern Paiute,
      Western Shoshone
  A. canescens   Fourwing saltbush
    Seeds   Utah Southern Paiute
  A. confertifolia   Shadscale
    Seeds   Gosiute, Nev. and Utah Southern Paiute
  A. lentiformis   Big saltbush
    Seeds   Utah Southern Paiute
  A. polygaloides
    Seeds   Gosiute
  A. powellii
    Seeds   Utah Southern Paiute
  A. serenana
    Seeds   Gosiute, Eastern Shoshone
  A. spinifera
    Seeds   Owens Valley Paiute

Table 1. Common Food Plants in the Great Basin
(*continued*)

Chenopodium album (introduced) Lamb's-quarters
  Seeds Owens Valley Paiute, Northern Paiute,
    Panamint, Western Shoshone, Gosiute, Northern
    Shoshone, Kawaiisu, Utah Shoshone Paiute
C. boytrys (introduced?) Jerusalemoa goosefoot
  Seeds Utah Southern Paiute
C. capitatum Blite goosefoot
  Seeds Gosiute
C. chenopodioides Red goosefoot
  Seeds Gosiute
C. fremontii Fremont goosefoot
  Leaves, seeds Owens Valley Paiute, Ore. Northern
    Paiute?, Utah Southern Paiute
C. incanum
  Seeds Owens Valley Paiute, Northern Paiute, Utah
    Southern Paiute
C. leptophyllum Slimleaf goosefoot
  Seeds Gosiute, Utah Southern Paiute
Salicornia europaea Rocky Mountain glasswort
  Seeds Gosiute
Sarcobatus vermiculatus Black greasewood
  Seeds Utah Southern Paiute
Suaeda depressa var. *erecta* Seepweed
  Seeds Washoe, Nev. Northern Paiute, Gosiute
S. diffusa Seablite
  Seeds Utah Southern Paiute
S. intermedia Seablite
  Seeds Oreg. Northern Paiute
S. torreyana var. *ramosissima* Bush seepweed
  Seeds Washoe, Panamint, Western Shoshone, Nev.
    and Utah Southern Paiute

Cucurbitaceae Gourd family
  Cucurbita foetidissima Calabazilla
    Seeds Utah Southern Paiute

Cupressaceae Cypress family
  Juniperus californica California juniper
    Seeds Kawaiisu
  J. occidentalis Western juniper
    Seeds Oreg. Northern Paiute, Kawaiisu?
  J. osteosperma Utah juniper
    Seeds Utah Southern Paiute

Cyperaceae Sedge family
  Carex douglasii Douglas sedge
    Seeds Kawaiisu
  Cyperus esculentus Chufa flat sedge
    Bulbs Owens Valley Paiute, Nev. Northern Paiute
  Eleocharis sp. Spike-rush
    Bulbs Owens Valley Paiute
  Scirpus acutus Tule bulrush
    Seeds, root Washoe, Owens Valley Paiute, Nev.
      Northern Paiute, Gosiute, Utah Southern Paiute
  S. californicus
    Seeds Owens Valley Paiute

Table 1. Common Food Plants in the Great Basin
(*continued*)

  S. maritimus Alkali bulrush
    Seeds Nev. Northern Paiute, Nev. and Utah
      Southern Paiute
  S. validus Softstem bulrush
    Stem, roots Oreg. Northern Paiute, Kawaiisu,
      Northern Ute

Elaeagnaceae Oleaster family
  Elaeagnus commutata Silverberry
    Fruit Owens Valley Paiute
  Shepherdia argentea Silver buffaloberry
    Fruit Northern Paiute, Western Shoshone, Gosiute,
      Utah Southern Paiute, Northern Ute
  S. canadensis Russet buffaloberry
    Fruit Oreg. Northern Paiute, Northern Shoshone,
      Eastern Shoshone

Ephedraceae Ephedra family
  Ephedra nevadensis Nevada ephedra
    Seed Owens Valley Paiute, Panamint

Ericaceae Heath family
  Arctostaphylos glauca
    Fruit Kawaiisu
  A. nevadensis Pinemat manzanita
    Fruit Oreg. Northern Paiute
  A. patula Greenleaf manzanita
    Fruit Owens Valley Paiute
  A. pringlei var. *drupacea*
    Fruit Utah Southern Paiute
  A. pungens Pointleaf manzanita
    Fruit Utah Southern Paiute
  Vaccinium membranaceum Big whortleberry
    Fruit Oreg. Northern Paiute
  V. ovalifolium Big whortleberry
    Fruit Oreg. Northern Paiute
  V. parvifolium
    Fruit Oreg. Northern Paiute

Fabaceae Pea family
  Acacia greggii Catclaw acacia
    Seeds Chemehuevi, Nev. Southern Paiute
  Dalea polyadenia Nevada dalea
    Seeds Owens Valley Paiute
  Phaseolus vulgaris Kidney bean (cultigen)
    Beans Nev. and Utah Southern Paiute, Chemehuevi,
      Panamint, Southern Ute
  P. acutifolius Tepary bean (cultigen)
    Beans Nev. and Utah Southern Paiute, Chemeheuvi
  Prosopis glandulosa Mesquite
    Beans Panamint, Chemeheuvi, Nev. and Utah
      Southern Paiute
  P. glandulosa var. *torreyana*
    Beans, fruits, seeds Kawaiisu, Utah Southern Paiute
  P. pubescens Screwbean
    Beans Owens Valley Paiute, Panamint, Chemeheuvi,
      Nev. and Utah Southern Paiute

Table 1. Common Food Plants in the Great Basin
(*continued*)

Psoralea castorea Beaverhead scurfpea
   Roots Utah Southern Paiute
P. mephitica Skunktop scurfpea
   Roots Utah Southern Paiute
Robinia neomexicana New Mexico locust
   Flowers Utah Southern Paiute
Trifolium tridentatum Clover
   Seeds, plants, leaves Owens Valley Paiute
T. wormskjoldii Cow clover
   Seeds, plants, leaves Kawaiisu

Fagaceae Beech family
  Castanopsis sempervirens Bush chinquapin
   Acorn Kawaiisu
  Quercus chrysolepis Canyon live oak
   Fruit Nev. Northern Paiute, Kawaiisu
  Q. douglasii Blue oak
   Fruit Kawaiisu
  Q. dumosa California scrub oak
   Fruit Kawaiisu
  Q. gambelii Gambel oak
   Fruit Utah Southern Paiute, Northern Ute
  Q. garryana Garry oak
   Fruit Ore. Northern Paiute, Kawaiisu
  Q. kelloggii California black oak
   Fruit Washoe, Owens Valley Paiute, Kawaiisu
  Q. lobata California white oak
   Fruit Kawaiisu
  Q. palmeri Palmer oak
   Fruit Owens Valley Paiute
  Q. turbinella Scrub liveoak
   Fruit Chemeheuvi, Nev. Southern Paiute

Table 1. Common Food Plants in the Great Basin
(*continued*)

  Q. undulata Wavyleaf oak
   Fruit Gosiute, Northern Ute
  Q. wislizenii Interior scrub oak
   Fruit Kawaiisu

Hippocastanaceae
  Aesculus californica California buckeye
   Fruit Kawaiisu

Hydrophyllaceae Waterleaf family
  Phacelia sp. Phacelia
   Leaves Nev. Northern Paiute
  P. distans Fern phacelia
   Leaves Kawaiisu
  P. ramosissima Branching phacelia
   Leaves Kawaiisu

Iridaceae Iris family
  Iris missouriensis Rocky mountain iris
   Roots Utah Southern Paiute

Juglandaceae Walnut family
  Juglans major Arizona walnut
   Nuts Chemeheuvi

Juncaceae Rush family
  Juncus balticus
   Seeds Owens Valley Paiute

Lamiaceae Mint family
  Agastache urticifolia Gitan hyssop
   Seeds Gosiute

 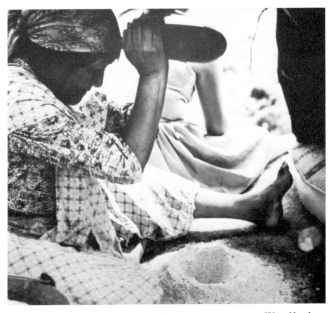

Fig. 5. Washoe women making acorn flour. left, Winnie Pete, her daughter, and granddaughter at a large bedrock mortar near Woodfords, Calif. right, Mrs. Pete using a stone pestle to grind the acorns to meal in the mortar pit. Photographs by John Price, 1961.

Table 1.   Common Food Plants in the Great Basin (*continued*)

Salvia columbariae   California chia
Seeds   Owens Valley Paiute, Panamint, Kawaiisu, Chemeheuvi, Nev. Southern Paiute

Lennoaceae   Lennoa family
Pholisma arenarium
Stem   Kawaiisu

Liliaceae   Lily family
Allium sp.   Onion
Bulbs   all groups except Northern Shoshone, Panamint, Western Ute
A. acuminatum   Tapertip onion
Leaves   Northern Paiute, Western Shoshone, Gosiute, Northern Shoshone, Eastern Shoshone, Northern Ute
A. anceps
Bulbs   Washoe, Northern Paiute
A. bisceptrum
Bulbs, leaves   Nev. Northern Paiute, Gosiute, Northern Ute
A. nevadense   Nevada onion
Leaves   Nev. Northern Paiute
A. parvum
Leaves   Washoe, Northern Paiute, Gosiute
A. platycaule
Bulbs   Nev. Northern Paiute
A. tolmiei   Tolmie onion
Bulbs   Ore. Northern Paiute
A. validum
Bulbs   Washoe
Calochortus sp.   Mariposa Lily
Bulbs   Owens Valley Paiute, Kawaiisu
C. flexuosus   Weakstem mariposa
Bulbs   Utah Southern Paiute
C. gunnisonii   Gunnison mariposa lily
Bulbs   Western Shoshone
C. invenustus   Plain mariposa lily
Bulbs   Western Shoshone
C. kennedyi   Desert mariposa
Bulbs   Panamint, Kawaiisu
C. leichtlinii   Smoky mariposa lily
Bulbs   Washoe, Nev. Northern Paiute, Western Shoshone, Gosiute, Utah Southern Paiute, Northern Ute
C. macrocarpus   Sagebrush mariposa lily
Bulbs   Ore. Northern Paiute
C. nuttallii   Sego lily
Bulbs   Washoe, Owens Valley Paiute, Northern Paiute, Western Shoshone, Gosiute, Northern Shoshone, Eastern Shoshone, Utah Southern Paiute, Northern Ute
C. venustus   Butterfly mariposa
Bulbs   Kawaiisu
Camassia quamash   Common camas
Bulbs   Washoe, Northern Paiute, Bannock, Northern Shoshone, Eastern Shoshone

Table 1.   Common Food Plants in the Great Basin (*continued*)

Chlorogalum pomeridianum   Soap plant
Bulbs   Washoe
Dichelostemma pulchellum   Purplehead brodiaea
Bulbs   Owens Valley Paiute, Nev. Northern Paiute, Kawaiisu?
Fritillaria atropurpurea   Purplespot fritillary
Bulbs   Nev. Northern Paiute, Utah Southern Paiute, Northern Ute?
F. pudica   Yellow fritillary
Bulbs   Northern Paiute, Northern Ute
Lilium columbianum   Columbia lily
Bulbs   Ore. Northern Paiute
L. parvum   Sierra lily
Bulbs   Washoe, Owens Valley Paiute, Ore. Northern Paiute
Triteleia grandiflora
Bulbs   Washoe, Ore. Northern Paiute
T. hyacinthina   Triteleia
Bulbs   Washoe, Northern Paiute

Loasaceae   Blazing star family
Mentzelia affinis   Valley stickseed
Seeds   Kawaiisu
M. albicaulis   White stem blazing star
Seeds   Washoe, Owens Valley Paiute, Nev. Northern Paiute, Western Shoshone, Gosiute, Kawaiisu, Nev. and Utah Southern Paiute
M. congesta
Seeds   Washoe, Ore. Northern Paiute, Kawaiisu
M. dispersa
Seeds   Kawaiisu, Utah Southern Paiute, Western Shoshone
M. laevicaulis   Big blazing star
Seeds   Owens Valley Paiute, Northern Paiute, Panamint, Western Shoshone, Nev. Southern Paiute
M. multiflora   Desert blazing star
Seeds   Utah Southern Paiute
M. nitens
Seeds   Panamint
M. vetchiana
Seeds   Kawaiisu

Lythraceae   Loosestrife family
Ammannia coccinea   Purple ammania
Seeds   Utah Southern Painte

Malvaceae   Mallow family
Sphaeralcea parvifolia   Glove mallow
Seeds   Utah Southern Paiute

Onagraceae   Evening primrose family
Oenothera biennis   Common evening primrose
Seeds   Gosiute
O. brevipes   Golden evening primrose
Seeds   Panamint
O. hookeri
Seeds   Owens Valley Paiute

Table 1.   Common Food Plants in the Great Basin
(*continued*)

Orchidaceae   Orchid family
  Spiranthes sp.   Ladies' tresses
    Bulbs   Owens Valley Paiute

Orobanchaceae   Broomrape family
  Orobanche sp.   Broomrape
    Plant   Panamint, Western Shoshone, Utah Southern
      Paiute
  O. californica
    Plant   Owens Valley Paiute, Nev. Northern Paiute,
      Western Shoshone, Utah Southern Paiute
  O. fasciculata
    Plant   Nev. Northern Paiute, Utah Southern Paiute
  O. ludoviciana
    Plant   Utah Southern Paiute, Chemehuevi

Pinaceae   Pine family
  Abies concolor   White fir
    Seeds   Kawaiisu?
  Pinus edulis   Piñon
    Seeds   Chemehuevi, Nev. and Utah Southern Paiute,
      Northern Ute, Southern Ute
  P. flexilis   Limber pine
    Seeds   Bannock, Northern Shoshone, Western
      Shoshone
  P. lambertiana   Sugar pine
    Seeds   Washoe, Kawaiisu
  P. monophylla   Single leaf piñon
    Seeds   Washoe, Owens Valley Paiute, Nev. Northern
      Paiute, Panamint, Western Shoshone, Gosiute,
      Northern Shoshone, Kawaiisu, Chemehuevi, Nev.
      and Utah Southern Paiute
  P. ponderosa   Ponderosa pine
    Seeds   Ore. Northern Paiute, Kawaiisu
  P. sabiniana   Digger pine
    Seeds   Kawaiisu

Poaceae   Grass family
  Agropyron sp.   Wheatgrass
    Seeds   Nev. Northern Paiute, Panamint
  A. repens (introduced)   Quackgrass
    Seeds   Owens Valley Paiute, Gosiute, Northern Ute
  A. trachycaulum   Slender wheatgrass
    Seeds   Owens Valley Paiute
  Agrostis sp.   Bentgrass
    Seeds   Nev. Northern Paiute, Western Shoshone
  Alopecurus aequalis   Short-awn foxtail
    Seeds   Ore. Northern Paiute
  Avena fatua (introduced)   Wild oat
    Seeds   Kawaiisu
  Bromus breviaristatus   Bromgrass
    Seeds   Gosiute
  Deschampsia caespitosa   Tufted hairgrass
    Seeds   Gosiute
  D. danthonioides   Annual hairgrass
    Seeds   Gosiute, Kawaiisu
  Echinochloa crus-galli (introduced)   Barnyard grass
    Seeds   Owens Valley Paiute

Table 1.   Common Food Plants in the Great Basin
(*continued*)

  E. muricata var. *microstachya*
    Seeds   Nev. Northern Paiute, Utah Southern Paiute
  Elymus canadensis   Canada wild rye
    Seeds   Ore. Northern Paiute, Gosiute, Northern Ute
  E. cinereus   Great Basin wild rye
    Seeds   Washoe, Owens Valley Paiute, Northern
      Paiute, Panamint, Western Shoshone, Gosiute,
      Northern Shoshone, Eastern Shoshone, Utah
      Southern Paiute
  E. triticoides   Beardless wild rye
    Seeds   Kawaiisu
  Eragrostis sp.   Lovegrass
    Seeds   Nev. Southern Paiute
  E. oxylepis
    Seeds   Owens Valley Paiute
  Glyceria borealis   Northern manna grass
    Seeds   Nev. Northern Paiute
  Hilaria jamesii   Galleta grass
    Seeds   Nev. Northern Paiute, Panamint
  Hordeum californicum   Barley
    Seeds   Nev. Northern Paiute
  H. depressum   Barley
    Seeds   Nev. Northern Paiute, Gosiute
  H. jubatum   Foxtail barley
    Seeds   Gosiute
  Melica imperfecta   Melic grass
    Seeds   Kawaiisu
  Muhlenbergia asperifolia   Scratchgrass
    Seeds   Kawaiisu?, Chemehuevi, Nev. and Utah
      Southern Paiute
  M. richardsonis   Mat muhly
    Seeds   Nev. Northern Paiute
  M. rigens
    Seeds   Panamint, Nev. and Utah Southern Paiute
  Oryzopsis hymenoides   Indian ricegrass
    Seeds   Washoe, Owens Valley Paiute, Nev. Northern
      Paiute, Panamint, Western Shoshone, Gosiute,
      Northern Shoshone, Kawaiisu, Chemehuevi, Nev.
      and Utah Southern Paiute
  O. miliacea
    Seeds   Owens Valley Paiute
  Panicum sp.   Panicum
    Seeds   Nev. Southern Paiute
  Poa arida   Plains bluegrass
    Seeds   Gosiute
  P. canbyi   Canby bluegrass
    Seeds   Gosiute
  P. nevadensis   Nevada bluegrass
    Seeds   Nev. Northern Paiute, Panamint, Nev.
      Southern Paiute
  Sitanium hystrix   Squirreltail
    Seeds   Owens Valley Paiute, Panamint, Western
      Shoshone
  S. jubatum   Big squirreltail
    Seeds   Kawaiisu
  Sporobolus sp.   Dropseed
    Seeds   Utah Southern Paiute

Table 1. Common Food Plants in the Great Basin (*continued*)

S. *airoides* Alkali sacaton
  Seeds Owens Valley Paiute, Panamint, Nev. and Utah Southern Paiute
S. *cryptandrus* Sand dropseed
  Seeds Utah Southern Paiute
Stipa speciosa Desert needlegrass
  Seeds Owens Valley Paiute, Kawaiisu
Triticum aestivum (introduced) Wheat
  Seeds Gosiute, Nev. and Utah Southern Paiute
Zea mays Corn (cultigen)
  Seeds Panamint?, Chemehuevi, Nev. and Utah Southern Paiute, Southern Ute

Polemoniaceae Phlox family
  Gilia leptomeria Gilia
    Seeds Owens Valley Paiute

Polygonaceae Buckwheat family
  Eriogonum angulosum Angle-stemmed buckwheat
    Seeds Kawaiisu
  E. *baileyi* Bailey buckwheat
    Seeds Kawaiisu
  E. *davidsonii*
    Seeds Kawaiisu
  E. *fasciculatum* Gray calyania buckwheat
    Seeds Owens Valley Paiute
  E. *inflatum* Desert trumpet eriogonum
    Seeds Kawaiisu, Utah Southern Paiute
  E. *nudum* var. *pubiflorum* Long trumpet buckwheat
    Flowers Kawaiisu

Table 1. Common Food Plants in the Great Basin (*continued*)

E. *plumatella* Yucca eriogonum
  Seeds Kawaiisu
E. *pusillum* Yellow turban buckwheat
  Seeds Kawaiisu
E. *roseum*
  Seeds Kawaiisu
E. *wrightii* Wrights buckwheat
  Seeds Kawaiisu
Fagopyrum esculentum (introduced)
  Seeds Utah Southern Paiute
Polygonum sp. Knotweed
  Seeds Ore. Northern Paiute
Rumex crispus Curly dock
  Seeds, stems, leaves Owens Valley Paiute, Nev. Northern Paiute, Panamint, Western Shoshone, Kawaiisu, Northern Ute
R. *hymenosepalus* Canaigre
  Seeds, stems Western Shoshone, Kawaiisu, Northern Ute

Portulacaceae Purslane family
  Claytonia lanceolata Lance leaf spring beauty
    Bulb Northern Shoshone, Eastern Shoshone, Utah Southern Paiute, Northern Ute
  C. *umbellata* Spring beauty
    Bulb Nev. Northern Paiute
  Lewisia rediviva Bitterroot lewisia
    Roots Washoe, Owens Valley Paiute, Northern Paiute, Western Shoshone, Gosiute, Northern Shoshone, Eastern Shoshone, Utah Southern Paiute, Northern Ute

Fig. 6. Emma Fox, Northern Paiute from Burns Reservation, Oreg., collecting roots. left, Digging yampa roots (*Perideridia bolanderi*), she uses a handled, pointed iron bar, a modern adaptation of the wooden digging stick. right, Washing roots in a rock-lined water catchment basin. Roots of bitterroot (*Lewisia rediviva*), yampa, and biscuit root (*Lomatium*) are drying in the sun. Photographs by Marilyn Couture, May 1978.

Table 1.   Common Food Plants in the Great Basin
(*continued*)

Montia perfoliata var. *depressa*   Miners' lettuce
  Leaves   Kawaiisu
Portulaca oleracea (introduced)   Common purslane
  Seeds, leaves   Utah Southern Paiute
P. retusa
  Seeds, leaves   Utah Southern Paiute

Ranunculaceae   Crowfoot family
  Aquilegia formosa   Sitka columbine
    Young plants   Washoe

Rhamnaceae   Buckthorn family
  Rhamnus californica   Coffeeberry
    Fruit   Owens Valley Paiute

Rosaceae   Rose family
  Amelanchier alnifolia var. *alnifolia*   Saskatoon
    serviceberry
    Fruits   Washoe, Oreg. Northern Paiute, Western
      Shoshone, Gosiute, Northern Shoshone, Utah
      Southern Paiute, Northern Ute
  A. alnifolia var. *cusickii*   Cusick serviceberry
    Fruits   Oreg. Northern Paiute
  A. alnifolia var. *pallida*
    Fruits   Nev. Northern Paiute
  A. utahensis   Utah serviceberry
    Fruits   Utah Southern Paiute
  Crataegus douglasii   Douglas hawthorn
    Fruits   Northern Paiute
  Fragaria spp.   Strawberry
    Fruits   Oreg. Northern Paiute
  F. vesca
    Fruits   Gosiute, Washoe
  F. virginiana
    Fruits   Oreg. Northern Paiute, Washoe
  Prunus subcordata   Sierra plum
    Fruits   Oreg. Northern Paiute
  P. virginiana var. *demissa*   Western chokecherry
    Fruits   Washoe, Northern Paiute, Western Shoshone,
      Gosiute, Northern Shoshone, Eastern Shoshone,
      Kawaiisu, Utah Southern Paiute
  P. virginiana var. *melanocarpa*   Black chokecherry
    Fruits   Washoe, Northern Paiute
  Rosa californica   California wildrose
    Fruits   Owens Valley Paiute, Northern Paiute
  R. pisocarpa
    Fruits   Owens Valley Paiute, Northern Paiute
  R. acicularis
    Fruits   Eastern Shoshone
  R. woodsii var. *ultramontanum*   Interior wildrose
    Fruits   Northern Paiute, Gosiute, Eastern Shoshone,
      Kawaiisu, Utah Southern Paiute, Southern Ute
  Rubus sp.   Raspberry
    Fruits   Oreg. Northern Paiute, Gosiute, Utah
      Southern Paiute
  R. leucodermis   Whitebark raspberry
    Fruits   Washoe, Western Shoshone

Table 1.   Common Food Plants in the Great Basin
(*continued*)

  R. parviflorus   Western thimbleberry
    Fruits   Washoe
  R. spectabilis
    Fruits   Oreg. Northern Paiute

Santalaceae   Sandalwood family
  Comandra pallida   Bastard toadflax
    Fruits   Utah Southern Paiute

Saxifragaceae   Saxifrage family
  Ribes aureum   Golden currant
    Fruits   Washoe, Owens Valley Paiute, Northern
      Paiute, Gosiute, Utah Southern Paiute, Northern
      Ute
  R. bracteosum   Stink currant
    Fruits   Oreg. Northern Paiute
  R. californicum   California gooseberry
    Fruits   Kawaiisu
  R. cereum   Squaw currant
    Fruits   Washoe, Owens Valley Paiute, Northern
      Paiute, Eastern Shoshone
  R. inerme   Whitestem gooseberry
    Fruits   Gosiute, Eastern Shoshone
  R. lacustre   Prickly currant
    Fruits   Oreg. Northern Paiute, Gosiute
  R. lasianthum
    Fruits   Washoe
  R. leptanthum   Trumpet gooseberry
    Fruits   Gosiute
  R. petiolare   Western black currant
    Fruits   Washoe
  R. quercetorum   Chaparral gooseberry
    Fruits   Kawaiisu
  R. roezlii   Sierra gooseberry
    Fruits   Washoe, Kawaiisu
  R. sanguineum   Redflowering currant
    Fruits   Oreg. Northern Paiute
  R. velutinum   Desert currant
    Fruits   Washoe, Nev. Northern Paiute, Kawaiisu

Scrophulariaceae   Figwort family
  Mimulus guttatus   Common monkeyflower
    Stalks   Eastern Shoshone

Solanaceae
  Lycium andersonii   Anderson wolfberry
    Fruit   Washoe, Owens Valley Paiute, Nev. Northern
      Paiute, Panamint, Western Shoshone, Utah
      Southern Paiute
  L. berlandieri
    Fruit   Utah Southern Paiute
  L. cooperi   Cooper wolfberry
    Fruit   Utah Southern Paiute
  L. pallidum   Pale wolfberry
    Fruit   Utah Southern Paiute
  L. torreyi   Torrey wolfberry
    Fruit   Owens Valley Paiute, Utah Southern Paiute

Table 1. Common Food Plants in the Great Basin
(*continued*)

Physalis ixocarpa   Ground cherry
   Fruit   Owens Valley Paiute

Typhaceae   Cattail family
   Typha domingensis
      Flower heads, seeds   Owens Valley Paiute, Nev.
         Northern Paiute, Kawaiisu, Utah Southern Paiute
   T. latifolia   Common cattail
      Roots, pollen, flowers, stalks   Washoe, Owens Valley
         Paiute, Northern Paiute, Panamint, Western
         Shoshone, Gosiute, Northern Shoshone, Kawaiisu,
         Chemehuevi, Utah Southern Paiute

Table 1. Common Food Plants in the Great Basin
(*continued*)

Valerianaceae   Valerian family
   Valeriana edulis   Edible valerian
      Roots   Nev. Northern Paiute, Bannock, Western
         Shoshone, Gosiute, Northern Shoshone, Utah
         Southern Paiute, Northern Ute

Verbenaceae   Verbena family
   Verbena bracteata   Bigbract verbena
      Seeds   Utah Southern Paiute

Vitaceae   Grape family
   Vitis arizonica   Canyon grape
      Fruits   Panamint, Nev. and Utah Southern Paiute

Mammals

Table 2 gives comparative data on mammal species commonly used in the region as food sources. The principal large game species were deer, pronghorn, and bighorn sheep. In a few selected areas, particularly in the north and east, moose, wapiti, and bison were also taken. On occasion in several areas bears were hunted for meat as well as furs.

Although reported as scarce in several areas, deer (*Odocoileus hemionus*) were hunted by all groups. In frequented habitats they were stalked and killed by solitary hunters or hunting partners using arrows dipped in poisons such as rattlesnake venom, rotted entrails or blood, or the juice of certain plant species. The wounded animal was then tracked until it either died or the hunter could take a killing shot. Blood placed in the track of a deer was considered by many Great Basin peoples as an effective means of tiring the animal and thus allowing it to be stalked more efficiently. Occasionally, solitary hunters also disguised themselves in a deer skin and horns so that they could move to within shooting distance of a deer or a small herd. This is referred to by Northern Paiute hunters as "putting on the horns." Hunters struck antlers together to simulate rutting battles, or imitated the foraging habits of deer. These strategies were to quiet if not attract the prey.

In suitable areas, deer were also corralled in small herds and then shot. Deer corrals were constructed of brush and rock in narrow canyons or at favored places along migratory trails. Several hunters cooperated in this form of hunting, some serving as drivers and others as bowmen. An alternative method in some areas was for hunters to drive deer along a frequented trail across which a low brush fence was built. A hunter, concealed in a pit behind the fence, shot the animals as they jumped the fence.

Deer surrounds and drives using fire were also used in some areas where suitable light brush cover made them effective. Northern Paiute in the area of Honey Lake, California, report that small herds of deer were occasionally driven to a low hill and then surrounded by several hunters. The brush around the hill was set afire and the deer moved either to the top of the hill or to an opening in the fire circle. They could then be shot from either vantage point (W. Z. Park 1933–1940). Burning the brush or grass in an area had the secondary advantage of improving forage for game for the next season. A number of Great Basin peoples recognized the relationship between fire and an increase in numbers of certain plants the following year.

Throughout the Great Basin, where they were available, people hunted pronghorns (*Antilocapra americana*), usually communally. Most communal hunts were directed by individuals with specific powers over these animals. They alone could call the pronghorns and keep them spiritually captive until they could be killed. They visited the herds, sang to the animals, and often slept among them for several nights. Often the animals were led to a brush corral built to contain them. An alternative was to make a corral by having people form a circle while holding a heavy sagebrush rope. In either case, the animals were run in the enclosure until they were tired and then shot with arrows or clubbed to death. It was normally the practice to take several antelope at a time or an entire small herd. Hunts were conducted only every 5 to 10 years in order to allow the pronghorn population to rebuild itself. Single pronghorns might also be taken on occasion by hunters using methods similar to those for deer.

Bighorn sheep (*Ovis canadensis*) were very important animals to native hunters and undoubtedly were more common than formerly suspected. Hunting them took several forms throughout the region. Techniques included stalking of individual animals, ambushing them along a favored trail, driving them with dogs toward

Table 2. Common Edible Mammals in the Great Basin

Antilocapridae   Pronghorn family
  Antilocapra americana   Pronghorn
    All but Panamint
Bovidae   Cattle, sheep, and goat family
  Bison bison   Bison
    Bannock, Northern Paiute, Northern Shoshone, Eastern
    Shoshone, Northern Ute, Western Ute, Southern Ute
  Oreamnos americanus   Mountain goat
    Northern Shoshone
  Ovis canadensis and subspp.   Mountain sheep
    All

Castoridae   Beaver family
  Castor canadensis   Beaver
    Washoe, Owens Valley Paiute, Northern Paiute, North-
    ern Shoshone, Bannock, Western Shoshone, Nev. and
    Utah Southern Paiute, Chemehuevi, Western Ute,
    Northern Ute, Southern Ute, Eastern Shoshone

Canidae   Dog family
  Canis familiaris   Dog
    Western Shoshone, Nev. Southern Paiute, Kawaiisu,
    Owens Valley Paiute
  C. latrans   Coyote
    Nev. Northern Paiute, Western Shoshone, Western Ute,
    Southern Ute, Kawaiisu, Owens Valley Paiute
  C. lupus   Gray wolf
    Western Shoshone, Western Ute, Southern Ute, Pana-
    mint
  Vulpes vulpes   Red fox
    Northern Paiute, Western Shoshone, Nev. Southern
    Paiute, Western Ute, Southern Ute
  V. macrotis   Kit fox
    Nev. Northern Paiute, Panamint, Western Shoshone, Nev.
    Southern Paiute, Western Ute
  Urocyon cinereoargenteus   Gray fox
    Panamint, Nev. Southern Paiute, Western Shoshone

Cervidae   Deer family
  Alces alces   Moose
    Northern Shoshone, Eastern Shoshone, Northern Ute
  Cervus elaphus   Wapiti (elk)
    Ore. Northern Paiute, Northern Shoshone, Bannock,
    Eastern Shoshone, Northern Ute, Southern Ute
  Odocoileus hemionus   Mule (or blacktail) deer
    All groups, but lacking or scarce in some areas
  O. virginianus   Whitetail deer
    Northern Shoshone, Bannock, Eastern Shoshone
  Rangifer tarandus   Caribou
    Northern Shoshone

Cricetidae   Mouse and rat (cricetid) family
  Neotoma albiqula   White-throated wood rat
    Southern Ute
  N. cinerea   Bushy-tailed wood rat
    Washoe, Northern Paiute, Northern Shoshone, Ban-
    nock, Western Shoshone, Northern Ute, Southern Ute,

Table 2. Common Edible Mammals in the Great Basin
(*continued*)

    Nev. and Utah Southern Paiute, Eastern Shoshone

  N. lepida   Desert wood rat
    Washoe, Owens Valley Paiute, Northern Paiute, Pana-
    mint, Western Shoshone, Northern Shoshone, Bannock,
    Utah Southern Paiute, Western Ute, Southern Ute,
    Northern Ute
  N. mexicana   Mexican wood rat
    Southern Ute
  Ondatra zibethicus   Muskrat
    Ore. Northern Paiute, Western Shoshone, Northern
    Shoshone, Bannock, Nev. Southern Paiute, Western Ute,
    Southern Ute, Northern Ute
  Microtus spp. (Meadow vole), *Onychomys* spp. (Grass-
  hopper mouse), *Peromyscus crinitus* (Canyon mouse),
  Reithrodontomys megalotis (Western harvest mouse), among
  spp. of "mice" eaten by many groups.

Erethizontidae   Porcupine family
  Erethizon dorsatum   Porcupine
    Washoe, Northern Paiute, Owens Valley Paiute, West-
    ern Shoshone, Northern Shoshone, Bannock, Utah and
    Nev. Southern Paiute, Western Ute, Northern Ute,
    Southern Ute, Eastern Shoshone

Felidae   Cat family
  Felis concolor   Mountain lion
    Nev. Northern Paiute, Western Shoshone, Bannock,
    Northern Shoshone, Utah Southern Paiute, Northern Ute,
    Western Ute, Panamint, Kawaiisu
  Lynx canadensis   Lynx
    Eastern Shoshone
  L. rufus   Bobcat
    All groups

Geomyidae   Pocket gopher family
  Thomomys spp.   Smooth-toothed pocket gophers
    Northern Paiute, Western Shoshone, Panamint, Nev. and
    Utah Southern Paiute, Western Ute, Southern Ute

Heteromyidae   Pocket mouse and rat family
  Dipodomys spp.   Kangaroo rat
    Washoe, Northern Paiute, Owens Valley Paiute, West-
    ern Shoshone, Panamint, Nev. and Utah Southern Paiute,
    Western Ute, Southern Ute, Northern Ute, Eastern
    Shoshone
  Perognathus spp.   Pocket mouse
    Owens Valley Paiute, Panamint, Western Shoshone, Utah
    and Nev. Southern Paiute, Chemehuevi, Southern Ute,
    Western Ute

Leporidae   Rabbit and hare family
  Lepus americanus   Snowshoe hare
    Washoe, Northern Paiute, Bannock, Northern Sho-
    shone, Nev. Southern Paiute, Northern Ute, Southern
    Ute, Eastern Shoshone

Table 2.   Common Edible Mammals in the Great Basin (*continued*)

L. californicus   Black-tailed jackrabbit
Washoe, Northern Paiute, Bannock, Panamint, Western Shoshone, Kawaiisu, Chemehuevi, Nev. and Utah Southern Paiute, Western Ute, Southern Ute

L. townsendii   White-tailed jackrabbit
Washoe, Northern Paiute, Western Shoshone, Northern Shoshone, Bannock, Western Ute, Northern Ute, Southern Ute, Utah Southern Paiute, Eastern Shoshone

Sylvilagus audubonii   Desert cottontail
Owens Valley Paiute, Western Shoshone, Nev. and Utah Southern Paiute, Panamint, Western Ute, Northern Ute, Southern Ute, Eastern Shoshone

S. idahoensis   Pygmy rabbit
Owens Valley Paiute, Northern Paiute, Northern Shoshone, Bannock, Western Shoshone, Utah Southern Paiute

S. nuttallii   Nuttall's cottontail
Washoe, Owens Valley Paiute, Northern Paiute, Western Shoshone, Northern Shoshone, Bannock, Utah Southern Paiute, Northern Ute, Southern Ute, Western Ute

Mustelidae   Weasel family
Lutra canadensis   River otter
Northern Shoshone, Bannock, Northern Ute, Southern Ute, Eastern Shoshone

Mephitis mephitis   Striped skunk
Nev. Northern Paiute, Western Shoshone, Bannock, Northern Ute, Southern Ute

Mustela vison   Mink
Northern Paiute, Western Shoshone, Utah Southern Paiute, Western Ute, Southern Ute, Northern Ute

Taxidea taxus   Badger
Washoe, Owens Valley Paiute, Northern Paiute, Western Shoshone, Bannock, Northern Shoshone, Eastern Shoshone, Western Ute, Southern Ute, Northern Ute, Nev. Southern Paiute

Ochotonidae   Pika family
Ochotona princeps   Pika
Washoe, Ore. Northern Paiute, Utah Southern Paiute, Northern Ute

Procyonidae   Raccoon family
Bassariscus astutus   Ringtail
Utah Southern Paiute, Southern Ute

Procyon lotor   Raccoon
Northern Paiute, Nev. Southern Paiute, Northern Ute, Southern Ute

Sciuridae   Squirrel family
Ammospermophilus leucurus   White-tailed antelope squirrel
Washoe, Northern Paiute, Owens Valley Paiute, Western Shoshone, Kawaiisu, Chemehuevi, Nev. and Utah Southern Paiute, Western Ute, Southern Ute, Northern Ute

Cynomys gunnisoni   Gunnison's prairie dog
Northern Ute, Southern Ute

Table 2.   Common Edible Mammals in the Great Basin (*continued*)

C. leucurus   White-tailed prairie dog
Utah Southern Paiute, Northern Ute, Southern Ute

C. parvidens   Utah prairie dog
Utah Southern Paiute, Northern Ute, Southern Ute

Eutamias spp.   Chipmunk
All groups

Glaucomys sabrinus   Northern flying squirrel
Washoe, Bannock, Northern Ute

Marmota flaviventris   Yellow-bellied marmot
Washoe, Northern Paiute, Owens Valley Paiute, Northern Shoshone, Bannock, Western Shoshone, Utah Southern Paiute, Eastern Shoshone, Northern Ute, Southern Ute

Sciurus aberti   Abert's squirrel
Utah Southern Paiute, Southern Ute

S. griseus   Western gray squirrel
Washoe, Nev. Northern Paiute, Owens Valley Paiute, Kawaiisu

Spermophilus armatus   Uintah ground squirrel
Northern Shoshone, Northern Ute

S. beecheyi   California ground squirrel
Washoe, Nev. Northern Paiute

S. beldingi   Belding's ground squirrel
Washoe, Nev. Northern Paiute, Western Shoshone

S. columbianus   Columbian ground squirrel
Northern Shoshone

S. lateralis   Golden-mantled ground squirrel
Washoe, Northern Paiute, Western Shoshone, Northern Shoshone, Bannock, Northern Ute, Southern Ute, Eastern Shoshone, Nev. and Utah Southern Paiute

S. richardsonii   Richardson's ground squirrel
Western Shoshone, Eastern Shoshone

S. tereticaudus   Round-tailed ground squirrel
Owens Valley Paiute, Panamint, Nev. Southern Paiute, Chemehuevi

S. townsendii   Townsend's ground squirrel
Washoe, Northern Paiute, Western Shoshone, Northern Shoshone, Bannock, Western Ute, Utah Southern Paiute

S. tridecemlineatus   Thirteen-lined ground squirrel
Eastern Shoshone, Northern Ute

S. variegatus   Rock squirrel
Western Shoshone, Utah and Nev. Southern Paiute, Western Ute

Tamiasciurus hudsonicus   Red squirrel
Northern Shoshone, Bannock, Eastern Shoshone, Utah Southern Paiute, Western Ute, Northern Ute, Southern Ute

T. douglasii   Douglas squirrel
Washoe, Ore. Northern Paiute

Ursidae   Bear family
Ursus americanus   Black bear
Washoe, Northern Shoshone, Bannock, Utah Southern Paiute, Northern Ute, Southern Ute, Eastern Shoshone

U. horribilis   Grizzly bear
Oreg. Northern Paiute, Northern Shoshone, Bannock, Northern Ute, Eastern Shoshone

Shoshone-Bannock Tribes, Media Center, Fort Hall, Idaho.

Fig. 7. Women cleaning buffalo tripe, probably in preparation for a tribal feast. A herd of buffalo is maintained by the Northern Shoshone-Bannock. Photographed on Fort Hall Reservation, Idaho, about 1976.

waiting hunters, and setting noose and net snares. Hunters reported that using disguises with these animals was sometimes dangerous as full-grown rams would charge hunters disguised as adult males or females. The hunters were safer in skins and horns of subadult males. Sheep were also attracted by hunters beating logs to simulate their rutting battles. Since bighorn sheep formerly ranged from the valley floor to the canyons and mountain peaks, hunting activities took place in a variety of natural settings.

The meat of large game animals was roasted in sections over the fire, or in some areas, in rock-lined pits. The body cavities of large mammals were sometimes filled with water and hot stones for cooking from within. Meat was cut into thin strips and dried in the shade, sometimes over a fire. True smoking of meat was reported only in certain areas of the region, principally in the north and east. Dried meat was pounded with berries, marrow, or fat to preserve it in several areas, but by no means all (Steward 1941, 1943a; O. C. Stewart 1941, 1942). Dried meat was stored in bags or grass- or bark-lined pits.

Many small game species were of equal if not more importance in day to day subsistence. Jackrabbits (*Lepus californicus, L. townsendii*) and cottontails (*Sylvilagus nuttallii, S. audubonii*), for example, were shot by hunters or taken with ingenious loop snares set in their runs (fig. 8). Large numbers of jackrabbits and occasionally cottontails were taken in communal drives in the fall for their meat and their furs. Nets measuring 300 feet or more in length were set in large semicircles or in a V-shaped formation into which the quarry was driven by men, women, and children working their way through the brush of the valley bottoms. The catch of these large drives was usually divided equally among

those who participated, but sometimes a larger share was offered to the hunt's organizer and leader or to the owners of the nets. Jackrabbits and cottontails were often split and dried after skinning for winter storage. The furs were twisted into long ropes and woven into blankets.

Several types of snares, deadfalls, pits, and traps were used to take small mammals, birds, and occasionally reptiles. Noose snares were used on cottontails (fig. 9). Figure-4 traps made with flat stones, sticks, and twine were also successful with a variety of small mammals (fig. 10). Property rights to trapping grounds for small mammals were apparently uncommon in the region, but were reported for at least the Pyramid Lake and Walker River Northern Paiute (W. Z. Park 1933–1940). Alternative techniques to trapping small game included drowning or smoking the animals from their burrows and extracting them by twisting a hooked stick into their fur (fig. 8).

Small mammals were variously processed for food. Rabbits, cottontails, marmots, badgers, woodrats, and others of similar size were often first placed on an open fire to burn off their fur. They might then have been pit roasted whole, sometimes eviscerated and stuffed with wild onions. Ground squirrels, tree squirrels, and mice were also boiled and pulverized in a mortar or on a metate. Bones and entrails of all mammals were also processed, either separately or as part of the general preparation of the species (Steward 1941, 1943a; O. C. Stewart 1941).

Birds

Table 3 lists by family the species of birds commonly taken as food by Great Basin peoples. Prominent among them were several types of land birds as well as numerous species of waterfowl. Both the western Great Basin and the eastern Great Basin had significant wetlands that supported waterfowl, and both areas are on major north-south flyways and thus subject to cyclical migrations of waterfowl and other species.

Bird hunting was thus a common Great Basin practice. Although the quarry differed from area to area, a set of standard techniques was generally employed across the region. Netting was a common means of taking both land and water birds. Sage grouse (*Centrocercus urophasianus*) were often taken by propping nets on sticks so as to cover part of the watering area. The birds entered under the net and when frightened by the hunter, flew up and entangled themselves. Large bag nets with a drawstring attached were set along runs in order to entangle the birds. Nets set on wickets to form a tunnel with brush wings converging at the net mouth were used in some areas. Often hunters using this device disguised themselves as antelope to gain the confidence of the birds and to move them slowly toward the opening of

82

a   b

top, Nev. Histl. Soc., Reno: 491; bottom, U. of Nev. Reno, Special Coll.: right, 2710/2859; a, Eastern Calif. Mus., Independence: A123; b. Smithsonian, Dept. of Anthr.: 14606.

Fig. 8. Rabbit hunt. top, Washoe encampment prior to a communal rabbit hunt. Women in the foreground are erecting a canvas windbreak. An Indian marching band is performing. Photographed about 1900. bottom left, Half of a rabbit net, originally over 300 feet long, made by Captain Wasson, Walker Lake Northern Paiute. The cordage of native hemp was tied to a mesh just large enough to catch a rabbit behind its ears as it tried to get through. Although all other possessions of Captain Wasson were destroyed at his death, this net was divided between his daughters (Wheat 1967:59). Photograph by Margaret M. Wheat, 1958–1962. bottom center, Washoe man, with his rabbit catch. Photograph by Lorenzo Creel, possibly Carson Valley, about 1920. a, Panamint Shoshone chuckwalla hook, a stick tipped with a bone point hafted in pitch, used to pull the large lizard (*Sauromalus obesus*) from its narrow rock crevice. Collected from a cave in the Saline Valley, Calif., 1931. b, Rabbit hook made of a willow stick and a square nail. The hook was inserted into the rabbit burrow, twisted to catch the animal's fur, and then withdrawn with the rabbit firmly attached. Collected by John Wesley Powell from the Southern Paiute in southern Utah, 1874. Total length 75.0 cm (length shown 10.0 cm), other same scale.

SUBSISTENCE

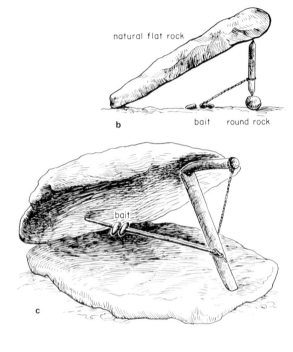

U. of Ill., Dept. of Anthr., Urbana.

Fig. 9. A Western Shoshone rigging a spring-pole trap for small game, such as squirrels, rodents, and sage grouse. Photograph by Julian Steward, 1936.

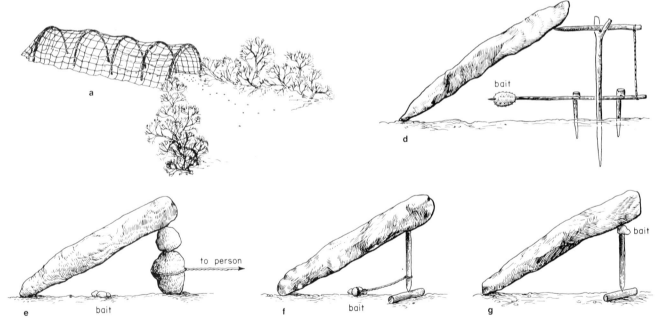

a, after Steward 1941:fig.1g; d, Harvard U., Peabody Mus.: 77–23–10/9444; e–f, after Steward 1943a:268, figs. a, c; g, after Steward 1941:fig.6n.

Fig. 10. Traps. a, Sage grouse trap consisting of a net set on willow wickets. Uprooted or broken sagebrush wings converge at the opening. Once under the net, the birds are flushed by the hunter. They fly up and entangle themselves in the net. Western Shoshone. b–g, Deadfall traps, illustrating different configurations and trigger mechanisms. All were used to take small mammals such as ground squirrels. b, Stick supported on a round rock trigger, commonly baited with pinenuts, Western Shoshone (Steward 1943a). c, Common figure-4 trap utilizing 2 flat stones (Wheat 1967:72–73), baited with pinenuts, Northern Paiute. d, Figure-4 trap baited with cholla fruit, Shivwits Southern Paiute. e, Deadfall, released by an individual hiding some distance away, Western Ute and Kaibab Southern Paiute. f, Two-stick trap, Northern Shoshone and Gosiute. g, Method of baiting a two-stick trap.

Table 3. Common Edible Birds of the Great Basin

Accipitridae   Kites, eagles, hawks and allies
  Accipiter gentilis   Northern goshawk
    Nev. Northern Paiute, Western Shoshone, Western
      Ute, Utah Southern Paiute
  A. cooperii   Cooper's hawk
    Nev. Northern Paiute, Utah Southern Paiute
  A. striatus   Sharp-shinned hawk
    Nev. Northern Paiute, Utah Southern Paiute
  Aquila chrysaetos   Golden eagle
    Western Shoshone, Nev. Southern Paiute, Western
      Ute
  Buteo jamaicensis   Red-tailed hawk
    Nev. Northern Paiute, Western Shoshone, Utah
      Southern Paiute
  B. swainsoni   Swainson's hawk
    Nev. Northern Paiute, Western Shoshone, Utah
      Southern Paiute
  B. lagopus   Rough-legged hawk
    Nev. Northern Paiute, Western Ute
  B. regalis   Ferruginous hawk
    Nev. Northern Paiute, Western Shoshone, Northern
      Ute, Western Ute, Utah Southern Paiute
  Circus cyaneus   Northern harrier
    Utah Southern Paiute, Western Shoshone
  Pandion haliaetus   Osprey
    Northern Shoshone

Alcedinidae   Kingfisher family
  Ceryle alcyon   Belted kingfisher
    Nev. Northern Paiute, Northern Shoshone

Alaudidae   Lark family
  Eremophila alpestris   Horned lark
    Nev. Northern Paiute, Utah Southern Paiute

Table 3. Common Edible Birds of the Great Basin
(*continued*)

Anatidae   Swan, goose, and duck family
  Aix sponsa   Wood duck
    Nev. Northern Paiute
  Anas acuta   Northern pintail
    Northern Paiute, Washoe, Utah Southern Paiute,
      Western Ute
  A. americana   American wigeon
    Northern Paiute, Western Ute
  A. clypeata   Northern shoveler
    Northern Paiute, Washoe, Northern Shoshone
  A. crecca   Green-winged teal
    Northern Paiute, Western Ute, Utah Southern Paiute
  A. cyanoptera   Cinnamon teal
    Washoe, Northern Paiute, Western Shoshone, Utah
      Southern Paiute
  A. platyrhynchos   Mallard
    Washoe, Northern Paiute, Western Shoshone, Western
      Ute, Utah Southern Paiute, Northern Shoshone,
      Eastern Shoshone, Northern Ute
  A. strepera   Gadwall
    Washoe, Northern Paiute, Western Ute, Utah
      Southern Paiute
  Aythya affinis   Lesser scaup
    Washoe, Northern Paiute, Western Ute
  A. americana   Redhead
    Washoe, Northern Paiute, Western Shoshone, Western
      Ute, Utah Southern Paiute
  A. valisineria   Canvasback
    Washoe, Northern Paiute, Western Ute, Utah
      Southern Paiute
  Branta canadensis   Canada goose
    Washoe, Northern Paiute, Western Shoshone, Western

left, U. of Nev. Reno, Special Coll.; right, Smithsonian, Dept. of Anthr.: 7127.

Fig. 11. Decoys. left, Jimmy George, Northern Paiute, with a duck decoy he made. The decoy's body is of twined tules, for buoyancy; the duck skin, with head attached, but minus the wings, is pinned to the body with sharpened greasewood pegs. Photograph by Margaret M. Wheat, 1958. right, Northern Paiute tule decoy covered with the skin of a male canvasback (*Aythya valisineria*). Collected at Carson Lake, Nev., about 1868; length 29.0 cm.

SUBSISTENCE

Table 3. Common Edible Birds of the Great Basin
(*continued*)

Ute, Northern Ute, Eastern Shoshone, Northern
Shoshone, Bannock, Utah Southern Paiute
Bucephala albeola Bufflehead
Nev. Northern Paiute
B. clangula Common goldeneye
Nev. Northern Paiute
Chen caerulescens Snow goose
Northern Paiute
Cygnus buccinator Trumpeter swan
Northern Paiute, Western Ute, Northern Shoshone
C. columbianus Tundra swan
Washoe, Northern Paiute, Western Ute
Mergus merganser Common merganser
Washoe, Northern Paiute, Northern Shoshone,
Western Ute, Utah Southern Paiute
M. serrator Red-breasted merganser
Northern Paiute

Ardeidae Heron and bittern family
Ardea herodias Great blue heron
Washoe, Owens Valley Paiute, Northern Paiute,
Western Shoshone, Northern Shoshone, Western
Ute, Utah Southern Paiute
Botaurus lentiginosus American bittern
Nev. Northern Paiute
Egretta thula Snowy egret
Northern Paiute, Western Ute, Utah Southern Paiute
Nycticorax nycticorax Black-crowned night heron
Nev. Northern Paiute, Western Ute, Utah Southern
Paiute

Charadriidae Plover family
Charadrius vociferus Killdeer
Nev. Northern Paiute, Utah Southern Paiute

Columbidae Dove family
Zenaida macroura Mourning dove
All groups

Corvidae Jay, magpie, and crow family
Aphelocoma coerulescens Scrub jay
Nev. Northern Paiute
Corvus brachyrhynchos American crow
Owens Valley Paiute, Nev. Northern Paiute, Western
Shoshone, Panamint, Nev. and Utah Southern
Paiute, Northern Ute, Southern Ute, Kawaiisu
C. corax Common raven
Nev. Northern Paiute, Western Shoshone, Kawaiisu,
Panamint, Owens Valley Paiute, Utah Southern
Paiute
Cyanocitta stelleri Steller's jay
Nev. Northern Paiute, Utah Southern Paiute
Gymnorhinus cyanocephalus Piñon jay
Nev. Northern Paiute, Utah Southern Paiute

Cuculidae Cuckoo and roadrunner family
86   *Geococcyx californianus* Greater roadrunner

Table 3. Common Edible Birds of the Great Basin
(*continued*)

Owens Valley Paiute, Panamint, Nev. and Utah
Southern Paiute, Chemehuevi

Emberizidae Warbler, meadowlark, blackbird, and oriole
family
Agelaius phoeniceus Red-winged blackbird
Northern Paiute, Utah Southern Paiute, Western Ute,
Western Shoshone
Euphagus cyanocephalus Brewer's blackbird
Nev. Northern Paiute, Utah Southern Paiute
Sturnella neglecta Western meadowlark
Northern Paiute, Utah Southern Paiute
Xanthocephalus xanthocephalus Yellow-headed
blackbird
Nev. Northern Paiute, Western Shoshone, Utah
Southern Paiute

Falconidae Falcon family
Falco mexicanus Prairie falcon
Utah Southern Paiute
F. sparverius American kestrel
Nev. Northern Paiute, Utah Southern Paiute

Gaviidae Loon family
Gavia immer Common loon
Washoe, Nev. Northern Paiute

Gruidae Crane family
Grus canadensis Sandhill crane
Washoe, Owens Valley Paiute, Northern Paiute, Utah
Southern Paiute, Northern Shoshone, Western Ute

Laridae Gull and tern family
Larus californicus California gull
Nev. Northern Paiute, Western Ute

Mimidae Mockingbird and thrasher family
Mimus polyglottos Northern mockingbird
Oreg. Northern Paiute, Owens Valley Paiute,
Panamint, Western Shoshone, Nev. Southern
Shoshone, Western Ute, Southern Ute

Muscicapidae
Sialia mexicana Western bluebird
Washoe, Nev. Northern Paiute
Turdus migratorius American robin
Washoe, Oreg. Northern Paiute, Utah Southern Paiute

Pelecanidae Pelican family
Pelecanus erythrorhynchos American white pelican
Washoe, Nev. Northern Paiute

Picidae Woodpecker family
Colaptes auratus Northern flicker
Washoe, Northern Paiute, Utah Southern Paiute
Picoides pubescens Downy woodpecker
Washoe, Nev. Northern Paiute, Utah Southern Paiute

Table 3. Common Edible Birds of the Great Basin (*continued*)

P. villosus   Hairy woodpecker
   Washoe, Nev. Northern Paiute, Utah Southern Paiute
Sphyrapicus varius   Yellow-bellied sapsucker
   Utah Southern Paiute

Phasianidae   Quail, pheasant, and grouse family
   Bonasa umbellus   Ruffed grouse
      Northern Shoshone, Bannock, Northern Ute
   Callipepla gambelii   Gambel's quail
      Utah and Nev. Southern Paiute, Chemehuevi
   Centrocercus urophasianus   Sage grouse
      Washoe, Northern Paiute, Northern Shoshone,
      Bannock, Western Shoshone, Utah Southern Paiute,
      Northern Ute, Western Ute, Southern Ute, Eastern
      Shoshone
   Dendragapus obscurus   Blue grouse
      Utah Southern Paiute, Western Shoshone, Northern
      Ute, Northern Shoshone
   Oreortyx pictus   Mountain quail
      Washoe, Northern Paiute, Northern Shoshone
   Tympanuchus phasianellus   Sharp-tailed grouse
      Northern Ute, Northern Shoshone, Bannock

Podicipedidae   Grebe family
   Aechmophorus occidentalis   Western grebe
      Nev. Northern Paiute, Western Ute

Table 3. Common Edible Birds of the Great Basin (*continued*)

Rallidae   Rails, gallinules, and coots
   Fulica americana   American coot
      Washoe, Northern Paiute, Western Shoshone,
      Northern Shoshone, Bannock, Utah Southern
      Paiute, Western Ute, Southern Ute, Northern Ute
   Gallinula chloropus   Common moorhen
      Utah Southern Paiute, Nev. Northern Paiute

Recurvirostridae   Avocet and stilt family
   Recurvirostra americana   American avocet
      Northern Paiute

Strigidae   Typical owl family
   Athene cunicularia   Burrowing owl
      Nev. Northern Paiute, Western Shoshone, Utah
      Southern Paiute
   Bubo virginianus   Great horned owl
      Northern Paiute, Western Shoshone, Utah Southern
      Paiute, Western Ute, Southern Ute, Northern Ute
   Otus kennicottii   Western screech-owl
      Panamint, Western Shoshone, Northern Shoshone,
      Bannock, Utah Southern Paiute, Northern Ute,
      Western Ute, Southern Ute

the trap. Blinds made of tule, and sometimes equipped with roosting poles, were set by water. Birds were either shot from these, or the hunter would reach up through an opening and grab a roosting bird.

Waterfowl were netted using similar principles. For example, long rabbit or duck nets were propped on sticks in the marsh and the sticks then angled toward the surface of the water. Ducks running on the surface preparatory to flight would hit the net and bring it down upon themselves. Hunters on shore or in the water would pull in the net, disentangle the birds, and kill them. American coots (*Fulica americana*), locally called mud hens, were often taken in this manner as well as in communal drives on land or in the marshes. While these and other waterfowl are flightless during mid to late summer, hunters and their families drove them from the water onto the land and either netted them as was done with rabbits or merely gathered them individually and killed them.

Waterfowl were taken by shooting them from blinds after the ducks had been lured to the area by floating tule duck decoys (fig. 11).

Disguised hunters also swam through the water and pulled the ducks under by their legs. Common disguises for this technique included placing a mound of tules resembling a beaver's lodge over one's head, wearing a duckskin helmet that protruded above the water, or

swimming under the surface while using a breathing tube of cane.

Some waterfowl, such as mud hens, were skinned, split, and dried for later use. Most others, however, were eaten while fresh after being pit roasted or boiled. Nearly all groups who took waterfowl also collected their eggs as food. Eggs were commonly boiled in baskets, added to mushes or stews, or buried in cold sand to preserve them.

Fish

Great Basin peoples fished most if not all the permanent streams and lakes of the region, using a variety of techniques (fig. 12). Table 4 lists the species commonly taken along with their general distributions. In major streams, such as the Truckee and Walker rivers in Nevada and the Snake River in Idaho, fishermen built platforms from the bank and fished with large dip nets, spears, and harpoons. Some streams were also dammed with rocks or brush fences to facilitate fishing with net and platform devices. Large gill nets were in use for trout, chub, whitefish, and other species along the Humboldt, Truckee, Carson, and Walker rivers in Nevada, along tributaries of the Snake in Idaho, and in the Sevier, Bear, and Virgin rivers in Utah. Weirs and various shapes and sizes of basket traps were also effective in these streams (fig. 13). The Northern Paiute along the Truckee and Walker rivers, for example, set cone-shaped traps in the openings of willow weirs and staked bipointed basketry minnow traps in the shallows of these streams. Women also fished the shallows and behind weirs and dams in low water. They used flat open-twined parching trays, dexterously scooping small fish from the water and spreading them on the shore to dry. Small streams and tributaries were also diverted, leaving fish stranded for gathering.

The Pyramid Lake and Walker River Northern Paiute fished their lakes with larger versions of gill nets as well as with a variety of set lines and trot lines made to the size of the quarry. Angled composite hooks of bone and wood (usually greasewood) (fig. 13) and bone pin or gorget hooks were made to take trout (*Salmo clarki henshawi*) or much smaller species such as speckled dace (*Rhinichthys osculus robustus*) or redsides (*Richardsonius egregius*). Smaller lines were cast out into the water while larger lines had to be placed by swimmers. Rock sinkers and floats secured the lines until the fisherman retrieved them. Favored bait was grubs, locusts, minnows, and the meat of other fish.

Fishing was not important everywhere in the region. Most of the large fisheries were connected with large lakes, such as Tahoe, Pyramid, and Walker lakes in Nevada and Bear, Utah, and Fish lakes in Utah. From these lakes major runs of fish took place each winter or spring or both. Fish also ran in other streams in the region, such as the Humboldt and Carson rivers, the Sevier River, and tributaries of the Colorado. The Snake River and its tributaries supported major runs of ocean-going salmon each year (Pavesic 1982). Elsewhere, small indigenous fish might be found in mountain and valley streams and ponds or even in large springs. Sometimes these smaller fish were taken; at other times they were ignored by the local population. The Western Shoshone are reported to have occasionally taken springfish (*Crenichthys* spp.) and poolfish (*Empetrichthys* spp.) by scooping them from springs with open-twined baskets (Steward 1941).

Fish were preserved by drying. Large fish were either filleted or split lengthwise and hung over racks in the shade (fig. 13). Small fish were dried whole and stored in sacks or in lined pits in that manner. The Northern Paiute of Pyramid Lake stacked dried fillets of cui-ui (*kuyui*)* (*Chasmistes cujus*) in the fashion of cordwood and then tied the bundles with twine. Cui-ui were then cached in pits or in sacks kept around the house. Fish were said to have kept reasonably well during the winter season. Dried fish were often pulverized and added to soups and stews. Whole fresh fish were baked in leaves in pits or roasted over an open fire.

Reptiles and Insects

Table 5 lists by genus as well as by general category the principal reptile and insect foods of Great Basin peoples. Data for both of these categories are poorly reported in the literature. In many cases, categories such as caterpillars, grasshoppers, frogs, and lizards are all that are represented, with little attempt at taxonomic accuracy; however, it does appear that certain species within these categories were quite widely taken (Steward 1941, 1943a; O.C. Stewart 1941, 1942).

Among the more important reptiles taken were the desert tortoise (*Gopherus agassizii*) and the chuckwalla (*Sauromalus obesus*). Both of these occur only in the southernmost areas of the region, in the Mojave and Sonoran deserts. Little specific information is available on the processing of either species. Apparently both were roasted in the fire prior to eating. Chuckwallas and other large lizards were extracted from crevices in the rocks by use of a special wooden skewer or hooked stick similar to those used for taking small mammals. Consumption of snakes, rattlesnakes, and other unidentified lizards and frogs is reported but seems rare other than in the harshest environments (Steward 1941, 1943a; O.C. Stewart 1941, 1942).

Similarly, the taking of certain species and classes of insects as food is also sporadically reported. Most widespread was the use of "caterpillars," cicadas, Mormon crickets, and ant eggs. In some localities, specific technologies developed around the taking of some of these

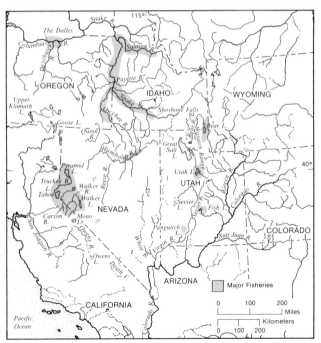

Fig. 12. Important aboriginal fisheries in the Great Basin.

*For the orthography of Indian words cited in italics see the orthographic footnotes in "Northern Paiute," "Western Shoshone," and "Southern Paiute," this vol.

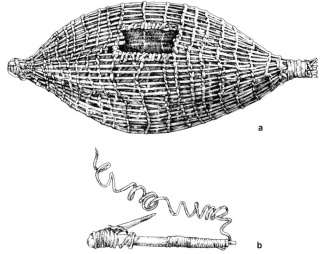

a

b

Milwaukee Public Mus., Wis: top left, 20023; center left, 20051; b, 21970; bottom left, Mus. of the Amer Ind., Heye Foundation, New York: 22378; top right, U. of Nev. Reno, Special Coll.: 2710/266; a, Harvard U., Peabody Mus.: 35–120–10/5166.

Fig. 13. Fishing. top left, Northern Paiute man with large dip or lifting net used to take trout in deep pools in rivers, usually from a platform. center left, Northern Paiute abandoned fishing platform, Walker River Reservation, Nev. Photographs by Samuel A. Barrett, 1916. bottom left, Northern Shoshone fish weir consisting of tripods of willow poles driven into the steam bed, across which heavy poles were lashed. Willow sticks were angled against the poles on the upstream side. Twined willow fences meant to channel the fish in front of waiting harpooners are at left. Photograph by DeCost Smith, Lemhi Reservation, Idaho, 1904. top right, Northern Paiute man with fillets of cui-ui scored and hung to dry, Pyramid Lake Reservation, Nev. Photograph by Lorenzo Creel, 1906–1922. a, Northern Paiute fish trap model of twined willow with a side entrance. Full-size traps are 0.5–1.0 m in length and are meant to be staked to the bottom of the river in the shallows. They are used to take minnows, trout, and carp. Collected by Willard Z. Park on the Walker River Reservation, 1935; length 38.0 cm. b, Northern Paiute composite fishhook with a greasewood hook and shank wrapped in native twine. It would have been suspended from a trotline set in the lake to take trout. Collected by Samuel A. Barrett in western Nev., 1916. Length 8.3 cm, a same scale.

Table 4. Common Edible Fishes in the Great Basin

Acipenseridae   Sturgeon family
  Acipenser transmontanus   White sturgeon
    Snake River system below Shoshone Falls. Bannock,
    Northern Shoshone

Catostomidae   Sucker family
  Catostomus ardens   Utah sucker
    Snake River system above Shoshone Falls, Bear River,
    Utah Lake, Bonneville system. Bannock, Northern
    Shoshone, Western Ute, Western Shoshone
  C. clarki   Desert sucker
    White River drainage, Colorado River system.
    Western Shoshone, Southern Paiute
  C. columbianus   Bridgelip sucker
    Snake River system below Shoshone Falls. Bannock,
    Northern Shoshone, Western Shoshone
  C. discobolus   Bluehead sucker
    Snake River system above Shoshone Falls, Bear River.
    Northern Shoshone
  C. fecundus   Webug sucker
    Utah Lake. Western Ute
  C. fumeiventris   Owens sucker
    Owens River. Owens Valley Paiute
  C. latipinnis   Flannelmouth sucker
    Colorado River. Southern Paiute–Chemehuevi,
    Southern Ute
  C. macrocheilus   Largescale sucker
    Snake River below Shoshone Falls. Northern
    Shoshone, Bannock, Western Shoshone
  C. platyrhynchus   Mountain sucker
    Utah Lake, Snake River, Bear River, Bonneville
    system. Western Ute, Northern Shoshone, Bannock,
    Western Shoshone
  C. tahoensis   Tahoe sucker
    Lake Tahoe, Pyramid Lake and Walker Lake systems.
    Washoe, Northern Paiute
  Chasmistes cujus   Cui-ui
    Pyramid Lake, lower Truckee River. Northern Paiute
  C. liorus   June sucker
    Utah Lake. Western Ute
  Xyrauchen texanus   Razorback sucker
    Colorado River system. Southern Paiute–Chemehuevi,
    Southern Ute

Cyprinidae   Minnow and carp family
  Acrocheilus alutaceus   Chiselmouth
    Snake River system below Shoshone Falls. Northern
    Shoshone, Western Shoshone, Bannock?
  Gila alvordensis   Alvord chub
    Small drainages of southeastern Oregon, northeastern
    Nevada. Northern Paiute
  G. atraria   Utah chub
    Snake River system above Shoshone Falls; Bear River;
    Utah Lake; Bonneville system. Western Ute,
    Western Shoshone, Northern Shoshone
  G. bicolor obesus   Lahontan tui chub
    Lahontan system (Walker, Carson, Truckee, Quinn,
    Reese, Humboldt rivers and associated lakes).
    Washoe, Northern Paiute

Table 4. Common Edible Fishes in the Great Basin
(*continued*)

  G. bicolor (and subspp.)   Tui chub
    Central Nevada; Owens River. Owens Valley Paiute,
    Western Shoshone, Chemehuevi
  G. copei   Leatherside chub
    South Fork of Snake River, Bear River, Utah Lake,
    Bonneville system, Sevier and Beaver rivers.
    Southern Paiute, Western Ute, Northern Shoshone,
    Western Shoshone?
  G. cypha   Humpback chub
    Colorado River system. Southern Paiute–Chemeheuvi,
    Southern Ute
  G. elegans   Bonytail chub
    Colorado River system. Southern Paiute–Chemeheuvi,
    Southern Ute
  G. robusta (and subspp.)   Roundtail chub
    Colorado River system; White River system. Western
    Shoshone, Southern Paiute–Chemeheuvi, Southern
    Ute
  Moapa coriacea   Moapa dace
    Moapa River. Southern Paiute
  Lepidomeda spp.   Spinedace
    Colorado River system. Southern Paiute
  Ptychocheilus oregonensis   Northern squawfish
    Snake River below Shoshone Falls. Northern
    Shoshone, Bannock, Northern Paiute
  Rhinichthys cataractae   Longnose dace
    Snake River system. Northern Shoshone, Bannock,
    Northern Paiute
  R. falcatus   Leopard dace
    Snake River system below Shoshone Falls. Northern
    Shoshone, Bannock, Northern Paiute
  R. osculus (and subspp.)   Speckled dace
    Lahontan system, Bonneville system, isolated locales in
    interior Basin, White River–Colorado River system,
    Amargosa–Death Valley system, Owens River,
    Sevier River, Snake River system. Washoe,
    Northern Paiute, Owens Valley Paiute, Western
    Shoshone, Bannock, Northern Shoshone, Southern
    Paiute–Chemehuevi, Ute
  Richardsonius balteatus (and subspp.)   Redside shiner
    Bonneville system, Snake River system, Bear River,
    Sevier River, Fish Lake. Western Ute, Northern
    Shoshone, Bannock
  R. egregius   Lahontan redside
    Lahontan system. Washoe, Northern Paiute

Cyprinodontidae   Killifish family
  Cyprinodon spp.   Pupfish
    Southern Basin. Panamint, Death Valley Western
    Shoshone, limited use.
  Crenichthys spp.   Springfish
    Central Basin. Western Shoshone, limited use.
  Empetrichthys spp.   Killifish
    Southern Basin. Panamint, Death Valley Western
    Shoshone, limited use.

Petromyzontidae   Lamprey family
  Lampetra tridentata   Pacific lamprey

90

Table 4. Common Edible Fishes in the Great Basin
(*continued*)

Snake River system below Shoshone Falls. Northern
  Shoshone, Bannock

Salmonidae Salmon and trout family
  Oncorhynchus kisutch Coho salmon
    Snake River system below Shoshone Falls. Northern
      Shoshone, Bannock, Northern Paiute
  O. nerka Sockeye salmon
    Payette, Little Payette, and Sawtooth lakes tributaries
      to the Salmon River. Northern Shoshone
  O. tshawytscha Chinook salmon
    Snake River system below Shoshone Falls, Weiser
      River. Northern Shoshone, Bannock, Northern
      Paiute
  Prosopium abyssicola Bear Lake whitefish
    Bear Lake. Northern Shoshone
  P. gemmiferum Bonneville cisco
    Bear Lake. Northern Shoshone
  P. spilonotus Bonneville whitefish
    Bear Lake. Northern Shoshone

Table 4. Common Edible Fishes in the Great Basin
(*continued*)

  P. williamsoni Mountain whitefish
    Upper headwaters of Lake Tahoe, Snake River
      system, Bonneville system, Colorado River system.
      Washoe, Northern Paiute, Northern Shoshone,
      Bannock, Ute
  Salmo clarki Cutthroat trout
    Snake River system. Northern Shoshone, Bannock,
      Northern Paiute
  S. c. henshawi Lahontan cutthroat trout
    Lahontan system. Washoe, Northern Paiute
  S. c. utah Utah cutthroat trout
    Bonneville system. Western Ute, Southern Paiute
  S. gairdneri (and subspp.) Rainbow trout
    Snake River system below Shoshone Falls. Subspecies
      in Tahoe, Pyramid Lakes. Washoe, Northern Paiute,
      Northern Shoshone, Bannock
  Salvelinus confluentus Bull trout
    Humboldt River system. Western Shoshone
  S. malma Dolly Varden
    Snake River system below Shoshone Falls. Northern
      Paiute, Northern Shoshone, Bannock?

and Owens Valley Paiute harvested the caterpillars of the Pandora moth (*Coloradia pandora*) by a system that involved the trenching of Jeffrey pine trees, the principal host of the larvae. For roughly a three-week period in late June and early July in alternate years, the larvae were collected in significant numbers as they descended the trees to pupate in the ground. The larvae were collected in special baskets, sand pit roasted, boiled, and dried in the shade. Special storage sheds were built to house drying larvae. The larvae of pandora moths contained roughly 12 percent protein, a significant measure of their nutritional value (Fowler and Walters 1982).

The use of linear trenches in open habitats is also reported as a means of taking "grasshoppers" and Mormon crickets (*Anabrus simplex*). These insects were driven into the trenches by beaters or with fire (Steward 1943a:270). Cicadas (*Okanagodes* spp.) apparently required less elaborate techniques, as they can easily be collected by hand early in the morning when dormant. Crickets, cicadas, and grasshoppers were usually parched in open-twined trays, then ground into meal. The meal was mixed with other foods when eaten. Ant and bee eggs were similarly treated.

The larval and pupal stages of the brine fly *Ephydra hiens* were also taken in the waters of saline lakes in western Nevada and eastern California by women using open-twined trays. These insects required little further preparation beyond drying and were said to preserve well because of their natural salt content (Heizer 1950).

Dietary Parameters

Little in-depth research has been done on protohistoric diets for Great Basin peoples, although some data are available on prehistoric diets. Some Great Basin foods have been analyzed for proteins, fats, carbohydrates, and various vitamins and minerals (Hilty et al. 1972; Keely 1980; Morris et al. 1981; Lawton et al. 1976; Simms 1983; Yanovsky 1936; Yanovsky and Kingsbury 1938).

Dietary change in the postcontact world has been even less well documented. Garner and Hawley (1950) and Garner (1954) have studied aspects of dietary adaptations among the Ute, Cook (1941) among the Washoe and Northern Paiute, and Malouf (1940) among the Gosiute. Other scattered references are also available, but general assessments and syntheses are lacking.

Given the differences in local environmental conditions across this vast region, as well as the cyclical nature of the availability of many foods, it is difficult to generalize about Great Basin diets prior to the time of contact. Each local area had somewhat different resources upon which to draw at different times of the year. For example, it can be estimated that the lake- and riverine-based peoples of Pyramid Lake and Walker River in Nevada probably obtained 50–60 percent of their livelihood from fish, 20 percent from large and small game, and 20–30 percent from wild plant products. The people of Owens Valley, on the other hand, probably obtained but 10 percent of their sustenance from fish, 30–40 percent from game animals, and

Table 5. Common Edible Reptiles, Amphibians, and Insects in the Great Basin

REPTILES
Crotalus viridis lutosus Great Basin rattlesnake
   Western Shoshone, Nev. Southern Paiute, Western
   Ute, Southern Ute
Gopherus agassizii Desert tortoise
   Panamint, Chemehuevi, Nev. Southern Paiute,
   Southern Ute
Phrynosoma spp. Horned lizard
   Panamint, Nev. Southern Paiute, Western Ute,
   Northern Ute, Southern Ute
Sauromalus obesus Chuckwalla
   Panamint, Owens Valley Paiute, Nev. Southern Paiute,
   Chemehuevi
large lizards
   Washoe, Nev. Northern Paiute, Owens Valley Paiute,
   Western Shoshone, Nev. and Utah Southern Paiute,
   Chemehuevi, Western Ute
small lizards
   Panamint, Western Shoshone, Western Ute

AMPHIBIANS
frogs
   Panamint, Western Shoshone, Utah Southern Paiute

INSECTS
Anabrus simplex Mormon cricket
   Washoe, Nev. Northern Paiute, Western Shoshone,
   Northern Shoshone, Bannock, Utah Southern
   Paiute, Western Ute, Southern Ute, Northern Ute
Coloradia pandora Pandora moth larvae
   Owens Valley Paiute, Nev. Northern Paiute

Table 5. Common Edible Reptiles, Amphibians, and Insects in the Great Basin (*continued*)

Diceroprocta spp. Cicada
   Panamint, Nev. Southern Paiute, Chemehuevi
Ephydra hians Brine fly larvae
   Washoe, Nev. Northern Paiute, Owens Valley Paiute,
   Panamint
Hyalopterus pruni Mealy plum aphis honeydew
   Washoe, Nev. Northern Paiute, Owens Valley Paiute,
   Panamint, Western Shoshone, Nev. and Utah
   Southern Paiute, Western Ute
Hyles lineata White-lined sphinx moth larvae
   Washoe, Nev. Northern Paiute, Nev. and Utah
   Southern Paiute, Western Shoshone, Western Ute
Okanagodes spp. Cicada
   Washoe, Nev. Northern Paiute, Owens Valley Paiute,
   Panamint, Western Shoshone, Northern Shoshone,
   Bannock, Nev. and Utah Southern Paiute, Northern
   Ute, Western Ute, Southern Ute
ants and larvae
   Nev. Northern Paiute, Western Shoshone, Nev.
   Southern Paiute, Northern Shoshone, Bannock,
   Northern Ute, Western Ute
bee larvae, often *Vespula diabolica* Yellow jacket
   Washoe, Nev. Northern Paiute, Western Shoshone,
   Northern Shoshone, Southern Ute
caterpillars
   Nev. Northern Paiute, Washoe, Western Shoshone,
   Northern Shoshone?, Utah Southern Paiute,
   Western Ute, Northern Ute, Southern Ute
grasshoppers
   Washoe, Western Shoshone, Northern Ute, Southern
   Ute

50–60 percent from plant products. And among the people of the Panamint district where large game was scarce and fish all but absent, the dietary proportions were made up of 60–70 percent plant foods and 30–40 percent animal foods.

On the whole a surprising proportion of the diet was derived from plants and plant products. The nutritional elements that occur in important quantities in plants are carbohydrates, including sugars and starches. Trace elements of iron, zinc, calcium, magnesium, manganese, and other minerals are also found. Berries and other fruits produce important quantities of ascorbic acid (Keely 1980). The cellulose and hemicellulose of plants may not be significant for its nutritive value, but they do aid digestion by providing necessary dietary bulk.

Most native plants are low in protein, thus requiring that this important dietary element be obtained either through meat or fish. In order to be utilized by human beings, protein must first be reduced to amino acids and then again synthesized to form the tissues of the body. Most of the protein provided by native game

animals and fish can be readily absorbed by people and contains most if not all the essential amino acids. Lean meat contains an average of 550 calories per pound of fresh weight, while fish can range from 450 to as high as 1,000 calories per pound of fresh weight. Lean meat averages 20–25 percent protein and 5–15 percent fat. The remainder is water and, on occasion, valuable trace elements. Fish ranges in protein content from 15–25 percent in the raw, boiled, or broiled states. Dry fish can run from 50 percent to as high as 90 percent protein depending on the species. The remainder of the nutrient content in dried fish is predominantly fat along with trace elements (Driver and Massey 1957; Morris et al. 1981).

Lack of sufficient fat in the diet can make the carbohydrates provided by plant foods much more important. The sugars and starches become valuable replacements for other nutrients under these circumstances. It has been suggested that both the protein and fat contents of Great Basin diets in some areas may have been low if not insufficient (Driver and Massey 1957:211). In light of this assumption it is perhaps significant that pine nuts, an important plant staple in much of the Great Basin region, are high in both fats and carbohydrates, ranging near 75 percent combined (Farris 1982). However, before generalizations can be substantiated about the overall character of Great Basin diets, much more work needs to be done.

Food taboos also played a part in Great Basin dietary adaptations. Most Great Basin peoples purposefully shunned at least bats and rattlesnakes as well as meat-eating birds, including eagles, hawks, owls, vultures, and magpies. Crows and ravens were also tabooed by several groups. Many groups did not eat wolf, coyote, and fox. Dietary taboos were in effect at various times during the life cycles of individuals. For example, deer heart, liver, and lungs were often taboo to young children and occasionally the elderly (Steward 1941, 1943a; O.C. Stewart 1941, 1942). Although not specifically tabooed, most groups also avoided taking frogs and small birds, lizards, and rodents. Except in the harshest environments, these may have been more trouble to take than they were worth.

Environmental Manipulation

Great Basin peoples were basically hunters and gatherers with only a few groups in the south practicing a supplemental form of garden horticulture; nonetheless, most groups manipulated or otherwise managed portions of their environments in various ways. Downs (1966a) has reviewed the most common practices, including burning to increase tobacco and wild seed harvests and possibly to provide fodder for game, broadcast sowing of wild seeds, and the watering and occasional irrigation of natural flora. To these can be added the pruning of plants to obtain desired forms or products, as well as certain hunting and fishing practices that seem to reflect a conservation ethic. Although varied, these procedures reflect a significant degree of environmental knowledge and awareness that is important to broader theoretical discussions of the origins of agriculture and animal domestication (Downs 1966a; Lawton et al. 1976).

Burning as a mechanism to increase natural plant production or as a preliminary process to broadcast sowing of wild seeds is reported in sporadic distribution throughout the Great Basin (Steward 1938, 1941, 1943a; O.C. Stewart 1941, 1942). However, the practice has not been studied in sufficient detail to understand its ramifications. Burning to increase natural yields of tobacco (*Nicotiana attenuata, N. bigelovii*) is the best attested procedure among all groups covered by this volume. In areas where it appears not to have been practiced, groups nonetheless recognized the association between tobacco yields and fires, frequenting naturally burned areas to harvest the plants (C.S. Fowler 1962–1984; O.C. Stewart 1941). Burning to increase yields of certain seed plants is also reported in the Culture Element

Distribution Surveys for the region, but in few cases are the plants that were the objects of these activities identified. The Western Shoshone of Ruby Valley, Nevada, burned to promote growth of *sunu* (*Artemisia argentia*), and those of Diamond Valley burned to increase growth of lamb's-quarters (*Chenopodium album*)† (Steward 1941:333). Burning of brush lands in the fall to increase spring yields of əpə (unidentified, but probably also lamb's-quarters) is likewise reported by W.Z. Park (1933–1940) for the Northern Paiute of the Walker River region, Nevada.

Burning to increase fodder for deer, antelope, or other animals has not been specifically verified for Great Basin peoples but is suspected. The Franciscan priest Silvestre Vélez de Escalante reported in September, 1776, that the Ute of Utah Valley had set many small fires in the pastures and meadows ahead of his party. He thought this was done to remove fodder for the intruders' horses—and thus discourage the intruders (Bolton 1950:179). But it is also possible that burning was a regular activity in grasslands, and that this was the season for the activity. Fires in grass and shrub lands would be beneficial to maintaining grass for fodder for game. Since several Great Basin groups hunted game with the fire surround, the same task may have been accomplished without direct intent (Steward 1941, 1943a; O.C. Stewart 1941, 1942; Downs 1966a:47).

Several Western Shoshone groups combined burning with broadcast sowing of wild seeds. Steward (1941:333) reports for the Humboldt Shoshone spring sowing of lamb's-quarters, stickleaf (*Mentzelia dispersa*), and unidentified wuꞏsia after fall burning of selected patches. The Diamond Valley Shoshone sowed *poina* (*Descurainia sophia*),‡ Indian ricegrass, and lamb's-quarters in the spring after fall burning. Other accounts are less specific, merely reporting sowing "wild seeds" (Steward 1941:281). Irrigation of wild seeds was specifically denied by all of O.C. Stewart's (1941) Northern Paiute and Washoe respondents. It was also denied by all of Steward's Western Shoshone respondents, with the exception of a Humboldt Valley individual who attributed the practice to the neighboring Diamond Valley people (Steward 1941:333). It was apparently unknown as well among the Northern and Eastern Shoshone, Southern Paiute, and Northern and Southern Ute, although it is difficult to tell from the extant literature whether the question was properly raised (Steward 1943a; O.C. Stewart 1941, 1942).

---

†Lamb's-quarters is listed as an adventive or introduced species from Europe by Munz and Keck (1963:272). Among most Western Shoshone and a few Northern Paiute groups it is called *iappi*, from the verb 'to plant'. Perhaps the original *iappi* was indigenous *Chenopodium fremontii* or a closely related species.

‡Listed as a species naturalized from Europe (Munz and Keck 1963:233). The term *poina* was probably first associated with a native species, such as *Descurainia pinnata*.

Ditch irrigation of wild plants is well attested for the Owens Valley Paiute; however, this issue has generated considerable discussion through the years. In 1930, Steward (1930) first made the case known, and speculated as to the origin of the practice. He rejected the notion that irrigation could have diffused independently of its associated cultigens from the Southwest, favoring instead the independent invention of the technique by the Owens Valley Paiute. Steward (1930, 1933b) described the system as extensive, with brush dams placed on natural streams and diverted water channeled into many ditches and feeders. Some ditches ran for miles and watered plots of several acres. The system was controlled by a leader or leaders, and focused only on native plants, two of which Steward identified as wild hyacinth (*Dichelostemma pulchella*) and *Eleocharis* spp. He suggested that the irrigation system may have originated from observations of the "swampy lowlands of the Owens Valley where it is obvious that moist soil—a natural irrigation—produced very prolific plant growth" (Steward 1933b:249). Later, he admitted the possibility that irrigation may have been introduced by the Spaniards or the Americans who moved into the region after 1850 (Steward 1938). Others have also proposed that "renegade neophytes" from Spanish missions or perhaps Owens Valley Paiutes resident for a time at the missions may have been responsible (see Lawton et al. 1976 for a review).

Documentary research by Lawton et al. (1976) seems to indicate that Owens Valley Paiute native irrigation practices predate by several years any actual American or Spanish penetration of Owens Valley and that it is unlikely, given the intensity of the practice, that renegade neophytes or any other indigenous individuals could have been the stimulus sources. Lawton et al. (1976) have carefully documented the extent of irrigation in the valley, which seems to have been much greater than was previously indicated. They also question Steward's (1930, 1933b) identification of the crops involved, suggesting that the principal focus was apparently the tubers of chufa flat sedge (*Cyperus esculentus*) as well as the corms of wild hyacinth, both of which seem to have been purposefully planted. Overflow encouraged the growth of other seed-producing species (Steward 1930:152, 1933b:247). Lawton et al. (1976) do not offer a solution to the question of the origin of irrigation in Owens Valley, but they suggest that observations of natural runoff in heavy snow years and the idea of stream diversion to obtain fish may have led to its development. Downs (1966a:51–55) had suggested the second possibility along with the notion that there may be a connection between the widespread Great Basin practice of diverting streams to flood rodents from their burrows and irrigating native plants (see also Tuohy 1984 for some support.)

94   Horticulture involving Southwest cultigens, and in historic times, European-introduced crops such as wheat and potatoes, was also a feature of the ethnographic Great Basin, especially in the south. Several groups of Southern Paiute were known to have cultivated corn in several colors, the common and tepary bean (*Phaseolus vulgaris, P. acutifolius*), several squash varieties, sunflowers, introduced wheat, and possibly amaranths at various times in the protohistoric period (Kelly 1932–1933, 1964; C.S. Fowler and D. Fowler 1981). The Death Valley Shoshone apparently adopted garden horticulture and some of these cultigens from the Ash Meadows Southern Paiute in early postcontact times (Steward 1938:89, 1941:232). Gardening seems to have spread as far west as Lida and Beatty, Nevada, during the same period. It also appears to have reached as far north as Spring, Snake, Antelope, and Steptoe valleys within Western Shoshone country, reportedly in the immediate precontact period, about 1840 (Steward 1938:122, 128). Planting corn, beans, and squash was also a practice of the Ute in the vicinity of Moab, Utah, in the immediate precontact period, about 1850 according to O.C. Stewart (1942:338). Additional research is needed to better document Great Basin horticulture, including the time of its adoption, the botanical identities of the crops involved, and the exact sources of its diffusion. It appears that horticulture was a supplemental rather than a primary subsistence means.

The pruning of native plants to achieve a desired product is sporadically reported in the Great Basin and is most commonly associated with growing tobacco. In Owens Valley and among the Kawaiisu, tobacco plants were irrigated, cultivated, and pruned to achieve hardier plants with larger leaves (fig. 14). Zigmond (1981:43–44) reports that the Kawaiisu pruned plants of *Nicotiana bigelovii* three times in late summer, at one-week intervals. Small leaves, flowers, and new growth near larger leaves were specifically removed. Patches were apparently weeded at the same time. Several groups in southern California also pruned and tended tobacco patches (Kroeber 1941).

Both intentional and unintentional pruning of willows (*Salix* spp.) and lemonade berry (*Rhus trilobata*) for basketry fibers also took place in most areas. In all areas with willows, women favored certain species and varieties in specific stands. They habitually cut first-year canes for baskets, thus in effect cultivating the patches, which in turn produced vigorous and straight canes the next year from the old root stock. Women at Walker River specifically recognized the efficacy of this process (C.S. Fowler 1962–1984). The San Juan Southern Paiute commonly burn patches of lemonade berry to promote hardy, straight growth (Pamela Bunte, personal communcation 1984). Martha Knack (personal communication 1980) reports that she was told by a Death Valley Shoshone woman of the practice of pruning piñon trees (*Pinus monophylla*). Part of routine maintenance ap-

left, U. of Nev. Reno, Special Coll.

Fig. 14. Caring for plants. left, Edna Jones, Walker River Northern Paiute, gathering willows. It was recognized that regular harvesting produced straighter and more vigorous canes. In some areas burning the patches produced the same results. Photograph by Margaret M. Wheat, about 1960. right, Sophie Williams, Kawaiisu, pruning wild tobacco to produce larger leaves. After the third pruning the tobacco leaves are harvested, dried, ground into powder, moistened, and molded into cakes. Tobacco is mixed with powdered lime and chewed by women. Men smoked tobacco without lime in cane cigarettes. Photograph by Maurice Zigmond, Piute Rancheria, 1936.

parently involved breaking the tips of the piñon branches. This would in effect produce more cones in subsequent years.

Activities involving environmental manipulation to the benefit of animals are less well documented than are those for plants. Beyond the possibility of burning areas to increase fodder (and possibly salt, see Lewis 1982) for game, one can cite only certain hunting and fishing practices that may have had positive effects on animal populations. For example, most Great Basin peoples report that females of game animals and rabbits were not hunted during the seasons when they were giving birth and rearing their young. Nor were ducks taken in large numbers while nesting or rearing young. The Pyramid Lake and Walker River Northern Paiute reported spearing only the redder male trout during their annual spawning runs, although netting of both sexes was reported (W.Z. Park 1933–1940). The Northern Shoshone were reported to have speared principally male trout and salmon on the spawning beds.

Downs (1966a:49) notes that the Washoe occasionally cut the upper limbs of browse plants to feed deer herds and thus encouraged the deer to remain in the vicinity during the winter. Steward (1933b:235) reported isolated instances where antelope were kept penned for several days and taken gradually as needed. Similarly, complex fish weirs may have prolonged fish runs by keeping migrating fish under a certain degree of control. Although these activities seem less related to proto-

domestication than do Great Basin activities involving plants, they are nonetheless of interest to theoretical discussions of the topic (see also Downs 1966a:50–51).

World View

Little has been written on the interesting topic of the roles that plants and animals played in the world views of Great Basin peoples. Yet it is clear that many species were important in native perception beyond the practical aspects of producing foods, medicines, and items for manufacture. In all areas, for example, respect was shown for animals and plants taken to meet human needs. Portions of large game animals, including the eyes, skulls, and sometimes organs such as pituitary glands and gall bladders were specifically set out in the brush or trees or buried after a kill. In addition to showing respect, these acts were a form of manipulation that would insure that game would be continually supplied. Slain game animals were often placed with their heads to the east and addressed with special terminology, again to show respect. In nearly all the Numic languages, names for game animals appear to derive from what may be older respect names: Northern Paiute *koipa* 'bighorn sheep', from *koi-* 'to kill (pl.)'; *winin·imidi* 'deer' from *wini-* 'to stand (sg.)', literally 'the one that moves about while standing', or 'the grazer'; perhaps also *tihiča* 'deer', from *tihoa-* 'to hunt'; Shoshone *tukku* 'bighorn sheep' from *tukku* 'meat, flesh'; and *wasippɨ* 'bighorn sheep' from *wasi* 'to kill (dl., pl. obj.)' (C.S. Fowler 1972a; Miller 1972).

Similarly, the taking of plants was often accompanied by prayers and occasionally offerings to the plant spirits to show respect. Northern Paiutes frequently buried a bead or a small stone in a hole left vacant by a root. Broken corms of spring beauty (*Claytonia lanceolata*) were also reburied by some Northern Paiute women so as not to bring on a thunderstorm. The taking of pine nuts, particularly the first harvesting of the fruit, was also marked by ceremony. Felling of piñon trees in historic times has brought outcries from many Great Basin peoples partly because of their potential food value but principally because the trees are sacred (Clemmer 1978; Malouf 1966).

Plants and animals, many but not all used for subsistence, played important roles in myths and tales. Zigmond (1972) has summarized aspects of their importance in Kawaiisu mythology, both as agents that set the scene and as objects that generate distinct story motifs. For example, the Kawaiisu, as do most southern and central Great Basin peoples, have a tale involving the origin of pine nuts. The tale is set in the myth-past or the time when animals were people. It involves the theft of pine nuts from a distant source (in this case from a well-guarded tree in Owens Valley) by a group of animals and birds. Their subsequent difficulties in dispersal of the seeds account for the presence or absence of nut-bearing trees in specific regions. Other myth themes account for the habits of certain plants, such as the afternoon closing of the flowers of evening snow, *Linanthus dichotomus* (Zigmond 1972:130–131) or the presence of certain geographic features, such as a cinder cone near Hurricane, Utah, that is said by the Southern Paiute to be Coyote's pile of *waʔai* (Indian ricegrass) seeds (C.S. Fowler 1962–1984). Many mammals, reptiles, birds, and occasionally insects and fish take prominent roles in mythological tales. Their adventures and misadventures account for the creation of the earth and people, the establishment of the seasons, the setting of food preferences and taboos, and the instituting of human birth, marriage, and death. They illustrate proper and improper social behavior. In tales in most areas, these actors have special myth names and other characteristics.

It seems clear that conceptualizations by Great Basin peoples of the activities and the actors in the myth-past were very closely related to ideas that animals, and to a lesser degree plants, were powerful and could thus help or hinder an individual's ability to progress through life. Animals were recognized as a major class of spirits from whom power in the shamanistic sense as well as in guardian and task-specific senses was readily obtained. Such relationships established special bonds between receiver and giver, often involving a complex set of mutual rights and obligations. Individuals with specific powers were known to have led antelope, deer, bighorn sheep, and rabbit hunts in most areas of the Great Basin, to have predicted the coming of fish among the Pyramid Lake and Walker River Northern Paiute, and to have overseen the roasts of agave among the Southern Paiute. Other subsistence activities were possibly assisted by individuals with powers, but such powers were not necessarily required. Power to cure disease also frequently came from animal spirits or from these in combination with personified spirits.

Goss (1967, 1972a) has discussed aspects of Ute world view in which animal spirits are related in a complex set of kinship relationships with the Utes themselves. These kin relationships are expressed in certain linguistic correlations between myth-names of the animal spirits and contemporary Ute kinship terms. Kin relations between and among the animal spirits and the Ute are also indicated in tales in which all actors stand in appropriate kinship positions to one another. This system of animal names and kinship terms does not seem to have exact equivalents elsewhere in the Great Basin, but there are certain other animal-kinship linkages. For example, it is common within the Numic-speaking groups to refer to Bear as "our father's sister," Coyote as "our father's brother," and Rattlesnake as "our father's father." These terms of reference and address appear to derive in part from a linguistic identity between the animal's present name and a kinship term (e.g., in Northern Paiute *togogʷa* 'rattlesnake' and *togo-* 'mother's father') and in part from a system of noa naming for these animals in myth. An additional aspect of the relationship of plants and animals, myth and world view is seen in the naming of constellations after animals and in tying these in turn to tales of their adventures and misadventures in the sky. Only Laird (1976) offers much documentation on this complex topic, although similar views are known to exist elsewhere in the region.

Flora and fauna, but particularly flora, play additional roles in world view by serving as sources of spiritual well-being. Of the more than 300 plant species used medicinally in the region (C.S. Fowler 1972a; Steward 1938; Train, Henrichs, and Archer 1941), certain ones stand out as more than incidental remedies. Fern-leaf lomatium (*Lomatium dissectum*) and hog fennel (*L. californicum*) in the western Great Basin, and fern-leaf lomatium and Porter's ligusticum (*Ligusticum porteri*) in the eastern Great Basin are cure-alls with a semisacred connotation. In the 1980s they were the most likely of all plants to be found in native households. They have also been given roles in new religious movements, such as the Sweat Lodge. Sacred datura (*Datura meteloides*) was also well recognized in the southern Great Basin and to some extent elsewhere as both powerful and dangerous. It seems not to have been the focus of initiation ritual in the Basin as it was in southern

California (see vol. 8:667–668). The introduction of peyote (*Lophophora williamsii*) and its influence and ritualism are treated in "Peyote Religion," this volume.

Big sagebrush (*Artemisia tridentata*) is another most respected plant. Its burning signifies purification of the living at the death of an individual or at times when ghosts may be present. It is often associated with girls' puberty ceremonies, being used as part of the costuming or as a wand with which girls are ceremonially sprinkled with water (Freed and Freed 1963a; W.Z. Park 1933–1940). Crushed sage can be a medium through which messages are taken to the spirits, for example, as an offering in the spring to ripen the pine nuts or as an offering for health after a specific illness.

People recognize the special importance of tobacco. It is respected for its role in shamanistic contact with the spirits, its own curative powers, and its recreational associations (W.Z. Park 1933–1940; Kelly 1932, 1964; Lowie 1924; Steward 1933b, 1941; O.C. Stewart 1941).

Another aspect of plants and animals and their roles in thought processes is the position both assume in native taxonomic classifications of the universe. In no instance in the region is there a native term clearly equatable with the English folk category label "plant" or "animal." Rather, plants and animals are variously treated as parts of larger schemes based more on use than morphology. Fowler and Leland (1967) have outlined the position of plants and animals in Northern Paiute taxonomic schemes, and C.S. Fowler (1972a) has presented various other schemes in which both are treated for the Northern and Southern Paiute and Western Shoshone. Chamberlin (1911) gives an account of Gosiute plant taxonomies as well as some notes on Gosiute principles of plant nomenclature. Zigmond (1981) treats plant taxonomies for the Kawaiisu, as do Couture (1978) for the Northern Paiute near Burns, Oregon, and Mahar (1953) for the people at Warm Springs, Oregon. All these studies were preceded by notes by John Wesley Powell taken in 1872 among the Northern Paiute of Pyramid Lake. Powell's attempt to obtain native principles of plant and animal taxonomy was the first in the Basin (see Fowler and Fowler 1971:241).

Summary

Plants and animals have played central roles as sources of food, but also as medicines and sources of manufacture throughout the region. They also have been the objects of environmental manipulations of various types, including focused burning, broadcast sowing, pruning, and irrigation for plants and various taking practices for animals. These manipulations are important considerations toward theoretical discussions involving the more complete knowledge of flora and fauna possessed by hunters and gatherers. Activities in this regard among Great Basin peoples have been frequently overlooked (Downs 1966a; Lawton et al. 1976). Plants and animals have also entered into many phases of the world views of Great Basin peoples, and probably to a much greater degree than has been documented. Plants and animals are subjects of myths and tales and are part of ceremony throughout the region. They are also important foci for present-day activities, including ceremonies and subsistence uses.

Sources

The data contained in tables 1–5 as well as in the discussion of plant and animal uses, processing, and storage are derived in general from the Culture Element Distribution Survey (Driver 1937; Drucker 1937; Steward 1941, 1943a; O.C. Stewart 1941, 1942), and from the following: Washoe, Schubert 1957; Owens Valley Paiute, Steward 1933b; Essene 1935; Nevada Northern Paiute, C.S. Fowler 1962–1983, 1972a; Kelly 1932; W.Z. Park 1933–1940; Wheat 1967; Oregon Northern Paiute, Couture 1978; Mahar 1953; Panamint, Coville 1892; Irwin 1980; Steward 1938; Western Shoshone, C.S. Fowler 1972a; Steward 1938; Gosiute, Chamberlin 1911; Eastern Shoshone, Shimkin 1947; Kawaiisu, Zigmond 1981; Nevada and southern California Southern Paiute, Bye 1972; C.S. Fowler 1962–1984, 1972a; Kelly 1932–1933; Utah Southern Paiute, Bye 1972; C.S. Fowler 1972a; Kelly 1932–1933, 1964; Northern Ute, Chamberlin 1909; Smith 1974; Southern Ute, Goss 1972a; Western Ute, Steward 1938.

Taxonomic usage and distributions generally follow Cronquist et al. (1972, 1977), Hitchcock and Cronquist (1978), Holmgren and Reveal (1966), Munz and Keck (1963), Munz (1968), and Welsh et al. (1981) for plants; Hall (1981) and Honacki, Kinman, and Koeppl (1982) for mammals; Behle and Perry (1975) and Ryser (1984) for birds; and Fowler and Koch (1982), Sigler and Miller (1963), and Simpson and Wallace (1978) for fishes. Key sources for the discussion of world view are C.S. Fowler (1972a), Laird (1976), and Zigmond (1972).

Numic Languages

WICK R. MILLER

Classification

Most of the languages of the Great Basin belong to the Uto-Aztecan language family, which is located in western America from southern Idaho through southern California, and in a second geographic area from southern Arizona through northwestern Mexico and into central America (vol. 10:113–124). The most northerly branch, Numic, is located primarily in the Basin (fig. 1). The Uto-Aztecan branches geographically closest to Numic are: Hopi, a single language in northeastern Arizona; Tubatulabal, a single moribund language, formerly spoken in a restricted area along the Kern River near Bakersfield, California; and the Takic branch, a diversified set of languages spoken in southern California.

The earliest adequate classification of the northern Uto-Aztecan languages (Kroeber 1907a, 1925:575) placed these four branches into a language family called Shoshonean, which was considered to be one of three branches of the larger Uto-Aztecan family. Kroeber labeled them the Plateau (Numic), Pueblo (Hopi), Kern River (Tubatulabal), and Southern California (Takic) branches of Shoshonean. Whorf (1935) suggested that these groups were separate branches of Uto-Aztecan, with "Shoshonean" and other larger subdivisions of Uto-Aztecan seen as geographic groupings that had no linguistic reality. This position was accepted by Lamb (1958, 1964) and Miller (1964, 1966, 1984), but the earlier view was maintained by Voegelin, Voegelin, and Hale (1962) and others (vol. 10:118). A shift to Whorf's position would make the term "Shoshonean" meaningless and is in part the motivation behind the shift in terms to Numic and Takic (Lamb 1958; Miller 1961), terms that have gained almost universal usage.

Kroeber's (1907a) classification was the first to deal with the internal relationships of Numic. He recognized three subgroups, which he called Mono-Paviotso, Shoshoni-Comanche, and Ute-Chemehuevi. Miller (1966:78) has suggested replacing these awkward terms with Western, Central, and Southern Numic. Because of inadequate information, some groups had to be shifted and the boundaries slightly redrawn once fuller information became available (Kroeber 1925:576–580; Steward 1938), but otherwise Kroeber's classification of Numic has stood the test of time and later work

(Lamb 1958, 1964; Miller 1964; Miller, Tanner, and Foley 1971; Goss 1968).

Lamb (1958) has described the dialect and language situation for Western Numic as follows. Throughout the northern region, among the Northern Paiute in Oregon and in Nevada north of Owens Valley and among the Bannock in Idaho, there are only slight differences from dialect to dialect. But between Mono Lake and Owens Valley there is a clear boundary with a number of important linguistic differences; the two varieties of speech on either side of this boundary are not mutually intelligible, and the differences are great enough for them to be considered two languages. Lamb further reports that dialect differences within the southern language and along the adjacent fringe of the northern language are of a much greater magnitude than within the northern language. The area covered by the southern language is fairly restricted and is in striking contrast with the very large area covered by the northern language.

Lamb (1958) notes some difficulty in providing appropriate names for these two languages. The southern language includes the Owens Valley Paiute (usually lumped together on the basis of culture with Paiute or Northern Paiute), along with the Monache, whereas the northern language includes the remaining Northern Paiute and Bannock. Lamb suggests that the languages be called Mono or Monachi, and Paviotso. He avoided the term Paiute or Northern Paiute, not only because the Owens Valley Paiute are speakers of the Mono language but also because the Southern Paiute belong to the Southern Numic group. The term Paviotso is also ambiguous in usage, and most linguists and anthropologists use Northern Paiute instead.

A similar division into two languages each for Central and Southern Numic was suggested. Lamb (1958) concurs with Kroeber's (1959:263–264) conclusion, based on unpublished data, that Kawaiisu is sufficiently distinct to be called a language separate from the rest of Southern Numic. The more easterly language, which Lamb calls Ute, covers a much greater area than Kawaiisu. The Ute language includes those people who are ethnographically known as Chemehuevi, Southern Paiute, and Ute. Goss (1965, 1966, 1968), who has collected dialect material for Southern Numic, agrees with Lamb's conclusions.

Lamb's data for Central Numic were scanty, but based

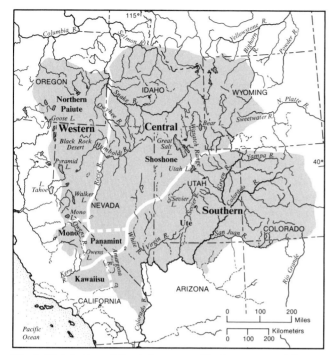

Fig. 1. Distribution of Numic languages. The languages and the names used for them are more inclusive than the corresponding ethnic units; for approximate location of the Comanche language, in the Plains area since the 18th century, see "Uto-Aztecan Languages," fig. 1, vol. 10.

on remarks of Panamint Shoshone speakers in Lone Pine, Lamb suggested that a similar situation obtained in this branch of Numic. Miller (1970, 1974; Miller, Tanner, and Foley 1971) showed that Panamint and Shoshone are distinct languages, but it proved difficult to find a language boundary, perhaps because there is no clear-cut boundary or perhaps because there are so few speakers left in the region where the boundary is expected. The best information available (Miller 1965–1969) would recognize Panamint as consisting of Panamint and Koso Shoshone (the Shoshone of the Amargosa Valley, along with what Kroeber 1907a:68 called Shikaviyam) and would recognize Shoshone as consisting of the Shoshone of the Kawich Valley, perhaps the Lida district, and all the remaining dialects to the north and east, including the Gosiute Shoshone.

Comanche, which belongs to the Central Numic group, is no longer in contact with the remaining Numic speakers. Comanche speakers left the Green River area in southwestern Wyoming in the eighteenth century, when they acquired the horse, and moved into the southern Plains in pursuit of the buffalo. Even though their move was a recent one, it broke the dialect chain, and set up a sharp boundary. The differences are great enough for it to be considered a third Central Numic language (Miller 1974).

This chapter will use the terms Mono, Northern Paiute, Panamint, Shoshone, Comanche, Kawaiisu, and Ute for the seven Numic languages. (In volume 10 the spell-

ing Shoshoni was used and Northern Paiute was referred to as Paviotso.) The ethnographic label will not always match the linguistic label, so that, for example, the Southern Paiute people speak the Ute language.

Dialects

The speech within each of the languages is not uniform: there is dialect differentiation and diversity. The greatest diversity is to be found in the southwestern section within Mono and Panamint. Within Northern Paiute, Shoshone, and Ute, the greatest dialect diversity is found in the southwestern extremities. Thus, within each of the three branches of Numic, there is increasing dialect diversity toward the southwestern limit of Numic in California (Lamb 1958; Miller 1966, 1970; Miller, Tanner, and Foley 1971; Goss 1965, 1966, 1968).

Most dialect differences can be classified into one of three types: lexical, phonological, or grammatical. Lexical differences are easiest to record, but they are also most susceptible to dialect borrowing and dialect contamination. Grammatical differences, on the other hand, are least obvious and least subject to dialect borrowing. Only Kroeber (1907a) and Steward (1938) have published comparative dialect lists from which lexical information can be derived. Some phonological information can be extracted from these lists, but more accurate recording will be needed before detailed work can be done. Miller (1970) had described the nature of the dialect differences for Shoshone; some of these are presented in Crapo and Spykerman's (1979) maps. Crapo (1970) has described the dialect variation found within and between individuals residing at Duckwater Reservation, a Western Shoshone community.

The term isogloss is used by dialectologists to indicate the boundary between two variants of a linguistic trait that shows dialect differentiation. Because of the high mobility of the Numic speakers, the mapping of isoglosses in the Numic area is difficult and often meaningless (Miller 1970). Nevertheless, the concept of isogloss can be a useful one. If the isoglosses bunch together, giving an "isogloss bundle," then it is sometimes possible to divide a language into dialects and to draw dialect boundaries. However, much more frequently the isoglosses intergrade in such a fashion that no dialects can be isolated, as no sharp boundaries can be drawn. In fact, in the few cases in which there are bundles of isoglosses and dialect boundaries, the dialect boundary is distinct in only part of the area.

Intergraded isoglosses can, however, show some pattern. In particular, they can show directionality. In Western Numic, they tend to run east and west (Sven Liljeblad, personal communication 1971; Michael J.P. Nichols, personal communication 1971), and in Central Numic they tend to run northwest and southeast (Miller

1965–1969). It is likely that Southern Numic will continue this pattern and show isoglosses running north and south, to give an overall picture in Numic of lines running in an arc, as on a fan. There are seldom sharp dialect boundaries within these languages. An exception is the boundary between the Oregon and Nevada dialects of Northern Paiute, which runs south of Surprise Valley, the Black Rock desert, and the Owyhee drainage (Michael J.P. Nichols, personal communication 1971). Nichols notes that the Oregon and Bannock dialects of Northern Paiute intergrade, even though they are physically separated.

Because of the distinct tribal appellations in the ethnographic literature, the intergrading nature of the dialects has often been overlooked. Thus, while there are dialect differences between the Utes in southern Colorado and the Southern Paiutes of southern Utah, the dialect grading is continuous so that no boundary can be drawn. The dialect differences are no greater than between the various Southern Paiute groups in southern Utah and southern Nevada. Similar remarks can be made about Gosiute and other Shoshone, about Bannock and Northern Paiute, and about Chemehuevi and Southern Paiute.

It should be noted that the direction of the dialect boundaries (more accurately, direction of the isoglosses) does not always match the direction of the cultural differences. Nor, for that matter, do the three major divisions, or their constituent languages normally match any cultural group (see Steward 1970:125–128). In fact, there are not always clear-cut territorial divisions between languages, as pointed out by Steward (1970:124) for the Shoshone and Northern Paiute where there is a zone as much as 100 miles wide of bilingualism and intermarriage. There is clearly more cultural similarity between the speakers of the two languages in this zone than between the southwestern and northeastern extremes of the Shoshone language.

There appear to be two examples of dialect isoglosses crossing language boundaries. In Panamint and in a restricted area of the bordering Shoshone the velar and labialized velar nasals /ŋ/ and /ŋʷ/ are phonemically distinct. Only neighboring Mono (and not all dialects of Mono), belonging to a different branch of Numic, shares this distinction. The second example pertains to the loss of initial /h/. Its loss is a feature of all Ute except Chemehuevi, as well as part of the bordering Shoshone (specifically Gosiute Shoshone) starting just west of the Utah-Nevada border near the Steptoe Valley, and extending east through Gosiute, Skull Valley, north along the west side of the Wasatch Mountains; how far north cannot be determined because this is the area of early intensive White settlement, and dialect information cannot be recovered. In areas to the north where dialect information is available, namely from Brigham City northward, the /h/ is present.

Glottochronology

A number of scholars have used glottochronology to estimate the ages of the prehistoric separations between various pairs of Numic languages, and between Numic and other Uto-Aztecan languages (Hymes 1960; vol. 10:122–123). This technique involves computing the number of words on a specified list that are inheritances shared by two languages and comparing this percentage of retention to the percentages found over various periods of time in a selected small number of literate languages with documented histories. There are a number of sources of potential error in the method and some specialists regard it as invalid, but others feel that it provides usable estimates at least of relative degrees of relatedness and particularly for the relatively recent time-depths of a closely related language group like Numic.

Glottochronological estimates of the age of the separation of various Numic languages from other northern Uto-Aztecan languages (conventionally given in "minimum centuries" of divergence) ranged from 29 to 46 centuries in one study (Swadesh 1954, 1954–1955) and from 22 to 41 centuries in another (K. Hale 1958–1959). Both studies found lower figures between Tubatulabal and Numic than between any other language and Numic, but they disagreed and must be considered inconclusive on the question of which branch of Numic is closest to Tubalutabal. Between languages and dialects that are in different branches of Numic the estimates in these studies ranged from 10 to 15 centuries for contiguous branches and from 13 to 19 centuries between the noncontiguous Western and Southern Numic. Between languages in the same branch estimates of six to nine centuries have been calculated. Between dialects of single languages (Panamint, Shoshone, and Ute) the estimates range up to four centuries, taking Goss's figures of two to four centuries for Ute as more reliable than Hale's figure of six centuries, on the grounds that Goss used his own word lists collected for this purpose while Hale relied on data from the publications of two different recorders (K. Hale 1958–1959; Goss 1965, 1966, 1968; Miller, Tanner, and Foley 1971; Miller 1984). While it is doubtful that these can be viewed as exact dates, this is a consistent picture that shows degree of diversity (partly a function of time, partly a function of degree of contact) between the Numic languages and dialects.

History of Research

Most of the early Numic material is represented by vocabulary collections of early travelers and adventurers. References to this early work are found in Lamb (1964:111–113) and Fowler and Fowler (1971:8). Not mentioned in either of these is the vocabulary of "Snake" (Northern Shoshone) collected by Ross (1855, 2:153–

154); the vocabulary of Fort Hall Northern Shoshone collected by Nathaniel J. Wyeth in 1832–1836 (Schoolcraft 1853–1856, 1:216); and the vocabulary of Comanche collected by R. S. Neighbors (Schoolcraft 1853–1856, 2:494–505). More systematic collection of vocabulary was done by John Wesley Powell (fig. 2) (Fowler and Fowler 1971), Albert Gatschet (1876, 1879), A.L. Kroeber (1907a, 1909a), and Julian Steward (1938). These early workers not only provided material for the classification of the languages but also gave some preliminary information about their phonetics.

Descriptive material on phonology as well as grammar did not appear until the twentieth century. St. Clair (1903) described the grammar of Eastern Shoshone, and for Western Numic there were publications by Waterman (1911), Marsden (1923), Natches (1923), and Angulo and Freeland (1929). Kroeber (1908, 1909) and J.P. Harrington (1911) have some early material for Southern Numic. Shimkin's material for Eastern Shoshone belongs chronologically to the later period (1949), but methodologically it belongs to the earlier period.

The modern period begins with Sapir's (1930–1931) classic study of Southern Paiute (fig. 3), which includes grammar, texts, and dictionary. Lamb (1958a) wrote a grammar and compiled a dictionary of North Fork Mono. Snapp, Anderson, and Anderson (1982) wrote a grammatical sketch of Northern Paiute. Nichols (1974) wrote a historical grammar of Northern Paiute. Miller prepared Shoshone texts, with a dictionary (1972). For a grammatical sketch of Shoshone see volume 17. Comanche has received considerable attention: Casagrande (1954–1955) wrote a linguistic sketch, and Canonge (1958) published a collection of texts that included a Comanche-English lexicon. Using primarily the notes of Canonge, Wistrand-Robinson (1980) prepared a dictionary to which Armagost (1980) appended a grammatical sketch. Zigmond (1975) prepared a Kawaiisu dictionary. There is a grammar and vocabulary of Chemehuevi (Press 1975), an additional grammar of Southern Paiute (Bunte 1979), and a dictionary and grammar of Ute (Givón 1979, 1980). Many other valuable studies, shorter or more limited in scope, have appeared since 1930; references to them can be found in the extensive bibliographies of McLaughlin (1983) and Langacker (1976, 1977).

Several treatments of Ute phonology have appeared,

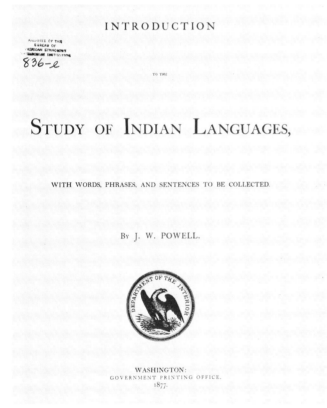

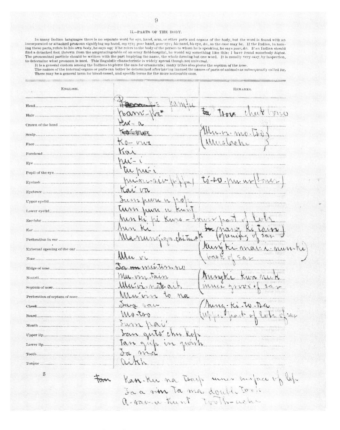

Smithsonian, NAA: 836–e.

Fig. 2. Vocabularies. left, Cover of vocabulary schedule developed by John Wesley Powell (1877) based in part on George Gibbs's vocabulary lists. Designed to provide standard selections of words for use in linguistic classification rather than materials for detailed analysis, it was used by many late 19th-century investigators. right, Weber River Ute vocabulary collected by Powell, Salt Lake, autumn 1877. The term Weber Ute is a misnomer for a linguistically mixed group who were probably speakers of a Shoshone dialect rather than a Ute dialect (Fowler and Fowler 1971:32).

101

Sapir 1930:opp. p.308.

Fig. 3. Tony Tillohash, Southern Paiute from Kanab, Utah, in his Carlisle Indian School uniform. Edward Sapir worked with Tillohash in Philadelphia from Feb. to May 1910 (Sapir 1930–1931, 2:299–300).

based not on original fieldwork but on Sapir's work with Southern Paiute: Harms (1966), Rogers (1967), and Chomsky and Halle (1968:345–351). Lounsbury (1955) considers the voiceless vowels of both Southern Paiute and Comanche. The extensive material on Numic lends itself to historical or comparative linguistic treatment: I. Davis (1966) on Numic consonants, Goss (1970) on the question of voiceless vowels, Nichols (1971, 1974) on Western Numic phonology, Klein (1959) on Mono and Kawaiisu, and Freeze and Iannucci (1979) on Numic classification. Iannucci (1973) studied Numic historical phonology.

Prehistory

There are a number of indications that the Numic-speaking people are relative newcomers to the Basin, moving from their homeland somewhere near Death Valley and the other Uto-Aztecan peoples in southern California.

Perhaps the best indication of recent movement is seen in the degree and nature of the diversity of the languages and dialects. It has been noted by linguists (for example, Sapir 1916a) that the area of greatest linguistic diversity is the area of longest occupation, and hence the homeland, since diversity is a function of

time. If a large area is covered by a uniform or nearly uniform language, then its occupation must be fairly recent. If, on the other hand, an area has diverse dialects or languages, the speakers must have remained in or near the same area for some time, in order for that diversity to have developed.

Applying this principle to the Numic languages, Lamb (1958) postulated that the southwest corner of the Basin was the homeland. He pointed out that each of the three Numic branches was divided into two languages with disproportionate areas. Those in the southwest corner of the Basin, centering around the Death Valley region—Mono, Panamint, and Kawaiisu—occupy a much smaller range than do Northern Paiute, Shoshone, and Ute, which spread out, fanlike, from the southwest corner of the Basin. Modern Kawaiisu, at any rate, does not display any noticeable dialect diversity (Maurice Zigmond, personal communications 1971), but the other two southwestern groups, Mono and Panamint, display greater diversity than the three geographically extended languages. Further, the greatest dialect diversity for the geographically extended languages is to be found where they border Mono, Panamint, and Kawaiisu in the southwest.

Lamb's interpretation has been supported by others (Miller 1966:92–94; Hopkins 1965; Jacobsen 1966a, 1968; Goss 1968:6–17). Moreover, very detailed evidence has been furnished for Central Numic (Miller, Tanner, and Foley 1971). W.W. Taylor (1961) and Swanson (1972: 9–15), both archeologists, have argued against this view; they would have the Numic peoples entering the Basin from the north. Goss (1977) has reversed himself, and in a unique interpretation of the data he now views the Basin as the homeland not only of the Numic but also the Uto-Aztecan ancestors.

Fig. 4. Sven Liljeblad, a long-time student of the Northern Paiute language, eliciting linguistic information from Wuzzie George, Stillwater, Nev., a speaker who has provided information to several linguists and anthropologists. Photograph by Wayne Suttles, summer 1964.

By tying in the glottochronological evidence, Lamb has the differentiation into the three branches take place about 2,000 years ago, which

> "gives us three Numic languages occupying only a small part of the Great Basin, until perhaps around one thousand years ago. At about this time, for some reason, there began a great movement northward and eastward, which was to extend the domain of Numic far beyond its earlier limits. Since the three branches of Numic were already distinct, this great spread must have been undertaken independently by each of the three groups. The separation in all of them, however, may have taken place at roughly the same time. This would indicate some kind of common influence present in the Great Basin, drawing these people farther into it" (Lamb 1958:99).

Archeologists have attempted to take Lamb's findings into account in the interpretation of the archeological record. The most noteworthy attempt is by Bettinger and Baumhoff (1982), who present a theoretical model for the Numic expansion.

Kroeber (1925:176–180) discussed the Numic languages in the broader context of the "Shoshonean" groups represented in California, that is, Takic, Tubatulabal, and Numic. He noted that the languages of the Takic branch are "sufficiently specialized to make it necessary to assume a considerable period for their development" (1925:578). The Numic languages, on the other hand, show a lesser degree of differentiation and "represent a much more recent stratum" (1925:580). But in what appears to be a non sequitur, he continued that "it is entirely conceivable that these tongues [the Numic languages] have been spoken in their present locations from time immemorial. Their territory is in the Great Basin; their speakers were actually part of the Plateau tribes; and there is no foreign element or anything else to indicate that they ever had any antecessors on the spot" (1925:580). Kroeber also points out that two Numic offshoots, Western Mono (spoken by the Monache) and Kawaiisu, "have crossed the Sierra and entered the true California valley system" (1925:580), and because of the lack of strong linguistic differentiation with Numic languages to the east of the Sierras, they must be latecomers. In most of the examples he discussed, Kroeber gave estimated dates (this work predates glottochronology); later work shows that the dates far underestimate the real time, but their relative chronology is correct.

Place-names give additional supporting evidence of recency and direction of movement. If the Numic-speaking peoples came out of the southwestern portion of the Great Basin, it would be expected that place-names near the homeland would more often be unanalyzable or opaque; people further removed from their homeland, hence more recent arrivals, would have place-names that would more often be translatable and transparent in meaning (see Sapir 1916a). This is the situation that obtains for Central Numic. Many Panamint place-names are transparent, but there are also many that are not, such as *si·napati* (Wild Rose Canyon), consisting of *si·*-'willow' and meaningless *-napati*; and *muatta* (Koso Hot Springs), with *mu-*, probably having to do with the mind (the hotsprings were used in curing), but otherwise meaningless (Miller 1965–1969). In Shoshone there are only a few meaningless place-names, like *wa·hkaima* ('Pilot Peak') and *pasimito?i* (name of the high plateau between Lost River Range and Lemhi Range). But there are many hundreds more like *tonopa·* (Tonopah), *tono-* 'greasewood', *pa·* 'water, springs'; *takkatoya* (Ruby Range), *takka-* 'snow', *toya-pin* 'mountain'; *pa·wa·kkati* (stream east of the Rockies in Wyoming), 'water-juniper-sitting'; *(h)u·kkati* (Oquirrh Mountains), 'sticks-sitting'; *mu·mpittsihokoe* (stream near Jackson's Hole), *mu·mpittsih* 'owl', *okoe* 'flowing'; *pohowia* (pass in western Wyoming), *poho-* 'sage', *wia* 'pass'; *isasonko* (The Dolly Varden), *isa* 'Coyote's', *sonko* 'lungs'; *pasawa·kkati* (Lone Butte in northeastern Nevada), 'dry-juniper-sitting' (Miller 1965–1969). A similar situation obtains in Western Numic: in Owens Valley and other Mono-speaking areas, a number of names are opaque or meaningless, while in the Northern Paiute–speaking area very few names are not analyzable. The one exception to this is found with the Bannock dialect of Northern Paiute, which is spoken in Idaho in areas that were primarily populated by Shoshone-speaking peoples. In this case, almost all the place-names were taken from Shoshone, with the result that the names were sometimes not meaningful in Bannock. For example, *si·wo·kki?i* 'willow-lined place' (name for the Boise-Weiser country) is clearly translatable in Shoshone, but only *si·*- 'willow' is meaningful in Bannock.

Sven Liljeblad (1971) has compared certain semantic domains of the Shoshone and Northern Paiute speakers in Idaho with those of the neighboring Nez Perce and has come to similar conclusions. His best example is with 'fish'. He finds that the Shoshone and Northern Paiute have only two root words for fish, and the many kinds of fish found in southern Idaho are given compound and descriptive names, such as Shoshone *ca·ppenkwi* 'trout' (literally 'good fish'), *patokwa* 'lamprey' (literally 'water snake') and Northern Paiute *pissáppakkwi* 'trout' (literally 'good fish') and *pakkwí papi?i* 'sturgeon' (literally 'the big brother of the fishes'). In all these instances, Nez Perce has a single, unanalyzable word. These facts again point to a recent arrival by the desert-dwelling Numic peoples, as opposed to the Nez Perce who lived in this environment for a greater period of time.

Reconstruction of vocabulary in order to determine semantic domains of the parent language has long been a fruitful activity in Indo-European and other well-studied language families. It has been attempted on a limited scale for Uto-Aztecan (see especially Miller 1966: 94–102) and Numic. Sven Liljeblad (1971:81–191; see also Jacobsen 1968:47) discusses the Numic words for fish, dog, buffalo, cactus, pine nut, camas, and various other plants, as well as for grinding implements, digging sticks, and planting. The items that are reconstructible point to a way of life for the Proto-Numic peoples similar to that of the present-day hunting and gathering people in the Great Basin and show a greater familiarity with things found in the southwestern Basin than with those in other parts of the Basin. C.S. Fowler (1972) has examined plant names, finding a southwestern focus for Proto-Numic.

Borrowings of words into or out of Numic give evidence of earlier contacts and interaction between neighboring peoples. The greatest number of such words is found between Numic and Washoe (Jacobsen 1966: 127–128) with the direction of borrowing being both ways. The items involved include: ant species, cui-ui sucker, muskrat, porcupine, fox species, buffalo or cow, Indian balsam, prickly pear cactus, White man, Achumawi, Shoshone, salt, shoe, and spirit. Dixon and Kroeber (1919:114–115) note a number of borrowings between the Uto-Aztecan languages of California and other California languages. They note that "for some reason borrowing appears to have gone on chiefly across the southern portions of this line" (1919:114), which is what would be expected if the Numic speakers spread from the southwestern portion of the Great Basin. The only word they note that involves a Numic language is the Mono word *nana* 'man'. Very likely the word is borrowed from Yokuts, but related forms are found in the Miwok languages, which are, like Yokuts, Penutian languages (Silverstein 1972:216–221). Apparently Maidu, another California Penutian language, has borrowed the Numic word for 'road'. The Maidu word *bó* has no apparent cognates in Penutian (Shipley 1963:91), while similar forms are widespread throughout Uto-Aztecan. Jacobsen (1966a:262) noted that the Southern Sierra Miwok word for 'sagebrush' was borrowed from Numic. Baumhoff and Olmsted (1964:12) suggest that the Achumawi word for 'sagebrush' and the Atsugewi word for 'juniper' are borrowed from Northern Paiute, but more accurate recordings from Northern Paiute and other Numic languages do not seem to support their suggestion.

There are fewer words borrowed between Numic and non-California languages. Some of these that involve Northern Paiute and languages to the north are discussed by Nichols (1971). Aoki (1975) notes borrowings from Numic (probably Northern Paiute since it is the closest language) into Nez Perce: *nimí·pu·*, the name for themselves, and *iceyé·ye* 'coyote'; compare Proto-Numic **nimɨ* 'person, Indian', and *ica* 'coyote' (the elements *-pu·* and *-yé·ye* are identifiable in Nez Perce). The Crow word for Old Man Coyote, *isipatu·ba*, may also be a borrowing, this time from Shoshone *icappɨ* 'coyote' or *isapaippɨh* 'Old Man Coyote'.

Cultural Setting

All languages display stylistic variation that is conditioned by things such as topic, setting, speaker, or audience. The greatest differentiation is found in the elevated or noncasual styles, such as used in oratory, story telling, and the like. In the Numic languages, it is poetry and song that have the greatest degree of elaboration (Crum 1980; Sapir 1910a).

In general, however, stylistic variation in Numic languages is not very great. There are no special conventions for linguistic play (as, for example, Pig Latin in Euro-American culture), no riddles, no special linguistic games, no specially developed conventions or lexicon for baby talk (except for the Ute, see J.L. Stewart 1960), no conventionalized difference between men's and women's speech. (For further discussion on Great Basin speech levels, see the chapter on the ethnography of speaking, in vol. 17).

Matching the low degree of stylistic variation is a relatively casual attitude toward language use, stylistic variation, and dialect differences (Miller 1970:32). No single language or dialect has developed into a prestige variety of speech, nor is there a feeling that one's own language or dialect is better than the other fellow's; language variation is recognized, but no special significance is attached to it. Historical contact has changed this picture somewhat, with English becoming a prestige language (Miller 1971).

Miller (1970) has attempted to reconstruct the aboriginal setting in which language socialization took place among the Shoshone. The situation was probably quite similar for other Numic-speaking groups. It has been shown that the peer group is important in the language development of the child in sedentary societies. However, there probably were less-permanent peer groups in the Basin, because the way of life could not support them. This has led Miller to suggest that the adult played a larger role than in other societies. Owen (1965) has speculated that the mother, who, he proposed, was normally a foreigner, played a disproportionate role in the child's linguistic acculturation. Steward (1965) took issue with Owen, primarily because he did not see the strong development of patrilocal bands that Owen postulated for the Basin. Miller (1970:30–31) points out that the mother is only one of the adults who are important in providing the linguistic environment for the child, but agrees that the mother (as well as other adults) is often a foreigner who speaks a different dialect or language, or speaks the local language with a foreign accent. Though the group surrounding the child is relatively small, not only does the composition vary through time, but also the hunting and gathering way of life in the Basin led to considerable linguistic variation within the small group. Hill (1978) has argued that these are factors that are conducive to maintaining maximum linguistic diversity in spite of a very low population density. This is the case not only in the Great Basin but also in other similar mobile societies. These factors present certain adaptive advantages in such societies.

Before the relocation caused by White settlement there were no bounded speech communities. This, along with the setting in which language socialization takes place, is seen by Miller (1970) as the major factor in the development of intergraded dialects with no sharp dialect boundaries (see also Steward 1970:126; Crapo 1970).

Steward (1970:124) noted that there was a wide band of bilingualism along the Northern Paiute–Shoshone language frontiers. It is likely that there was a considerable amount of bilingualism along all the language boundaries, but none or nearly none in the interiors of the large areas covered by Northern Paiute, Shoshone, and Ute. Most bilingualism was probably between Numic languages. Because of the close relationship and similarity between these languages, it is not difficult for a speaker of one Numic language to learn another. There was in the 1980s considerable passive bilingualism, and it seems reasonable to assume that it was present in past times, also. In addition to bilingualism, well-traveled individuals are often adept at dialect switching (Miller 1970:29–33).

Studies in ethnosemantics are represented by C. S. Fowler (1971, 1972), Fowler and Leland (1967), Zigmond (1971), and Hage and Miller (1976).

Linguistic Acculturation

There are several studies of linguistic acculturation, all of them limited to Central Numic (Casagrande 1954–1955; Miller 1971; Crapo 1974; Shimkin 1980; Shaul 1981).

Linguistic acculturation is an index to acculturation in general, though not a perfect one. Changes in a way of life are reflected in the vocabulary by formation of new words, extension of meaning of old words, and by changes or shifts in the meaning of words. Loanwords and loan translations normally come about through direct contact with the acculturating or donor language, though more rarely they can be passed through an intermediate language. Direct influence of the donor language, with a sizable number of bilinguals, is necessary for influence on phonological and grammatical rules.

There are a number of Spanish loanwords in the languages in or bordering on California. The distorted phonology suggests that some of them came via other Indian languages of California (see Shipley 1962), but some of the influence is probably direct since older Indians report learning at least some Spanish as children (Miller 1965–1969).

A few words from French are found in the north:

Bannock Northern Paiute *nappíassi* 'money', Lemhi and Fort Hall Shoshone *nappiasih* 'money, silver', from French *la piastre*; Northern Paiute *kossó*, Mono *kócci*, Lemhi and Fort Hall Shoshone *koso·h* 'pig', from French *cochon*; Oregon Northern Paiute *cú·ni* 'salt', from French *sel* (Miller 1965–1969). The words for 'pig' and 'salt' may have come from French by way of Chinook Jargon, since these words are found in this language (Nichols 1971:141).

Most influences on the Great Basin languages came either directly from English or indirectly from Anglo-American life. These influences are apparent in the changing state of vocabulary. Miller (1971:118) has described the situation for Shoshone, which is probably typical for other Numic languages. He divided the acculturated vocabulary into four groups. First, there is coinage of new terms, using native material. Examples are *pa·tikkappih* 'watermelon', literally 'water food'; *tu·hupa* 'coffee', literally 'black soup'. Some, like 'watermelon', are still in general use, but most have been replaced by English loans, such as *kappih* 'coffee'. Some items are covered by extension of meaning, for example, *eti*, the old word for 'bow' now used for 'gun', with a new coinage for the old item, *hu·ʔeti*, literally 'wooden gun'. Second is borrowing from English with native phonology preserved: *atammopih* 'automobile' and *tipoh* 'table'. Third is the use of English words for new items using English phonology: 'wrench', 'school', 'keys'. All age groups have been observed doing this, but it is more common with younger speakers. The fourth category is use of English words with English phonology, but for items that have Shoshone equivalents. Examples are 'salt', 'dog', 'wash', 'milk'. Again, this practice is more common with younger speakers.

Fig. 5. Beverly Crum, Western Shoshone, teaching a Shoshone song to children at the Utah Museum of Natural History, University of Utah, Salt Lake City. Photograph by Steven Crum, 1980.

In the 1970s only a few people were monolingual in the native language, and even these people knew some English words and phrases. As one moved to younger people, the quantity and quality of English improved, and often the quantity and quality of the native language decreased. Those people who were truly and fully bilingual were middle-aged. There were quite a number of people in the in-between generation, mostly young adults, whose first language was the native language, but whose primary language had become English. Their children normally did not speak the native language, though they may have understood it; very often their English was marked by an accent, presumably picked up by learning English from their parents and other Indian speakers of English.

The cut-off point for the native language varied from place to place and family to family. In the small colonies adjacent to towns and cities, which have greater access to Euro-American culture, and where the children form a minority of the school population, the cut-off age varied between 20 and 40 years. On the reservations, the majority of people over 20 and a sizable number of children spoke the native language in the 1970s. Perhaps the greatest preservation of language was found on the isolated Goshute Reservation, where almost all the children were learning the language. In other areas, the children were not normally learning the language except in households that had an older relative who felt most comfortable in the native language.

Crapo (1974) has studied English-Shoshone code switching. Code switching, the process of switching between two languages, is quite common among all the bilingual speakers who are fluent in English and a Numic language. Often the languages alternate within the same conversation or even the same sentence. Typically, one language is more common and more appropriate in certain settings than in others, for example, the native language in telling mythological tales and English in dealing with U.S. governmental affairs. Those settings in which English is appropriate are increasing in number and frequency, at the expense of settings in which the native language has been the appropriate one.

Unless the trend is arrested or reversed, the Numic languages are on the road to extinction and in the process of being replaced by English; however, in some areas the languages are viable and are still used as vehicles for social interaction. Thus, if they do die out, it cannot happen for some years to come. It is quite likely that these languages will survive into the twenty-first century.

Indian people have long been the objects of research. Since the 1970s there has been an interest in Indian cultures by Indians themselves. As a result, they are no longer passive objects of research. This concern can be seen in the development of language programs, both in the teaching of the language to younger Indians who do not speak it and in the development of literacy programs. Interest and involvement has come from the Indian communities but technical or expert assistance is required if the programs are to succeed. Malinda Tidzump (1970) prepared a thesaurus for Eastern Shoshone with the help of the Summer Institute of Linguistics at the University of North Dakota. Beverly Crum (fig. 5), a Shoshone speaker from Owyhee, has developed instructional material for both native speakers (Crum and Miller 1981) and nonspeakers. She has become involved in language programs at a number of communities in northern Nevada, Idaho, and Wyoming. In addition, she has undertaken Bible translation and ethnolinguistic research (Crum 1980).

Washoe Language

WILLIAM H. JACOBSEN, JR.

Classification

Washoe is the only Great Basin linguistic group that is not part of the Numic family. Located in a relatively circumscribed area centering on Lake Tahoe at the western edge of the culture area, it contrasts with the members of the Numic family in its minimal dialectal diversification and its isolation. It is not genetically related either to Numic or to the Maiduan and Miwokan stocks that are its California neighbors, nor does it have either a close or universally accepted relationship to any other language.

For a while after their discovery, the Washoe were thought to be linguistically similar to the Numic groups to their east (Bancroft 1886:469). Their linguistic distinctness was first pointed out by C.R. Collins (1876:467, 468). This was also noted by Gatschet (1882:254, 255), relying primarily on material collected by Powers in 1876, although Heizer (1966:12) suggests a possible influence of Collins through Hayden (1877). It was reaffirmed by Henshaw (1887a:xxx) on the basis of data he collected in 1883. A separate Washoan family was consequently recognized in the influential Powell (1891:131) classification, with credit given to Gatschet; the rival Brinton (1891) classification unaccountably omits any mention of this group.

Washoe is now commonly referred to as a member of the Hokan stock, or of larger groupings including Hokan, especially Hokan-Coahuiltecan (Hokaltecan) and Hokan-Siouan. Hokan contains 13 branches located in California and the Southwest, with an outlier in southern Mexico (Tequistlatecan or Chontal de Oaxaca) (vol. 8:85–87; vol. 9:172–173). Several linguists have detected diffuse but strikingly similar characteristics in the structures of these languages that give them reason to think that there may be a genuine, albeit distant, genetic relationship among at least several of these groups (Sapir 1925:526; Hoijer 1954a:637–638; Jacobsen 1979:570). In consequence, the established existence of a Hokan family has usually been taken for granted, so that it has been referred to with few reservations or as a probable entity (Lamb 1959:44; Voegelin and Voegelin 1965:12–14, 128–129, 141–142, 1966). However, through the years there have been dissenters claiming that sufficient evidence had never been adduced to validate even the narrower relationships of the Hokan group (Hoijer 1946:17–18, 1949:1, 1954:5; S. Newman 1954:632; Haas 1973:683; vol. 8:81). In the listing by Campbell and Mithun (1979:40–43), which purports to reflect a newer, more conservative consensus demanding a higher level of evidence in support of relationships, Hokan is shown as 13 unrelated branches. In the same book, Langdon (1979:592–596) advocates the retention of Hokan merely as a useful working hypothesis. The proposed wider connections such as with Coahuiltecan seem less likely (Haas 1967; Troike 1967; I. Goddard 1979; Jacobsen 1979:552–553; Campbell and Oltrogge 1980:222–223).

It is important to emphasize that potential relationships among the Hokan branches remain controversial and have none of the virtual certainty that applies, for example, to the relationship of Numic to the other Uto-Aztecan branches; consequently the Hokan construct must be used with the utmost caution in any inferences about prehistoric cultural contacts or migrations. Even the existence of a Hokan stock remains a debatable matter, given the absence of an agreed-upon methodology for establishing distant relationships. Due to the uncertainty of these relationships, and the complete uncertainty as to where a homeland for Hokan may have been located, there is no significant evidence either that Washoe may once have crossed the Sierras from California or that Washoe speakers represent an old, formerly more widespread Hokan-speaking area in the Great Basin. Both ideas were anticipated by S. Powers (1877:452, 453; in Fowler and Fowler 1970:119). The former is tentatively advanced by Kroeber (1925:569) and Sherzer (1968:272). W.W. Taylor's (1961) advocacy of the latter, in which he echoes Sapir (1920:290, 1921–1923:72), rests unduly on the presumed relationship of Hokan to Coahuiltecan, as well as on a now discredited relationship of Uto-Aztecan to Penutian (cf. Miller 1966:87–88; Jacobsen 1966:113–114, 1966a: 260, 1968:43–45; Goss 1968:9–11; Langdon 1974:73–75).

One can only assume that Washoe has long been in approximately the same area in which it is now found (similarly Price 1963:41). This is somewhat implied by a residue of unanalyzable place-names (Dangberg 1968:101–102 indicates 9 out of 25 for the periphery of Lake Tahoe) and of apparent older loanwords from the surrounding stocks.

Dialectal Differentiation

The Washoe language displays very little dialectal differentiation, implying the maintenance of a high level of intercommunication among its speakers. Differences in words mostly concern details of their pronunciation rather than completely different lexical items to express the same meaning, and other differences in the language structure are minimal (Jacobsen 1978:116–123, 1966:129). No sharp dialect boundary has been found. When there are two variants of a feature, generally one is found in a more northerly area and the other in a more southerly one, but the lines separating the two areas for the different features do not always coincide (table 1). Variant versions of a rule for vowel harmony account for some cases of *a* versus *e* in prefixes, and there is a tendency for vowel harmony patterns to take hold in borrowed words more in the northerly than in the southerly area. Other random vowel changes and assimiliations also occur. Some differences involve consonants, especially *ʔ*; some other consonants are involved in variant forms of borrowed words. A few lexical items show replacements: 'mosquito', 'husband'. For the introduced animals 'cow' and 'horse' there are alternative borrowings from other Indian languages as well as from Spanish, while for other introduced items there is a less geographically differentiated competition between older loanwords from Spanish and later loans from English (table 2). A few other differences concern alternative neologisms for new items ('chair') or borrowings opposed to neologisms.

Interaction with Adjacent Languages

A continuing contact of Washoe with languages of the surrounding stocks is attested to by the occurrence of a modest number of loanwords from all of them, as well as by the sharing of several phonological and grammatical characteristics that may have diffused among the contiguous groups.

Table 1. Variation in Washoe

Gloss	Northern area	Southern area
1. 'throw it over'	gašuʔmáwit	gešuʔmáwit
2. 'mosquito'	da(ʔ)muǩáyǩay	púˑieʔ
3. 'husband'	ʔméˑš	buméˑliʔ
4. 'cow'	gúsu (earlier 'buffalo'; from Northern Paiute)	báˑgaʔ (from Spanish *vaca*)
5. 'horse'	súkuʔ (earlier 'dog') from Nisenan	gawáˑyiʔ and variants (from Spanish *caballo*)
6. 'chair'	ʔitǩuláŋaʔ	ʔitgéˑgel

Table 2. Borrowings from Spanish and English into Washoe

Gloss	Older term	Newer term
1. 'sheep'	wudéˑguʔ and variants (from Spanish *borrego* 'lamb')	šíˑp (from English)
2. 'beans'	bihóˑliš and variants (from Spanish *frijoles*)	bíniši ʔ (from English)
3. 'gold'	ʔóˑdoʔ (from Spanish *oro*)	gúˑl (from English)
4. 'money'	biláˑdaʔ (from Spanish *plata* 'silver')	móˑniʔ (from English)

Borrowed words have the clearest cultural implications (cf. W. Bright 1973). Few borrowings are seen to have gone out from Washoe into other languages. However, at least 85 likely loanwords in Washoe are recognized, their sources being fairly evenly split between Miwokan languages (table 3) and Maiduan languages (table 4) on the west and varieties of Numic (table 5) on the east (Jacobsen 1984, 1978:118, 123–142, 1966:127–128, 1976:226–227, 232–233). Ten of the loanwords in Washoe may be older borrowings, considering that they do not reflect the contemporary forms or meanings in the contiguous languages but resemble more distant forms, on the west (table 3, nos. 1–3; table 4, nos. 1–2) and the east (table 5, nos. 1–5). The related words for 'hand game' in table 4 resemble both Maidu and Numic forms.

When the borrowings are grouped into semantic categories, certain patterns emerge. Among fauna, a few borrowings of words for insects and reptiles are primarily from the west. Two fish names seem to come from Numic. The limited number of likely borrowings of words for birds mostly stem from the forested regions to the west. Words for two large mammals, 'mountain lion' and 'black bear', come respectively from Miwokan and Maiduan. A Numic word 'buffalo' comes to mean primarily 'cow' in the northern area. The word for 'dog' (formerly and northern area also 'horse') is probably from Nisenan (Southern Maiduan), with similar forms in Miwokan and other languages to the west (noted already by Dixon and Kroeber 1903:16; cf. Shipley 1957:270; W. Bright 1960:231; Shipley and Smith 1979:68). A half-dozen words for smaller mammals have more varied origins, but the clearest cases ('muskrat', 'porcupine', 'red fox') involve Numic.

Turning to flora, a few borrowings are from Miwokan, most clearly words for two species of 'oak' and for 'green manzanita'. Perhaps a dozen words for plants or their products are from Numic, most of them being characteristic of a desert or marsh environment.

Among artifacts, a complex of words relating to wear-

Table 3. Washoe Words of Miwokan Origin

Gloss	Washoe	Source
1. 'lizard'	*píteliʔ*	cf. Lake Miwok *petéˑli*
2. 'hoop'	*púˑlul*	cf. Lake Miwok *polóˑlo* 'ball'
3. 'west'	*táŋlel*	cf. Central Sierra Miwok *tamal-* 'north', Bodega Miwok *támal* 'west, west coast'
4. 'mountain lion'	*hilíˑʒa*	Central Sierra Miwok *híˑliča-*
5. 'oak sp.'	*wíliši ʔ*	Central Sierra Miwok *wilˑiší-* 'California white oak'
6. 'oak sp.'	*šagáˑša ʔ*	Southern Sierra Miwok *hakaˑ-ha-* 'canyon live oak'
7. 'green manzanita'	*ʔeyéye ʔ*	Central Sierra Miwok *ʔeyˑe-*
8. 'to trade, exchange'	*damáˑli*	Central Sierra Miwok *temáˑl-* 'to trade', Southern Sierra Miwok *temaˑl-* 'to exchange'
9. 'snowshoe'	*šu ʔméˑli ʔ*	Southern Sierra Miwok *saˑwine-*
10. 'paternal grandfather'	*báˑba ʔ*	Central Sierra Miwok *páˑpa-* 'grandfather'
11. 'paternal grandmother'	*ʔáma ʔ*	Central Sierra Miwok *ʔamáˑ-* 'grandmother'

ing apparel has apparently come from Numic: 'shoe', 'stocking, sock', 'trousers', 'skirt, dress', and 'sack, bag, pocket' (from a word for 'stocking'). Nichols (1981:26) suggests that words for 'cave' and 'house' may be borrowed from older Uto-Aztecan. Trade relationships are implied by the borrowing of 'bead' from Maiduan (cf. Jacobsen 1976:226–227) and of 'knife' (from a compound word meaning 'white knife'), 'salt', and probably 'pitch' from Numic, as well as by the verb 'to trade, exchange' from Miwokan. Less certain candidates for borrowing are 'snowshoe' from Miwokan and 'close-weave tray basket' from Numic. Food processing is implied by 'to fish with hook and line' and 'to boil' from Maiduan. Other friendly relationships are suggested by the likely borrowing of two related words for 'hand game' from one or more of the contiguous groups. The likely borrowing of the two words for 'paternal grandparent' from Miwokan indeed suggests instances of intermarriage. A few other miscellaneous words, including 'to name', 'water baby', and 'spirit' from Numic, and a few words for ethnic groups, including 'White man' from Numic, complete the list of likely borrowings. On balance, it seems that the borrowings from Numic imply a more intimate cultural contact than those from the west. Numic has exchanged more loanwords with Washoe than with any other contiguous group.

Languages are often found to share structural characteristics with their neighbors thereby to constitute linguistic areas, and Washoe is no exception. Diffusion of traits is especially salient when, as in the case of Washoe, the neighbors are genetically unrelated. Since the early work of Kroeber (1907:253, 314–317) the general question has been whether Washoe displays greater structural similarities with languages to the east or to the west. Washoe features that have been cited as being of a California type include: certain syntactic characteristics (Dixon and Kroeber 1903:18; cf. Kroeber 1907:314); the pronominal dual (Dixon 1906); the quinary/decimal numeral system (Dixon and Kroeber 1907), which resembles one of two competing Maidu systems (Haas 1976:355–358); the absence of vowel-initial syllables; and the free stress pattern, which is most like that of Maiduan of the surrounding stocks (Jacobsen 1984). A different picture is found in a series of studies by Sherzer, who considered whether the culture areas of North America are also linguistic areas (areas over which at least some traits have diffused). Sherzer was

Table 4. Washoe Words of Maiduan Origin

Gloss	Washoe	Source
1. 'spider'	*číˑki*	cf. Konkow *číˑki*
2. 'bead'	*mák̓aw*	cf. Konkow *hówok̓o*, Maidu *wókkolò*
3. 'black bear'	*mí(ˑ)ʔde*	Maidu *míde* 'bear, brown bear'
4. 'to angle'	*p̓íʔli*	Nisenan *p̓ili*
5. 'to boil'	*mólmol*	Nisenan *molmol*
6. 'women's hand game' 'men's hand game'	*hináˑya* *hinayáwgi*	cf. Nisenan *helay* 'hand game' and Northern Paiute *naiyákʷi* 'to play the hand game'

Table 5. Washoe Words of Numic Origin

Gloss	Washoe	Source
1. 'medicine'	mú·ċuk	cf. Kawaiisu matasuk^wi, Southern Paiute musuttuk^wk^wi
2. 'sego lily'	kókšiʔ	cf. Kawaiisu kogosi(vi̱) 'Calochortus root'
3. 'skirt, dress'	ámuʔ	cf. Northern Paiute nak^wí 'dress', Southern Paiute nami 'apron'
4. 'cave'	káŋa	cf. Shoshone kahni, Southern Paiute kani 'house' (cf. no. 5)
5. 'house'	áŋal	cf. Tubatulabal hani·l 'the house' and no. 4
6. 'muskrat'	bá·muš	Northern Paiute pamúsi
7. 'porcupine'	séwi̱t	Northern Paiute cag^wídi̱
8. 'red fox'	wátʒiha, wásʒiha	Northern Paiute wacíʔa
9. 'shoe'	mókgo	Northern Paiute mokó
10. 'stocking, sock'	wé·ċi̱p	cf. Southern Paiute wičča-ppi̱ 'tied around, band, ribbon'
11. 'trousers'	wí·gis	cf. Northern Paiute wicá 'thigh', kus·á- 'breechclout, 'trousers'
12. 'sack, bag, pocket'	tóšap	Northern Paiute tas·ópa 'stocking'
13. 'knife'	táʔwiʔ	Northern Paiute tohák^wihi 'white (chalcedony) knife'
14. 'salt'	ʔuŋá·bi	Northern Paiute oŋábi
15. 'pitch'	šálaʔ	Northern Paiute saná-
16. 'close-weave tray basket'	mudá·l	Bannock Northern Paiute wi̱dán·u
17. 'to name'	díye	Northern Paiute nía- 'to call'
18. 'water baby'	meċuŋé·ʔ	cf. Northern Paiute paúŋa·ʔa
19. 'spirit'	ʒáʔaphu, ʒáʔbu	Northern Paiute coʔápa
20. 'White man'	dabóʔo, earlier dabibóʔo	Northern Paiute táiboʔo, earlier *tábiboʔo (recorded as tavivo by J.W. Powell in 1880—Fowler and Fowler 1971:245)

led to recognize a Great Basin linguistic area, subsuming Washoe and Numic (Sherzer 1968:266–288, 547–570, 634–637, 1973:782–783, 1976:153–167, 245–247; cf. also Bright and Sherzer 1976). However, this approach of starting out from culture areas seems to introduce some distortions as applied to Washoe, in that it minimizes the comparably great similarities to the California stocks (some of which Sherzer 1976:128, 164, 167, 238–239, 246 indeed notes). For example, considering the inventory of segmental phonemes, the two striking points of agreement with Numic, presence of i̱ and ŋ, are also shared with groups to the west, while other features of Washoe—presence of glottalized stops, l, and a s/š contrast, and absence of k^w—separate it from Numic and unite it with one or more of its western neighbors.

Other features show resemblances on both sides. Kroeber (1917:363–365) noted great similarities between the Washoe and Northern Paiute systems of kinship terminology, as well as similarities between these two and the Miwok and Yokuts systems. Jacobsen (1980b) has compared the Washoe reduplication pattern to a productive reduplication pattern of Numic and to a reduplicative shape for color stems in Maiduan and, less centrally, in Sierra Miwok.

Among grammatical characteristics, Washoe shares having instrumental verb prefixes with Maiduan, Shasta-Achumawi, and Numic (Kroeber 1907b:376–377, 1907:263, 268–269, 286, 314; Sapir 1916a:84), which is unique within Uto-Aztecan (Kroeber 1955:94); shares

a pronominal inclusive/exclusive distinction with Numic and Miwokan; and shares the syntactic device of switch-reference with Numic and Maiduan. The inclusive/exclusive distinction and switch reference are both found in contiguous languages over large areas (Sherzer 1968:522–523, 524–525, 540, 542, 553, 554–555, 562, 564, 569, 628–630, 635–636, 1973:779, 780, 782, 1976:120–121, 128, 161, 165; Bright and Sherzer 1976:255–256; Jacobsen 1980a:207–208, 212–214, 1966:127, 1967:259–261, 1978:134, 1979:574–575, 1983:172–174, 176–177; Oswalt 1976:298, 303; Langdon 1979:633–634). Diffusion of the former category was suggested by Sherzer (1968:553, 555, 564, 567, 1976:121, 131, 161, 166), while Jacobsen (1980a:208–212, 214–217) demonstrated its innovational status in both Washoe and Numic. Other commentary on areal features that include Washoe is that regarding instrumental verb prefixes and local verb suffixes (W.W. Taylor 1961:77; Jacobsen 1966a:262–263; Sherzer 1968:535–537, 542–543, 545–546, 560–561, 564–565, 566–567, 570, 630, 635, 1973:780, 783, 1976:125–126, 128, 130–131, 163–167, 238–239, 245–246; Bright and Sherzer 1976:260–262, 264).

On the other hand, Washoe differs from its neighbors in its lack of syntactic case suffixes (Dixon and Kroeber 1903:12; Kroeber 1907:263, 286, 314; Jacobsen 1966:127). It is only partly similar to Western Numic in its use of pronominal prefixes on nouns and verbs (Dixon and Kroeber 1903:9–10; Kroeber 1907:262, 316; Jacobsen 1966:127). The three-way genderlike classification imposed by the lower numerals is seen to be something of an anomaly for its area (Kroeber 1907:300; Sherzer 1968:556, 1976:162, 166, 246; Bright and Sherzer 1976:263; Jacobsen 1979b:77–78). A suggested diffusion of evidential suffixes into Washoe (Sherzer 1968:560, 564, 567, 1976:163, 166) has been called into question by Jacobsen (1985) on the grounds of a lack of match of the specific semantic areas. Gorbet (1977) suggested an areal diffusion of the pattern of headless relative clauses in the Southwest; although Washoe also displays this pattern, it is not close to the area in question (Jacobsen 1981, 1983:183).

Linguistic Acculturation

Some 20 words reflecting innovations introduced by Euro-Americans are ultimately from Spanish, considerably fewer than in languages to the west and south. Most of these are thought to have come to Washoe through Miwok (cf. Shipley 1962 for assumed trajectories, as well as phonemic substitutions). Most are listed by Jacobsen (1966:128, cf. 1978:122, 132–133; W. Bright 1960). They relate to domesticated mammals: 'horse', 'cow, bull', 'mule', 'sheep', and 'pig'; foods: 'beans', 'flour soup', 'chewing tobacco', and perhaps 'tortilla'; cash economy: 'dollar' (from 'peso'), 'money' (from 'silver'), and 'gold'; clothing: 'overcoat, coat'; ammunition: 'lead' (from 'bullet'); games: 'to play cards'; and the ethnic label 'Mexican' (from 'Spaniard').

Not surprisingly, there are numerous borrowings from English, which can be sorted to some extent into earlier and later strata on the basis of meanings and of the extent of phonological divergence from the English model. Jacobsen (1966:128–129) gives a sampling, of which seven are quite divergent ('quicksilver' also in Kroeber 1907:256) and nine less so. W. Bright (1960) includes five English borrowings for introduced mammals and two for fowls.

In a few cases, labels for newly introduced items have been obtained by a broadened application of words for indigenous items: 'bow' to 'gun', 'fire drill' to 'match', 'hoop' to 'wheel' to 'wagon' to 'automobile', 'dog' to 'horse' (Jacobsen 1966:129, 1978:122; W. Bright 1960:217).

Much more prevalent is the coining by affixation of new words descriptive of the appearance or the function of an item. W. Bright (1960) lists eight for introduced mammals. Jacobsen (1966:129, 1978:123) gives a few examples, mostly words for artifacts. Dangberg (1922:150) indicates two in translation.

In a unique study, Van Winkle (1977) demonstrates a largely shared residue of lexical items among Washoe whose major language is English.

A discussion of the status of the language in the 1980s is in "Washoe," this volume.

Sources

The earliest attestation of Washoe linguistic data comprises two words from 1844 in Frémont (1845:228), followed by 17 words from 1855 in Remy (1860, 1:41). Then follows the vocabulary of some 200 words collected in 1859 by C.R. Collins (1876). The most important nineteenth-century vocabulary, collected by Henshaw (1883, 1883a), remains unpublished, as do the shorter ones of S. Powers (1876a), Ridgway (1875) (cf. Ridgway and Powers 1880), and Keeler (1889).

The following are the principal twentieth-century field workers of linguistic interest, with the respective years in which they began their data gathering (see the characterizations in d'Azevedo 1963:1–7; Jacobsen 1964: 6–9, 1966:119): C. Hart Merriam 1903, Alfred L. Kroeber about 1905, Grace Dangberg 1917, Robert H. Lowie 1926, Walter Dyk 1931, John P. Harrington 1943, Gordon H. Marsh 1945, Fred W. Richards and Robert Young 1955, William H. Jacobsen, Jr. 1955, Otto J. Sadovszky 1964, and Barrik Van Winkle 1976. Much of their data remain unpublished, and for yet other field workers there is only symptomatic attestation in print: Roland B. Dixon in Dixon and Kroeber (1919:105–107), Paul Radin (1919), J.P. Harrington (1943).

Kroeber (1907) published a short morphological sketch, including brief texts and vocabulary, and he used his data in several typological, areal, and classificatory studies. Dangberg produced a brief statement about the language (1922), texts (1927, 1968), and a manuscript grammar (1925). Lowie prepared texts (1963) and an ethnographic manuscript containing linguistic data (1939). Jacobsen (1964) completed a dissertation on the grammar and various other studies, and data provided by him has also been used in comparative and descriptive studies by others.

The fullest description of the language is Jacobsen (1964), covering phonology, morphology, and some aspects of syntax. For brief summaries of Washoe structure, see Kroeber (1907:312–314), Dangberg (1922:150–151), and Jacobsen (1966:114–118). Descriptive treatment of some specialized grammatical topics is found in several other sources. Phonological topics include phoneme inventory (Jacobsen 1958:195–196; Haas 1963:43; Dangberg 1968: 99–100), vowel harmony (Jacobsen 1968a:822, 1978:117–118), and reduplication (Dangberg 1922:150; W. Winter 1970; Jacobsen 1980:86–87, 1980b; wrongly taken as suffixed by Kroeber 1907:271–273). Morphological topics separately treated are suffix orderings (Jacobsen 1973), pronouns (Kroeber 1907:260, 264–270, 274–286; Dangberg 1922:150; Jacobsen 1977:55–61, 1979a:146–152, 1980a:214–215), suppletive verb stems (Kroeber 1907:294–295; Jacobsen 1980:98), bipartite verb stems (made up of lexical prefixes and dependent verb stems) (Kroeber 1907:261, 286–287; Jacobsen 1980), numeral classifications

(Kroeber 1907:299–300; Jacobsen 1979b:75–77, 1980a:215–216), and evidentials (Jacobsen 1985). The purported examples of nominal compounding offered by Kroeber (1907:258–259, 1910:210) result from incorrect analysis; most are phrases. Syntactic topics discussed are voice relationships (Jacobsen 1979a:152–155), headless relative clauses (Jacobsen 1981), and switch-reference (Jacobsen 1967:242–248, 1981, 1983:159, 165, 176–177).

Texts have been provided by Kroeber (1907:302–306), Dangberg (1927, with further discussion and a rewritten translation 1968; cf. Jacobsen 1979b), and Lowie (1939:325, 1963, with English counterparts 1939:333–351).

For lexical information, general vocabularies are provided in manuscripts of Merriam (1903–1935, 1903–1935a, published 1979:109–111, 242–243, two words in 1955:146) and in publications of Kroeber (1907:297–298, 308–312), Curtis (1907–1930, 15:188–192), and Price (1962:61–66). Some sources on specialized lexical topics are as follows: numerals (Cohn 1902; Dixon and Kroeber 1907:677; Kroeber 1907:299–300; Curtis 1907–1930, 15:191; Haas 1976:356 on abstract pattern only), kinship terms (Kroeber 1907:309, 1917:362–363; Gifford 1922:230–232; Curtis 1907–1930, 15:191; Lowie 1939:311–314; Freed 1960:355–358, 1963:8–15), flora and fauna (Keeler 1889; Merriam 1979:109–111, 242–243; Kroeber 1907:311; Curtis 1907–1930, 15:189–192; Train, Henrichs, and Archer 1941; Murphey 1959; W. Bright 1960), games (Hudson in Culin 1907:199, 265, 322–323, 335, 396, 523, 664, 704; Lowie 1939:315–317), and place-names (Riddell 1960a:82–85; Freed 1966:78–82; Dangberg 1968:101–103; d'Azevedo 1978). Some ethnographic treatments additionally contain a sampling of vocabulary items (Barrett 1917; Kroeber 1925:569–573; Lowie 1939; Siskin 1941, 1983; Price 1962, 1963a; Freed 1963; Freed and Freed 1963, 1963a; Downs 1966; Fowler and Fowler 1970:119–120, 142; Nevers 1976; Van Winkle 1977). For ethnographic bibliography, see especially d'Azevedo and Price (1963), Jacobsen (1964:28–47), C.S. Fowler (1970:257–262), and Murdock and O'Leary (1975, 3:206–208).

Prehistory: Introduction

JESSE D. JENNINGS

The historic Indian cultures of the Great Basin and environs are the end products of a very long tradition. That rich heritage was still flourishing when the Great Basin tribes were first seen by Europeans in the seventeenth century. When first contacted and described by Europeans and Euro-Americans, the native peoples were practicing a close and intimate relationship to the land. Overall, the general culture of the aboriginal peoples can be characterized as a foraging or collecting one, selectively exploiting a wide range of plants and animals from an even greater range of available species. The people harvested available animals, grass seeds, tubers, nuts, and fruits without significantly modifying the landscape. Ecological exigencies required that groups, probably no larger than a family or extended family comprised of grandparents, parents, and children, moved about over a wide and well-known territory procuring the different species as they matured.

The accumulated archeological evidence reported in the following chapters indicates that this general cultural pattern had been carried on in prehistoric times for at least 10,000 years. The prehistoric peoples of the Great Basin were at a cultural stage called the Archaic tradition by North American archeologists. This denotes a level of technology generally lacking domesticated animals, horticulture, or permanent villages. In western North America, including the Great Basin, this stage of technological development is labeled the Western Archaic. Although generally similar all over the West, it is not a uniform entity. The detailed inventory of tools, the amount and range of annual mobility, and the major food and other resources vary from place to place throughout the West, including the Great Basin.

The term Great Basin has been used in several senses (see "Introduction," this vol.). It is derived from the geologic phenomenon of a large area of interior drainage often referred to as the hydrographic basin, which is part of a more extensive physiographic area known as the Basin and Range Province characterized by close-set mountain ranges that alternate with long narrow valleys and basins. The prehistoric Great Basin culture area, as defined in this volume, included all the hydrographic basin as well as portions of the Snake River Plain in Idaho, the Colorado Plateau of eastern Utah and northern Arizona, in addition to southern Nevada and California, where archeological subareas extend beyond the limits of the hydrographic drainage or even beyond the larger physiographic province (fig. 1).

The key to understanding prehistoric Great Basin human adaptation lies in the recognition of a myriad of microenvironments. Humans exploited spring- and stream-fed marshes, dry valleys, and the forested mountains. There were also precarious adaptations to the resources of chronically arid areas, such as the Mojave and Amargosa deserts.

Instead of being the uniformly uninviting desert so often visualized, the Great Basin consists of hundreds of special and often rich environments where a widely varying mix of desired plant and animal species was available for harvest. Generally, the resources were the same; what varied was the component species and the degree of abundance. Mehringer (1977, "Prehistoric Environments," this vol.) has described the nature and complexity of the sources of special environments or econiches with which the human populations coped through time. He has also emphasized the biologic changes in some of the local environments caused by frequent climatic variation over the past 10 millennia with attendant fluctuation in available moisture and temperature. In addition, the areal prehistory chapters provide descriptions of the climate, geomorphology, and resources.

The fundamental accuracy of the three climatic regimens proposed by Antevs (1948) is now generally accepted. Later studies merely modify the details and elaborate upon the many regional deviations from the broader trend. The first relevant climatic stage was the Anathermal, about 7000 to 5000 B.C., cooler and moister than the present. This was followed by the Altithermal, about 5000–2500 B.C., markedly hotter and drier, and then the Medithermal, 2500 B.C. to the present, similar to recent conditions. Since climatic changes directly affect the abundance or scarcity of plants, and therefore of animals, even subtle changes might require human adjustment so far as subsistence is concerned. The major climatic changes are well understood, and for some of the more local fluctuations there is also quite detailed knowledge (see Currey and James 1982 for the eastern Basin, and D.L. Weide 1982 for the southern Basin). But these changes are only roughly correlated or calibrated with cultural change, and specific changes in species occurrence or abundance at any

113

after Fenneman 1946; Morrison 1965.

Fig. 1. Key to the subareas discussed in the prehistory chapters. Overlapping areas indicate overlapping treatment.

given time have not been well established. There is more speculation than firm information about what precise effects climatic changes may have had on the human ecological balance in relation to available resources—particularly at the local or site level. This problem is reflected in several of the following chapters.

Archeological Subareas

As figure 1 indicates, the prehistoric cultures of the Great Basin were not restricted to the physiographic province itself; the same is true of the historic cultures. In fact, the Archaic cultures of the West were distributed over a vast area from Oregon to the central Mexican Plateau, and from the flanks of the Sierra Nevada to the western slopes of the Rockies. Typical artifacts—such as projectile points, basketry, and woven sandals—are also found in the western High Plains at sites such as Mummy, Pictograph, and Birdshead caves in Wyoming, as well as sites on the Snake River plain in Idaho, such as Wilson Butte Cave.

The archeological subareas shown on figure 1 are somewhat arbitrary in that they represent the concentration of research. They have, nonetheless, a certain reality in that they are distinguished on the bases of artifact inventories and, particularly, the variable adaptations made to local environments. The delineation of archeological subareas began with Cressman (1943). Heizer (1956) showed similarities between some of the artifacts from Humboldt Cave in Nevada and certain

types from the Anasazi area of the Southwest. Jennings (1957, 1964) described several subareal variants of the Western Archaic, including those within the Great Basin, and suggested their interpretation within a broad organizing concept or principle—the Desert (later Western) Archaic. (See Fowler 1980; Fowler and Jennings 1982 for general histories of Great Basin archeological classifications.)

Cultural-Chronological Frameworks

Because of the diversity of prehistoric cultural expressions, there is no currently accepted chronological framework that claims to present any detailed cultural connections across the entire Great Basin. The lack of consensus with regard to regional nomenclature reflects not only the "single scholar" tendency of those who have studied the archeology of the Great Basin, but the fact that much of the initial archeological work was done by enthusiastic, though untrained, excavators. Some of their work in the 1920s and 1930s was inspired by finds of early materials such as Clovis and Folsom points in the Plains; the search was for something as old or older in the Great Basin and elsewhere in the West. Hence the descriptions of finds were often unrestrained and the interpretations strove to establish great antiquity. Not until the late 1930s did a few professionals begin doing the more painstaking research that resulted in less flamboyant claims. Serious work began with Cressman's initial research in Oregon. At the same time, Steward began his study of the eastern Basin caves, and Heizer investigated sites in western Nevada. There matters rested until the late 1940s when more scholars became interested in the archeology of the Great Basin (though the southern portion was neglected until the 1960s). Because of the size of the area, full coverage is far from achieved. The archeological data tend to be spotty, and some areas are better understood than others.

In 1953 the Great Basin Archaeological Conference (now called Great Basin Anthropological Conference) was organized. Through that informal organization, an increasing number of researchers annually exchanged information. This stimulated a few tentative efforts to create a Basin-wide chronology that equated the scores of known local culture sequences within a 10,000-year time frame (for example, Bennyhoff 1958: table 9; Hester 1973: fig. 25; Heizer and Hester 1978b: fig. 6.1; James 1981: table 3). Nevertheless, actual research continued to be focused on small geographic areas such as a single valley or river drainage. The Reese River drainage (Thomas 1983, 1983a) is a good example.

The following chapters make it evident that a set of reasonable pan-Basin designators that distinguishes one region from another, yet links them all in a valid general system with a time-stage relationship, is not likely to be established very soon. Each author provides a time scale for the cultures of his area and explains the changes in prehistoric adaptation that warrant the sequence he uses. The nomenclature employed by the researchers in the several areas to label or distinguish the cultures of the local sequence from each other is not applicable Basin-wide. The paucity of excavated remains makes even local comparisons and correlations of site contents difficult. Moreover, many scholars tend to work a small area within their subregion in order to clarify the details of a local sequence. On a broader level, some are "splitters," giving great cultural importance to minor variations in the artifact inventories of local cultures, while others bring many manifestations together in larger, more inclusive categories. There are even those who question the desirability of having any Basin-wide cultural labels because the adaptive differences in each econiche seem to preclude the possibility that a broad classificatory scheme would be valid over such a large area. Nevertheless, the editors have superimposed a four-period sequence upon the periods named and used in each subarea chapter. Figure 2 shows the sequence of cultures defined in each subarea with four general prehistoric periods cutting across the entire Basin (except for the Western Basin, for which see "Prehistory of the Western Area," this vol.). Figures 3–4, which show the chronological framework defined by dated projectile point types, are intended as references for all the prehistory chapters.

Pre-Archaic Cultures

One of the more intriguing aspects of Great Basin prehistory is the dearth of good evidence for human use of the area before about 8000 B.C., though alleged finds of more ancient cultures have been and continue to be reported. Artifacts similar to those associated with the Paleo-Indian hunters of the Plains (such as Clovis fluted points) have been recovered all over the Basin, many in Utah and many in the western Basin. A number of extinct big game species also are represented in fossil localities: horse, camel, sloth, bison, and mammoth. But with the exception of Idaho ("Prehistory of the Snake and Salmon River Area," this vol.) no situation has been found where extinct mammals, stone tools or weapons, or evidence of fire, are credibly reported in good association. It is noteworthy that for each area there have been a few discredited claims of big game hunting, but acceptable evidence is lacking. The situation is puzzling. Several sites are evidently as old, by carbon-14 assays, as the classic Plains sites where fluted points and extinct fauna are found in close association. Numerous scattered surface finds of Clovis fluted points have been recorded, and the megafauna appear to have been abundant. Yet nowhere has a buried kill site or other firm association of human activity with bones of extinct prey been encountered in the physiographic Great Basin. Some argue that the big game animals became

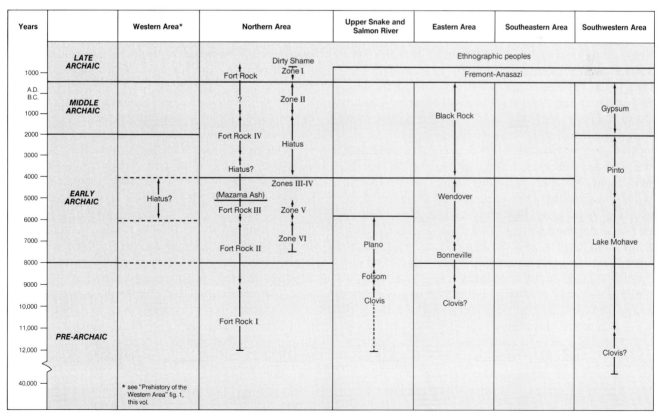

Fig. 2. Prehistoric chronology for the Great Basin.

PREHISTORY: INTRODUCTION

extinct earlier in the Basin than elsewhere, or that there were no human predators in the Basin when the animals were available. Whatever the reason, the fact remains that no big game hunter site has been accepted as valid except in Idaho. Discussion of these important problems concerning the Pre-Archaic period of Great Basin prehistory has been minimized in the chapters of this section due to the extensive and detailed exposition of these materials presented in volume 3 of the *Handbook*.

Interpretations

It is evident that since the 1950s scholarly perspectives have changed, and there is much more order and time-depth in the understanding of Great Basin prehistory. The scope of knowledge also has dramatically increased. There are detectable local variations in resources; the prehistoric record is quite clear as to some of these variations. For example, in the Humboldt Sink district of the western Basin, the prehistoric inhabitants focused on the marshes, with fish, waterfowl, and marsh plants looming large in their economy. In the eastern Basin, there is the same use of marsh resources where available (less commonly than in the west) but with much more emphasis on the collection of grass seeds and small animals in a far more diffuse wandering and collecting schedule. In Owens Valley, where conditions were favorable to extensive stands of grass, it has been asserted that there was a concentration of population in a semi- or fully sedentary mode similar to that of the historic period ("Prehistory of the Western Area," this vol.). Thus, the settlement system of the Great Basin ranged along a continuum from the near sedentary, where resources were concentrated, to the highly mobile, where the desired species were patchy and widely dispersed. The very fact of the survival of the population through all of recent time testifies to the flexibility and adaptive nature of the Basin cultures.

There is good reason for research preoccupation with the subsistence base and technology. Archeological data lend themselves best to an economic and ecological model because the artifacts recovered are most often tools and utensils used in food gathering and processing: milling stones (metates), chipped stone processing tools, winnowing baskets, and the like. Change may be inferred from changes in artifact styles, especially projectile points. Basketry techniques also change, with an early preference for twining giving way to a wide use of the coiling or stitching construction. Why changes in form occurred or how important they were to prehistoric peoples is a matter of debate. Yet artifact changes such as the shift from rather large heavy to small light projectile points at about the time of Christ may indicate increased procurement efficiency. That shift is believed to mark the introduction of the bow and arrow, a weapon that replaced the dart or lance used previously with the atlatl or spearthrower. It is presumed to have been more efficient: in effect, a rapid-fire weapon.

Another important aspect of the ecological perspective is the analysis of settlement patterns. The location of settlements—whether transient hunting camps, the summer gathering camps, winter encampments in piñon forests, or temporary camps by mineral outcrops where stone and pigment were secured—is utilized in developing an understanding of the full annual round of the food quest and the search for materials for manufacture. All habitation locations in one way or another are determined by resource locations.

The fact that the chapters in this section emphasize chronology, culture history, and settlement patterns in an attempt to explain cultural changes in environmental terms is an important measure of a growing consensus as to how raw archeological data are best employed to understand the adaptive behavior of successive Great Basin populations. The lack of a broader descriptive nomenclature for Great Basin prehistory becomes a very minor issue in the face of the higher level of interpretation being sought and steadily achieved.

Future Research Directions

The direction of prehistoric study in the Great Basin is difficult to predict. For the southwest subarea, even the culture history is incomplete. Is the break in the western subarea sequence at about 4000 B.C. real, or is it a mere lack of discovered evidence? Does the similar, but later, break in the northern subarea record a loss of population, or is it the failure to locate certain kinds of sites, a problem that more fieldwork should solve? In fact, until the entire Great Basin is as carefully studied as the Reese River Valley and environs, all scholars will be working with truly inadequate data. A prime example is Utah, where only five or six major Archaic sites (all caves) have been excavated since the 1930s; and these locations are distant, by as much as 200 miles, from each other. Thus the data base for the entire culture history of the Eastern Great Basin and Colorado Plateau ("Prehistory of the Eastern Area," this vol.) is derived from a few sites in at least three quite disparate ecological zones. Fortunately, the Fremont culture of Utah, based partly on horticulture, is better known, although problems in understanding it still exist. Therefore, one obvious need is more well-focused field research geared to expanding the data base, but not randomly. It should be guided by clearly defined problems and goals, including the collection of paleo-environmental evidence and specimens datable by radiocarbon and other techniques.

One can predict that climatological research will be biased toward greater precision in establishing a chronology of past climatic events, even minor ones. With

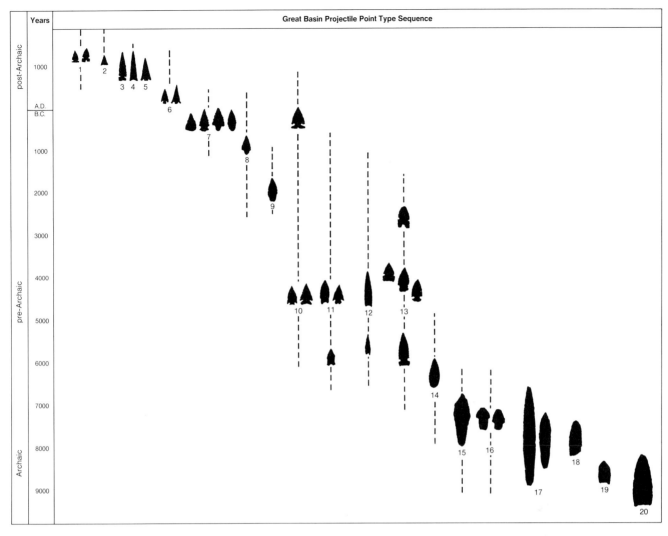

Type Name (Alternate Name)

1 Desert Side-notched Series
   Desert Side-notched
   Uinta Side-notched
   Bear River Side-notched
2 Cottonwood Triangular
3 Bull Creek Concave-base
4 Parowan Basal-notched
5 Nawthis Side-notched
6 Rose Spring–Eastgate Series
   (Rosegate Series)
   Rose Spring Corner-
     notched
   Rose Spring Side-notched
   Eastgate Expanding-stem
   Eastgate Split-stem
7 Martis Series
   Martis Triangular
   Martis Corner-notched
   Martis Stemmed-leaf
8 Gypsum

9 McKean Lanceolate
10 Elko Series
   Elko Corner-notched
   Elko Eared
   Elko Side-notched
   Elko Contracting-stem
11 Pinto Series
   (Gatecliff Series, Little Lake
     Series, Bare Creek Series)
   Pinto Square-shouldered
   Pinto Sloping-shouldered
   Pinto Shoulderless
   Pinto Willowleaf
12 Humboldt Series
   (Great Basin Concave-base
     Series)
   Humboldt Concave-base A
   Humboldt Concave-base B
   Humboldt Basal-notched
   Triple-T Concave-base

13 Large Side-notched
   Northern Side-notched
   (Bitterroot Side-notched)
   Hawken Side-notched
   Rocker Side-notched
   Sudden Side-notched
   San Raphael Side-notched
14 Cascade
15 Large unnamed stemmed
16 Large stemmed
   (Great Basin Stemmed Series)
   Lake Mohave
   Silver Lake
   Parman Series
   Windust
17 Haskett 1 and 2
18 Scottsbluff
19 Folsom
20 Clovis

Fig. 3. Temporal distributions of recognized Great Basin projectile point types. Projectile point outlines are placed on dashed lines, representing temporal span, at the times of maximum popularity. This chart is a generalization; in any given area within the Great Basin, the types present and their temporal occurrence may vary.

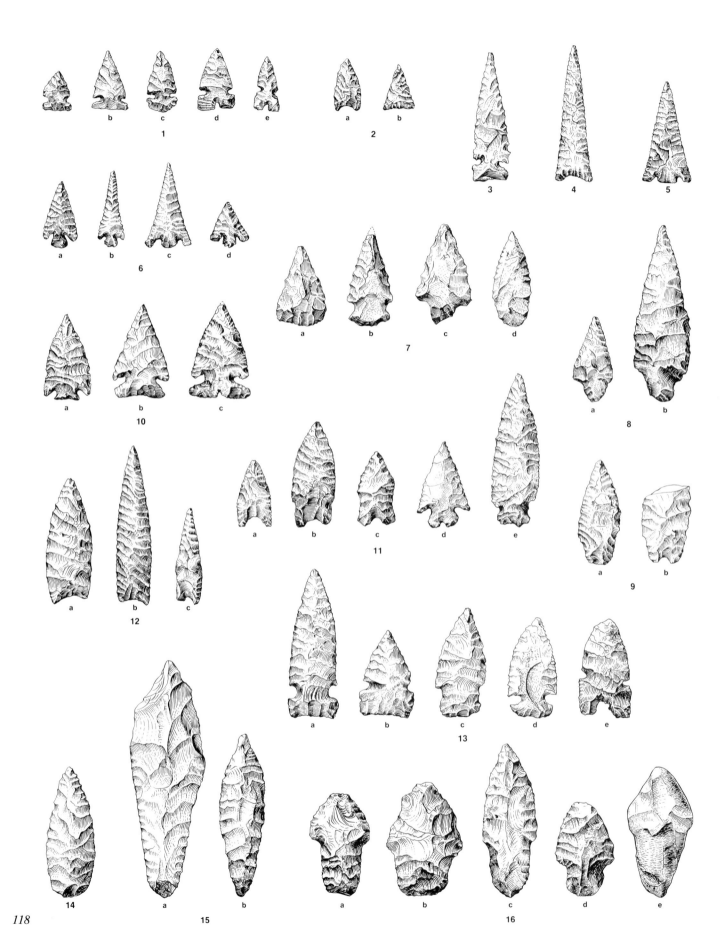

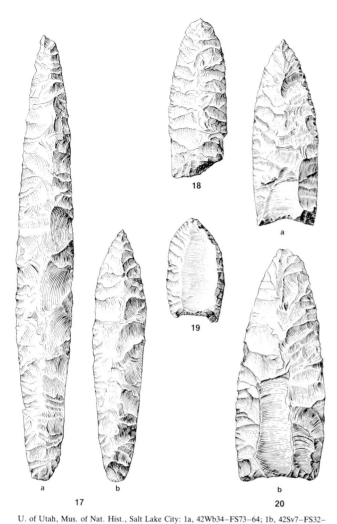

U. of Utah, Mus. of Nat. Hist., Salt Lake City: 1a, 42Wb34–FS73–64; 1b, 42Sv7–FS32–5142; 1c, 42Md180–FS225–V16; 1d, 4aBo268–FS226–127; 1e, 42Bo36–FS46–23; 3, 42Md180–FS289–111; 4, 42Ga34–FS425–1; 5, 42In124–FS208–8; 6a, 420Bo36–FS452–23; 6b, 42Wn420–FS27–12; 6c, 42In124–FS50–53; 8a, 42Wn420–FS843–11; 8b, 42Wn420–FS477w–5; 9a; 9b, 425V6–FST539–7; 10a, 42Bo36–FS717–43; 10b, 42Bo36–FS701–258; 10c, 42Bo36–FS39–11; 11a, 42Bo365–FS53–166; 12b, 42Bo365–FS48–4; 13c, 425V6–FS988–5; 13e, 48Sw101–FS779–3. Nev. State Mus., Carson City: 2a, 1403–G–678; 2b, 10–A–2; 6d, 42–B–036; 7a, 38–G–5207; 7b, 2395–G–859; 7c, 2395–G–2662; 7d, 235/0; 11b, 23109/3; 11c, 1003/26; 11d, 23350/1; 11e, 10–A–1; 12a, 22934/5; 12c, 1403–G–635; 13a, 23081/15; 13b, 1085–57; 13d, 23018/2; 15a, 50; 15b, 55; 16a, 1514–G–3; 16b, 819–G–134c; 16c, A92; 20a, 26Wa00/501; 20b, 26Wa00/500. 14, after Bedwell 1973:fig.12, P3; 16d–e, after Amsden 1937:pls.42, b, 41c; 17a–b, after Butler 1965:fig.9e, h; 18, after E.M. Davis 1962:fig.24; 19, after Butler 1978:fig.33.

Fig. 4. Great Basin projectile point types. Illustrated specimens show the range of morphological attributes subsumed under the type labels. Types are arranged from left to right as latest to earliest; the numbers refer to the key in fig. 3. Length of 10b 3.8 cm, rest same scale.

better control over the timing of such events, better grasp of the ecological problems confronting prehistoric populations can be expected with consequent improvement in the interpretations of perceived behavior; however, the correlation of climate and behavior will never be as close as archeologists might want. It is certain that a continued effort to intensify and refine the reconstruction of aspects of paleoecology other than the climate will be made. Here one would hope for fuller inventories of the species available and the conditions of their availability during any climatic regime, if this is indeed possible. The answers to most of the questions lie in imaginative research designs aimed at specific problems followed by intelligent and broad-spectrum field research.

Probably the most thorough effort toward the assessment of previous research in Great Basin prehistory and the projection of future needs in theory and method is provided by the collection edited by Madsen and O'Connell (1982). However, this work poses some problems that are directly relevant to the preceding discussion of Great Basin prehistory and research. The editors identify four emphases that have characterized research: the environment, cultural chronology, culture history, and settlement-subsistence patterns. Though they predict that these concerns will continue to be important, they also point out that the approaches are primarily descriptive and provide little explanatory power. It is suggested in summary critical review that "optimal foraging theory" might be the basis for a useful data synthesis (O'Connell, Jones, and Simms 1982:233–235). Some caution is in order here. The theory as posited argues that foragers collect those foods that offer the greatest amount of energy for the consumer with minimum energy expended on the gathering and processing effort. This is, essentially, the mechanical minimum effort–maximum gain model familiar to economists restated as a biological evolutionary model ("evolutionary ecology"). The theory is circular, and it is not clear what explanations it will offer to Great Basin archeologists, except that certain resources might have been favored while others were neglected. A more useful and appropriate theory needs to be developed and applied to Great Basin research.

Prehistory of the Northern Area

LUTHER S. CRESSMAN

Landforms and Environment

In contrast to the western and eastern sections of the Great Basin, each of which is dominated by a massive lake basin, the northern area consists of a series of smaller basins formed by displaced fault blocks (fig. 1). They are separated by highlands or mountains in the east ranging to over 9,000 feet in elevation. Each basin, with the exception of Klamath Lake basin on the extreme west, was the location of a pluvial lake. Large springs at the base of the escarpments of Summer, Abert, and Catlow basins provide dependable water from deep aquifers exposed by faulting. The region extends from the Cascade Mountains at 122° west longitude to the Owyhee Uplands at about 118° west longitude. On the north the Great Basin meets the Columbia Plateau at about 43° north latitude.

The alternating highlands and valley basins supported flora and fauna ranging from Upper Sonoran to Arctic-Alpine types on the Steens mountain range, providing a series of ecosystems centered on the lake basins. During postglacial climatic fluctuations, many species gradually shifted upward from their Pleistocene levels to reach a maximum elevation in the Altithermal and then to move somewhat lower again in the Medithermal. The highlands provided springs and in some cases small perennial streams that drained into the basins and probably persisted through even the warmest and driest phases of postglacial time (Cressman et al. 1942; Cressman 1956; Bedwell 1970).

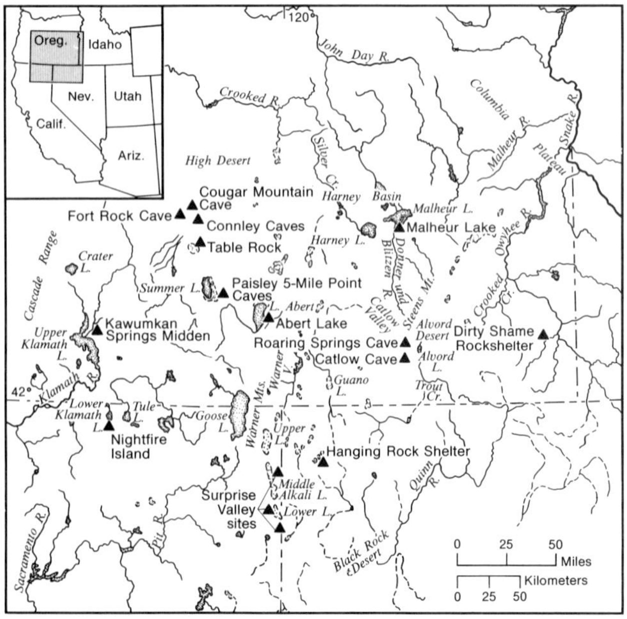

The Archeological Record

An interdisciplinary program of excavation in the northern Basin was conducted by Cressman and others from 1932 to 1940 (J.C. Merriam 1939). The program was extended to the Upper Klamath Lake area in 1947–1949 and 1951. Important sites excavated during this period were Catlow Cave (fig. 2) and Roaring Springs Cave in the Catlow Valley of east-central Oregon, the Paisley Five-Mile Point Caves (fig. 3) near Summer

Oreg. State Mus. of Anthr., Eugene: 12–10.
Fig. 2. Catlow Cave No. 1, a large overhang cut by Pleistocene lake wave action against the western escarpment of Steens Mountain, Catlow Valley, south-central Oreg. Wave-cut terraces can be seen on the slope below the cave. The cave faces southwest, and is just over 30 m wide at the mouth, 18 m deep, and 15 m high from the talus to the top of the overhang. The northern portion of the cave, choked with roof debris, held moisture by capillary action of the rocks, and failed to produce any quantity of perishable materials. Elsewhere in the cave deposits, preservation was good, with a perishables inventory that included basketry, matting, sandals, twine, rope, and fragments of leather. Semicircular windbreaks of piled up stones from roof fall attest to the windy conditions encountered in a high, broad, open cave by aboriginal inhabitants. Photographed in the 1930s.

Fig. 1. Selected archeological sites in the northern Great Basin.

Fig. 3. View from outside the mouth of Paisley 5-Mile Point Cave No. 1 across Summer Lake to the west. The escarpment in the distance is the Winter Rim, ethnographic boundary of the Northern Paiute and Klamath. The cave lies on a terrace on the west face of the scoriacious basalt east rim of Summer Lake. The entrance is 6 m tall and 4–5 m wide. The swing frame at right was used to support a large screen for sifting cultural deposits. Cultural stratigraphy preserved 2 definable occupations separated by a thick layer of Mt. Mazama ash, placing human presence in the area well before the eruption about 5000 B.C. Photographed by Luther S. Cressman, 1938.

Lake in south-central Oregon, and Fort Rock Cave (fig. 4) in the Fort Rock Valley northwest of Summer Lake. Extensive observations were also made of surface remains together with excavations to ascertain the stratigraphic position of materials eroding from exposed sediments at Lower Klamath Lake, in extreme south-central Oregon, and excavations were conducted at Ka-

Fig. 4. Inspection of Fort Rock Cave, Oreg., prior to testing in 1937, led by Luther Cressman. Excavation in 1938 showed a long occupation antedating the Mt. Mazama eruption about 5000 B.C. Excavation in 1966–1967 (Bedwell 1970) discovered a hearth radiocarbon dated at 11,200 B.C. ±720, the earliest well-documented evidence of man in the northern Great Basin. Photograph by Luther S. Cressman, 1937.

wumkan Springs Midden and village near Upper Klamath Lake (Cressman et al. 1942; Cressman 1956).

This program demonstrated that: the Northern Great Basin was occupied by humans at the same time as horse (*Equus*), camel, and bison (fig. 5) (Cressman et al. 1942, 1966); occupation had been continuous to historic time but intensity of occupation varied, probably due to climatic change; the Anathermal, Altithermal, and Medithermal climatic sequence defined by Antevs (1948) could be used as a working chronological device; palynology in conjunction with Antevs's climatic change model could provide a relative chronology; volcanic ash layers could provide valuable time-horizon markers; and the regional technology was highly developed in lithic manufacture and in fabrication of twined basketry and sandals. All dating, however, was relative.

In 1966 and 1967 further work was undertaken in Fort Rock Basin. This basin provided a situation unique in Great Basin studies: a series of six adjacent caves and rockshelters in the Connley Hills, and two other caves (Fort Rock and Cougar Mountain Cave No. 2) situated about 10 to 12 miles from each other and from the Connley Hills series. All were occupied concurrently, each contained a layer of Mount Mazama ash providing a common stratigraphic referent, and each yielded radiocarbon dates. With this evidence an absolute chronology was established in Northern Great Basin.

The cultural and paleo-environmental data preserved in the pluvial Fort Rock Lake basin serve as controls and referents for the development of stone tool technology in the northern Great Basin area (Bedwell 1970; Bedwell and Cressman 1971). Four periods of differing occupational intensity were established through statistical examination.

Period 1, 12,000–9000 B.C.

Bifacial flaking (by percussion) is typical. The two projectile points are unnotched specimens of different kinds. The blade-and-core technique appears to have been used; probably burins were known. Gravers and scrapers were part of the inventory. At this time pine trees identified as probably *Pinus edulis* or *P. monophylla* are documented from the Connley Caves charcoal, and grasses are known from opal phytoliths. A mano from the period is probably associated with the preparation of pine and grass seeds for food. All artifacts, except for use-reworked flakes, come from a hearth dated 11,250 B.C. ± 700 that was found under a rockfall at Fort Rock Cave.

Period 2, 9000–6000 B.C.

Seven different types of projectile points appear, one with a concave base continuing from Period 1. All points 121

Period 3, which terminates with the eruption of Mount Mazama (now Crater Lake) at about 5050 B.C., is marked by a decreasing use of the rockshelters; climate indicators suggest desiccation as the cause. Ground stone tools are represented by two manos and one mortar. A significant change in the lithic assemblage occurs with the appearance of the corner-notched projectile point. For the period as a whole, some 50 percent of all points are corner-notched, and two specimens are side-notched. A corner-notched point of basalt from the Klamath Lake area is also documented from before the Mount Mazama eruption (Cressman 1956:fig. 41, 6).

A change in stone flaking technology also occurs in this period. While the previous method continues, with flake scars at right angles to the long axis of the points, a technique of flaking at an oblique angle now appears in which the scar slopes toward the base. Analysis of flake scars indicates that this change may signify the appearance of pressure flaking. The points generally decrease in size, and a bone flaking tool appears. Use-reworked flakes make up 51 percent of the inventory knives and scrapers in Period 2 but 73 percent in Period 3.

A marked change occurs in the percentage of materials used for stone tools; in Period 2 basalt comprised 37 percent and obsidian 53 percent, but in Period 3 basalt drops to 8 percent and obsidian rises to 89 percent, a ratio carrying through the final period.

A cultural hiatus between 5000 and 3000 B.C. in the cave sequence does not represent abandonment of the country, only of the low-lying lake bed area. An infant burial dated at 3270 B.C. ± 210 from Table Rock Site No. 2 indicates that there was a population using the surrounding upland area. Further, Fagan (1973) has argued that springs at higher elevations in the eastern part of the area were occupied during the Altithermal and that their inhabitants carried on the lithic traditions of Period 3.

Period 4, 3000–1000 B.C.

Period 4 is correlated with the ameliorating Medithermal climate. A slender corner-notched projectile point type represents 70 percent of all points in this period, and 89 percent of all studied specimens of this type occur here; the remaining 11 percent occur in Period 3. Pressure flaking is dominant, represented on 56 percent of all points, as compared with 29 percent for Period 3 and 12 percent for Period 2. Textiles occur as grave goods. The rest of the lithic inventory is that common to the Great Basin for the period. In general, the lithic assemblage shows a continuation and amplification of the traditions of Period 3.

Statistical analysis indicates that the assemblages of

Oreg. State Mus. of Anthr., Eugene.

Fig. 5. Extinct faunal remains found with tools in Paisley 5-Mile Point Cave No. 3, Summer Lake area, south-central Oreg. Recovered fauna include horse and camel (presumed to have been extinct prior to the Holocene), bison, mountain sheep, wolf, fox, perhaps bear, and various modern bird species. a, fragments of worked obsidian; b, pieces of carbonized sagebrush; c. broken and partially worked long bones; d, unworked faunal remains. This association of man and extinct fauna implies human occupation prior to the Early Postpluvial defined by Antevs (1936) or pre-8000 B.C. (Cressman 1966; Cressman et al. 1942). Length of d bottom 24.0 cm, rest same scale.

are unnotched, and basal edges are typically ground. The large lanceolate Haskett point first appears at this time ("Prehistory: Introduction," fig. 3, this vol.). Multiple fluting on two points appears to be a thinning device; a single flake was removed for this purpose on the concave base points in this and the preceding period. This method of flake removal is not fully comparable to the technique observed elsewhere on Clovis Fluted points. The use of the core-and-blade technique is indicated, and flaking appears to be mostly by percussion. Manos, gravers, knives, scrapers, anvil stones, and the usual assortment of stoneworking tools occur. This is the period of the woven sandals from Fort Rock Cave and of basketry with false embroidery. The period represents the climax of cultural development in the Fort Rock Basin.

Period 2 shows a continued development of techniques and specimens found in period 1. Improvement in workmanship and modification of point types, suggesting experimentation with improved hafting methods, was the vogue. Successful adaptation to a favorable habitat is clear, and what change occurs appears to be internal and developmental.

each period differed from those of the preceding periods and that the resemblance between Periods 3 and 4 was closer than that between 3 and 2 and between 2 and 1.

The most important class of perishable artifacts was twined basketry, called Catlow Twine. Almost every variety of twining occurs, following a tradition of slanting the pitch of the weft stitch down to the right. Adovasio (1970) suggests that the northern Great Basin is the place of origin of this textile tradition; at any rate it is the place of highest development. It is not a part of the historic Northern Paiute inventory, but certainly the historic Klamath basketry is lineally descended from the fine basketry of the prehistoric period. Twining as a method of fabrication of textile products was a well-developed skill by 7000 B.C. as shown by the dated Fort Rock sandal (figs. 6–7), and there is a reasonable certainty that fragments of twined

Oreg. State Mus. of Anthr., Eugene: 12–735.

Fig. 6. Fort Rock Cave stratigraphy showing layers of ash, pumice, and occupation debris consisting largely of basketry and matting fragments. Two sandals (tag 7) are embedded in the silty basal layer of occupation. This layer yielded a radiocarbon date of 8200 B.C. ±230. An eroded hearth is atop a sterile layer of water-worn sand and gravel just below the sandal layer dated 11,200 B.C. ±720. Tag 5 marks the bottom of the ashy occupation layer resting on Mt. Mazama pumice; tag 6 marks the bottom of that bed. Definite cultural occupation below Mazama Ash at Fort Rock Cave and at Paisley 5-Mile Point enabled Cressman to establish the antiquity of humans in the northern Great Basin, a position substantiated by radiocarbon dating. Photographed 1935–1937.

Oreg. State Mus. of Anthr., Eugene: a, 1–31699; b, 1–33612.

Fig. 7. Fort Rock type sandals of twisted sagebrush bark shreds, of the type shown in the stratigraphic profile in fig. 6, radiocarbon dated at 8200 B.C. ±230. Front and back of a different sandal in each pair are shown. Soles are rectangular in outline, flat, and of uniform width. The sandals have no heel pocket but do have a squared toe flap. They were held to the foot by a long strap wound around the ankle several times and tied at either side of the sole. Other examples of sandal types from the Fort Rock area are in "Prehistoric Basketry," fig. 5, this vol. Length of bottom 24.0 cm, other same scale.

basketry with false embroidery were properly associated with the sandal and, therefore, carry the same date (Cressman 1951:308).

Additions to the Record

Logically, a Period 5, after 1000 B.C., should ensue to account for the remainder of prehistoric time in the Fort Rock basin. It is clear from the presence of late projectile point styles in the Connley Caves assemblages, and from surface sites in the area, that human occupation continued. But digging by vandals in the upper levels of the Connley Caves stirred or removed the deposits of the last 3,000 years, and no stratigraphically controlled and dated record of this period has been obtained for the Fort Rock area.

Excavations at Dirty Shame Rockshelter, in the far southeastern corner of Oregon, produced a record of human activity dated between 7500 B.C. and A.D. 1600 that supports the sequence from the Fort Rock Valley and extends it up to latest prehistoric times (Aikens, Cole, and Stuckenrath 1977). Projectile points from Zones 6 and 5, radiocarbon-dated between 7500 and 4500 B.C., included Lake Mojave, Windust, Northern Side-notched, Humboldt Basal-notched, Elko Eared, Elko Corner-notched, and Pinto Willowleaf types. Zones 4 and 3, which span the period from approximately 4500 to 3900 B.C., produced Humboldt Basal-notched,

Northern Side-notched, Elko Eared, Elko Corner-notched, and Wendover Side-notched types. At this point in the sequence the site was abandoned for over 3,000 years. The record resumed with Zone 2, dated between 800 B.C. and A.D. 800. Within this zone, excavation uncovered a series of circular pole-and-thatch huts or windscreens (fig. 8). Diagnostic artifacts include Eastgate- and Rose Spring arrowpoints. Zone 1, which accumulated between A.D. 800 and 1600, contained the same types, and in addition specimens of the Pinto and Desert Side-notched varieties. The data for the last 2,800 years at Dirty Shame Rockshelter complete the record of the final three millennia of prehistoric time that was not documented by the Fort Rock Valley studies.

The long persistence of individual northern Great Basin projectile point types, first documented in the Fort Rock Valley sequence, is borne out by the evidence from Dirty Shame Rockshelter. Supportive results have also been developed using the obsidian hydration method on a large series of points from Hanging Rock Shelter in extreme northwestern Nevada (Layton 1970), while stratigraphic and radiocarbon dating evidence from Surprise Valley in northeastern California (O'Connell 1971, 1975) lead to a similar conclusion.

Cressman's (1966a) assertion of the essentially stable character of the northern Great Basin culture over long periods of time is reinforced by the Dirty Shame data as reported by Hanes (1977:11). The few changes noted probably indicate some shifts in the relative intensity of certain activities at Dirty Shame, but they do not suggest any fundamental cultural changes.

The evidence from Dirty Shame Rockshelter also aids in understanding the chronology of the important Catlow and Roaring Springs Cave assemblages, which provided so much of the concrete picture of early northern Great Basin culture developed by Cressman et al. (1942) but which were excavated long before the radiocarbon dating method was developed and could not be fixed closely in time. Sandals of the Fort Rock type, and two related varieties referred to as Spiral Weft and Multiple Warp types, occur at both Dirty Shame Rockshelter and Catlow Cave ("Prehistoric Basketry," fig. 5, this vol.). The Fort Rock and Spiral Weft types at Dirty Shame are dated between 7500 and 3900 B.C. Further, projectile points of the Northern Side-notched, Elko Eared, Elko Corner-notched, Pinto Square-shouldered, Rose Spring Side-notched, and Desert Side-notched types also occur in both assemblages. The close parallels between the two sites suggest that Catlow Cave, like Dirty Shame, was probably occupied from about 7500 B.C. down to late prehistoric times. Roaring Springs Cave contained most of the same artifact types, but the Fort Rock sandal, earliest of the three kinds of footwear, is not present there, while the Multiple Warp type, latest of the three, is predominant. A span of occupation dating from about 4000 B.C. to late prehis-

124

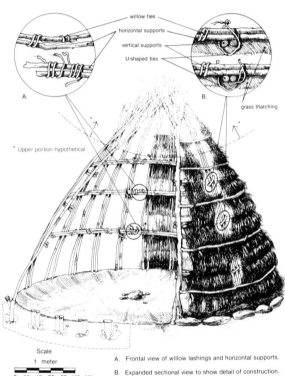

top, Oreg. State Mus. of Anthr., Eugene; bottom, Willig 1982.

Fig. 8. Pole-and-thatch dwellings exposed at Dirty Shame Rockshelter, southeastern Oreg. top, Set in a shallow alcove in a high rhyolitic cliff overhanging Antelope Creek, this structure is one of a series of perhaps 6 similar dwellings radiocarbon dated at 625 B.C. ±80 to A.D. 890±95. Paired vertical willow branches were placed at intervals around a shallow, dish-shaped depression about 5 m in maximum diameter, forming a circular framework. Bundles of grass, laid horizontally, were then attached by U-shaped willow pins to these uprights. Another layer of bundled thatch, set vertically, was shingled over the horizontal bundles by tucking upper ends under or into the lower bundles. Rock slabs placed around the perimeter anchored the superstructure. The doorway was probably on the east. The vertical willow branches may have been drawn together to form a dome or left upright, forming a simple windbreak. bottom, Reconstruction of dwelling. Aikens, Cole, and Stuckenrath (1977) suggest these structures were quite similar to ethnographic Northern Paiute dwellings (cf. Wheat 1967).

toric times is suggested for Roaring Springs Cave on the basis of these comparisons.

As in the Fort Rock Valley, human occupation ceased at Dirty Shame for a long interval of mid-Holocene time, between about 3900 and 800 B.C. The dates do not match precisely the dates conventionally assigned to the Altithermal period; nevertheless, it seems evident that warming or drying of the climate contributed to rendering both localities unprofitable for human exploitation for long spans of time.

An important aspect of early Great Basin lifeways is the extent to which lakeside adaptations flourished in certain times and places, giving rise to relatively sedentary settlements quite different from the largely temporary camps first investigated by archeologists. Many sites have been located around Malheur Lake, in east-central Oregon, of which at least two have been demonstrated to have deep middens rich in artifacts and food-bone debris (Newman 1974; Campbell 1980). One of these displayed a number of depressions on the surface, and test excavations indicated an occupation floor, suggesting that the depression may have been the base of a light semisubterranean structure. On the Blitzen River, a few miles away, test excavations revealed another apparent house floor associated with much bone refuse of marshland species (Fagan 1973).

Along the shore of Abert Lake, in south-central Oregon, intensive survey and limited excavation have brought to light a large series of sites, some displaying boulder-outlined house patterns on the surface, others with depressions that test excavations revealed to contain artifacts and occupation floors (Pettigrew 1980). Radiocarbon dates and projectile point cross-dating suggest that this occupation may have begun as early as 2500 B.C. and persisted until around A.D. 1500. Lake Abert is now a mineral-rich "dead sea," but clearly was, at times in the past, a productive freshwater lake attractive to human occupants.

Work in the Klamath country has also extended knowledge of prehistoric occupation there. The rich site at Nightfire Island, on the edge of Lower Klamath Lake, gives a record of waterside adaptation spanning the period from about 4000 B.C. to A.D. 1000 or later (Sampson 1985). Abundant faunal remains indicate Nightfire Island's importance as a fowling and fishing station throughout later Holocene time, and the occurrence of clay-lined pit house floors gives evidence that the site was occupied on a permanent or semipermanent basis between about 2300 and 1000 B.C. After 1000 B.C. lighter structures, perhaps signaling less intensive occupation, seem to have been in use, but significant exploitation of the locality continued until the site was abandoned some time after A.D. 1000. The site supports the interpretation of long-term waterside adaptation in the Klamath country that was arrived at by Cressman (1956) on the basis of work at Kawumkan Springs Midden but

Oreg. State Mus. of Anthr., Eugene: a, 1–10,001; b, 1–10,000; c, 1–7476; d, 1–7416; e, 1–8751.

Fig. 9. Atlatls, bow, and projectile shaft fragments recovered from Roaring Springs Cave, Oreg. a–b, atlatls with carved fingerholds and spurs; both were painted red and embellished by rows of white dots down the length of the board. Both may have had leather thongs tied over the carved fingerholds ("Prehistory of the Western Area," fig. 6, this vol.). For a more detailed description 32 of Great Basin atlatl assemblages see "Prehistory of the Southwestern Area," fig. 5, this vol. c–d, limb fragments of a finely made sinew-backed bow; remnants of sinew wrapping are lapped over the nocks on the belly of the bow. e, the nock end of a painted arrow, retaining sinew wraps at the nock and the points of feather attachment. Length of a, 60.0 cm, rest same scale.

adds many significant details and dimensions to the overall picture.

Finally, research in the Steens Mountain region of east-central Oregon has begun to measure systematically the extent to which the climatic and environmental fluctuations of Holocene time affected patterns of human occupation and settlement over a broad region through the millennia since the end of the glacial age (Aikens, Grayson, and Mehringer 1982). Multidisciplinary research has brought together pollen and sedimentary evidence from lake cores, site survey data, and the results of archeological excavation in a concerted attack on the problem; results indicate clearly the importance of environmental parameters in shaping patterns of human land-use in the region.

Subsistence

Subsistence patterns show no fundamental change through the entire record of occupation in the northern Great Basin deserts. The lake basin highland ecosystem provided a variety of faunal and floral resources within a relatively narrow compass. Climatic changes simply shifted biotic distributions, although in some cases earlier life forms became extinct and new ones, characteristic of a more arid environment, appeared. The large Pleistocene fauna, *Equus*, camel, *Bison* sp., and mammoth, early became extinct. In the Fort Rock Basin, piñon pine and the turkey, both identified from the Connley Caves, did not survive the dessication and the Mount Mazama eruption.* Elk, deer, and bison all continued as potential food resources and were used. The presence of manos in all periods at the Fort Rock Basin shelters reveals seed grinding as a method of food preparation as far back as 11,250 B.C. (Bedwell 1970). Given the ecosystem of the northern Great Basin, it is likely that the basic ethnographically known patterns of transhumance was already in use at the time of the first occupation of the caves. It then developed and increased its efficiency under the pressures of changing climatic conditions.

The economic development of the Klamath Lakes region shows an early emphasis on hunting similar to the basic early Great Basin pattern, and then an effective adaptation to the riverine, marsh, and lake environment. The riches of the food resources and the effective methods of exploitation made possible pit house villages and permanent settlements. Similar developments appear to have been present, at least during some periods, around Abert Lake and Malheur Lake as well.

Areal Relations

During the climax period, probably between 8500 and 7000 B.C., a far-flung similarity of artifacts and lithic fabricating techniques occurred from southeastern Washington, the Lower Snake River, and the middle

---

*Mehringer (1977) has questioned the identification of piñon pine on ecological grounds, while Grayson (1979) has questioned the identification of turkey on both ecological and osteological grounds. The charred wood from Connley Caves was originally identified by Robert C. Koppen, while the bird bones were identified by Robert W. Storer and Joseph G. Strauch, Jr.

Columbia River in the Plateau area in the north; through the Upper Snake and Salmon River region, the Northern, Western, and Southwestern areas of the Great Basin; to the San Diego County vicinity of the California culture area. Both ends of the Central Valley of California are also included. Obviously, historical connection of some sort along the eastern flanks of the Cascade-Sierra ranges is indicated. Bedwell (1970:23) proposed the name Western Pluvial Lakes tradition for this cultural manifestation.

Apparently by about 7000 B.C. the contact between the Columbia River drainage and the northern Great Basin began to lessen. The inhabitants of the former area were becoming more oriented economically toward the river system with the development of fishing techniques and the founding of their salmon economy. Likewise, in the Great Basin the development of economic and technological efficiency in exploitation of plant foods and small game made those activities a focus of attention. Under these circumstances major regional differences became accentuated. The Northern and Western Great Basin cultures seem to share much before 6000 B.C. and at the same time to differ somewhat from the Eastern. Thereafter, the Desert culture is common to the entire Great Basin with, of course, local but significant variations in certain components, such as textiles. The eastern part of the northern Great Basin (Catlow Valley Caves) seems to have had more contact with the Lovelock Cave area and the eastern Great Basin than did the Fort Rock Lake basin.

The prehistory of the Northern Great Basin is one of continuity and change in a distinctive ecosystem with changing climate. Cultural continuity is shown in the persistence of lithic and textile traditions and of subsistence patterns; change in the introduction of new methods of stone flaking, projectile point types, and some borrowed elements of culture.

The final stage of northern Great Basin prehistory is the occupation of all but the Klamath Lake area by the Numic-speaking Northern Paiute probably shortly after A.D. 1000. The archeological record is so far silent on this phase. Perhaps some few pottery sherds from Catlow Cave belong there (Cressman et al. 1942). The Northern Paiute tale of driving the Klamath westward (Kelly 1932) and the Tenino account (Ray et al. 1938) of fighting and driving back the Paiutes from the Columbia River area may be distant echoes of this last population expansion.

Prehistory of the Snake and Salmon River Area

B. ROBERT BUTLER

The cultural Great Basin extends beyond the physiographic Great Basin and includes portions of other physiographic provinces, such as the Columbia Plateau and the Rocky Mountains. The Upper Snake and Salmon River region serves as a natural corridor linking the northwestern Plains with the Intermontane area, a geographic position clearly reflected in the region's shifting cultural affiliations with the adjoining areas through time (fig. 1). These shifts appear to coincide with certain long-term trends and pronounced cycles in the regional climate as well as with the prevailing forms of large game animals. For example, an extinct form of elephant (*Mammuthus* sp.) was still to be found on the eastern Snake River Plain as late as 9000 B.C. (S.J. Miller 1982), and an extinct bison (*B. antiquus*) continued to occur in large numbers on the Plain until at least 6000 B.C., after which it was succeeded by the modern form of bison (*B. bison*) (Butler 1978a). Thus, although an Archaic way of life had already emerged in the physiographic Great Basin by 8000 B.C., big game hunting continued to be an important focal point in the cultures of peoples inhabiting the Upper Snake and Salmon River country long after that time. It was not until around 5800 B.C. that Archaic cultures became evident in the region. Even then, at least two different patterns were involved, one related to the Plains Archaic and the other to the Basin Archaic.

Systematic archeological investigation began in the region only in 1958. Highly stratified cave and rockshelter sites were selected for study because of their potential for yielding a broad range of biological and geological data bearing on the environment of the Upper Snake and Salmon River country and man's relation to it through time. One overriding concern was determining the antiquity of the Northern Shoshone in the region (Swanson 1972); another was elucidating the natural and cultural relationships between this region and the northwestern Plains and the Great Basin; and a third was establishing a reliably dated regional sequence to which an abundance of isolated cultural materials and components could be tied. A logical outcome of this approach to the prehistory of the region was the delineation of local cultural phases largely in terms of changes in the natural deposits, faunal remains, and projectile point styles supported by a modest number of radiocarbon dates (for example, Swanson 1972). For pur-

poses of synthesizing a regional sequence, the local phases can be grouped into three broad periods conventionally labeled, from earliest to latest, Early Big Game Hunting, Archaic, and Late. Each of these periods, in turn, can be divided into subperiods that embrace surface finds and isolated components, as well as materials recovered from the highly stratified cave and rockshelter sites.

Early Big Game Hunting Period, About 12,500–5800 B.C.

The hallmark of this period was the hunting of big-game animals that became extinct during the terminal phase of the Late Pleistocene or in the early Holocene. Chief among these were the elephants (*Mammuthus* sp.) and certain species of bison, especially *B. antiquus*. Also hunted were camel (*Camelops* sp.), horse (*Equus* sp.), mountain sheep (*Ovis* sp.), elk (*Cervus* sp.), and deer (*Odocoileus* sp.), some of which, including the mountain sheep, elk, and deer, were replaced by modern forms of the same animal that were hunted into the

Fig. 1. Archeological sites of the Upper Snake and Salmon River area.

127

Historic period. Others, such as the camel and horse, became extinct before the end of the Early Big Game Hunting period. Presumably, other foods were sought and utilized along with these big-game species. As Wedel (1978:190) has pointed out, the term "early big-game hunters" reflects what is believed

> about one of the principal activities of the early Plains people—the food quest. No implication is intended that their subsistence economy did not also include the seasonal or opportunistic use of vegetal products, small game, and perhaps other comestibles that may have been available from time to time but of which neither direct nor indirect evidence has yet been recognized in the material culture inventory as now known. The qualifier "early" distinguishes these ancient Americans from the later bison hunters of post-Altithermal times.

It is the forms of the game animals hunted and the distinctive spearpoints associated with the kills that are most conspicuous in the archeological record. On the basis of point types alone, the Early Big Game Hunting period can be divided into three subperiods—Clovis, Folsom, and Plano, a sequence that is characteristic of the early big-game hunting core area on the northwestern Plains (Jennings 1974) and of the Upper Snake and Salmon River country (Butler 1978a), but not of the Great Basin as a whole.

Clovis Subperiod, about 10,000–9000 B.C.

Evidence bearing on the Clovis subperiod in the Upper Snake and Salmon River country is of two kinds. One consists of cave deposits dating from this time period that contain indications of human activity but are lacking in diagnostic artifacts. Jaguar Cave, a limestone cavity in the mountains along the Continental Divide north of the Snake River Plain (Sadek-Kooros 1966), is a case in point. The butchered remains of 268 individual sheep larger than present-day mountain sheep were recovered from deposits ranging in age from 9580 B.C. ± 250 to 8320 B.C. ± 350 (Wright and Miller 1976). There were no chipped stone tools associated with the sheep remains; however, there were remains of domesticated dogs enclosed in the same deposits (Lawrence 1967). The presence of the dogs may indicate that dogs were employed in the hunting of wild sheep at least as early as 9000 B.C., presumably by the same peoples who hunted elephants on the open plains using spears tipped with Clovis fluted points. Examples of such points have been found in and around the eastern Snake River Plain, sometimes in apparent association with elephant remains (Butler 1978). None has been found in wholly undisturbed contexts.

The most striking Clovis find consists of 26–30 chipped stone bifaces accidentally uncovered at the Simon site near Fairfield, Idaho, at the foot of the Rocky Mountains northwest of Wilson Butte Cave (Butler 1963).

Among the bifaces was a series of finely made Clovis points closely resembling those found on the northwestern Plains (Butler 1963). Although a few biface fragments were subsequently found in place, no radiocarbon or other datable materials were ever recovered from the site. A similar cache of Clovis points and bifaces was discovered a decade later in Montana (Lahren and Bonnichsen 1974), but a detailed description of the discovery has yet to be published. Construction of fishponds along the Snake River below Twin Falls during the early 1980s has resulted in the extensive disturbance of deposits containing well-made Clovis points (Kelly Murphey, personal communication 1982). Curiously, neither Folsom nor Plano points have been noted at these sites.

Folsom Subperiod, about 9000–8600 B.C.

The Folsom subperiod is represented in the Upper Snake and Salmon River country by a combination of abundant widespread surface finds and a single well-excavated radiocarbon-dated component at a deeply infilled, highly stratified lava tube called Owl Cave (fig. 2) on the eastern Snake River Plain 120 miles northeast of Wilson Butte Cave (Butler 1978; S.J. Miller 1982). The component in question was found in the lowermost part of the lava tube, well below an 8,000-year-old *Bison antiquus* kill from which a series of Late Plano points were recovered. It consisted of a modest array of bone and stone tools, including parts of four Folsom points, and the remains of elephant, bison, and camel, all typical of the Late Pleistocene fauna found elsewhere on the eastern Snake River Plain (S.J. Miller 1982). Several radiocarbon determinations were made of the big-game animal bone associated with this component, ranging from 10,850 B.C. ± 150 to 8920 B.C. ± 150. Of these, the date of 8920 B.C. ± 150 is probably the most reliable (Butler 1978). Whatever the case, the Folsom occupation at Owl Cave clearly overlaps in time with the strong evidence of mountain sheep hunting found at Jaguar Cave. Thus, mountain sheep hunting would appear to have been characteristic of the entire time of human occupation in the region, for there is continuing evidence of mountain sheep hunting to be found through all subsequent prehistoric periods, including the Plano subperiod.

Plano Subperiod, about 8600–5800 B.C.

Of all the Early Big Game Hunting subperiods, the Plano is the most abundantly represented in the region, both in terms of surface finds and of excavated sites; it is also the longest lived. As on the northwestern Plains, there is a diversity of point forms and an occasional milling stone, for example, Wilson Butte II (Gruhn

Fig. 2. The Wasden site (Owl Cave), which held the butchered remains of *Bison antiquus* representing at least 2 separate episodes of human activity. Recovered diagnostic artifacts include Folsom and late Plano point types. top, Cave opening. center, Stratigraphic section cut through accumulation of loess and fine sandy loam. "a" marks a thin band of Mt. Mazama ash (5000 B.C.). "b" is the level of the 8,000-year-old bison kills. The carrotlike features in the loess below both levels are ice-wedge casts. bottom, Partially exposed bison bones. Photographs by B. Robert Butler, 1960–1966.

1961). However, the typical tool kit consists almost entirely of projectile points and is clearly oriented toward big-game hunting, especially bison (Butler 1978). In addition to bison (probably all *B. antiquus*, but the modern form, *B. bison*, may have begun to evolve locally), mountain sheep remains are common at sites in the higher mountain valleys surrounding the Snake River Plain, for example, levels 29–30 at Veratic Cave in Birch Creek Valley (Swanson 1972: table 18). On the basis of the accompanying projectile points alone, the Plano subperiod can be divided into two successive phases, Early and Late Plano.

Among the most remarkable of the Late Plano manifestations in the region is the sequence of well-preserved *Bison antiquus* kills that occurred at Owl Cave approximately 6000 B.C. (fig. 2), when the Archaic was already manifest in the physiographic Basin province. The complete skeletons of more than 70 individual bison, including bulls, cows, and calves of differing ages, comprise the sequence of kills (Butler, Gildersleeve, and Sommers 1971). Analysis of the under three-year-old bison jaws, along with the fetal remains, revealed that at least two separate kills were involved, one just before the onset of the calving season and one just after. A similar seasonal pattern is also evident in late Plano bison kills on the northwestern Plains (George C. Frison, personal communication 1978).

Apparently, each of the Owl Cave kills resulted from a well-planned and coordinated undertaking in which herds of 30 or more *Bison antiquus* were induced or driven into the cave, dispatched with spear thrust into the body cavities, and then systematically butchered. Individual bison were split open, the haunches detached, stripped of meat and stacked left and right: the head was detached and the lower jaw and tongue removed. Occasionally, a hole was chipped into the base of the skull and the brain removed, perhaps for later use in tanning the hides. Minute fragments of stone knives were evident in the many cut marks on the bones, but no such knives or other butchering tools were found among the skeletal remains; a single nasal-bone flesher and about 30 projectile points comprise the recovered tool kit (Butler 1978). The points were of a nondescript, generally lanceolate form, made from a variety of locally available materials, including basalt, chalcedony, and opalized wood. Two were reworked butt fragments of Birch Creek points (Butler 1978), a type characteristic of the earliest period of occupation at Veratic Cave, estimated to have ended around 6200 B.C. (Swanson 1972).

The Archaic Period, 5800 B.C. to A.D. 500

Shortly after 6000 B.C. the lanceolate spear points characteristic of the Plano period as a whole were almost completely replaced by new point forms characteristic of the Archaic period on the northwestern Plains as well as in the Great Basin ("Prehistory: Introduction," fig. 3, this vol.). These included the side-notched points found in the later occupations at Veratic Cave (locally referred to as Bitterroot and elsewhere as Northern side-notched; Swanson 1972) and the stemmed-indented base points in the layers immediately overlying the *Bison antiquus* kills at Owl Cave (Butler 1978) and the Wilson Butte III assemblage at Wilson Butte Cave (Gruhn 1961). However, the bulk of the tool kit remained essentially unchanged, at least at the more heavily utilized hunting sites in Birch Creek Valley (Swanson 1972). Thus, the Archaic in the Upper Snake and Salmon River country does not represent a major break with the Early Big Game Hunting period. Willey and Phillips (1958:107) define the Archaic in the Upper Snake and Salmon River country as "the stage of migratory hunting and gathering cultures continuing into environmental conditions approximating those of the present."

Although the horse, camel, and elephant had become extinct by this time, the modern forms of bison and mountain sheep had emerged and replaced the older forms in the region. The transition from Early Big Game Hunting to Archaic may have taken place while the modern forms of big game were evolving. In the archeological record, it mainly involved the appearance of a new weapon system, the atlatl and dart. The atlatl is inferred from the presence of the new types of points, particularly the stemmed-indented base and the larger side-notched, which are presumably dart rather than spear points. These may represent two different versions of the atlatl, one from the Basin represented by the stemmed-indented base points and one from the northwestern Plains represented by the large side-notched points (Gruhn 1961).

On the Snake River Plain, the older of these appears to be the stemmed-indented base form. It shows up in the deposits immediately overlying the last of the Plano points at Owl Cave, radiocarbon dated at 5750 B.C. ± 210 (Butler 1978) and also in the first post-Plano assemblage at Wilson Butte Cave, radiocarbon dated at 4890 B.C. ± 300 (Gruhn 1961). No large side-notched points occur at Owl Cave; however, they are characteristic of Wilson Butte IV, an assemblage estimated to date from about 4500 B.C. (Gruhn 1961). On the other hand, the earliest post-Plano point form at Veratic Cave (figs. 3–4) is the large side-notched type estimated to date from 6200 B.C (Swanson 1972), roughly contemporaneous with points of the same general type recovered from the Simonsen *Bison occidentalis* kill, an early Plains Archaic site in northwest Iowa (Wedel 1978).

Although a small number of stemmed-indented base and other Archaic point types occur in the succeeding Bitterroot phase occupations at Veratic Cave, the large side-notched type continues to be characteristic at that site until about 1450 B.C. (Swanson 1972). It is also

Fig. 3. View of Bison (at left) and Veratic (at right) Rockshelters, east-central Idaho. The overhangs were formed by the erosive action of Birch Creek in the limestone western face of the Bitterroot Mountains. Shelters open to the southwest, situated 3–6 m above the valley floor at an elevation of about 6,000 feet. Cultural deposits at Veratic Rockshelter are radiocarbon dated from 5222 B.C. ±229 to A.D. 1520 ±80, and at Bison Rockshelter, from 8340 B.C. ±850 to A.D. 1070±75. An extensive cultural inventory, consisting predominantly of stone artifacts and bone tools and scrap, was laid down in separable layers of occupation, interfingered with alluvial deposition, sandy loams, gravels, and episodes of rock fall. The stratigraphic record from these sites offered keys to the climatic history of the Birch Creek Valley, forming the basis for the definition of the Bitterroot phase, which Swanson (1972) proposed as ancestral to the ethnographic Northern Shoshone, a tradition of 8,000 years (see also Swanson 1962a; Swanson, Butler, and Bonnichsen 1964). Photograph by B. Robert Butler, 1960.

characteristic of the post-Plano occupations at high spring sites in the mountains north of the Snake River Plain (Richard Harrison, personal communication 1981).

South of the Snake River Plain at sites such as the Weston Canyon rockshelter, a highly stratified mountain sheep hunting station overlooking an arm of Lake Bonneville, there was an apparent alternation of occupations beginning as early as 6000 B.C. dominated first by stemmed-indented base points and then by large side-notched points, with the large side-notched points the predominant form between about 5800 and 3500 B.C. After 3500 B.C. another Basin point type, the Humboldt concave base, was dominant for a period of time (S.J. Miller 1972).

Another feature of the Archaic pattern in western Idaho is a distinctive burial pattern called the Western Idaho Burial complex (Pavesic 1983). The best-known site is the Braden burial site (Butler 1980; Harten 1980) near Weiser, Idaho (figs. 5–6). The burial offerings include large bifacially worked blades, some with distinctive notchings called "turkey tails;" large corner-notched points; large side-notched points; obsidian preforms; and red ocher. The complex dates around 2000–4000 B.C. and is contemporaneous with the early large pit houses at Givens Hot Springs. Whether the burial complex and pit houses are related is not known.

Although no Early Archaic houses have been found in the Upper Snake and Salmon River country, evi-

Fig. 4. Exploratory trench at Veratic Rockshelter, cut parallel to the cliff face and in line with the flow of alluvial sediments. Excavation was expanded by cutting blocks in toward the cliff, with deposits removed in natural levels first defined in the stratigraphic profile of the trench. Temporary blocks were left to preserve a record of site stratigraphy during the removal of excavation levels. Photograph by B. Robert Butler, 1960.

dence from excavations at Givens Hot Springs on the Snake River in southwestern Idaho indicates that large semisubterranean houses were being built there by at least 2300 B.C. (T.J. Green 1982). The houses are six to eight meters in diameter and have floors over one-half meter deep and multiple roof supports. Large side-notched and Humboldt concave base projectile points were found together on the house floors. Other artifacts

Fig. 5. The Braden site. This cache of obsidian blanks and preforms covering a large chalcedony turkey-tail point is part of the diagnostic artifacts indicative of Pavesic's (1983) Western Idaho Burial complex. Photograph by B. Robert Butler, 1968.

included large hopper mortars, knives, awls, and scrapers. Later Archaic houses date around 400 B.C. and have Elko series projectile points in association with hopper mortars and other artifacts. These appear to have been occupied seasonally during the winter; deer, rabbits, and river mussels (*Gonidea angulata*) are the most common food remains. There is no evidence to suggest that any of these houses represent the remains of large semipermanent villages. Evidence from survey and excavation indicates a pattern of groups of two or three houses each scattered up and down the Snake River Valley and the lower reaches of the major tributary streams in western Idaho. Extensive survey and testing in the upper Payette River drainage have yet to locate any house structures in the mountainous areas of the region (Ames 1982a).

Thus, there appear to be two distinctly different Archaic patterns in southern Idaho, one derived from the Plains and the other from the Basin. The former was dominant throughout much of southern Idaho and may have evolved into a Formative stage culture during the Late period.

The Late Period, A.D. 500–1805

More is known about the Late than any other period in southern Idaho prehistory, yet it remains the most perplexing. At least two distinctive sets of cultural manifestations are present, the Northern Fremont (a Formative stage culture) and the Shoshonean (an Archaic stage culture). These follow each other in time as they do in Utah ("Fremont Cultures," this vol.); however, the Northern Fremont persists to a much later date in southern Idaho than in northern Utah (Butler 1983).

Far less evidence of the northern Fremont has been found in southern Idaho than in the immediate vicinity of Great Salt Lake. This may be due to a much lower population level there than in northern Utah, though why that should be so is not clear, as similar food resources are found in both areas. Compounding the problem is the fact that Fremont material remains have gone unrecognized in southern Idaho or have been mistakenly identified as Shoshonean, as occurred in the case of the material remains recovered from Stratum A at Wilson Butte Cave. The latter formed one of the two components comprising the Dietrich phase in south-central Idaho; the other came from Pence-Duerig Cave (Gruhn 1961) and included fragments of several kinds of basketry identified as Fremont (Adovasio 1970). The Dietrich phase materials were originally believed to be Shoshonean, largely on the basis of an erroneous identification of the pottery recovered (Gruhn 1961). This pottery, called Wilson Butte Plain ware, was said to be Shoshonean when, in fact, it was Great Salt Lake Gray ware (Butler 1981). It is but one of a series of Great

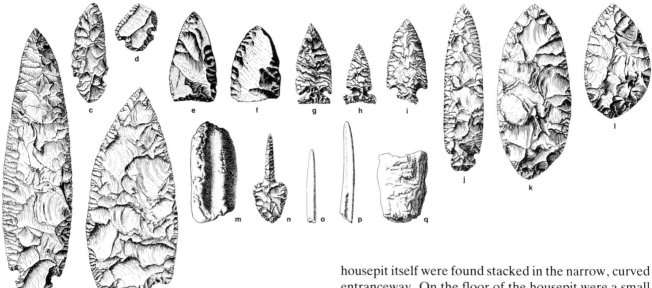

after Butler 1980:figs. 10–12.

Fig. 6. Diagnostic artifacts of the Western Idaho Burial complex recovered from the Braden site. a–b, Turkey-tail points; c–d, turkey-tail side and end scrapers; e–f, triangular obsidian blanks; g–h, side-notched points; i–j, large end-notched silica mineral points; k–l, ovate silica mineral blanks; m, stone abrader; n, stone drill or awl; o, bone point or awl; p, beaver incisor fragment; q, antler haft or socket. Length of a 22.0 cm, rest same scale.

Salt Lake Gray ware finds made in situ in the Upper Snake and Salmon River country (fig. 7). However, most of the others were not recovered from radiocarbon dated contexts. Among these is a sequence of Great Salt Lake Gray ware sherds recovered from a stratified housepit of uncertain size and shape at the Clover Creek site on the Snake River near King Hill (Butler 1982). The housepit deposits have not been radiocarbon dated, but on the basis of associated projectile point types, are estimated to have accumulated between A.D. 500 and 1350 (Richard N. Holmer, personal communication 1982), which would make them earlier than the Dietrich phase component at Wilson Butte Cave, radiocarbon dated at A.D. 1525 ± 150.

Great Salt Lake Gray ware pottery was also recovered from the entranceway of an undated, shallow, subrectangular housepit measuring 2.2 by 4.0 meters at the foot of Kanaka Rapids, some 35 miles up the Snake River from the Clover Creek site. There were vertical postholes around the perimeter of the housepit, as well as in the center of the pit, and a series of rock-lined cache pits at the upstream end of the housepit, from which sherds of Great Salt Lake Gray ware were recovered, along with a mano, pestle, several large, thick, ovoid bifaces, and a stone ball. The sherds from the

housepit itself were found stacked in the narrow, curved entranceway. On the floor of the housepit were a small scattering of projectile points and flake tools and parts of a "killed" pestle (Butler and Murphey 1983). The "killed" pestle on the floor of the house and the potsherds stacked in the entranceway of the house may indicate that the house had been abandoned as a result of the death of one of its occupants.

Great Salt Lake Gray pottery was also recovered from the single, circular, semisubterranean housepit at 10-EL-216, an open site on a broad, low terrace next to the Snake River a few miles upstream from the Clo-

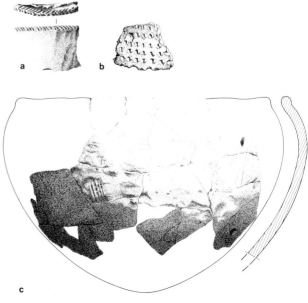

after Butler 1983:figs. 5, 7.

Fig. 7. Great Salt Lake Gray Ware sherds and vessel found in Idaho. a, Sherd from a stratum radiocarbon dated at A.D. 1525 ± 150 at Wilson Butte Cave; b, punctate sherd from the Dean site; c, bowl collected from the American Reservoir locality. Diameter of bowl about 29.0 cm, rest same scale.

ver Creek site. A few pieces of chipping detritus and a battered fragment of a Rose Spring corner-notched point were the only other artifacts recovered from the housepit; no radiocarbon datable materials were recovered (Butler and Murphey 1982).

Other Late period houses have been located farther west in southern Idaho. At Givens Hot Springs, three structures were located that date around A.D. 800 (T.J. Green 1982). These structures contained Rosegate projectile points, but no pottery. The largest structure was seven meters in diameter and 50 centimeters deep. It had a central roof support with beams radiating from the post to the edge of the pit. The roof was made of ryegrass thatch and was probably covered with dirt. Four mortars were excavated into the floor of the structure, and there were a central hearth and roasting pit. The other two structures at Givens Hot Springs dating to this time period were smaller (about 4.5 meters in diameter) and had saucer-shaped depressions.

Just upstream from Givens Hot Springs, at Swan Falls (10-AA-17), a small house was excavated containing Rose Spring projectile points and a few unidentifiable pottery sherds (Ames 1982). It was three meters in diameter with a shallow floor, and the roof of the structure was thatched with ryegrass. Mortars were excavated into the floor.

At Big Foot Bar (10-AA-166), an oval-shaped house approximately three by four meters in area and 30 centimeters deep was excavated. Small postholes were found around the perimeter of the structure, and Desert side-notched and Cottonwood projectile points were found in the house fill (Plew 1980a).

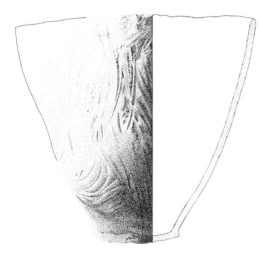

after Butler 1983:fig. 9.

Fig. 8. Flat-bottomed Shoshonean jar with characteristic flanged base and flowerpot shape. This pottery, also referred to as Intermountain Tradition pottery (Tuohy 1956; Coale 1963), shows a blend of Plains techniques (molding and patching, with coiling) and Basin techniques (paddle and anvil, with coiling and molding) (Butler 1983). An irregular undulating surface is common. Diameter 22.1 cm.

All the Late period structures from western Idaho, with the exception of a large semisubterranean house at Givens Hot Springs, are small wickiup-sized structures similar to those occurring after 1000 B.C. in Surprise Valley, California (O'Connell 1975). Their relationship to the Fremont culture and the Dietrich phase in south-central Idaho cannot be determined at this time.

However, if the dating of the Dietrich phase component at Wilson Butte Cave is correct, the Great Salt Lake Fremont may have survived far longer in southern Idaho than in northern Utah, where it was displaced by the culture of Numic-speaking peoples in the fourteenth century (Madsen 1975). Theoretically, the Numic speakers also should have expanded into southern Idaho in the fourteenth century, but there is no solid evidence of their presence in the region at that time. The earliest definite evidence of the Shoshone in eastern Idaho is the material culture remains comprising the Lemhi phase in Birch Creek Valley (Swanson 1972), which dates from the Early Historic period, about A.D. 1805–1840 (Butler 1981). However, it is very likely that small groups of Shoshone in northern Utah were extending their food-collecting activities into Idaho south of the Snake River Plain as early as the middle of the fifteenth century, with the main surge of Shoshone occupation coming in the late eighteenth century after their displacement from the High Plains by the newly horse-mounted and armed Blackfoot (Butler 1982a).

Because no evidence of Fremont culture has been found beyond the northern fringes of the Snake River Plain, there is a question as to what was happening in the region lying between the Snake River Plain and the Salmon River in central Idaho prior to occupation by the Shoshone in historic times. One possibility, based on a thin body of evidence recovered from caves and rockshelter sites in Birch Creek Valley, is that certain peoples on the northwestern Plains, moving along the Rocky Mountains after A.D. 300, may have extended their hunting territory across the Continental Divide into the mountains north of the Snake River Plain (Butler 1982a). It may have been the movement of these peoples, possibly ancestors of the Southern Athapaskans, that led to an infusion of Plains elements into the Great Salt Lake Fremont.

At present, there are no satisfactory explanations for the emergence of the Great Salt Lake Fremont, nor for its eventual demise or displacement. There is also no satisfactory explanation for the relatively rapid expansion of Numic-speaking peoples into areas formerly occupied by the Fremont and ultimately onto the northwestern Plains, where they became as much at home as they were in the western Great Basin. The two problems are closely interrelated; some writers (for example, O'Connell, Jones, and Simms 1982) have suggested that they are best solved by utilizing a model drawn from optimal foraging theory—those food-gathering efforts that produce the greatest return relative to time and effort expended will be favored over those that are less efficient. That model has been implicit in most of the archeological studies carried out in the Upper Snake and Salmon River country.

Summary

The archeological record in the Upper Snake and Salmon River country extends back to at least 12,500 B.C. by radiocarbon count. It reveals a considerable parallel if not direct relationship with the sequence of Early Big Game Hunting and big-game hunting weaponry and facilities found on the northwestern Plains. That is, the Upper Snake and Salmon River country appears to have functioned as a natural extension of the northwestern Plains west of the Continental Divide and as a corridor connecting the northwestern Plains area with the Intermontane area. Only with the advent of Shoshonean occupation, which began perhaps no earlier than the middle of the fifteenth century, can the region as a whole be viewed as a subarea of the Great Basin culture area. Prior to that, only the southern part of the region, from the foothills of the Northern Rockies southward, can be seen as an extension of the Great Basin, and mainly of the eastern part of the Basin, in which the Great Salt Lake Fremont flourished after A.D. 500. Thus, the Upper Snake and Salmon River country stands as a unique region within the Intermontane area, connected as much to the northwestern Plains as to the Great Basin.

Prehistory of the Western Area

ROBERT G. ELSTON

The development of the present chronological framework for the western Great Basin is discussed in Hester (1973), Heizer and Hester (1978a, 1978b), Thomas (1981), and J.O. Davis (1982). The framework is based on various geochronological data that have allowed the identification of temporally sensitive artifact types, including styles of basketry, marine shell beads, pottery, and projectile points (fig. 1). The projectile point chronology has the finest resolution, in large part because of the stratigraphic sequence from Gatecliff Shelter in central Nevada (Thomas 1981, 1983a).

Prior to the 1970s, archeological studies and dates tended to be site specific. With the advent of the regional approach to archeological research and the requirements of large-scale cultural resource management projects, it became necessary for archeologists to attempt broader correlations, which in turn required a more interdisciplinary interest in Quaternary stratigraphy, pedology, geomorphology, fossil pollen, and plant and animal macrofossils. Studies of this sort have made it possible to understand something of previous ecological systems and to determine the relative ages of land forms and provide fairly accurate limiting dates for various surfaces and deposits, along with the archeological remains on and in them.

Environment

The western Great Basin, as defined here, includes most of Nevada and parts of California along the Sierra Ne-

vada, which evidence suggests has been occupied for 11,000–12,000 years. It is divided into three subregions on the basis of differences in ecology and culture history: the central subregion, the Lahontan Basin, and the eastern slope of the Sierra Nevada (fig. 2).

Central Subregion

The central subregion of the western Great Basin lies between the Bonneville and Lahontan basins. It is characterized by long, roughly north-south trending mountain ranges and intervening valleys. Average elevation is the highest in the entire Great Basin: valley floors are all over 5,500 feet above sea level, and the mountains typically reach elevations above 10,000 feet. Vegetation is dominated by brush and grass communities with piñon-juniper woodland superimposed at middle elevations (although piñon is not found north of the Humboldt River). Sagebrush is the dominant species in the north; shadscale, in the south.

Lahontan Basin

The Lahontan Basin is the lowest area of northern Nevada and contains the sinks of all major streams in the western Great Basin. In the Pleistocene the Lahontan Basin was occupied by ancient Lake Lahontan. Because of the orographic effect of the Sierra Nevada, it is quite arid and contains a large area in which annual precipitation is less than four inches. Higher elevations just

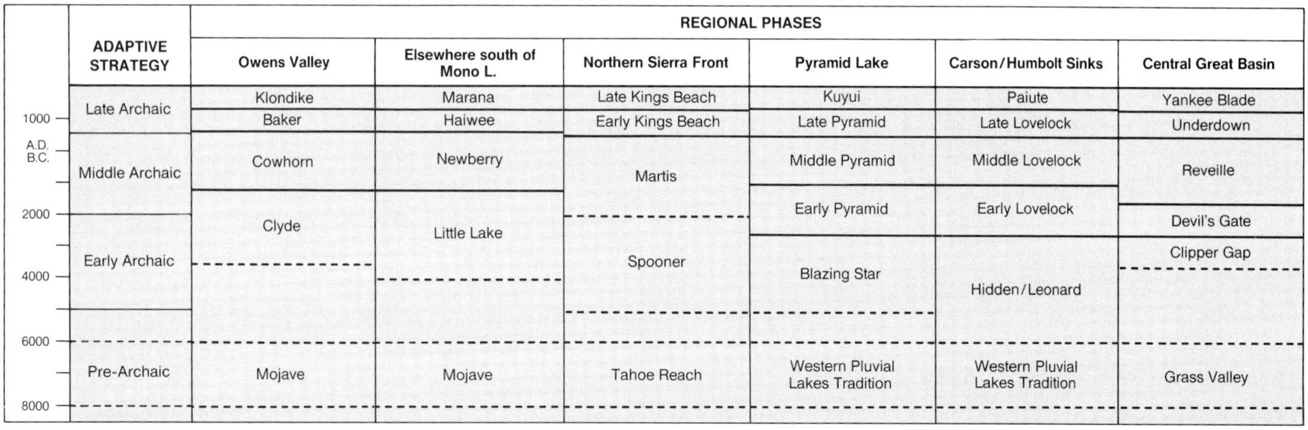

	ADAPTIVE STRATEGY	REGIONAL PHASES					
		Owens Valley	Elsewhere south of Mono L.	Northern Sierra Front	Pyramid Lake	Carson/Humbolt Sinks	Central Great Basin
1000	Late Archaic	Klondike	Marana	Late Kings Beach	Kuyui	Paiute	Yankee Blade
A.D. B.C.		Baker	Haiwee	Early Kings Beach	Late Pyramid	Late Lovelock	Underdown
	Middle Archaic	Cowhorn	Newberry	Martis	Middle Pyramid	Middle Lovelock	Reveille
2000		Clyde	Little Lake		Early Pyramid	Early Lovelock	Devil's Gate
4000	Early Archaic			Spooner	Blazing Star	Hidden/Leonard	Clipper Gap
6000							
	Pre-Archaic	Mojave	Mojave	Tahoe Reach	Western Pluvial Lakes Tradition	Western Pluvial Lakes Tradition	Grass Valley
8000							

Fig. 1. Chronological subdivisions of western Great Basin prehistory.

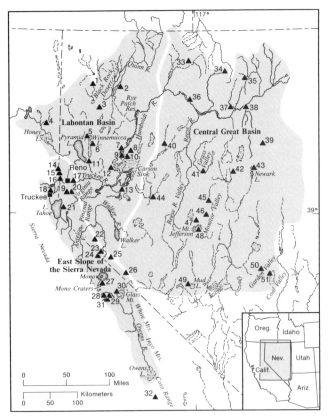

Fig. 2. Archeological sites and localities in the Western Great Basin. Lahontan Basin: 1, Silent Snake Springs; 2, Barrel Springs; 3, Trego Hot Springs; 4, Karlo; 5, Falcon Hill, Kramer Cave, Coleman locality; 6, Guano Cave, Cowbone Cave; 7, Granite Point locality; 8, Leonard Rockshelter; 9, Humboldt Lakebed; 10, Lovelock Cave; 11, Pyramid Lake burial, Marble Bluff locality; 12, Cocanour locality; 13, Hidden Cave, Hanging Rock Cave, Grimes Point. Eastern Slope of the Sierra Nevada: 14, Hallelujah Junction; 15, Bordertown; 16, Peavine Mountain; 17, Vista; 18, Alder Hill; 19, Steamboat Hills; 20, Steamboat Hot Springs locality; 21, Spooner Lake; 22, Pine Grove Hills; 23, Borealis locality; 24, Bodie Hills; 25, Mount Hicks; 26, Queen; 27, Mono Craters; 28, Casa Diablo; 29, Hot Creek Shelters; 30, Glass Mountain; 31, Mammoth Creek Cave; 32, Sugarloaf Mountain. Central Great Basin: 33, Ezra's Retreat; 34, Rossi Mine locality; 35, Saval Ranch; 36, Valmy; 37, James Creek Shelter; 38, South Fork Shelter; 39, Bronco Charlie Cave; 40, Painted Cave; 41, Horse Pasture Village; 42, Mount Hope; 43, Newark Cave; 44, Wagon Jack Shelter, Eastgate Cave, Marjo Shelter; 45, Toquima Cave; 46, Gatecliff Shelter; 47, Triple T Shelter; 48, Alta Toquima Village; 49, Lowe Shelter; 50, Slivovitz Shelter; 51, Civa Shelter II.

east of the Sierra Nevada support piñon-juniper woodland, but other upland areas are barren and treeless. The dominant vegetation throughout most of the region is sagebrush and shadscale. Extensive marshlands are found where major streams discharge into lakes and sinks.

East Slope of the Sierra Nevada

In addition to the Sierras, the East Slope subregion includes the valleys and mountain ranges to the east. In the southern end of the subregion, Owens Valley is a long, narrow trough, flanked by the steep escarpments of the Inyo and White mountains on the east and the Sierra Nevada on the west. All three ranges reach elevations of greater than 14,000 feet.

Both the valley floor and the Inyo-White mountains are in the Sierran rain shadow and are relatively dry. The valley floor is covered by desert shrubs and grasses except along the Owens River where riparian plants predominate. In the Sierra Nevada, a thin, discontinuous band of piñon-juniper woodland occurs below the coniferous forest of higher elevations. In the White and Inyo mountains, piñon-juniper woodland exists as a continuous zone to about 8,500 feet, above which are sagebrush and grass communities intermixed with stands of bristlecone and limber pine.

North of Owens Valley and south of Antelope Valley are a series of high basins including Long Valley Caldera, Mono Basin, and Bridgeport Valley. All are above 6,000 feet and are cold and snowbound all winter. The volcanism of this region has created a great deal of obsidian that was quarried at Bodie Hills, Queen, Mono Craters, Glass Mountain, and Casa Diablo (Bettinger 1982: fig. 17). Obsidian was also obtained from Sugarloaf Mountain in the Coso Range south of Owens Valley (Elston and Zeier 1984).

Farther north, the Sierra is broader, lower, and broken by block faulting and warping into a series of smaller ranges and intermontane basins such as the Tahoe Basin, the Truckee Basin, and Sierra Valley. These valleys are fairly low and could be occupied in mild winters. Valleys along the Sierra front are all traversed by the major streams draining the east slope, and they contained extensive wet meadows and riverine marshes. Piñon pine is found on all the ranges immediately east of the Sierra but does not extend north of the Truckee River.

Postglacial climatic and environmental changes have long been conceived in terms of Antevs's (1948) tripartite scheme, wherein the early Holocene (Anathermal) was cool and moist, the mid-Holocene (Altithermal) was hot and dry, and the late Holocene (Medithermal) roughly like today. Though generally consistent with recent evidence, this scheme is now recognized as too simple and does not accommodate phenomena such as large-scale, relatively short-term climatic events, seasonal variation in rainfall, or nonclimatic environmental change (volcanic activity, stream diversion or the dynamic interaction between the hydrology and geomorphology of lake basins), all of which may have been important to human populations (Mehringer 1977; J.O. Davis 1982; Weide 1982). It is also important to recognize that prehistoric Great Basin environments cannot be conceived in terms of modern plant communities with somewhat different distributions. At the end of the Pleistocene, and for nearly the first half of the Holocene, the types and distribution of Great Basin plants were very much different from today; changes of perhaps lesser magnitude have occurred up to the present time and are still in progress.

Changing Adaptive Strategies

Major divisions of western Great Basin prehistory are made on the basis of change in adaptive strategy, the most profound of which separates Pre-Archaic and Archaic. The Archaic itself is divided into three parts by changes of lesser magnitude. The most likely explanations for these changes involve some combination of local population pressure, environmental change, and possibly migration (Elston 1982; O'Connell, Jones, and Simms 1982).

Detailed treatment of the Pre-Archaic is given in volume 3 of this series, but its salient features are as follows. There are a few buried Pre-Archaic sites in the western Great Basin, but most are found on the surface. They range in size from an isolated artifact or two to scatters of artifacts that cover many acres. Pre-Archaic lithic technology is highly distinctive: it resembles that of the megafauna-hunting Paleo-Indians of the Great Plains much more than later Archaic cultures of the Great Basin. Pre-Archaic assemblages contain large bifacial knives, stemmed and concave base projectile points with edge grinding, crescentic objects, gravers, punches, choppers, and several types of scrapers with steep, well-formed edges (fig. 3). Tools with combinations of functional units (scrapers and gravers) are common. Many Pre-Archaic tools are worn and extensively resharpened. Seed-grinding implements are extremely rare or absent in Pre-Archaic assemblages of the western Great Basin, although they are present in early assemblages in the northern and eastern areas (Aikens 1982; Madsen 1982).

There is not so much functional differentiation among Pre-Archaic sites as there is among sites of Archaic cultures. A few Pre-Archaic sites are quarry-workshops, but most are diffuse scatters of lithic tools and debitage that lack structural remains or other archeological features. The larger sites are located on gravel bars or other high ground; when occupied, these were near marshy deltas of streams feeding shallow lakes or on terraces adjacent to floodplain marshes of the Humboldt River. Upland sites are also known but are smaller.

These features have triggered some lively debate concerning the nature of the Pre-Archaic adaptive strategy and its links to the Archaic, particularly with regard to exploitation of lacustrine resources (Tuohy 1968, 1974; Baumhoff and Heizer 1965; Heizer and Baumhoff 1970; Bedwell 1973). Present evidence suggests that people in Pre-Archaic cultures hunted big game (probably including extinct megafauna), utilized smaller animals, and (by extension) probably consumed easily gathered

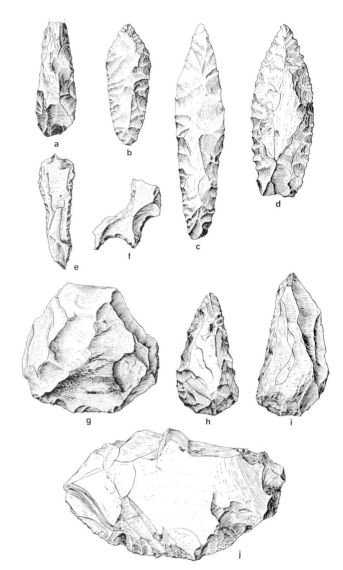

Nev. State Mus., Carson City: a, 2054; b, 52; c, 54; d, 2401; e, 2426; f, 2407; g, 2067; h, 2093; i, 1678; j, 2006.

Fig. 3. Sadmat site artifact assemblage, tools of a Pre-Archaic adaptation postulated to be closely related to the San Dieguito complex of the southwestern Great Basin (Tuohy 1968). Located in the Carson Sink, western Nevada, the site consists of a collection surface of about 2 square miles, littered with weathered tools and flaking debris. a, Leaf-shaped projectile point, bifacially flaked, highly polished and smoothed by exposure, with a broken tip. b, Lake Mohave type point, bifacially flaked basalt. c, Large, stemmed lanceolate point, bifacially flaked. d, Large, basally thinned, lanceolate basalt point with a serrated edge. e, Unifacially flaked chert blade, scraper-graver combination tool. f, Unifacially reduced chalcedony flake, multiple worked and retouched points and edges. g, Large, unifacially flaked core tool. h–i, Large, thick, triangular scrapers, unifacially percussion flaked, edges lightly retouched, plano-convex in cross-section. j, Large, bifacially flaked knife-chopper. Length of c 10.8 cm, rest same scale.

and processed lacustrine-marsh plant foods, such as cattail shoots, pollen, and green seeds. However, unlike people of Archaic cultures, they did not grind seeds, live on sites long enough to accumulate midden deposits, construct permanent structures, or store resources in facilities visible in the archeological record. However, it is good to remember that as intensive study of Pre-Archaic sites continues and more evidence accumulates, the Pre-Archaic adaptation is likely to appear more complex (R.L. Kelly 1978).

The transition to the Great Basin or Western Archaic (Jennings 1964, 1974; Elston 1982) was the major adaptive change in the western Great Basin, most likely in response to environmental variation and changing resources in the early Holocene. Compared to the Pre-Archaic adaptive strategy, the Archaic involves exploitation of a more diverse resource base, including the processing and storage of seeds. This was accomplished through the use of a more complex settlement pattern involving a home range or sequent home ranges (cf. Binford 1983; C.S. Fowler 1982), functional variation in site types (winter camps, seasonal base camps, task sites), and winter sedentism with substantial shelters and storage facilities. Hunting in the Archaic is often associated with game drives and ambushes using rock walls, lines of cairns, or brush fences. The production of rock art also begins in the Archaic and may be related to hunting cults or have served as territorial markers (T. Thomas 1983; Heizer and Baumhoff 1962; Nissen 1982; Dorn and Whitley 1983; Grant, Baird, and Pringle 1968).

Early Archaic

As the warming and drying trend of the early Holocene continued in the mid-Holocene, most of the lakes and marshes dried up. Brushy species such as shadscale, saltbush, and greasewood invaded lowland areas. Between 5000 and 3200 B.C., most precipitation fell in the summer (J.O. Davis 1982), probably promoting the advance of piñon-juniper woodland (dominated by juniper) into the western Great Basin where it arrived by 4000 B.C. (Thompson and Hattori 1983). Temperatures reached a maximum between 3100 and 2200 B.C., and Pyramid Lake may have been the only extant lake in western Nevada at this time (J.O. Davis 1982). After 2200 B.C. temperatures declined somewhat, and a series of shallow lakes may have appeared in the Carson Sink (Fallon Lakes of Morrison 1964), but Pyramid Lake seems to have remained low. Piñon-juniper woodland probably arrived at its northern limit along the Humboldt and Truckee rivers before 2000 B.C. (Madsen and Berry 1975; Thompson and Hattori 1983).

The origins of the Early Archaic in the western Great Basin are obscure since sites are rare and dates scarce. The Early Archaic apparently begins somewhat later in the west than in the north and east, sometime between 5000 and 4000 B.C. It does not become very visible in the archeological record until about 2500 B.C., and it terminates between 2000 and 1500 B.C.

Pinto and Gypsum projectile points (both subsumed in the Gatecliff series, Thomas 1981) and possibly Humboldt series points, all of which tipped atlatl darts, are diagnostic of the Early Archaic ("Prehistory: Introduction," fig. 3, this vol.). Although big game hunting remained a major focus of subsistence, projectile points and other hunting-related tools are smaller and less specialized than those of the Pre-Archaic. Intensive use of seeds processed with manos and metates as well as use of caves and rockshelters for the storage of goods and equipment are features of the Early Archaic.

There is a tendency for larger Early Archaic sites to be located in valley bottoms near permanent streams and springs possibly due to some specialization in lowland and riverine resources or as an adaptation to the warm, dry climate. However, uplands were also utilized. The scarcity of sites suggests that overall population was low, but the size of the few houses that have been excavated (Harrington 1957; Stanley, Page, and Shutler 1970) suggest that household groups could have been extended families.

Central Subregion

The earliest dated Archaic components in the central subregion are those of the first cultural strata in Triple T and Gatecliff shelters (figs. 4–5), both dated at about 3400 B.C. (Thomas 1983a), a few hundred years after the arrival of piñon-juniper woodland. These introduce the Clipper Gap phase (3500–2500 B.C.), marked by large, wide, concave-based Triple T projectile points (Pendleton 1979; Thomas 1981, 1983a). Population seems to have been quite low in the Clipper Gap phase, and very few sites of that age are known (Thomas 1982a:165). The small lithic scatters with large concave base points in Grass Valley, assigned by Clewlow and Pastron (1972) to the early Holocene, may actually belong to the Clipper Gap phase. The Clipper Gap strata of Gatecliff Shelter suggest occupation by small groups of hunters pursuing mountain sheep.

At Valmy on the Humboldt River (Elston et al. 1981; Rusco and Davis 1979), Humboldt points appear to mark a settlement or land use pattern in which the floodplain and valley floor were intensively used for hunting and, to a lesser degree, seed processing.

In central Nevada, the latter part of the Early Archaic is known as the Devils Gate phase (2550–1550 B.C.) and is marked by the use of Gatecliff series projectile points (Thomas 1981, 1983a, 1970). This series includes points with contracting stems that, in other places, have been called Gypsum or Elko Contracting Stem (Heizer and Baumhoff 1961), and bifurcated or split-stem points, elsewhere referred to as Pinto (Harrington 1957) ("Prehistory: Introduction," fig. 3, this vol.). Points of the Gatecliff series are relatively abundant in Reese River Valley and Monitor Valley (Thomas and Bettinger 1976;

Amer. Mus. of Nat. Hist., New York.

Fig. 4. Gatecliff Shelter (foreground), an overhang in the massive chert and dolomite Gatecliff Formation on the north side of Mill Canyon, Nev. On either side of the shelter are alluvial cones that head in chutes well above the site. This rocky debris periodically entered the shelter. Situated above an ephemeral stream, at an elevation of 2,319 m, the overhang served as a short term field camp, visited by hunting and plant-collecting task groups over the last 5,500 years. Excavations beginning in 1970 revealed 56 geologic strata and 11 separable cultural horizons spread out through 10 m of sediments that were laid down in a remarkably well-defined stratigraphic sequence. Dating of occupations is precise, with 46 radiocarbon assays and a layer of Mt. Mazama tephra. Photograph by Susan L. Bierwirth, 1975.

Amer. Mus. of Nat. Hist., New York.

Fig. 5. The deep stratigraphic sequence within Gatecliff Shelter. The alternating layers of colluvial rubble and fluvial beds of sand and silt are responsible for the varying colors and textures of the sediments, which demarcate different periods of geologic deposition. Photograph by Susan L. Bierwirth, 1978.

Thomas 1971a, 1983a), which to Thomas (1982a:165) indicates a sharp population increase and use of upland resources, possibly including the newly arrived piñon pine. If so, this may be a local phenomenon, since Gatecliff series points are not common in large-scale surveys of other areas such as the vicinity of Mount Hope (James and Elston 1983), the Saval Ranch (Crittenden and Elston 1981), Coal and Garden valleys (Busby 1979), and various valleys in White Pine County (James and Zeier 1981).

Lahontan Basin

Evidence for a transition between the Pre-Archaic and Early Archaic cultures of the Lahontan Basin subregion is as scant as it is in the central subregion. Although previously considered to be of Anathermal age, and the type site for the "Humboldt culture" (Heizer 1951; Roust and Clewlow 1968; Heizer and Hester 1978), work at Hidden Cave (Thomas 1970) failed to confirm such an early occupation. Evidence for the first part of the Early Archaic (Hidden phase or Carson phase in the Carson

Sink; Leonard culture in the Humboldt Sink) is also scarce.

There are very few cultural radiocarbon dates between 5300 and 3200 B.C.: 4780 B.C. from grass lining a cache pit at Shinners Site I in Falcon Hill, 4550 B.C. on organic debris from Guano Cave, and 3720 B.C. on a cedar-bark robe from a dessicated burial in Cowbone Cave, all at Winnemucca Lake (Heizer and Hester 1978b; Hattori 1982). An infant burial from Leonard Rockshelter was dated at 3787 B.C. (Grosscup 1958; Heizer and Hester 1978b). At the Silent Snake Springs site (Layton and Thomas 1979), located in the high rock country just outside the Lahontan Basin, occupation began at about 4100 B.C. when the site was used as a base camp for hunting, particularly mountain sheep.

After about 3000 B.C., evidence for occupation of the Lahontan Basin begins to increase. Intermittent use of

Lovelock Cave begins at about 2630 B.C., but intensive occupation there did not commence until 1500 B.C. Occupational episodes are thought to have coincided with high stands of Humboldt Lake (Heizer and Napton 1970:1–86).

Of particular interest are Kramer Cave in Falcon Hill at Winnemucca Lake (Hattori 1982) and Hidden Cave near Grimes point on the Carson Sink (Thomas 1970), both used intensively only at times when lakes occupied the Winnemucca Basin and Carson Sink and lacustrine-marsh resources appeared. Both were occupied during the period from about 1900 to 1600 B.C., and most projectile points from each site are in the Humboldt or Gatecliff series. These and other cave and rockshelter sites, such as Lovelock Cave and Hanging Rock Cave (Tuohy 1969), were seldom used as residential base camps, but rather for burials and as caches for equipment and goods to be used during the seasonal round. Consequently, they contained little debitage or food waste but large numbers of baskets, nets, fur and bird-skin robes, atlatls and darts (fig. 6), mats, cordage, and other perishable goods and equipment (fig. 7), finished

a–b, c (top 5), d, Nev. Histl. Soc., Reno; c (bottom 2), Nev. State Mus., Carson City: 15–A–12; 15–A–5.

Fig. 6. Atlatl, dart foreshafts, and carrying bag recovered from Cowbone Cave, Winnemucca Lake, western Nev. The pieces were wrapped in a fiber mat bundle tied with fiber cord (a). The atlatl is made from an unidentified dark brown hardwood, and its most distinctive features include a cylindrical piece of antler affixed to the proximal end behind a double leather thong finger grip, an elaborate, fiber-wrapped main grip, once completely inlaid with small feathers, and a keeled surface at the distal end carved to form a notch or hook for insertion of the concave base of the dart shaft (b). The central part of the throwing board is flat, sides parallel, except toward the distal end, where the shaft expands. A groove runs along the dorsal surface near the proximal end, interrupted by a small perforation that carries through to the ventral surface, and which, in conjunction with the groove, may have served for attachment of a weight. The wood foreshafts, some elaborately carved (c), would probably have tipped cane dart main shafts, the only part of the kit not recovered. Swollen proximal ends, some notched or spirally grooved, were shoved in the hollow cane shafts. Carved from a single hardwood shoot, the foreshaft tips are simple points, cones, and peculiar eyed hooks very like modern crochet hooks. The entire skin of a kit fox was used for a carrying bag, with only the posterior left open for insertion of foreshafts and atlatl. A number of atlatls have been found in the Great Basin (Loud and Harrington 1929; Cressman and Krieger 1940; Cressman 1944; Dalley and Peterson 1970; Tuohy 1982), but none is exactly like this specimen, nor were they found as a complete kit in so remarkable a state of preservation. The specimen shown is most similar to Basketmaker Anasazi examples from the Southwest in size, the presence of a dorsal groove in the distal portion of the board, and in having a double finger grip of leather thongs anchored over concave finger notches in the board. The antler section at the proximal end of the board is unique and appears to have served as a flaker for the manufacture and repair of stone projectile points. For the use of stone points with the Basin atlatl, as well as other items of the atlatl kit, and decoration, see "Prehistory of the Southwestern Area," fig. 5, this vol. Length of b 56.0 cm, c same scale; length of a about 58.0 cm, d same scale.

U. of Calif., Lowie Mus., Berkeley: 15–5509.

Fig. 7. Lovelock Cave, at the base of a concavity in a hinge fold of a massive limestone formation flanking the eastern margin of the Humboldt Sink, western Nev. The cavern, eroded by wave action of Pleistocene Lake Lahontan, overlooks the prehistorically rich marshes of the Humboldt Sink. The cave proved to be extraordinarily rich in perishable remains, cached there from about 2600 B.C. to A.D. 1850. Thousands of specimens were recovered in 1912, including human skeletal material and fiber artifacts (Loud and Harrington 1929), and in the 1960s, including chipped stone tools and bone and shell fragments (Heizer and Napton 1970). Reflecting the cave's marsh-side location, the artifact inventory contains tule duck decoys, fish nets, and fishhooks, as well as various baskets, basketry fragments, snares, and scapula and sheep horn sickles. Together with that of Humboldt Cave, the artifact assemblage from Lovelock Cave forms the basis of the Lovelock culture (2600 B.C.–A.D. 500), a prehistoric adaptation closely geared to extraction of the marsh resources of the Humboldt Sink (Cowan and Clewlow 1968; Heizer and Napton 1970). Photograph probably by Llewellyn L. Loud, about 1924.

lithic tools such as projectile points and knives, bone awls, and ornaments.

Residential base camps were open sites located around the margins of lakes and near permanent water. A single component site of this type is the Cocanour locality on the Humboldt Sink (Stanley, Page, and Shutler 1970) with two shallow, circular house depressions 2.4 to 3.4 meters in diameter, around which were scattered several manos and metates, Pinto points, some debitage, and large numbers of cores, choppers, bifaces, and scrapers. Small components of this age are suggested by the presence of a few diagnostic projectile points at sites such as the Humboldt Lakebed site (Cowan and Clewlow 1968), sites on the Humboldt River at Rye Patch Reservoir (Rusco et al. 1977; Rusco, Davis, and Firby 1979; Rusco and Davis 1982), the Karlo site (Riddell 1960) and the Trego Hot Springs site and other sites in the Black Rock Desert (Lohse 1980a; Seck 1980).

In spite of the excellent preservation in the dry deposits of caves and rockshelters, subsistence data for this period are sparse. A diet of fish, fowl, cattail seeds and shoots, and piñon nuts was revealed by analysis of coprolites from Hidden Cave (Roust 1967; Ambro 1967; Thomas 1970).

The presence of marine shell beads from many sites and obsidian from 22 different sources in western Nevada and California in Hidden Cave (Sappington 1985) indicates that trade and communication during the Early Archaic in the Lahontan Basin were well developed.

East Slope of the Sierra Nevada

As elsewhere, signs of the first portion of the Early Archaic are scarce. In the north, a date of 5150 B.C. from the Spooner Lake site (Elston 1971) is questionable, although Pinto points considered typical of the Spooner phase (5000–2000 B.C.) were recovered from the site (Elston 1971, 1979). Relatively small numbers of Pinto points are present at most residential base camps and larger field camps that also have later Martis components. Bettinger's (1975, 1977, 1977a, 1982; Bettinger and Taylor 1974) surveys of the Long Valley Caldera and Owens Valley show that Clyde phase (3500–1500 B.C.) residential base camps were located adjacent to rivers, while temporary field camps for hunting and gathering were in upland, desert scrub situations. Based on studies of Davis (1964), Meighan (1955), and Cowan and Wallof (1974), Bettinger (1977) suggests that this pattern is typical throughout the area south of Mono Lake. In the high country between Mono Basin and Antelope valley, most Early Archaic sites appear to be related to hunting and are located between 2,100 and 2,400 meters, while desert scrub and riverine environments are less favored (Kobori et al. 1980). It is possible, then, that the high region was used mostly for hunting by special task groups, and that it was seldom, if ever, occupied by residence groups.

Middle Archaic

The Middle Archaic spans the period from about 2000 B.C. to A.D. 500. The climate during this interval was cool and moist and has been described as neoglacial or neopluvial (J.O. Davis 1982; Weide 1982; "Prehistoric Environments," this vol.). Although it has been assumed that environmental productivity increased under such conditions, there is relatively little information regarding the ways ecosystems were actually affected. While neoglacial conditions might have made the exploitation of mountain meadows and other high altitude resource areas more difficult, this may have been balanced by the creation of meadows, marshes, and shallow lakes in places where they had not previously existed. *141*

The transition between the Early Archaic and Middle Archaic is gradual and not marked by large technological shifts; the major changes seem to be in settlement and subsistence patterns, stylistic elaboration, and apparent population density.

In many places, both winter sites and seasonal base camps were consistently re-occupied. Winter sites contain pit houses two to four meters in diameter with interior features such as hearths, storage pits, and burials. The character of such sites and the practice of caching tools at base camps and specialized cache sites in caves and rockshelters suggest that some groups regularly exploited a limited territory.

The diversity of utilized resources is greater during the Middle Archaic, possibly because of intensive exploitation of particular ecozones. Big game hunting remained important, but grinding stones and rabbit bones are abundant in most assemblages. Flaked stone technology is focused on the production of large bifaces from raw materials obtained at quarries. This technology generates large amounts of waste and increases the visibility of sites. Trade in exotic materials such as marine shell and obsidian becomes important. Diagnostic projectile points are Elko series and Martis series (the latter only on the northern east slope of the Sierra Nevada) ("Prehistory: Introduction," fig. 3, this vol).

Central Subregion

The Middle Archaic in the central subregion spans the time between 1500 B.C. and A.D. 500. It is marked by an apparent population boom and the beginning of intensive use and occupation at sites such as Ezra's Retreat (Bard, Busby, and Kobori 1979), South Fork Shelter (Heizer, Baumhoff, and Clewlow 1968), Wagon Jack Shelter (Heizer and Baumhoff 1961), Eastgate Cave (Elsasser and Prince 1961), Newark Cave (Fowler 1968a), Bronco Charlie Cave (Casjens 1974), and Lowe Shelter (Self 1980).

Big game hunting remains an important subsistence activity, focusing on mountain sheep (Pippin 1979) and to a lesser extent antelope and deer. Bison and elk remains are present in small numbers at Gatecliff Shelter (Thomas 1983a), Newark Cave, and South Fork Shelter. The intensity of use and variety of activities (including the production and use of bifaces, seed processing, and the manufacture of grinding slabs and scraper planes) at Gatecliff Shelter appear to increase at about this time (fig. 8) (Thomas 1983d). Excavations at the Horse Pasture Village sites in Grass Valley (Clewlow and Pastron 1972) revealed several shallow, circular house depressions that may have been occupied as early as 1500 B.C. Large-scale surveys in many areas show projectile points diagnostic of this period (Elko series) to be the most abundant (H. Wells 1981; Thomas 1971a, 1982, 1983a; Thomas and Bettinger 1976; James and

Elston 1983). However, at Valmy on the Humboldt River, intensity of occupation seems to decrease (Elston, Hardesty, and Clerico 1981). In central Nevada, this period is known as the Reveille phase, during which appears the first evidence for regional exchange in obsidian and marine shell beads, as well as an increase in the numbers and complexity of motif of portable rock art or incised stones (Thomas 1983d; T. Thomas 1983). The evidence from Gatecliff Shelter, Wagon Jack Shelter and South Fork Shelter and from high altitude sites such as those on Mount Jefferson (Thomas 1982) shows that big game hunting was an important subsistence activity throughout this period.

Lahontan Basin

The Middle Archaic in the Lahontan Basin is marked by a continuation and acceleration of trends established in the Early Archaic. During the period between 1500 B.C. and A.D. 500 (Transitional and Late Lovelock) sites seem to have been occupied intensively (Elston and Davis 1979; Roney 1978), but this may be partially a function of the increase in site visibility due to the lithic technology. Analysis of site distribution in the Black Rock Desert points to use of a more restricted range of environments than previously, with more sites in uplands and fewer in lowlands (Lohse 1980a). At the mouths of the Humboldt and Truckee rivers, the ex-

Amer. Mus. of Nat. Hist., New York.

Fig. 8. Hearth A, Horizon 8, at Gatecliff Shelter, part of the Devil's Gate component dated about 1350–1300 B.C. One of 7 hearths built during 3 different episodes of human activity concentrated on the primary dismemberment and processing of antelope and bighorn sheep, the manufacture of stone tools, and plant processing using grinding stones. The hearth shown is rock-lined, with fill containing artiodactyl long bones and tooth fragments, fire-fractured rocks, piñon charcoal, ash, and silt. Photograph by Susan L. Bierwirth, 1976.

ploitation of lacustrine resources continued, and intensive occupation began at villagelike residential base camps. Cache and burial sites such as Humboldt Cave, Lovelock Cave, and the Winnemucca Lake sites continued in use (Cowan and Clewlow 1968; Cowan 1967; Grosscup 1956, 1960; Hattori 1982; Heizer 1956; Heizer and Clewlow 1968; Heizer and Krieger 1956; Heizer and Napton 1970; Loud and Harrington 1929; Napton 1969; Napton and Heizer 1970; Orr 1974; Tuohy and Clark 1979).

The distinctive Lovelock Wickerware basketry ("Prehistoric Basketry," fig. 9, this vol.) is introduced at this time (Adovasio 1974), along with Elko series projectile points (Heizer and Hester 1978a; Thomas 1981), and possibly certain styles of rock art (Heizer and Baumhoff 1962). Trade in obsidian and marine shell remained widespread. Sites of this period have yielded esoterica such as the meadow mouse skin blanket and feathered tule duck decoys (fig. 9) from Lovelock Cave (Loud and Harrington 1929), the polychrome painted wooden "owl" effigy ("Portable Art Objects," fig. 8, this vol.) from Hanging Rock Cave (Tuohy 1969:57–58), and the stone sculpture accompanying a burial at Pyramid Lake (Tuohy and Stein 1969).

House pits at the Humboldt Lakebed site and near Marble Bluff at Pyramid Lake are about 2.5 meters in diameter and 40 centimeters deep, with central hearths, cache pits, and sometimes burials with grave goods in the floors. Dates for these houses range between 1065 and 130 B.C. (Grosscup 1958, 1960; Heizer and Napton 1970; Tuohy and Clark 1979; Tuohy and Stein 1969). The Karlo site (Riddell 1960), north of Honey Lake, contained houses defined by post-hole patterns about three meters in diameter, along with both cremations and pit burials. A radiocarbon date of 400 B.C. was obtained from this site.

Along the Humboldt River at Rye Patch Reservoir, people occupied a series of short-term base camps, processed seeds, and consumed a wide variety of animals ranging from minnows to large game, with an increase in the use of desert species from earlier times. A similar site was found on the southern margin of the Black Rock Desert at Trego Hot Springs (Seck 1980). It appears to be a temporary base camp occupied in the spring or early summer. Large numbers of grinding stones and crude knives with silica deposits on the edges suggest that seed collection and processing were important activities there. Most of the faunal remains are rabbits and small rodents (A. Dansie 1980). The site also contains patterns of post holes averaging 2.5 meters in diameter, hearths, and a shallow well. In contrast, fauna at the Barrel Springs site (Cowan 1972; Thomas 1972a) are dominated by mountain sheep, the production of large bifaces was a major activity, and relatively few seed processing tools were present.

East Slope of the Sierra Nevada

In the northern portion of the east slope, the Middle Archaic Martis complex dates from about 2000 B.C. to A.D. 500 (Heizer and Elsasser 1953; Elsasser 1960; Elston 1971, 1979; Elston et al. 1977). Martis residential base camps were situated on valley margins adjacent to a wide variety of resources; hot springs were particularly favored locations (Elsasser 1960; Elston 1970, 1979; Elston and Turner 1968; Elston and Davis 1972). Site density seems to have been highest in the southern Truckee Meadows–Steamboat Hot Springs area where many resources, including thermal waters and deposits of lithic raw materials, were available within a relatively small catchment. These sites, occupied during the winter (A. Dansie 1979), contained pit houses similar to those at Pyramid Lake and the Humboldt Sink, although at two to four meters in diameter they are somewhat larger. They contain internal features such as hearths and cache pits, as well as occasional burials. At the Bordertown and Hallelujah Junction sites, Martis houses were probably conical structures with a framework of juniper and pine over which was laid willow and grass thatching. Cobble-lined earth ovens and scatters of fire-cracked rock were found outside the houses. The size of these houses suggests that the household group may have been an extended family.

Martis field camps and task sites are found in a variety of situations. Seed-processing camps were located on valley margins near springs and creeks (Elston 1979). Multi-purpose camps for both seed processing and hunting are found on meadow margins in upland valleys of the Sierra Nevada (Heizer and Elsasser 1953; Elsasser 1960; Davis, Elston, and Townsend 1974; Elston 1971; Elston and Townsend 1974; Elston et al. 1977; James 1983a; Elston, Hardesty, and Zeier 1982; Rondeau 1982). Field camps for hunting in the Virginia Range, Pinenut Range, and Peavine Mountain are located on ridges and saddles overlooking streams and springs (Elston and Turner 1968; Aikens 1972a; Hagerty 1970). In the Sierra Nevada, there is some evidence for intensive use of rugged, mountainous terrain in the Early and Middle Martis, and less such evidence in Late Martis and Kings Beach phases (Turner and Hamby 1982; Elston 1982). This is supported by limited data from the Bordertown site (A. Dansie 1979), which suggest an emphasis on seed processing and big game (mountain sheep and mule deer) in Martis times.

Stone quarries were worked intensively in Martis times. Basalt was obtained at Alder Hill in the Truckee Basin and the Steamboat Hills in the Truckee Meadows, and chertlike sinter from the Steamboat locality, where the manufacture of large bifaces created vast amounts of lithic waste (Elston and Davis 1972; Elston et al. 1977; Elston, Hardesty, and Clerico 1981; Elston, Hardesty, and Zeier 1982). Obsidian was obtained from a few

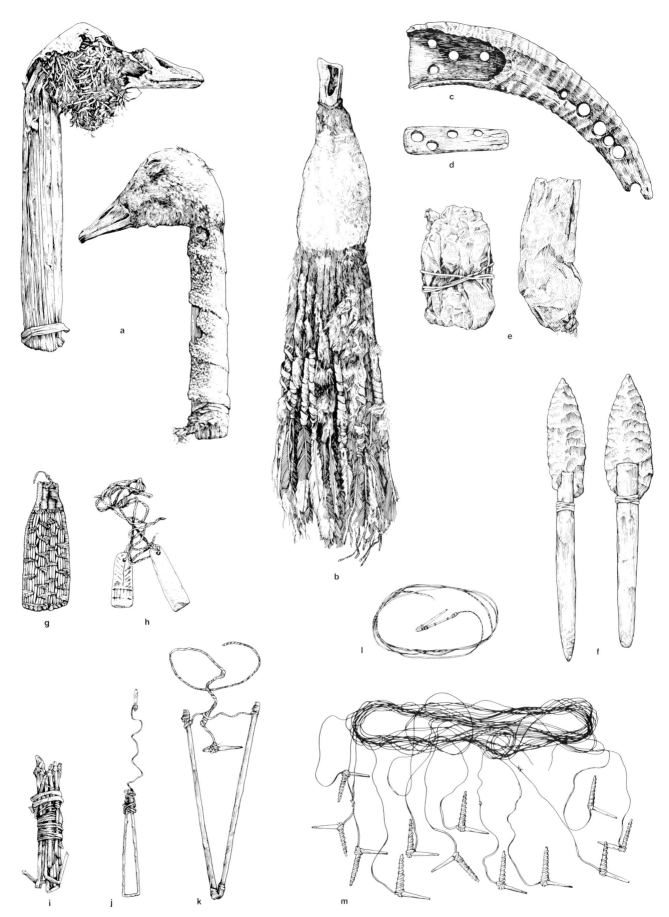

ELSTON

local sources of inferior quality, but most was imported from Bodie Hills, Pine Grove Hills, and Mount Hicks (Singer and Ericson 1977; James 1983a; M.C. Hall 1983), probably in the form of large flake blanks or bifaces.

The same emphasis on big game hunting and seed processing is seen all along the Sierra Front to Owens Valley. With the exception of the obsidian quarries mentioned above, Mid-Archaic sites between Antelope Valley and the Mono Basin are mostly small hunting camps at high altitudes (Kobori et al. 1980). It is not known whether the quarries were casually worked by hunting parties or by special task groups (Bettinger 1977:49; Ericson 1977; Ericson, Hagen, and Chesterman 1976; Singer and Ericson 1977; M.C. Hall 1983). Farther south, Middle Archaic sites of the Newberry period (Bettinger and Taylor 1974) with a seed processing and big game hunting focus have been excavated at Mammoth Creek Cave (Enfield and Enfield 1964) and the Hot Creek Shelters (Davis 1964).

Middle Archaic sites seem to be rare in the Borealis area (Pippin 1980), Casa Diablo (Cowan and Wallof 1974), and in the Long Valley Caldera (Bettinger 1977). Bettinger (1975, 1977a, 1977:49) has suggested that exploitation of these high upland areas may have become more difficult as the climate became cooler and moister during the Neoglacial interval, while the productivity of lowlands in the Mono Basin and Owens Valley may have increased. These changes may help to explain the shift from an emphasis on riverine resources during the Cowhorn phase to the later exploitation of desert scrub ecotones and the intensive use of upland seed resources within Owens Valley itself. However, since such changes in settlement and subsistence do not occur elsewhere until much later, local population increase seems the more likely explanation.

Late Archaic

The Late Archaic begins about A.D. 500 and, in the western Great Basin, lasts until shortly after White contact. Diagnostic artifacts are Rose Spring and Eastgate points (A.D. 500–1100), Desert series points, and brownware pottery (after 1100). A warming and drying trend, which began sometime before A.D. 1, reached a peak about 500, but this was relatively mild compared to that experienced during the Early Archaic. Nevertheless, important cultural changes occurred at about this time, which, although they may have been triggered by climatic change, probably had more to do with stress caused by increased population. The atlatl and dart were replaced by the bow and arrow, smaller and lighter projectile points (the Eastgate–Rose Spring type) were introduced, lithic technology emphasizing the production of bifaces and the use of quarried raw materials was replaced by an emphasis on the production of simple flake tools from locally available materials, and pottery was introduced after about A.D. 1100. At the same time, plant processing equipment became more elaborate and abundant. These technological changes accompanied the adoption of a subsistence strategy that entailed an increase both in the diversity of resources used and in the number of ecozones exploited. Plant foods and small game, especially rabbits, were emphasized at the expense of large game.

The fan-shaped distribution of the Northern Paiute, Western Shoshone, and Southern Paiute and their linguistic proximity suggested to Lamb (1958) that Numic speakers have expanded into the Great Basin from a common origin in southern California within the last 1,000 years. This putative spread would have occurred within the Late Archaic period. In contrast Goss (1977) believes that the linguistic evidence indicates in situ, long term development of Numic languages.

Each of these quite different views has important implications for the interpretation of the culture history of the Great Basin, but the problem is not easily resolved in archeological terms. Bettinger and Baumhoff (1982, 1983) have provided a theoretical discussion of the means by which invading Numic speakers could have out-competed preceding resident groups, but these speculations do not provide an operational or testable model (Simms 1983b). Moreover, there are serious problems in defining the material culture correlates of

U. of Calif., Lowie Mus., Berkeley: a, 1–21130; 1–21127; c, 1–9342; e, 43402; 43044; i, 1–21283; Mus. of the Amer. Ind., Heye Foundation, New York: b, 12–4151; d, 13–4189; g, 13–4570; h, 13–4575; j, 13–4517; k, 13–4517; l, 12–4177; m, 12–4181.

Fig. 9. Perishable artifacts from Lovelock and Humboldt Caves, Nev. a, Canada goose decoy heads mounted on tule foundations, found in a cache that contained 13 tule foundations, 7 stuffed heads, and 5 bills. b, Feather wand, elaborately decorated with a bone handle, cut and uncut feathers wrapped in strips of fur, and fringed with fiber cords. c, Shaft straightener of mountain sheep horn; graduated holes were used to scour and bend to shape wood projectile shafts, found with 4 scoured sticks of greasewood. d, Horn shaft straightener. e, Animal intestine bags tied with fiber cords. f, Hafted knives, attached to wood handles with pitch and sinew wrapping, part of a cache containing 2 other, similar, unshafted stone bifaces and 3 Eastgate type projectile points. g, Tiny, elaborate, paddlelike object of small twigs, tied and wrapped with fiber string. h, Pendants of large mammal bone, decorated with ocher-painted incised lines arranged in geometric patterns. i, Bundle of 8 complete sets of willow snares, each a single twig, bent, and attached by 20–30-inch-long fiber cord to a small wood pin. j, Bent willow twig snare and pin set as in i. k, Compound snares, 2 sticks, notched and closely tied at one end, the other end held by a fiber cord tied to a wood pin as in j. l, Composite fishhook, a bone point lashed to a socketed twig, and to a heavy fiber fishing line. m, Throwing line for fishing, consisting of 12 composite hooks, bone points set in twig shanks, wrapped and tied with fine fiber string to a coarser fiber line. Length of b about 40 cm, rest same scale. a–d, g–m, Lovelock Cave; e–f, Humboldt Cave.

linguistic and ethnic boundaries in the Great Basin (Elston 1982; Lyneis 1982; O'Connell, Jones, and Simms 1982).

Present understanding of the archeological record would not allow a firm conclusion as to whether the changes involved in the transition from the Middle to the Late Archaic are those that eventually culminated in the patterns observed for the ethnographic Numic speakers or the Hokan-speaking Washoe.

Central Subregion

In the Underdown phase (A.D. 500–1300) at Gatecliff Shelter (Thomas 1983a), overall numbers of artifacts decrease, and biface production declines. Similar trends were observed at South Fork Shelter (Heizer, Baumhoff, and Clewlow 1968), along with a reduction in numbers of bone awls and chert cores. At the same time at South Fork Shelter, there was a decrease in the absolute number of mammal bones, as well as an overall decrease in number of species, especially those associated with riverine habitats such as muskrat, beaver, and elk. However, cottontail rabbit bones remained abundant, and shellfish increased. Even so, a few bison and elk bones were found in Gatecliff Shelter, James Creek Shelter (Clerico 1983), and possibly at one of the Rossi Mine sites (Rusco 1982).

Some contact with the horticultural Fremont and Anasazi cultures to the south and east is indicated by a few pottery sherds at Newark Cave (Fowler 1968a), Lowe Shelter (Self 1980), Civa Shelter II and Slivovitz Shelter (Busby 1978, 1979), and Bronco Charlie Cave (Casjens 1974).

The end of the Late Archaic is marked by changes in technology, subsistence, and particularly in settlement patterns. Brownware pottery and Desert series (Desert Side-notched and Cottonwood) projectile points, which mark the Yankee Blade phase (A.D. 1300-Historic) of central Nevada are introduced. In Grass Valley, Clewlow and Pastron (1972) see an increased focus on gathering, which according to H. Wells (1981, 1983) includes an intensification of piñon exploitation. This is accompanied by increasing house size, settlement size, and sedentism, which culminates in the large valley floor villages documented for the Western Shoshone of the ethnohistoric period.

At the same time, there are changes in the use of previously occupied sites. South Fork Shelter and possibly James Creek Shelter are abandoned, and utilization of Newark Cave decreases. Conversely, intensity of occupation increases at Lowe Shelter, Toquima Cave (Thomas 1970), Painted Cave (Bard, Busby, and Kobori 1980), and sites in Coal Valley (Busby 1978, 1979).

Perhaps the most dramatic change is in the use of the high-altitude area on Mount Jefferson (Thomas 1982). The temporary hunting camps and facilities of the

Amer. Mus. of Nat. Hist., New York.

Fig. 10. Dense concentration of bighorn sheep bone in Horizon 2 at Gatecliff Shelter, part of the Underdown component dated about A.D. 1300. The excellent preservation and semi-articulated association of the bone is representative of the Horizon 2 bone bed as exposed throughout the site. Thomas (1983a) estimates that two dozen or so bighorn were killed and butchered at the shelter, perhaps as a single event. It seems likely that activity was focused on primary dismemberment of the carcasses preparatory to transport elsewhere, storage, or drying. Butchering marks on the bone and the nature of their association suggest careful skinning. The remains indicate a late winter–early spring hunt. The site during this time was being used solely as a kill-butchering station. Photograph by Susan L. Bierwirth, 1971.

Underdown and earlier phases were abandoned, and a residential base camp was established at Alta Toquima Village. This involved the construction of substantial circular rock-walled houses and storage features. An abundance of grinding stones associated with these structures indicates that processing seeds (perhaps limber pine nuts) was an important activity. Thomas (1982:113) comments that although the large numbers of Desert series projectile points suggest that hunting was also important at Alta Toquima Village, there is little evidence for hunting elsewhere in Monitor Valley during the Yankee Blade phase. In fact, Desert series points are much less abundant than Eastgate–Rose Spring and Elko points virtually everywhere in the western Great Basin. Why this is so remains to be discovered.

Lahontan Basin

In the Late Archaic, the villages at the mouths of the Truckee and Humboldt rivers continued to be occupied, but the houses there are smaller and shallower and lack internal features. A massive rockfall at Lovelock Cave

Mus. of the Amer. Ind., Heye Foundation, New York: 9453.
Fig. 11. Cache of 11 duck decoys at removal from Lovelock Cave, Nev., by Llewellyn L. Loud. Photograph by M.R. Harrington, 1924.

in A.D. 440 prevented much use of the interior thereafter, although occupation continued in the external shelters nearby. Humboldt Cave (Heizer and Krieger 1956), Granite Point Cave and Granite Point Shelter (Roust 1966), and several of the Winnemucca Lake sites continued to be used for burials and caches (fig. 11). A cache of feathered coiled baskets (fig. 12) from one of these sites was dated at A.D. 1040 (Tuohy 1974). In the Black Rock Desert all ecological zones continued to be exploited (Lohse 1980a) although certain sites, such as Trego Hot Springs, Barrel Springs, and Karlo, were abandoned. On the Humboldt River at Rye Patch Reservoir (Rusco and Davis 1982), occupation of temporary base camps continued, and the diet changed to include the greatest variety of fauna recorded at any time in the entire prehistoric sequence.

These changes in settlement and subsistence are accompanied by the same changes in lithic technology and projectile point style noted for the central subregion. Lovelock Wickerware begins to decline during this period (Grosscup 1960) but apparently is still present by A.D. 1370 (Tuohy 1974). Although the Numic expansion is supposed to have reached the Lahontan Basin during this time (Bettinger and Baumhoff 1982), the only really distinctive item of Northern Paiute material culture is the twill twined water bottle, which appears at about 1600 (Tuohy 1974).

East Slope of the Sierra Nevada

In the north, the Late Archaic is known as the Kings Beach complex, the precursor of the ethnographic Washoe Indians (Heizer and Elsasser 1953; Elsasser 1960; Elston 1971, 1979; Miller and Elston 1979; James,

Brown, and Elston 1982; James 1983a). Subsistence was based on seeds, fishing, and small game, particularly jackrabbits (A. Dansie 1979; Dansie and Ringkob 1979). Intensive exploitation of piñon appears to have started at this time (Hagerty 1970), and the bow and arrow replaces the atlatl as it does elsewhere. Although flaked stone technology becomes simplified, the equipment for plant food processing becomes more elaborate as various mortar forms come into use along with hullers. By late Kings Beach times (after A.D. 1100) houses are only about two meters in diameter, are not built on pits, and lack internal features except for an occasional hearth. The change from larger pit houses in early Kings Beach to the smaller, less complex type is not well dated. Major winter sites used during Martis times are still occupied but at less intensity, along with a number of sites in other locations. In the Truckee Meadows, occupation becomes more intense at sites along the Truckee River (Miller and Elston 1979; James, Brown, and Elston 1982). This pattern suggests some stress on resources, which perhaps resulted from demographic packing, with attendant loss of flexibility in movement.

Similar changes have been noted along the middle

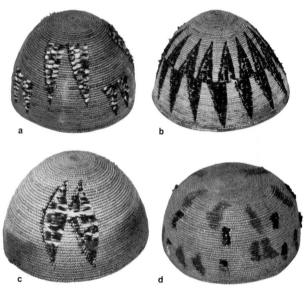

Nev. State Mus., Carson City: a, 25Pe00/a; b, 25Pe00/3; c, 25Pe00/4; d, 26Pe00/6.
Fig. 12. Close-coiled, feathered baskets, part of a cache from Brown Cave, Nev. (the other basket is in "Prehistoric Basketry," fig. 8, this vol). a–c, Coiled basket hats; d, coiled bowl. The feathers are secured by binding them with weft stitches to the exterior of the coils. Birds whose feathers were used include green-winged teal, cinnamon teal, yellow-headed blackbird, red-winged blackbird, and common merganser. Hats have quartered or halved design elements resembling bird wings. Bowls have geometric, zigzag, or simple linear patterns of feather decoration. In 3 specimens, the feather design layout is interrupted by single or double strands of split stitch overlays, or by a chain of triangles formed by weft splints with bark against a background of peeled splints and stitches. The warp rods and wefts are willow. a and d have been painted in bands of blue and white. a, Diameter of rim 18.1 cm, rest same scale.

and southern Sierra Front to, but not including, Owens Valley (Bettinger 1977; Cowan and Wallof 1974; Kobori et al. 1980; Pippin 1980). M.C. Hall (1983) suggests that trans-Sierran trade in obsidian obtained from the Mono Lake–Long Valley Caldera highlands may have been disrupted by a series of volcanic eruptions between A.D. 50 and 1450. Intensive piñon exploitation may have started earlier in the Bodie-Coleville area and in the Long Valley Caldera (Bettinger 1977; Kobori et al. 1980).

Owens Valley has a different pattern of change in the Late Archaic than the rest of the Sierra Front. Intensive exploitation of piñon from special base camps that were often occupied in mild winters began in the Baker phase between A.D. 550 and 1250. After about 950, most big game hunting was also done from these sites, and from high altitude sites in the White Mountains similar to Alta Toquima Village (Bettinger 1977a). Bettinger attributes these changes to dryer climatic conditions, which reduced the productivity of the desert scrub and riparian ecozones. However, increase in local population seems as likely and could also help explain the lack of sychroneity between events in Owens Valley and the rest of the western Great Basin. Although the shift toward piñon exploitation does occur elsewhere, it is not so intense and does not seem to involve hunting from piñon camps. The final change to the ethnographic Paiute patterns of settlement and subsistence in Owens Valley took place at about A.D. 1250 when a general decrease in big game hunting from upland and lowland sites occurred, probably because the inception of wild crop irrigation required sedentary life in lowland base camps for almost the entire year.

Summary

Adaptation to environmental variation is demonstrated by the ability of people to cope with changes in the abundance of resources. Such variation occurs at different time scales, but in climates with a dormant winter period, seasonal variation is critical (Binford 1982). In the late Pleistocene and early Holocene, upland and valley margin landscapes of the western Great Basin were dominated by expanses of sagebrush steppe, while valley floors contained lakes and marshes around which big game animals congregated. People lived in small, mobile groups, pursuing a seasonal round over very great distances. Seasonal variation may have been avoided by specializing in the exploitation of big game animals. Pre-Archaic sites all look alike because they are functionally similar: small field camps occupied for short periods of time. When the lakes and marshes dried up, the diversity of Great Basin ecosystems was reduced. As the large game animals became scarce, and then extinct, the pre-Archaic lifeway was no longer possible.

The Archaic adaptation was quite different. Rather than focused or specialized dependence on a few abundant and high-yield resources, it entailed intensive exploitation of whatever ecological diversity existed, obtaining a greater variety of resources in a smaller annual territory. Seasonal variability of resources was dealt with by gathering food surpluses that were specially processed and stored. This in turn required the construction of substantial shelters and the use of functionally different sites during the seasonal round. The Archaic strategy emphasized alternatives and opportunities. When a lake appeared on a formerly dry playa, the settlement pattern and usual seasonal round could be altered to exploit the new situation. When a lake or stream dried up, people apparently shifted their attention to upland areas with relatively little difficulty or stress. As ecological diversity and resource potential increased in the Great Basin after the mid-Holocene invasion of piñon-juniper woodland, flexibility and opportunism allowed Archaic cultures to prosper and populations to grow. Changing environmental conditions and high population levels contributed to shifts in technological, subsistence, and settlement pattern throughout the Great Basin after A.D. 500. In the western Great Basin, these were all variations of the Archaic strategy involving intensive use of a wide range of resources. Thus, resisting change through change, the Archaic way of life prevailed for 7,000 years or more and might have continued if it had not been overwhelmed by the expansion of European civilization.

Prehistory of the Eastern Area

C. MELVIN AIKENS AND DAVID B. MADSEN

This chapter describes a regional manifestation of the highly adapted and remarkably variable hunting-gathering culture that was characteristic of the intermontane west over many thousands of years. The prehistoric cultures of the eastern Great Basin and adjacent northern Colorado Plateau physiographic areas shared much in common in early times and hence are treated together here. More broadly, they represent variants of the distinctive Great Basin Desert Archaic culture that characterized a vast arid province in Utah, Nevada, California, Oregon, and Idaho. The narrative begins with the final phases of the Pleistocene and ends shortly after the beginning of the Christian era when horticulture, pottery, and related technology were added to the basic hunting-gathering pattern.

The geographic limits of the eastern Basin province are roughly marked on the north by the Goose Creek, Grouse Creek, and Raft River Mountains lying along the Utah-Idaho border; on the south by the Pine Valley Mountains of southern Utah; on the east by the Wasatch Range, which divides the western (Basin) portion of Utah from the eastern (Colorado Plateau) portion; and on the west by the Utah-Nevada boundary. The area can essentially be defined as the Bonneville Basin and the immediately adjacent mountainous terrain (fig. 1).

The eastern Basin, along with the Lake Lahontan area and Owens Valley in the far west, differs from the rest of the Great Basin in being relatively well watered by stored winter moisture from surrounding mountains. Freshwater sources of varying potability include the perennial feeder streams of the Great Salt Lake, Sevier Lake, and Utah Lake; freshwater Utah Lake itself; numerous ephemeral streams in the mountains, and seasonal playa lakes in the valley basins; and a number of springs, located usually along the bases of the mountain ranges. Water is most abundant along the Wasatch Front, but even in dryer areas water sources are sufficiently numerous and broadly distributed to have allowed the aboriginal inhabitants to range widely within the region.

Biotic resources include a considerable range of species, distributed from valley floor to mountain top. The variety of mammals is among the greatest in temperate North America due to the overlap in this area of several more northern and southern biotic communities. The variety of plants used by prehistoric people was also great; for example, 68 species or genera of plants were excavated from Danger Cave (Jennings 1957). Most of these species either have edible parts or could have been utilized for tools, fibers or medicines.

The Colorado Plateau country lies between the Wasatch Range and the Rocky Mountains ("Prehistory: Introduction," fig. 1, this vol.). Broad flat tablelands and deep, steep-walled canyons give a completely different aspect to the physiography. Nevertheless, quite similar biotic conditions prevailed. Since the material culture of early Colorado Plateau groups in eastern Utah and western Colorado is also similar to that of the Basin peoples, the ancient cultures of the northern Colorado Plateau are appropriately grouped with those of the eastern Basin.

The possible effect of post-Pleistocene climatic trends on environmental conditions and human occupation patterns in the Desert West has been the subject of much investigation. In the area of concern a semi-desert environment broadly similar to that of the present has persisted throughout the period of archeological record. However, within the context of this relatively stable

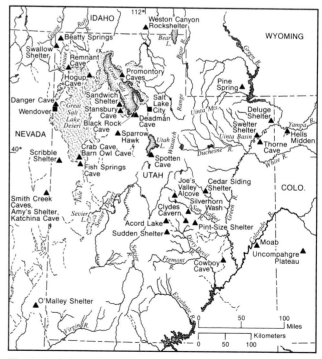

Fig. 1. Archaic period sites in the eastern Great Basin.

regional environment, there are documented locally important changes through both time and space in environmental conditions and correlative change in patterns of natural resource utilization (Mehringer 1977; Currey and James 1982).

At the end of the Pleistocene, before people arrived in the eastern Basin, the Late Wisconsin pluvial lakes on basin floors and the mountain glaciers in the uplands were rapidly reduced. But vegetation and the fauna dependent on it responded to the climatic changes much more slowly. The biotic record suggests that slightly cooler and moister conditions than at present prevailed until about 6000 B.C. A complex post-Pleistocene period of warmer and dryer conditions may have bracketed short periods of increased moisture and may have had different impacts from area to area. Beginning about 3500–3000 B.C. several Neoglacial episodes resulted in slightly elevated lake levels. With the exception of piñon pine, which may have arrived in the area sometime after about 4000 B.C. (Thompson 1979; Madsen 1985), the types of available flora and fauna did not change. However, the productivity of various communities was affected. This is particularly true of lake margins where fluctuating water levels alternately flooded and dessicated many lake-edge and marsh ecosystems.

The Nature of the Record

The archeological record of the eastern Basin is derived from excavations, primarily of caves and rockshelters, which provide chronological, typological, and subsistence data, as well as from formal sample surveys that have identified patterns of site distribution and the relationship of those distributions to the physical and biological environment. The greatest amount of data is derived from lake-margin cave sites around Great Salt Lake. The larger number of excavations at these dry cave sites appears, superficially, to bias the record, but survey data suggest that the earliest and most persistent focus of human occupation was around lake margins. The larger amount of data from these areas probably represents a reality, not a mere sampling bias.

Major Archaic sites in the eastern Basin and northern Colorado Plateau are plotted in figure 1. Three rich and well-documented habitation sites furnish the main chronological sequence around which the narrative of human prehistory in the region may be structured. These sites are Danger Cave (Jennings 1957) just northeast of Wendover, Utah, on the Utah-Nevada border (fig. 2); Hogup Cave (Aikens 1970) located near the western shore of the Great Salt Lake some 75 miles northwest of Salt Lake City (fig. 3); and Sudden Shelter (Jennings, Schroedl, and Holmer 1980) in the southern Wasatch Plateau east of Richfield, Utah.

Other important sites in the same general area are

U. of Utah Archeol. Center, Salt Lake City: 42TO13–80.
Fig. 2. Danger Cave, with a record of intermittent human occupation spanning the greater part of the Holocene, from about 8300 B.C. until after A.D. 1400. At the base of low limestone hills abutting Pleistocene Lake Stansbury and overlooking the Bonneville Salt Flats, the cave lies below a small cliff. The arched cavern is about 120 feet deep and averages 60 feet wide. Samphire-inkweed-pickleweed associations on the salt flat in front of the cave turn to salt grass–cheatgrass–greasewood–shadscale associations as one ascends the slopes of the hills. Danger Cave was a living site where worn-out tools, weapons, and other utensils as well as food bone, bone scrap, and plant parts were discarded on identifiable living surfaces and middens. Thirteen feet of cultural deposits represent 5 separate periods of occupation. Over 1,000 millingstones and fragments were found. The long record of occupation prompted Jennings's (1957, 1966a) formulation of the Desert culture concept—a basic hunting and gathering tradition of small, mobile groups who used a broad spectrum of desert resources. Photographed in 1950.

the Promontory caves located at the end of a long peninsula extending into the Great Salt Lake from the north (Steward 1937a); Black Rock Cave (Steward 1937a; Madsen 1983) and Deadman Cave (E.R. Smith 1941), both located at the southern end of the Great Salt Lake; Stansbury Cave 1 (Jameson 1958) and Sandwich Shelter (Marwitt, Fry, and Adovasio 1971), both in Stansbury Island at the southwest edge of the lake; the Sparrow Hawk site in the central Oquirrh Mountains southeast of Tooele, Utah (Janetski 1983); Spotten Cave, located near the southern tip of Utah Lake (Mock 1971); Crab and Barn Owl caves (Madsen 1982b) adjacent to Fish Springs southwest of the Great Salt Lake Desert; and Scribble Rock Shelter (Lindsay and Sargent 1979) in the Deep Creek Mountains south of Wendover, Utah.

Lying in an arc peripheral to this main cluster are, on the north and west, Weston Canyon Rockshelter (Delisio 1971), north of Bear Lake several miles north of the Utah-Idaho border; Swallow Shelter (Dalley 1976) in extreme northern Utah a few miles east of the Utah-Nevada state line; South Fork Shelter (Heizer, Baumhoff, and Clewlow 1968) near Elko, Nevada; and Amy's Shelter (Gruhn 1979) and Smith Creek Cave (Bryan 1979) in the Snake Range on the central Utah-Nevada

U. of Utah Archeol. Center, Salt Lake City: 42B036–48.

Fig. 3. Hogup Cave, Utah, a large limestone cavern about 50 feet deep, 30 feet wide, and 20 feet high at the portal. Excavation revealed 11–14 feet of cultural deposits, including 16 major occupational surfaces used from 6350 B.C. to A.D. 1470. The extensive multiple living surfaces document repeated use of the site as a hunting and seed processing camp. The excellent preservation of largely vegetal materials also provided the basis for reconstructing the local climatic record over much of the Holocene period (Aikens 1970). Combined with the cultural record from Danger Cave, which is similar in many ways, Hogup Cave constitutes the basis for the northeastern Great Basin cultural sequence (Jennings 1978).

U. of Utah Archeol. Center, Salt Lake City: 42Wn420–31.

Fig. 4. Walters Cave (left) and Cowboy Cave, Wayne Co., Utah, overlooking an ephemeral tributary of Spur Fork Canyon, part of the Barrier Canyon drainage running through Horseshoe Canyon. Human occupation of Cowboy Cave spanned the period from about 6000 B.C. to A.D. 500. Prehistoric use was confined to short-term activities, usually the summer harvesting and processing of plants, but with some hunting of both large and small game. This site, in conjunction with Sudden Shelter, supplies the basic chronological framework for the upper Colorado Plateau region (Schroedl 1976; Jennings 1978, 1980). Distinctive elements of the Cowboy Cave artifact assemblage include twig figurines found in everyday living contexts rather than in special caches; a large number of painted and incised stones; and early Archaic unbaked clay figurines that are quite distinct from later Basketmaker, Fremont, and ethnographic Southern Paiute and Ute forms. Photographed in 1975.

border. Northern Colorado Plateau sites that complete the eastern arc include Cowboy Cave in the Slickrock country northwest of the Green-Colorado River confluence (fig. 4) (Jennings et al. 1980); Clydes Cavern in east-central Utah (Winter and Wylie 1974); Hells Midden (Lister 1951), Deluge Shelter, Swelter Shelter (Leach 1970, 1970a), and Thorne Cave (Day 1964) in the Uinta Basin of northeast Utah–northwest Colorado; and several sites on the Uncompahgre Plateau of western Colorado (Wormington and Lister 1956). Three important sample inventories conducted in the western and southern portions of the region treated in this chapter (Lindsay and Sargent 1979; Janetski 1983; Janetski and Holmer 1982) supplement these records. Other sites and surveys provide important ancillary data.

All but a few of the sites mentioned are caves, several of them containing well-sheltered deposits that have remained utterly dry for thousands of years. As a result, the debris of their occupants has been remarkably well-preserved. Whereas the usual archeological site situated in the open and exposed to the elements commonly contains only the stone and sometimes bone artifacts of its past occupants, these cave sites have preserved whole ranges of artifacts made not only of stone and bone but also of hide, fur, feathers, horn, gut, sinew, grasses, wood, and bark. Additionally, both plant and animal food refuse, and even the identifiable remnants of actual human meals encapsulated in dessicated human feces are preserved for study (Fry 1976). These caves thus furnish an archeological record of unparalleled richness from which many details of the ancient Great Basin lifeway can be inferred.

The character of the cave deposits themselves is of importance both for understanding the kind of life that was lived at those sites, and for placing in proper chronological order the cultural events that the sites memorialize. Beyond the digging of the simplest storage caches and firepits (figs. 5–6) and the occasional movement of fill to level the living areas, the deposits exhibit no evidence of intentional construction; they can be understood as merely accumulations of the debris of daily living and the passage of time (fig. 7).

The materials in most of these cave deposits include small and large rock spalls from the cave ceilings; dust carried in by wind and in some cases—notably Sudden Shelter—colluvium carried in by water; droppings and other leavings of bats, pack rats, coyotes, sheep, and bobcats; and debris of many other kinds that results from human occupation. At Danger and Hogup caves, the greater bulk of the deposits (up to 11 feet deep at Danger, up to 14 feet deep at Hogup) was made up of vegetal material including grasses, twigs of woody plants, seed husks, and bulrushes (table 1), apparently carried in by humans during their visits. This occupational de-

U. of Utah Archeol. Center, Salt Lake City: 42Wn420-207.

Fig. 5. A square, slab-lined cist uncovered in the floor of Cowboy Cave. The cist is chinked with cedar bark bundles and surrounded by a floor or mat of grass 3 m in diameter. The bark lining and evidence of a stone cover plastered with adobe show concern with rodent-proofing, which is typical of both Basketmaker and Fremont storage structures. Photographed in 1975.

bris, revealed in excavation as thin, widespread lenses or layers of material endlessly accumulated one on another, suggests intermittent, repeated visits rather than continuous occupation of these sites. Overlying many of these minor strata at Hogup Cave were very thin but widespread and continuous layers of bat droppings deposited during brief intervals when people were not

U. of Utah Archeol. Center, Salt Lake City: 42Sv6-88.

Fig. 6. Slab-lined firepits in a stratum dating from 3777 B.C. ±90 to 3420 B.C. ±140 in Sudden Shelter, central Utah. Food, bone, and plant parts, lacking within the firepits, were common elsewhere in the midden. This, and a clear correlation of firepits and concentrations of ground stone, indicate that the firepits were used primarily in the roasting or cooking of plant foods. Average maximum diameter is 48.1 cm; average maximum depth, 25.9 cm. An emphasis on plant processing was confined in large part to this stratum; other occupation levels showed various degrees of emphasis on the taking of large game animals. Photographed in 1974.

152

U. of Utah Archeol. Center, Salt Lake City: 42T0-169.

Fig. 7. Cross-section of the Danger Cave cultural deposits, showing the finely detailed stratigraphic record. The gravels at the base of the section were left as Pleistocene Lake Bonneville receded below the level of the cave. The earliest evidence of human occupation lay on clean lacustrine sands, showing that people entered the cave soon after it was free of water. The finely layered character of much of the culture-bearing deposits reflects repeated, short-term occupation.

present at the site and the guano could accumulate undisturbed. Mountain sheep droppings showed a similar pattern in some areas. At Sudden Shelter the wet deposits exhibit a pattern of alternating cultural and natural depositions resulting from slope wash.

As these materials were scattered over the cave floors century after century, deep deposits were built up. The series of naturally deposited layers record the passage of time both in their natural stratigraphic succession and in the variations that are to be seen in the kinds and styles of artifacts contained in each layer. Samples of organic material for radiocarbon dating, taken from the same archeological layers as the artifacts, make it possible to calibrate the natural sequence of changes thus observed in terms of the approximate number of years elapsed since the artifacts of each period were used and then left to become incorporated into the slowly accumulating deposits.

Based on the sequences from Danger Cave, Hogup Cave, and Sudden Shelter, the history of early culture along the eastern edge of the Great Basin is here divided into three periods that are roughly equivalent to Basin-wide technological-chronological sequences (for example, Madsen and O'Connell 1982; Holmer 1983): the Bonneville period, 9000–7500 B.C.; the Wendover period, 7500–4000 B.C.; and the Black Rock period, 4000 B.C.–A.D. 500 ("Prehistory: Introduction," fig. 2, this vol.). Black Rock can in turn be subdivided into earlier and later phases of roughly 2,000 years each. The concluding post-Archaic periods dated after the beginning of the Christian era are treated in "Fremont Cultures," this volume.

Table 1. Biota of the Hogup Cave Deposits During Wendover and Black Rock Periods

PLANTS

Acer grandidentatum (bigtooth maple)[a]
Allenrolfea occidentalis (pickleweed)
Apocynum sp. (dogbane)
Artemisia spp. (sagebrush)
Asclepias speciosa (showy milkweed)
Astragalus sp. (locoweed)
Atriplex confertifolia (shadscale)
Betula occidentalis (water birch)
Celtis reticulata (hackberry)[a]
Cercocarpus ledifolius (leatherleaf mountain mahogany)
Chrysothamnus nauseosus (big rabbitbrush)
Cowania mexicana (cliffrose)
Delphinium (larkspur)
Distichlis spicata (salt grass)[a]
Elymus salina (salina wild rye)
Ephedra nevadensis (mormon tea)
Equisetum sp. (horsetail)[a]
Erigeron sp. (daisy)[a]
Juniperus osteosperma (Utah juniper)
Kochia vestita (gray molly)[a]
Liliaceae (bulb)[a]
Lomatium grayi (desert parsley)
Opuntia polyacantha (prickly pear)
Penstemon sp. (beard tongue)
Phragmites communis (reed grass)
Pinus monophylla (piñon pine)[b]
Poa spp. (bluegrass)[a]
Populus angustifolia (narrowleaf cottonwood)
P. tremuloides (trembling aspen)[b]
Prunus fasciculata (desert almond)[a]
Salix spp. (willow)
Sambucus caerulea (blue elderberry)[a]
Sarcobatus vermiculatus (greasewood)
Scirpus acutus (hardstem bulrush)
S. olneyi (olney's bulrush)
Shepherdia canadensis (russet buffaloberry)
Stipa sp. (needlegrass)
Tetradymia spp. (horsebrush)
Typha latifolia (cattail)[b]

MAMMALS

Ammospermophilus leucurus (antelope ground squirrel)
Antilocapra americana (pronghorn)
Antrozous pallidus (Pallid bat)
Bison bison (bison)
Canis latrans (coyote)
Cynomys parvidens (prairie dog)[b]
Dipodomys microps (chisel-toothed kangaroo rat)
D. ordi (Ord kangaroo rat)
Erethizon dorsatum (porcupine)[a]
Lepus californicus (jackrabbit)
Lynx rufus (bobcat)
Marmota flaviventris (marmot or rock chuck)
Microtus longicaudus (long-tailed meadow mouse)[a]

M. montanus (mountain vole)
Mustela frenata (long-tailed weasel)
Neotoma cinerea (bushy-tailed woodrat)
N. lepida (desert woodrat)
Odocoileus hemionus (mule deer)
Ovis canadensis (bighorn sheep)
Peromyscus crinitus (canyon mouse)[a]
P. maniculatus (deer mouse)
Spermophilus armatus (Uintah ground squirrel)[b]
S. townsendii (Townsend ground squirrel)
S. variegatus (rock squirrel)[a]
Spilogale putoris (spotted skunk)[b]
Sylvilagus audubonii (cottontail)
S. idahoensis (pygmy rabbit)
S. nuttallii (cottontail)[a]
Taxidea taxus (badger)
Thomomys bottae (southern pocket gopher)
T. talpoides (northern pocket gopher)[a]
Urocyon cinereoargenteus (gray fox)[b]
Vulpes macrotis (kit fox)[a]

BIRDS

Accipiter striatus (sharp-skinned hawk)[a]
Annas cf. acuta (pintail)[a]
A. carolinensis (green-winged teal)[a]
A. cyanoptera (cinnamon teal)[a]
A. platyrhynchos (mallard)
A. strepera (gadwall)[a]
Asio cf. flammeus (short-eared owl)[a]
Aquila chrysaetos (golden eagle)
Aythya affinis (lesser scaup)[a]
Bonasa umbellus (ruffed grouse)[a]
Bubo virginianus (great horned owl)
Buteo jamaicensis (red-tailed hawk)
Capella gallinago (common snipe)
Cathartes aura (turkey vulture)
Centrocercus urophasianus (sage hen)
Chlidonias niger (black tern)[a]
Colaptes sp. (flicker)[a]
Eremophila alpestris (horned lark)[a]
Falco columbarius (pigeon hawk)[a]
F. mexicanus (prairie falcon)[a]
F. peregrinus (duck hawk)[b]
F. sparverius (sparrow hawk)[a]
Larus californicus (california gull)[a]
Leucophoyx thula (snowy egret)
Leucosticte tephrocotis (gray-crowned rosy finch)[a]
Otus sp. (screech owl)[a]
Pica pica (magpie)[a]
Podiceps nigricollis (eared grebe)[a]
Podilymbus podiceps (pied-billed grebe)[a]
Spatula clypeata (shoveler)[a]
Speotyto cunicularia (burrowing owl)[a]
Rallus limicola (virginia rail)[a]
Recurvirostra americana (avocet)[a]
Xanthocephalus xanthocephalus (yellow-headed blackbird)[a]

[a] Lacking in Black Rock period.
[b] Lacking in Wendover period.

153

Bonneville Period, 9000–7500 B.C.

The Bonneville period takes its name from the Pleistocene Lake Bonneville, a now-dry basin that comprises the greater part of the eastern Basin province. Evidence of human activity at this period is scanty, and the character of the Bonneville culture is obscure.

The only excavated and dated materials from this period come from Danger, Smith Creek, and Deer Creek caves (Jennings 1957; Shutler and Shutler 1963; Bryan 1979). Danger and Smith Creek caves are located near the margins of early Lake Bonneville, but evidence (Currey 1980; Currey and James 1982; Spencer et al. 1984) suggests that lake waters had receded from these points by the time of earliest human occupation. Deer Creek and Smith Creek caves are located near permanent streams in mountainous areas of eastern Nevada; Danger Cave adjoins a salt marsh spring on the western margin of the Great Salt Lake Desert.

At Danger Cave a bed of beach gravel deposited by the lake inside the cave was covered by a thin layer of clean water-deposited sand. The first human occupants of the cave made camp on this clean sand floor. The remains of six small fires, several clusters of jasper and obsidian chips, several randomly utilized flake knives, one lanceolate knife or projectile point, three milling stones, and several fragments of handstones found lying on the sand constitute the known cultural inventory of these first people. Dates from this sand layer and from cultural deposits directly overlying it center around 9000 B.C.

At Smith Creek Cave there is a similar depositional pattern with chipped stone flakes, end scrapers, and the broken bases of large stemmed points reminiscent of the Lake Mojave type associated with hearths dating between 8000 and 9000 B.C. ("Prehistory: Introduction," fig. 3, this vol.). Little can be said of the early culture at Deer Creek Cave, since the stratigraphy is poorly controlled, but radiocarbon samples from two deeply buried hearths date human presence there slightly before and slightly after 8000 B.C. Limited subsistence data from the caves suggest that mountain sheep and possibly camels were hunted, but the plants and other animals perhaps used by these people are not yet documented.

Typologically diagnostic surface finds of Clovis and Folsom fluted points in the eastern Basin province and northern Colorado Plateau may belong to the Bonneville period or may immediately precede it (Tripp 1966; Gunnerson 1956; Hunt and Tanner 1960; Wormington and Lister 1956). Fluted points have not been found in any of the cave sites and are not directly dated in the Great Basin, but Clovis fluted points have been radiocarbon dated between 9000 and 9500 B.C. in the Southwest, with Folsom fluted points immediately following them in time (Haynes 1969). These dates would place the Clovis horizon slightly earlier than the first occupations of the Great Basin caves and make Folsom

contemporary with them if the dates are valid for the Great Basin as they are for the Southwest. Large stemmed points of Lake Mohave type, characteristics of the early Western Pluvial Lakes tradition in the western Great Basin, have also been identified in Utah (Madsen, Currey, and Madsen 1976; Janetski and Holmer 1982; Fike 1984). Many fluted and stemmed points have been found along the margins of early Holocene water bodies such as Sevier Lake, which at about this time was a freshwater mere draining into the Great Salt Lake basin (Madsen 1982).

The occurrence of early fluted and stemmed points in open surface sites along pluvial lakeshores is common throughout the Great Basin. It has been suggested that the large stemmed points found throughout the intermontane west derive from the Clovis horizon (Aikens 1978a) or, alternatively, that the Clovis and stemmed specimens represent two contemporary but independent cultural traditions with different origins (Bryan 1979). No archeological consensus has been achieved as to which is the proper interpretation, but the radiocarbon dates from Smith Creek Cave place Lake Mohave–like stemmed points there between 8000 and 9000 B.C., immediately postdating the established time span for the Clovis horizon.

The material culture remains of the Bonneville period are quite meager. The dated sites belong to a period when Pleistocene vegetation patterns were giving way to modern distributions, and it may be that human subsistence and settlement was correspondingly somewhat different from patterns established in Holocene times. Most sites of this period are found around lake margins, and it is probable that ecosystems along these margins were the focus of subsistence. To what extent this focus was on multiple ecosystems remains unclear, although it is known from evidence in the Southwest, Great Plains, and Eastern Woodlands that early fluted point makers were primarily hunters of mammoth, giant bison, and other extinct Pleistocene fauna. The Bonneville period may represent a time of transition between terminal Pleistocene Paleo-Indian big-game hunting and post-Pleistocene Desert Archaic foraging for plant foods and smaller game.

Wendover Period, 7500–4000 B.C.

The Wendover period corresponds to early Archaic phases defined elsewhere in the Basin. It is named after the town of Wendover on the Utah-Nevada boundary because the first rich and well-dated cultural assemblage of the period was found at Danger Cave, less than a mile northeast of town. More sites in a wider array of environmental settings allow a more detailed interpretation of prehistoric life than was possible for the Bonneville period. Dry cave sites adjacent to lake-edge marsh systems include Danger Cave, Hogup Cave, Deadman Cave, Sandwich Shelter, and Black Rock Cave (Jennings 1957; Aikens 1970; Steward 1937a; E.R. Smith 1941; Marwitt, Fry, and Adovasio 1971). Upland sites include Joe's Valley Alcove, Sudden Shelter, Cowboy Cave, Weston Canyon Rockshelter, and O'Malley Shelter (Madsen and Lindsay 1984; Jennings et al. 1980; Jennings, Schroedl, and Holmer 1980; Delisio 1971; Fowler, Madsen, and Hattori 1973). The occurrence of sites over a range of altitudinal and topographical settings implies a roving pattern of hunting and gathering, in which settlements were seasonally occupied. There was probably a shifting balance between hunting and plant collecting at different times of the year, with upland sites mainly oriented to hunting and lowland sites mainly oriented to plant food gathering. Both hunting and gathering activities were probably carried out in varying degrees at virtually all encampments.

The diet of Wendover period peoples was based on a wide range of vegetal foods. At Danger and Hogup caves, the tiny seeds of the pickleweed or burrowweed (*Allenrolfea occidentalis*) as well as the seeds of a variety of other species were major food resources. At Hogup the deposits dating to this period were literally golden with the chaff of the pickleweed. This plant is a low-growing succulent whose habitat is the edges of the salt pans ubiquitous in the Great Basin. In suitable local situations pickleweed may cover extensive areas along the edges of ancient lake beds, where it constitutes a readily available food resource. On slightly higher ground shoreward from the pickleweed zone there is typically a zone of saltgrass. Above that is a zone of greasewood and shadscale, and above that an extensive zone, extending to quite high elevations, with shadscale and sagebrush. Additionally, around the somewhat brackish springs near these sites the bulrush (*Scirpus*), cattail (*Typha*), and other marsh plants occur (Cottam 1942). The occasional gathering of all these species as well as many others is attested by the finding of actual remains of the plants within the cave deposits (table 1). Their consumption as food is demonstrated by the finding of their seeds (Fry 1976) or pollen (Kelso 1970) in desiccated human feces. At Cowboy Cave on the Colorado Plateau the dry deposits preserved plant macrofossil remains of grasses, composites, and other species that indicate a focus on summertime seed harvesting at that site (Jennings et al. 1980).

The tools used in exploiting these resources were simple and generally portable. Abundant fragments of coiled and, in lesser quantity, twined basketry indicate the presence of containers that could have served for gathering and carrying. Tough, tightly woven coiled trays, some of them with many small charred spots on their surfaces, suggest that the gathered seeds were either dried or parched by tossing them together with a few hot coals. Numerous handstones and nether milling slabs indicate the hulling and grinding of seeds, a process

further demonstrated by the finding in dessicated human feces of seeds with cases scored by milling and tiny fragments of stone worn from the mills during the grinding. Further preparation of the seed-meal as cakes or gruel is assumed but not directly demonstrated.

Animals both small and large were also important in the diet, but they were not so readily and consistently obtainable or storable as plant foods, and in that sense they constituted a secondary aspect of the diet. The species taken range from small mammals to birds large game such as deer, pronghorn antelope, mountain sheep, elk, and bison. In the Wendover period deposits at Hogup Cave, four species of large mammals, 32 species of small mammals (including carnivores), and 34 species of birds were represented. In all periods the large mammals provided the bulk of the meat obtained, if weight is used as the criterion. Nevertheless, smaller mammals also contributed signficantly and may have been even more important on a day-to-day basis. During the Wendover period at lake-edge sites, hares, rabbits, various small rodents, and birds were taken in much greater numbers than at any later time (Aikens 1970). During the same period large game is most important at upland sites like Sudden Shelter (Jennings, Schroedl, and Holmer 1980) and Weston Canyon Rockshelter (Delisio 1971).

Equipment that can be identified with the quest for small game is limited in kind, presumably reflecting the relative simplicity of the gear (such as nets and snares) needed to capture the small creatures (fig. 8). From the dry cave sites have come abundant fragments of netting and netting twine made of twisted fibers of Indian hemp (*Apocynum*) and other plants. At Hogup Cave in particular, in the Wendover period deposits there was a strong correlation between the abundance of jackrabbit and cottontail bones and the abundance of netting and cordage fragments. In later periods, when the quantity of rabbit bones declined, so did the quantity of netting fragments. Thus the Wendover period people, like those of historic times in the same region, probably stretched long nets to form broad cul-de-sac traps into which numbers of rabbits could be driven, trapped, and killed during communal hunts. In addition to fragments of netting, there were a few cords tied into a loop at one end that may represent small snares based on a running loop principle. Such devices may have been used in taking the small rodents that are so well represented in the cave deposits.

No special class of equipment used in catching birds has been identified and, presumably, at sites where birds were taken they were obtained without special apparatus. The abundance of waterfowl and shorebird bones in the faunal assemblages from lake-edge sites indicates (along with other evidence) that during the Wendover period there was still a good deal of open water nearby, probably in the form of marshlands that once covered now-barren salt flats (Currey and James 1982).

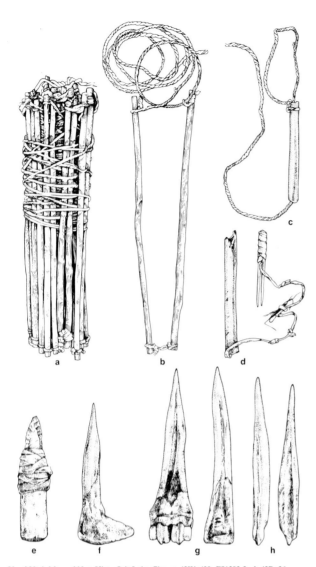

The numerous objects identifiable as hunting weapons and game processing tools relate chiefly to the quest for larger game. The characteristic projectile weapon of the Wendover and subsequent periods was the spearthrower and dart. This is well represented at Hogup and Danger caves by wooden dart foreshafts and both fragmentary and complete atlatls, and at these and many other sites of the region by numerous medium-to-large chipped stone projectile points, which were made in several styles, including the Pinto, Humboldt, Northern Side-notched, and Elko types ("Prehistory: Introduction," fig. 3, this vol.).

It is likely that some, perhaps many, of the objects identified as projectile points actually were used as knife blades. Hafted to a short handle, or even used as hafted at the tip of a dart foreshaft, they would have functioned well for butchering and skinning. Carved wooden hafts, notched to receive such points, are known from Hogup Cave and elsewhere (fig. 8e). Large, ovate chipped bifaces would have served effectively as hand-held cutting and skinning knives. Stone scrapers, chipped to a steeply beveled edge, are also abundant and indicate that working and utilization of the hides of food animals was an important emphasis. Most sites also contain heavy randomly chipped stone flakes and much lithic scrap. This material attests to the manufacture of chipped stone implements at the sites themselves, or rather to the final finishing of artifacts out of roughly shaped raw materials brought to the sites from quarries elsewhere.

Awls and needles made from split mammal long bones offer additional evidence of the utilization of game other than as food (fig. 8f–h). Awls would have served for the manufacture of both leather items and basketry. Needles, though only rarely found, attest to the sewing of soft hides into useful articles. Artifacts such as these appear to complete the cycle of hunting activity attested by all the objects just described—preparation for the hunt, killing of game, butchering for consumption as food, and utilization of animal by-products for essential manufactures.

Clothing is poorly represented. This lack in an otherwise rich archeological record makes it clear that clothing was simple and scanty. The basic item is the fur robe or blanket made of twisted strips of rabbit hide, either loosely twined, or laid out in long parallel strips and again twined together with transverse strands of cordage made of plant fibers. Such a robe would have served for both clothing and sleeping. The only footwear discovered in deposits of this period came from Cowboy Cave where a considerable number of woven plant fiber sandals (fig. 9), reminiscent of those known from the northern Great Basin were excavated (Jennings et al. 1980).

Hide pouches made of the skins of small mammals have been found at several sites; some of these may have served as wallets or purses carried on the person.

U. of Utah Mus. of Nat. Hist., Salt Lake City: c, 42Wn420–FS1393.2; d, 42Bo36–FS670.23; e, 42Bo36–FS581.18; f, 42Bo36–FS446.113; g, 42Bo36–FS160, 42Bo36–FS699; h, 42Bo36–FS149, 42Bo36–FS104.

Fig. 8. Artifacts found in Utah caves. a–b, Scissors snares, Cowboy Cave, dated about A.D. 100–500. Found as a bundle (a) of 23 snares, each snare (b) consisting of 2 greasewood sticks about 18 cm long joined at one end by a short section of cordage tied with overhand knots. At the other end, one stick has a short cord loop bound with sinew wrapping, while the other has a cord 90–100 cm long attached with an overhand knot. The cord passes through the sinew-bound loop so that the sticks are squeezed together when the line is pulled. The cordage is Z-twist, tied with a simple overhand knot to prevent unraveling. Spier (1955) discusses setting scissors snares. c, Noose snare made from a section of *Phragmites*. The 2-ply, S-twist cordage is 64.0 cm long. d, Ring-and-pin game from Hogup Cave, dated 6400–1250 B.C. This version consists of a long bone with a hide thong attached to one end that holds 2 well-smoothed bone pins. When found the pin was inserted in the bone tube. e, Hafted graver, Hogup Cave, dated A.D. 400–1350. The handle is of antelope or deer rib. The unifacially flaked stone point is wedged into the partially split rib and held in place by several wraps of a hide thong. f, L-shaped awl made from ungulate scapula, Hogup Cave, dated 6400–1250 B.C. g, Large awls with articular ends left intact as handles; ungulate long bones were split longitudinally, and then ground to shape; Hogup Cave. h, Splinter awls made from small linear sections of ungulate long bone; Hogup Cave. Length of e 9.0 cm, rest same scale.

AIKENS AND MADSEN

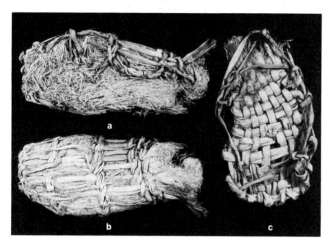

U. of Utah Mus. of Nat. Hist., Salt Lake City: a–b, 42Wn420–FS1980.1; c, 42Wn420–FS1413.1.

Fig. 9. Archaic open-twined (a, bottom view, b, top view) and plain-weave (c) sandals from Cowboy Cave, Utah. These are 2 of the 54 sandals found in strata dating from about 6575 B.C. to A.D. 100. The open-twined sandals are made of whole yucca leaves, with 2 or more leaves treated as one element to form the warps. Rows of Z-twist twining intersect the warps the length of the sandal, creating the markedly open weave. The inner soles are grass padding. The heels of both specimens are completely worn through. The plain-weave sandal was done in a basic over-one-under-one weave, with warp and weft elements of 2–4 yucca leaves. The weft elements are continuous and double back into the weave at the edge of the sandal. These were tied to the foot by thin yucca strips attached to the sole margins, which were pulled across the foot in the middle and knotted or looped together. Similar specimens are part of the Desha complex of northern Ariz., representative of the terminal Archaic or early Basketmaker II in the Southwest (Lindsay et al. 1968:95). Length of c, 20 cm.

Other accessories apparently worn as pendants, necklaces, or bracelets include small perforated bone tablets or mammal teeth, bone tubes (cut sections of small animal long bones) (fig. 10), and several perforated shells of olivella, a marine species imported from the Pacific Coast. Such objects, though present, are rare.

Small cobbles and pieces of stone with incised geometric designs similar to those on rock art sites may represent a form of hunting magic. These specimens are widespread in Great Basin sites. Painted stones have been found in the southernmost part of the area, most notably at Cowboy Cave (Jennings et al. 1980). Other reflections of the esthetic sensibilities of these ancient people are found in the fine workmanship seen on objects of everyday use, especially in the basketry and stone tool complexes, where a high order of technical competence was regularly achieved.

Black Rock Period, 4000 B.C.–A.D. 500

The Black Rock period is named after Black Rock Cave located near the southern end of Great Salt Lake at the base of the Oquirrh Mountains (Steward 1937a; Madsen

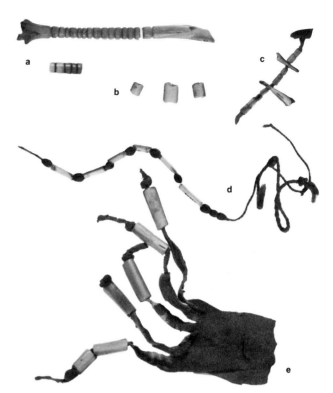

U. of Utah Mus. of Nat. Hist., Salt Lake City: a, 42Bo36–FS255.385; FS255.306; b, FS285.506; FS48.626; FS55.16; FS11; FS632.20; c, FS417; d, FS443.2; e, FS47.

Fig. 10. Tubular bone beads, made by incising the shafts of rabbit and bird long bones and then snapping off the scored sections. These specimens were found in cultural levels dating from 5865 B.C.–A.D. 1350 at Hogup Cave, Utah. Length of a, 11.2 cm, rest same scale. a, Rabbit long bone scored for bead production, with articular end still attached, and one smaller section, also scored, but without articular end. b, Unfinished tubular sections, snapped from the long bone, and ready for grinding to finished form. c, Perforated rodent teeth interspersed with short tubular bone beads. In one case, the scored bead was broken apart, forming two small ones. These beads are dated about A.D. 1450. d, Finished tubular beads strung on a length of 2-ply, S-twist Apocynum cordage, alternating with juniper berries, dated about 4250 B.C. e, Large beads strung on hide fringes, held in place by a single overhand knot at the loose end of each fringe, dated about A.D. 400.

1983). This culture is also well-represented at Deadman Cave several miles to the east, at Hogup and Danger caves west of the lake, and at a large number of localities elsewhere in the region. In conjunction with a dramatic increase in occupation sites during the early portion of this period, there was an apparent broadening of settlement patterns with a growing emphasis on the exploitation of upland zones. Projectile point styles also changed, with older types dropping out of the record and newer types becoming dominant.

During this period, occupation at ancient camps such as Danger Cave, Hogup Cave, and Sudden Shelter continued, but many new settlements became established as well. Of 23 sites in the eastern Basin whose initial occupations are dated, 12 were inhabited for the first time between 4000 and 2000 B.C. This pattern is sup-

U. of Utah Mus. of Nat. Hist., Salt Lake City.

Fig. 11. Bundle of painted gaming sticks from Danger Cave, Utah, dating between 3700 B.C. and A.D. 200. The sticks are serviceberry, 24.2–26.0 cm in length. The paint may be reddish brown organic material or vegetable dye. The sticks were found wrapped with cliff rose fiber. The nature of the game is unknown, but it can be assumed that it has parallels in the stick games recorded for Basin ethnographic groups.

ported by survey data that indicate a nearly 400 percent increase in the number of sites characterized by the Elko and Gypsum series projectile points of the Black Rock period, as compared to those characterized by the Humboldt and Pinto types of the preceding Wendover period (Intermountain Antiquities Computer System, at the University of Utah since 1982). Many of these new sites are located in upland regions away from the lake basins, in areas occupied previously only at low intensities, if at all. Information gathered from the Great Salt Lake region illustrates this development (Gruhn 1979; Lindsay and Sargent 1979; Fowler 1968a; Dalley 1976). Upland sites are situated in piñon-juniper zones in locations that allow access to sage and grass communities and higher montane resources. Many upland sites were primarily hunting camps, although grasses (such as Indian ricegrass, *Oryzopsis hymenoides*) were also collected. No site contains evidence of piñon utilization even though some are located in areas that presently have piñon (Heizer, Baumhoff, and Clewlow 1968; Shutler and Shutler 1963). As Madsen (1982:215) relates:

> The preferred (or perhaps the most abundant or the most readily procured) faunal resource was mountain sheep ([S.J.] Miller 1979). Deer and rabbit remains are also common,

and bison remains are occasionally recovered. Evidence from some sites (e.g., Dally 1976) indicates occupation by family groups rather than small male hunting parties. This strengthens the probability that most of these sites (some are far from lake margins) are related to the lake-edge sites through an occupational pattern often referred to as a seasonal or annual round. As noted, upland species such as mountain sheep in lake-edge sites after 5,000–6,000 years ago are indicative of a mobile subsistence-settlement system ([S.J.] Miller 1979).

The changes noted in the earlier part of the Black Rock period may be related to a mid-Holocene period of increased aridity that reached its greatest intensity at about that time (Antevs 1955; Baumhoff and Heizer 1965; Mehringer 1977). Diminishing lake margin resources and increasing population might have induced human groups to take greater advantage of upland resources than they had previously.

Later in the Black Rock period, Neoglacial climatic change brought about a regime in which effective moisture was at times significantly higher than the Holocene average (Currey and James 1982). The Neoglacial changes may have enhanced the productivity of local biotic communities and may have contributed to an overall increase of sites during the period, but at some lake-edge sites rising water levels resulting from this increased effective moisture appear to have actually diminished the local subsistence base by flooding springs and marshes on the lake periphery. At Hogup Cave, the later part of the Black Rock period saw a decline in the utilization of wild seed foods and the intensity of occupation at the site. The meal remains found in human feces indicate that a smaller range of plant species was being harvested. A marked decrease in the relative frequency of milling slabs and handstones is consonant with that observation. Jackrabbits, cottontails, and other small mammals all declined markedly as well, and the number of avian species shrank from 34 to 9 (table 1).

The virtual disappearance of waterfowl and shorebirds from the archeological record indicates the probable reason for the above shifts. Change in the marshland habitat that these birds require would also have wrought changes in the distribution and abundance of the other species that had previously been exploited at Hogup Cave, and it is clear from the avian evidence that marshy conditions on the lakebed near the cave had disappeared by the later Black Rock period (Harper and Alder 1970, 1972). Mehringer ("Prehistoric Environments," this vol.) mentions evidence that an episode of high water flooded the lakeside marsh below Hogup Cave and terminated the availability of shallow-water resources there around 1000 B.C. A similar event may have affected human occupation of Danger Cave at about the same time (Madsen and Berry 1975), but other lake-edge sites, such as the Fish Springs Caves (Madsen 1982b), adjacent to spring marshes above the level of the Neoglacial lake rise, continued to be in-

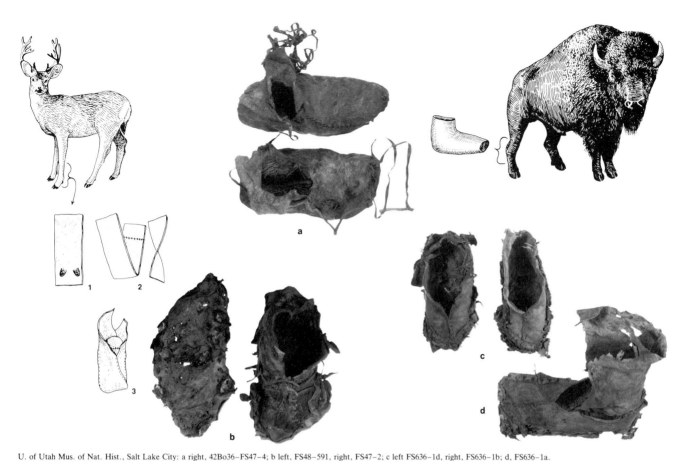

U. of Utah Mus. of Nat. Hist., Salt Lake City: a right, 42Bo36–FS47–4; b left, FS48–591, right, FS47–2; c left FS636–1d, right, FS636–1b; d, FS636–1a.

Fig. 12. Mocassin types recovered from Hogup Cave, Utah. a, One-piece moccasins cut from bison hide. These are termed "hock" moccasins because they were removed from the hock of the bison by girdling the leg at two points (diagram) and removing the hide as a skin tube. The tube was then sewn at one end, and the wearer's foot inserted into the opening at the opposite end, with the natural L-shaped angle of the hide at the joint serving as the heel. The string is a hide thong attached at the front of the ankle, taken around the back of the ankle above the heel, brought forward once again, and tied. Specimens are poorly tanned and sewed with 2-ply, S-twist sinew. They are dated about A.D. 420. b, The distinctive Fremont moccasin, made from hide cut from the forelegs of deer or antelope, with incisions made below the knee and just above the hoof (diagram), using 3 pieces of hide. The two upper pieces were sewn to a broad sole cut in the shape of the foot, and joined together along a seam running diagonally from the front of the ankle outward toward and over the third or fourth toe. The upper, longer piece was pulled back and around to at least the center of the heel. The 2 flaps formed by the ends of the uppers could be folded over one another at the back of the heel and ankle and held in place by wrapping the ankle with a tie string. The tie string was commonly a buckskin thong attached at the top of the diagonal seam near the ankle, and pulled straight downward to the juncture of the sole and upper on the outside of the foot, where it was held in place by being passed under a perforation near the bottom edge of the upper. From this point the tie string was threaded through additional perforations cut along the bottom edge of the upper and drawn around the back of the heel and brought forward again at the other side of the foot. The most conspicuous feature is the use of dewclaws on the soles as hobnails. Location of the dewclaws is variable, but they were usually placed at either side of the ball of the foot pointing toward the heel and at the heel or under the instep. Specimens are poorly tanned, sewed with 2-ply, S-twist sinew, and dated 650 B.C.–A.D. 420. The style was first defined by Morss (1931). c, Child's and d, an adult's moccasins, with attached legging. The moccasin proper is a single piece of hide, folded up and over the foot, sewed across the top along the center of the instep from the toes to the ankle, and up the back to about mid-ankle. To this basic footpiece was added a separate outer sole. A hide tie attached above the heel served to lash the moccasin below the ankle in the child's version, or around the ankle and the calf in the adult's pair. The child's moccasins have perforations along the top of the narrow ankle flap, perhaps indicative of an attached legging as in the adult's pair. Specimens are well-tanned, hair side turned in, and sewed with 2-ply, S-twist sinew. A yellowish to reddish cast on both pairs of moccasins suggests they were once painted with red pigment. Both pairs are dated at about 650 B.C. Length of a 22.0 cm, rest same scale.

habited. Occupation of higher altitude sites away from the lakebeds continued, and conditions for human existence in the uplands may even have been enhanced by an improved moisture regime.

The above data suggest that both demographic and dietary adjustments were made in the Desert Archaic lifeway in response to changing environmental conditions during the middle and later Holocene; however, the changes noted were not fundamental: they did not dramatically alter the desert adaptations established during the preceding Wendover period. Foraging and collecting a wide variety of plants and animals continued to constitute the food base. The ways in which these species were collected remained the same. Most of the tools used in the subsistence system were not substantially modified, and many of the same sites continued to be occupied at about the same time of year.

A few changes in the technical complex may be noted. New projectile point styles appeared early in the period. During the late Black Rock period the bow and arrow came into use and by the end of the period had fully replaced the older atlatl-and-dart weapon system. The new arrowpoints were very much smaller than the earlier dart points, but, particularly in the case of the corner-notched and stemmed Rose Spring and Eastgate series, were highly similar in form to the larger types that preceded them.

The basketry complex associated with seed gathering in the Wendover period continued without major change, but there were shifts in the relative frequencies of certain techniques, with one-rod-and-bundle foundation construction becoming dominant. Leather moccasins of a peculiar cut, fashioned so that the dewclaws of the animal that furnished the leather served like hobnails on the underside of the sole, appeared during this time (fig. 12). At Hogup Cave, small bundles of plant fibers were made into anthropomorphic or zoomorphic figurines, with bone splinters or porcupine quills protruding as horns from the plant fiber head, and feathers protruding below as the body of the specimen ("Portable Art Objects," fig. 4, this vol.). In the southeast, at Cowboy Cave and other sites, zoomorphic figurines made of split willows ("Portable Art Objects," fig. 5, this vol.), bent and bound to form representations of quadrupeds (probably deer and mountain sheep) relate to the so-called Grand Canyon Figurine complex centered outside the area of present concern (Schroedl 1977). All these types save the last became conspicious elements of the later Fremont culture, which dominated the eastern Basin province and northern Colorado Plateau in the succeeding phase.

Transition to Horticulture

Near the beginning of the Christian era a number of features characteristic of settled horticultural village life in the later Southwest were introduced into the Archaic cultures of the eastern Basin and northern Colorado Plateau. Earliest was the replacement of the atlatl or spear-thrower by the bow and arrow. Small projectile points of the Rose Spring and Eastgate types used to tip arrows began to occur in Archaic contexts (Holmer 1978, 1985). Elko series points, earlier used to tip atlatl darts, continued to occur after the transition to the bow and arrow was complete, probably as multipurpose tools hafted on handles and used as knives or similar implements (Wylie 1975). This technological shift presumably modified hunting patterns, but the nature of the change is poorly understood. There does seem to have been an increased emphasis on larger game, and bison and pronghorn antelope increased relative to other species.

About A.D. 400 to 500 limited amounts of pottery begin to appear in these same sites. Pottery sherds are occasionally accompanied by small amounts of maize, and it is probable that pottery and domesticated plants were introduced together. The immediate impact of this introduction was apparently limited, since the same sites continued to be occupied in much the same way as in earlier Archaic periods. Hunting and plant collecting continued and apparently still constituted the major subsistence base. The gathering of piñon nuts is well documented for the first time during this transitional period (Madsen 1985; Simms 1983a). Farther-reaching cultural change was in the offing.

By A.D. 800 settled Fremont cultural horticultural village sites characterized by pit houses, above- and below-ground storage features, and corn-beans-squash horticulture had begun to occur on the northern Colorado Plateau and in the eastern Basin (Madsen 1982; Marwitt 1970). Although some hunting and the collecting of wild plants continued, particularly in productive marsh areas, the advent of these settled farming villages finally marks the end of the Archaic.

For over 9,000 years the highly variable and highly adaptive Desert Archaic culture supported prehistoric peoples throughout the arid west. Through both time and space, societal variation probably ranged from relatively large, stable groups living within certain highly productive ecosystems, to very small familial groups moving from one temporary habitation spot to another and subsisting on a variety of sparse and scattered resources. This flexibility and adaptability allowed Archaic folk to survive and even flourish throughout the vicissitudes of environmental change that characterized late Quaternary times in the eastern Basin and northern Colorado Plateau.

Fremont Cultures

JOHN P. MARWITT

The Fremont culture label is applied to several culturally related but geographically widespread archeological complexes centered in the state of Utah. In terms of the overall culture history of the Great Basin, Fremont is an oddity, even an aberration, in that for a period of about 900 years (A.D. 400 to 1300), desert foragers were replaced by more or less sedentary horticulturalists who lived in scattered farmsteads and small villages. They made pottery, built substantial dwellings and storage structures, and developed a unique artistic tradition manifested in rock art and modeled clay figurines. After the Fremont culture disappeared in the late thirteenth or early fourteenth century, the Archaic type of lifeway continued to dominate the Basin until the arrival of Euro-American culture in the mid-nineteenth century.

Fremont culture developed in an area of considerable environmental diversity from an Archaic base that for thousands of years had become regionally specialized. Therefore, it is difficult to characterize in terms of a uniform set of cultural traits or a single cultural pattern. Even though a village farming pattern is broadly characteristic of Fremont, setting it off from both the preceding Archaic foraging cultures and the similar Shoshonean cultures that followed, horticulture and sedentary villages were never developed by the Fremont people to the extent that they were by their neighbors in the prehistoric Southwest. Hunting and gathering remained important economic activities for all groups during the entire span of the Fremont culture. This is especially true of the northern and western parts of the Fremont area, where reliance on game and wild plant foods appears to have outweighed the role of horticulture in subsistence, and where architecture was rather crude and insubstantial by comparison with the rest of the Fremont area.

This culture was influenced at various times and in various ways by the Southwestern cultures, but it is probably best viewed as the product of indigenous Basin traditions. Trade and other contacts with the Southwest do not seem to have been particularly close, and the culture traits that were introduced from the Southwest were modified and adapted by the Fremont peoples to suit the requirements of their own less hospitable environment.

Maize and pottery are ultimately of Mexican origin, but the route of their introduction into the Fremont area has not been established with certainty. Several radiocarbon dates from northern Utah in the A.D. 400 to 700 range (see Marwitt 1970) suggest that Fremont culture crystallized too early for Basketmaker influence from the Southwest to have played an important part in its genesis. Rather, the specific source of many Southwestern traits in Fremont may be the Mogollon area of Arizona and New Mexico, where there are a number of striking Fremont parallels in early Mogollon phases, including the very distinctive "Utah" type metate with a shelf on the end away from the operator (fig. 1) (Marwitt 1970; Jennings 1978).

Area and Environment

The archeological area described here includes most of the state of Utah north of the Colorado, Escalante, and Virgin rivers, as well as adjacent portions of eastern Nevada, western Colorado, and southern Idaho (fig. 2). Approximately 50 percent of this area lies within the physiographic Great Basin; most of the remainder is part of the Colorado Plateau. Separating the two

U. of Utah, Archeol. Center, Salt Lake City: left, 42Wn229–60; right, 42Wn229–37.
Fig. 1. Metates found at Gnat Haven, Utah, a San Rafael Fremont site radiocarbon dated A.D. 945±60. left, Characteristic Fremont type metate, with well-defined grinding trough and flat rest or shelf at the narrow proximal end nearest the user; right, typical Anasazi-style mealing bin consisting of vertically set slabs in a rectangular excavation and a flat grinding slab, which lacks both the trough and proximal shelf of the Fremont type. The presence of both types on a single Fremont site, which also yielded a relatively high proportion of Anasazi pottery types, indicates considerable interaction between the two cultural groups.

161

Fig. 2. Fremont sites and archeological regions: Great Basin variant—1, Great Salt Lake; 2, Sevier; 3, Parowan; Colorado Plateau variant—4, Uinta; 5, San Rafael.

physiographic provinces and their respective drainages are the north-south trending Wasatch Mountains and a series of high plateaus (Gunnison, Sevier, Panguitch, Paunsagunt) that form a curving line from the southern terminus of the Wasatch range toward the southwestern corner of Utah.

Both the eastern Basin province—a region of fault-block mountain ranges and alternating valleys—and the Colorado Plateau with its dissected highlands and narrow canyons are regions of great topographic and environmental diversity. Elevation ranges from approximately 3,000 feet on canyon floors to over 12,000 feet on the peaks of the highest mountains. Most of the land lies between 4,000 and 6,000 feet above sea level.

Precipitation, which is controlled by elevation, terrain, and temperature, is highly variable throughout the area. A reasonable average for valley floors of medium elevation would be five to eight inches annually. Much of the effective annual moisture results from winter snowfall and runoff, but the southwestern part of the area is also subject to summer rainfall from storms originating in the Gulf of California.

As a result of the variegated combinations of latitude, elevation, terrain, and precipitation, biomes are quite complex. Flora and fauna range from Upper Sonoran communities below 6,000 feet to arctic-alpine communities on high mountain peaks. Most valley floors and medium elevation uplands are arid to semiarid, but there is extensive freshwater and saltwater marshland bordering the eastern and northern edges of the Great

Salt Lake. Smaller desert marshes can be found in many of the valleys of the eastern Great Basin.

The environmental setting of Fremont culture is not rich but quite varied. Water, land suitable for small-scale horticulture, game, and wild plants were not abundant, nor were they uniformly distributed throughout the Fremont area. Along with cultural continuity from the regionally differentiated Archaic base, and the uneven assimilation of culture elements inspired by or introduced from the Southwest, variation in adaptation to regionally and locally different environmental conditions probably accounts for much of the marked regional flavor to be seen in Fremont culture.

Fremont Culture Origins

The Fremont culture was named by Morss (1931) based on his investigations in the Fremont River drainage of south-central Utah. Morss and many later investigators have recognized its generally Southwestern cast, to the extent that some have argued that Fremont developed almost wholly as a result of the diffusion of Southwestern culture elements such as pit houses, masonry architecture, pottery, and cultivated plants (fig. 3) to sparse populations of indigenes on the "northern periphery" of the Southwest. The hypothesis is that the local populations adapted these traits into their own

U. of Utah, Mus. of Nat. Hist., Salt Lake City.

Fig. 3. Varieties of corn commonly recovered from Fremont sites. These examples are from Harris Wash sites on the Escalante River drainage in south-central Utah. Fremont sites generally yield typical varieties of the Southwest corn series (a), a distinctive variety termed Fremont Dent (b, c), and forms intermediate between the 2 or weak dents (d, e, f). Fremont Dent has large, tapered cobs with wide butts, dented kernels, and rows that reach 14 in number rather than the 8 rows typical of Southwestern varieties. Winter (1973) argues that it represents an in situ development from nondented varieties of corn and that it thrived because it is very resistant to drought, extremes of climate, and a short growing season, all factors of the local climate (see also Galinat and Gunnerson 1963, 1969; Galinat and Campbell 1967). Confirmation of this view is found in a radiocarbon date of A.D. 525 ± 100 for a cultural unit with corn at Clydes Cavern, northern Utah, prior to development of the Fremont culture. Another view is that Mexican dents hybridized with Southwestern varieties and were transported into the Fremont culture area (Anderson 1948; Cutler 1966). Length of a about 14.6 cm, rest same scale.

cultural pattern, but some actual migration of Southwestern peoples may have been involved as well. Most advocates of this hypothesis of Fremont origins place the date of the Southwestern stimulus at a general Basketmaker III time level. But some view Fremont as the product of an Anasazi expansion beginning around A.D. 900. For detailed discussions of this general interpretation of Fremont origins, see Steward (1933), Wormington (1955), Ambler (1966), Gunnerson (1969), and Berry (1980).

Aikens (1966) has suggested that the early Fremont people were bison hunters of Athapaskan origin who entered the Utah region about A.D. 500, and who adopted and modified Pueblo ceramics, horticulture, and architecture. Fremont would thus be a synthesis of Plains and Southwest elements, with the Plains elements being more obtrusive on the northern frontier of Southwest influence. While this thesis is difficult to defend given the degree of Archaic-Fremont continuity, it is true that in the northern parts of its range Fremont does have a Plains flavor in both material culture and in subsistence.

More economical explanations for the genesis of Fremont culture are those of Rudy (1953), Jennings (1956), and Taylor (1957), who see it as an indigenous local development with roots in the Desert Archaic, but influenced to varying degrees in different regions and at different times by elements introduced from the Southwest. It can be shown that there is a great deal of cultural continuity in both subsistence techniques and material culture traits between Fremont and the antecedent Archaic (Aikens 1976; Holmer 1980; Madsen 1980a, 1982). Characteristic Fremont elements such as hide moccasins ("Prehistory of the Eastern Area," fig. 12, this vol.), one-rod-and-bundle basketry, incised stone tablets, and anthropomorphic figurines ("Portable Art Objects," fig. 9, this vol.) along with less diagnostic artifacts commonly found in Fremont contexts, all appear in pre-Fremont (Archaic) contexts well before A.D. 400. In some cases they appear as early as 2500 B.C. (Aikens 1970, 1972). There seems to be a greater degree of Archaic-Fremont cultural continuity in the Basin than there is on the Colorado Plateau (Holmer 1980).

The transition from Archaic to Fremont is clearest at Hogup Cave in northwestern Utah. There, the full Fremont complex appears only after A.D. 400, when pottery, maize, bone pendants, and other Fremont traits were simply added to the Archaic assemblage without replacement or marked cultural discontinuity.

Understanding Fremont culture origins is badly complicated by the fact that the complex seems to have emerged in a peculiar patchwork fashion, and no single beginning date can be made to fit Fremont over its geographic range. Recognizable Fremont patterns appear first in northern Utah, then a little after A.D. 400 in the Great Salt Lake region, and by A.D. 650 in the Uinta Basin. For eastern Utah south of the Uinta Basin,

there are single radiocarbon dates of A.D. 380 ± 60 from Cedar Siding Shelter (Martin et al. 1983) and A.D. 160 ± 100 from Pint Size Shelter (Lindsay and Lund 1976). Although both dates were obtained from hearths with associated Fremont artifacts, they are surprisingly early in view of the fact that elsewhere in this section of the state no Fremont occupation has been documented before A.D. 700. For the Great Basin south of the Great Salt Lake, the earliest radiocarbon dates cluster between A.D. 800 and 900 (Marwitt 1970).

The lack of a uniform date for the emergence of Fremont may be due to the fact that regional or even local populations could have had different ethnic origins in the Archaic of the Basin and Plateau, on the Great Plains, and in the Southwest. Madsen (1979) is of the opinion that all the origin theories that have been proposed (Plains, Southwest, and in situ Archaic) have some degree of merit. He suggests that there were two, or possibly three, separate groups that lived in the Fremont area and shared some rather minor traits acquired through trade or the spread of a religious cult expressed in rock art and anthropomorphic clay figurines (fig. 4). This theory is somewhat heterodox and has very little direct support, but it does have the advantage of being able to account for both the temporal unevenness of the Fremont emergence and the characteristic variability of Fremont material culture. For example, in Madsen's model, the late appearance of the Parowan variant in southwestern Utah, without local antecedents, as well as its relatively strong Southwest flavor, could be due to a northward expansion of Virgin branch Anasazi after A.D. 800. Similarly, the Plains elements present in northwestern Utah, southern Idaho, and the Uinta Basin would be explained if the post-Archaic populations of these areas were Plains-derived. However, even though there seems to be a blending of Plains traits with indigenous and Southwest-derived elements, the time and mechanism of their introduction has not been determined (Marwitt 1979).

Regional Variation

The degree of variation in Fremont culture is so great that some students have questioned the very existence of Fremont as a broad taxonomic unit. Madsen and Lindsay (1977), for example, restrict Fremont culture to the Colorado Plateau, employing the term Sevier to refer to the contemporaneous and related occupations of the eastern Basin province. This interpretation has the advantage of correlating major cultural differences in subsistence, settlement pattern, and material remains with the major physiographic and environmental provinces of the region, and it clearly has a considerable degree of utility in clarifying the broad differences between the Basin and Colorado Plateau cultural patterns. *163*

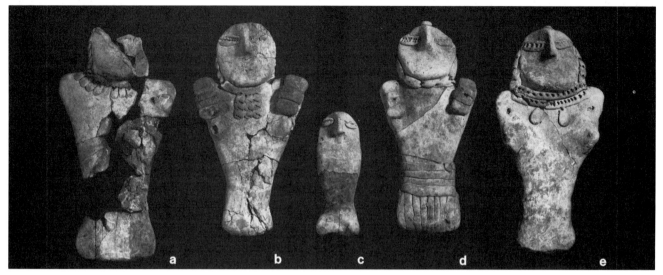

U. of Utah, Mus. of Nat. Hist., Salt Lake City.

Fig. 4. Five anthropomorphic fired clay figurines from the Old Woman site, south-central Utah. The clay lacks temper, and it is presumed that the figures were baked accidently when the dwelling burned. These specimens are typical of San Rafael variant figurines, having well-formed bodies, with modeled faces and anatomical features, hairdresses, necklaces, pendants, "bow tie" shoulder ornaments, and skirts and girdles of carefully applied clay pellets and strips of clay. a and d appear to be male representations, b and e, females, and c, perhaps a child. These lack the painting and backside basketry impressions of those in "Portable Art Objects" fig. 9, this vol. The figurines are dated A.D. 1100–1200. Their use is unknown, but they may have been used in fertility rites (cf. Taylor 1957; Morss 1954). Costume details and body form have close parallels in Fremont rock art. Height of far right about 11.3 cm, rest same scale.

It is also clear that the two patterns, whatever they are called, are culturally related. For this reason, many students retain the term Fremont, if only as a convenient label for the whole (Lohse 1980).

Distinct cultural variants or regional expressions appear to be present from the beginning of Fremont. Specific Archaic antecedents have not been identified for all the variants, but as Aikens (1972) suggests, Archaic assemblages at Hogup Cave and Deluge Shelter (Leach 1970) might represent basal traditions that developed into the regional Fremont cultures centered in northwestern Utah and the Uinta Basin, respectively. For the central and southern parts of the Fremont area, and especially for the western Colorado Plateau, specific Archaic antecedents have not been identified with certainty. Archaic assemblages from Clydes Cavern (Winter and Wylie 1974), Cowboy Caves (Jennings 1980), or Sudden Shelter (Jennings, Schroedl, and Holmer 1980) sites are presumably ancestral to later Fremont developments in eastern Utah and western Colorado, as may be the Uncompahgre complex of western Colorado (Wormington and Lister 1956).

Marwitt (1970) has distinguished five Fremont geographic variants, defined primarily on the basis of material culture trait distributions, subsistence, and settlement patterns. Three of these (the Great Salt Lake, Sevier, and Parowan variants) are restricted to the Basin province and are in effect subdivisions of the more inclusive unit termed Sevier by Madsen and Lindsay (1977). The other two variants (Uinta and San Rafael) are centered in the region east of the Wasatch Plateau and jointly comprise the Fremont proper, as recognized by Madsen and Lindsay. Each variant is a regional subculture with links to the others but with its own regional tradition and ecological correlates. Together with continuity from a regionally differentiated Archaic and the relative degree of interaction with non-Fremont populations, the requirements of adaptation to the special ecological circumstances of each area contributed to the distinctiveness of the Fremont variants.

Cultural boundaries between the variants are not well marked, and cultural transitions are gradual. Thus the center or "core" locality of each variant is the most distinctive when compared to other regions. It is also probable that the boundaries were not stable over time; however, as variable as Fremont is, the essential identity of the Fremont cultural tradition cannot be denied. All the regional variants have more in common with one another than does any of them with neighboring, non-Fremont areas. Fremont is best studied on its own terms rather than as a reflection of the Southwest.

Southwestern Utah

The Parowan Fremont variant, centered in the Parowan Valley of southwestern Utah, is best known from excavations at Paragonah (Judd 1917a, 1917, 1919, 1926; Meighan et al. 1956), Median Village (Marwitt 1970), Evans Mound (McKusick 1960; Ruby and Alexander 1962; Berry 1972, 1974; Dodd 1982), Beaver (Judd 1917a, 1926), Kanosh (Steward 1931, 1933a), Marysvale (Gillin 1941), and Garrison (Taylor 1954).

Parowan Fremont shows a significant amount of influence from the Virgin branch Anasazi located to the south. In part, this may be due to Proto-Basketmaker or Basketmaker-like antecedents. No Basketmaker occupation is known for the Parowan Valley or for any part of the Parowan Fremont region, but there are numerous sites of Basketmaker affiliation not far to the south (Nusbaum 1922; Judd 1926; Wheeler 1942; Shutler 1961).

Settlements are quite large by Fremont standards. The sites consist of closely spaced pit houses (fig. 5) and coursed adobe storage structures. They were occupied more or less continuously for periods of 100–200 years or perhaps even longer and tend to be situated on the floors of alluvial valleys near perennial streams, the waters of which could easily have been diverted for irrigation (fig. 6). The economy of the village inhabitants was based largely on maize horticulture, which was supplemented to an important extent by hunting of game and the collection of wild plant foods in several ecological zones. Outside the Parowan Valley, and especially in the western part of the subarea, settlements are quite small and most appear to have been occupied only seasonally, along with caves and rockshelters, for hunting and gathering.

Architecture and other aspects of material culture are quite uniform, especially in the core area of the Parowan Valley. Compared to other Fremont subcultures the Parowan variant is distinctive in several ways. Both circular and quadrilateral pit dwellings are found. These commonly include tunnel adjuncts interpreted as ventilators, with attached adobe or jacal deflectors. Ceramic artifacts include decorated and undecorated bowls and jars, almost all of which can be assigned to the sand-tempered Snake Valley Grayware series, which appears to have its center of manufacture in the Parowan Valley.

Other characteristic artifacts that distinguish this variant typologically from equivalent units elsewhere in the Fremont area include the distinctive Parowan basal–notched projectile point form ("Prehistory: Introduction," figs. 3–4, this vol.), flaked bone scrapers, lateral metapodial awls, and bone finger rings (fig. 7–9). With the exception of Parowan basal–notched points, which are commonly found in Virgin branch Anasazi sites but not in other Fremont areas, these artifact categories are rare or are absent outside the boundaries of the Parowan variant.

Sites outside the Parowan Valley do not show the uniformity characteristic of the core area. For example, pit houses at the Garrison site (Taylor 1954) lack ventilators and deflectors; the ceramic assemblage includes significant minority proportion of basalt-tempered Sevier Gray, and other artifact categories are stylistically more variable than they are in the Parowan Valley sites.

Two sequential cultural phases have been defined for

U. of Utah, Archeol. Center, Salt Lake City: top, 42In124–76; bottom, 42In124–92.

Fig. 5. A Summit phase (A.D. 900–1050) housepit at Median Village, Utah. The dwelling had a maximum diameter of 14 feet 7 inches, with essentially vertical pit walls cut a maximum of 14 inches into the ground. The structure had burned, as evidenced by a radial arrangement of charred roof timbers and clumps of burned adobe fragments on the floor, and intense reddening of the dirt walls (top). The roof was a flat-topped, quadrilateral framework of timbers supported on 4 or more interior posts, from which leaners were run down onto the exterior ground surface. This superstructure was covered over with small sticks laid horizontally, and grass, probably in the form of mats, which in turn were plastered with a thick coat of adobe. A crawlway-ventilator shaft (top of bottom picture) extended out from the northwestern sector of the dwelling for a distance of about 6 feet. The interior end of the crawlway was set off from the house interior by a jacal deflector 6 inches thick and as high as the dirt walls. The centrally placed firepit was circular, clay-rimmed, and sand-lined. Structure plan and construction design is typical of Fremont architecture, although details vary throughout the regions (cf. Lohse 1980).

the Parowan Valley (Marwitt 1970; Berry 1974). The earlier Summit phase (before A.D. 900 to 1100) is characterized by exclusively circular pit house architecture, crude anthropomorphic figurines made of unfired clay, and the absence of corrugated ceramics. In addition to Median Village, the type site, Summit phase compo-

U. of Utah, Archeol. Center, Salt Lake City: 42In124-3.

Fig. 6. View from Median Village, Utah, toward Summit Canyon about one mile to the south. This site location on a broad, sloping alluvial fan at the base of the Wasatch Plateau is typical of Fremont village settlement patterns in western Utah. Residents could take advantage of the water and nutrients supplied to fields by seasonal flooding.

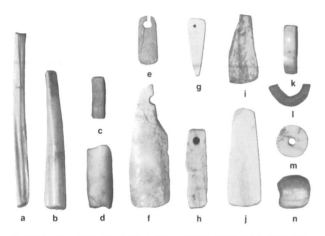

U. of Utah, Mus. of Nat. Hist., Salt Lake City: a, 42In124–FS497–187; b, FS477–219; c, FS149–91; d, FS465–225; e, FS398–96; f, FS167–62; g, FS149–92; h, FS309–8; i, FS521–75; j, FS281–3; k, FS156; l, FS528–52; m, FS156–77; n, FS136–3.

Fig. 7. Bone ornaments from Median Village, Utah, dated A.D. 900 ± 100 to 960 ± 100. a–d, Tubes of small mammal and bird long bones, with both ends cut and evenly ground. The surfaces are highly polished either through manufacture or use or both. Similar ornaments were found at Southwest burial sites (Kidder 1932:256–257; Hodge 1920:257) in direct association with more obvious ornaments. Bone tubes, common in the Fremont culture area, are relatively rare in Anasazi sites (Marwitt 1970). e–j, Pendants and blanks, made from sections of large mammal long bones, the sides and surfaces smoothed and polished. Holes for suspension were normally biconically drilled. Rectangular and subrectangular outlines are most common, although teardrop or triangular shapes are found (g). i–j are probably blanks, finished except for introduction of holes for suspension (i is partially drilled from both sides). k–l, Ring fragments made from round sections of large mammal long bones, most often humerii. The edges were ground smooth and the surfaces nicely polished. A similar ring was found in situ on the third finger, left hand, of a male skeleton at Evans Mound (Berry 1972). They are not common in Anasazi sites (Marwitt 1970). m–n, Beads. m is a flat disk bead, thin and tabular in cross-section and center-drilled. Both surfaces and the margins are ground and polished. n is a tubular bead that has been carefully sawed from a large mammal long bone, with both cut ends uniformly ground. Length of a about 7.1, rest same scale.

nents have been identified at Paragonah and Evans Mound.

The following Paragonah phase has a consistent series of radiocarbon dates clustering between A.D. 1100 and 1250. There is no discontinuity with the preceding phase; corrugated pottery and quadrilateral pit dwellings are new additions, and anthropomorphic figurines are larger, better made, and more ornate.

Central Utah

The Sevier Fremont variant of central-western Utah and adjacent portions of eastern Nevada is known from the excavated sites of Grantsville (Steward 1933a), Tooele (Gillin 1941), Hinckley Farm (Green 1961), Nephi (Sharrock and Marwitt 1967), Pharo Village (Marwitt 1968), Ephraim (Gillin 1941), and Backhoe Village (Madsen and Lindsay 1977). Snake Rock Village (Aikens 1967a) and the Old Woman and Poplar Knob sites (Taylor 1957) are also assigned by Marwitt (1970) to the Sevier Fremont. However, these three sites along with several others located nearby (Wilson and Smith 1976) have also been placed in the San Rafael variant (Schroedl and Hogan 1975) primarily on the basis of their ceramics. In any case, these sites lie on or near the poorly defined frontier between the Sevier and San Rafael areas and also near the transition from the Basin to the Colorado Plateau physiographic province. They exhibit a mixture of traits and are thus difficult to assign neatly to either variant.

Along the Basin-Plateau boundary, the typical Sevier Fremont site is a small hamlet or open settlement situated on an alluvial fan near a canyon mouth and convenient to a dependable source of water in the form of a perennial stream. With the exception of Snake Rock Village and the other sites of debatable classification discussed above, the settlements also tend to be relatively close to marshes. Although the average Sevier Fremont settlement does not compare in depth of deposits, concentration of structures, or length of occupation with Parowan Fremont sites to the south, the Richfield site, of which Backhoe Village is a part, appears to be even more extensive than the Parowan sites. Nawthis Village, near Salina, may be even larger. Excluding these atypically large villages, the sites generally include a few pit dwellings and associated coursed adobe storage structures, with occasional surface jacal dwellings. As with the Parowan variant, permanent village type settlements are almost entirely confined to the relatively well-watered eastern part of the area, with sites along the Utah-Nevada border representing only seasonal or transient occupation. The ratio of temporary camps to villages is roughly 10 to 1 (Madsen and Lindsay 1977).

The Sevier Fremont subsistence economy was mixed. Horticulture and wild food resources both played an

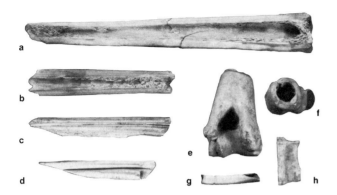

U. of Utah, Mus. of Nat. Hist., Salt Lake City: a, 42In124–FS263.6; FS2634; b, FS402–123; c, FS220–41; d, FS260–104; e, FS455–8; f, FS497; g, FS477–106; h, FS379–62.

Fig. 8. Scraps showing evidence of bone-cutting techniques at Median Village, Utah. Most manufacture appears to have occurred secondary to the routine breaking of all long bones for extraction of marrow. The common technique was simply grinding to shape, using varying grades of sandstone. Other methods included whittling and flaking, and less frequently sawing or incising with sections snapped off at the resultant groove. Sawing is illustrated here. a–b, Primary longitudinal splitting of large mammal metapodials, a technique used principally for the manufacture of awls. Bones were neatly grooved by sawing with a stone tool on both sides of the surface, often following the natural vascular channels, until the bone was completely cut through or sufficiently weakened to be snapped apart without splitting. c–d, Secondary longitudinal splitting, another technique used for the manufacture of awls. This method is the same as primary longitudinal splitting except that the sawing was done from the inside surface of a previously split bone. d is an awl blank nearly split out by longitudinal sawing. e–g, Transverse circumference sawing. This is the technique of sawing a groove around the circumference of a mammal, rodent, or bird long bone until the bone was either sawn through or was sufficiently weakened to be neatly snapped off. e and f are portions of deer humeri consisting of the distal articular end and a short length of the shaft. g is a section of rodent or bird bone with a smooth cut at one end and the start of a second cut 1 cm from the first. This is probably a blank for a small bone tube or tubular bone bead. h, Transverse sawing on tabular bone section, a technique that entailed cutting across the longitudinal axis of tubular bone scrap to create the desired object shape. This specimen is a section of artificially flattened bone with evidence of transverse sawing at or near the irregularly snapped ends, probably a blank for creation of an ornament. Length of a about 20.4 cm, rest same scale.

important part and the relative importance of each depended on local circumstances. At Backhoe Village and perhaps elsewhere in the Sevier area, marsh resources appear to have been the primary component in the subsistence economy and the most crucial factor that allowed sedentary villages to be present in the locality (Madsen and Lindsay 1977).

In architecture, Sevier Fremont is quite variable from site to site. Even a single site, such as Nephi, often has a variety of pit houses, surface adobe "coil" and "turtleback" dwellings, and storage structures. In the eastern part of the area, slab masonry storage structures are present at Pharo Village and Snake Rock, along with adobe structures (fig. 10). At Poplar Knob there

are no adobe structures, but slab masonry storage units are identical in size and shape to their adobe equivalents farther west.

This variant is typologically diffuse and the least uniform and cohesive of all the Fremont regional expressions. Artifacts such as flaked and ground stone implements are markedly heterogeneous. Perhaps the only trait found consistently in all sites is the locally made, basalt-tempered Sevier Gray pottery ("Prehistoric Ceramics," fig. 3, this vol.). But at Old Woman, Poplar Knob, and Snake Rock Village, Sevier Gray is a minority type, and most Sevier Fremont sites have a good representation of other Fremont grayware types. Ivie Creek Black-on-white pottery is common in Sevier sites, but it is also plentiful in collections from a number of eastern Utah sites assigned to the San Rafael variant by Marwitt (1970).

Sevier Fremont has radiocarbon dates ranging from the late ninth to the mid-thirteenth century A.D. There is very little change in material culture to be seen in the late sites compared to early ones, except that painted pottery, including Ivie Creek Black-on-white and intrusive Snake Valley Black-on-gray wares, increase in frequency after about A.D. 900. Snake Valley corrugated ceramics are also a time marker of sorts, appearing as tradeware from the Parowan variant after A.D. 1050.

Great Salt Lake

The Fremont subculture centered in the region of the Great Salt Lake is perhaps the most intriguing of all the variants. The usual Fremont pattern of mixed horticulture and foraging is replaced almost entirely by an

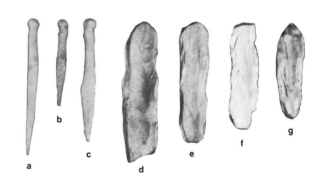

U. of Utah, Mus. of Nat. Hist., Salt Lake City: a, 42In124–FS379–63; b, FS525–142; c, FS521–68; d, FS309–3; e, FS309–28; f, FS204–10; g, FS345–191.

Fig. 9. Bone hide-working tools from Median Village, Utah, dated A.D. 900–1100. a–c, Lateral metapodial awls with distal ends ground to points. Metapodial bones have naturally tapering ends that required little work for conversion to serviceable awls (c is unmodified). d–g, Splinters of large mammal long bones, thinned by flaking one or both lateral margins, dulled and highly polished edges indicating use in the scraping and fleshing of hides. Length of a about 7.4 cm, rest same scale.

U. of Utah, Archeol. Center, Salt Lake City: 42Md180–25.

Fig. 10. Above-ground granary at Pharo Village, Utah, a site having 3 housepits, 6 surface granaries, several borrow pits, and 2 definable activity surfaces, dating A.D. 1190–1260. Differences in the color and composition of the coiled adobe walls indicate several building episodes. The original granary was a rectangular room about 20 feet by 13 feet. This was subdivided into 2 rooms by a clay partition through approximately the middle of the original structure. Still later, this 2-room granary was joined to an addition of comparable size. Adobe coils in the walls were about 1 foot wide, footed in a trench about 4 inches deep. Basal coils were wider than those above, lending stability to the walls. Flattening of the lower coils indicate that upper coils were laid on before the lower ones were dry. Judging from the amount of wall debris and the absence of postholes, excavators suggest a maximum height for the structure of 4–5 feet, with the roof probably flat and laid directly atop the walls. The floor was simply hard-packed sterile subsoil. The 2 large holes in the floor are looter's pits, not constructional elements. Since the fill contained general site debris of bone scrap and pottery fragments, and there was no roofing debris on the floor, the granary was probably dismantled sometime during site occupation, after which it was used as a dump.

economy based on the exploitation of wild flora and fauna, especially from marsh environments. Habitation sites in the Great Salt Lake subarea generally lack substantial dwellings. Stone masonry architecture is absent, and except at Willard (Judd 1917a, 1926) where there is a coursed adobe granary, pits are the only storage devices present. Major sites of this variant, such as Bear River No. 1 and Injun Creek (Aikens 1966), Bear River No. 2 (Shields and Dalley 1978), and the Levee and Knoll sites (Fry and Dalley 1979), are situated at an elevation of 4,212 feet above sea level. This is only slightly above the modern average stillstand of the Great Salt Lake, and the soil is too saline to support maize horticulture. These sites were apparently occupied only seasonally when waterfowl were abundant. Sheltered sites like Hogup Cave (Aikens 1970), the Promontory Caves (Steward 1937a), and Swallow Shelter (Dalley 1976) were also occupied by transient Fremont people as seasonal camps while harvesting seeds or hunting bison, antelope, and deer.

In addition to the strong emphasis on wild resources in the subsistence economy, the Great Salt Lake variant differs from the others in many items of material culture. Cylindrical ground stone pestles, slate knives, etched stone tablets, and side-notched projectile points are common only in northwestern Utah during the Fremont period and make their first appearance in Archaic levels at Hogup Cave. Knives or saws made of deer and mountain sheep scapulae, bone whistles, and harpoon heads tend to be restricted to the Great Salt Lake region (figs. 11–12).

The ceramic complex includes a sand-tempered grayware (Great Salt Lake Gray) as the dominant type. A unique minority ware is Promontory Gray, which is tempered with coarse calcite fragments and was made by a paddle-and-anvil method instead of the coil-and-scrape method of manufacture characteristic of Great Salt Lake Gray and all other Fremont pottery. Painted and corrugated pottery is found only in minute quantities in the form of trade ware from the Sevier and Parowan subareas.

Fry and Dalley (1979) have defined two phases for the Bear River locality on the northeastern edge of the Great Salt Lake. The earlier Bear River phase (represented by Bear River No. 1, Bear River No. 2, Bear River No. 3) and the early component village (42Bo110) at the Levee site are characterized by temporary hunting camps without structures and by small rancherias

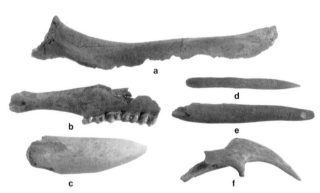

U. of Utah, Mus. of Nat. Hist., Salt Lake City: a, 42Wb34–FS392–71; b, FS451–10; c, FS388–12; d, FS70–1; e, FS54–3; f, FS525–6.

Fig. 11. Bone and antler tools from Injun Creek, Utah, radiocarbon dated A.D. 1365–1605. a, Scapula saw, made from a deer scapula broken longitudinally and worked along the thickened longitudinal axis to form an irregular, sawtoothed cutting edge; b, mandible saw, a deer mandible broken to form a sawlike implement with the teeth left in place to form the cutting edge; c, antler wedge, the midsection of an elk antler with one end bifacially cut and abraded to form the bit, the other crushed and fragmented from pounding; d, antler punch, a split and ground antler tine with a blunted, tapered point made by grinding; e, antler polisher, antler tine with a small, highly polished flat spot ground on one side of the tip through use; f, antler flaker, a tine attached to the beam, with marked abrasion at the tip and a surface highly polished from handling. Length of a about 22.2 cm, rest same scale.

U. of Utah, Mus. of Nat. Hist., Salt Lake City: top, 42Bo107–FS93–8; bottom, 42Bo107–FS38–16.

Fig. 12. Whistles made from sections of bird long bones. On the top specimen the hole is neatly drilled into the bone, while on the bottom one the hole was made by cutting across the long axis of the bone section. Both are unfinished forms, judging by the rough surface treatment and the lack of a stop within the chamber. Collected from the late component of the Great Salt Lake Fremont Levee site, and radiocarbon dated A.D. 1000–1300, these specimens are quite similar to ethnographic Eastern Shoshone and Ute examples. Length of top about 11.5 cm, other same scale.

with shallow, semipermanent structures. Rose Spring projectile points (a late Archaic type) dominate in these sites. Radiocarbon dates indicate an approximate timespan for the phase of A.D. 400 to 1000.

The Levee phase (A.D. 1000 to 1350) is best represented by the late component village (42Bo107) at the Levee site and by the Knoll site. It is characterized by the presence of Desert side-notched projectile points, intrusive pottery, and more substantial pit dwellings. The pit dwellings have long ventilator or crawlway tunnel adjuncts and adobe deflectors reminiscent of equivalent structures in the Parowan Valley. The dwellings of the Levee phase suggest a more sedentary population than in earlier times, but maize horticulture still seems to have played an unimportant part in the subsistence economy.

The Fremont complex represented by Unit 3 at Hogup Cave is easily accommodated in the Great Salt Lake variant, but the relationship of the Hogup complex to the phase sequence for the Bear River locality is not clear. It appears that the Hogup deposits cover the entire temporal span of Fremont culture in northern and northwestern Utah, from A.D. 400 to 1350. The Fremont occupation of the cave was seasonal, largely during the early autumn, apparently for the purpose of harvesting pickleweed seeds along the margins of the salt flats.

In an attenuated form, the Great Salt Lake variant is found as far north as the outliers of the Rocky Mountains on the north edge of the Snake River Plain in south-central Idaho (Butler 1979, 1981), where it may have persisted until as late as A.D. 1650. It is not known with any certainty whether these Idaho materials represent an extension of Great Salt Lake Fremont into the Snake River Plain on the same time level as the Fremont occupation of northern Utah or if they relate to a northward withdrawal of Fremont peoples following their abandonment of that area.

The Uinta Basin

Fremont occupation of the Uinta Basin of northeastern Utah lasted only from about A.D. 650 to 950 and was never very intensive, perhaps owing to the high average elevation of the region and the consequent short growing season. Most of the known sites are small hamlets or rancherias with no more than five or so shallow, circular pit houses occupied at any time; cultural deposits are thin and suggest rather short, possibly seasonal occupations. Surface storage structures are absent at open habitation sites, although storage pits are present. Small masonry granaries were occasionally constructed on rock ledges in the Dinosaur National Monument region. Habitation sites are typically located on knolls or buttes, or on hill slopes above creek flood plains.

The small size of the settlements, coupled with the absence of substantial storage structures, suggests that maize horticulture was not an important component of the subsistence economy as compared to related Fremont populations to the south and southwest. Gathering of wild plant products and hunting of deer, antelope, and small game seem to have been much more important subsistence activities.

A calcite-tempered grayware (Uinta Gray) dominates ceramic assemblages from Uinta Fremont sites to the virtual exclusion of all other types, and it appears to have been the only locally manufactured pottery. Small quantities of intrusive Fremont tradewares have been found at several sites, and a few sherds of Anasazi pottery are present at Caldwell Village (Ambler 1966). Surface-manipulated varieties of the basic grayware are relatively rare and are absent altogether at the earlier sites.

The Uinta variant is also characterized by the absence of the Utah–type metate and the anthropomorphic figurine complex, which are virtual hallmarks of Fremont culture elsewhere. These absences may be related in part to the geographically isolated location of the Uinta Basin with respect to the rest of the Fremont culture area, but there are no geographic barriers that would effectively prevent trade and exchange of ideas with other regional subcultures.

Two sequential cultural phases have been defined for the Uinta Basin (Marwitt 1970). The Cub Creek phase (A.D. 650 to 800) is represented by Boundary Village (Leach 1966), the Goodrich, Felter Hill, and Flattop Butte sites (Shields 1967), and a number of small habitation and campsites in the Cub Creek locality (Breternitz 1968). Surface structures are absent, and the only pottery present is undecorated Uinta Gray, with no bowl forms represented.

The later Whiterocks phase (A.D. 800 to 950) is represented by Whiterocks Village (Shields 1967) and Caldwell Village (fig. 13). There are no changes in the basic pattern of the variant and only a few new traits are added. At Whiterocks Village, masonry and coursed adobe dwellings are present; surface-manipulated varieties of Uinta Gray are introduced along with the bowl vessel form, and trade pottery from other parts of the Fremont area is present though rare.

It appears that Fremont groups withdrew from the Uinta Basin and Dinosaur National Monument regions before A.D. 1000. This is about 200 to 300 years before the disappearance of Fremont culture to the south and west. The reasons for this early abandonment are unclear, although a climatic change may be at least partly responsible. On the basis of changes in projectile points and grinding implements, coupled with an increase in faunal remains and a lack of evidence for horticulture, Leach (1970) concludes that the upper Fremont level at Deluge Shelter represents a shift in the local subsistence economy toward a foraging orientation. There is also a possibility that Fremont hunting parties continued to visit the Uinta Basin after permanent occupation came to an end, and Deluge Shelter may thus have been a campsite used by transient hunters.

U. of Utah, Archeol. Center, Salt Lake City: 42Wn95–90.

Fig. 13. Some of the 22 housepits at Caldwell Village, Utah, a Uinta Fremont site. The housepits were circular, from about 12 to 27 feet in diameter, and had been dug to a depth of 8–27 inches. They had unprepared dirt floors and walls, circular clay-rimmed firepits, storage pits, and quadrilateral roof supports. Crawlway-ventilator shafts were absent. Superposition of the dwellings was uncommon, leading Ambler (1966a) to suggest that they may have been occupied contemporaneously. If so, Caldwell Village is the largest village site yet reported on the Colorado Plateau and rivals or exceeds in size those excavated on the west side of the Wasatch Front. This is in clear contrast to the usual pattern of Fremont occupation on the plateau, where groups of families or individual families lived in rancherias or small self-sufficient compounds (cf. Jennings 1978; Jennings and Sammons-Lohse 1981). A date of A.D. 1050–1200 is estimated for Caldwell Village based on correlation of recovered pottery types with those types firmly dated in the Anasazi area to the south.

170

Eastern Utah

Fremont sites east of the Wasatch Plateau are assigned by Marwitt (1970) to the San Rafael variant. They are generally quite small, consisting of rancherias with a few pit houses and associated storage structures. Wet-laid and dry-laid masonry dwellings and granaries are also found. Permanent habitation sites such as Turner-Look (Wormington 1955), Innocents Ridge (Schroedl and Hogan 1975), Crescent Ridge, Power Pole Knoll, and Windy Ridge Village (Madsen 1975a), and the Bull Creek sites (Jennings and Sammons-Lohse 1981) tend to be located on low ridges or knolls near water and arable land. A few complexes of multiroom masonry structures resembling Anasazi unit pueblos are known from the Nine Mile Canyon locality, and it has been suggested, without much supporting evidence, that these were fortified (Gillin 1938).

Fremont groups in eastern Utah and extreme western Colorado also made extensive use of small caves, niches, and rockshelters, primarily for storage but also for habitation. Most sheltered sites have only flimsy brush shelters. This suggests temporary or intermittent use, and they are probably associated with hunting or seasonal collecting or both. Small dome-shaped masonry granaries were constructed in protected locations, and small niches and recesses were sometimes walled off for storage (fig. 14).

Although there is substantial evidence that procurement of wild resources played an important part in the subsistence economy of Fremont groups on the Colorado Plateau, it may be that cultigens, especially maize, were the crucial factor that permitted sedentary village life in the region (Madsen and Lindsay 1977). This is in contrast to much of the Basin province, where permanent settlements were made possible in large part by exploiting productive marshlands, which are lacking on the Colorado Plateau.

The extensive use of stone masonry is a characteristic of the eastern (San Rafael) Fremont, as are plastered interior walls and slab-floor firepits. The most common locally made ceramic variety is Emery Gray, which is tempered with crushed igneous rock. Surface-manipulated varieties of Emery Gray are common; painted pottery is present in the form of the indigenous Ivie Creek Black-on-white and intrusive (but Fremont) Snake Valley Black-on-gray. Anasazi trade pottery from the Mesa Verde and Kayenta areas is much more common than in any other part of the Fremont area.

Alcove sites in the Escalante River drainage show evidence of use by groups of both Fremont and Kayenta Anasazi affiliation. In the case of Harris Wash (Fowler 1963), the occupation seems to have been primarily by Fremont people; not far downstream (south) in Twentyfivemile Wash, Coyote Creek, and Davis Gulch, there is relatively more evidence of Kayenta utilization. In

U. of Utah, Archeol. Center, Salt Lake City: top, 42Wn996–39; bottom, 42Wn996–34.

Fig. 14. Hillside Cache, a San Rafael Fremont site in Utah, unique in being the only excavated open cache site in the Fremont culture area. It consists of 6 circular slab-lined storage cists set into the base of a low shale-sandstone hill. Three of the cists held no cultural material, evidently having been cleaned out; 2 others held corn cobs and seeds of amaranth, sunflower, and squawbush. The cist second from left was uncovered intact. It had 2 chambers, was bell-shaped in cross-section, lined with sandstone slabs, and caulked and rimmed with adobe. The roof was constructed of an initial layer of slender cottonwood branches, overlain with smaller willow branches, bark, matted grasses and corn husks, the whole covered with a thick coat of clay. This cist, 1.9 m in diameter, held a corn cob, sunflower seeds, whole and fragmented deer bones, fragments of bird bone, a small trilobed Sevier Gray pot, a pestle, 7 antelope phalanges, a broken chert blade, and the remnants of a reed cradleboard (bottom). A stick from the roof was radiocarbon dated A.D. 910±55. Photographed in 1977.

both localities there are considerable quantities of Fremont pottery in Kayenta sites, and vice versa. This would seem to indicate something more than casual contact and desultory trade between the two groups. The large Kayenta outpost of Coombs Village (Lister, Ambler, and Lister 1960) near Boulder, Utah, also has a large complement of Fremont ceramics. The nature of the relationship between San Rafael Fremont and Kayenta Anasazi is very poorly understood. This can be seen in the Bull Creek area (Jennings and Sammons-Lohse 1981), where the sites show such a mixture of traits that, although they were assigned to Fremont, they could as easily have been assigned to Kayenta Anasazi. And at Ticaboo Town Ruin (Madsen 1982a), grave goods associated with the burial of two juveniles

in a storage feature included Fremont moccasins, an Anasazi bowl, and Bull Creek projectile points that are common in both San Rafael Fremont and Kayenta Anasazi contexts. As Madsen observes, this illustrates the dangers of making what amount to ethnic identifications on the basis of material culture traits, and it may be that neither Fremont nor Anasazi may be a proper designator for sites in the southern San Rafael region.

Radiocarbon dates for the San Rafael variant range from about A.D. 700 to 1250 (Madsen 1975a; Jennings and Sammons-Lohse 1981). A few dendrochronology dates from Nine Mile Canyon and Hill Creek Canyon fall in the A.D. 915 to 1151 range. No temporal phases have been defined for the variant.

Demise of the Fremont Culture

Between A.D. 1250 and 1350, most of the Fremont population abandoned both the Great Basin and the Colorado Plateau provinces, although as noted above, there is limited evidence that an attenuated variety of Fremont may have persisted somewhat longer in the Snake River Plain of Idaho. The Uinta Basin seems to have been abandoned as much as 300 years earlier, except perhaps for transient hunters. There is no generally accepted explanation for this rather mysterious breakup of the long-lived Fremont pattern, but there are several hypotheses.

Some students (Rudy 1953; Taylor 1954; Gunnerson 1969) have taken the position that Fremont groups were ancestral to the Numic-speaking Shoshone, Ute, and Southern Paiute who were the inhabitants of the area at the time of Euro-American contact in the nineteenth century. They argue that these Proto-Fremont hunters and gatherers adopted a number of Southwestern culture traits including horticulture. But when a climatic change of some kind forced them to abandon farming, they simply returned to their ancient foraging lifeway and gradually lost their derived Anasazi elements, thus obscuring the evidence of their former identity with the Fremont. However, the majority opinion is that there is no evidence for cultural continuity between the prehistoric Fremont culture and the culture of the historic Numic speakers. Linguistic evidence suggests that the Numic languages diverged from a common ancestor only about 1,000 years ago (Miller 1966; Miller, Tanner, and Foley 1971; Goss 1968; C. S. Fowler 1972; Lamb 1958). In this view, Numic expansion into the eastern Great Basin began only a few years before A.D. 1000, rather than the A.D. 400 to 500 date that would be necessary for the Fremont people to have been ancestral Shoshone and Paiute.

Aikens (1966) has proposed that the Proto-Fremont people were bison hunters of northwestern Plains (Athapaskan) origin who entered Utah about A.D. 500, adopted some Southwest traits, and became village horticulturalists. He postulates that between 1400 and 1600, under pressure from the Shoshonean expansion into the Fremont area, they drifted back to the Plains to develop the culture represented by the Dismal River aspect of western Nebraska and Kansas, eastern Colorado, and Wyoming. Even though a northern Plains origin for the Fremont is doubtful in view of the demonstrated continuity from the Archaic, there are some striking parallels between Fremont manifestations in northern Utah and the northern and western Plains. In fact, some students are of the opinion that the Fremont affiliation of some Uinta Basin sites is open to doubt, and they may instead be of Plains origin. Wedel (1967) and others have expressed reservations about some of Aikens's evidence as it applies to the Dismal River aspect, but the post-fourteenth century location of the descendents of the Fremont culture has not been identified, and the Dismal River complex does appear rather suddenly without local antecedents. In any event, it would be unwise to aver that all Fremont populations shared a common fate, given the overall variability and flexibility in adaptation seen in Fremont or the differential exposure of the several regional variants to influences from non-Fremont cultural traditions.

Data from Hogup Cave and elsewhere support the proposition that the Fremont were replaced culturally and ethnically by Numic-speaking peoples. In Hogup Cave Unit 3, Great Salt Lake Gray ceramics and other diagnostic Fremont materials are replaced by a distinctly different pottery complex and other traits representing a population ancestral to the Western Shoshone who occupied the region in historic times. There is virtually no continuation of any Fremont trait into Shoshone levels. However, Shoshone pottery sherds were found in Fremont levels, especially in the upper strata. The same situation is present at several of the Great Salt Lake caves studied by Steward (1937a), at Pine Park Shelter (Rudy 1954), and elsewhere in western Utah (Madsen 1975a). A similar replacement of Fremont (and Virgin branch Anasazi) horticulturalists by Numic-speaking Southern Paiute groups is also reported for southern Utah and Nevada (Euler 1964).

There is a rather large number of sites with both Fremont and Shoshone-Paiute artifacts, which suggests that there was concurrent use of the same areas and a high degree of interaction between the two cultures. Even though this interaction seems to have been amicable, there was nevertheless a total replacement of Fremont artifact types. The reasons for this replacement and for the total disappearance of the Fremont pattern over its entire geographic range have not yet been determined.

Prehistory of the Southeastern Area

DON D. FOWLER AND DAVID B. MADSEN

The southeastern Great Basin archeological area lies between 114° and 115° 30′ west longitude and 36° and 38° north latitude. It includes portions of southeastern Nevada, southwestern Utah, and northwestern Arizona (fig. 1). Parts of the area are within the Colorado River drainage; the remainder is within the hydrographic Great Basin. The area lies beneath a major climatic gradation zone between the Gulf of Mexico–derived summer precipitation pattern and the Pacific Ocean–derived winter precipitation pattern (J. G. Houghton 1969). East-west fluctuations of this gradient in the past may have influenced the expansions and contractions of aboriginal horticulture in the area between A.D. 500 and 1150 (Aschmann 1958).

As is common throughout the Great Basin, the southeastern area contains a vertical succession of ecological life-zones (Dice 1943; Bradley and Deacon 1967; Mehringer 1965). The area is also marked by a transition zone between cold, northern desert vegetation and warm, southern desert vegetation (Shrieve 1942). In the northwestern portion of the area the two zones interdigitate on valley floors and lower upland slopes. Common fauna include mule deer and bighorn sheep, antelope, rabbits and numerous other rodents, small carnivores such as coyote and fox, and a variety of water and arboreal birds (Bradley and Deacon 1967; Austin and Bradley 1971). Elevations range from less than 400 meters in the lower Virgin River drainage to 3,000–3,600 meters in the high mountains.

The cultural chronology of the area is based on data from the O'Malley Shelter and Conaway sites in the upper Meadow Valley Wash area (Fowler, Madsen, and Hattori 1973), the Lost City complex and related sites in the lower Virgin River area (Shutler 1961), and the upper Virgin River area in southwest Utah (Aikens 1965, 1966a; Day 1966; Schroeder 1955).

Pre-Archaic Period

Evidence for Pre-Archaic (pre-8000 B.C.) occupations of the area is ambiguous. A number of "Clovis" fluted projectile points have been found at various surface locales (Davis and Shutler 1969) but none in stratigraphic contexts. Early reports of great antiquity of cultural materials in association with Pleistocene megafauna (camel, bison, horse) (Harrington and Simpson

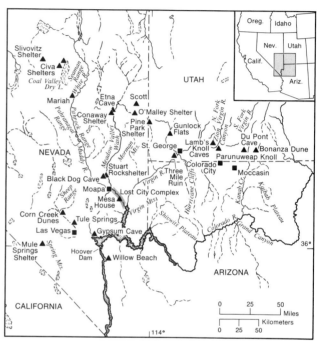

Fig. 1. Archeological sites in the southeastern Great Basin.

1961) have subsequently been disproved. Re-excavation of the Tule Springs site near Las Vegas, Nevada, produced minimal evidence of human occupation between 11,000 and 8000 B.C. but yielded no clear evidence of associations between artifacts and extinct faunal forms (Wormington and Ellis 1967). Gypsum Cave, excavated in 1931 (Harrington 1933), was thought to demonstrate a contemporaneity of human occupation of the cave with the Pleistocene ground sloth *Nothrotheriops shastensis*. Radiometric tests on sloth dung from the cave yielded dates between 9700 and 6500 B.C. However, when artifacts rather than sloth dung were radiocarbon-dated they fell in the range of 900 to 400 B.C. (Heizer and Berger 1970), precluding the contemporaneity of human and sloth occupation.

Archaic Period

The Archaic cultural period in the area dates between about 8000 B.C. and A.D. 1–500. As elsewhere in the Great Basin the Archaic cultural sequence is based primarily on projectile point chronologies (table 1) sup-

Table 1. Principal Projectile Point Types in the Southeastern Great Basin

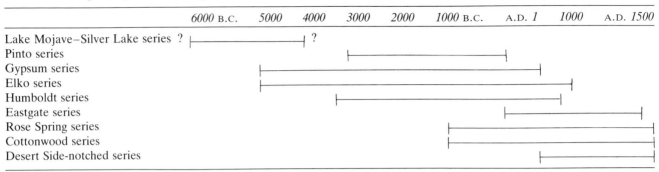

	6000 B.C.	5000	4000	3000	2000	1000 B.C.	A.D. 1	1000	A.D. 1500
Lake Mojave–Silver Lake series ?	⊢————————⊣ ?								
Pinto series				⊢————————————⊣					
Gypsum series		⊢———————————————⊣							
Elko series		⊢——————————————————————⊣							
Humboldt series				⊢——————————————⊣					
Eastgate series							⊢————————⊣		
Rose Spring series						⊢—————————————————⊣			
Cottonwood series						⊢—————————————————⊣			
Desert Side-notched series							⊢————————⊣		

SOURCE: Fowler, Madsen, and Hattori 1973.

ported by carbon-14 determinations. There are, however, a number of problems with the projectile point chronology, especially purported older types. Lake Mojave–Silver Lake and Pinto series types have not been found in secure stratigraphic contexts, with some few exceptions (Warren 1980a). Later types, those in the Gypsum, Elko, and Humboldt series, are more firmly dated (Fowler, Madsen, and Hattori 1973:20–28).

The principal Archaic sites in the area are Corn Creek Dunes (Williams and Orlin 1963), Stuart Rockshelter (Shutler, Shutler, and Griffith 1960), Gypsum Cave (Harrington 1933), Etna Cave (Wheeler 1942), and the lower levels of O'Malley and Conaway shelters (Fowler, Madsen, and Hattori 1973). Archaic-period artifacts occur in other sites, for example, Mule Springs Shelter (T. H. Turner 1978), and on many surface sites throughout the area. Most Archaic-period sites appear to represent temporary living stations occupied during an annual seasonal round, a pattern common throughout the Great Basin. Two examples demonstrate this pattern. O'Malley Shelter located in the upper Meadow Valley Wash drainage at an elevation of 1,615 meters was occupied by Archaic groups periodically between about 5200 and 4500 B.C. and again from about 2600 to 1000 B.C. (figs. 2–3). Faunal remains include minimal evidence of *Bison* in the lowest level, but the principal focus was on the taking of deer, mountain sheep, lagomorphs, and other small fauna. Botanical evidence was poorly preserved. Presumably the seed and root resources common to the surrounding piñon-juniper ecological zone were exploited, given the number of ground-stone processing implements found in the site (Fowler, Madsen, and Hattori 1973). Stuart Rockshelter, located in lower Meadow Valley Wash at an elevation of 530 meters, contained evidence of the taking of deer, antelope, jackrabbit, desert tortoise, and plant resources common to the local hot-desert setting of the site. The Archaic component is dated at about 2000 B.C. (Shutler, Shutler, and Griffith 1960). Unworked faunal and plant remains were not noted during the excavation of Etna Cave (Wheeler 1942). However, the site did yield a rich collection of Archaic, and later, textiles,

especially sandals and some basketry. The site also produced a number of split-twig figurines: small, enigmatic figures of deer, mountain sheep, and possibly other large animals (fig. 4). Split-twig figurines ("Portable Art Objects," fig. 5, this vol.), usually 10–11 centimeters tall and 13–16 centimeters long, occur in late-Archaic-period levels in nearly 20 rockshelters and cave sites in southeastern California, southern Nevada, central Utah, and the Grand Canyon and elsewhere in northern Arizona (Davis and Smith 1981: 56–71; Euler 1966a; Euler and Olson 1965; Farmer and DeSaussure

Desert Research Inst., Reno, Nev.
Fig. 2. O'Malley Shelter, a south-facing alcove in a 150-foot-high cliff face in Clover Valley, Nev. The shelter mouth is lost in shadow. This shelter, 26 m across at the face and 8.2 m from dripline to back wall, contains evidence of 3 cultural periods: Desert Archaic (A.D. 7150–3020 B.C.), Fremont-Anasazi (A.D. 950–1200 or 1300), and Shoshonean–Southern Paiute (A.D. 1100–historic). The major activity at the site in all periods was the production of chipped-stone tools geared to hunting and butchering large and small game. Cultural features consist entirely of ash lenses in the Desert Archaic period and large, deep, rock- and charcoal-filled firepits in the Fremont-Anasazi period. A major discovery was the occupational continuity between the Fremont-Anasazi and Shoshonean–Southern Paiute periods, culminating in documented use of the shelter by Southern Paiute groups in 1865. Photographed by David B. Madsen, 1970.

FOWLER AND MADSEN

Desert Research Inst., Reno, Nev.: top 42LN418–FS208/135; bottom, 42LN402–FS15/7.
Fig. 3. top, Spoon of mountain sheep horn from O'Malley Shelter, Nev., dated to A.D. 1100–1300. bottom, Wooden fire drill from Stine Canyon Shelter, Nev. Length of top 25 cm, other same scale.

1955; Janetski 1980a; Jett 1968; R. E. Kelly 1966; Olson 1966; Pierson and Anderson 1975; Schroedl 1977; Schwartz, Lange, and DeSaussure 1958; Wheeler 1937, 1939, 1942). A figurine fragment from the basal level of Etna Cave was radiocarbon-dated at about 1800 B.C. (Fowler 1973). The date falls within the range of other dated figurines from other sites, about 1000 to 2000 B.C. (Davis and Smith 1981:fig. 35). The function of the figurines is unknown, but their use in some form of "hunting magic" is often suggested.

The Archaic in the southeastern Great Basin was a period during which small groups of people foraged for floral and faunal resources within the various ecological zones available to them. However, data on settlement patterns in relation to subsistence systems remain sketchy since no intensive surveys of entire valleys and adjacent uplands have been undertaken in the area. Data at hand derive principally from specific rockshelter sites and partial surveys in various valleys and uplands.

Horticultural Period

After about A.D. 300–500, Archaic cultures are succeeded by horticultural cultures in the area. The term Puebloid used by some investigators refers to the fact that the cultures were characterized by small village sites with semisubterranean pit houses and masonry and adobe surface structures, ceramics, and some reliance on horticulture as part of the subsistence regime. Two such cultural traditions occur in the area.

Virgin Branch

Excavations by M.R. Harrington (Shutler 1961) and his associates, beginning in the 1920s, and subsequent ceramic analyses (Gladwin and Gladwin 1934; Colton 1952) defined a Virgin branch of the Kayenta Anasazi cultural tradition centered in the lower Virgin River drainage in southern Nevada. The southern Nevada manifestations were considered a branch of the Kayenta tradition because they evinced characteristic features—houses, storage structures, horticulture—and similarities in sequential design styles of painted ceramics. The general sequence of Kana'a/Lino, Black Mesa, and Sosi and Dogoszhi design styles, well-delineated in the Kayenta Anasazi heartland of the Four Corners region (vol. 9:108), is also found in the Virgin Valley (Lyneis 1982:178). Subsequent surveys and excavations extended the known range of Virgin branch sites eastward into the upper Virgin River area in southwestern Utah (Aikens 1965, 1966a; Day 1966; Gunnerson 1962; Pendergast 1962), onto the plateaus north of the Colorado River in the Arizona Strip as far east as the Kaibab Plateau (Abbott

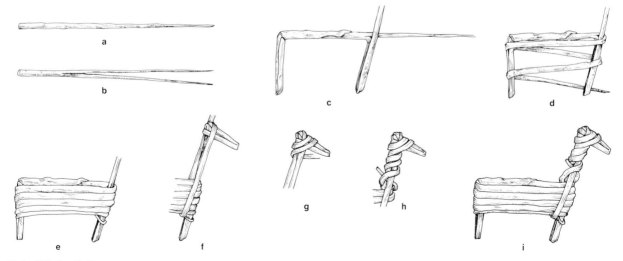

after Fowler 1973a:figs. 28–29.
Fig. 4. Construction of split-twig figurines found at Etna Cave, Nev.

1979; Holmer 1979; Lipe and Thompson 1979; Mc-Clellan and Phillips 1978; Moffit and Chang 1978; Thompson and Thompson 1978), and northward into the upper reaches of the Pahranagat Valley (Crabtree and Ferraro 1980) and Meadow Valley Wash (Fowler, Madsen, and Hattori 1973).

Although the term Western Anasazi is applied to Virgin branch cultures (R.A. Thompson 1978), the term Virgin branch is retained here to distingush a subregion within the Western Anasazi region as defined by the *Handbook* (vol. 9:108).

• CHRONOLOGY The Virgin branch has been divided into a variety of sequential phases and categories by different authors. The terminology used here has precedence in the literature and is correlated with the classic Pecos terminology used for the Western Anasazi region: Basketmaker I-III, Pueblo I-V. Virgin branch chronology is based primarily on ceramic cross-dating with the Kayenta core-area ceramic sequence. There is no dendrochronology sequence for the Virgin branch and a minimum of carbon-14 dates, which include a suite of dates on structures from the Lost City complex between A.D. 530 and 1070 (Soule 1975:18, 1976:12) and dates between A.D. 900 and 1080 from sites in upper Meadow Valley Wash (Fowler, Madsen, and Hattori 1973:tables 1, 19). Virgin branch sites are generally equated with Basketmaker II and III and Pueblo I and II phases in the Kayenta heartland. Nomenclature follows schemes advanced by Shutler (1961) and Aikens (1966a).

• MOAPA PHASE, A.D. 300–700 Basketmaker II sites include Dupont Cave in southwestern Utah (Nusbaum 1922) (figs. 5–6), Black Dog Cave near Moapa, Nevada (Shutler 1961:67), open clusters of pit houses in the Lost City complex (Shutler 1961), and a component of the Willow Beach site (Schroeder 1961), the last with a carbon-14 assay of about 300 B.C. ± 250 years. Settlement was apparently on mesa rims and in rockshelters; however, not enough is known about Moapa phase sites to delineate the full extent of settlement patterns.

• MUDDY RIVER PHASE A.D. 500–700 This phase is equated with Basketmaker III in the Kayenta core area. Most excavated sites are in the lower Virgin River drainage (Shutler 1961). Settlements are comprised of small clusters of pit houses situated on mesa rims overlooking river valleys or on knolls in them. The pit houses had prepared clay floors and fire basins; some had walls lined with wattle and daub or adobe and masonry. Slab basin metates were used for food processing. A variety of chipped stone tools was used, including small projectile points, indicating the use of the bow and arrow. Basketry, cordage, fur cloth, clay figurines, and bone tools were also manufactured. Ceramics were present and include Boulder Black on gray, a type with a Lino

Mus. of the Amer. Ind., Heye Foundation, New York: 6911, 6922.

Fig. 5. Cave DuPont, a Basketmaker II site in southwestern Utah. Fresh water was available for site inhabitants from a seep on the narrow sandstone ledge just below the base of the overhang. left, Cave, about 100 feet across the face, 60 feet from dripline to back wall, and 55 feet high. Over 24 cists had been constructed to store harvested crops of corn and other perishable and necessary items. One cist alone held 3.5 bushels of corn on the cob. Other cists held corn remains, wood, bone, horn, and fiber artifacts, including beds or nests of grass, cradleboards, nets and baskets, several kinds of snares, digging sticks, and bundles of raw materials for basketry. right, Cist 5, partially cleared. The cists had been roofed with juniper poles laid on top of slab walls and covered with a matting of grass and juniper bark. The floors were paved with sandstone slabs, and the interstices of floors and walls chinked with clay. The 2 small chambers within the cist each held a human burial and associated grave goods. Photographs by Jesse L. Nusbaum, 1920.

176

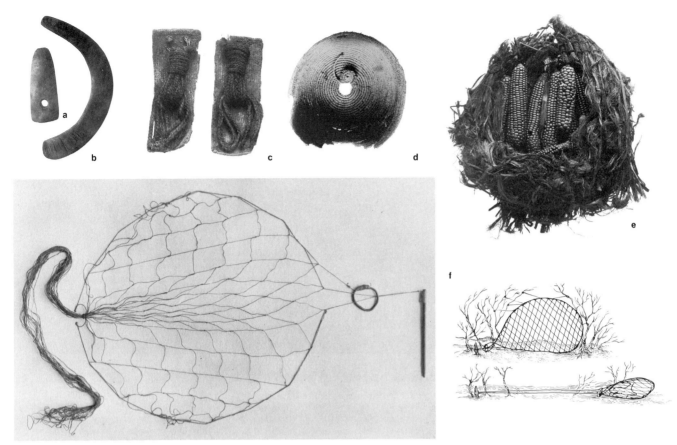

Mus. of the Amer. Ind., Heye Foundation, New York: a, 10/3929; b, 10/3930; c, 10/3891; d, 10/3999; e, 10/3972; f, top, 10/3973, bottom, after Nusbaum 1922:fig. 35.

Fig. 6. Perishable artifacts recovered from storage cists in Cave DuPont. a, Shaft straightener of mountain sheep horn used as a wrench, for straightening steamed sticks for dart shafts. b, Tool of moutain sheep horn, either a sickle for cutting grass or a flesher for working hides. c, Fiber sandals of twined work, with 24 warps. Loops of human hair string are for insertion of the second and third toes and the heel. The braided string is at least 10 feet long, twice carried backward and forward between toe and heel loops, then wrapped round and round itself over the instep, and finally knotted near the toe loop. d, Coiled basket found over the head of a burial in Cist 5. It has a flat base and steeply rising sides. "Ceremonial killing" of the basket may be indicated by the breaking inward of the first 3 coils of the base. e, Cache of seed corn, all ears fully developed. The number of kernel rows varies from 10 to 18, typical of hybrid variants from A.D. 1–1150 in the Southwest. The bag is crudely woven of crushed yucca leaves. f, Elaborate snare for small game. The edge cord of Apocynum fiber encloses a space about 106.5 cm in diameter; the net, of finer string, has a 7.5 cm mesh. The edge cord passes through a sinew-bound peeled twig ring and is fastened to a short pin. Presumably, the pin was driven into the ground and the net spread across an animal run over a burrow. When the animal or bird ran into the light mesh it would become entangled, and the net would gather, run up on the edge cord, and close about the victim. As the net pursed, the ring attached to it would be pulled up along the edge cord, shutting the mouth of the bag. Length of a 17 cm, b–e same scale, f not to same scale.

Black-on-gray design style (Shutler 1961:28, 67–68). During this phase horticulture was introduced into the lower Virgin River drainage, probably from the Kayenta region, by a presently undetermined route. Settlement seems to have concentrated in the lower Virgin River area, with some few sites in the upper drainage.

• LOST CITY AND MESA HOUSE PHASES A.D. 700–1150+   In the lower Virgin River area the Lost City phase is cross-dated A.D. 700–1100, followed by a brief Mesa House phase cross-dated A.D. 1100–1150 (Shutler 1961:68–69). In the upper Virgin River drainage, Schroeder (1955) and Aikens (1965) refer to the A.D. 700–1150+ period as Developmental Pueblo and distinguish Early and Late phases. These are more or less concordant with Pueblo I (A.D. 700–900 and Pueblo II (A.D. 900–1100) in the Kayenta sequence. Early phase

sites include a number of excavated sites in the upper drainage and Shutler's Lost City phase sites.

Early Developmental Pueblo phase sites are characterized by a continuation of circular semisubterranean earthen or slab-lined pit houses with prepared clay floors and slab-lined or clay-rimmed fire pits. Associated surface structures consist of contiguous blocks of small, rectangular masonry rooms arranged in a semicircular pattern (figs. 7–8). Associated ceramic types are listed in table 2 and illustrated in figure 9.

Late Developmental Pueblo phase sites have circular to square pit houses with clay-coated or slab-lined walls, deflector slabs for fire pits, ash pits, and clay ridges on floors adjacent to fire pits. Surface structures are contiguous rectangular rooms with stone-slab paved subfloors and adobe and masonry walls. Some surface rooms have

Mus. of the Amer. Ind., Heye Foundation, New York: 11367.

Fig. 7. Surface room blocks at House 47, a Lost City, Nev., site consisting of over 100 individual rooms, not all occupied contemporaneously. The pueblo unit was situated on a low knoll overlooking agricultural plots irrigated by diversion of the sluggish, shallow Muddy River. Rooms have walls of coursed adobe strengthened by inclusion of stones or walls of alternating adobe and stone courses. The larger rooms served as habitations, judging by the occurrence of fireplaces, metates, pieces of cooking pots, animal and vegetable remains, and other living debris. Smaller rooms without obvious habitation features were assumed to be storage structures. Rooms were laid out in U-shapes, straight lines, or blocks. House 47 was occupied during the Lost City phase, A.D. 700–1100, the period of maximum population density across the Lost City area, when the bulk of the large pueblo units were built. Photograph by M.R. Harrington, 1926.

fire pits; others do not (Day 1966:8). Late phase sites include Shutler's (1961) Mesa House sites and a number of excavated sites in the upper Virgin River area and in an affluent of Kanab Creek (fig. 10) (Aikens 1965; Gunnerson 1962; Pendergast 1962).

The Developmental (Pueblo I-II) period of Virgin branch Anasazi generally parallels that of the Kayenta outliers to the east in the Glen Canyon region (Jennings 1966). That is, there appear to have been initial, small-scale incursions into both areas of Basketmaker II-III peoples and cultures, followed by a population explosion and expansion of settlement in Pueblo I-II times. This was followed by a rapid population decline and areal abandonment in late Pueblo II–early Pueblo III times, about A.D. 1050–1250. In both areas at the peak of population and cultural development, villages were relatively small, from 3–4 to 10–15 rooms. However, this interpretation may be based only on extant archeological remains recorded in the twentieth century, at least in the Virgin area. There are a few poorly known and unexcavated late Virgin branch sites of 40–50 rooms, possibly with associated kivas, near Colorado City and Moccasin, Arizona (R.A. Thompson 1978). Other large Virgin branch sites were noted in the nineteenth century (Fowler and Matley 1978) but have been destroyed or built over by nineteenth-century Mormon settlements,

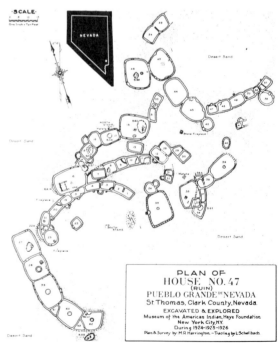

Shutler 1961: pl.30.

Fig. 8. Plan map of House 47, Lost City. Even if all rooms or room blocks were not inhabited at the same time, this site surely represents a village of considerable size, much larger than the village sites of Fremont neighbors to the northeast.

178

Table 2. Principal Virgin Branch Pottery Types

Pottery Type	Approximate date range (A.D.)
Boulder Gray	500–1150
Logandale Gray	500–700
North Creek Gray	500–1100
Shinarump Brown	700–1100
Washington Gray	700–900
Washington Corrugated	1000–1150
North Creek Corrugated	1000–1200
Moapa Corrugated	1000–1200
Boulder Black-on-gray	500–850
Washington Black-on-gray	600–900
St. George Black-on-gray	1000–1200
Moapa Black-on-gray	1000–1200
North Creek Black-on-gray	1000–1150
Hurricane Black-on-gray	1000–1150
Virgin Black-on-white	900–1200
Middleton Black-on-red	1000–1200

SOURCES: Colton 1952; Shutler 1961:28–29.

top left, Desert Research Inst., Reno, Nev.: 26Ln418–FS190/1; Smithsonian, Dept. of Anthr.: top right, 20961; bottom, 21146.

Fig. 9. Characteristic Virgin Anasazi pottery types and vessel forms. top left, Narrow-necked North Creek Gray olla from O'Malley Shelter, Nev., dated A.D. 1100–1300. The vessel, stoppered with a chert flake, held 2,318 grams of unidentified seeds. Appliquéd lug handles probably served to anchor perishable strap handles. top right, North Creek Gray corrugated olla, and bottom, North Creek Black-on-gray bowl, both collected by Edward Palmer from a mound near Santa Clara, Utah, in 1875. Diameter of bottom about 27.5 cm, rest same scale.

for example, those at Santa Clara and Saint George, Utah.

Most villages were concentrated along permanent water courses of the Virgin River drainage with foraging and hunting stations located in adjacent upland and plateau areas (Fowler, Madsen, and Hattori 1973; Lipe and Thompson 1978; McClellan and Phillips 1978). Evidence of horticulture from numerous sites includes maize, cucurbits, and beans and possibly sunflowers and amaranth, although the last two are uncertain (Soule 1979; Lyneis 1982). In addition, a variety of plant resources was gathered. By analogy with the Sevier Fremont area to the northeast and the Glen Canyon area to the east, the fraction of noncultigen plant resources gathered was probably high, perhaps half or more. Horticulture was thus an important but not dominant subsistence technique. As elsewhere, horticulture both permitted and required sedentary village occupation to irrigate and manage cultigens during the growing season.

Deer, antelope, mountain sheep, rabbits, and other small rodents were taken.

Sevier Fremont Culture

The second horticulturally based culture present in the southeastern area was the Sevier Fremont culture. Like the Virgin branch, the Sevier Fremont culture was characterized by small villages, ceramics, and some reliance on horticulture, although architectural forms and types of maize were somewhat different. The ceramics are typologically distinct from Virgin branch wares, although both have the general sequence of Kayenta design elements.

No Sevier Fremont village sites are known within the southeastern Great Basin; the nearest village sites are

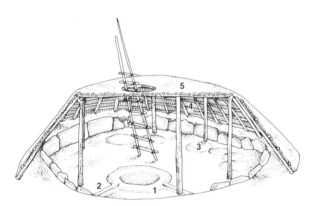

in Snake Valley to the north (Fowler 1968; Taylor 1954). However, ceramics occur widely on upland and in rock-shelter sites in the northern portion of the area and as occasional trade pieces in the southern portion. Other diagnostic elements include one-rod-and-bundle basketry, Fremont-style petrographs, distinctive maize varieties ("Fremont Cultures," fig. 3 this vol.), two-hand manos, and a particular moccasin type (Fowler, Madsen, and Hattori 1973; Wheeler 1942). The Sevier Fremont artifacts on and in sites, especially in the northern section of the area, probably represent remains left by hunting and foraging parties, rather than indicating permanent settlement. Radiocarbon dates document the presence of Fremont folk in the northern section between A.D. 900 and 1050 (Fowler, Madsen, and Hattori 1973:tables 1–19). The Sevier Fremont culture declined and disappeared in this area as well as to the east between A.D. 1100 and 1250, the same period as the general Anasazi decline to the south and east.

Trade

One function of the Virgin River settlements in the lower drainage area may have been as way-stations along

U. of Utah, Archeol. Center, Salt Lake City: top, 42Ka–1076–209; center, 42Ka–1076–147; bottom, after Aikens 1965:fig. 11.

Fig. 10. The Bonanza Dune site, Johnson Canyon, Utah. The architectural remains—11 Virgin Anasazi housepits, 3 large storage structures, and one kiva—represent at least 6 episodes of building from A.D. 900–1200. Site occupations probably never exceeded 4–5 households. top, Site view, with 5 people standing on different excavation levels to give some idea of scale. At the time of occupation, the site was no more than a few meters above the canyon floor. center, Five circular structures, visible in plan and profile along the excavation walls. All had clay floors, except storage cists, which had slab-paved or bedrock floors. All but one structure, which had clay-plastered walls, were lined with vertically set sandstone slabs. Sand-filled basins in floors served as heating pits. bottom, Reconstruction of structure 20. The clay-rimmed firepit (1) and flanking clay partitions (2) were not found in every dwelling. The sand-filled basins (3) are arranged against the far wall. Reed matting (4) covered the sloping walls, and adobe mixed with grass (5) covered the surface. The smokehole was also used as the entry.

Mus. of the Amer. Ind., Heye Foundation, New York: 9503.

Fig. 11. Entrance to Salt Cave No. 1, Lost City, Nev., on a cliff face on the west side of the Virgin River. The cave served as a salt mine, probably in use during the Lost City phase (A.D. 700–1100). Photograph by M.R. Harrington, 1924.

180

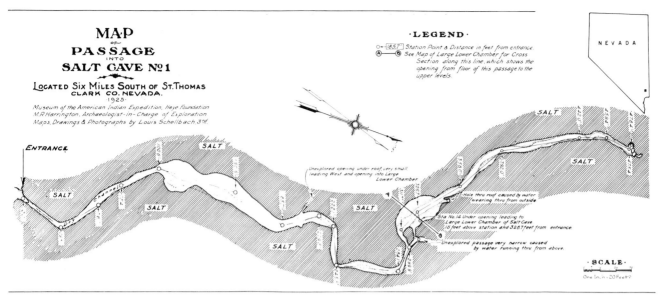

Southwest Mus., Los Angeles.

Fig. 12. Map of the passage into Salt Cave No. 1, Lost City, Nev. The north end of the cave was reached by passage through a long, low tunnel carved by an ancient watercourse. This route ended abruptly, at which point it was necessary to climb through a hole in the ceiling and proceed another 100 yards back into the salt vein, where a room 75 feet by 40 feet had been carved out. Five additional rooms, much smaller, were also found. Remains of torches were found in the tunnel and rooms. Hundreds of yucca quids were also found, chewed by miners to ease thirst while working in the salty environs of the close working space. This salt mine was no doubt a valuable resource for the Anasazi of the Virgin River area, as trade in salt and turquoise were thriving enterprises throughout the Southwest.

the Old Mojave Trail trading route connecting California and the Southwest (Heizer and Treganza 1944; Ruby 1970). Haliotis and olivella shells from coastal California, turquoise from aboriginal mines in the Mojave Desert and Nevada (Pogue 1915:46, 48–51; Morrissey 1968), and possibly salt from salt caves and open pit mines in the lower Virgin drainage (Harrington 1925, 1926; Shutler 1961:58–66) in southern Nevada (figs. 11–13) were traded eastward into Anasazi, Hohokam, and perhaps other regions in Puebloan times and possibly considerably earlier (Lyneis 1982:179). The Kayenta San Juan Red ware and Tsegi Orange ware ceramics found at Lost City (Shutler 1961:28) may represent items traded westward along the trail.

Shoshonean Tradition

The Virgin branch and Sevier Fremont cultural traditions were succeeded in the southeastern area, as elsewhere in the eastern Great Basin, by a tradition usually associated with the immediate ancestors of the historic Numic-speaking peoples. This tradition has generally been labeled Shoshonean, and later Numic, both linguistic rather than geographically derived terms. Distinct archeological manifestations of the tradition, which continued from A.D. 1000 into historic times, include a crude brownware pottery (Fowler 1968), twined and coiled basketry, and small side-notched projectile points. Mixed deposits of Shoshonean and Virgin branch ceramics were found in burials at Lost City (Shutler 1961)

and in Stuart Rockshelter (Shutler, Shutler, and Griffith 1960). In Pine Park Shelter, the O'Malley, Scott, and Conaway sites, Civa I and II and Slivovitz rockshelters, the Mariah site, and on the surfaces of numerous sites in southeastern Nevada and western Utah,

Mus. of the Amer. Ind., Heye Foundation, New York: a, 14/5334; b, 14/5363; c, 14/5336; d, 14/5411.

Fig. 13. Artifacts left behind by prehistoric miners of Salt Cave No. 1, Lost City, Nev. a, Hafted hammerstone used to chop out sections of salt up to 18 inches wide during the Lost City phase, A.D. 700–1100; b, fiber net bag for transporting blocks of salt; c, fiber sandals; d, corn cobs, the remains of miners' meals, along with mesquite beans and rabbit bones. Length of a 38.0 cm, rest about same scale.

Shoshonean ceramics were found mixed with Virgin branch and Sevier types, primarily Sevier (Brooks 1977; Busby 1979; Fowler, Madsen, and Hattori 1973; Rudy 1953).

The relationships, derivations, and fate of the three cultural traditions have been discussed since the 1940s. The archeological evidence from the southeastern area, especially the Conaway and O'Malley sites, indicates the coexistence for a time, about A.D. 1000–1200, of three distinct cultural traditions and presumably three distinct populations (Fowler, Madsen, and Hattori 1973). After A.D. 1200, only the Shoshonean tradition continues, carried into historic times by Numic-speaking peoples—the Southern Paiute bands that occupied most of the southeastern area in the ethnographic period.

Summary

In prehistoric times the southeastern Great Basin area was occupied by carriers of three sequential cultural traditions: Archaic, Horticultural, and Shoshonean. The Archaic tradition, 8000 B.C. to A.D. 1–500, was characterized by a hunting and foraging regime exhibiting an increasingly efficient adaptation to the various ecological zones of the area. There was a reliance on ungulates, lagomorphs and other rodents, birds, and a wide variety of seeds and roots. The atlatl and spear were used, and basketry and textiles were produced. Seed and root processing apparently became increasingly important after about 3000 B.C. as evidenced by an increasing number of ground-stone processing tools (Lyneis 1982). Settlements were in rockshelters and on open sites along streams and in upland areas, although Archaic settlement patterns are not well known.

The Horticultural tradition, A.D. 1–1200, was manifested in two variants—the Virgin branch along the Virgin River drainage and adjacent plateau and upland areas, and the Sevier Fremont tradition centered to the east but with incursions into the southeastern area. The Virgin branch tradition included pit houses, later with surface masonry storage and living structures, the growing of cultigens, and an increasing reliance on the bow and arrow. Sedentary or semisedentary villages developed along or adjacent to permanent stream courses. Foraging and hunting forays were made into areas of ephemeral streams and upland regions. Sevier villages have not been recorded in the area, only hunting and foraging stations. Both traditions declined sometime after A.D. 1050 and disappeared soon after 1200.

The Shoshonean tradition, A.D. 1000–historic times, was coexistent with the Horticultural traditions for approximately two centuries. The Shoshonean tradition had primarily a hunting and foraging subsistence base, although with minimal horticulture along the upper Virgin River (Euler 1966a). The horticulture was probably derived from the lower Colorado River (C. S. Fowler and D. D. Fowler 1981). The tradition continued into historic times, carried by Numic-speaking peoples.

Prehistory of the Southwestern Area

CLAUDE N. WARREN AND ROBERT H. CRABTREE

Environment

The southwestern Great Basin, as the term is used here, incorporates the large section of the Basin and Range physiographic province (Fenneman 1931) generally referred to as the Mojave Desert (Jaeger 1957). It extends mainly north of 34° north latitude and is bounded on the east by the Colorado-Virgin-Muddy river drainage and on the west by the southern Sierra Nevada Range and the Transverse Range (fig. 1). Most of Nevada south of Beatty and a large section of southeastern California north of Twenty-Nine Palms is within it, including Owens, Panamint, and Death valleys, and the Amargosa Desert straddling the California-Nevada border and centering on Ash Meadows. Except for relevant comparative material this chapter does not cover the area of the Lower Virgin River and Muddy River–Meadow Wash, which is dealt with in "Prehistory of the Southeastern Area," this volume.

The western and northern sections of this region are drained by three main river systems: the Mojave River, arising in the San Bernardino Mountains; the Amargosa River, arising in southwestern Nevada; and the Owens River deriving from the eastern slope of the Sierra Nevada Range. During pluvial times these rivers formed an integrated drainage system, along with several large lakes that ultimately drained into Death Valley, forming pluvial Lake Manly (Hubbs and Miller 1948:77–87).

For the most part, this area is over 2,000 feet above sea level except for the Mojave Sink and Death Valley, the latter being 282 feet below sea level. Adjacent mountain ranges have several peaks above 10,000 feet. The climate of this region is subarid, because evaporation exceeds precipitation, particularly below 5,000 feet elevation. Except in the higher elevations, mean annual precipitation for most of the area is less than 10 inches, and most of the precipitation generally occurs in the winter months (Aschmann 1958:25–27).

Several higher ranges receive sufficient precipitation to maintain permanent springs and short streams, and valleys and flatlands adjacent to these higher, better-watered mountains benefit from the increased ground water derived from them. Elevation and rainfall are important considerations for the plants and animals of the southwestern Great Basin, which is classified as the Mojavian biotic province. Biotic communities have been designated in terms of dominant plant types, and the distribution of these communities tends to coincide with altitude (Bradley and Deacon 1967:212–230; but also see Jaeger 1957:123–141).

Prehistoric Periods in the Mojave Desert

Archeology in the Mojave Desert has suffered from a plethora of named and renamed "cultures," "industries," "phases," and "periods." There has been a striking lack of agreement on taxonomic systems and terminology. This problem has become especially severe with the publication of the cultural overviews by the Bureau of Land Management as part of the California Desert Study (for example, Weide 1976; King 1981; Hall and Barker 1975; Stickel and Weinman-Roberts 1980; Garfinkel 1980; Warren, Knack, and Warren 1980; Davis, Brown, and Nichols 1980). Major temporal units or periods for the prehistory of the Mojave Desert are clearly established, but the absolute dates assigned to early intermediate periods remain points of contention.

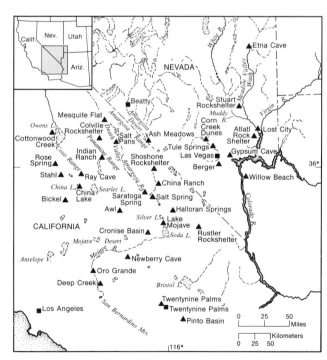

Fig. 1. Archeological sites in the southwestern Great Basin.

Bettinger and Taylor (1974) published a chronology in which temporal units were marked by distinctive projectile point types associated with radiocarbon dates. Warren and Crabtree developed a sequence of temporal units in 1972 that has served as the basis for other studies (for example, Warren 1980a, 1984). This sequence, also based on the temporal range of distinctive projectile points and associated radiocarbon dates, is similar to that of Bettinger and Taylor but differs significantly in the dates assigned to the early and intermediate periods.

The cultural sequence presented below is a modified version of Warren and Crabtree's 1972 chronology, organized on the basis of temporal units or periods that are marked by changes in distinctive artifact types (projectile points and pottery). These periods do not represent cultural units homogeneous in time or space; on the contrary, there are significant spatial and temporal variations in the cultural remains within each of these periods even where the variations cannot be detailed.

Lake Mojave Period, 10,000–5000 B.C.

Claims have been made for archeological assemblages dating to times earlier than the Lake Mojave period (for example, Simpson 1958, 1960, 1961; Schuiling 1979; Davis 1978), but all are controversial and have little or no known relationship to later cultural developments in the Mojave Desert. However, the Lake Mojave complex (Campbell et al. 1937), which is considered to be a Paleo-Indian assemblage by most archeologists, is also thought to be ancestral to the early Archaic cultures of the Pinto period and is therefore considered here.

This complex (fig. 2) has become the comparative unit for Early Man in the Mojave Desert, and similarities to sites in the western Great Basin and to the San Dieguito complex of southern California have been noted (Warren 1967; Bedwell 1970, 1973; Hester 1973). Included in it are various projectile point types, among them leaf-shaped forms, long stemmed points with narrow shoulders (Lake Mojave and Parman points), short bladed stemmed points with pronounced shoulders (Silver Lake point), and the rarer fluted point. Also present are crescents in simple lunate and more eccentric forms, small flake engraving tools with one or more very finely retouched points, specialized scrapers of distinctive types, leaf-shaped knives, drills, and a few heavy core tools that functioned as choppers or hammerstones. Milling stones are rare or absent.

Sites of the Lake Mojave period are nearly always limited to the surface, and it is possible that two or more assemblages are represented on these sites. Warren and Ranere (1968) suggested that the fluted points from this period represented a distinct occupation and that at Lake Mojave western Great Basin and southern California influences are represented. Southern California and the western Great Basin share a number of artifact forms but exhibit differences in point forms and in the lithic reduction technology of the bifaces. Davis (1969, 1978) proposed a Western Lithic cotradition and a Fluting cotradition to reflect this variety of cultural remains in the Mojave Desert during this period. Tuohy (1974) disagrees with these interpretations and argues for a single "Lake Mojave–Pinto Tradition" during the early part of which the fluted points were an element.

The Lake Mojave period incorporates both the fluted points and a variety of other large points and artifacts that may or may not belong to a single cultural unit. However, the similarity of these fluted points to Clovis points and the association of many of these sites with shoreline features of Pleistocene lakes is notable. Radiocarbon dates from Lake Mojave and sites with similar assemblages elsewhere (Hester 1973; Bedwell 1973) suggest dates of 10,000 to 5000 B.C. for the Lake Mojave period.

Warren (1967) postulated that the cultural assemblages of the Lake Mojave period were the remains of a widespread generalized hunting adaptation found throughout the western Great Basin. Bedwell (1970, 1973) and Hester (1973) interpreted these same assemblages as belonging to a Western Pluvial Lakes tradition, a more specialized adaptation to lacustrine resources of the pluvial lakes. Davis (1978) argues for a more generalized hunting and collecting economy for this early population in which the lakeside sites represent a "marsh orientation" during a portion of the seasonal round.

The nature of the cultural adaptation to the environments of the late Pleistocene–early Holocene transition in the Mojave Desert constitutes a problem area. It is becoming increasingly apparent that the cultural assemblages are representative of a technology and a subsistence system that is ancestral to those of the following Pinto period.

Pinto Period, 5000–2000 B.C.

The Pinto period, immediately following the desiccation of the Pleistocene lakes in the Mojave Desert, is not represented in the dated archeological remains. This is a period of major cultural adjustments, and it has been argued that conditions were so arid that the desert was essentially abandoned between 5000 and 3000 B.C. (Donnan 1963–1964; Wallace 1962; Kowta 1969). Others argue that an occupational hiatus of such magnitude would result in a disjuncture in the cultural sequence and that no such disjuncture occurs (Susia 1964:31; Tuohy 1974:100–101; Warren 1980a:35–44). Much of the debate centers around the definitions and dating of Pinto points ("Prehistory: Introduction," fig. 3, this vol.) and the association of sites containing Pinto points with dry lake beds and stream channels that suggest occupation during a wet period. The Pinto points that have been

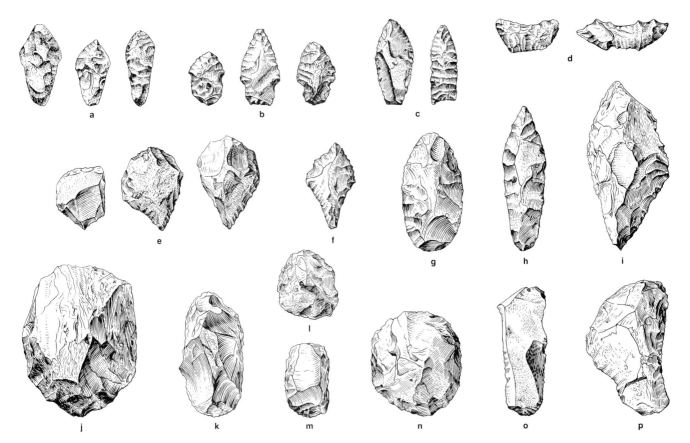

a, after Amsden 1937: pl. 41, a–c; Southwest Mus., Los Angeles: b, 498–G–3290; 498–G–3097; 498–G–2739–A; c, 498–G–270–D; 498–G–2748–A; d, 498–G–2293–A; 498–G–3096; e, 498–G–2771–F; 498–G–3278; 498–G–2735; f, 498–G–3342; g, 498–G–2288–B; h, 498–G–31; i; j, 498–G–2730; k, 498–G–2303–B; l, 498–G–2298–D; m, 498–G–2733; n, 498–G–2838; o, 498–G–2734; 498–G–2756–A.

Fig. 2. The Lake Mohave complex, an early artifact assemblage characterized by a wide variety of scraper forms and projectile points, ovate and lanceolate knives, crescents, and a limited range of large cobble choppers and hammers. Consisting mainly of surface collections from the shores of extinct lakes, this distinctive assemblage has not been found in good stratified context but has been radiocarbon dated at 8,270 ± 160 B.C. at a Lake Mohave site (Warren and Ore 1978; Ore and Warren 1971). a, Lake Mohave points, characterized by a long tapering stem and slight or sloping shoulders just below the center of the vertical axis. b, Silver Lake points, stems shorter, broader, and less tapering than on the Lake Mohave points, with well-defined shoulders. c, Unnamed lanceolate points. d, Crescents, form similar to scrapers, but more finely made and bifacially rather than unifacially chipped (photographs of these specimens are in vol. 8:27). e, Scraper-gravers, combination tools, usually somewhat smaller than single purpose scrapers. All suitable edges are modified by pressure or light percussion flaking. The distinctive feature is the well-developed graver point, usually plano-convex in cross-section. f, Drill, flat, thick flake with a point showing heavy wear. The shank has a markedly plano-convex cross-section. The lateral margins are retouched by pressure flaking. g, Ovate knife, well-controlled percussion flaking on both surfaces. h, Lanceolate knife or point, thin lenticular cross-section produced by careful percussion flaking, with pressure flaking for sharpening lateral margins. i, Large flake knife, bifacially flaked, tips and sides retouched by percussion. j, Larger scraper plane, big, thick flake, steeply percussion flaked around the periphery, with a distinctive, keeled appearance. k–l, Keeled scrapers, smaller and more definitely arched than the massive scraper planes, and varying from ovoid to rectangular in outline. m, Combination end and side scraper, rectangular outline, roughly plano-convex in cross-section, with secondary flaking on ends opposite the bulb of percussion. n, Ovoid side scraper, thick flake with a unifacially flaked convex scraping edge, an upper surface flattened rather than keeled, and including a broad flake channel that forms a convenient thumb hold. o, End scraper with blunt-nosed scraping end, showing little or no modification of the lateral edges. p, Side scraper, flaked on one side only, the thicker, nonworking edge serving as a convenient hand hold. Length of 2 (far left) 5.4 cm, rest same scale.

dated by radiocarbon are from the western Great Basin and appear to be typologically distinct from those of the Mojave Desert (Warren 1980). Warren (1980a) and Jenkins and Warren (1983) have also argued that since components containing Elko, Humboldt, and Gypsum points (but lacking Pinto points) date as early as about 1500 to 2000 B.C., the Pinto period should date between 5000 and 2000 B.C. An early period of more effective moisture in the Desert West also has been suggested

by Mehringer (1977) at about 4500–3500 B.C. Therefore, dates of 5000 to 2000 B.C. are assigned to the Pinto period.

Sites containing similar assemblages that may be assigned to the Pinto period with some confidence are the Pinto Basin site (Campbell and Campbell 1935), Salt Springs (M.J. Rogers 1939), the Stahl site (Harrington 1957), the surface component at Tule Springs (Susia 1964), the Awl site (Jenkins and Warren 1983), and

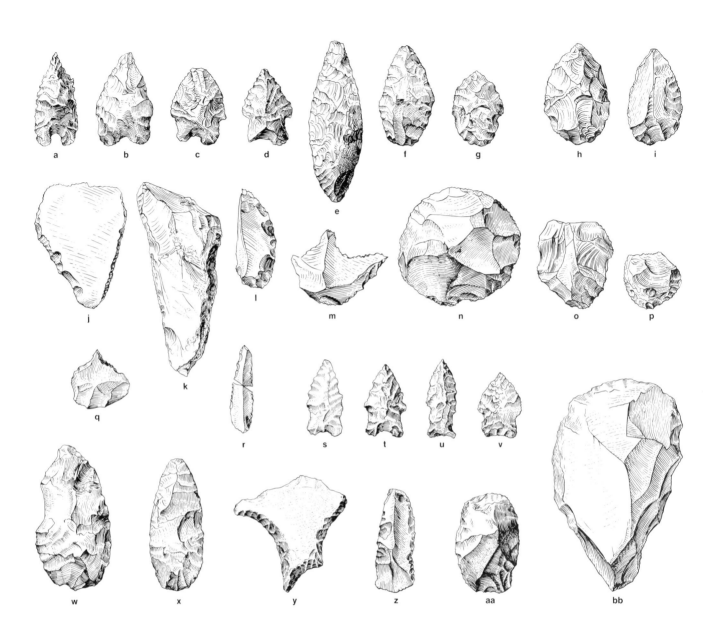

Southwest Mus., Los Angeles: a, 23–F–49; b, 23–F–318; c, 23–F–105; d, 23–F–119; e, 23–F–71; f, 23–F–52; g, 23–F–144; h, 23–F–186; i, 23–F–3091–A; j, 23–F–3011–D; k, 23–F–3290–B; l, 23–F–3285–F; m, 23–F–809; n, 23–F–347–C; o, 23–F–1203–B; p, 23–F–3098; q, 23–F–802; r, 23–F–3095; s, 498–G–2132–B; t, 498–G–2182–C; u, 498–G–2120–A; v, 498–G–2067; w, 498–G–2119; x, 498–G–2117–B; y, 498–G–2135–B; z, 498–G–2129–G; aa, 498–G–2141; bb, 498–G–2052.

Fig. 3. Pinto period tool assemblages, which includes variants of Pinto type projectile points, leaf-shaped points and knives, flake knives, and numerous kinds of scrapers and scraper-graver combination tools. Lake Mohave and Silver Lake points are often found in association with Pinto period artifacts. Shared characteristics in tool form and manufacture between Pinto and Lake Mohave assemblages have led some researchers to postulate an ongoing tradition of tool manufacture (Warren 1967; Tuohy 1974). Specimens a–r are from the Stahl site; s–bb are from the Pinto Basin, Calif. a, Pinto shoulderless point, crude, bifacially worked on a thick flake, with markedly serrated edges. b, Pinto sloping shoulder point. c, Pinto square shoulder point, well-defined shoulders, tip snapped off. d, Pinto barbed point, only one downward projecting shoulder left intact. e, Willow leaf point, lenticular cross-section, retouched edges. f, Leaf-shaped projectile point, regular lenticular cross-section with retouched edges. g, Silver Lake point, crude example, unifacially worked. h–i, Leaf-shaped knives, bifacially flaked, edges show heavy wear and retouch. j–k, Flake knives, unshaped except for bifacially flaked working edges. l–m, Retouched flakes, natural edges and points unifacially and bifacially trimmed. n, Large domed or humpbacked scraper. o, Small domed scraper, made on a thick primary flake, edges showing heavy attrition and retouch. p, Small oval or thumbnail scraper made on a thick primary flake, heavy attrition and retouch present on edge opposite the bulb of percussion. q, Graver, point and edges unifacially flaked. r, Perforator, made on a thin bifacially flaked prismatic blade, tip broken. s–v, Pinto type points, crude and variable in form. w–x, Lanceolate knives, bifacially flaked. y–z, Retouched flakes; y, with 3 usable points and a number of concave working edges, represents a classic spokeshave; z is a large blade with 2 unifacially retouched lateral edges, the edge opposite the striking platform showing heavy nibbling or attrition. aa, Keeled scraper, unifacially flaked. bb, Keeled scraper, also termed a "scraper plane," a hallmark of the Lake Mohave–San Dieguito complex. Length of s 3.8 cm, rest same scale.

WARREN AND CRABTREE

possibly the Corn Creek Dunes site (Williams and Or- lins 1963). The most characteristic artifacts at the sites are the several varieties of Pinto points, large and small leaf-shaped points and knives, domed and elongated keeled scrapers, and several forms of well made flake scrapers similar to those of the Lake Mojave period (fig. 3). Drills and engraving tools occur, as do occa- sional Lake Mojave and Silver Lake points. Few faunal remains have been recovered from Pinto sites; however, Artiodactyla (even-toed ungulates) and Lagomorpha (rabbits, hares, pileas) have been reported at the Stahl site and the Awl site, and both chuckwalla and desert tortoise occur at the Awl site (Harrington 1957; Jenkins, Warren, and Wheeler 1984).

Simple flat milling stones occur in Pinto period sites, as do occasional shallow-basined specimens and hand- stones. Wallace (1962) and Susia (1964) have argued that milling stones are rare or absent and that seed grinding is not an important economic activity. M.J. Rogers (1939:52–53) maintained that the polished, flat slabs were not milling stones but may have been "plat- forms upon which fibrous leaves or skins were scraped." At the Awl site where handstones and highly polished slabs occurred in a ratio of 1:16 it was suggested that the slabs were used for grinding only until the surface was smooth. When the surface became smooth, the milling stone was discarded and the handstone was car- ried away for use in conjunction with the next slab selected as a milling stone (Jenkins, Warren, and Wheeler 1984). The Stahl site is the only Pinto period site in which milling stones with well-developed circular basins are common.

The tool assemblage of the Pinto period sites suggests a generalized hunting and gathering subsistence system with only the beginnings of a technology for processing hard seeds. The lack of a well-developed seed grinding technology in the Mojave Desert contrasts sharply with the emphasis placed on seed grinding on the California coast (Warren 1968) and elsewhere in the Desert West (Jennings 1957) at that time. The seed processing tools were adopted in the Mojave Desert but were less im- portant to the economic system than elsewhere in the Desert West. This presents an interesting problem of adaptation to a desert environment, especially since the latter half of the Pinto period traditionally has been viewed as being the most arid of post-Pleistocene times.

The Stahl site (fig. 4), located at the south end of Owens Valley near the slopes of the Sierra Nevada, differs from other Pinto period sites in that it has a greater number and variety of artifacts and a deep mid- den containing house remains. In the central Mojave Desert the Pinto sites are most often limited to surface manifestation or have poorly developed middens with relatively low artifact density. They appear to be sea- sonal camps of highly mobile people. The small number of Pinto period sites, together with their apparent tem-

Southwest Mus., Los Angeles: 11224.
Fig. 4. The Stahl site, which held a detailed cultural record invaluable for reconstructing southern Great Basin prehistory. Seven housepits were dated by the occurrence of Pinto period artifacts to 2600 to 1200 B.C. (Harrington 1957). Postmold patterns were all that remained of these dwellings, which were small, pole- supported huts, circular to elliptical in outline, with doorways that faced east or southeast, and floors that had shallow firepits and deep storage pits. Faunal remains and tools evidence a mixed site economy based on hunting, primarily of deer, but also mountain sheep and rabbits, and the gathering and processing of wild plant seeds. Photograph by M.R. Harrington, 1943.

porary occupation, suggests that the population was small and poorly adapted to the desert environment. The people presumably followed a lifeway based on hunting large and small game and collecting vegetable resources. During arid periods they probably withdrew to the margins of the desert and to major oases, ex- panding their territory in the lower desert during the more moist periods to take advantage of the shallow lakes and the marshes and springs. During the later part of the Pinto period when the Mojave Desert was at its most arid, much of the lower desert may have been essentially uninhabited.

Gypsum Period, 2000 B.C.–A.D. 500

The Gypsum period begins at 2000 B.C. and continues to A.D. 500 and is characterized by medium sized to large stemmed and notched points. The most common forms are Elko Eared, Elko Corner-notched, Gypsum Cave, and Humboldt Concave Base points ("Prehis- tory: Introduction," fig. 3, this vol.). These points are dated at a number of sites and, in part, appear to rep- resent influences from outside the Mojave Desert. This period incorporates Bettinger and Taylor's (1974) New- berry period, the Gypsum portion of M.J. Rogers's (1939; Heizer and Berger 1970) Pinto Gypsum complex, Early and Middle Rose Spring (Lanning 1963; Clewlow, Heizer, and Berger 1970), Amargosa I (M.J. Rogers 1939), a portion of Wallace's (1962:176–177) Period III Amargosa, and Hunts's (1960) Death Valley II excluding the Pinto material, Harrington's (1933) Gypsum Cave culture, early levels of Stuart Rockshelter (Shutler, Shutler, and Griffith 1960), the Ray phase of the Coso Mountains (Hillebrand 1972), and Newberry Cave on the Mojave River (Davis and Smith 1981). The terminology involved in these reports is complex, inconsistent, and extremely confusing.

There are, fortunately, a number of sites dated by radiocarbon. These are highly variable in terms of quality of reporting and quantity of data, but they must form the basis for chronological interpretation. The Rose Spring site (Lanning 1963; Clewlow, Heizer, and Berger 1970) is a physically and culturally stratified site in the Owens Valley of the western Mojave. The cultural materials were relatively rich, but perhaps somewhat biased toward hunting activities and manufacture of obsidian artifacts. Through plotting depth and stratigraphic position of projectile points, it was possible to separate the midden into five successive units or phases. The artifact assemblages from the upper four units have been given phase names.

Five radiocarbon dates provide an age estimate of the three earliest cultural units. The lower three cultural units fall clearly in the Gypsum period, dating between 1950 and 290 B.C. (Clewlow, Heizer, and Berger 1970). The lowermost unit lacks diagnostic artifacts and has not been given a phase name. Early and Middle Rose Spring phases contain diagnostic points including Humboldt Concave Base, Elko Corner-notched, Elko Eared, Gypsum, and a large triangular point (or knife). Middle Rose Spring also contains the smaller Rose Spring Side-notched and Corner-notched types, which apparently signal the introduction of the bow and arrow.

On the Mojave River near Newberry, California, the Newberry Cave (Smith et al. 1957; Davis and Smith 1981; Davis, Taylor, and Smith 1981) excavation yielded Elko Eared, Elko Corner-notched, and Gypsum Cave points, and a suite of eight radiocarbon dates ranging from 1020 B.C. ± 250 (LJ-993) to 1815 B.C. ± 100 years (UCR-1094). Seven of the eight dates nearly overlap at about 1200 B.C. (in radiocarbon years), and the authors suggest that the cultural material was deposited in a very short interval that probably did not exceed 500 years.

At the eastern end of the Mojave in the Meadow Valley Wash, Shutler, Shutler, and Griffith (1960) excavated at Stuart Rockshelter. In the earliest levels they identified three "Shoulderless Pinto" points that would be classified as Humboldt Concave Base (or Humboldt Basal Notched) points. This level is dated by radiocarbon at 1920 B.C. ± 250 and 2100 B.C. ± 300. At successively higher levels are an Elko Eared point (identified as Basketmaker II), and Elko Corner-notched (identified as Basketmaker III), and what may be a Rose Spring Corner-notched point (identified as a Pueblo point).

The Price Butte phase at Willow Beach on the Colorado River contains large notched points similar to Elko Corner-notched and Elko Eared points that Schroeder (1961:89–90) regards as being similar to M.J. Rogers's (1939) Amargosa I and II prepottery points and to Basketmaker II materials of DuPont Cave and March Pass. The Price Butte phase is dated by radiocarbon at 250 B.C., which conforms comfortably to the Middle Rose Spring date.

Heizer and Berger (1970) have run dates for Gypsum Cave near Las Vegas, Nevada, and on the basis of radiocarbon assays on greasewood sticks from a fireplace and an atlatl dart shaft dates of 450 ± 60 B.C. (UCLA 1069) and 950 ± 80 B.C. (UCLA 1223) are indicated. These dates bring the Gypsum Cave points at Gypsum Cave in line with dates for them elsewhere in the Mojave Desert.

The Humboldt Concave Base, Elko Eared, Elko Corner-notched, and Gypsum Cave points apparently represent an overlapping sequence of point types. The Humboldt Concave Base seems to appear first about 2000 B.C. while Gypsum Cave, Elko Eared, and Elko Corner-notched points first appear between 2000 and 1500 B.C. and persist in decreasing numbers until after A.D. 500. The small projectile points had essentially replaced the larger Elko series and the Humboldt and Gypsum Cave points by A.D. 500, marking the end of the Gypsum period.

It is quite clear that points of the Gypsum period reflect a relationship with the western Great Basin and that interpretations of the prehistory of the western Mojave have been biased in that direction since the 1960s. But M.J. Rogers (1939), Wheeler (1942), Schroeder (1961), and Shutler, Shutler, and Griffith (1960) interpreted Gypsum period materials in terms of Southwest influence, which can be seen in the occurrence of pit houses along the eastern fringe of the Mojave during the late Gypsum period (Schroeder 1953, 1961; Shutler 1961), followed by the introduction of Basketmaker III pottery.

The split-twig figurine is another Southwest trait introduced during the Gypsum period. Figurines are reported from Newberry Cave, where they are dated at about 1800 to 1000 B.C. (Davis, Taylor, and Smith 1981); Etna Cave (Wheeler 1942) in a "Basketmaker III" deposit containing Gypsum Cave, Elko Eared, and Elko Corner notched points; and from an unidentified rockshelter in Moapa Valley (Schwartz, Lange, and DeSaussure 1958). Split-twig figurines, which are reported at no less than 13 sites in northern Arizona and southern Utah, range in age from 2145 B.C. ± 100 at Stanton Cave in the Grand Canyon to 1020 B.C. at Newberry Cave (Davis, Taylor, and Smith 1981; Schwartz, Lange, and DeSaussure 1958; Euler 1966a, 1967a; Schroedl 1977). Radiocarbon dates on material associated with the figurines at Cowboy Cave suggest their occurrence

188

as late as A.D. 455 in southwestern Utah (Schroedl 1977:261).

The context in which the figurines are found in Grand Canyon may have some significance for interpreting certain cultural elements in the Mojave Desert. Schwartz, Lange, and DeSaussure (1958:273) state that the figurines are always located in extremely inaccessible caves and that some of the specimens are pierced with small "spears." This suggests that the whole complex may be related to hunting ritual.

Smith et al. (1957) and Davis and Smith (1981) note that the data from Newberry Cave indicate use primarily for ceremonial activities rather than for occupation. Pictographs, weapons and figurines, paint, quartz crystals, the small painted stones, and sheep dung pendants or necklaces suggest ceremonial equipment used to insure success in hunting. Perhaps fashioning bighorn sheep from split twigs, the painting of some animal, or a symbol on the wall of the cave was part of a hunting ritual.

If a hunting ritual involving bighorn sheep is indeed represented at Newberry Cave, and bighorn sheep were among the most numerous faunal remains there (Smith et al. 1957; Davis and Smith 1981), then the beginnings of hunting ritual may be depicted in the elaborate petroglyphs of the Coso Range (Grant, Baird, and Pringle 1968; Hillebrand 1972). The postulated chronology for the Coso Range petroglyph, based on the change from depiction of atlatl, to atlatl and bow and arrow, to only bow and arrow, conforms closely to the dates suggested here.

During the early Gypsum period the projectile points are relatively large, suggesting the use of the dart and atlatl (fig. 5). This is further supported by the occurrence of dart shafts in Newberry Cave and Etna Cave. During the later part of the period small points of the Rose Spring series are introduced, all of which appear to be essentially the Elko series and Gypsum Cave point reduced in size. This probably represents the introduction of the bow and arrow. No precise date for development of the small point types can be given; however, they do occur during Middle Rose Spring, which has a date of 290 B.C. The small points replace the dart points by the beginning of Late Rose Spring and by about A.D. 500 at Willow Beach.

This transition from atlatl to bow and arrow would date the beginning of the Coso petroglyphs at some time in the Gypsum period and provide a terminal date of post-A.D. 500. The split-twig figurines and associated hunting ritual may have originated in northern Arizona about 2200 B.C. and reached the central Mojave a few hundred years later. The distribution suggests that the split-twig figurines and associated rituals diffused as a magico-religious system across cultural boundaries. The hunting rituals associated with petroglyphs may have been another aspect of the same magico-religious system that reached its climax in the Coso Mountains,

perhaps, as suggested by Grant, Baird, and Pringle (1968:58), because of the depletion of the bighorn sheep after the introduction of the bow and arrow.

Hunting continued to be an important economic pursuit during the Gypsum period, but milling stones and handstones became common during this period, indicating increased reliance on hard seeds. The mortar and pestle are reported at Mesquite Flat in Death Valley (Wallace 1977), at a Death Valley II site on the Amargosa River (Hunt 1960), and at Corn Creek Dunes in southern Nevada where they are dated between 2080 and 3250 B.C. (Williams and Orlins 1963). Each of these sites is located near or in mesquite groves, which suggests that the processing of mesquite pods with the mortar and pestle may have become an important element in the subsistence system during this period.

The beginning of the Gypsum period coincides with the beginning of the Little Pluvial about 2000 B.C., and it continues into the following arid period. The Gypsum period is a time of intensive occupation of the desert together with a broadening of economic activities, and increasing contact with the California coast and the Southwest. The bow and arrow was introduced late in this period, making hunting more efficient. The split-twig figurines and Coso petroglyphs suggest a rich ritual life was in existence. Generally the Gypsum period was a time in which the Mojave Desert population incorporated new technological items and ritual activities and increased socioeconomic ties through trade. Because of these new means of adaptation, the return of arid conditions toward the end of the Gypsum period had relatively little effect on the population density and distribution.

Saratoga Springs Period, A.D. 500–1200

The Saratoga Springs period, which is essentially the period of major Basketmaker III–Pueblo development and influence on the eastern Mojave Desert, begins about A.D. 500 and terminates about 1200. This period incorporates Late Rose Spring (Lanning 1963) and Bettinger's (1975) Baker phase in Owens Valley, Death Valley III in Death Valley and Ash Meadows (Hunt 1960; Hunt and Hunt 1964; Wallace 1958), the latter part of Amargosa II (M.J. Rogers 1939), Chapman I phase of the Coso Mountains (Hillebrand 1972), and Roaring Rapids phase and early Willow Beach phase at Willow Beach (Schroeder 1961). The initial occupation of the large village sites reported by Sutton (1981) in Antelope Valley date to this period, as do the Bickel site (McGuire, Garfinkel, and Basgall 1981) located to the north of Antelope Valley in the Western Mojave, the Saratoga Springs site in Death Valley (Wallace and Taylor 1959), the Oro Grande site on the Mojave River (Rector, Swenson, and Wilke 1979), and a portion of Rustler Rockshelter (J.T. Davis 1962).

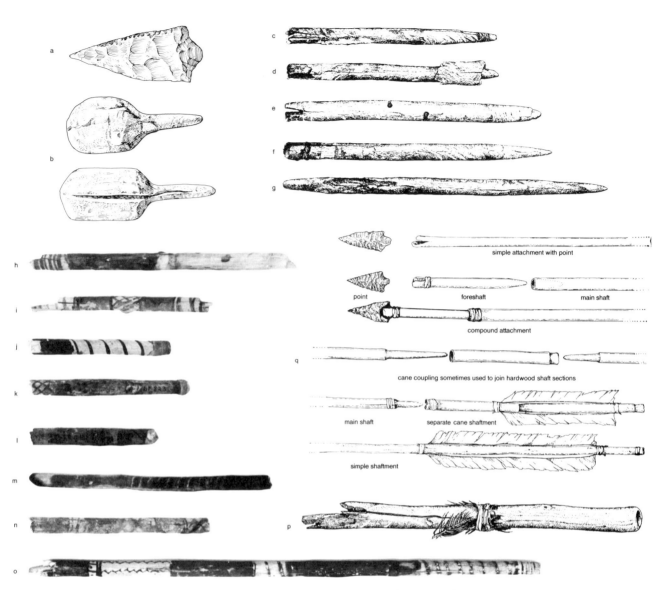

a–b, p–q, after Harrington 1933:figs.16, 51; c–g, Harrington 1933:fig.29; Southwest Mus., Los Angeles: h, 6–F–591; i, 6–F–428; j, 6–F–825; k, 6–F–823; l, 6–F–627; m, 6–F–113; n, 6–F–147; o, 6–F–164.

Fig. 5. Elements of the Middle Archaic atlatl dart assemblage from Gypsum Cave, southeastern Nev. The complete dart seems to have been some 4–5 feet long, fletched with 3 feathers, and armed with a large point of flaked stone, bone, or wood. Most examples were compound constructions consisting of a hardwood foreshaft inserted into a mainshaft of elder or arrowbrush. The darts were used with a throwing stick or atlatl, about 2 feet or less in length, with a handle at one end and a spur at the other. In use, the atlatl and dart were held in one hand, the butt of the dart shaft firmly engaged on the spur. The dart was thrown with a sweeping overhand motion. The atlatl effectively lengthened the arm of the thrower, thus increasing the velocity of the cast. a, Gypsum type stone point of fine-grained, light gray quartzite, once hafted to a dart foreshaft with pitch, some of which still adheres to the stem. b, Wooden bunts bearing traces of white pigment; the tapered proximal ends were shoved into the socketed dart shaft. c–g, Dart foreshafts. c–f have slots cut into the distal ends for attachment of projectile points, while the proximal ends are tapered for insertion into the dart mainshaft. c retains a portion of the stem of a flaked stone point and has remnants of a pitch and sinew binding. d retains a cylindrical portion of an elder mainshaft, and the distal slot is crammed with pitch impressed with marks of the original sinew seizing. e has a distinct shoulder cut below the distal slot and an abraded surface, features presumably designed to insure a firmer grip for the sinew wrapping. f has pitch inside and outside of the distal slot, and remnants of the binding sinew. g is a sharpened hardwood foreshaft-point, the tip blunted through use. h–o, Decorated dart mainshaft fragments. h and i are mainshaft fragments without proximal and distal ends. j–o have intact proximal ends with cups. j and k have sinew wraps just above the butts, ostensibly to help prevent splitting. o, the butt end of a mainshaft, with a proximal cup for engagement of the atlatl spur, shows marks from the sinew seizing that held feathers at the proximal end just above the cupped butt. All these specimens were painted with varying shades of red, brown, green, and blue. p, Dart butt of elder, close-up-view, showing coarse sinew binding just above the spur cup holding the tips of 3 unidentified brown feathers. The feathers on this example were not split or trimmed and were laid down tangentially with the ribs lengthwise along the side of the dart shaft. This is not characteristic of all fletching on the Gypsum Cave darts, since other proximal mainshaft fragments hold stubs of quills that were split, and numerous recovered bits of feathers show that these were commonly trimmed. q, Reconstructions of typical Gypsum Cave atlatl darts, simple and compound designs. Length of a 7.3 cm, rest same scale.

WARREN AND CRABTREE

In the northern Mojave, from Death Valley to the Sierra Nevada, the sites of the Saratoga Springs period appear to exhibit cultural continuity with the Gypsum period, change being most apparent in the size of projectile points. The Rose Spring series and the Cottonwood Triangular points dominate assemblages of this period, while milling stones and manos continue in use as do incised stones and slate pendants. The pestle and presumably the mortar are present.

Essentially the same assemblage is present across the Mojave Desert north of the Mojave River. However, Basketmaker–Pueblo influences increase with Anasazi occupation on the Muddy River. Hunt (1960:112–113) reports similarities between the burials and projectile points of Death Valley III sites and those of the Muddy River, as well as a number of other artifact types including olivine-tempered pottery from Ash Meadows (Hunt and Hunt 1964:10). M.J. Rogers (1929, 1939) reports Nevada-derived Anasazi pottery and mauls and picks in his Amargosa II assemblage. The mauls and picks are associated with turquoise mines near Halloran Spring in the east-central Mojave. Leonard and Drover (1980:251–252) report a sequence of pottery types from these turquoise mines supported to some extent by radiocarbon dates. This sequence suggests that the Anasazi controlled the mines between about A.D. 700 and 900 followed by Hakataya peoples who withdrew about A.D. 1200–1300. Finally, the Southern Paiute utilized the area in late prehistoric times. The mining of turquoise resulted in Anasazi influence in much of the eastern Mojave. The area of this influence can be mapped by the distribution of Anasazi sherds occurring in considerable frequency at sites in southern Nevada (Larson 1981), and in California as far west as the Cronise Basin (M.J. Rogers 1929). Anasazi influence sets the eastern Mojave apart from the remainder of the desert.

No adequate detailed accounts of excavated sites with Anasazi materials from southwestern Nevada exist, but the sites with Anasazi material from this area appear small and shallow, though widely distributed. They probably represent a more attenuated extension of the intermittent or seasonal foraging pattern that prevailed during the Gypsum period. The inference here is that relatively small parties of Muddy River villagers (Shutler 1961) periodically foraged through parts of this area. The extent of these forays is not as yet determined, but it appears to have been considerable, particularly in well-watered valleys such as Las Vegas Valley and Ash Meadows and in the Spring Mountains.

The cultural development of the Mojave Desert south of the Mojave River and Providence Mountains diverges from that in the northern area during this period. Few points of the Rose Spring series and virtually no Anasazi pottery occur in the southern Mojave. M.J. Rogers (1945:173–174) mentions a nonceramic Yuman pattern "which needs only the addition of native pottery to make it Yuman."

However, he fails to describe adequately the artifacts of this nonceramic Yuman pattern. Nevertheless, the artifact assemblage described for the Oro Grande site (Rector, Swenson, and Wilke 1979) on the Mojave River near Victorville supports Rogers's assertions. Of the 74 classifiable points, 67 are of the Cottonwood Triangular type, none is Desert Side-notched, and no pottery is present. Other artifact types, including knives, drills, milling stones, mortars and pestles, stone pipes, bone awls, and shell and stone ornaments, show close similarities to their counterparts in the later pottery-bearing sites along the Mojave River.

Radiocarbon dates ranging from A.D. 800 to 1300 place the occupation of the Oro Grande site in the later Saratoga Springs period, yet the artifact assemblage exhibits significant differences from the sites of this period north of the Mojave River. The Oro Grande site, together with later sites containing brown and buff, paddle and anvil pottery and Cottonwood Triangular and Desert Side-notched points (M.J. Rogers 1945; G.A. Smith 1963; J.T. Davis 1962; True, Davis, and Sterud 1966), seem to indicate that the Hakataya influence reported by vol. 9:100–107 from the lower Colorado River Valley and the Colorado Desert began to be felt in the Mojave River Valley as early as A.D. 800 and continued until historic contact. From the beginning of this cultural divergence the southern Mojave Desert is perhaps more properly placed within the Southwest sphere of influence than within that of the Great Basin.

Shoshonean Period, A.D. 1200–Contact

The Shoshonean period dates from about A.D. 1200 to the time of European contact. The diagnostic artifacts for this period are Desert Side-notched points and various poorly defined types of brownware pottery including Owens Valley Brownware. During this period, regional developments are more easily identified than in earlier periods, and three regional expressions may be tentatively identified. In the Mojave Desert south of the Mojave River the Hakataya influence continues (vol. 9:100–107). The assemblage reported from the Deep Creek site on the upper Mojave River (G.A. Smith 1963) includes brown, buff, and red-on-buff pottery apparently derived from the Colorado River, as well as Desert Side-notched and Cottonwood Triangular points. This same combination is found along the length of the Mojave River to the Mojave Sinks (G.A. Smith 1963; M.J. Rogers 1929; Drover 1979), and eastward through the Mid Hills and New York and Providence mountains to the Colorado River in southern Nevada (J.T. Davis 1962; Donnan 1963–1964; True, Davis, and Sterud 1966). The sites on the upper Mojave appear more elaborate: there are house pits, more abundant shell beads and ornaments, and the painting of utilitarian items such as metates with several different colors of pigment (G.A. Smith 1963). In southern Nevada, Colorado River wares are found on sites as far north as the Spring Mountains, often with Anasazi pottery or the coarse brown "Paiute ware" (Shutler 1961:29; Crabtree, Rodrigues, and Brooks 1970:9; Larson 1981; Warren 1974).

In the northwest Mojave the artifact assemblage continues from the Saratoga Springs period through the Shoshonean period with the addition of Desert Side-notched and Cottonwood Triangular points, Owens Valley Brownware pottery, and small steatite beads. This continuum can be seen in the Rose Spring sequence (Lanning 1963) and the Chapman I–II sequence of the Coso Mountains (Hillebrand 1972). In addition to Desert Side-notched and Cottonwood Triangular points and coarse brown pottery, the Shoshonean period assemblage of the northern Mojave includes large well-made triangular knives, unshaped manos and milling stones, incised stones, slate pendants, pestles and mortars, and shell beads. This northern Mojave assemblage extends from the Owens Valley on the west to the Valley of Fire on the east and is represented by the Klondike and Cottonwood phases in Owens Valley (Bettinger 1975; Lanning 1963); Chapman II phase in the Coso Mountains (Hillebrand 1972); the Indian Ranch site (True, Sterud, and Davis 1967) and Coville Rockshelter (Meighan 1953) in Panamint Valley; Death Valley IV sites (Wallace 1958; Hunt 1960) and the Panamint (Shoshone) culture (Wallace 1977; Wallace and Wallace 1978) in Death Valley; the China Ranch site (McKinney, Hafner, and Gothold 1971) and the Shoshone Rockshelter (Gearhardt 1974) in the Amargosa Valley; the Berger site in Las Vegas Valley (Crabtree 1978); and the most recent occupation of Atlatl Rock Shelter in southwestern Nevada (Warren et al. 1978).

The initial occurrence of this assemblage in southern Nevada is equated with ancestors of the historic Southern Paiute and is roughly contemporaneous with the terminal date for the Anasazi occupation of that area. The cultural continuity of the assemblages of the Saratoga Springs and Shoshonean periods in Owens Valley and the Coso Mountains suggests that this Shoshonean assemblage had its origin in that region. The restriction of this assemblage to the area north of the Mojave River corresponds roughly to the southern boundaries of the Numic languages. This suggests that the Shoshonean period assemblage in the northern Mojave may be identified with the expansion of the Numic speakers across the eastern Mojave (C.S. Fowler 1972).

Sutton (1980, 1981) summarizes data from a series of prehistoric sites including several cemeteries in Antelope Valley at the western edge of the Mojave Desert. The large sites with associated cemeteries are interpreted as major villages, and the small special purpose sites as seasonally occupied outliers. This has led Sutton to suggest that Antelope Valley supported a large population during the late prehistoric period and was not so marginal an area as indicated by the ethnographic data. Radiocarbon dates place the sites between 250 B.C. and A.D. 1650, while time-sensitive artifacts include Rose Spring and Cottonwood Triangular points and locally made undecorated brownware pottery.

Sutton (1980:220–221) attributes the large villages to the Kitanemuk, neighbors of the Tataviam in Antelope Valley, California, and interprets the differential distribution of wealth in the cemeteries as evidence of a system of prestige and status and a complex sociopolitical organization. The economic basis for such social complexity is attributed in part to well-developed trade systems in which the Antelope Valley people functioned as middlemen between coast and interior populations. This is supported by the relatively abundant shell beads, ornaments, and steatite from the southern California coast. This system appears to have declined rapidly after A.D. 1650, and the valley became a marginal area as reflected in the ethnographic record.

The sequence for Antelope Valley is poorly understood, but the available data appear to support the interpretation of cultural continuity since shortly before the time of Christ. Under the influence of the trade network between the coast and the interior, the cultural development of Antelope Valley diverged from that of the rest of the Mojave Desert. The cultural elaboration of Antelope Valley seems to parallel that of the Upper Mojave River but was less influenced by the Hakataya developments of the Southwest and more strongly influenced by contact with the southern California coast.

The north-south divergence in the cultural development of the Mojave Desert corresponds roughly to the boundaries between the Numic and the Takic speakers in the western Mojave and the Numic and Yuman speakers in the eastern Mojave. The Antelope Valley development is apparently the result of differentiation within the Takic-speaking groups and may reflect the separation of the Serrano and the Kitanemuk. The "boundary" between the Serrano and Yuman speakers in the central Mojave cannot be identified archeologically at this time. The regional differentiation identified for the Shoshonean period appears to correspond with major ethnographic and linguistic divisions of the historic period.

Conclusions

It is apparent that the available data relevant to Mojave Desert prehistory are unevenly distributed throughout the 10,000 years or so of documented human occupation. Occupation of the older Pleistocene period remains hypothetical because uncontrovertable evidence for the age of documented artifacts is lacking. The chronological placement of the fluted points as the earliest occupation of the Lake Mojave period is based on cross-dating and typological seriation and lacks firm radiocarbon dates and stratigraphic relationships. Some archeologists argue that the fluted points represent an element of the Western Pluvial Lakes tradition.

The Lake Mojave–San Dieguito assemblages represent the earliest occupation for which enough data are present to test the validity of various interpretations. Although some regional variation is present, the Lake Mojave–San Dieguito complex seems to belong to what has been called the Western Pluvial Lakes tradition, which is found throughout much of the western Great Basin and adjacent regions.

Dramatic environmental changes came to the Mojave Desert with the end of the Pleistocene. General desiccation set in, lakes and rivers dried up, and the resources available were much reduced. Human adaptation to these new environmental conditions appears to be represented by the Pinto period assemblages. The artifact assemblages of the Pinto period exhibit continuity with those of the Lake Mojave period in the use of heavy scraping implements. There was continued but reduced use of Lake Mojave and Silver Lake point types and an apparent emphasis on hunting. During the Pinto period the beginnings of a technology for processing hard seeds appeared, but it was not fully developed until late in the period or the beginning of the succeeding Gypsum period. The Pinto period occupation of the Mojave Desert appeared at this time as an unsuccessful attempt to continue hunting as a major subsistence activity. This was a poor adjustment to the arid conditions of the Altithermal. The population of the Mojave Desert seems to have decreased during this period, and some areas may have been abandoned.

The cultural continuity between the Pinto and Gypsum periods is less apparent than that of the Lake Mojave–Pinto transition. This may be due to the paucity of data for the Pinto period together with increased complexity of the cultural remains during the Gypsum period. The initial date of 2000 B.C. for the Gypsum period corresponds roughly to the beginning of a period of increased moisture, and environmental conditions are assumed to have improved by 1500 B.C. The Gypsum period is a time of increased contact with the Southwest as reflected in the early widespread distribution of the split-twig figurines and the later occurrence of Basketmaker II pit houses on the eastern fringes of the Mojave. Hunting continues as an important element of the subsistence as indicated by the abundance of hunting tools, the introduction of the bow and arrow, and the hunting rituals associated with the Coso petroglyphs, split-twig figurines, and the Newberry Cave artifact assemblage. Other subsistence activities also are further developed during this period as indicated by the introduction of the mortar and pestle and apparent increases in the occurrence of milling stones. The Gypsum period may be viewed as a time of increased

intensity of occupation with a broadening of economic activities and increased contact with the Southwest and the California coast.

Regional diversification can be identified as characteristic of the Saratoga Springs period (A.D. 500–1200) with strong Anasazi influence in the northeastern Mojave. The southern Mojave received the first impulses of the contemporary Hakataya developments along the lower Colorado River. Turquoise mining in the eastern Mojave and the Anasazi occupation of the lower Virgin and Muddy rivers indicate increased interaction with the Southwest. The Mojave River also developed as a trade route, and by the end of the Saratoga Springs period the Mojave River Valley shared a ceramic complex and projectile point styles with the lower Colorado Valley. Shell bead and ornament styles were shared with the California coast.

In the northwest Mojave, the Saratoga Springs period exhibits much continuity with the Gypsum period and can be distinguished by the reduction in size of projectile points. Changes in subsistence systems cannot be adequately identified, but reduction in artiodactyl hunting in the northern Mojave may be postulated. During the Saratoga Springs period there appears to be a refinement of adaptation to the arid environment of the northwest Mojave, and presumably the beginnings of the Numic expansion eastward across the Mojave.

The Shoshonean period (1200 to historic contact) is marked by the occurrence of crude brownware pottery and Desert Side-notched points. The Mojave River Valley and the southern Mojave continued to be influenced by trade between the California coast and the lower Colorado River with the brown, buff, and red-on-buff lower Colorado River pottery. California shell beads and ornaments occurred throughout much of the area. Villages, apparently in part dependent on trade, developed on the upper Mojave River. In Antelope Valley, farther to the west, similar villages date to this period and contain shell beads, ornaments, and steatite from the southern California coast, but the lower Colorado pottery types are rare or absent. In the northeastern Mojave the truncation of the Anasazi development marks the beginning of the Shoshonean period and corresponds roughly to the date assigned to the Numic expansion. The archeological assemblages from the whole of the northern Mojave, from Owens Valley to the Muddy River Valley, exhibit great similarity and are easily identified by the crude brownware pottery and Desert Side-notched points. These assemblages have been traditionally interpreted to represent the eastward expansion of the Numic speakers across the northern Mojave. Late in the Shoshonean period the trade networks involving both the Mojave River and the Antelope Valley appear to have been disrupted, bringing an end to the villages of Antelope Valley and reducing the intensity of activity along the Mojave River. *193*

Prehistoric Basketry

J. M. ADOVASIO

Few areas of North America have yielded more or better preserved prehistoric basketry remains than has the Great Basin. Controlled excavations in the abundant dry caves and rockshelters in nearly all sections of this area have yielded basketry collections that span more than 10,000 years of occupation. This is the longest and perhaps the best-controlled basketry sequence in the world due to the great number of radiocarbon dates on the perishables themselves and on directly associated materials.

As used here, the term basketry includes rigid and semirigid containers, matting, and bags. Matting is essentially two-dimensional or flat; baskets are three-dimensional. Bags are intermediate because they are more or less two-dimensional when empty but three-dimensional when filled. Driver (1961:159) observes that these artifacts can be treated as a unit because the overall technique of manufacture is the same; that is, all forms of basketry are manually woven without any frame or loom. Because basketry is woven it is properly a subclass of textiles (Emery 1966; Adovasio 1977; Kent 1983). Sandals can be included as they are made by using basketry construction methods.

Published analyses of prehistoric Great Basin basketry are numerous, but usually they are descriptive sections of larger site reports and limited in both the technological and cultural comparisons that they draw. Of particular interest are the works of Loud and Harrington (1929), Morss (1931), Steward (1937a), Cressman et al. (1942), Heizer and Krieger (1956), S.S. Rudy (1957), and Rozaire (1957). The emphasis in most later works is clearly culture-historical and comparative (Rozaire 1969, 1974; Adovasio 1970, 1970a, 1971, 1972, 1974, 1975, 1975a, 1976, 1979, 1980, 1980a, 1980b; Adovasio with Andrews 1985; Adovasio and Andrews 1980, 1983; Adovasio, Andrews, and Carlisle 1976, 1977; Adovasio, Andrews, and Fowler 1982; Andrews, Adovasio, and Carlisle 1984; Hewitt 1980).

Prehistoric Basketry Regions

As a result of comparative studies it has proved possible to identify at least three distinct prehistoric basketry manufacturing regions* within the Great Basin (Ado-

* What are here called regions were termed centers in Adovasio 1970; Adovasio and Andrews 1983.

vasio 1970). Each region has special characteristics and its own developmental sequence and shows fluctuating relationships to the others over time. The boundaries between the three Great Basin regions do not correspond to those of tribes or language families. The similarities in the basketry of each region represent instead shared technologies rooted in broad, environmentally related adaptive strategies that cut across many different ethnic groups (Adovasio with Andrews 1983).

Northern Basin Basketry Region

The Northern Basin basketry region is in south-central Oregon and includes adjacent parts of northern California and northwest Nevada (fig. 1). Principal sites where basketry was found in this area include Fort Rock Cave (Cressman et al. 1942; Cressman and Bedwell 1968; Bedwell and Cressman 1971; Bedwell 1973), Roaring Springs Cave (Cressman et al. 1942), Catlow Cave No. 1 (Cressman et al. 1942), the Paisley Five Mile Point Caves (Cressman et al. 1942), Table Rock No. 1 (Cressman and Bedwell 1968; Bedwell 1973), Seven Mile Ridge (Cressman and Bedwell 1968), Connley Cave No. 6 (Cressman and Bedwell 1968; Bedwell 1973), the Warner Valley Caves (Cressman et al. 1942), Guano Valley Cave (Cressman 1936; Cressman et al.

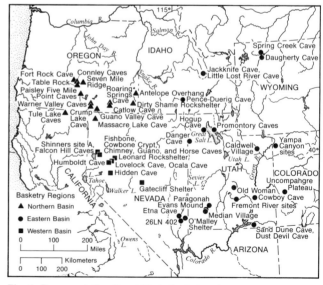

Fig. 1. Representative Great Basin basketry sites.

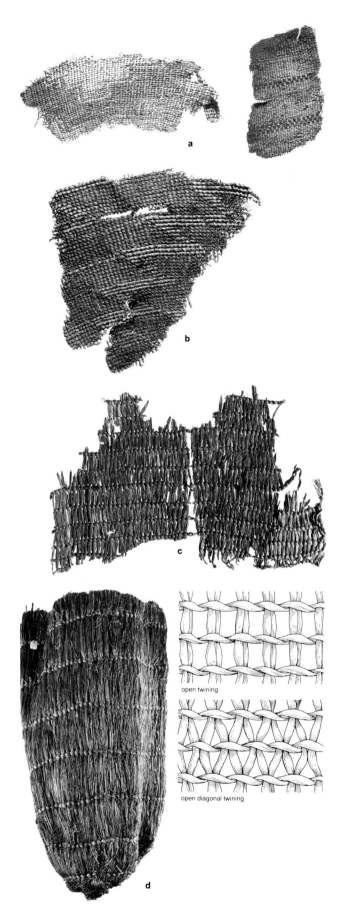

open twining

open diagonal twining

1942), Antelope Overhang (Adovasio 1970), Plush Cave (Cressman et al. 1942), Crump Lake Cave (Cressman et al. 1942), De Gorma Cave (Cressman et al. 1942), Massacre Lake Cave (Heizer 1942), the Tule Lake Caves (Heizer 1942), and Dirty Shame Rockshelter (Aikens, Cole, and Stuckenrath 1977; Adovasio, Andrews, and Carlisle 1976, 1977; Andrews, Adovasio, and Carlisle 1984; Adovasio with Andrews 1983).

Within the Northern Basin region, at least 13 different basket wall-construction techniques are known, including at least seven basic twining variations and six coiling types. The twined specimens are produced by one of three basic methods, close simple twining (plain two-element), close diagonal twining (twill twining), or open simple twining, all with Z-twisted wefts.

The forms of twined objects include large, semiflexible, conically and cylindrically shaped burden baskets (fig. 2a–c), bowls with rigid to semiflexible walls (fig. 3), rigid circular trays (or plaques) (fig. 4), elongate flexible bags (fig. 2e), and rectangular mats (fig. 2d), (Cressman et al. 1942:34–56; Adovasio, Andrews, and Carlisle 1977; Andrews, Adovasio, and Carlisle 1984). These forms served various functions, certainly including collecting, winnowing, and transporting, and dry storage of vegetal food stuffs. There is no direct archeological indication that twined forms were used for cooking, parching, or water storage in this area, but such functions cannot be totally precluded.

Twining was also used to produce at least three sandal types including the highly distinctive Fort Rock sandal (fig. 5a), the so-called multiple warp sandal (of several varieties), and spiral weft sandals (fig. 5b) (Cressman et al. 1942; Adovasio, Andrews, and Carlisle 1977; Andrews, Adovasio, and Carlisle 1984). Although rabbit fur strips have been recovered in several Northern Great Basin sites, twined rabbit fur robes are not documented in the archeological record for this area.

Twined objects commonly exhibit various decorative techniques in some Northern Great Basin sites, especially later in the sequence. These include several permutations of overlay, false embroidery, and wrapped twining, as well as the use of dyed weft elements.

According to Cressman et al. (1942:40–41), the basic design principle characteristic of prehistoric Northern

U. of Oreg., Oreg. State Mus. of Anthr., Eugene: 2, 1–3662; 1–8397; b, 1–8292; c, 1–8704; d, 1–31267.
Fig. 2. Twined basketry specimens, northern Great Basin. a, Fragments of semiflexible conical or cylindrical carrying baskets, close simple twining, Z twist weft, Roaring Springs Cave, Oreg. Overlay decoration in linear bands and geometric patterns is typical of this area. b, Fragment of a semiflexible conical or cylindrical carrying basket, close simple twining, Z twist weft, with overlay decoration, Catlow Cave No. 1, Oreg. c, Portion of a flexible rectangular mat, open simple and diagonal twining, Z twist weft, Roaring Springs Cave, Oreg. d, Coarse, elongate bag, open simple and diagonal twining, Z twist weft, Chewuacan Cave, Oreg. Length of d 76 cm, rest to same scale.

195

Great Basin twined work is the subdivision of the basket or bag into a series of zones or horizontal bands of varying size, each of which is treated as a unit within a decorative field. These zones may be beaded, or contain diagonal and step patterns, or consist of broken masses.

Coiling is present in the Northern Great Basin but is scarce. Both single- and multiple-rod foundations are known with interlocking, noninterlocking, and intentionally split stitches on the nonwork surface. The preferred work direction is right-to-left, but the reverse technique does occur. Coiled forms include wide-mouthed bowls, shallow trays, and pitched water vessels or jugs (the precise shapes of which are unknown). Decoration on coiled pieces is generally rare or absent and consists only of painting with red ocher, in the case of the pitched water vessels (Cressman et al. 1942:48–49), and apparently use the intentionally split stitches arranged to produce a simple V (or zigzag) pattern as seen on a coiled basket wall from Roaring Springs Cave. Coiling seems to have been employed, although rarely, in the prehistoric Northern Great Basin for vessels for storage, possibly for transport, and for water storage. There is no direct archeological evidence that it was ever used for cooking vessels.

There are fewer radiocarbon dates from the Northern Great Basin than from the other two regions, but it is possible to reconstruct a developmental sequence in basketry based largely on data from Dirty Shame Rockshelter (Andrews, Adovasio, and Carlisle 1984) and by examining other Northern Great Basin sites that have yielded textiles, expecially those that contain a layer of ash from Mount Mazama. This sequence is divided into three stages.

In Stage 1, about 9000 to 5000 B.C., basketry production is first evidenced in the Northern Great Basin in the form of open and close simple twined bags, mats, burden baskets, trays, and coarse receptacles of undetermined configuration. All the known specimens lack decorative embellishment of any sort despite Cressman et al.'s (1942:42) observations to the contrary. Only Fort Rock or spiral weft sandal types were made, and diagonal twining as well as coiling are absent.

In Stage 2, 5000 B.C. to A.D. 900, examples of diagonal twining, which are absent beneath the Mazama pumice (deposited about 5000 B.C.) at all the Northern Great Basin sites, appear above that marker bed and probably represent elaborations of the simple twining forms evidenced earlier in the sequence. Simple twining persisted and dominated the early portion of this stage. All the forms found in Stage 1 also continued into Stage 2. Spiral weft sandals dominated footwear early in this stage; the Fort Rock type was extinct by 3900 B.C. Later assemblages within Stage 2 include more diagonal twining, again in the same basic forms. Multiple warp sandals appeared. S-twisted wefts appeared early in this stage and increased in frequency after 2500 B.C. Decorated twining may have been produced early in this interval and was certainly well represented by the end of it. All basic decorative methods were in use, but coiling was absent throughout this stage. However catastrophic the Mount Mazama blast may have been in ecological terms, the basketry and related perishable industries of the Northern Great Basin continued without change.

In Stage 3, A.D. 900 to 1600, coiling appeared in minor quantities in the form of bowls and water bottles or jugs. Coiling appears never to have attained significant popularity, and most of the older twining forms persisted with several notable additions. These include the triangular winnowing tray and the seed beater. Most decorative embellishments so typical of the preceding period are rarely found within the meager twining as-

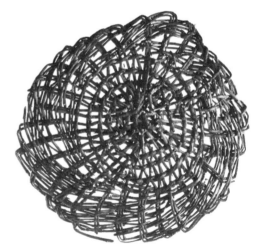

U. or Oreg., Oreg. State Mus. of Anthr., Eugene: 1–7976.
Fig. 4. Complete, flat, rigid circular plaque, open diagonal twining, S twist weft, Roaring Springs Cave, Oreg. The S twist wefts are not typical of the northern Great Basin but do occur. Diameter 18.0 cm.

10 cm

U. of Oreg., Oreg. State Mus. of Anthr., Eugene: 1–4709.
Fig. 3. Semiflexible circular tray, close simple twining, Z twist weft, Roaring Springs Cave, Oreg.

U. of Oreg., Oreg. State Mus. of Anthr., Eugene.
Fig. 5. Characteristic sandal types from the northern Great Basin, Catlow Cave No. 1, Oreg. left, Fort Rock type sandal; right, spiral weft type sandal, top and bottom views. Length of left 25.0 cm, rest to same scale.

semblages known from this stage. Few sites and assemblages are specifically ascribable to this period. However, Zone I at Dirty Shame Rockshelter clearly falls into this time range (Adovasio, Andrews, and Carlisle 1977; Andrews, Adovasio, and Carlisle 1984).

The Western Basin Basketry Region

The Western Basin basketry region encompasses much of west and central Nevada as well as contiguous portions of California (fig. 1). Principal sites include Lovelock Cave (Loud and Harrington 1929; Grosscup 1960, 1963), Humboldt Cave (Heizer and Krieger 1956), Leonard Rockshelter (Heizer 1951), Horse Cave (Rozaire 1974), Fishbone Cave (Rozaire 1974; Orr 1952, 1974), Chimney Cave (Rozaire 1974), Guano Cave (Rozaire 1974), Crypt Cave (Rozaire 1974), Cowbone Cave (Rozaire 1974), Ocala Cave (Adovasio 1970), the Falcon Hill Caves (Rozaire 1969; Hattori 1982), the Monitor Valley Caves (Adovasio and Andrews 1983), and Hidden Cave (Goodman 1985).

At least 16 basketry wall techniques or types are represented in the Western Basin region. Of these, seven are coiling variations, eight are twining, and one is a distinctive form of plaiting known as Lovelock Wickerware.

The range of twining forms represented in the Western Basin region is broadly comparable to that in the Northern Basin but is somewhat more extensive. Among the earliest and most persistent forms are open simple twined rectangular mats and flexible, probably conically shaped, bags or pouches (fig. 6d–f). These occur as early as 9300 B.C. ± 250 at Fishbone Cave, Nevada (Orr 1974), and 7590 B.C. ± 120 at Shinners Site A, Nevada (Hattori 1982). Other forms represented at one or another site in this area are semiflexible to rigid, generally shallow to round-bottomed conical bowls; large, rigid to semiflexible burden baskets of several shapes; elongate walletlike items (fig. 6c); flat, rigid circular plaques (fig. 6a); concave base, triangular-shaped trays;

and, later in the archeological record, seed beaters and close simple twined or, more often, diagonally twined, pitched water bottles (fig. 6b).

Other twined forms include open twined cradles (fig. 6g) and robes of rabbit or other small mammal fur, as well as of coot or other bird skin strips. Twined sandals appear early in this area, and an open simple twined multiple warp type (fig. 6h) not unlike that from the Northern Great Basin occurs sometime between 9300 B.C. ± 250 and 5880 B.C. ± 350 at Fishbone Cave (Orr 1974). Multiple warp sandal types also occur later with both open and close twined forms, some with diagonally twined weft rows. The spiral weft sandal form does not occur prehistorically in this region, nor are exact analogues of the Fort Rock sandal type known.

In the Western Basin basketry region twined goods were used for collecting, winnowing, transporting, and storage of both dry vegetal food stuffs and liquids. Cooking in twined baskets or bags may also have been practiced, as was the parching of large seeds and nuts.

The same range of decorative techniques as in twining in the Northern Basin basketry region is paralleled in the Western region, once again usually later in the cultural sequence. These include the use of warps and wefts of different colors as well as all known permutations of overlay, false embroidery, and wrapped twining (see Adovasio 1977 for definitions of these decorative techniques). Twining design styles in the Western region are more varied than those from the Northern region, but most are essentially geometric with triangles, zigzags, wavy lines, linear bands, and vertical bars. Anthropomorphic and zoomorphic motifs are absent.

Of the seven coiled basketry techniques, two multiple-rod foundation types (three-rod bunched; two-rod and welt bunched) are used in the great majority of coiled baskets known from the Western region. Noninterlocking, interlocking, and intentionally split stitch types are represented, but noninterlocking and, especially, interlocking stitches are rare. Right-to-left work direction is predominant, but the reverse technique is known.

The range of coiled basketry forms in the Western region is much more restricted than that for twining and includes large, flat, circular trays, and a limited variety of so-called hopper and bowl configurations (Heizer and Krieger 1956).

Circular trays of coiled basketry were used for parching or roasting (fig. 7). Deeper coiled baskets also were used for dry storage and as hoppers. Many specimens are impermeable by virtue of the tightness of the weave and possibly served as storage containers for liquids, though one cannot be certain of this function.

Decorative techniques used on coiling in the Western region include stitches of different colors (either dyed or painted) and the well-documented incorporation of feathers into the basket itself (fig. 8). Feathers were

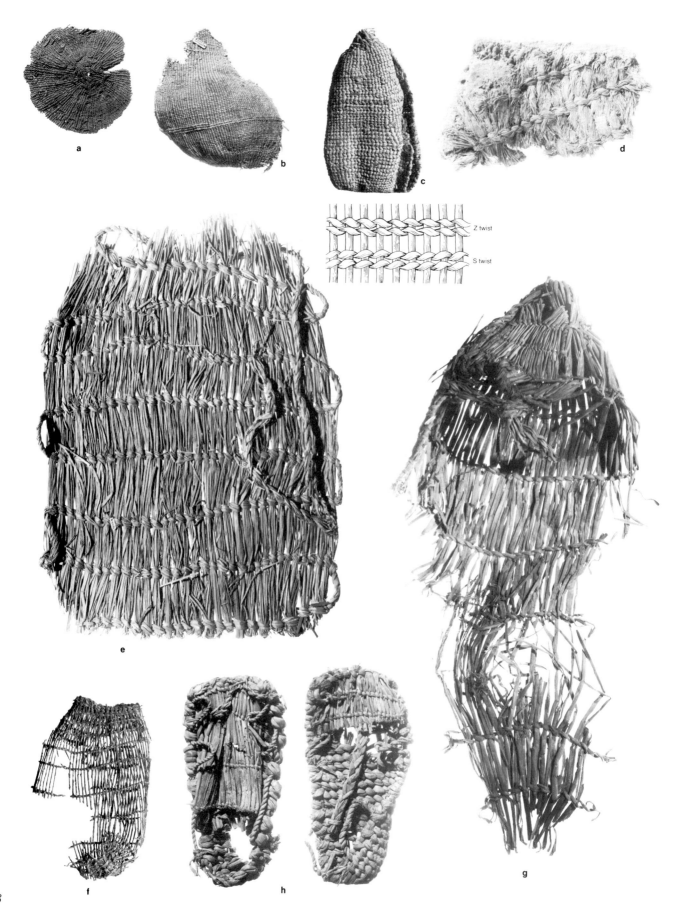

a

b

c

d

Z twist

S twist

e

f

h

g

198

ADOVASIO

U. of Calif., Lowie Mus. of Anthr., Berkeley: a, 1–44373; b, 1–20083; c, 1–43032; e, 1–43745; f, 1–42156; g, 1–42495; h, 1–42314; 1–42561; d, Orr 1974:fig. 7b.

Fig. 6. Twined basketry from the western Great Basin. a, Fragment of a rigid flat tray or plaque, close simple twining, Z twist weft, from Humboldt Cave, Nev. b, Fragment of a watertight globular vessel, close simple twining, S twist weft, from Lovelock Cave, Nev. Several courses of three strand wefts are used for decoration and reinforcement of the delicate side walls. c, Complete flexible wallet, close simple twining, alternate rows of Z and S twist wefts, from Humboldt Cave, Nev. d, Portion of a flexible mat, bag, or pouch, open simple twining, Z twist weft, from Fishbone Cave, Nev.; the oldest radiocarbon-dated textile in western North America, with a date of 9300 ± 250 B.C. (Orr 1974). e, Carrying case, open simple twining, Z twist weft, Humboldt Cave, Nev. f, Semiflexible, elongate carrying basket, open diagonal twining, Z twist weft, Humboldt Cave, Nev. g, Fragmented cradle, open diagonal twining, Z twist weft, Humboldt Cave, Nev. h, Two multiple-warp type sandals, open simple twining, Z-twist weft on toe flaps, top view, Humboldt Cave, Nev. Length of e 60.0 cm, rest same scale.

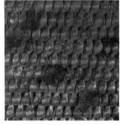

U. of Calif., Lowie Mus. of Anthr., Berkeley: 1–42147.

Fig. 7. Parching or roasting tray, close coiled, 3-rod bunched foundation, split stitch on both surfaces, Humboldt Cave, Nev. Diameter 52.0 cm.

Tuohy 1974a:figs 5a, 5b.

Fig. 8. Complete feathered bowl, close coiled, 3-rod bunched foundation, split stitch on the nonwork surface, Brown Cave, Nev. The zigzag design was produced with the brown and white feathers of the male eared grebe (*Podiceps nigricollis*).

generally obtained from local, usually lacustrine, birds and were used in making certain types of bowls (Tuohy 1974a; Baumhoff and Heizer 1958). Coiling designs with stitches of different colors are similar to those found on twining; they are wholly geometric, without anthropomorphic or zoomorphic motifs.

Feathered baskets are found in relatively small quantities at Lovelock, Humboldt, and several other western Nevada caves. Although they may have been made as early as 2,500 years ago, most known specimens are of far more recent age. Baumhoff and Heizer (1958:61) convincingly argue that these specimens are exotic imports from the Maidu-Washoe area. Tuohy (1974a:30–40) marshals equally convincing evidence that these items were produced locally, though perhaps with "foreign" models as prototypes. Whatever the origin, the decorative motifs are, once again, simple geometrics.

The most common textile technique represented in sites of the Western basketry region is semiflexible to rigid plaiting in the form of Lovelock Wickerware, at least after about 2000–1000 B.C. (see Loud and Harrington 1929:60–64; Heizer and Krieger 1956:37–45; Grosscup 1960, 1963). Lovelock Wickerware normally took the form of a large, conical burden basket (fig. 9). Some of these baskets had tumpline attachments or

straps and were again decorated with geometric designs using plaiting elements of different colors. Painting was rarely used to create this effect. More often, the contrast was effected by employing decorticated and undecorticated elements in the same piece. The principal functions of these specimens were collecting and transporting wild "produce" and other dry goods.

From the many radiocarbon dates available for the Western basketry region, the sequence of basketry development has been reconstructed in five stages.

In Stage 1, 9000–4500 B.C., twining dominated the complex. The earliest basketry types included both open simple twining and close simple twining, both with Z-twisted wefts. In general, these are mats and flexible bags, but semiflexible containers of several shapes were also produced. Multiple warp sandals also occurred early in this interval. Basketry with close simple twining and S-twisted wefts appeared by the end of this stage, as

199

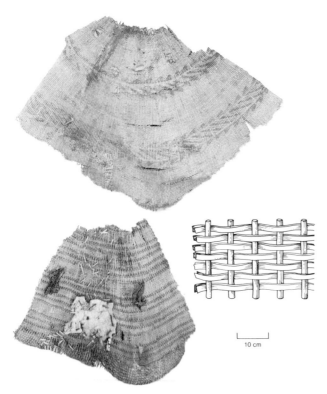

U. of Calif., Lowie Mus. of Anthr., Berkeley: 1–42426; 1–42442.
Fig. 9. Fragments of Lovelock Wickerware conical carrying baskets, Humboldt Cave, Nev. Plaited geometric designs are typical of the western Great Basin.

did diagonal twining. Once again, diagonal twining seems to represent an elaboration of the simple twining forms found earlier. Structural decoration on twining is known from this period but is not particularly common. Significantly, coiling and Lovelock Wickerware were absent throughout this stage.

In Stage 2, 4500–2000 B.C., coiling using multiple-rod foundations, generally with noninterlocking or intentionally split stitches, appeared in the form of parching trays as well as container forms of several types. This early Western Basin coiling resembles the far earlier Eastern Basin multiple-rod types but differs in splice patterns and other construction details. Decorated and undecorated twining of a variety of wall types and vessel or mat configurations and multiple-warp sandals persisted but seems to have declined steadily in frequency as well as in diversity. No Lovelock Wickerware was present.

In Stage 3, 2000–1000 B.C., the multiple-rod foundation coiling of Stage 2 continued to increase in apparent popularity. Twining of all types decreased, but no twining types disappeared completely. Burden baskets and rigid to semiflexible and flexible twined open work bags continued to be made as did rectangular mats. Several varieties of multiple-warp sandals were in use, and Lovelock Wickerware may have appeared at this time; however, Grosscup (1960) assigns it to a

transitional Lovelock phase, about 1000–1 B.C. The case for the earlier occurrence of Lovelock Wickerware may be supported by a specimen from Kramer Cave, which is tentatively ascribed to an occupation dated to 1800 B.C. (Hattori 1982).

In Stage 4, 1000 B.C.–about A.D. 1000, decorated and undecorated, rigid and flexible twining continued to be manufactured, though the range of forms was somewhat limited. Open twined containers and mats were produced but are not at all common in cave deposits, perhaps because they were simply not cached there. The principal construction medium for burden baskets was the highly localized and distinctive Lovelock Wickerware, the popularity of which peaked early in the period and may have been on the decline after A.D. 1 (Grosscup 1960). By the end of the stage, it was very rare. Coiling of the three-rod bunched variety, particularly with the central or apex rod split by the stitches, was common, and several other coiling wall types are represented. These include a restricted assortment of symmetrical and asymmetrical bunched foundation variants from Humboldt and several other dry caves, and at least three single-rod varieties from Lovelock Cave. Multiple-warp sandals continued to be made.

In Stage 5, about A.D. 1000–1800 or later, coiling, although present, no longer included the distinctive flat, circular parching tray. Lovelock Wickerware does not occur. Containers with bunched multiple-rod foundations produced early in this stage resemble, in most of their details, wares collected in historic times. Twining included open simple and diagonally twined forms, notably, the seed beater and triangular winnowing tray and multiple-warp sandal types. While few stratified sites fall into this time range, the perishable assemblages from Gatecliff Shelter and the other Monitor Valley sites (Adovasio and Andrews 1983) are clearly ascribable to this period. As a whole, the basketry and sandals of this period seem both technologically distinct and essentially unrelated to previous cultural developments.

Eastern Basin Basketry Region

The Eastern Basin basketry region encompasses the state of Utah north of the Colorado River and adjacent portions of western Wyoming, southern Nevada, southern Idaho, and northwest Colorado (fig. 1). Among the important Utah sites are Danger Cave (Jennings 1957), Hogup Cave (Aikens 1970), the Promontory caves (Steward 1937a), the Evans Mound (Marwitt 1970), Paragonah (Judd 1919), Caldwell Village (Ambler 1966a), Median Village (Marwitt 1970), Old Woman (Taylor 1957), the Fremont River area (Morss 1931), Antelope Cave (Adovasio 1970), Sand Dune and Dust Devil caves (Lindsay et al. 1968), and Cowboy Cave (Jennings 1980). In Colorado, one may include Yampa

Canyon (Burgh and Scoggin 1948) and the Uncompahgre Plateau (Wormington and Lister 1956). In Idaho are Little Lost River Cave, Pence Duerig Cave, and Jackknife Cave (Adovasio, Andrews, and Fowler 1982). Spring Creek Cave (Adovasio 1970) and Daugherty Cave (Adovasio 1970) are in Wyoming; Etna Cave (Wheeler 1942), 26LN402 (Adovasio 1970), and O'Malley Shelter (Fowler, Madsen, and Hattori 1973) are in Nevada.

The Eastern basketry region is represented by a minimum of 19 basket wall construction techniques or types. Eight of these types are twining variations; the remainder are coiling types. Plaiting in any form is absent.

Three twining variations are numerically important in the Eastern basketry region, at least for a limited period. These include close simple twining, S-twisted wefts; open simple twining, Z-twisted wefts; and open diagonal twining, Z-twisted wefts. All these were present by the early ninth millennium B.C. at Danger Cave (Jennings 1957).

Unlike the other two regions, the range of twining forms in the Eastern area is somewhat restricted, and decoration of any sort is rare. The earliest forms included both close and open twined rigid burden baskets; circular, flat, or nearly flat plaques of unknown extract configurations (fig. 10); as well as flexible bags of either pouch or conical shape. Open twined rectangular mats were also present (fig. 11).

Decoration was restricted to the occasional use of rows of three-strand wefts, apparently to work out simple linear bands and perhaps to provide structural reinforcement. Three strand weft decoration or reinforcement techniques particularly occur on close simple twined specimens. Of still rarer occurrence is the use of con-

Adovasio 1970a:fig. 99.
Fig. 11. Fragment of a large rectangular mat, open diagonal twining, Z twist weft, from Hogup Cave, Utah.

trasting natural color warp and weft elements in flexible bags.

Close simple rigid twining with S-twisted wefts, whatever its extract form, has no parallel in the earlier or later industries of the Western or Northern basketry regions and appears to be a local innovation in the Eastern region. The persistence of S-twisted twining throughout the known sequence is unique. In later prehistoric times, twined, triangular-shaped winnowing trays, and (usually) pitched water jugs occurred, as did seed beaters. The only twining forms that seem to have spanned the entire prehistoric sequence were mats and perhaps simple twined flexible bags. Interestingly, no twined sandals were produced in the Eastern region before the ethnographic period. Open twined rabbit fur robes are sporadically represented in collections through the period from about 7000 B.C. to the Historic period.

The twined forms were used for collecting, winnowing, transport, and storage of both dry and wet substances. There is no direct evidence that cooking was undertaken in twined containers, but some roasting or parching of large seeds and nuts may be documentable.

Of the very large number of known coiling types, single-rod foundations and variants thereof are by far the most numerous at all times before about A.D. 1200. Multiple-rod types did occur but, numerically at least, were clearly of secondary importance. Split stitches on the nonwork surface predominated as did right-to-left work direction; however, interlocking and noninterlocking stitch types did occur. Interlocking stitches were notably common in the earliest prehistoric period and persisted in varying percentages throughout the sequence.

The range of coiled basketry forms in the Eastern region is greater than in the others. The forms include flat to concave base parching trays (fig. 12), a variety of generally shallow bowl forms that grade into deep,

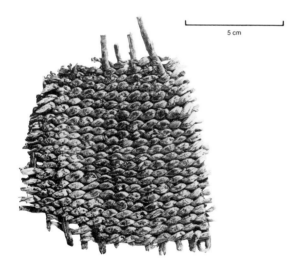

5 cm

S.S. Rudy 1957:fig. 219.
Fig. 10. Part of a rigid container or large, flat tray or plaque, close simple twining, S twist weft, from Danger Cave, Utah. The S twist wefts and the lack of decoration are typical of the rigid twining of the eastern Great Basin.

steep-sided containers, some of considerable size, and a few isolated specimens of open coiled sifter vessels. These were once presumed to be intrusive into this area (Adovasio 1970, 1974) but may in fact be quite ancient (Jennings 1980). All the early coiling is in the form of parching trays.

The decoration of coiled basketry forms in the Eastern region is very restricted and includes only the occasional use of false braid rims and the unique employment of feathers in simple chevron designs on a single specimen from Hogup Cave (fig. 12b). The use, on a single form, of stitches of different colors—a decorative technique so common in the adjacent Southwest—is virtually unknown in the Eastern basketry region.

Enough radiocarbon dates exist for the Eastern region that a detailed, five-stage developmental sequence can be postulated.

During Stage 1, 9000–6500 B.C., twining dominated the basketry produced in the Eastern region; coiling was absent. The principal basket wall techniques included the apparently indigenous close simple twining, S-twisted wefts. This was used in particular for rigid vessels or in making trays of various configurations. The technique known as open simple and diagonal twining, Z-twisted wefts, was used for making flexible bags, mats, and semiflexible burden baskets. The earliest twining type seems to be of the simple or plain variety; diagonal twining appeared later.

Early in Stage 2, 6500–4500 B.C., coiling was made in small amounts but was confined to what is now the state of Utah. This coiling from Hogup Cave and several other sites to the south is among the oldest coiled basketry recovered anywhere in the world. It has a close-coiled, one-rod foundation with interlocking stitches and was used almost exclusively for flat to slightly concave base, undecorated parching trays. By the end of this stage, one-rod and welt stacked foundations had appeared, and coiled bowls and trays had reached a percentage parity with twining. Twining, however, clearly dominated the early part of this period, and continued to be made in a limited repertoire of flexible to rigid forms, notably bags and mats.

In Stage 3, 4500–2000 B.C., coiling dominated in the Eastern basketry region, and twining was clearly on the decline. One-rod foundations and variants thereof (particularly the endemic and unique one-rod-and-bundle stacked foundation) were the most popular coiling variations, but multiple-rod types were also present and are the oldest examples of these wall types recovered in North America. Bowl and tray forms persisted, as did flexible twined bags and mats. Rigid twining was rare by Stage 3 times; its functions seem to have been usurped by coiling. Both the one-rod and multiple-rod coiling variants are interpreted as simple, progressive elaborations of the basic one-rod foundation technique.

In Stage 4, 2000 B.C.–about A.D. 1200, one-rod-and-bundle stacked foundation coiling dominated the entire Eastern region, but one-rod and one-rod variants as well as multiple rod coiling were present to different degrees. The fundamental coiled vessel forms of the preceding stage persisted, and limited amounts of flexible twining especially in the form of mats and bags continued to be made. Just after the beginning of the Christian era, Eastern region coiling techniques appeared in southern Nevada, eastern Idaho, and northwest Colorado as well as in parts of Wyoming; they are invariably associated with the spread of the Fremont formative culture.

In Stage 5, about A.D. 1200–1800 or later, one-rod-and-bundle basketry, the hallmark of the previous stage, and a Fremont culture diagnostic, disappeared completely, as did most of the previously favored one-rod coiling variants and vessel forms, specifically the parching tray. The twining that continued to be made included both open and close, simple and diagonal basket wall types in forms essentially identical to ethnographic wares from the same area. Coiling was dominated by

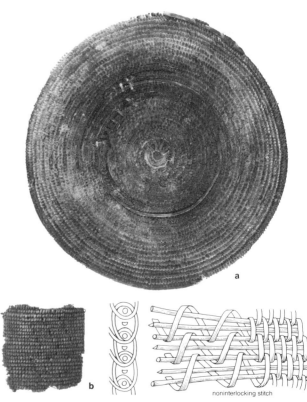

Adovasio 1970a:figs. 105, 111a.

Fig. 12. Coiled basketry specimens, eastern Great Basin. a, Classic flat parching tray typical of this area for more than 7,000 years, close-coiled, half-rod and bundle stacked foundation, split stitch on the nonwork surface, from Hogup Cave, Utah. b, Fragment of a deep-sided storage vessel of large size, close-coiled, half-rod and bundle stacked foundation, noninterlocking stitch, from Hogup Cave, Utah. Chevron design in feathers is highly unusual, decoration of any kind being rare on coiled baskets from this area.

ADOVASIO

multiple-rod foundation types, but some single-rod basketry also occurred. The only stratified site with basketry spanning this period is Hogup Cave (Adovasio 1970a) where the upper levels clearly document the Fremont-Shoshonean "succession." As with the twining, extant coiled specimens of this stage appear to be unrelated to previous cultural developments but do exhibit marked ties to the ethnographic wares known from the area.

Raw Materials

The prehistoric inhabitants of the Great Basin utilized a wide variety of plant sources in the manufacture of basketry, bags, and matting. These sources varied from region to region due to plant availability and different environment exploitation practices.

In the Northern Basin basketry region, the principal plant used for fine twined basketry varied among subareas. In the Fort Rock Valley, tule (*Scirpus acutis*) was utilized for both warps and wefts throughout the sequence, though occasionally cattail (*Typha latifola*) cords might be employed. In the Dirty Shame Rockshelter region, sagebrush (*Artemisia tridentata*) was selected early in the sequence and then replaced by tule. Throughout the region overlay decoration was crafted using turkey beard (*Xerophyllum* sp.; Cressman et al. 1942:41, 42). Coarsely twined baskets were made of tule, true rush (*Juncus* sp.), sagebrush, and occasionally willow (*Salix* sp.). In coiled basketry, willow was ordinarily used both for foundation and stitching, but other woods doubtless served on occasion. Matting was almost always made with tule; however, swamp grasses (including *Juncus* sp.) are also represented. Plants used in the Northern region were almost exclusively chosen from lakeside biomes. Other species were gathered rarely.

Aboriginal weavers of the Western Basin basketry region selected many of the same plant sources as did their contemporaries to the north, but different technical emphases altered the proportion of these raw materials. In the earliest Western Basin textiles tule of two species (*Scirpus acutis, S. nevadensis*) was the favored material followed by true rush. Other plant sources used for twining included cattail, cane (*Phragmites* sp.), and Indian hemp (*Apocynum* sp.). The use of these plants persisted throughout the textile developmental sequence despite the rapid diminution in the popularity of twining. Sagebrush, though presumably very common, was seldom if ever employed either for twining or any other basketry. With the appearance of coiled basketry, willow was heavily favored for both foundation and stitching, but other woods may have been selected in minor quantities. This was also the case for Lovelock Wickerware. Most of the plants drawn upon in the Western region for textile production were from lacustrine habitats.

In the Eastern Basin basketry region, weavers gathered a much more diverse range of plants. This probably reflects the scarcity of lacustrine sources and the geographically more wide-ranging adaptation of Eastern Great Basin human populations. By far the most common raw material throughout the period of textile manufacture was sandbar willow (*Salix exigua*) used alone or in combination with other plants for both twining and coiling. Among the many other species in the Eastern region plant repertoire were milkweed (*Asclepias speciosa*), Indian hemp, tule (*Scirpus americanus*), cattail, cedar (*Juniperus osteosperma*), cliff rose (*Cowania mexicana*), white sage (*Eurotia lanata*), and squaw bush (*Rhus trilobata*). Each of these plants was generally preferred alone or with willow for a particular type of textile. The relative degree of their exploitation fluctuated with the popularity of the textile type during a particular period. Jennings (1957, 1980) and Adovasio (1970, 1970a) give information correlating plant types and textile varieties.

Comparison of the Basketry Regions

A comparison of the three Great Basin basketry regions indicates that textile manufacturing in each extends back as far as the ninth millennium B.C. In each region the earliest technique was, to the exclusion of all others, twining. In the Northern area twining dominated the area into the Historic period. Early coiling was clearly restricted to the Eastern region and appeared there some 2,000 years earlier than in the other regions. This innovation would seem to reflect a functional necessity arising from a specialized economic adaptation predicated around the parching of very small seeds such as pickleweed (*Allenrolfea occidentalis*). Parching is a use for which most twining forms are ill-suited.

Although twined basketry was used both prehistorically and ethnographically to parch or to roast larger seeds and nuts, it is only with the appearance of coiling in the Eastern region around 6500 B.C. that there is substantial and unequivocal archeological evidence for the collecting, parching, and consumption of the small chenopods and their floral allies. This observation is strongly supported by well-dated and numerous human coprolites (Fry 1976). The appearance of coiling is probably related to a basic modification in the aboriginal subsistence strategy of the eastern Basin, to center on small seed processing.

After two millennia of change (which notably included the first use of three-rod bunched coiling types), coiling ultimately diffused from the Eastern region to the Western and from the Western to the Northern. Single-rod coiling variants dominated the Eastern region from 4500 B.C. until the Historic period. In the Western region multiple-rod coiling and Lovelock Wickerware were the dominant types after 4500 B.C.. *203*

Within each of the three Great Basin basketry regions there was a marked tendency toward regional specialization and technological divergence through time. At no period, however, is evidence for mutual influence entirely lacking. Throughout the period of textile evolution, or at least up to A.D. 900–1200, the Western and Northern regions were much more closely related than either was to the Eastern region. The only major exception to this was in the period during which coiling spread from the Eastern region.

Around A.D. 900–1200 or slightly later, major changes occurred in the textile inventories of all three Great Basin basketry regions. These changes reflect population or ethnic discontinuities that seem to be related to the dispersion of Numic-speaking peoples (see Adovasio with Andrews 1983).

External Comparisons

Textiles of an antiquity remotely comparable to those in the prehistoric Great Basin were unknown in the New World prior to research in areas as far removed as southwestern Pennsylvania (Stile 1982), Tennessee (Chapman and Adovasio 1977), Lower and Trans-Pecos Texas (Andrews and Adovasio 1980), and northern Peru (Adovasio and Lynch 1973; Adovasio and Maslowski 1980). These and similar efforts by other researchers indicate that the production of textiles is an exceedingly ancient craft in the New World and may well have been part of the technological repertoire of the first Americans.

The earliest textiles in the American Southwest, in California, and in contiguous parts of the Plains are all strongly reminiscent of Great Basin varieties. This may be the result either of diffusion or of a shared ancestry in the remote past. However, once established, the textile traditions in adjacent culture areas only occasionally shared basketry traits with contemporaneous traditions in the Great Basin. Indeed, as early as 6500–6000 B.C., the textiles of the eastern Great Basin, north of the Colorado and Virgin rivers, and those of the American Southwest were already so distinct that it is possible to delimit an artifactual frontier between them that persisted for the next seven millennia (Adovasio with Andrews 1985).

Ethnographic Continuities

Virtually all the aboriginal inhabitants of the Great Basin (except the Washoe) were Numic speakers by the onset of the Historic period. Nearly all these groups produced textiles and most of the prehistoric textile techniques discussed here are found somewhere among historic Numic-speaking groups. Yet, it does not appear that the textiles of the Numic speakers are "genetically" related to previous developments in any of the Great

Basin centers. There are a limited number of ways to produce basket walls, that is, by twining, coiling, or plaiting; thus, it is not surprising that many pre-Numic basket wall techniques also occur in the perishable assemblages of the Numic speakers. As useful as basket wall construction traits are for analysis and classification, collectively they are not the most culturally or ethnically diagnostic basketry manufacturing attributes. No single basketry attribute is restricted to a single human population, but the basketry of each population is characterized by a constellation of construction and finishing techniques that itself is usually unique. It is in this sense that one can say that although the basketry of the Numic speakers shares certain gross attributes of construction with that of pre-Numic groups, there are no demonstrated connections when the complex of culturally diagnostic attributes is examined as a whole.

Ethnographic research on trait distributions was conducted with many Numic and non-Numic aboriginal populations (for example, Steward 1941, 1943a; O. C. Stewart 1941, 1942; Drucker 1937; Driver 1937). Using these data, it is possible to construct "trait profiles" that effectively characterize the perishable industries of most of the Numic speakers and their immediate neighbors. (See, for example, the tables in Adovasio with Andrews 1985 that summarize select basketry and cordage construction attributes documented for both Numic and contiguous non-Numic groups. These tables also summarize data on preferred forms, selvages, raw materials, and other technical details.)

The trait profiles indicate that certain basket wall types and forms are almost "pan-Numic" in distribution; others are more restricted. It is clearly possible to distinguish the ethnographic basketry of the Numic speakers from that of their immediate neighbors and to extract salient taxonomic criteria for the closely related Numic cordage "industries." The twined seed beater, the twined triangular winnowing tray (and to a lesser degree the twined conical carrying basket), produced by simple or diagonal twining, and predominantly but not exclusively with S-twisted wefts, are the principal hallmarks of the Numic basketry assemblages. Simple twining and diagonal twining with S- and Z-twisted wefts are ancient basketry techniques in the Great Basin, but none of the diagnostic Numic forms seems to predate the posited arrival of the Numic groups themselves. Although starting techniques, rim finishes, splicing patterns, and raw materials can vary from one Numic-speaking population to another, the simple presence of these forms in so many Numic groups is itself culturally diagnostic (see Bettinger and Baumhoff 1982).

Although not nearly so widespread among Numic speakers, coiling is unique both in attributes and forms. The coiled, so-called water jug basket with a small or wide mouth, tapering spout, flat, round, or tapered bottom and a plaited center occasionally covered with buckskin has no precursors in pre-Numic assemblages. It differs radically from the normative coiling of pre-Numic Great Basin groups. Conversely, the nearly ubiquitous pre-Numic flat, circular coiled parching tray is rarely found in any Numic assemblages. So distinctive are the ethnographic Numic textile attributes that the products themselves can be clearly separated from those of earlier Great Basin groups.

The complete dissimilarity of Fremont and Shoshone basketry is treated at length by Adovasio, Andrews, and Fowler (1982). So different are these two industries that they cannot have been the products of the same cultural group. As pointed out by Bettinger and Baumhoff (1982), it has long been recognized that the basketry of the ethnographic Numic speakers (Kelly 1932, 1964; Steward 1934, 1941, 1943a; O.C. Stewart 1941, 1942; Smith 1974; Fowler and Matley 1979; Sapir 1910b) differs substantially from that made by members of the so-called Lovelock culture of the Humboldt and Carson Sink areas of the Western Great Basin (Grosscup 1960; Hester 1973; Heizer and Napton 1970a).

Basketry and other perishables of the Lovelock culture (the later stages of which are coeval in part with Fremont) are well-represented and analyzed (if differentially described) from a variety of sites including Lovelock Cave (Loud and Harrington 1929) and other closed site localities (for example, Heizer and Krieger 1956; Rozaire 1957, 1974; Hattori 1982).

Twining and coiling are present in the Lovelock perishable inventory, but the most diagnostic and common basketry type is Lovelock Wickerware, which first occurred between 2000 B.C. (Adovasio 1970, 1974) and about 1000–1 B.C. (Grosscup 1960, 1963). Indeed, so singular is this type in both its major (i.e., wall construction) and minor (i.e., finishing or selvage) attributes that it rivals the equally unique close coiling, half-rod and bundle-stacked foundation, noninterlocking stitch Fremont ware as the most distinctive prehistoric Great Basin basketry type.

The utter disappearance of Lovelock Wickerware, which is not known ethnographically among the Numic speakers or anyone else, signals (like the demise of Fremont basketry that, curiously, also becomes technologically extinct) one of those rare major "turnovers" in a regional basketry sequence attributable to population replacement rather than to intragroup stylistic or technological change. Some of the same simple and diagonal twining and bunched coiled basket wall foundation types found in the Lovelock culture also are known among Northern and Central Numic groups; however, minor attributes of construction, specifically method of starting, splicing techniques, and rim finishes, are totally different. Moreover, the highly distinctive and relatively common large, flat, circular coiled Lovelock parching tray also is absent from the inventory of the Numic groups (see Heizer and Krieger 1956). This also strongly suggests that whoever the makers of Lovelock Wickerware and associated Western Great Basin twining and coiling were, they were neither Northern Paiute nor any other Numic group, on typological and formal grounds alone. Other data could be cited (Adovasio with Andrews 1985), but it is apparent that textile data from the Great Basin support a major population change or shift about A.D. 1000. This shift correlates, not coincidentally, with the dispersal of the Numic speakers.

Prehistoric Ceramics

DAVID B. MADSEN

Three major cultural groups—Western Anasazi, Fremont, and Paiute-Shoshone—produced and used pottery within the Great Basin (fig. 1). Puebloan ceramics are discussed in *Southwest*, volume 9 of the *Handbook*; therefore only Western Anasazi pottery common in the Great Basin will be discussed here. Fremont and Paiute-Shoshone ceramics are more fully treated. While all three groups made fired clay figurines in addition to ceramic vessels (Fremont figurines are particularly elaborate), they are discussed in other chapters and will not be treated here.

Physical Characteristics of Pottery Types

Western Anasazi

A number of Western Anasazi pottery types and numerous tradewares from other areas are found in the Great Basin Pueblo area (Shutler 1961 lists 37 Pueblo pottery types from Lost City alone). The most common intrusive types are Lower Colorado River buffwares such as Pyramid Gray, a Yuman pottery type originating in the Lower Colorado River area. Many of the pottery types defined in the Western Anasazi area are decorative variants of a few major types. These include North Creek Gray, Moapa Gray, Shinarump Brown, and Logandale Gray. None of these named types is rigorously defined.

Western Anasazi ceramics are relatively uniform in construction and decorative techniques. Vessels were constructed by coiling, then scraped and smoothed. Vessel surfaces range from poorly smoothed to highly polished. In some cases a white slip was applied to vessels prior to application of painted designs. Decoration consists primarily of interior painted Sosi-Dogoszhi–style designs (an Anasazi motif) (Colton 1952) on bowls, exterior corrugation on jars, and exterior fugitive red staining on both forms. Vessels forms are primarily jars, bowls, and pitchers. Dippers, mugs, and colanders are rare.

North Creek Gray (Spencer 1934; Colton 1952) and its decorated variants constitute the major portion of most Western Anasazi ceramic collections ("Prehistory of the Southeastern Area," fig. 9, this vol.). Wong (1983) has suggested that North Creek Gray is essentially a locally made pottery intended to imitate Tusayan ce-

ramic types manufactured in Kayenta Anasazi areas. It is light to dark gray and was fired in a reducing atmosphere. Surface finishes range from well-smoothed to slightly polished. Temper is primarily fine quartz sand. Decorations include exterior red stain, exterior corrugation (usually indented), and Sosi-Dogoszhi painted designs.

Shinarump Brown (Spencer 1934; Colton 1952) is a dark gray to brown pottery fired in a poorly controlled oxidizing atmosphere. Surfaces are smoothed but not polished. Temper is primarily opaque angular fragments, with some quartz sand. Decoration is restricted to plain and indented exterior corrugation. A slipped and painted variant of Shinarump Brown (Virgin Black-on-white) has been defined (Spencer 1934; Colton 1952) but may well be a slipped version of North Creek Black-on-gray (Aikens 1965).

Moapa Gray and Logandale Gray are the only Pueblo pottery types whose primary distribution is within the Great Basin. These types are concentrated along the Moapa River and are distributed across southern Nevada and into extreme eastern California.

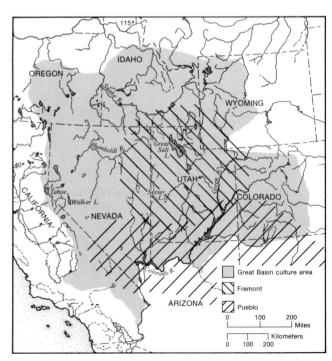

Fig. 1. Limits of Fremont and Pueblo pottery in the Great Basin.

Two varieties of plain Moapa Gray pottery (Boulder Gray and Moapa Brown) have been defined (Colton and Hargrave 1937; Colton 1952). However, the distinction appears to be only the result of poorly controlled firing atmospheres. Surfaces are light gray to brown with rough to smooth finishes. The tempering material is primarily quartz sand, with the addition of olivine (D.L. Weide 1978). Decoration includes exterior red staining, plain and indented corrugation, and Sosi-Dogoszhi painted designs.

Logandale Gray (Colton 1952) is gray to reddish-brown and was fired in an uncontrolled atmosphere. Surface finishes range from rough to smoothed. Crushed limestone temper makes it technically the poorest of Virgin branch Anasazi ceramic types. There are no decorated variants of this type.

Fremont

Within the Fremont area, regions of ceramic variation correspond roughly to Ambler's (1966) and Marwitt's (1970) definitions of five Fremont cultural variants. In fact, to a large extent the definition of these variants is based on differences in pottery (fig. 2). All five areas share general morphological and technological characteristics such as construction with a coiling and scraping technique (with the exception of Promontory pottery in northwestern Utah); smudging (which is generally better controlled in southern Fremont areas); smooth, slightly polished surface finishes (with the exceptions of Promontory and Uinta Gray pottery), and firing temperatures consistently near 800° C (again with the exceptions of Promontory and Uinta Gray). Beyond these general characteristics, marked variations occur.

The Parowan Fremont subarea is characterized by three ceramic types in the Snake Valley series (Rudy 1953; R.E. Madsen 1977). These include Snake Valley Gray, Black-on-gray, and Corrugated (fig. 3a,e,g). An untempered type, Paragonah Coiled (Meighan et al. 1956; Madsen 1970), is occasionally recovered. The pottery is tempered with quartz and feldspar particles of a relatively uniform size (R.E. Madsen 1977). Surface finishes are smooth and often highly polished. Vessel forms are generally restricted to bowls and globular, wide-mouthed jars with recurving rims; but vertically rimmed jars with loop handles, bulging rimmed jars, narrow-necked pitchers, composite bowls, and small "paint pots" are occasionally found. Designs consist primarily of interior Sosi-Dogoszhi and Black Mesa–style painting on bowls, exterior fugitive red washes on bowls and some jars, and exterior corrugation on both jars and bowls (the only "true" corrugation in the Fremont area). Tooled impressions and incising, along with some modeling and "coffee bean" appliqué are occasionally utilized on exterior surfaces of jars.

San Rafael Fremont is an east-central variant characterized by Emery Gray (Wormington 1955; Lister, Ambler, and Lister 1960; Gunnerson 1969; Madsen 1970), and Ivie Creek Black-on-white (Lister, Ambler, and Lister 1960; R.E. Madsen 1977). Emery Gray is a rarely decorated utility ware (fig. 3c). It is tempered with crushed gray basalt and quartz, a mineral frequently found in solid forms of basalt in the area (R.E. Madsen 1977). The pottery is smoothed, sometimes rather poorly, but rarely polished. Decoration is limited to fugitive red stain, appliqué, modeling, and some tooled impressions. There is some evidence of fugitive red painted designs (Madsen 1975a). Vessel shapes include globular, straight-rimmed, wide-mouthed jars, pitchers, and, more rarely, bowls.

Ivie Creek Black-on-white (Marwitt 1968; R.E. Madsen 1977) is common in the southwestern San Rafael and the southeastern Sevier areas (fig. 3b). The type is tempered with both light and dark gray crushed basalt and quartz and is both slipped and unslipped. Both varieties are often highly polished. The type is poorly defined, and it is probable that the unslipped varieties represent Sevier and Emery Gray vessels with painted designs and should properly be defined as Sevier and Emery Black-on-gray (for example, Madsen and Lindsay 1977). Vessel forms are predominantly bowls, with only a very few jars. Painted designs are restricted to bowl interiors (and rarely jar exteriors) and consist primarily of Chapin, Mancos, Sosi, Dogoszhi, and Black Mesa–style elements (Lister, Ambler, and Lister 1960; R.E. Madsen 1977). Fugitive red staining is often found on bowl exteriors.

Sevier Gray pottery (Steward 1936; Rudy 1953; R.E. Madsen 1977) is associated with the Sevier Fremont of central Utah (fig. 3h). It is a smooth, slightly polished, rarely decorated utility ware and is tempered with crushed dark basalt generally of a coarser and darker grade than is used in Emery Gray. Small percentages of quartz and mica are also occasionally present. Vessel shapes are primarily globular, wide-mouthed jars with straight to slightly outcurved rims; pitchers; "water bottles;" and rarely bowls. Loop handles frequently occur on all vessel shapes except bowls. Decorations are limited to incising, impressions, appliqué, modeling, and false corrugation. An exterior fugitive red wash is sometimes used, and occasionally broad lines of fugitive red wash are found. Steward (1936) and Madsen and Lindsay (1977) define a variety with mineral painted designs as Sevier Black-on-gray.

Uinta Gray (Wormington 1955; Lister, Ambler, and Lister 1960; Gunnerson 1969; Madsen 1970) is characteristic of the Uinta Fremont variant of northeastern Utah (fig. 3f). It is a plain gray utility pottery tempered with crushed calcite. Surfaces are poorly smoothed and often rough. Decorations are rare, primarily limited to appliqué. Major vessel forms include bowls; globular jars with vertical rims or wide mouths with opposing loop handles; and wide-bodied, narrow based, vertically rimmed narrow-necked jars or pitchers with a single loop handle.

The Salt Lake variant of Fremont is characterized by the presence of Great Salt Lake Gray (Steward 1936; Rudy 1953; R.E. Madsen 1977) and Promontory Gray (Steward 1937a; Rudy 1953; R.E. Madsen 1977). Other types (Malouf 1950; Madsen 1979a) have been described for the area but are apparently only variations of Great Salt Lake Gray. Plew (1979) has described a "Southern Idaho Plain" ware that may be Great Salt Lake Gray. A Great Salt Lake Black-on-gray was defined by Steward (1936) and Aikens (1966), but these sherds have been re-examined and are either Snake Valley Black-on-gray or Ivie Creek Black-on-white (R.E. Madsen 1977). Tempering materials include fine to coarse angular particles of quartz, mica, and occasionally rounded grains of sand. These inclusions are usually found mixed, but single sherds often appear to be tempered by only one of these minerals. Vessel walls range from thin and uniform to thick and undulating. Globular, wide-mouthed jars with outcurved rims are the dominant vessel form. Bowls and "seed jars" occur rarely. Decoration is rare but includes appliqué, impression, incising, modeling, fugitive red wash, and painted fugitive red designs.

Promontory Gray is predominantly tempered with large, angular particles of crushed calcite and constructed with a paddle-and-anvil technique (R.E. Madsen 1977; Madsen 1979a). The single extant vessel is a wide-mouthed jar with a thickened base and only a very slight constriction at the neck (fig. 3i). In form it resembles a cross between Southern Paiute and Northern Plains vessels and the more common Fremont jars. All rim sherds appear to be from jars of this type, and this may be the only vessel form. Exterior fingernail impressions are the primary decorative technique, along with limited use of appliqué and pinching. In construction technique, tempering inclusions, and vessel shape, Promontory pottery is distinct from other Fremont ceramics (there are some similarities with later Great Salt Lake materials) and may not be Fremont at all. Few investigators agree on the origins or affinities of Promontory Gray ware, but these traits, combined with the low percentages of this type at Salt Lake Fremont sites, suggest either an origin outside the Fremont cultural area or local production by non-Fremont groups.

While most Fremont ceramics can be readily distinguished from Paiute-Shoshone pottery, there is a small percentage that cannot be easily classified with either ware. In areas around the Great Salt Lake and northward into Idaho, limited definitive work on Paiute-Shoshone pottery has created problems in determining its distribution. In southern Idaho, for instance, pottery previously identified as Paiute-Shoshone has been reclassified as Great Salt Lake Gray (Butler 1979), while

Vessel Type	FREMONT POTTERY TYPES Vessel Form				
	Snake Valley Gray	Snake Valley Black-on-Gray	Snake Valley Corrugated	Paragonah Coiled	Sevier Gray
BOWLS					
OPEN MOUTH JARS					
JARS WITH HANDLES					
PITCHERS					
MUGS AND CUPS					

after Madsen 1977: figs. 4,7,11,22,25,28,31.

208   Fig. 2. Fremont and Paiute-Shoshone pottery vessel types and forms.

in the Great Salt Lake area some Great Salt Lake Gray is now considered to be Paiute-Shoshone (Dean 1983). Important questions involving relationships between Fremont and Paiute-Shoshone cannot be resolved unless these technical questions are investigated.

Paiute-Shoshone

Paiute-Shoshone pottery can, for the most part, be readily distinguished from most other Great Basin ceramic types on the basis of gross morphological and technological differences (Rudy 1953; Tuohy 1956, 1963; Coale 1963; Fowler 1968; Beck 1981; DeSart 1971). However, these types are the most poorly defined of all Great Basin ceramics, and in specific areas problems of identification remain unresolved. Unlike most Anasazi or Fremont pottery types, Paiute-Shoshone is highly variable in terms of manufacturing technique, presence or absence of tempering materials, type of tempering material, decorative technique and vessel shape (Beck 1981; DeSart 1971); and many of these identification problems may be the result of this broad range of variation. The use of the term Paiute-Shoshone implies that ceramic types found in archeological settings were in fact produced by ethnographically definable populations, and it should be made clear that in many cases this is an assumption. However, the pottery types are virtually identical with those known to have been produced eth-nographically, and it seems much better to assume that such pottery types are indeed Paiute-Shoshone rather than that they originate with some other, as yet undefined, prehistoric population.

Compared to both Anasazi and Fremont wares, Paiute-Shoshone pottery is relatively thick-walled and contains variably coarse inclusions. Basal portions of vessels were molded or impressed on a basket (Tuohy 1963; Tuohy and Palombi 1972). Coils were then added to complete the upper portion. After construction, the vessel was smoothed either by scraping or by using a paddle and anvil (Beck 1981). Owens Valley Brown was constructed with only the coiling and scraping technique (H.S. Riddell 1951; Riddell and Riddell 1956; Beck 1981). Surface treatment ranges from rough, poorly scraped to a well-smoothed finished. The exterior surface is often textured as a decoration. This is generally limited to fingernail punctation, although interior and exterior striations (possibly derived from scraping and smoothing) are common to Owens Valley Brown (H.S. Riddell 1951), Coale (1963), and Beck (1981) report some incised designs, and Larson (1981) reports the rare occurrence of corrugated varieties in areas of overlap with the Western Anasazi. Fingernail impressions sometimes cover the entire exterior of the vessel but are usually restricted to a few closely spaced bands around the rim. Crabtree (cited in Larson 1981) has described rare Paiute sherds with painted Anasazi designs.

FREMONT POTTERY TYPES					PAIUTE-SHOSHONE Vessel Form
Great Salt Lake Gray	Promontory Gray	Uinta Gray	Emery Gray	Ivie Creek Black-on-White	

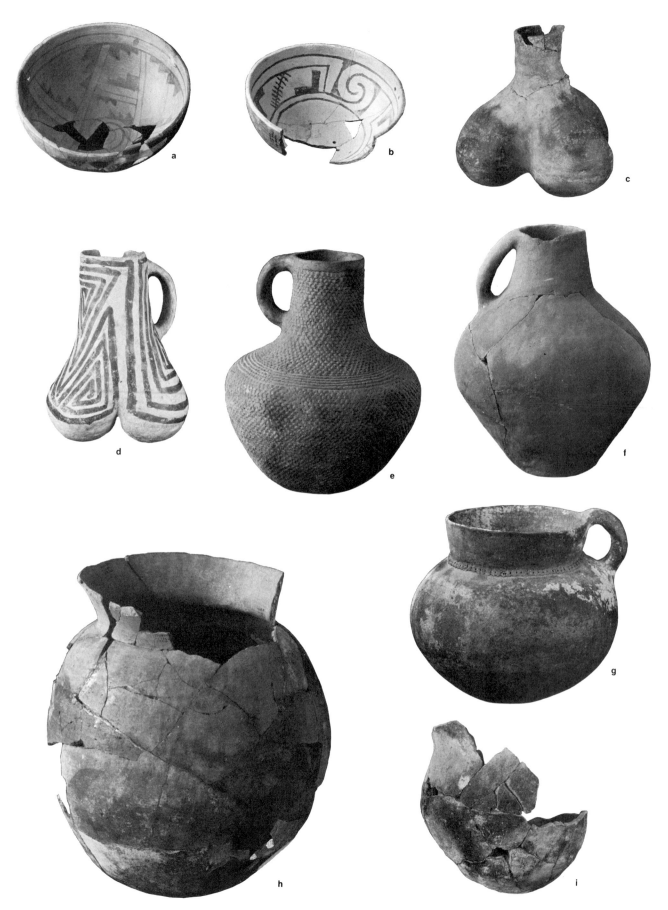

Tempering inclusions are, on the average, much more coarse than in other pottery types common to the Great Basin. Temper sizes range from very fine (0.1mm) to very coarse (2.0–10.0mm) but are predominantly coarse (0.5–1.0mm) (Coale 1963; Beck 1981; DeSart 1971). Firing temperatures and atmosphere are poorly controlled or even uncontrolled, producing multicolored vessels ranging from reddish-brown to brown to black. Areal variation of Paiute-Shoshone pottery is restricted primarily to vessel shapes. Three variants have been described: Shoshone pottery (Steward 1941, 1943a), Southern Paiute pottery (Baldwin 1950), and Owens Valley Brown ware (H.S. Riddell 1951). The predominant Shoshonean vessel form is a large wide-mouthed, flat-bottomed jar resembling a flowerpot in form. These vessels are usually straight-walled with no neck or shoulder. Jars with thick pointed bases and bowl forms occur rarely (Tuohy 1956; Rudy 1953). In the Southern Paiute area, wide-mouthed, conical jars with thick, pointed bases are the most common form. These vessels are straight-walled but often curve in slightly at the lip. Similar Promontory Gray vessels may also be a product of Paiute-Shoshone groups. Both pointed and flat base forms have been reported for the west-central Great Basin (Owens Valley Brown), as has a globular small-mouthed jar with re-curved rims (Riddell and Riddell

1956). With the exception of the Owens Valley area, bowl forms are rare throughout the Great Basin. Perforated Paiute-Shoshone jars resembling colanders have been reported from Grass Valley in central Nevada (Magee 1967), but these are more probably merely drilled repair holes.

Chronology and Distribution of Pottery Types

Great Basin ceramic distributions are often used to determine spatial and temporal distributions of cultural groups. This is made possible by the large number of variables involved in the selection of raw materials, construction, shaping, and decoration of pottery vessels. Most ceramic types can be readily distinguished from one another by one or more of these variables, making it easier (once the types have been defined within a cultural context) to distinguish specific cultural groups.

Western Anasazi

The earliest Western Anasazi pottery to be found in the Great Basin is Boulder Gray and Black-on-gray and Logandale Gray; all are representative of Basketmaker III occupations (Colton 1952, 1955). During the A.D.

U. of Utah, Utah Mus. of Nat. Hist., Salt Lake City: 2, FS 1236.5; b, FS 206.3; c, FS 42.1; d, 8639; e, 1714; f, FS 277; g, 13923; h, FS 189.3; i, FS 241.5.

Fig. 3. Characteristic pottery types of the Fremont culture area. a, Snake Valley Black-on-gray bowl, common in both the Summit and Paragonah phases of the Parowan variant, and dated A.D. 900–1200. Bowls are painted with mineral pigments. Designs usually involve 2 encircling lines around the tops and bottoms of bowls, with solid elements in the form of triangles, steps, and checkerboards. Design elements appear to be direct borrowings of Pueblo II types common in the Virgin and Kayenta areas of Arizona. Exteriors of vessels are often coated with a fugitive red wash. b, Ivie Creek Black-on-white bowl, San Rafael variant, dated A.D. 700–1200. Fired in nonoxidizing atmospheres, surface colors range from light to medium gray, with occasional brownish-orange specimens. Exterior fugitive red wash is common. Paint is organic pigments. Painted elements are found in various combinations, frequently occurring as repeated panels enclosed within one or 2 encircling lines around the tops and bottoms of bowls. Common elements are solid curvilinear motifs, open or interlocked scrolls, parallel lines, lines of dots, dots in squares, dots in outlined panels, squares, triangles, circles, steps, checkerboards, hatching, ticked lines, and comblike projections from linear and solid elements. Design elements are reminiscent of Pueblo I and II motifs from the Kayenta and Mesa Verde Anasazi areas to the south and east. It is the only slipped pottery in the Fremont area. c, Trilobed Emery Gray jar, San Rafael variant, dated about A.D. 900. Painting is limited to fugitive red wash designs, principally chevrons, and decoration consists of appliquéd, punched, incised, or modeled surfaces. This jar is the only example of this vessel form recovered in the Fremont area, although it is relatively common in Anasazi assemblages. d, Mancos Black-on-white trilobed jar with intact handle, Mesa Verde Anasazi, collected in Westwater Canyon, southeastern Utah. The obvious borrowing of the distinctive trilobed vessel form by Fremont potters in the creation of a vessel with typical Fremont temper and surface treatment (c) illustrates the close ties between the Fremont and Anasazi culture areas. e, Snake Valley Corrugated jar, Paragonah phase of the Parowan variant, dated A.D. 1100–1200. Surface colors range from medium to light gray, with vessels fired in a reducing atmosphere. Decoration consists solely of an elaborately corrugated surface, with horizontal and diagonal patterns of indentations and horizontal and diagonal series of grooves. A fugitive red wash occasionally covers the exteriors of these vessels. f, Uinta Gray jar, found in the Cub Creek and White Rocks phase of the Uinta variant, dated A.D. 650–950. Surface colors are largely medium to dark gray, although light brown and buff are also known. Decoration consists of incised, appliquéd, punched, or modeled surfaces. g, Snake Valley Gray jar, Summit and Paragonah phases of the Parowan variant, dated A.D. 900–1200, appliquéd with a single row of "coffee beans" encircling the neck. Surface colors are predominantly light to medium gray as a result of firing in reducing atmospheres. Seldom painted, decoration may consist of incised, punched, appliquéd, and modeled surfaces. A fugitive red wash is common on exterior surfaces. h, Sevier Gray jar, Sevier variant, of the type manufactured A.D. 800 to 1250. Fired in a reducing atmosphere, surface color is predominantly dark gray but ranges from light to dark gray and occasionally may be brown. Vessels are not slipped, but a fugitive red wash may be present on exterior surfaces. Decoration consists entirely of incised, punched, appliquéd, and modeled surfaces. i, Promontory Gray jar, Bear River and Levee phases of the Great Salt Lake variant, dated A.D. 1000–1300. Surface colors range from medium to dark gray, although brown is not uncommon. Vessels are not slipped. A fugitive red wash is sometimes applied to exterior surfaces. Decoration is confined to incised, appliquéd, and punched exterior surfaces. Unlike other Fremont pottery types, which are a product of coiling techniques, Promontory Gray is manufactured by paddle-and-anvil. This vessel is the most complete specimen recovered from the Great Salt Lake variant. a, 19.0 cm in diameter at the rim; rest same scale.

500–700 period, these types were restricted to the Virgin and Moapa Valley areas of southeastern Nevada (Shutler 1961). By about A.D. 1100–1200, the distribution of Western Anasazi ceramics covers most of the southern Great Basin. Ceramic types occurring during this period were primarily North Creek Gray and Shinarump Brown types along the northern edge of the Western Anasazi area on the Utah-Nevada border (Fowler, Madsen, and Hattori 1973), and Moapa Gray types along the western portion on the Nevada-California border. Temper for Moapa Gray appears to have been derived from a single source, probably the Mount Trumbull area of northern Arizona (D.L. Weide 1978), suggesting a relatively complex intercommunity ceramics industry. These various Western Anasazi ceramic types are found in hunting-gathering sites around the periphery of the main Puebloan occupation area, but they occur in quantities large enough to suggest occupation rather than trade. The pottery types described here occur as far north as southern Idaho (Butler 1979), but when found outside the limits described in figure 1, they probably have been traded.

Fremont

The regional distinctiveness of the Fremont culture is readily apparent in the distribution of pottery types. Pottery "core areas" (fig. 4) have been defined on the basis of varying percentages of ceramic types at sites within these regions. At sites within each core area, a single plain gray pottery type constitutes 50 percent or more of all plain gray pottery and reaches 90–100 percent at many sites. Outside these core areas no one type is dominant. The resulting "blending" effect may be the result of diffusion from the centers of regional development.

The distribution of Snake Valley pottery centers in the Parowan Valley of southwestern Utah. Snake Valley ceramics were evidently highly valued as trade items, since they have been recovered in limited quantities throughout much of the Fremont area (Aikens 1967a; Shields 1967; Marwitt 1968; Shields and Dalley 1978) and south to areas of Pueblo occupation (Shutler 1961). Technological analysis suggests that Snake Valley sherds from these peripheral areas were originally manufactured in the Parowan Valley and traded outward (R.E. Madsen 1977). Indigenous use extended from the Parowan Valley northwest to the central Utah-Nevada border (Rudy 1953; Taylor 1954), and southwest to Meadow Valley Wash in southern Nevada (Fowler, Madsen, and Hattori 1973). Snake Valley pottery is found rarely in small amounts west of this area (Fowler, Madsen, and Hattori 1973). Berry (1972) suggests a temporal range of A.D. 900–1250 for these pottery types.

The distribution of Sevier Gray centers in central and west-central Utah but extends to all other Fremont sub-

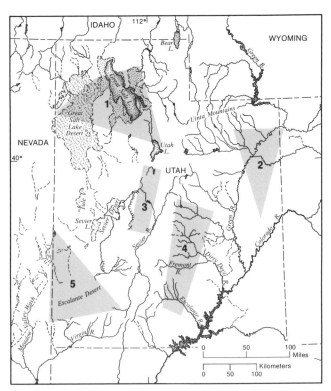

Fig. 4. Fremont gray ware core areas: 1, Great Salt Lake Gray; 2, Uinta Gray; 3, Sevier Gray; 4, Emery Gray; 5, Snake Valley Gray.

areas (Madsen 1970). It is found in small amounts as far west as the central Great Basin (Thomas 1983), and isolated sherds of a painted variety are found as far north as southern Idaho (Butler 1979). Acceptable radiocarbon dates associated with these pottery types range from A.D. 780 (Sharrock and Marwitt 1967) to 1260 (Marwitt 1968).

Great Salt Lake pottery distributions center around the Great Salt Lake extending west to the Utah-Nevada border, south to central Utah west of the Wasatch Front, and north to southern Idaho (R.E. Madsen 1977; Butler 1983). The temporal range of Great Salt Lake pottery is the most extensive of all Fremont ceramics: about A.D. 500 to 1300 (Marwitt 1970). Promontory Gray is restricted to the area defined for the Salt Lake Fremont (Madsen 1970). Its temporal range is poorly known.

With the exception of the Turner-Look site in east-central Utah (Wormington 1955), the distribution of Uinta Gray is restricted to the Uinta Basin. Uinta Gray constitutes 90–100 percent of all pottery from Fremont sites in this area. It is present in both the San Rafael and Salt Lake subareas. A temporal range of A.D. 650–950 (possibly 500–1200) is associated with this pottery type (Marwitt 1970).

Emery Gray and Ivie Creek Black-on-white are found primarily in east-central Utah. Emery Gray is occasionally found in limited quantities in the Uinta Basin (Ambler 1966; Shields 1967) and has been found on the surface within tepee-ring sites as far north as southwestern Wyoming (Sharrock 1966). The distribution of Ivie Creek Black-on-white centers along the boundary of the San Rafael and Sevier Fremont subareas in central Utah; it extends into northern Utah (Aikens 1967a; Shields and Dalley 1978) and south into areas of Anasazi occupation (Fowler 1963; Lister, Ambler, and Lister 1960). Dating in the San Rafael subarea is limited, but a range of A.D. 700 (Madsen 1975a) to about 1200 (Marwitt 1970) is associated with Emery Gray.

A source in the Puebloan area of southern Utah and a south to north diffusion pattern have been postulated for Fremont pottery (Ambler 1966; Lister 1959; Gunnerson 1969; Wormington 1955), but a review of radiocarbon dates associated with Fremont sites (Marwitt and Fry 1973) indicates otherwise. Fremont pottery is found in northern Utah by about A.D. 500 (Shields and Dalley 1978), in the Uinta Basin by 600 (Shields 1967) or possibly by 500 (Ambler 1966), and in central Utah by 900 at the earliest (Marwitt 1970). A north-to-south trend is clear and may suggest non-Pueblo origins.

Without question, Puebloan influence on Fremont pottery was great, especially in the southern areas during the later stages of Fremont development (fig. 3c-d). However, these shared ceramic traits do not necessarily imply Puebloan origins. Early Fremont pottery in northern Utah predates the earliest forms of Basketmaker III pottery, and the large intervening area between the two ceramic complexes argues against their being in early contact. The origin of Fremont pottery remains unresolved, but it is possible that both Fremont and Puebloan pottery originated from the same source, possibly from the Mogollon culture that reached the Four Corners area prior to A.D. 500 as suggested by Jennings (1966, 1978).

Paiute-Shoshone

Paiute-Shoshone pottery generally follows known ethnographic distributions. Southern Paiute pottery is found throughout southern Nevada, southeastern Utah, and extreme southeastern central California but does not extend into the Colorado Plateau area once occupied by the Southern Paiute (Euler 1964). Owens Valley Brown has a limited distribution centering around the Owens Valley in east-central California, and extending into Death Valley and east into Grass Valley in central Nevada. Shoshonean pottery is found throughout most of the rest of the Great Basin, primarily north and east of these other areas.

Paiute-Shoshone pottery has been dated at several central and eastern Great Basin sites. At Lost City in southern Nevada, Southern Paiute ceramics date (by correlation with Anasazi pottery) to A.D. 700–1000 (Shutler 1961). At Stuart Rockshelter Southern Paiute pottery was deposited in association with Anasazi ce-

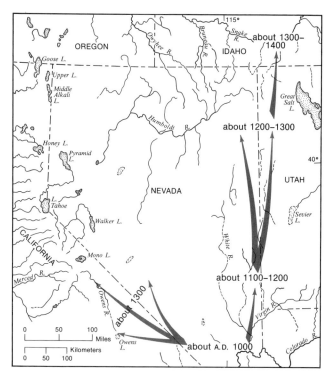

Fig. 5. Spatial-temporal distribution of Paiute-Shoshone pottery in the Great Basin.

ramics prior to 1150 (Shutler, Shutler, and Griffith 1960). Southern Paiute ceramics were recovered in a mixed Fremont, Anasazi, and Southern Paiute context at O'Malley Shelter (Fowler, Madsen, and Hattori 1973). Deposition occurred after about 1100 but before the disappearance of the Fremont about 1250. Fremont, Anasazi, and Southern Paiute pottery were also found mixed at Pine Park Shelter (Rudy 1954), Civa II (Busby and Seck 1977), and Slivovitz and Avacado shelters (Busby 1979). Fremont and Shoshonean ceramics were found in association on the surface of numerous sites along the central Utah-Nevada border (Malouf 1950;

Eastern Calif. Mus., Independence: 81.64.
Fig. 6. Panamint Shoshone pottery vessel, found in a cave at the northern end of Death Valley, Inyo Co., Calif.; height 21.5 cm; collected about 1975.

Rudy 1953; Taylor 1954; Fowler, Madsen, and Hattori 1973). At Gatecliff Shelter and high elevation sites on Mount Jefferson in the central Great Basin, Paiute-Shoshone pottery and other diagnostics appear about 1000 (Thomas 1982, 1983). In northern Utah, Aikens (1970) found mixed Fremont-Shoshonean pottery underlying a pure Shoshonean deposit at Hogup Cave. The Shoshonean deposit dates about 1500, but the Fremont-Shoshone association suggests the appearance of Shoshonean pottery prior to 1300.

Paiute-Shoshone ceramics have been inferentially dated in other Great Basin areas. Hunt (1960) and Wallace (1962) suggest a basal date of about 1000 for Paiute-Shoshone pottery in the Death Valley–Amargosa Valley area. An initial date of around 1300 has been suggested for Owens Valley Brown (Riddell and Riddell 1956; Lanning 1963). In the northern Great Basin, Swanson, Powers, and Bryan (1964) feel that Shoshonean pottery occurs in southwestern Idaho no earlier than 1700, while evidence at Wilson Butte Cave (Gruhn 1961) seems to indicate an initial date of 1300–1400 for the Shoshonean occupation of southern Idaho.

Based on these data Madsen (1975) has defined a tentative temporal-spatial sequence of the distribution of Paiute-Shoshone pottery throughout the Great Basin (fig. 5). The earliest appearance of this ware is about 1000 in southern Nevada and east-central California. In east-central Nevada and southern Utah, Paiute-Shoshone pottery appears in association with Fremont diagnostic traits at about 1100–1200. Shoshonean pottery reaches northern Utah and west-central Nevada by 1300, and southern Idaho by 1300–1400.

If the presence of Paiute-Shoshone pottery in these areas is the result of occupation by Numic-speaking peoples, it indicates that in less than 500 years, in the face of competition with groups already occupying the eastern and southern Great Basin, Numic groups expanded from southern Nevada to southern Idaho.

Rock Art

POLLY SCHAAFSMA

Rock art is an abundant archeological resource in the Great Basin. Hundreds of sites in the Great Basin physiographic province from eastern California across Nevada to central Utah have been documented where designs have been inscribed or painted on rock surfaces. Likewise, rock art sites are plentiful in the Colorado Plateau physiographic province in eastern Utah where sandstone cliffs, boulders, and rockshelters provide ideal situations for the rendering of designs. Rock art has been made by the occupants of these arid regions for the last several thousand years.

Rock art includes petroglyphs—designs pecked, scratched, abraded, or otherwise cut into surfaces of cliffs, boulders, bedrock, or any natural rock surface— and rock paintings—designs painted in similar situations. The term pictograph is also commonly used to denote painted designs or figures drawn on rocks with dry pigment.

As an important although often enigmatic archeological resource, rock art may illuminate culture history, as style and content reflect continuity as well as changes through time or between regions. The complex graphic imagery present in rock art is a manifestation of the ideational dimension of prehistoric cultural groups, ideologies that are often absent or expressed in restricted form in other parts of the archeological record. Although the meaning of what is expressed may often be inaccessible to the student of the past, archeologists have devised a number of methods for approaching an understanding of the art of preliterate societies and its numerous functions in economic, social, political, and ritual contexts (Schaafsma 1983). Meaning and symbolic concepts may be communicated through rock art images, but rock art was not intended and cannot be read as precise representations of speech; it is not writing.

Rock art sites were frequently noted in the accounts of early explorers in the Great Basin province (Bruff 1873; Loew 1876; J.H. Simpson 1876; Angel 1881; Fowler and Fowler 1970; A.S. Taylor 1860, 1861) and on the Colorado Plateau (Putnam 1876; Dellenbaugh 1877). Mallery's (1886, 1893) studies on the graphic expression of the American Indians include descriptions of a number of rock art sites in this culture area.

Steward (1929), who systematically surveyed the rock art of the West, defining its content and distribution, was the first to do a major study in the Great Basin. Heizer and Baumhoff (1959, 1962) described Great Basin rock art styles and, on the basis of site locations, developed a hypothesis to explain the function of Great Basin petroglyphs. Heizer and Clewlow (1973), Heizer and Nissen (1977), and Wellmann (1979a:54–62) synthesized other data for California and the Great Basin. The studies of Payen (1966) in the northern Sierra Nevada, Werlhof (1965) in the Owens Valley, Grant, Baird, and Pringle (1968) and Whitley (1982) in the Coso Range, Nissen (1982) in the western Great Basin, Heizer and Hester (1978) in southern Nevada, and Mary Rusco (1973) on anthropomorphic figure types in Nevada augment the basic research of Hejizer and Baumhoff.

Rock art of the northern Colorado Plateau in eastern Utah was discussed by Steward (1929), F. Beckwith (1931, 1934), Reagan (1931a, 1931b, 1931c, 1931d, 1932, 1933, 1935a), and Sleight (1946). It has been recorded and described in conjunction with the study of other archeological materials (Morss 1931; Hunt 1953; Gunnerson 1957, 1969; Taylor 1957; Jennings 1978; Wormington 1955). Schaafsma (1971) did an areal synthesis of Utah rock art sites and assigned stylistic designations on the basis of a study of rock art photographs in the Donald Scott File collection of the Peabody Museum, Cambridge, Massachusetts. Later surveys have added substantially to the knowledge of Utah rock art sites (Schaafsma 1970; Castleton 1978–1979; Hurst and Louthan 1979). A detailed synthesis of the Fremont area of Utah is by Wellmann (1979a:103–111).

Styles in the Great Basin Physiographic Province

Since around 9000 B.C. the Great Basin has been occupied by Western Archaic and Pre-Archaic populations participating in a hunter-gatherer economy. These groups are believed to be responsible for most of the rock art of the area within later prehistoric times (fig. 1); pit-and-groove and faceted boulders appear to have the most ancient origins. After about A.D. 1 the Basketmaker people and later Fremont and Anasazi horticulturalists also contributed to the stylistic inventory of Great Basin rock art sites.

215

Stillwater Faceted and Pit-and-Groove Styles

Neither the Stillwater Faceted nor Pit-and-groove style involves actual imagery or designs. Instead they represent specific types of manipulation of the rock surface. The Stillwater Faceted style is named after a phenomenon observed on 120 boulders at Carson Sink in western Nevada (Nissen 1975, 1982). The style, originally noted by Heizer and Baumhoff (1962:20) at the Grimes Point site (NV-Ch-3), consists of facets ground into the sides of boulders or across boulder angles. Although the distribution of the style appears to be very limited, it is likely to be more widespread than current documentation indicates. Because faceting is an inconspicuous feature only recently described, it may often have been unnoticed. Early Archaic dates are suggested for this style.

The Pit-and-groove style is distributed widely through many parts of the western United States and is well represented at several west-central Nevada sites (Heizer and Baumhoff 1962:209, pls. 1,3). Boulders with this type of modification may be covered with random depressions or pits, usually an inch or two in diameter but sometimes as large as 12 inches across (fig. 2). When grooves also occur, they may connect or encircle pits.

Churchill Co. Mus., Fallon, Nev.
Fig. 2. Pitted boulder from the Grimes site, Churchill Co., Nev.

Dates from 5500 B.C. to as late as 500 B.C. are suggested for this style.

Great Basin Abstract Petroglyph Styles

Great Basin rock art styles have traditionally been named, first, on the basis of the techniques employed in making them and, second, on the basis of element inventories. An analysis of the petroglyphs at the Lagomarsino site in western Nevada led Baumhoff, Heizer, and Elsasser (1958) to distinguish between the Curvilinear and Rectilinear styles within the Great Basin Pecked Abstract tradition (reprinted as Appendix D in Heizer and Baumhoff 1962:288–312). This tradition of abstract rock art dominates and characterizes the Great Basin from the Sierra Nevada on the west to the Wasatch Range in central Utah on the east. It also occurs sporadically in adjacent areas including the Southwest and the Plateau culture areas.

The Curvilinear style (fig. 3) is typified by the presence of circles, concentric circles, circle chains, sun disks, the curvilinear meander, wavy lines or snakes, and star figures (Heizer and Baumhoff 1962:200, table 3). "The circle, in one context or another, is the common element of this style but perhaps a more characteristic element is the curvilinear meander. These meanders have a vague sort of composition in that they tend to fill an area defined by the outline of a single boulder" (Baumhoff, Heizer, and Elsasser 1958:13).

The Rectilinear style is characterized by dots, rectangular grids, bird tracks, rakes, and crosshatching (figs. 4–5). According to Heizer and Baumhoff rectilinear elements are more limited in distribution than are curvilinear ones, occurring primarily in the western margins of the Basin; however, rectilinear style elements are prevalent in some eastern Nevada and western Utah sites (Schaafsma 1971).

However, curvilinear and rectilinear motifs often occur together and thus do not constitute distinct stylistic categories even at the Lagomarsino type site (Hedges

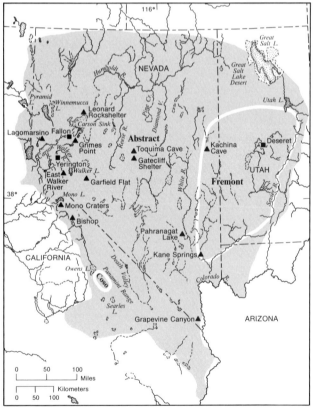

Fig. 1. Distribution of rock art styles. Abstract styles include both petroglyphs and paintings. Fremont and Coso Representational styles overlap the Abstract styles. Scratched and Pit-and-Groove styles occur throughout the Great Basin and are not mapped here.

Harvard U., Peabody Mus., Donald Scott Coll.

Fig. 3. Great Basin Curvilinear Style petroglyphs, Carson River, Lyon Co., Nev. Figures have been chalked, and to some extent chalking may reflect the judgment of the photographer. Other petroglyphs in this chapter have also been highlighted in chalk. Photographed 1927–1937.

Fig. 4. Great Basin Rectilinear Style petroglyphs, Lagomarsino site, Story Co., Nev. Photograph by Ken Hedges, 1983.

1982:207–209). Regional variations are also present within these broad categories, which, in fact, appear to underlie a variety of more specific styles (Hedges 1982). Such regional varieties of the Great Basin Abstract tradition have been described by Crotty (1979, 1981) for Tule Lake and Rector (1981) for the eastern Mojave region.

Great Basin Painted Style

Graphically related to the Abstract style petroglyphs are circles and parallel lines painted in mineral paints (McKee and Thomas 1973) found throughout central Nevada (Heizer and Baumhoff 1962:fig. 31,b). While Heizer and Baumhoff set these paintings aside as a separate style, other researchers have argued that stylistic distinctions should not be made on the basis of technique alone and suggest that these paintings are simply another expression of Great Basin Abstract art (McKee and Thomas 1973:112; Thomas and Thomas 1972).

Great Basin Scratched Style

Petroglyphs in the Great Basin Scratched style were made by a sharp rock that inscribed lines in a single stroke. Subject matter consists of straight lines, sun figures, and crosshatching. The style is distinguished by its limited subject matter as well as by technique. It usually appears to be of more recent manufacture than pecked glyphs (Heizer and Baumhoff 1962:208), and Bettinger and Baumhoff (1982:494) suggest that the scratchings represent the efforts of later, or Numic,

peoples to obliterate the earlier, or Pre-Numic designs. The distribution of Scratched style petroglyphs is uncertain, but they occur in general throughout Nevada (Heizer and Hester 1978:9).

Representational Styles

The Great Basin Representional style as defined by Heizer and Baumhoff (1962) is not a style as such, in that it is not a related visual complex with specific formal attributes and with given cultural, spatial, and temporal dimensions (Schaafsma 1983). Rather, it refers to various representational elements present in Great Basin rock art that are diverse in both formal characteristics and in origin (Schaafsma 1971:84, 117; Dewdney 1979:330; Hedges 1982).

In eastern Nevada and western Utah representational elements may be components of Virgin or Kayenta branch Anasazi or Fremont styles (Schaafsma 1971). Petroglyphs and rock paintings on the eastern edge of the Great Basin province in Utah with geometric pottery or textilelike fret designs, spirals, birds, tracks, hand and footprints, solidly pecked square-bodied mountain sheep, and above all, extremely stylized triangular or trapezoidal horned anthropomorphs (fig. 6) constitute a Sevier style attributable to the Sevier Fremont present

Fig. 5. Great Basin Rectilinear Style petroglyphs, Grapevine Canyon, Clark Co., Nev. Photograph by Ken Hedges, 1968–1969.

in the area between A.D. 750 and 1300 (see Madsen 1979 for discussion of cultural definitions of horticultural groups north of the Anasazi). Rock paintings in red ocher from Kachina Cave and upper Baker Creek in eastern Nevada consist of groups of distinctive very abstract angular horned human figures with tapered or triangular bodies (Schaafsma 1971:104–108; Tuohy 1979:figs. 3, 4, 5, and pp. 17–25). Some hold small shields. They are typologically similar to Fremont figures elsewhere, indicating that their cultural affiliations are with Basin Fremont. These paintings comprise Heizer and Baumhoff's (1962:208) Puebloan Painted style.

From the vicinity of Pahranagat Lake in southern Nevada (NV-Li-7), Heizer and Hester (1978) describe representational petroglyphs including mountain sheep and highly unusual stylized anthropomorphic figures that are suggested to be disguised hunters (fig. 7). These "hunters" are basically rectangular designs sometimes filled with lines of dots or other simple motifs, and they are sometimes fringed at the base. They have short arms and hold atlatls. These figures have typological features in common with certain highly stylized anthropomorphs in the Coso Range in eastern California.

Small stick, horned, and other types of human figures as well as mountain sheep are occasionally present in association with predominantly abstract elements in Basin rock art. The former are reviewed in an excellent article by Rusco (1973). In themselves they do not constitute a style but appear to be a part of what is otherwise an abstract style complex.

An important Great Basin rock art style in which representational elements predominate is the group of Coso Range petroglyphs described by Grant, Baird, and Pringle (1968:24, 57–58). Although not so designated by these authors, this group can be referred to as the Coso Representational style tradition, 1000 B.C.– A.D. 1000. This petroglyph tradition is distinguished by the presence of large numbers of mountain sheep, some of which are greater than life size and that have round, square, or boat-shaped bodies. Other elements of this style complex are sheep horns, dogs, deer, medicine bags, projectile points, and elaborately attired large human figures carrying atlatls or bows. In the Transitional (200 B.C.–A.D. 300) and Later phase (A.D. 300– 1000) there are shieldlike designs (figs. 8–10) and hunters with bows. Miscellaneous curvilinear and rectilinear patterns also are present throughout.

Chronology in the Great Basin Physiographic Province

Dating is a major problem in rock art research. Traditional methods of locating rock art in time involve

after Schaafsma 1971: p15.41, 52.

Fig. 6. Sevier Fremont representational style rock art. left, "Newspaper Rock," Clear Creek Canyon, Utah, where several hundred glyphs were pecked into a single stone face. right, Painted anthropomorphs, Kachina Cave, White Pine Co., Nev.

218

after Heizer and Hester 1978:figs. 14a, 4b.

Fig. 7. Representational rock art, Pahranagat Lake vicinity, Nev. left, Highly stylized anthropomorphic figures, holding atlatls, and figures of mountain sheep; right, ticked lines in combination with animal and other figures, which may represent diversion fences used in game drives (Heizer and Hester 1978).

analyses of superimpositions as well as studies of relative differences in weathering and the accumulation of patina, or desert varnish (a natural formation of brown or black stain composed of iron and manganese exides and hydroxides, clay minerals, and minor and trace elements) (Dorn and Whitley 1983:816). Stylistic analyses and studies of superimpositions and patina accumulation in concert yield relative chronologies. At the Grimes site (NV-Ch-3), Heizer and Baumhoff (1962:284,310) found clear evidence on the basis of patination that the Pit-and-groove boulders are older than Curvilinear style petroglyphs. At Iny-265 at Bishop, California, the superimposition of Curvilinear by Rectilinear designs indicates that at least at this site the Curvilinear motifs are older (Heizer and Baumhoff 1962:311). These factors, plus the observation of patina differences between curvilinear and rectilinear elements at the East Walker River site (NV-Ly-1), formed the basis for the temporal relationship between these styles in Heizer and Baumhoff's chronology. The Scratched

style usually occurs over both styles of the Pecked Abstract tradition.

Absolute dates and cultural relationships may be suggested by the position of rock art in relationship to cave deposits. In Leonard Rockshelter, Pershing County, Nevada, the position of Curvilinear and Rectilinear glyphs in relationship to midden deposits indicates that the petroglyphs are the product of the Lovelock culture. Heizer and Baumhoff (1962:231–233) suggest a beginning date of around 1000 B.C. for the Curvilinear style;

Fig. 8. Coso Representational Style petroglyphs with sheep superimposed over ceremonial figures. The figure above the sheep may be a medicine bag, endowed with anthropomorphic characteristics. Photograph by Campbell Grant, 1967.

Fig. 9. Elaborate anthropomorphic figures, Coso Representational Style, Coso Range, Calif. Photograph by Ken Hedges, 1983.

after Grant, Baird, and Pringle 1968:fig. 63 center.
Fig. 10. Shieldlike designs and medicine bags, Coso Representational Style, late period, Coso Range, Calif. Superimposed over earlier figures.

however, other studies of incised portable stones from datable levels in Gatecliff Shelter in the central Great Basin indicate that abstract rectilinear motifs resembling those found in both the Rectilinear and Scratched petroglyph styles were being made between 3300 and 1300 B.C. in this area (T. Thomas 1983). Thomas feels that such design comparisons suggest older dates for the petroglyph styles.

Grant, Baird, and Pringle (1968:48–55) propose dates for the Coso Range petroglyphs on the basis of the presence or absence of the bow in these representations, on the assumption that the bow first appeared in this region about 200 B.C.; however, Heizer and Hester (1978) suggest dates between 300 B.C. and A.D. 500 for the Coso-like elements at Pahranagat Lake in southern Nevada that lack representations of the bow.

Heizer and Baumhoff (1962) propose dates after A.D. 1000 for the Great Basin Painted style on the assumption that painted sites cannot be very old. Nevertheless, similar abstract paintings in the Southwest are believed to date from the Archaic, or prior to A.D. 1 (Schaafsma 1980:49–55). Further, Thomas and Thomas (1972) propose older dates for Great Basin paintings based on the presence of projectile points represented in paintings at Gatecliff and Toquima rockshelters in central Nevada. They assign the Toquima Cave paintings to the Great Basin Abstract style. The point types represented resemble those of the Eastgate series (A.D. 600–1300). Elements in the Gatecliff Shelter are largely representational, and the points depicted resemble those of the Pinto and Elko series (2500 B.C. to A.D. 600). Thus older dates for Great Basin paintings are both possible and likely.

Rock art in the eastern Great Basin with stylistic ties to the Virgin-Kayenta Anasazi (about A.D. 700–1100) and the Fremont (A.D. 750–1300) is dated by its cultural associations.

Methods of dating rock art directly are still in their experimental phases; nevertheless, they have produced some tantalizing results with Great Basin petroglyphs. Experimentation with neutron activation and X-ray fluorescence is suggestive and has corroborated the general style sequence proposed by Heizer and Baumhoff (Bard, Asaro, and Heizer 1978; Bard 1979). However, cation-ratio dating of patina from five Coso Range petroglyphs has yielded absolute dates that revise the earlier chronologies and suggests that petroglyphs in the Great Basin are almost twice as old as previously supposed. This method has provided "weak support for the previously hypothesized relative stylistic chronology" (Dorn and Whitley 1983:817). The earlier dates are supported by T. Thomas (1983) and Thomas and Thomas (1972).

Function of the Sites in the Great Basin Physiographic Province

Art functions in a variety of ways in the lives of preliterate peoples. Since the rock art described here predates historic times, and no knowledge of its meaning and purpose has been claimed by native peoples, the ethnographic record has provided little direct help in interpreting these sites. However, situational evidence, information present in the imagery itself, and models based on Great Basin ethnographic accounts have suggested that Great Basin petroglyph sites were related to the hunting of large game. This hypothesis was proposed by Heizer and Baumhoff (1959, 1962). Although its premises are open to question (Rector 1983), research in specific areas in the central and western Basin seems to support this contention (J.T. Davis 1962; Werlhof 1965; Grant, Baird, and Pringle 1968; T. Thomas 1976; D.E. Martin 1977; Heizer and Hester 1978; Wellmann 1979; Nissen 1982).

The rock art associated with hunting includes the petroglyphs of the Great Basin Abstract tradition and the Coso Range Representational style. Heizer and Baumhoff include the Scratched style in this category as well, but an alternative has been proposed for it by Bettinger and Baumhoff (1982). Heizer and Baumhoff (1962:219–225) found that in southern Nevada petroglyphs occur at sites especially propitious for game-taking: at points where animals coming to drink could be ambushed. They suggest that mountain sheep were the prime target. In northern Nevada where the ecology is more diverse and rainfall more plentiful, the pattern differs slightly, and deer and antelope were probably the object of the hunt. There, sites are located primarily along game trails over which animals moved during migrations or in changing foraging grounds. Petroglyphs are at good ambush spots in narrow draws or at points where corrals could be built and into which game might be driven. Archeological evidence for fences or corrals and hunting blinds still exists in some locations. None of these sites is near habitation remains or in a location associated with other types of subsistence activities such as seed collecting, rabbit hunting, or fishing.

Werlhof (1965) documented the location of Great Basin Abstract petroglyphs along deer trails in the Owens Valley and found that representational petroglyphs are found near winter feeding grounds. Further, he noted that along the trails the glyphs were oriented toward the passing animals. A similar observation was made by T. Thomas (1976) in the central Great Basin. Here detailed topographical recording, with specific attention to petroglyph faces, showed that only faces meeting oncoming game were pecked. Moreover, petroglyphs were made only on boulders in positions suited for attack or drive stations. Site situations of Coso Representational style petroglyphs, along with other archeological remains, further support the hunting hypothesis (Grant, Baird, and Pringle 1968). In the Coso Range petroglyphs are found in association with dummy hunters constructed of piled rocks and hunting blinds at ambush points, at gorge entrances, or on rocky points overlooking saddles between drainages. They are also found near springs.

The hunting hypothesis often seems to be supported by the content of the rock art itself. Near Yerington, Nevada, are depictions of sheep moving into V-shaped elements that resemble hunting corrals as described in Great Basin ethnographic accounts (Nissen 1974). Heizer and Hester (1978) propose that long ticked lines, present among petroglyphs strategically located for hunting, represent diversion fences for game drives (fig. 7).

The Coso Representational style in particular contains subject matter related to the hunt as well as to associated ritualistic activity. Hunting scenes are shown, as are impaled sheep and attacking dogs. In association with the numerous sheep, there are elaborately attired anthropomorphic figures carrying weapons and with horns, projectile point headdresses, and sun symbolism suggesting supernatural attributes. These figures may represent hunt shamans. It is suggested that atlatl weights exaggerated in size may have functioned as charmstones, enhancing the power of the weapon; the enigmatic shield designs and anthropomorphized medicine bags may be components of a hunting cult (Grant, Baird, and Pringle 1968). T. Thomas (1976) describes the presence of horseshoe-shaped vulva forms at hunting sites in central Nevada (see also Heizer and Baumhoff 1962:figs. 41x, 79h, 80b, 94d). Thomas proposes that these represent vulvas with specific associations with the hunt, signifying plenty and intended to replenish the game. As such they are a graphic indication of the shaman's role in maintaining balance and equilibrium.

There are ethnographic parallels for shaman-directed hunts. Prehistoric hunting ritual may have resembled shamanic hunting rites described in ethnographic ac-

counts of the Paiute. In these cases, the shamans directed the hunt, gave instructions on where to build corrals for animal drives, and told the people "how to act" (Nissen 1982:175–194). There is also an early account of a rock painting being made by two Southern Paiute hunters where they had killed a mountain sheep (Fowler and Fowler 1970).

Suggesting that superpositioning may have occurred as an aspect of ritual practice and was therefore intentional, Wellmann (1979) did a statistical analysis of these occurrences in the Coso petroglyphs. He found that sheep are superimposed over the anthropomorphic figures in statistically significant numbers, proposing that this nonrandom linkage probably signifies an important relationship between the sheep and the shaman figures.

Literal interpretations of the content of Great Basin rock art are questioned by some scholars. It has been suggested that the sheep depictions themselves may have a symbolic aspect, representing all big game animals (Nissen 1982:634–636). Or they may embody a variety of interrelated beliefs and values with broader connotations symbolizing plenty, well-being, and supernatural power (Hedges 1983). Whitley (1982) proposes on the basis of Western Shoshone oral traditions that the sheep may be a symbol of male virility and prowess in the hunt. He contends that this type of generalized symbolic interpretation involving personalized ritual is more consistent with what is known about aboriginal groups in the Great Basin than are formalized cult ceremonies.

Rector (1983), in a detailed reexamination of the evidence that has led to the formulation and support of the hunting magic hypothesis, challenges this explanation for Great Basin petroglyphs. In some localities, site contexts and associated archeological materials indicate that Basin petroglyphs were made for other reasons. In Death Valley, petroglyphs are found around the bases of alluvial fans near winter campsites and in the piñon forest near summer camps (D.E. Martin 1977:149). Crowley (1979) and Rector (1977) suggest multi-functional usage of petroglyphs in the Saline Valley in the eastern Mojave Desert, where petroglyphs are also associated with campsites and do not conform to a hunting ritual interpretation.

At Mono Craters is a petroglyph site consisting exclusively of horseshoe shapes, or vulva forms, carved in high relief at the summit of a volcanic cone. Davis (1961) proposes that these represent female genitalia that had magical and ritual associations and were made in connection with girls' adolescence ceremonies. Ethnographic accounts describe similar icons used in Diegueño initiation rites, where they were said to protect the initiates from evil forces and to ensure safe and easy childbirth. The fact that no other element is represented at the Mono Craters site and that the site is located in an isolated setting further supports this interpretation. *221*

Little information exists on the functions of other types of Great Basin province rock art. Painted sites in rockshelters are not appropriately located for use in hunting ritual (Heizer and Baumhoff 1962:221). The original purpose of the ancient Stillwater Faceted and Pit-and-groove boulders is unknown, although a historic use for the latter is reported: Northern Paiutes in Nevada placed offerings of pennies, beads, buttons, and safety pins in pits of anciently pecked boulders to solicit favors from supernaturals (Wheat 1967). In the California culture area, pitted boulders were actually made within the historic period. Among the Shasta of northern California they were referred to as rain-rocks, and ceremonies were performed at or near them to induce or stop rain. Among the Pomo such rocks, known as "baby rocks," were pecked by women wanting children (Heizer and Baumhoff 1962:237).

Styles in the Colorado Plateau Physiographic Province

Utah is centrally divided by the Wasatch Plateau, a high range that separates the Great Basin province on the west from the Colorado Plateau to the east. Unlike the Great Basin province, which is characterized by fault-block ranges and interior drainage basins, the Colorado Plateau is an area of high sedimentary plateaus dissected by major rivers and their associated canyon systems. Within historic times Numic speakers occupied the Colorado Plateau. Historic rock art of Ute origin on the Colorado Plateau has been documented by Castleton (1978–1979).

The Fremont culture predominated on the northern Colorado Plateau from approximately A.D. 500 or shortly thereafter to around 1250 (for local variability in dates see Jennings 1978:161, fig. 145). For several thousand years prior to this, Western Archaic hunter-gatherers occupied the Plateau province and, like the Fremont people, left a complex record of their ideologies and beliefs in the petroglyphs and rock paintings. This rock art, prevalent on the cliff walls and in rockshelters of the Colorado Plateau landscape, is for the most part quite distinct from that of the Basin province. Within this visual record several different styles have been identified.

Abstract Polychrome Paintings

Paintings in red, white, and black of abstract elements including ordered rows of parallel lines and dashes, rakes, tailed circles, zigzags of all sizes, lines of dots, plant forms, and bird tracks occur in a few central and southern Utah sites. Large fringed horseshoe-shaped elements are also present. These paintings have some affinities with abstract rock art in the Basin province and with the Polychrome Abstract paintings found in southern New Mexico (Schaafsma 1980:49–55), which is in the Southwest culture area.

The Barrier Canyon Style

Barrier Canyon style sites are located primarily along the western tributaries of the Green River in eastern and central Utah as well as in the White River drainage and its tributaries in northwestern Colorado. On the Colorado River it is found from Westwater Creek to the Escalante (fig. 11). The Barrier Canyon style in-

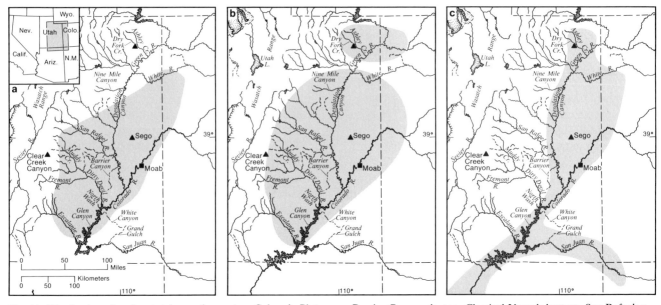

Fig. 11. Distribution of rock art styles on the western Colorado Plateau: a, Barrier Canyon; b, top, Classical Vernal; bottom, San Rafael; c, Glen Canyon Linear.

cludes both petroglyphs and rock paintings, with the paintings the more common form.

The dominant motif of this style is an elongated tapering anthropomorphic figure painted in dark red; the number of these present at a site may vary from one to dozens (fig. 12a-d). They are frequently ghostly in appearance, hovering in rows within arched sandstone alcoves and rockshelters. Very abstract heads, bulging heads with large staring eyes, and the absence or near absence of arms and legs serve to emphasize the spectral aspect of these beings. Headgear takes the form of horns or "antennae" painted in delicate thin lines. Some figures wear a crown of white dots, and occasionally white dot patterns applied by fingertips dipped in white paint decorate faces and bodies. Stripes and textile-like decorations are also depicted on the torso. Anthropomorphs with arms may hold snakes or plants, and they are sometimes flanked by tiny birds that fly toward them, animals, zigzags, and objects that defy identification. Large animals resembling dogs occur regularly (usually one per line of anthropomorphs or compositional group), and bears are represented on rare occasions (Schaafsma 1980:61–64).

A certain amount of stylistic variation is evident, although subject matter remains fairly consistent. In one stylistic version figures with flat bulging heads and enormous eyes are flanked by wavy serpent forms conveying a sense of the fantastic (Schaafsma 1980: pls. 4 and 5). Equally awesome are the somber paintings in the Great Gallery in Horseshoe (Barrier) Canyon (Schaafsma 1980:figs. 43–45) and the Bird site in the Maze in Horse Canyon (Schaafsma 1980:pls. 7 and 8) in which highly abstract life-size forms are painted in long rows and are accompanied by smaller, often exquisitely painted, birds and animals (Schaafsma 1971:figs. 75, 77). These sites contrast with those in which human figures are painted in bold lines on a smaller scale. As a group the anthropomorphs of this stylistic variant tend to be broad-shouldered and more triangular. They often have small heads and long necks and there is less accompanying detail (Schaafsma 1971:fig. 72). Overall they lack the emotional impact of the paintings first described. Whether or not these differences have temporal significance is not known, but they occur widely and thus do not seem to have regional connotations.

Fremont Styles

Fremont rock art on the Colorado Plateau is characterized by anthropomorphic figures that conform to a specific range of types but that as a rule are more lifelike than those of the Barrier Canyon style. Fremont anthropomorphs are sometimes extremely elaborate, and they may dominate in size and numbers the panels in which they occur. A variety of other elements, however, is present in Fremont rock art. Fremont type anthro-

pomorphs also appear in the Sevier style in eastern Nevada sites.

• CLASSIC VERNAL STYLE The Classical Vernal style of the Uinta Fremont region in northeastern Utah (fig. 12e) is dominated by large human figures. In a major site in the Ashley–Dry Fork Valley, nearly life-size anthropomorphs are pecked in rows across the cliff face. Their bold outlines contrast with their decorative detail. They are typically trapezoidal in shape and have large heads with facial features, including occasionally the weeping-eye motif. Feet are turned out to the side and fingers, when present, are splayed. Headgear is highly variable and individual. Body decoration as well as headgear is often indicated by areas of dots. Figures may wear earrings, heavy necklaces, kilts, and armbands. A few are shown carrying small circular shields and objects that look like heads, which may represent fetishes. Kidder and Guernsey (1919:190–192,pl. 87) describe a painted object of Basketmaker origin from northern Arizona made of the skin of a human head that is sewn together so that the eyes and nose as well as the hair are retained. At the top is a loop for suspension. Considering the continuities between San Juan Basketmaker and Fremont culture, this could be an example of the objects represented in the Fremont petroglyphs. There are also shield bearers with shields covering their entire bodies. Associated elements include spirals, other circular designs, mazes, one-pole ladder motif (a long line intersected at right angles by smaller ones), star elements, and various animals.

• SAN RAFAEL STYLE The highly decorative quality of the Classic Vernal style rock art occurs occasionally in the San Rafael style; however, San Rafael–style human figures tend to be simpler, are more frequently solidly pecked, and are found often in a context with many other elements (fig. 12f). Earbobs, heavy necklaces, and sashes grace their forms. Horns, antlers, or a single feather are the standard headgear. Large arcs, probably representing rainbows, may be pecked or painted over the heads of San Rafael anthropomorphs. Other associated elements include wavy lines, rows of dots, netlike patterns, spirals, wading birds, snakes (some of which are horned), and scorpions. But the predominant adjunct figure is the mountain sheep, which is prominent in Fremont rock art throughout the San Rafael region (fig. 12g). Hunting scenes in which horned human figures with bows and arrows pursue sheep are depicted. Human figures are also commonly shown carrying or bearing shields.

Distinctive, at some sites, are highly abstract anthropomorphs that are painted or pecked (or both) in simplified form. In these examples, only heads and triangular or trapezoidal torsos lacking appendages are portrayed, and decoration is minimal. Other elements are few or lacking altogether (Castleton 1978–1979,1: 85; Schaafsma 1971:pls. 22, 26).

a

b

c

e

f

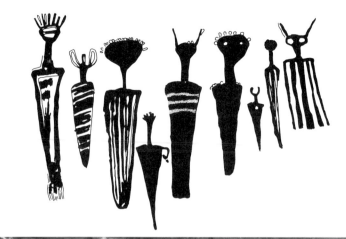

d

g

h

224

Glen Canyon Linear Style

Glen Canyon Linear style petroglyphs (originally described by C.G. Turner 1963:708 as Glen Canyon style Five) are also present on the northern Colorado Plateau (fig. 12h). This style consists of large outline representational figures and various other seemingly abstract linear motifs pecked with less than geometric precision. Outline deer, elk, and mountain sheep with small heads, legs, and tails and vaguely rectilinear elongated human forms are filled with bold crosshatching or stripes. The human forms typically have two straight "horns" on either side of the head. Arms and legs may be absent or rudimentary. The style is further characterized by the presence of animal tracks, snakes, long wavy lines, ticked lines, lines of dots, rakes, zigzags, ladders, wide grids, sunbursts, and squiggle mazes.

Other Colorado Plateau Rock Art

Rock art on the northern Colorado Plateau displays an extremely complex spectrum of imagery. Although the Glen Canyon Linear style, the Barrier Canyon style, and Fremont rock art styles are generally distinct, there are ambiguous sites. At some sites painted human figures displayed typological features of both Barrier Canyon and Fremont styles; at others confusion exists between Glen Canyon Linear and Barrier Canyon style anthropomorphic types. Also equivocal are petroglyphs and paintings of rectangular-bodied anthropomorphs with fringed torsos and with short outstretched arms and splayed fingers. These figures occur frequently in east-central Utah and in western Colorado sites and may have typological features of Barrier Canyon style as well as Fremont and Southwest Basketmaker anthropomorphs.

Chronology in the Colorado Plateau Physiographic Province

Both the Abstract Polychrome and Glen Canyon Linear styles have been ascribed to Western Archaic cultural affiliations preceding the horticultural Fremont and Anasazi (Schaafsma 1980:72–76). A latest date for the Abstract paintings is suggested by their position in a Grand Gulch rockshelter south of the area under discussion, where the paintings are on a now-inaccessible cave roof formerly reached by a ledge that has collapsed. Basketmaker II (San Juan Anthropomorphic Style) paintings (A.D. 100–400) are present in the ledge scar, indicating that the abstract paintings above were made before the collapse, that is, before A.D. 100. Southwest Abstract Polychrome paintings may date to 2000 B.C. Similarly, superimposed Basketmaker figures and the position of Glen Canyon Linear style petroglyphs relative to dune scars in which Basketmaker rock art is present demonstrate that the Glen Canyon Linear Style (the oldest art style in the Glen Canyon sequence) preceded Basketmaker art (Schaafsma 1980:75–76). Its beginnings may go back beyond 4000 B.C.

On the basis of superimpositions, stylistic affiliations, and the lack of depictions of the bow, the Barrier Canyon style is also assigned to an Archaic horizon (Schaafsma 1971:128–135). Stylistic continuities with both Fremont and Basketmaker rock art at some sites led to the proposal that the Barrier Canyon style dates between 500 B.C. and A.D. 500; however, typological similarities between Barrier Canyon style painted anthropomorphs from the Great Gallery and clay figurines found in an early context in a nearby cave (Hull and White 1980:122–125) suggest that much older dates are possible, perhaps as early as 5500 B.C.

Dates for the Classic Vernal and San Rafael styles are suggested by the age of the Fremont culture in the Colorado Plateau area, which occurs there as a discrete entity between A.D. 450 or 500 and 1250. Although later beginning dates have been proposed (Marwitt 1970:137–145), stylistic continuities between Fremont and Basketmaker rock art argue for the earlier dates. For the Classic Vernal style a final date is proposed at around A.D. 950 (Marwitt 1970; Jennings 1975).

Chronological evidence indicates that these styles are affiliated with both the Archaic cultural horizon and the later horticultural Fremont culture. Stylistic ambiguities and interrelationships indicate that Colorado Plateau rock art is a continuous record made over a long period of time. This, in turn, argues for an indigenous cultural development from the Archaic to the Basketmaker and Fremont horticulturalists in eastern Utah.

Functions of the Barrier Canyon and Fremont Style Sites

Studies of northern Colorado Plateau rock art site locations, aimed at determining site function, have not

c, after Schaafsma 1980:fig. 122; d, after Schaafsma about 1982; e, g, Harvard U., Peabody Mus.

Fig. 12. Western Colorado Plateau rock art styles. a, Barrier Canyon Style paintings in red and white, "The Great Gallery," Barrier Canyon, Utah, the largest figure about 2 m high; b, Barrier Canyon Style figures, Barrier Canyon, Utah; c, San Rafael Fremont anthropomorphs painted and incised figures with rainbow arcs, Barrier Canyon, Utah; d, anthropomorphs, White Canyon drainage, Colo. e, Life-sized Classical Vernal Style anthropomorphs from Dry Fork Canyon, Utah. f, San Rafael Style petroglyphs, Capitol Reef National Park, Utah. g, San Rafael Style petroglyphs, Nine Mile Canyon, Utah. h, Glen Canyon Linear Style petroglyphs, Desolation Canyon, Green River, Utah. Human figures with short, outstretched arms are typical of the northern Colorado Plateau version of this style. a–b, Photographed by David Noble, 1982; e and g photographed by Donald Scott, 1927–1937; f, photographed by Curtis Schaafsma, about 1974.

been done. Interpretation is thus based mainly on the imagery itself. The nonrepresentational content of the Abstract Polychrome style by itself communicates little to the modern viewer. The Glen Canyon Linear style combines similar abstract elements with representational figures. The highly stylized anthropomorphic forms with their various types of horned headdresses, occasional sun symbolism, and skeletal characteristics convey the impression of the supernatural and shamanic practices. The deer and mountain sheep may have symbolic significance. Even more obviously, however, the content of the Barrier Canyon style and Fremont rock art appears to be an expression of shamanic ritual.

The Barrier Canyon Style has numerous attributes that suggest it is shamanic art. The abstract quality of the anthropomorphs, the very focus of the style, is basic to this interpretation. Ambiquity and abstraction contribute to the esoteric nature of an element, thereby increasing its power. This is a cross-cultural, nearly universal, principle of artistic expression (Vastokas and Vastokas 1973:116, 134), and there is every reason to believe that the principle is operative here. In the Barrier Canyon style the anthropomorphic figure is reduced in form, a graphic device that subtracts from its human or earthly qualities and conveys a sense of the supernatural or otherworldliness. Horns and elaborate headgear are further indications of special powers.

Shamanic implications seem to be present in the animals depicted and in their relationships to the anthropomorphic figures. Tiny mountain sheep and birds perch on their shoulders and heads. In some examples, birds fly around or toward the heads of these beings. Snakes are also significant in Barrier Canyon style imagery, where anthropomorphs are flanked by them or hold them in their hands.

Likewise, Fremont art is replete with imagery that may be interpreted within a shamanic framework. The ceremonial attire of the anthropomorphs, especially their horned and other types of ornate headdresses, suggest that these are figures with supernatural powers. The high degree of abstraction in some of the Fremont examples also signifies their otherworldly status. Snakes occasionally appear in close association with Fremont anthropomorphs (Castleton 1978–1979,1:119; Schaafsma 1971:pl. 12). Rainbow imagery at San Rafael sites (Schaafsma 1971:fig. 42, 1980:fig. 122) may symbolize a bridge between earth and sky.

Overall, Fremont rock art is less mysterious than the Barrier Canyon style. In the rock art of the San Rafael and Sevier regions, the association of horned anthro-pomorphs or shamans with mountain sheep and the presence of actual hunting scenes in which horned men participate suggest a specific function for some Fremont rock art. It would appear that, as in the central and western Basin province, these petroglyphs are involved with rituals associated with hunting large game. In spite of the horticultural adaptation of the Fremont culture, archeological remains confirm that large game hunting was an important aspect of Fremont economy (cf. Bettinger and Baumhoff 1982:499). Rock art connected to shamanic ritual with hunting associations would be consistent with this observation. However, there is no indication that these rock art sites occur at the actual scene of the hunt itself, as in the case of the Basin province.

On the other hand, Fremont rock art in which shield-bearers are prominent or in which abstract anthropomorphs alone are represented may have different functional connotations. Classic Vernal style rock art featuring elaborate anthropomorphs often carrying "fetish" heads, and associated with shields or other large circular devices and spirals have definite ceremonial implications that lack hunting symbolism.

Conclusion

The rock art of the Great Basin represents several thousand years of graphic expression produced primarily by hunter-gatherers in the Western Archaic tradition. In the two physiographic provinces involved, there are two major rock art traditions or series of related styles with culture-historical implications—the Great Basin Abstract tradition, which is present in a limited number of sites in painted form on the Colorado Plateau, and the Anthropomorphic tradition that dominates the rock art of the northern Plateau from the Archaic through Fremont times. The Anthropomorphic tradition becomes manifest in later prehistoric times in the Basin province via the Fremont culture there. Important exceptions to this scheme are the ancient faceted and pit-and-groove boulders as well as the Coso Representational style in the Basin area of eastern California.

In addition to providing the archeologist with a sensitive tool for illuminating culture history via style and content, rock art is the graphic expression of prehistoric ideologies and ritual practices. Both locational and graphic evidence exists to indicate that the rock art styles in the Great Basin culture area functioned in some capacity in connection with hunting ritual and in other shamanic contexts.

Portable Art Objects

DONALD R. TUOHY

Hunter-gatherers of desert areas the world over share a relatively simple material culture and a rich spiritual life frequently reflected in abundant and often magnificent rock art. The high latitude deserts of the Great Basin are no exception and people who lived there throughout millennia have left their mark upon the natural environment. In addition to the fixed petroglyphs and pictographs widespread in the Basin ("Rock Art," this vol.), there are many portable objects made of stone, bone, wood, clay, fiber, feathers, reeds, bark, and other plant parts. They were sculptured, modeled, bent, tied, twisted, incised, perforated, and sometimes painted or otherwise embellished to create visual images. Since these mobiliary artifacts are not a set of related forms, and because they range in age from the late nineteenth century to as old as 6000 B.C., their functions within a particular prehistoric society are usually unknown; however, in some cases functions can be inferred or suggested.

Freestanding Stone, Bone, and Wood Sculpture

The first description of an effigy found in the western Great Basin was Harrington's (1927; see also Loud and Harrington 1929:44, fig. 10b), who called the miniature carving in slate that he had found on the Humboldt lakebed a "composite monster . . . [with] the head and the fins of a fish with the markings and the tail of a rattlesnake" (fig. 1). Harrington excavated other art objects in Lovelock Cave, including a horn object, a snakelike figure with eyes (Loud and Harrington 1929:fig. 10a, pl. 15f), incised bird bones, bone pendants (one with abstract punctate designs, ibid.:pl. 12c–d, h–i), a small zoomorphic or phallic image made of wood and incised with dots (ibid.:pl. 50b), and a bird-shaped scoria ring, possibly a club head (ibid.:pl. 57a). Thus the first major published excavation report on the archeology of the western Great Basin included examples of all major subtypes of sculpture later recovered in abundance throughout the region.

Information on 133 freestanding sculptures of stone, bone, and wood from the western Great Basin has been compiled (Tuohy 1978). Most of them were archeological finds without recorded associations, preserved in amateur collections. The majority came from basins in

Mus. of the Amer. Ind., Heye Foundation, New York: 13/4115.

Fig. 1. Slate effigy found on the dry Humboldt Lake bed near Lovelock Cave, Nev. by M.R. Harrington. Grooves around the middle of the effigy and above the tail may have served for suspension. Length 8.3 cm.

western Nevada—the Humboldt Sink, the Carson Sink, the Lower Truckee Basin, Carson Valley, and others. Freestanding forms in the Nevada area are of four subtypes: miniature, phallic, utilitarian, and abstract forms (fig. 2). A wide variety of freestanding sculpture has been recovered elsewhere in the Great Basin (table 1).

The functions of this class of portable art objects are conjectural, although the shape and size of some suggest particular uses known for historic cultures of the area. Some smaller effigies may well represent pieces palmed by sucking shamans and then shown to the patient as the cause of illness. Some pieces were evidently utilitarian, such as phallic or zoomorphic pestles. Small zoomorphic bowls may well have served as pigment palletes or mortars. Several anthropomorphic figurines

Nev. State Mus., Carson City: left, 12–A–1/122; right, 11–A–1/25.

Fig. 2. Stone effigies from western Nev. left, Zoomorph found in the lower Truckee River Basin; a head, complete with mouth, eyes and ears, and a stylized torso, have been pecked into a piece of vesicular basalt. right, "Grasshopper" found on the surface of the Humboldt Sink. Length of right 6.7cm, other same scale.

227

Table 1. Freestanding Sculpture

Region	Objects	Sources
Eastern Great Basin		
Danger Cave, Utah	clay effigy fragments	Jennings 1957:207–208, fig. 188
Castle Valley, Utah[a]	clay, wood, and fiber figurines	Gunnerson 1962a:67–91
Levee Site, Utah	clay effigy, slate figurine	Fry and Dalley 1979:58, fig. 42a
Bear River No. 2, Utah	slate effigies	Aikens 1967a:52, fig. 42f–g
Pharo Village, Utah	clay and bone figurines	Marwitt 1968:39, 53, figs. 50, 67
Western Great Basin		
Western Great Basin[a]	miniature effigies	Strong 1969:231–232, figs. 105–106
Stick Cave, Nev.	stone rabbit effigy	Orr 1952:13, fig. 6
Karlo site, Calif.	crescents, clay figurines, stone disks, bone spatulates	Riddell 1960a: figs. 10–21
Lovelock Cave, Nev.	wooden grasshopper, etc.	Jones, Weaver, and Stross 1967
Humboldt Sink, Nev.	stone owl, horned toads, etc.	Cowan and Clewlow 1968:202–203, fig. 4
Humboldt Sink, Nev.	abstract and zoomorphic pieces	Dansie 1973:1–4
Pyramid Lake, Nev.	stone fish and other effigies	Tuohy and Stein 1969:121–128, figs. 3–10
Grimes Point, Nev.	painted wooden owl	Tuohy 1969:57–58, figs. 4–5
Hallelujah Junction, Calif.	clay and stone heads, clay disks; incised stones, decorated pestle	Elston 1979:149–174, figs. 45, 50–51, 53–57
Glendale site, Nev.	stone head, stone cylinder	Miller and Elston 1979:175–177, fig. 15a–b
Carson River, Nev.	stone mountain sheep	Clewlow and Wells 1981:292, fig. 1
Falcon Hill, Nev.	olivella-topped wand, sheep effigy	Hattori 1982:50, fig. 21a–h
Northern Great Basin		
Wildcat Canyon, Ore.	zoomorphic effigies, decorative objects, clay figurines	Dumond and Minor 1983:212, 227, pls. 2, 9
Klamath Area, Ore.	henwas figurines	Howe 1968:137–142, figs. 108–110; Carlson 1959:93, pl. 1

[a] Inadequate archeological documentation for these pieces.

resemble henwas figurines, stone sculptures said to be used by Klamath shamans during healing ceremonies (Carlson 1959:89). The elaborate and sophisticated anthropomorphic Fremont figurines from Castle Valley, Utah (on the Colorado Plateau), may have been connected with fertility rituals and other ceremonial practices in this agricultural area, although the documentation must be considered largely uncontrolled (Gunnerson 1962a).

Soft Sculpture

Soft sculpture made from plant fiber, although not abundant, was highly developed in the Great Basin. Dry caves with nearly ideal preservation environments contain superb examples of both representational and abstract soft sculpture made of plant fiber as well as bone splinters, twigs, cactus spines, feathers, and other usually perishable materials. Such pieces are known primarily from the western, eastern, and southern portions of the Great Basin.

The most notable group of soft sculptures from the western Great Basin is the bundle of waterfowl decoys recovered in Lovelock Cave in 1924 (Loud and Harrington 1929:pl. 7a–b; Heizer and Krieger 1956:76; Napton 1969:54, pls. 7, 9). These decoys presumably had only a utilitarian function, but they are classic sculptural expressions deserving consideration as art forms. Although the forms of decoys changed over the centuries, their use persisted and has had a wide ethnographic distribution in the west (Heizer and Krieger 1956:76). The known prehistoric specimens date to the Transitional to Late Lovelock culture phases from about 1000 B.C. to A.D. 500 (Grosscup 1960:fig. 10).

The prehistoric examples, totaling 17 complete decoys and numerous fragments, were described by Loud and Harrington (1929:114) as either "painted" or "stuffed." They are known only from the Humboldt Sink area of western Nevada at Lovelock, Ocala, and Humboldt Caves (Loud and Harrington 1929; Harrington 1941; Heizer and Krieger 1956; Grosscup 1960; Napton 1969). The painted type differs from the stuffed type largely in the construction of the head and neck. Only ducks are represented by the painted type, and heads and necks are artfully constructed of rushes smoothly bound to bodies in a realistic pose (fig. 3). The stuffed type of decoy that imitates ducks, geese, mud hens, and gulls is usually a waterfowl skin with the head and neck intact, mounted on a body made of bent and bound tule stems cut at one end to simulate a tail ("Prehistory of the Western Area," fig 9, this vol.). In historic Northern Paiute decoys of this type the earlier fibrous neck stuffing was augmented with a single stick support (Wheat 1967:52).

Two other outstanding classes of soft sculpture zoomorphs, known primarily from the eastern Great Basin, in the Grand Canyon of the Colorado River, and the adjacent southern Great Basin are "horned" anthropomorphic figurines (Aikens 1970:121, 124, fig. 83) and zoomorphic split-twig figurines (Schroedl 1977). Both classes have distinct cultural and temporal affiliations.

Horned figurines were recovered in Hogup Cave in four excavation levels. They are bundles of wrapped plant fiber made from either reeds or sagebrush bark, with projecting "horns" at one end made of bone splinters, twigs, or cactus spines (Aikens 1970:121). Feathers are attached to the ends opposite the horns on four specimens (fig. 4). Because they resemble the horned anthropomorphic figures that are a common element of Fremont rock art and are of equivalent age (A.D. 400–1350), the Hogup Cave figures are believed to be directly related to the Fremont rock art style ("Rock Art," fig. 12, this vol.).

Another type of zoomorphic soft sculpture made from plant fiber is the split-twig figurine in the form of large game animals (fig. 5). Originally described by Wheeler (1937) who also worked out the construction technique (1939, 1942, 1949), these figurines have a distribution summarized by Schroedl (1977), who also inferred their function. Over 300 figurines are known from 16 caves and rockshelters (table 2), with 1,049 fragments from one rockshelter alone (Newberry Cave in the western Mojave Desert, Davis and Smith 1981). The split-twig figurine apparently developed as an Archaic cultural trait during the second millennium B.C. in the Grand Canyon area of Arizona where it appears to have been associated with hunting ritual. Later Archaic contexts— at 11 sites in Arizona, California, Nevada, and the east-

Mus. of the Amer. Ind., Heye Foundation, New York: 13/4512.
Fig. 3. Tule decoy made to resemble a canvasback drake, recovered from Lovelock Cave, Nev. It was part of a prehistoric cache that held 10 other finished decoys, 3 incomplete specimens, a rush bag full of feathers, some feathers wrapped in a piece of matting, a bunch of feathers tied to a string, and 2 bundles of snares, all covered over with a rush mat. The cache is radiocarbon dated to about 200 B.C. The body of the decoy was formed by bending a bundle of 25–30 large tule stems and binding them together. The ends were trimmed to simulate the duck's tail. A head constructed of rushes and smoothly bound with split rush stems was stitched fast to the body, care being taken to obtain a realistic pose. Bent rushes of the breast were also bound with split tule stems. The head, breast, and tail were then painted to represent the actual bird, using black and reddish-brown pigments. A final touch was covering the body with white feathers, the quills of which were stuck under the breast wrappings and held fast with fine cords of Indian hemp. Length 28.5 cm.

U. of Utah, Archeol. Center, Salt Lake City: left to right, 42Bo36–FS47.117; FS583.19; FS125.70; FS452.28; FS431.
Fig. 4. Horned anthropomorphic figurines recovered from levels of Fremont occupation in Hogup Cave, Utah. Labeled anthropomorphs because they resemble the horned anthropomorphic figures characteristic of Fremont rock art, these are simply wrapped bundles of sagebrush bark or reed, with projecting horns of bone splinters, twigs, or cactus spines, and tiny feather tails. Compare the anthropomorphs in "Rock Art," fig. 12d, this vol. Length of right 10.4 cm, rest same scale.

top, U. of Utah, Mus. of Nat. Hist., Salt Lake City: a, 42Wn420–FS4261; b; c, 42Wn420–FS1693; d.

Fig. 5. Zoomorphic split-twig figurines from Cowboy Cave, Utah. The figures were made by splitting, folding, and wrapping green twigs of *Salix* sp. or *Rhus trilobata*. Particularly well-made specimens have heads, ears, and muzzles. In general, these figures have inordinately long legs and necks and squat, thick bodies. a, Long-legged figurine with head a simple knob, loosely wrapped with grass fiber; radiocarbon dated about 2020 B.C. b, Largest of the figures recovered, typical in construction technique except for the short neck. c, Figure whose front legs have been charred. The muzzle is well formed as in b, while body configuration is very similar to a. Radiocarbon dated about 1990 B.C. d, Figurine with the elongated neck and long back legs of a and c, but with prominent ears and muzzle, neck and front legs wrapped with grass, radiocarbon dated about 2020 B.C. Length of a 4.5 cm (front to back), rest same scale.

ern Great Basin in Utah—suggest a more secular role, perhaps as recreational items such as toys or playthings (Schroedl 1977:263).

Less dramatic woven fiber objects also have been recovered in Great Basin caves and rockshelters. These are usually abstract objects such as button-shaped and linear fiber artifacts from Cowboy Cave (Hewitt 1980:72, fig. 33) and from the Fremont River area (Morss 1931:74). There are also woven spoon-shaped artifacts from Lovelock Cave (Loud and Harrington 1929:pls. 43f, 48), one of which possibly served as a pendant. Other woven enigmas found in the Great Basin may well have functioned as balls for the ball-and-pin game (Cressman et al. 1942:fig. 93h, 93k).

Incised Stones

Incised stones with etched linear, geometric, and circular designs were reported for the Great Salt Lake region in a pioneering archeological study by Steward (1937a:77–79). During the next four decades more specimens were recovered in modern cave excavations (fig. 6), as well as from unexcavated open sites.

The technique of incising bone, wood, and stone is an ancient one, prominent in the Upper Paleolithic of the Old World. By at least 6000 B.C. the incising tra-

dition had been firmly established in the New World (T. Thomas 1983:246; Schuster 1968). The Great Basin apparently was a center for the proliferation of incised stone rock art. In one excavated site alone, Gatecliff Shelter, 428 stones, three fragments of incised bone, and two pieces of incised sun-dried clay were recovered (T. Thomas 1983:246, table 59). Two private collections made in the vicinity of Las Vegas totaled 676 specimens (Santini 1974:4). These totals for excavated and surface specimens in Nevada are the largest known from anywhere in the New World (for other Great Basin sites and peripheral areas see table 3). Materials used for incising vary from area to area, but generally sedimentary or metamorphic rocks were chosen.

There are three stylistic zones of incised stones within the Great Basin (T. Thomas 1983a:342, fig. 180). A Northern style is centered on the Great Salt Lake and includes major portions of the Bonneville Basin; a Central style extends discontinuously from west-central Utah across central Nevada and southward into California; and a Southern style occurs in southern Nevada as well as in the Death Valley area of southeastern California. The Southern and Northern incising styles tended to integrate curvilinear elements and to append disparate motifs, unlike the Central style. But all three styles organize the same basic elements into identical rectilinear motifs.

230

Table 2. Split-Twig Figurine Sites

Site	Dates of collection	Number of figurines	Radiocarbon dates	Sources
Arizona				
Luka Cave[a]	1933	3		Wheeler 1949
Stantons Cave[a]	1934	15		Wheeler 1949; Reilly 1966
Stantons Cave[a]	1939	32		Reilly 1966
Stantons Cave[a]	1950	9		Schwartz, Lange, and DeSaussure 1958; Gunnerson 1955
Stantons Cave[a]	1959	1		Reilly 1966
Stantons Cave[a]	1960s	3 +		Jett 1968:344
Stantons Cave[a]	1962	9		Reilly 1966
Stantons Cave	1963	20	2145 ± 100 B.C.	Euler and Olson 1965
Stantons Cave[a]	1966	3 +		Reilly 1966
Stantons Cave[a]	1966	5 +		S.C. Jett, personal communication 1977
Stantons Cave[a]	1967	10		Jett 1968
Stantons Cave[a]	1967	1		Reeder 1967
Stantons Cave[a]	1968–1969	74		Euler 1977
Stantons Cave	1969–1970	65		Euler 1977
Tse-An-Sha[a]	1954	3		Schwartz, Lange, and DeSaussure 1958
White Cave[a]	1954	8		Schwartz, Lange, and DeSaussure 1958
Tse-An-Kaetan[a]	1954	23	1150 ± 100 B.C. 1580 ± 300 B.C.	Schwartz, Lange, and DeSaussure 1958
Sycamore Canyon[a]	1930s	15		Wheeler 1949; R.E. Kelly 1966
Walnut Canyon	1963	31	1930 ± 90 B.C. 1550 ± 100 B.C.	Olson 1966
California				
Newberry Cave	1957	5 +		G.A. Smith 1963a
Newberry Cave	1975	1		Anonymous 1975
Newberry Cave			1020 ± 250 B.C.	
Newberry Cave			1255 ± 170 B.C.	
Newberry Cave			1370 ± 180 B.C.	
Nevada				
Moapa Valley[a]	1950s	1		Schroeder 1953
Etna Cave	1935	12	1800 ± 300 B.C.	Fowler 1973, 1973a
Utah				
Cottonwood Cave[a]	1930	1		Gunnerson 1969
Moonshine Cave	1960	3		Pendergast 1961
Green River[a]	1966	2		Tripp 1967
Moab	1973	1		Pierson and Anderson 1975
Walters Cave	1975	1		Jennings 1975
Cowboy Cave	1975	20		Jennings 1975

[a] Inadequate documentation.

U. of Utah, Mus. of Nat. Hist., Salt Lake City: a, 42Bo36–FS429.222; b, 42Bo36–FS114.45; c, 42Wn420–FS2098.2; d, 42Bo36–FS412; e, 42Wn420–FS1591.5; f, 42Wn420–FS1020.3; g, 42Wn420–FS609.2; FS1600.1; h, 42Wn420–FS2013.2; j, 42Bo36–FS86.102; FS86.101; i, Mus. of the Amer. Ind., Heye Foundation, New York: 13/4560.

Fig. 6. Incised and painted stones and bones found in Hogup and Cowboy Caves, Utah, and Lovelock Cave, Nev. Most of the stones are tabular shapes of sandstone. Etched designs were made by incising the surface with a sharp instrument or by "walking" the edge of a chisel-like tool across the stone. Painting probably was done with a chewed, frayed stick or a small, soft brush of plant fiber. a, Rectangular slab with 4 chevrons. At each end of the slab is a triangle with its apex toward the center of the design field, filled with faint lines. b, Thin slab with 5 horizontal bands; at the rounded end, cross-hatching forms a grid of tiny rectangles; at the opposite end, the apex of a triangle points to the sharp end. c, Rectangular slab with scratched zigzag lines. d, Flat pebble with irregular zigzag lines deeply incised. e, Thin, flat slab with narrow zigzag lines made by walking a chisel-like tool across the surface. f, Thick, tabular slab decorated with a crude cross and a broad band painted in black. g, Oval slab with 3 painted thin lines radiating from the narrow end and a pattern of interconnected lines and dashes across the bottom half. h, Both sides of lozenge-shaped slab, painted at the top with a red cross covered in black and below with 5 red stripes and 3 black stripes that encircle the stone. i, Carved bone "feather," incised lines and dots filled with ocher. j, Ungulate bone splinters painted with bands of red hematite. Length of a 7.0 cm, rest same scale.

The Gatecliff Shelter incised stones are dated by radiocarbon assays on associated materials from 3300 B.C. to A.D. 1480. Motifs utilized from 3300 B.C. to 1300 B.C., according to T. Thomas (1983a:352), are directly related to the Great Basin Scratched and Rectilinear Abstract rock art styles defined by Heizer and Baumhoff (1962), who estimated the age of the Rectilinear Abstract style at A.D. 1000. Curvilinear motifs were introduced at Gatecliff apparently by 1250 B.C. together with new incising techniques and design arrangements.

Painted Objects

Painting on stone slabs, incised or not, tends to have a southern and eastern distribution in the Great Basin. One of three limestone slabs from Granary Cave in the Moapa Valley in southern Nevada was decorated with black dots (York 1973:22). These slabs date to A.D. 500. At Cowboy Cave and Walter Cave in eastern Utah, 23 painted stones were recovered, ranging from 2.4 to 19.0 centimeters long and from 0.3 to 3.4 centimeters thick, dating from 6425 B.C. to A.D. 515 (Jennings 1980:19; Hull and White 1980:120). The stones were striped primarily in red and black (fig. 6 f-h), although white pigment was used on one. Faded designs in black, difficult to discern, occurred on four tabular stone pieces from Swallow Shelter (Dalley 1976:46, fig. 22n), also in the eastern Great Basin. In the same area Hogup Cave yielded 12 ungulate bone splinters and one jackrabbit scapula that were painted with red hematite (fig. 6j). Some were merely coated or blotched with pigment, while other bones had the paint applied in bands across their widths or lengths (Aikens 1970).

Similar alternating red and black bands are on one of the wood pendants from Lovelock Cave (Grosscup 1960:36–37, fig. 8c-d), while another was painted with red ocher. These painted spatulate wooden pendants with knobs at one end are believed to date to the Early Lovelock phase, 2000–1000 B.C.

Several different pigments also were applied to freestanding zoomorphic sculpture in wood such as the grasshopper (fig. 7) from Lovelock Cave (Jones, Weaver, and Stross 1967:127, pl.1) and the painted owl effigy (fig. 8) from Hanging Rock Cave (Carson Sink), and also in the western Great Basin (Tuohy 1969:37–38, 57–58, figs. 4–5). Holes in the grasshopper were filled with piñon pine (*Pinus monophylla*) pitch, while the red pigment was iron oxide (red ocher). The pitchlike substance adhering to the owl effigy from Hanging Rock Cave was not analyzed, but it, too, appeared to be piñon pine pitch.

Pigments also were used on unfired clay figurines recovered in the eastern Great Basin Fremont sites. San Rafael figurines were beautifully modeled with hairdress, necklaces, pendants, ornaments, skirts, and gir-

Table 3. Incised Stones

Region	Total Recovered		Sources
	Surface sites	Excavations	
Eastern Great Basin			
Skull Valley, Utah[a]	b	b	Warner 1979, 1979a
Promontory Caves, Utah		17	Steward 1937a:77–79
Great Salt Lake region[a]	b		Holliman 1967, 1969
Hogup Cave, Utah		30	Aikens 1970:79–84
Danger Cave, Utah		1	Jennings 1957:219
Danger Cave, Utah		1	James 1983:1–12
Cowboy and Walters Caves, Utah		22	Hull and White 1980
Swallow Shelter, Utah		63	Dalley 1976:46–48
Thomas Shelter, Nev.		8	Dalley 1976:88
White River area (42Un371), Utah	1		Berry and Berry 1976:29
Bear River No. 2, Utah		1	Aikens 1967a:52
Southwestern Utah	1		Fowler and Matley 1978:31
Stansbury Cave II, Utah			Jameson 1958
Nephi Mounds, Utah			Sharrock and Marwitt 1967
Spotten Cave, Utah			Mock 1971
Millard and Toole Cos., Utah			Rudy 1953
Central Great Basin			
Ruby Cave, Elko Co., Nev.	1	53	T. Thomas 1981
Gatecliff Shelter, Nev.		428	T. Thomas 1983
Central Nevada, near Gatecliff	8		McKee and Thomas 1972
Western Great Basin			
Sierra Valley, Calif.	1		Elsasser 1978
Douglas Co., Nev.[a]	1		Tuohy 1967
Placer Co., Calif.	1		Elston et al. 1977:99
Lassen Co., Calif.	1		Pilling 1957
Mono Co., Calif.	1		Elsasser 1957
Southern Great Basin			
Clark Co., Nev. (Dixon coll.)[a]	203		Santini 1974
Clark Co., Nev. (Santini coll.)[a]	564		Santini 1974
Clark Co., Nev. (Lost City Museum)	3		Perkins 1967
Inyo Co., Calif.	1		Lathrap and Meighan 1951:24
Inyo Co., Calif.		5	Lanning 1963:248
Owens Valley, Calif.	2		Steward 1933b:275
Western Mojave Desert, Calif.	b		M.J. Rogers 1939:63
Panamint Mountains, Calif.	4		Ritter 1980:103–105
Wildrose Canyon, Calif.	2		Wallace and Taylor 1955
Colville Rockshelter, Calif.		3	Meighan 1953:184–185
Death Valley, Calif.	b		Hunt 1960:267–268
Northern Great Basin			
Southeast Oregon (Vail)	1		Bennyhoff 1957
Umatilla region, Ore.[a]		17	Osborne 1957:65–69
Coyote Lake, Ore.	1		Huntley and Nance 1979
Owyhee uplands, Idaho	2		Plew 1977
Boise Valley, Idaho	2		Huntley and Nance 1979
Gooding Co., Idaho		1	Plew 1981b
Northern Idaho	12		Plew and Cupan 1981
Cassia Co., Idaho		1	J.P. Green 1972:89
Southeastern Idaho		1	W.R. Powers 1969:35

[a] Inadequate documentation.
[b] Unknown total.

Nev. State Mus., Carson City: file no. E–115.

Fig. 7. Grasshopper effigy from Lovelock Cave, Churchill Co., Nev. A head, body, and rear legs have been carved in cottonwood. The body is painted in an unidentified black pigment, the legs in iron oxide or ocher. Pairs of holes at the shoulders and at the forehead are filled with weathered resin, probably piñon pitch, embedded with microscopic bits of feathers. Presumably, the feathers once represented wings and antennae. Two holes at the underside of the abdomen indicate that the figure may have topped a stick or wand or perhaps was mounted on a base. Length 9.5 cm.

dles formed of appliquéd pellets, and with heads and bodies decorated with red, yellow, and lime-green pigments (fig. 9) (see also "Fremont Cultures," this vol.).

Clay Objects

Two classes of figurines are clay: crudely modeled and poorly fired figurines of animals, birds, human figures, miniature vessels, and carrying baskets, presumed mud toys for children of historic Great Basin Indians and their immediate ancestors; and unfired, modeled clay figurines, often elaborately painted and most anthropomorphic, found in Utah in Fremont sites, and also from other parts of the Great Basin.

Two historic figurines from Grass Valley in central Nevada (Magee 1966; Ambro 1978) are similar to those described among the Ute and Southern Paiute (O.C. Stewart 1942:273; Fowler and Matley 1979:84) and Northern Paiute (O.C. Stewart 1941; S.W. Hopkins 1883:57; Riddell 1960:54, 79). Typical Shoshone historic figurines (Steward 1943a:375) include animal effigies with twig limbs (fig. 10). Clay animal figurines are not part of the Basketmaker effigy complex but do occur among Fremont forms.

Nev. State Mus., Carson City: file no. E–114.

Fig. 8. Owl effigy from Hanging Rock Cave, Nev. An associated mat was radiocarbon dated at about A.D. 250. Unusually large, this figure was carved from a half-round section of a cottonwood log. Two pits in the head represent eyes. Four organic-base paints were applied to the convex surface: red ocher to paint the tail; an unidentified white pigment over the body and head; a resinous black pigment (probably *Pinus monophylla* mixed with carbon) to paint the tail, zigzag designs on the head and body, a straight midsagittal line, and peripheral lines on the head and wings; and an unidentified green pigment to the neck groove and the head. Only red and black pigments were used on the concave surface: a thick coat of red ocher and then black pigment to paint the tail and zigzag body lines. Length 44.6 cm.

Unfired clay anthropomorphic cylinders are commonly recovered from sites on the peripheries of the Great Basin. The Furnace Creek fan in Death Valley, California (Hunt 1960:224) yielded 57 figurines and other objects from 27 sites. These pieces are said to be most similar to those from Basketmaker III sites in northeastern Arizona (Morss 1954) and those from Lost City, Nevada (Shutler 1961:pl. 78–79). Similar figurines also were reported by Wallace (1965) and Knight (1973).

Cigar-shaped and female clay figurines also occur in western Nevada and northeastern California. The Karlo site (Riddell 1960) yielded 12 fragmentary examples of

College of Eastern Utah, Prehistoric Mus., Price: A–141.

Fig. 9. Fremont clay figurines, unbaked and untempered, found in a low, shallow overhang in Range Creek Canyon, a tributary of the Green River, Utah. Eleven figures were found lying in a row on a shelf overlooking a small coursed sandstone slab structure with a collapsed pole roof and near a white pictograph of an anthropomorphic figure with an inverted trapezoidal head, broad shoulders, and narrow waist, very like the figurines, and typically Fremont. Water color painting on faces and torsos probably reflects body paint. It is likely that all or most of the figurines were once painted. Sexes are clearly distinguished in anatomy and dress: females have breasts and aprons; men wear breechclouts, except for b, which appears to be wearing a kilt. Womens' hair is dressed in heavy bobs, bound with cords hanging down over the shoulders. Morss (1954) postulates that the figurines were made by a single artist at different times and as separate male and female pairs (one badly preserved figure is not included here). Use of the figurines is uncertain but could be related to increase rites known throughout the Southwest (Parsons 1919, 1939) or to "bewitching" practices (Hawley 1950; Kluckhohn 1944; Morris 1951) or to a general aboriginal concern with ensuring fecundity (Spinden 1928; Renaud 1929). The paired figurines could also represent beliefs akin to the modern Pueblo use of male and female pairs for each of the 6 world directions (Parsons 1933, 1939). Their occurrence as male and female pairs and very careful attention to details of costume seem to indicate a strong ritualistic component in Fremont society, and perhaps, direct association with the well-being of the people as a group. Height of a 15.7 cm, rest same scale.

PORTABLE ART OBJECTS

Smithsonian Dept. of Anthr.: 11297.

Fig. 10. Baked clay horse and buffalo, probably from the Uintah Ute. The horse has a Mexican-style saddle; commercial purple string serves as a bridle. Collected by J.W. Powell in 1872. Length of top 9.0 cm, other to scale.

fired and unfired human figurines crudely fashioned and undecorated. A pregnant female figurine comes from Plumas County, California (Stephenson 1968). Other shaped clay objects from the region were reported by Layton (1970a) who relates them to his organic stratum in Hanging Rock Shelter, postdating A.D. 700. Another odd piece, a fragment of a globular-shaped miniature vessel with punctate designs similar to those in Death Valley, was a surface find in the Humboldt Sink (Cowan and Clewlow 1968:207).

Fremont style anthropomorphic figurines are restricted to the eastern Basin province and the Colorado Plateau in Utah. These ornate clay figurines, dating from A.D. 500 to 1250, show the regional variations present among other Fremont traits (Jennings 1978:155–234). Nearly all are trapezoidal anthropomorphs, often lacking arms and legs. They are very similar to anthropomorphs depicted in Fremont style rock art (Schaafsma 1971:104). There is also a Nevada variant.

A yucca fiber sandal possibly associated with an unfired clay figurine (fig. 11) from Walters Cave in Utah has been dated at 6925 B.C. (Hull and White 1980:123). While this is the earliest, Archaic period figurines from Sudden Shelter range in age from 4720 to 2720 B.C. Thus, the making of poorly fired clay figurines has deep roots in the Great Basin, as well as in the Southwest.

Stone Disks

A fairly numerous class of artifacts recovered more commonly in the eastern and western Great Basin than in other subareas is the centrally perforated stone disk, usually biconvex in cross-section, up to 10 centimeters in diameter, and frequently less than 3 centimeters thick. Heizer (1974) recorded 50 examples, all surface finds from the Lower Humboldt Valley in western Nevada, of two types, decorated and undecorated. Elston (1967:11) suggests some of the latter are the products of natural weathering.

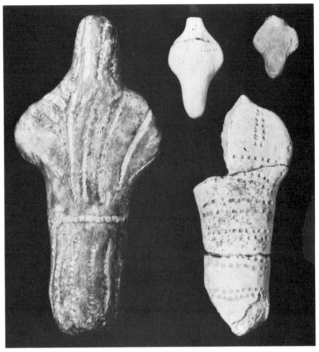

U. of Utah, Mus. of Nat. Hist., Salt Lake City: a, FS307; b; c.

Fig. 11. Archaic clay figurines from Cowboy and Walters Caves, Utah. Of the so-called "handle terminus" type (cf. Morss 1954), these have rudimentary heads and shoulders and bodies that end in straight bars that are slightly rounded at the bottom. Although similar in configuration to later Southwest figures, these are distinct in having decorative punctations or incisions across the body and in lacking facial and sexual details and body ornamentation. The largest figure is radiocarbon dated about 7000 B.C. At Sudden Shelter, Utah, a similar figurine is radiocarbon dated about 4700–4300 B.C. (Jennings et al. 1980). Height of a 10.5 cm, rest same scale.

Stone disks attract attention and therefore often occur in private collections made in the Lower Truckee Basin (Strong 1969:228, fig. 94), the Carson Sink (R.L. Kelly 1983, fig. j), and elsewhere in the western Great Basin. Excavated disks have been reported for Lovelock Cave and Falcon Hill, Nevada, the Karlo site in northeastern California, and the northern Great Basin at Laird's Bay on Lower Klamath Lake (Loud and Harrington 1929:107; Hattori 1982:54, fig. 22a; Riddell 1960a:47, 58, fig. 21e–f, h; Cressman et al. 1942:101). Their chronology is poorly known, but they could date to as early as 2000 B.C. (Hattori 1982:30).

The possible function of stone disks in the western Great Basin remains unclear. They have been interpreted as "wand heads" (Hattori 1982:54 after Henshaw 1887:28–30, figs. 14–18), "part of a top" (Cressman et al. 1942:101), a "pendant" (Strong 1969:228, fig. 96f), "a transit" (Dansie 1973:1 after John T. Reid's notes), and "a flywheel for a pump drill" (Miles 1963:88, figs. 3.70, 3.73, 3.75). Plain ovate and rectilinear forms occur as well as disks that are also perforated near an edge, and these types were undoubtedly ornaments (R.L. Kelly 1983:fig. i; Strong 1969:228, fig. 94a).

Problems of functional interpretation are less confusing in the eastern Great Basin, where undecorated stone disks were frequently spindle whorls. In the excavation of Cowboy Cave 23 spindle whorls were recovered (Hull and White 1980:117), some of stone but most of clay or other material. Several of the clay whorls still had parts of the central spindle stick remaining in them. However, when diameters of perforations in stone disks are larger than 0.7 to 1.0 centimeters (as in the case of 23 examples from Swallow Shelter (Dalley 1976:45–46, fig. 23i–k), are off center, or are multiple, the disks presumably served as pendants. The disks are widespread throughout the Great Basin and intermontane region, and functional criteria are often unclear. Stone and ceramic disks are found in Fremont contexts throughout Utah dating from about A.D. 500 to 1300, and they occur in possible Archaic levels in sites on Stansbury Island in the Great Salt Lake (Lindsay 1976:115; Jameson 1958).

Miniature Eccentrics of Flaked Stone

Flaked stone eccentrics, apparently ornaments, have unusual geometric or zoomorphic shapes. They are not peculiar to the Great Basin but range throughout North America as far north as Point Barrow, Alaska (Jordan 1980) where they serve as hunter's amulets.

The largest collection of obsidian eccentrics reported for the western Great Basin came from the Carson Sink. The pieces are intricately flaked, zooform, crescentic, or geometrically shaped miniatures all under 10 centimeters in length (R.L. Kelly 1983:11, fig. h). Eccentrics also come from the western and northern Great Basin in Nevada and Oregon. Three from Nevada were tightly curved pieces shaped like crescents, identified as nose ornaments (Strong 1969:196; Arment 1961:pls. 7, 13). Similar pieces also ground smooth were recovered in the Karlo site (Riddell 1960a:135, fig. 10). Other examples from the western Great Basin and southeastern Idaho include two bird-shaped forms made of obsidian (Tuohy 1980:1; Hutchinson 1982; J.C. Woods, personal communication 1984), and curious, medially joined pieces from the Carson and Humboldt Sinks (Tuohy 1978).

Bird or butterfly eccentrics have also been found in the eastern Great Basin, notably by Gunnerson (1962) in Castle Valley, central Utah, and by Jennings and Sammons-Lohse (1981:66, fig. 35i) at Bull Creek. Both are Fremont cultural manifestations dating from about A.D. 500 to 1300.

Early Trade

RICHARD E. HUGHES AND JAMES A. BENNYHOFF

Compared to the attention devoted to trade in adjoining culture areas—California (L. L. Sample 1950; J.T. Davis 1961; vol 8:690–693), the Southwest (Beaglehole 1937; W.W. Hill 1948; Ford 1972; vol. 10:711–722), the Plains (Jablow 1951; Ewers 1954; Wood 1972, 1980), and portions of the Plateau (Teit 1930; Spier and Sapir 1930; Griswold 1970)—relatively little has been written on the subject of trade in the Great Basin (Malouf 1939, 1940c).

In this chapter, the ethnographic data will be briefly reviewed, but major emphasis will be given to the available information on two nonperishable trade items as examples of foreign versus internal Great Basin trade. An inevitable unevenness in the areal coverage within the Great Basin is apparent because most research on prehistoric trade has been undertaken in the western portion, using shell and obsidian. Shell artifacts made from Pacific coast species represent the most widely distributed commodity (at least five trade networks) in western North America, extending in time back to the early Holocene (fig. 1). Obsidian was a major raw material that can be traced to a minimum of 10 localized sources within the Great Basin, the trade of which also extends back to the early Holocene, for example, in Danger Cave (fig. 2). A variety of other nonperishable trade items (pottery, turquoise, lignite, catlinite, pigments) lack specific source data; all, except pigments, appear to be Late Archaic or Historic in time.

The study of prehistoric and protohistoric exchange begins with identification of the sources of material, specifying the distribution of these materials in space within particular periods of time. It is one thing to determine the geographic source area for a commodity, but it is quite another matter to infer the social mechanism responsible for the occurrence of that material at an archeological site. Because the presence of non-local material in a site does not, by itself, provide unimpeachable evidence for long-distance trade (cf. Heizer 1944), it is necessary to review some of the ways in which resources and other goods may have been obtained. The three major mechanisms are: direct access, indirect access by trade, and scavenging.

Most goods were secured through direct access when they were located within a group's home territory, or when amicable relations with neighboring social groups permitted unimpeded access to desired resources. In the case of indirect means, commodities were procured by one group at the source, then transferred to their ultimate destination through a series of intermediate transactions. These transactions may have involved more than one exchange , sometimes with middlemen (Farmer 1935; Heizer 1941). Objects also were procured by scavenging from abandoned sites (Barrett 1910:246, 253; Kelly 1932:141; Lowie 1924:246; O.C. Stewart 1941:431, no. 809, 1942:340, no. 1506; Riddell 1960a:50; Smith 1974:111). This form of commodity acquisition is difficult to evaluate in Basin-wide perspective. The assumption is that the more distant a commodity is from its point of origin the more likely it is that the commodity was obtained through trade. However, due to the limitations of available evidence, direct access cannot be ruled out in many instances.

Information scattered throughout ethnographies, culture element distribution lists, and diaries of early explorers and missionaries (for example, Lewis and Clark in 1804 and 1805 in Thwaites 1904-1905; Escalante in 1776, see Euler 1966; Fowler and Fowler 1971) documents that trade took place on a casual basis whenever contacts were made with neighbors. The principal redistributive mechanism for goods during the ethnographic period occurred during the festival, when individuals from neighboring valleys congregated for periods ranging from a few days to a week or more to visit, dance, gamble, and trade during periods of temporary resource abundance (cf. Davis 1965:21–22; Fowler and Fowler 1971:248). Depending on local conditions, there was considerable mobility and contact between peoples living in adjacent valleys, which could have further dispersed objects traded at the festivals. In some places, exchanges of shell bead money for food goods may have taken place, serving to buffer the effects of local resource shortages (cf. Steward 1933b:257–258; Bettinger and King 1971).

By the time intensive ethnographic research was being conducted in the Great Basin during the early 1930s, precontact economic patterns had been affected by nearly a century of interaction with Anglo-American, English, French, Spanish, and Mexican explorers, missionaries, and settlers. This contact occurred much earlier in the eastern Great Basin, where Eastern Shoshone and Ute peoples had frequent encounters with North West Company fur traders as early as 1800. Horses could have

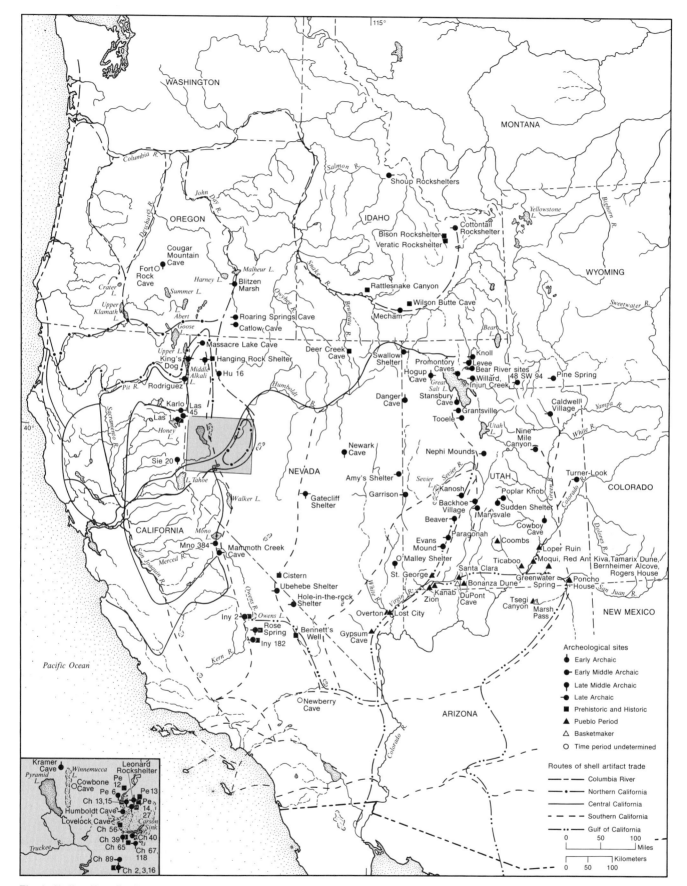

Fig. 1. Shell artifact distribution: major sites and trade routes (after Tower 1945; J.T. Davis 1961).

EARLY TRADE

Fig. 2. Obsidian trade routes.

What Was Traded

A wide variety of perishable and nonperishable goods circulated among Great Basin groups at the time of early European contact. By far the most common commodities were perishable resources. These included buckskins, buffalo skins, beaver and buffalo robes, rabbitskin blankets, deer hides, antelope hides, elk hides, beaver and otter skins, rabbit fur "rope," women's skin dresses, moccasins, serviceberry and horn bows, arrows (some eagle-feathered), camas and other roots, soaproot, seeds, dried crickets, dried fish, salmon (fresh and dried), acorns, pine nuts, fly larvae, red, white, and yellow paint, *Apocynum* nets, firewood, mescal, mescal fiber brushes, maize, beans, wheat flour, wafer bread, rugs, blankets, saddle blankets, medicinal plants, redbud stem for baskets, dogs, tobacco, salt, and knife handles. The most frequently mentioned "perishable"

been components of Northern Shoshone existence as early as the late 1600s (Driver and Massey 1957:285, map 85; cf. Steward 1938:201), by which time Southern Utes were already using horses (Fowler and Fowler 1971:102). While the horse clearly revolutionized local economies of many Basin groups, other more isolated peoples appear to have been less affected (Steward 1938:201–202). Long distance slave trade also was facilitated by the horse, beginning as early as 1813 (Fowler and Fowler 1971:103–105).

resource exchanged among eastern and southern groups was the horse.

Nonperishable resources traded included shell beads, dentalium shells, small univalve shells, abalone ornaments, clamshell disk beads, glass beads, frog-shaped shell pendants, obsidian, pottery, metal arrow points, catlinite and other stone pipes, stone knives, turquoise, guns, steel axes and knives, horse bridles, bullets, percussion caps, Navajo silver shoe buttons, steel fishhooks, brass bracelets, and pumice arrowshaft smoothers.

Lists of specific commodities exchanged between Great Basin groups are provided in tables 1–4, which show that perishable materials make up the vast majority of trade items. This fact has obvious implications for the study of prehistoric trade. The importance of the horse as an item of exchange is reflected especially among the southeastern and northeastern groups who were among the first to acquire these animals. The tables also indicate other items introduced about the same time as the horse, such as metal artifacts, glass beads, and munitions. The Muache Ute, for example, obtained Monitor pipes "from eastern Indians just before white people settled in the area," while the Pahvant Ute Monitor pipes were "traded from Uintah after [the] Mormons arrived" (O.C. Stewart 1942:344, no. 2899).

Of particular importance to archeological studies is Ewers's (1954:435, 440) observation of a shift in the types of materials exchanged following the introduction of the horse; aboriginal patterns featured "primarily an exchange of perishables—food and leather goods," while in post-horse days "commerce was largely in imperishables." Except under special circumstances (in caves and rockshelters) the objects preserved in Great Basin archeological sites are exclusively nonperishables, representing only a fraction of the material culture described in the ethnographies. Because of this, the interpretations made about prehistoric trade in the Great Basin, are, of necessity, derived primarily from nonperishable materials—particularly shell and stone. Both shell and stone artifacts are especially suited for use in the study of prehistoric trade because it is often possible to trace them to their geographic points of origin. Ocean shells can have been procured in only a few places, and modern techniques of chemical analysis can be applied to "fingerprint" the source outcroppings for stones (particularly obsidian) used in prehistoric tool manufacture.

Uses of Shell and Obsidian

Clam disk beads from California functioned as money among four Northern Paiute bands adjacent to the Washoe (O.C. Stewart 1941:402; Curtis 1907–1930, 15:80, 82), in Owens Valley, and among the western-

Table 1. Items Traded By Southern Paiute and Ute

	Items Traded	Items Traded For	Group Traded With
Southern Paiute Kaibab	buckskins	*Proboscidea louisianica* (basket material), and beans(?)	Shivwits
	mescal fiber brush, buckskins, hides, bows	bows, arrows, red paint	Kaiparowits
	buckskins	rugs (Navajo?)	San Juan
	buckskins, blankets	maize, beans	Saint George
	buckskins(?), blankets	pipes, maize and beans(?)	Cedar
	Apocynum nets	rabbitskin blankets, buckskins, serviceberry canes, dogs	Panguitch
	buckskins, horses, Navajo blankets, moccasins, woman's skin dress	horses, buffalo robes, white paint, dogs	Koosharem
	buckskins, horses	horses, knives, guns, yellow paint	Ute
	buckskins, horses, small hides	blankets, beads, and earrings	Navajo
	horses	Hopi and Navajo rugs, maize	Hopi
Kaiparowits	buckskins	blankets	Navajo
San Juan	arrows	buckskins, buffalo hides	Ute
	antelope hides, "wedding baskets," buffaloskin blankets	blankets, $5 for a "wedding basket"	Navajo
	rabbit-fur rope, buffalo-skin blankets, firewood	maize, wafer bread, salt, horses	Hopi
	eagle-feathered arrows, red paint	mescal	Havasupai
Saint George	guns	horses, blankets, skins	Walapai
Panguitch	buckskins, rabbitskin blankets	moccasins with badger soles	Cedar
	Artemesia seeds	pine nuts	Beaver
Shivwits	?	Apocynum nets, salt	Moapa
		catlinite(?) pipes	Plains groups
Ute	hatchets, knives	mescal	Walapai
	horses	leggings, beaded blankets, porcupine quills	Arapaho
	buckskins, buckskin clothing, elk hides, elk hide storage sacks, buffalo robes, saddle bags, horses, bandoliers, beaded bags, tweezers, beaver and otter skins, buffalo generative organs, pitch for ceremonial whistles, "wedding baskets"	chief blankets, saddles, bridles	Navajo
	red ocher, blue dye; buffalo, deer, and antelope meat; hides; horses; backed bows; beaded vests; leggings; Navajo blankets	corn, corn meal, wheat flour, wheat bread, dried fruit, tobacco, sugar, coffee, pottery, woven goods, iron knives	Tewa Pueblos
	guns, black powder, bullets, percussion caps, Navajo silver shoe buttons	blankets, buckskins	Havasupai
		maize	Hopi
		catlinite pipes	Plains groups

SOURCES: Beaglehole 1937:84; Drucker 1941:172; Ford 1972:31–32; vol. 10:711–713; W. W. Hill 1948:377, 380; Kelly 1964:66, 86, 90–91, 159, 165, 173–174, 188; Mook 1935:166; Smith 1974:252; Spier 1928:361–362, 370; O. C. Stewart 1938:759, 1942:293, 337–338, 340–342, 344–345.

most Shoshone (Steward 1941:308). Olivella and haliotis necklaces as well as ear ornaments of shell were universal among the Northern Paiute (O.C. Stewart 1941:390–391) and the Western Shoshone (Steward 1941:297), but their use was denied by Northern Shoshone (Steward 1943a:321) and Ute–Southern Paiute consultants (O.C. Stewart 1942:276–277). Northern Paiute men also attached shell ornaments to their double hair braids (Curtis 1907–1930,15:69; Loud and Harrington 1929:106).

A variety of stringing methods was utilized for necklaces in the prehistoric period (Loud and Harrington

Table 2. Items Traded by Northern Paiute, Owens Valley Paiute, Northern Shoshone, and Western Shoshone

	Items Traded	Items Traded For	Group Traded With
Northern Paiute			
Pyramid Lake	moccasins, beads, dentalia		Honey Lake
	fish	pine nuts	Lovelock and Fallon areas
		horses, drums	Bannock
		pine nuts	Walker Lake
Honey Lake	buckskin, dried fish	small univalve shells	Maidu
		pine nuts	Walker Lake
Walker Lake	fish		Lovelock and Fallon areas
		fly larvae	Mono Lake
Fallon area	pine nuts		Honey Lake
Owens Valley Paiute	shell money, buckskins	salt, rabbitskin blankets	Western Shoshone
Northern Shoshone	buffalo skins, beaver and buffalo robes, salmon, deer hides, camas roots	horses	Nez Perce
	horses	metal arrow points	Crow
	horses	catlinite pipes	Blackfoot
	dried salmon		Flathead

SOURCES: Park 1933–1940; J. T. Davis 1961; Steward 1938:45, 78, 90, 91, 191, 203, 206; Lowie 1909:175, 191, 212; Teit 1930:358.

1929:105; Carroll 1970:fig. 1; Hattori 1982:fig. 23). Occasionally olivella beads were sewn on garments as pendants (Loud and Harrington 1929:14) and on moccasins (fig. 3), while fragmentary pieces were appliquéd on pipes (Grosscup 1960:14; Loud and Harrington 1929:pl. 52a). Haliotis Square beads were sometimes sewn to flexible twined basketry (Loud and Harrington 1929:14). Olivella Spire-lopped beads also were sewn to feather plumes (Loud and Harrington 1929:118, pl. 20) or attached to the tips of wooden wands (fig. 4).

Obsidian was employed as raw material for manufacturing chipped stone implements such as projectile points, large knives and bifaces, and drills. The Lemhi and Snake River Northern Shoshone and Owens Valley

Table 3. Washoe Exchange with Other Tribes

From Washoe	Items Traded to Washoe (Tribe received from)
piñons, salt, obsidian, rabbitskin blankets, buffalo hides, hand game bones	acorns, clam disk beads, yew wood, yew bows, soaproot, medicinal plants, redbud bark for basketry (Miwok, Nisenan)
piñons, salt, obsidian, rabbitskin blankets	redbud bark (Nisenan)
shell jewelry, ritual objects, deer hides, pumice arrowshaft smoother	antelope hides, buffalo hides, fish (Northern Paiute)

SOURCES: Barrett and Gifford 1933:193, 221, 273; Curtis 1907–1930, 15:93–94, 171, 190; d'Azevedo 1966:330–332; Downs 1966:11, 29, 36–37; Freed 1966:78; Kroeber 1925:571; Layton 1981:133; Long, Love, and Merrill 1964:56–57; Lowie 1939:328; Price 1962:51.

Paiute used obsidian to fashion arrow points and knives (Thwaites 1904–1905, 3:12; Lowie 1909:173; Steward 1933b:262, 277, 1943a:368, 370); the Snake River Northern Shoshone also used unmodified obsidian flakes as knives, sometimes insetting obsidian bifaces into wooden or horn handles. Promontory Point Western Shoshone used large pieces of obsidian from springs north of Washakie, Utah, to fashion obsidian bifaces, 8 to 10 inches long, with one end wrapped to serve as a handle (Steward 1943a:368). Obsidian arrow points affixed to arrowshafts and a hafted obsidian knife (Fowler and Matley 1979:65, 69) have been attributed to Moapa and Kaibab Southern Paiute and unspecified Southern Paiute of southern Utah. The Surprise Valley Northern Paiute recognized advantages for different physical properties of obsidians; red obsidian was favored over the black variety because it was scarcer and because it did not break so easily (Kelly 1932:144).

The prehistoric use of obsidian largely parallels the uses documented in the ethnographic record. Obsidian arrow points and darts have been recovered archeologically still attached to weapon tips (Fenenga and Riddell 1949:fig. 58s; Tuohy 1980a:fig. 2, 1982:fig. 2d, 2e; Hattori 1982), and knives and bifaces have been recovered from dry cave deposits (Loud and Harrington 1929; Thomas 1985). Most uses for obsidian were utilitarian, but uses in ceremonial contexts are possible. Large obsidian bifaces (manufactured from Great Basin obsidian source materials) similar to those documented ethnographically in northwestern California ceremonial activities (Goddard 1903:pl.30) have been recovered archeologically at Nightfire Island in the northern subarea of the Great Basin and at Gold Hill, outside the Great

Table 4. Selected Units of Equivalent Value in Great Basin Exchange

Commodities	Groups	Source
6 measures of beads: 50¢	unspecified	Steward 1938:45
12 measures of beads: 50¢	unspecified	Steward 1938:45
5 gallons of pine nuts: 10 strings of beads	unspecified	Steward 1938:45
One sinew-backed bow: about 24 strings of beads	unspecified	Steward 1938:45
Moccasins: 10–40 strings of beads	unspecified	Steward 1938:45
A wife: 100 strings of beads	unspecified	Steward 1938:45
25 dentalium shells: $7.00	Pyramid Lake Northern Paiute–Honey Lake Northern Paiute	O. C. Stewart 1941:435
3 deer hides: a horse	Snake River Northern Shoshone–Nez Perce	Steward 1938:45
½ bushel of yams or camas roots: a colt	Snake River Northern Shoshone–Nez Perce	Steward 1938:45
20 lengths of twisted rabbit skin rope: $5.00	unspecified	Steward 1938:45
4 bags of salmon: one horse	Lemhi Northern Shoshone–Nez Perce	Lowie 1909:191
10 sheep skins: one horse	Lemhi Northern Shoshone–Nez Perce	Lowie 1909:191
2 bear skins: one horse	Lemhi Northern Shoshone–Nez Perce	Lowie 1909:191
One dried salmon: one straight awl and a small fishhook	unspecified	Lowie 1909:191
10 fish: one butcher knife	unspecified	Lowie 1909:191
Rabbitskin blanket: arm's length of clam disk beads	Mono Lake Northern Paiute–Sierra Miwok	Barrett and Gifford 1933:250

Basin area (fig. 5). The obsidian bangles, or bipoints, from Kramer Cave (Hattori 1982:44–48) may have been employed as clothing decoration (vol.8:128–136); the sinew wrap suggests that they were suspended (fig. 6).

The Archeological Record

In the last quarter of the nineteenth century, while United States government geologists remarked on the presence of obsidian in the Great Basin (S.F. Emmons 1877; Hague and Emmons 1877; C. King 1878; see also Iddings 1888), its use among native peoples also was attracting attention (Rau 1873:357; Holmes 1879; B.B. Redding 1879). These volcanic glasses can be used to investigate prehistoric trade. The remarkably uniform chemical composition of obsidians makes it possible to characterize them on the basis of unique combinations of trace and rare earth elements using either X-ray fluorescence or neutron activation techniques. Once the parent sources have been fingerprinted, archeological artifacts are analyzed and matched with the geological sources. In addition to chemical characterization, it also has been possible in some cases to employ obsidians as time markers (Friedman 1977; Hughes 1982, 1983a:168–169), providing archeologists with a useful method of dating specimens that may not be typologically distinctive. While obsidian sourcing research has a comparatively long history in California (Parks and Tieh 1966; Jack and Carmichael 1969; T.L. Jackson 1974; Jack 1976; Hughes 1978; Ericson 1981), it is only since the late 1970s that it has been applied successfully to Great Basin research (cf. Hughes 1984a).

The acquisition and use of Pacific coast shells by California and Great Basin peoples first evoked comment in the 1870s (Barber 1876a, 1877a; Stearns 1877, 1877a; Yates 1877). Although some later researchers (Brand 1937; Tower 1945; Gifford 1947, 1949) recognized the potential of these marine shells to reconstruct prehistoric routes of commerce and to provide cross-dates from Southwest archeological sites, it remained for Bennyhoff and Heizer (1958) to propose refined dating schemes for a wide variety of olivella, haliotis, dentalium, and clamshell beads and ornaments manufactured in California and traded into the Great Basin. Bennyhoff and Hughes (1984) expanded and revised this work

U. of Calif., Lowie Mus., Berkeley: 1–21640.
Fig. 3. Child's leather moccasin from Lovelock Cave, Nev., ornamented with olivella shell beads, stitched to the leather with twine. Length 24.3 cm.

Nev. State Mus., Carson City: 26Wa196–412.

Fig. 4. Shell-tipped ceremonial wand from Kramer Cave, Nev. This specimen has a carved greasewood shaft with 5 raised bands and is capped by a spire-lopped olivella shell bead tied with sinew to a projection at the end. The bands were left the natural color of the wood, while the rest of the shaft was painted red. Sinew wrapping at the end of the wand holds a tiny remnant of leather thong, which may have suspended a pendant. Length of shaft 16.2 cm, diameter 0.9 cm.

for the western Great Basin (figs. 7–9). This chapter summarizes this work, adding information from the Upper Snake and Salmon River, northern, eastern, southeastern, and southwestern subareas (fig. 1, table 5).

More than 7,000 artifacts made from ocean shells have been recovered from the six subareas of the Great Basin (85% represent the western subarea). The different species indicate that the occupants of the Great Basin participated in five major exchange networks involving Pacific shell beads and ornaments traded from manufacturing centers in northern, central, and southern California as well as on the Gulf of California and the Oregon-Washington coast (vol. 8:60). While two freshwater shells from the Missouri-Mississippi drainage indicate slight contact with the Plains, no Atlantic species have been found north of the Anasazi area (cf. Tower 1945: frontispiece). In addition to the occasional use of local freshwater shells in the Great Basin, the imported beads and ornaments were often reworked.

Because many shell beads and ornaments recovered from Great Basin archeological sites lack meaningful context, temporal spans were assigned to these speci-

mens by cross-dating them with typologically equivalent forms manufactured in California. Because the dating schemes applied to shell bead and ornament types in California are of comparatively short duration, they do not correspond to the longer cultural periods outlined for the Great Basin. Comparison between the California and Great Basin dating schemes is shown in fig. 10 (cf. Moratto 1984: fig. 4). In general, dating scheme B1 has been followed because it is the most consistent with recent radiocarbon dates from central California.

Upper Snake and Salmon River Subarea

Trade during the Early and Middle Archaic along the Snake River is uncertain. The five distinctive notched shell ornaments assigned to the Birch Creek phase (pre-5000 B.C.) at the Veratic Rockshelter (Swanson 1972:128) presumably represent local freshwater shells. A possible haliotis ornament from the Shoup Rockshelter (Swanson and Sneed 1966:fig. 26s) may represent the Middle Archaic period, but no provenience or description was provided in the published report. The single "tabular shell" ornament assigned to the Beaverhead phase (1000 B.C.–A.D. 400) at the Veratic Rockshelter (Swanson 1972:128) presumably represents local freshwater shell but was not distinguished from the older Birch Creek specimens.

A definite increase in Pacific coast shell bead trade is evident in the Late Archaic along the Snake River and the tributary Birch Creek of the Columbia Plateau.

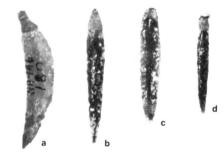

Nev. State Mus., Carson City: a, Wa196–180; b, Wa196–3373, c,Wa196–1195; d, Wa196–1196.

Fig. 6. Bifacially flaked, bipointed obsidian pendants from Kramer Cave, Nev. The sinew wrappings at the base hold fragments of leather cord that probably served for suspension from a garment or necklace. Several examples showed ocher stain on the sinew and the leather cord. Length of b, 5 cm, rest same scale.

Oreg. State Mus. of Anthr., Eugene: a, 1–266; b, 1–264; c, 1–249; d, 1–251.

Fig. 5. Obsidian bifaces from Gold Hill, Oreg. Length of a, 32.8 cm, rest same scale.

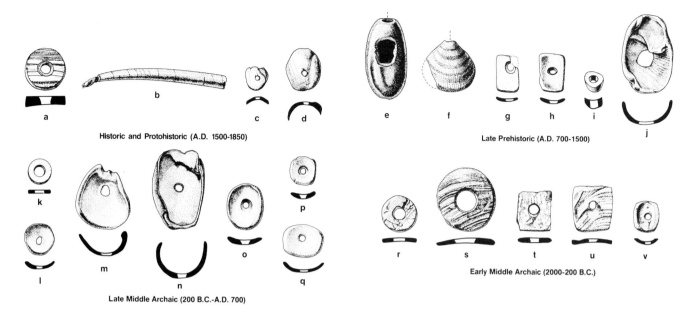

Historic and Protohistoric (A.D. 1500-1850)

Late Prehistoric (A.D. 700-1500)

Late Middle Archaic (200 B.C.-A.D. 700)

Early Middle Archaic (2000-200 B.C.)

U. of Calif., Lowie Mus. of Anthr., Berkeley: a, 1–66305; b, 2–26101; c, 1–188250a; d, 1–65714a; e, 1–45062; g, 2–39552a; h, 1–65717b; j, 1–65708a; k, 1–46120; l, 2–39552b; m, 1–65708c; n, 1–101436b; o, 1–101595c; p, 1–65717a; q, 1–65715; r, 1–164689; s, 1–188227; t, 1–196870a; u, 1–196870b; v, 1–196896. Nev. State Mus., Carson City: f, 1–41–4; i, 1–41–182.

Fig. 7. Shell bead marker types. Historic and protohistoric types: a, *Saxidomus* clam disk, Pe13; b, dentalium, Pe12; c, Olivella Rough Disk, Iny–372; d, Olivella Thin Lipped, Ch15. Late Prehistoric types: e, pine nut bead type II, Ch35; f, *Glycymeris* bead, Ch39; g, olivella pendant, Pe67; h, Olivella Sequin, Ch15; i, Olivella Cupped, Ch39; j, Olivella Shelved Punched, Ch15. Late Middle Archaic types: k, Olivella Ring, Pe66; l, Olivella Saucer, Pe67; m, Olivella Scoop, Ch15; n, Olivella Split Drilled, Las–1; o, Olivella Oval, Las–1; p, Olivella Square Saddle, Ch15; q, Olivella Full Saddle, Ch15. Early Middle Archaic types: r, *Macoma* clam disk, Mod–204; s, *Haliotis cracherodii* ring, Iny–372; t, Haliotis Square, Las–7; u, *Mytilus* Square, Las–7; v, Olivella Thick Rectangle, Las–7. Diameter of a, 1.1 cm, rest same scale. Site designations with 2 letters are in Nev., those with 3 are in Calif.

The Mecham Rockshelter burial near Shoshoni Falls yielded 28 Pacific coast shell beads (27 Olivella Spire-lopped and one tiny section of *Dentalium pretiosum*) along with 10 cylindrical bone beads (Gruhn 1960:9–10). Projectile point types suggest a date of A.D. 700–1200 for this burial. The contemporaneous Blue Dome phase (A.D. 400–1200) on Birch Creek (at the Cottontail Rockshelter) featured an *Olivella biplicata* Spire-lopped bead (type A1b), a *Dentalium pretiosum* section bead, and two freshwater mussel notched pendants (Swanson, Butler, and Bonnichsen 1964:86).

The Shoshonean period (Dietrich phase) on the Upper Snake River is represented in stratum A at Wilson Butte Cave by one complete *Dentalium pretiosum* and two *Olivella biplicata* Spire-lopped beads (type A1a), associated with 12 Shoshone ware sherds (Gruhn 1961:97–98).

The Historic period witnessed an increase in wealth, facilitated by acquisition of the horse and visits by fur traders. The cremations at Rattlesnake Canyon in southwest Idaho (Bonnichsen 1964:31–33) yielded 282 shell artifacts, 149 stone points, 76 bone artifacts, and other offerings. *Olivella biplicata* was represented by 214 specimens—210 Spire-lopped (types A1a, A1b, and A1c) and four centrally perforated circular to oblong beads. *Dentalium pretiosum* was represented by 48

specimens (one complete and 47 sections); at least nine were incised. The two clam disk beads are not identified as to species; these could be from California because the Walla Walla may have visited the Sacramento Valley as early as 1800 (Heizer 1942a:5, note 2), and by this time the Klamath were participating in the Dalles slave trade (Layton 1981:127–130). The remaining 22 shell ornaments (Bonnichsen 1964:fig. 5m-w) appear to include both California abalone and local freshwater shell. The two pieces of copper were the only European artifacts and the absence of glass beads suggests a very early date within the fur trade period. Glass beads and pottery also define the Lemhi phase on Birch Creek at sites 10-BT-51 and 10-CL-100 (Swanson, Butler, and Bonnichsen 1964:82, 96), but no shell beads were in association. The Lemhi phase at Veratic Rockshelter is represented by five glass beads, one whole *Dentalium pretiosum*, and a local freshwater pendant. Bison Rockshelter yielded 16 glass beads and a local gastropod bead (Swanson 1972:127, 143).

Obsidian source analysis has documented some shifts in the nature of prehistoric trade in the Upper Snake and Salmon River region. Jack (1974) conducted an analysis of archeological obsidians from Garden Creek Gap (10-BK-39), Weston Canyon Rockshelter (10-FR-4), and the Rock Creek site (10-CA-33). At Rock Creek,

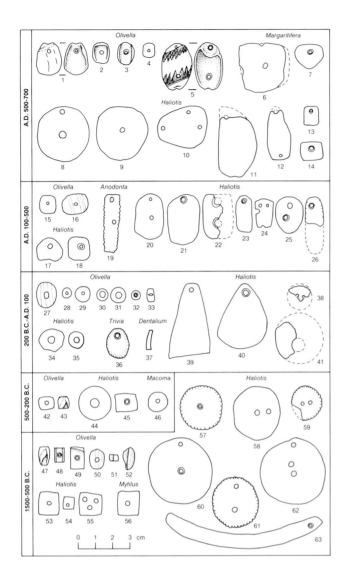

Fig. 8. Shell beads and ornaments of the Middle Archaic period. 1–14 (A.D. 500–700): 1, Olivella Scoop (type C5) Ch15; 2, Olivella Split Drilled (type C2), Ch18; 3, Olivella Oval (type C3), Las–1; 4, Olivella Square Saddle (type F3a), Ch15; 5, Olivella Split Double-perforated incised (type C6i), Ch15; 6, *Margaritifera* bead type 4b, Ch18; 7, *Margaritifera* bead type 3, Las–1. 8–13, Haliotis ornaments: 8, Type uCA2j, Ch18; 9, Type uCA6j, Las–7; 10, Gifford type Q11aII, Iny–372; 11, Type uTA3j, Las–7; 12, Gifford type AC5a, Iny–372; 13, Type uBA3j, Las–1; 14, Haliotis bead type 4c, Las–1. 15–26 (A.D. 100–500): 15, Olivella Square Saddle (type F3a), Las–1; 16, Olivella Full Saddle (type F2a), Las–1; 17, Haliotis bead type 4d, Ch18; 18, Haliotis bead type 4a, Las–1; 19, *Anodonta* ornament type BB6f, Ch13. 20–26, Haliotis ornaments: 20, Type uBA6j, Ch13; 21, Type cBA3j, Las–1; 22, Type cBA8j, Las–1; 23, Type cBB3j, Las–1; 24, Type uPA5j, Las–1; 25, Type rSA6j, Las–1; 26, Type cS(B3)a, Las–1. 27–41 (200 B.C.–A.D. 100): 27–33, Olivella beads—27, Oval (type C3) Wa1016; 28, Small Saucer (type G2a), Ch15; 29, Large Saucer (type G2b), Ch15; 30, Small Ring (type G3a), Pe66; 31, Large Ring (type G3b), CH15; 32, Ground Saucer (type G4), CH18; 33, Small Grooved Rectangle (type N2), Ch18. 34, Haliotis bead type 3a, Wa1016; 35, Haliotis bead type 3c, Ch18; 36, *Trivia* bead, Wa1016; 37, dentalium section, Las–194. 38–41, haliotis ornaments: 38, Type uCA4j, Wa1016; 39, Type cFA3j, Ch18; 40, type cOJ3j, CH18; 41, Type cCC1j, Ny301. 42–46 (500–200 B.C.): 42, Olivella Oval Saddle (type F1), Iny–372; 43, Olivella Barrel (type B3b), Las–7; 44, Haliotis bead type H9, Iny–372; 45, Haliotis bead type la, Ny301; 46, *Macoma* clam disk, Las–7. 47–63 (1500–500 B.C.): 47–52, Olivella beads—47, End-ground (type B2b), Las–7; 48, Small Thick Rectangle, non-shelved (type L2b), Las–7; 49, Large Thick Rectangle, shelved (type Lla); 50, Oval (type C3), Las–7; 51, Cap (type B4a), Ch18; 52, Oblique Spire-lopped (type A2b), Ch13. 53–54, Haliotis bead type la, Las–7; 55, Haliotis bead type 2b, Las–7; 56, *Mytilus* bead type la, Las–7; 57–63, Haliotis ornaments: 57, Type uCA2n, CH18; 58, Type uCA4j, Ch18; 59, Type uCA4n, Las–7; 60, Type uCA6j, Ch18; 61, Type uCA6n, Ch18; 62, Type CA20j, Ch18; 63, Type uAA3j, Las–7.

Jack's analysis of 361 specimens showed that local welded tuff glass was the predominant obsidian employed during the earliest use of the site (J.P. Green's 1972:29 Occupation I, 8500–5900 B.C.). Beginning during the Early Archaic period about 5900 B.C., but peaking in Occupation III and IV times, about 5900 B.C.–A.D. 1, significant quantities of obsidian from Malad, Idaho, were imported to the site, along with lesser amounts of other volcanic glasses from distant Timber Butte and Big Southern Butte. These data also suggest a significant diminution of distant obsidian source procurement at Rock Creek during Late Archaic times. Practically all (97%) of the 85 pieces of obsidian analyzed from Archaic deposits at Weston Canyon Rockshelter came from the nearby Malad source, as did the entire sample (n = 41) of surface-collected artifacts from Garden Creek Gap (J.P. Green 1982:table 12). Sappington (1981, 1981a) has provided compilations of obsidian and vitrophyre source locations that should be invaluable in sourcing research in this area.

Northern Subarea

Prehistoric exchange in shell in the northern subarea is represented by 10 sites, which produced 33 Pacific coast shell artifacts (four genera, six species), four freshwater shell specimens (one genus), and one pine nut bead. Both lack of grave lots and less intensive trade in shell are reflected in these northern data. While the *Olivella baetica*, pine, nut, and many of the *O. biplicata* Spire-lopped beads probably came from northern California, the Olivella Cupped, Sequin, *Macoma* Disk, and Haliotis Square beads probably came from central California. It is hypothesized that the Middle Archaic period dentalium (about 200 B.C.) came from southern California while most of the Late Archaic period dentalium cane from Vancouver Island in the Northwest Coast.

Two northern Great Basin sites document exchange with western groups extending back to 3000–500 B.C. (nine beads). Single Haliotis Square beads (type H1a)

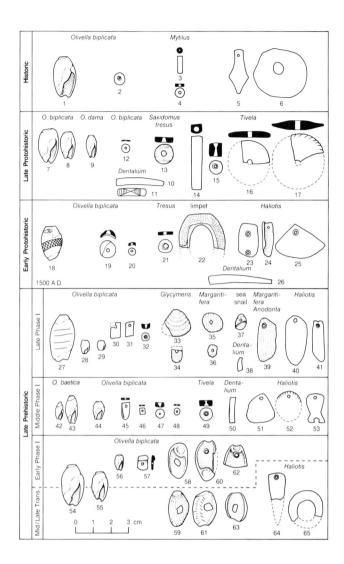

Fig. 9. Shell beads and ornaments of the Late Archaic period. 1–6, Historic (A.D. 1800–1850): 1, Olivella Large Spire-lopped type A1c, site Las–7; 2, Olivella Rough Disk type H2, Ny754; 3, *Mytilus* tube, Death Valley 30–56; 4, *Mytilus* disk, Ny754; 5–6, Haliotis types uNA3j, Ch15, and CD1j, Ch13; 7–17, Late Protohistoric (A.D. 1700–1800): 7–9, Olivella Large, Medium, and Small Spire-lopped, types A1c, A1b, A1a from Ch16, Ch18, Iny–2; 10, dentalium, Ch39; 11, incised dentalium section, Ch15; 12, Olivella Ground Disk H1a, Ch39; 13, *Saxidomus* Medium Disk A2a, Ch15. 14–17, *Tivela*: 14, tube, Death Valley 12–56; 15, thick disk, Iny–2; 16, large disk, Iny–2; 17, large disk, incised, Iny–2. 18–26, Early Protohistoric (A.D. 1500–1700): 18, olivella type A1ciII, Ch39; 19, Olivella Round Thin Lipped E1a, Ch15; 20, Olivella Bushing K2, Ch15; 21, *Tresus* Small Disk A1c, E125; 22, Limpet ring, Death Valley 46A–56; 23, haliotis type uBA8j, Las–1; 24, haliotis type AR1 (Gifford 1947), Death Valley 68–56; 25, haliotis type U4b (Gifford 1947), Death Valley 26–56; 26, whole dentalium, Pe12. 27–41, A.D. 1300–1500: 27–32, olivella: 27, type A1ciI; 28, End-ground B2b, Ch18; 29, Barrel B3a, Ch18; 30, Pendant M2a, Pe67; 31, Rhomboid M2b, Ch39; 32, Cupped K1, Ch39. 33–34, *Glycymeris* whole shell and pendant, Ch39; 35–36, *Margaritifera* types 1 and 2, Las–1, Roaring Springs Cave, Oreg.; 37, sea snail, Iny–372; 38, dentalium section, Ch39; 39, *Margaritifera* pendant, Las–1; 40–41, haliotis types rsB3j, Ch36, and uBB3j, Pe67. 42–53, A.D. 1100–1300: 42–48, olivella: 42, Small Spire-lopped A1a, Las–7; 43, Medium Spire-lopped A1b, Las–7; 44, End-ground B2b, Ch18; 45, Pendant M2a, Ch39; 46, Sequin M1a, Ch39; 47, Cupped K1, Ch39; 48, Tiny Saucer G1, Wa385; 49, *Tivela* Thin Disk, Iny–372; 50, dentalium section, Ch39; 51–53, haliotis: 51, type rOA3j, Las–7; 52, type rCA3a, Pe27; 53, type uJB3j, Wa385. 54–60, A.D. 900–1100. 54–60, olivella: 54, Large Spire-lopped A1c, Las–1; 55, Medium Spire-lopped A1b, Las–1; 56, Small Spire-lopped A1a, Pe67; 57, Sequin M1a, Ch39; 58, Shelved Punched D1a, Ch15; 59, End-perforated C4a, Ch15; 60, End-perforated Segment C4b, Ch15. 61–65, A.D. 700–900: 61–63, olivella: 61, Shelved Punched D1a, Ch15; 62, Shelved Punched Incised D1ai, Ch15; 63, Oval Punched D3, Pe27; 64–65, haliotis types u(E)B3j and uCC1j, Las–1.

occurred in the Silent Snake phase (4000–1500 B.C.) at Hanging Rock Shelter (Layton 1970:101), and in the Bare Creek phase (2000–500 B.C.) at the King's Dog site (O'Connell 1971:121). This type is diagnostic of the Early period (3000–500 B.C.) in central and southern California (see fig. 10) and also was traded into the western Great Basin (Bennyhoff and Hughes 1984). Spire-lopped *Olivella biplicata* (n = 5) and *O. baetica* (n = 2) were stratigraphically associated with these Early beads at Hanging Rock Shelter. Single *Macoma* clam disks at these same two sites are diagnostic of the Transition phase between the Early and Middle periods (500–200 B.C.) in central California.

Some seven beads from three Basin sites represent trade with Middle period groups of central California (200 B.C.–A.D. 700). In addition to four *O. biplicata* Spire-lopped beads (Rodriguez and Cougar Mountain Cave sites), there is one Olivella Square Saddle (site 26Hu16), one Olivella Small Saucer (Rodriguez site), and a worked olivella (Rodriguez). A single dentalium section from a level dated 200 B.C. at the Rodriguez site probably came from southern California.

Trade in the Late Archaic period (A.D. 700–1500) is represented by 13 beads from six Basin sites (Bennyhoff and Hughes 1984). There are four Olivella Spire-lopped beads (at King's Dog, Massacre Lake Cave, and Catlow Cave No. 1), and one Olivella Cupped bead and one Olivella Sequin from Hanging Rock Shelter. Single dentalium sections were found at Massacre Lake Cave, Catlow Cave No. 1, and Blitzen Marsh (Fagan 1974:85), while one pine nut (*P. sabiniana*) bead was found at Roaring Springs Cave. The four *Margaritifera* beads from Roaring Springs Cave are considered local manufactures. The three *O. biplicata* Spire-lopped beads from Fort Rock Cave (n = 2, one incised; Bedwell 1970:168) and 26Hu17 (Bennyhoff and Hughes 1984) cannot be placed in time. It should be noted that there is presently no evidence for Protohistoric (A.D. 1500–1816) or Historic specimens in these northern Great Basin sites. Shoshonean period avoidance of caves and reduced trade with central California are possible explanations. The total absence of haliotis pendants in any period is another indication of limited trade in shell.

A considerable number of obsidian artifacts have been

Table 5. Sources of Great Basin Shell Imports

Gulf of California
  Busycon perversum
  Certithidea californica
  Glycymeris maculatus
  Olivella dama

Southern California
  Amphissa versicolor
  Conus californicus
  Diadora aspera
  Haliotis fulgens
  Megathura crenulata
  Mitra catalinae
  Olivella pedroana
  Tivela stultorum
  Trivia solandri
  Turbinidae
  Turridae
  Haliotis bead type H5, H9
  Haliotis ornament[a] AC5a, AR1, J2aIV, Q11aII, U4b
  Mytilus disk
  Mytilus tube
  Olivella bead type B3, B4, G4, H1a, H2, N2

Central California
  Macoma nasuta
  Saxidomus nuttalli
  Tresus nuttalli
  Olivella bead class F, M
  Olivella bead class C5, G3

Southern and Central California
  Haliotis cracherodii
  Haliotis rufescens
  Haliotis bead type 1, 2, 3
  Mytilus Square bead
  Olivella bead class E, J, K, L
  Olivella bead type A2, B2, C2, C3, D1, G1, G2

Southern California and Vancouver Island
  Dentalium pretiosum

Northern California
  Glycymeris subobsoleta
  Olivella baetica
  Pinus sabiniana

Pacific Coast
  Olivella biplicata bead type A1

Mississippi Drainage
  Lampsila ?
  Lasmigona ?

---

[a] Gifford (1947) typology; other types from Bennyhoff and Hughes (1984).

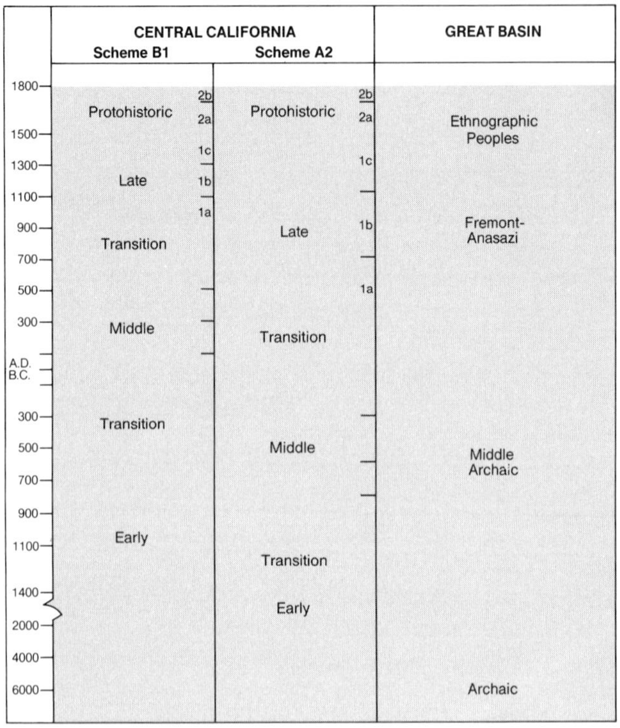

after Bennyhoff and Hughes 1984.

Fig. 10. Correspondence between California and Great Basin cultural periods.

analyzed from the northern area. The principal sites are located in Surprise Valley, northeast California and Nightfire Island in the Lower Klamath Basin.

Source characterization research has been completed on 381 obsidian projectile points from King's Dog (n = 175), Menlo Baths (n = 70), the Rodriguez site (n = 54) (O'Connell 1971, 1975; O'Connell and Ambro 1968), and Bare Cave (n = 82; Brown 1964) in Surprise Valley. The chronological dimension of this study was controlled by using time-sensitive projectile point types marking local phases defined by O'Connell (1971); all obsidian points were stratified by type, and a simple random sample was drawn from each type at each site (Hughes 1983a:197–257). During the Menlo phase, marked by Northern Side-notched points (4500–2500 B.C.), the Warner Mountains obsidian source deposits that border Surprise Valley on the west were the dominant choices for raw material. When Northern Side-notched points were supplanted at the beginning of the Bare Creek phase (about 2500 B.C.) by examples of the Gatecliff series (Split Stem forms, comparable to O'Connell's 1971 Bare Creek Eared), a shift was observed in the source of raw material. There was a greater percentage of obsidian from areas to the east and southeast of the valley at distances of 30–50 kilometers. At the start of the Emerson phase (about 1000 B.C.), Gatecliff Split Stem forms were replaced by the Elko series. Source-specific frequencies of Elko Eared points were essentially identical to those recorded for Gatecliff

Split Stem projectiles, but Elko Corner-notched points were manufactured much more frequently from western Warner Mountains obsidian. Following Elko times, when Rose Spring–Eastgate series specimens were employed during the Alkali phase (A.D. 500–1500), the source-specific frequencies for this type were statistically indistinguishable from Elko Corner-notched frequencies, although they contrasted with those registered for Elko Eared points.

Because of the close proximity of these Surprise Valley sites to obsidian source deposits, the temporal contrasts observed in source use may relate not so much to shifts in trade relations (although this cannot be conclusively ruled out) as to adjustments in response to broader scale environmental and social changes postulated for the valley. For example, the results of obsidian source analysis of Gatecliff Split Stem points would be consistent with what one would expect if, as O'Connell (1971, 1975) postulated, the inception of the Bare Creek phase reflects either a population replacement from the east or a change in the previous settlement-subsistence pattern encouraged by climatic factors unrelated to population change. The source use dichotomy within the Elko series may monitor shifts in the frequency or intensity of prehistoric use of environmental zones in and adjacent to the valley, perhaps reflecting exploitation of game animals residing in different habitats.

A sample of 347 projectile points was analyzed from the Nightfire Island site (Sampson 1985), situated in the Lower Klamath Basin about 145 kilometers west of Surprise Valley, again employing projectile point types for temporal control (Hughes 1983a:118–171). During the time Northern Side-notched points were being used at the site, the obsidian procurement pattern was consistent with what would be expected if Nightfire Island folk enjoyed direct access to the nearest available obsidian outcroppings about 20 miles to the south in the Medicine Lake Highland. When Northern Side-notched points were replaced by examples of the Elko series, distant volcanic glass source materials (probably obtained through trade from the north and northeast) were much more frequently represented. When Gunther series points were introduced, following the period of Elko series point use, there occurred a shift back to high frequencies of Medicine Lake Highland glass, indicating that the obsidian acquisition pattern during the Gunther temporal episode was similar to that registered during Northern Side-notched times.

Western Subarea

The western subarea is represented by more than 6,000 shell specimens from 51 archeological sites (see Bennyhoff and Hughes 1984 for details). An additional 142 specimens lack site provenience (Strong 1969:154–157; Aikens 1972a:9; R.L. Kelly 1983a). No quantification

was given for Cowbone Cave (Orr 1972:125) or Wa525 (Hester 1973:53). Some 16 genera (19 species) represent Pacific coast imports, while two species from the Gulf of California are represented by single specimens (*Olivella dama* and Busycon). *Olivella biplicata* (57%) and haliotis (36%) dominate the collection. *Mytilus californianus* constitutes only 2.4% while all other species represent only 1–33 specimens. Some 193 pine nut (*P. sabiniana*) beads represent imports from northern California.

Three burial sites (Las-7, Ch-18, and Iny-372) yielded 63 percent of the total imported shell artifacts, and the larger collections came from sites near Honey, Pyramid, Winnemucca, Humboldt, Carson, and Mono lakes. Of 3,316 shell specimens associated with 25 burials, 56 percent occurred with six infants and children.

The Early Archaic period in the western subarea is represented by 52 *Olivella biplicata* Spire-lopped specimens assigned to the Humboldt culture at Leonard Rockshelter, dated to 5100 B.C. (Heizer 1951). The most extensive trade between California and the western Great Basin (65% of all phased imported shell) occurred during the early portion of the Middle Archaic period, contemporaneous with the Early period of central and southern California (fig. 10). Early (1950–1650 B.C. dominance of southern California (*Haliotis fulgens, H. cracherodii*; *Amphissa*; Olivella Barrel beads) is evident at Kramer Cave (Hattori 1982), with a later (1500–200 B.C.) shift to central California emphasis (Haliotis Square beads, Olivella Thick Rectangles) at 10 sites, including Lovelock Cave and the Karlo site (Bennyhoff and Hughes 1984).

A dramatic decline in shell trade occurred during the late Middle Archaic period (200 B.C.–A.D. 700), which corresponds to the Middle period in central California. Some 20 sites produced only 9.5% of the phased shell artifacts, particularly Olivella Scoops, Ovals, Saddles and Saucers. Both central and southern California types occur, with local emphasis on freshwater shells.

The Late Archaic period witnessed an increase in trade (20% of the phased specimens at 34 sites), particularly with the San Joaquin Valley (Olivella Shelved Punched) and central California (Olivella Thin Rectangles). After A.D. 1300 there was a shift in emphasis to the northern exchange network, featuring dentalium, Glycymeris, and pine nut beads.

A very sharp reduction in shell trade marks the Protohistoric to early Historic periods (A.D. 1500–1880), when 16 Great Basin sites produced only 4 percent of the phased specimens. Olivella Thin Lipped beads were the most abundant type, but Full Lipped beads and the central California *Saxidomus* and *Tresus* clam disks were unusually rare. Steatite disk beads from the southern Sierra foothills were frequently imported into Owens Valley. Eleven sites yielded a total of 121 glass beads, and a copper pendant was recovered at Pyramid Lake (Ting 1968).

Evidence for obsidian trade comes primarily from two sites, Gatecliff Shelter and Hidden Cave. Very little obsidian was recovered from Gatecliff Shelter (Thomas 1983a), despite the site's proximity to local sources of obsidian nodules. All three flakes recovered from Horizon 12 (3050–2300 B.C.), were from the nearby Box Spring nodule source. No obsidian was analyzed from Horizons 11 or 10, but virtually all the specimens examined from Horizons 9 and 8 (dated to 1450–1300 B.C.) were fashioned from obsidian source materials situated over 175 kilometers to the southwest in the Mono Lake area of California (Hughes 1983). Beginning during Horizon 7 times (1300–1250 B.C.) and continuing through the remainder of the sequence, local Box Spring obsidian was the dominant source represented, though it was accompanied by occasional specimens from Queen, Bodie Hills, a specimen from Casa Diablo, and specimens from unknown sources. These unknown source materials were confined to late temporal contexts (Horizons 1–4; post-A.D. 600). Despite the rather small sample analyzed by X-ray fluorescence (n = 54), the results at Gatecliff suggest that the period between about 1450 and 1300 B.C. witnessed the most intensive contact between users of the site and folk in the Mono Lake area in California. This conclusion is consonant with that reached on the basis of shell bead and ornament analysis (Bennyhoff and Hughes 1984), further supporting the existence of a widespread exchange system during this time.

Analyses of 176 obsidian artifacts from Hidden Cave (Hughes 1985) provided evidence for sustained social contact between groups in the Carson Sink, the Humboldt Sink to the north, and the Mono Lake area to the south. Hidden Cave was utilized primarily as a cache cave, with radiocarbon dates indicating that most cultural debris was deposited between 1800 and 1500 B.C. (Thomas 1985). Nearly 70 percent of the 152 typable obsidian projectile points recovered from excavations were attributable to the Gatecliff series (cf. Thomas 1981), 12 percent were Humboldt Basal-notched forms, while the remaining 18 percent was composed of Elko series, Rose Spring–Eastgate series, and concave base points.

Obsidian came to Hidden Cave from two directions: south and north. Most of the projectile points, finished tool fragments, and unmodified flakes were traced to Mount Hicks and Bodie Hills sources to the south in the Mono Lake area, while lesser amounts of Queen, Pine Grove Hills, Casa Diablo, and Garfield Hills glass accounted for the remainder of the southern total. Primarily during the time that Gatecliff series points were deposited, obsidian from Majuba Mountain to the north also was conveyed to the site, along with a few specimens from more distant sources in northwestern Nevada (Homecamp A and C). No significant north versus south distinctions by projectile point type were ob-

served at the site, with the exception of Humboldt Basal-notched forms. All but one of these Humboldt Basal-notched points were fashioned from southern Mono Lake area obsidians.

About 110 kilometers northwest of Hidden Cave, Hattori (1982) has reported on a series of caves at Falcon Hill at the north end of Winnemucca Lake. On the basis of radiocarbon dates and artifact similarities, it appears that Kramer Cave (the major Falcon Hill site) and Hidden Cave were utilized at the same time (2000–1500 B.C.). If so, human groups using these sites might have been participants in a common interaction network, possibly involving trade in obsidian. However, preliminary analysis of the Kramer Cave assemblage indicates that only one specimen (out of 29 analyzed) was fashioned from southern Mono Lake area obsidian, the majority having been manufactured from volcanic glasses nearer to the site. Thus despite the typological and radiometric correspondences between these Winnemucca Lake and Carson Sink sites, it appears that obsidian was not a typical unit of exchange between these contemporaneous social groups. One implication of this finding for studies of prehistoric Great Basin exchange is that shell beads and obsidian were subject to different principles of procurement and transmission.

Contrasts in obsidian source use also have been observed between different categories of contemporaneous artifacts. In the Mono Lake area, Hughes and Bettinger (1984) found that projectile points were more frequently fashioned from distant source materials, while debitage samples consistently displayed higher frequencies of obsidian from the closest source. Elsewhere, Bettinger (1982a) used contrasting frequencies of Fish Springs obsidian debitage to demarcate a prehistoric territorial boundary in Owens Valley.

Although turquoise outcrops occur in Monitor Valley, including the Indian Blue mine with evidence of prehistoric use (Kramer and Thomas 1983:239), and near Battle Mountain (Crabtree 1974:89), turquoise artifacts are extremely rare. At Gatecliff Shelter a small fragment occurred in Horizon 8 (1300 B.C.) and a possible bead blank was found in Horizon 1 (A.D. 700-historic); other worked pieces occurred at surface sites (Kramer and Thomas 1983:239). A milling slab found on the surface near Battle Mountain retained traces of crushed turquoise and cinnabar (Crabtree 1974), indicating that this blue-green stone may have been used for pigment rather than jewelry.

Eastern Subarea

The two shell ornaments found in the deep levels of Stansbury Cave II represent the Deadman/Wendover phase (Jameson 1958:29) of the Early Archaic (8000–4000 B.C.), but no species identification has been published; the edge incision and exfoliation suggest abalone. The Early Archaic at Danger Cave is represented by two *Olivella biplicata* Spire-lopped (type A1b) or End-ground (type B2) beads from Stratum D III (5150–4620 B.C., Jennings 1957). No other ocean shell was found in the later strata IV–VI. Another early olivella shell was found in Stratum 6 (4010–4450 B.C. at Hogup Cave (Aikens 1970:91), but the type cannot be identified. A fragment of haliotis from Sudden Shelter (Plimpton 1980:153) and at least one *Olivella biplicata* Spire-lopped bead from Cowboy Cave (Lucius 1980:97–98) may represent the Early Archaic.

Middle Archaic specimens from Hogup Cave include an abalone ornament from Stratum 8 (2660–1250 B.C.; Aikens 1970:29, 91), which probably came from the Windmiller culture in central California (sites CA-SJo-112 and CA-SJo-142 have the same type). A pendant from Stratum 9 (1000 B.C. ?) might be *Tivela* clam from southern California (cf. Aikens 1970:fig. 53c). It is likely that the Stratum 12 (970 B.C. ?) *Olivella biplicata* specimen from Hogup Cave was the Split-Drilled bead illustrated in Aikens (1970:fig. 53b). A single Olivella Thick Rectangle (an Early period marker type in California) was found in Shallow Shelter Stratum 4, about 900 B.C. (Dalley 1976:12, 50, 56).

Archaic period obsidian trade was first investigated in the eastern subarea when Condie and Blaxland (1970) analyzed a sample of 92 artifacts from Hogup (n=76) and Danger (n=16) Caves. Because few of the existing source deposits were then known, the authors were unable to assign the artifacts to sources, concluding that "it is probable that the major source represented at Hogup Cave was also the nearly sole source at Danger Cave" (ibid.: 281). Archaic obsidian projectile points from Hogup (n = 20) and Danger (n = 4) caves have been matched with the trace element fingerprinting of Malad, Idaho, obsidian (Hughes 1984), confirming an earlier suggestion by J.P. Green (1982). However, few of the artifacts from Hogup and Danger caves analyzed by Condie and Blaxland (1970:280) possess elemental concentrations similar to those published for Malad (Hughes 1985:table 3; Nelson 1984), suggesting that the source for these specimens must be elsewhere. Nevertheless, the source data indicate that quantities of Malad obsidian reached northwestern Utah (over 250 kilometers from Danger Cave; over 130 kilometers from Hogup Cave) during the Archaic period although it is uncertain how important this source was through time at either site. To determine whether prehistoric exchange relations at Hogup Cave during this period involved importing finished artifacts or blanks to be reduced at the site (cf. Aikens 1970:65–67) will require source analysis of chipping detritus as well as finished artifacts.

Data on the Fremont culture will be presented in terms of the five variants proposed by Marwitt (1970:fig. 84). While shell artifacts have been reported for all five variants, the analyzed sample of obsidian comes primarily from Sevier. Turquoise and lignite beads and pendants have scattered occurrences.

Madsen (1970:69–75, figs. 49–50) has summarized the occurrence of five major plain gray Fremont wares in terms of core areas and distributional limits. All wares except Emery Gray (San Rafael variant) had signficant frequencies in adjacent districts. Fremont wares probably were traded into Anasazi areas, where they were much more common on the Escalante River (Kayenta Anasazi) than on the upper Virgin River (Holmer and Weder 1980:63, 65, tables XVI, XXI). Anasazi trade wares are always rare but were widely distributed, particulary Tusayan Black-on-red (A.D. 1050–1150), which reached Utah Lake (Malouf 1940c:120). The highest frequencies occur at the western border of the Parowan variant, where Virgin series pottery constitutes 8–29 percent of the pottery at Conaway and O'Malley Shelters (Holmer and Weder 1980:66, table XXIV). At Median Village (southern Parowan variant), Kayenta wares represented only 0.4% of the ceramics, while Mesa Verde wares constituted 0.7% (Madsen 1970). Most of the Anasazi wares at the Evans Mound came from within a 120-kilometer arc to the south, while foreign Fremont types came from districts over 160 kilometers to the north and northeast (W.A. Dodd 1982:57). Kayenta wares usually outnumbered Fremont wares on the Lower Muddy River (Area IV of Holmer and Weder 1980:65, table XIX), and Mesa Verde wares ranged from 1 to 4 percent of the ceramics.

More than 187 shell artifacts were found in 23 sites distributed through the five Fremont variants (Bennyhoff 1985). If a necklace (of 79 type C3 beads) is reduced to one occurrence, a less distorted frequency distribution is evident, by which the Parowan variant received the greater share of imported shell. A total of 15 *Anodonta* or *Margaritifera* pendants represent local freshwater shells, all from the Great Salt Lake variant. Another seven specimens represent unidentified shell. If these 22 specimens are omitted some 101 occurrences represent definite imports, and the Great Salt Lake variant was clearly the most isolated.

Some seven genera (at least 11 species) of ocean shells are represented. By far the greatest number of shell artifacts came from the Pacific Coast (143 specimens), with 137 beads representing *Olivella biplicata*. Most of these probably came from southern California, but the center of Punched bead manufacture (for types D1, D2, n=4) appears to be in the San Joaquin Valley. Both these regions were served by the Mohave trade route. The single *Olivella baetica* came from northern waters, while the *O. pedroana*, *Mitra*, and *Tivela* specimens are southern California species.

Definite Gulf of California species were much less frequent (n = 19), but Judd (1919:19) provided no count for the *Olivella dama* beads at Paragonah. At *251* least 17 *O. dama* were documented, while the single *Cerithidea californica* and the single Large Bilobed bead represent unique Great Basin occurrences. These beads apparently moved along the Colorado River route. The absence of Glycymeris is a major contrast with Southwest shell ornaments (Jernigan 1978:figs. 9, 20, 53, pl. 1).

The three freshwater naiad shells (one *Lampsilia* ? and two *Lasmigona* ?) from two southwest Colorado sites (Pine Spring and 48 Sw94, Sharrock 1966:95, 109, 111) were unmodified but had to have been traded in from their native Missouri-Mississippi drainage. Although Tower (1945:frontispiece) placed the southeastern portion of the Colorado Plateau within the limits of trade from the Gulf of Mexico, no Atlantic species have been reported from Fremont sites.

The 165 imported shell beads represent at least 21 types. Bead types and the context indicated that 101 specimens (of 165 imports) represent the early period of Fremont occupation (A.D. 450 to 900). Early types include all the *Olivella biplicata* types B3, C2, C3, C7, *Mitra*, and *Olivella pedroana* as well as the A1 bead from Caldwell Village, and the single Olivella Shelved Punched bead from Backhoe Village. The remaining 64 specimens or 60 occurrences represent the late period of Fremont occupation (A.D. 900 to 1300).

Based on the frequency of occurrence, there is a slight increase in shell trade with the south and west, although the change is not so dramatic as the influx of decorated and corrugated Anasazi pottery. Most, if not all, Gulf of California specimens (*O. dama*, *Cerithidea*, Bilobed) date from the late period. Whereas all five variants received shell beads in the early period, no beads reached the Great Salt Lake or Uinta variants in the late period. This difference strengthens the conclusion that most of the shell beads imported by Fremont peoples came from the south, rather than from the west or north across the Great Basin.

Fremont peoples occasionally reworked the imported *Olivella biplicata* Spire-lopped beads. The Spire-lopped End-perforated bead (type A6; Judd 1926:pl. 46f) from Paragonah is a unique form that has been drilled for suspension. At least two beads from Marysvale (Gillin 1941:pl. Vb, 10, 11) appear to be nonstandardized reworked specimens. The seven type C4, along with eight from the western Great Basin (Bennyhoff and Hughes 1984), represent a type not found in California.

The extent of Fremont trade in turquoise will require geochemical analyses before secure statements about exchange can be advanced. Malouf (1939:5, 1940c:121) indicates that no turquoise deposits are known in Utah, suggesting that early collectors may have confused turquoise with verisite (outcroppings at the south end of Toole Valley and at Lucin) or scorodite (found at Gold Hill, Utah). Therefore, Steward's (1936:48) and Malouf's (1939:5, 1940c:121) reporting of "turquoise" spec-

imens might be questioned. Since only Alexander and Ruby (1963) have reported turquoise artifacts (Evans Mound, n = 2), it may be that many of the early reports cited refer to other blue-green minerals, possibly of local origin.

While locally made bone beads were the most common Fremont ornaments, 21 lignite disk beads were found in three of the variants. The Paragonah site in the Parowan variant yielded nine specimens (F.D. Davis 1956:74; Harrison 1956:103; McBain 1956:54). Backhoe Village in the Sevier variant also yielded nine disk beads (Madsen and Lindsay 1977:67), and the Nephi Mounds produced two (Sharrock and Marwitt 1967:33). A single bead from Oak Creek site 27 represents the San Rafael variant (Morss 1931:60). One possible lignite pendant (edge-perforated disk) from Grantsville represents the Sevier variant (Steward 1936:48). No specific source for this material is documented, but coal deposits exist in Cedar Canyon, 25 miles south of Paragonah (F.D. Davis 1956:74).

Based on extensive sampling and quantitative analysis of obsidian source materials, Nelson (1984; Nelson and Holmes 1979) has begun investigation of Fremont obsidian source use patterns within the eastern subarea. Nelson's research indicates that the Topaz Mountain, Black Rock area, Mineral Mountains, and Modena source areas served as the principal sources for Fremont obsidian artifact manufacture. The majority of archeological artifacts analyzed were fashioned from obsidian from the nearest available occurrence. Although the sample of Fremont period obsidian artifacts is small, (n = 70), there may be emerging contrasting patterns of obsidian acquisition, especially around Utah Lake and south of the Great Salt Lake. Of particular interest is an apparent local shift from use of distant Black Rock area obsidian at the Goshen site during this period to higher frequencies of Malad, Idaho, obsidian recorded at the nearby Williamson site during Shoshonean times. If this is not simply a result of small sample size, the change is significant because the nearby Topaz Mountain obsidian is not well represented at sites around Utah Lake and Great Salt Lake, while it made up the majority of obsidian analyzed only a few miles farther west and southwest. However, the vast majority of specimens so far studied by Nelson have come from Sevier Fremont sites, and few Shoshonean or Middle period site collections have been analyzed.

The Late Archaic period of Shoshonean (A.D. 1300-historic) occupation in the eastern subarea is a single *Tresus* clam disk bead (type Alc) from central California (A.D. 1500–1700) found at Deer Creek Cave in northeast Nevada (Shutler and Shutler 1963:49). The rarity of clam disks, and absence of the contemporaneous Olivella Full or Large Lipped beads and *Saxidomus* clam disks, is one indication of a decline in California–Great Basin shell bead trade during the Protohistoric

252

period. Deer Creek Cave also produced one glass bead and an iron knife blade of the late nineteenth century. One catlinite pipe found on the surface at Kanosh (Steward 1936:50) probably represents the historic period when acquisition of the horse greatly expanded contacts with the Plains. It is of interest that all Southern Ute and Southern Paiute people interviewed by O.C. Steward (1942:277) denied the importation of haliotis necklaces or pendants, as well as (anciently) turquoise. Likewise, the Promontory Point Western Shoshone and Gosiute denied haliotis pendants and olivella and dentalium beads (Steward 1943a:356).

Only 10 samples of eastern subarea obsidian (10% of the subarea total) can be attributed to the Shoshonean period, and all 10 pieces came from two sites (Nelson and Holmes 1979; Nelson 1984). However, of nine specimens analyzed from the Williamson site, five came from the Malad source, two possibly were derived from the Yellowstone National Park area in Wyoming, while two other objects may have come from sources farther south in Utah. The sole Shoshonean specimen analyzed from Fish Spring came from the nearby Topaz Mountain source. Clearly, much more work focusing on Shoshonean sites needs to be done in the eastern subarea before any patterns of resource acquisition and distribution can be discerned.

Southeastern Subarea

Only one site in the southeastern subarea provides evidence for trade in shell during the Archaic period, although extensive evidence exists farther south (Haury 1950). The three "Olivella shells" (probably *O. biplicata* Spire-lopped) from O'Malley Shelter probably date from the Middle Archaic, about 2680–1790 B.C. (Fowler, Madsen, and Hattori 1973:14–15).

A sample of 26 sites occupied between Basketmaker II and Pueblo III times (A.D. 1–1300) yielded a total of 395 shell, turquoise, and lignite beads. Most of these sites display a mixture of Fremont and Anasazi traits, although the ceramics are predominantly Virgin-Kayenta. From the point of view of trade, there can be little question that these sites belong to the Anasazi sphere (cf. Madsen 1982a:23, 25); the southern "boundary" proposed for Fremont by Marwitt (1970, "Fremont Cultures," this vol.) is fully supported by a shift in mortuary and trade patterns. Only one Fremont burial north of this "boundary" had a shell bead; in contrast, 10 burials from six sites (Basketmaker II through Pueblo III) south of this boundary yielded 334 shell, turquoise, and lignite specimens. Some 84.6% of northeast Anasazi imported goods occurred with burials, in contrast to 0.5% of Fremont imported wealth. The richest site in the sample, the Coombs site where two grave lots contained 119 specimens, is just south of the Fremont area (Lister, Ambler, and Lister 1960:263).

Because several large grave lots distort the average frequencies, adjusted frequencies will be given in terms of occurrences in which any necklace or bracelet is counted as a single trading transaction. The 1,011 tiny stone cylindrical beads from a Coombs site burial will be considered local manufactures. Of 58 occurrences of imported wealth, 59 percent are shell items. The majority of these are olivella, and the Gulf of California species (*O. dama*) was more important than the Pacific species (*O. biplicata*; cf. Tower 1945:20); the species frequencies are reversed in the eastern subarea, suggesting the operation of different exchange networks. Haliotis is remarkably rare in both subareas, but only the southeastern subarea obtained "standard" Southwestern types such as Glycymeris and Conus ornaments (both Gulf of California species) as well as the rare *Diadora* (from the Pacific). Despite the large number of shell beads, the southeastern subarea is represented by only five genera (eight species), thus displaying less variation than the eastern subarea (seven genera, 11 species), and far less than the Southwest where 140 sites yielded 82 species as of 1945 (Tower 1945:13).

Perhaps the most striking contrast between the southeastern and eastern subareas is provided by the relative abundance of turquoise in the south. Although represented by only 10 percent of the 58 occurrences, and confined to two Pueblo II–III sites in the sample, the near absence of turquoise in the eastern subarea at sites excavated since 1940 indicates a lack of wealth and different exchange networks. Lignite, on the other hand, was apparently more important in the eastern subarea.

Jack's (1971) study of 217 artifacts from 16 sites in north-central Arizona documented the importance of the Government Mountain–Sitgreaves Peak obsidian source as the dominant one used in obsidian tool manufacture in the vicinity of Flagstaff. Government Mountain obsidian may have been represented at Tyende Mesa, near Kayenta, more than 130 miles to the northeast of the source, although the sample analyzed from Paria Plateau and Cummings Mesa probably was derived from obsidian sources in southern Utah. Nelson's (1984) analysis of a small sample (n = 9) of obsidian from Little Creek Mountain, Utah, the Kaibab Paiute Reservation, Arizona, and the Grand Canyon National Park, Arizona, shows that obsidian from the Modena source in southern Utah was the principal obsidian used at these sites, although the time period represented by these specimens was not identified. No material from Government Mountain–Sitgreaves Peak was identified in Nelson's sample, although the Arizona sites are within the area apparently supplied by this source (Findlow and Bolognese 1982:figs. 3–5). Findlow and Bolognese (1982) delineate three major periods of intensity in obsidian use in the subarea, beginning between A.D. 1 and 700, when moderate amounts of glass circulated. The most intense period of obsidian use apparently occurred about A.D. 700–1150, followed by a significant decline A.D. 1150–1350.

Southwestern Subarea

No clear evidence is available for shell trade in the southwestern subarea during the Archaic period. The two abalone (or freshwater clam ?) pendant fragments from Newberry Cave lack provenience and are not temporally diagnostic (Davis and Smith 1981:79). Some of the "saucer" beads (unquantified) reported by Hunt (1960:270) could represent Middle Archaic specimens, but the associations of most specimens support a Protohistoric placement.

The period from A.D. 900 to 1100 provides good evidence for shell bead trade to judge from the Pueblo II point associations reported for Death Valley. None of the eight *Olivella biplicata* specimens found with two burials at Ubehebe Shelter (Wallace 1978a:129) or Hole-in-Rock Shelter (Wallace 1957:150) can be classified into specific types (five "disk" and three "Olivella beads"). Hunt (1960:123, 146) reports Pueblo II points and one *O. biplicata* Barrel (type B3a, from the Channel Islands) associated with a Death Valley III burial mound.

The period of Shoshonean occupation has the best evidence for trade in shell beads, but Hunt (1960) neither quantified nor classified these late beads. Site occurrence (a maximum of one bead has been counted herein) and rare illustrations allow placement of eight sites and 63 shell specimens from the Channel Islands in the early Protohistoric period, A.D. 1500–1700 (Bennyhoff and Hughes 1984). The Bennett's Well burial had 54 Olivella Thin Lipped beads and two limpet rings in association; seven other sites produced at least four Thin Lipped beads, one limpet bead, and two southern California haliotis ornaments.

The Late Protohistoric period, 1700–1816, may be represented by 16 sites that produced at least 22 specimens. Hunt (1960:144) assigned all olivella "saucers" to the Death Valley IV period; most of these probably represent Wall Disks (type J), but some could be Middle Archaic type G Saucers. Quantification was provided for only one site, so a minimum of one "saucer" bead has been assigned to 15 sites. Two *Tivela* (?) tubes and a haliotis ornament also came from the Pacific, while two *Olivella dama* Spire-lopped beads originated in the Gulf of California.

At least four glass beads, two olivella "saucers," and a Mytilus tube place two of Hunt's Death Valley sites in the Historic period. Cistern Cave produced one Olivella Rough Disk (type H2, an Historic period marker) and a Mytilus disk (Bennyhoff and Hughes 1984). Despite quantification problems, a protohistoric peak in shell bead trade with southern California seems indicated, with a sharp decline in the Historic period. Trade with the Gulf of California was of minor importance.

The southwestern subarea also produced evidence of prehistoric turquoise mining by the Anasazi, beginning perhaps A.D. 400–700 and continuing into the Historic period (Pogue 1915; M.J. Rogers 1929; Ball 1941; Leonard and Drover 1980; Drover 1980). Colberg-Sigleo (1975) matched 13 turquoise beads recovered from the fill in house 8 (a Gila Butte phase structure) at Snaketown to the trace element composition of the Himalaya group of mines in the Halloran Springs area in San Bernardino County, California, over 350 kilometers northwest of the site. The Gila Butte phase has been dated to A.D. 550–700 at Snaketown (Haury 1976:338, table 16.1), suggesting that long-distance trade in turquoise had its roots during the Anasazi period.

The chief sources of obsidian exchanged during prehistoric times in the southwestern subarea were Cosa Hot Springs, near Little Lake (Farmer 1937; Harrington 1951), and Obsidian Butte, near the south end of the Salton Sea (Treganza 1942; Heizer and Treganza 1972:305). Coso Hot Springs obsidian was widely exchanged; it has been identified at Malibu (CA-LAn-324) on the southern California coast nearly 240 kilometers from the source (Meighan 1978; Ericson 1981:191–192), and on Santa Rosa Island off the southern California coast more than 300 kilometers distant (Jack 1976:194). Jack's (1976) data show that Coso Hot Springs glass was used exclusively at sites up to 44 kilometers south and southwest of the source. Work conducted near Fort Irwin in northern San Bernardino County over 135 kilometers southeast of the source provides further documentation for the predominance of Coso obsidian and evidence for occasional importation of specimens from the Queen source. The eastern distribution of Coso Hot Springs obsidian is presently unknown. Obsidian Butte volcanic glass appears to have a much more restricted archeological distribution, confined mainly to Late (California) period sites in the vicinity of the source and westward into San Diego County (Hughes 1986; Hughes and True 1985).

Summary

Trade in Pacific coast shells has been documented archeologically in the Great Basin since Early Archaic times (about 5000 B.C.), represented by specimens from western Nevada and northwestern Utah. Obsidian from southern and southwestern Idaho also may have reached northwestern Utah during this time.

A major trade network is evident in the early Middle Archaic (2000–200 B.C.), when beads and ornaments from southern and central California appear at Honey Lake, Surprise Valley, and Mammoth Creek Cave in California; Carson and Humboldt Sinks, Hanging Rock Shelter, and Gatecliff Shelter in Nevada; and Hogup Cave in Utah. This period also provides the best evidence for obsidian trade, when volcanic glasses from the Mono Lakes area were conveyed northward into the Carson and Humboldt Sinks eastward into Gatecliff Shelter, with occasional pieces reaching Lovelock Cave, Kramer Cave, and sites around Pyramid Lake. Diachronic studies in Surprise Valley and at Nightfire Island revealed shifts in source use patterns during this and subsequent portions of the Late Archaic period.

While the quantity of Pacific shell artifacts declined sharply in the late Middle Archaic (200 B.C.-A.D. 700), the geographic extent of trade expanded to include southern Oregon, southern Utah, and northern Arizona. An increase in the trade of shell artifacts in the Late Archaic period (A.D. 700–1500) is associated with the widest dispersal of Pacific coast shell species, extending to southern Oregon, southern Idaho, and all of Utah as well as northern Arizona. During this time in the eastern subarea, obsidian appears to have been procured primarily from nearby sources, with little evidence for extensive trade. Conversely, the early portion of this period (A.D. 700–1150) in the southeastern subarea witnessed widespread obsidian trade, while a dramatic decrease occurred during the later part (A.D. 1150–1350). Little work has been done on this period in the western subarea, but Gatecliff Shelter results indicate that obsidian trade may have been less widespread than it had been during the early Middle Archaic.

The Protohistoric period (A.D. 1500–1816) witnessed a sharp decline in trade of Pacific coast shell artifacts; Oregon, Idaho, Utah, and northern Arizona were no longer part of the trade networks. However, limited obsidian source analysis indicates that Shoshonean peoples in Utah still obtained volcanic glasses from Idaho and Wyoming.

The Historic period (A.D. 1816-) represents a climax in trade on the Snake River, but a sharp retraction in shell artifact trade in the rest of the Great Basin. Southern California supplied shell beads to Owens Valley, Death Valley, and southern Nevada while central California supplied beads to western and northeastern Nevada. Aboriginal patterns were clearly influenced by acquisition of the horse.

This generalized summary of evidence for prehistoric trade has made it apparent that, although general patterns can be outlined for certain subareas, serious gaps in available knowledge still exist. However, the evidence from the western subarea is complete enough to allow some fairly specific inferences about trade relationships during certain periods of time, particularly in the early Middle Archaic. During this period, it appears likely that obsidian and shell artifacts were transferred through the same trans-Sierran network, probably along the same trails. Whether this pattern applies to later periods and other subareas is unknown. Shell data are available, but only a bare beginning has been made on obsidian source analysis.

Contract Anthropology

DONALD L. HARDESTY, THOMAS J. GREEN AND LA MAR W. LINDSAY

After 1960 the nature of Great Basin archeological and ethnological research was changed by the passage of preservation laws intended to manage archeological sites and other cultural resources (see Fowler 1982 and King, Hickman, and Berg 1977 for a review of this legislation). Cultural Resource Management research goes back at least to the federally funded river basin and reservoir, pipeline, and highway emergency salvage programs of the 1950s and 1960s. Significant examples, if somewhat peripheral geographically, are the Glen Canyon (Jennings 1966), Columbia Basin (Caldwell and Mallory 1967; Sprague 1973), and Watasheamu Reservoir (J.T. Davis 1958; Elsasser 1957a; Rusco 1977) projects. Within the Basin heartland, the earliest significant salvage projects were surveys and excavations of endangered sites within the rights-of-way of highways, pipelines, and reservoirs. These include the Bureau of Reclamation project at Gunlock Flats in southwestern Utah (Day 1966), the Northern Nevada Natural Gas Pipeline right-of-way survey in Nevada and Idaho (Tuohy 1963), and a number of pioneering site excavations sponsored by the Department of Transportation, Federal Highway Administration (Gunnerson 1962; Pendergast 1962; Ranere, Ranere, and Lortz 1969; Swanson and Dayley 1968). These surveys and excavations provided important information about the distribution and content of archeological sites in a few areas, especially southern Idaho, and contributed to various syntheses of Great Basin prehistory (for example, Butler 1978; Swanson 1972, 1974).

Cultural resource management, as such, was effectively launched on a large scale during the 1970s. The passage of key preservation laws by congress (table 1) laid the groundwork for much greater federal involvement in the protection of cultural resources. Because of the vast amount of land under federal ownership, Executive Order 11593, issued in 1971 to implement the 1966 Historic Preservation Act, was the principal stimulus to work in the Great Basin. Following this directive, federal agencies were obligated to sponsor inventories and evaluations of cultural resources on a regular basis. Subsequently, archeologists and ethnologists in the Great Basin became involved with "compliance" studies. The compliance process requires surveys and inventories of the area to determine what resources are likely to be jeopardized, damaged, or destroyed by construction or other activities. Determination of eligibility for listing in the National Register of Historic Places, if cultural resources are located, and the "mitigation" of adverse impacts upon those resources were an integral part of survey assignments. Land-holding agencies, such as the Department of the Interior, Bureau of Land Management and the Forest Service, were required by Executive Order 11593 to inventory cultural resources on the land they administered. Pursuant to this order, summaries of site records and literature, called Class 1 Overviews, were prepared for Idaho (Franzen 1981; Gehr et al. 1982; Wildesen 1982), Nevada (Bard et al. 1981; Bowers and Muessig 1982; Hauck et al. 1979; James 1981; Pendleton, McLane, and Thomas 1982; Smith et al. 1983; Rafferty 1984), Utah (Hull and Avery 1980; James and Singer 1980; Thompson et al. 1983), California (Busby, Findlay, and Bard 1980; Gallegos 1979; Theodoratus Cultural Research 1979; Warren, Knack, and Warren 1980; Warren and Roske 1978), and Oregon (Cultural Resource Consultants 1979; Minor, Beckham, and Toepel 1979). A few surveys also resulted (Bard, Findlay, and Busby 1979; Cinadr 1976; Lindsay and Sargent 1979; Rusco and Munoz 1983). The State Historic Preservation Offices, charged by the 1966 Historic Preservation Act with assisting in the compliance process, have supported some large-scale survey and testing programs (Hardesty, Firby, and Siegler 1982; Pavesic 1979; Plew 1981a);

Table 1. Key Federal Preservation Laws

1906, Antiquities Act (U.S. Code 34 Stat 225)
1935, Historic Sites Act (U.S. Code 49 Stat 666)
1960, Reservoir Salvage Act (U.S. Code 88 Stat 174–175)
1966, Historic Preservation Act (U.S. Code 80 Stat 915, 94 Stat 728)
1966, Department of Transportation Act (U.S. Code 80 Stat 933)
1969, National Environmental Policy Act (U.S. Code 83 Stat 852)
1976, Federal Land Policy and Management Act (U.S. Code 90 Stat 2743)
1978, American Indian Religious Freedom Act (U.S. Code 92 Stat 469)
1979, Archeological Resources Protection Act (U.S. Code 93 Stat 728)

however, most contract anthropology in the Great Basin has been on a much smaller scale, limited to actual impact areas. Typical of these studies are short cultural resources reports issued by the Bureau of Land Management and the Forest Service in the Department of the Interior and by state highway departments evaluating oil, gas, and geothermal leases; seismic lines; reseeding of burned areas; timber sales; development of springs; fenceline erosion; highway construction and repair; housing developments; pipeline and transmission line right-of-ways; and recreational events and facilities.

Unlike traditional academic research, the location of contract anthropology studies is controlled not by research problems but by sponsor needs. For this reason, information about the Great Basin, originating in the provisions of preservation laws and policies, does not give a good geographical cross-section but tends to be clustered in certain areas. Table 2 lists major cultural resource management projects by geographical locality. A few factors stand out as especially important in influencing where these studies take place. For example, the presence of large tracts of marketable timber in southern Idaho has resulted in a large number of surveys. Likewise, the major river systems in the same area have been associated with hydroelectric power plant construction, resulting in projects at specific archeological sites. The search for new energy and mineral sources has been particularly important throughout the Great Basin. In the geological overthrust belt region of eastern Nevada and Utah, many oil, gas, and geothermal leases and drilling projects were begun in the 1970s; these have generated a tremendous volume of reports mostly containing survey data. The dramatic rise in gold and silver prices during the same period encouraged the redevelopment of old mining areas throughout the Great Basin, as well as new exploration and a corresponding activity in research (for example, Berge 1974; HCRS/NAER 1980; Janetski 1983; Madsen 1983; Pippin 1980). Population growth was another factor. The Great Basin has also experienced an accelerated immigration of new industries and retired citizens; consequently, some rapidly growing cities and towns required surveys and mitigation for housing developments, highway construction, waste disposal, and energy.

Unique historical events may be determinants of where contract anthropology takes place. For example, perhaps the largest project ever planned in the Great Basin emerged from the proposed installation of the MX ballistic missile system. In the 1970s the U.S. Air Force developed plans to build a system of 2,300 missile shelter sites, along with related logistical support such as roads and housing complexes, in 32 hydrologic basins in Nevada and Utah. Cultural resources in an area of about 20,000 square miles would have been affected. Although the Nevada-Utah MX basing plan was elim-

Table 2. Major Cultural Resource Management Projects in the Great Basin

IDAHO
Weiser River Valley (Bowers 1967, ISHS; Pavesic 1979; Ruebelman 1973; Warren, Wilkinson, and Pavesic 1971)
South Fork of Salmon River (Boreson 1979)
Middle Fork of Salmon River (Knudson, Jones, and Sappington 1982; Pavesic 1978; Rossillon 1980; Wildesen 1982; IMUSFS)
South Fork Payette River (Ames 1982a)
Sawtooth Valley (Gallagher 1979, IMUSFS; O'Connor 1974; Sargeant 1973)
Boise Basin (Jones, Davis, and Ling 1979)
Boise River (Jones 1980, 1982; Knudson, Jones, and Sappington 1982; Sappington 1981b)
Bennett Hills (Cinadr 1976)
Snake River Canyon (Ames 1983, ISHS; Carley and Sappington 1982; T.J. Green 1982, ISHS; Keeler and Koko 1971, ISHS; Landis and Lothson 1983; Lothson and Virga 1981; Ostrogorsky 1981, ISHS; Ostrogorsky and Plew 1979, ISHS; Pavesic and Meatte 1980; Plew 1981a; Tuohy 1958, ISHS)
Owyhee Mountains (Moe 1982)
Owyhee Plateau (Plew 1980, 1981; Tuohy 1963)
Bruneau River (Pavesic and Hill 1973, ISHS)
Rosevear/Deadman/Saylor Creek (Western Snake River Plain) (Bucy 1971, ISHS; K. A. Murphey 1977; Pavesic and Moore 1973, ISHS)
Salmon Falls/Devil's Creek (K. A. Murphey 1977a; Tucker 1976)
Twin Falls/Burley (Eastern Snake River Plain) (Butler and Waite 1978)
Cassia Hills (Bousman, Cheek, and Leonhardy 1979, ISHS; J. P. Green 1972; Skinner 1981, IMUSFS)
Little Lost River–Birch Creek (Kingsbury 1977)
Challis (Epperson 1977)
Eastern Snake River Plain (Franzen 1980, 1980a, ISHS; Kimball 1976; Ranere, Ranere, and Lortz 1969; D. G. Roberts 1976)
Island Park (MacDonald 1982, ISHS; Pippin and Davis 1980, ISHS, DRI)
Willow Creek (Butler et al. 1976; W.R. Powers 1969)
Blackfoot Reservoir (Miss 1974, ISHS; Neudorfer 1976)
Bannock Mountains (Franzen 1977; Swanson and Dayley 1968)
Southwest Idaho Transmission Line (Moe, Eckerle, and Knudson 1980)
Obsidian Research Project (J.P. Green 1982, ISHS; Sappington 1981)
U.S. Forest Service Timber Sale Program (Wylie and Flynn 1977, IMUSFS; Wylie 1978, IMUSFS; Wylie and Ketchum 1979, 1980, IMUSFS; Gallagher 1981, 1983, IMUSFS)
Idaho Transportation Department Projects (Gaston 1981, 1982, 1983, IDOT, ISHS)
Rocky Mountain Cabin Project (M.A. Wilson 1981)
Lieu Lands Survey (Harrison, Green, and Burnett 1978, IBLM)

NEVADA
Moapa Valley (Ellis 1982, NSM, UNLV; Warren 1982, NSM, UNLV; Kirkberg 1980, NSHPO; Lyneis 1980, UNLV; Warren et al. 1978, NSM, UNLV; Brooks et al. 1977, UNLV; McClellan, Phillips, and Belshaw 1980)

Las Vegas Valley (Page and Associates 1978, NSHPO; Rafferty 1984)

Spring Mountains (Brooks et al. 1981, NSM, UNLV)

Rossi Mine (Rusco 1982, NSM)

Yucca Mountain/Nevada Test Site (Pippin and Zerga 1981, DRI; Pippin, Clerico, and Reno 1982, DRI)

Black Rock Desert (Jones 1980, NBLM; Lohse 1979, NSM; Seck 1980; Clewlow 1983, NSM)

Black Rock Range (Clewlow 1981, NSM; Elston and Davis 1979, UNR, NSM)

Rye Patch Reservoir (Rusco et al. 1977, 1979, 1982, NSM)

Valmy (Bard 1980, NSM; Napton and Greathouse 1979, NSM; Davis, Fowler, and Rusco 1976, DRI; Busby and Bard 1979, NSM; Elston et al. 1981, DRI; Ancient Enterprises 1980, NSM)

Carson Desert/Carson Sink (Bard, Busby, and Findlay 1981; Hardesty 1979, NSM, NBLM; Bard, Findlay, and Busby 1979, NBLM; Busby, Kobori, and Nissen 1975, NBLM; Hattori and McLane 1980, DRI; Bard, Busby, and Kobori 1980; Hatoff and Thomas 1981)

Carlin (Clerico 1983, IMR; Rusco, Davis, and Jensen 1979, NSM)

Pine Forest Range (Elston, Covington, and Davis 1978, UNR, NSM; Roney 1977, NSM; James 1978, NSM)

Railroad Valley (Elston, Davis, and Clerico 1979, UNR)

Lovelock (Hattori, Rusco, and Tuohy 1979, NSM)

Smokey Valley (U.S. Forest Service project at Jefferson City)

Sheldon National Wildlife Refuge (Elston and Earl 1979, UNR, NSM)

Walker River/Wassuk Range (Rusco and Dansie 1977, NSM; Pippin 1980; Pippin et al. n.d., DRI; E. Seelinger 1978, NSM)

Desatoya Mountains (Tuohy 1974b; Hardesty 1979, NSM, NBLM)

Dixie Valley (Botti 1981, NSM)

Washoe Valley/Carson Range (Elston 1976, NSM; Hardesty and Elston 1979, NSM; Turner and Turner 1979, NSM)

Virginia Range (Hardesty, Firby, and Siegler 1982; HCRS/NAER 1980)

Lake Tahoe/Truckee River (Miller and Elston 1979, UNR; Turner et al. n.d., NDOT; Fowler, Elston, and Hamby 1981, UNR; Elston et al. 1977, UNR)

Pyramid Lake (Tuohy and Clark 1979, NSM; Seelinger, Brown, and Rusco 1979, NSM)

Cortez (Hardesty and Hattori 1982, NBLM)

Carson River (Rusco 1977; Turner 1980, NSM; Hattori 1978, NSM; Elston 1979, UNR, CT)

Bird Springs Range (Clewlow and Wells 1980, NSM)

Mormon Mountains (Rusco and Munoz 1983)

Pine Valley (Turner, Stearns, and Turner 1979, NSM)

Schell Creek (Seelinger 1978, NSM; Fowler 1975, DRI; 1976, NSM)

Mt. Moriah/Snake (Seelinger 1978a, NSM; Wylie 1974, IMUSFS)

Tonopah (McGonagle and Waski 1978, NBLM; Thomas 1977, NSM)

Wilson Creek/White River (James 1979, NSM; Brooks et al. 1977, UNLV)

MX Project (HDR Sciences 1980, 1980a)

Intermountain Power Project (Fowler et al. 1978, DRI; Fowler, Pippin, and Budy 1978, DRI; Stoffle and Dobyns 1983; Tucker 1982, NSM)

Nellis Air Force Base Project (Bergin 1979, UNLV, NBLM; Bergin and Roske 1978, UNLV, NBLM; Crownover 1981, UNLV, NBLM)

Nevada State Historic Preservation Plan (Lyneis 1982, NSHPO)

U.S. Department of Energy Survey of Historic Structures (Kensler 1981, DRI)

White Pine Power Project (Zeier 1981)

Navajo-McCullough Transmission Line (Brooks et al. 1975, UNLV)

Allen-Warner Valley Energy System (Barker, Rector, and Wilke 1979, NSM, NBLM; Bean and Vane 1979, NBLM)

CALIFORNIA

Mojave Desert (Brooks, Wilson, and Brooks 1980, DPU; Coombs 1979, 1979a, DPU; King and Casebier 1976, DPU; Gallegos 1979; Lyneis 1980, UNLV; Warren and Roske 1978)

Death Valley National Monument (Craib 1978, WAC-NPS; Greene and Latschar 1980, DVNM; Hardesty 1981, UNR, DVNM)

Owens Valley (Busby, Findlay, and Bard 1980)

Lava Beds (Hardesty and Fox 1974, UNR)

Hallelujah Junction/Stead (Elston 1979; UNR, CT)

Joshua Tree National Monument (King 1975, WAC-NPS; Parker 1980)

Intermountain Power Project (Bean and Vane 1982; Macko et al. 1982)

Allen-Warner Valley Energy System (Barker et al. 1979, NSM, NBLM; Bean and Vane 1979, NBLM)

OREGON

Lake Abert (Pettigrew 1981, OSPHO)

Fort Rock Basin

Burns District BLM Reseeding Projects

Pacific Power and Light Transmission Line Surveys

Bonneville Power Administration Transmission Line Surveys

UTAH

Wasatch Plateau (Aikens 1966b; Berge and Nielson 1978, IMUSFS; Holmer 1978a, UUDA; Jennings, Schroedl, and Holmer 1980; Nielson 1976, 1976a, BYU; Simms 1979, 1979a, UDSH)

Wah Wah Mountains (Berge 1974)

St. George Basin (Day 1966)

Santa Clara River (Gunnerson 1962; Pendergast 1962)

Salt Lake Valley (Hawkins 1981, UDSH)

Clear Creek (Hawkins and Dobra 1982, UDSH; Lindsay 1979, UDSH)

Escalante Desert (Holmer and Janetski n.d. UDSH; Janetski 1981, UDSH)

Oquirrh Mountains (Janetski 1983; Madsen 1983)

Colorado River (Jennings 1966)

Deep Creek Mountains (Lindsay and Sargent 1979)

Boulder Mountain (Lister and Lister 1959–1961, UDSH)

Table 2.   Major Cultural Resource Management Projects in the Great Basin (*continued*)

Fish Springs (Madsen 1982b)

Sevier Valley (Madsen and Lindsay 1977, UDSH)

Parowan Valley (Marwitt 1970)

MX Project (Woodward-Clyde Consultants 1980, UDSH; Holmer and Janetski n.d., UDSH)

Intermountain Power Project (Janetski and Holmer 1982, UDSH; Stoffle and Dobyns 1982)

BLM Pony Express and Historic Railroads Project (Fike and Headley 1979; Raymond and Fike 1981)

Key to Report Repositories

AMNH	American Museum of Natural History, New York
BBLM	Bakersfield District, Bureau of Land Management, Department of the Interior, Bakersfield, California
BYU	Brigham Young University, Department of Anthropology and Archaeology, Provo, Utah
CT	CALTRANS, California Department of Transportation, Sacramento
DPU	Desert Planning Unit, Bureau of Land Management, Department of the Interior, Riverside, California
DRI	Desert Research Institute, University of Nevada, Reno
DVNM	Death Valley National Monument, Death Valley, California
IBLM	Idaho State Office, Bureau of Land Management, Department of the Interior, Boise
IDOT	Idaho Department of Transportation, Boise
IMR	Intermountain Research, Silver City, Nevada
ISHS	Idaho State Historical Society, Boise
IMUSFS	Intermountain Region Office, U.S. Forest Service, Department of Agriculture, Ogden, Utah
NBLM	Nevada State Office, Bureau of Land Management, Reno
NDOT	Nevada Department of Transportation, Carson City
NSHPO	Nevada State Historic Preservation Officer, Carson City
NSM	Nevada State Museum, Carson City
OBLM	Oregon State Office, Bureau of Land Management, Department of the Interior, Portland
OSHPO	Oregon State Historic Preservation Officer, Salem
UO	University of Oregon, Department of Anthropology
UBLM	Utah State Office, Bureau of Land Management, Department of the Interior, Salt Lake City
UDSH	Utah, Division of State History, Antiquities Section, Salt Lake City
UNLV	University of Nevada, Museum of Natural History, Las Vegas

Table 2.   Major Cultural Resource Management Projects in the Great Basin (*continued*)

UNR	University of Nevada, Special Collections Library, Reno
UUDA	University of Utah, Department of Anthropology, Salt Lake City
WAC-NPS	Western Archeological Center, National Park Service, Tucson, Arizona

NOTE: References followed by acronyms are unpublished works that may be found in the repository indicated; they are not in the volume bibliography.

inated in 1981, some planning and surveys preliminary to the evaluation of the project's impact upon cultural resources did take place (for example, Desert Research Institute 1981; Fowler et al. 1980; HDR Sciences 1980, 1980a). Unlike energy and population growth, unique projects such as the MX system have no predictable geographical locations; therefore, many cultural resource management studies are rather randomly scattered across the Great Basin.

While the search for archeological sites has been the overriding concern of cultural resource management efforts in the Great Basin, the legal definition of "cultural resource" has been expanded by legislation to include all significant historic, cultural, and natural aspects of the national heritage (Laidlaw 1982). In response to this change, a few ethnographic studies have been done under the auspices of preservation laws and policies to identify and document cultural resources that are important to contemporary people. Both the Intermountain Power Pipeline project (Stoffle and Dobyns 1982, 1983) and the MX project (HDR Sciences 1980, 1980a) include such studies. Ethnographic contract anthropology is centered upon the comments and interpretations of participants in contemporary cultures. For example, the interpretation of the American Indian Religious Freedom Act of 1978 defines Native American religious leaders and practitioners as the appropriate group to review and comment upon the management of ritual and sacred properties. Some difficulty has been encountered in finding people who are willing to play this role. Since about 1970 Native Americans in the Great Basin have increasingly acted in the political arena in matters concerning land, water, and other scarce natural resources (Clemmer 1974; Hanes 1982; Stoffle and Dobyns 1982, 1983), though such activity has not been so intensive as in California, the Plains, or the Southwest. A series of court decisions against the provisions of the American Indian Religious Freedom Act and other Native American religious claims may have had some effect in this regard. For example, both the federal district court and the court of appeals rejected the claim by some members of the Navajo tribe

259

Utah State Histl. Soc., Antiquities Section, Salt Lake City: 425v–662.

Fig. 1. Salvage excavation at Backhoe Village, a Sevier Fremont site in western Utah. Excavation proceeded while Sevier Valley Technical School was constructed. The site was named from the use of backhoes to test the broad extent of the site surface and remove overburden from cultural features. Photographed in 1976–1977.

U. of Nev., Dept. of Anthr., Nev. Archaeol. Survey, Reno.

Fig. 2. Excavation prompted by construction on U.S. 395 near Hallelujah Junction, Nev. Because the work was done under deadlines, backhoes were used to test site deposits. Cultural features, once exposed, were meticulously examined. As in most contract work, the rule was to use the coarsest possible tool consistent with the time problem and the judicious allocation of effort and money. Photographed in 1975.

that the federal government's operation of the Glen Canyon Dam and management of the Rainbow Bridge National Monument denied the Navajo access to a sacred prayer place and attracted tourists, which prevent conduct of traditional religious ceremonies (*Badoni* v. *Higginson* 1980); however, the U.S. District Court of Northern California ruled in favor of a similar claim (*Northwest Indian Cemetery Protective Association and Others* v. *Peterson and others* 1983). The claim challenged a decision by the Forest Service to complete a section of paved road from Gasquet, California, to Orleans, California, and to implement a plan to harvest timber in one part of the Six Rivers National Forest. Both projects, it was argued, would violate a region traditionally used for religious purposes by the Yurok, Karok, and Tolowa tribes of California. This decision may well bring sacred sites and similar cultural resources in the Great Basin further into the political arena, as well. The principal reason is that the role of sacred places as symbols around which Native American traditionalists can rally is greatly strengthened by the legitimacy of the American Indian Religious Freedom Act in the federal courts.

Although cultural resources management research in the Great Basin is a major source of data upon which archeological interpretation is anchored, there are several key problems with it. Perhaps the most immediate of these is data retrieval—gaining rapid access to what information is already gathered. Nearly all reports are unpublished typed manuscripts stored in local and regional repositories (see table 2). For example, the Idaho State Historical Society, Boise, the Nevada State Museum, Carson City, and the Utah Division of State History, Salt Lake City, have copies of most cultural resource management documents for their respective states. Additional copies of some literature can be found in district offices of the Department of the Interior Bureau of Land Management and Forest Service, as well as state highway departments, among others. Retrieving the information that these reports contain is time consuming and expensive; paradoxically, it is precisely this information that is used in making decisions about site significance and the like. To alleviate this problem, several federal and state agencies and universities in the Great Basin have experimented with the Intermountain Antiquities Computer System, administered by the University of Utah, to facilitate data retrieval. Another response to the data retrieval problem is a change in policy in the state historic preservation offices. They have shifted their granting and staff priorities away from surveys and toward data retrieval systems and long-range planning, especially the development of regional predictive models.

A second major problem with contract anthropological research in the Great Basin is the lack of integration of data coming from surveys and data coming from excavation projects. Survey data are by far the most abundant but are of limited value for understanding Great Basin prehistory and ethnology, although information about the kind of archeological sites and where they occur can be obtained. Both types of information are useful for comparative studies and for studies of site distribution. At the same time, it is clear that most surveys yield information only about surface manifestations and not about the buried portion of sites. Furthermore, the often random scattering of studies raises questions about the geographical coverage of survey data. Finally, artifacts visible on site surfaces are sometimes removed from their original archeological context. Without context, functional and diachronic interpretations of artifacts and archeological sites are next to impossible. All these limitations can be overcome by combining survey data with detailed information from excavations of particular sites. Unfortunately, cultural resource management excavation projects are few and far between and for the most part do not occur in places where the best survey data are available. The most likely solution is the detailed investigation of sites carefully selected to provide linkages to survey data. Such investigations would generally have to be undertaken by academic institutions and traditional academic research efforts.

The final problem with contract anthropology that is likely to affect its future viability is the quality of data gathered by such projects. Severe time and money limitations have always attended these projects, raising questions about the care with which data have been collected. Questions have also been asked about the professional qualifications of some researchers, many of whom have not completed traditional academic training programs. The emergence of professional societies, such as the Utah Professional Archeological Council and the Nevada Council of Professional Archaeologists, is a positive response to this problem.

Western Shoshone

DAVID HURST THOMAS, LORANN S.A. PENDLETON, AND STEPHEN C. CAPPANNARI

The Western Shoshone (shō'shōnē) inhabited one of the last areas in the continental United States to be settled by Euro-Americans, and the persistence of much native culture into relatively recent times has added greatly to ethnographic and theoretical interest in these tribes.

Territory

Western Shoshone country extended from the arid reaches of Death Valley inhabited by the Panamint Shoshone, through the mountainous highlands of central Nevada into northwestern Utah, where it encompassed the area of the Gosiute of Tooele and Skull valleys and Deep Creek and the "Weber Ute." The northern boundary is rather arbitrarily taken as roughly the divide separating the Humboldt River drainage from the Snake and Salmon River area, where the Northern Shoshone lived; the people of the Duck Valley Reservation are also included (fig. 1). The Snake and Boise river groups, including the Bannock Creek people, who extended as far south as the northern end of Great Salt Lake, fall within the scope of the chapter "Northern Shoshone and Bannock." Western Shoshone territory was sparsely inhabited in historic times, and boundaries tended to be fluid, engendering continuing debate (see particularly Kroeber 1925; Steward 1937b, 1938, 1939; Driver 1937; Park et al. 1938; Malouf 1940; Grosscup 1977).

Despite a high incidence of intermarriage with Ute neighbors, the Gosiute remained culturally and ecologically similar to, if somewhat more impoverished than, the Western Shoshone of Nevada, and accordingly they are treated here (Steward 1937b:627, 1938:123, 133–135, 1940:474–475, 1943a:263; Malouf 1940:52; see also Collins in J.H. Simpson 1876:467, App. P). The Indian Claims Commission in 1962 found the Gosiute to be a landholding entity separate from the Western Shoshone (O.C. Stewart 1978).

Language

The Western Shoshone peoples all spoke varieties of Central Numic, a component of the Numic ('numik) branch of the widespread Uto-Aztecan family. Central Numic comprises three languages, Panamint, Shoshone, and Comanche, of which Panamint was spoken by the Panamint Western Shoshone and Shoshone by the other Western Shoshone (including the Gosiute), the Northern Shoshone, and the Eastern Shoshone. The Western Shoshone are therefore not a discrete linguistic group but strictly a culturally delimited ethnic entity. There is some dialectal diversity within Shoshone,* but the local speech varieties tend to intergrade, and even the separate Panamint language† is not sharply distinct

*The phonemes of Shoshone are: (stops and affricate) *p, t, c, k, k^w, ?*; (continuants) *s, h*; (nasals) *m, n*; (semivowels) *w, y*; (short vowels) *i, e, a, o, u, i*; (long vowels) *i·, e·, a·, o·, u·, i·*. The pronunciation of the consonants varies greatly in some cases depending on the environment. In initial position the oral stops are voiceless and unaspirated; in other positions they are pronounced as follows: (between vowels) [β], [r], [z], [γ], [γʷ]; (with preceding nasal) [mb], [nd], [nʒ], [ŋg], [ŋgʷ]; (geminated) [p·], [t·], [t̯·s], [k·], [k·ʷ]; (with preceding *h*) [ɸ], [R], [s], [x], [xʷ]. After a front vowel (*i, i·, e,* and *e·*) the following different pronunciations of *t* and *c* occur: *t* [δ], *c* [ž]; *nc* [nʒ]; *cc* [č·]; *ht* [θ], *hc* [š]. *s* is [s·] between vowels, [š·] after a front vowel. The word-medial pronunciations of the nasals are: (between vowels) *m* [w̃] (nasalized [w]), *n* [n ~ ỹ] ([ỹ] is nasalized [y]); *mm* [m·], *nn* [n·]; *hm* [hw̃], *hn* [hn ~ hỹ].

The pronunciation of Shoshone words often differs in different parts of the extensive territory over which it is spoken and even from speaker to speaker. For example, there is a great deal of variation between *ai* and *e*; in Gosiute Shoshone word-initial *h* is dropped; intervocalic *m* is often replaced by *w*; other examples are given by Miller (1972:15–16). Sources differ on the analysis and transcription of word-final voiced vowel or [?] followed by an echo vowel as -?, ? plus vowel, or nothing and in the use of word-final -*h* to indicate vowel devoicing, and the *Handbook* transcriptions have not resolved these inconsistencies.

In the practical orthography used by Miller (1972) the phonemes of Shoshone are spelled as follows: p, t, ts, k, kw, '; s, h; m, n; w, y; i, *ai*, a, o, u, e; ii, *aai*, aa, oo, uu, ee.

Information on Shoshone phonology is from Miller (1972; see the sketch on the Shoshone language, vol. 17); Shoshone words appearing in italics in the *Handbook* have been written in the phonemic orthography by Wick R. Miller and Sven Liljeblad (communications to the editors 1985).

†The phonemes of Panamint are: (stops and affricate) *p, t, c, k, k^w, ?*; (continuants) *s, h*; (nasals *m, n, ŋ, ŋʷ*; (semivowels) *w, y*; (short vowels) *i, e, a, o, u, i*; (long vowels), *i·, e·, a·, o·, u·, i·*; (diphthong) *ai*. The word-medial pronunciations of the consonants are generally like those of Shoshone. Information on Panamint phonology and the transcriptions of Panamint words cited in the *Handbook* in italics are from McLaughlin (1984).

from adjacent Shoshone dialects ("Numic Languages," this vol.).

History

Euro-American Contact

Jedediah Strong Smith traversed Western Shoshone territory in 1827 (G.R. Brooks 1977), establishing initial Euro-American contact with many Western Shoshone groups, including the Gosiute of Deep Creek and Skull Valley (Malouf 1940:59). Peter Skene Ogden, who traveled in the northern Great Basin from 1828-1829, also briefly mentioned the Shoshone (Cline 1963).

In 1830-1831, Zenas Leonard (of the Benjamin Bonneville–Joseph Reddeford Walker party) scornfully recorded the absence of the horse among the natives near the Humboldt River and described the heavy burdens that the women had to carry (Leonard 1904). Horses, of course, would have consumed the same staple grasses that the Shoshone harvested in great abundance for themselves. John C. Frémont (1845, 1887) crossed central Nevada in 1845, camping in Big Smoky Valley among other places, noting various aspects of Indian life; Frémont also passed through northern Gosiute territory in 1845 (Malouf 1940:62). The detailed accounts of James H. Simpson (1869, 1876) for 1849 and 1869 and Egan (1917) for 1847 are perhaps the earliest ecologically and ethnographically relevant statements on the Western Shoshone.

Euro-American settlers of the mid-nineteenth century had a far greater impact upon the Western Shoshone than did earlier explorers and trappers (Rusco 1976). The Gosiute were heavily impacted by the establishment of the Church of Jesus Christ of Latter-day Saints, the Mormons, in their territory as early as 1847 (Egan 1917; Malouf 1940:63, 77). Euro-American penetration into and through Western Shoshone territory was accelerated by the discovery of gold in California in 1848 and at Gold Canyon on the Carson River the next year. But the greatest single impetus to the Euro-American settlement of Nevada was the discovery of the Comstock lode in 1857.

Reservation Period

There were no true reservations in the Great Basin prior to 1860, although reserves (or "farms" as they were called) had been established in Ruby Valley and Deep Creek Valley as early as 1858 (Egan 1917; Forbes 1967:3; Inter-Tribal Council of Nevada 1976b:33-35). During the early 1860s a few Western Shoshones engaged in hostilities against the settlers moving along the Humboldt River and along the Overland Stage route. There is some evidence that occasionally local Euro-American farmers encouraged and even directly assisted the West-

ern Shoshone in their raids upon the emigrant caravans (Forbes 1967:48). Fort Ruby was established in part to curtail such activities, and the federal government began negotiating treaties with the tribes of the Great Basin.

The Treaty of Ruby Valley was signed on October 1, 1863, and the Treaty of Tooele Valley with the Gosiute was signed on October 12. Gov. James Nye of the Nevada Territory and Gov. James D. Doty of the Utah Territory represented the United States government, and 12 "captains" or chiefs represented the Indians, collectively termed the "Western Bands of Shoshone" to distinguish them from the Gosiute Shoshone to the east and the Northern Shoshone in Idaho and Utah (O.C. Stewart 1978, 1980:253).

As part of the 1863 treaty, the Western Shoshone agreed to cease hostilities against immigrants and officers of the federal government. The treaty further formalized the settlers' right to establish various forms of commerce. The Western Shoshone also agreed to "abandon the roaming life" and live upon reservations at an unspecified time to be determined by the president of the United States. In return for these concessions, the Treaty of Ruby Valley promised the Shoshone 10 annual payments of $5,000 each, to be delivered in provisions, clothing, and livestock. It is significant that, although the captains agreed to tolerate further White incursions, at no time did the Western Shoshone actually surrender their lands (O.C. Stewart 1978). The work of the Indian Claims Commission, established in 1946, underscores the complexity of the problem. When the commission was dissolved in 1978, the unresolved cases were transferred to the U.S. Court of Claims, later the U.S. Claims Court.

Within the next few years, the U.S. government began a new policy of "rounding up" the Indians. Major Henry Douglas held a series of councils including meetings in Austin with over 500 Shoshones whose representatives requested parcels of good farming land with adequate water, preferably near Grass Valley. Douglas concurred that their requests were just and promised to arrange what he could. But no reservations in Grass Valley or anywhere else were forthcoming during the 1870s, and several Shoshones joined Bannock and Northern Paiute parties in waging sporadic warfare. Forbes (1967:8) estimates that in 1878, about 1,000 Shoshones were living on the Carlin Farms Reserve near the Humboldt River, in Ruby Valley, and in 19 other places. About this time, the order came that the Shoshone were to travel to the Idaho border to join the Duck Valley Reservation. On March 24, 1879, a delegation of 16 Shoshone captains unanimously expressed their strong displeasure at the order and refused to move.

In an independent action, a governmental commission under John Wesley Powell told the Shoshone that

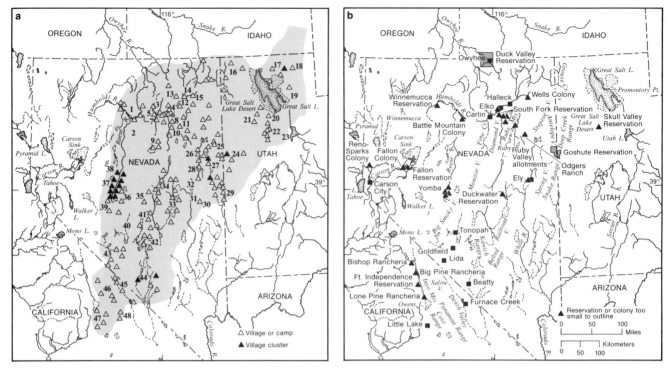

Fig. 1. a, Nineteenth-century territory with subgroups, as given by Steward (1937b, 1938): 1, White Knives; 2, Crescent Valley; 3, Independence Valley; 4, Elko; 5, Carlin; 6, South Fork; 7, Palisade; 8, Dixie Valley; 9, Diamond Valley; 10, Huntington Valley; 11, Ruby Valley; 12, Halleck; 13, North Fork; 14, Mary's River; 15, Clover Valley; 16, Pine Nut Eaters; 17, Huki Eaters; 18, Fish Eaters; 19, Weber Ute; 20, Tooele Valley Gosiute; 21, Skull Valley Gosiute; 22, Rush Valley Gosiute; 23, Cedar Valley Gosiute; 24, Trout Creek Gosiute; 25, Deep Creek Gosiute; 26, Cherry Creek; 27, Spring Valley; 28, Steptoe Valley; 29, Snake Valley; 30, Cave Valley; 31, White River; 32, Jakes Valley; 33, Railroad Valley; 34, Little Smoky Valley; 35, Fish Springs Valley; 36, Big Smoky Valley; 37, Reese River; 38, Smith Creek Valley; 39, Ione Valley; 40, Ralston Valley; 41, Hot Creek Valley; 42, Kawich; 43, Lida; 44, Beatty; 45, Death Valley; 46, Saline Valley; 47, Little Lake; 48, Panamint Valley. For information on these names see the Synonymy. b, Twentieth-century towns and reservations.

they would not receive the payments stipulated in the treaty of 1863 unless they took up residence on the Fort Hall Reservation in Idaho. Despite such incidents, the situation of the Western Shoshone changed little until after 1900, when federal land was set aside for "Indian colonies" in Reno, Carson City, Battle Mountain, Elko, and elsewhere.

The year 1935 marked the beginning of the "Indian New Deal," when Western Shoshone were encouraged to organize their own legally constituted tribes on newly established reservations (Clemmer 1973:8).

In the 1930s many groups of Western Shoshone joined to elect a traditional council to arbitrate their demands. The council, although informally selected, considered Chief Temoak and his descendants as leaders (see O.C. Stewart 1980). Several groups, including the White Knife and Reese River bands, did not participate in the council (Clemmer 1973:8). The U.S. government refused to recognize the traditional Te-Moak council as a legally constituted tribe and organized a government-sponsored Te-Moak Bands Council. This council was not particularly popular with many of the more traditional Western Shoshone, resulting in 1974 in the establishment of the United Western Shoshone Legal Defense

and Education Association (now called the Sacred Lands Association) (E.R. Rusco 1982:46-48).

The traditionalists went before the Indian Claims Commission arguing that the Te-Moak Bands Council did not represent the interests of the Western Shoshone and that title to Western Shoshone lands had never legally passed into government hands. Their claims, and subsequent appeals, were rejected in a 1979 court decision, wherein the Indian Claims Commission ruled that the Western Shoshone lost title to their land in the Treaty of Ruby Valley of 1863. A 1980 court decision ruled that whereas the Western Shoshone had not lost title to their lands in 1863 or in subsequent years, they lost title as of December 6, 1979, when the judgment of the Indian Claims Commission was delivered (E.R. Rusco 1982). The tribe appealed to the U.S. Supreme Court, which ruled in 1985 that the $26 million paid to the Indians in 1979 extinguished their title to the 24 million acres of land.

Population

Forbes (1967:10) points out that the Western Shoshone have never been "reservation Indians" in the ordinary

264

Inter-Tribal Council of Nevada, Reno: 845.

Fig. 2. Vaccination of the Western Shoshone against typhoid. Some of the individuals are: Dr. J.B. Henneberger, John Wiley, Bessie Crow Harney, Big Foot Dick, Maggie Dick, Alice Tom Cleveland, and Pappy Dodge (Ollie). Photographed at Owyhee, Duck Valley Reservation, Nev., 1914.

Fig. 3. Anees Tommy, last traditional chief of the Gosiute (d. 1940). He was active in encouraging the Gosiute to vote to organize under provisions of the Indian Reorganization Act of 1934. Photograph by Carling Malouf, 1940.

sense. Prior to 1877, fewer than 20 percent of the aboriginal population lived on reserves, and by 1927 this figure had only increased to about 50 percent. Since that time, despite the addition of new reservation land, the reservation population has consistently declined.

No accurate census of aboriginal Western Shoshone population is available (Leland 1976), and best estimates derive from early settlers' accounts, government surveys, and informant testimony of the 1930s. Estimates of aboriginal population in the Reese River Valley, for instance, range from 250 to 1,000 people. For historic population figures, see "Population," this volume. Steward (1938:48) computed an overall population density for all aboriginal Nevada at one person per 13 to 15.8 square miles. But population density was variable (Thomas 1983). Steward (1937b:628) suggests that even in well-watered areas population was restricted to about one person per two square miles; in the desert, this figure dropped to one person per 50-60 square miles. It is clear that rather different cultural geographic strategies were employed by various Western Shoshone groups. Although the factors contributing to this population mosaic were complex, key determinants were available water, relative abundance and distribution of wild plants, availability of various lacustrine resources, overall elevation, microtopographic variability, and proximity to individual procurement areas (Thomas 1972b, 1983).

In 1873 the Western Shoshone population was 2,405 (Powell and Ingalls in ARCIA 1874: 41–75, as modified by Leland 1976:table 1). In 1970 the number living on or near reservations, colonies, and rancherias in California, Nevada, and Utah was 2,034 (U.S. Bureau of Indian Affairs. Statistics Division 1970, 1970a); in 1980, it was 2,923 (U.S. Bureau of Indian Affairs. Financial Management Office 1981).

Culture

The elemental technology of the Western Shoshone provoked many deprecatory comments from early explorers, traders, trappers, soldiers, and settlers (Murphy 1970; Steward 1939a). The truth is that the Western Shoshone adaptation was marvelously complex, and students of ecological and social evolution are only now beginning to comprehend the diverse adaptive processes that articulated the Shoshone pattern to the Great Basin ecosystem (Bettinger 1978; Thomas 1981a, 1983, 1983b; Madsen and O'Connell 1982; C.S. Fowler 1982).

Subsistence

Western Shoshones employed markedly diverse strategies of procurement and economic organization, which spanned much of the so-called forager-collector continuum (Binford 1980). Knowledge of Western Shoshone economy, ecology, material culture, and world view derives largely from the works of Steward (1938, 1941, 1943a), supplemented by other accounts (C.S. Fowler 1977, 1982; Thomas 1981a, 1983). This discussion emphasizes mainstream subsistence activities, necessarily minimizing both spatial and temporal variability, and also various backup strategies relied upon in lean years.

Families and family clusters commonly foraged in relatively small groups from the spring through the fall. Group movements were keyed largely to the availability of low bulk and patchy resources, and carefully coordinated harvesting strategies (Wheat 1967). The greatest residential stability occurred in the winter, when villages of several families were typically established in the relatively warmer places, not far from caches of pine nuts, seeds, dried meat, and other foods (Steward 1937b:628). Western Shoshone in areas such as the Reese River, Ruby, Spring, and Big Smoky valleys tended to have traditional winter villages, with fairly stable populations. In more marginal areas, such as the Kawich Mountains, eastern California, Battle Mountain, and Gosiute territory, the Shoshone varied winter village location to coincide with the more productive piñon areas or other seasonal crops (Steward 1938).

Plant procurement provided the economic mainstay for the Western Shoshone people, and the variability within that technology is well documented by several ethnographic and ethnohistoric sources (for example, Coville 1892; Dutcher 1893; Chamberlin 1911; Egan 1917; Steward 1938, 1941, 1943a; Fowler and Fowler 1971). These collection strategies varied with the crops being exploited and the nature of the cultural geography. After winter stores were spent, people relied on early spring resources, such as the edible greens that ripened in the lowlands. By summer, seeds and berries were ripe in the valleys and low foothills.

Seeds were generally knocked loose with a seed beater or wrapped stick; entire seed heads were sometimes cut and tied into bunches (figs. 4-5). Small seeds were transported in twined carrying baskets, as were piñon nuts (*Pinus monophylla*). A long hooked pole was often used to pull down the piñon cones. The ubiquitous digging stick was used for roots. Coiled basketry ollas coated with pine pitch for waterproofing became portable water caches, enabling families to gather seeds far from sources of water (Coville 1892:353, 358).

Once gathered, seeds were often transported to residential bases or field camps for threshing with sticks and wooden paddles. Smaller seeds were roasted on parching trays by adding charcoal and ashes, then vigorously shaking and agitating them to prevent scorching. Cooked seeds were winnowed to remove remaining chaff and charcoal. Manos and metates were generally used to mill seeds, although some were simply boiled without milling. The prepared seeds were either eaten immediately or cached for later consumption. The nature and location of the caches depended on both the bulk of specific resources and also the overall subsistence strategy being employed (see discussion of caching strategies in Egan 1917:242).

In areas of abundant piñon—south of the Humboldt River, generally between 5,000 and 8,000 feet elevation—caches and winter residential sites were commonly positioned in the low foothills (Steward 1939a:531-532). In less abundant areas, temporary camps were established in the groves in early fall while nutting was in progress (Dutcher 1893:377). The abundant piñon groves of Reese River Valley were owned by individual families, the only record of this practice among the Western Shoshone (Steward 1938:105).

Steward (1938:27) estimated that a typical Western Shoshone family of four could gather about 1,200 pounds of pine nuts during the few weeks in the fall when the nuts were available; several bushels could be garnered in a day (Egan 1917:242; Dutcher 1893:380). This sup-

U. of Ill., Dept. of Anthr., Urbana.
Fig. 4. Gathering (left) and threshing rice grass. The grass is beaten with sticks (right), and the seeds separated by shaking and tossing them in a winnowing basket. Photographs by Julian H. Steward, 1935–1936.

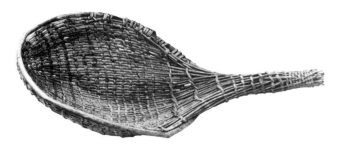

Harvard U., Peabody Mus.: 35–78–10/5010.
Fig. 5. Seed beater of twined willow with an outer rim of serviceberry. Made by Maggie Mose, Steptoe Valley, Nev. Collected by Julian Steward in 1935; length 43.7 cm.

ply was sufficient to last the family about four months. Because the bulky seeds were not easily transported, winter villages were often situated near the caches (Coville 1892:353; Steward 1939a:532). In relatively well-watered areas with abundant piñon (such as Reese River), piñon trees in the foothills behind the camp afforded the winter staple while the marshy valley floor yielded additional resources in the spring and summer (Steward 1938:101). Judicious choice of winter village caches could provide the natural products of several microenvironments within a journey of one or two hours from camp. In areas lacking local piñon (such as the Humboldt River), the Shoshone cached their piñon stores up to several days' walk from their winter village, then gradually transported supplies to camp over a period of months (Steward 1938:158).

The Death Valley Shoshone relied heavily upon mesquite pods, which were ground into flour with a mortar and pestle and readily transported as cakes (Driver 1937:68–69). Salvia seeds were also important in the south, as were several species of cactus, crucifers, agave, and gourds (Coville 1892:353-355; Chalfant 1930:77; Driver 1937:64).

Groups such as the Reese River and Ruby Valley Shoshone (and to a lesser extent people of Railroad and Little Smoky valleys and the Gosiute) broadcast wild seeds, especially Chenopodium and Mentzelia. Steward (1940:482) attached little overall economic significance to this technique of intensification, and ownership of seed plots was recorded only among the Reese River Shoshone (Steward 1938:105).

Although hunting contributed far fewer calories than did plant procurement, several species were regularly hunted. Bighorn sheep, the most important artiodactyl in the prehistoric Western Shoshone economy, was secured several ways (Thomas 1983:40–71). During the summer, hunters monitored diurnal movements (daily foraging shifts, trips to water, etc.) to determine those sufficiently predictable to allow interception at a pre-designated spot. Permanent hunting facilities might be constructed to help with ambush, and dogs often assisted in summertime bighorn hunting (Muir 1894:322; Lowie 1924:195; Driver 1937:61; Steward 1941:220–221).

With the first snowfall, bighorn procurement shifted to migration hunting. This may have been the time of greatest potential return, particularly in areas of marked vertical relief. Hunters concealed themselves behind rock walls, lines of stone cairns, and hunting blinds, particularly along the side canyons that provided the change of pace and funneling factors necessary for successful intercept strategy hunting (Chalfant 1930:96; Pendleton and Thomas 1983).

Bighorn were also taken in the winter range, probably on a simple encounter basis (Thomas 1983:46). At such times, rams could be attracted by thumping together logs to simulate the sounds of fighting (Steward 1941:220). Local factors, such as adequacy of precipitous terrain, played a significant role, contributing to the variability in bighorn procurement throughout Shoshone territory (Thomas 1983:47). Although bighorn were available throughout Shoshone territory during the ethnohistoric period, communal hunts persisted only in Ruby Valley (Steward 1938:148).

Antelope, which probably ranked second to bighorn in importance to aboriginal populations, was the largest game in Gosiute territory (Malouf 1940:94). Living in large herds in open terrain, antelope were most profitably hunted by communal driving (Egan 1917:238-241; Steward 1941:218). Many Western Shoshone groups had such drives, but the far western groups such as Lida, Beatty, Death Valley, and Panamint Valley had to travel considerable distances for these get-togethers (Steward 1940:483). The precise location of the antelope drive depended on several factors including permanent hunting facilities, the local availability of an antelope shaman or director, and the local herd abundance. Such communal drives provided one of the few occasions during which large groups of people gathered for festivals (Steward 1938:237).

Antelope were driven along a V-shaped runway into a corral constructed of brush, stone, and poles. To help with the drive, a shaman acquired the power to capture antelopes' souls through dreams, songs, and other ritual activities, charming the animals into the center of the corral. Once a herd was driven into the corral, the gate was "closed," sometimes by fire (Steward 1938:82, 1939a, 1941:220, 272); archers then dispatched the animals. For some years thereafter, antelope could not be hunted in that locale, since considerable time was required for the herd to recover (Egan 1917:240; Steward 1938:33; see Steward 1941:218–220 for variations within this communal hunting system). Individuals sometimes hunted antelope using as disguises skins and masks with male antelope horns (Driver 1937:62).

Although not abundant in aboriginal times, deer were hunted occasionally; deer were particularly scarce in the southern regions (Steward 1941:258). Communal deer hunts were generally rare or unimportant, having some significance only among the Ruby Valley, Steptoe, Battle Mountain, and Little Smoky groups (Steward 1938). Deer were pursued either by low-density intercept hunting or encounter strategy stalking. Deer disguises were used, and an antelope shaman was sometimes employed to charm deer.

Shamanism played no part in hunting rabbits, an important source of food and fur. The fall rabbit hunt was another major social occasion during which people assembled. Jackrabbits were most commonly hunted communally by both sexes who drove them into long nets of twisted grass twine (Chamberlin 1911:336; Egan 1917:235–237; Steward 1941:220–222). The black-tailed jackrabbit (*Lepus californicus*) could be taken throughout Western Shoshone territory, but less abundant white-tailed rabbits (*L. townsendii*) were found only north of Tonopah.

Two allopatric species of cottontail were also available to the Western Shoshone. *Sylvilagus nuttallii* was common north of Goldfield while *S. audubonii* was restricted to the southern deserts. Cottontail behavior dictates a different mode of hunting: unlike jackrabbits, who flee when frightened, cottontails generally hide in a nearby burrow. Since cottontails could not be driven, snares and deadfalls were used.

Burrowing rodents such as pocket gophers and ground squirrels were dug out with rodent skewers, or flooded and smoked out (J.H. Simpson 1876:53; Frémont 1845; S. Powers 1877:450; Coville 1892:351; Egan 1917:237, 245–246; Steward 1941:224). Spring pole traps and deadfalls were also used (Driver 1937:61). While ethnohistoric sources document a wide range of procurement techniques, each resulted in a low yield with relatively little effect on settlement patterns.

Use of reptile hooks was restricted to the southern areas, coinciding somewhat with the distribution of the chuckwalla (Coville 1892:352; Steward 1940:483). The data are somewhat conflicting, as Driver's (1937:62) informants denied eating chuckwalla.

Fishing was restricted among the Western Shoshone, adding substantially to the diet only in the well-watered areas such as Reese River, Humboldt River, Ruby Valley, Spring, Snake, and Antelope valleys, and Pine and Grouse creeks (Steward 1938). Although minor fish resources could be obtained from the small creeks and springs throughout the territory, fishing had no substantial impact in most areas; fishing techniques were apparently absent in the southern sectors (Driver 1937:63). Several groups (Gosiute, eastern Californians, Pine and Grouse creek people) traveled considerable distances to fish (Steward 1938; Malouf 1940:111).

The Western Shoshone ate many other creatures. They commonly hunted dove, mockingbird, sage hen, and quail; owl, hawk, and crow were captured less frequently. Waterfowl were communally hunted particularly in Ruby, Snake, Spring, and Antelope valleys and at Little Lake (Steward 1938, 1941:224; O.C. Stewart 1980:250). Panamint Shoshone constructed rush beehive-shaped blinds to hunt ducks, sheep, and quail at springs (Birnie 1875, in Chalfant 1930:95–96). Also consumed were bee eggs, larvae, grasshoppers, and crickets. When plentiful, the swarms of large black Mormon crickets provided a temporary, but important food source (Egan 1917:230–238; Steward 1941:228, 277; Malouf 1940:112).

Despite the diversity of natural foodstuffs, Western Shoshone economy was grounded in a systematic and rather predictable seasonal round. Specific resources varied spatially, seasonally, and annually; but the long-term cultural geography of Western Shoshone people shared a basic structural similarity with that of other Numic groups, particularly the Northern Paiute (J.H. Simpson 1876:80; Steward 1940:475; see also Thomas 1983:72–91).

Structures

The relatively high degree of residential and logistic mobility, coupled with a lack of adequate transportation facilities, favored dwellings that were temporary and unambitious affairs (Thomas 1983:72–91; C.S. Fowler 1982:134). Local diversity of such dwellings was determined by several factors: projected use, difficulty in procuring timber, and duration of stay (Steward 1940:485).

The typical winter house was a conical hut, housing a family of about six. The light frame was covered with slabs of bark, sometimes surrounded with a single tier of stones to keep the supports firmly planted (Steward 1941:238). Since few Western Shoshone structures involved subterranean construction, the only vestiges of such structures are often stone circles, sometimes erroneously considered tepee rings.

In Death Valley, Zigmond (1938a) reports that gabled houses were constructed in which the roof was supported by two vertical uprights; but Driver (1937:66) denies the presence of this building style in the area. Remy and Brenchley (1861) suggest that the more mobile Shoshone dispensed with constructed houses altogether, seeking shelter in caves. Steward (1943a:307) also found this practice among some of the Gosiute. Shelter during the hot Great Basin summer was often merely a semicircular sun shade (fig. 6) (Driver 1937:68). J.H. Simpson (1876:36, 64) noted circular brush dwellings were used by the Gosiute and Ruby Valley Shoshone summer and winter (see also Steward 1940:485). The Kawich Mountain Shoshone built domed wikiups both summer and winter (Steward 1941:282–283), but such structures were absent among the Gosiute (Malouf 1940:142).

The sweathouse was nearly universal among Western Shoshone groups. In the south, sweathouses were generally conical; they were domed in the northern areas

top, U. of Nev. Reno, Special Coll.; center, Natl. Park Service, Death Valley Natl. Monument, Calif.: F-5120; bottom, U. of Utah, Special Coll., Salt Lake City: PO 244, #1258A.

Fig. 6. Dwellings. top, Camp at Ruby Valley, Nev. Photograph by Lorenzo D. Creel, about 1917. center, Camp at Furnace Creek, Calif., with tent on far right and brush sun shades. The tallest boy is Charlie Shoshone. Photographed about 1925. bottom, Indian colony on the north side of Elko. Houses on the left are Indian houses. The larger one on the right, with a water tank, was the Indian agent's residence; only the agent had running water. Photographed 1935.

(Driver 1937:67; Steward 1940:485, 1941:233). Similarly, most Western Shoshone, except those in Death Valley and Beatty, constructed menstrual huts (Driver 1937:97; Steward 1941:284–285).

Clothing and Adornment

Clothing varied according to age, sex and the ability of a hunter (Steward 1940:486). Nudity was not uncommon (especially in the summer), being more frequent for prepubescent boys than for girls, who wore a front apron. Even in subzero temperatures, clothing was scarce, and the most common protection against cold was a woven or sewed robe of fur. Rabbitskin fur was most popular, but clothing made of bighorn, antelope, or deer hides was worn when available. Women wore hats or helmets of twined sage bark or willow (fig. 8a) and, in winter, preferred a long gown of two skins. Whenever skin clothing was scarce, women wore skirts of skin, bark, or grass (fig. 8b); (Egan 1917:238: Driver 1937; Zigmond 1938a; Malouf 1940; Steward 1943a; Grosscup 1977). Men preferred tailored garments of tanned hide, but unsuccessful hunters wore a breechclout of fur or twined bark with a robe for warmth. In winter or rough terrain both sexes wore moccasins of fur or twined sagebark stuffed with bark, fur, or grass (fig. 8c). The garment choice was left to individual preference and circumstances (Steward 1940:486).

Ears of both sexes were often pierced to receive ornaments. Necklaces of shell beads and bone tubes were common, as were fur belts. Mineral pigment mixed with marrow was applied to the face and body, especially the former. Facial tattooing using a wood charcoal pigment was practiced, especially among young adults.

Technology

The Western Shoshone were part of the Numic basketry complex characterized by some coiled baskets, the twined seed beater, the twined triangular winnowing tray, and, to a lesser extent, the twined conical carrying basket (fig. 12). Western Shoshone also made a wide variety of less diagnostic forms, detailed in Steward (1941, 1943a), Mason (1904), Driver (1937), Zigmond (1938a), Kirk (1952), and Grosscup (1977). Nevada Shoshone generally made twined basketry; coiling was basically abandoned in northeastern Nevada but was retained by the Skull Valley Gosiute (Steward 1940:482; Malouf 1940:155).

Women used twined conical baskets for seed gathering in the west (Steward 1940:484; Coville 1892:357) and carried their infants on oval or Y-framed cradles (fig. 13) (Zigmond 1938a; Grosscup 1977; Steward 1943a). Among men the sinew-backed bow of juniper using horn glue was widely distributed (Coville 1892; Driver 1937:70; Steward 1943a:313), and the Gosiute also made bows of mountain mahogany (Chamberlin 1911:346). Quivers were most often made of wildcat skin. Hunting nets were specially constructed in the southern areas and made from old rabbit nets in the north (Steward 1940:484). In the Panamint area, arrowshafts were made from reed and willow with hardwood foreshafts; these were straightened with double-grooved heated stones (Coville 1892:360; Driver 1937:71) or horn wrenches (Malouf 1940:136).

Relatively low-quality pottery, termed Shoshone ware (Rudy 1953), was manufactured from local clays con-

Nev. Histl. Soc., Reno: 550.

Fig. 7. Camp at Bullfrog, Esmeralda Co., Nev. One woman wears a basketry hat over her scarf, and the man behind the fire holds a double barreled shotgun. They are standing in the middle of a brush windbreak, which is similar to the circular shelters observed among the Western Shoshone in 1859 ("Euro-American Impact Before 1870," fig. 7, this vol.). Photographed in 1906.

taining residual temper. The outer surface was occasionally decorated with indentations (Driver 1937:80; Zigmond 1938a; Steward 1940, 1941; Tuohy 1956, 1973; Coale 1963; Madsen 1975).

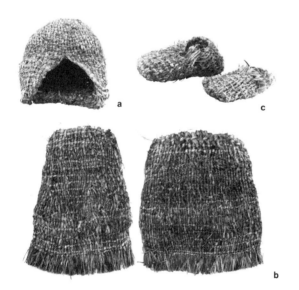

Harvard U., Peabody Mus.: a, 35–78–10/5014; b, 35–78–10/5024; c, 35–78–10/5022.

Fig. 8. Clothing of twined sagebrush bark. a, Winter hat; b, front and back parts of a woman's apron; c, moccasins, the larger, a man's, the smaller, a woman's. All were made by Renie Bill and collected by Julian Steward in 1935, at or near Elko, Nev. Height of a 27 cm, rest same scale.

Life Cycle

"Birth, girl's puberty, and death entailed more ritual than any other activities" (Steward 1941:255). Ritual at childbirth was a practical affair, performed for the benefit of parents rather than the newborn. Supernatural measures were taken to insure welfare of the child, including the selection of a shamanistic midwife, and disposal of afterbirth and umbilical cord (Steward 1941:255, 1943a:280). The rituals involved with childbirth were widely distributed among the Western Shoshone, differing only in the duration (varying from 5 to 90 days) (Steward 1941:314–316).

Only the Death Valley and Big Smoky groups report killing of one twin, although infanticide (of unwanted infants) was fairly widespread in the western part of the territory (Steward 1941:316).

Puberty rites were restricted to females. Observance of first menstruation was an individual rather than a group ritual in which the girl spent a few days in near isolation, attended by her mother who admonished her "to arise early, work hard, and be restrained in talking and laughing" as such behavior would insure her future conduct (Steward 1941:255). These rites were widespread among the Shoshone, from Death Valley to the Gosiute (Steward 1941:317–318, 1943a:280–281).

Death customs were locationally variable. In Death Valley, Lida, Elko, and sometimes in Big Smoky Val-

Rose Sherman Hanson, Mountain City, Nev.

Fig. 9. Women's clothing. left, One woman wears a fringed buckskin dress similar to Plains garments, while the others wear cloth dresses with blanket shawls. right, Girls home for the summer from Carlisle Indian School, Pa. At school they often took sewing courses where they made their own clothes in Euro-American styles. Photographs by James Sherman, Duck Valley Reservation, 1906.

ley, bodies were cremated (Driver 1937:99; Steward 1941:256). In mountain areas, the dead were buried in rock slides or talus slopes (Steward 1943a:343), and cave burials were reported among the Gosiute (Yarrow 1881:129, 181). The deceased were also sometimes abandoned or burned in their dwellings (Yarrow 1881:143, 153–154; Driver 1937:99). The eastern California groups and several Gosiute deviated from the typical Western Shoshone mortuary pattern by observing an annual mourning ceremony replete with singing, oratory, and destruction of the clothing and valuables of the deceased (Steward 1938:74, 1943a:344).

Occasionally in the spring, when the food supply was virtually exhausted, the aged and infirm were abandoned with sparse food and water (Steward 1939a:529). A case of suttee is reported for the Western Shoshone in which the prettier of the deceased man's two wives was killed and buried with him by his brother (Remy and Brenchley 1861; see also MacLeod 1931:209). In precontact times, mourning by both sexes involved the cutting of the hair and a minimum period of 12 months before remarriage (Steward 1941:257).

The ghost, believed to leave the body immediately at death, was feared by eastern California and central Nevada groups, and dreaming about a dead person was regarded as a bad omen (Driver 1937:100; Steward 1941:323). Steward's (1941:257) informants felt that mentioning the name of the dead person was taboo, yet they demonstrated no hesitation in doing so themselves.

Religion

Western Shoshone religion involved a simple direct relationship with the supernatural. There was no formal priesthood, but acquisition of supernatural powers was possible through visionary and dream experiences.

Steward (1941:257) defines three kinds of shamans: specialists able to cure specific ailments, individuals who used their powers only for their own benefit, and those who had general curing ability. There were two types of dreamed power: one involving a spirit helper, usually an animal or bird, but sometimes a natural object; and a second invoking dreamed capabilities, rather than spirits. The common term for shaman, *puhakanti* (dialectally *pohakanti*), is derived from *puha* (*poha*) 'power' by a suffix *-kanti* 'one who possesses or uses'. Although it was widely accepted that women could be shamans, only men are known to have actually practiced; the Shoshone around Ely and Spring Valley deny the presence of shamans (Steward 1941:320, 1943a:344).

Curing

Typical cures involved laying hands on the patient and exhibiting his lost soul, and sucking out foreign objects such as a stick, or some blood. Killing a shaman for declining a case was not unknown; the unsuccessful shaman usually returned his fee in the western sections,

Nev. State Mus., Carson City: top, 551-G-21c; bottom, 551-G-22g.

Fig. 10. bottom, Beaded moccasins, pan-Indian style, made by a Western Shoshone during or before the 1950s. top, Beaded and fringed buckskin gauntlets, made by Mary Stanton before 1950. Both are items commonly made for sale to Whites. Length of bottom about 19 cm, other same scale.

U. of Nev. Reno, Special Coll.

Fig. 11. Tim Hooper making white paint from a naturally occurring mineral. Gathered from specific sites, the mineral is ground fine, mixed with water, and compacted by squeezing water out through a bag. Photograph by Margaret M. Wheat, Monitor Valley, Nev., 1959.

but not in the east (Driver 1937:102–103; Steward 1941:320–321, 1943a:347).

Those bruises, injuries, cuts, and intestinal disorders not considered to be caused by supernatural agencies were treated with herbal remedies. Chamberlin (1911) collected ethnobotanical information from the Gosiute, and much of these data related to the use of specific plants as herbal medicine (see also Steward 1941). In 1940, Train, Henrichs, and Archer (1941) made an intensive study of medicinal uses of plants by the Indians of Nevada. Several hundred plant species are listed to which remedial powers for a wide variety of ailments are ascribed. Fifty-two plants are said to constitute medicine for "colds," 57 for venereal diseases (with occasional distinctions between gonorrhea and syphilis), 44 for "swellings," 34 for diarrhea, 37 for rheumatism, and 48 for various stomach indispositions including "stomachache." Obviously the Western Shoshone were thoroughly at home in their floral environment. The

Western Shoshone pharmacopoeia is described by J.H. Smith (1972).

Ceremonies

Relative to other Native American groups, ceremonial life was relatively meager. The only traditional dance in most localities was the Round Dance (*nikkappih*). This dance, which was still practiced on reservations and elsewhere in the 1980s, was widely known in the Great Basin (Steward 1941:265, 323).

Festivals, which generally included the Round Dance, were held whenever they coincided with times of abundant food supply—especially the piñon harvest, rabbit drives, and antelope hunts. Although primarily performed for pleasure, the Round Dance afforded opportunity for courtship and, in various localities, was thought to produce rain. The Round Dance was performed as part of the annual Mourning ceremony in eastern California (Steward 1938:74). Most Western Shoshone groups (except those around Lida, Spring Valley, and Battle Mountain) held their dances in the fall, in conjunction with the piñon harvest or with communal rabbit hunts. Summer festivals were also held by the Reese River, Railroad, and Ruby Valley Shoshone, and by the Gosiute. Most eastern groups held another festival in the spring coinciding with communal antelope drives (Steward 1938:237, 1941:323, 1943a:349).

Games and Music

Many games and forms of gambling distributed widely throughout Native North America were also found in the Great Basin (fig. 15). Games were played mostly for pleasure and, except for games such as shinny (which required a number of persons), most lacked social or religious significance.

The ball race was a men's game in which opposing sides raced, kicking a stuffed skin ball to a line at the end of the course; this game was absent in the western part of the territory. Shinny was basically a women's game in which 5 to 10 persons on each side attempted to propel a braided skin puck or ball toward a goal using a short stick. Shinny was fairly widespread, although absent in Death Valley. These games involved betting.

So did the hoop and pole game, played in the western areas as far east as Big Smoky Valley (Steward 1941) and also by the Skull Valley Gosiute (Malouf 1940:175). Hand (fig. 16), dice, and four-stick guessing games also furnished the opportunity for gambling (Driver 1937:80–83; Steward 1941:302–306; Malouf 1940:176). Other forms of competition and amusement were juggling stones, playing with jacks and tops, making cat's cradles, and shooting arrows at a target (Steward 1941:306–307).

The four-holed elderberry flute was the only musical

Harvard U., Peabody Mus.: 35–78–10/5020.

Fig. 13. Cradle of twined willow holding a twined sagebrush bark and rabbit fur blanket. Model of an old style made by Renie Bill, near Elko, Nev. Collected by Julian Steward, 1935; length about 80 cm.

instrument capable of producing a melody. Musical bows were used occasionally around eastern California, Lida, and Reese River, but the whistle had a wider distribution along with the bull-roarer (fig. 17). During the

top right, Smithsonian, Dept. of Anthr.: 220, 420; bottom right, Natl. Park Service, Death Valley Natl. Monument, U.S. Borax & Chemical Corp. Coll., Calif.

Fig. 12. Baskets. bottom left, Grandma Dock making a close twill-twined basket used for harvesting seeds for the Southwest Museum, Los Angeles. The basket was left unfinished to show the technique. At the time this was made, few individuals still knew how to make this type of basket. Photograph by Ruth Kirk, 1950–1952. bottom right, Panamint woman making a close-coiled basket. Photographed at Furnace Creek, Calif., about 1920s. top right, Panamint coiled bowl decorated with 6 vertical cruciform elements in brown. Collected by C. Hart Merriam, Saline Valley, Calif., 1902; height 17.7 cm.

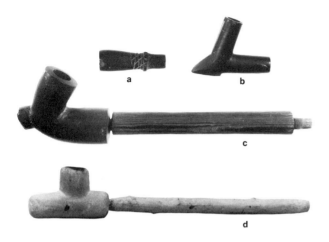

Smithsonian, Dept. of Anthr.: a, 16788; b, 16782; c, 16781; d, Harvard U., Peabody Mus.: 35–78–10/5008.

Fig. 14. Pipes. a, Black slate straight or "cloud blower" pipe, decorated with a crenate collar and cross-hatched lines, presumably the older style of Gosiute pipe; b, black slate elbow pipe with a pronounced 8-sided prow at the base of the elbow; c, black slate elbow pipe, with a short wooden stem, filed smooth, and undecorated except for a projection at the elbow that carries a crude cross filed into its face; d, plain stone pipe and wooden stem made by Stick Frank, near Mineral Hill, Nev. Length of d 25.5 cm, rest to same scale. a–c, Collected by J.W. Powell from the Deep Creek Gosiute, 1875; d, collected by Julian Steward near Ely, Nev., 1935.

hand game, two bones were struck together as a percussive accompaniment to singing. Hoof rattles may have been used by shamans, but they are reported from only Lida and Big Smoky Valley (Driver 1937:85; Steward 1941:307–310). Steward (1941:309) reports that the

split-stick rattle and the musical rasp spread to several localities in the south in postcontact times.

Social and Political Organization

Western Shoshone sociopolitical structure has been a topic of interest and debate, particularly in various formulations of ecological and cultural evolution (for example, Steward 1955; Service 1962, 1966; Fried 1967; Y.A. Cohen 1968:49; Lee and DeVore 1968; Damas 1969; Sahlins 1972:236–266; Harpending and Davis 1977; Lomax and Arensberg 1977). Archeologists have likewise employed a Western Shoshone analogy to explain prehistoric social organization and cultural ecology (for example, Jennings 1957:8; Butzer 1964:230; MacNeish 1964, 1972; Flannery 1966; Wilmsen 1970:82; Flannery and Marcus 1976:207).

Initial interpretations of Western Shoshone social organization were proffered by Powell (ARCIA 1874), based on firsthand observations in the early 1870s. Powell thought that the Western Shoshone were organized into unilineal kin groupings with descent through the male line. He described these groupings as "own[ing] land" and considered this social unit to be directly comparable to the gens as defined by Lewis Henry Morgan (Fowler and Fowler 1971:244–245, 286).

Powell's interpretation persisted until the 1920s. In 1927, 1935, and 1936 Julian H. Steward carried out ethnographic fieldwork in the Great Basin that led to the publication of a classic monograph on sociopolitical organization (Steward 1938). Although his fieldwork

left, Nev. Histl. Soc., Reno: 557.

Fig. 15. Recreation. left, Men and women playing a game, probably a card game, Tonopah, Nev. Photographed about 1905. right, Men playing pool at the "Rec Hall," a cafe and game room on the Duck Valley Reservation, Nev. Photograph by Diane Hagaman, 1981.

left, Nev. Histl. Soc., Reno: 535; right, Harvard U., Peabody Mus.: 35–78–10/4990.

Fig. 16. The hand game, in which one wrapped bone and one plain are given to each of 2 players on the same team to conceal in their hands. left, Player at left center is positioning her bones under the blanket; others are preparing to beat time on plank in foreground. Opposing team must guess the position of the plain bone. The game was accompanied by singing, guessing by motion, and keeping score with counters (Steward 1941:248). Photographed at a Duck Valley Reservation fandango, about 1940s. right, Hand game bones made by Wilbur Patterson, Saline Valley, Calif. Length about 6 cm; collected by Julian Steward, 1935.

followed Powell's by more than half a century, the mean birthdate of Steward's informants was 1868 ± 2.6 years (data taken from Steward 1941). The baseline for Steward's reconstructions was thus about 1880, but his data and interpretations were in direct conflict with those of

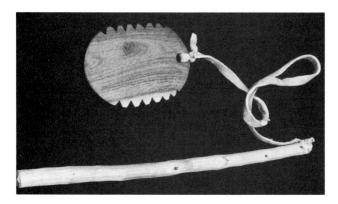

Harvard U., Peabody Mus.: 35–78–10/4991.

Fig. 17. Bull-roarer, used only as a boy's toy, made by Wilbur Patterson, Saline Valley, Calif. Length of stick 20.5 cm; collected by Julian Steward, 1935.

Powell. While granting Powell "major kudos as a redoubtable soldier, intrepid explorer and promotional genius," Steward (1970:138) argued that "an examination of his unpublished manuscripts . . . revealed incredible ethnographic naiveté. Powell simply held the views about bands that were current during his period."

According to Steward (esp. 1938:241), Western Shoshone social practices were best characterized in terms of "quantitative simplicity" (Steward 1955:102ff.): absence of sharp dialectal, cultural, and political boundaries; absence of well-defined groups transcending the simple village; absence of men's institutions; absence of age grades and women's societies; absence of significant ceremonialism, extensive recreational activities, and warfare. In this broad view, the Great Basin lifeway was characterized as a "negative fact," distinguished by "the absence of nearly all the more intensive cultural manifestations" (Kroeber 1939:49–50). The Western Shoshone social system became "the inevitable response to areas of meager resources, low population density, and an annual cycle of nomadism" (Steward 1970:115).

Rose Sherman Hanson, Mountain City, Nev.

Fig. 18. Foot race as part of a Fourth of July celebration at Duck Valley Reservation, Nev. Photograph by James Sherman, 1906.

Steward's extensive field data (1938, 1941, 1943a) provide the empirical basis for generalizing the beliefs and practices that, to one degree or another, characterized all Western Shoshone groups. Steward (1937b:628–629) stressed that political organization was a direct function of social and economic conditions.

Families usually belonged to small, local geographic districts within the general expanse of Western Shoshone territory and were frequently centered about a single valley or cluster of winter villages (Steward 1937b:629). The group name was commonly derived from a distinctive geographic feature or a prominent food resource, emphasizing the territory rather than a unified group occupying it (Steward 1938:154, 1939:262).

The White Knife Shoshone, for instance, were so called because of a distinctive local white chert they used to manufacture stone tools. Harris (1940:39) noted that the term White Knife Shoshone "was primarily geographical, designating a shifting membership of Indians who were also known by a number of other names depending upon their temporary location or their principal food supply." Steward recorded similar naming practices among a number of other Western Shoshone peoples (see synonymy), but this practice was less common among the Western Shoshone than among their neighbors, leading Steward (1938:100) to suggest that the naming of groups after prominent resources had been borrowed from the Northern Paiute or perhaps the Northern Shoshone.

Local food-named groups were not "bands" or "tribes" in the strict sense, for membership fluctuated considerably. No descent or rigid kinship structures were involved, and no territorial limits were recognized, families frequently foraging from area to area in the course of an annual seasonal round.

The structural flexibility within Shoshone society may have been related to the density and distribution of critical resources: stable social units tended to occur in areas of stable resources such as the Reese River Valley.

The same families could generally winter together, harvesting in traditional locations. In areas where resources were less predictable (the Kawich Mountains, the Gosiute and Panamint areas) families had to travel to distant resource patches, and group composition in any given year was dependent on who chose which patch.

C.S. Fowler (1982a) concluded that these food-named designations played a key role for the Northern Paiute in defining rights to resources in more densely populated zones. Although individuals moved freely between home districts, they were expected to "check in" with local residents. A network of relationships was hence created across space, granting new rights and establishing reciprocal obligations, thus reducing pressure on local resources.

Larger groups formed briefly during crop harvests when others from neighboring districts with poor crops shared more plentiful harvest areas. But except in particularly abundant resource areas, these associations were rarely comprised of the same individuals in successive years. Other communal activities, such as rabbit and antelope drives, did little to promote large group cohesion. Headmen, variously referred to as chiefs or directors (*tek^wahni*), enjoyed power generally restricted to periods of communal activity.

Group composition was situational, based on the proximity of individual families to these activities (Steward 1937b:629). The small winter village with its shifting population and informal headman was the most stable political group. But even this village cohesion was loose and the headman had little authority. Although O.C. Stewart (1980) has argued for prehistoric band organization in Ruby Valley, Steward (1937b:630) felt this innovation was clearly the result of Euro-American politico-economic pressure.

To Steward, kinship terms (fig. 19) were not merely terms of address. Kin terms were a basic ingredient of sociopolitical organization, reflecting a fundamental division of labor: men mostly hunted and women pri-

276

THOMAS, PENDLETON, AND CAPPANNARI

marily gathered, so marriage became an essential institution strictly on economic grounds.

Social organization followed from the sexual division of labor. Good hunters could take more than one wife and polygyny was usually sororal, the oldest sister being married first. Bride price, common among the western groups, was virtually unreported among the Shoshone east of the Humboldt. Polyandry, both fraternal and temporary, was absent west of Reese River Valley. Marriages established strong bonds between families, and brothers in one family frequently married sisters in another, or a brother and sister in one family might marry a brother and sister in another family.

The strong relationship between families formed by marriage was manifested in a universally expressed preference for the levirate and sororate. Divorce was common, and many adults remarried several times. Postmarital residence was variable. In general, old and handicapped persons looked after children while parents were out obtaining food. In central and eastern

Nevada, a man occasionally obtained a wife by abducting a woman—married or not—from her home. He might be aided by friends, and a fight with the husband might ensue. But weapons were not used, and there was no intent to kill. This practice was absent among the eastern California groups and the Grouse Creek and Promontory Point Western Shoshone (Steward 1941:311, 1943a:337).

Such economic organization was not conducive to armed conflict, since food was generally collected by persons who were related to each other, and the communal hunts included sharing of the spoils (Cappannari 1960). Accordingly, warfare was not common prior to contact, although killing of individuals, especially strangers, did occur. Steward (1938:107, 140) describes a fight between Reese River Western Shoshones and some Northern Paiutes who had stolen two Shoshone girls. There was also conflict over the efforts of the Ute to sell Gosiutes into slavery.

Steward's view assumed a holistic unity within West-

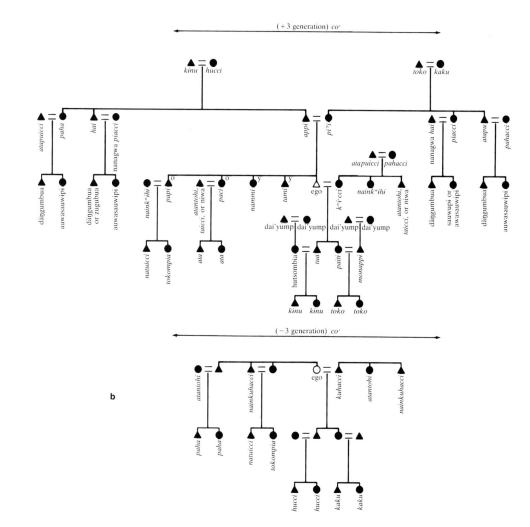

Fig. 19. Consanguineal kinship system of the Reese River Western Shoshone (Steward 1938:284–305). a, Male ego; b, female ego. Terms for omitted or unlabeled kin types are the same as for male ego.

WESTERN SHOSHONE

ern Shoshone social organization. This picture is accurate when viewed against the perspective of Native American culture in general. But Steward's Great Basin publications, particularly the later ones (especially Steward 1955:101–121), seemed to create the impression of universal coverage, implying that the family band model applied to all Numic groups. Neither impression is correct. Steward (1938:ix–xi, 1941:210–211, 1943a:264) worked with relatively few informants and spent scant time with each. Few of these informants came from riverine areas, and apparently none from lacustrine adapted groups. Steward's data thus reflected little of the variability known to exist within Western Shoshone ecological and social patterning (see Service 1966; O.C. Stewart 1939, 1966; Kelly 1934, 1964; C.S. Fowler 1977; Thomas 1983b).

"It should be clear that on one level—the *actualized* level—[patterns] were quite varied and variable, while on another—the generalized level—they were all also basically the same" (C.S. Fowler 1982:134; see also C.S. Fowler 1977, 1982a; Thomas 1981a, 1983). Without denying the considerable homogeneity within Western Shoshone society, it is perhaps more enlightening to explore the implications of actualized diversity. The nature of variation in Western Shoshone social organization can be roughly subdivided into three sets, based on density, distribution, and responses to resource variability. Eggan (1980:186–187) has explored the social ramifications of this Basin-wide diversity, concluding that "at the simplest levels of subsistence the social systems are sensitive to small variations in the underlying ecology so that a simple basic pattern may not exist over a wide area until the subsistence problems are solved by more favorable conditions for gathering or hunting, or by the development of agricultural or pastoral activities that provide greater certainty."

Parts of Western Shoshone territory include relatively infertile areas characterized by widely dispersed resources and very sparse populations (generally one person per 20 square miles or so): for instance, the Shoshone of Panamint and Death Valley, those near Lida, Beatty, and Little Smoky Valley, plus the Gosiute. Such areas typically contained adequate but distant and unpredictable resource patches, commonly separated by wide expanses of waterless desert. Subsistence strategies favored a highly fluid social organization. Several such groups lived near piñon woodland, and others lived in relatively abundant seed areas; but annual acquisition of an adequate diet involved extensive travel. These patchy resources were rarely sufficient for local communal hunts or festivals, and these groups traveled to other, fertile areas for those occasions. The Deep Creek Gosiute "possessed the most impoverished culture so far recorded in the Great Basin" (Steward 1943a:263).

In such extreme environments—habitats with low population densities and residentially mobile settlements—the kinship system functioned primarily as a social network, disseminating information regarding details of resource availability. Near Death Valley, marriage was exogamous and kin terms defined a wide network of relatives to be counted on for critical information regarding resource availability, such as the condition of particular seed patches, areas of high piñon production, location and condition of game herds, and availability of surface water. In such cases "marriage was an economic alliance in a very real sense," just as Steward (1938:241) said it was.

But the greater the unpredictability of resources, the stronger became the built-in restrictions on sharing (Eggan 1980:177). Women "owned" seed harvests and, in the winter residential camps, were responsible for the welfare of the camp group. There was, however, no automatic right to share between brothers and sisters. Areas of low population density and low resource predictability are precisely where Steward's "family band" seemed to occur.

The Gosiute developed a variant of cross-cousin marriage. Although population densities were low, the valleys were sufficiently isolated one from another so that intermarriage was encouraged as a regional integrating mechanism. Eggan (1980:179) refers to this system as "incipient patrilateral cross-cousin marriage."

A second resource constellation is found in Big Smoky, Railroad, Pine Creek, and Diamond valleys, along the Humboldt River, and in eastern California around Little Lake, the Coso Mountains, and Saline Valley. While more fertile, these areas have a certain degree of built-in temporal or spatial incongruity: acquisition of key resources involved more travel time or higher transportation costs, so residential stability was sacrificed for logistic mobility. The resource base in such areas tends to be somewhat dispersed and still quite unpredictable:

Eastern Calif. Mus., Independence.

Fig. 20. George Hanson (d. 1943), leader of a group in Panamint Valley, Calif. His Indian Ranch became a reservation in 1928 and was terminated in 1958. Photograph by Mark Kerr, Nov. 1936.

water resources were commonly restricted to semipermanent streams and rather dispersed springs. Plant resources typically consisted of abundant local piñon woodland or relatively fertile valley grasses, but rarely both. Social organization tended toward fluidity, with group composition varying from year to year. Communal activities were generally restricted to the fall, with fairly dispersed settlements for the remainder of the year. Resource structure in such areas fostered somewhat lower population densities, averaging one person for every five to nine square miles.

For the Humboldt River Shoshone, fish and seed resources functionally compensated for absence of local piñon. Although the intensity of land use near the Humboldt River approached the highest in the Basin, many key resources required extensive travel. Similar adaptations, in somewhat sparser locales, were noted among the Cave Valley, Kawich Mountain, Grouse Creek, Promontory Point, Steptoe Valley, and Battle Mountain Shoshone who generally needed 10 to 15 square miles to feed a person.

But a rather different social pattern emerged in those areas where gross elevation, microtopographic variability, and fertility simultaneously increased. Portions of Western Shoshone territory—most notably the Reese River, Spring, Snake, Antelope, and Ruby valleys—are blessed with relatively predictable, locally abundant stands of piñon, dense patches of valley seeds, and large game. These resources tend to be spatially constricted with both summer and autumn staples typically located within a few hours of the winter village. These valleys are well watered, with permanent streams flowing from side canyons to valley bottom and numerous springs in the uplands. In these areas, both residential stability and population densities increased markedly (approaching one person per three square miles). Here, there was less need for the social system to provide a kinship network for monitoring ecological conditions and sharing information.

These Western Shoshone people evolved a series of social institutions that increased local group integrity. Cross-cousin marriage became common, continuing brother-sister exchange into the next generation where possible. This marriage alliance system increased intracommunity bonds while minimizing ties to neighboring areas. Multiple marriages became more common, and the levirate and sororate became optional. The importance of sororal polygyny and fraternal polyandry increased.

Kin terms in such areas were modified to facilitate cross-cousin marriage, particulary in ego's generation (fig. 19) (Eggan 1980:179–180). The new marriage practices intensified within-group bonds by reducing the incest boundary and proliferating the ties between relatives.

To summarize, Western Shoshone subsistence strategies and social practices can be viewed along a steplike, interrelated continuum: as residential stability increases, the social system correspondingly shifts away from an inward-looking "family level" of organization that shares information (but not necessarily subsistence resources) toward institutions that increase the degree of local and corporate integration.

Synonymy‡

The name Shoshone was first applied to a group of the Eastern Shoshone (see the synonymy in "Eastern Shoshone," this vol.) and was extended to include the Western Shoshone in the course of the nineteenth century, as the affinity of these peoples became known. Earlier a distinction was frequently made between the equestrian Northern and Eastern Shoshone, referred to as Shoshone (Shoshonee, Shoshoni) or Snakes, and the nonequestrian Western Shoshone, called Shoshocoes (Shoshoko, Shoshoki), Walkers, Root-Diggers, or Diggers (Henshaw 1910:554); but the application of these terms was by no means consistent (Steward 1938:264). For example, Western Shoshones of the Humboldt River–eastern Nevada area were referred to as Shoshokoes, 1826; Bonarch Diggers (that is, foraging Bannocks), 1848; Snake Diggers, 1860; and Shoshonee Diggers, 1864. They are called Shoshoni by 1852 and Western Shoshonee by 1860, and after 1865 are referred to con-

Natl. Arch., Bureau of Ind. Affairs Coll.

Fig. 21. House under construction through the Mutual Help Housing Program, a federal program established in 1962. Under this program, prospective homeowners agree to provide contributions of cash, labor, land, and materials for the housing project. There is a long-term lease, with monthly payments based on family income. The Duck Valley Housing Authority operates the program. From 1962 to 1984 160 units were built (Dorese Vasques, communication to the editors 1985). Photographed on the Duck Valley Reservation, Nev., 1965.

‡This synonymy was written by Ives Goddard.

sistently by variants of one of these two terms (Steward 1938:268–269).

The Western Shoshone refer to themselves in Shoshone as *niwi* (dialectally *nimi*), also used for 'person' ('people') and 'Indian' ('Indians'); there is an explicit plural form *niwini·*. The Gosiute are reported to have called the Nevada Shoshone ko-its´ (Powell in Fowler and Fowler 1971:258), presumably the same as the name koets used by the Southern Paiute for the Panamint (Steward 1938:71). A Northern Paiute name for the Shoshone was tovomb (Steward 1938:154).

Subgroups

Steward's (1937b:626) mapping of Western Shoshone groups divides the area among 43 groups; 9 of these are indicated as "bands" and 34 as "districts," but the differences reflected in this distinction appear to be ecologically determined rather than based on political or social organization (Steward 1937b:629, 631). Most of these groups are referred to by geographical terms; for 13 of them Shoshone names are attested that are based on a prominent local food resource, but these can also be regarded as fundamentally territorial rather than ethnic designations.

The following list includes references and variants for all Steward's band and district names plus entries for Gosiute, Panamint, and Panamint Valley district; the numbers correspond to those on figure 1. Where Steward's map uses an abbreviated form of the name this is given in parentheses. Some parts of the Western Shoshone area, the more extensive of which Steward (1937b:map, 1938:ix) labels "largely desert" (and "deserts—few camps") or "desert/little occupied" (and "intermontane semideserts/little occupied") were not assigned by him to any band or district; the people in the larger of these unassigned areas are discussed in Steward (1938:145–146).

Beatty (44). One "band" is given on the map in Steward (1937b), but the discussion in Steward (1938:93–99) is under the heading Beatty and Belted Mountains and suggests the possibility of two linked bands, one concentrated in the Beatty area and one at the south end of the Belted Range.

Big Smoky Valley (Smoky Valley) (36). The Shoshone name for the people here is *wiʔyimpihtikka* 'eaters of buffalo berry' (Steward 1938:100, phonemicized).

Carlin (5). This district is discussed under this name in Steward (1938:155) and is delimited but not named on the map in Steward (1937b). Steward's discussion suggests that it was only partly distinct from the Elko district.

Cave Valley (30). This district is indicated but not named on the map in Steward (1937b); it is discussed in Steward (1938:125, 131).

Cherry Creek (26). This district is inhabited by the people of Egan Canyon, near the modern town of Cherry Creek (Steward 1938:125, 145–146).

Clover Valley (15). This district is delimited on the map in Steward (1937b) to include the groups discussed separately under the headings Wells and Clover Valley in Steward (1938:157). The people of the Halleck, Mary's River, and Clover Valley districts along the Humboldt River were called in Shoshone *kuyudikka* 'eaters of bitterroot' (Steward 1938:156–157, phonemicized). This name is the same as that for the Smith Creek Valley people, except for the dialectal variation between *kuyu* and *kuya* as the word for *Valeriana edulis* (Steward 1938:30).

Crescent Valley (2). As delimited on the map in Steward (1937b) this district appears to include Crescent and Grass valleys, in which no villages are located in Steward (1938:ix).

Death Valley (45). This group is discussed in Steward (1938:85) under the name Northern Death Valley, which distinguishes them from a Southern Death Valley group who were Kawaiisu. A village at Furnace Creek between these two is reported to have spoken "Shoshoni," Southern Paiute, and Kawaiisu (Steward 1938:91–92). Driver (1937:58) lists two Panamint subgroups in Death Valley, the oʹhya and the tŭ´mbïca.

Deep Creek Gosiute (25). This district is discussed under the name Deep Creek Valley in Steward (1938:137); the people of Antelope Valley are included here (Steward 1938:125, 128). See also under Gosiute in this list.

Diamond Valley (9). These people were discussed under the heading "Pine Creek and Diamond Valley" by Steward (1938:141). The "Pine Valley people" (presumably those of the Diamond Valley district) were called in Shoshone *pasiatikka* 'eaters of redtop grass' (Steward 1938:154, phonemicized).

Dixie Valley (8). Steward (1938:155) concluded that "a small, somewhat distinct group" probably lived on Dixie Creek; this district is delimited but not named on the map in Steward (1937b).

Elko (4). This district is named and discussed in Steward (1938:155); it is delimited but named only by the indication of the modern town name on the map in Steward (1937b). Northern Shoshones on Snake River called the people in the Elko region tsogwiyuyugi, a name Steward (1938:154) analyzed as including tsogwi, the name of an unidentified root, and the verb *yuyuki* 'shake (like jelly)'. See also the discussion of the Carlin and Palisades districts, to the west of Elko on the Humboldt River.

Fish Eaters (18). Steward (1937b) referred to this group as Fish Eaters on his general map, but he discusses them under the heading Cache Valley (Pängwidüka) in Steward (1938:218). Their Shoshone name was *painkwitikka* (dialectally *penkwitikka*) 'eaters of fish' (Steward 1938:218, phonemicized).

Fish Springs Valley (35). These people are discussed by Steward (1938:101, 114) but are not indicated on the map in Steward (1937b).

Gosiute ('gōsh, yōōt). The name Gosiute has been applied to impoverished Western Shoshone living around the southern edges of the Great Salt Desert and Great Salt Lake. There is no complete agreement on which groups are to be classified under this label, but Steward (1937b, 1938:135–137, 178) uses the term for the Deep Creek Gosiute, the Skull Valley Gosiute, and the Trout Creek Gosiute, as well as for the poorly known people to the east of the Skull Valley band between them and the Weber Ute. These poorly known people are given as an unnamed probable "band" on the map in Steward (1937b) but are separately labeled in Steward (1938:178) as the Tooele (tōō'ĕlu) Valley Gosiute (20), the Rush Valley Gosiute (22), and the Cedar Valley Gosiute (23).

Extensive lists of the variant forms of the name Gosiute in the historical literature are in Steward (1938:132–133) and Hodge (1907–1910, 1:496–497). These include Go-sha-Utes, Goshee Utes, Goshoots, Go-shutes, and Gosh Yuta; they are also referred to as Go-ship-Utes and Goships. This name is officially spelled Goshute in the name of the Goshute Reservation. The Shoshone form is kusiutta (Miller 1972:115), written kucyut (= [kušyut]) by Kroeber (1909a:267); this is usually analyzed as derived from kusippih 'ashes' in the secondary meaning 'dry earth', but the details of the derivation are obscure. An alleged connection with the name of a chief Goship was denied by Chamberlin (1909:27–28).

Halleck (12). This district is given the name Halleck, after the modern town, in Steward (1938:156); it is delimited but not named on the map in Steward (1937b). For the Shoshone name, see the discussion of Clover Valley.

Hot Creek Valley (Hot Creek) (41). This district is delimited on the map in Steward (1937b) to encompass Hot Creek Valley and the northern end of Reveille Valley; it corresponds to the area of Hot Creek, Tybo Creek, and Hot Springs, which is discussed in Steward (1938:111) together with the Kawich district under the heading Kawich Mountains.

Huki Eaters (17). This band is treated in Steward (1938:177–178) under the names Promontory Point and Hukundüka, a name interpreted as 'eaters of porcupine grass seeds'. The same name was also used for the neighboring Bannock Creek Northern Shoshone (see the entry Kammedeka in the synonymy in "Northern Shoshone and Bannock," this vol.). Steward (1938:30, 177) gives the Shoshone word for porcupine grass (Stipa sp.) as huki, but Steward (1937b:633) has the band name as Hükün düka, derived from hüki; the phonetics of the name appear to be against this interpretation. Equated by Steward (1938:267–268) with his Hukundüka are Hokan-tíkara (Gatschet in G.M. Wheeler 1879:409), and Hokandika, a form apparently based on the terms Hokandikahs or Salt Lake Diggers (Bancroft 1886, 1:463) and Ho´handi´ka 'earth-eaters' (Hoffman 1886:298); Hodge (1907–1910, 1:556) adds a variant Ho-kan-dik´-ah. Hoffman's gloss 'earth-eaters' suggests an interpretation as Shoshone hukkuntikka 'eaters of dust'; the nineteenth-century recordings could support an interpretation as Shoshone hukkantikka 'eaters of pickleweed (Allenrolfea occidentalis)' (Wick R. Miller, communication to editors 1985).

Huntington Valley (10). This district is named and discussed in Steward (1938:ix, 155–156) but is unnamed, probably for lack of space, on the map in Steward (1937b).

Independence Valley (Independence) (3). There was a small group here on Maggie (or Magpie) Creek (Steward 1938:155).

Ione Valley (Ione) (39). People in the vicinity of Cloverdale were called in Shoshone waitikka 'eaters of ricegrass' (Steward 1938:100, phonemicized).

Jakes Valley (32). Steward (1938:147) groups together the little-known inhabitants of Jakes Valley and "White Sage Valley"; no "White Sage Valley" can be located on Steward's maps or in other sources, and this may be an error for White River Valley.

Kawich (42). This district is discussed under the heading Kawich Mountains in (Steward 1938:111–112).

Lida (43). The marginal distinctness of the people of this district is discussed in Steward (1938:68).

Little Lake (47). These people are indicated as forming a "band" on the map in Steward (1937b), but elsewhere, in discussing them under the heading Little Lake and Koso Mountains, Steward (1938:81) says that the inhabitants lived in three winter villages and "lacked sufficient intervillage cohesion to constitute a true band." Driver (1937:58) refers to them as the Koso, in a restricted sense; the name he gives as pawo´nda is Steward's village name pagunda. See further under Panamint in this list.

Little Smoky Valley (34). The people of this district had no name for themselves, but the Railroad Valley people called them yuwinai 'dwellers in the south' (Steward 1938:113).

Mary's River (14). This district is called Deeth in Steward (1938:156), Mary's River on the map in Steward (1937b). Northern Shoshones of Snake River called the people here tu·kkoi 'black peak' (Steward 1938:154, phonemicized). For the Shoshone name, see the discussion of the Clover Valley district.

North Fork (13). The name refers to the North Fork of the Humboldt River; the people are discussed in Steward (1938:156).

Palisade (7). This district is named in Steward (1938:155) and delimited but not named on the map in Steward (1937b). Steward's informants disagreed about whether the people here were part of the Pine

Creek people (of the Diamond Valley district) or were more closely associated with other Humboldt River people.

Panamint ('pănə,mĭnt). The people in the southwesternmost extremity of the area treated in this chapter speak a variety of Central Numic that is distinct from Shoshone and have often been given the separate designation Panamint or Koso ('kōsō) (Kroeber 1925:589–592). The Panamint can conveniently be defined as the Central Numic speakers within the present area of California; they include the "bands" or "districts" given on the map in Steward (1937b) as Little Lake, Saline Valley, and Death Valley and are discussed under the heading Eastern California in Steward (1938:70–93), where the people of the northern half of Panamint Valley are also explicitly included. Driver (1937:58) lists five subgroups. Steward (1938:71) thought that linguistically the people of the Lida district also went with members of this group, but Kroeber does not treat these people, who are just over the line in Nevada. Kroeber (1925:589) lists as additional synonyms Kosho, Shikaviyam, Sikaium, Shikaich, Kaich, and Kwüts, but he does not say what languages these are from. The first is apparently Tubatulabal ši·gawiyam (C.F. Voegelin 1958:226). The Southern Paiute called the Panamint koets, and the Northern Paiute and Owens Valley Paiute referred to them by various expressions meaning '(people of the) east' (Steward 1938:71). The name Panamint was applied to the Kawaiisu of the southern end of Panamint Valley by Panamints of Death Valley and, in the form panümünt, by Southern Paiutes immediately to the east (Steward 1938:71), and because a variant was applied also to the Vanyume, a group of Serrano, Kroeber preferred Koso to Panamint as the name for the Central Numic speakers of California.

Panamint Valley (48). This district is not clearly delimited on the map in Steward (1937b), but the Central Numic inhabitants of the valley north of Ballarat are discussed in Steward (1938:84). Driver (1937:58) gives the name Haita for them.

Pine Nut Eaters (16). These people are discussed under the heading Grouse Creek in Steward (1938:173). The Northern Shoshone called them *tipatikka* 'eaters of pinenuts' (Steward 1938:174, phonemicized), "because they are the northernmost Shoshoni in the pinenut area." The Fort Hall Shoshone also include them among those referred to as tutwanait 'beyond people' or 'below people'. The Northern Shoshone are also reported to have applied the term *tipatikka* to the Shoshones of "the southern interior of Nevada" generally (Hoffman 1886:298).

Railroad Valley (33). The distribution of the people of this district is given in Steward (1938:101, 117–118). The people at Duckwater were called tsaidüka 'eaters of tule'.

Ralston Valley (40). Although delimited and named

on the map in Steward (1937b), no information on occupation is given for this area in Steward (1938:101).

Reese River (37). The Shoshone self-designation for this group is mahaguadüka 'eaters of Mentzelia seeds' (Steward 1938:100).

Ruby Valley (11). The Ruby Valley people are called in Shoshone *watatikka* 'eaters of ryegrass seed' (Steward 1938:144 phonemicized). Powell obtained the Northern Paiute name pa-hi´-ka for 'Utes in Ruby Valley' (Fowler and Fowler 1971:215).

Saline Valley (46). The people of the three subdivisions of this group "associated with one another at least more often than with people from elsewhere," but they had no joint self-designation (Steward 1938:77). The names of the three subdivisions from north to south were pauwü'ji (or pauwü'jiji and other variants); ko'önzi, the people of the main village ko'o and sigaitsi, the people of a mountaintop area called sigaiwatü. Sigaitsi is evidently the same as the name Shikaich given by Kroeber as a synonym for Panamint; see Panamint in this list.

Skull Valley Gosiute (21). This group included the Gosiute of Skull and Sink valleys (Steward 1938:136–137, 178).

Smith Creek Valley (Smith) (38). In Shoshone the people were called *kuyatikka* 'eaters of bitterroot'; Steward (1938:100) gives this name as Kuivadüka, but his analysis shows that this is a misprint for Kui[y]adüka. The Clover Valley, Mary's River, and Halleck people have a dialectal variant of the same name.

Snake Valley (29). The people of this district are discussed in the section headed Spring, Snake, and Antelope Valleys in Steward (1938:123, 129–130).

South Fork (S. Fk.) (6). This district is delimited and named (S[outh] Fork V[alley]) on the general map in Steward (1938:ix), but the village indicated there does not appear on the larger scale map or in the accompanying discussion (1938:141, 155–156), though there is a reference to "people from South Fork."

Spring Valley (27). The people of this district are treated in the section headed Spring, Snake, and Antelope Valleys in Steward (1938:123–128).

Steptoe Valley (28). The people of this district are separately discussed in Steward (1938:121, 125).

Trout Creek Gosiute (24). The people in this valley are treated in Steward (1938:137, 178).

Weber Ute ('wēbər,yōot) (19). Steward (1938:220–221) reviews the early references to the Weber Ute and presents evidence that despite their popular name they were Shoshones, not Utes. Variant names are also listed in Hodge (1907–1910, 1:371–372), under the heading Cumumbah. These include Weber River Yutahs and Kumumbar; the source cited for the second has the phrase "Goship or Kumumbar bands" (Doty in ARCIA 1865:175), as if to make it a synonym of Gosiute, but this is inconsistent with the use of this name in other sources. What is evidently the Shoshone form of the name Weber Ute is given by Miller (1972:148) as *wipayutta* 'Skull Valley Gosiute' (the easternmost band of Gosiute, nearest the Weber Ute); perhaps this is used on the Goshute Reservation to refer indistinctly to a group or groups formerly living to the east near Great Salt Lake.

White Knives (1) or White Knife. This name is a translation of the Shoshone designation *tosawi·ccih*, dialectally *tosawi·* and *tosawihi*. According to Steward (1938:154) it was "usually applied only to a small group at Iron Point, near Battle Mountain, where good white flint occurred, though there was no consistency in its application." The people in this area are discussed under the heading "Battle Mountain and vicinity" in Steward (1938:161).

In addition to being used in the narrow sense, this name is applied in some sources to Indians along a considerable stretch of the Humboldt River, including in some cases those of Diamond Valley and even as far east as the Goose Creek Mountains, on the Nevada-Utah border. In 1863 the Tosowitch were described as one of the two principal bands of the "western Shoshonees" (Doty in ARCIA 1865:175). A Shoshone born near Elko told Kroeber (1909a:267) that this was the name of the Indians there. Citations of the use of variants of the English and Shoshone names of this group in the historical literature are in Hodge (1907–1910, 2:854), under the form Tussawehe, and in Steward (1938:162). Other variants include To-sow-witches, To-sa-witches, To-si-witches, To´-sa wee, and To-so-ees.

White River (31). This is given as a district on the map in Steward (1937b), but although Steward (1938:ix, 125) assigns it to "Shoshoni" he locates no villages there.

Sources

The primary ethnographic sources on the Western Shoshone are by Steward (1936c, 1937b, 1938, 1939, 1939a, 1940, 1941, 1943, 1943a, 1955, 1970), and Eggan (1980). Primary data on the Panamint may be found in E.W. Nelson (1891), Coville (1892), Dutcher (1893), Kroeber (1925), Driver (1937), and Zigmond (1938a); Grosscup (1977) has reviewed the pertinent literature including Merriam's unpublished notes on the Panamint. The Gosiute have been extensively documented by Egan (1917), Steward (1943), Chamberlin (1908, 1911, 1913), and Malouf (1940).

Euro-American contact with the Western Shoshone is recorded by Cline (1963), Malouf (1940, 1966, 1974), Forbes (1967), Thomas (1982b, 1983: 118–138), and C.S. Fowler (1982). The historic Shoshone lifeway, including detailed reservation data and tribal claims, is described in publications by the Inter-Tribal Council of Nevada (1976b), O.C. Stewart (1966, 1978, 1980), and Clemmer (1973).

Northern Shoshone and Bannock

ROBERT F. MURPHY AND YOLANDA MURPHY

The Northern Shoshone and Bannock ('bănək) Indians occupied an area roughly coincidental with the political boundaries of the state of Idaho, south of the Salmon River (fig. 1). The names Northern Shoshone and Bannock do not refer to discrete political or social entities. The term Northern Shoshone has arisen in anthropological usage only as a general means of distinguishing Shoshones of the upper Columbia River drainage from the Western Shoshone of Nevada and Utah and the Eastern Shoshone of western Wyoming. The Western Shoshone differed from both the eastern and northern populations in lack of horses and access to the buffalo hunting areas of the Plains; a by-product of this difference in subsistence and location was the abundance of Plains Indian cultural and social features among the Eastern and Northern groups and their relative absence among the Western people. The Eastern and Northern Shoshone are less easily distinguished from each other. The conventional division made between them rests primarily upon their separate locales and the importance of salmon fishing to the Northern Shoshone diet. The Indians themselves made no recognition of the Eastern, Northern, and Western distinction; and actual social units among the Northern Shoshone varied in type from composite, mounted bands to isolated families or small clusters of families uninvolved in larger political units. Consistent with this variety and fragmentation, there were no clear cultural boundaries, and the Northern Shoshone blended into and merged with the other Shoshone to the south and east.

The distinctiveness of the Bannock rests on a basis different from that of the Northern Shoshone. The Bannock were Northern Paiute speakers who had migrated from Oregon into the general area of the Snake River plains, where they lived among Shoshone speakers in peaceful cooperation. The Bannock became differentiated from their fellow Northern Paiutes to the west through the acquisition of the horse and participation in organized buffalo hunts, but the populations continued to interact socially, and the separation was not deep enough or long enough to result in substantial linguistic divergence.

Language

The distinction between Shoshone and Bannock was noted as a social phenomenon by early travelers who reported the Bannock as one of a number of Snake "bands." It is quite remarkable that none of the chroniclers noted, or thought fit to mention, that the difference between the groups was less social and cultural than linguistic. A.L. Kroeber (1907a) was the first to report that they spoke separate and mutually unintelligible languages. Both the Shoshone and Bannock languages are members of the Numic branch of the larger Uto-Aztecan family.* The Bannock speak a dialect of Northern Paiute, in the Western Numic division, which is quite similar to the Northern Paiute of Oregon, whence they had originally migrated. Their speech is mutually intelligible with other Northern Paiute dialects scattered as far south as Mono Lake basin, California. The Northern Shoshone speak a Central Numic dialect that is easily comprehensible to the Western Shoshone of Nevada and to the Comanche of the southern plains, who separated from the main population of the Shoshone in the seventeenth century. The Pohogwe dialect, used by some speakers on the Fort Hall Reservation, is identical to the Green River dialect, spoken by the Eastern Shoshone on the Wind River Reservation, Wyoming (Sven Liljeblad, communication to editors 1985).

The spread of the Numic languages in the Great Basin, with the consequent separation between Western and Central Numic, was recent enough so that Bannock and Shoshone remain quite similar languages, and there was considerable Bannock-Shoshone bilingualism among both groups in southern Idaho. The inherited linguistic similarities were reinforced by heavy lexical borrowing between the two languages. Another consequence of the recency of the spread of the Numic languages is the absence of major dialect differences, whose development was retarded by continual contacts among the highly mobile seminomadic groups (Liljeblad 1957:21). This is a most important point, for one of the characteristics of Shoshone and Bannock groups was their openness, their interchangeability of members, and the continual move and flux of people. This tended to minimize dialect differentiation, just as it did cultural separation. On both the linguistic and cultural levels, the Shoshone and Northern Paiute, including the Bannock,

*For the transcription of Shoshone words, see the orthographic footnote in "Western Shoshone," this vol.; for the transcription of Bannock words, see the orthographic footnote in "Northern Paiute," this vol.

evidenced small and incremental change from area to area. The absence of sharp discontinuities was a function of their social life.

Prehistory

The prehistory of the southern Oregon-Idaho region is not well known, and evidence is incomplete regarding the possible spread of Shoshonean speakers throughout the Great Basin area in the last millennium. Most archeological sites are either in caves and rockshelters or at the sites of what were probably winter camps along river bottoms ("Prehistory of the Snake and Salmon River Area," this vol.). Excavations, especially those conducted at Birch Creek, Idaho, have altered the previously held view that Great Basin culture was relatively homogeneous and unchanging over many millennia. Butler (1972) has argued that culture change has been significant over the past 12,000 years due to the progressive dessication of the Great Basin region, climaxed by a shift to relative impoverishment of flora and fauna at the beginning of the fifth millennium B.C. The past 2,000–3,000 years were, according to present knowledge, quite stable, though hardly unchanging, and it may be inferred that the general patterns of social life showed greater persistence than was the case for most parts of North America.

Environment

The Northern Shoshone and Bannock occupied an area of Idaho that belongs physiographically to the Columbia Plateau province. This southern Idaho region is marginal to the Plateau culture area and merges into the Great Basin. Although it is drained by waters of the Columbia River, precipitation is generally low, and the vegetation is characteristic of regions farther south. Except for the Sawtooth Mountains, where small and scattered groups of Shoshone resided, the average rainfall of the region is under 15 inches a year.

The two most prominent physical features of southern Idaho are the Sawtooth and Bitterroot ranges and the Snake River plains. The Sawtooths rise to a height of over 12,000 feet in the watershed between the Snake and Salmon rivers, both Columbia River tributaries; and the Bitterroots, and their Beaverhead Range extension, pose a barrier of up to 11,000 feet between the Columbia waters and the Missouri River drainage. Precipitation is higher in the mountain zones, and heavy winter snows block the passes during several months of the year. In certain of the broader valleys, such as that of the Lemhi River, grasses are abundant, and rich areas of edible roots provided an important source of subsistence for the residents. The high mountains provided an ecological diversity that ranged from semi-arid valley floors of sagebrush through coniferous zones to alpine environments above the tree line.

The Snake River runs through a lava plateau, cutting more deeply into it as it flows toward the Columbia. The plain slopes from some 6,000 feet in the east to 2,150 feet at Weiser, Idaho. Rainfall in the upper Snake River plain is higher than in its lower reaches, and grasses and edible roots are accordingly more abundant in the east and near the mountain ranges. Most of the Snake River plain lies north of the river, and the region to the southeast and east of the present city of Pocatello, Idaho, is mountainous with peaks rising to 9,000 feet. South of the Snake River, the countryside rises toward the watershed of the Snake and Humboldt rivers, where typical Great Basin landscape and vegetation become predominant.

Cattle grazing has resulted in the replacement of grasses by sagebrush in much of the region. In the past, grasses were sufficiently rich to have supported buffalo, which were hunted in the Lemhi Valley and the upper Snake River plains until about 1840. These areas and the upper Boise River valley, which also enjoyed a higher rainfall than neighboring districts, were accordingly centers for equestrian groups. Mounted hunting parties also traveled annually beyond the present location of Bozeman, Montana, or joined with the Eastern Shoshone of southwestern Wyoming for the fall hunt.

Fish constituted an important part of Northern Shoshone and Bannock subsistence. Trout, perch, and other fish were found in streams throughout the region, but the most important fish, the salmon, was restricted to the Snake River below Shoshone Falls, to the lower Boise and Weiser rivers, and to the southern tributaries of the Salmon River, including the Lemhi. The principal season for salmon fishing was during the spring spawning run; the fish were not so abundant as on the lower reaches of the Columbia system, but they formed an essential component of the diet during the lean times at the end of winter, and, for some groups, into the fall.

As one moves north from the Great Basin proper, into the southern fringes of the Columbia Plateau, grasses diminish in dietary importance, and wild roots become the major source of vegetable food. The chief of these was the camas (*Camassia quamash*), which was found in abundance in certain prairies immediately south of the Sawtooth Range and in the valley bottoms of these mountains. The most notable of the root districts was Camas Prairie, in the vicinity of modern Fairfield, Idaho. Another important feature differentiating southern Idaho from the Nevada Basin was the absence of the piñon tree (*Pinus monophylla*), a principal source of subsistence among the Western Shoshone. Northern Shoshone from the Snake River often collected pine nuts in the Grouse Creek Mountains in northwestern Utah.

Resources and environment are the principal criteria

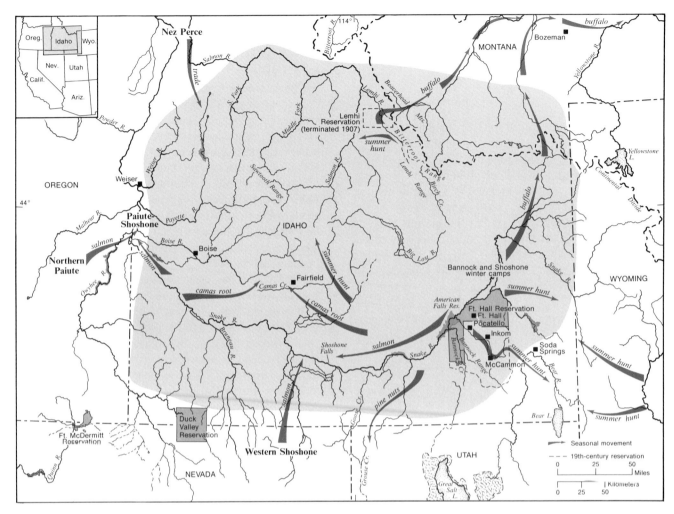

Fig. 1. Nineteenth-century territory. Labeled arrows show seasonal movement and acquired food resources. Modern reservations and major reservoirs are indicated in tone.

by which one may distinguish a Northern Shoshone population from others. The Snake River was a focus of the population, for its waters provided fish, its plains yielded roots, its upper reaches gave pasture lands for horses and, formerly, buffalo, and its bottoms afforded protection for winter camps. Subsistence was richer than among the Western Shoshone, and dependence upon the buffalo was less complete than among the Eastern Shoshone. The country was peripheral to the Basin, the Plateau, and the Plains, and it enjoyed many of the benefits, and liabilities, of life in each area.

External Relations

By historic times, the Shoshone of the Lemhi and upper Snake valleys pursued buffalo into Montana but retreated beyond the Continental Divide after the hunt for protection from the Blackfeet to the northeast. In contrast to their enmity with the Blackfeet, relations with the Flathead to the north were generally amicable.

Meriwether Lewis and William Clark noted that the Lemhi Shoshone and Flathead buffalo parties joined at the Three Forks of the Missouri River for mutual protection from the Blackfeet during the hunt (Lewis and Clark 1904–1905, 2:324). The Nez Perce, the other northern neighbors of the Shoshone, were also on generally friendly terms with them in the mid-nineteenth century, though earlier hostility is indicated by the Nez Perce term for Shoshone, *tiwélqe*, which is also used to mean 'enemy'. The Nez Perce joined the Cayuse, the Umatilla, and the Shoshone at an annual trading market on the Weiser River (Liljeblad 1959:52). Steward (1938:188–189, fig. 1), lists several winter camps on the southern tributaries of the Salmon River in the Sawtooth Range and maps the Shoshone on the Lemhi River and Middle and East Forks of the Salmon River; the Nez Perce are allotted the lower Salmon River area and the upper waters of the Weiser River. The Shoshone population of the Salmon River waters was small and scattered, and some mixed villages of Nez Perce and Shoshone were reported.

MURPHY AND MURPHY

Territory

Northern Shoshone and Bannock social groups reflected their intermediate status between Plains and Great Basin; they were at once larger and more organized than was typical among most Numic speakers and more fluid and open than those of the Plains Indians. This looseness of social organization makes the delineation of subgroups in the area difficult and renders impossible the distinction of strictly demarcated territoriality. No boundaries, as such, can be drawn between the Northern Shoshone and those Shoshone to the south in Utah and Nevada. Similarly, the distinction between Eastern and Northern Shoshone rests entirely on respective loci of activity and not upon cultural grounds or fixed memberships in social groups. Shoshone occasionally wandered from the Snake River into Nevada and Utah for pine nuts, and northern Utah and Nevada people sometimes traveled to the Snake River for salmon fishing (Murphy and Murphy 1960:322). The lack of winter camps in the highlands between the Humboldt and Snake watersheds and the gravitation of population toward the two streams, however, made for some discontinuity of interaction between Idaho and Nevada Shoshone. Drift of population from one area to another did occur. The Eastern Shoshone of Wyoming conducted most of their buffalo hunting in the region beyond South Pass, into the valleys of the Wind and Big Horn rivers. Their winter camping grounds were generally in the area of the Green River. During the spring and summer small parties sought subsistence in the mountains of northern Utah and southwestern Idaho, and their routes often took them through the same country traveled by similar small groups of Snake River people (cf. Shimkin 1947:247–248; Murphy and Murphy 1960:329–332). Families and small groups of Northern and Eastern Shoshone not only wandered into each other's orbits, but also sometimes remained. The rubric of Northern Shoshone, then, did not refer to a stable political or social aggregate, but to a locus of population, a center of gravity so to speak, in the Snake River plains and the mountains to the north.

The western neighbors of the Northern Shoshone were the Northern Paiute, and the question of distinguishing their respective limits is complicated by two factors. First, despite the linguistic difference, early travelers and chroniclers did not recognize the distinction and tended to lump the two populations together as "Snakes." Second, an important component of the Idaho population was the Bannock, a group that had immediately derived from the Northern Paiute but were found in varying degrees of amalgamation with the upper Snake River (or Fort Hall) Shoshone. Though the Bannock commonly wintered in the neighborhood of Fort Hall, they often visited the Northern Paiute, and accounts are sometimes unclear as to the origins of the group

mentioned. Moreover, relations between the Shoshone and Northern Paiute were friendly, and their settlements were interspersed in the lower Payette and Weiser River valleys (Liljeblad 1959:48).

Steward's research assigned the Boise, Payette, and Weiser rivers to the Shoshone (1938:172), though his map (ibid: fig. 1) gives a boundary somewhat above the mouths of these streams, probably reflecting the leavening of the essentially Shoshone population with Paiute from the west bank of the Snake River. Steward's conclusions are essentially substantiated by Murphy and Murphy's (1960:316–319) research on Boise and Weiser River Shoshone settlement patterns and land use, which found the Northern Paiute to be somewhat mingled with Shoshone on the lower reaches of these streams, but otherwise found only in a small corner of southwest Idaho. Omer C. Stewart (1939:133) places most of the Boise River valley and a very substantial portion of southwest Idaho in the territory of a Northern Paiute band called the "Koa'aga'itöka" (Trap Salmon Eaters), but no further documentation has been found for such a group.

Local Groups

Within the Shoshone region, the identification of local groups has been greatly complicated by the existence of names designating the people of certain areas by foods commonly eaten by the inhabitants. This practice is found among both Shoshone and Northern Paiute groups of the Basin and Plateau, leading some scholars to believe that the food names represented stable sociopolitical units, or bands. Thus, for example, the inhabitants of the Boise River were called Yahandeka (Groundhog Eaters), those of the Snake River Agaideka (Salmon Eaters), and the inhabitants of the Sawtooths were named Tukudeka (Sheepeater); the last is the only one of the food names that passed into English nomenclature for an Indian group (Steward 1938:172; cf. Lowie 1909:206). Indicative of the looseness of this nomenclature, multiple names were sometimes attached to the people of a single district, the same names could be found given to the people of widely separated areas, and a single group could be known by a series of names as they traveled from an area characterized by one kind of food to another named sector (cf. Liljeblad 1957:54–56, 1959:47). One ethnographic report gives "People Eater" as a term that was jokingly given by a Shoshone informant (Liljeblad 1970:2); however, the same designation was reported by Blyth (1938:404) as denoting a mixed Shoshone-Paiute band in Idaho. It can be concluded that the concurrence of the food names with actual social groups was adventitious and largely a function of the degree of stability and lack of mobility of the population in question.

The major focuses of population in the Idaho region were: the upper Snake River valley in the general region surrounding Fort Hall; the Lemhi River valley; the Sawtooth Range; the Boise, Payette, and Weiser valleys; and the valley of the Bruneau River. Turning first to the upper Snake River, it is necessary to clarify the position of the Bannock as Northern Paiute speakers living in close association with the mounted Shoshone of southeastern Idaho. This was clearly recognized by Steward (1938:200) and has been corroborated (Liljeblad 1957:81–90; Murphy and Murphy 1960:326; O.C. Stewart 1970). The drift of population from Oregon to eastern Idaho probably began with the introduction of the horse, which made buffalo hunting a more attractive pursuit and was part of a more general movement of Numic peoples to the northeast. Since the Shoshone probably had acquired the horse by the end of the seventeenth century (Haines 1938:435), the peaceful coexistence of Northern Paiute and Shoshone must have endured for at least a century and a half. That the Paiute language and identity had not disappeared into the numerically superior Shoshone population would seem to be a result of the continuing migration of Oregon Paiute to the Bannock ranks and of the strong positions of leadership often assumed by individual Bannocks.

The point of initial mixture and entry of Northern Paiute into Idaho was probably along the Snake River, where it forms the border of Idaho and Oregon, and the lower reaches of the Boise, Weiser, and Payette rivers (Liljeblad 1957:85). Paiute inhabitants and visitors could well have been attracted by the wealth and power of the mounted Shoshone visiting this region from Fort Hall, and it required only the acquisition of horses to join them. Their Shoshone hosts may have extended the hospitality of their ranks in order to build up their military strength, for the pressure of the Blackfeet, equipped with firearms, had pushed the Shoshone back from the buffalo grounds they had inhabited in Montana in the eighteenth century into the fastnesses of the Rocky Mountains (Murphy and Murphy 1960:294–295).

The Fort Hall, or upper Snake River, Shoshone and Bannock formed into large composite bands of shifting composition and leadership. The Shoshone speakers were always the majority, but the chieftaincy was sometimes held by a Bannock. Most of the Fort Hall people formed into a single group each fall to hunt buffalo east of Bozeman, Montana, and returned to the Snake River bottomlands near Fort Hall for the winter. If snows closed the passes early, they wintered in the valleys on the east slope of the Continental Divide and returned to the Snake River in the spring. The large bands split into smaller units for spring salmon fishing below Shoshone Falls, and summer was spent digging camas roots in Camas Prairie and other favored places. Deer and elk were hunted in the mountains of southeastern Idaho and northern Utah. Information is lacking on the composition of the smaller hunting and fishing groups of spring and summer, but it is quite possible that Shoshone and Bannock camp clusters separated during these periods, further contributing to the persistence of the division of language and identity.

The second of the two centers of buffalo-hunting peoples in Idaho was in the Lemhi River valley, where the large composite band that cooperated in the hunt was also composed of both Shoshone and Bannock. One of the great Lemhi chiefs of the mid-nineteenth century, Tendoy, was said to be half Shoshone and half Bannock (Lander 1860:125). Significantly, Lewis and Clark, who were acute observers, made no mention of Bannocks in the valley in 1805, and it may be that much of the Bannock influx occurred during the nineteenth century. The Lemhi people hunted buffalo on the upper waters of the Missouri and eastward beyond Bozeman and utilized other areas immediately east of the Divide, except when Blackfeet hostilities forced them back into the Salmon River drainage. Like their neighbors to the south, they took salmon in the spring and into the summer and hunted in the adjoining mountain ranges. Their round of activities was, therefore, much like that of the Fort Hall people, as was the degree to which they were influenced by Plains culture.

The Shoshone of the Boise, Payette, and Weiser rivers in southwestern Idaho occupied an environment that was favored by superior fisheries, a milder climate, and good grasses. The grass supported horses, which gave them the mobility to travel to Camas Prairie in the summer and to join the Fort Hall people occasionally in the buffalo hunt, but most of their subsistence depended upon the spring and fall salmon runs and hunting in the mountains to the east of their valley winter camps. Winter camps were somewhat larger than among the foot-going Shoshone and political organization more developed, but neither at any time reached the scale of the Fort Hall Shoshone and Bannock. Although there was some interpenetration of Northern Paiute in the lower waters of these streams, they remained a minority at all times.

The remainder of the Idaho population was Shoshone with little or no Northern Paiute intermixture. Unlike the above-mentioned groups, they were largely unmounted, did not participate in the buffalo hunt, lived a largely peaceful existence, and were found in small and scattered groups reminiscent of the settlement pattern of the Western Shoshone. The Sawtooth Range was frequently entered by hunting parties of the mounted peoples, but it was the permanent home of a Shoshone population loosely grouped under the rubric of Sheepeaters. The mountain sheep was an important source of food, but deer and salmon were also key elements in the diet, as were roots and berries. The population was widely scattered in the subsistence search, and winter villages were small. Steward (1938:193) reports chieftainship and larger forms of political consolidation to have been absent.

A similarly dispersed Shoshone population was found south of the Snake River, between the watershed separating the Owyhee and Bruneau rivers and the area of Bannock Creek. This area was also roamed over by mounted Shoshone and Bannock from the east, but the resident population was mostly unmounted until after 1850. The people subsisted on salmon, small game, occasional deer, roots, and berries. Pine nuts were gathered in Utah by the people west of Bannock Creek (Murphy and Murphy 1960:324), but this population was closely associated with Shoshone living in northern Utah (Steward 1938:217). The people of the Bannock Creek area, or Kammedeka (Jackrabbit Eaters), had frequent contact with the Western Shoshone of the Grouse Creek district, an area important for its pine nuts. Shoshone from Grouse Creek occasionally visited the Snake River for salmon, but they also maintained contact with other Shoshone living north of the Great Salt Lake. In this area it is difficult to draw a line between distinct Western and Northern Shoshone types of economy and settlement pattern.

Population

There are no reliable demographic data for this region in prereservation times. The population was nomadic and scattered, making such an assay dubious under the best of circumstances. The sources were also notoriously unreliable, as in the fur trapper Alexander Ross's (1956:167) early estimate of 36,000 "Snakes." Steward (1938:49), using figures gathered mainly from early Indian agents' reports, gives a total population of 3,000 Shoshone and Bannock in Idaho during the 1860s. Averaging some rather discrepant figures, this total is divided as follows: Fort Hall Shoshone and Bannock, 1,200; Lemhi (including Shoshone, Bannock, and Sheepeaters who had been settled at the Lemhi agency), 1,200; Boise Shoshone, 245; Bruneau Shoshone, 355. This count is more in the nature of an estimate, and it should be remembered that it was taken after disease and White hostilities had taken a severe toll of the population. A 1873 census enumerated 1,037 Northern Shoshone and Bannock on the reservation, and estimated 900 others (ARCIA 1874:61). In 1981 the Shoshone-Bannock Tribes reported 3,100 enrolled tribal members (U.S. Bureau of Indian Affairs. Enrollment Office, communication to editors 1985); in 1983 the local resident Indian population for the Fort Hall Agency and Reservation was about 3,900 (U.S. Bureau of Indian Affairs. Financial Management Office 1983:18).

Culture

Just as the environment and resources of southern Idaho were varied and transitional to other physiographic areas, so also was the culture of the Shoshone and Bannock diverse. The most striking feature of this variation was the presence of strong Plains Indian influences among the Fort Hall and Lemhi inhabitants, as contrasted to a way of life in areas of southwestern Idaho that approximated that of the Nevada Great Basin. Since the distinction between Shoshone and Bannock was seldom recognized in the early sources, it is important to note that Steward's (1938:200) research showed only slight cultural differences between the Shoshone and Bannock of Fort Hall.

One of the basic sources for Northern Shoshone culture, especially material culture, art, folklore, and religion, is Lowie's (1909) monograph, which was based on material collected at Lemhi in 1906. Knowledge of the Idaho Shoshone is thus weighted heavily in the direction of Plains influences. The picture is corrected with respect to political and social organization by Steward's (1938) classic work, which shifted attention to the Basin affiliations of the Northern Shoshone. The overall picture is that of varying degrees of blend of Plains, Plateau, and Basin culture, as conditioned by the economic life of peoples of different areas.

Political and Social Organization

The chief characteristic of Northern Shoshone and Bannock social life was a looseness and lack of definition of groups that bespoke the Basin origins of the people. Liljeblad (1957:90) has noted that there was a stronger tendency toward the exercise of and submission to leadership among the Northern Paiute, and their Bannock offshoots, than among the Shoshone, whom he characterizes as "extreme individualists." Whatever the reason for this may be, the Bannock exerted leadership functions disproportionate to their numbers in the buffalo-hunting bands, whereas the institution of chieftaincy was almost absent among the purely Shoshone groups farther west. But the presence or absence of bands and chieftains was not a result of Bannock initiative; rather it depended upon the type of pursuit in which the people were engaged. It was necessary to enter the plains buffalo country in organized force, both as a means of protection against hostile Blackfeet and Crows in Montana and because of the requirements of buffalo hunting itself. It was necessary to hunt the buffalo in numbers, to flank herds with many men mounted on swift buffalo ponies. This required discipline and coordination. The chiefs took care of the defense of the people, and functioned also in the organization of the hunt and maintenance of order in the large parties. Of equal importance in the last two functions were "po- *289*

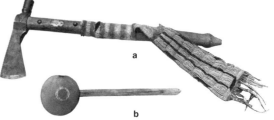

a

b

MURPHY AND MURPHY

lice." Lowie (1909:208) writes that policemen armed with quirts preserved order at hunts and dances among the Lemhi Shoshone, and Steward (1938:211) reported that four or five middle-aged men, either Bannock or Shoshone, carried out this function in the Fort Hall area without direction from the band chief. However, informants denied the existence of police or soldier societies, or sodalities, common among the Plains Indians (Murphy and Murphy 1960:333).

The power of the chiefs was limited by camp or band councils, which had become established among the buffalo hunters (Lowie 1909:208–209; Steward 1938:210–211). These councils took a direct part in decision making. There were also "announcers" or "criers" in these bands. Although there were many notable Shoshone and Bannock chiefs, such as Tendoy, Tagee, Peiem, the Horse (Horn Chief), and Pocatello, the reader of the early chronicles is struck by the fact that the names of many chiefs are mentioned for only a few years and then drop from the records. This was probably due in some cases to death, but just as frequently it was because the chieftainship shifted to other persons. The office was not firmly institutionalized anywhere among the Shoshone, and it was quite possible for a chief to lose his following to a rising new leader. The office was also nonhereditary, and anyone who showed qualities of leadership and bravery could become a chief. Just as bands had unstable and shifting membership, so also did chiefs lack a fixed following. Their powers were limited by the essential egalitarianism of Shoshone society and by the fact that it was a simple matter for any Shoshone to move his camp and attach himself to another leader.

It is not certain how many buffalo-hunting bands existed. There was probably only one in the Lemhi Valley, but the evidence for the upper Snake River plains is not clear. Steward (1938:210) says that the Bannock and Shoshone had separate band chiefs, but Liljeblad's (1957:90) research suggests greater consolidation. The size and number of bands probably depended heavily upon situational factors. All the evidence indicates changing leadership and shifting amalgamations resulted from outside threats and changing economic pursuits. The larger bands, in any event, were seasonal, for during the spring and summer seasons groups split up into smaller components that foraged the rivers, mountains, and valleys of the region in search of subsistence. This splitting was more pronounced in the Idaho area than among the Plains Indians because of the variety of resources available and the diversity of their locations.

The high degree of political development of the buffalo hunters diminished rapidly to the west. Band organization in the rest of the region was almost nonexistent. Murphy and Murphy (1960:318–319) reported the names of two chiefs for the Boise River, Captain Jim and Eagle Eye, but obtained no data on their functions. The largest social unit in the Boise-Weiser area, the Sawtooths, the Bruneau drainage, and the region south of the Snake River appeared to have been the winter camp, and it is not clear to what degree these were stable membership units. Very temporary band organizations grew up during hostilities with Whites on the Oregon Trail in the 1860s, a phenomenon that had its counterpart among the Western Shoshone along the California Trail. One of the more important of these bands was formed under the leadership of Pocatello, a Bannock Creek Shoshone. This group was actively hostile from about 1860 to 1863 in an area from the Great Salt Lake to the Snake River (cf. Lander 1860:137); these activities ended with the massacre of Shoshones by militia at the Bear River in Utah in January 1863 (Doty in ARCIA 1865:173).

In summary, the Northern Shoshone and Bannock evidenced a wide range of types of political organization and grouping, from the bands of Fort Hall and Lemhi Valley through the large villages of the Boise River to the scattered groups composed of a few foot-going families living in the Sawtooths and south of the Snake River. The need for cooperation in economic activities and war underlay the mode of organization and leadership, but beneath this was the basic Shoshone characteristic of loose and shifting association and individual autonomy.

This fundamental looseness and diffusity of Shoshone social institutions reaches its ultimate expression among

top, Smithsonian, NAA: 1704-b; bottom left, Church Archives, The Church of Jesus Christ of Latter-Day Saints Archives, Salt Lake City: P1300/633; bottom right, Helen Wrensted Sherwood, Bellflower, Calif.; Mus. of the Amer. Ind., Heye Foundation, New York: a, 10/5496; b, 11/5120.

Fig. 2. Nineteenth-century leaders. top, Delegation of Lemhi and Fort Hall Reservation Northern Shoshone and Bannock who visited Washington, D.C., May 1880. standing, left to right: Tyhee (Bannock), leader of delegation; John A. Wright, Indian Agent; Charles Rainey, interpreter. sitting, left to right, Jack Tendoy (Uriewici), Captain Jim, Tendoy (leader of the Lemhi band), Grouse Pete, Jack Gibson, and Tesedemit. The delegation signed the Agreement of May 14, which: ceded lands on the Fort Hall Reservation (including Marsh Creek valley, long in contention), surrendered Lemhi Reservation in return for lands in severalty at Fort Hall, and guaranteed annuities for 20 years. All provisions were modified or nullified (Madsen 1980: 109–111, 114–116). Photograph by Charles M. Bell, 1880. bottom left, Part of Pocatello's band in a studio portrait. The man second from left holds a carte de visite photograph, probably of himself. Photograph by Charles William Carter, Salt Lake City, 1870s. bottom right, Arimo or Edmo, Bannock subchief in the McCammon and Inkom areas of southeastern Idaho. Photograph by Benedicte Wrensted, Pocatello, 1890–1914. a, Bannock brass pipe tomahawk. The wooden handle is decorated with inlaid metal shields, tacks, and a buckskin wrap and pendant sewn with lazy-stitched seed beads. Collected before 1921. b, Unusual disk-shaped stone pipe with plain wooden stem. The bowl is inlaid on both sides with a ring of lead. Collected by William Wildschut from Bannock in Idaho before 1922. Length of b 24 cm, other same scale.

the Nevada Shoshone, whom Steward (1955:101–121) characterized as being at a "family level of integration." In later analysis Steward (1970:129–130) more precisely defined the basic unit of all Shoshone society to be the bilateral "family cluster," composed of four or five nuclear families that maintained relatively close and continuing association. Moreover, it must not be inferred that Shoshone families or family clusters were isolates living outside a realm of broader association, for Steward implied only that stable, formalized, and continuing social units of broader scope were absent. In Northern Shoshone society, this was not the case among the buffalo hunters. Even among the foot-going people another component of Shoshone social life emerges. A broad network of ties resulted from shifting residence, intermarriage, feasting, visiting, and extensive migration. Just as there were no firm group or territorial boundaries, so also were there few barriers to communication and interaction (cf. Murphy 1970:158–159). Among the foot-going Shoshone, there was considerable flux and movement in and out of neighborhoods, and the neighborhoods had no strict boundaries. The mounted people coursed back and forth through the territory, from the buffalo grounds of Montana and even Wyoming to the fisheries of the Snake and Boise rivers, from the root fields of Camas Prairie to the Bear River of Idaho and the Green River waters in Wyoming. Perhaps their very lack of large, stable political groupings made the Shoshone a "people" in the truest sense of the word, for the social networks of individuals were widely ramified and interlocking.

Consistent with the composite nature of their bands and the fractured quality of settlement in southeastern Idaho, the Shoshone were both bilateral and bilocal. There were no descent groups or rules of ascribing membership in social units, nor were there strict rules on postmarital residence. People usually lived with the relatives of either mate but sometimes located with more remote kinsmen. Steward (1938:195, 214) reported a tendency toward matrilocality in Lemhi but found bilocality at Fort Hall; the latter was probably the more general mode among all the Northern Shoshone. Most marriages were monogamous, but polygamy was possible. This usually took the form of polygyny (cf. Lowie 1909:210), but polyandry was practiced informally in arrangements of sharing one wife (Steward 1938:215). Polyandry was certainly more common among the Western Shoshone than in Idaho. Sororal polygyny occurred throughout the area, though not universally, and the practices of levirate and sororate were common, though not required, forms of union.

Lowie's (1909:210) Lemhi informants told him that marriage with first cousins was permitted, but Steward's (1938:285) information indicates that marriage with first degree cross-cousins (mother's brother's or father's sister's children) occurred only in Nevada and Utah. In Idaho the preferred union was with a "pseudo cross-cousin" (father's sister's stepchildren, mother's brother's stepchildren, and stepmother's brother's children). Beyond these preferences, the network of possible marriage partners was apparently as broad as the social orbits of these nomadic peoples and contributed to the diversity of kinship ties in the area. There were clusters of kin allied to each other through the pseudo cross-cousin marriage form, but these clusters were also connected to other groups in other areas through more extended marital and kinship links.

Divorce, like marriage, was simple and unformalized and apparently common. Despite customs such as bride abduction, relations between the sexes were relatively egalitarian, and the high status of women may be noted even in the 1980s on the Fort Hall Reservation. Equality and the value on individual autonomy were cardinal principles of Shoshone society, as seen in both the total absence of systematic social stratification and in the marital relationship and the position of the woman.

Kinship Terminology

Kinship terminology among the Northern Shoshone showed a fairly consistent pattern of terminology merging of the mother's sister with the mother and of the father's brother with the father. The mother's brother and father's sister were each denoted by a separate term. There was no distinction, however, between cross and parallel cousins, and all were addressed by brother

Mus. of the Amer. Ind., Heye Foundation, New York: 22407.

Fig. 3. Man on Lemhi Reservation hunting muskrats. The hunter has a spearlike instrument that he used to break into the den and a pipe-tomahawk through the belt at his waist. Photograph by De Cost Smith, 1904.

292

and sister terms. The terminology was thus Dakota on the first ascending generation and Hawaiian on ego's own generation. The Northern Shoshone also shared the general Shoshone pattern by which grandparents and grandchildren addressed each other by the same terms, distinguished only by sex (Lowie 1909:209–210; Steward 1938:284–306).

Property

As can be inferred from their migratory life and the amorphous nature of their social groups, the Shoshone "lacked any form of ownership of land or resources on it" (Steward 1938:54). This lack of corporate or individual ownership extended to fishing sites; root, seed, and pine nut resources; and hunting grounds both within Idaho and east of the Continental Divide, where access to the buffalo belonged to the strongest. All Shoshone had rights to subsistence-yielding natural resources, and even the Northern Paiute were able to share in their fruits. There was private property in tools, weapons and other artifacts, and in foods after they were taken.

Subsistence

Buffalo were hunted in groups by the common Plains technique of flanking the herds on swift horses and dispatching the animals with bow and arrow. Lowie (1909:185) states that the Blackfeet method of driving the herd over a cliff was not practiced, a report contradicted by Butler's (1971a) account of a buffalo jump site on the upper Salmon River. Antelope were taken by stalking by individual hunters wearing antelope skin disguises and also by running the animals on horses. Steward (1938:205) reports the occasional use of antelope corrals. Elk, mountain sheep, and deer were taken by individual hunters or by small parties.

Salmon fishing was important throughout the area and constituted the principal source of subsistence of the Shoshone living below Shoshone Falls and in the western Idaho region. The fish were taken by a harpoon with a detachable head used by individuals standing on platforms or wading in the water. Another important technique was the building of weirs across small streams or channels. The weirs were built of stone and brush and, at times, woven willows. Basketry traps were occasionally set within them. Wyeth (1851, 1:213–214) also reported the use of seines and hand nets. Some degree of cooperation was necessary in the use of weirs and seines, but on a far smaller scale than in buffalo hunting. Other fish caught above Shoshone Falls included sturgeon, suckers, perch, and trout.

The principal vegetables eaten were the camas bulb, the yampa root (*Perideridia gairdneri*), the tobacco-root

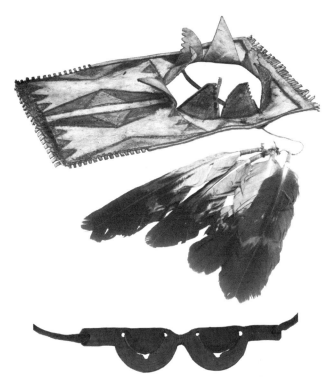

top, U. of Pa., U. Mus., Philadelphia: 38078; bottom, Smithsonian, Dept. of Anthr.: 153, 545.

Fig. 4. top, Bannock headdress of rawhide. The bill and open crown are painted with earth pigments in a parfleche motif. Eagle feathers are attached by a thong to the rear of the crown. The headdress was secured on the wearer's head by a leather thong tied under the chin. Length 47 cm. bottom, Shoshone-Bannock snow goggles, crudely cut from commercial harness leather, with half-circle slits for the eyes, and shallow incised lines as surface decoration. Blue cloth tied the goggles to the wearer's head. Length 22 cm. top and bottom, Collected at Fort Hall, Idaho, about 1892.

(*Valeriana edulis*), and the bitterroot (*Lewisia rediviva*), all of which were taken from the ground with sharpened and fire-hardened digging sticks by the women. The roots were either boiled or steamed in pits dug in the ground, into which hot rocks were placed and covered over with earth. Some residents of Bannock Creek relied on pine nuts (Murphy and Murphy 1960:324). A variety of berries, seeds, and other roots were also collected in the summer, but these activities were usually incidental to hunting expeditions.

Trade

Trade was extensive throughout the region and beyond. It was probably through the intermediary of trade with the Shoshone that the horse reached the Plateau groups, and regular exchange with them into the historic period has been noted to have taken place on the Weiser River. Lewis and Clark noted the presence among the Lemhi people of metal arrow points that had been ob-

294

tained from the Crow in exchange for horses (Lewis and Clark 1904–1905, 3:19). By the 1820s, the Shoshone and Bannock entered the fur trade in varying degrees, and trade with the White trappers took place within their region and at the great summer rendezvous in the Green River country of southwestern Wyoming. The chief participants in the trade appear to have been the mounted people.

Structures

Most information on housetypes, clothing, and artifacts of the Northern Shoshone and Bannock comes from Lowie (1909), who, fortunately, visited the Lemhi at a time when the traditional culture was still alive in the minds of his informants. The Fort Hall and Lemhi people generally lived in tepees (fig. 5), a dwelling type they had borrowed from their Plains neighbors. Throughout the rest of the area, the standard dwelling was a small conical lodge made of sagebrush, grass, or woven willow branches. Small versions of these grass lodges were still built in Lemhi, at the time of Lowie's visit, as sweathouses and menstrual huts (Lowie 1909:183).

Clothing

Clothing varied according to degree of Plains influence (fig. 8). Among the mounted people, both sexes wore buffalo robes in the winter. Dressed elk skins, with hair removed, were worn in the summer. Both men and women at Lemhi wore leggings, but breechclouts were also worn by both sexes. Breechclouts and robes of lesser animals such as the rabbit were standard raiment for the Shoshone farther west (Irving 1837:209). Footgear consisted of moccasins made of elk, deer, and buffalo hide, though people often went barefoot.

Technology

Household artifacts included crude clay vessels, but basketry containers were more common and important. These were of both the coiled and woven variety. Their functions included use as water and cooking vessels, hats, roasting trays, gathering trays, and fans. Water containers and cooking vessels were made watertight by applying pitch to their interior surfaces. Boiling was done by dropping hot stones into a water-filled basket; roasting over open fires or in underground ovens were the other principal means of cooking. Steatite bowls and cups were also made, and the same material was used to make pipe bowls. Rawhide containers became increasingly important with the spread of equestrianism. Infants were carried on the back in cradleboards having backings of willow sticks and white buckskin covers (fig. 9).

The principal weapon of the Northern Shoshone and Bannock was the Great Basin wooden bow backed with sinew, though bows of bighorn sheep and elk horns were also made (fig. 10). Arrow points were made of obsidian, and of metal in later times, and knives were also fashioned from obsidian flakes. Arrow quivers, made of otterskin, were used to carry the fire drill and soft wood hearth by which fires were kindled (fig. 11). In warfare, both men and horses were protected with armor made of folds of antelope skin held together with glue and sand. The war club was made of stone lashed by thongs to a two-foot-long wooden handle, and both head and handle were covered with dressed skin.

Art and Music

The chief medium of graphic art among the mounted Shoshone and Bannock was rawhide, or parfleche, painted design work. Geometric designs were most common, and rectangles, triangles, diamonds, and lineal borders were only occasionally interspersed with curvilinear motifs. Beadwork was by necessity carried out in geometric designs. Plains influences were dominant in this art, but less so among the pedestrian Shoshone to the west. Little is known of realistic art among the Shoshone, except for petroglyphs and Irvings's account of painted Shoshone lodges (Lowie 1909:199).

Musical instruments consisted of the drum, the notched board, and the Indian flageolet. There were two types of drum: one was a small Plains-derived hand drum, and the other was a larger instrument made of a hollowed cottonwood log and covered with elk hide. A notched stick was employed as a rasp in a courting dance (*wihinikkakkinna*); it is widely distributed on the Plains and known in other parts of the Intermontane area. The flageolet was mainly used in courting.

Idaho State Histl. Soc., Boise: top, 77–69.4; center right, 77–69.9; center left, Smithsonian, NAA: 1716-b; bottom left, Natl. Arch.: 75–A0–171–66–101; bottom right, U. of Ill., Dept. of Anthr., Urbana.

Fig. 5. Dwellings. top, Winter residence of canvas tepees with windbreaks of sagebrush. The high-wheeled wagon was the chief means of transportation from about 1880 until the 1940s. Photographed about 1900. center left, Tepees of canvas near Snake River Agency, Fort Hall Reservation, Idaho. A drying rack is in front of the tepee to right. Photograph by William H. Jackson, 1872. center right, Summer tepee made of interwoven rushes and willows. Photographed about 1900. bottom left, Log cabin on the Fort Hall Reservation, which frequently had a rectangular, 4-post summer shade adjacent to it. Photographed in 1966. bottom right, Lemhi menstrual hut, sometimes called a moon house, on Fort Hall Reservation. Such structures were usually large enough for only a single person and were located about 20 feet from the main dwelling. Photograph by Julian Steward, 1936.

left, Natl. Arch.: 75–A0–171–67–21.

Fig. 6. Preparation of deerhide. left, Louella Pocatello fleshing hide with a serrated iron fleshing tool. In earlier times, the hair was removed with an elkhorn scraper with iron blade secured by a thong or with a horse's rib. The brains and bones of the animal were boiled and the mixture used to soften the hide. The deerskin was then soaked in cold water, wrung and scraped, repeatedly, until the material was white and smooth. After being scraped the hide was smoked (Lowie 1909:175–176). Photographed in 1967. right, Dora Hammer Pondzo, a Northern Paiute originally from Oregon, who lived most of her life with the Northern Shoshone in Idaho, placing a tanned hide over a pit with a smoldering fire (smoking the hide). The process gave the material a golden color and special fragrance. Durable gloves and moccasins could then be made from it. Photograph by Sven Liljeblad, 1940.

Religion, Mythology, and Ceremony

Lowie (1909) reported that the basis of Shoshone religion was the belief in the efficacy of dreams and visions, and their use in acquiring the aid of tutelary spirits. In a general way the Northern Shoshone shared in the vision quest of the Plains Indians, though without the element of self-inflicted torture and suffering. In common with the Plains, the tutelary spirit usually instructed the individual in the acquisition and preparation of "medicines," which were used to implement the power granted by the supernatural. The tutelary spirits also imposed certain food taboos and other requirements upon their devotees as a condition of the granting of power. A variety of benefits derived from the spirits. They cured illness, protected the individual from arrows, and could even be used to wreak harm on others.

To a certain extent, all Shoshone and Bannock men were "shamans," but there was also a category of medicine men who specialized in the art to varying degrees. In addition to the services of the medicine man, the Shoshone also used a variety of medicinal herbs and roots. Amulets and charms were believed to have supernatural efficacy.

Although the Shoshone expressed belief in a creator, referred to as *appɨ* 'father', the principal figures in Shoshone mythology are Wolf and Coyote. Wolf is generally believed to have created man and the solar system and is regarded as serious and benevolent. In contrast, Coyote is a trickster who opposes Wolf's efforts and brings disorder to the world. Out of their struggle, the world as man knows it took shape. Other myths relate to ogres and animal creatures. Both the latter and the Coyote-Wolf stories have wide distribution in North America, but their chief affinities are to Great Basin and California mythology (Lowie 1909:235–236).

Most of Northern Shoshone and Bannock ceremonialism took the form of dances, which commonly followed the pattern of the Great Basin Round Dances. The most important at Lemhi was the *nuakkinna*, or ta-nū´in (Lowie 1909:217), which was celebrated in early spring to insure the return of the salmon and the regeneration of the food supply. Another ceremony was held at the time of the actual arrival of the salmon. The

296

Smithsonian, Dept. of Anthr.: left, 22, 294; center 27, 817; right, Idaho State U. Idaho State Mus. of Nat. Hist., Pocatello: 3525.

Fig. 7. Northern Shoshone and Bannock feathered headdresses. left, Headdress with a forked trail that would have reached the ground behind the wearer. The headband is of red stroud covered with a buckskin band with seed beads lazy-stitched in triangles of dark blue, light purple, green, and yellow, with edge bands of dark green and yellow. Erect rough-legged hawk and peacock feathers are attached, as are antenna-like wires strung with tan linen yarn, anchored behind buttons with green ribbon pendants. Below the headband is a scalp lock with a tuft of split red-tailed hawk feathers. The red stroud trailer is edged with blue stroud affixed by zigzag interlocking stitches of yellow yarn. On the edges are brass buttons with red, green, and yellow ribbon pendants; hawk bells and brass buttons alternate along the fork edges. The trailer once had 3 parallel lines of pendants: red-tailed hawk feathers, the quills wrapped with dark blue, red, and green and white seed beads, attached to hawk bells. At the apex of the fork are a magpie feather, a swan feather, and small red-dyed plumes, stuffed under a hawk bell. Collected on the Fort Hall Reservation, Idaho, in 1876. center, Northern Shoshone headdress. A fur turban, most likely horsehide, supports 2 antelope horns and a cluster of split eagle and magpie feathers and grouse tail feathers tipped with strips of ermine. Split turkey vulture feathers decorate the top of the trailer. Below them are red-tailed hawk tail feathers and 2 sets of golden eagle tail feathers tipped with downy underplumage. Collected by J.W. Powell, Utah, 1875. right, Bannock feathered bonnet. A cap of brown felt is the foundation for a lazy stitch beaded front band, on both sides of which are round mirrors and 3 ermine-skin pendants. Red stroud, edged with blue stroud, forms the double trailer. The golden eagle tail feathers are tipped with bits of ermine and gold and white tassels of dyed horsehair. Collected from Charlie Bell, Fort Hall, about 1950. Length of right 177 cm, rest same scale.

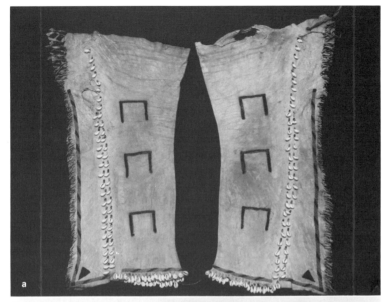

a

b

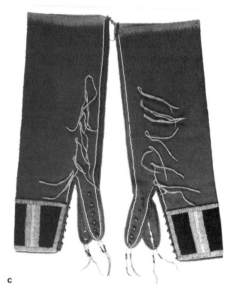

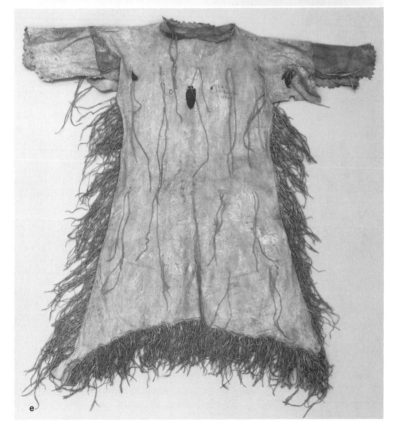

c

d

e

opposite page top right and this page, top left, Natl. Arch.: 75–SEI–19, 75–SEI–10; a, U. of Ariz., Ariz. State Mus., Tucson: E-3717a, b; Smithsonian, Dept. of Anthr.: b, 19,876; d, 22,001; e, 19,828; f, 19,855; g, 19,834; h, 19,858; c, Harvard U., Peabody Mus.: 40–79–10/22619.

Fig. 8. Clothing. opposite page, top right, Frank George (b. 1866, d. 1939) and his wife Pohena (b. 1861, d. 1931). She wears a beaded buckskin dress, and a leather belt decorated with metal studs. He wears a cloth shirt, leggings, and waist blanket, and beaded armbands and carries a beaded, fringed pouch. Photograph by Benedicte Wrensted, Pocatello, 1890–1914. this page, top left, Young woman from Fort Hall Reservation wearing stroud dress decorated with cowrie shells, small round disks, and beads. She also wears a leather belt with metal studs, hair pipe choker, and bead and metal bracelets. Photograph by Benedicte Wrensted, Pocatello, 1890–1914. a, Pair of straight-bottom leggings, a style common throughout the Plains after 1850 (cf. Schneider 1968), buckskin, smoked yellow, cut in the pattern introduced with trade stroud. Rows of cowrie shells are strung on buckskin thongs with green and brown glass "bugle" beads. Length 78 cm; collected at Fort Hall, 1913. b, Man's tunic made from a single hide, with fringed strips added. Bullet holes in in the back hide were patched aboriginally with buckskin. Length 36 cm; collected by J.W. Powell from Goose Creek Northern Shoshone, Utah Terr., 1871–1879. c, Fine red flannel "panel legging" with beaded cloth sewn onto legging bottoms (Koch 1977). The hide fringes of aboriginal sewn leggings are here replaced by the long side flaps and the thongs along the outside seam and on the flaps. Brass buttons line the cuff panels and side flaps. The blue stroud panels and leggings are edged with seed beads. Trade stroud quickly replaced skin for leggings. Length 66 cm; collected from the Bannock, 1869–1880. d, Three-piece woman's mocassin-leggings stitched with sinew. The sole is rawhide, the upper, well-tanned buckskin. Height 48 cm; collected by J.W. Powell from Northern Shoshone at Bear Lake, Utah Terr., 1871–1879. e, Woman's buckskin dress of 2 hides with separate patches applied as sleeves, stitched with sinew. An Elko Corner-notched stone projectile point hangs from at the front yoke; a bird beak hangs from one shoulder, and a bird foot and claws hang from the other. Length 83.5 cm; collected by J.W. Powell from Goose Creek Northern Shoshone, Utah Terr., 1871–1879. f, Elaborate feathered buckskin skirt made from two pieces of hide, with separate fringed strips. Two rows of buckskin thongs on the front and back of the skirt hold split feathers, deer hooves, and squirrel and chipmunk tails. Length 63.5 cm; collected by J.W. Powell from Goose Creek Northern Shoshone, Utah Terr., 1871–1879. g, Boy's tunic of beaver skin, tanned with fur on. Length 38 cm; collected by J.W. Powell from Goose Creek Northern Shoshone, Utah Terr., 1871–1879. h, Girl's fawn skin dress made from 2 skins, buckskin fringes added. Buckskin thongs, front and back, sport fawn hooves. Length 58 cm; collected by J.W. Powell from Goose Creek Northern Shoshone, Utah Terr., 1871–1879.

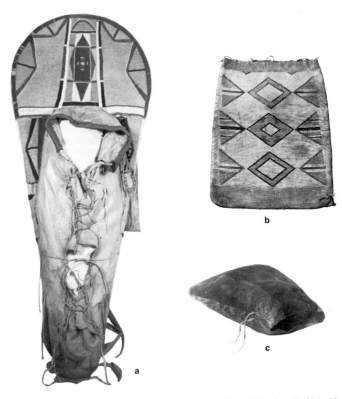

left, Harvard U., Peabody Mus.: H 5355; a, Riverside Municipal Mus., Calif.: A1–587; b, Mus. of the Amer. Ind., Heye Foundation, New York: 20/1356. c, Idaho State U., Idaho Mus. of Nat. Hist., Pocatello: 5938.

Fig. 9. Cradleboards and containers. left, Family of Bannock Indians at Ross Fork, Fort Hall Reservation, Idaho. The small child is in a buckskin-covered cradleboard that has an elaborately beaded headboard. Photograph by Scott, 1915–1916. a, Elaborately beaded, buckskin-covered cradleboard with buckskin carrier. Backboard is a flat piece of pine. The buckskin cover, decorated in geometric motifs of lazy-stitched blue, yellow, green, black, and red seed beads, is Crow-Nez Perce style. A beaded leather pouch, probably to hold butterfly pupae for medicine, and 10 large, blue trade beads hang from the side of the board. Collected before 1911, perhaps as early as the 1870s. b, Nez Perce–style woven carrying bag collected from Bannock at the Lemhi Reservation, Idaho. c, Salmon-skin bag for chokecherries and other berries. It was carried over the shoulder by holding the buckskin straps. Made by Cora George of Blackfoot, Idaho. Length of a 113 cm, rest same scale.

blessings of the Round Dance were also sought in the fall and in time of adversity at other periods of the year (Steward 1938:193).

The Shoshone shared in the warfare practices of the Plains, counting coup and taking the scalps of enemies. They also borrowed the scalp dance from the Plains, and scalps were brought to the village and placed on a long pole, which formed the focus of the dance. Other borrowed dances include a Cree dance introduced during the reservation period and the Sun Dance. Dances were also carried out for purposes of enjoyment in times when food was abundant and large numbers of people congregated at a single locale, such as at Camas Prairie during the summer. These were also the periods during which the hand game and other gambling pastimes so common in the Great Basin and Plateau areas were played.

The lack of elaborate ceremonial or of highly specialized religious practitioners was congruent with the nomadic and shifting nature of Shoshone society and with its egalitarianism. Everybody was to some degree a shaman, just as everybody was to some degree a chief. Their religion was, of course, just as deeply important

for them as for other peoples, but the forms that it took were simple, in keeping with their way of life.

History†

The effect of the European colonization of the New World had profound impact upon Shoshone and Bannock society a century before European knowledge of them, and long before they, themselves, had even encountered a European. It is estimated that the horse reached the Shoshone in the late seventeenth century, filtering northward along the west flanks of the Rocky Mountains from the Spanish settlements of the Southwest. By that time, the Shoshone had completed their millennium-long spread through the Basin and into the southern fringes of the Plateau, and equipped with their new mounts and equestrian abilities, they spread beyond the Rockies into Montana as far as Canada in search of the now accessible buffalo (D. Thompson

†Important contributions by Joseph Manzione are incorporated in the section on History.

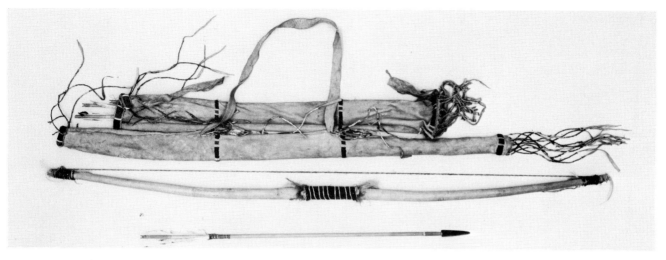

Smithsonian, Dept. of Anthr.: top, 203, 809; bottom, 9044.

Fig. 10. Archery equipment. top, Ornate bow, arrow, and bowcase-quiver set. The bowcase and quiver are smoke-tanned buckskin, stitched with sinew, and decorated with quill-wrapped buckskin fringes, dyed red, turquoise, and white, and bands of red, green, blue, yellow, and white seed beads. The bow is a thick, heavy, double-curved self-bow with red-dyed, quill-wrapped buckskin strips below each nock end holding tufts of yellow-dyed horsehair. The 4 arrows, with slightly flaring V-shaped nocks, are painted red and green above the tips and below the nocks. The shafts are tipped with steel points, held with heavy sinew wraps. The bow, arrows, and style of the bowcase-quiver are characteristic of the Northern Shoshone, Bannock, and Eastern Shoshone. Length of bow 128 cm; collected by Emile Granier in Wyo., before 1899. bottom, Elaborate 2-piece bowcase-quiver made from a single dog skin. Pieces of beaded green felt, bordered with red ribbon, backed with trade cloth, and sporting ribboned rosettes of beaded buckskin sewn over canvas were stitched to the insides of the paws. Beading was done in light purple, white, red, dark blue, black, and green, on the rosettes. Two rosettes supporting fringes of white rabbit fur wrapped in beaded red stroud were sewn to the bandelier. Strips of white rabbit fur were also used to fringe the bowcase flaps. An eagle feather, the quill wrapped in red stroud and top notched, hangs by a short leather thong from the quiver flaps. This is an early documented example of the classic Plains 2-piece bowcase-quiver combination, which emphasized minimal alteration of the natural shape of the hide, even to use of the tail as a pendant from the mouth of the quiver. The general style is common from the Blackfeet to the Apache (Holm 1981). Use of a dog skin is unusual, although this pelt is particularly luxurious (Mason 1894 misidentified it as bear); more usual is otter or mountain lion skin. Arrows collected with the quiver are crudely shaped hardwood shafts, lacking in decoration except for 3 "blood grooves." These are fletched with closely trimmed, split red-tailed hawk feathers, and tipped with metal points. The bow is sinew-backed, highly reflexed, with a thick, 3-strand string, and buckskin thong grip. Length of bow 97 cm; collected in the Idaho Terr. before 1869.

1916:328ff: Wissler 1910:17; Shimkin 1940:22; Ewers 1955:16–17; Hultkrantz 1958:150). The Blackfeet, first armed with the gun and later mounted, pushed them back from the Plains by the mid-eighteenth century to their approximate area at the time of contact. The beginnings of the equestrian period also saw the splitting off and migration southward of other Shoshone who became known as the Comanche.

The horse, firearms, and the push of the White settlers westward caused turmoil in the Plains and adjoining areas as the newly mounted populations fought for hunting territories and horses. The dislocation became even more severe with the penetration of the region by fur trappers and traders in the early nineteenth century. British trading interests pushed south and west from Canada, and by 1809 David Thompson established posts on Pend Oreille Lake in northern Idaho. At the same time the American traders moved westward up the Missouri waters, following the route of Lewis and Clark. The North West Company founded a post at the junction of the Big Horn and Yellowstone rivers in 1807. Andrew Henry located a post in 1810 on Henry's Fork of the upper Snake River, in the heart of the Fort Hall Shoshone and Bannock country. John Jacob Astor's Pacific Fur Company established a post at Astoria on the mouth of the Columbia River in 1811, and steamboats began service to his Fort Union, on the upper Missouri River, in 1832. The Snake drainage had been thoroughly penetrated and exploited by the North West Company after 1818 and, shortly after that date, by Peter Skene Ogden of the Hudson's Bay Company. The Rocky Mountain Fur Company began operations in 1823, its trappers ranging through western Wyoming, southern Idaho, and northern Utah. The only positive results of the ensuing disruption of native life and destruction of the beaver was that the more literate of the traders and factors left behind journals that are the major sources of knowledge of the Indians of the region (Beckwourth 1931; Bryant 1885; Farnham 1843; Ferris 1940; Irving 1837; Leonard 1904; O. Russell 1921; R. Stuart 1935; Townsend 1905).

The Shoshone did not become involved in the fur trade to the same extent as the Algonquians and Athapaskans of Canada, although they did do extensive business with the Whites at the annual summer rendezvous that took place on the Green River in Wyoming, Cache Valley, Utah; Pierre's Hole in southeast Idaho; and other locations. The fur trappers and the Indians also hunted out the remaining buffalo herds west of the Continental Divide during this period, and by 1840 they were gone from the Green and Snake River areas; by 1860, they were scarce even in Montana. Also, the fur trade had collapsed by 1840; the beaver had been hunted out of the region, and the fashion for beaver hats had declined.

302   The end of the fur trade brought no quietude to the area, for the 1840s saw the beginning of the White emigration to California and Oregon. The Oregon Trail went over South Pass, Wyoming, passed either through or north of Fort Bridger, ascended the Bear River to Soda Springs, Idaho, and then cut westward along the Snake and Boise rivers. Beginning as a trickle in 1841, and growing with the Marcus Whitman group in 1843, the White emigration became a flood by 1850. There was some predation upon the emigrant parties by groups such as Pocatello's band, but most of the Idaho Shoshone and Bannock were scattered in hunting activities during the summer emigration season and did not often encounter the White travelers.

The end of autonomous life for the Shoshone and Bannock began in the 1860s with the virtual disappearance of the buffalo herds and the beginning of White settlement. Mormon pioneers settled the Bear River valley in 1860, and the rest of the decade saw settlers enter the Boise River valley and other areas of southern Idaho. Farther north, gold miners penetrated the Sawtooth Range. There were many minor clashes between Indians and Whites, ending with the Bannock War of 1878, which began in Idaho but culminated among the Northern Paiute of Oregon, and the infamous Sheepeater War of 1878–1879, perpetrated by White miners in the Salmon River district. The United States pursued a policy of treaty making with the Indians in the 1860s, and pacts were concluded in 1863 at Fort Bridger, Box Elder, and Soda Springs, with the Boise Shoshone at Fort Boise in 1864 and with the Bruneau River Shoshone in the same year. The Fort Hall Reservation was established in 1867 for the Boise and Bruneau people, and the Fort Bridger Treaty of 1868 located the Fort Hall Shoshone and Bannock on the same reserve. The Lemhi and Sheepeater populations were assigned a reservation in the Lemhi valley in 1875, but the reservation was terminated and the Indians removed to Fort Hall in 1907.

The Fort Hall Reservation, originally some 1,800,000

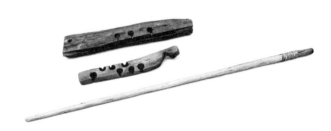

Mus. of the Amer. Ind., Heye Foundation, New York: 13/1501.

Fig. 11. Wooden fire hearths and drill. Rubbed vigorously between the palms, the hardwood drill spinning in the hearth would ignite dry tinder placed to the side. Collected by William Wildschut at the Fort Hall Reservation, Idaho, sometime before 1924; length of drill 47 cm.

acres in size, had been reduced to 524,000 acres by the 1950s due to a series of cessions, but a program of reacquisition reversed the losses. The first major encroachment on the reservation came with the building of the Union Pacific Railroad from Ogden, Utah, through the reservation to the mines of western Montana in 1877, followed two years later by the extension of the railroad to Oregon (Madsen and Madsen 1980). As a result of the railroad cessions, and the growth of the city of Pocatello as a transportation hub and center for White squatters, the boundaries were renegotiated in 1881; by 1900 the reservation acreage was halved (U.S. Office of Indian Affairs. Land and Law Division 1880–1887).

Further shrinkage of reservation lands was brought about by the Dawes Severalty Act of 1887 and the allotment of reservation lands to individual Indian families during the years 1911 to 1916. Aridity and poverty of soil made small holdings infeasible, and the program was largely a failure. Allotment in severalty was terminated by the Indian Reorganization Act of 1934, and as of 1956, there were 277,900 acres of land in allotment, 204,600 acres in tribal ownership, and 41,400 acres in government holdings. The land problems were exacerbated by the lack of irrigation water and the fact that the Fort Hall Irrigation Project of 1912 and sub-

sequent water developments mainly benefited White farmers. Add to this the flooding of Snake River bottomlands by the American Falls Reservoir, the inroads of timber and phosphate mining interests, and further cessions for highway and other rights-of-way, and it becomes clear that the integrity of the Fort Hall Reservation had been seriously compromised.

The Indian Reorganization Act of 1934 was a profound change in direction of U.S. government policy toward Indian peoples. Whereas previously policy had been assimilationist and was characterized by the active suppression of Indian language and culture, the New Deal initiative sought to promote reservation autonomy and self-determination and to encourage the preservation of Indian cultures and values. To that end, reservations were urged to elect tribal councils and establish business corporations to manage tribal funds and resources. The Shoshone and Bannock of Fort Hall approved a constitution and by-laws in 1936 and ratified a corporate charter in 1937 (Council Minutes, July 9, 1940).

Although Northern Shoshone and Bannock culture change since the nineteenth century has been generally in the direction of loss of the aboriginal ways and the adoption of Euro-American culture, two important postreservation innovations have come from other Indian tribes. One of these, the Plains Indian Sun Dance, was adopted by the Eastern Shoshone of the Wind River Reservation, Wyoming, in 1890 and diffused to Fort Hall a few years later (Liljeblad 1972:95). The Sun Dance unites humans with the domain of holiness through mortification of the flesh and is entered into as a way toward curing of illness, restoration of harmony and the promotion of spiritual and physical well-being. The Sun Dance gatherings have become great public celebrations that attract other Shoshones from Wyoming, Utah, and Nevada, as well as an audience of people from other tribes and Whites. As such, the rites are expressive of Indian unity and the active perpetuation of native life. The Sun Dance has been closely associated with Plains Indians, even in reservation times, and it did not spread westward from Fort Hall.

Another native religious movement, the Peyote religion, has spread from its precontact origin in Mexico to most of the Indian reservations of the United States. It first appeared at Fort Hall in 1915 (Liljeblad 1972:103) and has remained important since that time. A sacramental religion, Peyotism incorporates significant elements of Christian belief while remaining jealously guarded as an exclusively Indian cult. Much more so than the Sun Dance, it is pan-Indian in spirit and content, despite its syncretistic nature. One of the principal means of transmission of Peyote music is through records and tapes, an example of the uses of modern technology in diffusion and in the preservation of a distinctively Indian way of life.

Fig. 12. Shoup Deepwater preparing native hemp for cordage twining. The cordage, usually plied, was used in netting, for binding, and in heavier gauges for rope. Exceptionally strong, plied cordage lasted indefinitely. Photograph by Sven Liljeblad, Fort Hall Reservation, Idaho, 1940.

303

NORTHERN SHOSHONE AND BANNOCK

left, Idaho Histl. Soc., Boise: 77-69.7; top right, Mus. of the Amer. Ind., Heye Foundation, New York:23/8993; bottom right, Amer. Mus. of Nat. Hist., New York: 50/1181.

Fig. 13. Grass Dance, a Plains-derived dance similar to the *nuakkinna*, in which the men sometimes used white clay on their foreheads and hair. The object of the *nuakkinna*, and Grass Dance, celebrated in early spring, was to ensure plentiful food, such as salmon, berries, and grasses (Lowie 1909:217). left, Performers. The elaborate costumes include beaded vests, bandoliers, kilts, mocassins and leggings. The man in the center holds a feather wand. Photographed at Ross Fork, Fort Hall Reservation, Idaho, about 1900. top right, Golden eagle feather hair ornament. Small dyed tufts decorate the top and bottom of each feather, and midway up the quill. Strands of braided, beaded hair are anchored to the base of the quills. This may be a braid wrap ornament or a decorative element for a hair roach. Collected from the Northern Shoshone, Idaho, before 1966. bottom right, Beaded moccasins, Bannock; collected by A.L. Kroeber on the Fort Hall Reservation, Idaho, in 1900. Length of top right 33 cm, other same scale.

By the twentieth century most of the Northern Shoshone and Bannock were located on the Fort Hall Reservation, with a small number living among the Western Shoshone and Northern Paiute of the Duck Valley Reservation. There has been extensive intermarriage between Paiute and Shoshone speakers on both reservations, but to a surprising degree people identified themselves in the 1980s as either Bannock or Shoshone, and both languages were still in constant usage. Liljeblad (1958) reported that in 1950, 750 adults, or almost half the adult population, could neither read nor write English, and some 200 could not speak it. Education of the ensuing generations has reduced these figures.

The people of the Fort Hall Reservation have income far below the norm for the region, and unemployment is an endemic problem. Educational levels have shown improvement, but Indian children still perform at a lower level than their White classmates, into whose schools they have been integrated since the 1950s. This is wholly explicable by the language barrier, frequent lack of parental involvement, and the fact that school is commonly a child's first encounter with Euro-American society (Liljeblad 1972a).

On the positive side, tribal income from leases and mineral rights has increased greatly, agriculture has shown increased profitability, and improved public health has been a contributing factor in the growth of on and off-reservation populations. The award of $15,700,000 to Northern and Eastern Shoshone by the Indian Claims Commission in 1968 also strengthened the tribal economy. The Northern Shoshone and Bannock are assiduously defensive against outside threats to their economic, political, and cultural autonomy, a stance that bodes well for tribal persistence. The people of Fort Hall, with their own constitution and under the leadership of a competent elected business council, have attained political, economic, and educational status closer to their White neighbors than is usually realized. At the same time, they preserve valued parts of their traditional heritage promoting bilingual education, keeping their own library, museum, weekly newspaper, and having their traditional festival dress patterns and dances adapted to the annual festivals of a modern calendar (fig. 15). Accordingly, their future is contingent upon their ability to balance economic integration with cultural distinctiveness.

304

Bureau of Ind. Affairs, Washington.
Fig. 14. Men playing Indian monopoly, a game played only in the daytime (Bonnie Teton, communication to editors 1984). Photographed at Fort Hall Reservation, Idaho, about 1936.

Synonymy

For the origin of the name Shoshone, see the synonymy in "Eastern Shoshone" (this vol.).

Early reports on the Indians of the southern Oregon and Idaho area are complicated by loose and contradictory identifications, one of the most common of which was the failure to distinguish the speakers of Shoshone and Northern Paiute. Alexander Ross, who had entered the service of the Pacific Fur Company in 1810 and spent the next 15 years in the area, identified the "Ban-at-tees" as a branch of the "great Snake nation," which he found to be synonymous with the "Sho-sho-nes" (Ross 1956:166). The term "Snake" had variable application, sometimes being used to denote all Shoshone and Northern Paiute speakers of the region and sometimes to distinguish the mounted buffalo hunters, as opposed to the Diggers or Root Diggers of the Nevada and Utah deserts (cf. Bryant 1885:137, 168, 211; Wilkes 1845, 4:471). The labeling of Shoshones as Snakes was apparently widely employed by other tribes in the region. The two sons of the explorer Pierre Gaultier de Varenne, Sieur de la Vérendrye, were told of the existence of a people whom they reported on as Gens du Serpent after their 1742 tour of the northern plains, although it is not entirely certain that the reference is to Shoshones (Margry 1888:601). Lewis and Clark identified their hosts in the Lemhi River valley as "Sho-shonees," but were later told by Indians on the Columbia River of their fear of a "Snake" tribe in central Oregon (Lewis and Clark 1904–1905, 3:147). Both Work (1945:6) in 1832 and Ogden (1909–1910:206) in 1826 encountered Indians whom they termed "Snakes" in the Harney Basin of Oregon. Ogden in the same year also found a "Snake" camp of 200 on the Raft River in southern Idaho (Ogden 1909–1910:357). The equation of Snake and Shoshone was carried into the ethnographic literature by Albert Gallatin, who placed the "Shoshonees proper" east of the Snake River, the "Western Shoshonees, or Wihinasht" to the west, presumably in Oregon, and the "Ponasht or Bonnacks" along the banks of the Snake and Owyhee rivers (Hale 1848:18). The term Snake was gradually displaced by the designation Shoshoni or Shoshone during the second half of the nineteenth century. Henshaw (1910:557), who lists numerous variants and synonyms, noted the official restriction of "Snake" to the Yahuskin and Walpapi groups of Northern Paiute in Oregon; however, other contributors to Hodge (1907–1910) continued to refer to these Northern Paiutes as Shoshoni.

Despite the multiplicity of names such as Snakes, Diggers, Bannocks, Shoshocos, Shoshonees, Mountain Snakes, and so forth, given them by other Indians and by early travelers, none of these terms or their Shoshone equivalents was used as a self-designation. In common with most of the Shoshonean speakers of the Great Basin area, the Shoshone and Bannock both call themselves *nimi*, with the predictable stress on the first syllable in Shoshone and on the second in Bannock (Kroeber 1907a:102; Liljeblad 1957:23; Lowie 1909:206). These terms mean simply 'the people' and were used to refer to that collectivity of persons having common language and customs who formed a part of each individual's network of social relations. Although the term has the connotation of 'human being', it does not deny humanity to other ethno-linguistic groups, but merely rel-

Shoshone-Bannock Tribes, Sho-Ban Media Center, Fort Hall, Idaho.
Fig. 15. Give-away by the Pahvitse family in honor of Lori Pahvitse, who was concluding her year as Miss Shoshone-Bannock 1977–1978, at the annual Shoshone-Bannock Festival and Rodeo, Fort Hall Reservation, Idaho. left to right, Sophronia Poog, Richard Johnson, Alceodine Pahvitse, Randall Pahvitse, Lori Pahvitse, Natahn Jim, and Andrew Punkin.

egates them to a generalized "they" category as opposed to the "we" of the inner social world.

The term Bannock and its variants are English corruptions of Shoshone *pannaitti* or Northern Paiute *pan·ákwati*. Liljeblad (1957:22) gives the first term as the Northern Shoshone designation for the Northern Paiute living among them, and the second as the term the Bannock use to distinguish themselves from their Shoshone fellows and neighbors; the Gosiute dialect of Shoshone has the variants *paʔanehti* and *paʔanepiccih* for 'Bannock, Northern Paiute' (Miller 1972:125). Conversely, the Bannock called the Shoshone *wihínakwati*, and the Northern Shoshone referred to themselves as *wihinaitti* to distinguish themselves from the Bannock. Liljeblad (1957:23) states that "these terms were not tribal designations but referred to a linguistic dichotomy in a bilingual group." Although the term for Bannock became standardized, *wihinaitti* and its variants appears only sporadically in the literature (cf. Hale 1848:18). This is congruent with the fact that the Bannock always constituted a minority in the area, and their separate status was noted by the term that distinguished them from the predominantly Shoshone population.

Subgroups‡

The names of the local groups of the Northern Shoshone are discussed here; these groups, often identified by a type of food commonly eaten in a given area, are not regarded as political divisions.

Agaideka. This name, from Shoshone *akaitikka* 'eaters of salmon', is applied in this chapter to the Northern Shoshones on the Snake River below Twin Falls. In Shoshone it is also used for the groups in central Idaho here called Lemhi and Tukudeka (Steward 1938:165, 186–187); Steward's spelling was Agaidüka.

Kammedeka. The *kammitikka* 'eaters of jackrabbits' were the Indians who ranged from the Snake River, between Bannock Creek and the Raft River, to Great Salt Lake. Steward (1938:177, 216–217) distinguished the Kamudüka from the Promontory Point group he called Hukundüka (see the synonymy in "Western Shoshone," this vol.), but other sources use *kammitikka* and *hukkantikka* 'eaters of wild wheat' as synonymous names (Steward 1938:216–217; Sven Liljeblad, communication to editors 1985).

Lemhi. The Lemhi ('lem,hī) Shoshone are those of the Lemhi River valley and the upper Salmon River; they were also one of the groups called *akaitikka* (Steward 1938:186–187). The name Lemhi is a local place-name of White origin derived from the *Book of Mormon*.

Pohogwe. The Shoshone and Bannock of the upper Snake River are referred to as *pohokʷi* 'people of sagebrush butte', referring to The Ferry Butte on the Fort Hall Reservation (Steward 1938:198). This group is also referred to as the Fort Hall Shoshone and Bannock.

Tukudeka. The mountain-dwellers of central Idaho, southern Montana, and the Yellowstone area of Wyoming were the *tukkutikka* 'eaters of mountain sheep'; they were also one of the groups called *akaitikka*. Steward (1938:186–187) used the spelling Tukadüka, and Hodge (1907–1910, 2:835) lists additional early variants under the heading Tukuarika. The name Sheep-Eaters also appears in English (ARCIA 1865:175). The name Mountain Shoshone is among a few given by Hoffman (1886:297).

Yahandeka. The Yahandeka (*yahantikka* 'eaters of groundhogs'; Steward's Yahandüka) were the Shoshone on the lower Boise, Payette, and Weiser rivers (Steward 1938:165, 172). This country was called *si·wo·kkiʔi* 'willow-striped'; the same notion is reflected in the French name Boisé 'wooded', which appears in Shoshone in borrowed form in the alternative self-designation *poisi nimi* (Sven Liljeblad, communication to editors 1985). Hoffman (1886:298) listed the Ya·handi·ka, and his reference appears in Hodge (1907–1910, 2:982) under the heading Yahandika.

Sources

The two principal sources on Northern Shoshone and Bannock culture are Lowie (1909) and Steward (1938). Lowie (1909) is an invaluable repository of data on material culture, mythology, and certain aspects of social organization collected among the residents of the Lemhi Reservation before their move to Fort Hall. Lowie (1930) described Bannock kinship terminology, and Hoebel (1939) did the same for Northern Shoshone in comparison with Comanche. Steward's (1938) classic monograph, based on fieldwork throughout Nevada and Utah and at Fort Hall in 1933–1934 complements Lowie's (1909) study by providing detailed descriptions of economic life, domestic groups, and sociopolitical institutions; some analytical refinements are in Steward (1977). Steward (1938b) also gathered data on Lemhi native remedies and practices of physical therapy. The distribution of culture elements, except mythology, among the Northern and Gosiute Shoshone is dealt with by Steward (1943a) on the basis of fieldwork in eastern Idaho and northern Utah.

Liljeblad (1972) is part of the yield of a lifetime's work at Fort Hall. Another monograph combining ethnographic and historic research is Murphy and Murphy (1960), which focuses on social organization and subsistence patterns up to the settlement of the Indians on

‡This section was written by Ives Goddard, incorporating Shoshone forms and other information supplied by Sven Liljeblad (communication to editors 1985).

reservations about 1868. Based largely on the above sources is a brief discussion of Shoshone-Bannock culture and subsistence in Walker (1973). For the archeology and prehistory of the region consult Butler (1978).

Hultkrantz (1954) focuses on the relationship between nature and the religion and culture of the Northern Shoshone bands in Yellowstone Park, while an ethnohistory of the Shoshone presence in the Rockies is given by Hultkrantz (1957a, 1974) and Trenholm and Carley (1964). On the Lemhi in particular see B.D. Madsen (1979) and Crowder (1969), the latter mostly a biography of Lemhi chief Tendoy, and again B.D. Madsen (1958) on the Bannock. A comprehensive history of the Northern Shoshone and the Fort Hall Reservation from the mid-1800s to 1970 is by B.D. Madsen (1980). For another study on the history of Fort Hall see Zimmerman (1959). Two other studies were conducted at Fort Hall: one on federal Indian land policy (S.J. Laidlaw 1960), and the other on the overall economy and living conditions (Nybroten 1964).

There are a number of primary historical sources on the Northern Shoshone and Bannock, beginning with the journals of Lewis and Clark (1904–1905). Irving's (1837) account of the adventures of Capt. B.L.E. Bonneville, the journals of fur trappers Peter Skene Ogden (1909–1910), Alexander Ross (1956), and John Work (1945), and the report of Commander Charles Wilkes (1845) encompass the fur trade period from 1810 to the 1830s. The chief historic sources for the 1850s and after are contained within the annual Reports of the Commissioner of Indian Affairs (ARCIA 1846–). These embody correspondence with field agents and are primary documents for the reservation period and the 10 years preceding it. Drawn mostly on these sources are W.C. Brown's (1926) account of the Sheepeater War of 1879, and Brimlow's (1938) history of the Bannock War of 1878.

A number of museums hold important collections of Northern Shoshone and Bannock artifacts. The Idaho State Museum of Natural History, Pocatello, has a large and extensive collection. Well-documented collections by A.L. Kroeber and R. H. Lowie are housed at the American Museum of Natural History, New York. Baskets collected by W. Wildschut around 1900 are at the Museum of the American Indian, Heye Foundation, New York, which also holds other important collections. The Utah Museum of Natural History, Salt Lake City, has a small collection of Bannock basketry. The holdings at the National Museum of Natural History, Smithsonian, are not large but do contain a singular collection assembled for the 1876 centennial celebration.

Eastern Shoshone

DEMITRI B. SHIMKIN

The Eastern Shoshone have occupied western Wyoming and, periodically, adjoining areas since A.D. 1500 or earlier. Throughout this period, they have combined Great Basin cultural traditions with those of the pre-horse and horse-period Plains, while restructuring their culture by borrowing from Spanish, Métis, and Anglo-American sources. In these processes, the Eastern Shoshone have manifested continuing creativity, particularly in the domains of politics and religion. Although they suffered great losses of persons and wealth in the nineteenth century, falling from a population of perhaps 3,000 in 1840 to 800 in 1900, they had recovered to about 2,400 men, women, and children of a quarter-blood or more by 1981 (U.S. Bureau of Indian Affairs. Enrollment Office, communication to editors 1985).

Language

Eastern Shoshone speech clearly belongs within a west-east continuum of closely related dialects (Miller, Tanner, and Foley 1971), showing particular affinities with other northern dialects, including those of Fort Hall, Owyhee, Ruby Valley, and Skull Valley Gosiute.* Morphologically, the similarities with materials from the Gosiute (Miller 1972) and Big Smoky Valley, Nevada (Crapo 1976), are systematic.

To the east, data are less extensive and of varying quality. Nevertheless, only trivial differences in vocabulary and phonology are found in the comparison of Eastern Shoshone with data from Saskatchewan in 1800 (Shimkin 1980:210–211), the Upper Yellowstone in 1805 (Burpee 1910:72), and the Great Bend of the Arkansas in 1819–1820 (E. James 1823, 2: lxxix). Eighteenth-century Comanche name lists (A.B. Thomas 1932:325–328) also display a compatible phonology; the loss of preconsonantal nasals characteristic of modern Comanche is not evident until the mid-nineteenth century.

For vocabularies, grammatical sketches, and texts of the Eastern Shoshone see W.J. Jones (1875); Shimkin (1947a, 1949); Tidzump (1970); Miller, Tanner, and Foley (1971); and Vander (1983).

A survey by T.L. Haynes (1976:87) indicated that, among women aged 15–49, 43 percent retained use of the Shoshone language.

Territory

Several lines of evidence support the hypothesis of a Shoshone entry into western Wyoming about 1500, with migration far out into the northern Plains subsequently (Shimkin 1940; Wright 1978). Archeological data indicate a concurrent depopulation of the Central Rocky Mountains area, with resettlement ensuing about 1800, as part of the great Shoshone westward retreat. This is supported by the discovery in central Wyoming of a cleft, bundle burial of distinctly Shoshone type, dated A.D. 1430 ± 110 (Wright 1978; Miller and Gill 1981). It is also consistent with Rehrer and Frison's (1981) analysis of changes between 1400 and 1600 at the Vore bison killing site in the Wyoming Black Hills.

Keyser's (1975) attribution of the Plains shield-bearing warrior motif to Shoshone origins is plausible. However, a direct relationship to Dinwoody and related western Wyoming pictographs ethnographically attributable to the Eastern Shoshone has yet to be shown (Gebhard 1951, 1969; Gebhard and Cahn 1950). It is also unclear how the steatite vessel tradition noted as early as A.D. 720 at Mummy Cave, northwestern Wyoming (Wedel, Husted, and Moss 1968), entered and was maintained in Eastern Shoshone culture.

Decisive proof of the great Shoshone advance and retreat in the northern Plains came with David Pentland's 1976 discovery of the Shoshone word list of Peter Fidler, the Hudson's Bay Company factor at Cumberland House, Saskatchewan, in 1800 (Shimkin 1980:208–209). These findings had been anticipated by Teit's (1930:303–305) reports from Salishan informants (see also Hultkranz 1968).

In 1805, Meriwether Lewis and William Clark (Thwaites 1904–1907, 6:82, 106–107) reported from hearsay that the Shoshones ranged on both sides of the Rockies from the Missouri to the Arkansas rivers and

---

*For the transcription of Shoshone words, see the orthographic footnote in "Western Shoshone," this vol. Shoshone words in italics are in phonemic transcription, transcribed on the advice of Wick R. Miller and Sven Liljeblad (communications to editors 1985). Nonitalicized Shoshone words could not be transcribed into the phonemic orthography on the basis of the information available to the editors and have been left in the orthography of the source.

were divided into "three large tribes" who wandered at a considerable distance from one another.

Other observers of the early nineteenth century encountered the Shoshone over a wide area, often in the company of other tribes. In 1805 Larocque (Burpee 1910:22–37) met 20 Shoshone lodges visiting the Mandan with a much more numerous Crow party. They traveled together to the Big Horn River. In 1821 Jacob Fowler (Coues 1898:51–54) saw Shoshones in a large trading rendezvous dominated by Comanches on the upper Arkansas. In 1826 James O. Pattie (Thwaites 1904–1907, 18:138–139) met a large party of Shoshones, clad in buffalo robes, equipped with muskets, and provided with horse and mule transport, on the Little Colorado, in Navajo country. They had recently destroyed a company of French hunters on the headwaters of the Platte.

O. Russell (1921:144–145), who traveled with the Shoshone in 1837, stated: "Their country comprises all the regions drained by the head branches of Green and Bear Rivers and the east and southern head branches of the Snake River. . . . They seldom stop more than eight or ten days in one place." A similar territory is delineated by Hamilton's (1905:63, 71–73) recollections for 1842.

Shimkin's (1947) data define a complex pattern of land use for the nineteenth century, about 1825–1880. The Eastern Shoshone may be differentiated into Buffalo Eaters (Sage Brush People) and Mountain Sheep Eaters (Mountaineers). The Buffalo Eaters, in particular, did not have a single set of specified boundaries, but a hierarchy of different boundaries with pragmatic and religious significance. In this hierarchy the valleys of the Green and Wind Rivers (fig. 1) had a core value, with other plains and mountains being exploited episodically. Moreover, the Eastern Shoshone, like many other plains and mountain people, had a pattern of annual movement with concurrent tribal concentration or dispersal (fig. 2). Finally, the whole area was under continuing assault from plains tribes, first the Blackfeet and later the Arapaho and Sioux, who had been displaced by the advancing Western frontier.

The Mountain Sheep Eaters occupied the central Rocky Mountain region, including the area around Yellowstone Lake, but also interacted with the Buffalo Eaters; in the 1980s they were concentrated at Sage Creek on the Wind River Reservation. Dominick (1964) and Hultkrantz (1954, 1966–1967) cover the scanty literature available on these people.

History

Eastern Shoshone protohistory and history since about 1500 can be described in seven phases, beginning with pre-horse penetration of the High Plains and adoption

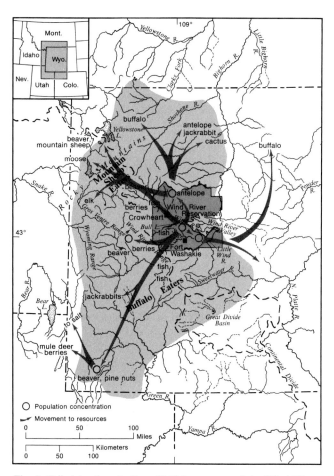

Fig. 1. Tribal territory in the mid-19th century and the Wind River Reservation in 1975. Arrows show seasonal movement to food resources.

of large-scale buffalo hunting, 1500–1700. During this period, the Comanche-Shoshone attained high competence as a militaristic, buffalo-hunting people. With the acquisition of horses came the second phase, of widespread raiding throughout the Plains, 1700–1780. In this period, it is certain that strong chiefly leadership and considerable protocol and sumptuary rights prevailed. The third period, 1780–1825, was marked by defeat by the Blackfeet, who had firearms, by smallpox, and by retreat to the west, with some cultural reorganization but much instability. A key development, about 1800, was the introduction of the Sun Dance by the Comanche Yellow Hand (Shimkin 1953; Hultkrantz 1971a).

The fourth period, 1825–1880, was one of White alliances and renewed tribal vitality under Washakie (Shimkin 1942; T.H. Johnson 1975). Early reservation life, intense hardship, population losses, and slow cultural restitution characterized the fifth period, 1880–1910 (Shimkin 1942). In the sixth period, 1910–1945, there was cultural and demographic stabilization and renewed innovation, especially in religious institutions (Shimkin 1953; Voget 1948, 1950). Since 1945, Eastern

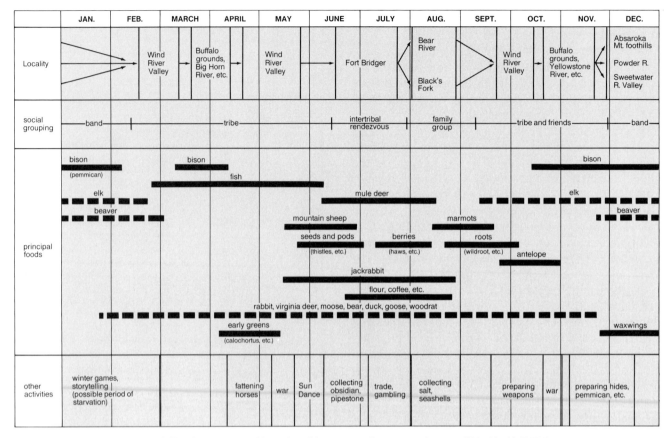

Fig. 2. Annual subsistence round. Foods are arranged in order of importance from top to bottom (Shimkin 1947:279).

Shoshone have experienced population growth, new occupations, cultural stabilization, urban adaptation, and growing Arapaho political dominance on the reservation (U.S. Bureau of Indian Affairs 1960; Schutz, Baker, and Vanvig 1960).

Trenholm and Carley (1964) provide a comprehensive, documented, but somewhat uncritical overview of Eastern Shoshone history.

Culture

Political Organization

The key to Shoshone survival in the Plains was effective leadership in the bison hunt, warfare, trade, and winter shelter. During Washakie's ascendancy after 1842, and in earlier prosperous times such as the chieftainship of Mawoma (fig. 4), the Shoshone were a tribe of 1,500–3,000 people, at least seasonally. This assemblage decomposed into three to five bands in the winter and early spring. Each had a loose association with a particular region of western Wyoming but was neither spatially bounded nor named. Membership in each also fluctuated, with extended family groups now joining one and then another, or sometimes another tribe such as the Crow (Shimkin 1947; Larocque in Burpee 1910:22–37).

In the tribe and, to a varying extent, in each band, the conduct of chieftainship was aided by two military societies, and by a variety of largely temporary aids, such as heralds. There is little evidence of an active tribal council.

Of key importance was the chief (*te·kʷahni*), a middle-aged or older man of military and shamanistic distinction who gave orders affecting the tribal march or a collective hunt and who gave counsel on issues of joint decision (cf. *te·kʷa-* 'to talk, to order'). He had various assistants, usually temporary, such as the game scout (*kuʔiawappi*), and control of the two military-police societies (Lowie 1915). A number of sumptuary signs marked his status. His tepee was painted, usually with a broad yellow band. He wore a special feathered headdress, and his place in a battle charge might be marked by an eagle standard (Bourke 1891:337). The Shoshone chief met visitors, often with a preliminary smoking ritual. He had little to do with internal disputes (Hoebel 1940:131–134).

Tribal viability in the bitter contest for access to buffaloes demanded critical numbers for both military effectiveness and large-scale killing and carcass processing, the disciplined control of military societies, and the moral integration given by the Sun Dance. The two Shoshone military societies, the Yellow Brows and the Logs, were complementary rather than competitive. The

310

Joslyn Art Mus., Omaha, Nebr.: 163.

Fig. 3. *Woman of the Snake Tribe,* a Shoshone who was the wife of an American Fur Company employee at Fort McKenzie, La. Terr. Her dress is typical of Blackfeet women: "a long leather shirt . . . [with] short wide sleeves, ornamented with a good deal of fringe . . . thin leather strips, [and] with broad diversified stripes of sky-blue and white glass beads" (Maximilian 1843, 2:249). There were several Shoshone women among the Blackfeet camped near Fort McKenzie, probably prisoners from raids (Maximilian 1843, 2:228). Watercolor by Karl Bodmer, Fort McKenzie, Sept. 1833.

Yellow Brows, so named for their yellow painted cockscomb hairdo, were a group of 100–150 brave young men, recruited by a ritual involving "backwards speech," in which, for example, "no" meant "yes." Committed to fearlessness, they acted as vanguards on the march. In combat, their officers, the bravest of the brave, might plant their otterskin-wrapped staves on the ground and not give way even at cost of death. The Yellow Brows prepared for battle with a dance that brought man and horse into sacred ecstasy, the Big Horse Dance. The Logs were middle-aged men who acted as rear guards. All were honored for their military deeds, which entitled them to blacken their faces (see also Lowie 1915, 1924).

The Shoshones went through periods of tribal strength and weakness. In 1837, the leadership of the Buffalo Eaters Pah-da-hewakunda and Mawoma over 3,000 Shoshones was beginning to break up. By 1842, after their deaths, divisiveness prevailed (O. Russell 1921:114–

115, 144–146). Washakie (fig. 5), already prominent in 1837, was a band chief, as is evident from Hamilton (1905). In 1852, when Brigham Young brought representatives of the Ute and the Shoshone to Salt Lake City to negotiate peace and to permit expanded Mormon settlement, Washakie went as the leading Shoshone chief. From this time on, Washakie's status was strengthened by his key role as negotiator between White and Shoshone (see also Murphy and Murphy 1960:310–314).

Social Organization

In general, the traditional roles of Shoshone women embodied several paradoxes (Shimkin 1947b). On one hand, women were socially subordinated to men. Menstruation stigmatized women as sources of dangerous ritual pollution. Polygyny involved conflicts and the economic exploitation of the younger wife or wives; almost never sororal, its stresses were inherently high. Widowhood was marked by mourning and dispossession. On the other hand, women possessed critical skills in plant gathering, household crafts, household transportation, child care, and other areas. Women gained status from successful husbands but also as individuals. In middle and older ages, midwifery, curing, or gambling earned prestige. But their roles were particularly transformed by the advent of the fur trade. As T.H. Johnson (1975) has shown, daughters and sisters became the key instruments of alliance with White and Métis trappers and traders. Interethnic ties through these marriages became prominent very early (O. Russell 1921).

Age and sex largely determined roles and statuses within traditional society; inheritance also played a modest role. Otherwise, social positions were earned, attributed to the acquisitions or nonacquisitions of supernatural power (Shimkin 1947b).

Infants in the cradleboard, little girls, and boys too young to shun their mother's menstrual hut were dependents undifferentiated by sex. They were rarely chastised but kept quiet through fears of monsters and enemies. Larger boys joined peer groups, spending their time in horse riding and care, hunting, and rough play, with aggression much encouraged by their elders, as in the Magpie ceremony of the Sun Dance. Adolescence was not formally marked. The search for supernatural power began at this time. Marriage and joining a military society connoted a man's status, *tennappi* meaning both man and husband. Grandchildren, a second or third wife, rising prestige as a shaman, a growing reputation for wise advice and for skill in storytelling, perhaps chieftainship, marked the successful old man.

A girl would stay with her mother, helping in household chores, caring for younger siblings, and playing girls' games, until marriage. Menarche required isola-

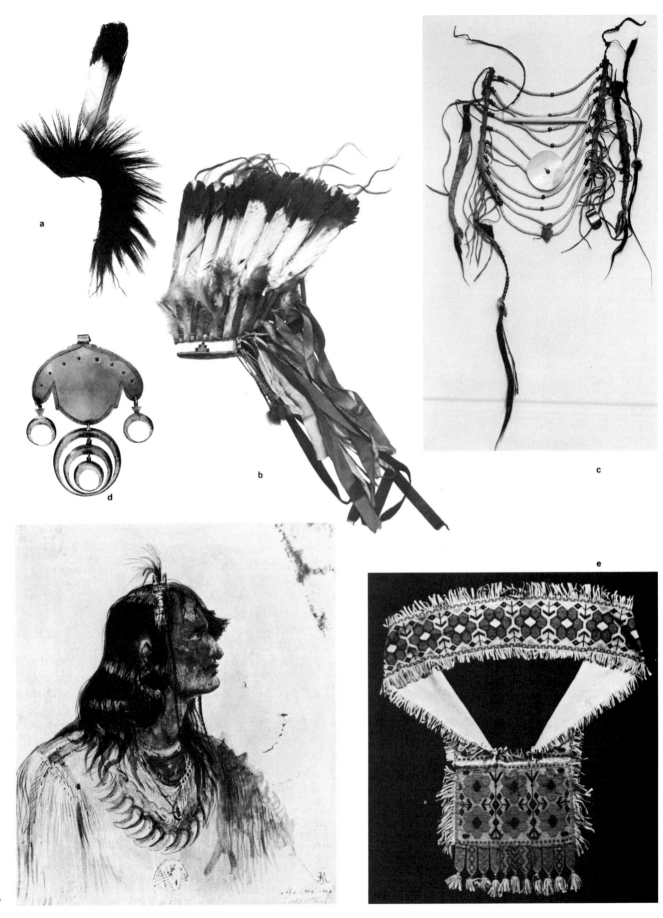

a

b

c

d

e

bottom left, Thomas Gilcrease Inst. of Amer. Hist. and Art, Tulsa, Okla.: 0236.1095; a, Field Mus., Chicago: 60748; Amer. Mus. of Nat. Hist., New York: b, 50/2440; e, 50.1/1271; c, Smithsonian, Dept. of Anthr.: 200, 934; d, Denver Art Mus., Colo.: 1956.154.

Fig. 4. bottom left, *Ma-wo-ma or Little Chief*. The name Little Chief "was somewhat of a misnomer, the subject of it standing nearly six feet in his moccasins" (Miller in M.C. Ross 1968:pl. 35). Watercolor by Alfred Jacob Miller, Green River, near Wind River Mountains, Oreg. Country, 1837. a, Porcupine hair roach. Dyed in bright colors, and flying eagle or other feathers from a wood or bone spreader, roaches were an essential part of male dance costumes ("Northern Shoshone and Bannock," fig. 13, this vol.). b, Feathered bonnet with golden eagle feathers, tufted with dyed horsehair and wrapped in stroud holding downy plumes, placed around a buckskin cap. The headband is ornamented with lazy-stitched seed beads. This headdress was intended for men's dances or other public displays. c, Breast ornament attributed to Dick Washakie, son of Washakie. Ten strands of white ceramic beads are strung between side bars of commercial harness leather. The free ends of the thongs stringing the beads were passed through the side bars, knotted, split, and left as decorative fringes. Hair (mostly horsehair, some human) wrapped in cloth, rabbit fur, or brass barrel beads was hung from the lateral fringes. Attached to the center of the bead strings is a shell moon, with a brass barrel bead at the center tie. Above this is a shell hairpipe 15.5 cm long, and below, a stone projectile point. Both the hairpipe and the moon are probably *Strombus gigas*, a West Indian conch, popular trade items throughout the 19th century. The shell hairpipe was replaced by cheaper, more durable, bone hairpipes in the 1880s (Ewers 1957). The point is of the Elko Side-notched type, dated 2000 B.C.–A.D. 1000. Beaded breast ornaments of this style were characteristic of the Eastern and Northern Shoshone, Nez Perce, and other northwestern tribes until about 1900, when they were in large part replaced by Plains hairpipe breastplates. d, Pectoral of German silver, dated to the late 19th century. The form may derive from the faceplate of Spanish bridles (Conn 1982). Designs were engraved into the metal by stamping or by walking or rocking a metal chisel across the surface. e, Beaded bandolier, an article of clothing favored by males throughout the northwestern Plains. The beadwork was done on a beading loom and is only tacked to the skin. The floral design was borrowed in the 19th century from Northeast and Plains Indians. Made by an Eastern Shoshone woman with the surname Spoonhunter, a family still active in the 1980s in the production of native crafts, particularly fine beadwork. a, Collected on the Wind River Reservation, Wyo., about 1901; b, collected on the Wind River Reservation, in 1901; c, collected at Fort Washakie, Wyo., before 1910; e, collected in Wyo. before 1899. Length of a 47 cm; b, c, e same scale. d, 10.5 by 17.8 cm.

tion in the family menstrual hut, the avoidance of meat and of daytime sleeping, and the obligation to gather firewood. Shortly after menarche, a girl's parents or, if they were dead, her older brother or maternal uncle would arrange her marriage. These relatives sought a good hunter, a stable and reliable although often much older man.

Kinship

In the kinship terminology, which was still used in the 1980s, distinctions are evident between primary and descriptive terms (fig. 7). Moreover, collective and quasi-kin terms indicate, respectively, focal and indefinitely extended relationships. Except for three male affines

Smithsonian, NAA: left, 85–1372; center, 42,023-e; right, Southwest Mus., Los Angeles:196–L–2.

Fig. 5. left, Washakie; photograph probably by Charles W. Carter, 1860s. center, grandson of Washakie wearing hairpipe breastplate and small-bead collar; photograph by Baker and Johnston, about 1882. right, Beaded chief's boy's saddle. A wood frame underlays the rawhide cover. White beads from the background; decorative elements are in blue, rose, yellow, and green seed beads. The hide-covered wooden stirrups are attached to the saddle with beaded heavy rawhide straps. The cinch is undecorated commercial harness leather. The lavish expenditure of effort to create this beading is typical of the love and status bestowed on favored children of important families in Indian societies of the northern Plains. Collected at Fort Washakie, Wyo., before 1930.

313

EASTERN SHOSHONE

314

(husband, son-in-law, brother-in-law) and for wife, the primary morphemes refer to consanguinal kin. They distinguish the kinsman's line of descent and generation and, in part, the sex of the speaker. The grandparental, cross-avuncular, and cross-amital terms are self-reciprocal. The descriptive terms provide alternate, more specific labels for some consanguinal relationships and are particularly developed in the affinal vocabulary, with female teknonymy being the major analytical base. For certain affines, descriptive terms have replaced the extended use of primary terms recorded by Lowie (1924).

Collective terms group relationships of special social closeness: *nanatua* 'son and father' (*nana-* 'reciprocal' + *tua* 'son'), *nanapapi* 'two brothers' (*nana-* + *papi* 'older brother'). They are found only for parent and child of same sex, parents, parents and children, spouses, and siblings of the same sex. Quasi-kin terms bring distant relatives and friends into the domain of kinship: *naniwi* 'relative', *taka* 'man's close friend', *ti?i* 'woman's close friend'. Such extensions link not only individuals but also kindreds in alliances (T.H. Johnson 1975). From such ties come pseudo-sibling terms and, as frequent consequences, the pseudo cross-cousin marriages also known among other Numic peoples (Eggan 1980). The marriage of true cousins is regarded as incestuous; the anomalous affinal terms noted particularly by Lowie (1924) reflect extended, not literal, usages.

Life histories and mythological stereotypes illuminate Eastern Shoshone kinship behavior in the past and, to a considerable extent, in the twentieth century (Shimkin 1947 a, 1947b). Both parallel and cross-cousins are deemed to be more distant siblings. Other consanguinal relations rest upon those of parent and child, and of siblings. If these are close, then the more extended grandparental, avuncular, and amital relations also are close.

In the past bride service was common, especially a young groom living initially with his bride's parents.

During the nineteenth century, a number of kinship behaviors changed. O. Russell (1921), Hamilton (1905), and Brackett (1880) agree on the high frequency of polygyny among the Eastern Shoshone. It is also likely that sibling exchange marriages were common, as is indicated by the kinship terminology. However, Shimkin's (1947b) genealogical data, covering the period 1850–1930, report only three cases of polygyny, two of sibling exchanges, and three of marriage with consanguinal kin, in a total of 239 marriages. Christian influences are likely causes of such change.

Wealth and Property

The buffalo-hunting Shoshone of the nineteenth century enjoyed some economic surplus (Farnham 1843:28–29). This is clear even for the period of retreat to the West. Chiefs could be wealthy. In 1874–1878 the 1,250 Eastern Shoshones had 3,300 horses and 1,400 cattle, but of these the subchief Taboonshiya owned 100 head of cattle and about 50 head of horses (ARCIA 1875: 132–133, 1877: 209, 1878: 150).

Shamanistic curing and midwifery also commanded important incomes, while the successful gambler, male or female, and the fast runner profited significantly. Good hunters and trappers and shrewd traders (particularly, partners with Whites or Métis) likewise accumulated resources, which gave both prestige and obligations (T.H. Johnson 1975).

In general, Eastern Shoshone society was both differentiated and commercialized to a degree. Its terminology recognized chief or master (*te·k^wahni*), trading partner (*tattakanti*), servant or slave (*titewappi* worker); the rich (*canahkanti*) and poor (*tittannahkanti*); hire (*titenai*), sale (narenwak), debt (nagacaxan), gambling (tivhakwa), gambling winnings (*kwakkuppi*), and theft (*titikappi*) (Shimkin 1937–1938, 1966–1975; Tidzump 1970). Money (ohapuwi 'yellow metal') was well

Glenbow-Alberta Inst., Calgary, Alta.: 349/291 AE-X-4.
Fig. 6. Elk hide painted about 1880, supposedly by Washakie. It serves as a fine representation of traditional Shoshone society, emphasizing the importance of the Sun Dance in ensuring successful buffalo hunting and warfare, and hence, the health of the people. Top-center on the hide (top entire hide painting; bottom detail) is a depiction of the Sun Dance center pole, adorned with a buffalo bull's head, backstrap and tail, hung over a willow bundle tied in the fork of the cottonwood tree. When so displayed during the Sun Dance, the bull's head faced west and the backstrap-covered willow bundle hung down on the east side of the pole. That this arrangement does in fact represent the Sun Dance is confirmed by the placement of the large drum and musician-singers to the southeast of the center pole, as they would be placed in the actual ceremony. However, the dancers' positions, costumes, and orientation to one another and to the center pole indicate that the artist was juxtaposing cultural elements to express his view of his society's well-being. Sun Dance dancers would have been clad only in breechclouts or aprons and would have had rattles and eagle-bone whistles; none of these elements is present. Also, in the Sun Dance, the dancers would be facing the center pole, or arranged around it facing east. These dancers are arranged in rows, without regard to the center pole, engaged in what appears to be a rapid alternating step dance, clothed in elaborate costumes that include hair roaches and eagle feathers, belts, and cloth breechclouts that trail long in the rear, leggings with bells, shirts, metal armbands, breast ornaments, and chokers with small mirrors. The dancers' positions, orientation, and costumes may well reflect the War Dance described by Lowie (1909), which also involved a forked cottonwood tree in the middle of the dance area. Surrounding this composite central scene is painted a marvelously detailed buffalo hunt, with depictions of thrown riders and various aspects of butchering. Since the oldest known form of Shoshone Sun Dance was performed to ensure the ongoing success of the buffalo hunt and dominance in war (Shimkin 1953), one may assume that the painter placed Sun Dance elements in the center of his composition to relate these two very importance aspects of Shoshone society— buffalo in number to meet the people's needs, and the ability to fend off enemies in war—thereby guaranteeing the long-term survival of the Shoshone. Hide is 157 by 152 cm; collected about 1880.

315

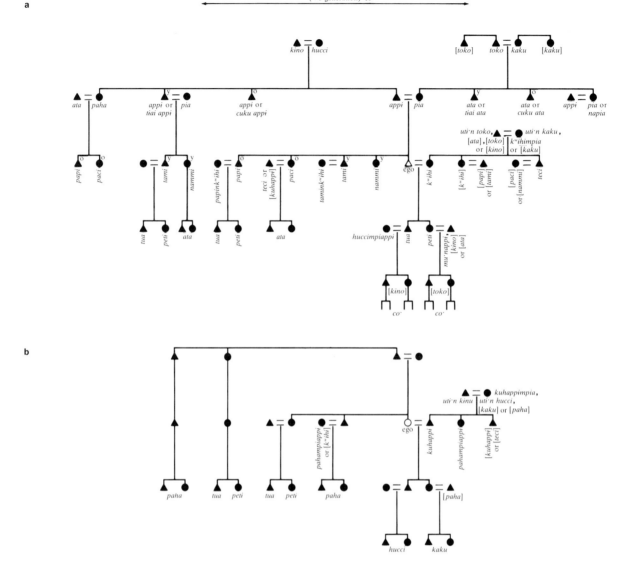

Fig. 7. Eastern Shoshone kinship terminology. a, Male ego. b, Female ego. Terms for omitted or unlabeled kin types are the same as for male ego. Bracketed terms were reported by Lowie (1924) but were not in general use in the 1930s. Sources: Lowie (1924), Shimkin (1937–1938, 1966–1975, 1941, 1947a), Tidzump (1970).

known. Economic relationships were enhanced when trading partners became formal older and younger brothers, with corresponding extensions of kin networks.

Economic calculations were aided by a decimal system of up to 100,000, supported by counting sticks of varying unit value.

At the same time, a number of forces limited economic ordering. In Shoshone theory, all significant accomplishment was (and is) a shamanistic gift through vision quest, dream, or, rarely, transfer from kin. This gift is accompanied by highly specific and personal taboos, for example, the limitation of curing payments to particular ritual articles. Generosity is an abiding ex-

pectation; in the 1980s the public announcement of meritorious deeds was still accompanied by a giveaway of valuables (Vander 1978). And, up to World War II, death required extensive property destruction or abandonment.

Subsistence

The Eastern Shoshone were favored by a large and diverse inventory of faunal resources. These were supplemented by berries and roots, with seeds of minor importance. Access to these resources was limited by natural conditions and the actions of hostile tribes. Hunters had rights to their kill, with a sequence of sharing followed for buffalo. Sites for fish weirs or game traps involved only temporary property rights; plant gathering, none. Food was ritualized only to a minor extent, the most important practice being a taboo on meat eating by women in menstrual or birthing retreat.

Staples of the Shoshone diet were the buffalo, fish (especially trout), elk, beaver, and mule deer. Major but periodic game included the antelope, jackrabbit, mountain sheep, marmot, and sage hen. These were supplemented by many minor food sources, from moose to wood rat. The lynx, mink, otter, and weasel were valued as furbearers but not eaten. A few people, particularly in the Green River area, ate lampreys, ants, locust, crickets, and owls. Women, especially in late summer and fall, picked currants, rose berries, hawthorns, and gooseberries. They dug up wild roots, camass, and wild onions. Greens, pistils and leaves, and the sugary content of honey plants, gilia, cinquefoil relieved dietary monotony. Thistles and some kinds of sunflowers served as the only sources of seeds (Shimkin 1947:265–270).

The seasonability of foodstuffs governed the annual aggregation, movement, and dispersal. The buffalo was by far the greatest resource, an animal that weighed 1,200–1,800 pounds when adult and provided a virtually endless list of edible parts and industrial products. But, certainly after 1840, it was available to the Shoshone only for a brief period in the spring and a longer season in the fall, and then at great risk from hostile tribes. Although the Shoshone women were skilled, rapid butchers and were also efficient in drying buffalo meat into strips easily packed into leather parfleches carried by pack horses, they were able to use buffalo products only with low efficiency. The primary limitation was the vulnerability of their horses. These, on one hand, quickly consumed available fodder in short-grass prairies; on the other, could not be too widely dispersed for fear of theft. In consequence, the Shoshone could rarely gain as much as half their annual food supply from the buffalo.

The buffalo hunt itself demanded considerable discipline, enforced by persuasion and scolding from the Yellow Brows. First, two or three scouts would be sent out to locate a herd grouped close together. These men would signal the camp by loping back and forth. All hunters then mounted their fast buffalo-hunting horses. The herd would not flee but tend to move closer together. Then, some hunters sought to shoot their prey; others, to hamstring it with lances. What had to be watched for beforehand was untoward sound that would alert the buffalo's keen hearing.

The principal food fishes of western Wyoming are cutthroat trout, Montana grayling, and Rocky Mountain whitefish. They were taken primarily in the spring, when other food supplies were low, and were either eaten fresh or preserved by sun-drying or smoking. The

characteristic method was weir and driving: "The Shoshone dammed a stream with wattle work and rocks, leaving a gap where a gunny sack might be placed to catch the fish. Then others entered the stream below the dam on horseback, to move upstream while lashing the surface with poles, the whole accompanied by song. The frightened fish were driven to the gap and captured en masse" (Bourke 1891:340).

Next in importance to buffalo and fish were elk, denizens of upland valleys and forests. The elk was less migratory than the buffalo, with many browsing alternatives. Elk in herds were run down like buffalo; single elk were tracked like mule deer. They were specially vulnerable in winter snow drifts to hunters on snowshoes. Of the other game, mountain sheep and beaver were most important, although the beaver was virtually eliminated by trappers in the 1830s.

For floral resources, the upland forest and high prairies, the sources of berries and roots, were most important. Berries were eaten fresh, or in soups, or were pounded with buffalo or elk meat and fat to be preserved as pemmican. Roots were commonly cooked in the earth oven. In the drier steppe and desert, the prickly pear was prized as a source of glue and paint stock. It was rarely eaten.

Technology

Animal products, woody materials, and minerals (flint, obsidian, slate, steatite, salt, mineral paints) provided all the important industrial raw materials except iron. This metal, widely used for arrow heads, knives, lance points, scrapers, chisels, and other tools, was entirely imported from traders. The products were either pur-

Field Mus., Chicago: 53160.
Fig. 8. Steatite vessel. Height 24.7 cm. Collected at Little Warm Spring Creek, Wyo., 1896.

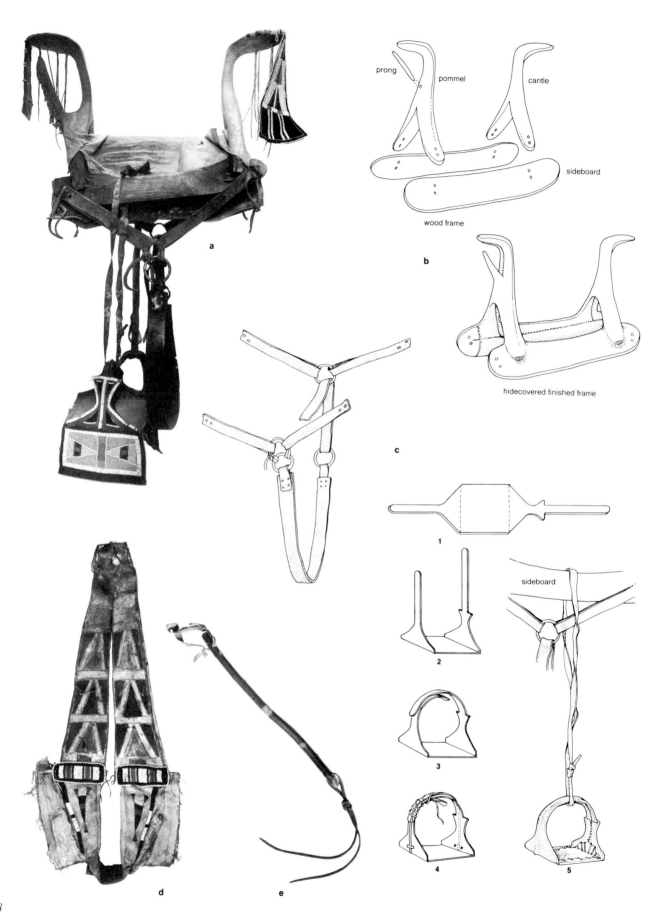

a

b

prong   pommel   cantle

sideboard

wood frame

hidecovered finished frame

c

1

2

sideboard

3

4

5

d

e

318

SHIMKIN

chased or cold-worked; blacksmithing (Gebow 1868) was known but evidently not practiced.

A major problem of Shoshone household operation, prior to extensive trade, was the supply of firewood. The gathering of twigs and branches for cooking and heating was one of the most exhausting of women's and girls' chores, especially in winter.

While family level exchanges must have been ubiquitous, and there was generosity toward the hungry, no systematic approach to the procurement, storage, and distribution of foodstuffs or industrial materials appears to have been practiced. Each took care of his own.

By far the most important items of manufacture were those of transport and leather goods. While horse breaking, horse guarding, and the care of buffalo horses were strictly for men and boys, women rode and cared for pack and riding animals. Again, while most leatherwork was woman's work, men prepared shields, hide drums, and rattles. The skills involved in Shoshone crafts were widely shared, but part-time specialists also were evident. Such persons usually directed the cutting of hides for tepee construction. Women gained prestige and profit from well-made, well-decorated parfleches; men, from excellent bows, arrows, and lances. Distinct patterns of art, geometric versus naturalistic, were characteristic for women and men.

The Shoshone prized horses and dogs as aids in transportation, hunting, and war; neither animal was eaten except in direst need, nor were the hides and bones of either animal put to economic use. Horsehair, however, was a valued fiber. Horses, particularly those wounded in combat, would be decorated with paint and feathers in mane or tail. Buffalo horses were regularly curried by their masters. While dogs had no ritual associations, at least the buffalo horse was sacrificed on a man's grave, horses participated in the Big Horse Dance of the Yellow Brow society, were protected by special horse medicines, and provided omens. For example, three rapid pawings of a front hoof which left a column of half-moon marks signified the owner's forthcoming death.

A substantial continuity is evident between the Shoshone horse culture observed in 1805 (Thwaites 1904–1907, 2: 329–383, 3: 19–32; Larocque in Burpee 1910) and Eastern Shoshone practices of later periods. This includes high skill in riding by men, women, and children; abundant horses and a few valued mules; men caring for war horses, women for pack animals and baggage; distinct men's and women's saddles, the former a simple pad and the latter of Spanish type with high pommel and cantle, and with stirrups; bit-halters with reins on either side of the horse's head; painting and feathering; lassoing; shields, bows, lances, and maces as cavalry equipment; column and charging line led by chiefs as basic tactical formations (see also Frémont 1845:147; Bourke 1891:312, 337); and horses as payments for marriage. Only the practice of ear cutting and antelope hide armor disappeared.

Eastern Shoshone horse culture fits in well with Ewers's (1955:323–327) general model. For example, the Shoshone used rawhide-lashed wood-handled whips but not spurs, transported the infirm with horse travois, had horse raids with formal recruitment, drumming and singing of war songs prior to departure, and valued horses as stakes in gambling and as prestigious giveaways.

Amer. Mus. of Nat. Hist., New York: a, 50/2289; d, 50/2291; e, Smithsonian, Dept. of Anthr.: 200, 798; b, after Ewers 1980:fig. 52; c, after Wissler 1915:fig. 10.

Fig. 9. Riding equipment. a, Woman's saddle, with flat-headed pommel and cantle, heavily beaded pommel and cantle flaps, and elaborate stirrup flaps. Design elements consist of light blue, orange, and green triangles within light blue and dark blue fields outlined in white. Beads were sewn to red stroud stitched over buckskin, except for the beads sewn directly to the hide cover of the stirrups. Rigging straps are native tanned leather or rawhide, to which are tied the cinch rings and commercial leather girth. b-c, Saddle and rigging construction. The saddle was built of green cottonwood, used for the sideboards, about one-half inch thick, 16–20 inches long, and 4 inches wide (Ewers 1980), and often curved, and for the pommel and cantle. The pommel and cantle were lashed to the sideboards by buckskin thongs. The final step in construction of the saddle frame was the addition of a buffalo rawhide cover. Stretched over the wooden framework, the hide was fitted and cut, and seams sewn with a rawhide cord on the underside of the sideboards. After the saddle had dried, two holes werre burned into the ends of each sideboard, for tying on grass-stuffed pads, which ran parallel to and underneath the boards. Stirrups were made from a single piece of cottonwood, cut, grooved, and bent to shape. A strip of prepared buffalo hide was stretched around the outside of the stirrup, and stitched with rawhide lacing through the bottom of the foot rest. The stirrup from here is characteristic of women's saddles among the Eastern Shoshone, Crow, and Blackfeet (Wissler 1915). The saddle was secured to the horse by a single cinch strap. Rawhide rigging straps were attached to the opposite ends of the sideboards. Indians saddled and mounted horses from the right (Euro-Americans prefer the left), and the manner of rigging is reversed from that of Whites. The rigging straps on the left are tied to the cinch ring. Early on, a a rawhide tie would have sufficed for the cinch ring, but later, as metal rings became available, these were preferrred. Cinch bands, if Indian-made, were about four fingers wide or wider (the cinch is of commercial harness leather). The stirrups were adjustable, not only in length but also in placement along the saddle. d, Typical Plains-style crupper, which appears to be a direct borrowing of the Spanish crupper introduced into the Southwest in the early 17th century. Its function was to keep the saddle from sliding frontward. The broad panels of painted hide ran back from the saddle over the horse's rump, where the 2 attached buckskin and canvas pads were held by the strap under the horse's tail. The long hide straps are painted with yellow and red triangles in panels outlined in blue and green. Stroud patches covering the seams between the straps and rump pads are beaded in light blue, red, dark blue, yellow, and red seed beads. Buckskin sections sewn over the heavy canvas backing of the rump pads are beaded with triangles of dark green, red, light blue, purple, gold, and dark blue seed beads. e, Cherry branch quirt with a patched buckskin wrist thong and a commerical harness leather lash. Use of undecorated wood or antler handles was common among Basin groups, although lavishly decorated specimens are also known. e, Length 49 cm; rest same scale. a and d, collected at Fort Washakie, Wyo., 1900; e, collected in Wyo. before 1899.

Fig. 10. A reconstructed camp circle during the centennial of Wind River Reservation, Wyo. In the foreground is a woman in semi-traditional dress with cradleboard on her back. Photograph by Thomas H. Johnson, 1968.

Amer. Mus. of Nat. Hist., New York: 50.1/1294.

Fig. 11. Hunting shield, plain rawhide with a white buckskin cover painted with 2 buffalos, one blue, the other black and yellow, above an eagle within a red circle. A circle has been drawn within the body of each buffalo, and a small leather medicine bag tied at the neck of the eagle. Two eagle feathers and 4 northern flicker feathers hang from buckskin thongs. Collected at Fort Washakie, Wyo., before 1910; diameter 33 cm.

A few special features might be noted. Gelding was primarily to make for gentle mounts, not to control breeding per se. Horse training emphasized multiple gaits and responsiveness to riders' knees for buffalo horses, while pack horses were trained only to walk and trot. The surcingle (Ewers 1955:62) was used in combat to permit greater rider maneuverability and survival of the wounded (Hamilton 1905:82–83). Conversely, the Shoshone had relatively low incorporation of the horse into religion and formal social structure.

While the Buffalo Eaters kept dogs for hunting and as guards, the Mountain Sheep Eaters used dog transport—a Plains, not a Basin tradition—on a substantial scale. O. Russell (1921:31–32) met six men, seven women, and 8–10 children accompanied by 30 pack dogs. These people were well fed and well clothed, and thus must have produced a reliable margin of meat for their animals. The Mountain Sheep Eaters used dog transport both with parfleche-type packs and with the travois, in which a rawhide case or a basket of willow was seated. Food and goods but not children were carried. The dog's harness, it may be noted, was primarily a cinch around the chest, secured by breast and hindquarters straps. There was no leash, the dog being directed entirely by voice.

The Shoshone made a wide array of leather goods. Except for shields, bowstrings, drums, and rattles, all of rawhide, leather working was woman's work. Tepees, clothing, and containers, as well as hides or furs primarily for trade, were the major manufactures.

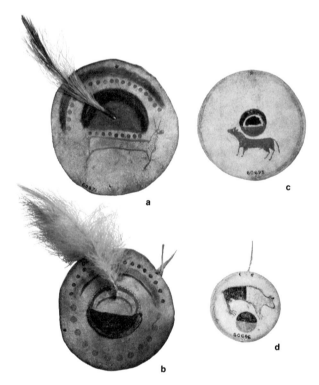

Field Mus., Chicago: a, 60871; b, 60870; c, 60895; d, 60696.

Fig. 12. Tiny buckskin shields or charms, decorated with painted animals, dots, circles, and crescents. Down has been attached to a and b in the same manner as the eagle feathers tied to the hunting shield in fig. 11. Painting was done in blue, green, red, yellow, and purple. c, Diameter 11.4 cm. rest to same scale; collected on the Wind River Reservation, Wyo., in 1900.

320

To make a tepee, men killed at least 10 adult buffalo for fresh hides, then found and cut 12 major and about 20 shorter poles for the supports, "ear" flap regulators, lock pins, and stakes. All poles had to be straight, knotless pines. The buffalo hides were placed on tripods for scraping with a stone or iron scraper, then placed in a shallow creek for one and one-half or two days. The soaked hides were again scraped to remove all hair, which was saved to stuff pillows and saddles. Then the hides were placed on level ground and pounded with a heavy rock to soften them, a task requiring at least a day. Again, each hide was hung, now on a stand, and scraped with a sharp, split cobble. At this time, the hides were covered with buffalo brains, and again soaked

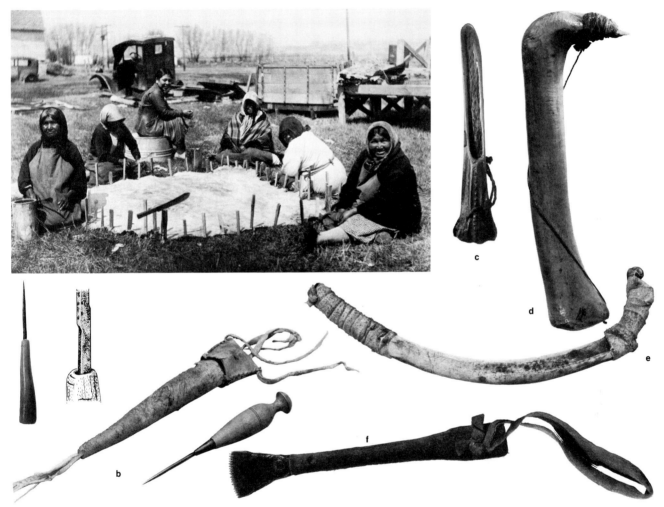

top left, Natl. Arch.:75–RAS–67; Smithsonian, Dept. of Anthr.: a, 200, 521; c, 200, 520; d, 200, 305; f, 200, 306; Amer. Mus. of Nat. Hist., New York: b, 50/2335a, b; e, 50/2313.

Fig. 13. Hide preparation. top left, Women tanning an elk hide as part of a Works Progress Administration project, Wind River Reservation, Wyo. The knife (on one stake) was used for scraping and thinning the skin. Photograph by H.L. Denler, before Aug. 1936. Antler, bone, and steel tools were used to scrape, thin, and stitch hides. a, Steel awl with a nicely crafted handle of antler tine. The surface retains a sheen and red hematite at the butt end. The tine holds an offset steel awl. Having a double tapered steel shaft of square cross-section, with a pronounced offset at the middle of the blade, the awl would not pass through the handle if too much force were applied. These "Indian awls" were important elements of exchange. A hole and impression at the butt end of this specimen indicate that a somewhat larger awl blade had been mounted at that end. b, Sewing awl and leather case stitched with sinew. c, Bone scraper-flesher made from a large mammal long bone split and carved to form a long, thin working edge, with the articular end left as the butt of the handle. A structural ridge extending from the intact articular end has been carved into a series of notches, perhaps a functional element ensuring a better grip, perhaps purely decorative. d, Elk antler scraper. The butt of a single tine at one end was cut down to form a right angle to the handle and filed flat on the underside to receive the steel bit that was secured by a buckskin wrapping and tied to the haft with buckskin thongs. Bits were common elements of the Indian trade, often made at the trading post from stock bars of steel. Indians also fashioned their own from scrap iron and steel. This tool was used to dress, thin, and dehair large, thick hides, and as such, was the one multi-purpose tool essential to every woman's kit. It was not uncommon for antler handles and steel bits to be passed down over several generations. e, Scraper made from a section of horse rib, with ends wrapped in buckskin as handles. f, Characteristic Plains-style flesher, made from a bar of scrap iron, folded to form a handle and flattened to create the flanged working end. The scraping edge has been serrated with a file, and the handle wrapped in hide sewn with sinew. f, Length 34.5 cm, rest to same scale. a, c, e, f, Collected in Wyo. before 1889; b, d, collected on the Wind River Reservation, Wyo., 1901–1906.

overnight to soften and whiten them. Next followed squeezing out of water, added scraping, pulling, and tugging for elasticity (fig. 13).

The next stage, guided by an expert, was laying out the hides to fit them together in a tepee cover without waste. The cover was attached to one pole, which was placed upon the four-pole foundation and the five supplementary poles. For this purpose, a kind of tripod step ladder was used. The critical point came in aligning the cover so that the hides overlapped neatly and permitted accurate placing of eight pairs of pin holes for the forked-stick lock pins. Then came the making of the door. The final step, prior to furnishing, was painting, which varied according to the husband's coups but usually included a black bottom band and black "ears" to regulate smoke. Furnishings (fig. 4) included beds with back rests, a central fireplace with a tripod for suspending kettles, numerous parfleches, and a decorated antelope hide or two in back of the master's bed. Sacred and military objects were either suspended from tepee poles or placed on tripods outside. The tepee was secured with pegs, about 15 inches long, placed about three feet apart.

Among other manufactures, special note should be taken of the shield, which was prepared from the thick shoulder hide of a two-year buffalo bull. The process has been described for the Northern Shoshone (Thwaites 1904–1907, 3: 20). In essence, a group of shamans and old warriors prepared a hole of the diameter of the intended shield. Red hot stones were thrown into the hole, then water to generate steam. The hide was placed over this to be dehaired and shrunk. Stamping with heels compressed the hide. The process continued for several days with feasting until the shield had become impervious to arrows. Each shield had a handle, a buckskin cover decorated with "medicine" decorations, and a fringe of feathers.

Shoshone manufactures were of three standards. The highest was for sumptuary, ritual, and craft products governed by careful design and production, often decorated, such as the beading of moccasins or the adornment of women's festive dresses with drilled elk's teeth. There was also a large class of utilitarian objects, of adequate technical standard but without distinction. Characteristic of this class were the coiled basketry used for eating and gambling trays, utensils such as drinking and sage-tinder horns, and much working equipment, such as the bear-paw snowshoes used to pursue game in winter snows. Finally, the Shoshone were expert in improvised, expedient production. This third category included temporary brush-covered housing, weirs and antelope enclosures, bullboats, hide toboggans, nail-head arrowpoints, crowbars made into digging sticks, scrapers from split cobbles, and many other artifacts designed for quick manufacture and disposal after use.

Games and Gambling

Games were an avenue for prestige and wealth, a means of social integration within the tribe and intertribally, and a tool for improving cognitive and physical skills.

The widespread hand game (Culin 1907:267–326) was (and is) the Shoshone's principal game of chance. As Wislizenus (1912:86–88) observed in 1839: "Men and women are so carried away by the game, that they often spend a whole day and night at it." Stakes were large—horses (signified by sticks), hides, buffalo robes. Betting might be person against person, or the wager could be pooled on both sides and entrusted to a man who did not otherwise participate.

The game is played with any number of persons on each side, sitting on their heels, facing each other. Each side has 10 counters to start with. The bones are two in number, one plain, the other marked with a black strip.

A leader on each side, replaced by another if he has bad luck, does either the hiding or guessing. The side holding the bones sings everyday songs, accompanying itself by beating with short sticks on the long pole that lies in front of each side; swaying and grimacing, folding both arms across the chest, holding them outstretched to the front, and repeating the performance. At any moment, the leader of the other side might make his guess: with arms folded across the chest, both hands closed, he will extend a forefinger in the direction of

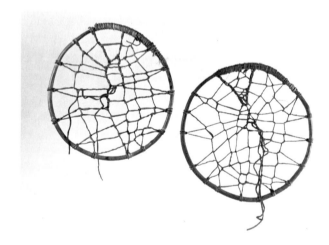

U. of Pa., U. Mus.: 36772.

Fig. 14. Models of boy's snowshoes. A circular peeled sapling frame, 29 cm in diameter, is spliced and coarsely wrapped with leather thongs. A thong webbing, with meshes created by half-hitch wraps, has been attached to the frame by double loops in thongs tied around the perimeter. Doubled and twisted thongs at the front form foot rests or slings. The foot was tied into the snowshoe by leather thongs at the center of the webbing. This form of snowshoe is similar to ones collected among the Ute and is characteristic of the area north and west of the Rocky Mountains (Mason 1896a:pls. 21, 91). These specimens were collected by Stewart Culin on the Wind River Reservation, Wyo., in 1900.

SHIMKIN

the unmarked bone. A correct guess is rewarded by gaining possession of the bones. A miss is penalized by the loss of a counter, the game continuing until all the counters have been won by one side.

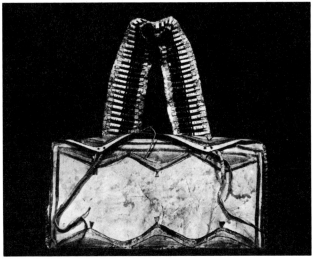

Amer. Mus. of Nat. Hist., New York: top, 50.1/1298; center, 50.1/1293; bottom 50.1/1289.

Fig. 15. Porcupine quillwork. top, Elaborately ornamented pipe and stem. The bowl is Wind River pipe stone, the surface smoothed but undecorated. Strands of multicolored braided quillwork are wrapped tightly around a wooden stem. Beaded fringes sewn over buckskin hide the juncture of pipe bowl and stem. center, Buffalo horn spoon. Split longitudinally through the outer curve of the horn, and then carefully carved to shape, these were common on the northern Plains. They were used on special occasions, to serve honored guests. Strands of braided, multicolored quillwork are wrapped around the fringed buckskin cover on the handle. Quilled fringes sport two deer toes. bottom, Painted rawhide pouch with a quilled carrying strap. Rawhide thongs passed through the double holes in the triangular-cut flap and, tied, sealed the envelope. Collected at Fort Washakie, Wyo., before 1910. Length of top 32 cm, center same scale; bottom width 37 cm.

Intertribal games of hand were frequent, especially in the summer months when the Shoshone were camped in the mountains. Opposing them would be the Bannock. Sweating in the sweathouse often preceded play.

Second only to the hand game as a sedentary pastime for both sexes and all ages was the four-stick-dice game, also reported for the Northern Shoshone, Bannock, and Skull Valley Gosiute (O.C. Stewart 1942:275–277). It too inspired heavy gambling. The game required four split-willow dice, painted red on the round side, and a scoreboard of rawhide, in the center of which was a round rock.

Foot races were normally between young men and over fairly long courses, half a mile and longer. Two or three pairs of partners would compete. Only first place counted, and the winning pair would take everything bet, which was often a very considerable amount. Onlookers also bet heavily. Races were held with other tribes, occasionally, with the Bannock at their summer meetings in the mountains.

Double-ball shinny was a popular women's game played by teams of about 10 (see also Culin 1907:647–665). A field roughly 75 yards long was chosen, and two goal lines were marked off or indicated. Two starters met in the center of the field, their teammates bunched behind them. As all watched, one of the starters threw the ball up into the air, and the teams started scrimmaging for its possession. It might be touched, pushed along rather than tossed, only with the sticks, which were straight and about five feet long. The purpose of the game was to toss or carry the ball over the opponents' goal line. Doing this once won, but that might take all afternoon.

The ball, really two connected buckskin balls, and the sticks were looked after by old men and women. The ball might also be a single sphere, some three inches in diameter. In that case J-shaped bats were used, and the ball was thrown into the air rather than being pushed along the ground. Both variants were equally popular.

Warfare

War was a continuing state among the Eastern Shoshone, and war gains and losses directly affected tribal viability.

An account of 1735 (D. Thompson 1916:327–332) shows the Shoshone assembling over 300 warriors, conducting formal battle with champions backed by a line of shield-bearing warriors armed with sinew-backed bows, obsidian-tipped arrows, and short clubs.

In the early nineteenth century, the Shoshone, battered by smallpox and the onslaughts of tribes displaced by American frontier advances, were gravely threatened by Sioux, Cheyenne, and Gros Ventre raiders from the Plains (Frémont 1845:47). Shoshone resistance was spirited (Hamilton 1905:72–73). Washakie formed alliances with fur traders and the U.S. government that increasingly gave the Shoshone military capabilities. By 1874–1876 the Eastern Shoshone were key parts of governmental campaigns against the Sioux, Cheyenne, and Arapaho. They were well drilled, armed with late-model .45 caliber rifles, and advised by cavalry men, especially Thomas Cosgrove, a former Confederate captain (Bourke 1891:303–319, 334–340). Nevertheless, enemy raids took an appreciable toll of small parties. Some reached official notice (ARCIA 1877:209); many did not.

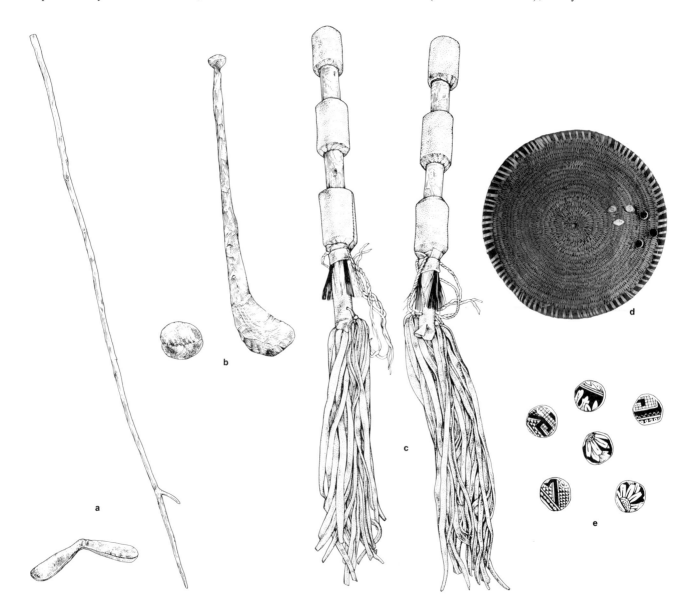

U. of Pa., U. Mus., Philadelphia: a, 36875; 36876; b, 36878; c, Amer. Mus. of Nat. Hist., New York: 50/2443; 50/2442; Field Mus., Chicago: d, 60624; e, 60596.

Fig. 16. Gaming equipment. a, Double ball and stick. The game of double ball, like shinny, was widespread throughout the North American continent and, except for some northern California groups, was exclusively a women's game (Culin 1907). The one-piece buckskin double ball, with its constricted mid-section, and the plain, unadorned forked stick are typical of this game in the Great Basin. The stick is a peeled willow branch. b, Shinny stick and ball. The shinny stick has a broad, curved playing end and a knot carved as a handle. The buckskin ball has a puckered median seam and flattened cross-section. c, Ring game clubs, wood wrapped with buckskin "knobs." The first of the knobs is painted red, the second yellow, and the third red. The buckskin knobs and fringe on one club are painted yellow; on the other, red. Black and white horsehair is bound by strips of buckskin to the handles, which also have 4 twisted buckskin thongs attached to the band on the side nearest the knobs. A 34.2 cm diameter hide-covered ring, sewn with sinew, and stuffed with cotton cloth, and 6 willow counting sticks, 34.9 cm long (2 painted yellow, 2 red, and 2 green) are part of the set (Culin 1907). d, Gaming tray and dice. Six dice are present, 3 diamond-shaped, flat pieces of bone marked with burnt-in lines, and 3 circular, flat pieces of non-Indian pottery. The tray is of close coiled construction, rimmed with red and blue stroud. Dice were tossed and caught within the tray, winning throws assessed by specific combinations of dice. Counters were used to record winning throws. A game was over when one of the opposing sides won all the counters. e, Six dice (2 sets of 3) made from blue and white china. These were probably used with a tray. All collected on the Wind River Reservation, Wyo., in 1900, except c, collected in 1901. Length of a, 118 cm, b-d same scale; diameter of e about 1 cm.

SHIMKIN

Six features were evident in Shoshone warfare: war honors, the greatest source of prestige, memorialized in many ways, such as black finger marks on both sides of a warrior's tepee door, with red finger marks below; suicides in combat, although death in battle was not a favored goal; berdaches, male roles of isolation and low status, without shamanistic connotations; horse-stealing raids on foot, the basic form of offensive; chiefs in charge of large actions and peace-making; and shamanism, whether shamans foretold the events or were wound or horse doctors (Bourke 1891:308, 314, 319, 343).

The demographic effects of warfare on the Eastern Shoshone were severe. The gap between resources and population, the low adult sex ratio, and the impelling need to recruit trappers, Métis, and Indians from other tribes into marriages all reflected the continuing attrition of war.

Religion

In the mid-nineteenth century, prior to extensive Christian proselyting and to the introduction of the Peyote religion, the Eastern Shoshone practiced two complementary forms of religious belief and behavior. One was directed toward personal success and survival through the acquisition of supernatural powers from a generally dangerous world of spirits that demanded compliance with individual taboos. The most basic of these prohibitions was against the contact of fetishes with blood, especially menstrual blood. The other aspect of religion, designed for the welfare of the community and of nature and to ward off impending, prophesied disasters, was group ceremonials led by persons with supernatural power. These ceremonials, the Father Dance, the Shuffling Dance (sometimes called Ghost Dance), and the Sun Dance, properly, Standing Alone in Thirst, were supplications addressed to beneficent beings, particularly Our Father.

While both ceremonials shared common objectives and sacred powers and had common ritual features such as a center pole, they were complementary in many respects. The Father Dance or Shuffling Dance was usually a night-time event of the fall, winter, or spring participated in by both men and women, in which the central feature was the singing of sacred songs. Secondary features such as feasting were minimal. The Sun Dance was a day and nighttime event of the summer restricted to men, with dancing and thirsting to exhaustion being central. Secondary features focused upon were generosity, intergeneration relations, intertribal participation, and feasting. The Father or Shuffling Dance was particularly a tradition of the Mountain Sheep Eaters; the Sun Dance was intimately related to the Plains tradition of the Shoshone.

The exposition below expands on these generalizations, based on Shimkin (1947a, 1953), O. Russell (1921), W.J. Jones (1875), Brackett (1880), Lowie (1924), John Roberts (Olden 1923), Hultkrantz (1951, 1954, 1962, 1968), and Vander (1983).

The mythological beings and animations of nature and their powers (*poha*) are of central importance; the shaman is called *pohakanti* '(one who) has power'. The relation between shaman and power is not one of control but of supplication and dependency. Although power may come in the unsought dreams of late adolescence and is sometimes transfered from shaman to acolyte, it is commonly the fruit of efforts, either in the Sun Dance or through sleeping in sacred places, to gain the blessing or pity of a source of power through quasi-compelling petition or prayer. A successful quest is expressed by a vision in which the *poha* appears, often transforming itself from one form to another, and bestows skills or protections, fetishes to call forth the power, a song, and individual taboos. The *poha* often resides within the shaman and may be coughed out, then transfered to another by blowing. Sometimes a person's *poha* departs, perhaps because of a breach of taboo. This is deadly; a shaman must come to track the *poha*, capture it, and then blow it back into the sufferer lest he die.

The most sacred of places are the sites of pictographs (*poha kahni* 'house of power'), particularly in the vicinity of Dinwoody Canyon, on the Wind River Reservation. There are hundreds of pictographs, clearly accumulated over a long period (Gebhard and Cahn 1950; Gebhard 1951). The later representations are peculiarly important. They include large panels representing the feared Water Ghost Beings and Rock Ghost Beings.

In addition to Dinwoody Canyon, Bull Lake remains both fearful and attractive. It is reported to be the home of monsters; those who kill and eat them will change into Water Buffalo and disappear. It is also the place where ghost people play the hand game.

The domain of ghosts includes not only Ghost Beings, but old women, great-grandparents, and apparitions. Whirlwinds come into this class. All are feared; up to World War II, houses where death had taken place were often abandoned. Death, danger, fear, illness are all semantically linked. Curiously, enemy scalps and hands did not come into this dread class. They were trophies handled with impunity.

Illness is visualized in both supernatural and pragmatic terms. Other than through breach of taboo, illness comes from malevolent dwarf people, who shoot magic arrows into people to cause rheumatism, pneumonia, and heart attacks; also, Water Ghost Beings both cause and cure epilepsy. Sorcery acts through intrusions of worms and pus, sometimes through the contagion of the deadly *toyarotuwora* plant (Shimkin 1953:433; see also Lowie 1924:297). Evil doers may also steal supernatural power; the relation of such acts to soul theft is unclear (Hultkrantz 1951). Conversely, the Shoshone have always been pragmatic about childbirth, the handling of snake bites, minor ailments, and, particularly, wounds and fractures.

While legerdemain is inherent in cures of extraction, Shoshone theory distinguishes the shaman (*pohakanti*) from the magician or wonder worker (*timapanti*). Reported magic includes wondrous transformations of moccasins into buffalo tongues, exhibitions of living birds as personal powers, antelope charming; weather control to make snow, rain, or thaw; invulnerability to gunshot; deaths of women attracted to sorcerors. Magic is often mediated through a compelling instrument, an eagle feather to chase away clouds, a bull-roarer to bring about a thaw, antelope-hoof rattles to charm herds, or the toyarotuwora plant to place in victims' footsteps.

Ritual objects and acts ceremonialize religion. In the 1980s purification through bathing in running water or through sweating, addresses of respect to the supernatural, and censing with burning pine boughs or other aromatics were needed preliminaries for sacred events. In the past, smoking wild tobacco in a sacred, rock-bowled pipe was essential to curing. Other key objects are feathers, best of all eagle down feathers, which are used to transmit power. Shamanizing is done barefoot and, for men, bare chested; sacred paints, often white, adorn the healer. Songs, usually in groups of four; touching, sucking of the poison through hand or shoulder; often, a trance; chest hitting to release the captured entity; and a final exhibition of the intruding object formed the traditional sequence.

Ceremonialism

The Eastern Shoshone held a complex of belief and ritual comprising faith in Our Father; prayer songs eliciting visions, welfare for people, animals, and plants, and relations with the dead; and a Round Dance for men and women usually repeated for four or five nights. This complex has varied over time.

An ancient form, reported by hearsay by two informants (Polly Shoyo, b. 1845, d. 1938) and Moses Tassitsie (b. 1852, d. about 1940), was associated with smallpox epidemics in the late eighteenth (about 1781) and early nineteenth centuries (about 1837). According to Polly Shoyo, the Father Dance warded off smallpox. A sponsor's dream initiated the dance, usually in the spring. They started in the morning when the sponsor and his two assistants gave each dancer two bundles of big-leafed sage to hold in each hand. The dancers formed a circle, men and women alternating. In the center, facing east, was the sponsor who prayed 10 prayers and sang 10 prayer songs, so that the children would have no illness. These invocations were addressed to the Sun, Moon, Trees, Queerly Shaped Rocks, Mountains, Berries, Sage, Sky, Waters, and finally Earth. The people

Field Mus., Chicago: top, 60563; center, 60795; bottom, U. of Calif., Lowie Mus., Berkeley:2–15756.

Fig. 17. Musical instruments. top, Double-headed drum. The side shown is painted with fleur-de-lys and stars within a quartered design field. The opposite side has a picture of a crane. The skin drum heads are laced onto the wood frame with buckskin thongs. Several instances of head repair are obvious, the split skin stitched with slender rawhide thongs or sinew thread. center, Courting flute of bamboo with a carved wooden block in the form of a stylized bird, and ornamented with wraps of otter fur and an end pendant of sage grouse and other feathers. Use of bamboo is nontraditional; usual is the split and pitched wood or reed chamber. bottom, Traditional courting flute of split wood, the seams pitched, and the chamber tied with buckskin thongs. A carved wooden zoomorphic block is near the mouth piece, and several wraps of ermine skin at the other end. Made about 1860s. top, Drum diameter 57 cm, rest to same scale. top and center, Collected by George A. Dorsey on the Wind River Reservation, Wyo., 1900; bottom, collected by Demitri B. Shimkin on the Wind River Reservation, 1937.

stood quietly as he prayed, then hopped up and down with their sage bundles as he sang. In the evening, they quit.

The Shuffling Dance enters into Shoshone mythology in the story of the Hoodwinked Dancers. Coyote comes to his prey, saying: "We should shake off disease to send this illness away, having shaken our blankets."

And that night, they stood around a bonfire with Coyote in the center.

Reported Shuffling Dance performances, the last being prior to World War II, conform to this pattern. Only three men knew the songs needed. The dance was held at full moon in the three winter months, four (sometimes three) nights in succession. A fire, a cedar, and the principal singer were in the center; the leaders would change around, each leading one to four songs. Some time in the night, they would end, shaking disease away with their blankets, and finally circling the fire twice to an exit.

The songs that were sung were musically varied within a small range, and consisted of pairs of couplets subtly indicating visions, and promoting the good. Vander's (1983) collection of 17 songs as well as Shimkin's (1947a:350–351) data bring out the great importance of water and fog imagery in these songs. Significant also is the suggestion of movement.

For the Eastern Shoshone, the Ghost Dance of the 1890s, although remembered and associated with Bannock proselytizing, was no more than a variant in a deep tradition (see also Olden 1923:37). Nor did the religious excitement and intense Mormon missionizing of 1879–1880 have lasting effects (Brackett 1880; G.E. Wright 1982).

The Wolf Dance (fig. 18) or War Dance, as it was called by Whites, was invented about 1890 as an adaptation of the Hot Dance of the Crow, according to Moses Tassitsie. Dancers were painted with realistic representations of bears or snakes below their breasts standing for bear or snake medicine. Certain elements of painting were symbols: right angles or angular horseshoes represent horse tracks; wavy lines running the length of the arms and legs symbolize the rainbow; short lines, whether horizontal, curved, oblique, or vertical, indicate people killed by the wearer; broad painted bands record hand-to-hand encounters with the enemy (Culin 1901).

The origin of the Sun Dance is ascribed to a former Comanche shaman, Yellow Hand, about 1800 (Shimkin 1953; Hultkrantz 1971a). A brief explicit description of the Eastern Shoshone Sun Dance (W.P. Clark 1885:363) stresses the four days and nights of fasting and thirsting, "religious zeal," and a structure with a center pole on which a buffalo head was mounted, and 10 outer poles. Other accounts describe the Sun Dance in the twentieth century (Shimkin 1953:474–475; Lowie 1915; Voget 1948, 1950, 1953; T.H. Johnson 1968; Jorgensen 1972).

The Sun Dance, in the nineteenth century and even in the twentieth, may be best understood as a political event with important religious elements. The Sun Dance expressed variable themes of communal and personal welfare. More than that, it symbolized the cultural standing, wealth, prowess, and alliances of the tribe. It marked both expressions of manhood and of intergenerational ties. It was the scene of visionary experiences and shamanistic contests. And the sacred joy of the occasion was shared by participant and onlooker, adult and child.

In the winter, a shaman and experienced Sun Dancer announced a vision requiring him to perform the ritual on pain of death. By spring, invitations would be sent.

The Sun Dance leader, his chosen assistant or assistants, and distinguished warriors conducted a series of preparatory rituals, including preparation of a Sun Dance doll, ceremonial practice, and the building of the lodge. Another key step was hunting and killing the ceremonial buffalo whose head and back hide were to be placed on the center pole. Following this was a drama, involving both men and women, that comprised a sham battle to locate, "hunt," and "kill" the trees used for the lodge.

The Sun Dance (fig. 20) proper lasted four nights and three days. The dancers joined in formal secrecy, although the ceremonial regalia—eagle bone whistle with down attached, eagle down for each little finger, ceremonial apron, and, often, fetishes—constituted family treasures made available for the occasion. Each dancer bathed in running water or sweated before coming to the sponsor's tepee for initial songs and ritual entry into the lodge. Each danced in place except once or twice during the day, when they would dance to the center pole and back. Each dancer had a sponsor urging him to dance to fainting and vision. The greeting of the sun at dawn marked a ritual climax, particularly on the third day, when visions, curing, and power transfers were likeliest. Blessings by sponsors, water drinking, and ritual vomiting concluded the ceremony.

Then followed a great, communal feast on buffalo tongues. Most important was the charge of little boys to seize tongues. Old men sponsored this act; on its conclusion the boys bathed and ate. After the feasting, sickly people came to tie old clothes to the center pole as magical means of discarding illness. Up to World War II such clothes remained on center poles until they rotted away. Other parts of the Sun Dance lodge were quickly disassembled.

The Sun Dance has retained great vitality. Since the 1930s the Sun Dance has changed appreciably, even disregarding various short-term innovations such as the post-World War II flag-raising rite or the re-introduction of the Sun Dance doll. The site is explicitly christianized, with the center pole representing Jesus, and the 12 posts, the apostles (Hultkrantz 1969). The Sun Dance joins together the range of beliefs, from Mormon to Peyotist, and has a partial endorsement from Christian ministers. It is also intertribal, with dancers coming and going as far as the Cree of Canada. Themes vary; in 1965 and 1966 Tom Wesaw prayed to end the Vietnam war. Finally, old elements of battle and heroism have been replaced by honors for the aged as such.

327

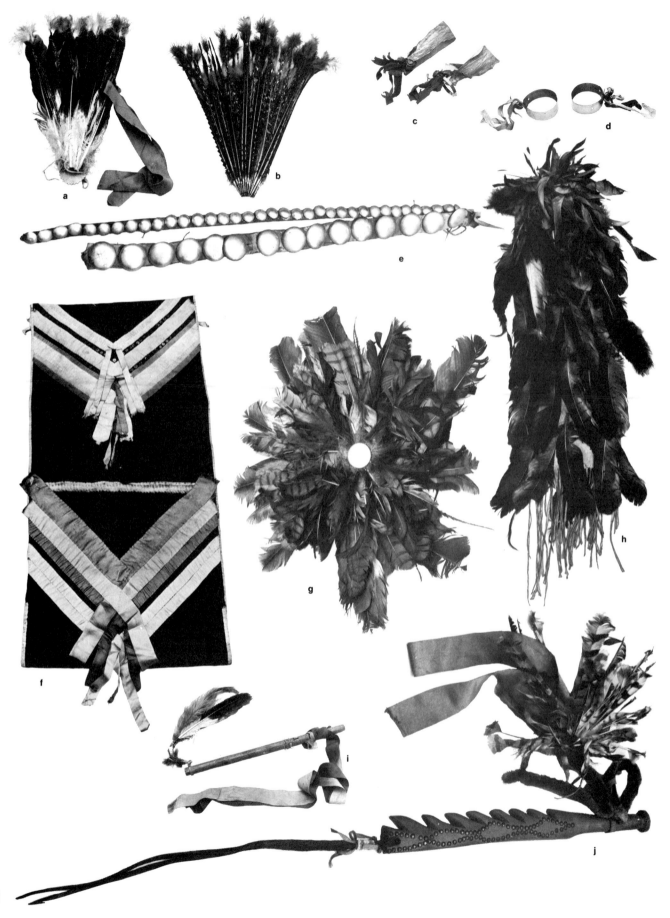

Amer. Mus. of Nat. Hist., New York: a, 50/2339i; b, 50/2339j; c, 50/2339F; d, 50/2433A, B; e, 50/2417B; f, 50/2417A; g, 50.1/1278A; h, 50/1278B; i, 50/2354; j, 50/2353.
Fig. 18. Wolf Dance paraphernalia. These items represent at least three different dancers' outfits. Though variable in material and design, they reflect the overriding characteristic of Wolf Dance costumes: intense elaboration reflected in the use of bright colors, encompassing the liberal use of beadwork, body paint, multicolored satin ribbons, and delicately cut feathers from a wide variety of bird species. a, Eagle feather fan, eagle tail feathers mixed with grouse tail feathers, tied to a serrated abalone plate and bedecked with a satin ribbon. b, Feather fan of serrated grouse and other feathers with tufts of dyed down. c, Leather arm or ankle bands, decorated with ribbons, a quilled ring, and sleigh bells. d, Metal armbands trailing brightly colored ribbons. e, Concho belt. f, Wolf Dance apron, stroud ornamented with ribbon chevrons. g, Feather bustle, without trailer, mirror at the center. h, Elaborate feather bustle with trailer of feathers affixed to a piece of fringed hide. i, Whistle with ribbon and feather trailers. j, Wolf Dance leader's whip, carved wood handle, decorated with tacks, and having a wrist thong of fur trailing a cluster of feathers and ribbon. The lash is commercial harness leather, beaded below the juncture with the wood handle. All collected at Fort Washakie, Wyo., a-f, i-j, in 1901; g-h, before 1910. a, Length 30 cm, others same scale.

Reservation Life: 1937, 1966, 1980

After the collapse of the buffalo economy in the 1880s and up to World War II, the Eastern Shoshone faced and gradually won a struggle for physical and cultural survival under the pressures of extreme poverty, governmental paternalism, and isolation. The processes of adaptation, especially in the critical years up to 1910, are described in Shimkin (1942). See also U.S. Census Office. 11th Census (1894:627–634).

Field Mus., Chicago: a, 60819; b, 60564; c, 60746; d, Amer. Mus. of Nat. Hist., New York: 50.1/1317.
Fig. 19. Dance wands. a, Crane's head carved on a short stick of wood. This specimen may be complete, or it may represent only the tip of a wand meant to slide into a socketed wood shaft or reed handle. b, Complete crane's head wand. The snakelike wooden shaft is topped by a carved crane's head adorned with red-dyed feather plumes. c, Dance wand of slender, elaborately cut feathers mounted on a red-painted stick. Quilled circles, one a cross, the other a crescent within a circle surmounted by a long-tailed zoomorph, probably a lizard, are affixed to the center of the feathers and the stick. d, Forked dance stick, decorated with seed beads, brightly quilled tassels with tin tinklers and dyed horsehair, and eagle tail feathers. With less decoration, this specimen would be quite similar to the forked sticks used in the pole and ring game. Length of a 31.5 cm; b, 91 cm, c and d same scale. a-c, Collected on the Wind River Reservation, Wyo., 1900; d, at Fort Washakie, Wyo., before 1910.

Fig. 20. John Trehero (1887–1985), an important shaman who reintroduced the Sun Dance to the Crow in 1941. On the third day of the Sun Dance, initiating a prayer at the center pole. Photograph by Joseph Hemphill, July 1968.

1937

In 1937 the Shoshone were all but destitute, deprived both of the grazing land north of Wind River and the fertile, irrigable land given to the Arapaho on the eastern side of the reservation. They lacked the resources, moreover, to open up the high-mountain timberland and pastures. A few people, especially on Sage Creek, were independent through a combination of gardening, hay raising, animal husbandry, hunting, fishing, and crafts. For most families, the basis of survival was the reservation's Indian Agency, which provided work through New Deal programs, at wages of $30 to $50 per month, and also disbursed rations to the elderly and indigent. A few former Indian scouts received pensions. Average household income ran $300–$400 annually. Transportation difficulties and White prejudice effectively blocked off-reservation employment.

A rather typical economic inventory (in a three-generation household of nine, including four small children) was the following: 40 acres of grazing land, 30 beef cattle, 3 horses, 5 poultry; one man employed at $44 a month, 1936 truck being purchased; two tents and unpainted, chinked log house with dirt roof and dirt floor, factory door and windows; one steel, double bedstead, two mattresses on floor, six blankets and comforters, one lumber table, benches, and a box cupboard, sewing machine, one oil lamp, meager furnishings in tents; water from stream, no privy.

The prevailing diet was flour, meat, coffee, sugar, and some canned fruit, supplemented in season by fish, roots, and berries. Only 15 out of 228 households supplemented this with fair amounts of cow's milk, garden vegetables, and extra supplies of protein, such as eggs or poultry. At the same time, maternal nursing for at least a year was universal. Also, the 153 children at the government day school received a balanced lunch (Shimkin 1947b).

The overall youthfulness of the Shoshone population and the major differences between its full and mixed blood components are shown in table 1. For the full-blood population, the peculiar sex ratios appear to reflect a shortage of females, probably the result of systematic neglect or even the killing of girl children plus female age misstatements related to early marriage. Correspondingly, the evident excess of mixed-blood girls may reflect a movement of unwanted females from full blood to mixed blood families.

Partial vital statistics for 1928–1937 and standard demographic analysis (United Nations. Department of Economic and Social Affairs 1968) permit reconstructing population dynamics. The median age at death (approximating life expectancy at birth) was 22 years. Birth rates exceeded 40/1,000 and gave a natural increase rate of about 10/1,000. The heavy toll of tuberculosis must be stressed; about 10 percent of the entire population in 1937 was actively tubercular, subject to prolonged infectivity and declines in health prior to death. About 30 percent of the adult population was infected with trachoma, a disease of the external eye leading to substantial blindness. One 35-bed hospital served the reservation.

White people and a few Sioux Indians employed by the Indian Service controlled the key resources and decisions affecting Eastern Shoshone life; at this time the Bureau superintendent, not the tribal council, held power. Specifically, the Indian Agency controlled work and welfare, health, law enforcement, and education. Although some of the work developed tribal resources through road building and brush clearance, it was viewed

Fig. 21. Moses Tassitsie's house, one of the most substantial on the Wind River Reservation, Wyo. Photograph by Demitri Shimkin, 1930s.

Table 1. Enrolled Shoshone at Wind River Reservation, 1930

	Total Population			Full-blood			Mixed-blood		
	Total	Male	Female	Total	Male	Female	Total	Male	Female
Under 1 yr	32	17	15	13	7	6	19	10	9
1–3	95	52	43	23	15	8	72	37	35
4–9	170	81	89	54	31	23	116	50	66
10–19	204	97	107	69	29	40	135	68	67
20–29	152	73	79	48	25	23	104	48	56
30–39	121	65	56	60	34	26	61	31	30
40–49	81	48	33	44	28	16	37	20	17
50–59	74	40	34	40	23	17	34	17	17
60–69	42	20	22	31	17	14	11	3	8
70–79	37	23	14	32	20	12	5	3	2
80–89	9	2	7	7	2	5	2	0	2
Totals	1,017	518	499	421	231	190	596	287	309

SOURCE: U.S. Congress. Senate 1934: 14, 460.

as a relief operation, disbursed on the basis of need rather than merit. The money provided subsistence but often at the cost of neglecting livestock and homesteads, a procedure that increased dependency upon the Agency. At the same time, the Agency exercised social control: old people received rations fortnightly but their younger relatives were obliged to do work in recompense. No special provisions existed for dependent children, except for the minor efforts of the Episcopal Mission; otherwise, they were cared for as well as possible by relatives.

Law enforcement was handled by an Indian judge, elected by the tribal council, who tried misdemeanors, and the Federal District Court in Cheyenne, which tried felonies or cases in which a jury trial might be desired. Executive power rested in the U.S. Deputy Special Officer (for the entire reservation) and (among the Shoshone) two Indian policemen as assistants. Violations were few; out of 54 criminal cases in 1936–1937, all but six involved drunk and disorderly or malicious conduct.

The curriculum of the government day school was conventional but mildly enriched by the use of folklore in English composition and art. About three-fourths of the students finished the seventh grade, perhaps half the tenth grade.

Ceremonial activity served as the basic means through which men and, to a much more limited degree, women were able to express hope and relieve sorrow and to form alliances of mutual support.

The Ghost Dance of 1890 was explored but rejected. Early contacts with Peyotism via the Comanche and Quanah Parker were also unproductive. However, about 1900, Charley Washakie began to practice Peyotism as learned primarily from the Arapaho.

Early in his ministry, Reverend John Roberts (fig. 22) worked with Shoshone to translate elements of the book of Common prayer (Lajoe and Roberts 1899) and a Shoshone catechism (Enga-Barrie and Roberts 1900).

This translation integrated into a new context pre-existing theological concepts, such as Our Father, "soul," and "spirit." It added to these new ideas, some of which had limited acceptance, for example, Heaven, commandment, and similar guides to conduct.

In 1937–1938 participation in religious groups, apart from Catholicism and apart from the Ghost Dance Peyote schism, tended to be multiple. Out of 336 men above age 16, 167 were active in such groups; 89 belonged to 1 organization, 57 to 2, 17 to 3, 5 to 4, and one person to five. Most broadly based was participation as a leader, dancer, singer, or drummer, or in the Sun Dance. Women's roles remained minor, as auxiliaries in singing, as cooks, or in the case of old women, as recipients of giveaways. All parts of the reservation

Natl. Arch:75–RAS–20A.

Fig. 22. John Roberts (right), Episcopal missionary to the Eastern Shoshone, 1883–1949, at the Ft. Washakie cemetery on Memorial Day with the BIA agent, Forrest R. Stone. Photograph by H.L. Denler, before Aug. 1936.

participated, although the representation from the heavily mixed-blood northern areas was light. Northern Shoshones, Bannocks, and Arapahos attended (Shimkin 1953:456–472).

The great reversal in Shoshone fortunes started in 1938 and in 1939, when successful suit against the federal government and the Act of June 27, 1939, restored alienated lands and provided money compensation as well. The reservation, through the re-acquisition of lands north of Big Wind River, rose from 808,500 to 2,268,008 acres; nearly $3.5 million became available for economic development (Schutz, Baker, and Vanvig 1960:6–7). Concurrently, the tribal council, hitherto a passive organization, began to have major authority and responsibilities connected with the new resources, the legal enrollment of persons as Wind River Shoshone, relations with the Arapaho, and pressure on oil companies to start production from dormant oil and gas leases. Between 1938 and 1941, political dependency had basically ended (Hemphill 1970).

During this same period, major advances were realized in improving health. A tribal Board of Health, which was in operation by 1952, pressed for the eradication of tuberculosis, venereal diseases, and other acute problems. By 1956, when a thorough examination was undertaken of children under 12 in every fifth Shoshone and Arapaho family, health conditions had become fairly satisfactory (Perkins and Church 1960).

1966

The postwar decades created a complex and contradictory social environment for the Shoshone. On the one hand, new economic resources, better health, housing, and food, better education, increased migration, and the acquisition of real power by the Shoshone Business Council opened new perspectives. The young people especially began to think of themselves as citizens of rural Wyoming, as well as Indians. On the other hand, job and social discrimination by Whites, limited job skills, a lack of economic development on the reservation, fear of the growing numbers and political cohesiveness of the Arapaho, and conflicts in goals adversely affected the Shoshone.

Data for this section were drawn from Conklin (1967, 1975), De Riso (1974), Hemphill (1970), and T.H. Johnson (1968). Use has also been made of L. Fowler's (1982) and T.L. Haynes's (1976) excellent works, as well as reports of the U.S. Bureau of Indian Affairs (1960) and the other government agencies.

In 1957, a year characteristic of the postwar years, 385 Shoshone households resident on the reservation had a median income of $3,272; 25 percent of these households received $500–1,499, while 22 percent received over $6,000. Almost three-fourths of this income came from per capita payments for oil and gas leases on the reservation; 22 percent from wages, and only 3 percent from self-employment in agriculture. The labor force totaled 330; of these, 86 were self-employed in agriculture, 37 combined agriculture and wage work, and 127 were full-time wage workers, while 80 or nearly one-fourth had been unemployed the previous year (U.S. Bureau of Indian Affairs 1960). Shoshone employment was almost entirely on the reservation; job and housing discrimination, and the necessity of long travel to work blocked participation in the growing mining and industrial economy of western Wyoming.

Between 1934 and 1957, the enrolled Shoshone population rose at the rate of 2.0 percent per year; its growth rate then fell to 1.6 percent. Underlying data are both incomplete and contradictory, but the most likely model for this growth is a birth rate of 30–35/1,000, a death rate of 15–20/1,000, and a life expectancy at birth of 40–45 years. A sharp rise in violent deaths and an increasing toll from chronic cardiovascular diseases and diabetes seemingly account for this high mortality (U.S. Department of Health, Education and Welfare 1974). Distrust of Indian Health Service practitioners and poor compliance by patients with chronic ailments appear to have been contributory (Conklin 1975).

Migration, like natural increase, was at high rates in the years 1934–1957 and at lower rates in 1957–1976. In 1957, only one-third of the enrolled out-migrants resided in Wyoming; the remainder were widely scattered in pursuit of jobs and education. Most of the out-migrants returned periodically for family gatherings and the Sun Dance. In-migration come practically to a standstill after 1957.

By the 1960s the reservation's Joint Business Council and its component Shoshone Business Council had become dominant political powers. This reflected national legislative and policy changes; the growing experience of a stable, representative group; new resources from oil and gas leases, federal grants, and logging; and the transfer of several functions, notably education and health, from agency to state or contract authority. The Bureau superintendent's role had become largely advisory (Hemphill 1970).

The Business Council had a major role, from 1960 on, in the building of housing, water supplies, and sewerage facilities. It handled a budget of nearly $300,000 yearly, supervising a range of operations from fish and game, to the new Rocky Mountain Hall, to funeral expenses for the indigent. Its greatest difficulties were in gaining contact and cooperation with local White business and political interests, who saw the Indians and their land basically as objects of exploitation.

After World War II, education was transferred to state school districts, with partial federal re-imbursement, while the Fort Washakie health facility was reduced in status to an ambulatory clinic. The changes in education had mixed successes; there was better school attendance and performance at the expense of cohesion. In 1957, in grades 1–8 there was relatively full attendance, an average of 40 per grade. In grades 9–12, the average attendance was 20. The average educational attainment of adults aged 19–28 was 10 years, compared to 6 for those aged 60 or more. Twenty-six Shoshones were in college (U.S. Bureau of Indian Affairs 1960).

Along with kin-based cohesion (T.H. Johnson 1975) Shoshone society underwent changes in residence, role, and self-image among the elderly, women, and adolescents. An important element has been the right of each enrolled Shoshone to his share of tribal disbursals. Improved housing, including a development for the elderly, practically eliminated extended households. By 1957 mean household size for the resident enrolled and nonenrolled population had fallen to 3.7 persons.

The central role of religious activity and the implied premise of personal supernatural power have remained as meaningful forces. In the 1960s and later, both personal motivation and family pressure led to repeated participation in tribal rituals such as Peyotism and the Wolf Dance, and in the Sun Dance particularly. T.H. Johnson (1968) has argued convincingly on the key function of the old in a new setting. The Sun Dance is a public ritual, placing the Shoshone on display. It is flexible in the concerns attacked and in ritual details. It is a medium of both fellowship and rivalry.

1980

Although housing in the 1980s was bungalow style, shades are built outdoors for summer, and canvas-covered tepees remain for Peyote religion and Sun Dance assemblies. Hunting and fishing are at most auxiliary pursuits, with ranching, industrial crafts and clerical skills predominating. Women, no longer subject to the heavy control of father, brother, and husband, may be prominent in politics, or even reign at the newly instituted powwow (fig. 23). Accidents related to cars, alcohol, and Valium have replaced warfare and tuberculosis as primary killers. And, while some youngsters attend the Wyoming Indian High School—dominated by Arapaho—most go to Lander High School, off-reservation and integrated.

But within this context there are many important continuities. The most significant relate to religion, and especially sacred dreams as sources of skill and invention, such as personal songs to be sung when sick (Vander 1978:20). Associated with these are venerated regalia, above all, eagle feathers and eagle-bone whistles. The Sun Dance, in its quasi-Christian form, has great vitality, on an intertribal level. On the other hand, the complex of belief surrounding the Shuffling Dance was only a tradition held by a few Mountain Sheep Eaters. The popular cult for contemplation and the relief of ills

was Peyotism, introduced early in the twentieth century (Shimkin 1942).

Ceremonialism has had a complex development. Dancing styles, costumes of quasi-traditional nature, drumming, and music continue in a sequence that can be traced back to the Big Horse Dance of the Yellow Brows (Vander 1978). But contexts vary, with powwows coming in after World War II. Elements from one ritual context have been transferred to others; for example, the giveaway customary in the public counting of coups has become a separate ceremony used variously to end mourning or to celebrate a powwow queen (Vander 1978:42–44).

The kinship system maintained structural distinctions such as those between mother's mother and father's mother or between father-in-law, man speaking or woman speaking; or between elder and younger brother, elder and younger sister. It maintained collective terms for relatives and parents. But kin-term extensions, such as

Fig. 23. The Crowheart powwow, Crowheart, Wyo. top, The grand entry with Bernadine Shoyo, Crowheart princess, leading the procession. bottom, Shoyo giveaway in honor of their daughter. Photographs by Judith Vander, 1982.

the self-reciprocal use of the term 'father's father' for 'son's child,' appear to be obsolescent. The term for paternal uncle no longer extends from that of 'father'; rather the old mother's brother's term is applied. The same shift has taken place with 'mother's sister' (Tidzump 1970; Shimkin 1941, 1947b:323–324).

At the same time, better survival, more stable co-residence, and the accumulation of property have made large, bilateral kindreds key sociopolitical elements. Marriage alliances and, conversely, coalitions against the concentration of power in single hands have become characteristic (T.H. Johnson 1975). In 1980 there were 2,851 Eastern Shoshones at Wind River Reservation (U.S. Bureau of Indian Affairs. Financial Management Office 1981).

Although oral artistry (Shimkin 1947a) was in jeopardy, native tape recordings notwithstanding, as the great storytellers have been dying, Shoshone language use and understanding were still widespread in the 1980s.

And the hand game, with its singing and drumming, still was a source of fun, skill, and gambling risk.

Synonymy†

The name Shoshone first comes to notice in reports of encounters with an Eastern Shoshone group associated with the Crow in 1805 (Meriwether Lewis in Thwaites 1904–1907, 2:345; F.A. Larocque in Burpee 1910:73). Lewis also refers to these people as Shoshonees, Sosone, and "Sosonees or snake Indians" (Thwaites 1904–1907, 2:364, 329, 244). Although Larocque specifies that this name was what they called themselves, subsequent investigators have not found it to be used by any Shoshones as a self-designation, except perhaps as a very recent borrowing from English (Liljeblad in Beal and Wells 1959:38). Some Shoshone speakers have speculated that the name may have been derived from *sonippih* 'high-growing grass', but although such a form would have regular reduplication and is grammatically possible it has not been attested in use (Sven Liljeblad, communications to editors 1982, 1985).

Gallatin (1836:120, 133, 306) used the spelling Shoshonee, and Hale (1846:199, 218, 569) introduced in addition Shoshóni, defined as "Snakes, Bonnaks, &c.," which Gatschet (1877:426) gave as Shóshoni. The spelling Shoshoni was used in Hodge (1907–1910, 2:556) and in volumes 8, 9, and 10 of the *Handbook*, but Shoshone has been adopted as standard in this volume since it is the preferred spelling used by the Shoshone people.

†This synonymy was written by Ives Goddard, incorporating information supplied by Demitri B. Shimkin.

Most sources equate the Shoshone and the Snake (in French *les Serpents*), a name widely used especially for the Northern and Eastern Shoshone; early uses are by Fidler, 1800 (Shimkin 1980:208), and Tabeau, 1806 (Abel 1939:160–161). The different uses of these names in the nineteenth century are discussed in the synonymies in "Western Shoshone" and "Northern Shoshone and Bannock," this volume. Washakie's band of Eastern Shoshone were called Green River Snakes by G. Stuart (1865:80). The people called *Serpents* encountered in 1741 by the sons of Pierre Gaultier de Varennes, Sieur de la Vérendrye (Burpee 1927:412) are probably to be regarded as undifferentiated Shoshone-Comanche.

In other Indian languages the Shoshone are often called by names that literally mean 'snake people': Blackfeet *pi·ksí·ksinaitapi·wa* (Allan R. Taylor, communication to editors 1974); Ojibwa *kine·piko·nini* (Baraga 1878–1880, 2:136); Gros Ventre *si·sí·yɛ·nin* (Allan R. Taylor, communication to editors 1983); Hidatsa *wa·púksa rupá·ka* (phonetically [ma·púkša nupá·ka]), glossed 'Snakes' by Long (1823, 2:lxxxiv) but in the 1970s believed to be the Kiowa (Douglas Parks, communication to editors 1975); Lakota *zuzéča wičʰáša* (Bushotter in Hodge 1907–1910, 2:558); Mandan *wákruxka rúwąkaki* (phonetically [wákuruxka númąkaki]) (Robert C. Hollow, communication to editors 1975); Omaha-Ponca (Hodge 1907–1910, 2:558). Curtis (1907–1930, 5:154) glosses the Gros Ventre name 'rattlesnake men' and this is the meaning of the alternate Lakota term *sįtéxla wičʰáša* (Buechel 1970:454, 733).

Another set of names has the meaning 'grass-house people' or the like: Arapaho e-wu-xa´-wu-si (F.V. Hayden 1862:326, slightly normalized); Cheyenne moiéomīnī´tan (Mooney 1907:422); Crow bik-ta´-she (F.V. Hayden 1862:402), micʰkyashé (Curtis 1907–1930, 4:180); Gros Ventre wasöinhiyeihits (Kroeber 1916:132); Hidatsa miká-ațí (Curtis 1907–1930, 4:186); Kiowa *sóntò·dɔ̀* (Laurel Watkins and Parker McKenzie, communication to editors 1979); Lakota *pʰeží-wokʰéya-otʰí kį* (Buechel 1970:440, 733). Of these, the Gros Ventre term is said to be applied to a particular Shoshone group, and the Cheyenne term is reported to be that of a distinct people "cognate with the Shoshoni, but farther northwest, beyond the mountains. . . . Probably some of the so-called Snake bands of Idaho" (Mooney 1907:422).

Some languages use names that appear to be borrowed from English: Arapaho *sósoní ʔi* (Salzmann 1983), Cheyenne *sósoné ʔeo ʔo* (Glenmore and Leman 1984), Lakota *súsuni* (Buechel 1970:459, 733).

In the Plains Indian sign language the Shoshone are indicated by the sign for 'snake': the right hand is moved forward in a sinuous motion with the index finger (or the first and second fingers) extended to the front; they were also sometimes referred to by the signs for 'bad lodge' or 'brush lodge' (W.P. Clark 1885:336–337, 353).

Subgroups

Buffalo Eaters. The *kuccuntikka* 'eaters of buffalo' are also referred to as the *poho?ini·* 'sagebrush people'; the Lemhi and Pohogwe Northern Shoshone also called themselves *kuccuntikka* (Sven Liljeblad, communication to editors 1985).

Mountain Sheep Eaters. The *tukkutikka* 'eaters of mountain sheep' are also called *toyahini·* 'mountaineers'; other *tukkutikka* joined the Lemhi Shoshone and are hence included in the Northern Shoshone, as arbitrarily delimited in the *Handbook*.

Sources

Trenholm and Carley (1964) present a historical and cultural overview. For linguistics, Shimkin (1949), Tidzump (1970), Miller, Tanner, and Foley (1971), and Shimkin (1980) are basic; for archeology, Shimkin (1940) and Wright (1978), and for rock art, Gebhard (1969). Early ethnographic reports include Larocque in Burpee (1910), O. Russell (1921), M.C. Ross (1968), and Hamilton (1905); for the terminal Plains period, Bourke (1891), W.A. Jones (1875), and Brackett (1880) are useful. The reservation period prior to World War I is dealt with by Shimkin (1942), U.S. Census Office. 11th Census (1894), and Mooney (1896).

Key modern ethnographies include Lowie (1915, 1919, 1924), Olden (1923), Shimkin (1947, 1947b, 1953), Voget (1948, 1950, 1953), Hultkrantz (1971a, 1981a), Dominick (1964), and T.H. Johnson (1975). Folklore and music are partially covered by St. Clair and Lowie (1909), Shimkin (1947a), and Vander (1978, 1983). Important data on the post–World War II period may be found in U.S. Bureau of Indian Affairs (1960), Schutz, Baker, and Vanvig (1960), Hemphill (1970), and T.L. Haynes (1976).

The Shimkin, Conklin, DeRiso, Hemphill, and Johnson files at the University of Illinois Department of Anthropology are to go to the State of Wyoming Archives, Cheyenne. The major collections of Eastern Shoshone artifacts are those of H.H. St. Clair at the American Museum of Natural History, New York, and Stuart Culin, in the University Museum, University of Pennsylvania, Philadelphia. The ethnographic paintings of Alfred Jacob Miller (1837) at the Walters Gallery, Baltimore, are also noteworthy.

Ute

DONALD CALLAWAY, JOEL JANETSKI, AND OMER C. STEWART

Language and Territory

The Ute ('yōot), together with the Southern Paiute and the Chemehuevi, speak one of the two languages of the Southern Numic branch of Uto-Aztecan. There were regional differences in Ute speech, but all dialects were mutually intelligible (T.J. Warner 1976:60; Miller 1966:78; Smith 1974:23).*

In the 1830s, before Europeans arrived in any considerable number, Ute bands occupied over 130,000 square miles between the Oquirrh Mountains on the west, the Uintah Mountains and the Yampa River on the north, the San Juan River on the south, and through the Middle Park of the Colorado Rockies to the Front Range on the east (fig. 1).

Environment

In the eastern range of Ute territory the Colorado Rockies form rank upon rank of ridges and peaks (some to 14,000 feet), generally extending along a north-south axis. The central portion is a montane region cut by deep river valleys. On the west the Wasatch Front is a massive block-fault mountain range that marks the eastern edge of the Basin physiographic province and the western edge of the Colorado Plateau. Peaks over 10,000 feet are fairly common with several over 12,000. This physiographic barrier traps the winter-spring storms streaming across the Great Basin, resulting in consid-

erable accumulations of snow in the peaks, which in turn feed the many streams and rivers that drain the Wasatch (cf. P.A. Kay 1982). Because the Basin has no outlet, these streams wind their way into lakes, sinks, and marshes such as the Great Salt Lake, Utah Lake, and Sevier Lake.

The southwestern portion of Ute aboriginal range consisted of sedimentary plateaus more than a mile above sea level. As a result of several river drainage systems these high plateau areas contain deeply sculptured canyons and mesas.

The beauty of these granite mountains, sculptured mesas, shaded deep river valleys, and pristine lakes created a spiritual attachment still evident in Ute attitudes toward mineral development.

Much of Ute aboriginal territory lay within the confines of the Colorado Plateau. The Plateau is a geological anomaly characterized by sedimentary rocks that have been lifted during the last 10 million years a mile or more above sea level. The Plateau is a semi-arid region; clouds coming from west lose much of their moisture to the Sierra Nevada range. However, with the exception of the western fringe of their territory, the physiographic character of the Ute area differed from the Great Basin proper. Annual average precipitation varied from 10 to 20 inches for the Uintah on the north and Weeminuche on the south to 20 to 40 inches for the Uncompahgre on the east (Jorgensen 1980:380). This rainfall pattern was in contrast to other Great Basin groups, for example Reese River and Battle Mountain Western Shoshone, who might experience less than 10 inches per year.

Valleys in the north such as Uinta were bunchgrass dominated while southern valleys among the Weeminuche and Uncompahgre were short-grass dominated (Jorgensen 1984b:17). Most valley systems received 10 to 12 inches of precipitation per year, while the high montane coniferous forests and alpine communities that rose from valley floors might average 20 to 40 inches per year. Snow packs of 200 inches were not uncommon in the Utah areas of the central Rocky Mountains. Spring runoffs benefited the valleys, which were often covered with camass, yampa, bitterroot, and wild potatoes.

Southerly Ute bands might forage in New Mexico during the winter, whereas other bands would spend

---

*The Ute words appearing in italics in the *Handbook* are written in the phonemic system of Givón (1979, 1980), with certain substitutions of phonetic symbols to conform to the standard Technical Alphabet of the *Handbook* (see p. x): (voiceless stops) $p, t, č, k, ?$; (voiced fricatives) v ([v] or [β]), r (tap), γ; (voiceless fricatives) s, x, h; (nasals) m, n; (semivowels) w, y; (short voiced vowels) i, e (perhaps not a phoneme), a, o ([ö]; [ɔ] next to the back allophone of a velar), $u, ɨ$; (short voiceless vowels) $I, A, O, U, ɨ̦$; (long vowels) $i·, a·, o·, u·, ɨ·$. The velar consonants (k, γ, x) have back velar allophones ([q], [ɣ], [x]) if between two a vowels or adjacent to one or two o vowels. Additional details of pronunciation are given by Givón (1979:3–13, 1980:2–15).

In the practical orthography used by the Southern Ute Tribe the phonemes are written as follows: p, t, c, k (back variant q), '; v, r, g (back variant ĝ); s, x (back variant x̂), h; m, n; w, y; i, e, a (fronted variant a̧), ǫ (back variant o), u, ṳ (variant i̧); i̠, a̠ (a̧), ǫ̠ (o̠), u̠, ṳ̠ (i̠); ii, aa, ǫǫ, uu, ṳṳ.

336

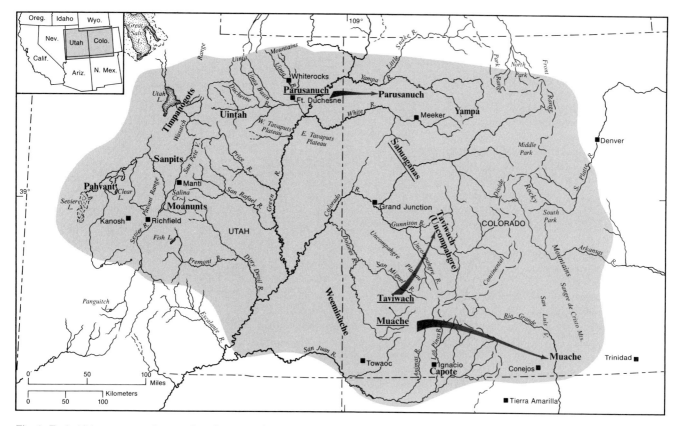

Fig. 1. Early 19th-century territory and modern town locations. Underlined band names are in approximate 18th-century locations; those not underlined are prereservation, 19th-century locations.

the winter months in sheltered valleys at lower elevations. Winters were considerably colder in the Uinta Basin than along the Wasatch Front (Eubank and Brough 1979) and, as it lies in the rain shadow of the Wasatch Mountains, the area is drier with the primary oases being along the river bottoms.

January temperatures averaged between 10 and 20° F, although frequent sunny days made living more comfortable than these temperatures would suggest. Average July temperatures ranged from 60 to 70° F for most of the Ute range; however, Weeminuche bands at somewhat lower elevations might average 10 degrees more. Daytime temperatures might reach the high 90s; however, because of the high altitude of most summer camps (4,500–8,500 feet) night temperatures were regularly in the 50s (Jorgensen 1980:320).

Western bands had slightly fewer species of grasses available than eastern bands. On the other hand, western groups had greater resources of roots, nuts, lilies, and berries. The short-grass grasslands of the Weeminuche and Uncompahgre had at least 12 species of available grasses; the bunchgrass grasslands of the Uintah had 9–10 species available. Most of these yielded tiny but edible seeds.

Utes had access to pigweed, lamb's-quarter, Indian millet, and broomrape.

Throughout the Uintah area well-watered valleys and

prairies produced large fields of wild potatoes, yampa, and camass. Nearly all Ute groups had access to wokas and brake fern (table 1). O.C. Stewart (1942:250–251) noted that mesquite was not available and that only the Weeminuche, on occasion, utilized mescal. Nearly all groups ate the blossoms and fruit of the yucca (various species) and used its root for soap. Jorgensen (1984b:19) generalizes that "all plant resources considered, the Utes had as many species of edible grasses as their Basin counterparts, but they had them in greater quantities than elsewhere. They also had more berry-producing shrubs and dense and productive root grounds (easily harvested in considerable quantities)."

Along with the periodic availability of large quantities of crickets, grasshoppers, and locusts, Ute territories had a plethora of available land mammals. With the exception of the Weeminuche, who had 11–15 major types, most Ute bands had upward of 19 major types available, such as buffalo, jackrabbits, cottontails, mountain sheep, mule deer, whitetail deer, elk, antelope, and moose.

Buffalo occurred everywhere in Colorado except the southwestern part of the state. "Herds of bison on the plains prior to settlement were immense. . . . In the mountains, bison occurred in parks and valleys, and apparently, ranged above timberline frequently. . . . A few bison from the southern end of South Park (were

337

Table 1. Major Flora Collected

Berries

Shepherdia argentea, silver buffaloberry: fruits eaten raw; more often cooked as sauce to flavor buffalo meat; also dried for winter use.

Shepherdia canadensis, soapberry: whipped into a froth used as a dessert (Harrington 1967:285).

Prunus virginiana, chokecherry: somewhat dried, mashed, then dried in cakes (Dawson 1978, 1:42).

Ribes aureum, currants: used only raw.

Ribes spp., gooseberries: eaten fresh.

Juniperus scopulorum, juniper berries: eaten raw or cooked; dried into cakes; used with young shoots and leaves in teas.

Rubus strigosus, red raspberries: eaten raw; dried into cakes.

Amelanchier alnifolia, serviceberry: eaten raw; cooked and dried into cakes.

Prunus americana, wild plum: eaten raw; sun dried for winter use.

Sambucus spp., elderberry: eaten raw; dried for storage.

Fragaria vesca, wild strawberry: eaten fresh (although not abundant).

Roots

Calochortus nuttallii, sego lily: dug in July, eaten immediately or baked in earth oven; seeds ground as food, flower buds eaten raw.

Camassia quamash, camas: bulbs steamed, then eaten or dried for storage; important resource where found, but not available to most eastern bands.

Perideridia gairdneri, yampa: probably the favorite tuber of Eastern Ute; eaten raw; baked in earth oven and dried, ground on metate, and stored in buckskin bags.

Cymopterus spp., biscuit root: in spring, eaten raw; in summer, peeled, boiled, baked, or roasted and ground.

Orogema linearifolia, Indian potato: eaten all year around.

Allium spp., wild onion: used extensively.

Pteridium acquilinum, brake fern: collected in autumn, dried and ground; young shoots eaten raw in spring.

Solanum jamesii, wild potato: eaten raw, boiled, or baked.

Nuphar polysepalum, wokas (yellow pond lily): boiled or roasted, then peeled; seedcups cooked, ground, and winnowed for flour.

Seeds

Amaranthus retroflexus, A. graecizans, pigweed: collected in autumn, winnowed, parched, then either eaten or ground into flour for cakes or boiled mush; or boiled, mashed, dried, then ground; young shoots and stems eaten raw or boiled.

Cleome serrulata, guaco: seeds treated like pigweed; shoots and leaves long boiled, sometimes stored, for dye or plant.

Oryzopsis hymenoides, Indian ricegrass: parched to remove scales, winnowed, ground into meal for cakes or mush.

Helianthus annuus, sunflower: parched and eaten, or hulled and ground; roots sometimes roasted or boiled.

Nuts

Pinus edulis, P. monophylla, piñon: cracked, meat eaten raw; or roasted and stored, then ground for cakes and gruel, sometimes mixed with sunflower seeds; important but sporadic, with bumper harvests every few years.

reported) in 1871 . . . Bison were taken in Middle Park in 1873 and were present in North Park in 1879" (Armstrong 1972:308).

Although not present in the valley at the time of the Francisco Atanasio Domínguez–Silvestre Vélez de Escalante visit in 1776, buffalo were clearly present (in small numbers) along the eastern periphery of the Great Basin in relatively recent prehistoric times (Currey and James 1982:43; O. Russell 1921; Pratt 1849; Beeley 1946). In the east, mountain buffalo were probably most important in prehistoric times. Along with immense herds of buffalo that might be found during the winter months, large herds of 500 or more antelope could also be hunted. Elk, deer, and mountain sheep usually moved in small herds throughout the year. "In terms of both the number of mammal species and the quantity of their distribution, the Utes and Northern Shoshones had more access to mammals than all Indians in Western North America except for the northwesterly dwellers of the Fraser and Columbia Plateaus" (Jorgensen 1984b:20).

In general, Ute territory was richer both in abundance and available species than that of most groups occupying the Great Basin. The physiographic diversity "coupled with the diversity of plant and animal forms, even though diffusely distributed and often relatively scarce, probably always provided food resources of some sort, no matter what period of the year" (Jorgensen 1984b:21).

Despite this relative abundance of fauna within the Great Basin culture area, Ute bands had fewer resources when compared with other cultures in western North America, such as the incredibly fish-rich areas of the Northwest Coast or the abundant acorn and fish areas of northern California. Resources in those areas supported much higher aboriginal population densities than were found among the Ute. In fact, even with population densities of up to one person per square mile 70 percent of the 172 Western North American Indian societies studied by Jorgensen (1980:447) had higher population densities than the Ute. On the other hand, Ute population densities are higher and in contrast to other cultures in the Great Basin with densities of less than one person per five square miles. While Western Ute groups had population densities similar to Eastern Ute bands their major concentrations occurred along the Wasatch Front, especially in Utah Valley and in the Pavant Valley and lower Sevier River area (Clayton 1921:278; T.J. Warner 1976:52–67).

Ute Bands

A definitive listing of the numerous Ute bands is made difficult by their fluid membership, the high mobility of most of them in the historical period, and the shifts and inconsistencies in the names used for several of them (Steward 1938:222–230, 1974; O.C. Stewart 1942:235–237). Here 11 bands are distinguished, six originally eastern bands with ranges primarily in present Colorado (Muache, Capote, Weeminuche, Uncompahgre, Parusanuch, Yampa), and five western bands of present Utah (Uintah, Timpanogots, Pahvant, Sanpits, Moanunts). New groupings and designations came into use after the settlement of the Ute on reservations. The descendants of the Muache and Capote bands are on the Southern Ute Reservation in Colorado, and the descendants of the Weeminuche are on the adjacent Ute Mountain Reservation; the residents of these reservations are generally referred to as Southern Utes and Ute Mountain Utes, respectively. The people known as Northern Utes are descendants of the other eight bands and live on the Uintah-Ouray Reservation in northeastern Utah, which combines two earlier reservations. The original Uintah Valley Reservation was set aside in 1861; after 1864 most of the Utes from central Utah were eventually made to settle there with Utes already in the Uintah Basin area, and after 1880 the White River Utes (Parusanuch and Yampa) were relocated there from Colorado. The adjacent Ouray Reservation was established for the relocated Uncompahgre in1882.

Muache

In the southeastern and south-central portion of the Ute aboriginal range were two bands. The Muache resided north of Trinidad, Colorado, to the Denver region. On the east they occupied areas east of the Sangre de Cristo and Culebra mountain ranges to as far south as Santa Fe. After the adoption of the horse the Muache were said, in association with the Jicarilla Apache, to have ranged southeastward as far as the panhandle of Texas (Schroeder 1965:54).

Capote

The other southeastern band was the Capote, who ranged east of the Continental Divide (and in the mid-nineteenth century west of the Divide near the Animas River), south of the Conejos River, and east of the Rio Grande to the west side of the Sangre de Cristo Mountains. They occupied areas in the San Luis Valley in Colorado and around what are now the towns of Chama and Tierra Amarilla, New Mexico. Both the Muache and Capote came into conflict with Plains tribes.

Weeminuche

The Weeminuche occupied territory west of the Continental Divide, from the Dolores River in western Colorado through the Blue Mountains and including the fringe of the mesas and plateaus in the canyonlands of eastern Utah. Their southern boundary extended to the valley of the San Juan River in northwestern New Mexico.

Uncompahgre (Taviwach)

The Taviwach were located in an area including the Gunnison River, the Elk Mountains, and the Uncompahgre River, with what is now Grand Junction at approximately their western boundary. Eastward they occupied territories through the South Park of the Colorado Rockies. The 1863 Treaty of Conejos established a reservation for them, along the Uncompahgre River, which was largely included in the Confederated Ute Indian Reservation set aside by the treaty of 1868. The agency for the Taviwach was moved to the Uncompahgre in 1876, and they came to be referred to as the Uncompahgre Utes. In 1880 after the so-called Meeker Massacre (in which they played no part) a government treaty council forced the Uncompahgre to sell all their land in Colorado. Under armed escort they were then moved to an area just south of the Uintah Reservation in Utah. There a new reservation was established by executive order in 1882 and named Ouray after the Uncompahgre chief.

White River (Parusanuch and Yampa)

Originally the Parusanuch and Yampa Utes occupied the river valleys of the White and Yampa rivers and North Park and Middle Park in the mountains of northern Colorado, with their territories extending westward to eastern Utah. Under the 1868 treaty the Parusanuch and Yampa bands, then called the Yampa and Grand River Utes, came under the jurisdiction of an agency at Meeker, Colorado, called White River. These two northern Colorado bands later came to be known as the White River Utes. In the 1880 treaty council the White River Utes, who had participated in the Meeker Massacre, were forced to sell all their land in Colorado and were moved under armed escort to live on the Uintah Reservation.

Uintah

Originally the Uintah band resided from Utah Lake east through the Uinta Basin to the Tavaputs Plateau in the Green and Colorado river systems. In the 1850s and 1860s after two prolonged wars, the Mormons displaced the Utes from their territory west of the Wasatch Mountains and with federal help began to remove and restrict them to the Uintah Reservation, an area considered valueless for farming or ranching.

Pahvant

The Pahvant band ranged the deserts surrounding Sevier Lake west of the Wasatch Mountains almost to the Nevada border, where Steward (1938) notes they were somewhat mixed with Gosiute. The government removed many to the Uintah Reservation, but small remnants remained in their old territory and in the 1980s their descendants survived at Kanosh, Koosharem, and other small settlements in Utah, where they were largely intermixed with Southern Paiutes in groups known officially as Utah Paiutes.

Timpanogots

Prior to the 1850s the Timpanogots band lived around the southern and eastern perimeter of Utah Lake in the Utah Valley, north-central Utah. They were displaced southward by Mormon settlement in the 1850s and later merged with the Uintah and other western Utes on the Uintah Reservation.

Sanpits

The Sanpits of the San Pete Valley in central Utah (Powell and Ingalls in ARCIA 1874:104) wintered in the Sevier River valley where there was less snow and where they could take deer, rabbits, ducks, and geese and trap beaver and mink (Steward 1938:228). In the spring they camped west of Manti. This band did not adopt the horse-riding pattern. They were among the Utes who eventually amalgamated with the Uintah.

Moanunts

The Moanunts lived in the upper Sevier River and Otter Creek regions south of Salina, Utah (O.C. Stewart 1942:236; Steward 1938:229, 1974:62). The importance of Fish Lake as a spring-summer residence contributed to the term Fish Ute to refer to this group. Gottfredson (1919:327–329) suggests that two groups of Moanunts were present in this area, one centered at Fish Lake, the other in the Marysvale area. Their fate was the same as that of the Pahvant.

External Relations

There are nearly 100 reports of eastern and southern Utes raiding Pueblo, Apache, Hopi, and Navajo settlements in what is now New Mexico and Arizona (Schroeder 1965). Utes and Navajos were at war in 1748 and 1770 but were considered friends in the 1780s, 1818, 1833, 1844, and 1850. In 1858 Utes joined the Americans and Mexicans in the war against the Navajo that ended in the Navajo removal of 1863. Peaceful relations between Ute and Navajo were restored with the return of the Navajo following their release from Bosque Redondo in 1868. Initially, a similar ebb and flow characterized Ute relations with Plains groups such as the Comanche. However, in the middle eighteenth century as Plains groups felt continual pressure from the north and east, relations became uniformly hostile.

The Western Ute groups maintained cordial relations with each other and with the Eastern Ute.

Ute relations with the Northern and Eastern Shoshone were generally poor (T.J. Warner 1976:46,58). Conflicts between the Ute and Shoshone continued sporadically into the late 1850s (Steele 1933:691; Ferris 1940:210).

Relations with the Western Shoshone were amiable and occasionally involved intermarriage (J.H. Simpson 1876:52), and Utes also interacted with the Southern Paiute (Ferris 1940:219). However, with the onset of the Spanish demand for slaves, Utes on horseback began to raid unmounted Western Shoshone and Southern Paiute (Malouf 1966).

Culture

Ute culture in the period just before 1850 in the west and 1870 in the east—that is, prior to the decimation of their population and the loss of their traditional lands—can be described from depositions and conversations conducted by ethnographers with elderly Ute informants in the 1930s and 1940s (especially Smith 1974 and O.C. Stewart 1942) and from ethnohistorical materials (see especially Jorgensen 1964, 1972; Janetski 1983a).

Subsistence

Key gathering, hunting, and fishing sites were not owned among the Ute. Access was communal and granted to all, within both the local and extralocal Ute communities. Good form might expect visitors to request the use of resource areas, but there was little etiquette or ceremonialism involved. Locally, reciprocity was balanced; strangers were bargained with but gift-giving prevailed among friends and relatives. Between communities trade was always conducted within a bargaining atmosphere.

Throughout Ute territories variable environments led to differential exploitation of resources. In general, the Western Ute had access to greater fish resources, Eastern bands had greater access to land mammals, while the Weeminuche, with lesser amounts of both fish and mammals, relied more heavily on plant resources (table 2).

• HUNTING Smith's (1974) informants stated that deer was the preferred meat (fig. 2); only one informant, from the White River band, mentioned that her band had more buffalo than deer. However, it seems likely, especially after the introduction of the horse, that the bands that eventually coalesced into the Uncompahgre Ute received a majority of their animal protein from buffalo. Western bands may have preferred deer meat, but a significant proportion of their diet involved smaller land mammals and fish. Deer, elk, and antelope were hunted by individuals stalking their prey in all bands. In addition, every group used drives, forcing animals into narrow areas where they were usually ambushed and killed.

Pitfalls were used by game-rich Utes, and their use is also mentioned for the Weeminuche. Only the Weeminuche used deadfalls (Jorgensen 1984b:36; O.C. Stewart 1942:247; Smith 1974:53).

Only Western groups used a deer skin as an animal disguise, while these same groups and the Weeminuche were the only ones to use poison arrows. In contrast, Eastern bands were the only ones to have a formal hunt chief. All O.C. Stewart's (1942) informants stated that they hunted buffalo (which prior to the arrival of the Americans were run down on horseback), but only the Eastern bands reported using a horse surround or driving buffalo over a precipice.

Yarded elk were hunted by surrounding them in deep snow. "Sometimes a small group of hunters on snowshoes would stalk elk, killing them when the elk tired, floundering in deep snow" (Smith 1974:54).

Unlike the Northern Paiute (O.C. Stewart 1941) or other Basin groups, no Ute hunter used charms in hunting antelope. Smith (1974:55) has a detailed discussion of an antelope drive in which a number of hunters, without women participants, would drive up to 200 antelope into a V-shaped funnel. The wings of the V were composed of piles of brush with men standing between and in front. The antelope were then driven over a cliff camouflaged with branches. Antelope and mountain sheep were hunted by individuals as well as communally in all bands. Task groups organized to hunt game were usually composed of several men, kin and affinally related, directed by a hunt leader.

All bands had communal rabbit drives but only West-

Milwaukee Public Mus., Wis.: 44386.
Fig. 2. Hunters with a load of deer meat, which became scarce as Whites began hunting in Ute territory, forcing Utes to hunt farther from their homes (Matteson 1901:29–36). "Chief" John McCook (right) was involved in the original secret burial of Ouray and acted as a pallbearer at Ouray's reinterment some 45 years later. Photograph by Sumner W. Matteson, Rio Blanco Co., Colo., Oct. 1898.

ern Ute used nets. Women made the cordage of sagebrush, juniper bark, milkweed, or dogbone fibers from which the men wove the nets, and only among the Western Ute did women participate in the communal rabbit drives (Smith 1974:56). Only the Western bands had a special leader to direct these drives, and he was usually the net owner.

Sage grouse were captured with nets near springs, while other birds and ground squirrels were usually shot with the bow and arrow (Smith 1974:58,60). Crickets and grasshoppers were gathered in large numbers in drives such as that observed by the first Mormon settlers entering Salt Lake Valley in July 1847 (Egan 1917:230–231). They were dried and mixed with berries to make a storable food called desert fruit-cake (Bryant 1967:141).

Waterfowl, especially ducks and mud hens, were hunted individually and in communal drives by the Eastern Ute who clubbed and shot them with bow and arrow. However, waterfowl were more plentiful, hunted more assiduously, and with a greater variety of techniques among the Western Ute, who herded them into shallow water or onto dry land, sometimes using balsas of tule, where they could then be captured by hand or shot with arrows (Smith 1974:60; O.C. Stewart 1942:244). Waterfowl drives were probably carried out in the early summer when young birds were not yet able to fly and adults were in molt. Waterfowl egg gathering may have been an important spring subsistence activity (O. Russell 1921:125).

Only the Western Ute and the Weeminuche were reported to eat reptiles such as rattlesnakes and lizards (chuckwalla and horned toad). All Ute bands gathered

Table 2.   Percentage Contribution to Diet of Subsistence Pursuits

	Agriculture	Fishing	Gathering	Hunting
Eastern Ute				
Weeminuche	0	20	45	35
Uncompahgre	0	15	35	50
Western Ute				
Uintah	0	25	40	35
Timpanogots	0	30	40	30

341

U. of Pa., U. Mus., Philadelphia: NA 2101.

Fig. 3. Snowshoes and accompanying moccasins. Living in a mountain environment, Utes could not afford to let winter snows curtail hunting or group movement. Snowshoes consist of a circular bent stick frame, a rawhide lattice work, the thongs retaining fur, and a buckskin loop and tie system for anchoring the foot. Circular snowshoes seem to be the traditional form, though Smith (1974) presents informants' recollections of bearpaw and trail shoe type snowshoes in the late 19th and early 20th centuries. Diameter 41 cm; collected in Utah in 1909.

insects such as cicadas and crickets, but only the Western Ute and Weeminuche stated that they ate ants.

In general, the Eastern bands had a greater variety of animal and food taboos than did the Western Ute. For example, eating the hearts of big game animals was taboo to Eastern Ute women. In accord with their use of rabbit nets, only the Western bands used a variety of snares and nets to capture birds (including grouse), rodents, and other small mammals.

All Ute groups cut meat in thin strips and dried them in the sun; however, only the Eastern Ute pulverized meat on a parfleche. While pulverized meat might be mixed with fat, all O.C. Stewart's (1942:329) informants denied mixing it with berries or seeds to make pemmican. Meat was also cured by placing it on a domed willow drying frame and slowly smoking it with a fire underneath.

• FISHING   Fish were eaten by all the groups but were more important in the diet of Western bands. Most Western bands, the Weeminuche, and Eastern bands from the Grand, Green, and Colorado drainages were reported to have used weirs, traps, and harpoons. Utah Lake, which was perhaps the single most impressive fishery in the eastern Great Basin, and all the streams and rivers draining the Wasatch contained significant

populations of fish, as did the freshwater and brackish marshes formed where the fresh water discharged into marshes and playa lakes. Fish and Panguitch were upland lakes containing significant fisheries as well. Domínguez and Escalante (T.J. Warner 1976:69) in the vicinity of Clear Lake in Pavant Valley describe the lakes and marshes as "abounding in fish." Others, such as Pratt (Hafen and Hafen 1954–1961,2:74), D.S. Jordan (1891), Bryant (1967), J. Sharp (1898) and T.J. Warner (1976:50), have documented the fish populations in the streams and rivers of the Wasatch and the rivers flowing into the Uinta Basin. The economically important fish species in these lakes and streams were Bonneville cutthroat trout (*Salmo clarki utah*), Utah chub (*Gila atraria*), suckers (*Catostomus* spp., *Chasmistes liorus*), and whitefish (*Prosopium williamsoni*) (Heckman, Thompson, and White 1981).

The specialized technology developed by the Utes to harvest fish resources included fish arrows, bone or wood gorgets attached to lines, greasewood fish spears, weirs of brush or saplings, woven dip nets, cordage nets, and basket traps (Smith 1974:61–63; O.C. Stewart 1942:249–250, 337; Stansbury 1852:148). Lowie's (1924:200) Uintah Ute informants said fish were shot with barbed arrows, occasionally from grass (tule?) rafts. G.W. Armstrong (in ARCIA 1855:202) noted that trapping and shooting with the bow and arrow were the "usual" ways for the Utes to take fish. Fish were also commonly caught by hand (Pratt 1849; Gottfredson 1919:326). Fish were also captured through the ice by erecting a small shelter on the ice, cutting a hole, and spearing or shooting the fish with arrows (Smith 1974:63). R.L. Campbell (1850) reported Pahvant Utes fishing in February.

Fish were prepared for immediate consumption by cutting them into pieces and boiling them in earthen vessels (Lowie 1924:200). Others "were split down the middle, the backbones removed, and then laid across two poles to dry. The drying poles were raised from the ground so that the dogs would not get the fish. Fish were stored in round sacks made of buckskin or elkskin. These were shaped like flour sacks, but rounded on the bottom . . . The sacks were stored in a hole dug in the side of a hill" (Smith 1974:64). Similar methods are reported by O.C. Stewart (1942:253), Madsen and Madsen (1900), and Lowie (1924:200) who notes that the dried fish were eaten in the fall. Timpanogots gave the members of a Spanish expedition dried fish for their journey from Utah Lake southward (T.J. Warner 1976:57). Frémont also obtained dried fish from the Ute in 1843 (Preuss 1958:129).

Technology seems more focused on the capture of fish in streams than in lakes, although both were exploited. The Utah Valley Ute had a special fishing chief (O.C. Stewart 1942:300) who apparently directed group fishing efforts, perhaps as a rabbit or antelope boss directed drives for those resources, suggesting that co-operative efforts were more important at certain times of the year, such as spring. Communal use of dams and weirs probably took place primarily during the spawning seasons. As the spawning season waned, individual strategies such as fishing with gorgets, bow and arrow, and spearing through the ice would have been more common (Follett 1982).

• GATHERING   All groups collected and ate sunflower seeds, grass seeds, cactus blossoms and fruit, roots, tubers, berries, and thistles. A Weeminuche informant also reported removing the leaves and eating the core of mescal plants. Table 1 provides details on the major flora collected by Ute groups. Gathering was done by women although men might help in the gathering of piñon nuts. In most cases gathering was not carried out by task groups, although females from an extended family might join together in gathering berries or seeds. All Northern Ute groups used a great variety of seeds that ripened from early spring to late fall (Smith 1974:65). Acorns were gathered.

Although not equally abundant at all locations each year, the piñon groves were sufficiently scattered in Western Ute territory that some good crops of piñon nuts were found by nearly all Western Ute each year. Hunters regularly kept watch on the piñon trees to report the prospective harvests. Fall gathering of piñon nuts was combined with deer hunting. The piñon groves took on a festive air if the crops were extremely abundant so that several families or even several bands might congregate and live mostly on piñon nuts and venison until deep snow forced a retreat to lower elevations. Piñon nut stores were revisited to carry supplies to camps at lower elevation (O.C. Stewart 1942:250). While all groups used a straight pole in the gathering of piñon nuts, only the Western bands also used a hooked pole (see Steward 1941:279).

All groups gathered wild tobacco, recognizing that it grew better in burned-over areas. Some Eastern and Western bands purposefully burned off areas to affect its growth.

O.C. Stewart's (1942:254) Weeminuche informant claimed that exceptional families among his band planted varieties of maize just prior to the arrival of White settlers in the early 1860s. Men cleared the fields, planted the corn, and harvested the crop. Women weeded the fields, and both sexes aided in the irrigation of the small plots. While all other reports on this topic indicate that the southerly bands certainly traded meat and buckskins for agricultural products with the Pueblos, none mentions the cultivation of crops prior to the reservation period. The fact that the Weeminuche informant stated that only maize but not beans, squash, melons, or sunflowers were cultivated indicates that this one instance of agriculture was probably a very recent introduction.

• STORAGE   Food was cached in a variety of places,

top, Denver Public Lib., Western Hist. Dept., Colo. 11439; Amer. Mus. of Nat. Hist., New York: bottom, 50.1/6985a, b.

Fig. 4. Women's clothing and adornment. top, Tannah with facial paint, dark circles on cheeks, and white circle on forehead and a painted hair part. The pin on her bodice says "souvenir." Photograph by John K. Rose and Benjamin S. Hopkins Studio, Denver, Colo., 1899. bottom, Pair of beaded buckskin half-leggings. These are part of traditional women's apparel, tied below the knee, with the plain top portion covered by the hem of the dress. Nickel-plated buttons are sewed along the margins. This is the most common half-legging style, simply an open square of buckskin tied up on the side and lashed at the top to the leg. All sewing was done with sinew thread. Collected by R.H. Lowie, Navajo Spring, Colo., 1912. Length 33 cm.

including storage platforms in coniferous trees with branches thick enough to protect it from rain and snow and in grass- or bark-lined pits. Pits were dug under cliff overhangs, lined with bark, and filled with sacks of food, which were then covered with bark, grass, rocks, dirt, and more rocks. A fire was built on top to conceal the pit. Even so, bears occasionally found and robbed the caches (Smith 1974:67).

Clothing and Adornment

In 1776 Veléz de Escalante noted that the Eastern Ute had surplus deer skins to trade. He also noticed marked differences in clothing between Colorado Utes and Utah Lake Utes. The former were better dressed and fully clothed in buckskin while the latter were partially dressed in buckskin. Smith (1974:80) remarks that "buckskins tanned by Utes were recognized as being exceptionally well done and were frequently used as trade articles with other tribes, and with the Spanish colonists of New Mexico."

Western Ute women often wore a woven bark or fiber apron (O.C. Stewart 1942:281). Sanpits women wore a "piece of skin, reaching from the middle to the knees, and instances are not uncommon where they possess complete leather skirt, but no other articles of dress" (Alter 1941:94). In the colder seasons blankets of tanned fur, especially of rabbit but also of muskrat, badger, marmot, coyote, and wolf were commonly worn (Smith 1974:72). Other clothing, especially a poncho-like shirt,

was occasionally made of sagebrush bark and tule fibers.

Women from Eastern groups wore a long gown usually made from two deerskins (preferably doe); less commonly antelope or mountain sheep skins were used. Eastern Utes had some rabbit skin robes, but they preferred robes constructed of buffalo that had been tanned on one side. See Smith (1974:69–79) for details on the construction of Ute clothing.

In the east men usually wore a breechclout, leggings, and shirt of buckskin. They also wore a two-piece hard-sole moccasin sometimes over a sagebrush stocking for warmth during the winter. The sole might be of buffalo hide with an upper of deer or elk hide. Muskrat and beaver were also used as insoles in hide moccasins or yucca sandals. Initially shirts were without ornamentation, but during the period of increased contact with Plains tribes elaborated decoration began to be adopted. Decorations included paint, fringe, beads, deer ankle bone, elk teeth, porcupine quills, and scalps. These styles were apparently less common along the Wasatch Front (O.C. Stewart 1942:281).

A Spanish journal describes the Pahvant or Sanpits Ute as wearing in their "nostril cartilage . . . a tiny polished bone of deer, fowl, or some other animal" (T.J. Warner 1976:64). The Utes also wore necklaces, especially of animal claws, bone beads, fish vertebrae, stones, and juniper seeds (O.C. Stewart 1942:277). Painted and braided belts and straps were sometimes decorated with feathers. Paint in white, black, red, yel-

bottom left and right, Utah State U., Merrill Lib., Logan; Smithsonian, Dept. of Anthr.: a, 210,986; g, 200,965; Colo. Histl. Soc., Denver: b, E 1324; c, E 2005; Mus. of the Amer. Ind., Heye Foundation, New York: d, 2/3115; f, 2/7280; Denver Mus. of Nat. Hist., Dept. of Anthr.: e, 11725.

Fig. 5. Men's clothing and body decoration. Both men and women painted their face and hair with designs that appear to have had no symbolic significance (Smith 1974:78). bottom left, Studio portrait of man with feather headdress and horizontal lines painted on his loose hair. He has animal skin containers for his bow and quivers and a pipe-tomahawk with flap. bottom right, Young man with several colors of facial paint. He wears a shell bead breast ornament. bottom left and right, Photographs by Charles Ellis Johnson, at Uintah-Ouray Reservation, Utah, about 1898. a, Yellow buckskin shirt cut and machine sewn on a European pattern. Under each arm is tied a cloth medicine bundle, one red, the other blue. Seed beads, dark blue and red triangles on a light purple background, are sewed along the shoulder and arm seams. Painted green lines run down the front. On the back are painted lines and rosettes in imitation of quilled or beaded blanket strips; the lines are black, the interior colors, blue, green, and red. One ermine skin hangs from the left shoulder. Collected in Utah before 1901. b, Robe of blue stroud with scalloped white cloth borders and an ornate beaded blanket strip with rosettes done in white, blue, green, and yellow seed beads. A small medicine bag of red and brown print cloth is tied to the lower rosette with a buckskin thong. Common on articles of clothing and elements of personal adornment, these bags often carried owner's amulets or sweet-smelling herbs and grasses. Width 147.5 cm; collected 1900–1905. c, Cloth scalp shirt of Severo (d. 1916), a chief of the Capote Ute. The fabric is green calico and pink calico, cut and ornamented in the traditional style of buckskin shirts, decorated with beaded strips of white background with blue and yellow geometric motifs. Scalplocks of dark brown hair are attached to the sleeve and shoulder strips. The shirt is sewn with sinew and cotton thread. d, Beaded bandolier or men's shoulder bag. Beads and strouding are sewn over a thick leather foundation. Usually, the bags also have a red or blue stroud flap that hangs down from the bottom seam. Bandolier bags were worn by Ute men from the 1870s on; around 1900 they were taken up by women and worn or displayed at parades, sometimes hung on cars or around the necks of horses (cf. Loeb 1980). Basic form and decoration has remained consistent. Design motifs, including elongated geometric shapes, a preference for light blue or pink backgrounds, and sparing use of white except to outline major shapes, are very similar to defined Crow design (cf. Wildschut and Ewers 1959). Great Basin affiliation is evident only when these characteristics are combined with the "red finger" design on the shoulder strap and, to a lesser extent, diamond and triangle motifs on the pouch as the major foreground shapes (Loeb 1980). This specimen is unusual in that the seed beads have been applied in a very loose lazy stitch, arranged both vertically and horizontally, whereas in most examples, stitching is done in overlay beading or in the Crow stitch, both of which yield flat, smooth, beaded surfaces. Collected before 1909. e, Man's beaded elkskin moccasins with hard soles, the cuffs lined with red stroud. Made in early 1900s. f, Pair of quilled buckskin moccasins, the ankle top bordered in stroud, and the inside in cloth. Collected before 1910. g, Breast ornament of shells strung on buckskin thongs suspended between commercial leather side bars. A blue glass trade bead is at the center of the shell moon. The ornament was tied around the wearer's neck by means of the red printed cloth tied to the top buckskin thong. Collected before 1899. a Length, 80 cm, c–d same scale; e, length 29.8 cm; f–g same scale.

left, Colo. Histl. Soc., Denver: E 1350; right, U. of Utah Lib., Special Coll., Salt Lake City: P2014 #5.

Fig. 6. Bead work. left, Beaded and fringed ration ticket pouch, probably made in the period 1880–1900. The front of the buckskin pouch is beaded in a turtle design surrounded by stepped triangles, all geometric figures done in yellow, trimmed in royal blue, mauve, red, and green, on a light blue background. The turtle motif seems to have been borrowed during the late 19th century from the Sioux or other tribes of the northern Plains. Ration ticket pouches reflect the requirement that heads of families present ration tickets at reservation depots to draw supplies. Length, 27 cm; collected before 1923. right, Uncompahgre men, women, and children on the Uintah-Ouray Reservation, Utah. The woman on the left is beading a small piece of skin, probably part of a moccasin. Photograph by Edward Sapir, summer 1909.

low, blue, and green was applied to the face for special occasions, while red and white paint and feathers were used to decorate the hair. Facial tattooing was done with cactus thorns dipped in cedar (juniper?) leaf ashes (Smith 1974:79).

Technology

• LEATHERWORK The well-regarded Ute buckskin was tanned by women. The fleshy side of the hide was usually scraped off first using a notched deer canon bone with the proximal end wrapped with buckskin. The skin was then soaked overnight in a pit filled with water before the hair was removed. Brains, which had been boiled or baked and stored in a piece of intestine, were then applied as a tanning agent. Next the hide was left in the sun for a few days, then soaked in water for a short period, stretched (a time-consuming process), and then smoked over a fire on one side. A buffalo hide might be cut in half to facilitate tanning and the tanning agent applied to the fleshy side only, thus preserving the hair side for insulation. Heavy hides were softened by rubbing with a stone or pulling them briskly over a rope.

• BASKETRY Baskets were produced in a variety of forms, especially for gathering seeds and berries (Smith 1974:89–94; O.C. Stewart 1942:269–271). Round-bottomed, wide-mouthed forms of various sizes were the most prevalent, although conical baskets, traps, cradles, seed beaters, small and large-mouthed water jugs, ladles or dippers, and fish traps were also manufactured. Preferred materials were willow (*Salix* sp.) and especially squawbush (*Rhus trilobata*) twigs, which were dampened and usually coiled, sometimes twined. Twining was more common among the Western Ute, although the Weeminuche made a twined conical carrying basket, and most groups manufactured a twined seed beater or "sunflower hammer."

Baskets were occasionally decorated with paint, especially since the early 1900s, or by rubbing the exterior with white clay or seed paste. Water jugs were waterproofed by smearing with pitch on the inside. Baskets sometimes had attached handles of buckskin or human, buffalo, or horse hair (O.C. Stewart 1942:271).

• WOODWORK AND CORDAGE Other containers were made of wood (cups, ladles, platters), stone (usually steatite cups), horn (ladles or spoons of mountain sheep and bison horn) (fig. 8), and skin (both rawhide and tanned bags) (Smith 1974:96). Skins were occasionally

left, Denver Pub. Lib., Western Hist. Dept., Colo.: H463; center, Mus. of the Amer. Ind., Heye Foundation, New York: 10/5444; right, Colo. Histl. Soc., Denver: F-15456.

Fig. 7. Cradleboards. left, Woman identified as Peearat, with child in cradleboard. Smith (1974:101–104) and O.C. Stewart (1942:274–275) detail at least 2 different types of cradle construction; the oldest, using willow in the frame, was still in use in 1936. This one is probably the later type, a board cradle, made for a girl. The boy's cradle was painted white using white clay mixed with water, while the girl's cradle was painted yellow, using yellow clay mixed with water. The cradle was usually carried with a strap across the chest. Cradles were most often made by the baby's maternal grandmother, but if she were not available the father's mother or the mother would make it. The baby would be kept in the cradleboard during the day but would usually be removed from it at night and placed on bedding or put to sleep in a soft buckskin bag that could be laced up the front. Babies were bathed each morning prior to being placed in the cradle. Frequently, shredded bark was used as a diaper. Photograph by John K. Rose and Benjamin S. Hopkins Studio, Denver, Colo., 1899. center, Board cradle, with a shaped section of wood as the frame. This style replaced the traditional Ute cradle frame of bent and woven willow shoots. Both styles made use of a fitted buckskin cover and an awning of twined willows. This specimen has elements characteristic of a boy's cradle. There is a penis hole in the center of the leather flap tied over the pouch lacings, which allowed the infant to urinate outside the buckskin pouch. A girl's cradle was laced up the front a lesser distance, allowing for insertion of a soft pad between the infant's legs. The beaded and fringed buckskin band at the top of the carrying pouch was tied across the infant's chest. Use of elaborate beading at the top of the board is also a postcontact trait. Height 101 cm; collected in Utah before 1921. right, Bessie Box, with a doll on a play cradleboard, Sally Box, and Bessie Tobias. Photograph probably by H.H. Tammen, before 1902.

stretched over a willow frame made in the shape of a deep bowl and used for burden baskets.

Cordage was made from fibers of sagebrush (*Artemisia tridentata*) bark, juniper (*Juniperus osteosperma*) bark, dogbane (*Apocynum androsaemifolium*), yucca (*Yucca* sp.), and nettle (*Urtica* sp.). O.C. Stewart's (1942) informants demonstrated the process of twisting the Apocynum fibers on their thighs and then rolling together two or three strings for greater strength. Animal cordage was made of sinew, rawhide, and hair. Cordage uses included nets, traps, ropes, and bowstrings. Plant parts and fibers were also used in the manufacture of rafts or balsas made of bundles of tules or bulrushes. Tules were also used to make mats and blankets.

• POTTERY All Ute bands did not make pottery (Smith 1974:84 to the contrary). Weeminuche women may have made some coiled pottery (Driver and Massey 1957:340, 343), but it is apparent that most Eastern Ute groups did not use pottery. Instead, they boiled food by dropping heated stones into coiled baskets (O.C. Stewart 1942; Jorgensen 1980).

Pottery was made by coiling techniques, of clay tempered with sand or vegetable material (Opuntia cactus leaves and juice), and fired in an open fire (Smith 1974:84–88; O.C. Stewart 1942:273). Vessel forms were limited but may have included conical shapes as well as flat-bottomed, parallel-sided pots and mugs. The impression from ethnographic reports is that pottery was not important. However, archeological excavation of apparent Ute sites in Utah Valley has recovered pottery in considerable quantities (Beeley 1946), thereby suggesting that pottery may have been fairly common in late prehistoric times in some areas.

The ethnographic literature on the Western Ute was obtained primarily during the 1930s when many of the traditional crafts were little more than a memory. Be-

Amer. Mus. of Nat. Hist., New York: a, 50/1308; Mus. of the Amer. Ind., Heye Foundation, New York: b, 2/7432; c, 16/9587.

Fig. 8. Eating utensils, traditionally made from knots of juniper, pine, and cottonwood (Smith 1974) and from the horns of mountain sheep. To make utensils from a knot, the craftsman charred the wood with hot coals, and then carved the desired form with a knife, repeating this process as often as necessary to complete the utensil. Horn also had to be heated before working, the piece placed near the fire or in hot water until malleable, then shaped with a knife. Cut to form, the horn was then placed in a prepared mold in the ground and filled with dirt so that it would retain its shape upon cooling. Outer surfaces were smoothed by rubbing with an abrasive stone, and polished through the application of oil or grease. As metal utensils became available, traditional forms quickly declined in popularity, though some, like the horn spoons, were reserved for ceremonial or special social occasions. a, Wood cup or ladle with a buckskin carrying thong; b, metal spoon ornamented with quillwork, tin bangles, and thread; c, horn spoon with a handle carved in the form of a bird's head. a, Diameter 11 cm; rest to same scale. a, Collected by A.L. Kroeber at Whiterocks, Utah, 1900; b, collected before 1910; c, collected before 1930.

cause of the superiority of metal trade pots, pottery vessels were one of the first items of material culture to be abandoned.

• STONEWORK Before metal was introduced the Western Ute made a variety of chipped and ground stone tools. Among the former were knives, unshaped stone flakes used for skinning animals, scrapers, drills, and arrow and spear points, including small arrow points of various shapes but especially a corner-notched type (O.C. Stewart 1942:264, 267). Preferred materials for chipped tools were fine-grained cherts and obsidian. Ground stone tools included round or oval manos and thin slab and deep trough metates used to grind seeds, nuts, tubers, and berries. Mortars and pestles, which were rarer, consisted of a bowl-shaped cavity pecked into a stone into which the elongate, rounded pestle fit.

Mortars and pestles were used more for mashing meats, berries, and nuts rather than for grinding. Grinding tools were often collected from prehistoric sites (Smith 1974:98; O.C. Stewart 1942:262).

Structures

Only the Western Ute occupied domed willow houses throughout the year. Among the Eastern bands only the Weeminuche built domed willow houses (usually by stream beds) but occupied them only during the summer; these were about eight feet high and 15 feet in diameter and were covered with willow boughs (but without a smoke hole). All groups made tripod or conical houses with a three or four-pole foundation and a circular ground plan some 10–15 feet in diameter with coverings of brush or bark. Only Western bands mentioned coverings of tule. Occasional canvas coverings are suggested by archeological evidence (Smith 1974:35; O.C. Stewart 1942:256; Janetski 1983a:94).

Southern Utes (probably Muache) living north of Santa Fe were reported in 1720 to carry with them and dwell in "tents made of bison hide" (A.B. Thomas 1935:171). Escalante, in a visit to the Uncompahgre in 1776, noted not only the presence of "huts" (probably conical houses), but also the use of tepees and horses. O.C. Stewart's (1942) informants appear to confirm these sources. Some informants indicated that some Western bands had one or two skin tepees even before the band had horses. His Timpanogots informant stated they were not used by his band until after the Mormons had arrived. However, Jedediah Smith (G.R. Brooks 1977:42) recorded lodges of skins used by Utah Valley Utes in Spanish Fork Canyon in 1826. The Pahvants denied their use, while the Weeminuche recounted that they were an introduction after the Anglos had entered their territory; however, all other Eastern bands claimed their use prior to the arrival of the Americans. The Muache said that they had traded with the Mexicans prior to their adoption of tepees from the Plains tribes.

Tepees, used in both summer and winter, used 6 to 10 elk or buffalo hides (fig. 9). Smith's informants note that elk was used more frequently than buffalo hides, although this was probably not the case for the easternmost bands. Western Ute tepees rarely exceeded 15 feet in height, while those of the Eastern bands were commonly up to 17 feet high. In addition, only Eastern Ute informants (O.C. Stewart 1942:258) claimed the packing of the heavy cover on horses prior to the arrival of the Anglos. The Moanunts packed the cover on a travois pulled by men. Naturalistic decoration and designs were a later phenomenon. A tepee cover was usually constructed by a group of several women. It might take three or four days to sew the hides using sinew from the back of a deer or buffalo (which provided the longest thread). Smith (1974:38–42) gives a

Smithsonian, NAA: top left, 1506; top right, 1547; bottom, Rell G. Francis Coll.

Fig. 9. Dwellings. top left, Encampment. Within the camp, tepees were usually scattered, with access to wood and shade being a primary consideration. When the camp was to be moved, tepee poles were bundled and fastened to the side of a horse with another horse usually carrying the tepee cover. Although the travois was known it was rarely used. With the exception of an area around the fireplace, the interior of a tepee was covered with brush or bark. Beds were made from willows stacked and formed and then covered with a buffalo robe. A tripod on the right was used to hold bags, shields, and other items. A metal cooking pot lies on the ground under the tripod. Photograph by William H. Jackson, near Denver, Colo., 1874. top right, Home of Chief Tavaputs, a conical brush house, with drying rack to left loaded with Indian corn. Conical houses were usually constructed on a 4-pole foundation. Additional poles made a circular ground plan with a diameter of 10–15 feet. Coverings of brush, bark, or tule were added to the frame. This house type probably predates the skin tepee among the Ute and shows that they retained this typical Great Basin house into the 1870s. Photograph by John K. Hillers, Uinta Valley, Utah, 1873. bottom, Camp of Western Ute at Kanosh, Utah, with both brush and canvas structures. Photograph by George E. Anderson, about 1900.

349

detailed description of tepee construction, decoration, and interior organization.

A wickiup-type sweathouse was commonly used by all Ute groups, but only the Eastern bands used the conical type. A sweathouse was heated with rocks carried from a fire outside, although some groups also poured or sprinkled water on the rocks to generate steam. Sweating served for bathing at any time and in addition was considered efficacious in the cure of sickness, with or without a shaman. Men usually took sweat baths with other men, and less frequently women with women. Among several Eastern Ute groups and the Pahvant a husband and wife might bathe together (Smith 1974:44). In 1936 "while its use was not common, some men still used the sweat house" (Smith 1974:45). In 1982 on the Southern Ute Reservation during mild weather it was not uncommon to hear of a sweatbath every week or so.

Weapons

Ute wooden bows were both single and double curve with the latter sinew-backed. Preferred materials were chokecherry and mountain mahogany, although juniper and serviceberry were also used. Most bows measured three to four feet long. Bows were also manufactured

Mus. of the Amer. Ind., Heye Foundation, New York: 16/6137.
Fig. 10. Warrior's shield of two thicknesses of buffalo hide with a deer skin cover painted white and ornamented with eagle feathers. Anchored to the forearm and hand or wrist by leather straps, the buffalo hide shield offered reasonable protection against arrow or lance and was an essential part of a prominent warrior's kit. Decoration was variable, ranging from none to painted designs (Smith 1974). The shield had a sacred connotation, and ritual was associated with its use and display. In camp, it was commonly displayed outside the owner's tepee. Diameter 46.5 cm; collected by J.W. Powell, Colo. Terr., 1871.

from the horns of mountain sheep, by heating the horn, splitting it, and splicing the two pieces into a single curve using sinew wrapping. Such bows were still found among Great Basin Indians as late as the mid 1800s (J.H. Simpson 1876:52).

Arrows, both single and composite, 22 to 24 inches long, were made using serviceberry and other hardwoods. Composite arrows were made with cane mainshafts and hardwood foreshafts tipped by sharpening, with stone points or with crossed sticks for birds. Fletching consisted of the split wing feathers of a large bird such as magpie, eagle, hawk, or owl, with three equally spaced feathers tied near the proximal end of the arrow with sinew and glue.

O.C. Stewart's (1942:269) informants from Utah and Colorado described the use of thrusting spears, but Smith (1974:112–113) states that only Colorado Utes used these weapons. The use of a warclub made of a rawhide-covered stone was claimed by at least one band in Utah and at least one band in Colorado (O.C. Stewart 1942:269; Smith 1974:112).

Spears were used for hunting and fishing. Composite fishspears four to five feet long and tipped with sharpened greasewood foreshafts were made only by the Utah groups.

Music

All Ute groups used a notched rasp called a morache for the Bear Dance, rawhide and hoof rattles, and a single-headed drum; men used a wooden flute in courting. Gourd rattles and the water drum came to the Ute with the Peyote religion (O.C. Stewart 1942:294).

Life Cycle

A pregnant woman had to observe several taboos including the avoidance of fattening foods, coitus after the first sign of pregnancy (this seems to have been more of a theoretical admonition), and the avoidance of sitting any place where a gopher had dug. There were many food taboos: "certain animals whose 'power' was strong should not be eaten by pregnant women nor hunted by their husbands, for fear the baby might be killed. Mountain lion and the badger, which was thought to be a former Ute shaman, were taboo; also bob-cat and fox" (Smith 1974:137). Beaver meat was to be avoided, as was mole or gopher. Timpanogots, Uncompahgre, and Weeminuche informants noted that the husband had to observe the same taboos as his wife (O.C. Stewart 1942:303).

Delivery never occurred in the dwelling but in a special house or windbreak constructed for that purpose. The woman's husband collected firewood and a fire was kept continuously in the birth house (Smith 1974:138). During delivery a woman knelt and was usually assisted

top, Smithsonian, Dept. of Anthr.: 315,168; bottom, Colo. Histl. Soc., Denver: E 1023.

Fig. 11. Ute courtship flutes. top, Flute decorated with buckskin ties, buckskin pendants trailing green- and red-dyed plumes, purple satin ribbon, painted chamber with alternating yellow and red bands covering the 7 holes, and an animal effigy carved atop the regulator painted red with black stripes. A young man would leave camp in the late afternoon or early evening, and playing a special tune known to his sweetheart, would await her arrival (Smith 1974). bottom, Flute of 20th-century manufacture, made along traditional lines, with 6 holes, buckskin thongs tying the halves of the chamber together, and a buckskin thong anchoring the unadorned regulator. The designs, incised, and painted in red, orange, green, yellow, blue, and black, are not traditional motifs; they are probably adapted from late 19th-century Plains beadwork. Use of these motifs to decorate an otherwise traditional flute is characteristic of modern manufacture, which combines traditionally distinctive elements of form and decoration in the creation of pan-Indian artifacts usually intended for sale to non-Indians. Length of bottom, 89 cm; other same scale. top, Collected in northeastern Colo. before 1920. bottom, Collected in Towoac, Colo., before 1935.

by a female relative, a mother or grandmother, or in some cases by an experienced woman or woman with special powers. Husbands also assisted during the delivery. In the case of a difficult delivery a shaman would be called in, would press his or her forehead on the woman's stomach, and sing power songs.

After delivery the mother was bathed and might squirt some of her milk on a hot rock to insure a sufficient supply. During a month-long postpartum confinement a new mother might be attended by a relative; she drank warm water, avoided grease and meat, and could not scratch her hair or body with her fingers.

The child's umbilicus was cut with a stone knife, stored in a skin pouch, and attached to the child's cradle for one or two years or until the child began to walk. Ul-

timately a girl's umbilicus might be placed in a red-ant nest to promote industriousness on her part.

After his child's birth a father might bathe himself, be rubbed with sage or juniper boughs, and then run strenuously to insure the child's industriousness. Until the navel cord dropped off, the father would avoid cold water, eating meat or grease, scratching his hair or body, smoking, and gambling.

"Twins were not welcome; in fact, they were considered rather a disgrace and a sign of impending bad luck. A taboo on eating deer (which frequently give birth to twins) was reported, but the usual cause of having twins was said to be having had intercourse with more than one man during pregnancy, or having had too frequent intercourse with the husband. Another reason advanced for the birth of twins was that somebody had used evil power (bad power) against the mother. One twin was

left, Center of Southwest Studies, Fort Lewis College, Durango, Colo.: IV-411; right, Smithsonian, Dept. of Anthr.: 1879.

Fig. 12. Hair plates. left, Ute dancers at Ignacio, Colo. Male dancer to right wears hair plates of German silver. Photographed 1900–1920. right, Hair ornament of braided buffalo hair and brass plates and buttons (detail). Attached to the wearer's own hair, it would have reached well below the waist. The plates are engraved with small angular tracks. Of the brass buttons, the uppermost button with the embossed eagle and wreath is a flat, 2-piece great coat button, of the type issued to regular army enlisted men and cavalry prior to 1839 (cf. Albert 1969). Sheets of brass and tin and finished hair plates were traded to Indians west of the Mississippi River by 1800, with brass and tin largely replaced by German silver after the 1860s (Feder 1962). Popularity of these ornaments fell off dramatically after the 19th century. The specimen, collected before 1869, is the oldest set of hair plates in any museum collection (cf. Bushnell 1909; Feder 1962). Its date of manufacture could be even earlier given the great coat button. Length 94 cm; collected on the Green River, Utah Terr.

usually neglected and left to die; frequently the other twin died, also" (Smith 1974:138).

Children were highly desired and adults welcomed all children whether family members or not. Attitudes toward children were permissive. Babies were often cared for by other children, sometimes only 9 or 10 years old, who carried them on their backs, in a cradleboard or a folded shawl (Smith 1974:144).

An individual might be named after birth, after weaning, when walking began, or even through adulthood. Names might refer to some action of personal characteristic or some material object, animal, bird, or plant; examples are Blue Hummingbird and Deer Leg Fur. Later in life a name might be changed or a new name given for some deed committed by the individual; for example, "lying in pit" was a name given to a man who had intercourse with his wife when she was still in the birth hut (Smith 1974:276). Names were not kept secret. Everyone had nicknames (sometimes several) given by friends or as a result of some idiosyncrasy.

When a young woman began to menstruate she was confined or secluded in a hut separate from the family dwelling. Then and during subsequent menstrual confinements the woman was subject to several restrictions: she had separate eating and drinking receptacles; meat, cold water, and (only among the Weeminuche) salt were taboo; she could only scratch herself with a wooden scratcher; and she must avoid hunters, gamblers, and the sick.

O.C. Stewart's (1942:311) and Smith's (1974:146–148) informants stated there was no public recognition of a girl's puberty, but Jorgensen's (1980:536) indicated that menstrual huts were sometimes located near Bear Dance grounds during which newly pubescent females danced in public recognition of their new status. These ceremonies were akin to those performed during the Jicarilla Apache Holiness Rite. There was no formal puberty rite for boys, although it was taboo for a young man to eat his first big game kill.

Most of Smith's (1974:128–137) informants in 1936 had been married several times, and marriage was "a tenuous and temporary bond in all Ute groups." Choosing a spouse was usually an individual decision although parents had some influence in the selection for first marriages. Jealousy, bad temper, and sterility were the usual causes of divorce.

A dying person might be removed from the dwelling and placed in a willow shade during summer. After death a corpse was washed, its face painted, and then dressed in its best clothes. The extended body was usually buried in a rock crevice or cave with the head toward the east. O.C. Stewart's (1942:313) informants also report cremation. Personal property was usually burned, although some might be distributed. O.C. Stewart's (1942:313) informants report burning of the deceased's dwelling, but Smith (1974:151) says that val-

uable tepees were not burned. Surviving relatives might crop their hair and abstain from dancing. A year's wait was considered proper before remarriage. Stewart notes a taboo on speaking the name of the dead in the presence of a decedent's kin. Smith found no formal taboo but did note a reluctance to discuss the dead for fear of ghosts.

Social Organization

• DEMOGRAPHY. For the Ute the year-around residence groups usually numbered from 50 to 100 people, although higher populations were not uncommon during the summer, especially after the acquisition of the horse. Winter camps in the Uintah Basin and the Utah Lake areas were estimated at 20 to 30 households (100–150 people), although no mention is made of the number of such camps in an area at any one time (Smith 1974:124).

Population densities along the Wasatch Front region were estimated by Steward (1938:47) to be 0.1 to 0.3 persons per square mile in aboriginal times. However, Jorgensen (1980:447) notes that a number of Ute bands may have reached population densities of one person per square mile. Even with a range of 0.2 to 1.0 person per square mile, these densities are considerably higher than most estimates for other groups in the Great Basin.

• MARRIAGE AND RESIDENCE First and second cousin marriage was disapproved of and there existed a marked preference for band exogamy. General polygyny existed for the Uintah and Uncompahgre, while the Weeminuche preferred sororal polygyny. Polygamous marriages probably never exceeded 10 percent of the total. Only the Uncompahgre, probably influenced by intermarriage with Plains groups, are reported to have accompanied marriage with gift-giving. This was a prenuptial unequal exchange of goods and services between relatives of the bride and groom that approached being a bride price. Bride service after marriage is not reported for any Ute group. The predominant form of postnuptial residence was matrilocal. Independent nuclear households were the prevalent household form.

• KINSHIP The Utes had separate terms for each of the four grandparents and used these terms self-reciprocally for grandchildren, and they distinguished among siblings and cousins according to sex and relative age.

> Utes differentiated the relative age of uncles, on the maternal and paternal sides and aunts on the maternal side, but they did not distinguish the relative ages of paternal aunts (skewed bifurcate collateral) . . . . the Utes were making more careful distinctions among their aunts on the matriside than they were on the patriside, and they were making finer distinctions among nieces than was true for other Basin people. The emphasis on distinguishing mother's sisters while lumping father's sisters, and also distinguishing mother's sister's daughters by the relative ages of

their mothers, was compatible with the matrilocal emphasis of Ute demes (Jorgensen 1984b:54).

Ute kin units or demes were mobile exogamous year-round residence groups composed of several families that were usually related through the matriline and resided matrilocally. They owned no property. In most cases, individual families would occupy separate dwellings and would be autonomous with regard to whether they desired to leave camp and move to another relative's camp. Families were held together by their respect for the deme headman whose status was usually derived from his hunting prowess and from his successful direction of the camp's movements.

Ute demes were kin units that demonstrated descent from a common ancestor and, in addition, were united by common residence. Relationships within the deme were egalitarian; internal statuses were solely based on age, sex, and generation. Matridemes within the band were not ranked in prestige or privilege (Jorgensen 1980:466, 468, 474).

Political Organization

There is evidence for the existence of bands among the pre-equestrian Ute and for Ute trading and raiding parties throughout the Puebloan Southwest in the sixteenth and seventeenth centuries before they received horses (Schroeder 1965). The relative abundance of subsistence resources in the summer implies that bands formed then, allowing ad hoc groups to leave the main en-

Denver Mus. of Nat. Hist., Dept. of Anthr., Colo.: 756/1.

Fig. 13. Painting on muslin depicting the Sun Dance and Bear Dance, by an unknown Ute artist, presumably done in the 1890s. The top half shows the Sun Dance underway within the brush-walled lodge, with partitions to segregate spectators and dancers, canvas wall cover to shield dancers from the wind, and stalls for individual dancers separated by sheets. The date of the Sun Dance coincided with the full moon, usually being held in late July, and organized by a man who had a vision to do so, with dancers pledged to participate. Shamans cured dancers and spectators during the last day of 3 days and 3 nights of dancing. Five of the dancers in this painting carry eagle-feather fans, which commonly marked the shamans in attendance. The lower half depicts the Bear Dance, with 3 scenes probably representing Ute myths. Men and women danced facing one another to the accompaniment of music from a notched rasp. Performed in early spring, the dance was intended to conciliate the bear, who had given the dance to the Ute. In practical terms, the dance was a social occasion, when women took the initiative, selecting male partners, and directing the elements of the dance. The Sun Dance and the Bear Dance were of utmost importance in the health and continuance of Ute society, one a formal attestation of faith and promise of hope, the other, a time for festivity and opportunity to establish and renew social ties. Dimensions 165 by 190 cm.

campments to carry goods for trade with the Pueblos and Southern Paiute (Jorgensen 1984b:56).

The persistence of Ute bands and the prominence of many of their chiefs imply that the acquisition of horses in the seventeenth century greatly strengthened Ute band organization.

Bands were usually composed of several residential units (matridemes) joined under the leadership of a headman who solicited advice from a council of other deme leaders. Bands provided a common defense against Plains raiders, and arbitrators mediated disputes between demes or individuals within a band. However, the political functions of Ute bands were limited: they did not form alliances nor did they punish individual crimes.

Bands readily moved to new locations, and individuals easily changed band membership.

Warfare

The Eastern Ute, who raided and were raided frequently, had ceremonies for activities both before and after conflicts. Raids were mainly initiated for economic booty, but they were also conducted for captives to trade as domestics to the Spaniards, for women who were sometimes married and adopted within the band, for poaching, and for avenging the death of a warrior.

Shamanism

As with the rest of the Great Basin, Utes had a basic belief that all living things required some supernatural force in order to exist. This supernatural power, which was diffuse and impersonal, was not sought but came with life. Like other Great Basin tribes and unlike almost all the rest of western North America, the Ute had an equal proportion of men and women shamans. But a few Ute shamans, unlike those in the rest of the Great Basin, undertook vision quests, a practice probably borrowed from Plains tribes.

Comparative Culture Among Bands

Jorgensen's (1980) comparative analysis indicates that the Weeminuche band was culturally intermediate between the Uintah and Uncompahgre. In technology, for example, of 204 attributes of 46 variables the Weeminuche and Uintah shared 63 percent with each other but only 45 percent with the Uncompahgre. No doubt a significant part of these differences is due to the diffusion of Plains and Northern Shoshone material culture to the Uncompahgre.

In subsistence economy (30 variables, 182 attributes) the Uncompahgre and Weeminuche, who occupied contiguous territory and overlapping environments, are more similar to each other (80%) than to the Uintah (62%).

The differences are less in economic organization (67 variables, 409 attributes): the Uncompahgre and Weeminuche share 97 percent while the Uintah share only 87 percent with the Uncompahgre and Weeminuche. Fundamental Great Basin egalitarian ideals of open access to resources probably account for the great similarities between these bands, while the greater emphasis on trade (surpluses of the hunt for agricultural products and later barter in horses) for the Weeminuche and Uncompahgre probably account for the differences.

Slight differences exist between the groups in social and political organization, whereas almost no differences exist in ceremonial organization, and in measures of shamanism they are virtually identical.

In mythology, from a sample of 37 folk tales known to various Ute bands, 18 were known to both Eastern and Western Ute informants and 18 others were told by Eastern Ute informants alone (Smith 1940). Seven of the tales known to both Eastern and Western Ute were also known to tribes of the Plains who were neighbors of the Ute. Eight other Eastern Ute folk tales not recorded among Western Ute were known to either Jicarilla Apache or Arapaho or both. Thus of the 18 Eastern Ute tales not recorded from Western Ute eight were shared with Plains tribes, but the Eastern Ute shared 27 tales with other Great Basin groups.

History

From roughly 1650 to 1850 Ute groups were organized into large summer hunting bands named either for a geographic feature of the territory they inhabited or for a particular subsistence resource that they exploited. The time of face to face contact with and actual settlement by Europeans was very different for the Eastern and Western Ute groups. Eastern Utes were in contact with Spaniards at least by the early 1600s and were early participants in the Plains equestrian lifeway. The Western Ute did not receive European visitors until the mid-1700s, and their involvement with the Plains pattern was relatively late, around 1800.

During the seventeenth and eighteenth centuries southern and eastern Ute bands raided New Mexico, stealing horses from the Spaniards and various goods from the Pueblos. They also traveled as far south as Arizona, where they harassed Hopi villages, and as far east as the Plains where they hunted buffalo (Schroeder 1965:53–61). Utes raided unmounted Western Shoshone and Southern Paiutes to steal women and children, which they sold to the Spaniards in New Mexico for use as domestics or shepherds (Malouf 1966:11; Fowler and Fowler 1971:181). Western Ute bands were unmounted at this time. By about 1750 Plains tribes such as the Arapaho, Sioux, Cheyenne, and Comanche (the last previously a Ute ally) acquired horses in sufficient quantities to begin exploiting Ute hunting territories in the mountain valleys.

In Colorado, up until 1850, the hunting and raiding life of Eastern Ute bands had been little affected by White expansion, but in Utah major conflicts between Mormon settlers and Western Ute bands had begun. By the early 1870s the population of Utah Utes had been decimated and displaced from their traditional hunting and gathering areas and moved east of the Wasatch Range.

Utah Utes participated in the Ghost Dance of 1870 but by then were no longer actively resisting Mormon encroachment. However, members of some Colorado bands who had also participated in the Ghost Dance returned to Colorado and offered resistance to White expansion for the next decade.

Loss of Lands in Colorado

In Colorado, from their aboriginal range of 56 million acres (about 85% of Colorado) Ute tribal lands were reduced to about 18 million acres in 1868 (about 9 million apiece for Southern Ute and Ute Mountain Ute). By 1934, due primarily to the Dawes Severalty Act of 1887, the original Southern Ute Reservation had been reduced by 99 percent to 40,600 acres (fig. 14). In the same period, the Ute Mountain Reservation had been reduced (94%) to 513,000 acres. Since 1934 allotment and heirship-status lands have been purchased by tribal corporate entities so that in 1984 Southern Ute tribal lands stood at about 305,000 acres, whereas Ute Mountain lands, which were not allotted prior to 1934, remained at about 533,000 acres.

In 1855 the governor of New Mexico Territory negotiated the Treaties of Abiquiu with Colorado Ute bands. In exchange for 2,000 square miles north of the San Juan River and east of the Animas, the Utes would absent themselves from New Mexico. These treaties were never ratified, and after increasing violence between miners and Utes in Colorado a major treaty council was convened in 1863. The government intended to convince these bands to move to the Four Corners area and to farm. On the whole the Colorado Ute bands resisted the treaty. The Weeminuche band sent word that they would not attend. The Capote band did attend but refused to sign the treaty, making it clear that they, like the Weeminuche, would not farm or be relocated. No representatives from the Muache band attended. Only several Taviwach chiefs and three lesser chiefs from White River signed the 1863 treaties whereby all Utes (regardless of whether they refused to attend or sign) would relinquish "all mineral rights, all mountain areas settled by whites and the San Luis Valley" in exchange for a reservation that totaled about 18 million

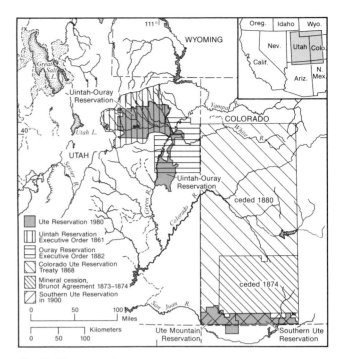

Fig. 14. Ute reservations and land cessions.

acres. By signing, these representatives had preserved their own hunting territories, while ceding lands of those bands that had refused to attend or sign the treaty.

In 1868, a treaty was signed by most Colorado Ute bands (fig. 15) that reduced their lands to about 15 million acres and established two new agencies—Los Pinos (moved to the Uncompahgre River in 1876) and White River. Almost immediately, huge mineral deposits were found in the San Juan Mountains, and in 1873, the government, under the prodding of mining interests, negotiated the Brunot Agreement, ceding an additional 3,450,000 acres from the Colorado reservation by the 280 Ute signers. This was to be "the last request the government would ever make of the Ute" (Petit 1982:60).

In 1880, following the Meeker Massacre in Colorado, 665 Utes from the White River Agency were forced to relocate to the Uintah Reservation where they found 800 Utes from several bands. After being forced to sell their lands, 361 Uncompahgre Utes were also relocated, under armed escort, to Ouray, a new reservation eventually established by executive order in 1882. The Ouray Reservation was adjacent to the southern boundary of the Uintah Reservation.

The intent of the Dawes Severalty Act of 1887, which so powerfully affected Ute landholding, was to provide allotments of land to Indian individuals: family heads were to receive 160 acres, spouses nothing, single individuals 60 acres, although in practice the allotments were much more haphazard. In theory, with land of their own, individual Indian families could enter the mainstream of American life. A small part of the land

Colo. Histl. Soc., Denver: 905-WPA.

Fig. 15. Some of the participants in the signing of the Treaty with the Ute, Washington, 1868. left to right: Ankatosh, Piah, Suriap, Uriah M. Curtis (interpreter), George M. Chilcott (delegate to Congress from Colo.), Sowwachwiche, Col. Albert G. Boone (grandson of Daniel Boone), Gov. A.C. Hunt of Colo., Nicaagat, Hiram P. Bennet (first delegate to Congress from Colo.), Lafayette Head (Indian agent), Guero, Daniel C. Oakes (Indian agent), Ouray (Chief of Uncompahgre), Edward H. Kellogg (Indian Bureau employee), Severo (Chief of Capote), and William G. Godfrey. The delegation was known as the Kit Carson delegation, because Carson accompanied it and was a party to the signing of the treaty. The Whites shown were witnesses to the treaty signing (Kappler 1904–1941:993). The 1868 treaty ceded 3 million acres. In compensation, the Utes were promised a reservation; assurances of education, clothing, and rations; and protection from White trespassers. Photograph by Matthew Brady, Washington, Feb. 1868.

remaining after the allotment process was set aside for the tribe, but most of the land reverted to the public domain where ensuing acts (Desert Land Acts of 1877 and 1891, Timber and Stone Act of 1878) turned it over to homesteading Americans at minimal prices.

Ignacio, a Weeminuche leader, and the rest of the Weeminuche resisted the act (successfully to some extent because their land was less desirable); however, 375 Muache and Capote Utes were allotted land totaling about 74,100 acres. The original 74,100 allocated acres of the Southern Ute had been reduced to 40,600 by 1934. The land had been alienated through sales, patents in fee, and certificates of competency.

In response to the Meriam report of 1928, which described the appalling conditions on Indian reservations, the Indian Reorganization Act of 1934 was passed. This act ended the allotting of tribal lands and provided for tribes to consolidate Indian lands and acquire non-Indian lands. Under the provisions of the Indian Reorganization Act Southern Ute tribal lands increased from 40,600 in 1934 to 304,700 in 1966; however, because of a variety of problems, including heirship status, ownership of allotted lands had dropped to 5,000 acres by 1966. Since the 1950s when alienation of their allotments began, the Ute Mountain had lost about 20 percent of their original allotted acres.

Loss of Lands in Utah

Western bands originally occupied about 23.5 million acres (about 45% of Utah). By the 1870s Utah Utes had been restricted to the 2,039,400-acre Uintah Reservation. In the 1880s after the forced relocation of the White River band to the Uintah Reservation and the creation of Ouray Reservation for the Uncompahgre band who had also been forcibly relocated, Ute holdings in Utah stood at slightly over four million acres. After the Dawes Severalty Act, Utah lands were opened to mineral exploitation—asphalt, gilsonite, and oil. By 1930, 113,000 of the remaining 350,000 acres were allotted to individuals, and 30,000 of these allotments had been alienated through sales. Two-thirds of the non-alienated acres were tied up in heirship status (Jorgensen 1971:96).

In Utah, the Uintah Reservation had already been established as early as 1861 by the executive order of Abraham Lincoln. The area in question was described in a survey ordered by Brigham Young as "one vast 'contiguity of waste' and measurably valueless, except for nomadic purposes, hunting grounds for Indians and to hold the world together" (Jorgensen 1972:36). Hence, there was no Mormon objection to the establishment of the reservation. During the 1860s, Mormons continued to displace Utes from their territory west of the Wasatch Mountains and from farms established in the 1850s by the federal government near Utah Lake in what is now Sanpete County. In the 1870s, through Mormon and government suasion, Utah Utes became increasingly restricted to the Uintah Reservation. Thus by the mid-1870s these Utes had been restricted to about 9 percent of their aboriginal range.

Following provisions of the Indian Reorganization Act of 1934, the federal government began to purchase Indian land sold to non-Indians, in large part using scarce Indian capital (in accounts under federal control)

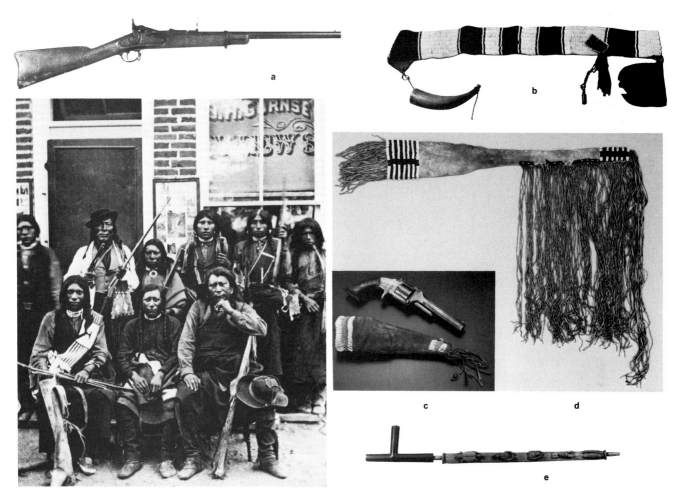

bottom left, Colo. Histl. Soc., Denver: F-7051; a, e, The White River Mus., Meeker, Colo.; Mus. of the Amer. Ind., Heye Foundation, New York: b, 24/1957; Smithsonian, Dept. of Anthr.: c, 200, 482; d, 14, 849.

Fig. 16. left, Chief Colorow (seated, right) and other White River band members in front of Benjamin H. Gurnsey's photography studio in Colorado Springs, Colo. Colorow, who had been insistent in his resistence to White encroachment, had been ignored as a spokesman for the Northern Ute by the United States government during negotiations of the 1868 treaty. Ouray, who had been selected as spokesman and who was attacked by his brother-in-law Sapinarvo for signing the treaty, later proclaimed his unhappiness with its terms (Steward 1974:37). Photograph by B.H. Gurnsey, 1873–1880. a, 1863 Allin breechloader said to have belonged to Colorow. Utes, by the end of the Civil War, had little trouble in getting the best quality firearms. b, Bandolier with powder horn, cartridge shell powder measure, and leather bullet pouch. The strap is leather completely covered in dark blue and white seed beads, lazy-stitched. Collected by J.W. Powell in Colo. Terr., probably 1869–1872. c, Pistol and holster attributed to Shavanaugh, a Southern Ute subchief. The beaded buckskin holster, which carries a Smith and Wesson revolver made 1863–1865, is stitched with buckskin thongs, and decorated with light and white seed beads. Collected before 1899. d, Buckskin gun case, decorated with patches of red stroud, and beaded with pony beads. Collected by J.W. Powell, Colo. Terr., probably 1869–1872. e, Catlinite pipe said to have belonged to Colorow. On wooden stem are carved a turtle, buffalo, mountain sheep, deer or elk, and what appear to be rattlesnake rattles. The turtle, buffalo, and elk are characteristic of Sioux effigy pipes, but the mountain sheep and the rattles are unusual, as are the collars at the ends of the stem; these additional elements may mark Ute manufacture. Collected in Colo., 1886. Length of a 101.1 cm, rest to same scale.

to buy land from White farmers who had gone bankrupt. Thus, through repurchase and transfer of nonallocated lands, by 1950 the Northern Ute owned about one million acres (Jorgensen 1971:98). By 1969 two-thirds of all the original allotments in Utah had been sold to non-Indians or through repurchase by the tribe. Of the 38,000 allotment acres that had not been alienated 97 percent were tied up in heirship status disputes (Jorgensen 1971:99).

Population, 1880–1980

A number of factors make exact figures difficult to obtain. For example, from their nadir of 334 in 1920, Southern Ute tribal membership grew to 939 in 1980 (table 3). Prior to 1960 most tribal members resided on the reservation, but since then there has been an increased rate of emigration, and in 1980 slightly over one-fourth of all tribal members lived off-reservation.

357

top, Smithsonian, NAA:1553; Colorado Histl. Soc., Denver: bottom left, H 5830.1; bottom right, H 5830.4.

Fig. 17. Ouray (d. 1880), an important leader of the Uncompahgre Utes. He participated in negotiations with the Whites from the early 1860s and visited Washington, D.C., several times during this period. top, Ouray and his wife, Chipeta. Photographed in Washington, 1880. bottom left, Desk and gun cabinet built for Ouray by order of the U.S. government, 1876–1877. The desk held his calling cards (bottom right). Height of desk only 96.5 cm. Size of calling card 5.5 by 8.9 cm.

358

Emigration occurs for a number of reasons, but perhaps the most important is the paucity of jobs within the reservation economy.

For the Northern Ute persistent problems arise in the definition of tribal membership. In 1980 there were 2,104 enrolled members as defined by the tribe's standards, that is, five-eighths Ute blood quantum. However, there were another 1,000 Ute persons of one-half or less Ute blood quantum who are members of families in which one of the parents is an enrolled tribal member.

Based on legislation enacted in 1954, the BIA informed the Northern Ute tribe that for their purposes one-half quantum is sufficient for enrollment and the BIA will not recognize the tribe's more stringent standard of five-eighths.

The 1954 legislation also separated a group of Ute mixed-bloods, the Affiliated Ute Citizens, whose blood quantum was less than one-half, from the Northern Ute tribe. However, court decisions have declared that the Affiliated Ute Citizens retain their treaty rights to hunting, fishing, water, and other resources not specifically denied to them by the termination legislation. In addition mixed-bloods may still have other reserved rights to the Uintah-Ouray Reservations. This dispute is not simply an enumeration problem among the tribe, the BIA, and mixed-bloods. The Northern Ute tribe in 1984 provided *enrolled* Ute members $400 per month in dividend payments. The tribe also provided additional payments and services to elderly and incapacitated members. Revenues to provide for these dividend payments are in large part derived from the leasing of tribal mineral resources. Given the unemployment problems and income levels, the divisive nature of these disputes is profound (Jorgensen 1984c).

Sociocultural Situation in 1980

Age

Over half the Ute population was under the age of 18 in 1980 whereas for Colorado and the United States in general only about one-fourth of the population was younger than 18. Utah, with the youngest median age in the United States, formed an exception.

The high proportion of the Ute population in younger age cohorts (table 4) has important implications for future employment demands, the demand for social services, and the economic strain placed on families who have few resources but contain a great number of dependent individuals.

Education

One of the major difficulties faced by Ute adults in making a living in an already depressed rural economy

Table 3.   Ute Population, 1880–1980

Year	Southern Ute	Ute Mountain Ute	Northern Ute
1880	500	650	2,825
1890	428	530	1,854
1900	420	528	1,660
1910	353	463	1,150
1920	334	462	1,005
1930	369	485	917
1940	440	493	1,000
1950	479	570	1,150
1960	679	813	1,498
1968	711	1,099	1,611
1980	939	1,534	2,104
1983	1,107	1,554	2,244

SOURCES: Jorgensen 1972:91; U.S. Department of Labor. Employment and Training Administration 1982:5 [four counties], except 1983, which is from the U.S. Bureau of Indian Affairs. Financial Management Office 1983.

is their educational attainment. Although the percentages vary, there is a constant 2:1 ratio between Utes and Whites over 25 years in educational attainment. Proportionally, Utes have twice the number of individuals who do not complete high school. And while median years of eduation may vary by up to two years, proficiency, as measured by achievement scores, may vary by as much as four years. There is a significantly higher dropout rate for young adult Utes, with two reservations having half their adults 18–24 not completing high school (Hacker 1983:250–251; U.S. Department of Labor. Employment and Training Administration 1982:8–10).

A consistent difference in Ute reservations is apparent in language usage: Ute Mountain, Northern Ute, and then Southern Ute reservations increase in this order in the proportion of individuals who speak English

top, Smithsonian, NAA: 1484–a; center, Natl. Arch., 75N UIN-631; bottom, Utah State Histl. Soc., Salt Lake City: 970.77.
Fig. 18. 19th and 20th century leaders. top, Kanosh (b. about 1821), leader of the Pahvant Utes from the 1850s until his death in 1884. He represented the Pahvant at the signing of the treaty at the end of the Walker War in 1854 and was described as a man of "ability" and "influence" by John Wesley Powell and George W. Ingalls in 1873. He successfully argued for the Pahvants to be allowed to remain in their traditional homeland but also was pro-acculturation and encouraged farming. Photograph probably by Charles R. Savage & George M. Ottinger Studio, Salt Lake City, 1860s. center, Capt. Perank or Andrew Frank, leader of Uintah band on Uintah–Ouray Reservation, who led the Ute exodus to S. Dak. in 1906 (Hodge 1907–1910, 2:876) and remained an important figure through the 1950s. He was the main informant of Anne Smith in 1936, who also identfied him as a shaman (Smith 1974:iii) and of Omer Stewart in 1937. Photograph by Morrow, May 1951. bottom, Posey (d. 1923), a Southern Paiute who legally became Ute after enrolling in the Southern Ute Reservation (Parkhill 1961:45), known for his involvement in Ute-White conflicts in 1915 and in 1923. Photograph by Lyman Hunter, 1921.   *359*

Colo. Histl. Soc., Denver: F-1614.

Fig. 19. Women playing shinny on the Ute Mountain Ute Reservation, Colo. Shinny was a team sport usually played by women; sometimes there were all-male teams and infrequently teams of both sexes. A field approximately 250 ft. long was cleared and a goal established at either end. Teams were composed of 10 to 25 individuals. Each contestant used a 3–4-foot stick curved at the bottom. The "ball" was 3–4 inches in diameter and made from buckskin stuffed with deer hair. Hitting or kicking the ball was allowed, although carrying it with the stick was frowned upon. The game would begin with the throw of a "ball" into the air between two players standing in the middle of the field. The object was to hit (or kick) the ball over the opponents' goal line. One goal was sometimes enough to win the game (O.C. Stewart 1942:285). However, others report that once a goal was scored, the teams changed sides (Smith 1974:234). If the team that scored the initial goal scored again, then the game was over. If, however, the score was tied at one to one, then a third and deciding goal was played. Games of shinny might begin in spring and be played every day for a month or more. Wagers of deerskins or other objects could be bet on the game and often play was rough and very intense. Photograph by S.F. Stacker, at Towaoc, Colo., summer 1908.

only. The same ordering holds true for individuals 14–24 years of age who speak English only. For the proportion, albeit low, of individuals five years of age and older who speak English poorly the ordering is reversed with Southern Ute having the smallest proportion of non-English speakers. Southern Utes are concerned, as evinced in their Tribal Comprehensive Plan, that the use of Ute language is being lost to younger tribal members. Less than one-third of Southern Ute tribal members between the ages 14–24 speak Ute, whereas nearly two thirds of Ute Mountain Utes of the same age speak languages other than English (predominantly Ute).

The proportion of individuals who speak little or no English is very low, with Ute Mountain having the most with 5 percent of the population, most of them middle-aged or older.

Households and Families

The categories of the U.S. Census (which are not necessarily appropriate) show that Ute households are, on the average, about 40 percent larger than the typical U.S. household and are from one-fourth to one-third larger than their rural White counterparts (Utah being the state with the largest mean household size in the U.S.).

A telling comparison is the percentage of households with dependent children that are headed by women (table 5). With the exception of the anomalous and highly suspect findings for Ute Mountain, the Ute population has proportionally about four times as many such households as do White populations living in the same counties.

An indirect indicator of the stresses faced by Ute families can be found in table 6. Except for Ute Mountain Ute, there are high proportions of single-parent families when compared to the inhabitants of surrounding counties.

All reservations have a high proportion of minor children living with neither parent. This is due in part to cultural expectations in child raising—grandparents and extended kin being regarded as suitable parent surrogates—but it is also unfortunately an indicator of deaths

360

left, Amer. Mus. of Nat. Hist., New York: 50.1/6944; right, U. of Pa., U. Mus., Philadelphia: 37112.

Fig. 20. Games. left, Buckskin-wrapped darts and ring for a hoop-and-pole game, commonly played by 2 males, though more often joined in. The target ring was rolled across the ground, and the darts, spears, or arrows thrown at the ring. Contestants accumulated points by spearing the ring, having the ring come to rest on the darts, or by proximity of the dart to the ring. Decoration of the ring served in scoring, as did some agreed upon proximity measure. Players kept score by means of counting sticks. Length of dart 31 cm; collected by R.H. Lowie at Ignacio, Colo., 1912. right, Stick dice for a Uintah Ute basket dice game. Dice are rectangular slips of willow, flat on one side, rounded on the other. The flat side is painted red, the rounded branded with diamonds. Essential elements of the game are a shallow, circular tray or basket and a set of counting sticks. A typical game involved throws of the dice, either within the basket or on a playing surface, and the taking of counters for winning throws, which were determined by specified combinations of the marked dice. The game would end when one side held all of the counters. Wagering among participants and spectators was spirited. Smith (1974) describes several variants of the basket dice game, explaining throws and methods of counting. Length 10 cm; collected at Whiterocks, Utah, 1900.

and disability in the parental generation due to alcohol abuse.

Lack of income and fluctuations in the sources of income also account for differences between Ute and White families in the proportion of "nuclear" families (table 5). Ute households increase in membership as resources become less stable and less predictable and "near kin, affines, and often distant kin, join together under the same roof to pool their resources and share their skills" (Jorgensen 1972:116).

Economic Situation in 1980

Employment

All Ute Reservations have labor force participation rates significantly lower than national averages. Among the reasons accounting for these differences are lack of employment opportunities in economically depressed rural areas, lack of job skills, discrimination, poor educational attainment, and a high proportion of workers aged 16–20. Equally important is the high proportion

Table 4. Age of Population, 1980

	Younger than 18	65+	Median Age
Southern Ute	38%	3.9%	20.6
La Plata County	25	8.9	28.2
Ute Mountain Ute	40	2.4	21.1
Montezuma County	31	11	30.8
Northern Ute	45	3.9	19.7
Uintah and Duchesne Counties	39	6.6	23.0
Total Ute Population	42	4.1	about 20
Utah	37	7.5	24.2
Colorado	27	8.6	28.6
United States	28	11.3	30.0

SOURCES: U.S. Bureau of the Census 1984:31, 34; U.S. Department of Labor. Employment and Training Administration 1982.

of female-headed households with dependent children. Finally, disabilities due to childhood morbidities and social pathologies (including alcoholism) also depress rates of participation in the labor force (table 7).

Unemployment rates at 15–17 percent in 1980 were over twice the national average and about three times that experienced by residents of surrounding communities. With the exception of the Southern Ute (at 13%) unemployment for men runs 19–24 percent—four to five times surrounding community averages (U.S. Bureau of the Census 1984:405; U.S. Department of Labor. Employment and Training Administration 1982:16). However, even these statistics are entirely misleading, being based on a ridiculously broad definition of employment used by the Bureau of Labor Statistics that

Table 5. Household Characteristics in 1980

	Mean household size	"Nuclear" households	Families headed by women
Southern Ute	4.47	56%	40.2%
La Plata County	3.09	87	10.9
Ute Mountain Ute	4.88	96	4.1
Montezuma County	3.18	88	10.8
Northern Ute	5.00	71	24.7
Uintah and Duchesne Counties	3.75	92	6.8
Colorado	2.65	52	9.7
Utah	3.20	61	7.7
United States	2.75	50	9.9

SOURCES: U.S. Bureau of the Census 1984:51; U.S. Department of Labor. Employment and Training Administration 1982:9.

Table 6. Living Arrangements of Children Under 18, 1980

	Two Parents	Living With One Parent	Neither Parent
Southern Ute	50%	38%	12%
La Plata County	85	11	4
Ute Mountain Ute	81	6	13
Montezuma County	85	12	4
Northern Ute	57	22	21
Uintah and Du- chesne Counties	91	7	2
United States	76.7	19.7	3.7

SOURCES: U.S. Bureau of the Census 1984:53; U.S. Department of Labor. Employment and Training Administration 1982:9.

does not distinguish between part-time and full-time employment nor does it include "discouraged workers" (a high proportion of the possible labor force on all Ute reservations). When underemployment is considered— those who because of seasonal or sporadic jobs worked less than six months out of the year—between one-third and one-half of all those individuals counted as employed by the Bureau of Labor Statistics were actually unemployed more than six months out of each year. The Southern Ute Tribe's Comprehensive Plan (Southern Ute Tribe 1982:121) draws the conclusion, based upon a 1980 BIA survey, that the effective unemployment rate for resident Southern Ute tribal members was 57 percent, a much more realistic appraisal of the situation.

The reservation economies are unstable. Lack of jobs in the private sector, the Indian Self-Determination Act of 1975, lack of training and skills in appropriate industrial sectors, federal budget cuts, and discrimination in hiring have all caused tribal governments to become the major source of employment for Utes. Between

Table 7. Labor Force Participation Rate in 1980

	Total[a]	Men	Women
Southern Ute	50.1%	64.5%	36.8%
La Plata County	64.2	72.5	55.7
Ute Mountain Ute	51.6	61.2	42.6
Montezuma County	62.0	76.8	48.4
Northern Ute	55.0	65.0	37.0
Uintah and Duchesne Counties	61.0	83.0	39.0
United States	63.8	77.4	51.5

SOURCES: U.S. Bureau of the Census 1984:407; U.S. Department of Labor. Employment and Training Administration 1982:13.
[a]Civilian noninstitutional population.

362

one-half and two-thirds of employed Utes work for government agencies. This contrasts sharply with employment in surrounding communities where one-fifth of non-Indians work for some level of government. Between 50 and 60 percent of those Utes employed by government work for the tribe, the majority of the remainder work for federal agencies, and less than 5 percent work for state, county, and local government (U.S. Department of Labor. Employment and Training Administration 1982:17).

As federal grants and programs are cut back, more tribal revenues (from mineral royalties, right-of-way payments, and investments) must be used to support the existing work force. A number of services formerly provided by federal grants are funded in this way, but as tribal work forces are cut back this already enormous unemployment problem is exacerbated.

Due to their sources of employment, the occupations and skills exhibited by Ute workers are concentrated in the services and public administration sectors; about two-thirds of all Ute jobs come from these sectors. In 1980 less than 10 percent of Utes were employed in sales. Hardest hit by unemployment are general laborers, two-thirds of whom are unemployed at any one time. For detailed analyses of the economy see Jorgensen (1971, 1972, 1984b).

In general Ute families have about half the average income of other American families. In addition, the number of Ute families below the poverty level is three times national averages. Ute families have about two-thirds the average income of families who live in surrounding rural counties, but they have three to five times the number of families living below the poverty level. Southern Ute female-headed households have about half the income of other Ute families (tables 8–9).

Changes occurred in Ute and non-Indian Colorado family incomes between 1950 and 1980. In 1950 Ute families, on the average, had two-thirds less income than their rural counterparts. By 1962 this gap in income had been reduced to 40 percent for the Northern Ute and 15 percent for the Southern Ute, and Ute Mountain family income actually exceeded the average non-Indian Colorado family income by 18 percent. By 1980 the gap had widened again and Ute families had from one-half to two-thirds an average non-Indian Colorado family's income.

The gains in Ute family income in the decade 1955 to 1965 were not due to improved reservation economic conditions but rather were the result of per capita or dividend payments made to individual tribal members. The dividend payments were from land claims settlements ($6 million to the Southern Ute), royalties accrued from the lease of mineral resources, and rents for rights of way. For example, in 1966 an average Ute Mountain family received $6,000 in dividend pay-

Table 8. Household Income, 1980

	Median income	Mean income	Female head, mean income	Families below poverty level	Individuals below poverty level
Southern Ute	$ 8,773	$11,287	$ 5,722	37.0%	39.9%
La Plata County	$15,874	$19,191	$11,464	7.3	11.4
Ute Mountain Ute	$10,115	$10,197	$10,498	36.4	37.3
Montezuma County	$15,097	$17,889	$10,553	8.5	11.6
Northern Ute	$12,846	$14,308	$13,388	30.0	27.0
Uintah and Duchesne Counties	—	$20,021	$10,768	9.0	11.8
United States	$21,023	$23,974	$10,408	11.2	—

SOURCES: for national figures, Hacker 1983:142, 144, 147; all others, U.S. Department of Labor. Employment and Training Administration 1982:27–30.

ments—nearly 80 percent of the average family's income. Enrolled Northern Ute tribal members received $400 per month, and similar payments were made to Southern Ute tribal members, although they tended to receive distributions three times a year.

There was a drop in the proportion of earned family income from about 75 percent in 1950 to about 50 percent in 1980. Much unearned income is from payments accrued from the sale of nonrenewable resources.

Tribal Economies

In the 1980s all three Ute reservations were located in rural areas where economic activity was very slack compared with the high rates in metropolitan areas in Colorado and Utah. The region occupied by the two Colorado reservations was heavily dependent on energy extraction (coal and gas) and on tourism, both industries vulnerable to outside economic forces such as declines in the price of energy on the world market or in the strength of the national economy. Agriculture and forestry exhibited little growth. New jobs tended to be concentrated in the low-paying trade and service sectors or in the seasonal and volatile construction and mining industries.

For the Northern Ute in 1978 approximately 70 percent of tribal revenues were internally generated, with

Table 9. Average Family Income, 1950–1980

	Colorado Non-Indians	Southern Ute	Ute Mountain	Northern Ute
1950	$ 3,080	$ 900[a]	$ 900[a]	$ 1,525
1962	$ 6,928	$ 5,900	$ 8,400	$ 4,000
1980	$21,279	$11,287	$10,917	$14,308

[a] Includes BIA estimates of cash value of animals hunted, crops and animals raised and consumed, and timber utilized.
SOURCES: U.S. Bureau of the Census 1984:467; Jorgensen 1972:115; U.S. Department of Labor. Employment and Training Administration 1982:27–30.

about 30 percent coming from federal grants (Stillwaggon in Jorgensen 1984c). For fiscal 1984 the Northern Ute tribal budget was about 16 million dollars, with almost all the nonfederal portion coming from oil and gas royalties. In 1983 out of the 100 million dollars generated by the sale of oil and gas from tribal lands, the Northern Ute received about 17 million dollars. In summary, in an environment of decreasing federal support (mandated by treaty agreement) and pressure on tribal revenues to replace these discontinued services, tribal budgets were dependent on royalties from nonrenewable resources. Attempts to capitalize future business ventures faced the problem that revenues from mineral royalties flowed through the tribe to its members as employment income and dividends and hence were not available for capital information and investment.

Tribal attempts at economic diversification were mostly failures. On the Northern Ute Reservation in 1984 there were four enterprises: an expanding tribal water system, a bowling alley that showed a marginal profit, a restaurant and motel that lost over one-half million dollars in 1983, and a cattle operation (fig. 21) that had turned one profit in 22 years but lost $500,000 in 1983. A chemical industry, a furniture industry, a sheepskin-vest production firm, and an industrial park were all defunct. Similar failures could be documented for the Southern Ute with a motel-restaurant and a race track requiring a tribal subsidy of about $500,000 in 1982.

The reasons for these failures are manifold and in part inherent in the rural setting: distance from markets, poor federal planning, the difficulties faced in applying management techniques to a workforce of kin-based polities, tribal factionalism, depressed local economies, an unskilled work force, and high rates of alcoholism.

Factionalism

Not only do elected officials face the dilemma of combined legislative and administrative functions, but also

U.S. Dept. of Interior, Bureau of Reclamation, Upper Colo. Region, Salt Lake City, Utah: P987–400–119.

Fig. 21. Northern Ute enterprises—the Ute Fab. Co., the Ute Tribal Water System, and the Ute Tribal Livestock Enterprise. The Ute Fab. Co., which manufactured cabinets and fixtures, ceased operation in the late 1970s. In 1984 the facility was converted into a tribal adult vocational center. The Ute Tribal Water System, which was started in 1963–1964 with a grant from the BIA, was operating and expanding in the 1980s. The Ute Tribal Livestock Enterprise is a cattle-raising business that the Northern Ute invested in in 1962. The Utes, like other cattle ranchers, faced strong competition from feed-lot operators, and in 1985 the Enterprise herd, which had stood at 6,000 head in 1971, was reduced to 1,300 (Jerome Cuch, communication to editors 1985). Photograph by Vern Jetley, at Ft. Duchesne, Utah, 1975.

they face the problems of factionalism in a strongly divided polity. Disputes centered on the divisive nature of tribal membership criteria are only the end product of a number of confrontations fueled by government policy. For example, in the 1880s on Uintah-Ouray Reservation, Uncompahgre Utes were angry with White River Utes because although the Uncompahgre had not been involved in the Meeker Massacre they had been forced to sell their land in Colorado and had been relocated to Utah. For their part the White River Utes were furious that they had been removed from their territory simply because they had tried to defend it and were incensed with the Uncompahgre because they had refused to join in the common cause. Uintah Utes, who had to relinquish half their reservation without compensation, were angry at the White River Utes for their intrusion. Uintah feelings were exacerbated when they realized White River band members were receiving per capita payments while they received nothing. These payments came from funds established as part of the agreement in which the White River Utes relinquished all their lands in Colorado. Further animosity was engendered between White River and Uncompahgre Utes when the former received half the per capita payments of the latter. The White River band was forced to pay pensions to the families of agency and military personnel injured or killed in the Meeker Massacre.

364   During the allotment procedure under the Dawes

Act, federal officials decided that there was not enough suitable farming acreage available on the Ouray Agency for the Uncompahgre Utes, so over the protests of all three groups (all of whom had fought the allotment process) lands were taken from the Uintah and White River Utes and alloted to the Uncompahgre. Similar processes involving different disputes also encouraged antagonisms between Weeminuche, Muache, and Capote bands. For a detailed account of the federal role in these disputes see Jorgensen (1972).

Synonymy†

The English name Ute is a shortening of earlier Utah. The status of the two terms was indicated by the Indian agent at Provo in 1857, who referred in an official letter to "a band of Utah Indians, (commonly called Utes,)" (G.W. Armstrong in ARCIA 1858:308). Hodge (1907–1910, 2:876) cites an 1846 use of the form Ute by Charles Bent, but the source indicated does not use this spelling (U.S. Congress. House 1850:192–193). Two other possible 1846 uses are in the journals of Edwards (1936:212) and Gibson (1935:252), but this spelling has not been confirmed from the manuscripts. Other spellings of Utah (Utahs) in English are: Utaws, 1827 (D.T. Potts in Frost 1960:63); Eutaw (Ferris 1940:266); Eutahs (Schoolcraft 1851–1857, 5:498); Utahn (Egan 1917:146); and Yutas (Gregg 1844, 1:285). Ute (Utes) also is found as Yute, 1850 (Garrard in Hodge 1907–1910, 2:876) and Youts, 1843 (de Smet in Hodge 1907–1910, 2:876).

English Utah was an oral borrowing from New Mexican Spanish Yuta (pl. Yutas), a term in use since the seventeenth century. An early attestation is in a 1680 letter of Antonio de Otermín (Hackett 1942, 1:206). A treatise of 1686 describing events of 1630 refers to the Yuta and presumably takes this name from documents of the period (Hackett 1931–1941, 1:503). This Spanish name must be a loanword from an Indian language, but its precise origin is uncertain. A similar name for the Ute is found in a number of neighboring Indian languages, and presumably one of them is the source: Jicarilla yóta (Curtis 1907–1930, 1:135); Hopi yóta, pl. yótam (Whorf 1936:1323); Jemez yítaǫ́, pl. yítaǫ́š (Joe Sando, communication to editors 1978); Comanche yú·hta (Gatschet in Hodge 1907–1910, 2:876); Shoshone youtah (Gebow in Hodge 1907–1910, 2:876); Southern Paiute yu·tta·ci, pl. yu·tta·mmi, yu·tta·cimi, yu·cimi, also yu·tta·nimimi 'Ute people' (Sapir 1930–1931:214, 586, 726, 730, phonemicized). Mooney (1898:167) alludes to a Ute form yútawáts, apparently not otherwise recorded. Although some of these might be borrowings from Spanish, it seems unlikely that all of them are.

†This synonymy was written by Ives Goddard.

CALLAWAY, JANETSKI, AND STEWART

Names for the Ute in other Indian languages include: Navajo *Nóóda'í* (Young and Morgan 1980:677); Havasupai *úta* (Leanne Hinton, communication to editors 1981); Kiowa *í·tàgɔ̀*, pl. (Laurel J. Watkins, communication to editors 1979), iätägo (Mooney 1896:1043), íätä(go) (Mooney 1898:167); Lakota *sápa wič^háša*, literally 'black person', *wič^háša yúta*, related by folk etymology to *yúta* 'eat' (Buechel 1970:452, 580, 733, phonemicized); Cheyenne *mo'óhtávéhetaneo'o* pl., literally 'black people' (Wayne Leman, communication to editors 1984); Omaha and Ponca maščiŋgeha wai^n, literally 'rabbitskin robes' (Dorsey in Hodge 1907–1910, 2:876).

The Utes call themselves *nú·čI* 'Ute, Indian, person', pl. *nú·čiu* (Givón 1979:20, 147). Earlier recordings like no-vïntc (Chamberlin 1909:31) and no-o-chi, no-ónch (Hrdlička in Hodge 1907–1910, 2:876), show that this term is cognate with Southern Paiute *niminci* 'person, Indian' (phonetically [niŋ^wincI], Sapir 1930–1931:585). The suggestion of J.P. Harrington (1911a) that this term is the source of Spanish Yuta is refuted by the phonetics of the two words.

Bands

A list of Western Ute band names found in early sources has been compiled by Steward (1938:224–225). O.C. Stewart (1942:236–237) gives variant names for Ute bands obtained in 1937–1938, and Schroeder (1965) gives a number of Southern Ute band names found in the sources in his historical discussion. Additional variants are given in the respective entries in Hodge (1907–1910). The following alphabetical listing of the bands gives major variants and alternate names but is not exhaustive.

Capote. Capote is the spelling used in the Treaty of 1868, with "Ca-po-tas Utes" appearing after the signatures (Kappler 1904–1941, 2:990, 995). Ute *kapú·ta*, *kApú·ta*, is assumed to be a borrowing from Spanish *capote* 'cloak' (Givón 1979:119, 224). The name also appears as Kapota (O.C. Stewart 1942:233; Jorgensen 1972:30), and there are minor variants in Hodge (1907–1910, 1:203). Schroeder (1965:54) interpreted a 1626 mention of Indians the Jemez called Guaguatu or Guaputu as a reference to the Capote.

Moanunts. O.C. Stewart (1942:236) has this name as Moavinunts 'mountain-pass Utes' (a reference to the pass at the head of Salina Canyon, Utah; cf. Ute *miá·* 'gap') and recorded the Pahvant name as pagogowatsnunts. Steward (1938:228) gives pavógowunsiŋ and also, apparently less accurately, pavogogwunsin (Steward 1938:225), which Cooke (in W.Z. Park et al. 1938:629) identifies as "the group known as Black Hawk's band," in Ute pavɨ́·wats and tú·paránovits. Stewart's informants also referred to this band as uintahnunts ('Uintah Utes') and pagónunts, names applied by them to the Timpanogots as well. Historically the Moanunts were

called Fish Utes (ARCIA 1870:142) and Fish-Utes (ARCIA 1868a:148).

Muache. Muache is the spelling in the 1868 treaty (Kappler 1904–1941, 2:990). The Ute form is *moɣwáčI* (Givón 1979:136). They are also referred to as Moguache (J.P. Harrington 1911a), Mowatsi (W.Z. Park et al. 1938:632), Möwatci (O.C. Stewart 1942:237, 238), Mouaches (Steward 1974:138), Muwach (Jorgensen 1972:30), Moache (Hodge 1907–1910, 1:915), Muhuaches (Vélez de Escalante in Bolton 1950:144) and Yutas Mogoachis (Miera y Pacheco in Josephy 1961:130–131); among the variants given by Hodge are Maquache, Moquaches, Moguachis, Mohuache, and Mouuache. The occasional designation Cimarron Utes refers to their agency at Cimarron, New Mexico (ARCIA 1874:258). The members of the Muache and other southern bands that used to camp near Taos Pueblo in the nineteenth century were sometimes referred to as the Taos Utes (Taos Yutas).

Pahvant. The Ute designation is also given as pahvá·ntits (Cooke [Smith] in W.Z. Park et al. 1938:629), pavandüts (Steward 1938:227), and pahvantinunts and pahvanduts (O.C. Stewart 1942:236). Shoshone has *pa·panti* (Miller 1972:125). Historical variants include Pah-Van, Pahvontee, Parant, Paravan Yuta, Pavant, Pohbantes, Povantes (Steward 1938:224; Hodge 1907–1910, 2:185). The "Kanosh band of Paiutes," named after their chief (Sapir 1930–1931:629; W.R. Palmer 1933:91–92, 96–97), and the "Koosharem Ute" (Kelly 1964:103) are historically mixed groups of Pahvant Utes and Southern Paiutes from several bands. The Pagampachi of 1776 (Vélez de Escalante in Bolton 1950:220) were incorrectly identified as the Pahvant in Hodge (1907–1910); they were a Southern Paiute group located near the Colorado River (O.C. Stewart 1942:237).

Parusanuch. The Parusanuch (Jorgensen 1972:30) and the Yampa were the two components of the White River Ute, or White River Indians, known among the Utes as taviwatsiu (O.C. Stewart 1942:237) or kaviawach (Hrdlička in Hodge 1907–1910, 2:946). The name White River Utes derives from that of the agency established for these groups at Meeker, Colorado (Jorgensen 1972:43), and Jorgensen's term Parusanuch, which is not found in historical sources, appears to be a literal Ute translation of this English name. Variants of taviwatsiu are also applied to the Uncompahgre. The White River group included the Grand River Ute (Hodge 1907–1910, 1:503), who are mentioned under that name in the Treaty of 1868 (Kappler 1904–1941, 2:990, 994), and the Akanaquint or Green River Ute (Beckwith 1855, 2 [pt. 1]:61; Hodge 1907–1910, 1:32).

Sanpits. Variants include Sanpet, used by Hodge (1907–1910, 2:451), who also lists Sampeetches, San-Petes, and others; and Sampiche (Humfreville 1903:205), Sanpitc (O.C. Stewart 1942:233), San-pitch, 1834, Sampits and sampí·viwants (W.Z. Park et al. 1938:629), and the misprinted Land Pitches, 1839 (in Steward 1974:90). Steward (1938:224, 228) was told that Sampits meant 'cane people'.

Timpanogots. This band is referred to by Vélez de Escalante as the Timpanogotzis, Timpanocutzis, Timpanois, Lagunas 'Lake (People)', and Come Pescados 'Fish-Eaters'; the name Timpanogotzis is explained as derived from Timpanogó, the Ute name for Utah Lake (Bolton 1950:153, 154, 184, 186, 187). Miera y Pacheco called them Timpanogos (Bolton 1950:243), and later recordings include Timpenaguchyǎ (Burton in Hodge 1907–1910, 2:751), Tinpay nagoots (Gebow in Hodge 1907–1910, 2:751), Tempanahgos (in Schroeder 1965:66), and tümpa'nogots (Steward 1938:224, 225), as well as the derived nickname Tenpenny Utahs (Wilson in ARCIA 1850:67). O.C. Stewart (1942:236) used the name tömpanöwotsnunts and also reported the use of pagöwadziu, pagönunts, and Fish-eaters (note Ute payí 'fish'); Smith (1974:iii-iv; Park et al. 1938:628–629) was told that the Utes on Utah Lake were called both timpá·nanunc and payí·anunc and were considered Uintahs (cf. Goss in Smith 1974:iv). Jorgensen (1972:30) refers to the Timpanogots as Tumpanuwach. The name Timpaiavats used by Hodge (1907–1910, 2:751) is based on a form recorded by J.W. Powell. Hodge gives additional variants, but the forms of Tirangapui he lists refer to a different, presumably Southern Paiute, group to the south.

Uintah. Variants include Ewinte (Wilson in ARCIA 1850:67) and Uinta, used by Hodge (1907–1910, 2:863), who lists others; the Southern Paiute name is yipinti·cimi 'pine canyon-mouth people' (Sapir 1930–1931:725). O.C. Stewart (1942:236) was told that the name Uintah or Uintahnunts 'Uintah Utes' was applied to both the Moanunts and the Timpanogots but that there was no separate band by this name. The Ute name paywánú·čI, now glossed 'Uintah Ute', literally 'water-edge Ute' (Givón 1979:154), was also obtained by O.C. Stewart (1942:236) as a name for the Moanunts and the Timpanogots; his spelling is pagönunts, which suggests Ute payí 'fish'. The same name appears as pag-wa-nu-chi, obtained by Hrdlička (in Hodge 1907–1910, 2:863) as one of the Uintah Utes' names for themselves; his translation 'people with a little different language and dress' must have actually been a descriptive explanation.

Among the groups eventually absorbed into the Uintah were the Seuvarits Ute, who ranged between the Sevier and Green rivers in southeastern Utah (Powell in ARCIA 1874:42; Hodge 1907–1910, 2:514); variants of their name include Sheberetches (ARCIA 1870:142), She-ba-retches (ARCIA 1868a:148), and Asivoriches (ARCIA 1861:125).

Uncompahgre (Taviwach). The Uncompahgre Ute take their name from the reservation established by the Treaty of 1863, which was sometimes referred to as the Uncompahgre reservation, after the Uncompahgre River.

This name comes into use particularly after their removal to Utah beginning in 1881 (ARCIA 1881:19, 1882:151); earlier expressions like "Uncompahgre Utes" (ARCIA 1865:241) and "the Uncompagre tribe" (ARCIA 1870:266) refer just to those actually in the Uncompahgre valley. The spelling Uncompaghre has been used by some (ARCIA 1888:map; Smith 1974:v; Jorgensen 1972). The Ute name for this band appears as möwataviwatsiu (O.C. Stewart 1942:237). The same name is found in Southern Paiute muk"attapi'mancimi [moɣwat·aviŋ'wantsiŋWɨ] pl. (Sapir 1930–1931:574, 669), but in modern Southern Ute the equivalent moɣwá-taví'waačI is apparently a general term for the Northern Ute (Givón 1979:136); these sources give widely differing interpretations of the analysis and meaning. Ute tawiwatsu, used for the White River Ute, is said to be a shortening of möwataviwatsiu (Hrdlička in Hodge 1907–1910, 2:664), and the two terms are hard to distinguish in the literature. To judge by their location, the Tabehuaches of Vélez de Escalante (Bolton 1950:148), the Yutas tabeguachis on the map of Miera y Pacheco (Josephy 1961:130–131), are to be identified as the Uncompahgre, and Tabeguache was in fact the usual earlier name of the Uncompahgre (Hodge 1907–1910, 1:664), appearing also as Tabaguache, Tobawache (Schroeder 1965:68), Tabbywatts (Jorgensen 1972:39), and in other spellings given by Hodge. The Treaty of 1868 has the spellings Tabaquache, Tabequache, and Tabaguaches (Kappler 1904–1941, 2:990, 994), the italicized letters being uncertain readings. Jorgensen (1972:30, 39, 43) uses Taviwach as the name for the historical antecedents of the Uncompahgre and has suggested (personal communication 1985) that möwataviwatsiu may have been applied to the same people when they traveled east of the Rocky Mountains.

The Yutas Sabuaganas, living in 1776 in the area between the Gunnison River and the upper Colorado (Vélez de Escalante in Bolton 1950:153–165), called Zaguaganas on the Miera y Pacheco map (Josephy 1961:130–131), were equated with the Uncompahgre Ute by O.C. Stewart (1942:137) and, with a query, by Schroeder (1965:60). Hodge (1907–1910, 1:32), who gives variant spellings, equated them with the White River Ute, who lived considerably to the north.

Weeminuche. Weeminuche is the spelling used in the text of the Treaty of 1868, and "We-mi-nu-ches Utes" after the signatures (Kappler 1904–1941, 2:990, 995). O.C. Stewart (1942:237) uses Wimönuntsi and also gives wimönuntci. Weminutc is used by Opler (W.Z. Park et al. 1938:632); Jorgensen (1972:30) has Wiminuch and Jorgensen (1980:4) Wimonuch. Hodge (1907–1910, 2:956) uses Wiminuche and gives a number of variants, including Guibisnuches, Guiguimuches, Nomenuches, Wemenuche, Wamanuche, and Womenunche. The Weeminuche were sometimes referred to by variants of the name Paiute: "Wamenuches (also known as Pa-

Uches)," 1862 (Schroeder 1965:71); "the *Wemenuche* band, or *Pah Utes*" (ARCIA 1864:151). Jorgensen (1972:29, 30) refers to the "Payuchis—mixed Wiminuch Ute–Southern Paiutes."

Yampa. O.C. Stewart (1942:233) has Yamparkau and Jorgensen (1972:30) Yamparka. Some minor variants are given by Hodge (1907–1910, 2:987) and Steward (1938:225, 228), who calls them the Yampah Utes.

Sources

Ethnohistoric materials containing firsthand descriptions of the Ute at the time of contact are highly variable in terms of their reliability but provide important contributions to knowledge of prehistoric patterns. The Domínguez-Escalante journals (Bolton 1950; T.J. Warner 1976) and the several versions of the map made of the expedition route by Miera y Pacheco (Alter 1941a; Auerbach 1943; C.I. Wheat 1957–1963, 1) contain valuable insights into pre-1800 Ute lifeways and distribution. Other Spanish journals and documents include descriptions of Utes in the seventeenth century (see L.S. Tyler 1951 and O.C. Stewart 1966 for reviews). Records left by mountain men such as Jedediah Smith (G.R. Brooks 1977) and Osborne Russell (1921), government explorers (Frémont 1845, 1848, 1887; Stansbury 1852; Beckwith 1855; Powell and Ingalls in ARCIA 1874), emigrants and settlers (Bean 1945; Bryant 1967), and Indian agent reports all provide scattered but useful ethnographic data. Jorgensen (1964, 1971) provides detailed ethnohistories of the Northern Ute.

The two most detailed descriptions of Ute culture as remembered by elderly informants were compiled by Anne M. Smith (1974) and Omer C. Stewart (1942). Both did their research during the 1930s, Smith with the Northern Ute and Stewart with all Ute groups. Earlier but less extensive work was performed by Lowie (1924) on the Uintah-Ouray Reservation, Opler (1940) with the Southern Ute, and Steward (1938) on the Western Ute based on historic records.

The best single analysis of Ute history, economy, and religion is Jorgensen (1972). Brief histories of the Southern Ute include Schroeder (1965) and Jefferson, Delaney, and Thompson (1972); other historical material may be found in F.L. Swadesh (1974). Reports on Northern Ute history include Lyman and Denver (1970) and Conetah (1982). For a brief general history of the Ute with a number of excellent photographs see Pettit (1982). The Northern Ute Tribe has published books on Ute culture and history (Uintah-Ouray Tribe 1977, 1977a, 1977b, 1977c, 1977d). Reaction of Utes to contact is considered in Opler (1940), Lang (1953), O.C. Stewart (1966a), and Jorgensen (1972).

Peyote religion is described by O.C. Stewart (1948), Aberle and Stewart (1957), and Opler (1940a, 1942). On the Sun Dance, see Jorgensen (1972), Lowie (1919), Opler (1941), and J.A. Jones (1955). The Bear Dance is treated by Reed (1896), Steward (1932), and Opler (1941a).

Analysis of Ute personality and psychology derived from the tri-ethnic project of the 1950s can be found in Jessor et al. (1968). A formal analysis of Ute language may be found in Givón's Ute dictionary (1979) and grammar (1980). O.C. Stewart (1971a, 1982) provides detailed bibliographies on Ute ethnohistory and ethnography.

Southern Paiute

ISABEL T. KELLY AND CATHERINE S. FOWLER*

Language and Territory

The people to be considered here generally are known as the Southern Paiute ('suðərn 'pī͵yо̄ōt) and include the Chemehuevi (͵chemə'wāvē), a closely related group. The Southern Paiute–Chemehuevi, as well as the adjacent Ute, belong to the Southern Numic branch of the Uto-Aztecan linguistic family.†

Sixteen identifiable groups of Southern Paiute once occupied a broad strip of territory extending across southern Utah and southern Nevada and, following the sharp bend in the Colorado River, southward into California, along the right bank (fig. 1). Only one group, the San Juan, lived south and east of the Colorado.

On the northeast and north, the Southern Paiute merged with the Western and Southern Ute, who could be close to indistinguishable from Paiute if stripped of their overlay of Plains traits (Kelly 1964:34). One group (Antarianunts), which Kelly thought Ute, has been considered Southern Paiute by O.C. Stewart (1942:237;

Kelly 1964:144–145, 168) and as such is included here. As a matter of fact, the Cedar group was called Ute by some of its Paiute neighbors, and to one person from the Cedar area, the Beaver group was Pahvant,who are usually considered to be Western Ute (O.C. Stewart 1942).

It is quite possible that the Antarianunts, Beaver, Cedar, and Kaiparowits groups should be considered transitional Southern Paiute–Ute. Elsewhere, the Paiute were bounded by neighbors who were distinct linguistically and culturally. The western groups, especially the Chemehuevi, were strongly influenced by the Mohave.

There was no overall "tribal" organization. Territorial subdivisions often are called bands, although definition of that term is flexible. The groups discussed here are those outlined by Kelly (1934), with minor changes and with the addition of the Antarianunts. Each group was a geographic unit associated with a definite territory. Some differed slightly in speech. Except for two, each territory was self-sufficient economically; only the Gunlock and Saint George groups had to go outside their own areas for certain staples.

Mutual aid and economic collaboration—often considered band diagnostics—are not implied. If such a definition were used, Southern Paiute "bands" would be extremely numerous, each composed of a small number of camps. Probably a "band," so defined, would correspond pretty well to what have been designated previously as "economic clusters" within each of the larger units (see, for example, Kelly 1964:8, 22–24, map 1). The 16 larger units are here called groups, not bands. Some of the names for these are indigenous; others are labeled for convenience with non-Native designations.

External Relations

Several Southern Paiute groups (Moapa, Shivwits, Saint George, Pahranagat) accused others (Beaver, Cedar, Gunlock, Panguitch) of capturing women and children for sale as slaves. In particular, the Shivwits suffered these depredations yet were themselves accused by the Moapa of similar practices. There was resentment but no resistance. Otherwise, the several groups north of the Colorado were on friendly terms. They visited, hunted, and gathered in one another's territory, occa-

---

*The first part of this chapter, on aboriginal culture, was written by Kelly in 1972 based on field studies in 1932–1933. Minor corrections and additions were made by Fowler after Kelly's death in 1982. The section beginning with history was written by Fowler, based in part on field studies intermittently from 1967–1980 and in part on the literature.

†The phonemes of Southern Paiute are: (stops and affricate) *p, t, c* (phonetically [c], [č]), *k, k^w, ʔ*; (continuants) *s* ([s], [š]), *h;* (nasals) *m, n, ŋ;* (semivowels) *w, y;* (short vowels) *i, a, o* ([ɔ]), u ([o], [u]), *i·;* (long vowels) *i·, a·, o·, u·, i·. h*, which is only word-initial, is found only in the Chemehuevi dialect, though Sapir recorded some marginal examples for the Kaibab dialect. Several consonants have distinctly different pronunciations when between two vowels: *p* is [β], *t* a "lightly trilled" [r], *k* [γ], *k^w* [γ^w], and *m* [ŋ^w]. Word-final vowels are devoiced, as are the vowels of non-penultimate odd-numbered moras (counting from the beginning of the word) before geminates or *s*. The geminate stops and affricate (*pp* and so forth) are long and voiceless ([p·]) after a voiced vowel and preaspirated ([hp]) after a voiceless vowel. Southern Paiute words cited in italics in the *Handbook* have been transcribed into this phonemic system by the editors on the basis of the transcriptions and detailed phonetic explanations of Sapir (1930–1931). Single *s* and *n* have been written even though intervocalically these behave like geminates, since there is no contrast with nongeminates; *ʔ* has been written where Sapir indicates it phonetically, but the analysis of its occurrence is incomplete. Words in roman could not be found in Sapir and have been left unphonemicized. Words and pronunciations in some Southern Paiute dialects differ from the forms given in the *Handbook* in some instances.

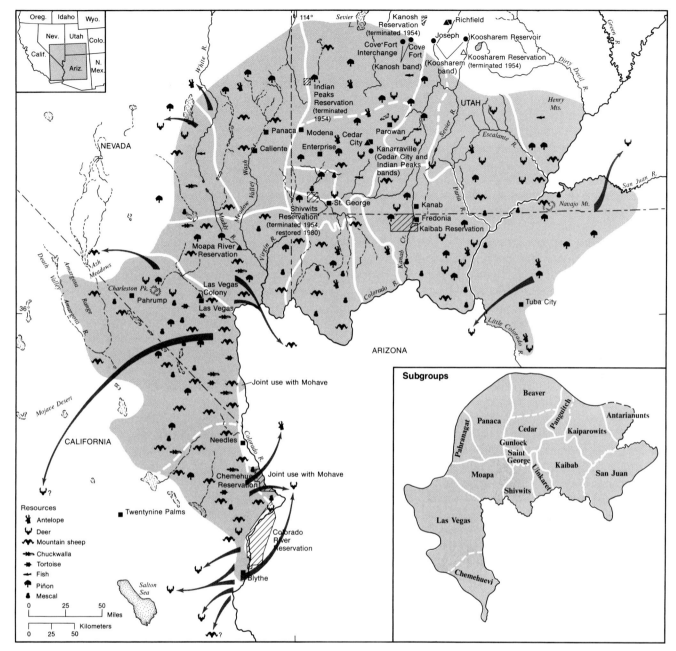

Fig. 1. Nineteenth-century territory (after Kelly 1934) with approximate locations of subgroups and important precontact subsistence resources. Triangles and striped pattern indicate colonies and reservations. Circles locate lands restored to bands under the Paiute Indian Tribe of Utah Restoration Act of 1980.

sionally intermarried and, on a small scale, traded. About 1900, gatherings that were almost pan–Southern Paiute were held in connection with the Mourning ceremony (Sapir 1912; Kelly 1964:95). But even in the early 1930s, the Kaibab were vague about the country west or south of the Moapa, and the Chemehuevi knew little of the area east of the Moapa.

Relationships with non-Paiute peoples varied with proximity. The San Juan at times had limited contact with fellow Paiutes. They were friendly with the Havasupai, yet they also lived in chronic fear of the Navajo

although they outwardly adopted modes of dress, housing, and to some degree language from them. Not only were the Ute and "Mexicans" aggressive slave raiders, but also the Navajo forded the Colorado to steal women, children, and horses (Malouf and Malouf 1945).

Ute-Paiute relations were ambivalent. On the one hand, Ute slave raids in historic times caused fear and indignation. On the other, the Kaibab, who seem not to have suffered such aggression, spoke admiringly of the Ute. They were credited with the introduction of the Bear Dance, and they knew the Sun Dance.

With the Western Shoshone on the north and northwest, relations were friendly. Some Las Vegas people spoke Shoshone, and there was mention of visiting, economic cooperation, intermarriage, and borrowing of Shoshone dances. In contrast, the *nimikko?ici* 'those who killed people'—apparently the Panamint—were described as "mean."

The Chemehuevi and Las Vegas people traveled widely and had amicable contact not only with Shoshone but also with the Kawaiisu, Serrano, Vanyume, Cahuilla, and Diegueño. The Chemehuevi were in direct touch with several Yuman peoples. It was said that generations ago, before the Chemehuevi and Las Vegas separated and Chemehuevi acquired separate identity, they exterminated the Desert Mohave and thereafter moved into much of the territory thus left vacant (see Kroeber 1959; Roth 1976). Occasionally, the Chemehuevi joined the Mohave and Quechan in skirmishes with the Cocopa and Halchidhoma and intermittently were at war with the Mohave themselves (Roth 1976). Seldom did the Chemehuevi fight with the Quechan; they hunted deer in Quechan territory, and several culture traits from the south may have been funneled through Quechans: cane cigarettes, dogs and horses from Sonora, and several Old World cultigens (cf. C.S. Fowler and D.D. Fowler 1981).

The Chemehuevi and, on a lesser scale, the Las Vegas people, took over much of Mohave culture: vocabulary, floodplain farming and some associated crops, the earth-covered house in modified form, basic features of the song series, emphasis on dreams, and a complex of elements related to warfare (Laird 1976). A few specific Mohave traits adopted were: the squared metate, balsas, ferrying pots, ceramic forms and ornaments, paddle-and-anvil pottery techniques, and hair dye.

The Moapa, Shivwits, and Saint George sometimes crossed the Colorado and encountered Walapai hostility (cf. Kroeber 1935a:179–180). The Chemehuevi hunted routinely in Yavapai country and reported specific cases of trade, intermarriage, and game playing. Laird (1976:17) also notes that Chemehuevi routinely hunted in western Walapai territory.

Culture

Subsistence

Southern Paiute terrain ranges from the high Colorado Plateaus west and southwest, through canyon country through Basin and Range, into the Mojave Desert (C.S. Fowler 1966:15–16). There is a corresponding shift in vegetation from spruce and fir, through pine, through juniper, piñon, and sage, to creosote and mesquite. Such differences in elevation and vegetation are reflected in local resources. Diet was varied and subsistence often precarious; practically all groups named starvation foods. Stored provender lasted through the winter, but spring might be a time of stint.

Small game was the chief source of protein. Rabbits were hunted individually and in drives. Other small game included wood rats, mice, gophers, squirrels, chipmunks, and birds. Some groups ate certain lizards and snakes. In the Mojave Desert, chuckwalla and tortoise were eaten, but not the Gila monster. Bird eggs and baby birds, locusts, ant larvae (Beaver, Pahranagat), and caterpillars were gathered. Only among the Panguitch Lake group were fish important, although several groups occasionally fished. Only the Chemehuevi specifically disdained fish (Laird 1976:46–47).

Of large game, bear and elk were not significant. Deer apparently moved into the central areas of the region during the nineteenth century but elsewhere were general. About half the groups had access to antelope, and most to mountain sheep. Such game was stalked individually or by several men, sometimes under the direction of a hunt leader. Marksmen using bow and arrow (fig. 2) were stationed at strategic spots and others drove the game past them.

Magical devices insured luck in hunting. Some (Chemehuevi, Las Vegas, Pahranagat) made gifts to the mountain spirits. The San Juan had a shaman for antelope (O.C. Stewart 1942:241), and some (Chemehuevi, Las Vegas, Moapa, Pahranagat, and Shivwits) had "dreamers" for large game. Laird (1976:33) states that Chemehuevi men had inherited rights to hunt large game (deer, mountain sheep) within certain tracts of their territory. Songs seem to have defined these tracts through recurrent references to place-names within the territories. One either must have the proper song (i.e., rights) or else be in the company of one who had in order to hunt.

A great variety of plant foods was utilized. More important than game, they were largely the women's responsibility. On the plateaus, roots and berries were plentiful. Pine nuts were a staple among many groups. In early fall, the cones were roasted to force opening, and the small nuts extracted and dried for winter. The best pine nuts were said to come from Indian Peak (Beaver-Panaca boundary) and Charleston Mountain (Las Vegas), undoubtedly from single-leaf piñon (*Pinus monophylla*). Elsewhere they were "greasy" but, even so, extensively exploited (nuts of *Pinus edulis*). Agave (*Agave utahensis*), available all year, was a mainstay especially in the canyon lands and when pine nuts were scarce. The base of the stalk was cut with a wooden chisel, the leaves cut off with a stone knife, and the resulting "head" baked in an earth oven.

Seeds were basic. Most were swept with a basketry beater into a conical container. Thereafter, they were winnowed, parched, ground on a flat stone, and prepared as mush or as bread baked in the ashes.

A few decades before occupation by the Whites, Southern Paiute economy was bolstered by the introduction of native agriculture. Distribution was spotty; some groups (Antarianunts, Kaiparowits, Panguitch) remained nonagricultural; Uinkaret planted adjacent to one spring only; of the Beaver group only those in the vicinity of Indian Peak had fields. The Cedar group was mainly nonagricultural, but the earliest reported center of Paiute planting lay near the mouths of Ash and LaVerkin creeks, and in adjacent territory of the Saint George group along the Virgin River. There, Silvestre Vélez de Escalante (Bolton 1950:205ff.) reported fresh corn, cultivated squash, and irrigation ditches.

Maize and squash seem to have reached at least Kaibab Southern Paiute from the Pueblo area. A number of crops were also taken over in the west from the Mohave, Quechan, and Halchidhoma (C.S. Fowler and D.D. Fowler 1981). Inasmuch as Old World cultigens moving north from Mexico appeared about the same time as native agriculture, several of them were considered indigenous.

Red and white flour corn were common; few groups (Chemehuevi, Kaibab) reported yellow maize. The Moapa claimed to have blue corn from the Walapai in post-Mormon times. Squash or pumpkin had about the same distribution as corn and included thin- and hard-shelled varieties. There were mush melons and watermelons, both thought native. Gourds were limited to the Chemehuevi, Las Vegas, and Shivwits groups. Beans were of restricted distribution; several specimens have been identified as teparies (*Phaseolus acutifolius*). The introduced cowpea (*Vigna* sp.) was thought to be native. The sunflower (*Helianthus annuus*) was widely cultivated as was an amaranth (kumutɨ).

Winter wheat (*Triticum vulgari*) was planted by some (Chemehuevi, Las Vegas, Moapa, Saint George), and the Chemehuevi took over the semicultivated grasses reported for the Mohave (Stewart 1966:9). The Pahranagat burned a plot and scattered seeds of an unidentified plant called *iappɨ* ('what is planted'; 'corn' in some dialects); the Shivwits did the same with one named *ko·* (*Chenopodium* sp.). Devil's claw (*Proboscidea* sp.) for basket decoration was grown by the Chemehuevi and Las Vegas. Tobacco was not cultivated, but a plot was burned to encourage its growth. There was no wild-plant irrigation.

Floodplain farming was practiced where feasible and dominated Chemehuevi agriculture, which followed Mohave patterns (Stewart 1966). The Pahranagat planted along the edges of lakes and, as the lakes dried, watered by hand. Elsewhere, water from a spring or stream was carried to the garden by a ditch, with laterals. Informants' statements suggest irrigation on a modest scale. A "small" garden might cover about an acre; larger plots were the joint responsibility of brothers or other relatives. Ordinarily, women helped in the fields, and widows might farm without assistance. Implements included a dibble and, among most groups, a "flat stick" or "spade."

Annual Cycle

The annual cycle varied with habitat. Some chose to winter at high elevations, where snow was deep, fuel plentiful, and pine nut stores at hand. If pine nuts were not a staple, winter was passed at the foot of hills or in protected canyons, where snows were light, fuel abundant, caves handy as dwellings, and agave available. Water was not a problem; potholes were full and snow could be melted.

Cached stores could run out in late spring. Then unpalatable plant foods (juniper berries, Joshua tree shoots) were eaten; caterpillars and locusts were gathered; and rattlesnakes captured as they came out of their dens (Panaca). Valley seeds began to ripen, and those who farmed prepared their fields. The seasonal cycle was little altered by the adoption of agriculture; gardens were left before plants sprouted or were tended until danger from birds had passed. Then most of the camp left on the usual collecting and hunting trips, leaving the elderly to watch the fields.

In summer, big game was hunted, and seeds, fruits and berries were gathered. In late summer and fall, farmers and nonfarmers gathered at the gardens, for it was customary to share produce. Even before the harvest was completed, some people left for the mountains to have an early start on pine nut gathering; others remained to finish collection and storage of crops.

For most, fall was a time of plenty and one of great mobility, with shuttling from high to low country and from one spot to another where collecting and hunting were most favorable. Many moved to the mountains to cache pine nuts and hunt large game, returning to the valleys for rabbit drives. Highland seeds and berries were available, as was yucca fruit. All groups stored as much food as possible against the winter and recurrent spring famine.

Structures

The "winter" house was conical or subconical (fig. 3). Usually the doorway faced east, to receive the morning sun, and most houses had a smoke hole (Watkins 1945). A San Juan respondent (O.C. Stewart 1942:257) described the standard house as gabled, with the limb of a tree serving as ridgepole. Only among the Chemehuevi and on Cottonwood Island (Las Vegas) was there an approximation of the Mohave earth-covered dwelling but built without front wall. Caves were favored as winter quarters in some areas.

In hot weather, many "lived under the trees," perhaps tossing brush on them, to provide denser shade.

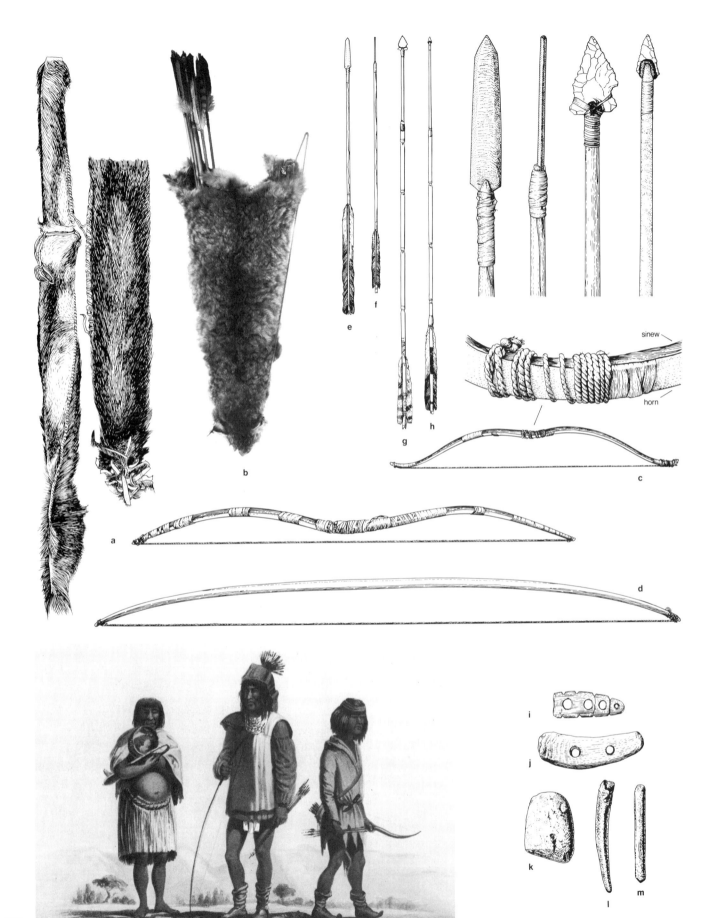

A variety of auxiliary structures—shades and windbreaks—was described, and a good many individuals, but not all, considered the widely distributed, flat-roofed shade to be "recent."

Ute influence accounts for the canvas- or skin-covered tepee, introduced as early as 1855 among the Cedar (Euler 1966:67) and popular about 1900. A few innovators copied the sweathouse from Ute, Shoshone, Walapai, and Navajo neighbors, and construction followed that of the source.

Clothing and Adornment

Occasionally a simple wraparound "kilt" was mentioned for both sexes, but the basic Southern Paiute garment was the double apron of skin or vegetable fiber (fig. 4). Though universal among women, it was mentioned specifically for men among the Beaver, Cedar, Kaibab, Pahranagat, and Panguitch groups. The butcher-style variant of double apron (Chemehuevi, Las Vegas, Shivwits) relates to a similar garment among Yavapai, Walapai, and Havasupai (for example, Kroeber 1935a:99–100). A bark "dress" was reported by only the Shivwits. In winter, both sexes wore twined bark leggings.

Skin clothing, beyond simple poncholike shirts for men and single or multiple-skin capes for both sexes, is not aboriginal. Elaborately fringed men's shirts, leggings, and full-length women's dresses probably date from the early to mid-nineteenth century (fig. 4) and are of designs introduced by the Ute. Several of the pieces photographed by J.K. Hillers for John Wesley Powell in 1872 and 1873 are in fact Ute (Fowler and Matley 1979:3). Prior to these introductions, men (particularly elderly men) sometimes went naked in hot weather, but a skin breechclout was more usual. Simple short leggings were worn by some in cooler weather or while hunting. In addition to the skin cape or throw, rabbit-skin robes were worn by both sexes in all groups.

Men wore a skin cap whose pattern varied. The most prestigious one was of tanned hide, with a tuft of quail feathers on the crown (Chemehuevi, Gunlock, Las Vegas, Moapa, Pahranagat, Shivwits); it was affected by chiefs and good hunters. The woman's basketry cap was general.

At least part of the year, individuals in warm areas went barefoot. Traditional footgear seems to have been sandals or "moccasins" (fig. 5) of bark or yucca; for use in snow, a slab of the inner wood of the Joshua tree served as a sole (Pahranagat). A rawhide sandal for summer wear (Chemehuevi, Las Vegas) probably was copied from Yuman peoples. A foot "mitten" was made from the entire skin of a squirrel or small badger. Both sexes wore tailored skin moccasins of various styles, which some declared a "recent" innovation.

Men, it was said, pulled the hair back and tied it at the nape, a style not confirmed by Hillers's plates (Fowler and Fowler 1971), which show the men with fairly short hair, worn loose, sometimes with a part. Braids were "new style"; occasionally the Chemehuevi and Las Vegas people affected Mohave-style curls. Eagle down was applied to the hair for special occasions (Las Vegas), and one or more eagle feathers were worn (Fowler and Fowler 1971:fig. 25). Upright feathers presumably represent Hillers's or Powell's idea of "Indian" headdress (Fowler and Matley 1979:3). Women wore the hair loose, sometimes with a part.

Red paint was smeared on face and body for skin

bottom left, Smithsonian Lib.: Ives 1861: pl. 3; Smithsonian, Dept. of Anthr.: a, 14,886; c, 12,028; d, 14,511; e, 11,219; f, 10,792; g, 14,540; h, 14,610; i, 14,340; j, 14,423; k, 14,341; l–m, 14,346; b, Harvard U., Peabody Mus.: 34–24–10/3713.

Fig. 2. Hunting equipment. a, Bow and horsehide quiver and bowcase. The bow is hardwood, double-curved when strung, lightly reflexed, and sinewed-backed; string is 2-strand sinew. Sinew-backed bows like this one were the mainstay of the Southern Paiute arsenal, stronger than the simple self-bow and less costly than the horn bow (Kelly 1964). b, One-piece quiver of wildcat skin, a very old quiver form in the Great Basin (see "Prehistory of the Western Area," fig. 6, this vol.). c, Mountain sheep horn bow, strongly reflexed, double-curved with working recurved ears, and heavily sinew-backed, made from 2 thinned strips of horn, overlapped at the grip, and held by several thick wraps of sinew. Wraps of 2-strand sinew cord at the grip are probably a spare bowstring. d, Moapa self-bow, bowstring 2-ply Indian hemp. The simple self-bow is probably the oldest bow form. e–h, Arrow types. Arrows were commonly made of serviceberry or cane, less frequently of currant or wild rose. Wooden wands were scraped clean, dried about a week, stuck in hot ashes, straightened between the teeth or with a wrench of antelope or mountain sheep horn, and smoothed between two stones. Cane arrows were straightened on large, flat stones heated in the fire. Two or 3 split feathers fletched either type of shaft. Arrow points were made from stone, wood, metal, and bottle glass (Kelly 1964; Fowler and Matley 1979). e, Kaibab wood arrow, shaft tipped with a triangular iron point, secured with sinew lashing. Fletching is golden eagle tail feathers. f, Kaibab wood arrow, shaft tipped with heavy gauge brass wire. Fletching may be turkey vulture feathers. g, Moapa cane arrow, tipped with a hardwood foreshaft and scavenged chalcedony Elko Corner-notched projectile point. Fletching is red-tailed hawk tail feathers. h, Moapa cane arrow, tipped with a hardwood foreshaft and chert point hafted in pitch. Fletching is golden eagle tail feathers. i–m, Arrow-making equipment. i, Thin, triangular shaft straightener–diameter gauge of mountain sheep horn. j, Shaft straightener–gauge of mountain sheep horn. Remnants of black pitch perhaps indicate use of this tool to spread pitch evenly onto the shaft for fletching. k, Soft, white, gritty stone, with abrasion facets, for "smoothing bows and arrows" (Powell 1873). l–m, Shivwits antler flakers. l is a tine with wear at the narrow tip; m is ground at both ends, one sharp, the other blunted. l may have been used for fine, finishing flaking; m for rougher, preparatory work. Length of bow a, 109 cm; b–h to same scale. Length of i, 7.2 cm; j–m to same scale. a, c–m, Collected by J.W. Powell, southern Utah, 1871–1873; b, by Isabel T. Kelly from Chemehuevi, 1933. top right, Arrow details. bottom left, Chemehuevis. Man in center holds a simple bow; man on right carries a double-curved, sinew-backed horn bow; both wear traditional skin caps. The men's tunics and moccasins are postcontact styles; the woman's skirt, cape, and cradle are traditional styles. Lithograph after a drawing by Heinrich B. Möllhausen, Jan. 1858.

protection and for esoteric reasons (boy's first game; girl's first menses; birth). Black, white, yellow, and blue pigments were used, and the Chemehuevi commonly applied black coloring about the eyes. For festivals, young people painted designs on the face. The Kaibab, Kaiparowits, and San Juan denied tattooing; otherwise, both sexes tattooed their faces, but rarely their arms and chests.

The ears of recalcitrant children were perforated (Chemehuevi, Las Vegas, Moapa). Moreover, Coyote ruled that without pierced ears it would be impossible after death to cross the chasm to the other world. An added inducement was the association of ear perforation with longevity. Small sticks, stones, or shells were used as earrings. A few "high-toned" men among the western groups perforated the nasal septum, wearing as an ornament a stick, bone, or pendant of haliotis shell or turquoise.

Technology

The chief craft was basketry, whose products were admirably suited to local needs. All the usual Great Basin forms were present: conical burden basket, fan-shaped tray for winnowing and parching, seedbeater, water jug with piñon pitch coating (fig. 6). Baskets generally were twined, but the Cedar and Kaibab had both coiled and twined burden baskets; about half the groups coiled the water jug, considering this more durable. Most seedbeaters were twined, but one of wicker work was used for berries. The basket for stone-boiling—absent among the Chemehuevi, Las Vegas, Moapa, Panaca, and Panguitch groups—was coiled, as was the mush or eating bowl. Also coiled was a circular winnowing or parching tray. The woman's cap was twined and was either hemispherical or mammiform. Agave was hauled in a wrapped-stitch carrying frame ("Subsistence" this vol.).

A Paiute infant had three or four successively larger basketry cradles. Forms are well known (Lowie 1924:figs. 33a, 34a; Kelly 1964:pl. 5). The Chemehuevi and Las Vegas adopted a near-Mohave type (fig. 7) with inverted-U frame and transverse bars, but closely spaced. With it, instead of the usual shade, they used a narrow, twined band. The Moapa had a similar bandlike shade but combined it with the traditional cradle frame.

Men and women wove strips of rabbit or other fur into rectangular or trapezoidal capes, which served also as bedding. The warps were twisted fur strips, held together in twined stitch by vegetable-fiber cordage, strips of buckskin, or, since the late nineteenth century, torn strips of commercial cloth. Warping varied.

Cordage was two- or three-ply, of apocynum (*Apocynum cannabinum*), cliffrose bark (*Cowania mexicana*), or milkweed fiber (*Asclepias fascicularis*). Yucca (*Yucca* spp.) fiber was favored for rope. Chemehuevi specialties were agave rope and "bean" (cowpea) fiber string. The bowstring was two- or three-ply and of sinew. Women made twine and light cordage; men, rope.

Netting was a man's job. The Saint George people did not make nets. The Shivwits made few, and obtained others in trade from the Moapa, and when they were worn, passed them on to the Saint George people. Products included the rabbit net, a baglike device for catching cottontails or birds, and the man's burden net of cordage (fig. 8) or strips of mountain-sheep hide. The Chemehuevi and Las Vegas made their nets double, so they could be opened and expanded to accommodate bulky loads.

Men were the tanners, scraping both sides of the skin with the sharpened cannon bone of a deer or mountain sheep and applying, as tanning agents, brain and marrow from the spinal cord. The skin was wrung with the aid of a stick, then rubbed and pulled. To improve the color, some groups soaked the hide with a dye plant or smoked it.

Not all groups made pottery. It was absent among the Antarianunts (O.C. Stewart 1942:273), Gunlock, and San Juan. The Kaibab occurrence was ephemeral (Kelly 1964:77–78); some (Beaver, Panaca, Panguitch) shaped vessels, using them sun-dried and unfired. Even so, there was heavy reliance on ceramics, and not all groups had cooking baskets. Pahranagat respondents had never heard of stone-boiling. Usually women were the potters, but a man made his own tubular tobacco pipe, and children formed unfired effigies and miniature vessels as toys (fig. 9). There was also limited use of archeological vessels (Fowler and Matley 1979:84).

Clay was pounded on a stone or ground on the metate. Some used no temper; others, dry yucca root or the mucilaginous juice from one of several cacti. The

---

Smithsonian NAA, top left: 1635; top right, 1634; center left, 72,593; Calif. Histl. Soc., Los Angeles: Title Insurance Coll.: center right, 3524; bottom left, 3515; bottom right, 3527.

Fig. 3. Structures. top left, Winter lodge near St. George, Utah. Circular in ground plan (10–15 ft. diameter), the house had a 3–4 pole foundation, usually of juniper. The poles interlocked at the top producing a height of 10–15 ft. Additional poles were added over the framework, and covered with juniper bark, grass, brush, rushes, or arrowweed. A man is sleeping in the shade of the lodge. top right, House of Tapeats near St. George, Utah, a summer house or windbreak, open at the top. In the foreground is an open twined burden basket containing clothing. top left and top right, Photographs by John K. Hillers, 1873. center left, Chemehuevi gabled house, a style adopted from the Mohave but without the front wall. The framework of horizontal and vertical poles is covered with willow and arrowweed and often earth. Photograph by Edward S. Curtis, 1907. center right, Chemehuevi granary of willow and arrowweed, set on four-post frame. This type of structure, adopted from the Mohave, was used to store corn, beans, and squash. bottom left, Chemehuevi flat-topped shade, common in several communities until the 1940s. bottom right, Chemehuevi field house, a temporary shade usually built adjacent to cultivated fields. center right and bottom, Photographs probably by Charles C. Pierce, 1890s.

top left, Smithsonian, NAA: 1609; Smithsonian, Dept. of Anthr.: a, 14,594; b, 14,601; c, 11,200; d, 14,368.

Fig. 4. Men's and women's skin clothing. top left, An arrowmaker and family wearing buckskin clothing. Manufactured for John W. Powell in 1872 (Fowler and Matley 1979:28–30), the shirt and calf-length dress do not depart markedly from mid-19th-century patterns described for the Kaibab (Kelly 1932–1933; Sapir 1910b:66–68; O.C. Stewart 1942:280–281). The shirt is poncho-style with wrist-length sleeves; the dress is made of 2 skins with short sleeves added. The fringing follows Ute patterns and may be atypical of Southern Paiute. The man's moccasins have a welted sole seam and tongue, the tongue perhaps a postcontact innovation (Sapir 1910b:90–91). The tunic on the child at right is probably more typical of earlier skin clothing. The man is holding a hafted knife that he may be reworking. Photograph by John K. Hillers, near Kanab, Utah, 1872. a–b, Men's skin caps. a, Las Vegas cap of buckskin folded in the middle and stitched down the sides with sinew. At the top the skin is bunched and wrapped to simulate ears or horns. The feathers are red-tailed hawk from the tail and wing. b, Moapa cap, buckskin, with a long flap at the back. The front edge is laced with a buckskin drawstring for tying. Horns of wrapped rawhide are colored black with red tips. Red and black lines are accented at the front by a series of small holes. Width 20 cm; a is to same scale. c, Kaibab man's buckskin shirt, the body made of 2 skins and the sleeves, of separate pieces of skin. d, Kaibab girl's buckskin dress, made from 2 skins, probably fawn, and 2 separate pieces of hide sewn into the yoke. This is a scaled-down version of the woman's whole skin dress. The cut of the body is very distinctive, markedly flaring at the hem. The border of the yoke, front and back, is accented by blue and white seed beads and rows of perforated elk teeth. This dress style is of general Plains type, similar to those worn by Eastern Shoshones and Utes. Length of c 80.6 cm, d same scale; a–d collected by J.W. Powell, 1872–1874.

376

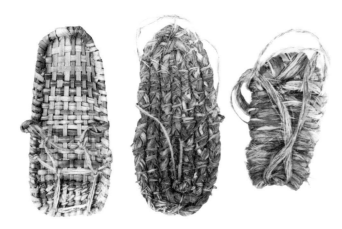

Amer. Mus. of Nat. Hist., New York: left, 50.2/3441; right, 50.2/3512; center, Mus. of N. Mex., Santa Fe: 874/12.

Fig. 5. Sandals. left, Plaited sandal with plain twining at the toe and simple netted upper. center, Sandal with continuous warp of 3-strand braid and open plain twining between warp rows; ties went between toes and fastened to a separate heel loop. right, Sandal on a U-shaped warp, ultimately knotted at the toe to form ties that would intersect a separate heel loop; weft of sandal is unwrapped at top of warp to form a heel pad and then is continuous in figure-8 over the 2 warps to toe. Length of left, 28 cm; all collected by I.T. Kelley, 1932.

Moapa and Panaca people described a spiral start, but usually the bottom was a single lump to whose edge rolls of clay were added as concentric circles, while one hand was held, anvillike, against the inside wall. The chief vessel was a cooking pot, flat bottomed (Beaver, Gunlock, Kaibab, Panguitch), conical, or subconical (Moapa, Panaca, Pahranagat, Shivwits); the Cedar and Shivwits reported both forms (fig. 10e). The cooking vessel was about one foot high.

In ceramics, the Chemehuevi and Las Vegas people showed strong Mohave influences. They alone used stone temper, baked and ground; the paddle-and-anvil technique, with a small cobble as anvil; and painted wares. Forms included a cooking pot; a similar vessel for pre-planting germination of seeds; a spoon or scoop; and a water jar, often used for seed storage. The Chemehuevi made a large pot for ferrying children across the river. There were no canteens, duck pots, rattled handles, or clay cones used as vessel supports.

Transport

The Southern Paiute were foot travelers who packed their burdens. The annual cycle required great mobility, and men seem also to have traveled rather widely for hunting, trade, and pleasure. Men carried burdens in the shoulder net, with a chest tumpline. Women used the conical burden basket; the wrapped-stitch frame, especially for agave; and a conical skin-covered frame, for seeds and pine nuts. These were supported by a head tumpline that, to prevent chafing, rested on the

basket cap. Burdens were not borne directly on the head.

For easterly groups, the Grand Canyon was an effective barrier, but from the Shivwits downstream, the river was crossed almost casually, swimming with a log tucked under the arm. The Chemehuevi copied the Mohave in making log rafts and reed balsas, both poled, and in ferrying children in pots. They crossed the river frequently, hunting on the east shore; about five families habitually planted directly across the river from Chemehuevi Valley.

The Chemehuevi and Las Vegas liked to travel, traversing the Mojave Desert to hunt in the Tehachapi area and farther south, possibly in the San Bernardino Mountains. Men from both groups went to the Pacific Coast "just to look around" and to obtain haliotis shell. Upon rare occasions, eight or 10 men journeyed to the Hopi villages: "perhaps two Moapa, two from Vegas, two Chemehuevis, and two Walapais" (Kelly 1932–1933). They forded the Colorado by Cottonwood Island, crossed Walapai country, among the Havasupai were joined by two local men, apparently as guides. The round trip took about two months and was not a trading venture, although gifts were exchanged.

Kinship

Kinship terminologies have been published for Antarianunts and Shivwits (O.C. Stewart 1942:350–351), Kaibab (Gifford 1917:245–246; Kelly 1964:121–130), Moapa, and Shivwits (Lowie 1924:287–288). Although terms for cousins, parallel and cross, were the same as those for siblings, those for parents did not apply to parents' siblings. A series of terms reflected the levirate and sororate, which, among some groups, were obligatory following the death of a spouse. Emphasis on age differences was marked, and there were distinctions based on the sex of the speaker.

Life Cycle

Most marriages were monogamous. Some polygyny was reported, usually with sisters as co-wives; polyandry was less frequent, but specific cases were cited (Gunlock, Pahranagat, Panaca), and some on hearsay (Shivwits, Saint George). Exchange marriages, with a brother, were fairly common. Young people married early; it was immaterial if a girl married before or after her first menses, provided she was competent in domestic chores. The chief requisite for a husband was hunting skill.

Birth usually took place in a circular brush enclosure. The parturient knelt, sometimes clutching a post. The cord was cut with a stone knife and tied with string or sinew, and the placenta was buried without ceremony. When the stump dropped off, it might be tied to the cradle but eventually it was taken to the mountains by

377

a

c

b

e

f

g

d

h

KELLY AND FOWLER

Smithsonian, Dept. of Anthr.: a, 11,806; c, 14,680; Amer. Mus. of Nat. Hist., New York: b, 50.2/3506; f, 50.2/3509; h, 50.2/3590; Mus. of N. Mex., School of Amer. Research Coll., Santa Fe: g, 9965–12.

Fig. 6. Basketry. bottom left, Winnowing pine nuts in a close twill twined tray. Photograph by Isabel Kelly, Beaver, Utah, 1932. a, Close-coiled burden basket, 2–3-rod stacked foundation, single rod coiled to rim. The tumpline is 2-ply, Z-twist, fiber cordage. b, Shivwits open twill twined winnowing and parching tray. c, Close twill twined winnowing and parching tray. d, Chemehuevi close coiled tray used to sift mesquite meal. It has a grass bundle foundation and characteristic devil's claw design. e, Las Vegas seed beater, open twill twined, with an elongated, tubular handle. f, Shivwits wicker seed beater of the type used for berries. A cottonwood slat blade is attached to the rim. g, Unpitched Moapa close twill twined water bottle. The diagonal checked pattern is made by alternating peeled and unpeeled wefts. h, Pitched Moapa close twill twined water bottle. Length of e (model) 9.5 cm; length of f, 24 cm, rest to same scale. a, c, Collected by J.W. Powell, Utah, 1873–1874. b, d–h, collected by Isabel T. Kelly, 1932–1933.

the father. He faced east (Chemehuevi) and left a boy's cord in the hole of an antelope squirrel or on the track of a mountain sheep to insure ability to hunt. A girl's cord he placed in an anthill or in the hole of a pocket gopher or kangaroo rat, so that she might be industrious.

Following childbirth, a woman remained on a slightly excavated "hotbed" for several days. Her husband spent the night in the enclosure, keeping the fire going; only the Chemehuevi stated that he too occupied a hotbed. Seclusion lasted from four to 30 days. The husband shared the postpartum practices: use of a hair fillet, a scratching stick, and a tooth stick, and a taboo on meat, salt, and drinking cold water. Restrictions were lifted gradually and attendant practices included bathing, washing and trimming the hair, singeing the infant's hair, and rubbing red paint (Moapa only: white paint) on the body of both parents and the infant.

The nearest approximation to boys' puberty rites focused on hunting. Until he was old enough to marry, a boy and his parents did not eat the game he killed, nor did any young woman. It was given to old people, often the grandparents, or traded to other boys, who could eat it. Failure to follow restrictions made the boy

left, Calif. Histl. Soc., Los Angeles: Title Insurance Coll.: 3502; center, Harvard U., Peabody Mus.: 34–24–10/3726; right, Mus. of N. Mex. School of Amer. Research Coll., Santa Fe: 879/12.

Fig. 7. Cradles. left, Chemehuevi basketmaker repairing cradle. The shade has been removed and is to the right. Photograph probably by Charles C. Pierce, 1890s. center, Chemehuevi cradle, inverted U-shaped frame of mesquite root and slatted back of willow. The shade twined in paired rows and the use of feathers as ornamentation mark this as a boy's cradle. For girls, the cradle was decorated with beads. Collected by Isabel T. Kelly, 1933. right, Canvas-covered cradle with open, plain twined back and pointed shade fastened to a single willow bar. The canvas cover is a 20th-century adaptation of the skin cover, ideas borrowed from the Western Shoshone or Ute. The frame or foundation is traditional. Collected by Isabel T. Kelly from Cedar subgroup, 1932. Length of center 54 cm, right same scale.

379

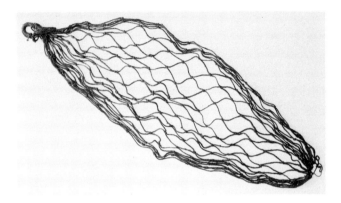

Smithsonian, Dept. of Anthr.: 11244.
Fig. 8. Carrying net. Length 125 cm.

weak, lazy, and unable to sight the quarry. When the ban was lifted, the boy was bathed, painted red, his hair trimmed, and he was made to run.

The girls' puberty rite followed the patterns outlined for childbirth. If she married prior to the first menses, her husband shared the restrictions: seclusion, use of the hotbed at night, use of the scratching and tooth sticks, and a taboo on meat, salt, and drinking cold water. The conclusion was marked by bathing, washing and trimming the hair, and painting the face or body red.

Relatives prepared a corpse for burial. For four days thereafter, they bathed and abstained from meat, salt and, apparently, intercourse. Some (Cedar, Chemehuevi, San Juan, Shivwits; conflicting data for Las Vegas) reported cremation to be traditional. The Panaca cremated when there was nobody to help carry the corpse or frozen ground prevented interment. A shift to burial—that is, depositing the body in a rock cleft or shallow wash—apparently coincided with colonization by the Mormons (Cedar, Chemehuevi, Shivwits).

Property was destroyed at death. Eagles—an important form of personal property—were killed, as were the dog and horses of the deceased. Immolation of a relative provided company for the deceased (Gunlock, Shivwits, Saint George, Kaibab, and Uinkaret reported by a Shivwits individual). The Shivwits held a family discussion; none "wanted 'to go'; there were no volunteers." The group selected the victim, who had no recourse and was then hit with a club or shot, or an evil shaman was hired to shoot him figuratively.

Following a death, the family, or sometimes the entire camp, moved at least temporarily. Gardens were taken over by others, and the site shifted slightly. Women cut the hair in mourning, and there was a permanent taboo on the name of the dead.

Political Organization

There was no central political control within any of the groups designated here. Nor were their boundaries so rigid as to prevent exploitation of resources by people of neighboring groups, in the guise of "visiting." Some of these groups were named, some not. Some were composed of a number of economic units, some of few. These were assemblages of individual households that tended to move together on hunting and gathering trips, returning to the same spring or the same agricultural site. Settlement was mobile and scattered, but with recurrent residence in at least one fixed area. Houses seem to have been closely grouped (Fowler and Fowler 1971: fig. 22), and occupants were usually related by blood or marriage. Size varied from one or two households to "many," which seems to have meant about 10; the maximum number reported was 20 (Kelly 1932–1933).

Commonly, springs were said to be private property and inherited. Married siblings—especially males, but sometimes also females—tended to camp at the same springs, with one of the brothers regarded as the owner; occasionally a woman was so cited. Despite temporary matrilocal residence at marriage, a strong patrilocal tendency was evident. One economic cluster within the Beaver group had 13 individual camps, of which eight were headed by brothers.

The basic unit was the nuclear family, with some cases of polygyny and polyandry. A good many camps consisted of a lone man or a childless couple. Number of children varied; infant mortality must have been high, yet one Las Vegas settlement had 16 households, of which 13 were headed by or included full siblings.

Most large economic clusters had a headman, who was more advisory than authoritative. From the doorway of his house, he addressed the people, telling them when to move and where to go for certain wild products. He urged the men to hunt, not to fight or steal; he received visitors and admonished thieves.

Chiefly succession tended to run in the family, but not from father to son. The office might go to a brother, or father's sister's husband, a sister's son, or a grandson. Personality was a deciding factor, and the elder men of the group chose a new headman, after lengthy deliberations, sometimes in consultation with people from neighboring economic clusters.

Most individuals could state flatly which chiefs were native and which were Mormon-appointed. To complicate matters, early White travelers tended to designate as "chief" any man willing to deal with them, and some names that appear in early accounts as chiefs were not mentioned as such by local people.

As usual, the Chemehuevi and Las Vegas groups were atypical. Among them, a chief was succeeded by his son, preferably the eldest. He must be a good man: "generous, not mean; smart; not lazy; able to talk well." He should be "wealthy," with a large camp and an ample shade; he must be ready to go without eating to provide for others. Only the Chemehuevi and Las Ve-

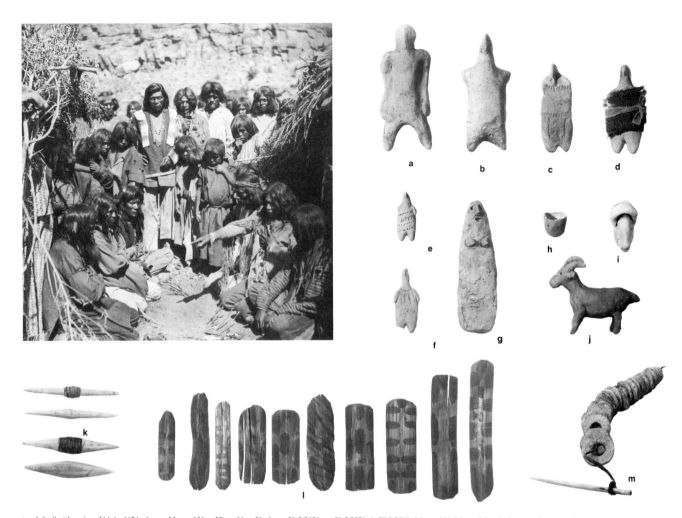

top left, Smithsonian, NAA: 1624; Amer. Mus. of Nat. Hist., New York: a, 50.2/3458; g, 50.2/3571; i, 50.2/3518; Mus. of N. Mex., School of Amer. Research Coll., Santa Fe: b, 895/12; j, 892/12; Smithsonian, Dept. of Anthr.: c–f; h, 11,297; l, left to right, 11,970; 11,959; 11,217; m, Mus. of the Amer. Indian, Heye Foundation, New York: 11–6844.

Fig. 9. Toys and games. top left, Hand game. Two players of the team on the left are hiding the bones (one marked, one unmarked) while the team on the right is guessing their positions. Each side's counters are in the foreground. The man in the center, in beaded shirt, is the Kaibab chief, Chuarumpeak. Photograph by John K. Hillers, near Kanab, Utah, 1872. a–j, Unfired clay figurines, toys. Decoration usually consisted of fingernail impressions or sharp punctations, wrapping the figure in cloth, or painting with red pigments. a–f are human figures, undecorated (a–b), impressed with fingernails to simulate buckskin fringe on clothing (c), wrapped in commercial tweed-weave cloth secured by blue denim and having bands of red paint down both cheeks (d), embellished with series of punctate lines representing clothing and ornamentation (e–f). g may be a woman with breasts, a person with short arms, or an upright animal with protruding forelegs. h, Basket or bowl; i, cradleboard; j, mountain sheep. Length of a 12.6 cm, b–j same scale. k, Hand game bones in 2 styles, one a full set, the other a single pair. l, 10 juniper-bark playing cards, with red designs (Fowler and Matley 1979). Powell (Culin 1898:749–750), said these were dice and described their use in a game similar to the basket dice game. m, Chemehuevi ring and pin game of pumpkin rinds strung on a leather thong tied to a pin. It is similar to ring and pin sets used by the Mohave (Kroeber 1925). More typical of Southern Paiute games were a tube of bone or reed, a rabbit skull, or a button, strung on leather and attached to a wooden pin. Length of k about 7 cm, l–m same scale. a–j, l, Collected by J.W. Powell, Utah, 1871; k, collected by J.W. Powell from the Kaibab and Uinkaret, Utah, 1871; m, collected at Beaver Lake, southeastern Nev., before 1923.

gas mentioned dreaming in connection with chiefs. One Chemehuevi individual dreamed of "Earth's son, who spoke good things. It rained whenever this child was mentioned." Another Las Vegas man dreamed of the sayings of Earth's son; years later, the son of this chief spoke in the same vein. Still another Las Vegas chief dreamed of "good earth," and of giving sound advice; after such a dream, he addressed the camps morning and evening (Kelly 1932–1933). Laird (1976:24) also notes the possibility that Chemehuevi chiefs used spe-

cial language in speaking to one another and at gatherings.

Warfare

The Southern Paiute were notably pacific. The Chemehuevi were more warlike, undoubtedly reflecting Mohave influences. The reputedly cannibalistic Desert Mohave were exterminated by the still-united Chemehuevi–Las Vegas, presumably in the late eighteenth

top right, Calif. Histl. Soc., Los Angeles, Title Insurance and Trust Co. Coll.: 3495; Smithsonian, Dept. of Anthr.: a, 14,455; b, 14,471; c, 11,865; d, 14,452; e, 20,956.
Fig. 10. Household utensils. a, Spoon made from steamed and scraped mountain sheep horn. b, Kaibab tortoise shell bowl. c, Coiled mush bowl, noninterlocking simple stitch with a 2-rod stacked foundation. The carrying loop consists of knotted buckskin thongs and a strip of cloth. d, Kaibab carved wooden bowl with slight rim extensions as handles. e, Clay pot, paddle and anvil construction, with crude surface finish and undulating rim. Fingernail indentations follow the top of the rim and form a band below it. Length of a, 37.5 cm; rest to same scale. a–d, Collected by J.W. Powell, 1872–1874. e, Collected by Edward Palmer near St. George, Utah, 1875. top right, Chemehuevi girls making a drink from mesquite pods and beans. They are grinding the materials in a painted pottery bowl. Photograph probably by Charles C. Pierce, 1890s.

century. Subsequently, the Chemehuevi fought occasionally as Mohave allies and, upon occasion, with the Mohave themselves; such hostilities are reflected in a "peace treaty" signed in 1867 (Heizer and Hester 1970; see Roth 1976 for details on conflicts).

Probably battle casualties were light. With a war party went a "peacemaker," usually a half-blood related to the opponents. After one or two had been killed, he halted combat. One individual remarked there was little real fighting before guns were available (Kelly 1932–1933).

There is some mention of battle formation in two opposing lines about 20 feet apart. Nevertheless, Chemehuevi warfare was essentially a matter of predawn raids, in which sleeping victims were clubbed. Nobody

was spared and no captives taken. Scouts surveyed at night, and women worked as lookouts: "They were good runners, able to give signals, and trained so their voices would carry" (Kelly 1932–1933).

Warriors—called "brave men"—were those who had favorable dreams of traveling to the east; of the Pleiades, Orion's belt, or the morning star; of the sunrise; of riding on the moon. Other themes were of luck in battle and of the face painted black, and the hair red, for combat. Warrior-dreamers wore Cooper's hawk feathers in the hair and carried a wooden (fig. 11) or a stone club. Among them were the war leaders who bore feathered pikes, with sharpened tip, which were hurled as spears and involved no-flight obligations. Those whose dreams were not promising were the archers. On arrowshaft and point they rubbed poison made from the dried heart of deer or mountain sheep, mixed with salt. For four days after returning to camp, all who had participated in battle bathed and ate unsalted food.

Both War-incitement dances and Scalp dances were Round Dances. A "scalp" apparently comprised the entire head, and none was taken unless a scalp dreamer were present. If so, following the fight, at stopping places back to home camp, and once there, a dance was held with the "scalp" mounted on a central pole (Laird 1976:43–44).

Shamanism and Curing

Illness was attributed to disease-object intrusion as the consequence of a malevolent shaman or ghost; to ghost intrusion; or to soul loss (Kelly 1936, 1939). Practitioners were men or women, the women often considered malicious. Power came in dreams, from one or more tutelaries, usually in animal form, who provided instructions and songs. Dreams could be obtained by spending a night alone in one of several caves (Chemehuevi, Las Vegas) (Laird 1976:38), and unsolicited dreams might be rejected.

There was almost no association between datura (*Datura stramonium*) and shamanism (cf. Laird 1976:39), as there was among several California groups, nor was the trance part of Southern Paiute doctoring, as elsewhere in the Great Basin. Soul loss necessitated pursuit and restoration of the wandering soul: disease-object intrusion, the removal of the object through sucking. During this operation, the shaman lay supine on the ground beneath the prone body of the patient. Paraphernalia was scant: a crooked cane, thought by some to have occult powers of its own (Laird 1976:31), and eagle feathers whose function remains unclear. O.C. Stewart (1942:315) also lists tobacco and paint as important accompaniments. Specilizations included the power to cure rattlesnake bites and wounds, control the weather, and aid in childbirth.

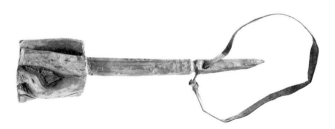

Smithsonian, Dept. of Anthr.: 14,447.
Fig. 11. Moapa "war club," a bludgeon made from a single piece of hardwood cut from the lower section of a tree trunk, after a Mohave style. The wrist thong is buckskin. Length 39 cm; collected by J.W. Powell, 1873.

Games

Games were a major diversion (fig. 9), and in some (hand game, four-stick game) the participants sang. Gambling was associated chiefly with the hand game, but bets were laid on the hidden-object and four-stick games, shinny, and hoop-and-pole game. Beads, Hopi shirts, horses, and local products were wagered. Games were played between various groups and with non-Paiute neighbors. Target games were "best . . . because you can't cheat" (Kelly 1932–1933).

Of the four-stick game (Culin 1907:327–335), there were 8- and 12-stick variants. Games of chance included stick or cane dice and women's basket dice. Probably all Southern Paiute played ring and pin, usually with a rabbit skull, but the Chemehuevi and Las Vegas speared disks of pumpkin rind (see Culin 1907:528 for Pima and Mohave).

In addition to the field games, there was competitive kicking of two balls of stone or buckskin over a course about a mile long. These were reported only by the Chemehuevi, and Mohave influence is likely.

For children, there were target games and races. Youngsters made clay dolls and painted figures on the inner bark of juniper (Kelly 1964:pl. 6). The wooden bull-roarer was a boy's toy; one of mountain-sheep horn was associated with wind, storm, and the mountain-sheep dreamer.

Ceremonies

The Mourning ceremony or Cry (*yakappi*) (called also Burning and Powwow) is presumably related to that of southern California. Nevertheless, the Chemehuevi and Las Vegas people declared that "we always had it." The Kaibab group related that Coyote held the first Cry (Sapir 1930–1931,2:347), but the Chemehuevi said that the Locusts(?) (usíwanabi) were the originators, although Coyote gave specifications for the "orator's" headdress. Associated songs were in part traditional, taught only to family members; in part, they were dreamt and evidently related to the southern California song series. Associated speeches, probably recitative, were unintelligible to many (Sapir 1910a:455, 468). According to one account, a visiting Mohave introduced the Cry to the Moapa people, whose two associated songs were clearly in the Mohave language; a late extension eastward, spread chiefly by the Moapa and Saint George people, has been discussed by Sapir (1912).

Prosperous relatives of a deceased person sponsored a Cry "to save themselves"; otherwise they could not eat or sleep well. The Cry occurred from three months to a year after the death of a relative. The outlay for food and goods was enormous, hence such ceremonies were infrequent. Several families who had lost members since the last Cry might cooperate. Invitations were sent by knotted cord or a bundle of small sticks. Specimens for the ceremonial burning were accumulated over a period of time by families involved. Buckskins, eagle feathers, weapons, rabbitskin blankets, nets, and baskets were destroyed. By the 1930s, objects destroyed were primarily baskets made for the occasion. By the 1970s, the Cry and the funeral were often combined, at least among the Chemehuevi (Laird 1976:246). The Southern Paiute Cry did not involve the burning of effigies or sham battles as among Yuman groups (Kroeber 1959).

The Ghost Dance of 1870 did not touch the Southern Paiute, although that of the 1890s affected some groups. The data suggest an essentially western and northwestern distribution (Chemehuevi, Las Vegas, Moapa, Panaca, Pahranagat); on Walapai evidence, the Saint George had the dance in 1889 (Kroeber 1935a:198). For the central groups there is no specific information. Kaibab people disclaimed knowledge of the Ghost Dance although, years before, Sapir obtained a detailed account from Tony Tillohash, a Kaibab, who must have been a very small boy when he viewed the gathering he described (Kelly 1964:106–107). Absence of the dance among the Kaibab, Shivwits, and San Juan is attested by O.C. Stewart (1942:322), who reports it for the Antarianunts, who received the dance from the Ute.

In the west, the first group affected was the Panaca. Pahranagat and Moapa people went to Panaca country to observe procedures; there they learned the songs and returned home to organize their own dances. The Moapa constituted a second center of dispersal and both directly and indirectly were the source of the Ghost Dance among the Chemehuevi and Las Vegas.

Certain songs came with the Ghost Dance and, through dreams, supplementary local ones were added. Emphasis was on the return of dead relatives; songs contained messages from the dead but seem also to have followed the pattern of naming geographical features.

The Round Dance (dialectally *nikkappi* and *kiyappi*) (called also harvest, pine nut, rabbit, or squaw dance) was fundamental, and the War-incitement, Scalp, and Ghost dances had the same formation ("Music," fig. 5, this vol.). Typically, men and women, especially young people, alternated in a circle, each facing inward, arms linked (interlocking fingers considered "new style"; Saint George), and moved clockwise (Kelly 1964:104–106). Men—seldom women—took turns singing, without accompaniment.

There seem to have been Deer and Mountain-sheep songs of two kinds, one for diversion and one for success in the chase, although this may hold for Chemehuevi and Las Vegas only (cf. Laird 1976:11ff.). After a run of bad luck, hunters asked a game dreamer to sing. They gathered at night, ate, then formed an incomplete circle about the singer, the men in an arc on the east, the women, on the west. Each hunter laid his bow across his belly, holding it in place with his arms, which hung down and forward, fingers turned inward, to simulate hooves. In this position, men and women marked time and, at the conclusion, the dreamer-singer directed them to a spot where they would find game. The Moapa are said to have copied the Las Vegas dance for mountain sheep, but "they jumped around, imitating sheep." The Pahranagat and Shivwits sang to attract sheep, but there is no description of a related dance (Kelly 1932–1933).

These seem to be all the dances that might be considered Southern Paiute, but within memory of individuals in the 1930s several intrusive dances have been adopted. In the early 1900s, the Ute Bear Dance reached the Kaibab (Sapir 1930–1931,2:473; Kelly 1964:107–112), whence it spread westward to the Moapa and beyond (W.Z. Park 1941).

Another noncircle dance (manakɨpɨ, mankɨpɨ) apparently reached the Moapa, Panaca, and Pahranagat from the Western Shoshone. A woman sang, accompanied by two men, each with a pair of sticks approximating a split-stick rattle, while two girls, each with a burden basket on her back, danced between the two lines of men. The men were expected to deposit beads or coins in the baskets, and contributions were divided among the performers.

Possibly of the same provenience was a dance accompanying the Prophecy song (kotóubiabɨ; cf. *upiapɨ* 'song'). Again, two women danced between two lines of men. The chief singer was male and held a near split-stick rattle. During the performance he "dropped dead and traveled" afar; upon recovery, he related events transpiring "there."

There are scraps of information concerning other dances. A Turkey Dance, thought to be Ute, was known but seldom performed (Cedar, Shivwits; O.C. Stewart 1942:349). Something (else?) called a War Dance was taken over 10–20 years prior to 1932 by the Pahranagat from the Shoshone. It began with a mock fight between the dance sponsor and an opponent he had selected as "quick and active." They approached one another, shooting arrows; when they met, all present joined in a Round Dance. Ties with mourning are confusing; the sponsor wanted to "free" himself after his wife's death, and elderly women who had lost relatives scattered food and "all cried and cried" (Kelly 1932–1933).

Art and Music

Aesthetic expression focused on song, recitative, and folk tales. Graphic art was almost nonexistent. The Chemehuevi and Las Vegas alone painted simple motifs on some of their pots. Other groups spoke admiringly of Moapa basketry.

Unfortunately, no one has continued the study of song recitative, so promisingly launched by Sapir (1910a). Information concerning songs is uneven, and most applies to the westerly groups, where southern California influence was strong. As a consequence, themes centered on travels, with the naming of places, natural phenomena, and animals, and with no action save the journey itself. Of this type were the following songs: Funereal, Deer and Mountain sheep, Bird, Salt, Quail, and Coyote (Laird 1976:11). Songs associated with some of the introduced dances may have followed other patterns. Nothing is known of shamans' songs nor of those sung during games.

Most songs were derived from dreams, and this holds even for the Kaibab, remote from southern California. Shamans dreamt the songs provided by their tutelaries. Some of the Round Dance songs were learned but new ones, dream-inspired, were added (Kelly 1964:106). Deer and Mountain-sheep singers dreamed of killing game; of deer food, such as "grass and bitter stuff," of foods eaten by mountain sheep; of rocky country. A sheep singer also dreamed of rain, quail caps and bull-roarers, of a bow and arrows, the arrows turning into male mountain sheep. Women learned game songs but never dreamed them.

For a dying person, those present tried to sing his own songs; if he had none, the Salt song was suitable. Funereal songs, both dreamed, were two: the ampau-biabɨ (cf. *ampaka-* 'to talk', *upiapi* 'song'), in part recitative, and the ampagapɨ ubiabɨ (cf. *ampakappi* 'sound of talking', *upiapi* 'song'), wholly so. These were reserved for burials (presumably also cremations) and the Cry (Chemehuevi, Las Vegas, Moapa).

Some remarked that the Chemehuevi–Las Vegas people had but four songs: Bird, Salt, Deer, and Mountain sheep. Of these, the first two were not dreamed. All songs could be learned from a relative, but the last two had to be validated, so to speak, through dreams. These came unsolicited or could be sought by spending the night alone in certain caves (Laird 1976:38).

In addition to these four songs, there was a Quail song (Chemehuevi, not Las Vegas); a Coyote song (Las Vegas, not Chemehuevi), and a Prophecy song. Songs were borrowed freely. The Bear Dance song was in Ute; the Cry songs, partly in Mohave, as was the Salt song; the Bird and Quail songs in Cahuilla (cf. Laird 1976:19). The Coyote song was in Southern Paiute, but certain individuals thought it had been translated from either Vanyume or Cahuilla.

Traditionally, the Southern Paiute had no musical instruments. None was used with the Round Dance nor with the Deer and Mountain sheep songs. The flageolet—a length of elder with the pith removed—was mentioned by the Chemehuevi, Las Vegas, and Pahranagat. Young boys played for pleasure, and there was no notion of love songs.

The rasp was introduced with the Bear Dance; and an approximation of the split-stick rattle with the manakɨpɨ Dance and Prophecy song (cf. Steward 1941:251). Two sticks were knocked together to keep time, but on high notes both were held in the same hand and shaken. The basket drum came from the Cahuilla with the Quail song. A gourd rattle was used with Bird, Salt, and Coyote songs and spread eastward to the Kaibab in association with the Cry. A woman did not use the rattle.

World View and Mythology

Little is known of Southern Paiute world view, but one individual (Chemehuevi–Las Vegas) volunteered his idea of the universe (Kelly 1932–1933): "The world is round, like a basketball; thus it was in the beginning. It turns to the west; this is the way Coyote started to turn it. It floats in the air but is attached by a heavy cord to another earth . . . . if it should break, we'd all be dumped off. The ocean belongs to the earth too, but it is separate; there is more ocean than land." This description is supplemented by data from Southern Paiute tales, contained in Fowler and Fowler (1971), Kroeber (1908a), Laird (1976, 1984), Lowie (1924a), and Sapir (1930–1931). Various tales refer to the time "when the world was young." Then Coyote and other animals had human attributes, and even Wood, Water, and Salt were anthropomorphized. Coyote (*sinamapi*, dialectally *sinawapi*) and his elder brother Wolf (*tipaci*) were the protagonists, but the former had the more prominant role.

There seems to have been no outright creation story. Primeval water was mentioned (Chemehuevi, Moapa), also continuous daylight. Indirectly, through Wolf's "medicine," night came into being. There seems to be no account of the origin of the sun, but several concern the moon. Animals were made of mud and were named by Coyote. He bungled, in a sort of Pandora's-box episode, and thus established tribal and linguistic diversity (Chemehuevi, Kaibab, Moapa, Pahranagat, Shivwits) (Kroeber 1908a:240).

Coyote—trickster and seducer of women—was unable to think for himself and consulted his tail (Chemehuevi, Kaibab, Moapa) or another part of his body. Yet he stole fire for the benefit of mankind (Kaibab, Moapa, Shivwits) and he, or he and Wolf, were instrumental in introducing agriculture. Among Coyote's other contributions were the establishment of menstrual and birth customs; of game restrictions for boys; of food offerings to the four directions, so as to avoid illness referable to ghosts. He showed the people how to tie the bowstring, to make pottery, to make a buckskin dress. He and his family and other figures were linked to the identification of constellations (see "Oral Tradition: Content and Style of Verbal Arts," this vol.).

Many women knew the tales, but men were the narrators. Of an evening during the winter months (to recite tales in summer might result in snakebite) the traditional stories were related (Kelly 1964:120). Often they involved mimicry, song, and participation of various persons. Powell (Fowler and Fowler 1971:73) was sufficiently discerning to note the importance of such recitals in the transmission of social norms, and it is clear that they so functioned. These and other aspects of the oral tradition also related people to their territories and to the subsistence resources contained therein. They set the tone for precontact socioeconomic life.

Prehistory

Archeological manifestations of the Southern Paiute, principally in the form of brownware pottery and certain types of twined basketry, are in evidence in the western part of the region no earlier than A.D. 1000 to 1200. This suggests a rather late movement of these peoples into their present territory, coincident with the proposed spread of other Numic-speaking peoples into the rest of the Great Basin ("Numic Languages," this vol.). Gunnerson (1962b), Euler (1964), Madsen (1975), and C.S. Fowler and D.D. Fowler (1981) provide reviews of various theories of movement.

History

The Spanish *entrada* into the Southwest, beginning in the 1540s, seems to have had little direct impact on the Southern Paiute and Chemehuevi for roughly 250 years. Undoubtedly, there were indirect impacts, and the people were probably aware of the presence of the Spaniards long before actual contact. Through the Ute and Navajo, who were in close proximity to Spanish settlements in the seventeenth and eighteenth centuries, the Southern Paiute probably learned of their presence and may have acquired a few items of their material culture. Spanish-introduced diseases may also have preceded actual contact (C.S. Fowler and D.D. Fowler 1981:150). However, when in 1776 the Spanish priests Francisco T.H. Garcés, Francisco Atanasio Domínguez, and Escalante documented the first direct contacts with the Southern Paiute, they noted little evidence of any foreign presence among them (Coues 1900; Bolton 1950). They described instead what were largely aboriginal conditions (Euler 1966:32–38).

By the early nineteenth century, Spanish impacts on the Southern Paiute were more direct and devastating. The Spanish colonies of what are now northern New Mexico and southern California had institutionalized slavery and other forms of servitude. Based on extensive archival research into early Spanish documents, Brugge (1968) has suggested that Southern Paiutes may have been slaves in Santa Fe and outlying communities as early as the late 1700s. Certainly by 1810 their presence is documented, with persons specifically identified

as Paiutes being baptized in the Spanish settlements on the upper Rio Grande (Brugge 1968:19). Ute and Navajo slave raiders, as well as in later periods Spanish expeditions and American trappers were the sources of most if not all of these individuals (Malouf and Malouf 1945). The Southern Paiute were in the unfortunate position of being between Ute raiders on the north and east and Navajos on the south. They were also astride a portion of the Old Spanish Trail, which opened to commerce in the 1830s and became a route for slaving activities. In 1839, the trader Farnham (1843:11) reported that "Piutes" were: "hunted in the spring of the year, when weak and helpless, by a certain class of men, and when taken, are fattened, carried to Santa Fe and sold as slaves during their minority. 'A likely girl' in her teens brings often-times £60 or £80. The males are valued less." Captives were also sold at settlements in southern California, being transported there by Ute captors or sold to traffickers on the Old Spanish Trail. The first record of a baptism in California of a person definitely identified as a Paiute is dated 1844 and took place in Los Angeles (Smith and Walker 1965:11–14).

Although it is difficult to assess the total impact of the slave trade on the Southern Paiutes, certain effects seem probable. Euler (1966:46ff.) has suggested that several historic documents noting the total absence of Southern Paiutes from some ecologically favorable but heavily traveled areas within their territory in the 1830s and 1840s may reflect a fear of slavers. He also notes that reports of open aggression and hostility by some Southern Paiutes in the 1840s may show last-ditch efforts against the traffickers (Euler 1966:47). This behavior is in marked contrast to the nonwarlike temperament reported for the Southern Paiute in the precontact period. The slave trade also seems to have led to population depletion for the Southern Paiutes. The Indian agent Garland Hurt (1876:462) noted that prior to 1860, because of the slave traffic, "scarcely one-half of the Py-eed children are permitted to grow up in a band; and a large majority of these being males, this and other causes are tending to depopulate their bands very rapidly." And slave raiding may have inhibited the expansion of Southern Paiute horticulture in the early postcontact period, again by forcing people from favorable ecological settings (C.S. Fowler and D.D. Fowler 1981:151).

Whatever its effects, slave raiding on the Southern Paiutes came to an end soon after the advent of the Mormons into northern Utah in 1847. Initially, the Mormons became unwilling participants in the trade, purchasing Indian children from the Utes who threatened to kill the children if the Mormons did not buy them. But active measures by Brigham Young and the territorial legislature ultimately ended the trade by the mid-1850s (Malouf 1966:14).

However, the positive effects for the Southern Paiute

of ending the slave trade were soon offset by the negative effects of a permanent Morman presence. The decade of the 1850s was a settling-in period for the Mormons in much of Utah. By 1855, there were several Mormon communities within the territory of the Cedar people and a mission among the Moapa and Las Vegas. By the mid-1860s, there were also settlements among the Shivwits, Panaca, Beaver, Kaibab, Panguitch, and Uinkaret (Inter-Tribal Council of Nevada 1976:83). Non-Mormon miners and traders were on most of the Colorado River within the territory of the Chemehuevi (Roth 1976:101). Mormon settlements and farms, in particular, displaced Southern Paiutes from their best gathering and horticultural lands. Before long, traditional food supplies throughout the region were further depleted by livestock, timbering, and other activities.

Some Southern Paiutes, particularly those with horses, retaliated by raiding settlements and travelers during the late 1850s and the 1860s. Navajos added to the settlers' problems by raiding them as well. Some Chemehuevis, alone or with Mohave allies, raided miners in northern Arizona and travelers along southern California desert trails from the 1850s to the early 1870s. In the middle and late 1860s the Chemehuevi were also engaged in war against the Mohave, a conflict that was not settled until 1871 (Roth 1976:111). In short, throughout the region sporadic troubles were continually reported during the first two decades after settlement (Euler 1966:67ff.). But for southern Utah, at least, major confrontations were prevented by the activities of Mormon missionaries among the Southern Paiute. Most notably, Jacob Hamblin, "the Buckskin Apostle," averted several serious confrontations through his considerable powers of persuasion and compromise (Little 1966; Inter-Tribal Council of Nevada 1976:83ff.).

Apart from some of the official and quite favorable policies toward Utah Indians by Brigham Young, individual Mormon and non-Mormon settlers held varying opinions about the Southern Paiute quite in keeping with general American views of the period. These ranged from common stereotypes about laziness and stealing to positive attitudes noting their basic industry, intelligence, and educability (Euler 1966:64). Many felt that although Indians were basically "savages," they could and should be taught "civilized" ways (Euler 1966:61). Few Whites advocated a policy of direct integration of the two cultures, as they were held to be too distinct and separate. Mormon ideology regarding the origin and identity of the Indians as descendants of the Lost Tribes of Israel generally was responsible for some favorable attitudes and policies toward them, but it may also have been a contributing factor in maintaining a degree of social distance between the groups (C.S. Fowler and D.D. Fowler 1971:107–108).

By the 1870s most Southern Paiutes had been under some form of direct and sustained contact with settlers for at least a decade. Some groups had responded by forming larger and more stable residence units in proximity to the towns. Here they attempted to combine aspects of aboriginal subsistence with menial labor and other pursuits. Some groups had spokesmen who acted as go-betweens with the settlers. Some of these were individuals who might have been chosen local headmen by former procedures; others were those who learned a little English early; and yet others were chosen by the Whites (Euler 1966:66). By the 1870s as well, most groups had various items of non-Indian manufacture, including metal-tipped arrows, iron and brass buckets, pans, and cast-off clothing from the settlements (C.S. Fowler and D.D. Fowler 1971; Fowler and Matley 1979:10; Euler 1966:115). Some individuals had been baptized Mormons ("Euro-American Impact Before 1870," fig. 6, this vol.), or were otherwise Christianized, although the ideological impact was probably slight. Loanwords from English were added to earlier loans from Spanish and the process of linguistic accommodation had begun (C.S. Fowler and D.D. Fowler 1981:152).

The Reservation Period

During the mid-1860s, as troubles escalated in various Southern Paiute areas, some thought was given by the federal government to confining the Southern Paiutes to reservations. In 1865, Utah Superintendent of Indian Affairs O.H. Irish suggested that problems in southern Utah and southern Nevada might best be solved by removing the Southern Paiute to the Uintah Reservation in northeastern Utah. In September 1865 Irish negotiated the Treaty of Spanish Fork with six Southern Paiutes (proportedly headmen) by which the "Pi-ede and Pah-Ute bands of Indians" would relinquish all "right of occupancy in and to all of the lands heretofore claimed and all occupied by them . . . within the defined borders of the Territory of Utah" (Irish 1865:1). In exchange for their lands, the Southern Paiute would be given instruction in farming and the equipment and supplies. Although six individuals signed the document on behalf of the Southern Paiutes, no one actually moved to Uintah. Fear of the Ute, their old enemies in the slaving days, was cited as the general reason; but attachment to their homelands was also a factor. The treaty was never ratified, thus making the proposal even less tenable (Inter-Tribal Council of Nevada 1976:87).

In 1869 the first local agent for the Southern Paiute, R.N. Fenton, was appointed through the Nevada superintendency of Indian affairs. He immediately recommended that a reservation be "located on the Upper Muddy [river] in Nevada, about 25 or 35 miles above this point [St. Thomas], containing from 700–1000 acres of fine farming land, also a good range for stock" (Fenton 1869:646). On it would be settled all the Southern

Paiute of southern Utah, Arizona, Nevada, and California. In 1872 President Ulysses S. Grant issued an executive order establishing a reservation of approximately 3,900 square miles. The Moapa were the first to settle on Moapa Reservation. Few others followed.

In 1873 the commissioner of Indian affairs sent a special commission to Utah and Nevada to look into certain Indian matters, especially suggestions for removing Indians to areas away from the settlements. This commission was headed by John Wesley Powell, famed Colorado River explorer who was well acquainted with the Southern Paiute, and George W. Ingalls, then Indian agent for southern Nevada (fig. 12). Their report consisted of a summary of conditions, a census of Indian "tribes," and recommendations for removal of the Indians to reservations. They initially proposed that the Southern Paiute be sent to Uintah, but on reconsidering the question of Southern Paiute–Ute emnity, suggested instead that they be sent to Moapa. They further suggested that the Moapa Reservation be expanded to provide more farmland and access to timber (Powell and Ingalls in ARCIA 1874:20). This recommendation was followed, and on February 12,1874, President Grant issued an executive order expanding the reservation boundary 8 miles to the east and 20 miles to the west. The Utah Southern Paiute reluctantly agreed to move to Moapa, on condition that they be given sufficient aid to establish themselves. The commissioners recommended specific amounts for this purpose as well as to buy out White farmers who controlled some of the best lands in the district and most of the water. These appropriations were not forthcoming in proportion and after a year only a few Utah Southern Paiutes had actually moved there. Agitation from the settlers in the area further complicated the issue, and in 1875 the reservation was reduced to 1,000 acres. From that time until after 1900 conditions at Moapa Reservation deteriorated, until very few people remained (Inter-Tribal Council of Nevada 1976:97ff.).

Farther south, on the Colorado River, similar abortive efforts were made to settle the Chemehuevi on the Colorado River Reservation, to which a specific piece was added for the purpose in 1874 (Roth 1976:146). However, periodic conflicts with the Mohave who also resided there were a factor in Chemehuevi reluctance to move to this location. Although there were several forced as well as peaceful removals of various Chemehuevi groups to the Colorado River Reservation through the years, it was not until the nineteenth century and early twentieth century that many Chemehuevi agreed to reside there. They preferred to remain in their historic locations near Blythe, Needles, Beaver Lake, and in Chemehuevi Valley. In these places, they had combined wage work, agriculture, some mining, and wood cutting along with traditional hunting toward a good adjustment (Roth 1976:114, 124). However,

Smithsonian, NAA: 1662-A.

Fig. 12. Council with the Southern Paiutes near St. George, Utah. John Wesley Powell (standing at left) was sent out to look into the "conditions and wants" of the Utah and Nevada Indians. George W. Ingalls and Powell spent the summer and autumn of 1873 traveling and investigating (Powell and Ingalls in ARCIA 1874). In addition Powell used this visit to collect much ethnographic and linguistic information, which is preserved in the Smithsonian's National Anthropological Archives. Photograph by John K. Hillers, Sept. 1873.

changes in government policies toward consolidation of Indian populations and allotment of lands finally forced the issue. During the war between the Chemehuevi and the Mohave from 1865 to1871, some Chemehuevi also took refuge among the Cahuilla near Banning and the Serrano at Twenty-Nine Palms. After 1911, the population at Twenty-Nine Palms was consolidated with that near Banning on the Morongo Reservation (Roth 1976:111).

Meanwhile, the situation in southern Utah continued to deteriorate. It is quite clear that after failing to induce the people to go to Moapa, the federal government felt little further obligation to provide the Southern Paiute with aid. For the next several years, people in and around Saint George, Utah, attempted with some help from the Mormons to remain in their old districts. A few also moved south into the Arizona Strip in one last attempt at aboriginal subsistence. Yet others went north to farms and ranches around Cedar City for wage work. People around Kanab, Utah (the aboriginal Kaibab), were in the same situation, and despite repeated appeals to the federal government from the local citizenry, little help was forthcoming. The government still believed that removal to Moapa or Uintah was the only answer (C.S. Fowler and D.D. Fowler 1971:110–111).

In the late 1880s, Anthony W. Ivins, prominent rancher in southwestern Utah, succeeded in obtaining a federal appropriation to remove the Shivwits from their lands on the Arizona Strip to a new location on the Santa Clara River just west of Saint George. This move set up the first Southern Paiute reservation in Utah, the Shivwits Reservation. In addition to the Shivwits people, those from Gunlock, Saint George, and the Uinkaret areas also moved there in 1891, although the land was not officially federal property until 1903 (Inter-Tribal Council of Nevada 1976:114). Ivins established a school and bought teams, wagons, and farming tools with the remaining federal monies. The government took little direct interest beyond operating the school.

In 1916 and again in 1937, the Shivwits Reservation was expanded to ultimately contain 28,160 acres (Inter-Tribal Council of Nevada 1976:117). At various times it was administered out of the Deep Creek and Uintah-Ouray reservations, which caused problems because of distance. It was apparently never sufficient in land base and resources to meet the needs of the people. It was reported that only 85 of the 28,160 acres were considered suitable for homesites and tillage (U.S. Congress 1954:13). This plus repeated conflicts over water and cattle trespasses forced many people to seek wage work off the reservation. Gradually the population dwindled, with Shivwits families moving to Enterprise, Saint George, Cedar City, Moapa, and elsewhere.

Between 1870 and 1900, the Kaibab population was able to depend less and less on native subsistence and thus moved into proximity of the Mormon settlement of Kanab, Utah. Several families also settled at Moccasin Spring 25 miles southwest of Kanab. Around 1900, the Mormon Church at Kanab obtained the rights to one-third of the flow of Moccasin Spring for the Kaibab, and a small farm was started. In 1907 the Kaibab Reservation of roughly 20,000 acres was established by executive order at that place. A day school was begun, an irrigation system installed, and several buildings constructed. The land base was expanded in 1913 and again in 1917 to include 120,413 acres (Euler 1972:82, 92; Farrow 1930:58). The day school was maintained into the 1930s. A fairly successful cooperative cattle business was under way by 1930 (Farrow 1930:58).

Other Southern Paiute reservations were established late as well: the Chemehuevi Reservation, in Chemehuevi Valley on the Colorado River north of Parker, Arizona, in 1907; the Las Vegas Colony, near the city of Las Vegas, Nevada, in 1911; the Indian Peaks Reservation (primarily Beaver, Cedar, Panaca), northwest of Cedar City, Utah, in 1915; the Koosharem Reservation (Panguitch, northern Kaibab, Kaiparowits) east of Ritchfield, Utah, in 1928; and the Kanosh Reservation (Beaver, Pahvant Ute) near Kanosh, Utah, in 1929 (U.S. Congress 1954). Land bases for each varied, but none was large enough to support the population by agriculture, the subsistence enterprise preferred by the federal government. In addition, in 1899 and again in 1925, federal funds were appropriated to purchase land for Southern Paiutes at Cedar City. However, the funds were not expended for this purpose because the Mormon Church had already purchased 10 acres on the outskirts of town and established the people there. A rancher at Richfield, Utah, had also allowed people to settle on a small tract of his land near that town, and the Mormon Church had constructed some houses and other community facilities there (L.M. Hill 1968:8). These two "villages" along with the federal reservations thus became the permanent locations available to the various Southern Paiute groups in the region after aboriginal land reduction. A few individuals continued to reside at other locations, but without federal sponsorship or assistance.

Utah State Histl. Soc., Salt Lake City: 970.64 P.4.
Fig. 13. Wattle housing typical of the Shivwits, Moapa River, and Chemehuevi reservations in the 1930s. The girl is Nellie Snow and the toddler is Lucis John. Photograph by D.E. Beck, Shivwits Reservation, Utah, 1930s.

U. of Calif., Bancroft Lib., Berkeley: C. Hart Merriam Coll. 1978.8 misc. P. 17 #19.
Fig. 14. Hauling water, Kaibab Reservation, Ariz. Photograph by C. Hart Merriam, 1932.

Each village, colony, and reservation has a complicated history, usually involving more failures than successes in economic development (Inter-Tribal Council of Nevada 1976; Roth 1976; Euler 1972). A few families in Chemehuevi Valley, for example, had limited success in the cattle business until 1939 when Parker Dam was built and the bulk of their lands flooded (Roth 1976:172). Las Vegas Colony, lacking any significant land base, continued to be an urban settlement for people engaged in wage work in the nearby town. Troubles with its water system and access plagued the group well into the 1970s (Inter-Tribal Council of Nevada 1976:124ff., 1974:19). Indian Peaks Reservation had a small resident population supporting itself on gardens and with a few cattle for roughly 15 years, but lack of sufficient income ultimately sent families to other areas for wage work. By 1935 the reservation was largely abandoned. The people at Kanosh tried some cooperative farming, using a government loan for equipment and seed. However, by 1953, the supervisors reported that the Kanosh group was "hardly more than meeting expenses and interest, and is not building a backlog to retire their loan" (U.S. Congress. House. Committee on Interior and Insular Affairs 1954:87). By the mid-1950s, the entire Koosharem Reservation was being worked by two families, while the others had moved to the village at Richfield (U.S. Congress. House. Committee on Interior and Insular Affairs 1954:86). The Shivwits had also attempted to manage a small farm and livestock enterprise for several years but had gone farther into debt. Few of these groups had much more than token assistance over the years from resident and nonresident Indian agents or other federal officials. They were too small and too isolated to be of much concern.

Termination

In 1953 Congress passed House Concurrent Resolution 108, declaring that it was the policy of the government to terminate its trust responsibility over the Indian people of the United States. After hearings on the matter, but with little evidence that the action was fully understood or justified, four Southern Paiute reservations were terminated from federal control in 1954. These were Shivwits, Indian Peaks, Koosharem, and Kanosh reservations (U.S. Code 68 Stat. 1099–1104).

Although the official termination policy was first to establish the readiness and willingness of groups to assume the rights and duties of full U.S. citizenship (U.S. Congress 1954:8–9), it seems quite clear that in the Southern Paiute case this policy was not actually followed. Investigations prior to the termination hearings (U.S. Congress. House. Committee on Interior and Insular Affairs 1954) as well as the hearings themselves (U.S. Congress 1954) repeatedly reported that these groups were in exceedingly poor economic condition. The average per family income was one-third to one-half that estimated for non-Indian families in the same areas. Only a few families were self-supporting; most depended totally or partially on public or church assistance (O. Lewis 1954:8–9). Most lived in substandard housing, had low educational levels (English illiteracy averaged above 20%), lacked the skills to take advantage of any but minimal job opportunities, and showed little more than minimum participation in the broader social and economic activities of the surrounding non-Indian communities (U.S. Congress 1954:13–16; Witherspoon 1955; L.M. Hill 1968). Harry Gilmore, superintendent of the Uintah-Ouray Agency and special

left, State of Nev., Transportation Dept., Carson City; right, Natl. Arch.: 75–N–CARS–321–M–4.

Fig. 15. Harvesting and loading radishes, Moapa River Reservation, Nev., under a federally sponsored agricultural rehabilitation program. Photographs by Arthur Rothstein, 1940.

special investigator into the conditions of these groups, added that without special help the groups would probably lose their lands to taxation after termination (U.S. Congress. House. Committee on Interior and Insular Affairs 1954:432). Yet in spite of a demonstrated lack of readiness and some conflicting evidence as to willingness, federal control was terminated over 232 individuals and 44,530 acres of land, the act taking effect in 1957. The principal justification appears to have been the small size of the communities and the minimal federal involvement in their affairs to that time. The motivation of Utah Sen. Arthur Watkins, Chairman of the Subcommittee on Termination, in providing a demonstration case for this new federal policy has also been suggested (Jacobs 1974:22; Knack 1980:13).

Almost immediately the effects of termination were felt on the population. Termination made former trust lands liable to federal and state taxation. This posed an additional financial burden on people already unable to meet individual financial commitments. In 1956, a trust agreement was authorized by the secretary of the interior between Walker Bank and Trust in Salt Lake City and the terminated Southern Paiutes for supervision of tribal lands (Jacobs 1974:34). All lands other than those previously allotted or otherwise set aside for individual residences or other uses were included under the agreement. Immediately the bank negotiated leases with non-Indians for some of the lands, principally for grazing. As of 1967, leases for 26,680 acres of Shivwits land returned $2,075 per year, which after taxes provided each individual with $5 per year (L.M. Hill 1968:13). By 1968, less than one-half of the original Kanosh lands remained under Indian ownership. Over 2,000 acres had been parceled out to individuals who later sold or lost their holdings to non-Indians. Much of the remainder was leased to non-Indians, but the income was little over and above taxes. Approximately 400 acres of Koosharem holdings were returned to the people by the bank after a few years and were ultimately lost for nonpayment of taxes. The two remaining members of the reservation continued to make a living from their former allotments plus additional land purchases. The Indian Peaks band sold its reservation and used the money to establish members in Cedar City and other areas (L.M. Hill 1968:13). Under the terms of termination, tribal governments established under the Indian Reorganization Act of 1934 at Shivwits and Kanosh were disbanded. And the minimal medical, dental, and social services that the groups had been receiving were discontinued.

In conjunction with termination, the federal government entered into an agreement with the University of Utah for manpower training for eligible Southern Paiutes. A survey of conditions prior to initiation of the program indicated that very few individuals had ever been involved in technical training of any type (Witherspoon 1955). From 1956 to 1957, 12 individuals were enrolled at the Salt Lake Area Vocational School in programs of auto mechanics and repair, practical nursing, and cosmetology. None of the 12 completed the course of study (Osborn 1959:106), nor did any find employment in the field in which they were at least partially trained (Knack 1980:42). By all indications, termination had failed to improve the lives of many (if any) Southern Paiutes. In effect, it left them in worse condition than before.

Claims and Restoration

In 1957, the Southern Paiutes filed a suit with the Indian Claims Commission for compensation for their aboriginal lands. The Chemehuevi initially filed a separate action, but it was later combined with the Southern Paiute claim for the purposes of hearings and awards. In 1965, the Indian Claims Commission made its final judgment, awarding the groups $8,250,000 for roughly 29,935,000 acres (27¢ per acre). In 1968, a social and economic survey of the Southern Paiute of Utah was undertaken to suggest ways that the claims monies might be distributed. With little land base in which to invest, per capita payment seemed advisable for terminated groups. However, the study revealed that the economic situation of the Southern Paiutes since termination had not appreciably improved (table 1) and thus that the proposed $8,000 to $10,000 per person payments would likely be little more than a temporary windfall (L.M. Hill 1968).

In 1971, the terminated Southern Paiute without a remaining land base received $7,522 per capita in land claims monies (U.S. Code 82 Stat. 1147–1148). Funds for minor children were put in trust until they reached 21 years of age. Groups with a land base voted on various other plans of distribution. The Kaibab, for example, allocated 15 percent to per-capita distribution (slightly over $1,000 per person), an additional 15 percent to help families pay off past debts and make new purchases and the remaining 70 percent to tribal concerns (education, 10%; tribal enterprises, 35%; community development, 15%; and administration, 10%) (Euler 1972:94). The Moapa people put 60 percent of their award into a perpetual capital fund for improvements on the reservation and economic development (J. Mitchell 1979:2). Although the per-capita money went quickly for those in need, it did provide some funds for improved housing and living conditions. In addition, and at roughly the same time, the economic situation for many Southern Paiute families began to turn around because of a number of new federal programs and policies.

In the early 1970s, Southern Paiute reservation communities participated in successful self-help housing programs through Department of Housing and Urban

Table 1. Employment and Average Family Income for Terminated Southern Paiutes, 1968

	Shivwits	Kanosh	Koosharem	Indian Peaks	Cedar City	Totals
Full-time employees	18	8	2	4	9	41
Part-time employees	15	5	7	2	6	35
Unemployed	17	8	5	6	9	45
Unemployable	16	6	5	5	8	40
Number of families	50	21	14	12	24	121
Total income	$150,736	$61,194	$27,159	$26,576	$66,574	$332,239
Average per family	$ 3,015	$ 2,914	$ 1,940	$ 2,215	$ 2,744	$ 2,746

SOURCE: L.M. Hill 1968.

Development grants or other financing. The Kaibab, Moapa, and Colorado River Reservations were first, with Cedar City, Shivwits, Kanosh, Richfield, and Chemeheuvi reservations and colonies following. With new housing available, a number of families returned to reservations and villages.

On-reservation economic development has been aided since the early 1970s as well. In 1973, the Utah Southern Paiute received a large federal grant to build three multi-purpose complexes to house businesses and industries at Richfield, Cedar City, and Kanosh (fig. 16). Although not overly successful, the enterprises that have used these facilities have given the tribes some income. The Moapa Reservation has also had funds for a cooperative farm, leather goods business, and tomato greenhouses (J. Mitchell 1979). Again, although not wholly successful, the enterprises have aided tribal members in learning practical and managerial skills along with providing some tribal income. Other business ventures include a very successful smoke-shop at Las Vegas Colony and a boat landing and campground at Chemeheuvi Reservation. In the late 1970s, the Kaibab had started a cattle cooperative and had plans for a tourist center (Euler 1972; Stoffle, Last, and Evans 1979).

The most important single piece of legislation affecting the Southern Paiute is the Paiute Indian Tribe of Utah Restoration Act, signed into law in 1980 (U.S. Code 94 Stat. 317–322). Under this act, the Shivwits, Kanosh, Koosharem, and Indian Peaks groups were restored to federal trust relationships, and the Cedar City group, long under uncertain status, was confirmed as under trust. The act restored all federal services and benefits to these groups. And it proposed the acquisition of up to 15,000 acres in southwestern Utah as tribal lands (the latter in partial compensation for loss of lands by Koosharem, Kanosh, and Indian Peaks). By 1984 some lands had been acquired by Koosharem, Kanosh, Indian Peaks, and Cedar City, and a council representing all groups was headquartered in Cedar City. The San Juan group of Arizona, never officially recognized, were in 1983 petitioning the Federal Acknowledgement Program in the BIA for federal status (Pamela Bunte, personal communication 1983).

Many of the cultural traditions that were current in the aboriginal period and in the early phases of contact were remembered in the 1980s only by a few older individuals. A number of specific practices, such as shamanistic curing, or seclusion of women during childbirth or menstruation, were all but gone. Others, such as funeral observances, gaming, and vestiges of religious belief were still followed. Some traditional subsistence items were still sought, including game animals, pine nuts, and berries. A few natural medicines were still gathered and used. Native language skills varied from area to area, but in general, persons younger than 50 years of age had limited fluency. Some traditional visiting patterns were maintained, and spring and summer activities such as the Bear Dance, the Ute Sun Dance, and rodeos were well attended by Southern Paiutes. A few native artisans practiced traditional handicrafts, particularly beadwork. There have also been attempts at tribally managed cultural and language awareness programs (Benioh 1980).

In 1980 Southern Paiutes numbered 1,400, including 625 in Arizona, 124 Chemeheuvi in California, 339 in Nevada, and 312 in Utah (U.S. Bureau of Indian Affairs. Financial Management 1981).

Fig. 16. Cedar City tribal building under construction. The structure, a result of a federal grant to stimulate economic development, was occupied by various businesses until it became the headquarters of the Paiute Tribe of Utah in 1980. Photograph by Martha Knack, 1973.

392

Synonymy‡

The name Paiute is a modification of a form borrowed into English in the early nineteenth century, but its ultimate origin is uncertain.

The earliest attestation of any variant of Paiute may be in the name Yutas Payuchis located vaguely at the northern edge of New Mexico on some versions of the Nicolás de Lafora (1958) map ostensibly dated 1771. However, this name may reflect knowledge later than this date, as it is absent from the version that appears to be the original map of the Lafora series (no. 151 in C.I. Wheat 1957–1963, 1:87–89). The first definitely located and dated use was by Francisco Garcés, who recorded in 1776 that the Havasupai used a name he hispanicized as Payuches for some people living north of the Colorado River opposite them (Coues 1900, 2:351). Garcés used the spelling Payuchas in reporting information about these people from the Yavapai and Quechan (Coues 1900, 2:405, 434). A few months later in the same year the Domínguez-Escalante expedition learned of a group they called Payuchis, whose territory lay south of the Colorado River in the San Juan River area (Bolton 1950:226, 228; Miera y Pacheco in Josephy 1961:130–131). Escalante classified the Payuchis as one of five "provinces" of the "nation" of the Yutas ('Utes') and accordingly also uses the expression Yutas Payuchis ('Payuchi Ute'). Escalante classified the Indians in Southern Paiute territory north of the Colorado River as a distinct province called the Yutas Cobardes ('timid Ute') (Bolton 1950:227). Later Spanish sources also have a variant Payutas, showing contamination with Yutas.

The first English uses of any variant of the name Paiute are in letters by two trappers that were published in newspapers in 1827. On the Virgin River in 1826, Jedediah Smith encountered Indians whose name appears as Pa-Ulches and Pa Ulches (Dale 1918:188–189; D.L. Morgan 1953); this is presumably to be taken as Pa-Utches (Merriam 1955:160). D.T. Potts refers to the Pie-Utaws on the Sevier River in 1827 (Frost 1960:63). Like Spanish Payutas, Pie-Utaws reflects contamination by the name of the Ute, which was earlier Utah, spelled Utaw by Potts. Subsequently, when Ute replaced Utah as an ethnic name, Paiute (variously spelled) replaced Pie-Utaw (Pah-Utah, etc.). Merriam (1955:160–162) gives an extensive list of variants of these names, notably including Pah-Utes, Paiuches, Pa-utes, Pey-ute, Pieutes, Pi-u-chas, Piute, and a number of the type Pah-Edes, Pi-Edes, Pi-eeds, and Py-eeds, specifically for those of southern Utah.

Both Smith and Potts reported that the variants of Paiute they give were used as a self-designation by the Indians, and Sapir (1930–1931:610) obtained the

‡This synonymy was written by C.S. Fowler and Ives Goddard.

Southern Paiute form *payu·cimi* 'Paiute Indians'. However, this word has no clear derivation within Southern Paiute and is generally thought to be of non-Paiute origin. Similar forms are found in a number of other Indian languages as names for the Southern Paiute: Ute *payó·čI* (Givón 1979:159); Hopi *payóci* (Whorf 1936:1278), Third Mesa *páyowci* (Voegelin and Voegelin 1957:49); Navajo *Báyóodzin* (Young and Morgan 1980:967); Arizona Tewa *payuči* (Paul V. Kroskrity, communication to editors 1977); Jemez *pá·yíce* (Joe Sando, communication to editors 1978); Havasupai *payúč* (Leanne Hinton, communication to editors 1985). If the name is of non-Paiute origin, it is likely that the Southern Paiute knew that this is what other Indian groups called them and gave it to outsiders as the name for themselves for that reason. The early recordings and the Indian language forms make it clear that the name originally had nothing to do with the name of the Ute, and hence interpretations like 'water Ute' or 'true Ute' cannot be correct (Henshaw and Mooney in Hodge 1907–1910, 2:186). Paiute and other variants that contain forms of Ute are innovations that arose after a name resembling that used in the Indian languages had come into use in English (or Spanish).

The name Cuajala, applied to part of the Southern Paiute by Garcés in the expression Chemegué Cuajála (Coues 1900, 2:444), appears to be matched by Mohave *kohwáilče* '[Southern] Paiute' (Curtis 1907–1930, 2:114, normalized), 'Virgin River Paiute' (Kroeber in Hodge 1907–1910, 2:188).

Although the name Paiute was originally applied only to the Southern Paiute, as the exploration of the Great Basin proceeded it was extended to additional groups. The linguistic and geographical distinctness of these other groups, and hence the need to differentiate among them, was recognized at least by the mid-nineteenth century; some of these early attempts at differentiation are surveyed in the synonymy in "Northern Paiute" (this vol.).

Loew (1876:323) used "Southern Payutes" to differentiate vocabularies taken from people in southern Nevada from those in southern California (Owens Valley Paiute) and western Nevada (Northern Paiute). In the same year, Powers also referred to "Southern Paiute," but he used the term for the "Paiute of Inyo County, California [Owens Valley Paiute] and Southwestern Nevada," thus adding confusion (Fowler and Fowler 1970:135). By 1907 Kroeber (1907a:107) was speaking of "southern Paiute," as was Waterman (1911:14): "The southern or 'true' Paiutes." Kroeber (1907a:109) incorporated the Chemehuevi into his treatment, although their linguistic and cultural affinities had been recognized by Turner (1856:76). Sapir (1913) seems to have made capitalization of "Southern" official in his "Southern Paiute and Nahuatl," although apparently there was still enough confusion in the public and anthropological literature in 1920 for Merriam (1955:152)

393

to call for a standardization of the terms Northern Paiute and Southern Paiute (for him Piute) to end it. He noted as well additional problems with usages for the Owens Valley Paiute and Mono Lake Paiute as holdovers of the early historical literature (see synonymies in "Owens Valley Paiute" and "Northern Paiute," this vol.). Lowie (1924:193) distinguished between Paiute and Paviotso for the two major groupings, as had been proposed by Powell. But Kroeber (1925:593) adopted Southern Paiute (including Chemehuevi), a proposal followed by Kelly (1932–1933, 1934, 1964). The popular literature remains confused, with the unmodified term Paiute being used indiscriminately for the Northern Paiute, Owens Valley Paiute, and Southern Paiute peoples and their languages.

Besides the term *payuˑcimi*, whose status is uncertain, there is no inclusive self-designation in Southern Paiute other than the general noun *nimi* 'person, Indian', in some dialects perhaps *niwi;* another singular form is *niminci*, and the plural is *nimincimi* (Sapir 1930–1931:585–586).

Subgroups

The delimitation and naming of the 16 Southern Paiute subgroups in this chapter follows Kelly (1934), with the addition of the Antarianunts (O.C. Stewart 1942). Kelly (1934:550) felt that these were the primary "sub-groups, bands, or tribes if you like . . . dialectic units with political concomitants," though the nature of their political integration was never clearly documented, and the dialectal differences can no longer be confirmed. Powell (Powell and Ingalls in ARCIA 1874:50–51, 53; Fowler and Fowler 1971:104, 107) gave the names of 31 local groups (not including the Chemehuevi, mentioned separately), and Kelly gives a correlation between these groups and hers. Powell's names all appear as separate entries in Hodge (1907–1910), with suppression of his hyphens and accents and other minor changes, except for Kau-yaiˊ-chits, which was erroneously listed as a synonym of Cahuilla. W.R. Palmer (1933) maps and discusses many named groups; here only the names on his map are given. Not synonymized here are the modern Ute names for Southern Paiute groups given by O.C. Stewart (1942).

Antarianunts. The name of this group, near the Henry Mountains in Utah, is from O.C. Stewart (1942:239). It appears to be a Ute form, as it ends with a form of the Ute self-designation nunts, but the etymology is otherwise unknown. The Southern Paiute name is given by Kelly (1964:107, 144–145) as yantarii.

Beaver. This group is named after the town of Beaver, Utah. Their Southern Paiute name is *kʷiʔumpaˑcimi* 'kʷiʔu-spring people' (Sapir 1930–1931:598, 651), *kʷiʔu* being an edible root identified by Kelly (1934:558) as *Frasera speciosa;* equivalent are Kwi-umˊ-pus (Powell

and Ingalls in ARCIA 1874:50) and Qui-ump-uts (W.R. Palmer 1933). The translation 'bear river people' (Hodge 1907–1910,1:748) wrongly assumes a connection with *kʷiaci* 'grizzly bear' (Sapir 1930–1931:648). Palmer also puts in this area the Tu-roon-quints, Toy-ebe-its, "Indian Peak Tribe," and Pa-moki-abs.

Cedar. The name is taken from that of Cedar City, Utah. The Southern Paiute name for the group is *ankappaˑnukkicicimi* 'red-stream people' (Sapir 1930–1931:69, 590, 598), a reference to Coal Creek. Equivalent is Un-kaˊ-pa-Nu-kuintsˊ (Powell and Ingalls in ARCIA 1974:50). W.R. Palmer (1933) gives kumo-its and wahn-quints in this area, and farther south Tave-at-sooks and Toquer-ats. The Parowan Paiutes (near Parowan, Utah) are included in the Cedar group by Kelly (1934), but Palmer (1933) gives the "Pa-ra-goons & Pa-gu-its" as a composite group (cf. Panguitch, below). Sapir (1930–1931:597, 607) gives their name as *patukunancimi* 'Indians of Parowan Lake', based (irregularly) on the lake name *patuˑkanti*, and Pa-raˊ-guns was used by Powell and Ingalls (in ARCIA 1874:50). The people at Rush Lake Kelly puts in the Cedar group, but Palmer associates them with the Panguitch, giving their name as Pa-rup-its. Escalante gives the name of this group as Huascaris, also appearing as Hauscari (Bolton 1950:204, 227).

Chemehuevi. This name is not a self-designation but may be of Yuman origin. It was first used by Garcés, who learned it from his Mohave guides in 1776; he initially recorded it as Chemebet but generally uses the form Chemeguaba, other variants being Chemeguagua and Chemegué (Coues 1900, 1:219, 224, 2:353, 444). Garcés also used Chemegué in the names Chemegué Cuajála and Chemegué Sevínta for Southern Paiute groups to the north of the Chemehuevi (Coues 1900, 2:444; Kroeber 1925:593). In the twentieth century the Mohave form has been recorded as *čamowév* (Curtis 1907–1930, 2:114, normalized) and as *ʔačiˑmuˊéˑv*, literally 'those who do something with fish' (Pamela Munro, personal communication 1983). Translations that appear to be folk etymologies are 'all mixed up' (Laird 1976:3) and 'always moving around' and 'roadrunners' (C.S. Fowler 1970a). However, since Garcés's recordings do not match the Mohave forms very well, the exact historical filiation of the name remains open to question. Variant spellings are in Hodge (1907–1910, 1:242–243) and Merriam (1955:163–164).

A number of languages have names that resemble Chemehuevi: Cahuilla *čemewáva* (Seiler and Hioki 1979:29), a form that exactly matches Garcés's Chemeguaba; Havasupai *čmwav* (Leanne Hinton, communication to editors 1981); Quechan *camawéˑv* (Abraham M. Halpern, communication to editors 1985); Southern Paiute *cimmoayapi*, apparently a borrowed term (Sapir 1930–1931:700).

Powell reported täˊn-taˊwats, which he glossed

'southern men', as a Chemehuevi self-designation (in Hodge 1907–1910, 1:243), and he also recorded Las Vegas dialect tan-ta-waits 'people who live to the south' (Fowler and Fowler 1971:156); this name is found in the historical literature as Tantawait and in other spellings. Others have found this used for the Chemehuevi by more northerly Southern Paiute groups, such as those of Las Vegas and Moapa, and for the Las Vegas group by the Moapa (Lowie 1924:193, Kroeber 1925:595; Kelly 1932–1933). It is formed on a stem *tantipai-*, which in the Kaibab dialect means 'far west' and is used to refer to the Mohave (Sapir 1930–1931:665); probably the meaning should be taken as 'far down', in reference to the course of the Colorado River.

Other names used for the Chemehuevi include: Pima ah'alakát 'small bows' (ten Kate in Hodge 1907–1910, 1:242), Quechan mat-hat-e-vátch 'northerners' (Whipple in Hodge 1907–1910, 1:243), and Serrano Yu-akayam (Kroeber 1925:595).

Gunlock. The name of this group is from that of the town of Gunlock, Utah. W.R. Palmer (1933) gives their name as Ma-toosh-ats; this matches matisatï, a name used by the Saint George Paiute for the Gunlock group and by the Gunlock group for people to their northwest (Kelly 1934:552); see the entry for Panaca.

Kaibab. The group is named after the Kaibab Plateau in northern Arizona (Southern Paiute *kaipaʾpici*), as also in their self-designation *kaipaʾpicicimi* (Sapir 1930–1931:75, 118, 627). Variant recordings are Kaiʾ-vav-wits (Powell and Ingalls in ARCIA 1874:50), Kaibab-its (W.R. Palmer 1933), and Qaiвáвitc (Lowie 1924:193); Hodge (1907–1910, 1:641) used Kaibab. Another group, in Long Valley, was the *ankakkaniʾkacimi* 'red-cliff-base people' (Sapir 1930–1931:549, 631); other recordings are Un-ka-kaʾ-ni-guts (Powell and Ingalls in ARCIA 1874:50) and Unka-kanig-its (W.R. Palmer 1933). A third group, near Moccasin, Arizona, was called the Pa-spiʾ-kai-vats by Powell (Powell and Ingalls in ARCIA 1874:50), who wrongly located them near Toquerville, Utah; their name is based on *paʾcippikkaina* 'Moccasin Spring' (Sapir 1930–1931:597, 701). W.R. Palmer (1933) has Pa-spika-vats as a synonym of Unka-kanig-its. The people near Kanab, Utah, are the *kanatiʾcimi* 'Kanab people', whose name is based on that of Kanab Canyon; this is a modern name for the Kaibab group (Sapir 1930–1931:202, 472–473, 564, 629). Lowie (1924:193) recorded Qanáвi, probably derived from the English form of the place-name. W.R. Palmer (1933) also has the Timpe-sha-wa-gots-its in this district. The Pagampachis, who are associated with the Uinkarets in Escalante's narrative (Bolton 1950:220), seem to be placed, as the Paganpachi, on the east side of the Kaibab Plateau on Miera y Pacheco's map, but W.R. Palmer (1933:100) locates the Pa-gaump-ats west of the Uinkarets. The Ytimpabichis seem to be located in the northern part of this area (Escalante in Bolton 1950:227);

they appear on the map as Itimpachis (in Josephy 1961:130–131). Palmer also puts here the I-oo-gune-intz and Pa-epas.

Kaiparowits. The name is from that of the Kaiparowits Plateau, near Escalante, Utah. This is probably the group referred to as the "Escalante band of Paiutes" by Sapir (1930–1931:548–549).

Las Vegas. The name of this group is from that of Las Vegas, Nevada. Their Southern Paiute name is *nipakanticimi* 'people of Charleston Peak' (Sapir 1930–1931:586), given as Nu-aʾ-gun-tits by Powell (Powell and Ingalls in ARCIA 1874:50). Powell gives the names of 10 other groups in the area, most of which can be analyzed as based on nearby place-names: Pa-gaʾ-its, Kwi-enʾ-go-mats, Mo-vwiʾ-ats, No-gwats, Pa-roomʾ-pats, Mo-quats, Ho-kwaits, Tim-pa-shauʾ-wa-got-sits, Kau-yaiʾ-chits, Yaʾ-gats. The Pa-roomʾ-pats, Parumpats in Hodge (1907–1910, 2:204), are the Pahrump of Steward (1938:182–185); the Kau-yaiʾ-chits (at Ash Meadows) and Yaʾ-gats (Amargosa) were partly Western Shoshone (Steward 1938:93, 183).

Moapa. The group is named after the valley in southeastern Nevada. Sapir (1930–1931:572, 574–575) gives two Southern Paiute names that he glosses 'Muddy Creek Paiute', a reference to the same valley: *muappa*, pl. *muappacimi* (with no etymology), and *muʾtiʾci*, pl. *muʾtiʾcimi*, either based on the name for Muddy Creek, *muʾtiʾnukkinti* (literally 'bean stream'), or directly 'bean person (people)', in either case a reference to the raising of beans by the Indians. C.S. Fowler collected the place-name as [moɣʷaʾpaʾ] (Fowler and Fowler 1971:134). Powell gives the name of this group as Mo-a-pats (Fowler and Fowler 1971:161) and (assuming this is equivalent) Mo-a-pa-riʾ-ats, which is listed as being in the Moapa Valley together with the Sau-wonʾ-ti-ats, Nau-wanʾ-a-tats, Pinʾ-ti-ats, Pa-roomʾ-pai-ats, Iʾ [-]chu-arʾ-rum-pats, and U-tumʾ-pai-ats (Powell and Ingalls in ARCIA 1874:50). Lowie (1924:193) gives Moʾápa and Mu-ápötsⁿ, and W.R. Palmer (1933) has Moa-pariats, Pa-weap-its, and Tan-tib-oo-ats, a general term for the southern Nevada people used by Southern Paiutes farther north (see under Chemehuevi).

Pahranagat. This group is named after the Pahranagat Valley in Nevada. Their Southern Paiute name is *pataʾnikici*, taken to mean 'person who sticks his feet in the water', pl. *pataʾnikicimi* (Sapir 1930–1931:584, 597); Sapir refers to them as the "Corn Creek band of Paiutes," a label that seems to show confusion with the Pahvant Ute, the group actually on Corn Creek. Other renditions are Pa-ran-i-guts (Powell and Ingalls in ARCIA 1874:50) and Paranagats (W.R. Palmer 1933). Lowie (1924:193) says that this name ("Paránö, Put-foot-into-the-water") was formerly used by the Shivwits for Moapa; Kelly (1934:554) thought that Ingalls's (1913, 1:187) explanation of a connection with the word for watermelon might in fact reflect a possible connection with the word for pumpkin. Palmer records the alternate name Sau-wan-du-its, which seems to be the same as Powell's Sau-won´-ti-ats (see the entry for Moapa).

Panaca. The name is from that of Panaca, Nevada. Powell locates the Tsou-wa´ -ra-its in Meadow Valley in this area. W.R. Palmer (1933) names the group Ma-tis-ab-its, and Lowie (1924:193) confirms the application of such a name, reporting that the "ᵐᵃᶜtü´ sats . . . used to live near Panaka, from Enterprise, Utah, northward"; compare the discussion of Matisatï in the entry for Gunlock. Lowie also recorded the apparently directional expression tö´ intesà-ᵘ (cf. ti·in-'up') used by the Moapa for the people toward Caliente, Nevada (near Panaca).

Panguitch. The name of this group is taken from that of the town of Panguitch, Utah, and Panguitch Lake. In Southern Paiute they are *pakiucimi*, literally 'fish people', so named because of the abundance of fish in Panguitch Lake (*pakiupa* 'fish water') (Sapir 1930–1931:118, 638); the group name is the ultimate source of the English place-name. Other renderings are Pa-gu´-its (Powell and Ingalls in ARCIA 1874:50) and Pa-gu-its (W.R. Palmer 1933). Palmer also puts in this area the small As-sich-oots group and the Pa-rup-its of Rush Lake, but Kelly assigns Rush Lake to the Cedar area.

Saint George. This name is from that of the town of Saint George, Utah. Powell lists the U´ -ai-Nu-ints as being in the area (Powell and Ingalls in ARCIA 1874:50); elsewhere he glosses this name 'people who live by farming' and also gives the form U-en-u-wunts 'Santa Clara [River] Indians' (Fowler and Fowler 1971:156, 161). W.R. Palmer (1933:95) has the spellings U-an-nu-ince and U-ano-intz, with the same explanation, and the synonym Pa-roos-its; he gives Tono-quints as the name of a second group in this area. Pa-roos-its can be identified with Parussi, obtained by Escalante (Bolton 1950:205) for the Indians along the Virgin River, called *patusa* (phonetically [parúšA]) in Southern Paiute (Sapir 1930–1931:597, 689). According to Lowie (1924:193) Moapa and Shivwits Paiutes called the Saint George group suwü´ntsu and sü´вüts, apparently variants of the name of the Shivwits in the meaning 'eastern people' or 'upper people' (see Shivwits).

San Juan. This group is named after the San Juan River of northern Arizona. Powell gives their name as Kwai-an´ -ti-kwok-ets (Powell and Ingalls in ARCIA 1874:50); this appears to mean 'people being over on the opposite side', judging from the recording of a similar form in Sapir's (1910b) field notes, but this is not published in Sapir (1930–1931), and there are some problems in determining the correct phonemic Southern Paiute transcription. Sapir (1930–1931:685) gives the name of this group as *toi'oippicimi* 'San Juan River people'.

Shivwits. The name is that of the Shivwits Plateau in Arizona, which is based on the Southern Paiute name

for these people: *sipicimi* (Sapir 1930–1931:656). Other versions are Shi´-vwits (Powell and Ingalls in ARCIA 1874:50), She-bits (W.R. Palmer 1933), and Süвü´ts (Lowie 1924:193); Sapir used the English designation Sibit Paiutes. This name has no etymology in Kaibab Southern Paiute but may be based on an element that shows up as *sibi-* 'east' in Mono; compare Powell's gloss of Las Vegas Southern Paiute si-vints´ 'people who live to the east' (Fowler and Fowler 1971:156). It is possibly also to be seen in the name Sevinta, appearing in the labels Cajuala Sevinta and Chemegué Sevínta applied by Garcés (Coues 1900, 1:224, 2:444) to a group beyond the great bend of the Colorado River (where it runs between Nevada and Arizona). Palmer also locates in this area the Shin-ava and the Pa-gaump-ats (see under Kaibab).

Uinkaret. This name matches that of the Uinkaret Plateau in northwestern Arizona. The Southern Paiute name for this group is *yipinkatiticimi* 'people of Mt. Trumbull' (Sapir 1910b), which like Uinkaret is based on *yipinkatiti* 'Mt. Trumbull', literally 'ponderosa-pine peak' (Sapir 1930–1931:634, 725). Other recordings are Yubuincariris (Escalante in Bolton 1950:212, 227), U-in-ka´-rets (Powell and Ingalls in ARCIA 1874:50), and Uint-karits (W.R. Palmer 1933). Palmer also has the Timpe-ab-its in this area.

Sources

Ethnographic work among the Southern Paiute was begun in 1870 by John Wesley Powell, whose ethnographic and linguistic data, principally from the Kaibab, were edited and published by Fowler and Fowler (1971). In 1875 Edward Palmer worked briefly among the Shivwits; his notes were published by Heizer (1954). In 1910, based on extensive interviews with a single Kaibab individual, Edward Sapir made ethnographic notes (Sapir 1910b), analyzed the Southern Paiute language, and prepared texts and a dictionary (Sapir 1930–1931).

Robert H. Lowie worked briefly among the Moapa and Shivwits groups in 1914, making general observations (Lowie 1924) and collecting myths and tales (Lowie 1924a). In 1916 S.A. Barrett gathered a museum collection from these two groups.

The most comprehensive ethnographic work among the Southern Paiute, carried out by Isabel T. Kelly, 1932–1933, remains unpublished except for extensive data on the four eastern groups (Kaibab, San Juan, Kaiparowits, and Panguitch) (Kelly 1964) and overviews on group distributions and shamanism (Kelly 1934, 1936, 1939). Laird (1976) compiled notes on the Chemehuevi from 1919 to 1940.

In 1942 Omer Stewart provided culture element distributions for four groups (Antarianunts, Kaibab, Shivwits, and San Juan) (O.C. Stewart 1942). Drucker (1937, 1941) added like data for the Shivwits and Chemehuevi. Although lacking much synthesis, these studies provide needed detail for these groups.

Pertinent documentary sources toward a Southern Paiute ethnohistory were drawn together and analyzed by Euler (1966, 1972) and the Inter-Tribal Council of Nevada (1976). Roth (1976) did the same for the Chemehuevi while also providing an analysis of their interactions with the Mohave and other ethnic groups along the lower Colorado River. Knack (1980) gives important data and analyses of the socioeconomic conditions for the Utah Southern Paiute, especially since termination. Additional data on specific topics are found scattered in a diverse literature (see C.S. Fowler 1970; O.C. Stewart 1982).

Significant museum collections of Southern Paiute material culture include: the American Museum of Natural History, New York (I.T. Kelly and R.H. Lowie collections); Museum of New Mexico, Laboratory of Anthropology, and School of American Research Collections, Santa Fe, (I.T. Kelly collection); Lowie Museum of Anthropology, University of California, Berkeley (I.T. Kelly collection); Milwaukee Public Museum (S.A. Barrett collection); Peabody Museum, Harvard University (Edward Palmer and I.T. Kelly collections [the latter Chemehuevi only]); U.S. National Museum of Natural History, Smithsonian (Edward Palmer collection and the extensive J.W. Powell collection). A large Chemehuevi basket collection is located at the Colorado River Indian Tribes Museum near Parker, Arizona (Birdie Brown collection).

Kawaiisu

MAURICE L. ZIGMOND

Territory and Environment

The Kawaiisu (kə'wäyī͟,so͞o) in the *Handbook* are assigned to the Great Basin culture area, but, like their northern neighbors the Tubatulabal, they might also be considered Californian (Kroeber 1925:601). Their homeland straddles the southern end of the Sierra Nevada watershed generally regarded as a boundary line between the two culture areas, and their culture is related to both.

The core area of the Kawaiisu is located in California in the Sierra Nevada and the nearby Piute and Tehachapi mountains (fig. 1). Their habitat thus formed a low mountainous ridge between the Mojave Desert and the San Joaquin Valley. Explorers and missionaries traversed Kawaiisu territory while proceeding from the one to the other. Several passes, especially Tehachapi, Oak Creek, and Walker, provide natural routes through the region. In altitude, the terrain spans some 7,500 feet, from below the 1,000-foot level on the west (near the Kern River) to an elevation of 8,432 at the top of Piute peak. This broad differential accounts for a wide variety of fauna and flora. Twisselmann (1967) distinguishes among 17 "plant associations" in Kern County, California, which embraces the tribe's primary habitat. Forest, desert, and grassland were ready at hand, but forays were made into areas beyond for needed materials and certain foods not locally available.

The Kawaiisu were bordered to the north by the Tubatulabal, to the west by Southern Yokuts groups, and to the south by the Kitanemuk and Serrano, all California groups. The Kawaiisu were separated from the Chemehuevi and the Panamint by the desert to the east and northeast respectively. Steward (1938:84, figs. 1, 7) assigns the southern half of the Panamint and Death valleys to the Kawaiisu, but implies temporary rather than permanent residence: "The [Panamint] valley proper was so low. . .and so arid that the native population was extremely sparse. There is virtually no water in the valley where winter villages could have been located. The Panamint and Argus Ranges. . .had few residents." These observations find support in some recollections of Refugia Williams, a Kawaiisu, who remembered "spring migrations from the Piute Mountains across Indian Wells Valley to the Argus Range where

'surrounds' were made of antelope and mountain sheep" (Walker 1971:8).

A telling factor in determining the extent of the permanent settlement area is to be found in the basic food habits. The Kawaiisu were acorn eaters, and their usual habitat provided them with seven species of oak. There were other important nutritious floral resources, of course, but only a minor role was played by typical desert plants such as mesquite and screwbean. Some items necessitated travel, but such trips were followed by a return to the normal domicile. The concept of territory was weakly developed, and the idea of boundary was probably nonexistent. There was recognition of a home base, but knowledge of regions and resources far beyond indicates that the people moved about to satisfy their needs (Cappannari 1960:135). Conversely, other groups were not likely to meet with resistance when they came into the Kawaiisu homeland in quest of essential commodities. The characteristic shifting about in relation to the seasons makes it impossible to devise a static map of land occupation. The range of movement depended upon the availability of supplies and thus inevitably varied from year to year.

Language

Kawaiisu is the westernmost branch of the Southern Numic division of Uto-Aztecan. The division covers most of the Great Basin from the Kawaiisu homeland to central Colorado and western Wyoming, and there is remarkable uniformity of speech throughout. It has been widely held that the speech differences with Southern Numic are of the level of dialects (Sapir 1930–1931:5, 300). However, as Kawaiisu has become better known, there are some linguists (for example, Goss 1966:266) who classify it as a separate language.* The locus of origin and the age and spread of Southern Numic are the subject of debate. The area from which

*The phonemes of Kawaiisu (Zigmond 1981:6) are: (voiceless stops and affricates) *p, t, c, č, k, kʷ, ʔ;* (voiced stops) *b, d, g, gʷ;* (voiceless spirants) *s, š, h, hʷ;* (voiced spirants) *v, z, ž;* (tap) *r;* (nasals) *m, n;* (semivowels) *w, y;* (short vowels) *i, e, a, o, u, i;* (long vowels) *i·, e·, a·, o·, u·, i·.* In addition, *l* is found in loanwords. The voiced stops, voiced spirants, and tap are not found word-initially.

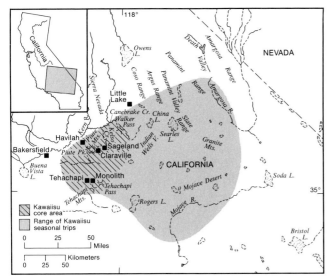

Fig. 1. Tribal territory.

both Proto-Numic and Southern Numic dispersed has been placed "in the vicinity of the southern Sierra Nevada, perhaps in the foothills above the Mojave Desert" (C.S. Fowler 1972:110), that is, in or near the Kawaiisu area. If this theory is valid, the Kawaiisu have been in the vicinity of their present location for at least 2,000 years. It should be noted that the Kawaiisu lack migration tales (Zigmond 1972:134). In historic times the tribe has been separated from other members of its linguistic division by the Mojave Desert and has been wedged between non-Numic speakers to the north (Tubatulabal) and south (Takic), and non–Uto-Aztecan speakers (Yokuts) to the west.

External Relations

Both modern consultants and the archeological evidence portray the Kawaiisu as friendly, peaceful people whose group conduct was not violent or warlike.

There were commodity exchanges with other tribes. Sources confirm that trade was carried on with the Western Shoshone of Little Lake from whom "obsidian and salt were procured in return for acorns" (Garfinkel, Schiffman, and McGuire 1979:49). An archeological site at Twin Oaks (near Loraine) contained obsidian and shell beads and "it would appear most likely that (the) obsidian was procured through trade, and not by direct acquisition, from either the Tubatulabal acting as middlemen or the Panamint-Shoshone in whose territory the Coso quarry is located" (Garfinkel and Schiffman 1981:128). The Southern Valley Yokuts traded local items for Kawaiisu acorns (Schiffman and Garfinkel 1981:2–3).

An intertribal game drive is mentioned by Latta (1949), who names as participants the Chumash, Yokuts, Tubatulabal, and Kawaiisu. Voegelin (1938:13) reports that once a year in July the Tubatulabal joined with the Kawaiisu, Chumash, and Yokuts for an antelope drive in Yokuts territory near Bakersfield. Such events would indicate intertribal friendliness and cooperation. At least one Kawaiisu consultant referred to hostility between the Kawaiisu and the Southern Yokuts though it is not clear whether this attitude was chronic or sporadic. There is a story about Kawaiisu hunters who descended into the San Joaquin Valley to join the Southern Yokuts in an antelope surround that ended in a fight between the participants (Zigmond 1936–1940, 1970–1974).

Culture

Subsistence

Agriculture was lacking in the hunting-gathering economy of the Kawaiisu. Aside from the pruning of stands of wild tobacco and perhaps the firing of dry brush in late summer (to make the next season's growth more abundant), no physical techniques for manipulating the environment were employed. The varied character of the terrain offered a wide variety of floral resources. An ethnobotanical survey (Zigmond 1981) lists 233 plant species to which utility was attributed. Of these, 112 provided food and beverage, 94 medicine, 87 miscellaneous products and services, while 27 had supernatural and mythological connotations.

The following 20 floral genera, comprising at least 36 species, were among the important sources of vegetal foods: *Amsinckia* (fiddleneck), *Arctostaphylos* (manzanita), *Calochortus* (mariposa), *Calyptridium* (sand cress), *Coreopsis* (tickseed), *Descurainia* (tansy mustard), *Juniperus* (juniper), *Lepidium* (peppergrass), *Lomatium* (wild celery and wild parsley), *Lycium* (box thorn), *Melica* (melic grass), *Mentzelia* (stickweed), *Oryzopsis* (ricegrass), *Perideridia* (Indian carrot), *Pinus* (pine, piñon), *Quercus* (oak), *Salvia* (chia), *Stanleya* (prince's plume), *Stipa* (speargrass), and *Yucca* (yucca, Joshua tree).

Despite the large number of items that provided nourishment, it is not to be assumed that an abundance of edibles was always at hand. There were lean winter months, and, if a major food source such as oak trees had a meager crop, suffering, and perhaps starvation might ensue. Efforts were made to conserve sufficient foodstuffs to carry through nonproductive periods, but a poor yield and the pillaging of rodents might reduce available stores to dangerous levels.

Gathering and preparing food involved a number of basketry types: seedbeaters, burden baskets, and containers of several sizes (for collecting acorns, seeds, nuts, berries, and roots), winnowers (both concave and flat), trays, and hoppers (fig. 2). There were pointed digging sticks, flat-ended poles, long poles—sometimes

U. of Calif., Lowie Mus., Berkeley: top, 1–19701; bottom, 1–9692.

Fig. 2. Characteristic Kawaiisu basketry. top, Twined burden basket, collected at Loraine, Calif., 1915; bottom, openwork twined winnowing–parching tray, collected at Piute Rancheria, Calif., 1915. Height of top, 48 cm, other to same scale.

hooked—and a brush (primarily for sweeping meal together). Stone items for food preparation were principally the bedrock mortar (fig. 3) and a pestle about a foot and a half long and rounded at the ends, the portable metate and accompanying mano, and the obsidian knife. Of less importance were portable mortars and bedrock metates.

Some foods, especially spring greens and some seeds and berries, were consumed as gathered. Others required pounding or grinding, leaching (acorns and buckeye nuts), boiling (usually stone-boiling), parching (with live coals on a flat basketry tray), roasting in a pit oven on the surface or in hot ashes, frying (a modern technique), drying, and molding into cakes. Diverse ingredients were at times combined, and the meal of several kinds of acorns was often mixed to achieve the desired taste.

Invariably, deer meat was mentioned as the favorite animal food, but a large number of faunal species, including large and small game, rodents, birds, and insects, were considered edible. Some, like the chuckwalla, could be obtained only in the desert. The caterpillar of the pandora moth and a white "worm" found in dead trees were commonly eaten, the latter fed to children to "fatten" them. There is some difference of opinion as to which species were rejected, but at least some informants named skunk, grizzly bear (brown bear was eaten), rattlesnake, buzzard, bat, roadrunner, eagle, crow, and grasshopper. Coyote was apparently an emergency food as was dog, though it was also asserted that the dog was sometimes purchased to be eaten. Fish was a minor dietary item since fish-bearing streams are few in the region, but the catching of fish with bone hook and by stupefaction was known. The latter procedure was effected by casting the mashed root of false solomon's seal (*Smilacina* sp.) on the water. There was disagreement as to the edibility of freshwater mussels, but their shells constituted a minor source of lime (to be mixed with tobacco).

Animals and birds were usually hunted with the bow, and hunters at times used decoys and blinds. Nets, several types of traps, brush fire surrounds, and deadfalls were employed in snaring game. The first kill called for the ceremonial use of wild chrysanthemum (*Artemisia douglasiana*), and a "brotherhood" was established between man and animal if sand from the tracks of the latter were mixed in the food of the former. Of several men involved in a hunt, the one whose arrow actually brought the deer down received the meat and hide "al-

Maurice Zigmond, Belmont, Mass.

Fig. 3. A shelf of bedrock mortars at Nettle Spring, west of Sand Canyon and northeast of Tehachapi, Calif. Photograph by Judy Barras, 1970.

though its flesh was evenly apportioned" (Cappannari 1960:138).

Structures

The winter house (*tomokahni*) was built on a ground-level circular base with vertical forked poles, usually of willow, bound together at the top to form a smoke hole. Transverse poles were tied both inside and outside the vertical shafts, and the intervening space tightly filled with brush. Bark and tule mats are said to have made the structure waterproof, and a tule mat served as a door. The occupants slept with their feet toward the fire built at the center. In the summer the women worked in an open, flat-roofed shade house (*havakahni*) (fig. 4). A sweathouse (*tivikahni*), located near water, was earth-covered. Circular brush enclosures served as windbreaks for temporary encampments and particularly large ones as celebration areas for festive occasions. Small granaries, built two feet or more above the ground, were used to store acorns, nuts, and seeds.

Technology

The bow was commonly of juniper wood and sinew-backed, the bowstring of twisted sinew. A three-piece arrow was utilized in hunting large game. The mainshaft was of the bamboolike carrizo grass (*Phragmites australis*). The foreshaft was made of some straight stem—desert almond (*Prunus fasciculata*), choke cherry (*Prunus virginiana* var. *demissa*), golden bush (*Haplopappus palmeri*), or serviceberry (*Amelanchier ulnifolia* var. *pallida*)—to which an obsidian point was bound. Small game and birds were hunted with one- and two-piece arrows, the latter of *Phragmites* into which a pointed foreshaft was fitted, the former of any of the woods listed above in addition to willow (*Salix* spp.) and winter fat (*Baccharis glutinosa*). To bring down birds, an attachment of small twigs was tied near the arrowpoint.

The presence of shards around some old settlements gives evidence of the manufacture of a crude, undecorated pottery, but no whole vessel has been found. In all likelihood pottery-making was never an important industry, and, in any case, seems to have been abandoned long ago. Pottery may have been traded in, rather than made locally, for example, Owens Valley Brown ware (Griset 1981).

Basketry was an ever-present art among the Kawaiisu until the end of the 1950s. In common with neighboring people, Kawaiisu employed two basic weaves—twined and coiled—but developed a unique variant of the coiled for which nothing similar is to be found in the Great Basin or California areas. This distinctive Kawaiisu coiled basket is designated by the word *wičikadi* 'wrapped around' (Zigmond 1978). The normal coiling stitches are interrupted by occasionally wrapping the coils around the foundation without anchoring them to the previous row. No reason for this procedure was suggested, and

left, U. of Calif., Bancroft Lib., Berkeley: C. Hart Merriam Coll. 1978.8 23w–P1.

Fig. 4. Rancheria of Fred Collins and family at Kelso Creek, Kern Valley, Calif. left, Open, flat-roofed shade houses for summer work next to the small Euro-American house with chimney. Photograph by C. Hart Merriam, Oct. 1934. right, Martina Collins (b. about 1850), mother of Fred Collins, beside a traditional shade house on the rancheria. Photograph by Maurice Zigmond, 1936.

one can only surmise that the purpose was to achieve diversity.

With the exception of the flat tray that served both utilitarian and decorative purposes, workware was twined (fig. 5), of unsplit willow for the warps and split willow for the wefts. The rims of burden baskets might be of unsplit willow, oak, or rosebush stems. The only pattern element occasionally introduced in twined basketry was achieved through variation in stitching. Water bottles and other receptacles holding liquids required tight stitching and were usually daubed with pitch. Containers intended for seed-gathering were often lined with cloth.

In coiled basketry greater diversity in materials, shape, and design was possible, but the foundation was invariably of multiple shoots of deergrass (*Muhlenbergia rigens*). The usual coiling material was split willow. Color patterns could be achieved through the use of other elements: the core of the rootstock of the Joshua tree (red-brown) or of the yucca (orange), and the stems of the squawbush (light brown). Black color formerly came from the midrib of the leaves of the bracken fern (*Pteridium aquilinum*), but, within the memory of older informants, a substitute was found in the split black "horns" of the unicorn plant (*Proboscidea louisianica*). The quills of two birds were infrequently integrated into the patterns of coiled baskets, as were the crests of quails.

Cordage, usually three-ply, was made in various strengths depending upon the purpose intended. The common material was the fiber of milkweed stems (*Asclepias* spp.) whose native name, *wiʔivi*, is generic for cordage. Other materials included pondweed (*Potamogeton*), nettle (*Urtica*), and slippery elm (*Fremontodendron*). Beside the usual function of tying and binding, cordage was used in the making of nets, as warps in tule mats, and as bowstring for small-game hunting.

Handles for obsidian blades and awls (of bone or thorn) were fashioned out of lac gum deposited by aphids on sagebrush (*Artemisia tridentata*) and creosote bush (*Larrea tridentata*). A brush and a starchy "soap" were derived from the soap plant (*Chlorogalum pomeridianum*). There were stone arrow-straighteners (heated when used) and small stone bowls and pestles for mixing and serving moistened tobacco and crushed limestone. Elderberry wood (*Sambucus*) provided a six-holed flute as well as a container for holding an individual supply of tobacco-lime meal. Split sections of cane (*Phrag-*

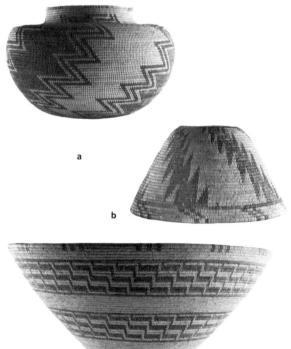

U. of Calif., Lowie Mus., Berkeley: a, 1–28023; b, 1–19711; c, 1–20930.

Fig. 5. top, Emma Williams making a twined winnower. She wears a coiled basketry hat. Photograph by Maurice Zigmond, near Piute Rancheria, Calif., 1936. a, Close-coiled burial offering basket, made by Mary Keyes before 1929. b, Close-coiled woman's hat made before 1915. c, Close-coiled basketry bowl, occasionally used in a burial to cover the face of the deceased; collected 1893–1908. Height of a, 14.2 cm, rest same scale.

a

b

c

402

mites) constituted clappers, while cocoons and deer hooves served as rattles.

Two cradle types, one oval and the other Y-shaped (the latter could be stuck in the ground and rocked), were of willow except that on the basis of a myth sandbar willow (*Salix hindsiana*) was never employed for this purpose. It is said that quail had lost all her children until she stopped making their cradles of this wood.

Clothing and Adornment

Clothing was scanty. Infants were wrapped in the skins of wildcat, jackrabbit, or young deer. Diapers were of shredded tule.

The tanning of skins involved the soaking of rawhide in a solution of deer brains and pine nuts. After drying, the hide was scraped to remove the hair and then worked between the hands to make it soft and pliable.

Young children were usually naked; older children wore a two-piece buckskin skirt. A breechclout and the two-piece skirt were worn by the women with nothing above the waist. In winter a rabbitskin blanket might be bound about the neck. Breechclouts sufficed for the men, with a blanket added in cold weather. On hunting trips a wildcat-skin muff protected the forearms. Shoes were of tanned deer hide; for long trips, the soles might be reinforced with piñon pitch and stomped in ashes. For walking in snow there were shoes made with heavy twined cord and lined with pounded sagebrush bark.

The hair of young people was burned short. Adults let their hair grow long, parted in the middle and often braided. Bangs were popular among women, and they wore coiled basketry hats outdoors.

Piercing of ears and nasal septum was usual with women who suspended a string of beads from their ears and wore a tubular nose plug. Both men and women were commonly tattooed on the hands, arms, and face. Several colors of paint were used for personal adornment. Women might paint themselves daily if the ingredients were available. Men restricted such activities to festive occasions. At celebrations women put red pigment on their faces and eagledown in their hair, while men wore eagledown aprons and daubed their bodies with white paint.

Tobacco

Two species of tobacco grow in the Kawaiisu area: *Nicotiana attenuata* (*koʔopi*), the common tobacco of the Great Basin, and *N. bigelovii* (*soʔodi*), dominant in most of California. To the Kawaiisu, *soʔodi* is the preferred tobacco and *koʔopi* a poor and weak substitute. Wild tobacco is apparently the only plant that received care during its period of growth. It was pruned three times before its mature leaves were plucked. There followed a process of drying, pounding, and curing. After

being moistened with a solution prepared by boiling some tobacco, a few pine nuts, and perhaps a leaf or two of the bush poppy (*Dendromecon rigida*), the tobacco was molded into plugs.

Only men smoked, and at night. The usual pipe was a short section of cane, though buckwheat (*Eriogonum* spp.) stems could also serve. Men and women chewed and often ate a tobacco-and-lime mixture. The lime normally came from slaked limestone. While the use of the mixture may be conceived as recreational, it also had medicinal and magical implications. Taken internally, it was emetic and soporific. Applied externally, it relieved pain, stopped bleeding and itching, and eased parturition. Blown into the air or tossed on a stone into the night, it drove away bothersome supernatural beings.

Medicine

Many plants were regarded as therapeutic. An expert in their utilization was called a *matasuk^wigadi* 'one who has medicine'. The Kawaiisu believed that in the beginning of time four primary medicines were given to man: jimsonweed, tobacco, nettle, and red ants (swallowed live in balls of eagledown). There was great confidence in traditional medical procedures. About 1910 a Kawaiisu man wrote out the amazing curative powers of holly-leaf buckthorn (*Rhamnus crocea*) and considered obtaining a patent on it (Zigmond 1981: frontispiece). Among other things, it was said to cure boils and disorders of the stomach, kidneys, spleen, bowels, liver, and blood (Zigmond 1981:58–59). Remedies for the more obvious indispositions were probably quite effective, and the principle of counter-irritation was well established. Non-Indian neighbors were often impressed with the effectiveness of "Indian medicine."

Life Cycle

The birth of a child was generally considered a happy event. There seems to have been a slight preference for males. Twins were unwelcome and, to avoid bearing them, women did not eat eggs with double yolks, twin fruit, or twin piñons. Infanticide was practiced when, for economic or social reasons, survival posed a problem. One of twins might be killed. Abortions could be effected in the early months of pregnancy by drinking a brew of mistletoe growing on blue oak (*Quercus douglasii*). The swallowing of piñon pitch was said to stop menstruation and thus prevent conception. A sterile woman might become fertile by drinking a decoction prepared from the powdered paw of a mouse.

An infant might be named after someone dead, but the names of those recently deceased were avoided lest the child also die. The navel cord was cut with a sharp edge of cane and, when fallen off, placed in a small basket that could serve as a rattle. The infant was washed in warm water and not fed for one to three days. Nursing could continue for three to four years unless another pregnancy intervened. When a cradle was outgrown it was hung on a tree—a ponderosa pine for a boy's cradle, any tree for a girl's. The child would die if a jealous person found and destroyed the cradle.

With the onset of puberty a girl was subject to a number of restrictions that in part continued at each subsequent menstrual period. No meat, fat, or salt could be eaten. A head scratcher was used; scratching the face would bring wrinkles. Since the girl's activities at this time were indicative of her behavior later in life, she was exhorted to rise early, run mornings and evenings, and be industrious. The period ended with bathing in a wild chrysanthemum solution.

Marriage was monogamous, though an instance of a man marrying two sisters could be recalled. A suitor brought gifts to a young woman and her parents and, if these were not rejected, he was deemed acceptable. Payment to the parents might be considered the only formal act of marriage. There was no fixed rule about residence: the location depended upon circumstances and could be easily shifted. A female rival (woho-) for a husband's attention was fairly common, though the woman was usually blamed for the relationship. Gifford (1917:231) translates the term woho(ni) as 'co-wife/co-husband'. Divorce involved little more than separation, but some details were contingent upon whether the husband or the wife initiated the action.

A pregnant woman came under restrictions that, for the most part, were a continuation of those instituted at adolescence. She kept away from foods and objects that symbolized closure or stoppage. She refrained from eating the feet of animals lest her infant be born feet first, and from stepping over a mole tunnel lest the child be born blind. She might toughen her body for the ordeal ahead by taking cold baths every night or by beating her stomach with nettles. During the last month of pregnancy she ate no meat, fat, or salt, drank only warm water, did not cook or indulge in intercourse. If labor were prolonged, a tobacco-lime mixture was rubbed on the stomach. When labor started, she was given nothing to eat or drink.

Following delivery, the mother lay on earth and wild chrysanthemums placed over heated rocks. There were postparturition restrictions for both parents. They were bathed in a wild chrysanthemum solution, submitted to the familiar food prohibitions (the mother for a longer time than the father), and they ran uphill so that they would be light and vigorous. The mother was subject to hair-combing, scratching, and drinking taboos for three months. There could be no sexual relations during this period.

Death was due either to natural causes or to bewitching, though the two could be interrelated. The body, wrapped in a tule mat, was usually placed in a rock

cleft, covered with a split burden basket, and heaped over with rocks. Burial took place on the same day as the demise, but not after sunset. Some vague information indicates that when a mother died her children, or at least her youngest child, stepped on her body to avoid death. The deceased's house was burned or abandoned, and the family moved elsewhere. Personal property might be interred with the corpse, abandoned, or burned. Some items, however, might be retained by relatives or friends. Members of the family wailed morning and evening, burned off their hair, and left their faces unwashed for a designated period after the death.

There is tentative evidence that, when a death involved a marriage between a Kawaiisu and a Tubatulabal, two special procedures were required. The first concerned a face-washing ceremony (Voegelin 1938:68). Only after a mourner's face was washed by one with whom he had established a reciprocal face-washing agreement could he again eat meat. Also, a female mourner, after having her face washed, could let her hair grow and remarry. No data indicated that the Kawaiisu observed the custom independent of the Tubatulabal. The second procedure involved the making of a payment to the Tubatulabal parents-in-law if their son or daughter died. The amount paid was apparently not fixed, but stinginess would be the subject of gossip. Until this obligation was fulfilled, the surviving spouse could not eat meat or remarry, and, if it were neglected altogether, might suffer death. The name of the recent dead was not mentioned, but a word derived from 'spirit, ghost' was substituted. Burial places were avoided. Coming upon human bones was a bad omen; grave goods somehow uncovered were not touched. The deceased's spirit might seek to linger around familiar places, but before long it had to embark upon the journey to the spirit world. The trail led eastward across the desert. If one saw tracks on that trail, one knew that someone had died.

Ceremonies

Though informants did not specifically associate datura with a life cycle period, it seems commonly to have been taken a year or two after puberty by both boys and girls (Kroeber 1922:314). There were a number of ritualistic aspects to the procedure. The root of *Datura wrightii*—probably shredded—was soaked from sunrise to sunset in a small, decorated basket that was moved during the day in a westerly direction. Festive beads were worn. For a girl, some of the puberty-pregnancy taboos were invoked and, prior to imbibing, her hair was washed in wild chrysanthemum solution. The drink was administered by an older person who told about the old days and scattered beads as he or she led the drinker to bed. Thereafter, the drinker was under constant watch and, if necessary, physically subdued, remaining in a stupor at least until the next morning and often longer. In the meantime relatives and friends gathered for a celebration that included eating, dancing, and the scattering of beads, seeds, and berries. The next day the drinker was induced to vomit by the swallowing of warm water. A meat-eating prohibition was observed for a week. Datura brought on visions. These might call for immediate action on the part of the drinker or of those who had appeared in the vision. Aside from its ceremonial role, datura was deemed effective medicine.

At about the age of 14 young people might be subjected to the ant-ordeal. After swallowing live ants in balls of eagle-down, the participants were bidden to lie quietly in the sun all day. Then warm water was drunk and the ants, dead or alive, were vomited. Like datura, the ant-ordeal was looked upon as preventive therapy.

At irregular intervals a mourning ceremony, usually commemorating the death of several persons, was held. It took the form of an intertribal celebration in which each tribe was assigned space within a large circular brush enclosure. In the center was a pit of fire. Images constructed of brush and bark, representing the dead, were dressed in clothing previously worn by the deceased. Carried on a pole frame, the images, amid the wailing of women, were tossed into the fire. Beads, piñons, and other items were also thrown in, but some were caught by children. There followed a night of dancing during which the Kawaiisu, as mourners, were spectators rather than participants. The occasion ended with a feast and payment to the celebrants. The event marked the termination of the mourning period. The bereaved ceased their weeping, and widows were free to marry again.

Recreation

Pastimes varied with the seasons. For children there were out-of-doors games like tag (called Bear—the one who was "it" was the Bear), see-saw, shooting practice with small bow and arrow for boys, dolls for girls. Tops were made of acorn cupules. A split willow spiral could be made to travel along a cord. Wing charms were suspended within houses. They would fascinate an infant, but also served to frighten away the *inipi* (spirit).

Among men's games were hoop and dart, shinny, ring and pin, a hit-the-target throwing game, and concealed stick (usually played in the sweathouse and accompanied by song). Playing with shell dice was a woman's diversion.

Informants were vague as to the nature of Kawaiisu dancing, but it is clear that this activity might bring together large numbers of people and extend over several days. The dance steps seem to include a slow-moving circle dance and a shuffling of the feet on one spot.

Singing was a usual accessory and cane clappers might serve to beat time.

Winter was the season for telling stories and making string figures. If stories were related in summer, rattlesnakes might come and snow and rain could fall. Among the string figures were: man with shoes, man without shoes, boy, coyote running, fox running, metate, and muller. It is said that, if the cord broke as a figure was being made, a hot coal would be applied to the back of the hand of the performer.

Social Organization

Social and political organization was minimal beyond the family group. Some families, usually related, tended to dwell in close proximity and to cooperate in food quests and other expeditions. Such groups can be considered bands only in an informal sense.

Kinship terminology takes into account both age and sex, and utilizes a diminutive suffix, *-ci* (*-zi*), to express reciprocity. Thus there are four terms for siblings, four for grandparents and great-grandparents (without age distinctions), and seven for uncles and aunts (without age distinctions for 'father's sister'). The diminutive suffix indicates endearment rather than reciprocity when used with words designating members of the nuclear family (*muwa-* 'father', *muwaci-* 'little father'), but prefixes attached to such words denote in-law relationships (*adamuwa-* 'wife's brother', 'sister's husband'). Bereaved fathers and mothers are called 'father's older brother' and 'mother's older sister' respectively. The diminutive form of 'younger brother' and 'younger sister' refer to great-grandfather and great-grandmother and of 'older brother' and 'older sister' to great-grandson and great-granddaughter respectively. There are, in addition, generalized terms without sexual distinctions for children, parents, parents-in-law, children's parents-in-law, grandparents, and great-grandparents.

Chieftainship

The concept of chieftainship was recognized, but a chief became such simply through tacit acknowledgment of the people about him. Since the Kawaiisu had little consciousness of tribal unity, several leaders might be accepted locally. The important qualifications were wealth and generosity. The term for chief is *niya·gadɨ* 'he who has a name'; but one informant, seeking to express the idea of 'braggart', came up with the same word. A chief was expected to sponsor celebrations, and his reputation grew if he were especially lavish with food and festivities. There was no occasion for a chief to serve as war leader (Driver's 1937:134 suggestion is based on a misunderstanding). Violent conflict was ordinarily an individual matter involving at most a few men and a single incident or retaliation for one. Upon   *405* the death of a chief the same informal recognition of a successor followed. A chief's son might succeed him, but this was not an automatic procedure. Acceptance was dependent upon personal endowment. One of the last chiefs recalled was a berdache. He dressed like a woman and did women's work, but he was popular and obviously possessed those talents required of a leader. No woman was known to have achieved the office.

Shamanism

Three kinds of shamanism were well developed among the Kawaiisu even though the techniques involved are not clearly delineated. Curing and bewitching shamans and, presumably, weather shamans obtained their power through dreams and visions. Since the distinction between benevolent and malevolent shamans was not always obvious, parents sought to discourage a child whose dreams suggested proclivities in either direction. He might be urged to go off and "talk to the mountains" so that the telltale visions might cease to come; however, if early tendencies persisted, he could be expected to acquire the power and procedures required for his vocation.

The name of a curing shaman, *huviyagadi* 'one who has song', points to the prominence of singing as a healing technique. Touching the body, locating the affected part, removing a foreign object, and blowing tobacco smoke were elements in the process. The factors that led an ailing person to consult a *huviyagadi* rather than a *matasuk^wigadi* are not evident. Presumably those disabilities seemingly impervious to physical medication, or suspected of having been caused by a witch, needed the skills of a curing shaman, who had a dual responsibility both to diagnose and to heal. If convinced that the illness was the work of a witch, he sought to identify the guilty party. The witch might be unaware of his evil power and therefore be willing to nullify its baneful effect. But he might refuse to admit that he was in any way involved. Such an attitude could call for counteraction and, if the patient died, relatives might seek to avenge his death. To complicate matters, there could be a difference of opinion, depending upon the results of treatment, as to whether a shaman was a curer or a witch (Kroeber 1922:314).

Like the *huviyagadi,* the evil shaman (*pohagadi* 'one who has evil power') acquired his talent through dreams. Visions of rattlesnake, grizzly bear, coyote, the Rock Baby, and other supernatural beings could be the prelude to a pernicious career. A *pohagadi* was not always conscious of his power, but with it his unfriendly feelings toward anyone might result in that person's illness or death. To attack his victim, the *pohagadi* might secure something belonging to him, or the bewitching might be effected through a supernatural agent such as an *inipi*. The cure, if any, had to come through the efforts of a powerful *huviyagadi.*

Weather manipulation seems to have been a Kawaiisu specialty (Steward 1933b:311; Voegelin 1938:64). Kroeber (1925:604) notes: "As to Kawaiisu shamans, nothing is on record except that they had powerful rain doctors. Thus, one member of the profession, while lying on a summer's day with a wound in his neck . . . made a light rain to ease his pain and reduce the inflammation." The weather shaman, *uwapohagadi* ('one who has rain-power'), was secretive about his procedures, but the rainmaking material most widely known was a tree moss, probably *Ramalina menziesii.* (A Kawaiisu myth associates the moss with Coyote's hair.) When gathered fresh and submerged in water, it could produce either rain or snow. Bob Rabbit, celebrated Kawaiisu weather shaman, said the "people all over the country would try to use it. It invariably made trouble and also kept the rain shamans out of work" (Cappannari 1947–1949).

The Supernatural

The world of the supernatural was a real world to the Kawaiisu and has persisted even when other aspects of their culture have vanished (Zigmond 1977). The manifestations of the unseen are manifold: there are beings and nonbeings, the latter taking the form of dreams, omens, signs, and unexplained events.

The best known and most commonly experienced supernatural creature is the *inipi*. Every human being—and probably every animal—has its own *inipi*, identifiable and indestructible. The *inipi* can wander off when one is asleep and continues to exist when one is dead. When a person is doomed to die, his *inipi* may act as though he is already dead and thus betray his forthcoming demise to the living. An *inipi* is visible on occasion but is not easily recognized. At times it is described as having horns, though this may be a borrowed concept. It may mingle with people as an ordinary human being but is apt to reveal itself by superhuman behavior such as suddenly flying off or showing imperviousness to bullets. As a ghost, it might return to old haunts and, in one way or another, attack those who mistreated it in life. Or, it may be playfully mischievous. Sometimes an *inipi* carried out the evil designs of a witch who controlled it. When heard approaching at night, it can be frightened off by the blowing of tobacco powder, ashes, the smoke of dried wild celery root (*Lomatium californicum*) or of the blue sage (*Salvia dorrii*).

Another supernatural being is the *ya·hwe^ʔera,* sometimes indistinguishable from the *inipi*. In mythology it is associated with a cave that leads to the underworld. In the rocks there dwells the Rock Baby who makes pictographs. Since it is continually at work on them, one should not be surprised to see them altered with each visit. Touching the pictographs and then rubbing one's eyes will produce sleeplessness and death. To photograph the pictures will bring disaster—at least to the camera. But the Rock Baby itself is an omen of doom. To see it or (more commonly) to hear it is a sure sign of tragedy. There are other creatures who figure in myths and, when seen or heard, foreshadow bad luck or death.

Dreams are understood as a source of information, as conveying power, or as bearing messages for good or ill. Despite the dangers inherent in them, dreams were sought in the hope that the revelation might be of benefit to the dreamer. Datura, the ant ordeal, the application of nettles on bare flesh, the eating of tobacco-lime mixture (or tobacco alone), and the quest for visions in the mountains at night resulted in "dreams" that were to be taken literally and might call for direct and immediate action.

The custom of "talking to the mountains" may be construed as the Kawaiisu form of prayer. Its purpose was to gain visions or to initiate counteraction against them. It also represented a hunter's effort to persuade "the mountains" to let him see deer and no rattlesnakes. The scattering of beads, eagledown, acorns, and other offerings was another common procedure. It apparently served as a protective measure or to insure the success of a venture and was an integral element in ceremonials and celebrations.

The foreshadowing of ominous events might come not only through visions but also through signs and omens. These are called *tu·waru·gidi* 'premonition (of death)'. Almost any unusual or unexpected sight or sound might be a *tu·waru·gidi*. The disaster might already have occurred or be about to occur. The formula might be expressed thus: "I heard a strange sound (or saw a strange sight); a few days later he died (or, I learned of his death)." When a non-Indian rancher died in a brush fire, his Kawaiisu neighbors insisted that they knew of his impending fate since, some days before, they had heard his riderless horse galloping through the night. Such instances were frequently recalled.

Mythology

Kawaiisu mythology (Zigmond 1980) participates in a broad folklore area. Some of the tales refer to localities beyond Kawaiisu country. The time setting is the old days, and the characters almost invariably consist of animals who, with a few exceptions, speak Kawaiisu. Occasionally a man or woman appears in the tale, but the central character is usually Coyote—cunning, foolish, lecherous—who regularly manages to come to grief. Many of the plots are repetitive: Coyote sees someone doing something; he boasts that he can do it too; he tries, fails, and dies. When darkness prevails because the Sun has been extinguished, Coyote pleads to be

Fig. 6. John Nichols (left) and Sam Willie standing in front of Red Rock Canyon. In Kawaiisu mythology the vertical-ribbed rock formation in the background represents the bones of the giant, man-carrying bird, *nihnihno·vi*. Nichols, who lived on the Piute Rancheria, now abandoned, was an important Kawaiisu informant (Zigmond 1977:59). Photograph by Maurice Zigmond, 1938.

admitted into the winter house in which the animals are huddled. "If you don't let me in," he argues, "who will think for you?" But, when the crisis is over, he goes out and urinates on a food plant (*Coreopsis bigelovii*).

There are a number of brief origin myths—origin of fire, of sexual intercourse, of hunting (or how the Kawaiisu were recognized as the greatest hunters)—as well as some just-so tales: why yucca leaves have brown tips, why the titmouse has a crest, why the flowers of evening snow (*Linanthus dichotomus*) are closed during the daylight.

Cultural Position of the Kawaiisu

The Sierra Nevada Range is generally considered the dividing line between the aboriginal cultures of the Great Basin and those of California. Since the Range runs through the Kawaiisu area, it is to be expected that Kawaiisu culture should exhibit aspects of both. The *407*

Fig. 7. John and Louisa Marcus, near Monolith, several miles east of Tehachapi, Calif. John Marcus was an important informant on many aspects of Kawaiisu culture, including mythology. Photograph by Maurice Zigmond, about 1938.

cultural position of the Tubatulabal, similarly situated, is described by Voegelin (1938:6) as "of the borderline variety, showing affiliations in its material, social, and religious aspects with the Great Basin, (South) Central California, and Southern California cultures."

The composite character of Kawaiisu culture is to be seen in distributional surveys that have been made of specific traits. In some of these studies the Kawaiisu are found to participate in the typically Great Basin pattern, in others in that of central California, and in still others in a cultural pattern of contiguous peoples living along the Sierra Nevada Range from Oregon to southern California. In her analysis of folktales, Gayton (1935:595) indicates that "the Basin mythologic area makes inroads into California. . . . The penetration . . . becomes the dominant factor in the mythology of the Tübatulabal, and of the Kitanemuk, Serrano, and Chemehuevi so far as it is known." Data point to the inclusion of the Kawaiisu in that group as well. Gifford (1918:216, map) finds that the California area in which moieties are prevalent is interrupted by a nonmoiety "wedge composed of [Uto-Aztecan] (Tübatulabal and Kawaiisu) and [Southern] Yokuts peoples . . . which has all the appearance of driving asunder the northern and southern moiety groups." In tracing the usage of mixing natural lime with tobacco, Kroeber (1941:18, map 10) shows that the trait is found in "a solid block of tribes stretching from southwestern Nevada to the Coast from Central to Southern California."

But the Kawaiisu are characteristically Californian as acorn eaters (with pine nuts as important but secondary) and as users of the dominant California species of tobacco, although the typical Basin species was also available to them.

Some of the culture configurations in which the Kawaiisu participated are neither distinctively Great Basin nor Californian. Thus the utilization of tobacco as an offering, the pruning of tobacco plants, the tabooing of the use of salt in connection with certain ceremonies (usually life-cycle occasions), and the eating of dogs are, as mapped by Kroeber (1941), irregular in extent but include the Kawaiisu in each instance. Klimek's (1935) conclusion that the Kawaiisu are culturally very like the Tubatulabal and Foothill Yokuts appears to be substantiated.

Prehistory

While no comprehensive account of archeology in the Kawaiisu area has been published, many surveys and test digs have been undertaken. Even without excavation, two types of remains of the aboriginal past are to be found scattered through the region: pictographs and bedrock mortar holes. The holes vary in size from shallow depressions to cavities some 10 inches deep and more than six inches across the top. These holes, numbering in the thousands, offer a clue to the size of a community and its duration. As holes became too deep for convenient use, they were apparently abandoned and new ones started. A test site on Phillips Ranch, three miles from Tehachapi Pass, uncovered 300–500 mortar holes in addition to 16–20 house rings and many artifacts (Schiffman and Garfinkel 1981:3, 22). Sand and Horse canyons, northeast of the town of Monolith, have been subjected to several archeological investigations, and many prehistoric settlement sites have been exposed. One site is estimated to contain at least 250 mortar holes. A survey reported 14 occupational locations in the Sand Canyon–Horse Canyon area (Schiffman and Garfinkel 1981:3, 23).

North of the town of Tehachapi several campsites have been analyzed. McGuire and Garfinkel (1980) have reported on the part of the Pacific Crest Trail that runs along the approximate boundary line between Kawaiisu and Tubatulabal settlements. Sutton (1982) has explored Teddy Bear Cave east of Tehachapi to establish a relationship between its rock art and Kawaiisu mythology.

The pictographs are generally in red, but there are polychrome areas in a shallow cave in Horse Canyon and in a large rockshelter near Sand Canyon. The rock art is gradually fading, and except those in well-sheltered locations, the paintings seem doomed to disappear. Traditionally the Kawaiisu have denied responsibility for the rock art. The pictographs were held to be the work of the dreaded Rock Baby and were therefore a supernatural phenomenon.

History

The earliest mention of the Kawaiisu is in the diary of Francisco Garcés—if they are indeed the people referred to by his Mohave guides as Cobaji. He was crossing the high terrain that separates the San Joaquin Valley and the Mojave Desert in May 1776 when he came upon a "a rancheria of a people of a different language from the Noches [Yokuts] and Quabajais [Kitanemuk?] . . . and . . . discovered them to be those whom the Noches themselves call by the name of Noches Colteches. There were none but women and children who made us presents of meat, seeds and even of two baskets to take along with us. There are here firs, oaks, and many other kinds of trees . . . the women told me that they regaled me solely because we were so needy; that their nation was generous . . . not stingy like that on the west. . . . These people are very robust, the women at least, who are the only ones I saw, as the men were out hunting" (Coues 1900, 1:304–305). Font's map of 1777 seems to place the Cobaji in the Kawaiisu areas (Coues 1900, 1:frontispiece).

In 1844 John Charles Frémont traveled from the valley to the desert, and there is evidence that he used Oak Creek Pass (H.W. Johnson 1927). In 1853 the Indians, possibly Kawaiisu, were harvesting carrizo grass along Canebrake and Kelso creeks (Twisselmann 1967:180).

Trappers, stockmen, and farmers had meanwhile penetrated the region, and with the report of gold discoveries in the early 1850s there was a rush of prospectors that "surpassed everything that had preceded it" (Comfort 1934:18). Soon the very center of Kawaiisu habitation was dotted with mining claims around Havilah, Piute, Claraville, and Sageland. There were occasional clashes between the natives and the newcomers, but the physical penetration of the land was not, at least in the beginning, the usual basis for the disputes. Of more immediate concern was the alleged thievery of the Indians, especially of cattle and horses (for food), and the "stealing" of women by the non-Indians. Reports that an intertribal group of Indians was gathering near Keysville in Tubatulabal territory brought a detachment of soldiers under the command of Capt. Moses A. McLaughlin to the scene. The result was the Massacre of 1863 when 35 unarmed Indians were killed. The captain, in his official report, refers specifically to "the Tehachapie and Owens River Indians." The prevailing opinion among Indians and non-Indians is that there was no justification for the slaughter (B. Powers 1974:55).

A different picture of the Kawaiisu is to be found in reminiscences of Nanna Ramkin who moved to Kawaiisu territory as a child. She wrote that the "Indians were generally friendly and peaceable. . . . They had a high standard of integrity and honesty and were hon-

U. of Calif., Lowie Mus., Berkeley: left, 1–20934; center, 1–20942; right, 1–20935.

Fig. 8. Unusual, elaborate Kawaiisu baskets. left, So-called apostolic basket, with 13 figures said to represent Christ and the apostles (Zigmond 1978:212ff). center-right, Fancy baskets decorated with red yarn and quail crests. The zigzag pattern and encircling human figures are unusual motifs in Kawaiisu basket decoration. Diameter of left 37.5 cm, others to same scale. left, Collected at Piute Peak, Calif., about 1893–1908; center-right, in Kelso Valley, Calif., about 1893–1908.

orable men and women" (in B. Powers 1974:54). A number of stable interracial marital unions are recorded, and the names of some of the pioneers are borne by Kawaiisu descendants down to the present time.

Population

Admitting that "for modern times the census, and for the older period even estimates, fail us," Kroeber (1925:603) notes that "the aboriginal population may have been 500" and "there seem to be nearly 150 of them," probably in 1910. Who is to be deemed a Kawaiisu Indian in the 1980s poses a question since all manifestations of tribal life disappeared by the 1960s. Some supernatural concepts, a few myths, and the knowledge of some edible and medicinal plants are still vivid in the minds of a few older people, but any kind of corporate existence is impossible. The only criterion for a modern census is language. On this basis there appeared to be about 30 Kawaiisus scattered throughout southern California in 1984 with no more than nine in any one locality and a few individuals in several western states. There was only one married couple where both members were Kawaiisu. Children were no longer taught the language since, as one mother said, "they have no one to talk to." It may be assumed that, in the 1980s, no one under the age of 35 participated in Kawaiisu culture, however defined.

As a tribal entity, the Kawaiisu have ceased to be. All group activities—the coordinated hunting "surrounds," the mourning ceremony, the acorn, piñon, and tobacco expeditions—have vanished. The custom of burying corpses in rock clefts has been replaced by interment in cemeteries. And the individual arts such as basketmaking, the gathering of roots, seeds, and berries have also disappeared. There is nothing in the day-to-day life of the modern Kawaiisus that would identify them as Indians.

Synonymy†

The name Kawaiisu was introduced in this form by Hodge (1907–1910, 1:666); it is the name used in one of the Yokutsan languages, as recorded by A.L. Kroeber. Kroeber (1925:602) did not know the further etymology of the word. Other renderings are Kâ-wi´-a-suh (S. Powers 1877a:393), and Kah-wis´-sah and Kow-ā´-sah (C.H. Merriam in Hodge 1907–1910, 1:666).

The Kawaiisu do not apply this name to themselves, using instead the self-designation niwi 'person', niwiwi 'people' (Kroeber 1925:602; Zigmond 1936–1940, 1970–1974); the plural form is what Merriam rendered as Newoo´-ah (Hodge 1907–1910, 1:666). However, this

†This synonymy was written by Ives Goddard, incorporating materials from Maurice L. Zigmond.

Fig. 9. Lida Girado, an important linguistic informant in the 1970s. Photograph by Maurice Zigmond, Aug. 1972.

designation does not have exclusive reference but is employed generally to mean 'person' or 'Indian' without further specificity. Kawaiisus interviewed in the 1970s referred to their people in English as Paiute, showing a recognition of their relationship to other Numic groups (Zigmond 1936–1940, 1970–1974).

Names for the Kawaiisu in other Indian languages were given by Kroeber (1925:602): Tubatulabal kawishm; Chemehuevi hiniima or hinienima; Serrano agutushyam, agudutsyam, or akutusyam; Mohave kuvahya, earlier given as kubakhye (in Hodge 1907–1910, 1:666). The Panamint called them mugunüwü, said to mean 'people of the point' (Steward 1938:71). Stephen Powers (1877a:393) reported that the Kawaiisu in the Tehachapi Pass called themselves ta-hi-che-pa-han´ -na and were called by the Tubatulabal ta-hichp´.

Francisco Garcés encountered a people in 1776 whom his Mohave guides called by a name he wrote Cobaji and whom the Yokuts called Noches Colteches (as if 'Colteche Yokuts';); these people are assumed to be Kawaiisu on the basis of Garcés's statement that their language was distinct, their location, and the resemblance of Cobaji to the Mohave name for the Kawaiisu recorded by Kroeber (Coues 1900, 1:295, 304, 2:445). The Indians Garcés referred to as Cuabajay, Cuabajái, and Cobajais (Coues 1900, 1:269–273, 2:445, 489) are a distinct group, variously identified as Kitanemuk or Tataviam (vol. 8:537, 569).

Sources

No wide-ranging account of Kawaiisu culture has been published. Gifford (1917) published on kinship terms, and Kroeber (1925:601–605) on the tribe. In 1929

Theodore D. McCown spent a few days in the area and his notes (on file at the Department of Anthropology at the University of California, Berkeley) touch upon various cultural aspects (Zigmond 1977:59). Stephen C. Cappannari (1947–1949) did fieldwork during parts of three summers.

Driver (1937) included a Kawaiisu trait list. Zigmond's Kawaiisu research spanned two periods (1936–1940, 1970–1974). Based primarily on this fieldwork, papers were published on Kawaiisu geography (1938, 1972), ethnobotany (1941, 1972a, 1981), mythology and beliefs (1977, 1980), and basketry (1978). B. Powers (1981) has written popular books on the pioneering days that make references to the Indians but especially to the Tubatulabal. Booth, Munro, and Zigmond (1984) are writing on the Kawaiisu language.

Owens Valley Paiute

SVEN LILJEBLAD AND CATHERINE S. FOWLER

The people who are called Owens Valley Paiute once controlled a narrow valley that encompasses the headwaters and terminus of the Owens River and parallels the eastern slope of the southern Sierra Nevada (fig. 1). Owing in large measure to favorable ecological conditions in their piedmontane homeland, the Owens Valley Paiute in precontact times developed a degree of stability in settlements and durability and cooperation in social units unmatched elsewhere in the Great Basin. Through important trade relationships with their Monache and Yokuts neighbors west of the mountains, they also carried aboriginal California culture elements and modes of living to groups in the southern part of the Great Basin.

Prehistory

Julian Steward, principal ethnographer of the Owens Valley Paiute, conducted some of the pioneering work into their prehistory (Steward 1933b). He identified protohistoric and some prehistoric sites and mapped the location of petroglyphs (Steward 1928, 1929, 1933b). Both protohistoric and prehistoric sites have been excavated (H.S. Riddell 1951; Riddell and Riddell 1956; Bettinger 1975, 1976, 1977a, 1982). The record of occupation for the region is a long one, with several sites suggested to predate 3500 B.C. and many more after then; however, it is a matter of speculation to tie any but the protohistoric sites to the Owens Valley Paiute. Bettinger (1982:69) cautiously suggests that certain changes in adaptive strategies reflected in the archeological record at A.D. 600 or 1000 may mark the spread of Numic-speaking peoples into the area.

Language

The Owens Valley Paiute speak dialects of Mono, which along with Northern Paiute makes up the two-fold division of the Western Numic segment of the Numic branch of Uto-Aztecan. Speakers of Northern Paiute in the southernmost extension of its range call the Mono dialects (as well as their speakers) collectively *pitan·agʷ·adɨ*, that is 'southern' or 'southerners', and

claim that they cannot understand their speech.* This assertion indicates two distinct languages, an assumption that has never been fully verified but is supported by a considerable difference in grammatical structure, even though the phonemic and lexical inventories of the two divisions are quite similar. Semibilingualism prevails on either side of the vague boundary separating the two, as for example in the communities of Bishop, Benton, and Schurz. Otherwise, the northernmost speakers of Owens Valley Mono live in the 1980s in Bishop and vicinity, and formerly lived in Long Valley on the upper course of the Owens River and in Fish Lake Valley, Nevada. The southernmost speakers of Northern Paiute, who formerly lived in the Mono Lake Basin, now live in Bridgeport, Lee Vining, and Benton. The forested divide between these two water systems separates one speech area from the other. In addition to the people of Owens Valley, Mono speakers are also found west of the Sierra Nevada crest in a contiguous area. Groups on that side of the divide, although showing various degrees of dialect affinity with those in Owens Valley, are treated separately as the Monache (vol. 8:426–436) within the California culture area.

Internally, the Mono language shows a much greater and more deep-rooted dialect diversity than Northern Paiute. An environment more favorable than conditions prevailing elsewhere in the Great Basin enabled the Owens Valley Paiutes to live a semisettled life that was possible for no other Numic-speaking people. Permanent settlements and subgroupings of longer duration gave rise to local dialects that despite shifts in population have proved to be remarkably stable. On the basis of phonology, Lamb (1958a:14–16) classified Mono speech forms on both sides of the Sierra into three dialect groups: Northwestern Mono, spoken west of the

---

*The phonemes of Mono (Owens Valley Paiute dialects) are: (fortis stops and affricates) *p, c, t* (alveolar), *č, k, kʷ, ʔ*; (lenis stops and affricates) *b, ʒ, d, g, gʷ*; (lenis spirants) *s, h*; (fortis spirant) *s·*; (lenis nasals) *m, n, ŋ, ŋʷ*; (fortis nasals) *m·, n·, ŋ·*; (glides) *w, y*; (short vowels) *i, e, a, o, u, ɨ*; (long vowels) *i·, e·, a·, o·, u·, ɨ·*. Forms containing the stop *gʷ·* and affricate *ʒ* are recognized dialect variants.

Information on the phonology of the Owens Valley Paiute dialects of Mono was provided by S. Liljeblad, who along with C. Fowler has transcribed the words in this language cited in italics in this volume. Lamb (1958a) provides an alternative solution and orthography for Mono (Northfork dialect and generally); see the orthographic footnote in "Monache" (vol. 8:426).

mountain divide and containing the San Joaquin and the Kings River dialects, each split into two subdialects separated by the rivers (all Monache people); Northeastern Mono, in the 1980s still heard in the neighborhood of Bishop and formerly spoken in three subdialects, two in the northern part of Owens Valley and one northeast of that locality, in Deep Springs and Fish Lake valleys (all Owens Valley Paiute people); Southern Mono, once the most widespread dialect, distributed on both sides of the Sierra Nevada, which had one subdialect in southern Owens Valley still known to a few speakers in Big Pine, Fort Independence, and Lone Pine (Owens Valley people) and another branch west of the mountains, on the Kameah River (Monache people). In the 1980s the few from different places who were familiar with one dialect understood the others without much difficulty.

In the populations of small isolated groups attached to White municipalities, native speech was near extinction in 1985. In Owens Valley, presumably 4–5 percent of the Paiute population retain any appreciable speaking knowledge of Mono, whereas an estimated 7–8 percent of the tribal population on the major reservations might be regarded as competent speakers of Northern Paiute, although often in a substandard form with anglicized phonetics, English lexical substitutions, and an increasingly simplified grammar. All Western Numic speech, Mono and Northern Paiute alike, occurred in the 1980s on some level of bilingualism, usually with English as the dominant tongue.

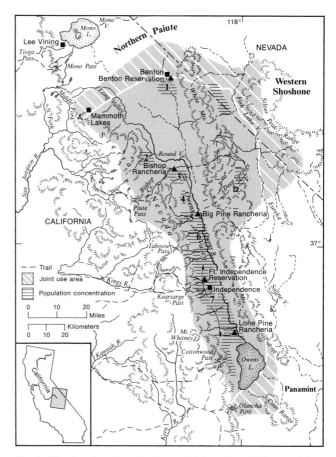

Fig. 1. Nineteenth-century territory with locations of districts (after Steward 1933b: maps 1–2): 1, *itiʔitiwiˑti*; 2, *kwiˑnapaˑti*; 3, *pitanapaˑti*; 4, *itiʔitiwiˑti*; 5, *tobowahamati*; 6, *panati*; 7, *tinihuˑwiˑti*.

Environment

Where the southern range of the Sierra Nevada abruptly puts an end to the monotony of the Mojave Desert, the highest mountain and the lowest depression in the continental United States, both situated in Inyo County, are within view of each other, barely 80 miles apart. The prominent top of Mount Whitney reaches a height of almost 14,500 feet; Badwater, the lowest point in Death Valley, is nearly 300 feet below sea level. Between these extremes and separated by the Inyo and the White Mountain ranges, there are parallel defiles of a very different character: Owens Valley, watered by streams from the Sierra Nevada and densely populated now as in precontact time; and east of the divide three narrow wastelands, the Panamint, the Saline, and the Eureka valleys, and a northward extension in Deep Springs and Fish Lake valleys, which have always been sparsely inhabited.

The leading culture center of this region is Owens Valley. This remarkable, strikingly beautiful place, surrounded by high mountains, is an enormous, amply watered glen. Owens Valley is more than 80 miles long and between 4 and 10 miles wide. The valley floor,

walled in on the east by the Inyo and White mountains, skirts the Sierra Nevada escarpment and broadens toward the north.

For most of its course the Owens River is a clear stream, which in precontact time averaged "50 feet in width and 15 feet in depth" (Wilke and Lawton 1976:25). When it was first described in 1859 Owens Lake measured "nineteen miles long and four to eight broad," the depth varying depending on the seasons (Wilke and Lawton 1976:24). Like Mono Lake to the north, its water was strongly saline—a dead sea supporting no conspicuous fauna except the brine fly and the brine shrimp on which migratory aquatic birds fed seasonally. However, since the 1930s, with the diversion of more and more water from the Owens River and its watershed to Los Angeles, Owens Lake has become little more than a playa, and the river, half to one-quarter of its former size, dries up several miles before reaching the former lake bed.

North of Owens Valley are Round Valley and Long Valley; both were mentioned by early explorers as a country of plenty and a refuge in times of trouble (Chalfant 1933). Beyond these points, there were no settlements in precontact times, although foraging parties

413

from Owens Valley and occasionally Deep Springs came to gather the ricegrass seed and the larvae of the pandora moth and penetrated into the mountainous country north of Long Valley, which was also part of the summer range of the Mono Lake Northern Paiutes (Steward 1933b:256, 325, 1934:425–426, 1938; Davis 1965:29, 32).

Although the steep eastern slopes of the Sierra Nevada are dominated by a mixed coniferous forest with a poor representation of piñon (Bettinger 1982:9–11), the people of Owens Valley and adjacent eastern valleys had immediate access to the important piñon tracts of the White and Inyo mountain ranges. The lower slopes of these ranges, although steep and generally drier than the Sierran side of the valley, supported a varied Great Basin flora and fauna. In the southern end of Owens Valley as well, various plant and animal species characteristic of the Mojave Desert were accessible as the transition to this drier, low-lying region was gradually made. In sum, Owens Valley was exceedingly varied environmentally, and these varied habitats were accessible to the native inhabitants within relatively short distances from a home base.

Settlement Pattern

Unlike other Great Basin groups at the time of White contact, the native population of Owens Valley and the adjacent lesser depressions occupied semipermanent base camps of some durability, named for topographic features. These are here called villages after Steward's (1933b) suggestion, the term to be understood in a sociopolitical sense. These hamlet-sized communities did not qualify as villages, properly speaking, but rather were transitory and unstructured settlements temporarily occupied from year to year by the same families, loosely coordinated for social purposes: ceremonial, religious, and recreational. Thus, there are no references to symmetrical order in the clustering of family camps, nor was foraging activity or family economy subject to any public control beyond voluntary sharing and assistance. Consisting of a population ever on the move, shifting from one gathering place to another, these villages cannot be called sedentary in the ordinary sense of the word, although they were permanently localized and intermittently occupied throughout the year, especially in times when the pine nut crop failed. Periodically, individual families went to gather seeds and pine nuts during the summer and late fall and spent the winter in the piñon-juniper belt, away from the river, near the new pine nut crop. Within a village, which in most instances would be endogamous (Steward 1933b:294), a family was completely independent, even though individuals adhered to widespread kindreds.

The size and population of permanent villages varied

considerably. The only places where detailed census reports referring to a given approximate date in aboriginal time were recorded (Steward 1938:58–59, 62–65) are Deep Springs Valley, where the only village housed five camps or families totaling 23 persons, and Fish Lake Valley, which had a population of 107 individuals, partly Western Shoshone, living in eight villages of one to four families each. For two of these sites, which Steward called "family or camp clusters," that is, villages dominated by one kindred, he gave genealogically arranged census data: one totaled 22 persons, the other 20; both consisted of four siblings each (the oldest generation), their spouses, descendants, and descendants' spouses, mostly from distant villages (Steward 1977:386). The villages listed and mapped by Steward (1933b:325–328, maps 1 and 2, 1938:51–52, fig. 7) for Owens Valley proper were allegedly much larger, some with a population estimated at 200 people and, judging from the site distribution on his map, better called "districts" than "villages." Marriage exchange occurred across district boundaries, and there was constant travel between villages and valleys (Steward 1934, 1938).

The distribution of village sites in Owens Valley depended on the courses of the streams from the Sierra Nevada and the volume of water that each stream carried. In the southern portion of the valley, each village, regardless of size, was a self-supporting autonomous unit, situated on a creek or near the waning water of the rivulet below the alluvial fan spreading out from the mouth of each canyon. In northern Owens Valley, where the water courses were larger and included many branches, which reached the river through swampy meadows, villages and camps were more numerous, dispersed over a larger territory, and closer to the river. In remote parts of the area where there were no major streams, that is, in the southernmost portion of Owens Valley and in Deep Springs and Fish Lake valleys, semipermanent settlements were restricted to the vicinity of the springs and streamlets at the foot of the mountains.

Within Owens Valley proper, Steward (1933b:237) noted that the villages and camps of certain areas were organized into "composite land-owning bands," and he mapped five such units in northern Owens Valley and two more widely dispersed ones in the south (fig. 1). These units seem to correspond in various ways to the "tribelets" of the trans-Sierran Foothill Yokuts (Gayton 1948) as well as to those of other California groups (Kroeber 1955a). The nature of intragroup cohesion and cooperative activities varied, with groups in the north displaying more unity.

Population

The earliest official report on Owens Valley and its aboriginal population before White settlement estimated the population at "about 1,000" in 1855 (Chalfant 1933:120–122). In 1858 Indian Agent J.R. Vineyard reported the stationary population in "the region of Owens Lake east of the Sierra," apparently including the Mono Lake Northern Paiutes, about 1,500, a figure that may have indicated an average (Chalfant 1933:123). Other estimates in the 1850s were 2,000 people (Wilke and Lawton 1976:46) and 1,200 (Wilke and Lawton 1976:29). J.P.H. Wentworth, the Indian Agent for the Southern District of California in 1862 and 1863, apparently obtained his figures from military estimates, which varied from 1,500 to 2,000, inclining more to the larger figure (Chalfant 1933: 172–173). The last official census record for Owens Valley and vicinity before the U.S. Census Bureau took over was made in 1870 by Major H.C. Egbert, the commander of Fort Independence. Egbert's estimates were: Round Valley, 150; Bishop Creek, 150; Big Pine, 200; Independence, George's Creek, and Lone Pine, 400 to 500; for a total of 900 to 1,000. He added 400 for some Western Shoshone, who were camping at that time in the desert southeast of Owens Lake (Chalfant 1933:44).

Steward (1933b:237) approximated "about 1,000 for Owens Valley proper," referring to the figure 970 from the 1930 Indian Service record with the explanatory note that "the population has been maintained at close to 1000 with relatively little decrease—about 2.5 persons per square mile." Yet additional calculations based on Steward's figures for the distribution of precontact habitations in Owens Valley (Steward 1933b:237, 325–326, maps 1 and 2, 1938:48, 51–52, fig. 7), yield a population between 1,700 and 2,000. Although in the absence of detailed data for all but the southern part of Owens Valley the size of each village and each individual camp must remain a statistical abstraction, the higher figure seems warranted. Steward (1933b:325–326, map 2) localized roughly 50 "villages or camps" for the northern section of the valley as far south as Taboose Creek. With 15 persons per campsite as a probable average—12.5 is Steward's (1977:385) figure for the adjacent Deep Springs and Fish Lake valleys in an environment somewhat less favorable—the total for northern Owens Valley would be 750. Based on more detailed data for the southern section of the valley, Steward (1938:51–52, fig. 7) lists 15 sites, four with "possibly 200 inhabitants" and one with "perhaps 25 people." Using his own average from the neighboring valleys for the remaining 11 yields a total of 962 for that region. Combining the two figures gives a total of about 1,700 inhabitants, which, by the time additional isolated sites are counted, might mean for the piedmont at large a population of 2,000 people.

In 1971, the public school system reported a population of about 1,100 individuals on the tribal rolls of the "Owens Valley Paiute-Shoshone Band of Indians." In 1981 the total enrollment was approximately 1,900, of whom presumably about half still lived in the valley, the rest having moved to Los Angeles and elsewhere in California. Most of the Owens Valley Paiutes lived in 1985 in settlements adjacent to the towns. The Paiutes in Deep Springs and Fish Lake valleys, who used to intermarry with people from Owens Valley, moved to Big Pine and Bishop after 1880. The Lone Pine Indian Colony is partly Shoshone, descendants of Panamint Shoshone groups from Saline Valley, Death Valley, and the slopes of the Sierra Nevada and the Coso Range south and southeast of Owens Lake (Steward 1938:71, fig. 7).

External Relations

The Owens Valley Paiutes, influenced by their California neighbors, developed a cultural regime and a social order that in some respects differs from that of other Great Basin groups, including the kindred Northern Paiutes. On the North Fork of the San Joaquin River lived the Northfork Mono (a Monache subgroup), who were the cultural mediators between the Owens Valley Paiutes on the one hand and the Eastern Miwok and the Yokuts on the other. The Owens Valley Paiutes intermarried and traded with the Yokuts, Miwok, and Tubatulabal. The westward trade in products ultimately reached the San Joaquin Valley Yokuts with the Monache acting as middlemen (Gayton 1948:160).

The reciprocal dissemination of culture elements across the Sierra Nevada seems to have been taking place for centuries. "The magnitude of the crest of the Sierra" (Steward 1935:2) was no "cultural barrier," for, between the California and the Great Basin cultural provinces, there was a third one with a mixed polyglot population, the Sierra Nevada highland tribes. These groups shared equally in the cultural inventory of both sides, united as they were by the upland trails crossing the mountains at every possible defile (Davis 1965). The uniformity of aboriginal culture on either side of the Sierra Nevada notwithstanding, it still must be emphasized that those on the eastern side were still subject to a much more dispersed pattern of food resources than those to the west. Thus, seasonal movement for subsistence purposes, as in other parts of the Great Basin, was still required.

The frequent summer traffic across the Sierra often resulted in intermarriage. Movement over the passes between Mono Lake Northern Paiute country and Yosemite Miwok areas continued even in the winter: men from the east side crossed the mountains on snowshoes and remained in the Mono villages on the San Joaquin River until the early salmon runs.

The right to fish in the streams on the hilly eastern side of the San Joaquin Valley was explicitly intertribal and attracted visitors from various quarters (Gayton

1948:143). Women from east of the mountains crossed over on foot in order to participate in the autumn acorn harvest and remained in the highland villages over the winter (Steward 1933b:246). They often brought piñon to exchange. An additional impetus to westward movement was the active trade in salt from Saline Valley (in Panamint Shoshone country). In this, as well as in other transactions, strung shell bead money (*nacibuhidi*) was a medium of exchange.

Eastward trans-Sierran movement was in the main restricted to the summer expeditions of the Northfork Mono via Mammoth Pass. In the Northfork villages a tradition prevailed that the first tribal antecedents came from the Bishop region east of the Sierra Nevada (Gifford 1932:16). In agreement with this view more recent information from people in Owens Valley stressed the Bishop area as a center for migratory enterprises westward. Actually, most people going west for trade or visiting left from Bishop via various passes through the mountains.

The lasting result of all these activities was a widespread bilingualism and a bilateral diffusion of culture rather than migration of a people. Movement from one valley to the other dictated by the annual round occurred also eastward from the Sierra Nevada piedmont, for example, over the Benton range of the Inyo Mountains between Long Valley and Hammil Valley by Mono-speaking groups equally at home in both places (Essene 1935a). Likewise the Fort Independence Paiutes continued roaming in Saline Valley into historic times (Hulse 1935:153). Panamint Shoshone people likewise moved back and forth in southern Owens Valley.

Culture

Subsistence

The seasonal food-gathering activity depended upon the cycles of ripening of the wild seed and root crops that provided food resources the year around. Steward (1933b) lists some 40 food plants, mostly seed crops, harvested in Owens Valley. Five species of roots and bulbs and six species of berries, as well as pine nuts and acorns, were also in common use.

Paramount among all the products that these mountain valleys afforded was the pine nut, the seed of *Pinus monophylla*, far and away the most important single food, which all Numic-speaking peoples called by cognates of the same word: Owens Valley Paiute *tiba*, Western Shoshone and Southern Paiute *tipa*, for example (fig. 2). The influence of native California culture can be seen in the great value that the Owens Valley Paiutes placed upon the acorns as a most important food; when it was available, they preferred it even to the pine nut. Great Basin people living on the border

416

of California, not only the Washoe but also the Northern Paiute (O.C. Stewart 1941:374, 427), regularly shared in the trans-Sierran acorn economy; the acorn is a more dependable crop than the pine nut. Because pine nuts and acorns mature in succession in the fall, people could harvest both crops before winter. Although acorns usually had to be imported, a few oaks grew in the territory east of the Sierra Nevada. The California black oak grows higher up the eastern slopes of the Sierra. The acorns of this species (*wiya*) were the most highly praised food prepared the same way as usually done among California tribes: pounded in bedrock mortars, leached with hot water in sand pits lined with grass for removing the tannic acid, boiled and stirred in clay pots into a thick mush for immediate consumption or coagulated to solid cakes by being poured into cold water while still hot (Driver 1937:64, 113). Most of the supply of acorns was obtained through trans-Sierra trade and distributed eastward as far as Fish Lake Valley (Steward 1938:28–29). The Owens Valley Paiutes traded salt and pine nuts to their Monache kin in exchange for acorns and acorn flour (Gayton 1948:258–259). Despite the incomparably greater bearing which the pine nut harvest had on the annual food supply, the equality between the two staples in terms of popular evaluation is in Mono dialects reflected in the term *ikibi*, indiscriminately for both pine nut and acorn mush, a term derived from the verb *igi-/iki* 'to scoop up with the forefinger and the middle finger and lick' (cf. Northern Paiute *igin·u* for a modern spoon). In Mono dialects it means 'to eat acorn or pine nut gruel'.

Nat. Hist. Mus. of Los Angeles Co., Western Hist. Coll.: 2399.

Fig. 2. Mary Lent sorting unshelled pine nuts in an open, plain-twined tray. Nuts were winnowed twice—first, after they were taken from the cones to remove debris and shells not containing nut meats. After shelling a second winnowing separated the shells from the nut meats. A storage sack for nuts is to the left, and additional winnowing trays are in the foreground. Photograph by Andrew A. Forbes, Bishop, Calif., 1903–1916.

Chief among the grain-producing food plants furnishing the main diet, particularly in years when the pine nut failed, was Indian ricegrass. Of equal importance, although less common, was the high-growing wild rye (*Elymus cinereus*). Most commonly used were Desert needlegrass (*Stipa speciosa*) and the blazing star (*Mentzelia laevicaulis* or *M. dispersa*). So were also chia, an important southern desert plant, and *mono*, the seed of *monopɨ* or lovegrass (*Eragrostis* sp.), as well as a multitude of other species. Harvesting the seed crops was finished by midsummer, and the food-gathering families drifted back to the nuclear villages in the home valley. Late in the summer, edible roots began to mature, but these mostly grew in the swampy lowlands in the immediate vicinity of major permanent camping sites where they were artificially irrigated. The most important of these plants were probably the corm of the wild hyacinth, small bulbs of nutgrass (*Cyperus*) (Essene 1935a), and spikerush (*Eleocharis*), a seed-bearing plant (Steward 1933b:245, 1938:24, 308; cf. Lawton et al. 1976).

In Owens Valley and Round Valley hydrophytic species were grown by a system of irrigation, which was not used in seed-producing areas. On the basis of archeological evidence Bettinger (1976, 1977a:13–15) has concluded that, in early prehistoric times, these crops, rather than pine nuts, were the mainstay of the local food supply. There must have been an intensive use of lowlands, and the soil seems adapted to tuberose plants (Wilke and Lawton 1976:29). Surface irrigation of wild (noncultivated) food crops in aboriginal times in Owens Valley, Round Valley, and presumably also in Fish Lake Valley, not attested by convincing reports anywhere else in the area, has attracted considerable attention in the ethnographic literature. Documents are few and incomplete; the practice was discontinued after the exodus of Owens Valley people to Fort Tejon in 1863 and the subsequent depopulation of the border regions. Davidson (Wilke and Lawton 1976:19–20), describing the great value that the population of the valley placed upon nutgrass, continues: "Whole fields, miles in extent, of this grass are watered with great care. Digging the tubers, destroys the fields, and the 'nuts' are reproduced by planting." Aboriginal irrigation in Owens Valley was described as "*acequias* from the mountain affluents of the River, spread over the land like threads of the spider's web" (Wilke and Lawton 1976:19–20). The most detailed reports come from Steward's (1933b:234, 1934:432–438) interviews, which refer to a time around the year 1850.

When the water from the mountains increased in early summer, it inundated the low-lying meadows near the river, where the vegetation consisted mostly of bulbous plants. It seems clear that the people flooded these already water-logged grounds artificially in order to increase the productivity of the natural vegetation there.

Bishop Creek, the largest tributary to the river, was dammed near the mountains every year, and the water was diverted down to the marshy fields near the river, where the people dug roots in the fall. There, as elsewhere in the valley, the primitive water control that the people practiced made use of a simple device, a temporary check dam across the stream and feeder ditches to conduct the water to the swampy grounds. From the lower end of the ditch, or directly from the dammed brook, the surface water spread out on both sides over the sloping valley floor. The irrigator then manipulated the distribution of water by continuous damming with boulders, sod, brush, and mud, placed at a right angle to the direction of the flow. In the fall, before any root-digging was allowed, the dams were destroyed so that the water resumed its natural course. Irrigation ditches at *pitanapa·ti* were maintained by extensive teamwork, but sustained watering was done by one man for each district, a publicly elected irrigator. The tool he used, called *pabodo* 'water-staff', was a long, heavy pole-shaped wooden bar used as a lever but unsuitable for digging. Harvesting the irrigated root crops was communally controlled (Steward 1933b:305) and open to the women of the district in the traditional competitive way. The unirrigated seed areas, however, were open also to visiting gathering parties when the seeds, notably ricegrass and wild rye, were plentiful. It was chiefly the swampy areas, overgrown with bulbous plants and lovegrass growing in patches, and covering large areas, which were artificially watered, whereas a variety of gramineous seed plants, sunflower, pigweed, bulrush and other hydrophytes, growing downstream from the intentionally irrigated plots, also happened to benefit from the final uncontrolled run-off (Steward 1930:150–152, 1933b:243–245, 247–250, map 2).

At the time of European contact, artificial irrigation of wild crops in Owens Valley was an integral part of communal activity and an essential feature of traditional village organization. In the most complete description Steward (1933b) suggested, as an alternative to the other possible explanations of the practice, that it might have originated locally, "the original idea probably coming from the swampy lowlands of Owens Valley." Steward later (1938:53) expressed doubt, preferring the hypothesis that irrigation had been introduced by Americans or Spaniards by the middle of the nineteenth century. The same conclusion was drawn by Treganza (1956). Such a theory is contradicted by Steward's (1934:423, 432–433) own data and seems even less likely in view of the fact that, after a few decades of itinerant explorers, prospectors, and migrant Mexican herdsmen visiting the secluded valley, White men did not settle in the area until 1861 (Chalfant 1933:93–145), nor are any Spanish settlements in the valley known from an earlier date. Eventual diffusion of the feature is discussed by a number of authorities (Steward (1930:153–

156, 1977:372–373, 376–377; Patch 1951:51; Treganza 1956; Downs 1966a:45–46; Lawton and Bean 1968:20; and Lawton et al. 1976). Returning to his original opinion, Steward (1977:376–377) maintained that the people of Owens Valley were practicing irrigation "before the whites came," that dams and irrigation ditches in the Bishop subarea (the part of Owens Valley that is best known ethnographically) "had been constructed in native time," and that "irrigation augmented the naturally flooded areas." At the time of White penetration into the area, this custom, unique to Owens Valley and the immediate vicinity, was a communally organized effort, evidently of long standing, the execution of which had become both a duty and a privilege. The position of communal irrigator was much sought after.

The irrigation question is of considerable importance for reconstructing the unique and dramatic history of the Owens Valley Paiute. Although they were food gatherers and did not practice agriculture in settled communities, their system of spreading the summer floodwaters over communally exploited water meadows, whether that system was borrowed or independently invented, constituted a human intervention in the ecosystem of the valley, imitating and enhancing previously existing natural conditions. The method of overflowing described by Steward (1930) was part of a perfected gathering complex, a spontaneous extension and prolongation of an observable natural process, resulting from an intimate knowledge of the plant life of the region that was well within the scope of the hunter-gatherer adaptations and utterly unlike any other horticultural development in the region before the advent of White immigration.

The heavy dependence of the Northern Paiutes on waterfowl had no counterpart in Owens Valley. Decoys, nets (other than the rabbit net also used for catching fish), and communal duck hunting were generally unknown in the Sierra Piedmont. Balsas were known but were apparently not in common use (Steward 1933b:258; Driver 1937:68, 115). Like quail and sage hens, aquatic game birds were shot by individual hunters equipped with feathered arrows.

Fishing played an unimportant part in the tribal economy. Weirs, fishing scaffolds, and the dipnet have not been reported in this subarea. It is doubtful whether the Owens Valley people had the harpoon, which was well known elsewhere in the Great Basin, although they did use the fish spear with fixed point. In addition to the native sucker, the only species of fish endemic to the water courses were the tiny cyprinodont, the Owens pupfish, which the people sun-dried for winter use after catching them in large quantities by damming and poisoning the streams, and two species of minnows (Steward 1933b:251; Driver 1937:63, 112; Wilke and Lawton 1976:47–48).

418   As long as Owens Lake existed, its shallow and strongly alkaline water was barren of fish and, as far as is known, supported only saltwater algae, brine shrimp (Aldrich 1912:90), presumably also some diaptomid copepods (miniature crustacea) (Light 1938:74), and, first and foremost, the larvae and pupae of a small brine fly (*Ephydra hians*). This fly formerly bred in heavily alkaline waters in the Great Basin, although it was not important as a staple food anywhere except Mono and Owens lakes (Steward 1933b:256; O.C. Stewart 1941:373, 426–427; Heizer 1950:35–41; Davis 1965:33). Both the larvae and the pupae of the brine fly, known by separate names, were prepared, as different kinds of food. The pupae, called *iŋ·ada* in Mono, after being washed ashore and deposited in windrows in late summer, were gathered by the hundreds of bushels, dried, shelled by manual rubbing, and stored for winter food; under the trade name kutsavi (Western Numic *kuʒabi*), they were brought northward to other related groups and to the Washoe (Wilke and Lawton 1976:30). A pinkish maggot-sized life form (*pis·awada*) also came ashore at certain times of the year, a food ready to be boiled and consumed; this may have been the larvae of the brine fly, the brine shrimp (*Artemia monica*), or the very minute copepods, or possibly a combination of all three. When it drifted ashore, the people scooped it up from the water with winnowing trays or conical carrying baskets in the same way as they fished for pupfish (Liljeblad 1965; Wilke and Lawton 1976:49).

Hunting, when possible, was fortuitous. Individual hunting was a prerogative of men predisposed to life in the mountains and given to the chase. A hunter had usually made a covenant with a supernatural power (*puha*) supplying the aid he needed, but hunting as such was void of ritualism except for a few food taboos and the necessity to share with the village population (Driver 1937:62–63; Steward 1938:186, 193). Communal hunting was limited to the home district or to the territorial periphery of no-man's land. Teams of hunters recruited from several districts hunted deer in the high Sierra, sometimes crossing the summit as the Miwok did from their side (Muir 1916–1924, 1:92–93, 2:219). Occasionally communal drives for mountain sheep and deer with intervillage participation occurred in precontact time both in the Sierra and in the White and Inyo mountains. On rare occasions antelopes were caught in bagging corrals in the open country east of Owens River and by intertribal effort on the Long Valley flats, but as far as known without shamanistic assistance. As elsewhere in the Great Basin, the rabbit was the most common game, sometimes taken with bow and arrow (fig. 3). Rabbit drives with nets usually in connection with a fall festival attracted visitors from neighboring districts. Rabbits were also caught in snares set on game trails and smaller rodents in figure-4 traps. For these and other hunting methods, see Muir (1916–1924, 2:204–205, 5:39, 54–55), Steward (1933b:252–255, 1934,

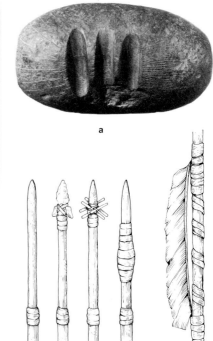

left, U. of Ill., Urbana, Dept. of Anthr.; center, Southwest Mus., Los Angeles: 6729; a, U. of Calif., Lowie Mus., Berkeley: 1–27024; b–c, after Steward 1933b:fig. 3.

Fig. 3. Bows and arrows. left, Jack Stewart, Big Pine, Calif., placing blunt arrow on bowstring in order to demonstrate shooting method. Photograph by Julian H. Steward, 1927–1928. center, Demonstrating the use of a heated grooved steatite arrow straightener on a cane arrow shaft (Harrington 1932:72). Bow and feathered arrows are in the foreground. Photograph by Mark R. Harrington, San Fernando Mission fiesta, Calif., May 1932. a, Stone shaft straightener. b, 4 principal compound arrow types of the Owens Valley Paiute: left to right, a simple greasewood foreshaft for taking rabbits, a wood foreshaft tipped with an obsidian projectile point for hunting large game, a wood foreshaft with a crosshatch frame of sticks below the point for birds, and a wood foreshaft wrapped with a ball of sinew that caused the arrow to skip across the water when hunting waterfowl. c, Sinew at the nock end of the arrow, the wraps below the nock and feathers said to prevent the shaft from splitting. Length a, 11.5 cm; b and c, no scale.

1938:53–54, 1955:110), Driver (1937:61–62), and Davis (1965:12, 27–28, 32).

The gathering and storage of varied plant and insect foods secured survival and relative comfort through the winter months. Next to pine nuts the largest bulk of food was the crop of caterpillars of the pandora moth (*Coloradia pandora*) gathered in large quantities every second year (within a 20-year peaking cycle) in the extensive pine forests covering the high plateau between the Mono Lake and the Owens River drainages and the nearby foothills of the Sierra Nevada at an altitude of about 7,000 feet (fig. 4). These fleshy larvae (*piagi*) feed on the needles of the Jeffrey pine (yellow pine). The larvae descend the trees to pupate in late June and early July. Families from the surrounding valleys moved up into the deep pine forest and camped near springs and water courses while the pupation lasted. The infested trees were encircled with trenches in which the caterpillars were trapped in great numbers. The larvae were gathered in diagonally open-twined round-bottom carrying baskets of a special type used on both sides of the Sierra, baked in hot ashes, sun-dried, and stored in bark shelters on a high elevation to prevent spoilage.

For the groups living close to the Jeffrey pine forests this food was an important source of fat and protein. A single gathering party could in short time put up a ton or more. In preserved form the *Coloradia* larvae were traded widely (Aldrich 1921:36–38; Steward 1933b:238, 256, 1934:436; Driver 1937:62; O.C. Stewart 1941:373, 426–427; Essig 1958:670–671; Davis 1965).

Technology

Although Owens Valley and the Sierra Nevada piedmont as a native cultural province is in some ways marginal to the Great Basin, the ethnography of the Owens Valley Paiute rests on Basin tradition. Often on the move from one camping place to another, a family traveled lightly, also when taking their possessions along. The indispensable item they carried was the fire smoldering in long, cigar-shaped slow matches (*kosobi*) with tinder wrapped in juniper bark. The fire drill (fig. 5) was used by men with the dexterity of long practice. In the winter, people dressed and slept in fluffy rabbitskin blankets woven on a vertical frame (not a horizontal frame as did other Basin people). Game was hunted

419

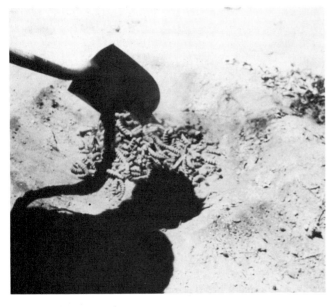

bottom right, Field Mus., Chicago: 59029.

Fig. 4. Gathering and preparing caterpillars of the pandora moth. top left, Caterpillars roasting in a pit under hot sand for about 1 hour. top right, Caterpillars removed from the pit and sifted using a screen. In earlier times, an open, plain twined winnowing basket was used. bottom left, Caterpillars then boiled in water for about 1 hour. bottom center, Drying and storage shed for caterpillars after they have been pit roasted and boiled. They are ready to eat at this stage. This site predates the 1920s. Photographs by Catherine S. Fowler, Inyo National Forest, Mammoth Lakes, Calif., 1980, 1982. bottom right, Open twined basket of the type used to contain live caterpillars and other insects. Length 40 cm; collected by J.W. Hudson in Long Valley, Calif., 1900.

with sinew-backed self-bows of juniper (in Owens Valley proper occasionally of oak). Woven products, garments of sagebrush bark like sandals and socks, and baskets, twined and coiled in rich variety, made up the greater part of the property. Next to baskets and grinding implements, a woman's most important tool was her digging stick (*podo*) made of mountain mahogany. In Owens Valley, where digging for roots on previously irrigated but later dry and hard soil continued until snow covered the ground, the digging stick usually had a step and was called *tapodo* 'foot *podo*'. Heavier articles,

metates and mortars, pottery vessels, and prepared food, were cached at habitual camping places.

Long before any elements of European culture were known, the Owens Valley Paiutes had adopted various marginal features otherwise foreign to the Great Basin peoples, and therefore generally classified as borrowed elements. In the last millennium at least, for certain traits presumably earlier, the piedmontane valleys received innovations from both California and the Southwest.

Among the datable culture elements introduced into

420

U. of Ill., Urbana, Dept. of Anthr.

Fig. 5. Jack Stewart, Big Pine, Calif., demonstrating the use of the fire drill. He kneels on the end of the pitted hearth and twirls the cane drill in his hands. Photograph by Julian H. Steward, 1927–1928.

the highlands in protohistoric time, the art of pottery making has attracted particular interest. Pottery making in the Sierra Nevada piedmont seems to have begun in the mid-seventeenth century. After flourishing for 200 years and decaying for a brief period under the impact of European culture, the pottery disappeared as abruptly as it began. Pottery, like basket making, was always a woman's task. Old potters explained the procedure, which was partly observed and fully recorded in 1925–1930 by Steward (1928, 1933b) for Owens Valley, by Gayton (1929) for the Monache and the Yokuts, and by Voegelin (1938) for the Tubatulabal. In all three instances the methods were strikingly similar. Clay, preferably reddish in color and containing natural sand temper, was selected from quarries open to everybody, pulverized by shifting through winnowing baskets, wetted to a dough, and pounded in bedrock mortars to make it viscid. The vessels were built up by clockwise coiling, smoothed over by hand, and sun-dried before being fired in an open pit for a day or two. Then the pots, while still hot, were coated inside and out with a

decoction, which had been prepared from *Sphaeralcea*, a plant of the mallow family, or from acorns boiled to a thin mush. This syrupy substance produced a glossy, nonabsorbent surface. Depending on the quality of the clay and the duration and intensity of the fire, the color of the finished ware varied from gray or dull red to brownish gray or black. The motley coloring suggested the term Owens Valley Brownware, used indiscriminately for all pottery types in the area (fig. 6).

During its short time of existence the manufacturing of pottery in Owens Valley and vicinity developed a great variety of shapes and utility purposes, all modeled on previously existing types of basketry. Most specimens had flat bottoms with curveless straight or flaring sides, sometimes with an incurved rim. The size varied from small, pan-shaped, low-walled pots, to medium-size bowls used as dippers and for keeping food to large cooking vessels with a rim diameter of 20 centimeters or more. Meanwhile the old-fashioned food baskets kept their place in the household until modern times, and food continued to be eaten from baskets, not from clay dishes. Most common among the clay vessels were the round-bottomed and curve-sided or bell-shaped containers used for boiling. The pointed shape of these pots indicates that they could be stuck in the ground with fire built around them, which explains the early transition from stone-boiling in baskets, categorically denied in Owens Valley, to direct fire boiling. The term *apo*, cognate with Northern Paiute *opo*, for an old-fashioned boiling basket was remembered in the 1980s although in the generic meaning 'basket'. Stone-boiling in clay pots was reported from Big Pine, apparently the most productive center for pottery making in Owens Valley (Steward 1933b:266; Driver 1937:65, 78). After the introduction of clay pots, the practice of boiling in baskets disappeared.

An indication of the relative recency of pottery in the Sierra piedmont, about 200–300 years later than among

Eastern Calif. Mus., Independence: A1275.

Fig. 6. Owens Valley Brownware vessel. This specimen was found in the Inyo Range, southeastern Calif.; height 16 cm; collected before 1971.

the Southern Paiute and Western Shoshone, is that only some women manufactured it, a feature otherwise foreign to Great Basin economy. Whereas basketry and woven articles were manufactured in techniques and types known and practiced by everybody, not every woman knew how to make pottery. The few women who practiced this specialty bartered some of their products for food, basketry, or shell money. Whereas the terminology that has to do with basketry is rich and varied, no analogous terminology for pottery developed. Thus, there is no generic term for clay vessels in Mono other than *winabi* 'clay'; special names for clay vessels of different shapes and usage are lacking.

Both in ethnographic and archeological terms the distribution of Owens Valley Brown was limited to the Sierra piedmont and adjacent regions. East of the Sierra Nevada these localities are, beside Round Valley and Owens Valley proper, the Hammil, Deep Springs, and Fish Lake valleys formerly with a predominantly Mono-speaking population, and Panamint and Death valleys once with a population speaking Shoshone (Irwin 1980:28–29). Traces of this pottery have also been found in the Mono Lake Basin (Davis 1964:277). Among the Monache and the Foothill Yokuts, brown wares continued to be manufactured until the 1920s and 1930s (Gayton 1929, 1948:80–81, 134, 161, 226, 265). The pottery as produced on either side of the Sierra Nevada differs markedly from that of southern California. Since the use of pottery was more important east of the Southern Sierra, where stone-boiling in baskets already had disappeared, while it was retained among the Monache and Yokuts (Driver 1937:65, 122), diffusion must have occurred from east to west. Evidently the connecting link with the Pueblos, perhaps the ultimate point of departure, is to be found in the undecorated pottery produced by Shoshone-speaking neighbors in Nevada and Utah, several hundred years earlier (Fowler 1968:10–13). Descriptions of Sierra Nevada pottery with detailed discussions of distribution and historical relation to the Southwest ceramic tradition are provided by Steward (1928, 1933b), Gayton (1929, 1948), Voegelin (1938), H.S. Riddell (1951), Riddell and Riddell (1956), Elsasser (1960:30–31, map 7), Tuohy (1973), and C.S. Fowler and D.D. Fowler (1981).

Among culture elements that migrants from Owens Valley brought across the mountains to the Monache and Yokuts villages on the headwaters of San Joaquin River, basketry is most conspicuous. A common and doubtlessly ancient feature was the twined, necked, and small-mouthed water container, in various sizes, which occurred in plain twine west of the mountains, but typically in twill twine in the Great Basin, Owens Valley included. The twined conical carrying baskets made by the Owens Valley Paiute occurred in different size and tightness (Steward 1933b:272). A coarse, open twine, cone-shaped burden basket was used for gathering firewood and transporting large articles. A seed-gathering woman was equipped with a smaller, tightly woven type with cloth-covered bottom and a basketry seed beater. The winnowing trays were made in tightly woven twill twine, but the parching trays for use with live coals in open plain twine.

An unusual item known only among the Yokuts, the Tubatulabal, Kawaiisu, Owens Valley Paiute, and the Panamint Western Shoshone was the finely coiled, narrow-necked and flat-shouldered "treasure" basket, the receptacle for shell-bead money. The distribution center of these basketry jars, often ornamented with feathers and other finery, evidently is in the Yokuts territory as implied by the description "Tulare bottleneck." Yet, the prototype is either the versatile water olla of the Great Basin or the Southern Paiute treasure basket, although manufactured in a different technique, that is, Yokuts coiled ware replaced Mono and Southern Paiute twined. The Yokuts called their decorated money jar *osa* (Gayton 1948:19), a word borrowed from Mono *os·a,* which referred to narrow-necked and pitched water bottles, sometimes in the derivation *paʔos·a,* literally meaning 'water basket'. The historical course of events is obvious: the perfected flat-bottomed Yokuts bottleneck basket, the most elaborate in the area, was derived from the Great Basin, later to reverberate as eastbound trade goods associated with an entirely new concept, namely that of wealth, the diffusion of clamshell currency, and payment of bride price (Kroeber 1925:531–532; Driver 1937:78, 121; Voegelin 1938:31–32; Gayton 1948:17–19).

This participation in two different culture systems, whether on the one or the other side of the Sierra, appears in the local inventory of milling implements. In Owens Valley, as everywhere in the Great Basin, grinding of wild seeds, including pine nuts, was done on a portable, lightweight metate with a flat or slightly concave grinding surface, using a roundish or nearly oblong muller or mano of hard stone, smoothed on both sides from long usage. In certain localities of the Sierra piedmont the portable stone mortar and pestle had replaced the metate as the most important tool for milling under the influence of Sierra highland tradition. This shift in milling techniques, pounding instead of grinding, was a consequence of participation in the California acorn complex, which was characterized by the use of bedrock mortars.

Structures

The habitation pattern, the most consequential domain of local ethnography, provides diagnosis and theoretical control both of the yearly cycle of tribal economy and of social organization. Aboriginal dwellings in Owens Valley required an extensive terminology. In Numic languages there are three localisms for 'house' used in different areas, all of which occur in Owens Valley Mono to designate particular house types. The most widespread term is that of Shoshone *kahni* and Southern Paiute *kani*, an old Uto-Aztecan word (Miller 1967) that occurs as the Owens Valley compound base *-kani/ -gani*. Next in frequency and diffusion is *nobi*, derived from *no-* 'to camp, to dwell', a common Western Numic term and the generic name of a human dwelling in Northern Paiute. In Mono spoken in Owens Valley and occasionally west of the Sierras, there is also the term *toni*, but with unknown etymology. Possibly *toni* (also pronounced *to·ni*) is a contraction of Proto–Western Numic **tomonobi*, which would have meant 'winter-house' corresponding to the Mono Lake Northern Paiute term *tomogani* for the cone-shaped winter dwelling. In Owens Valley the form *to·nobi* has been recorded in this meaning. In contemporary Mono the root for 'winter' is *to·-* (*to·wani* 'to be winter'). The word *toni*, unknown in other Numic languages, may also relate to an enigmatic name, *tõti* or *tõthi*, recorded in Panamint Shoshone (Driver 1937:114) for a conical or domed dwelling. Steward (1933b:263–266) and Driver (1937:66–68, 113–115) independently interviewed informants on aboriginal house types. Driver's classification was based on form and Steward's on function. For other subareas in the Great Basin Steward (1941:232–234) applied Driver's classification. Material and construction of a structure varied depending upon the length of time and when during the annual round it was used. Thus, in late precontact time the Owens Valley Paiutes erected at least seven types of structures.

The most durable building was the communal assembly lodge, in English the sweathouse, an obviously secondary function. There is no aboriginal equivalent term in Mono. In the 1980s the Owens Valley Paiutes called this structure *mu·sa*, a presumably recent loan from the Yokuts and Monache, who both call it *mu·sa*, a Penutian word. The last house of this type (fig. 7) described by Steward (1933b:265–266), was a relatively spacious, "nearly circular" (tending toward the elliptical, cf. Driver 1937:114), semisubterranean house. Unlike the Plains form of sweathouse, sporadically occurring elsewhere in the Great Basin, or the introduced ceremonial sweatlodge, it was heated by direct fire built immediately inside the low entrance, not by steam from heated stones. The building, ownership, and maintenance of the lodge was closely associated with tribal chieftainship. The district or village chief sponsored, supervised, and presumably to no small degree supported the erection of such a structure, which in proportion to the means of this society was an enormous public undertaking. The excavation was done with digging sticks and carrying baskets, and the poles were shaped by fire since cutting tools were lacking.

The *toni* or *siwanobi*, similar in construction but without ridge pole, was a cone-shaped and in comparison to other local house types fairly roomy dwelling, "15 to 20 feet in diameter" built around a central smokehole on a frame of high poles over an excavation "about 2 feet deep" (Steward 1933b:264). The cover was mats of tule or other grass overlapping like shingles, sometimes with earth added. This house was erected by several men in cooperation and built to last. Steward called the structure a "winter valley house," thereby stressing its function as a family dwelling for people remaining in the valley during the winter, which suggests perennial occupation. Such a house might also be used throughout the year as a men's meetinghouse in lieu of a complete *mu·sa* but would not serve as a sudatory (Driver 1937:114).

The third type comprised a variety of conical to dome-shaped (Driver 1937:114), thatched or mat-covered dwellings built on level ground mostly without earth cover (fig. 8). The framework consisted of willow posts bent or brought together at the top. As elsewhere in the Great Basin, the hemispherical frame with closely spaced, pliable posts might once have been the predominant type. Later the conical form with straight willow poles dominated house construction along the

top, Eastern Calif. Mus., Independence; bottom, after Steward 1933b:fig. 4.

Fig. 7. The *mu·sa* at Big Pine Creek, Calif. The structure served as a communal assembly house, a place for the men to sweat, and a dormitory for young unmarried men. top, George Robinson and Ben Tibbets in the doorway of the *mu·sa*. Behind them can be seen the chimney of a wood burning stove. Photographed about 1930. bottom, Plan of the *mu·sa*. It was roughly 25 feet in diameter, excavated 2 feet, and had a central ridge pole supported by 2 forked posts set in the ground. The framework of closely spaced poles with the butt ends stuck in the ground and the top ends converging around a smokehole was covered with grass and then a thick layer of earth. It had a central fire pit and a smoke hole before the wood burning stove was added. The doorway faced east.

western border and sporadically everywhere in the Great Basin. The term *saibi toni* 'house of tule' in Big Pine Mono for houses of this type guarantees that they occurred as a perennial structure in villages near the swampy bottomlands in the north.

The most archaic-looking building was the fourth type, a crudely shaped circular wooden structure (*wogadoni*), a conical pole lodge composed of dead timber, since green trunks could not be felled. The poles were placed close together, slanting inward over a shallow excavation and covered with bark slabs and conifer boughs.

The Owens Valley Paiutes and the Mono Lake Northern Paiutes, as well as other tribes in the Great Basin, knew of this kind of house built on a four-pole foundation. As a winter house, the type prevailed throughout the Sierra highlands. East of the mountains it was exclusively used at the sites for pine nut gathering on an elevation of 6,000 to 8,000 feet from late October to the end of winter.

Remnants of developed, gabled variants of the timbered winter house (*wogani*), the fifth type, have been found scattered throughout the piñon-juniper zones on

Nat. Hist. Mus. of Los Angeles Co., Western Hist. Coll.: top, 5900; bottom left, 5459; bottom right, 5881.

Fig. 8. Dwellings. top, Temporary open camps with individual fire areas clustered near the fence at the edge of a circular dance ground at Five Bridges area, north of Bishop, Calif. Two women are sleeping in the center; bedding and cooking equipment hang from the fence. bottom left, Woman near Sand Hill, Inyo Co., Calif., carrying grass for the house walls in a burden basket supported with a forehead tumpline, balanced also by grasping the rim. Women carried burdens long distances, even crossing the Sierra Nevada while trading. bottom right, A shade at Big Pine Creek, Calif., used as protection from the summer heat and winter winds. Mary Bell is at left, Tom Bell at right; Teha, Mary's mother, at center, wears a rabbitskin blanket and basket cap. Owens Valley basket caps were larger and covered more of the head than those of other Great Basin tribes. Photographs by Andrew A. Forbes, 1903–1916.

LILJEBLAD AND FOWLER

the western slopes of the White and the Inyo mountains and for all at the extensive piñon groves in the Benton Range north of Bishop. This house is described as a "mountain house" (Steward 1933b:263) and as "a dwelling with a single ridgepole. . .either a double lean-to with gabled ends or with ends rounded and slanting (hip-roofed)" (Driver 1937:66–67, 113–114). Building materials were the same as for the conical pole lodge, timber lodges with roofing of bark and pine boughs. The Owens Valley Paiutes used these houses only in winter in association with pine nut storage in faraway localities where such building material was available. Although built on unexcavated ground and without grass or earth covering, the construction with its ridge pole supported by two forked posts set 15 feet apart is remotely suggestive of a *mu·sa*.

The sixth type was a four-sided shade of ramada type (*haba*) used at the height of summer, the frame usually remaining from year to year. This structure was in principle a rectangular willow roof supported by four crotched willow posts with long poles resting lengthwise and crosswise, forming a horizontal support for a cover of willow, brush, other foliage, or tule. The ramadas were in former days the main living quarters in summer time and a place to cook.

Finally, there was the semicircular brush windbreak, also a general Great Basin type. This consists of broken limbs of sagebrush or willow, or uprooted sagebrush plants placed vertically so that they stand waist-high and slightly incurve. Such structures were ordinarily temporary, being built most often in summer at harvesting localities. A fire might occasionally be built in the center, if the structure were large enough. However, it was probably more common to have the fire for cooking outside this structure.

As a nucleus of sociopolitical integration, the assembly lodge or eventually some other permanent structure in the community served both as an assembly hall and as a dormitory for old or unmarried men, a place for gossip, gambling, storytelling, and singing, sometimes as a forum for discussing common enterprises and practical communal undertakings, but never for serious ritual or ceremonial occasions like annual festivals, dances, and shamanistic performances. In precontact time no houses were built for these purposes anywhere in the Great Basin, although huge lodges meeting these needs were erected later by modern means on some reservations in the north, in a pan-Indian style inspired from the Plains. Traditional dance grounds were elaborate open structures in densely populated areas and served an entire district as a ceremonial center. Here people congregated for intertribal dances and for the tribal mourning ceremony, an annual death festival celebrated in the fall. For Owens Valley, Driver (1937:101, 139–140) described a round or elliptical roofless brush enclosure (fig. 8, top), serving both for ceremonials and for temporary camping ground for guests from other villages.

Kinship

The constituent unit of social integration was the nuclear family. The members of a domestic unit, no matter how it was composed, considered themselves as close relatives, though not necessarily as a "family," the latter a group in theory but without name in Western Numic and mentioned only periphrastically. Prolonged, consistent solidarity and mutual support beyond the family level prevailed only within the ego-centered kindred, the totality of somebody's consanguineous kin.

With the nuclear family as a point of reference, bilateral terminology (fig. 9) covers a lineal range of seven generations, three ascending and three descending from ego's collateral line, allowing for a greater range of identification of individuals within his or her kindred than actually known, given that they are dispersed over an unlimited area. Held together by genetic ties in ego's own and descending generations, but ignoring affinal ones, the kindred did not exist as a land-using or property-owning body, nor as a cohesive corporate group. From the viewpoint of an individual, the kindred was a group of people cognate with him or her but without consideration to lineage or locality rules whether matri- or patri-oriented. Thus, it cannot be said that ego was a member of a discrete descent group existing "in perpetuity." Within the framework of Owens Valley society, there never were formally segmented groups of cognatic descent beyond the nuclear kindred of siblings (cousins inclusive), their parents, children, and grandparents, that is, as far as reciprocal terminology distinguishing sex and bifurcation would reach. Within this range, the Mono dialects had a greater variety of synonymous relationship terms than any other Numic language.

The system is fundamentally the same as in other Numic languages, but displays traits unique for the Mono dialects. Mono east of the Sierra Nevada distinguishes each one of the four types of parental siblings under separate designations. Only Mono and Bannock (both marginal) extend terms for ego's lineal offspring collaterally to children of his first parallel cousins, whereas Northern Paiute keeps these distinct. Bilateral descent is reflected in the bifurcate terminology for grandparent-grandchild relationship ignoring polarity. Likewise, grandparental status and authority appears in these terms, which recognize the sex of the senior alternant but not the sex of the junior. These words are derived from old Uto-Aztecan roots with known etymology (Miller 1967:67). All four terms imply the same degree of intrafamilial relation between alternating generations. Lateral extension of these terms for ego's grandparents is acknowledged, but evidently seldom applied. Bifur-

425

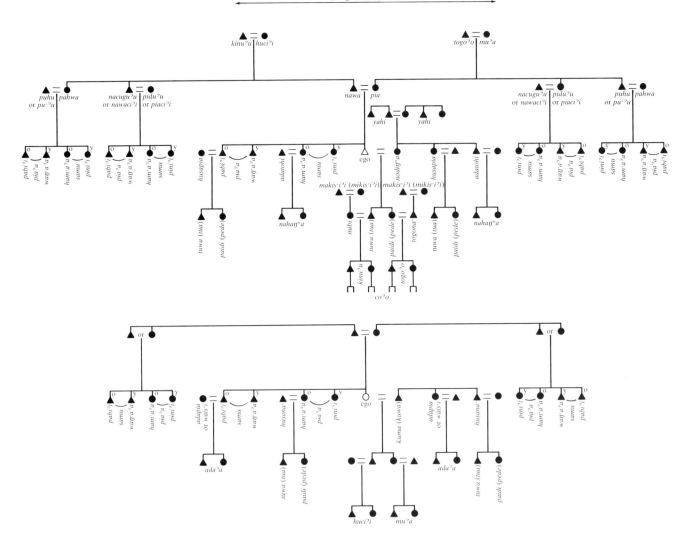

Fig. 9. Owens Valley Paiute kinship terminology. top, Male ego; bottom, female ego. Terms for omitted or unlabeled kin types are the same as for male ego.

cation, which otherwise characterizes the system, is ignored for the two terminal generations, that is, beyond the second ascending and the first descending. No components other than sex and relative age keep individual types of the sibling generation apart. Collaterals on this level were not terminologically distinguished; that is, sibling terms are extended to close cousins on both father's and mother's side, but no formal rules for degree of further extension exist. How far a line would be acknowledged as kin seems to have varied with local conditions, personal sentiment, and with the social influence exerted by a group of siblings acting in consort.

In the Mono-speaking community, the consanguineal kindred was exogamous. Terminology for affinal relation is less detailed and lacks an inclusive label. The closest generalization is the bound plural form *-yahimi*, for example, *iyahimi* 'my parents-in-law and their brothers and sisters', that is, all relatives by marriage

of the first ascending generation, each one called somebody's *yahi*. Affinal terms occur only on ego's own and on his first ascending and descending generations.

The dominant genetic and the weak affinal aspect of Shoshonean kin terminology was stressed by Shimkin (1941:236–237): "The exclusion of all blood kin from marriage might be a clue to the careful reckoning of descent in the terminology, and to the secondary nature of affinal terms. Possibly affinal relatives are not regarded as kin at all." Affinal terminology, which developed by extension of cognate kin terms, occupies in modern times a conspicuous symbiotic lexical position in relation to genetic terminology.

Although interdependent with the consanguineal system, but secondary to it, affinal kinship terminology is consistent and applicable to traditionally favored marriage forms. Any traceable blood relation closer than third cousins prevented marriage with the consequence

426

that villages, with the exception of major population centers, were exogamous. Both parallel and cross siblings from two unrelated families preferably entered into exchange marriage, under the same rules as in the Great Basin generally.

One feature of great consequence in Owens Valley kinship was borrowed from speakers of Penutian languages. It strengthened the affinal relationship between two unrelated families for ceremonial exchange and other mutual interests. Parents of marriageable children would join in a relationship called *makis·i* (or *mikis·i*), a word derived from Miwok and Yokuts (cf. Southern Sierra Miwok *maksi?* 'child's parent-in-law'), *makis·i?i* being the mutual term of address between parallel children's spouses' parents. Since the children are double cross-cousins, the bond is closed with the second generation.

Sociopolitical Organization

The Owens Valley Paiutes moved about as gatherers in spring and summer. In years with an ample supply of pine nuts most of them did not spend the winter in the base camps in the lowlands, a semi-desert where fuel was scarce and food supplies soon would be exhausted. Solid log-dwellings for winter use were scattered throughout the highlands east and northeast of the valley, where both the piñon crop and, in years when that crop failed, the Indian ricegrass seed, were cached. But in spring, in time for the meadow irrigation, and in early fall for the social activities, each family or cluster of consanguineally related families returned to their customary dwelling place in the valley. The seasonal increase of population at the sites of the traditional ceremonial centers was a consequence of the calendrical nature in this society of public ritualism and ceremony. It was the coordination of seasonable events between the otherwise autonomous and independently foraging local groups that necessitated organized leadership of each district or cluster of villages. Thus, when speaking about "permanent villages" in the aboriginal Owens Valley, one should remember that most frequently only some individuals remained at the village site throughout the year.

An individual or a family sometimes shifted allegiance from one village or district to another, in either case from the dependence on a politically dominant family, but usually because of marriage into another group.

Each one of the districts (fig. 1) was originally ascribed by Steward (1933b:304) to a land-owning band under the control and leadership of a headman. Later, recognizing the nuclear family as a self-sufficient group, Steward (1977:366, 393) rejected the term "band" in favor of "incipient or proto-bands" for aggregates of population. The interaction between villages within a delimited area involved frequent intermarriage, community irrigation, cooperative hunting and rabbit drives, and common use of the *mu·sa*. Steward (1933b:305) at first believed the population of a district claimed hunting, fishing, seed-gathering, and root-digging rights within their boundaries and that piñon groves in the White and Inyo ranges were held by Owens Valley districts immediately west of them. He revised his view, stating that group exploitation of the same territory each year did not imply "exclusive claims to or defense of its resources" (Steward 1938:20, 1977:375–376.)

Formal cooperation among district groups was limited to occasional common enterprises and to exchange of rituals. Because of relationship by marriage or for other reasons, individuals from different districts in Owens Valley assisted each other at funerals, with the face-washing ceremony, as part of the annual mourning rituals, and on other festive occasions, a custom unheard of among other tribes of the Great Basin. However,

Eastern Calif. Mus., Independence.

Fig. 10. Men's hoop and pole game. left, The field, which was 50 ft. long, had 2 brush fences at either end, between which a small hoop (3–12 in. in diameter) was rolled. right, A man aims at the hoop with an 8 ft. pole, hoping to throw it through the hoop and pin it to the ground. Photographs possibly by Harry W. Mendenhall, Big Pine, Calif., 1920s.

Eastern Calif. Mus., Independence.
Fig. 11. Women's shinny or double ball game. A knotted or stuffed buckskin strip is moved with sticks between 2 goals. Photograph possibly by Harry W. Mendenhall, Big Pine, Calif., 1920s.

perhaps the most important introduction of trans-Sierran cultural elements over the centuries was the apparent adoption of the Yokuts system of tribal division, first by the enclaves in the Sierra highlands, and later by the natives in Owens Valley. Among the Monache, almost the entire Yokuts system prevailed, including even tribal names and territorial independence, as well as patrilineal cross-tribal division in totemic moieties; the latter, however, held true only in ceremonial rituals, since they were not exogamous. To a lesser extent, this order is also found among the Owens Valley Paiutes. Thus, people who camped every year around a cult center on the Independence and George creeks in the southern part of Owens Valley were sometimes called "the Eagles." This epithet corresponds to the nickname "the Magpies" for people living farther north in the valley. These bird names for locally defined groups, used only as sobriquets, as they presumably always were, seem to be a faint echo of the division terminology of the moiety-possessing California tribes.

Common enterprises such as meadow irrigation, group hunting or rabbit drives, and ritual exchange were shared by the tribelets. The tribelet was unquestionably the maximum social unit. However, the kindred of any individual of the group, because it was more widely dispersed and was looked upon as more important and enduring, cut across the boundaries of the tribelet.

Since districts in the northern part of the valley and principal villages in the south were independent political units, the administrative power of a "chief" or headman was limited to a few communal activities. His title in Mono was *poginabi* derived from the verb *pogi-/poki-* 'to announce, to give orders'. His duties were to direct irrigation and rabbit, antelope, and deer drives; to conduct fall festivals, dances, and mourning ceremonies; to supervise the building and maintenance of the assembly lodge; and to keep people informed about the ripening of pine nuts and forthcoming common enterprises. It was his obligation to approve or veto the killing of a shaman accused of witchcraft. Chieftainship was hereditary; that is, an aged headman chose his own successor, subject to public approval. The preferred succession was from father to son; but a sister's son was acceptable or an unrelated person. The main reason for selecting community leaders from the same family was apparently economic. A politically leading family did in a generation or two accumulate a considerable wealth counted in shell-bead money, and the headman was ultimately responsible for the economy of the entire group.

Ceremonialism

After a wandering life of gathering activity during summer, people assembled each fall for the traditional Round Dances, gambling, and festivity. Professional singers were hired, and skilled dancers, men dressed in elaborate dance regalia, performed individually in the center of the spacious dance corral enclosed by a willow fence. Communal enterprises were preceded and followed by dances, called fandangos in postcontact time. Before or after the pine nut harvest, the headmen of districts or major villages called people together to celebrate the pine nut festival for days, also attended by visitors from distant places (Steward 1933b:320–323).

The only festival that attracted people from Owens Valley as a whole was the annual Mourning ceremony held in the fall for those who died during the year past, usually called the Cry. It served the purpose of terminating the obligatory year of mourning that the spouse of a deceased person must observe. A mourner's sorrow was symbolically ended after his face had been washed by a ceremonial partner of the same sex. This act was one of the major functions of the *makis·i?i* but was not necessarily performed by a person with that relationship. Given that the spouse of the deceased had not washed his face since the death of the loved one as a show of respect, the face washing also ended any public display of mourning on the individual's part. Clothing and other personal property of the deceased person was burned together with costly offerings from his family. The Cry complex in Owens Valley is related to the more widespread complex of southern California and may have arrived via the Monache from the Yokuts.

Shamanism among the Owens Valley Paiutes, even though primarily doctoring, assumed a social control unknown among most Great Basin Indians. Whereas political leadership was inheritable, shamanistic power was individual and usually obtained in dreams brought about by culturally determined expectation. Both sexes acted as doctors, but shamans were seldom headmen (Steward 1933b:308–316). A doctor could, however,

Southwest Mus., Los Angeles: 6725.

Fig. 12. Men performing a dance at the San Fernando Mission fiesta, Calif. The dancing was "a marvelous contrast to the fake 'Indian dances'—with orchestra accompaniment—usually seen at pageants. The 'tom-tom' was not heard, nor even rattles. Our Owens Valley dancers used nothing but their own characteristic split-stick clappers to mark the time" (Harrington 1932:76). They wear skirts of twisted eagle down and magpie feathers, hats of erect magpie feathers encircled by head rings of eagle down ("Southern Valley Yokuts," fig. 11, vol. 8), and carry eagle feathers, sometimes attached to the waist by a long cord. The dance and costume were introduced to the Owens Valley Paiute by California Indians about 1850 (Steward 1933b:321). Photograph by Mark R. Harrington, May 1932.

by making a village or district chieftain depending on his service, eventually as a witch, in a clandestine manner exercise an influence upon family disputes or other public affairs.

History

Documentary evidence of early exploration of Owens Valley by non-Indians is scant. Although Spaniards from California may have entered the area in the early 1800s, there seems to be no record of such incursions. Fur trappers and prospectors seem to have left the first records, and their references to the native inhabitants of the valley are few. Most comment on the generally arid and cold conditions in the region, news of which may have kept permanent settlers from the area and thus spared the Indian people disruption until the early 1860s (Busby, Findlay, and Bard 1979:53).

In 1855 A.W. von Schmidt was contracted by the state of California to survey the public lands on the eastern slope of the Sierra south of Mono Lake. Although on the whole not favorably impressed by the potential for White exploitation, he did characterize Round Valley and Long Valley as being "splendid land for any purpose" (Chalfant 1922:73). His detailed data on water resources, including those utilized by the Indians "for the purpose of raising grass and roots on which they subsist," constitutes the first and most important description of irrigation by these groups (Lawton et al. 1976:23). Although von Schmidt seems to have had a few clashes with the Indians, he describes them as generally peaceable, "a fine looking set of men," who subsist "principally on pinenuts, fish and hares, which are very plenty" (Chalfant 1922:72).

In 1859 Capt. J.W. Davidson led a military reconnaissance from Fort Tejon (Wilke and Lawton 1976).

Davidson was sent to the valley on a punitive expedition to catch suspected Indian livestock thieves and return the stock to ranchers west of the mountains. He was also to ascertain the suitability of the valley for an Indian reservation. Davidson found no evidence that the Indians were involved in the thefts, or that there was much White influence in any aspect of their lives. He described aboriginal irrigation practices in the valley, commented upon the harvesting of brine fly pupae in Owens Lake, and recommended that a large section of the tract be set aside for a reservation and that the Indians be protected by the government (Wilke and Lawton 1976:29, 31). In February 1859, 22,300 acres near Independence in southern Owens Valley were withdrawn pending a decision about establishing a reserve. In 1864 the order was revoked (Walter 1984).

In 1861 the first permanent White settlers arrived in the valley. They were cattlemen from Nevada and California settlements intent on supplying pasturage for their herds (Chalfant 1922:88–90). Ranches and trading stations were established in Round Valley and near the present sites of Bishop, Independence, and Lone Pine. Produce from these areas fed miners both north and south of the valley.

Almost immediately, there were skirmishes with the Indians over rights to their irrigated lands. As the White population increased, took up more meadow areas, and began to fell piñons for fuel, the clashes increased. Indians stole cattle to replace depleted game, and the Whites retaliated by killing several Indians. By joining forces under several leaders, most prominent among them Captain George from Southern Owens Valley and Joaquin Jim from the north (a Yokuts), the Indians, by superior numbers, were in undisputed control of the valley by early 1862 (Chalfant 1922:121).

On July 4, 1862, Camp Independence was founded as a military outpost to quell the disturbances (Chalfant 1922:123). The fighting soon broke out again as the military food supplies for the Indians were exhausted. Mineral strikes in the valley also brought more settlers to the district. In spring 1863 local and nonlocal Indians under Joaquin Jim increased their depredations in the northern part of the valley. Several major battles resulted, with fighting continuing into late spring and early summer. The military under Capt. Moses A. McLaughlin ultimately engaged in a "scorched earth" campaign against the Indians, burning all their stores, houses, and equipment (Chalfant 1922:146–147). One June 4, roughly 400 people surrendered at Camp Independence, including many of the followers of Captain George and Joaquin Jim. Others soon followed. On July 11, 1863, over 900 prisoners, including men, women, and children, were marched from Camp Independence to San Sebastian Reservation near Fort Tejon for internment. Nearly 100 people either died or escaped along the way. But the reservation and fort were ill-equipped

to hold the people, and within three years, most were back in the valley. By this time more of their lands and resources had been appropriated, and they were left to settle around the emerging towns, on ranches (figs. 13–14), or in mining camps. There men and women worked as laborers, while attempting to supplement their subsistence with some natural products. An 1870 census reported 1,150 Indians in the valley, although one in 1877 gives the count at 776 (Busby, Findlay, and Bard 1979:57).

The federal government began to take a more active role in providing services to Owens Valley people after this time. By 1897, Indian schools were in operation at Big Pine and Bishop (ARCIA 1897:12). One at Independence opened a few years later. Although Indians were living in several places in the valley, reservations were not actually established until after 1900. In 1902, a portion of Camp Independence was officially set aside for use by local Indians. In 1912, additional tracts were reserved in the valley for the purpose of setting up reservations at Bishop, Lone Pine, and Big Pine. A small reserve was also established at Benton in 1915, and in that same year the Fort Independence Reservation, including the lands reserved earlier, was established (U.S. Bureau of Indian Affairs 1975:53–55). Although most reserved lands were not large enough for ranching, small-scale farming and gardening were practiced. Families also continued to reside on nonreservation lands in the valley. Western Shoshone families from southern Owens Valley and valleys to the east also moved to the reservations and other settlements.

In 1905, the city of Los Angeles began to take an interest in the water resources of Owens Valley. It purchased all the available water rights and much of the irrigated land in the southern half of the valley and in 1913 finished a 233-mile aqueduct to the city. These initial purchases apparently included lands belonging to

Eastern Calif. Mus., Independence: 9837.

Fig. 13. Indian dwellings at Benton Dude Ranch, Calif., where Indians worked as domestics and ranch hands. Dome-shaped structures using nontraditional materials are next to modern-style house made of sawed lumber. Photograph by Burton Frasher, about 1910–1915.

430

U.S. Geological Survey Photographic Lib., Denver, Colo.: 78.
Fig. 14. Group at Oasis in Fish Lake Valley, Esmeralda Co., Nev., where they were employed on White ranches. They wear ranch clothing of the period, and 2 women also wear traditional basketry caps. Photograph by Henry W. Turner, 1899.

19 Indians (Kahrl 1982:354). In the 1920s, the city began to expand its holdings to the northern part of the valley, leading to hostilities and open conflicts with White citizens. Despite opposition, by 1933 the city owned 95 percent of the farmland and 85 percent of all town property in the valley (Busby, Findlay, and Bard 1979:83; Kahrl 1976:114; Ostrom 1953:127). The resulting destruction of the economy of the region placed further burdens on the Indian people who found their jobs on farms and as laborers abolished.

In the early 1930s, in an effort to obtain additional rights to lands and water, the city of Los Angeles also proposed various plans for either consolidating or re-

Nat. Hist. Mus. of Los Angeles Co., Western Hist. Coll.: 1590.
Fig. 15. Fort Independence, Calif., Indian band, which performed in parades and other festivities throughout Owens Valley. back row, left to right: Fred Glenn, Tony Harris, Alex Patton, Happy Jack, Cleveland Buff, Harrison Diaz, and Jim Reynolds. front row, Johnny Symms, Pete Thomas, Ben Hunter, Ed Lewis, and Jim Earl. Photograph by Andrew A. Forbes, about 1912–1916.

Fig. 16. The Paiute-Shoshone Cultural Center and Museum, Bishop, Calif. The Center, dedicated in 1981, houses temporary exhibits and promotes cultural activities for Indians throughout Owens Valley. Photograph by Catherine S. Fowler, 1984.

moving the remaining Indian people in the valley. Special right-of-way and land agent A.J. Ford (1930, 1932) alternately proposed expanding and relocating existing reservations to contain all the people and removing the population entirely to another area west of the Sierra. Perhaps with duplicity, the Department of Water and Power of the city of Los Angeles also appropriated funds to hire Indians on maintenance crews for city-owned properties. Before action could be taken on either proposal, a new agent was installed and an additional assessment made. Under E.A. Porter's tenure, an agreement was reached between the Department of the Interior and the city of Los Angeles for a series of land exchanges involving the Bishop, Lone Pine, and Big Pine reservations. Fort Independence, also initially involved, rejected the agreement and retained its initial holdings. In 1937 Congress provided for the exchanges, and the majority of Indian people also voted in favor of the plan (Walter 1984:5–7).

The federal government built new housing and installed sewer and efficient irrigation systems on the new tracts in the 1940s. Fort Independence and the small Benton reserve continued to operate without these improvements.

In the 1970s and 1980s other improvements have been made, including the addition of new houses, tribal buildings, and businesses, and at Bishop, a museum-cultural center. Each of the reservations in the valley is governed by an elected council, with further consolidation being provided by the Owens Valley Paiute-Shoshone Band of Indians, an administrative unit with representatives from Big Pine, Lone Pine, Bishop, and Fort Independence (the last if a quorum is needed). This body administers federal, state, and private grant funds and programs for the valley as a whole, while the local councils continue to take responsibility for local funds and programs (Busby, Findlay, and Bard 1979:180). *431*

Cultural awareness programs and some attempts at language maintenance have been sponsored independently on valley reservations and by the combined administrative unit. The museum at Bishop (fig. 16) sponsors exhibits and dances, and beginning in 1982 has been involved with the Bishop Reservation and the Owens Valley Paiute-Shoshone Band in sponsoring a summer rodeo and powwow (fig. 17). Several individuals continue to participate in traditional subsistence activities, such as the harvest of pandora moth larvae and pine nut gathering. In the early 1980s, valley elders were effective in persuading the U.S. Forest Service not to spray the pine trees in the Inyo National Forest to prevent a pandora moth infestation. They seek to protect other aspects of their cultural heritage as well.

Synonymy

The people of Owens Valley, when first contacted and described in the 1840s, seem to have been referred to merely as Indians (for example, Kern 1876:482). However, in 1856 both the names Paiute—as Pah-Utahs—

Fig. 17. Children's Indian dress contestants at the Powwow at Bishop, Calif. Photograph by John W. Walter, 1982.

and Mono (earlier applied to the Monache and the Mono Lake Northern Paiute) were being used for them (Merriam 1955:167–172; Chalfant 1933:121). In 1859 Davidson referred to the people as Wokopee Indians in the mistaken belief that this was their name for the Owens River (Wilke and Lawton 1976:33–34). By the 1860s spellings of the name Monache were in use for both the Monache and the Owens Valley Paiute (Merriam 1955:170, 172).

As with other applications of Paiute to Great Basin peoples (see synonymies for Northern Paiute and Southern Paiute, this vol.), the term as used here has no obvious etymology and was not a self-designation until the early twentieth century, when it was adopted from English. Steward (1933b:235) gives popular etymologies.

Loew (1876:541) differentiated the Owens Valley Paiute as Western Payutes, and in 1876 Powers applied the term Southern Paiute to the "Paiute of Inyo County, California and Southern Nevada" (Fowler and Fowler 1970:135). However, although the need for a distinctive name for the Owens Valley Paiute was early expressed by Gatschet (1879:411), throughout the late nineteenth and early twentieth centuries variations of Paiute, Mono, and Monache continued in the literature (Merriam 1955). Eventually Steward (1933b:235, 1938:50) introduced Owens Valley Paiute, although he did not recognize a sharp linguistic distinction between them and the Northern Paiute, referring to the people as the "Northern Paiute of Owens Valley."

The names Mono and Monache ultimately reflect terms used by Penutian-speaking groups of the Sierras for their Western Numic–speaking neighbors: Nisenan Moan´-au-zi for the Northern Paiute (Powers 1877a:320), given as Maidu monozi by Kroeber (1925:584, 1959:267), Wikchamni Yokuts Mona´či 'Owens Valley Paiute' (Gayton 1948:56). Lamb (1958a:97) suggests that popularized Monache, as applied to all Mono speakers, is probably from Yokuts; Kawaiisu mo-na-che 'Owens Valley Paiute' (Merriam 1955:171) must also be a borrowing. Mono resembles Southern Sierra Miwok mo·na? 'Mono person or language' (Broadbent 1964:257; cf. Merriam 1955:168). Wheeler-Voegelin (1957) suggests that from these various native applications of the terms, Mono at least came to be equated by Americans in California by the mid-1850s with wild or unacculturated peoples, at that time principally in the mountains to the east of permanent settlements.

The etymologies of Mono and Monache are uncertain. Kroeber (1925:584–585, cf. 1959:267–268) dismisses the suggestion that Mono is from the Spanish term for 'monkey' and equally discounts that it derives from Yokuts monai, monoyi 'flies' said to be applied to Mono speakers because of their ability to scale cliffs (see also Hodge 1907–1910, 1:932). However, Karpenstein (1945) suggested that the Yokuts name meant 'fly people' as an allusion to the Owens Valley Paiute and Mono Lake Northern Paiutes as gatherers of brine fly pupae, and this suggestion has received some acceptance (Heizer 1950:39).

Merriam (1902–1942, 1955) favored the terms Monache or Owens Valley Monache. Kroeber (1907a:114–119) used Mono for the language, although he professed some confusion as to the exact extent of this speech form. Gifford (1916:293) attempted some differentiation by applying the term Inyo Mono to the Owens Valley Paiute and distinguishing them from the Bridgeport Mono (a Northern-Paiute-speaking group), with whom they were often confused. Kroeber (1925:584) added the distinction Eastern Mono for Owens Valley versus Western Mono for the Monache. Following Lamb (1958a), Kroeber (1959:268) wrote on behalf of the proposal that the linguistic differentiation be recognized by using the terms Northern Paiute and Mono and the ethnic distinction by Paviotso and Monache.

The name Mono has gone out of use for the Owens Valley Paiute for several reasons: the term was never recognized by the people so designated; it was never made official by the United States Indian Service as their name (Paiute is used instead); the Penutian source words were used to refer to various local groups of both Mono and Northern Paiute speakers, and not exclusively for the populations of Owens Valley; and it was used imprecisely by ethnologists for the Mono speakers, or the Northern Paiute speakers of Mono Lake Basin, or both.

In common with all other Great Basin Indian people with the exception of the Washoe, the Owens Valley Paiute called themselves *nimi*, which means 'person' or 'the people' in their native language. In historic times they have also called themselves Paiutes, a term borrowed from English. Any one who lived in Owens Valley was called *payahuˑciʔi*, a nickname with a diminutive or affectionate implication derived from *payahuˑpi* 'Owens Valley'. There was no other collective name for the native valley population, and no group self-denomination.

Other terms by which the Owens Valley Paiute are known by their neighbors include: yówač, by the Wobonuch and Entimbich Monache and yóʔowəts or yóʔots by the Michahai and Waksachi, transitional Yokuts-Monache groups (Gayton 1948:214, 228, 258). The Tubatulabal name for them is given as iˑwiˑnaŋhal (Voegelin 1938:40) and ʔiwinaŋhal (C.F. Voegelin 1958:223). Numic-speaking groups often apply directional or orientational terms to each other, and these have included the Owens Valley Paiute in various ways. Thus, Panamint Shoshone east of Owens Valley call the Owens Valley Paiute *panˑaŋʷiˑti* 'westerners' or '(those) in the direction of the water', while Panamint south of Owens Lake used *kʷinˑagʷiˑti* 'being on the north' for the Owens Valley people near Bishop. The Monache some-times called the Owens Valley Paiute *sibiti* 'being on the east side'. Northern Paiute groups as far north as Pyramid Lake called them *pitanˑagʷˑati* 'being on the south', which is the source of Petonoquats (Merriam 1904:910) and Petenegowats (Hodge 1907–1910, 2:236).

Subgroups

Steward (1933b, 1938) lists several subgroups for the Owens Valley Paiute, the most important of which are those for the seven districts: *kwiˑnapaˑti*, *pitanˑapaˑti*, *tobowahamati*, *panati*, *tinihuˑwiˑti*, and two groups named *itiʔitiwiˑti*. The last of these is the basis for the English designation Utu Utu Gwaiti (earlier also Gwaitu) used by the Benton group. In addition, people might also be referred to internally within the valley by directional terminology or as the inhabitants of a specific place. Steward (1933b:325, 1938) lists several such names: e.g., tupūˊsi witü (*tipusiwiˑti*) 'people in nutgrass place', a site south of present-day Independence, California; and tsigūhūˊmatü (*siguhuˑmati*) 'people on rabbitbrush creek'. Merriam (1920) adds yet other sites and names of this type (see also Swanton 1952:377; Tohaktivi in Hodge 1907–1910, 2:771). Food names, a common device for speaking of people among both the Northern Paiute and Western Shoshone, were apparently little used here. Examples include: *čakisadikaʔa*, 'interior live oak (acorn) eaters' for the people on Division and Oak creeks in southern Owens Valley and *piagitikaʔa* 'pandora moth larvae eaters' for the people of Long Valley north of Owens Valley (cf. Merriam 1955:170–171).

Sources

The principal published ethnographer of the Owens Valley Paiutes is Steward (1933b, 1934, 1936b). Driver (1937) also obtained two culture element distribution survey lists and many miscellaneous notes. The work conducted in the 1930s through the State Emergency Relief Administration by F.J. Essene and F.S. Hulse, resulting in some 2,700 typed and manuscript pages that remain unpublished, is also very important (Valory 1971).

Topical treatment of oral tradition is provided by Steward (1936b). He also collected brief autobiographies (Steward 1934, 1938a). Native irrigation practices, of much interest since first described by Steward (1930), have figured in numerous theoretical works on the region, the data from which have been summarized by Lawton et al. (1976). Little has been done on ethnohistory in the region although the historical work by Chalfant (1922, 1933) and the paper by Walter (1984) contain much useful information. Busby, Findlay, and Bard (1979) have also provided a historical and ethnographic overview of the area.

Unpublished field notes, other than those by Hulse and Essene, include those of Liljeblad (1961–1980) involving several months of linguistic and ethnographic work in the communities of Lone Pine, Fort Independence, Big Pine, and Bishop; Walter (1978–1984) on Big Pine and Bishop; and C.S. Fowler (1980–1983) on Bishop. Other documentary repositories for ethnohistoric data include: the National Archives, Washington; the Federal Records Centers at Los Angeles and San Bruno, California; and the Bancroft Library, University of California, Berkeley.

Principal museum collections include those made by Steward and Gifford on deposit at the Lowie Museum of Anthropology, University of California, Berkeley; the C. Hart Merriam Basketry Collection at the University of California, Davis, Department of Anthropology Museum; and the very extensive holdings of the Eastern California Museum, Independence, California.

Northern Paiute

CATHERINE S. FOWLER AND SVEN LILJEBLAD

Territory and Language

The people who are today called the Northern Paiute ('norðərn 'pī,yōōt) consisted, at the time of Euro-American contact, of several linguistically homogeneous but culturally and politically distinct populations. Included among them were numerous geographically and ecologically defined subgroups for whom a consciousness of common language and a general appreciation of the geographic extent of that language constituted the principal tie. The recognition of a Northern Paiute people or nationality is thus based principally on linguistic evidence; that is, these groups all spoke the Northern Paiute language. They were not for any practical purpose politically integrated, nor did they constitute a single "tribe."

The vast area over which the Northern Paiute were distributed is outlined in figure 1. On the west, for some 600 miles, the perimeter followed the western edge and occasionally the crest of the Sierra Nevada and the watershed separating the Pit and Klamath rivers from the interior draining northern sector of the Great Basin. On the north, for roughly 300 miles, it continued through an undetermined territory beyond the summits dividing the drainage systems of the Columbia and Snake rivers (Park in Park et al. 1938; Ray et al. 1938; O.C. Stewart 1939). Over most of these two frontiers the Paiutes faced various foreign peoples all of whom spoke either Hokan or Penutian languages and with whom they were often in conflict. The eastern limit of their territory continued from the east side of Mono Lake diagonally north through central Nevada, following in that region the crest of the Desatoya Range. It further coincided approximately with the present Oregon-Idaho state line as far north as the outlets of the Weiser and Powder rivers beyond the great bend of the Snake River. However, unlike the western and northern borders, this limit was the boundary between closely related languages—Northern Paiute and Shoshone. It thus constituted a zone of some overlap that widened toward the north. Over much of this border bilingualism prevailed as it still did in the 1980s, and there was and continues to be a considerable exchange of population chiefly through intermarriage.

The same was true of the narrow southern border area. South of Mono Lake and extending east to west across a 50-mile strip lived groups of Owens Valley Paiute, close linguistic kin of the Northern Paiute. With these groups as well communication and exchange were common, and a number of cultural features were shared. However, the Owens Valley Paiute achieved a degree of sociopolitical integration unmatched by their northern neighbors.

Northern Paiute, the native language of the peoples in this region, and Mono are the two languages that constitute Western Numic, an offshoot of the Uto-Aztecan linguistic family. At the time of major field studies of the language, 1940s to 1970s, it showed some internal diversity but insufficient to affect mutual intelligibility. Lexical items, pronunciations, and an occasional grammatical feature differ from north to south, as would be expected over so vast an area. However, known movements of individuals, families, and groups (probably also typical in prehistoric times) have blurred major subareal distinctions. Most noticeable in the 1980s were the differences in phonemic inventories between speakers generally south of Pyramid Lake and those north of it—although speakers with these differences were also found elsewhere. Nichols (1974:5) makes a similar two-way division of the language into superdialects labeled Oregon Northern Paiute and Nevada Northern Paiute. He adds several subdialect divisions of the language based on additional contrastive sound features.*

---

*The phonemes of Northern Paiute are: (fortis stops and affricates) p, c (dental), t (alveolar), č, k, kʷ, ˀ; (lenis stops and affricates): b, ʒ, d, g, gʷ; (lenis and fortis sibilants) s, sˑ; (glottal spirant) h; (lenis nasals) m, n, ŋ; (fortis nasals) mˑ, nˑ, ŋˑ; (glides) w, y; (short vowels) i, a, o, u, ɨ; (long vowels) iˑ, aˑ, oˑ, uˑ, ɨˑ. The Southern dialect also has the following: (fortis voiced stops and affricates) bˑ, ʒˑ, dˑ, gˑ, gʷˑ. Bannock is the same language as Northern Paiute but lacks the Southern dialect series. Loanwords show some additional segments.

Wycliffe Bible Translators, Inc., uses the following practical orthography, equivalent to the above: p, ts, t, ch, k, kw, '; b, tz, d, g, gw; s, ss; h; m, n, ng; mm, nn, nng; w, y; e, a, o, oo, u; ee, aa, o, oo, uu; in most publications vowel length is not distinguished for o or u; i is used for the diphthong ai; ow for au. Southern dialect: bb, dds, dd, gg, ggw.

Information on Northern Paiute phonology was provided by S. Liljeblad and C.S. Fowler and follows Liljeblad (1966). They also transcribed the Northern Paiute words cited in italics in the Handbook, except that the forms in the chapter "Numic Languages" are given in an orthography that uses the same principles as the Shoshone orthography, to facilitate comparison between the languages.

In historic times Northern Paiute speech extended beyond the area outlined. In the north there has been since protohistoric times a continuous movement eastward of Northern Paiute speakers from their territory in Oregon to the Snake River Plain in southeastern Idaho—predominantly Shoshone territory. This outward migration has left the Northern Paiute-speaking Bannock outside Northern Paiute territory as a minority intermixed with the Northern Shoshone. Likewise, as a reminder of groups once freely roaming beyond the confines of the Great Basin, there were in the 1980s some Northern Paiutes living on the Warm Springs Reservation in Oregon together with the Tenino and Wasco of the Plateau. In addition, a small number of Northern Paiute descendants, scattered remnants of former warring bands, lived with the Achumawi in northern California, the Klamath on the Sprague River in southern Oregon, the Umatilla at Pendleton in northern Oregon, and the Yakima in Washington.

Regional Subdivisions

Northern Paiute groups were seminomadic and made their living by hunting, gathering, and fishing. Their precontact communities in most areas consisted of semi-annually united clusters of individual families, *nanobia?a* ('neighbors together'), who seasonally occupied a home tract or district, *tibiwa*. When not together, individual households or "camps" (*nogadi*) formed smaller camp clusters (*nanan·ogadi*, pl. of *nogadi*) whose composition varied seasonally and also through the years. The contingency of this pattern is apparent from the derivation of the term *nogadi* (on the root *no-* ~ *no·-* 'house, dwell', but also 'pack and carry', 'camp temporarily'; and the verb *kati* 'to sit', actually 'being settled for a time in a certain place'). The term *tibiwa* referred not to the people themselves but to a resume of preferred camping places where maximal congregation seasonally occurred. It included as well the foraging districts associated with these camping places. The derivative *tibiwaga?yu* 'possessor of a home district' was used to denote the migrant population that habitually returned to each named region for seasonal concentration, but especially for winter encampments.

The size and extent of home districts varied widely within Northern Paiute territory. In several areas, the *tibiwa* was defined relative to the foraging range of the groups radiating from a point of reference, such as a mountain or some other topographically prominent detail, toward an indefinite periphery. Not of necessity conflicting with this view was the suggestion that certain home districts in the topographically dissected west-central portion of the region were defined as valley centered and delimited although somewhat vaguely by the crests of adjacent ranges. But whatever the basis for definition, home districts overlapped to a certain degree and sharing of local resources habitually occurred. Well-established patterns of "visiting," still in effect in the 1980s, brought individuals, families, and occasionally even camp clusters into the *tibiwa* of others.

Group names used both within as well as outside home districts vary in principle across the region. Some are quite transient, referring to small kin groups that could and did lose the name if they moved elsewhere. Others might label several unrelated groups, often engaged in a similar economy. Yet others are at once fixed as to group, place, or both. The most common types of group names are: food-named designations, toponyms, and names for authoritative figures. With the possible exception of the last, none of these refers to units that can be called "bands" even though they have sometimes been so characterized (cf. O.C. Stewart 1939; Steward and Voegelin 1974). Groups of varying size, composition, and stability can be and were designated by any of these principles. Names can be multiple for a single population or apply to different groups across Northern Paiute territory.

Food-named designations are by far the most common group names in the region. The food designated is usually one quite common in a local area, but by no means its only food resource. The names are derived from the verb *tika* 'to eat', participialized in the south with *-di* and in the north with *-?*. These group names, continually recorded in the ethnographic and historic literature, are prevalent in both Western and Central Numic languages. They are increasingly common and more overlapping in territory the farther north one moves in the Great Basin (see the synonymy). Some food-named designations, such as *tibadika?a* 'pine nut eaters', used by the peoples of the north to designate those to the south with access to piñons, or *kucutikadi* 'bison eaters', used by people in the south to designate the Bannock and Northern Shoshone, had much broader geographical implications. Economics is in part implied in all these names, but often the terms are little more than handy resource labels with minor rather than major economic implications.

Toponyms often overlap with food-named units or in some cases serve as distinct alternatives (see the synonymy). Many of these terms contain the form *tibiwaga?yu*, designating the home district. With potentially hundreds of local place-names, groups of varying size, composition, economic pursuit, and degree of permanency could be designated in several ways.

The band names after chieftains presumably do not antedate White immigration and have gone out of usage. Names of men who by the mid-nineteenth century acted as leaders of dispersed local groups or loosely connected families or camps are well represented in the literature (Fowler and Fowler 1971:229–234). O.C. Stewart (1939:131–143) traced the names of several individuals and groups in the oral tradition of the 1930s. The group names themselves derive from the name of the individual with the addition of the form *atuam·i*, meaning 'his children'. Individuals such as Winnemucca, Egan, and Oitsi lent their names to such groupings. The only one to survive in 1984 was the designation *pedikepe tuam·i* 'Paddy Cap's children' a name used by the Miller Creek Paiutes, who for many years since they moved with this man have been settled on the Duck Valley Reservation and have kept together as a self-conscious minority.

Using the most commonly occurring group names as a principle of division but with the warning that "interband divisions were often vague and indefinite," O.C. Stewart (1939:130) isolated 21 terms naming bands under known chieftains within delimited geographic borders, which, however, "were not always conceived so precisely" as his map indicates (fig. 1). Pointing to the comparative independence of the small family-centered subsistence groups and to the extreme recency of band formation in the Northern Paiute population (only about 30 years before relocation on reservations made this type of organization impossible), Steward (1955:116, 1977) warned against the common mistake of explaining Stewart's groups as aboriginal bands and the casual leaders of post-White composite and predatory bands as aboriginal chiefs. Despite far-reaching generalization and apparent eclecticism, O.C. Stewart's (1939, 1941) survey of group distribution and the culture elements for each remains the only comprehensive study of cultural relationship between major Northern Paiute population centers. O.C. Stewart's (1939) map, supported by other cartographic work (O.C. Stewart 1966:204–223, 1970), is and will doubtless continue to be generally used for orientation in ethnographic studies of the area.

Environment

The vast area occupied by Northern Paiute speakers was environmentally diverse, offering over its more than 70,000 square miles varied subsistence choices and settlement alternatives to hunters, gatherers, and fishermen. Although all groups foraged broadly within their home districts, as well as to some degree in the districts of their neighbors, some had access to richer or more specialized localities than did others. Some were better able to concentrate for a season or at least part of a season on procuring one or a related set of resources, while others followed a more mobile or generalized seasonal round.

Piedmont Subarea

The southernmost district of Northern Paiute territory, that occupied by the Mono Lake people, was a relatively high district on the shoulder of the Sierra Nevada. Base elevation in the interior-draining Mono Lake basin is

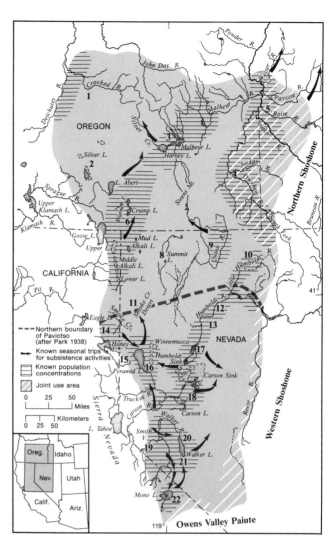

Fig. 1. Maximum area of Northern Paiute speech, about 1800–1830, with approximate locations of subgroups given by O.C. Stewart (1939): 1, Hunipuitöka (Walpapi); 2, Yahuskin; 3, Wadatöka; 4, Tagötöka; 5, Koa'aga'itöka; 6, Kidütökadö; 7, Tsösö'ödö tuviwarai; 8, Aga' ipañinadökadö; 9, Atsakudöka tuviwarai; 10, Yamosöpö tuviwarai; 11, Kamodökadö; 12, Sawawaktödö tuviwarai; 13, Makuhadökadö; 14, Wadadökadö; 15, Tasiget tuviwarai; 16, Kuyuidökadö; 17, Küpadökadö; 18, Toedökadö; 19, Tövusidökadö; 20, Aga'idökadö; 21, Pakwidökadö; 22, Kutsavidökadö. For information on these names see the Synonymy.

approximately 6,400 feet. The Sierra, which rises abruptly on the west, ranges from 9,000 to 13,000 feet elevation. To the east and northeast, lower, rounded mountains and rolling hills grade more gently. At the center of the basin is Mono Lake, highly saline and harboring only the brine fly (*Ephydra hians*) from which the group takes its name (*kucadikadi* 'brine fly pupae-eaters') and brine shrimp. Several species of waterfowl, often in great numbers, were also found on its surface as well as nesting on its islands. Vegetation ranges from halophytic grasses at the margin of the lake through xerophytic communities on the floor of the basin to and through a series of associations on the surrounding hill-

437

sides and mountains (piñon/juniper, jeffrey pine, lodge-pole pine). Each has associated faunal species (deer, bighorn sheep, quail, marmots). Jeffrey pine forests south of the basin in areas jointly used with the Owens Valley Paiute provided the larvae of the pandora moth (*Coloradia pandora*), harvested on a two-year cycle. Given altitudes and the continental-interior position of the region, temperatures are cool, and frost can be expected in any month (Logan 1965).

In addition to these environmental features, to which the local population adapted a transhumant subsistence-residence system (Davis 1965), this region is also of interest in that its groups freely associated with their neighbors, the Eastern Miwok and the Owens Valley Paiute. Various cultural exchanges occurred among these groups, and all show similar subsistence patterns and overall adaptive strategies. Thus, the groups on the Sierran slope, whether speakers of Numic languages or others totally unrelated, were similar in orientation.

Lake-Riverine Subarea

Two regions within Northern Paiute territory contained large freshwater lakes with major inlet streams—Walker Lake with associated Walker River and Pyramid Lake with associated Truckee River. Groups centered around these lakes and rivers were able to take advantage of the large and abundant fisheries that both provided. Particularly attractive were large (15–30 pounds) winter and spring migrating cutthroat trout (*Salmo clarki henshawii*), suckers (*Catostomus* spp.), and in Pyramid Lake, the cui-ui (*Chasmistes cujus*). Other smaller species of chub, redsides, and dace were also frequent quarry. Groups in these areas took their names from fish species. Their seasonal attention to these resources also colored aspects of their settlement patterns (often semi-sedentary during the fishing season) and material culture (elaboration of fishing gear, such as nets, hooks and lines, harpoons, spears, basket traps, and weirs). The areas served as focal points for groups in other and especially less favorable winter subsistence areas. Populations concentrated in these districts seasonally for fishing, trading, feasting, and dancing. In addition to fish, both areas offered seeds and roots, small game, and to some degree, large game. Waterfowl frequented the lakes and stream margins.

Freshwater Marsh Subarea

Four areas within Northern Paiute territory, as well as provisionally two others, can be characterized as distinctive for the extensive freshwater marshes they contained. These are the Carson Sink, Humboldt Sink, middle Walker River, and Malheur Basin, as well as the Silver Lake and Warner Valley districts. While a marsh-oriented material culture and subsistence pattern can be clearly documented for the first four, the last two are less well known due to historic contingencies, that is, changes in overall subsistence and cultural orientations brought about by adoption of the horse as well as by early group displacement.

The freshwater marshes of western Nevada that serve as focal points for groups were characterized by extensive stands of tules and cattails (*Scirpus* spp., *Typha* spp.), and were seasonal as well as permanent residence areas for many species of waterfowl. Marsh resources were also used for technology: people built cattail houses and tule balsa boats and made duck decoys, matting, bags, sandals, skirts, and dresses of tule and other marsh plants. The margins of the marshes were often winter residence areas because of the seasonal abundances the areas produced. The marshes of southern Oregon are assumed to have been equally productive, but the pre-contact subsistence and technological patterns there are less clearly defined. The Nevada marsh areas have drier surrounding country and less potential for large game. But unlike those in Oregon, the Nevada areas were also in proximity to piñon reserves.

Columbia–Snake River Drainage Subarea

The Columbia-Snake drainage was home district to several groups who concentrated their subsistence efforts on anadromous fish (*Salmo* spp.), collecting roots and bulbs (*Lomatium* spp., *Perideridia* spp., bitterroot, camas), and hunting large game (deer, elk, occasionally buffalo and moose). The country is relatively high (about 5,500 feet base elevation) and well watered. In some areas it is also deeply dissected by tributaries of the Snake River.

The subsistence pattern here had similarities to that of the Plateau culture area, and some groups interacted with Plateau peoples, especially in the historic period, through participation in great trading fairs. The horse was introduced from this direction as well as from the east. This region became one of the last refuges in the historic period for people displaced through White contact and settlement.

Generalized Subarea

The remainder of the region lacks resource specificity; it is characterized instead by a more generalized Basin and Range topography and a flora and fauna typical of "cold deserts" (Shelford 1963). In these areas, subsistence pursuits were about equally divided among the taking of small game and large game, numerous seeds, berries, and some roots, upland game birds and occasional waterfowl, insects, and sometimes fish. The details of the regimes varied by area, but little resource

438

specialization was apparent. These districts constitute the major portion of the region and serve in many senses to define the base pattern for the others.

Culture

Subsistence

• HUNTING   Techniques and equipment for taking large and small game, for fishing, and for collecting plants and plant products differed in these various subareas. Deer, antelope, and desert bighorn sheep, the principal large game animals in most of the region, were hunted either singly by individuals or in small herds by groups of men ("Subsistence," this vol.).

Hunting implements used to take large game, and to some degree, smaller game, included the bow and arrow and traps and corrals. Bows (*adi*) were made of hard, straight-grained woods and were sinew-backed in most areas. Bows for shooting large game were four to five feet long; those for small game, about three feet long. Individuals knew of the fine bows the Northern Shoshone manufactured of mountain sheep horn, and occasionally they obtained them in trade.

Straight-stemmed plants were chosen for arrows (*paga, poṇos·a*). Arrows were made with or without foreshafts and were tipped with stone, bone, and wooden points depending on quarry. Fletching was with hawk, owl, sagehen, eagle, goose, or woodpecker feathers depending on area and availability. Shafts usually bore the maker's mark in color striping. Individuals could always recognize their own arrows, an important matter if a kill were in dispute.

Various devices were employed in arrow manufacture, including shaft smoothers and polishers made of grooved stones and shaft wrenches (*pa'abi*) made of curved stone. Stone straighteners were usually heated in the fire to make the task of shaft straightening easier, a warmed shaft being more pliable.

Quivers for arrows were made of the whole skins of coyote, desert fox, or bobcat, or of sections of the skin of deer, mountain lion, antelope, or bear. In addition to a bow and arrows, a man often carried his fire making kit (*wa'i, manimugi*) (fig. 2) in the bottom of his quiver.

Knives, made of obsidian, chert, or other stone in several styles, were carried by hunters for dispatching and bleeding game as well as skinning and butchering (fig. 3). Sometimes these were wrapped with a skin pad to prevent cutting the hand.

Traps, corrals, and other types of game enclosures were built of uprooted sagebrush, rocks, and tree limbs. They sometimes consisted of converging wings in a narrow or box canyon or of actual corrals or enclosures in more open areas. Traps and corrals were considered private property in the Walker River district, a group

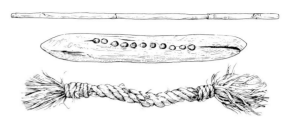

Milwaukee Public Mus., Wis.: 21836.

Fig. 2. Fire-making kit. Kept in the bottom of a man's hunting quiver, the typical kit consisted of a cane drill, a sage wood hearth, and a roll of fibrous tinder. The drill was placed on the hearth and twirled rapidly between the hands, friction serving to light the tinder. Note the singed holes running along the center of the hearth. Collected by Samuel Barrett, Pyramid Lake Reservation, Nev., 1916; hearth length 34.3 cm.

of men passing down use rights to their sons (W.Z. Park 1933–1940).

Smaller mammals such as hares and rabbits, marmots, and porcupines, when hunted individually, were either shot or caught in noose snares or deadfalls. Hares and rabbits were also netted in large cooperative drives held in the autumn in most areas. At this season the animals were fat and their pelts were in good condition for making rabbitskin blankets. Small mammals were either pit roasted or boiled. The meat might also be dried for storage.

Ground squirrels and other burrowing mammals were often taken in figure-4 traps or by bringing them from their burrows by directing water or smoke down the entrance. W.Z. Park (1933–1940) reports that ground squirrel trapping areas were considered private property at Pyramid Lake and Walker River, the rights passing from a father to his sons. As many as 20 to 30 traps were set at a time.

top, Milwaukee Public Mus., Wis.: 21955/5294; bottom, Harvard U., Peabody Mus.: 35–120–10/5185.

Fig. 3. Stone knives. top, Hafted knife, the basalt blade set in a carved willow handle, secured with buckskin. This type of knife was a common part of men's hunting equipment, carried in the quiver, and used in the butchering of game. Collected by Samuel Barrett, Pyramid Lake Reservation, Nev., 1916. bottom, Basalt blade used to flesh hides and cut meat. Collected by Willard Z. Park, Pyramid Lake Reservation, 1934. Length of top 13.2 cm, bottom same scale.

top left, top right, bottom left, U. of Nev., Reno, Special Coll.; bottom right, Mus. of the Amer. Ind., Heye Foundation, New York: 13/4188.

Fig. 4. Tule technology. Tules provided the Northern Paiute with raw material not only for shelter and clothing but also for boats, bags, matting, and decoys. top left, Boat, made of 2 large bundles of tules secured with cattails and supplied with tule rails. This craft rarely lasted more than one season (Wheat 1967:41). Jimmy George holds the boat, and Wuzzie George is in the foreground. top right, Jimmy George kneeling in the boat in the traditional poling position. bottom left, Wuzzie George braiding a handle on an open, plain twined bag of tules, used when collecting duck eggs. These tule gathering bags had no set form of construction, the mesh being fine or coarse depending on the food being collected (Wheat 1967:84). Photographs by Margaret M. Wheat, near Stillwater, Nev., 1956–1962. bottom right, Male canvasback decoy collected at Carson Lake, Nev., probably in 1859 (J.H. Simpson 1876:83). Decoys were commonly stored and carried to the water in woven tule baskets ("Prehistory of the Western Area," fig. 11, this vol.). They were placed on areas of open water surrounded by stands of cattails from which hunters could shoot or net attracted birds. However, other decoys collected with this one were equipped with 8-in. "crutch-top" handles, wired to the underside of the float, which were probably used by underwater swimmers to manipulate the decoys in a lifelike manner. Length 15 cm.

440

Bird hunting was important in some regions, and various techniques were used on land birds and waterfowl. Sage grouse and blue grouse were shot individually or were netted around springs. Waterfowl were driven into nets set at an angle to the water or decoyed for individual hunters to shoot. The favorite subjects of decoy hunting were canvasbacks (*Aythya valisineria*), and decoys were made of tules and cattails to resemble them (fig. 4). American coots (*Fulica americana*), locally called "mud hens," were driven from the marshes onto land during their period of molt and captured and killed. Boats were constructed of bundles of tules (fig. 4) for this purpose, as well as for collecting duck eggs in the marshes, duck hunting, and fishing. They were used extensively in the freshwater marsh subareas as well as at Pyramid Lake and Walker Lake (O.C. Stewart 1941:381).

• FISHING   Fishing was a very important subsistence activity in the inland lakes and the Snake River drainage subareas. It was of lesser importance elsewhere, although all groups fished to some degree. At Pyramid Lake and Walker Lake, locations with major fisheries, fishing was a year-round activity, but with intensive fishing occurring during seasons of major runs (late fall, winter, spring). Fishing techniques in these areas depended on the quarry and also on whether lake or river fishing was the major mode. For river fishing during spawning runs, groups in both areas built fishing platforms into the rivers and fished from these with large dip nets (fig. 5e) or with single or double-headed harpoons (*kʷatin·u*) (fig. 5b). Weirs and platforms (*pas·oni*) were private property, owned and used by the builders. Others fished in these localities only with permission. At times when large fish such as cutthroat trout, Tahoe suckers, or cui-ui were not running, shallower weirs were constructed across the river with various types of basket traps attached. These would take smaller trout and also quarry such as dace, chub, and redsides. Gill nets were set in the river for chub, as were several types of basket traps. Large fish were speared with two-pronged leisters or harpooned at times of low water (Fowler and Bath 1981).

Fishing in the lakes likewise depended on quarry and conditions. Trout were gill netted or taken on long set lines with either gorges or angled hooks (fig. 5c). Occasionally they were speared or harpooned from the shore in shallow water. Throwing lines were set out into the lake to take chub, dace, and redsides (fig. 5a). And women sometimes fished along the shore for small fish with their open twined winnowing trays. All nets used for fishing were made of native cordage (*wiha*) and in the inland lakes subareas, made with a shuttle and gauge (fig. 5d).

Platform and weir fishing were also practiced along tributaries of the Snake and Columbia rivers where the quarry was migrating salmon, sturgeon, and lamprey.

Single barbed harpoons were apparently favored, although the use of leisters is also reported. Weirs were used to hold fish for spearing and harpooning, or they might be set with large conical or elongated basket traps. Less is known about the fishing techniques of the Northern Paiute in these districts, although they are assumed to be similar to those of the Northern Shoshone and Bannock. It was principally an early spring and summer activity. In all areas, game and fish were dried and stored for winter use in bark- or grass-lined pits.

• GATHERING   Seed and other plant product collecting was very important everywhere in the region, with roughly 150 species sought. South of the Humboldt River, all groups were involved in the piñon complex. A few groups north of that area came south for nuts or traded for them. Principal implements involved in piñon collecting and processing included large, single-rod open twined conical baskets for collecting cones, single-rod open twined trays (*yata, yad·a*) for parching raw nuts, and double-rod open twined trays (*saʔyadima*) for winnowing cracked shells from nut meats. Manos and metates were used for shelling nuts as well as for grinding the nuts into flour. In west-central Nevada, wooden or stone mortars and stone pestles were also used for grinding pine nuts (fig. 6). Close twined trays (*tima*) were then used for sifting and refining the ground flour. The meal was mixed with water and made into a cold mush in close twined cooking baskets.

North of the Humboldt, and especially in the Oregon district, groups were increasingly involved in the root collecting complex. The primary tool used for extracting roots was often the handled and sometimes curved digging stick, like that of Plateau peoples. Root digging south of this district in Northern Paiute country was less intensive and was done with the straight hardwood digging stick. Pit roasting of camas (*Camassia quamash*), a technique of some elaboration on the Plateau (Downing and Furniss 1968), is reported only in Oregon where camas was common. Elsewhere roots of various types were either eaten raw when collected or dried in hot sand and stored.

Small and large seeds were collected in all districts of Northern Paiute country using a variety of tool types. For seeds and seed heads that shatter on impact, the twined seed beater (*sigu*) or a straight stick was used to dislodge the material. It fell into a close twined tray or close twined conical basket. Other seeds, such as Indian ricegrass (*Oryzopsis hymenoides*), were cut from the plant with stone or bone knives and flash burned over hardened ground surfaces to remove the chaff. Yet others were collected and sorted by hand.

Hard-shelled seeds were ground on the metate (*mata*) with a flat circular handstone (*wikʷan·u*)or muller. Larger seeds, such as sunflowers, had their seed coats cracked on the metate with an elongated mano (*tusun·u*) and then were winnowed and ground into flour. Soft-shelled

441

top right, U. of Nev. Reno, Special Coll.; a, Smithsonian, Dept. of Anthr.: 19047; b, Amer. Mus. of Nat. Hist., New York: 50.2/3730; Harvard U., Peabody Mus.: c, 34–114–10/3962; d, 34–114–10/3963; e, Milwaukee Public Mus., Wis.: 21712/5293.

Fig. 5. Fishing. top right, Katie Frazier cleaning and filleting cui-ui on the shores of Pyramid Lake, Nev. Photograph by Margaret M. Wheat, about 1964. a, Throwing line, tiny hooks of sharpened rabbit bone in folded willow splints, bound and attached with native cordage to a fiber main line. The line, hooks baited with grubs, would be set in the shallows of a lake, one end anchored by a cane shaft on the beach, the other, by a stone sinker. Collected by Stephen Powers at Pyramid Lake, Nev., in 1876. b, Detail of a double-pronged harpoon model used to take trout and other large fish in rivers or lake shallows. Two greasewood foreshafts are lashed to a 3–4 m pole with native string. The points are sharpened fragments of deer or coyote long bone, socketed with pelican quill sheaths that are lashed to the bone points with native string and cemented with piñon gum. Collected by Willard Z. Park on the Pyramid Lake Reservation, Nev., 1934. c, Bone gorge hook and line. It would be baited with grubs and tied to a set line to take minnows; larger versions, baited with pieces of sucker meat, were used for trout. Collected by Willard Z. Park on the Pyramid Lake Reservation, 1934. d, Model of a fish net shuttle and gauge. Mesh size varied according to the size of the fish being taken. Collected by Willard Z. Park on the Pyramid Lake Reservation, 1934. e, Chub net, made to be attached to poles and used as dip net during seasonal fish runs. Collected by Samuel Barrett on the Pyramid Lake Reservation, 1916. a, Length of cane shaft 57.2 cm; b, d, same scale. c, Length of hook 3 cm. e, Unfolded size of net 292 by 286 cm.

Field Mus., Chicago: 58474.

Fig. 6. Wooden mortar and stone pestle used to grind pine nuts and acorns into meal. Collected by J.H. Hudson in Smith Valley, Nev., 1902. Length of pestle, 28 cm.

seeds were processed without the intermediate cracking and winnowing steps. Seed meal mushes stone-boiled in twined cooking baskets usually resulted. Several seed species as well as seed and berry cakes were sun-dried and stored in bark- or grass-lined pits.

Berries of many varieties were common in most of the region. They were often seeded using a twined basketry sieve or ground with seeds and pulp on the metate. Dried whole berries were added to soups and stews, and dried berry cakes were often taken on journeys away from camp. Other equipment associated with food processing included spoons and dishes, storage bags, stirring sticks, and hot rock lifters.

Structures

House types and house construction details varied throughout the region, with some of the variation attributable to the availability of suitable materials, some to genuine subregional differences in form, and some to historical influences. Houses also varied as to season, with at least some differences noted in all areas between winter and summer structures.

In the north, from roughly Surprise Valley into Oregon, winter houses (*kahni*) were conical in form and tule or grass covered. They were built over a framework of willow poles, truncated and fastened to a willow hoop at the top. Twined or sewn mats of a single layer of tule covered these houses where this material was available. Otherwise, houses were covered with bundles of long-stemmed grasses sewn together. A smoke hole was left at the top, and the doorway was skin covered. According to Kelly (1932:104), the conical structure was attributed by individuals in Surprise Valley to influences from the north, particularly from the Northern Shoshone and Bannock. In protohistoric times, prior to the introduction of the horse and with it the skin-covered tepee, the Bannock–Northern Shoshone lived in conical tule- and grass-covered houses.

The dome-shaped, mat-covered house (*kani, nobi*) was the most common winter structure for most of the Nevada Northern Paiute groups (fig. 7). A smoke hole was left in the top and a doorway in one side, usually facing east or away from prevailing winds. A fire for cooking and warming was in the center inside. The size of the house varied according to the size of the family, but 8 feet to 15 feet in diameter seems to have been the standard. Houses at Pyramid Lake, Walker River, Mono Lake, and Yerington were often equipped with a mat-covered vestibule or tubular entryway, reminiscent of those found on houses made by the Washoe and other Sierran groups.

W.Z. Park (1933–1940) reports that when people in this central area elected to winter in the mountains near piñon caches, they built a more substantial semi-subterranean conical house. For this house, a pit was excavated one to two feet deep and 10 to 15 feet in diameter. The butt ends of large juniper poles were placed near the walls of the pit and leaned against each other at center to form the top. Smaller juniper and piñon poles were placed in between. Branches of these same trees, as well as willows and rye grass, were added over the framework and dirt was placed over these to complete the construction. A space was left near the center of the roof for a smoke hole. These houses might also have tunnel entrances made of the same materials. Such houses were built to be occupied for several winters. An alternative winter house in the Mono Lake district was similar in construction, although much taller and lacking earth covering (Steward 1933b:264). This shape is similar to that of the houses of other Sierran groups.

Occasionally groups occupied mat-covered houses the year around, although the more common pattern was to move out of these structures in the summer and into cooler brush windbreaks or shades. People ate, worked, and slept in these structures, although cooking was usually done elsewhere. The four- to six-pole flat-roofed shade (*haba*), considered by some individuals interviewed in the 1930s to be recent, was mat- or brush-covered on the top only (W.Z. Park 1933–1940; O.C. Stewart 1941:430). It doubled as a storage platform for foodstuffs in some localities, although some groups (Pyramid Lake, Walker River) also built a smaller version specifically as a storage platform.

Houses seem not to have been closely spaced in a "village" pattern in any area within the region. Rather, winter camps and houses of two to three related families were dispersed in favored camping spots, so as not to put undue pressure on fuel or water supplies. Figures on the size of typical winter camps are infrequently recorded, but something on the order of 50 persons at a good site was typical. Summer camps were smaller, reflecting separate foraging rounds for related families.

Clothing among the Northern Paiute was quite varied, with some of the variation being attributable to the availability of materials, some to individual preferences, and some to season of the year. There are vague hints at regional styles, and at historical influences from surrounding areas.

Throughout the region, there were differences in women's and men's dress. In the summer, and in some areas in winter if skins were scarce, women wore a single or double apron (*nak*^{w}*i*). Single aprons were knee-length and covered women in front only; double aprons had a duplicate flap behind. Both were suspended from a belt. Both were made of twisted and twined sagebrush bark, rushes, or lengths of duck or coot skins. The people near inland lakes and freshwater marshes used the last three materials most frequently. Aprons were

also made of tanned coyote, badger, or rabbit skins elsewhere. This costume, along with appropriate footwear and a basket cap, is probably the oldest in the region for women and was basic in areas where large game was scarce. It was also the costume of women without hunters to provide for them or with husbands too lazy or unskilled (W.Z. Park 1933–1940).

Women in better circumstances wore calf-length dresses (*k*^{w}*as·i*) of buckskin, or occasionally of antelope or bighorn sheep skins. These were made of two skins sewn together at the sides and around the neck. If there were enough skins, elbow-length sleeves were added. Fringe might be added to each side, across the bodice, and to the sleeves. Bone and shell beads and porcupine quill–wrapped strips might be added to the fringe (Kelly 1932:107; W.Z. Park 1933–1940). Buckskin dresses were more common in the northern or Oregon sector than in any other, although good hunters in other areas kept

bottom, Smithsonian, NAA: 1655-A; top, U. of Calif., Bancroft Lib., Berkeley: C. Hart Merriam Coll. 1978.8 ×/23a/P6.

Fig. 7. Winter dwellings of domed-shaped houses covered with cattail mats. Mats are roughly 2–3 m long and made of cattails placed at right angles to paired willow poles (2 on top surface, 2 underneath). The poles are tied to 2–4 horizontal hoops of decreasing diameters to form a dome. The mats are tied shingle fashion and secured. bottom, House with adjacent windbreak-shade used in summer for cooking and sleeping. Photograph by James Mooney, Walker River Reservation, Nev., Jan. 1892. top, Large dwelling with twined baskets at either side of the doorway used for seed harvesting. Photograph by C. Hart Merriam, Pyramid Lake, Nev., July 1903.

U. of Nev. Reno, Special Coll.
Fig. 8. Wuzzie George in tule dress. Skirt and aprons were more common than full-length dresses and were worn with a short rabbitskin or tanned hide cape in winter. Photograph by Margaret M. Wheat, Stillwater, Nev., about 1958.

Milwaukee Public Mus., Wis.: 22007/5294.
Fig. 9. Man's buckskin shirt with golden eagle feathers at the neck. This shirt was used in the Bannock or War Dance but is similar to patterns designed for everyday use. Collected by Samuel Barrett, Pyramid Lake Reservation, Nev., 1916; length, 76 cm.

their wives clothed in this manner as a matter of pride. Alternatives for winter to the skin dress in the inland and marsh subareas were dresses of tule (fig. 8), twined sagebrush bark, or twisted and twined coot skin.

Men's costume consisted of a breechclout (*sasinubɨ*) or loin cloth (*topada*) in the summer and the same plus a buckskin shirt (fig. 9) in cooler weather. Shirts were normally of buckskin, but rabbitskin and twined sagebrush bark are also reported (O.C. Stewart 1941:394). Shirts (*kʷasˑɨ*) were either of one skin, worn poncho style with the sides seamed, or of two, seamed at the shoulder. Elbow-length sleeves were added if there were sufficient materials. Shirts were sometimes fringed and had their seams painted red. Rabbitskin robes or tanned hides with the fur side out were added as capes in winter. The hides were by preference in all areas either of bighorn sheep or deer, although coyote, marmot, and bobcat robes were reported (O.C. Stewart 1941:393). Rabbitskin robes, whether worn as capes or used as blankets, were woven on a two- or four-bar horizontal loom. The skins were twisted into long chains for warp, and native cordage was twined between as weft.

In the winter, and also when out hunting and gathering in thick brush, both men and women added leggings or leg wrappings to their attire. Leggings (*kusa*) were of buckskin and either full or knee length. Leg wrappings (*wisa wipaʔaga*) were of long strips of buckskin, badger skins, or twined sagebrush bark. Skin leggings more common in areas with good supplies of game, as in Oregon, the Sierran piedmont, and some parts of western Nevada.

Both sexes wore hide or buckskin moccasins, normally cut from a single piece of skin (Wissler 1910: pattern #8). A two-piece moccasin is also reported as normal footwear for men (O.C. Stewart 1941:394). Men's moccasins were ankle high; women's might have additional flaps to make them calf high, especially in winter. In areas where skins were scarce, both sexes wore twined or braided sagebrush bark, tule, or rush moccasins. Overshoes of twined sagebrush bark were added in winter and were often worn with rabbitskin socks. Badgerskin boots were made for winter wear.

Women wore basket caps in all but the Oregon district (O.C. Stewart 1941:392). These protected the head from the sun and the tumpline. They also kept pitch out of the hair during pine nut harvesting. Men wore fur caps, particularly in northern Nevada and Oregon. These were of muskrat, beaver, badger, bobcat, or coyote skin, or of the skin of a young deer, antelope, or bighorn sheep. They were decorated with quail top-

left, Milwaukee Public Mus., Wis.: 22059/5294; right, Smithsonian, Dept. of Anthr.: 19,065.
Fig. 10. Hairbrushes. left, Porcupine tail, the hair trimmed short by fire, and the skin stuffed with sagebrush bark and laced shut. Collected by Samuel Barrett on the Pyramid Lake Reservation, Nev., 1916. right, Stalks of Great Basin wild rye, held together by wraps of cloth. Collected by Stephen Powers, Pyramid Lake Reservation, 1876. Length of left 19 cm; right same scale.

Nev. Histl. Soc., Reno: 595.
Fig. 11. Woman with face tattooed or painted. When Indians moved to towns, change in clothing to long cotton dresses, scarves, and commercial blankets was typical. Photographed at Lovelock, Nev., about 1886.

knots or other feathers and occasionally with the horns of young game (O.C. Stewart 1941:396). Both sexes wore headbands of buckskin, rabbit or duck skin, and twisted sagebrush bark or rushes, depending on available materials. Single hawk, eagle, or magpie feathers were also tied to the hair.

Men and women ordinarily wore their hair loose. By the 1880s braids had become the fashion in much of the region, particularly in the north from whence the influence came. Men wore them more than women, but both sexes participated in the innovation. Hair brushes (*winasu*) were made of the tail of the porcupine, the roots of wild rye grass, or rabbit brush stems (fig. 10).

Both sexes used simple facial and body tattoos (fig. 11). Women, and occasionally men, wore shell or stone pendants suspended from pierced ears. Men plucked their eyebrows to a straight line (Pyramid Lake, Honey Lake) and also removed any beard hairs. Face and body painting (red, black, yellow, white) was ordinarily reserved for dances (fig. 12). Bone and shell necklaces were worn by both sexes, again most often at dances.

Social Organization

From birth until death, an individual was surrounded by a network of kinsmen and friends that included the immediate family, a larger group of close relatives (the kindred), the camp group of which the family was a part (expanded or contracted with the seasons), associated camp groups in the district, and individuals (kin, nonkin) who resided outside the local area, and at times, even outside the general distribution of the Northern Paiute language.

Of all these units, the most effective for social integration was the family (*nanodik*ʷ*a*, element-by-element 'together with wife'), at base nuclear and independent, but at times variously modified to allow for inclusion of fractional elements. Ideally, it included parents and siblings, but at various points in time a parent might be absent through death or divorce and one or more siblings might be resident elsewhere. Time depth added additional spouses and children, some temporarily, so that the core expanded and contracted continually. Typical families included: nuclear (parents and children) plus unmarried, widowed, divorced siblings of either spouse; nuclear plus widowed parents of spouses; nuclear plus any other consanguineal relative of either spouse, most commonly children by former marriages. Three and in some cases four generations might sometimes be present. Lateral extension (two sibling couples plus children) also produced a special family type. Families might occupy a single household or expand into two or three adjacent structures. They were economically self-sufficient, although they did enter into various cooperative ventures with other nearby units.

Beyond this immediate unit, there was from the individual's point of view his or her bilaterally based personal kindred, *nanimi*, literally 'co-people', usually verbalized *un·animi* 'the totality of somebody's consanguineal kin'. This was not normally a residence unit, even if the *tibiwa* were considered; nor was it corporate in any sense. It was an informal linkage of primary relatives whose ties could be activated if need be. Given that siblings shared the same *nanimi*, its support base could be enhanced by sibling exchange marriages, a frequent occurrence. Figure 13 lists the primary or core kinship terminology for the kindred and gives their genealogical positions.

Genealogical depth for the kindred was based on three ascending and three descending generations. At the third generation, the discrete terminology merges to single terms and these were extended to generation

four and beyond. By the same token, lateral extension of discrete terminology was maximally through parents siblings' children. Beyond these relatives, the terms merge and were laterally extended without change. But in practice, genealogical links were rarely traced more specifically, except for the general purpose of marriage prohibition. An individual's personal kindred, a set of relatives known specifically to him or her, rarely extended beyond this point. The primary function of this unit for the individual was support. It was among relatives of this unit that the child would go for adoption if need be or if the natural parents wished to share a child with a barren close relative. The kindred also functioned at funerals, providing food and related services. And it served in matters of inheritance of property, minimal though this was, given that in Northern Paiute society consanguinity superseded affinity.

The camp group (*nogadɨ,* or *nɨmɨ manipin·i* 'people shifting for themselves') of which a person's family was a part also changed size and composition. Often two or three related families camped together rather contin-

top and bottom left, Huntington Lib., San Marino, Calif.: bottom right, Smithsonian, Dept. of Anthr.: 19,113.
Fig. 12. "War" Dance, said to have been the last performed at Walker River Reservation, Schurz, Nev. The War Dance, sometimes called fandango, was introduced by the Yokuts to the Owens Valley Paiute and thence to the Walker River Northern Paiute. bottom left, Dance ground with Indian police and other officials in the foreground, spectators surrounding the dancers, and shades in the background. top, Dancers. The 2 men on the right wear magpie feather caps with eagle down head rings. Both carry magpie feather dance wands. One wears skirt and collar and twisted eagle down trimmed with magpie feathers. The man on the left wears local adaptations of feathered dance headdresses. Face and body paint patterns are characteristic of several dances. Photographed Aug. 1906. bottom right, Dance wand of two golden eagle feathers with magpie feathers clustered at the base. Crimson pony beads and a loom-beaded strip of blue and white seed beads wrap the handle. White seed beads are tied along the midrib of each feather. Collected by Stephen Powers, Pyramid Lake, Nev., 1876; length 42.5 cm.

NORTHERN PAIUTE

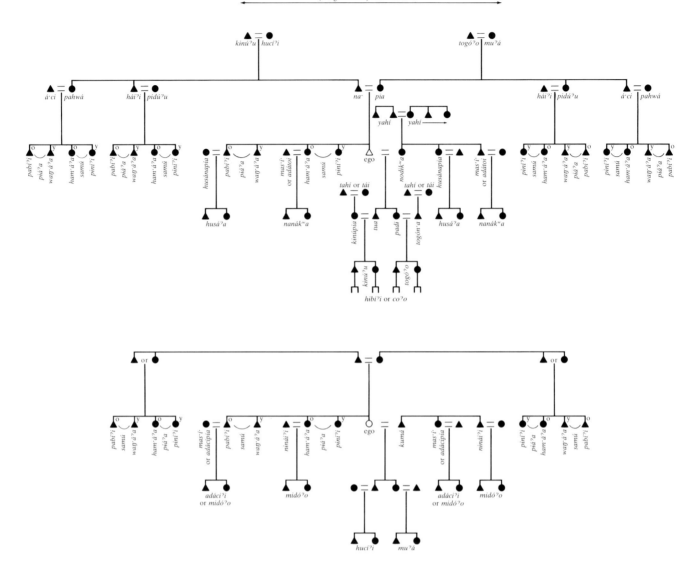

Fig. 13. Kinship terminology. top, Male ego; bottom, female ego. Terms for omitted or unlabeled kin types are the same as for male ego.

uously, foraging together and sometimes pooling resources if necessary. It was from this group that hunting and fishing partners were normally drawn. From it as well women managed child care and gathering activities, even though each woman was free under normal circumstances to keep her harvest for her immediate family. Larger camp groups, such as in winter, were less effective as cooperative units, although they might undertake communal activities such as rabbit, coot, or antelope drives. These "task groups" were temporary economic alliances, however, and the next task might be organized with different membership. Although winter camps often contained families related to each other in various ways, this was by no means a requirement. They might contain camps of "visitors," individuals or families who for various reasons were temporarily attached to a different home district. (Visitors often became permanent residents.) Winter camp sizes were

undoubtedly environmentally dependent to some degree, although few concrete data are available to demonstrate the functioning of this or any other contingent factor. At Pyramid Lake, in winter, individual camps were scattered all along the Truckee River from the lake to its great bend (W.Z. Park 1933–1940).

An individual's orientation to others on the level of the home district was nebulous at best, as these districts were not sociopolitical or economic units. A person was familiar with the camping spots and their patrons in his district, but probably equally familiar with places and individuals in immediately adjacent districts. Some individuals were also known to have traveled widely, sometimes for the purpose of trade, but often also just out of curiosity. These individuals had friends and often relatives (kindred or more extended) even more widely spaced. District names, including the various alternatives, were known to individuals over broad expanses of Northern Paiute territory, probably as a result of visiting, and to some degree, foraging patterns.

Life Cycle

When it came time for an individual to marry, usually in the middle to late teen years for both sexes, parents often arranged a suitable match. They wanted a boy for their daughter with proven hunting and fishing skills, a generous person, and someone of genial character. They wanted a girl for their son with good gathering skills and one not known to be lazy or irritable. Parents might also look to arrangements that brought suitable economic alliances, often outside the home district. Their role in matchmaking was considered advisory, with the young people's wishes in the matter normally being considered. The only bar to marriage was proven genealogical linkage of the families, traced as broadly as the individuals could remember.

An important type of marriage arrangement among the Northern Paiute as well as in the Great Basin generally (Steward 1933b, 1938; Hoebel 1939) was what can be termed intrafamilial or sibling exchange marriage. In this type, two or more brothers from one family married sisters from another, or a brother and sister from one married a sister and a brother from another. Although sometimes called "sister exchange" marriages, this term is misleading as there was no male prerogative implied or involved. Such arrangements were made to further cooperation, and they terminated after one generation. Since the sibling sets also shared personal kindreds, these marriages strengthened bonds between two separate sets of relatives by doubling ties. An added advantage to them was that they also set up situations in which secondary marriages (after the death of a spouse) could more easily follow the levirate or sororate. These in turn would lead to sororal polygyny or fraternal polyandry (W.Z. Park 1937; O.C. Stewart 1937, 1941; Kelly 1932). These types of multiple spouse households were not uncommon. Sibling exchange marriages might result in a single household, although more commonly the pairs lived adjacent to each other and habitually cooperated.

Marriage was not marked by ceremony. After a period during which the boy made his intentions known through visiting the girl's household, he merely moved in his belongings at her consent. Parents of the couple might then exchange gifts, especially if not well known to each other. The new couple typically resided in her parents' household for the first year or until the birth of their first child. During this time, he hunted and fished for the household, usually being incorporated with other male relatives into their subsistence plans. After this period, the couple was free to establish a new residence in the vicinity, or return to the boy's camp or district. Either choice seemed equally likely.

Birth took place inside the living quarters, no special house being constructed for the purpose (W.Z. Park 1933–1940). Three or four women, preferably with experience, attended the parturient. She was supine with her body slightly elevated on a bed of hot ashes covered with sagebrush bark. The baby was received by one of the attendants, who cut the umbilical cord. A piece of the cord was saved and placed in a small bag (si·magoʔo) to be attached to the cradle. The baby was bathed and placed with the knees flexed in a receiving cradle (fig. 14 left). He was wrapped in a piece of rabbit skin or coot skin. Softened sagebrush bark or cattail fluff was used for a diaper. The mother was bathed, as she and her child would be every five days for the next 20 days, the period of confinement. At each bath, the baby received a new cradle. During her confinement, the mother did little work and remained on the bed of ashes. She drank only warm water (cold would kill her) and ate sparingly. After her confinement, she gathered firewood to prove her future industriousness.

The woman's husband was also under food taboos after birth (especially against meat). He bathed almost immediately, leaving his old clothes by a stream along with an offering of bone or shell beads. He gave away his first kill and his first gambling winnings. His wife did likewise with her first winnings.

In cases of difficult birth, a shaman might be called. In some areas (Pyramid Lake, Fallon) he was specifically supposed to have the power of Water Baby. Other techniques held effective in difficult births were: rubbing the parturient with a weasel skin so that the swiftness with which the weasel moves would be transferred to the woman or passing a baby that had been born quickly over the woman. Stillborn infants were buried in their cradles face up if the parents wanted another child soon or face down if they did not. The placenta could be interred with cord-side up or down for the same intended results.

When the infant was old enough to hold its head up, it was transferred to a flat cradle with a shade (fig. 14 right). All previous cradles were hung together high in a juniper tree away in the mountains. The new cradle was marked for the sex of the child: slanted lines twined into the shade for a boy and zigzag lines for a girl. Cradles were not buckskin covered until the late nineteenth century, such a style being attributed to Northern Shoshone–Bannock influences. The child's umbilical cord was ultimately placed in a mole hole if a girl (to insure good root digging and seed gathering skills) and in a bushy tailed woodrat's nest if a boy (to insure good hunting) (W.Z. Park 1933–1940).

Puberty observances varied to some degree in the region (O.C. Stewart 1941; Driver 1941). A typical practice for girls involved running to and from a local hill each morning for 5–10 mornings and then making five piles of dry brush at places along the path. The girl

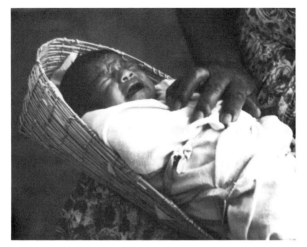

left, U. of Nev. Reno, Special Coll.; right, Nev. Histl. Soc., Reno: 752.

Fig. 14. Cradles. left, Receiving cradle made of open twined mat of willow around which an open twined protection for the infant's head is added. After swaddling the infant is secured to the cradle by buckskin strips passed through loops at the sides. Photograph by Margaret M. Wheat, about 1964. right, Woman, possibly from Pyramid Lake, working on a bead loom, a 19th-century introduction. Beaded strips decorated clothing and occasionally cradles. The open, plain twined willow cradles on the left, similar to the Washoe style, are of the oldest type. The buckskin-covered one with the baby in it is a style diffused from Bannock and ultimately Plateau sources. Shades on the 3 cradles in diamond or zigzag pattern indicate the child is a girl; parallel lines are for boys. Photograph by Esther L. Linton, Goldfield, Nev., about 1905.

was accompanied in this by an older woman, usually her mother, but also a person who could run with her. She might carry a staff painted white and decorated with sagebrush and beads (W.Z. Park 1933–1940).

After the time of running, the girl was bathed by the older women of the camp while she was seated on a pile of sagebrush. In some areas, she jumped over this pile or over a fire made from it. No public dance was held (Pyramid Lake and Honey Lake may have been exceptions), and apparently there was no ceremony the following month. The girl avoided meat, fish, and salt for from 15–20 days and drank only warm water. Special menstrual houses were reported from northern Nevada and Oregon groups only, probably as influenced by the Western and Northern Shoshone (O.C. Stewart 1941:410).

For boys, a puberty observance (*nadikawi*) was held at the time of his first large game kill (usually deer). At this time, his father, often accompanied by another skilled hunter, made a pile of sagebrush bark for the boy to stand upon. They chewed meat from his kill along with sagebrush and placed it on each of his joints to make him strong. In the Pyramid Lake area, the men also passed a willow hoop wrapped with meat from the first kill from his head to his feet and back again. He was then fed a choice cut from the animal, and henceforth the family could eat the game that he killed.

Death brought a period of mourning to family and friends, normally lasting a year. Close relatives, especially women, wailed and cut their hair to signal bereavement and smeared their faces with ashes and pitch. The body of the deceased was removed from the house, wrapped in skins with legs flexed in front or behind, and taken to the hills for burial. It might be placed in a rock crevice or cave, or it might be buried on a hillside. The person's personal goods were interred as well. Seeds and beads were often sprinkled over the grave. At Walker River and Mono Lake, the possessions of the deceased might be burned at the graveside. Burning of the deceased was reserved for individuals suspected of witchcraft. The house of the deceased was either torn down and moved or burned. The name of the deceased was never mentioned again. Spouses were free to marry after roughly a year. Some never remarried.

Political Organization

The principal social as well as political units within Northern Paiute society were the independent families. Decisions affecting their livelihood as well as their internal and external relations were made by the senior family members in consultation. Beyond these units, local camp groups also had headmen (*poinabi*) who acted as camp advisors, commonly giving speeches encouraging good virtue and industriousness. They served as focal points for group discussion of matters of mutual concern, such as moving camps for subsistence purposes, treatment of witches, and difficulties with neighbors. For such discussions they called the people together in their house and passed a smoking pipe to all senior members (fig. 15). After smoking, each was free to discuss the point at issue. The headman summarized the discussion of such topics and helped the group to reach a consensus. In some areas (Pyramid Lake, Or-

450

FOWLER AND LILJEBLAD

top, Nev. State Mus., Carson City: 760–G–1; bottom, Milwaukee Public Mus., Wis.: 21842/5293a,b.

Fig. 15. Pipes. top, Pipe-tomahawk given by Numaga in 1862 to Warren Wasson, federal deputy and advocate of peace between Northern Paiutes and Whites, as a token of personal friendship. bottom, Precontact style straight pipe of catlinite with wood stem. The weasel bag contains native tobacco. Collected by Samuel Barrett on the Walker River Reservation, Nev., 1916. Length of top, 45.7 cm; bottom same scale.

egon), headmen had persons who acted as "repeaters" (*nani·kʷikidi,*) giving the words of the headman so all could hear and understand. This idea may have been borrowed through the Bannock from the Northern Shoshone.

Headmanship seems not to have been inheritable in this region, with most groups reporting that upon the death of such an individual, another was selected by consensus. Headmen were not the same as subsistence task group leaders (antelope, coot, rabbit, deer drives; fish runs), although the same term (*poinabi*) was used to designate them (*kam·i poinabi* 'rabbit [drive] leader'). These task positions fluctuated according to the assessed skills and luck of the individuals. They were chosen as temporary leaders only, the next time the task possibly being assigned to another. While in charge, they directed daily activities connected with the particular task by group agreement. With the exception of antelope drives, these individuals need not have specific powers over the quarry being sought. Dances and battles were additional occasions when task group leaders or directors were chosen.

Supernatural Beliefs

The Northern Paiutes believed that power (*puha*) could reside in any natural object, including animals, plants, stones, water, and geographic features, and that it habitually resided in natural phenomena such as the sun and moon, thunder, clouds, and wind. Any individual could seek power for purposes such as hunting or gambling, but only shamans (*puhagam·i*) acquired it in sufficient strength to call upon it to do good, and on occasion, harm to others. Individuals other than shamans maintained highly personal and individualistic relation-

ships with power sources, if indeed they had them. The details of these relationships were often unknown to friends and family. Leaders of rabbit, coot, or deer drives or of fish runs might be chosen by others for their known power, but their skill was also considered—perhaps the two being interchangeable at times. Whatever instructions had been given to the person by the power source (for example, food taboos or a special way of handling the remains of hunted animals) had to be followed to the letter or the power would withdraw its support—a seemingly frequent occurrence (W.Z. Park 1938). Although O.C. Stewart (1941:415) reported a concept of "guardian spirit" as universal among the Northern Paiute, it is more likely these special power associations that were intended.

For the shaman, power associations were much clearer and more critical. Both men and women could be shamans, and both seem to have acquired power in roughly the same ways. It was most common for power, in the form of a mammal, bird, snake, rock, or spirit such as Water Baby, to come to the individual unsought in a dream. The dream might start in childhood, but it would be repeated into the late teen years or adulthood. The power source ordinarily also instructed the individual in the dream as to what paraphernalia would be required for doctoring—eagle tail feathers and down, tobacco, a pipe, a rattle of deer's dew claws (fig. 16) or ears (*wisabaya?a*), and possibly a stone. These were kept in a special bag of weasel, otter, badger, deer or other skin. The power also gave the individual a song or songs through which the power could be called (fig. 17). For an individual to ignore these dreams and their instructions or refuse to accept the power being offered meant certain illness and possibly death.

In addition to this means, power could also be inherited from a close relative, usually deceased. Again, the dream was normally the vehicle, although the relative might also offer some of his or her power directly. Normally after the initial offer in either context, the real power source would come to the individual per-

Amer. Mus. of Nat. Hist., New York: 50.2/3616.

Fig. 16. Shaman's rattle of deer dewclaws and abalone shell beads strung on buckskin thongs. Collected by Willard Z. Park, Pyramid Lake Reservation, 1934. Length of stick 25 cm.

Fig. 17. Jimmy George, a singing shaman, wearing twisted and twined sagebrush bark shirt and leggings, and with some of the symbols of his power as a doctor (kit fox skin, straight pipe, skunk, magpie feather hat). He was active as a healer in Nev. and Calif. until near his death in 1969. Photograph by Sven Liljeblad, Stillwater, Nev., 1967.

sonally. Paraphernalia were rarely transferred directly on these occasions as it was considered very dangerous for another person to retain the materials of a deceased shaman or even handle these materials without consent while the shaman was alive.

Lastly, power could be deliberately sought by visiting specific caves scattered throughout Northern Paiute territory. An individual was required to spend the night in such a location, where he would be visited by powers if the powers so chose. Instructions as to paraphernalia and other procedures would be given at this time. Some individuals were unlucky in such quests and rarely tried a second time (W.Z. Park 1938).

After two or three years of preparation, a shaman was ready for his first doctoring. Ordinarily, the person would first apprentice himself to an older and more experienced shaman to learn more about the craft (W.Z. Park 1938; Olofson 1979). He might act as an interpreter (or "repeater") for this doctor, translating the language, songs, and activities of the senior shaman to those assembled for the cure.

Shamanistic curings normally lasted two days. The family of the person to be treated went to the shaman's house early in the morning to request services unless it were an emergency. The shaman smoked about the subject and considered whether to take the case, although normally his powers would not let the person refuse. The shaman then made a short staff of willow to which he attached one of his eagle feathers. This was placed outside the house of the sick person for the day to retard any additional bad influences. That evening, the shaman, the interpreter, and for some, a woman (*witadi*) especially chosen to dance during the night, went to the patient's house. The doctor arranged the patient with head to the south and placed the eagle feather wand beyond the head. The doctor then summoned his power through song and attempted to ascertain the cause of illness (soul loss, breaking a taboo set by a power or mishandling power, dreaming, or sorcery). Normally this was done while in a trance state. If soul loss were responsible, the shaman's soul attempted to retrieve the soul before it wandered far or before it actually entered the afterworld. If successful, the individual would recover. Other causes of illness (especially sorcery) might result in the intrusion of an object into the patient, and this the shaman must retrieve by sucking the affected part. If successful, the shaman spat the object (an insect or a small stone) into a specially prepared hole in the ground or otherwise disposed of it. Prescriptions of foods, herbal medicines, or specific activities were then made for the patient's recovery. Normally the doctoring lasted from dusk to dawn with a break for a meal around midnight (see "Oral Tradition: Content and Style of Verbal Arts," this vol., for discussion of the shaman's night). If the patient did not immediately improve, a second night of doctoring would be required. The family was also free to call in another shaman (they sometimes worked in teams on difficult cases) if things were not going well. Otherwise they paid the shaman a fee in beads or hides. If an individual lost a number of patients, it was thought that he no longer had power. But if suspected of sorcery in these dealings, the shaman might be killed by the group.

All shamans were to some degree specialists in that their powers differed and thus did their abilities. However, some individuals were also known for their ability to cure rattlesnake bites (also wounds from poisoned arrows), to control the weather, to be clairvoyant, and to be invulnerable (W.Z. Park 1938). Antelope shamans were a special class of individuals, thought to have more power than ordinary individuals with power of deer or rabbit, but also not as powerful curers. All shamans could acquire multiple powers, and most did.

Classes of spirits who might help shamans but who also were of more general reference in supernatural beliefs were Sun and Moon, Thunder, especially as

Thunder Brothers (*tukimɨna, hino*), Wind, Clouds, and Stars. Of all, Sun was the most powerful and most respected. Many people addressed morning prayers to the Sun, asking that it have a good journey through the sky and that it take their troubles with it as it entered the "big water" to the west. Prayers to the Moon were less frequently addressed. Thunder and particularly Thunder Brothers were feared and respected as those that controlled the rain. Certain individuals with power from them could bring rain or stop it (W.Z. Park 1933–1940), but ordinary individuals also addressed them for rain or for it to cease. Rainbows and lightning were considered to be the symbols of power for the Thunder Brothers, and to point at either would make one paralyzed. To mock Thunder would bring death by lightning or floods.

Clouds and Stars were similarly powerful and could be sources of power to shamans. Stars were also thought to cause illness, particularly to boys or young men through their desires to have them as husbands. All these phenomena and their spirit aspects were the objects of narratives and tales, and thus myth and legend blend with these concepts so that no clear-cut boundary exists. With the notable exception of Coyote, and possibly also Wolf as well, nearly all the animal, plant, and other natural objects that were actors in myth could also serve as sources of power. Coyote did not because of his trickery and treachery, undesirable qualities for a doctor or other person of power. Other spirits normally personified were Water Babies (*paʔohaʔa*), creatures greatly feared and respected that inhabited most permanent bodies of water, dwarfs (*ninɨʔi*), which were especially active at night, and creatures of legend and myth such as the "bone crusher" (*pahiʒ·oʔo*) and "water snake" (*pa·togogʷa*). Strength of belief in all these varied, so that each person put together personal approaches to the supernatural.

Group approaches to the supernatural were limited. In all areas, dances and prayers were offered prior to communal food-getting efforts, such as antelope and rabbit drives. In areas with lakes and marshes, coot drives were also celebrated communally. Pyramid Lake and Walker River peoples likewise held dances and offered prayers for fall, winter, and spring fish runs; and all groups within the distribution of piñon had a fall festival in preparation for the harvest and normally offered special prayers early in the season to "set" the crop. Although each of these activities was under the direction of a specialist, it was not uncommon for that person to call upon another person much respected to offer the prayers. Prayers over antelope were the province of the antelope shaman alone. All times of group prayer and dancing were also times of merriment. Night dances were followed by gambling, foot races, and other forms of secular entertainment.

Concepts of an afterworld varied considerably in the region. According to some, souls (*mugua* 'life soul') of the deceased journeyed to an underworld where night was day and day night, but otherwise life was as on earth. Others felt that the soul went to another world in the south by means of the Milky Way (*kus·ipo·* 'dusty trail'). They were tempted to delay or stray along the way by Coyote and did not make a successful passage until they entered between two constantly opening and closing clouds. Once in this land, they hunted and gathered as before, but in a situation of abundance. There was also much time for dancing and gambling (W.Z. Park 1933–1940).

Ghosts (*coʔapa*) could remain in this world and plague the living, often causing illness. However, specific ghosts could also act as power sources for shamans (W.Z. Park 1938). Disembodied human spirits (*caʔabɨ*) roamed the earth in whirlwinds; thus to look at one was potentially dangerous to health and well-being.

Games

Games of chance and skill as well as other forms of amusements were well known in Northern Paiute country. Most were widely distributed, being played in essentially similar versions over the entire area. A few have regional variants (Culin 1907; Kelly 1932; W.Z. Park 1933–1940; O.C. Stewart 1941).

The most popular and widespread were the hand game, the related four-stick game, and various dice games (fig. 18). Of these, the hand game has been the most persistent historically and was likely to be seen in the 1980s at Northern Paiute gatherings for any type of older social or religious purpose. In the most common version of the hand game (*naiyakʷi*), four "bones" (*tipo*) were used, two wrapped or painted at the center and two plain. Five or 10 willow sticks per team were used as counters. Two teams of players, all male or all female (although sometimes of mixed sexes in the 1980s), sat facing each other on the ground. A log was in front of each team, and each member beat the log and sang in unison with other teammates during their team's turn to hide the bones. The object was to guess the position of the unmarked bones being hidden by the opposing team. Various correct and incorrect guesses brought forfeitures of bones or counters. Play continued until one team captured all the counters. Side bets, magic, and mirth made for lively competitions.

The four-stick game (*witaciʔi*) was probably a derivative of the hand game, although it was played with wooden billets rather than bones. These were hidden under a close-twined basket, arranged in the same possible order as in the hand game. Individuals or small teams played against each other, exchanging counting sticks for correct and incorrect guesses.

Various versions of dice games were played. Most popular was *wokʷokotasaŋa*, played with cane dice, painted on the interior and plain on the exterior.

Women's basket dice (*nabogoibi*) was also a popular game, often being played for amusement around a campfire at night. Women kept track of their scores on the dice by color or surface texture. The one with the highest for a given round won.

Games of skill included men's football (*wacimo?i*), women's double ball or shinny (*naʒicaka?a*), men's hoop and pole (*pici*), as well as arrow shoots, foot races, and relays.

Children's games included variants of ring and pin (fig. 18), jacks (girls only), and "flipper"—a game in which mud balls were thrown at each other from the ends of sticks (boys only). Boys walked on stilts, made whistles of willow or cane, and swung bull-roarers. Girls played with clay dolls and miniature baskets in imitation of female activities.

Prehistory

A clear archeological record for the various Northern Paiute peoples does not extend beyond about A.D. 1000.

top left, U. of Nev. Reno, Special Coll., 217; bottom left, Catherine S. Fowler, Reno; Smithsonian, Dept. of Anthr.: a, 19,058; b, 19,044; c, 19,045.
Fig. 18. Games and gaming equipment. top left, Hand game. Women at the right are hiding the "bones" while the other team members are preparing to beat the plank and sing. A team facing them will attempt to guess the order of the 2 unmarked bones. Photograph by Margaret M. Wheat, Walker River Reservation, Schurz, Nev., about 1964. bottom left, Cane dice game platform made of packed earth with scoring pegs at the edge. Eight to 12 painted split-cane dice are thrown on the platform and the color recorded by placing a stick marker between the appropriate counting pegs. Markers of opposing players landing in the same space force the first in the space to start at the beginning. One full circuit of the board (both directions) wins the game. Photograph by Willard Z. Park, Pyramid Lake Reservation, Nev., 1934. a, Pin and bundle game, a tule bundle tied to a wood pin by fine fiber string. The object was to toss the bundle and spear it with the pin. b, Four-stick game, consisting of 4 playing sticks painted red (one with corn stalks on the ends) and 10 cottonwood counting sticks sharpened at one end. c, Cane dice. Length of a 12 cm, rest same scale; a–c, collected by Stephen Powers, Pyramid Lake, Nev., 1875.

454

However, some investigators have suggested that there are interesting continuities (and discontinuities) between the material culture of the Northern Paiute of west-central Nevada and that of the archeological Lovelock culture (Grosscup 1974). Similarities and differences in the historic and archeological records in southeastern Oregon prior to A.D. 1000 have been noted as well (Aikens, Cole, and Stuckenrath 1977).

History

The culture of the Northern Paiute peoples described here is reconstructed from ethnographic and historic accounts to the period roughly 1800 to 1830. After that time, and in some areas even before, a series of events that occurred elsewhere in western North America set in motion changes that affected the aboriginal cultures in various ways. The first of these was the introduction of the horse into the southern Plains and Southwest in the sixteenth century and into California in the eighteenth century. The second was the "opening of the West" by non-Indians—Spaniards, French, British, and Americans—as they searched for furs and other riches. And the third was the discovery of gold and silver in California, Oregon, and ultimately Nevada, which brought numerous travelers to Northern Paiute country and finally permanent settlers.

Although the documentary sources are far from clear on the matter, Northern Paiute speakers from eastern Oregon, and perhaps principally those in contact with the Northern Shoshone in the Owyhee-Snake-Weiser river basin, first obtained horses sometime in the mid to late 1700s. Once in possession of horses, they joined with their Northern Shoshone cousins, traveling widely through the Snake River plain and well beyond. Ultimately known as Bannocks, but also identified in the historical literature as "Snakes" (as were the Northern Shoshone with whom they habitually traveled), they became the first Northern Paiute speakers to change their culture in response to this animal. They developed fully mounted "bands" with shifting leadership and personnel that habitually made forays beyond the Rocky Mountains to the Plains for buffalo. They also became involved in a raiding complex for horses and other booty, and they generally took on the appearance in material culture of their Plains neighbors (Steward 1938; O.C. Stewart 1970).

But not all Oregon Northern Paiutes became involved in the horse complex this early. In 1805 Meriwether Lewis and William Clark learned of "Snakes" (in all likelihood Northern Paiutes) living in large numbers on the Deschutes River in north-central Oregon, but seemingly without horses (Thwaites 1904–1905, 3:147–149). Peter Skene Ogden, Hudson's Bay Company trapper and the first individual to document in detail his traverses of Northern Paiute territory, noted that in 1826 most of the "Snake" groups he met in Oregon were either unmounted or had but few horses (Ogden 1909–1910:349–350).

But other activities involving horses may have affected some Northern Paiutes. In 1827 the trapper Jedediah Strong Smith encountered 20 to 30 horsemen at Walker Lake, far south of the Oregon country. Ogden had a similar encounter in 1829 with an estimated 200 Indians at the Humboldt Sink, at least some of whom were mounted. Layton (1981) suggests from various lines of evidence that these groups may have been traders or raiders from elsewhere (California, Oregon) using western Nevada as a base of operations, or else locals involved in a much wider complex. Whichever the case, the people encountered by Smith and Ogden were in possession of Spanish blankets, buffalo robes, and Euro-American goods, indicating at least some outside influences on the material culture of the region by this time.

Mounted parties are rarely mentioned by trappers and explorers in these same areas in the 1830s and 1840s. Rather, documents from the period suggest that at this time Northern Paiutes in most areas were still unmounted and carrying on traditional subsistence pursuits. For example, the Joseph Reddeford Walker party found numerous Indians in 1833 and 1834 at the Humboldt Sink and on the Carson River, seemingly with neither horses nor firearms, but subsisting "upon grass-seeds, frogs, fish, &c.-" (Leonard 1904:166). John C. Frémont (1845:218) visited a large village of fishermen at the mouth of the Truckee River in 1843. He described the people as living quite well on large salmon trout they caught behind numerous weirs in the river. Although he observed horse tracks at the lake, this group was apparently not involved in the horse complex. They did have several items of Euro-American manufacture (Frémont 1845:11–12).

The period of marked local expansion of the use of the horse and seemingly also consolidation of mounted raiding groups coincided with the time of marked increase in traffic through Northern Paiute country, roughly in the late 1840s through the 1850s. Although some trappers were undoubtedly responsible for the beginnings of hostile encounters between Indians and Euro-Americans, for example, the Walker party massacred nearly 100 Northern Paiutes in 1833 and 1834 (Leonard 1904), other factors were also at work by this time. As American emigrants began to flow across the Great Basin on their way to Oregon and California, ecological impacts became more noticeable. Trapper bands, sometimes with 100 to 200 horses and occasionally cattle and sheep, had important but probably only temporary effects on the local forage and game supplies (Rusco 1976). Sustained movements of wagons and livestock were more devastating.

The opening of Oregon to settlement in the early 1840s and the discovery of gold in California in 1848 brought continuous streams of traffic across fragile ecosystems. Although the Oregon Trail actually touched only a small portion of Northern Paiute territory in the north, the California Trail came straight through the heartland of the region in Nevada (fig. 19). In 1849, undoubtedly the year of heaviest traffic, it has been estimated that some 6,200 wagons, 21,000 people, and 50,000 head of livestock passed over the Overland Trail down the Humboldt River to California (G.R. Stewart 1962:231ff.). The impact of this mass migration on the distribution of Northern Paiute groups in the region was undoubtedly significant. Native subsistence resources, particularly seed plants and large game, were virtually destroyed for miles on either side of the road. Fuel supplies were exhausted and water holes were fouled or drained. Even though the peak period of traffic was the summer, little would have been left in most of these areas for winter residents. Some groups reacted by with-

drawing from the region and seeking refuge in Oregon. Others found new opportunities in misfortune: wagons and stock offered alternatives for subsistence and exploitation of the region.

Steward and Voegelin (1974) provide documentary evidence for the rise of mounted predatory bands among the Northern Paiute in parts of Nevada and Oregon during this and later periods. It seems clear from the data that the increased presence of non-Indians, and particularly emigrants during the late 1840s and 1850s, as well as damage to subsistence resources, were factors of importance in the transition. An additional factor may have been the encouragement offered the Indians by unscrupulous White traders, several of whom set up temporary headquarters along the Humboldt and Carson river routes to service the emigrants. Government agent Jacob Holeman, sent to investigate reports of increased depredations in 1852 and 1853, reported that he was told by the Indians that traders had suggested to them that they steal stock and sequester the animals in adjacent valleys until after the emigration season. Then the traders would exchange guns, ammunition, and blankets for the stolen animals. Holeman concluded that "the whites who infest the country are far more troublesome than the Indians" (Holeman 1853:447).

During the late 1840s and early 1850s more and more Nevada and Oregon Northern Paiutes acquired horses, so that by the end of the decade, a number of mounted groups under named leaders were operating in the region. Not all these mounted groups preyed on emigrants or on the isolated stations and ranches or the small number of permanent settlements. Some clearly used the horse for greater mobility in aboriginal subsistence pursuits or for an economy that included only occasionally taking livestock (including horses) for food (Layton 1978). Yet others seem not to have adopted the horse at all, but rather began to attach themselves to ranches and the small settlements. A number of these groups, too, began to have spokesmen or "chiefs," a postcontact solidification of the older pattern of headmanship. Table 1 lists the leaders and population figures given by Indian agent Frederick Dodge in 1859 for west-central Nevada. A number of these groups lacked horses in any numbers. Winnemucca (fig. 20), who would continue to play a role during the 1860s and 1870s, is listed as "Chief of Nation," an unlikely role but one promoted by his daughter Sarah Winnemucca (C.S Fowler 1978; Heizer 1960).

In 1859, gold and silver were discovered in two areas in Northern Paiute territory: the Virginia Range in western Nevada and the Owyhee basin in Oregon and Idaho. These discoveries led to new emigrations along old and new trails, and to the founding of large settlements such as Virginia City, Nevada; Canyon City, Oregon; and Silver City, Idaho. Ranches to support the

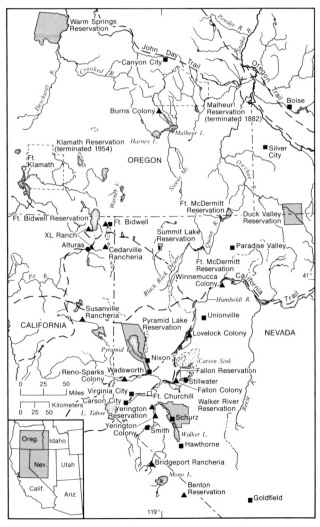

Fig. 19. Historic trails and primary reservations, colonies, and communities with Northern Paiute population.

456

Table 1. Northern Paiute Bands in Western Nevada, 1859

Chief	Location	Population
Winnemucca	Smoke Creek, near Honey Lake	155
San Joaquin	Carson Valley, at forks of river	170
Had-sa-poke	Gold Canyon on Carson River	110
Wa-hi	big bend of Carson River	130
O-duk-e-o To-sarke Pe-tod-se-ka	the lakes and sinks of Carson River	1,625 (848 men, 372 women, 405 children)
To-no-yiet	below big bend of Truckee River	280
To-Repe	near lower crossing of Truckee River	360
Ge-nega	mouth of Truckee River	290
Wat-se-que-order	Pyramid Lake	320
Numaga	Lower Mud Lake	300
	Total visited	3,740
	Paiute Nation (estimated)	6,000

SOURCE: Dodge in ARCIA 1860:373–374.

larger population base also usurped good grazing lands in outlying areas. Individual miners or small parties were in many surrounding places seeking potential strikes. Depredations increased on both sides until major conflict was inevitable.

On May 12, 1860, Northern Paiutes at Pyramid Lake killed 43 members of a volunteer unit sent to avenge a justified raid on Williams' Station on the Carson River (F. Egan 1972). Two weeks later, a large force from California routed the groups in several additional skirmishes. Later that summer, Col. Fredrick West Lander, special government envoy, held a council with some of the leaders—Numaga (fig. 20), Winnemucca—and quieted the troubles. The Pyramid Lake War thus ended. Some of the people involved returned to Pyramid Lake to be settled on newly set aside lands. Others, including Winnemucca, withdrew to northern Nevada and southeastern Oregon where they were involved in later conflicts. Additional skirmishes occurred throughout the 1860s in northern and western Nevada, often involving troops stationed at Fort Churchill, established on the Carson River in 1860 as a result of the Pyramid Lake War (Angel 1881). The post operated until 1869, by which time most of the conflicts in the region had ceased.

Similar circumstances existed in Oregon during the same period. By 1863 an estimated 10,000 settlers were in the Malheur mining district, with supporting ranches usurping most of the good forage lands (Steward and Voegelin 1974:237). Many groups throughout the region had been displaced, and were operating in small groups as predatory bands on emigrants, miners, and ranchers, who were also taking reprisals on any Indians encountered. The mounted groups often covered vast distances, at one point being in localities in eastern Oregon and a few weeks later being in western or southern Oregon, Nevada, or Idaho. Although the groups were probably always small and certainly highly mobile, they were involved in many encounters through the years until 1868. Steward and Voegelin's (1974) documentary compilation of conflicts demonstrates the overlapping ranges of some of the band leaders. Men such as Paulina, Wewawewa, Oitsi (these three were classificatory brothers), Egan, Winnemucca, and Ocheo apparently commanded varied followings at various seasons and times, not all of whom were local people. Peoples from Idaho (Bannock–Northern Shoshone) and individuals from Plateau tribes may also have been involved in some of these skirmishes. Trade with Snake River groups and probably from the north as well brought guns, although by no means all were armed with these weapons.

Military campaigns waged from Fort Klamath and Fort Boise as well as from local posts established in Warner Valley and Harney Valley finally pacified most of the region in late 1868. Campaigns waged by Capt. George Crook between 1866 and 1868, known as the Shoshone or Snake Wars, were particularly decisive. Treaties negotiated in 1864 (Klamath Lake) and in 1868 (J.W.P. Huntington's treaty, unratified) laid the foundation for the beginnings of reservation life in the district (Wheeler-Voegelin 1955–1956).

Reservation Period

Due to continued local agitation, reserved lands were set aside for Northern Paiute people by the federal government beginning in 1859 (fig. 19). The first to be proposed were Pyramid Lake and Walker River reservations in Nevada (each initially set aside in 1859 but not formally established until 1874) and Malheur Reservation in Oregon (established in 1871). Although it was thought that those three areas would be quite sufficient for all the people, and at times attempts were made to settle all groups on any one of the three, this solution proved unworkable. In the end, many people refused to go to any of these places, so that well into the twentieth century additional colonies and small reservations were being established throughout the region. In some cases, these additional reservations were within old home districts little affected by the period of the rise of predatory bands (Lovelock Colony, Yerington Colony, Fallon Reservation and Colony). In others, they were the result of displacement and disruption of

left, U. of Nev. Reno, Special Coll., 217-B; right, Natl. Arch.: 75–IP–3–26.

Fig. 20. The Winnemucca family. left, Numaga, or Young Winnemucca, a leader during the Pyramid Lake War of 1860 and a man of considerable influence in western Nevada until his death in 1871. Photograph by J.K. Sutterley, Wadsworth, Nev., 1870. right, Delegation to Washington, D.C., which met with Secretary of the Interior Carl Schurz to discuss the restoration of reservation lands at Malheur, Oreg., and conditions at Pyramid Lake Reservation, Nev. left to right, Sarah Winnemucca, Winnemucca (d. 1882), Natches, Captain Jim, and an unidentified White youth. Sarah Winnemucca lectured in western Nevada, San Francisco, Boston, and Washington, D.C., 1879–1886, and wrote *Life Among the Piutes: Their Wrongs and Claims* (S.W. Hopkins 1883). Natches, son of Winnemucca, lived on a farm in Lovelock. Captain Jim was a headman in western Nev. and southern Oreg. Photographed in 1880.

native groups during the period of wars (Burns Colony, Duck Valley Reservation—Miller Creek extension, Fort McDermitt, Fort Bidwell). Each reservation and colony has its own separate and often complicated history (Houghton 1973; Inter-Tribal Council of Nevada 1976a; Johnson 1975; Lynch 1971).

Malheur Reservation was initially established to contain "all the roving and straggling bands" in southeastern Oregon after the ending of hostilities in 1868 (Walker in ARCIA 1872:102). In the end it was occupied only between 1871 and 1878, when, through a long series of circumstances (C.S. Fowler 1978; Steward and Voegelin 1974:262ff.), groups abandoned the locality to participate in the Bannock War of 1878 (Brimlow 1938). This conflict, initially started by troubles at Fort Hall Reservation and on the Camas Prairie of southwestern Idaho, involved Bannocks and Northern Shoshones under Buffalo Horn and Northern Paiutes under Egan, Oitsi, and others. The short-lived campaign ended in the death of Egan (Howard 1887) and the surrender of Oitsi at Malheur. Winnemucca, who

spent most of the campaign in the Steens Mountains of southeastern Oregon, was apparently an unwilling participant (S.W. Hopkins 1883). But a number of his people, together with others who were not participants, were interned for several years on the Yakima Reservation in Washington (S.W. Hopkins 1883). In 1883 most of these groups returned to Nevada on their own, some settling at Fort McDermitt, some at Pyramid Lake, and the remainder at Miller Creek on the Duck Valley Reservation (Inter-Tribal Council of Nevada 1976a:48). Other Oregon people from the war went to Fort Klamath and ultimately Fort Bidwell, California (Ocheo's group), to Warm Springs Reservation (remnants of Wewawewa's group), to Umatilla Reservation, or remained in the Malheur district. In 1933 lands were finally purchased for people who had been living in this vicinity for many years, and the Burns Colony was established.

Pyramid Lake and Walker River reservations as well as Malheur were intended as areas where the former hunting, gathering, and fishing Northern Paiutes would

458

learn to be farmers. The degree to which this was ever accomplished was limited, largely due to the unsuitability of the areas chosen for agriculture and to the lack of water. Both Pyramid Lake and Walker River have been involved in major conflicts with non-Indians through the years for adequate water rights. Knack and Stewart (1984) outline in detail the issues involved in the various Pyramid Lake cases, some of which were pending in 1984. They also give an excellent account of the encroachment of Whites on that reservation and of the destruction of Pyramid Lake's fishery in the postcontact period (see also F.M. Dixon 1980 for detailed discussion of the land trespass issue). Johnson (1975) and Inter-Tribal Council of Nevada (1976a) discuss the recurrent water problems at Walker River. Lands originally allotted at Fallon (Stillwater) Reservation in 1891 at the rate of 460 acres per head of family but without water were exchanged for 10 acres per head of family with water in 1910 (Inter-Tribal Council of Nevada 1976a).

In the late 1870s and early 1880s day schools were established at Pyramid Lake and Walker River. Sarah Winnemucca established and ran a school for Northern Paiute children at Lovelock from 1885 to 1887 under partial sponsorship of Elizabeth Palmer Peabody, noted pioneer in kindergarten education (C.S. Fowler 1978). Boarding schools were established at Pyramid Lake in 1883 and at Carson City (Stewart Institute) in 1890. Paiute children from several areas in western Nevada were encouraged to attend both, the latter also being a school for other Great Basin tribes. Some children attended other federal boarding schools, such as at Grand Junction, Colorado, and Carlisle, Pennsylvania.

Day schools were not established at colonies and other reservations until much later: Lovelock in 1907, Fallon Reservation in 1908, Reno-Sparks in 1928, Burns in 1931. People had lived at these locations for many years prior to this time and in most cases well prior to the formal establishment of these areas as federal lands. Many began to work in their local areas for food and wages early during the settlement period. Some attached themselves by families to ranches, others clustered on the outskirts of developing towns. Hittman (1973:48), who has discussed the history of Smith and Mason valley Northern Paiutes, most of whom reside either at Yerington Colony or on Yerington Reservation in the 1980s, lists the types of jobs commonly held in 1880 as follows: for women, dishwashing, laundering, housekeeping, harvesting and stacking hay; for men, chopping wood, farm chores, driving cattle to and from summer pastures, feeding livestock, digging irrigation ditches, planting, irrigating, harvesting and stacking hay. Men in other areas also bounty hunted rabbits and squirrels in pastures and took game and fish for sale.

With reservation confinement and education came changes from the precontact past. Many traditional subsistence modes had to be abandoned, particularly ac-

U. of Nev. Reno, Special Coll.: 2710/106.
Fig. 21. Capt. Dave Numana and family. Numana was an important, often controversial, headman and Indian policeman from the 1870s until his death in 1919. Photograph by Lorenzo D. Creel, Pyramid Lake Reservation, Nev., 1906–1919.

tivities such as harvesting seeds and in some cases roots and berries as well. Either the resources had been destroyed, or people no longer had access to them. For a number of years, Pyramid Lake and Walker River remained as active fisheries, making good individual profits for the fishermen through the sale of fish to nearby towns. However, the 1920s diversion of water by upstream users and poaching on the lakes and in the rivers by non-Indians had led to a major decline in fish supplies (Knack and Stewart 1984; Johnson 1975). Large and small game and waterfowl were in short supply on most reserved lands, although some people continued to take game in season elsewhere. Knowledge of the former range and diversity of subsistence pursuits was gradually reduced to memory by the 1930s when most ethnographers worked in the region (Kelly 1932; W.Z. Park 1933–1940; O.C. Stewart 1941). In the 1980s a number of Nevada families still gathered pine nuts, buckberries, and chokecherries. A few families at Burns took various roots and berries (Couture 1978). Men at Pyramid Lake took cui-ui and trout, both species showing signs of recovery. And various individuals hunted game and fowl or went after other resources as much for enjoyment as necessity.

Other subsistence pursuits replaced those of earlier days. During the 1930s families at Fort McDermitt ran a successful cattle ranching enterprise, which continued in part in the 1980s (Houghton 1973). People at Pyramid Lake and Walker River engaged in stock raising partly through the support of government loans (fig.22). Haying has likewise been productive for some families. In the 1980s tribally owned, operated, or leased businesses brought income to the reservations and colonies. *459*

U. of Nev. Reno, Special Coll.: 2710/53.

Fig. 22. Indian cowboys branding a horse near a brush corral, Pyramid Lake Reservation, Nev. Native cowboys managed small tribal and individually owned cattle herds on reservation lands beginning about 1900. Photograph by Lorenzo D. Creel, near Nixon, Nev., 1906–1922.

Social organization has not changed drastically. Independent families remain the most cohesive units in Northern Paiute society. Although intertribal marriages have brought many new individuals to reservations and colonies, other marriages are still contracted locally. Houghton (1968) provides excellent data to show that most precontact family types are still operative and functional at Fort McDermitt, and the same is true elsewhere. Although active knowledge of kinship terms and patterns was declining along with language proficiency generally, a number of middle-aged and most elderly people still remembered proper reckonings.

Political organization has changed considerably, from a precontact system of headmanship through the development of chiefs and leaders during the 1840s through 1870s to what was a return to the headmanship system in early reservation years after the breakup of mounted bands. Most groups in 1984 were organized under the Indian Reorganization Act of 1934 and elected tribal councils. Councils handled tribal funds, often oversaw law and order in communities, planned for tribal and economic development, and had many functions of business corporations.

Although shamanism declined to some degree through White influence and the presence of physicians and clergy on reservations, it was still active in the 1930s, when W.Z. Park (1938) noted more than 20 individuals practicing at Pyramid Lake, Walker River, and Yerington. Whiting (1950) found several shamans active at Burns in the mid-1930s. People still received and sought power through traditional means and held cures of one or two nights duration. Many individuals also received medical treatment from nonnative sources, although medical care on most reservations and colonies was not necessarily common or routine. Shamanism has gradually declined since that time, although at least a few practicioners operated into the 1960s and 1970s.

Other religious activities have commanded the attention of Northern Paiutes since contact. In 1869, a Ghost Dance was initiated at Walker River by Wodziwob, who came from Fish Lake Valley to the south (Hittman 1973b). The newly established Walker River Reservation was not producing sufficient food for the people and droughts followed by floods had made conditions much worse. Wodziwob preached that if the people would dance the traditional Round Dance five nights in succession, eventually the Whites would disappear, and game, fish, and plant foods would return in abundance. Dead relatives would also return. Under converts such as Frank Spencer (Weneyuga), the 1870 Ghost Dance spread to the adjacent Northern Paiute, Washoe, Klamath, and into California (Du Bois 1939; W.Z. Park 1933–1940; Spier 1935). After about two or three years, the followers seemed to lose interest, although Wodziwob continued to practice as a shaman on the Walker River Reservation (Hittman 1973b).

In 1887, another Ghost Dance movement was initiated by Wovoka (Jack Wilson) of Mason Valley, Nevada. In a few years it became popular, known as the Ghost Dance of 1890. Wovoka's father had been a follower of Wodziwob, and Wovoka was additionally influenced by Christian teachings. Like Wodziwob, Wovoka preached that if the people danced the traditional Round Dance and prayed, the Whites would be removed, their dead relatives would return, and native resources would be restored. Although the dance only lasted a short time among the Northern Paiutes, Wovoka continued to be a much respected shaman, practicing until near his death in 1932 (Dangberg 1957, 1968).

O.C. Stewart (1944) has written about the Native American Church among the Northern Paiutes and adjacent Washoes, among whom it was actively promoted in the 1930s and 1940s. It was not accepted by Paiutes in all areas, nor by all individuals in those areas where it was active. During the 1950s and 1960s it was less active than among the Washoe. In 1984 Peyotists remained at Fort McDermitt, Duck Valley, and Coleville. Meetings drew participants from several localities.

In the 1960s another religious movement diffused to some Northern Paiute people from sources to the north. Under the leadership of Raymond Harris of the Wind River Reservation in Wyoming, the Sweat Lodge movement became active in several localities in western Nevada. Harris's movement is closely related to that of Mark Big Road, introduced into Wind River in the 1950s (Hultkrantz 1962a). It is a variant of the Spirit Lodge practices of the Sioux and groups in Canada. It and the Sun Dance introduced in 1981 at Fort McDermitt reflect increasing contacts between Northern

Table 2. Northern Paiute Reservations and Colonies, 1980

Locality	Population 1950	Population 1970	Population 1980	Land Acreage
Benton Reservation, Calif.			25	160
Bridgeport Colony, Calif.			81	40
Burns Colony, Oreg.	149	149	194	40
Cedarville Reservation, Calif.	15	13	16	17
Duck Valley, Nev.	288[a]	263	331	294,242
Fallon Reservation (Still-water) and Fallon Colony, Nev.	148	159	481	5,480 and 60
Fort Bidwell Reservation, Calif.	99	54	162	3,335
Fort McDermitt Reservation, Nev.	233	359	620	35,183
Lovelock Colony, Nev.	135	117	163	20
Alturas, Calif.		12	10	
Lee Vining and Coleville, Calif.	123	251		
Pyramid Lake Reservation, Nev.	603	414	776	475,162
Reno-Sparks Colony, Nev.	231[a]	282	302	28
Summit Lake Reservation, Nev.	48	1		10,208
Susanville Reservation, Calif.	42[a]	5	42	30
Walker River Reservation, Nev.	371	385	862	320,512
Warm Springs Reservation, Oreg.	47	320	384	563,305
Winnemucca Colony, Nev.	26	41	81	340
Yerington Reservation and Colony, Nev.	155	290	342	1,156 and 9.5
Total	2,590	2,987	5,123	

Sources: U.S. Bureau of Indian Affairs. Statistics Division 1970, 1970a; U.S. Bureau of Indian Affairs. Financial Management 1981; Leland 1976; Frankson et al. 1980–1981; U.S. Congress. House. Subcommittee on Indian Affairs of the Committee on Public Lands 1950.
[a]Figures include other tribes on the reservation.

Paiute people and the religious practitioners of other tribes ("Ghost Dance, Bear Dance, and Sun Dance," this vol.). Participation in them also reflects a rising concern on the part of many Northern Paiute people, especially the young, for establishing a firmer ethnic identity.

Reservation communities and colonies changed drastically during the 1970s. Most groups have undertaken successful federal housing programs and have basic services such as electricity and sewer systems. Tribal buildings, often used for recreation as well as economic development and general tribal management, are pres-ent on most Indian-owned properties. Tribal businesses bring in some funds to supplement the few earned by agriculture and cattle ranching on the bigger reservations. An increasing number of people also maintain off-reservation jobs in nearly all areas of the private sector. More and more children are completing grade school and high school and are going on for higher education. Population figures for reservations are given in table 2.

Poverty and health problems were still significant in 1985 (Leland 1980). Colonies, especially near urban centers, were overcrowded, underserved, and in need of additional lands and resources. Out-migration throughout the historical period has led to a significant nonreservation and noncolony population scattered throughout the West. Northern Paiutes were part of a much larger national scene while still retaining a unique legal position common to all Native Americans.

Synonymy†

The name Paiute, in many variants, was first applied to the Southern Paiute (see the synonymy in "Southern Paiute," this vol.). The earliest evidence for its being extended to include the Northern Paiute is in the reminiscences of trappers. Leonard (1904:166–167), who was in western Nevada in the mid-1830s, referred to Indians near the Humboldt Sink (who he says called themselves Shoshocoes) as "Pai-utes or Root Diggers (Diggers) sometimes called Snake Indians" (first published in 1839). Hamilton (1905) and Farnham (1850), who were in the area in the mid-1840s, used Pah Utes and Paiuches. By the 1850s the name Paiute was in common use for the Northern Paiutes, examples being Pah Utah for those of Mono Lake, 1850 (Hoffmann 1868, in Merriam 1955:155), Pi-utah for those on the Carson River (Holeman in ARCIA 1852:151), Py-ute for those in Humboldt Sink (Hurt in ARCIA 1857:228), and Pah-Utah for those in western Nevada generally, 1859 (Bishop in Merriam 1955:155).

The name Paiute continued to be the usual name in local and popular usage into the twentieth century, referring to the Northern Paiute, Owens Valley Paiute, or Southern Paiute without distinction. Usages and spelling variants are listed by Merriam (1955:155–157). Borrowed from English as names for the Northern Paiute are Northern Paiute *payu·di* and Shoshone *payutih*.

In 1860 Hurt (in J.H. Simpson 1876:459–460) used variant spellings to differentiate the Northern Paiutes ("Py-Utes") from the "Pah-Utahs" (undefined) and the "Py-eeds" (Southern Paiutes, or a segment of them). However, contrary to Merriam's claim (1955:151), Hurt did not "definitely adopt" this usage in an earlier report

†This synonymy was written by Catherine S. Fowler and Ives Goddard.

The Native Nevadan, Reno–Sparks Indian Colony.

Fig. 23. Katie Frazier from Pyramid Lake Reservation, Nev., with the dancers from Natches School, Wadsworth, Nev. The children, largely under her direction, learn traditional music and dance and perform in western Nev. as part of their cultural heritage program. Photographed in 1983.

in which he had used "Py-ute" for the Northern Paiute of Nevada (ARCIA 1857:228). J.H. Simpson (1876:34–38) gives an explicit presentation of Hurt's classification, distinguishing the "Pi-Utes" or "Py-utes" (Northern Paiute), "Pah-Utes" ("Diggers or Pah-Utes, who are of Sho-sho-nee origin"—a segment of the Western Shoshone), and "Pi-eeds" (Southern Paiute, or a segment of them), and Gatschet (1876:80–81) notes a distinction between the "Pā-Utes (Payutes, Pyedes, Paï-Utes)" on the Colorado River and the "Pi-Utes" of northwestern Nevada, perhaps following the differentiation of Pai-Utes and Pi-Utes made by Cooley (in ARCIA 1866:28–29). These attempts to differentiate the two groups by artificial distinctions of spelling met with little success.

Waterman (1911:14) used the expression "Northern Paiute Language" in his title and clearly distinguished it from the language of the "southern or 'true' Paiutes," but in his text he uses "northern Paiute" or simply "Paiute." Kroeber (1925:581–582) effectively established the designation Northern Paiute, though he discussed the people of the Mono Lake area together with the Owens Valley Paiute under the label Eastern Mono (Kroeber 1925:586). Merriam (1955:152, 166), who (in a paper completed in the 1930s) was the first to draw the linguistic boundary between the Mono Lake Northern Paiute and the Owens Valley Paiute (Kroeber 1959:268), argued for a terminological distinction between "Northern Piute" and "Southern Piute." O.C.

Stewart (1939, 1941:361) and Steward (1938:ix, 50) used Northern Paiute but included under this label the Owens Valley Paiute. Northern Paiute has been used in a series of tribal histories prepared for use in public schools by the Inter-Tribal Council of Nevada (1976a).

Northern Paiutes, especially those in Oregon, were sometimes referred to as Snakes. Lewis and Clark used this name for people living in large numbers on the Deschutes River in north-central Oregon in 1805 (Thwaites 1904–1905, 3:147–149); in all likelihood these were Northern Paiutes, making this the earliest written reference to them. Ogden (1909–1910) used this name for Northern Paiutes encountered in eastern and southeastern Oregon in 1826 and 1828, and it continued to be used in the literature until these people were settled on reservations in the 1870s (Wheeler-Voegelin 1955–1956, 1:116–117). The name Snake was earlier applied to the Eastern Shoshone on the Plains and was extended to other Numic groups as the fur trade expanded westward (Fowler 1965:46–54; Steward 1938:263–272; synonymies in "Eastern Shoshone" and "Western Shoshone," this vol.).

J.W. Powell proposed that the Northern Paiute be called "Pa-vi-o-tsoes," stating that this was what they were called by themselves and neighboring Indians (ARCIA 1874:53; Fowler and Fowler 1971:107); he refers only to those of western Nevada. In fact Paviotso is Western Shoshone pa·piocco (Miller 1972:125); related forms are used in Owens Valley Paiute (pabioʒoʔo) and Panamint, but not in Northern Paiute itself. The groups that use this name apply it only to the Northern Paiutes of Nevada and California, not to those of Oregon, who are unknown to them. Kroeber (1907a:114) adopted the name Paviotso from Powell for its convenience and extended it to all Northern Paiute; he also used it in the compound name Mono-Paviotso, which he introduced to designate Western Numic and replaced by Mono-Bannock two years later (Kroeber 1909:267, 1925:577). Lowie (1924:192) used Paviotso for the Northern Paiute generally, including those he referred to as "the Oregon Paviotso." Only W.Z. Park consistently restricted the name Paviotso to those Northern Paiutes specifically called this in Shoshone; the boundary he drew between what he called "the Paviotso" (to the south) and "the Northern Paiute" (to the north), admittedly "quite vaguely defined" (Park in Park et al. 1938), approximates the dialectal and cultural demarcations presented in this chapter. Some writers have argued against using Paviotso on the grounds that in Indian usage it is not a self-designation and not used for all Northern Paiutes (Waterman 1911:14; Merriam 1937–1938:1; O.C. Stewart 1966:192–193). Furthermore, it is slightly derogatory among those for whom it is idiomatic.

The Mono Lake Northern Paiute have often been referred to as Mono and classified under this name with the Owens Valley Paiute and the Monache; Merriam (1955:167) gives an extensive list of instances dating from the 1850s to the 1930s. Only a few writers used unambiguous compound names like Mono Pi-Utes (Campbell in ARCIA 1866:119) or Cozaby Pah-Utes (Campbell in ARCIA 1870:113); for Cozaby, see the entry Kutsavidökadö, below. The confusion stems ultimately from the similar names used in Yokuts and Miwok, for example Southern Sierra Miwok *monʔayˑaʔ* 'Mono Lake Northern Paiute; Northern Paiute (in general)' and *moˑnaʔ* 'Monache, Owens Valley Paiute' (Broadbent 1964:257). The name Mono and its variants are discussed in the synonymy in "Owens Valley Paiute" (this vol.).

The Sai´-du-ka given by Hodge (1907–1910, 2:606) as a synonym of Snakes, also misrendered Saidyuka (Hodge 1907–1910, 1:932), is a misunderstanding of Powers (Fowler and Fowler 1970:123); see the entry Kupadökadö, below.

The only self-designation used in Northern Paiute is *nimi* 'people'; this has been used in the spelling Numa as an English name, beside Northern Paiute, by the Inter-Tribal Council of Nevada (1976a). Names for the Northern Paiute in other languages include: Western Shoshone *paʔanetti, paʔanepiccih,* and *pappanaihti* (Miller 1972:125, 127); Northern Shoshone *pannaihti;* Washoe *báʔlew* (William H. Jacobsen, Jr., personal communication 1985); Nez Perce *tiwélqe,* applied to the Northern Paiute, Bannock, and Shoshone and sometimes translated 'enemies' (Haruo Aoki, communication to editors 1985); Umatilla *kpúspał* 'rattlesnakes'; Achumawi *áˑpʰùy* (James Bauman, communication to editors 1985); Atsugewi *henna* 'strangers' (Olmstead 1984:237); Klamath *saˑt* (Barker 1963:350); Maidu *tolómma* (Shipley 1963:180); Nisenan *moan´-au-zi* (Powers 1877a:320), rewritten monozi by Kroeber (1925:582, 1959:267) but perhaps the same as *mo´-nă-mus-se* 'Mono Lake Northern Paiute', and *koyoʔiyemise* (Uldall and Shipley 1966:268); Northern Sierra Miwok koi´-yu-wak or koi-aw´we-ek; Central Sierra Miwok mo-nahk or mo-nok (Kroeber 1925:582; Merriam 1955:158–159, 168).

Subgroups

A large number of subgroup names have been recorded for the Northern Paiute, many of them of quite uncertain status. The list that follows uses as headings the names of the groups delimited by O.C. Stewart (1939:146–147); under each are its variants and apparent equivalents, as judged by similarity of form and location. The numbers refer to figure 1; referred to by name alone are Powell (in Fowler and Fowler 1971:229–234), Powers (in Fowler and Fowler 1970), Kelly (1932:70, 72), Loud and Harrington (1929), Park (in Park et al. 1938), and the alphabetical entries in Hodge

(1907–1910). Some of these names are compounded of the word for a type of food and *-tikadi* 'eater'; most of the rest are derived from place-names and in full Northern Paiute form end with *tibiwa* 'home district' or *tibiwagaʔyu* 'home-district possessor'. (In some sources these elements are confused or used inappropriately.) A few subgroup names are directional terms, such as 'northerners', which have variable referents depending on who is using them. In the historical literature a number of groups are named after men in authority (see table 1) (Powell in Fowler and Fowler 1971:229–234); names of this type in Northern Paiute were formed by suffixing the headman's name with *-tuamˑi* 'children'.

Aga´idökadö (20). The Northern Paiute name is *agaidikadi* 'trout eaters', also written A´-gai-ti-kut´-teh (Powers), A-gai-du-ka (Powell), Agai´tükədᵃ (Park), see the next entry; Campbell (ARCIA 1866:119) has "Walker River or Ocki Pi-Utes."

Aga´ipañinadökadö (Moadökadö) (8). The Northern Paiute name *agaipaniˑnˑadi* 'Summit Lake (literally, trout lake) person' does not contain the 'eater' element; this is Powell's A-gai-va-nu´-na. Kelly has *agaidikaʔa* 'trout eaters' for both this group and Stewart's Aga´idökadö, at Walker Lake. Moadökadö is Northern Paiute *moadikaʔa* 'eaters of wild onion sp.'.

Atsakudöka tuviwarai (9). This name is Northern Paiute *acakudakʷa tibiwagaʔyu* 'red butte dwellers'. Located in the same area are the kwi´naduvaᵃ, kwi´nodub (*kʷiˑnodiba* 'Quinn River') of Kelly and the ko-yu-hon of Powell, given as Ko-yu-how´ in Hodge.

Hunipuitöka (Walpapi) (1). The name is Northern Paiute *hunipuitikaʔa* 'eaters of *Lomatium* sp. roots'. Based on this is the name Hoo-ne-boo-ey (ARCIA 1865:466), misprinted Hoo-ne-boo-ly (ARCIA 1865:471), the source of Hoonebooey (Hodge; Wheeler-Voegelin 1955–1956:241). Walpapi is not a Northern Paiute word but presumably from Klamath; as Walpápi it was introduced by Gatschet (1879:410) as a normalization of spellings used in official reports, like Woll-pa-pe (ARCIA 1866:77) and Woll-pah-pe (ARCIA 1865:466, 1866:344; Wheeler-Voegelin 1955–1956:95, 117).

Kamodökadö (11). The Northern Paiute name is *kamˑidikadi* 'jackrabbit eaters'.

Kidütökadö (6). These are in Northern Paiute *kiditikadi* 'marmot eaters', rendered gidü´tikadᵘ by Kelly. Their area has been assigned to the tu-zi´-yam-mos and kai-va-nung-av-i-dukw (Powell).

Koa'aga´itöka (5). A shorter variant of this name is Northern Paiute *agaidikaʔa* 'salmon eaters'. For the Northern Shoshone partially overlapping this area, see the entry Yahandeka in the synonymy in "Northern Shoshone and Bannock" (this vol.).

Küpadökadö (17). The Northern Paiute name is *kiˑpadikadi* 'ground squirrel sp. eaters', also given as Kuh´-pat-ti-kut´-teh, located to the north in the area assigned by Stewart to the Sawawaktödö tuviwarai

(Powers), and kepA-tekade (Loud and Harrington). Also recorded for this area are the Sai´-du-ka Du-bi´-wa (Powers) and Sai-du-ka tu-wi-wait (Powell), miscopied as Lai´-du-ka-tu-wi-wait in Hodge; this name signifies 'possessors of the Saiduka territory', the Saiduka being a legendary group described as the predecessors of the Northern Paiute in some areas. Uses of names like Sidocaw (Campbell in ARCIA 1866:119) for this group result from a misunderstanding. The legendary Saiduka (Northern Paiute *saiduka* 'under tule', that is 'tule-mat-house dwellers') are variously identified with the ancestors of the Nez Perce, Achumawi, or Klamath (O.C. Stewart 1939:140; Fowler and Fowler 1970:143).

Kutsavidökadö (22). The recorded Northern Paiute form is *kucadikadi* 'eaters of brine fly pupae'; Stewart's form and the Ko-za´-bi-ti-kut´-teh of Powers show a compounding with the free form *kucabi* that is less idiomatic. Powell has Kots-a´-va. An extensive treatment of names used for the Mono Lake Northern Paiute is in Merriam (1955:164–168).

Kuyuidökadö (16). The Pyramid Lake people are in Northern Paiute *kuyuidikadi* 'cui-ui eaters', also rendered Ku´-yu-wi-ti-kut´-teh (Powers), Ku yu-i-di ka and Ku yu i´ di ka (Powell), kuyui-yekade (Loud and Harrington), Kuiyui´tikad^ü (Kelly), and Kuyui´tükəd^ə (Park); Campbell (ARCIA 1866:119) has Coo-er-ee.

Makuhadökadö (Pauide tuviwarai, Pauida tuviwarai) (13). The Northern Paiute forms and translations of these names are uncertain. Powell located in this area the It-sa´-a-ti-a-ga 'coyote canyon' (Fowler and Fowler 1971:232), given as idza'a-teaga-tekade by Loud and Harrington (1929:153).

Pakwidökadö (21). The Northern Paiute word is *pak^widikadi* 'chub eaters', also given as Pa´-gwi-ho tu[viwagaiyu] (Powell). Steward (1933b:236) locates the pahumu witü and ozavdika in this area.

Sawawaktödö tuviwarai (Sawakudökwa tuviwarai) (12). The Northern Paiute names refer to those living near Winnemucca Mountain, called *sawagatidi* 'sagebrush mountain' or *sawagudak^wa* 'sagebrush butte'; other renderings are sawa-kate (Loud and Harrington 1929:153) and Sa-wa´-ga-ti-ra (Powell), which appears as Sawagativa in Hodge. The Ha´pudtükəd^ə have been placed partly in this area (Park).

Tagötöka (4). This is Northern Paiute *tagitika'a* 'eaters of *Lomatium* sp. roots'.

Tasiget tuviwarai (15). The Northern Paiute name denotes the dwellers at *tasig^waiti* 'middle place'. Park locates in this area the kamu´tükəd^ə, who are placed immediately to the north, as the Kamödökadö, by Stewart.

Toedökadö (18). The name is Northern Paiute *toidikadi* 'cattail eaters', also rendered Toy´-yu-wi-ti-kut´-teh (Powers), To-i-wait (Powell), toi-tekade (Loud and Harrington), To´itikad^ü (Kelly), and Toi´tükəd^ə (Park

in Park et al.); Campbell (ARCIA 1866:119) has Toy Pi-Utes. People in this area were also designated as dwellers at Carson Lake (*kus·iba'a*): Ku´-si-pah (Powers), Ko-si-pa tu-wi-wa-gai-yu (Powell). Park locates the ko·si´patükəd^ə in this area but gives a different explanation of the name.

Tövusidökadö (19). The Northern Paiute name is *tib·us·idikadi* 'Cyperus bulb eaters', which Powers gives as Tu-pūs´-ti-kut´-teh; these are placed in Mason and Smith valleys. In Antelope Valley were the *poʒidadikadi* 'clover eaters', given as Poat´- sit-uh-ti-kut´-teh (Powers) and Po-tsid´-a tu[viwagaiyu] (Powell). Also placed in this area are the Pam´-mi-toy (Powers) and the *oŋadikadi* 'salt eaters' (Liljeblad).

Tsösö'ödö tuviwarai (7). These are in Northern Paiute *iʒicidi tibiwaga'yu* 'dwellers in the Steens Mountains (literally, cold ones)'; another rendering is Tsitsiadi (Whiting 1950:16). They are possibly the tübu´iuitikad^ü 'berry-eaters (?)' reported by Kelly.

Wadadökadö (of Honey Lake) (14). In Northern Paiute this name is *wadadikadi* 'eaters of *Suaeda* seeds'; this is the same as the name of the group in the Malheur Lake area (following entry). Other renderings are Wada´tikad^ü (Kelly), Wará-tikárû (Curtis 1907–1930, 15:66, 170), Wada´tükəd^ə (Park), Wadátkuht (Riddell 1960a:3).

Wadatöka (of Malheur Lake) (3). The Northern Paiute name is *wadadika'a* 'eaters of *Suaeda* seeds', appearing as wada´tikad^ü (Kelly); this is the same as the name of the group at Honey Lake (preceding entry). A spelling of this, or a Klamath borrowing (Wheeler-Voegelin 1955–1956, 2:257), is Wah-tat-kin (ARCIA 1865:466). Powell located the To-gwing´-a-ni, Egan's band, in this area in 1881 (Fowler and Fowler 1971:232); this is Hodge's Togwingani.

Yahuskin (2). This name is not Northern Paiute but presumably from Klamath. It was first used, as Yah-hoos-kin, Ya-hoos-kin, "the Yahooskin band of Snakes," and "the Yahooskin Band of Snake Indians," in connection with the Klamath Lake Treaty of 1864 (ARCIA 1865:102, 466, 471; Wheeler-Voegelin 1955–1956, 1:98); subsequently it appears only in Office of Indian Affairs reports, not in Army reports or other primary sources. Gatschet (1879:410) normalized the name as Yahúskin. Wheeler-Voegelin (1955–1956, 1) demonstrated that the "Yahooskin Snakes" were not a distinct group and that the people so referred to were Surprise Valley Northern Paiutes (Kidütökadö); a group later referred to as Yahooskins were Klamaths from the upper Sprague River Valley. According to Kelly (1932:72, 1938:364) the "Beatty band" (the Northern Paiutes at the Klamath Reservation) were known in their earlier territory as dühü´tcyatikad^ü 'deer eaters', and later, on the reservation as go'y´atikad^ü 'crawfish eaters' (a name derived from Klamath *goy̓a* 'crawfish').

Yamosöpö tuviwarai (10). The name means 'dwellers

in Paradise Valley'; cf. Northern Paiute *yam·os·uk^waiti* 'flat valley place' and the recordings Yam-mūs´ (Powers) and Yäm mōs tu we wa gai yu (Powell). In this area Liljeblad locates the *payapadikaʔa* 'angelica root eaters' and the *wiyitikaʔa* 'buckberry eaters'.

Groups given by Hodge (1907–1910) as Paviotso but now considered Western Shoshone (including Panamint) are: Koeats, Nahaego, Nogaie, Olanche, Pagantso, Sunananahogwa, Tonawitsowa, and Toquimas. The names Lohim and Loko, given for Northern Paiute groups in early sources, have no known etymology.

Sources

Ethnographic work began among the Northern Paiute with the brief surveys of Powers in 1876 (Fowler and Fowler 1970) and Powell in 1880 (Fowler and Fowler 1971). Lowie (1924) was next to visit the region, providing notes on the Northern Paiute of western Nevada as part of his more general Great Basin ethnographic reconnaissance. In the 1930s, several able students worked on basic cultural descriptions, including Kelly (1932) on the Surprise Valley Paiute and W.Z. Park (1933–1940) on the Pyramid Lake, Walker River, Dayton, and Honey Lake groups. O.C. Stewart (1939, 1941) was also in the field in the 1930s completing a culture element distribution survey (see also Steward 1941). Works by Riddell (1960a) on the Honey Lake area, Davis (1965) on the Mono Lake area, and Heizer (1970) on the Lovelock area helped to fill the gaps. Underhill (1941) also provided an overview.

Topical works included W.Z. Park (1938) and Whiting (1950) on shamanism; O.C. Stewart (1944) on Peyotism; Wheat (1967) on material culture; Lowie (1924a) and Kelly (1938) on mythology; Steward and Voegelin (1974), Wheeler-Voegelin (1955–1956), Hittman (1973), Lynch (1971), Houghton (1968, 1973), Shimkin and Reid (1970), and Knack and Stewart (1984) on ethnohistory. Tribal histories include those by Johnson (1975) and the Inter-Tribal Council of Nevada (1976a). Additional bibliography is in C.S. Fowler (1970).

Unpublished manuscripts on various aspects of Northern Paiute ethnography, linguistics, and ethnohistory are in several repositories. The Special Collections Department of the Getchell Library, University of Nevada, Reno, has the following: Lorenzo Creel Collection (extensive photographs, some diaries, miscellaneous reports and correspondence of a federal Indian agent and inspector, 1910–1930); Margaret M. Wheat Collection (extensive photographs, tape-recorded interviews by a talented amateur ethnographer, 1950s–1970s); Omer C. Stewart Collection (documents and field data on Peyotism, 1930s–1950s); Pyramid Lake Tribal Council Records (1940s–1970s); Robert Leland Collection (tribal attorney, legal consultant on many cases, 1950s–1970s); and the Sven Liljeblad Collection (extensive linguistic and ethnographic notes, tape recordings, photographs; Bannock, Northern Paiute, Shoshone; 1940 intermittently to 1980s). University Archives, Bancroft Library, University of California, Berkeley, has the W.L. Marsden linguistic records for Burns, Oregon, Northern Paiute (1900–1915); the C. Hart Merriam Collection of photographs and miscellaneous notes (1900–1935); and a collection of linguistic notes made by A.L. Kroeber and Gilbert Natches around 1915. The Nevada Historical Society, Reno, has the John T. Reid Collection (popular ethnography, interviews, correspondence, from Lovelock, Nevada, 1910–1930); and extensive photographs. The National Archives, including regional repositories in Seattle and San Bruno, California, has Office of Indian Affairs and Bureau of Indian Affairs records from the region, as well as extensive military records. Major libraries with Western Americana collections, all of which are important for ethnohistorical work, include the Bancroft Library, University of California; the Huntington Library, San Marino, California; the Newberry Library, Chicago; Yale University; Nevada Historical Society; Oregon Historical Society, Portland. Unpublished field notes include those by Park and Liljeblad cited above, as well as those of Omer C. Stewart (1930s–1980s, intermittently, on ethnography in 1930s–1940s; documentary toward various litigations, 1950s–1980s) and Catherine S. Fowler (1964 intermittently to 1980s; ethnobotanical, miscellaneous ethnography, linguistics). The University of Nevada Department of Anthropology Archives has unpublished field notes from 20 graduate students' summer field projects on western Nevada reservations and colonies, 1964–1965. Some of these students, including Ruth Houghton, Robert Lynch, and Michael Hittman wrote dissertations from these and later field experiences, and have additional field notes.

Material culture collections for the Northern Paiute are housed at the National Museum of Natural History, Smithsonian Institution (Powers collection); Milwaukee Public Museum (Barrett collection); Lowie Museum, University of California, Berkeley (Kelly collection); American Museum of Natural History, New York (Park and Lowie collections); Peabody Museum of Harvard University, Cambridge (Park collection); Field Museum of Natural History, Chicago (Hudson collection); University of California, Davis (Merriam collection); and Museum of the American Indian, Heye Foundation, New York (Harrington collection). The Nevada State Museum, Carson City, also has miscellaneous provenienced pieces, as do many other public repositories.

Washoe

WARREN L. D'AZEVEDO

The Washoe ('wä͵shō) are the only people of the Great Basin whose language is not Numic (see "Washoe Language," this vol.).* There can be little doubt that the Washoe people have had long tenure in their known area of historic occupation and that their presence predates the arrival of their Numic-speaking neighbors.

Origins

The tribes to the west of the Washoe represented California-type cultures and subsistence economies, while those to the east were typically Great Basin. The Washoe, though geographically a Great Basin people, nevertheless reveal strong cultural affinities to both regions (Barrett 1917:5–6; Lowie 1923; Kroeber 1920:168, 1925:571; Heizer and Elsasser 1953:4; Downs 1966:65–71). Yet Kroeber (1957:209–212) found the Washoe to be the most culturally divergent group in the western Great Basin, suggesting that their most ancient ties were to California rather than with the Northern Paiute and that this might indicate that they came into contact with Numic speakers much later or that their relatively rich environment afforded them a degree of isolation and independence from neighboring peoples. One hypothesis of Washoe origins traces them to the Martis archeological complex of the Sierra Nevada, which spread eastward into the historic Washoe area about 4000 B.C. (Elston 1971:10–11; Price 1962a:92; Moratto 1984). This interpretation coincides with Washoe lore concerning an ancient range extending over the crest of the Sierra Nevada into the acorn belt of the western foothills, from which they were slowly driven back by the Maidu on the northwest. There is some archeological evidence that efficient acorn-processing techniques developed after about A.D. 500, leading to intensive occupation of the western Sierra Nevada slopes by ancestors of the historic occupants of that region (Moratto 1972).

About A.D. 500 a Late Archaic culture known as the Kings Beach complex began to emerge in the Lake Tahoe region and along the northern Sierra Nevada front (Heizer and Elsasser 1953:19–21; Elston 1982:198–199). This culture has been generally equated with the Washoe and continued to historic times. Although Heizer and Elsasser (1953:4; Elsasser 1960:72–74) considered the Kings Beach and Martis complexes to be geographically and culturally exclusive, others have pointed out that materials diagnostic of each complex are often found in the same sites, so they may represent overlapping traditions (Elston 1971:10–11, 1979:46; Elston et al. 1977:167–168; C.S. Fowler et al. 1981:88). During Kings Beach times the climate became somewhat drier, and the environment may have been less productive than during the Martis period. The settlement pattern shifted to numerous smaller and more dispersed winter habitation sites, indicating the possibility of demographic stress and the exploitation of a wider range of resources and ecological niches. The substantial Martis pit house gives way to the conical bark slab house and the temporary brush shelters identified with the historic Washoe. Small projectile points made of obsidian replaced heavy Martis basalt implements. The bow and arrow appears to have replaced the atlatl and dart, while fishing, intensive seed gathering, and the procurement of small animals such as rabbits began to replace the Martis emphasis on hunting of larger game along with seed processing. The concentrated exploitation of piñon probably did not begin until these times, and the increased use of bedrock mortars throughout the area indicates the intensification of seed processing technology. The culture of the early historic Washoe people, as reconstructed from ethnographic investigation, was clearly a continuation of these precursive developments.

Environment

The area occupied or used by the Washoe in early historic times was part of the Sierra Nevada region, "a special culture province, characterized by seasonal movements within its borders of the inhabitants, who, for most of the year, including the winter time, utilized its lower altitude eastern and western slopes" (Elsasser 1960:2). It contains three major life-zones providing

*The phonemes of Washoe are: (voiceless stops) p, t, k, ʔ; (voiced stops and affricate) b, d, ʒ, g; (glottalized stops and affricate) ṗ, ṫ, ċ, k̓; (voiceless fricatives) s, š, h; (voiced nasals) m, n, ŋ; (voiceless nasals) M, N̦; (voiced semivowels and lateral) w, l, y; (voiceless semivowels and lateral) W, ł, Y; (short vowels) i, e, a, o, u, i; (long vowels) i·, e·, a·, o·, u·, i·; (stress) v́.

Washoe words appearing in italics in the *Handbook* have been transcribed in this orthography by William H. Jacobsen, Jr.

abundant and varied plant and animal species. The Boreal zone around Lake Tahoe and along the crest of the Sierra Nevada at elevations of from 6,000 to 10,000 or more feet has forests of Jeffrey pine, fir, sugar pine, and hemlock, and numerous lakes, streams, and mountain meadows. Though deep snows cover most of the mountain sections in the winter, large game such as mountain sheep, deer, and antelope were plentiful, as were many species of smaller animals. Fish were abundant in all the waters and were one of the most important sources of food. Over the crest of the Sierra Nevada the tributaries of many rivers such as the Feather, Yuba, American, Cosumnes, Mokelumne, and Stanislaus flowing into California were the routes along which Washoe traveled to the western foothills to procure acorns in the late summer and fall.

In the Transition zone along the lower elevations of the Sierra Nevada at about 4,500 to 6,000 feet, Jeffrey pine and fir forests merge with the piñon, juniper, and sage brush belt in the Pine Nut Mountains, which divide the region from the drier and more extensive Upper Sonoran zone. A chain of large valleys extends from north to south on the Sierra slope, presenting a piedmont environment. Three lakes—Honey Lake, Washoe Lake, and Topaz Lake—with interior drainage and seasonal marshlands provided abundant resources of fish, waterfowl, and a variety of plants, as well as small and large game attracted to their shores. The climate is warm in the summer with some rains through July; winter snows are light. At higher elevations, such as at Lake Tahoe, heavy winter snow packs form between November and April, though these vary in depth from year to year and some winters are relatively mild.

A number of specialized altitudinal vegetation zones each supported relatively distinctive animal and plant communities (J. Jack 1978:3–12): the sagebrush steppe just east of the Sierra slope valleys; the piñon-juniper woodland of the Pine Nut Mountains; the ponderosa shrub forest, including stands of Jeffrey pine on the low altitude eastern and western Sierra foothills; the forests of mixed conifers, fir, and lodgepole pine on ascending mountain altitudes intermingled with various species of shrubs; the high alpine zone above the timberline containing short grasses, sedges, and farbs providing forage for some large mammals such as bighorn sheep; the chaparral and oak woodlands of the western foothills of the Sierra Nevada; high mountain meadows rich in tubers, seeds, and berries; and extensive marshlands around mountain lakes as well as around the lakes and playas of large lowland valleys where tules and rushes once grew in profusion and numerous species of waterfowl thrived.

Thus the area occupied by the Washoe contained a great variety of climatic conditions, topography, and biota in close geographic proximity (Downs 1966:8–11). All major vegetation belts are represented (Oost-

ing 1958:312), and the area is a center of differentiation for more than 68 species of mammals, 12 of which do not occur elsewhere in the region (R.E. Hall 1946:34,44). Fish, as well as large and small game, were plentiful, and herds of antelope were frequently sighted (though antelope disappeared before the end of the nineteenth century).

Territory

The major habitation centers of the Washoe were on the floors of the large valleys averaging about 4,500 feet elevation, where water, vegetation, and game were abundant in a relatively mild climate. There the Washoe had permanent settlements identified with traditionally acknowledged subgroups and geographic features (fig. 1). Year-round settlements were also maintained in small valleys at altitudes around 5,500 feet, such as at Woodfords and Markleeville in Alpine County, the upper reaches of the Truckee River near Donner Lake, and in eastern Sierra Valley. Notions of firmly bounded territory and "exclusive use" imposed by Euro-Americans and, ultimately, as criteria for judgments in the Indian Claims Commission proceedings of the mid-twentieth century have tended to obscure the fact that the Washoe (and their neighbors) occupied an essentially open range. There is no evidence that the Washoe regularly defended or excluded others from their territory. Reports of hostilities are of localized events involving aggression or the threat of aggression by others in the vicinity of their settlements or of established hunting and gathering locations in current use. Moreover, much of the Washoe range, including the core area, was jointly used by adjacent non-Washoe peoples or provided a corridor of trade and travel. Such trespass was usually accommodated by negotiation or the prior withdrawal of one group from confrontation. Many of the so-called wars between the Washoe and the Northern Paiute, Miwok, or Maidu were of this nature and represent skirmishes between small parties whose general associations were peaceful (Downs 1966:51–54, 69).

The extensive Washoe territorial range beyond the core area was clearly open to joint use by the Washoe and adjacent peoples, subject to traditional understandings of priority and affected by the current state of relations between groups. Even the ostensible core area itself was a discontinuous entity, crossed by corridors of tolerated access (d'Azevedo 1966:334). This does not mean the actual lands required for subsistence were minimal. On the contrary, the economy necessitated the exploitation of large areas beyond what might be considered the area of exclusive occupancy (Price 1962a:v, 1; Nevers 1976:90; O.C. Stewart 1961:185–189), without which it is unlikely that the richly complex and interdependent cultures of the region could have survived.

467

The homogeneity of Washoe culture may be attributed to the close proximity of the groups residing in and identified with various geographic sections within an area less than 120 miles long and 40 miles wide. This area comprises about 4,000 square miles within a more extensive range of seasonal exploitation that totals 10,000 square miles or more (Price 1962a:3).

Subgroups

A convention has developed among students of the Washoe concerning a division of the territory and the tribe into sections supposedly representing concrete subareas of distribution (Lowie 1939:301; Curtis 1907–1930, 15:90; Freed 1960:350; Price 1962a:1; Nevers 1976:3). These are usually identified as the *wélmelti⁷* 'northerners', the *ṕá·wa⁷lu⁷* 'valley dwellers' (Carson Valley), and the *háŋalelti⁷* 'southerners'. Downs (1966:49) has added the *táŋlelti⁷* 'westerners', though this designation is no clearer than the others with reference to specific areas or peoples. One might as well contribute the additional term *ṕéwlelti⁷* 'easterners', which is occasionally used for peoples residing on the eastern side of the valleys, or for the Northern Paiute.

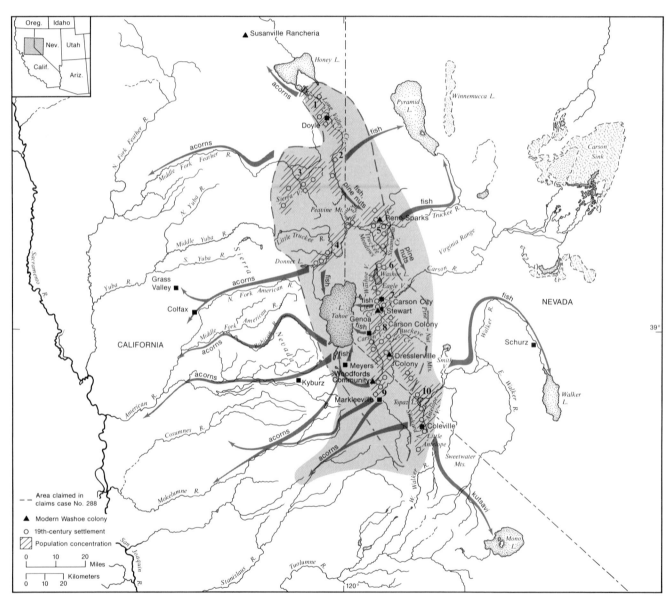

Fig. 1. Early 19th-century Washoe core area (tone) with regional communities: 1, *dísem dá⁷aw detdé⁷yi⁷* 'seepweed(?) lake dwellers'; 2, *čó⁷ya⁷ wáła detdé⁷yi⁷* 'tule river dwellers'; 3, *⁷múčim detdé⁷yi⁷* 'grass-place dwellers'; 4, *⁷áłabi⁷ wáła detdé⁷yi⁷* 'fish river dwellers'; 5, *⁷á⁷waku wáła detdé⁷yi⁷* 'cui-ui river dwellers'; 6, *čó⁷ya⁷ dá⁷aw detdé⁷yi⁷* 'tule lake dwellers'; 7, *⁷ušéwi wáła detdé⁷yi⁷* '(rabbit-) drive river dwellers'; 8, *ṕá·wa detdé⁷yi⁷* 'valley dwellers'; 9, *dačilgá·š dewbeyúmewe⁷ detdé⁷yi⁷* 'dwellers in the corner where rivers flow away out'; 10, *⁷uŋá·biya detdé⁷yi⁷* 'salt-place dwellers'. Arrows show routes to important resources within the total Washoe range. Dashed line delimits the area claimed for the Washoe before the Indian Claims Commission (Docket No. 288), after O.C. Stewart (1966:map 21). Southwestern extension of the core area after Barrett (1917: map1) and Kroeber (1925: pl. 37, 570).

However, these terms were not applied by the Washoe themselves as designations for precisely defined geographic sections or tribal divisions. Usage often depended on what part of the Washoe area an individual had grown up in, and the designation of the geographic placement of groups elsewhere was usually relative to one's own location. For example, the people of Truckee Meadows and northward to Honey Lake recognized themselves as *wélmelti?* only in a comparative or explanatory context, and all the peoples to the south of them in Washoe, Eagle, Carson, and Antelope valleys were referred to as *háŋalelti?*. Yet the people of Washoe and Eagle valleys were usually called *wélmelti?* by those to the south of them. The *pá·wa?lu?* of Carson Valley (a term that might be applied to any residents of large, flat valleys) were also *háŋalelti?* to all peoples north of them. The Washoe of Antelope Valley were *háŋalelti?šému* 'real southerners', a term also applied to those residing in the mountains of the Woodfords area who had close associations with the Antelope Valley people. But the people of Woodfords were also called *táŋlelti?*, a term also applied to the Miwok and Maidu or any Washoe people who might be living among them. The term has come to be synonymous with "California side." Downs (1966:49) is correct in pointing out that people were usually identified with the location of their winter residences, which were often the places where they were born and had lived most of their lives. However, these were not strictly kin-based or exogamous settlements, for families and individuals frequently shifted residence and might eventually become identified with groups in other localities. Therefore, the prominence given to the so-called tribal divisions of the Washoe seems to be an artifact of the historical period and the tendency of observers to overstate the case. As early as 1859, for example, Indian Agent Frederick Dodge (in ARCIA 1860:374) reported that the "Wa-sho nation" was "divided into three different bands," led by "Captain Jim," "Pos-Souke," and "Deer Dick."

The three leaders whom Dodge names are identified in Washoe historical narrative as prominent headmen who were selected by Whites as spokesmen and who eventually became known as "Captains" with a jurisdiction and authority greater than their traditional status had afforded. Captain Jim (*he?nú·ƙeha*) (d. 1868) was headman of a large family near the trading station at Genoa in Carson Valley. He figured in early settler lore as the chief negotiator for his people in the area and was soon to be pronounced "Captain Jim, chief of all the Washoe," an unofficial title he and his successor, also Captain Jim (*gúmelaŋa?* or Epésua) (fig. 2) held until the early twentieth century. Deer Dick (*bá?lew hé·ʒi?* or *bá?lew Mí·ƙi?* 'little Paiute' or 'looks like a Paiute') was headman of a group that camped in Honey Lake, Sierra, and Long valleys and had a similar role with regard to early settlers in the northern area, as did

"Pos-Souke" (*póšok*; George Pasuk), whose group lived in the Woodfords-Markleeville area. These men were not considered by the Washoe to be "chiefs" in the sense that Whites had defined them. Their traditional roles were as temporary headmen of major family units that were the core of larger collections of families making up the settlement clusters of particular areas. In aboriginal times such men might attain a degree of respect and trust that gave them some wider influence in organizing group activities, the settlement of grievances, or leadership in times of war. But each family or localized group had its own headman and retained a high degree of independence in decision-making and movement. The "Captain" phenomenon produced by White contact crystalized what had been a fluid and tentative process by singling out certain individuals for patronage and brokerage roles and, in effect, elevating them to a kind of sectional leadership. This precipitated deep resentments and competitive struggles among major families of local groups whose headman were ignored by the new system, and much of the factionalism in Washoe society during the late nineteenth and early twentieth centuries can be attributed to the disruption of traditional egalitarian principles of organization. The divisional chieftaincies defined by Dodge, representing primarily a convenience of Whites in dealing with widely scattered and mobile groups, gained a degree of influence and permanence that could not have obtained in former times. Despite the continued objections of other traditional headmen of the various local groups, the vaguely defined tripartite division of tribal territory and major leaderships became a reality in both White and Washoe perceptions.

Another effect of White contact was the notion that the Washoe had been unified under a dominant "tribal chief" (Lowie 1939:303; Freed 1960:353). This role was often ascribed to the Captain Jims of the Carson Valley area where Whites had made first contacts with the Washoe, and in the vicinity of the early concentration of White settlement, mining activities, and ranching that attracted impoverished Washoe dependents and laborers from other sections. In the 1890s the increasing role of the Indian agency and the opening of the Stewart Indian School near Carson City made the area a focal point of Washoe habitation and population. It was in this context that the Captain Jims of that area came to be known as chiefs of the entire tribe, *gúmelaŋa?* earning the reputation by a remarkable persistence and selflessness in pursuit of the interests of his people. But this status was never recognized by all Washoe groups, who firmly held to a fading assertion of local independence, and who acquiesced to the idea of a politically unified tribe and primary spokesman only as an expediency of relations with White society. Moreover, by the late nineteenth century the "Washoe tribe" was conceived by Whites to be essentially the Washoe pop-

Smithsonian, NAA.

Fig. 2. Washoe leaders. left, Captain Heel (*dadóˑ ̣koyiˀ*), who succeeded Deer Dick as headman of the Honey Lake group. The canvas structure has rabbitskin strips around it. Photograph by Clark, near Doyle, Calif., 1904. right, Captain Jim (*gúmelaŋaˀ*) (d. 1911), wearing a military coat. Photographed at Genoa, Nev., about 1905.

ulation converging around Carson City and Carson Valley, while the remnant groups and leaders of the northern area were scarcely known or mentioned.

Intra-Washoe Relations

The relations among Washoe local groups were consistently peaceful and cooperative. The pattern was one of extensive interaction, rather than the insulation or exclusiveness implied by ethnographic accounts that stress the defense of boundaries and the ostensible atomism of the social organization.

Sustaining good relations with other groups was a valued attribute of local headmen. They usually had close kinship connections with other groups and often maintained polygynous unions in which wives might continue to reside among their own people. Kinship networks linked groups and encouraged continual visiting and the sharing of resources. Visiting and festivals were occasions for arranging marriages and for the exchange of gifts. Old people recall that a messenger was sent through distant settlements with a knotted string (*baˀlóˑgo*) to indicate the number of days before a festival or other large gathering to which all were invited or to request assistance from volunteer warriors when hostilities threatened (Downs 1966:52).

The extensive seasonal mobility of individuals and groups allowed the effective communication of news of events and of good hunting and gathering locations.

Goods were exchanged at the periodic gatherings for rabbit hunts, fish runs, and pine nut or acorn harvests.

Yet some mutual suspicion sometimes existed between groups. The Washoe in the foothills near Woodfords and Markleeville were closely related to those of Antelope Valley, with whom they shared the hunting and gathering resources of Heenan Lake and Slinkard Valley. They also shared productive piñon groves with the Carson Valley Washoe, less than 10 miles away, and assembled with them for annual harvest rites. But the Carson Valley people considered the mountain Washoe to be somewhat aloof and mysterious, or less like real Washoe than like the non-Washoe people to their west with whom they had longstanding relations (Dangberg 1918–1922; d'Azevedo 1956). In southern lore they figure as adept hunters in the Sierra Nevada, as the source of rare medicinal plants, and as a rough warlike people often called on for aid in defense or retaliatory raids. These attitudes were manifested during a schism over Peyotism in the 1930s and 1940s (Merriam and d'Azevedo 1957:615–616) and played a subtle role in the political factionalism of the nineteenth century that carried over into the development of the formal tribal organization after the 1930s.

External Relations

Intermarriage between Washoe subgroups and adjacent peoples such as the Pyramid Lake and Walker River

Northern Paiute, the Miwok, and even the less trusted Maidu and Nisenan were not uncommon in aboriginal and early historic times in sections where these peoples regularly shared ranges (Beals 1933:366; Riddell 1960a:75; Downs 1966:51). Such contacts also involved trade, visiting, and, in a few reported instances, co-operation in defense against intruders (d'Azevedo 1952–1955, 1963–1984). Relations of this kind never involved the participation of Washoes from all segments of the tribe, but usually only from those subareas where such contacts had been long established and where Washoe groups were closely connected by common land use and the proximity of winter settlements.

In the southern Washoe area, there is little indication that non-Washoe people made any regular use of Carson Valley in aboriginal times. There was little direct contact between the valley-dwelling Washoe of this area and the Northern Paiute immediately to the east; the Pine Nut Mountains provided an effective material boundary between them. Both peoples tolerated some access over the crest of the mountains when resources were plentiful, but such joint use seems to have been rare.

In the northern Washoe area, the important black oak acorn resources of the western Honey Lake Valley were shared with the Northern Paiute and Maidu under generally peaceful conditions of accommodation (Riddell 1960a:32,37). The Washoe and Northern Paiute also jointly used fishing and gathering sites around Honey Lake and eastward to Pyramid Lake. Northern Paiutes were allowed to hunt and fish in Truckee Meadows and apparently made extensive use of sites near Peavine Mountain for deer hunting and for gathering (W.Z. Park 1933–1940; C.S. Fowler 1969:12).

Although northern Washoe traditions reveal a distrust of the Maidu, who were said to be hostile and aggressive, the Maidu and Washoe shared use of sections of Sierra Valley and Honey Lake Valley (Dixon 1905:125–126), and the Washoe regularly trekked for acorns as far west on the American River as what are now Colfax and Grass Valley in Nisenan country (Nevers 1976:12), where some often wintered and even intermarried (d'Azevedo 1952–1955, 1963–1984). The reports of friction and occasional skirmishes seem to be with the Konkow near what is now the town of Oroville. Consistent and more intense hostility was expressed toward Achumawi and Atsugewi, who were said to have frequently raided Washoe camps in Honey Lake Valley, and against whom the Washoe and Northern Paiute sometimes joined together in retaliation.

Price (1962a:26–27) notes that the Washoe had little trade with non-Washoe peoples and attributes this to language differences, a degree of geographic isolation, and a habitat that supplied most of the resources required. He points out that of 83 items listed by J.T. Davis (1961) as traded among groups in California, all but five were gathered or made by the Washoe in their own area. Though actual exchange was more extensive than this might indicate, the items listed by Sample (1950) and J.T. Davis (1961) as either imported or exported by the northern Washoe are notably sparse even as compared with recorded exchanges by the southern Washoe. The main items indicated as imports from the Nisenan and Wintu are papam bulbs, acorns, skins, sea shells, and kutsavi (a grub of the fly *Ephydra hians*), while the Washoe are said to have exported salt, obsidian, pine nuts, and rabbitskins to the Maidu. There are many Washoe place-names for locations in California as far west as the Sacramento and San Joaquin rivers, and legends are told of expeditions to the Pacific Ocean for shells (d'Azevedo 1956, 1952–1955, 1963–1984; Downs 1966:37). Little information exists on trade between the northern Washoe and the Northern Paiute, who sought deer skins (Price 1962a:28). The Washoe also traded other items to them, such as acorns, shells, and obsidian, in exchange for antelope skins and the prized cui-ui fish from Pyramid Lake and the lower Truckee River (d'Azevedo, 1952–1955, 1963–1984). In view of the fact that the Washoe area provided a major corridor between east and west, it may be assumed that they were in a position to transfer a number of desirable goods between the Great Basin and California (Downs 1966:37).

Although Antelope Valley was excluded from Washoe territory on the map submitted to the Indian Claims Commission (O.C. Stewart 1966:199), there is substantial evidence that the Washoe occupied at least the western side of the valley as well as southwestward to Little Antelope Valley on the upper reaches of the west fork of the Walker River (Forney in ARCIA 1860:364; Dodge in ARCIA 1860:374; Mooney 1896:1051; Creel 1875–1945; Hudson 1902:242, 251; Dangberg 1918–1922:48; Dewitt-Warr 1913:144; Curtis 1907–1930, 15:89; Siskin 1938:626–627; d'Azevedo 1966:330; Muhs 1981; Fred I. Green, personal communication 1964). Most commentators also agree that the Northern Paiute of Smith Valley hunted and sometimes camped on the eastern side of Antelope Valley, and that there was little friction between them and the Washoe in that area. The valley and its vicinity were important to the Washoe as a source of salt and flint, and the marshes around Topaz Lake provided waterfowl, fish, and abundant plant life. It was, moreover, a corridor through which both Washoe and Northern Paiute groups often trekked to Mono Lake in late summer to gather or trade kutsavi. They also were able to procure a type of sandstone there for making smoking pipes and arrow smoothers. In consequence, considerable intermarriage and bilingualism obtained in the extreme southern Washoe area, and there was a tendency for individuals and groups to shift tribal identity or to be ambiguous about their allegiance. This often led the Carson Valley Washoe to refer to them disparagingly as "half-breeds" (d'Azevedo 1956; Downs 1966:51). Some tension was also generated by the regular attendance of these Washoe groups (often with their Northern Paiute relatives and neighbors) at the fall pine nut gathering rites at Double Springs or in southern Carson Valley. But relations were generally peaceful and cooperative, and many of the southern Washoe made use of the privilege granted by the adjacent Northern Paiute for fishing along the Walker River. Contact with the Miwok was particularly intensive in the vicinity of Big Trees (known as p̓á·l 'juniper' or 'incense cedar' by the Washoe) on the upper Stanislaus River, where both peoples gathered acorns, often camped together and sometimes intermarried (Barrett 1906, 1908:347, 1917:6; d'Azevedo 1966:331). Some Washoe individuals and families also wintered over if the harvest had been good and relations with the Miwok remained friendly.

Similar, though less intensive, intercourse with the Nisenan is reported by Beals (1933:365–366), who indicates that there had been friendly relations and some intermarriage in aboriginal as well as historic times. Ben James, a prominent Woodfords Washoe in the late nineteenth century, regularly invited Nisenan friends to "big times" near the present sites of Kyburz and Myers. Headman George Pasuk, who was an older relative of Ben James's, spent considerable time among the Miwok around what is now West Point.

Culture

Settlement Pattern

Permanent settlements were located on high ground near rivers and springs, close to a variety of ecological zones, each seldom more than one or two days away. Houses were usually separated from one another for protection and privacy.

Small groups ranged in highly divergent and independent strategies of subsistence during the seasonal cycle of procurement. Temporary mobile camps might be utilized anywhere in the region at different times of the year, and it was not uncommon for individuals or family units to visit with relatives and friends for one or more winters in other Washoe settlements, or even among neighboring peoples such as the Miwok and Northern Paiute if conditions were favorable. The permanent settlement sites were not abandoned during intensive periods of hunting or gathering, for elderly persons and young children might remain there while other members of families moved about on the food quest, living in temporary camps in the valleys and mountains. This was true of the annual use of Lake Tahoe as well, or of the family gathering plots in the Pine Nut Mountains, or the oak groves over the Sierra Nevada where some members of families might choose to remain during the winter (Freed 1966:75; Downs 1966:12–37). The Washoe appear to have been less compelled to continual movement over vast stretches of land in the food quest than was the case for many of the Northern Paiute and Western Shoshone.

Subsistence

Though the Washoe had a detailed knowledge of a vast region around them and made frequent treks to distant places for desired foods and other materials, there was a large variety of predictable resources close at hand. Seasonal movements occurred regularly involving aggregations of people from different subareas at locations of predictable abundance, such as Lake Tahoe, Honey Lake, the fish runs on major rivers and streams, rabbit and antelope drives in the valleys, the harvests of acorn in western Honey Lake Valley, and the piñon groves in the Pine Nut Mountains. Yet most groups hunted and gathered in the vicinity of their traditional habitation sites, from which they dispersed during the summer and fall to temporary and shifting camps. Some individuals and small units ventured into the mountains or into other areas to known locations of good hunting or special plant growth. The distribution of resources was similar in all the major valleys of Washoe habitation so that in times of scarcity in one area or abundance in another the sharing of ranges diminished the threat of crises. There is no evidence that the Washoe suffered periodic starvation or severe winter "hungry times" prior to the disruption of their core habitation areas by White intrusion in the nineteenth century, though periods of shortage undoubtedly occurred due to unusual climatic changes or the occasional failure of a major crop. The reports of almost continuous or imminent starvation that appear in early settler accounts (Price 1962a:33) refer to conditions or recollections of conditions that obtained in the historic period when a way of life had been all but destroyed and the meager rations supplied by the federal government were insufficient to sustain the population.

Nevertheless, the aboriginal Washoe, though "seldom actually starving," were compelled by their environment and level of technology to a rigorous and continual search for food (Downs 1966:37). Yet the "seasonal round" was not a universal pattern of procurement affecting the entire tribe at any time during the year, nor did groups in any one of the subareas carry out a concerted or rigidly defined sequence of activities. Rather, each unit (as well as individuals) made independent decisions concerning the resources to be utilized at any time, resulting in a highly adaptive dispersal of peoples over fairly limited ranges of considerable topographical and ecological diversity. This fluid and optional pattern of movement during the spring, summer, and fall months is described by Freed (1960:350–351) for the southern Washoe, whose families split up to pursue various strategies of the food quest while at the same time sharing the diverse resources obtained. This was true of the Washoe of the northern sections as well, who concentrated their efforts in different ranges with slightly different emphases such as the reliance on local acorn harvests, the plants and game of large higher altitude valleys between Donner Lake and Sierra Valley, and the plentiful fish of Honey Lake and the Truckee River and its tributaries.

Although there was a tendency for peoples to move from lower to higher elevations in the spring and summer, to find relief from the heat of the lowland valleys and to exploit the mountain environment, this movement was not undertaken by all the population nor was it of the same degree or duration from year to year. It depended largely on the availability and relative abundance of alternative resources in an area.

• FISHING   The numerous lakes and streams contained many species of fish that could be procured at any time and that became available in particular abundance during frequent spawning runs (Snyder 1917; LaRivers 1962). Major fish runs in the streams surrounding Lake Tahoe involved varieties of trout in May and June, Tahoe suckers in late June, Lahontan tui chub later in the summer, as well as other species.

The tributaries and rivers emptying into Walker, Pyramid, and Honey lakes provided numerous fish runs at intervals throughout the year. The Lahontan sucker (*Pantosteus lahontan*) spawned profusely up Long Valley Creek from Honey Lake in the spring and early summer and was harvested by the northern Washoe, who congregated there in large numbers for first-fish rites and festivals (d'Azevedo 1952–1955, 1963–1984). The Truckee River flowing from Lake Tahoe to Pyramid Lake was a prime fishery of the northern Washoe, involving runs of trout from April to June and also from October to December, often lasting through the winter. Tahoe sucker and mountain whitefish attracted peoples from the surrounding region whom Snyder (1917:53) observed catching the fish in such large numbers that "tons of them are dried for later use." Runs of cutthroat trout and mountain whitefish also occurred in the spring and fall in the Carson and Walker rivers; especially large-sized fish of these species spawned in Walker Lake and along the Walker River in October where many southern Washoe shared a late-year abundance with the Northern Paiute. Fishing was possible in these waters even in severe winters, and spearing, netting, or angling through ice-holes were common practices (d'Azevedo 1952–1955, 1963–1984; Downs 1966:16).

The prominence of fishing in Washoe life is indicated by the relatively large inventory of implements and techniques used for this purpose: spears, cordage lines with bone fishhooks, harpoons with detachable point, dams for stream diversion, nets of cordage and basketry, weirs, and fishtraps of many types (Hudson 1902:248; Dangberg 1918–1922:21–22; Freed 1960:351–352; Downs 1966:16–17). Early White travelers through the area report having observed "floating houses" for fishing on the Truckee River (Johnson and Winter 1846:103; Camp 1960:207). These reports may actually refer to the covered fishing platforms that the Washoe and other peoples of the region constructed over streams or on lake margins, giving the impression of "floating." On the other hand, rafts of cedar bark and tule bundles were made for fishing along lakeshores and for crossing rivers, some said to have been large enough to hold as many as 15 people (Lowie 1939:329).

Large fish were caught by men using spears, hook and line, nets, traps, and weirs, while women used twined baskets for scooping up minnows and fish eggs. Though most fishing seems to have been done by individuals and small family units for themselves, larger aggregates of people during fish runs frequently participated in cooperative efforts for driving and taking great amounts of fish for communal distribution. Cooking was usually done by placing larger fish on coals or pit roasting; small fish, fish eggs, and roe were pit roasted, stone-boiled in baskets, or dried. Surplus big fish were split open and hung on poles or in the trees to dry. The smoke of fires was sometimes employed to speed drying and discourage insects. Great bundles of dried fish on strings were carried back to winter habitation sites where, during the colder months, preservation was ensured until they were eaten. Fishing provided the most predictable and consistent source of year-round food in the aboriginal and early historic Washoe diet.

• GATHERING   The gathering of plant products was pursued intensively from early spring until late fall. The irregularity of such crops, and their brief seasonal readiness for harvesting in many different locations, was the major factor in the dispersal of local population and frequent movement over a larger range (Downs (1966:19). J. Jack (1978:13–33) has listed over 170 plants occurring in the area, drawn from the ethnographic literature but primarily from plant terms collected by Jacobsen (1955) and identified by Schubert (1957). The remarkable retention of names for specific plants and the information about their uses on the part of older Washoe people in the mid-twentieth century attests to the focal importance of vegetation in Washoe subsistence. Not only did plant products provide a substantial part of Washoe diet through the growing year, but also they were the sources of medicinal substances and the materials of most manufactures.

In the spring and early summer numerous bulbs and roots became available in scattered locations in the valleys and the mountain meadows. As early as March, camas was gathered in the Sierra Nevada foothills, and it is reported in one source to have been eaten raw (Camp 1960:206). Bitterroot and sego lily were among the major roots gathered. Also there were a number of species of "wild onions," some of which were roasted in pits and formed into cakes for storage (Dangberg 1918–1922:4). Several types of "Indian potatoes" (dé·guš, golsísi', má'al, and others) also prized as food were abundant in the valleys and mountains. Tule and cattail, which grew in profusion in mountain and low valley marshes, constituted major staples during the summer. The roots were roasted or boiled; new shoots and seed-heads were eaten raw; the ripe heads were singed to loosen the seeds, which were milled and cooked as a gruel or baked into cakes; large quantities of pollen were taken to use as a sweetener with other foods or mixed with water and baked as cakes in sand pits (Hudson 1902:245–250). The roots of many plants used for medicinal purposes were also gathered, among them Indian balsam (*Leptotaenia dissecta*), which older Washoe people still search for in the spring as a highly regarded remedy for colds and body aches. The digging stick was the universal implement for procuring roots; this task was entirely undertaken by women.

A great variety of seeds and nuts were gathered and processed, mainly by women. Special attention was given to growths of dísem and 'múčim, two grasses prevalent at Honey Lake and Sierra Valley, respectively, after which these places are named. In the foothills and in the southern area the seeds of sunflowers, wild mustard, and wild rye were gathered, as well as those of pigweed and many other plants. A handled seed beater was used to knock off seeds into a tightly woven container basket. Seeds with hard shells were ground on a flat portable metate with a mano, or in a bedrock mortar with a pestle, then winnowed and made into a flour for cakes or boiled gruel. If the seeds were very small or soft-shelled they might be cooked without grinding.

In years of normal productivity or predictable crop fluctuation, pine nuts (tá·gim) and acorns (máliŋ) constituted staples, particularly in late fall and winter when other plant resources were becoming scarce. Traditionally, each major family unit held harvesting privileges on strips of land ('má·š) from which others were excluded from picking unless permission had been granted, or in the case of usufruct rights claimed by ties of kinship and marriage (Lowie 1939:303; Price 1962a:19, 34). When the crop was ripe, each family held brief propitiatory rites before going to the groves. However, this also was done collectively at large assemblies of people from which families would proceed to their traditional plots. Cones were knocked from the trees with hooked poles by men, while women and children gathered them into conical burden baskets or spread them out to dry. Most of the cones were stored on the spot in large brush and pine-bough-covered caches. Price (1962a:34) estimates that each household might have four such caches, each with 300–600 pounds of pine nuts. Some cones were roasted in fires until they had opened sufficiently to release their contents. The nuts were then parched over coals in flat basketry trays in preparation for storage or further processing. To prepare them for eating, the shells were cracked by rolling a mano over the nuts on a metate and then winnowing until the kernels were clean. They were eaten in this state but, more commonly, were ground into a fine flour for making a soup by stone-boiling in a close-coiled basket (Barrett 1917:13–14). Quantities of flour might also be prepared for future use or household storage. The gathering of pine nuts continued for three or more weeks in September and October while people moved from lower to higher elevations as the crop matured. In normal years there was enough carried back to winter residences or accumulated in caches to last for many months and, in some years, more was collected than could be consumed before the next crop was ready or before spoilage or animals destroyed the remainder (Price 1962a:34).

For the northern Washoe acorns assumed a role similar to that of pine nuts among the people to the south. Only a few of the southern groups made the arduous trek over the Sierra Nevada to the oak groves in the California foothills, from where acorns were carried back in burden baskets. Frequently, a method of relay-caching was employed by which a contingent of a party backtracked to bring up previously cached supplies to where the others were camped. In this way, more could be transported over the summit before winter snows set in than if each member of the group had carried a single burden. Some caches were left along trails to be returned for in the spring. Each person could carry a single large burden basket of unshelled acorns, which would yield about four or five pounds of flour. If shelling or flour processing had been done at the gathering site, the kernels or flour would be carried, while the unshelled acorns were brought by relay-caching (d'Azevedo 1952–1955, 1963–1984). Thus it is clear that acorns, though considered a great delicacy, were not a staple for the southern Washoe (Lowie 1939:326). It is possible that consumption may have increased somewhat in the late nineteenth and early twentieth centuries after the introduction of pack animals, wagons, and motor cars, though Cook (1941:54) estimates an average of less than two sacks of acorns annually for Carson Valley Washoe families, while a few might collect much more and share them with others (d'Azevedo 1952–1955, 1963–1984).

There is no information about whether the northern Washoe assembled for acorn harvest rites and festivals as they did for the major fish runs at the mouth of Long Valley Creek, though Curtis (1907–1930, 15:97) reports an "acorn dance."

The processing of acorn (fig. 3) for food involved a technology that the Washoe shared with California, where it apparently originated (Gifford 1936:87–89). Kernels were removed from the shell by use of mortar and pestle and rubbed to remove the skin. Then they were pounded to a rough consistency and finally ground into a fine flour by metate and mano. The flour was placed on a closely woven tray (or cloth) within a circle of rocks in the shallows of a stream for initial leaching, then leached for about an hour in a sand pit by pourings of warm water. The leached flour was cooked in water by stone-boiling in tight woven coiled baskets, stirred with a paddle, and the hot rocks were removed and replaced by a looped stick. During leaching and boiling, sprigs of juniper (*Juniperus osteosperma, J. occidentalis*) or incense cedar (*Libocedrus decurrens*) might be included as a flavoring. When sufficiently cooked, the gruel was dipped up in small amounts and dropped into cold water to form gelatinous dumplings, *megedí·dit*, called "biscuits" (Price 1980:47). These are usually eaten as a condiment with meat but were also eaten alone or with other foods. Information is inconclusive concerning other uses of acorn, such as rock or pit roasting of cakes.

Berries of many kinds were plentiful and eagerly sought as they ripened in the valleys and mountains. Among the most commonly found were western chokecherry,

elderberry (*Sambucus glauca*), buckberry (*Shepherdia argentea*), Saskatoon serviceberry, desert and golden currants, Sierra plum, and Sierra gooseberry. Varieties of wild strawberries were picked in mountain meadows and were highly prized. Manzanita berries were gathered in the Sierra Nevada and often traded from the Miwok. Many berries could be eaten fresh, but usually they were pounded into a pulp and cooked into soups with other foods, or baked or dried into cakes for storage or travel. Some were seeded through a sieve and mixed with water for a beverage; for example, manzanita berries were made into a cider similar to that used by the Miwok. The prominence of berries in the diet during the summer is generally noted by older Washoe people, especially western chokecherry and elderberry. Chokecherries were consumed in such large quantities that their discarded seeds eventually produced compact clumps of bushes which are said to mark the sites of old camps (Downs 1966:19).

The leafy and tender parts of some plants could be eaten raw, though often cooked or dried. Watercresses (*Rorippa curvisiliqua, R. sinuata, Barbarea vulgaris*) grew along many streams, and some varieties were available through the winter; the leaves were eaten as picked, though sometimes cooked with salt. This was also the case for miner's lettuce and wild rhubarb (*Peltiphyllum peltatum*). Mushrooms of a number of unidentified varieties were gathered under trees after spring rains. Mormon tea (*Ephedra*) was used as a stimulating tea and also for medicinal purposes.

Many of the plants used for food and other purposes

U. of Nev. Reno, Veronica Pataki Coll.

Fig. 3. Acorn processing. left, Leaching the acorn flour in a clothlined sand pit, with juniper sprigs for flavoring. right, Preparing the acorn gruel. The initial leaching basin is in the stream. Photographed in Carson Valley, Nev., 1966–1967.

also were collected for their medicinal properties, and knowledge of their processing and application was considered to be a particular skill of older women. There were also many inedible plants, such as wild parsnip and death camas, which were used as poisons and for ritual purposes. Others were difficult to find or had to be traded from surrounding peoples. Various mineral and faunal substances were utilized as well. A partial inventory of these materials is contained in Jacobsen (1955) and Schubert (1957), and an especially detailed list including location and therapeutic use was prepared by G.E. Montgomery (1965).

The smoking of tobacco (*Nicotiana attenuata, N. bigelovii*) was prevalent among men: a pipe was made with a soapstone and hollow reed stem or, sometimes, merely a straight reed tube (Wier 1901:47). Women smoked to a lesser extent and, it is said, mainly for medicinal purposes. Potions and poultices of tobacco were applied for various ailments, and the smouldering leaves (as with cedar and juniper) were commonly used incense. There is no conclusive evidence for the sowing of tobacco seed or the burning over of areas to increase growth (Lowie 1939; d'Azevedo 1952–1955, 1963–1984).

Insects of various kinds were a highly nutritious supplement to the diet. Though the Washoe in the mid-twentieth century continued to make some use of insects, the practice was often denied by them because of the negative reaction expressed by Whites. Yet in aboriginal times, and well into the historic period, swarms of locusts and grasshoppers were occasions for intensive gathering activity. Women and children and sometimes entire families drove the insects into ditches by beating or burning the brush. These were roasted in coals or sand pits, or dried and ground for storage and to be mixed with other foods (Downs 1966:35). Women and children often went out early in the morning with seed beaters and baskets to gather grasshoppers while they were still inactive (Dangberg 1918–1922:2). In earlier times, women carried a small jar-shaped, lidded basket for this purpose in which they also collected larvae (Hudson 1902:247). At least two types of worm were taken (Freed 1966:81; Dangberg 1918–1922:22; G.E. Montgomery 1965); both were roasted in sand pits or dried and stored. Large amounts of fly grub known generally as kutsavi (and to the Washoe as *mačibá·baši?*) were gathered during treks to Mono Lake in the late summer or procured from the Northern Paiute of that area through trade. The grub was scooped up on the shores of the lake with basketry sieves, dried, and could be stored for long periods. Different fly pupae, referred

left, Smithsonian, Natl. Mus. of Amer. Hist., Warshaw Coll.: 9758; center, Field Mus., Chicago: 58368; right, Nev. State Mus., Carson City: 38–6–411.

Fig. 4. Utilitarian baskets. left, "Washoe Indians—The Chief's Family." Two seed beaters, 2 conical open twined burden baskets, and a globular cricket basket are to the left of the standing woman. Both women have cradles. The clothing is Euro-American, but the hairstyles—the women's bangs and the man's side-braids—were traditionally Washoe. The elaborate bone and shell necklaces may be Miwok and Maidu pieces. Stereoscopic photograph by Charles Leander Weed, 1862, published by the Lawrence and Houseworth Company, San Francisco. center, Girl's willow cradle with badger skin swaddling. The narrow triangular outline and open twined shade are typical though often more elaborate. Collected by J.W. Hudson at Lake Tahoe, Calif., 1902; length, 95.2 cm. right, Open twined cricket basket, collected before 1900, height 20 cm.

to by the same name, were gathered in small shallow lakes. Honey was collected, as well as bee larvae (Downs 1966:35). In addition to honey, which was eaten directly from the comb or mixed with cooked foods, sweeteners included the sap of the piñon tree and of the sugar pine, the latter also used as a medication for colds and sore throat. The gathering of seeds, roots, berries, and greens was almost exclusively women's work, and they also participated with men in the harvesting of pine nuts and acorns as well as in some fishing and hunting activities. Moreover, they were the processors of most foods and were entirely relied upon for their skills in cooking and the scheduling of meals from the family hearth. Their focal role in subsistence is expressed in the popular lore that without women men would go hungry except for meat, fish, and raw foods found on the spot: thus a man with more than one wife or daughters was fortunate. A particularly important activity of women was the preparation of foods for preservation and winter use. These are often referred to by women as "real food" (*démlušému*) in contrast to those consumed when taken and not susceptible to processing for storing.

Except for the large assemblies and collective rites occasioned by the annual pine nut and acorn harvest, or by fish runs and special animal drives in which both men and women participated, most food procurement was carried out by individuals or small groups. Downs (1966:22) suggests that gathering, a predominantly female activity, was less ritualized than hunting or other pursuits engaged in mainly by men. However, ethnographers have tended to overlook the religious and social aspect of women's subsistence activities. Prior to any gathering task, women (usually led by an elder member of the group) offered prayers to the plants and for the blessing of their utensils and other equipment. There

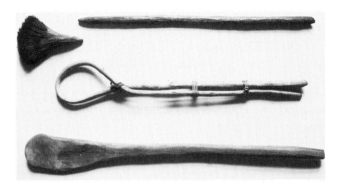

Milwaukee Public Mus., Wis: 18368, 18375, 18366, 18365.
Fig. 5. Cooking implements. top to bottom: Wooden fire poker; meal brush, used to gather up the bits of meal during the grinding process, of soaproot fiber, the fiber traded from the Miwok (Barrett 1917); the handle was formed by gluing the fibers together with the sticky gum of the roasted soaproot; looped stick used for stirring mush during cooking and for lifting hot stones out of the cooking basket; wooden stirring paddle. Length of poker 62.6 cm, rest same scale; collected by Samuel Barrett, 1915.

were traditional restrictions on the amount that could be harvested from a given area, to insure future growth; and debris was removed out of "respect" for the local species. Of particular significance was the consecration of the female role in the girls' puberty rites in which symbolic acts connected with gathering and domestic chores were given emphasis as well as taboos against eating meat and fish (Freed and Freed 1963a:27; Downs 1966:36; Price 1980:22–23).

• HUNTING   The principal large mammals hunted by the Washoe were mule deer, pronghorn antelope, and mountain sheep (*Ovis canadensis*). The basic weapons used were bow and arrow (fig. 6). Bows were made of even-grained woods and might be of a simple type for hunting small game, or the longer and heavier sinew-backed bow with sharply curved ends used for large game (Wier 1901:41; Hudson 1902:244; Barrett 1917:12). Bowstrings were usually of deer sinew. Arrows were of cane or other straight-stemmed plants, sometimes merely sharpened at the end and feathered for small animals. A poison made from rattlesnake venom and other ingredients was sometimes applied to arrow points (Lowie 1939:325). Stone knives for killing, butchering, and other tasks were made in many forms and of various lithic materials.

The most usual method of fire making was on a pitted hearth of cedar pine with single or double drills and particles of fiber. A piece of bone was spliced or bound to the drill, or a hollow cane was filled with charcoal dust or dry pith (Powers 1876; Dangberg 1918–1922:10; O.C. Stewart 1941:381, 431). Wier (1901:70) notes that fire was also struck from two pieces of flint, though O.C. Stewart (1941:381) found this method absent in the region. Stewart reports the preservation of fire by burying embers in earth or burning into sagebrush roots. Embers covered with sand or earth also could be carried wrapped in a damp skin (d'Azevedo 1952–1955, 1963–1984).

Deer and mountain sheep were hunted at high altitudes by parties of men on snowshoes, which were constructed of a circular hoop of manzanita or piñon about 18 inches in diameter. Strips of buckskin were plaited horizontally and vertically, and the feet were lashed to the middle of this web by thongs (Lowie 1939:329; Price 1962a:64). A long pole was used for support. A type of ski made of bark or wood slabs was also employed for snow and marsh walking (d'Azevedo 1952–1955, 1963–1984). Though deer might be hunted at any time, late summer and fall were preferred, when the animals were fat and the herds were moving down from the mountains. Individuals or pairs of men made frequent sorties in search of deer. When herds were reported in the nearby mountains, parties of 5–10 men pursued them and set up ambushes along known trails, sometimes building rock-sided blinds topped with poles and brush (Dangberg 1918–1922:23). Such parties often were

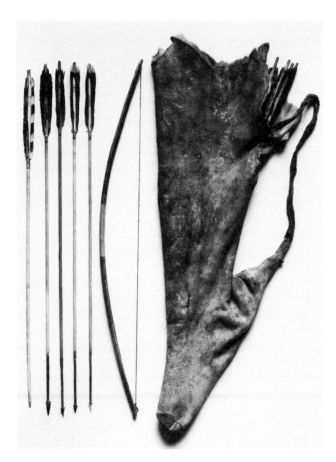

Milwaukee Public Mus., Wis.: left to right, 18386b, 18385, 18384, 18383, 19382, 18386a, 18386f.

Fig. 6. Self-bow, arrows, and one-piece deerskin quiver (hair to the inside), typical of the Washoe of ancient times. Bow length, 82.5 cm; collected by Samuel A. Barrett, 1916.

led by an admired hunter or one who had dreamed of deer (Hudson 1902:247; Dangberg 1918–1922:24; d'Azevedo 1952–1955, 1963–1984; cf. Lowie 1939:326). Antler and deerskin cloak disguises were also used for stalking (Freed 1960:351; Downs 1966:28). Skinning, bleeding, and butchering were done on the spot and the meat divided equally. Each man might carry as much as 200 pounds of boned meat (Downs 1966:30), some of which was further processed for storage by women. Other hunts in the vicinity of habitation sites often involved 100 or more people, including women and children. The children would form a wide circle at some distance from a herd and slowly drive the deer toward the hunters, who shot them with bows and arrows. This method was supplemented frequently by setting fires in the undergrowth, though this was never done near pine nut groves (Dangberg 1918–1922:24).

Antelope were rarely stalked by individual or small parties, but large groups of people drove the animals into V-shaped corrals or sagebrush or rock for the hunters to shoot. They were sometimes driven over cliffs and killed in great numbers (d'Azevedo 1952–1955,

1963–1984). Dangberg (1918–1922:34–35) records occasions where women joined the men in the slaughter of fallen and maimed animals using stone knives and clubs (see also Lowie 1939:325). Mountain sheep were generally stalked by individual hunters or ambushed along the trails where they came down to drink. Few were taken, and the return of a successful hunter was celebrated with dancing (Dangberg 1918–1922:30; Downs 1966:32). Black bear and the grizzly were considered to be animals of great magical power. They were rarely hunted purposively, though parties of men might arouse and kill a hibernating bear. The meat might be eaten by the hunters, but it was not distributed to others (Downs 1961:380–381, 1966:33). Bears provoked fear and respect, and killing one required acts of propitiation and the ritual burial of unused remains.

By far the most plentiful and important game animals in Washoe subsistence were hares and rabbits. The two major species taken were white-tailed jackrabbit and cottontail, though the less abundant snowshoe hare was also hunted in the mountains. In the autumn the population of jackrabbits and cottontails was so great in the lowland valleys that thousands of them could be taken in drives involving large numbers of people. These drives were organized by an elected "rabbit boss" who called together all able-bodied people from local groups at a site usually on the upper end of large flats. Instructions and exhortations were given by the leader, and the people, in a wide semicircle, slowly drove the rabbits into long nets where they were killed by arrows or clubbed within the circle (Wier 1901:40; Barrett 1917:11–12; Dangberg 1918–1922:29; Freed 1960:351; Nevers 1976:14–16). Though most families had rabbit nets (Downs 1966:27), certain old men owned especially long nets that were used for large drives, and the owner was compensated by receiving an extra portion of the catch (d'Azevedo 1952–1955, 1963–1984). Barrett (1917:11) and Kroeber (1925:572) estimate these nets to have been about 30 inches wide and, in some cases, as much as 300 feet long. The rabbits were divided among the participants and skinned immediately; the pelts were cut for the weaving of blankets (fig. 7). The carcasses were roasted and boiled for a feast of celebration, and the remainder was dried to be cooked into stews or pounded into a meal for winter use.

Other small mammals were taken as well. Porcupine and beaver were sought for their succulent flesh. Chipmunks, gophers, squirrels, woodchucks, and badgers were taken by snares, traps, or bows and arrows. Mice, rats, shrews or moles, were caught mainly by women and children using sticks or smoke to drive them from their holes.

All birds were eaten with the exception of scavengers or predators (such as eagle, hawk, magpie, owl, or crow), or very small species. Among the most important were valley quail, mountain quail, sage grouse, blue grouse, and mourning dove. They were shot with small bows and arrows (merely sharpened or with very small obsidian points) from blinds erected near springs, or caught in nets spread on poles into which they were flushed while drinking (Dangberg 1918–1922:26). Numerous waterfowl were attracted to the lakes and marshes, where mallard duck, Canada goose, and whistling swan were the largest and favored species. Duck and goose decoys of twisted and bound tule were used, as well as marsh-walkers (made of bark slabs or constructed like snow-shoes), and there were tule and willow rafts for driving birds or reaching nests. Bird eggs were gathered wherever found.

The golden eagle was never killed or eaten, for it was believed to have extraordinary supernatural attributes. The tail feathers had great value, particularly in trade (Downs 1961:371). Certain individuals (often shamans) were said to have dreamed of eagle and to have derived power from the tutelary connection. Such a person might have exclusive access to an aerie where particular birds allowed him to remove dropped feathers or a prescribed number from their tails: a gift must be left in the nest and no other human being was to approach it (d'Azevedo 1952–1955, 1963–1984). Feathers might be taken from a dead bird if its death was known not to have been caused by human violence. O.C. Stewart (1941:370) reports that the young were often taken from the nest

and raised in a cage, though this practice is questioned by Downs (1966a:50). The feathers of magpie were also prized. The use of feathers from these and other birds for ritual or adornment purposes is an aboriginal practice that has continued as an aspect of cultural identity and religious expression in the twentieth century (Freed 1960:371; d'Azevedo 1978a:22–26).

Reptiles of all kinds were apparently avoided as food, though Downs (1966:35) reports that certain large lizards were eaten. However, most Washoe respondents consider the idea repugnant and attribute the practice to Whites and other tribes.

Structures

The basic forms and construction techniques of Washoe dwellings have been described in some detail by Price (1962a:66–70; cf. Barrett 1917:10–11). The winter house (*gális dáŋal*) (fig. 8, center left) was the relatively substantial and permanent home built in the traditional habitation sites and returned to during the winter, but it was often occupied by some members of families the year around. Though the form might vary, it was usually constructed by setting a number of long poles into the ground in a circle of about 12–15 feet in diameter and interlocking them at the top. Hudson (1902:241) reports that a shallow house-pit was dug first. The classical

left, Southwest Mus., Los Angeles: 20,647; right, Nev. Histl. Soc., Reno: 1033.

Fig. 7. Rabbitskin clothing. left, Skins cut into strips, hanging from tree, and being woven into a blanket on a 2-bar horizontal loom. Photograph possibly by Charles F. Lummis, in Carson Valley near Dresslerville, Nev., about 1919. right, Rabbitskin blankets worn as cloaks by John Anthony and Wama Anthony. Also used as bedding, the fur made a warm covering but wore out quickly. Photograph about 1920.

top left, U. of Calif., Bancroft Lib., Berkeley; top right, Smithsonian, NAA: 79–4656; Southwest Mus., Los Angeles, center left: 20,667; center right: 1624; bottom left, Milwaukee Public Mus., Wis.: 20159.

Fig. 8. Dwellings. top left, Encampment of Chief Bohala's group, in the Calaveras Big Tree Forest on the Stanislaus River. Dwellings are made of bark and branches against a crossed stick framework (Vischer 1870). Drawing by Edward Vischer, summer 1862. top right, Bark slab winter house with entrance passage at Tallac, Lake Tahoe, Calif. Photographed 1905. center left, Canvas-covered *gális dáŋal* near Lakeside Park, Lake Tahoe, Calif. A woman is making a basket on the left and the man on the right appears to be working on a wire screen. Acorns are drying in the foreground. Photograph possibly by George Wharton James, before 1914. center right, Canvas-covered windbreak being set up by a man in the background. A woman tends to her daughter's hair. A boy's cradle, small carrying basket, and utensils are in the foreground. Photograph by Warren Dickerson, near Lake Tahoe, Calif., before 1933. bottom left, Summer brush shelter with a windbreak near Woodfords, Calif. A pine nut gathering ladder leans against the entrance. Photograph by Samuel Barrett, 1916. bottom right, Frame dwellings in Dresslerville Colony, Nev. Photograph by Edgar Siskin, 1938.

D'AZEVEDO

conical dwelling was made by leaning lengths of bark slab against the poles and tying them firmly with strands of willow or deer skin thongs but, depending on availability, other materials also might be utilized, such as bundles of grass, tule, and willow for thatching, or sometimes deer-hide covering. Fireplaces were set in the center, and a small smoke hole opened at the top. Doorways always faced eastward and, in some instances, involved a short passageway extending from the house. As many as seven or more persons might inhabit such a dwelling, sleeping in a circle with feet to the fire; some privacy was provided by hanging skins or other materials. In early historic times, variant forms of this dwelling appeared with a discarded lumber, canvas or sack covering and, sometimes, with additional rooms (Wier 1901:35–36).

The dome-shaped summer house (*gá·du*) (fig. 8, bottom left) was a temporary dwelling constructed of tule or brush woven together with willow for use by mobile groups while hunting and gathering. Some, however, were substantially and skillfully made for use near the winter dwellings. Simple windbreaks and sunscreens were assembled by leaning limbs and brush against horizontal poles, or on a frame placed on four posts. The lean-to was the most common type for seasonal trekking.

Reports of sweating practices or sweathouses among the Washoe are contradictory. Powers (1876) and O.C. Stewart (1941:379, 430) deny their existence; Wier (1901:66), Kroeber (1925:572), Curtis (1907–1930, 15:94), Lowie (1939:324), Price (1962a:70), and Siskin (1941:5) claim various structures for sweating. Isolated instances of the practice may have been present among the Washoe at various times during the historical period; however, neither sweathouse nor induced sweating was general among the aboriginal Washoe, and sweating was known historically only as a practice introduced by a few persons who learned of it elsewhere. Even the vigorous westward spread of the Sweat Lodge religious movement in the late twentieth century has had little direct impact upon Washoe communities. Older persons deny that sweathouses were built or used locally, though they agree that shamans sometimes had made small enclosures heated with direct fire or hot stones for ritual preparation and the treatment of patients. Cold and hot springs were extensively used for purification and therapeutic bathing.

Similar doubts remain about the occurrence of large ceremonial structures ("dance houses"), which the Washoe deny that they used in the early historic period. Despite reports implying the contrary (Siskin 1941:68; Barrett 1917:11; Kroeber 1925:72), only a few such structures seem to have been built, one at Woodfords, California, about 1893 (Dangberg 1918–1922) by George Pasuk after an assembly house he had learned to build while living among the Miwok. For a few years it was used for council meetings, doctoring sessions, and public theatricals where Washoe and Miwok songs and dances (including so-called War Dances) were performed to both White and Indian audiences who paid admission. In the 1930s a nine-sided structure was built in Antelope Valley by the Peyotist leader, Ben Lancaster, for meetings of the Native American Church (Price 1962a:70).

Clothing and Adornment

Early Whites described the Washoe as very scantily clad even in the severest weather (Frémont 1845:224–229; Remy and Brenchley 1861:45–46). Clyman in 1846 (Camp 1960:206) said they did not complain of the cold, though "nearly naked." Dodge (in ARCIA 1860:373–374) reported that "they have no clothing except the merest apology of a breech-cloth." Such comments are curious in view of the fully clad Washoes in the few photographs and drawings of the period.

Traditional Washoe attire involved a number of elements whose use depended on circumstance and the availability of materials. Deerhide and other skins were used for breechclouts, aprons, capes, and leggings. Sagebrush bark and other basts were used for the same purposes (Hudson 1902:236, 240, 250; Curtis 1907–1930, 15:93; O.C. Stewart 1941:393–394). Skins were prepared by soaking in water (often hot springs), scraping and then tanning with cooked brain; sinew was taken from the loin of deer or antelope (Price 1962a:63). Sinew-sewn tailored clothing was probably a late introduction (Kroeber 1925:572). Most persons went barefoot, though moccasins were made of untanned deerhide and, sometimes, included a lining of sage or other bast for winter use (O.C. Stewart 1941:394; Price 1962a:64).

The rabbitskin blanket or robe (fig. 7) was one of the most important and widely used items for both clothing and sleeping; some people continued to make and use them in the mid-twentieth century. It was constructed of narrow strips of fresh pelt in lengths of eight feet or more. A warp of these strips was wound around a horizontal loom of parallel poles. The weft of buckskin thong or plant fiber was twined in two interlocking strands across the rabbitskin warp (Price 1962a:60–62). A large blanket might require the skins of 30 or more rabbits (Lowie 1939:327). The tendency of the fur to become infested by lice was dealt with by placing the blankets on ant hills during the summer where they would be thoroughly cleaned before winter (Dangberg 1918–1922:25).

Men usually wore their hair parted in back and tied into a loose braid over each shoulder. The hair was sometimes tucked into a net of milkweed or wild flax fibers while working. Face hair was plucked out. A headband of buckskin was worn, often with a feather or two. Women's hair was cut about shoulder length, and bangs were common. Longer hair might be braided. A hairbrush of soaproot and a comb of bound grease-

481

wood stems were personal items (Wier 1901:29; Dangberg 1918–1922:1; O.C. Stewart 1941:392; Price 1962a:65). Hats are not reported.

Ornaments of many kinds were made of bone (fig. 9), claws, berries, cedar knots, seeds, and shells (olivella, dentalium, haliotis through trade, and local freshwater shellfish). Earlobes were pierced by both men and women (O.C. Stewart 1941:391; Price 1962a:65). Beadwork was done on a handloom stretched on a bowed stick (fig. 10) (Wier 1901:20).

Women sometimes rubbed grease and red ocher on their skin for softening and protection from wind and sun. Designs in white, red, and black stripes were painted on body and face, and there were distinctive styles for men and women for specific activities (Price 1962a:66). Red and white paints might have had a special significance in distinguishing moietylike divisions of people at large gatherings (Lowie 1939:304) and were extensively used in competitive games as team insignia. Tattooing also was common and, apparently, was purely decorative. The pigment was usually black soot mixed with grease and applied with thorn prickers. Boys and girls were often tattooed between the ages of 9 and 15 (Price 1962a:65). Women decorated their wrists, and a common face design involved three vertical lines on the chin and a horizontal line across each cheek from mouth to ear (Wier 1901:33). Hudson (1902:249) observed the most general design to be a small cross on each cheek, but he also estimated that 20 percent of the people had a straight line down the nose ridge while 5 percent had vertical bars on the lower lip. Many men had five parallel bars tattooed on their calves, which were said to be means of measurement.

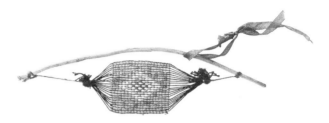

Smithsonian, Dept. of Anthr.: 395,470.
Fig. 10. Bead loom model. Light blue, turquoise, orange, white, and light red seed beads are suspended between ends of a thin curved stick, around which is also wrapped a red satin ribbon. Collected in Nev. about 1956; length 17 cm.

The transition to White styles of clothing was rapid, so that they became almost universal within a few decades after the 1850s. However, there were frequent fandangos and public performances of dances and games where some individuals decked themselves out in what were purported to be "Indian outfits." Dangberg (1918–1922) gives a rare account of a dance organized by George Pasuk in the 1890s where the men wore black trunks, feathered aprons and headdresses, and painted their legs and torsos with white, red, and black stripes. The women wore their usual settler-style garments but also elaborate shell ornaments and broad black bands with white dots painted across their faces. Both men and women wore moccasins. Some of these features were said to have been copied from the Miwok.

Basketry

Traditional weaving involved a variety of techniques and forms for the production of utensils that were essential to Washoe subsistence and food preparation. Both coiled and twined weaves were employed: the former similar to those of the Miwok and Maidu of California, and the latter apparently derived primarily from the Numic peoples of the Great Basin (Barrett 1917:17; Kroeber 1925:571–572). N.C. Kern (1969) and Cohodas (1979, 1983) discuss form and design (see also "Ethnographic Basketry," this vol.).

The importance of traditional basketry in Washoe economic and ceremonial life is clear, but the late nineteenth century saw the beginning of a period that Cohodas (1979:12) has referred to as a florescence in basket making among the southern Washoe that coincided with the emergence of new styles and an intensive demand from White traders and patrons (fig. 11). This was the period in which a number of expert weavers including Louise Keyser (Datsolalee), responded to the new demand by creating remarkably fine-coiled baskets of innovative form and design. The artists were besieged with requests for their work, and to commemorate events (fig. 12).

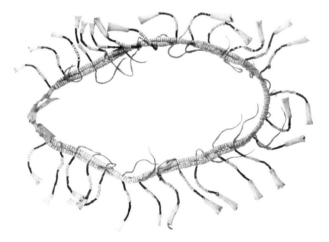

Field Mus., Chicago: 58454.
Fig. 9. Belt of a double strand of ground and polished bone disk beads, fringed with strings of glass trade beads, bone disk beads, and deer phalanges. All stringing was done with buckskin. Collected by J.W. Hudson, Eagle Valley, Nev., 1902. Length 17 cm.

Smithsonian, NAA: 79-4660.
Fig. 11. Maggie Mayo James (d. 1952), who produced classic basketry styles about 1900–1930s. Her decorative patterns included both geometric designs and naturalistic ones using butterfly, horse, eagle, and human motifs. Her work was commercially successful (Cohodas 1979:53–58). Photographed at Lake Tahoe about 1913.

Social Organization

There is some evidence that a weak moietylike system existed in the late nineteenth century. Its major expression appears to have been at the fall pine nut harvesting events organized by the southern Washoe. As families arrived at the festival, the presiding leader assigned them to one of three or four camping sections that formed a U-shaped enclosure. Lowie's (1939:304) discussion suggests that these camp groups represented patrilineal moieties, possibly borrowed from the Miwok, but without exogamy. Individuals were identified by the "side" in which they were placed and the paint color associated with it: *péwlel táyadi⁷* 'east side' or *díṗek gumiánu* 'white paint people'; *táŋlel táyadi⁷* 'west side' or *sawásaŋ gumiánu* 'red paint people'; *dačilgá·š táyadi⁷* 'in the corner side' with optional paint; and *ṗal⁷áša táyadi⁷* 'cedar people' with optional paint (d'Azevedo 1952–1955, 1963–1984; Freed 1960:361). The first two sides were most important, thus giving the system a dual orientation. However, the question of patrilineal inheritance of membership is not clearly substantiated by the available data, nor is it possible to define the actual functions of the divisions. Apparently the notion of "sides" designated by paint color was commonly used for competing teams in various games and sports, but the choice of paint and sides often seemed to be optional. Northern Washoe respondents claimed no knowledge of the practice of camp divisions at communal gatherings but recalled the use of red and white paint for opposing teams at most games. Two older southern Washoes indicated that the camp organization at harvest festivals represented affinal or potentially affinal divisions of peoples between whom the relationship was not too close and thus marital arrangements could be anticipated (d'Azevedo 1952–1955, 1963–1984). Downs (1966:49–50) questions whether these divisions should be considered moieties rather then merely reflections of Washoe "ethnogeography" in the context of changing demographic patterns and population concentration in the historic period. Though the temporal depth of this phenomenon among the Washoe cannot be ascertained, the possible influences from California cultures provide a more likely basis for explanation. The southern Washoe had close ties with the Miwok and other California groups where loose "pseudo-moieties" obtain (Gifford 1916a:140–148; Driver and Massey 1957:411; Bean and Blackburn 1976:105–106). The use of paint colors for geographically designated divisions in games and some ritual activities, as well as the absence of strict exogamous rules between the divisions, are sufficiently similar among all these groups to suggest a significant relationship.

• THE LOCAL COMMUNITY   The basic viable unit of social organization was a cluster of closely related households, sharing the same or nearby winter camps and identified with its own leader. This is the kind of group that Downs (1966:44–46) and the Washoe themselves refer to as "the bunch" or *gumiánu lákalélew⁷áŋali⁷i* 'many people living near one another'.

The nuclear family involving a married couple and their children was not perceived as an isolate or independent unit, but as part of an extended family of close relatives living in a single dwelling or cluster of houses and constituting the core of the "bunch" or local community. Price's (1962a:15, 71–73) reconstruction of the composition of 15 households in the late nineteenth century reveals great variation in membership and changing structure over time. The local community might include a number of married or unmarried siblings of either spouse, parents or grandparents, children, and grandchildren. Some affinal relatives were often in residence, as well as more distant relatives or nonrelatives who were either visiting or attached to the group with some degree of permanence. Individuals or segments of the group might shift residence temporarily or permanently to the households of other relatives in the same or a distant community, or they might construct their own dwelling. This pattern of visiting and shifting association was a pervasive feature of Washoe social

left, Smithsonian, NAA; right, Warren L. d'Azevedo, Reno, Nev.

Fig. 12. The Woodrow Wilson presentation basket, a large degikup. left to right, Capt. Pete Mayo of Woodfords, Calif., Sarah Jim Mayo (who made the basket), Agnes Jim Pete, and Captain Pete of Carson Valley, Nev. The basket, made in 1913, was presented as a gift along with a petition to President Wilson, March 1914, for redress of Washoe grievances, including the lack of suitable lands for homes, the restrictions on hunting and fishing rights, and the fact that other tribes who had been hostile to the Whites had received more recognition from the government than the peaceful Washoe (Nevers 1976:72–74; Cohodas 1979:47). The basket depicted the first Captain Jim turning over guns and ammunition of the Washoes to the White settlers in Nev. in the early 1860s. It contains both representational figure design and textual material, unique features in early Washoe baskets. The President acknowledged receipt of the gift, but the petition was unsuccessful, and the basket disappeared (d'Azevedo and Kavanagh 1974). Photograph probably by Margaretta Dressler, 1913.

relations. It was common for a household to break up due to disaffection, abandonment of a dwelling after a death, or insufficient range of production among its members. However, there was a strong inclination on the part of those representing the core families of the local community to remain in the area traditionally identified as their place of relatively permanent habitation. Such communities were generally small, consisting of two to three or as many as 10 winter houses and temporary structures. It was this local community, comprised primarily of close kin, that the Washoe perceived as "household" rather than the personnel of the separate dwellings. Moreover, it may be considered the minimal effective unit of Washoe social organization for "the bunch consisted of a minimal number of families that could cooperate to do those things which an individual family could not do for itself" (Downs 1966:45). Though the composition of its membership was fluid and often heterogeneous, its continuity and informal leadership was maintained by a dominant local kin group. The community provided the basis for essential cooperation in communal hunts, drives, defense, and occasional group rites. At the same time, individuals or families also moved about independently on subsistence and other pursuits, particularly during the major seasons for gathering or fishing. But the sites of local communities were seldom completely abandoned during these periods, for the very old and the very young, as well as

caretakers, usually remained behind. The most stable phase of residence was during the winter months, which the Washoe associate with returning "home," with group intimacy, storytelling, domestic tasks, and the sharing of stored provisions.

The concept of ʔišgéʔeš 'moving about', associated with seasonal mobility and temporary camps, refers to small groups separating off from the winter communities to form gathering contingents or a hunting party. These groups might vary in size from two or three individuals to as many families who chose to travel together for a specific subsistence task or, if successful, for a longer period of wandering during the year. These mobile contingents, so essential to Washoe economic life during a greater part of the annual cycle, were nevertheless only temporary extensions of relatively permanent local communities, which provided the primary units of orientation.

• THE REGIONAL COMMUNITY The regional community was comprised of the local communities in a recognized subarea of traditional habitation, who were united by identification with place and by loose ties of consanguinal and affinal kinship, and constituted a population of hundreds of persons with whom there was some degree of familiarity and mutual trust who could be relied on for some cooperative efforts. The five or six local communities near what are now Woodfords and Markleeville were such a regional community. This

Nev. State Mus., Carson City: a, 38–G–233; b, 38–G–Lee; c, 38–G–5680; d, 38–G–1449b.

Fig. 13. Items made by Poker Charley (d. 1934), one of "the last of the Washoe arrowhead makers" (S.L. Lee 1939). a, Antler flaker for the manufacture of stone projectile points. It consists of a section of deer antler tied atop a rabbitbrush stick with wraps of buckskin. b, Straight pipe of serpentine with short wooden stem. c, Obsidian, chert, and glass projectile points, all of the very late small triangular style, with straight-sided blades, markedly concave bases, and narrow, shallow side notches for hafting with sinew to the arrow shaft. d, Snowshoe model, a sapling bent to roughly circular shape, the overlapped edges secured with buckskin, and the web and foot tie formed with interlaced buckskin thongs. Length of a, 21.6 cm, b–c same scale, d, 39.5 cm.

was also true of the numerous small communities of Carson Valley and the nearby valleys of the Pine Nut Mountains; and a similar situation obtained for all the major valleys to the north. Price (1962a:4) refers to the regional communities as "bands," while they may represent what Steward (1970:138–141) called "incipient or proto-bands" (revising his earlier concept of "bands" and "composite bands").

Ties beyond these regional communities, though more tenuous, existed through extensive intermarriage, overlapping ranges of subsistence procurement, a system of communication, and cooperation in defense or joint festivals. These ties were closer with the people of regional communities in adjacent valleys. Yet the Washoe had a distinct sense of being part of a larger community of persons of the same culture and speaking the same language. All Washoe of all sections are considered to be related by some degree of kinship and, therefore, have never instigated aggression against one another or conspired with non-Washoe to do so. This view of a

"Washoe world" within which one could move freely by exploiting a lore of common origin and the hospitality accorded distant or putative kin was a cohesive element in Washoe life that is tantamount to a normative sense of "tribe" without centralization or the concomitant institutions of cohesion.

Kinship Terminology

Though an individual's personal kindred was formed primarily from among his or her consanguinal kin in a local community, adoption, visiting, and task group participation vastly extended the range of significant relatives.

Early contributions to the study of Washoe kinship terminology were made by Kroeber (1907, 1917) and Lowie (1939), but the work of Freed (1960) stands as the most comprehensive. Kinship reckoning was bilateral, though the orientation of an individual's personal kindred often expressed greater emphasis on the relatives of one or the other parent depending on the side of the family that had performed the most intensive role in early socialization. Generational depth was limited to those relatives known during a lifetime and seldom extended beyond grandparents and grandchildren. Siblings of grandparents and their descendants were rarely identifiable, but parents' siblings and their children were important consanguinal relatives with whom association was potentially as close as with parents and one's own siblings. In a person's own generation, the terms for male and female siblings are extended laterally to all known cousins, though rarely beyond the children of one's parent's siblings. These terms merely distinguish older and younger siblings or cousins depending on the relative ages of their parents; however, there is a tendency among younger people in the late twentieth century to apply the terms relative to their own ages (Freed 1960:355, 358, 360). There is also a trend toward using alternate terms for cousins (distant male/female relative, friend) to distinguish them from true siblings. Such changes reflect the influence of the American kinship system, as does the common usage of "cousin-brother" or "cousin-sister" among older Washoes when speaking English.

On the parental generation father, father's brother, father's sister, mother, mother's sister, and mother's brother are each given distinct terms. The spouses of aunts and uncles are not designated as relatives except where two brothers have married two sisters, in which case the spouses are consanguinals of the nephews and nieces, who refer to them by the appropriate kin terms (Freed 1960:358). The terms for sons and daughters are distinguished from those for brothers' or sisters' children, and the latter are extended outward to all known collaterals of the generation. Reciprocal terminology is used between grandparents and grandchildren: all relatives of the third ascending generation are denoted by a single term (*dipísew*), while those of the third descending generation are referred to by a term with the same stem (*lepísewiʔ*). There are, apparently, no separate terms for reference and address, and there are a number of terms in the first and second descending generations that are specific to male or female usage (Freed 1960:358, 1963:10–13). Special terms were employed for affinal relatives, including a set of deferential teknonymous terms. Freed (1960) has noted significant changes in Washoe kinship terminology, which, in the late twentieth century, evidences a consistent tendency toward the lineal type. These changes are tentatively attributed to the impact of a money economy and the diminishing importance of a network of cooperating relatives. Moreover, old Washoe terms have become adapted to the American kinship system, and this is consistent with changing role behavior between related persons.

Life Cycle

Every phase of Washoe life was marked by specific beliefs and rites intent upon the protection of the community and the fostering of healthy and productive individuals. Many of these observances are retained in modified form among the Washoe of the late twentieth century (Freed 1960:352; Freed and Freed 1963:25–39).

• BIRTH   A woman delivered in a temporary shelter where a shallow trench of heated earth covered with sagebrush bark or cedar boughs served as a bed. An older woman of the family or a midwife attended her: she was kept warm and washed with warm sage water. A belt was bound above the abdomen and worked downward to produce pressure (Hudson 1902:251; Dangberg 1918–1922:12). During delivery, prayers were offered encouraging the child to emerge quickly (Price 1963a:97).

The umbilical cord was cut about four inches from the child and tied at the navel with sinew. After washing in warm water a poultice of medicinal root and bast was applied and the child's abdomen bound with a belt of deerskin: swaddling was a deerskin or the first groundhog pelt procured by the father. The first cradles were simple oval baskets lined with bast padding and changed frequently. For the child's first permanent cradle (fig. 4), the hood exhibited a design of parallel diagonal lines for boys and rhomboids for girls (Wier 1901:56; Dangberg 1918–1922:15; Kroeber 1925:572; Price 1963a:100).

The husband was not to be present during childbirth and he shared his wife's fast for a short period after the delivery, avoiding meat, salt, and gambling. Immediately following the birth, the father bathed and gave away gifts of his old clothing and first kill. The couple abstained from sexual intercourse for a period

of 8 to 12 months, and children were sometimes nursed until four or five years of age (Wier 1901:57; Lowie 1939:305; Price 1963a:98–99). Naming took place when the child was ready to walk, the name usually derived from a mispronounced word or some aspect of personal behavior. Berutti (1965) discusses naming practices.

• PUBERTY   One of the most important ceremonies in Washoe society was the puberty ceremony for girls (*teʔwéʔweʔ*), which persisted with little alteration into the late twentieth century (Freed 1960:352; Downs 1961:375–376; Freed and Freed 1963a:29–32; Price 1963a:107–108). It is very similar to the ceremony among neighboring California tribes (Garth 1953:161; Riddell 1960a:56–59; Cartwright 1953:140–142).

At first sign of menses a Washoe girl was lectured by her mother concerning the duties of womanhood and the significance of the rite through which she must pass. She was advised to avoid salt, meat, fish, and fat and must bathe in warm water; otherwise her menstruation would be prolonged (Hudson 1902:252; Dangberg 1918–1922:15, 44; Price 1963a:101). She was expected to run daily, fetch firewood, help with domestic chores, sleep only briefly, not lie down in the daytime, and avoid gambling and the sick as well as hunters and their equipment (Freed and Freed 1963a:27–28; Price 1963a:102). Though she was not secluded, she slept in a shallow pit warmed by ashes (Lowie 1939:306) and must not comb her own hair or scratch herself with her fingers. O.C. Stewart (1941:410) reports the use of a scratching stick. She carried an elderberry staff painted with bands of red ocher for support; the staff must not fall or break for it symbolized erect posture and strength (Price 1963a:103).

At the end of the third day of fasting the girl lit a fire on a hill to signal that the rite was about to begin. A fire was built at the dancing ground near the family camp, and the ceremony commenced with the chanting of the girls' puberty songs (*ʔuwíya Míšim*) by a closely packed group of women relatives and friends who swayed back and forth facing the fire and eastward. The girl's staff and another pole were planted on each side of the girl and her assistant who held a pole in one hand while placing their other arms on one another's shoulders. The dance of the girls before the swaying and singing women is called "the jumping dance" (*melehéheʔ*) and is believed to encourage the flow of menstrual blood (cf. Price 1963a:103–104; Freed and Freed 1963a:28).

After the *ʔuwíya*, all the men and women present joined in the Round Dance (*teʔwéʔweʔ ʔló·š*), interlocking fingers and stepping to the left: in former times it is said that men and women danced separately in opposite arcs of the circle. As the dance proceeded it became more lively with short hopping steps similar to that of the girls in the opening rite. Occasionally, the girl, supported by a female attendant, entered the circle and performed the back-and-forth hopping dance while holding out small gifts of shell, beads or coins to the circle of dancers; they utter short bilabial trills ("br-r-r" sounds). A feast was usually held at midnight, but the dancing continued. Just before sunrise, the girl was brought before the crowd, stripped of most of her clothing, painted with ashes or ocher on face and body while the sponsoring female relative offered prayers and advice for her health and productivity. A basketful of water was poured over her head for the "washing," and she threw the basket into the crowd to be kept by the one who caught it. The girl's staff was hidden by her father or other male relative in a place where it would stand upright to aid the girl throughout life. She was given a little pine nut soup and a piece of meat to chew and spit out. This concluded the ceremony, though the guests might stay to visit, relax, or to dance the slow Morning Round Dance (sešiši) until "breakfast" and departure. The ceremony was repeated at the girl's second menses. At a final rite her hair was cut, the dietary restrictions were lifted, and she was considered eligible for marriage (Dangberg 1918–1922:36–43; Price 1963a:104–108; Freed and Freed 1963a:28–34).

• MARRIAGE   Marriage or sexual contact between consanguinally related persons was strongly discouraged. In that descendants of the collaterals of great-grandparents—or even of grandparents—were rarely traceable, the prohibition operated largely within the context of the consanguinal group comprised of first cousins and their children, though theoretically applying universally. In aboriginal times marriage partners were arranged for a young person of the family by parents or other older relatives whose task it was to find an eligible candidate. A primary criterion was that there be no question about the possible relatedness of a prospective partner. Sometimes a kinship connection was discovered after a marriage had taken place, causing profound embarrassment and a sense of dishonor to both families, as well as fear of supernatural sanction: it was believed that the offspring of such unions would suffer deformity or death. Every effort was made to "forget" the facts of the kinship connection and to diminish gossip by avoidance of the subjects. Persons who knowingly entered into a sexual or marital alliance with a relative were ostracized by ridicule and avoidance.

Though monogamy appears to have been the most common arrangement in early times (and exclusively so in the late twentieth century), polygyny did occur (Barrett 1917:9; Curtis 1907–1930, 15:97; Freed 1960:362). Spring (1967, 1967a) defines the most prevalent form as "serial monogamy" in which individuals marry early in life but eventually may have from two to five spouses due to death or separation. It was economically essential for all adults to be married. The occurrence of polygyny depended to a large extent on special circumstances; a man who had proved his ability as a provider

or showed qualities of leadership was encouraged to accept additional wives. In some instances two brothers might marry two sisters, creating a particularly cohesive family that might live in the same or adjacent houses. Both sororate and levirate were practiced to some extent as a means of providing continuity to the care of children and interfamilial relations, though the levirate was less frequent due to the tendency toward matrilocal residence (Spring 1967a:23). It is doubtful that polyandry existed as a recognized practice (Price 1962a:110–111; Spring 1967a:23–24).

First marriages were ideally arranged by parents who were concerned that a potential mate for their son or daughter be a good worker and that the connection between the two families be an advantageous one. Prospective mates from the local or regional community were preferred in order to insure the proximity of the couple, but sometimes unions with more distant persons were approved for purposes of establishing useful alliances, even though this might result in the long absence of a daughter or son. The soliciting family brought gifts that if accepted, indicated agreement. Reciprocal gifts were given and courtship began (Lowie 1939:308; Freed 1960:352; Spring 1967a:28–41). Courtship and marriage might also be initiated by the prospective pair themselves by approaching their parents for agreement (Wier 1901:51; Dangberg 1918–1922:18, 31, 44). Older or widowed individuals usually arranged their own marriages and established co-residence at any time (cf. Price 1962a:22; Spring 1967a:33). An extensive investigation of mate preferences and the criteria for eligible partners is summarized by Spring (1967a:47–58).

Residence patterns were generally bilocal with a strong tendency to matrilocality for newly married couples; however, patrilocal, neolocal, and alternating residence occurred with considerable frequency (Lowie 1939:308; Curtis 1907–1930, 15:97; Freed 1960:360–361). Initial residence with the wife's family was attributed to a woman's desire to remain among her female relatives for assistance with childbirth and childcare. There was also an expectation on the part of her parents for a degree of service from the son-in-law as a provider. However, decisions about residence were dependent upon circumstances such as the size and composition of either family, or personal preference (Spring 1967a:40). After birth of the first child couples usually shifted residence either to the households of other close relatives or built their own dwellings nearby (Freed 1960:361). In former times, the practice of arranged marriages contributed to a strong cooperative relation between affines, often resulting in the parents or other close relatives of intermarried families setting up residence in proximity to one another (Dangberg 1918–1922:9; Price 1962a:28–29; Spring 1967a:43).

Separation was obtained easily by either spouse. The major reasons given for divorce were incompatibility, infidelity, laziness, and friction with a spouse's relatives (Spring 1967a:58–68; Price 1980:29).

• DEATH Methods for disposing of the dead include tree or scaffold exposure together with belongings (Powers 1876; Dangberg 1918–1922:5), burial under logs, burning with possessions in a dwelling or wherever death occurred, and extended or flexed burial in remote places (cf. Wier 1901:66; Hudson 1902:239; Price 1963a:112). Most sources agree that cremation, the most common practice in early times, was slowly replaced by ground burial in the late historical period (Wier 1901:66; Dangberg 1918–1922:44, 62; Barrett 1917:9; Lowie 1939:310; Curtis 1907–1930, 15:97; Freed 1960:352; C. Fowler et al. 1981:19–20). Some suggest that cremation was more common in winter when the ground was frozen (Price 1963a:112; Dressler 1972:12–13).

The belongings of the deceased, along with gifts of food and other items, were either burned or buried with the body: this was done to dissuade the spirit from returning. Prayers were offered exhorting the spirit to think well of the living, to note the sorrow of the mourners, and to go away and not trouble the people. Mourning continued for several days, but the spouse and close relatives might mourn for a much longer period. The observance was concluded by prayers, bathing, and the change of clothing worn by the participants (Dangberg 1918–1922:9, 44; Price 1963a:112–113, 1980:31–32; Freed 1960:352; Freed and Freed 1963a:32). Though Barrett (1917:9) and Curtis (1907–1930, 15:97) report an annual mourning ceremony, Freed and Freed (1963a:25–26) discount it for lack of sufficient evidence.

Property

There is no firm evidence of the existence of specific rules of inheritance in precontact times. Descent was bilateral, and children and close relatives generally shared equally in family resources and rights. Personal property such as implements, clothing, or ornaments was usually destroyed at death because of the view that there was an intimate connection between persons and the objects used or manufactured by them: even items given to others might be placed in graves of the deceased for this reason. There were, however, many things that had been jointly used by a group of relatives that though contributed by a deceased person, were considered to be shared and were not disposed of. This was often the case with nets, traps, fishing platforms, blankets, and stored food, but the house in which an individual had died was usually abandoned or burned. Individuals and families established prerogatives with regard to certain fishing and gathering sites (sometimes, eagle aeries) by current or continuous use, but if these were not visited for a season or longer others could use them until they were reclaimed (Freed 1960:361; Price 1962a:9).

This was also the case with regard to the pine nut gathering plots, for which certain families claimed a degree of exclusive use. In the twentieth century these were parallel strips of piñon lands in the Pine Nut Mountains sometimes marked off by lines of rocks (Lowie 1939:303; Price 1962a:34), resulting from the Dawes Severalty Act of 1887 when sections of the range were mapped and haphazardly assigned to heads of families who applied for them (Nevers 1976:52–63). Early in the nineteenth century as well as in aboriginal times the groves were used primarily by the southern Washoe whose families had established picking rights in certain areas that had little relationship to government allotments. Rights were maintained by regular seasonal use and the discouragement of intrusion by others except by invitation—a pattern of local group prerogative that was effective with regard to all traditionally confirmed hunting, fishing, or gathering sites within the recognized range of a regional community. In precontact times the piñon groves were more extensive, and families had a number of locations depending on variable harvest conditions (Dangberg 1918–1922:60). Washoe from other areas might regularly visit adjacent grounds or request usufruct privileges.

Leadership

Anyone in a position of leadership was called *detúmu* 'the one in front'. The headman (or occasionally headwoman) of a family unit living in a single dwelling or a cluster of dwellings was usually a respected and trusted older person to whom others came for advice. As with all other special statuses among the Washoe, this position was not hereditary or necessarily permanent: a family might shift its preference to a better qualified close relative at any time. A particularly able male leader of a large family often emerged as the spokesman and head of a local community of related families and attached nonkin. The recognition of such a person as leader and representative was often based on the fact that he had traveled widely and had useful connections with other Washoe areas or adjacent tribes. It was his responsibility to maintain communication among groups and between sections.

Sometimes a leader of this kind was the informal representative of a regional community or even a number of such entities, as appeared to have been the case in the early historical period when a few regional "chiefs" had the role of intermediaries between sections of their people and the Whites. However, such men, referred to as "Captain" by the Whites, were called *detúmu* by the Washoe only when the conditions of their recognition as leaders had been validated by consensus. Otherwise an alternate term (*dewbéyu*) apparently derived from English and meaning literally 'the one who pays out' was usually employed, possibly referring to redistribution of payments received from Whites. Over time, the word became general and is sometimes used for any leader (d'Azevedo 1952–1955, 1963–1984).

In times of threatened attack from alien groups, or in preparation for retaliatory raids, a war leader would be selected from among the best fighters. His tenure lasted only as long as the specific danger persisted or until a war party under his guidance returned, but during that period he enjoyed a degree of authority and importance often greater than that of the local headman. As men of renowned courage and aggressiveness these leaders were allowed, while performing the warrior role, to exhort the public to anger against enemies, to strut about, give orders, and brag of their own prowess in a way that would not be tolerated in others under normal circumstances.

Another important leader was the man selected to lead rabbit drives (*pélew ʔušéwi*) and called *pélew detúmu*. This position was not hereditary, as Barrett (1917:12) and Kroeber (1925:572) suggest, but was a temporary (though sometimes continuing) assignment to a skillful and experienced rabbit hunter who might be succeeded by a son or younger relative because of the knowledge transmitted by close association. As with other leadership positions, the most successful persons were considered to be guided by dreams, which gave them knowledge of proper procedures and endowed them with the power to make appropriate prayers, though this was not an essential attribute of their roles. Any unusually talented individual, whether hunter, warrior, or artisan, was thought to have some access to supernatural powers.

Lowie (1939:303, 324–325) states that there was a distinctive "antelope charmer" who gained the right to lead through dreaming and was, thus, tantamount to a shaman. This is denied by Siskin (1941:118) and Downs (1966:30–32), who hold that the leadership of antelope drives was essentially secular and could be held by any proficient hunter. Though no antelope drives have been held since the nineteenth century, Lowie's detailed description of a leader's dreams and ritual procedures (as reported to him by a respondent who had witnessed a drive) cannot be discounted: a few older Washoes in the 1950s knew traditional accounts of special individuals who led antelope drives and were designated by the term Lowie had elicited (*ʔáyis gumómʔliʔ* 'antelope doctor or shaman') (d'Azevedo 1952–1955, 1963–1984). Moreover, Dangberg (1918–1922:27) reports that one of the last "antelope dreamers" in the nineteenth century was a woman whose ritualized behavior was identical with that reported for shamans in their adjunctive role in hunting and warfare. It is possible, however, that such practices were elements borrowed from other Great Basin groups where elaborate shamanistic rituals were connected with antelope hunting (Steward 1938:34–35; O.C. Stewart 1941:366–367; Downs 1966:32).

Some individuals were noted for their expert knowledge in matters of health. Among these were male and female curers who were adept at the use of herbs or other medicinal substances and female midwives. Many of them were persons believed to have a special relationship with their medicinal materials and to be dreamers who received spiritual support in their work. However, most people denied such direct guidance because of the danger and responsibility thought to be associated with it.

Despite the high priority given to able leadership and special skills, any claim to superiority or unique endowment was likely to arouse suspicion and disapproval in others. The strong Washoe orientation to egalitarian social relations required that admired individuals exhibit self-depreciation, unassertiveness, and generosity in the sharing of assets. Violations were controlled by ridicule and, if not corrected, the person might be accused of evil intentions and avoided.

Religion

Spirits of the dead or ghosts were greatly feared as the cause of illness and misfortune: such spirits were thought to travel in whirlwinds seeking their former places of abode. Other important classes of spirits were Water Babies, small humanlike creatures of great power who inhabited waters and caves, and various monsters such as the one-eyed giant *hanawíywiy* living in the Pine Nut Mountains and the great bird *ʔá·ŋ* of Lake Tahoe.

Many classes of spirits and special beings were objects of personification in numerous mythic and legendary tales. However, the principal figures in the creation tale are Old Woman, who in a version recorded by Hudson (1902:238–239) is a female mallard duck, and two sets of "brothers"—Long-tailed Weasel and Short-tailed Weasel, and Wolf and Coyote. To these beings is attributed the transformation of the primeval world into its present form and the creation of human beings.

• SHAMANS Though fear of sorcery was deeply embedded in Washoe culture and was the basis for most explanations of sickness and ill fortune, the disruption of traditional Washoe social organization in historic times and the ascendant role of the shaman in the fragmented postcontact communities cannot be taken to represent the aboriginal situation, where a greater degree of social cohesion and effectiveness of normative sanctions obtained. Nevertheless, a profound ambivalence concerning shamans is a fundamental aspect of Washoe world view. Their crucial function in curing, divining, and directing the forces of nature on behalf of individuals or groups was complicated by their capacity for doing harm (Leis 1963:59). As expert manipulators of specific powers and secrets inaccessible to other persons, their social behavior could not be regulated by ordinary means, but only by the threat of assassination or by soliciting the services of a rival practitioner. They were often braggarts and aggressively acquisitive persons who demanded exorbitant payment for their work, contrary to the normative values of reticence and sharing in social relations. A "good doctor" could be distinguished from an evil one only by deeds and reputation, but this was not always possible for each had the power to do good or bad. Though shamans were never political leaders, their services were solicited by headmen for all events affecting the community and they often accompanied hunting and war parties. A successful shaman might be commissioned by distant peoples, thus acquiring the unique status of itinerant specialist, which accentuated the perception of autonomy and possible improbity associated with the role.

The shaman is a person who has accepted a special intimate relationship with spirit power (*wegeléyu*). This power manifests itself in various forms and many people—especially children—are said to have been approached by unsolicited spirits in dreams or visions, but most feared the consequences and sought the aid of an experienced practitioner to rid themselves of such importunities (Siskin 1941:40–41; Freed and Freed 1963:42; Downs 1961:369–370). It took three to five years to become a shaman, during which the neophyte became familiar with the complex nature of the particular tutelary and submitted to the guidance of a senior shaman. Once embarked on this path, there is no escape other than death. In recurrent dreams the spirit power imposed strict regulations with regard to diet and ritual procedures and also implanted an object that the novice must succeed in removing from his or her own body before completion of training as a curer (Siskin 1941:49–50). A novice was instructed that the exact identity of the power must not be revealed and that secrecy must be maintained concerning the significances of ritual procedures and paraphernalia. But the sources of a shaman's power are usually known through observation and reputation. A shaman might have multiple tutelaries, but the principal remained the one that first came to him or her in dreams. It is from this chief helper that the main songs and prayers were learned and from whom sustaining power was derived throughout life.

The preparation and care of paraphernalia was a sacred obligation for every shaman. These were the basic objects and emblems of the profession—a cocoon rattle made under the guidance of a dream, and eagle feathers bound with buckskin. Other items might be miniature baskets or stone mortars, bird-bone whistles, tobacco pouch and tubular stone pipe, red and white body paint, decorative headdress and personal ornaments. Elaborate costuming on most public occasions was a mark of the shaman (Dangberg 1918–1922:22).

A curing ceremony was arranged by the family of the ill person who paid in advance with either a fine basket or the equivalent value in deerskins and ornaments. (In historic times payment was supplemented in money and the increasing amounts demanded became a source of bitterness.) The shaman usually came to the house of the patient; the curing ritual lasted for four nights and was open to the public. The patient was placed with head to the west; smoke was blown over the entire body and the face was washed periodically with cold water. The shaman danced while shaking a rattle and singing special songs at intervals between smoking, speaking to his or her spirit power, and exhorting the sickness to leave the patient. The rite culminated when the shaman succeeded in luring the disease object or objects out by the sound of a whistle, or by applying his mouth to the affected part and sucking. He then spit out the object and held it in his hand for all to see. Sometimes, however, some of the sickness passed into the shaman and caused him to become unconscious for a time, during which he or she must not be disturbed. After reviving, the shaman smoked and eventually coughed up the disease objects, which were shown to those present. The patient was washed with water and sage leaves and advised how to recover. A small feast was prepared by the family for the assembled guests (Siskin 1941:95–114; Freed 1960:353; G.E. Montgomery 1965). These practices persisted until the decline of Washoe shamanism in the 1940s (Siskin 1941) and were retained in a much modified form by the man considered to be the last of the Washoe shamans (whose life and work has been discussed by Handelman 1967, 1967a, 1976).

If a patient died during the curing session, payment was returned by the shaman, but if death occurred even shortly thereafter there was no reimbursement. Should too many patients die or remain ill (particularly in the same community), a shaman might be suspected of sorcery. The only control over a shaman was either to hire another to seek out and subdue the source of evil action

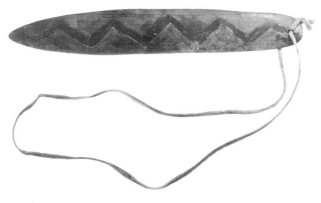

Field Mus., Chicago: 58425.

Fig. 14. "Thunder stick" or bull-roarer, used by shaman in ceremonies. The thong is caught in the hand, and the stick twirled rapidly through the air, causing a whirring or low roar that sounded like thunder. The stick is painted in a zigzag or lightning design, in red and yellow native paints, the yellow made from cattail pollen. Collected by J.W. Hudson, Carson Valley, Nev., 1902. Length about 37 cm.

Field Mus., Chicago: 58442.

Fig. 15. Shaman's garb, a hat, apron, necklace, headband, armbands, and kneebands, of magpie tail feathers, sage grouse feathers, and eagle down. The necklace has a shell disk at the center. This attire is very like that used by Southern Valley Yokuts, Owens Valley Paiute, and Northern Paiute in dances. Collected by J.W. Hudson, Carson Valley, Nev., 1902.

or to kill him. Assassination of unsuccessful shamans and other persons suspected of sorcery is said to have been frequent in aboriginal times, and newspaper and other accounts in the nineteenth and early twentieth centuries, supported by the reminiscences of older Washoes, reveal such homicide (Wier 1901:63–66).

Shamans usually accompanied war parties to divine the intentions of enemies and to direct a repertoire of dangerous powers against them. They frequently participated in hunts involving animals associated with their spirit power and were called upon to perform preliminary rites for the protection and success of any major communal activity. Shamans sometimes tested their powers in contests in which each attempted to prove superiority by deflecting arrows or bullets, enduring fire, invisibility, inflicting pain or ailments from a distance, and other marvelous acts. A poor showing could result in loss of power and public ridicule, whereas the demonstration of exceptional power enhanced the shaman's reputation and brought pride to his local group.

Numerous individuals were acknowledged to have a special relationship with sources of *wegeléyu* and used these powers in their exceptional performance of tasks, or to enhance success in any group endeavor. The distinction between them and persons identified as shamans was ambiguous or a matter of degree. The shaman was usually one who declared himself or herself to be such, who exacted a prescribed fee, whose behavior validated public perception of a direct connection with a tutelary, and who had the credentials of a formal apprenticeship or record of successful curing and other feats. In this sense the shaman was a professional who controlled and manipulated certain powers, while other semispecialists and endowed persons exercised a less intensive and compelling involvement. Respected older people were thought to have the faculty for making effective prayers and blessings that were essential propitiatory rites in any communal activity. Those who were known to have special power of the appropriate kind were selected by consensus to consecrate the proceedings as prayer leaders (*dagumsabá?yi?*). Though shamans might be asked to participate in such events as diviners and protectors against malevolent forces, they were not chosen as *dagumsabá?yi?*, for the role required the services of honored and trusted elder members of families whose exhortations were listened to with respect and whose dreams and prayers emanated from a character of proven good will and social responsibility. Such persons represented the community in its efforts to achieve internal harmony and cooperation from the spirits of nature whose resources were necessary to survival. Prayers were directed to the spirits of plants, animals, and other desired products of the environment, beseeching them to allow human beings to procure them and thanking them for their generosity and continued productivity. However, in the sacred context of prayer and propitiation, these natural phenomena are addressed by the generalized names of species and classes of things, rather than as the personified beings of myth and fable. Beings such as Wolf, Coyote, Water Baby, or other characters that figure so prominently in creation myth are absent from communal supplication, for these appear to be associated with the more secularized and individualistic approaches to the supernatural in shamanism and story telling. Reference to a vague Creator or Supreme Being is frequently made, but it is not certain that these concepts represent precontact Washoe views.

• CEREMONIES   Propitiatory prayers and other ritual observances were an integral part of all individual and group subsistence activities (see Downs 1961:379–383), but their major expression occurred at the large gatherings of people that took place in connection with communal harvesting, hunting, or fishing at times of particular abundance. These also were occasions for social interaction among groups throughout a regional community as well as visitors from afar, and involved feasting, dancing, games, exchange of information, gift giving, and the making of marital arrangements. Festivals of this kind, referred to as *gumsabáy?*, had basically a ritual purpose and were distinguished from purely social events.

Among the southern Washoe, the major annual ceremony took place in the fall of any year that the pine nut crop was good. This was usually preceded by individual family or local group observances in the spring when the pinecones had formed. A branch with young cones was broken off and buried on the banks of a stream to insure against premature drying of the crop. Prayers were then offered for an abundant harvest and there was dancing for one or two nights (Dangberg 1918–1922:56–59). When the pine nuts were ripe, word was sent out by a prominent headman for the people to assemble at a specified place for harvest observances. Prior to harvesting there were four nights of dancing in which each person carried the gathering implements to

be used such as hooked poles, burden baskets, manos and metates, and stirring paddles, and thus these objects also received the blessings of the accompanying prayers and songs. During the day, rabbit drives were organized, and each family was allowed to pick some pine nuts for a feast on the last night of dancing. But this food was considered to be an offering: what was prepared by each family must not be eaten by them but distributed to others. The leader prayed over the food and exhorted the people to good behavior, warning that failure to follow prescribed procedures would affect the future productivity of the trees. After the fourth night, the people bathed and families separated to their traditional gathering sites (Dangberg 1918–1922:56; Curtis 1907–1930, 15:95; Freed and Freed 1963a:34–36). After the death of Captain Jim (*gúmelaŋa?*), who had been a diligent activist on behalf of Washoe claims to the pine nut lands, the ceremonies were held less frequently and on a smaller scale. By the mid-twentieth century they no longer occurred except for occasional attempts at revival, though individual families frequently carried out their own rites.

Important as the pine nut observances were in former times, similar first-fruit and harvest celebrations were common in connection with any major resource whose seasonal exploitation could be anticipated with some regularity.

Several extinct dances and songs are reported in the literature. Lowie (1939:329–330) refers to a Scalp Dance that may have been associated with the Miwok-derived War Dance of Woodfords around 1900. Hunting and shaman's songs are described by Siskin (1941:95–114, 118).

Games

The hand game is the major game surviving among the Washoe. Formerly played by men's and women's teams, mixed teams have become common.

Men played hockey or football, ran footraces, and held contests in darts, bow and arrow, and spears. Women played a game with staves in which they attempted to push a buckskin strap to goal posts at opposite ends of a field. All games involved intensive betting and brought great prestige to winners (Hudson 1902:248–249; Culin 1907; Price 1962a:24; Freed and Freed 1963a:34–36; Nevers 1976:23).

Population

Estimates of Washoe population from the mid-nineteenth to the mid-twentieth centuries have been contradictory and inexplicably low (d'Azevedo 1966:323–325). Kroeber (1925:570) suggested an aboriginal population of 1,500, double what it was reported to be in the 1920s. Mooney (1928:20) posited a population of 1,000 in 1845.

The high estimates made for aboriginal Washoe population attest to their relatively abundant environment. Their adaptation apparently produced one of the highest population densities in the Great Basin. Figures proposed by Kroeber (1925:944, 1939:137) and Price (1962a:3) suggest a density of between 2.4 and 2.7 square miles per person (Downs 1966:4, 11 gives even higher estimates). Mooney (1928:20) gives 300 for 1907, but the 1910 census states 819 (Curtis 1907–1930, 15:91; Swanton 1952:384; Freed 1960:350). A sharp reversal of the population decline occurred in the 1930s, and there was a particularly rapid recovery after the 1950s during the period of tribal reorganization, unprecedented government aid programs, Indian rights movements, and the anticipation of new opportunities.

By 1973 tribal census data showed 520 persons residing in the colonies and reservation of whom approximately 35 percent were over 30 years old and 65 percent under, with slight preponderance of males over females. Roughly 600 persons were thought to reside outside the colonies (Washoe Tribe of Nevada and California 1973:15–28, 1980:20–22). BIA figures, which exclude off-reservation Washoes, are slightly different (table 1).

Data compiled by the Washoe tribe in 1984 gave an unadjusted figure of 1,530 persons on the tribal rolls who met the minimal requirements of one-quarter blood (JoAnn Nevers, personal communication 1984).

History

The Washoe and their territory were unknown to Americans before the 1850s, except for sparse reports by trappers and explorers (d'Azevedo 1963:2–3; Price 1962a:49–50; Hamilton 1905; Nevers 1976:38–46; Schallenberger 1953:46–84). The first reports seem to have been made by Jedediah Strong Smith and a party of trappers who crossed the Sierra Nevada over Walker Pass in 1825–1826. Early in the 1830s, Joseph Reddeford Walker led a party of trappers up the Truckee River to California; a diary of the trip was kept by Zenas Leonard (1904). In 1841 J.B. Bartleson and John Bidwell guided an immigrant party to California over Sonora Pass (Bidwell 1928:51–60); this may have been the group that Indians in Antelope Valley (possibly Washoe) described a few years later (Nevers 1976:39). More immigrants were guided over Walker Pass to California by Walker in 1843 and, in the same year, Johnson and Winter (1846) came down the Truckee River noting briefly the conditions of Indians they encountered. John C. Frémont and Kit Carson discovered Carson Pass in 1844, and Frémont's (1845) report of the expedition was the first to provide some description of the inhabitants in the vicinity of Carson Valley; the

Table 1. Population

Location	1970	1980
Woodfords, Calif.	250	173
Dresslerville, Nev.	152	172
Carson, Nev.	157	199
Reno-Sparks, Nev.	141	151
Nev. allotments	25	0
	725	695

SOURCES: U.S. Bureau of Indian Affairs. Statistics Division 1970, 1970a; U.S. Bureau of Indian Affairs. Financial Management Office 1981.

report also contained an indirect identification of the people by recording the single word "Mélo" for the name of his local guide (in Washoe the man's term for 'my male friend or relative' is diMílu). In 1849 Wistar (1914:110) "surprized and caught two Indians, both naked as they were born, and without arms, which they had probably concealed. . . . We treated them gently and gave them a little of our vanishing hard tack . . . and released them."

The record of American penetration into Washoe territory for the three decades preceding actual settlement is noteworthy for the paucity of comment about the aboriginal inhabitants. Washoe legends of early contact underscore their practice of abandoning their camps and taking refuge in nearby hills when warned of approaching strangers. Moreover, their scattered settlements were purposely constructed in settings whose natural camouflage hid them from view (Hudson 1902). In the late eighteenth and early nineteenth centuries, Washoes had contact with Spaniards, had seen or heard of horses, cattle, and European clothing, and a few are said to have been conscripted as laborers in Spanish mines (Downs 1966:73; Nevers 1976:38; d'Azevedo 1952–1955, 1963–1984). Cook (1960:251, 275) has documented Spanish expeditions into the Sierra Nevada, Indian "escapes" to the mountains, and the Spanish impact upon Indian settlements (see also Cook 1943:56–90; Elsasser 1960:7). In the foothill territories of the Miwok and Maidu, Indian warriors raided both Indian camps and European ranches. Among these was a Washoe headman from Lake Tahoe (Widding 1983:83, 89, 116, 181, 304, 320–322, 355).

Thus the Washoe apparently were familiar with the existence of Europeans in California during the early nineteenth century, but it was the Whites in the mid-nineteenth century with wagon trains and numerous animals that were an unexpected and frightening experience (Nevers 1976:44–47). Within a few years, many of these intruders had established trading posts and settlements in the area and had begun to fence the lands and water holes for ranches. By the early 1850s trading posts and camps appeared at Woodfords (Brannan Springs or Carey's Mill), Genoa (Mormon Station), Eagle Station (later to be Carson City), Reno, and in Sierra Valley. Ranches and cattle-holding corrals formed a network of claimed lands throughout most of the valleys. A peculiar fragment of White folklore in this period is the claim that Col. John Reese "bought" the lands around present-day Genoa from Captain Jim (*heʔnúˑḱeha*) for two sacks of flour (DeQuille 1877:20; see also Price 1962a:10).

A persistent figment of settler lore is the purported conquest of the Washoe by the Northern Paiute (Dodge in ARCIA 1860:375; S.W. Hopkins 1883; S.P. Davis 1905; Hodge 1907–1910,2:920; Fairfield 1916:13–14; Kroeber 1925:570; Curtis 1907–1930, 15:90; Swanton 1952:384). It is alleged that the Washoe were defeated in a war sometime before 1860 and that "the Paiutes" imposed a treaty denying them the right to have guns or horses. The restriction supposedly was lifted at a so-called council of peace about 1890. There is no credible evidence that any such events took place, though a few Washoes have incorporated them as historical "facts" transmitted through White sources. Most Washoes flatly deny the tales. Friction between the Washoe and Northern Paiute increased during the 1850s as the mounted war parties from Pyramid Lake became more aggressive toward the intruding Whites. They made frequent forays into Washoe territory and accused them of having allowed settlers to take their lands. The Northern Paiute chief Numaga is said to have sold nine miles of Long Valley south of Honey Lake to Col. Warren Wasson in 1858; the Washoe headman Deer Dick protested to Wasson and demanded payment for these misappropriated "Washoe lands" (Angel 1881:533–534).

The Washoe were often blamed for depredations instigated by both Northern Paiute and White brigands. Under continuing pressure, they were forced to seek protection of the White settlers who had appropriated their lands and to cooperate with them against the Northern Paiute in the Pyramid Lake War of 1860. Captain Jim (*heʔnúˑḱeha*) even is said to have urged his fellows to give up their arms so that they would not be taken for hostiles (Downs 1966:88). This situation contributed to a deepening antagonism between the Washoe and the Northern Paiute and is, perhaps, the major basis for the tales of Paiute conquest and dominance.

White perception of the Washoe as submissive and backward appears to have been largely conditioned by the scarcity of horses among them as compared with the equestrian Pyramid Lake Northern Paiute. Yet numerous reports exist of Washoe attempts in the early 1850s to drive off the settlers or to demand compensation for the use of lands and resources. These sporadic expressions of resistance usually met with patronizing amusement or, when deemed a serious threat, aroused ruthless retaliation. By 1860 the Washoe were dismissed as more of a nuisance than a danger, and the last re-

ported incident of open conflict was the "Potato War" of 1857 near Honey Lake where a small group of Washoes were routed and some killed for gathering potatoes on the farm of a White resident (Fairfield 1916:13–14; Nevers 1976:49–50). Though there is some indication that a few Washoes may have used horses for riding and packing in the early contact periods, by 1859 Dodge (in ARCIA 1860:374) wrote that "there was not a horse, pony or mule in the whole nation" (see also Maule 1938:10). Most commentators assert that these and other domesticated animals usually were stolen for food (DeQuille 1877:23–24; Hamilton 1905:159–162; Price 1962a:48–51). Downs (1963a:138–150) has presented a cogent case for what he considers to be a culturally based Washoe aversion to animal husbandry and agriculture. However, this argument tends to present the Washoe as a unique case of cultural incompatibility in the region rather than taking into account other factors in the acculturative process. The Washoe were the first people of the region to experience massive invasion of their lands by White settlers, during the period when intensive equestrian practices were just beginning to be adopted by some Northern Paiute groups. And, though the Washoe were used as farm laborers and ranch hands by the settlers, they were not given reservations on which to develop independent enterprise. The remnant lands available to them were largely devoid of water or other necessary conditions for animal husbandry or cultivation, a fact commented on by many early Indian agents. As conditions changed in the late nineteenth century, many Washoe men became proficient procurers of wild ponies and expert "bronco busters" and cowboys (fig. 16) (Creel 1875–1945; d'Azevedo 1952–1955, 1963–1984; cf. Downs 1963a:145, 1966:97–98).

After the discovery of the Comstock Lode at Virginia City in 1858, more than 20,000 miners and entrepreneurs rushed into the area within a two-year period. Grasses and other plants were trampled by grazing herds of cattle, game became scarce, and large sections of forest on the eastern slopes of the Sierra Nevada and in the Pine Nut Mountains were denuded. In the early 1850s the Washoe had strongly resisted White incursions into their fishing area around Lake Tahoe, but by the end of the decade a commercial fishery appeared at Tahoe City, and Whites were taking thousands of tons of trout from the lake to be sold in the valley settlements. Some Washoes attempted to compete by selling to settlers in the towns, but as Whites gained control over the area, traditional fishing practices were strenuously discouraged; with the later enforcement of fish and game laws, only a few Washoes continued to summer at Lake Tahoe (Price 1962a:54–55; Downs 1966:79–81).

As early as 1859, Indian Agent Dodge (in ARCIA 1860:375–377) proposed the establishment of Indian reservations at Pyramid and Walker lakes to which the

U. of Nev. Reno, Special Coll.

Fig. 16. Washoe cowboys branding cattle in Antelope Valley, Calif. Photograph by Lorenzo D. Creel, about 1917.

Washoe would be moved among the Northern Paiute, but this was dismissed as unfeasible due to Washoe objections and Paiute hostilities. A number of agents subsequently recommended a separate reservation for the Washoe without results, for the view prevailed that no available lands remained for such a purpose and that, at any rate, the tribe was on the verge of extinction (Nevers 1976:53–55). In 1880 Captain Jim (*gúmelaŋaʔ*) and a number of other Washoe "captains" met in Carson Valley to prepare a written appeal to the governor of Nevada in which they complained of the damage done to the pine nut trees and the depletion of the fishery at Lake Tahoe, concluding with a demand for compensation. In 1891 Captain Jim again met with Washoe leaders to prepare a petition to take to Washington, and a subscription was circulated requesting donations from local Whites for the trip. Captain Jim and

U. of Nev., Reno, Special Coll.

Fig. 17. Women washing clothes on the Carson River near Dresslerville, Nev. Photograph by Lorenzo D. Creel, about 1920.

his "interpreter" Dick Bender met with Nevada and California senators and congressmen, appeared before the Indian Commission, and saw President Benjamin Harrison in 1892. They returned empty-handed except for the promise of $1,000 for the "immediate relief" of the old and infirm. The funds were never received by the Washoe (Wier 1901:48; d'Azevedo 1973:4–6; Nevers 1976:56–61).

Weneyuga (Frank Spencer), the first Northern Paiute prophet recalled by the Washoe, "converted" them to the Ghost Dance in the early 1870s (Du Bois 1939:1–7). Dances were held at Reno, Black Springs, and Carson City where large numbers of Washoes are said to have attended. Though there can be little doubt that some Washoes were involved in the Ghost Dance movement of 1890 (Mooney 1896:1051), twentieth-century Washoes vigorously deny its importance and attribute attendance to mere curiosity (Wier 1901:48; d'Azevedo 1978; Downs 1966:94).

Under provisions of the Dawes Severalty Act of 1887 the Washoe had expected to be awarded large sections of land in the Pine Nut Mountains and around Lake Tahoe, but the allotment parcels were limited to the waterless and sometimes barren sections undesirable to Whites. Despite the protestations of Washoe leaders, the allocation of largely worthless lands continued intermittently from 1893 to 1910 while the pine nut groves were further depleted by White timber cutters and sheep grazing (Nevers 1976:62–66).

During the early twentieth century poverty and dislocation were extreme among the Washoe population. Some men were employed as ranch hands (fig. 18) and construction workers, and many women worked as household servants and laundresses for White families. But most endured a precarious existence in scattered camps on the outskirts of towns or in more isolated sections. Meager government subsidies were barely sufficient to ward off starvation for those few who received them. They were denied the right to vote, schools and public facilities were largely segregated, and White law enforcement was repressive. U.S. citizenship was not granted until 1924, and separate schooling continued in most areas until the 1950s.

Washoe protests continued with regard to the alienation of their lands and resources (fig. 12) (Wier 1901:26–27). Periodically the Nevada legislature debated a series of resolutions for the relief of the Washoe and the purchase of lands with water rights for them, but no bills were passed because it was said that no suitable areas remained that had not been claimed and developed by Whites. Cattle ranchers began to lease grazing privileges on the allotments, though the ridiculously low rates seldom brought Washoe families more than two or three dollars a year.

In 1917, despite some local opposition, the government provided the first funds for purchase of a small

Natl. Arch.: 75–N–CARS–233.
Fig. 18. Indians from Dresslerville, Nev., at haying time on the Heidtman Ranch, Gardnerville, Nev. Photograph by Arthur Rothstein, 1940.

tract near Carson City for the Washoe; this became Carson Colony. In the same year, a Carson Valley rancher donated 40 acres of land near Gardnerville to be held in trust for the Washoe as long as they should reside there; this became Dresslerville Colony. An additional 20 acres set aside near Reno for both Washoe and Northern Paiute families became the Reno-Sparks Indian Colony. Each of these sites involved poor lands with inadequate water or power (Mordy 1966; Downs 1966:99–101; Nevers 1976:79–81). During the 1920s the superintendent of the Reno Agency discouraged customs such as the pine nut harvest, girls' puberty dance, hand games, and Indian curing (Nevers 1976:81–82). Nevertheless, these and other elements of Washoe culture have demonstrated a remarkable persistence through time (Freed and Freed 1963, 1963a; Price 1963; Downs 1966:108–109).

The Washoe had known of the Peyote religion from meetings that had been held among the neighboring Northern Paiute as early as the 1920s, but it was not introduced to them until 1932 when Raymond Lone Bear, a Uintah Ute Peyotist, married a Washoe woman and began to hold meetings in Carson Valley. He taught his songs and procedures to Sam Dick, a Washoe shaman. These meetings declined as Lone Bear became less involved. In 1936, Ben Lancaster, a relative of Sam

Dick, returned to Carson Valley and organized meetings among the Washoe as well as in Northern Paiute communities. By 1938 Peyotism had spread to 14 communities (O.C. Stewart 1944:68–77). The movement was seriously disrupted by schisms among its adherents, and by the strenuous opposition of local Whites and some of the traditional shamans (Siskin 1941). Ben Lancaster left the area and the religion appeared to have died out. However, it continued quietly under the leadership of Roadchiefs who declared themselves followers of "the New Tepee Way" affiliated with the Native American Church (Merriam and d'Azevedo 1957). The religion, practiced by small groups of Washoe in the 1980s, is accepted as a positive expression of traditional Indian practices and values in a changing world.

The Indian Reorganization Act of 1934 provided the Washoe with the opportunity for recognition as a legally constituted tribe. A constitution and by-laws were ratified on December 16, 1935, and approved by the secretary of the interior on January 24, 1936 (U.S. Bureau of Indian Affairs 1944). The tribe was able to procure additional lands in the Carson Valley area, including a 795-acre parcel on the Carson River known as the Washoe Ranch. A small dairy herd was developed, a few hogs and sheep were raised, and crops of potatoes and peaches were harvested. When production declined in the 1950s the land was leased to White farmers (Nevers 1976:89, 92).

The Washoe were inexperienced in tribal organization, and tribal councils from the 1930s to the mid-1960s were ineffective in uniting the tribe around issues crucial to welfare and development. There were charges of mismanagement of funds, family rivalries often disrupted council meetings, and relations with the Bureau of Indian Affairs and other agencies were strained. Poverty remained severe and the general employment and living conditions imposed a sense of hopelessness throughout the Washoe settlements (MacGregor 1936; Downs 1966:104–106; Nevers 1976:89).

In 1948 tribal members agreed to prepare a claim for the Indian Claims Commission (O.C. Stewart 1966:196–203). The Washoe of California and Nevada were included in the same case, a move that was important for the emergence of a stronger sense of tribal unity. In 1951 the case of the Washoe Tribe of Nevada and California was filed with the Indian Claims Commission, demanding a compensation of $42.8 million for 9,872 square miles of appropriated land and resources. In 1970 the Washoe were awarded about $5 million for their ancient lands, which had become one of the richest and most desirable locations in the American West (d'Azevedo and Kavanagh 1974:60; Nevers 1976:90–91). John Henry Dressler, an organizer and the first chairman of the Inter-Tribal Council of Nevada from 1963 to 1969, helped effective liaison between Indians and state and federal agencies. Largely due to his efforts, a Nevada Indian Affairs Commission was formed, which greatly enhanced attention to Indian interests in the state (Dressler 1972; Inter-Tribal Council of Nevada 1974a:1–3; Nevers 1976:87). Since 1966 the tribal council has been a nine-member body composed of two representatives from Dresslerville Colony, two from Woodfords Colony, one from the Washoe of Reno-Sparks Colony, and two from off the reservations. For the first time, all Washoes were under a central tribal administration coordinating the activities and programs of the various local community councils. The council obtained federal funds for new housing in Dresslerville, Carson Colony, and Woodfords Colony. "The impact of a strong and determined Council to established self-rule has seen a lessening of the role of the Bureau of Indian Affairs over Washoe destiny in recent times" (Washoe Tribe of Nevada and California 1973:5–7).

Of their claims case settlement, the Washoe voted to invest 70 percent of the funds for tribal operations and programs and to provide the remainder as per capita payments to older members of the tribe (Nevers 1976:91). A general plan was prepared that stated among its objectives the further consolidation of the tribe, the development of Washoe lands, improvement of housing and public services to the colonies, and raising the standards of living through education and the creation of jobs. Land holdings increased steadily through purchase and award. State and federally funded aid programs under sponsorship of the Inter-Tribal Council of Nevada were undertaken and supplemented by Washoe tribal funds (Nevers 1976:27–28). New Washoe tribal council headquarters were built near Gardnerville, including a smoke shop and Indian crafts enterprise. A park with camping facilities on the Carson River, the Washoe Health Center, and Senior Citizens' Center (fig. 19) and a Housing Authority office in Dresslerville were operated by the tribe. A tribal police force (fig. 20, right), a construction company, aquaculture (brine shrimp at Hobo Hot Springs), and the Washoe Ranch offered employment. Washoe Tribe of Nevada and California (1982, 1982a) details tribal organization and programs. In 1978 the Washoe Tribe Hunting and Fishing Commission was formed to regulate wildlife resources on Washoe lands, and in 1980 the tribe won jurisdiction in federal court over deer herd control as well as hunting and fishing in the pine nut allotments, over state of Nevada objections.

In the past, degrees of fluency in speaking Washoe—involving knowledge of ritual procedures, myths, legends, and the old way of life—were primary criteria for determining "Washoeness." However, since the early twentieth century all Washoe children have learned English from early childhood, and the use of Washoe has steadily declined. In the late 1950s the number of speakers was estimated at 100 to 200 (Jacobsen 1964). Two decades later there were said to be less than 100 speakers in a population of about 1,450 (Van Winkle

Fig. 19. Theresa Jackson and Marie Kizer (on right) making baskets at the Senior Citizens Center, Dresslerville, Nev. The center, operated by the tribe under a federal program started in 1975, provides daily meals at the center and delivered to homes. Photograph by Kenneth L. Miller, Oct. 1984.

1977), while by 1983 there were less than 50 recognized to be fluent speakers, almost all of them older than 55 and living in or near the traditional settlement. Over half those over 45 years old were judged to be semi-speakers or passive bilinguals (Barrik Van Winkle, personal communication 1984), while the tribal enrollment officer and historian counted 138 frequent users of the language (JoAnn Nevers, personal communication 1984). Most tribal council and other activities were conducted in English in the 1980s.

Synonymy†

The name Washoe is derived from the Washoe self-designation *wá·šiw*. This name does not have a transparent interpretation in Washoe, but Jacobsen has tentatively suggested that the original meaning could have been 'people from here' (William H. Jacobsen, Jr., personal communication 1984). There is an optional plural *wašíšiw*.

The earliest use of the name Washoe appears to have been in 1846 by James Clyman (in Camp 1960:206–207), who used the spellings Washee, Washew, and Waushee. Merriam (1907:343, 1910:213, 1926:map) used Washoo or Wahshoo. Other spellings include Was-saws (Hurt in ARCIA 1857:228), Washaws (Holeman in ARCIA 1852:152), Wah-shoes (Hurt in J.H. Simpson 1876:460), and Wa-sho (Dodge in Hodge 1907–1910, 2:920). The spelling Washo was established as standard for the anthropological and linguistic literature by Hodge (1907–1910, 2:920) and Kroeber (1907:252, 1925:569), who gives Washoe as a variant. The spelling Washoe, which has generally prevailed locally and is used by the

†This synonymy was written by Warren d'Azevedo and Ives Goddard.

Fig. 20. Contemporary life. left, Recreational vehicle and mobile home park along the Carson River, Nev. right, Eugene Frank, a tribal policeman. Photographs by Kenneth L. Miller, Oct. 1984.

Washoe Tribe, has been adopted in the *Handbook;* it was used by J.H. Simpson (1876:38). In this spelling the second syllable was originally pronounced like the English word shoe, and this pronunciation ('wä‚shoō) could still be heard from older residents of the area in the 1950s and 1960s.

There are no distinctively named Washoe subgroups. The view that there was a Pao "tribe" of Carson Valley (Hudson in Culin 1907:227, 335) appears to reflect a misunderstanding of the geographical designation ṗá·waʔluʔ; in this interpretation the Washoe "tribe" is assigned to the Lake Tahoe area.

Names for the Washoe in other languages include: Achumawi mah´-nah´-tse´-e (Merriam 1926:49), Atsugewi ok-pis-se´ (Merriam 1926:49), Maidu čáysi, literally 'ones away from here' (Shipley 1963:97), Nisenan mo´nasa (Beals 1933:366), Northern Sierra Miwok hisatok, histoko, literally 'easterners' (Kroeber 1925:570), Southern Sierra Miwok waš·iwiʔ (Broadbent 1964:282), Northern Paiute wá·šiu (Sven Liljeblad, personal communication 1984), Pyramid Lake Northern Paiute mánaᶜts (Curtis 1907–1930, 15:171).

Sources

The major ethnographic sources on the Washoe are as follows: Powers (1876, see also Fowler and Fowler 1970); Hudson (in Culin 1907), Barrett (1917), Kroeber (1925), Dangberg (1927), Curtis (1907–1930, 15), Lowie (1939, 1963), Siskin (1941), O.C. Stewart (1941, 1944), Freed (1960), Downs (1961, 1961a, 1966), Price (1962a, 1980), d'Azevedo (1963, 1978a), Spring (1967a), Handelman (1976), Nevers (1976), C.S. Fowler et al. (1981), Cohodas (1983). Unpublished field notes and manuscripts of considerable importance are those of Wier (1901), Hudson (1902), Kroeber (1903–1907), Barrett (1906, 1908a), Dyk (1931–1932), and d'Azevedo (1952–1955,

1963–1984). Extensive ethnographic data is contained in the field notes and reports of the field training projects conducted by the Department of Anthropology at the University of Nevada, Reno (Handelman 1964; L.C. Klein 1964; Mordy 1964; Berutti 1965; Lerch 1965; G.E. Montgomery 1965; Spring 1965).

Principal museum collections are to be found in the Field Museum of Natural History (J.W.H. Hudson collection), Chicago; Nevada State Museum (S.L. Lee Collection), Carson City; and University of California, Lowie Museum of Anthropology, Berkeley (G. DePeu Collection). Smaller collections exist at the Smithsonian Institution Museum of Natural History, Washington; Heard Museum of Primitive Art, Phoenix; Southwest Museum, Los Angeles; and the Peabody Museum of Harvard University. Major archival collections of unpublished notes and manuscripts are those of the Smithsonian Institution National Anthropological Archives; the National Archives; and the University of California, Bancroft Library, Berkeley. The extensive papers of Omer C. Stewart are deposited in the University of Colorado Library at Boulder, and his field notes and schedules of Washoe–Northern Paiute Peyotism research were donated to the University of Nevada Reno, Special Collections, which also maintains a repository of manuscripts and rare resources, including the complete file of the Washoe Claims Case. The papers and correspondence of George W. Wright, Washoe Claims Case attorney, are deposited in the archives of the Department of Anthropology, University of Nevada Reno. A small but valuable archival and museum collection is maintained by the Nevada Historical Society, Reno. A collection of films, photographs, and surveys exists in the offices of the Historical Project of the Inter-Tribal Council of Nevada in Reno and at the headquarters of the Washoe Tribal Council in Gardnerville, Nevada, where the tribal rolls, genealogical research files, and reports of tribal organization and programs are kept.

Euro-American Impact Before 1870

CARLING I. MALOUF AND JOHN M. FINDLAY

Relations between Euro-Americans and Native Americans in the Great Basin generally followed the disintegrative course of interaction that prevailed in most other parts of North America. Growing numbers of European and American newcomers constituted an increasing threat to the security and integrity of aboriginal ways and forced Indians to modify their cultures in order to persist. In the intermontane West Native Americans were able to survive early contact with Euro-Americans in relatively better shape than many other North American tribes and bands. From the seventeenth century through the mid-nineteenth century, they were able to develop responses to the disruptive pressures exerted by Whites on native peoples. Thus, by the beginning of the reservation period, in the 1860s, traditional societies, which had been severely threatened by the impact of newcomers bent upon taming the lands of the region and dominating its inhabitants, had adopted methods of resistance and acculturation that permitted much of their traditional autonomy to survive. As a result, the Great Basin in the late twentieth century contains smaller but nonetheless vital Indian groups that retain an identity in a region where Euro-Americans have come to prevail.

Interaction between Native Americans and Euro-Americans in the Great Basin took place in a unique setting that shaped the outcome of cultural contact extensively. On the one hand, the generally limited resources of the region slowed the pace of nonaboriginal incursion and minimized the extent and diversity of immigrant settlement. As the last broad region of the 48 states to be fully explored, and as one of the most lightly inhabited parts of the American continent, some parts of the intermontane West offered native peoples more leeway to resist Euro-American incursions and sustain ethnic identity.

On the other hand, the sparse resources of the Great Basin in some instances accounted for a fragile ecology that could not recover from historic-period exploitation of natural resources. Beginning in the early nineteenth century, Euro-American development of the Basin came in intense bursts of activity that seriously altered environmental settings in selected areas, undermining native subsistence patterns and provoking conflict between Whites and Indians. Whites eventually won the competition for control over natural resources such as the few sources of water that had sustained Indians for so long. Yet, Great Basin native societies were able to absorb many new elements of culture with sufficient speed to enable them to adapt to the Euro-American world while retaining much of their ethnic identity. They achieved this cultural synthesis only after struggling to adjust to changes imposed by European and American immigrants, and only by altering their traditional ways of life. Material culture and subsistence patterns were especially modified, while traditional elements of social organization and religion endured more successfully.

For the purposes of this essay, Euro-American history has been divided into three phases of contact with Great Basin tribes, each eliciting certain responses from natives (cf. Steward and Wheeler-Voegelin 1974:301–327). The Spanish period, from the seventeenth century through 1820, was a time of minimal contact between Europeans and Native Americans but saw the adoption of the horse by some Indian groups as well as the start of trade relations, including traffic in Indian slaves.

During the Mexican period, from 1821 to 1846, there was increased contact between natives and newcomers. Trading and slaving continued, but by then it was accompanied by activities related to the Anglo-American fur trade, exploration, and overland migration. Although non-Indians tended merely to pass through the region, developments in this era posed the first serious environmental threat to Basin Indians and laid the groundwork for the more intensive Euro-American settlement and development of the intermontane West during the American period.

Pressures on indigenous peoples increased sharply after 1847 as routes of travel received growing use, White settlements appeared for the first time, and mining rushes concentrated Euro-Americans in parts of the region. Mormons inhabited portions of the eastern Great Basin, and discoveries of precious minerals encouraged occupation of the western Basin. By the early 1860s the tensions resulting from Whites' more permanent presence had erupted into several prolonged conflicts throughout the region. The subjugation of Native Americans at this time assured Euro-American predominance and ushered in a troubled era of treaties and reservations. Basin Indians had to sustain their cultures within a context established and regulated by unreliable agents of the United States government.

The Spanish Period

The earliest Euro-American impacts on Great Basin native cultures stemmed from Spanish colonization of Mexico and the North American Southwest beginning in the sixteenth century. The Spaniards introduced new elements, most notably the horse, into the cultures of Native Americans residing east of the Rocky Mountains, south of the Colorado River, and west of the Sierra Nevada. European influences steadily made their way from these areas into the Great Basin by exploration and trade.

The Horse

By the time the first Spanish explorers entered the intermontane West during the 1770s, native cultures had already received European influences through contacts with Plains, California, and Southwest tribes. During the mid-seventeenth century groups of Shoshone and Ute were exposed to Plains Indians' adaptation to the horse. These groups gradually adopted the horse for their own transportation. By approximately the mid-seventeenth century, Utes living in Colorado reportedly used horses and some Eastern Shoshones had apparently brought horses into their habitat. Over the next two centuries the horse loomed large in the life of several Indian groups in the Basin and contributed to the disruption of aboriginal cultures.

Indian adaptation to the horse in the Great Basin varied from place to place and from group to group. In many barren areas the environment could not support the animal, so it was looked upon as food rather than as a beast of burden. The Northern Shoshone adopted the horse for transportation, while the Western Shoshone, with the exception of the White Knife, resisted adaptation to the horse because it did not suit their habitat and their way of life. Similarly, while most Northern Paiutes continued to live as before, one group, which became known as the Bannock, took to the horse, moved into Northern Shoshone territory, and developed Shoshone-like patterns of subsistence (Dewey 1966:8–9, 18–19; B.D. Madsen 1980:18–19). Utes in Colorado had highly developed the use of the horse by 1776, according to the first well-documented description by the Spanish padre Silvestre Vélez de Escalante, while those in Utah did not make extensive use of the animal until the 1820s. And even then, only those Utes who lived in grassland regions (the Uintah Basin and Wasatch Piedmont or along the lower Sevier River) where horses could find ample feed used the horse for transportation. Other groups killed the animal and ate it (Steward 1974:39–44; O.C. Stewart 1952:47).

Possession of horses frequently modified traditional cultural patterns and rearranged political relationships between indigenous groups. Those peoples that acquired the horse, such as the Northern and Eastern Shoshone, the Bannock, and the Ute, developed more complex societies. The "kin-clique" or extended family was often replaced as the primary unit of subsistence in these tribes by the band, a form of social organization that better suited predatory activities facilitated by horses. Groups that acquired domesticated beasts traveled farther to reach sources of subsistence, increasingly journeying to the High Plains of Wyoming and even beyond in pursuit of buffalo. The horse thus exposed Native Americans to additional outside cultural influences. Meanwhile, societies like the Gosiute and Southern Paiute that did not adopt the horse, even though they had traditionally resembled the Ute and Shoshone in culture, grew weaker by comparison, sometimes becoming targets for slave raids by mounted Indians (Steward 1974:94–98; Malouf 1966:9). The use of horses introduced lasting distinctions between Great Basin tribes as well as promoted cultural changes.

Acquisition of the horse also involved Native Americans in new trade relationships. Horses were imported from the south probably at first from Southwest Indians in contact with White colonists. Then Spanish and Mexican traders gradually began to traffic in horses and other commodities themselves. Most trading expeditions were unauthorized, so little is known about their chronology and extent. Nonetheless, they provided additional goods that Great Basin Indians absorbed into their cultures.

Exploration

The insubstantial record of Spanish activities in the Great Basin in large part reflects the weakness of Spain's claims to the territory. From their New World base in Mexico City, colonizers moved northward along two main routes, one into New Mexico and Arizona and the other into California. In both regions isolated missions, forts, and settlements served as outposts of the Spanish empire; however, no enduring routes of travel connected Spanish colonies in California and New Mexico because portions of the intervening territory were deserts peopled by tribes hostile to the Europeans. Although the Spanish were the first Euro-American people to penetrate much of the Far West of North America, they generally lacked the resources to establish lasting colonies at any great distance from their New World stronghold in Mexico. By the time Spaniards turned their attention to systematic exploration and colonization along the northern frontier during the late eighteenth century, their North American empire had become moribund.

One of the challenges that Spanish colonizers faced on their northwestern frontier was to provide communications between their far-flung settlements. Attempts to find an overland route from Santa Fe to Alta California resulted in the first significant Euro-American penetration of the Great Basin. Spanish expeditions like that of Juan María de Rivera in 1765, which explored the plateaus at the southeast corner of the Basin, provided a degree of familiarity with the geography of the area and encouraged illicit trading expeditions.

Three Franciscan priests were in large part responsible for the initial official expeditions into the intermontane West. In early 1776, a party led by Father Francisco Tomás Hermenegildo Garcés and Juan Bautista de Anza entered the very southern tip of the Great Basin in California, crossing from the Colorado River to the Mojave River in about two weeks (fig. 1a) (Cline 1963:35–38). On this occasion Anza and Garcés encountered a number of Chemehuevi Indians, the southernmost Great Basin group (Euler and Fowler 1973:36).

Six months after Garcés and Anza traversed the southern tip of the Great Basin, another Spanish expedition led by Fathers Francisco Atanasio Domínguez and Silvestre Vélez de Escalante arrived in the Basin from the east (fig. 1a). Guided both by Ute Indians and by Spaniards such as Pedro Mora, Gregorio Sandoval, and Andres Muñoz, who had traveled all along the Colorado Plateau, Domínguez and Escalante entered the area near Utah Lake, moved southward past present-day Cedar City, Utah, and returned to the Colorado Plateau of Arizona and New Mexico. Like Garcés and Anza, the two priests were searching for an overland route from Santa Fe to Monterey, the capital of Alta California. They had chosen a path through Utah because their knowledge of the area suggested that the Ute Indians were friendly and would permit them to pass (Cline 1963:37, 43–48; Bolton 1950:9). Unable to accomplish its goal, the Domínguez-Escalante party nonetheless added to Euro-American understanding of the West and pioneered part of the route that became the Old Spanish Trail from Santa Fe to Los Angeles.

Escalante's journal not only depicted Indians' material goods and discussed trading experiences but also commented on Ute and Southern Paiute subsistence activities such as gathering pine nuts, seeds, and prickly pear foods; growing corn in southern Utah; and fishing. Escalante noted that some natives feared the Spanish travelers and suspected their motives for entering the country. Some had perhaps heard of Europeans, and a few had already seen them in New Mexico and southern Colorado. Escalante tried to reassure Native Americans that Spaniards came as friends. He and Domínguez preached to the Indians regularly and promised to return soon to establish missions among them (Bolton 1950:77–80, 188–189). Near Cedar City, Escalante noted that Southern Paiutes preferred to trade "'only for red clothes,' an indication that the Indians had been in some contact with Europeans, probably indirectly, before 1776" (Euler and Fowler 1973:32).

Trade

Domínguez and Escalante did not return to Utah or central Colorado. Indeed, the Spaniards conducted no further official exploration of the Basin, as colonizers focused their attention elsewhere; however, by 1800 Spaniards had gained a better understanding of the region between Santa Fe and Utah Lake as a result of unauthorized expeditions into the area. Some of these trips may have been efforts by Spaniards in New Mexico and their Indian allies to recover horses stolen by Utes, but most of the expeditions likely developed for commercial purposes. Colonial officials forbade commerce between private parties and Indians in the Basin and prosecuted those who were caught breaking the law (Twitchell 1914, 2:263,291,297,384), but prospects for profitable trade apparently tempted numerous Spanish adventurers.

Commerce between Indians and Spanish colonists was documented in early American accounts of contact with natives in the Great Basin. In 1805 Shoshones told William Clark, leader with Meriwether Lewis of the exploring expedition, about "the white people with whom they traded for horses mules cloth metal beads and the shells which they woar as ornament" (D.L. Morgan 1968:11). In writing about his epic crossing of the basin of 1826 and 1827, Jedediah Strong Smith implied that several tribes had been in direct or indirect contact with Mexican or Anglo-American traders. The Utes wore buffalo robes and carried Spanish guns, the Southern Paiutes had acquired blue cloth and iron, and the Northern Paiutes at Walker Lake possessed "buffalo robes, knives, and Spanish blankets" (G.R. Brooks 1977:42–43,64–65, 176). Some of the commerce apparently took place around Utah Lake, where traders from New Mexico acquired pelts. Spanish-speaking people followed the Old Spanish Trail into the area (J.J. Hill 1930:3,16–17).

Trade between Hispanics from New Mexico and Indians in the Basin increasingly included traffic in slaves captured from indigenous tribes. It has been suggested that this commerce in humans began as early as the 1770s, but the first definite record of the activity dates from 1813, when an expedition of seven men under Mauricio Arze and Largo García left Abiquiu, New Mexico, for a trading expedition into the Utah Lake country. In court proceedings that followed their return to New Mexico, the men testified that natives had insisted they purchase Indian captives as part of their transaction. When the Spaniards declined the offer, Ute tribesmen killed several horses and a mule before their chief was able to quiet them (Malouf 1966:7, 11). Over the next 40 years the sale of Indians as bondsmen continued. Slavers sought women and children in particular because Indian men were difficult to manage. Many of the captives were taken to ranches in New Mexico. As *501*

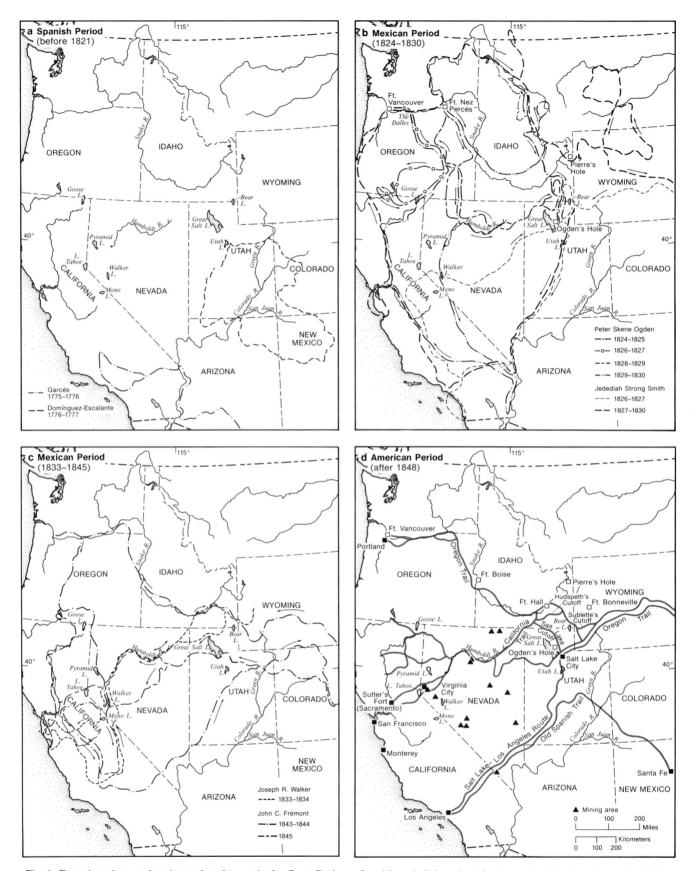

Fig. 1. Euro-American exploration and settlement in the Great Basin; a, Spanish period; b and c, Mexican period; d, American period with overland routes, mining centers, and forts.

in California, Mexicans became especially prominent in the commerce in slaves after Spain lost its North American holdings in 1821. With the extension of the Old Spanish Trail to Los Angeles in the late 1820s, the trade grew larger (J.J. Hill 1930:20; Inter-Tribal Council of Nevada 1976:36; Creer 1949: 174,179; Twitchell 1914, 2:227).

The development of the slave trade during the early nineteenth century mirrored the shifting balance of power among Great Basin tribes that had proceeded since Euro-American influences were first felt by native cultures. Whites who traded for Native American slaves, including Spaniards, Mexicans, and Anglo-Americans, did not often capture the slaves themselves but rather relied on other natives to supply them. Among those Great Basin groups victimized by slave raids, some kin-cliques were decimated; the peoples who had lost so many of their numbers in slave raids were described by travelers as timid. Meanwhile, other groups, mounted and armed, thrived. Bands of Utes on horseback, including the followers of Wakara (or Chief Walker), became notorious for their raids on other tribes (Snow 1929:69–70,78–79; Creer 1949:180).

The Gosiute and Southern Paiute especially were victimized by this trade. Indeed, repeated slave raids may have accounted for the fearful character of the Southern Paiutes with whom White travelers came into contact. Jedediah Strong Smith noted in 1826 that these natives were afraid of horses and White men and had concealed their women and children as his party approached. Accounts from later years reported that Southern Paiutes had actually begun to sell their children to slavers (Euler and Fowler 1973:46–47; Malouf 1974:32; G.R. Brooks 1977:49–53, 60). Along with the horse, the slave trade in the southern Great Basin served to make native groups less equal. By supporting activities such as the slave trade and by introducing new elements such as the horse into native cultures, Euro-Americans had begun to alter traditional ways of life in the Great Basin.

The Mexican Period

Euro-American influence on native cultures increased after 1820. In 1821 the Spaniards lost control of their North American possessions in Mexico. In sharp contrast to European colonizers, Mexican authorities assumed a more permissive attitude toward foreigners in their Far Western territories. Moreover, Anglo-Americans were taking a growing interest in the lands and resources of the intermontane West. Like the Spaniards, the Mexicans were never able to assert more than nominal control over Basin lands that they claimed. They managed to operate only on the fringes of the Basin. Mexican traders, joined by their American counterparts, continued to operate in the southern part of the region, traveling over the Old Spanish Trail to California during the 1830s and 1840s, but the swelling tide of British and Yankee interest in the area ensured that trappers, explorers, and emigrant parties soon invaded the domain of the Great Basin Indians, too. These newcomers heightened the disruption of native cultures by upsetting the fragile environment of the region.

Anglo-American entrepreneurs initially had no threatening designs on the Mexican lands, but increasingly they came to embody the spirit of Manifest Destiny that drove Americans to the edge of the continent by the mid-nineteenth century. Trappers' penetration of the intermontane West was not very extensive at first, for they relied on trade with Indians to procure furs. Even after organized trapping expeditions began to replace trade as a source of beaver skins, mountain men continued to look upon their activities in the Basin and on adjacent plateaus as a transient phase in their lives. But trappers' trails gradually became heavily traveled overland routes to the Pacific coast. Explorers, migrants, and eventually the transcontinental railroad all made their way through the Basin in the wake of trappers, undermining the ecological balance that supported Indian societies and ensuring that Native American cultures would never be the same.

The Fur Trade

Canadian and American trappers pushed up the Missouri and Columbia rivers during the first two decades of the nineteenth century. In 1811 and 1812 members of overland Astoria expeditions actually set foot in the northern Great Basin, hunting through the Bear River area. In 1819 and 1820 Donald Mackenzie led trappers of the Canadian Northwest Company into the same vicinity on the very first Snake River expeditions. Thereafter, the pace of exploration and hunting by trappers quickened, largely as the result of the work of two companies. The Hudson's Bay Company, based in England and Canada, bought out Mackenzie's firm and dispatched trappers into the area from its headquarters along the Columbia, while members of the American Rocky Mountain Fur Company, based in Saint Louis, came into the area from the north and east. As a result of the wanderings of these mountain men, the contours of the Great Basin came to be identified (Cline 1963:77–163).

From 1824 on several trappers of the Rocky Mountain Fur Company entered the Great Basin and plateaus in search of new sources of fur. The party of Étienne Provost was attacked by either Northern Shoshones or Utes in north-central Utah, and 8 or 10 trappers were killed. The Americans blamed the hostility of the natives on a British trapping party that had earlier killed a chief in a skirmish over horses (D.L. Morgan 1947:147; Greer et al. 1981:103). Another mountain man, Jedediah Strong Smith, traversed the basin in both directions in a legendary journey of 1826–1827, undertaken for exploration and for acquiring pelts (fig. 1b). Smith distinguished between the timid and horseless Gosiutes, who refused to come near his party, and the stronger, equestrian Bannocks who offered food to the explorers. He also attempted to settle a dispute between Utes and Northern Shoshones in the vicinity of the Great Salt Lake, and signed a "treaty" with one tribe that allowed Americans to trap and hunt in the area. In several instances Smith's men acquired food from the natives that helped to sustain them on their journey (G.R. Brooks 1977:41–42,57; Malouf 1974:102–103).

Meanwhile, from the Pacific Northwest Peter Skene Ogden led a series of four expeditions through portions of the hydrographic basin and the Snake River plateau between 1824 and 1830, locating the Humboldt River as well as other features for the first time (fig. 1b). Ogden made detailed observations of Native Americans in the area. Near Humboldt Sink, for instance, he described a mounted party of Indians (probably Northern Paiute), armed with rifles believed to have been taken originally in an attack on Jedediah Strong Smith's party in Oregon. Of the Northern Shoshone in the Bear River country Ogden noted that, except for knives, Indians had little interest in trading for the White man's goods

(Malouf 1966:9; Cline 1963:107, 123–124; Greer et al. 1981).

Accounts such as Smith's and Ogden's help to delineate the many-sided impact of the fur trade on indigenous cultures between 1810 and the 1840s (Murphy and Murphy 1960:295–296; Rusco 1976). Ogden routinely employed local Indians as guides through parts of the Great Basin, indicating that Whites relied on natives' knowledge of the West to make their way about the unknown territory and to locate fur and food resources. Moreover, mountain men commonly engaged in trade with Indians (fig. 2), usually for beaver pelts but sometimes for food as well. This doubtless had a profound effect on traditional economies. Goods acquired from Anglo-American fur companies in some cases supplanted elements of aboriginal material culture. Trade also exposed Indians to liquor, which was used by traders to facilitate deals, as well as to firearms (fig. 3). Acquisition of such items probably had an impact akin to that of the horse by helping to undermine ancient patterns of subsistence, social organization, and social control. Some Euro-American trappers not only took Indian wives but also participated on occasion in the Indian slave trade in the southern Great Basin. Finally, mountain men introduced Old World diseases to Great Basin and Plateau peoples, although natives

Elizabeth Waldo Dentzel, Northridge, Calif.

Fig. 2. Northern Shoshone and Eastern Shoshone encampment during a fur trade rendezvous in the Wind River Mountains, Oreg. Country, at which over 3,000 Indians assembled. Indian and White trappers and traders gathered to exchange goods such as buffalo robes and pelts for dry goods, ammunition, and tobacco. They also planned the next year's hunt and participated in sports such as horse races. The annual rendezvous were important occasions for accommodation during the Mexican period. Pen and ink with gray wash on pink card by Alfred Jacob Miller, 1837.

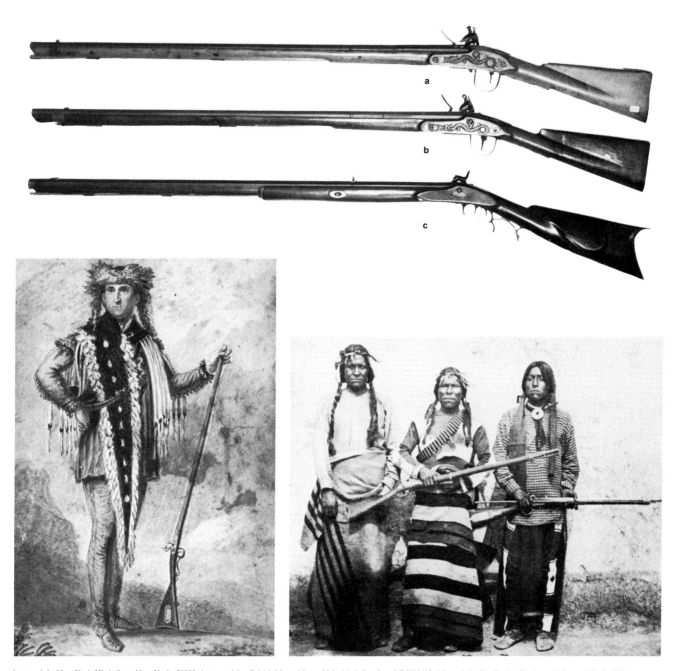

bottom left, New-York Histl. Soc., New York: 51322; bottom right, British Mus., Mus. of Mankind, London: MM018413; Mus. of the Fur Trade, Chadron, Nebr.: a, 931; b, 521A; c, 4336.

Fig. 3. Types of guns traded to Great Basin tribes during the early 19th century. Fusils, or smoothbore muskets, the standard trade gun of the major fur trading companies, decreased in popularity only in the 1860s, with the increased sale of shotguns, cheap muzzle-loading rifles, and breech-loading carbines. Fusils were made on a standard pattern, used simple, replacement parts, were relatively inexpensive, light in weight, and used an efficient 30 gauge ball or shot. Barnett, the name of the principal English supplier, became a standard for the Indian trade, as did the decorative serpent side plate, and both trademarks of the early English Northwest gun were quickly adopted by Belgian and U.S. manufacturers. Somewhat later, percussion rifles, often made by St. Louis manufacturers, were sold to the Indians. a, English Northwest gun stamped "Barnett 1833." This type, distributed by the Hudson's Bay Company throughout the American Northwest, represents the standard copied by Belgian and American gun manufacturers. b, Belgian Northwest gun stamped "Burnett 1844." After 1836 Belgian guns were given out by the U.S. government by the thousands in treaty payments. c, Albright percussion rifle of the type sold to Great Basin tribes by the Mormon traders in Utah in the 1850s, one of the earliest examples of percussion rifles sold to the Indians. bottom left, Capt. Meriwether Lewis wearing a beautiful otter tippet, most likely presented to him by Northern Shoshones on August 18, 1805 (Thwaites 1904–1905, 7:138, 2:378). Ermine fur decorated the edge of the tippet; down the center were attached small abalone shell ornaments. Watercolor by Charles B.J.F. de Saint-Mémin, 1807. bottom right, Utes in N. Mex., probably to trade. The man in the center holds an 1841 percussion rifle, .54 caliber, paper cartridge. The man on the right carries a Springfield rifle, .50 caliber, made about 1870, commonly given as a treaty payment. Photograph possibly by John K. Hillers, 1879.

in the intermontane West tended to be so dispersed that diseases did not travel between them so quickly as in more densely settled regions such as California.

While many fur trappers reached a modus vivendi with the Great Basin Indians, they also represented a source of tension because the pursuit of beaver belts inevitably altered the delicate environmental balance that had sustained the native cultures. Competition between companies of trappers and traders—Canadians and English, Yankees, and French-Canadians—heightened the destructive impact on the environment as each expedition tried to take all the beaver from a watershed before its rivals arrived. For many Indians who lived near or along streams, depletion of the beaver supply was catastrophic. It not only deprived them of a food and fur resource but also endangered other forms of wildlife upon which they depended (Nissen 1982: 66,107). The decrease in the supply of beaver and other game in Northern Shoshone territory was observed in 1843 by Charles Preuss, cartographer for John C. Frémont: "The white people have ruined the country of the Snake Indians and should therefore treat them well. Almost all the natives are now obliged to live on roots, game can scarcely be seen any more" (Gudde and Gudde 1958:86).

Relations between White and Red men deteriorated as a result of Euro-American destruction of the native habitat. Indians apparently responded to changes in the ecology by stealing the fur companies' traps (Inter-Tribal Council of Nevada 1976b:14–15), and mountain men responded violently to this threat (Angel 1881:145). The most significant clashes, notorious for poisoning relations between Indians and Whites for years to come, were those between Joseph Reddeford Walker's party and Northern Paiutes along the lower Humboldt River. Walker guided an expedition down the Humboldt and over the Sierra Nevada in 1833, returning via Owens Valley, California, and the Humboldt the following year (fig. 1c). On both trips through the Humboldt Sink Walker's men fought with Indians. These clashes contrasted sharply with Ogden's experience in the same vicinity. Ogden depicted the natives as quite "daring and bold," but he managed to negotiate skillfully with them (Cline 1963:8, 1974:89–90). Walker's party, on the other hand, was less restrained.

Troubles began upstream on the Humboldt after Whites responded on two occasions to theft of their traps by killing "several" Indians. Walker disciplined the murderers because he feared that such actions placed his outnumbered band in jeopardy. When his party encountered between 800 and 900 Indians at the Humboldt Sink, he responded by giving them an ultimatum to disband or be attacked. The Indians refused to disperse, and Walker's men charged and killed between 25 and 39 natives. Zenas Leonard, a member of Walker's party, argued that the purpose of the attack was to scare the Indians away. Although the attack was thus presented as an act of self-defense, White motives may have better been expressed in the ruthless scalping and killing of wounded natives as they lay on the ground. The act appears to have been more of a "punitive measure" aimed at "savages" with whom the Whites did not expect to be able to reason (Leonard 1904:163–165; Watson 1934:50–55; D.L. Morgan 1943:51; Napton 1970: 113,123; B. Gilbert 1983:129–133). Walker's party repeated their actions the following year on their return journey through central Nevada, this time killing about 15 natives (Cline 1963:174, 176–177; D.L. Morgan 1943:60; B. Gilbert 1983: 146–147).

The violent conflict and ecological destruction that accompanied Anglo-Americans into the Great Basin heralded a new era of cultural contact. Tensions did not characterize White relations with all tribes, since many groups, such as the Gosiute (Malouf 1974:107), remained outside the area of White influence. Trappers tended primarily to encroach upon native groups that dwelled near where beaver could be trapped. Along the Virgin, Muddy, Humboldt, and other streams, new modes of interaction characterized relations between Euro-Americans and Indians. Clashes between Euro-American travelers and indigenous peoples apparently encouraged Native Americans to withdraw from intensive occupation patterns in areas of heavy travel and beaver trapping. By the time that explorer Edward Kern reached the Humboldt Sink in 1844, Indians who had first stood up to Walker's men seemed "much more indigent and shy, hiding from us on our approach" (Kern 1876:478). The activities of fur trappers and traders had clearly reduced the Native American's security in his traditional homeland.

Exploration and Emigration

Spaniards and Mexicans had primarily limited their penetration of the Basin to trading expeditions that did not push deeply into the territory, but Anglo-Americans sought to exploit the area's natural resources more fully and became much more familiar with the entire Basin. At the same time, Americans began to view the Far West in a new way. Trappers were gradually replaced in the Basin by nationalistic explorers intent upon conquest and by overland travelers interested only in passing through the area. Without much stake in maintaining friendly relations with natives, neither of these groups treated the Indian very sensitively.

The exploring parties of John C. Frémont were one expression of American interest in territory claimed by Mexico. During the early 1840s Frémont guided expeditions through Utah, Nevada, and eastern California, finally putting to rest the suspicion that a waterway connected the eastern half of the continent with the western half (fig. 1c). In early 1844 he had the first recorded sighting of Pyramid Lake in western Nevada, reporting impoverished natives as well as a relatively wealthy group that resided in the vicinity. The Indians described the surrounding terrain to Frémont but refused to guide his men beyond the shores of the lake (J.U. Smith 1911:120–124). Later on the same expedition, while crossing southern Nevada and Utah, one of Frémont's guides, Christopher (Kit) Carson, purchased a Southern Paiute boy from the Ute as an "apprentice" (Gudde and Gudde 1958:134).

Expeditions such as Frémont's, along with the explorations of Anglo-American fur trappers, helped to open routes of travel across the Great Basin to California. As overland migration increased, natives and Whites came into ever more frequent contact. Euro-Americans thus continued to weaken Native American patterns of subsistence and autonomy.

The Old Spanish Trail and the California Trail along the Humboldt River tended to channel overland travel to the Pacific coast (fig. 1d), and along each of them emigrants threatened native cultures. Most early parties followed the northern route to California. The stream of migrants, which swelled steadily until it peaked after the discovery of gold in the foothills of Sierra Nevada, placed increasing pressure on Indian food sources along the Humboldt. Overland travelers ravaged the ecology of the Humboldt River valley. They grazed their livestock on the grasses that lined the river and permitted their animals to trample the turf to a hard shell. At the Humboldt Sink grasses were actually harvested for the dangerous trip across the Forty Mile Desert, so that in later years emigrants found very little feed there for their horses, cattle, and oxen. Moveover, the travelers' livestock may have passed Old World diseases on to game animals such as rabbits and deer, poisoning the food for Indian consumption. Additionally, emigrant trains hunted wild game or drove it away. They also were responsible for introducing a cholera epidemic that killed "hundreds" of Northern Paiutes in 1850 (Nissen 1982:66–69, 115–116, 125–126).

In the face of such powerful destructive forces, many Native Americans simply withdrew from their former habitations along the river. However, some attempted to remain along the overland trail, and resorted to begging or taking goods from emigrant parties. Although the Indians were clearly trying to replace lost food sources, Whites often interpreted their thefts as "ambushes" and, following the example set by Walker's party, responded accordingly. After Indians stole some oxen from an 1846 party, migrants retaliated by burning down the natives' tule huts (Napton 1970:114,116,123–124; Mordy and McCaughey 1968:11; Remy and Brenchley 1861, 1:58,76,85–86,95–99). Into the late 1840s and the 1850s, streams of overland travelers continued to erode the supply of native food resources that had supported large groups of Indians along the Humboldt.

The Huntington Lib., San Marino, Calif.
Fig. 4. Fort Hall on the Snake River. The growing number of Whites traveling through the Great Basin encouraged the development of trading posts and provoked conflict with natives that led to the development of a series of military bases for the protection of both emigrants and Indians. The artist purposely passed by Fort Hall "to see the mountaineers there, for information about the travel after crossing the pass in the Sierra Nevada" (Read and Gaines 1949:94) on his way to the California goldfields. The presence of an Indian camp at the site, which was not uncommon at military fortifications, express stations, trading posts, and other points of White occupation, foreshadowed the conversion of Fort Hall into the headquarters of an Indian reservation during the 1860s. Colored chalk drawing by J. Goldsborough Bruff, Aug. 1849.

Depletion of natural resources also took place along the Old Spanish Trail. The impact on natives' subsistence patterns was not so great as along the Humboldt route, but Indians nonetheless felt the effects of Euro-American contact. Southern Paiutes living along the Muddy, Virgin, and Santa Clara rivers were hardest hit, while away from trails and streams traditional culture remained more intact. One native response to the invasion by emigrants and traders was to adopt some elements of Euro-American material culture; another was to raid the herds of livestock that were trampling native grasses and taking over water holes (Euler and Fowler 1973:54, 97–98; Euler 1972:49, 54; Inter-Tribal Council of Nevada 1976:39–40). Still another was to withdraw from the brunt of these new forces, a response that Southern Paiutes had adopted since the first slave raids on their people.

Groups like the Southern Paiute that continued to travel by foot responded more timidly to cultural changes, and newcomers noticed the differences. Horses served to create lasting distinctions between Basin Indians in White minds. Mounted tribes seemed more impressive and civilized to Euro-Americans, while groups that traveled by foot were commonly viewed as slovenly "diggers" (G.R. Brooks 1977:42–43, 185; Euler 1972:46; Dewey 1966:13; Euler and Fowler 1973:43–45, 48–49; Murphy and Murphy 1960:296–298). Such stereotypes served to simplify White perceptions of native cultures. As a result, discoveries of the complexities of Basin ways of life, such as Capt. J.W. Davidson's realization in 1859 that the Owens Valley Paiute practiced a form of agricultural irrigation (Wilke and Lawton 1976:19–20), almost invariably came as surprises.

The horse was but one element of European culture that Basin peoples adopted. Other material goods and domestic plants were acquired as a result of contact with Euro-Americans. The Southern Paiute reportedly incorporated numerous new elements—iron, clothing, firearms, and horsemeat—into their culture, but traditional subsistence patterns were not fundamentally altered in most areas (Euler and Fowler 1973:116). B.D. Madsen (1980:23, 25) argues that the limited Northern Shoshone contact with fur traders and trappers produced a short-lived "cultural golden age" by adding new elements to their way of life, without seriously disrupting traditional patterns.

As long as contact between the two peoples was not too extensive and ecological destruction did not overwhelm native subsistence patterns, Great Basin tribes withstood early contacts quite well. In areas of heavy Euro-American activity, Indians suffered greater cultural loss. In most parts of the intermontane West, Indian populations were widely scattered over barren terrain that offered few attractions for non-native peoples. In a few places with more substantial natural resources, such as at the Humboldt Sink and along the Virgin, Muddy, and Santa Clara rivers on the Old Spanish Trail, native groups were more concentrated. These areas also attracted Anglo-American trappers and emigrants who undermined the fragile desert ecology of such oases and severely disrupted the Indians' subsistence patterns (Nissen 1982:198–199; Euler and Fowler 1973:50).

Indians affected by extensive Euro-American activities in these areas sometimes responded by stealing beaver traps and raiding herds of livestock. Such retaliations generally required a higher degree of social organization than was common before contact with Euro-Americans, and it encouraged the development of "bands" where only loosely organized groups had existed before. The introduction of the horse had already altered traditional forms of social organization among those peoples who adopted the animal as a form of transportation. As Whites placed more pressure on existing resources, even "foot" Indians responded by forming bands to prey on the livestock of overland travelers (Euler and Fowler 1973:99–104). As Euro-Americans came to tax native resources even more after mid-century, bands became still more prominent as a form of social organization that represented a response to the arrival of Whites. In addition, then, to upsetting the balance of power between traditional societies, disrupting traditional subsistence practices, and causing ecological changes, Euro-Americans prompted new forms of social organization among Native Americans in the Great Basin. Each of these changes became even more pronounced after 1847 as a new era of development began.

The American Period

The United States acquired the territory of the Great Basin as a result of the Treaty of Guadalupe Hidalgo in 1848, which concluded the Mexican–American War. Migration through the region increased decisively after the discovery of gold in California in 1848, and in 1847 Mormons became the first of several groups of settlers and miners to put the lands of the Basin to extensive use. Each of the new developments heightened pressure on Native American cultures and quickened the pace of social and ecological change. Between the late 1840s and the early 1860s Indians responded to increased pressures on their territory by attempting to find a means of coexisting peacefully with the newcomers while retaining traditional cultures, incorporating elements of Euro-American civilization into their ways of living, and resisting the Whites who threatened their cultural integrity. After about 1860, these reactions were played out increasingly within the context of "protective" policies developed by the United States government, including the establishment of reservations.

Mormon Settlement

Mormons (members of the Church of Jesus Christ of Latter-day Saints) were the first Euro-American group to come to the Great Basin with the intent to settle. They located in the intermontane West in 1847 because they thought that, as a remote part of Mexican territory, the region would serve as a refuge from the harassment they had received at the hands of Americans. They also understood that the Salt Lake Valley, where they built their headquarters, was a no-man's land situated between feuding groups of Ute and Shoshone (J. Brooks 1944:3), and they hoped to avoid provoking Indian hostilities by locating there.

By taking up lands in Utah the Mormons automatically increased the pressure on native cultures that were already threatened by White emigrant trains (Wilson in ARCIA 1850:67; Hoopes 1932:136–137). Skirmishes between the Latter-day Saints and Ute and Shoshone Indians took place during the initial years of the settlers' occupation, but by the early 1850s Mormon leaders had developed a careful Indian policy that minimized conflict between the two groups for about 10 years (Remy and Brenchley 1861, 1:446–447, 466–467; Inter-Tribal Council of Nevada 1976b:23–24,26; Malouf 1974:110; Greer et al. 1981:103). The Saints' policy consisted of elements of diplomacy, trade, education, missions, and protective benevolence.

508

Unlike trappers and emigrants who had no permanent stake in the Great Basin, Mormons intended to stay in Utah and therefore needed to develop a stable relationship with Native Americans. Brigham Young enunciated a policy of friendliness toward Indians that was designed to minimize tensions between settlers and natives. Official policy did not prevent disputes between Indians and individual settlers, but it seemed to reduce tensions by ensuring that the natives' welfare was attended to (J. Brooks 1944:18, 22–23). The practical-minded Mormon doctrine was summarized: "We always consider it cheaper to feed and clothe the Indians than to fight them, and so long as we can get access to them to feed them &c. we have no trouble with them; but when they get out of the settlements into the mountains there is danger of depredations &c. by them" (D.H. Wells 1933:126). In caring for the welfare of the Indians, the Mormons tried to convince them that they would receive better treatment from the Saints than from other Americans, and to some extent Indians tended to accept this distinction (Hunt in ARCIA 1858:593; Remy and Brenchley 1861, 2:408; Carvalho 1857:218). Mormon policy toward the Indians thus not only reflected doctrinal teachings but also came to be intertwined with the Saints' antipathy toward Americans in general.

When the Mormons determined to abolish the Indian slave trade and continued to encroach on Ute territory, a series of clashes between Whites and the Indians, including Wakara's band and the Pahvant, occurred in 1853 throughout central Utah (D.H. Wells 1933:127–130; Hoopes 1932:136–137; Manners 1974:215–217; Greer et al. 1981:103). The fighting died down in part because the Mormons had established their hold on the territory and in part because the Indians gained concessions from White leaders (Christy 1979). Mormon leaders visited Wakara (fig. 5) and made peace by promising protection and distributing rifles. Young, who had previously opposed arming the Indians, reasoned that the Ute were already acquiring guns from traders and emigrants, and that the Mormons wanted to encourage the natives to shoot their own game rather than steal from Mormon herds and towns (Carvalho 1857:187–199, 253–266; Dewey 1966:16–18). The Saints' policies represented a practical approach to the problem of peaceful coexistence with this powerful group of natives. The Mormons also coexisted with less threatening groups—the Gosiute and Southern Paiute—by drawing them into the orbit of their agricultural settlements where Indians were provided with food, clothes, and work (Carvalho 1857:213; Malouf 1974:114–115). The apparent cooperation between Mormons and Indians in the Mountain Meadows Massacre, an event during September 1857 in which most members of a party of overland emigrants were slaughtered, seemed to constitute additional evidence of a relatively strong bond between

The Thomas Gilcrease Inst. of Amer. Hist. and Art, Tulsa, Okla.
Fig. 5. Wakara, also known as Chief Walker, leader of the Timpanogots Ute band, which dominated much of the present state of Utah during the Mexican and early American periods. The artist painted this portrait after witnessing negotiations between Wakara and Young on the Sevier River, May 1854. Wakara died soon afterward. Oil painting by Solomon Nuñes Carvalho, 1854.

Saints and Indians (Forney in ARCIA 1860:362–373; J. Brooks 1950).

The institution of the mission formalized Mormon Indian policy in areas more removed from nuclei of White settlement. Brigham Young established the first mission in 1854, and by 1855 six more sites had been added, but most of these agricultural experiments were short-lived, in part because natives refused to farm (Forney in ARCIA 1859:209–213). Seeing that Indians generally preferred their independence to "the benefits of civilized life," Young instructed Mormon missionaries to reach the natives by living in their world as much as possible (Remy and Brenchley 1861, 2:414–415; J. Brooks 1944:10–14; Euler and Fowler 1973:65–70).

The impact of the Mormon missionaries upon Native Americans was limited; however, missionary activity was one avenue by which numerous Mormon families acquired Indian children. The "adoption" of these children seems ironic in light of the Saints' attitudes toward the Indian slave trade. The Mormons were quick to outlaw the traffic in Indian captives, which annoyed some of the Indians who had participated in the commerce. However, natives occasionally pressured the Mormons to buy an Indian captive by threatening to kill the child if he was not purchased (Bancroft 1889:266; Malouf and Malouf 1945:389). After the first few such

Church Arch., Church of Jesus Christ of Latter Day Saints, Salt Lake City: P 500–79–3.

Fig. 6. Mormon baptism of Shivwits Southern Paiutes. Performing the baptism is Daniel P. McArthur, President of the St. George Stake. The White man standing on the right is Sheriff Augustus P. Hardy. Nearly 200 men, women, and children were baptized in the pool at Mount Hope (Alter 1944:67). Mormon settlers provided work and welfare and tried to convert Indians through missions, schools, and other means. Photograph by Charles R. Savage, St. George, Utah, March 1875.

transactions, the Saints began to acquire more and more Indian children, and justified the practice by arguing that these "servants" and "apprentices" would grow up in a civilized environment and eventually attain freedom. Many of the children simply ran away from their "godfathers" and "godmothers," and others died after being exposed at close range to Euro-American diseases. The Indian children and their "half-breed" offspring were never truly accepted as equals in Mormon society (Armstrong in ARCIA 1858:308–309; J. Brooks 1944:6–7, 13–14, 33–34, 48; Inter-Tribal Council of Nevada 1976:63,67).

Mormon attitudes were unique in the history of Indian-White relations in the Great Basin. More than other Euro-American settlers, the Latter-day Saints tried to get along with natives of the area, and to a certain extent they succeeded. However, by the early 1860s several influences undermined the pattern of coexistence that had been established. One was the arrival of federal troops and Indian agents, who replaced the Mormons as sources of welfare and protection for Indians. Another was the growing numbers of the Mormons themselves. Despite official policies of peaceful coexistence, too many settlers crowded into the region, introducing foreign diseases and depleting Indians' traditional resources. Prior to the White man's arrival, Utes had regularly burned brush away from meadows "in order to provide open, clean, grassy pastures to attract wild game and thereby facilitate hunting" (O.C. Stewart 1952:48–49). Mormons halted this practice, and meadows turned into sagebrush-covered valleys or came to be cultivated as agricultural fields.

This and other methods of destroying traditional sources of subsistence had reduced many natives to extreme poverty by 1860, according to Indian agent Jacob Forney. Put in a position where they had either to "*steal* or *starve*," many Indians simply elected to take livestock, particularly during severe winters, and raid Mormon settlements (Forney in ARCIA 1860:362–373). Hostilities between the Whites and Indians increased during the early 1860s, culminating in a massacre of Bannock and Northern Shoshone men, women, and children, by federal soldiers under Col. Patrick E. Connor at Bear River in 1863 (Inter-Tribal Council of Nevada 1976:59–61; Arrington 1966:151; Dewey 1966:16; B.D. Madsen 1980:30–31, 35–36; R.C. Colton 1959:164:166).

Non-Mormon Settlement

If Mormon settlement encouraged the decline of Native American cultures, non-Mormon activities in the Great Basin after 1847 proved even more destructive. Unlike the Latter-day Saints, most of the Euro-Americans who came to the intermontane West around the mid-nineteenth century had little interest in settling permanently and thus saw less need to come to peaceful terms with Indians. In addition, they were more inclined than the Mormons to summon federal troops at the slightest hint of trouble with natives. These Whites tended to become involved in either ranching or mining, and both activities jeopardized Indians' traditional habitats.

Ranches in the Great Basin were generally located in level, relatively well-watered areas that had previously served as important sources of native foodstuffs. Herds of cattle tended to trample grasses and deplete supplies of seed upon which some aboriginal diets had depended (Downs 1963:122). Ranching did not take up so much of the Basin that it displaced a great many Native Americans; most were able to retreat to more remote locations where they could avoid extensive contact with Euro-Americans. And some attached themselves to the White settlers, working as ranch hands (Malouf 1974:126).

In the vicinity of Austin, Nevada, during the mid-1860s, natives were working on ranches, riding horses, and living in White-style housing. The local newspaper, the *Reese River Reveille*, seemed convinced that Euro-American civilization had only a positive effect on native cultures: "The occupancy of the country directly benefits the Indian even without cost to the white. The cast off clothing and waste provisions, that he as a scavenger appropriates, are greater luxuries than he ever before enjoyed" (Clewlow, Wells, and Ambro 1978:15–16,18–22). Native Americans did not always prefer the amenities of White society, however. Groups of Indians from western and central Nevada traveled to California in order to work on ranches or in the mines, learning

510

MALOUF AND FINDLAY

English enough so that one Indian agent could speak of them as "domesticated" (Nissen 1982:129), but they frequently returned to their native habitat. Native Americans were commonly not satisfied with working for Whites and, to the dismay of many Euro-Americans, simply would not adapt to new means of subsistence so long as they could get by in some other way (J.H. Simpson 1876:85–86, 106; Malouf 1966:22–23).

American settlers were disappointed when Indians did not adopt "civilized" styles of living and complained that the natives often expected too much from the White men. Some had learned from the Euro-Americans how to beg, to demand a "toll" from Whites who passed through their territory, and to offer their services at exorbitant fees. Most Whites scorned such behavior, but a few realized where new habits had been learned. When William Wright's party traveled the Carson Sink and came to a Northern Paiute village, the Indians demanded payment for access to their drinking water. One old chief explained bitterly where the custom had originated: "'It was a *dirty whiteman's trick*, and he would see that it was not again repeated.' He said that they had caught the idea by seeing water sold at some of the wells on the deserts" (W. Wright 1963:10, 38, 140–142).

This incident typified the dilemma faced by Indians in the 1850s. On the one hand their traditional culture was being undermined in a variety of ways—disease, depletion of food sources, military conflicts, introduction of White material culture. On the other hand, few could respect or adapt to the new culture introduced by Euro-Americans, and those that did accept White civilization were often scorned. Indian ways of life had not been appreciably threatened by Spaniards' and Mexicans' weak claims to the Great Basin. When the United States began to claim and occupy the Great Basin, natives had either to resist the newcomers or to adapt to survive within the strange culture.

A clear record of escalating Indian–White interaction is the sequence of shifts seen in aspects of native material culture, entailing changes in form, design, technique of manufacture, and range of materials used (fig. 8). In many instances, traded goods simply replaced native counterparts. In other instances, whole new classes of artifacts with no aboriginal forerunners were made entirely from imported materials. Metal was highly sought after by the Indians for everything from jewelry to weapons and tools. White traders were also quick to procure and supply stone, shell, and other traditional materials and finished products, reaping profits upon restoration of disrupted native routes of supply.

Mining

The discovery of silver on the Comstock lode launched a tremendous migration to western Nevada in the late 1850s and 1860s that disrupted Indian cultures far more

Natl. Arch.: top, Cartographic Branch, RG 77, 120–2; bottom, 77–F–149–9–11.
Fig. 7. Capt. James H. Simpson's expedition in Utah, 1859. top, Gosiute brush dwelling in Pleasant Valley near the present Utah-Nev. border encountered while exploring for wagon routes. Although he commented that these "wretched looking creatures" relied mostly on traditional means of subsistence, Simpson complained of their "thievish disposition" toward Whites' livestock, an indication that aboriginal sources of food were becoming scarce. He also noted that the Gosiutes "have until recently recognized no chief. Now, at the instigation of the government, they have elected one, but as yet do not know how to respect him" (J.H. Simpson 1876:52–54). Watercolor by H.V.A. Von Beckh, 1859. bottom, Utes including Arrapene (Sinnearoach), the head chief of the tribe, and Luke the interpreter. This is one of the earliest surviving photographs of Great Basin people (J.H. Simpson 1876:8). Photographed on the outskirts of Camp Floyd, Jan. 1859.

quickly and thoroughly than previous Euro-American influxes to the Basin. Trappers and Mormons had also come upon the scene suddenly and seriously undermined native patterns of subsistence, but they had been more careful to cultivate friendly relations with Indians as they went about remaking the landscape. Miners, in contrast, pursued their fortunes in a more single-minded fashion. Their goal was to dig the ore from the earth as rapidly as possible, using as much of any local natural resources as they needed. They generally had no intention of remaining in what they regarded as a barren environment, and they consequently saw little need to protect the natural setting or maintain peaceful relations with Native Americans. And while trappers and Mormons had generally relied upon their own resources in their dealings with Indians, miners depended upon federal troops and Indian agents to cope with the problems that mining generated. A new era of strained re-

top left, U. of Calif., Bancroft Lib., Berkeley: 1905.16894. 21-Pic; Smithsonian, Dept. of Anthr.: a, 200,954; b, 200,948, 200,953; c, 200,949; d, 200,950; e–f, 211,049; g, 200,465; h. 200,463; i, 200,464; j, 272,213; k, 210,987; l, Colo. Histl. Soc., Denver: H-A3.2–2.9.

Fig. 8. Postcontact changes in material culture. top left, Indian agent John Moss with Southern Paiute chief Tercherrum. The Indian's attire—rabbitskin cloak, fringed leggings, cloth shirt—and rifle indicate the extent to which Euro-American goods had modified traditional material culture. Photograph by d'Heureuse at Camp Mohave, on the Colorado River, Ariz., about 1866. a, Tin earrings strung on brass wire. Called danglers, tinklers, cones, or earbobs, these ornaments were common trade items. Collected from Eastern Shoshone before 1899. b, Earrings strung on brass wire (left to right): brass bullet button, brass pendant plated in silver, cowrie shell. Collected from Eastern Shoshone before 1899. c–d, Abalone pendants strung on brass wire. Abalone, a valued trade item in aboriginal times, was also an important item supplied by White traders. Collected from Eastern Shoshone before 1899. e–f, Beaded pouches of commerical leather designed to hold mirrors, strike-a-lights, and ration tickets. Pouch on left has bone or antler buttons, and one on right, a commercial metal button inscribed "Mode de Paris." Collected from Eastern Shoshone before 1899. g, Trade butcher knife and ornamented sheath. The blade bears the mark "J. Ward Atlas Works." The wooden handle is probably Indian-made. The sheath is rawhide, riveted with brass tacks. The stroud strip and seed beads are sewed with both sinew and commercial cotton thread. Collected from Eastern Shoshone before 1899. h, Hand-wrought bowie knife and painted and beaded rawhide sheath. The knife has a wooden handle, iron guard, and false edge, with no maker's mark. Collected from Eastern Shoshone before 1899. i, Trade butcher knife with a belt and sheath of harness leather. The wooden handle is probably aboriginal. Collected from Eastern Shoshone before 1899. j, Ute woman's panel belt of saddle leather, ornamented with seed beads and brass tacks. Panel belts, which do not seem to have any native prototype, are characteristically made entirely of trade goods. Collected in Utah before 1912. k, Ute man's concho belt. The conchos are German silver; the belt, harness leather. As the custom of wearing hairplates declined in the 1870s, the plates or conchos came to be mounted on leather belts, men's belts lacking the added pendant of conchos displayed on the women's. Collected in Utah about 1900. l, Iron-handled brass kettle, one of a lot issued as annuities in the 1870s to Utes at the White River Agency, Colo. Length of f, 12.0 cm; a–e to same scale. Length of knife, g, 25.5 cm; h–l to same scale.

lations between indigenous peoples and newcomers in the Basin had begun.

Comstock miners affected Indian societies in many ways (fig. 9), but their most important impact was the depletion of resources upon which the Washoe and Northern Paiute had relied for subsistence. The sudden appearance of an urban mining settlement drained the countryside of its natural wealth. Mountain slopes were deforested as lumbermen felled trees in order to provide wood for mine shafts, railroad tracks, housing, and fuel. Heavy logging increased the extent of erosion, flooding, and fires, depleted the stock of pine nuts, destroyed the habitat of the mountain sheep, and drove away large game animals that Indians had hunted. Miners also reduced freshwater resources through the overfishing, damming, diverting, and silting of local streams. As the need to feed miners produced a sizable market for foodstuffs, farmers and ranchers also came to the Comstock and occupied lands that Indians had once used for gathering food resources. Ranchers' herds trampled and consumed wild grasses until they died off, often to be replaced by sagebrush and non-native weeds. The number of livestock in Nevada grew tremendously when a drought in California in the early 1860s drove large herds of sheep into the Basin for the first time (Nye in ARCIA 1862:111; Nissen 1982:70–75, 136; Downs 1966:76–77). In the short space of a few years, these events altered an ecology that had supported Native Americans for centuries.

The development of Comstock mining was felt most strongly by Indians in western Nevada and eastern California, but it had repercussions throughout the Great Basin. The sudden influx of Euro-Americans heightened the pressure on virtually all native cultures. It was no accident that the rapid increase of mining coincided with an era of intensified military hostilities between Whites and Indians throughout the intermontane West,

from Owens Valley, California, to the Bear River in Idaho. Fighting was not the only Indian reaction to incursions into their territory. Some responded by fleeing, others by accepting aspects of White civilization. Additionally, the increase in tensions generated new government efforts to contain and protect Native American tribes, resulting in the establishment of new forts, Indian agencies, and reservations. In short, the rise of mining on the Comstock had an enormous impact on Indians throughout the Great Basin.

In the immediate vicinity of the silver mines around Virginia City, the responses of native groups varied. Often faced with the prospect of substantially reduced food resources, many Northern Paiutes were able to resist and flee the White influx, but some Northern

Nev. Histl. Soc., Reno.: 704.

Fig. 9. Northern Paiute village, Virginia City, Nev., with mine dump in the background. Indian settlement, adjacent to the railroad (tracks in foreground) and apparently away from White residences, attests to the participation of Indians in developing the Comstock Lode in western Nev. Photograph by William Cann, 1891.

513

Paiutes and numerous Washoes accommodated the new culture and joined the White economy (Downs 1966:78–85, 1963:122–123, 130–131). The rapidly growing society of the Comstock absorbed many Indians who labored on farms and ranches, cut trees and sold timber, hunted and fished for the market, and sometimes begged, stole, and scavenged in order to sustain themselves. Indians in some respects thus became partly acculturated to White ways. However, by assigning Indians to the most menial positions (fig. 10), segregating their housing, and failing to provide for their welfare, Comstock society served notice that Indians would be regarded as inferior (Downs 1966:76–84; Hattori 1975:16–17).

Conflict and Accommodation

Like other Basin Indians who had begun to participate in the Euro-American economy, natives subsisting on the Comstock foreshadowed the eventual acceptance of Euro-American society that all tribes reached. However, around 1860 numerous Indian groups determined to resist the inroads of Whites. This widespread response was epitomized by the actions of Northern Paiutes in the vicinity of Pyramid Lake and the Humboldt Sink. These groups had lost substantial portions of their traditional bases of subsistence over the years, and as increasing numbers of Whites poured into Nevada, they felt even more threatened by the presence of newcomers. By late 1859, one Indian agent reported, depletion of traditional food sources had reduced the Indians to either thieving from Whites or dying from hunger (Dodge

Nev. State Mus., Carson City: 1867–G–84 P-1.
Fig. 10. Susie, a Western Shoshone, washing clothes. She worked for the Maute family from 1876 until 1900. Photographed in Belmont, Nev., about 1890s.

514

in ARCIA 1860:376); but the Whites continued to abuse the Indians without regard for their plight. The harsh winter conditions of 1859–1860 reduced the availability of food even further, prompting raids on White settlements. Tensions eventually erupted into the two battles known as the Pyramid Lake War of 1860, which did not prove Euro-American military superiority but did assert White domination over the Indians in western Nevada and prompted the formation of reservations for them (Nissen 1982:133–134; Angel 1881:149–163; F. Egan 1972; Hays 1860:89).

Two Indian–White conflicts that occurred in the central and western Great Basin around the same time, for roughly the same reasons, ended similarly. Construction of 22 stations of the overland stage route at watering holes located throughout Gosiute territory, and continued migration and settlement along the upper Humboldt River in Western Shoshone territory, prompted Indian attacks on settlers, stations, and soldiers in 1860 and 1863. The disputes were settled by the Treaty of Tooele Valley in 1863 (Johnson 1975:32; Greer et al. 1981:103; Malouf 1974:124–134). In the Owens Valley, the sudden appearance of miners and stockmen with large herds during the early 1860s led to diminished food resources. The "Owens Valley War" broke out between 1862 and 1864 and resulted in the removal of Indians to a reservation at Fort Tejon, California (Steward and Wheeler-Voegelin 1974:128–129,156; Nissen 1982:137–138; Angel 1881:166–168).

In each case of military conflict, Whites had placed increasing pressure on natives' natural resources and cultural integrity, and Indians had responded by raiding stations and settlements. In each case, a series of small attacks developed into a "war" of two or more pitched battles, usually won by soldiers who had been summoned to the area to protect White settlers and miners. Hostilities commonly prompted the establishment of forts to ensure a strong military presence in the Great Basin, and federal authorities repeatedly suggested that reservations would solve the problems that settlers and Indians faced.

The organization of Indians into military parties marked the culmination of the development of "predatory bands" in the Great Basin, a common Indian response to Euro-American incursions. Acquisition of the horse had permitted a few groups of Utes and Eastern Shoshones to develop mounted bands by the eighteenth century, helping to recast the balance of power among indigenous tribes, but most Great Basin peoples retained their comparatively loose social organization until the arrival of large numbers of Whites during the mid-nineteenth century. As Whites took over increasing amounts of land, Indians were forced onto smaller parcels and thus compelled to cooperate with one another more extensively. In addition, as the Indians lost more of their traditional subsistence resources, they formed both mounted and unmounted bands in order to raid White settlements for food and other resources. Finally, Whites themselves encouraged the formation of predatory bands by viewing Indian groups as "nations" and attempting to recognize "chiefs" as their leaders (Manners 1974:33–35, 212–214, 267; Euler 1972:71; Steward and Wheeler-Voegelin 1974:20–22, 75, 115–116, 241; Steward 1974:44, 47; Harris 1940:76–84).

Indians, naturally, did not see their society as being as rigidly ordered as the newcomers did; leaders whom the Whites recognized as "chiefs" tended to have much less influence than Whites supposed (Remy and Brenchley 1861, 1:146; Steward and Wheeler-Voegelin 1974:320–323). Nonetheless, in resisting the incursions of Whites, Indians devised new levels of social organization that strengthened their response to changing conditions. The important role of horses in these bands decreased after the military defeats of the early 1860s (Downs 1966:70), and the band generally declined as a form of social organization at that time. In many cases Indians reverted to the small groups they had known prior to the introduction of the horse.

Armed conflict between Whites and Indians brought the plight of Basin Indians to the attention of federal authorities. Prior to 1860 the government had spent money primarily to pacify the natives, not to secure their welfare (Malouf 1974:113). Now, the conclusion of several battles resulted in treaties that promised reservations. Indians generally sought a reservation land base within their traditional territory (Euler and Fowler 1973:92–93; O.C. Stewart 1978:81, 84), expecting secure title to the lands they were assigned; however, the process of establishing reservations and guaranteeing the provisions of treaties often worked against natives' hopes. The quality of federal officials assigned to the Indians varied from very good to very bad, and agents often did not have much support from the Office of Indian Affairs or from other bureaus of national and local government. Indian agents pleaded constantly for more resources, and, as the territorial governor of Nevada noted, led the Indians "to expect more from the government than it would be possible to perform" (Nye in AR-CIA 1862:109–110). In addition, reservations and Indian agents could not stop the outbreak of hostilities, as the Bannock War of 1878 illustrated. Growing numbers of Whites continued to threaten Native Americans, treaties were disregarded, Indian agents often proved unpopular and ineffective, and resentment between Euro-Americans and Indians persisted (Brimlow 1938:211–212).

Of the many groups that suffered from unenforced or unratified treaties and appropriation of lands assigned to them (for example, B.D. Madsen 1980:40; S.W. Hopkins 1883:76–87; Danziger 1974:62–63; Malouf 1974:120–140; Johnson 1975:28, 105), the experience of the Western Shoshone may have been typical. Garland Hurt's treaty of 1855 promised the Western

U. of Nev. Reno, Special Coll.: 217-A.
Fig. 11. Carte de visite of the Northern Paiute Chief Winnemucca. Used as business and calling cards, these photographs were popular in the 1860s. Although Winnemucca is shown in a Napoleonic pose wearing a military uniform, feather headdress, and nose ornament, Indian chiefs generally had neither the authority nor the warlike character that Whites believed they possessed. Photographed about 1860s.

Shoshone a reserve in Ruby Valley, Nevada, but was never ratified by Congress; another document signed in 1863 promised to establish two reservations on traditional lands, but the properties were not set aside until 1877, years after Whites had already taken some of the better parcels for themselves. Then, the reserve that stood inside traditional Western Shoshone territory was gradually given away to Whites, leaving the natives with one plot of land that lay outside the Indians' former homelands (Inter-Tribal Council of Nevada 1976b:45–46,67; Harris 1940:79–80,86–87). Reservations hardly delivered the security and separation from Whites that had been promised.

Prospects for Indians in the Basin thus remained uncertain as they entered the reservation era. The influence of Euro-American groups over more than two centuries left Indian groups in a precarious position as they grew increasingly dependent on White society. Di-

515

minished by war and disease and threatened by the subversion of ancient ways of life, Indians struggled to retain traditional cultures at the same time that they adapted to the permanent presence of Whites. While some groups adjusted by scattering to remote locations in order to subsist in old fashions, others lived on reserves and among Whites and responded to environmental changes by participating in the White economy and adopting several Euro-American customs. No longer able to migrate, hunt, and gather successfully, the majority of Basin Indians became increasingly sedentary. They worked for ranchers, mine owners, and farmers, accepted more elements of White civilization, and looked for niches in White society that permitted them the most latitude for sustaining their autonomy (Malouf 1974:139–141; Hattori 1975:5; Euler and Fowler 1973:65–69; Clemmer 1978:62–63; Laird 1976:19–20,44). Retention of traditional ways proceeded best in those parts of the Basin where the impact of Whites was least felt and in those aspects of society least influenced by White material culture.

The limited resources of the region served both to help and to hinder the natives' cause. Because Whites viewed much of the Basin as a barren area, they did not penetrate it very thoroughly through the nineteenth century, leaving some pockets of space for Indians. The Gosiute locality of Deep Creek, for example, served as a focus for traditional social life among the Western Shoshone and Gosiute because it did not initially attract much Euro-American attention (Malouf 1974:152–153).

The impact of Euro-American cultures on the Great Basin Indians differed from group to group and from region to region, but in every instance White activities disrupted and ultimately weakened traditional cultures in the basin. As the presence of Euro-Americans grew stronger, from the indirect introduction of the Spanish horse to the rapid influx of Comstock miners, threats to native peoples mounted until conflicts of the 1850s and 1860s resolved tensions in favor of White society. In responding to each new historic activity in the Great Basin, Indian groups distanced themselves increasingly from their precontact heritage. After the defeats of the early 1860s, only one paradoxical course of action seemed available to Indians striving to preserve their ethnicity. In order to survive as distinct cultural entities in a drastically modified world, they were compelled to accept certain elements of White economic life and political organization.

The Introduction of the Horse

DEMITRI B. SHIMKIN

The history of the horse in the Great Basin can be divided into four periods: initial dispersion (1640–1706), the rise of equestrian societies on the High Plains (1706–1752), the rise of the horse and trading cultures in the Great Basin (1753–1830), and the epoch of collapse (1830–1911).

Initial Dispersion

Juan de Oñate's establishment of Spanish rule in New Mexico, 1597–1610, was facilitated by the importation of several hundred horses and, later, by the extensive use of Indian, especially Pueblo, slaves as herdsmen. Horses were rapidly dispersed by Spanish settlement, by escaped Indians, and by being captured by unconquered tribes. It is likely that Ute captives obtained knowledge of horses by 1637–1641 (Forbes 1959:200) and that Utes escaping from Spanish peonage first spread horses north of the Colorado River. In any case, by the 1650s the Utes were using pack horses as well as dog travois as groups of a thousand or more people followed buffalo herds on the High Plains, although they did not yet ride the horses (S.L. Tyler 1951:161).

The Pueblo Revolt of 1680 provided a major opportunity for the Utes to acquire livestock from the Eastern Pueblos (Twitchell 1914, 2:277) and resulted in the accelerated dispersion of horses to their neighbors. To the west, between 1683 and 1698 Father Eusebio Kino established extensive stock ranching throughout the Papago and Pima country south of the Gila River (Bolton 1919, 1:56–57).

Equestrian Societies on the High Plains

On the High Plains the use of horses characterized two closely related peoples of Basin origin who early developed equestrian societies, the Shoshone in the north and the Comanche in the south. The Comanche-Shoshone peoples, who had already been moving onto the High Plains in the protohistoric period, had horses by the early eighteenth century and expanded eastward over a vast area that ultimately extended from the South Saskatchewan River in the north to the Red River in the south. This mass migration was accompanied by the adoption of additional elements of Plains culture, by the acceptance of elements of material and social culture from the Spaniards and later the northern fur traders, and by increasingly bitter intertribal warfare.

The Comanche–Shoshone shift to an equestrian society appears to have taken place very rapidly. In the 1720s the Shoshone in southern Saskatchewan were still fighting their enemies the Blackfeet entirely on foot, but by the 1730s besides fighting on foot behind lines of three-foot shields, they were using horses in raids. Within a few more years warfare shifted entirely to a pattern of ambushes and mounted raids and skirmishes as the Blackfeet acquired guns and metal weapons as well as increasing number of horses captured from the Shoshone themselves (D. Thompson 1916:327–335). By the 1740s the Shoshone (or undifferentiated Comanche-Shoshone) of north-central Wyoming were using horse-mounted warriors in full-scale attacks on villages (Burpee 1927:411–412; Hultkrantz 1968:63–65). Comanches, initially accompanying Utes on trading and raiding expeditions against the Spaniards, first became known in New Mexico in 1706. After acquiring horses beginning about this time, by 1727 they dominated the High Plains between the Arkansas and the Missouri, displacing the Apache (Auerbach 1943:24–26; A.B. Thomas 1966:61, 209–217).

By the end of the eighteenth century the horses and guns of their enemies and the devastation of smallpox

Natl. Park Service, Capitol Reef Natl. Monument, Torrey, Utah.
Fig. 1. Historic pictographs of horses, mounted riders, and figure with shield and lance or spear, Grand Wash, Capitol Reef National Monument, Torrey, Utah. Photographed in 1971–1972.

had so weakened the northeastern groups of Shoshone that their range had contracted considerably, and entire bands had disappeared. The Flathead and Nez Perce had traditions, referring apparently to the eighteenth century, of Shoshone on the upper Yellowstone and east to the Bighorn Mountains, "or beyond." A large Shoshone band was said to have lived at one time near Fort Benton on the Upper Missouri (about 47°50′ north latitude, 110°30′ west longitude) and another one "still farther north" (Teit 1930:303–305). The tradition of Shoshone on the Yellowstone is confirmed by Larocque's firsthand account of 1805 (Burpee 1910:42). In that year the Northern Shoshone were already taking refuge in the Columbia River Basin during the summer (Thwaites 1904–1905, 2:373).

Meriwether Lewis and William Clark provide detailed information on the use of the horse and associated aspects of culture among the Northern Shoshone of the Missouri–Columbia divide at this time, perhaps at the inception of their retreat to the west (Thwaites 1904–1905, 2:329–383, 3:19–32). This band, numbering about 400, had nearly 700 horses and about 20 mules, many with Spanish brands.

Each warrior kept one or more horses tied to a stake near his tepee, day and night, to be ready to fight at a moment's notice on horseback. For horsegear, the young men rarely used more than a bit-halter and a small pad of dressed leather stuffed with hair, which was cinched around the horse's belly. However, favorite horses were frequently painted, their ears cut into various shapes, and their manes and tails, which were neither drawn nor cut, decorated with feathers and other ornaments. The Shoshone were excellent horsemen, skilled in lassoing running animals. In battle, riders and horses were protected by a kind of armor formed of many folds of antelope hide joined by glue and sand. Warriors used tactical mounted formations including column and charging line, the line led by chiefs.

Saddles for women and the elderly were of Spanish type. Two flat thin boards that fit along the horse's back were joined front and back by the pommel and cantle, which were set on edge so as to flare outward. A buffalo

Yale U., The Beinecke Rare Book and Manuscript Lib., Western Americana Coll.

Fig. 2. *Racing—near Wind River Mountains*. Horse racing was one of the main recreational events at the annual Green River, Wyo., trade rendezvous, which was attended by some 3,000 Indians, mostly Eastern and Northern Shoshones. Riders were usually young men who wore only breechclouts and rode bareback. Mawoma, in the foreground wearing an eagle feather headdress, was a prominent Eastern Shoshone chief. Cropped view; pencil, pen and ink, and watercolor by Alfred Jacob Miller, 1837.

hide with the hair on served as saddle blanket. The saddle might also be furnished with leather-covered wooden stirrups and a loose leather covering. Bits and stirrups were obtained from the Spaniards. The women were in charge of the pack animals.

The Shoshone assigned particular value to horses in certain contexts. War honors were given for individually stealing enemy horses, and the bride price given in the marriage of infant girls was usually in horses or in mules, which were considered much more valuable.

The Horse in the Great Basin

By the end of the eighteenth century a series of equestrian Numic peoples having a variety of contacts and interactions extended from the Comanche on the High Plains through the Shoshone to the Northern Paiute in the Great Basin, and by 1830 horses and horsemanship had spread in the Basin to all ecologically possible areas. The factors that brought about this situation were the conclusion of peace between the Spaniards and the Comanche in 1786, the westward movement of the Plains Shoshone and the attendant development of extensive trade networks, military pressures from mounted Plateau tribes of the Columbia River, the opening of the southeastern Great Basin in 1776 by the Silvestre Vélez de Escalante–Francisco Atanasio Domínguez expedition, and the Spanish colonization of California after 1769.

A distant consequence of the conclusion of peace with the Comanche was the re-establishment of at least intermittent Spanish trade contacts as far north as the Shoshone bands on the Snake River of Idaho and on the Yellowstone (Thwaites 1904–1905, 2:347; Burpee 1910:42). But the locus of Eastern Shoshone society from the beginning of the nineteenth century until the secondary advance of the 1850s was deep in the Rocky Mountains (Murphy and Murphy 1960; Shimkin 1947). Occasionally, the Eastern Shoshone even had their fall encampments as far west as Great Salt Lake, where Beckwourth (1931) observed an encampment of 600 lodges of "Snake" Indians and the construction of a large "medicine lodge," perhaps an early Sun Dance.

As early as 1805, Lewis and Clark found that the Shoshone, Nez Perce, Yakima, Wishram, and a number of other tribes between the headwaters of the Columbia River drainage and the great Indian trading center at The Dalles had immense numbers of horses of "excellent race" (Thwaites 1904–1905, 4:76). At least in some cases the Columbia Basin tribes obtained their horses by raiding the Shoshone (Thwaites 1904–1905, 4:280–281).

In general, the horse stimulated trade, raiding, and slaving as far west as the Klamath of Oregon (Spier 1930:39–43). Through these hostile actions the Columbia River tribes began to press southward against the Northern Paiute and Shoshone. By the 1820s the Shoshone had been displaced into adverse brushland and were harassed by continuing raids (Ray et al. 1938).

left, Kansas State Histl. Soc., Topeka; right, Colo. Histl. Soc., Denver: E 463.

Fig. 3. left, Eastern Shoshone man on horseback, with what appears to be a bow and quiver. He is using a blanket but no saddle. Photograph by Albert Bierstadt, Nebr. Terr., 1859. right, Navajo saddle blanket of handspun, single ply wool in blue, red, indigo, cochineal, and natural white. Twill weave saddle blankets were common items of exchange among the Ute. Eastern Shoshone–Navajo trade was reported for 1826 (Thwaites 1904–1907, 18:138–139) and for 1842 (Hamilton 1905:97). This specimen is said to have belonged to Ute chief Colorow in the 1870s. Length 117 cm.

a

b

c

d

e

top right, Smithsonian, NAA: 1511; Colo. Histl. Soc., Denver: a, E 1325; b, E 1854; Denver Mus. of Nat. Hist., Colo.: c, 4083; e, 158; d, Idaho State U., Idaho Mus. of Nat. Hist, Pocatello: 5336.

Fig. 4. Horse equipment. top right, Ute man at the Los Pinos Agency, Colo., wearing a long eagle feather headdress, a type associated with travel on horseback. His horse equipment includes a non-Indian saddle with leather stirrups and a quirt. Photograph by William Henry Jackson, 1874. a, Saddle bag, buckskin with a canvas back, lazy-stitched with blue, red, green, yellow, and white seed beads. Tin jinglers holding red-dyed horsehair line the side panels and the cover flap. The bag has bands of quillwork, dyed in alternating orange, purple, and yellow sections. Said to have belonged to Southern Ute chief Ignacio, collected on the Southern Ute Reservation, Colo., 1890–1915. b, Ute double saddle bag of beaded and fringed buckskin sewn over a thick canvas backing. Red stroud tacked down by silver-colored studs outlines the side and top, and brass hawk bells line the bottom. The design is in glass seed beads and metal faceted beads with background in white and elements in red, dark and light blue, translucent green, waxy yellow, and green. The beaded band at the top-back of the saddlebag is white, with cross motifs in orange, dark blue, and light blue seed beads, and faceted brass beads. Presumably made before 1915. c, Beaded armband-quirt combination. The quirt is braided leather and buckskin. Collected from the Ute in Utah. d, Incised and carved elk antler quirt. Rattlesnakes, elk, antelope, bison, eagles, coyotes, and deer are portrayed on the handle, and the head of a squirrel carved on the stub of the prong. Collected before 1900, Fort Hall Reservation, Idaho. e, Rawhide horse hobble, braided and twisted, with knots at one end. Collected from the Ute in Utah. Width of a 49 cm, rest same scale.

Peter Skene Ogden reported encountering in 1828 and 1829 mounted parties of 200 and 300 non-Numic warriors in the environmentally adverse areas on the Humboldt River in Nevada and near the Humboldt Sink (Williams 1971:108–109, 153). Layton (1981) has plausibly conjectured that pressure from the ecological competition of horse bands and, above all, the impact of slaving depopulated parts of the northwestern Basin by the 1820s.

Apparently for ecological reasons, the Gosiute Shoshones near the Great Salt Lake and other groups of the desert and desert margins were little affected by the spread of equestrianism, with the possible exception of some growth of political leadership (Chamberlin 1908; Steward 1943a). In such areas the maintenance of relatively large populations required a flexible economy based on a full range of plant exploitation that was not compatible with the ecological wastefulness of equestrianism and the concentration of power necessary for the effective use of horses in warfare (Euler 1966; Shimkin 1947; Shimkin and Reid 1970).

Nevertheless, the explorations into just such marginal-subsistence areas by the Escalante-Domínguez expedition—in part following old Hopi trade routes (Hunt 1953:18)—were particularly important in opening the Great Basin to trade and to horses. The region near Utah Lake reached by the expedition in September 1776 was just beyond the equestrian frontier, but the presence of a "chief leader" among the Utes there suggests that influence from horse-using groups may have led to an increased complexity in political organization (Auerbach 1943:66–68).

The Escalante-Domínguez expedition reached the Virgin River in southwestern Utah, intersecting aboriginal trade routes to both the Colorado River Yumans and the Hopi. Its findings were promptly disseminated, and Francisco Garcés evaluated their implications for communications between New Mexico and California in 1777, pointing out that the Utes encountered by the expedition were in contact with the Chemehuevi (Coues 1900:475). Moreover, while the Ute country remained officially closed to travel and trade for 40 more years, clandestine trade, centered in the *genízaro* village of Abiquiu, New Mexico, thrived. What were called Jedediah Strong Smith's discoveries in the 1820s and the formal opening of the Spanish Trail between Santa Fe and Los Angeles in 1830 simply gave official recognition and sanction to longstanding communication routes.

On the opposite side of the Great Basin there was some diffusion of horses into the area from the Spanish settlements in California or through Indian groups in contact with them. There were no horses in Alta California before the founding of San Diego in 1769. In his reconnaissance of 1775–1776 Francisco Garcés found that although some horses were present on the lower Colorado, the Diegueño and apparently the Mohave

and Chemehuevi lacked them, the Mohave declaring that "the nations of the north" had them; to the south and east the Pima had horses and the Yavapai had some from the Hopi (Coues 1900:104, 197, 337–339, 428, 466). However, horses quickly increased in number in California and diffused to Indians in the San Joaquin Valley and beyond, who often used them for food (Chapman 1916:427; Cook 1960:255, 267, 270). The Panamint Shoshone stole horses for food from their neighbors the Tubatulabal, who bought them in the Chumash missions on the coast (Voegelin 1938:22).

In consequence of these factors the horse was apparently an element of Great Basin Indian culture, even in marginal areas, by the early nineteenth century. The horse stimulated cultural elaboration, trade, and warfare but also depleted limited range capacities, often competing directly for the Indians' seed supplies. Mobile bands, cavalry warfare, chieftainship, and allied traits were present as an unstable admixture to the simpler institutions of foot Indians. Except in a few localities, equestrianism was limited by shortages of fodder and water. Its most destructive ultimate effect was the facilitating of Anglo-American trapping and settlement, and it was to be eliminated or transformed into a vehicle of hopeless resistance as trappers penetrated and devastated the area (Hafen 1965, 1).

Collapse

The establishment of the great routes of commerce and emigration, beginning with the formal opening of the Spanish Trail in 1830, accelerated this process of destruction. The Spanish Trail burdened the uplands and deserts with the grazing and watering of as many as 5,000 animals in a season, and after 1847 Mormon settlement pre-empted prime Indian lands, precipitating futile conflict and general Indian depopulation. By 1853, peaceful Mormon colonization and conciliation had been replaced by war, in which Wakara's Utes were crushed (P.D. Bailey 1954:98, 128, 137–149). The Utes, as well as the hapless Southern and Northern Paiutes, began increasingly to be subjugated. In some eastern areas hostilities, the reduction of food supplies, and diseases virtually eliminated the Indian population (Woodbury 1944:122).

Environmental differences and antecedent subsistence patterns shaped particular courses of history in different areas. The upper reaches of the Yellowstone and Sweetwater rivers and the broad zone between the Bear River and Klamath Lake to the west are shrub and grassland areas of moderate bearing capacity for grazing herds (Küchler 1964). Subsistence patterns mixed hunting, root gathering, and fishing in varying proportions. There, the advent of the horse led to equestrian societies engaged in long-distance hunting migrations, trade, and warfare. Pedestrian societies suffered from

a

b

c

d

e

f

g

the competition of mounted hunters (Wyeth 1851:208) and increasingly from Indian slave-raiding for local use and for The Dalles market on the Columbia (Spier 1930:39–40). By the 1820s horse transportation, largely supplied by mounts and pack animals from the Columbia River grasslands, permitted the rapid penetration of the Great Basin by British and American trappers, who all but exterminated the beaver and were a major factor in causing the disappearance of the buffalo in the Rockies and Great Basin within barely 20 years. After 1840 the development of the Oregon Trail burdened grazing resources with large numbers of livestock, killed off game, and displaced native groups from prime areas. This led to desperate acts of reprisal, which in turn justified the destruction of Indian "predatory bands."

In the central region of desert and shrubs, only the Humboldt River provided a convenient passageway between the Snake River country and California for Indian and White mounted parties. However, even in remote desert uplands native seed plots were vulnerable to the grazing of horses, mules, and later cattle and sheep (Shimkin and Reid 1970:174). Ecological vulnerability, political powerlessness, susceptibility to imported diseases, and the active assaults of settlers and miners reduced the native population by 1890 to remnants on tiny reservations, urban fringes, and White ranches.

The Colorado River Basin, settled by native farmers and plant gatherers, has been an area of longstanding equestrianism despite its limited pasture capacity. For a considerable period, the use of horses was seemingly on

a small scale, for clandestine trade, warfare, and especially slaving for the Spanish market (L.R. Bailey 1966:139–172), but after about 1820 it increased rapidly.

During the 1830s and 1840s the improvement of communications, the greater availability of game and other trade goods, and the personal influence of Anglo-American and New Mexican trappers and traders provided cultural stimulation to the Utes and the Eastern Shoshone. At the same time these tribes were faced with a sharp decline in buffalo and other game. Slave raiding and trading, the theft of horses from California, and hazardous expeditions on the Great Plains provided substitute resources, but at the price of ever more costly conflicts with the Californians and with the Arapaho, Cheyenne, and Sioux (P.D. Bailey 1954:58, 63, 64; Frémont 1845:47, 174). The Ute were pressed westward from the High Plains grasslands by the advancing Arapaho, their mounted bands raiding under Wakara's leadership as far west as Los Angeles.

The Eastern Shoshone alone, under the astute leadership of Washakie, retained a relatively favorable military, economic, and demographic status until the 1870s. Then even they fell into severe decline (Shimkin 1942). By 1890, the U.S. government itself said: "The material condition of the Shoshones is easily summed up: they are poor as they can be and live" (U.S. Census Office. 11th Census 1894:631).

The last echo of the equestrian culture of the Shoshone was encountered in the tiny bands of Indians that maintained up to the eve of World War I a wild independence involving an increasing amount of stock rus-

a, Colo. Histl. Soc., Denver: E 1853; b, Smithsonian, Dept. of Anthr.: 11,035; U. of Pa., U. Mus., Philadelphia: c, 38191; f, L–73–4; Mus. of the Amer. Ind., Heye Foundation, New York: d, 23/4022; g, 15/6994; e, Milwaukee Public Mus., Wis: 21988/5293.

Fig. 5. Indian saddles and accoutrements. a, Nontraditional woman's saddle with a rawhide-covered wood frame incorporating pieces of western saddles. Traditional elements include buckskin fringes and brass tacks at the pommel and cantle. The stirrups are Indian-made, attached to the saddle by commercial harness straps, and the pattern of rigging is typically Indian. A skirt of tooled, machine-stitched leather replaces the grass-filled pads tied below the saddle frame. The 2-piece cinch is canvas. This combination of Indian and White saddle and rigging elements is indicative of the rapid changes in native material culture during the late 19th century. Made before 1915. b, Typical Ute woman's frame saddle, covered with rawhide, thick hide brace or pad attached underneath the sideboards, commercial harness straps on the sideboards supporting harness rings, to which is attached a cloth-lined leather cinch, and wood frame stirrups covered in rawhide and suspended from rawhide straps. This saddle is also rigged with a poitrel, a leather strap with a padded collar that was passed around the horse's neck to keep the saddle from slipping backward. The pommel has the characteristic prong for suspension of a quirt or baggage. Collected by J.W. Powell among the Seuvarits Ute (west of the Green River, Utah), early 1870s. c, Buffalo-hide saddle cloth, ornamented with seed beads and buckskin fringes. Fancy saddle cloths were used by women of the Eastern Shoshone and some Plains tribes (Wissler 1915). Collected from the Southern Ute, 1891. d, Traditional man's pad saddle, the oldest form of Indian saddle, which probably diffused northward with the horse (Wissler 1915; Ewers 1980), perhaps modeled after a Spanish pack saddle that consisted of rawhide cushions stuffed with hay. The typical pad saddle consists of tanned hides cut in an hourglass shape sewn down the midline, and stuffed with buffalo or deer hair. Many pad saddles were also furnished with a rectangular piece of rawhide across the center of the pad to which could be attached stirrup straps. Beadwork replaced earlier use of porcupine quillwork. Collected from the Northern Shoshone. e, Northern Paiute pad saddle of less traditional form, incorporating a number of western saddle rigging elements. The pad is constructed as in d, but covered with a rectangular piece of canvas. The rigging is makeshift, utilizing a fender to which a rigging ring has been laced for attachment of the woven cinch and leather stirrup straps, probably of Indian manufacture. Collected by Samuel Barrett at Walker Lake, Nev., 1916. f, Crupper, beaded red stroud and buckskin sections sewn over a rawhide base, the edges hung with tin bangles and self fringes. The thong at the top would have been attached to the woman's saddle cantle, and the thongs at the bottom placed above and below the horse's tail, the fringes falling over the rump. Collected from the Ute, northeastern Utah, about 1875. g, Bridle with iron Spanish style ring bit and long, curved shanks. The headstall is buckskin with a loom-beaded band sewn over it. The reins are missing. Collected before 1927. a, 75 by 63 cm, b–f same scale; length of g, 11 cm.

tling and killing. Such a band was that of the Western Shoshone Mike Daggett and his family, which was pursued and destroyed in 1911 at Little High Rock Canyon, northwest Nevada, by a posse avenging the killing of four ranchers by Indians. Daggett was killed fighting in a Plains-style feathered war bonnet. At the Indians' camp was a willow-stake horse corral, and the children's toys found included in addition to dolls, toy horses made of baked clay (Layton 1977).

Sources

The standard treatments of the diffusion of the horse among the North American Indians are by Haines (1938, 1938a) and Secoy (1953). This chapter expands on the findings of Steward (1938:201–202, 248–250) for the Northern Shoshone, but the impact of the horse in the western and southern Great Basin was earlier and more profound than Steward believed.

Treaties, Reservations, and Claims

RICHARD O. CLEMMER AND OMER C. STEWART

The lands in the Great Basin were organized into United States territories in the mid-nineteenth century, beginning with Oregon in 1839 and ending with Wyoming in 1868. When each territory was established the federal government assumed the task of regulating relations with the Indians in that area. The officially declared Indian policy of the period was based on the premise that most western lands would be alienated from Indian occupancy or use and emphasized the establishment of reservations, in or near the Indians' aboriginal territories, as enclaves where they could be insulated from the influx of homesteaders, miners, and entrepreneurs while acquiring the agricultural and stock-raising skills necessary to survive as self-sufficient citizens. On the frontier, in contrast, reservations were regarded as providing containment for people whose cultures and even presence were considered a hindrance to the development of the local economy, and even so there was continual pressure to settle on or mine Indian land or to remove the Indians altogether to other parts of the country. By the same token, some Great Basin groups on land considered undesirable were left alone and have persisted to the present as sociopolitical and cultural entities without having reservations.

By 1855 several forces of change and disruption had thrust their way deeply into portions of the Great Basin. Caravans of homesteaders and later gold-seekers had turned the Oregon and Humboldt Trails and their offshoots into roads. Mormon settlement of Utah had been so successful that some politicians in Washington considered the State of Deseret to be a potential threat to the United States. And the official U.S. takeover of the Santa Fe Trail had accelerated a steady drift of traders and soldiers of fortune into the southeastern Basin. In this situation the U.S. government's first intention was to secure the loyalty of Indian groups that some feared might be swayed to allegiance with the Mormons (AR-CIA 1858:305–314) or with "hostile" Southwest and Plains Indians, such as Apaches, Sioux, Cheyennes, or Arapahoes, or might pose threats to U.S. citizens intruding into their territories.

A prerequisite for securing Indian loyalty was the identifying of the character, leadership, whereabouts, and territories of various groups. Therefore, the Bureau of Indian Affairs appointed some roving agents whose duty was to gather information and to maintain the good will of groups within their jurisdictions. A concurrent development was the establishment of military garrisons in major settlements and erection of permanent forts in more isolated areas that were on major routes of travel and also usually in the heart of aboriginal territories. Except for the occasional use of these forts for distribution of presents and later treaty annuities, there was never any particular coordination of military with Indian policy. In many instances, Indian agents and military authorities openly disagreed. On more than one occasion, military authorities negotiated agreements with Indian groups that went unacknowledged by civil authorities (table 1).

Many factors complicated the situation, including the varying backgrounds and motivations of the agents and other officials, and the influence of settlers, traders, and entrepreneurs. Many early agents had been trappers, traders, or army scouts. Some had religious backgrounds. Often, in the absence of guidelines, the personal predilections of agents had more impact than policies promulgated in Washington. Where there were substantial settlements, the settlers and traders often appealed to the nearest military garrison when they felt threatened or affronted by Indians, rather than to the Indian agent. Early policy toward the Indians in the Great Basin was thus extremely variable in its effects from place to place and even from month to month. Federal authority was present wherever U.S. military personnel were stationed, and local Indian policy was in principle an extension of federal policy to the extent possible, but beyond federal control local power groups acted out of narrower interests.

A consequence of this administrative unevenness was that different Basin groups received quite different treatments. A few were favored with distributions of material goods, while others received nothing at all. Some groups' leaders were accorded a diplomatic status akin to that of head of state and were visited by agents as if they were roving ambassadors, while other groups found themselves arbitrarily placed under the aegis of chiefs whom they did not acknowledge. Some groups were treated with promises and threats pertaining to cessions of land, protection from encroachment, creation of reservations, and government services, while other groups accommodated to situations that were unaccompanied by formal negotiations. Some groups lived

Table 1. Treaties and Agreements, 1846–1906

Year	Treaty	Group	Bands	Provisions
1846	Treaty of Santa Fe, unratified	Ute	Muache, Capote	peace and friendship
1849	Treaty of Abiquiu, ratified	Ute	Muache, Capote	peace and friendship, concessions
1852	Agreement of Salt Lake City	Eastern Shoshone	Washakie's	peace and friendship
1855	Garland Hurt's treaties, unratified	Ute	Pahvant, Sanpits, Timpanogots	peace and friendship, reservations, presents, concessions
		Gosiute	Deep Creek	
		Western Shoshone	White Knife	
1855	Treaties of Abiquiu, unratified	Ute	Muache, Capote	presents, reservations
1859	Jacob Forney's agreement, unratified	Western Shoshone	White Knife, Ruby Valley	peace and friendship, reservations, concessions, presents
1859	William Lander's agreement, unratified except for Eastern Shoshone	Northern Shoshone Bannock	Tukudeka, Snake River	peace and friendship, presents, annuities
		Northern Paiute Eastern Shoshone	Winnemucca's Washakie's	
1862	Warren Nye's agreement, unratified	Western Shoshone	Tutuwa's	equal sharing of resources between Indians and Whites
1863	Treaty with White River Utes, unratified	Ute	White River	concessions, presents
1863	Treaty of Conejos (with the "Tabeguache band"), ratified	Ute	Uncompahgre	peace and friendship, concessions, annuities
1863	Treaty of Tooele ("Tuilla") Valley, ratified	Gosiute	Deep Creek	peace and friendship, concessions, annuities
1863	Treaty of Ruby Valley, ratified	Western Shoshone	White Knife, others	peace and friendship, concessions, annuities
1863	Agreement of Ogden, unratified	Northern and Western Shoshone	Little Soldier's	peace and friendship, concessions, annuities
1863	Treaty of Soda Springs, ratified	Northern Shoshone, Bannocks	Snake River	peace and friendship, cession, annuities
1863	Treaty of Box Elder, ratified	Northern and Western Shoshone	Pocatello's, Sanpits's	peace and friendship, concessions, annuities
1863	Treaty of Fort Bridger, ratified	Eastern Shoshone	Washakie's	peace and friendship, concessions, annuities
1863	Treaty of Fort Churchill, unratified	Northern Paiute	Pyramid Lake, Walker River, others	peace and friendship, reservations
1864	Caleb Lyon's treaty, unratified	Northern Shoshone	Snake River	cession, reservation, annuities, procurement rights
1864	Treaty of Klamath Lake, ratified	Northern Paiute	Yahuskin	cession, reservation, annuities
1865	Treaty of Sprague River Valley, ratified	Northern Paiute	Walpapi	cession, reservation, presents
1865	Treaty of Spanish Fork, unratified	Ute, Southern Paiute	Pahvant, Uintah	cession, removal
1866	Caleb Lyon's treaty, unratified	Bannock	Bruneau Valley	cession, reservation, annuities, procurement rights
1866	Treaty of Hot Springs, Colo., unratified	Ute	Yampa	cession, annuities
1868	Treaty with the Ute, ratified	Ute	Uncompahgre, Muache, Capote, Weeminuche, Yampa, Parusanuch, Uintah	cessions, reservation, annuities

Table 1.   Treaties and Agreements, 1846–1906 (*continued*)

Year	Treaty	Group	Bands	Provisions
1868	Treaty of Fort Bridger, ratified	Northern Shoshone, Bannock Eastern Shoshone	Tukudeka, Snake River Washakie's	cession, reservation, annuities, procurement rights
1868	J.W.P. Huntington's treaty, unratified	Northern Paiute	Burns, Camp Smith, Ft. McDermitt	peace and friendship, reservation, annuities
1872	Brunot Agreement of Sept. 26, ratified	Eastern Shoshone	Washakie's	cession, annuities
1873	Brunot Agreement (San Juan Cession), ratified	Ute	Uncompahgre, Muache, Capote, Yampa, Parusanuch, Weeminuche, Uintah	cession, annuities
1878	Agreement of Pagosa Springs, unratified	Ute	Capote, Muache, Weeminuche	cession, reservation
1879	Agreement of Colorado Park, unratified	Ute	Uncompahgre	cession, removal, annuities, reservation
1880	Ute Cession, ratified	Ute	Uncompahgre, White River, Muache, Capote, Weeminuche	cession, removal, annuities
1880	Agreement of May 14, ratified	Northern Shoshone, Bannock	Lemhi, Fort Hall	cession, removal, annuities
1881	Agreement of July 18, ratified	Northern Shoshone, Bannock	Fort Hall	cession, annuities
1887	Agreement of May 27, ratified	Northern Shoshone, Bannock	Fort Hall	cession, annuities
1888	Agreement of Nov. 13, repealed Feb. 20, 1895	Ute	Weeminuche, Muache, Capote	cession, removal, annuities
1896	Agreement of April 21, ratified	Eastern Shoshone		cession, annuities
1898	Agreement of Feb. 5, ratified	Northern Shoshone, Bannock	Lemhi, Fort Hall	cession, reservation, annuities
1904	Agreement of April 21, ratified	Eastern Shoshone		cession, annuities
1906	Agreement of July 20, ratified	Northern Paiute	Walker River	cession, allotment

SOURCES: Abel 1915:92–96, 127–132, 208–209; Brunot et al. in ARCIA 1874:83–112; Bancroft 1889:313, 477, 634–635; Canfield 1983:27, 58–59; Hebard 1930:215; J.T. Hughes 1848:127; Institute for the Development of Indian Law 1973, 1975, 1975a; Inter-Tribal Council of Nevada 1976b:105–111; Johnson 1975:36; Kappler 1904–1941:585–587, 848–853, 856–860, 865–868, 876–878, 990–996, 1020–1024; Keleher 1952:80; Madsen 1980:31–32; Manners 1974:21–99; Nye in ARCIA 1862:217–228; Rockwell 1956:64, 66, 69–70; U.S. Congress. Senate 1914; ARCIA 1865, 1875.

amidst a welter of military and entrepreneurial activity, while others remained isolated. While some groups began to acculturate to Euro-American frontier society, others maintained ways of life that were relatively uninfluenced by Whites. And while some groups managed to avoid the wrath of punitive military expeditions through their diplomatic status, less fortunate groups were, at times, subjected to forced marches, harassment, and massacre (Clemmer 1974).

The Treaty Period, 1846-1870

As early as 1849 agencies were established, and the first treaty with Great Basin groups that was ratified was the 1849 Treaty of Abiquiu with the Muache and Capote Utes (table 1). Between 1855 and 1868 a number of treaties made by officials of the U.S. government were never approved by the Senate, usually because they had not been authorized in advance as required.

In 1855 two more treaties were negotiated with the Muache and Capote Ute, but these were not ratified because the descriptions of these bands' territories did not follow any landmarks (Keleher 1952:80). In 1859, agent Jacob Forney (ARCIA 1860:365–367) distributed presents to Western Shoshones in Ruby Valley and promised them a six-mile-square reservation in return for their pledge of peaceful intentions. In 1862, Nevada's territorial governor, James Warren Nye (AR-

CIA 1863:215–217) negotiated an agreement with Tutuwa, leader of Western Shoshones around the mining town of Austin. Although only a fragment of Nye's report survives in the National Archives, it seems that he agreed to equal ownership and occupation of land and resources for Shoshones and U.S. citizens.

In 1859, William Lander, a surveyor with the Army Corps of Engineers acting as special agent, authorized presents to the Washakie band of Eastern Shoshone, the Snake River and Tukudeka bands of Northern Shoshone, and the Bannock in the amount of $8,856, although records show that only the Washakie band received its goods in the amount of $3,321 (Madsen 1980:31–32). Lander also acted as "peace negotiator" among Winnemucca's band of Northern Paiutes at Pyramid Lake (Canfield 1983:27). Caleb Lyon, governor of Idaho, took it upon himself to negotiate a treaty with the Boise River Northern Shoshone in 1864 that would have ceded all lands 30 miles either side of the river plus all lands drained by its tributaries, leaving the band with only a pledge of "equal hunting and fishing rights" with non-Shoshone and the promise of a reservation. In 1866 Lyon negotiated a similar treaty with the Bruneau bands of Bannock that would have ceded all land south of the Snake River between Goose Creek and the Owyhee River in return for the promise of a 14-mile-long reservation in the Bruneau Valley (Madsen 1980:45).

In 1865 O.H. Irish negotiated treaties with Utes at Spanish Fork, and with six purported Southern Paiute headmen, in an attempt to obtain from them their rights of occupancy to their aboriginal lands and to guarantee their relocation to the Uintah Basin Reservation (Manners 1974:21–99; Bancroft 1889:634–635). In 1868 Oregon superintendent Huntington negotiated a peace treaty with "wandering" Northern Paiutes under the auspices of Sarah Winnemucca and her brother, Natches, at three locations (Canfield 1983:58–59).

None of these treaties and agreements was ever ratified by the U.S. Senate, but it is not unlikely that the groups in question took the negotiations and promises quite seriously. Western Shoshones living around Austin and Battle Mountain, Nevada, in the 1970s were aware of Nye's agreement with Tutuwa and spoke of the "Nye Treaty."

In general the treaty period brought the development of two powerful opposing forces into the political lives of many Great Basin Indian groups—local interest groups and the federal government (figs. 1–3). Treaties affirmed federal suzerainty on the frontier, but local in-

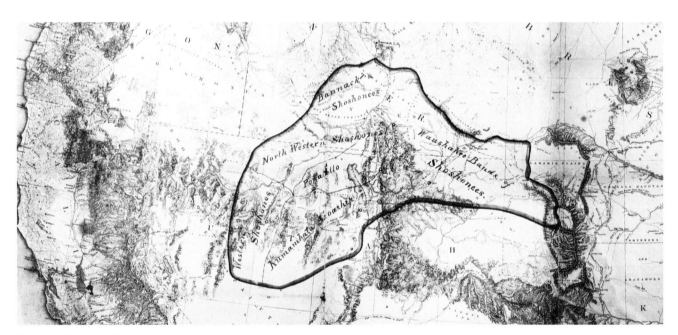

Natl. Arch.: RG 46, Sen. 38B-C8.

Fig. 1. Official map of the General Land Office (Madsen 1980:37) used by Superintendent James D. Doty during treaty negotiations with the Northern, Western, and Eastern Shoshone in the summer and fall 1863. Doty drew in red ink the boundaries of the territories occupied by all of Northern Shoshone, Western Shoshone, and part of Eastern Shoshone. The map shows 6 groups, but Chief Pocatello's band joined the other Northern Shoshone in the Treaty of Box Elder, July 30, 1863. Chief Washakie and the Eastern bands signed at Fort Bridger, on July 2, the Western Shoshone at Ruby Valley on Oct. 1, Gosiute at Tooele Valley on Oct. 12, and, the Northern Shoshone–Bannock at Soda Springs on Oct. 14. The locations where the treaties were signed were marked by Doty with small circles on the map. The Senate ratified the 5 treaties on March 7, 1864, including an amendment concerning Indian title or interest in lands under former Mexican law (Madsen 1980:37). All bands formally approved the amended treaties, except the Northern Shoshone–Bannock, who for logistical reasons never assembled to give their consent to the ratified version. Size of map 60 by 120 cm.

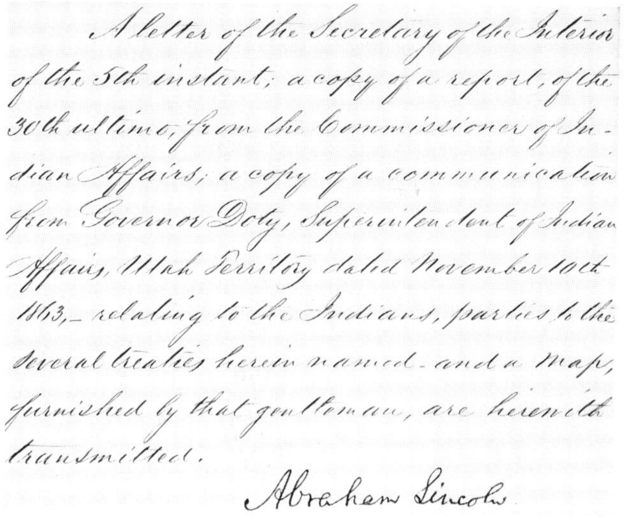

A letter of the Secretary of the Interior of the 5th instant; a copy of a report, of the 30th ultimo, from the Commissioner of Indian Affairs; a copy of a communication from Governor Doty, Superintendent of Indian Affairs, Utah Territory dated November 10th 1863,_ relating to the Indians, parties to the several treaties herein named, and a map, furnished by that gentleman, are herewith transmitted.

Abraham Lincoln

Natl. Arch.: RG 46, Sen. 38B-C8.

Fig. 2. Last paragraph of manuscript letter signed by President Abraham Lincoln, Washington, D.C., Jan. 1864, transmitting to the Senate for ratification the 5 Indian treaties negotiated in 1863. As part of the documentation Lincoln sent the map used by Superintendent James Doty (fig. 1).

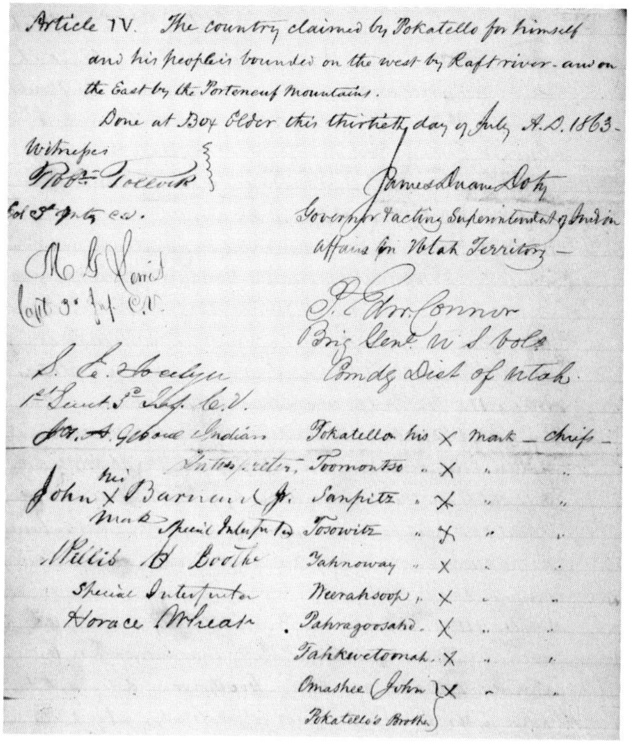

Article IV. The country claimed by Pokatello for himself and his people is bounded on the west by Raft river and on the East by the Porteneuf mountains.

Done at Box Elder this thirtieth day of July A.D. 1863.

Witnesses

Robt. Pollock
Col 3 Infy CV.

James Duane Doty
Governor & acting Superintendent of Indian Affairs for Utah Territory —

M. G. Lewis
Capt 3 Inf CV

P. Edw. Connor
Brig Genl. U S Vols
Comdg Dist of Utah

S. E. Jocelyn
1st Lieut 3 Infy C.V.

Jas. A. Gebow Indian Interpreter — Pokatello his X mark — chief —
Toomontso " X "
John his X mark Barnard Jr. Special Interpreter — Sanpitz " X "
Tosowitz " X "
Willis H. Boothe Special Interpreter — Yahnoway " X "
Weerahsoop " X "
Horace Wheat — Pahragoosahd " X "
Tahkwetoonah " X "
Omashee (John X Pokatello's Brother)

Natl. Arch.: RG 11, Ratified Ind. Treaty No. 325.

Fig. 3. Signatures on the Treaty with the Northern Shoshone, Box Elder, Utah Terr., July 30, 1863. Heading the U.S. delegation was Utah Terr. Gov. James D. Doty accompanied by Brig. Gen. Patrick Edward Connor, commanding the District of Utah, whose signatures appear on the upper right. The Indian delegation was headed by Chief Pocatello, who was "so anxious to participate that he sent word he would give ten horses to prove his sincerity" (Madsen 1980:37), in order to relieve his people from their destitute status caused by the war. The other Northern Shoshone "chiefs" who signed included: Toomontso, Sanpits, Tosowitz, Yahnoway, Weerahsoop, Pahragoosahd, Tahkwetoonah and Omashee (John), brother of Pocatello. On the left are the signatures of the witnesses, 3 of whom were army officers in the California Volunteers, and 3 interpreters. In return for annuities, the chiefs agreed to open their country to wagon roads, military posts, the telegraph, and railroads.

terest groups began to modify treaty provisions effectively almost as soon as they were ratified. For example, a clerk's error resulted in the "Kamas Prairie" being written as the "Kansas" Prairie, and settlers in Idaho seized upon the error as justification for denying Northern Shoshones' and Bannocks' rights to this desirable area in violation of the Treaty of Fort Bridger. Although the Treaty of Ruby Valley affirmed Western Shoshones' aboriginal possession of their territory, ranching and mining interests in Nevada assumed that Indians had no property rights at all and that the entire state was basically wide open for development (Clemmer 1974).

In 1871 Congress passed an act that ended the policy of treaty making. Thereafter, the results of negotiations between the federal government and Indian tribes were referred to as agreements. This is a distinction of form, as agreements have the same binding value as treaties.

The Development of Reservations, 1855–1870

Table 2 lists, chronologically, land set aside for Great Basin Indians. In cases where the dates of Indian residence, executive order, and congressional action are different, the earliest date has been used. For this reason, dates in table 2 may be different from those mentioned in the tribal chapters. Figure 4 outlines reservations established for Great Basin groups before 1922. The following summary, based largely on reports of agents and government farmers, sketches the status of Great Basin groups at the end of the first 25–30 years of formal contact with the United States and its citizens.

Eastern Shoshone

Although on friendly terms with the State of Deseret headed by Brigham Young, Eastern Shoshones under Washakie were not drawn into the Mormon War of 1856–1857 and maintained their political independence until the mid-1870s. Because they were long-time enemies of the Sioux, Arapahoe, Cheyenne, Blackfeet, and Crow (cf. Hebard 1930:180; Bourke 1891:303, 350–356; O.C. Stewart 1965:3; E.N. Wilson 1910; Trenholm and Carley 1964:172), Washakie's Shoshones were probably, of all Great Basin groups, the most receptive to friendship and even alliance with the Americans. In many ways, Eastern Shoshones held the balance of power in the transition zone between the Great Basin and the Plains. Shoshone warriors constituted a formidable military force and, because they were well-organized as a distinct band with many features of the mounted bands of the Plains, Eastern Shoshones were treated with far more deference and consistency than were other Basin groups.

During the mid-1850s, Pocatello, a Northern Shoshone, was unsuccessful in persuading Washakie to join him in opposing settlers who were encroaching on the Cache, Bear, Bruneau, and Snake valleys (E.N. Wilson 1910). Pocatello acknowledged the hegemony of Washakie and the Eastern Shoshones while their two bands traveled together (O.C. Stewart 1965:28), but Pocatello's band and another group of Shoshones seem to have separated from Washakie's band over disagreement with his political strategy (E.N. Wilson 1910; Steward 1938:212).

Eastern Shoshones were the only group in the Great Basin that were not militarily conquered, displaced, encroached upon, or totally ignored during the early reservation period. With minimum disruption of their social integrity or way of life, they seem to have withdrawn to their reservation where they pursued a life based on hunting buffalo and other game, gathering, and fishing, until the arrival of Arapahoes in 1878 and disappearance of the buffalo in the late 1880s (cf. Bourke 1891:341; ARCIA 1881:184).

Avoidance of much of the trauma experienced by other Great Basin groups may have been due to the Eastern Shoshones' military prowess and the sagacity of their principal chief, Washakie, "whose unusual personality seems to have welded the Wyoming Shoshoni into a single band" (Steward 1938:211–212; cf. Hebard 1930). Washakie requested a reservation in 1858, "making choice of the valley of Henry's Fork, about 40 miles south of Fort Bridger, and asking that a farm be opened there" (Hebard 1930:91). Neither reservation nor farm was established, and in 1867–1868, the Union Pacific Railroad was pushed through Eastern Shoshone territory, bringing several thousand construction workers and accompanying boom towns. In 1867 Washakie again requested a reservation, this time in the Wind River Valley (Hebard 1930:118).

The Treaty of Fort Bridger set aside the Wind River Valley Reservation in 1868, but, in the first cession of reservation lands in the Great Basin, Washakie had to sign away a large tract in 1872 for a payment of $25,000 due to an apparent surveying error, which had included a substantial number of previously homesteaded ranches within the reservation's boundaries (Hebard 1930:118–143; Trenhom and Carley 1964:318). Continued favor with the federal government was assured when Washakie volunteered to assist Gen. George Crook in his campaign against the Sioux in 1876; Washakie showed up with 112 warriors and was later joined by about 40 Utes, who saw some action against the Sioux, as well as providing scouts (Bourke 1891:334–357). Two years later, Washakie refused to join Egan and other Northern Paiute and Bannock bands in the Bannock War, and again supplied a contingent of warriors who, along with Arapahoes, served as scouts hunting down Bannocks that had been chased east nearly to the boundary of the Wind River Reservation (Trenholm and Carley 1964:264).

However, Eastern Shoshones eventually came to experience the consequences of the expediency that characterized the U.S. government's reservation policy elsewhere in the Great Basin. Northern Arapahoes had refused to be settled with Southern Arapahoes in a reservation in Oklahoma; they retreated to Wyoming and Montana, and petitioned the government for a reservation in their familiar territory, which included parts of Colorado, Kansas, Wyoming, and Montana (Elkin 1940:229–230). The government reluctantly acceded to the Arapahoes' refusal to be located in Oklahoma, moving them to the Wind River Reservation by military escort (Hebard 1930:208). Eastern Shoshones were apparently not happy that their old enemies, the Arapahoes, were to be located on their reservation; however, they understood that the arrangement was temporary, and that eventually Arapahoes would be moved to a reservation of their own. That event never happened; Arapahoes were granted de facto about half the reservation for their exclusive use.

Northern Shoshone and Bannock

As Mormon settlers moved north from Salt Lake City into the Bear River area, they pushed the remnants of the Fish Eater (Cache Valley) Western Shoshones out of their traditional areas. These Indians were under the nominal protection and leadership of Pocatello, whose mounted band was allied with the influential Washakie to the northeast, but the massacre of 368 of them in 1863 left a remnant population that seems to have become refugees in their own country.

To the west, Northern Shoshone and Bannock bands along the Boise and Bruneau rivers were experiencing similar difficulties with settlers. More than 400 members of these bands were forced to depend on rations meted out by territorial officials during the winter of 1867. The Bannock to the east, probably numbering around 1,500, continued to hunt, gather, and fish along the Snake River and on the Camas Prairie until the Fort Hall Reservation was established in 1867.

From 1868 through 1877, the hostility of settlers and the inadequate facilities of Fort Hall made life virtually impossible for the Bannocks and Snake River Shoshones that had been targeted for relocation to the reservation. For one thing, the reservation had been illegally settled by homesteaders, and the town of Pocatello had become entrenched. For another thing, although Bannocks and Shoshones had been guaranteed access to traditional hunting, gathering, and fishing areas, the hostility of settlers off the reservation was as great as that of those encroaching on Fort Hall, and many Indians were so fearful of reprisals that they did not leave the reservation to gather foodstuffs for the winter (Madsen 1980:54). Inadequate rations at various times forced Indians either to starve on the reservation or to risk punishment for leaving to gather food. Finally, although Fort Hall was established as a farming reservation, inadequate supplies of seed and farming implements coupled with plagues of insects made it impossible for reservation-based resources to be a dependable source of sustenance. In 1872, an agent reported 6,000 Indians (probably an exaggeration) camped in Cache Valley, just below the Idaho line, who were supposedly living off supplies that they exacted from settlers as rent for their land.

The Lemhi Reservation was established for the Tukudeka and Salmon River Northern Shoshones in 1873. By the Agreement of May 14, 1880, the Lemhi Indians were to move to Fort Hall. But they objected, and the move did not take place until 1907. A few families remained at Lemhi on nonreservation land, at the sufferance of settlers who had dispossessed them (Madsen 1980:110; Royce 1899:898–899).

Three small bands of Paiute and Shoshone speakers continued to live in the lower Bruneau Valley and did not locate on either the Lemhi or Fort Hall reservations. Between 1882 and 1886, about 300 people under Bruneau John, Big Jim, and Panguitch consented to locate permanently at Duck Valley under threat of being sent to the Yakima Reservation.

With the defeat of the Bannock and Northern Paiute warriors under Egan, Buffalo Horn, and Paddy Cap in late summer 1879, and the movement of the lower Bruneau bands to Duck Valley, the off-reservation life of Indians ended in Idaho. From 1886 on, reservation life, rather than treaty provisions or aboriginal lifeways, became the focus for people whose aboriginal territories had encompassed most of southern Idaho (Madsen 1980:36–95; O.C. Stewart 1965; McKinney 1983:17–31, 58–68).

Despite the ambivalent relationship between Mormons in northern Utah and Ute and Shoshone bands, it seems that even as late as the 1870s, Mormons were still anxious to secure the allegiance of Indians. For a brief period, Mormons distributed rations to the Fish Eater Western Shoshone and Pocatello's band of Northern Shoshone. When Pocatello relocated to Fort Hall in 1874, a delegation from the Fish Eaters visited Fort Hall and picked out spots for homesites, but it was nearly a century before they relocated. They returned to the mouth of Bear River, where a Mormon missionary established a farm and baptized 574 Shoshones, including some who had come from Fort Hall. About half the neophytes were rounded up and brought back to Fort Hall by the army, but the Mormons managed to hold about 300 and finally purchased 1,700 acres near Portage, Utah, on which to settle them. Thus the remnants of the Fish Eaters became wards of the Church of Jesus Christ of Latter-day Saints, rather than of the U.S. government, and by 1880 they were being schooled in the tenets of Mormonism as well as in the methods of cash-crop farming (Madsen 1980:94–98).

Ute

In 1855 Indian Agent Garland Hurt convinced some Western Utes, probably the Pahvant, Sanpits, and Timpanogots, to settle on three reservations, at the mouth of Spanish Fork River. The Sanpits remained in the San Pete Valley. The Pahvant remained at Kanosh. Mormons, who competed for farmland in these areas, lobbied for removal of the Indians. Despite the success of two of these reservations, slightly over two million acres were set aside in the Uintah Basin, and the Spanish Fork Agency was moved there in 1865. Utes resisted attempts to remove them from Spanish Fork, where they had 800 acres under cultivation, and from San Pete. Between 1865 and 1870 the Black Hawk War was pursued by Utes who periodically raided settlements that were encroaching on these reservations (Stewart and Janetski 1983).

Congress did not confirm the amount of acreage withdrawn for the Unitah Reservation until 1879, and by 1873, only 556 Utes had moved there. Pahvants eventually split into two groups—one that relocated to the Uintah Basin, and the other, under the leadership of Kanosh, that remained in the south and subsequently became amalgamated with the Southern Paiute around what is now Meadow, Kanosh, and Richfield, Utah. The Sanpits seem to have dissolved as a distinct entity following their eviction from the San Pete Valley and may have settled with Pahvants at Meadow and Southern Paiutes and other Utes at Koosharem and Richfield. Some may have joined the Fish Eater Western Shoshones, who became known as "Sanpitch Shoshones" in the late 1860s and 1870s and threw in their lot with Pocatello, and some Little Soldier's band, which probably also included speakers of two Shoshone dialects and was variously referred to as Shoshone, Gosiute, and Weber Ute (Utah Superintendency 1855–1861; cf. O.C. Stewart 1954).

Mounted, and ranging between the Green River and Utah Lake, the Uintahs were able to retreat from military incursions better than their more westerly affiliates. Tabby was acknowledged by government officials as their chief. The Uintahs experienced pressure from Mormon settlers around Salt Lake and west of the Wasatch Mountains, especially on their farms at Spanish Fork, and after 1858 there were pressures from miners seeking gold in the deep interior of the Rockies. A

Table 2. Reservations, Colonies, Homesteads, and Allotments Established 1855–1980

Date	Name	Group	Acreage at Founding	Acreage Added
1855–1865	Spanish Fork, Utah	Timpanogots Ute	a	
1855–1865	Deep Creek, Utah	Gosiute	a	
1855–1865	San Pete, Utah	Sanpits Ute	a	
1855–1865	Corn Creek, Utah	Pahvant Ute	a	
1859	Walker River, Nev.	Northern Paiute	329,692	277,100
1859	Pyramid Lake, Nev.	Northern Paiute	493,962	
1859–1870c	Washoe-Paiute Timber Reserve, Nev.		20,531	
1861	Uintah Valley, Utahb	Ute	2,039,400	675,000b
1863–1880	Ute, Colo.	Ute	14,730,000	
1867	Fort Hall, Idaho	Northern Shoshone, Bannock	1,566,718	
1868	Wind River, Wyo.	Eastern Shoshone	2,800,000	1,459,508
1873	Moapa, Nev.	Southern Paiute	3,900	70,889
1873–1882	Malheur, Oreg.	Northern Paiute	1,778,560	
1873–1907	Lemhi, Idaho	Northern Shoshone, Bannock	64,000	
1875–1879	Carlin Farms, Nev.	White Knife Western Shoshone	52	
1877	Duck Valley, Nev.	Western Shoshone and Northern Paiute	289,667	4,007
1880	Southern Ute, Colo.	Ute	475,000	266,510
1882	Ouray, Utahb	Ute	1,912,320	b
1884–1922	Paiute Strip, Utah and Ariz.	San Juan Southern Paiute	498,202	
1887	Woodfords Colony, Calif.	Washoe	580	80
1889	Burns allotments, Oreg.	Northern Paiute	14,519	
1892	Fort McDermitt allotments, Oreg.–Nev.	Northern Paiute, Western Shoshone	34,787	23
1893–1930	Allotments, Calif., Nev.	Washoe	63,000	3,000
1897–1917	Fort Bidwell, Calif.	Northern Paiute	3,335	
1902	Fallon Reservation, Nev.	Northern Paiute, Western Shoshone	2,680	3,480
1906	Fallon Allotments, Nev.	Northern Paiute, Western Shoshone	1,960	
1907	Chemehuevi, Calif.	Chemehuevi	28,233	10,430
1907	Skull Valley, Utah	Gosiute	17,745	
1910	Lovelock Colony, Nev.	Northern Paiute	20	
1911	Las Vegas Colony, Nev.	Southern Paiute, Chemehuevi	10	3
1913	Bishop Colony, Calif.	Owens Valley Paiute, Western Shoshone	875	1,000
1913	Summit Lake, Nev.	Northern Paiute	10,208	846
1914	Cedarville Colony, Calif.	Northern Paiute	17	
1914–1925 1926–1954c	Cedar City, Utah	Southern Paiute	13	
1915–1954	Indian Peaks, Utah	Southern Paiute	10,240	
1915	Fort Independence, Calif.	Owens Valley Paiute, Western Shoshone	320	36
1915	Benton, Calif.	Northern Paiute	160	
1915	Ute Mountain, Colo.	Ute	525,000	81,787
1916	Carson Colony, Nev.	Washoe	160	
1917	Dresslerville Colony, Nev.	Washoe	40	
1916–1954	Shivwits, Utah	Southern Paiute	28,160	

Table 2. Reservations, Colonies, Homesteads, and Allotments Established 1855–1980 *(continued)*

Date	Name	Group	Acreage at Founding	Acreage Added
1917	Yerington Colony, Nev.	Northern Paiute	10	10
1917	Fallon Colony, Nev.	Northern Paiute, Western Shoshone	40	
1917	Reno-Sparks Colony, Nev.	Northern Paiute, Washoe, Western Shoshone	20	9
1917	Kaibab, Ariz.	Southern Paiute	120,453	
1917	Battle Mountain, Nev.	Western Shoshone	680	6
1917	Goshute, Nev.	Gosiute	34,560	75,792
1918(1938)[d]	Elko Colony, Nev.	Western Shoshone	193	
1922	Big Pine Colony, Calif.	Owens Valley Paiute, Western Shoshone	279	
1923	Susanville allotments, Calif.	Northern Paiute, Washoe, Atsugewi, Achumawi, Maidu	30	
1928	Winnemucca Colony, Nev.	Northern Paiute	340	
1928–1954	Koosharem, Utah	Ute, Southern Paiute	440	
1928–1958	Indian Ranch, Calif.	Western Shoshone	?	
1929–1954	Kanosh, Utah	Southern Paiute, Ute	5,290	8,047
1930s–1954	Gandy Homestead, Utah	Southern Paiute	160	
1931	Ely Colony, Nev.	Western Shoshone	10	101
1936, 1941	Campbell Ranch and Yerington Reservation	Northern Paiute	1,156	
1937	Yomba, Nev.	Western Shoshone	4,718	37
1937	Odgers Ranch, Nev.	Western Shoshone	1,197	
1938	XL Ranch, Calif.	Northern Paiute, Achumawi, Atsugewi	560	8,695
1938–1941	South Fork, Nev.	Western Shoshone	11,064	2,775
1939	Lone Pine Colony, Calif.	Owens Valley Paiute, Western Shoshone	237	
1940[e]	Ruby Valley, Nev.	Western Shoshone	1,240	120
1940–1944	Duckwater, Nev.	Western Shoshone	3,785	142
after 1972	Bridgeport Colony, Calif.	Northern Paiute, Owens Valley Paiute	?	
1977	Wells Colony, Nev.	Western Shoshone	80	
1980	Utah Paiute, Utah	Southern Paiute	15,000	

SOURCES: U.S. Congress. House. Committee on Interior and Insular Affairs 1953:500–506, 593–636, 687–718, 728–731, 837, 964–1009, 1131; U.S. Department of Commerce 1974; E. Taylor 1931; Nevada Indian Commission 1980; Brophy and Aberle 1966:193–196; Jefferson, Delaney, and Thompson 1972; Johnson 1975:190–201; Knack and Stewart 1984:192–195; Madsen 1980:111–125.
[a] Four Utah reservations totaled 291,000 acres.
[b] Combined in 1883 as Uintah-Ouray Reservation.
[c] City lots under trust status, but land owned by Mormon Church.
[d] A small allotment in 1918 was taken from trust status in 1937, and specific lots were patented to individuals. The land not patented was then sold or exchanged and a larger reservation was formed in 1938, approximately .75 miles north within the city of Elko.
[e]The original reservation, a 6-mile-square area, was set aside in 1859 but never confirmed by Congress or executive order. In 1940 several allotments were placed under trust status by Congress.

reservation was designated for them in the Uintah Basin by executive order in 1861, but some Uintahs elected to join the Yampas, with whom they had close ties, and head south, rather than following the rest of the band onto the reservation in 1865. Thus, although ostensibly located on a reservation in their own territory, the Uintahs were actually destroyed as an integral group and,

like the Bannocks, Northern Shoshones, and Western Utes, became refugees in their own land.

By the time that the Uintah Reservation was finally in operation in 1870, many of its inhabitants had already experienced, within 20 years, the full range of contradictory and vacillating actions that eventually affected all Great Basin groups in the nineteenth century: ineffective treaties; harassment by settlers and military; denial of traditional culture, relocation from homelands, inadequate infrastructure for establishment of reservation-based farming communities; and further relocation to a reservation meant only as a dumping ground.

In 1863 a reservation was set aside for the "Tabeguache" (Taviwach) band of Utes west of the Wasatch Mountains between the Uncompahgre, Gunnison, and Grand rivers. This was superseded in 1868 by the Confederated Ute Indian Reservation, encompassing nearly 40 percent of Colorado, established for the Muache, Capote, Weeminuche, Taviwach, Yampa, and Grand River bands. A large segment of this reservation was ceded in 1873 for mining, and except for a strip that became the Southern Ute and Ute Mountain reservations, the remainder was ceded in 1880 in the aftermath of the Meeker Massacre. After these cessions the Yampa and Grand River Utes (then collectively called the White River Utes) and the Taviwach (then called Uncompahgre) were relocated to what eventually became the combined Uintah-Ouray Reservation in Utah.

The Meeker Massacre grew out of a minor confrontation between a Ute and a White farm employee who was working under agent Nathan C. Meeker at the White River Agency. Meeker panicked and, breaking a promise to the Utes, called in a detachment of 160 U.S. Army troops. When the troops advanced on the reservation community contrary to the agreements their commanding officer had also made with Ute headmen, the Utes attacked them, killing 12, and besieged the agency for six days, killing all 10 men and taking all the women captive (O.C. Stewart 1984b).

During treaty negotiations starting in 1863 a Jicarilla Apache–Ute leader named Ouray rose to prominence. From 1868 until his death in 1880, he was designated "Chief of the Colorado Utes," having been appointed to that previously nonexistent position by government officials. As "chief" Ouray was able to argue for and obtain favorable treatment for himself and his band far exceeding that accorded to the Utah Utes or any other Great Basin group except for the Eastern Shoshone under Washakie. Although unsuccessful in opposing the clamor of the Coloradans for removal, which increased after the Meeker Massacre, Ouray was able to secure not only the Southern Ute Reservation in Colorado but also a separate reservation, established in northern Utah by executive order in 1882, for the Uncompahgre bands. Although the fiction of a pan-Ute chief was not maintained after Ouray's death, the tradition of strong chieftaincy was maintained by the bands of the Southern Ute Reservation well into the second half of the twentieth century.

Western Shoshone

Chieftaincy never became strongly developed among Western Shoshones. Only four chiefs are mentioned with any consistency in reports of Indian agents: Shokub, Buck, Temoak, and Tutuwa. Shokub and his successor, Buck, appear to have been leaders of the White Knife Shoshone. The White Knives were living in four different communities by 1873—Carlin Farms, Battle Mountain, Wells, and Elko—and had abandoned band integrity by that time.

Both Tutuwa and Temoak were sought by Indian agents as spokesmen. However, while treaty commissioners seriously sought approval of the treaty of 1863 as it was to pertain to Western Shoshones, they negotiated only with Temoak, Buck, and others near Ruby Valley. Indian agents' correspondence conveys the impression that personnel of the Utah and Nevada superintendencies had no inkling that the leaders of the White Knives and the leaders of other Western Shoshone communities were not one and the same. Even Powell and Ingalls's (ARCIA 1874) carefully constructed list of "bands" and "band chiefs" seems to have had little influence on the government's policy toward Western Shoshone leadership. On the very rare occasions that treaty annuities were supposedly distributed, they were shipped to the Indian agents in Ruby Valley or in Elko and used mostly to defray administrative costs.

The Western Shoshone agent was headquartered as often at Carson Valley, Walker River, or Pyramid Lake as at Elko. However, around 1870 an itinerant preacher named Levi Gheen was appointed special agent to the Western Shoshone, probably to distribute treaty annuities. In 1871 a government farmer was appointed. By that date, however, Ruby Valley, the original site of the "Government farm" recommended by Agent Forney in 1859, had never been established as a reservation, and the land had been taken first by the Butterfield Stage Line, then by the U.S. Army, and finally by settlers. Gheen was the only government employee who attempted to visit all Western Shoshone communities regularly; and in his capacity as either agent or farmer, he submitted periodic reports that form the only basis for a picture of the Western Shoshone during the 1870s and 1880s (Clemmer 1972:340–349, 1974:27–31).

In 1873 some Western Shoshones, probably White Knives, under Captain Sam, established a small settlement north of Palisade and began to farm. A farmer was appointed specially for them, and 52 acres were set aside by executive order in 1877 as the Carlin Farms Reserve. Almost as soon as the reserve was set aside, two settlers claimed they had filed on the land prior to its withdrawal. In spite of considerable opposition to their claim by Shoshones, their agent, the state's governor, and other settlers who thought Indians should be encouraged in the "civilized" pursuits of farming, Shoshones were evicted from Carlin Farms when the land was restored to the public domain in 1879.

A much larger reservation, Duck Valley, had also

been set aside in 1877. This reservation was intended for all Western Shoshones outside of Carlin Farms, although it was well outside Western Shoshone aboriginal territory. When the time came to move, few Carlin Farms residents wanted to relocate. A meeting at Battle Mountain produced a petition requesting that Indians there and at Carlin Farms be allowed to stay where they were. Temoak announced that those who wanted to move to Duck Valley could do so but he would not support the move and instead would retire to his homestead east of Ruby Valley. Apparently government officials had invested most of their persuasion in Captain Sam as leader without anticipating the fragmentary response that Western Shoshones would give to the relocation proposal. A temporary agent was assigned to Elko in 1878, probably to facilitate the move, but by April 1879, only 1,000 Indians (about 25% of the enumerated Western Shoshones) were living there (Mc-

Kinney 1983:55). The Western Shoshone Agency was moved to Duck Valley in the same year, but most of the people under its jurisdiction were acknowledged to be in more than a dozen communities outside Duck Valley.

By 1882, a combination of low selling prices for reservation crops and high purchase prices for supplies, nondelivery of government-promised rations, lack of support and expertise from the BIA, and a corrupt agent caused more than two-thirds of the residents of Duck Valley to leave. Some went to Fort Hall; others headed west to Jarbidge, North Fork, and other mining districts of north-central Nevada; and still others probably headed back into the heart of Western Shoshone territory. By 1884, only about 300 people remained at Duck Valley (McKinney 1983:79–86). A proposal to relocate Southern Paiutes from Moapa was made but never pursued, and an attempt to close Duck Valley

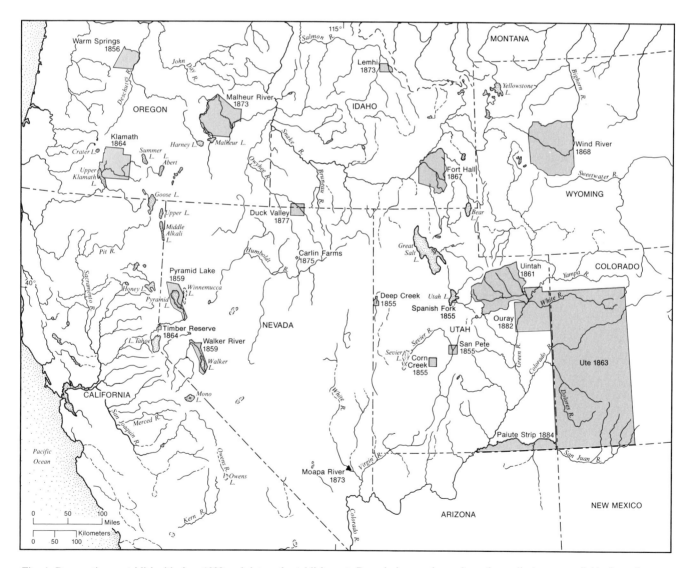

Fig. 4. Reservations established before 1922 and dates of establishment. Boundaries are drawn from the earliest maps available from the Department of the Interior, Bureau of Indian Affairs, cartographic records but may not always reflect the reservations as first created.

and move its residents to Fort Hall in 1884 failed. Finally, enlargement of the reservation and relocation of Malheur and Bruneau Valley Northern Paiutes stabilized the Duck Valley population at around 600 by 1886.

Although the Gosiute were not a separate ethnographically documented band, the Gosiutes of Deep Creek were treated as a distinct entity by BIA agents beginning in 1855 and throughout the treaty period. Farms were established at Deep Creek and Skull Valley, but assistance from government farmers was inadequate or nonexistent, and no agent was ever assigned regularly to Deep Creek. The Treaty of Tooele Valley in 1863 acknowledged a vast area as Gosiute territory; and as the focus of non-Indian interest coalesced to the west along the Humboldt River and its tributaries, and to the east along the western slope of the Wasatch Range, the Deep Creek Gosiute were left to pursue a mixed subsistence strategy based on a modified aboriginal way even after the reservation policy had long become entrenched in other parts of the Great Basin (Clemmer 1972:293–295; ARCIA 1861:128–134; Chamberlin 1911:335–337).

By 1930, about 35 or 40 Panamint Shoshone had settled in Death Valley around Scotty's Castle and, between then and the early 1980s, combined traditional subsistence strategies with sale of crafts and occasional wage work. Other Panamint seem to have become associated with other Western Shoshones in eastern California who settled around Fort Independence. Until 1910–1930 between 700 and 1,000 Northern Paiute and Western Shoshone people continued to live in small groups and extended families in mining towns and in enclaves nearby, maintaining closed linguistic and cultural communities and combining traditional subsistence strategies with wage work. Eventually, government colonies were set up for all these groups except Panamint, Kawaiisu, and Yosemite Valley Northern Paiute.

After 25 years of sporadic, inconsistent, and largely ineffective actions by federal officials, Western Shoshones were largely cut loose from federal influence for the next half-century. Duck Valley as the "Western Shoshone Reservation" was maintained for only about one-tenth of the identifiable group; the remaining Shoshones continued to combine a transhumant hunting, gathering, and collecting way of life with seasonal wage work in mining towns or other relationships of dependency with mining and agricultural settlements of the dominant society.

Northern Paiute

In 1859 the Utah Superintendency established an agency in the Carson Valley and reservations at Walker Lake and at Pyramid Lake. However, gold was discovered at Genoa, at the foot of the eastern Sierras, in the same year, and with gold-seekers came homesteaders who settled the most agriculturally desirable lands, including those on the Walker River Reservation. Federal authorities neither acted decisively in favor of the Paiutes nor admitted their powerlessness amidst a fluctuating and peripatetic population of 10,000 homesteaders, miners, and entrepreneurs.

Despite a successful history of fishing and gathering supplemented by hunting, Walker River Northern Paiutes were encouraged to farm rather than fish. Without local markets, the growing of cash crops proved futile, and even after local markets improved, the ambiguous legal status of the reservation and dearth of farming implements and expert agricultural advice made farming tenuous. Good land was usurped by non-Indians; farming was supported in word but not in deed. Between 1873 and 1877 proposals were circulated to relocate all Paiutes in Nevada to either Pyramid Lake or Duck Valley. Reservation boundaries were not confirmed by executive order until 1874, and a number of Paiutes found it impossible to live at Walker River without becoming involved in the cash economy, which non-Indian squatters had imported onto the reservation. When the government finally attempted to apply its uniform reservation policy to Walker River, it found a situation already compromised by the intrusion of local interests that would put to a severe test the legal principle of exclusive federal jurisdiction over Indian nations (Johnson 1975).

Pyramid Lake Northern Pauites also had no treaty with the U.S. government, and thus Pyramid Lake was also not a treaty reservation. Its boundaries, too, were confirmed by executive order only in 1874, 15 years after its creation and long after non-Indian encroachment had taken many of the best lands in its southern portion. The Pyramid Lake War of 1860 was precipitated when Paiutes killed traders whom they accused of kidnapping Paiute girls. Only two battles ensued and neither the local militia nor the Paiute claimed a decisive victory (Knack and Stewart 1984:70–72).

Pyramid Lake Paiutes were primarily fishers, collectors, and hunters; however, by 1871 the first of a series of events had occurred that modified and then crippled the Paiutes' fishing. In 1905 a dam built on the Truckee River (Canfield 1983:68–69) was in accord with agents' desires to develop agriculture by using water from Pyramid Lake for irrigation. Until well into the 1940s, the BIA continued to build dams and irrigation ditches. These dams at first discouraged and finally prevented the migration of anadromous fish to their spawning grounds. Paiutes' advice against such procedures went unheeded. Even occasional non-Indian opposition had little impact (Knack and Stewart 1984).

The most respected and feared Northern Paiute opposition to manipulation came from leadership that had neither treaty nor reservation as a base from which to argue. Winnemucca and three of his children, Numaga

536

(Young Winnemucca), Natches, and Sarah Winnemucca, represented themselves to Indian agents, military personnel, settlers, and state authorities as representatives for all Northern Paiutes in Nevada, but they actually represented no more than a few hundred people, who were either originally part of Winnemucca's band or elected to be represented by members of the Winnemucca family on various occasions. Nonetheless, Winnemucca's participation in the Pyramid Lake War of 1860 and apprehension that he might join in the Bannock War of 1878 caused him to be feared and respected. The services of Winnemucca and Sarah Winnemucca were sought as negotiators and peacemakers through the 1860s and 1870s, and the mobility of the Winnemucca band made them a valuable liaison with the Northern Paiutes of the Burns area. When the Malheur Reservation was established in 1873, Winnemucca's band was among those designated to relocate there (Canfield 1983:178–179).

Eventually, the Winnemucca band became fragmented and dispersed. Band members had neither a reservation of their own nor rights at Pyramid Lake. Winnemucca Paiutes eventually ended up at Pyramid Lake, in Lovelock Colony, at Fort McDermitt, and in Susanville, California.

The Oregon Northern Paiutes probably numbered about 1,100. The Yahuskin band signed a treaty of cession in 1864, and the Walpapi in 1865. Oregon Paiutes were, at various times, assigned to the Yakima, Klamath, and Warm Springs reservations (which they shared with Plateau Indians), and the Malheur and Duck Valley reservations in the Great Basin.

The Malheur Reservation was established at Fort Harney in 1872 for all Oregon Paiutes except the Yahuskins plus Winnemucca's band and for Northern Shoshone bands under Panguitch, Big Jim, and Bruneau John. However, troops arrested the remnants of Egan's Bannocks plus the Paddy Cap, Panguitch, and Leggins bands, escorted them to the Yakima Reservation in Washington, and confined them there until 1884. Since Winnemucca refused to go to Malheur without Leggins, less than 20 percent of Malheur's intended residents were living on the reservation in 1880. When the incarcerated bands were finally released, they found that their own reservation had been abolished in 1882 under pressure from settlers who argued that the allocation of so much land for so few Indians was not justified. A few Malheur Paiutes were settled at Warm Springs Reservation, but the majority remained on allotted land near Burns, Oregon. The remaining Paiutes drifted to Fort McDermitt and Pyramid Lake but found no actual reservation at Fort McDermitt and no place for them at Pyramid Lake. Some remained at Fort McDermitt anyway. Under Paddy Cap, most finally moved to a 6-by-20-mile addition to the Duck Valley Reservation in 1885, after having suffered nearly a 40

percent population loss due to deaths from malaria and measles at Yakima (McKinney 1983:57–70).

The Yahuskins, numbering probably fewer than 200, were located on the Klamath Reservation in 1864. The agent's report for 1890 insisted that distinctions among the Plateau Klamaths and Modocs and Great Basin "Snakes" (Northern Paiutes) and other ethnic groups on the reservation had been obliterated by intermarriage. However, a report listed 151 "Paiute Indians" at Klamath in 1950. Walpapi Paiutes under Ocheo were among those who were rounded up in 1879 as a result of the Bannock War. Originally incarcerated at Yakima, about 40 eventually ended up at Warm Springs after being held briefly at Klamath, where 25 of them died (cf. Canfield 1983:86–87). Altogether, the Walpapi Paiutes probably numbered around 150 when they signed the Treaty of Sprague River Valley in 1865. Their band integrity was virtually destroyed in 20 years, and they seem to have been reduced to about 80 by the 1880s, with half remaining at Klamath and half living at Warm Springs.

Many Paiutes never joined Winnemucca or any other chiefs, while also feeling no affiliation with either Pyramid Lake or Walker River. Although these two reservations were set aside as the official Paiute reserves for two bands in Nevada, they were never intended to have had more than one-quarter, at best, of the Nevada Northern Paiute population. The remaining Paiutes combined traditional subsistence strategies with increasing dependence on mining and ranching economies in more than a dozen clusters for the next half-century (Steward 1938). Some Northern Paiutes began moving south into the desert areas around Las Vegas and Barstow. Others went to Fort McDermitt. In 1892, allotments were granted to Shoshones and Paiutes living around the Fort, after the military post had been dissolved (U.S. Department of Commerce 1974:313).

Owens Valley Paiute

Owens Valley was a fertile and well-watered oasis that attracted settlers, largely from the Los Angeles area, and by 1862 these settlers had encroached on Indian lands to the point that altercations had begun to occur. The Owens Valley people had probably adopted introduced and native cultigens prior to the government's efforts to establish Indian farms in the Great Basin and had utilized flood irrigation methods in stimulating the growth of desired species such as tobacco. Thus, settlers and Indians came into direct competition not only for land but also for water. Indian agents from Nevada recommended that they be encouraged in these endeavors (Johnson 1975:34), but troops from Los Angeles under inept and uncompromising leadership entered the valley in spring 1862, when they were promptly defeated by a force of Paiutes. Although agents operated out of Bishop from time to time, Owens Valley Indians had to extricate themselves from one difficulty after another stemming from the decision of the City of Los Angeles and its citizens to treat Owens Valley as its own rural resource. In 1939, Los Angeles executed an agreement with Owens Valley Indians that affirmed Los Angeles's taking of the water from what had been Owens Lake, setting up a governing body, the Owens Valley Board of Trustees, that resembled the federally organized tribal councils.

Washoe

Although among the first of the Great Basin groups to experience the full impact of the westward migrations of the 1840s, the Washoe remained outside the purview of treaty commissions, Indian agents, and advocates of the reservation policy.

Nearly 1,000 Washoes were identified as living in three "bands" between Honey and Carson lakes in 1859 (Johnson 1975:28). A "timber reserve" of 22,000 acres was ostensibly set aside for Northern Paiutes on the eastern slope of the Sierra Nevadas, to which the Washoe were also supposed to have access, according to early Indian agents' reports. Originally, this reserve was intended as a pine nut gathering area. But a logging and sawmill operation was set up under private contract and, by 1865, the sawmill had been sold for $30,000 worth of milled lumber that was never delivered to Washoes, to Paiutes, or to the Agency, and the timber reserve was lost (Canfield 1983:50). A recommendation to move the Washoe to Pyramid Lake was never taken seriously, but neither was another recommendation for two small half-section reservations in the Carson and Washoe valleys. No land was reserved for Washoes until the 1880s (table 2), and Washoes combined traditional subsistence strategies with seasonal and occasional wage labor in lumber camps and mining towns until well into the twentieth century.

Southern Paiute

It is extremely difficult to distinguish Southern Paiutes from Southern Utes in some parts of southern Utah. There was a great deal of interchange among these groups in the early to mid-nineteenth century. Although Southern Paiutes distinguished groups among themselves more on the basis of locality than by ethnic or linguistic affiliation (Manners 1974), chieftainship as an institution seems to have been absent or minimally developed.

The most consistent influences affecting Paiutes in Utah and northern Arizona came from Mormons and Navajos. Although Paiutes took up agriculture independently before 1800, the overtures of missionaries from the Mormon settlement of Saint George, Utah,

greatly encouraged Paiutes to become dedicated farmers. By 1885 there seem to have been three sedentary communities subsisting almost entirely by farming under Mormon influence: one at Santa Clara, Utah, later known as the Shivwits Reservation; one in the Moenavi-Willow Springs area near Tuba City, Arizona (cf. Hamblin 1909); and another south of Kanab, Utah. Mormons were evicted from Tuba City in 1903 when the Western Navajo Reservation was established (Nagata 1970:34), but Paiutes have continued to live and farm there and at Gap, Arizona, and near Mexican Hat, Utah. The Paiutes' agricultural settlement at Santa Clara has also endured.

In the mid-1800s, Utes in the Sevier Valley were under the leadership of Kanosh, a Pahvant Ute, and may also have absorbed remnants of the Moanunts Utes and some Southern Paiutes. This group seems to have maintained a less sedentary pattern until the 1890s, when some of the group went to the Uintah Reservation and others joined Southern Paiute groups around Richfield and Cedar City. Some of these Paiutes eventually came under the influence of Mormons in Cedar City in the early twentieth century (A. Spencer 1973; Knack 1980). Southern Paiutes southwest of Bluff, Utah, came under the protection of the Weeminuche under Ignacio in the 1880s and 1890s. A number of Southern Paiutes who moved from Arizona to Allen Canyon in the mid-1920s, perhaps to take up allotments, became known as the Allen Canyon Paiute or Ute. Although they agreed officially to join the Ute Mountain band in 1925, the BIA has continued to distinguish them from other Ute Mountain tribal members. They continue to be culturally distinct from the Ute Mountain Utes, who refer to them as "White Mesa" people or simply Paiutes. They hold their own Bear Dance separate from Ute Mountain Utes. The Kaibab, just south of Kanab, Utah, seem to have pursued a subsistence pattern relatively independent of government or Mormon influence even after their reservation was established in Arizona in 1917 (Manners 1974:21–99; Bunte and Franklin 1983:64–65).

An agency established at Moapa in 1873 for all Southern Paiutes was abolished in 1876. The 3,000-acre Moapa Reservation was set aside as a farming reservation, but no provisions were made for adequate irrigation or infrastructural support. Under pressure from settlers, the reservation was reduced to 1,000 acres in 1875 (Royce 1899:862, 882). An agency seems to have operated on and off out of either Panguitch, Utah, or Moapa, Nevada, between 1905 and the early 1920s for all Southern Paiute in southern Utah, southern Nevada, and northern Arizona, but it does not seem to have had much impact. In 1927, operating out of Moapa, the agency was transferred to Cedar City, Utah, and in 1939 it was closed entirely (Bunte and Franklin 1983:64–65; Indians at Work 1934–1935, 5, 6).

Probably 500–600 Southern Paiutes continued to live

538

in small groups and enclaves near mining towns and in isolated rural areas, combining traditional subsistence strategies with seasonal wage work. At times, various groups and extended families moved in and out of the Moapa Reservation. Mormons established a mission station at Las Vegas in 1855 (Jensen 1926), and by the early 1900s, Las Vegas and Pahrump had become focuses of permanent settlement. In 1911 a government colony was established at Las Vegas.

Although distinguishable from other Southern Paiutes, Chemehuevis were often lumped with other Southern Paiutes or with Mohaves in the BIA censuses. However, an agent's report of 350 Chemehuevi in 1875 is probably accurate (cf. Manners 1974:99–116). Although some Chemehuevis seem to have lived at Moapa and in other Southern Paiute communities in Nevada for a while, most apparently associated themselves with Mohaves politically and economically and eventually moved onto either the Mohave or the Colorado River Indian Reservation.

The Pan-Reservation Policy, 1870–1890

Beginning with Ulysses S. Grant's administration in 1869, there was an attempt to streamline the administration of Indian matters and to apply a uniform policy to all reservations. The purpose of this policy was to de-Indianize the Indians: to make them into rural farmers of Christian faith, literate in English (and preferably speaking no other language), "unfettered" by ancient traditions and customs, and skilled in blue-collar professions that would turn Indian communities into approximations of rural American towns. The cornerstones of this policy were: a resident agent for each reservation; one or more Christian missions for each community; establishment of farming as the dominant economic strategy, regardless of the pre-existing expertise of their inhabitants; removal of all Indians to reservations or creation of reservations around them; and implementation of behavioral codes meant to encourage acculturation. Between 1890 and 1929, the effort to "stamp out nativism" was especially acute. The effort aimed at banning religious ceremonies, prohibiting Native doctoring, and mandating sectarian Christian instruction in government-operated schools. Those who defied the bans and prohibitions were punished, often with imprisonment for weeks or months.

In various contractual arrangements between 1870 and the late 1880s, Christian missionary sects were selected to supply either agency personnel or educational facilities, or both, as well as to establish churches. By 1890, most of these contracts had been replaced by personnel who came directly under the newly formed federal civil service provisions. By 1910 all reservations had at least one and usually two or more mission churches;

one or more government-operated day schools; a boarding school operated on a military model by non-Indian teachers; a physician; a government farmer; an agency with non-Indian support staff; an all-Indian police force answerable to the BIA; and a Court of Indian Offenses, usually with a non-Indian chief judge (often the local agent or superintendent) and one or more Indian associate judges. The BIA also developed the tradition of off-reservation schooling during this period. Before about 1890, a few Utes were sent to the Good Shepherd Boarding School in Denver, and the Colorado Industrial School in Grand Junction collected Ute, "Shoshone," and "Paiute" pupils. Stewart Indian School near Carson City, Nevada (fig. 5), started enrolling Paiutes, Shoshones, and Washoes in 1890. Later, other Great Basin Indian youngsters were sent to the Sherman Institute in Riverside, California, to Santa Fe Indian School, to Chemawa Indian School in Oregon, to Haskell Institute in Lawrence, Kansas, to Carlisle Indian School in Pennsylvania, and to other schools.

The "pan-reservation" policy must be judged a failure on nearly all counts. First, it should be noted that fewer than 60 percent of all Great Basin Indians were actually on reservations. Even for well-settled reservation groups, several factors intervened between the implementation and accomplishments of the government goals. One factor was the significant resistance to acculturation and domination, ranging from the Bannock War of 1878 to institution of the Ghost Dance, Cry, and Sun Dance in many communities. A second factor was the fact that most reservations were only marginally suited to agriculture: many lacked adequate water or had water usurped by non-Indian users upstream. Those that did have adequate water were far removed from transportation facilities and had precariously short growing seasons. Third, local non-Indian interests often worked against the goals of reservation administrators, hoping either to dislodge Indians from desirable lands or to divert water or mineral resources from Indian control. In many cases, administrators and Indians were powerless to halt outright encroachment. In Colorado, gold-seeking miners had already overrun the central portion of eastern Ute territory by the time the Treaty of Conejos, guaranteeing the inviolability of that territory, was signed in 1868.

Another reason for failure was the variability in length of contact and of reservation-based experiences among groups. Mere placement of several different ethnic groups on one reservation did not automatically melt away differences or fuse the groups into a single reservation community. Often there were vast disparities among ethnic groups in their responses to implementation of policies. Also, there was still a great deal of inconsistency in agents' implementation of policies promulgated in Washington. Finally, the ostensible attempt to create reservation communities of farmers was predicated on *539*

top left, Clayton B. Sampson, Reno, Nev.; Natl. Arch.: top right, 75–N–CARS–236; bottom right, 75–N–CARS–213; center left, Rose Sherman Hanson, Mountain City, Nev., Nat. Hist. Mus. of Los Angeles Co., Western Hist. Coll.: center right, 5906; bottom left, 5898.

Fig. 5. Schools, a powerful force for acculturation. top left, Stewart Indian School near Carson City, Nev., also known as Carson Indian School and Stewart Institute. Authorized by the Nevada legislature in 1887, it was the only nonreservation Indian boarding school in Nev. and emphasized vocational skills as well as athletic competition. In 1899, the first known newspaper by and about Indians in Nevada, *The Indian Advance,* was printed by some of its students (Johnson 1985). The boys are entering the dining hall. At right is the main boys' dormitory. Photograph by Harry Sampson, 1920s or 1930s. top right, Washoe students Kenneth Peters and Tommy Smokey in the Stewart Indian School shoe shop. Photograph by Arthur Rothstein, 1940. center left, Western Shoshone students and their teacher at the day school on the Duck Valley Reservation, Owyhee, Nev. Photograph by James Sherman, 1906. center right, Owens Valley Paiute school built in 1906 at Big Pine, Calif. A school had been in operation there since 1891. It served until 1924 when public schools were opened to Indian students. Photograph by Andrew A. Forbes, 1909. bottom left, Owens Valley Paiute students at the Bishop Indian School, Calif., all of whom have been identified. Clara Goodale Symmes, second row, third from left, wears a beaded collar. Photograph by Andrew A. Forbes, about 1910. bottom right, Northern Paiute and Western Shoshone boys at a day school on the Fallon Indian Reservation, Nev. Photograph by Arthur Rothstein, 1940.

CLEMMER AND STEWART

a dependency model that set up the agent and his staff as wholesalers of seeds and farming implements, marketers of agricultural products, and caretakers of Indians' financial affairs. For example, despite the relative success of the farming program on the Southern Ute Reservation, proceeds from agricultural sales were routinely placed in individuals' bank accounts by the agent, who then issued scrip to the individuals for purchases at local stores that would, in turn, use the scrip to draw cash against the particular individuals' accounts. At the same time, the world in which Indians were expected to operate was based on a capitalist model that assumed a primary drive on the part of all human beings to acquire and accumulate wealth naturally and to affix a monetary value to all goods and services. Often, both the dependency and capitalist models violated Indian systems of ethics and social relationships. Such contradictions resulted in patronized and beleaguered communities that were anything but self-sufficient.

Agricultural life does appear to have grown in importance and become entrenched on some reservations between 1880 and 1900. For example, at Wind River, a prosperous economy based on the sale and trade of buffalo products (ARCIA 1881:184) collapsed in 1884 when the last buffalo herd passed out of the Wind River area. A year later, the Indian Office cut rations, and Indians were expected to purchase supplies from traders with annuity money and cash earned from government employment and sale of crops or to depend on donations from missions. Graft was also a problem at Wind River (L. Fowler 1982:80–81, 85–86). But in spite of problems, Wind River seems to have provided, by far, the most successful experiment in reservation agriculture (ARCIA 1890:478–479).

On other reservations, agriculture had poor results. Trespassing by non-Indians became a mounting problem on all reservations but was especially acute at Fort Hall, Pyramid Lake, Walker River, Malheur, and Wind River (Madsen 1980:144–146; Knack and Stewart 1984:140–209; ARCIA 1880:147–150; Johnson 1975; L. Fowler 1982:81). For example, the Malheur Reservation, Oregon, was a disaster from the very start. Only seven years after its creation, its agent reported in 1880 that 32 non-Indian stock-owners had overrun the reservation with 18,000 head of cattle and 600 horses. No Indians farmed, and the reservation's entire production of 2,400 bushels of wheat and 1,900 of oats resulted from efforts of the agency's non-Indian employees on about 200 cultivated acres (ARCIA 1880:140, 141). In 1890 the agent at Lemhi reported that only 45 Indians (probably less than half the adult population) actually farmed, and at Duck Valley the agent noted that he had "succeeded in inducing forty-seven heads of families to plant gardens, but these Indians are failures as gardeners. . . . They will work faithfully during the planting season, but that done they must have a

Nev. Histl. Soc., Reno: 402.
Fig. 6. A Northern Paiute trial in progress on the Walker River Reservation, Nev. Photographed about 1890s.

ramble in the mountains; their gardens go to destruction" (ARCIA 1890:79, 151).

At most reservations, wage labor and capitalism were introduced by the BIA. Wagons were provided to Indians on an installment plan, whereby Indians would pay for the wagons by contracting to haul crops and freight for the agency. Without transportation provided by agency-owned wagons, farmers could not get crops to markets. Thus the agent had almost total control over the Indian economy. Paradoxically, Northern Paiute attempts to market large quantities of fish at Walker River and Pyramid Lake went unassisted by the agency and were eventually thwarted by restrictive state legislation implemented between 1885 and 1891 and by dam construction.

Uintah and Uncompahgre were the only Utes who farmed. The Los Pinos agent reported that 30 Indians farmed 75 acres and sold part of the produce to U.S. troops and other Whites. Although the Capote, Muache, and Weeminuche had small herds of sheep, goats, horses, and cattle, the Southern Ute agent reported in 1880 that "none of these Indians make any attempt at farming; they refuse all offers of schools; none speak English; a greater portion understand some Spanish. . . . They live in tents or brush lodges, and frequently move from one portion of the reservation to another" (ARCIA 1880:17). By 1890 "progress" seems to have been made: 600 acres were cultivated in oats, wheat, barley, corn, melons, squash, pumpkins, and potatoes, and 14 children were in school (ARCIA 1890:22).

However, nearly half the Southern Utes had little contact with farming. By 1885 nearly all the Weeminuche had followed their chief, Ignacio, west of the La

Plata Mountains to the unirrigated, more barren, western portion of the reservation. From there, the Weeminuche frequently ranged into eastern Utah and seem to have taken some Southern Paiutes into association with them. Although continuing to camp along the La Plata River, the Weeminuche under Ignacio refused farming allotments between 1895 and 1910, and although Ignacio did not, most of the Weeminuche as well as some Capotes and Muache retreated permanently to the nonirrigated portion of the reservation. By 1915, band affiliation and leadership had been submerged under a government-inspired dichotomy: Utes who farmed, and those who did not farm. The nonfarmers west of the La Platas eventually became known as the Ute Mountain band and eked out a living on sheepherding, hunting, gathering, government rations (fig. 7), and trading some craft items to Navajos. The Southern Ute east of the La Platas lived by farming,

top left, Oreg. Histl. Soc., Portland: 44161; top right, Denver Mus. of Nat. Hist., Colo.: OL78–015; bottom left, U. of Utah, Special Coll., Salt Lake City: P2014, #17; bottom right, U. of Pa., U. Mus., Philadelphia: 45–15–779.

Fig. 7. Rations at the reservations. Tribal members were commonly issued annual rations such as beef, flour, blankets, or money for a certain length of time. top left, Northern Paiutes, possibly at Burns, Oreg., being issued tents, blankets, and money by Agent Heinlein. Photograph by Benjamin A. Gifford, about 1900. top right, Ute woman cutting up ration meat while a dog attempts to make off with part of it. Photograph by Stephen Olop, Ute Mountain Reservation, Colo., 1915. bottom left, Utes with their wagons converging on Whiterocks, Utah, for ration day. Photograph by Edward Sapir, summer 1909. bottom right, Ration ticket pouch, with ticket dated 1886, issued to a Shoshone man named Dutch Charley at the Western Shoshone Agency, Nev. Pouch, of smoke-tanned buffalo or elk skin with an elkskin strap, is decorated with green, navy blue, and white seed beads. Length 14.5 cm.

CLEMMER AND STEWART

sheepherding, hunting, and government rations. Although a lawsuit filed in the Court of Claims in 1909 resulted in a three-million dollar judgment for lands taken from Utes of Colorado after the Meeker Massacre, these funds were placed in a bank account that could be drawn upon only in small amounts with the written permission of the agent until the late 1940s.

The Allotment Period, 1890–1933

Between 1870 and about 1910, there were continued attempts by local interests to abolish the Southern Ute, Walker River, Lemhi, Malheur, and Fort Hall reservations and either to allot all reservation lands to Indians in severalty with no restrictions on alienation of the allotments, or to have the Indians moved to some other reservation. In the case of Malheur and Lemhi, these attempts were successful. The Dawes Severalty Act of 1887 partially pacified these local interests with regard to many of the other reservations in the Great Basin. The act was also strongly supported by some Indians, such as Sarah Winnemucca, who felt that private ownership of an agricultural homestead was a necessary step in the process of Indians' achievement of legal and cultural parity with non-Indians. Thus, while agents were ostensibly struggling to introduce farming to their wards, reservation lands were being eaten away by the allotment, alienation, and homesteading processes. Between 1887 and 1933, the disastrous allotment policy resulted in Indians being restricted to farming plots that, even in the late nineteenth century, were too small to support them adequately, and the best lands were being taken by non-Indian farmers. Only Duck Valley, Ute Mountain, and Wind River reservations remained safe from encroachment because of their inadequate water supplies.

The year 1906 marked the acceleration of allotment (table 3). At the same time that reservations were being cut into allotments and parceled out to non-Indian homesteaders, ostensibly in preparation for the day when fully acculturated Indians would no longer require reservations, off-reservation Indians were being gradually concentrated onto small parcels that became known as "camps" or "colonies" (fig. 8). A few of these had been treated as exclusive Indian country by the BIA despite never having been withdrawn by executive order or congressional act; one of these was the camp at Wells, Nevada (cf. U.S. Congress. House. Committee on Interior and Insular Affairs 1953:968).

These smaller reservations, on the outskirts of towns or cities or within city limits, were colloquially called "colonies" sometimes in BIA reports. They have the same status of "Indian country" as reservations. Paiutes and Shoshones generally refer to them as "camps;" the term reflects their historic and cultural origins. The BIA

also used the term colony to refer to settlements that Indians called camps, which did not have official status as "Indian country," and sometimes the BIA referred to these settlements as reservations despite their unofficial status. For example, the Western Shoshone settlement at Wells, Nevada, was listed as "Wells Reservation" by the BIA long before it became an official reservation (U.S. Congress. House. Committee on Interior and Insular Affairs 1953:969; Nevada Indian Commission 1980:35–36).

Allotments were carved from reservations during the period in which the Dawes Severalty Act was in force—1887 to 1933—and were maintained as "Indian country" only as long as their trust status was maintained. Trust status, in which land was held in trust for its Indian owners by the U.S. government and could not be alienated, was supposed to be maintained for 25 years following allotment; following expiration of the 25-year period, the allotments would become the private property of the allottee and could be sold or taxed. During the 25-year trust period, allotments could not, in theory, be sold or taxed. However, in actual fact, many allotments were sold, either by the local agency on behalf of their Indian owners upon presentation of justification to the commissioner in Washington, or by their Indian owners after an agent issued "certifications of competency" attesting to their attainment of a sufficient degree of "civilization" to enable them to dispose of their property competently (cf. Jorgensen 1972:97).

Allotments generally went to heads of households or to adults, and varied in size from 40 acres to a full section (640 acres), depending upon the tract's suitability for agriculture. Nonirrigated tracts were larger; choice tracts in bottom lands were smaller. Allotments were made on all Great Basin reservations except at Pyramid Lake, Duck Valley, and Ute Mountain, between 1905 and 1915 (Jorgensen 1972:93–97; Johnson 1975: 99–116; Knack and Stewart 1984:236). Parcels of land on the former Malheur Reservation in Oregon were patented to Northern Paiutes living there as "trust allotments" under provisions of the Dawes Severalty Act, and in eastern Nevada some portions of nonreservation lands were apparently designated as "Indian allotments" on survey plats, though their actual status is confused as recorded in records of the General Land Office (O.C. Stewart 1980).

Additionally, a few Indians in Nevada homesteaded under provisions of the Dawes Severalty Act and the Homestead Act of 1891. A quarter-section was homesteaded in Crescent Valley and 1,141.19 acres were homesteaded in Ruby Valley (Clemmer 1972). Other isolated tracts of 40 to 750 acres (cf. Clemmer 1972:294) were placed under trust status in California, Utah, and Nevada. In some rural portions of Nevada, especially near Beowawe and Austin, isolated Western Shoshones continued to live on small plots of land that were not

Table 3. Alienation of Unallotted Reservation Lands 1863–1954

Reservation (establishment)	Year	Acreage	Cause of Alienation[a]
Idaho			
Fort Hall (1867)	1888	1,840	Taken by Union Pacific Railroad
	1889	297,000	Taken by Marsh Valley homesteaders
	1900	418,000	Taken by Congress for homesteading, the city of Pocatello, and mining under the Dawes Act
	1907	325,000	Taken by BIA for Lemhi Indians, Agreement of May 14, 1880
	1924	28,000	Taken by Congress for American Falls Reservoir
	1950–1971	864	?
Lemhi (1873)	1907	64,000	Taken for homesteading.
Nevada			
Pyramid Lake (1859)	1870	20,531	Timber Reserve abandoned by BIA
	1863–1867	773	Taken by Central Pacific Railroad
	1867	120	Taken by state of Nevada for townsite
	1867–1872	421	Taken by state of Nevada for highways, school, and other purposes
	1872–1906	19,186	Taken by city of Wadsworth and surrounding homesteaders
	1889–1933	2,100	Illegally homesteaded by non-Indians
Walker River (1859)	1882	372	Ceded to Colorado and Carson Railroad
	1906	286,000	Taken for homesteading under the Dawes Act
Moapa River (1873)	1876	2,900	Taken by Congress for homesteaders
Carlin Farms (1875)	1879	52	Adverse claim by homesteaders
California			
Chemehuevi (1907)	1912	7,776	Inundated by Lake Havasu
Fort Bidwell (1897)	1950–1971	5	?
Arizona			
Paiute Strip (1884)	1922	498,202	Taken by Department of Interior for public domain for cattlemen, then added to the Western Navajo Reservation at Navajos' request, 1929–1933
Kaibab (1917)	1950–1971	50	?
Utah			
Deep Creek, Corn Creek, Spanish Fork, and San Pete reservations (1855)	1865, 1878	291,000	Ceded by Treaty of Spanish Fork, 1865; confirmed by Congress, 1878
Uintah-Ouray (1861, 1882)	1890–1933	523,079	Taken for homesteading under the Dawes Act
	1906	973,777	Added to Uintah National Forest
Gandy Homestead (1930)	1954	160	Terminated
Indian Peaks (1915)	1954	10,240	Terminated
Kanosh (1929)	1954	7,730	Terminated
Koosharem (1928)	1954	840	Terminated
Shivwits (1916)	1954	27,520	Terminated
Cedar City (1914)	1925	13	?
Colorado			
Ute Reservation (1863)	1873	3,450,000	Taken by the Brunot Agreement for mining
	1880	11,280,000	Agreement of cession and removal resulting from lobbying by local interests after the Meeker Massacre
Southern Ute (1880)	1890–1933	523,079	Taken for homesteading under the Dawes Act
Wyoming			
Wind River (1868)	1872	710,000	Taken by Brunot Agreement for mining
	1878	1,045,000	Occupied by Arapahoe (Trenholm and Carley 1964:314–317)
	1896	64,000	Taken by state for resort
	1906–1911	719,317	?
Oregon			
Burns (1889)	1950–1971	2,734	?

544   NOTE: In most cases in which land is described as "taken" or otherwise alienated, payment of some sort was made.

U. of Nev. Reno, Special Coll.

Fig. 8. Northern Paiutes moving from Sparks, Nev., to the Reno-Sparks colony. Except for some irrigation ditches no improvements were provided (Inter-Tribal Council of Nevada 1976a:76–77), and the Indians had to move their own houses. Photograph by Lorenzo D. Creel, about 1917.

under trust status. These actual homesteads and off-reservation allotments and isolated living places were called "homesteads" or "allotments" by the BIA.

Thus, although a comparison of reservation populations in the Great Basin in 1880 with those in 1928 (U.S. Congress. Senate. Committee on Indian Affairs 1934) might indicate a prospering growth rate, in actuality, the population increase was due to reservations being created where Indians happened to be living. A few reservations experienced population increases due to in-migration: 450 Lemhi residents were moved to Fort Hall in 1907, and after 1910, Western Shoshone families gradually drifted to Duck Valley and Fort McDermitt as many of the mining districts in northern Nevada closed down. In 1911, the killing of 8 of 12 members of a band under the Western Shoshone Mike Daggett by a sheriff's posse north of Golconda, Nevada, was the last confrontation between off-reservation In-

dians and Whites in the Great Basin (Madsen 1980:110; Hyde 1973:210–257).

The severe population decline that affected American Indians generally also prevailed in the Great Basin. In 1880 the Fort Hall agent reported "quite a percentage of deaths in the last year," apparently from syphilis. Syphilis was also reported for Western Shoshones in the 1870s, and malaria and measles ravaged Leggins's band of Northern Paiutes while they were at Yakima. High infant mortality, tuberculosis, syphilis, and smallpox were also reported for Fort Hall, and the influenza epidemic of 1918–1919 was felt among the Northern Ute (Gheen 1873; ARCIA 1881, 1890; Swanton 1952; McKinney 1983:69; Madsen 1980:140).

As the "allotment period" neared its end in 1930, few, if any, Great Basin Indians approximated the image that government policy had fixed as the ultimate goal of its administration of reservations. Despite the

Smithsonian, NAA: 84–4924.

Fig. 9. Northern Shoshones and Bannocks in council, Fort Hall Reservation, Idaho, discussing the disposition of the funds received from the sale of the Snake River bottomland. Despite the opposition of the Fort Hall Indians, in 1924 Congress passed legislation that secured 28,000 acres of Snake River bottomland for the American Falls Reservoir project (Madsen 1980:167), paying $700,000 to the Indians, of which $100,000 was for improvements and repairs on the reservation. At the council meeting, the Indians denounced the sale of the land, as the land had economic and religious significance for them, and they requested immediate payment of the funds in full. The reservoir was begun in 1925 and completed in 1927. Photograph by Flora Warren Seymour, 1926.

destruction of some groups and dissolution of some prereservation sociopolitical entities, "Indianness" was hardly dissolved; if anything, it was strengthened, and new reservation-based sociopolitical entities were formed. Despite prohibitions against speaking Indian languages in most schools, there was little language loss during this period. As the land base on some reservations shrank, as water resources on others were diverted, and as the economies of the more isolated reservations suffered from increasingly distant markets and centers of distribution, their inhabitants came to rely heavily on mixed strategies combining subsistence farming and miniscule cash-cropping with animal husbandry, traditional hunting and collecting, and government assistance.

Northern Paiutes were selling between 70,000 and 90,000 pounds of fish from Pyramid Lake throughout the 1890s, garnering anywhere from $5,000 to $9,000 for their harvests, but in 1891 the Nevada legislature outlawed seines, gillnets, set-lines, spears, grab-hooks, weirs, and traps, which Paiutes had used, and made it illegal to transport "trout or land-locked salmon" between October 1 and April 1. These regulations were aimed specifically at destroying Indian dominance of the commercial fish market, and they were largely successful. The Derby Dam on the Truckee River, completed in 1905, also led to the decline of fishing in Pyramid Lake (Hulse 1981; Knack and Stewart 1984:269–272).

As off-reservation groups found themselves provided with official, government-sanctioned residence plots in either traditional areas of habitation or on the outskirts

of mining towns and cities where a group of core families lived, the "landless" Indians of the Great Basin came to resemble other rural poor: wage-workers with few jobs and no land base to which to retreat. The creation of government camps and colonies encouraged sedentism and tended to increase dependence on non-Indian towns as Indians trickled into the colonies to live among relatives or to establish a base from which to secure wage work.

With the collapse of all but five or six of the major mining districts in Nevada during the 1920s and 1930s, some of the newly created colonies became pockets of extreme poverty, while others in boomtowns such as Austin and Ely bulged with population increases. Housing in the colonies consisted of shacks; on the reservation, it consisted of deteriorating houses of log or clapboard, some of which had been constructed by the BIA in the early reservation period. At Southern Ute and Ute Mountain, there were some adobe houses and Navajo-style hogans. Tents were in common use in all seasons on all reservations. The majority of families on all reservations and colonies had no access to plumbing of any kind. Although some families had been fortunate enough to obtain regular wage work and dependable cash-cropping, such families were rare in the reservation and colony contexts.

The "Indian New Deal," 1933–1945

Upon being appointed Commissioner of Indian Affairs, John Collier hoped to institutionalize many of the reforms that he had advocated during the 1920s as a private citizen (cf. L.C. Kelly 1983; Philp 1977:1–112). Although Collier did not accomplish all these reforms, he did lay the foundation for the Indian New Deal, which included: a halt to the allotment of Indian lands and to their alienation; restoration of former reservation lands that had not been homesteaded to tribal ownership; provision to tribes of the capability of consolidating allotments under tribal ownership; purchase of desirable lands for Indians where feasible and appropriate, and creation of reservations for Indians that had none; lifting of bans on Indian religious and ceremonial activities; encouragement of indigenous customs and traditions; encouragement of indigenous crafts and art forms; federal programs of employment, community development, college scholarships, and loans for individuals and tribes; improvement of health care; and reinvigoration of "tribalness" through the codification of the powers of self-government vested in elected tribal councils and tribal chairmen (G.D. Taylor 1980:18–31; Philp 1977:113–134; L.C. Kelly 1983:347–348; S.L. Tyler 1964:66–73; T.H. Haas 1957:19–22).

Introduction of the tribal council system was made through the Indian Reorganization Act of 1934, which all recognized groups were asked to adopt by referendum. Even the groups that did not adopt the act, or that actually rejected it (L. Fowler 1982:167–190), such as the Eastern Shoshone, exercised the principles of self-government provided by the act through business councils with elected council members and a chairman elected either from the council or at-large. Between 1936 and 1980, virtually every group, community, band, tribe, and reservation in the Great Basin became incorporated into some sort of tribal council system, with the exception of the Skull Valley Gosiutes and fewer than 800 Western Shoshones and Southern Paiutes living in widely scattered clusters around Crescent Valley, Ruby Valley, Austin, Eureka, and Pahrump, Nevada; around Gap and Willow Springs, Arizona; and in Death Valley, Yosemite Valley, and northern Kern and southern Inyo counties, California.

For Great Basin Indians, provisions of the Indian New Deal resulting in improved health, guaranteeing freedom of religion and custom, providing for return and improvement of land, and introducing the tribal council system have had the greatest impacts. Economic improvements were important but tended to be short-lived. At all three Ute reservations and at Duck Valley, Fort Hall, and Wind River, sheepraising cooperatives and cattlemen's associations were established, and credit unions under BIA management were formed to provide capitalization of farming and ranching ventures. At Duck Valley, construction of Wild Horse Reservoir greatly increased the irrigable land and initiated an accelerated attempt by the BIA to use its facilities to improve ranching and cattle-raising. Tables 2 and 3 summarize the land areas that were added to, or subtracted from reservations. A total of 2,234,005 acres were withdrawn for reservation lands during the New Deal era.

Throughout the early reservation period and the New Deal era, prereservation political institutions continued to exist on some reservations and were even strengthened. The deaths of noted chiefs such as Black Hawk, Peanum, Little Soldier, Buck, Leggins, Egan, Buffalo Horn, Ouray, Winnemucca, and Washakie seem to have brought the demise of chieftaincy among Northern Utes, Bannocks, Northern Paiutes, Northern Shoshones, and Eastern Shoshones by 1900. But chieftaincy not only survived but also seems to have grown more important in the "entrenched reservation" and New Deal eras among the Skull Valley Gosiutes, Kanosh Ute-Southern Paiutes (southern Utah), Ute Mountain and Southern Utes, Western Shoshones, and Duck Valley Northern Paiutes.

Chieftaincy survived as an institution among Southern Paiutes through the 1950s. Skull Valley Gosiutes vested representative authority in a traditionally sanctioned chief through the early 1970s. Ignacio and Buckskin Charlie (fig. 10) were important leaders among the Southern Ute until about 1910, when Ignacio seems to have retired. Buckskin Charlie continued to be extremely influential and, under conditions in which Indian agents maintained strict control over Southern Utes' lives and in which their best lands and irrigation ditches were being usurped by ever larger numbers of non-Indian homesteaders, Buckskin Charlie maintained cohesiveness among a geographically scattered population by supporting cultural institutions such as Peyote and the Sun Dance. His son, Antonio Buck, who inherited the chieftaincy, was elected as the first chairman of the Southern Ute under the Indian Reorganization Act.

Muchach Temoke, who inherited the Western Shoshone chieftainship, emerged in the 1920s as spokesman for a group of Shoshones who advocated the official return of abandoned homesteads and unoccupied lands to Shoshone hegemony. But the Western Shoshone did not have a political body that could accomplish that goal (E.R. Rusco 1982a:196).

The New Deal administration gave legal sanction to the configuration of land-based tribal entities that had begun to develop in the early reservation period and removed some of the ambivalence that had always enshrouded the government's relationship to Indian leadership in the Great Basin. However, the mechanics of recognizing those tribal entities were sometimes affected by the pressing haste with which the Indian Bureau sought to ameliorate the errors of the past. For example, in Nevada, Bureau personnel recognized the fact that Western Shoshones were scattered on several different reservations but did not initially realize that a substantial portion did not live on reservations at all. When referenda were conducted on the Indian Reorganization Act, "the places at which elections were held did not include more than a fraction of the Western Shoshone population" (E.R. Rusco 1982a:181–182).

After explaining the IRA to Western Shoshones in 1936, Superintendent Alida Bowler received a petition from Muchach Temoke and 80 other Western Shoshones opposing "self-government" and, instead, requesting land. Even following Bowler's meeting with Muchach to explain the advantages of organization, Western Shoshones seem to have maintained a high degree of skepticism. Western Shoshones from Ely, Ruby Valley, Battle Mountain, Elko, and South Fork were selected for a "constitutional committee" and requested the name "Te-Moak Western Shoshone" for the yet-to-be-formed council, but after the constitution had been drafted and sent to Commissioner Collier, the Nevada superintendency apparently discovered that not all Western Shoshones felt strong affiliation with the bands that had been loosely organized under old Temoak. In October 1936 the BIA rejected the draft constitution because the Western Shoshone, "scattered over several communities," did not constitute a "recognized tribe" and therefore had no legitimate basis for organizing as

top, Denver Public Lib., Western Hist. Dept.: F2797; bottom left, U. of Nev. Reno, Special Coll.; bottom center, Rose Sherman Hanson, Mountain City, Nev.; bottom right, Colo. Histl. Soc., Denver: F-43386.

Fig. 10. Prominent 19th- and 20th-century leaders. top, Buckskin Charlie, Capote Ute, Southern Ute Reservation, Colo., wearing a buckskin shirt decorated with beads, probably horsehair and eagle feathers, an eagle-feather bonnet, a hairpipe choker, a German silver necklace, and a Benjamin Harrison peace medal issued in 1889. This was the last Indian peace medal issued. Buckskin Charlie was a subchief or advisor of Ouray and became, at Ouray's request shortly before his death, "chief" of the Southern Ute. He had accompanied Ouray in a delegation to Washington, D.C., in 1880 and with 350 other Utes had marched in Theodore Roosevelt's inaugural parade in 1905. Photograph by Horace S. Poley, 1890s. bottom left, Ben James, Washoe, who was one of those instrumental in creating the Dresslerville Colony (JoAnn Nevers, communication to editors, 1985); photograph by Lorenzo D. Creel, Woodfords, Calif., about 1918. bottom center, Paddy Cap, Northern Paiute, Duck Valley Reservation, Owyhee, Nev., photograph by James Sherman, 1906; bottom right, Ignacio (b. 1828, d. 1913), leader of the Weeminuche band of Utes and an important member of 1880 and 1886 Ute delegations to Washington. Through his perserverance the Weeminuche band was granted a 525,000-acre reserve within the Southern Ute Reservation that became, in 1915, the Ute Mountain Ute Reservation. Photograph probably by Frank Balster, Colo., 1906.

CLEMMER AND STEWART

one. In addition, Julian Steward (1936d:10), who had done extensive ethnographic work among Western Shoshones, argued against creation of a pan-Western Shoshone tribal council and suggested, instead, that Nevada Shoshones be organized in "a series of smaller groups, based upon the present geographical distribution of the people, in which actual neighbors and kinsmen would cooperate in organization and new land units." Eventually, a compromise constitution was proposed which created a "Te-Moak Bands Tribe"; this was adopted by the Elko Colony in 1937 and by the South Fork community in 1941 following creation of the South Fork Reservation. The constitution provided for an unlimited number of separate reservations and colonies to join the Te-Moak Bands Tribe as constituent communities, but none did until Battle Mountain joined in 1977 and Wells in 1981.

The constitution also provides for creation of a Western Shoshone council with a chief, subchief, and members elected by constituent communities, but the BIA requirement that the individual colonies and reservations become separate "Western Shoshone tribes" has rendered creation of such a council quite unlikely. Although the descendants of Austin Shoshones continued to distinguish themselves from other Western Shoshones a general "Western Shoshone" identity has persisted, confirming the Nevada superintendency's insistence that the descendants of the signatories to the Treaty of Ruby Valley of 1863 regard themselves as a distinct nation still in possession of their aboriginal territory (E.R. Rusco 1982a:192; Clemmer 1970–1975). Until the late 1960s a "traditional council," convened sporadically by Muchach Temoke and later by his son, Frank Temoke, was the only political entity that drew representation from nearly all Western Shoshone communities. This council gathered and disseminated information but assumed no legislative, judicial, or executive responsibilities.

World War II cut short the implementation of New Deal policies on virtually all reservations. By 1943, the Indian Office headquarters had been moved to Chicago, where it had little influence with Washington legislators, and its budget had been eviscerated. Most of the programs initiated by Collier were no longer in existence by 1950.

Though the BIA seems to have recognized the need for employment on reservations, most new jobs were provided through the Indian Office's share of New Deal programs such as the Work Projects Administration and the Indian Civilian Conservation Corps. When these and other programs were curtailed, jobs disappeared. While the Indian Office made some effort to eject squatters and illegal users of reservation lands for stock-grazing, little change was effected in the leasing system, which often provided vast tracts to non-Indian permit-holders for a fraction of their actual value. The Indian Office recognized this problem as acute at Fort Hall (U.S. Congress. House. Committee on Interior and Insular Affairs 1953:598). Thus, where non-Indian rural economies held their own, Indian economies continued to stagnate despite some temporary improvement.

On the more positive side, the paternalistic control of Indian agents had ended. The land bases of some reservations had been greatly increased, and much progress had been made in eradicating endemic and chronic conditions of disease and malnutrition. Thus, by the middle of World War II some new directions had been set for nearly all Great Basin groups that permanently reversed the declines evident during the entrenched reservation period. Improved health care, for example, resulted in a rapidly growing population. The rise in infant survival rates and decreases in the incidence of dysentery, tuberculosis, and pneumonia increased the proportion of the population in the younger age groups.

Termination and Claims, 1946–1964

For the second time in two decades, federal policy changed course. In a complete reversal following World War II, the thrust of federal dealings with Indians was directed toward preparing all Indians for termination of federal trust responsibility; abolishing reservations; and providing assistance for nuclear families, rather than communities, to become integrated into the dominant society. Several developments contributed both to the acceleration of this thrust and to Indians' successful opposition to it (Lurie 1957:56–70; H.L. Peterson 1957:118–120; A.V. Watkins 1957:47–55; Zimmerman 1957:39; Clemmer 1970–1975; Jorgensen 1972:144–145, 150–152, 1978:22–25).

Senators Patrick McCarran (Nevada) and Arthur B. Watkins (Utah) were among those who pushed hardest for termination legislation. Thus, it can be said that the termination policy was at least partially constructed by policymakers who had a keen awareness of the history and contemporary situations of Great Basin Indians. Watkins and McCarran also supported establishment of the U.S. Indian Claims Commission in 1946. The Claims Commission acted as a separate tribunal with special rules that processed claims for monetary compensation pressed by Indian groups and tribes. The Court of Claims served as the first court of appeal, from which appeals could be made to the Supreme Court on questions of law. The enabling legislation provided that an expenditure plan be drawn up either by the particular tribe or by the secretary of the interior, and each tribe's plan was different. It is clear from remarks published in the *U.S. Congressional Record* (1946:5312–5317) that some legislators thought that disbursement of claims monies would eventually aid the termination process by either enabling tribes to finance all their own programs or by providing individuals with sufficient capital and investment funds to make them economically self-sufficient.

A second postwar development was mineral leasing. Coal, oil, and other mineral leases had been let on the Wind River Reservation as early as 1907 (ARCIA 1909:54). But between 1947 and 1955, large leases were negotiated for oil and gas at Northern Ute; for uranium, oil, and gas at Ute Mountain; for oil and gas at Southern Ute and Wind River; and for phosphates at Fort Hall.

A third development was the dismal failure of the BIA's relocation program. Intended to relieve the unemployment problem on reservations, this program was aimed especially at returning veterans. Provided with an apartment, job training, and employment in one of several cities—Denver, Salt Lake City, Chicago, Cleveland, Oakland, San Francisco, Los Angeles—the Indian client was expected to become an average, urban-dwelling wage-earner. But by the late 1950s, many relocatees from Fort Hall, Wind River, Northern Ute, and Southern Ute had returned home from experiencing layoffs, discrimination, inadequate preparation for city life, and alienation from kin and culture.

These younger heads of families—in their 30s, 40s, and 50s—sought alternatives within stagnating reservation milieus and unpromising economies. Termination, however, was not one of those alternatives. The Duck Valley Western Shoshones and Northern Paiutes, the Eastern Shoshones, the Northern Utes, and the Southern Utes were all asked to draw up termination plans. All refused to do so except for the Northern Utes, whose lawyer drew up a plan whereby the criterion for tribal membership would be raised from one-quarter to one-half Northern Ute blood quantum, and those of one-quarter or less would be given shares in the corporate assets of the tribe that would expire after a specified time period. The shares were similar to shares of stock and could be, and were, sold or given away by some "terminated Utes." The only other groups in the Great Basin to be terminated were bands of Southern Paiutes in southeastern Utah, and they had never been asked their opinions on termination at all.

Except for those on the Duck Valley and Klamath reservations, Western Shoshones and Northern Paiutes were not slated for termination. Both groups were rated on an "acculturation index" by the Bureau in 1950 and determined to be "unsuited" for termination at that time. Neither group had control over tracts of mineral-rich land and were among the last to be awarded financial settlements by the Indian Claims Commission. However, the results of lawsuits in the Court of Claims and later before the Indian Claims Commission brought many millions of dollars to Great Basin Indians between 1938 and 1962. In addition, mineral leasing brought millions more. Thus, tribal councils that had initially

had no budgets to administer and few decisions to make suddenly found themselves wielding huge sums and making expenditure priorities similar to those made by stockholding corporations. Individuals and families who had been poverty-stricken received several thousand dollars a year in per-capita distributions and dividend payments. Family incomes increased tenfold in some cases. At one point, family income at Wind River Reservation was substantially above that of Wyoming in general.

The implementation of the "Rehabilitation Plans" developed by the three Ute reservations for the use of their claims monies basically accomplished many of the unrealized goals of the BIA's New Deal policy. Tribal councils became the overseers of tribal governments that, by 1964, each employed 40–60 people, thus providing steady employment in much the same manner as the agencies had done in the 1930s and 1940s. Per capita income was increased to adequate levels. Attempts were made to improve reservation infrastructures through heavy investment in tribal cattle herds and improvement of range lands. Monies were set aside for distribution to minors when they reached age 18. Tribal scholarship programs for college attendance were started. Housing improvement committees were formed and dilapidated housing was finally repaired or replaced. Tribal welfare departments were funded in order to pick up where BIA and county welfare payments left off. With transfer of responsibility for sanitation and health care from the BIA to the Public Health Service in 1955, joint tribal-federal sewerage and water projects were undertaken.

By 1964, then, Great Basin groups found themselves in one of four situations: high-income reservations with large tribal budgets and households with a majority of their income from nongovernment sources; low-income reservations where a mixed strategy of wage labor, welfare, subsistence farming, and ranching and assistance from kin continued to predominate and households were poor or destitute; colonies, small reservations, and off-reservation communities in which households supported themselves by combining wage work with government assistance; and terminated groups, or those in the process of termination.

Claims Cases

Passage of the Indian Claims Commission Act in 1946 brought to fruition the efforts of various advocates over at least a 40-year period. Although Commissioners of Indian Affairs Francis Leupp, 1905–1908, and Collier, 1933–1945, as well as the authors of the Meriam Report of 1928 had advocated establishment of a special court or commission to adjudicate Indian claims, the final push for passage of the act came largely from attorneys for several Great Basin tribes, for example, Ernest L.

Table 4.   Great Basin Cases filed in U.S. Court of Claims 1863–1945

Plaintiff	Date Filed	Amount Claimed	Nature of Claim	Court Action
Ute (Confederated Bands)	Mar. 9, 1909	Not stated	Accounting for lands lost in Colorado after Meeker Massacre, 1880	Claim allowed May 23, 1910 $3,516,231.05
Klamath, Modoc, and Yahuskin Northern Paiutes	May 21, 1925	$7,810,549.05	Inadequate price paid for ceded land, 1864	Dismissed April 4, 1938
Klamath, Modoc, and Yahuskin Northern Paiutes	May 23, 1925	Not stated	Value of 87,000 acres of land and timber	Claim allowed June 7, 1937 $5,313,347.32 with interest
Klamath, Modoc, and Yahuskin Northern Paiutes	May 25, 1925	$970,000	General accounting on treaty session, Oct. 14, 1864	Dismissed Oct. 20, 1931
Eastern Shoshone	May 27, 1927	$37,150,279.90 plus interest	Alleged violation of treaty by settling Arapahos on Wind River Reservation	Dismissed May 5, 1930
Shoshone (Northwestern bands)	March 31, 1931	$15,070,000	Compensation for land taken and nonfulfillment of treaty, 1867	Dismissed Mar. 2, 1942
Ute (Confederated Bands)	Nov. 22, 1941	Not stated	Additional value due from land lost 1880	Claim allowed June 1950 $31,938,473.43
Ute (Confederated Bands)	Dec. 12, 1942	Not stated	Accounting suit	Claim dismissed Mar. 4, 1946
Ute (Confederated Bands)	Oct. 15, 1945	Not stated	Accounting suit	Dismissed ?

SOURCE: U.S. Congress. House. Committee on Interior and Insular Affairs 1953:1563–1571.

Wilkinson, who participated in drafting the act and testified at hearings regarding its passage. At the time, Wilkinson represented the Ute, the Klamath (including the Yahuskin band of Northern Paiutes), the Northern Shoshone and Bannock, and the Warm Springs Indians (including some Northern Paiutes) of Oregon.

Although in theory Indian tribes had had the right of submitting claims to the U.S. Court of Claims since 1863, in fact each tribe that desired to do so had to follow the same procedures as a foreign nation: it had to secure a congressional jurisdictional act giving that specific tribe permission to sue. Few tribes were able to muster the political influence necessary to do so. Great Basin tribes were authorized by Congress to sue the U.S. nine times before the passage of the Indian Claims Commission Act (table 4). By 1950, only 34 tribes in the United States had recovered any compensation from the Court of Claims; by far the most successful claim was by the Ute Indians of Colorado, who were awarded $31 million resulting from a suit filed in 1932 (Lurie 1957:56–57).

Congressional advocates of the Indian Claims Commission Act argued that (1) the U.S. should pay its "just debts" to the Indians by correcting mistakes that might have been made in securing some tracts of land through treaties in the past; (2) the U.S. had an obligation to apply "standards of fair and honorable dealings" to Indian tribes; (3) settlement of claims in a quick and efficacious manner should encourage the "progress of

the Indians who desire to be rehabilitated at the white man's level in the white man's economy"; and (4) if the claims were not settled, continuation of this situation would "perpetuate clouds on white men's titles that interfere with the proper development of the public domain" (U.S. Congressional Record 1946:5312–5317).

Five years were allowed after August 13, 1946, for "any Indian tribe, band, or other identifiable group of American Indians residing within the territorial limits of the United States or Alaska" to hire attorneys and to file petitions setting forth claims. The Commission early decided that it did not have the authority to return land, although it could, in response to proper arguments, declare that the Indian title to particular tracts had never been extinguished.

The Commission determined at what date specific parcels of Indian land were taken, how much was taken, and the value of the land at the time it was taken, in response to legal briefs and arguments filed by attorneys for various Indian groups and for the U.S. government. Its assumption was that Indian title was extinguished in any of the following ways: by negotiation of a treaty of cession, by the settling or homesteading of land by Whites, by the federal government taking or disposing of land, by reservations being created, or by states being created. More often than not, the lawyers for the government and for the Indians reached compromises between their two positions to stipulate the date of extinguishment. The dollar value of the land at the time of   *551*

Table 5. Great Basin Indian Claims Cases at the Indian Claims Commission

Tribe	Docket Number	Final Judgment	Disposition
Chemehuevi	351, 351-A	Jan. 18, 1965	$996,834.81 for land
Confederated Bands of Ute	327	Feb. 18, 1965	7,908,586.16 for land
Eastern Shoshone ("Shoshone of Wind River")	63 157	April 22, 1957 Feb. 24, 1965	433,013.60 for land 120,000.00 for gold removed from reservation
Eastern Shoshone and Northern Shoshone–Bannock ("Shoshone–Bannock," "Bannack," and "Shoshone")	326-D,E,F,G,H; 366, 367	Feb. 13, 1968	15,700,000.00 for land and accounting
Gosiute ("Goshute Shoshone")	326-B,J	Nov. 5, 1975	7,300,000.00 for lands and minerals
Klamath, Modoc, and Yahuskin band of Northern Paiute ("Yahooskin Band of Snake Indians")	100 100-A 100-B-1 100-C	Jan. 31, 1964 Sept. 2, 1969 Jan. 21, 1977 Jan. 21, 1977	2,500,000 for land 4,162,992.80 for land 18,000,000.00 for accounting 785,000.00 for accounting
Lemhi Northern Shoshone	326-I	Aug. 5, 1971	4,500,000.00 for land
Nev. Northern Paiute (of "Paviotso Tract")	87	Nov. 4, 1965	15,790,000.00 for land
Northern Paiute	87-A	March 2, 1978	Transferred to Court of Claims
Northern Paiute (not attached to Klamath), Oreg.	87	July 3, 1961	3,650,000.00 for land
Northern Paiute ("Snake or Piute") of former Malheur Res., Oreg.	17	Dec. 4, 1959	567,000.00 for land
Owens Valley Paiute (of "Mono Tract")	87	Nov. 4, 1965	935,000.00 for land
Pyramid Lake Northern Paiute	87-B	July 23, 1975	8,000,000.00 for deprivation of water
Southern Paiute	88, 330, 330-A	Jan. 18, 1965	7,253,165.19 for land and accounting
Southern Ute	328	July 14, 1971	Dismissed
Uintah Ute	44, 45	June 13, 1960	7,700,000.00 for land
Uncompahgre Ute	349	Feb. 18, 1965	300,000.00 for land not received
Western Shoshone (Temoak Bands)	326-K	Aug. 15, 1977	26,145,189.89 for land and minerals (refused)
Washoe	288	Dec. 2, 1970	4,959,350.00 for land
Western Shoshone (Temoak Bands) and Northern Shoshone–Bannock	326-A 326-C	May 8, 1976 Dec. 15, 1976	Transferred to Court of Claims Transferred to Court of Claims

SOURCE: U.S. Indian Claims Commission 1980.

extinguishment was also sometimes established in this manner. Once the Commission made a decision, either the government or the Indian group had three months to appeal the decision to the Court of Claims, but there was no further channel of appeal.

There were several stages in the process of awarding claims to Indians. After the Commission had determined the amount of money to be awarded, Congress had to pass an act authorizing the deposit of the money in the U.S. Treasury. The burden then shifted to the Bureau of Indian Affairs to hold meetings with each group named to determine how the awards should be paid and to prepare, or to submit if it was already prepared, a roll of all descendants of the group on whose behalf the lawsuit was filed. In some cases, a tribe was given the money with a few general guidelines for its expenditure, such as a percentage for new homes, for education, for farm loans. In other cases, the entire award was divided equally. The BIA ruled that an individual could receive an award for membership in only one group.

In the majority of successful cases, lawyers received a commission of 7–10 percent of the awards. Once the award was made and the money was in the hands of the Indians, such payment disposed "of all rights, claims or demands which said petitioners. . . could have asserted with respect to said tract. . . and said petitioners,. . . [were] barred thereby from asserting any such rights, claims, or demands against" the U.S. government in the future (*9 Ind. Cl. Comm. 417*; Forbes 1965:45).

The Northern Paiute Indians of the former Malheur Reservation, Oregon, were the first Great Basin group to file a claim. By December 29, 1950, the case had been heard and dismissed without award. On December 28, 1956, the Court of Claims reversed the 1950 ruling and remanded the Malheur docket for rehearing, attaching it to the Northern Paiute claim. Eventually, all Great Basin tribes filed claims (table 5).

In determining territorial boundaries of Great Basin groups as a basis for compensating the taking of land, the Commission gave more weight to the maps prepared under the supervision of James D. Doty (fig. 1) than to any other source. These maps, drawn up during the negotiations for the treaties of 1863, which were treaties of peace, not land cession, were intended to illustrate to Congress the extent of the territories of groups with which Congress was treating. However, the testimony of Anne Cooke Smith, Omer Stewart, and other anthropologists who served as expert witnesses for Great Basin tribes was often important in providing ethnohistorical data with which attorneys could counter the government's arguments that the groups in question had never existed, that they had come into existence long after the lands in question had been taken, or that their territorial boundaries were so vague that accurate bases for compensation could not be determined. In many cases, anthropological theory and interpretation accounted for many hours of testimony in the courtroom and resulted in some of the more contentious proceedings (Steward 1968, 1969; Clemmer 1970–1975).

The funds made available to Great Basin tribes as compensation for lands (fig. 11) and other resources taken without payment reached the total of $137,206,129, out of the total $818,172,606.64 authorized for all awards in the U.S. This includes the $26,145,189 awarded to the Western Shoshone but refused by them.

The Self-Determination Era, 1964–

President Lyndon Johnson's social programs were combined with adoption of a BIA policy, later enacted into law by the Indian Self-Determination Act of 1975, known as the "Buy Indian Contract." The "war on poverty" brought on-the-job training programs for youth and adults; housing developments financed and constructed through the Department of Housing and Urban Development; grants and programs from the Economic Development Administration; community action programs that did everything from emergency medical assistance to publication of community newspapers; Headstart centers; and various educational and rehabilitational programs that could be administered by lo-

Fig. 11. Tracts of land for which "original tribal occupancy" was recognized as a result of cases before the U.S. Indian Claims Commission or the U.S. Court of Claims (U.S. Indian Claims Commission 1980:map and ceded reservation areas in Colorado for which the Utes were compensated (U.S. Indian Claims Commission 1980:103; Royce 1899:pl.CXVI).

cal entities. The "Buy Indian Contract" philosophy initially meant that tribal governments were encouraged to submit bids to operate various BIA-funded programs, from road maintenance to welfare assistance. On reservations, tribal governments were to be given first choice in bidding to operate any number of federally funded programs. Those tribal governments that had the longest experience in administering large budgets were the first to take advantage of these opportunities. While at first these moves placed the three Ute tribes and Eastern Shoshone ahead of other Great Basin groups in services, standard of living, and income, the award of Bannock and Northern Paiute claims monies between 1964 and 1972 resulted in Fort Hall, Pyramid Lake, and Walker River Reservations developing profiles similar to the other large reservations: major employment was provided by federal agencies or tribal governments; unearned income accounted for a high proportion of household resources; and annual tribal budgets, including administered grants and contracts, soared into the hundreds of thousands of dollars.

The rise in population, income, life expectancy, and living standard has been accompanied on some reservations by rises in alcohol consumption and addiction, drug use, suicide, and homicide. These were reported as severe problems in the 1960s, 1970s, and 1980s among the Northern, Mountain, and Southern Ute; Fort Hall Northern Shoshone–Bannock; and Eastern Shoshone. 553

Data from the 1980 census indicate that despite efforts by tribal and federal programs to improve the economic infrastructures of reservations, all groups except the Dresslerville Washoe and the Walker River Northern Paiute had substantially larger proportions—1.5 to 5 times as large—of persons below poverty level than surrounding non-Indian populations in the late 1970s. Except for the Kaibab Southern Paiute, Warm Springs Reservation, and Bishop Colony, all reservations with Great Basin populations had substantially lower female labor force participation rates than the United States as a whole. On no reservation did per capita income exceed 70 percent of the average U.S. per capita income, and on some reservations, per capita income was less than 30 percent of the U.S. average. The incidence of female-headed families on the majority of Great Basin reservations far exceeded the incidence of female-headed families in the U.S. in general.

Although nearly all the larger tribes had at least one tribal enterprise by 1970, few have showed profits in the subsequent 10–15 years, or even met operating expenses, with the exception of Moapa. Farming and ranching were still popular pastimes on most reservations, but produced only a fraction of total household incomes. Leasing of reservation lands to non-Indian ranchers was still widespread. Mineral development continued to be entrenched at Fort Hall, Northern Ute, Ute Mountain, Southern Ute, and Wind River Reservations. Three hundred oil and gas rigs operated on the Northern Ute Reservation, but only seven Utes were working for these firms in 1982. A similar situation prevailed at Southern Ute. The bulk of the Northern Ute Tribal Council's operating budget of 17 million dollars derived from oil and gas royalties (Jorgensen 1984c).

The tribal governments of all reservations administered sums of federal monies to varying degrees in the 1970s. Even small reservations and colonies were administering grants and contracts. In the 1980s, the dependence of these smaller communities on local economies seemed to be giving way to a strategy based on securing nonlocal funding sources.

Wind River and the three Ute reservations were generating 60–70 percent of their incomes from internal sources—mineral royalties, investment dividends, or leases. This capability permitted the Northern Ute tribe, for example, to have 420 tribal members on its payroll in the early 1980s (Jorgensen 1984c). Thus, in 30 years, these tribes reversed the trend of the previous 70 years: instead of merely absorbing federal dollars year after year, they were able to use federal and private dollars to generate a considerable local multiplier effect, and thus to contribute substantially to local economies.

After more than two decades in which the reservation land base in the Great Basin actually shrank through termination of the Utah Southern Paiutes, the self-de-

termination era witnessed the addition of 123,261 acres to 14 reservations and colonies. In 1980, long after a federal commission had revealed abysmal economic and educational conditions and total lack of informed consent in the termination process (cf. Brophy and Aberle 1966), the four Southern Paiute bands as well as other non-reservation Paiutes in southern Utah were restored to trust status, and a 15,000-acre reservation was established. This reservation included most of what was still under nominal Paiute ownership through a trustee arrangement outside the BIA purview, but it was less than half the original reservation acreage (table 2). The Utah Paiutes formed an interim council, and by 1984 were operating under a tribal council form of government. In 1983 Congress passed legislation adding 160 acres to the Burns, Oregon, allotments and 3,840 acres to the Las Vegas Colony. The San Juan Southern Paiutes, most of whom lived at Gap and Willow Springs, Arizona, had a petition before Congress to be recognized as a separate tribe and to have their homesteads and surrounding land, officially part of the Navajo Reservation, as well as the "Paiute Strip" placed under separate trust status. Reservations in 1980 are shown in figure 12.

Two longstanding legal issues could drastically affect the resource base of Great Basin Indians. One issue is that of water resources. After a series of legal challenges ending before the Supreme Court, the Pyramid Lake Paiutes failed in 1983 in their attempt to guarantee their rights to the Pyramid Lake fishery that had been an integral part of their resource inventory in aboriginal and early reservation times.

The second issue is that of Western Shoshones' legal control over their aboriginal territory. Well-defined in the 1863 Treaty of Ruby Valley, Western Shoshone land includes many abandoned mines and homesteads as well as vast tracts administered as "public domain" by the Bureau of Land Management. Although the treaty permitted establishment of mines and of ranches, homesteads, roads, rail lines, timber industries, and towns to support the mining industry, it did not extinguish aboriginal title or convey title to either the U.S. government or any other entity. When Congress purchased abandoned homesteads and ranches in the 1930s and 1940s and turned them into reservations, many Shoshones considered the action to be a token gesture to mask the government's real failure to adhere to its treaty obligations.

When Western Shoshones were asked to submit a claim to the Indian Claims Commission, only four groups—Duck Valley, Elko, South Fork, and Battle Mountain—participated in the deliberations, and later Battle Mountain withdrew its representative. Rather than asking for monetary compensation, many Shoshones boycotted the claims proceedings because they felt that, again, the government was attempting to sidestep

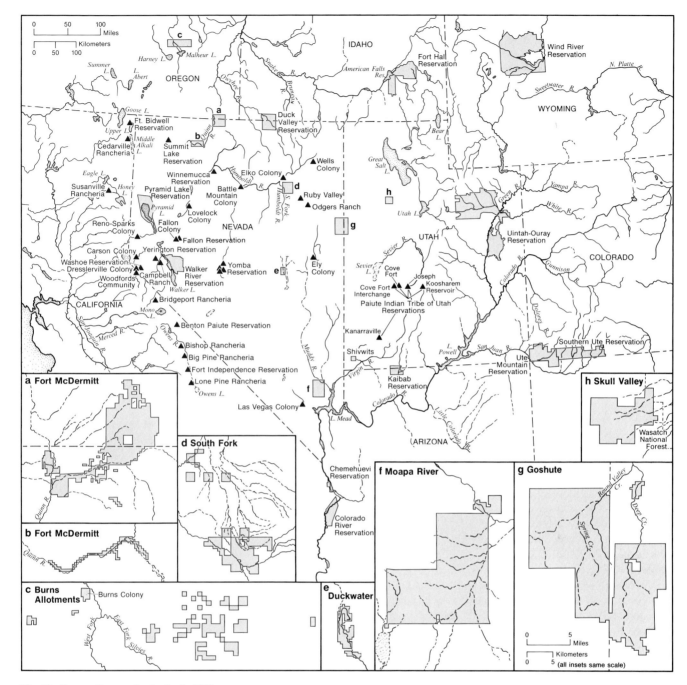

Fig. 12. Reservations and colonies in 1980.

its treaty obligations and to pay them off rather than to return their land. Efforts to enforce the Ruby Valley Treaty became the basis for formation of a "traditionalist" revitalization movement in the 1950s and 1960s (Clemmer 1972).

The Te-Moak Bands Tribal Council was eventually elected by representatives from the four participating groups to represent the "Western Shoshone Identifiable Group." Although only a fraction of Western Shoshones, perhaps 30 percent, were members of these groups, the Te-Moak Bands Council was duly certified as the

Western Shoshone government to participate in all stages of the claims process, since federal legislation made no stipulations concerning the exact composition, nature, or origins of the particular Indian government asking for compensation on behalf of an identifiable group or tribe.

Throughout the 1960s and 1970s state and federal authorities came into conflict with Western Shoshones over control and use of land in eastern Nevada. Regulation of hunting seasons, license and tag requirements for hunting deer and sage hen, and the Bureau of Land

Management's destruction of piñon-juniper stands ostensibly to improve wildlife habitats and grazing lands were all opposed by Western Shoshones.

In 1974 Shoshones at Battle Mountain formed the Western Shoshone Legal Defense and Education Association as part of the community's participation in making a documentary film favorable to the traditionalists' position. The association, along with Frank Temoke, attempted to intervene in the Claims Commission proceedings to reopen the Western Shoshone case, but the Commission refused. At the same time, the Bureau of Land Management brought a trespass suit against two Western Shoshones, Carrie Dann and Mary Dann, who refused to pay grazing permits for horses and cattle that, they said, were grazing on Shoshone land, not on public domain. In 1976 the Legal Defense Association was replaced by the Western Shoshone Sacred Lands Association (fig. 13) which mounted an educational campaign to convince Shoshones and non-Indians alike of the importance of pressing for return of land rather than accepting the Claims Commission's monetary award.

In 1979 the government made its disposition in the Western Shoshone claims case by depositing the final award, 26 million dollars, in a "Western Shoshone Account" in the U.S. Treasury in Washington, D.C. Enabling legislation, however, required that, for an award to be valid, it had to be officially accepted by vote, and the awardees had to be given the opportunity to draw up a distribution plan for the money. In a meeting convened by the BIA, Western Shoshones rejected the award by majority vote in 1980 and refused to draw up a distribution plan. This action followed by a year the ruling of a federal judge in Reno that, until the award had been deposited in the Western Shoshone Account the Danns had been within their rights in not paying grazing fees since Western Shoshone aboriginal title was still in force, but as soon as the award had been deposited Western Shoshones, and therefore the Danns, had lost rights to the land because depositing the money in the bank effectively constituted an extinguishment of title by the government. The Danns appealed the decision, but it was upheld by the Supreme Court in February 1985.

Sources

Many of the sources of data on which the summaries and tables in this article are based, especially for the period 1859–1960, are reports and papers that were originally published in very small quantities or were not published at all. Citation of all these sources has not been attempted in the text; some of them are listed in O.C. Stewart (1978).

556   Much unpublished information is in the various doc-

Fig. 13. Leaders of the Western Shoshone Sacred Lands Association, which sued the federal government for control of their traditional territory in Nev. left to right, Sandy Dann, Glenn Holley, Kathleen Holley, Mary Dann, Carrie Dann, and Clifford Dann. Photograph by Ilka Hartman, near Beowawe, Nev., 1979.

uments, reports, and theses generated by the Tri-Ethnic Research Project, which produced studies on subjects ranging from demography to ethnohistory. Some of these works are available on microfilm and are reviewed by O.C. Stewart (1982). The major summary of the project's findings is Jessor et al. (1968); works that are especially relevant to this chapter are Collins (1971), C.C. Johnson (1963), Lang (1953, 1954, 1961–1962), O'Neil (1971), and O.C. Stewart (1971a).

The following sources were especially valuable in the reconstruction of the early reservation period: for the Southern Paiute, Bunte and Franklin 1983; Knack 1980; A. Spencer 1973; O.C. Stewart 1984b; for the Northern Paiute, McGreehan 1973; Knack and Stewart 1984; J.W. Hulse 1981; Canfield 1983; S.Hopkins 1883; for the Gosiute, Reagan 1934a; Malouf 1940b; for Duck Valley Reservation, McKinney 1983; for the Northern Shoshone and Bannock, Madsen 1980; for the Western Shoshone Mack 1968; Patterson 1973; Hyde 1973; O.C. Stewart 1978; and for the Ute, Jorgensen 1964, 1972, 1978, 1984c; Opler 1940; Stillwaggon 1979. Herman (1972) is valuable only for its photos and anecdotes of Northern Paiutes. Important sources of specific information on treaties, population, reservation acreage, and early reservation life are the reports of the commissioners of Indian affairs, as well as letters from agents and farmers to the commissioner, filed by state superintendency and housed in several repositories of the National Archives. Other works are also important for discussion of the treaty and early reservation periods (Abel 1915; E.E. Hill 1974; Kappler 1904–1941; Powell and Ingalls in ARCIA 1874; Royce 1899; U.S. Department of the Interior 1866; ARCIA 1865, 1875; U.S. Congress. Senate 1914; U.S. Indian Claims Commission 1954).

For the entrenched reservation, New Deal, and termination periods, Dobyns (1948), d'Azevedo et al. (1966), Euler and Naylor (1952), U.S. Indian Claims Commission (1972), Mizen (1964), E.R. Rusco (1982a), O.C. Stewart (1961, 1979), U.S. Congress. House. Committee on Interior and Insular Affairs (1953), and U.S. Congress. Senate. Committee on Indian Affairs (1934) were important. Population and acreage figures were drawn from comparisons among Royce (1899),

U.S. Congress. House. Committee on Interior and Insular Affairs (1953), U.S. Department of Commerce (1974), and U.S. Bureau of the Census (1980a). Events of the self-determination era are impossible to summarize for all groups, but the following sources are valuable: Knack 1980; Houghton 1973, 1973a; Lynch 1971; U.S. Department of Commerce 1974; Nevada Indian Commission 1980; Jorgensen 1972. For discussion of land issues among the Western Shoshone and Southern Paiute see Forbes (1965, 1967), Shattuck (1981), Clemmer (1972, 1974), Clemmer-Smith (1981), Thorpe (1981), E.R. Rusco (1982), Widener (1984). For political events among the Western Shoshone in the 1960s and 1970s see Forbes (1967), Clemmer (1972, 1973, 1978), Clemmer-Smith (1981), and E.R. Rusco (1982a). For economic developments, see Clemmer (1972), E.R. Rusco (1982a), and Christensen (1967).

Tribal Politics

ELMER R. RUSCO AND MARY K. RUSCO

Political life for Great Basin Indians in the 1980s has both external and internal dimensions. The relationships with the wider Euro-American society are crucial to the survival of Native Americans as culturally distinct, self-governing peoples, and because of this status Native governments make many decisions of crucial importance within their own societies. The literature about these aspects of Great Basin Indian life is small and contradictory. How much of the disagreement results from the fact that each tribe or reservation is in a sense unique and has a unique set of relationships with Euro-American society and how much is due to inadequate understanding on the part of scholars is unclear.

Until the 1970s almost all literature about Great Basin Indians was produced by anthropologists, who seldom focused on contemporary conditions. Early anthropological work on Native Americans aimed to preserve information about societies as they existed before Euro-American contact, or at least before recent changes resulting from contact, because the cultures of such societies were believed to be disappearing. While some anthropologists have concerned themselves with contemporary conditions, as have a few scholars in other fields, scholarship has not yet produced a comprehensive picture of modern Native American politics in the Great Basin.

Theoretical Frameworks

Three theoretical constructs dealing with the nature of Indian and Euro-American interaction are helpful in understanding Great Basin political life in the late twentieth century: the legal, neocolonial, and interaction theories.

The legal theory, brilliantly explicated by Felix Cohen (1941), describes the historic interaction of Native with European or Euro-American groups, which created a pattern of legal rights that gives Indians a unique position in the general American polity. In some part, this legal structure was created by treaties between Indian and Euro-American societies, but it was also in part the product of decisions by the United States Supreme Court and the executive branch. This model explains much of the interaction of recognized Indian societies with the federal government. Administrators concerned with Indian affairs have not always conformed their policies to the theory as recognized by the courts, but the existence of this legal structure has nevertheless had an impact.

Several aspects of the legal model are of great significance. First, although Congress may limit their sovereignty by explicit action, Indian societies still retain the right to govern themselves in many areas and are not bound by the United States Constitution in several respects; in fact, they are legally separate from both the federal government and the states. Second, the model restricts the authority of states over Indian societies except where Congress has specifically permitted state jurisdiction; hence, Indians deal primarily with the federal government. Third, the federal government has trust responsibilities toward Indians that are unique; these include protecting Indian land and resources.

The neocolonial theory, one of the best formulations of which was developed out of a study of Great Basin Indians, sees Native peoples as victims of a colonial system that subjects them to inconstant but massive assaults on their remaining resources and cultures. Jorgensen (1972) studied the Sun Dance religion as it was practiced in the 1950s and 1960s on five predominantly Ute, Northern Shoshone, and Eastern Shoshone reservations in Colorado, Utah, and Wyoming, and in doing so developed neocolonial theory to describe Indian–Euro-American interactions in general.

Jorgensen's approach, which is complex and intertwined with a great deal of information about the several groups he studied, is based upon the postulate that, chiefly for economic gain, the governing structures of general American society push steadily toward the destruction of Native American societies. He documents conquests of various groups, the forcible taking of Indian-owned lands, the past confinement of Indians to reservations, racist-ethnocentric attempts to destroy Indian cultures, and contemporary attempts to secure control over Indian lands, water, or other resources. As a result, Indians have been and are poor; their poverty, health, and other problems derive from their position within the economy of the general society. The nature of the forces within the general society is variously described. The basic categories are "metropolis" and "satellites," but the meaning of these terms seems to vary. At times, Jorgensen seems to suggest that Indians are a special case of the general "underdevelopment" of rural areas, which is the underside of urban "development," but in another publication he cites the "concentration of economic and political power and political influence" within the overall society as the basic fact; it is happenstance that this concentration is physically located in urban areas (Jorgensen 1971:84–85). In another article, he identifies financial and corporate structures ultimately owned by the "ruling class" as the decision-makers (Jorgensen, Davis, and Mathews 1978:10). In any case, his central argument is that attempts to deprive Indians of their land and resources and to keep them "underdeveloped" result from the domination of non-Indian governments by groups that benefit from exploitation of Indians, and apparently he believes that it is inevitable that the "metropolis" will prevail.

By implication, the neocolonial theory assigns little importance to the legal structure of Indian rights and to the various changes in orientation of Congress and the federal bureaucracy that have characterized Indian policy. For example, Jorgensen notes the reversal of the allotment policy during the Indian New Deal and recognizes that Bureau of Indian Affairs Commissioner John Collier during the 1930s attempted to conform administrative policy to the legal structure by acknowledging tribal sovereignty. The Indian Reorganization Act of 1934 "in many respects . . . made Indian tribes into small states within states" (Jorgensen 1972:98). However, he does not see this development as a basic change in the nature of Indian–Euro-American interaction, arguing that "with the adoption of charters and constitutions under the provisions of the IRA, Indians were supposed to begin to exercise *some* power over the disposition of their lands and the direction their reservation lives would take, but ultimate approval and control always rested with the Secretary of the Interior" (Jorgensen 1972:100). In fact, he concluded, "the IRA actually *increased* the power that the federal bureaucracy held over" Indians because of departmental authority "to review nearly all ordinances they passed, whether they were financial, legal, or other" (Jorgensen 1972:139). Further, other agencies of the federal government and Congress can still control Indian lives. Finally, he asserted that while the BIA from the Collier era on promoted Indian self-government in part, its policies also pressed on Indians two sets of values that were at odds with traditional Indian values: federally urged collectivism and Protestant-ethic individualism. Both of these he sees as different from Indian collectivism, and he explains the persistence and growth of the Sun Dance religion among the Great Basin groups he studied as being due to its religious embodiment of Indian collectivism.

Another view, the interaction theory, asserts that relations between Indians and non-Indians are best explained by mutual influence. In this view, Native American societies are not passive victims of forces in the wider society. Instead, the present position of Indians is the result of their responses to Euro-American efforts to dominate, exploit, or change them and also of Indian responses to changed conditions facing both societies. The cultures and societies that have emerged from this interaction are neither purely aboriginal nor purely Euro-American. There seems to be no example of this theory that can match either the legal or the neocolonial theory in complexity and sophistication. However, such a model is outlined in a study of the Northern Arapahoe, who are Plains Indians, sharing the Wind River Reservation with the Eastern Shoshone (L. Fowler 1982).

Lynch (1973) asserted that a simpler patron-client model of mutual influence best described the situation of the residents of "Brownsville," a small urban colony of Northern Paiute, at the end of the 1970s. The BIA is the patron and the colony is the client. Since this model was developed to describe other types of social systems, its strict applicability to the Great Basin is doubtful, but Lynch's major point is that the people of Brownsville are in a position to exercise some control over their lives and practice some self-determination. He showed that they have not been forced to give up their social identity and all aspects of their previous culture. A more complete interaction model would presumably identify the factors that affect the relative strength of the two parties to the interaction.

Evaluation of the Theories

Although the data for systematic testing of the adequacy of these theories are scarce, some tentative conclusions about their relative explanatory power may be drawn. Elements of all three help to explain the position of Indians in the Great Basin since the nineteenth century.

First, as the neocolonial theory predicts, many of the most important problems facing Indians concern retaining ownership of land and other resources. Although not all Great Basin groups were conquered in a military sense, all experienced substantial loss of land as Euro-Americans moved into the area. Reservations are the remnants of vast areas once owned by Indians. In most cases, surviving Indian groups have accepted monetary awards for the loss of their lands. The land base by the 1980s was clearly too small to provide sufficient resources for the Indians who still desired to live on it. Moreover, assaults on Indian land and resources are ongoing, and not just of historical interest. This is particularly the case with respect to water rights and the development of nonrenewable resources.

On the other hand, the ability of Indians to protect and even to enlarge their resources in some cases is substantial, and at least part of this capacity is due to their legal position. The land base of several Nevada tribes was increased during the 1930s. After 1970 trust

left, Colo. Histl. Soc., Denver; right, Shoshone–Bannock Tribes, Sho-Ban Media Center, Fort Hall, Idaho.

Fig. 1. Indian policemen. left, Southern Ute tribal police; left to right: Dick Charley, wearing an unofficial peace medal bearing a likeness of George Washington of the kind widely distributed to Indians in the late 19th century (Prucha 1976:69), Rob Richards and Severo wearing Indian police badges, and Bob Richards wearing a neck scarf pin with an Indian on it, possibly an exposition or fair souvenir. Photograph by Harry Buckwalter, Colo., 1890s. The establishment of uniformed Indian police followed the creation of the reservations (Hagan 1966). Indian agents hired local chiefs and warriors to serve as a police force; their duties included arresting intruders and squatters on reservations; driving out cattle, horse, or timber thieves; guarding rations and agency property; making arrests; and returning truants to school (U.S. Bureau of Indian Affairs. Division of Law Enforcement Services 1975:10). In the 1980s law enforcement on reservations was the responsibility of BIA or tribal police. Since 1969 the BIA-operated Indian Police Academy has offered training for both BIA and tribal police. In 1984 the Indian Police Academy, Marana, Ariz., trained 44 cadets representing 18 tribes (U.S. Bureau of Indian Affairs. Office of Public Information 1985:3). right, Larry Neaman, an Eastern Shoshone born in Ft. Washakie, Wyo., who became a member of the Northern Shoshone–Bannock tribe, Fort Hall, and a tribal policeman. Photograph by Bill Richmonds at Fort Hall Reservation, 1976.

land was established by Congress for Washoes living near Woodfords, California, and for Western Shoshone at Wells, Nevada; and the Fallon Paiute-Shoshone Tribe and the Las Vegas and Moapa groups of Southern Paiutes had significant additions to their reservations. Also, the several Southern Paiute bands in Utah, terminated during the 1950s, were extended recognition as the Paiute Indian Tribe of Utah by a Congressional statute, and their land base was enlarged.

While the evidence is incomplete and subject to varying interpretations, it seems that there are enough instances in which the federal government has honored its legal obligation to protect Indian resources to justify the conclusion that this government is not automatically or necessarily part of an assault on Indian rights. Another example is government support for the water rights of the Pyramid Lake Northern Paiute tribe. Also, during the 1970s the federal government significantly increased funding for Indian programs while reducing federal government control over the spending of these funds. For most Great Basin groups in the 1970s there was both a meaningful increase in employment for Indians on reservations and increased services and moneys available to individual Indians as a result of these federal government policies. The extent to which these developments have advanced the long-run economic viability of reservation economies is less clear. There has been an apparent reduction in Indian poverty since 1970 in the Great Basin as a result of federal policies, but unemployment and poverty rates on reservations remain high.

The role of tribal governments since the 1930s remains a matter of controversy. For many groups BIA control over tribal decision-making has probably declined as a result of deliberate federal policy and the entry of Indians into top-level positions within the BIA, at the same time as the increased tribal resources have strengthened the capacities of tribal governments to function effectively, but hard evidence on this point is difficult to secure. On the Uintah-Ouray Ute reservation, during the 1950s, the tribal council increased its competence and resources, even though a portion of the tribe withdrew from it. By 1960 "agency personnel tacitly acknowledged the fact that power and authority had shifted almost imperceptibly to the Utes" (Lang 1961–1962:171).

Case Histories of Interaction

There is substantial scholarly writing on the relations between the Pyramid Lake Paiute Tribe (Northern Paiute) and non-Indians. Non-Indian settlement of northwestern Nevada resulted in the creation of the reservation in 1858–1859. In addition to a brief violent conflict in 1860 (the Pyramid Lake War), the Paiutes

560

experienced numerous assaults on their reservation and its resources. Non-Indian ranchers illegally took up some of the best farmland and others grazed cattle on the reservation, commercial and sports fishermen utilized the lake without compensation to the tribe, and a railroad and accompanying town were built on part of the reservation without tribal consent. The Pyramid Lake fisheries declined as a result of upstream sawdust dumping by lumber companies and the diversion of stream flow to the Truckee-Carson Irrigation District. In addition, the state of Nevada was able to curb the tribe's commercial fishing. In the long run, then, the tribe has certainly experienced the assault on its resources predicted by the neocolonial theory (Knack and Stewart 1984).

The federal government's role is complicated. Since the 1930s it has most often attempted to protect the interests of the Pyramid Lake Paiutes, in part because of the strength of their legal rights. In the 1920s Congress passed legislation allowing squatters to purchase lands seized on the reservation; when some of the ranchers failed to make payments under the provisions of this law, the government moved to take possession of the lands for the Indians. Although the struggle took a long time, eventually the tribe recovered this land. Attempts, beginning in the 1930s, by Nevada's powerful United States Sen. Patrick McCarran to enact legislation to award the land to the non-Indian ranchers were consistently thwarted. F. M. Dixon (1980) and Underdal (1977) conclude that the tribe's efforts were aided substantially by the tribal council organized in the 1930s under the Indian Reorganization Act.

During the 1970s there was a conflict between the Pyramid Lake Paiute Tribe and a commission representing ranching and other non-Indian interests in Nevada and California (Haller 1981). The commission negotiated an interstate compact governing water of several interstate rivers, including the Truckee. The tribe believed that ratification of the compact by the state legislatures and Congress would result in the loss of waters to which it was legally entitled. Tribal opposition did not prevent passage by the legislatures (although it did result in some amendments), but in 1984 the compact had not yet been ratified by Congress, at least partly because of tribal opposition.

A complicated struggle by the tribe to secure legal rights to enough water to maintain the lake's present level continued in 1985. One federal district court ordered the secretary of the interior to manage diversions to the Truckee-Carson Irrigation District in such a way as to protect Pyramid Lake and its fisheries, but a federal district court in Nevada turned down a tribal challenge to a 1944 decree allowing it only enough water from the Truckee for irrigation of a small part of the reservation. Federal moneys permitted the restoration of much of the fishery, a federally financed dam near

Inter-Tribal Council of Nevada, Reno: 590.
Fig. 2. Boundary sign of the Goshute Indian Reservation, Nev. and Utah (Western Shoshone), evidence of the jurisdictional reality of tribal government. Photograph by Bob Shaw, 1971.

the mouth of the river provided protection from erosion for Indian lands as well as protection for the fisheries, and the legal struggle continued (Knack and Stewart 1984). In short, since the 1930s the tribe has been unusually aggressive and effective, often with support by the federal government. Although the outcome has been loss of some resources, others have been saved and the outcomes are dramatically better from the Indian point of view than in earlier periods.

In another conflict of national importance, a group of traditionalist Western Shoshone persistently asserted, through litigation, its legal title to most of the lands within aboriginal Western Shoshone territory (*U.S.* v. *Mary Dann and Carrie Dann*) (E. Rusco 1982) ("Treaties, Reservations, and Claims," this vol.). Clemmer (1972) gives an elaborate account of the efforts of the Western Shoshone traditionalists over many years to assert their claim. The claim is based on the Ruby Valley Treaty of 1863, which provided for peace with the Western Shoshone and the United States, the establishment of a reservation within the treaty territory, annuities for 20 years, and the cession of lands for specified purposes but did not provide explicitly for the transfer of the bulk of Western Shoshone lands to federal control. In addition to asserting the land claim, traditionalists also opposed the destruction of pine nut forests within the treaty territory and asserted their right to hunt and fish off-reservation; they also continued aboriginal religious and other beliefs and practices. In the late 1970s they cooperated extensively with various non-Indian groups to oppose plans to deploy the MX missile system (fig. 3) in Utah and Nevada (Wilcox and Eubank 1982).

Clemmer (1973) described a stable though informal structure, which he called the traditional council, made up of Western Shoshone from many places within the

561

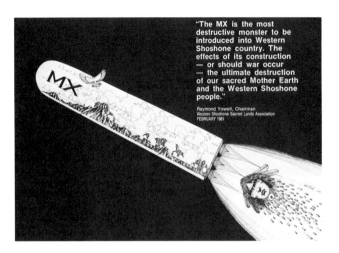

"The MX is the most destructive monster to be introduced into Western Shoshone country. The effects of its construction — or should war occur — the ultimate destruction of our sacred Mother Earth and the Western Shoshone people."

Raymond Yowell, Chairman
Western Shoshone Sacred Lands Association
FEBRUARY 1981

Jack R. Malotte, Reno, Nev.

Fig. 3. Poster protesting the proposed installation of multiple-warhead intercontinental ballistic missiles (MX), by the Western Shoshone artist Jack R. Malotte, 1981.

treaty territory; he viewed this council as an alternative to tribal councils organized on several Western Shoshone reservations under the IRA. However, the traditionalists have shown that they are flexible on strategy and tactics for achieving their goals. A study of the writing of the Te-Moak Bands' constitution during the 1930s found that the traditional council probably attempted at this time to organize under a written constitution. This move was blocked by the Washington office of the BIA, which ruled that the Te-Moak Bands were not a tribe or based on a reservation. As a result, the proposed constitution was rewritten to apply to the Elko Colony and any subsequently created reservations (E. Rusco 1982a).

The traditional council continued largely outside the Te-Moak Bands structure for many years but in the 1970s incorporated under Nevada state law. Later, the traditionalists re-entered the Te-Moak Bands Council and, after the favorable court decision in 1983, joined in creating a new structure to include all Western Shoshone, whether they lived on or off reservations (*Reno Gazette-Journal*, February 5, 1984). A group within the Western Shoshone tribe has thus adopted various organizational forms and joined with other Western Shoshone to accomplish its objectives. What is constant is the set of objectives, not organizational forms. At times, even Indian Reorganization Act constitutional structures have been used by the traditionalists. Forbes (1967) documents similar independent action, taking various forms, by other Nevada tribes seeking to protect their rights over several decades.

During the early 1960s, the Inter-Tribal Council of Nevada was organized as an umbrella group to provide services to many reservations. Although the Walker River Tribe of Northern Paiute was designated a Community Action Agency by the Office of Economic Op-

portunity and thus received federal poverty funds, most reservations and colonies in Nevada had populations too small to permit separate funding. The Inter-Tribal Council was the poverty agency for most Nevada Indian groups and received many other federal and some private grants, with the result that for years it was the largest single employer of Indians in the state.

In 1969 the Inter-Tribal Council, deeply involved in administering several governmental programs, initiated a study that sought to increase Indian involvement still further. Funded by the Department of Health, Education, and Welfare, this program was conducted by the Inter-Tribal Council with technical assistance from Warren d'Azevedo and Elaine Walbroek, a community development specialist. The director of the project was John Dressler (fig. 4), chairman of Council's executive board; except for three part-time employees, it was staffed by Indians. The planning of a new program to improve the delivery of government assistance involved a community self-study (Dressler and Rusco 1970). The project provided information about six Nevada colonies and reservations and included studies of how the tribal councils interacted with the non-Indian communities surrounding them.

The genesis and findings of this study illustrate the process that seems to have been going on then throughout the Great Basin. Indian-controlled agencies were assuming a more vigorous role in the provision of services to Indian people, and at the same time the BIA and Indian Health Service were staffed at higher levels by Indians. Until this process was reversed after 1980, federal funds available for Indian programs steadily increased. Clearly, conditions changed on most Great Basin reservations; many new homes were built, roads were paved, water systems were improved, community buildings were constructed, educational and health programs were expanded, and there were a number of attempts at economic development.

Another aspect of change during the 1970s was that formal organization within reservations became more elaborate (fig. 5). In addition to strengthened tribal councils, which after 1975 received federal funds for purely administrative costs, a network of advisory committees and authorities was built on many reservations. One change was the shift of membership of these committees from largely non-Indian to all or predominantly tribal members. Although staffing these committees undoubtedly placed a strain on small tribal groups, it clearly increased local control (Dressler and Rusco 1970).

Another change was the extension of legal services to more Nevada groups and individuals through the Office of Economic Opportunity and later through Legal Services Programs. In 1984, a statewide Legal Services office served Nevada Indians as well as non-Indians outside Washoe County.

In brief, at least in Nevada, the late 1960s and 1970s

left, Clayton B. Sampson, Reno, Nev.; center, *Native Nevadan,* Reno-Sparks Indian Colony.

Fig. 4. Some prominent Basin natives. left, Harry Carl Sampson and Dewey Edward Sampson, Northern Paiute brothers. Harry, a founder of the Reno-Sparks colony, served it in various capacities. Dewey Sampson was involved in organizing both the Pyramid Lake Paiute Tribal Council and the Reno-Sparks Tribal Council in the 1930s. Photograph probably taken at Stewart Indian School, Carson, Nev., 1920s. center, Linda Howard, Chairman of the Yerington Northern Paiute, 1970s–1980s, and of the Inter-Tribal Council of Nevada in 1984. Photographed in Reno, June 1984. right, John Dressler, Chairman of the Washoe Tribe during the 1960s and 1970s. He was the first Chairman of the Inter-Tribal Council of Nevada and of the Nevada Indian Affairs Commission. Photograph by Tom Dressler, about 1967.

saw increased resources coming to tribal governments and the Inter-Tribal Council. The overall result was a strengthening of tribal governments in many areas, although the extent of BIA control of these governments is not entirely clear.

Increased funds to tribes have not come from increased strength in state and local elections. Indian participation in non-Indian elections is probably less than the participation of other groups. Jorgensen (1972:136) reported very low registration and voting in non-Indian elections on five Ute, Northern Shoshone, and Eastern Shoshone reservations. Cedar City Southern Paiutes did not participate in non-Indian elections; in spite of a registration effort there were no registered voters in this community in the late 1970s (Knack 1975:40–41). C.C. Johnson (1963:4) reported that, as of 1960, only about 15 percent of the tribal electorate on a Ute reservation was registered for non-Indian elections.

There is only one study of how Indians vote in non-Indian elections, reporting voting behavior in primary and general elections from 1950 through 1964 for three largely Indian precincts in Nevada (E. Rusco 1966). While voting participation in these precincts was less than in the state as a whole, there was significant participation in each election. Nixon (Pyramid Lake) was strongly Democratic during these years while Schurz (the Walker River Reservation) was less Democratic, and Owyhee (the Duck Valley Reservation) was slightly more Republican than Schurz was Democratic. Further, although Nixon's voters reacted sharply against Senator McCarran after he introduced bills to prevent the return

of reservation land to the tribe (his share of the vote at Nixon fell from 55 percent in 1932 to 8 percent in 1938), there is no indication that the other two reservations joined Nixon in opposing McCarran. There is also no evidence of coordination among the three reservations in primary elections or proposition campaigns. The Inter-Tribal Council of Nevada made efforts to increase politial cooperation of Indians on a statewide basis in the 1970s, but the effect of this effort is not known. Tribal members interviewed reported a relatively high level (57%) of participation in tribal elections, but much less participation in state and national elections (37 and 35% respectively) (Dressler and Rusco 1970:33).

A partial measure of Indian impact in elections would be the number of Indians elected to non-Indian offices. Evidently only two Great Basin Indians have been elected to state legislatures. In 1938, Dewey E. Sampson (fig. 4), a Northern Paiute then living at the Pyramid Lake Reservation, was elected to the Nevada Assembly. Sampson was chairman of the Military and Indian Affairs Committee and served on two other committees. A Sampson resolution asking greater federal support for old-age pensions for Indians was adopted by the Assembly, but his resolution in support of the Pyramid Lake Paiute Tribe in its conflict with squatters and Senator McCarran failed. Scott Ratliff, an enrolled Eastern Shoshone with a master's degree in counseling from the University of Wyoming who had been a counselor for Native American students at Central Wyoming College for nearly 10 years, was elected to the Wyoming House

of Representatives in 1980 and 1982. He was a member in 1983 of the Corporations, Elections, and Political Subdivisions and the Labor, Health and Social Services committees; during the 1983–1984 interim session he served on a joint committee concerned with legislative oversight audits of executive agencies (Ralph E. Thomas, personal communication 1983; Scott J. Ratliff, personal communication 1984).

State governments have little authority in Indian affairs and have shown little interest, but probably this interest is increasing. In 1983 all Great Basin states except Wyoming and California had state agencies dealing with Indian affairs (Elwood Mose, personal communication 1984; Governors' Interstate Indian Council 1982).

Internal Political Organization

In spite of tribal differences, several generalizations may be made about precontact tribal politics. No Great Basin groups had written constitutions before the twentieth century. Authority, for the most part, was not identified with formal governmental positions; instead, individuals gave advice about specific areas of group life, which the group was free to reject. In a few cases, leadership may have been inherited. The ideal rule for decision-making was consensus.

By the 1980s the majority of recognized groups within the Great Basin had governments based on written constitutions (table 1). It is difficult to say what impact a written constitution alone may have had. If the constitutions established the structures desired by the Indians, the fact that a constitution was written matters little. Taken as a whole, the constitutions clearly represent a shift toward investing authority in positions rather than individuals; a tribal council and its officers are given the right to make decisions.

Much literature about internal political life uses the concept of factionalism, apparently as defined in an influential article by Siegel and Beals (1960) as "overt, unregulated (unresolved) conflict which interferes with the achievement of goals of the group." It is distinguished from "conflict between groups" and "party conflict." In fact most literature about the Great Basin describes group conflict, which though not institutionalized in political parties competing for control of government, is also not so disruptive to the group as factionalism. Apparently in only one modern case has group conflict led to disruption of the group: the withdrawal of the mixed-blood Northern Ute from the tribal council of the Uintah-Ouray Reservation. Hence, the concept of group conflict better describes the internal divisions discussed in the literature, even though the more common term is factionalism.

One obvious source of group conflict is that tribes or peoples who lived separate lives before Euro-American contact were in several instances placed together on the same reservation by decisions of the federal government. For example, in various ways the Colorado River Indian Reservation came to be the home of Mohave, Chemehuevi, Navajo, and Hopi Indians (Roth 1976). Similar situations exist on other reservations: the Wind River Reservation, the Duck Valley Reservation, the Reno-Sparks Colony, and the Uintah-Ouray Reservation. The Fort Hall Reservation, which is the home for both Western Shoshone and Bannock, continues a preexisting relationship.

Indian response to this source of group conflict has been varied. Roth (1976) found that a sense of identification with the reservation developed on the Colorado River Reservation; however, in the 1960s some Chemehuevis on that reservation joined with tribal members living off-reservation to reorganize the Chemehuevi Tribe and reactivate the Chemehuevi reservation. At Wind River, for most purposes the two tribes

top, Inter-Tribal Council of Nev., Reno: WS-123; center left, Southern Ute Tribe, Ignacio, Colo.; center right, *Native Nevadan*, Reno-Sparks Indian Colony; bottom left, U. of Nev. Reno, Publications and Graphics; bottom right, Shoshone–Bannock Tribes, Sho-Ban Media Center, Fort Hall, Idaho.
Fig. 5. Tribal councils. top, Duck Valley Reservation Council, Nev.-Idaho. left to right, front row: unidentified, Kelly Shaw, Sr., Joe Gibson, Sr., Jack Sims, Thomas Premo, George Prentice, Tommy Thacker, Guy Manning. back row: 2 unidentified men, Extension Agent Charles Spencer, Hoke Dick, John Dick, Superintendent E.E. McNeilly, Louis Dave, Willie Wines, Willie Pretty, Frank Dutch, and Frances Charles. Photograph by Benson Gibson, Duck Valley Reservation, Nev., 1930s. center left, Southern Ute council meeting with U.S. Sen. Gary Hart. Elected for 3-year terms, this body conducts all the business of the tribe, from passing tribal ordinances to considering future business enterprises. left to right, Erwin Taylor, Vice-chairman Chris A. Baker, Eddie Box, Sr., Tribal Chairman Leonard C. Burch, Senator Hart, Joe Mestas, Thelma Kuebler, and John E. Baker, Sr. Photographed at Southern Ute Reservation, Colo., 1976. center right, Washoe Council, the governing body for Dresslerville, Carson City, Woodfords, and Washoe tribal members living elsewhere. front row: left to right, Vice-chairman Jean Dexter, Tribal Chairman Robert Frank, Secretary Clare Smokey, Catherine Fillmore; back row: Beverly Frank, Ann Wade, Wayne Snooks, Vernon Wyatt, Romaine Smokey, Sr., and Eugene Frank. Photographed by John J. Nulty, Nov. 1978. bottom left, Inter-Tribal Council of Nevada executive board at an annual meeting. Names with asterisks are chairmen of the groups they represent. left to right, front row: Whitney McKinney* (Duck Valley), Dena Austin* (Lovelock), Larry Piffero (Elko), Elvin Willie, Jr.* (Walker River), Chairman of ITC; middle row: Roy Garcia* (Pyramid Lake), Leslie Blossom (Battle Mountain), Murry Barr* (Summit Lake), Lawrence Astor* (Reno-Sparks); back row: William Rosse, Sr.* (Yomba), Cheryl Mose (South Fork), Felix Ike* (Te-Moak Bands), Jerry Millett* (Duckwater), Wesley Allison* (Ely), Robert Frank* (Washoe), Romaine Smokey, Jr.* (Dresslerville), Clifton Surrett* (Moapa). Photographed in Reno, Nev., Nov. 1984. bottom right, Northern Shoshone–Bannock council at Fort Hall Reservation, Idaho, 1984. standing, left, Marvin Osborne and Darrell Shay; seated, left to right, Layton Littlejohn, Frank Papse, Sr., Kesley Edmo, Sr. (Chairman), and Willis Dixey. Photograph by Susie Farmer.

565

Table 1. Constitutions of Great Basin Tribes

Entity	Date of Election	Date of Approval	Percent Voting Yes on Constitution
Bridgeport Indian Colony	April 9, 1976	July 21, 1976	100.0
Burns Paiute Indian Colony[a]	May 16, 1968	June 13, 1968	98.6
Carson Colony	May 27 1967	June 16, 1967	73.2
Cedarville Rancheria	Aug. 17, 1977	Feb. 1, 1978	100.0
Chemehuevi Indian Tribe	Feb. 14, 1970	June 5, 1970	94.0
Amended Apr. 16, 1977		Oct. 30, 1976	86.0
Confederated Tribes of Goshute Reservation Amended Feb. 7, 1964	Nov. 9, 1940	Nov. 25, 1940	85.7
Dresslerville Community	Oct. 21, 1969	Nov. 14, 1969	
Duckwater Shoshone Tribe of the Duckwater Reservation	Nov. 30, 1940	Nov. 28, 1940	100.0
Ely Indian Colony	Feb. 19, 1966	April 8, 1966	80.8
Fort Bidwell Indian Community of the Fort Bidwell Reservation Amended July 12, 1940, May 6, 1942, July 23, 1971	Dec. 21, 1935	Jan. 28, 1936	51.7
Fort Independence Indian Community[a]	Jan. 9, 1965	May 7, 1965	88.9
Fort McDermitt Paiute and Shoshone Tribe	May 30, 1936	July 2, 1936	83.1
Kaibab Band of Paiute Indians of the Kaibab Reservation Amended	May 15, 1951	June 15, 1951	83.9
Las Vegas Tribe of Paiute Indians	June 24, 1970	July 27, 1970	92.9
Lovelock Paiute Tribe	Feb. 10, 1968	March 14, 1968	68.3
Moapa Band of Paiute Indians of the Moapa River Reservation	March 15, 1942	April 17, 1942	96.5
Paiute Indian Tribe of Utah[a,b]	Oct. 1, 1981	Oct. 8, 1981	88.4
Paiute-Shoshone Tribe of the Fallon Reservation and Colony[a]	Dec. 18, 1963	June 12, 1964	64.5
Pyramid Lake Paiute Tribe of Nevada Amended Feb. 3, 1956, Feb. 23, 1962, Feb. 6, 1973, Nov. 3, 1976	Dec. 14, 1935	Jan. 15, 1936	67.0
Reno-Sparks Indian Colony	Dec. 16, 1935	Jan. 15, 1936	98.1
Amended June 8, 1974	Dec. 5, 1970	Feb. 8, 1971	75.0
Shoshone–Bannock Tribes of the Fort Hall Reservation	March 31, 1936	April 30, 1936	80.6
Shoshone-Paiute Tribes of the Duck Valley Reservation of Nevada Amended May 20, 1966	March 21, 1936	April 20, 1936	76.3
Southern Ute Tribe of the Southern Ute Reservation Amended Feb. 2, 1943, Feb. 28, 1946	Sept. 12, 1936	Nov. 4, 1936	88.4
Summit Lake Paiute Tribe	Oct. 24, 1964	Jan. 8, 1965	100.0
Susanville Indian Rancheria	Jan. 11, 1969	Mar. 10, 1969	92.0
Te-Moak Bands of Western Shoshone Indians, Nevada	May 31, 1938	Aug. 24, 1938	95.9
Ute Indian Tribe of the Uintah-Ouray Reservation	Dec. 19, 1936	Jan. 19, 1937	96.7
Ute Mountain Tribe of the Ute Mountain Reservation, Colorado, New Mexico, Utah	May 8, 1940	June 6, 1940	88.3
Utu Utu Gwaitu Paiute Tribe, Benton Paiute Reservation	Nov. 22, 1975	Jan. 20, 1976	100.0
Walker River Paiute Tribe of Nevada Amended July 12, 1945, June 28, 1973	Feb. 20, 1937	March 26, 1937	87.2
Washoe Tribe of Nevada and California[c]	Dec. 16, 1935	Jan. 24, 1936	100.0
Amended Oct. 13, 1969	May 14, 1966	June 20, 1966	
Winnemucca Indian Colony, Nevada	Dec. 12, 1970	March 5, 1971	100.0

Table 1. Constitutions of Great Basin Tribes (*continued*)

Entity	Date of Election	Date of Approval	Percent Voting Yes on Constitution
Yerington Paiute Tribe Amended May 20, 1964, Jan. 5, 1976	Dec. 12, 1936	Jan. 4, 1937	93.3
Yomba Shoshone Tribe of the Yomba Reservation, Nevada	Dec. 22, 1939	Dec. 20, 1939	100.0

NOTE: Amendments adopted only through the end of 1978 are shown.

[a] Non–Indian Reorganization Act documents.

[b] The Paiute Tribe of Utah consists of five bands—Cedar City, Indian Peaks, Kanosh, Koosharem, and Shivwits—all of which except Cedar City had been recognized tribes before being terminated in 1954 by act of Congress. Prior to termination, Kanosh and Shivwits had adopted constitutions under the Indian Reorganization Act. The termination statute eliminated the authority of the secretary of the interior over these two bands and abrogated such powers granted by these constitutions as were inconsistent with the termination act. However, the constitutions were still binding insofar as they were not inconsistent with the termination act and insofar as actions under them did not require secretarial approval (68 Stat. 1099, Section 10). The 1981 constitution superseded the previous constitutions of Kanosh and Shivwits.

[c] Articles of Association for the Woodfords Community Council were drawn up, apparently in 1969, but were never adopted.

live separate lives, although occasionally a joint general council is convened to decide issues affecting the entire reservation. At Reno-Sparks, there is a single tribal government, but conflict between Northern Paiute and Washoe residents has been apparent at various times since the 1930s. At Duck Valley there is a single tribal government; conflict between Western Shoshone and Northern Paiute members of the reservation is not reported in the literature.

On the Uintah-Ouray Reservation, the most extensive report discusses tribal politics from the mid-1950s to the mid-1960s. Jorgensen (1972:140) stated that there was factionalism during this period but that "the composition of the factions changes from issue to issue. Sometimes people align, more or less, along historic band lines—or some combination of them—and sometimes they align along 'nativist' versus 'not-so-nativist' dimensions." Among the conflicts are differences among the three Ute bands settled on the reservation during the nineteenth century, opposition to the tribal council by a traditionalist group (the True Utes) that at times advocated dissolution of the tribal council and a return to traditional governing structures, and disputes over economic policies (such as conflict over the distribution of claims moneys between advocates of per capita payments and advocates of spending the money on tribally run projects). One of these disputes became defined as between mixed-bloods and full-bloods; between 1954 and 1960 this became so intense that the mixed-bloods withdrew from the tribal council, formed a new organization (Affiliated Ute Citizens), and were terminated (see also Lang 1961–1962).

On some reservations, group conflicts are based on differing attitudes toward acculturation to the dominant society. At times, differences between more and less acculturated individuals have been reported on Great Basin reservations. However, probably most Great Basin Indians who have remained on reservations wish to retain their cultural differences from the general society; they are not involved in a one-way process of abandoning one culture for another. Further, many of the changes that have taken place among these peoples are peculiarly Indian responses to the conditions created by Euro-Americans; while the resulting cultural patterns differ from aboriginal ones, they also differ from contemporary general American patterns.

Some writers have asserted the existence of conflict between traditionalists and tribal pragmatists (to use the terms suggested by Forbes 1973), but others have not. Harris (1940) reported two clear-cut groups among the Western Shoshone on the Duck Valley Reservation in the mid-1930s: "These factions have no roots in the aboriginal life. One group is led by the 'educated, White-talking' Indians and the other group, much larger, is termed the 'conservative.' " In spite of the names, he believed that division between the two groups was not based on degree of interest in "retention of the old culture" but on "a deep-seated resentment against the Whites, and particularly the agency officials."

> It is significant that the 'progressive' group is led by the three principal Indian families on the reservation who are the richest, the best educated, who are 'church' Indians and who hold the commanding positions in the native councils, school board and associations. . . . The 'progressive' Indians themselves have no great liking for the agency officials, but because they honestly believe that they are working for the good of the reservation by holding positions in the councils and by working with the agency officials rather than by maintaining the sullen resentment or passive resistance which the 'conservative' group manifests, the dichotomy became inevitable (Harris 1940:100–101).

The "conservatives" won Duck Valley elections until the 1920s, but the "progressives" took over in the 1930s (Crum 1983).

The main division at the Southern Ute Reservation at the end of the 1930s was between older, traditional men and younger men who served on the tribal council   *567* and were more highly assimilated to Euro-American culture. While he used the words "progressive" and "conservative" to describe these groups, Opler (1940) believed that the basic difference was that the younger men had become farmers. "The conflict between generations at Ignacio, while not sharp, is always precipitated by the economic independence of the younger generation and their real stake in current policies made possible by a brand new mode of living" (Opler 1940:188). C.C. Johnson (1963) reported for one Ute reservation that during the 1950s the tribal council was dominated by more highly educated, more acculturated members.

Lynch (1971) reported in detail on eight tribal council meetings held during 1968 at a small urban colony he calls Brownsville, with less detailed information about tribal politics in this community from the 1930s to the late 1960s. Brownsville voted to accept the Indian Reorganization Act but failed to adopt a constitution at that time, partly because one group opposed it. An elected tribal council came into being in 1940, but a written constitution was not drawn up and adopted until 1966–1967, then partly at the urging of the BIA. Lynch reported little change in the way that the council operated after adoption; Brownsville politics were explained chiefly by the fact that there were two factions loosely based on kinship.

Knack (1975) studied the political life of bands in Utah (cf. Knack 1980). Four bands (Indian Peaks, Kanosh, Koosharem, and Shivwits) were terminated by Congress in 1954. The status of a fifth band, Cedar City, was ambiguous before 1954. The land on which it is located was not trust land but was owned by the Mormon church, although band members were treated as Indians by the BIA. The members of all bands considered themselves to be one people during the period of termination. They founded a Utah Paiute tribal corporation and a housing authority at the tribal level, and when Congress restored them (including the Cedar City band) in 1980 it provided for a single tribal council with representation from each band (94 Stat. 317). Utah Paiute tribal politics were found to involve factions that "tend to follow kinship lines, because these are the courses of most intercourse between households"; however, factions "remain unfixed and fluctuate with the day-to-day events of the community" (Knack 1975:173).

On the rural "Rye Meadow Reservation" in northern Nevada the preferred economic activity is cattle-raising (Houghton 1973). Although the amount of land available is too small for more than one-tenth of the households to make a good living raising cattle, nearly one-third of the households engaged in this activity. Rye Meadow has a tribal council elected under an Indian Reorganization Act constitution adopted in the 1930s. Houghton concluded that this council had been dominated since the beginning by a few families from the cattle-raising minority. These families used political power

to favor themselves in dispensing the few jobs controlled by the council as well as in the allocation of self-help housing and land assignments.

This reservation saw extensive intervention efforts during the 1960s by government and private groups to overcome severe health and economic problems (Dressler and Rusco 1970:47–50). Only one of three major objectives was achieved: "by late in 1971 most households in the community evidenced striking improvements in the living conditions" (Houghton 1973:4). A second goal, to "increase the scope of the leadership pool and to strengthen community unity," was not achieved, because of the domination of reservation politics by the leading families. Houghton's data indicate, however, that the pattern of preferential treatment for core family members in many other areas did not apply to the antipoverty effort. Families identified as "not in Kinship Core and not Politically Powerful" comprised 48 percent of the reservation adult population in 1971. Yet 58 percent of the men and 65 percent of the women in the work training program for the full three years were from this group, and 75 percent of the men and 66 percent of the women ever enrolled in the program were from this group. Likewise, 48 percent of factory workers employed in November 1971 and 61 percent of the total number of persons employed in the factory were from this group (Houghton 1973:380). The third objective, to increase the employment rate, was also not met (ibid.:63).

Although family was the main basis of factionalism, Houghton (1973:108) noted the existence of a "treaty Indian" faction, which was traditionalist in orientation.

Tribal politics in the Yerington Paiute Tribe (Northern Paiute) were dominated for many years by a group based upon a major economic division created by federal action (Hittman 1973a). The Yerington Colony, founded in 1917, is purely residential, with no agricultural land or other economic resources; Campbell Ranch, a small area of irrigated ranchland purchased by the BIA during the 1930s, provides the economic base for a few resident families. Both comprise the Yerington Paiute Reservation.

Conflicts between Campbell Ranchers and Colony residents have affected council elections and deliberations for many years. Moreover, the minority Ranch group dominated the council, which adopted an election rule guaranteeing that three of the five members would be elected from Campbell Ranch regardless of the number of votes cast for candidates. In the 1960s colony residents gained control of the tribal council and abolished the election rule.

There are no reports of group conflict among the Washoe. A study of the formation of the Washoe tribal constitution in the 1930s, based on data from the National Archives, did not disclose any group conflict over this development in tribal politics (E. Rusco 1983).

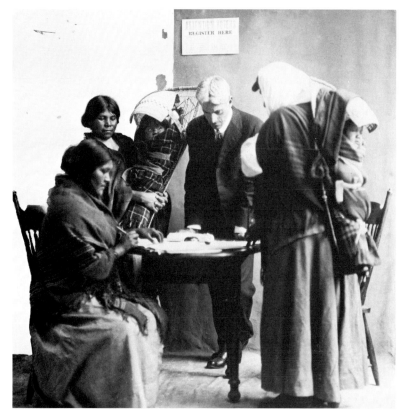

left, Nat. Hist. Mus. of Los Angeles Co.: 5396; right, U. of Utah, Special Coll., Salt Lake City: PO 127 #89.

Fig. 6. The right to vote. left, Owens Valley Paiute women registering to vote. left to right, Amy Yandell, Susie Kane, Mr. Von Blon, and Emma Willis. About two-thirds of all U.S. Indians were citizens even before the Indian Citizenship Act of 1924, and California gave women the right to vote in 1911, one of several states to have instituted universal suffrage before the ratification of the 19th Amendment in 1920. Photograph by Andrew A. Forbes, 1916, Owens Valley, Calif. right, Marie Victor voting in a Ute tribal election on Uintah-Ouray Reservation, Fort Duchesne, Utah. Photographed about 1950.

The Chemehuevi, living on the Colorado River Indian Reservation and in southern California, had no group conflicts until the 1960s (Roth 1976). A movement to establish a tribal council and restore the Chemehuevi Reservation, abandoned in the 1930s when flooded by Parker Dam on the Colorado River, created conflict between members who wished to remain at the Colorado River Reservation and those who wished to move to the Chemehuevi Reservation. It also made existing divisions of other kinds politically relevant.

On the Walker River Reservation in the 1960s and early 1970s tribal politics were reported by Brengarth-Jones (1976) to involve two main groups—the traditional "'06ers" and the "newcomers" (differing in degree of acculturation) and a third group, "marginal men," persons culturally Northern Paiute but able to function very well in the Euro-American world. The most important tribal leaders were described as "marginal men" although the '06ers won most elections for the tribal council.

A traditionalist–tribal pragmatist division was reported among the Eastern Shoshone of the Wind River Reservation, but T.H. Johnson (1975:5) found this rel-

atively insignificant to tribal politics because "the underlying structure of Wind River Shoshone society is based upon an elaborate series of socio-political family alliances . . ." cutting across this and other divisions. In brief, "leadership has been drawn from the same families for at least a century, but these families have formed marital alliances with almost every other Shoshone family. . . . Shoshone society manages diversity by developing mediating links between distinct social groups" (T.H. Johnson 1975:8).

In summary, there were several sources of group conflict among Great Basin Indians in the 1980s. Jorgensen (1972) and Knack (1975) report that bases of group conflict change over time and are diverse. Traditionalist–tribal pragmatist divisions are reported for Duck Valley, "Rye Meadow," Walker River, Wind River, and Uintah-Ouray; however, the significance of this varies, and in some groups this division is only partly or occasionally the source of conflict. Houghton (1973) and Lynch (1971) report kinship structures as the primary basis of group conflict at Rye Meadow and Brownsville, and Knack (1975) finds kinship a partial basis for group conflict among the Southern Paiute. *569*

Conflict on the Reno-Sparks Colony and the Uintah-Ouray Reservation has developed at times on the basis of the different tribal groups that live there; however, on the Duck Valley and Colorado River Reservations, this circumstance has not created conflict. Traditionalist–tribal pragmatist conflict among the Western Shoshone on the assertion of treaty rights has assumed national importance in Indian country, but alignments over this question have taken different forms at different times. Nor is it clear that group conflict always exists. No significant conflict has been reported for the Washoe or for the Colorado River Reservation before the 1960s. Group conflict is thus as variable and complex as it is for general American society, although some sources of tribal conflict are not present in the wider society.

It is sometimes assumed that written constitutions necessarily replaced consensual with majority rule, but several writers note that consensual decision-making is still followed by some tribal groups. For example, Lynch (1971:264) concluded that the influential political principles in Brownsville were:

> —a desire to reach a consensus and to avoid open breaches of the peace leading to a public confrontation,
> —a willingness to try new ideas or modes of behavior, coupled with a dogged determination to uncover all facets of an issue presented in public meetings of the council, and
> —a tendency to rely on individuals who have proven their worth over a period of time in a variety of situations, together with assignment of authority to these individuals rather than to a position or a procedure.

These and similar traits are continuations of earlier political practices and beliefs.

Similarly, among the Southern Paiute "public decisions are based on consensus. This is as true in the new business corporation as in the household. Every attempt is made to assure that all persons partaking in the decision agree with the results" (Knack 1975:168). Leadership is by "suggestion" and voluntary adherence by followers to actions recommended by leaders. Houghton (1973:192) agrees that "political decisions are the product of the traditional process, consensus, despite the presence of a representative form of government since 1936" and apparently also in spite of family-based group conflict.

Another question is the extent to which tribal governments are effective, fully legitimate in the sense that their right to make decisions is widely accepted, and stable. Few writers have addressed themselves specifically to these points, but Brengarth-Jones (1976:2) concluded that "a majority of the Walker River Reservation residents regard the Tribal Council as the means by which their important political needs are met. They usually accept its authority, regard its rules as binding, and view it as a legitimate channel for communication between themselves and the Federal system, particu-

larly the Bureau of Indian Affairs." Following adoption of a written constitution and charter in the 1930s, the Southern Ute Tribe saw "a steady development of tribal responsibilities and functions, a formalization and differentiation of the tribe's internal organization, and a process of institutionalization of business procedures" (Clifton 1965:322). This is surely true of many other Great Basin groups; even the traditionalist–tribal pragmatist split does not seem so deep or so disruptive as is the case among several other Native American groups, such as the Hopi or the Sioux of Pine Ridge Reservation, South Dakota. Conflict over traditionalist–pragmatist policies among Western Shoshone did not preclude the setting up of a tribal-wide political structure in 1983–1984, after the traditionalists' court victory.

Tribal Government

From a governmental standpoint, there are several types of Indian groups in the Great Basin. The recognized groups on reservations are most obvious and important, because of their status in the legal system of the United States. Recognition has been extended in the past by a number of means, but chiefly since 1978 under BIA regulations; in 1982 the Death Valley Western Shoshone were recognized. Congress may still create a tribe by statute, and it did so in 1980 by restoring the Southern Paiutes of Utah.

There are still nonrecognized groups in the Great Basin that have one or more of the characteristics required for recognition. These include Northern Paiute and Shoshone groups living at Coleville and Antelope Valley in California, which applied for recognition in 1983 (Frances Munsey, personal communication 1984). Although little is known about the government of unrecognized groups, at least one, the Southern Paiutes in Pahrump, Nevada, had a tribal council with a chairman in 1982 (Stoffle and Dobyns 1983:271).

Recognized Groups

Although the Indian Reorganization Act acknowledged unextinguished tribal sovereignty and the BIA acknowledges traditional governments without written constitutions, most recognized groups in the 1980s have such constitutions. As of July 21, 1981, the BIA recognized six "traditional organizations," defined as groups "without formal federal approval of organizational structure" in the Great Basin (Simmons 1981). The largest is the Eastern Shoshone tribe of the Wind River Reservation, which shares its reservation with the Northern Arapahoe; neither has a written constitution. Each meets separately and governs itself, with ultimate authority in a general council of all adult voting members. Councils meet annually and elect business councils to transact business between meetings. Joint meetings are occasionally held to decide matters affecting the entire reservation (for the Shoshone councils, see L. Fowler 1982:92–86, 142–148, 250–251; C.C. Johnson 1963:146, 156, 289, 400–2).

Three traditional organizations consist of bands of Owens Valley Indians: the Big Pine band of Owens Valley Paiute-Shoshone Indians, the Paiute-Shoshone Indians of the Bishop Community, and the Paiute-Shoshone Indians of the Lone Pine Community. They have a joint structure based on a Trust Agreement for Relief and Rehabilitation Grant to Organized Tribes approved by the BIA in 1936, which established an Owens Valley Board of Trustees with five trustees from Bishop plus one each from Big Pine and Lone Pine. The Agreement requires that their successors be elected "by a resolution adopted at a general meeting called for this express purpose." Each community has an informally chosen council, and Bishop has a Utility Organization.

The governmental structure of the Ute Mountain Reservation in the late 1930s was described as strongly dominated by conservative older leaders who rejected Euro-American culture, political forms, and practices. Opler (1940:186) referred to "the refusal of these people to accept a tribal constitution similar to that of the Ignacio [Southern] Ute, or to function through a tribal council other than a most informal gathering of prominent elders and shamans under the leadership of a conservative chief." However, the Ute Mountain Utes have had a written constitution since 1940.

Constitutions

Most recognized groups have written constitutions. Twenty-one of these were adopted under specific statutory authority (the Indian Reorganization Act except for the Paiute Indian Tribe of Utah), but three (the Fort Independence Indian Community, the Burns Colony, and the Paiute-Shoshone Tribe of the Fallon Reservation and Colony) were adopted "outside of specific federal statutory authority" (Simmons 1981). In addition, the Carson Colony and the Dresslerville Community, technically part of the Washoe tribe, have constitutions approved by the colonies and the Washoe tribe. In 1983, 34 written constitutions were in force (table 1). Three more constitutions (the Death Valley group of Western Shoshone, Big Pine and Lone Pine bands of Owens Valley Paiute) had been submitted to the BIA for approval and were pending in 1984 (Frances Munsey, personal communication 1984).

In addition to these governing structures, Great Basin Indians have increasingly resorted to incorporation under state law, for various purposes. Most striking is the fact that two traditionalist groups, United Paiutes, Inc. and the Western Shoshone Sacred Lands Association, have followed this route. In addition, there are several incorporated groups of urban Indians and several intertribal groups that have incorporated under state law.

Conclusions

Great Basin Indians in the 1980s continued to confront difficulty in retaining their land and resource bases; they were still to some extent subject to various forms of pressure from elements of the wider society that desired Indian-owned land, water, or minerals. On the other hand, since about 1970 there has been an increase in the land base of several groups, and the federal government, which in the past has often led the assault on Indian resources, has sometimes performed the trust responsibility required by the legal position of Indians. Therefore, neither the neocolonial theory nor the legal theory of Indian–Euro-American interaction is adequate alone, but each helps explain the place of Indians in the general society and polity. If this is correct, the view that Indians are powerless to control their fate is not correct, though doubtless most Native American societies would prefer greater control over their lives.

The extent to which Great Basin Indians are losing their cultural identity is less than clear. A number of observers of these groups have reported that conflicts between traditionalists and tribal pragmatists were among the most important kinds of group conflict during the 1950s–1980s. However, it by no means follows that traditional orientations are dying out and that most Native Americans will soon be fully assimilated into general American society. The traditionalist Western Shoshone, for example, have shown remarkable ability to adapt organizational strategies to changed conditions in order to assert more effectively their traditionalist orientation. Further, the traditionalist–tribal pragmatist split has not been reported for all groups, and the way in which this split affects group politics apparently varies. Furthermore, other divisions apparently exist within Great Basin Indian societies, as they do in the general society, and the earlier conception that group differences threatened the survival of these societies is clearly exaggerated. Factionalism defined as highly disruptive conflict seems to apply only partially to the Northern Utes, who did experience the secession of a portion of reservation society.

The extent to which tribal governments actually utilize the authority that their legal status gives them is unclear; however, the creation of Indian governments based on written constitutions, which is the path followed by most recognized groups since the 1930s, has apparently strengthened Native government. Increased financial resources available to tribal governments beginning in the 1960s and the federal policy of self-determination have increased the ability of such governments to make their own decisions. The extent of control by the BIA over tribal governments and the effectiveness of Indian governments remain questions that need study.

One element that affects answers to these questions is the extent to which the written constitutions reflect Indian desires or, alternatively, represent Euro-American impositions on traditional societies. In legal theory, the BIA, when it assisted groups to draw up and adopt such constitutions, was helping them to embody in a written document decisions that represented their own choices. It is clear from a look at the constitutions themselves that they are far from identical and that some of their provisions have clear relevance to specific situations. Further, the documents themselves neither impose majority rule nor require BIA approval of all decisions of tribal councils. The biggest changes from aboriginal practices are probably the movement to written constitutions themselves and the placement of authority in institutions (usually the tribal council) rather than individuals.

The question of how tribal governments operate in fact is interesting. Several authors report that tribal governments actually operate on the basis of consensus rather than majority rule; in this respect they are clearly continuing aboriginal practices. The formal structures of tribal governments provide for more democratic governments, in the sense of governments that vest authority in the entire community, than is the case with most non-Indian governments in the United States.

Finally, formal organizations based on state law are becoming increasingly common in the Great Basin, as a supplement to the governments of recognized groups. While these structures do not have the legal standing of recognized governments, urban Indians, intertribal groups, and even traditionalist groups have increasingly resorted to them. Native Americans have evidently become increasingly sophisticated about strategies for pursuing their objectives, which seem still to be to retain their cultural identity and such sovereignty as is left to them.

Indian Economies, 1950–1980

MARTHA C. KNACK

The nineteenth century brought economic chaos to all Great Basin groups. Tribes that put up military resistance were defeated and forced onto reservations far smaller than their previous ranges and often far from homelands (Jorgensen 1972:27–85). Those who did fight were also defeated, crowded out by non-Indian control of critical subsistence resources—grasslands, piñon forests, springs, and streams (Downs 1966:72–110; Clemmer 1974). Reduction of the land base assured that subsistence could not be gained by traditional means, and new needs required contact with the non-Indian economy, for rations (Garner and Hawley 1950), employment, or trade goods. Although reservation economies were themselves stagnant and unproductive, not even reservations had been provided in much of Nevada and western Utah. There the pattern became what ethnohistorians often call "attachment to scattered ranches," individual families working for ranchers in varying capacities for room, board, goods, and a little cash (C.S. Fowler and D.D. Fowler 1971). Throughout the Great Basin, Indians were in a position of economic marginality and poverty.

In the early twentieth century small reservations were established primarily to provide homesites for often transient populations, for instance Dresslerville (40 acres) in 1917, Ely (10 acres) in 1931, Las Vegas (10 acres) in 1911, and Lovelock (20 acres) in 1907, all in Nevada. These were obviously too small to support the population by the regional system of mixed farming and ranching. Even with the establishment of tribal governments under the Indian Reorganization Act of 1934 the availability of revolving credit funds and the addition of lands in some areas, the situation did not change structurally before 1950.

In the 1950s, anthropologists, economists, and other scholars began to view Indian tribes not as remnants of a past to be sought through the living, but as ongoing, contemporary societies to be studied in their own right. It was not until then that there were any serious studies of observable Great Basin economies, certainly in a number sufficient for comparison, and in a depth greater than bare bureaucratic statistics.

The more statistical data available for Indian studies, the greater the disagreement among sources, even on matters such as population and reservation land base, and most certainly on income and unemployment rates.

Sources from the same agency published in the same year can differ 10–15 percent. Tribal, Bureau of Indian Affairs, Indian Health Service, and other sources are often widely divergent. Although all the figures cited in this chapter should be taken as approximations, a very clear overall pattern does emerge.

Uintah-Ouray Reservation

About 1950 only half the one million acres of Uintah-Ouray Reservation, Utah, were useful for range grazing, 53,334 were irrigable, and the rest were forest, mountain, or alkaloid waste (Lang 1954). Livestock ownership was fundamental to the Northern Utes' economy, and 165 persons owned stock, running 5,000 cattle and 7,000 sheep. In the Uintah band most men owned a few head, but in the Uncompahgre band ownership was concentrated in the hands of five men; only these five owned enough cattle to approach family support through ranching. Indians used 62 percent of the available grazing, while the remaining 38 percent was leased to non-Indians (Jorgensen 1964:191, 203, 221, 224, 1972:108; Hoffmeister 1945:610–611; cf. Schutz, Baker, and Vanvig 1960:10–26; Houghton 1973:184; Hittman 1973a:20; American Indian Policy Review Commission 1976:42; Knack and Stewart 1984:326–327).

In 1951 Northern Utes farmed 7,044 acres of the irrigable land, producing a product value of $17.54 per acre.* Non-Indians farmed 21,558 reservation acres that year, producing $19.33 per acre (U.S. Congress. Sen-

---

*Monetary figures can be misleading in the period 1950–1982 because of the rapid inflation of the dollar. The consumer price index, based on 1967, allows conversion ratios to be constructed to standardize figures of specific interest for longitudinal comparison (U.S. Bureau of the Census 1982:452):

1950	1.387	1960	1.127	1970	0.860	1980	0.406
1951	1.285	1961	1.116	1971	0.824	1981	0.367
1952	1.258	1962	1.104	1972	0.799	1982	(June)
1953	1.248	1963	1.091	1973	0.752		0.348
1954	1.242	1964	1.076	1974	0.678		
1955	1.247	1965	1.058	1975	0.621		
1956	1.229	1966	1.029	1976	0.587		
1957	1.186	1967	1.000	1977	0.551		
1958	1.155	1968	0.960	1978	0.512		
1959	1.145	1969	0.911	1979	0.461		

Natl. Arch.: 75–N–VIN–638.
Fig. 1. Ute Indians stacking lumber. The wood was cut from the Uintah forest on the Uintah-Ouray Reservation and processed at a non-Indian-owned sawmill near Fort Duchesne. The wood was used for housing programs funded by the Bureau of Indian Affairs. Photograph by Morrow, Uintah-Ouray Reservation, Utah, May 1951.

ate. Committee on Interior and Insular Affairs 1951:46). Since tribal land assignments in 1950 averaged 60 acres per household, few Utes could support families through farming. Alfalfa was a major crop, often fed to a few head of cattle rather than sold. Many families had gardens and actively hunted game, fished, and gathered wild plants.

Many families turned to wage labor to supplement household income. Of 829 adults on the reservation in 1950, the Bureau of Indian Affairs considered 54 percent unemployable, that is over 65 years of age, sole parent of dependent children, physically disabled, or mentally handicapped. All others were defined as in the labor force. Of these 83 were employed full time, 166 were underemployed, and 131 unemployed. Thus, 16 percent of all adults were unemployed, but if calculated as a proportion of the available labor force this rises to 35 percent, and 78 percent were unemployed or underemployed (part-time or seasonal). Of those Utes finding employment, 43 percent worked for the federal government directly, 33 percent for tribal government, and 24 percent for other types of employers, primarily ranchers, farmers, and private homeowners. Almost none were employed by commerce or industry in non-Indian towns adjoining the reservation (Jorgensen 1972:110–111). A 1950 survey of 160 adults concluded, "Few Utes had skills which would aid them in securing jobs, particularly jobs on or near the reservation" (Jorgensen 1964:193). The most frequently self-reported skills were beadworking, farming, and ranching, and even these were listed by only one-third of the sample. Only two persons in this sample had stable employment, one working for the tribe, the other for the agency. The BIA reported that same year that 54 percent of all adults were illiterate, 7 percent had grad-

uated from high school, and there were only four college graduates in the entire tribe (Jorgensen 1972:134).

This pattern of high unemployment, lack of salable skills, and marginal involvement in agriculture resulted in 1950 in an average annual income of $1,525 for a family of six, including an agency estimate of the value of farm, hunting, and gathering products. In 1948 a researcher had estimated annual family income at $1,160, or $190 per capita. For comparison, the average cash income of nearby non-Indians in 1949 was $3,300 (Jorgensen 1972:115–117). Fully 40 percent of the Ute average came from unearned income, mostly payments from tribal leases and royalties, a source that had not been available to them before 1946. In addition, a number of families qualified for county, tribal, or BIA welfare assistance. In Lang's (1954) sample, 35 percent of families received some such aid (cf. Schutz, Baker, and Vanvig 1960:8, 25).

This low cash income was reflected in housing. A 1948 survey of 52 houses in White Rocks, Utah, found them about equally divided between cabins and wood frame and clapboard. Only 8 percent had doors, insulation, and windows, and these were most often the log cabins, by far the best housing on the reservation. Frame houses were often army surplus shacks. Only 11 percent of the sample had water piped inside, and all the rest used water from ditches or streams. Over 96 percent had coal or wood stoves, and only 11 percent had electricity, even though power mains ran through the community (Lang 1954:193).

The overall economic pattern was one of primarily unskilled labor, intermittent employment in marginal agriculture, and great dependence on federally funded jobs. The result was poverty, both absolutely and in comparison to surrounding non-Indians. Families utilized as many sources of income as possible—farm land, cattle, wage labor when available, and unearned income. Relatives shared their small and unstable income as well as houses, labor, and cars, producing large complex households of interdependent kinsmen.

Fort Hall Reservation

Other large, land-based reservations repeated this economic pattern. At Fort Hall Reservation, Idaho, in 1963 Indians used only 26 percent of tribally owned grazing land, 5 percent of tribally owned irrigated farmland, and 20 percent of irrigated allotment land, the rest being leased to non-Indians. Indians had far less of their land in valuable cultivated row crops and grains and more in hay and fodder, with the result that their land produced an average value of $31.93 per acre, while reservation land leased to non-Indians produced $136.64 per acre. One reason for this high rate of alienation and differential production was the size of parcel; Indian farms averaged 49 acres, and half were less than

Shoshone–Bannock Tribes, Sho-Ban Media Center, Fort Hall, Idaho.

Fig. 2. Lee Bear, a Northern Shoshone farmer on land he was leasing from the Shoshone–Bannock tribe. This potato field is part of 320 acres he had under irrigation in the Michaud Flats area. Photograph by Bill Richmonds, Fort Hall Reservation, Idaho, about 1976.

20 acres, while plots that non-Indians leased averaged 172 acres, with only one-quarter less than 20 acres. Even in the 1950s small western ranches and farms were not so profitable as larger ones, which became increasingly true in later years. Much of the differential product value of Indian farms was explained by choice of low-value fodder crops, which in turn was the result of another economic fact. In 1960 to produce a $4,700 net income on a farm of 1,000 acres, an Idaho farmer would have to put in row crops. That would require an investment of over $43,000 for specialized equipment, above and beyond the cost of land. Indians simply did not have access to capital on this scale, since borrowing from banks was forestalled by the nonforecloseable nature of their trust-status land, nor would they have enough personal property to place as collateral for such a loan. Although smaller farms did require somewhat smaller investment, a basic set of equipment was needed regardless of size of farm, while profits declined rapidly. There was no cooperative or tribal farming at Fort Hall to attempt to pool equipment and no tribal livestock association (Nybroten 1964:12–20; cf. Roth 1976:380).

In a sample of approximately one-third (190) of the adult population in 1960, 42 were farmers or ranchers, of whom 10 percent reported no income for 1959. Of 34 skilled laborers, 41 percent had no income; and of 25 unskilled laborers, none reported cash income. Half the 16 professional and clerical workers had no income that year, while two-thirds of all housewives reported earning some cash through craft sales. Thus, it would appear that the more highly skilled workers were least unsuccessful in finding employment, while the agriculturally based occupations were most successful. Employed workers averaged 14 years older than unemployed workers, hinting at the difficulty young people had in supporting their families.

The average cash income per employed worker was $1,780, or $540 per capita. Furthermore, as in many other Indian societies, the distribution of income over the population was very uneven. Over 12 percent of the population had an annual income of less than $100, and 42 percent earned less than $300 per year. The next income group was the $500–599 bracket, with 12 percent of the population. Thus, Fort Hall had one large group in extreme poverty and another sizable percentage slightly better off, with a very long and thin statistical "tail" stretching into the higher income brackets (Nybroten 1964:150–158). In 1950, the income of Idaho non-Indians was 36 percent greater than the average at Fort Hall, and in 1967 it was more than twice the Indian average (Jorgensen 1972:117; U.S. Congress. House. Committee on Interior and Insular Affairs 1972:21).

The social consequences of this economic situation were plain, as they had been at Uintah-Ouray 10 years earlier. Only 5 percent of Fort Hall housing was rated as comparable to that of surrounding rural non-Indians. Three-quarters of all Indian houses were substandard wood frame in need of repairs, and 13 percent were log cabins. Five percent were renovated box cars, and 3 percent floored tents. Over 34 percent had only one room, while only 5 percent of dwellings in the state of Idaho did; only 5 percent of Fort Hall homes had five or more rooms, while 42 percent of Idaho homes did. In these smaller houses Fort Hall Indians had 6.12 persons per household, while Idahoans averaged 3.25. Combined, these facts meant that Indians averaged 2 people per room, and Idahoans generally 0.74. Thus, Fort Hall houses were small, substandard, and crowded.

In Idaho, only 4 percent of farm houses lacked indoor water in 1960, while 80 percent of the reservation homes did. Only 15 percent of the Indian population drank water that had passed state health standards. Over half hauled their own water or drank from surface sources such as ditches and streams. Only 65 percent of reservation homes had electricity, which was nearly universal in non-Indian homes in the state (Nybroten 1964:73, 80–86).

The Fort Hall study documented another social result of the economic situation, its effects on the health of the people. While, like Indians generally, they had lower than state and national rates of death due to cancer and heart disease, many other categories were disproportionately high—3.66 times the Idaho rate of accidents, 4.25 times the influenza and pneumonia, 15.5 times the tuberculosis, 89 times the dysentery, 29 times the meningitis, and 29 times the deaths due to measles. All these categories can be attributed to poor and uninsulated housing, unsanitary water sources and waste disposal, and inadequate and untimely health care. In short, "the worst single factor found in relation to diseases at Fort

575

Denver Mus. of Nat. Hist., Colo.: left, 1098/3; right, 1218/6; center, Mus. of the Amer. Ind., Heye Foundation, New York: 24/4148.

Fig. 3. Modern handicrafts. left, Pair of modern, soft-soled, smoked elkhide moccasins from the Fort Hall Reservation, Idaho. These moccasins are machine sewn. This pan-Indian design is typical of pieces made for sale, as is the simple, sparse application of beadwork. More elaborately beaded pieces of both traditional and innovative artistry are also made for sale and personal use. Collected in 1970. center, Beaded bottle, cork stopper, and buckskin bottom. Beadwork done in a blue field of seed beads, with red, white, dark blue, and yellow geometric design elements. Collected in Nev. before 1971. right, Ute necklace of plastic red, white, yellow, and blue beads and hairpipes and cowrie shells. Part of a Ute Mountain costume for the 1967 Miss Indian America Pageant. Length of left, 25.4 cm; rest to same scale.

Hall is the general living condition of the people" (Nybroten 1964:90).

Small Reservations in Utah

It is useful to compare the situation of reservations with large land and population bases, such as Uintah-Ouray and Fort Hall, with smaller reservations lacking these natural and human resources, such as the Western Shoshone and Southern Paiute groups marked for termination from federal trust responsibility in the mid-1950s (U.S. Congress. Joint Committees on Interior and Insular Affairs 1954).

According to the BIA report in the termination hearings, the Skull Valley Reservation of Western Shoshone contained 19,665 acres and supported one Indian family. The rest of the land was leased for a total annual rental of $1,350. Of the other 11 families of enrolled members, three were deemed self-supporting through wage work in the town of Grantsville, 50 miles away, and the remaining eight were dependent on church and public welfare assistance. Family income was estimated to be one-third that of neighboring rural non-Indians. BIA services were provided out of the Uintah-Ouray Agency 200 miles away.

Of the Southern Paiute bands, the largest was at Shivwits, with 97 members and 28,160 acres of land. None of the 24 families was self-supporting, five being totally dependent on welfare. From 1941 to 1949 the tribe attempted to operate the Shivwits Farm and Livestock Enterprise with revolving credit funds available through the Indian Reorganization Act of 1934. The cooperative was never profitable and ceased operation deeply in debt. The entire reservation was leased to a non-Indian cattleman for $1,500 per year. By 1954 all family income was from wage work and was estimated to be one-third that of surrounding non-Indians. School-age children composed 47 percent of the Shivwits population, but fully one-third had dropped out of school "because of home conditions, marriage, or employment" (U.S. Congress. Joint Committees on Interior and Insular Affairs 1954:13), reflecting the families' need for their children's labor and whatever cash contribution they could make to the household. This reservation, like the other four Southern Paiute ones, was administered by the Uintah-Ouray Agency 450 miles away, making BIA services practically unavailable.

Koosharem had an enrolled membership of 27 and land holdings of 280 acres, two-thirds of which was individual allotments. One family partially supported itself by farming the entire reservation, and the remaining eight lived in Richfield, 45 miles away. Oral history relates the late 1940s and early 1950s as a time of migrant agricultural labor, frequent moving, living in tents in the fields of employers and wintering in those same tents on a parcel of private land in town

(Knack 1973–1982). The hearings describe the living conditions as "unsatisfactory." The BIA reported that two families were self-supporting, three combined wages with welfare assistance from church and public sources, and three were totally welfare dependent. Income was estimated to be one-half that of surrounding non-Indians.

The Indian Peaks Reservation contained 10,240 acres and had an enrolled membership of 26. The 1954 BIA report stated that no one had lived there in the last 10 years, but oral history described the last family sliding down 40 miles of dirt road in an autumn blizzard with all their possessions and two children piled into a Model T pickup, which would seem to date the abandonment somewhat earlier. Reasons cited for leaving were the inability to make a living ranching the land, complete lack of wage work, and fear of being snowed in for another winter (Knack 1973–1982). Indian Peaks families moved to Cedar City and other small towns along the Wasatch Front to seek wage employment. In this they were only partially successful, for the BIA reported only two families self-supporting in 1954 and the remaining four combining wage and welfare income. Even so, their income was estimated at half that of surrounding non-Indians. The entire unoccupied reservation was let for grazing at $525 per year. The conditions on the Northern Shoshone allotments at Washakie and at Kanosh followed a similar pattern.

For all these groups, the land base failed to provide an adequate living for more than a very small minority of the population. The overwhelming majority had to leave the reservation to find work. What labor they found was often menial, intermittent, and low-paying, so that it had to be supplemented by a variety of public and private agencies. In all regards, the economic picture on these small reserves parallels that of large ones, except that the lack of land base forced much higher rates of outmigration.

Between 1950 and 1965, 85 to 100 percent of the enrolled population of the large reservations lived on them (Jorgensen 1972:93), but for the small and remote reservations in Nevada, less than half and sometimes none of the members lived on tribal lands (U.S. Department of Commerce 1974; Facilitators 1980; Washoe Tribe of Nevada and California 1981:31, 39). There is no systematic data for these off-reservation populations at this period, and very scanty information at other times. The impression from brief statements in the anthropological literature, historical references, and the oral record, was of a thinly scattered population living through manual labor jobs in agriculture, mining, and transport, which were often temporary and at low rates of pay. Cash income was supplemented by hunting, gathering, and welfare. This population was apparently mobile, of necessity moving to wherever jobs were available.

Summary

Throughout the Great Basin, the economic situation of Indians in the 1950s was grim. Agriculture and ranching were the only productive enterprises on the reservations, and that only on the few with substantial land bases. Even there these activities were hampered by the small size of land assignments, factionated heirship status of allotments, and the lack of individual credit sources. Limited funds were available from the BIA under the revolving credit program, and bureau policy emphasized range improvement and individual or co-operative stock raising as the appropriate investment for an Indian economy. On some reservations, such as Uintah-Ouray and Southern Ute, there were cooperative herding associations, while on others, such as Ute Mountain, and among Eastern Shoshone at Wind River, herding was done individually (Hoffmeister 1945; Jorgensen 1964:221; Schutz, Baker, and Vanvig 1960). All studies show that ownership of livestock was very unevenly distributed with the vast majority of adults owning few if any stock, that the income from livestock was equally skewed with very few individuals earning a viable income, and that the reservation land base could never have supported more than a very small minority of members at full-time ranching. On smaller reservations even this option was not available.

None of the reservations except Southern Ute had light industry or other manufacturing on their lands, and there were no tribally owned or operated enterprises. Only a very few reservations, such as Wind River and Northern Ute, had mining activities, and all these were by non-Indian corporations, which simply paid lease and royalty fees to the tribe. Rates of Indian unemployment were very high and salaries low. Few could find full-time employment, and most jobs were seasonal, short-term, or part-time. These jobs were either provided by the BIA and other government agencies operating on the reservation or by the surrounding non-Indian economy. In seeking jobs off-reservation, Indians were faced by negative stereotypes of their behavior as workers (Nybroten 1964:159–160), lack of salable skills valued by the non-Indian economy, and a competitive disadvantage in language and education against non-Indian laborers. For instance, in 1954, 25–50 percent of Southern Paiute adults in the four bands in southern Utah could not read or write English (U.S. Congress. Joint Committees on Interior and Insular Affairs 1954:12–15), and in 1960, 87 percent of all family heads at Fort Hall Reservation had less than eighth-grade education, with 56 percent of all adults illiterate (Nybroten 1964:76; Jorgensen 1972:134). Put at such a competitive disadvantage, the employment Indians found was often manual, agricultural labor—migrant crop harvesting in Utah, potato processing in southern Idaho, cattle roundup and hay baling in Nevada. The resulting income was well below that of surrounding non-Indians, but even these averages hide the large percentage of people with only a few hundred dollars a year.

As a result, Indians relied on multiple income sources, combining stock ownership, wage labor, welfare, unearned tribal income, and other sources whenever these were available. Further, kinsmen pooled labor, property, and resources. Housing was in poor condition and crowded to the point of affecting public health. The community infrastructure common in non-Indian towns was lacking on reservations; for instance, the only paved roads on the huge Uintah-Ouray Reservation were the federal highways that crossed it, all other roads being dirt, unplowed in winter and deep with mud in the spring (Jorgensen 1964:199).

In short, the economic situation in the 1950s was one of a marginal agricultural–ranching economy on large reservations, complete dependency on equally marginal off-reservation wage work on small reservations, poverty, weak community infrastructure, little cash and less credit.

Changes in the 1960s

The decade of the 1960s produced many economic changes. Among these were the initial influx of major amounts of capital from land claims settlements and mineral royalties, training programs, federal grants to tribes, the policy of contracting through tribal governments services previously provided by the BIA, and growth of tribally owned production and service-oriented enterprises.

Land Claims Settlements

Northern Utes were the first in the Great Basin to receive large land claims settlements—one million dollars in 1931. Since then, each tribal group has been awarded multimillion-dollar settlements ranging from five million dollars for Washoes to almost 50 million dollars for various Ute groups (Jorgensen 1964:205, 1972:113; U.S. Congress. House. Committee on Interior and Insular Affairs 1972:1; Western Shoshone Sacred Lands Association 1982:19; Inter-Tribal Council of Nevada 1976:150, 1976a:89–91; Johnson 1975:153). Many people thought that such large blocks of money would provide working capital in sufficiently large amounts to improve, develop, and modernize reservation economies.

The actual effects of land claims monies were best documented at Uintah-Ouray, but scanty references from elsewhere showed a similar pattern at Wind River, Southern Ute, and Ute Mountain Ute reservations. Large proportions of the funds were allocated on a per capita basis. Between 1951 and 1959, Northern Utes each received over $11,000, more than quadrupling household income of the previous decade and making unearned income by far the largest cash source on the reservation. The marginally rewarding activities of part-time wage labor and livestock herding were dropped, so that by 1960 many families were totally dependent on unearned income. When the per capita payments dwindled after 1963, state welfare became the major source of support (Jorgensen 1972:159–161).

The amount of money received by each Indian varied according to the amount of the judgment, the number of enrolled members, and the portion the tribe decided to expend on per capita payments. Eastern Shoshones distributed 85 percent of their award on a per capita basis, while Kaibab Southern Paiutes, having learned from the history of earlier awards, spent only 15 percent in per capita payments and another 15 percent in family plan accounts. Terminated Southern Paiutes and landless Western Shoshones voted for complete expenditure on an individual basis (U.S. Congress. House. Committee on Interior and Insular Affairs 1972:1; Inter-Tribal Council of Nevada 1976a:89–91).

Individual use of per capita funds was often not a matter of free choice; rather, the BIA placed money in Individual Indian Money (IIM) accounts and released only a small fraction, $100 of the initial Wind River award of $2,450 for instance (Jorgensen 1972:112). The rest would be authorized after the Indian presented the agency or the tribal government with an approved plan for expenditure (Bennett 1961–1962; Knack 1973–1982). Further attempts to control Indians' use of these funds were made, such as paying Indians' outstanding debts to local merchants, often extended in anticipation of the award, or directly paying merchants for goods rather than giving the Indians cash for their own purchases (Lang 1961–1962). Funds for minors were often shielded from use by their parents (Jorgensen 1964:206).

Per capita monies at Uintah-Ouray were used for goods that would increase the quality of life for the individual rather than for investments that would later be income-producing. Down payments for houses and cars, too expensive to be bought outright, were initiated. Clothes, radios, televisions, travel to visit relatives or dances, household appliances, and daily living expenses absorbed much of the rest (Jorgensen 1964:206). There was virtually no long-term benefit except elevated expectations of a standard of living that, once unearned sources were removed, could not be supported by the wage labor of the Indians.

Use of the tribal portion of the Uintah-Ouray land claims settlement was in accordance with BIA policy. Land was purchased to reinforce the flagging stock industry, consolidate tribal boundaries, resolve fractional ownership of allotments, and prevent tax sales. A tribal livestock enterprise was begun that never showed a profit and employed only a few men. Other expenditures were for infrastructure and service, including construction of buildings to house the tribal government, recreational facilities, and welfare programs (Jorgensen 1972:113; Euler and Naylor 1952). As the local and regional value of agriculture declined, stock raising and farming decreased on all reservations except in a few unusually favorable locations such as Fort Hall and Colorado River reservations (Jorgensen 1972:105; Jorgensen, Davis, and Mathews 1978; American Indian Policy Review Commission 1976:33, 41; Roth 1976:343; U.S. Congress. House. Committee on Interior and Insular Affairs 1972:26; Facilitators 1980:2.123; U.S. Bureau of Indian Affairs. Phoenix Area Office 1980:2–44).

Tribes receiving later judgment funds tended to diversify their investments more. Washoes budgeted 70 percent of their settlement for education and tribal development, but in fact, like Kaibabs, managed to build tribal enterprises from grant funds, saving much of the land claims money in reserve for future needs (Inter-Tribal Council of Nevada 1976a:89–91; Euler 1972:94). On the whole, few expenditures have been of a productive nature, with massive amounts being spent to ameliorate immediate conditions of poverty without altering the causes. Tribal welfare and social services expanded dramatically, as did numbers of tribal employees, putting some money back into the communities in the form of salaries (table 1). For instance, by 1963 the Uintah-Ouray tribal government had grown to 45 full-time and 60–80 part-time positions, of which 20 full-time and 40 part-time were filled by non-Indians or mixed-bloods, soon to be expelled. Like income, jobs were unevenly distributed, and 12 of the remaining full-time positions were controlled by three families. Ute Mountain tribal government became employer to 97 percent of the work force (Jorgensen 1972:156).

The other major result of land claims settlements was intensification of political factionalism. In some cases this was merely a predictable dispute over the appropriate use of the funds and a challenge to the leadership of those administering the monies, while in other cases the issues were more profound. At Uintah-Ouray questions rose concerning who had legitimate right to benefit from the money, which, crystalizing on old issues of blood admixture, band membership, and tribal history, led to the expulsion of the mixed-blood faction from the reservation (Jorgensen 1972:151–155; Bennett 1961–1962; Lang 1961–1962). In Nevada, Western Shoshones were split on the moral legitimacy of land claims compensation, when traditionalists opposed distribution of the judgment funds on religious grounds and won a tribal vote to halt payment (Western Shoshone Sacred Lands Association 1982).

Vocational Training Programs

Lack of working capital was one factor many analysts had used to explain the condition of reservation economies in previous decades; lack of salable skills was another. In accordance with long-standing BIA emphasis on education, the relocation program of the 1950s included a job-training element. While it is unclear how many Great Basin Indians participated in this program over the years, it appears to have touched most reservations. Between 1961 and 1967, the BIA relocated 56 workers from Wind River, 58 percent of whom returned to the reservation within a few years. In the decade ending in 1967, the BIA provided adult vocational training to 177 persons on that reservation, of whom 52 percent completed the course (U.S. Congress. House. Committee on Interior and Insular Affairs 1972:31). When federal relations with Utah Southern Paiutes were terminated in 1954, the government provided vocational training focusing on manual skills to 12 adults, none of whom completed the course (Knack 1980:42). A survey of Pyramid Lake Northern Paiutes in 1962, just before the initiation of major federal programs, discovered that 43 percent of adult men and 27 percent of women had already had formal vocational

Table 1. **Sources of Indian Employment on Some Reservations**

Reservation, Year	Federal Agencies	Tribal Government	Tribal Enterprises	Other	Source
Southern Ute, 1962	28%	72%		0	Jorgensen 1972:111
Wind River, 1962	55	40		5	Jorgensen 1972:111
Uintah-Ouray, 1966	58	37		7	Jorgensen 1972:164
Colorado River, 1971[a]	36	62		2	Roth 1976:378
Utah Southern Paiutes, 1974[b]	7	0	0	93	Knack 1973–1982
Kaibab, 1978	67	23		10	Kaibab Paiute Tribe 1980:48
Moapa, 1980	10	20	48	22	Facilitators 1980:5.40
Battle Mountain, 1980	18	29	12	41	Facilitators 1980:3.52
Elko, 1980	31	25	4	40	Facilitators 1980:3.75
South Fork, 1980	23	16	0	61	Facilitators 1980:3.139
Las Vegas, 1980	3	10	10	77	Facilitators 1980:5.76

[a] The majority of residents of this reservation are members of Southwest tribes.
[b] Not a reservation, but a group that retained tribal identity during termination.

Nev. Histl. Soc., Reno: 1024.

Fig. 4. Western Shoshone and Northern Paiute women assembling electronics equipment and transistors, Duck Valley Reservation, Nev. Photographed about 1973.

training at some time, about half while attending BIA secondary schools and most of the remainder through the relocation program (Brink 1969:189; Gomberg and Leland 1963:36–37). Training was overwhelmingly manual and sexually stereotyped, without preparation for management or executive positions that would enable people to initiate and control enterprises of their own.

Federal anti-poverty programs, designed to enable the poor to become competitive in the labor market, were active throughout the Great Basin by the mid to late 1970s—Job Corps, Mainstream, Manpower, and the Comprehensive Employment Training Act. Again, skills provided were low-level ones, such as truck driving and cooking, or in the manual trades, such as carpentry and secretarial work. These programs were open to Indians, along with other poor.

Terminated Southern Paiutes participated in these programs and others. By 1973, 31 of a sample of 73 adults had been in one or more vocational programs (Knack 1980:37–39). Training seemed to be unsuccessful, as it increased neither chances of employment nor income (Knack 1978). Most participants were young, while greatest unemployment continued being among these same young adults. Much of the ineffectiveness of training programs seems to have been a result of the generally stagnant rural economies surrounding reservations. There were few jobs for semiskilled and skilled workers; those were already held by long-term employees, and few new openings were being created. The

580

situation seemed similar in northern Utah and may have been general throughout the Great Basin (Jorgensen 1972:167).

Mineral Royalties and Leases

Elsewhere in the West, much of the economic growth of tribes in the 1980s was built on the independent income base of mineral leases and royalties from large energy corporations. In the Great Basin, such sources were important on only a few reserves, but in those cases provided much-needed cash. In 1952–1953 Uintah-Ouray received $3.7 million from mineral extraction, but this decreased rapidly until, by the 1962–1963 fiscal year, the amount was only $775,000 (Jorgensen 1964:206). On the other hand, Wind River had $1.3 million from mineral leases in 1956, and that increased steadily over the next two decades until oil and gas royalties formed by far the major sources of income for this reservation (U.S. Congress. House. Committee on Interior and Insular Affairs 1972:26). By 1980 most Ute Mountain tribal income also came from oil and gas leases (U.S. Congress. Senate. Select Committee on Indian Affairs 1980:38–40). Wind River, Southern Ute, Uintah-Ouray, Walker River, and Ute Mountain joined the Council of Energy Resource Tribes (CERT) in an attempt to improve their negotiating position with the multinational corporations, reduce dependency on the BIA for technical advice, and improve management of financial resources. While some argued that tribes that allowed their nonreplaceable natural resources to be extracted for the benefit of non-Indian industry were being exploited (Jorgensen et al. 1978), CERT declared that money acquired from mineral leases "could be used for economic development purposes. If carefully managed it could become a foundation for the overall economic development needs of the tribe. We look to projects that could result from energy production which could bring revenues to tribal government, jobs, income for tribal members, and for incentives for businesses to locate on the reservation" (U.S.Congress. Senate. Select Committee on Indian Affairs 1980:38).

By comparison, reservations elsewhere in the Great Basin acquired little income from minerals. In 1967 Fort Hall Reservation (fig. 5) received only $150,000 from mineral leases and Walker River Reservation got $8,000 from exploration leases in 1979 (U.S. Congress. House. Committee on Interior and Insular Affairs 1972:21; Facilitators 1980:2.125). Other reservations received next to no income from this source, except an occasional gravel extraction contract.

Federal Grants and Tribal Contracts

By 1955 it was federal policy to diffuse Indian services from administration by the BIA to handling through

Shoshone–Bannock Tribes, Sho-Ban Media Center, Fort Hall, Idaho.
Fig. 5. Northern Shoshone Virgie Fisher, working in the parts room at the Simplot Gay Mines, Putnam Mountains, Fort Hall Reservation, Idaho. Fisher was one of the first Native women to be hired at the open pit phosphate mine. Photograph by Bill Richmonds, 1970s.

other federal agencies. The Indian Health Service was moved into the Department of Health, Education, and Welfare, and many community and small-business support programs were specifically opened to tribes. After 1970 reservations with corporate charters were encouraged to subcontract for services previously provided by the BIA, such as law enforcement, child adoption, and senior care.

Some of the more aggressive Great Basin reservations went further. Through their tribal councils, in cooperation with the Inter-Tribal Council of Nevada, or with planning consultants hired independently of the BIA, many applied for and won grants from various federal agencies. Among the most successful grant-ac-

quiring groups was the Kaibab Southern Paiute (fig. 6) who, in 1979 alone, had $410,000 in active grants for tribal administration, planning, provision of social services, and vocational training. Even the tiny Ely colony had won nearly the same amount between 1973 and 1980, for housing, street construction, electrification, and sewer development. Duckwater Reservation, Nevada, acquired over $2 million in grants in 1978–1980 (Kaibab Paiute Tribe 1980:28; Facilitators 1980:3.96, 3.221). Some other groups received almost no grant income. There is no data comparing success of tribes and rural towns in exploiting this income source.

Some groups, such as Lovelock (Facilitators 1980:2.37) and Cedar City Southern Paiute (Knack 1973–1982), acquired access to federal revenue sharing funds, and a very few, such as Moapa (Facilitators 1980:5.44), combined grants with loans from commercial banks. The vast majority of this revenue was in the form of outright grants, rather than loans or mortgages.

Most grants were used for one of two purposes: to construct a community infrastructure—housing, roads, sewer and water systems, indoor plumbing, buildings for tribal council offices and community meetings, and gymnasiums; or to plan and construct tribally owned enterprises and to train workers.

Exemplifying the first category was the Las Vegas colony community center, which opened in 1981. The colony incorporated a construction company that then contracted for the project funded by the Department of Housing and Urban Development. Moapa, Washoe, and other groups used this same strategy with housing and other contracts in order to retain the wage benefits within the Indian community. Las Vegas paved streets, built curbs and sidewalks, and connected with city water and sewer facilities on federal grant money. Lovelock

The Native Nevadan, Reno-Sparks Indian Colony.
Fig. 6. Southern Paiute tomato-growing enterprise, Moapa Reservation, Nev. The greenhouses were built with a $1.5 million grant from the Department of Housing and Urban Development in 1978. From that time until 1980, when the greenhouses were destroyed by hail, the tomato operation was run by the tribe. In 1981 the greenhouse was leased for one year to a non-Indian. Since then the enterprise has not been re-activated. left, Greenhouses. Photograph by Arlene Fisher, 1981. right, Preston Tom, Chairman of Moapa tribe and U.S. Sen. Howard Cannon at dedication ceremonies for Jackpot Brand tomatoes. Photographed in Feb. 1979.

Northern Paiutes built a tribal administrative building with funds from the Department of Commerce Economic Development Administration and renovated water and sewer delivery in 1980 with a HUD grant. Fallon constructed a new water system in 1966 and upgraded it 11 years later, got a planning grant for law enforcement coordination with state and federal jurisdictions in 1976, built a community building in 1976, and added an educational wing the next year. Each one of these grants was between $200,000 and $400,000; similar instances could be cited for nearly all Great Basin reservations (Facilitators 1980:2.41, 2.80, 5.78). There would have been no hope of such improvements on the basis of tribal or personal incomes or self-taxation; external funding sources were necessary.

Tribal Enterprises

The second major use of grant funds was to plan and develop tribal enterprises in order to create jobs for members. Private non-Indian industries had generally failed to establish themselves on reservations because of distance from raw materials sources and markets (which increased transportation costs in each direction), lack of skilled labor, poor condition of highways, and, until the 1970s in some areas, lack of electricity, natural gas, and suitable buildings. In the 1960s the BIA had begun a national campaign to encourage non-Indian industry to locate on reservations, with minimal results. Tax incentives, tribal subsidies of building construction, and federal subsidies of wages for trainees did create jobs but did not solve the problems. When tax waivers lapsed, industries relocated elsewhere, leaving tribes

with their limited funds tied up in unusable, customized buildings. When trainee salary payments expired, new trainees were taken on instead of permanently hiring those already trained. The BIA insisted that leases specify Indian hiring preferences, that given equal skills, Indians would be hired before non-Indians. But with the limited education of most Indians and work experience often restricted to agricultural or manual labor, employers argued that qualified Indians were unavailable. Sixty percent of the jobs created went to non-Indians, including the majority of more technical, highly paid, and decision-making positions (Jorgensen 1978:61–63).

Between 1965 and 1975, the Economic Development Administration granted over $185 million to reservation groups for infrastructural development and tribal enterprises (see table 2). Because of federal laws supporting minority businesses, these nascent industries were able to win contracts from defense and other federal agencies. Many reservations located near major highways invested in recreation-related enterprises aimed primarily at the non-Indian traveler. Unlike the BIA programs that encouraged non-Indian industries to utilize the availability of cheap production costs, unskilled labor, and tax advantages, this approach held the promise of developing Indian-owned and -controlled enterprises.

Such, however, was not always the actual result. For example, in 1973, the then-terminated Southern Paiute bands of Utah acquired an Economic Development Administration grant to construct three industrial buildings near their residential areas. Incipient Paiute enterprises were given first priority in leasing, other tribes'

left, Smithsonian, NAA: 85–7026; right, U.S. Dept. of Interior, Water and Power Resources Service, Montrose, Colo.: P71–427–148 NA.
Fig. 7. Ute Mountain Ute pottery, a tribal enterprise begun in 1970. The modern plant on the Ute Mountain Ute Reservation, Towaoc, Colo., employs about 30 native artisans. The pottery is shipped to gift shops throughout the world. left, Cover of advertisement brochure, published 1980. right, Susie Mills, using a pottery wheel, hand painting a mug. Each piece is signed by the artist. Photograph by Verne Jetley, 1975.

582

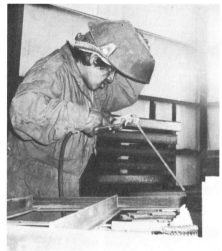

Native Nevadan, Reno-Sparks Indian Colony.
Fig. 8. Gosiute Western Shoshone welding enterprise, Ibapah, Utah. left, Cattle guards stored outside plant. right, Native employee. Photographs by Arlene Fisher, 1981.

industries next, and third, non-Indian companies. A short-lived beadwork cooperative rented one room of the largest building but went out of business within the year as a result of internal disputes. The only other Indian lease was a partnership between one Paiute and a non-Indian in garment finishing, which deteriorated within three years amid accusations of fraud. Thereafter that building burned down. The largest building had at least five major tenants in its first five years, including a mushroom grower, lumber yard, and roller disco. It stood empty at least half the time, until the tribe regained federal status and took it over for a tribal headquarters. The third building was leased by a small local non-Indian company for several years, providing some rent income, but it too was soon unoccupied. Other than the tribal government itself, the only lessor who hired any Paiutes was the clothing enterprise, which provided five to seven jobs with a very high rate of turnover and a modest salary. In spite of their proximity to commercial centers, the benefits of this grant to the Indian community have been minimal (Knack 1973–1982).

Despite their lack of business experience and political unity, which hindered effective utilization of the buildings, the Utah Southern Paiutes had had a large grant and new resources virtually thrust upon them by the federal government and the active intervention of the state Office of Indian Affairs, which coordinated the grant proposal. Other Great Basin groups observed such overambitious projects and retained professional planners, some of whom recommended beginning on a small scale and risking little of the limited tribal capital while members gained managerial skills. Later, with the seed money and expertise produced, more elaborate enterprise could be initiated on new grant funds and another group of trainees begun in the old project, thus safely expanding the industrial base without overextending tribal resources. Throughout, tribal members were to be actively involved in idea development, planning, grant seeking, and execution, rather than having decisions made for them by others. The long-term plans of Moapa and Kaibab Paiutes were of this nature; both groups began with the familiar skills of ranching and farming and gradually introduced more commercial enterprises (J. Mitchell 1979; Turner 1981a). Other groups initiated more ambitious projects, such as the two fish hatcheries and fish biology training program at the Pyramid Lake Northern Paiute Reservation (fig. 9) associated with their complex series of legal suits to regain water resources necessary for economic development (Knack and Stewart 1984; Cerveri 1977).

Tribal sale of cigarettes deserves special mention (fig. 10). Because of the federal trust status of reservation lands, often sizable state taxes on cigarettes were, for a long time, not believed applicable to sales on reservations. Thus, entrepreneurs there could undersell off-reservation retailers by $1.25 to $2.00 per carton. Coupled with low overhead and low pay scales, such businesses built massive trade by 1977, particularly in Nevada where several reservations were near urban markets. In the Las Vegas Colony a non-Indian was first to identify the opportunity and he obtained a five-year lease to an old building there. Despite lack of direct access to public streets, he was soon doing extensive business. The tribe set up its own competitive smokeshop across the street two years later. After grossing an estimated $4 million, the non-Indian's lease expired and the tribe took over his location as well. While tribes do not release income figures, in 1979 the state tax commission estimated that the Las Vegas colony grossed $1 million

Table 2. Housing, Tribal Enterprises, and Tribal Incomes, 1982

Reservation	New houses	Total houses	Improvement projects	Tribal enterprises	Other income sources	Sources
ARIZONA						
Chemehuevi [a]		10	[a]	campground	lease lakeshore	
Colorado River[b]	270	424	[a]	industrial park leased, clock factory, marina, 2 trailer parks, airline	land leases for homesites, 90 business leases, irrigated farm, recreation and agricultural leases	Roth 1976:389–393
Kaibab	10(1962) 15(1980)	46	6	visitors center, trailer park and campground, store, laundry	irrigated agriculture	Euler 1972:92; Turner 1981:162; Kaibab Paiute Tribe 1980:36, 47
COLORADO						
Southern Ute	[a]	[a]	10	motel, horse training stable, campground, hunting guide service	oil and gas leases; right of way, agricultural land leases	Richard Clemmer, communication to editors 1983
Ute Mountain	20(1983)	[a]	[a]	industrial park leased, park and guide service, pottery factory, campground	oil and gas leases	Ute Mountain Ute Tribe 1980; U.S. Congress. Senate. Select Committee on Indian Affairs 1980:40
IDAHO						
Fort Hall	78(1968) 75(1975)	556	60	2 resource industries, a commercial establishment	mineral leases	American Indian Policy Review Commission 1976:122
NEVADA						
Battle Mountain	28(1982)	62	15(1972) 17(1975)	smokeshop	none	Facilitators 1980:3.57; Sharon Kay, personal communication 1985
Duck Valley	70(1975)	368	18	motel, laundry, store, gas station	none	American Indian Policy Review Commission 1976:80
Duckwater	12	29	0	none	none	
Elko	10 23(1972) 11(1976) 23(1981) 58(1982)	130	15	smokeshop, electronic assembly, fly fishing manufacture	building rental	Facilitators 1980:3.77; Richard Clemmer, personal communication 1983; Sharon Kay, personal communication 1985
Ely	17(1973)	39	0	none	none	Facilitators 1980:3.101
Fallon	26(1971) 49(1980) 22(1974)	151	[a]	leased smokeshop, industrial park	crops and livestock	Facilitators 1980:2.52
Ft. McDermitt	15(1968) 30(1973) 35(1976)		43	none	lease to electrical parts manufacturers	Houghton 1973:89
Goshute	30(1978)	35	0	welding shop	none	Facilitators 1980:3.265
Las Vegas	0	25	0	construction company (inactive), 2 smokeshops	none	U.S. Congress. Senate. Select Committee on Indian Affairs 1982:2; Facilitators 1980:5.73
Lovelock	16(1973) 10(1980)	43	0	none	none	

Table 2. Housing, Tribal Enterprises, and Tribal Incomes, 1982 (*continued*)

Reservation	New houses	Total houses	Improvement projects	Tribal enterprises	Other income sources	Sources
Moapa	15(1970) 17(1972) 10(1978) 40(1981)	87	0	farm, leather shop, construction company, general store, tomato greenhouses	none	U.S. Congress. Senate. Committee on Energy and Natural Resources 1980:6; Facilitators 1980:5.44
Pyramid Lake	40	160	0	2 fish hatcheries, campground, industrial park leased	fishing permits	
Reno-Sparks	20(1970) 65(1974)	141	a	mini-mall leased	none	American Indian Policy Review Commission 1976:80
Ruby Valley	0	7	0	none	none	
South Fork	7(1974) 4(1977)	39	15	none	none	Facilitators 1980:3.143
Summit Lake	0	4	0	none	grazing leases; fishing permits; trout egg sales	
Walker River	20(1965) 80(1973–1980)	148	19	smokeshop, arts and crafts coop, general store, motel	mineral, airport, and building leases	Johnson 1975:158; Facilitators 1980:2.129
Washoe-Dresslerville	14	121	a	mini-market, smokeshop, farm, trailer park, construction company		Washoe Tribe of Nevada and California 1981:36
Winnemucca	8(1981)	9	0	none	none	Facilitators 1980:2.155
Yerington	44(1970)	53	0	none	none	
Yomba	16(1980)	29	10	none	none	Facilitators 1980:3.177
UTAH						
Skull Valley	0	4	0	none	lease rocket site	Facilitators 1980:3.281
Southern Paiute	10(1974) 11(1976) 25(1977) 10(1980) 7(1982)	88	0	none	gravel, grazing and building leases	Facilitators 1980:4.25–80
Uintah-Ouray	182(1972) 70(1976)	a	13	resort, furniture factory, research lab, cattle, guided hunting trips, laundry	oil and gas royalties	Bennett 1961–1962:160
WYOMING						
Wind River	a	a	a	none	oil and gas royalties	

SOURCE: U.S. Bureau of Indian Affairs, Phoenix Area Office 1976, unless otherwise noted.
a No information.
b The majority of residents of this reservation are members of Southwest tribes.

that year, and that Walker River Reservation made $76,000 profit, Fallon $71,000, and even Battle Mountain cleared $3,000 in its first three months. For the last two tribes, this was their sole source of income, and Walker River had only an $8,000 mineral lease, plus whatever grants they successfully competed for. In 1980, a U.S. Supreme Court decision (*Washington et al. v.*

Confederated Tribes of the Colville Indian Reservation et al.) declared that tribes must collect state tobacco and sales taxes from their non-Indian customers. Many tribal shops remained competitive by cutting their profit margin. The state of Nevada claimed in 1980 that it was losing $2 million in tax revenues annually and tried to force the reservations to collect a tribal tax equal in

center and bottom, *Native Nevadan,* Reno-Sparks Indian Colony.

Fig. 9. Pyramid Lake, Northern Paiute, fish hatchery enterprise. In 1985 there were 2 tribally owned fish hatcheries operating on the reservation. They bred local endangered species, which had been in precontact times an important resource. top, The Captain Dave Numana Hupa-Agai hatchery. Photograph by Martha C. Knack, 1982. center, Pyramid Lake Indian Tribal Enterprises (PLITE) employee with trout; photographed about 1983. bottom, PLITE employee with cui-ui; photographed about 1983.

Fig. 10. Washoe smokeshop. top, Advertisement sign with smoke from the Indian Creek forest fire in the distance. bottom, Interior of shop, tended by Madelina Henry, where cigarettes are purchased at a savings to the buyer and a profit to the Washoe. Photographs by Kenneth L. Miller, July 1984.

amount to the state levy. As the depression in the early 1980s deepened and state tax income shriveled, pressures increased to close off Indian tax-free cigarette sales (Anonymous 1980).

The 1970s

The processes outlined above took place at varying rates and to differing degrees on reservations of various size, isolation, and resource possession. By 1980, some had made solid beginnings toward local development, while others continued to rely on an ever less viable agricultural base. None had attained economic self-sufficiency or total employment.

Comparative data show that Indians in the Great Basin continued to earn significantly lower wages than their non-Indian neighbors. At Fort McDermitt, Nevada, in 1970, the median family income was $3,100 while surrounding Humboldt County was $10,000 (Houghton 1973:73, 189). The per capita income at

Yomba Reservation in 1977 was $800; in Nye County, Nevada, it was $5,801 (Facilitators 1980:3.175). And at Battle Mountain Reservation in 1980, the median family income of $4,800 contrasts with $23,435 for Lander County, Nevada (Facilitators 1980:3.54). On-reservation household income consistently ran from one-half to one-fifth that of the non-Indians in surrounding counties, who were participants in the same regional economy. The income differential existed regardless of the size of reservation or proximity to towns.

By 1980 Indian populations were characteristically young. Between 45 pecent and 55 percent of most on-reservation populations were below 15 years of age, due to high birth rates, lowered infant mortality, and out-migration of mature adults to seek jobs (Facilitators 1980). Furthermore, the statistical patterns of unemployed young adults and of women working, but at lower pay rates than men, continued (Knack 1980:33). Unemployment remained disproportionately high. For instance, Skull Valley had an unemployment rate of 27 percent in 1980 when surrounding Tooele County as a whole had 5 percent; Ely colony had 49 percent and Duckwater Reservation 57 percent, while White Pine County had 11 percent; Moapa had 39 percent, while Clark County had 8 percent; and urban Las Vegas colony had 31 percent while the city had 7 percent (Facilitators 1980:3.286, 3.51, 5.76).

The accumulated effect of there being few people able to find jobs, many who could not, and great numbers of children, was a very large number of people depending on the income of every worker. This resulted

socially in large, extended families, cooperative networks, and resident kinsmen, and statistically in dependency ratios ranging from 0.8 to over 1.0, and average household sizes of 5 to 6 persons in some areas (Knack 1980).

A partial cause of low income was the type of jobs Indians were able to acquire. Table 3 summarizes the studies that detail Indian employment, using U.S. Census standard categories and paired for comparison with census data for the surrounding counties. A consistent pattern emerges of Indians being employed far below regional averages in professional, managerial, decision-making, commercial, public contact, and skilled labor positions, and statistically above average in labor, service, and domestic jobs. In other words, Indians in the Great Basin found employment most often in the least prestigious and lowest paying jobs, which held little future for career growth or advancement to positions of control and ownership.

Mean income figures hide another continuing characteristic of Indian economy, the uneven distribution of available cash. Because of high unemployment, welfare and other forms of public and BIA assistance formed the sole income of large numbers of families, creating a group that existed on the barest subsistence level. For instance, in 1973, 23 percent of Utah Southern Paiute families depended on state or private welfare, in an area where the county-wide welfare rate was 4 percent (Knack 1980:44). In 1970, 65 of the 81 households at Fort McDermitt Reservation received tribal, BIA, or county welfare, and the average income from this source

Table 3. Percentage of Adults in the Labor Force by Job Category

Reservation/County	Date	Sample Size	1	2	3	4	5	6	7	Sources
Pyramid Lake, Nev.	1963	60	8%	6%	3%	3%	27%	32%	20%	Gomberg and Leland 1963:app.11
Washoe County	1960	30,144	28	16	15	1	12	5	23	U.S. Bureau of the Census 1963:table 84
Walker River, Nev.	1976	99	7	1	7	65	7	6	7	Facilitators 1980:2.124
Mineral County	1970	2,823	19	17	30	1	14	4	14	Facilitators 1980:2.124
Fallon, Nev.	1973	231	11	4	59	13	7	5	1	Facilitators 1980:2.77
Churchill County	1970	3,324	23	20	18	6	9	10	14	Facilitators 1980:2.77
Duckwater, Nev.	1980	56	7	12	13	23	30	14	0	Facilitators 1980:3.220
White Pine County	1980	4,104	12	14	19	3	21	19	12	Facilitators 1980:3.220
Washoe-Dresslerville, Nev.	1973	70	13	1	4	2	31	39	10	Murray-McCormick Environmental Group 1973:51
Douglas County	1970	3,168	25	20	10	3	5	5	32	U.S. Bureau of the Census 1973b:table 122

Job category code:
1. Professional, nurses, teachers, technicians, managers except farm, administrators.
2. Retail sales workers, bookkeepers, secretaries, and other clerical workers.
3. Craftsmen, foremen, and kindred workers.
4. Farmers and farm managers.
5. Manufacturing, transport, and nonmanufacturing operatives.
6. Laborers, farm laborers, farm foremen, and construction workers.
7. Service workers, including health, food, cleaning, protective, personal and household workers.

Table 4. Distribution of Family Income of 4 Groups

	Year	Sample Size	Less than $1,000	1,000–1,999	2,000–2,999	3,000–3,999	4,000–4,999	5,000–5,999	6,000–6,999	7,000–7,999	8,000–8,999	9,000–9,999	Over 10,000	Sources
Pyramid Lake, Nev.	1962	59	15%	24%	14%	5%	8%	14%	8%	5%	7%	0	0	Gomberg and Leland 1963:6
Fort McDermitt, Nev.	1965	63	8%	34%	35%	9%	8%	6%	0	0	0	0	0	Houghton 1973:190
Washoe-Dresslerville, Nev.	1970	117	9%	7%	16%	12%[a]	13%[a]	8%[a]	8%[a]	8%[a]	8%[a]	8%[a]	5%	Murray-McCormick Environmental Group 1973:24
Utah Paiutes	1973	31	0	10%	10%	18%	7%	18%	15%	10%	5%	2%	5%	Knack 1980:39

[a] Averaged from grouped data.

was nearly identical to that which working members could earn in wages (Houghton 1973:189). Virtually all studies showed that Indians adopted a strategy of multiple income sources—wages combined with welfare, tribal income distribution where available, livestock raising, and continued hunting (Jorgensen 1972; Knack 1980; Houghton 1973; Facilitators 1980:3.210). Income in the late 1970s showed the same distribution that it had a generation earlier, with a large group very low on the income scale, and a smaller group at or slightly above the federally designated poverty line (table 4). Numbers of workers and their family incomes are shown in table 5.

The source of employment is outlined in table 1. In urban colonies and the tiny reservations typical of much of Nevada, where there was little BIA presence, few federal agencies, and little or no tribal enterprise, Indians relied on the private sector for employment, which meant working off-reservation for non-Indians. Large reservations with active BIA agencies and federal programs showed high dependency on these sources of employment and decreasing reliance on distant off-reservation sources. Interestingly, the Utah Southern Paiute distribution shifted dramatically toward the large-reservation pattern following reinstatement and the funding of a substantial tribal bureaucracy. However, for most groups, as for Washoes, "existing tribal enterprises provide[d] employment and increased economic opportunities to only a small percentage of tribal members" (Washoe Tribe of Nevada and California 1981:36), and federally funded programs tended to be unreliable economic bases because of their fluctuation following political shifts.

By 1980 the housing on reservations had improved dramatically, not because of expansion of the local economy or higher incomes to support a higher standard of living, but because of massive federal investment over the previous decade (table 2). The majority of standard quality housing on Great Basin reservations was built through the Department of Housing and Urban Development self-help program, which substituted construction labor contribution for a down payment by the individual owners, or through grants to the tribe, which would own and rent the houses at nominal fees to individual members. Crowding was relieved and household size declined. The number of nuclear family households increased and extended family households decreased, an arrangement that had previously been a function of amount and reliability of income (Jorgensen 1972; Knack 1980). Almost half the houses built on most reservations went to families previously living elsewhere. The return of these migrants often increased the population of small reservations 30–60 percent or more (Facilitators 1980), putting added pressure on an economy experiencing at best weak growth.

Accompanying these new housing projects were water and sewer systems, facilitated by compact cluster development (which changed both the physical shape of communities and the social relationships between neighbors). Substantial grants through the Indian Health Service of the Department of Health and Human Services put older houses on septic systems and improved individual wells. These improved sanitary conditions affected public health; incidence of hepatitis and other such diseases declined, but other health conditions related to the economy remained unchanged (U.S. Congress. House. Committee on Interior and Insular Affairs 1972:26–27; Murray-McCormick Environmental Group 1973:23). The most commonly reported illnesses in Indian Health Service records were influenza, upper respiratory infections, and diabetes and its related complications (U.S. Bureau of Indian Affairs. Phoenix Area Office 1976). Alcoholism and accompanying high rates of accidents and suicide were consistently reported and thought to be "essentially" a result of the continued depressing economic prospects on most reservations (Berman 1980:28). Except for the largest reservations, many lacked clinics. They were visited by mobile units periodically, or private doctors' services were obtained in local non-Indian communities. The nearest Indian Health Service full-service hospital was frequently hundreds of miles away. Thus emergency and specialists' services were not readily available.

Nonreservation Communities

A substantial Great Basin Indian population continued to live off reservations in 1980. Some lived in very re-

Table 5. Employment and Income by Reservation and Sex, 1975

Reservation	Enrolled Members	Resident Members	In Work Force			Unemployed		Approximate Family Income
			Men	Women	Total	Men	Women	
ARIZONA								
Chemehuevi	312	37	a	a	17	a	a	a
Colorado River[c]	a	1,767	423	256	679	127	173	a
Kaibab	161	75	a	a	61		27[b]	$3,021
COLORADO								
Southern Ute	a	751	a	a	279		98[b]	a
Ute Mountain	a	1,380	a	a	438		168[b]	a
IDAHO								
Fort Hall	a	2,782	a	a	1,142		389[b]	a
NEVADA								
Battle Mountain	163	83	38	18	56	11	12	4,800
Duck Valley	959	a	233	135	368	63	73	5,600
Duckwater	a	84	11	12	23	3	5	3,200
Elko	420	a	109	99	208	60	45	4,800
Ely	157	23	25	27	52	6	20	3,500
Fallon	a	347	75	76	151	30	45	5,100
McDermitt	407	372	90	67	157	55	27	4,900
Goshute	a	126	42	4	46	24	0	3,000
Las Vegas	a	97	23	24	47	12	15	5,000
Lovelock	a	88	27	4	31	6	1	5,600
Moapa	165	128	36	40	76	12	26	5,000
Pyramid Lake	a	626	221	176	397	80	91	5,500
Reno-Sparks	a	503	122	113	235	67	81	6,190
South Fork	120	78	27	13	34	6	1	3,000
Summit Lake	66	0			a			a
Walker River	a	452	121	48	191	17	20	5,000
Washoe-Dresslerville	a	489	114	98	212	55	69	5,100
Winnemucca	106	26	9	1	10	3	0	4,460
Yerington	a	190	37	46	83	2	26	6,700
Yomba	a	66	19	17	36	9	14	4,600
UTAH								
Skull Valley	62	15	a	a	13		4[b]	a
Uintah-Ouray	1,640	1,405	308	265	573	112	132	a
WYOMING								
Wind River	a	4,538	a	a	1,076		516[b]	a

SOURCE: U.S. Bureau of Indian Affairs. Phoenix Area Office 1976; U.S. Department of Commerce 1974.
[a] No data.
[b] Total.
[c] The majority of residents of this reservation are members of Southwest tribes.

mote, rural areas, as did the San Juan Southern Paiutes located near Navajo Mountain and Willow Springs within the Navajo Reservation. Subsistence farmers, they cultivated native and introduced crops in usufruct-held fields, and they pastured sheep, cattle, and horses on adjoining rangeland. They got cash through periodic sales of beef, wool, and fine baskets, especially those needed for customary Navajo weddings. Like Southern Paiutes in southwestern Utah, San Juan people did migrant harvesting during World War II but were replaced in this occupation by other ethnic groups. Their local economy offered no opportunities for wage labor in 1980 due to very depressed agricultural conditions. Southern Paiutes were unsuccessful in competing with Navajos for the available jobs within the federal and tribal bureaucracies, and industry was nearly nonexistent. Although a few families moved to the town of Blanding to obtain jobs, on the whole, this Paiute community lived on a marginal subsistence base with little cash income, in one-room houses without electricity or plumbing, unsupported by federal agencies, which did not recognize their tribal status (Pamela Bunte, personal communication 1983).

In other rural areas, small clusters of Great Basin

Indians combined small-scale livestock production with occasional agricultural and railroad-maintenance wage labor, welfare, and tribal distributions when these were available. In such a way, a group of 25 Northern Shoshones lived on the site of the old Lemhi Reservation near Salmon, Idaho, at the sufferance of the non-Indian private owners of the land (U.S. Congress. Senate. Committee on Interior and Insular Affairs 1971). Until 1977, 75 Western Shoshones lived on private land in Wells, Nevada, in one- and two-room frame houses without indoor plumbing or electricity. At that time Congress granted them an 80-acre reservation and with such land title they could then qualify for federal housing and economic development grants (U.S. Congress. Senate. Select Committee on Indian Affairs 1977a:1,7).

Another small group in a once-remote area had the unusual experience of finding themselves enclosed in a national park. In 1936, the Civilian Conservation Corps built timber and adobe houses for the Western Shoshones of Death Valley. Despite Park Service efforts to encourage outmigration, 25 Shoshones continued to live there into the 1980s. Until then, they were refused the right to build new houses or bring in trailers, and electricity was denied as a fire hazard in the substandard dwellings. Some worked in menial capacities for the park and tourist concessions (Knack 1973–1982).

Access to a small town economy did not seem to improve the standard of living for Indians in the Great Basin. A study of town-dwelling Southern Paiutes in southwestern Utah showed that even amid a prosperous agricultural, commercial, and recreational economy, Indians remained disproportionately poor and underemployed (tables 3, 4) (Knack 1980). Even in urban areas, Indians fared no better. A 1972 federal survey of 64 Washakie Northern Shoshone households who had moved into Salt Lake City from their Utah allotments revealed that 34 had at least one member with a full-time job, 18 only part-time or short-term wage earners, and 11 no wage earner at all. Forty-seven employed persons had full-time jobs and 30 part-time, with 11 being professional and clerical (primarily employed by federal agencies), 18 in the skilled trades, and 48 manual laborers. Only one-third of the households were self-supporting, all others mixing wage income with public assistance, pensions, social security, and other sources. Average income was $5,424, with exactly half the families below the federal poverty line (U.S. Congress. House Committee on Interior and Insular Affairs 1972:10).

In addition to groups and individual families of Great Basin Indians, the urban areas of Salt Lake City, Reno, and Las Vegas each had a substantial Indian population by 1980. Drawn from Eastern as well as Western tribes, some had moved into the middle class and others followed the pattern of poverty documented for urban Indians elsewhere. In Las Vegas, the pan-Indian group had formed several culturally oriented clubs, as well as organized an Indian Center concerned with grant acquisition, job training, and aiding in migrant adjustment. All these urban Indian organizations had cool relations with the local Southern Paiutes (Knack 1973–1982). On the other hand, Nevada Urban Indians, a Reno pan-tribal organization, rented office space from the Reno-Sparks colony when they established their arts and crafts shop (Nevada Urban Indians Incorporated 1983).

Conclusion

By 1983, Indian economies in the Great Basin differed from their own condition at mid-century, remained distinctive from the non-Indian economies around them, and yet were strikingly similar to each other. Despite differences in the amount of land, resources, and commercial opportunity available to the various groups, their twentieth-century history and the resulting economic situation were uniform. The first large-scale infusion of capital, lack of which had previously stultified tribal development, resulted from successful land claims by each tribe. Large proportions of these funds were dissipated in per capita payments that had little lasting effect other than to increase dependence on unearned income. Some claims funds were spent for social services for temporary alleviation of oppressive conditions, and a few groups invested in income-producing enterprises. Reliance on livestock production declined through these years, not so much out of choice but from the general depression of ranching in the West. The infrastructure and physical appearance of most reservations improved dramatically as roads were paved and homes and community centers were built with federal grants won by the tribes.

However, this new infrastructure rested on a weak economic base. With a very few exceptions Indians earned significantly less than non-Indians in their area, and they were more likely to be employed in low status, manual labor jobs, be employed only part-time, or be unemployed. Tribally owned and operated enterprises had made minimal impact on most reservations, hiring far fewer workers than did the federally subsidized tribal governments. Household economies remained combinations of wage and unearned income, home production, and welfare.

Although the problem of capital for tribal development had been overcome by several of the reservation groups, other economic problems remained unchanged from earlier periods. Some were unchangeable, such as distance from urban markets, which increased production costs. Lack of skilled and experienced personnel, especially in managerial and professional fields, both hampered economic development and was hampered by the current conditions. Tribes in the Great Basin, as elsewhere, lacked access to the specialized business and legal information possessed by large, established non-Indian corporations. The BIA did not provide comparable data to assist Indians to break into these markets or to negotiate successfully with corporate giants who wished to develop reservation resources. The desperate need for jobs often forced reservation groups to make short-term decisions, many times without the experience, data, or foresight to anticipate long-term detrimental impacts. The federal trust relationship led to BIA oversight of businesses operating on the reservations, bureaucratic regulations, and multiple levels of approval with delays in decision-making. Questions of legal jurisdiction, confused by the adoption of Public Law 83–280 by Nevada on some reservations and not others, the *Oliphant* v. *Suquamish Indian Tribe* (435 U.S. 191) decision and other events (see "Issues: The Indian Perspective," this vol.), made the status of non-Indian employees on reservations complicated. Even should a tribe establish its own business, because of the lack of local Indian control of commerce, wages earned by Indian employees moved rapidly into the non-Indian economy as they purchased necessary goods. Great Basin Indian economies remained, in 1983, marginal and delicately poised on the thin edge of viability.

Issues: The Indian Perspective

EDWARD C. JOHNSON

Tribal leadership in the Great Basin is concerned with issues that have affected Indian people and their lands in the 1970s and 1980s—treaty and agreement rights, water rights, jurisdiction, economic development, and educational and social needs.

Treaties and Agreements

Tribal homelands have been reserved by treaties and agreements between tribes and the federal government. These records are of supreme importance because they have become the basis of Indian rights. Tribes, in some cases, ceded land to the United States government and retained reservations and certain rights. However, not all Indian tribes live on land reserved for them by these means, "lands which they received for tax-free use in compensation for other lands they ceded" (Liljeblad 1972:41), and many continue to claim aboriginal rights they do not believe were surrendered. For example, a Fort McDermitt Reservation tribal chairman commented in 1975 that "We have been denied our rights....The Indians are still owners of the fish and game and all of the land here" (Ryan 1975). Citing the Ruby Valley Treaty of 1863, Pacheco Gibson of Elko, Nevada, vowed to appeal his conviction in the Elko Justice Court for hunting deer out of season and off the South Fork Indian Reservation:

> Gibson and other Shoshone claim they have the right to hunt anywhere in the state, any time....
> "Under the 1863 Treaty of Ruby Valley we are entitled to this," Gibson insisted. "We have every right that's in the treaty, including hunting and fishing," said Gibson, as long as it's done to provide for their own families. "The Indian only takes what he needs," Gibson said with conviction. "They hunt for subsistence only," he said contrasting that with white hunters, who are only after a trophy head to put above the mantle.
> Gibson said he frequently comes across deer carcasses left by white hunters, who only take the hindquarters, or sometimes only the antlers, leaving the rest of the animal to rot. The attorney (John O'Connell) said the issue is "separate but related" to the land claims the Western Shoshone have been battling through the federal courts, claiming that the government never gained title to aboriginal lands (McMillan 1984).

Of the more than 20 Great Basin treaties and agreements, the Ruby Valley Treaty of 1863, the Fort Bridger Treaty of 1868 with the Eastern Shoshone, Northern Shoshone, and Bannock, the Shoshone-Bannock Agreement of 1898, and the Brunot Agreement of 1873 with the Utes are important because they established certain lands and rights for the Indian people that were still important in the 1980s.

The pressure of the Civil War brought about several Great Basin treaties and agreements. The federal government wanted to protect shipment of gold and silver from Nevada Territory's Comstock lode mines for the war effort in the east and to protect settlers moving through Indian lands. According to one interpretation of this ambiguous treaty, the Western Shoshone allowed non-Indians to move into their territory, but the remaining unsettled land was returned to the Western Shoshone. Instead, the federal government has acted as though all the lands within the treaty territory had become federal property (Deloria 1976:16–20).

Western Shoshones who opposed the attempt to gain a monetary settlement for the land gained control of the Te-Moak Bands tribal council in the 1970s. They fired their claims attorney and tried to halt the process in the Indian Claims Commission. The tribal council decided independently to reject over $26 million awarded to the Western Shoshone by the Indian Claims Commission for 16 million acres of land. This was considered to be a mere pittance, and it was determined to wait until the legal cases determining title to the land are decided in federal courts.

Several Western Shoshone tribal groups opposed the establishment of the MX missile system ("Tribal Politics," fig. 3, this vol.) in Nevada and Utah on their treaty lands in 1980 and 1981. A confederation of Great Basin tribes was formed to deal with this issue: the Duckwater, Gosiute, Ely Colony, and Yomba Western Shoshone, and the Moapa and Utah-Paiute Southern Paiute.

State governments and private interests began in the late 1970s and early 1980s to press for title to extensive federal lands in the far West. In Nevada alone, the federal government holds title to 86 percent of the land. This movement has been called the Sagebrush Rebellion, comprising a coalition of White landholders and state and local officials whose aim was to acquire control of federal holdings.

The business council of the Fort Hall Northern Shoshone–Bannock tribes, stressing their off-reservation

Jack R. Malotte, Reno, Nev.

Fig. 1. *Used and Abused.* Pencil and ink drawing by a Western Shoshone artist, Jack R. Malotte, 1982.

treaty rights established by the Fort Bridger treaty of 1868 and the Agreement of 1898, objected to the turnover of federal lands to the states. In testimony before the Subcommittee on Mines and Mining of the U.S. House Committee on Interior and Insular Affairs on November 22, 1980, representatives stated that:

> The Shoshone Bannock Tribes, like many other Indian tribes, possess extensive off-reservation federal treaty rights to use federal lands, primarily National Forest and Bureau of Land Management areas for a variety of purposes. The Shoshone-Bannock use rights include hunting, fishing, trapping, gathering of wild foods, grazing of livestock, and cutting of timber.... Exercise of these traditional use rights...reaches to the essence of the Shoshone-Bannock culture and subsistence economy. These traditional activities remain sacred to the Shoshone-Bannock today, just as they were at least 6,000 years before the birth of Christ.... Advocates of the "Sagebrush Rebellion" have not carefully considered the disastrous consequences that will follow generally from any state takeover of federally owned lands. Even less consideration has been given to the specific legal, social, and cultural impact of such a takeover upon Indian tribes. Such consideration must consist of more than uninformed verbal

"guarantees" that Indian treaty rights must be respected. The history and nature of those treaty rights must be understood. Overriding federal law and the honor of this Nation as well as the states demand no less (Echohawk 1980).

Hunting and Water Rights

Relying on the Brunot Agreement of 1873, the Ute Mountain Ute tribe, with the assistance of the Native American Rights Fund, succeeded in 1978 in obtaining recognition of off-reservation treaty hunting rights in a consent decree in a U.S. District Court in Colorado. The court held that:

> Authorized tribal hunters may hunt deer and elk for subsistence, religious or ceremonial purposes in the Brunot Agreement Area under tribal hunting regulations which shall provide for season, manners of taking, and bag limits which are identical to those required by the state of Colorado, except that tribal members need not obtain a state hunting license. In addition to the privilege of hunting deer and elk free of state license fees, authorized tribal hunters

may hunt deer and elk at other times of the year when non-Indian hunting is prohibited (*Ute Mountain Ute Tribe of Indians* v. *The State of Colorado Department of Natural Resources, Division of Wildlife Commission*, September 21, 1978).

These hunting rights apply in an area ceded to the United States.

Many reservations in the Great Basin were created on lands adjacent to rivers and lakes. Groundwater underneath the reservations has also proved to be very important in this arid region. Development of the reservations is impossible without water (Veeder 1969:480–511). Indians find themselves in increasing competition with non-Indian agricultural and urban users.

When the reservations were established "there was reserved or confirmed not only the land but also the right to enough water to irrigate the irrigable portions of the reserved lands or otherwise fulfill the purposes of the reservations" (*Winters* v. *United States*, 202 U.S. 564). This decision, which became known as the Winters Doctrine, was issued in 1908 by the U.S. Supreme Court. Because in many cases Indian reservations were established prior to non-Indian development, Winters Doctrine rights usually have higher priority than non-Indian rights in the West. Furthermore, the Ninth Circuit Court of Appeals determined in 1908 that as the Indian need grows, their water rights grow, because Indians are entitled to water to meet future as well as present needs (*Conrad Investment Company* v. *United States*, 161 Fed. 829).

The Winters Doctrine was extended to other than treaty reservations in 1939 by the Ninth Circuit Court of Appeals in its *U.S.* v. *Walker River Irrigation District* decision. The court held that a water right was established for the Walker River Reservation, Nevada, in 1859 when the reservation was created, even though an executive order establishing the reservation was not proclaimed until 1874 (Johnson 1975:145).

Perhaps one of the most significant cases involving Winters Doctrine water rights, other than those for irrigation purposes, has been the case between the Pyramid Lake Northern Paiute and non-Indian interests over the Truckee River waters in Nevada. The Pyramid Lake Reservation, established in 1859, entirely surrounds Pyramid Lake. Since time immemorial the Pyramid Lake Paiutes have been dependent on their fishery (Harner 1974:22). In 1905 a dam built on the Truckee River, Pyramid Lake's primary source of water, by the Newlands Federal Reclamation Project diverted water to the project and lowered the lake some 80 feet.

The tribe's right to water for irrigation purposes had been determined in *U.S.* v. *Orr Water Ditch Company* in 1944, but the tribe had not secured recognition of its right to water to maintain the Pyramid Lake fishery. The tribe filed suit against the Truckee-Carson Irrigation District, the state of Nevada, Sierra Pacific Power

U.S. Dept. of Interior, Bureau of Reclamation, Upper Missouri Region, Billings, Mont.: P 285–600–1255 A.

Fig. 2. Boysen Dam, Wyo., at the south end of Wind River Canyon near the border of the Eastern Shoshone Wind River Reservation. Constructed by the Department of the Interior Bureau of Reclamation in 1952, the dam provides flood control, irrigation, recreation, and hydroelectric power. According to Robert Harris, Chairman of the Shoshone Tribal Council (communications to editors 1985), the Shoshone and Arapahoe Indians of the reservation have opposed the dam, built on Indian land for which they believe they were not adequately compensated. Photograph by Lyle C. Axthelm, 1967.

Company, and over 17,000 water users in 1973 (Reynolds 1975). In 1981 the Ninth Circuit Court of Appeals upheld the right of the tribe to assert its water rights claim for a fishery against the Newlands Reclamation Project but dismissed the suit against other users. The Appeals Court directed the district court to determine whether a water right for the Pyramid Lake fishery exists against the project. On June 24, 1983, the U.S. Supreme Court overruled the Ninth Circuit Court of Appeals and refused to overturn the 1944 decree.

One of the opinions noted that the Pyramid Lake Paiute Tribe could sue for damages, "but our decision today is that thousands of small farmers in northwestern Nevada can rely on specific promises made to their forebears two or three generations ago, and solemnized in a judicial decree, despite strong claims on the part of the Pyramid Lake Paiutes" (*Pyramid Lake Paiute Tribe* v. *Truckee-Carson Irrigation District* et al., No. 82–38). The Pyramid Lake Paiute Tribe applied to the Nevada state engineer on May 25, 1984, for 477,851 feet of unappropriated Truckee River water "for protective purposes, as well as to enable the tribe to continue to operate the Marble Bluff Dam and the Pyramid Lake Fishway; to provide sufficient flows to protect the Lahontan cutthroat trout and cui-ui as well as recreational uses; and to maintain water quantity and quality of Pyramid Lake" (Adler 1984). Other water users, including Washoe County and Sierra Pacific Power Company, filed requests for unappropriated Truckee River water prior to the Pyramid Lake Paiute application.

Because of a little-known aspect of federal water law contained in the McCarran Water Rights Suits Act of 1952, competitors with Indians for water rights have succeeded in getting federal water rights decided in state courts in the first instance before possible final determination in the federal courts (*U.S.* v. *District Court for Eagle County*, 401 U.S. 520, 1971). Since state courts have generally not favored Indian rights, this development has added another obstacle and could delay the establishment of Indian water rights. For instance, water rights on Wind River Reservation, Wyoming, were adversely affected when a state judge ruled on May 11, 1983,

> that water rights of the Shoshone and Arapaho Tribes.... were limited to agricultural use only. The tribes claimed rights of 1.3 million acre-feet of water from the Wind and Big Horn Rivers and the judge gave them 500,000—or less than half.... The judge said that the tribes' original claims demonstrated "an avaricious appetite on the part of the tribes for practically all the water in the Big Horn River system." The Court ruling was significantly more restrictive than the recommendation made by Special Water Master Teno Roncalio in January, which proposed granting the tribe half of what they originally had claimed (U.S. Bureau of Indian Affairs, Office of Public Information 1983:3).

Appeals through the state and federal court systems can last for many years. Tribal leaders, realizing this fact, have considered negotiations and entered into compacts with state governments. The Northern Utes agreed on September 20, 1965, to defer its claim "to approximately 60,000 acre-feet in order to create a viable cost/benefit basis for diversion of water from the Uintah Basin to the Bonneville Project. That deferral was made by the Ute Indian tribe on the condition that its Winters Doctrine water right entitlement would be recognized without resort to litigation" (Chairperson Ruby Black to Utah Gov. Scott Matheson, November 12, 1981). Later a Ute Indian Compact (including the Ute Tribe of Utah, the State of Utah, and the federal government) was developed involving water rights and including the earlier agreement. In 1985 the compact had not been approved by the Northern Ute. The tribe hired consultants to review its water resources in order to develop a series of specific water storage and irrigation alternatives for the Ute Reservation. There were claims made that the Ute tribe was holding up approval of the Ute Indian Compact, but the tribal chairperson did not think that the tribe's review of the Ute Indian Compact was delaying matters. The Utah state legislature had taken two sessions to approve the compact. And the United States representative had also taken considerable time to review and approve the compact.

Chairperson Ruby Black felt that the tribal business council should take all the time it needed to review this important document. The tribal business council should then refer the document to the members of the tribe for their review and approval. Water in arid Utah is crucial, and the Northern Utes have first claim to water under the Winters Doctrine.

One Ute leader, on hearing that a dam would not be built, commented: "I think the tribe is rejoicing over no dam in the Uintah. When our people see things as the Creator did, let the water run" (Anonymous 1980a).

Recreation interests have also sought to infringe upon Indian water rights. As an example, Indian farmers and ranchers on the Duck Valley Reservation, Nevada, have been affected by the demands of local and state governments for recreational uses of Wild Horse Reservoir on the Owyhee River. A tribal spokesperson wrote: "In recent years, Elko County and the State of Nevada have begun efforts to restrict the amounts of water that farmers at Duck Valley can draw. They argue that Wild Horse Reservoir has become one of the greatest outdoor recreational areas in the state. The tribes, in reaction to these threats, have hired an attorney and have begun efforts to have Wild Horse annexed to the reservation in order to insure the future of (the) people. There is great potential for agricultural expansion" (Manning 1980:92). The land around Wild Horse Reservoir is primarily owned by the federal government, not the Duck Valley Western Shoshone and Northern Paiute.

There are many competitors for water in the arid Great Basin. The federal government in the 1980s endorsed negotiation of Indian water rights rather than determinations by the courts. State and urban interests pressed for changes in their favor.

Jurisdiction

Most tribal governments in the Great Basin have adopted constitutions under the Indian Reorganization Act of 1934. The jurisdiction of tribal governments has been stated in constitutions and by-laws. Treaties and agreements also established tribal jurisdiction (Berkey 1976:17). Without congressional consent, states may not exercise jurisdiction over reservations. A law enacted by the Congress in 1953, during the termination era, allowed states to exercise state criminal jurisdiction over Indian land, reservations, and colonies, without the consent of tribal governments. As a result of a Nevada law passed to implement that act, many of the small reservations and colonies in Nevada went under state criminal jurisdiction at the option of the counties. In the 1970s the tribes were given the right by the Nevada state legislature to decide whether they wanted to be under state or federal jurisdiction, and almost all the tribes chose federal jurisdiction.

Conflicts between state governments and tribal governments have occurred over jurisdiction. The U.S. Supreme Court in *Oliphant* v. *Suquamish Indian Tribe* (435 U.S. 191) ruled that tribal governments do not

U. of Calif., Lowie Mus., Berkeley: 25–1261.

Fig. 3. "No-Tresspassing/Indian/Allotments/No Cutting Trees," warning sign on Washoe land protecting the pine nut trees in Douglas County, Nev. Photograph by Jack L. Reveal, 1939.

Natl. Arch.: 75–CL–3–15.

Fig. 4. The American Indian Movement (AIM), an Indian political organization founded in the 1960s. In November 1972 AIM organized a demonstration in Washington, D.C., known as the Trail of Broken Treaties. The participants arrived the week of the presidential elections to deliver a 20-point proposal on Indian rights. When AIM spokesmen were not granted meetings with top administration officials, they occupied the Bureau of Indian Affairs building for 5 days. During this time the occupants barricaded themselves in the building and dotted the walls with political graffiti. At one point there may have been as many as 300 Indians inside the building, some of whom evidently were Ute members of AIM. Photographed in the Tribal Operations Area, Room 130 of the Bureau of Indian Affairs, 1972.

have criminal jurisdiction over non-Indians. The decision can be expected to pose serious difficulties for tribal leaders on reservations where many non-Indians reside, such as the Walker River, Wind River, Southern Ute, Northern Ute, and other allotted reservations.

In some instances courts have upheld tribal jurisdiction in "Indian country." The Federal District Court for Nevada in 1980 ruled in favor of Washoe tribal jurisdiction over the pine nut allotments (fig. 3), which were established in the 1890s. The court held that "regulation of hunting within the pinenut allotments has been preempted by Federally authorized tribal assumption of regulatory authority and responsibility" (*Washoe Tribe* v. *Joseph Greenley, Director, Department of Wildlife, and William Parsons, Chief of Law Enforcement, Department of Wildlife, State of Nevada*). On April 16, 1980, the District Court permanently enjoined the state of Nevada from restricting the right of the Washoes to hunt in the pine nut allotments. The Ninth Circuit Court of Appeals then disallowed the state's appeal on the ground that the suit was brought against state officials and not against the state. According to the Washoe tribal attorney the Washoe jurisdiction suit was important because it was "the first case to hold that states are without jurisdiction to regulate hunting and fishing by tribal members on off-reservation allotments" and because it "upheld the tribe's right to regulate (such) hunting and fishing... pursuant to an amendment of the tribal constitution. This was significant because most of these allotments were individual and not tribal" (Peter Sferrazza, personal communication 1982).

The Northern Utes won a jurisdictional dispute when Federal District Judge Bruce Jenkins ruled on June 19, 1981, that the Uintah-Ouray Reservation is a continuing reservation and is Indian country. The Northern Utes wanted to establish their jurisdiction over towns within their reservation. However, the ruling excluded the forest lands, the Gilsonite Strip, and the Strawberry Reservoir. The tribe appealed the exclusions in the decision to the Tenth Circuit Court of Appeals (Anonymous 1981) and instituted a review of its taxing power and licensing authority over business within the reservation as a result of the decision.

In an important case involving civil jurisdiction over non-Indians, the Tenth Circuit Court of Appeals ruled in *Dry Creek Lodge et. al.* v. *Arapahoe and Shoshone Tribes* that a non-Indian corporation and non-Indian plaintiffs could sue the Arapahoe and Eastern Shoshone tribes in federal district court for damages incurred where the tribe blocked access to a parcel of real estate wholly owned by non-Indians within the Indian reservation. The tribes claimed sovereign immunity to suit in federal court pursuant to *Martinez* v. *Santa Clara Pueblo*; however, the court held that this was a matter external to the tribe, unlike *Martinez*, which involved internal matters. The judges stated that "there has to be a forum where the dispute can be settled" and "to hold that they [the non-Indian plaintiffs] have access to no court is to hold that they have constitutional rights but have no remedy" (N. Anderson 1981:2).

The Walker River Northern Paiutes in 1984 won a jurisdictional dispute over the Southern Pacific Railroad when the U.S. Supreme Court declined to review a decision of the Ninth Circuit Court of Appeals that held that the railroad must obtain the approval of the Walker River Paiutes for a right-of-way across the Walker River Indian Reservation. According to the Native American Rights Fund, "The Tribe will now go back to the district court for a determination of past damages and ejectment of the railroad" since Southern Pacific was found to be in trepass in 1976 and its various appeals have failed (Native American Rights Fund 1984:13).

While some jurisdictional issues have been settled in court systems, tribal and other governmental leaders often have developed mutually acceptable agreements to solve jurisdictional disputes. On the Southern Ute Reservation, where half the residents are non-Indians, state highway patrolmen and tribal police for years have worked closely together and met regularly. "State police turn over any apprehended Indian offenders to tribal authorities and tribal police release non-Indian offenders to state officials" (Commission on State-Tribal Relations 1981).

States have given grants or endorsed grants to tribal governments to strengthen tribal jurisdictional efforts. For example, Oregon state Law Enforcement Assistance Administration planning agencies have assisted the Burns Northern Paiute with a grant to support a voluntary counseling and recreation program. Previously, it was granted funds for manpower and housing and equipment for a small criminal justice system.

Concern about the pollution in nearby rivers, nuclear waste storage, industrial development, and urban growth caused Fort Hall Northern Shoshone–Bannock leaders to have the Idaho governor designate the reservation as a separate planning area and to appoint the tribal business council as the planning agency. A jurisdiction question concerning liquor control by the state of Colorado led Southern Ute tribal leaders to license a tribally owned resort motel and restaurant under tribal ordinance, coordinated with state rules and regulations (Commission on State-Tribal Relations 1981). The Pyramid Lake Northern Paiutes have adopted taxation ordinances affecting non-Indian businesses within the Pyramid Lake Reservation.

Economic Development

Tribal leaders have been dependent on federal grants for the economic development of Indian land. Economic alliances have been formed, such as the Inter-Tribal Council of Nevada, the Inter-Tribal Council of Arizona, the Inter-Tribal Policy Board of Idaho, the United Ute Tribes, the Council of Energy Resource Tribes, and the Smoke Shop Tribes of Nevada. Perhaps the most successful alliance has been the Inter-Tribal Council of Nevada.

Several Great Basin tribes have become members of

Fig. 5. Little Pete, a Northern Paiute, stirring a boiling cauldron at Fallon, Nev. The sign over the pot reads "E.C.W. Stew," referring to the Emergency Conservation Work program set up in the 1930s under the Civilian Conservation Corps to give Indians employment on reservations. Photograph by Lucile Hamner, 1937.

the Council of Energy Resource Tribes, including the Northern Ute, the Pyramid Lake and Walker River Northern Paiute, the Ute Mountain and Southern Utes, and the Fort Hall Northern Shoshone–Bannock. CERT was formed in 1976 "to insure that the Indian people receive an equitable return for their resources, and are able to utilize those resources as a foundation upon which to develop stable tribal economies." In 1979 CERT received a $1,200,000 grant that was used to strengthen its Washington, D.C., office and to open a regional technical office in Denver. CERT provides technical assistance to member tribes.

In the view of Ernie Stevens, a former director of the Office of Economic Development of the U.S. Bureau of Indian Affairs, "Indian people suffer from the colonialism of the past. They still haven't been able to break past the barrier of negative conditioning which has been forced on them over the last 200 years" (Stevens 1981:2–3). He posed some questions concerning business development and energy cartels and other business on Indian trust land in an address at the 1981 mid-year meeting of the National Congress of American Indians at Spokane, Washington.

> What are some of the current energy and economic issues that need to be discussed? Is it possible for real reservation energy self-sufficiency? What are the rules for capital formation? How available is private financing and under what conditions? What is the role of the entrepreneur in tribal society? How do you implement technical assistance and the transfer of technology? Can Indians manage business enterprises? (Stevens 1981:2–3).

This problem is exemplified by the fact that Great Basin tribes with oil and gas deposits have been able to develop their reservations to a much greater extent than other tribes. However, several tribes, including those on the Wind River Reservation and the Northern Utes, have been affected by illegal diversion of their resources by private companies.

Another economic alliance that has proved to be successful is the Smoke Shop tribal organization of Nevada. In 1983 the Smoke Shop tribes with the assistance of professional lobbyists defeated attempts in the state legislature to amend the Nevada law that allows the tribes to collect their own excise tax on cigarettes. An unsuccessful attempt was made to allow the tribes to keep only the taxes paid by their own members (Minutes, Assembly Committee on Taxation, Nevada State Legislature, March 11, 1983). The Reno-Sparks Colony and the Las Vegas Colony, located in Nevada urban centers, have used several million dollars in annual smoke shop revenue to improve their land basis and to support social programs. Several other Nevada tribes have also established smoke shops (Amicus Curiae Brief, *Washington State* v. *Colville Confederated Tribes* et. al., 447 U.S. 134).

Among other economic developments in the Great Basin, Moapa Southern Paiutes established a greenhouse vegetable industry in southern Neveda ("Indian Economies: 1950–1980," fig. 6, this vol.).

With limited resources, planned economic development will continue to be important. However, whether the federal government will adequately assist tribal governments is questionable. Funds in the past have been made available on a piecemeal basis.

Social Development and Education

Indian leadership has been deeply concerned with the social development and education of their people in the Great Basin. The following tribes and communities have constructed tribal and community centers with federal government assistance: Walker River, Yerington, Las Vegas, Yomba, Fallon, Duck Valley, Goshute, Lovelock, South Fork, Moapa (fig. 6), Reno-Sparks, Elko, Washoe tribe, Dresslerville, Carson City, Pyramid Lake, in Nevada; Fort Hall, Idaho; Wind River, Wyoming; Southern Ute and Ute Mountain Ute, Colorado; Woodfords, Bishop, Bridgeport, California; and Kaibab, Arizona. These projects have been important in providing a focus to community identity and pride. For many Indians such centers are concrete evidence of their progress.

Most Indian children in the Great Basin in the 1980s attended public schools. Some attended private schools and U.S. Bureau of Indian Affairs boarding schools. A few tribes have taken over management of schools on their reservations because the school authorities were not successfully educating their children. The head of the Education Division of the Northern Utes stated in May 1984 that "the facts and charges that I make suggest that Ute students are not receiving an equitable education in various schools in the local area." He stated that:

The Native Nevadan, Reno-Sparks Indian Colony.

Fig. 6. Contemporary life. left, Northern Paiute and Washoe Reno-Sparks Indian Colony mall. It is located in the 28-acre colony, which had a population of about 600, modern housing, and tribal businesses. Photograph possibly by Shane del Cohen, 1985. right, Moapa tribal community center, located on the Moapa Indian Reservation, built in 1976 with funds provided by the Department of Housing and Urban Development, the tribe providing most of the labor for its construction. The center houses the offices of the tribal council, a business office, and a tribal community store. Photograph by Arlene Fisher, 1981.

top left, Natl. Arch: 75–N–CARS–305; top right, *The Native Nevadan*, Reno-Sparks Indian Colony; bottom left, Reno-Sparks Ind. Colony Coll.; bottom right, Shoshone–Bannock Tribes, Sho-Ban Media Center, Fort Hall, Idaho.

Fig. 7. Education. top left, Max Chapoose, a Ute, welding in the auto shop class at the Stewart Indian School, Carson, Nev. Photograph by Arthur Rothstein, 1940. top right, Western Shoshone class at Duckwater, Nev., tribal school with their cultural studies curriculum books. Photographed May 1983. bottom left, Northern Paiute and Washoe children in the Reno-Sparks Indian Colony Headstart program. Photograph possibly by Shane del Cohen, 1984. bottom right, Making a video tape called "Living with Indian Ways," at the Northern Shoshone Sho-Ban Alternate School. Seated left is Brenda Honea and on the far right is Donna Honea. Photograph by Bill Richmonds, 1977.

Only 25% of the Ute secondary students have graduated from Union High School during the 11-year period 1972–1983.

Comparison of standardized achievement scores for the years 1956 and 1976 by an independent research group indicates no significant gains in average academic achievement.

While Ute student attendance is quite high (91–93% for elementary and 83–84% for secondary) in comparison to other Indian tribes, Ute students remain 2–4 years behind their Anglo peers in average academic achievement (Cuch 1984).

Several Indian-operated schools have been organized including the Duckwater Shoshone Elementary School, the Pyramid Lake High School, the Wyoming Indian High School, and the Fort Hall Sho-Ban Alternate School (fig. 7). All but the Pyramid Lake High School, which opened in 1980, were established in the 1970s. Stewart Indian Boarding School, near Carson City, Nevada, which had been operated by the U.S. Bureau of Indian Affairs since 1890, was closed in 1980. Inter-Mountain Boarding School, Utah, also operated by the U.S. Bureau of Indian Affairs, was closed in 1984.

Tribal Leadership

In the 1980s women increasingly joined the ranks of tribal governmental leadership. During 1980 both the Ute Mountain Utes and the Northern Utes had female chairpersons for the first time. The tribal councils of Summit Lake, Yerington, Lone Pine, Fort Bidwell, Big

Pine, and the Utah Paiutes also had female chairpersons in 1980 as well as the community councils at Battle Mountain, Dresslerville, Woodfords, and Carson Colony. And the entire Big Pine tribal council has been made up of women (O. Anderson 1981:2).

New or revitalized tribal governments have been formed, such as the Paiute Indian tribe of Utah, consisting of the previously terminated bands of Southern Paiute Indians and the Utu Utu Gwaitu Band of Northern Paiutes near Benton, California. The Antelope Valley Indian Community (Washoes and Northern Paiutes) in California is seeking federal recognition as a tribe (Grace Dick, personal communication 1981).

Urban growth in areas far removed from reservations will continue to be a threat to tribal resources. Examples are water needs and the growth of Los Angeles, which has affected the Western Shoshone and Owens Valley Paiutes; Salt Lake City and urban Utah expansion, which has affected the Northern Utes; the growth of Pocatello, Idaho, which has affected the Northern Shoshone-Bannock; and Reno-Sparks expansion, which has affected the availability and quality of the Truckee River, the primary source of Pyramid Lake Reservation water.

Tribal leadership will continue to wrestle with treaty and agreement rights, jurisdiction, water rights, economic development, educational and social needs, and increasing the land base, in order to protect Indian rights and build a better life for Indian people.

Tribal Historical Projects

JOHN R. ALLEY, JR.

A Native Voice

A long-needed voice began to find its place in American Indian studies during the late twentieth century, as more Indians took part in research and writing about their history and culture. This was nowhere more evident and more productive than in the Great Basin. Tribal histories and historical projects were manifestations of a broader revival of Indians' interest in their heritage. This was by no means a new concern, but Native American voices had been stifled since the beginning of European colonization by an official policy that sought first to separate and exclude and later to submerge and assimilate them. Without resources, largely nonliterate, without access to print media, and often punished for expressing traditional cultural values or even speaking their languages, Indians had little opportunity to speak out about their history, let alone do research and publish accounts. It took a great deal of effort by older people to preserve an oral tradition that offered a point of view separate from the officially prescribed history their children learned in school.

To say that the problem with literature about American Indians has been that most of it was written by White Americans alien to the culture they studied would be to draw the anti-intellectual conclusion that people of one nationality cannot write accurately about those of another. The problem instead was twofold. First, much of that literature was written from an ethnocentric point of view that glorified the achievements of European culture at the expense of American Indians. Second, every nation, people, or ethnic group has its own points of view about its past, a unique perspective that is fired by inherited values. A people's past, because it is at the core of identity, has a meaning that is often not readily understood or accepted by others. To suppress that perspective not only robs those people of part of their identity but also robs the rest of mankind of one of its multitudinous voices.

Despite such barriers, the Great Basin produced several strong native voices that were disseminated in print. Most of them were heard through the medium of non-Indian writers, generally anthropologists or explorers. Cameahwait, a Lemhi Northern Shoshone and brother of Sacajawea, gave Meriwether Lewis and William Clark and, through their journals, White America and Europe, the first indigenous description of Numic life (Coues 1893,2:382–434). No nineteenth-century American Indian voice carried more impact than that of Wovoka, the Northern Paiute Ghost Dance prophet. His message, a forceful example of Indian efforts to interpret historical change in terms of native values, reached Indians by word of mouth. Thanks especially to James Mooney of the Bureau of American Ethnology, it also reached a literate public (Mooney 1896). With a few exceptions, the written record of the Great Basin Indians' understanding of their history and culture in the nineteenth and early twentieth century is found in ethnological accounts. These accounts were not intended to provide a forum for Indians; most anthropologists did not identify their Indian contributors or allow individuals to elaborate their points of view. Yet these studies did help preserve and disseminate handed-down cultural tradition. Some of the informants, such as the Ute Richard Komas (fig. 1) who worked with John Wesley Powell (Conetah 1982:71; Fowler and Fowler 1971), and the Southern Paiute Tony Tillohash, who worked with Edward Sapir (Sapir 1930–1931; Fowler 1980:10), have since become well known at least among specialists and their own people. Another, the Northern Paiute Annie Lowry (fig. 2), had her story recounted in Scott's *Karnee: A Paiute Narrative* (1966). Forbes in his book *Nevada Indians Speak* (1967) specifically set out to rectify some of this anonymity by providing a forum for many of the lost, hidden, or ignored voices of Great Basin Indians.

The only early book on Great Basin Indians written, directed, published, or controlled in any way by Indians (and one of only a few such nineteenth-century histories anywhere) was *Life Among the Paiutes: Their Wrongs and Claims* (1883) by Sarah Winnemucca Hopkins (fig. 3). An unusual woman in many ways, Sarah Winnemucca was the daughter of Winnemucca, an important Northern Paiute leader during the early years of White settlement. Having learned to read and write at an early age, she served as an interpreter and army scout, became a popular lecturer in the East, and acquired influential friends, such as Mrs. Horace Mann and Elizabeth Peabody (Canfield 1983). She established an Indian school near Lovelock, Nevada, that was supported fi-

601

Smithsonian, NAA: 1520–b–1.

Fig. 1. Richard Komas (d. 1875–1876), a Northern Ute who attended the preparatory program at Lincoln University, Pa., from 1870 to 1874. He was an official interpreter to Indians from Utah who visited Washington, D.C. Photograph by Alexander Gardner, 1872.

nancially by her White associates. Her book remains an important primary source on her people's relations with Whites in the nineteenth century.

Opportunities for Indians to follow Sarah Winnemucca's precedent emerged gradually in the twentieth century. With the New Deal, official attitudes toward

Nev. Histl. Soc., Reno: 582.

Fig. 2. Annie Lowry and John T. Reid. Lowry's narrative documents her and her mother's lives on the frontier. Reid was a friend of many Indian people in the Lovelock area. Photographed at Lovelock, Nev., late 1920s.

Smithsonian, Natl. Portrait Gallery.

Fig. 3. Sarah Winnemucca Hopkins (b. 1844, d. 1891). The outfit was probably made as a lecture costume and is not traditional in ornamentation. Studio portrait by Noral H. Busey, Baltimore, Md., about 1882.

native culture changed, and Indians were finally allowed, even encouraged, to take an interest in their heritage. Educational opportunities for Indians expanded, especially after World War II. Well-read Indians, finding few books that presented their history as they understood it, began to search for ways to supply those materials. In the 1960s, while correctly insisting that their situation was unique, many Indians also took advantage of the general rebirth of ethnic consciousness and pride. In civil rights legislation and Great Society social programs, Indians found tools to broaden school curricula, bring their concerns before the general public, and preserve the traditional elders' knowledge of the past.

One of the first information tools employed by Great Basin Indians was the newspaper. In the 1980s most of the larger tribes had such an organ, for example: *The*

Desert Breeze in Nixon, Nevada; *Warpath* in Stewart, Nevada; *The Native Nevadan* in Reno, Nevada; *Elko Community News* in Elko, Nevada; *Duck Valley Roundup* in Owyhee, Nevada; *Ute Bulletin* in Fort Duchesne, Utah; *Wind River Journal* in Fort Washakie, Wyoming; *American Indian News* in Fort Washakie, Wyoming; *Sho-Ban News* in Fort Hall, Idaho; *The Southern Ute Drum* in Ignacio, Colorado, and *Echo* in Towoac, Colorado (National Native American Cooperative 1982; National Congress of American Indians 1975).

The Tribal Projects

In the 1970s, Great Basin tribal communities sponsored and directed a series of historical research projects that resulted in tribal history texts, archives, and curriculum materials (fig. 4). Each project approached the needs of its sponsoring community differently, but all shared certain goals and characteristics. All the histories intended to present a clear point of view, that of "the People," the particular tribe studied. This often meant not just supplementing, but also countering, previous published accounts. In most cases, however, so little had been written about the postreservation history of Great Basin Indians that there was not a great deal to counter. Students had grown accustomed to reading a short account of Indians, placed right after the description of natural resources and before the "real" history began. While the tribes' universal priority was to provide a sense of their own past for their own children, the projects were also educational in the broader sense of creating a public resource. All the tribally published histories were grade-leveled, generally for use in secondary schools, but they were designed to appeal to adult readers as well.

In most of the tribal histories, the tribe is credited as publisher and owns the copyright. This makes it all the clearer that these books present the Indian version of their history, a point of view that is supported by thorough research and careful documentation. These histories were among the first on the Great Basin to make full use of U.S. National Archives documents. In addition they drew on published government documents in the serial set and elsewhere, as well as the significant body of oral history collected in the course of the projects.

The tribes employed expert help to attain their goals. In a majority of cases, the American West Center at the University of Utah worked as a consulting partner in the undertaking from beginning to end, providing professional support in fund-raising, planning, research, writing, and publication. Floyd A. O'Neil directed these efforts. Tribal authors also took advantage of expert advice at nearby colleges, such as the University of Nevada. The Institute of the American West in Sun Valley, Idaho, provided support services for the Duck Valley project. Producing books or conducting a major research project required money. Some tribes had limited funds to employ, but, in general, financially strapped councils had to look to outside sources. The National Endowment for the Humanities, the Donner Foundation of New York, the Research and Cultural Studies Development Section of the Bureau of Indian Affairs, and the Fund for the Improvement of Post-Secondary Education in the U.S. Department of Education were major contributors. Many other organizations gave smaller sums to Great Basin projects.

left, Inter-Tribal Council of Nevada, Reno: NP 194; right, Beverly Crum, Salt Lake City.

Fig. 4. Tribal people involved in projects that benefit their tribe. left, Gussie Williams, Lulu Jim, and Lena Wright, Northern Paiute, examining historical photographs collected by the Inter-Tribal Council of Nev. Photograph by Dorothy Nez, 1974. right, Beverly and Earl Crum, Western Shoshone, translating English sentences into Shoshone. Photograph by Steve Crum, Salt Lake City, Utah, 1980.

While the centerpiece of most tribal projects was a published volume of history, the collection and indexing of tribal archives were of equal, perhaps greater, long-term value, for they provide the foundation for the histories and other publications. They reflect a common goal of the projects: to acquire a tribal record to which tribal officials and members and concerned lawyers and scholars could refer. Every tribe that did produce a history used the accumulated documentation as the core of an archive. The archives had many components, varying from tribe to tribe. One of the larger ones was collected by the Inter-Tribal Council of Nevada to represent the history and culture of its four member tribes, the Southern Paiute, Northern Paiute, Western Shoshone, and Washoe. In addition to the National Archives in Washington, D.C., documents came from the Federal Records Centers at Denver, Colorado, and San Bruno, California, and from the Nevada Indian Agency at Stewart, Nevada. The archives included an extensive photograph collection from the National Archives, the Smithsonian Institution, the Library of Congress, Washington; the Nevada State Museum, Carson City; the Nevada Historical Society, Reno; the University of Nevada, Reno; and the collections of Indian and non-Indian people throughout the state. Many Indians also contributed to an excellent selection of native plants and artifacts. The oral history program was one of the most valuable components. Hundreds of tapes and transcripts are stored in the collection. Albeit on a smaller scale, most of the tribal archives contain these types of materials. In a very real sense, archives represent a transfer to Indian communities of some measure of power over their own lives. Rather than having someone tell them how it was, they can look it up for themselves in their own body of records. Moreover, archives can grow with the tribe and its resources. Some tribes have taken the process a step farther toward cultural centers or museums, which not only preserve history and culture but also earn income. The Washoe, for example, planned an elaborate complex at Lake Tahoe to include craft demonstrations, a gallery and museum, preservation programs, and an archives.

The Peoples' Histories

The publication programs of tribes varied from a 30-page history published by the Las Vegas Paiutes to the multivolume efforts of the Inter-Tribal Council of Nevada and the Uintah-Ouray Utes. The Inter-Tribal Council produced four volumes under the direction of Winona Manning Holmes, a Western Shoshone, who replaced Norman Rambeau, a Northern Paiute. Holmes's staff worked closely with the staff of the American West Center, notably Laura Bayer, the principal editor. All the books drew on the cooperative labor of many individuals; no authors are listed on the title pages. But major writers for each volume can be identified (table 1). These histories, like many of the others, use either a native name, such as Numa, or the phrase "the People" in place of the usual English names for the groups covered. In the Inter-Tribal Council books these names also serve as titles.

The Inter-Tribal Council of Nevada also published two smaller volumes. *Life Stories of Our Native People: Shoshone, Paiute, Washo* (1974a) is a selection of short biographies of outstanding Great Basin Indians. *Personal Reflections of the Shoshone, Paiute, Washo* (1974) is a collection of essays and reminiscences by Nevada Indians that deal primarily with modern issues and problems. Finally, a motion picture and a filmstrip were produced on each of the member tribes.

The Northern Ute of the Uintah-Ouray Reservation in Utah sponsored an equally extensive project. Many Utes played a role in this, but Forrest Cuch, the tribal education director, and Fred A. Conetah, the tribal historian, were especially important. Their publications included a wide selection of curriculum materials geared to children in grades one through twelve. The first of these was a collection of traditional Ute literature published as *Stories of Our Ancestors: A Collection of Northern Ute Indian Tales* (Uintah-Ouray Ute Tribe 1974). The Ute released *A Brief History of the Ute People* (Uintah-Ouray Ute Tribe 1977), *Ute Ways* (Uintah-Ouray Ute Tribe 1977a), *The Ute People* (Uintah-Ouray Ute Tribe 1977b), *The Ute System of Government* (Uintah-Ouray Ute Tribe 1977c), *The Way It was Told* (Uintah-Ouray Ute Tribe 1977d) and other materials including a coloring book, a map series, and slide presentations. The culmination was *A History of the Northern Ute People* (Conetah 1982). The evolution of a model for tribal histories can be seen by comparing this work with a predecessor, *Ute People: An Historical Study* (Lyman and Denver 1970), which was the first regional tribal history developed for use in schoolrooms. Although it helped encourage many tribes to try something similar, it was not itself sponsored by or controlled by the Ute tribe. Rather, it was a project of the Uintah School District in Utah. Its content, while attempting to offer an Indian-oriented alternative to students, has neither the topical range or interpretative scope of *A History of the Northern Ute People*, which benefits both from reliance on more extensive source material and from the participation of Fred Conetah and the tribal council he represented.

It should be understood that what is meant by a "tribal history" varies considerably from one such book to another. Edward C. Johnson's (1975) *Walker River Paiutes: A Tribal History* and the Inter-Tribal Council of Nevada's *Newe: A Western Shoshone History* (1976b) are examples of histories in the commonly understood sense of examining important topics and events in a straight-

Table 1. Tribally Published Histories

Tribe, Date	Title	Contributors
Southern Ute Tribe, 1972	*The Southern Utes: A Tribal History*	James Jefferson (Southern Ute), Robert W. Delaney, Gregory Thompson
Walker River Paiute Tribe, 1975	*Walker River Paiutes: A Tribal History*	Edward C. Johnson (Northern Paiute)
Inter-Tribal Council of Nevada, 1976	*Nuwuvi: A Southern Paiute History*	John R. Alley, Anne Shifrer, Jack Rice (Southern Paiute), Maureen Frank (Southern Paiute), Robert J. Eben (Northern Paiute)
Inter-Tribal Council of Nevada, 1976	*Numa: A Northern Paiute History*	Robert J. Eben (Northern Paiute), Randy Emm (Northern Paiute), Dorothy Nez (Northern Paiute), Winona Holmes (Western Shoshone), Edward Johnson (Northern Paiute), Michael Kane (Western Shoshone)
Inter-Tribal Council of Nevada, 1976	*Wa She Shu: A Washo Tribal History*	JoAnn Nevers (Washoe)
Inter-Tribal Council of Nevada, 1976	*Newe: A Western Shoshone History*	Beverly Crum (Western Shoshone), Richard Hart, Nancy Nagle, Winona Holmes (Western Shoshone), Larry Piffero (Western Shoshone), Mary Lou Moyle (Western Shoshone), Lillie Pete (Western Shoshone), Delores Conklin (Western Shoshone), Robert J. Eben (Northern Paiute), Michael Red Kane (Western Shoshone)
Fallon Paiute–Shoshone, 1977	*After the Drying Up of the Water*	Cheri Robertson (Paiute–Shoshone)
Las Vegas Tribe of Paiute Indians, 1977	*The Las Vegas Paiutes A Short History*	John R. Alley
Uintah-Ouray Ute Tribe, 1982	*A History of the Northern Ute People*	Fred A. Conetah (Northern Ute) with Kathryn L. MacKay, Floyd A. O'Neil
Duck Valley Shoshone–Paiute Tribe, 1983	*A History of the Shoshone–Paiutes of the Duck Valley Indian Reservation*	Whitney McKinney (Western Shoshone) with E. Richard Hart, Thomas Zeidler

forward chronological order. While they raise ethnographic points and discuss culture in historical context, events rather than traits are the focus. Johnson, a Paiute himself, is very thorough in this regard. He discusses everything from the Ghost Dance to Indian agents, from conflicts with farmers over water and railroads over land, to the accomplishments of native sports heroes. Walker River's history project, under the direction of Melvin D. Thom, also prepared a teacher's guide and a student workbook to supplement the text.

Some of the books focus especially on specific aspects of the tribe's history. Western Shoshone historian Whitney McKinney's *A History of the Shoshone-Paiutes of the Duck Valley Indian Reservation* (1983) devotes considerable attention to the Garland Hurt treaty of 1855 and the treaties of 1863, printing the text of three 1863 treaties (fig. 5). Other volumes either balance the historical narrative with lengthy cultural descriptions or concentrate almost exclusively on the culture. The earliest example in the Great Basin of a tribally sponsored

history was *The Southern Utes: A Tribal History* (Jefferson, Delaney, and Thompson 1972). In this book, Robert W. Delaney and Gregory C. Thompson, professional historians who are not Indians, wrote the history section, describing the Muache and Capote bands of Utes after contact with Euro-Americans. James Jefferson, a historian as well as a Southern Ute, wrote the chapters on Ute economy, government, intertribal relations, religion, recreation, songs and dances, medicine and cures, and story telling.

The Fallon Paiute-Shoshone Tribe published *After the Drying Up of the Water* (1977), which is entirely composed of cultural description and discussion. Drawing primarily on original interviews supplemented by secondary literature, the book addresses topics ranging from clothing and housing through subsistence practices to dances and celebrations in the Carson-Humboldt Sink region of Nevada. The reliance on oral interviews for documentation is a significant aspect of all the tribal histories. This book, for example, prints excerpts from   *605*

The Native Nevadan, Reno-Sparks Indian Colony.
Fig. 5. Whitney McKinney, a Western Shoshone, autographing copies of his book on the reservation history of the tribe. Photographed at Owyhee, Nev., 1983.

some interviews. The title *After the Drying Up of the Water* is a reference to a creation tale told by Tom Austin to Robert H. Lowie in which the Sun as he dried up the flood instructed that "Anything that comes to the world after the drying up of the water shall be your relative" (Lowie 1924a). *Numa: A Northern Paiute History* (Inter-Tribal Council of Nevada 1976a), contains a unique account of the Pyramid Lake War of 1860 based on interviews conducted by the Inter-Tribal Council staff. Traditional literature is also incorporated in many of the books. *Nuwuvi: A Southern Paiute History* (Inter-Tribal Council of Nevada 1976) uses traditional tales taken from John Wesley Powell's manuscript collections to set off chapters of chronological history. *Wa She Shu: A Washo Tribal History* (Inter-Tribal Council of Nevada 1976c) by JoAnn Nevers, Washoe tribal historian, includes a chapter on traditional literature with most examples provided by Harold Wyatt.

Great Basin Indians have participated in other tribal histories besides these published by the tribes. The Kaibab Southern Paiutes participated in the publication by the Indian Tribal Series of *The Paiute People* (Euler 1972). While emphasizing the eastern bands, this is a general history of the Southern Paiute based on Euler's extensive work in Paiute ethnohistory. Another work in the same series is Robert W. Delaney's (1974) *The Southern Ute People* published with the cooperation of the Southern Ute tribe. Individual Great Basin Indians also have written and published accounts of their people independently. Nellie Shaw Harner, a Northern Paiute,

wrote *Indians of Coo-yu-ee Pah: The History of the Pyramid Lake Indians* (1974). Rupert Weeks, an Eastern Shoshone from the Wind River Reservation in Wyoming, authored *Pachee Goyo, History and Legends from the Shoshone* (1961), a fictionalized rendering of Shoshone traditional history.

The tribally sponsored books do have their limitations. They are not and should not be expected to be everything to everybody. Partly because of their strengths and partly because they were all that was available, they have been used in contexts for which they were never intended. It should be remembered that they have almost all been grade-leveled for younger readers and were directed at a general audience, not specialists. The books vary in quality, in approach, in subjects discussed, in thoroughness of research. Questions have arisen about their objectivity because of tribal government sponsorship. It is true that some controversial, particularly modern, issues are not discussed. Many of the histories end at World War II and thus do not address the problems that confront and divide current tribal communities. On the other hand, the appropriateness of airing such disputes in a forum designed above all to instill a sense of cultural heritage in school children may be questioned.

The authorship of the histories has been criticized either because non-Indian expertise was too extensively employed or because Indian authors and researchers had insufficient training and qualifications for their tasks. Non-Indians did play a considerable role in producing many of the books, usually to strengthen and support the work of Indians new to historical writing, but the goals of most tribes had less to do with the ethnic background of those doing the work than with correcting the imbalance they saw in existing literature about their people. What eventually saw print was subject to the tribe's approval, and, regardless of who did what, it had to meet the goals that the tribal governing body had defined. In such a process, cooperation among numerous individuals was beneficial since the more the participation from tribal officials, community members, elders, Indian students, and outside consultants, the closer these, in essence, "official" statements on their past would come to representing both the tribe's perspective and the historical facts, a combination that can be difficult to achieve in any community. The success of these efforts can be best judged by examining the documentation of each book; in the majority of cases it is quite thorough. The training of the participants was not always what might be desired (although a number of the Indian authors such as James Jefferson and Edward Johnson were qualified historians), partly because qualified tribal scholars were not always available, but also because these projects were part of a learning process by design and necessity. They set out to train tribal representatives in the skills and methods of historical research and writing. They provided on-the-job training to numerous young Indian and White historians.

Since the early Great Basin histories had few precedents to draw upon, those involved had to feel their way along to a workable model. Each history drew on the experience gained by predecessors, and while it cannot be said that progress always resulted, an increased sophistication can definitely be seen in some of the later Great Basin works and in books done by groups in other regions. Certainly the variation in histories already published indicates that there is more than one approach and that continued improvement is possible.

What did these books contribute? They offered the historical values and perspectives of a varied people, the Indians of the Great Basin. But anyone looking for a polemic should look elsewhere, for above all these books were meant to inform, to fill wide gaps in the written history of the Great Basin. This dearth of information was most evident in schoolrooms, where the books have found permanent residence. In many cases, they also have been virtually the only works published on a particular tribe's history. Often, the average reader's only alternative has been technical works addressed to a scholarly audience or passing notice in more general histories. As reference tools they have proved useful to more serious researchers as well. Having enriched the literature on Great Basin Indians, they stand as a tribute to the many Indians whose desire for a voice in the discussion of their own affairs, whose hope that they would have a chance to express their own sense of history, led to their publication.

Population

JOY LELAND

The 1980 population of Great Basin Indians was estimated at about 29,000. This number includes Indians identified with all Indian groups who inhabited the Great Basin in aboriginal times as well as those who live within or adjacent to a reservation, rancheria, or colony where these groups predominated in 1980. Some people from other tribal backgrounds are included where it has not been possible to estimate their numbers to separate them out. In addition, the Kawaiisu, whose 1980 population was very small, are not separately identified in the sources used here and are therefore excluded.

In 1890, Great Basin Indians comprised about 8 percent of the Indian population nationwide. This decreased to about 5 percent by 1910 and to about 2 percent in 1980. The failure of the Great Basin Indian population to grow at a rate comparable to the total Indian population reflects two circumstances. First, while the population of U.S. Indians as a whole had stopped decreasing by 1900 (some sources say 1920; see fig. 1), the number of Great Basin Indians continued to decline until 1930, by which time there were only about 12,000—barely half as many as in 1873. This three-decade lag behind the overall U.S. Indian population in the reversal of the population downtrend is not surprising, since the Great Basin was part of the last frontier of westward expansion. Second, the Great Basin Indian population has increased at a much slower pace than Indians nationwide, whether calculated from the first available figures in the 1870s (35% versus 335%) or from the point of downtrend reversal (139% since 1930 versus 475% since 1900, close to the all-races increase of 487%).

Explanations for the failure of Great Basin Indians to keep pace with the growth of all U.S. Indians undoubtedly are complex. The relatively poor resources of the Great Basin areas that most of them still inhabit may have contributed. However, environmental influences vary greatly, both among and within subgroups of Great Basin Indians, along continua from locations within cities to extremely isolated rural areas, from high altitude to low, from cold to very hot, etc. It therefore is likely that the overall mosaic of Great Basin Indian population experience since the late nineteenth century is the product of widely differing circumstances, intricately combined for each subgroup.

Even though Great Basin Indian population growth

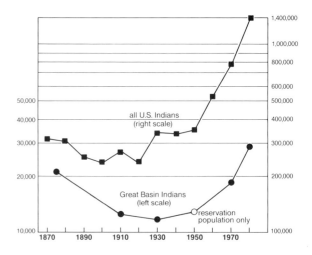

after Leland 1976: 29.

Fig. 1. Population of Great Basin Indians and of all Indians in the continental United States plotted on a semilogarithmic scale.

has not kept pace with Indians nationwide, their average increase nevertheless has been accelerating dramatically since the 1930 low: 11 percent per decade between 1930 and 1950, 16 percent between 1950 and 1970, and 48 percent from 1970 to 1980.

Population Decrease and Increase

According to estimates herein, the Great Basin Indian population level in 1873 (the first comprehensive figures of acceptable reliability) was finally surpassed in the 1970s and by 1980 was about 35 percent higher. However, significant declines had occurred before 1873. Indians of Utah provide one example. Powell and Ingalls's (in ARCIA 1874) 1873 population figure for Southern Paiute, Western Shoshone, and Ute subgroups living in Utah was 1,474, a 79 percent decrease from Schoolcraft's (1853–1856, 1:522) 1850 figure of 7,000 which Demitri B. Shimkin (personal communication 1983) considers a real change reflecting "the pathetic histories of various Southern Paiute and Ute groups." The Northern Shoshone and Bannock of Idaho decreased by 35 percent from an 1860s estimate of about 3,000, after that population already had been devastated by disease and White depredations (Steward 1938:49), to an 1873 figure of 1,937 (table 1).

In the absence of adequate estimates of the aboriginal Great Basin Indian population levels, it is only a guess whether these have yet been regained. Mooney (1928:20, 22) estimates 18,644* as of 1845, when he says the aboriginal period terminated; since the 1873 figure is higher, this one is surely too low and it excludes Great Basin Indians in California except for 200 Northern Paiutes. Kroeber (1934) estimates 26,700 (2.47 per square mile) without specifying a date; his figure is, without explanation, 8,056 higher than that of Mooney, on whom Kroeber said he relied; it also seems to exclude California Great Basin Indians. Dobyns (1966) has argued that Kroeber's North American aboriginal estimates are in general too low, and that Mooney's dates chosen to represent aboriginal population conditions are much too late (see also Ubelaker 1976:288). However, the hemisphere-wide average depopulation ratio of 20 to 1, between initial contact and the lowest population point, suggested by Dobyns as a basis for estimating aboriginal levels, is inappropriate for regional projections, as he acknowledges, and this seems particularly likely in the case of hunter-gatherers, especially in the Great Basin where the wide dispersal of population probably provided more protection from epidemics than in more densely settled areas and where contact occurred quite late. It was Mooney's (1928:20) opinion that these Indians had suffered less than those of any other large section of the United States.

Extrapolation of the 1930 (nadir) population into the past, in a straight line through the 1873 figure, yields an estimate of about 27,000 for 1850, when it could be argued the greatest effects of contact had begun to be felt; about 37,000 in 1830, when Euro-American penetration had first become intense; about 47,000 in 1810, when the central Basin had first been entered; and about 57,000 in 1776, when White explorers had first come into the Great Basin at the eastern edge. However, a straight line undoubtedly distorts the true course of depopulation in the region, particularly in the earliest periods. More probable is an aboriginal Great Basin Indian population of about 40,000 (a depopulation ratio of about 3.4 to 1), which had not yet been regained by 1980.

Since the first census count of all Indians in 1890, they always have made up less than 1 percent of the total U.S. population; their proportion decreased from

Table 1. Population of Great Basin Indian Groups, 1873

Northern Paiute (with Owens Valley Paiute)	
Walker River and Pyramid Lake Reservations[a]	800
Malheur Reservation[a]	500
uncollected groups in western Nev. and northeastern Calif.	1,000
Yahuskin and Walpapi, Klamath Agency, Oreg.	[b]
Snakes of Oreg., not on reservations	200[c]
Total	6,500
Southern Paiute (with Chemehuevi)	
Utah	528
Northern Ariz.	284
Southern Nev.	1,031
Southeast Calif.	184[a]
Chemehuevi	300[d]
Total	2,327
Western Shoshone (with Gosiute)	
Gosiutes of Nev.	204
Gosiutes of Utah	256
Western Shoshones of Nevada	1,945
Total	2,405[e]
Northern Shoshone (with Bannock)	
Cache Valley, Goose Creek, Bear Lake	400
Fort Hall Reservation[a]	1,037
Salmon River tribes[a]	500
Total	1,937[e]
Eastern Shoshone	1,000
Ute	
Uintah Reservation	526
Pahvants of Corn Creek	134[f]
Taviwach band, Los Pinos Agency, Colo.	3,000
Yampa, Grand River, and Uintah bands, White River Agency, Colo.	800
Muache band, Cimarron Agency, N. Mex.	650
Weeminuche and Capote bands, Abiquiu Agency, N. Mex.	870
Total	6,010[g]
Washoe	1,365
Total	**21,544**

Sources: Powell and Ingalls in ARCIA 1874; Fowler and Fowler 1971:97–119; ARCIA 1872–1873:391–459. In cases of conflict within the BIA source, the figures used are from the text of the report; the summary tables (ARCIA 1872–1873:456–459, 776–782) contain what appear to be errors of transcription and interpretation.
[a] Figures Powell and Ingalls obtained from secondary sources, such as agents' estimates.
[b] The U.S. Commissioner of Indian Affairs (ARCIA 1872–1873:453) reported about 4,000 "Klamaths, and Modocs, and the Yahooskin and Wal-pah-pee band of Snakes" at the Klamath Agency but provided no breakdown among these tribes. The proportion of Northern Paiute at this time is unknown; it was 11% in 1944–1945 (U.S. Congress. House 1953:837). The Yahuskin figure in 1873 was 448 (ARCIA 1874:344).
[c] "Upon the edge of Grande Ronde reservation" (ARCIA 1872–1873:454).
[d] An estimate given to Powell and Ingalls by a delegation of Chemehuevi they met at Las Vegas (Fowler and Fowler 1971:107).
[e] ARCIA (1868:174) in 1867 listed 2,000 Western Shoshone, 1,800 "Northern" Shoshone, plus 3,500 in tribes where "Shoshone" predominate.
[f] ARCIA (1868:174) listed 1,500 Pahvants in 1867.
[g] ARCIA (1868:174) lists (by bands) 11,300 Ute.

*1,000 Bannock, 4,500 Western, Northern, and Eastern Shoshone, 4,500 Ute (including Gosiute), 7,500 Paiute (Northern and Southern), 1,000 Washoe, and 144 Chemehuevi. Ubelaker (1976:285–286) details the sources (all from Annual Reports of the Commissioner of Indian Affairs) from Mooney's notes, stored in the National Anthropological Archives, Smithsonian Institution, Washington.

1890 (.39%) to 1950 (.24%) but by 1980 this figure had more than doubled (to .6%), reflecting the fact that Indians have increased much more (281%) since 1950 than the general population (50%) and also much more than Great Basin Indians (95%).

Census officials have expressed the opinion (Anonymous 1972) that willingness of persons to identify themselves as Indian has increased since the 1960s. The basis for this judgment is not stated, but if it is true, part of the apparent increase in U.S. Indians may result from this fact, rather than from natural increase. If Indians of Great Basin groups have for some reason not become as willing as those of other tribal backgrounds to identify themselves as Indian, this would artificially deflate their apparent growth relative to other Indians.

Shoshone

Among Great Basin Indians, the Shoshone population dynamics are unique (fig. 2). The initial Shoshone decline of 20 percent from 1873 to the all-time low was less drastic than the Great Basin group average (44%) and climaxed two decades earlier (1910) than the others (1930 for all except the Washoe, whose rebound point was delayed until 1950). Above all, the 1980 Shoshone population represented a much more dramatic increase than the Great Basin group average, whether calculated from 1873 (124% versus 35%) or from their all-time low (181% versus 139%). The Shoshone account for 89 percent of the Great Basin Indian population increase from 1873 to 1980 (6,633 of 7,445 additional people). (Note that the semilogarithmic scale used in figs. 1–2 causes equal vertical distances to indicate equal percentage change, regardless of the absolute size of the

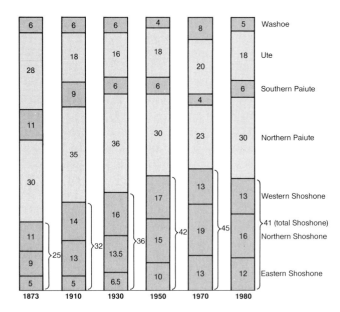

Fig. 3. Relative size population (in percent) among Great Basin tribes, compiled from tables 1–5.

numbers; thus, an equal angle of slope indicates an equal rate of change.)

In 1873, the Shoshone had comprised only 25 percent of Great Basin Indians; by 1980 they represented 41 percent (fig. 3). However, this 1980 Shoshone proportion was down from their all-time high of 46 percent in 1970; the 1970–1980 Shoshone increase of 35 percent was below the Great Basin Indian average of 48 percent. Thus, until 1970, the Shoshone had managed somehow to be more "successful" than their Great Basin Indian neighbors in recouping population losses; since then, their record has weakened slightly compared to the other groups (tables 2–3). However, the apparent Shoshone success relative to the other Great Basin groups in maintaining their numbers could merely reflect a greater propensity than the other groups to remain on reservations, where they are more likely to continue to be counted as Indians than those who no longer inhabit Indian land. Some age evidence suggests that this may be the case.

Each of the three Shoshone groups declined far less from 1873 to their all-time low than the Great Basin group average of 44 percent (fig. 2). Furthermore, from 1873 to 1980, each Shoshone group grew much more than the Great Basin combined average of 35 percent. The increase from all-time low to 1980 was 182 percent for the Northern Shoshone and 398 percent for the Eastern Shoshone, both far above the Great Basin average of 139 percent, while the Western Shoshone increase of 97 percent was the only Shoshone group to fall short of that average.

The population downtrend reversal point was 1910 for the Western and Eastern Shoshone; the Northern Shoshone rebound point was delayed until 1930. In 1873,

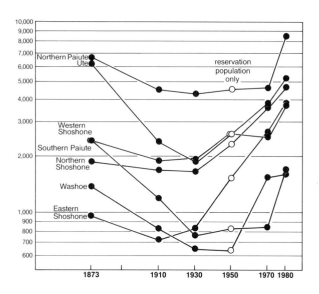

Fig. 2. Population of Great Basin Indians by tribe compiled from tables 1–5.

610

Table 2. Population in 1890

Northern Paiute (with Owens Valley Paiute)	
Pyramid Lake Reservation	485
Walker River Reservation	481
Duck Valley Reservation	203
Snakes of Warm Spring Reservation	80
Total	1,249
Southern Paiute (with Chemehuevi)	
Moapa Reservation	30
Southern Nev.	350
Chemehuevi, Colorado River Agency	200
Total	580
Western Shoshone (with Gosiute)	
Western Shoshone Agency	383
Gosiute not under an agent	256[a]
Total	639
Northern Shoshone (with Bannock)	
Bannock of Fort Hall Agency	514
Bannock of Lemhi Agency	75
Shoshone of Fort Hall Agency	979
Shoshone of Lemhi Agency	249
Tukudeka	108
Total	1,925
Eastern Shoshone of Shoshone Agency	916[b]
Ute	
Pahvant, not under an agent	134
Capotes, Muaches, and Weeminuches of Southern Ute Agency	985[a]
Uncompahgre at Ouray Agency	1,021
Uintah at Uintah Agency	435
White River at Uintah Agency	398
Total	2,973
Washoe	200
Total reservation Indians	8,482
Nonreservation Indians, not identified by tribe, almost all of which are Great Basin:	
Colo.	107
Nev.	3,599[c] or 6,815[d]
Utah	608
Wyo.	22[e]
Total	4,336 (7,552)
Great Basin Indians comprise unknown proportion of census totals for:	
Ariz.	102[f]
Calif.	1,762[g]
Idaho	75[h]
Oreg.	25[i]
Total	1,964
Total	14,782 (17,998)

SOURCE: U.S. Census Office. 11th Census 1894:98,102,106, which incorporates figures from U.S. Department of the Interior 1890.
[a] ARCIA 1890:462.
[b] Counted at 833 by the U.S. Department of the Interior (ARCIA 1890:242).
[c] Indians "subject to tax" (U.S. Census Office. 11th Census 1894:381).
[d] U.S. Department of the Interior (ARCIA 1890:456).
[e] Estimated from 43 nonreservation Indians counted for the state; the Eastern Shoshone proportion of about 51% is estimated on the basis of their proportion relative to the Northern Arapahoe counted *on* reservations (U.S. Census Office. 11th Census 1894:627).
[f] 1910 figure used as a conservative 1890 estimate.
[g] 1910 figures used as a conservative 1890 estimate for the Owens Valley Paiute (1,388), Northern Paiute (101), and Washoe (273).
[h] Estimate based on the assumption that the number of Great Basin nonreservation Indians is in the same proportion to the total number of nonreservation Indians (159) as the corresponding on-reservation Indian figures (1,925/4,062 = 47%).
[i] Estimate based on the assumption that the number of Great Basin nonreservation Indians is in the same proportion to the total number of non-reservation Indians (1,258) as the corresponding on-reservation Indian figures (80/3,708 = 2%).

the Western Shoshone were proportionately the largest Shoshone group (fig. 3); by 1980 the Northern Shoshone held this distinction. As a proportion of Shoshone combined, between 1873 and 1980, the Western group declined, while the other two increased. Because the breakdown of population figures into these three groups is rough from 1950 onward, confidence in the validity of the apparent differences is insufficiently strong to warrant attempts to explain them. The population figures in table 4 include only Indians on reservations because the 1950 census did not include an enumeration of Indians by tribe (see also table 5, notes [c] and [f]).

Incidentally, an alternative picture of early Eastern Shoshone population history emerges from different sources incorporating some closer data points (Demitri B. Shimkin, personal communication 1983). U.S. Bureau of Indian Affairs (ARCIA 1885:354) reports an 1885 Eastern Shoshone population of 887, sharply down from 1,250 in 1878 (ARCIA 1878:150), where the numbers leveled out for some time (births and deaths fluctuating around 40/1,000). In 1867 the estimate was 2,000 (ARCIA 1868:174). By 1910–1911, a low of 830 was reached (ARCIA 1910), but the downtrend reversed, and by 1930 the population had increased to 1,017 (U.S. Congress. Senate. Committee on Indian Affairs 1934:14460).

Ute

The Ute population at its lowest point in 1930 was only one-third its 1873 level (fig. 2), while Great Basin groups combined bottomed the same year at 56 percent of the 1873 level. The Ute population in 1980 was still 14 percent lower than in 1873. On the other hand, the Ute increase from its all-time low in 1930 was 160 percent, higher than the Great Basin average of 139 percent. Between 1970 and 1980, the Ute population increased by 35 percent, about the same as the Great Basin combined average of 48 percent.

Table 3. Population of Great Basin Indian Groups in 1910 and 1930

Group	1910	1930
Northern Paiute (with Owens Valley Paiute)		
Owens Valley Paiute	1,448	
Northern Paiute	3,038	
Total	4,486	4,304
Southern Paiute (with Chemehuevi)		
Chemehuevi	355	
Southern Paiute	780	
Total	1,135	756
Western Shoshone (with Gosiute)		
Panamint	10	
Shoshone	1,840	
Total	1,850	1,926
Northern Shoshone (and Bannock)		
Bannock	413	415
Northern Shoshone	1,286	1,273
Total	1,699	1,688
Eastern Shoshone	714	795
Ute		
Pahvant	37	
"Ute"	440	
Capote	64	
Grand River	1	
Muache	156	
Southern	237	
Uintah	373	
Uncompahgre	412	
White River	320	
Weeminuche	241	
Total	2,281	1,980
Washoe	819	668
Total	12,984	12,117

SOURCE: U.S. Bureau of the Census 1915:17–21, 1937:63–64.

Southern Paiute

Like the Ute, the Southern Paiute–Chemehuevi population decreased by about two-thirds from 1873 and reached the lowest point in 1930. By 1980 their population was still 25 percent below 1873, making them the only other Great Basin group beside the Ute that had not regained and exceeded 1873 levels by 1980. The Southern Paiute–Chemehuevi population increase from all-time low to 1980 of 131 percent was about the average for Great Basin Indians combined.

In the 1950s Southern Paiute reservations in Utah were terminated—an occurrence unique among Great Basin Indians. Perhaps this circumstance discouraged natural increase. More likely, however, in view of the reliance on Bureau of Indian Affairs figures for Indians

within and adjacent to reservations as the basis for estimating 1970 and 1980 population, the decrease in the Southern Paiute population is at least in part an artifact of the termination. From 1970 to 1980 the Southern Paiute–Chemehuevi population increased by 113 percent, about half of which is accounted for by the addition to the population of the "Paiute Indian Tribe of Utah," comprised of formerly terminated Indians (hence not included in the 1970 reservation population), who were reinstated in 1980.

Northern Paiute

The Northern Paiute population decreased by only about one-third from 1873 to the all-time low in 1930. Their population experience is distinctive for its relative stagnation between 1910 and 1970 and for the dramatic increase of 90 percent since 1970, as compared to an average Great Basin Indian increase of only 48 percent from 1970 to 1980. The Northern Paiute 1873–1980 increase of 2,076 people contributed 28 percent of the growth experienced by Great Basin Indians combined, over that period.

Washoe

The aboriginal languages of all the groups discussed so far were closely related, classified as Numic. The Washoe are the only Great Basin tribe whose language (classified as Hokan) is unrelated to Numic; such linguistic distance suggests genetic distance from the other groups as well. Nevertheless, responses to a common environment have created more cultural similarity to the other Great Basin groups than this linguistic and genetic difference would imply.

The Washoe also are the only Basin group for which there are no population data from either of the 1873 sources, so their baseline figure has had to be estimated

Table 4. Population of Reservation Groups in 1950

Northern Paiute (with Owens Valley Paiute)	4,400
Southern Paiute	827
Western Shoshone (with Gosiute)	2,542
Northern Shoshone (with Bannock)	2,292
Eastern Shoshone	1,512
Ute	2,626
Washoe	633
Total	14,832

SOURCE: U.S. Bureau of Indian Affairs data compiled from U.S. Congress. House. Committee on Interior and Insular Affairs 1953:1085–1366.
NOTE: A few figures actually were for 1944–1945; they are included to make the coverage more complete in the absence of later figures. The identifications of Paiute and Shoshone have been made on the basis of geographic location.

Table 5. Population in 1970 and 1980

Groups	Population on and adjacent to reservations 1970[a]		1980[b]			Total Population 1970	1980[f]
	Number	Percentage of Paiute–Shoshone total	Number	Percentage of Paiute–Shoshone total	Percentage Change 1970–1980		
Northern Paiute	3,617	31.69	6,872	38.46	+ 90	4,515[c]	8,576
Southern Paiute and Chemehuevi	656	5.75	1,400	7.84	+134	819[c]	1,748
Western Shoshone	2,034	17.82	2,923	16.36	+ 44	2,539[c]	3,648
Northern Shoshone	3,038	26.61	3,820	21.38	+ 26	3,791[c]	4,768
Eastern Shoshone	2,070	18.13	2,851	15.96	+ 38	2,583[c]	3,559
Total—all Shoshone and Paiute	11,415	100	17,866	100	+ 57	14,248	22,299
Ute	3,347		4,514		+ 35	3,815[d]	5,147
Washoe	725		695		− 1	1,500[e]	1,543
Total	15,487		23,075		+ 49	19,563	28,989[g]

[a] U.S. Bureau of Indian Affairs, Statistics Division (1970, 1970a).

[b] U.S. Bureau of Indian Affairs, Financial Management Office (1981).

[c] Since the 1970 census provided no separate figures for Northern Paiute, Southern Paiute and Chemehuevi, and Shoshone, these numbers are estimates based on the assumption that each tribe's proportion of the "reservation" population also represents its proportion of the total U.S. population of these groups. The total of 14,248 (U.S. Bureau of the Census 1973:188–189) for these groups has been multiplied by each of the tribal percentages of the Paiute–Shoshone total. Obviously, this assumption is open to challenge. For one thing, among the tribal grouping totals for which both figures are available, the BIA "reservation" population as a percentage of the U.S. Census total population of these groups varies from .8012 to .877. For the Washoe the BIA reservation population as a percentage of the tribe's estimate of total population is only .483. Even more puzzling, the U.S. Bureau of the Census (1973:188–189) estimates of the "reservation" population as a percentage of the total population of these groups are much lower than those dervied from taking the BIA "reservation" population as a percentage of the U.S. Census totals. Even by subtracting from the BIA figures the people living "adjacent" to Indian land, this does not account for the discrepancy of 7,333 between the BIA and the census "reservation" populations (table 8). The same is true for the Ute. The Census estimates that only 2,471 Ute live on reservations, which is only 64.8% of the 3,815 Ute they counted nationwide. In contrast, the BIA estimates that 3,347 live on or near reservations, 87.7% of the census total. One possibility is that the census undercounted the reservation population and hence the total population of Great Basin Indians.

[d] U.S. Bureau of the Census 1973:188–189.

[e] Estimate by the Washoe tribe.

[f] 1980 census enumerations of the U.S. Indian population by tribe were not yet available when this was written, so the U.S. population of Great Basin Indians has been estimated, as follows.
A total of 22,299 for all Paiute and Shoshone is derived from the 1980 "reservation" population of 17,866 divided by .8012 based on the assumption that the "reservation" population represents the same proportion of the total U.S. population of these groups in 1980 as in 1970. This assumption is even shakier than the one described in footnote[c] by which subgroups were estimated for both 1970 and 1980. The resulting total figure probably understates the 1980 total population of Great Basin Indians, since the off-reservation population probably was greater in 1980 than in 1970. The Ute total is derived in the same way. The Washoe figure is again a tribal estimate. If it had been derived in the same way as the others the total would have been 1,438; the tribal estimate is 7% higher. The judgment roll for the Washoe land claims case included 1,560, according to the tribe, i.e., 17 additional people who qualified as Washoe by those criteria, beyond the 1,543 on the tribal roll.

[g] This figure is within .005% of the estimated 29,135 that would have resulted from dividing the 1980 reservation total by .792, which is the 1970 proportion of "reservation" to total U.S. population of Great Basin Indians.

(table 1), extrapolated from the 1910 census figure (table 3) on the basis of the 40 percent average decrease of Great Basin Indian groups during that period. Clearly, this baseline figure and the subsequent trends figured therefrom are the least reliable of all the groups. The U.S. Bureau of Indian Affairs (ARCIA 1868:69) listed only 500 Washoes in 1867.

The Washoe population history is remarkable for the length and magnitude of its initial decline—two decades longer and 10 percentage points greater than the Great Basin group average. The 1873 to 1980 Washoe population increase was only 178, or 13 percent. By 1980 the Washoe comprised only 5 percent of the Great Basin Indian population (fig. 4).

Comparisons

In 1873, the largest proportion of Great Basin Indians had been in Nevada (30%), followed by California (21%), Colorado (18%), Idaho (9%), New Mexico and Utah (7% each), Wyoming (5%), Oregon (3%), and Arizona (1%). In 1980, the order was Nevada (32%), Idaho (17%), California and Wyoming (12% each), Colorado and Utah (11% each), and Oregon and Arizona (2.5% each).

Age and Sex

Because 1980 census data on age and sex by tribe were

613

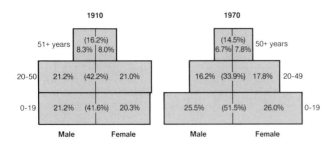

Fig. 4. Age and sex of population of Great Basin Indians, 1910 and 1970, compiled from table 6. The 1970 figures do not include Washoe.

not available in November 1984 for the total U.S. population of Great Basin Indians, 1970 figures must suffice. Although there are such 1980 figures for Great Basin Indians who live within and adjacent to reservations (U.S. Bureau of Indian Affairs. Financial Management Office 1981), the age cohorts do not correspond to, and hence cannot be compared to, data for earlier years. Such frustrating inconsistencies are typical of Great Basin Indian population figures.

Age

The Great Basin Indian population was considerably younger in 1970 than in 1910 (fig. 4, table 6); over half were 19 years old or younger, while only about 42 percent were that young in 1910. Over the same period, the all-races U.S. population became somewhat older; the proportion 19 years old or younger was smaller in 1970 (37.9%) than in 1910 (42%). By 1970, Great Basin Indians were much younger than the general U.S. population; their median age that year was 18.9 years, compared to 28.1 years for all races.

Among nine reservations in which the 1970 median age cohort (20–24) was above the average for 25 Great Basin groups (16–19), four were predominately Shoshone (Leland 1976:72). This is consistent with the idea that Shoshone may tend to remain on reservations more than other Basin groups. If so, this could contribute to the apparent trend of an increasing proportion of Shoshone relative to other Basin Indian groups, which culminated in 1970 (fig. 3), since reservation dwellers are more apt to retain their Indian identity than people who move into the general population.

The relative youth of the 1970 Great Basin Indian population, compared to all races, is consistent with the fact that these Indians experienced a much greater increase (48%) from 1970 to 1980 than the average for the country (11%). A relatively young population (with a high proportion of members who have not yet passed their reproductive years) is likely to exhibit a greater natural increase than an "older" population, if other influences are equal.

However, influences other than relative age of population evidently were *not* equal during this period when Great Basin Indians are compared to U.S. Indians combined. Despite the fact the Great Basin Indians were younger (18.9 years median age) than U.S. Indians (20.4 years) in 1970, their population increased far less over the subsequent decade (48% versus 72%). In contrast to Great Basin groups (and like all races combined), the population of U.S. Indians aged slightly between 1910 and 1970. The proportions who were 19 years old or younger decreased from 51.7% in 1910 to 49.2% in 1970.

Neither are differences in rates of natural increase consistent with differences in population increase between Great Basin and U.S. Indians 1970–1980. Deaths minus births per 1,000 population (i.e., the rate of natural increase) were almost identical for all U.S. Indians (32.5) and for Indians in the Great Basin states (31.98) during this period (Leland 1976:78); both were about three times the all races rate of 11.8%.

It is possible that this anomaly reflects a greater propensity among U.S. Indians as a whole than among Great Basin Indians to retain their Indian identity. An alternative explanation is that the 1970–1980 Great Basin Indian population increase is understated as an artifact of the estimation methods made necessary by the absence of 1980 census data for the total U.S. population of Great Basin Indians, which assume that the proportion of off-reservation Indians was the same in 1980 as in 1970 (table 5). Actually, this proportion may have increased 1970–1980, and the census figures, when they appear, may be closer to 35,000 for the Great Basin Indians (the estimate that results from using the U.S. Indian 1970–1980 increase as a basis) than the estimate herein (28,989) derived from the 1970 off-reservation proportion.

Indians in the three states (Idaho, Wyoming, and Nevada) that together account for 96 percent of the 1980 Shoshone population and in which the Shoshone comprise 68 percent of the Indian population ranked among the highest in death rates and lowest in birth rates and rates of natural increase in the eight Great Basin states during the years just before 1970. This foretold that the days of relative increase of Shoshone over other Great Basin groups soon would end (Leland 1976:10), as the 1980 figures have confirmed.

Sex Ratios

The sex ratio picture among Great Basin Indians is puzzling. In 1910, males outnumbered females among Great Basin Indians (102.9 per 100), but by a smaller margin than among U.S. Indians combined (103.5) and among all races (105.9) as shown in table 7. However, this Great Basin group average leveled great variation among tribal groupings, whose sex ratios ranged from

Table 6. Age and Sex of Great Basin Indian Population, 1910 and 1970

	Male				Female				Total			
	0–19	20–50	51+	Total	0–19	20–50	51+	Total	0–19	20–50	51+	Total
1910[a]												
Northern Paiute (with Owens Valley Paiute)												
Owens Valley Paiute	319	277	86	682	331	318	100	749	650	595	186	1,431
Northern Paiute	574	614	261	1,449	575	696	254	1,525	1,149	1,310	515	2,974
Total	893	891	347	2,131	906	1,014	354	2,274	1,799	1,905	701	4,405
Southern Paiute (with Chemehuevi)												
Chemehuevi	64	77	36	177	75	68	35	178	139	145	71	355
Southern Paiute	176	162	67	405	164	142	59	365	340	304	126	770
Total	240	239	103	582	239	210	94	543	479	449	197	1,125
All Shoshone												
Bannock	79	93	42	214	70	83	46	199	149	176	88	413
Shoshone	822	829	316	1,967	767	781	327	1,875	1,589	1,610	643	3,842
Total	901	922	358	2,181	837	864	373	2,074	1,738	1,786	731	4,255
Ute	540	491	193	1,214	477	417	147	1,041	1,017	898	340	2,255
Washoe	156	199	64	409	155	193	53	401	311	382	117	810
Total	2,730	2,722	1,065	6,517	2,614	2,698	1,021	6,333	5,344	5,420	2,086	12,850
Percent of total Basin	21.2	21.2	8.3	50.7	20.3	21.0	8.0	49.3	41.	42.2	16.2	
Percent[b] of total U.S. Indians	26.2	18.6	6.1	50.9	25.5	17.6	6.0	49.1	51.7	36.3	12.1	

	0–19	20–49	50+	Total	0–19	20–49	50+	Total	0–19	20–49	50+	Total
1970[c]												
All Shoshone and Paiute	3,498	2,341	970	6,809	3,620	2,633	1,186	7,439	7,118	4,974	2,156	14,248
Ute	1,103	577	237	1,917	1,083	586	229	1,898	2,186	1,163	466	3,815
Total	4,601	2,918	1,207	8,726	4,703	3,219	1,415	9,337	9,304	6,137	2,622	18,063
Percent of total Basin	25.5	16.2	6.7	48.6	26.0	17.8	7.8	51.7	51.5	33.9	14.5	
Percent of Total U.S. Indians	24.6	17.3	7.2	49.1	24.6	18.1	8.1	50.8	49.2	35.5	15.3	

	Male	Female	Total
Median Age[d] in 1970			
Shoshone	19	21	19
Ute	14	17	17
Combined	18.5	19.3	18.9
All U.S. Indians	19.9	20.9	20.4
All races	26.8	29.3	28.1

SOURCES: U.S. Bureau of the Census 1913:303, 1915:58, 142–144, 160, 1973:157, 1973a:263.
[a] 1910 totals differ from table 3 by exclusion of people of unknown age.
[b] These age by sex percentages are calculated based on net population (total minus those of unknown age, U.S. Bureau of the Census 1915:58, table 4) and so differ slightly from table 39 therein.
[c] 1970 totals differ from table 5 by omission of Washoe.
[d] No median age is provided for U.S. Indians in 1910, but it must be very near the top of the 0–19 age cohort, since it comprises 51.7% of the population.

117 males per 100 females among the Ute to 93.7 among the Northern Paiute; however, males did predominate in all groups except the Northern Paiute and the Chemehuevi.

The 1910 census warned of three possible sources of distortion in the Indian population figures by sex (U.S. Bureau of the Census 1915:43). The first, sex bias in omissions, would be expected to undercount men, rather than women who are the more likely to be at home when the census taker calls. Second, the census mentioned sex bias in tribal assignment of people of mixed tribal background; no data are provided on numbers of

Great Basin Indians of mixed tribal heritage, but it is hard to imagine any systematic source of bias toward reporting one sex or the other with one or another subgroup. Third was sex bias in misreporting of mixed-bloods as Whites or Blacks instead of as Indians, especially the tendency to report as White Indian women of mixed blood who were married to White men (U.S. Bureau of the Census 1915:46). The overall proportion of Indian/non-Indian mixed-bloods was small among Great Basin Indians in 1910: 11 percent average as compared to 35 percent for U.S. Indians combined. The Eastern Shoshone proportion of mixed-bloods, 28 per-

Table 7. Sex Ratios in 1910 and 1970

Group	1910				1970			
	0–19	*20–50*	*50+*	*Total*	*0–19*	*20–49*	*49+*	*Total*
Owens Valley Paiute	96.4	87.1	86.0	91.1				
Northern Paiute	99.8	88.2	102.8	95.0				
Chemehuevi	85.3	113.2	102.9	99.4				
Southern Paiute	107.3	114.1	113.6	111.0				
Bannock	112.9	112.0	91.3	107.5				
All Shoshone	107.6	106.7	96.0	105.2				
All Shoshone and Paiute	102.6	98.3	98.4	100.1	96.6	88.9	81.8	91.5
Ute	113.1	115.9	133.6	117.0	101.8	98.5	103.5	101.0
Washoe	100.6	97.9	120.8	102.9				
Total, Great Basin Indians	104.4	100.9	104.3	102.9	97.8	90.6	85.1	93.5
All U.S. Indians	102.8	105.4	100.7	103.5	100.2	95.7	89.7	96.7
All races	101.6	108.8	110.4	105.9	103.5	94.8	82.9	94.8

SOURCE: Table 6.
NOTE: Ratios not calculated for totals under 35. See U.S. Bureau of the Census 1915:48 for some detailed breakdowns by state and full- and mixed-blood in 1910.

cent, was highest; the Ute proportion, 5 percent, was smallest (U.S. Bureau of the Census 1915:31, 33–34). Since the proportion of mixed-bloods was much lower among Great Basin Indians than among U.S. Indians, they would have been less subject to the distortion of counting Indian females in mixed marriages as non-Indians. This is consistent with the fact that males outnumbered females less among Great Basin Indians than among Indians nationwide. However, such a large difference in proportion of mixed-bloods should have produced a greater difference in sex ratios than actually occurred, if that were the governing variable. If Great Basin Indian females (whether mixed-blood or full-blood) in mixed marriages did tend to be counted as non-Indians more than males in mixed marriages, or if more females than males entered mixed marriages, then sex ratio differences might provide an index of differential subgroup propensity to mixed marriages. Unfortunately, data to test this hypothesis are not available.

Variation among age cohorts in 1910 sex ratios assumed different patterns in the three comparison groups in table 7. The preponderance of males over females increased from the youngest to the oldest age cohort among all races but was highest in the 20–50 age group among U.S. Indians and lowest in the same age group among Great Basin Indians, perhaps reflecting the relative recency of White incursion into their territory. Presumably the results of White contact had a greater effect on the male population now in this age group than the female.

By 1970, males were outnumbered by females in all three comparison groups, most among Great Basin Indians (93.5 per 100), next among all races (94.8), and least among U.S. Indians combined (96.7). Possible

reasons for these differences are obscure. The pattern of sex ratios among age cohorts was more similar in the three groups in 1970 than in 1910, with males outnumbered by females most in the oldest age cohort and least (or not at all) in the youngest. No subgroup breakdown by sex is available for 1970.

Data Sources and Problems

Most of the Indian population data herein are from the U.S. Bureau of the Census and the U.S. Bureau of Indian Affairs. Though probably less accurate than ethnographic sources for individual groups at a particular time, these government figures have the advantage of covering many groups at several different times. Nevertheless, the data present vexing problems of reliability and comparability, requiring tortured adjustments to produce a time series. The 1860 census was the first to enumerate American Indians as a separate group, but excluded those in Indian territory or on reservations, who were not included in the official population count of the United States until the 1890 census (U.S. Bureau of the Census 1973:x). However, the 1870 census included a figure for Indians, of which 61 percent was estimated. Even the 1873 baseline figures for table 1 (chosen as the first reasonably complete and accurate data with subgroup detail, though too late to approximate aboriginal population levels) contain problems. The most important 1873 source is an enumeration of Indians by Powell and Ingalls (in ARCIA 1874) in their report to the commissioner of Indian affairs on the condition of Indians in portions of Arizona, California, Idaho, Nevada, and Utah. The report is reproduced by Fowler and Fowler (1971:97–119). Powell and Ingalls

616

evaluate their population figures as "accurate" for the groups they visited, except for the Western Shoshone, which data they describe as a "fair approximation" (Fowler and Fowler 1971:107).

Estimates earlier than 1873 are available for some Great Basin groups (see, for example, the compilation of Steward 1938:48–49). However, the Powell and Ingalls data for 1873 represent the first enumeration that covers a major portion of Great Basin groups, gathered at the same time, by the same observers, and hence presumably under standard conditions. The "tribal" subcategories used in the sources for the 1873 baseline population have been arranged to correspond as closely as possible to the groups delineated in this volume. The components of the summary categories used by Powell and Ingalls are shown in detail in their report (Fowler and Fowler 1971:104–105).

Unfortunately, Powell and Ingalls did not provide figures for all the groups defined as Great Basin Indians in this volume. For example, they do not provide population estimates for "a number of Indians known as Ko-eats, Pan-a-mints, etc." "in Western Nevada and on the Eastern slope of the Sierra Nevada in California" (Fowler and Fowler 1971:107). The identity of the Ko-eats is not clear; the Panamint are considered Western Shoshone in this volume.

Some of the groups defined as Great Basin Indians by this volume that were not covered by Powell and Ingalls have been added to figure 1 by using population data from the Annual Report of the Commissioner of Indian Affairs. For example, U.S. Bureau of Indian Affairs provides an estimate of 4,000 Owens Valley Paiute (ARCIA 1872:393), part of the western Nevada and eastern California groups mentioned but not enumerated by Powell and Ingalls. This estimate seems extremely high in light of Steward's (1933b:237) estimate of 1,000 as the aboriginal population of this group and the BIA's 1867 estimate of only 1,600. The BIA supplies no figures for the balance of the groups in their geographical area of "Western Nevada and the Eastern slope of the Sierra Nevada in California;" these are lumped into the large (20,000) category, California "Indians not on reservations" (ARCIA 1874:344). This omission is not a major one in terms of the total population involved. Five years earlier, the BIA listed 2,800 Northern Paiute: 600 on the Truckee River and Pyramid Lake, 600 on Humboldt Lake, 1,500 on the Carson Sink, 600 on the Walker River and Lake, and 100 Ya-huskin at Klamath (ARCIA 1868:168,62).

The BIA estimate for the Ute of Colorado and New Mexico (5,320) also seems high in light of other evidence. The margin of error seems smaller than that for the Owens Valley Paiute. However, the combined error introduced into the 1873 baseline population by these two figures may be large enough to distort the total seriously.

On the other hand, the Eastern Shoshone figure (1,000) seems rather low, in view of the 1910 estimate of 714. The total for the nonreservation "Snakes" of Oregon is so small that it would not greatly distort the 1873 total even if it were off by 100 percent. Generally speaking, the direction of error in the BIA figures seems to be upward. This evaluation is based on the fact that the total population figure reported by the BIA is 17,174 for the groups counted by Powell and Ingalls as 9,659. The effect of overstatement of 1873 population figures would be to overstate the subsequent declines. The "trends" over the years should be viewed in the light of the possible errors in the baseline data.

The long interval between the first (1873) and second (1910) data points is unfortunate. However, although the 1890 Indian census is a rich source of data about many aspects of Indian history (including a summary of enumerations from 1759 to 1890), its 1890 population figures for most of the Great Basin Indian groups are unsuitable for the purposes of this discussion. For completeness, the 1890 census figures, which for most Great Basin groups seem to have been copied from the BIA figures (ARCIA 1890), are presented in table 2, but they do not appear in figures 1–2 or the calculations based thereon.

For the 1890 population of reservation Indians ("not subject to tax") enumerated in the special Indian census, the figures probably are fairly accurate as far as they go (total = 8,482); they are for the most part identical to those in table 2 from the Report of the Commissioner of Indian Affairs (ARCIA 1890).

On the other hand, the nonreservation Indian ("subject to tax") figures are much less accurate, because of the difficulties stemming from the fact that the general census did not identify them by tribal background. Even so, in the states (Colorado, Nevada, and Utah) where the nonreservation Indian totals are almost entirely comprised of Great Basin Indians, plus in Wyoming, where there is a reasonable basis for judging the Eastern Shoshone proportion of nonreservation Indians, it is possible to add in these state totals, to arrive at a figure of 16,034. However, the lack of tribal identification makes it impossible to separate out accurately Great Basin Indians in the four states where the nonreservation Indian totals include many other tribal groups (Arizona, 1,512; California, 11,517; Idaho, 159; and Oregon, 1,258). In the last two, however, there is a reasonable basis for estimating the Great Basin proportion. The 1890 Great Basin Indian population of Arizona was undoubtedly small and the 1910 figure is used as a conservative estimate. The one big problem is presented by California because the estimated total is large enough to introduce a considerable margin of error in the total of 17,998. Incidentally, this estimate is only about 800 lower than the trendline in figure 1 that connects the 1873 and 1910 estimates. Given the tenuousness of the manipulations of the 1890 census figures required to arrive at a total, the trendline figure of about 18,800 seems to provide the more straightforward (and accurate) 1890 estimate.

Even if the census figures were used to arrive at the total for figure 1, it remains impossible to separate out the tribal groups from nonreservation Indian state totals for inclusion in figure 2. In Nevada, for example, the nonreservation proportion constitutes 70 percent of the census total, among whom the relative proportions of Northern and Southern Paiute, Western Shoshone, and Washoe are unknown.

The population figures in table 3 are based on special enumerations of Indians in 1910 and 1930 by the U.S. Bureau of the Census (1915, 1937). The census figures have been chosen in preference to those provided by the Commissioner of Indian Affairs for these years because the census attempts to cover all Indians, while the BIA reports are generally restricted to "reservation" Indians. Furthermore, the census provides figures by "tribe," while the BIA reports totals for reservations, which may include several tribes.

Disadvantages of the census data include the lumping under cover terms of groups that spoke different languages and that this volume treats separately. One vexing case is the 1930 combination of Northern Paiute (Western Numic speakers) and Southern Paiute (Southern Numic speakers) under the cover term Paiute. Although subgroup detail is relatively good in the 1910 and 1930 censuses, the distribution between these groups has had to be roughly estimated on the basis of geographical location (counties), as detailed in the source. Another problem is that different categories and cover terms are used in the two censuses. However, the 1930 census arranges categories used in the two years into approximate equivalents, and these summary categories have been used in table 3 (U.S. Bureau of the Census 1937:48–49, 51).

In general, the 1910 census presented a breakdown that is more detailed and in keeping with the categories used here than the 1930 census. The 1950 census included no enumeration by tribe, so for that year the BIA figures were used, which omit nonreservation Indians; no reasonable basis exists for estimating the nonreservation portion of Great Basin Indians for that year. Subgroup figures for the 1970 total population of Indians have had to be estimated on the basis of reservation proportions in BIA data, because of census category combinations in that year (see table 5, note ᶜ).

The 1980 census enumerations of the Indian population by tribe were still unavailable in November 1984; even the categories to be used therein had not yet been revealed. Therefore, the nonreservation U.S. population of Great Basin Indians, as well as the subgroup proportions, have had to be estimated for 1980 (see table 5, note ᶠ). Rates of natural increase (from Leland

Table 8. Off-Reservation and On-Reservation Population 1970: Two Estimates

Group	Total	Off-Reservation[a]	On-Reservation	Percent Living on Reservation
Shoshone			6,010	
Northern Paiute			3,356	
Southern Paiute and Chemehuevi			549	
BIA		4,333	9,915	69.6
U.S. Census	14,248	10,165	4,083	28.7
Ute				
BIA		723	3,092	81.0
U.S. Census	3,815	1,344	2,471	64.8
Washoe				
BIA			700	47.0
Estimate	1,500	800		
Total				
BIA		5,856	13,707	70.1
U.S. Census	19,563	12,309	7,254	37.1

SOURCES: U.S. Bureau of the Census (1973:188–189) and U.S. Bureau of Indian Affairs. Statistics Division (1970, 1970a).
ᵃ Calculated by subtracting on-reservation figures from U.S. Census total.

1976) had to be calculated from Hill and Spector (1971:231, 232 and supplementary data supplied by the authors) by subtracting calculated weighted average birth rates (1959–1967) from crude death rates (1957, 1960, 1963, 1965, 1966). The Great Basin weighted average is corrected from Leland (1976:78). Note that the time periods for the birth and death rates vary slightly, so the rates of natural increase per 1,000 population are only approximations. More important, the data refer to Indians of all tribes in the Great Basin states and therefore do not correspond exactly to the category of Great Basin Indians.

The most frequently recurring difficulties in studying Great Basin population stem from the gradual combination of groups into linguistically and culturally hybrid categories, the broad outlines of which can be traced in the tables; a detailed treatment of the evolution of Great Basin Indian group categories would make an interesting study in itself. The latest, and perhaps most dismaying, combination was the 1970 Census lumping into one population figure the "Shoshone, Northern and Southern Paiute and Chemehuevi." Students of Great Basin Indians of course need separate totals for each of these subgroups, which in turn represent lumpings that sacrifice useful information. Similarly, the Bureau of Indian Affairs reports of reservation population often lump Great Basin Indians with those of other tribal backgrounds sharing the same land. The age and sex data from the Indian Health Service (Hill and Spector 1971) are reported by state and thus include many Indians from tribes outside the Great Basin.

Other problems stem from changes over the years in methods of enumeration and in criteria for the designation Indian, both by the U.S. Bureau of the Census (1973:x-xi summarizes these) and the Bureau of Indian Affairs. When the census has not specifically inquired as to tribal background (in 1940, 1950, and 1960), many potential Indians have not been so identified, and of course tribal subgroup totals have not been provided. The BIA has sometimes included in its population counts only people residing on reservations, sometimes people living both within and adjacent to reservations combined, and sometimes people enrolled in the tribe, regardless of where they live. Where independent figures are available from both sources, the BIA figures for reservation Indians invariably are higher than the census (table 8). Enrollment eligibility requirements, such as degree of Indian blood or parental affiliation, have been tightened gradually over the years. All such variations affect the size of the population reported as Indian.

In addition to the discussion of the limitations of the data here and in the figures and tables, general caveats concerning population figures for Indians and summaries of the problems therewith should be consulted, such as discussions by the U.S. Bureau of the Census (1913, 1937, 1973), U.S. Office of Indian Affairs (1935), De Lien and Hadley (1952), Hadley (1957), Owl (1962), and Leland (1976).

Kinship

JUDITH SHAPIRO

Presenting an overview of kinship patterns in the Great Basin is, in some respects, easier than presenting such an overview for other ethnographic areas of native North America. Although significant local variations in kinship organization are found, there is a considerable degree of similarity among the closely related peoples of the region.

On the other hand, the information one can draw on for such an overview is limited. Earliest sources on the Great Basin provide little useful information about kinship. The ethnographies that provide most of the available material were written after decades of invasion and disruption. Analyses of kinship were based on data gathered from a small number of older informants. The historical dimension of the material collected was usually not assessed in a systematic manner; the present tense was commonly used both as a convention for the timeless description of traditional customs and for accounts of what was actually observed during the period of research. Investigation of native ideas about kinship was largely limited to obtaining lists of kin terms. Little is known about how these terms were actually used in social situations and how kinsmen behaved toward one another in everyday life.

Given these limitations, what follows is a discussion of the best documented aspects of kinship organization in the Great Basin. The major focus will be on patterns that appear to have been widely characteristic of the region before the time when the horse was adopted by some groups and before major incursions of Whites transformed indigenous societies.

Kinship and Local Groups

Great Basin society was at one time described by its major ethnographer, Julian Steward (1955), as typifying the "family level of socio-cultural integration." The term family referred to the nuclear family—what Steward also called the "biological family"—composed of a man, a woman, and their children (Steward 1938:230–231, 1955:103). This description of Basin society was based on the absence of wider kinship groupings such as patrilateral or matrilateral extended families, lineages, clans, or moieties. Groups of families that came together for certain subsistence activities, ceremonies, and recreational events were not based on any principle of fixed membership, and they shifted in their composition from year to year. There were no permanent local settlements in which the same group of people remained together over time.

Ethnographers of the Great Basin have come to emphasize the importance of kin-based groupings above the level of the individual family. Fowler (1966:62), for example, has used the term "kin clique" for the co-resident group of related families that he sees as the most significant social unit in Basin society. Steward (1968, 1970), spoke of clusters of intermarried families as the basic components of Basin social organization. Steward's general account of these kin clusters echoes Harris's (1940:46, 55) description of the "camp group" among the White Knife Western Shoshone, which was composed of "related persons of one to three, and seldom more than five families" and constituted the "basic political, economic and social unit . . . a practically self-sufficient entity with shifting and temporary ties to other camp groups."

The most important kinship groupings in Basin society, then, were families and family clusters. Families grouped together to form residential clusters on the basis of bilateral kinship. A set of married siblings formed the core of the local community (Eggan 1980). The size and composition of these groups varied from one year to another and also seasonally, in accordance with the availability of food resources. During the greater part of the year, the sparseness of food supplies in most areas required a scattering of the Basin population into relatively small groups; however, at certain times some resources would be available in sufficient quantity to permit larger numbers of people to come together. The most important of these resources was pine nuts. At harvest time, large groups of families gathered in fall and winter camps that might include as many as 20 to 30 families within easy visiting distance of one another (Steward 1955:106). The typical Washoe winter camp group, referred to in English as the "bunch," consisted of 4–10 households (Downs 1966:44–45).

During the pine nut season, families cooperated in communal subsistence activities, such as rabbit drives, and enjoyed a time of heightened ceremonial and recreational activity. Large groups of people were also able to come together in areas where fish were an abundant resource—Lake Tahoe, and Walker and Pyramid lakes. Relatively stable year-round settlements may have been possible in these areas. Among the equestrian groups of the northern and eastern Basin large seasonal camps formed for buffalo hunting, and groups split into smaller units during the winter. Population density and degree of sedentarization varied in different areas (C.S. Fowler 1977; Eggan 1980; Bettinger 1983; Thomas 1983b).

Ethnographers of the Basin have debated the significance of social units larger than the family or family cluster. For a time, the discussion centered around the question of whether "bands" were a characteristic feature of aboriginal sociopolitical organization. Much attention was devoted to this issue, largely in the context of attempts to use Basin ethnography in support of general theories of the evolution of human social organization.

Steward (1938), a major contributor to the evolutionist approach in anthropology, used the term band in his earlier writings to designate the largest cooperating unit in Basin society. "Bands" were contrasted with the "villages" found in a few areas of the Basin, where the relative abundance of resources made possible the adoption of a less nomadic, more settled mode of life. Steward's (1936a:343) view of band organization in the Basin was influenced by the theoretical assumption that "All peoples in an area of low population density have some form of politically autonomous, land-owning band, which is greater than the bilateral family." Over the years, Steward refined and revised his use of the term band. He later emphasized the flexible relationship between named territories and the populations found within them. He reserved the term band for the kinds of sociopolitical units that emerged in the Basin after the introduction of the horse, which made possible activities such as buffalo hunting and retaliatory raiding against White intruders.

These revisions of Steward's were formulated in the course of disagreements with other anthropologists about the nature of Great Basin society. One such interchange was with Elman Service, who described Basin peoples as being organized into patrilocal bands, that is, bands formed according to a rule of postmarital residence with the husband's father. This description, apparently based on a misreading of Steward's data, allowed Service (1962) to consider the Basin as a case supporting his own theory that patrilocal bands were typical of groups at a hunting and gathering stage of subsistence, a theory that has been superseded by comparative research on foraging peoples. The fact that Steward and Service were both evolutionists and that both used the Basin to illustrate their respective theories led to considerable confusion. Steward had repeatedly to call attention to the fact that he was not using the term band to designate a patrilocal group; in his view, Basin bands were bilateral, or "composite," in structure. Downs (1966), for

example, mistakenly attributed to Steward the idea that patrilocal bands were characteristic of the Basin, whereas Steward (1938:265) described patrilocal bands only for some southern California Uto-Aztecan-speaking groups. And Fowler (1966:71–72) did not distinguish between bands in general and patrilocal bands in particular. There is, in effect, no ethnographic evidence for patrilocal bands among Basin peoples. Steward, for his part, virtually abandoned the use of the term band in his descriptions of indigenous Basin society. He noted, moreover, that it was problematic as a comparative term for cross-cultural analysis, since it failed to designate a specific set of co-occurring social structural features (Steward 1970:115).

Another side of the debate over band organization in the Basin involved Omer Stewart, also a Basin ethnographer. Steward and Stewart held different views on the political nature of larger social groupings in the Great Basin and their relationship to territory in aboriginal times. O.C. Stewart (1939, 1959) contended that named regions of the Basin constituted bounded territories communally owned by the peoples living within their borders. He called these landholding units bands and emphasized their importance in Great Basin sociopolitical organization. Steward (1968, 1970), on the other hand, insisted that the relationship between people and land in the Basin was a flexible one, that the composition of groups—particularly larger ones—was highly variable, and that social organization in the Basin is more properly analyzed in terms of smaller units like families and family clusters.

Ethnographically, it is Steward who is correct. Indigenous patterns of social organization throughout most of the Basin revolved around families and family clusters. Larger aggregates were temporary and seasonal. Relatively stable local groups did emerge in certain areas of the Basin, for example, among the Owens Valley Paiute and the Reese River area Northern Paiute (Steward 1938:50–56, 104–105; Bettinger 1983), but these were the exceptions rather than the rule. As for regional names, the consensus is that they referred primarily to territories defined in terms of major food resources and only secondarily to the people living there at any particular time. The association between a particular group and a fixed territory is problematic even for the hunting and predatory raiding bands that developed in certain areas of the Basin.

The essential features of Great Basin kin group organization outlined thus far are closely related to the ecology of the region. Given the features of Basin environment and the technology of its inhabitants, the most efficient unit of consumption and production throughout much of the area was the small family group. Scarcity and unpredictability in the food supply militated against the formation of larger stable groupings. Subsistence practices, for the most part, were such that collective labor presented no advantage over individualized labor. Seed gathering, the major activity of women, was no more efficiently carried out by women working together than by one woman working alone. The family, organized around the sexual division of labor, "was able to carry out most activities necessary to existence" (Steward 1955:117). The Washoe family, a self-contained unit, contained the number of people that could most efficiently exploit the environment; sharing within the family accounted for 70–90 percent of all Washoe economic distributions (Price 1962). Even during the harvesting of pine nuts,which was the occasion for large gatherings of people, families tended to operate on their own; "each family could harvest more if it worked alone" (Steward 1955:105). Individual families owned pine nut territories among the Washoe (Price 1962:34). Subsistence activities that involved cooperation among larger numbers of people—rabbit drives, for example—were occasional events; family-centered activities constituted the daily routine.

Although social life seems to have revolved largely around the small family group in most areas of the Basin, families did not exist in isolation. They came together to form larger units that provided various forms of social and economic support. Bilateral kinship ties served as a flexible basis for local group affiliation, providing families with a range of alternatives. Moreover, in some parts of the Basin, there were relatively stable groups above the level of the individual family or family cluster. This was the case among the Owens Valley Paiute, for example, who were organized into villages and districts (Steward 1933b; Bettinger 1983). According to Bettinger's (1983:49–50) reconstruction of the available evidence, there was a hierarchy among families within these villages and districts based on family ownership of important resources. In most discussions of variation in kinship and social organization within the Basin, the emphasis is on local environmental features, and an attempt is made to account for variation in ecological terms. Bettinger's analysis of the Owens Valley Paiute, on the other hand, centers around processes of contact and diffusion, underlining the similarities between Owens Valley Paiute society and patterns of social organization among tribal groups of the California culture area.

Marriage

Given the structure and significance of the family unit in Great Basin social organization, the conjugal relationship was a central one. At the same time, marriage involved more than the husband and wife themselves; it was also a union between wider family groups, or sibling sets.

The most general rule governing choice of spouse among Basin peoples was that marriage to anyone within one's bilateral kindred was forbidden. Since the reckoning of effective kinship appears to have been variable, it would probably be a mistake to think of the marriage prohibition as involving a fixed degree of genealogical distance. Insofar as camp groups were composed of close relatives, it was necessary to marry outside the group. The ratio of endogamous to exogamous marriage is estimated as 1:6–7. Endogamous marriages probably involved second or third cousins (Steward 1970:131).

Marriage in the Great Basin was not regulated by negative rules alone. Certain forms of preferred marriage were found throughout the area. These included the levirate (marriage of a woman to her deceased husband's brother), the sororate (marriage of a man to his deceased wife's sister), the marriage of two brothers to two sisters, and the marriage of a brother and a sister to a sister and a brother. The levirate and sororate have been variously described as obligatory, preferential, or merely optional.

A form of preferred union found among some Basin groups, but not others, was cross-cousin marriage, which took two forms: "true" cross-cousin marriage and "pseudo" cross-cousin marriage, the latter being marriage with a step relative (that is, a cross-cousin by marriage).

Though most marriages were monogamous, plural unions did occur. Preferential forms of polygamy included sororal polygyny (marriage of a man to two or more sisters) and, less commonly, fraternal polyandry (marriage of a woman to two or more brothers). An important point to note about these two types of polygamy is that such marriages, like the other forms of preferred union, connected families or sibling groups by multiple conjugal bonds.

Ethnographic data on polygyny reveal variation both in the general incidence of the practice and also in the degree to which it was sororal. Among the White Knife Western Shoshone, for example, nonsororal polygyny was reported to be extremely rare (Harris 1940:50). On the other hand, the few cases of polygyny described for the Eastern Shoshone were nonsororal (Shimkin 1947b:293). Among the Surprise Valley Northern Paiute, both forms were common (Kelly 1932:165). Unfortunately, there is little information on attitudes toward such marriages or on the various factors that entered into individual cases.

Cases of polyandry have been reported for many Shoshone (Steward 1936c; Lowie 1948), for the Northern Paiute (W.Z. Park 1937; O.C. Stewart 1937), and for the Washoe (Price 1963a:110; Downs 1966:40–41). True polyandrous marriages appear to have been rare. A more common situation was for a man to have temporary access to the domestic and sexual services of an older brother's wife prior to acquiring a wife of his own

(Steward 1938:164, 195–196, 215, 1943a:278–279; Lowie 1948:115; Harris 1940:49–50).

Other forms of marriage reported in the literature include stepdaughter marriage, found among some Ute, Southern Paiute, and Northern Shoshone groups (Opler 1940:151–152; Steward 1938:215; Kroeber 1940) and wife's brother's daughter marriage, found among the Owens Valley Paiute, and Panamint Western Shoshone (Kroeber 1940). Such practices are further instances of unions between individuals who are already linked to one another as the result of a previous marriage. They appear only sporadically and do not form part of a general Basin pattern, as do the other forms of preferred marriage discussed so far.

The most significant variation in marriage practices within the Basin concerns the appearance among some groups of a preference for cross-cousin marriage (marriage between the respective offspring of a brother and sister). Cross-cousin marriage is common elsewhere in the world and in many other North American Indian societies; however, in the Basin, it presents an exception to the widespread rule prohibiting unions with kinsmen. It is perhaps for this reason that cross-cousin marriage in the Great Basin often took the form of what has been called pseudo cross-cousin marriage (marriage with a father's sister's or a mother's brother's stepchild). This practice, unusual from a cross-cultural perspective, may be seen as particularly appropriate in the context of Basin kinship, since it preserves the taboo on marriage between genealogically close relatives.

Basin groups reported to have practiced true cross-cousin marriage include the Gosiute, Elko, Egan, Steptoe Valley, Ruby Valley, and Humboldt River Western Shoshone (Steward 1943a:278–279, 1941:311–2, 1938:123, 140, 150, 151). Pseudo cross-cousin marriage has been reported for the Eastern Shoshone (Shimkin 1947b:294), for most of the Northern Shoshone and Gosiute (Steward 1943a:278–279), and for Western Shoshone groups (Steward 1938:285; Hoebel 1939:456). Thus, groups that practiced true cross-cousin marriage generally practiced pseudo cross-cousin marriage as well, while others practiced the latter type exclusively. Cross-cousin marriage was generally bilateral, although a patrilateral preference (that is, for the father's sister's daughter or stepdaughter) has been reported for a number of groups. Eggan (1980:179) has suggested that this preference grew out of a man's responsibility to his sister, which here took the form of his providing her with a son-in-law who would take care of the sister and her daughter.

The emergence of cross-cousin marriage in certain areas of the Basin has been explained as a response to a more secure resource base. The need for a widely dispersed kinship network to provide information about resource availability in different locales gave way to the possibility of greater local group integration, and cross-cousin marriage served as an important means of consolidating ties within the community (Eggan 1980:178). Eggan has also addressed the relationship between true and pseudo cross-cousin marriage, noting a shift in the northern part of the Basin from the first to the second type of preferred union. In his view, pseudo cross-cousin marriage developed out of true cross-cousin marriage because the former was too restrictive, whereas the latter offered the possibility of creating ties with a wider range of families (Eggan 1980:182–183). It should be noted, however, that cross-cousin marriage, as it is commonly encountered cross-culturally, involves not only one's genealogically close relatives, but a wider range of kin who are classified under the cross-cousin category. If the Basin system did not operate in this more generally classificatory manner, it is important to keep in mind when comparing the role of cross-cousin marriage in the Basin with its form and function in various other societies in which it is found.

While cross-cousin marriage was a practice that emerged only in certain areas of the Basin and represented a departure from marriage patterns that were generally characteristic of the region, there is nonetheless a connection between cross-cousin marriage and other forms of preferred union found among Basin peoples. Its particular relationship to the marriage of a brother and a sister to a sister and a brother was noted by Harris (1940:50) for the White Knife Western Shoshone:

> Brother–sister exchange in marriage was frequently practiced and two such couples, with their respective children, would usually combine to form a distinct camp group. There was a marked desire to keep the children in the same camp after marriage both because of strong kinship bonds and of the advantage of retaining members who were familiar with food possibilities of the camp range. This was accomplished by cross-cousin marriage. This marital arrangement was often preferred, even when potential mates of this category were not in the same camp group, for they were commonly represented in the larger winter community.

Among the Owens Valley Paiute, families wanting to maintain a tie through marriages of their offspring, sometimes even before having children, entered into a relationship called *makis·i'i*, "the kinship term used between fathers-in-law, signifying potential marriage connection. It entailed close friendship, mutual regard, aid, and gifts of food and other things" (Steward 1933b:294–295).* Such practices, which are common in societies with cross-cousin marriage, indicate that affinity not only follows upon marriage but also may precede and determine it.

Cross-cousin marriage constituted a departure from more general marriage patterns in the Great Basin in that it perpetuated affinal relationships across the gen-

---

*The term *makis·i'i* comes from Yokuts. Gayton (1948:167, 235) discusses the term and the relationship it designates.

erations. What it had in common with the other forms of preferred marriage found in the region was that it multiplied the conjugal bonds uniting two families. Taken together, the various marriage preferences found among Basin peoples reveal a view of marriage as a relationship between families, in which the significant units are sibling sets rather than individuals (Steward 1936c:562, 1955:118–119; Hoebel 1939:446–448; Eggan 1980:175). Reinforcing the ties between particular families through plural marriages served to counterbalance the otherwise dispersed pattern of social ties and the high mobility of minimal family units.

Marriage was generally accompanied by exchanges of goods between the bride's family and the groom's family. These exchanges might continue for varying periods of time; among the Washoe, they were said to go on for several months (Lowie 1939:308). Marital exchanges were usually symmetrical; however, among certain Shoshone groups, particularly in the north, gift-giving by the groom's people predominated to the point of constituting a virtual bride price (Steward 1938:108–109, 1943a:278–279).

There was no formal ceremony of marriage in traditional Great Basin society. Common practice was for the boy to begin visiting the girl and spending nights in her house until he came to be acknowledged as her husband. Similarly, the dissolution of a marriage was accomplished without any official proceedings, but merely by the departure of one of the spouses. Whereas in some societies, marriages are brought into being (and ended) through particular acts, in other societies, including those of the Great Basin, marriage is more appropriately understood as a process. Research on Washoe concepts of marriage and divorce has revealed that conjugal relationships were spoken of in terms of degree (Spring 1967). This was probably the case more generally throughout the Basin, but comparable studies have not been carried out.

Marriage by capture, either ritual or actual, has been reported for some Ute and Shoshone groups (Steward 1938:109). This practice, which is not characteristic of the Basin, seems a clear case of Plains influence.

Postmarital residence patterns were generally flexible. It appears to have been common for the newly married couple to live for a while with the wife's people, during which time the husband commonly worked for his affines. Aside from this tendency toward an initial period of uxorilocality, there was no rule of postmarital residence. The couple was free to settle where they chose, usually with close kin, and also to change residence. Tendencies toward unilocality may have been stronger among some groups than among others. Steward (1933b:294) claims that the Owens Valley Paiute favored permanent uxorilocal residence after a period of alternation between the wife's and the husband's people. Kelly (1964) reports that among the Kaibab

Southern Paiute, uxorilocality was said to prevail, but this was not revealed in census data. Miller (1970:25), referring to Basin groups in general, suggests that "residence had (and still has) a matrilocal [i.e., uxorilocal] bias." On the other hand, a preference for virilocality, for example, among the Little Smoky Valley Western Shoshone, is occasionally reported (Steward 1938:116). In general, statements about resident patterns in the Great Basin must be viewed with caution. Census data are sparse, and accounts often fail to specify whether the generalization offered designates a cultural norm or a behavioral frequency. It should be kept in mind, in this context as in others, that ethnographic accounts of the Basin are usually extrapolations from work with a small number of informants.

In sum, throughout most of the Basin, residence appears to have been governed not by any general rule of postmarital residence, but by a variety of practical and personal considerations, notably the availability of resources and the proximity of various kinsmen (Steward 1938:243).

The marital relationship itself has been described in various Basin ethnographies as being "brittle" or "unstable." In the absence of quantified data, it is difficult to say exactly how Basin groups compare with other societies in this regard. It is true that marriages were created and dissolved in a relatively informal manner and that serial monogamy was common, as revealed in the individual marital histories that have been recorded. Moreover, while parents seem to have had an important say concerning the first marriages of their children, subsequent unions were more purely a matter of the individual partners' discretion and could be entered into and terminated with little pressure from kinsmen. Relationships between the sexes were sufficiently egalitarian for divorce to be as easily initiated by a woman as by a man.

In considering the stability of marriage in the Great Basin, it is important to distinguish between the perpetuation of particular unions and the importance of the conjugal bond itself. On one hand, Basin society lacked the kinds of institutions that contribute toward holding particular marriages together in other societies: status groups or classes that depend on arranged unions to maintain or promote their social position; corporate kin groups with vested interests in the alliances that marital unions create; authority patterns that place women under the control of their husbands. On the other hand, the structure of Basin society placed great emphasis on the relationship between husband and wife. Since small family units spent a good part of the year in relative isolation, spouses were highly dependent on one another as economic partners and social companions. As Steward (1938:242) has pointed out, the fact that a particular marriage may be of short duration does not mean that individuals are likely to remain single for

624

any length of time. A relatively high divorce rate can still combine with the social centrality of the conjugal, or quasi-conjugal bond, which is the closest of relationships in societies characterized by extreme individualism and geographical mobility.

Kin Classification

Knowledge of how Great Basin Indians themselves thought about kinship is largely limited to lists of kin terms. In the earlier sources, these terms appear as isolated items in vocabularies; they are useful mainly for purposes of linguistic comparison, though the close relationship among Basin terminologies permits inferences to be drawn about the rest of the classificatory system. Later sources present more complete and systematically organized sets of kin terms elicited by the genealogical method. Informants were asked what terms they used for particular relatives that appeared in their family trees and were also requested to give native terms as answers to questions like "What would you call your mother's brother's wife?" What this reveals is how the kin terminology sorted genealogical positions into referential categories, which is now considered only a part of the study of kinship as a conceptual system and of the investigation of how kin terms function in a social context.

The kin terminologies that have been collected show a great degree of similarity in their semantic structures and also, with the exception of the non-Numic Washoe terminologies, in the linguistic forms themselves.† There are certain significant local variations—such as those corresponding to the presence or absence of cross-cousin marriage—but the same general features characterize most of the kin classificatory systems of the region.

The most basic and pervasive ordering principles are sex, generation, and relative age. Kinsmen of one's own generation are usually distinguished by sex and relative age only; all cousins are classified together with siblings. Thus, there are four terms in all: older sister/female cousin, younger sister/female cousin, older brother/male cousin, younger brother/male cousin. Terms for adjacent generation relatives most frequently follow a bifurcate-collateral pattern, that is, distinctions are made on the basis of sex, lineality, and the sex of the relative

---

†Comparison of Numic terminologies with those of linguistically related peoples outside the Great Basin can be found in Hoebel (1939), Gifford (1917, 1922), Kroeber (1917), and Shimkin (1941). Some comparative information on kinship terminology is also available in Miller's (1967) collection of Uto-Aztecan cognate sets. Many of the features of Basin Numic terminologies outlined here are characteristic of California Uto-Aztecan groups as well, and of the larger Uto-Aztecan family. For information on typological similarities between Basin terminologies and those of linguistically unrelated native groups in other areas of North America, see Spier (1925).

through whom the relationship is traced. Parents are distinguished from parents' siblings, and maternal aunts and uncles are distinguished from those on the father's side. In the terminologies of many Basin groups, terms for first ascending and descending generation kinsmen are self-reciprocal, that is, the relatives in question call each other by the same term.

The classification of second ascending and descending generation relationships follows the principles of sex and laterality. Self-reciprocal terms are commonly used between relatives of alternate generations. The ascending generation terms depend on the sex of the relative and the sex of the parent through whom the relationship is traced. The descending generation terms depend on the sex of the speaker and the sex of the child through whom the relationship is traced. No distinction is made between lineal and collateral relatives. Thus, an individual has four terms for second ascending generation relatives: male relative, mother's side; female relative, mother's side; male relative, father's side; female relative, father's side. Given the self-reciprocal pattern, the term used by the senior relative depends on his or her own sex. A woman uses one term for the children of her daughters and another for the children of her sons; a male speaker makes the same distinction, but uses two different terms.

A single self-reciprocal term is used for all third ascending and descending generation relationships.

Relative age distinctions and self-reciprocal terminology, while characteristic of Basin kin classification in general, show varying patterns in different regions of the Great Basin. In Southern Numic terminologies, relative age distinctions are commonly applied not only to same-generation kinsmen but also to first ascending generation kinsmen; collateral relatives, with the exception of the paternal aunt, are distinguished not only by sex and laterality but also according to whether they are older or younger than the linking parent. Terms for first descending generation relatives are structured correspondingly (Kelly 1964:127–128; Steward 1938:301–302; Goss 1972a:14–30). Terms that differentiate maternal aunts by relative age are reported for some Central Numic groups (Steward 1938:302).

Relative age on the first ascending generational level serves as the basis for choosing appropriate sibling/cousin terms in a number of terminologies. Thus, for example, the term for older brother/cousin would be used for the son of a parent's older classificatory sibling. Such patterns have been giving way to the reckoning of relative age within the sibling/cousin generation. The Ute are one such example: according to Powell's early schedules, terms for same-generation relatives depended on the relative ages of the linking relatives, whereas the later studies of Steward and Opler report the practice of determining relative age within the sibling/cousin generation itself (Goss 1961a:12–13). The latter pattern is the one generally encountered among Western and Central Numic groups. Sources are not always explicit on this point, and the historical depth of the pattern may be questioned. In the traditional Washoe system, relative age terms for siblings and cousins were based on the respective ages of the linking relatives, but these first ascending generation relatives were not themselves terminologically distinguished according to relative age (Freed 1960:355, 1963:9). By the 1950s the trend among younger speakers was to choose terms on the basis of relative age on the speaker's own generation (Freed 1960:356), a shift similar to the one outlined for Numic groups.

The use of self-reciprocal terminology between relatives of adjacent generations is a characteristic feature of Southern and Central Numic terminologies and distinguishes them from those of Western Numic groups (for examples, see Kelly 1964:127–128; Goss 1972a:14–30; Steward 1938:287, 301–302; Lowie 1909:209–210; Shimkin 1947b:323, Hoebel 1939:442). The occurrence of self-reciprocal adjacent generation kin terms in other Uto-Aztecan systems of classification (Shimkin 1941:224, 227) suggests that the Western Numic terminologies represent a later divergence from an earlier shared pattern closer to that of Central and Southern Numic.

The most significant variation among Great Basin terminological systems is the appearance of bifurcate-merging features in the kin classifications of certain Central Numic groups. On the first ascending generational level, bifurcate-merging terminology involves a classification of the paternal uncle with the father and the maternal aunt with the mother. This pattern is sometimes found together with the generational sibling/cousin terminology described above; this is the case, for example, in Kammedeka Northern Shoshone kin classification (Hoebel 1939:441). Some Shoshone terminologies merge the maternal aunt with the mother but distinguish the paternal uncle from the father. Such a system is reported for the Elko, Battle Mountain, and North Fork Western Shoshone (Steward 1938:284). Other Shoshone groups have bifurcate-merging terminology on ego's generation—that is, parallel cousins are merged with siblings, and cross-cousins are designated by separate terms. In some of these cases, bifurcate-merging features are limited to ego's generation, while in others they are found on all three central generational levels (see Steward 1938:284 for a presentation of these variations in chart form). This bifurcate-merging kin terminology found among Central Numic groups is often associated with true or pseudo cross-cousin marriage (Steward 1938:284, 288; Eggan 1980:178). However, data do not show a complete overlap between the marriage rule and the terminological system. The two Gosiute groups that Steward (1938) reports on, for example, have cross-cousin marriage and a generational cousin terminology, but Wick R. Miller (personal communi-

cation 1975) found bifurcate-merging cousin terminology among the Gosiute.

A terminological variation found only among the Washoe is a distinction between lineal and collateral relatives of alternate generations. Thus, for example, the Washoe term for the father's mother is different from the term for the father's father's female siblings/cousins (Freed 1960:356; Lowie 1939:311).

Though most of the data on the reckoning of kin ties among Basin peoples concern the kind of genealogical distinctions outlined thus far, there is some indication that degree of relationship was an important dimension in Basin concepts of kinship. Material collected among the Northern Paiute reveals a set of terms used in conjunction with particular kin terms, and also with the general term for "relative," that indicate how close or distant the kin tie was reckoned to be (Shapiro 1965). Some evidence for distinctions of this kind can be found in kinship data from other groups, but the approaches to kinship current at the time most of the available ethnographic material on the Basin was being gathered made it unlikely that such lines of inquiry would be pursued. The focus on degree of relationship encountered in the Northern Paiute system of kin classification is reminiscent of the Washoe concepts of marriage, which involve attention to the degree of the marital relationship, and not just to its presence or absence.

Affinal terminology is not highly elaborated among Basin peoples. In addition to terms for husband and wife, there is usually a single term for parent-in-law and another for grandparent-in-law, which are extended to the spouse's collateral relatives. Terms for spouse's siblings are the same as terms for sibling's spouse and depend both on sex of the relative and sex of the speaker.

Terms for relatives by marriage on the first ascending generation—spouses of aunts and uncles—show the following common pattern: the paternal aunt's husband is classified with the mother's brother and the paternal uncle's wife with the mother's sister; the mother's brother's wife is classified with the paternal aunt and the mother's sister's husband with the paternal uncle. Thus, the terms that designate consanguineal collateral relatives on one side of the family designate the spouses of consanguineal relatives on the other side. Relatives by marriage on the second ascending generation are merged with consanguineal relatives of the same side; thus, for example, the same term is used for a mother's father, a mother's father's sibling/cousin, and a mother's mother's husband. Terms for spouses of descending generation relatives, including children-in-law, are usually teknonyms.

The affinal terminologies of groups with cross-cousin marriage show certain special features, notably the frequent equation of mother-in-law and father-in-law with paternal aunt and uncle respectively (Steward 1938:284, 301). More widespread secondary marriage patterns like

626

the levirate, sororate, and sororal polygyny accord with terminological features such as the equation of the paternal uncle with the stepfather and the equation of the maternal aunt with the stepmother. Terms for siblings-in-law of the opposite sex sometimes reflect their status as potential marriage partners (see, for example, Steward 1938:300–305; Shimkin 1947b: 323; Shapiro 1965:38, 41–42; Kelly 1964:129; Goss 1972a:14–30). Kin terms for first ascending generation relatives also accord with brother–sister exchange marriage. In general, the extent to which Basin marriage practices revolved around sibling sets is clearly revealed in the systems of kin classification.

While one can see various correspondences between aspects of Great Basin social organization and features of the region's kin terminological systems,‡ it would be a mistake to look for too direct a correlation between the structuring of referential kin terms and social practice. As Steward (1938:285) points out, "Peculiar features of the terminologies seem to have developed in response to social custom in some localities and not in others and to have spread to groups not possessing those customs. In certain instances there was a possible choice of several terminologies, any of which would have been consistent with social usage. And, finally, some features of the terminologies have no relation whatever to social practice." Freed (1960) has attempted to find a correspondence between the structure of kin categories and social behavior by administering a social role profile test to informants, having them describe the behavior patterns and attitudes that go along with each pair of kin statuses; however, the results do not indicate that it is profitable to think of each terminologically distinct relationship as being correlated with a clear-cut set of role expectations.

In general, highly stereotyped behavior patterns between particular categories of kinsmen were not characteristic of traditional Basin society. There were exceptions to this, commonly among groups that were influenced by the cultural institutions of neighboring peoples and adopted formalized patterns of avoidance and joking between affines or potential affines. Such patterns were often associated with cross-cousin marriage. Among the White Knife Western Shoshone, cross-cousins of the opposite sex who were potential mates joked in a sexual manner with one another; such behavior also characterized the relationship between a man and his wife's sister, and between a woman and her husband's brother (Harris 1940:68–69). Joking between brothers-in-law and between true or pseudo cross-

‡Eggan (1980) correlates variations in kin classification with variations in social organization and explains both in terms of microenvironmental differences. Thomas (1983b), who discusses variability in Great Basin organization from an archeological perspective, attempts to incorporate Eggan's suggestions, but his approach to kinship and kin terminology is somewhat confused.

cousins of the same sex was found among several Northern Shoshone and Ute groups (Steward 1938:197, 216; O.C. Stewart 1942). Among the Eastern Shoshone, joking occurred between siblings-in-law and between cousins of the opposite sex (Shimkin 1947b:306–307). Strict parent-in-law avoidance has been reported for the Owens Valley Paiute (Steward 1933b: 295), for the Fort Hall Northern Shoshone, Skull Valley Gosiute, and Bannock (Steward 1943a), and for the Fish Springs and Fishlake Northern Paiute (Steward 1941). The strong mother-in-law taboo among the Lemhi Northern Shoshone has been attributed to the influence of Crow and Blackfeet neighbors (Lowie 1909).

Another way of investigating the meaning of kinship and kinship categories among Basin peoples is to look into the use of kin terms in contexts other than the reckoning of genealogical relationships among persons. The use of relationship terms for the anthropomorphized animal figures of myths and folk tales, for example, provides a window into the moral universe of kinship. The most complete information of this sort comes from ethnolinguistic studies of the Ute, which show how the spiritual representatives of various culturally significant animal species are related to the human community and to one another (Goss 1967, 1972a). In addition to providing information about how the Ute conceived of their ties to the world around them, these mythical genealogies and the stories in which they figure reveal Ute attitudes toward dimensions of kin roles such as relative age, generation, and gender. The activities of spirit animals, like those of the Ute themselves, take place in a social world of sibling sets linked to one another through ties of marriage.

Theoretical Context of Great Basin Kinship Studies

In comparison to other areas of native North America, the Great Basin stands out not only in its degree of homogeneity but also in the extent to which anthropological knowledge of the area has been influenced by the work of a single scholar. There are, to be sure, other cases of an individual leaving his mark on the study of a particular North American culture area, but Julian Steward's influence on Great Basin studies is distinctive because of the explicitness with which he focused attention on certain aspects of culture and viewed them within a clearly defined theoretical framework.

Steward's approach to Great Basin ethnography was ecological and evolutionist: he was interested in how social institutions functioned to adapt human groups to their environments, and the conditions under which such adaptations change. The Basin was particularly suited to this approach. Given the simple technology of the area's aboriginal inhabitants, environmental constraints on social arrangements were readily apparent. It was also tempting to look at these peoples, whose way of life seemed more "primitive" than that of any other North American Indians, for clues to earlier phases of human history. Local developments within the Basin—for example, the proto-irrigational system found in Owens Valley or the adoption of the horse by groups in the eastern and northern areas—provided opportunities to study the evolution of new social forms. In brief, the direction of Basin studies has reflected a productive convergence of regional features and theoretical outlook; as one anthropologist observed, "the intimate relations between social organization, habitat and technology have, to my knowledge, been nowhere better expressed than in Steward's intensive studies of the Basin-Plateau region. . ." (Manners 1959:188).

In accordance with his overall approach to Basin society, Steward viewed kinship institutions primarily in terms of their adaptational significance. The structure of the family was considered to be a direct outcome of techno-environmental pressures. Attention was focused on its economic functions, how it, and other social groupings, served as a mode of organizing labor. Kin groups were seen as task forces, designed to meet the needs of survival. The image of Basin society that emerged was one of peoples so entirely preoccupied with the food quest that virtually all their social and cultural institutions were directly deducible from the material conditions of their existence (Steward 1938:46).

At the same time, Steward's evolutionist concern with arriving at a theory of general stages of human history had its effect on the interpretation of Great Basin kinship and social organization. This theoretical orientation influenced his early ideas about bands and his subsequent views about the family level of sociocultural integration. Since Steward's own ideas on human social evolution continued to evolve in the course of his scholarly career, his final formulations reflect the influence of later comparative research on the social organization of hunting and gathering peoples. Here, he develops a concentric model of social organization, "starting analysis with the smallest cohesive groups . . . and then tracing the interaction of these groups in expanding spheres" (Steward 1970:114).

Great Basin society has thus tended to be viewed within the perspectives of ecological functionalism, on the one hand, and evolutionist typology, on the other. Much has been written about the adaptive significance of Basin kinship patterns and the degree to which they are representative of a general stage in the development of human society. While these lines of inquiry have been productive, the result has been a comparative neglect of other approaches to kinship. Relatively little is known about the cultural dimensions of kinship, the way in which Basin peoples' own ideas about kin relations formed part of an indigenous world view.

The literature on Great Basin kinship also reflects certain assumptions current in the anthropological study of kinship during the period when fieldwork was being carried out. The attention given in kinship studies to institutions such as moieties, clans, and lineages made kinship organization in the Basin appear relatively formless and led to a tendency to characterize it negatively, in terms of what it lacked. An analytic prejudice in favor of bounded groups with fixed rules of membership made it difficult for anthropologists to talk about the principles governing kinship in societies like those in the Basin and also, as it turned out, in the societies to which the anthropologists themselves belonged.

The focus on the nuclear family in descriptions of Great Basin kinship must be understood in this context. Steward (1955:103) used the term "nuclear family" for the fundamental unit of Basin social structure even though he recognized that the domestic unit was commonly enlarged through polygynous unions and also tended to include additional relatives like "a grandparent, aunt or uncle who would otherwise be homeless." He refrained from using the term "extended family" to describe Basin domestic groups, since he equated this term with a norm of unilateral recruitment (Steward 1938:236). Even in his latest writings, Steward (1970:115) continued to speak of Great Basin societies in terms of "the remarkable absence of any traditional institutions other than nuclear families." He made this statement in the same article in which he argued for the importance of larger kin clusters in Basin social organization.

Steward's continuing focus on the nuclear family does not mean that he considered the individual family to be an isolate. His approach should rather be understood in the context of an insistence that all larger groupings in Basin society were flexible and open-ended. He wished to note the general absence of bounded social groups and to emphasize that one should think of Basin society in terms of a continuous web of social ties that became increasingly diffuse as one moved outward from the immediate domestic group (Murphy 1970:158). Nonetheless, the focus on the nuclear family is problematic since it represents an attempt to identify and accord priority to a social unit with a clear principle of composition (spouses and children) and a stable membership, an approach that is at odds with the essential nature of Great Basin society as Steward himself described it. Steward's difficulty seems to have been in fitting his ethnographic insights into the habitual grooves of anthropological kinship studies.

In the years since most of the sources of Basin kinship were written, anthropologists working in other areas of the world have turned their attention to describing and theorizing about bilaterally organized kinship systems. This research can help to understand better the kinship systems of Basin peoples. What kinship provided was not a model for the formation of bounded social groups, but a network of possible social ties and a moral idiom for creating and maintaining loyalties.

The Twentieth Century

This overview of Basin kinship has focused on indigenous custom, as reconstructed from ethnographic interviews with older informants. While studies dealing explicitly with kinship in the postcontact period are few, the research that has been done in this area reveals interesting patterns of cultural persistence and change. Among the Washoe, for example, the civil and Christian marriage customs brought into the area by Whites have been added to the indigenous repertoire of marriage types, and they combine with more traditional criteria for classifying and evaluating particular conjugal unions (Spring 1967). In the Carson River Basin area, where the local Northern Paiute population has been augmented by many Western Shoshones, traditional kinship patterns have been revitalized because of their adaptiveness to a new set of economic conditions. Heirship problems associated with the multiple ownership of land and the benefits of cooperation between those living on the reservation and those living away have led to a strengthening of extended families and bilateral kin ties (Shimkin and Reid 1970:190–192).

The general features of Great Basin kinship contributed to continuity in social life. Absent from Basin society in aboriginal times were the kinds of structured kin groupings that succumbed to the colonial situation in many other areas of North America. When drastic social change took place in the Great Basin, it turned out that a family-centered, bilateral kinship system was adaptive to the people's new economic conditions, as it had been in the past. The Great Basin Indians in the 1980s might seem, on the surface, to have a kind of family life and network of kin ties not unlike those of rural Whites living in the region. In fact, there are certain similarities between the kinship systems of the Basin and those of many sectors of White America. But beneath the general structural parallels are different cultural worlds.

Mythology and Religious Concepts

ÅKE HULTKRANTZ

The religious concepts and mythology of the Great Basin peoples are perhaps less well known than other religious and mythological systems of native North America but they have attracted much interest from scholars. The pioneer was John Wesley Powell, founder of the Bureau of American Ethnology. The main sources of his mythological collections were the Southern Paiute, Northern Paiute, and Ute. Powell's theoretical sketch of the development of mythology (a typical product of late nineteenth-century anthropological evolutionism) was founded on this material (Powell 1881; cf. Hultkrantz 1966a:100–101). Kroeber (1901) and J.A. Mason (1910) concentrated on Uintah Ute mythology. Lowie (1908, 1909, 1909a, 1924a, 1939) collected tales from all the Basin groups. Sapir (1930–1931) was the first scholar to present Numic mythology in its original language. Other early researchers were Steward (1936b, 1943) and Kelly (1938).

The nature of the myth collections varies. Some are of a less technical nature (W.R. Palmer 1946) but remain valuable in many respects. Some purported tales are unfortunately free inventions of unscrupulous White authors (Hultkrantz 1970:255). Large mythological collections in the original languages, Shoshone or Bannock, by Willard Park, Sven Liljeblad, and Demitri B. Shimkin remain unpublished (cf. Liljeblad 1969; Shimkin 1947a). A general analytical survey of Great Basin myths and tale motifs is contained in a thesis by Anne Cooke Smith (1940).

W.Z. Park (1934, 1938) issued important analyses of Northern Paiute shamanism and Basin shamanism in general. He also studied the Round Dance (W.Z. Park 1941). Short general surveys of Basin religion have been published by Liljeblad (1969), Fowler and Fowler (1974), and Hultkrantz (1976). There are local investigations (Steward 1932; Whiting 1950; Downs 1961; Freed and Freed 1963a; Hultkrantz 1970a, 1981a; Smith 1974; Zigmond 1977) as well as studies encompassing the Great Basin as part of a larger area (Driver 1941; Elmendorf 1952). Beginning with Mooney's (1896) study of the Ghost Dance some scholars have elucidated the acculturative forms of religion in the Great Basin (see "Ghost Dance, Bear Dance, and Sun Dance," this vol.).

Great Basin Indian myths and beliefs make up a pattern closely corresponding to the prerequisites and possibilities of the Basin culture in general. However, there is little agreement among specialists as to the exact nature of this pattern.

Steward (1938:46) found the basic orientation of Basin culture "gastric" and reported few signs of organized religious activity. He repeatedly pointed out that ritual had practically no attachment to economic pursuits. He accepted the theory that ceremonialism dedicated to objectives of group interest only characterizes complex and cohesive societies, while shamanism, in a broad sense, satisfies individual religious interests in simple hunting and gathering societies (Steward 1938:45–46, 1940:490–493, 497, 1955a:113–114; Steward and Voegelin 1974:50–51). In the realm of individual religion, guardian-spirit beliefs, shamanism, and crisis rites were prevalent. Lucky individuals received power in unsought dreams from spirit protectors—supernatural power that enabled them to achieve success in gambling and hunting. Some were instructed by their guardian spirits to cure diseases and may be termed medicine men (shamans). Birth, puberty, menstruation, and death were surrounded by separate rites, such as food restrictions, isolation, and mourning customs.

As for group ceremonialism, the Round Dance, primarily a dance for social recreation, in some places secondarily assumed the character of a religious ceremony of fertility. Among the Northern and Eastern Shoshone true collective ceremonialism started with the creation of mounted bands and the introduction of the Sun Dance.

Contrary to many other writers, Steward (1940:450) emphasized the distinctive features of Basin shamanism and mythology; however, he insisted that religion was not an integrative factor in Basin culture and that the shaman did not play an integrating social role. Owens Valley Paiute autobiographies reveal to what extent the individual's religious world is based on personal visionary experiences (Steward 1934, 1938a). The successful hunter or the satisfied individual was considered to be blessed by the spirits; the unsuccessful man who scarcely filled his place in society was one who had never been granted such blessings. Steward thus seems to suggest that there was some integration between the guardian-spirit complex and Basin society.

Malouf (1966:4) observes that simplicity certainly dominated many aspects of Great Basin life, but he contends that "their religious practices had more in common with the complexities of some societies in better endowed areas which surrounded the Great Basin, particularly in matters which concerned the hunting of big game animals." He delineates the Basin system of religion as "essentially shamanism." By shamanism he means the complex of rites and beliefs developed around the recipient of supernatural powers in spontaneous dreams or sought visions. Malouf puts much weight on the shaman's functioning in group ceremonies and sees a meaningful relation between shamanism and hunting rites. Steward (1941:228, 1940:482), to the contrary, considered supernatural observances in connection with hunting "dispensable or functionally unnecessary."

Liljeblad (1957:38–39) finds that among the Northern Shoshone and Bannock religion centers around the belief in guardian spirits. However, mythology constitutes part of the religious system, although not invariably so (Liljeblad 1969).

These interpretations of Great Basin religion and mythology only partly coincide. Steward's reconstruction has been the most influential in professional circles. However, the three views complement each other, two of them being mainly concerned with the outer aspects of the religious systems, the rites in their interaction with culture and the ecological setting. The third is more closely connected with intrinsic religious values and ideas.

Mythology and religious concepts deserve to be treated as parts of a larger complex that may be called "supernaturalism" (Lowie 1924b:xvi–xvii). In most collections myths and other tales are not separated but discussed simply as "tales." Many of the narratives function virtually as myths, if myths are defined as tales that describe the action of supernatural beings in a distant time and that are believed to be true. Specifically myths deal with cosmogony and the origins of natural conditions and human institutions. There are such myths among the Basin people, although they are not many in comparison with surrounding areas. There is no sharp distinction among myths, legends, and tales of entertainment (Liljeblad 1969:49). The mythical element is sometimes hidden behind a hedge of incidents that may have grown out of the original myth, or it is concentrated in short explanatory notices at the end of tales or tale-motifs (Waterman 1914). Still, a functional treatment of the tales demands differentiation among myths, legends, and other stories (Ray 1947:411; Hultkrantz 1960). Legends are narratives of meetings between human and supernatural beings in historical or recent times and are believed to be true. Other stories are narratives that may contain supernatural motifs but are not necessarily believed.

It is important to observe that Great Basin Indians do not make these distinctions themselves. If they categorize their narratives at all they do so according to content. Eastern Shoshone for instance, separate Coyote tales, monster tales, "White man's tales," and so on (Hultkrantz 1960:554–556). When questioned they may disagree as to the "truth" of different narratives. It is possible that the distinction between "true" and "imagined" stories is late, a result of the secularization process.

The mythic components are part and parcel of the tales and occur as epic elements or mythic concepts. The mythic element may be found in the epic framing of the tale, or in isolated motifs ("explanatory tales"). By mythic concepts is meant persons, things, and events that refer to a mythic world (cf. Boas 1940:483–490). In many mythologies, such as those of the ancient Near East, the persons of the mythic plots and the gods and spirits of the religion are identical. This is not always the case among Great Basin Indians. The acting personages of the mythology are supernatural and to a certain extent play a divine role, but many of them do not appear in general religious concepts.

Religious Concepts

Basin religious concepts and mythology are relatively independent. The supernatural beings are not the same in both realms, or only partly so. There are many levels of religious belief. A Northern Paiute Indian can simultaneously believe in shamanism, Peyotism, and Christianity but practice them at different occasions. The situations as determined by social, traditional, and ecological factors recreate the religious configurations.

An understanding of Great Basin religion requires analysis of two main themes: ecology and tradition. The Great Basin is an excellent field for culture studies from an ecological point of view, including religion. The basic pattern of religion was adjusted to the demands of climate, natural resources, and physiographic environment on a sparse hunting and collecting population. The supernatural powers assumed the shapes of the animals and birds of the area. The goals of religious activity were integrated with the needs and patterns of subsistence and the small nomadic social units that prevailed (Hultkrantz 1976). Basin religion is thus the result of a unique fusion of ecological and traditional factors.

Traditional Great Basin religion was structured on five main levels: cosmology, the beliefs in supernatural beings supposed to control nature and man, social and individual rites connected with collective and individual survival, visions and shamanism, and crisis rites (with practices and beliefs referring to life after death). These patterns were sometimes interconnected, sometimes not. In any case there was no unitary religious system and no world view that provided a dogma of supernatural sanctions. Religious ideas and practices were diffused through the culture but did not constitute a set of defined beliefs, values, and rites.

Cosmology

Cosmology changed contours from one group to another and even within the same group (Liljeblad 1969:51). Sometimes the physiographic features of the surrounding landscape strongly influenced its configuration. The Kaibab Southern Paiute, for instance, thought that the Kaibab Plateau was the middle of the world and that in the west, behind the ocean, the earth was bounded by a line of towering cliffs resembling those surrounding the plateau. The edge of the sky rested upon the brink of the cliffs, which were so irregular that at many places people could fall through (Fowler and Fowler 1971:38, 73–75, 161). The Milky Way had a conspicuous place in the Great Basin cosmos. It was conceived alternatively as the "sky path" or "ghost road" or "dusty road"—the road that the spirits of the dead had to travel on their way to the hereafter—and as the backbone of the sky. Ultimately both these concepts merge, or they have perhaps always been the two sides of the coin.

Supernatural Beings

Among the supernatural beings there was one that may have represented a cosmic order—the supreme being, known among the Numic peoples as "Our Father" or Wolf in postcontact times.

There has been some doubt whether the anthropomorphic concept of a god was at all aboriginal. Steward (1941:267) thinks that the father concept was introduced from Plateau tribes who had been subjected to mission influences. Liljeblad (1969:48–49) considers that the structure of Shoshone society impeded the rise of "high-god" concepts, and that, where they existed, they were purely mythological. Garvin and Schmitt (1951:249) opine that the Shoshone had "multiple gods" and a belief in "an indefinite all-pervading supernatural power."

Much can be said in favor of a late, postcontact introduction of the anthropomorphic concept of a supreme being; for instance, its relative absence in the guardian-spirit or power quest. Other circumstances speak for a truly aboriginal conception such as the fact that Christ does not appear at all, except in late acculturative situations (cf. Hultkrantz 1969:35–37). In particular, the appelation of the high god ("father"), his identification with the sun, his roles as recipient of prayers (cf. Densmore 1948:96–97) and as protector of the annual dances are features that recur in a fixed combination at many places distributed all over the Great Basin area. Schmidt (1912–1955, 6:392–393) has pointed out how common the term "father" is for this deity among North American Indians—in north-central California as well as among Algonquian Indians and some Sioux. Shoshone statements may indicate that the appellation "father" preceded Christian missionary influence (Shimkin 1942:458; Hultkrantz 1948–1958).

In addition to an apparent supreme being, there was a host of other spirits, some of whom belonged to the sky and atmosphere, and these fulfilled functions similiar to those of a high god. In particular this was the case with the sun. The sun may be a manifestation of the supreme being. In the words of an Eastern Shoshone, "they claim that the sun might be God himself, looking over the world every day" (Hultkrantz 1948–1958). In many places the people turned to the sun in their morning prayers. The Northern Paiute believed that an eclipse of the sun was the sun dying, or the sun being eaten by a snake (Kelly 1932:200; Fowler and Fowler 1971:243). Such inconsistencies reflect the attitude of the religious man: he sees the powers as aspects of either a unitary or a divided supernatural world, depending upon the circumstances (Hultkrantz 1971).

Other heavenly bodies figure more in mythology than in general religion. Reports exist from the Ute and some other groups of rites at the appearance of the new moon (O.C. Stewart 1942:324; cf. Fowler and Fowler 1970:137).

Next to the heavenly powers ranked those of the atmosphere, thunder and lightning, the winds, and the eagle. Among the Northern Paiute, according to Powell, the winds were produced by the blowing of four gods, three of whom had a birdlike appearance (Fowler and Fowler 1971:243). This is obviously an instance of the common North American idea that the winds represent the four world corners and cardinal directions (cf. Alexander 1916:286–287). Throughout the area the whirlwind was supposed to be the ghost of a dead person, whether on his way to the realms of the dead or as a wandering being. Southern Paiutes appeased whirlwinds by smoke offerings (Steward 1941:309, 348).

The conceptions of thunder and lightning were most varied. The Washoe thought that the creator, This Man Up Here, once owned thunder and lightning (Lowie 1939:319). Numic Indians did not conceive of Thunder as an anthropomorphic being, except in myths (Fowler and Fowler 1971:92). The Southern Paiute imagined the lightning to be a red snake whose voice was thunder (Fowler and Fowler 1971:243). In Northern Paiute beliefs Thunder or "rain chief" lived on the clouds. He was a kind of badger who, when lifting his head to the sky, made the rain come (Marsden 1923:185). According to the Northern Shoshone thunder was the noise caused by a small mouse rushing through the clouds (Lowie 1909:231). Many Ute, Southern Paiute, and Eastern Shoshone believed thunder was brought about by a bird. Among the Eastern Shoshone the Thunderbird was like a small hummingbird, or a blackbird; however, it was also thought of as an eagle with lightning in its flashing wings, possibly a Plains Indian idea (Hultkrantz 1948–1958). Among the Washoe the eagle was considered a messenger to the spirit world (Downs 1966:41). The same idea prevailed among the Eastern

Shoshone, particularly in connection with the Sun Dance: the eagle has a nest at the top of the center post.

There are mythical notions of a union between a male heaven and a female earth among the Gosiute, and Shoshone myths know of Mother Earth as owner of water and fish (Clark 1966:175–177). However, there is very little evidence of an aboriginal religious belief in Mother Earth, except among the eastern groups who make offerings to her in the Sun Dance (Hultkrantz 1956:204–207). Wherever Peyotism has been accepted the Mother Earth concept has been disseminated, and it is also present in the Ghost Dance (Spier 1935:11, 21).

The dominant religious concept of most hunting peoples, the master of the animals (Hultkrantz 1961b), held a less conspicuous position in Basin religion. The best information on the subject comes from the Ute and Southern Paiute who believed that all animals such as bears, mountain sheep, elk, and deer were controlled by a snow-white being who lived high in the mountains, walked about in cloudy weather, and was able to transform himself into a raven. The hunter who had slain an animal left some portions of the carcass on the spot to propitiate the spirit (O.C. Stewart 1942:243, 246, 337; Fowler and Fowler 1971:66, 75). Other masters of the animals were the coyotelike spirit of the Western Shoshone (Steward 1941:230), and the Shoshone dwarf spirit (Steward 1943a:271). Among the Eastern Shoshone the buffalo was believed to be a master of the animals (Hultkrantz 1961a).

As often was the case in North America the "high god" represented functions usually associated with lower divinities: the White Knife Western Shoshone "father" provided man with game animals (Harris 1940:56).

Some conspicuous localities of nature also had their masters or rulers. Thus, mountains, lakes, and hot springs were known to have their spirits. For example, one Owens Valley Paiute had a mountaintop as his guardian spirit who promised him successful deer hunting on the slopes (Steward 1934:428). The mountains were the common area of ogres and evil giants who took delight in throwing human beings over the rocks. They are the weird actors in many legends. Most lakes also were inhabited by Water Babies, usually small people with long hair ("Oral Tradition: Content and Style of Verbal Arts," fig. 6, this vol.). Some of them lived in springs and made the waters hot (hot springs). According to some reports the Water Baby was half woman, half fish. She carried away children and tortured them, among other evil acts (Fowler and Fowler 1971:66, 75–76, 224–225, 241, 243). Other mysterious beings—a great serpent in Pyramid Lake, white water buffaloes in Bull Lake (Eastern Shoshone country), frogs in wells—have been mentioned as water sprites, all of an evil disposition. The Washoe in particular seem to have feared the Water Babies in Lake Tahoe and surrounding waters;

there is even talk of a "king" of the Water Babies (Downs 1966:58, 62–63). The Ute made offerings to the hot springs in their area (O.C. Stewart 1942:318). The hot springs basins in the Yellowstone Park were avoided by groups other than the Mountain Sheep Eater Eastern Shoshone (Hultkrantz 1954, 1979a).

The Numic peoples dreaded most of all, besides ghosts, the little dwarf spirit with poisonous arrows. This little being lived everywhere—in mountains, among bushes, in caves, around wells—and was mostly unseen. Its arrows caused pneumonia. The beliefs in the dwarf spirits were very uniform over the Numic area and, to judge from reminiscences and legends, attracted more attention than any other religious beliefs. Although ideas of similar pygmy spirits existed in surrounding culture areas—particularly the Plateau and the Plains—they were most typical of the Numic religions, especially in the north.

Many of the spirits (particularly spirits in animal disguise) were the supernatural beings from whom the hunter's individual guardian spirits were recruited. Guardian spirits appear to represent another level of conception than the other spirits; contrary to some assumptions they were rarely identical with the "owners" of species and places (Hultkrantz 1970a:77). Indeed, the individual guardian spirits bestowed upon their clients the success in hunting that in other quarters was granted them by the masters of the game.

The specific forms of supernatural belief were molded by social and economic factors. Thus, the organization of spirits followed the loose and fluid organization of social groups, and the position of the master of the game reflected that of the leader of the local group. Likewise, the animals appearing in visions all represented species known to local inhabitants. The White Knife Western Shoshone, for instance, recognized as the foremost animal spirits eagle, elk, antelope, and buffalo, all well-known Basin animals (Harris 1940). The high-god concept, on the other hand, did not reveal any integration with the environment though this is a matter of diverse opinion.

Ritual Practices

It has long been observed that the small, seminomadic Great Basin population had few opportunities to conduct group rituals of a greater scope. Still, there were certain occasions each year when larger groups assembled, such as the communal hunts, the fish runs, and the piñon harvest. On these occasions simple Round Dances took place. The lack of ceremonialism characterizes the Great Basin area as a whole in comparison with adjacent culture areas (Fowler and Fowler 1971:8). Apparently there was no functional need for ceremonialism dedicated to group purposes (Steward 1955a:114).

Nevertheless, certain dances had a strong ritual char- *633*

U. of Calif., Dept. of Anthr., Archaeol. Research Facility, Berkeley: 69787.
Fig. 1. Johnny Shoshone (d. 1952 or 1953), the last Panamint shaman, singing a song. Photograph by Ruth Kirk, Death Valley, Calif, 1951.

acter and were not merely recreational in purpose with a secondary religious aspect as suggested by Steward (1939:265). The annual thanksgiving ceremonies are a case in point.

Sources are contradictory and often vague, with regard to the various Round Dance rites. Different names of the same dance, diffusion of local dance forms, and modern desacralization are some reasons for this confusion. A further complication may have been changing ecological motivations (seed dance, pine nut dance, grass or spring dance). Finally, the later Ghost Dance has been superimposed on the old Round Dance and blurred its native forms.

All over the area ceremonials were held marking the beginning of seasonal economic activities and aiming at the increase of food supply. They had a clear religious purpose: the first day was often dedicated to prayers that in most cases were directed to the supreme being (the "father"). Information that the main purpose was recreational only probably reflects progressive secularization (W.Z. Park 1941:186, 196). The idea that the religious motivation was secondary is less convincing.

In intent and purpose these ceremonies corresponded to the great annual rites in surrounding areas. However, the divided economic activities called for more diversity than in the highly specialized Plains area: the Snake River Northern Shoshone had one rite in May to make the plants green, another in late summer and fall to produce a good harvest of seeds and pine nuts. On the other hand, the ritual elements were few and simple: dancing, a prayer performed in most cases by the dance leader, and, in some places, offerings to the powers (Fowler and Fowler 1970:137).

Among the White Knife Western Shoshone, the Northern Shoshone, and the Pyramid Lake Northern Paiute, Round Dances included prayers for the fish. First Salmon ceremonies, which were principally distributed on the North Pacific coast, on the Plateau, and in northern California (Gunther 1928:131), appeared in the Great Basin area among the Snake River Northern Shoshone (Lowie 1909:218) and probably the Northern Paiute (Speth 1969:236). The general thanksgiving ceremonies in the north had the character of first-fruit rites: the Northern Shoshone along Grouse Creek offered the first pine nuts to the "father" (Steward 1943a:288), and the Northern Paiute pine nut feast opened the season (Speth 1969:237). Indeed, Powell says that the Northern Paiute offered "the first fruits of the forest, the meadows, the chase" as thanksgiving to the powers (Fowler and Fowler 1971:246). There is a close connection between first fruit rites and first fish-run rites in western North America (Gunther 1928:166–167; M. Schuster 1964:613).

There are traces of cosmological ideas in the religious Round Dances. First, thoughts on cataclysms and world renewals have been reported from some Western Shoshone groups (Steward 1941:267). They are reminiscent of the world renewal rites in connection with the salmon catch among the Hupa and Karok of California (Kroeber and Gifford 1949). It is as yet difficult to tell whether the Basin flood myths should be included in this perspective. Second, the Round Dance took place around a pole—a cedar tree, a pine tree, or a willow pole—among many Basin groups. The symbolism of the pole is never explained in the sources; however, in other American culture areas the pole stands for the axis of the world, the world pillar that carries the universe and connects man with God (Haekel 1955). The Southern Ute thought that the sky was supported by one cottonwood tree in the west and another in the east (Lowie 1924:293). The cedar tree of the Eastern Shoshone Round Dance was, like the dance itself, transmitted to the Ghost Dance (Mooney 1896:809; Hultkrantz 1981a:264–281).

The ceremonial Round Dance has been called "one of the most important socio-religious events" in the Great Basin (W.Z. Park 1941:198). It also appears among the Yuman tribes in the Southwest. Its general emphasis on rain and vegetation, as well as its diffusion, may suggest its affinity with archaic Desert cultures (W.Z. Park 1941:194, 199–200).

In addition to the great collective rites aimed at promoting the growth of seeds and plants, and occasionally

Fig. 2. Tayoni, a Lemhi Northern Shoshone shaman with face paint. Photograph by Åke Hultkrantz, 1955.

Fig. 3. Mike Dick, recognized as the most powerful Washoe shaman in the 1930s (Siskin 1983:xix). He became a shaman at age 50; "after his father died, power came to him. It told that it wanted him to be a good doctor, to cure people" (Siskin 1983:31). He is leaning on a shaman staff on which are notched the number of patients he had attended. In his other hand is one end of a 2-man saw. Photograph by Edgar Siskin, Meyers, Calif., 1938.

general welfare, there were individual rites for hunting of animals. Hunting rituals were irregularly resorted to in specific situations to ensure good success (Downs 1966a:49). Among these was the antelope ritual in which the medicine man charmed the curious antelopes into a corral, a procedure that has been well described by a Northern Paiute (S.W. Hopkins 1883:55–57; cf. Lowie 1924:302–305; Anell 1969:48–54). Antelope hunting is known from the Washoe to the Eastern Shoshone and involves the singing and hypnotizing power of a medicine man.

Visions and Shamanism

The Great Basin vision complex was structured along lines known from other parts of North America and was strongly developed (Steward 1940:492). Individuals who did not receive guardian spirits through dreams or visions were sometimes considered less successful in their lives (Steward 1934), or even lost their faith in the supernatural (Shimkin 1947b:309). The vision and guardian-spirit complex did not have the same intensity as on the Plateau, and there were some distinguishing aspects. The spontaneous dream often replaced the sought-for vision as the source of spirit power. The Great Basin shared this peculiarity with California and the Southwest (Spier 1930:251). In the northern and eastern Great Basin the vision quest was more usual, possibly as a result of Plains and Plateau influences

(Lowie 1923:154). Dreams sometimes imparted supernatural power without implying the visit of a supernatural being. This pattern may be generically akin to the visions of the Southwest culture area (Benedict 1923:36). Few Gosiute visionaries possessed guardian spirits (Malouf 1974:84). The powers granted in dreams and visions were those that for ecological and social reasons were important to the Basin Indians: longevity, gambling luck, running and hunting powers, and, of course, doctoring powers. The introduction of the Plains war complex added new types of power; among the White Knife Western Shoshone, for instance, the power of the wolf that gave cunning in the hunt was reinterpreted as war power (Harris 1940:78).

Among the Northern Paiute at least, supernatural power was not an outright gift once and for all, but the beginning of a continuing relationship with the supernatural being (R. Flannery 1952:187). This continuing-contact type of power was fairly characteristic of the Great Basin as a whole.

Some dreamers or visionaries were shamans, that is, they had powers for curing the sick, and usually had more and stronger powers than other men (W.Z. Park 1938). In contradistinction to other visionaries it was their obligation to serve the community. Although most shamans were men, female shamans were quite common. The shaman usually received his powers in dreams describing the ways he should cure the sick. Where spirits appeared in the dreams they could force the dreamer to accept the shamanistic profession (Washoe, Northern Paiute). The spirit could be inherited, as among the Gosiute, and was sometimes among the Northern Paiute the ghost of an ancestor (W.Z. Park 1934: 101–102).

The shamans cured diseases due to two main causes: intrusion of a foreign object, usually indicated by an acute pain, and loss of the soul, usually indicated by unconsciousness (Steward 1941:259–260). This etiology holds good for other parts of North America as well (Hultkrantz 1953:451). The soul loss idea is unevenly emphasized in different parts of the continent but clearly has a strong position on the Northwest Coast and in the Great Basin (Elmendorf 1952:106).

Therapy corresponded to the cause of the disease. Intrusion of an object or spirit was cured by sucking, blowing, brushing, and other measures aimed at expelling the disease agent. Among the Chemehuevi the medicine man sang a song in which he described the approach of his guardian spirit for the operation (Laird 1976:32). Some "sucking shamans" (fig. 4) had spe-

cialized powers, for example, those shamans who cured bites of rattlesnakes, prominent among the Northern and Southern Paiute (Kelly 1936:136; O.C. Stewart 1941:414, 1942:317). Soul loss, provoked by the wanderings of the soul in dreams or by the theft of ghosts who carry it off to the land of the dead, could be treated in different ways, but the most common method was for the shaman to go into a trance and dispatch his own soul to hunt the fugitive one. Such expeditions into the spirit world were sometimes dramatically described in songs (Natches 1923:259; "Oral Tradition: Content and Style of Verbal Arts" this vol.).

Medicine men who refused to cure sick persons, or who too often failed to cure them, were suspected of witchcraft and ran the risk of being killed. The fear of sorcerers was common in the Basin and may be related to similar beliefs among the Navajo and Pueblo peoples in the Southwest. Whiting (1950) has shown how in societies lacking means for social control, like the Northern Paiute, sorcery carried out this function.

The extinction of the old rituals and the perdurability of shamanism into modern times has created an exaggerated impression of the role of shamanism in traditional Basin religion. Indeed, although the shamans were influential they carried no specific authority, and they did not conduct group ceremonies (Steward 1955a:114).

Life Crises, Soul Beliefs, and Afterlife

Driver (1941:37) concludes that, except for the Washoe, there was little public celebration of most life crises events in the area (in contrast to the Northwest Coast, California, and the Southwest). He also states that nearly all the elements of the girls' puberty rites were shared with surrounding areas (except the Plains).

Although religious beliefs surrounded all life crisis rituals they were particularly well represented at death. The ritual precautions aimed at preventing the return of the dead person, for the fear of the dead was great. The destruction of the dwelling of the deceased person and of his belongings, as well as the moving of the camp from the place of death, testify to this fear. The ghost was dreaded because it wanted to fetch the living and take them to the other world for good. Ghosts appeared in dreams, but also in daily life, and took the forms of human beings, animals, and whirlwinds, the last an idea spread all over the Basin.

Parallel with the belief in wandering ghosts was the conviction that the soul at death went to the land of the dead. Among the Eastern Shoshone and the Northern Paiute, it is thought that there are two souls for each person, one a free soul able to leave the body in dream, the other a soul bound to the body and giving it life. When the free soul leaves for good, the body soul also goes, and that means death (Hultkrantz 1951; Fowler and Fowler 1971:242; O.C. Stewart 1942:319).

Fig. 4. Tom Wesaw, Eastern Shoshone shaman, father of George Wesaw (who lived among the Northern Shoshone and Bannock at Fort Hall), both of whom were famous sucking shamans. They were very influential as doctors, Sun Dance leaders, and Peyote roadchiefs. Photograph by Thomas H. Johnson, Wind River Reservation, Wyo., Jan. 1970.

Interest in an afterlife was slight and usually founded on reports from persons who had been in the land of the dead and returned, such as shamans and individuals in coma (Steward 1941:265; Lowie 1909:226). Another source was the Orpheus tradition, the tale of a man who tries to rescue his deceased wife from the realm of the dead but fails in the Basin version; this tale is recounted from the Southern Paiute (Fowler and Fowler 1971:69, 76–77), Northern Paiute (Gayton 1935a:277–278), and possibly the Fort Hall Northern Shoshone (Steward 1943a:287). A Lemhi Northern Shoshone tale about a man's marriage with a supernatural spirit also follows an Orpheus pattern (Hultkrantz 1957:30).

The path to the other world followed the Milky Way but was sometimes described as an underground passage ending with a bridge over a terrific chasm, a well-known motif in North American eschatology (Hultkrantz 1957:78). Also the so-called Symplegades motif (the skies that go up and down at the edge of the world as the traveler passes by) as found among the Northern Paiute has a wide distribution in North America (S. Thompson 1929:275–276; Hultkrantz 1957:79–80). The Fort Hall Northern Shoshone know of the bush with berries that should not be eaten by anyone wishing to return from the realm of the dead, a frequent motif in tales of journeys to the dead.

The domains of the dead lie in the south, north, or west and are situated on the other side of the ocean or, most frequently, up in the sky. The place is described as delightful and happy, with green grass for the Washoe, pine nuts for the Owens Valley Paiute, and buffalo for the Lemhi Northern Shoshone and Eastern Shoshone. Its ruler is "Our Father" (Bannock, some Northern Shoshone, Northern Paiute, Washoe), Wolf (Ute, Southern Paiute, some Northern Shoshone, and Smith Creek Western Shoshone), or Bat (Southern Paiute). It seems that Wolf and the Father have here been interchangeable concepts. A curious idea possibly echoing Christian baptism occurs among the Fort Hall Northern Shoshone and the Ute: Wolf has to wash the newly dead and even to escort them to the other world.

Mythology

The cultural and social systems described in the myths are of precontact Great Basin society. Powell (1881:30, 39) defined the Numic tales as "zootheistic," that is, representing the gods as animals. It is apparent that few anthropomorphic beings figure in mythology. However, as in other parts of North America, the mythological animals talk and behave as human beings, except that they can accomplish supernatural feats. At the same time they preserve their animal nature: the Skunk is painfully stinking, and Coyote has the same voracious appetite as in real life. The difference between common

Fig. 5. Dick Mawee, Northern Paiute, with his doctoring paraphernalia. Photograph by Omer C. Stewart, Nixon, Nev., 1936.

animals and the mythological animals is clearly perceived in the Southern Paiute language, which has different sets of names for them (Fowler and Fowler 1971:172; Sapir 1949:465).

Powell and other authors have taken it for granted that mythological animals were supposed to be the progenitors of today's animals. No doubt there was some connection, for Lowie reported a Lemhi Northern Shoshone storyteller who identified the Cottontail Rabbit that once shot the Sun with a cottontail that he had hunted (Lowie 1959:13, cf. 1909:252–253). An analysis of Eastern Shoshone myths reveals that one of the theriomorphic myth figures, Coyote, corresponds to the master of animals (Hultkrantz 1961a:210–215; cf. Pettazzoni 1956:370). The age of these primeval beings came to an end when, through Coyote's magic, they were transformed into the animals they are today (cf. Alexander 1916:294). Some myths describe how certain personages became stars and constellations or even figures on the moon (Kelly 1932:200). The most well-known of these myths narrates how the trickster's wife and daughters make their escape from his sexual desires and turn into stars (Lowie 1909:250, 1924a:28–30; Sapir 1930–1931:463–465). Data from both the Americas and Siberia suggest that the transformation of mythical animals into stars is a widely diffused and probably very ancient idea (Jettmar 1962:336).

Two mythological characters are of paramount importance, Wolf and Coyote (Malouf and Smith 1942). Their nature is well illustrated by Kaibab Southern Paiute beliefs as recorded by Sapir (Kelly 1964:133). Wolf, "the powerful one," was the most prominent of all beings. He was the "people's father" because he had made heaven and earth. His brother, Coyote, "comic fellow," was the next most powerful being. He was told by Wolf to assist in making the earth, but he could not do so. It was Coyote who introduced death on earth, and since prayer was called "Coyote-talk" he apparently had taught people how to pray.

The theme of the two brothers is spread over the Great Basin area with some variations. Contrary to other Numic groups some Southern Paiute make Wolf the younger brother instead of Coyote. Among the Eastern Shoshone Wolf occasionally appears as a trickster. Other mythological pairs also enter the scene, such as Mink and Weasel; Weasel has a trickster character. In Numic mythology the brothers are known as the big and the little wolf (that is, coyote), or "the wolf brothers."

Wolf appears occasionally as a culture hero and is generally a benign and responsible fellow, a kind of a mythological counterpart to the supreme being. Coyote, besides being the greedy and licentious character described in the myths, is responsible for many cultural institutions and natural conditions: he secured the fire and the pine nuts, released the game impounded in a cave, caused death to occur, and imparted to man knowledge of arts and crafts. He set the example for all future generations to follow. Among the White Knife Western Shoshone, for instance, a newborn child was held up toward the east while the grandmother blew upon it and wished it good health and a good life, just as Coyote did in the beginning of times. One who had Coyote power could break all taboos like Coyote. However, present-day Indians often refer to Coyote's behavior to explain bad manners and ill fortune (Harris 1940:55, 60, 63, 111–112).

In comparison with Wolf and Coyote, other mythological beings play a less prominent role. Porcupine, Skunk, and the Weasel brothers figure large in some tales, but their mythological significance is slight (except among the Washoe where the Weasel brothers transform the landscape). There is, on the other hand, a series of traditions dealing with monsters such as the mountain and water monsters and the Cannibal Bird. These stories belong partly in the category of myths since they also introduce mythological characters like the Weasal brothers and Mosquito, and partly in the category of legends since they sometimes introduce human actors (as in the story of the child or man carried away by the Cannibal Bird). Tales that concern experiences with ghosts and other-world journeys of human beings are purely legendary.

Creation

The creation myth has two variants, the primeval waters or Earthmaker and the flood myth. Both myths occur throughout the Great Basin.

The myth of primeval waters is found among the Northern Shoshone. After a world conflagration the whole earth was flooded and "Our Father" floated alone on the waters calling on different animals to fetch mud from the bottom of the sea. Muskrat succeeded (although he succumbed). The Father flattened and stretched out the mud thus creating a new earth (Clark 1966:172–174; Liljeblad 1969:50). Similar variants are found among the Eastern Shoshone (Lowie 1909a:273), the Southern Paiute (Lowie 1924a:157–158), and the Northern Paiute (Marsden 1923:185–187; Steward 1936b:364; Kelly 1938:365) for whom Sun and Gray Wolf, or Wolf and Coyote, take part as creators. In all these variants the myth ends with the creation of vegetation and animals.

The myth of the primeval waters is combined with the Earth Diver motif. The Northern Shoshone have a version where Wolf and Coyote, from an upper world, throw down the soil into the world ocean (Liljeblad 1969:50–51). In Chemehuevi mythology Ocean Woman stretches out the land and commands Wolf and Coyote to find out its extension (Laird 1976:148–149).

In the flood variant of the creation myth the world exists, but some being wishes the flood to drown everything. This being may act from vengeance, as did the Water Baby among the Washoe and the water ogre among the Western, Northern, and Eastern Shoshone, or for other reasons such as among the Northern Shoshone where Coyote wants to wash the world (Lowie 1909:247). The Northern Paiute relate that fire was saved from the deluge by a sage hen who retreated to a mountain top protruding above the waters.

Origin of People

Besides short, enumerating notices with Our Father as creator (Lowie 1909a:272–273), most myths describe how people were born as the result of a sexual union between Coyote and two women, or between Wolf or Coyote and their wives. Coyote's approach to the women is first prevented by their having teeth in their vagina. This is the *vagina dentata* motif, widespread in North America (S. Thompson 1929:309; Hatt 1949:85–87). The end of this tale tells how Coyote is sent away with

Fig. 6. John Trehero, Eastern Shoshone medicine man, who among other powers is reputed to have received the cure of epilepsy from the Water-Ghost-Being (Shimkin 1947a:332). He is dressed for the Sun Dance wearing a wig and face paint. Photograph by Åke Hultkrantz, Wind River Reservation, Wyo., 1955.

a bag that he opens out of curiosity, whereupon the ancestors of all Indian tribes (whom he had conceived with the women) jump out and people the world.

Regulation of Birth and Menstruation

Lesser myths describe how Coyote puts blood on his sister or his daughters and confines them in a hut, thereby instituting menstruation; and how he either himself experiences, or decrees, that a child should be born by the swelling of the mother's body and through physical pains.

Theft of Fire

Coyote and his people steal the fire from Crane's or some other being's camp. The pursuers kill all the thieves except the fastest of them who succeeds in bringing fire to Coyote's camp. This myth is distributed over North America but is concentrated on the west coast where it appears in different forms: as theft of the sun, of the light, and of the water (S. Thompson 1929:281–282, 289–290; Rooth 1957:504–506).

Theft of Pine Nuts

Wolf, Coyote, and their followers steal the pine nuts from the mountain dwellers and distribute them over the valleys. A curious detail is that all the thieves are caught except for the loose leg of a bird that manages to save the nuts. This myth may be combined with the theft of fire into one tale (Lowie 1909:244–247).

Cottontail and the Sun

The Sun scorches the ground and makes it hot, so Cottontail Rabbit kills him with his arrows or, in some variants, with a fire drill. Cottontail's neck is burned at the same time (which shows today). He throws back the Sun's gall to the sky, and it becomes a new, less fierce sun (in some variants both sun and moon).

Origin of Death

Wolf wants people to live, but Coyote says they must die. When Coyote's own son dies Wolf refuses to change what Coyote had ordered. This myth type is characteristic of the Great Basin area and occurs, with different actors, in most of western North America (Boas 1917; S. Thompson 1929:284–285; Hultkrantz 1955).

Regulation of the Seasons

Coyote wants the year, or one season of the year, to be very long; in his absence the other mythical beings decide on a shorter span of time. This myth also has a wide distribution in western North America (S. Thompson 1929:288).

Release of the Game Animals

Coyote opens the pen or cave where Wolf keeps the wild animals, and they run away to Wolf's dismay. In some variants other actors are mentioned: the Ute, for example, tell that Crow and his people had the animals secluded, and Weasel liberated them (Lowie 1924a:62–64). Here the deed is regarded as a benefit to the people, but in other Basin variants it is an antisocial action that makes the animals difficult to hunt (Steward 1936b:372–373). In those variants where Coyote appears as a positive being, smarter than Wolf, the motif is often added that Coyote reshapes the animals, gives them mouths, ears, eyes (S. Thompson 1929:292–293).

Origin of Star Constellations

Coyote pretends to be another person and induces sexual relations with his sister, daughter, or mother-in-law. The offended female relatives flee away or become stars. This tale was widespread in the Great Basin, on the Plateau, and on the Plains (S. Thompson 1929:304–305; Schmerler 1931). There are other tales that describe how mythic beings such as mountain sheep and jackrabbits have turned into constellations.

639

War Between Birds and Water Monsters

The Western, Northern, and Eastern Shoshone tell stories of fights between huge serpents and eagles, dwarfs and eagles, witches and eagles, and even monster beings (cannibal or water giants) and mythical birds. Southern Paiutes relate that Rabbit, father of Wolf and Coyote, shoots arrows into the sea (Fowler and Fowler 1971:78). A similar theme seems to underlie the legend of the Cannibal Bird, when it is said that water beings help the hero who has been carried away by this bird to return home. Often this cannibal bird is identified with the eagle, or thunderbird (S. Thompson 1929:318).

Beside these myths there are other tales of more or less fictional character that contain mythological motifs. The Star Husband tale is widely spread in North America in a number of versions (S. Thompson 1953). A simple version appears among the Northern and Eastern Shoshone, and a more complicated version among the Washoe. On the Plains this story is a myth, integrated with the Sun Dance ritual (Hultkrantz 1973:8, 15); in the Great Basin it is a marginal tale without connection with the rest of the mythology.

True mythological tales also are told for entertainment, and where they have lost their explanatory function they have become sheer adventure stories (Coffin 1961:xvi). There is evidence that new "origin myths" have been fabricated in fairly recent times, for instance, the tales of Coyote's meeting with the Whites (Harris 1940:112), but these "myths" are rather jocular stories. The majority of genuine myths have an ambivalent character: "what at one moment appears to be a jest, at another is a solemn fact" (Fowler and Fowler 1971:73).

Other characteristics have been referred to in authoritative efforts to delineate a particular Basin mythological province. Steward (1940:497) considered the prosaic Great Basin mythology to be a survival from an early period. J.A.Mason (1910:299) judged the preponderance of animal stories and relative absence of cosmogonies as a distinct feature of Ute, Northern Shoshone, and Comanche mythology. Lowie (1923:155–156) found that California and Basin mythology had much in common both in actual myths and in "general cast and spirit," a point of view also taken by Liljeblad (1957:25).

Oral Tradition: Content and Style of Verbal Arts

SVEN LILJEBLAD

Utterances that in one way or the other surpass everyday speech constitute the expressions of verbal art produced by speakers of Great Basin languages. In their simplest structure they are limited to a single phrase or to one cryptic word. In each of these one-word phrases there is a double meaning: one specific, literal, and openly manifest, and another connotative in a figurative sense. As a general rule in native tradition, a metaphorical aspect permeates the entire inventory of formal expressions that come under the heading "oral literature," including the mythological tales. The semantic play in much of this metaphoric fiction is sometimes difficult to detect. The use of figurative speech verbalizing values and attitudes once dominant in the society has followed every turn of culture change and therefore cannot always be explained even by the speakers themselves. Figurative speech, common in the Numic languages, can seldom be interpreted by simply analyzing the literal meaning of a verbal sequence. The social context is decisive.

Metaphor could be used by any member of the culture capable of handling the necessary idiomatic rules. Since there was neither an anthropomorphic deity nor a permanent suprafamily social order to take into consideration, everybody was free to develop his own association with the supernatural and to form his own concept of the animal nature of man or the human character he would spontaneously find in natural phenomena. The use of metaphor is enhanced by the continued use of free composition, creating new, unexpected "words" and ideas, producing compounds and phrases not otherwise found in the lexicon.

Epigrammatic Forms

Pronounced individualism prevailed in the societies of the Great Basin, and tribal and band organization developed in but a few areas. Since membership in any identifiable group was constantly shifting as a consequence of aboriginal social fragmentation into nuclear family units, attendance at group ceremonials such as the autumn pine nut festival was conspicuously irregular (Steward 1938:45, 1955:111–115, 1977:369). Community size was limited to the localized kinship group, and the seminomadic peoples of the Great Basin did not convene into large summer or winter groups (Jorgensen 1980:154–163, 250–257, 270–271). However, among the Washoe the annual pine nut festival involved major assemblages, and the initiation rites for girls continued in the 1980s to be an important social event (Lowie 1939:304–308, 314; Freed and Freed 1963a:27–36). Religious observances mainly concerned individual health and healing rather than imperative formulas and patterned prayers or inheritance of specific and definitely worded incantations. A notable exception is the shamanistic songs for health and weather control that were sometimes passed on to a child or grandchild (W.Z. Park 1934:101–102, 1938:29; Laird 1976:19–21). However, Steward (1933b:311) questions whether the Owens Valley Paiutes had inherited songs and other shamanistic rituals that had been acquired by individual members of the society. Supplicating the supernatural was a matter of personal discretion rather than a fixed usage of formulaic convention. Formalized prayers collectively practiced were therefore lacking even at shamanistic séances. A supplicant communicating with the source of his supernatural power would develop a prayer style of his own, sometimes with an amazing eloquence heard still at funerals, at Pine Nut Prayer and Sun Dance, or at Peyote meetings. There was also the free use of metaphor in sympathetic magic; for example, when a plant used for medicine was addressed as a person in a prayer.

Elaborate public speech in free form was also practiced by village headmen and band leaders, called Mono *pogínabi*, Northern Paiute *póinabi*, Shoshone *tek^wahni*, or some similar title meaning 'talker'. Deplorably little of this oratory has reached print, but the original stylistic features of oral tradition in prose and verse are described and exemplified by Shimkin (1947a) for the Shoshone in the only comprehensive study of this topic. A noteworthy exception of free style is the appellatives used in prayers to the heavenly bodies, improvised charms with more or less formalized invocations to the sun and, less commonly to the moon, usually appealing for aid in removing disease. In Northern Paiute the sacral name of the sun (ordinarily *tabá*, Shoshone *tábe*) was *pú·sa·ti*,

641

and the moon (*mihá*, Shoshone *mía*), when prayed to, was called *ikinúˀu wákoyoci* ('your father's father, the Moon'). Both these sacral names, used only in prayer, are archaic and etymologically unexplained. Another enigmatic term still used in Northern Paiute prayers to the sun is *pitín·aˀa*, as, for example, in the formulary appeal included in an extemporaneous prayer to the sun for the recovery of an ailing person: *pitín·aˀa í· / í· adimáʒaikʷí í·*. ('You, Sun! You will help him, you'). Likewise, the earth as a personified entity is addressed as Northern Paiute *ibiá tiípi* ('my Mother Earth'), as still today in the Peyote tepee.

Cosmology in general but also various other inanimate phenomena and abstract ideas were subject to personification, creating an imaginary world of animate beings. The stars in the winter sky were well known, and the movements of the four brightest planets were observed. In Northern Paiute the North Star was called *kái yicíŋ·adi pá·tusuba* ('not moving star'). Only a few of the constellations as perceived by the Great Basin Indians have been recorded, and those in a terminology that is far from consistent, but there was a story told about each one. A common name of the Pleiades was in Northern Paiute *iʒáˀa padími* ('Coyote's Daughters'). The Big Dipper was Northern Paiute *wakʷánagaˀyu*, which means 'the ones having nets'. The five stars to the left, so the story tells, were five men who held the catching net the proper way, whereas the two stars to the right were two men who did not and therefore were called *waˀímikʷapi* ('the Failures'). The Morning Star, always personified, was prayed to, and in rare cases still is. In Mono, the Morning Star is *tabiháˀa* and a star in general *taʒínu*, and Shoshone has respectively *ta·ttaciˀumpi* and *taciˀumpi*. For relevant terminology, see Goss's (1972a:38–47, 1972:124) review of "cosmological animate nouns" in Ute. The sun, moon, and stars were power-endowing entities in Northern Paiute shamanism (W.Z. Park 1938:17). A woman of the Owens Valley Paiutes communicated with the Morning Star, who advised her in gambling (Essene 1935a:87B). In a mythological tale, the hero calls upon the Wind, the Rain, and a named mountain for help (Essene 1935a).

The same attitude is found in various biographical materials, as, for example, in a detailed account of the life and ideas of an Owens Valley Paiute with a life-long dependence on one of the most majestic mountains of the Sierra Nevada (Steward 1934:428–432). Unlike the guardian-spirit concept among neighboring tribes to the north and east, this kind of association with the supernatural was unsought and was conveyed only in dreams unless needed for shamanistic purpose. Personification was the productive principle when appealing to nature for aid in everyday affairs. The mythological tales representing centuries of metaphoric fiction remained a never-failing repository of allegorical ideas.

For example, in stories of famine scrapings of food, Northern Paiute *tí·kidapi*, occur personified as a hunger demon. It was in this vein that frost in the allegorical saying *husíaba tóˀisabui kóiuˀyakʷi* ('Frost killed the chokecherries') was thought of as a personage having life and movement. Salt came to the Moapa Southern Paiutes in the shape of a man traveling through the country and putting his hand in the boiling food (Lowie 1924:199–200). Kawaiisu *soˀodi* 'wild tobacco' appeared as a man roaming the world and warding off various evils (Zigmond 1980:199, 1981:43–44). Typical also are the anecdotes about quarrels between different food plants (for example, Natches 1940:15) and the prayers for success addressed to herbs with pharmaceutical properties. Viewing nature under the aspect of human conditions appears in a variety of comic sayings, as, for example, when the Northern Paiutes greet the chickadee with the allocution *haˀún·iˀyu supiá* ('how is your mother?').*

Special aptitude for producing and interpreting figurative speech in connection with concepts of power seems to have been a traditional predisposition rather than a spontaneous personal inclination. This aptitude is reflected in the noa names used in lieu of ordinary nouns that were taboo under certain conditions (Liljeblad 1940–1983). For example, conservative Northern Paiutes moving about in the bush would avoid ordinary *togókʷa* 'rattlesnake' but use instead *waˀyáʒiʒiˀi* 'dear little waving one', or a similar appellation. Etymological evidence suggests that the ordinary term, and its cognates throughout Numic, was itself a noa name, substituting for a now forgotten generic term. It can be explained as derived either from a stem for 'long' (Sapir 1930–1931:688) or from one meaning 'mother's father', given the habit of using kinship terms as names of myth animals (Catherine S. Fowler, personal communication 1984). Thus, a substitute, once it became commonly used, would itself be subject to replacement. The generic name for a bear (Northern Paiute *wida*, Shoshone *wita*), when security so required, was replaced by Northern Paiute *mipahwá*, Shoshone *uti·n paha* 'their father's sister'. Gradually these substitutes became so familiar that in many places new noa words were adopted, such as Mono *pahabiʒíˀi* 'dear swimmer', Northern Paiute *paduáˀa* 'water-son', Shoshone *piatappa* 'big sole', Northern Paiute *anínadikadi* 'ant-eater'.

Proverbial Aphorisms

Though most authorities hitherto have commented upon the absence or the very sporadic occurrence of proverbs

---

*Examples unless otherwise given are quoted from manuscript, phonograph, and tape collections in the University of Nevada Reno, Library, Special Collections Division.

among the North American Indians, their presence in the pre-Caucasian oral tradition of the Great Basin cannot be denied (cf. Fower and Fowler 1971:96, 127). As elsewhere in the world, proverbial expressions in Numic fall into two classes: the hortatory type directly or indirectly requesting something, advising social behavior, or warning against misconduct or danger; and commonly repeated sayings generalizing a situation, an individual habit, a desire, a social custom, or a natural phenomenon. In either case, it is a figure of speech, built on a metaphor or a metonym. Proverbial imagination is still a living process apparent from examples referring to social changes in the historic period, such as the ironical remarks in Northern Paiute *kapíta· kai tidíaidi* 'chiefs don't work' (the word for 'chief' being borrowed from the Spanish or French for 'captain'), or *táibo pikúbatu nabás·aʔyain·a* 'White people would kill each other over a dollar bill'. On the other hand, there are truly metaphorical proverbs still in use but so out-of-date that the logical link between the designative or literal meaning and the connotative or figurative conclusion has become incomprehensible. There is, for example, in Northern Paiute the popular expression *nikúba timánagahu* 'draw a picture on top of me', which actually means 'pay for me' (on a bus or at a fair). Or there are old ideas that have been recast, such as *kái im·ugúa can·ágipa·na* 'don't chase your soul', (that is, 'do not drive so fast as to endanger your life'); or the common assertion, with a humorous tenor today, *iča·ís·i itimágak^wi* 'I shall pay you when you die', originally referring to the lavish gift giving at funerals. The allusion is sometimes so remote that the speaker himself is uncertain about the idea implied. All he may know is the applicability of the conventional formula in a given situation. For example, a Bannock may urge a person to dance with the warning *kái niká, widáʔa ikigíuk^wi* 'if you don't dance, the bear will bite you', but the association with the old Bear Dance has vanished. Disobedient children are still reproved with sayings such as Northern Paiute *niníʔi hunák^wa* 'the Stranger is outside' and *niníʔi ikigíuk^wi* 'the Stranger will bite you'; Bannock *kái itináka, waʔíci páiuk^wi, in·aká cihíuk^wi* 'if you don't obey I will call the old man and he will pierce your ear'.

The communicative message, the hidden meaning in word play, can best be classified in a social context. Most of these standardized utterances disclose the speaker's critical or disapproving attitude, often with a sarcastic touch: Northern Paiute *suʔiʒáʔa kim·áʔasu tibíwawaitu, kim·ás·i pis·á nimíyaduʔa* 'when Coyote arrives at a place, he speaks the people's language well', implying "do not trust an outsider." As would be expected, proverbs reflecting family relationship are aimed at present-day conditions: (Northern Paiute) *nabóinagati inobík^waiti* 'I am boss in my own house'. With the radical change in culture and social order, old proverbs might have been replaced by new images serving the same idea; or the concrete scene from which a generalization is made might be maintained but reinterpreted according to new habits. Thus, there is a common saying (Bannock) *itigúhanin·a cihán·i* 'stir your cooking' or Northern Paiute *itigúhaninasiʔmi han·í* 'tend to your own cooking', said by a man to his wife to mean 'mind your own business!' The reference is to the female task of former days of stirring the seed-gruel in a boiling basket. Other common proverbial admonitions are, for example, Northern Paiute *iwá kucás·i, yáis·i natínidui* 'after gathering enough wood, you might tell tales', alluding to the taboo against telling stories by daylight but used as a way of saying 'first think about it, then talk it over'. Fixed phrases in daily conversation regarding people's behavior occur as reciprocal correlation or as a simile: Northern Paiute *pis·á suwáʔidi, sik^wíapa sag^wá·ʔidi* 'the one who laughs well is quick to anger'; *muák^wiʔna·ʔwaniʔyu, iní· tin·obís·upiča* 'like an old chicken, he or she likes his or her own house' (that is, 'always stays home'). Metonymy and wellerism occur with proverbs referring to weather and season but as far as possible avoiding any mention of winter and cold: Northern Paiute *tohátinia* 'white falls down' or Bannock *tohátiniačak^wi* 'white falls slowly', 'it is snowing'; Northern Paiute *kái tomók^wi, kidí maʔnáʔwi, mís·u muán·imi* '"it will not be winter, when the ground hogs are out," the oldtimers said'.

Ritualism

Fixed sentences formulated in rhythmic or metric patterns for ritual action are rare in Numic languages and were limited mostly to weather control. A commonly used Bannock formula was the following: *ní·da taʒáti taʒáwi·pi/ tičuíno ní· wí·pi/ yán·o·su pis·á yuípin·i* 'I was summer-born in the summer; I was born in our warm weather; hence, it will be nice and warm from now on'. Variants of this charm with accompanying ritual procedures are published by Kelly (1932:201–202) from the Surprise Valley Northern Paiutes. Charms used for luck in gambling, including formulas, are widely reported from western North America (Jorgensen 1980:298, 575, 621), although records of the actual wording are lacking. Annually recurring rites are associated with first pine nut picking, first fishing, or any other subsistence activity were informal, as was the prayer offered to a plant used for medicine before the specimen was gathered. The supplicant went out at sunrise, sat facing east on the shady side of the plant, telling about his need and asking for cure and protection.

Personification of natural phenomena was closely associated with individual access to supernatural aid and patronage, the principal doctrine in the religious system of the Great Basin Indians. Supernatural power, sought by some and feared by others, was everywhere a source of individual competence, mental and physical ability, health, and success; for this the Numic languages use cognate forms of a single term: Mono and Northern Paiute *puha*, Shoshone *puha* and *poha*, Kawaiisu *puhwa*, Southern Paiute *pua-*, Ute *puwávi*. Derivatives are used in a wide range of expressions referring to praying and doctoring. The Washoe term, *wegeléyu*, is noteworthy, usually occurring possessed, *dewgeléyu* 'his power', thus stressing its shamanistic qualities (William Jacobsen, personal communication 1984). In anthropological literature supernatural power has usually been discussed within one of two distinct frames of reference. It has either been counted as a manifestation of animism, at least as spiritual representation of nature (hence, the commonly used term "spirit power"), or with due regard to its impersonal character in other connections has been classified as mana. Both views could be justified, but neither would be sufficient, given the broad applicability of the term.

Plurality of spirit power in a doctor's possession depended on his status. If he was a general practitioner, he usually had special power in addition to his main power; if he was a specialist, he had but one (Kelly 1932:189–193, 1939; Steward 1933b:312, 1941:258–259, 320, 1943a:281–286; W.Z.Park 1938:16–19; O.C. Stewart 1941:413; Siskin 1983:25). A person who was convinced that he possessed supernatural power, whether from animate or inanimate nature, knew where his power (or powers) emanated from (W.Z. Park 1934:99–102; Lowie 1939:318–321; Kelly 1939; Downs 1961:369–372; Freed and Freed 1963:42–49; Jorgensen 1980:560–561, 619). Spirit power was a personal experience, acquired in secrecy (W.Z. Park 1938:20–32). It revealed its physical character in dreams and visions. When a practicing shaman was called on duty, he sometimes brought along visual representations of each one of his spirit powers, a custom presumably borrowed from neighboring peoples, inasmuch as shamanistic costume and emblems were more common in the Plateau and in northern California than in the Great Basin (W.Z. Park 1938:33–36, 129–130, 149). His professional power was therefore neither "unseen" nor ubiquitous, as has sometimes been said. It was an entity at the disposal of the owner when called upon in a prayer.

In California, west of the Sierra Nevada sources of spirit power for treating sickness mostly were from animals, whereas east of the Sierra they were often inanimate objects (fig. 1) and phenomena: mountains, trees, and peculiarly shaped rocks (fig. 2) as well as meteorological forces and mythical beings living in nature (Steward 1933b:308ff.; Driver 1937:142; W.Z. Park 1938:15; O.C. Stewart 1941:444). When doctoring, a shaman might have talked to Wind, Cloud, and Rain; but the prime example of attaching personal power to physical nature in shamanistic practice among Numic-speaking peoples was the personification of "Darkness"

Fig. 1. Sacred places of the Eastern Shoshone of Wind River Reservation, Wyo., areas of supernatural power and thus sources of danger. top, Bull Lake, home of a mysterious, malevolent water buffalo (Shimkin 1947a:349) and meeting place of ghostly hand game players who sometimes gave power to those who sought it. bottom, Pictographs representing Ghost Beings at Dinwoody Canyon. Photographs by Demitri Shimkin, top, 1937, bottom, 1966. .

(W.Z. Park 1938:19). The preferred time for shamanistic activity was night. If the shaman could not complete the ritual in one night, then he must wait until another night had elapsed and finish his work on the third night (W.Z. Park 1938:48). Shortly before daybreak, "behind the night," some increased darkness was thought to occur, noticed only by those few endowed with spirit power. This was "the second night" described in some detail by Park's informants, when the power of the shaman grew in proportion to the depth of darkness, called *natógacabihu* 'concentrated darkness'. A Northern Paiute speaker compared the sudden onset of "the second night" with swarming bees landing on a dry tree. Thus although the common belief that a Northern Paiute doctor got his power confirmed by the "spirit of the night" is somewhat imprecise, the fact remains that "Darkness" appeared to the shaman as a living advisor and source of healing power.

Extemporaneous public prayers in Shoshone dialects

U. of Calif., Dept. of Anthr., Archaeol. Research Facility, Berkeley: 7000.
Fig. 2. Dan Voorhees, Northern Paiute, standing next to a rock with pictographs said to have supernatural powers. Photograph by Omer C. Stewart, near Schurz, Nev., 1936.

displaying remarkable rhetorical diction have been studied by Shimkin (1947a:351–352, 1953). Unpublished records of Northern Paiute prayers from seasonal dances and other festivals await transcription and translation. The elaborate oral rituals involved in shamanistic healing, the most common ceremonialism among the Great Basin Indians in precontact times, are virtually unknown. Beside Park's well-known works, there is a detailed study of shamanistic practice in general, well exemplified when it was still a living tradition (Kelly 1939). But formal study of incantation, songs, and dialogues at shamanistic séances has been deplorably neglected, although there are phonographic records of a few accidentally recorded shamanistic songs. Steward (1933b:278–279) published two such song texts from Owens Valley, one of which, sung by a Panamint shaman, is set to a melody reminiscent of the local Round Dance songs in repeated phrases but with nonsense syllables. Three samples in English translation appear in Natches (1923:258–259).

The shaman had learned his song at some secret place at the same time as he obtained his spirit power; however, he was under the obligation to "forget" his song between the times when it was needed. When treating a sick person, the shaman was accompanied by his assistant interpreter, the only one familiar with his practice and manner of talking. This person, called Northern Paiute *póinabi* 'talker' or Shoshone *tek*ʷ*awapi*, best translated 'speech master', acted as the doctor's manager, arranging time and place of doctoring and in various ways mediated between him and his audience. People present used to join in the shaman's song together with the assistant interpreter. Without his (or her) comments, the shaman would not have been understood (Kelly 1932:189–195; Steward 1933b:315, 1941:260–261; W.Z. Park 1938:50, 95, 97, 126–129; O.C. Stewart 1941:413). In most places, the term for a practicing shaman was the same, Shoshone *pohakanti*, Northern Paiute *puhága'yu*, Mono *puhágetu*, Kawaiisu *pohagadɨ*, all meaning 'possessor of power'. An interesting exception occurred in the lake area of the northwestern Great Basin. Here the individual shaman was called in Northern Paiute *puhágam·i*, the plural form of the same noun. That is, when talking about the doctor, both he and his assistant had to be mentioned, which seems to point to a more firmly developed shamanistic institution in this subarea. Here also, a shaman of advanced age often possessed multiple spirit powers obtained in different revelations, presumably the primary reason for employing the plural suffix (Catherine S. Fowler, personal communication 1984).

The radically independent self-expression inherent in Great Basin shamanism prevented the development of fixed ritual patterns and standardized shamanistic song texts. The only exception is the shaman's incantations at the communal antelope drives, traditional songs and formulas remembered long after the custom was dropped. These antelope drives, held at irregular intervals of many years, temporarily brought together a larger number of people than any other communal activity and were controlled by a shaman with power to charm the antelopes (Lowie 1924:302–305, 1939:324–325; Steward 1938a). In Northern Paiute he was called *tin·á timádaidi* ('antelope wonder-worker'). As antelope power was a rare gift, competent antelope shamans were often summoned from distant places. During the nights preceding the drive, the shaman sang, accompanying himself by bowing a stick over a rawhide bundle. The following song was recorded in 1962 from a 92-year-old Northern Paiute speaker from the Fort McDermitt Reservation, who had learned it in the 1890s from an antelope shaman at Summit Lake. Even though the text is set to a melody typical of Great Basin song style and follows the same rhythmic pattern, it is a magic formula in mode and function. It is given here in phonetic transcription (the letters ẓ and ᶎ mark voiced apical and front-dorsal positional allophones of the /s/ phoneme):

haya·wiai, haya·wiai
haya·wiai, haya·wih

ʔiẓíẓayukaβi káupaẓumina kim·ákaiku
ʔiẓíẓayukaβi káupaẓumina kam·ákaiku.

This stanza was repeated ad infinitum. The first two lines are exhortative but otherwise meaningless vocalizations, and the words in the second two are: *ʔisi-* 'gray' + *sayúkabi* 'dried up sagebrush'; *káupa* 'leg' or 'legs' + *-sumina* (an archaic utterance of uncertain meaning); and *kim·ákaiku* 'begin(s) to approach gradually'. The esoteric meaning was explained to be: The singing shaman imagines and wishes that the legs of "the gray one" (the gray buck who used to lead a large herd) would become "like dried up sagebrush." Unaware of this, the antelope would gradually approach leading the herd, whereupon they would be captured in a previously built sagebrush enclosure and killed by the hunters.

Siskin (1983:79) denies the existence of Washoe shamans specializing in antelope charming, in conformity with the general "lack of specialization which marks the Washo spirit world." However, it seems that the Washoe "antelope chief" (Lowie 1939:325) had the same power to capture the soul of the animal as did his Northern Paiute counterpart. As long as it lasted, antelope shamanism among the Washoe evidently retained its share of verbal magic, presumably more or less informal judging from the following apparently extemporaneous formula recorded in 1926 (Lowie 1963:15–16; William Jacobsen, personal communication 1984):

gaʔlóǩašé·s   ʔáyis,   ke hamómoyaŋ gepíʔšuk.
Don't get scared   antelope,   slowly   come here.

gapá·šuk máŋala.   gaʔlóǩašé·saʔ.   máŋal
Come in to your house.   Don't get scared. Your house

ke ǩéʔle.   ladámaléʔweʔ.
  it is.   Obey me.

Poetry and Verse

There has been a tendency among anthropologists to suggest that most Indian songs in the Great Basin, as elsewhere, contained only meaningless vocables. This is true of certain widely diffused song styles: the gambling songs; songs borrowed across linguistic boundaries in the twentieth century, many of them of a religious or ritualistic character like the Sun Dance or the Peyote songs, and the Round Dance songs among the Washoe; and the Plains-style war-dance songs, sung by a chorus of men to the rhythm of a big drum with which they accompany solo dancers in fancy costumes. On the other hand, there are songs incontestably of Great Basin origin, and limited to that area, that have meaningful texts, including even the songs of shamans, although the shaman and his interpreter may well be the only ones who know the meaning of his cryptic words.

Formal verse with meaningful words served as lyrical song texts, usually with dances or in other social con-

nections, sometimes as songs spontaneously composed by the singer. Very little pertinent field data has appeared in print, although there are substantial collections of sound recordings both in archival and in private holdings awaiting scholarly attention. A detailed analysis of Shoshone song texts is Shimkin's (1947a) study. Although brief and precisely worded, these song texts display a formal structure of considerable complexity. Hymes's (1965) analysis of selected poems for the Northwest Coast also has direct bearing on the Round Dance poetry of the Great Basin Indians. Crum (1980) has published a short but thorough study of four representative Shoshone songs; a phonological appendix by Wick R. Miller supports her analysis.

Most recorded song texts with poetic themes were sung to ancient dances, local variants of the Round Dance, the fundamental choreographic form in the Great Basin and the only one distributed throughout the area. Among the multitude of sacral and secular dances practiced by the aboriginal population in early contact times, only this form and the more spectacular "back-and-forth" or Bear Dance, which originated among the Utes, were truly indigenous. Both types antedate the use of drums; but the Bear Dance songs were sung to the accompaniment of the musical rasp (a notched stick with a basket resonator) and had incoherent texts that seldom rose to the level of structural compositions. At a late date verbalized song texts disappeared entirely, as the dance, together with the songs, spread into other Numic speech communities. The Round Dance, on the other hand, everywhere retained its musical style: songs with meaningful texts chanted in unison without instrumental accompaniment. This singular and indeed noteworthy dance was presumably the only one originally known to the Great Basin Indians. It has been described by Steward (1933b:320–321, 1941:265–267, 352–353, 1943a:287–288, 349–350) as "the old, native Great Basin dance" but locally "specialized in several forms." With joined hands, moving clockwise in a circle, facing one another, the dancers slightly flex the right knee while stepping to the left. The name of the dance depends on which aspect of dancing is emphasized in the particular area where the inquiry was made. The most common term for the Round Dance is formed on the Numic verb 'to dance': Northern Paiute *nigába*, Shoshone *nikappih*, and Southern Paiute *nikkappi*. Southern Paiute also has *kiyappi* (Sapir 1930–1931:636) and *kwinunip* (Kelly 1964:104), apparently a literal translation of English Round Dance. In Shoshone, there is also the descriptive term *nataya·ti*, literally 'lifting feet together'. The Washoe term *sešíši* is from a verb *íši* 'to drag or to shuffle one's feet' (William Jacobsen, personal communication 1984). A variant of the Round Dance is called Northern Paiute *naníẓakana naníka*, literally 'dancing together holding each other around the shoulders'. In Mono (and sporadically elsewhere) this dance is also called *waigi nigati* 'side dance'. Northern Shoshone also has *nuakkinna*, based on a verb *nua-* 'to move' cognate with what Miller (1972) gives as *numa* 'to do the circle dance'; from the same verb comes *nuahupia* 'Round Dance songs'. Nowadays, this old dance in some places is called "squaw dance" in English, because the women choose their partners (cf. Lowie 1915:832–833), but this is not a direct translation of a native term. Local choreographic style is reflected in the rhythmic patterns of the dance songs and indirectly in the poetry in general.

The Round Dance songs have been thoroughly studied by Herzog (1935) in connection with the 1889–1890 Ghost Dance. The Northern and Eastern Shoshone acted as intermediaries in spreading the movement from its distribution center among the Northern Paiute of western Nevada to the Plains tribes, and with it the musical form and compositional patterns of the Round Dance songs (Mooney 1896; Jorgensen 1972). Although this last resurgence of the Ghost Dance as a religious movement did not last long, was mostly disregarded in the Great Basin even at that time, and was completely forgotten in the 1980s (Kelly 1932:179–180, 1964:105–106; Du Bois 1939; Steward 1941:325, 1943a:288; O.C. Stewart 1941:445), the songs associated with it were remembered. In the absence of other choreographic types, the Round Dance, as well as its musical style, assumed at times a devout character that it had presumably never had before. But expressions for this genre based on the stem *coa-* 'ghost' in certain marginal districts (Owens Valley Pauite *coahubia* and Northern Shoshone *coahupia* 'ghost dance songs', Northern Shoshone *coanikkappi* and Eastern Shoshone *coanikakkinna* 'Round Dance') do not represent ancient Great Basin tradition, and the oft-repeated belief that the genre originated with the Ghost Dance religion is a misconception. It did so among the Indians of the Plains, but not in the Great Basin. Here the Round Dance and the related songs remained secular, occurring at any festival occasion (for a different interpretation, see W.Z. Park 1941:198–202). As this old dance type spread to the east with the Ghost Dance movement and adapted to its new ritualistic function, in a different cultural setting and in another linguistic environment, the songs retained their unique melodies but with different lyrics.

Along with a great similarity in musical style, all extant Great Basin Round Dance songs have one thing in common: unless a song refers directly to the dance as such, each song is an image in miniature of a scene from nature. To use Sapir's (1910a:455) term they are "non-ceremonial," devoid of ritual. "Dances were danced largely for immediate satisfaction" (Steward 1941:216), and their popularity points to entertainment rather than a sacral function. The songs express the delight in dancing and the beauty of nature, not its usefulness. But

the Ghost Dance songs of the Plains are concerned with economic and political problems of the day (the reservation life with its misery and distress) no less than with the newly introduced faith: the spirit host advancing with the buffalo at the will of a heavenly Father providing a new earth for his Indian children (Mooney 1896:1061–1103).

This introduced religion gave rise to a new term, *appinikkappi* or *appinikkanna* 'father-dance', among the Northern and Eastern Shoshone (Lowie 1915:817; Steward 1943a:287–288; Shimkin 1947a:350). The dance as such kept its identity regardless of distribution, purpose, or the occasion of performance. It is remembered in association with festivity, enjoyments, and courtship, seldom as a ritual act with religious or sacral implications. Once the songs reached the Plains, they came to express a spiritual abstraction unknown west of the mountains. None of the nine "songs of the Paiute" quoted by Mooney (1896:1052–1055) as samples of Ghost Dance songs alludes to piety, nor does any one of those known from the Great Basin today. These brief ditties, always in one uniform and continually repeated strophe, invariably contain a single clearly outlined picture of animate or inanimate nature, never any abstractions, social or religious ideas, nor health-seeking, as in the Sun Dance. Whereas other verbal art forms include sequences of motifs combined in composition, a Round Dance song contains only one situation, or scene from nature, vividly described in one or two repeated lines. The mode is intuitive rather than contemplative, involving no conscious symbolism or personification. In this respect, such a poem is strikingly similar to a classic Japanese haiku, with the difference that in a Numic dance-song the subject is always impersonal. The Round Dance poet never expressed himself in the first person, as the Ghost Dance singer among the Plains Indians commonly did. These songs constitute the core of Great Basin poetry. Hundreds of them are known in the 1980s although seldom heard, because the Round Dance at tribal festivals is accompanied by hand drums in a new song style borrowed from the Plains.

The pronunciation of words in Numic songs differs from that in ordinary speech in certain systematic ways. In Northern Paiute, the voiced stops, *b*, *d*, *g*, etc., are pronounced as the corresponding fricatives [β, r, γ], etc. In Shoshone, the phonemic geminated consonants, *pp*, *tt*, *kk*, etc., are heard in verse sonorously prenasalized [mb, nd, ŋg], etc., exactly like the phonemic nasal-plus-stop sequences, *mp*, *nt*, *nk*, etc. This occurs in all Shoshone singing quite regularly and occasionally in Northern Paiute, where phonemic nasal-plus-stop sequences do not occur. The trait has been observed elsewhere in American Indian song style. In Ute and Southern Paiute whispered vowels in ordinary speech are restored to their voiced quality in verse. Another poetic license is the prosodic lengthening of short vowels and *647* the breaking of long ones, if the melody so demands. As a consequence, in verse the stress may shift freely from one syllable to another. Most important, the uniformity in style of traditional (not borrowed) song of the Great Basin Indians derives above all from the radical symmetry of parallel construction. The Round Dance songs are strophic, with paired verses of various lengths; a repeated phrase or metric unit occurs with identical verbal and musical content except at the ending of the strophe. This doubling of phrases or entire sentences is sometimes replaced by or complemented with parallelism, that is, rewording in variant forms. For further information about construction of Round Dance song in "paired pattern" see Herzog (1935) and "Music," this volume. The melodic range of these songs is narrow, usually a fifth, sometimes a fourth or a third, as compared to the Ghost Dance songs of the Plains, which have an average range of "an octave or above" (Herzog 1935:410). Seldom does a song text composed for the Round Dance contain more than two lines of meaningful verse, albeit repeated; but within this unassuming verbal range numerous poems of supreme beauty are found, usually anonymous.

Some of these songs have a wide distribution across language boundaries. The following three examples of Round Dance song texts in Northern Shoshone have been chosen for illustration because they are representative in style and are matched by variants on the same themes elsewhere. In these songs the entire poem consists of only one stanza, which for the sake of parallel construction has four, six, or eight verses or lines. The fully developed stanza in this conservative song style usually begins with two cola held together in one musical phrase ending on the tonic and repeated at least once, often three times with the additional vocable fillers in the context. The final syllable of the last verse of the strophe is abbreviated by apocopation. Alternatively, one or two syllables may be added to the last verse in order to denote the end of the stanza. Any reiteration of the stanza is separated from what precedes by a caesura representing one dance step. The texts are in phonetic transcription to illustrate the phonetic modifications of verse, which would not be apparent in a phonemic transcription.

I. pí·a·ʔáŋginándɨ óhandóŋgimbínʒi
   pí·a·ʔáŋginándɨ óhandóŋgimbínʒi
   pábu·ndí·diná·nʒi
   pábu·ndí·diná·nʒi
   hí:na
   pábu·ndí·diná·nʒi
   hí:na
   pábu·ndí·dinà·nd

The large sunflower, the fully yellow flower spreading out
The large sunflower, the fully yellow flower spreading out
From the water-clear root

From the water-clear root
Heena!
From the water-clear root
Heena!
From the water-clear root.

This song begins with two hexasyllabic phrase cola, each one under one principal stress on the first syllable, forming one syntactic nominal sentence repeated once and followed by three identical hexasyllabic verses, a final abbreviated pentasyllabic line, and the expletive emphatic particle *hi·na* or *he·na*, which often occurs in both Numic and Washoe poetry (Warren L. d'Azevedo, personal communication 1984). In phonemic transcription the words in this song are: *piaʔakkinnanti* 'being a large sunflower'; *ohattokipicci* 'fully yellow' *papu·ntitinacci* 'pretty transparent root'.

II. nanás·u·yáγɨ húumbi, nanás·u·yáγɨ húumbi
    nanás·u·yáγɨ húumbi, nanás·u·yáγɨ húumbi
    cinámboŋgóombi éŋgandɨ
    túduwán·ɨ
    cinámboŋgóombi éŋgandɨ
    túduwàn·

Pretty one, the bush; pretty one, the bush
Pretty one, the bush; pretty one, the bush
Root above the ground and rose hips
In string of red
Root above the ground and rose hips
In string of red.

The nominal phrase [cinámboŋgóombi] is apparently a contamination, typical of verse, of [nanámboŋgó·mbi] (found in a variant of this song; with *nana-* 'togetherness' or 'hanging together') and *ciampih* 'wild rose hip'; *pokompih*, elsewhere 'currant(s)', here means 'berry' or 'berries'.

III. tí·sidó·yací·ya· tó·yaní·ga·rúŋga
     tí·sidó·yací·ya· tó·yaní·ga·rúŋga
     tí·sidɨkwá·ruŋgíu
     tí·sidɨkẃa·ruŋgíugìn·a

Freely translated: 'Bluegrass hill, under the side of the hill, the bluegrass waves [in the wind]'. The *-kinna* added to the last line indicates 'motion toward the speaker'. The song was recorded also in an eight-line stanza by the same singer.

The structure in "paired progression" of the examples given above (x representing the metric filling particle) are:

(1) aabbxbxb
(2) aabcbc′
(3) aabb′

Naturally, this does not exhaust the occurrences of paired patterns in Shoshonean poetry, metrical configurations that are well nigh uncountable (Herzog 1935:406–408). Variants with the same motifs as the second and third song texts were widely known and remained popular into modern times (cf. Mooney 1896:1054; Shimkin

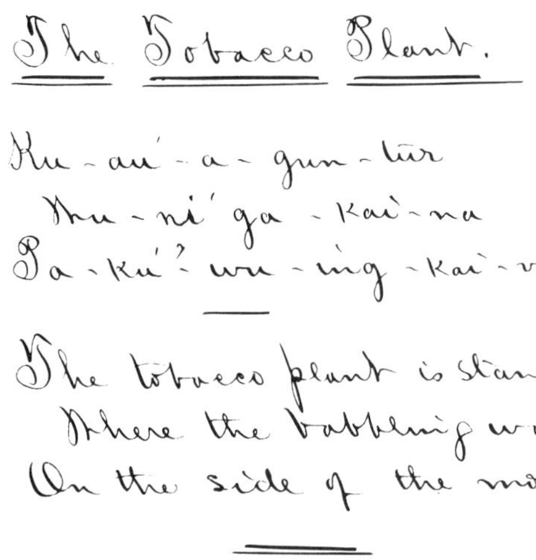

The Tobacco Plant.

Ku-au'-a-gun-tur
Nu-ni' ga-kai-na
Ba-ku'? wu-ing-kai-va.

The tobacco plant is standing
Where the babbling water runs
On the side of the mountain.

Smithsonian, NAA: 831-c.
Fig. 3. A Southern Paiute song used in the Round Dance. Collected in southern Utah. Manuscript by John Wesley Powell, 1870s.

1947a:350). Such songs were among the first recorded and occur in epitomized versions in John Wesley Powell's field records from the Southern Paiutes in the early 1870s (Fowler and Fowler 1971:128). Most songs in Powell's classic collection (fig. 3) prove to be "song-recitatives," that is, songs with mythological association detached from the tale types to which they originally belonged (Fowler and Fowler 1971:121–128). Nevertheless, an indefinite number of Powell's "Songs and Chants" are to all appearance abridged Round Dance song texts with repetitive verse excluded. Generally, the dance songs evoke a purely poetic sentiment with pictures visualized for their own sake (the red clouds at sunset, the trout in the blue water, the hawk on the wing floating in the air). It is a colorful poetry but without abstraction. This subject matter lends additional credence to the observation that dance and song served a social rather than a religious or ritualistic end, at least for most people attending. The social nonritual function of the Round Dance among the Washoe is vividly illustrated in "Various instructions about a Dance," recorded in 1926 (Lowie 1963:7–8). When the dance appeared among the Havasupai and Chemehuevi, the purpose was public entertainment only (Spier 1928:261; Laird 1976:44–45).

Like the shaman, a Round Dance poet (Shoshone *hupiakanti* 'song-owner') was thought to have received his inspiration in dreams. The principal singer leading the dance must have known a fair number of songs, inasmuch as a dance festival lasted four or five nights. After a day of gambling, the dance began toward evening at flaming bonfires and lasted for two or three hours. Dances were held any time of the year but were most common in the fall, when people congregated for communal drives of rabbit or antelope or for the open-

ing of the brief season of picking pine nuts. At Pyramid Lake, the Round Dance was a nightly entertainment during the cui-ui fishing in May, when visitors from other places arrived in order to participate in the catch. The Bannock and the Northern Shoshone lit their dance fires in the evenings of early summer and therefore called the dance respectively *tamánika* and *tawanikka* 'spring-dance'. It is said to promote health in man and fertility in nature, to make grass, seeds, and pine nuts grow, to melt snow and produce rain. The English name Grass Dance is an allusion to this function. Ritualism was incidental and varied and may be looked upon as a matter of afterthought. Any distinction between poetic play and rationalization would be futile, for each participant took an attitude of his own (Lowie 1909:216–223, 1924:298–307, 1939:315; Kelly 1932:178, 1964:103–106; Steward 1933b:320–323, 1941:265, 323–324, 352–353, 1943a:287–290, 349–350; O.C. Stewart 1941:415–416, 444; W.Z. Park 1941:183–198; Downs 1961:382–383; Crum 1980:3, 5).

Songs with meaningful texts sung by people in gatherings vanished simultaneously with the gradual extinction of the native dialects and the adaptation of dances and art forms borrowed from neighboring peoples, using song styles with meaningless vocalization. However, a variety of lyric poetry formerly in vogue has mostly been overlooked or omitted in the ethnographic literature of the area or has remained buried in unpublished collections. Samples known are less complex than the fully developed dance songs, but the same poetic devices in doubling phrases and verses are used. There was, for example, in the northeasterly sector of the area a category of songs featuring humorous or sarcastic allusions seemingly composed for a particular occasion and sung in chorus by young men about a peer at odds with the group. The following text is translated from the Shoshone original but with the repetitive lines excluded: 'When we were going up [to the mountains] to chop pinewood for making cups, you did not want to go, my friend'. Under the telling title "mocking songs," Shimkin (1947a:350–351) quotes a more artful variant in 14 lines. Another class of poetry expressing common sense and social control consists of versified proverbial utterances, for example, the warning to a disobedient child: "Coyote might carry you off on his tail." Crum (1980:5–8) has analyzed a poem relating to this topic in two versions, one of them translated as follows:

> Furry Wolf
> On his tail
> He carries him away
> Carries him away
> Carries him away
> Upon his tail
> He carries the child away.

Three or four songs with proverbial themes occur in   *649*

Powell's collection from the Southern Paiute (Fowler and Fowler 1971:127).

The people themselves used to classify their secular lyrics not by form or by content but according to the occasion of use. There were songs for nightly entertainment performed as duets, Shoshone *k^wapihupia* 'lying-down songs' and others called *titayotihupia* 'waking-up songs'. In the same northeasterly subarea there were also *mahimiahupia* 'going-to-war songs', and unlike the other songs the relative age of these can be dated. The warfare referred to is the horse-stealing raiding parties into territories of neighboring tribes during the late eighteenth and early nineteenth centuries. These songs, remembered in the 1980s, are said to have been sung not by the young adventurers themselves but by people waiting for them to return. The content of the texts seems to verify this assumption. The following samples are free translations from Northern Shoshone originals:

I. I wonder who went to war
   Leaving his little brother behind,
   Standing alone.

II. Her brother went away.
    She took his ring and kept it.
    She cried when he left.
    She heard her brother coming back.
    His sister took the ring and came out.
    Then he began to smile.

III. Wake up, wake up!
     Start walking, friends!
     I guess our sisters are sitting thinking.
     Take rest for a day!

This poetry contains the same denigration of bravery and heroism as in the later historical legends. This is to be expected in any sector of Great Basin culture, even when overlaid with traditions from the Plains.

Storytelling

The content of narrative forms is of two kinds: legendary stories about experiences and events supposed to have occurred in times still remembered, and stories about events happening in a timeless mythological age. This distinction is recognized by the raconteurs themselves. Any claim to excellence as a traditional storyteller depended on mastering the system of narrative techniques regardless of topic. The term for storytelling whether public or private is Shoshone *natik^winappi*, Northern Paiute *nadí·g^winaba*, literally 'telling each other stories', a reciprocal pursuit. After finishing a detail of the plot, the storyteller used to pause for response or questions, whereupon he repeated or rephrased his utterance. Thus, an episode or a single phrase would recur in the same or in a slightly different form, as the narrator continued his story step by step. Repetition also gave the narrator an opportunity to elaborate an incident with epic embellishment. The fact that storytelling used to occur within the frame of conversation between the narrator and his audience is obscured in published tale collections, owing either to incomplete recording or to omission of repetition. Later, when phonographic recording became available, it sometimes happened that a storyteller refused to cooperate unless another speaker of the language was present to "answer" him properly. Another obstacle in former days to recording storytelling verbatim was the dependence on an interpreter. The mythological tales, told by an artistically skilled person, depicted the course of events in pictorial style. The storyteller depended on eidetic imagery, a clear visualization of the sequence. Interrupted by interviewer and interpreter, he sometimes complained that he "lost sight" of what happened as the story unfolded in his vivid imagination.

Few persons professed to know the lore of the ancients, and most were either incapable or reluctant to tell a mythological tale as it should be told. Men and women were equally well informed, but in mixed company old men assumed the leadership each excelling in his own narrative style; occasionally two narrators exchanged stories. The importance attached to storytelling, not only as entertainment but also for its presumed educational value, made the storyteller an indispensable member of the local group. Yet his audience was modest, often consisting only of the members of the family and a neighbor or two who might drop in for the evening. In the flickering light of the tiny fire in the center of the flimsy winter dwelling, people huddled in their rabbitskin blankets, listening to stories they had known since childhood but never tired of hearing again. Storytelling, an important social event, was hedged about by strict rules and taboos. For all, it was seasonally restricted. The proper time was after the pine nut harvest in the late fall and winter. In the southern part of the Great Basin, violation of this rule was punished by people in the community being bitten by rattlesnakes; in the north, violent storms might occur. Good manners would not only prevent people from taking food after dark, but also from telling tales by daylight. Storytelling as well as shamanistic practice must occur in the late evening, "in darkness," when people were resting from the hardships of the day but before falling asleep. The storyteller continued as long as he received an answer; but the story must be brought to an end or be resumed the following night.

Fig. 4. Andrew Johnson, a Northern Shoshone storyteller from Ft. Hall Reservation, Idaho. He is relating a mythological tale using a rhythmic language and a succession of tones in speech covering a full octave. The constant motion of his hands, a narrative technique that he shared with most professional storytellers, is not a sign language but gesticulatory symbolism paralleling the spoken word. Photograph by Sven Liljeblad, 1941.

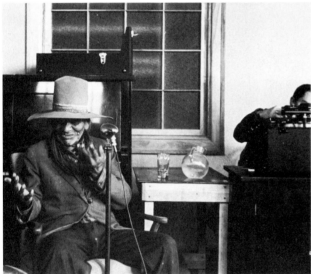

Legendary Narratives

There are no boundaries between verifiable historical memories and legendary fiction. Sometimes these stories are localized and regarded as the incorporeal property of people descended from the principal actor in the story; however, identical realistic stories with human characters do occur as migratory legends in places far apart. The ultimate horizon of personal history coincides with the time-depth of known genealogy. In most cases this is the grandparental generation of the speaker. Most historical legends recorded by 1900 would therefore refer to early postcontact time. There is an emotional keynote of privation and misfortune in many of these narratives. Typical examples are the often recurring almost identical stories about cannibalism sometimes told as having been committed by a relative of the victim, by early White travelers, or by man-eating shamans (witches) practicing ritual cannibalism (Kroeber 1901:280–285; Lowie 1909:290–292, 1939:347; Steward 1938a:190; Smith 1940:109–118; Miller 1972:33–37; Laird 1976:32–33, 1977:100; Zigmond 1980:205). That these stories of anthropophagy, even when recorded in autobiographical accounts, are legendary, is further borne out by their having been characterized as the act of a "cannibal witch" and as "unwitting," "occasional," or "deliberate cannibalism," motifs *G11.3*, *G60*, *G70*, (*77* and *79*) in S. Thompson's (1955–1958) motif index. The entire complex—the realistic stories in their relation to legends about man-eating ogres (Motif *G11.2*)—is treated by Smith (1940:60–75).

Historical memories became traditional legends to the extent that they adapted to standardized motifs, varying in different subareas. Wherever they occur, these stories tell about individuals or families in conflict with hostile groups (Lowie 1924a:78–84, 242). As distinguished from the mythological tales, they are epic in a realistic sense and told at some length in a matter-of-fact style. The stories of any actual historical value concern memories from the time of incipient band-formation, of people in the process of militarization (Steward 1938:202, 258–260). Their distribution seems limited to the northern frontier, and they are told in Northern Shoshone and Northern Paiute (Bannock), though in the mid-twentieth century they were told usually in colloquial English. Recurring themes are of intertribal conflicts and calamities caused by raiding parties of northern Plains Indians crossing the mountains in order to rob the equestrian Shoshones of horses and women. The advent of the horse, perhaps in the 1690s and surely by the mid-eighteenth century, gives a terminus a quo for the historical events upon which these narratives are based. In spite of some obvious anachronisms, names of persons and topographic details are sometimes sufficient for ethnohistoric identification. Both bow and gun are mentioned. Details told in the journals of the

651

fur hunters recur as motifs in these family sagas in which women invariably are the heroines, foreseeing and warning of approaching disaster, as in the following epitome of a detailed epic narrative recorded in Bannock in 1950:

> Darkness closed in on an isolated camp of Bannock hunters—three men, two young women and a small child. They had pitched their tipi near a pine grove in a sheltered glade facing a willow-fringed river. The night was moonlit, with drifting clouds throwing dark shadows over the glen. The women thought they could discern human figures in the shade of the willows, shapes darker than the dusk in which they crawled. The dog was barking furiously. The frightened women cautioned the men, who slothfully continued to warm their backs at the fire. The camp leader, an old man and their father-in-law, admonished the two women to calm down: now was the time when the coyotes were mating, and it was at them that the dog was barking. The women dared take no chance. After caching their few belongings and loosening the bottom of the tipi cover opposite the entrance, they went to bed with their moccasins on. Toward daybreak, which is the darkest time of night, when enemies operating in secret would be most active, the attack came, anticipated by no one except the women, who escaped with the child into the woods. The sun was high in the sky when the two fugitives looked down on their camp from the heights beyond. The camp was in flames. They could see the raiders burning utensils and supplies and bringing in the horses. The men selected the horses they wanted to ride; and, with three Bannock scalps waving in the wind, the riders disappeared over the ridges. When evening came, the braver of the two women returned to the devastated camp to dispose of the bodies and pick up what little was left to save. As she dumped the mutilated body of her father-in-law into the river, the girl muttered to herself: "How badly bitten you are by those mating coyotes." Then followed the lonesome journey of the two women back to their people, to inform them of the outcome of the hunting expedition. The abandoned women concluded with the remark, "Those men did not take warning." (Liljeblad 1971a).

A warning by women of approaching danger, disregarded by the men but proved in the event to be real, is a common theme (cf. Lowie 1924a:83). Common also are stories about women escaping from their Piegan and Assiniboine abductors. These exciting adventures describe the perilous homeward journeys of the heroines, the escapes always successfully completed in the stories. But such accounts are not always consistent with those of the fur trade journals.

Historical legends are rare in published collections. A variety of stories about supernatural beings is more common. These narratives represent aboriginal cosmological beliefs, a world view very different from that of the mythological tales and logically incompatible with it. The legends are usually localized within one tribal territory and are assumed to be the recollection of a known individual. They reflect autochthonous but still productive folk belief, in contrast to mythological tale types, which are composed of chimerical motifs of universal distribution. As the storyteller did not have an established cosmology that could integrate the borrowed motifs, stories with contradictory motifs were often told on the same occasion. Yet a basic concept of existence held in common was definitely expressed as a simple dichotomy: there is no world above the one we live in, but there is a populated underground, a dogma stated in the Northern Paiute formula *ibí tam·íduha nimí tiwás·u ibíhu mi²í* 'it is told that under us there are people, too'. The fabulous idea of an otherworld or a secluded place from which game animals emerge (Motif *F127*) or are finally released by the culture hero (Motif *A1421*) (S.Thompson 1955–1958) was commonly held in most parts of native North America and can be assigned to the same category of mythological tales as other cosmogonic mythology (see S.Thompson 1929:348). Independently of mythology, the belief in accidental visits to the mysterious world below was found throughout the Great Basin (Motif *F102*), reflected in a particular class of testimonial legends describing subterranean existence.

The prototype of these legends, with local variants, relating visits to the lower world (Motif *F100*), occurs throughout a common culture area comprising the western Great Basin (W.Z. Park 1933–1940,2:43, 44, 64, 3:63–68, 108, 4:28–29; Gayton and Newman 1940:17, 74; Zigmond 1980:175–178). Caves and other named localities, which remained sacred sites for the shamanistic power quest (fig. 5), are believed to have served formerly as entrances to the legendary underground pathway. The recurrent theme in these stories is the adventures of a hunter following a wounded animal to the lower world and his return after a time spent with the dwellers down below. The legendary underworld was no Hades but a delightful place, a populated, beautiful valley with plenty of game, green grass, and streams flowing from the mountains lined with willows and cottonwood, an idealized copy of human life on earth. Thus, the gloomy underground passage wrapped in obscurity leading to "the land to which the dead go" mentioned by Powell in his field notes from Southern Paiute (Fowler and Fowler 1971:67–69) is a unique record, although the idea, presumably a postcontact feature, was voiced elsewhere (Lowie 1909:301–302; W.Z. Park 1933–1940,3:108). Another type occurs with the Kawaiisu: health, shamanistic singing, and inexhaustible food (Motif *F166*) are procured from the patron of the underworld, but the entrance is blocked by rocks that open and close (the Symplegades Motif *D1553*). In other variants of the same story (see for example, W.Z. Park 1933–1940) people down below have no mouths and subsist by inhaling the smoke from frying meat. This secondary so-called bizarre motif (*F513.0.3*) borrowed from mythology marks the incongruity between the natural and supernatural. In all other respects, everything told is true to real life, a concretization of the belief in a populated underworld, a cosmic duality at the bottom

Catherine S. Fowler, Reno, Nev.

Fig. 5. A cave in western Nev. where shamanistic power is sought. Photograph by Willard Z. Park, about 1934.

of all existence, though with time in reversed order: day prevailing with them, when there is night in the world of man. Persons who made the adventurous journey could return only by observing the taboos neither to speak to the people below (Motif *C405*) nor to eat their food (Motif *C211*) (S. Thompson 1955–1958). Among Great Basin peoples these stories, often supported by details claimed to be memories of historically named persons, have remained the most common legends. The same world view is reflected in the belief that wind arises from cavities or depressions thought to be connected with the netherworld (Northern Paiute *hikʷápa tó·* 'holes of the wind') known in most localities.

The relative paucity of indigenous mythological tale types (as compared to the folkloristic inventory of surrounding culture areas) is compensated for by an extremely rich tradition of localized narratives about supernatural beings that populate nature. The greater part of these stories, still considered to be factual (cf. Miller 1972:27), tell about localized encounters with anthropomorphic characters, whose appearance and behavior, even when eidetically observed, are dictated by legendary tradition. Mostly apparitions of this kind appear

either as diminutive images of man or as giants. There are throughout the intermontane region a multitude of persistent testimonial stories about a water sprite of evil disposition, a creature still observed today by old and young, called the Water Baby, a literal translation of Shoshone *páʔohma·ʔa* and *páuhna·* and Northern Paiute *paúŋa·ʔa*. The Washoe equivalent *meċuŋéʔ* (William Jacobsen, personal communication 1984) was apparently borrowed from Northern Paiute, with the replacement of the prefix *pa-* 'water' by the equivalent Washoe prefix *me-*. In English, this small but immensely powerful and greatly feared personage is referred to as "he" or "she" indiscriminately, because in the native languages neither nouns nor pronouns are inflected for gender. People who had seen and associated with the Water Baby (for example shamans with water-baby power) describe it as female, and it has remained so in the minds of most people. In the mythological tales, supernatural water beings also may appear in various anthropomorphic shapes. There is, for example, Ute Pánaputc or Pā·ᵃpatsi, Water-boy, who wrestles with various mythological characters (J.A. Mason 1910:319; Lowie 1924a:27). The Owens Valley Paiutes knew about *pacugucíʔi* (*pa-* 'water' + *cugucíʔi* 'old man') and *pahibicíʔi* 'the dear old water-woman'. Another term occurring in Mono folklore, but always in the plural, is *paʒiʒíʔa* 'water little girls', that is, little girls living in the Owens River. The Water Baby is usually a solitary sprite, dwelling in streams, lakes, or springs, making nightly visits to people's camps and stealing babies left unguarded by their mothers or pulling people into the river (Motif *K1022.2.1*). Water Babies may, however, be seen trooping. In Washoe lore, they occur as social beings, both male and female (Motif *F420.2.2*) (S.Thompson 1955–1958), living in houses in the depths of Lake Tahoe (Lowie 1939:322). No other legendary beings in Great Basin oral tradition have attracted such popularity as this persistent belief in water sprites. The Owens Valley Paiutes tell that even *ninimís·i*, the man-eating giant, was dragged down into the water and drowned by *paúha*, alias *pacoʔáŋʷa*, the Water Baby (Steward 1936b:424–425). For further references see W.Z. Park (1938:15–19, 77–78), Smith (1940,1:111–116, 2:97–100), O.C. Stewart (1941:444), Downs (1961:366–367, 1966:62–63), Freed and Freed (1963:44), Kelly (1964:159–160), Fowler and Fowler (1971:66, 75–76, 224–225), Siskin (1983:23–25, 30–31, 70–71).

The Water Baby concept is found in the Great Basin, California, and the Plateau. The Nez Perce, living immediately north of the Northern Shoshone, knew the Water Baby as a benevolent figure by the name of *papyú·mes* (Liljeblad 1960). At second dentition, a child was expected to offer each discarded milktooth to the Water Baby while uttering the formula:

papyú·mes tít takláynim,
papyú·mes tít takláynim.

'Water Baby, trade a tooth with me!' The Northern Paiute had the same custom, but *kaŋí tibízoni*, the Old Sage Woman, a personification occurring only in this connection, was substituted for the evil Water Baby. The change of name and character is easily explained: the purple sage (*Salvia carnosa*) was used for tooth medicine (W.Z. Park 1933–1940, 2:55–70, 3:98–99). The Chemehuevis observed the same practice, but the water sprite there is replaced by *hucipama·ʔipici*, Old Ocean Woman (Laird 1974:21, 1976:45–46), a personage of mythological dignity, apparently a loan from southern California, who figures in cosmogonic tales and is also the Old Woman of the Sea of Southern Paiute mythology (Fowler and Fowler 1971:73, 78, 160). The Water Baby and the man-eating ogres (fig. 6, right) are the only mythological personages that both play the role of adversary in conflict with characters from the myth age and come as apparitions to persons endowed with "second sight" (Jorgensen 1960:111–112).

In the past, when preparing a communal rabbit drive, the Owens Valley Paiutes used to sing what is called today a "prayer song to nature," beginning:

[tóyazúgunímicíʔ ní·dí·pi]
"The little old man in the mountain—I am."

The epithet is one of several noa names—another is Shoshone *toyanimi* 'mountain-man' for the dwarf commonly called Southern Paiute *inippici* or Shoshone *ninimpi* (fig. 6, left) or some other name based on the root *ini-*, or *nini-*, words suggesting something terrifying or harmful (cf. Goss 1967:8; Crapo 1976:62; Zigmond 1977:63–69). Northern Paiute *nini·ʔi* 'bogeyman' is used as a word of warning when disciplining children. In legends and memorates, conceptions of the mountain dwarf (Motif *F451:5.2*), who leaves footprints as long as a finger, are best summed up by Steward (1943a:282–286, 367). "The little fellow, traveling at the timberline" (Owens Valley) and armed with bow and arrow, has remained a central figure in Numic folklore. Both solitary and trooping, he sometimes shows himself as a pygmy less than five inches tall (Motif *F535*). He may then occur as a bright green miniature, as microoptically perceived imaginary beings often do (Motif *F451.2.7.2*). In his relation to man, *ninimpi* displays the same ambivalent attitude as the Water Baby. An invisible arrow from his quiver (Motif *D1655.1.1*) would cause sickness in man and animals, and people are reluctant to utter his name (Lowie 1909:234–235). The equestrian Northern Shoshone and Bannock blamed *ninimpi* for driving the horses up into the mountains. On the other hand, as the patron of animals, he would help hunters locate game; and he bestowed his spirit power only upon "good men," assuring successful shamanistic doctoring (W.Z. Park 1938:77–79; Steward 1943a:282).

Unlike mythological personages characterized as animals, the legendary beings whom people might meet face to face in everyday life are with few exceptions anthropomorphic and can be appeased by informal offerings of game or other food (Steward 1941:263). Exceptions are certain legendary motifs also adapted to mythology and therefore no longer widely believed in. For it is the possible reality of supernatural beings that constitutes the great difference between the legends and the mythological tales of a chimerical and timeless ex-

U. of Nev. Reno, Sven S. Liljeblad Coll.

Fig. 6. Representations of mythological beings. left, Water Baby and the mountain dwarf (Shoshone *ninimpi*); right, man-eating ogre carrying its human victim. Drawn in color by Smoke, Northern Shoshone storyteller from Ft. Hall Reservation, Idaho, 1941.

654

istence. Overlapping does occur between current legend and mythology, however. There are legends about man-eating ogres of superhuman size, who also figure as frightening characters in the mythological tales. The Owens Valley Paiute called the dreadful giant roaming their valley *Ninimís·i*. The Mono Lake Northern Paiute told of two such monsters, Tse´nahāhā and Pü´wihi (Steward 1936b:428); their names imitate the weird chanting the giants make when approaching their victims. The latter term, Northern Paiute *piwihi* or *pikʷihi*, was apparently a noa word (cf. W.Z. Park 1933–1940, 1:32–33); the current expression, *páiʒa*, is a colloquialism from the generic term *pahíco²o*, of unknown origin and etymology. The Shoshones envision this class of supernatural beings, still common in Great Basin folklore, as a solitary figure, named in the literature Tsoavits (*coapicci*), a term etymologically related to Shoshone *co²appi* 'ghost'. They still call the Sawtooth Mountains in south-central Idaho *coapiccan kahni* 'the giant's house', just as the Washoe call a peak overlooking Topaz Lake *hanawíywiy ²áŋal*, meaning the same thing (Dangberg 1968:20). In Washoe folklore, the various manifestations of this cyclops, who is at home in the Sierras, differ in many details; he occurs as several different characters under a variety of names (William Jacobsen, personal communication 1984). Thus, *hanawíywiy* and *wé·²muhu* are proper names referring to his chanting call. Avoiding these terms, people also used descriptive noa names, for example *saw²móŋo* (*saw²-* 'limping'), because the legends picture the giant as a one-legged monster (Motif *F331.1.3.3.1*), or *beyuwéwiš* (-*wewiš-* 'digging around'—in search of something). Despite the variety of terms applied, the conceptions were largely the same throughout the common area; hence Lowie (1909:234–235) defines a "Dzō´avits cycle" of stories. The theme is the abduction of people by the man-eating ogre (Motif *G440*), in Ute tradition represented by a fabulous race of humanlike creatures, living in a society of their own, and variously called Sī´′ats (Lowie 1924a:74–76) or Siants (Smith 1940,2:101–105, 193–195; Jorgensen 1960:54–55, 110). Elsewhere in the area, the giant appears with only one eye or with large, glowing eyes (Motif *F531.1.1*). People hear his ominous song from a distance, a constant repetition of his own name (Motif *G652*), or his whistling as he enters (Motif *G653*). He paralyzes everybody with his glance (Motif *D2071*), catches his victim with a harpoonlike hook, and carries him off in a conical gathering basket lined with thorns or pine resin (Motif *G441*) (S. Thompson 1955–1958).

Present-day Northern Paiute and Shoshone classification of supernatural beings uses the generic name Northern Paiute *cóabici* and Shoshone *coapicci* in an extended sense. In the plural, this term, particularly in the alternative Northern Paiute form *ticóabi*, is translated 'monsters', 'devils', or 'cannibals'. Northern Paiute has the compound form *sanático²abi*, derived from the stem *sana-* 'pitch', 'pine resin', 'rubber' and translated by competent speakers as 'rubber devils'. The belief in these monsters, who could be killed only by fire (Motif *G512.3*), is firmly rooted in Great Basin mythology. They appear under different names both in the legends and the mythological tales as characters from a pre-human era or as cannibals once living in caves in the mountains but now extinct. Thus, the Northern Paiutes used to call these mythological giants *ni²míʒoho²o* 'people-crushers' from their habit of pounding human victims in mortars, or *wi²wímuhu²u*, a term that imitates their call. The Chemehuevis called them *tutusiwi* and considered them ancestors of the neighboring Mohaves (Laird 1976:160, 256). This mysterious race was also known as Northern Paiute *sáiduka²a* 'under the tule'. Originally, this term was applied to the tribes on the Columbia River who lived in tule-covered longhouses and were often in conflict with the Oregon Northern Paiutes. Ultimately, it came to mean 'foreign enemy'. In anthropological literature, this term has been confused with the group name *sáidika²a* 'tule-eaters' applied to certain local groups who have a marsh-culture economy (cf. O.C. Stewart 1941:431, 440–441). On the other hand, stories about the mythological *sáiduka²a*, their hostility to man, and their final extermination were still popular in the 1980s. These tales tell about people setting on fire the covering of the giant's cave or the hiding place of the resinous monsters and burning them to death.

As often happens with folk beliefs, these mythical tales were rationalized to conform to local reality: the monsters might be depicted as a former population. Most writers on the subject have accepted this latter rationalization of an old mythological motif when interpreting these stories, even though it seems clear that the process is the exact opposite: the idea of supernatural opponents in general is rooted in mythology, not in history. Conventional storytelling in Basin tradition disregards all considerations of chronology; therefore, it would probably not occur to the storyteller to place his or her story in a historical continuum. Moreover, the stories about burning the ogres to death in their own abode (Motif *K812*) have a much wider distribution than the popular quasi-historical interpretation of these stories, which is a secondary erratic tradition told in English and limited to a few localities in western Nevada. The matter has been debated (S.W. Hopkins 1883:73–75; Loud and Harrington 1929:163–168; O.C. Stewart 1941:440–441; Heizer 1966a:245, 1970a:241–242; Fowler and Fowler 1970:123, 143, 1971:218, 285; K.C. Warner 1978). This whole subject has been largely ignored in published reports. There continues to be sporadic mention of encounters with such legendary figures (Lowie 1909:254–262, 1924a:202–205, 242, 1939:347–348; Steward 1936b:429–431, 1941:261; Kelly

1938:366, 369; Natches 1940:11–14; Downs 1961:367–368, 1966:61–63).

Legendary fiction in the Great Basin represents the very image of prevailing folk beliefs and is thoroughly integrated with cultural forms, as the mythological tales are not. Throughout the area, an abundance of ghost stories pictures a ghastly afterlife in the same milieu where life was passed. On the other hand, indigenous stories about a credible afterworld are lacking, a gap in the aboriginal belief system barely filled by postcontact borrowing from biblical motifs. The best-known tale about life and death, the Orpheus myth about a hero who journeys to the land of the dead to bring back his wife, a motif with a world-wide distribution, is conspicuous by its absence (S. Thompson 1929:337–338, 1946:351, 1955–1958; Gayton 1935a; Hultkrantz 1957). Two fragmentary versions recorded from a Pyramid Lake Northern Paiute informant are annotated as unknown to other members of the community (W.Z. Park 1933–1940, 5:98–99, 3:63, 65–68, 1:29, 45–51) and are evidently borrowings from the Plains (Gayton 1935a:277). Powell cited another atypical example from the Southern Paiute (Fowler and Fowler 1971:69); the story is also reported from the Chemehuevis (Laird 1976:40–41).

Any reference to the soul as the seat of life, a clear animistic conception called in Northern Paiute *mugua* (with cognates in the sister languages), is limited to shamanism. The spirit of the shaman would follow the soul of a dying person southward and if possible intercept it before it passed into oblivion. The soul may appear materialized in a variety of forms and, if so, is called Shoshone *coʔappi* or Northern Paiute *coʔapa*; for example one must never follow a butterfly, which, like the apparition of a dead person, is called *coʔappi* in some dialects of Shoshone. The term has a wide range of implications and figure extensions. Miller (1972:145) translates the Shoshone as 'ghost, spirit of a dead person' and relates it to a verb *coʔa* 'to be stunned'; in contemporary Bannock, *coʔápa tamá* means 'false teeth', *coʔapa napíasˑi* 'life-insurance money', and so on. The Panamint Shoshone form of the related term *coapicci*, the man-eating ogre, also means 'the spirits of deceased people' (Kerr 1980:30). The name of the mountain dwarf (Kawaiisu *ʔinipi*, Southern Paiute *inippici*, as well as other Numic cognates) is commonly used as a blanket term for various supernatural beings, but mainly for visible specters. The Washoe, who believed that "the spirits of the dead were to be greatly feared and avoided" (Downs 1966:59–60), used the term *dewYúʔliʔ* (from the root *yúli* 'to die') to mean 'ghost' (William Jacobsen, personal communication 1984).

In aboriginal times, ghost stories were evidently told more frequently than any other kind of fiction. And yet, in the plentiful Northern Paiute narrative material recorded by Willard Park and others there are no stories that suggest the belief in an afterworld or a future life other than the existence of spectral revenants. The realm of the dead was vaguely comprehended, rarely mentioned, and of no mythological importance. The only time when dead people come together is to dance at night, but where this might occur is never made clear. The ghost lurking at the roadside is conceived of as real and described as such; the giant roaming the valley is not. A conservative speaker of Numic is a confirmed realist. He respects everybody's opinion about a future life, even when expressing his own agnosticism.

Mythological Tales

Great Basin mythology constitutes a large body of indigenous local folk narratives. Only those folkloristic features that are unique to each subarea are reviewed here. In the border regions, there are tales with transcontinental distribution, presumably recent borrowings. Thus, the best known of all Northern American Indian stories, the Star Husband tale, told from coast to coast in six different subtypes, is conspicuously rare in the Great Basin and the Southwest. The generalized version, the basic subtype, occurring in both the East and the West, tells about two girls who agree late one evening that each will marry her own favorite star and next morning find themselves in the upper world with their star husbands, their marriages ending in tragedy as the consequence of a broken taboo. Only six versions, all from marginal areas, are reported for the Great Basin: one from the Owens Valley Paiutes, two from the Washoe, two from the Northern Shoshones, and a variation from the Southern Utes. The Mono and the two Washoe versions are evidently derived from Californian tradition represented by a known Maidu record; the two Shoshone records go back to a Plateau prototype, presumably Flathead, and the Ute text is a fragmentary story that must once have been a full-blown Plains version (Reichard 1921; S. Thompson 1946:345–348, 1953; Young 1970; Rich 1971; Catherine Fowler, personal communication 1984). Commonly occurring also among the neighboring Plateau tribes but missing in Great Basin folktale tradition is the universally distributed motif of the hero who reaches the upper world on a chain made of his discharged arrows (S. Thompson 1929:333). The absence of hero tales in the Great Basin also indicates that widespread tale motifs are less often shared with isolated culture areas; as for example, the Twin Heroes begotten by the sun and born to a human mother, a tale motif of worldwide distribution recorded in fragmentary versions from Ute speakers on the southern border but nowhere else in the Great Basin (Wycoco 1951:198–203). These and a few other tales with related motifs are marginal to the area at large. This may be explained by the importance attached by the storytellers among Great Basin peoples to an imaginary underworld, whereas no formal narratives depict a heavenly sky. Nevertheless, heavenly bodies are personified in anecdotal starlore as, for example, the three stars in the Belt of Orion, which are called in Northern Paiute *kóipa kumámi* 'the mountain-sheep husbands' (of Sirius, regarded as a woman called *tinágidi* 'The Chaser'). This inconsistency has led thoughtful storytellers to rationalize that "the stars were people long before the animals were; they had the form of animals then" (W.Z. Park 1934–1940,6:14).

It is certainly true that a speaker of Northern Paiute might say *ʔisˑá kadíˑpi madúkupitu* 'Wolf created the earth', although he would not have any actual story about world creation on which to base his statement. In the Great Basin, it is world-transformation that accounts for human life, in contrast to the extensive development of cosmogony by the Southwest Indians. Great Basin peoples were less concerned with how it all began than with cosmological order and how it might end. All known creation myths had the same didactic value and were accepted as equivalent but alternative views of an unknown and imaginary cosmos. A mythological tale was regarded less as a matter of faith than as one reasonable explanation among several of the mystery of existence. The raconteurs themselves were fully aware that their long and embellished mythological stories were fictitious but defended their own versions as having traditional acceptance, in itself a sufficient proof of validity.

The storyteller's conception of life is determined by the mythical belief that the present life is connected to and somehow grows out of a former mythological age. Conditions now reflect what happened "away back on the first earth," which the Northern Paiutes variously called *múidiˑpi*, *múʔasˑu tíˑpi*, or *múigasˑu tiípi*, all three phrases meaning literally 'early earth' or 'the old earth', which preordained once and for all happenings in nature and set bounds to man's capabilities. Man must die because it was so decided in the first world; he will never succeed in his attempt to reach the stars because none of the birds in the tales did; flowers that open first in the shades of night do so because in that earlier world they were people who were too lazy to get up in the morning. The cosmic order results from the tension inherent in a duality that is personified as the two mythological brothers, Wolf and Coyote, transformers rather than creators. In the cosmological tales, Wolf, the elder and wiser of the two, represents perfection, leaving it to the capriciousness of his younger brother Coyote to make a virtue of grim necessity. Man cannot live forever; he must labor to hunt for game and to collect food; there must be starvation, sickness, and death. The style of the mythological tales combines narrative form with dramatic art; the characters ought rather to be called actors. With few exceptions they have animal

names and mostly animal forms in conformity with the elementary idea common everywhere that etiological stories are set in an earlier world that had a theriomorphic population. Nevertheless, in Shimkin's (1947a:331) view, "Shoshone mythology is pre-eminently realistic," combining imagination with realistic details in a mythological framework. The heroes change shape at will and take on anthropomorphic features, in unceasing alternation, as the action demands.

To what extent the theriomorphic pantheon of the Great Basin Indians formed a closed system, with kinship terminology interlocked with other cultural subsystems, is debatable. In an important introductory study of Southern Ute, Goss (1967) demonstrated "a multidimensional folktaxonomy," that is, that consanguinal kinship terms and the mythological ancestors are nearly homonymous with their present-day zoological equivalents. Goss (1972a) described how the mythological cosmos ensued from the hierarchy of animal characters of a former age, as the Ute apprehended the world. Possibly owing to oversight by linguists, this aspect of mythology is not known from other Numic speech communities. Elsewhere in the common area, Wolf, whether animal or culture hero of the past, appears under one and the same name, for example Northern Paiute *isˑá*, Shoshone *isa*. The coyote, as an animal, is Northern Paiute *iʒáʔa*, Shoshone *icappi*, but Coyote, the trickster in the tales, is Northern Paiute *iʒábui*, Shoshone *isapaippi*; Southern Paiute *sinamapi* is related to *sinaʔapi* 'wolf, dog'. Despite the traditional form that characterized each principal role, a storyteller would sometimes intensify the plot by reshaping a configuration, often introducing a drastic metamorphosis. A giant flays Weasel and wraps himself in the skin (W.Z. Park 1933–1940,5:57–59). Coyote and Mountain Lion escape from the Bears through a hollow elderberry-wood tube (Zigmond 1981:63). Rolling Rock chases Coyote, who has stolen his blanket, and turns into an Indian (J.A. Mason 1910:306–307). Coyote is enabled to fly with the Geese by borrowing a feather from each of them; he hunts with bow and arrow or sits at home mending his fishing net. The principal animal actor is sometimes represented in a brief song or rhythmic formula that refers to the story but is more often included as an ornamentation that characterizes this particular figure independently of the plot. The texts of these songs and formulaic miniatures are sometimes obscure or archaic and difficult even for a competent speaker of the language to translate. This style, best known from Southern Paiute, is more common than it appears from the published tale collections. Under the title "song recitative," it is described by Sapir (1910a) and represented in his contextual records of Southern Paiute and Uintah Ute (1930–1931:414–448).

The classic folktale of the Great Basin is perhaps best characterized as one in which "ritual, symbolism, and   *657* art attain little intensity, and monotonous simplicity takes the place of a rich growth" (Kroeber 1925:583). Truly indigenous mythological material includes several types about "the first parents" and the dispersal of the tribes (Motif *A1620*) but also includes independent parallels of universally known tale motifs, such as, for example, "Hero carried away by Giant Bird" (*B31.1*) and "Pursuit by Rolling Head" (*R261.1*). Presumably the most common and elaborate of all autochthonous Great Basin folktales is The Theft of Pine Nuts, a story on the same pattern as the widespread tale type, The Theft of Fire (Motif *A1415.2*) (S.Thompson 1955–1958); these two stories are combined into one by the Northern Shoshones, who live outside the piñon belt. The greatest part of the folktale inventory among the Basin tribes consists of trickster stories, which these peoples brought to an unsurpassed variety of narrative patterns and animal characters, at the expense of other themes and styles. The leading characters are Coyote and Cottontail, both acting also as transformers of nature and as culture heroes who benefit mankind.

The trickster tales are cyclical only on a selective basis. The narrator combined independent motifs as episodes in paratactic composition, resulting in cumulative stories that may provisionally be called "chain tales" but in a different and wider meaning than that term has been applied to European folktales (see S.Thompson 1946:230–234). The sequence of motifs incorporated into a composition of this magnitude occurs within the frame of a background story that may also occur independently. For example, Coyote meets Badger carrying Whirlwind in a bag and insists on looking into it. Badger opens the bag, and Whirlwind carries Coyote off to the end of the world. On his way back he has a series of adventures, each time freeing mankind from some evil. Cottontail sets out to kill the Sun in order to make a new one, a well-known story called in Shoshone *tapepekkappi* 'sun-being-killed' and classified among tales about sun-catching (*A728*) (S.Thompson 1929:290). Although the incident has been recorded and published in tale collections innumerable times as an independent story, no storyteller of repute would have told it as a complete and finished narrative. This story as told anywhere in the Great Basin is a framework including a series of incidents—not always the same— about Cottontail as a transformer and trickster. The trickster characters are neither "good" nor "evil." No such attributes exist in Great Basin Indian ideology. The tension is between foresight and thoughtlessness, wisdom and erratic behavior, seriousness and frivolity.

Neo-Mythology and Contemporary Narration

All existing records of Great Basin mythological tales were made long after these peoples came under the cultural influence of fur hunters, traders, Jesuit missionaries, and Mormon settlers. It was during this early period, antedating any treaty-making with the United States and concomitant government Indian agencies, that a considerable number of family names, chiefly French-Canadian, were adopted. A surprisingly large number of European folktales and biblical borrowings also were incorporated into traditional narratives and told in Numic and Washoe vernaculars. Many such tales have been recorded in the field since Stith Thompson (1919) published his study of European folktales among North American Indians. It was much later, about the time of the Indian Reorganization Act of 1934, that a radical change in economy, political participation in communal affairs, and the new public educational system eroded the fundamental support of aboriginal tribal traditions that had been provided by the common use of the native languages and by the authority of the grandparental generation in family life. The new order on the reservations and access to modern communication coincided with the sudden growth of intertribal dance festivals, powwows, and pan-Indian political and religious associations. Storytelling in the old style, reduced to occasional exchange of memories between old men, unobserved and even scorned by young people, continued for a few decades. Tales of traditional types known to native informants have become few and rudimentary, and even the oldtimers have lost the rhetorical power which as recently as the early twentieth century could hold an audience spellbound. However, the gradual disappearance of traditional folktales did not leave a void in Great Basin folklore. Stories of an anecdotal type began to change. Although there is now easy access to archival audiotaped material in unprecedented abundance, variety, and linguistic accuracy, there is very little published material available to the general reader. Jorgensen (1960:83–135) has described the changes in content and style in the oral tradition of the Northern Utes during clearly defined periods of acculturation. The influence of Christianity is obvious, although the tales themselves are all primarily Ute. The use of colloquial American idioms has changed the style of contemporary narration, which now consists chiefly of etiological tales explaining "life and creation," legends about the origin of the Bear Dance, encounters with the Water Baby, and ghost stories of historic times that have survived in Ute lore. Another study of contemporary narrative art from the Ute is Milspaw's (1975:251–330) draft of 46 narratives, chiefly historical memories from postcontact time, autobiographical sketches, oral essays on religious and socioeconomic affairs on the reservation, and some survivals of the trickster cycle.

Eloquence in the use of the native languages, in which many individual speakers formerly took great pride, was vanishing in the 1950s to the extent the dialects became extinct. Nevertheless, outstanding excellence in oratorical skill, albeit in English, continued to be heard at intertribal Peyote meetings. Peyotism, the most esoteric of pan-Indian movements, arrived in the Great Basin late in its history and reached its zenith in the 1940s. As the number of adherents dwindled, the remaining circle of devotees strengthened their union, even across tribal boundaries, and despite the bitter opposition of the shamans (cf. Siskin 1941; O.C. Stewart 1944; Lieber 1972). Variants of the new gospel, founded in the main upon Christian tenets but tolerant of other creeds, were gradually integrated into a maturing system of metaphysical ideas. In the ethnographic literature on the Great Basin, it is best known as it has been practiced among the Washoe (O.C. Stewart 1944; d'Azevedo 1978a). D'Azevedo's (1984) narratives consist of 23 testimonial records made in the 1950s by members of the Native American Church. Some of these narratives are accounts of personal experiences in the Peyote tepee, while others are detailed accounts of the attitude to the common doctrine embraced by members of the group in their collective striving for personal and social integrity.

Despite the obvious encroachment of biblical teaching upon the domains of neo-mythology, Numic-speaking storytellers have been fastidiously selective in regard to morality. The ethical dichotomy of good and evil had no place in the aboriginal value system of the Great Basin Indians. "Right" is in the Northern Paiute verbalized *togí*, synonymous with 'adequate, enough'. A newcomer would be introduced with the standard phrase *pis·á?yu naná*, *kái iʒá*, which literally means 'a beautiful man, not Coyote'. The Shoshone synonym is *ca·nti* 'beautiful, right, good'. A "beautiful man" is a person of equity, prudence, and foresight, one who obeys the rule, a trustworthy man. Coyote, the trickster, is not evil. He is thoughtless but cunning and impersonates the character who disobeys the rule. No contemporary narrator familiar with old-time tradition would call Coyote "the devil." There was no such power to overcome. On the other hand, Wolf, Coyote's wise and provident elder brother, is in the mythological tales entitled "Our Father" (in Shoshone *tammin appi*). It is, however, mainly in terms of mythological chronology and world view that storytellers have made use of the Euro-American way of looking at things. The firm belief remains that nothing may happen in the present world that is not a reflection of occurrences in a former mythological age; but, there is also the idea that the world people now live in is doomed to destruction in the year 2000, in Northern Paiute called *wahámano nawá?iciyaidi* 'twenty old men's death all together'.

Sources

The most complete accounts of narrative forms in the Great Basin tradition are found in the classic tale collections, mostly recorded in English prior to 1940. The underlying imaginary world of supernaturalism and deeply rooted beliefs show much the same characteristics throughout the culture area. Tale typology, on the other hand, varies considerably from one subarea to another. None of the early, comprehensive collections covers the entire area. The most important of these from a comparative point of view is John Wesley Powell's report on his field studies in the 1870s in Utah, Arizona, and Nevada (Fowler and Fowler 1971). The most comprehensive collection of tale-type variants is Lowie's (1924a) detailed and exhaustive records of Ute, Southern Paiute, and Northern Paiute myths and folktales. Lowie's (1909) account of Northern Shoshone folklore describes a marginal area with culture elements in part borrowed from the Plains. Other major early collections are Kroeber's (1901) and J.Alden Mason's (1910) on the Utes and Kelly's (1938) on Northern Paiute. Steward's (1936b) compilation of Owens Valley Paiute myths shows cultural borrowings from the trans-Sierran tribes in central California, an influence that reached farther east into the southern Great Basin; on the other hand, his collection of Western Shoshone myths (Steward 1943) represents the very core of Great Basin folktales. Sapir's (1930–1931) work on the Kaibab Southern Paiute and the Uintah Utes has served as a model for later collections inasmuch as it was the first time that Great Basin folktales were recorded in the narrators' vernaculars with careful linguistic analysis, a method that has been followed ever since. The folklore of the Chemehuevi is described by Laird (1984).

ORAL TRADITION: CONTENT AND STYLE OF VERBAL ARTS

Ghost Dance, Bear Dance, and Sun Dance

JOSEPH G. JORGENSEN

The Ghost Dance religion has been explained as a response of many American Indians to the deep poverty and ubiquitous oppression they had suffered during prolonged contact with Whites (Mooney 1896). Indian populations had been depleted by warfare, epidemics, starvation, and exposure. Native Americans had been corralled on reservations and denied access to the majority of resources on which they once lived. Indians had also become dominated by federal bureaucrats, the U.S. Cavalry, and local entrepreneurs, farmers, and stockmen. As there was no place to flee, and as treaties with the federal government brought dole at best and broken promises eventuating in death at worst, Indians were left with few options. Many became adherents of religious movements that promised a better world or better lives (Jorgensen 1972). Some movements have been short-lived, only a year or so, and some have had great endurance, 90 or 100 years. Only three of the major religious movements that diffused among Great Basin native peoples will be treated here—the so-called Ghost Dance, the Bear Dance, and the Sun Dance.

The Ghost Dance was the first recorded religious movement in the Great Basin, and it has been the focus of much controversy about the origins and meanings of religious movements. In 1890 the Ghost Dance began to attract the attention of anthropologists and federal officials. The so-called Sioux Outbreak of 1890 (or the Battle at Wounded Knee) in which 49 federal troops, state militiamen, Indian police in the service of the federal government (6 of the 49), and a herder were killed while taking the lives of 370 Sioux Indians, 250 of whom were women and children, drew more attention to the religion. The "outbreak" followed a year-long period of intense participation in the Ghost Dance religion and was attended by a belief that Sioux adherents of the religion who wore "ghost shirts" were immune to bullets (Mooney 1896: 868–872).

The creator of the movement in 1889 was Wovoka, also known as Jack Wilson, a Northern Paiute prophet whose vision instructed him to create the religion. Yet Mooney (1896:701) learned that the Ghost Dance of 1889 was not the first. Two decades earlier another Northern Paiute prophet received a vision to start the first Ghost Dance religion.

The Ghost Dance of 1869

The Ghost Dance of 1869 (Gayton 1930; Du Bois 1939; Hittman 1973) spread to the northern California tribes in 1870. Du Bois suggested that Wodziwob, a Walker Lake–Walker River Northern Paiute prophet not related to Wovoka, was first to dream of the dance. Hittman (1973), in the most complete investigation of the origin and meaning of the religion, suggests that Wodziwob (also known as Fish Lake Joe) was born and raised among the Fish Lake Valley Northern Paiute 90 miles southeast of Walker Lake.

The precontact Northern Paiute of the Fish Lake area and the Owens Valley Paiute were among the few Great Basin peoples to practice mourning ceremonies and cremations in honor of the deceased. Such observances were widespread in California, especially among the California neighbors of the Owens Valley Paiute. Furthermore, the natives of Walker Lake, Mason Valley, and Fallon were the only Northern Paiute who sought the return of the dead (Du Bois 1939:6). Thus, the milieu in which Wodziwob was reared and in which he spent his adult life was not ideologically opposed to the message of his visions, particularly to the return of the dead.

Wodziwob's visions, which began in the mid-1860s, taught that men, women, and children should join in a circle of alternating men and women, interlock fingers with dancers on each side, shuffle to the left, and sing special songs. The dance was to be performed at night for at least five nights in succession. The sessions were to recur regularly, perhaps 20 times or so throughout the year. During the dancing the participants would become exhausted and, at the proper time, some would receive visions that were to give them new Ghost Dance songs and, ultimately, would restore the resources on which Indians once lived. Deceased Indians but no Whites would be restored to life, a new and happy existence. Hittman's (1973) analysis of the context of oppression and deprivation in which Wodziwob created the Ghost Dance is convincing and lends credence to the notion that religious movements are, in part, responses to deprivation. He shows how (in the 1860s and 1870s) the Northern Paiute were devastated by epidemics, prohibited from using most of their aboriginal territory due to White encroachment, suffering from starvation, and discriminated against.

The 1869 Ghost Dance swept northwest and southwest through the struggling Indian communities of California (Gayton 1930; Du Bois 1939). It also was carried by proselytizers throughout the Great Basin. Among the Northern Paiute it is known to have been performed by the people at Owens Valley, Fish Springs, and Fish Lake (Steward 1933b:322–323, 1941:325); at Walker River, Walker Lake, and Mason Valley (Hittman 1973:81–88); at Pyramid Lake, Truckee River, and Surprise Valley (O.C. Stewart 1941:445; Kelly 1932:179); and in the Carson Sink and McDermitt–Quinn River areas (O.C. Stewart 1941:445). It is probable that most Northern Paiute attended some Ghost Dance performances, even if each group did not sponsor dances.

The first Ghost Dance was accepted and sponsored by the Kaibab and other Southern Paiute of southwestern Utah who learned it from Indians (unspecified) in Nevada (Mooney 1896:703; Sapir 1909). Dellenbaugh (1908:178) seems to have observed part of a Ghost Dance performed by the Kaibab on January 6, 1872. It is known that the Southern Paiute, like the Northern Paiute, performed the religion for about two years before discontinuing it.

Among the Western Shoshone only those people at Morey are known to have sponsored dances, and they too terminated the religion after a short period (Steward 1941:267). The Deep Creek, Ibapah, and Skull Valley Gosiute participated in Ghost Dances cosponsored by Bannock, Northern Paiute, and Northern Shoshone (Jorgensen 1964, 1972).

By May 1870 the severely deprived Northern Shoshone and Bannock from the Fort Hall Reservation and the Eastern Shoshone from Wind River Reservation had become active proselytizers for the religion. Ghost Dances were cosponsored by the Pohogwe Northern Shoshone, Eastern Shoshone, and Bannock in both the Bear River Valley of Utah and Idaho and in the Bridger Basin of Wyoming. Uintah, Taviwach, and Yampa Utes, Gosiutes, and Navajos attended. The Ghost Dances of the early 1870s represent the first joint ceremonial undertakings of Ute and Northern Shoshone. Extreme mutual deprivation may have contributed to the willingness of Shoshone and Ute to convene in hopes of restoring their territory, culture, and deceased ancestors while excluding Whites (Jorgensen 1964, 1972).

The Ghost Dance religion fell out of use among the Utes during the mid-1870s, but it was performed by Shoshone and Bannock at Wind River, Wyoming, through the early 1880s. The religion persisted at Fort Hall, Idaho, through the 1890s (Jorgensen 1972). It seems paradoxical that the Northern Paiute people who originated and missionized the religion dropped it after two or three years of unfulfilled expectations, whereas a few recipients of the religion continued to perform it

fervently. Heidenreich (1967), following Jorgensen (1964), demonstrated that societies that had been structurally complex (as measured by numbers and types of kinship organizations, annual and sporadic rituals, levels of jurisdictional hierarchy, and the like) were more likely to accept and perform the dance intensively (as measured by relative number of participants, length and number of dances, and so forth).

All the societies in Heidenreich's sample represented deprivation; however, only the least complex groups rejected the dance or performed it briefly. The Ute and Northern Shoshone exhibited more complex social organization than their western neighbors—Northern Paiute, Southern Paiute, and Western Shoshone. This complexity, especially in performance of annual rituals linked to the social-political groups, might well explain why the Ghost Dance persisted in the eastern Great Basin and Rocky Mountains after it had disappeared in the area of origin (Jorgensen 1972). Fear of ghosts, a factor often used to explain rejection of the dance, does not seem to be of much importance in explaining acceptance or rejection of the dance, but the mourning ceremony and propitiation of the deceased in the Owens Valley–Fish Lake area might help to explain the origin of the dance by Wodziwob.

Wodziwob's Ghost Dance religion of 1869 and the manifestations of that religion elsewhere in the Great Basin represented a synthesis of the traditional belief in visions, the traditional practice of circle dancing associated with antelope charming and other subsistence pursuits, and, perhaps, a borrowing from Sahaptian or Salishan Indians of the Plateau and Northwest Coast of the belief in prophets, prophecies, and return of the dead (see Spier 1935; Aberle 1959; Spier, Suttles, and Herskovits 1959; cf. Hittman 1973). Yet Wodziwob's religion represented a radical departure from tradition.

The Ghost Dance religion of 1869 can be understood as a transformative movement (Aberle 1966:318–320; Jorgensen 1972). It was sponsored and participated in by people who actively sought a transformation of the social and natural order in their own lifetimes. The adherents radically rejected things as they were and had some perception of the enormous force necessary to transform things to what they should have been. By supernatural means the world was to be rid of Whites, Indian land and resources were to be restored, and deceased Indians were to be resurrected so as to restore Indian life unhindered by Whites. It is interesting that prominent members of the Church of Jesus Christ of Latter-day Saints (Mormons) interpreted the religion as a harbinger of the millennium, and in the 1870s because of the superficial compatibilities of Mormon and Ghost Dance doctrines, the Mormons had some success in proselytizing the Bannock and Northern Shoshone from Fort Hall (Mooney 1896:703–704) and the Eastern Shoshone (Shimkin 1942:456) to be baptized into the Church and to be baptized for deceased Indians. Mormons, too, believed in resurrection of all deceased and a radical transformation of the social and natural order. Furthermore, Mormons performed proxy baptisms for the dead in order to step up the date for the millennium.

The Ghost Dance of 1889

In 1889, well after the Ghost Dance religion had died among most Northern Paiute, Western Shoshone, Southern Paiute, and Ute groups, Wovoka ("History of Research," fig. 9, this vol.), the Northern Paiute prophet from Mason Valley (Yerington, Nevada), received a series of visions instructing him to revive the Ghost Dance religion. His message was interpreted differently outside the Northern Paiute area, especially throughout the Plains (Hittman 1973:92–114; Du Bois 1939:7). Wovoka's Ghost Dance ideology preached living in peace with Whites, encouraged industry and work, besought Indians to live together without quarreling, and eschewed war. If Indians would but perform the Ghost Dance and love one another while observing these other loose guidelines "they would at last be reunited with their friends in this other world, where there would be no more death or sickness or old age" (Mooney 1896:772).

Wovoka's Ghost Dance, then, called for both accommodation to Whites and the strengthening of the Indian community. It called for adjustment to odious conditions in this world, the here and now, so that eternal happiness could be achieved in the "other" world in the future.

This shift of focus from immediate transformation by supernatural means to coping with the present through supernatural means is critical to an understanding of Wovoka's version of the religion. The 1889 Ghost Dance did not seek to change the total natural and social order, but sought new individual states: people should not bicker, people should work, and so forth. A new and loose code of ethics found evil in the world as well as in the individual and sought to overcome these evils to gain happiness in the present life as well as the future. The focus on individual change in a group context so that the transformed individuals changed their relationships toward one another in the face of resistance is called "redemptive" in Aberle's (1966:320–322) typology. The second Ghost Dance was in this sense a redemptive social movement at its place of origin.

Regardless of Wovoka's message about the meaning of the Ghost Dance (Du Bois 1939; Hittman 1973), the Ghost Dance religion that swept east out of Nevada was interpreted and reinterpreted so as to proclaim that Wovoka's vision had guaranteed an immediate transformation. This interpretation motivated the Southern

Paiute in Utah, for instance, but it was nowhere more evident than among the Bannock and Shoshone at Fort Hall, Idaho, who had not stopped sponsoring Ghost Dances since 1870. Indeed, these peoples again became the most energetic missionaries for the religion when they learned of Wovoka's vision, sending emissaries to the Eastern Shoshone (Shimkin 1942:456–457) and the Northern Ute in Utah (Jorgensen 1972). They received emissaries in Pocatello, Idaho, from many Plains tribes (Mooney 1896:807). The message promulgated by the Fort Hall adherents contradicted Wovoka and alleged that the world would be rid of Whites and that the Indian dead would be resurrected (Shimkin 1942:456).

The transformative version of the dance was not revived among the Eastern Shoshone or the Ute groups, but all these people began to dance a modified version of the Ghost Dance that promised only good health (Shimkin 1942:457; Jorgensen 1964, 1972). The philosophy of the modified version was much the opposite of the 1869 version and considerably different from the 1889 version as taught by Wovoka as well. Blankets were used to cover the dancers, and at the end of each dance the participants shook the blankets in order to bring good health and to get rid of any lingering ghosts (Jorgensen 1964). Ghost Dances of this form were added to other ceremonials as adjuncts to the main event. These dances were performed among the Ute groups, the Northern Shoshone and Bannock, Eastern Shoshone, and the Southern Paiute groups in Utah through 1983 with no signs of abating.

The Bear Dance

About the time that the Ute became disillusioned with the transformative promise of the Ghost Dance religion, they altered their traditional Bear Dances to focus more on the pursuit of good health than had been the traditional practice (Jorgensen 1964). The altered version of the Bear Dance may have been performed for 15 years or so.

The precontact Bear Dance probably was created by the Ute. The exact locus is not known because it was practiced by all Ute bands at first contact as their grandest ritual (Reed 1896:237–244; Lowie 1915; Spier 1928:267–273; Steward 1932). It was performed in the late winter, usually toward the end of February or the beginning of March, and each band invited others to participate. The sponsoring band provided food, built the large, circular brush enclosure, and organized the dance. Bear Dances lasted about 10 days during which time an all-male orchestra played musical rasps (notched and unnotched sticks) on the top of a drum resonator (fig. 1) ("Music," fig. 6, this vol.) to charm the dancers and to propitiate bears. This is analogous to the extensive practice of using musical rasps to charm antelopes.

Amer. Mus. of Nat. Hist., New York: 118667.

Fig. 1. Southern Paiute Bear Dance. Musicians use an inverted metal washtub and notched rasps to accompany dancers on the right. Photograph by Robert Lowie, Moapa, Nev., summer 1915.

Bear Dances were directed by a dance chief and two or more assistants. These officials stopped people from gambling, encouraged women to choose male dance partners, and as the dance progressed, used long whips to stimulate the dancers. The dancing was conducted throughout the days, and gambling and fraternizing occurred throughout the nights. During the dance sessions women selected male partners and danced opposite them—men forming one line and women forming another (fig. 2) ("Music," fig. 5, this vol.). The line dance originally was peculiar to the Utes in the Great Basin, although they also performed Round Dances prior to the Ghost Dance movement of 1869. By the final day of the dance the lines had begun to break down into several smaller lines, perhaps four men facing four women, the women advancing while the men retreated and, then, the men advancing while the women retreated. Finally couples broke off from their respective lines and, while the man put one arm around the woman's waist and she one arm around his, the dancing became very athletic—the men trying to exhaust the women completely and vice versa. Eventually a young woman, usually pubescent, would fall along with her young male partner. The dance chief then revived both of them by rubbing the musical rasp on their bodies. The dance terminated with a feast sponsored by the host band.

The Ute had no bear taboo and had no specific bear shamans. On the other hand, they believed that a Ute hunter once saw a bear dancing outside a cave in the spring. The bear instructed the Ute hunter that he would gain sexual and hunting prowess if he propitiated bears by performing the dance (Jorgensen 1964). It seems clear that the aboriginal Ute dance was performed to propitiate bears, to make Ute hunters more successful, and to make men and women successful in their sex lives. It was also used as the public announcement of the completion of the girls' puberty ritual. Utes equate the dance with the girls' puberty ceremony of the Apache (Jorgensen 1969).

Some time before extensive White contact the Bear Dance was adopted by the Lemhi and Pohogwe Northern Shoshone and Eastern Shoshone (Lowie 1909:219; Steward 1943a:288). It is not known to have been adopted by Western Shoshone, Southern Paiute, or Northern Paiute prior to 1880. The more puzzling diffusion of the Bear Dance began during the late 1880s and continued for about 30 years, being followed by another modest diffusion of the dance in 1930.

The diffusion of the Bear Dance seems to have begun when the reservation Utes in Utah and Colorado dropped the Ghost Dance religion and modified the Bear Dance. In February 1876 the Bear Dance participants on the Tabeguache reservation in Colorado were observed to fast for four days, seek spiritual power and good health, and desire protection from "the Great Spirit" (Bond in ARCIA 1876:20; Anonymous 1884). As the 200 or so dancers swayed back and forth, many dancers collapsed and were revived by shamans using musical rasps. At the dance's conclusion the fast was ended with a feast. The dance was shorter than in prereservation times and had come to emphasize spiritual healing on a massive scale in Ute terms.

Apparently in the 1890s an Antarianunts Southern Paiute named Tom taught the Bear Dance to the Kaibab, San Juan (who attended but did not sponsor the dance), and Shivwits Southern Paiute (Sapir 1930–1931:472–473, 533; Kelly 1964:107–110).

The Bear Dance was spread subsequently to the Moapa and Las Vegas (documented for Ash Meadow) Southern Paiute, the Koosharem Ute–Southern Paiute, and the Walapai, Havasupai, and Mohave tribes of the Southwest (Lowie 1924:299; Spier 1928:267–273; Steward 1941:266, 353). Among the Yuman-speaking groups the Bear Dance became known as the Mohave dance (Spier 1928).

The westward diffusion of the Bear Dance coincides with, or follows shortly after, the second Ghost Dance movement. The Southern Paiute accepted the transformative version of Wovoka's Ghost Dance and transmitted it to the Havasupai and Walapai (Dobyns and Euler 1967:14–17). The Havasupai, Walapai, Mohave, and Southern Paiute in southwestern Utah performed the Ghost Dance for a couple of years but then dropped it much as the other Southern Paiute had terminated the dance two decades earlier.

top left, U. of Utah, Special Coll., Salt Lake City: PO244, #1322A: top right, Smithsonian, NAA: 84–3839; Colo. Histl. Soc., Denver: bottom left, E 1900; bottom right, 1894.170.

Fig. 2. Ute Bear Dances. top left, Dance corral with the Bear Dance flag. Photographed at Whiterocks, Utah, 1948. top right, Dance at Uintah Agency. The female dancers include several White women and the male dancers are predominantly White men, some in military uniforms. The "cat man" is in the foreground. Photographed about 1870s. bottom left, Cotton Bear Dance flag painted with brown bears and an Indian man in a supplicative posture, probably dated 1880–1920. bottom right, Bear Dance scene painted on buckskin. The detailed painting shows the corral, people seated at a table playing moraches, 12 pairs of men and women in facing dance lines with male "whippers" at either end, seated spectators on both sides of the corral entrance, fruit on a table beneath a leafless tree, a White man facing the spectators, and a girl clothed in a blanket peering into the corral at the right of the entrance. Collected about 1890–1900 by Thomas McKee. Size 115.5 by 30.5 cm.

The Mourning Ceremony

Between 1892, following the rejection of the second Ghost Dance, and about 1915, the Havasupai and Walapai; the Mohave; the Kaibab, Moapa, Shivwits, Las Vegas (Ash Meadow), and Cedar (Cedar City) Southern Paiute; the Koosharem Ute–Southern Paiute; and the Death Valley Western Shoshone began sponsoring nightlong "Cries" for the deceased following cremation—a part of the Yuman Mourning ceremony—in conjunction with Bear Dances (Spier 1928; Steward 1941; Lowie 1924:279; Kelly 1964). The fusion was made in

the Southern Paiute area, did not spread farther west than the Death Valley Shoshone, and did not spread back north and east to the Ute and Northern Shoshone. Yet about 1930 the Cry and the Bear Dance, replete with cremation of the dead, were passed from Southern Paiute to the Deep Creek and Skull Valley Gosiutes, and thence to the Lemhi Northern Shoshone at Fort Hall (Steward 1943a:288, 350, 388). It is probable that the Cries and Bear Dances were used to revere the dead and to bring good health and camaraderie to the living in what were odious and oppressive conditions. There is no evidence that Cries diffused with either Wodzi-

664

wob's or Wovoka's Ghost Dance religion, although Wodziwob was reared in the only Great Basin area where the Mourning ceremony was a precontact practice.

In another wave beginning sometime in the early 1890s, the Ute Bear Dance was diffused west to the Huki-Eater Western Shoshone from the Uintah Ute. It was carried to the Deep Creek and Skull Valley Gosiute (Steward 1943a:288, 350); the Duck Valley Western Shoshone (Lowie 1909:219); the Western Shoshone at Elko, Ely, Humboldt, Morey, Ruby Valley, Egan, Reese River, and Smith Creek (Steward 1941:266); and the Northern Paiute at Quinn River–McDermitt, Winnemucca–Middle Humboldt, and Humboldt Sink (O.C. Stewart 1941:416). The more westerly Northern Paiute at Surprise Valley knew about the line dance but did not sponsor it (Kelly 1932:178–179), and the Owens Valley Paiute only had the California-type bear shamanism (Steward 1933b:322–323).

The sweep of the Bear Dance from east to west among Western Shoshone and Northern Paiute was independent of the Yuman-Southern Paiute ritual package that eventually got all the way to Fort Hall in 1930, but it is probable that the Bear Dance movement through Western Shoshone areas was not independent of Wovoka's Ghost Dance religion. As a matter of fact, the Western Shoshone and Northern Paiute Bear Dances were held in conjunction with Round Dances, if not in conjunction with Wovoka's redemptive Ghost Dance religion. The Southern Paiute, Walapai, Havasupai, Yavapai, and Mohave, on the other hand, had interpreted the 1889 Ghost Dance message as transformative and then dropped the religion two years later, partly because of disillusionment. The redemptive version of the Ghost Dance religion accepted by Northern Paiute and Western Shoshone was compatible with the focus of the Bear Dance to have a good time, good health, and happy relations in the here and now.

By the 1940s Bear Dances were not performed by any Shoshone or Northern Paiute. They were performed annually through 1983 by each band on all Ute reservations, and intermittently among the Kanosh Ute–Southern Paiute near Fillmore, Utah, Cedar City Southern Paiute, and Koosharem Ute–Southern Paiute near Richfield, Utah. The dances are sponsored so as to avoid scheduling conflicts and so that Indians from all nearby reservations can participate. The form is almost identical to the precontact version of the dance except that menstrual lodges for pubescents are no longer constructed near the brush-enclosed dance grounds.

The puzzlement about the Bear Dance among the Ute, especially the way in which it was slightly altered in the 1870s and 1880s, only to be restored to a form close to the original in the 1890s, is removed after consideration of the Sun Dance religion. At the time Southern Paiute, Yumans, Western Shoshone and the like

were borrowing the revised Bear Dance and joining it with a version of the Mourning ceremony, Utes and Eastern Shoshone were creating a new redemptive movement, the modern Sun Dance religion.

As the promise of the Ghost Dance began to wane among the Eastern Shoshone, they began paying greater attention to the tenets and to the missionaries of the Church of Jesus Christ of Latter-day Saints, who had been proselytizing among Fort Hall, Bear River, and Lemhi Northern Shoshone for three decades. Mormon doctrine held that baptism by immersion remitted persons of all sins and prepared them for the millennium, at which time deceased ancestors would be resurrected and united with the living wherein peace and harmony would be restored. Mormons, furthermore, were charismatics, preaching and practicing faith healings through the power of the Holy Ghost, which they claimed any lay elder could invoke.

Eastern Shoshones began requesting baptism by Mormon elders, and in 1880 they sent word to church headquarters in Salt Lake City "that they wanted a Latter-day Saint to preach to them" (A.R. Wright 1982:28). Wright (1982:30–34), a Shoshone speaker, was dispatched as a missionary to them for one month. Though fearful of agency, military, and settler intervention because of the large movements of Indians from agency settlements to his mountain hideaways, Wright baptized and "administered" ("laying on of hands" and calling on the Holy Ghost to heal the sick) to several hundred Shoshones (120 on one day, 87 another, 17 on a special trip to Chief Washakie and his family, and so forth). The preachings and acts of the Mormon missionaries focused on total transformations of persons (through baptisms by immersion), faith healings, acquisition of the authority to call the Holy Ghost to assist in solving specific problems, and preparing for the millennium. These concepts coincided with, and may have influenced, changes made by Eastern Shoshone shamans to the Sun Dance religion, which became the preeminent means to gain and control supernatural power, to heal one's self, to administer to the sick, and to restore supernatural power to economically and politically powerless communities.

The Sun Dance Religion

Except for the Eastern Shoshone, the Sun Dance is a postreservation phenomenon in the Great Basin. In a thorough analysis of the Eastern Shoshone dance, Shimkin (1953:436) shows that the ritual was greatly altered in purpose and practice during the early years of reservation life. The focus of the Sun Dance was changed from insuring successful buffalo hunts and warfare to an increased concern over illness and community misery. The early Ute and Fort Hall dances (about 1890 for Northern Ute, 1900 for Ute Mountain Ute, 1907 for

Lemhi Northern Shoshone–Bannock at Fort Hall) stressed the same themes and had the same ritual organization as the revised Eastern Shoshone dance of 1890. The case is a strong one for selective change in the Wind River ritual as a response to absolute and relative deprivation during the early reservation period, as is the case for diffusion of the Wind River ritual to Utes and Fort Hall Shoshone and Bannock during the oppressive early years of reservation existence.

Evidence suggests that the Sun Dance was invented by Plains Algonquians, perhaps the Cheyenne, as early as 1700 (Spier 1921:498; Driver and Kroeber 1932:235; Shimkin 1953:406–407). After 1750 this ceremony diffused rapidly throughout the Plains by channels created by the nomadic plainsmen.

From the late eighteenth to the mid-nineteenth century the Sun Dance ceremony was the grandest of all the aboriginal religious ceremonies performed by Plains tribes. These tribes varied greatly in how they performed, when they performed, and the reasons they gave for performing the ceremony (Spier 1921:453–527; Shimkin 1953:403–417); however, all were complex group ceremonies complete with singers, dancers, musicians, and spectators. It was common for a complex mythology to be associated with the ceremony. The dance was usually vowed by some individual who planned to avenge a death, lead a successful hunt, or insure a bountiful supply of buffaloes. Because dances were usually performed only after vows were made, the ceremonies were not necessarily annual affairs. In brief, men danced for three or four days and nights to the accompaniment of drumming and singing. The dancers often underwent various tortures such as ritual fasting, thirsting, and mutilations, in a quest for power, good health, success in wars and on hunts, and the general welfare of the group.

By the end of the nineteenth century this spectacular ceremony had all but vanished from the Plains (Shimkin 1953:403). The Plains Indians were living upon reservations, and this intense ceremony, indeed all native religious ceremonies, had been suppressed by Indian agents, the U.S. military, and other federal employees.

The Eastern Shoshone, from whom the Ute borrowed the dance, had themselves learned it as early as 1800 from a Comanche, Yellow Hand, who learned it from the Kiowa. Yellow Hand joined the easternmost Shoshone and became the Sun Dance leader. The leadership of the dance was retained primarily among his descendants for over 100 years (Shimkin 1953:409–417). It is reasonably well confirmed that the Shoshone were performing the ceremony in a rather stable form by 1820 or 1830 (Shimkin 1953:417). From the 1820s on, the historical record is full of accounts of contacts between various Ute, Shoshone, and Bannock bands, including trade relations and intermarriages (Jorgensen 1964, 1972).

In the 1880s, following the last big Eastern Shoshone buffalo hunt and even their last warfare with other Plains tribes, at a time when they had lost access to the strategic resources on which they once subsisted, when their movements were restricted, when their death rate greatly outstripped their birth rate, and when many Shoshones had lost faith in the transformation promised by the first Ghost Dance, a few Eastern Shoshone shamans began to revise the Sun Dance ritual. Shimkin (1953:436–437) demonstrates that many war and buffalo-hunt features were dropped from the dance, and some Christian-like concepts were accreted to the dance. For instance, the number of corral posts was increased from 10 to 12. Finally, there was a notable shift of concern toward the curing of illness and the maintenance of communal unity as the dance was reshaped. This change in focus is obviously the key to the entire restructuring of the dance: a few Shoshone shamans sought a solution to the illness, death, and petty factionalism that became pervasive in the 1870s and 1880s. The Sun Dance religion became a redemptive religious movement performed once or twice annually at Wind River Reservation (Jorgensen 1972).

The post-1880s version of the Sun Dance, which persisted in most respects through the 1980s, was sponsored by a Sun Dance chief who had received a vision instructing him to direct the new dance (Shimkin 1953:437–451). He appointed subchiefs and a committee to help him. The dancers and all other participants worked hard at the dance in order to nourish the public good. The dancers, for instance, suffered to achieve power and to cure the sick (fig. 3, center right). Before the dancing began, the chief selected a center pole to be cut and had a hole dug for it. Often a sham battle, with Shoshones and visitors dressed in warrior clothing, preceded the erection of the center pole. Shortly after the sham battle was completed the corral was constructed. Its boundaries consisted of 12 side poles and they encompassed the center pole hole. The center pole was carried to the center of the corral and erected on the fourth ritualized attempt to raise it. Twelve roof rafters were then put in place, and branches were placed around the outside of the corral (fig. 3, top left).

Singers and drummers sat in the southeast section, spectators in the northeast section, and dancers occupied the rest of the corral. While in the corral the men danced to and from the center pole (fig. 3, top right) for three days and nights without water. The singers and drummers accompanied the dancing. Some dancers, especially powerful shamans, pursued visions. If men fell in the process of the dance, they were administered to by the Sun Dance chiefs. Falling often signified that a man was receiving his vision.

When the dancing terminated the dancers received blessings from respected shamans (fig. 3, center left). In turn they paid shamans with shawls, blankets, and

666

horses (later money) for their services. The hosts (Wind River Reservation residents) contributed gifts to the visitors (fig. 3, bottom left), and a feast of beef and bread followed. The modified Ghost Dances to prevent sickness and pacify ghosts were often performed as well. These dances became much attenuated and were performed only as a nightlong adjunct to other rituals beside the Sun Dance after about 1890.

The Northern, Southern, and Ute Mountain Ute, the Fort Hall Bannock and Northern Shoshone, and the Elko Western Shoshone at Star Valley and Steptoe Valley adopted this ritual while living under conditions similar to those of the Wind River people. As among the Eastern Shoshone, it became the major redemptive movement on all these reservations, save Elko, and was sponsored to promote inter- and intrareservation well-being.

Jorgensen's (1972) political, economic, historical, and dialectical (structural) analysis of the Sun Dance movement in the Great Basin shows that the Uintah Ute were the first Ute group to begin sponsoring Sun Dances, probably in 1889 or 1890 (see also Lowie 1915, 1924; Spier 1921; O.C. Stewart 1942). The Ute Mountain and Southern Utes must have attended Northern Ute dances in the 1890s, though this history is somewhat murky. The most prominent Southern Ute Sun Dance chief in the past quarter-century says it was first performed there in 1904 but that it was learned from the Ute Mountain Ute. The first Ute Mountain Ute dance, then, must have been earlier. Northern and Ute Mountain Utes concur that a Ute Mountain shaman was the first man to sponsor a Sun Dance among his people and that he learned the dance from the Northern Utes. The Ute Mountain Utes, in turn, taught a Southern Ute shaman how to sponsor dances.

The modern Sun Dance was introduced to the Fort Hall Shoshone-Bannock by a shaman, Bear, who had attended previous dances at Wind River (Hoebel 1935:578). Bear had failed to cure an ailing woman and he attributed this to an inadequacy of his powers. He dreamed to sponsor a dance and did so in 1901. Sun Dances were held annually after that time. Steward (1937) in 1927 was the first anthropologist to observe and describe a Sun Dance at Fort Hall, and his (1943a:290) account makes it clear that the religion was borrowed from the Eastern Shoshone.

The Lemhi Northern Shoshone-Bannock were moved to the Fort Hall Reservation in 1907 and did not participate in Sun Dances until that time. A few years later, it is not clear when, they began sponsoring their own Sun Dances at Fort Hall (Hoebel 1935:578). Although the oldest established Fort Hall version of the dance incorporated women as dancers and assistant chiefs (fig. 3, bottom right), the Lemhi version did not follow suit.

The Western Shoshone at Elko, who perhaps performed one dance about 1918, but definitely performed one in 1935, never generated the momentum to sustain sponsorship of the religion, although some Western Shoshones, especially women, have danced at Fort Hall over the decades (Jorgensen 1972).

The Sun Dance religion is a redemptive movement that was born of misery and oppression and has persisted in that context (Jorgensen 1972). A communitarian ethic is preached at Sun Dances that eschews narrow, individualistic behavior—whether hedonistic, witchcraft, withholding help and resources from kin and friends, or the like. Each participant, whether committeeman, dancer, singer, or spectator-adherent, sacrifices pleasures and endures hardships giving of himself or herself so that other Indians, living and dead, might have happier conditions. An interreservation Sun Dance community has developed among Wind River Shoshone, Fort Hall Shoshone, Northern Ute, Southern Ute, and Ute Mountain Ute. Adherents on these reservations sponsor dances, and Southern Paiutes and Western Shoshones attend them.

The Traditional-Unity Movement

An Oglala Sioux version of the Sun Dance religion has been performed in conjunction with Sacred Pipe, Peyote, and Sweat Lodge* rituals at the Northern Paiute–Shoshone Fort McDermitt Reservation, Nevada and Oregon. All these rituals, except Peyote, are very recent introductions to the western Basin (the short-lived Elko Western Shoshone Sun Dance being the exception). The first performance of this package of rituals at the McDermitt Reservation occurred August 1–4, 1979, and it has been sponsored annually on those dates since. The McDermitt version of the Sun Dance was introduced and directed for two years by a Sun Dance chief from the Pine Ridge Reservation in South Dakota, Eddie Whitewolf. He was invited to do so by a McDermitt religious leader, Stanley Smart. Smart, long a Roadman and formerly a Drummerman and Fireman in the Native American Church (Peyote), had introduced his version of a sweating ritual to the McDermitt Reservation during the late 1970s. In 1981, upon the death of Eddie Whitewolf, Smart became the Sun Dance chief at McDermitt (Smart 1981).

Some background for the introduction of the Sun Dance among the Northern Paiute and Western Shoshone is necessary inasmuch as the context in which it

---

*Ritualized sweating has been practiced by some Northern Paiutes since the 1960s. It was introduced to them by an Eastern Shoshone, who, in turn, probably learned the ritual from the Crows whose version it resembles and with whom they participate in ritual sweats. The Crow–Eastern Shoshone version of the Sweat Lodge ceremony is different from the Traditional-Unity version, not being integrated with the Sacred Pipe, Sun Dance, or Peyote. The Sweat Lodge is discussed in "Northern Paiute," this vol.

668

JORGENSEN

occurred is similar to the context in which the Sun Dance has persisted among the Ute and Northern Shoshone. There have been longstanding Indian grievances about treaty land and hunting rights and also widespread poverty and personal misery. The Northern Paiute and Western Shoshone of Nevada began pushing for their sovereignty and the enforcement of their treaty rights in the 1960s through several acts, such as hunting wherever and whenever they chose and denouncing bills in the Nevada legislature that would have affected them and their resources (Lieber 1972; Clemmer 1973). On one occasion White hunters on Indian land were detained by tribal members dressed in feathers and beating drums and emphatically told that they were not welcome to hunt on Indian land. In 1971 Western Shoshone and Northern Paiute condemned a Bureau of Land Management project that had cleared 40,000 acres of piñon-juniper forest on treaty land. Western Shoshones and Northern Paiutes refused monetary awards from the Indian Claims Commission and the U.S. Court of Claims for land claims settlements, demanding return of their treaty land instead and seeking to enjoin the federal government from paying the attorneys' fees from the award (Jorgensen 1984a).

According to Smart (1981), during the early 1970s some Northern Paiutes and Western Shoshones were attracted to the activities of the American Indian Movement (AIM), particularly the Trail of Broken Treaties which, in 1972, took AIM members and supporters to Washington, D.C. to protest treaty violations, poverty, and poor health among Indians and to restore Indian tribal sovereignty. The AIM occupation of Wounded Knee, South Dakota, in 1973, which also protested treaty violations and sought the restoration of treaty rights, followed soon after the Trail of Broken Treaties and was prompted by the federal government's failure to respond immediately to the desires of the protestors. The young Indian leaders of that occupation were counseled by traditional Sioux religious leaders. As the Traditional-Unity movement took shape, it joined respected elders, religious leaders, and political activists in the pursuit of common goals. The younger activists began to study the religious teachings of the elders and to seek the elders' advice.

From the rebellious acts and litigation of the early 1970s, many Indian activists joined with Sun Dance (Sioux), Long House (Iroquois), Dream Drum (Menominee, Chippewa), and Peyote (Kickapoo, Potawatomi, Winnebago) religious leaders from across the country and, in 1977, embarked on "The Longest Walk" from Seattle to Washington, D.C. (Smart 1981; Jorgensen 1984). Again the intention was to focus attention on Indian problems, to seek redress of grievances, and to unify Indian people. Stanley Smart joined the Walk and was asked by its leaders to be the Roadman for Peyote meetings for participants.

In 1977 Smart visited the Crow Dog family's religious camp (known as a "center") in South Dakota so as to participate in the group of rituals that the several Sioux religious leaders of the Pine Ridge and Rosebud reservations had drawn together. The rituals—Sacred Pipe, Peyote, Sweat Lodge, and the Sun Dance—are integrated into a spiritual and ideological program that is known as the Traditional-Unity movement. That movement is political, seeking national and international recognition of tribal sovereignty, as well as religious. Leaders of the movement, such as Leonard Crow Dog and Russell Means, are frequent participants at international tribunals and conferences (Jorgensen 1984). A film made in 1977 and released in 1983, *Crow Dog's Paradise*, provides a graphic introduction to the Traditional-Unity ideology.

Upon his return to McDermitt Reservation Smart established Sweat Lodges there, and they became used for ritual sweating either following, or independent of, Peyote meetings. Smart was soon invited to direct Sweat Lodge ceremonies for other Western Shoshones and Northern Paiutes, among whom the practices continued in 1984 under the direction of religious leaders.

Stanley Smart was beckoned back to the Crow Dog

Sven S. Liljeblad, Reno, Nev., top left and bottom right; top right, Mus. of the Amer. Ind., Heye Foundation, New York: 32207; center left, © Natl. Geographic Soc., Washington; center right, U. of N. Mex., Maxwell Mus. of Anthr., Albuquerque: 5.55; bottom left, Smithsonian, NAA: 56791.

Fig. 3. Sun Dance. top left, Northern Shoshone–Bannock dance enclosure, Fort Hall Reservation, Idaho. Photograph by Fritiof Fryxell, 1927. top right, Inside an enclosure, the Eastern Shoshone participants advancing toward and retreating from the center pole while blowing eagle-bone whistles. The dancers concentrate on the acquisition of power, the primary religious focus of this ritual. Photograph by William Wildschut, Wind River Reservation, Wyo., 1927. center left, Eastern Shoshone dancers being blessed by the shaman prior to the termination of the dance (Voget 1953:495). Male singers are seated around a double-headed bass drum in the foreground; some dancers blow eagle-bone whistles toward the pole, which bears a buffalo head that "issues" challenges to the dancers (Jorgensen 1972:319). Photograph by B. Anthony Stewart, Fort Washakie, Wind River Reservation, Wyo., Sept. 1944. center right, Eastern Shoshone shaman, using an eagle feather to perform a blessing for the sick at the center pole, which is a conduit of supernatural power. The patient usually stands between the center pole and the shaman and both face the pole (Voget 1984:178–179). The ash altar, which represents "life-giving" soil, is at the base of the pole. Photograph by Williard William Hill, probably at Wind River Reservation, about 1938. bottom left, Eastern Shoshone participants, 2 painted with white clay to keep the dancer cool and dry (Jorgensen 1972:324). They are praying during the accumulation of gifts, at their feet and around the base of the center pole, which will be distributed to the visitors at the end of the dance. Photographed at Fort Washakie, Wind River Reservation, Wyo., 1902. bottom right, Northern Shoshone and Bannock dancers blowing eagle-bone whistles at the sunrise ceremony where the warm, drying power of the sun is greeted and its power sought. Women were first allowed to participate in the Sun Dance in 1944. The shaman stands with his back to the center pole. Photographed at Bannock Creek, Fort Hall Reservation, Idaho, 1944–1945.

GHOST DANCE, BEAR DANCE, AND SUN DANCE

Colo. Histl. Soc., Denver: E 1894.171

Fig. 4. Ute Sun Dance ceremony painted on buckskin 1880–1890. Details include: dancers in stalls; 2 dancers with eagle-bone whistles at the center pole; 2 men, presumably shamans, with eagle-feather fans; 2 men with grass bundles; partitions segregating the dancers from the musicians and the spectators; drummers to the left of the entrance; spectators; and 2 males in ceremonial robes observing, one inside the corral at the right of the entrance, the other outside, looking into the enclosure. Collected by Thomas McKee. Size 153 by 200 cm.

Center in 1979. Earlier he had been taught by the Sioux leaders that the Sun Dance was originally Wovoka's Ghost Dance and had been given to the Sioux by Wovoka himself. Now Smart was told that he should reinstitute the Sun Dance in the western Great Basin from whence it came. The Sun Dance, of course, was a pre-contact ritual that predated the Ghost Dance by at least one century, probably two. It had a corpus of songs, ritual acts, pledges, and beliefs different from the Ghost Dances of both 1870 and 1890 (the former transformative, the latter redemptive as originally preached). Yet in the late 1970s the messages and performances of the two were interpreted by the Oglala Sioux as the same thing, indeed of a single origin. The purpose of the Sun Dance at McDermitt was to purify the body and the spirit, to bring good health to self and others, to acquire spiritual power for good, and to honor and protect Mother Earth.

The version of the Sun Dance performed at McDermitt varies significantly from Northern Ute, Southern Ute, Ute Mountain Ute, Fort Hall Northern Shoshone, and Eastern Shoshone practices. These differences are described in this account; similarities are not mentioned. At McDermitt during the five-day period before

the Sun Dancers enter the corral there is a Pipe ceremony, followed by a Peyote ceremony, and then a three-day Sweat Lodge ceremony. Participation in the Pipe ritual entails the obligation to keep a pure heart and to pledge oneself to maintenance of Mother Earth.

The ritual sweats are conducted in four tepees, two each for men and women. During the sweating, participants are physically, emotional, and spiritually challenged to withstand the power of the heat, and to shake the perspiration from their bodies, thereby purifying themselves. (This ritual act is analagous to the simulation of horses shaking sweat from their bodies, which is done by Sun Dancers.) Visions, usually from an animal spirit, can be acquired during the sweating that bring spiritual power and assurance to the dancer that he or she can complete the dance. The ritual sweat, like the Sun Dance proper, oppose hot, drying power to cool, thirst-quenching power.

The Sun Dance corral is built from cottonwoods on the fifth day. Each dancer makes a pledge or vow before entering, such as to acquire power to assist an ailing relative. Vows are made by Ute and Northern Shoshone dancers, but at McDermitt pledges differ significantly in one respect, namely: a dancer can pledge to dance

670

as few as one or as many as four days of the Sun Dance. Children younger than 10 years of age have participated for one day at McDermitt with the intention of increasing their dancing days in subsequent years.

Women dance at McDermitt unless they are menstruating or pregnant. A woman in either condition cannot so much as attend the McDermitt dance (similar proscriptions apply at the Ute and Northern Shoshone dances) because menstrual flow and pregnancies are believed to be fatally contaminating, causing hemorrhaging, or severely debilitating, causing leg cramps, stomach cramps, uncontrollable nose bleeds, and the like. Contact with a woman in either condition—touch, smell, sight, or touching something touched by the woman—is believed to be a major cause of illness and death. (Women can dance at the Bannock Creek Sun Dance at Fort Hall, but at no other Ute or Northern Shoshone dance.)

During the performance dancers at McDermitt can, from time to time, drink either wild cherry juice or white sage tea. And also during the dancing two dancers must keep two sacred pipes going. They cannot rest until they pass the pipes in their possession to two other dancers. The pipes must be kept going through the duration of the dance. Rests are necessary according to this version of the dance so that the spirit will charge the dancers' minds and bodies and make it possible for them to continue the dance.

The most spectacular difference between the McDermitt version and the Ute-Northern Shoshone versions is "piercing." Following the Sioux tradition (Spier 1921; Driver and Kroeber 1932), men can pierce themselves if they wish. Sharpened hardwood sticks about four inches long and $\frac{3}{8}$ inch in circumference are driven through each side of the man's chest and attached to a $\frac{3}{8}$ inch nylon rope. The rope is attached to the center pole. Dancers dance forward toward the sun and then run backwards challenging the heat and the rope. Although dancers pray for help to withstand both, they also seek the strength to break through the skin. All who pierce do not have the hardwood pins torn through their bodies.

Women, too, can pierce. But their offerings are chunks of flesh dug from their arms.

The McDermitt Reservation Sun Dance is followed by a second sweating ceremony to purify all those who participated.

The connection among the amalgam of religious rituals and native ideology that comprise the Traditional-Unity movement is explicit. AIM leaders and traditional religious leaders have created a movement for sovereignty, redemption, curing, and the good of all Indians. Missionaries proselytize so as to spread the ideology and the ritual. The Pipe-Peyote-Sweat Lodge-Sun Dance ritual has been performed annually at D-Q University (a Native American–Chicano institution funded by Congress) in Davis, California, since 1978, and at Big Mountain on the Navajo Reservation since 1983 (Shebala 1983). Big Mountain is a center of controversy over the compulsory relocation of Navajo persons and families from their homeland.

Stanley Smart is explicit as to why he became a Roadman, a sweat leader, and a Sun Dance chief. He became ill from mercury poisoning after nine years as a mercury miner in mines near McDermitt. While struggling with ill health he often drank too much alcohol. As a Peyotist he was told to stop drinking. During a Peyote session he dreamed that he was "wrong to have raped Mother Earth [as a miner]," learning that a "hex of poisoning" had been put on him for his actions against Mother Earth.

Some of Smart's Indian friends continued to work at the mines and died. Others continued to drink heavily. The context at McDermitt required some changes. Poverty and fear of termination of federal treaty obligations plagued the McDermitt people (Houghton 1973). Smart heeded the admonitions of his fellow Peyotists and avoided alcohol. He counseled with tribal elders and eventually became a Peyote Roadman, participated in local Indian and pan-Indian political and religious movements, brought ritual sweating to McDermitt in 1977, and in 1979 assisted in establishing the Traditional-Unity movement in the western Basin. He pledged the ritual to help "Indian brothers and sisters who are hurting themselves and don't even know it," and to "protest against the rape of 'Mother Earth'." The Sun Dance has subsequently been pledged to stop the deployment of the MX missile system on Shoshone-Paiute lands, to stop the poisoning of all living things, and to take care of the earth so that the earth will be good to Indian people. The eruption of Mount St. Helens in 1980, earthquakes, and airplane crashes are all messages that the spirits' instructions have not been followed and that Indian persons should pay heed.

Conclusions

If the future is like the past, the adoption of ritual sweating in some western Great Basin communities will persist. But the sponsorship of the Pipe-Peyote-sweating-Sun Dance ritual at McDermitt probably will not persist in its current form. The package of rituals comprising the Traditional-Unity movement requires considerable organization, considerable resources (trees, food and water for guests, hauling, construction of Sun Dance grounds), and considerable efforts from hundreds of people. Ritual sweating, like Peyote, requires much less, and its redemptive purposes, being the same as those fostered by the Sun Dance, will probably survive.

There is little doubt that the Ghost Dance transformative movement was more successful among the Northern Shoshone and Ute than it was among the

Southern Paiute, Northern Paiute (who created the religion), and Western Shoshone. Furthermore, the large, highly structured redemptive movements were more successful among the Utes and Northern Shoshone than they were among other Basin groups. Although all native peoples of the Great Basin were deprived, and although in one form or another transformative or redemptive movements were generated in the northern (Sun Dance), eastern (Bear Dance), southern (Mourning-Bear Dance), and western (first and second Ghost Dances) reaches of the Basin, the largest, most complex movements persisted only among those people who were the most complexly organized prior to reservation subjugation.

The Peyote Religion

OMER C. STEWART

The Peyote religion, which uses a small spineless cactus called peyote, *Lophophora williamsii,* as a divine medicine, as a symbol of the supernatural, and as a means of communicating with the supernatural, was discovered in use in the Valley of Mexico when the Spaniards arrived there in the sixteenth century. The cactus grows naturally only in north-central Mexico and in a limited area on the dry rocky hills north of the Rio Grande River in the vicinity of Laredo, Texas. Supplies of the cactus have been cut and dried for shipment to communicants of the Peyote religion in the United States since the 1880s. The ritual of the Peyote religion in the United States was first reported in 1886 by J.L. Hall and was first described by Mooney (1892). The religion first reached the eastern Great Basin, Colorado, in 1896. In 1914 it was established on Uintah-Ouray Reservation, Utah. La Barre (1938) wrote the first general historical and comparative study, which has remained the principal source.

In 1950 estimates of the number of adherents of the Peyote religion in the Great Basin obtained from several sources included:

Eastern Shoshone	235
Bannock and Northern Shoshone	450
Washoe and Northern Paiute	115
Gosiute	90
Southern Paiute	40
Ute	500
Western Shoshone	100
Total	1,530

The total amounts to little more than 10 percent of the estimated 1950 Great Basin Indian population of 13,527 (Tax and Stanley 1960). But such a calculation is misleading. Peyotists are concentrated in about 10 of the more than 50 Indian communities in the region, varying from about 90 percent of the 538 Utes on the Ute Mountain Reservation, the only place where Peyotism is the dominant religion, through about 50 percent of the Gosiute, to only 1 or 2 percent of the Northern Paiute or Western Shoshone. By 1972 the proportions were about the same as in 1950 except that membership had increased at McDermitt and Duck Valley Reservations,

Nevada, while it had declined at Fallon, Gardnerville, and Coleville.

The Peyote Ritual

Two Ute Peyote (O.C. Stewart 1948; Aberle and Stewart 1957) rituals at Whiterocks, Utah, in 1935 and 1972 were remarkably similar, and they were like others in Nevada in 1938 and in 1972, although the one at McDermitt, Nevada, was held in a dwelling (O.C. Stewart 1972). At Whiterocks, the tepee had been prepared Saturday afternoon, including the forming of the sand half-moon altar on the west side of the center of the tepee opposite the doorway opening to the east. Although the fire had been started inside the tepee, the congregation assembled at the entrance and the Roadman, or Chief of the ceremony, offered prayer to Jesus, God, Mary, and Peyote before leading the group into the tepee, everyone passing left of the fire. The ceremonial direction is clockwise, and four is the sacred number.

Prayer remains one of the activities that takes up most of the time of the Peyote meeting. After the congregation is seated, the Roadman opens the service with prayer, followed by the assembling of the paraphernalia for the service. From an equipment box decorated with Peyote symbols, the Roadman removes a gourd rattle (fig. 1), demounted staff, fan, eagle-bone whistle, Chief Peyote, and a bag of cedar leaves. The Chief Drummer, seated to the right of the Roadman, has carried in a water drum, already tied with buckskin head, and a carved wooden drumstick.

There are slight variations in meetings, but the order of service is similar everywhere in the United States. First the Chief Peyote is placed on the altar, then a small bundle of stocks of sagebrush is passed around the tepee, and each person can take a few leaves to rub on hands and clothing. This is followed by one or two sacks of Bull Durham tobacco. Cigarettes are rolled of corn husks or of regular cigarette papers. Each adult has a cigarette, which is lighted when the Doorman or fireman passes around a special fire stick lit from the ceremonial altar fire. When all cigarettes have been lit, the Roadman prays for the congregation, for known sick people, and for the welfare of the world. Following

673

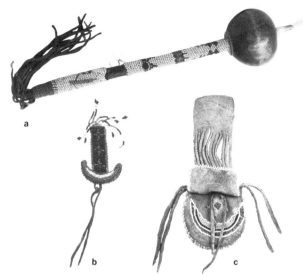

a, Mus. of the Amer. Ind., Heye Foundation, New York: 24/4342; Colo. Histl. Soc., Denver: b, E 1894.71; c, E 1894.20.

Fig. 1. The Peyote ritual. top left, Sam Dick (third from left) and his wife (second from left), Washoes, the morning after a Peyote meeting that was attended by Washoe and Northern Paiute, Mono Lake, Calif., July 1938. center left, Washoe and Northern Paiute canvas-walled "corral" with participants dancing around the Peyote altar after a meeting, Mono Lake, Calif., July 1938. bottom left, Northern Shoshone participants in the Peyote tepee, seated around the fire. The sand half-moon altar is in the foreground. Photographed at Fort Hall Reservation, Idaho, in 1938. bottom right, Jeanne Long Hair, Ute Peyotist with paraphernalia, Uintah-Ouray Reservation, Utah, Oct. 1937. top left, center left, and bottom right, Photographs by Omer C. Stewart. a, Ute Peyote rattle, a gourd with rawhide-covered wood handle wrapped in seed beads. b, Ute Peyote charm of buckskin beaded in the crescent and star motif characteristic of the Peyote religion. The beading is lazy stitch in red, blue, and white seed beads and faceted silver and brass beads. c, Ute Peyote pouch of beaded buckskin, with a crescent and star design in mauve, royal blue, metallic gold, and white seed beads, bordered in light blue, yellow, and white. The cover flap is sewed shut. a–c probably made about 1900. Length of a 37 cm, others same scale.

the prayer, all cigarette butts are placed at the two ends of the altar.

At this point Peyote is distributed in several possible forms. The dried buttons may be passed in a sack, for each person to take four buttons. A "tea" may be passed, and each participant may take four sips. The Peyote may have been ground to a fine powder and then passed around either dry or mixed with water to form a paste and taken with a spoon. In 1972 the form in which the Peyote was consumed appeared to be of no significance. The period of Peyote eating is quiet and solemn.

After the officials have consumed their first serving of Peyote, the Roadman takes up his staff, fan, and gourd rattle and sings the opening song, and then three others with the accompaniment of the drum, beaten by the chief drummer. All present may join in the singing. After the first four songs by the Roadman, the Roadman's staff, rattle, and fan are carefully passed clockwise, followed by the drum and drumsticks. Each male sings four songs and then accompanies his neighbor on the drum.

At midnight the ritual is interrupted by special songs and by the bringing in of a bucket of water to be blessed by a favored woman, usually the wife of the Roadman or the woman of the house where the ritual is taking place. Communicants may go outside for a short intermission if they desire. When the ritual is resumed the Roadman goes outside to blow his whistle and pray to the cardinal directions.

During the ritual, especially after midnight, participants may ask for and receive additional servings of Peyote to eat and may be accorded the opportunity to make a personal prayer while smoking a Bull Durham cigarette, lit by the special fire stick. Such prayers frequently include confessions of personal failures to adhere to the rule against the use of alcohol and prayers for future strength. Much of the service appears oriented to curing physical and mental illness.

The ceremony ends with special prayers and blessings connected with a ceremonial meal of water, maize, meat, and fruit. The singing, drumming, and praying last all night (10–14 hours) and are followed by a feast an hour or two later, as soon as the women can prepare it.

Thus the Peyote religion serves as an important social event as well as an impressive religious experience. It strengthens Indian self-respect and group identity. It is a pan-Indian movement that helps the Indians keep a strong group identity while adjusting to the national culture of the United States.

Peyote Art

As elsewhere where the Peyote religion is followed seriously, in the Great Basin a special Peyote art has been known as long as the religion has been present. Sam Lone Bear, an early Peyote missionary, and his followers produced paintings on cloth that served as altars. His carefully manufactured Peyote staff or cane was decorated with incised and painted lightning symbols. Beads were used to decorate handles of gourd rattles, handles of feather fans, joints of demountable staffs, buckskin bags to hold cedar incense, as well as small skin bags to wear suspended from the neck in which to carry a protective Peyote button. These bags were popular with Peyotists in the army in World War II, in Korea, and in Vietnam. Beaded broaches with Peyote symbols are popular items in Indian stores and are frequently purchased by Whites who are unaware of the meaning of the symbols. The same is true of metal ornaments—bolo ties, earrings, pins, and pendants. At least one Great Basin artist has gained national recognition as a painter in oils specializing in Peyote themes. Clifford Duncan, President of the Native American Church of the Uintah-Ouray Reservation, Utah, has exhibited widely (fig. 2).

Syncretism

Nearly all Great Basin Indians had been vigorously proselytized by Mormons or traditional Christian denominations for at least a half-century before Peyotism came among them. By then Anglo-American culture was everywhere in the Great Basin a powerful force, in addition to the remnants of aboriginal values and beliefs. The mixing of aboriginal religious culture and Christianity had already occurred in the Ghost Dance before the Peyote religion arrived in the Great Basin, and such syncretism continued after its introduction.

Peyotism has often been bracketed with the Ghost Dance. Thus the Ghost Dance is said to have prepared the way for the spread of the Peyote religion, which "flowed easily along the newly opened channels of friendship" (Shonle 1925:57). "The Ghost Dance messianism may be considered to have paved the way for this sudden diffusion of the use of the vision-giving drug in the religions of the reservation tribes of the United States" (MacLeod 1928:530). "With the dying out of the Ghost Dance . . . the use of peyote . . . spread from group to group" (La Barre 1947:294). Although many other authors have repeated the idea set forth by Shonle, historical documents establish that Peyotism had become an active ritual among at least 20 tribes in Texas, Oklahoma, and Nebraska (O.C. Stewart 1971) before Wovoka (Jack Wilson) had directed the first Ghost Dance among the Northern Paiute people in western Nevada about 1889 (Mooney 1896:784).

Both the Ghost Dance and the Peyote religion taught the value of peaceful intertribal relations. Both taught that Jesus is a living God who can appear anytime on earth. But since both religions existed during the entire 675

period of the Ghost Dance in Oklahoma, and since many individuals participated in both almost simultaneously, the interpretation that one prepared the way for the other or that one greatly influenced the other seems unwarranted. More than 20 years intervened between the end of the Ghost Dance in Nevada and the acceptance there of the Peyote religion. A letter from the Nevada Agency of the Bureau of Indian Affairs written in 1917 states that Wovoka:

> is the "Messiah" and the originator of the "Ghost Dance". He . . . apparently has considerable influence among distant tribes and he seemingly keeps in close touch with them; that he is corresponding with certain individuals in Montana, South Dakota, Wyoming, and Oklahoma. It is also learned that some few Indians from a distance have called upon him at his home. . . . It was learned that upon a recent trip to Oklahoma he raised about $400.00 in cash, besides valuable gifts. . . . After careful inquiry I am satisfied that Jack Wilson does not use peyote or mescal, nor has he encouraged its use by others. . . . he is constantly advising the Indians to abstain from the use of all drugs and intoxicants (O.C. Stewart 1977).

From childhood Wovoka had received "religious and moral training" in Christianity (Dangberg 1957:284). Similar experience with Christianity continued among the Northern Paiute in Nevada and could have prepared others for an Indian religion with a number of Christian elements. For example, Northern Paiute shaman Joe Green became a deacon of the Episcopal Mission at Pyramid Lake while still an Indian doctor. He maintained both religions when he also became a Peyote religion convert. Two Colorado Ute Peyotists also reported being shamans and Peyotists at the same time that they accepted traditional Christianity (Aberle and Stewart 1957:41). For example, Uintah Ute John Duncan (fig. 3) became a Peyotist and was devout for 20 years yet remained an active Episcopalian.

On the other hand, many features of the Peyote religion are similar to Great Basin Indian aboriginal religious patterns, parallels that might have made the new religion acceptable to some. Among the Ute Mountain Ute, where Peyotism is the dominant religion, there were many parallels between ancient Ute religion and Peyotism: "curative, prophetic and moral functions . . . inducing dreams and visions of power . . . pooling of shamanistic power . . . fanning people . . . with eagle-tail feather wands . . . clockwise circuit . . . shamanistic

top, Omer C. Stewart, Boulder, Colo.
Fig. 2. Peyote structures. Canvas tepees are the most desirable place to conduct the Peyote ritual, but other structures may be used (O.C. Stewart 1982a:201). top, Oil painting symbolizing the water bird and Peyote tepee. By Ute artist Clifford Duncan, Whiterocks, Utah, 1971. center, Western Shoshone tepee, Goshute Reservation, Ibapah, Utah, used for Peyote meeting. Photograph by Omer C. Stewart, Nov. 1939. bottom, Washoe "corral" enclosure for the Peyote ceremony, Coleville, Calif. Photograph by Edgar Siskin, Aug. 1939.

676

top, Smithsonian, NAA: 1516-A; bottom, Nev. Histl. Soc., Reno: 386.

Fig. 3. Peyotists. top, John Duncan, Uintah Ute, Whiterocks, Uintah-Ouray Reservation, Utah. Photograph by DeLancey Gill, Bureau of American Ethnology, Washington, D.C., 1905. bottom, Louise Byers Lancaster (left), Western Shoshone from Fallon, Nev., and her husband Ben Lancaster (d. 1953), Washoe leader. Photograph by Arthur Rothstein, Stewart, Nev., 1940.

cane . . . eastward orientation of the tipi,'' and others (Opler 1940a:465, 476). Among the Washoe, less than 10 percent of whom became Peyotists, there were also similarities between Peyotism and shamanism: "Both are curing ceremonies combining social as well as religious features. The session in both cases begins around nine o'clock in the evening; no one is excluded, men and women are accorded equal status, and all participate in the singing and smoking. . . . lasts all night and

is concluded with a feast. Eagle feathers, rattle, and a bird-bone whistle are used in both. So it is with the pattern number 4 and the clockwise circuits. . . . Both the shaman and peyote diagnose sickness. . . . In a word, both constitute a medicoreligious complex'' (Siskin 1983:137).

But differences in the similarity between Peyotism and shamanism in the individual Indian communities in the Great Basin do not appear to explain varying acceptance of the Peyote religion. The total rejection of Peyotism at Yomba, a conservative Western Shoshone community in central Nevada, where "peyote has been integrated into the traditional cognitive system" (Lieber 1965), can be contrasted with Goshute Reservation, a conservative Western Shoshone community in eastern Nevada where about 50 percent became Peyotists.

For a small minority of Great Basin Indians, Peyotism appears as a welcome native religion that serves as a focus for Indian spiritual life and as an aid to resist the temptations of alcohol. As a Christianized Indian religion, Peyotism can serve as a bridge between the ancient and modern belief systems for that relatively small number of Indians who have accepted Peyotism and who live by its strict rules of conduct.

History

Indians of the Great Basin learned of Peyotism via several different routes and at various times. The two sects of the Peyote religion are the Half-Moon or Tepee Way of the Comanche, Kiowa, Southern Cheyenne, and Southern Arapahoe, which appears to have been formalized by the Comanche in the 1880s, and the Big Moon or Cross-Fireplace rite, originated by the Caddo Indian, John Wilson, near Anadarko, Oklahoma, also about 1880, which spread to the Delaware, Osage, Quapaw, Winnebago, Sioux, and to the Great Basin.

The Half-Moon Way was learned by the Utes of southern Colorado during two visits to Oklahoma. Ute informants in 1948 remembered that Buckskin Charlie, a Ute chief at Ignacio, Colorado, had learned of Peyote while visiting the Cheyenne in 1900 and before, and said that an Arapahoe Peyotist, Henry Lincoln, also visited the Colorado Ute to conduct Peyote meetings in 1900. A Cheyenne Indian is reported to have returned to Colorado with Buckskin Charlie in 1896 and lived with the Ute (Woodson 1896). Taos Indians remembered that Taos Indians accompanied Utes to Oklahoma and also learned of the Peyote religion there (Parsons 1936:62).

The Half-Moon rite was also taught to the Eastern Shoshone about 1909 by the Northern Arapahoe, who share the Wind River Reservation in Wyoming, who had learned it 15 years earlier. A Southern Arapahoe Peyote leader and proselytizer, Jock Bull Bear, of Oklahoma, corresponded with Charles Washakie about the fine points of the ritual in 1919, and several Shoshones traveled to the Cheyenne and Arapahoe reservation to receive instruction in the ritual and theology of Half-Moon Peyotism (Stenberg 1946). The Western Shoshone Sam Nipwater, who moved to the Wind River Reservation, taught Half-Moon rites to Northern and Western Shoshones and to Southern Paiutes in Utah from 1930 at least until 1971. He participated in Half-Moon rituals with the Southern Paiute in Cedar City, Utah, in 1970 but was not the first to teach Peyotism to them. Southern Paiutes originally learned from the Gosiute and in 1972 continued to travel to Ibapah and Skull Valley, Utah, and to Nevada, to attend meetings.

Sam Lone Bear, a Sioux from South Dakota, was the principal Peyote missionary to the Great Basin tribes, starting with the Ute in 1914. Lone Bear participated in Big Moon Peyote rituals with Winnebagos and Oglala Sioux. He had become a Peyote supplier by means of trips to Oklahoma and Texas and by receiving shipments by mail or express before going to Utah. In late summer 1914 Lone Bear arrived with a large supply of Peyote on the Uintah-Ouray Reservation and settled at Dragon, Utah, among Uncompahgre Utes in one of the most isolated parts of the reservation, far from the Bureau of Indians Affairs agency. But he soon visited other parts of the reservation to spread the religion.

Federal government employees on the Uintah-Ouray Reservation were so upset about Lone Bear and his activities that they began to exert vigorous political pressure on the Colorado and Utah legislatures to outlaw Peyote. Both states passed laws prohibiting Peyote in February 1917. The Chief Special Officer of the Bureau of Indian Affairs, Henry A. Larson, was also recommending state legislation against Peyote.

In 1916, responding to a nationwide questionnaire from the Bureau of Indian Affairs, Superintendent Kneale (1916) reported "possibly 40% or 50% of the Indians" of Uintah-Ouray Reservation were Peyotists, that is, over 1,000 adherents. He wrote that Peyote was introduced into Uintah-Ouray "in 1914 by a Sioux Indian [who] interested some of our very best men." The superintendent of the Wind River Reservation forwarded a 1916 report that said about 30 Eastern Shoshones used peyote. White observers there "admired the ritual of the lodge and . . . saw nothing reprehensible at the meetings" (J. Roberts 1916). Colorado Indian agents denied the use of Peyote among the Ute Mountain Ute and the Southern Ute in 1916, as it was also denied for tribes of the Fort Hall Reservation, Idaho, and the other tribes of the Great Basin.

Sam Lone Bear is given credit by Bannock and Northern Shoshone informants at Fort Hall and by a Northern Paiute Peyotist from Fallon, Nevada, for introducing the Peyote religion into Idaho about 1915–1920 (Sven Liljeblad, personal communication 1971; John Wright,

personal communication 1938; O.C. Stewart 1971). That Lone Bear was an active proselytizer was further confirmed by Colorado Ute Indian reports in 1936, 1937, and 1938 (Opler 1940a:468; O.C. Stewart 1938a), which place Lone Bear in southern Colorado as a Peyote missionary in 1917. That year he was arrested and spent 15 days in a Grand Junction, Colorado, jail for violation of the Colorado anti-Peyote law.

The Gosiute Shoshone of the Deep Creek Reservation, 60 miles south of Wendover, Utah, first received the attention of Sam Lone Bear in 1925 according to Hayes (1940:34), but other research has dated the first peyote there at 1929 (Lily Pete, personal communications 1937, 1972, 1980). Although Lone Bear taught his Big Moon rite, he told the Gosiute that "within a short time the 'Tipi Way' [Half-Moon Way] or orthodox procedure of the Native American Church" would come to them. The Gosiute reported "that in Lone Bear's meetings tobacco was never used" (Hayes 1940:34). Malouf (1942:93) reported two Peyote sects among the Gosiute. He recorded the Half-Moon rite, and by 1937 a written order-of-service of the Half-Moon Way had been supplied to the Gosiute by "an Oklahoma Indian" (O.C. Stewart 1944:121). In 1972 Sam Lone Bear was remembered by the Gosiute and by the Ruby Valley Western Shoshone. A staff left by Lone Bear in 1929 was cared for and used as a sacred object by a Western Shoshone near Elko, Sammy Long.

In 1937 the Gosiute Tribal Council (1937) sent a letter to Commissioner of Indian Affairs John Collier that said the Gosiute were killing themselves with Peyote. Correspondence followed between the superintendent in charge of the Gosiute, and the Bureau of Indian Affairs in Washington. In 1938 a Gosiute tribal councilman wrote again to Commissioner Collier, this time through the office of Joseph Chez (1938), attorney general of Utah, who added: "I suggest that you . . . take up the complaint and take diligent steps to protect the Indians from Peyote." At the same time Arthur Johnson and Clyde McGill were requesting the Indian agent and school teacher at Deep Creek, Utah, A.L. Robertson, to protect their rights to practice their religion. A.L. Robertson (1938) estimated that of the total of 158 Gosiutes at Deep Creek, 71 were Peyotists.

Other Nevada Shoshones became aware of Peyote via the Fort Hall Reservation (O.C. Stewart 1982a). A tribal council letter from the Western Shoshone Agency, Duck Valley Reservation, Owyhee, Nevada, March 6, 1939, to Commissioner Collier (Premo, Thacker, and Davis 1939) outlined the history of Peyotism on that reservation. A Shoshone named Dan Dick had brought Peyote to Owyhee in 1915 to be used to try to cure an abscess. The treatment did no good and Dan Dick was "reprimanded for bringing peyote on to the reservation by the tribal council." In 1936, three men came the 200 or so miles from Fort Hall to visit Owyhee for a celebration when the community hall was dedicated. The men had brought Peyote and stayed long enough to instruct a local group in its use. Jessie Little, a Northern Paiute on the Duck Valley Reservation, said in 1972 that the first Peyote meeting at Owyhee was held in her home in 1937 as a curing ritual for her husband, George Little. George was healed and became a leader and missionary for Peyote until his death about 1955. By 1939, of a total of about 1,000 Indians on the Duck Valley Reservation, the tribal council estimated "175 members who use peyote to some extent."

In 1939, the Duck Valley Tribal Council wished to enact a tribal ordinance to make use of Peyote on the reservation a criminal offense but were dissuaded from doing so by a letter from Commissioner Collier (1939). About the same time Peyote was "just beginning to filter down from the Fort Hall Agency" to the White Knife Western Shoshone of Owyhee but it "never reached ceremonial proportions, and [was] used only individually by a few Indians" (Harris 1940:108).

A 1944 report from the Western Shoshone Agency, Duck Valley Reservation, stated that "a small percent . . . profess adherence to the belief in the Native American Church" (U.S. Congress. House. Committee on Indian Affairs 1953:597). In 1963, Douglas Little was leader of Peyotists at Owyhee (Sven Liljeblad, personal communication 1971). Reuben Hardin, Northern Paiute, was leading Peyote meetings in 1956 at McDermitt Reservation, and Stanley Smart was leader there in 1968 and 1972. In 1972 the Northern Paiute of McDermitt gave credit to George Little as the first Peyotist to conduct services in their community; since then Roadmen have visited Oklahoma in order to learn the Peyote ritual. The ritual observed in 1972 was designated "pure Comanche."

Anti-Peyote attitudes were recorded among the Western Shoshone at Yomba Reservation, near Austin, Nevada, in the summer of 1964, but the number of Peyotists there, if any, was not mentioned (Lieber 1965).

The Northern Paiute were also missionized by Sam Lone Bear. During 1929 he was reported in Montana, Wyoming, and Nevada. In 1938 he was the first Peyotist proselytizer remembered as being with the Northern Paiute of Pyramid Lake, Reno, Fallon, and elsewhere (O.C. Stewart 1944:69). The Big Moon ritual he practiced at Fallon disappeared with his departure. John Wright of Fallon had learned this ritual at Fort Hall in 1920 but later spent several weeks each winter in Oklahoma participating in Half-Moon rituals among the Cheyenne and Arapahoe (U.S. Bureau of Indian Affairs 1943; Mrs. Lone Bear, personal communication 1971; O.C. Stewart 1938a).

In 1932 a Uintah Ute Peyotist, Ralph Kochampanaskin, sometimes also called Lone Bear, arrived in western Nevada. He married a Washoe woman and settled in the Washoe community. Although a much-traveled and experienced Peyotist, his rituals had limited appeal, even though he taught them to the Washoe medicine man Sam Dick (fig. 1), who later became a director of Peyote ceremonies (O.C. Stewart 1944:69, pl. 1a).

In October 1936 a Washoe Indian, Ben Lancaster (alias Chief Gray Horse) (fig. 3) returned to his home near Gardnerville, Nevada, with a large supply of Peyote and the ritual paraphernalia and knowledge to run Peyote meetings. During 20 years away from home, Ben Lancaster had traveled widely and acquired a good command of English, plus the techniques of an experienced patent-medicine salesman, which he had in fact been for several years. His personal history and the history of the Peyote religion he introduced to the Washoe and Northern Paiute of Nevada and eastern California were recorded by O.C. Stewart (1944) and Siskin (1941, 1983). Ben Lancaster's ritual was a typical Half-Moon rite.

Although only about 5 to 10 percent of the Washoe and Northern Paiute who were proselytized during the first two years became converts, Stewart found no social, cultural, or economic conditions that united the converts or explained their acceptance of the new religion. Peyotists represented a cross-section of Nevada Indian society.

The intertribal nature of Peyote religion in Oklahoma is well known (La Barre 1938). It has also become the major pan-Indian institution in the Great Basin. Several Peyotists from the East have been resident missionaries in Great Basin communities, and Oklahoma Peyote leaders have been frequent visitors to the Ute at Towaoc, Colorado, as well as to communities in Utah, Idaho, and Nevada. Among these visitors between 1920 and 1970 were Alfred Wilson and Sam Standing Water (Southern Cheyennes), Baldwin Parker and Thomas Black (Comanches), Truman Dailey and Edgar Moore (Otos), Allen Dale (Omaha), and Joe Kaulaity (Kiowa). In 1972 a Southern Arapahoe Peyotist lived with his Washoe wife in Carson City, Nevada. Two Sioux Peyotists were married to Northern Shoshone women and supervised Peyote affairs there from 1950 to 1972. Two Southern Arapahoe brothers married to Navajos, and their father, frequently visited nearly every Peyote congregation in the Great Basin.

Great Basin Indians have often visited Oklahoma and Texas in search of the peyote cactus and also to gain understanding of the Peyote ritual.

In 1913 a Bannock was living in Lawton, Oklahoma, and learning of Peyote from a famous Comanche Roadman, Post Oak Jim (Wallace and Hoebel 1952:109). Both Ute and Gosiute reported traveling to visit the Eastern Shoshone and Northern Arapahoe Peyote meetings with Sam Lone Bear during the 1920s. An Eastern Shoshone started periodic visits to the Comanche in Oklahoma in 1937. By 1972 he was married to a Bannock and living at Fort Hall, Idaho. He had visited Lawton, Oklahoma 20–30 times, and had attended Peyote meetings with adherents of many Plains tribes in Oklahoma, Montana, and Alberta.

In 1972 Peyotism was strong among the Washoe and Northern Paiute only in three communities. At Woodfords, California, Ramsay Walker and two adult sons conducted meetings at home and served as visiting leaders in other Nevada and California communities. Walker learned from Ben Lancaster, and attended meetings with the Washoe Sam Dick, and with George Little and Jim Humpy (Northern Paiutes of Owyhee, Nevada), and John Two Eagles (Sioux) at Fort Hall, Idaho. He has been host to Truman Dailey (Oto), Ralph Turtle and John Pedro (Southern Arapahoes) from Oklahoma as well as participating in meetings in Oklahoma. With Frank Takes Gun (Crow) in 1958, Ramsey Walker was an incorporator of the Native American Church of California. In 1972 he was invited frequently to be Roadman for Peyote meetings held almost weekly near Healdsburg, California, for members of the Native American Church of the San Francisco area.

Nevada and Idaho Peyotists reported in 1972 that there had been an active congregation of Peyotists at Burns, Oregon, but that no local Roadman developed so that meetings were infrequent. At Nixon, Nevada, a Northern Paiute Peyotist from Warner Valley, California, reported in 1972 that there had been an active group in that community that had disappeared for want of leadership.

Peyotists from the Great Basin have not been noted frequently as participants in Native American Church conventions. Orin Curry, a Ute Indian of Utah, attended a convention at Calumet, Oklahoma, on June 6, 1925 (Haag and Wilson 1925). John Pokeebro (Bannock) and Sam Nevada (Northern Shoshone) attended the 1946 meeting at White Oak, Oklahoma. At the 1950 convention at Apache, Oklahoma, John Pokibro was appointed to the NAC Board of Directors by President Allen Dale. In 1952, another convention at Apache, Oklahoma, was attended by the following Indians from the Great Basin: Harvey and Edward Natches and David Colorow (Utes), John Two Eagles (Sioux of Fort Hall), and Willie Jim (Northern Shoshone). In 1972 an informal intertribal meeting to discuss Peyote problems was called at Ashland, Montana. From the Great Basin were Clifford Duncan and Harvey Natches and John Two Eagles.

Peyote and the Law

Laws prohibiting the use of peyote were passed in Colorado, Utah, and Nevada in 1917, in Wyoming in 1929, and in Idaho in 1935. Very few court cases resulted. The Utah law was declared unconstitutional by a Uintah County judge about 1930 and was repealed in 1935 (O.C. Stewart 1948:5) yet in 1938 two Ute Indians were arrested, tried, convicted, and given a suspended sentence by a judge of the District Court at Monticello, San Juan County, Utah (Collier 1938). The Nevada law was dropped from the law books, so that an amendment to it passed in 1941 was ruled invalid; this was the basis for the dismissal, on March 17, 1942, of charges of illegal possession of peyote brought against Ben Lancaster when he was arrested in Reno on Oct. 24, 1941 (*Washington Daily News,* March 19, 1942). The Idaho law was repealed in 1937.

In part as a defense against such laws, the Peyote religion was incorporated in various states as the Native American Church. It was evidently the Bannock and Northern Shoshone who first filed papers of incorporation in March 1925, listing among their purposes to recognize "the sacramental use of the Peyote . . . with its teachings of morality, sobriety, industry, kindly charity and right living, and to cultivate a spirit of self-respect and brotherly union among . . . Indians" (Diggie et al. 1925).

Frank Takes Gun, vice president of the NAC, was very active in helping Peyotist groups incorporate under state laws. In June 1945 the Navajo of southeastern Utah filed the articles of incorporation of the NAC for Utah. Such articles, of course, also served for the Ute, Gosiute, and Southern Paiute Peyotists of Utah. The Ute of Colorado incorporated in April 1946, and the Northern Paiute and Washoe of California and Nevada filed articles in those states in May 1958. Record of the incorporation of the NAC in Wyoming has not come to light, although Peyotists in all states came under the charter of the NAC of the United States in 1944 (when the NAC incorporated in 1918 in Oklahoma broadened its charter). In 1955 the NAC of the U.S. became the NAC of North America.

In March 1965 the Nevada state legislature reconsidered prohibiting Peyote. Testimony by members of the Native American Church, supported by Warren d'Azevedo as an expert witness, convinced the legislature that the NAC was a bona fide religion and should be allowed under the provisions for freedom of religion guaranteed by the constitution of Nevada.

California was the last to legislate against Peyote, in 1959. Nevertheless, the legal history there assumes extra importance. Stimulated by stated opinions of constituents who thought the California anti-Peyote law was unconstitutional, Assemblyman Nicholas C. Petris requested an opinion by Stanley Mosk, attorney general of California. In April 1962, before the opinion of the attorney general was prepared, a Navajo Peyote meeting in San Bernardino County, California, was raided; and Jack Woody, Dan Dee Nez, and Leon B. Anderson, all Navajos, were arrested. The case became known as Woody *et al.* and was tried in San Bernardino, California, in November 1962 with Frank Takes Gun, NAC President, Truman Dailey, Gordon A. Alles (University of California at Los Angeles pharmacologist), and Omer C. Stewart (University of Colorado anthropologist) as expert witnesses for the defense. With the opinion of Attorney General Mosk justifying the Peyote prohibition in hand, Superior Judge Carl B. Hilliard found the Peyotists guilty, December 2, 1962. The case reached the California Supreme Court, where on August 24, 1964, Judge J. Tobriner delivered an opinion reversing the lower court, thus freeing Woody *et al.* (California Supreme Court 1964). Peyotism was declaired protected by the First Amendment of the U.S. Constitution, and the Native American Church was allowed to use Peyote, even when it might be prohibited for other use. The 1964 California Supreme Court opinion would, of course, protect the religious freedom of Washoe and Northern Paiute in California, but it has had a much wider influence.

In fact, the U.S. Drug Abuse Act of 1972 included an exemption for the Native American Church. All the states of the Great Basin have followed suit. Thus in 1972, the Native American Church use of Peyote was legal in Colorado, Nevado, Idaho, Wyoming, and Utah, following the legal opinion of the California Supreme Court and the laws of the U.S. Congress.

Despite protection of the law, Peyotists continued to be subject of "discriminatory harassment . . . being arrested for possession and use of peyote. And unlike consideration given other religions, they were often under the burden of having to prove . . . their legitimate membership in the Native American Church" (Native American Rights Fund 1979:5). In response to a growing concern for the lack of a clear federal policy safeguarding Indian aboriginal and constitutional rights to freedom of religion, in 1978 Congress passed the American Indian Religious Freedom Act (P.L. 95–341). Although the Peyote religion was not mentioned explicitly in the act, it is protected under the following provision: "henceforth it shall be the policy of the United States to protect and preserve for American Indians their in-

herent right of freedom to believe, express, and exercise the traditional religions . . . including but not limited to access to sites, use and possession of sacred objects, and the freedom to worship through ceremonials and traditional rites" (P.L. 95–341 in Native American Rights Fund 1979:4).

Sources

Published sources on Peyotism in the Great Basin are relatively few and date mostly from the 1940s. Malouf (1942) discusses the presence of two Peyote cults, both of Plains origin, among the Gosiute; he draws in part from Hayes's (1940) seminal article. Peyotism among the Washoe and its impact on shamanism is Siskin's (1941, 1983) subject. For a critical review of Siskin's works see O.C. Stewart (1984a). On Washoe Peyote songs see Merriam and d'Azevedo (1957), and d'Azevedo (1973, 1978a) on Washoe Peyote narratives. O.C. Stewart's (1944) history of the diffusion of Peyotism among the Washoe and Northern Paiute includes an element distribution list for the two groups and other Great Basin and Plains tribes and statistical information on Great Basin Peyotism. For a divergent interpretation of the Peyote religion among the Southern Ute compare O.C. Stewart (1941a) and Opler (1942). O.C. Stewart's (1984) lifetime association with Ute Peyotism is discussed in an autobiographical article, part of a larger work on Peyotism in the West (Stewart and Aberle 1984).

Unpublished sources on Great Basin Peyotism include articles of incorporation of the Native American Church (Diggie et al. 1925); letters to the commissioner of Indian affairs (Gosiute Tribal Council 1937; Chez 1938; Premo, Thacker, and Davis 1939); letters from the commissioner to local tribal councils (for example, Collier 1939); and correspondence on Peyote in possession of anthropologists (for example, A.L. Robertson 1938).

Music

THOMAS VENNUM, JR.

As is universal in American Indian music, traditional Great Basin music consists almost exclusively of songs performed by individuals or groups singing in unison, with or without percussion accompaniment they provide themselves. Songs are recognized as having specific uses, be they curative, magical, or essential components of dances and religious ceremonies.

In distinguishing among the various song styles, students of American Indian music have come to recognize the salient traits of the prototypical Great Basin style as the following: narrow melodic ranges, a relaxed vocal performance, undulating melodic contours with frequent returns to the tonic, a limited number of rhythmic values, and a tendency toward paired phrase structure (see Nettl 1954:297–301). These traits are evident in song 1a, a Northern Paiute Badger song. Presumably it is sung by Badger, who in legends brings on winter; the paired texts and general structure suggest it to be a Round Dance song, performed during the pine nut harvest. The text alludes to the onset of winter: people move among the mountains, knowing that the pine nuts, a Paiute staple, will have ripened (C.S. Fowler, personal communication 1983). A typical Basin melody, it conforms to the traits mentioned: a limited range—it moves within the interval of a 4th; a performance style lacking vocal tension—the singer comfortably places the song in her lower register; an absence of vocal pulsation—in part due to the assignment of different syllables to almost every tone, a pervasive Basin practice. The melodic movement of the Badger song is descending with some undulation, and the tendency for most phrases to end on the tonic (D in all transcriptions here), is clear. Rhythmic variety is restricted essentially to three durational values. Like many Basin melodies, it is tritonic (see song 2) (Crum 1980:6, 14), and the internal repetition in the doubled text in phrase A exhibits the tendency toward paired-phrase structure that is often claimed for the majority of Basin songs, although it is only one of several structural types.

While the Badger song exhibits those characteristics thought most typically to represent Basin music, other styles present in Basin repertoires diverge sufficiently from this prototype to suggest the need for a reassessment of the Great Basin as a single musical culture area. A reconstruction of the history of Great Basin music awaits a full analysis of archival holdings of sound recordings and accompanying documentation. Early collecting in the Basin, even more than elsewhere in North America, was uneven and sporadic; almost no information has surfaced for the central area. The task is further complicated by the fact that religious movements, such as the Ghost Dance and Peyote religion, diffused quickly and exposed Basin people to new musical repertoires and styles. Still, with present evidence it is possible tentatively to recognize at least three distinct music culture areas—the northeastern, western, and southwestern sectors (fig. 1)—even though boundary lines are difficult to draw, particularly on the peripheries of the Basin where hybrid styles are found. These distinctions are based on musical instrument distribution, song genres or use categories (table 1), and musical styles. Generally speaking, the farther north and east one moves, the greater the infusion of Plains styles and practices, while on the southwestern fringes much of the musical culture is virtually indistinguishable from that of California tribes, such as the Yokuts or Monache.

Musical Instruments

Areal distinctions are reflected in the instrument inventories of Basin tribes, although compared to other culture areas in North America, the Great Basin is striking in its limited use of musical instruments. Except for shamans' rattles and sticks beaten during hand games, musical instruments widely distributed elsewhere on the continent were either lacking in the Great Basin or comparatively late borrowings from adjacent peoples. Where almost universally Indian songs were accompanied by some form of percussion provided by the singer, the older layer of Basin music is best represented by the Round Dance, the oldest and most widespread style in the Basin, known by many names (W.Z. Park 1941) in which the performers' voices were the only regulators of dance steps. Songs for the Ghost Dance, the Uintah Ute Woman's Dance, the Washoe Girl's Puberty Dance, the Northern Paiute Hump Dance, and the Lemhi Northern Shoshone early spring *nuakkinna*, to name but a few, were all unaccompanied, as were the songs of Ute medicine men and an Owens Valley basketgame hider, who kept time to the music simply

Fig. 1. Great Basin music culture areas.

by raising and lowering the back edge of his basket (Steward 1933b:286).

Chordophones (stringed instruments) were nonexistent in the Basin, except possibly for some use of

top, Catherine S. Fowler, Reno, Nev., bottom, Harvard U., Peabody Mus.: 34–114–10/3961.

Fig. 2. Flageolets. top, Nick Downington, a Northern Paiute from Honey Lake, Calif., playing an elderberry flageolet used for doctoring. Photograph by Willard Z. Park, 1935. bottom, Simple 4-holed flageolet. Collected by Willard Z. Park, Honey Lake, Calif., 1934; length 36 cm.

the musical bow by antelope shamans. Excluding toys, the two aerophones known in the northeastern Basin were the eagle-bone Sun Dance whistle and the courting flute, an end-blown flageolet common to many North American tribes and probably imported to the Basin via the Crow (Joseph G. Jorgensen, personal communication 1983). Both were restricted in distribution principally to the northeast (cf. Steward 1933b:278, 316). A section of elderberry (or willow), as long as 24 inches, an inch or more in diameter, was split, its pith removed, and the pieces glued back together (fig. 2). A smaller, shorter (8 inch) flute was used for doctoring in the western and southwestern sectors. Although some Basin (mostly southwestern) flutes had four holes, most had six. Little flute music was recorded in the Basin. Steward collected one simple, tritonic flute melody at Mono Lake, although his illustration of the instrument shows seven holes, rare for an instrument from this area (Steward 1933b:277, fig. 9). While Ute were still making and playing the flageolet in 1914, by then it had disappeared from Northern Shoshone culture (Lowie 1909:206).

The single-hole Sun Dance whistle was made from the humerus bone of an eagle with an eagle pin-feather attached as decoration. Tied around the dancer's neck, it was held between his teeth ("Ghost Dance, Bear Dance, and Sun Dance," fig. 3, this vol.). Capable of

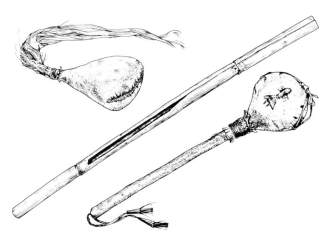

Mus. of the Amer. Ind., Heye Foundation, New York: top, 8/7410; bottom, 13/1465; center, Eastern Calif. Mus., Independence: 12 571.51.

Fig. 3. Rattles. top, Rawhide rattle. The skin is shaped while wet, filled with pebbles, and then allowed to dry. It becomes increasingly hard and resonant. From the fringed and bead-wrapped handle trails a shank of dyed horsehair. Collected from the Ute before 1918. center, Split-stick rattle, a section of cane split up through one joint to a point just below the other joint. Collected from the Owens Valley Paiute maker, Tom Stone, 1962. bottom, Rawhide rattle, with a rawhide-covered stick handle. The juncture between rattle and handle is fringed and wrapped with multicolored strands of seed beads. Painting on the rattle depicts a dancing woman in traditional dress. Buckskin thongs sport home-made metal cones enclosing tufts of dyed horsehair. Collected by W. Wildschut on the Fort Hall Reservation, Idaho, before 1923. Length of center 53 cm, others same scale.

VENNUM

only one tone, the whistle was used percussively by the dancers, who gave it shrill blasts in time to the music. Occasionally they might sing through it (Opler 1941:564). Such whistles were used in the 1980s in the Sun Dance and Peyote ceremonies and by some Ute and Eastern Shoshone shamans.

Several types of idiophones were known; the materials from which they were fashioned generally indicate their provenance. The few cocoon rattles were trade items from California, found among the Washoe and Owens Valley Paiute. They were a shaman's instrument, as was the deer's ear rattle, made by sewing ears together to form a sphere containing pebbles. In Owens Valley they were used in the sweathouse after a rabbit drive (Steward 1933b:278); elsewhere, in the western Great Basin, they were used by shamans in doctoring. In the northeastern Basin, rattles made from gourds or rawhide were shaken in the Sun Dance and in the Ute chinúanhkaγa dance, where participants had rattling objects attached to their costumes as well (Lowie 1915:832; normalized). The Ute Deer Hoof Rattle Dance was accompanied by deer or antelope dewclaws strung on the ends of long sticks. The cleft-stick rattle widely used by California tribes (Merriam and Spier 1959:614) was found only in the southwestern Basin. This rattle spread northeast from Owens Valley or Death Valley with the South or Exhibition Dance (Steward 1941:251; see illustration in Pietroforte 1965:54–55). The notched rasp, for which Densmore (1922:26) introduced the term morache, was used to accompany the Bear Dance wherever it was practiced in the Basin.

Membranophones, or drums, probably even absent aboriginally, were restricted at least historically to the northeastern Basin. They were unknown, for example, in Owens Valley as recently as Steward's (1933b:278) fieldwork. Their later arrival farther west is reflected in the Bannock word for drum, witua, which originally referred to a clay bucket. Historically the drum reached only the easternmost Western Shoshone via the Ute (Steward 1941:251), while Surprise Valley Northern Paiute date its arrival from the northeast at the same time as Whites (Kelly 1932:147). Before the introduction of actual drums to the Basin, singers in the northeastern sector simply beat with sticks on a stiff buffalo rawhide, which they held by a thong threaded through holes in its perimeter. Snake River Northern Shoshone–Bannock women performed in this fashion for an outer circle of warriors dancing around them (Sven Liljeblad, personal communication 1983) as did the Ute in their Begging Dance (Lowie 1915:833) and Northern Shoshone in recruiting members for a horse raid, a musical custom they shared with the Nez Perce (Lowie 1909:194).

The large dance drum, two to three feet in diameter (fig. 4), was probably diffused with the Plains warrior societies into northeastern regions in the late nineteenth century. Made of hollowed cottonwood, the frame was covered with two heads of elk rawhide laced together. The upper head might have some symbolic design painted on it, such as a bird (see Lowie 1909:fig. 19 for an Eastern Shoshone example). As elsewhere in North America, it was being replaced with the commercial bass drum about 1900. The most common drums in the northeastern Basin were the single-headed hand drums, 12 inches in diameter, with crossed holding thongs on the back (fig. 4). They were played on by four or five singers, usually standing in a line facing the dancers (Densmore 1922:106, 156), to accompany nearly every dance except the Sun Dance, Ghost Dance, Bear Dance, and Basin versions of the Grass Dance. They could also be carried on horseback (Densmore 1922:166). The Peyote water drum was introduced to the Great Basin about 1900.

Song Texts

Great Basin songs are performed to meaningful texts, lexically meaningless syllables called vocables, or some combination of the two (song 2). Vocables are fixed for each song and may include sounds not otherwise present in the spoken language. In some instances they represent archaic texts that have lost their meaning, or texts in a language unintelligible to the singer due to song

top, Smithsonian, NAA: 74–11005; center left, Idaho State Histl. Soc., Boise: 77–69.8; bottom left, U. of Pa., U. Mus., Philadelphia: 13573; bottom right, Smithsonian, Dept. of Anthr.: 22301.

Fig. 4. Drums. top, Utes with a commercial marching band drum at one of the 3-day festivals sponsored by the Mountain and Plain Association of Denver businesses. Photograph by Harry Heye Tammen, 1894–1901. center left, Northern Shoshones and Bannocks with a Grass Dance drum, which was played suspended above the ground for more resonance. Support stakes held the drum by rawhide handles. The man to the right of the drum holds the fourth support stake. Photographed at Ross Fork, Fort Hall Reservation, Idaho, about 1890s. bottom left, Utes accompanying the Coyote Dance (at right) on a double-headed bass drum resting on blocks. Photograph by Edward Sapir, Whiterocks, Uintah-Ouray Reservation, Utah, Aug. 1909. center right, Tommy Sopes, a Western Shoshone, playing a hand drum and singing a prayer honoring the land. Photograph by Dianne Hagaman, Duck Valley Reservation, Nev., 1981. bottom right, Northern Shoshone–Bannock hand drum and drum stick. The painted hide is stretched over a circular machined and stapled wood frame, probably part of a cheese box. Water colors of red and brown depict a tepee, a meat-drying rack, a man smoking a pipe, a strongly recurved bow, 2 more pipes or pipe-tomahawks, a knife and scalp, and a highly stylized war bonnet. A strip of blue stroud has been tacked down around the circumference of the drum with a double row of brass tacks. Red and blue stroud and fringes of furred hide are affixed at the 4 points of attachment for hand thongs. The drum stick beater is rectangular machined wood stock, wrapped in blue stroud and partly covered in furred hide strips. Length of drum stick 16.5 cm; collected before 1876.

borrowing. In 1949 Lone Pine Owens Valley Paiute had Ute and Mohave songs, and Owens Valley singers could not translate many songs because their texts were foreign (Randle 1953:158). Walker River Northern Paiutes in 1891 sang a Mohave hand game song but did not understand the words (Mooney 1896:1009). Over time, most foreign texts disintegrate and survive as vocables.

Even meaningful words in the singer's language are subject to changes when sung. Sapir (1910a:458) noted that voiceless, whispered, and murmured vowels otherwise inaudible in spoken Southern Paiute are clearly heard when set to a sung tone and can even be lengthened or broken. There is also a tendency to prenasalize consonants (see the Shoshone song texts in "Oral Tradition: Content and Style of Verbal Arts," this vol.). Normal accentuation in the spoken language may be violated in its musical setting, particularly in songs cast in triple meter. Frequently the most common arrangement of note values—long-short—(in the transcriptions, quarter note followed by eighth) is reversed, and a text whose stress in normal speech falls on the first syllable will find it shifted to its second. In some cases, special words are substituted in songs: Owens Valley Paiute *paba* 'large' becomes *kida* in a song text (Steward 1933b:279), and at places where a singer takes a breath or reaches a cadence, final syllables of a word may be dropped (song 1a, phrase E). Animal sounds may also be incorporated into song performances (song 1b); during hand games in Lone Pine, California, singers emitted cries of mice and squirrels who are considered "helpers" in hiding the die (Randle 1953:156).

Many song texts, particularly those of doctors and shamans, are obscure in meaning, even if intelligible to native speakers; others contain figurative references. Received supernaturally, they become powerful formulas to recite during the shaman's endeavors to heal, to control weather, or to charm animals. The phonetic transcriptions in roman with the music are in many cases only approximations based on indistinct recordings; they are included to give an idea of the relation of the verbal text to the music and to aid in following the recordings.

Western Basin

If there is in fact a definite Great Basin style, its traits are most discernible in the western area and found with the greatest regularity in the music of Northern Paiute and Washoe. (The recorded sample for the Western Shoshone, while very small, conforms to this style as well.) Their indigenous songs appear to be relatively free of California or Plains influences.

Kroeber's (1914) wax cylinder recordings of Gilbert Natches (table 1) performing 55 Indian songs comprise one of the most valuable early collections of American Indian music. Natches's personal repertoire suggests

Table 1. Selected Collections of Great Basin Music on Wax Cylinders

WESTERN AREA

Songs of Gilbert Natches, Pyramid Lake–Lovelock Northern Paiute, recorded by A.L. Kroeber, December 1914. (Lowie Museum of Anthropology, U. of Calif., Berkeley:24–2257 to 24–2325).

14 hand game songs (6 women's, 4 men's, 1 men vs. women, 3 Shoshone)
13 War songs (4 Bannock)
9 doctoring songs (1 Shoshone)
9 Bear Dance songs (6 Shoshone)
3 ă´no 'Cree' song (Rabbit Dance)
1 Peace Dance song
1 Capt. John's Old-fashioned Paiute song
1 unspecified song
1 Shoshone Dance song
1 Song of Frog (Modoc)
1 unspecified song (Modoc)
1 Agaitsi 'little salmon, trout' tribal dance song

SOUTHWESTERN AREA

Songs recorded by Julian H. Steward at Owens Valley (singers: Ed Lewis, Tom Stone, Billy Murphy, Jack Stewart) and Mono Lake (singers: Harry Tom, Joe McBride, Johnson Charlie, Bridgeport Tom, Tom Stone), 1927–1928 (Lowie Museum of Anthropology, U. of Calif., Berkeley:24–2866 to 24–2924).

Owens Valley Paiute

6 circle dance songs (1 Bishop, 1 Washoe jumping, 1 Round Valley)
5 hand game songs (2 Bishop, 2 Shoshone, 1 Round Valley)
5 legend songs
4 ghost songs ("night songs")
3 war dance songs (1 Round Valley, 1 Monache)
2 doctoring songs (1 Shoshone, 1 saida-mudhe)
2 dance songs from the south
2 Bear songs (1 Kern County, sung by cub; 1 going through the mountain)
2 fandango songs (Bishop and Owens Valley)
2 basket-hiding songs
2 cry dance songs (Bishop, Round Valley)
1 Bear Dance song (NOT northeastern)
1 fishing song (partly whistled)
1 Tuhukimi's song
1 Tuhukimi's wife's song
1 hunting-lonesome song
1 hukunumuni sikumuka (shooting dance, bow and arrow)
1 Devil's song for driving away devil after bad dream

Mono Lake Northern Paiute

7 hand game songs (1 Yosemite Miwok, 1 Shoshone)
5 Round Dance songs (1 Yosemite Miwok)
2 war dance songs sung while fighting
1 Pyramid Lake Paint dance song (war)
1 doctor's song
1 doctor's flute melody associated with doctor's song
1 Bear Dance song (NOT northeastern)

NORTHEASTERN AREA

Northern Ute songs recorded by Frances Densmore, 1914 and

1916 (25 singers listed in Densmore 1922:17) (Library of Congress, Archive of Folk Culture, AFS 10,583A to 10,596B).
18 Bear Dance Songs
15 War songs (4 scalp dance songs, 2 for washing the wounded, 1 scout song)
13 doctoring songs
12 Parade songs
9 Sun Dance songs
8 hand game songs
6 Turkey Dance songs
4 story songs
3 Lame Dance songs
3 Dragging Feet Dance songs
3 Tea Dance Songs
3 undetermined dance songs
2 Woman's Dance songs
2 Double line dance songs
1 Iron Line Dance song
1 dream song
1 Begging Dance song
1 welcoming song
1 serenade
1 song around a rawhide

several things about Northern Paiute music about 1914; for example, the War Dance and Bear Dance were the two most frequent social dances, and Plains influences had penetrated the western sector through the Northern Shoshone and Bannock. The music of the Sun Dance, absent from Natches's repertoire, had apparently not diffused this far west.

Because his songs are so carefully labeled, Natches's western Basin repertoire is easily extricated for analysis. His Indian material shows several styles, two of which are the most prominent and seem the most indigenous to the area.

The first style is represented by hand game songs, the genre most frequently recorded in the Basin. Except for their percussion accompaniment, stylistically these songs are indistinguishable from the Round Dance songs of the area. Formerly, they were performed during the daytime when people congregated for five-day Round Dance festivals, the evenings taken up with dancing (W.Z. Park 1941:184). These game songs are still enormously popular, probably because they are easily learned and the game still very viable. They provide the hiding team one means of distracting their opponents from guessing which hand contains the unmarked bone die. The excitement of the event is reflected by its singers, who pepper their performance with yelps and other ejaculations, even when recording out of context (song 1b). Some Basin people believed the team that sang the loudest would win (Pietroforte 1965:52). Although

Natches recorded his hand game songs without accompaniment, in a game he would have beaten a stick on a board commensurate with the beginning of each melodic pulse (triplet).

Natches's Walker Lake hand game song (song 1b) should be compared to the Badger song. Although it has a wider range and different tonality, it, too, is almost exclusively syllabic, the text closely wedded to the melodic rhythm; it also shows the frequent return to the tonic and the transposition of melodic sections as a compositional device.

The other western Basin hand game songs show similar small ranges, averaging a 7th, rarely exceeding an octave. Two-thirds of them are also cast in triple meter and contain two or three phrases (sometimes four) that are related through repetitions of text and rhythmic motifs. But it is also common for half of each of two phrases to be identical, either in their beginnings or endings. The so-called paired phrase structure (AABB) of Basin music is also apparent in some but not many examples. Thus it is probably more correct to assume that this particular type of hand game song may have served as the model for Ghost Dance song form rather than the Paiute hand game song generally (Herzog 1935).

Similar in style to the hand game songs are western Basin songs for the Round Dance. Almost universally the dance was unaccompanied, men and women dancers alternating in a circle holding hands and moving slowly clockwise; however, counterclockwise movement is attested by Lowie (1909:219) for the dū´munö´kakin and by Crum (1980:15). They sang in unison, while the dance "boss" would walk around outside the circle praying aloud (W.Z. Park 1941:186).

Lead singers of the dance were those who knew many songs. Dellenbaugh's (1908:178) description of a Kaibab Southern Paiute Round Dance in 1872 (fig. 5) suggests that there may once have been some sort of antiphonal call and response pattern in performing its songs. Round Dance songs, far more than hand game songs, show a high incidence of paired phrase structure. Dellenbaugh gives texts for two Kaibab songs also collected by Powell (Fowler and Fowler 1971:127). Because each line of Powell's text is given twice in succession by Dellenbaugh, the latter may have been describing the actual performance, whether responsorial or full choral repetitions of melodic phrases. This paired phrase structure became the hallmark of songs of the Ghost Dance, the most famous of Basin Round Dances (see Herzog 1935).

Similar to the Northern Paiute examples are the songs of the Washoe girl's puberty dance (ʔuwíya). Performed by the girl's female attendants the evening of the final day of the ceremony, these songs demonstrate additional principles of song composition common to the western Basin. The melodies are brief and move within a narrow range (song 3a), usually a major 6th or less and never more than an octave. Their repetition an

top left, Smithsonian, NAA: 1623; top right, Colo. Histl. Soc., Denver: F-41942, bottom, Mus. of the Amer. Ind., Heye Foundation, New York: 34858.

Fig. 5. Round Dance, Bear Dance, and War Dance. top left, Round Dance performed in winter clothing of rabbitskin cloaks by Kaibab Southern Paiutes, probably requested by John Wesley Powell (at left). In the Ghost Dance, for instance, the circle moved clockwise to the unaccompanied songs performed by the dancers. The two-motion step—left, right brought to meet it—was coordinated, one motion to each pulse (usually a triplet) of the melody. Photograph by John K. Hillers, 1872. top right, Ute Bear Dance. The man in right background, wearing a badge and carrying a staff, is the "cat man," who acts as a tomcat or bear coming out of hibernation, looking for a mate. (Jorgensen 1964). In the Bear Dance a line of women faces their male partners. Locked into position by the dance step, each line does the opposite of the other—two steps forward, followed by three (presumably) smaller steps back, the same then repeated beginning with the other foot. The Ute name for the dance, *mamákwAnhkápi* (lit. 'woman-step dance') refers to this backward and forward movement of the lines. Other Ute line dances were the Lame Dance and the Double Dance (Densmore 1922:106, 118). Photograph by Harry Buckwalter, Durango, Colo., 1890s. bottom, Eastern Shoshone War Dance. Individuality of dance style and to some degree costuming were stressed. The male dancers, following no prescribed direction, were free to meander, dancing erect or in a semi-crouch, and struck poses as they wished. Chief Washakie holding a pipe-tomahawk is at left. Photograph probably by Baker and Johnston studio, Ft. Washakie, Wyo., 1884.

688

indefinite number of times comprises a song. Melodic motion is undular, frequently dipping beneath the tonic. Despite their brevity, internally the melodies show the general Basin tendency toward repetition. Variety is achieved through several means: contraction (song 3b), phrase B created from phrase A by omitting the second and third beats in its repetition; substitution of neighboring tone (or other pitches) at the end of a phrase (song 3c); transposition (song 3a)—phrase A repeated, is then essentially transposed to a lower level (phrase B) and repeated. The songs are set syllabically to vocable patterns that sometimes incorporate the syllables of the word ʔuwíya (song 3a).

Washoe hand game melodies show a style similar to the ʔuwíya songs, though the latter are never performed outside the context of the puberty dance. The typical hand game melody is divided into two phrases of approximately equal length. These phrases are usually of contrasting material and do not exhibit the varied repetitions of the ʔuwíya songs. More than half of them are in duple rhythm, which is less prominent in the puberty dance songs. Like the ʔuwíya songs, some have paired phrases. In both genres a fair degree of isorhythm results from the repetition of the text. Although the distinction was made between women's and men's hand game songs in the western Basin, as in California, stylistic differences between them are not apparent.

Also within this general style are the unaccompanied dance songs from the annual Pine Nut Dance (táˑgim gumsabáyʔ ʔlóˑš), once sung early in the morning after an all-night dance but now rarely performed. One dance song, called a sešíši, was recorded while a prayer was being spoken. Tonally quite simple, of the two collected one exhibits paired phrases, and the other lacks them but begins with a kind of introductory formula with heavily aspirated downward portamentos.

In contrast to the style represented by Northern Paiute hand game and Round Dance songs are the doctors' songs—the second indigenous style represented in Natches's repertoire. Each shaman had a number of them received supernaturally in dreams and used magically to cure rattlesnake bites, control the weather, or diagnose some affliction. These unaccompanied songs are generally more formulaic than melodic, characteristically narrow in range (but not always), and move by whole and even half steps. Some are cast in triple meter, but when sung rubato, as they usually are, meter is imperceptible and song form obscured. Even if the range is wide and meter is clear, the formulaic character is evident, as in the tetratonic doctor's song with its constant descents from B to D (song 4). Also formulaic is one Washoe ʔuwíya song performed by a man (song 3d), which contrasts greatly in style with the women's singing of ʔuwíya songs. Its fragmentary melodic construction and limited range are curiously similar to Ute hand game songs recorded by Densmore (1914–1916).

Southwestern Basin

A mixture of California and Basin music that can be characterized as transitional is evident all along the Basin's western periphery, as far north as Mono Lake (Northern Paiute). In this sector a singer's repertoire rarely lacked songs originating farther west. Thus Harry Tom, recorded by Steward (1927–1928a) at Mono Lake, knew two Miwok War Dance songs—a Madera County hand game song and a Yosemite Miwok dance song—and Billy Murphy at Owens Valley recorded a Monache War Dance song, while funeral songs in that community were believed to have come from Indians to the west, probably Miwok or Foothill Yokuts.

The difficulty in distinguishing between California and Basin styles in the southwestern Basin can be seen by comparing a Yosemite Miwok hand game song recorded at Mono Lake with a Northern Paiute Round Dance Standing song (songs 5a–b). Aside from differences in tonality and melodic rhythm, they share the following: two four-beat phrases, repeated an indefinite number of times; a narrow range, restricted to a 4th or 5th constant reiteration of the tonic, heavily weighted at ends of phrases; isorhythm through repetition of vocable patterns in each phrase, with slight variations in its repetition; melodic similarity between phrases, the Miwok phrases varying at their beginnings, the Paiute near their ends.

On the western edge of the Basin sharing went in both directions. Just as the central California cleft-stick rattle was taken up by Basin singers, the paired phrase structure affected some California music, such as some Monache Round Dance songs. It characterizes most Yokuts songs and may have been a Paiute influence through the Monache (Richard Keeling, personal communication 1983).

While a repertoire in the southwestern sector had its western Basin components (Round Dance and hand game songs), certain elements mark it as transitional, specifically the presence of genres otherwise absent in the Basin, such as Cry songs, fandango songs, basket-hiding songs, and bear shaman songs and stylistic traits, such as the "Yuman rise" (cf. Herzog 1928), which characterizes much of southern California music. Also, only in this sector do War Dance songs conform to the general western Basin style, with narrow ranges and pendular or undular motion.

Steward's Owens Valley sample is particularly rich in legend (story) songs ordinarily sung unaccompanied within the context of trickster tales (song 6), their melodies among the briefest in the Basin, their tonal material among the simplest. He also recorded the southwestern Basin bear shaman's songs—not to be confused with northeastern Basin Bear Dance songs, being unaccompanied and lacking their paired phrase structure. Reflecting the California bear complex in their performance, shamans dressed in grizzly bear skins would rattle claws and growl, while jumping sideways or dancing in a slow bear walk; some were believed capable of transforming themselves into bears (Steward 1933b:284, 309, 322–323).

Steward's recordings of Owens Valley Cry songs are similar to later ones from this genre made at Bishop but lack the heavy aspirations that conclude each strophe (song 7). Performed while the clothes of the deceased were burned on his grave, the Owens Valley Paiute songs by two different singers show a consistency in their style. The pendular motion is evident in all songs collected from this category. A contextual simulation is suggested by Steward's recording of Billy Murphy singing a Round Valley Cry song, as he speaks preceding and throughout the song, perhaps in the manner of a funeral leader. The singer hired for the Cry would occasionally stop the circle of dancers by clapping his hand and instructing them to wail (Steward 1933b:298).

A special dance song performed during fandangos throughout Owens Valley incorporates what seem to be animal (deer?) sounds at the end of each strophe (song 8). Some sort of mimed hunt seems suggested by the dance, in which men with bows shot dull arrows at people, while singers wearing buckskin on their backs would run and hop around. A western Basin version of this dance is suggested by the Surprise Valley Northern Paiute tobo´nigü, where two singers dressed as antelopes ran around in the circle pretending to be angry (Kelly 1932:179). The song for this dance illustrates the isorhythmic structure enforced by text repetition.

The Owens Valley ranges are about average for the Basin generally. However, some are enlarged by "Yuman rise" (Herzog 1928), evident in songs said to be "from the south," in Bishop and Owens Valley festival dance songs (fandango), and in some War Dance, Cry, and Night songs (coahubia 'ghost dance songs'). These particular songs have two phrases; the first, sung to vocables, may be repeated as many as seven times before the second. Usually with a text, this phrase is sung once only before returning to the first phrase. It stands out by interrupting the general melody with material pitched higher than the first phrase, "the rise." A similar use of two phrases is found in two Mono Lake dance songs said to be used also by the Miwok.

Steward's seven hand game songs include Shoshone and Yosemite Miwok examples. Song 9 is fairly typical of the hybrid of southwestern and western styles: triple meter, mostly syllabic setting with some pulsation. After the long sustained tonic, the leap to A in measure 3 may represent the Yuman rise.

The introduction of drum accompaniment to four Mono Lake dance songs seems recent and clearly from the east. One was said to be a Pyramid Lake Northern Paiute song, performed on horseback before going to war, the other two while fighting. The war songs were pitched high, performed loudly in a tense voice and concluded with yelps—more characteristic of eastern and western Basin music.

Bridgeport Tom's doctor's song covers the wide range of a 10th in a slow descent performed in a bel canto style—the rubato reminiscent of Ute doctors' songs. This contrasts with the western Basin doctoring songs, which have very limited ranges and are rhythmically more active.

Northeastern Basin

Music in the northeastern sector is distinguished from that in the other two subareas by the pervasive use of percussion accompaniment, the vitality of its Sun Dance and Bear Dance rituals, and the large portion of the repertoire associated with warfare.

Densmore's (1922) study of White River, Uintah, and Uncompahgre Ute music in 1914 and 1916, based on her analysis of 114 songs by 25 singers, was the first and remains the most extensive study of a single Great Basin music. Her data largely corroborate Lowie's (1915) for the Ute Mountain Ute in 1912 and Northern Ute in 1914.

A number of genres Densmore recorded had become obsolete, including songs for several social dances (Iron Line, Dragging Feet, Lame, and Double dances). The natural contexts for songs associated with warfare began to disappear when the Utes were settled on reservations in the 1860s. Occasions calling for songs from the war complex were similar to those of most northern Plains tribes, such as songs for the scout to indicate sighting the enemy—apparently a special function assigned to members of the Dog Company (Lowie 1915:823). Some songs served multiple purposes: for example, a Scout song was later used as a Parade song.

Whenever a large group of Utes was encamped, each morning there would be a parade headed by two men with hand drums and followed by men and then women, all on horseback and joining in the singing. The pattern of their hand drum accompaniment—a rapid tremolo moving to a slow, stately single stroke—is peculiar to this genre. The style of singing is equally distinctive. During the relatively long durations between drum strokes (MM = 60 to 66), the singer indulges in a lively ornamental style, with considerable tossing and sliding of the voice over wide intervals, the textless melody punctuated by glottal stops, its tones often raspy. The tradition of virtuosic song performance on horseback continued in the 1980s (Joseph G. Jorgensen, personal communication 1983).

What Densmore calls war songs can be assumed from the duple beat of the accompaniment to be dance songs used, for example, in the War Dances the evening prior to the war party's departure. Although rich in syncopations, they lack the vocal style of the Parade songs and are performed in a less ornamental manner. Their formal structure tends toward paired phrases.

Doctoring songs were solely the property of shamans and herbalists. Densmore (1922:127–131; normalized) recorded two Ute doctors: Mrs. Washington (Sakwia-gant), who received her songs supernaturally from an eagle and performed them in succession, and Teddy Pageets (Pagich), who had received his power from "a little green man" who was believed to shoot his arrows into those who offended him; all show a great consistency in style. Without texts and unaccompanied, they are sung to open vowels, pitched fairly low and delivered slowly in a crooning, almost lullabylike fashion, reminiscent of love songs of other tribes. The effect is one of a meandering, quasi-improvisational performance, with long sustained tones beginning and ending phrases. In scale, the songs are tetra- or pentatonic, and melodic motion tends to be undular, often a result of simple alternations of two adjacent tones.

Ute hand game songs contrast greatly with those elsewhere in the Basin. They are in duple meter over a fairly rapid double beat of the percussion, unlike the slow, lilting single stroke that typifies west-central hand game accompaniment. Sparse in tonal material and narrow in range, their melodies consist of brief fragmentary phrases separated from each other by short rests. Sung exclusively to vocables, the tones have a nasal quality. Often a phrase may consist of only a single tone quickly released on the tone a half or whole step higher. (Densmore 1922:175 notes a "sliding upward" characteristic.) The frequent breath expirations and use of only two or three tones often combine to produce a complicated melodic rhythm with considerable syncopation, such as in the tritonic hand game melody of song 10.

Various forms of the War Dance were performed principally in the northeastern Great Basin. The Turkey Dance is one, the Ute version of the Grass Dance, rapidly diffused throughout the Plains in the late nineteen and early twentieth centuries. The Ute received the dance from the Eastern Shoshone (fig. 5), who probably learned it from the Kiowa or Comanche (Joseph G. Jorgensen, personal communication 1983). All the novel elements of the Grass Dance are present in the Ute Turkey Dance: the accompaniment—a single large bass drum at one side of a dance ring, surrounded by as many as a dozen singers in contrast to the older practice of individual hand drummers in consort performing in a row; the choreography—a leader circling clockwise, thereafter meandering in the middle of the dance ring, as others followed him using the standard War or Grass Dance step, toe-heel alternating left and right feet. The novel body motions spread with the Grass Dance seemed clearly unusual to each new tribe receiving the dance. In Ute the name given it was 'jigging dance', the Turkey Dance being a White appel-

lation to describe the strutting of the dancers, thrusting and wagging their heads.

Turkey Dance songs, like Plains songs, are pitched high in the singer's range and begin at their highest tone, descending gradually over a wide range, frequently a 12th or more. The phrases are longer and less undular or arc shaped than in western and southwestern Basin songs. The tonic, frequently touched in every phrase of a western Basin song (see song 1a) is not established until the end of the melodic descent. Their melodies are sung in a tense manner to open vowels, and the rhythmic pulsations of the singer's voice divide sustained tones into syncopations, a Grass Dance trait even in the 1980s. Most indicative of Plains influence is their formal structure: the double introductory phrase and incomplete repetition (AABC/BC) (song 11).

Just as the Turkey Dance is the Ute version of the Grass Dance, so is the Ute Woman's Dance the equivalent of the Woman's Dance or Squaw Dance of the Plains. The Ute received the Woman's Dance from the Eastern Shoshone and probably at the same time. Accompanied by a duple beat with alternate accentuation, the melodies have smaller ranges than the Turkey Dance songs, are briefer and, like Round Dance types on the northern and southern Plains, have a brief cadential formula used to conclude each strophe.

The one other "modern" Ute dance about 1915 was the Tea Dance for couples (Densmore 1922:20). By 1893, next to the Bear Dance, it was already the largest social occasion (Reed 1896:244). Because in the Tea Dance men donated bracelets and other jewelry to their partners (?), just as gift exchange fairly often accompanies the Woman's Dance of many tribes, some sort of round dance is suggested. Additionally, the accompaniment pattern is similar to that of the Ute Woman's Dance, and the cadential formulae are present. The vocal style present on the recordings is the simplest and seems the most acculturated in their entire repertoire— an extremely regular melodic rhythm to open vowels completely synchronous with the even duple drumbeat pattern.

The music for the older social dances (Iron Line, Lame Dance) seems more typically Basin than what was current during the 1910s. The range of the Double Dance song, for example, is generally smaller than that for the other secular dances, and there is considerable degree of phrase repetition within the melody. On the other hand, the presence of the incomplete repetition in some of these dance songs suggested them to be hybrid Plains-Basin forms.

Of great importance to Densmore (1922:200–205) was her discovery of what she called "rudimentary song," by which she meant songs that lacked any discernible form and simply meandered from phrase to phrase. These were said to be narrative songs to which a story would be recited in which various animals played the principal roles. Because some of the doctoring songs seemed to Densmore to be just as meandering, she noted particularly that the Utes made a distinction between the two genres, using the word "song" to describe what an herbalist sang, but in the case of story tellers, only that "they sing this way when they tell stories."

The Ute doctor Weeyutchee recorded his four unaccompanied story songs, for the most part with a slightly nasal open vowel tone. (In places the singer lapsed into humming.) It is not clear how an entire story would be recited to these melodies, for three of the four seem to be textless.

There may be some early connection between the Ute story songs and the Southern Paiute recitative. There is little published data for their music, although Adams (1976) used J. Sapir's transcriptions of Southern Paiute songs for a discussion of melodic typology. Until a full analysis of Sapir's collection (1910c) is available, its assignment to any of the three sectors is impossible. Like the Northern Paiute, in their western sector the Southern Paiute were susceptible to California traits; "the rise," for example, occurs in a Sapir recording of a Southern Paiute Bird song.

The Kaibab Southern Paiute repertoire was the earliest Basin music to be collected in depth, when in 1910 Sapir recorded Tony Tillohash, then a student at Carlisle School. Many of the genres he performed are found in the northwest sector: Bear, Round, Ghost, and Scalp Dance songs, as well as those for doctoring and gambling. Still, the largest portion was taken up by 125 mourning songs in some non-Numic language unintelligible to the singer, apparently Mohave or another Yuman language (Sapir 1910a:472). Tillohash sang mourning songs in both an old and a new style, the differences being rhythmic, not melodic according to Sapir (1910a:469). The large number of songs from this genre is not surprising: the Southern Paiute all-night Cry dances can last two to three days.

The Southern Paiute recitative seems restricted in the Basin to that tribe, although its idea perhaps was also borrowed from the Mohave. Sapir distinguishes between simple story songs (see Crum 1980) occurring within the context of Ute or Kaibab myths among others, and speech sung to rhythmic-melodic formulae. The narrative portions of Kaibab myths were spoken but the conversations of certain characters were always performed to recitatives. When playing the role of Porcupine, Skunk, Chipmunk, or Badger, the teller used his speaking voice; but for Wolf, Eagle, Lizard, Badger Chief, Red Ant, and others, their words were set to melodies. The Kaibab fixed formula for a given character follows him from story to story. While the text is improvised by the narrator, the tactus remains unbroken because the singer may subdivide beats to accommodate more syllables or, with a short text, fill out the melody with vocables. The contrasts in the musical setting help to distinguish one character from another. Thus Wolf's 16-beat recitative is pentatonic, moving within the range of a major 6th, where Badger Chief's is simple, based on 6 beats and using only the two tones of a minor third. By contrast, Rattlesnake's formula has real melodic shape, rising a full octave at the beginning of its second phrase. Sapir's theory is that these formulae originated as elaborations of simple story songs.

Generally speaking, the same genres are found in Northern Shoshone music as in Ute. Certain dances, however, were diffused to them from the north and west that apparently did not reach the Ute. For example, the Lemhi received the Jackrabbit Dance from Fort Hall Shoshone, who had learned it from people to their west; likewise, the Warm Dance was introduced to them about 1880 by visiting Nez Perce (Steward 1943a:287).

The Plains stylistic traits evident in Ute music also permeate the Northern and Eastern Shoshone repertoires, particularly their dance songs. The Woman's Dance, Crazy Dog Society Dance, Pushing from Behind Dance, Sun Dance, and all war dances have wide ranges and are performed in the Plains vocal style. Most of the Bear Dance songs, however, like those of the Ute, show the Basin paired phrase structure and smaller ranges; similarly, they have only partly meaningful texts (song 12). Hybrid Plains-Basin styles are also found. In the Scalp Dance song (song 13) the Plains elements are its opening at the top of the melody, gradual descent to the tonic with frequent sustaining of tones, essentially pentatonic scale, and wide range. The Basin characteristics are its paired phrase and syllabic text setting.

By the late 1970s the few vestiges of older dance practices of the Shoshone were disappearing or had at least lost their association with warfare. The Eastern Shoshone Chokecherry Dance, once belonging to the Nose Poke Society organized in the early 1900s, derived its form from old Crow and Shoshone war societies. Dancers would move three times toward a pot of chokecherry gravy, then circle it with raised arms, while a leader presented it to the cardinal directions (Vander 1983:92). The ritual feigning and central pot of food seem analagous to portions of the Dog Feast celebrated among Plains warrior societies and ultimately incorporated in the Grass Dance, as does the Pointing Stick Dance, last performed at Wind River Reservation in 1968. The War Bonnet Dance in that community died out about 1975; one reason given for its demise was the difficulty in finding enough bonnets for the women to wear (Vander 1983:90).

The Ghost Dance

The musical practices of adherents to the Ghost Dance, Bear Dance, Sun Dance, and Peyote religion differ sufficiently in matters of style, dancing, and instrumental

692

accompaniment to merit separate consideration. To varying degrees their repertoires were alive in the Great Basin in the 1980s.

Mooney's (1896) study of the 1890 Ghost Dance devoted as much attention to the ritual as it did to its historical milieu; his published transcriptions, however, are exclusively from tribes outside the Basin. The musical style of Ghost Dance songs was analyzed on a comparative basis by Herzog (1935), who concluded they show the persistence of musical form even across tribal boundaries.

The Ghost Dance is typical of the many circle dances in the Basin that predated the movement. The various names given to the dance almost always describe some aspect of its choreography: Northern Paiute nänigükwa, said to mean 'dance in a circle' (Mooney 1896:791); Eastern Shoshone nataya·ti, literally 'lifting feet together'. The circle began to move after the song, begun by the lead singer, had been performed once through. Its size apparently determined the number of repetitions of the melody: the smaller the circle the more strophes performed. A circle of 200 dancers would terminate the song and rest briefly once the leader arrived at his starting point (Mooney 1896:920).

Some Western Shoshone insist that the Ghost Dance was not practiced by them but has been confused with the tan nataya· nikkanna 'the dance to uplift oneself', which was performed to open an all-night Round Dance. It could be danced in a straight line or a circle (Beverly Crum, personal communication 1984).

Initially, Wovoka himself exercised musical control of the 1890 Ghost Dance, as pilgrims traveled from distant tribes to learn carefully the songs and rituals. As a messenger of peace, Wovoka prohibited the War Dance and others like it, thus encouraging the spread of the new music, some of which he composed himself. As the movement grew beyond Wovoka's control, dances led to trances in which new songs were received. Consequently the Paiute repertoire was continually added to or supplanted, while the newer songs were assured circulation through regular rehearsals of song leaders. The ability of Vander's (1977–1981) informant to recall 147 songs learned a half-century earlier from this one genre alone suggests the repertoire was enormous at one time.

The absence of any percussion accompaniment in the Ghost Dance and the fact that all dancers sang relate it to older traditions in the Basin. Such communal unaccompanied singing was uncommon elsewhere in North America, where most Indian music is provided by specialists using drums or rattles, usually apart from the dancers.

The characteristic Ghost Dance melody contains two sections of equal or unequal length, each of which is repeated (song 14a); a narrow range, moving within a 5th or 6th; short descending or undular melodic con-

tours, with many phrases ending on the tonic. Additional Basin traits are the pervasiveness of triple meter melodies (13 of 17 in Vander's sample) and melodic variation through substitution of neighboring tones. From performance tempos it can be assumed that, in dancing, a foot was moved for each duplet or triplet. Many musical sections are organized in odd meters (5/4, 7/4), which end the singer-dancer in mid-cycle of the step, but because each section was repeated, by its conclusion the dancers would begin the new phrase on the "correct" (left) foot. Although the average tempo was relatively slow, there were certain faster songs used to induce the desired trances (Mooney 1896). A characteristic that may be exclusive to Shoshone Ghost Dance songs is the elided endings and beginnings of sections.

Beyond Vander's, the sample for Great Basin Ghost Dance songs is quite small. The Northern Paiute example (song 14b) is far less elaborate than the Shoshone (and other tribes') melodies. Mooney (1896:1050) found Walker River Northern Paiute Ghost Dance songs to have a "monotonous, halting movement" that made them inferior to Plains melodies.

Presumably other tribes adopted Paiute songs intact with their texts (see Mooney 1896:804, 814, 919); however, very soon, they began to compose songs in their own language. Still, borrowing continued everywhere, as songs of some tribes became particularly popular.

Like most vision-received songs, Ghost Dance texts are often obscure in meaning; archaisms and dialectal differences offer problems even to native speakers. One singer, having trouble translating her text, explained it as "Something like singing and a white thing standing up. I don't really know that. That song's from Nevada. Some of the words are a little bit different from ours. It means something, they know" (Vander 1983:71).

The song texts are typically brief and usually divided into two phrases, each repeated at least once and as many as four times. (Paired lines of text occur in 122 of the 137 texts given by Mooney.) This practice may have originated in a pattern of Paiute conversation in which the listener repeats each phrase he hears including its inflection to get the speaker's approval before he continues (Mooney 1896:770–771), or, as suggested, it may reflect an antiphonal performance in earlier Round Dances.

The nine Paiute texts published by Mooney are replete with nature imagery, mentioning briefly, among other things, cottonwoods, rocks, an antelope, and weather phenomena, such as fog, snow, lightning, and whirlwinds. Vocables are used to fill out a phrase if a text is brief (see song 14b). For example, Mooney gives as one of the favorite Paiute Ghost Dance songs the text: "The snow lies there ro-ra-ni/The Milky Way lies there." Eastern Shoshone texts describe similar phenomena. More than half have references to the Wind River Mountains or to a mountain setting, such as tammin

693

toyapin tuanci 'our small mountains', literally 'our mountain children', or to beliefs concerning the afterlife. The "whirlwind," for instance, was believed caused when someone dies, or the text "soul fog, soul floating" hinting at the Eastern Shoshone belief that the soul rises to Wolf's house in the form of a cloud (Vander 1983:72–73). The attention to various forms of water is found as well in Southern Paiute texts collected by Powell, suggesting they may have been the forerunners of Ghost Dance texts: "Rainwater at the foot of the mountain; rainwater singing;" "the blue water [clouds] rolls on the mountain" (in Fowler and Fowler 1971:127–128). Wovoka, a weather shaman, was said to have five songs to control the elements: the first to bring on mist (possibly song 14b), the second to cause a snowfall, the third rain, and so on.

The Bear Dance

The music for the Bear Dance is provided by as many as a dozen male singers each with a rasp made by women. This instrument consists of a notched stick held upright in the left hand, resting on some object enclosing or covering a cavity to serve as resonator, and a second smaller stick or short cattle bone rubbed quickly up and down across the notches in rhythm to produce the characteristic raspy sound (fig. 6; "Ghost Dance, Bear Dance, and Sun Dance," fig. 1, this vol.).

At one time symbolism surrounded this instrument and supernatural powers were ascribed to it (it was used to charm antelope, for example). In the Bear Dance they were meant to symbolize the bear's jawbone, and the raspy noise, especially the sharp downward glissando, was said to resemble a bear sound. The initial tremolo on the rasp that characterizes the opening of all Bear Dance songs was believed to create the noise of thunder in the bear's cave and awaken him from hibernation. Should someone fall from exhaustion in the course of a Ute Bear Dance, the music would stop while the person was "revived" with the rasp. A musician, the lead dancer, or a medicine man would touch the rasp to the feet, knees, shoulders, and head of the fallen, assuring him that the bear was listening and would dispel any pain by "blowing it away."

The Bear Dance (fig. 5) commences as follows: while a song begins over rasp tremolos, as many as 50 women select their partners, then form their line, interlocking arms and facing the singers. The music stops, then the tremolo begins anew while the men move out to face their partners forming their line holding hands. The song continues over the tremolo until both lines are in place, at which point the singers begin their duple strokes on the rasp signaling the dancers to begin their steps (Steward 1932:268).

Because there are no recordings of Bear Dance songs before 1914, it is impossible to determine whether there were attendant shifts in its style with the diffusion of the dance or when it was appended to mourning ceremonies. Southern Ute recordings show that the style has remained fairly constant over the past 60 years.

Bear Dance songs are sung in a manner so different from other songs that they are easily recognized, even without the characteristic rasp accompaniment. There is considerable portamento of the voice, tones are attacked emphatically from below using a nasalized vowel (ą), that vocable remaining constant throughout the song, perhaps in imitation of a bear sound. This nasalization is applied especially to long sustained tones at the beginnings of melodies. Except for recent songs, they show an average range of an octave or less. Additional Basin characteristics are the predominance of triple rhythms in the melody over the duple beat of the rasp and its song form: structurally the songs nearly all show paired phrases (songs 2, 12). Another consistent stigma is a concluding tag-on formula (x), such as is found in Woman's Dance songs. As it, too, is doubled the form of a typical Bear Dance song is AABBxx (repeated a number of times). Finally, in all of Basin music the Ute Bear Dance songs have the highest incidence of tonal structures based on double thirds—the so-called triadic melodies (song 2).

Although most are textless in the 1980s, apparently at one time all Bear Dance songs contained meaningful words. Those texts received in dreams are brief and abstruse in meaning, such as "eagle down," or "yellow hair sticking up" (Densmore 1922:59). Their full significance may be known only to the vision recipient. Even with his explication, the meaning may be obscure.

More common were texts pertaining to the dance itself or incorporating local gossip. Formerly, after the winter hunt, when the time of the Bear Dance was determined, song composers convened to create new songs to the Bear and dead spirits; but they gave much more attention to reviewing the year's hearsay and picking the best tidbits to set to tunes (Reed 1896:239). Apparently, there was a stock of melodic formulae, and new songs were simply created out of old by changing their texts. Still, there were Saturday night song rehearsals to establish the new songs, and old songs were performed only if the singers ran out of the new ones (Steward 1932:267).

In keeping with the social nature of the occasion, it was also common for song texts to comment on the dancing—often with vulgar allusions to bears' mating—or to encourage the participants: thus the text "swing weaselskin hard" urged dancers to perform more vigorously (Densmore 1922:61). Customarily singers would tease and ridicule the men for succumbing to the aggressive behavior of the women, in texts such as (see also song 2): "What kind [of man] are you, being pushed like that?" "She is pushing Wind-bird around, she's grabbing at him all over" (Givón and Smith 1981). Be-

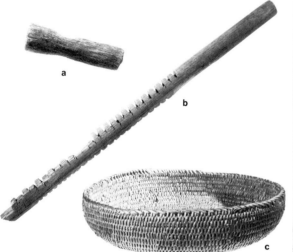

top left, Smithsonian, NAA: 1550; top right, Southern Utah State College, Special Coll., Cedar City; bottom right, U. of Ill., Urbana, Dept. of Anthr.; Smithsonian, Dept. of Anthr.: b, 287,230a; a, 287,230b; c, 287,229.

Fig. 6. Musicians for the Bear Dance. top left, Ute man demonstrating a notched rasp used with an inverted basket, a traditional resonator. Photograph by Frances Densmore, 1914. top right, Southern Paiute musicians at a dance: Crockett Kanosh, Mose Jack, Grant Pete, Clifford Jake, and Ray Mike. They use a metal washtub as a resonator. Photograph by William Rees Palmer, Cedar City, Utah, 1936. bottom right, Ute musicians at a dance. Bear Dance rasps were crudely made; the "teeth" of the rasp often broke and rubbing sticks eventually wore thin; when broken they were often discarded in the pit below the trough. Dance leaders (at left) directed the activities and shouted encouragement to the participants. Photograph by Julian Steward, Whiterocks, Uintah-Ouray Reservation, Utah, 1932. a, Rubbing stick; b, rasp; c, basket resonator—all specimens shown in top left. Collected by Frances Densmore, northeastern Utah, 1915. Length of b 63.5 cm, others same scale.

tween verses of the song the singers would shout at dancers, often by name, yelling, "That's the way!" or emitting a whinnylike laughter.

The Sun Dance

Initially the Sun Dance (Shoshone *takunikka, takuwini,* Ute *tagúnhkápɨ*) (Miller 1972:136; Givón 1979:183) was held during the first full moon in July, when the sun was at its strongest, its date among the Utes being always announced after the Bear Dance. The dance flourished in the 1980s although the ritual had changed somewhat, and the repertoire had become pan-Indian. By

1890 Eastern Shoshone dancers were participating in Sun Dances of the Ute, to whom they gave the dance, and by 1906 to the Crow and Northern Shoshone. By 1937 more than a quarter of those dancing at Wind River were from outside the reservation (Shimkin 1953:470).

Unlike the Bear and Ghost Dances, the Sun Dance was exclusively danced by males, except at Bannock Creek and Fort Hall. The number of dancers taking part varied, depending upon how many were pledged to fast. Two types of dancing were used in the Sun Dance. What may have been the older practice was dancing in place: facing east and concentrating on the

Sun Dance pole, the dancer kept time with the song by simply raising and lowering the heels slightly and flexing the knees, while blowing on the bone whistle on alternate drumbeats. By about 1880 the practice of dancing to the pole and back was observed (Shimkin 1953:436). After one dancer had "cleared a path" to the pole with his feet, dancers were free by themselves to run, dance, or hop to the pole and back again or advance toward the pole together with another dancer (Shimkin 1953:445).

In addition to the Sun Dance songs performed in the lodge were those accompanying preliminary or ancillary activities. War songs were borrowed for "capturing," taunting, and bringing back to camp the forked tree the day before the dance. Victory and parade songs were used while the horseback procession circled the corral and when the pole was decorated. During each of the three ritual feints while raising the pole a song was repeated (Opler 1941:557). In the evenings, social dancing, Ghost Dances, and hand games might be held outside the corral (cf. Densmore 1922:80), and sometimes a Dragging Feet Dance would follow a mock battle held before the Sun Dance began (Densmore 1922:80).

Although it was claimed Sun Dance songs were very old and had never been changed (Shimkin 1953:463), it is evident that their style of performance at least derived from War Dance songs of the Plains. Conceivably the songs of the Deer Hoof Rattle Dance (Lowie 1915:832)—in its decline about the time the Sun Dance was borrowed by Northern Utes from the Eastern Shoshone about 1890 (Opler 1941:571)—were simply retooled to the new style. For instance, the specially preserved Morning songs performed each day were likened by the Ute to old songs from the Deer Hoof Rattle Dance (Opler 1941:561). Still, new Sun Dance songs were made up each year.

The songs recorded are sung to a limited stock of vocables, mostly nasalized vowels (song 15) (cf. Densmore 1922:81), perhaps a further indication that they were imported. A distinction was made between dancing and resting songs, and singers were instructed before a dance how to space them. Otherwise, except for opening and closing songs, there was no prescribed order for songs, a participant being free to request his personal song when he danced. While all singers performed around the drum in unison, one had a rattle to regulate the tempo by watching the dancers (Shimkin 1953:423–444). Waving bunches of sagebrush or willow branches in rhythm, the women "helped" with the singing, probably joining the melody partway through each repetition, singing an octave higher than the men, the general practice on the northern Plains. They would also emit shrill ululations of encouragement to the dancers and perform a single sustained tone at a high pitch (Shimkin 1953:444).

696   Eastern Shoshone Sun Dance songs of about 1937 as

described by Shimkin (1938) conform to standard Grass Dance practice of the 1980s: a solo lead singer began the first phrase in a high shrill voice and the phrase was then repeated by the group. After a number of repetitions of the melody over an even duple drumbeat accompaniment, five emphasized offbeats (Shimkin's "slow ponderous beats") introduced a shift to a slightly faster tempo sung at increased volume (according to Shimkin, MM-130 to 160). The strophes were repeated for as long as it took the last dancer to return to his booth for rest. To conclude the song, a "tail" was added, which was simply an additional incomplete repetition of the melody. Typically, as with all songs associated with warfare, singers emitted war whoops and yelps after the final drumstroke.

Several characteristics are evident in the musical style of Basin Sun Dance songs. Unlike older Basin music, the songs have very wide ranges—never less than an octave and usually a 10th or 12th. They are pitched very high in the singer's voice and performed in a very emphatic manner that frequently causes the voice to lag somewhat behind the drumbeats. Melodic rhythm is exclusively duple in contrast to the more characteristic Basin triple meter. Tonally almost all of them can be considered in the minor mode, that is, the tone next above the tonic forms a minor rather than a major third with it. Like Plains melodies, they begin with the uppermost tones and descend to the tonic over several phrases. Unlike Plains music, the descent in Great Basin Sun Dance songs appears to be more abrupt; often in quartal chains tones are sustained with little or no pulsation, particularly at the melody's beginning.

Peyote Religion

The Peyote rite was diffused to the Basin beginning in 1910. Participation in the ritual was restricted to singing (without dancing), praying, and eating peyote buttons. From its inception the repertoire spread rapidly from one tribe to the next. For example, Gosiute attended Fort Hall Northern Shoshone and Ute meetings, while Western Shoshone and Northern Paiute visited Gosiute rites at Ibapah (Malouf 1942:102). New songs were continually brought back from intertribal Peyote meetings and their composer or tribal source always acknowledged. Thus the Ute Mountain Ute repertoire in 1936 was mostly from other tribes, much of it consisting of Mescalero Apache songs, while all Basin tribes knew songs from Oklahoma, the mecca of the Peyote religion. This also accounts for a Mono Lake singer knowing a Ute Peyote song and the name of its creator (song 16).

The Peyote ceremony begins in the evening with introductory prayers outside the tepee. Participants then enter, circling clockwise to their places. Once seated, the leader begins the singing, accompanying himself with a rattle in the right hand, while a drum is beaten by the person to his right. Each person performs a cycle of four songs in succession, during which no one may leave. Then the two instruments are passed clockwise to the next performers, taking care the drum does not touch the ground. If the new singer is in the midst of prayer, he is allowed to finish. Newcomers may have others sing for them, and formerly women sang, although many groups no longer permit them to.

Songs fall essentially into two categories: fixed songs that must be performed in context—opening and closing songs, for instance, and special midnight songs before a break at that time—and general songs, whose selection is up to the singers who may use them outside a ceremonial. There is some variation in the cycles: the Southern Ute could repeat an opening or closing song four times or combine it with three others (O.C. Stewart 1941a:305). Because of a limited repertoire, one Washoe group fell into the custom of repeating a song four times to form a cycle (Merriam and d'Azevedo 1957:622).

The Basin Peyote water drum and gourd rattle are vital ritual paraphernalia related to their Kiowa and Comanche counterparts. The rattle is a pear-shaped four-inch gourd shell impaled on a handle that protrudes a few inches beyond, where it is tufted with horsehair or feathers. The shell cavity contains seven stones or other rattling substances. Some Washoes use brass balls from a key chain (Merriam and d'Azevedo 1957:619). The handle may be carved or covered with beadwork in designs symbolic to the religion.

A three-legged cast-iron pot 6–12 inches in diameter serves as a drum frame. For performance, singers fill it three-quarters full of water and affix an Indian-tanned deerskin head over its top, lashing it firmly with seven pebbles (or marbles) under the edges of the head. The criss-cross lacing is brought under the belly of the pot where it forms a "star." In singing, the drum is held slightly tilted between the knees and beaten with a curved drumstick.

The characteristic high-pitched tone of the water drum is achieved by keeping the head moistened and using the thumb of the left hand to depress it, thereby raising the pitch. Although songs begin and end over percussion tremolos, the rattle and drum move to the same rapid duple beat of accompaniment for the sung portion. Washoe singers (and possibly others in the Basin), however, take liberties with the rattle and perform slightly different rhythmic patterns against the drumbeats, although the tactus remains the same (cf. Merrian and d'Azevedo 1957:628).

A complete analysis of Basin Peyote music is needed before substyles can be discerned—particularly in matters of range, form, and tonality. Because of the constant exchange of songs it is difficult to sort out any repertoire for its indigenous material. Singers may learn songs from many sources, including commercial recordings, and are free to compose them or learn them

The Native Nevadan, Reno-Sparks Indian Colony.
Fig. 7. Dance of Northern Paiutes at a powwow. Photographed at Pyramid Lake, Nev., summer 1983.

in some supernatural fashion. Washoe singers may receive a song "all at once in a moment of great emotional intensity" (Merriam and d'Azevedo 1957:623); archival notes identify one Washoe example as "Peyote song taught to Sam Dick by his automobile generator as he drove to peyote meeting" (O.C.Stewart 1938c).

Still, some general characteristics of Peyote melodies may be noted in the Basin sample: a relatively relaxed vocal style, though slightly more tense and pitched higher than normally in the western Basin; exclusively duple rhythm (quarter and eighth note durations) (song 16) concurrent with the drumbeats; a general downward melodic motion terminating on the tonic; a cadential formula to the vocables [he ne yo we] or something similar to them; the use of special Peyote vocables, usually one per eighth note, which may or may not occur in the language of the singer (see Nettl 1953). The vocable patterns are different but fixed and usually repeated within each song, resulting in some isorhythm. They may incorporate meaningful words in English referring to Christ ("Jesus," "Jesus only one," "Jesus save me").

697

Sources

Nettl (1954) was the first to consider the Great Basin to constitute a distinct musical culture area. He based his conclusions mainly on earlier studies, which had focused on the music of one tribe—the Northern Ute (Densmore 1922), one intertribal genre—the Ghost Dance (Herzog 1935), or music within the general ethnography of one tribal division—the Owens Valley Paiute (Steward 1933b). Nettl's sample included some Plateau material as well. Since 1954 many early wax cylinder collections of Basin music have been transferred to tape for preservation and study; these and more recent recordings permit a reassessment of earlier work, particularly published transcriptions.

Before historical recordings were accessible, scholars relied on musical transcriptions of Basin music. Because accurate stylistic analysis must be based on the actual performance or sound recordings of it, conclusions drawn from transcriptions without recourse to their source must be treated with caution. For example, the earliest published notation of a Basin melody is by Barber (1877). His transcription of a Yampa Ute hand game song is highly suspect in light of what is known of Basin music generally and Ute hand game songs specifically. Barber (or someone with him) must have taken the melody down by ear, because his Utah visit predates by more than a decade the earliest use of the cylinder recorder in the field. The melodic range of a 13th—enormous by Basin standards—contrasts with the very limited ranges of Densmore's 1914–1916 recordings (the first) of eight Ute hand game songs by four different singers. It is unlikely that such an abrupt shift in traditional Ute hand game song style would have occurred in 30 years.

Major repositories of Great Basin field recordings are the Lowie Museum of Anthropology, University of California, Berkeley; the Department of Anthropology, University of Nevada, Reno; Archives of Traditional Music, Indiana University, Bloomington; and the Archive of Folk Culture, Library of Congress. The Northern Paiute were recorded early and in some depth, principally by Waterman (1910), Kroeber (1914), and W.Z. Park (1934a). Sapir (1910d) and Adams (1966–1967) recorded the Southern Paiute. Except for Peyote and hand game songs, the sample for the Washoe has been relatively small and recent. Principal collectors have been O.C. Stewart (1938c), Rhodes (1937–1952), Jackson (1955), and d'Azevedo (1954–1964), while traditional Washoe hand games, and pinenut and puberty dances were filmed by Pataky (1969). Stewart's (1927–1928, 1927–1928a) Owens Valley Paiute and Mono Lake Northern Paiute recordings and Pietroforte's (1959) of the Owens Valley Paiute comprise the data for the discussion here of the southwestern sector. Densmore's wax cylinder collection of Northern Ute songs (1914–1916) and collections of Eastern Shoshone music by Shimkin (1938), Liljeblad (1940–1943), and Vander (1977–1981) support the analysis here of northeastern Basin music.

The music of the Sun Dance has received little attention, although its ritual is discussed in detail by Jorgensen (1972:177–205, 305–340). The only study of a single Basin Ghost Dance repertoire has been Vander (1983). Her data, 147 Ghost Dance songs from the 1920s and 1930s recorded by an Eastern Shoshone woman from 1977–1981 essentially substantiate earlier findings. In his study of Peyote music McAllester (1949:54–56) included an analysis of Washoe Peyote songs. The only focus exclusively on a Basin repertoire has been Merriam and d'Azevedo (1957), who discuss the Washoe ritual, its history, the construction of their musical instruments, song sources, and performance practices. They present a complete analysis of five Tepee Way song cycles recorded by three Washoes in Woodfords, California, in 1954. O.C. Stewart collected Mono Lake Northern Paiute, Uintah Ute, and Washoe Peyote songs (1938c, 1938d, 1938e), and Shimkin, Eastern Shoshone songs (1938). Commercially produced disk and tape recordings of contemporary music in the Great Basin are available from Canyon Records, Indian Records, Everest Records, Folkways Records, and the Motion Picture, Broadcasting, and Recorded Sound Division, Library of Congress.

Song 1a. Northern Paiute Badger Song

Recorded by Catherine S. Fowler, 1979
Singer: Wuzzie George
Text transcription and translation: Sven Liljeblad
(communication to editors 1985).

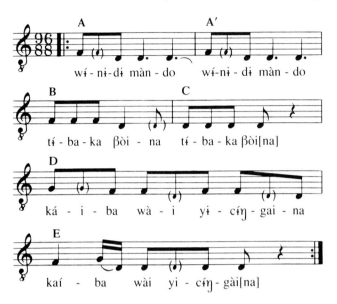

A

A′

wí - ni - dɨ màn - do   wí - nɨ - dɨ màn - do

B

C

tí - ba - ka βòi - na   tí - ba - ka βòi[na]

D

ká - i - ba   wà - i   yɨ - cíŋ - gai - na

E

kaí - ba   wài   yi - cíŋ - gài[na]

TEXT:

winɨdɨmad·u/ tɨbakabuina/ kaibawai yɨcɨgaina.

'Toward the tree (with) pine nut cone seeds, in the mountains (we) move about'.

The song is repeated continuously.

Song 1b. Walker Lake Northern Paiute Hand Game Song

Recorded by A.L. Kroeber, 1914
Singer: Gilbert Natches

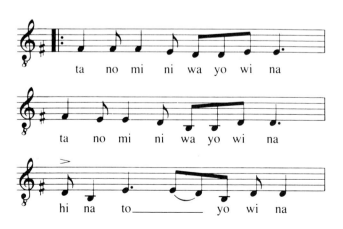

ta   no   mi   ni   wa   yo   wi   na

ta   no   mi   ni   wa   yo   wi   na

hi   na   to_____   yo   wi   na

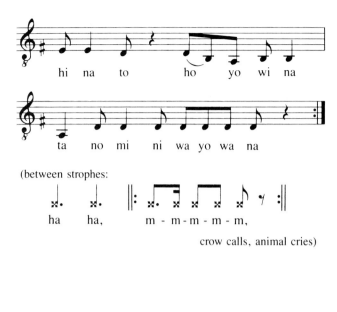

hi   na   to   ho   yo   wi   na

ta   no   mi   ni   wa   yo   wa   na

(between strophes:

ha   ha,   m - m - m - m - m,

crow calls, animal cries)

Song 2. Northern Ute Bear Dance Song

Recorded by Frances Densmore, 1914-1916
Singer: Isaacs
Text transcription and translation: Talmy Givón and Sunshine
Cloud Smith (personal communication 1981).

A

háy   áy   pú·-pa   pɨ-ní-wɨ-nɨ́-tay/

B

2

tú· - kwi - yá - ɣa - tɨ   ʔɨ́

pú· - pa   wh - čɨ́ - ɣwa - na - tay

X   2   2   2

ʔɨ́:   (ɯ)

TEXT:

[háy áy] *pú·pa pɨníwɨnɨtay/ tú·kwiyáɣatɨ/ pú·pa whčɨ́ɣwanatay.*
[ʔɨ́:]

(vocables) 'The way they all are standing and watching the black bear, the way he is being pressed.' (vocables)

Song 3. Washoe Girl's Puberty Song
Song 3a.

Recorded by Warren d'Azevedo, 1954-1964
Singer: Clara Frank, lead

♩ = 60

he - yai ho-wi-ya he-yai ho-wi-ya he-yai

ho - wi-ya he - yai ho - wi-ya he - yai

ho - wi-ya he - yai

ho - wi-ya he - yai ho-wi he - yai

ho - wi-ya he - yai ho - wi-ya he - yai

ho - wi he - yai ho - wi-ya he - yai

ho - wi - ya he yai ho - wi he - yai

Song 3b.

Recorded by Warren d'Azevedo, 1954-1964
Singer: Clara Frank, lead

♩ = 66

he ya-wi no hi - na he ya-wi

no hi - na he - ya-wi - no

he - ya-wi no hi - na he ya-wi-no

Song 3c.

Recorded by Warren d'Azevedo, 1954-1964
Singer: Clara Frank, lead

♩ = 56

ho wi-na he-no win

ho wi - na wi ho wi-na-win

Song 3d.

Recorded by Warren d'Azevedo, 1955
Singer: Hank Pete

accompaniment: (foot stamping)

♩ = 70

ha wi na hə na wi ha wi na

he - ya he - ya he - ya he - ya - he

hin-ai ya - o - wi-na hi - ai ha - o - wi-na

hi-ye ke-a he - a ha - e - a he ya

hi - ai ha - o - wi - a hi - ai ETC.

Song 4. Doctor's Song

Recorded by Willard Z. Park, 1934
Singer: Nick Downington

ba - u ka - a ba - a

me wa - a do na me no yo wis

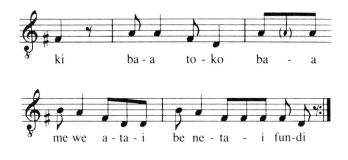

ki ba - a to - ko ba - a

me we a - ta - i be ne - ta - i fun-di

Coyote's Song for Magpie

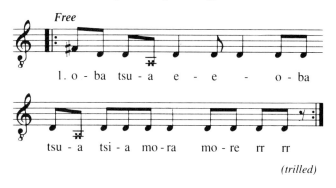

Free

1. o - ba tsu - a e - e - o - ba

tsu - a tsi - a mo - ra mo - re rr rr

(trilled)

Song 5a. Yosemite Miwok Hand Game Song

Recorded by Julian H. Steward, 1927-1928
Singer: Harry Tom

hə - ne hi - ya hi - ya - na ha hə - ne

begins:

hi - ya hi - ya - na ha hə - ne hi - ya

Pamakwaju's Song

pa ma kwa ju wa - i ni wi - i du

pa ma kwa ju wa i ni wi du

Song 5b. Round Dance Standing Song

Recorded by S.A. Barrett, 1907
Singer: Edmon Wata

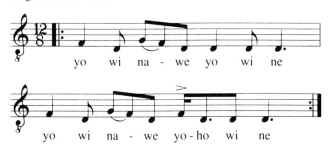

yo wi na - we yo wi ne

yo wi na - we yo - ho wi ne

Song 7. Owens Valley Cry Songs

Recorded by Catherine Fowler, Sven Liljeblad, 1981
Singer: Sam Kinney

yo ya - na he a yo ya na

he a na whi - a (breath)

Song 6. Owens Valley Legend Songs

Recorded by Julian H. Steward, 1927-1928
Singer: Tom Stone

Magpie's Song

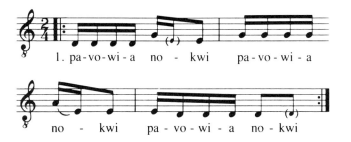

1. pa - vo - wi - a no - kwi pa - vo - wi - a

no - kwi pa - vo - wi a no - kwi

Recorded by Alfred Pietroforte, 1959
Singer: Molly Pomona

yo wi ya he he a ha na wi - ya - ha

yo wi a he a ha - na wi ya - ha (breath)

Song 8. Owens Valley Fandango

Recorded by Julian H. Steward, 1927-1928
Singer: Jack Stewart

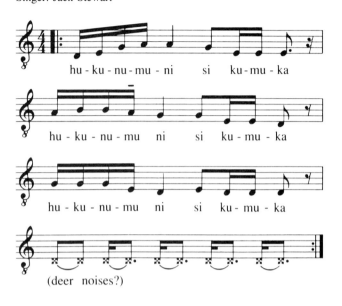

hu - ku - nu - mu - ni   si   ku - mu - ka

hu - ku - nu - mu   ni   si   ku - mu - ka

hu - ku - nu - mu   ni   si   ku - mu - ka

(deer noises?)

Song 9. Northern Paiute Hand Game Song

Recorded by Julian H. Steward, 1927-1928
Singers: Joe McBride, Harry Tom

ho - wi yo - wi yo - wi yo

i - yo no - a - a kwe - a no - a - na

ha - yo - a   yo - win yo - wi - na ha - yo - wi

yo   ya - wa - na me - a no - a - na

kwe - a - na me - a - no kwe - a no - a - na ha - yo - i

yo - o - o yo - wi - na ha - yo - wi yo

Song 10. Northern Ute Hand Game Song

Recorded by Frances Densmore, 1914-1916
Singer: Quinance

Accompaniment:

Song 11. Bannock War Dance Song

Recorded by A.L. Kroeber, 1914
Singer: Gilbert Natches

Drum:

A
he - a - yo kwai - e - e de - a - da yo-

e - da kwai - e kwai - e - e de - e - e ke-

A
da whe - e - ya wha - e - e he - e - e yo - o

whe - da whai - e   wha - e - e de - e - e e - e

B
yo - wa - pe - e - e - e - e - e ya - hi - i

C
pi - i - ta ha - i - i i - i - i   yo - hi

ti - to ko - i - i - i - i - i i - i

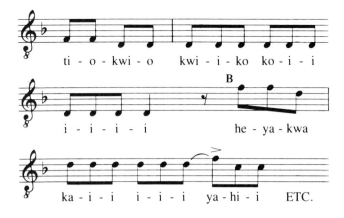

ti - o - kwi - o   kwi - i - ko   ko - i - i

B

i - i - i - i   he - ya - kwa

ka - i - i   i - i - i   ya - hi - i   ETC.

Song 12. Shoshone Bear Dance

Recorded by A.L. Kroeber, 1914
Singer: Gilbert Natches

Accompaniment: 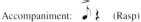 (Rasp)

A

pe   pim - zi   wa - da   wa - ho   ka - ma-

A

te - o   te   pim - zi   wa - da   wa - ho

B

ka - ma - te[o]   a - e   i - ya - a

B

e - a - e   ha - ha   a - e   i - ya - a

X

e - a[e]   ha   ka - na - tse - o

Song 13. Scalp Dance Song

Recorded by Sven Liljeblad, 1941
Singer: Andrew Johnson

Accompaniment: ♩♩   *Voice slightly behind drum throughout.*

A

po - jo   ma - yun - ga   yo - a - a - wi   ga - na

po - jo   ma - yun - ga   yo - a - wi   ga - na

B

po - jo   ma - yun - ga   yo - a - wi

B'

ga - na   po - jo   ma - yun - ga   yo - a - wi

C

ga - na   ya - na - kwa - dji   ya - ga - na

wun - de - o - wi - ga   fe - za-

du - ya

Song 14. Ghost Dance Songs

Song 14a. Northern Shoshone Ghost Dance Song

Recorded by Sven Liljeblad, 1943
Singer: Zurick Buck
Text transcription and translation: Sven Liljeblad
(communication to editors 1985)

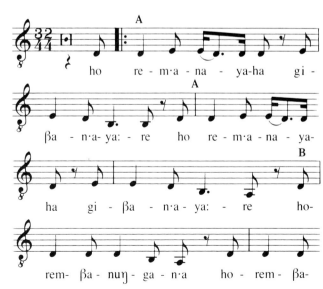

A

ho   re - m·a - na - ya - ha   gi -

A

βa - n·a - ya: - re   ho   re - m·a - na - ya-

B

ha   gi - βa - n·a - ya: - re   ho-

rem- βa - nuŋ - ga - n·a   ho - rem - βa-

TEXT:

kusippancaya'a kipantaya·tɨ/ kusippɨnnunkanna/ hupianna.
'Grayhawk is turning on stiff wings—gray one, his whirling—
  as the song goes.'

Song 14b. Northern Paiute Ghost Dance Song

Recorded by T.T. Waterman, 1910
Singer: Dick Mawee

TEXT:

vocables plus *pakɨnna* 'fog, cloud on the ground'.

Song 15. Sun Dance Song

Recorded by Edward S. Curtis, 1909
Singer: Dick Washakie

Song 16. Clark Tanner's Ute Peyote Song

Recorded by Julian H. Steward, 1927-1928
Singer: Harry Tom

[Water drum and rattle ♩♫]

Ethnographic Basketry

CATHERINE S. FOWLER AND LAWRENCE E. DAWSON

Basketry has long been regarded as one of the technological hallmarks of archeological and ethnographic Great Basin groups. Twined, coiled, and to a lesser degree wicker-plaited varieties have long and complex histories in the region (see "Prehistoric Basketry," this vol.). Relationships of Great Basin archeological and ethnographic basketry complexes to those of surrounding areas are clear in some cases, less so in others. In all, the data to be derived from studies of basketry are very important for culture-historical reconstructions and ultimately overall interpretations.

Ethnographic baskets, unlike most archeological pieces, which are fragmentary, can more readily be classified as to form and function as well as to means of construction. The living link between makers and uses, still intact in some areas, or retrievable from the elderly in others, has been studied (for example, Barrett 1917; Kelly 1932, 1964; Lowie 1909, 1924; Merriam 1902–1942; W.Z. Park 1933–1940; Steward 1933b, 1941, 1943a; O.C. Stewart 1941, 1942; Zigmond 1978). Although collection dates for baskets in museums are principally after 1900, when carefully combined with the field data they can aid in the characterization of pre- and postcontact complexes.

Traditional Basketry

Traditional baskets are those pieces, their forms, functions, and techniques of construction that appear most clearly to approximate the pre- or immediate postcontact situation. Each group in the Great Basin had several classes of baskets attributable to this time, and there were often subgroup differences as well. The generalizations that follow do not account for all basket types and variants but illustrate the common core of forms and techniques within the groups. Examples of traditional baskets arranged by type are in figures 1–6.

Washoe

Traditional Washoe baskets were made in a variety of twined and coiled weaves. The twined openwork pieces included: conical piñon cone gathering baskets (fig. 3h); slightly smaller burden baskets; small conical gathering baskets; parching trays (fig. 4c); fish baskets or traps; seed beaters (fig. 5a); pinenut roasting scoops; gathering scoops (fig. 5d); insect gathering baskets; and cradles. The close-work twined baskets included seed gathering baskets (fig. 3c), seed winnowers-parchers (fig. 4h), and water bottles (fig. 7). Baskets made on a three-rod coiled foundation included mush boilers, dipper–soup drinking bowls, and fancy baskets for keeping small articles. One-rod coiled work was used for bowl baskets of various shapes and nonstandardized uses. Table 1 gives the Washoe terminology, weave type, and dimensions for these baskets.

Washoe twined weaves were of two classes: whole peeled willow shoot wefts on whole willow shoot warp sticks, and split peeled willow shoot wefts on whole peeled willow shoot warp. Class 1 was used only for openwork and always had down-to-the-right twining turns. Class 2 was used for both open and close work and had up-to-the-right slant of twining turns. Both plain twining over single warps and twill twining over two warps were used for both classes, but twill twining was uncommon with whole shoot wefts. Except for scoop or fan-shaped baskets, twining proceeded as a single continuous row around the radially arranged warp sticks, the work direction normally to the weaver's right as it is in all Great Basin twined ethnographic baskets. Occasionally a left-handed weaver's basket was made leftward and with the opposite slant of turns in twining. Scoop or fan-shaped baskets were woven from edge to edge, turning the basket over at the end of each row so that the weaver would not have to change work direction. The round face of split strands was always kept facing the weaver. Close twill twined winnower-parchers were nearly always woven two weft rows at a time.

A common warp selvedge for twined baskets was made by turning every second to sixth warp rod or a pair of warp rods horizontally and doing one turn of twining with them over the next two to six warps (fig. 3h). The ends used as wefts were trimmed on the work face; those serving as warp were trimmed directly above the twining row. A gap of two to three centimeters was left between the last row of twining and the selvedge in order to leave space for the lashing strand used to bind on the reinforcing rod, which was bound either rightward or leftward. In the case of seed beaters, the handle was the warp selvedge, which had a spiral row

Table 1. Washoe Baskets

Type	Name	Manufacture	Size
piñon cone gathering basket	ʔitmáˑguʔ 'for gathering'	openwork, plain twine, Class 1	76 cm deep
burden basket	máˑmayʔ	openwork, twill twine, Class 2	60 cm deep
small gathering basket	máˑmayʔ ŋáʔmiŋ 'small máˑmayʔ' wáˑš daŋáˑm 'son of wáˑš'	openwork, Class 1 or 2	40 cm deep
fish basket	meċiyéyil̦ or máˑmayʔ	openwork, Class 2	70 cm long
seed beater	i̦ugéˑbil̦ or i̦ápil̦iʔ i̦ugéˑbil̦ 'handled i̦ugéˑbil̦'	openwork, Class 1 or 2	27–57 cm
pine nut roasting scoop	i̦ugéˑbil̦ or i̦ugíˑs	openwork, Class 1 or 2	60–77 cm
gathering scoop	?	openwork, Class 1 or 2	24–46 cm long
cradle	bík̦us	openwork, Class 1 for back; Class 2 for shade	79 cm long, 26 cm wide
seed gathering basket	mugíwiț	close work, twill	40–55 cm deep
seed winnower-parcher	mudáˑl	close work, twill	40–55 cm
water bottle (?)	k̦étep	close work, twill	24–68 cm long
mush boiler or bowl (?)	guyánda	close work, twill	24 cm diameter
mush boiler	gíwlew	close coil, 3-rod foundation	12–45 cm deep
dipper or mush bowl	ʔitmahadáˑš 'for pouring in' or čiŋáˑm 'basket'	close coil, 3-rod foundation	8.5–9.5 cm deep and 19.5–21.5 diameter
trinket basket	degíˑk̦ip 'globular'	close coil, 3-rod foundation	18–19 cm diameter
bowl	deyul̦áțiyiʔ or bayul̦áți	open or close coil, 1-rod foundation	varies

of twining around it, ended by a row of warp ends twined over other warp sticks.

An underselvedge was frequently used on close-twined baskets that consisted of several rows of plain twining over paired warps, sometimes using two different colored wefts so that the rows appeared checkered. On many close-twined baskets decorative gaps in the twining one centimeter or so wide were left at intervals. The warp slant averaged about 10 degrees to the left of vertical.

The close-twined baskets were done exclusively in twill twining and were apparently always decorated, the designs nearly always in horizontal bands. Also used for decoration were regularly spaced narrow bands of openwork about one centimeter wide.

The Washoe coiled work utilized both three-rod and one-rod willow shoot foundations, but the large majority of home use baskets had three-rod bunched foundations. The work direction was to the weaver's left. The side on which the awl was inserted was the convex or exterior face. Besides the simple self-rim, Washoe coiled baskets were frequently ornamented with a num-

ber of different kinds of rim overstitching. None of the Washoe rim overstitchings had its own foundation.

Coiled baskets on a three-rod foundation, which far outnumber those on a one-rod foundation, are standard for mush boilers, dippers, and trinket baskets (fig. 1g). So far as known they are always decorated, and these appear to be of a tradition different from those of twill twined baskets. The differences in technique are definitely not the cause of the design differences, but historical factors may account for them. A few design names recorded by Barrett (1917) follow the general California practice of naming the designs casually after familiar objects in the environment. Trinket baskets were also sometimes decorated in duck feathers (fig. 6d).

The Washoe twined mush boiler seems doubtfully recorded. Few are known from museum collections, and descriptions are inconsistent (for example, Price 1962; Lee 1912). The close twined tub-shaped boiler was listed by Barrett (1917) but denied by those interviewed by O.C. Stewart (1941). Given that the Washoe regularly boiled food in a coiled basket of which there are many examples in collections, the case looks weak

a, Harvard U., Peabody Mus.: 08–4–10/72986; Nev. State Mus., Carson City; b, 38–6–1363; i, 38–G–1353; c, Smithsonian, Dept. of Anthr.: 11,831; d, U. of Calif., Lowie Mus., Berkeley: 1–26992; Field Mus., Chicago: e, 59039; f, 110704; h, 58462; g, 58385.

Fig. 1. Basket hats, bowls, and boilers. a, Panamint Shoshone woman's close-coiled basket hat, made before 1908. In addition to protecting the head from the tumpline attached to carrying or burden baskets, Panamint caps were also used as a standard unit of measure for seeds and other foods. b, Western Shoshone woman's twill-twined basket hat, collected in 1876. Three-strand twining is in the finish row. c, Southern Paiute close-twined mammiform basket hat, with 3-strand twining as underselvedge and warp bundle selvedge. Collected from Uinkaret or Kaibab Southern Paiute, 1870s. d, Owens Valley Paiute woman's close-twill-twined basket hat. It has 3-strand twining to start and is overpainted with a 2-band pattern. Collected in 1927. e, Northern Paiute close-twill-twined basket hat/food bowl, with an overpainted 2-band pattern and 3-strand twining in the final row. Collected on the Walker River Reservation, Nev., 1904. f, Northern Shoshone–Bannock twill-twined food bowl, with decorative bands of 3-strand twining. Collected before 1925. g, Washoe close-coiled boiling basket with overstitching on the rim, of the type also used to leach acorn meal. Collected in 1902. h, Northern Paiute close-coiled boiling basket, collected in 1902. i, Northern Paiute twill-twined boiling basket, a reinforcing rod coiled to the rim. Collected in 1899. Diameter of a, 24 cm; rest to same scale.

707

ETHNOGRAPHIC BASKETRY

for twined ones. There may have been occasional boilers obtained in trade from neighboring Northern Paiutes.

Northern Paiute

Northern Paiute basketry is predominantly twined. Principal wares in twining include: winnowing-parching trays, burden baskets, boiling-mixing baskets, eating bowls, seed beaters–sieves, water bottles, hats, and cradles. Less common, or restricted to a limited area, are fish traps, insect baskets, and scoops. Coiling is confined to eating bowls, trinket baskets, and in some areas boiling baskets. Additional types in coiled ware were made for sale in the historic period.

Northern Paiute twining can be either plain, normally over one warp, or twill, normally over two warps. Of the two, twill twining is by far the most common, being used for all close work and a majority of openwork. Plain twining over one warp is limited to openwork. The slant of turns in twining is predominantly up-to-the-right, although Kelly (1932:129–130) reports some down-to-the-right work in Surprise Valley along with pieces of mixed slant. The Burns, Oregon, area also shows a limited amount of down-to-the-right work, especially in plain twined pieces. Work with whole rod wefts, common in Washoe plain twining, is very rare in Northern Paiute work.

Most Northern Paiute groups, at least from Mono Lake to Surprise Valley, recognize from two to four grades of twined trays based on weave type, size, and tray function. Common are: large and small close twill twined over two rods, large open twill twined over two rods, and large open plain twined over one rod. Table 2 gives native terms.

Small close twined trays average 30 centimeters long by 22 centimeters wide while large trays are roughly 60 centimeters long by 45 centimeters wide. Both are characteristically shallow (4–8 cm deep). All are twill twined. The weaver works across the front of the tray and then turns the tray over and works in the same direction across the back. Occasionally two weft rows are woven from one edge to the other before the tray is turned. Trays are woven from the tip, or small end, thus facilitating warp rod additions and truncations.

Many close twined trays are decorated and probably also reinforced by multiple bands of plain twining over two rods worked along the sides and occasionally across the tips (fig. 4g). Ends, particularly on trays from the central Northern Paiute area, are also finished with plain twining over two or three warps and a one- or paired-rod twined selvedge, resembling the Washoe edge treatment. Baskets north and south of this core area may show this selvedge but also may differ. In the south, around Mono Lake, coiled selvedge bundles similar to those on Owens Valley and adjacent Western Shoshone trays are common. In the north, simple truncation of the warp rods occurs. Trays are rimmed with single and multiple-edge rods. Rods may be wrapped or occasionally coiled in place with a simple overcast stitch. Often the rod is carried to the back to support the tip. An additional rod may be added to the end.

Open twined trays vary in size and shape, but most tend to be shallower and broader than those of the adjacent Owens Valley Paiute and Western Shoshone (see "Subsistence," fig. 3b, this vol.) Large trays are often one meter or more in length. Starts, selvedges, and finishes are similar to those on close twined trays. A final two or three rows of close twining, either plain over one or two rods, or twill, serves as a foundation for attaching the rim rod.

Plain twined trays are used primarily for the preliminary winnowing of pine nuts, while the twill twined openwork variety is used for secondary parching and cleaning shelled pine nuts and for parching or winnowing other large seeds or berries. They may also serve as sifters to separate seeds of different sizes, or alternatively, seeds from chaff. Close twined trays are multipurpose: gathering, sorting, cleaning, winnowing, and parching small and larger seeds and catching meal at the end of the milling stone. They also double as serving platters. In those Northern Paiute areas with both plain and twill twined openwork trays, the plain twined type is associated primarily with pine nut processing. In Surprise Valley, which is outside the principal distribution of piñon, plain twined trays are smaller and are used to grate the skin from roots (Kelly 1932:128).

Burden baskets as well come in roughly four grades or sizes: small (33 cm deep) and large (55 cm deep) close twined, and large (65 cm deep) twill and plain twined openwork. All are begun with three-strand twining before the dominant stitch used to complete the basket walls. Leather patches may cover starts of burden baskets. The bases of close twined varieties apparently wear out easily, and they are then treated as a repair. Close twined baskets, large and small, are finished with an underselvedge of four or five rows of plain twining over two rods, sometimes also with a second set offset by one rod (fig. 3d). The twined warp rod selvedge, as described for trays, completes the basket. To this a single or double rim rod is added with simple wrapping. Open twined baskets lack the plain twine top underselvedge but are usually finished with the same twined edge. A few plain twined baskets have a bundle selvedge instead. Close twined baskets are usually decorated with from two to five horizontal bands of design elements.

Large close twined and open twined burden baskets have tumplines for carrying. These are secured to the basket by two loops that intersect an interior reinforcing rod, the rod usually being placed halfway down inside the basket and being half the circumference of the basket. The baskets are meant to fit comfortably on the

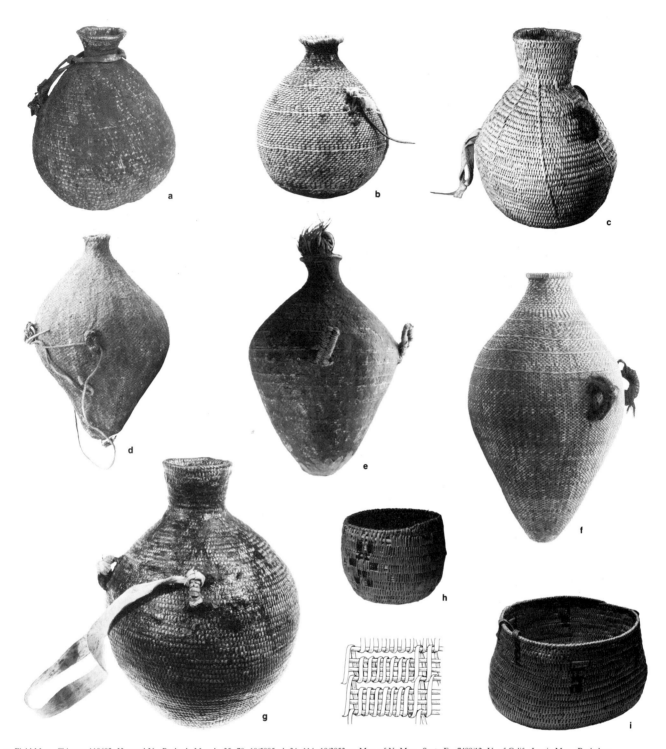

a, Field Mus., Chicago: 110692; Harvard U., Peabody Mus: b, 35–78–10/5005; d, 34–114–10/3953; c, Mus. of N. Mex., Santa Fe: 7498/12; U. of Calif., Lowie Mus., Berkeley: e, 1–191713; f, 1–21718; g, Smithsonian, Dept. of Anthr.: 11,874; h, Denver Mus. of Nat. Hist., Colo.: 11249; i, U. of Utah, Mus. of Nat. Hist.: 4079.

Fig. 2. Water bottles and utility baskets. a, Northern Shoshone–Bannock open twill-twined water bottle in the personal canteen style, heavily pitched. There is one central band of 3-strand twining. Collected before 1925. b, Western Shoshone twill-twined water bottle decorated with bands of 3-strand twining and plain twining over paired warps, pitched inside and out. Collected about 1935. c, Ute close-coiled water bottle decorated with the supplementary weft technique and false braid rim finish. Collected about 1935. d, Northern Paiute pointed-bottom water bottle in twill twining, of the size used at a residence. Collected 1934. e, Kawaiisu twill-twined water bottle with bark stopper. Several bands of 3-strand twine constitute decoration. Collected in 1915. f, Owens Valley Paiute water bottle, close twill twining, with a band of plain twining over paired warps below the neck, and rows of 3-strand twining. Collected in 1918. g, Southern Paiute close-coiled water bottle, pitched inside and out, with a 2-rod stacked foundation, and a 3-strand overcast rim. Collected in the 1870s. h, Northern Shoshone–Bannock close-coiled utility basket, with 3- and 4-rod stacked foundation, and coil wrapping for decoration. Probably made in the 1920s. i, Ute utility basket, close-coiled, 3-rod stacked foundation decorated with false rim braid and coil wrapping. Collected in 1920. Height of a, 29 cm; rest to same scale.

back and to be easily emptied by dumping them forward. Small close twined baskets may have a strap attached to the rim. This is looped over the wrist, and the basket is held when gathering. Contents are then dumped periodically into the burden basket on the gatherer's back. Large, openwork baskets were frequently used to collect pine cones or nuts. They also functioned in the transport of household items when camp was being moved.

Close twined boiling baskets (fig. 1i) with flattened or slightly rounded bases and roughly cylindrical walls are also common among most groups. Techniques of manufacturing these paralleled those for close twined burden baskets, including techniques for starts, twill twining of the body, underselvedges, and selvedges. Occasionally these baskets are lightly pitched on the exterior to make them watertight. However, the mushes usually boiled in them also render them watertight. Two or three bands of decoration in motifs similar to those on burden baskets are added. Twined eating bowls (fig. 1e) are miniatures of the cooking baskets, but without the underselvedge and selvedge. Instead, the warps on these are cut close to the last row of twill twining. A row or overcast stitch or, more often, a row of three-strand twining might be added to finish. Eating and drinking bowls often doubled as women's hats, and the two forms are indistinguishable.

Northern Paiute water bottles were made in three sizes. Small bottles were for individual use as canteens; medium, for carrying water to a locality to be used temporarily by a few people; and large (fig. 2d), for use at the base camp. Medium and large bottles are bipointed, although the large bottles have a more elongated basal section relative to the top section. Small bottles have a rounded, occasionally indented or flattened, base and cordage loops for attaching a handle on opposite sides above the shoulder. Loops on large bottles are just above the shoulder and on the same side, to facilitate attaching a tumpline. The form of large bottles kept the water from spilling when they rested sideways. Medium-sized bottles were of either shape.

Water bottles were constructed in the same way as were burden baskets. The narrow neck of each bottle might be finished in plain twining over two warps or less frequently with several rows of coiling. A simple overcast selvedge over truncated warp ends completed the neck. Juniper or sagebrush bark stoppers were often provided. Piñon pitch was applied inside and out, over a coating of red ocher and ground chaff. Bottles are otherwise undecorated. Unpitched bottles were used to store seeds.

Most Northern Paiute seed beaters are fairly large, elongated, and made in open twining. They have short handles in comparison to seed beaters in the adjacent Western Shoshone country. The warp rods gathered together to form the handle are secured with open twin-

ing on the exterior of the bundle. The end of the handle may have a twined warp selvedge or simply be truncated. A single rim rod encircles the body of the beater continuing behind the handle. Seed beaters often show staining, a result of their use as sieves in pitting small berries (such as *Lycium* sp., *Shepherdia* sp.). A few are charcoal stained, evidence of use as parchers. Some have nearly vertical short handles and are probably best described as scoops for processing pine nuts and other large seeds.

Northern Paiute cradles before the twentieth century consisted of a flat, roughly rectangular base made in open twining and with both top and base wrapped with an overcast stitch. The shade was made of parallel warp rods usually secured with twill twining, often in paired rows. To this were attached several additional rods to support the shade above the child's head. Patterns on the shade indicated the sex of the child: diagonal lines for a boy, zigzags or diamonds for a girl. After 1900 people in most areas added a buckskin cover to their cradles. The perimeter of the old style cradle was rimmed with a chokecherry rod that protruded above and below the older foundation to give the new shape. These cradles were highly decorated with beads, shells, and other ornaments, with overall design layouts resembling those of the Plateau, a probable source ("Northern Paiute," fig. 14, this vol.).

Twined fish traps and baskets were confined principally to lake and riverine fishing groups among the Northern Paiute ("Subsistence," fig. 13a, this vol.).

Northern Paiute coiled basketry is limited in form and function in most areas except Mono Lake where it is diverse. Present in most areas are small serving and eating bowls made on three-rod foundations using non-interlocking stitches, a leftward work direction, and an exterior work surface. Similar open-stitch varieties on a single-rod foundation are sometimes referred to as trinket baskets, used to store personal items such as paints and beads (although a twined trinket basket is also known). Coiled cooking baskets (fig. 1h) are also reported for a number of areas (O.C. Stewart 1941) but are uncommon except at Mono Lake. They may have been traded from there and from the Washoe into other areas. Multi-rod foundation coiling, as seen in Oregon, probably is an introduction from the Northern Shoshone–Bannock. An older coiling tradition may have been present but is undescribed.

Owens Valley Paiute

Owens Valley Paiute basketry includes both twined and coiled wares with twined predominating. Principal types in twining include: burden baskets, collecting baskets, winnowing-parching trays, seed beaters, water bottles, hats, cradles, and, perhaps in former times, cooking or boiling baskets. Those in coiling include mixing-boiling

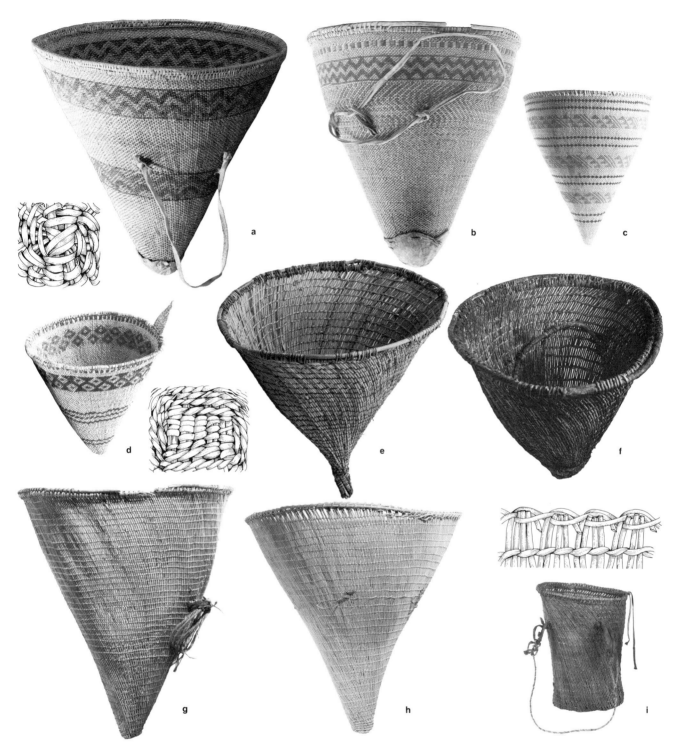

a, Mus. of N. Mex., School of Amer. Research Coll., Santa Fe: 9970/12; U. of Calif., Lowie Mus., Berkeley: b, 1–19675; c, 1–70724; g, 1–19680; h, 1–10493; d, Mus. of the Amer. Ind., Heye Foundation, New York: 13/4419; e, Harvard U., Peabody Mus.: 35–78–10/5025; f, U. of Utah, Mus. of Nat. Hist.: 18712; i, Field Mus., Chicago: 110713.

Fig. 3. Burden baskets and seed gathering baskets. a, Moapa Southern Paiute close-twill-twined seed gathering basket, with bundle selvedge and single rim rod. Collected in 1932. b, Owens Valley Paiute close-twill-twined seed gathering basket, with bundle selvedge and single rim rod. Collected in 1915. c, Close-twill-twined seed gathering basket made by Washoe Scees Bryant Possock (d. 1918). Selvedge is warp twined. d, Northern Paiute close-twill-twined seed gathering basket; start in plain twining over paired warps plus 4 rows of 3-strand twining; underselvedge of plain twining over paired warps for checkered band; twined warp selvedge; designs overpainted. Collected in 1924. e, Western Shoshone conical carrying basket, with warp-bundle selvedge and rim rod coiled in place at intervals. Collected in 1935. f, Gosiute openwork twill-twined burden basket, stained with piñon pitch, collected in 1939. g, Owens Valley Paiute, openwork plain twined burden basket; bundle selvedge; 3-strand twining at base; collected in 1915. h, Washoe openwork, twill-twined gathering basket with twined warp selvedge and 3-strand twining at the base; collected in 1906. i, Northern Shoshone–Bannock openwork twill-twined gathering and burden basket with warp bundle selvedge, collected before 1925. Height of a 65 cm; rest to same scale.

baskets, eating bowls, treasure baskets, cups or dippers, and flat sifting-gambling trays. Specialized baskets were also made in open twining for harvesting the larvae of the pandora moth. Because of the pivotal position of the Owens Valley Paiute in trans-Sierran trade, their basketry shows several south-central California as well as Great Basin features.

Burden baskets were in open, plain twining (fig. 3g). Several rows of three-strand twining around the start facilitated the introduction of new rods to form the body of the basket. Two-strand twining in rows roughly five centimeters apart continued throughout the body of the basket and had an up-to-the-right slant of turns. The warp rods whirled slightly to the left of vertical and were ultimately bent to the left (some truncated) to form a bundle at the rim. The bundle was secured by lashing, and an additional rim rod was coiled to the top of the bundle. Although most open, plain twined baskets were conical, some had a large and more curved upper section resembling Monache baskets (Driver 1937:78). The Washoe and Northern Paiute twined selvedge was absent.

Gathering baskets were made in both open and close twill twining (fig. 3b). Open twined baskets were larger (roughly 45 cm) with rows roughly one centimer apart. Unlike burden baskets, which were undecorated, gathering baskets had three or more bands of simple checked, striped, or zigzag designs, often worked in dyed willow or bracken fern root (table 3). Finishes are the same as for burden baskets. Gathering baskets and burden baskets were equipped with tumplines for carrying, usually with attachments half-way down on the outside of the basket. The interior supports for attaching the tumpline were small sticks lashed to the surface. Smaller (25 cm) close-twined gathering baskets were meant to be carried in the hand and emptied periodically into the large baskets. A looped strap for grasping was secured just below the bundle rim to two short sticks. An underselvedge of plain twining over paired warps, as in Northern Paiute and Washoe baskets, is present on these. One large band of zigzag lines or another simple motif decorated the small baskets.

Owens Valley winnowing-parching trays are of several grades and sizes, with clear-cut differentiation difficult (Driver 1937:78). All are deeper on the whole than Northern Paiute trays, a feature shared with Monache trays. The larger, plain twined tray has slightly protruding warp rods at the tip or start. The finish is a warp bundle, but occasionally the method of gathering it differs from the norm in that the rods are not bent at a sharp angle, but rather, more gently. This produces a distinctive crossing of rods on the exterior surface. The trays are also reinforced with a single rod running across the exterior, lashed to the basket surface. It protrudes slightly on either side. For winnowing or parching the basket is grasped at the intersection of the rod with the plain rim rod. A like feature characterizes Panamint Shoshone open twined trays.

Close and medium close twined trays (fig. 4f) of a more rounded shape and deeper (almost scoop-shaped) are also characteristic of the region. Warp rods may protrude at the tip of these as well, and short bundles characterize the selvedge. A band of several rows of plain twining over paired warps occurs at the point of rod reductions 7 to 10 centimeters from the top. A rim rod is lashed to the entire perimeter, passing under the warp rods at the tip for support. The deeper, scoop shape of these and the plain twine trays may be related to the manner in which they are held—large end to the processor. A flatter, close twined, and more fan-shaped tray was also made in the area.

Seed beaters vary from nearly circular with a short handle as among the Washoe, to more elongated or paddle-shaped (fig. 5c). They are plain twined over one warp. A single rim rod encircles the blade of the basket, passing over the junction with the handle. Handles on elongated beaters are tubular and finished with twill twining. The usual selvedge is a simple overcast stitch.

Water bottles (fig. 2f) are exclusively twill twined, and most have rounded bases. The canteen-size bottle has a single loop at the side, while larger ones may be handleless. A few bottles seem to have been finished without a neck, although this may merely be a technique of repairing and reusing a bottle after the narrow neck has broken. Some bottles are decorated with bands of three-strand twining, usually in the lower section, at mid-line, and as the bottle narrows to a neck.

Women's twined basket caps (fig. 1d) are also characteristic. They are rounded at the base and apparently designed to cover the whole head (Steward 1933b:273). They are started in three-strand twining and completed in twill twining. A band of three-strand twining is added to the rim before the warp rods are cut flush. Two wide and possibly a third narrow band of dyed willow (overpainted) is added to decorate. A string loop may be added to the top of the cap, perhaps to facilitate holding. However, these caps are not reported as being used as food bowls, as among the Northern Paiute. Zigzags and positive and negative diamonds are common motifs.

Although the evidence is slim, the Owens Valley Paiute may once have had a twined mush boiler similar to that of the Northern Paiute. The Mono Lake Northern Paiute, immediately to the north, had them, and the related Monache to the west made them as well (often in large sizes). If present, they were probably displaced by the introduction of pottery to the valley in the 1600s or before. The limited use of coiled boiling baskets is also reported by Steward (1933b:271).

Cradles are of two styles. The first style is reminiscent of Northern Paiute and Washoe cradles: an open, plain or diagonally twined flat back with a twined shade added.

a

b

c

d

e

f

g

h

top right, Mus. of the Amer. Ind., Heye Foundation, New York: 22367; Field Mus., Chicago: a, 60973; d, 110743; Harvard U., Peabody Mus.: b, 35–78–10/4987; e, 35–78–10/4989; g, 34–114–10/3919; U. of Calif., Lowie Mus., Berkeley: c, 1–53990; f, 1–26828; h, Smithsonian, Dept. of Anthr.: 204,842.

Fig. 4. Winnowing and parching trays. a, Ute close-twill-twined tray, collected in 1900. b, Panamint Shoshone open, plain twined tray used for pine nuts and small seeds; warp rods project at start; warp bundle selvedge; exterior lateral reinforcing rod. Collected in 1935. c, Washoe openwork, plain-twined tray for roasting pine nuts; whole rod wefts, twined selvedge, rim rod beneath tip. Collected before 1930. d, Northern Shoshone–Bannock close-twill-twined tray with coiled perimeter; 4-rod stacked foundation; collected before 1925. e, Panamint Shoshone close-twill-twined tray used for small seeds; warp rods project at tip; warp bundle selvedge. Collected 1935. f, Owens Valley Paiute twill-twined seed winnower, bands of plain twining over triple warps, with warp bundle selvedge. Collected before 1927. g, Northern Paiute close-twined winnowing tray with tabular tip in plain twining over paired warps and multiple bands and rows of plain twining over paired warps around the edges, above overpainted design band, and under selvedge; twined selvedge; white circle in native paint possibly a marker for tossing basket dice. Collected in 1934. h, Washoe tray of close twill twining, plain twining over paired warps at edges and as underselvedge, with twined warp selvedge. Collected before 1900. Length a, 43 cm; rest to same scale. top right, Northern Shoshone woman winnowing. Photograph by De Cost Smith, Lemhi Reservation, Idaho, 1904.

713

The second type has a double layered back, with the exterior layer of horizontal rods and the interior one of vertical rods. The two layers are then lashed together. This feature is also characteristic of Monache cradles. The shade remains as in Northern Paiute cradles and is decorated similarly to indicate the sex of the child: slanted lines for boys, zigzag or diamonds for girls.

Coiling in the area around Bishop is predominantly on a three-rod bunched foundation, with a leftward work direction and an exterior work surface. There are few standardized forms in coiling, perhaps suggesting that coiling is late in this area. The work direction seems to tie it more to the Monache area than to the Panamint Shoshone, whose work direction is primarily rightward. However, there are indications from C.H. Merriam's collection that the Paiute around Lone Pine may have practiced a different kind of coiling that is almost exactly like Panamint work.

Large coiled mixing and cooking bowls are in the form of a truncated cone with a flat base. They are used to mix pine nut soup, served cold and without boiling. Other large bowls are shaped with rounded bases and slightly incurving sides. Although some of both shapes were apparently made in the valley, most appear to have been traded from the Monache and yet others from the Panamint. Eating bowls (smaller versions of the mixing-cooking baskets) were also made, as were handled cups and dippers (Steward 1933b:271).

The large, flat, coiled tray seems to have been used in the Lone Pine area, but none has been reported from northern Owens Valley. As with groups to the west and east, the Owens Valley people apparently used the tray as a sifter and winnower as well as for tossing basket dice.

The people of Owens Valley made coiled and necked treasure baskets similar to the Yokuts and Monache style, to contain shell bead money and other personal valuables. Designs on these are also trans-Sierran, even though the original basket type from which the form was developed was probably either the Southern Numic treasure basket or the Great Basin water bottle. Merriam (1902–1942) reports that these baskets were used as mortuary offerings with food being placed inside and the basket being placed at the head of the deceased before burial. Although they were occasionally given away at the annual Mourning ceremony for the deceased, there is doubt that they were ever used as Merriam records.

The remaining Owens Valley basketry type, also of special use, is the globular open twined basket used to collect the larvae of the pandora moth ("Owens Valley Paiute," fig. 4, this vol.). The open twining was meant to assist in keeping the insects alive until they could be processed. These baskets are also reported for the contiguous Mono Lake Northern Paiute and the Washoe.

Western Shoshone

Data on Western Shoshone basketry are scant and documented pieces in museum collections few. However, basketry seems to be quite variable in technique and function with the following kinds most mentioned: in open twining, the burden basket, gathering basket, winnowing-parching trays, seed beater, berry basket, and cradle; and in close twining, winnowing-parching trays, the boiling basket, hat, water bottles, and eating bowls. Coiled wares include eating bowls and around Beatty a boiling basket. Other shapes are documented for the historic period.

The large, conical burden basket in this region is in plain twining over one warp and with slant of turns up-to-the-right as is all Western Shoshone twining. Ten to 15 rows of three-strand twining secure the warp rods in a conical shape. Open twining continues around the basket to the top, which is finished with a warp rod bundle selvedge. An additional single rim rod is coiled in place. The reinforcement rod for the tumpline is lashed in place so that it forms an upward curve (fig. 3f), a feature shared with the Panamint.

Open twill twined gathering baskets are of two forms, one conical in shape as is the burden basket and a second in which the warp rod ends protruded at the start (fig. 3e). The function of this unusual base is unknown, although it was suggested by a Shoshone woman that the basket could more easily stand in the sand. Rim finishes on both types are the same as for burden baskets but with a tendency for the warp bundle selvedge to be somewhat heavier. The rim rod lashing is spaced at intervals, like that of the Tubatulabal, Kawaiisu, Panamint, and Southern Yokuts.

Winnowing-parching trays in this region are quite variable as to shape and size. Steward (1941:238) illustrates some of the variation with outlines and admits that there appears to be little pattern to it. Open twined trays were made in both plain twining over one warp and twill twining over two warps. Occasionally both techniques occur on the same tray, usually with the twill twining at the top quarter of the basket. Selvedges on open twined trays may include small warp bundles, warp rods (usually single) twined over each other in a fashion similar to Washoe and Northern Paiute selvedges, and simple truncation of the warp after a twining row. Rim rods encircle the trays and are coiled in place at intervals. Occasionally coiling on the rim rod is continuous and close. Open twined trays are not decorated.

Seed beaters are also variable in shape but tend to be more rounded than linear and to have finished handles ("Western Shoshone," fig. 5, this vol.). Twill twining then covers the full surface of the beater. The warp ends are joined with twill twining on the surface to form a finished handle. The tip is not overcast. A rim reinforcing rod encircles the blade of the beater, passing

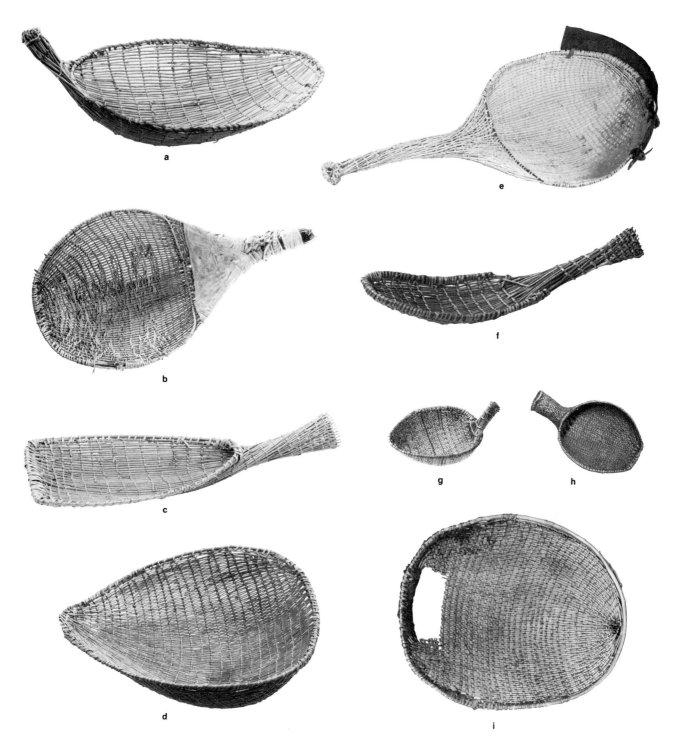

U. of Calif., Lowie Mus., Berkeley: a, 1–10478; b, 1–19708; c, 1–26983; d, 1–10482; Eastern Calif. Mus., Independence: e, A1149; h, B247; f, Idaho State U., Idaho Mus. of Nat. Hist., Pocatello: 5446; g, Smithsonian, Dept. of Anthr.: 19,034; i, Field Mus., Chicago: 110728.

Fig. 5. Seed beaters and scoops. a, Washoe seed beater in openwork plain twining, using whole rod wefts, with rim rod coiled to interior of the handle; collected in 1906. b, Kawaiisu plain twined seed beater with cloth-wrapped handle and rim rod coiled to the interior of the handle; repaired and reinforced surface; collected in 1915. c, Owens Valley Paiute seed beater in plain and twill twining; collected in 1927. d, Washoe openwork twill twined food gathering scoop, collected in 1906. e, Panamint Shoshone seed beater with metal cutting blade tied in place, and a wire rim, collected in 1950s. See "Southern Paiute," fig. 6f, this vol., for Southern Paiute seed beater with wooden blade. f, Northern Shoshone–Bannock twill twined seed beater with a tubular handle, collected before 1930. g, Northern Paiute close-twined ladle, used as cup or dipper, patterned after the seed beater. Collected 1875–1876. h, Death Valley Panamint Shoshone seed beater in close twill twining with tubular hollow handle. Seeds were also cleaned into it and poured into containers through the handle. Made before 1930. i, Northern Shoshone–Bannock seed beater tray with interruption of warp and weft at center for handle. Smith (1974:90) describes similar beaters for the Ute. Collected before 1925. Length of a, 51 cm; rest to same scale.

715

behind the handle or splitting the warp bundle at the handle, except for Panamint beaters, where it passes in front.

According to Steward (1941:241), a few groups of Western Shoshone made a special, round-bottomed, open twined basket similar to the caterpillar collecting baskets of the Owens Valley Paiute, Mono Lake Northern Paiute, and Washoe, but in this case for collecting berries. If truly like these counterparts, the narrow-mouthed opening of these might better suggest their use in collecting insects (cicadas, crickets). Most berry baskets made by the Northern Shoshone–Bannock or by the Ute were wide mouthed and probably more related in shape to the Southern Paiute trinket basket than to the insect collectors.

Western Shoshone cradles are variable in shape, with versions that have elliptical exterior rods, ones in which the encircling rod is wider at the top and with a narrower base, ones nearly square, and variations between ("Western Shoshone," fig. 13, this vol.) (Steward 1941:341). Cradles vary in the treatment of the back, with some being of the ladder style, with horizontal slats, others with horizontal rods closely twined together, and yet others with vertical rods also closely twined. In all cases, a twined shade is apparently attached. Some cradles were buckskin covered in whole or in part at least in historic times, but the dating on the addition of a buckskin cover is not clear. The supports for the shades on Western Shoshone cradles appear to be kept to the exterior edge of the basket if it is skin covered rather than tucked into the interior as in Northern Paiute cradles.

Various Western Shoshone groups made close twined winnowing-parching trays as well as ones in open twining. Close twined trays were essentially the same in outline as the open twined varieties with a slight tendency to be more fan-shaped. They were also decorated. Common decorative techniques included the use of bands of plain twining over paired warps or, occasionally, near the tip, plain twining over a single warp. Close twined trays may have warp bundle selvedges or twined selvedges as do open twined varieties. Steward (1941:238–239) reports that trays were sometimes decorated with two to four simple narrow bands of unpeeled willow wefts.

Little is known of Western Shoshone boiling baskets beyond what Steward (1941, 1943a) records. He notes the presence of twined boiling baskets among two groups: the Grouse Creek and the Beatty Shoshone. The form and technique of manufacture is unknown. It is likely that pottery had largely displaced basketry boilers.

Close twined women's hats (fig. 1b) are reported for most groups as far north as central Nevada (Steward 1941:292). One version, at least, was finished with three-strand twine over two warps before the warps were truncated. Hats seem not to have been decorated.

Water bottles (fig. 2b) were known in large and small varieties with pointed bases, rounded bases, and a nearly bipointed style represented. All have narrow necks and are most frequently decorated with bands of three-strand twining near the shoulder and neck. Rims are finished with overcast stitch, and loops are then added at the shoulder line for attaching a carrying strap. Bottles are covered with a mixture of red ocher and crushed vegetable material and then pitched, with pitch on the inside surface and the outside of the bottom most commonly mentioned. Pitched bottoms may also be leather or canvas covered.

Close twined eating and mixing bowls are also reported sporadically in the region (Steward 1941). They appear to be similar in outline to Northern Paiute boiling baskets but lack the rim rod. They have several rows of three-strand twining at the base and may have bands of it as well in the body of the basket. They may also be decorated with plain twining over two warps in alternating peeled and unpeeled willow.

Western Shoshone coiling appears to be limited to rounded food bowls and possibly a boiling basket. Both forms were found in but a few areas by Steward (1941). Work direction appears to be leftward over a three-rod bunched foundation. Moving ends are caught under the top rod of the bundle and fag ends turned to the left and carried in the coil. Steward (1941:241) remarked that coiling appeared to be recent in the Wells area. Gosiute coiled water bottles are also assumed to be recent and, by shape, probably derived from the Ute. Several additional coiled shapes were made for sale in the twentieth century.

• PANAMINT Panamint Shoshone basketry has both coiled and twined forms. Based on scant records, the traditional basket types made by the Panamint appear to include the following: in open twining, the burden basket, winnowing-parching tray, seed beater, and the roasting scoop; in close twining, the gathering basket, winnowing-parching tray, woman's hat, water bottle, and necked treasure basket. Coiled baskets, all essentially of one technique, included the shallow circular winnowing tray, eating bowl, woman's hat, and a necked, jar-shaped form, possibly associated with cremation. Panamint cradles, about which there seems to be some disagreement, were said by Driver (1937:79) to be of the forked-stick variety, similar to those of the Kawaiisu and Yokuts, while Steward (1941:295, 341) suggests an oval frame. Merriam said that both were used (Grosscup 1977:128–129). Both apparently had horizontal slats at the back and a twined mat pad.

Panamint openwork plain twined burden baskets, used principally in gathering piñon cones and nuts, are similar in shape and size to those of the Kawaiisu. They are roughly 35 centimeters long and 40–45 centimeters wide. They are in plain twining, with a slant of turns up-to-the-right. Starts are usually obscured by a patch

Smithsonian, Dept. of Anthr.: a, 14,700; e, 10,751; i, 14,739; b, U. of Calif., Dept. of Anthr. Davis: 601; U. of Calif., Lowie Mus., Berkeley: c, 1–26838; d, 1–70634; g, 1–19690; f, Field Mus., Chicago: 110740; h, Harvard U., Peabody Mus.: 35–78–10/5001.

Fig. 6. Treasure baskets, berry baskets, coiled trays and bowls. a, Southern Paiute close-twill-twined treasure basket, made to hang inside the house to store personal property. Collected in 1870s. b, Panamint twill-twined hanging treasure basket, with overpainted design. Collected in 1935. c, Panamint coiled treasure basket, noninterlocking stitch on a 3-rod foundation. Collected 1917–1927; d, Washoe close-coiled treasure basket, 3-rod foundation and duck feather decoration, collected before 1944. e, Ute berry basket, a type perhaps related in shape to the Southern Paiute treasure basket; open to close coiling over a 2–3 rod stacked foundation; stitches intentionally split on the work surface. Collected probably 1867–1868. f, Northern Shoshone–Bannock twill-twined berry basket with bundle selvedge, paired rows of 3-strand twining as decoration, and cordage handle. Collected before 1925. g, Kawaiisu flat, close coiled tray, used to sift coarse from light meal. Collected in 1915. h, Panamint Shoshone flat, close coiled tray, used for winnowing-parching and casting stick dice. Collected in 1935. i, Southern Paiute close-coiled bowl, 2-rod stacked foundation, simple asymmetrical petal design. Collected in 1870s. Height of a, 20 cm, b–d to same scale; e, 22 cm, f to same scale; g, 49.5 cm, h–i to same scale.

717

of canvas or leather at the base, but they appear to be more rounded than conical. A small warp bundle selvedge, turned to the left, is used. A separate rim rod is coiled over the bundle, with coil stitches grouped at intervals rather than continuously. Coiling in a leftward direction opposite that of normal Panamint coiling probably is the result of the direction of the warp rod lean and bundle. Attachments for the tumpline are sustained by a curved stick on the inner wall of the basket.

Open, plain twined trays (fig. 4b) for the Panamint are similar in style to those of Owens Valley, with the warp rods protruding at the start, a horizontal reinforcing rod often lashed to the back midsection of the tray, and similar features of finishing. They are less scoop-shaped than Owens Valley trays. Both large and small trays apparently made for winnowing and parching pine nuts and large seeds are undecorated.

Seed beaters are also made in openwork plain twining over one warp and have finished, long handles. The paddle is oval and somewhat deeper at the side opposite the handle than those of their neighbors. Most interesting is the attachment of a wooden slat or metal blade to the front edge of the beater, making it in effect a cutting tool as well as a more effective beater (fig. 5e). This is also a feature of Southern Paiute beaters.

An additional open twined basket type was a scoop-shaped basket that may have doubled as a roaster. These small (17–30 cm long), deep (10 cm) baskets were in twill twining, and finished with a warp rod bundle as are close-twined trays. A rim rod encircles to add stability.

Panamint close twined seed gathering baskets are similar in overall shape to those of the Kawaiisu and Southern Paiute but lack the underselvedge of those baskets. They are slightly wider at the mouth than long. The end is more rounded than pointed as were those of the Kawaiisu, and it is ordinarily leather or cloth covered. The rim finish is a coiled warp rod bundle to which is attached a rim rod coiled on separately at intervals. A broad design band is placed near the top of the basket and the tumpline immediately below it. The reinforcing rod for the tumpline loops is a single stick curved upward.

Closed twined trays are variable in outline, from nearly circular to more elongated (fig. 4e). The broad trays resemble in shape those of the Southern Paiute while the more elongated versions are more like those of the Owens Valley Paiute or other Western Shoshone. Unfortunately, there are too few documented trays to say much about their characteristics other than that they have warp bundle finishes at the top and for the elongated version, protruding warp ends at the tip. Several decorative rows of plain twining over two warps may appear near the top. Twined trays were also decorated with bands of small designs worked in red Joshua tree root.

Panamint twill twined hats are decorated with two design bands, one small near the top of the hat and the other large near the base. Hats are finished with three-strand twining over one or two warp rods before the rods are truncated. Water bottles are described by Merriam (Grosscup 1977:128) as of three sizes, with the small and medium apparently rounded at the base, resembling those of the Tubatulabal, and the large ones pointed, resembling those of other Western Shoshone.

A close twined version of the seed beater was made in at least some areas. The blade of the basket narrows near the handle, and the warp rods are formed into a tube that is completed in close twining. Small seeds were apparently poured through the tubular handle into narrow necked containers.

The twined, necked treasure or trinket basket (fig. 6b) of the Panamint is very similar in outline to those of the Southern Paiute. It differs primarily in the use of plain twining over two warp rods at the neck and in retaining a warp rod bundle selvedge. A separate rim rod is coiled to the bundle as well. These vessels have a large horizontal design band that is overpainted, as are those of the Southern Paiute.

The Huntington Lib., San Marino, Calif.

Fig. 7. Washoe camp with woman pitching water bottles. The bottle is held by a stick inserted in its neck, while hot piñon pitch is applied on the outside with a paddle. The pitch seals the close, twill twined bottle, making it watertight. Photograph possibly by George W. Ingalls, about 1900.

Panamint coiled work was done on either a three-rod bunched foundation (fig. 9) or one combining rods and grass stems (*Muhlenbergia rigens*). The stitch type was noninterlocking, with a minor number of stitches accidentally split on the back face. The work direction was almost invariably to the right; leftward work direction in this case is interpreted as the work of left-handed weavers. On open forms such as bowls and trays, the awl was inserted as often on the convex side as on the concave. On narrow necked shapes, the convex side is always the work face. The edges of coiled baskets are always self-rims, never overstiched, and the coil endings were simply tapered.

Coiled forms include circular winnowing trays, bowls, hats, and necked jars. Circular trays (fig. 6h) are similar to those of the Kawaiisu and Tubatulabal (Grosscup 1977:128). They may be plain or carry a simple geometric design band. Roughly 35 centimeters in diameter, they can be used for winnowing and for tossing basket dice (Driver 1937:78).

Bowl-shaped baskets, basically truncated cones with narrow, flat bases, are of various sizes. The largest may once have been boiling baskets, although Driver (1937:78) does not list boilers for the Panamint (pottery was preferred for cooking). Smaller sizes served as mixing and eating bowls. Coiled women's hats (fig. 1a) are conical, but the sides flare less than those of eating bowls. The necked treasure baskets (fig. 6c), most with flat shoulders but some also rounded like the treasure baskets of the Southern Paiute and Chemehuevi, are reminiscent of Kawaiisu, Tubatulabal, and Yokuts styles.

Designs on coiled baskets consist principally of vertical and diagonally ascending bands. A single black coil near the base of the basket starts the design. A second black coil ends it three coils below the rim on large bowls or just below the neck on necked forms. After a plain light-colored coil, the rim is finished with alternating dark and light stitches spaced at intervals. Panamint designs appear to be most similar to those of the Tubatulabal, which in turn are likely Yokuts derived. There is a further link to Tubatulabal designs in the use of concealed asymmetry, that is, in placing diverse marks in the background or in designs or on the edge of designs. These are often in different colors, including white or pink feather quills in historic times. Some baskets have many such marks, others only one. Small baskets or two-color baskets may lack them, but they are nearly always found on three-color baskets.

Northern Shoshone–Bannock

Collection data for the Northern Shoshone and Bannock are insufficient to allow differentiation of the baskets of these two groups. The principal types that they made are: in twining, winnowing-parching trays, burden baskets, water bottles, hats, berry baskets, seed beat-

ers, fish traps, and cradles; in coiling, water bottles, a variety of utility baskets, and in former times, the boiling basket. Basket types are fewer due to loss of function and replacement by Plains-type containers.

Winnowing-parching trays occur in both open and close twill twining, but open twined ones are rare. Trays are in two sizes: small, at roughly 25 to 30 centimeters long and nearly as wide; and large, at roughly 40 centimeters long and the same wide. Both types are rounded at the tip and straight to slightly rounded at the broad end. Twining proceeds with an up-to-the-right slant of turns, incorporating new warps. Open twined trays have paired weft rows separated by 0.5 to 1.0 centimeters space and are undecorated. Close twined trays may have three to four bands of four to five rows of plain twining over two rods to decorate, with or without alternating design bands of autumn peeled versus fully peeled wefts. Ends are finished with a small bundle of broken warp tips or splints on both front and back faces. Occasionally a row of three-strand twining is below the bundle. Rim rods are attached by coiling, often very tightly. A few trays may have additional rows of close coiling at the edges of the top of the tray before addition of the rod. One tray has three rows of close coiling over a four-rod stacked foundation around the perimeter (fig. 4d). Both open and close twined trays may have a single buckskin loop attached to the edge rod at the side or slightly above the top to facilitate grasping.

Seed beaters from this region are variable in shape: round in open twining with a short (6 cm) handle of warp rods; oval in close twining with a short (3 cm)

U. of Nev. Reno, Special Coll.
Fig. 8. Wuzzie George, Northern Paiute, splitting willow for weft. She holds one element in her teeth and uses her hands to separate the remaining 2 and stabilize the third. Pith will be removed from the interior of each strip with a fingernail, and each strand trimmed with a knife to even it. The outer bark will also be removed, although scraping may not follow if a darker surface is desired for decoration. Photograph by Margaret M. Wheat, Stillwater, Nev., about 1954.

handle finished in open twining; curved, paddle-shaped in open twining with a longer (18 cm of overall 42 cm length) handle also in open twining (fig. 5f); and fan shaped, constructed as are open twined trays with the center warp rods truncated two-thirds of the way to the top and the remaining twined rods bent toward the center to form a handle (fig. 5i). Nothing is known of the functions of these different styles of implements.

Burden baskets and berry baskets are constructed similarly in most instances and differ only as to size. Berry baskets are roughly 28 centimeters tall by 20 centimeters wide, and burden baskets 40 centimeters tall by 33 centimeters wide (fig. 6f). Both are made in open and close twill twining, with up-to-the-right slant of turns. Burden baskets are characterized by broad bases (fig. 3i), unlike those to the south. Selvedges vary from a small warp bundle attached to the outside in overcast stitch with rim rod added in a second coil, to various degrees of close coil rims. Some of the latter have two to three coil rows over a two to three-rod stacked foundation. Normally burden baskets have a reinforcing rod around the entire interior of the basket, half-way from the rim. To this are attached loops that go to the outside where the tumpline is fastened. Berry baskets have a variety of rim loops for suspension or grasping in the hand. Close twined versions of the berry basket may be decorated with three to four double bands of three-strand twining, or darkened autumn-peeled willow, or both.

Small (15 cm high by 19 cm rim diameter), close twined bowls (fig. 1f) are an additional type. Some of these may be eating bowls, some basket hats, reportedly worn by the Fort Hall Northern Shoshone but not by the Lemhi or Bannock (Steward 1943a:317), and some collecting baskets. Plain or twill twining forms the body of the basket. They may be decorated with bands of plain twining over two rods, or bands of three-strand twining, or a row or two of dyed or painted wefts. Baskets since the 1920s are decorated with aniline-dyed wefts.

Water bottles (fig. 2a) in close twill twining are also characteristic of this region. They vary from 20 to 35 centimeters high. Rounded bases and narrow necks are typical. Rims are finished in overcast stitch. Decoration may be a band of three-strand twining or of plain twining over paired warps. Pitch is applied both inside and out but apparently not over a coating of red ocher or chaff as with the Northern Paiute. Loops for carrying larger baskets are above the shoulder on the same side, to which a tumpline or handle is attached. Smaller bottles have a single loop on one side to which a buckskin strap is applied and then fastened around the neck of the bottle. Smaller bottles are for personal use, larger ones for water storage and camp use.

Northern Shoshone–Bannock cradles vary in design, owing to different protohistoric contacts. The oldest

bottom, Eastern Calif. Mus., Independence: 82.32.

Fig. 9. top, Susie Wilson, Panamint Western Shoshone, finishing the rim of a coiled necked basket, using a 3-rod foundation, a rightward work direction, and exterior work surface. Work direction rarely varies in Panamint work, but the work surface changes depending on the shape of the basket. The remains of moving ends of wefts on the interior surface of the basket have been left to be trimmed after a few coils are completed. Basketry materials around her include additional weft material soaking in the pan in the foreground, weft coils and warp rods, and a tin can lid with holes poked through it for evening the weft material. The cloth rags in narrow strips were used for tying up the coils and bundles of weft and warp materials. Photograph by Ruth Kirk, Death Valley, Calif., 1950–1952. bottom, Basketry making tools, including a perforated can lid used to trim wefts to desired sizes, awls made from spines of cottontop cactus (*Echinocactus polycephalus*) embedded in lac from creosote, and a granitic stone used in the final shaping of baskets. Very fine wefts, especially characteristic of Panamint baskets after 1900, were made with can lid gauges rather than trimming knives. Collected by Ruth Kirk, Death Valley, Calif., 1950–1952.

types appear to have been similar to those of the Western Shoshone and Northern Paiute: an elliptical frame of willow upon which a mat of warp rods is placed. Reinforcement bars run horizontally across the back and the warp rods were laced to these. Either a single rod hoop, to be buckskin covered, or a twined shade completed the cradle (Steward 1943a:376). These cradles were then buckskin covered, with the sack being split down the middle to receive the child. It is not known when in Northern Shoshone–Bannock history this buckskin covering became typical. Yet two additional cradle types, the board-backed buckskin-covered cradle ("Northern Shoshone and Bannock," fig. 9, this vol.) and the rawhide cradle, are known to be more recent and due to Plateau and Plains influences.

Northern Shoshone–Bannock coiled basketry is variable in shape, size, and function but difficult to assess historically. Coiled water bottles, rounded at the base and with narrow or slightly flaring necks, are found among both the Fort Hall Northern Shoshone and Bannock (Steward 1943a:317). In overall shape and design they are similar to Ute styles. Three-rod stacked and bunched foundations seem typical. Single or two-strand overcast stitching on the last coil finishes the bottles. Double horsehair loops on the same side above the shoulder secure the strap handle. The capacity is roughly one to two gallons.

Other coiled wares include a variety of utility baskets, as well as (in former times) the boiling basket (Steward 1943a:317). All lack reported specific uses, but storage and food collection can possibly be inferred from the shape and the attachment of carrying straps. Most are on two- to four-rod stacked foundations and have an exterior work surface and noninterlocking stitches. Many are lidded, a feature reported to Steward (1943a:317) as precontact. Several coiled baskets show decorative wrapped stitch coiling (fig. 2h) as do Ute wares.

Eastern Shoshone

Based on admittedly meager data, the Eastern Shoshone appear to have five documentable basket types: close twined winnowing-parching trays, both twined and coiled berry baskets, flat coiled gambling trays, and coiled water bottles. Apparently most of the basketry types still functional among the Northern Shoshone–Bannock are no longer so among Eastern Shoshone. They have been replaced by Plains-type hide containers and other implements.

Twined trays resemble those of the Northern Shoshone–Bannock. They have oval tips and straight to slightly rounded tops. Twining proceeds from the tip across alternate faces of the tray, incorporating warps added periodically to widen the tray. Occasionally four to six rows of plain twining occur at the point of regular warp introduction or deletion. Warp rods are thinned at the top of the tray, some broken, and then some folded to the interior from each side to form a bundle. A row of coiling over this bundle secures it to the top of the tray. A single rim rod is added to the edge of the basket with a simple overcast stitch. Trays are undecorated, except for occasional plain twining in peeled versus unpeeled willow or a band or two of twining in unpeeled willow. Trays show stains from berries and charcoal.

A single large (54 by 43 cm) tray that combines twining and coiling was collected on the Wind River Reservation in 1924. The central area of the tray is plain twine over one rod with a full twist up-to-the-right slant of turns. The rim consists of three rows of coiling on a three rod stacked foundation, exterior work surface, rightward work direction, and non-interlocking stitch. A single rim rod is coiled to the exterior.

Twined berry baskets are similar to corresponding Northern Shoshone–Bannock baskets. These containers are started in twill twining over two rods and have a distinctive flattened shape. The remainder of the basket, roughly two-thirds, is finished in plain twining over two to three warps. Some twining especially at the base has a full twist between the warps. The rim of the basket consists of a twisted bundle of some of the remaining warp rods in a down-to-the-left direction and is on the exterior only. This is secured in place with a simple overcast stitch. A rim rod is attached to the bundle, also with a simple overcast stitch.

An additional category of Eastern Shoshone basketry is the flattened, close coiled tray used for gambling, resembling that of the Plains ("Eastern Shoshone," fig. 16d, this vol.) (Weltfish 1930). Eastern Shoshone gambling trays are made on a two- or three-rod stacked foundation and are 30 to 40 centimeters in diameter. Work direction is leftward with an interior work surface, although occasionally a single basket may show both work surfaces. Wefts either split the top rod or incorporate it fully in the new coil. Some baskets have red or blue stroud incorporated into the last coil and may also be finished with a single row of widely spaced overcast stitch. Tossing basket dice is the only known use of these baskets.

The coiled water bottle is poorly represented. Small (14 cm high) and large (27 cm high) versions are known. Both are rounded at the base and have straight to slightly flaring necks. Both three-rod bunched and two-rod stacked foundations are known. A leftward work direction, exterior work face, and a simple overcast selvedge are present. Double pairs of loop handles are just below the shoulder. Some of these bottles may be Ute trade pieces.

Kawaiisu

Kawaiisu basketry is a mixed twined and coiled industry with both California and Great Basin affinities. According to Zigmond (1978), it includes the following principal types: in twined openwork, burden baskets, gathering baskets, winnowing-parching trays, and seed beaters; in close twining, gathering baskets, water bottles, and an acorn meal drying tray. Types in coiling include the flat sifting tray, eating bowls, necked treasure baskets, the basket hat ("Kawaiisu," fig. 5b, this vol.), the hopper for a mortar, and possibly a boiling basket, mortuary basket ("Kawaiisu," fig. 5a, this vol.), and a special basket for drinking jimsonweed juice.

Burden baskets are in open twill twining with an up-to-the-right slant of turns, as is all Kawaiisu twining

Table 2. Comparative Numic Basketry Terminology

	Owens Valley Paiute	Northern Paiute	Bannock	Panamint Shoshone	Western Shoshone	Kawaiisu	Southern Paiute	Ute
Twining								
1. close-twined winnowing-parching tray	*tima*	*tima* *saʔyadima*	*tima*		*tima*		*takʷkʷiˑʔu* *takoiyu*	*takʷio* *takoʔi*
2. open-twined winnowing-parching tray	*pacoˑ*	*yadˑa* *yata*	*wosˑa*	*yantu*	*yantu* *wiˑttahai*	*yaduci* *saˑzowinibi*	*yantu* *yantuppi*	
3. close-twined burden basket	*kakadusi* *kudusi*	*kakudusi*		*hiˑppi wosa* *kakkuˑsi*	*kakkutuˑ*		*aisi* *kabono*	*asiʔaipi*
4. open-twined burden basket	*wonu* *kawonu*	*wono* *kudusi*	*siˑwosˑa* *siˑwitua*	*wosa*	*wosa*	*aniši* *woʔnizi*	*aisi*	*aˑsa* *tanikʷu* *ʔaipi*
5. close-twined hat	*poʔno*	*cotia*	*cotia*	*siˑccappo*	*ticoi*		*kaiccoko*	*kacakupi*
6. close-twined cooking basket		*sanˑu* *opo*	*wosˑa*					
7. seedbeater	*cigu* *taniku*	*cigu*		*tannehu*	*tanihku* *ciŋgu*	*taniku*	*tikanimpi* *tanikkimpi*	*akʷukʷu-* *pitunipi*
8. water bottle	*osˑa* *paʔosˑa*	*osˑa* *siˑosˑa*	*wosˑa*	*osa* *paʔosa*	*woˑta,* *occa*	*sanaʔoˑcozi* *navaʔakurazi*	*occa* *osa*	
9. treasure basket							*sibanoci* *sopoto*	
10. berry basket			*siˑwosˑa*		*toˑnampi wosa* *kappippo*			
11. eating bowl		*cida* *siˑʒida*	*siˑʒida*					
12. fish trap								
13. insect harvester	*kunu* *piagi kudusi*							
14. cradle	*huˑpi*	*huˑpi*	*huˑpi*	*kohno*	*kohno*	*kohnoci*	*kono*	*kʷuni*
Coiling								
1. burden basket								
2. winnowing-parching tray	*saku*			*toda*		*saguci*	*sakuʔu* *koci*	*patunipi* *tukʷai*
3. gambling tray								*siawoci*
4. treasure basket	*apo*			*opo*		*šivoron(i)ži* *tsoponazi*	*sopoto*	
5. boiling basket	*apo*	*waboi* *opo*		*opo*		*muruwasi(?)*	*koci* *siˑkicici*	
6. woman's hat						*iki(ci)* *ikibizi*		
7. water bottle							*occa*	*paˑcici usa* *sitaci* *paʔakʷuci*
8. eating bowl	*apo*	*cida*				*mučiži* *kʷičizi*	*koci* *siˑkicici*	*akʷuci* *siici*
9. mortuary basket						*muruwasi*		
10. hopper for mortar						*ikibiga(zi)ka*		
Other								
1. wrapped-stitch carrying frame							*kaŋwabi*	

SOURCES: Zigmond 1975, 1978; Miller 1972; Crapo 1976; C.S. Fowler (1970–1982, 1962–1984, 1980–1983; J. McLaughlin, personal communication 1984; Merriam 1902–1942; McCown 1929; Stewart 1942; Kelly 1932–1933.

("Kawaiisu," fig. 2, this vol.). They are generally wider at the mouth than deep and have more rounded than pointed bases. Twill twining at intervals of one to two centimeters was used for the sides of the basket up to the top where a row of three-strand twining serves as an underselvedge. The selvedge consists of a bundle of warp ends folded to the left. Some warps are cut at the selvedge and the tips added to the bundle. This bundle is held together by simple coiling. A rim rod is coiled to the top of the bundle for added reinforcement. The tumpline may be attached to loops one-third of the way down, connecting with single horizontal reinforcing rod on the interior.

Gathering baskets (two sizes) are similar in shape and construction with the exception that they are reported to be somewhat smaller, to occur in both open and close twill twining, and to have a looped carrying strap attached to the rim that can be wrapped around the forearm for carrying (McCown 1929). They may also have one large or two small bands of decoration usually merely alternating colors or simple geometrics.

Twined winnowing-parching trays are in open, plain twining over one warp rod. They vary in length from 30 to 60 centimeters and are oval and shallow. Truncated warp rods project at the tip or start. Twining rows are roughly one centimeter apart. Near the top of the tray a few rows of twill twining may gather the rods for the finish. A very thin warp rod bundle serves as a selvedge, or truncated warp rods may be wrapped with a simple coil stitch. A rim rod reinforces the perimeter of the tray, being added by spaced segments of coiling separated by blanks. The same implement served as a cleaning tray for large seeds and nuts as well as a winnower and parcher.

Kawaiisu seed beaters (fig. 5b) have rounded blades and unfinished warp rod handles. They are also worked in open twining over single warp rods. A few rows of twill twining over two to four rods serve to gather the rods into a bundle for the handle. A rim rod may reinforce the perimeter, crossing the handle on the inside of the beater. Beaters are shallow rather than scoop-shaped.

Water bottles (fig. 2e) are of several shapes and sizes, but all are made in close twill twining. Small canteen-sized bottles have rounded bases and narrow necks, and either single or double loops for attaching a handle. Larger bottles are more pointed at the base, but none so pointed as Northern Paiute types. Necks are finished with a simple overcast stitch, and single or paired rows of three-strand twining may occur over the bottle's surface for decoration. Loops are at the shoulder and on the same side. Bottles are pitched both inside and out.

A rare type of water bottle is the double bottle, or one with a marked constriction at the mid-section. Zigmond (1978:211) reports that one weaver, a transvestite, manufactured this type. Double bottles, also twill twined, are recorded for the Havasupai (Spier 1928:128) and other Southwest groups. The Ute made a coiled version in historic times.

Equally rare but reported to Zigmond (1978:211) was a special tray type basket made for leaching and drying acorn meal. It was said by some to be twined and by others coiled. Absent from museum collections are Kawaiisu cradles. They were reported by McCown (1929) and Driver (1937) to be of Valley Yokuts type (a forked stick with horizontal slats and a twined mat of rushes).

Kawaiisu coiling is almost universally over a foundation of a bundle of grass stems (*Muhlenbergia rigens*). It is also universally rightward in work direction, but the work surface may vary according to the shape of the basket.

The flat coiled tray (fig. 6g) is most frequently worked from the concave or interior surface and may be from 30 to 60 centimeters diameter. Patterns woven into these trays consist of small geometric figures in encircling bands. They have simple self rims, usually in the light background material of the tray or one-strand over-stitching between the stitches of the last coil. These trays are used for sifting and winnowing but apparently not for tossing basket dice (Driver 1937:78).

Bowl-shaped baskets with flat bases and flaring sides or more rounded sides were apparently used for eating bowls and possibly also as cooking baskets, although their use in cooking was said to have been abandoned long ago (McCown 1929; Driver 1937). These were also most frequently worked on the concave surface, and they display a variety of simple geometric designs. A few are decorated with more elaborate multicolored vertical and diagonal bands, similar to Yokuts and Tubatulabal patterns. These designs were probably acquired later in connection with trans-Sierran trade. Zigmond (1978:205) reports that larger baskets of this type were used only in association with death; they were placed inverted over the head of the deceased.

The Kawaiisu made a coiled version of the necked treasure basket. These pieces were highly decorated with bands of vertical or horizontal zigzag motifs and occasionally with quail crests around the rim or shoulder. They were meant to contain shell bead money and other personal valuables. A version of this basket with a more rounded shoulder was also made at least in historic times in spaced coil wrapping. Wrapped coils were joined periodically by regular stitches incorporating the coil above. Coil wrapping is known only among the Ute and Northern Shoshone in the Great Basin, but it also occurs in Mexican trade baskets in historic times. Its antiquity here as with the other groups is unknown.

The woman's basket cap among the Kawaiisu was exclusively coiled and flat based. The work surface on caps is about equally likely to be the interior surface as

723

Table 3. Materials Used in Ethnographic Basketry in the Great Basin

	Warp	Weft	Design	Other
Washoe	willow (*Salix* sp.)	willow (*Salix* sp.)	bracken fern root; redbud (R)(T)	mallard feathers
Owens Valley Paiute	willow (*Salix*; sp.); rye-grass (*Elymus* sp.)	willow (*Salix* sp.)	root (*Scirpus* sp.); devil's-claw (R); Joshua tree root (R)(T) (*Yucca brevifolia*); bracken fern (R); Northern flicker quills (*Colaptes auratus*) (R)	overpainting quail crests (R) mallard feathers (R) meadowlark feathers (R)
Northern Paiute	willow (*Salix* sp.)	willow (*Salix* sp.)	bracken fern foot (R) (T); redbud (R)(T)	overpainting
Panamint Shoshone	willow (*Salix lasiandra*); sumac (*Rhus trilobata*); bunchgrass (*Muhlenbergia rigens*)	willow (*Salix lasiandra*) sumac	bulrush root (*Scirpus nevadensis; S. robustus*); Joshua tree root; devil's claw (R); Northern flicker quills (R); American crow quills (R) (*Corvus brachyrhynchos*)	overpainting
Western Shoshone	willow (*Salix* sp.)	willow (*Salix* sp.)		aniline dyes (R)
Northern Shoshone/ Bannock	willow (*Salix* sp.); sumac	willow (*Salix* sp.); sumac		aniline dyes (R)
Eastern Shoshone	willow (*Salix* sp.)	willow (*Salix* sp.)		
Kawaiisu	willow (*Salix lasiolepsis, S. laevigata, S. hindsiana*); bunchgrass (*Muhlenbergia rigens*)	willow (*Salix lasiolepsis, S. laevigata, S. hindsiana*)	Joshua tree root; root (*Yucca whipplei*) sumac; bracken fern; devil's claw (R); rush (*Juncus balticus*) (?); Northern flicker quills	overpainting (?); quail crests; yarn (R)
Chemehuevi	willow (*Salix* sp.)	willow (*Salix* sp.)	devil's claw; rush root (*Juncus* sp.); rush (*Juncus textilis*) (R); Northern flicker quills (R)	quail crests
Southern Paiute	willow (*Salix* sp.); sumac	willow (*Salix* sp.); sumac	devil's claw (R); Joshua tree root (R)(T); rush root (*Juncus* sp.)	overpainting
Ute	willow (*Salix* sp.); sumac	willow (*Salix* sp.); sumac		overpainting

R indicates recent; T, trade.

the exterior. Designs were in vertical or oblique zigzag bands, and rims show no special treatment.

Other specialized baskets made by the Kawaiisu included the coiled hopper for the stone acorn mortar, often said to be made from broken larger baskets as well as purposefully manufactured (Zigmond 1978:205); and a specialized basket, perhaps a miniature of the necked treasure basket, for drinking liquid from soaked jimsonweed root. Other vessel shapes, derived from surrounding areas, were also manufactured for sale in the historic period. The use of human figures in coiled baskets seems to be associated with the historic period, perhaps first being used in the late nineteenth century.

Southern Paiute

Although not represented in all groups, the common Southern Paiute (including Chemehuevi) basketry types include, in twined wares, winnowing-parching trays, seed beaters, and basketry cradles; in both twined and coiled wares, water jugs, hats, burden baskets, and treasure baskets; and in coiled wares, circular parching trays, cooking baskets, and eating bowls ("Southern Paiute," fig. 10c, this vol.). To these may be added in some areas the wrapped-stitch carrying frame, the conical twined fish trap, and the bipointed twined pitch container. In historic times several other varieties of coiled bowls, baskets, and plaques were made for trade or sale to Whites or other Indian groups. In all, Southern Paiute twining is predominantly twill woven over two rods with an up-to-the-right slant of turns. Coiling is predominantly two- and three-rod stacked (limited use of three-rod bunched), noninterlocking stitch and in a leftward work direction. However, a fair number of Chemehuevi coiled baskets have a rightward work direction.

Southern Paiute winnowing and parching trays exhibit the dominant type of twining in both open and close work ("Southern Paiute," fig. 6, this vol.). On openwork trays the first pair of rim rods becomes a set of warp rods and twining continues around them alternately across the convex and concave sides of the tray. The second pair of rim rods is coiled to the finished basket with a simple overcast stitch. Warp rod ends are usually cut on open twined trays, and one to two rows of three-strand twining secures the edge. An additional reinforcing rod may be coiled across the lip surface. Open twined trays are approximately as wide at the lip as they are long, yielding the distinctive fan shape. Elsewhere in the Great Basin they are elongated in overall outline. Throughout the area, open twined winnowing-parching trays are associated with the pine nut complex and with the processing of large seeds.

Close twined trays have similar features and differ principally in the tightness of weft rows and in selvedge treatment. Often a single rim rod encircles these trays, producing a more rounded overall shape. Finishing may include a double bundle, made by folding the warp ends toward the interior surface from both ends of the tray, and then coiling each bundle separately. Additional coil rows may be added to contain the rim reinforcing rods.

Southern Paiute seed beaters ("Subsistence," fig. 3a, this vol.) closely resemble those for other Great Basin groups except in three features: the lack of a finished handle, the use of the butted start, and the use of a wooden (usually oak or cottonwood) slat to reinforce the lip. The wooden slat edge occurs principally among the Shivwits and Kaibab (Kelly 1964:83) although Panamint Shoshone and Southern Ute examples are also known. The same type with a metal rim was collected by Kelly in 1933 from the Kaibab.

Two variant forms of seed beaters are reported. One is the whole rod wicker work style, very similar to Havasupai and Walapai forms (Spier 1928; Kroeber 1935a), and the other is of similar shape but with a close twined blade surface. This second form is also reminiscent of a Western Shoshone variant (Steward 1941). Both forms probably represent intrusive ideas. The common Southern Paiute term for seed beater, at least among the western groups, has cognates in other Numic languages (table 2). The Kaibab Southern Paiute term does not have apparent cognates.

Southern Paiute water bottles are of four types: bipointed twined ("Southern Paiute," fig. 6g–h, this vol.), flat based twined, bipointed (or nippled base) coiled, and round-based coiled (fig. 2g). Mouth and neck shapes and sizes of all varieties vary. Twined bottles have warp rod bundle selvedges, similar to other close twined finishing procedures. Coiled bottles have simple self-finish rims. All bottles have two multistrand braided loops, of milkweed fiber or horsehair or both for attaching a carrying strap. Bipointed twined bottles are found only among the westernmost groups.

Kelly (1932–1933) provides evidence that coiled water bottles are "late" (late nineteenth century) in several western Southern Paiute areas. Some western groups did not adopt the technique at all. Otherwise, coiled water bottles are principally found among southern and eastern Great Basin groups (fig. 10).

Basket hats display some variation across the Southern Paiute area. Apparently a bell-shaped coiled variety was once made (Sapir 1910b:86; Lowie 1924); however, the most common varieties are the conical and peaked (mammiform) twill twined caps (fig. 1c). Selvedges for these vary across the area and include: warp bundle plus simple coil stitch, three-strand twine plus cut warp ends and a single rod coiled to the rim, and cut warp plus a simple overcast stitch. Designs include simple bands of both dyed and unpeeled weft, and multiple rows of the same in diamond pattern.

Both close and open twined burden baskets (fig. 11) are characteristic Southern Paiute types. Selvedges on open twine baskets generally include a whole or partial warp bundle plus a single rim rod, or cut warps plus a single rim rod. Rim rods in both cases are added with simple coiling. There often is a decided whirl to the left for the warp rods in these baskets. Close twined burden baskets (fig. 3a) are similar in both starts and selvedges, although the bundle rim is more typical and a row of three-strand twining may occur as an underselvedge. Close twined burden baskets are roughly as wide across the rim as they are deep. They are similar in outline to Walapai and Havasupai types except that these can have distinctive nipple-shaped bases. Selvedges serve to distinguish one tradition from the other (Spier 1928:125). Coiled burden baskets ("Southern Paiute," fig. 6a, this vol.) were barely remembered by Kaibabs in 1933 (Kelly 1964:78).

Southern Paiute circular coiled parching trays are generally made on a three-rod foundation with a self or wrapped start and a self rim. Overall, these are found

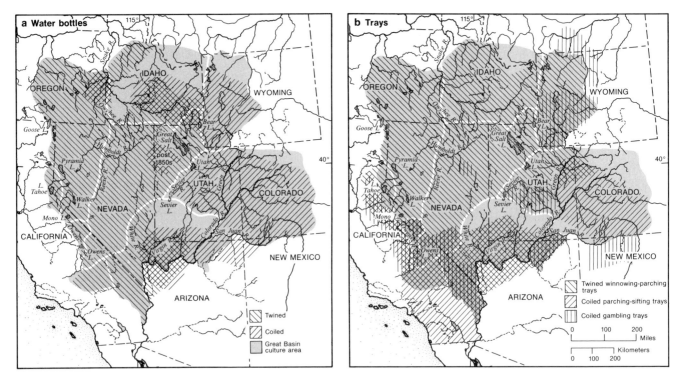

Fig. 10. Distribution of twined and coiled basketry in the Great Basin: a, water bottles; b, trays (Driver 1937; Steward 1941, 1943a; O.C. Stewart 1942; Kelly 1932–1933, 1964).

only among southern Great Basin groups, among whom cognate terminology for them seems to be shared (table 2). They are also a well-known part of southern California complexes (vol. 8:621–641), and they occur in the adjacent Southwest (fig. 10).

Southern Paiute coiled cooking baskets are difficult to categorize, as few documented examples are described in the literature or are available in museum collections. It is assumed that they were coiled on a two-rod stacked or three-rod bunched foundation, as were most other Southern Paiute coiled wares, but their exact shape is open to question (conical with rounded base seems most likely). Since pottery vessels served several Southern Paiute groups for cooking, it is possible that cooking baskets were uncommon in these localities. They were also rapidly replaced in historic times by metal containers. Various coiled food bowls (fig. 6i), most on two-rod stacked foundations, some with buckskin or cloth handles, were collected by John Wesley Powell in the 1870s. Larger coiled bowls on two-rod stacked or three-rod bunched foundation, some with simple decorations, were also collected (Fowler and Matley 1979).

Of the other remaining Southern Paiute forms, the globular or jar-shaped treasure basket (fig. 6a), either twined or coiled depending on area, requires special comment. According to Kelly (1932–1933), these baskets were hung inside the house and meant to contain personal items such as paint, beads, awls, and head scratchers. They were called sopoto, a term that appears

to have cognates only in related Kawaiisu among Great Basin languages (but see Yokuts in Gayton 1948, 1:19). They are similar in shape to Ute coiled "berry" baskets.

Fowler and Matley (1979:21, fig. 5f–g) illustrate Southern Paiute bipointed twined pitch containers. The wrapped-stitch carrying frame was used by the Southern Paiute principally for gathering agave ("Subsistence," fig. 4a, this vol.). For cradles see "Southern Paiute," fig. 7, this volume.

Ute

Ute basketry has not been the subject of much systematic research. According to Smith (1974:98ff.), the principal Northern Ute (Uintah, White River, Uncompahgre) and Western Ute (Pahvant, central Utah) basket types include: for twined wares, conical burden baskets and berry baskets ("Subsistence," fig. 3, this vol.), seed beaters, conical fish traps, and cradles; and for coiled wares, cooking baskets, eating bowls, berry baskets, winnowing-parching trays, and water bottles. A wicker fish trap is also reported for some subgroups (Smith 1974:62). O.C. Stewart (1942) adds for the Western Ute twined winnowing trays, water bottles, and basket hats, and coiled "tublike" burden baskets, seed beaters, and handled dippers. For the Northern Ute he includes the twined winnowing-parching tray and the coiled burden basket and handled dipper. For both, he lists apart from the coiled winnowing-parching tray an additional circular tray. O.C. Stewart's (1942) Southern Ute basketry

726

left, Calif. Histl. Soc., Los Angeles: Title Insurance Coll.: 3497; right, Milwaukee Public Mus., Wis.: 2895.

Fig. 11. Southern Paiute basket makers. left, Chemehuevi woman stripping bark from split wefts. A decorated, close twined seed gathering basket is to her left and a close twined winnowing tray to her right has some ground flour in it. Photograph probably by Charles C. Pierce, 1890s. right, Harriett Blaine Holmes working on an open, twill twined burden basket. Photograph by Samuel A. Barrett, Moapa River Reservation, Nev., 1916.

list includes the twined seed beater and burden basket and coiled winnower-parcher, circular tray, berry basket, water bottle, eating bowl, and cooking basket.

Coiled burden baskets, listed by O.C. Stewart (1942), are undescribed but may have been similar to those of the Southern Paiute. Smith (1974:90) characterizes the Northern Ute seed beater as open twined, roughly oval in shape, and handleless. A space was left in the weave on the narrow end for the fingers to grasp the implement (similar to the Northern Shoshone–Bannock type shown in fig. 5i).

Open and close twined berry baskets are known for several Ute subgroups. They are often plain twined if in openwork and twill twined in close work, both with an up-to-the-right slant of turns. Several warps cross or are butted together to form the base, and there may be a full reinforcing rod lashed halfway down in the interior of the basket. Selvedges include a single rod coiled onto the basket with a simple overcast stitch. Coiled berry baskets (fig. 6e), by far the most common, appear to be related in shape to the globular, flared rimmed treasure basket of the Southern Paiute–Chemehuevi. Most are laced with buckskin strips across or just below the rim, apparently to secure a covering of leaves to keep the berries fresh (Smith 1974:91).

Coiled cooking baskets, although replaced among most Ute groups by pottery vessels, were apparently round bottomed with slightly flaring sides. Eating bowls were the same shape or flat bottomed, but smaller. A flat-

tened, somewhat traylike version similar in shape to deeper Navajo wedding baskets was said to have been used to mash berries (Smith 1974:90). Coiled winnowing-parching trays appear to be similar to those of the Southern Paiute. The additional flat coiled tray noted by O.C. Stewart (1941) for most Ute groups may have been a gambling tray. Twined trays are basically triangular in outline, twill twined, and undecorated (fig. 4a). O.C. Stewart (1942:270) lists both open and close twine varieties for the Pahvant Ute.

Water bottles are most commonly coiled among the Ute, although J.W. Powell collected one pointed-bottomed twined and heavily pitched example among the White River Ute (Fowler and Matley 1979: fig. 5b), and O.C. Stewart (1942:271) reports the twined water bottle among one Southern Ute group. Coiled bottles have slightly convex bottoms, sometimes pitch covered, and are basically spherical in shape. The necks of bottles flare slightly. Bottles are most frequently pitched on the interior only, and some are coated with white clay on the exterior. They have horsehair handles and sagebrush stoppers. Of all Ute basketry they are the most common and have been the most persistent.

Northern and Southern Ute cradles since at least the second half of the nineteenth century are buckskin-covered and heavily beaded ("Ute," fig. 7, this vol.). Smith (1974:101ff.) describes an additional older style of the Northern Ute that was less elaborate. This cradle consisted of an elongated oval of willow with vertical

727

willow "slats" tied at top and bottom. Willow bark was plaited between the slats. The cradle was then placed in a buckskin bag to which lacing was added. An additional piece of buckskin might be placed over the child before lacing. An alternative cradle was a stiffened piece of rawhide into which the child could be laced.

Although twining and coiling appear to be roughly equal in the Ute basketry inventory, in terms of kinds and numbers of wares, Ute materials are predominantly coiled. Most coiled wares are two-rod stacked in foundation, with a leftward work direction and an exterior work face. Some are intentionally split stitched on the surfaces. A very limited number of one-rod and three-rod stacked pieces may be of recent manufacture. Selvedges may be plain, of two-strand wrapping, or of false braid (Fowler and Matley 1979; Smith 1974). False braid predominates on water bottles.

Most Ute baskets are undecorated. Cooking and eating bowls and wares made for sale have some simple geometric design elements. Smith (1974:90) reports that the Northern Ute preferred to paint designs on baskets rather than weave in dyed splints. Baskets in museum collections, most of which date to 1900 or later, also show short decorative sections of coil wrapping (fig. 2i). Seemingly unique to the Ute, but perhaps shared in part with the Jicarilla Apache (Tanner 1983:fig. 5.1), is the technique of adding surface interest to a coiled basket by carrying separate splints up the sides so that they override the coil. Each supplementary weft is incorporated only a vertical stitch at a time as the basket walls are built (fig. 2c). The antiquity of the technique is unknown.

Internal and External Relationships

The ethnographic basketry of the Great Basin exhibits considerable diversity while at the same time sharing a number of features, permitting speculation about internal and external relationships that may have culture-historical implications.

Twined basketry typical of the Numic-speaking groups in the region is nearly uniform in forms, weaves, functions, and nomenclature. It contrasts sharply with the work of surrounding tribes on all sides except in California, where there appears to be a close and ancient relationship with Tubatulabal and Yokuts twined basketry. There are two minor exceptions to this rule. One, the Havasupai, Walapai, and Yavapai of the Southwest have a pitched twined water bottle and a burden basket that are closely similar to Numic forms. This sharing may have taken place while their ancestors were in southern California near the ancestors of the Numic-speaking peoples (as hypothesized by the linguist Leanne Hinton, and L.E. Dawson). Two, the Washoe appear to have adopted some of the Numic twined baskets together with Numic designs. Forms include the winnowing basket, the pine nut tray, the seed gathering basket, and possibly the water bottle. Most other Washoe baskets are different from Numic analogues.

Minor differences in bases and underselvedge weaves between the Western and Southern Numic groups suggest later differentiation of the Numic twined complex along the lines of present linguistic groups. For example, the Southern Numic peoples (especially the Kawaiisu and Southern Paiute) used three-strand twining for an underselvedge and made more broadly rounded bases on their burden baskets and bottles, whereas the Western Numic peoples (Owens Valley Paiute and Northern Paiute) used plain twining over paired warp elements for the underselvedge (on winnowers and seed gatherers) and made more pointed bases on burden baskets and bottles. Central Numic types also show patterns of divergence in starts and selvedges of twined wares.

There is evidence that coiled basketry was not made by Numic-speaking peoples earlier in their history. First, the Northern Paiute apparently lacked it, or at least they had few standard forms in coiling. The northernmost Western Shoshone are also said to have lacked standardized coiled types (Steward 1941:238). The Northern Paiute and to a lesser degree the Western Shoshone had twined mush boilers that had not been displaced by coiled forms or pots even in relatively recent times. Second, the Monache of California appear to have acquired coiling after moving across the Sierra, probably in the eighteenth century. In the twentieth century they had had it for such a short time that twined boilers and coiled ones were both used. The Owens Valley Paiute appear to have received coiling from the Monache, not from the Panamint Shoshone, as determined by the presence of leftward work direction and rim overstitching. Third, the Kawaiisu and Chemehuevi, closely related Southern Numic speakers, have very different kinds of coiling. Kawaiisu coiling resembles that of the Yokuts and Tubatulabal of California, whereas Chemehuevi coiling resembles Anasazi work in forms and techniques. The two types are so disparate that the most likely explanation is that they were acquired from separate sources, one to the west and the other to the east. Fourth, the Numic-speaking groups that have coiling adhere to strict rules in placing designs on twined baskets but are more cavalier with coiled baskets, as though there were no rules for them. They freely adapted designs from twined basketry to the stitch work of coiled basketry but seem never to have attempted to apply coiled basketry designs to twined work, even though there were no technical hindrances. This attitude suggests that coiled basketry was regarded as a rule-free foreign medium open to experimentation. Fifth, the tribes closest to the sources of coiling in southern California and the Southwest show the greatest displacement of twined forms by coiled ones, and those farthest away show the least (figure 10).

Washoe coiled basketry appears to have a third separate history, including some apparent links to the basketry of the archeological Lovelock culture of western Nevada. Washoe coiled basketry is similar to Sierra Miwok work in many ways and suggests a common background for the two derived either by adoption or by descent from the Lovelock tradition. There are a few technical differences from Lovelock coiling, which may represent divergence over a long span of time. The Washoe practice of making designs in duck feathers is also unlike Pomo or Yokuts work but does resemble Miwok and Lovelock feathering. A few designs in Washoe coiled basketry also appear to have been adopted from the Maidu over an undetermined period of time. The Washoe lack of the flat coiled seed winnower-parchers so common in Lovelock tradition may have resulted from displacement by the radical acceptance of Northern Paiute twined winnower-parchers. An additional link between Washoe basketry and that of the Lovelock tradition can be seen in openwork twining with whole willow shoot wefts. It is definitely neither Northern Paiute nor Miwok inspired. In addition to general techniques, it shares the down-to-the-right slant of turns with Lovelock examples.

In the remainder of the Great Basin, few links are suggested between the archeological basketry and that documented ethnographically. Lamb (1958) hypothesized, based on linguistic evidence, that the Numic-speaking groups expanded into the Great Basin only about 1,000 years ago from a homeland in southern California. Although one must be cautious in equating artifact types or technologies with linguistic groups and especially with suggested migrations, the evidence from ethnographic basketry fits this hypothesis. It favors the expansion of twined complexes into the region from southern California, followed by later acquisitions of coiled techniques and forms. However, many more well-dated archeological occurrences of basketry from widespread localities will be required before technological replacement can be demonstrated and a time-frame and correlations to proposed linguistic movements can be determined.

Several features associated with coiling in the southern Great Basin appear to link Southern Paiute and Ute wares to those of the Pueblos, both ancient and modern. The flat coiled tray form, for example, goes back to at least Basketmaker III times, A.D. 600, in the region, although this early its foundation type and decoration are unlike Southern Paiute–Ute forms. By Pueblo III times, A.D. 1200, similarities are greater, although never identical. Coiled trays in southern California appear to have yet another origin. However, given that the distribution of these is nearly continuous from northern Arizona to California, more work needs to be done

before Southern Paiute–Ute sources and time of adoption can be determined with certainty. Wrapped-stitch coiling similar to that on Ute baskets is also a known Basketmaker III–Pueblo III technique (Morris and Burgh 1941).

Modern Pueblo features seen in Southern Paiute–Ute baskets include the false braid selvedge and the double bottle (Ute only) and coiled water bottle forms, although the last two are more widely distributed in the Southwest. Historic exchange of baskets is known to have been common in the Southwest, and it often included the Ute wares (Tanner 1983:83; Mason 1904:500). It appears that borrowing is responsible for these similarities, but the time-frame is unknown.

The distribution of coiled water bottles on the southern, eastern, and northern fringes of the region suggests the possibility that this form was acquired from the south after introduction of the horse. Other Northern Shoshone–Bannock and Eastern Shoshone coiling techniques may also be Ute-derived. Wrapped-stitch coiling, found as a decorative technique on some Northern Shoshone–Bannock pieces, is reminiscent of Ute techniques. Multirod stacked foundations appear to link these wares to each other as well as to Oregon Northern Paiute coiled products. Contact and commerce are known to have been common among these groups after the acquisition of the horse. However, coiling in the northern area is known from analysis of specimens collected well after contact and also well after groups began manufacturing cruder products for trade or sale to Whites.

Historic Period

Permanent settlement by Whites of the Great Basin region ushered in a new period of basketry development among most groups. With the introduction of new tool types by Whites, wares that in the precontact period were associated with specific functions such as cooking, water or food storage, or plant food processing were altered and even disappeared. Early historical photographs of native camps show a mixture of baskets along with metal utensils. This replacement process was probably faster in some areas than others, but in all aboriginal basketry types suffered a decline.

Paralleling the decline in certain types of utility wares was an increase in basket types made to trade with Whites. Prior to 1900 many White households throughout the region used Indian-made laundry baskets, sewing baskets, and small trinket baskets. Native women ordinarily traded these wares for food, clothing, or cloth but also in many cases for the metal utensils that were replacing their baskets. Although these wares differ from area to area within the region, most are characterized by a certain crudeness of workmanship often uncharacteristic of precontact products. Also the shapes val-

top, Smithsonian, NAA: 56793; Nev. State Mus., Carson City: bottom left, 412; bottom right, 38–G–457.

Fig. 12. Washoe basketry made for sale. top, Louisa Keyser (d. 1925) surrounded by some of her fine baskets. She holds a mush stirrer and a nontraditional carved walking stick. Photograph by Amy Cohn, Carson City, Nev., 1897. bottom left, "The Talesman," a close-coiled work in the shape of a traditional seed gathering basket that was always twined. Woven by Louisa Keyser, July 10, 1914, to April 17, 1915. bottom right, close-coiled basket, degikup shape, in willow with bracken fern and redbud as decoration. Woven by Lena Frank Dick, 1921. Height of bottom left 58.5 cm, other to same scale.

ued by Whites usually differed from those made aboriginally, the oblong laundry basket being the most obvious example. In all areas coiling predominated as the technique for these wares, leaving aboriginal twining complexes most vulnerable to loss or decay. In some areas, as for example among the Northern Paiute of northern Nevada and Oregon, and possibly among the Northern Shoshone and certain Western Shoshone, the manufacture of these specific trade wares seems to have led to the spread of coiling into areas where little or none was found before. After 1900 and well into the 1930s in rural parts of the Great Basin, this trade continued.

Sale of Baskets to Whites

In the late nineteenth century, weavers began to make baskets to sell in the growing tourist or curio market. Prominent in this trade were Washoe, Mono Lake Northern Paiute, Owens Valley Paiute, Panamint Shoshone, and Chemehuevi weavers. Tourist access to Lake Tahoe, Yosemite Valley, and Death Valley was instrumental in developing markets for most weavers. Only belatedly has the true artistry of some of these weavers been recognized.

Most is known about the Washoe weavers of the late nineteenth and early twentieth centuries (G.W. James 1902; Gigli 1967; Cohodas 1976, 1979, 1979a, 1981, 1982, 1983, 1985). From 1895 to 1935, which Cohodas refers to as the period of Washoe "fancy basketry" (as well as the time of Washoe basketry florescence), several weavers rose to prominence. Among them were Louisa Keyser or Datsolalee (fig. 12), Sarah Jim Mayo, Maggie Mayo James, Tootsie Dick, Lena Dick, Scees Bryant, and Tillie Snooks (Cohodas 1976, 1979, 1979a, 1981). All worked principally in the close coil technique over a three-rod foundation, producing bowl-shaped baskets, some with incurving rims (degikup style).

Louisa Keyser's fame was gained largely through the patronage of Abe and Amy Cohn, owners and operators of a store in Carson City, Nevada, and later a shop at Lake Tahoe. The Cohns supported Mrs. Keyser and her husband in exchange for most of her baskets. Publicity about her and her wares, often fanciful and inaccurate, as well as a careful registry of her baskets and a certificate of authenticity to the buyer, helped to promote Mrs. Keyser as the "Queen of the Basket Weavers" (Cohodas 1982, 1985). She may have invented the degikup (*degí·kip* 'globular') style for which she and other Washoe weavers became famous during this period (Cohodas 1982; but see Bates 1982). If not, she surely perfected the style, embellishing it with simple but highly effective and integrated geometric designs. She is known to have borrowed design elements from Pomo and Maidu work as well as from introduced beadwork. Some of the other Washoe weavers introduced or perfected in their pieces pictorial images (Sarah Jim Mayo), complex floral motifs (Lena Dick, Tootsie Dick), and refined multicolored designs (Maggie Mayo James). Few enjoyed the support (and at the same time the degree of exploitation) that characterized Mrs. Keyser's career, but all produced exceedingly fine products (fig. 12).

After 1935, with the deaths and advancing ages of these weavers, Washoe basketry gradually declined. Most surviving weavers turned to the manufacture of single-rod close or open coil baskets. These were less time-consuming to produce, and more likely to sell in the market without the support of patrons. Miniature close twined burden baskets and open twined miniature and full-size cradles were also produced for sale after this time. Some utilitarian pieces, such as open twined burden baskets and winnowing-parching trays were made for home use.

Similar developments in a fancy basket tradition were taking place in the Mono Lake–Yosemite Valley area at about the same time. Bates (1979, 1982, 1982a) has documented the history of these developments among the Mono Lake Northern Paiute and adjacent Yosemite Valley Miwok with whom they were closely linked. Around 1900 women from these groups began to produce baskets with new designs and shapes and an added neatness (Bates 1982:10). The designs were influenced by the introduction of loom beading, so that forms such as eight-pointed stars, serrate diamonds, arrowheads, arrows, and crosses entered the repertoire. Two-color

motifs in native bracken fern (*Pteridium aquilinum*) and traded redbud (*Cercis occidentalis*) also make their appearance. By 1912 yet newer motifs and shapes were introduced, particularly by the Mono Lake Paiute–Miwok weaver Lucy Parker Telles. Her finely woven three-rod foundation baskets included her adaptation of the traditional Miwok gift basket including some with locked lids. Her designs were bold and elaborate but well balanced. Other Mono Lake weavers soon began weaving extremely fine baskets; among them Leanna Tom, Mrs. Louis Charlie, and Suzie and Sally Jackson. In 1916, 1920–1926, and 1929, these and other weavers were aided by competitions held in Yosemite Valley in which cash prizes were given for the best baskets and basketry displays (fig. 13) (Bates 1982:15). The competitions were also attended by Washoe weavers, people from Owens Valley, and Monache and Miwok women, further influencing the cross-fertilization of ideas, styles, and designs of the Sierran weavers. During this time, Bates (1982:15–16) identified as active 13 prominent Mono Lake Paiute–Yosemite Miwok weavers. After 1930 several of these weavers continued to do fine three-rod coiling for the market, seemingly more than did the Washoe weavers. However, in the 1950s most turned to single-rod baskets and model cradles. Carrie Bethel and her sister Minnie Mike continued to weave fine three-rod baskets until their deaths in the mid 1970s (Bates 1982:19).

The origin of beaded baskets, another type made for sale principally in western Nevada and adjacent Cali-

Natl. Park Service, Yosemite Natl. Park, Calif.: left, 2122; right, 4547.

Fig. 13. Mono Lake Northern Paiute–Sierra Miwok weavers and their baskets. left, Indian Field Days, Yosemite Valley, Calif., which featured competitive displays of baskets and other items of contemporary native manufacture. left to right, Tina Charlie, Carrie Bethel, Alice Wilson, Leanna Tom, and Maggie Howard. The men behind Tom and Howard are Forest Tounsley and James H. Schwabacker, who organized these events (Bates 1982:13). Photographed 1929. right, Close coiled basket by Carrie Bethel, Mono Lake Northern Paiute, woven over the course of 4 winters, completed about 1935. The complexity of design in sedge root, bracken fern and redbud is one of the outstanding features of baskets from the Mono Lake–Yosemite region. Design motifs show influence of loom beadwork patterns. Height 50.8 cm.

a, Nev. State Mus., Carson City: 2176–G–1; b, Denver Mus. of Nat. Hist.: 6874.

Fig. 14. Beaded baskets. left, Northern Paiute beaded basket with lid, single rod close coiled construction. The beads are added in a netlike covering beginning at the rim of the basket and finishing at the bottom. The background is white with geometric designs done in red, black, blue, and orange. Purchased at Wa-Pai-Shone Craftsmen, Inc., Pyramid Lake Reservation, Nev., 1964. right, Pyramid Lake Northern Paiute beaded basket with lid in figurative pattern, with birds, flowers and abstract motifs. Beaded figures are far less common than simple geometric patterns. Height of left, 7.5 cm; other to same scale.

fornia, is also suggested as traceable to the Mono Lake area (Bates 1979a). Whatever their origin, by the 1920s baskets covered with thread-sewn network or beads were being produced by Mono Lake, Walker River, and Pyramid Lake Northern Paiute, Washoe, and Western Shoshone weavers in significant numbers (fig. 14). They were occasionally made by Owens Valley Paiute weavers (Steward 1933b:271). These baskets were still made in the 1980s by a few weavers of these groups, although beadworkers sometimes obtained their baskets for beading from other individuals, including persons from other tribes (Cohodas 1983:27–28).

Less is known about the development of marketable styles of baskets among the Owens Valley Paiute. However, it is clear that from 1900 to the late 1930s, Owens Valley weavers were making a number of excellent coiled pieces. Lacking markets such as those that the Washoe and Mono Lake weavers enjoyed, these weavers sold their products principally to local collectors. Shapes included varieties and sizes of round bowls and necked vessels resembling those of the Monache and Yokuts. Designs were principally geometric, although natural-

istic figures such as deer, dogs, and mountain sheep as well as alphabetic letters and words were also woven. Cross-fertilization in designs, principally geometric, also took place between the Owens Valley Paiute weavers and Panamint Shoshones, especially after 1900 when more Panamint people began to reside in the southern part of Owens Valley. Harvest festivals featuring displays and sales of fine baskets were held in the valley in the 1910s and 1920s (fig. 15). Among the fine Owens Valley Paiute weavers were Joe Eugley (a transvestite), Mattie and Jennie Horton and Mary Yandell of Bishop, Mary Gorman of Fort Independence, and Minnie Sullivan of Big Pine.

Panamint Shoshone baskets made for sale include styles with geometric motifs, probably elaborated from precontact patterns, as well as ones with pictorial images. As with other Great Basin groups, the Panamint offered for sale principally fine coiled wares. Between 1910 and 1940, and continuing to some degree after then, pictorial images introduced included butterflies, birds, mountain sheep, flowers, and an occasional anthropomorph. According to Bernstein (1979:69), weavers say that they were responding specifically to White requests for these motifs, especially at Death Valley National Monument, California. However, it seems clear from collections that they added other figurative motifs from their own imaginations and experiences. Basket shapes showing pictorial motifs most commonly are small flat-based bowls with flaring sides or flat-topped necked jars (fig. 16).

Chemehuevi baskets made for sale are also of fine workmanship, but little has been written of their history. All are close coiled over a three-rod foundation. Favorite shapes made between roughly 1900 and 1945 were the globular jar, large and small shallow bowl, and rounded bowl. The globular jar is probably derived from the indigenous treasure basket style, the shallow and rounded bowls from the coiled eating and serving-mixing bowls. However, unlike the early wares of these types, which were largely undecorated, these show new and multiple design patterns. Tanner (1983:219ff.) characterizes Chemehuevi geometric designs as crisp and controlled, with evidence of well-planned layouts (fig. 17). Designs are more in spots than totally covering a form (although trays may have designs connected by solid bands). Outlining as opposed to solid multicolored patterns predominates. Many Chemehuevi baskets made for sale are decorated with pictorial designs. Favored motifs are snakes (especially rattlesnakes), butterflies, rabbits, lizards, birds, insects, flowers, vines with leaves, and occasional anthropomorphs. Many of these patterns are worked in miniatures (0.75 cm to 12.0 cm high), a specialty of Chemehuevi weavers. Well-known weavers include Maggie Painter, Kate Fisher, Mary Lou Brown, and Mary Snyder, although there were undoubtedly others (Collings 1979).

Eastern Calif. Mus., Independence: right B206.

Fig. 15. Baskets for sale. left, Owens Valley Paiute, Harvest Festival, Bishop, Calif., which attracted weavers from various groups, encouraging basket making and fostering exchanges of designs among the weavers. Photograph possibly by Harry W. Mendenhall, about 1920. right, Basket in figurative style by Mary Gorman, Owens Valley Paiute, close-coiled on 3-rod foundation and lidded. Decoration features an "ibex," a boy, and a dog, each labeled, as well as geometric motifs. Woven before 1930; height 17 cm.

Nev. Histl. Soc., Reno: a, H132; b, H137; c, Smithsonian, Dept. of Anthr.: 220,421.

Fig. 16. Panamint basketry made for sale. Figurative motifs, such as the parade of elephants (left), or deer worked in two tones of black devil's claw and yellow rush (center), characterize Panamint baskets made for sale after 1900. Shouldered baskets (right), related to Yokuts styles and with geometric motifs similar to those of Kawaiisu, Tubatulabal, and Yokuts, are also common during this period. Lids, including locking lids, are a common feature of baskets made for sale. Height of left, 10.8 cm; others to same scale.

Chemehuevi, Panamint Shoshone, and Owens Valley Paiute weavers used as the black element in designs in baskets made for sale fiber strips taken from the fruits of devil's-claw (*Proboscidea parviflora*). This plant, with a true domesticated form as well as wild varieties, was first traded into the southern Great Basin from sources on the lower Colorado River (Nabhan et al. 1981). Although the dates for the introduction of the material into baskets in the southern and western Great Basin are far from clear, the domesticated variety (with longer fruits) seems to have been in use by at least 1900. It

(or a wild form) may have been cultivated by the Panamint as early as the 1860s (Jaeger 1941:248). It is identified in Owens Valley baskets collected in 1901 by Merriam (1902–1942). Other fibers seemingly introduced into baskets made for sale include northern flicker and American crow feather shafts and fibers from rush (*Juncus textilis*) (table 3).

Elsewhere in the Great Basin changes in basketry made for sale are less well documented. Although certain individual weavers became prominent in other areas, they seem to have been fewer and not part of specific

local trends in excellence or marketing. Some did specialized work, as for example Mary Hall, Western Shoshone from Elko, who produced among her other coiled products, fine baskets using horsehair weft (fig. 18). Several Northern Paiute women in western Nevada are well known for their buckskin-covered and beaded cradles. Among them are Louise Dick, Lena Wright, and Flora Smith of Pyramid Lake, and Mammie Nez of Reno-Sparks Colony. Northern Paiute weavers must have produced many unpitched water bottles for sale, judging by the numbers of these in museum and private collections.

Western Shoshone and Northern Shoshone–Bannock weavers introduced aniline-dyed wefts into their coiled baskets some time after 1900. Lidded baskets, baskets with basal rims, cups, and broad-brimmed hats were among the innovations in shape. Many sizes of coiled bowls and trinket baskets were made by these weavers, often on from two- to four-rod stacked foundations.

Western Nevada basketry as well as other crafts received a marketing boost in the 1930s and 1940s with the founding of the Wa-Pa-Shone coop. Native run, it marketed Washoe, Northern Paiute, and some Western Shoshone materials from outlets at Stewart Indian School in Carson City, Pyramid Lake Reservation, and Walker River Reservation. It faltered after the 1960s and periodically ceased operation.

Intergroup Sales

Although various types of informal exchanges of baskets can be suggested between groups for the precontact period, the only well-documented postcontact exchange is that developed by the Southern Ute and San Juan Southern Paiute with the Navajo. The baskets involved are primarily Navajo wedding baskets, featuring multipointed bands in black, brown (red), and natural weft colors and a vertical design break or doorway (fig. 19). Beginning before 1900 (Fishler 1954:211), and seemingly correlated with a decline in the production of baskets by the Navajo for a complex set of reasons (Tschopik 1938, 1940), Southern Ute and San Juan Southern Paiute weavers began to make these baskets for sale to Navajo reservation traders or directly to Navajos. In order to conform to Navajo requirements for baskets used in ceremonial contexts (not just weddings), the Ute and Southern Paiute weavers produced the baskets

Smithsonian, Dept. of Anthr.: a, 220,463; b, 220,467; c, 220,474; d, 220,480.
Fig. 17. Chemehuevi baskets made for sale. top, Mary Lou Brown, working on a close-coiled bowl. Photograph by Jerry Jacka, Colorado River Reservation, Ariz., 1977. a–c, Close-coiled bowls, evidencing the balanced design layouts characteristic of Chemehuevi work. d, Globular jar in the shape of a treasure basket. All collected in 1904; diameter of a 41.8 cm, rest to same scale.

FOWLER AND DAWSON

left, Northeastern Nev. Mus., Elko: 17–L–2 NF 2532; Idaho State U., Idaho Mus. of Nat. Hist., Pocatello: top right, 3030; bottom right, 3171.

Fig. 18. left, Mary Hall, Western Shoshone, with one of her prize-winning baskets (at Northeastern Nev. Mus., Elko), which typically used horsehair weft on a 1- or 3-rod foundation. Photograph by A.J. Hood, Beowawe, Nev., 1933–1934. top right, Lidded, finely woven coiled basket decorated with a flower pattern in red and green aniline-dyed wefts. Made by Nellie Pokeebro, Bannock, Fort Hall Reservation, Idaho, before 1927. bottom right, Coiled hat in Euro-American style, made by Old Mauite, Northern Shoshone–Bannock, Fort Hall Reservation, Idaho, before 1932. Similar innovations in hats are documented for the Ute, Chemehuevi, and Northern Paiute. Height top right, 11.5 cm; other to same scale.

with an interior work surface, a new design, a new form (30–35 cm in diameter; 7.5–10.0 cm deep), and a new selvedge treatment (false braid). Although some of the departures can be seen in older products of early Southern Paiute and Ute weavers, the combination represents change for this specific purpose (O.C. Stewart 1938b). Weavers in the late 1930s were Utes from Towaoc and Ignacio, Colorado, Southern Paiutes and Utes from Blanding, Utah, and Southern Paiutes from near Tuba City and Navajo Mountain, Arizona. In the 1980s there were some weavers in all these areas, but the most active appeared to be the Southern Paiutes near Tuba City. They also wove other baskets of new and eclectic designs for collectors.

The 1980s

Although no figures are available, it is generally felt that basketry production in all Great Basin areas (except perhaps among the San Juan Southern Paiute) has been declining since 1945. Cohodas (1985) states that there were four active Washoe weavers of one-rod coiled baskets in 1983. There were 10–20 active weavers in all of Northern Paiute country. Similar figures are suggested for other areas. On the average, two to three persons wove in each Great Basin Indian community, and most were elderly. The Washoe and the Walker River and Pyramid Lake Northern Paiutes held classes for children and young adults in the 1980s in an attempt to stimulate interest in basketry.

Sources

Washoe. Published sources include Barrett (1917), Price (1962), and G.W. James (1902) on ethnographic or precontact basketry as well as Cohodas (1976, 1979, 1979a, 1981, 1982, 1983, 1985) and Gigli (1967, 1974) on those made in historic times or on known weavers. Unpublished sources include the field notes of J.W.H. Hudson (1902, 1904). Principal museum holdings with well-documented Washoe collections include: the Field Museum

Fig. 19. Southern Ute close-coiled "wedding basket," a type made for trade or sale to the Navajo. Collected by Robert Lowie at Colorado Springs, Colo., before 1912; diameter 35 cm.

of Natural History (J.W.H. Hudson Collection), Chicago; the Lowie Museum of Anthropology, University of California, Berkeley (G.B. DePue Collection; S.A. Barrett Collection); Milwaukee Public Museum (S.A. Barrett Collection), Wisconsin; Nevada State Museum (S. Lee Collection), Carson City; and the Department of Anthropology Museum, University of California, Davis (C.H. Merriam Collection).

Northern Paiute. Published sources include Bates (1982, 1982a), Kelly (1932), and Lowie (1924). Unpublished field notes by Merriam (1902–1942) and W.Z. Park (1933–1940) also contain much useful data. Principal museum collections include: American Museum of Natural History (R.H. Lowie Collection; W.Z. Park Collection), New York; Field Museum of Natural History (G.O. Dorsey Collection); Lowie Museum of Anthropology, University of California, Berkeley (I.T. Kelly Collection; W.Z. Park Collection; and general); Milwaukee Public Museum (S.A. Barrett Collection); Museum of the American Indian, Heye Foundation (M.R. Harrington Collection; E.H. Davis Collection), New York; Peabody Museum, Harvard University (W.Z. Park Collection); Department of Anthropology Museum, University of California, Davis (C.H. Merriam Collection); Nevada State Museum; Southwest Museum, Los Angeles; National Park Service, Yosemite.

Owens Valley Paiute. Published sources include Steward (1933b) and Driver (1937). Museum collections include those at California State Indian Museum (C.P. Wilcomb Collection), Sacramento; Eastern California Museum (M. Black Collection and general), Independence; Field Museum of Natural History (J.W.H. Hudson Collection); Lowie Museum of Anthropology, University of California, Berkeley (J.H. Steward Collection; M.C. Randolf Collection); Department of Anthropology Museum, University of California, Davis (C.H.

Merriam Collection); Los Angeles County Museum of Natural History.

Western Shoshone. Published sources include Steward (1941, 1943a) and Malouf (1940). Principal collections are in the Peabody Museum, Harvard University (J.H. Steward Collection); the Nevada State Museum; Nevada Historical Society, Reno; and the Utah Museum of Natural History, Salt Lake City.

For Panamint, published sources include Coville (1892), Driver (1937), Grosscup (1977), Kirk (1952), Kroeber (1925), Mason (1904), O.C. Stewart (1941), Wallace (1954), and Wallace and Wallace (1979). Unpublished field notes include those by Merriam (1902–1942). Bernstein (1979) discusses historic basketry and its protohistoric antecedents. Principal museum collections include those at the California State Indian Museum (C.P. Wilcomb Collection); Eastern California Museum (M. Black Collection); National Park Service, Scotty's Castle, Death Valley, California; Department of Anthropology Museum, University of California, Davis (C.H. Merriam Collection); Lowie Museum of Anthropology, University of California, Berkeley.

Northern Shoshone. Published sources are primarily Lowie (1909) and Steward (1943a). Collections include those at the Field Museum of National History (G.O. Dorsey Collection, W. Wildschut Collection); American Museum of Natural History (A.L. Kroeber Collection, R.H. Lowie Collection); Idaho Museum of Natural History (E.O. Leonard Collection, DeArmond Collection), Pocatello; and the Museum of the American Indian, Heye Foundation (W. Wildschut Collection).

Eastern Shoshone. Principal museum collections include those at the American Museum of Natural History (H.H. St. Clair Collection); Field Museum of Natural History (G.A. Dorsey Collection); and the Museum of the American Indian, Heye Foundation (W. Wildschut Collection).

Kawaiisu. Published sources include Driver (1937) and Zigmond (1978). Unpublished field notes include those by McCown (1929) and Gifford (1915). Major museum collections include Lowie Museum of Anthropology, University of California, Berkeley (E.W. Gifford Collection, T.D. McCown Collection, E.L. McLeod Collection); G.A. Steiner Museum, Portersville, Pennsylvania; University of California, Department of Anthropology Museum, Davis (C.H. Merriam Collection).

Southern Paiute. Principal published sources include Collings (1979), Fowler and Matley (1979), Kelly (1964), Lowie (1924), Mason (1904), O.C. Stewart (1942), and Tanner (1983). Unpublished field notes include those by Kelly (1932–1933). Museum collections include those located at the American Museum of Natural History (I.T. Kelly Collection, R.H. Lowie Collection); Colorado River Indian Tribes Museum (B. Brown Collection), Parker, Arizona; Lowie Museum of Anthropology, University of California, Berkeley (G.B. DePue Collection, I.T. Kelly Collection); Milwaukee Public Museum (S.A. Barrett Collection); Laboratory of Anthropology, Museum of New Mexico (I.T. Kelly Collection), Santa Fe; Peabody Museum, Harvard University (I.T. Kelly Collection); and the Smithsonian Institution National Museum of Natural History (J.W. Powell Collection).

Ute. Principal published sources include Fowler and Matley (1979), Smith (1974), O.C. Stewart (1942, 1938b), and Tanner (1983). Important museum collections include those of the Field Museum of Natural History (G.O. Dorsey Collection); American Museum of Natural History (R.H. Lowie Collection, A.L. Kroeber Collection); Museum of New Mexico, School of American Research Collection; Utah Museum of Natural History; Smithsonian Institution, Museum of Natural History.

Contributors

This list gives the academic affiliations of authors at the time this volume went to press. Parenthetical tribal names identify Indian authors. The dates following the entries indicate when each manuscript was (1) first received in the General Editor's office, (2) accepted for the first time by the General Editor, and (3) sent to the author (or, if deceased, a substitute) for final approval after revisions and editorial work.

ADOVASIO, J.M., Department of Anthropology, University of Pittsburgh, Pennsylvania. Prehistoric Basketry: 4/18/72; 5/29/84; 7/5/84.

AIKENS, C. MELVIN, Department of Anthropology, University of Oregon, Eugene. Prehistory of the Eastern Area: 6/16/72; 2/14/84; 6/29/84.

ALLEY, JOHN R., JR., Department of History, University of California, Santa Barbara. Tribal Historical Projects: 8/22/83; 8/16/84; 4/4/85.

BENNYHOFF, JAMES A., Department of Anthropology, Sonoma State University, Rohnert Park, California. Early Trade: 3/16/84; 6/18/84; 9/7/84.

BUTLER, B. ROBERT, Idaho Museum of Natural History, Idaho State University, Pocatello. Prehistory of the Snake and Salmon River Area: 4/25/73; 9/9/83; 7/5/84.

CALLAWAY, DONALD G., Institute on Aging, Portland State University, Oregon. Ute: 9/11/84; 11/5/84; 4/1/85.

CAPPANNARI, STEPHEN C. (deceased), Department of Psychiatry, Vanderbilt University Medical Center, Nashville, Tennessee. Western Shoshone: 5/22/72; 10/23/84; 3/15/85.

CLEMMER, RICHARD O., Department of Anthropology, University of Denver, Colorado. Treaties, Reservations, and Claims: 12/21/84; 2/14/85; 5/13/85.

CRABTREE, ROBERT H., Bureau of Land Management, Tonopah, Nevada. Prehistory of the Southwestern Area: 6/20/72; 5/22/84; 7/6/84.

CRESSMAN, LUTHER S. (emeritus), Department of Anthropology, University of Oregon, Eugene. Prehistory of the Northern Area: 7/5/72; 5/23/84; 6/28/84.

DAWSON, LAWRENCE E., Lowie Museum of Anthropology, University of California, Berkeley. Ethnographic Basketry: 1/22/85; 1/25/85; 5/17/85.

D'AZEVEDO, WARREN L., Department of Anthropology, University of Nevado Reno. Introduction: 9/28/84; 9/29/84; 12/11/84. Washoe: 2/8/85; 5/14/85; 5/17/85.

ELSTON, ROBERT G., Intermountain Research, Silver City, Nevada. Prehistory of the Western Area: 11/25/83; 5/29/84; 8/11/84.

FINDLAY, JOHN M., Department of History, Pennsylvania State University, University Park. Euro-American Impact Before 1870: 5/22/72; 9/5/84; 4/12/85.

FOWLER, CATHERINE S., Department of Anthropology, University of Nevada Reno. Subsistence: 7/5/83; 3/14/84; 7/6/84. Southern Paiute: 7/20/72; 4/5/84; 4/16/85. Owens Valley Paiute: 1/11/85; 1/17/85; 4/18/85. Northern Paiute: 9/11/84; 10/19/84; 5/3/85. Ethnographic Basketry: 1/22/85; 1/25/85; 5/17/85.

FOWLER, DON D., Department of Anthropology, University of Nevada Reno. History of Research: 3/28/77; 3/12/84; 6/29/84. Prehistory of the Southeastern Area: 6/16/72; 9/27/83; 7/6/84.

GREEN, THOMAS J., Idaho State Historical Society, Boise. Contract Anthropology: 7/29/83; 2/10/84; 8/13/84.

HARDESTY, DONALD L., Department of Anthropology, University of Nevada Reno. Contract Anthropology: 7/29/83; 2/10/84; 8/13/84.

HARPER, KIMBALL T., Department of Botany and Range Science, Brigham Young University, Provo, Utah. Historical Environments: 10/30/72; 5/30/84; 6/28/84.

HUGHES, RICHARD E., Department of Anthropology, University of California, Davis. Early Trade: 3/16/84; 6/18/84; 9/7/84.

HULTKRANTZ, ÅKE, Institute of Comparative Religion, University of Stockholm, Sweden. Mythology and Religious Concepts: 5/9/72; 11/26/84; 4/18/85.

JACOBSEN, WILLIAM H., JR., Department of English, University of Nevada Reno. Washoe Language: 5/29/84; 8/30/84; 8/31/84.

JANETSKI, JOEL C., Museum of Peoples and Cultures, Brigham Young University, Provo, Utah. Ute: 9/11/84; 11/5/84; 4/1/85.

JENNINGS, JESSE D. (emeritus), Department of Anthropology, University of Utah, Salt Lake City. Prehistory: Introduction: 8/16/72; 7/5/84; 7/31/84.

JOHNSON, EDWARD C. (Northern Paiute), Stewart Indian Museum, Carson City, Nevada. Issues: The Indian Perspective: 2/28/83; 1/29/85; 4/16/85.

JORGENSEN, JOSEPH G., Program in Comparative Culture, University of California, Irvine. Ghost Dance, Bear Dance, and Sun Dance: 4/28/72; 8/20/84; 5/15/85.

KELLY, ISABEL T. (deceased), Tepepan, Mexico. Southern Paiute: 7/20/72; 4/5/84; 4/16/85.

KNACK, MARTHA C., Department of Anthropology, University of Nevada Las Vegas. Indian Economies, 1950–1980: 7/14/83; 10/16/84; 4/3/85.

LELAND, JOY, Social Sciences Center, Desert Research Institute, Reno. Population: 6/9/75; 9/19/84; 4/17/85.

LILJEBLAD, SVEN, Department of Anthropology, University of Nevada Reno. Owens Valley Paiute: 1/11/85; 1/17/85; 4/18/85. Northern Paiute: 9/11/84; 10/19/84; 5/3/85. Oral Tradition: Content and Style of Verbal Arts: 10/19/84; 10/19/84; 4/26/85.

LINDSAY, LA MAR W., Utah State Historical Society, Salt Lake City. Contract Anthropology: 7/29/83; 2/10/84; 8/13/84.

MADSEN, DAVID B., Antiquities Section, Utah State Historical Society, Salt Lake City. Prehistory of the Eastern Area: 6/16/72; 2/14/84; 6/29/84. Prehistory of the Southeastern Area: 6/16/72; 9/27/83; 7/6/84. Prehistoric Ceramics: 11/17/72; 2/10/84; 6/28/84.

MALOUF, CARLING I., Department of Anthropology, University of Montana, Missoula. Euro-American Impact Before 1870: 5/22/72; 9/5/84; 4/12/85.

MARWITT, JOHN P., Department of Sociology, University of Akron, Ohio. Fremont Cultures: 6/16/72; 2/28/84; 7/3/84.

MEHRINGER, PETER J., JR., Departments of Anthropology and Geology, Washington State University, Pullman. Prehistoric Environments: 4/2/84; 4/4/84; 8/13/84.

MILLER, WICK R., Department of Anthropology, University of Utah, Salt Lake City. Numic Languages: 5/22/72; 3/12/84; 7/5/84.

MURPHY, ROBERT F., Department of Anthropology, Columbia University, New York. Northern Shoshone and Bannock: 5/22/72; 6/20/84; 3/27/85.

MURPHY, YOLANDA, Empire State College, State University of New York, Nanuet. Northern Shoshone and Bannock: 5/22/72; 6/20/84; 3/27/85.

PENDLETON, LORANN S.A., Department of Anthropology, American Museum of Natural History, New York. Western Shoshone: 5/22/72; 10/23/84; 3/15/85.

RUSCO, ELMER R., Department of Political Science, University of Nevada Reno. Tribal Politics: 6/18/80; 10/24/84; 3/29/85.

RUSCO, MARY K., Department of Anthropology, Nevada State Museum, Carson City. Tribal Politics: 6/18/80; 10/24/84; 3/29/85.

SCHAAFSMA, POLLY, Laboratory of Anthropology, Museum of New Mexico, Sante Fe. Rock Art: 5/1/72; 2/10/84; 6/28/84.

SHAPIRO, JUDITH R., Department of Anthropology, Bryn Mawr College, Pennsylvania. Kinship: 9/22/76; 8/14/84; 4/10/85.

SHIMKIN, DEMITRI B. (emeritus), Department of Anthropology, University of Illinois, Urbana. Eastern Shoshone: 8/15/83; 2/12/85; 3/28/85. Introduction of the Horse: 3/28/77; 1/29/85; 4/10/85.

STEWART, OMER C. (emeritus), Department of Anthropology, University of Colorado, Boulder. Ute: 9/11/84; 11/5/84; 4/1/85. Treaties, Reservations, and Claims: 12/21/84; 2/14/85; 5/13/85. The Peyote Religion: 12/7/71; 3/19/85; 5/10/85.

THOMAS, DAVID H., Department of Anthropology, American Museum of Natural History, New York. Western Shoshone: 5/22/72; 10/23/84; 3/15/85.

TUOHY, DONALD R., Department of Anthropology, Nevada State Museum, Carson City. Portable Art Objects: 7/5/83; 2/29/84; 7/6/84.

VENNUM, THOMAS, JR., Office of Folklife Programs, Smithsonian Institution, Washington, D.C. Music: 7/14/83; 12/14/84; 5/10/85.

WARREN, CLAUDE N., Department of Anthropology, University of Nevada Las Vegas. Prehistory of the Southwestern Area: 6/20/72; 5/22/84; 7/6/84.

ZIGMOND, MAURICE, Belmont, Massachusetts. Kawaiisu: 12/2/72; 6/21/84; 3/22/85.

739

List of Illustrations

This list identifies the subjects of all illustrations, organized by chapter. All artists, photographers, and some individuals depicted (but not collectors) are included. Every identified individual depicted is found in the index, which also covers the captions. Tables are not listed here.

LIST OF ILLUSTRATIONS

Bibliography

This list includes all references cited in the volume, arranged in alphabetical order according to the names of the authors as they appear in the citations in the text. Multiple works by the same author are arranged chronologically; subsequent titles by the same author in the same year are differentiated by letters added to the dates. Where more than one author with the same surname is cited, one has been arbitrarily selected for text citation by surname alone throughout the volume, while the others are always cited with added initials; the combination of surname with date in text citations should avoid confusion. Where a publication date is different from the series date (as in some annual reports and the like), the former is used. Dates, authors, and titles that do not appear on the original works are enclosed by brackets. For manuscripts, dates refer to time of composition. For publications reprinted or first published many years after original composition, a bracketed date after the title refers to the time of composition or the date of original publication.

ARCIA-Commissioner of Indian Affairs
1849-   Annual Reports to the Secretary of the Interior. Washington: U.S. Government Printing Office. (Reprinted: AMS Press, New York, 1976-1977.)

Abbott, David R.
1979   An Introduction to the Cultural Resources of the Kaibab Plateau. *Western Anasazi Reports* 2(2):126-140. Cedar City, Utah.

Abel, Annie H., ed.
1915   The Official Correspondence of James S. Calhoun, While Indian Agent at Santa Fé and Superintendent of Indian Affairs in New Mexico; Collected Mainly from the Files of the Office of Indian Affairs. Washington: U.S. Government Printing Office.

————, ed.
1939   Tabeau's Narrative of Loisel's Expedition to the Upper Missouri. Norman: University of Oklahoma Press.

Aberle, David F.
1959   The Prophet Dance and Reactions to White Contact. *Southwestern Journal of Anthropology* 15(1):74-83.

1966   The Peyote Religion Among the Navaho. *Viking Fund Publications in Anthropology* 42. New York.

Aberle, David F., and Omer C. Stewart
1957   Navaho and Ute Peyotism: A Chronological and Distributional Study. *University of Colorado Studies, Series in Anthropology* 6. Boulder. (Reprinted: *University of Utah Anthropological Papers* 108:129-265, Salt Lake City, 1984.)

Adam, David P.
1967   Late Pleistocene and Recent Palynology in the Central Sierra Nevada, California. Pp. 275-301 in Quaternaray Paleoecology. Edward J. Cushing and Herbert E. Wright, Jr., eds. New Haven, Conn.: Yale University Press.

Adams, Charles R.
1976   Melodic Contour Typology. *Ethnomusicology* 20(2):179-215.

————, coll.
1966-1967 Southern Paiute Songs. (Cat. No. 67-148-F in Archives of Traditional Music, Indiana University, Bloomington.)

Adler, Lee
1984   Paiutes Apply for Unappropriated Truckee River Water. *Reno Gazette-Journal*, June 13:3D. Reno, Nev.

Adovasio, James M.
1970   The Origin, Development and Distribution of Western Archaic Textiles. *Tebiwa: Journal of the Idaho State University Museum* 13(2):1-40. Pocatello.

1970a   Textiles. Pp. 135-153 in Hogup Cave, by C. Melvin Aikens. *University of Utah Anthropological Papers* 93. Salt Lake City.

1971   Some Comments on the Relationship of Great Basin Textiles to Textiles from the Southwest. Pp. 103-108 in Great Basin Anthropological Conference 1970, Selected Papers. C. Melvin Aikens, ed. *University of Oregon Anthropological Papers* 1. Eugene.

1972   Basketry as an Indicator of Archaeological Frontiers. (Paper

presented at the 37th Annual Meeting of the Society for American Archaeology, Miami, Fla.)

1974   Prehistoric North American Basketry. Pp. 98-148 in Collected Papers on Aboriginal Basketry. D.R. Tuohy and D.L. Rendall, eds. *Nevada State Museum Anthropological Papers* 16. Carson City.

1975   Prehistoric Great Basin Textiles. P. 141 in Irene Emery Roundtables on Museum Textiles, 1974 Proceedings. Patricia L. Fiske, ed. Washington: The Textile Museum.

1975a   Fremont Basketry. *Tebiwa: Journal of the Idaho State University Museum* 17(2):67-76. Pocatello.

1976   Textiles from Swallow Shelter, Utah. Pp. 167-169 in Swallow Shelter and Associated Sites, by Gardiner F. Dalley. *University of Utah Anthropological Papers* 96. Salt Lake City.

1977   Basketry Technology: A Guide to Identification and Analysis. Chicago: Aldine.

1979   [Comment on] The Fremont and the Sevier: Defining Prehistoric Agriculturalists North of the Anasazi, by David B. Madsen. *American Antiquity* 44(4):723-731.

1980   Fremont: A Postscript. *Utah State Historical Society, Antiquities Section Selected Papers* 7(16):73-74. Salt Lake City.

1980a   Prehistoric Basketry of Western North America and Mexico. Pp. 341-362 in Early Native Americans: Prehistoric Demography, Economy, and Technology. David L. Browman, ed. The Hague: Mouton.

1980b   Fremont: An Artifactual Perspective. *Utah State Historical Society, Antiquities Section Selected Papers* 7(16):35-40. Salt Lake City.

Adovasio, James M., and R. L. Andrews
1980   Prehistoric Basketry and Related Perishables from the Upper Levels of Dirty Shame Rock Shelter and Gatecliff Shelter: Evidence for the Arrival of the Numic Speakers? (Paper presented at the 17th Great Basin Anthropological Conference, Salt Lake City, Utah.)

1983   Material Culture of Gatecliff Shelter: Basketry, Cordage and Miscellaneous Fiber Constructions. Pp. 279-289 in The Archaeology of Monitor Valley, 2: Gatecliff Shelter, by David H. Thomas. *Anthropological Papers of the American Museum of Natural History* 59(1). New York.

Adovasio, James M., with R.L. Andrews
[1983]   Artifacts and Ethnicity: Basketry as an Indicator of Territoriality and Population Movements in the Prehistoric Great Basin. In Anthropology of the Desert West: Essays in Honor of Jesse D. Jennings. Carol J. Condie and Don D. Fowler, eds. Salt Lake City: University of Utah Press. In press.

Adovasio, James M., and Gary F. Fry
1972   An Equilibrium Model for Culture Change in the Great Basin. Pp. 67-71 in Great Basin Cultural Ecology: A Symposium. Don D. Fowler, ed. *University of Nevada, Desert Research Institute Publications in the Social Sciences* 8. Reno.

Adovasio, James M., and Thomas F. Lynch
1973 Preceramic Textiles and Cordage from Guitarrero Cave, Peru. *American Antiquity* 38(1):84-90.

Adovasio, James M., and Robert F. Maslowski
1980 Cordage, Basketry, and Textiles. Pp. 253-290 in Guitarrero Cave: Early Man in the Andes. Thomas F. Lynch, ed. New York: Academic Press.

Adovasio, James M., R.L. Andrews, and R.C. Carlisle
1976 The Evolution of Basketry Manufacture in the Northern Great Basin. *Tebiwa: Journal of the Idaho State University Museum* 18(2):1-8. Pocatello.

1977 Perishable Industries from Dirty Shame Rockshelter. *Tebiwa: Miscellaneous Papers of the Idaho State University Museum of Natural History* 7. Pocatello.

Adovasio, James M., R.L. Andrews, and C.S. Fowler
1982 Some Observations on the Putative Fremont "Presence" in Southern Idaho. *Plains Anthropologist* 27(95):19-27.

Ahlbrandt, Thomas S.
1974 Dune Stratigraphy, Archaeology, and the Chronology of the Killpecker Dune Field. Pp. 51-60 in Applied Geology and Archaeology: The Holocene History of Wyoming. Michael Wilson, ed. *Geological Survey of Wyoming, Report of Investigations* 10. Laramie.

Aikens. C. Melvin
1965 Excavations in Southwest Utah. *Glen Canyon Series* 27, *University of Utah Anthropological Papers* 76. Salt Lake City.

1966 Fremont-Promontory-Plains Relationships, Including a Report of Excavations at the Injun Creek and Bear River Number 1 Sites, Northern Utah. *University of Utah Anthropological Papers* 82. Salt Lake City.

1966a Virgin-Kayenta Cultural Relationships. *Glen Canyon Series* 29, *University of Utah Anthropological Papers* 79. Salt Lake City.

1966b Excavations at Snake Rock Village and the Bear River No. 2 Site. *University of Utah Anthropological Papers* 87. Salt Lake City.

1967 Plains Relationships of the Fremont Culture: A Hypothesis. *American Antiquity* 32(2):198-209.

1967a Excavations at Snake Rock Village and the Bear River No. 2 Site. *University of Utah Anthropological Papers* 87. Salt Lake City.

1970 Hogup Cave. *University of Utah Anthropological Papers* 93. Salt Lake City.

1972 Fremont Culture: Restatement of Some Problems. *American Antiquity* 37(1):61-66.

1972a Surface Archeology of Southwestern Washoe County: The G.W. Smith Collection. *University of Nevada, Desert Research Institute Publications in the Social Sciences* 9. Reno.

1976 Cultural Hiatus in the Eastern Great Basin? *American Antiquity* 41(4):543-550.

1978 Archaeology of the Great Basin. *Annual Review of Anthropology* 7:71-87. Palo Alto, Calif.

1978a The Far West. Pp. 131-181 in Ancient Native Americans. Jesse D. Jennings, ed. San Francisco: W.H. Freeman.

1978b Indian Petroglyphs from White Pine County, Nevada. Pp. 3-15 in *Miscellaneous Papers* 19, *University of Utah Anthropological Papers* 99. Salt Lake City.

1982 Archaeology of the Northern Great Basin: An Overview. Pp. 139-155 in Man and Environment in the Great Basin. David B. Madsen and James F. O'Connell, eds. *Society for American Archaeology Papers* 2. Washington.

1983 The Far West. Pp. 149-201 in Ancient North Americans. San Francisco: W.H. Freeman.

Aikens, C. Melvin, and Y.T. Witherspoon
1984 Great Basin Numic Prehistory. In Anthropology of the Desert West: Essays in Honor of Jesse D. Jennings. Carol J. Condie and Don D. Fowler, eds. Salt Lake City: University of Utah Press. In press.

Aikens, C. Melvin, David L. Cole, and Robert Stuckenrath
1977 Excavations at Dirty Shame Rockshelter, Southeastern Oregon. *Tebiwa: Miscellaneous Papers of the Idaho State University Museum of Natural History* 4. Pocatello.

Aikens, C. Melvin, Donald K. Grayson, and Peter J. Mehringer, Jr.
1980 Steens Mountain Prehistory Project, Eastern Oregon: A Progress Report. (Paper presented at the 17th Great Basin Anthropological Conference, Salt Lake City.)

1982 Final Project Report to the National Science Foundation on the Steens Mountain Prehistory Project. (Report in Department of Anthropology, University of Oregon, Eugene.)

Albert, Alphaeus H., comp.
1969 Record of American Uniform and Historical Buttons 1775-1968. Boyertown, Pa.: Boyertown Publishing Company.

Aldrich, J.M.
1912 The Biology of Some Western Species of the Dipterous Genus Ephydra. *Journal of the New York Entomological Society* 20(1):77-99.

1921 Coloradia Pandora Blake: A Moth of Which the Caterpillar Is Used as Food by Mono Lake Indians. *Annals of the Entomological Society of America* 14(1):36-38. Columbus, Ohio.

Alexander, Hartley B.
1916 North American Mythology. *The Mythology of All Races* 10. Cambridge, Mass.: Archaeological Institute of America.

Alexander, Wayne, and Jay W. Ruby
1963 1962 Excavations at Summit, Utah: A Progress Report. Pp. 17-32 in 1962 Great Basin Anthropological Conference. *Nevada State Museum Anthropological Papers* 9. Carson City.

Allison, Ira S.
1966 Fossil Lake, Oregon: Its Geology and Fossil Faunas. *Oregon State Monographs, Studies in Geology* 9. Corvallis.

1979 Pluvial Fort Rock Lake, Lake County, Oregon. *Oregon State Monographs, Studies in Geology* 7. Corvallis.

1982 Geology of Pluvial Lake Chewaucan, Lake County, Oregon. *Oregon State Monographs, Studies in Geology* 11. Corvallis.

Alter, J. Cecil
1941 W.A. Ferris in Utah, 1830-1835. *Utah Historical Quarterly* 9(1-2): 81-108. Salt Lake City.

1941a Father Escalante's Map. *Utah Historical Quarterly* 9(1-2):64-72. Salt Lake City.

1944 The Mormons and the Indians. *Utah Historical Quarterly* 12(1-2):49-67. Salt Lake City.

Ambler, J. Richard
1966 Caldwell Village and Fremont Prehistory. (Unpublished Ph.D. Dissertation in Anthropology, University of Colorado, Boulder.)

1966a Caldwell Village. *University of Utah Anthropological Papers* 84. Salt Lake City.

Ambro, Richard D.
1967 Dietary-technological-ecological Aspects of Lovelock Cave Coprolites. *University of California Archeological Survey Reports* 70(3):37-47. Berkeley.

1978   A Second Clay Animal Figure from Grass Valley Nevada: Implications for the Distribution and Interpretation of Great Basin Figurines. Pp. 105-118 in History and Prehistory at Grass Valley, Nevada. C. William Clewlow, Jr., Helen F. Wells, and Richard D. Ambro, eds. *University of California, Institute of Archaeology Monograph* 7. Los Angeles.

American Indian Policy Review Commission
1976   Task Force Seven: Reservation and Resource Development and Protection. Washington: U.S. Government Printing Office.

Ames, Kenneth
1982   Management Report: Archaeological Excavations at Site 10-AA-17, Swan Falls, Idaho. (Manuscript in Department of Anthropology, Boise State University, Boise, Idaho.)

1982a   Archaeological Investigations in the Payette River Drainage, Southwestern Idaho, 1979-1981. *Boise State University, Department of Anthropology Archaeological Reports* 11. Boise, Idaho.

Amsden, Charles A.
1937   The Lake Mohave Artifacts. Pp. 51-95 in The Archaeology of Pleistocene Lake Mohave, by E.W. Campbell et al. *Southwest Museum Papers* 11. Los Angeles.

Anderson, Edgar
1948   Racial Identity of the Corn from Castle Park. Pp. 91-92 (App. 1) in The Archaeology of Castle Park, Dinosaur National Monument, by R.F. Burg and C.R. Scoggin. *University of Colorado Studies, Series in Anthropology* 2. Boulder.

Anderson, Ned
1981   Litigation Report: The Effect on Tribal Sovereignty of Mitchell, Jicarilla, Bertelson, and Dry Creek. (Paper presented at the Mid-Year Meeting of the National Congress of American Indians, Spokane, Wash.)

Anderson, Owanah
1981   Today, 67 Indian "Chiefs" Are Women. *OHOYO* 9 (July):2. Wichita Falls, Tex.: OHOYO Resource Center.

Andrews, R.L., and James M. Adovasio
1980   Perishable Industries from Hinds Cave, Val Verde County, Texas. *Ethnology Monographs* 5. Pittsburgh, Pa.

Andrews, R.L., James M. Adovasio, and R.C. Carlisle
1984   Perishable Industries from Dirty Shame Rockshelter. *University of Oregon Anthropological Papers*. Eugene. In press.

Anell, Bengt
1969   Running Down and Driving of Game in North America. *Studia Ethnographica Upsaliensia* 30. Uppsala, Sweden.

Angel, Myron, ed.
1881   History of Nevada, with Illustrations and Biographical Sketches of Its Prominent Men and Pioneers. Oakland, Calif.: Thompson and West. (Reprinted: Howell-North, Berkeley, Calif., 1958.)

Angulo, Jaime de, and Lucy S. Freeland
1929   Notes on the Northern Paiute of California. *Journal de la Société des Américanistes de Paris* n.s. 21(2):313-335.

Anonymous
1878   A Trip Across the Continent; The Frank Leslie Excursion to the Pacific: A Noonday's Ride to Winnemucca. *Frank Leslie's Illustrated Magazine* 45 (1163):321-323.

1884   A Scene Among the Utes: A Reminiscence. *Gunnison Sun*, March 1. [Colorado State Historical Society, Dawson Scrap Book, Vol. 10:321.]

1972   U.S. Indians Increase 51% Over Decade. *Los Angeles Times*, December 14, Pt.9:5.

1975   Student Discovers Second Major 'Find.' *Treasure* 6(8):47.

1980   State Eyes Indian Cigarette Vendors. *Las Vegas Review Journal*. June 11:1B, col. 2-5.

1980a   Tribal Leaders Meet Governor on Water. *The Ute Bulletin* 15(6):1,7. Fort Duchesne, Utah.

1981   Jurisdiction Declared. *The Ute Bulletin* 16(4):1. Fort Duchesne, Utah.

Antevs, Ernst
1936   Pluvial and Postpluvial Fluctuations of Climate in the Southwest. *Yearbook of the Carnegie Institution of Washington* 35:322-323. Washington.

1948   Climatic Changes and Pre-White Man. Pp. 168-191 in The Great Basin with Emphasis on Glacial and Postglacial Times. *Biological Series* 10(7), *University of Utah Bulletin* 38(20). Salt Lake City.

1952   Cenozoic Climates of the Great Basin. *Geologische Rundschau* 40:94-108. Berlin.

1955   Geologic-climatic Dating in the West. *American Antiquity* 20(4):317-335.

Aoki, Haruo
1975   Northern Plateau Linguistic Diffusion Area. (Manuscripts in Aoki's and Wick R. Miller's possession.)

Armagost, James L.
1980   Comanche Language. Supp. to A Comanche-English, English-Comanche Dictionary and Grammar, by Lyla Wistrand-Robinson. (Unpublished manuscript in Armagost's possession.)

Arment, Horace L.
[1961]   Indian Artifacts of the Upper Great Basin. Ontario, Oreg.: George P. Ward.

Armstrong, David M.
1972   Distribution of Mammals in Colorado. *University of Kansas, Museum of Natural History Monograph* 3. Lawrence.

Arnow, Ted
1980   Water Budget and Water-surface Fluctuations of Great Salt Lake. Pp. 255-263 in Great Salt Lake: A Scientific, Historical and Economic Overview. J. Wallace Gwynn, ed. *Utah Geological and Mineral Survey Bulletin* 116. Salt Lake City.

1983   Water-level and Water-quality Changes in Great Salt Lake, Utah, 1847-1983. *U.S. Geological Survey Circular* 913. Washington.

Arrington, Leonard J.
1966   Great Basin Kingdom: An Economic History of the Latter-Day Saints, 1830-1900. Lincoln: University of Nebraska Press.

Aschmann, Homer
1958   Great Basin Climates in Relation to Human Occupance. Pp. 23-40 in Current Views on Great Basin Archaeology. *University of California Archeological Survey Reports* 42. Berkeley.

Askew, Bonny, and Sylvester T. Algermissen
1983   An Earthquake Catalog for the Basin and Range Province, 1803-1977. *U.S. Geological Survey Open-File Report* 83-86. Denver.

Auerbach, Herbert S.
1943   Father Escalante's Journal, 1776-77. Newly Translated with Related Documents and Original Maps. *Utah Historical Quarterly* 11(1-4). Salt Lake City.

Austin, George T., and W. Glen Bradley
1971   The Avifauna of Clark County, Nevada. *Journal of the Arizona Academy of Science* 6(4):283-303. Tucson.

Bacon, Charles
1983   Eruptive History of Mount Mazama and Crater Lake Cal-

dera, Cascade Range, U.S.A. *Journal of Volcanology and Geothermal Research* 18(1-4):57-115. Amsterdam.

Bailey, D. K.
1970   Phytogeography and Taxonomy of *Pinus* subsection *Balfourianae*. *Annals of the Missouri Botanical Garden* 57(2):210-249. St. Louis.

Bailey, Lynn R.
1966   Indian Slave Trade in the Southwest: A Study of Slavetaking and the Traffic of Indian Captives. Los Angeles: Westernlore Press.

Bailey, Paul D.
1954   Walkara, Hawk of the Mountains. Los Angeles: Westernlore Press.

Bailey, Roy A., Brent Dalrymple, and Marvin A. Lanphere
1976   Volcanism, Structure and Geochronology of Long Valley Caldera, Mono County, California. *Journal of Geophysial Research* 81(5):725-744.

Baldwin, Gordon C.
1950   The Pottery of the Southern Paiute. *American Antiquity* 16(1):50-56.

Ball, Sydney H.
1941   The Mining of Gems and Ornamental Stones by American Indians. *Anthropological Papers* 13, *Bureau of American Ethnology Bulletin* 128:1-78. Washington.

Bancroft, Hubert H.
1886   The Native Races of the Pacific States. (The Works of Hubert Howe Bancroft) 5 vols. San Francisco: The History Company.

———
1889   The History Utah: (The Works of Hubert Howe Bancroft 26) San Francisco: The History Company.

———
1890   The History of Nevada, Colorado and Wyoming 1540-1888. (The Works of Hubert Howe Bancroft 25) San Francisco: The History Company.

Baraga, Friedrich
1878-1880 A Dictionary of the Otchipwe Language, Explained in English. New ed. 2 vols. Montreal: Beauchemim and Valois. (Reprinted: Ross and Haines, Minneapolis, 1973.)

Barber, Edwin A.
1876   Language and Utensils of the Modern Utes. *Bulletin of the U.S. Geological and Geographic Survey of the Territories* 2(1):71-76. Washington.

———
1876a   Bead Ornaments Employed by the Ancient Tribes of Utah and Arizona. *Bulletin of the U.S. Geological and Geographical Survey of the Territories* 2(1):67-69. Washington.

———
1877   Gaming Among the Utah Indians. *American Naturalist* 11(6):351-353.

———
1877a   Stone Implements and Ornaments from the Ruins of Colorado, Utah, and Arizona. *American Naturalist* 11(5):264-275.

Bard, James C.
1979   The Development of a Patination Dating Technique for Great Basin Petroglyphs Utilizing Neutron Activation and X-ray Fluorescence Analyses. (Unpublished Ph.D. Dissertation in Archaeology, University of California, Berkeley.)

Bard, James C., F. Asaro, and R. F. Heizer
1978   Perspectives on the Dating of Prehistoric Great Basin Petroglyphs by Neutron Activation Analysis. *Archaeometry* 20(1):85-88. Oxford, England.

Bard, James C., Colin I. Busby, and John M. Findlay
1981   A Cultural Resources Overview of the Carson and Humboldt Sinks, Nevada. *Nevada Bureau of Land Management, Cultural Resource Series* 2. Reno.

Bard, James C., Colin I. Busby, and Larry S. Kobori
1979   Ezra's Retreat: A Rockshelter/Cave in the North Central

Great Basin. *Center for Archaeological Research at Davis Publication* 6. Davis, Calif.

———
1980   Test Excavations at Painted Cave, Pershing County, Nevada. *Nevada Bureau of Land Management, Contributions to the Study of Cultural Resources, Technical Report* 5. Reno.

Bard, James C., John M. Findlay, and Colin I. Busby
1979   A Class II Cultural Resource Inventory of the Bureau of Land Management, Cinnebar Hill Project Area, Pershing and Churchill Counties, Nevada. Carson City: Nevada Bureau of Land Management, Carson City District.

Barker, M.A.R.
1963   Klamath Dictionary. *University of California Publications in Linguistics* 31. Berkeley.

Barrett, Samuel A.
1906   [Washoe Vocabulary: Washo-Miwok Ethnographic Notes.] (Unpublished manuscript No. CU-23.1, Item 7, in Ethnographic Documents, Museum of Anthropology Archives, Bancroft Library, University of California, Berkeley.)

———
1908   The Geography and Dialects of the Miwok Indians. *University of California Publications in American Archaeology and Ethnology* 6(2):333-368. Berkeley.

———
1908a   [Geographic Notebooks—Miwok, Yokut, Washoe, Mono.] (Manuscript No. 216, dated April 12, 1908 in Lowie Museum of Anthropology, University of California, Berkeley.)

———
1910   The Material Culture of the Klamath Lake and Modoc Indians of Northeastern California and Southern Oregon. *University of California Publications in American Archaeology and Ethnology* 5(4):239-292. Berkeley.

———
[1916] [Fieldnotes and and Field Catalog, Washoe, Pyramid Lake, and Walker Lake Northern Paiute, Shivwits Southern Paiute.] (Manuscripts in Lowie Museum of Anthropology, Berkeley, and the Milwaukee Public Museum, Milwaukee, Wis.)

———
1917   The Washo Indians. *Bulletin of the Public Museum of the City of Milwaukee* 2(1):1-52. Milwaukee, Wis.

Barrett, Samuel A., and Edward W. Gifford
1933   Miwok Material Culture. *Bulletin of the Public Museum of the City of Milwaukee* 2(4):117-376. Milwaukee, Wis.

Barrett, S.W.
1980   Indians and Fire. *Western Wildlands* 6(3):17-21. Missoula, Mont.

Barrett, Stephen, and Stephen F. Arno
1982   Indian Fires as an Ecological Influence in the Northern Rockies. *Journal of Forestry* 80(10):647-651.

Barry, R.G.
1983   Late-Pleistocene Climatology. Pp. 390-407 in Late-Quaternary Environments of the United States. Vol. 1: The Late Pleistocene. Herbert E. Wright, Jr. and Stephen C. Porter, eds. Minneapolis: University of Minnesota Press.

Bartlett, Richard A.
1962   Great Surveys of the American West. Norman: University of Oklahoma Press.

Batchelder, George L.
1970   Post-glacial Ecology at Black Lake, Mono County, California. (Unpublished Ph.D. Dissertation in Zoology, Arizona State University, Tempe.)

Bates, Craig D.
1979   Miwok-Paiute Basketry 1920-1929: Genesis of an Art Form. *American Indian Art Magazine* 4(4):54-59.

———
1979a   Beaded Baskets of the Paiute, Washo and Western Shoshoni. *Moccasin Tracks* 5(1):4-7.

———
1982   Yosemite Miwok/Paiute Basketry: A Study in Cultural Change. *American Indian Basketry* 8:4-22. Portland, Oreg.

————
1982a   Lucy Telles: A Supreme Weaver of the Yosemite Miwok/ Paiute. *American Indian Basketry* 8:23-29. Portland, Oreg.

Baumhoff, Martin A.
1958   History of Great Basin Ethnography. Pp. 1-6 in Current views on Great Basin Archaeology. *University of California Archaeological Survey Reports* 42. Berkeley.

Baumhoff, Martin A., and J.S. Byrne
1959   Desert Side-notched Points as a Time Marker in California. *University of California Archaeological Survey Reports* 48(72):32-65. Berkeley.

Baumhoff, Martin A., and Robert F. Heizer
1958   Outland Coiled Basketry from Caves of West Central Nevada. Pp. 49-59 in Current Views on Great Basin Archaeology. *University of California Archaeological Survey Reports* 42. Berkeley.

————
1965   Postglacial Climate and Archaeology in the Desert West. Pp. 697-707 in The Quaternary of the United States. Herbert E. Wright, Jr., and David G. Frey, eds. Princeton, N.J.: Princeton University Press.

Baumhoff, Martin A., and David L. Olmsted
1964   Notes on Palaihnihan Culture History: Glottochronology and Archaeology. Pp. 1-12 in Studies in Californian Linguistics. William Bright, ed. *University of California Publications in Linguistics.* 34. Berkeley.

Baumhoff, Martin A., Robert F. Heizer, and Albert B. Elsasser
1958   The Lagomarsino Petroglyph Group (Site 26-St-1) Near Virginia City, Nevada. *University of California Archaeological Survey Reports* 43(2):1-17. Berkeley.

Beaglehole, Ernest O.
1937   Notes on Hopi Economic Life. *Yale University Publications in Anthropology* 15. New Haven, Conn.

Beal, Merrill D., and Merle W. Wells
1959   History of Idaho. 3 vols. New York: Lewis Historical Publishing Company.

Beals, Ralph L.
1933   Ethnology of the Nisenan. *University of California Publications in American Archaeology and Ethnology* 31(6):335-414. Berkeley.

Bean, George W.
1945   Autobiography of George Washington Bean, a Utah Pioneer of 1847, and His Family Records. Flora D. Bean, Horne comp. Salt Lake City: Utah Printing.

Bean, Lowell J., and Thomas C. Blackburn
1976   Native Californians: A Theoretical Perspective. Socorro, N.M.: Ballena Press.

Bean, Lowell J., and S.B. Vane
1982   Intermountain Power Project: Intermountain Adelanto Bipole I Transmission Line. Ethnographic (Native American) Resources. Fullerton, Calif.: Applied Conservation Technology.

Beck, Colleen M.
1981   Shoshoni Brownware from Grass Valley, Nevada. *Annals of the Carnegie Museum of Natural History* 50(1):1-29. Pittsburgh, Pa.

Beckwith, E.G.
1855   Report of Explorations for a Route for the Pacific Railroad on the Line of the 41st Parallel of North Latitude. *U.S. Congress. House. 33d Cong. 2d sess., House Executive Document* No. 91. (Serial No. 791-801). Washington.

Beckwith, Frank
1931   Some Interesting Pictographs in Nine Mile Canyon, Utah. *El Palacio* 31(14):216-222.

————
1934   A Group of Petroglyphs Near Moab, Utah. *El Palacio* 36(23-24):177-178.

Beckwourth, James P.
1931   The Life and Adventures of James P. Beckwourth [1856]. T.D. Bonner, ed. New York: A.A. Knopf.

Bedwell, Stephen F.
1970   Prehistory and Environment of the Pluvial Fort Rock Lake Area of Southcentral Oregon. (Unpublished Ph.D. Dissertation in Anthropology, University of Oregon, Eugene.)

————
1973   Fort Rock Basin: Prehistory and Environment. Eugene: University of Oregon Books.

Bedwell, Stephen F., and Luther S. Cressman
1971   Fort Rock Report: Prehistory and Environment of the Pluvial Fort Rock Lake Area of South-central Oregon. Pp. 1-25 in Great Basin Anthropological Conference 1970: Selected Papers. *University of Oregon Anthropological Papers* 1. Eugene.

Beeley, Stephen J.
1946   The Archeology of a Utah Lake Site. (Unpublished M.A. Thesis in Anthropology, University of Utah, Salt Lake City.)

Beget, James E.
1982   Recent Volcanic Activity at Glacier Peak. *Science* 215(4538):1389-1390.

Behle, William H., and Michael L. Perry
1975   Utah Birds: Check-list, Seasonal and Ecological Occurrence Charts and Guides to Bird Findings. Salt Lake City: Utah Museum of Natural History.

Benedict, Ruth F.
1923   The Concept of the Guardian Spirit in North America. *Memoirs of the American Anthropological Association* 29. Menasha, Wis.

Benioh, Travis N.
1980   The Paiute Language for Beginners. (Multi-cultural Center, Title III SDIP Grant.) Cedar City: Southern Utah State College.

Bennett, Robert L.
1961-1962 Building Indian Economies with Land Settlement Funds. *Human Organization* 20(4):159-163.

Bennyhoff, James A.
1957   An Incised Tablet from Oregon, Pp. 26-28 in Papers on California Archaeology, 50-62. *University of California Archaeological Survey Reports* 38. Berkeley.

————
1958   The Desert West: A Trial Correlation of Cultures and Chronology. Pp. 98-112 in Current Views on Great Basin Archaeology. *University of California Archaeological Survey Reports* 42. Berkeley.

————
1985   Fremont and Northwest Anasazi Shell Beads and Ornaments. *University of Oregon Anthropological* Papers 83. Eugene.

Bennyhoff, James A., and Robert F. Heizer
1958   Cross-dating Great Basin Sites by Californian Shell Beads. Pp. 60-92 in Current Views on Great Basin Archaeology. *University of California Archaeological Survey Reports* 42. Berkeley.

Bennyhoff, James A., and Richard E. Hughes
[1984]   Shell Bead and Ornament Exchange Networks Between California and the Great Basin. In The Archaeology of Monitor Valley, 5: Regional Synthesis and Implications, by David H. Thomas. *Anthropological Papers of the American Museum of Natural History*. In press.

Benson, Larry V.
1978   Fluctuation in the Level of Pluvial Lake Lahontan During the Last 40,000 Years. *Quaternary Research* 9(3):300-318.

Berge, Dale L.
1974   Preliminary Report on Archaeological Investigations in the Southern Wah Wah Mountains, Beaver County, Utah. Provo, Utah: Museum of Archaeology and Ethnology, Brigham Young University.

Berkey, Curtis
1976   The Inherent Powers of Indian Governments. *American Indian Journal* 2(5):15-18.

Berman, Alan L.
1980   Indian Suicide: The Duck Valley Reservation. *Nevada Public Affairs Review* 1:24-31.

Bernstein, Bruce
1979   Panamint Shoshone Coiled Basketry: A Definition of Style. *American Indian Art Magazine* 4(4):68-74.

Berry, Michael S.
1972   The Evans Site. (Special report in Department of Anthropology, University of Utah, Salt Lake City.)

1974   The Evans Mound: Cultural Adaptation in Southwestern Utah. (Unpublished M.A. Thesis in Anthroplogy, University of Utah, Salt Lake City.)

1980   Fremont Origins: A Critique. Pp. 17-24 in Fremont Perspectives. David B. Madsen, ed. *Utah Division of State History, Antiquities Section Selected Papers* 7(16). Salt Lake City.

Berry, Michael S., and Claudia F. Berry
1976   An Archaeological Reconnaissance of the White River Area, Northeastern Utah. *Utah State Historical Society, Antiquities Section Selected Papers* 2(4):1-42. Salt Lake City.

Berutti, Betty
1965   [Fieldnotes and Report: Washoe Naming Practices; University of Nevada Ethnographic Archives 13, National Science Foundation Graduate Field Training Project June 7 to Sept. 7, 1965.] (On file, Department of Anthropology, University of Nevada, Reno.)

Betancourt, Julio L.
1984   Late Quaternary Plant Zonation and Climate in Southeastern Utah. *Great Basin Naturalist* 44(1):1-35.

Betancourt, Julio L., and Owen K. Davis
1984   Packrat Middens from Canyon de Chelly, Northeastern Arizona: Paleoecological and Archaeological Implications. *Quaternary Research* 21(1):56-64.

Bettinger, Robert L.
1975   The Surface Archeology of Owens Valley, Eastern California: Prehistoric Man-land Relationships in the Great Basin. (Unpublished Ph.D. Dissertation in Archaeology, University of California, Riverside.)

1976   The Development of Pinyon Exploitation in Central Eastern California. *Journal of California Anthropology* 3(1):81-95.

1977   The Surface Archaeology of the Long Valley Caldera, Mono County, California. *University of California, Archaeological Research Unit Monograph* 1. Riverside

1977a   Aboriginal Human Ecology in Owens Valley: Prehistoric Change in the Great Basin. *American Antiquity* 42(1):3-17.

1978   Alternative Adaptive Strategies in the Prehistoric Great Basin. *Journal of Anthropological Research* 34(1):27-46.

1979   Multivariate Statistical Analysis of a Regional Subsistence-settlement Model for Owens Valley. *American Antiquity* 44(3):455-470.

1982   Archaeology East of the Range of Light: Aboriginal Human Ecology of the Inyo-Mono Region, California. *Monographs in California and Great Basin Anthropology* 1. Davis, Calif.

1982a   Aboriginal Exchange and Territoriality in Owens Valley, California. Pp. 103-127 in Contexts for Prehistoric Exchange. Jonathon E. Ericson and Timothy K. Earle, eds. New York: Academic Press.

1983   Aboriginal Sociopolitical Organization in Owens Valley: Beyond the Family Band. Pp. 45-58 in The Development of Political Organization in Native North America, by Elisabeth Tooker and Morton H. Fried. *Proceedings of the American Ethnological Society*, 1979. Washington.

Bettinger, Robert L., and Martin A. Baumhoff
1982   The Numic Spread: Great Basin Cultures in Competition. *American Antiquity* 47(3):485-503.

1983   Return Rates and Intensity of Resource Use in Numic and Pre-Numic Adaptive Strategies. *American Antiquity* 48(4):830-884.

Bettinger, Robert L., and Thomas F. King
1971   Interaction and Political Organization: A Theoretical Framework for Archaeology in Owens Valley, California. *Annual Reports of the University of California Archaeological Survey* 13:139-150. Los Angeles.

Bettinger, Robert L., and R.E. Taylor
1974   Suggested Revisions in Archaeological Sequences of the Great Basin in Interior Southern California. *Nevada Archeological Survey Research Papers* 5:1-26. Reno.

Biddle, Nicholas, ed.
1962   The Journals of the Expedition Under the Command of Capts. Lewis & Clark to the Sources of the Missouri, Thence Across the Rocky Mountains and the River Columbia to the Pacific Ocean, Performed During the Years 1804-5-6 [1814]. New York: The Heritage Press.

Bidwell, John
1928   Echoes of the Past About California. (The Lakeside Classics [26]) Chicago: R.R. Donnelly and Sons.

Billings, W.D.
1950   Vegetation and Plant Growth as Affected by Chemically Altered Rock in the Western Great Basin. *Ecology* 31(1):62-74.

1978   Alpine Phytogeography Across the Great Basin. Pp. 105-117 in Intermountain Biogeography: A Symposium. Kimball T. Harper and James L. Reveal, eds. *Brigham Young University Great Basin Naturalist Memoirs* 2. Provo, Utah.

Binford, Lewis R.
1980   Willow Smoke and Dog's Tails: Hunter-gatherer Settlement Systems and Archaeological Site Formation. *American Antiquity* 45(1):4-20.

1982   The Archaeology of Place. *Journal of Anthropological Archaeology* 1(1):5-31.

1983   In Pursuit of the Past: Decoding the Archaeological Record. London: Thames and Hudson.

Birkeland, Peter W.
1968   Correlation of Quaternary Stratigraphy of the Sierra Nevada with that of the Lake Lahontan Area. Pp. 469-500 in Means of Correlation of Quaternary Successions. Roger B. Morrison and Herbert E. Wright, Jr., eds. Salt Lake City: University of Utah Press.

Black, Charles A.
1968   Soil-plant Relationships. 2d ed. New York: Wiley.

Blinman, Eric, Peter J. Mehringer, Jr., and John C. Sheppard
1979   Pollen Influx and the Deposition of Mazama and Glacier Peak Tephra. Pp. 393-425 in Volcanic Activity and Human Ecology. Payson D. Sheets and Donald K. Grayson, eds. New York: Academic Press.

Blyth, Beatrice
1938   Northern Paiute Bands in Oregon. *American Anthropologist* 40(3):402-405.

Boas, Franz
1917   The Origin of Death. *Journal of American Folk-Lore* 30(118):486-491.

1940   Race, Language and Culture. New York: Macmillan.

Bohrer, Vorsila L.
1983   New Life from Ashes: The Tale of the Burnt Bush (*Rhus trilobata*). *Desert Plants* 5(3):122-124. Superior, Ariz.

Bolen, Eric. G.
1964   Plant Ecology of Spring-fed Salt Marshes in Western Utah. *Ecological Monographs* 34(2):143-166.

Bolton, Herbert E., ed.
1919   Kino's Historical Memoir of Pimeria Alta, 1683-1711. 2 vols. Cleveland: Arthur H. Clark. (Reprinted: University of California Press, Berkeley, 1948.)

————, ed.
1950   Pageant in the Wilderness: The Story of the Escalante Expedition to the Interior Basin, 1776; Including the Diary and Itinerary of Father Escalante. *Utah Historical Quarterly* 18(1-4):1-265. Salt Lake City.

Bond, H.F.
1876   [Report from] Los Pinos Indian Agency, Colorado. Pp. 18-20 in Report of the Commissioner of Indian Affairs for the Year 1876. Washington: U.S. Government Printing Office.

Bonnichsen, Robson
1964   The Rattlesnake Canyon Cremation Site, Southwest Idaho. *Tebiwa: Journal of the Idaho State University Museum* 7(1):28-38. Pocatello.

Booth, Curtis, Pamela Munro, and Maurice L. Zigmond
[1984]   A Kawaiisu Dictionary. In press.

Boreson, Keo
1979   Archaeological Test Excavations at 10-VY-165 South Fork Salmon River Satellite Facility, Valley County, Idaho. *University of Idaho Anthropological Research Manuscript Series* 57. Moscow.

Born, Stephen M.
1972   Late Quaternary Historic, Deltaic Sedimentation, and Mudlump Formation at Pyramid Lake, Nevada. Reno: University of Nevada, Desert Research Institute, Center for Water Resources Research.

Bourke, John G.
1891   On the Border with Crook. New York: C. Scribner's Sons.

Bowers, Janice E.
1982   The Plant Ecology of Inland Dunes in Western North America. *Journal of Arid Environments* 5(3):199-220.

Bowers, Martha H., and Hans Muessig
1982   History of Central Nevada: An Overview of the Battle Mountain District. *Nevada Bureau of Land Management, Cultural Resource Series* 4. Reno.

Brackett, Albert G.
1880   The Shoshonis, or Snake Indians, Their Religion, Superstitutions, and Manners. Pp. 328-333 in *Annual Report of the Smithsonian Institution for 1879*. Washington.

Bradley, W. Glen, and James E. Deacon
1967   The Biotic Communities of Southern Nevada. Pp. 201-295 in Pleistocene Studies in Southern Nevada. *Nevada State Museum Anthropological Papers* 13. Carson City.

Brakenridge, G. Robert
1978   Evidence for a Cold, Dry Full-glacial Climate in the American Southwest. *Quaternary Research.* 9(1):22-40.

Brand, Donald D.
1937   Southwestern Trade in Shell Products. *American Antiquity* 2(4):300-302.

Brengarth-Jones, Dorothy J.
1976   Development of Paiute Marginal Man. (Unpublished Ph.D. Dissertation in Sociology, Colorado State University, Fort Collins.)

Breternitz, David A.
1968   Archeological Excavations in Dinosaur National Monument, Colorado-Utah, 1964-1965. *University of Colorado Studies, Series in Anthropology* 17. Boulder.

Bright, Robert C.
1966   Pollen and Seed Stratigraphy of Swan Lake, Southeastern Idaho: Its Relation to Regional Vegetational History and to Lake Bonneville History. *Tebiwa: Journal of the Idaho State University Museum:* 9(2):1-47. Pocatello.

Bright, Robert C., and Owen K. Davis
1982   Quaternary Paleoecology of the Idaho National Engineering Laboratory, Snake River Plain, Idaho. *American Midland Naturalist* 108(1):21-33.

Bright, William
1960   Animals of Acculturation in the California Indian Languages. *University of California Publications in Linguistics* 4(4):215-246. Berkeley. (Reprinted: Pp. 121-162 in Variation and Change in Language: Essays by William Bright, Anwar S. Dil, ed., Stanford University Press, Stanford, Calif., 1976.)

————
1973   North American Indian Language Contact. Pp. 713-726 in *Linguistics in North America*. Current Trends in Linguistics. Thomas A. Sebeok, ed. Vol. 10. The Hague and Paris: Mouton. (Reprinted: Pp. 59-72 in Native Languages of the Americas, Vol. 1, Thomas A. Sebeok, ed., Plenum Press, New York, 1976.)

————
1976   Variation and Change in Language: Essays by William Bright. Anwar S. Dil, ed. Stanford, Calif.: Stanford University Press.

Bright, William, and Joel Sherzer
1976   Areal Features in North American Indian Languages. Pp. 228-268 in Variation and Change in Language: Essays by William Bright. Anwar S. Dil, ed. Stanford, Calif.: Stanford University Press.

Brimhall, George W.
1889   The Workers of Utah. Provo, Utah: Enquirer Company.

Brimlow, George F.
1938   The Bannock Indian War of 1878. Caldwell, Idaho: Caxton Printers.

Brink, Pamela J.
1969   The Pyramid Lake Paiute of Nevada. (Unpublished Ph.D. Dissertation in Anthropology, Boston University, Boston.)

Brinton, Daniel G.
1891   The American Race: A Linguistic Classification and Ethnographic Description of the Native Tribes of North and South America. New York: N.D.C. Hodges. (Reprinted: Johnson Reprint Corporation, New York, 1970).

Broadbent, Sylvia M.
1964   The Southern Sierra Miwok Language. *University of California Publications in Linguistics* 38. Berkeley.

Broecker, Wallace S., and Aaron Kaufman
1965   Radiocarbon Chronology of Lake Lahontan and Lake Bonneville II, Great Basin. *Geological Society of America Bulletin* 76(5):537-566.

Broecker, Wallace S., and Phil C. Orr
1958   Radiocarbon Chronology of Lake Lahontan and Lake Bonneville. *Geological Society of America Bulletin* 69(8):1009-1032.

Brooks, George R., ed.
1977   The Southwest Expedition of Jedediah S. Smith; His Personal Account of the Journey to California, 1826-1827. Glendale, Calif.: Arthur H. Clark.

Brooks, Juanita
1944   Indian Relations on the Mormon Frontier. *Utah Historical Quarterly* 12(1-2):1-48. Salt Lake City.

————
1950   The Mountain Meadows Massacre. Stanford, Calif.: Stanford University Press.

Brooks, Richard H.
1976   The Fort Mojave Cultural Resource Inventory, Southern Clark County, Nevada. (Manuscript in University of Nevada Archaeological Research Center, Las Vegas.)

Brooks, Richard H., Daniel O. Larson, Joseph King, Robert Leavitt, and Kathryne Olson
1977   The Archaeology of the Mariah Site, 26-Ln-618, White River Narrows, Lincoln County, Nevada. *Nevada Bureau of Land Management, Cultural Resources Report* 4-48. Las Vegas.

Brophy, William A., and Sophie D. Aberle
1966   The Indian, America's Unfinished Business: Report of the Commission on the Rights, Liberties and Responsibilities of the American Indian. Norman: University of Oklahoma Press.

Brown, David E., ed.
1982   Biotic Communities of the American Southwest—United States and Mexico. *Desert Plants* 4(1-4). Superior, Ariz.

Brown, James H.
1978   The Theory of Insular Biogeography and the Distribution of Boreal Birds and Mammals. Pp. 209-227 in Intermountain Biogeography: A Symposium. Kimball T. Harper and James L. Reveal, eds. *Brigham Young University Great Basin Naturalist Memoirs* 2. Provo, Utah.

Brown, Walter R.
1964   The Prehistory of Surprise Valley. (Unpublished M.A. Thesis in Anthropology, University of California, Davis.)

Brown, William C.
1926   The Sheepeater Campaign, Idaho 1879. Boise, Idaho: Syms-York.

Bruff, Joseph G.
1873   Indian Engravings on the Face of Rocks Along Green River Valley in the Sierra Nevada Range of Mountains. Pp. 409-412 in *Annual Report of the Smithsonian Institution for 1872*. Washington.

Brugge, David M.
1968   Navajos in the Catholic Church Records of New Mexico, 1694-1875. *Navajo Tribe Parks and Recreation Department, Research Section Research Report* 1. Window Rock, Ariz.

Bryan, Alan L.
1979   Smith Creek Cave. Pp. 162-253 in The Archaeology of Smith Creek Canyon, Eastern Nevada. D.R. Tuohy and D.L. Randall, eds. *Nevada State Museum Anthropological Papers* 17. Carson City.

Bryan, Kirk
1941   Pre-Columbian Agriculture in the Southwest, as Conditioned by Periods of Alluviation. *Annals of the Association of American Geographers* 31(4):219-242. Washington.

Bryant, Edwin
1885   Rocky Mountain Adventures: Bristling with Animated Details of Fearful Fights of American Hunters with Savage Indians, Mexican Rancheros, and Beasts of Prey . . . New York: Hurst and Company.

————
1967   What I Saw in California: Being the Journal of a Tour by the Emigrant Route and South Pass of the Rocky Mountains, Across the Continent of North America, the Great Desert Basin, and Through California in the Years 1846, 1847. Minneapolis, Minn: Ross and Haines.

Bryson, Reid A., and Thomas J. Murray
1977   Climates of Hunger: Mankind and the World's Changing Weather. Madison: University of Wisconsin Press.

Bryson, Reid A., David A. Baerreis and Wayne Wendland
1970   The Character of Late-Glacial and Post-Glacial Climatic Changes. Pp. 53-75 in Pleistocene and Recent Environments of the Central Great Plains. Wakefield Dort and J. Knox, eds. Lawrence: University of Kansas Press.

Bucknam, R.C., and Paul C. Thenhaus
1983   Great Basin Seismic Source Zones—Summary of Workshop Convened October 10-11, 1979. Pp. 4-9 in Summary of Workshops Concerning Regional Seismic Source Zones of Parts of the Conterminous United States Convened by the U.S. Geological Survey, 1979-1980 at Golden, Colorado. P.C. Thenhaus, ed. *U.S. Geological Survey Circular* 898.

Buechel, Eugene
1970   A Dictionary of the Teton Dakota Sioux Language; Lakota-English: English-Lakota. Pine Ridge, S. Dak.: Red Cloud Indian School.

Bunte, Pamela
1979   Problems in Southern Paiute Syntax and Semantics. (Unpublished Ph.D. Dissertation in Linguistics, Indiana University, Bloomington.)

Bunte, Pamela, and Robert Franklin
[1983]   San Juan Southern Paiute Ethnohistory and Federal Acknowledgement. (Unpublished manuscript in Omer C. Stewart's possession.)

Burgh, Robert F., and Charles R. Scoggin
1948   The Archaeology of Castle Park, Dinosaur National Monument. *University of Colorado Studies, Series in Anthropology* 2. Boulder.

Burke, R.M., and P.W. Birkeland
1983   Holocene Glaciation in the Mountain Ranges of the Western United States. Pp. 3-11 in Late-Quaternary Environments of the United States. Vol. 2: The Holocene. Herbert E. Wright, Jr., ed. Minneapolis: University of Minnesota Press.

Burpee, Lawrence J., ed.
1910   Journal of Larocque from the Assiniboine to the Yellowstone, 1805. *Publications of the Canadian Archives*. 3. Ottawa.

————, ed.
1927   Journals and Letters of Pierre Gaultier de Varennes de la Vérendrye and His Sons. (*Publications of the Champlain Society* 16) Toronto: The Champlain Society.

Burton, Richard F.
1862   City of Saints, and Across the Rocky Mountains to California. New York: Harper and Brothers.

Busby, Colin I.
1978   The Prehistory and Human Ecology of Garden and Coal Valleys, Southeastern Nevada. (Unpublished Ph.D. Dissertation in Anthropology, University of California, Berkeley.)

————
1979   The Prehistory and Human Ecology of Garden and Coal Valleys: A Contribution to the Prehistory of Southeastern Nevada. *University of California Archaeological Research Facility Contributions* 39. Berkeley.

Busby, Colin I., and Susan M. Seck
1977   Archaeological Investigations at Civa Shelter II, Lincoln County, Nevada: Report of Field Activities, 1976. *Nevada Archaeological Survey Reporter* 10(5):1-5. Carson City.

Busby, Colin I., John M. Findlay, and James C. Bard
1979   A Culture Resource Overview of the Bureau of Land Management Coleville, Bodie, Benton and Owens Valley Planning Units, California. Bakersfield, Calif.: Basin Research Associates.

Buschmann, Johann C.E.
1859   Die Spuren der aztekischen Sprache im nördlichen Mexiko und höheren amerikanischen Norden. Pp. 512-576 in *Abhandlungen der Königlichen Akademie der Wissenschaften*, 1854. Suppl. Vol. 2. Berlin.

Bushnell, David I., Jr.
1909   The Various Uses of Buffalo Hair by the North American Indians. *American Anthropologist* 11(3):401-425.

Butler, B. Robert
1963   An Early Man Site at Big Camas Prairie, South-central Idaho. *Tebiwa: Journal of the Idaho State University Museum:* 6(1):22-33. Pocatello.

————
1965   A Report on Investigations of an Early Man Site Near Lake Channel, Southern Idaho. *Tebiwa: Journal of the Idaho State University Museum* 8(2):1-21. Pocatello.

————
1967   More Haskett Point Finds from the Type Locality. *Tebiwa:*

Journal of the Idaho State University Museum 10(1):25. Pocatello.

1971   The Origin of the Upper Snake Country Buffalo. *Tebiwa: Journal of the Idaho State University Museum* 14(2):1-20. Pocatello.

1971a   A Bison Jump in the Upper Salmon River Valley of Eastern Idaho. *Tebiwa: Journal of the Idaho State University Museum* 14(1):4-32. Pocatello.

1972   The Holocene or Postglacial Ecological Crisis on the Eastern Snake River Plain. *Tebiwa: Journal of the Idaho State University Museum* 15(1):49-63. Pocatello.

1978   A Guide to Understanding Idaho Archaeology: The Upper Snake and Salmon River Country. 3d ed. Pocatello: Idaho Museum of Natural History, Special Publication.

1978a   Bison Hunting in the Desert West Before 1800: The Paleoecological Potential and the Archaeological Reality. Pp. 106-112 in Bison Procurement and Utilization: A Symposium. Leslie B. Davis and Michael Wilson, eds. *Plains Anthropologist Memoir* 14.

1979   A Fremont Culture Frontier in the Upper Snake and Salmon River Country? *Tebiwa: Miscellaneous Papers of the Idaho State University Museum of Natural History* 18. Pocatello.

1980   The 1968 Excavations at the Braden Site (10-WN-117), an Early Archaic Cemetery in Western Idaho. Pp. 117-129 in Anthropological Papers in Memory of Earl H. Swanson, Jr. Lucille B. Harten, Claude N. Warren, and Donald R. Tuohy, eds. Pocatello: Idaho Museum of Natural History, Special Publication.

1981   Late Period Cultural Sequences in the Northeastern Great Basin Subarea and Their Implications for the Upper Snake and Salmon River Country. *Journal of California and Great Basin Anthropology* 3(2):245-256.

1982   A Closer Look at the Clover Creek Site. (Paper presented at the 10th Annual Conference of the Idaho Archaeological Society, Boise State University, Boise, Idaho, October 16.)

1982a   Numic Expansion and the Demise of the Fremont in Southern Idaho. (Paper presented at the 18th Biennial Meeting of the Great Basin Anthropological Conference, September 30-October 2, Reno, Nev.)

1983   The Quest for the Historic Fremont and a Guide to the Prehistoric Pottery of Southern Idaho. *Occasional Papers of the Idaho State University Museum of Natural History* 33. Pocatello.

Butler, B. Robert, and Kelly Murphey
1982   A Further Delineation of Cultural Resource Loci within the Proposed Dike Hydroelectric Project Impact Area. *B.R. Butler Associates Report* 82-2. Pocatello, Idaho.

1983   Kanaka Rapids Hydroelectric Project, Phase II Cultural Resource Evaluation. *B.R. Butler Associates Report* 83-2. Pocatello, Idaho.

Butler, B. Robert, and Philip R. Waite
1978   Final Report on Sampling and Evaluation of Archaeological and Historical Sites in or near Bureau of Reclamation's Authorized Salmon Falls Division, Twin Falls and Cassia Counties, Idaho. *Archaeological Reports of the Idaho State University Museum of Natural History* 17. Pocatello.

Butler, B. Robert, Helen Gildersleeve, and John Sommers
1971   The Wasden Site Bison: Sources of Morphological Variation. Pp. 126-152 in Aboriginal Man and Environments on the Plateau of Northwest America. H. Stryd and Rachel A. Smith, eds. Calgary, Alta.: The University of Calgary Archaeological Association.

Butler, B. Robert, Giovanna Neudorfer, Madelyn Walter, and Chris Torp
1976   Final Report on Archaeological Salvage Excavations and Survey of the Blacktail Park Site, Ririe Lake, Bonneville County, Idaho. *Archaeological Reports of the Idaho State University Museum of Natural History* 7. Pocatello.

Butzer, Karl W.
1964   Environment and Archeology: An Introduction to Pleistocene Geography. Chicago: Aldine.

1983   Human Response to Environmental Change in the Perspective of Future Global Climate. *Quaternary Research* 19(3):279-292.

Bye, Robert A., Jr.
1972   Ethnobotany of the Southern Paiute Indians in the 1870's: With a Note on the Early Ethnobotanical Contributions of Dr. Edward Palmer. Pp. 87-104 in Great Basin Cultural Ecology: A Symposium. Don D. Fowler, ed. *University of Nevada, Desert Research Institute Publications in the Social Sciences* 8. Reno.

Byrne, Roger, Colin I. Busby, and Robert F. Heizer
1979   The Altithermal Revisited: Pollen Evidence from the Leonard Rockshelter. *Journal of California and Great Basin Anthropology* 1(2):280-194.

Caldwell, Warren W., and Oscar L. Mallory
1967   Hells Canyon Archaeology. *River Basin Surveys, Publications in Salvage Archaeology* 6. Lincoln, Neb.

Camp, Charles L., ed.
1960   James Clyman, Frontiersman: The Adventures of a Trapper and Covered-wagon Emigrant as Told in His Own Reminiscences and Diaries. Portland Oreg.: Champoeg Press.

Campbell, Elizabeth W. Crozer, and William H. Campbell
1935   The Pinto Basin Site: An Ancient Aboriginal Camping Ground in the California Desert. *Southwest Museum Papers* 9. Los Angeles.

1937   The Lake Mohave Site. Pp. 9-44 in The Archaeology of Pleistocene Lake Mohave: A Symposium. *Southwest Museum Papers* 11. Los Angeles.

Campbell, Elizabeth W. Crozer, William H. Campbell, Ernst Antevs, Charles A. Amsden, Joseph A. Barbieri, and Francis D. Bode
1937   The Archeology of Pleistocene Lake Mohave: A Symposium. *Southwest Museum Papers* 11. Los Angeles.

Campbell, Lyle, and Marianne Mithun
1979   Introduction: North American Indian Historical Linguistics in Current Perspective. Pp. 3-69 in The Languages of Native America: Historical and Comparative Assessment. Lyle Campbell and Marianne Mithun, eds. Austin: University of Texas Press.

Campbell, Lyle, and David Oltrogge
1980   Proto-Tol (Jicaque). *International Journal of American Linguistics* 46(3):205-223.

Campbell, Robert L.
1850   Journal of Robert L. Campbell. (Microfilm on file at Latter-Day Saints Church Archives, Salt Lake City, Utah.)

Campbell, Sarah
[1980]   Draft Report of Test Excavations at the Headquarters Site (35HA403), Malheur National Wildlife Refuge. (Report at U.S. Fish and Wildlife Service, Portland, Oreg.)

Canfield, Gae Whitney
1983   Sarah Winnemucca of the Northern Paiutes. Norman: University of Oklahoma Press.

Canonge, Elliott
1958   Comanche Texts. Norman: University of Oklahoma, Summer Institute of Linguistics.

754

Cappannari, Stephen C.
[1947-1949] [Ethnographic Notes from Fieldwork Among the Kawaiisu, California.] (Manuscript in Cappannari's and M.L. Zigmond's possession.)

1960 The Concept of Property Among Shoshoneans. Pp. 133-144 in Essays in the Science of Culture in Honor of Leslie A. White. Gertrude E. Dole and Robert L. Carneiro, eds. New York: Thomas Y. Crowell.

Carley, Caroline D., and Robert L. Sappington
1981 Archaeological Survey of the Clear Lakes Project on the Snake River, South Central Idaho, 1981. With Appendix by Madeline Buckendorf. *University of Idaho, Anthropological Research Manuscript Series* 71. Moscow.

Carlson, Roy L.
1959 Klamath Henwas and Other Stone Sculpture. *American Anthropologist* 61(1):88-96.

Carroll, John
1970 Notes on Bead Stringing at Lovelock Cave, Nevada. Pp. 39-43 in Papers on Anthropology of the Great Basin. *University of California Archaeological Research Facility Contributions* 7. Berkeley.

Cartwright, Willena D.
1953 A Washo Girl's Puberty Ceremony. Pp. 136-142 in *Proceedings of the 30th International Congress of Americanists, Cambridge, 1952*. London: Royal Anthropological Institute.

Carvalho, Solomon Nunes
1857 Incidents of Travel and Adventure in the Far West; with Col. Fremont's Last Expedition Across the Rocky Mountains; Including Three Months' Residence in Utah, and a Perilous Trip Across the Great American Desert to the Pacific. New York: Derby and Jackson. (Reprinted: Jewish Publication Society of America, Philadelphia, 1954.)

Casagrande, Joseph B.
1954-1955 Comanche Linguistic Acculturation: I, II, III. *International Journal of American Linguistics* 20(2):140-151, (3):217-237; 21(1):8-25.

Casjens, Laurel
1974 The Prehistoric Human Ecology of Southern Ruby Valley, Nevada. (Unpublished Ph.D. Dissertation in Anthropology, Harvard University, Cambridge, Mass.)

Cass, Lewis
1823 Inquiries, Respecting the History, Traditions, Languages, Manners, Customs, Religion, etc., of the Indians Living within the United States. Detroit, Mich.: Sheldon and Reed.

Castetter, Edward F., Willis H. Bell, and Alvin R. Grove
1938 The Early Utilization and the Distribution of Agave in the American Southwest: Ethnobiological Studies in the American Southwest. Pt. VI. *University of New Mexico Bulletin, Biological Series* 5(4). Albuquerque.

Castleton, Kenneth B.
1978-1979 Petroglyphs and Pictographs of Utah. 2 vols. Salt Lake City: Utah Museum of Natural History.

Castleton, Kenneth B., and David B. Madsen
1981 The Distribution of Rock Art Elements and Styles in Utah. *Journal of California and Great Basin Anthropology* 3(2):163-175.

Cerveri, Doris
1977 Pyramid Lake: Legends and Reality. Sparks, Nev.: Western Printing and Publishing.

Chalfant, Willie A.
1922 The Story of Inyo. Chicago: Published by the Author.

1930 Death Valley: The Facts. Palo Alto, Calif.: Stanford University Press.

1933 The Story of Inyo. Rev. ed. Los Angeles: Citizens Print Shop.

Chamberlin, Ralph V.
1908 Animal Names and Anatomical Terms of the Gosiute Indians. *Proceedings of the Academy of Natural Sciences of Philadelphia* 60:75-103. Philadelphia.

1909 Some Plant Names of the Ute Indians. *American Anthropologist* 11(1):27-40.

1911 Ethno-botany of the Gosiute Indians of Utah. *Memoirs of the American Anthropological Association* 2(5):329-405. Lancaster, Pa.

1913 Place and Personal Names of the Gosiute Indians of Utah. *Proceedings of the American Philosophical Society* 52(208):1-20. Philadelphia.

Chapman, Charles E.
1916 The Founding of Spanish California: The Northwestward Expansion of New Spain, 1687-1783. New York: Macmillan.

Chapman, J.B., and James M. Adovasio
1977 Textile and Basketry Impressions from Icehouse Bottom, Tennessee. *American Antiquity* 42(4):620-625.

Chez, Joseph
1938 [Letter to the Commissioner of Indian Affairs, Dated January 10.] (Manuscript in Letters Received, Record Group 75, National Archives, Washington.)

Chitwood, Lawrence, Robert A. Jenson, and Edward A. Groh
1977 The Age of Lava Butte. *The Ore Bin* 39(l0): 157-164. Portland, Oreg.

Chomsky, Noam, and Morris Halle
1968 The Sound Patterns of English. New York: Harper and Row.

Christensen, L. Clair
1967 Economic Development Plan, Duck Valley Indian Reservation, Owyhee, Nevada. Reno: University of Nevada, Agricultural Cooperative Extension Service.

Christy, Howard A.
1979 The Walker War: Defense and Conciliation as Strategy. *Utah Historical Quarterly* 47(4):395-420. Salt Lake City.

Cinadr, Thomas J.
1976 Mount Bennet Hills Planning Unit: Analysis of Archaeological Resources. *Archaeological Reports of the Idaho State University Museum of Natural History* 6. Pocatello.

Clark, Ella E.
1966 Indian Legends from the Northern Rockies. Norman: University of Oklahoma Press.

Clark, William P.
1885 The Indian Sign Language, with Brief Explanatory Notes . . . Philadelphia: L.R. Hamersly.

Clayton, Lee, and Stephen R. Moran
1982 Chronology of Late Wisconsinian Glaciation in Middle North America. *Quarternary Science Reviews* 1(1):55-82.

Clayton, William
1921 William Clayton's Journal: A Daily Record of the Journey of the Original Company of "Mormon" Pioneers from Nauvoo, Illinois, to the Valley of the Great Salt Lake. Salt Lake City: Clayton Family Association; The Desert News.

Clemmer, Richard O.
[1970-1975] [Fieldnotes from Approximately 14 Months of Ethnographic and Ethnohistorical Research on the Western Shoshone.] (Manuscripts in Clemmer's possession.)

1972 Directed Resistance to Acculturation: A Comparative Study of the Effects of Non-Indian Jurisdiction on Hopi and Western Shoshone Communities. (Unpublished Ph.D. Dissertation, in Anthropology, University of Illinois, Urbana-Champaign.)

1973 Channels of Political Expression Among the Western Shoshone-Goshute of Nevada. Pp. 8-19 in Native American Politics: Power Relationships in the Western Great Basin Today. R.M. Houghton, ed. Reno: University of Nevada, Bureau of Governmental Research.

1974   Land Use Patterns and Aboriginal Rights: Northern and Eastern Nevada, 1858-1971. *The Indian Historian* 7(1):24-49.

1978   Pine Nuts, Cattle, and the Ely Chain: Rip-off Resource Replacement vs. Homeostatic Equilibrium. Pp. 61-75 in Selected Papers from the 14th Great Basin Anthropological Conference. Donald R. Tuohy, ed. *Ballena Press Publications in Archaeology, Ethnology and History* 11. Socorro, N.M.

Clemmer-Smith, Richard O.
1981   Western Shoshone Oppose MX. *New Life News* 2(7):12. Santa Fe: New Life Co-op.

Clerico, Robert
1983   Report on an Archaeological Reconnaissance in the Vicinity of James Creek, Eureka County, Nevada. (Federal Antiquities Permit No. 83-NV-167; report prepared for Carlin Gold Mining Company, Carlin Nevada, by Intermountain Research, Silver City, Nevada.)

Clewlow, C. William, Jr., and Allen G. Pastron
1972   Preliminary Investigations. Pp. 11-32 in The Grass Valley Archeological Project: Collected Papers. C. William Clewlow, Jr. and Mary Rusco, eds. *Nevada Archeological Survey Research Papers* 3. Reno.

Clewlow, C. William, Jr., and Mary Rusco, eds.
1972   The Grass Valley Archeological Project: Collected Papers. *Nevada Archeological Survey Research Papers* 3. Reno.

Clewlow, C. William, Jr., and Helen F. Wells
1981   Notes on a Portable Rock Art Piece from Western Nevada. *Journal of California and Great Basin Anthropology* 3(2):290-294.

Clewlow, C. William, Jr., Robert F. Heizer, and Rainer Berger
1970   An Assessment of Radiocarbon Dates for the Rose Spring Site (CA-Iny-372), Inyo County, California. Pp. 19-27 in Papers on Anthropology of the Great Basin. *University of California Archaeological Research Facility Contributions* 7. Berkeley.

Clewlow, C. William, Jr., Helen F. Wells, and Richard D. Ambro
1978   History and Prehistory at Grass Valley, Nevada. *University of California, Institute of Archaeology Monograph* 7. Berkeley.

Clifton, James A.
1965   The Southern Ute Tribe as a Fixed Membership Group. *Human Organization* 24(4):319-327.

Cline, Gloria G.
1963   Exploring the Great Basin. Norman: University of Oklahoma Press.

1974   Peter Skene Ogden and the Hudson's Bay Company. Norman: University of Oklahoma Press.

Clokey, Ira W.
1951   Flora of the Charleston Mountains, Clark County, Nevada. Berkeley: University of California Press.

Coale, George L.
1963   A Study of Shoshonean Pottery. *Tebiwa: Journal of the Idaho State University Museum* 6(2):1-11. Pocatello.

Coffin, Tristram P., ed
1961   Indian Tales of North America: An Anthology for the Adult Reader. Philadelphia: American Folklore Society.

Cohen, Felix S.
1941   Handbook of Federal Indian Law. Washington: U.S. Government Printing Office. (Reprinted: Michie Bobbs-Merrill, Charlottesville, Va., 1982.)

Cohen, Yehudi A.
1968   Man in Adaptation: The Cultural Present. Chicago: Aldine.

Cohn, C. Amy
1902   [Washoe Numerals, 1 to 100. Carson City, Nevada.] (Manuscript No. 4368 in National Anthropological Archives, Smithsonian Institution, Washington.)

Cohodas, Marvin
1976   Dat so la lee's Basketry Design. *American Indian Art Magazine* 1(4):22-31.

1979   Degikup: Washoe Fancy Basketry, 1895-1935. Vancouver: University of British Columbia, Fine Arts Gallery.

1979a   Lena Frank Dick: An Outstanding Washoe Basket Weaver. *American Indian Art Magazine* 4(4):32-41, 90.

1981   Sarah Mayo and Her Contemporaries: Representational Design and Washoe Basketry. *American Indian Art Magazine* 6(4):52-59.

1982   Dat so la lee and the *Degikup*. *Halcycon: A Journal of the Humanities*: 4:119-140, Reno.

1983   Washoe Basketry. *American Indian Basketry* 3(4) [Whole Issue No. 12]:4-30. Portland, Oreg.

[1985] Washoe Innovators and Their Patrons. Pp. 203-220 in The Arts of the North American Indians. Edwin L. Wade, ed. Tulsa, Okla.: Philbrook Art Center. In press.

Colberg-Sigleo, Anne
1975   Turquoise Mine and Artifact Correlation for Snaketown Site, Arizona. *Science* 189 (4201):459-460.

Cole, Kenneth
1982   Late Quaternary Zonation of Vegetation in the Eastern Grand Canyon. *Science* 217(4565):1142-1145.

1983   Late Pleistocene Vegetation of Kings Canyon, Sierra Nevada, California. *Quaternary Research* 19(1):117-129.

Collier, John
1938   [Letter of July 27 to Omer C. Stewart.] (In Omer C. Stewart's possession.)

1939   [Letter to Duck Valley Tribal Council.] (Manuscript in Letters Received, Record Group 75, National Archives, Washington.)

Collings, Jerold L.
1979   Profile of a Chemehuevi Basket Weaver. *American Indian Art Magazine* 4(4):60-67.

Collins, C.R.
1876   Report on the Languages of the Different Tribes of Indians Inhabiting the Territory of Utah. Pp. 467-474 (App. P) in Report of Explorations Across the Great Basin of the Territory of Utah ..., by J.H. Simpson, Engineer Department, U.S. Army. Washington: U.S. Government Printing Office.

Collins, Thomas W.
1971   The Northern Ute Economic Development Program: Social and Cultural Dimensions. (Unpublished Ph.D. Dissertation in Anthropology, University of Colorado, Boulder.)

Colton, Harold S.
1942   Archaeology and the Reconstruction of History. *American Antiquity* 8(1):1-33.

1952   Pottery Types of the Arizona Strip and Adjacent Areas in Utah and Nevada. *Museum of Northern Arizona Ceramic Series* 1. Flagstaff.

1955   Pottery Types of the Southwest. *Museum of Northern Arizona Ceramic Series* 3A. Flagstaff.

Colton, Harold S., and Lyndon L. Hargrave
1937   Handbook of Northern Arizona Pottery Wares. *Museum of Northern Arizona Bulletin* 11. Flagstaff.

Colton, Roy C.
1959   The Civil War and the Western Territories: Arizona, Colorado, New Mexico, and Utah. Norman: University of Oklahoma Press.

Comfort, Herbert G.
1934   Where Rolls the Kern: A History of Kern County, California. Moorpark, Calif.: The Enterprise Press.

Commission on State-Tribal Relations
1981   State-Tribal Agreements: A Comprehensive Study. (Report prepared for the Commission on State-Tribal Relations by the National Conference of State Legislatures and the American Indian Law Center, Albuquerque, N.M.)

Condie, Kent C., and C.K. Barsky
1972   Origin of Quaternary Basalts from the Black Rock Desert Region, Utah. *Geological Society of America Bulletin* 83(2): 333-352.

Condie, Kent C., and Alan B. Blaxland
1970   Sources of Obsidian in Hogup and Danger Caves. Pp. 275-281 (Appendix 9) in Hogup Cave, by C. Melvin Aikens. *University of Utah Anthropological Papers* 93. Salt Lake City.

Conetah, Fred A.
1982   A History of the Northern Ute People. Kathryn L. MacKay and Floyd A. O'Neil, eds. Salt Lake City: Uintah-Ouray Ute Tribe.

Conklin, Elizabeth
1967   Shoshone Teen-agers 1966: A Study of the Contemporary American Indian Adolescent. (Manuscript in Department of Anthropology, University of Illinois, Urbana.)

———
1975   An Overview of Health Care on the Wind River Shoshone Reservation: Summer 1975. (Manuscript in Department of Anthropology, University of Illinois, Urbana.)

Conn, Richard
1982   Circles of the World: Traditional Art of the Plains Indians. Denver: Denver Art Museum.

Cook, Sherburne F.
1941   The Mechanism and Extent of Dietary Adaptation Among Certain Groups of California and Nevada Indians. *Ibero-Americana* 18:1-59. Berkeley, Calif.

———
1943   The Conflict Between the California Indian and White Civilization. 2 Pts. *Ibero-Americana* 21-22. Berkeley, Calif.

———
1960   Colonial Expeditions to the Interior of California: Central Valley, 1800-1820. *University of California Anthropological Records* 16(6):239-292. Berkeley.

Cooke, Anne M., *see* Smith, Anne M. Cooke.

Cottam, Walter P.
1942   The Flora of the Great Salt Lake. *News Bulletin of the Mineralogical Society of Utah* 3(2):33-35. Salt Lake City.

———
1961   Our Renewable Wild Lands: A Challenge. Salt Lake City: University of Utah Press.

———
1961a   The Impact of Man on the Flora of the Bonneville Basin. (Advancement of Learning Series Lecture, Feb. 20, 1961) Salt Lake City: University of Utah.

Coues, Elliott, ed.
1893   The History of the Expedition Under the Command of Lewis and Clark. 4 vols. New York: Francis P. Harper.

———, ed
1898   The Journal of Jacob Fowler, Narrating an Adventure from Arkansas Through the Indian Territory... 1821-22. New York: F.P. Harper.

———, ed.
1900   On the Trail of a Spanish Pioneer; The Diary and Itinerary of Francisco Garcés (Missionary Priest) in His Travels Through Sonora, Arizona, and California, 1775-1776. 2 vols. New York: Francis P. Harper.

Couture, Marilyn Dunlap
1978   Recent and Contemporary Foraging Practices of the Harney Valley Paiute. (Unpublished M.A. Thesis in Anthropology, Portland State University, Portland, Oreg.)

Coville, Frederick V.
1892   The Panamint Indians of California. *American Anthropologist* 5(4):351-361.

Cowan, Richard A.
1967   Lake-margin Ecological Exploitation in the Great Basin as Demonstrated by an Analysis of Coprolites from Lovelock Cave, Nevada. Pp. 21-35 in Papers on Great Basin Archaeology. *University of California Archaeological Survey Reports* 70. Berkeley.

Cowan, Richard A., and C. William Clewlow, Jr.
1968   The Archaeology of Site NV-Pe-67. *University of California Archaeological Survey Reports* 73:195-236. Berkeley.

Cowan, Richard A., with David H. Thomas
1972   The Archeology of Barrel Springs Site (NV-Pe-104) Pershing County, Nevada. Berkeley: University of California, Archeological Research Facility, Department of Anthropology.

Cowan, Richard A., and Kurt Wallof
1974   Final Report: Fieldwork and Artifact Analysis; Southern California Edison No. 2 Control—Casa Diablo 115 kv Transmission Line. (Report at the Archaeological Research Unit, University of California, Riverside.)

Crabtree, Don E.
1974   Unusual Milling Stone from Battle Mountain, Nevada. *Tebiwa: Journal of the Idaho State University Museum* 17(1):89-91. Pocatello.

Crabtree, Robert H.
1978   Archaeology of the Berger Site. (Manuscript in Crabtree's possesion.)

Crabtree, Robert H., and David D. Ferraro
1980   Artifact Assemblages from the Pahranagat Unintentional Trespass Act Land Sales Parcels: Lincoln County, Nevada. Compiled for the Bureau of Land Management, Las Vegas District Office. Las Vegas: University of Nevada, Museum of Natural History, Archaeological Research Center.

Crabtree, Robert H., Raymond J. Rodrigues, and Richard H. Brooks
1970   Interim Report on the Red Rock Area, Clark County, Nevada. Las Vegas: University of Nevada, Desert Research Institute, Archaeological Survey. Mimeo.

Crapo, Richley H.
1970   The Social Dynamics of Language Replacement and Linguistic Acculturation Among the Duckwater Reservation Shoshone of Nevada. (Unpublished Ph.D. Dissertation in Anthropology, University of Utah, Salt Lake City.)

———
1974   Code Switching in Shoshoni. *University of South Florida Language Quarterly* 13(1-2):2-4.

———
1976   Big Smokey Valley Shoshoni. *University of Nevada, Desert Research Institute Publications in the Social Sciences* 10. Reno.

Crapo, Richley H., and Bryan R. Spykerman
1979   Social Variation in Shoshoni Phonology: An Ecological Interpretation. *Human Ecology* 7(4):317-332.

Creel, Lorenzo D.
[1875-1945] [Papers.] (In Special Collections Department, Reno Library, University of Nevada, Reno.)

Creer, Leland H.
1949   Spanish-American Slave Trade in the Great Basin, 1800-1853. *New Mexico Historical Review* 24(3):171-183.

Cressman, Luther S.
1933   Contributions to the Archaeology of Oregon: Final Report on the Gold Hill Burial Site. *University of Oregon Publication, Studies in Anthropology* 1, *Bulletin* 1. Eugene.

———
1933a   Aboriginal Burials in Southwestern Oregon. *American Anthropologist* 35(1):116-130.

1936   Archaeological Survey of the Guano Valley Region in Southeastern Oregon. *University of Oregon Monographs, Studies in Anthropology* 1. Eugene.

1937   Petroglyphs of Oregon. *University of Oregon Monographs, Studies in Anthropology* 2 Eugene.

1943   Results of Recent Archaeological Research in the Northern Great Basin Region of South Central Oregon. *Proceedings of the American Philosophical Society* 86(2):236-246. Philadelphia.

1944   New Information on South-central Oregon Atlatls. *The Masterkey* 18(6):169-179.

1951   Western Prehistory in the Light of Carbon-14 Dating. *Southwestern Journal of Anthropology* 7(3):289-313.

1956   Klamath Prehistory: The Prehistory of the Culture of the Klamath Lake Area. *Transactions of the American Philosophical Society* n.s. 46(4):375-513. Philadelphia.

1962   The Sandal and the Cave: The Indians of Oregon. Portland, Oreg.: Beaver Books.

1966   Man in Association with Extinct Fauna in the Great Basin. *American Antiquity* 31(6):866-867.

1966a   Comments on Prehistory. Pp. 275-293 in The Current Status of Anthropological Research in the Great Basin: 1964. Warren L. d'Azevedo et al., eds. *University of Nevada, Desert Research Institute Social Sciences and Humanities Publications* 1. Reno.

1977   Prehistory of the Far West: Homes of Vanished Peoples. Salt Lake City: University of Utah Press.

Cressman, Luther S., and Stephen F. Bedwell
1968   Report to the Secretary, Department of the Interior, on Archaeological Research on Public Lands in Northern Lake County, Oregon, Under Permit for 1967 and to the National Science Foundation, as Annual Report—June 30, 1968. Grant No. GS1652. (Manuscript in National Anthropological Archives, Smithsonian Institution, Washington.)

Cressman, Luther S., and Alex D. Krieger
1940   Atlatls and Associated Artifacts from Southcentral Oregon. Pp. 16-49 in Early Man in Oregon, by L.S. Cressman, H. Williams, and A.D. Krieger. *University of Oregon Monographs, Studies in Anthropology* 3. Eugene.

Cressman, Luther S., F.C. Baker, H.P. Hansen, P. Conger, and R.F. Heizer
1942   Archaeological Researches in the Northern Great Basin. *Carnegie Institution of Washington Publication* 538. Washington.

Crittenden, Laurel, and Robert G. Elston
1981   A Class II Cultural Resource Reconnaissance of the Saval Ranch Research and Evaluation Area, Elko County, Nevada. Reno: University of Nevada, Department of Anthropology.

Crittenden, Max D., Jr.
1963   New Data on the Isostatic Deformation of Lake Bonneville. U.S. *Geological Survey Professional Paper* 454-E. Washington.

Cronquist, Arthur, Arthur H. Holmgren, Noel H. Holmgren, and James L. Reveal, eds.
1972   Intermountain Flora: Vascular Plants of the Intermountain West, U.S.A. Vol. 1: Geological and Botanical History of the Region, Its Plant Geography and a Glossary; The Vascular Cryptograms and the Gymnosperms. New York: Hafner.

Cronquist, Arthur, Arthur H. Holmgren, Noel H. Holmgren, James L. Reveal, and Patricia K. Holmgren
1977   Intermountain Flora: Vascular Plants of the Intermountain West, U.S.A. Vol. 6: The Monocotyledons. New York: The New York Botanical Garden and Columbia University Press.

Crotty, Helen K.
1979   Rock Art of the Modoc Territory. (Paper presented at the 5th Annual A.R.A.R.A. Symposium, The Dalles, Oregon, May 27, 28, 29, 1978. Frank G. Bock, et al., eds.) *American Indian Rock Art* 5:22-37. El Toro, Calif.

1981   Petroglyph Point Revisited: A Modoc County Site. Pp. 141-168 in Messages from the Past: Studies in California Rock Art. Clement W. Meighan, ed. *University of California, Institute of Archaeology Monograph* 20. Los Angeles.

Crowder, David L.
1972   Tendoy, Chief of the Lemhis. Caldwell, Idaho: Caxton Printers.

Crowley, M. Suzzane
1979   The Rock Art of Saline Valley, Inyo County, California. (Paper presented at the 5th Annual A.R.A.R.A. Symposium, The Dalles, Oregon, May 27, 28, 29, 1978. Frank G. Bock et al., eds.) *American Indian Rock Art* 5:37-49. El Toro, Calif.

Crum, Beverly
1980   Newe Hupia—Shoshoni Poetry Songs. *Journal of California and Great Basin Anthropology, Papers in Linguistics* 2:3-23.

Crum, Beverly, and Wick R. Miller
1981   How to Read and Write Shoshoni: A Book of Spelling Lessons, Readings, and Glossary for Shoshoni Speakers. (Manuscript in Miller's possession.)

Crum, Steven J.
1983   The Western Shoshone of Nevada and the Indian New Deal. (Unpublished Ph.D. Dissertation in History, University of Utah, Salt Lake City.)

Cuch, Forrest S.
1984   Injustice in Local Schools. *The Ute Bulletin* 18(5):3. Fort Duchesne, Utah.

Culin, Stewart
1898   Chess and Playing Cards: Catalogue of Games and Implements for Divination..... Pp. 665-942 in *Report of the United States National Museum for 1896.* Washington.

1901   A Summer Trip Among the Western Indians: The Wanamaker Expedition. *Bulletin of the Free Museum of Science and Art of the University of Pennsylvania* 3(1-3). Philadelphia.

1907   Games of the North American Indians. Pp. 3-809 in *24th Annual Report of the Bureau of American Ethnology for the Years 1902-1903.* Washington.

Cultural Research Consultants
1979   Cultural Research Overview for the Bureau of Land Management, Vale District, Oregon. *Cultural Resource Management Reports* 3. Portland, Oreg.

Cummings, Byron
1910   The Ancient Inhabitants of the San Juan Valley. *University of Utah Bulletin* 3(3). Pt 2. Salt Lake City.

1915   Kivas of the San Juan Drainage. *American Anthropologist* 17(2):272-282.

Currey, Donald R.
1980   Coastal Geomorphology of Great Salt Lake and Vicinity. Pp. 69-82 in The Great Salt Lake, a Scientific, Historical and Economic Overview. J. Wallace Gwynn, ed. *Utah Geological and Mineral Survey, Department of Natural Resources Bulletin* 116. Salt Lake City.

1982   Lake Bonneville: Selected Features of Relevance to Neotectonic Analysis. *U.S. Geological Survey Open-File Report* 82-1070. Denver, Colo.

Currey, Donald R., and Steven R. James
1982   Paleoenvironments of the Northeastern Great Basin and Northeastern Basin Rim Region: A Review of Geological and Biological Evidence. Pp. 27-52 in Man and Environment in the Great Basin. David B. Madsen and James F. O'Connell, eds. *Society for American Archaeology Papers* 2. Washington.

Currey, Donald R., Genevieve Atwood, and Don R. Mabey
1983   Major Levels of Great Salt Lake and Lake Bonneville. *Utah Geological and Mineral Survey, Department of Natural Resources Map* 73. Salt Lake City.

Curtis, Edward S.
1907-1930   The North American Indian: Being a Series of Volumes Picturing and Describing the Indians of the United States, and Alaska. Frederick W. Hodge ed. 20 vols. Norwood, Mass.: Plimpton Press. (Reprinted: Johnson Reprint, New York, 1970.)

Cutler, Hugh C.
1966   Corn, Cucurbits and Cotton from Glen Canyon. *Glen Canyon Series* 30, *University of Utah Anthropological Papers* 80. Salt Lake City.

Dale, Harrison C., ed.
1918   The Ashley-Smith Explorations and the Discovery of a Central Route to the Pacific, 1822-1829. Cleveland, Ohio: Arthur H. Clark.

Dalley, Gardiner F.
1970   Faunal Remains. Pp. 127-133 in Median Village and Fremont Culture Regional Variation, by John P. Marwitt. *University of Utah Anthropological Papers* 95. Salt Lake City.

1976   Swallow Shelter and Associated Sites. *University of Utah Anthropological Papers* 96. Salt Lake City.

Dalley, Gardiner F., and Kenneth L. Petersen
1970   Additional Artifacts from Hogup Cave. Pp. 283-286 (App. 10) in Hogup Cave, by C. Melvin Aikens. *University of Utah Anthropological Papers* 93. Salt Lake City.

Damas, David, ed.
1969   Contributions to Anthropology: Band Societies. Proceedings of the Conference on Band Organization, Ottawa, August 30 to September 2, 1965. *Anthropological Series* 84, *National Museum of Canada Bulletin* 228. Ottawa.

Dangberg, Grace M.
[1918-1922]   [Fieldnotes on the Washoe.] (Folders in possession of W.L. d'Azevedo.)

1922   The Washo Language. *Nevada State Historical Society Papers* 3:145-152. Reno.

[1925]   Washo Grammar. (Unpublished manuscript in Department of Anthropology, University of California, Berkeley.)

1927   Washo Texts. *University of California Publications in American Archaeology and Ethnology* 22(3):391-443. Berkeley.

1957   Letters to Jack Wilson, the Paiute Prophet, Written Between 1908 and 1911. *Anthropological Papers* 55, *Bureau of American Ethnology Bulletin* 164:283-296. Washington.

1968   Washo Tales: Three Original Washo Indian Legends. Carson City: Nevada State Museum Occasional Paper.

1968a   Wovoka. *Nevada Historical Society Quarterly* 11(2):1-53. Reno.

1972   Carson Valley: Historical Sketches of Nevada's First Settlement. Carson City: Carson Valley Historical Society.

Dansie, Amy
1979   Analysis of Faunal Material from Sites 4LAs317 and 26WA1676. Pp. 373-402 (App. B) in The Archeology of US 395 Junction, California, by Robert G. Elston. (Report submitted to the California Department of Transportation (CalTrans) and Nevada Department of Highways by University of Nevada, Reno.)

1980   Notes on 26Pe118 Fauna. App. C in The Archeology of Trego Hot Springs: 26Pe118, by Susan M. Seck. (Unpublished M.A. Thesis in Anthropology, University of Nevada, Reno.)

Dansie, Amy, and Thomas Ringcob
1979   Faunal Analysis of the Glendale Site Assemblage. Pp. 181-207 in The Archeology of the Glendale Site (26WA2065), by Margaret M. Miller and Robert G. Elston. (Report submitted to the Nevada Department of Highways by the Nevada Archeological Survey, University of Nevada, Reno and the Nevada Department of Highways, Carson City.)

Dansie, Dorothy P.
1973   Some Artifacts Found in the Humboldt-Carson Sink Area Half a Century Ago. *Chippings* 7 (December): 1-4. Reno.

Danziger, Edmund J., Jr.
1974   Indians and Bureaucrats: Administering the Reservation Policy During the Civil War. Urbana: University of Illinois Press.

Daubenmire, Rexford F.
1979   Plants and Environment: A Textbook for Plant Autecology. 3d ed. New York: Wiley.

Davidson, Daniel S.
1937   A Preliminary Consideration of Aboriginal Australian Decorative Art. *Memoirs of the American Philosophical Society* 9. Philadelphia.

Davis, C. Alan, and Gerald A. Smith
1981   Newberry Cave. Redlands, Calif.: San Bernardino County Museum Association.

Davis, C. Alan, R.E. Taylor, and Gerald A. Smith
1981   New Radiocarbon Determinations from Newberry Cave. *Journal of California and Great Basin Anthropology* 3(1):144-147.

Davis, Emma Lou
1961   The Mono Craters Petroglyphs, California. *American Antiquity* 27(2):236-239.

1963   The Desert Culture of the Western Great Basin: A Lifeway of Seasonal Transhumance. *American Antiquity* 29 (2):202-212.

1964   An Archaeological Survey of the Mono Lake Basin and Excavations of Two Rockshelters, Mono County, California. Pp. 251-392 in *Annual Reports of the University of California Archaeological Survey for 1963-1964*. Los Angeles.

1965   An Ethnography of the Kuzedika Paiute of Mono Lake, Mono County, California. *Miscellaneous Paper 8, University of Utah Anthropological Papers* 75:1-55. Salt Lake City.

1969   The Western Lithic Co-tradition. Pp. 11-78 in The Western Lithic Co-Tradition, by Emma L. Davis, C.W. Brott, and David L. Weide. *San Diego Museum Papers* 6. San Diego.

1978   The Ancient Californians: Rancholabrean Hunters of the Mojave Lakes Country. *Natural History Museum of Los Angeles County, Science Series* 29. Los Angeles.

Davis, Emma Lou, and Richard Shutler, Jr.
1969   Recent Discoveries of Fluted Points in California and Nevada. *Miscellaneous Paper 7, Nevada State Museum Anthropological Papers* 14:154-169. Carson City.

Davis, Emma Lou, C.W. Brott, and David L. Weide
1969   The Western Lithic Co-tradition. *San Diego Museum Papers* 6. San Diego.

Davis, Emma Lou, Kathryn H. Brown, and Jacqueline Nichols
1980   Evaluation of Early Human Activities and Remains in the California Desert. *California Bureau of Land Management, Cultural Resources Publications, Anthropology-History*. Riverside.

759

Davis, E. Mott
1962   Archeology of the Lime Creek Site in Southwestern Nebraska. *University of Nebraska State Museum, Special Publication* 3.

Davis, Frank D.
1956   A Pit House at Mound B. Pp. 60-87 in Archaeological Excavations in Iron County, Utah, by Clement W. Meighan et al. *University of Utah Anthropological Papers* 25. Salt Lake City.

Davis, Irvine
1966   Numic Consonantal Correspondences. *International Journal of American Linguistics* 32(2):124-140.

Davis, James T.
1958   The Archaeology of Three Central Sierran Sites. Report on a Joint Archaeological Project Carried out Under Terms of a Contract (No. 14-10-434-202) Between the U.S. National Park Service and the University of California. (Manuscript on file, National Park Service, San Francisco, Calif.)

————
1961   Trade Routes and Economic Exchange Among the Indians of California. *University of California Archaeological Survey Reports* 54. Berkeley.

————
1962   The Rustler Rockshelter Site (SBr-288): A Culturally Stratified Site in the Mohave Desert, California. *University of California Archaeological Survey Reports* 57(2):25-56. Berkeley.

Davis, Jonathan O.
1978   Quaternary Tephrochronology of the Lake Lahontan Area, Nevada and California. *Nevada Archaeological Survey Research Papers* 7. Reno.

————
1982   Bits and Pieces: The Last 35,000 Years in the Lahontan Area. Pp. 53-75 in Man and Environment in the Great Basin. David B. Madsen and James F. O'Connell, eds. *Society for American Archaeology Papers* 2. Washington.

————
1983   Geology of Gatecliff Shelter: Sedimentary Facies and Holocene Climate. Pp. 64-87 in The Archaeology of Monitor Valley, 2: Gatecliff Shelter. David H. Thomas, ed. *Anthropological Papers of the American Museum of Natural History* 59(1). New York.

————
1983a   Level of Lake Lahontan During Deposition of the Trego Hot Springs Tephra About 23,400 Years Ago. *Quaternary Research* 19(3):312-324.

————
1985   Sediments and Geological Setting of Hidden Cave. Pp. 80-103 in The Archaeology of Hidden Cave, Nevada. David H. Thomas, ed. *Anthropological Papers of the American Museum of Natural History* 61(1). New York.

————
1985a   Correlation of Late Quaternary Tephra Layers in a Long Pluvial Sequence Near Summer Lake, Oregon. *Quaternary Research* 23(1):38-53.

Davis, Jonathan O., and Robert Elston
1972   New Stratigraphic Evidence of Late Quaternary Climatic Changes in Northwestern Nevada. Pp. 43-55 in Great Basin Cultural Ecology: A Symposium. Don D. Fowler, ed. *University of Nevada, Desert Research Institute Publications in the Social Sciences* 8. Reno.

Davis, Jonathan O., and Lonnie C. Pippin
1979   Pike's Point Site Geology. Pp. 32-58 in Archaeological Investigations at the Pike's Point Site (4-LAS-537) Eagle Lake, Lassen County, California, by L.C. Pippin, J.O. Davis, E. Budy, and R. Elston. *University of Nevada, Desert Research Institute, Social Sciences Center Technical Report* 7. Reno.

Davis, Jonathan O., Robert Elston, and Gail Townsend
1974   Preliminary Archeological Reconnaissance of Fallen Leaf Lake Area, Eldorado National Forest, California. (Report to U.S. Forest Service, San Francisco; manuscript on file, Special Collections, Getchell Library, University of Nevada, Reno.)

————
1976   Coastal Geomorphology of the South Shore of Lake Tahoe: Suggestion of an Altithermal Lowstand. Pp. 40-65 in Holocene Environmental Change in the Great Basin. Robert Elston and Patricia Headrick, eds. *Nevada Archaeological Survey Research Papers* 6. Reno.

Davis, Jonathan O., Wilton N. Melhorn, Dennis T. Trexler, and David H. Thomas
1983   Geology of Gatecliff Shelter: Physical Stratigraphy. Pp. 39-63 in The Archaeology of Monitor Valley, 2: Gatecliff Shelter. David H. Thomas, ed. *Anthropological Papers of the American Museum of Natural History* 59(1). New York.

Davis, Owen K.
1981   Vegetation Migration in Southern Idaho During the Late-Quaternary and Holocene. (Unpublished Ph.D. Dissertation in Botany, University of Minnesota, Minneapolis.)

Davis, Samuel P.
1905   The Nevada Piutes. *Sunset Magazine* 15(5):458-460. San Francisco.

————, ed.
1913   The History of Nevada. 2 vols. Reno, Nev.: The Elms Publishing Company.

Day, Kent C.
1964   Thorne Cave, Northeastern Utah: Archaeology. *American Antiquity* 30(1):50-59.

————
1966   Excavations at Gunlock Flats, Southwestern Utah. *Miscellaneous Collected Paper* 11, *University of Utah Anthropological Papers* 83:1-48. Salt Lake City.

d'Azevedo, Warren L.
[1952-1955,
1963-1984]   [Ethnographic Notes and Unpublished Manuscripts on Fieldwork among the Washoe of Nevada and California.] (Manuscripts in d'Azevedo's possession.)

————, coll.
1954-1964   [18 Washoe Songs, 7 Paiute Songs, 1 Shoshone Song; Accompanying Notes.] (In Department of Anthropology, University of Nevada, Reno.)

————
1956   Washo Place Names. (Manuscript, in Department of Anthropology, University of Nevada, Reno.)

————, ed.
1963   The Washo Indians of California and Nevada. *University of Utah Anthropological Papers* 67. Salt Lake City.

————
1966   Comments on Tribal Distribution, Pp. 315-334 in The Current Status of Anthropological Research in the Great Basin: 1964. Warren d'Azevedo et al., eds. *University of Nevada, Desert Research Institute Social Sciences and Humanities Publications* 1. Reno.

————
1973   The Delegation to Washington: A Washoe Peyotist Narrative. *The Indian Historian* 6(2):4-6.

————
1978   Ethnohistorical Notes on Eagle Valley, Carson City, Nevada. Pp. 69-75 (App. 2) in The Archaeology of the Stewart Dump Site (260R121), by Eugene M. Hattori. Carson City, Nev.: Carson City Department of Public Works.

————
1978a   Straight with the Medicine: Narratives of the Washoe Followers of the Tipi Way. Reno, Nev.: Black Rock Press. (Reprinted: Heyday Books, Berkeley, Calif., 1985).

[1984]   [Roadchiefs and Members.] (Manuscript in d'Azevedo's possession.)

d'Azevedo, Warren L., and Thomas Kavanagh
1974   The Trail of the Missing Basket. *The Indian Historian* 7(4):12-13, 60, 64.

d'Azevedo, Warren L., and John A. Price
1963 An Annotated Bibliography of Washo Sources. Pp. 153-201 in The Washo Indians of California and Nevada. Warren L. d'Azevedo, ed. *University of Utah Anthropological Papers* 67. Salt Lake City.

D'Azevedo, Warren L., Wilber H. Davis, Don D. Fowler, and Wayne Suttles, eds.
1966 The Current Status of Anthropological Research in the Great Basin: 1964. *University of Nevada, Desert Research Institute Social Sciences and Humanities Publications* 1. Reno.

Dean, Patricia W.
[1983] Black Rock Cave Ceramics. In Black Rock Cave Revisited, by D.B. Madsen. *Bureau of Land Management, Utah Cultural Resource Series* 15. Salt Lake City. In press.

Delaney, Robert W.
1974 The Southern Ute People. Phoenix, Ariz.: Indian Tribal Series.

De Lien, H., and J. Nixon Hadley
1952 How to Recognize an Indian Health Problem. *Human Organization* 11(3):29-33.

Delisio, Mario P.
1971 Preliminary Report of the Weston Canyon Rockshelter, Southeastern Idaho: A Big Game Hunting Site in the Northern Great Basin. *University of Oregon Anthropological Papers* 1:43-57. Eugene.

Dellenbaugh, Frederick S.
1877 The Shinumos: A Pre-historic People of the Rocky Mountain Region. *Bulletin of the Buffalo Society of Natural Sciences* 3(4):168-180. Buffalo, N.Y.

————
1908 A Canyon Voyage: The Narrative of the Second Powell Expedition Down the Green-Colorado River from Wyoming, and the Explorations on Land, in the Years 1871 and 1872. New York: G.P. Putnam's Sons. (Reprinted in 1962).

Deloria, Vine, Jr.
1976 The Western Shoshones. *American Indian Journal* 2(1):16-20. Washington.

Denny, Charles S., and Harold Drewes
1965 Geology of the Ash Meadows Quadrangle, Nevada-California. *U.S. Geological Survey Bulletin* 1181-L. Washington.

Densmore, Frances
1914-1916 [114 Northern Ute Songs: Uintah and Ouray.] (Nos. AFS 10, 583-AFS 10, 596 in Archive of Folk Culture, Library of Congress, Washington.)

————
1922 Northern Ute Music. *Bureau of American Ethnology Bulletin* 75. Washington.

————
1948 Notes on the Indian's Belief in the Friendliness of Nature. *Southwestern Journal of Anthropology* 4(1):94-97.

DeQuille, Dan (William Wright)
1877 History of the Big Bonanza: An Authentic Account of the Discovery, History, and Working of the World Renowned Comstock Silver Lode of Nevada. Hartford, Conn.: American Publishing Company. (Reprinted: Alfred A. Knopf, New York, 1947.)

De Riso, Michel
1974 Female Activism Among the Wind River Shoshone, 1966. (Unpublished M.A. Thesis in Anthropology, University of Illinois, Urbana.)

DeSart, Dennis J.
1971 A Study of Paiute and Shoshone Pottery Temper. (Manuscript in Western Studies Center, Desert Research Institute, University of Nevada, Reno.)

Desert Research Institute
1981 Technical Proposal: M-X Historical Regional Research Design. (Proposal submitted to ERTEC Northwest, Inc., Seattle, Wash.)

Dewdney, Selwyn
1979 Verbal versus Visual Approaches to Rock Art Research. Pp. 325-339 in CRARA '77: Papers from the 4th Biennial Conference of the Canadian Rock Art Research Associates, Oct. 27-30, 1977, Victoria. Doris Lundy, ed. *Heritage Record 8.* Victoria: British Columbia Provincial Museum.

Dewey, John R.
1966 Evidence of Acculturation Among the Indians of Northern Utah and Southeast Idaho: A Historical Approach. *Utah Archaeology: A Newsletter* 12(3):3-10, (4):12-21.

DeWitt-Warr, Vernille
1913 Destitute Nevada Indians. Pp. 132-152 in History of Nevada. Sam P. Davis, ed. 2 vols. Reno, Nev.: Elms Publishing Company.

Dice, Lee R.
1943 The Biotic Provinces of North America. Ann Arbor: University of Michigan Press.

Diggie, Eugene, Grant Martin, Peter Jim, and Jack Attidmo
1925 [Articles of Incorporation, Native American Church, Filed on March 25 in the District Court, Blackfoot, Idaho, and on April 1 with the Secretary of the State of Idaho.]

Dixon, Faun M.
1980 Native American Property Rights: The Pyramid Lake Reservation Land Controversy. (Unpublished Ph.D. Dissertation in Political Science, University of Nevada, Reno.)

Dixon, Roland B.
1905 The Northern Maidu. *Bulletin of the American Museum of Natural History* 17(3):119-346. New York.

————
1906 The Pronominal Dual in the Languages of California. Pp. 80-84 in Boas Anniversary Volume: Anthropological Papers Written in Honor of Franz Boas. Berthold Laufer, ed. New York: G.E. Stechert.

Dixon, Roland B., and Alfred L. Kroeber
1903 The Native Languages of California. *American Anthropologist* n.s. 5(1):1-26.

————
1907 Numeral Systems of the Languages of California. *American Anthropologist* n.s. 9(4):663-690.

————
1913 New Linguistic Families in California. *American Anthropologist* 15(4):647-655.

————
1919 Linguistic Families of California. *University of California Publications in American Archaeology and Ethnology* 16(3): 47-118. Berkeley.

Dobyns, Henry F.
1948 The Indian Reorganization Act and Federal Withdrawal. *Applied Anthropology: Problems of Human Organization* 7(2):35-44.

————
1966 Estimating Aboriginal American Population, 1: An Appraisal of Techniques with a New Hemispheric Estimate. *Current Anthropology* 7(4):395-416.

Dobyns, Henry F., and Robert C. Euler
1967 The Ghost Dance of 1889 Among the Pai Indians of Northwestern Arizona. *Prescott College Studies in Anthropology* 1. Prescott, Ariz.

Dodd, Walter A.
1982 Final Year Excavations at the Evans Mound Site. *University of Utah Anthropological Papers* 106. Salt Lake City.

Dodge, Richard I.
1882 Our Wild Indians: Thirty-three Years' Personal Experience Among the Red Men of the West. Hartford, Conn.: A.D. Worthington.

Dominguez, Francisco A.
1976 The Dominguez-Escalante Journal: Their Expedition Through Colorado, Utah, Arizona, and New Mexico in 1776. F.A.

761

Chavez, trans., and T.J. Warner, ed. Provo, Utah: Brigham Young University Press.

Dominick, David D.
1964 The Sheepeaters. *Annals of Wyoming* 36:131-168. Cheyenne.

Donnan, Christopher B.
1963-1964 A Suggested Culture Sequence for the Providence Mountains (Eastern Mojave Desert). *Annual Reports of the University of California Archaeological Survey for 1963-64*:1-23. Los Angeles.

Dorn, Ronald I.
1983 Cation-ratio Dating: A New Rock Varnish Age-determination Technique. *Quaternary Research* 20(1):49-73.

Dorn, Ronald I., and David S. Whitley
1983 Cation-ratio Dating of Petroglyphs from the Western Great Basin, North America. *Nature* 302(5911):816-818.

Doty, James D.
1865 Reports (No. 63 and 65) of Governor Doty to the Commissioner of Indian Affairs. Pp. 317-320 in *U.S. Congress. House. 38th Cong. 2d sess. House Executive Document* No. 1220. Washington.

Douglas, Frederic H.
1936 Plains Beads and Beadwork Designs. *Denver Art Museum Leaflet* 73-74. Denver, Colo.

Downing, Glenn R., and Lloyd S. Furniss
1968 Some Observations on Camas Digging and Baking Among Present-day Nez Perce. *Tebiwa: Journal of the Idaho State University Museum* 11(1):48-59. Pocatello.

Downs, James F.
1961 Washo Religion. *University of California Anthropological Records* 16(9):365-385. Berkeley.

————
1961a The Effect of Animal Husbandry on Two American Indian Tribes: Washo and Navaho. (Unpublished Ph.D. Dissertation in Anthropology, University of California, Berkeley.)

————
1963 Differential Response to White Contact: Paiute and Washo. Pp. 115-137 in The Washo Indians of California and Nevada. Warren L. d'Azevedo, ed. *University of Utah Anthropological Papers* 67. Salt Lake City.

————
1963a Washo Response to Animal Husbandry. Pp. 138–152 in The Washo Indians of California and Nevada. Warren L. d'Azevedo, ed. *University of Utah Anthropological Papers* 67. Salt Lake City.

————
1966 The Two Worlds of the Washo, an Indian Tribe of California and Nevada. New York: Holt, Rinehart and Winston.

————
1966a The Significance of Environmental Manipulation in Great Basin Cultural Development. Pp. 39-56 in The Current Status of Anthropological Research in the Great Basin: 1964. Warren L. d'Azevedo et al. eds. *University of Nevada, Desert Research Institute Social Sciences and Humanities Publications* 1. Reno.

Dressler, John H.
1972 Recollections of a Washo Statesman. (Oral History Project, University of Nevada, Reno.)

Dressler, John H., and Mary Rusco
1970 Communication and Community Organization on Nevada Indian Reservations: Testing the Feasibility of a New Delivery System Model. Reno: Inter-Tribal Council of Nevada.

Driver, Harold E.
1937 Culture Element Distributions, VI: Southern Sierra Nevada. *University of California Anthropological Records* 1(2):53-154. Berkeley.

————
1941 Culture Element Distributions, XVI: Girls' Puberty Rites in Western North America. *University of California Anthropological Records* 6(2):21-90. Berkeley.

————
1961 Indians of North America. Chicago: University of Chicago Press.

Driver, Harold E., and Alfred L. Kroeber
1932 Quantitative Expression of Cultural Relationships. *University of California Publications in American Archaeology and Ethnology* 31(4):211-256. Berkeley.

Driver, Harold E., and William C. Massey
1957 Comparative Studies of North American Indians. *Transactions of the American Philosophical Society* n.s. 47(2):165-456. Philadelphia.

Drover, Christopher E.
1979 The Late Prehistoric Human Ecology of the Northern Mohave Sink, San Bernardino County, California. (Unpublished Ph.D. Dissertation in Anthropology, University of California, Riverside.)

————
1980 The Ethnohistory of Turquoise Mining in Southern California. *Journal of California and Great Basin Anthropology* 2(2):257-260.

Drucker, Phillip
1937 Culture Element Distributions, V: Southern California. *University of California Anthropological Records* 1(1):1-52. Berkeley.

————
1941 Culture Element Distributions, XVII: Yuman-Piman. *University of California Anthropological Records* 6(3):91-230. Berkeley.

Du Bois, Cora A.
1939 The 1870 Ghost Dance. *University of California Anthropological Records* 3(1):1-151. Berkeley.

Dumond, Don E., and Rick Minor
1983 Archaeology in the John Day Reservoir: The Wildcat Canyon Site 35-GM-9. *University of Oregon Anthropological Papers* 30. Eugene.

Dunn, F.L., and R. Watkins
1970 Parasitological Examinations of Prehistoric Human Coprolites from Lovelock Cave, Nevada. *University of California Archaeological Research Facility Contributions* 10(5):176-185. Berkeley.

Du Ponceau, Peter S., Samuel Brown, R.M. Patterson, and Robert Walsh
1819 Heads of Enquiry and Observation Among Each of the Indian Tribes of the Missouri. (Manuscript [Freeman] No. 1408 in American Philosophical Society Library, Philadelphia.)

Durrant, Stephen D.
1952 Mammals of Utah: Taxonomy and Distribution. *University of Kansas, Museum of Natural History Publications* 6. Lawrence.

————
1970 Faunal Remains as Indicators of Neothermal Climates at Hogup Cave. Pp. 241-245 (App. 2) in Hogup Cave. C. Melvin Aikens, ed. *University of Utah Anthropological Papers* 93. Salt Lake City.

Dutcher, B.H.
1893 Pinon Gathering Among the Panamint Indians. *American Anthropologist* 6(4):377-380.

Dyk, Walter
1931-1932 [Washoe Fieldnotes.] (Unpublished manuscript in Department of Linguistics, University of California, Berkeley.)

Eardley, Armand J.
1962 Gypsum Dunes and Evaporite History of the Great Salt Lake Desert. *Utah Geological and Mineralogical Survey, Special Studies* 2. Salt Lake City.

Eardley, Armand J., Vasyl Gvodetsky, and R.E. Marsell
1957 Hydrology of Lake Bonneville and Sediments and Soils of Its Basin. *Geological Society of America Bulletin* 68(9):1141-1201.

Echohawk, Larry J.
1980   Statement of the Shoshone-Bannock Tribes of the Fort Hall Indian Reservation Before the Subcommittee on Indian Affairs, U.S. House of Representatives, Salt Lake City, Utah, November 22.

Edwards, Marcellus B.
1936   Journal of Marcellus Ball Edwards, 1846-1847. Pp. 107-280 in Marching with the Army of the West, 1846-1848. Ralph P. Bieber, ed. (*The Southwest Historical Series* 4) Glendale, Calif.: Arthur Clark.

Egan, Ferol
1972   Sand in a Whirlwind: The Paiute Indian War of 1860. Garden City, N.Y.: Doubleday.

Egan, Howard R.
1917   Pioneering the West, 1846-1878: Major Howard Egan's Diary. Richmond, Utah: Howard R. Egan Estate.

Eggan, Fred
1980   Shoshone Kinship Structures and Their Significance for Anthropological Theory. *Journal of the Steward Anthropological Society* 11(2):165-193. Urbana, Ill.

Eliade, Mircea
1964   Shamanism: Archaic Techniques of Ecstasy. Princeton, N.J.: Princeton University Press.

Elkin, Henry
1940   The Northern Arapaho of Wyoming. Pp. 207-255 in Acculturation in Seven American Indian Tribes. Ralph Linton, ed. New York: D. Appleton-Century.

Elmendorf, William W.
1952   Soul Loss Illness in Western North America. Pp. 104-114 in Indian Tribes of Aboriginal America: Selected Papers. Sol Tax, ed. Chicago: University of Chicago Press.

Elsasser, Albert B.
1957   A Decorated Stone Implement from Mono County, California. *University of California Archaeological Survey Reports* 38(52):7-9. Berkeley.

————
1957a   Report of an Archaeological Survey of Three Reservoir Sites of the Washoe Project, Lahontan Basin, California. San Francisco: National Park Service.

————
1960   The Archaeology of the Sierra Nevada in California and Nevada. *University of California Archaeological Survey Reports* 51:1-93. Berkeley.

————
1978   Two Unusual Artifacts from the Sierra Nevada of California. *Journal of California Anthropology* 5(1):73-78.

Elsasser, Albert B., and E.R. Prince
1961   The Archaeology of Two Sites at Eastgate, Churchill County, Nevada. *University of California Anthropological Records* 20(4):139-149. Berkeley.

Elston, Robert G.
1967   Notes on Stone Discs, Site 26LC215. *Nevada Archaeological Survey Reporter* 1(4):11-13. Reno.

————
1970   A Test Excavation at the Dangberg Hot Springs Site (26D1). *Nevada Archaeological Survey Reporter* 4(4):3-5. Carson City.

————
1971   A Contribution to Washo Archaeology. *Nevada Archaeological Survey Research Papers* 2. Reno.

————
1979   The Archaeology of U.S. 395 Right-of-Way Corridor Between Stead, Nevada and Hallelujah Junction, California. (Report submitted to the California Department of Transportation and the Nevada Department of Transportation; on file, Special Collections, Getchell Library, University of Nevada, Reno.)

————
1982   Good Times, Hard Times: Prehistoric Culture Change in the Western Great Basin. Pp. 186-206 in Man and Environment in the Great Basin. David B. Madsen and James F. O'Con-

nell, eds. *Society for American Archaeology Papers* 2. Washington.

Elston, Robert G., and Jonathan O. Davis
1972   An Archeological Investigation of the Steamboat Hot Springs Locality, Washoe County, Nevada. *Nevada Archaeological Survey Reporter* 6(1):9-14. Reno.

————
1979   An Overview of Cultural Resources in the Lahontan Cutthroat Trout Study Area, Black Rock Range, Humboldt County, Nevada. (Report submitted to the Winnemucca District, Bureau of Land Management; on file in Special Collections, Getchell Library, University of Nevada, Reno.)

Elston, Robert G., and Gail Townsend
1974   An Intensive Archeological Investigation of Sites in the U.S. 395 Right-of-way Corridor Between the Stead Interchange and the State Line. (Manuscript on file, Archeological Survey, University of Nevada, Reno.)

Elston, Robert G., and David Turner
1968   An Archaeological Reconnaissance of the Southern Truckee Meadows, Washoe County, Nevada. (Unpublished manuscript on file, Archeological Survey, University of Nevada, Reno.)

Elston, Robert G., and Charles D. Zeier
[1984]   The Sugarloaf Obsidian Quarry. (Report prepared for Phillips, Brandt, Reddick, Irvine on Behalf of Naval Weapons Center, China Lake.) In press.

Elston, Robert G., Donald Hardesty, and Sheryl Clerico
1981   Archaeological Investigations in the Hopkins Land Exchange. (Contract No. 53-91U9-0-80077; report submitted to U.S. Department of Agriculture, Forest Service, Tahoe National Forest, Nevada City, Calif., by Intermountain Research, Silver City, Nev.)

Elston, Robert G., Donald Hardesty, and Charles Zeier
1982   Archaeological Investigations on the Hopkins Land Exchange. Vol. II: An Analysis of Archaeological and Historical Data Recovered from Selected Sites. (Report prepared for U.S. Department of Agriculture, Forest Service, Nevada City, Calif., by Intermountain Research, Silver City, Nev.)

Elston, Robert G., Jonathan O. Davis, Alan Leventhal, and Cameron Covington
1977   The Archeology of the Tahoe Reach of the Truckee River: A Report to the Tahoe-Truckee Sanitation Agency. Reno: University of Nevada, Northern Division of the Nevada Archaeological Survey.

Elston, Robert G., Jonathan O. Davis, Sheryl Clerico, Robert Clerico, and Alice Baker
1981   Archeology of Section 20, North Valmy Power Plant, Humboldt County, Nevada. *University of Nevada, Desert Research Institute Social Sciences Center, Technical Report* 19. Reno.

Emery, Irene
1966   The Primary Structures of Fabrics: An Illustrated Classification. Washington: The Textile Museum.

Emmons, S.F.
1877   Goose Creek Hills to Tucubits Mountains. Pp. 515-527 in Descriptive Geology, by Arnold Hague and S.F. Emmons. *U.S. Geological Exploration of the Fortieth Parallel.* Vol. 2. Washington: U.S. Government Printing Office.

Enfield, Rollin, and Grace Enfield
1964   Mammoth Creek Cave, Mono County, California. Pp. 393-424 in *Annual Reports of the University of California Archaeological Survey, 1963-1964.* Los Angeles.

Enga-Barrie, and John Roberts
1900   Questions and Answers in Shoshone. Nanidevin des Nanarwink. Fort Washakie, Wyo.: Episcopal Mission.

Epperson, Terrence W.
1977   Final Report on Archaeological Inventory of the Challis Planning Unit, Bureau of Land Management. *Archaeological Reports of the Idaho State University Museum of Natural History* 11. Pocatello.

Ericson, Jonathon E.
1977 Egalitarian Exchange Systems in California: A Preliminary View. Pp. 109-126 in Exchange Systems in Prehistory. Timothy K. Earle and Jonathon E. Ericson, eds. New York: Academic Press.

1981 Exchange and Production Systems in Californian Prehistory: The Results of Hydration Dating and Chemical Characterization of Obsidian Sources. *British Archaeological Reports, International Series* 110. Oxford, England.

Ericson, Jonathon E., Timothy A. Hagan, and Charles W. Chesterman
1976 Prehistoric Obsidian in California, II: Geologic and Geographic Aspects. Pp. 218-239 in Advances in Obsidian Glass Studies - Archaeological and Geochemical Perspectives. R.E. Taylor, ed. Park Ridge, N.J.: Noyes Press.

Essene, Frank
[1935] Paiute and Shoshone Plant Uses. (Manuscript 86A-B in University Archives, Bancroft Library, University of California, Berkeley.)

[1935a] [Ethnographic Notes from Fieldwork Among the Owens Valley and Mono Lake Paiutes.] (Manuscripts in Department and Museum of Anthropology, University of California, Berkeley.)

Essig, Edward O.
1958 Insects and Mites of Western North America. New York: Macmillan.

Eubank, Mark, and Clayton Brough
1979 Mark Eubank's Utah Weather. Salt Lake City: Weatherbank.

Euler, Robert C.
1964 Southern Paiute Archaeology. *American Antiquity* 29(3):379-381.

———, ed.
1966 Southern Paiute Ethnohistory. *Glen Canyon Series* 28, *University of Utah Anthropological Papers* 78. Salt Lake City.

1966a Willow Figurines from Arizona. *Natural History* 75(3):62-57.

1967 Ethnographic Methodology: A Tri-chronic Study in Culture Change. Informant Reliability, and Validity from the Southern Paiute. Pp. 61-67 in American Historical Anthropology: Essays in Honor of Leslie Spier. C.L. Riley and W.W. Taylor, eds. Carbondale: Southern Illinois University Press.

1967a The Canyon Dwellers. *The American West* 4(2):22-27. Salt Lake City, Utah.

1972 The Paiute People. Phoenix, Ariz.: Indian Tribal Series.

1978 Archeological and Paleobiological Studies at Stanton's Cave, Grand Canyon National Park, Arizona - A Report of Progress. Pp. 141-162 in National Geographic Society Research Reports: Abstracts and Reviews of Research and Exploration Authorized under Grants from the National Geographic Society During the Year 1969. Washington: National Geographic Society.

Euler, Robert C., and Catherine S. Fowler
1973 Southern Paiute Ethnohistory. *University of Utah Anthropological Papers* 78. Salt Lake City.

Euler, Robert C., and Harry L. Naylor
1952 Southern Ute Rehabilitation Planning: A Study in Self-determination. *Human Organization* 11(4):27-32.

Euler, Robert C., and Alan P. Olson
1965 Split-twig Figurines from Northern Arizona: New Radiocarbon Dates. *Science* 148(3668):368-369.

Ewers, John C.
1954 The Indian Trade of the Upper Missouri Before Lewis and Clark: An Interpretation. *Bulletin of the Missouri Historical Society* 10(4):429-446. St. Louis.

1955 The Horse in Blackfoot Culture; with Comparative Material from Other Western Tribes. *Bureau of American Ethnology Bulletin* 159. Washington.

1957 Hair Pipes in Plains Indian Adornment: A Study in Indian and White Ingenuity. *Anthroplogical Papers* 50, *Bureau of American Ethnology Bulletin* 164:29-85. Washington.

1980 Saddles of the Plains Indians. Pp. 72-84 in Man Made Mobile: Early Saddles of Western North America. Richard E. Ahlborn, ed *Smithsonian Studies in History and Technology* 39. Washington.

Facilitators Incorporated
1980 MX/Native American Cultural and Socio-economic Studies—Draft. Las Vegas, Nev.: Facilitators.

Fagan, John L.
1973 Altithermal Occupation of Spring Sites in the Northern Great Basin. (Unpublished Ph.D. Dissertation in Archaeology, University of Oregon, Eugene.)

1974 Altithermal Occupation of Spring Sites in the Northern Great Basin. *University of Oregon Anthropological Papers* 6. Eugene.

Fairfield, Asa M.
1916 Fairfield's Pioneer History of Lassen County, California.... Also Much of the Pioneer History of the State of Nevada. San Francisco: H.S. Crocker.

Fallon Paiute-Shoshone Tribe
1977 After the Drying Up of the Water. Fallon, Nev.: Fallon Paiute-Shoshone Tribe.

Farmer, Malcom F.
1935 The Mojave Trade Route. *The Masterkey* 9(5):154-157.

1937 An Obsidian Quarry Near Coso Hot Springs, California. *The Masterkey* 11(1):7-9.

Farmer, Malcolm F., and Raymond DeSaussure
1955 Split-twig Figurines. *Plateau* 27(4):13-23.

Farnham, Thomas J.
1843 Travels in the Great Western Prairies, The Anahuac and Rocky Mountains, and in the Oregon Territory. New York: Greeley and McElrath. (Reprinted: Vols. 28-29 of Early Western Travels. Reuben G. Thwaites, ed. Arthur H. Clark, Cleveland, Ohio, 1906).

1850 Life, Adventures, and Travels in California...to Which Are Added the Conquest of California, Travels in Oregon, and a History of the Gold Regions. New York: Nafis and Cornish.

Farris, Glenn J.
1982 Pine Nuts as an Aboriginal Food Source in California and Nevada: Some Contrasts. *Journal of Ethnobiology* 2(2):114-122.

Farrow, E.A.
1930 The Kaibab Indians. *Utah Historical Quarterly* 3 (2):57-59. Salt Lake City.

Faust, Ernest C., and Paul F. Russell
1964 Clinical Parasitology. 7th ed. Philadelphia: Lea and Febiger.

Feder, Norman
1962 Plains Indian Metal-working with Emphasis on Hair Plates. *American Indian Tradition* 8(2):55-76.

[1969] American Indian Art. New York: Henry N. Abrams.

1971 Two Hundred Years of North American Indian Art. New York: Prager.

1980 Plains Pictographic Painting and Quilled Rosettes: A Clue to Tribal Identification. *American Indian Art Magazine* 5(2):54-62.

Fenenga, Franklin, and Francis A. Riddell
1949   Excavation of Tommy Tucker Cave, Lassen County, Cali-
            fornia. *American Antiquity* 14(3):203-214.

Fenneman, Nevin M.
1931   Physiography of Western United States. New York: Mc-
            Graw-Hill.

————
1946   Physical Divisions of the United States. Washington: U.S.
            Geological Survey.

Fenton, R.N.
1869   [Report from], St. Thomas, Nevada, October 14, 1869. Pp.
            645-646 in Papers Accompanying the Annual Report of the
            Commissioner of Indian Affairs, 1869. *U.S. Congress. House.
            41st Cong., 2d sess., House Executive Document* No. 1(3).
            (Serial No. 1414) Washington.

Ferguson, Charles W.
1968   Bristlecone Pine: Science and Esthetics. *Science* 159(3817):839-
            846.

————
1969   A 7104-year Annual Tree-ring Chronology for Bristlecone
            Pine, *Pinus aristata,* from the White Mountains of California.
            Tree-Ring Bulletin 29(3-4):3-29. Tucson, Ariz.

————
1970   Dendrochronology of Bristlecone Pine, *Pinus aristata:* Es-
            tablishment of a 7484-year Chronology in the White Moun-
            tains of East-central California, U.S.A. Pp. 237-259 in Ra-
            diocarbon Variations and Absolute Chronology. Ingrid U.
            Olsson, ed. New York: John Wiley.

————
1979   Carbon Dioxide and Climate: Dendrochronology of Bristle-
            cone Pine, *Pine longaeva. Environment International* 2(4-
            6):209-214.

Ferguson, Charles W., and D.A. Graybill
1983   Dendrochronology of Bristlecone Pine: A Progress Report.
            Radiocarbon 25(2):287-288.

Ferris, Warren A.
1940   Life in the Rocky Mountains: A Diary of Wanderings on the
            Sources of the Rivers Missouri, Columbia and Colorado from
            February 1830 to November 1831. C. Phillips, ed. Denver:
            F.A. Rosenstock, Old West Publishing.

Fike, Richard E.
[1984]   Fluted Points from Utah. *Utah Bureau of Land Management,
            Cultural Resource Series.* Salt Lake City. In press.

Fike, Richard E., and John W. Headley
1979   The Pony Express Stations of Utah in Historical Perspective.
            Utah Bureau of Land Management, Cultural Resource Series
            2. Salt Lake City.

Findlow, Frank J., and Marisa Bolognese
1982   A Preliminary Analysis of Prehistoric Obsidian Use within
            the Mogollon Area. Pp. 297-316 in Mogollon Archaeology:
            Proceedings of the 1980 Mogollon Conference. Patrick H.
            Beckett, ed. Ramona, Calif.: Acoma Books.

Fishler, Stanley A.
1954   Symbolism of a Navajo "Wedding" Basket. *The Masterkey*
            28(6):205-215.

Flannery, Kent V.
1966   The Postglacial "Readaptation" as Viewed from Mesoamer-
            ica. *American Antiquity* 31(6):800-805.

————
1969   Origins and Ecological Effects of Early Domestication in Iran
            and the Near East. Pp. 73-100 in The Domestication and
            Exploitation of Plants and Animals. Peter J. Ucko and G.W.
            Dimbleby, eds. London: Gerald Duckworth.

Flannery, Kent V., and Joyce Marcus
1976   Evolution of the Public Building in Formative Oaxaca. Pp.
            205-221 in Cultural Change and Continuity: Essays in Honor
            of James Bennett Griffin. Charles E. Cleland, ed. New York:
            Academic Press.

Flannery, Regina
1952   Two Concepts of Power. Pp. 185-189 in Indian Tribes of
            Aboriginal America: Selected Papers. Sol. Tax, ed. Chicago:
            University of Chicago Press.

Follett, W.I.
1982   An Analysis of Fish Remains from Ten Archaeological Sites
            at Falcon Hill, Washoe County, Nevada, with Notes on Fish-
            ing Practices of the Ethnographic Kuyúidikadi Northern Paiute.
            Pp. 179-203 (App. A) in The Archaeology of Falcon Hill,
            Winnemucca Lake, Washoe County, Nevada, by Eugene M.
            Hattori, *Nevada State Museum Anthropological Papers* 18.
            Carson City.

Forbes, Jack D.
1959   The Appearance of the Mounted Indians in Northern Mexico
            and the Southwest, to 1680. *Southwestern Journal of An-
            thropology* 15(2):189-212.

————
1965   The "Public Domain" of Nevada and Its Relationship to
            Indian Property Rights. *The Nevada State Bar Journal* 30(3):16-
            47.

————
1967   Nevada Indians Speak. Reno: University of Nevada Press.

————
1973   The Anishinabe Liberation Movement. *Harvard Civil
            Rights - Civil Liberties Law Review* 8(1):217-222.

Ford, A.J.
1930   Owens River, California, Indian Problem. (Manuscript, on
            file, Right of Way and Land Agent, Department of Water
            and Power, City of Los Angeles, June 1930; copy in Special
            Collections Department, Getchell Library, University of Ne-
            vada, Reno.)

————
1932   Statement Regarding Condition of the Indians of Owens Val-
            ley, California. (Manuscript, on file, Right of Way and Land
            Agent, Department of Water and Power, City of Los An-
            geles; copy in Special Collections Department, Getchell Li-
            brary, University of Nevada, Reno.)

Ford, Richard I.
1972   Barter, Gift, or Violence: An Analysis of Tewa Intertribal
            Exchange. Pp. 21-45 in Social Exchange and Interaction.
            Edwin N. Wilmsen, ed. *University of Michigan, Museum of
            Anthropology Anthropological Papers* 46. Ann Arbor.

Fowler, Catherine S.
1962-1984   [Ethnographic Notes, from Fieldwork Among the Northern
            and Southern Paiute, Intermittently and Totalling Approxi-
            mately 30 Months.] (Manuscripts in Fowler's possession.)

————
1966   Environmental Setting and Natural Resources. *Glen Canyon
            Series* 28, *University of Utah Anthropological Papers* 78:13-
            31. Salt Lake City.

————
1969   The Black Springs Site (26WA1200), Washoe County, Ne-
            vada. *Miscellaneous Paper* 1, *Nevada State Museum Anthro-
            pological Papers* 14. Carson City.

————, comp.
1970   Great Basin Anthropology: A Bibliography. *University of
            Nevada, Desert Research Institute Social Sciences and Hu-
            manities Publications* 5. Reno.

————
1970a   [Chemehuevi Fieldnotes; Approximately 2 Weeks, Ethnog-
            raphy, Ethnobotany, Las Vegas, Nev.] (Manuscript in Fow-
            ler's possession.)

————
[1970-1982] [Southern Paiute Fieldnotes on Various Ethnographic Top-
            ics.] (Manuscripts in Fowler's possession.)

————
1971   Some Notes on Comparative Numic Ethnobiology. Pp. 147-
            154 in Great Basin Anthropological Conference 1970: Se-
            lected Papers. C. Melvin Aikens, ed. *University of Oregon
            Anthropological Papers* 1. Eugene.

1972   Some Ecological Clues to Proto-Numic Homelands. Pp. 105-121 in Great Basin Cultural Ecology: A Symposium. Don D. Fowler, ed. *University of Nevada, Desert Research Institute Publications in the Social Sciences* 8. Reno.

1972a   Comparative Numic Ethnobiology. (Unpublished Ph.D. Dissertation in Anthropology, University of Pittsburgh, Pittsburgh, Pa.)

1976   The Processing of Ricegrass by Great Basin Indians. *Mentzelia: Journal of the Northern Nevada Native Plant Society* 2:2-4. Reno.

1977   Ethnography and Great Basin Prehistory. Pp. 11-48 in Models and Great Basin Prehistory: A Symposium. Don D. Fowler, ed. *University of Nevada, Desert Research Institute Publications in the Social Sciences* 12. Reno.

1978   Sarah Winnemucca, Northern Paiute, 1844-1891. Pp. 33-44 in American Indian Intellectuals. Margot Liberty ed. (*Proceedings of the American Ethnological Society, 1976*) St. Paul, Minn.: West Publishing Company.

1980-1983   [Ethnographic Fieldnotes, Owens Valley Paiutes of Bishop, Calif., One Month Total Time.] (Manuscripts in Fowler's possession.)

1982   Settlement Patterns and Subsistence Systems in the Great Basin: The Ethnographic Record. Pp. 121-138 in Man and Environment in the Great Basin. David B. Madsen and James F. O'Connell, eds. *Society for American Archaeology Papers* 2. Washington.

1982a   Food-named Groups Among the Northern Paiute in North America's Great Basin: An Ecological Interpretation. Pp. 113-129 in Resource Managers: North American and Australian Hunter-gatherers. N.M. Williams and E.S. Hunn, eds. *American Association for the Advancement of Science Selected Symposium* 67. Boulder, Colo.

Fowler, Catherine S., and Joyce E. Bath
1981   Pyramid Lake Northern Paiute Fishing: The Ethnographic Record. *Journal of California and Great Basin Anthropology* 3(2):176-186.

Fowler, Catherine S., and Don D. Fowler
1971   Notes on the History of the Southern Paiutes and Western Shoshonis. *Utah Historical Quarterly* 39(2):95-113. Salt Lake City.

1974   North American Great Basin Indians. *Encyclopedia Britannica*, 15th ed., Vol. 13:204-207.

1981   The Southern Paiute: A.D. 1400-1776. Pp. 129-162 in The Protohistoric Period in the North American Southwest, A.D. 1450-1700. David R. Wilcox and Bruce Masse, eds. *Arizona State University Anthropological Research Papers* 24. Tempe.

Fowler, Catherine S., and Joy Leland
1967   Some Northern Paiute Native Categories. *Ethnology* 6(4):381-404.

Fowler, Catherine S., and Nancy Peterson Walters
1982   Harvesting Pandora Moth Larvae with the Owens Valley Paiute: Optimal Foraging? (Paper presented at the Great Basin Anthropological Conference, Reno, Nev.)

Fowler, Catherine S., et al.
1981   An Ethnohistoric and Ethnoarchaeological Study of a Washoe Cemetery at Camp Richardson, Lake Tahoe. Placerville, Calif.: U.S. Forest Service, Eldora National Forest.

Fowler, Don D.
1963   1961 Excavations, Harris Wash, Utah. *Glen Canyon Series* 19, *University of Utah Anthropological Papers* 64. Salt Lake City.

1965   Cultural Ecology and Culture History of the Eastern Shoshoni Indians. (Unpublished Ph.D. Dissertation in Anthropology, University of Pittsburgh, Pittsburgh, Pa.)

1966   Great Basin Social Organization. Pp. 57-73 in The Current Status of Anthropological Research in the Great Basin: 1964. *University of Nevada, Desert Research Institute Publications in the Social Sciences* 1. Reno.

1968   Archaeological Survey in Eastern Nevada, 1966. *University of Nevada, Desert Research Institute Social Sciences and Humanities Publications* 2. Reno.

1968a   The Archeology of Newark Cave, White Pine County, Nevada. *University of Nevada, Desert Research Institute Social Sciences and Humanities Publications* 3. Reno.

_____, ed.
1972   Great Basin Cultural Ecology: A Symposium. *University of Nevada, Desert Research Institute Publications in the Social Sciences* 8. Reno.

1973   Dated Split-twig Figurine from Etna Cave, Nevada. *Plateau* 46(2):54-63.

_____, ed.
1973a   S.M. Wheeler's The Archeology of Etna Cave, Lincoln County, Nevada: A Reprint. *University of Nevada, Desert Research Institute Publications in the Social Sciences* 7. Reno.

1975   Notes on Inquiries in Anthropology: A Bibliographic Essay. Pp. 15-32 in Toward a Science of Man: Essays in the History of Anthropology. Timothy H.H. Thosesen, ed. The Hague: Mouton.

_____, ed.
1977   Models in Great Basin Prehistory: A Symposium. *University of Nevada, Desert Research Institute Publications in the Social Sciences* 12. Reno.

1980   History of Great Basin Anthropological Research, 1776-1979. *Journal of California and Great Basin Anthropology* 2(1):8-36.

1982   Cultural Resources Management. Pp. 1-50 in Advances in Archaeological Method and Theory. M.B. Schiffer, ed. New York: Academic Press.

Fowler, Don D., and Catherine S. Fowler
1969   John Wesley Powell, Anthropologist. *Utah Historical Quarterly* 37(2):152-172. Salt Lake City.

_____, eds.
1970   Stephen Powers' "The Life and Culture of the Washoe and Paiutes." *Ethnohistory* 17(3-4): 117-149.

_____, eds.
1971   Anthropology of the Numa: John Wesley Powell's Manuscripts on the Numic Peoples of Western North America, 1868-1880. *Smithsonian Contributions to Anthropology* 14. Washington.

1981   Museum Collections and Ethnographic Reconstruction: Examples from the Great Basin. Pp. 177-199 in The Research Potential of Anthropological Museum Collections. A.M. Cantwell, J.B. Griffin, and N.A. Rothschild, eds. *New York Academy of Sciences Annual* 376. New York.

Fowler, Don D., and Jesse D. Jennings
1982   Great Basin Archaeology: A Historical Overview. Pp. 105-120 in Man and the Environment in the Great Basin. David B. Madsen and James F. O'Connell, eds. *Society for American Archaeology Papers* 2. Washington.

Fowler, Don D., and David Koch
1982   The Great Basin. Pp. 7-66 in Reference Handbook on the Deserts of North America. Gordon L. Bender, ed. Westport, Conn.: Greenwood Press.

Fowler, Don D., and John F. Matley
1978   The Palmer Collection from Southwestern Utah, 1875. *Miscellaneous Paper 20, University of Utah Anthropological Papers* 99. Salt Lake City.

———
1979   Material Culture of the Numa: The John Wesley Powell Collection 1867-1880. *Smithsonian Contributions to Anthropology* 26. Washington.

Fowler, Don D., David B. Madsen, and Eugene H. Hattori
1973   Prehistory of Southeastern Nevada. *University of Nevada, Desert Research Institute Social Sciences and Humanities Publications* 6. Reno.

Fowler, Don D., et al.
1980   M-X Cultural Resources Studies, Preliminary Research Design. San Francisco: Woodward-Clyde Consultants.

Fowler, Loretta
1982   Arapahoe Politics, 1851-1978: Symbols in Crises of Authority. Lincoln: University of Nebraska Press.

Frankfort, Henri, H.A. Frankfort, John A. Wilson, and Thorkild Jacobsen
1973   Before Philosophy: The Intellectual Adventure of Ancient Man. Baltimore, Md.: Penguin Books.

Frankson, Yvonne, Pat Dumais Anderson, Deborah Goodwin, Judith A. Kinney, and Barbara Karshmer
1980-1981   Paiute, Shoshone, Washoe Children, Our Greatest Resource: A Feasibility Study for the Tribes of Inyo, Mono and Alpine Counties to Implement the Indian Child Welfare Act of 1980 (# J50G14 20CW04-1980-81) Bishop, Calif.: Toiyabe Indian Health Project.

Franzen, John G.
1977   A Preliminary Analysis of the Bissel Springs Site (10-0A-20) and Some Related Materials from Southeastern Idaho. *Archaeological Reports of the Idaho State University Museum of Natural History* 12. Pocatello.

———
1981   Southeastern Idaho Cultural Resources Overview, Burley and Idaho Falls Districts: Final Report R-2196. Jackson, Mich.: Commonwealth Associates for U.S. Bureau of Land Management.

Freed, Stanley A.
1960   Changing Washo Kinship. *University of California Anthropological Records* 14(6): 349-418. Berkeley.

———
1963   A Reconstruction of Aboriginal Washo Social Organization. Pp. 8-24 in The Washo Indians of California and Nevada. Warren L. d'Azevedo, ed. *University of Utah Anthropological Papers* 67. Salt Lake City.

———
1966   Washo Habitation Sites in the Lake Tahoe Area. Pp. 73-84 in Notes on Western Nevada Archaeology and Ethnography. *University of California Archaeological Survey Reports* 66(3). Berkeley.

Freed, Stanley A., and Ruth S. Freed
1963   A Configuration of Aboriginal Washo Culture. Pp. 41-56 in The Washo Indians of California and Nevada. Warren L. d'Azevedo, ed. *University of Utah Anthropological Papers* 67. Salt Lake City.

———
1963a   The Persistence of Aboriginal Ceremonies Among the Washo Indians. Pp. 25-40 in The Washo Indians of California and Nevada. Warren L. d'Azevedo, ed. *University of Utah Anthropological Papers* 67. Salt Lake City.

Freeze, Ray A., and David E. Iannuci
1979   Internal Classification of the Numic Languages of Uto-Aztecan. *Amerindia* 4:77-92.

Frémont, John C.
1845   Report on the Exploring Expedition to the Rocky Mountains in the Year 1842 and to Oregon and Northern California in the Years 1843-1844. Washington: Gales and Seaton.

———
1848   Geographical Memoir Upon Upper California, in Illustration of His Map of Oregon and California. *30th Congress, 1st sess., Senate Miscellaneous Document No. 148 (Serial No. 511)* Washington.

———
1887   Memoirs of My Life, Including the Narrative of Five Journeys of the Western Exploration During the Years 1842, 1843-4, 1845-6-7, 1848-4, Together with a Sketch....2 vols. Chicago: Belford, Clarke.

Fried, Morton H.
1967   The Evolution of Political Society. New York: Random House.

Friedman, Irving
1977   Hydration Dating of Volcanism at Newberry Crater, Oregon. *Journal of Research of the U.S. Geological Survey* 5(3):337-342.

Friedman, Irving, and John Obradovich
1981   Obsidian Hydration Dating of Volcanic Events. *Quaternary Research* 16(1):37-47.

Fritts, Harold C.
1971   Dendroclimatology and Dendroecology. *Quarternary Research* 1(4):419-449.

———
1976   Tree Rings and Climate. New York: Academic Press.

———
1982   An Overview of Dendroclimatic Techniques, Procedures, and Prospects. Pp. 191-197 in Climate from Tree Rings. M.K. Hughes et al., eds. Cambridge, England: Cambridge University Press.

Fritts, Harold C., Robert Lofgreen, and Geoffrey A. Gordon
1979   Variations in Climate Since 1602 as Reconstructed from Tree Rings. *Quaternary Research* 12(1):18-46.

Frost, Donald McKay
1960   Notes on General Ashley: The Overland Trail and South Pass. Barre, Mass.: Barre Gazette. (Original: *Proceedings of the American Antiquarian Society* 54(2):161-312, 1945.)

Fry, Gary F.
1970   Prehistoric Human Ecology in Utah: Based on the Analysis of Coprolites. (Unpublished Ph.D. Dissertation in Anthropology, University of Utah, Salt Lake City.)

———
1970a   Preliminary Analysis of the Hogup Cave Coprolites. Pp. 247-250 (App.3) in Hogup Cave, by C. Melvin Aikens. *University of Utah Anthropological Papers* 93(3). Salt Lake City.

———
1976   Analysis of Prehistoric Coprolites from Utah. *University of Utah Anthropological Papers* 97. Salt Lake City.

———
1978   Prehistoric Diet at Danger Cave, Utah, as Determined by the Analysis of Coprolites. *Miscellaneous Paper 23, University of Utah Anthropological Papers* 99. Salt Lake City.

———
1980   Prehistoric Diet and Parasites in the Desert West of North America. Pp. 325-339 in Early Native Americans. David L. Browman, ed. The Hague: Mouton.

Fry, Gary F., and Gardiner F. Dalley
1979   The Levee Site and the Knoll Site. *University of Utah Anthropological Papers* 100. Salt Lake City.

Gale, Hoyt S.
1915   Salines in the Owens, Searles and Panamint Basins, Southeastern California. Pp. 251-323 in Contributions to Economic Geology, 1913. *U.S. Geological Survey Bulletin* 580. Washington.

Galinat, Walton C., and Robert G. Campbell
1967   The Diffusion of 8-Rowed Maize from the Southwest to the Central Plains. *Massachusetts Agricultural Experiment Station Monograph Series* 1. Amherst.

Galinat, Walton C., and James H. Gunnerson
1963   Spread of 8-Rowed Maize from the Prehistoric Southwest.

Harvard University Botanical Museum Leaflets 20(5). Cambridge, Mass.

1969 Fremont Maize. Pp. 198-206 in The Fremont Culture: A Study in Culture Dynamics on the Northern Anasazi Frontier, by James H. Gunnerson. *Papers of the Peabody Museum of American Archaeology and Ethnology, Harvard University* 49(1). Cambridge, Mass.

Gallatin, Albert
1826 A Table of Indian Tribes of the United States East of the Stony Mountains, Arranged According to Languages and Dialects. Washington: U.S. Office of Indian Affairs. (Printed copy with: Albert Gallatin to Thomas L. McKenney, March 4, 1826. Letter book 125:731-735. Letters Received. Office of Indian Affairs, Record Group 75, National Archives, Washington.)

1836 A Synopsis of the Indian Tribes within the United States East of the Rocky Mountains, and in the British and Russian Possessions in North America. *Archaeologia Americana: Transactions and Collections of the American Antiquarian Society* 2:1-422. Cambridge, Mass.

————, ed.
1848 Hale's Indians of North-west America and Vocabularies of North America. *Transactions of the American Ethnological Society* 2:1-130. New York.

Gallegos, Dennis
1979 Cultural Resources Inventory of the Central Mojave and Colorado Desert Regions, California. San Diego, Calif.: WESTEC Services. (Prepared for U.S. Department of the Interior, Bureau of Land Management, Riverside, Calif.)

Galloway, Robert W.
1970 The Full-glacial Climate in the Southwestern United States. *Annals of the Association of American Geographers* 60(2):245-256. Washington.

1983 Full-glacial Southwestern United States: Mild and Wet or Cold and Dry. *Quarternary Research* 19(2):236-248.

Garfinkel, Alan P.
1980 A Cultural Resource Management for the Fossil Falls/Little Lake Locality. Bakersfield: California Bureau of Land Management, Bakersfield District Office.

Garfinkel, Alan P., and Robert A. Schiffman
1981 Obsidian Studies at the Ming Ranch (CA-Ker-983). Pp. 125-129 in Obsidian Dates, III: A Compendium of the Obsidian Hydration Determinations Made at the UCLA Obsidian Hydration Labratory. Clement W. Meighan and Glenn S. Russell, eds. *University of California, Institute of Archaeology Monographs* 16. Los Angeles.

Garfinkel, Alan P., Robert A. Schiffman, and Kelly McGuire
1979 Archaeological Investigations in the Southern Sierra Nevada: The Lamont Meadow and Morris Peak Segments of the Pacific West Trail Crest. *California Bureau of Land Management, Cultural Resources Publications - Archaeology*. Bakersfield, Calif.

Garner, Beatrice M.
1954 Ute Acculturation and Dietary Adaptation. (Unpublished M.A. Thesis in Anthropology, Michigan State University, East Lansing.)

Garner, Beatrice M., and Florence Hawley
1950 Changing Foods and Food Habits. Pp. 324-331 in Culture Process and Change in Ute Adaptation. Pt. 1. Florence Hawley, ed. *El Palacio* 57(10).

Garth, Thomas R.
1953 Atsugewi Ethnography. *University of California Anthropological Records* 14(2):129-212. Berkeley.

Garvin, Paul L., and Karl Schmitt
1951 [Review of] Der Urmensch und sein Weltbild, by Wilhelm Koppers. *American Anthropologist* 53(2):249.

Gatschet, Albert S.
1876 Zwölf Sprachen aus dem Südwesten Nordamerikas (Pueblos- und Apache-Mundarten; Tonto, Tonkawa, Digger, Utah). Weimar, Germany: Hermann Böhlau.

1877 Indian Languages of the Pacific States and Territories. Pp. 416-447 in The Indian Miscellany. W.W. Beach, ed. Albany, N.Y.: J. Munsell.

1879 Classification into Seven Linguistic Stocks of Western Indian Dialects Contained in Forty Vocabularies. *Report Upon United States Geographical Surveys West of the 100th Meridian, in Charge of 1st Lt. George M. Wheeler.* Vol. 7:403-485. Washington.

1882 Indian Languages of the Pacific States and Territories, and of the Pueblos of New Mexico. *Magazine of American History* 8(April):254-263.

Gayton, Anna H.
1929 Yokuts and Western Mono Pottery-making. *University of California Publications in American Archaeology and Ethnology* 24(3):239-255. Berkeley.

1930 The Ghost Dance of 1870 in South-central California. *University of California Publications in American Archaeology and Ethnology* 28(3):57-82. Berkeley.

1935 Areal Affiliations of California Folktales. *American Anthropologist* 37(4):582-599.

1935a The Orpheus Myth in North America. *Journal of American Folk-Lore* 48(189):263-293.

1948 Yokuts and Western Mono Ethnography. 2 Pts. *University of California Anthropological Records* 10(1-2):1-302. Berkeley.

Gayton, Anna H., and Stanley S. Newman
1940 Yokuts and Western Mono Myths. *University of California Anthropological Records* 5(1). Berkeley.

Gebhard, Davis S.
1951 The Petrolyphs of Wyoming: A Preliminary Paper. *El Palacio* 58(3):67-81.

1969 The Rock Art of Dinwoody, Wyoming. Santa Barbara Calif.: University of California, The Art Galleries.

Gebhard, David S., and Harold A. Cahn
1950 The Petroglyphs of Dinwoody, Wyoming. *American Antiquity* 15(3):219-228.

Gebow, Joseph A.
1868 A Vocabulary of the Snake or Sho-Sho-Nay Dialect. 2d rev. ed. Green River City, Wyo. Terr.: Freeman.

Gehr, Elliott, Evelyn Lee, Gretchen Johnson, J. Donald Merritt, and Steven Nelson
1982 Class I Cultural Resources Overview for the Bureau of Land Management, Boise and Shoshone Districts, Idaho. 2 vols. Eugene, Oreg. Professional Analysts.

Gerhardt, Patricia L.
1974 Shoshone Shelter Cave Number Two: A Preliminary Report. *Pacific Coast Archaeological Society Quarterly* 10(2):35-50. Santa Ana, Calif.

Gheen, Levi
1873 Letter from the Government Farmer for the Western Shoshone to the Commissioner of Indian Affairs. (In Letters Received by the Office of Indian Affairs, 1824-1880, Nevada Superintendency, Microfilm Roll M-234-540, April 28, National Archives, Washington.)

Gibbs, George
1863 Instructions for Research Relative to the Ethnology and Philology of America. *Smithsonian Miscellaneous Collections* 7(160). Washington.

768

Gibson, George R.
1935   Journal of a Soldier Under Kearny and Doniphan, 1846-47. *Southwest Historical Series* 3. Glendale, Calif.

Gifford, Edward W.
[1915] [Unpublished Ethnographic Notes on the Kawaiisu (including Basketry).] (Manuscript on file, Lowie Museum of Anthropology, University of California, Berkeley.)

1916   Dichotomous Social Organization in South Central California. *University of California Publications in American Archaeology and Ethnology* 11:(5):291-296. Berkeley.

1916a   Miwok Moieties. *University of California Publications in American Archaeology and Ethnology* 12(4):139-194. Berkeley.

1917   Tübatulabal and Kawaiisu Kinship Terms. *University of California Publications in American Archaeology and Ethnology* 12(6):219-248. Berkeley.

1918   Clans and Moieties in Southern California. *University of California Publications in American Archaeology and Ethnology* 14(2):155-219. Berkeley.

1922   Californian Kinship Terminologies. *University of California Publications in American Archaeology and Ethnology* 18(1):1-285. Berkeley.

1932   The Northfork Mono. *University of California Publications in American Archaeology and Ethnology* 31(2):15-65. Berkeley.

1936   Californian Balanophagy. Pp. 27-98 in Essays in Anthropology Presented to Alfred L. Kroeber in Celebration of His Sixtieth Birthday. Berkeley: University of California Press.

1947   Californian Shell Artifacts. *University of California Anthropological Records* 9(1):1-114. Berkeley.

1949   Early Central Californian and Anasazi Shell Artifact Types. *American Antiquity* 15(2):156-157.

Gigli, Jane G.
1974   Dat So La Lee, Queen of the Washo Basket Makers. *Nevada State Museum Anthropological Papers* 16: 1-27. Carson City. (Originally published as *Nevada State Museum Popular Series* 3, 1967.)

Gilbert, Bill
1983   Westering Man: The Life of Joseph Walker. New York: Atheneum.

Gilbert, Grove K.
1890   Lake Bonneville. *Monographs of the Geological Survey* 1. Washington.

Gillin, John P.
1938   Archeological Investigations in Nine Mile Canyon, Utah. *Bulletin of the University of Utah* 28(11). Salt Lake City.

1941   Archaeological Investigations in Central Utah. *Papers of the Peabody Museum of American Archaeology and Ethnology, Harvard University* 17(2). Cambridge, Mass.

1955   Archaeological Investigations in Nine Mile Canyon, Utah: A Re-publication. *University of Utah Anthropological Papers* 21. Salt Lake City.

Givón, Talmy, comp.
1979   Ute Dictionary. Prelim. ed. Ignacio, Colo.: Ute Press, The Southern Ute Tribe.

————, ed.
1980   Ute Reference Grammar. Ignacio, Colo.: Ute Press, The Southern Ute Tribe.

Givón, Talmy, and Sunshine Cloud Smith
1981   [Two Ute Bear Dance Song Texts Nos. 691, 693; Recovered from Frances Densmore Field Recording.] (Manuscript in Thomas Vennum's possession.)

Gladwin, Winifred, and Harold S. Gladwin
1934   A Method for Designation of Cultures and Their Variations. *Gila Pueblo, Medallion Papers* 15. Globe, Ariz.

Gleason, Henry A., and Arthur Cronquist
1964   The Natural Geography of Plants. New York: Columbia University Press.

Glenmore, Josephine Stands in Timber, and Wayne Leman
1984   Cheyenne Topical Dictionary. Busby, Mont.: Cheyenne Translation Project.

Goddard, Ives
1979   The Languages of South Texas and the Lower Rio Grande. Pp. 355-389 in The Languages of Native America: Historical and Comparative Assessment. Lyle Campbell and Marianne Mithun, eds. Austin: University of Texas Press.

Goddard, Pliny E.
1903   Life and Culture of the Hupa. *University of California Publications in American Archaeology and Ethnology* 1(1):1-88. Berkeley.

Goetzmann, William H.
1966   Exploration and Empire: The Explorer and the Scientist in the Winning of the American West. New York: Alfred Knopf.

Gomberg, William, and Joy Leland
1963   "We Need to Be Shown": A Study of the Talents, Work Potential and Aspirations of the Pyramid Lake Indians. [Washington]:U.S. Bureau of Indian Affairs.

Goodman, Stacy
1985   Material Culture: Basketry and Fiber Artifacts. Pp. 262-298 in The Archaeology of Hidden Cave, Nevada. David H. Thomas, ed. *Anthropological Papers of the American Museum of Natural History* 61(1). New York.

Gorbet, Larry
1977   Headless Relatives in the Southwest: Are They Related? Pp. 270-278 in *Proceedings of the Third Annual Meeting of the Berkeley Linguistics Society, February 19-21, 1977.* Kenneth Whistler et al, eds. Berkeley: Berkeley Linguistics Society.

Gosiute Tribal Council
1937   [Letter to the Commissioner of Indian Affairs, dated November 5.] (Manuscript in Letters Received, Record Group 75, National Archives, Washington.)

Goss, James A.
1961   A Short Dictionary of the Southern Ute Language. Ignacio, Colo.: The Southern Ute Tribe.

1961a   Ute Social Organization. (Unpublished manuscript in Goss' possession.)

1965   Ute Linguistics and Anasazi Abandonment of the Four Corners Area. Pp. 73-81 in Contributions of the Wetherill Mesa Archeological Project. Douglas Osborne, ass. *Memoirs of the Society for American Archaeology* 19. Salt Lake City.

1966   Comments on Linguistics: Internal Diversity in Southern Numic. Pp. 265-273 in The Current Status of Anthropological Research in the Great Basin: 1964. Warren L. d'Azevedo et al., eds. *University of Nevada, Desert Research Institute Social Sciences and Humanities Publications* 1. Reno.

1967   Ute Language, Kin, Myth, and Nature: A Multi-dimensional Folk Taxonomy. *Anthropological Linguistics* 9(9):1-11.

1968   Culture-historical Inference from Utaztekan Linguistic Evidence. Pp. 1-42 in Utaztekan Prehistory. Earl H. Swanson, Jr., ed. *Occasional Papers of the Idaho State University Museum* 22. Pocatello.

1970   Voiceless Vowels (?) in Numic Languages. Pp. 37-46 in Languages and Cultures of Western North America: Essays in

Honor of Sven S. Liljeblad. Earl H. Swanson, Jr., ed. Pocatello: Idaho State University Press.

1972   A Basin-Plateau Shoshonean Ecological Model. Pp. 123-128 in Great Basin Cultural Ecology: A Symposium. Don D. Fowler, ed. *University of Nevada, Desert Research Institute Publications in the Social Sciences* 8. Reno.

1972a   Ute Lexical and Phonological Patterns. (Unpublished Ph.D. Dissertation in Linguistics, University of Chicago, Chicago.)

1977   Lingustic Tools for the Great Basin Prehistorian. Pp. 49-70 in Models and Great Basin Prehistory: A Symposium. Don D. Fowler, ed. *University of Nevada, Desert Research Institute Publications in the Social Sciences* 12. Reno.

Gottfredson, Peter, ed.
1919   History of Indian Depredations in Utah. Salt Lake City: Skeleton Publishing.

Gould, Richard A., Don D. Fowler, and Catherine S. Fowler
1972   Diggers and Doggers: Parallel Failures in Economic Acculturation. *Southwestern Journal of Anthropology* 28(3):265-281.

Grant, Campbell, James W. Baird, and J. Kenneth Pringle
1968   Rock Drawings of the Coso Range, Inyo County, California. *Maturango Museum Publications* 4. China Lake, Calif.

Grayson, Donald K.
1977   A Review of the Evidence for Early Holocene Turkeys in the Northern Great Basin. *American Antiquity* 42(1):110-114.

1979   Mount Mazama: Climatic Change, and Fort Rock Basin Archaeofaunas. Pp. 427-457 in Volcanic Activity and Human Ecology. Payson D. Sheets and Donald K. Grayson, eds. New York: Academic Press.

1982   Toward a History of Great Basin Mammals During the Past 15,000 Years. Pp. 82-101 in Man and Environment in the Great Basin. David B. Madsen and James F. O'Connell, eds. *Society for American Archaeology Papers* 2. Washington.

1983   The Paleontology of Gatecliff Shelter: Small Mammals. Pp. 99-135 in The Archaeology of Monitor Valley, 2: Gatecliff Shelter. David H. Thomas, ed. *Anthropological Papers of the American Museum of Natural History* 59(1). New York.

Green, Dee F.
1961   Archaeological Investigations at the G.M. Hinckley Farm Site, Utah County, Utah. Provo, Utah: Brigham Young University Press.

Green, James P.
1972   Archaeology of the Rock Creek Site, 10-CA-33, Sawtooth National Forest, Cassia County, Idaho. (Unpublished M.A. Thesis in Archaeology, Idaho State University, Pocatello.)

1982   XRF Trace Element Analysis and Hydration Measurement of Archaeological and Source Obsidians from the Northeastern Great Basin. (Unpublished manuscript in Green's possession.)

Green, Thomas J.
1982   House Form and Variability at Givens Hot Springs, Southwest, Idaho. *Idaho Archaeologist* 6(1-2):33-44. Caldwell.

Greer, Deon C., Klaus D. Gurgel, Wayne L. Wahlquist, Howard A. Christy, and Gary B. Peterson
1981   Atlas of Utah. Ogden, Utah: Weber State College.

Gregg, Josiah
1844   Commerce of the Prairies: Or, The Journal of a Santa Fe Trader....2 vols. New York: H.G. Langley.

Griset, Suzanne
1981   Ceramic Artifacts. In Archaeological Investigations in the Southern Sierra Nevada: The Rockhouse Basin Segment of the Pacific Crest Trail. (Unpublished manuscript on file at U.S. Forest Service, Porterville, Calif.)

Griswold, Gillett
1970   Aboriginal Patterns of Trade Between the Columbia Basin and the Northern Plains. *Archaeology in Montana* 11(2-3). Missoula.

Grosscup, Gordon L.
1956   The Archaeology of the Carson Sink Area. Pp. 58-64 in Papers on California Archaeology, 37-43. *University of California Archaeological Survey Reports* 33. Berkeley.

1958   Radiocarbon Dates from Nevada of Archaeological Interest. Pp. 17-31 in Archaeological Radiocarbon Dates from California and Nevada. *University of California Archaeological Survey Reports* 44(1). Berkeley.

1960   The Culture History of Lovelock Cave, Nevada. *University of California Archaeological Survey Reports* 52:1-71. Berkeley.

1963   Lovelock, Northern Paiute and Culture Change. *Nevada State Museum Anthropological Papers* 9:67-71. Carson City.

1974   Northern Paiute Archeology [1954]. Pp. 9-51 in Paiute Indians, IV. (*American Indian Ethnohistory: California and Basin-Plateau Indians*) New York: Garland

1977   Notes on Boundaries and Culture of the Panamint Shoshone and Owens Valley Paiute. *University of California Archaeological Research Facility Contributions* 35:109-150. Berkeley.

Gruhn, Ruth
1960   The Mecham Site: A Rockshelter Burial in the Snake River Canyon of Southern Idaho. *Tebiwa: Journal of the Idaho State University Museum* 3(1-2):3-19. Pocatello.

1961   The Archaeology of Wilson Butte Cave, South-central Idaho. *Occasional Papers of the Idaho State University Museum* 6. Pocatello.

1961a   A Collection of Artifacts from Pence-Duerig Cave in South-central Idaho. *Tebiwa: Journal of the Idaho State University Museum* 4(1):1-24. Pocatello.

1979   Excavation in Amy's Shelter, Eastern Nevada. Pp. 90-160 in The Archaeology of Smith Creek Canyon, Eastern Nevada. Donald R. Tuohy and Doris L. Rendall, eds. *Nevada State Museum Anthropological Papers* 17. Carson City.

Gudde, Erwin G., and Elisabeth K. Gudde, eds. and trans.
1958   Exploring with Frémont: The Private Diaries of Charles Preuss, Cartographer for John C. Frémont on His First, Second, and Fourth Expeditions to the Far West. Norman: University of Oklahoma Press.

Gunnerson, James H.
1955   Archeological Evidence of Hunting Magic. *Utah Archeology: A Newsletter* 1:5-8.

1956   A Fluted Point Site in Utah. *American Antiquity* 21(4):412-414.

1957   An Archeological Survey of the Fremont Area. *University of Utah Anthropological Papers* 28. Salt Lake City.

1959   The Utah Statewide Archaeological Survey: Its Background and First Ten Years. *Utah Archaeology: A Newsletter* 5(4):3-16. Salt Lake City.

1960   The Fremont Culture: Internal Dimensions and External Relationships. *American Antiquity* 25(3):373-380.

1962   Highway Salvage Archeology: St. George, Utah. *Miscella-*

770

neous Collected Paper 3, *University of Utah Anthropological Papers* 60:45-65. Salt Lake City.

1962a   Unusual Artifacts from Castle Valley, Central Utah. *Miscellaneous Collected Paper* 4, *University of Utah Anthropological Papers* 60:67-91. Salt Lake City.

1962b   Plateau Shoshonean Prehistory: A Suggested Reconstruction. *American Antiquity* 28(1):41-45.

1969   The Fremont Culture: A Study in Culture Dynamics on the Northern Anasazi Frontier. *Papers of the Peabody Museum of American Archaeology and Ethnology, Harvard University* 59(2). Cambridge, Mass.

Gunther, Erna
1928   A Further Analysis of the First Salmon Ceremony. *University of Washington Publications in Anthropology* 2(5):129-173. Seattle.

HCRS/NAER
1980   A Search for Balance, Conservation and Development on the Historic Comstock. Washington: Heritage Conservation and Recreation Service, National Architectural and Engineering Record.

HDR Sciences
1980   Environmental Characteristics of Alternative Designated Deployment Areas: Native Americans (Nevada/Utah). *U.S. Air Force Ballistic Missile Office, MX Environmental Technical Report* 21. Norton Air Force Base, Calif.

1980a   Environmental Characteristics of Alternative Deployment Areas: Archaeological and Historical Resources. *U.S. Air Force Ballistic Missile Office, MX Environmental Technical Report* 23. Norton Air Force Base, Calif.

Haag, Mack, and Alfred Wilson
1925   General Report of the President and Minutes of the 6th Annual Convention of the Native American Church, Calumet, Oklahoma. (Manuscript, copy in O.C. Stewart's possession.)

Haas, Mary R.
1963   Shasta and Proto-Hokan. *Language* 39(1):40-59.

1967   On the Relations of Tonkawa. Pp. 310-320 in Studies in Southwestern Ethnolinguistics: Meaning and History in the Languages of the American Southwest. Dell H. Hymes with William E. Bittle, eds. (*Studies in General Anthropology* 3) The Hague: Mouton.

1969   Grammar or Lexicon? The American Indian Side of the Question from Duponceau to Powell. *International Journal of American Linguistics* 35(3):239-255.

1973   American Indian Linguistic Prehistory. Pp. 677-712 in *Linguistics in North America*. Current Trends in Linguistics. Thomas A. Sebeok, ed. Vol. 10. The Hague and Paris: Mouton. (Reprinted: Pp. 23-58 in Native Languages of the Americas, Vol. 1, Thomas A. Sebeok, ed., Plennum Press, New York, 1976.)

1976   The Northern California Linguistic Area. Pp. 347-359 in Hokan Studies: Papers from the First Conference on Hokan Languages Held in San Diego, California, April 23-25, 1970. Margaret Langdon and Shirley Silver, eds. (*Janua Linguarum Series Practica* 181) The Hague: Mouton. (Reprinted: Pp. 353-369 in Language, Culture and History: Essays by Mary R. Haas, Anwar S. Dil, ed. Stanford University Press, Stanford, Calif., 1978.)

Haas, Theodore H.
1957   The Legal Aspects of Indian Affairs from 1887 to 1957. Pp. 12-22 in American Indians and American Life. George E. Simpson and T. Milton Yinger, eds. *Annals of the American Academy of Political and Social Science* 311. Philadelphia.

Hack, John T.
1942   The Changing Physical Environment of the Hopi Indians of Arizona. *Papers of the Peabody Museum of American Archaeology and Ethnology, Harvard University* 35(1). Cambridge, Mass.

Hacker, Andrew, ed.
1983   U/S: A Statistical Portrait of the American People. New York: Viking Press.

Hackett, Charles W., ed.
1931-1941   Pichardo's Treatise on the Limits of Louisiana and Texas....3 vols. Austin: University of Texas Press.

————, ed.
1942   Revolt of the Pueblo Indians of New Mexico and Otermín's Attempted Reconquest, 1680-1682. Charmion Shelby, trans. 2 vols. Albuquerque: University of New Mexico Press.

Hadley, J. Nixon
1957   The Demography of the American Indians. Pp. 23-30 in American Indians and American Indian Life. G.E. Simpson and J. Milton Yinger, eds. *Annals of the American Academy of Political and Social Science* 311. Philadelphia.

Haekel, Josef
1955   Zur Problematik des heiligen Pfahles bei den Indianern Brasiliens. Pp. 229-243 in *Proceedings of the 31st International Congress of Americanists*. Sao Paulo, 1954.

Hafen, LeRoy R., ed.
1965   The Mountain Men and the Fur Trade of the Far West. 10 vols. Glendale, Calif.: Arthur H. Clark.

Hafen, Leroy R., and Ann W. Hafen, eds.
1954-1961   Addison Pratt's Diary [1850]. Pp. 66-85 in Vol. 2 of The Far West and the Rockies Historical Series, 1820-1875. 15 vols. Glendale Calif.: Arthur H. Clark

Hagan, William T.
1966   Indian Police and Judges: Experiments in Acculturation and Control. New Haven, Conn.: Yale University Press.

Hage, Per, and Wick R. Miller
1976   'Eagle' = 'Bird': A Note on the Structure and Evolution of Shoshoni Ethnoornithological Nomenclature. *American Ethnologist* 3(3):481-488.

Hagerty, Donald J.
1970   Archeology and Ecology in the Pine Nut Mountains, Nevada. (Unpublished M.A. Thesis in Anthropology, University of California, Davis.)

Hague, Arnold, and S.F. Emmons
1877   Region of the Mud Lakes. Pp. 775-800 in Descriptive Geology, by Arnold Hague and S.F. Emmons. (*U.S. Geological Exploration of the Fortieth Parallel,* 2) Washington: U.S. Government Printing Office.

Haines, Francis
1938   The Northward Spread of Horses Among the Plains Indians. *American Anthropologist* 40(3):429-437.

1938a   Where Did the Plains Indians Get Their Horses? *American Anthropologist* 40(1):112-117.

Hale, Horatio E.
1846   Ethnography and Philology. United States Exploring Expedition During the Years, 1838, 1839, 1840, 1841, 1842 Under the Command of Charles Wilkes, U.S.N. Vol. 6. Philadelphia: Lea and Blanchard. (Reprinted: The Gregg Press, Ridgewood, N.J., 1968.)

1848   Hale's Indians of Northwest America, and Vocabularies of North America. *Transactions of the American Ethnological Society* 2:xxv-130. New York.

Hale, Kenneth
1958-1959   Internal Diversity in Uto-Aztecan: I and II. *International Journal of American Linguistics* 24(2):101-107; 25(2):114-121.

Hall, E. Raymond
1946   Mammals of Nevada. Berkeley: University of California Press.   *771*

———
1981   The Mammals of North America. 2d ed. 2 vols. New York: John Wiley.

Hall, Henry J.
1972   Diet and Disease at Clyde's Cavern, Utah: As Revealed via Paleoscatology. (Unpublished M.A. Thesis in Anthropology, University of Utah, Salt Lake City.)

———
1977   A Paleoscatological Study of Diet and Disease at Dirty Shame Rockshelter, Southeast Oregon. *Tebiwa: Miscellaneous Papers of the Idaho State University Museum of Natural History* 8. Pocatello.

Hall, Matthew C.
1983   Late Holocene Hunter-gatherers and Volcanism in the Long Valley-Mono Basin Region: Prehistoric Culture Change in the Eastern Sierra Nevada. (Unpublished Ph.D. Dissertation in Anthropology, University of California, Riverside.)

Hall, Matthew C., and James P. Barker
1975   Background to Prehistory of the El Paso/Red Mountain Desert Region. (Report in California Bureau of Land Management, Desert Planning Staff, Riverside.)

Haller, Timothy G.
1981   California-Nevada Interstate Water Compact: A Study in Controversy. (Unpublished Ph.D. Dissertation in Political Science, University of Nevada, Reno.)

Hamblin, Jacob
1909   Jacob Hamblin, a Narrative of His Personal Experiences as a Frontiersman, Missionary to the Indians and Explorer...by James A. Little. 2d ed. Salt Lake City, Utah: The Deseret News.

Hamilton, William T.
1905   My Sixty Years on the Plains, Trapping, Trading, and Indian Fighting. New York: Forest and Stream. (Reprinted: University of Oklahoma Press, Norman, 1960.)

Handelman, Don
1964   [Fieldnotes and Report - Carson Indian Colony; University of Nevada Ethnographic Archives 2. National Science Foundation Graduate Field Training Project - June 7 to Sept. 7, 1964.] (On file, Department of Anthropology, University of Nevada, Reno.)

———
1967   Transcultural Shamanic Healing: A Washo Example. *Ethnos* 32(1-4):149-166. Stockholm.

———
1967a   The Development of a Washo Shaman. *Ethnology* 6(4):444-461.

———
1968   Shamanizing on an Empty Stomach. *American Anthropologist* 70(2):353-356.

———
1976   The Development of a Washo Shaman. Pp. 379-407 in Native California: A Theoretical Retrospective. Lowell J. Bean and Thomas C. Blackburn, eds. Socorro, N.M.: Ballena Press.

Hanes, Richard C.
1977   Lithic Tools of the Dirty Shame Rockshelter: Typology and Distribution. *Tebiwa: Miscellaneous Papers of the Idaho State University Museum of Natural History* 6. Pocatello.

———
1982   Cultural Persistence in Nevada: Current Native American Issues. *Journal of California and Great Basin Anthropology* 4(2):203-211.

Hansen, Henry P
1947   Postglacial Vegetation of the Northern Great Basin. *American Journal of Botany* 34(3):164-171.

———
1947a   Postglacial Forest Succession, Climate, and Chronology in the Pacific Northwest. *Transactions of the American Philosophical Society* n.s. 37(1): 1-130. Philadelphia.

Hardesty, Donald, Valerie Firby, and Gretchen Siegler
1982   An Archaeological Survey of the Virginia City National His-toric Landmark. Carson City: Nevada Division of Historic Preservation and Archaeology.

Harding, Sidney T.
1965   Recent Variations in the Water Supply of the Western Great Basin. *Bulletins and Reports of California State Water Agencies, Archives Series Report* 16:1-226. Berkeley.

Hardman, George, and Cruz Venstrom
1941   A 100-Year Record of Truckee River Runoff Estimated from Changes in Levels and Volumes of Pyramid and Winnemucca Lakes. *EOS, American Geophysical Union Transactions* 22:71-90.

Harms, Robert T.
1966   Stress, Voice, and Length in Southern Paiute. *International Journal of American Linguistics* 32(3):228-235.

Harner, Nellie Shaw
1974   Indians of Coo-yu-ee Pah: The History of the Pyramid Lake Indians, 1843-1959, and Early Tribal History, 1825-1834. Sparks, Nev.: Dave's Printing and Publishing. (Reprinted: Western Printing and Publication, 1978.)

Harner, Richard F., and Kimball T. Harper
1973   Mineral Composition of Grassland Species of the Eastern Great Basin in Relation to Stand Productivity. *Canadian Journal of Botany* 51(11):2037-2046. Ottawa.

Harpending, Henry, and Herbert Davis
1977   Some Implications for Hunter-gatherer Ecology Derived from Spatial Structure of Resources. *World Archaeology* 8(3):275-286.

Harper, Kimball T.
1967   The Vegetational Environment of the Bear River No. 2 Archeological Site. Pp. 61-65 in Excavations at Snake Rock Village and the Bear River No. 2 Site, by C. Melvin Aikens. *University of Utah Anthropological Papers* 87. Salt Lake City.

———
1968   The Ecological Perspective, Pp. 25-43 in The Future of Utah Environment. M. Treshow and C.M. Gilmour, eds. Salt Lake City: University of Utah Center for Environmental Ecology.

Harper, Kimball T., and G.M. Alder
1970   The Macroscopic Plant Remains of the Deposits of Hogup Cave, Utah, and Their Paleoclimatic Implications. Pp. 215-240 (App. 1) in Hogup Cave. C. Melvin Aikens, ed. *University of Utah Anthropological Papers* 93. Salt Lake City.

———
1972   Paleoclimatic Inferences Concerning the Last 10,000 Years from a Resampling of Danger Cave, Utah. Pp. 13-23 in Great Basin Cultural Ecology: A Symposium. Don D. Fowler, ed. *University of Nevada, Desert Research Institute Publications in the Social Sciences* 8. Reno.

Harper, Kimball T., D. Carl Freeman, W. Kent Ostler, and Lionel G. Klikoff
1978   The Flora of Great Basin Mountain Ranges: Diversity, Sources, and Dispersal Ecology. Pp. 81-103 in Intermountain Biogeography: A Symposium. Kimball T. Harper and James L. Reveal, eds. *Brigham Young University, Great Basin Naturalist* Memoirs 2. Provo, Utah.

Harrington, Harold D.
1967   Edible Native Plants of the Rocky Mountains. Albuquerque: University of New Mexico Press.

Harrington, John P.
1911   The Phonetic System of the Ute Language. *University of Colorado Studies Series in Anthropology*. 8(3):199-222. (Reprinted: *Santa Fe School of American Research Papers* 24.) Boulder.

———
1911a   The Origin of the Names Ute and Paiute. *American Anthropologist* 13(1):173-174.

———
1943   Hokan Discovered in South America. *Journal of the Washington Academy of Sciences* 33(11):334-344. Washington.

Harrington, Mark R.

1925   Ancient Salt Mine Near St. Thomas, Nevada. *Museum of the American Indian, Heye Foundation, Indian Notes* 2(3):227-231. New York.

1926   Another Ancient Salt Mine in Nevada. *Museum of the American Indian, Heye Foundation, Indian Notes* 3(4):221-232. New York.

1927   Some Lake-bed Camp-sites in Nevada. *Museum of the American Indian, Heye Foundation, Indian Notes* 4(1):40-47. New York.

1932   Museums and Fiestas. *The Masterkey* 6(3):72-77.

1933   Gypsum Cave, Nevada. *Southwest Museum Papers* 8. Los Angeles.

1933a   A Cat-tail Eater. The *Masterkey* 7(5):147-149.

1934   A Camel Hunter's Camp in Nevada. *The Masterkey* 8(1):22-24.

1934a   American Horses and Ancient Men in Nevada. *The Masterkey* 8(6):165-169.

1936   Smith Creek Cave. *The Masterkey* 10(5):192.

1941   Ancient Hunters of the Nevada Desert. *Desert Magazine* 4(4):4-6. El Centro, Calif.

1948   An Ancient Site at Borax Lake, California. *Southwest Museum Papers* 16. Los Angeles.

1951   A Colossal Quarry. *The Masterkey* 25(1):14-18.

1957   A Pinto Site at Little Lake, California. *Southwest Museum Papers* 17. Los Angeles.

Harrington, Mark R., and Ruth D. Simpson

1961   Tule Springs, Nevada, with Other Evidence of Pleistocene Man in North America. *Southwest Museum Papers* 18. Los Angeles.

Harrington, Mark R., Irwin Hayden, and Louis Schellbach, III

1930   Archeological Explorations in Southern Nevada: Report of the First Sessions Expedition, 1929. *Southwest Museum Papers* 4. Los Angeles.

Harris, Jack S.

1940   The White Knife Shoshoni of Nevada. Pp. 39-116 in Acculturation in Seven American Indian Tribes. Ralph Linton, ed. New York: Appleton-Century.

Harten, Lucille B.

1980   The Osteology of the Human Skeletal Material from the Braden Site, 10-WN-117, in Western Idaho. Pp. 130-148 in Anthropological Papers in Memory of Earl H. Swanson, Jr. Lucille B. Harten, Claude N. Warren, and Donald R. Tuohy, eds. Pocatello: Idaho Museum of Natural History, Special Publication.

Hatoff, Brian W., and David H. Thomas

1981   The Hidden Cave Archaeological Project: A Case Study in Creative Funding. *Contract Abstracts and CRM Archeology* 2(3):7-9.

Hatt, Gudmund

1949   Asiatic Influences in American Folklore. *Danske Kongelige Videnskabernes Selskab, Historiskfilologiske Meddelelser* 31(6). Copenhagen.

Hattori, Eugene M.

1975   Northern Paiutes on the Comstock: Archaeology and Ethnohistory of an American Indian Population in Virginia City, Nevada. *Nevada State Museum Occasional Papers* 2. Carson City.

1982   The Archaeology of Falcon Hill, Winnemucca Lake, Washoe County, Nevada. *Nevada State Museum Anthropological Papers* 18. Carson City.

Hauck, F.R., D.G. Weder, L. Drollinger, and A. McDonald

1979   A Cultural Resource Evaluation in Clark County, Nevada. Pt. I: Cultural Resource Overview. *Archaeological-Environmental Research Corporation Paper* 17. Salt Lake City.

Hauck, Paul A.

1955   Ute Rorschach Performances with Notes on Field Methods. *University of Utah Anthropological Papers* 23. Salt Lake City.

Haury, Emil W.

1950   The Stratigraphy and Archaeology of Ventana Cave, Arizona. Tuscon: University of Arizona Press.

1976   The Hohokam: Desert Farmers and Craftsmen; Ecavations at Snaketown, 1964-1965. Tucson: University of Arizona Press.

Hawley, Florence M.

1950   The Mechanics of Perpetuation in Pueblo Witchcraft. Pp. 143-158 in For the Dean. Santa Fe: Hohokam Museum Association and Southwestern Monuments Association.

Hawley, John W., and William E. Wilson, III

1965   Quarternary Geology of the Winnemucca Area, Nevada. *University of Nevada, Desert Research Institute Technical Report* 5. Reno.

Hayden, Francis V.

1862   Contributions to the Ethnography and Philology of the Indian Tribes of the Missouri Valley. Philadelphia: C. Sherman and Son.

Hayden, H.E.

1877   Indian Languages of the Pacific. *Magazine of American History* 1:331.

Hayes, Alden

1940   Peyote Cult on the Goshiute Reservation at Deep Creek, Utah. *New Mexico Anthropologist* 4(2):34-36. Albuquerque.

Haynes, C. Vance, Jr.

1967   Quaternary Geology of the Tule Springs Area, Clark County, Nevada. Pp. 15-104 in Pleistocene Studies in Southern Nevada. H.M. Wormington and Dorothy Ellis, eds. *Nevada State Museum Anthropological Papers* 13. Carson City.

1968   Geochronology of Late-Quarternary Alluvium. Pp. 591-631 in Means of Correlation of Quarternary Successions. Roger B. Morrison and Herbert E. Wright, Jr., eds. Salt Lake City: University of Utah Press.

1969   The Earliest Americans. *Science* 166(3906):709-715.

1982   Great Sand Sea and Selima Sand Sheet, Eastern Sahara: Geochronology of Desertification. *Science* 217(4560):629-633.

Haynes, Terry L.

1976   Contraceptive Behavior Among Wind River Shoshone and Arapahoe Females. (Unpublished M.A. Thesis in Anthropology, Colorado State University, Fort Collins.)

Hays, John C.

1860   Report to Governor A. Cumming of Utah. Pp. 89-92 in Report of the Secretary of War, December 3, 1860. *36th Cong., 2d sess. Senate Executive Document* No. 1 (Serial No. 1079). Washington: George W. Bowman.

Hayward, C. Lynn, D. Elden Beck, and Wilmer W. Tanner

1958   Zoology of the Upper Colorado River Basin, I: The Biotic Communities. *Brigham Young University Science Bulletin, Biological Series* 1(3). Provo, Utah.

Hebard, Grace Raymond

1930   Washakie: An Account of Indian Resistance of the Covered Wagon and Union Pacific Railroad Invasions of their Territory. Cleveland, Ohio: Arthur C. Clark.

Heckman, Richard A., Charles Thompson, and David A. White
1981   Fishes of Utah Lake. Pp. 107-127 in Utah Lake. *Great Basin Naturalist Memoirs* 5. Provo, Utah.

Hedges, Ken
1982   Great Basin Rock Art Styles: A Revisionist View. *American Indian Rock Art* 7-8:205-211. El Toro, Calif.

————
1983   Shamanic Origins of Rock Art. Pp. 46-59 in Ancient Images on Stone: Rock Art of the Californias. Jo Anne Van Tilburg, ed. Los Angeles: University of California, Institute of Archaeology.

Heidenreich, Charles A.
1967   A Review of the Ghost Dance Religion of 1889-90 Among the North American Indians and Comparison of 8 Societies Which Accepted or Rejected the Dance. (Unpublished M.A. Thesis in Anthropology, University of Oregon, Eugene.)

Heiken, Grant H.
1981   Holocene Plinian Tephra Deposits of the Medicine Lake Highland, California. Pp. 177-181 in Guides to Some Volcanic Terranes in Washington, Idaho, Oregon, and Northern California. David A. Johnston and Julie Donnelly-Nolan, eds. *U.S. Geological Survey Circular* 838. Alexandria, Va.

Heizer, Michael, comp.
1979   Bibliography of Published Writings of Robert F. Heizer, 1937-78. Berkeley, Calif.: Privately printed.

Heizer, Robert F.
1941   Aboriginal Trade Between the Southwest and California. *The Masterkey* 15(5):185-188.

————
1942   Massacre Lake Cave, Tule Lake Cave and Shore Sites. Pp. 121-134 in Archaeological Researches in the Northern Great Basin, by L.S. Cressman et al. *Carnegie Institution of Washington Publication* 538. Washington.

————
1942a   Walla Walla Indian Expeditions to the Sacramento Valley. *California Historical Society Quarterly* 21(1):1-7. San Francisco.

————
1944   Artifact Transport by Migratory Animals and Other Means. *American Antiquity* 9(4):395-400.

————
1949   The California Archaeological Survey. *American Antiquity* 14(3):222-223.

————
1950   Kutsavi: A Great Basin Indian Food. *Kroeber Anthropological Society Papers* 2:35-41. Berkeley, Calif.

————
1951   Preliminary Report on the Leonard Rockshelter Site, Pershing County, Nevada. *American Antiquity* 17(2):89-98.

————, ed.
1954   Notes on the Utah Utes by Edward Palmer, 1866-1877. *University of Utah Anthropological Papers* 17:1-8. Salt Lake City.

————
1956   Recent Cave Explorations in the Lower Humboldt Valley, Nevada. Pp. 50-57 in Papers on California Archaeology, 37-43. *University of California Archaeological Survey Reports* 33(42). Berkeley.

————
1960   Notes on Some Paviotso Personalities and Material Culture. *Nevada State Museum Anthropological Papers* 2. Carson City.

————, ed.
1962   Notes on the Utah Utes by Edward Palmer, 1866-1877. *Utah Archeology: A Newsletter* 8(3):7-14. Salt Lake City.

————
1966   Languages, Territories, and Names of California Indian Tribes. Berkeley: University of California Press.

————
1966a   General Comments. Pp. 239-247 in The Current Status of Anthropological Research in the Great Basin, 1964. Warren L. d'Azevedo et al., eds. *University of Nevada, Desert Research Institute Social Sciences and Humanities Publications* 1. Reno.

————
1967   Analysis of Human Coprolites from a Dry Nevada Cave. *University of California Archeological Survey Reports* 70(1):1-20. Berkeley.

————, ed.
1970   An Anthropological Expedition of 1913, or Get it Through Your Head, or Yours for the Revolution. Correspondence Between A.L. Kroeber and L.L. Loud, July 12, 1913 - October 31, 1913. Berkeley: University of California Research Facility.

————
1970a   Ethnographic Notes on the Northern Paiute of Humboldt Sink, West Central Nevada. Pp. 232-245 in Languages and Cultures of Western North America: Essays in Honor of Sven S. Liljeblad. Earl H. Swanson, Jr., ed. Pocatello: Idaho State University Press.

————
1974   Decorated Stone Discs from the Lower Humboldt Valley. Pp. 65-70 in Four Papers on Great Basin Anthropology. Robert F. Heizer, ed. *University of California Archaeological Research Facility Contributions* 21(4):65-70. Berkeley.

Heizer, Robert F., and Martin A. Baumhoff
1959   Great Basin Petroglyphs and Prehistoric Game Trails. *Science* 129(3353):904-905.

————
1961   The Archaeology of Wagon Jack Shelter. *University of California Anthropological Records* 20(4):119-138. Berkeley.

————
1962   Prehistoric Rock Art of Nevada and Eastern California. Berkeley: University of California Press.

————
1970   Big Game Hunters in the Great Basin: A Critical Review of the Evidence. Pp. 1-12 in Papers on the Anthropology of the Western Great Basin. *University of California Archaeological Research Facility Contributions* 7. Berkeley.

Heizer, Robert F., and Rainer Berger
1970   Radiocarbon Age of the Gypsum Cave Culture. *University of California Archaeological Research Facility Contributions* 7:13-18. Berkeley.

Heizer, Robert F., and C. William Clewlow, Jr.
1968   Projectile Points from Site NV-CH-15, Churchill County, Nevada. Pp. 59-88 in Papers on Great Basin Prehistory. *University of California Archaeological Survey Reports* 71. Berkeley.

————
1973   Prehistoric Rock Art of California. 2 vols. Ramona, Calif.: Ballena Press.

Heizer, Robert F., and Albert B. Elsasser
1953   Some Archaeological Sites and Cultures of the Central Sierra Nevada. *University of California Archaeological Survey Reports* 21. Berkeley.

Heizer, Robert F., and Thomas R. Hester
1970   Document 3c: Treaty Between Mohave and Chem-e-huevis Tribes, 1867. P. 111 in Papers on California Ethnography. *University of California Archaeological Research Facility Contributions* 9. Berkeley.

————
1978   Two Petroglyph Sites in Lincoln County, Nevada. Pp. 1-44 in Four Rock Art Studies. William C. Clewlow, Jr., ed. *Ballena Press Publications on North American Rock Art* 1. Socorro, N.M.

————
1978a   Great Basin Projectile Points: Forms and Chronology. *Ballena Press Publications in Archaeology, Ethnology, and History* 10. Socorro, N.M.

————
1978b   Great Basin. Pp. 147-199 in Chronologies in New World Archaeology. R.E. Taylor and Clement W. Meighan, eds. New York: Academic Press.

Heizer, Robert F., and Alex D. Krieger
1956   The Archaeology of Humboldt Cave, Churchill County, Ne-
            vada. *University of California Publications in American Ar-
            chaeology and Ethnology* 47(1):1-190. Berkeley.

Heizer, Robert F., and Lewis K. Napton
1969   Biological and Cultural Evidence from Prehistoric Human
            Coprolites. *Science* 165(3893):563-568.

————   Archaeological Investigations in Lovelock Cave, Nevada.
1970   *University of California Archaeological Research Facility
            Contributions* 10(1). Berkeley.

1970a   Archaeology and the Prehistoric Great Basin Lacustrine Sub-
            sistence Regime as Seen from Lovelock Cave, Nevada. *Uni-
            versity of California Archaeological Research Facility Con-
            tributions* 10. Berkeley.

Heizer, Robert F., and Karen M. Nissen
1977   Prehistoric Rock Art of Nevada and California. *IPEK: Jahr-
            buch für prähistorische und ethnographische Kunst* 24:148-
            157. Berlin.

Heizer, Robert F., and Adan E. Treganza
1944   Mines and Quarries of the Indians of California. *California
            Journal of Mines and Geology* 40:291-359.

————   Mines and Quarries of the Indians of California. Ramona,
1972   Calif.: Ballena Press.

Heizer, Robert F., Martin A. Baumhoff, and C. William Clewlow, Jr.
1968   The Archaeology of South Fork Shelter (NV-El-11), Elko
            County, Nevada. *University of California Archaeological Sur-
            vey Reports* 71:1-58. Berkeley.

Hemphill, Joseph A.
1970   The Development of Tribal Government on the Wind River
            Indian Reservation. (Unpublished M.A. Thesis in Anthro-
            pology, University of Illinois, Urbana.)

Henshaw, Henry W.
1883   Washoe. (Vocabulary). Carson City, Nevada. (Unpublished
            manuscript No. 963-a in National Anthropological Archives,
            Smithsonian Institution, Washington.)

1883a   Washoe - Washoan Family - (Vocabulary). Carson City, Ne-
            vada. (Unpublished manuscript No. 963-b in National An-
            thropological Archives, Smithsonian Institution, Washing-
            ton.)

1887   Perforated Stones from California. *Bureau of American Eth-
            nology Bulletin* 2. Washington.

1887a   [Linguistic Field Work: Work of Mr. H.W. Henshaw on
            Washoe, October-November, 1883]. P. xxx in *5th Annual
            Report of the Bureau of American Ethnology for the Years
            1883-1884*. Washington.

1910   Shoshoni. Pp. 554-558 in Vol. 2 of Handbook of American
            Indians North of Mexico. Frederick W. Hodge, ed. 2 vols.
            Bureau of American Ethnology Bulletin 30. Washington.

Hermann, Ruth
1972   The Paiutes of Pyramid Lake: A Narrative Concerning a
            Western Nevada Indian Tribe. San Jose, Calif.: Harlan-Young
            Press.

Herzog, George
1928   The Yuman Musical Style. *Journal of American Folk-Lore*
            41(160):183-231.

1935   Plains Ghost Dance and Great Basin Music. *American An-
            thropologist* 37(3):403-419.

Hester, Thomas R.
1973   Chronological Ordering of Great Basin Prehistory. *University
            of California Archaeological Research Facility Contributions*
            17. Berkeley.

Hewitt, Nancy J.
1980   Fiber Artifacts. Pp. 49-74 in Cowboy Cave, by Jesse D. Jen-
            nings. *University of Utah Anthropological Papers* 104. Salt
            Lake City.

Hill, Charles A., Jr., and Mozart I. Spector
1971   Natality and Mortality of American Indians Compared with
            U.S. Whites and Non-Whites. U.S. Health Services and Men-
            tal Health Administration Reports 86(3):229-246. Washing-
            ton.

Hill, Edward E.
1974   The Office of Indian Affairs, 1824-1880: Historical Sketches.
            New York: Clearwater.

Hill, Jane H.
1978   Language Contact Systems and Human Adaptations. *Journal
            of Anthropological Research* 34(1):1-26.

Hill, Joseph J.
1930   Spanish and Mexican Exploration and Trade Northwest from
            New Mexico into the Great Basin, 1765-1853. *Utah Historical
            Quarterly* 3(1):2-23. Salt Lake City.

Hill, Leonard M.
1968   Social and Economic Survey of Shivwits, Kanosh, Koosha-
            rem, Indian Peaks and Cedar City Bands of Southern Paiute
            Indians, by the U.S. Department of the Interior, Bureau of
            Indian Affairs. (Manuscript in possession of Catherine S.
            Fowler.)

Hill, Mary R.
1972   The Great Owens Valley Earthquake of 1872. *California Di-
            vision of Mines and Geology, California Geology* 25(3):51-
            54. Sacramento.

Hill, W.W.
1948   Navaho Trading and Trading Ritual: A Study of Cultural
            Dynamics. *Southwestern Journal of Anthropology* 4(4):371-
            396.

Hillebrand, Timothy S.
1972   The Archaeology of the Coso Locality of the Northern Mo-
            jave Region of California. (Unpublished Ph.D. Dissertation
            in Anthropology, University of California, Santa Barbara.)

Hilty, Ivy E., Jean H. Peters, Eva M. Benson, Margaret A. Edwards,
and Lorraine T. Miller
1972   Nutritive Values of Native Foods of the Warm Springs In-
            dians. *Oregon State University Extension Service Circular* 809.
            Corvallis.

Hitchcock, C. Leo, and Arthur Cronquist
1978   Flora of the Pacific Northwest: An Illustrated Manual. Se-
            attle: University of Washington Press.

Hittman, Michael
1972   An Ethnohistory of Smith and Mason Valley Paiutes. (Draft
            copy of Ph.D. Dissertation, Department of Anthropology,
            University of New Mexico. Albuquerque, N.M.; copy in pos-
            session of Joseph G. Jorgensen.)

1973   Ghost Dances, Disillusionment and Opiate Addiction: An
            Ethnohistory of Smith and Mason Valley Paiutes. (Unpub-
            lished Ph.D. Dissertation in Anthropology, University of New
            Mexico, Albuquerque.)

1973a   Factionalism in a Northern Paiute Tribe as a Consequence
            of the Indian Reorganization Act. Pp. 20-37 in Native Amer-
            ican Politics: Power Relationships in the Western Great Basin
            Today. R.M. Houghton, ed. Reno: University of Nevada,
            Bureau of Governmental Research.

1973b   The 1870 Ghost Dance on the Walker River Reservation: A
            Reconstruction. *Ethnohistory* 20(3):247-278.

Hodge, Frederick W., ed.
1907-1910   Handbook of American Indians North of Mexico 2 vols. *Bu-
            reau of American Ethnology Bulletin* 30. Washington. (Re-
            printed: Pageant Books, New York, 1960; Rowman and Lit-
            tlefield, New York, 1971.)

1920   Hawikuh Bonework. *Museum of the American Indian, Heye Foundation, Indian Notes and Monographs* 3(3). New York.

Hoebel, E. Adamson
1935   The Sun Dance of the Hekandika Shoshone. *American Anthropologist* 37(4):570-581.

1938   Bands and Distributions of the Eastern Shoshone. *American Anthropologist* 40(3):385-415.

1939   Comanche and Hɜkandika Shoshone Relationship Systems. *American Anthropologist* 41(3):440-457.

1940   The Political Organization and Law-ways of the Comanche Indians. *Memoirs of the American Anthropological Association* 54. Menasha, Wis.

Hoffman, Walter J.
1878   Miscellaneous Ethnological Observations on Indians Inhabiting Nevada, California, and Arizona. Pp. 461-478 in *10th Annual Report of the U.S. Geological and Geographical Survey of the Territories for the Year 1876*. F.V. Hayden, ed. Washington: U.S. Government Printing Office.

1886   Remarks on Indian Tribal Names. *Proceedings of the American Philosophical Society* 23(122):294-303. Philadelphia.

Hoffmann, C.F.
1868   Notes on Hetch-Hetchy Valley. *Proceedings of the California Academy of Science* 3(5):368-370. San Francisco.

Hoffmeister, Harold
1945   The Consolidated Ute Indian Reservation. *Geographical Review* 35(4):601-623.

Hogan, Patrick F.
1980   The Analysis of Coprolites from Cowboy Cave. Pp. 201-211 in Cowboy Cave, by Jesse D. Jennings. *University of Utah Anthropological Papers* 104. Salt Lake City.

Hoijer, Harry
1946   Introduction. Pp. 9-29 in Linguistic Structures of Native America. *Viking Fund Publications in Anthropology* 6. New York. (Reprinted: Johnson Reprint Corporation, New York, 1963.)

1949   An Analytical Dictionary of the Tonkawa Language. *University of California Publications in Linguistics* 5(1):1-74. Berkeley.

1954   Some Problems of American Indian Linguistic Research. Pp. 3-12 in Papers from the Symposium on American Indian Linguistics Held at Berkeley July 7, 1951. *University of California Publications in Linguistics* 10. Berkeley.

1954a   [Comment on] Newman's American Indian Linguistics in the Southwest, 1954. *American Anthropologist* 56(4):637-639.

Holeman, J.H.
1853   Report No. 64 of, Indian Agent, Utah Territory, to His Excellency Brigham Young, Superintendent of Indian Affairs, Utah Territory. Pp. 439-447 in Report of the Commissioner of Indian Affairs for 1852. *32d Cong., 2d sess., Senate Executive Doc.* No. 1 (Serial No. 658). Washington.

Holliman, Rhodes B.
1967   Engraved Basalt Stones from the Great Salt Desert, Utah. *Southwestern Lore* 32(4):86-87.

1969   Further Studies on Incised Stones from the Great Salt Lake Desert, Utah. *Southwestern Lore* 35(2):23-25.

Holm, Bill
1981   Crow-Nez Perce Otterskin Bowcase-quivers. *American Indian Art Magazine* 6(4):60-70.

Holmer, Richard N.
1978   A Mathematical Typology for Archaic Projectile Points of the Eastern Great Basin. (Unpublished Ph.D. Dissertation in Anthropology, University of Utah, Salt Lake City.)

1979   Archeological Survey of Exxon Mineral Leases, Lake Mead National Recreation Area. *Western Anasazi Reports* 2(1):3-38. Cedar City, Utah.

1980   Fremont versus Archaic Subsistence: Is There a Difference? (Paper presented at the 17th Great Basin Anthropological Conference, Salt Lake City.)

1985   Projectile Points of the Intermountain Region. In Anthropology of the Desert West: Essays in Honor of Jesse D. Jennings. Carol J. Condie and Don D. Fowler, eds. Salt Lake City: University of Utah Press.

Holmer, Richard N., and Dennis G. Weder
1980   Common Post-Archaic Projectile Points from the Fremont Area. Pp. 55-68 in Fremont Perspectives. David B. Madsen, ed. *Utah Division of State History, Antiquities Section Selected Papers* 7(16). Salt Lake City.

Holmes, William H.
1879   Notes on an Extensive Deposit of Obsidian in Yellowstone National Park. *American Naturalist* 13(4):247-250.

1886   Pottery of the Ancient Pueblos. Pp. 257-360 in *4th Annual Report of the Bureau of American Ethnology for the Years 1882-1883*. Washington.

1914   Areas of American Culture Characterization Tentatively Outlined as an Aid in the Study of Antiquities. *American Anthropologist* 16(3):413-446.

Holmgren, Arthur H., and James L. Reveal
1966   Checklist of the Vascular Plants of the Intermountain Region. *U.S. Forest Service Research Paper* INT-32. Ogden, Utah.

Honacki, James H., Kenneth E. Kinman, and James W. Koeppl
1982   Mammal Species of the World: A Taxonomic and Geographic Reference. Lawrence, Kans.: Allen Press and the Association of Systematics Collections.

Hooke, Roger LeB.
1972   Geomorphic Evidence for Late-Wisconsin and Holocene Tectonic Deformation, Death Valley, California. *Geological Society of America Bulletin* 83(7):2073-2098. Boulder.

Hoopes, Alban W.
1932   Indian Affairs and Their Administration, with Special Reference to the Far West, 1849-1860. Philadelphia: University of Pennsylvania Press.

Hoover, J.D.
1974   Periodic Quaternary Volcanism in the Black Rock Desert, Utah. *Brigham Young University Geological Studies* 21. Provo, Utah.

Hopkins, Nicholas A.
1965   Great Basin Prehistory and Uto-Aztecan. *American Antiquity* 31(1):48-60.

Hopkins, Sarah Winnemucca
1883   Life Among the Piutes: Their Wrongs and Claims. Mrs. Horace Mann, ed. Boston: Cupples, Upham. (Reprinted: Chalfant Press, Bishop, Calif., 1969).

Houghton, John G.
1969   Characteristics of Rainfall in the Great Basin. Reno, Nev.: Desert Research Institute.

Houghton, John G., Clarence M. Sakamoto, and Richard O. Gifford
1975   Nevada's Weather and Climate. *Nevada Bureau of Mines and Geology, Special Publication* 2. Reno.

Houghton, Ruth M.
1968   The Fort McDermitt Indian Reservation: Social Structure and the Distribution of Political and Economic Power. (Unpublished M.A. Thesis in Anthropology, University of Oregon, Eugene.)

1973   Adaptive Strategies in an American Indian Reservation Community: The War on Poverty, 1965-1971. (Unpublished Ph.D. Dissertation in Anthropology, University of Oregon, Eugene.)

————, ed.
1973a   Native American Politics: Power Relationships in the Western Great Basin Today. Reno: University of Nevada, Bureau of Governmental Research.

Howard, Oliver O.
1887   Indian War Papers: Causes of the Piute and Bannock War. *Overland Monthly* 9(53):492-498.

Howe, Carrol B.
1968   Ancient Tribes of the Klamath County. Portland, Oreg.: Binfords and Mort.

Howell, Paul W.
1960   Interpretation of the Past Climate Represented at Stuart Rockshelter from the Soluble Salt Content of Its Strata. Pp. 23-25 (App. A) in Stuart Rockshelter: A Stratified Site in Southern Nevada, by Dick Shutler, Jr., Mary E. Shutler, and James S. Griffith. *Nevada State Museum Anthropological Papers* 3. Carson City.

Hubbs, Carl L., and Robert R. Miller
1948   The Zoological Evidence: Correlation Between Fish Distribution and Hydrographic History of the Desert Basins of the Western United States. Pp. 17-166 in The Great Basin, with Emphasis on Glacial and Postglacial Times. *Bulletin of the University of Utah* 38(20), *Biological Series* 10(7). Salt Lake City.

Hubbs, Carl L., Robert R. Miller, and Laura C. Hubbs
1974   Hydrographic History and Relict Fishes of the North-central Great Basin. *Memoirs of the California Academy of Sciences* 7:1-259.

Hudson, J.W.H.
[1902] [Unpublished Fieldnotes on the Washoe, Northern Paiute, Owens Valley Paiute, etc.] (Unpublished manuscript and collections catalog in Field Museum of Natural History, Chicago.)

[1904] [Unpublished Fieldnotes on the Washoe, Northern Paiute, Owens Valley Paiute, etc.] (Unpublished manuscript at the Sun House, Ukiah, Calif.; copy in possession of Lawrence E. Dawson).

Hughes, John T.
1848   Doniphan's Expedition: Containing an Account of the Conquest of New Mexico; General Kearney's Overland Expedition to California; Doniphan's Campaign Against the Navajo; His Unparalleled March Upon Chihuahua and Durango...Cincinnati, Ohio: J.A. and U.P. James.

Hughes, Richard E.
1978   Aspects of Prehistoric Wiyot Exchange and Social Ranking. *Journal of California Anthropology* 5(1):53-66.

1982   Age and Exploitation of Obsidian from the Medicine Lake Highland, California. *Journal of Archaeological Science* 9(2):173-185. London.

1983   X-ray Fluorescence Characterization of Obsidian. Pp. 401-408 in The Archaeology of Monitor Valley, 2: Gatecliff Shelter, by David H. Thomas. *Anthropological Papers of the American Museum of Natural History* 59(1). New York.

1983a   Exploring Diachronic Variability in Obsidian Procurement Patterns in Northeast California and Southcentral Oregon: Geochemical Characterization of Obsidian Sources and Projectile Points by Energy Dispersive X-ray Fluorescence. (Unpublished Ph.D. Dissertation in Anthropology, University of California, Davis.)

1984   Notes on Hogup Cave and Danger Cave Obsidian. (Unpublished manuscript in Hughes' possession.)

1984a   Obsidian Studies in the Great Basin. *University of California Archaeological Research Facility Contributions* 45:1-19. Berkeley.

1985   Obsidian Source Use at Hidden Cave. Pp. 332-353 in The Archaeology of Hidden Cave Nevada. by David H. Thomas. *Anthropological Papers of the American Museum of Natural History* 61(1). New York.

1986   Trace Element Composition of Obsidian Butte, Imperial County, California. *Bulletin of the Southern California Academy of Sciences* 85. In press.

Hughes, Richard E., and Robert L. Bettinger
1984   Obsidian and Prehistoric Sociocultural Systems in California. Pp. 153-172 in Exploring the Limits: Frontiers and Boundaries in Prehistory. Suzanne P. De Atley and Frank J. Findlow, eds. *British Archaeological Reports, International Series* 223. Oxford.

Hughes, Richard E., and D.L. True
1985   Perspectives on the Distribution of Obsidians in San Diego County, California. *North American Archaeologist* 6(4):325-339.

Hull, Frank W., and Alec Avery
1980   Cultural Resources Existing Data Inventory, Richfield District, Utah. Salt Lake City: Utah Bureau of Land Management.

Hull, Frank W., and Nancy M. White
1980   Spindle Whorls, Incised and Painted Stone, and Unfired Clay Objects. Pp. 117-125 in Cowboy Cave, by Jesse D. Jennings. *University of Utah Anthropological Papers* 104. Salt Lake City.

Hulse, F.S., comp.
1935   Fort Independence Paiute Ethnographic Notes. (Unpublished manuscript in Bancroft Library, University Archives, University of California, Berkeley.)

Hulse, James W.
[1981] The Pyramid Lake Fishery (1874-1944) and the Case of United States v. Orr Water Ditch Company et al. (1913-1944): A Historical Narrative. (Unpublished manuscript in Omer C. Stewart's possession.)

Hultkrantz, Åke
[1948-1958] [Wind River Shoshone Fieldnotes.] (Manuscripts in Hultkrantz's possession.)

1951   The Concept of the Soul Held by the Wind River Shoshone. *Ethnos* 16(1-2):18-44. Stockholm.

1953   Conceptions of the Soul Among North American Indians: A Study in Religious Ethnology. *Statens Ethnografiska Museum, Monograph Series Publications* 1. Stockholm.

1954   The Indians and the Wonders of Yellowstone: A Study of the Interrelations of Religion, Nature and Culture. *Ethnos* 19(1-4):34-68. Stockholm.

1955   The Origin of Death Myth as Found Among the Wind River Shoshoni Indians. *Ethnos* 20(2-3):127-136. Stockholm.

1956   Configurations of Religious Belief Among the Wind River Shoshoni. *Ethnos* 21(3-4):194-215. Stockholm.

1957   The North American Indian Orpheus Tradition: A Contribution to Comparative Religion. *Statens Ethnografiska Museum, Monograph Series Publications* 2. Stockholm.

1958   Tribal Divisions within the Eastern Shoshoni of Wyoming. Pp. 148-154 in *Proceedings of the 32d International Congress of Americanists*. Copenhagen, 1956.

1960   Religious Aspects of the Wind River Shoshoni Folklore Literature. Pp. 552-569 in Culture in History: Essays in Honor of Paul Radin. Stanley Diamond, ed. New York: Columbia University Press.

1961   The Shoshones in the Rocky Mountain Area. *Annals of Wyoming* 33(1):19-41. Cheyenne.

1961a   The Masters of the Animals Among the Wind River Shoshoni. *Ethnos* 26 (4):198-218. Stockholm.

1961b   The Owner of the Animals in the Religion of the North American Indians: Some General Remarks. Pp. 53-64 in The Supernatural Owners of Nature: Nordic Symposium on the Religious Conceptions of Ruling Spirits and Allied Concepts. Åke Hultkrantz, ed. *Acta Universitatis Stockholmiensis: Stockholm Studies in Comparative Religion* 1. Stockholm.

1962   Religion und Mythologie der Prärie-Schoschonen. Pp. 546-554 in *Proceedings of the 34th International Congress of Americanists*. Vienna, 1960.

1962a   Spirit Lodge, a North American Shamanistic Seance. Pp. 32-68 in Studies in Shamanism: Papers Read at the Symposium on Shamanism, Turku, Finland, 1962. Carl Martin Edsman, ed. *Scripta Instituti Donneriani Aboensis* 1. Stockholm.

1966   An Ecological Approach to Religion. *Ethnos* 31(1-4):131-150. Stockholm.

1966a   North American Indian Religion in the History of Research: A General Survey. Pt. 1. *History of Religions* 6(2):91-107.

1966-1967   The Ethnological Position of the Sheepeater Indians in Wyoming. *Folk* 8-9:155-163. Copenhagen.

1968   Shoshoni Indians on the Plains: An Appraisal of the Documentary Evidence. *Zeitschrift für Ethnologie* 93(1-2):49-72.

1969   Pagan and Christian Elements in the Religious Syncretism Among the Shoshoni Indians of Wyoming. Pp. 15-40 in Syncretism. Sven S. Hartman, ed. *Scripta Instituti Donneriani Aboensis* 3:15-40. Stockholm.

1970   The Source Literature on the "Tukudïka" Indians in Wyoming: Facts and Fancies. Pp. 246-264 in Languages and Cultures of Western North America: Essays in Honor of Sven S. Liljeblad. Earl H. Swanson, Jr., ed. Pocatello: Idaho State University Press.

1970a   Attitudes to Animals in Shoshoni Indian Religion. *Temenos: Studies in Comparative Religion* 4(2):70-79. Helsinki.

1971   The Structure of Theistic Beliefs Among North American Plains Indians. *Temenos: Studies in Comparative Religion* 7:66-74. Helsinki.

1971a   Yellow Hand, Chief and Medicineman Among the Eastern Shoshone. Pp. 293-304 in Vol. 2 of *Proceedings of the 38th International Congress of Americanists*. Stuttgart-München, 1968.

1973   Prairie and Plains Indians. *Iconography of Religions* 10(2). Leiden, The Netherlands: E.J. Brill.

1974   The Shoshones in the Rocky Mountain Area. Arne Magnus, trans. Pp. 173-214 in Shoshone Indians. (*American Indian Ethnohistory: California and Basin-Plateau Indians*) New York: Garland.

1976   Religion and Ecology Among the Great Basin Indians. Pp. 137-150 in The Realm of the Extra-human: Ideas and Actions. A. Bharati, ed. The Hague: Mouton.

1979   The Fear of Geysers Among Indians of the Yellowstone Park Area. Pp. 33-42 in Lifeways of Intermontane and Plains Montana Indians. Leslie B. Davis, ed. *Museum of the Rockies Occasional Papers* 1. Bozeman, Mont.

1981   Accommodation and Persistence: Ecological Analysis of the Religion of the Sheepeater Indians in Wyoming, U.S.A. *Temenos: Studies in Comparative Religion* 17:35-44. Helsinki.

1981a   Belief and Worship in Native America. Syracuse, N.Y.: Syracuse University Press.

Humfreville, James L.
1903   Twenty Years Among Our Hostile Indians. 2d ed. New York: Hunter.

Hunt, Alice P.
1953   Archeological Survey of the La Sal Mountain Area, Utah. *University of Utah Anthropological Papers* 14. Salt Lake City.

1960   Archeology of the Death Valley Salt Pan, California. *University of Utah Anthropological Papers* 47. Salt Lake City. (Reprinted: Johnson Reprint Corporation, New York, 1971.)

Hunt, Alice P., and Charles B. Hunt
1964   Archeology of the Ash Meadows Quadrangle, California and Nevada. (Manuscript on file, Dealth Valley National Monument, Death Valley, Calif.)

Hunt, Alice P., and Dallas Tanner
1960   Early Man Sites Near Moab, Utah. *American Antiquity* 26(1):110-117.

Hunt, Charles B.
1967   Physiography of the United States. San Francisco: W.H. Freeman.

_____, ed.
1982   Pleistocene Lake Bonneville, Ancestral Great Salt Lake as Described in the Notebooks of G.K. Gilbert, 1875-1880. *Brigham Young University Geology Studies* 29(1). Provo, Utah.

Hunt, Charles B., and Don R. Mabey
1966   Stratigraphy and Structure, Death Valley, California. *U.S. Geological Survey Professional Paper* 494-A. Washington.

Hunt, Charles B., T.W. Robinson, Walter A. Bowels, and A.L. Washburn.
1966   Hydrologic Basin, Death Valley, California. *U.S. Geological Survey Professional Paper* 494-B. Washington.

Huntley, J., and W. Nance
1979   More Incised Cobbles. *Idaho Archaeologist* 3(2):8-9.

Hurst, Winston, and Bruce D. Louthan
1979   Survey of Rock Art in the Central Portion of Nine Mile Canyon, Eastern Utah. *Brigham Young University Publications in Archaeology*, n.s. 4. Provo, Utah.

Hurt, Garland
1876   Indians of Utah. Pp. 459-464 (App. O) in Report of Explorations Across the Great Basin of the Territory of Utah for a Direct Wagon-route from Camp Floyd to Genoa, in Carson Valley in 1859, by Captain James H. Simpson. Washington: U.S. Government Printing Office.

Hutchings, Selar S., and George Stewart
1953   Increasing Forage Yields and Sheep Production on Intermountain Winter Ranges. *U.S. Department of Agriculture Circular* 925. Washington.

Hutchinson, Phil W.
1982   Bird Shaped Artifact. (Paper presented at the 18th Great Basin Anthropological Conference, Reno, Nevada, September 30-October 2, 1982; manuscript in Department of Anthropology, Nevada State Museum, Carson City.)

Hyde, Dayton O.
1973   The Last Free Man: The True Story Behind the Massacre of Shoshone Mike and His Band of Indians in 1911. New York: Dial Press.

Hymes, Dell H.
1960   Lexicostatistics So Far. *Current Anthropology* 1(1):3-40.

1965   Some North Pacific Coast Poems: A Problem in Anthropological Philology. *American Anthropologist* 67(2):316-341.

Hyne, Norman J., Paul Chelminski, James E. Court, Don S. Gorsline, Charles R. Goldman
1972   Quaternary History of Lake Tahoe, California-Nevada. *Geological Society of America Bulletin* 83(5): 1435-1448. Boulder.

IAW = Indians at Work
1934-1945   Indians at Work. 12 vols. Washington: U.S. Department of the Interior, Office of Indian Affairs.

Iannucci, David E.
1973   Numic Historical Phonology. (Unpublished Ph.D. Dissertation in Linguistics, Cornell University, Ithaca, N.Y.)

Iddings, Joseph P.
1888   Obsidian Cliff, Yellowstone National Park. Pp. 249-295 in *7th Annual Report of the U.S. Geological Survey for the Years 1885-1886.* Washington.

Ingalls, G.W.
1913   Indians of Nevada, 1825-1913. Pp. 20-189 in History of Nevada. Sam P. Davis, ed. 2 vols. Reno, Nev.: Elms Publishing Company.

Institute for the Development of Indian Law
1973   A Chronological List of Treaties and Agreements Made by Indian Tribes with the United States. Washington: Institute for the Development of Indian Law.

1975   Treaties and Agreements of the Indian Tribes of the Pacific Northwest. Washington: Institute for the Development of Indian Law.

1975a   Treaties and Agreements of the Indian Tribes of the Southwest; Including Western Oklahoma. Washington: Institute for the Development of Indian Law.

Inter-Tribal Council of Nevada
1974   Personal Reflections of the Shoshone, Paiute, Washo. Reno: Inter-Tribal Council of Nevada.

1974a   Life Stories of Our Native People: Shoshone, Paiute, Washo. Reno: Inter-Tribal Council of Nevada.

1976   Nuwuvi: A Southern Paiute History. Reno: Inter-Tribal Council of Nevada.

1976a   Numa: A Northern Paiute History. Reno: Inter-Tribal Council of Nevada.

1976b   Newe: A Western Shoshone History. Reno: Inter-Tribal Council of Nevada.

1976c   Wa She Shu: A Washo Tribal History. Reno: Inter-Tribal Council of Nevada.

Irish, O.H.
1865   Articles of Agreement and Convention Made and Concluded at Pinto Creek in the Territory of Utah this Eighteenth Day of September, Eighteen Hundred and Sixty-Five, by O.H. Irish, Superintendent of Indian Affairs for Said Territory, and the Undersigned Chiefs, Head-men and Delegates of the Pi-ede and Pah-Ute Tribe or Band of Indians Occupying Lands within Utah Territory. In Utah Superintendency, 1849-80, Letters Received by the Office of Indian Affairs, 1824-80, Reels 897-906. *National Archives Microfilm Publications* 234. Washington.

Irvine, C.A.
1969   The Desert Bighorn Sheep of Southwestern Utah. *Utah State Department of Natural Resources, Division of Fish and Game Publication* 69-12. Salt Lake City.

Irving, Washington
1837   The Rocky Mountains; or Scenes, Incidents, and Adventures in the Far West...: The Journal of Captain B.L.E. Bonneville, U.S.A. 2 vols. Philadelphia: Carey, Lea and Blanchard.

Irwin, Charles N., ed.
1980   The Shoshoni Indians of Inyo County, California: The Kerr Manuscript. *Ballena Press Publications in Archaeology, Ethnology and History* 15. Socorro, N.M.

Ives, Joseph C. *see* U.S. Army. Corps of Topographical Engineers

Izett, Glen A.
1981   Volcanic Ash Beds: Recorders of Upper Cenozoic Silicic Pyroclastic Volcanism in the Western United States. *Journal of Geophysical Research* 86(11):10200-10222.

Izett, Glen A., Ray E. Wilcox, H.A. Powers, and G.A. Desborough
1970   The Bishop Ash Bed, a Pleistocene Marker Bed in the Western United States. *Quaternary Research* 1(1):121-132.

Jablow, Joseph
1951   The Cheyenne in Plains Indian Trade Relations, 1795-1840. *Monographs of the American Ethnological Society* 19. New York.

Jack, Jennifer
1978   Analysis of the Resources Used by the Washo Indians. (Unpublished manuscript, in Department of Anthropology, University of Nevada, Reno.)

Jack, Robert N.
1971   The Source of Obsidian Artifacts in Northern Arizona. *Plateau* 43(3):103-114.

1974   Final Results of the Northwest Obsidian Analyses. (Unpublished report in Jack's possession.)

1976   Prehistoric Obsidian in California, I: Geochemical Aspects. Pp. 183-217 in Advances in Obsidian Glass Studies: Archaeological and Geochemical Perspectives. R.E. Taylor, ed. Park Ridge, N.J.: Noyes Press.

Jack, Robert N., and I.S.E. Carmichael
1969   The Chemical 'Fingerprinting' of Acid Volcanic Rocks. *California Division of Mines and Geology Special Report* 100:17-32. San Francisco.

Jackson, Donald, ed.
1962   Letters of the Lewis & Clark Expedition with Related Documents, 1783-1854. Urbana: University of Illinois Press. (Second revised edition in 1978.)

Jackson, Thomas L.
1974   The Economics of Obsidian in Central California Prehistory: Applications of X-ray Fluorescence in Spectrometry in Archaeology. (Unpublished M.A. Thesis in Anthropology, San Francisco State University, San Francisco.)

Jackson, W., coll.
1955   [14 Washoe Songs; Ray James, Hank Pete, Singers.] (In Department of Anthropology, University of Nevada, Reno.)

Jacobs, Mary Jane Threlkeld
1974   Termination of Federal Supervision Over the Southern Paiute Indians of Utah. (Unpublished M.S. Thesis in History, University of Utah, Salt Lake City)

Jacobsen, William H., Jr.
1955   [Washo Terms for Plants and Animals.] (Unpublished manuscript in Jacobsen's possession.)

1958   Washo and Karok: An Approach to Comparative Hokan. *International Journal of American Linguistics* 24(3):195-212.

1964   A Grammar of the Washo Language. (Unpublished Ph.D. Dissertation in Linguistics, University of California, Berkeley.)

1966   Washo Linguistic Studies. Pp. 113-136 in The Current Status of Anthropological Research in the Great Basin: 1964. Warren L. d'Azevedo et al., eds. *University of Nevada, Desert Research Institute Social Sciences and Humanities Publications* 1. Reno.

1966a   Comments on Linguistics. Pp. 259-264 in The Current Status of Anthropological Research in the Great Basin: 1964. Warren L. d'Azevedo et al., eds. *University of Nevada, Desert Research Institute Social Sciences and Humanities Publications* 1. Reno.

1967   Switch-reference in Hokan-Coahuiltecan. Pp. 238-263 in Studies in Southwestern Ethnolinguistics: Meaning and History in the Languages of the American Southwest. Dell H. Hymes with William E. Bittle, eds. (*Studies in General Anthropology* 3) The Hague: Mouton.

1968   Comment on James A. Goss's "Culture-historical Inference from Utaztekan Linguistic Evidence." Pp. 43-52 in Utaztekan Prehistory. Earl H. Swanson, Jr., ed. *Occasional Papers of the Idaho State University Museum* 22. Pocatello.

1968a   On the Prehistory of Nez Perce Vowel Harmony. *Language* 44(4):819-829.

1973   A Rhythmic Principle in Washo Morphotactics. (Paper presented to the Symposium on California Indian Linguistics, Annual Meeting, Southwestern Anthropological Association, San Francisco.)

1976   Observations on the Yana Stop Series in Relationship to Problems of Comparative Hokan Phonology. Pp. 203-236 in Hokan Studies: Papers from the First Conference on Hokan Languages Held in San Diego, California, April 23-25, 1970. Margaret Langdon and Shirley Silver, eds. (*Janua Linguarum Series Practica* 181) The Hague: Mouton.

1977   A Glimpse of the Pre-Washo Pronominal System. Pp. 55-73 in Proceedings of the Third Annual Meeting of the Berkeley Linguistics Society, February 19-21, 1977. Kenneth Whistler et al., eds. Berkeley, Calif.: Berkeley Linguistics Society.

1978   Washo Internal Diversity and External Relations. Pp. 115-147 in Selected Papers from the 14th Great Basin Anthropological Conference. Donald R. Tuohy, ed. *Ballena Press Publications in Archaeology, Ethnology and History* 11. Socorro, N.M.

1979   Hokan Inter-branch Comparisons. Pp. 545-591 in The Languages of Native America: Historical and Comparative Assessment. Lyle Campbell and Marianne Mithun, eds. Austin: University of Texas Press.

1979a   Why Does Washo Lack a Passive? Pp. 145-160 in Ergativity: Toward a Theory of Grammatical Relations. Frans Plank, ed., London: Academic Press.

1979b   Gender and Personification in Washo. *Journal of California and Great Basin Anthropology, Papers in Linguistics* 1:75-84.

1980   Washo Bipartite Verb Stems. Pp. 85-99 in American Indian and Indoeuropean Studies: Papers in Honor of Madison S. Beeler. Kathryn Klar, Margaret Langdon, and Shirley Silver, eds. (*Trends in Linguistics, Studies and Monographs* 16). The Hague: Mouton.

1980a   Inclusive/Exclusive: A Diffused Pronominal Category in Native Western North America. Pp. 204-227 in Papers from the Parasession on Pronouns and Anaphora, Chicago Linguistic Society, April 18-19, 1980. Jody Kreiman and Almerindo E. Ojeda, eds. Chicago: Chicago Linguistic Society.

1980b   Reduplication in Washo: An Alternative Hypothesis. (Paper presented to the History West and East Session, 19th Conference on American Indian Languages, 79th Annual Meeting of the American Anthropological Association, Washington.)

1981   Headless Relative Clauses in Washo. (Paper presented to the Conference on the Syntax of Native American Languages, Calgary, Alta.)

1983   Typological and Genetic Notes on Switch-reference Systems in North American Indian Languages. Pp. 151-183 in Proceedings of a Symposium on Switch-reference and Universal Grammar, Winnipeg, May, 1981. John Haiman and Pamela Munro, eds. (*Typological Studies in Language* 2) Amsterdam: John Benjamins Publishing Company.

1984   Washo Linguistic Prehistory. (Paper presented to the 1984 Hokan-Penutian Workshop, Berkeley, Calif.)

1985   The Heterogeneity of Evidentials in Makah. Pp.75-77 in Evidentiality: The Linguistic Coding of Epistemology, Wallace L. Chafe and Johanna Nichols, eds. Norwood, N.J.: Ablex. In press.

Jaeger, Edmund C.
1941   Desert Wild Flowers. Palo Alto, Calif.: Stanford University Press. (3d ed. in 1969.)

1957   The North American Deserts. Stanford, Calif.: Stanford University Press.

James, Edwin
1823   An Account of an Expedition from Pittsburgh to the Rocky Mountains Performed in the Years 1819 and '20, by Order of the Hon. J.C. Calhoun, Sec'y of War: Under the Command of Major Stephen H. Long. 2 vols. Philadelphia: Corey and Lea.

James, George W.
1902   Indian Basketry, 2d ed. Pasadena, Calif.: Privately Printed for the author.

James, Steven R., ed.
1981   Prehistory, Ethnohistory, and History of Eastern Nevada: A Cultural Resources Summary of the Elko and Ely Districts. *Nevada Bureau of Land Management, Cultural Resource Series* 3. Reno.

1983   An Early Incised Stone from Danger Cave, Utah. (Manuscript in Department of Anthropology, Nevada State Museum, Carson City.)

1983a   Test Excavations at the Indian Creek Archaeological Sites, Alpine County, California. *Intermountain Research Reports, CR Report* 3-831(P). Silver City, Nev.

James, Steven R., and Robert G. Elston
1983   A Class II Archaeological Survey in the Mt. Hope Vicinity, Eureka County, Nevada. (Report prepared for Exxon Minerals Corporation, Houston, Texas; manuscript on file at Intermountain Research, Silver City, Nev.)

James, Steven R., and David J. Singer
1980   Cultural Resources Existing Data Inventory, Salt Lake District, Utah. Salt Lake City: Utah Bureau of Land Management.

James, Steven R., and Charles D. Zeier
1981   The White Pine Power Project: Cultural Resource Considerations Vol. 2: An Archaeological Reconnaissance of Eight Candidate Siting Locations in White Pine County, Nevada. (Report prepared for Dames and Moore, Inc., Los Angeles, by Intermountain Research, Silver City, Nev.)

James, Steven R., Bonnie Brown, and Robert G. Elston
1982   Archaeological Investigations at the Vista Site (26WA3017), Washoe County, Nevada. (Report on file at Intermountain Research, Silver City, Nev.)

Jameson, Sydney J.S.
1958   Archeological Notes on Stansbury Island. *University of Utah Anthropological Papers* 34. Salt Lake City.

Janetski, Joel C., ed.
1980   MX Cultural Resources Studies: Regional Cultural Re-
            sources Survey Area C. (Draft report) Santa Barbara, Calif.:
            HDR Sciences.

1980a   Wood and Reed Artifacts. Pp. 75-95 in Cowboy Cave, by
            Jesse Jennings. *University of Utah Anthropological Papers*
            104. Salt Lake City.

————, ed.
1983   Preliminary Report of Archaeological Investigations at Spar-
            row Hawk (42To261) in Tooele County, Utah. *Brigham Young
            University, Department of Anthropology Technical Series* 89-
            5. Provo, Utah.

1983a   The Western Ute of Utah Valley: An Ethnohistoric Model
            of Lakeside Adaptation. (Unpublished Ph.D. Dissertation in
            Anthropology, University of Utah, Salt Lake City.)

Janetski, Joel C., and Richard N. Holmer, eds.
1982   The Intermountain Power Project Cultural Resource Survey.
            Intermountain - Adelanto Bipole I Transmission Line Right-
            of-way, Utah Section. *University of Utah, Archaeological
            Center Report of Investigation* 81-20. Salt Lake City.

Jefferson, James, Robert W. Delaney, and C. Gregory Thompson
1972   The Southern Utes: A Tribal History. Floyd A. O'Neil, ed.
            Ignacio, Colo.: The Southern Ute Tribe.

Jefferson, Thomas
[1792]   Vocabulary. [Blank schedule of 276 words on a broadside.]
            (Manuscript No. 185(18), Freeman No. 2051, in American
            Philosophical Society Library, Philadelphia.)

1964   Notes on the State of Virginia [1782]. New York: Harper
            and Row.

————, et al.
1799   Circular Letter. *Transactions of the American Philosophical
            Society* 4:xxxvii-xxxix. Philadelphia.

Jenkins, Dennis L., and Claude N. Warren
1983   Obsidian Hydration and the Age of Pinto Points. (Paper
            presented at the Southwest Anthropological Conference, San
            Diego, Calif.)

Jenkins, Dennis L., Claude N. Warren, and Thomas Wheeler
1984   Test Excavation and Data Recovery at the Awl Site, SBr-
            4562: A Pinto Site at Fort Irwin, San Bernardino County,
            California. (Fort Irwin Archaeological Project Research Re-
            port. Prepared for Interagency Archaeological Services, Na-
            tional Park Service, Western Region, San Francisco.)

Jennings, Jesse D.
1953   Danger Cave: A Progress Summary. *El Palacio* 60(5):179-
            213.

————, ed.
1956   The American Southwest: A Problem in Cultural Isola-
            tion. Pp. 59-127 in Seminars in Archaeology, 1955. Robert
            Wauchope, ed. *Memoirs of the Society for American Ar-
            chaeology* 11. Salt Lake City.

1957   Danger Cave. *University of Utah Anthropological Papers* 27.
            Salt Lake City.

1964   The Desert West. Pp. 149-174 in Prehistoric Man in the New
            World. Jesse D. Jennings and Edward Norbeck, eds. Chi-
            cago: University of Chicago Press.

1966   Glen Canyon: A Summary. *Glen Canyon Series* 31, *University
            of Utah Anthropological Papers* 81. Salt Lake City.

1966a   Early Man in the Desert West. (Proceedings of the 7th Con-
            gress of the International Association for Quaternary Re-
            search, Vol. 15) *Quaternaria* 8:81-89. Rome.

1973   The Short Useful Life of a Simple Hypothesis. *Tebiwa: Jour-
            nal of the Idaho State University Museum* 13(1):1-9. Pocatello.

1974   Prehistory of North America. 2d ed. New York: McGraw-
            Hill.

1975   Preliminary Report: Excavation of Cowboy Cave. (U.S. De-
            partment of the Interior, Bureau of Land Management Per-
            mit No. 74-UT-011) Salt Lake City: University of Utah, De-
            partment of Anthropology.

1978   Prehistory of Utah and the Eastern Great Basin. *University
            of Utah Anthropological Papers* 98. Salt Lake City.

1980   Cowboy Cave. *University of Utah Anthropological Papers*
            104. Salt Lake City.

Jennings, Jesse D., and Edward Norbeck
1955   Great Basin Prehistory: A Review. *American Antiquity* 21(1):1-
            11.

Jennings, Jesse D., and Dorothy Sammons-Lohse
1981   Bull Creek. *University of Utah Anthropological Papers* 105.
            Salt Lake City.

Jennings, Jesse D., Alan R. Schroedl, and Richard N. Holmer
1980   Sudden Shelter. *University of Utah Anthropological Papers*
            103. Salt Lake City.

Jennings, Jesse D., Erick K. Reed, James B. Griffin, J. Charles Kelley,
Clement W. Meighan, Stanley Stubbs, Joe Ben Wheat, and Dee C.
Taylor
1956   The American Southwest: A Problem in Cultural Isolation.
            Pp. 59-128 in Seminars in Archaeology: 1955. R. Wauchope,
            ed. *Memoirs of the Society for American Archaeology* 11. Salt
            Lake City.

Jensen, Andrew
1926   History of Las Vegas Mission. *Nevada State Historical Society
            Publications* 5:117-284. Reno.

Jernigan, E. Wesley
1978   Jewelry of the Prehistoric Southwest. Albuquerque: Univer-
            sity of New Mexico Press.

Jessor, Richard, Theodore Graves, Robert C. Hanson and Shirley L.
Jessor
1968   Society, Personality and Deviant Behavior: A Study of a Tri-
            ethnic Community. New York: Holt, Rinehart and Winston.

Jett, Stephen C.
1968   Grand Canyon Dams, Split-twig Figurines, and "Hit-and-
            Run" Archaeology. *American Antiquity* 33(3):341-351.

Jettmar, Kael
1962   Die Aussage der Archäologie zur Religionsgeschichte Nord-
            eurasiens. Pp. 305-356 in Die Religionen der Menschheit.
            Vol. 3. Christel Schröder, ed. Stuttgart, Germany: W. Kohl-
            hammer Verlag.

Johnson, Charles C.
1963   A Study of Modern Southwestern Indian Leadership. (Un-
            published Ph.D. Dissertation in Anthropology, University of
            Colorado, Boulder.)

Johnson, Edward C.
1975   Walker River Paiutes: A Tribal History. Schurz, Nev.: Walker
            River Paiute Tribe. (Reprinted in 1978.)

[1985]   A Brief History of Stewart Indian School. Mimeo.

Johnson, Henry W.
1927   Where Did Frémont Cross the Tehachapi Mountains in 1844?
            *Annual Publication of the Historical Society of Southern Cal-
            ifornia* 13:365-373. Los Angeles.

Johnson, Overton, and William H. Winter
1846   Route Across the Rocky Mountains, with a Description of
            Oregon and California; Their Geographical Features, Their
            Resources, Soil, Climate, Production, etc. Layfayette, Ind.:
            John B. Semans, Printer.

Johnson, Thomas H.
1968   The Wind River Shoshone Sun Dance, 1966 and 1967. (Un-

published M.A. Thesis in Anthropology, University of Wisconsin, Stevens Point.)

1975   The Enos Family and Wind River Shoshone Society: A Historical Analysis. (Unpublished Ph.D. Dissertation in Anthropology, University of Illinois, Urbana-Champaign.)

Jones, A.C., J.R. Weaver, and F.H. Stross
1967   Note on Indian Wood Carving in the Form of a Grasshopper Found in Lovelock Cave, Nevada. *University of California Archaeological Survey Reports* 70(8):123-128. Berkeley.

Jones, John A.
1955   The Sun Dance of the Northern Ute. *Anthropological Papers* 47, *Bureau of American Ethnology Bulletin* 157. Washington.

Jones, Timothy W.
1980   Archaeological Test Excavations in the Boise Redevelopment Project Area, Boise, Idaho. (With Chinese Artifact Analysis by George Ling, and Boise History by Michael Ostrogorsky.) *University of Idaho Anthropological Research Manuscript Series* 59. Moscow.

1982   Excavation of the Foote Site Dump (10AA96). *University of Idaho Anthropological Research Manuscript Series* 68. Moscow.

Jones, Timothy W., Mary Anne Davis, and George Ling
1979   Idaho City: An Overview and Report on Excavation. *University of Idaho Anthropological Research Manuscript Series* 50. Moscow.

Jones, William A.
1875   Report Upon the Reconnaissance of Northwestern Wyoming Including Yellowstone National Park Made in the Summer of 1873. *43d Cong., 1st sess., House Executive Document No.* 285. Washington: U.S. Government Printing Office.

Jordan, David S.
1891   Report of Explorations in Colorado and Utah During the Summer of 1889, with an Account of the Fishes Found in Each of the River Basins Examined. *Bulletin of the United States Fish Commission for 1889.* Vol. 9:1-40. Washington.

Jordan, Richard H.
1980   The University of Pennsylvania Museum Collection of Chipped Stone Amulets from Point Barrow, Alaska. *Anthropological Papers of the University of Alaska* 19(2):33-41. Fairbanks.

Jorgensen, Joseph G.
1960   The Functions of Ute Folkfore. (Unpublished M.A. Thesis in Anthropology, University of Utah, Salt Lake City.)

1964   The Ethnohistory and Acculturation of the Northern Ute. (Unpublished Ph.D. Dissertation in Anthropology, Indiana University, Bloomington.)

1969   [Fieldnotes on Bear Dance at Southern Ute, Ute Mountain Ute, and Northern Ute, Memorial Day Ceremonies at Wind River Shoshone, April 19-June 30.] (Manuscripts in Jorgensen's possession.)

1971   Indians and the Metropolis. Pp. 66-113 in The American Indian in Urban Society, by Jack Waddell and Michael Watson. Boston: Little, Brown.

1972   The Sun Dance Religion: Power for the Powerless. Chicago: University of Chicago Press.

1978   A Century of Political Economic Effects on American Indian Society, 1880-1890. *Journal of Ethnic Studies* 6(3):1-82.

1980   Western Indians: Comparative Environments, Languages, and Cultures of 172 Western American Indian Tribes. San Francisco: W.H. Freeman.

1985   Religious Solutions and Native American Struggles: Ghost Dance, Sun Dance and Beyond. In Religion/Rebellion/Revolution: An Interdisciplinary and Cross-cultural Collection of Essays. Bruce Lincoln, ed. New York: Macmillan and St. Martin's Press. In press.

1984a   Native American Claims to Resources in the Lower 48, and United States' Policies. (Paper read at the Alaska Native Review Commission Overview Hearings Roundtable, March 6, Anchorage.)

1984b   Great Basin Language, Culture and Environment. (Manuscript in D. Callaway's possession.)

1984c   The New Federalism and the Northern Ute. (Manuscript in Jorgensen's possession.)

Jorgensen, Joseph G., Shelton H. Davis, and Robert O. Mathews
1978   Energy, Agriculture, and Social Science in the American West. Pp. 3-16 in Native Americans and Energy Development, by Joseph G. Jorgensen et al. Cambridge, Mass.: Anthropology Resource Center.

Jorgensen, Joseph G., Richard O. Clemmer, Ronald L. Little, Nancy J. Owens, and Lynn A. Robbins
1978   Native Americans and Energy Development. Cambridge, Mass.: Anthropology Resource Center.

Josephy, Alvin M., Jr., ed.
1961   The American Heritage Book of Indians. New York: American Heritage Publishing Company.

Judd, Neil M.
1916   Archaeological Reconnaissance in Western Utah. *Smithsonian Miscellaneous Collections* 66(3):64-71. Washington.

1917   Evidence of Circular Kivas in Western Utah Ruins. *American Anthropologist* 19(1):34-40.

1917a   Notes on Certain Prehistoric Habitations in Western Utah. Pp. 119-124 in Proceedings of the 19th International Congress of Americanists. Washington, 1915.

1919   Archaeological Investigations at Paragonah, Utah. *Smithsonian Miscellaneous Collections* 70(3). Washington.

1926   Archeological Observations North of the Rio Colorado. *Bureau of American Ethnology Bulletin* 82. Washington.

1940   Progress in the Southwest. *Smithsonian Miscellaneous Collections* 100:417-444. Washington.

1954   The Material Culture of Pueblo Bonito. *Smithsonian Miscellaneous Collections* 124. Washington.

Julander, Odell
1962   Range Management in Relation to Mule Deer Habitat and Herd Productivity in Utah. *Journal of Range Management* 15(5): 278-281. Denver.

Kahrl, William L.
1976   The Politics of California Water: Owens Valley and the Los Angeles Aqueduct, 1900-1927. *California Historical Society Quarterly* 55(1):2-25, (2):98-120. San Francisco.

1982   Water and Power: The Conflict Over Los Angeles' Water Supply in the Owens Valley. Berkeley: University of California Press.

Kaibab Paiute Tribe
1980   Kaibab-Paiute Overall Community Development Plan, 1980. (Manuscript, copy in possession of Pamela Bunte, University of New Mexico, Las Cruces.)

Kappler, Charles J., comp.
1904-1941   Indian Affairs: Laws and Treaties. 5 vols. Washington: U.S. Government Printing Office. (Reprinted: AMS Press, New York, 1971.)

Karpenstein, Katherine
1945   Mono Lake. *California Folklore Quarterly* 4(1):90-92. Berkeley.

Kay, Paul A.
1982   A Perspective on Great Basin Paleoclimates. Pp. 76-81 in Man and Environment in the Great Basin. David B. Madsen and James F. O'Connell eds. *Society for American Archaeology Papers* 2. Washington.

Keeler, Charles A.
1889   [A Vocabulary of Washoe Indian Names of Birds. Carson City, Nevada.] (Manuscript No. 952 in National Anthropological Archives, Smithsonian Institution, Washington.)

Keely, Patrick B.
1980   Nutrient Composition of Selected Important Plant Foods of the Pre-contact Diet of the Northwest Native American Peoples. (Unpublished M.S. Thesis in Nutritional Science and Textiles, University of Washington, Seattle.)

Keleher, William A.
1952   Turmoil in New Mexico, 1846-1868. Santa Fe, N.M.: The Rydal Press.

Kelly, Isabel T.
1932   Ethnography of the Surprise Valley Paiute. *University of California Publications in American Archaeology and Ethnology* 31(3):67-210. Berkeley. (Reprinted: Krauss Reprint, New York, 1965.)

———
1932a   Fundamentals of Great Basin Culture. (Unpublished Ph.D. Dissertation in Anthropology, University of California, Berkeley.)

———
[1932-1933] [Unpublished Fieldnotes (Ethnographic) from the Southern Paiute and Chemehuevi.] (Manuscripts in University Archives, Bancroft Library, University of California, Berkeley.)

———
1934   Southern Paiute Bands. *American Anthropologist* 36(4):548-560.

———
1936   Chemehuevi Shamanism. Pp. 129-142 in Essays in Anthropology Presented to A.L. Kroeber in Celebration of His Sixtieth Birthday. Robert E. Lowie, ed. Berkeley: University of California Press.

———
1938   Northern Paiute Tales. *Journal of American Folk-Lore* 51(202): 363-438.

———
1939   Southern Paiute Shamanism. *University of California Anthropological Records* 2(4):151-167. Berkeley.

———
1964   Southern Paiute Ethnography. *Glen Canyon Series* 21, *University of Utah Anthropological Papers* 69. Salt Lake City.

Kelly, Lawrence C.
1983   The Assault on Assimilation: John Collier and the Origins of Indian Policy Reform. Albuquerque: University of New Mexico Press.

Kelly, Robert L.
1978   Paleo-Indian Settlement Patterns at Pleistocene Lake Tonopah, Nevada. (Unpublished B.A. Honors Thesis in Anthropology, Cornell University, Ithaca, N.Y.)

———
1983   The Carson-Stillwater Archaeological Project: Public Domain Collections. (Report submitted to the Bureau of Land Management, Carson City District, Nevada; copy in Department of Anthropology, Nevada State Museum, Carson City.)

———
1983a   An Examination of Amateur Collections from the Carson Sink, Nevada. *Nevada Bureau of Land Management, Contributions to the Study of Cultural Resources, Technical Report* 10. Reno.

Kelly, Roger E.
1966   Split-twig Figurines from Sycamore Canyon, Central Arizona. *Plateau* 38(3):65-67.

Kelso, Gerald
1970   Hogup Cave, Utah: Comparative Pollen Analysis of Human Coprolites and Cave Fill. Pp. 251-262 (App. 4) in Hogup Cave. C. Melvin Aikens, ed. *University of Utah Anthropological Papers* 93. Salt Lake City.

Kent, Kate P.
1983   Prehistoric Textiles of the Southwest. Santa Fe: School of American Research; Albuquerque: University of New Mexico Press.

Kern, Edward M.
1876   Journal of Mr. Edward M. Kern of an Exploration of the Mary's or Humboldt River, Carson Lake, and Owens River and Lake, in 1845. Pp. 475-486 (App. Q) in Report of Explorations Across the Great Basin of the Territory of Utah for a Direct Wagon-route from Camp Floyd to Genoa, in Carson Valley, in 1859, by Captain J.H. Simpson. Washington: U.S. Government Printing Office.

Kern, Norval C.
1969   A Presentation of Sculpture: A Synthesis of a Design Alphabet Derived from the Art Forms of a Primitive People. (Unpublished Ph.D. Dissertation in Education, New York University, New York City.)

Kerr, Mark
1980   The Shoshoni Indians of Inyo County, California: The Kerr Manuscript. Charles N. Irwin, ed. *Ballena Press Publications in Archaeology, Ethnology and History* 15. Socorro, N.M.

Keyser, James D.
1975   A Shoshonean Origin for the Plains Shield Bearing Warrior Motif. *Plains Anthropologist* 20 (69):207-215.

Kidder, Alfred V.
1924   An Introduction to the Study of Southwestern Archaeology. *Phillips Academy Southwestern Expedition Papers* 1. New Haven, Conn.

———
1927   Southwestern Archaeology Conference. *Science* 66(1716):489-491.

———
1932   The Artifacts of Pecos. *Phillips Academy Southwestern Expedition Papers* 6. New Haven, Conn.

Kidder, Alfred V., and Samuel J. Guernsey
1919   Archeological Explorations in Northeastern Arizona. *Bureau of American Ethnology Bulletin* 65. Washington.

Kilbourne, Richard T., Charles W. Chesterman, and Spencer H. Wood
1980   Recent Volcanism in the Mono Basin-Long Valley Region of Mono County, California. Pp. 7-22 in Mammoth Lakes, California Earthquakes of May 1980. Roger W. Sherburne, ed. *California Division of Mines and Geology Special Report* 150. Sacramento.

Kimball, Patricia C.
1976   Warm Creek Spring: A Prehistoric Lithic Workshop. *Archaeological Reports of the Idaho State University Museum of Natural History* 8. Pocatello.

King, Chester
1981   Part 1: Background to Prehistoric Resources of the East Mojave Planning Unit. Pp. 3-53 in Background to Historic and Prehistoric Resources of the East Mojave Desert Region, by Chester King and Dennis G. Casebier. *California Bureau of Land Management, Cultural Resources Publications, Anthropology-History*. Riverside.

King, Clarence
1878   Systematic Geology. (*U.S. Geological Exploration of the Fortieth Parallel* 1.) Washington: U.S. Government Printing Office.

King, Guy Quintin
1978   The Late Quaternary History of Adrian Valley, Lyon County, Nevada. (Unpublished M.S. Thesis in Geography, University of Utah, Salt Lake City.)

King, Thomas F., Patricia P. Hickman, and Gary Berg
1977   Anthropology in Historic Preservation: Caring for Culture's Clutter. New York: Academic Press.

783

Kingsbury, Lawrence A.
1977 Final Report of the 1976 Cultural Resources Inventory of the Little Lost River - Birch Creek Planning Unit. *Archaeological Reports of the Idaho State University Museum of Natural History* 10. Pocatello.

Kirk, Ruth E.
1952 Panamint Basketry - A Dying Art. *The Masterkey* 26(3):76-86.

Kittleman, Laurence R.
1979 Tephra. *Scientific American* 241(6):160-177.

Klein, Jeffrey, J.C. Lerman, P.E. Damon, and E.K. Ralph
1982 Calibration of Radiocarbon Dates: Tables Based on the Consensus Data of the Workshop on Calibrating the Radiocarbon Time Scale. *Radiocarbon* 24(2):103-150.

Klein, Lauren C.
1964 [Fieldnotes and Report - Dresslerville Community; University of Nevada Ethnographic Archives 4, National Science Foundation Graduate Field Training Project - June 7 to Sept. 7, 1964.] (On file, Department of Anthropology, University of Nevada, Reno.)

Klein, Sheldon
1959 Comparative Mono-Kawaiisu. *International Journal of American Linguistics* 25(4):233-238.

Klimek, Stanislaw
1935 Culture Element Distributions, I: The Structure of California Indian Culture. *University of California Publications in American Archaeology and Ethnology* 37(1):1-70. Berkeley.

Kluckhohn, Clyde
1944 Navaho Witchcraft. *Papers of the Peabody Museum of American Archaeology and Ethnology, Harvard University* 22(2). Cambridge, Mass.

Knack, Martha C.
1973-1982 [Fieldnotes from Approximately 18 Months' Fieldwork among the Southern Paiute of Utah; 2 Months in the Las Vegas Urban Indian Community, Nevada; and 1 Month among the Death Valley Shoshones, California, and the Moapa Southern Paiute, Nevada.] (Manuscripts in Knack's possession.)

1975 Contemporary Southern Paiute Household Structure and Bilateral Kinship Clusters. (Unpublished Ph.D. Dissertation in Anthropology, University of Michigan, Ann Arbor.)

1978 Beyond a Differential: An Inquiry into Southern Paiute Indian Experience with Public Schools. *Anthropology and Education Quarterly* 9(3):216-234. Washington.

1980 Life Is With People: Household Organization of the Contemporary Southern Paiute Indians. *Ballena Press Anthropological Papers* 19. Socorro, N.M.

Knack, Martha C., and Omer C. Stewart
1984 As Long as the Rivers Shall Run: An Economic Ethnohistory of the Pyramid Lake Indian Reservation. Berkeley: University of California Press.

Kneale, Albert H.
1916 [To Henry A. Larson, in Reply to BIA Questionnaire Dated November 17.] (Manuscript in Letters Received, Record Group 75, National Archives, Washington.)

Knight, Lavinia C.
1973 A Figurine from China Ranch (4-INY-962). *Pacific Coast Archaeological Society Quarterly* 9(3):48-51. Costa Mesa, Calif.

Knudson, Ruthann, Timothy W. Jones, and Robert L. Sappington
1982 The Foote House (10-AA-96): An Historic Archaeological Complex in the Boise River Canyon, Idaho. *University of Idaho Anthropological Research Manuscript Series* 72. Moscow.

Kobori, Larry S., Colin I. Busby, James C. Bard, and John M. Findlay
1980 A Class II Cultural Resources Inventory of the Bureau of Land Management's Bodie and Coleville Planning Units, California, Vol. 1. (Basin Research Associates report to the Bureau of Land Management, Bakersfield, California, District Office.)

Koch, Ronald P.
1977 Dress Clothing of the Plains Indians. Norman: University of Oklahoma Press.

Kowta, Makoto
1969 The Sayles Complex: A Late Milling Stone Assemblage from Cajon Pass and the Ecological Implications of Its Scraper Planes. *University of California Publications in Anthropology* 6. Berkeley.

Kramer, Karen, and David H. Thomas
1983 Ground Stone. Pp. 231-246 in The Archaeology of Monitor Valley, 2: Gatecliff Shelter, by David H. Thomas. *Anthropological Papers of the American Museum of Natural History* 59(1). New York.

Krieger, Herbert W.
1928 A Prehistoric Pit House Village Site of the Columbia River at Wahluke, Grant County, Washington. *Proceedings of the United States National Museum* 11:1-29. Washington.

Kroeber, Alfred L.
1901 Ute Tales. *Journal of American Folk-Lore* 14(55):252-285.

[1903-1907] [Washoe Field Notebook.] (Unpublished manuscript No. C-B 925, Carton 6: Washoe, Alfred L. Kroeber Correspondence and Papers, Manuscript Division, Bancroft Library, University of California, Berkeley.)

1907 The Washo Language of East Central California and Nevada. *University of California Publications in American Archaeology and Ethnology* 4(5):251-316. Berkeley.

1970a Shoshonean Dialects of California. *University of California Publications in American Archaeology and Ethnology* 4(3):65-165. Berkeley.

1907b The Yokuts Language of South Central California. *University of California Publications in American Archaeology and Ethnology* 2(5):165-377. Berkeley.

1908 Notes on the Ute Language. *American Anthropologist* 10(1):74-87.

1908a Origin Tradition of the Chemehuevi Indians. *Journal of American Folk-Lore* 21(81-82):240-242.

1909 Notes on Shoshonean Dialects of Southern California. *University of California Publications in American Archaeology and Ethnology* 8(5):235-269. Berkeley.

1909a The Bannock and Shoshoni Languages. *American Anthropologist* 11(2):266-277.

1910 Noun Composition in American Languages. *Anthropos* 5(1):204-218.

———, coll.
1914 [55 Northern Paiute Songs: Pyramid Lake; Gilbert Natches, Singer.] (Nos. 24-2257-24-2325 in Lowie Museum of Anthropology, University of California, Berkeley.)

1916 Arapaho Dialects. *University of California Publications in American Archaeology and Ethnology* 12(3):71-138. Berkeley.

1917 California Kinship Systems. *University of California Publications in American Archaeology and Ethnology* 12(9):339-396. Berkeley.

1920 California Culture Provinces. *University of California Publications in American Archaeology and Ethnology* 17(2):151-169. Berkeley.

1922   Elements of Culture in Native California. *University of California Publications in American Archaeology and Ethnology* 13(8):259-328. Berkeley.

1923   Anthropology. New York: Harcourt, Brace.

1925   Handbook of the Indians of California. *Bureau of American Ethnology Bulletin* 78. Washington.

1931   The Culture-area and Age-area Concepts of Clark Wissler. Pp. 248-265 in Methods in Social Science: A Case Book. Stuart A. Rice, ed. Chicago: University of Chicago Press.

1934   Native American Population. *American Anthropologist* 36(1):1-25.

1935   Preface. Pp. 1-11 in Culture Element Distributions, I: The Structure of California Indian Culture, by S. Klimek. *University of California Publications in American Archaeology and Ethnology* 37(1). Berkeley.

―――, ed.
1935a   Walapai Ethnography. *Memoirs of the American Anthropological Association* 42. Menasha, Wis.

1939   Cultural and Natural Areas of Native North America. *University of California Publications in American Archaeology and Ethnology* 38(1):1-242. Berkeley.

1940   Stepdaughter Marriage. *American Anthropologist* 42(4):562-570.

1941   Culture Element Distributions, XV: Salt, Dogs and Tobacco. *University of California Anthropological Records* 6(1):1-20. Berkeley.

1955   Linguistic Time Depth Results So Far and Their Meaning. *International Journal of American Linguistics* 21(2):91-104.

1955a   Nature of the Land-holding Group. *Ethnohistory* 2(4):303-314.

1957   Ethnographic Interpretations, 1-6. *University of California Publications in American Archaeology and Ethnology* 47(2):191-234. Berkeley.

1959   Ethnographic Interpretations, 7-11. *University of California Publications in American Archaeology and Ethnology* 47(3):235-310. Berkeley.

Kroeber, Alfred L., and Edward W. Gifford
1949   World Renewal: A Cult System of Native Northwest California. *University of California Anthropological Records* 13. Berkeley.

Küchler, August W.
1964   Potential Natural Vegetation of the Conterminous United States. *American Geographical Society Special Publication* 36. New York.

Kuntz, Mel A., et al.
1980   Geological and Geophysical Investigations and Mineral Resources Potential of the Proposed Great Rift Wilderness Area, Idaho. *U.S. Geological Survey Open-File Report* 80-475. Denver, Colo.

La Barre, Weston
1938   The Peyote Cult. *Yale University Publications in Anthropology* 19. New Haven, Conn. (Reprinted: Schocken Books, New York, 1975.)

1947   Primitive Psychotherapy in Native American Cultures: Peyotism and Confession. *Journal of Abnormal and Social Psychology* 42(3):294-309.

1960   Twenty Years of Peyote Studies. *Current Anthropology* 1(1):45-60.

Lafora, Nicolas de
1958   The Frontiers of New Spain: Nicolas de Lafora's Description, 1766-1768. Lawrence Kinnaird, ed. *Quivira Society Publications* 13. Berkeley, Calif.

Lahren, Larry, and Robson Bonnichsen
1974   Bone Foreshafts from a Clovis Burial in Montana. *Science* 186(4159):147-150.

Laidlaw, Robert M.
1982   Cultural Resource Management, Regulations and Policy: Potential Roles for Cultural Anthropologists. (Paper presented at the 1982 Meeting of the Southwestern Anthropological Association, Sacramento, Calif.)

Laidlaw, Sally J.
1960   Federal Indian Land Policy and the Fort Hall Indians. *Occasional Papers of the Idaho State College Museum* 3. Pocatello.

Laird, Carobeth
1974   Chemehuevi Religious Beliefs and Practices. *Journal of California Anthropology* 1(1):19-25. Banning.

1975   Encounters with an Angry God: Recollections of My Life with John Peabody Harrington. Banning, Calif.: Malki Museum Press.

1976   The Chemehuevis. Banning, Calif.: Malki Museum Press.

1977   Behavioral Patterns in Chemehuevi Myths. Pp. 97-119 in Flowers of the Wind: Papers on Ritual, Myth and Symbolism in California and the Southwest. Thomas C. Blackburn, ed. *Ballena Press Anthropological Papers* 8. Socorro, N.M.

1984   Mirror and Pattern: George Laird's World of Chemehuevi Mythology. Banning, Calif.: Malki Museum Press.

Lajoe, Charles, and John Roberts
1899   Shoshone Prayer Service. Fort Washakie, Wyo.: Episcopal Mission.

LaMarche, Valmore C., Jr.
1973   Holocene Climatic Variations Inferred from Treeline Fluctuations in the White Mountains, California. *Quaternary Research* 3(4):632-660.

1974   Paleoclimatic Inferences from Long Tree-ring Records. *Science* 183(4129):1043-1048.

1978   Tree-ring Evidence of Past Climatic Variability. *Nature* 276(5686):334-338.

LaMarche, Valmore C., Jr., and Katherine K. Hirschboeck
1984   Frost Rings in Trees as Records of Major Volcanic Eruptions. *Nature* 307(5947):121-126.

LaMarche, Valmore C., Jr., and Harold A. Mooney
1972   Recent Climatic Change and Development of the Bristlecone Pine (*P. Longaeva* Bailey), Krummholz Zone, Mt. Washington, Nevada. *Arctic and Alpine Research* 4(1):61-72.

Lamb, H.H.
1982   Reconstruction of the Course of Postglacial Climate Over the World. Pp. 11-32 in Climatic Change in Later Prehistory. A.F. Harding, ed. Edinburgh, Scotland: Edinburgh University Press.

Lamb, Sydney M.
1958   Linguistic Prehistory in the Great Basin. *International Journal of American Linguistics* 24(2):95-100.

1958a   Northfork Mono Grammar. (Unpublished Ph.D. Dissertation in Linguistics, University of California, Berkeley.)

1959   Some Proposals for Linguistic Taxonomy. *Anthropological Linguistics* 1(2):33-49.

1964 The Classification of the Uto-Aztecan Languages: A Historical Survey. Pp. 106-125 in Studies in Californian Linguistics. William Bright, ed. *University of California Publications in Linguistics* 34. Berkeley.

Lander, F.W.
1860 Report of F.W. Lander, Superintendent, ..., to the Commissioner of Indian Affairs. *36th Cong., 1st sess., Senate Executive Document* No. 1033:121-139. Washington.

Landis, Daniel G., and Gordon A. Lothson
1983 Phase III Archaeological Test Excavations, Hagerman National Fish Hatchery, Site 10GG176, Gooding County, Idaho. *Eastern Washington University Reports in Archaeology and History* 100-28. Cheney.

Lang, Gottfried O.
1953 A Study in Culture Contact and Culture Change: The Whiterocks Utes in Transition. *University of Utah Anthropological Papers* 15. Salt Lake City.

1954 The Ute Development Program: A Study of Culture Change in an Underdeveloped Area within the United States. (Unpublished Ph.D. Dissertation in Anthropology, Cornell University, Ithaca, N.Y.)

1961-1962 Economic Development and Self-determination: The Northern Ute Case. *Human Organization* 20(4):164-171.

Langacker, Ronald W.
1976 Non-distinct Arguments in Uto-Aztecan. *University of California Publications in Linguistics* 82. Berkeley.

1977 An Overview of Uto-Aztecan Grammar. Studies in Uto-Aztecan Grammar. Vol. 1. Ronald W. Langacker, ed. (*Publication in Linguistics* 56) Arlington: Summer Institute of Linguistics and the University of Texas.

Langdon, Margaret
1974 Comparative Hokan-Coahuiltecan Studies: A Survey and Appraisal. (*Janua Linguarum Series Critica* 4) The Hague: Mouton.

1979 Some Thoughts on Hokan with Particular Reference to Pomoan and Yuman. Pp. 592-649 in The Languages of Native America: Historical and Comparative Assessment. Lyle Campbell and Marianne Mithun, eds. Austin: University of Texas Press.

Lanner, Ronald M.
1981 The Piñon Pine: A Natural and Cultural History. Reno: University of Nevada Press.

1983 The Expansion of Singleleaf Piñon in the Great Basin. Pp. 167-171 in The Archaeology of Monitor Valley, 2: Gatecliff Shelter. David H. Thomas, ed. *Anthropological Papers of the American Museum of Natural History* 59(1). New York.

Lanning, Edward P.
1963 Archaeology of the Rose Spring Site INY-372. *University of California Publications in American Archaeology and Ethnology* 49(3):237-336. Berkeley.

LaRivers, Ira
1962 Fishes and Fisheries of Nevada. *Nevada State Fish and Game Commission, Biological Society of Nevada Memoirs* 1. Carson City.

Larson, Daniel O.
1981 A Study of the Settlement Patterns of Southern Nevada as Reflected by the Archaeological Record. *Western Anasazi Reports* 3(1). Cedar City, Utah.

Latham, Robert G.
1856 On the Languages of Northern, Western and Central America. *Transactions of the Philological Society of London* 17:57-115. London.

Lathrap, D.W., and Clement W. Meighan
1951 An Archaeological Reconnaissance in the Panamint Mountains. Pp. 11-32 in Papers on California Archaeology:10-12. Robert F. Heizer, ed. *University of California Archaeological Survey Reports* 11(12). Berkeley.

Latta, Frank F., ed.
1949 Handbook of Yokuts Indians. Bakersfield, Calif.: Kern County Museum.

Laudermilk, J.D., and Philip A. Munz
1934 Plants in the Dung of *Nothrotherium* from Gypsum Cave, Nevada. Pp. 29-37 in Contributions to Palaeontology. *Carnegie Institution of Washington Publication* 453. Washington.

Lawrence, Barbara
1967 Early Domestic Dogs. *Zeitschrift für Säugetierkunde* 32(1):44-59. Hamburg and Berlin.

Lawton, Harry W., and Lowell J. Bean
1968 A Preliminary Reconstruction of Aboriginal Agricultural Technology Among the Cahuilla. *The Indian Historian* 1(5):18-24, 29.

Lawton, Harry W., Philip J. Wilke, Mary DeDecker, and William M. Mason
1976 Agriculture Among the Paiute of Owens Valley. *Journal of California Anthropology* 3(1):13-50.

Layton, Thomas N.
1970 High Rock Archaeology: An Interpretation of the Prehistory of the Northwestern Great Basin. (Unpublished Ph.D. Dissertation in Anthropology, Harvard University, Cambridge, Mass.)

1970a Evidence for Pottery Manufacture on the North Western Periphery of the Great Basin. *The Masterkey* 47(1):23-27.

1977 Indian Rustlers of the High Rock. *Archaeology* 30(6):366-373.

1978 From Pottage to Portage: A Perspective on Aboriginal Horse Use in the Northern Great Basin Prior to 1850. *Nevada Historical Society Quarterly* 20(4):241-251. Reno.

1979 Archaeology and Paleoecology of Pluvial Lake Parman, Northwestern Great Basin. *Journal of New World Archaeology* 3(3):41-56.

1981 Traders and Raiders: Aspects of Trans-Basin and California-Plateau Commerce, 1800-1830. *Journal of California and Great Basin Anthropology* 3(1):127-137.

Layton, Thomas N., and David H. Thomas
1979 The Archaology of Silent Snake Springs, Humboldt County, Nevada. *Anthropological Papers of the American Museum of Natural History* 55(3):249-270. New York.

Leach, Larry L.
1966 The Archaeology of Boundary Village. *Miscellaneous Paper* 13, *University of Utah Anthropological Papers* 83: 85-129. Salt Lake City.

1970 Archaeological Investigations at Deluge Shelter in Dinosaur National Monument. (Unpublished Ph.D. Dissertation in Archaeology, University of Colorado, Boulder.)

1970a Swelter Shelter, 42 UN40. Pp. 127-135 in Archaeological Excavations in Dinosaur National Monument, Colorado-Utah, 1964-65. David A. Breternitz, ass. *University of Colorado Studies, Series in Anthropology* 17. Boulder.

Lee, Richard B., and Irven DeVore
1968 Man the Hunter. Chicago: Aldine.

Lee, Shirley W.
1967 A Survey of Acculturation in the Intermontane Area of the United States. *Occasional Papers of the Idaho State University Museum* 19. Pocatello.

Lee, Simeon L.
1912   [Manuscript Catalogue of Indian Work and Baskets.] (In Department of Anthropology, Nevada State Museum, Carson City.)

1939   [Dr. S.L. Lee Collection.] (In Nevada State Museum and Art Institute. Carson City.)

Leis, Philip E.
1963   Washo Witchcraft: A Test of the Frustration-aggression Hypothesis. Pp. 57-68 in The Washo Indians of California and Nevada. Warren L. d'Azevedo, ed. *University of Utah Anthropological Papers* 67. Salt Lake City.

Leland, Joy H.
1976   Great Basin Indian Population Figures (1873 to 1970) and the Pitfalls Therein. *University of Nevada, Desert Research Institute Publications in the Social Sciences* 11. Reno.

1980   Native American Alcohol Use: A Review of the Literature. Pp. 1-56 in Tulapai to Tokay: A Bibliography of Alcohol Use and Abuse Among the Native Americans of North America. Patricia D. Mail and David R. McDonald, comps. New Haven, Conn.: HRAF Press.

Leonard N. Nelson, III, and Christopher E. Drover.
1980   Prehistoric Turquoise Mining in the Halloran Springs District, San Bernardino County, California. *Journal of California and Great Basin Anthropology* 2(2):245-256.

Leonard, Zenas
1904   Leonard's Narrative; Adventure of Zenas Leonard, Fur Trader and Trapper, 1831-1836. W.F. Wagner, ed. Cleveland, Ohio: Burrows Brothers.

Leopold, A Starker
1950   Deer in Relation to Plant Succession. Pp. 571-580 in Transactions of the 15th North American Wildlife Conference, March 6-9, 1950, San Francisco. Ethel M. Quee, ed. Washington: Wildlife Management Institute.

Lerch, Oliver
1965   [Fieldnotes and Report - Camps in the Settlement Pattern of the Washoe Population of Wood Fords, Calif.; University of Nevada Ethnographic Archives 18, National Science Foundation Graduate Field Training Project - June 7 to Sept. 7, 1964.] (On file, Department of Anthropology, University of Nevada, Reno.)

Lewis, Henry T.
1973   Patterns of Indian Burning in California: Ecology and Ethnohistory. *Ballena Press Anthropological Papers* 1. Ramona, Calif.

1982   Fire Technology and Resource Management in Aboriginal North America and Australia. Pp. 45-67 in Resource Managers: North American and Australian Haunter-gatherers. Nancy M. Williams and Eugene S. Hunn, eds. *American Association for the Advancement of Science Selected Symposium* 67. Boulder, Colo.

Lewis, Meriwether, and William Clark
1904-1905 Original Journals of the Lewis and Clark Expedition, 1804-1806. Reuben G. Thwaites, ed. 8 vols. New York: Dodd, Mead. (Reprinted: Antiquarian Press, New York, 1959.)

Lewis, Orme
1954   [Letter of], United States Department of the Interior, Office of the Secretary, Washington, D.C., February 15, 1954, to Hon. Hugh Butler. Pp. 8-9 in Termination of Federal Supervision Over Certain Tribes of Indians. Joint Hearing Before the Subcommittees on Interior and Insular Affairs. *83d Cong., 2d sess. S.2670 and H.R.7674 (Pt. 1: Utah)*. Washington: U.S. Government Printing Office.

Libby, Willard F.
1952   Radiocarbon Dating. Chicago: University of Chicago Press.

Lieber, Michael D.
1965   The Case Against Peyote: A Native Point of View. (Paper read at the Annual Meeting of the American Ethnological Society, Lexington, Ky. April 15, 1965.)

1972   Opposition to Peyotism Among the Western Shoshone: The Message of Traditional Belief. *Man* n.s. 7(3):387-396.

Light, Sol F.
1938   New Subgenera and Species of Diaptomid Copepods from the Inland Waters of California and Nevada. *University of California Publications in Zoology* 43(3):67-78. Berkeley.

Liljeblad, Sven
1940-1983 [Ethnographic and Linguistic Manuscripts and Tapes on Various Great Basin Numic Groups.] (In Special Collections Department, Getchell Library, University of Nevada, Reno.)

1957   Indian Peoples in Idaho. Pocatello: Idaho State College. Mimeo.

1958   Epilogue: Indian Policy and the Fort Hall Reservation. *Idaho Yesterdays* 2(2):14-19

1959   Indian People of Idaho. Pp. 29-59 in History of Idaho. S. Beal and M. Wells, eds. Pocatello: Lewis Historical Publishing.

1960   [Nez Perce Ethnohistoric and Folkloristic Fieldnotes and Tape Recordings from Lapwai and Kamiah, Idaho.] (Unpublished manuscripts in Liljeblad's possession.)

[1961-1980] [Unpublished Fieldnotes, Linguistics and Ethnography, Approximately 6 months, Owens Valley (Paiute), California.] (Manuscript in possession of Sven Liljeblad and Special Collections Department, Getchell Library, University of Nevada, Reno.)

1965   [Fieldnotes, Vol. 3: Fort Independence.] (Unpublished manuscript in Special Collections Department, Getchell Library, University of Nevada, Reno.)

1966   Northern Paiute Manual, I: Grammatical Sketch of the Northern Dialects. (Unpublished manuscript in Liljeblad's possession.)

1969   The Religious Attitude of the Shoshonean Indians. *Rendezvous: Idaho State University Journal of Arts and Letters* 4(1):47-58. Pocatello.

1970   Shoshoni and Northern Paiute Indians in Idaho. (Manuscript in Idaho Historical Society, Reference Series No. 484, Boise.)

1971   The History of Indian Tribes in Idaho: Languages. (Manuscript in Liljeblad's possession.)

1971a   The Oral Traditions of the Shoshoni and Bannock Indians of Idaho. *Rendezvous: Idaho State University Journal of Arts and Letters* 6(1):2-3. Pocatello.

1972   The Idaho Indians in Transition, 1805-1960. Pocatello: Idaho State Museum Special Publication.

[1972a]   Some Observations on the Fort Hall Indian Reservation. (Unpublished manuscript in Liljeblad's possession.)

1984   Northern Paiute and Mono. (Unpublished manuscript in Liljeblad's possession.)

Lindsay, Alexander J., Jr., J. Richard Ambler, Mary Anne Stein, and Philip M. Hobler
1968   Survey and Excavations North and East of Navajo Mountain, Utah, 1959–1962. *Glen Canyon Series* 8, *Museum of Northern Arizona Bulletin* 45. Flagstaff.

Lindsay, La Mar W.
1976   Unusual or Enigmatic Stone Artifacts: Pots, Pipes, Points, and Pendants from Utah. *Utah Division of State History,*

787

Antiquities Section Selected Papers 2(8):107-117. Salt Lake City.

1980 Pollen Analysis of Cowboy Cave Cultural Deposits. Pp. 213-224 (App. 10) in Cowboy Cave, by Jesse D. Jennings. *University of Utah Anthropological Papers* 104. Salt Lake City.

Lindsay, La Mar W., and Christian K. Lund
1976 Pint Size Shelter. *Utah Division of State History, Antiquities Section Selected Papers* 3(10). Salt Lake City.

Lindsay, La Mar W., and Kay Sargent
1979 Prehistory of the Deep Creek Mountain Area, Western Utah. *Utah Division of State History, Antiquities Section Selected Papers* 6(14). Salt Lake City.

Linton, Ralph, ed.
1940 Acculturation in Seven American Indian Tribes. New York: D. Appleton-Century.

Lipe, William D.
1960 1958 Excavations, Glen Canyon Area. *Glen Canyon Series 11, University of Utah Anthropological Papers* 44. Salt Lake City.

Lipe, William D., and Richard A. Thompson
1979 A Cultural Resource Assessment of the Grand Wash Planning Unit of the Arizona Strip District of the Bureau of Land Management. *Western Anasazi Reports* 2(1):39-74. Cedar City, Utah.

Lipe, William D., et al.
1960 1959 Excavations, Glen Canyon Area. *Glen Canyon Series 13, University of Utah Anthropological Papers* 49. Salt Lake City.

Lister, Robert H.
1951 Excavations at Hells Midden, Dinosaur National Monument. *University of Colorado Studies, Series in Anthropology* 3. Boulder.

1959 The Coombs Site. Pt. 1. *Glen Canyon Series 8, University of Utah Anthropological Papers* 41. Salt Lake City.

Lister, Robert H., J. Richard Ambler, and Florence C. Lister
1960 The Coombs Site. Pt. 2. *Glen Canyon Series 8, University of Utah Anthropological Papers* 41. Salt Lake City.

Little, James A., ed.
1966 Jacob Hamblin: A Narrative of His Personal Experience, as a Frontiersman, Missionary to the Indians, and Explorer [1909]. 2d ed. Salt Lake City: The Desert News Press.

Loeb, Barbara
1980 Mirror Bags and Bandoleer Bags: A Comparison. *American Indian Art Magazine* 6(1):46-53, 88.

Loew, Oscar
1876 Notes Upon the Ethnology of Southern California and Adjacent Regions. Pp. 541-547 in *Annual Report of the U.S. War Department, Report of the Chief of Engineers for 1876.* Vol. 23, (App. J.J.) Pt. H.14. Washington.

Logan, Richard F.
1965 The Setting of the Mono Lake Area. Pp. 22-25 in An Ethnography of the Kuzedika Paiute of Mono Lake, Mono County, California, by Emma Lou Davis. *Miscellaneous Collected Paper 8, University of Utah Anthropological Papers* 75. Salt Lake City.

Lohse, Ernest S.
1980 Fremont Settlement Pattern and Architectural Variation. Pp. 41-54 in Fremont Perspectives. David B. Madsen, ed. *Utah Division of State History, Antiquities Section Selected Papers* 7(16). Salt Lake City.

1980a Prehistoric Adaptation in the Black Rock Desert-high Rock Country of Northwestern Nevada. (University of Utah Archeological Center report to the Bureau of Land Management, Winnemucca District, Nev.)

Lomax, Alan, and Conrad M. Arensberg
1977 A Worldwide Evolutionary Classification of Cultures by Substistence Systems. *Current Anthropology* 18(4):659-708.

Long, Austin, and Paul S. Martin
1974 Death of American Ground Sloths. *Science* 186 (4164):638-640.

Long, Ileen Price, Mabel C. Love, and Angie T. Merrill
1964 Alpine Heritage: One Hundred Years of History, Recreation and Lore in Alpine County, 1864-1964. Markleeville, Calif.: Alpine County Museum.

Long, Stephen H.
1823 Account of an Expedition from Pittsburgh to the Rocky Mountains Performed in the Years 1819 and '20 by Order of the Hon. J.C. Calhoun, Sec'y of War: Under the Command of Major Stephen H. Long. Philadelphia: Cary and Lea.

Lothson, Gordon A., and Keith Virga
1981 Archaeological Test Excavations Phase II Testing at the Hagerman National Fish Hatchery, Hagerman Valley, Idaho. *Eastern Washington University Reports in Archaeology and History* 1-2. Cheney,

Loud, Llewellyn L.
1918 Ethnogeography and Archaeology of the Wiyot Territory. *University of California Publications in American Archaeology and Ethnology* 14(3):221-436. Berkeley.

Loud, Llewellyn L., and Mark R. Harrington
1929 Lovelock Cave. *University of California Publications in American Archaeology and Ethnology* 25(1):1-183. Berkeley.

Lounsbury, Floyd G.
[1955] Voiceless Vowels in Cayuga, Comanche, and Southern Paiute: Their Phonological Status and Conditioning Factors. (Manuscript in Lounsbury's possession.)

Lowie, Robert H.
1908 The Test-theme in North American Mythology. *Journal of American Folk-Lore* 21(81-82):97-148.

1909 The Northern Shoshone. *Anthropological Papers of the American Museum of Natural History* 2(2):165-306. New York.

_____, ed.
1909a Shoshone and Comanche Tales. H.H. St. Clair, II., coll. *Journal of American Folk-Lore* 22(85):265-282.

1915 Dances and Societies of the Plains Shoshone. *Anthropological Papers of the American Museum of Natural History* 11(10):803-835. New York.

1919 Sun Dance of the Shoshoni, Ute, and Hidatsa. *Anthropological Papers of the American Museum of Natural History* 16(5):387-431. New York.

1923 The Cultural Connections of Californian and Plateau Shoshonean Tribes. *University of California Publications in American Archaeology and Ethnology* 20(9):145-156. Berkeley.

1924 Notes on Shoshonean Ethnography. *Anthropological Papers of the American Museum of Natural History* 20(3):185-314. New York.

1924a Shoshonean Tales. *Journal of American Folk-Lore* 37(143-144):1-242.

1924b Primitive Religion. New York: Boni and Liveright.

1930 The Kinship Terminology of the Bannock Indians. *American Anthropologist* 32(2):294-299.

1939 Ethnographic Notes on the Washo. *University of California Publications in American Archaeology and Ethnology* 36(5):301-352. Berkeley.

1948 Social Organization. London: Routledge and Kegan Paul.

1959 Robert H. Lowie, Ethnologist: A Personal Record. Berkeley: University of California Press.

1963 Washo Texts. *Anthropological Linguistics* 5(7):1-30.

Lucius, William A.
1980 Bone and Shell Material. Pp. 97-107 in Cowboy Cave, by Jesse D. Jennings. *University of Utah Anthropological Papers* 104. Salt Lake City.

Lurie, Nancy Oestreich
1957 The Indians Claims Commission Act. *Annals of the American Academy of Political and Social Science* 311:56-70. Philadelphia.

Lyford, Carrie A.
1940 Quill and Beadwork of the Western Sioux. (*Indian Handcrafts* 1) Washington: U.S. Office of Indian Affairs, Education Division.

Lyman, June, and Norma Denver
1970 Ute People: An Historical Study. Floyd A. O'Neil and John D. Sylvester, eds. 3d ed. Salt Lake City: Uintah School District and the Western History Center, University of Utah.

Lynch, Robert N.
1971 Politics in a Northern Paiute Community. (Unpublished Ph.D. Dissertation in Anthropology, University of Minnesota, Minneapolis.)

1973 The Role of the B.I.A. on the Reservation: Patron or Client. Pp. 46-59 in Native American Politics: Power Relationships in the Western Great Basin Today. R.M. Houghton, ed. Reno: University of Reno, Bureau of Governmental Research.

1978 Cowboys and Indians: An Ethnohistorical Portrait of Indian-White Relations on Ranches in Western Nevada. *Ballena Press Publications in Archaeology, Ethnology and History* 11:51-60. Socorro, N.M.

Lyneis, Margaret M.
1982 Prehistory in the Southern Great Basin. Pp. 172-185 in Man and Environment in the Great Basin. David B. Madsen and James F. O'Connell, eds. *Society for American Archaeology Papers* 2. Washington.

1982a An Archaeological Element for the Nevada Historic Preservation Plan. (Prepared for the Nevada Division of Historic Preservation and Archaeology Project No. 230-0580 by the University of Nevada, Las Vegas.)

Mabey, Don R.
1971 Geophysical Data Relating to a Possible Pleistocene Overflow of Lake Bonneville at Gem Valley, Southeastern Idaho. *U.S. Geological Survey Professional Paper* 750-B. Washington.

McAllester, David P.
1949 Peyote Music. *Viking Fund Publications in Anthropology* 13. New York.

MacBain, E. Heath
1956 Excavation of Mound B. Pp. 39-59 in Archaeological Excavations in Iron County, Utah, by Clement W. Meighan et al. *University of Utah Anthropological Papers* 25. Salt Lake City.

McClellan, Carole, and David A. Phillips, Jr.
1978 Archeological Survey North of Lake Mead, Arizona: Wahl-Yee and Mobil Mineral Leases Final Report. Tucson: U.S. National Park Service, Western Archeological Center.

McClellan, Carole, David A. Phillips, Jr., and Mike Belshaw
1980 The Archeology of Lake Mead National Recreation Area: An Assessment. *U.S. National Park Service, Western Archeological Center Publications in Anthropology* 9. Tucson.

McCown, Theodore D.
[1929] [Unpublished Fieldnotes on the Ethnography of the Kawaiisu.] (Manuscript in the Lowie Museum of Anthropology, University of California, Berkeley.)

MacDonald, Angus A.
1970 The Northern Mojave Desert's Little Sahara. *California Division of Mines and Geology, Mineral Information Service* 23(1):3-6. Sacramento.

McGreehan, Albert J.
1973 Burns Paiute Indian Reservation Resource Development Survey. Portland, Oreg.: Portland State University, Urban Studies Center.

MacGregor, Gordon
1936 Washo Indians of the Sacramento Jurisdiction. Washington: U.S. Office of Indian Affairs, Applied Anthropology Unit. Mimeo.

McGuire, Kelly R., and Alan P. Garfinkel
1980 Archaeological Investigations in the Southern Sierra Nevada: The Bear Mountain Segment of the Pacific Crest Trail. *U.S. Bureau of Land Management, Cultural Resources Publications - Archaeology.* Bakersfield, Calif.

McGuire, Kelly R., Alan P. Garfinkel, and Mark E. Basgall
1981 Archaeological Investigations in the El Paso Mountains of the Western Mojave Desert: The Bickel and Last Chance Sites (CA-Ker-250 and 261); report prepared by Far West Anthropological Research Group, Inc. for U.S. Bureau of Land Management, Riverside, Calif.)

Mack, Effie M.
1947 Mark Twain in Nevada. New York: Charles Scribner's Sons.

1968 The Indian Massacre of 1911 at Little High Rock Canyon, Nevada. Sparks, Nev.: Western Printing and Publishing Company.

McKee, Edwin D., ed.
1979 A Study of Global Sand Seas. *U.S. Geological Survey Professional Paper* 1052. Washington.

McKee, Edwin H., and David H. Thomas
1972 Petroglyph Slabs from Central Nevada. *Plateau* 44(3):85-104.

1973 X-ray Diffraction Analysis of Pictograph Pigments from Toquima Cave, Central Nevada. *American Antiquity* 38(1):112-113.

McKenzie, Don
1982 The Northern Great Basin Region. Pp. 67-102 in Reference Handbook on the Deserts of North America. Gordon L. Bender, ed. Westport, Conn.: Greenwood Press.

McKinney, Aileen, Duane Hafner, and Jane Gothold
1971 A Report on the China Ranch Area. *Pacific Coast Archaeological Society Quarterly* 7(2):1-48. Costa Mesa, Calif.

McKinney, Whitney
1983 A History of the Shoshone-Paiutes of the Duck Valley Indian Reservation. Salt Lake City: The Institute of the American West and Howe Brothers.

Macko, M.E., et al.
1982 Class III Cultural Resource Survey, Intermountain Power Project (IPP), Intermountain Adelanto Bipole I Transmission Line Right of Way, California Section. Fullerton, Calif.: Applied Conservation Technology.

McKusick, Marshall B.
1960 Expedition Reports, 1960 Archaeological Field School, U.C.L.A. (Manuscript in Department of Anthropology. University of California, Los Angeles.)

McLaughlin, John E.
1983 A Working Bibliography of the Languages of (Roughly) the Western United States ([-Athapaskan] [+ Haida, Tsimshian, Wakashan]). (*Studies in Native American Languages* 2) *Kansas Working Papers in Linguistics* 8(2):247-367. Lawrence.

1984   Notes on Panamint Phonology. (Paper read at the Friends of Uto Aztecan Working Conference, San Diego, Calif., June 1984.)

MacLeod, Norman S., David R. Sherrod, Lawrence A. Chitwood, and Edwin H. McKee
1981   Newberry Volcano, Oregon. Pp. 85-103 in Guides to Some Volcanic Terranes in Washington, Idaho, Oregon, and Northern California. David A. Johnston and Julie Donnelly-Nolan, eds. *U.S. Geological Survey Circular* 838. Alexandria, Va.

MacLeod, William C.
1928   The American Indian Frontier. New York Alfred A. Knopf.

1931   The Distribution and Process of Suttee in North America. *American Anthropologist* 32 (2):209-215.

McMillan, Doug
1984   Shoshone Claims Right to Hunt Deer Anywhere, Anytime. *Reno Gazette-Journal* March 25:7A. Reno, Nev.

MacNeish, Richard S.
1964   Ancient Mesoamerican Civilization. *Science* 143(3606):531-537.

1972   Summary of the Cultural Sequence and Its Implications in the Tehuacan Valley. Pp. 496-504 in Vol. 5 of Prehistory of the Tehuacan Valley. R.S. MacNeish, M.L. Fowler, A.G. Cook, F.A. Peterson, A. Nelken-Terner, and J.A. Neely, eds. Austin: University of Texas Press.

Macomb, J.N.
1876   Report of the Exploring Expedition from Santa Fe, New Mexico to the Junction of the Grand and Green Rivers of the Great Colorado of the West, in 1859. Washington: U.S. Government Printing Office.

McVaugh, Rogers
1956   Edward Palmer: Plant Explorer of the American West. Norman: University of Oklahoma Press.

Madsen, Betty M., and Brigham D. Madsen
1980   North to Montana! Jehus, Bullwhackers, and Mule Skinners on the Montana Trail. *University of Utah Publications in the American West* 13. Salt Lake City.

Madsen, Brigham D.
1958   The Bannock of Idaho. Caldwell, Idaho: Caxton Printers.

1979   The Lemhi: Sacajawea's People. Caldwell, Idaho: Caxton Printers.

1980   The Northern Shoshone. Caldwell, Idaho: Caxton Printers.

Madsen, David B.
1970   Ceramics. Pp. 54-75 in Median Village and Fremont Culture Regional Variation, by John P. Marwitt. *University of Utah Anthropological Papers* 95. Salt Lake City.

1972   Paleoecological Investigations in Meadow Valley Wash, Nevada. Pp. 57-65 in Great Basin Cultural Ecology: A Symposium, Don D. Fowler, ed. *University of Nevada, Desert Research Institute Publications in the Social Sciences* 8. Reno.

1975   Dating Paiute-Shoshone Expansion in the Great Basin. *American Antiquity* 40(1):82-86.

1975a   Three Fremont Sites in Emery County, Utah. *Utah Division of State History, Antiquities Section Selected Papers* 1(1). Salt Lake City.

1979   The Fremont and the Sevier: Defining Prehistoric Agriculturalists North of the Anasazi. *American Antiquity* 44(4): 711-722.

1979a   Great Salt Lake Fremont Ceramics. Pp. 79-100 in The Levee Site and the Knoll Site, by Gary F. Fry and Gardiner F. Dalley. *University of Utah Anthropological Papers* 100. Salt Lake City.

_____, ed.
1980   Fremont Perspectives. *Utah Division of State History, Antiquities Section Selected Papers* 7(16). Salt Lake City.

1980a   Fremont/Sevier Subsistence. Pp. 25-33 in Fremont Perspectives. David B. Madsen, ed. *Utah Division of State History, Antiquities Section Selected Papers* 7(16). Salt Lake City.

1980b   The Human Prehistory of the Great Salt Lake Region. Pp. 19-31 in Great Salt Lake, a Scientific, Historical and Economic Overview. J. Wallace Gwynn, ed. *Utah Geological and Mineral Survey, Department of Natural Resources Bulletin* 116. Salt Lake City.

1982   Get It Where the Gettin's Good: A Variable Model of Great Basin Subsistence and Settlement Based on Data from the Eastern Great Basin. Pp. 207-226 in Man and Environment in the Great Basin. David B. Madsen and James F. O'Connell, eds. *Society for American Archaeology Papers* 2. Washington.

1982a   Salvage Excavations at Ticaboo Town Ruin (42Ga2295). In Archaeological Investigations in Utah at Fish Springs, Clay Basin, Northern San Rafael, South Henry Mountains. *Utah Bureau of Land Management, Cultural Resource Series* 12. Salt Lake City.

1982b   Prehistoric Occupation Patterns, Subsistence Adaptations, and Chronology in the Fish Springs Area, Utah. In Archaeological Investigations in Utah. David B. Madsen and Richard E. Fike, ass. *Utah Bureau of Land Management, Cultural Resource Series* 12. Salt Lake City.

1983   Black Rock Cave Revisited. *Utah Bureau of Land Management, Cultural Resource Series* 14. Salt Lake City.

[1985] Great Basin Nuts: A Short Treatise on the Distribution, Productivity and Prehistoric Use of Pinyon. In Anthropology of the Desert West: Essays in Honor of Jesse D. Jennings. Carol J. Condie and D.D. Fowler, eds. Salt Lake City: University of Utah Press.

Madsen, David B., and Michael S. Berry
1975   A Reassessment of Northeastern Great Basin Prehistory. *American Antiquity* 40(4):391-405.

Madsen, David B., and Donald R. Currey
1979   Late Quaternary Glacial and Vegetation Changes, Little Cottonwood Canyon Area, Wasatch Mountains, Utah. *Quaternary Research* 12(2):254-270.

Madsen, David B., and La Mar W. Lindsay
1977   Backhoe Village. *Utah Division of State History, Antiquities Section Selected Papers* 4(12). Salt Lake City

1984   Joe's Valley Alcove. *U.S. Forest Service, Intermountain Region Cultural Resource Reports* 15. Ogden, Utah.

Madsen, David B., and James F. O'Connell, eds.
1982   Man and Environment in the Great Basin. *Society for American Archaeology Papers* 2. Washington.

Madsen, David B., Donald R. Currey, and James H. Madsen, Jr.
1976   Man Mammoth and Lake Fluctuations in Utah. *Utah Division of State History, Antiquities Section Selected Papers* 2(5). Salt Lake City.

Madsen, David H., and C. Elmer Madsen
[1900] Utah Lake, the Western Sea of Galilee. (Manuscript in Alfred E. Madsen's possession, Lakeview, Utah.)

Madsen, Rex E., comp.
1977   Prehistoric Ceramics of the Fremont. *Museum of Northern Arizona Ceramic Series* 6. Flagstaff.

Magee, Molly
1966 The Grass Valley Horse: A Baked Clay Head of a Horse Figurine from Central Nevada. *Plains Anthropologist* 11(33):204-207.

1967 A Report on Perforated Sherds from Central Nevada with a Tentative Suggestion for Their Use. *American Antiquity* 32(2):226-227.

Mahar, James M.
1953 Ethnobotany of the Oregon Paiutes of the Warm Springs Indian Reservation. (Unpublished B.A. Thesis in History and Social Science, Reed College, Portland, Oreg.)

Malde, Harold E.
1964 The Ecologic Significance of Some Unfamiliar Geologic Processes. Pp. 7-13 in The Reconstruction of Past Environments: Proceedings of the Fort Burgwin Conference on Paleoecology, Ranches of Taos, N.M., 1962. James J. Hester and James Schoenwetter, ass. *Fort Burgwin Research Center Publications* 3.

1968 The Catastrophic Late Pleistocene Bonneville Flood in the Snake River Plain, Idaho. *U.S. Geological Survey Professional Paper* 596. Washington.

Maley, J.
1977 Paleoclimates of the Central Sahara During the Early Holocene. *Nature* 269(5629):573-577.

Mallery, Garrick
1886 Pictographs of the North American Indians: A Preliminary Paper. Pp. 3-256 in *4th Annual Report of the Bureau of American Ethnology for the Years 1882-1883.* Washington.

1893 Picture-writing of the American Indians. Pp. 3-822 in *10th Annual Report of the Bureau of American Ethnology for the Years 1888-1889.* Washington.

Malouf, Carling
1939 Prehistoric Exchange in Utah. *University of Utah, Museum of Anthropology Archaeology and Ethnology Papers* 1. Salt Lake City. (Reprinted: *University of Utah Anthropological Papers* 1-8:1-6, 1950.)

1940 A Study of the Gosiute Indians of Utah. (Unpublished M.S. Thesis in Sociology and Anthropology, University of Utah, Salt Lake City.)

1940a The Archaeology of the Deep Creek Region, Utah. *University of Utah, Museum of Anthropology Archeology and Ethnology Papers* 5. Salt Lake City.

1940b The Gosiute Indians. *University of Utah, Museum of Anthropology Archaeology and Ethnology Papers* 3:29-36. (Reissued in 1950 as *University of Utah Anthropological Papers* 3, Salt Lake City.)

1940c Prehistoric Exchange in the Northern Periphery of the Southwest. *American Antiquity* 6(2):115-122.

1942 Gosiute Peyotism. *American Anthropologist* 44(1):93-103.

1944 Thoughts on Utah Archaeology. *American Antiquity* 9(3):319-328.

1950 The Archaeology of Sites Along Fifteen-Mile Creek. Pp. 41-56 in The Archaeology of the Deep Creek Region, Utah. Carling Malouf, Charles E. Dibble, and Elmer R. Smith, eds. *University of Utah Anthropological Papers* 5. Salt Lake City.

1966 Ethnohistory in the Great Basin. Pp. 1-38 in The Current Status of Anthropological Research in the Great Basin: 1964. Warren L. d'Azevedo et al., eds. *University of Nevada, Desert Research Institute Social Sciences and Humanities Publications* 1. Reno.

1974 The Gosiute Indians. Pp. 25-172 in Shoshone Indians. (*American Indian Ethnohistory: California and Basin-Plateau Indians*) New York: Garland.

Malouf, Carling, and A. Arline Malouf
1945 The Effects of Spanish Slavery on the Indians of the Intermountain West. *Southwestern Journal of Anthropology* 1(3):378-391.

Malouf, Carling, and Elmer R. Smith
1942 Some Gosiute Mythological Characters and Concepts. *Utah Humanities Review* 1(4):369-377. Salt Lake City.

Manners, Robert A.
1959 Habitat, Technology and Social Organization of the Southern Paiute. *América Indígena* 19(3):179-197.

1973 Julian Haynes Steward, 1902-1972. *American Anthropologist* 74(3):886-903.

1974 Southern Paiute and Chemehuevi: An Ethnohistorical Report. Pp. 21-300 in Paiute Indians, I. (*American Indian Ethnohistory: California and Basin-Plateau Indians*) New York: Garland.

Manning, Winona
1980 Pressures on Duck Valley; I Will Die an Indian. Sun Valley, Idaho: Institute of the American West.

Margry, Pierre, ed.
1888 Journal du voyage fait par le Chevalier de la Verendrye. Pp. 598-601 in Vol. 6 of Découvertes et établissements des Français dans l'Ouest et dans le sud de l'Amérique septentrionale, 1614-1754. 6 vols. Paris: Maisonneuve et Cie, Libraries-Editeurs. (Reprinted: AMS Press, New York, 1974.)

Marsden, W.L.
1911 Some Shoshonean Etymologies. *American Anthropologist* 13(4):724-725.

1923 The Northern Paiute Language of Oregon. *University of California Publications in American Archaeology and Ethnology* 20(11):175-191. Berkeley.

Martin, Curtis W., H.J. Armstrong, S.M. Crum, B.J. Kutz, and L.A. Wheeler
1983 Cedar Siding Shelter: Archaeological Excavation of a Multi-aspect Overhang, Emery County, Utah. *Utah Bureau of Land Management Cultural Resource Series* 15. Salt Lake City.

Martin, Donald E.
1977 Introduction to the Rock Art of Death Valley: Paper presented at the Third Annual A.R.A.R.A. Symposium. A.J. Bock et al., eds. *American Indian Rock Art* 3:144-150. Whittier, Calif.

Martin, Paul S.
1961 Southwestern Animal Communities in the Late Pleistocene. Pp. 56-61 in Bioecology of the Arid and Semiarid Lands of the Southwest. Lora M. Shields and Linton J. Gardner, eds. *New Mexico Highlands University Bulletin* 212. Las Vegas, N.M.

1963 The Last 10,000 Years: A Fossil Pollen Record of the American Southwest. Tucson: University of Arizona Press.

Martin, Paul S., and Richard G. Klein, eds.
1984 Quaternary Extinctions: A Prehistoric Revolution. Tucson: University of Arizona Press.

Martin, Paul S., and Peter J. Mehringer, Jr.
1965 Pleistocene Pollen Analysis and Biogeography of the Southwest. Pp. 433-451 in The Quaternary of the Unites States. Herbert E. Wright, Jr. and David G. Frey, eds. Princeton, N.J.: Princeton University Press.

Martin, Paul S., Bruno E. Sabels, and Dick Shutler, Jr.
1961 Rampart Cave Coprolite and Ecology of the Shasta Ground Sloth. *American Journal of Science* 259(2):102-127.

Martin, S. Clark
1983   Responses of Semidesert Grasses and Shrubs to Fall Burning. *Journal of Range Management* 36(5):604-610. Denver.

Marwitt, John P.
1968   Pharo Village. *University of Utah Anthropological Papers* 91. Salt Lake City.

1970   Median Village and Fremont Culture Regional Variation. *University of Utah Anthropological Papers* 95. Salt Lake City.

1979   [Comment on] The Fremont and the Sevier, by David B. Madsen. *American Antiquity* 44(4):732-736.

Marwitt, John P., and Gary F. Fry
1973   Radiocarbon Dates from Utah. *Southwestern Lore* 38(4):1-9.

Marwitt, John P., Gary F. Fry, and James M. Adovasio
1971   Sandwich Shelter. Pp. 27-36 in Great Basin Anthropological Conference, 1970: Selected Papers. *University of Oregon Anthropological Papers* 1. Eugene.

Mason, J. Alden
1910   Myths of the Uintah Utes. *Journal of American Folk-Lore* 23(89):299-363.

Mason, Otis T.
1894   North American Bows, Arrows and Quivers. Pp. 631-679 in *Annual Report of the Smithsonian Institution for 1893*. Washington.

1896   Influence of Environment Upon Human Industries or Arts. Pp. 639-665 in *Annual Report of the Smithsonian Institution for 1895*. Washington.

1896a   Primitive Travel and Transportation. Pp. 239-593 in *Annual Report of the U.S. National Museum for 1894*. Washington.

1904   Aboriginal American Basketry: Studies in a Textile Art without Machinery. *Annual Report of the United States Museum for 1902*. Vol 1:171-784; Vol. 2: 1-248. Washington.

1907   Environment. Pp. 427-430 in Vol. 1 of Handbook of American Indians North of Mexico. Frederick W. Hodge, ed. 2 vols. *Bureau of American Ethnology Bulletin* 30. Washington.

Matteson, Sumner W.
1901   Red Man and White Man in Colorado's Game Fiekds. *Outing* 38:29-36. Albany, N.Y.

Matthai, Howard F.
1979   Hydrologic and Human Aspects of the 1976-77 Drought. *U.S. Geological Survey Professional Paper* 1130. Washington.

Maule, William M.
1938   A Contribution to the Geographic and Economic History of the Carson, Walker and Mono Basins in Nevada and California. San Francisco: U.S. Department of Agriculture, California Regional Forest Service.

Maurer, Evan M.
1977   The Native American Heritage: A Survey of North American Indian Art. Chicago: The Art Institute of Chicago.

Mawby, John E.
1967   Fossil Vertebrates of the Tule Springs Site, Nevada. Pp. 105-128 in Pleistocene Studies in Southern Nevada. H.M. Wormington and Dorothy Ellis, eds. *Nevada State Museum Anthropological Papers* 13. Carson City.

Maximilian, Prince of Wied
1843   Travels in the Interior of North America. 2 vols. H. Evans Lloyd, trans. London: Ackermann.

Mehringer, Peter J., Jr.
1965   Late Pleistocene Vegetation in the Mohave Desert of Southern Nevada. *Journal of the Arizona Academy of Science* 3(3):172-188. Tucson.

1967   The Environment of Extinction of the Late-Pleistocene Megafauna in the Arid Southwestern United States. Pp. 247-266 in Pleistocene Extinctions: The Search for a Cause. Paul S. Martin and Herbert E. Wright, Jr., eds. New Haven Conn.: Yale University Press.

1967a   Pollen Analysis of the Tule Springs Area, Nevada. Pp. 129-200 in Pleistocene Studies in Southern Nevada. H.M. Wormington and Dorothy Ellis, eds. *Nevada State Museum Anthropological Papers* 13. Carson City.

1977   Great Basin Late Quaternary Environments and Chronology. Pp. 113-167 in Models and Great Basin Prehistory: A Symposium. Don D. Fowler, ed. *University of Nevada, Desert Research Institute Publications in the Social Sciences* 12. Reno.

Mehringer, Peter J., Jr., and Charles W. Ferguson
1969   Pluvial Occurrence of Bristlecone Pine (*Pinus aristata*) in a Mojave Desert Mountain Range. *Journal of the Arizona Academy of Science* 5(4):284-292. Tucson.

Mehringer, Peter J., Jr., and John C. Sheppard
1978   Holocene History of Little Lake, Mojave Desert, California. Pp. 153-176 in The Ancient Californians: Rancholabrean Hunters of the Mojave Lakes Country. Emma Lou Davis, ed. *Natural History Museum of Los Angeles County, Science Series* 29. Los Angeles.

Mehringer, Peter J., Jr., and Claude N. Warren
1976   Marsh, Dune and Archaeological Chronology, Ash Meadows, Amargosa Desert, Nevada. Pp. 120-150 in Holocene Environmental Change in the Great Basin. Robert G. Elston and Patricia Headrick, eds. *Nevada Archeological Survey Research Papers* 6. Reno.

Mehringer, Peter J., Jr., William P. Nash, and Richard H. Fuller
1971   A Holocene Volcanic Ash from Northwestern Utah. *Proceedings of the Utah Academy of Sciences, Arts, and Letters* 48(1):46-51. Salt Lake City.

Mehringer, Peter J., Jr., John C. Sheppard, and Franklin F. Foit, Jr.
1984   The Age of Glacier Peak Tephra in West-central Montana. *Quaternary Research* 21(1):36-41.

Meighan, Clement W.
1953   The Colville Rock Shelter, Inyo County, California. *University of California Anthropological Records* 12(5). Berkeley.

1955   Notes on the Archeology of Mono County, California. Pp. 6-28 in Papers on California Archaeology, 27-29. *University of California Archeological Survey Reports* 28. Berkeley.

1976   Stone Effigies in Southern California. *The Masterkey* 50(1):25-29.

1978   Obsidian Dating of the Malibu Site. Pp. 158-161 in Obsidian Dates, II: A Compendium of the Obsidian Hydration Determinations Made at the UCLA Obsidian Hydration Laboratory. Clement W. Meighan and P.I. Vanderhoeven, eds. *University of California, Institute of Archaeology Monograph* 6. Los Angeles.

Meighan, Clement W., Frank J. Findlow, and Suzanne P. De Atley
1974   Obsidian Dates, I: A Compendium of the Obsidian Hydration Determinations Made at the U.C.L.A. Obsidian Hydration Laboratory. *University of California, Institute of Archaeology Monograph* 3. Los Angeles.

Meighan, Clement W., N.E. Coles, F.D. Davis, G.M. Greenwood, W.M. Harrison, and E.H. MacBain
1956   Archeological Excavations in Iron County, Utah. *University of Utah Anthropological Papers* 25. Salt Lake City.

Meinzer, Oscar E.
1922   Map of the Pleistocene Lakes of the Basin-and-Range Province and Its Significance. *Geological Society of America Bulletin* 33(3):541-552. Boulder, Colo.

Melhorn, Wilton N., and Dennis T. Trexler
1983   'Geology of Gatecliff Shelter: Stratigraphic and Climatic Interpretations. Pp. 88-98 in The Archaeology of Monitor

Valley, 2: Gatecliff Shelter. David H. Thomas, ed. *Anthropological Papers of the American Museum of Natural History* 59(1). New York.

Meltzer, David J., and Jim I. Mead
1983   The Timing of Late Pleistocene Mammalian Extinctions in North America. *Quaternary Research* 19(1):130-135.

Meriam, Lewis
1928   The Problem of Indian Administration. Baltimore: Johns Hopkins Press.

Merriam, Alan P., and Warren L. d'Azevedo
1957   Washo Peyote Songs. *American Anthropologist* 59(4):615-641.

Merriam, Alan P., and Robert F.G. Spier
1959   Chukchansi Yokuts. Pp. 611-638 in Vol. 2 of *Proceedings of the 33d International Congress of Americanists*. San Jose, Costa Rica, 1958.

Merriam, C. Hart
[1902-1942] [Basketry Collections Catalog Cards.] (On file, Department of Anthropology Museum, University of California, Davis.)

————— 1903-1935 [Vocabulary of Washo Flora and Fauna.] (Unpublished manuscript in Department of Anthropology, University of California, Berkeley.]

————— 1903-1935a [Washo Vocabulary.] (Unpublished manuscript in Department of Anthropology, University of California, Berkeley.)

————— 1904   Distribution of Indian Tribes in the Southern Sierra and Adjacent Parts of the San Joaquin Valley, California. *Science* 19(494):912-917.

————— 1907   Distribution and Classification of the Mewan Stock in California. *American Anthropologist* n.s. 9(2):338-357.

————— 1910   The Dawn of the World: Myths and Weird Tales Told by the Mewan Indians of California. Cleveland, Ohio: Arthur H. Clark.

————— [1920]   [Lists of Tribes, Synonymy, Southern Paiute, Chemehuevi (Includes Owens Valley) from His Own Notes and Published Sources.] (Manuscripts, X23W-2/N8 in Bancroft Library, University of California, Berkeley.)

————— 1926   The Classification and Distributions of the Pit River Indian Tribes of California. *Smithsonian Miscellaneous Collections* 78(3):1-52. Washington.

————— [1937-1938] [Notes on Indian Tribal Names: Paviotso, Bannock Bands, Northern Piute, Shoshonean Tribes and Bands.] (Manuscript in C. Hart Merriam Collection, Anthropology Museum, University of California, Berkeley.)

————— 1955   Studies of California Indians. The Staff of the Department of Anthropology of the University of California, eds. Berkeley: University of California Press.

————— 1966   Ethnographic Notes on California Indian Tribes. Robert F. Heizer, ed. *University of California Archaeological Survey Reports* 68(1). Berkeley.

————— 1979   Indian Names for Plants and Animals Among Californian and Other Western North American Tribes. Robert F. Heizer, ass. *Ballena Press Publications in Archaeology, Ethnology and History* 14. Socorro, N.M.

Merriam, John C.
1939   Paleontology, Early Man and Historical Geology. *Carnegie Institution of Washington Year Book* 38:301-310. Washington.

————— 1941   Paleontology, Early Man, and Historical Geology. *Carnegie Institution of Washington Year Book* (40): 316-333. Washington.

Metcalfe, Duncan W.
1982   Worked and Unworked Faunal Remains. Pp. 79-92 in Final Year Excavations at the Evans Mound Site, by Walter A. Dodd, Jr. *University of Utah Anthropological Papers* 106. Salt Lake City

Mickelson, D.M., Lee Clayton, D.S. Fullerton, and H.W. Borns, Jr.
1983   The Late Wisconsin Glacial Record of the Laurentide Ice Sheet in the United States. Pp. 3-37 in Late-Quaternary Environments of the United States. Vol. 1: The Pleistocene. Herbert E. Wright, Jr. and Stephen C. Porter, eds. Minneapolis: University of Minnesota Press.

Mifflin, Martin D.
1968   Delineation of Ground-water Flow Systems in Nevada. *University of Nevada, Desert Research Institute Technical Report Series H-W, Hydrology and Water Resources Publication* 4 Reno.

Mifflin, Martin D., and Margaret M. Wheat
1979   Pluvial Lakes and Estimated Pluvial Climates of Nevada. *Nevada Bureau of Mines and Geology Bulletin* 94, *Mackay School of Mines, University of Nevada*. Reno.

Miles, Charles
1963   Indian and Eskimo Artifacts of North America. New York: Bonanza Books.

Miller, Margaret M., and Robert G. Elston
1979   The Archaeology of the Glendale Site (26Wa2065). (Report submitted to the Nevada Department of Highways, Carson City; report on file Special Collections, Getchell Library, University of Nevada, Reno.)

Miller, Mark E., and George W. Gill
1981   A Late Prehistoric Bundle Burial from Southern Wyoming. *Plains Anthropologist* 25(89):235-246.

Miller, Robert R.
1950   Speciation in Fishes of the Genera *Cyprinodon* and *Empetrichthys*, Inhabiting the Death Valley Region. *Evolution* 4(2):155-163.

Miller, Susanne J.
1972   Weston Canyon Rockshelter: Big-Game Hunting in Southeastern Idaho. (Unpublished M.A. Thesis in Anthropology, Idaho State University, Pocatello.)

————— 1979   The Archaeological Fauna of Four Sites in Smith Creek Canyon. Pp. 272-292 in The Archaeology of Smith Creek Canyon, Eastern Nevada. D.R. Tuohy and D.L. Rendall, eds. *Nevada State Museum Anthropological Papers* 17. Carson City.

————— 1982   The Archaeology and Geology of an Extinct Megafauna/Fluted-Point Association at Owl Cave, the Wasden Site, Idaho: A Preliminary Report. Pp. 81-95 in Peopling of the New World. Jonathon E. Ericson, R.E. Taylor, and Rainer Berger, eds. *Ballena Press Anthropological Papers* 23. Ramona, Calif.

Miller, Wick R.
1961   [Review of] The Sparkman Grammar of Luiseño, by A.L. Kroeber and George William Grace. *Language* 37(1):186-189.

————— 1964   The Shoshonean Languages of Uto-Aztecan. Pp. 145-148 in Studies in Californian Linguistics. William Bright, ed. *University of California Publications in Linguistics* 34. Berkeley.

————— 1966   Anthropological Linguistics in the Great Basin. Pp. 75-112 in The Current Status of Anthropological Research in the Great Basin: 1964. Warren L. d'Azevedo et al., eds. *University of Nevada, Desert Research Institute Social Sciences and Humanities Publications* 1. Reno.

————— 1967   Uto-Aztecan Cognate Sets. *University of California Publications in Linguistics* 48. Berkeley.

1970   Western Shoshoni Dialects. Pp. 17-36 in Languages and Cultures of Western North America: Essays in Honor of Sven S. Liljeblad. Earl H. Swanson, Jr., ed. Pocatello: Idaho State University Press.

1972   Newe Natekwinappeh: Shoshoni Stories and Dictionary. *University of Utah Anthropological Papers* 94. Salt Lake City.

1974   What Went Wrong with the Growth of the Central Numic (Uto-Aztecan) Tree? Or: Leaf Your Language Alone. (Paper presented at the 41st International Congress of Americanists, Mexico City, 1974.)

1984   The Classification of the Uto-Aztecan Languages Based on Lexical Evidence. *International Journal of American Linguistics* 50(1):1-24.

Miller, Wick R., James L. Tanner, and Lawrence P. Foley
1971   A Lexicostatistic Study of Shoshoni Dialects. *Anthropological Linguistics* 13(4):142-164.

Milspaw, Yvonne J.
1975   An Analysis of Folklore: Theories as Applied to Great Basin Indian Oral Narratives. (Unpublished Ph.D. Dissertation in Folklore, Indiana University Bloomington.)

Minor, Rick, Stephen D. Beckham, and Kathryn A. Toepel
1979   Cultural Resource Overview of the BLM Lakeview District, South-central Oregon: Archaeology, Ethnography, History. *University of Oregon Anthropological Papers* 16. Eugene.

Mitchell, Jacqueline
[1979]   Moapa Band of Paiute Indians. Moapa [Nevada]: Privately printed.

Mitchell, Val L.
1976   The Regionalization of Climate in the Western United States. *Journal of Applied Meteorology* 15:920-927.

Mizen, Mamie L.
1964   Federal Facilities for Indians. Report of Sept. 5-15, 1963 [for the] Senate Committee on Appropriations. Washington: U.S. Government Printing Office.

Mock, James M.
1971   Archaeology of Spotten Cave, Utah County, Central Utah. (Unpublished M.A. Thesis in Archaeology, Brigham Young University, Provo, Utah.)

Moe, Jeanne M.
1982   Prehistoric Settlement and Subsistence in Reynolds Creek, Owyhee County, Idaho. *University of Idaho Anthropological Research Manuscript Series* 73. Moscow.

Moe, Jeanne M., William P. Eckerle, and Ruthann Knudson
1980   Southwestern Idaho Transmission Line Archaeological Survey, 1979. *University of Idaho Anthropological Research Manuscript Series* 58. Moscow.

Moffitt, Kathleen, and Claudia Chang
1978   The Mount Trumbull Archeological Survey. *Western Anasazi Reports* 1(3):185-250. Cedar City, Utah.

Montgomery, George E.
1965   [Fieldnotes and Report on Washoe Health and Disease; University of Nevada Ethnographic Archives 20, National Science Foundation Graduate Field Training Project-June 7 to Sept. 7, 1965.] (On file, Department of Anthropology, University of Nevada, Reno.)

Montgomery, Henry
1894   Prehistoric Man in Utah. *The Archaeologist* 2(8):227-234, (10):289-306, (11):335-342. Waterloo, Iowa.

Mook, M.A.
1935   Trade and Transportation. Pp. 164-167 in Walapai Ethnography. A.L. Kroeber, ed. *Memoirs of the American Anthropological Association* 42. Menasha, Wis.

Mooney, James
1892   Eating the Mescal. *The Augusta Chronicle*, January 24:11. Augusta, Ga.

1896   The Ghost Dance Religion and the Sioux Outbreak of 1890. Pp. 641-1136 in *14th Annual Report of the Bureau of American Ethnology for the Years 1892-1893*. Pt. 2. Washington. [Abridged version reprinted: University of Chicago Press, 1965.]

1898   Calendar History of the Kiowa Indians. Pp. 129-445 in *17th Annual Report of the Bureau of American Ethnology for the Years 1895-1896*. Pt. 2. Washington.

1907   The Cheyenne Indians. *Memoirs of the American Anthropological Association* 1(6):357-442. Lancaster, Pa.

1928   The Aboriginal Population of America North of Mexico. John R. Swanton, ed. *Smithsonian Miscellaneous Collections* 80(7). Washington.

Moore, J.G., G.F. Fry, and E. Englert, Jr.
1969   Thorny-headed Worm Infection in North American Prehistoric Man. *Science* 163(3873):1324-1325.

Moore, J.G., A.W. Grundman, H.J. Hall, and G.F. Fry
1974   Human Fluke Infection in Glen Canyon at A.D. 1250. *American Journal of Physical Anthropology* 41(1):115-117.

Moratto, Michael J.
1972   A Study of Prehistory in the Southern Sierra Nevada Foothills, California (Unpublished Ph.D. Dissertation in Anthropology, University of Oregon, Eugene.)

1984   California Archaeology. New York: Academic Press.

Mordy, Brooke D.
1964   [Fieldnotes and Report on Carson Indian Colony; University of Nevada Ethnographic Archives 9, National Science Foundation Graduate Field Training Project-June 7 to Sept. 7, 1964.] (On file, Department of Anthropology, University of Nevada, Reno.)

1966   A Conflict Over Right of Residence. (Unpublished M.A. Thesis in Anthropology, University of Nevada, Reno.)

Mordy, Brooke D., and Donald L. McCaughey
1968   Nevada Historical Sites. Reno: University of Nevada, Desert Research Institute.

Morgan, Dale L.
1943   The Humboldt, Highroad of the West. New York: Rinehart.

1947   The Great Salt Lake. Indianapolis, Ind.: Bobbs-Merrill.

1953   Jedediah Smith and the Opening of the West. New York: Bobbs-Merrill.

1968   Utah Before the Mormons. *Utah Historical Society Quarterly* 36(1):3-23. Salt Lake City.

Morgan, Lewis H.
1862   Circular in Reference to the Degrees of Relationship Among Different Nations. *Smithsonian Miscellaneous Collections* 2(10). Washington.

Morris, Earl H.
1951   Basketmaker III Human Figurines from Northeastern Arizona. *American Antiquity* 17(1):33-40.

Morris, Earl H., and Robert F. Burgh
1941   Anasazi Basketry: Basket Maker II Through Pueblo III. A Study Based on Specimens from the San Juan Country. *Carnegie Institution of Washington Publication* 533. Washington.

Morris, Elizabeth A., W. Max Witkind, Ralph L. Dix, and Judith Jacobson
1981   Nutritional Content of Selected Aboriginal Foods in Northeastern Colorado: Buffalo (*Bison bison*) and Wild Onions (*Allium* spp.). *Journal of Ethnobiology* 1(2):213-220. Flagstaff, Ariz.

Morrison, Roger B.
1964   Soil Stratigraphy: Principles, Applications to Differentiation and Correlation of Quaternary Deposits and Landforms, and Applications to Soil Science. (Unpublished Ph.D. Dissertation in Geology, University of Nevada, Reno.)

1964a   Lake Lahontan: Geology of Southern Carson Desert, Nevada. *U.S. Geological Survey Professional Paper* 401. Washington.

1965   Quaternary Geology of the Great Basin. Pp. 265-285 in The Quaternary of the United States. Herbert E. Wright, Jr., and David G. Frey, eds. Princeton, N.J.: Princeton University Press.

1970   Conflicting Pluvial-Lake Evidence on Climatic Changes Between 14 and 9 Millenia Ago, with Particular Reference to Lakes Lahontan, Bonneville, and Searles. (Abstracts of the First Meeting of the American Quaternary Association, Bozeman, Mont.)

Morrison, Roger B., and John C. Frey
1965   Correlation of the Middle and Late Quaternary Successions of the Lake Lahontan, Lake Bonneville, Rocky Mountain (Wasatch Range), Southern Great Plains, and Eastern Midwest Areas. *Nevada Bureau of Mines Report* 9. Reno.

Morrissey, Frank R.
1968   Turquoise Deposits in Nevada. Reno: Nevada Bureau of Mines and Geology.

Morss, Noel M.
1931   The Ancient Culture of the Fremont River in Utah. *Papers of the Peabody Museum of American Archaeology and Ethnology, Harvard University* 12(3). Cambridge, Mass.

1954   Clay Figurines of the American Southwest. *Papers of the Peabody Museum of American Archaeology and Ethnology, Harvard University* 49(1). Cambridge, Mass.

Muhs, Martha
1981   [Washoe-Paiute Presence in Antelope Valley.] (Manuscript, copy in Warren L. d'Azevedo's possession).

Muir, John
1894   The Mountains of California. New York: The Century Company.

1916-1924 The Writings of John Muir. Manuscript edition. 10 vols. Boston: Houghton.

Mullineaux, Donal R., and Ray E. Wilcox
1980   Stratigraphic Subdivision of Holocene Airfall Tephra from the Climatic Series of Eruptions of Mount Mazama, Oregon. EOS, *American Geophysical Union Transactions* 61(6):66.

Mullineaux, Donal R., and Dwight R. Crandell
1981   The Eruptive History of Mount St. Helens. Pp. 3-15 in The 1980 Eruptions of Mount St. Helens, Washington. Peter W. Lipman and Donal R. Mullineaux, eds. *U.S. Geological Survey Professional Paper* 1250. Washington, D.C.

Mundorff, James C.
1971   Nonthermal Springs of Utah. *Utah Geological and Mineralogical Survey, Water-Resources Bulletin* 16. Salt Lake City.

Munz, Philip A.
1968   Supplement to A California Flora. Berkeley: University of California Press.

Munz, Philip A., and David Keck
1963   A California Flora. Berkeley and Los Angeles: University of California Press. (Reissued in 1973.)

Murdock, George P.
1960   Ethnographic Bibliography of North America. 3d ed. New Haven, Conn.: Human Relations Area Files.

Murdock, George P., and Timothy J. O'Leary
1975   Ethnographic Bibliography of North America. 4th ed. 5 vols. New Haven, Conn.: Human Relations Area Files.

Murphey, Edith Van Allen
1959   Indian Uses of Native Plants. Palm Desert, Calif.: Desert Printers.

Murphey, Kelly A.
1977   An Archaeological Inventory of Devils Creek, Owyhee and Twin Falls Counties, Idaho. *University of Idaho Anthropological Research Manuscript Series* 35. Moscow.

1977a   The Archaeological Survey of the Tuanna Desert Land Entries Project - Southcentral Idaho. *University of Idaho Anthropological Research Manuscript Series* 37. Moscow.

Murphy, Robert F.
1970   Basin Ethnography and Ecological Theory. Pp. 152-171 in Languages and Cultures of Western North America: Essays in Honor of Sven S. Liljeblad. Earl H. Swanson, Jr., ed. Pocatello: Idaho State University Press.

1977   Introduction: Pp. 1-39 in Evolution and Ecology: Essays on Social Transformation, by Julian H. Steward, Jane C. Steward, and Robert F. Murphy, eds. Urbana: University of Illinois Press.

1981   Julian Steward. Pp. 171-204 in Totems and Teachers. Sydel Silverman, ed. New York: Columbia University Press.

Murphy, Robert F., and Yolanda Murphy
1960   Shoshone-Bannock Subsistence and Society. *University of California Anthropological Records* 16(7): 293-338. Berkeley.

Murray-McCormick Environmental Group
1973   Washoe Nation General Plan. Reno, Nev.: Murray-McCormick Environmental Group.

Nabhan, Gary, Alfred Whiting, Henry Dobyns, Richard Hevly, and Robert Euler
1981   Devil's Claw Domestication: Evidence from Southwestern Indian Fields. *Journal of Ethnobiology* 1 (1):135-164.

Nagata, Shuichi
1970   Modern Transformations of Moenkopi Pueblo. *Illinois University Studies in Anthropology* 6. Urbana.

Napton, Lewis K.
1969   Archaeological and Paleobiological Investigations in Lovelock Cave, Nevada: Further Analysis of Human Coprolites. *Kroeber Anthropological Society Special Publication* 2. Berkeley, Calif.

1970   Archaeological Investigations in Lovelock Cave, Nevada. (Unpublished Ph.D. Dissertation in Anthropology, University of California, Berkeley.)

Napton, Lewis K., and Robert F. Heizer
1970   Analysis of Human Coprolites from Archaeological Contexts with Primary Reference to Lovelock Cave, Nevada. *University of California Archaeological Research Facility Contributions* 10(2):87-129. Berkeley.

Napton, Lewis K., and Gerald K. Kelso
1969   Preliminary Palynological Analysis of Lovelock Cave Coprolites. *Kroeber Anthropological Society Special Publication* 2(3):19-27. Berkeley, Calif.

Natches, Gilbert
1923   Northern Paiute Verbs. *University of California Publications in American Archaeology and Ethnology* 20(14):243-259. Berkeley.

1940   Northern Paiute Myths. Saul Reisenberg of Lovelock, Nev., recorder. (Manuscript in possession of Catherine S. Fowler.)

National Congress of American Indians
1975   National Indian Directory. Washington: National Congress of American Indians.

National Native American Co-operative
1982   Native American Directory: Alaska, Canada, United States. San Carlos, Ariz.: National Native American Co-operative.

Native American Church of Idaho
1925   [Articles of Incorporation.] (Manuscript filed with the Sec-
            retary of State, Boise, Idaho.)

Native American Rights Fund
1979   "We Also Have a Religion:" The American Indian Religious
            Freedom Act and the Religious Freedom Project of the Na-
            tive American Rights Fund. *Announcements* 5(1). Boulder,
            Colo.

_____
1984   Supreme Court Declines Review in Walker River Right-of-
            Way Case. *NARF Legal Review* Spring:13. Washington.

Nelson, Bernard C.
1972   Fleas from the Archaeological Site at Lovelock Cave, Nevada
            (Siphonaptera). *Journal of Medical Entomology* 9(3):211-214.

Nelson, David L., and Charles F. Tiernan
1983   Winter Injury of Sagebrush and Other Wildland Shrubs in
            the Western United States. *U.S. Department of Agriculture,
            Forest Service Research Paper* INT-314. Ogden, Utah.

Nelson, E.W., Jr.
1891   The Panamint and Saline Valley (Cal.) Indians. *American
            Anthropologist* 4(4):371-372.

Nelson, Fred W., Jr.
1984   X-ray Fluorescence Analysis of Some Western North Amer-
            ican Obsidians. Pp. 27-62 in Obsidian Studies in the Great
            Basin. Richard E. Hughes, ed. *University of California Ar-
            chaeological Research Facility Contributions* 45. Berkeley.

Nelson, Fred W., Jr., and Richard D. Holmes
1979   Trace Element Analysis of Obsidian Sources and Artifacts
            from Western Utah. *Utah Division of State History, Anti-
            quities Section* Selected Papers 6(15):65-80. Salt Lake City.

Nelson, Michael E., and James H. Madsen, Jr.
1980   A Summary of Pleistocene, Fossil Vertebrate Localities in
            the Northern Bonneville Basin of Utah. Pp. 97-113 in Great
            Salt Lake: A Scientific, Historical and Economic Overview.
            J. Wallace Gwynn, ed. *Utah Geological and Mineral Survey
            Bulletin* 116. Salt Lake City.

Nettl, Bruno
1953   Observations on Meaningless Peyote Song Texts. *Journal of
            American Folklore* 66(260):161-164.

_____
1954   North American Indian Musical Styles. Pt. 3: The Great
            Basin Area. *Journal of American Folklore* 67(265):297-307.

Neudorfer, Giovanna M.
1976   Poison Creek (10-BM-50): A Study in Methodology and Site
            Structure in Southeastern Idaho. *Archaeological Reports of
            the Idaho State University Museum of Natural History* 3. Po-
            catello.

Nevada Indian Commission
1980   Directory of Indian Organizations. Reno: State of Nevada.

Nevada Urban Indians, Incorporated
1983   [Arts and Crafts.] *The Reno Talking Leaf* 5(5):1. Reno, Nev.

Nevers, Jo Ann
1976   Wa She Shu: A Washo Tribal History. Reno: Inter-Tribal
            Council of Nevada.

Newman, Stanley
1954   American Indian Linguistics in the Southwest. *American An-
            thropologist* 56(4):626-634.

Newman, Thomas M.
1974   Archaeological Reconnaissance of the Malheur National
            Wildlife Refuge, Harney County, Oregon, 1974. (Manuscript
            at Malheur National Wildlife Refuge, Burns, Oreg.)

Nichols, Michael J.P.
1971   Linguistic Reconstruction of Proto Western Numic and Its
            Ethnographic Implications. Pp. 135-145 in Great Basin An-
            thropological Conference 1970: Selected Papers. C. Melvin
            Aikens, ed. *University of Oregon Anthropological Papers* 1.
            Eugene.

_____
1974   Northern Paiute Historical Grammar. (Unpublished Ph.D.
            Dissertation in Linguistics, University of California, Berke-
            ley.)

_____
1981   Old California Uto-Aztecan. *Survey of California Indian
            Languages, Report* 1:5-41. Berkeley.

Nickens, Paul B., and Kenneth L. Kvamme
1981   Archaeological Investigations at the Kanab Site, Kane County,
            Utah. In Excavations of Two Anasazi Sites in Southern Utah,
            1979-1980. *Utah Bureau of Land Management, Cultural Re-
            source Series Monograph* 9. Salt Lake City.

Nielson, Asa S.
1978   Proposed Subsistence Models for the Sevier Culture, Sevier
            River Drainage, West Central Utah. (Unpublished M.A.
            Thesis in Anthropology, Brigham Young University, Provo,
            Utah.)

Nissen, Karen M.
1974   The Record of a Hunting Practice at Petroglyph Site NV-
            LY-1. Pp. 53-81 in Four Great Basin Petroglyph Studies.
            *University of California Archaeological Research Facility
            Contributions* 20(2). Berkeley.

_____
1975   A New Style of Rock Art in the Great Basin: The Stillwater
            Facetted Style. *Nevada Archaeological Survey Reporter* 8(2):10-
            11. Reno.

_____
1982   Images from the Past: An Analysis of Six Western Great
            Basin Petroglyph Sites. (Unpublished Ph.D. Dissertation in
            Anthropology, University of California, Berkeley.)

Nusbaum, Jesse L.
1922   A Basket-maker Cave in Kane County, Utah. *Museum of
            the American Indian, Heye Foundation, Indian Notes and
            Monographs, Miscellaneous Series* 29. New York.

Nybroten, Norman, ed.
1964   Economy and Conditions of the Fort Hall Indian Reserva-
            tion. *University of Idaho, Bureau of Business and Economic
            Research Report* 9. Moscow.

Oakeshott, Gordon B., Roger W. Greensfelder, and James E. Kahle
1972   One Hundred Years Later. *California Division of Mines and
            Geology, California Geology* 25(3):55-61.

O'Connell, James F.
1971   The Archeology and Cultural Ecology of Surprise Valley,
            Northeast California. (Unpublished Ph.D. Dissertation in
            Archaeology, University of California, Berkeley.)

_____
1975   The Prehistory of Surprise Valley. *Ballena Press Anthropo-
            logical Papers* 4. Ramona, Calif.

O'Connell, James F., and Richard D. Ambro
1968   A Preliminary Report on the Archaeology of the Rodriguez
            Site (CA-Las-194), Lassen County, California. *University of
            California Archaeological Survey Reports* 73:95-193. Berke-
            ley.

O'Connell, James F., Kevin T. Jones, and Steven R. Simms
1982   Some Thoughts on Prehistoric Archaeology in the Great Ba-
            sin. Pp. 227-240 in Man and Environment in the Great Basin.
            David B. Madsen and James F. O'Connell, eds. *Society for
            American Archaeology Papers* 2. Washington.

O'Connor, Frank A.
1974   Final Report of the Dancing Cat Site (10-CR-233). *Archae-
            ological Reports of the Idaho State University Museum of
            Natural History* 2. Pocatello.

Ogden, Peter S.
1909-1910   Journals of the Snake Expedition, 1825-1827. T.C. Elliott,
            ed. *Oregon Historical Society Quarterly* 10(4):331-365;
            11(2):201-222. Portland.

Olden, Sarah E.
1923   Shoshone Folk Lore, as Discovered from the Rev. John Rob-
            erts, a Hidden Hero, on the Wind River Indian Reservation

in Wyoming. Milwaukee, Wis.: Morehouse Publishing Company.

Olmstead, D.L
1984   A Lexicon of Atsugewi. *Survey of California and Other Indian Languages, Report* 5. Berkeley.

Olofson, Harold
1979   Northern Paiute Shamanism Revisited. *Anthropos* 74(1-2):11-24.

Olson, Alan P.
1966   Split-twig Figurines from NA5607, Northern Arizona. *Plateau* 38(3):55-64.

O'Neil, Floyd A.
1971   The Reluctant Suzerainty: The Uintah and Ouray Reservation. *Utah Historical Quarterly* 39(2):129-144. Salt Lake City.

Oosting, Henry J.
1958   The Study of Plant Communities. San Francisco: W.H. Freeman.

Opler, Marvin K.
1940   The Southern Ute of Colorado. Pp. 119-206 in Acculturation in Seven American Indian Tribes. Ralph Linton ed. New York: D. Appleton-Century. (Reprinted: Peter Smith, Gloucester, Mass., 1963.)

_____
1940a   The Character and History of the Southern Ute Peyote Rite. *American Anthropologist* 42(3):463-478.

_____
1941   The Integration of the Sun Dance in Ute Religion. *American Anthropologist* 43(4):550-572.

_____
1941a   A Colorado Ute Indian Bear Dance. *Southwestern Lore* 7(2):21-30.

_____
1942   Fact and Fancy in Ute Peyotism. *American Anthropologist* 44(2):151-159.

Ore, H. Thomas, and Claude N. Warren
1971   Late Pleistocene-Early Holocene Geomorphic Hsitory of Lake Mojave, California. *Geological Society of America Bulletin* 82(9):2553-2562. Boulder, Colo.

Orr, Phil C.
1952   Preliminary Excavations of Pershing County Caves. *Nevada State Museum, Department of Archeology Bulletin* 1. Carson City.

_____
1972   The Eighth Lake Lahontan (Nevada) Expedition, 1957. Pp. 123-126 in National Geographic Society Research Reports, 1955-1960. Washington: National Geographic Society.

_____
1974   Notes on the Archaeology of the Winnemucca Caves, 1952-1958. Pp. 47-59 in Collected Papers on Aboriginal Basketry. Donald R. Tuohy and Doris L. Rendall, eds. *Nevada State Museum Anthropological Papers* 16. Carson City.

Osborn, Harold W., Jr.
1959   Evaluation of Counseling with a Group of Southern Utah Paiute Children. (Unpublished Ph.D. Dissertation in Anthropology, University of Utah, Salt Lake City.)

Osborne, Douglas
1957   Excavations in the McNary Reservoir Basin Near Umatilla, Oregon; With Appendixes by Marshall T. Newman, Arthur Woodward, W.J. Kroll, and B.H. McLeod. *River Basin Surveys Papers* 8, *Bureau of American Ethnology Bulletin* 166. Washington.

Ostrom, Vincent
1953   Water and Politics: A Study of Water Policies and Administration in the Development of Los Angeles. Los Angeles: The Haynes Foundation.

Oswalt, Robert L.
1976   Switch Reference in Maiduan: An Areal and Typological Contribution. *International Journal of American Linguistics* 42(4):297-304.

Owen, Roger C.
1965   The Patrilocal Band: A Linguistically and Culturally Hybrid Social Unit. *American Anthropologist* 67(3):675-690.

Owl, Frell M.
1962   Who and What is an American Indian? *Ethnohistory* 9(3):265-284.

Palmer, Edward
1871   Food Products of the North American Indians. Pp. 404-428 in *Report of the Commissioner of Agriculture for the Year 1870.* Washington.

_____
1876   Exploration of a Mound in Utah. *American Naturalist* 10(7):410-414.

_____
1878   Plants Used by the Indians of the United States. *American Naturalist* 12(9):593-606, (10):646-655.

_____
1878a   Cave Dwellings in Utah. Pp. 269-272 in *11th Annual Report of the Trustees of the Peabody Museum of American Archaeology and Ethnology* 2(2). Cambridge, Mass.

_____
1878b   A Review of the Published Statements Regarding the Mounds at Payson, Utah, with an Account of Their Structure and Origin. *Proceedings of the Davenport Academy of Natural Sciences* 2:167-72. Davenport, Iowa.

Palmer, William R.
1933   Paiute Indian Homelands. *Utah Historical Society Quarterly* 6(3):88-102. Salt Lake City.

_____
1946   Pahute Indian Legends. Salt Lake City: Deseret Book Company.

Park, Susan
1975   The Life of Stephen Powers. *University of California Archaeological Research Facility Contributions* 28:1-44. Berkeley.

Park, Willard Z.
1933-1940   [Ethnographic Notes on Approximately 15 Months of Fieldwork Among the Northern Paiute of Pyramid Lake, Walker River, Reno, Dayton, Carson Sink, Yerrington.] (Manuscript in Catherine S. Fowler's possession.)

_____
1934   Paviotso Shamanism. *American Anthropologist* 36(1):98-113.

_____, coll.
1934a   [14 Northern Paiute Songs, Nos. ATL 1066.1 ATL 1066.17] (In Archives of Traditional Music, Indiana University, Bloomington.)

_____
1937   Paviotso Polyandry. *American Anthropologist* 39(2): 366-368.

_____
1938   Shamanism in Western North America: A Study in Cultural Relationships. *Northwestern University Studies in the Social Sciences* 2. Evanston, Ill.

_____
1938a   The Organization and Habitat of Paviotso Bands. Pp. 622-626 in Tribal Distribution in the Great Basin, by Willard Z. Park and others. *American Anthropologist* 40(4).

_____
1941   Cultural Succession in the Great Basin. Pp. 180-203 in Language, Culture and Personality: Essays in Memory of Edward Sapir. Leslie Spier, A.I. Hallowell, and Stanley S. Newman, eds. Menasha, Wis.: Sapir Memorial Publication Fund.

Park, Willard Z., Edgar Siskin, Anne M. Cooke, William T. Mulloy, Marvin K. Opler, Isabel T. Kelly, and Maurice L. Zigmond
1938   Tribal Distribution in the Great Basin. *American Anthropologist* 40(4):622-638.

Parker, Patricia
1980   One Hundred Years of History in the California Desert: An Overview of Historic Archaeological Resources at Joshua Tree National Monument. *U.S. National Park Service, Western Archaeological Center, Publications in Anthropology* 13. Tucson, Ariz.

Parkhill, Forbes
1961   The Last of the Indian Wars. New York: Crowell-Collier.

Parks, George A., and Thomas T. Tieh
1966   Identifying the Geographical Source of Artefact Obsidian. *Nature* 211(5046):289-290.

Parry, C.C.
1877   Exploration of a Mound Near Utah Lake, Utah: Report from a Correspondent in Utah, Miss Julia J. Wirt. *Proceedings of the Davenport Academy of Natural Sciences* 2:28-29. Davenport, Iowa.

1877a   Further Reports on a Mound Near Payson, Utah from Miss Julia J. Wirt. *Proceedings of the Davenport Academy of Natural Sciences* 2:82. Davenport, Iowa.

Parsons, Elsie Clews
1919   Increase by Magic: A Zuni Pattern. *American Anthropologist* 21(3):279-286.

1933   Hopi and Zuni Ceremonialism. *Memoirs of the American Anthropological Association* 39. Menasha, Wis.

1936   Taos Pueblo. *General Series in Anthropology* 2. Menasha, Wis.

1939   Pueblo Indian Religion. 2 vols. Chicago: University of Chicago Press.

Pataky, Veronika, producer
1969   Washoe (Film, 55 minutes, black-and-white, sound). Santa Barbara, Calif.: Western Artists Corporation.

Patch, Richard W.
1951   Irrigation in East Central California. *American Antiquity* 17(1):50-52.

Patterson, Edna B.
1973   This Land Was Ours: An In-depth Study of a Frontier Community. Springville, Utah: Art City Publishing.

Pavesic, Max G.
1978   Archaeological Overview of the Middle Fork of the Salmon River Corridor, Idaho Primitive Area. *Boise State University Archaeological Reports* 3. Boise, Idaho.

1979   Public Archaeology in the Weiser Basin and Vicinity, a Narrative Report. Boise: Center for Research, Grants and Contracts, Boise State University.

1982   Shoshonean Salmon Procurement in Southern Idaho. (Paper presented at the Northwest Anthropological Conference, Boise, Idaho; in possession of Catherine S. Fowler.)

1983   The Western Idaho Archaic Burial Complex; Abstracts of Papers, 34-36. (Paper presented at the 36th Annual Northwest Anthropological Conference, Boise, Idaho.)

Pavesic, Max G., and Daniel S. Meatte
1980   Archaeological Test Excavations at the National Fish Hatchery Locality, Hagerman Valley, Idaho. *Boise State University Archaeological Reports* 8. Boise, Idaho.

Pavesic, Max G., Mark G. Plew, and Roderick Sprague
1979   A Bibliography of Idaho Archaeology, 1889-1976. *Northwest Anthropological Research Notes, Memoir* 5. Moscow, Idaho.

Payen, Louis A.
1966   Prehistoric Rock Art in the Northern Sierra Nevada, California. (Unpublished M.A. Thesis in Anthropology, Sacramento State College, Sacramento, Calif.)

Peck, Eugene L., and E. Arlo Richardson
1966   Hydrology and Climatology of Great Salt Lake. Pp. 121-134 in *Guidebook to the Geology of Utah* 20. William Lee Stokes, ed. Salt Lake City: Utah Geological Society.

Pendergast, David M.
1961   1960 Test Excavations in the Plainfield Reservoir Area. Addendum to 1960 Excavations, Glen Canyon Area. *Glen Canyon Series* 14, *University of Utah Anthropological Papers* 52. Salt Lake City.

———
1962   The Frei Site, Santa Clara, Utah. *Miscellaneous Collected Paper* 7, *University of Utah Anthropological Papers* 60. Salt Lake City.

Pendleton, Lorann S.
1979   Lithic Technology in Early Nevada Assemblages. (Unpublished M.A. Thesis in Anthropology, California State University, Long Beach.)

Pendleton, Lorann S., and David H. Thomas
1983   The Fort Sage Drift Fence, Washoe County, Nevada. *Anthropological Papers of the American Museum of Natural History* 58(2). New York.

Pendleton, Lorann S., Alvin McLane, and David H. Thomas
1982   Cultural Resource Overview, Carson City District, West Central Nevada. *Nevada Bureau of Land Management, Cultural Resource Series* 5. Reno.

Peng, T.H., J.G. Goddard, and W.S. Broecker
1978   A Direct Comparison of ^{14}C and ^{230}Th Ages at Searles Lake, California. *Quaternary Research* 9(3):319-329.

Perkins, Georgia B., and Gertrude M. Church
1960   Report of Pediatric Evaluations of a Sample of Indian Children - Wind River Reservation 1957. *American Journal of Public Health* 50:181-194.

Perkins, R.F.
1967   Engraved Stones of Southern Nevada. *Nevada Archaeological Survey Reporter* 1(7):11-13. Reno.

Peterson, Frederick F.
1980   Holocene Desert Soil Formation under Sodium Salt Influence in a Playa-margin Environment. *Quaternary Research* 13(2):172-186.

Peterson, Helen L.
1957   American Indian Political Participation. Pp. 116-126 in American Indians and American Life. George E. Simpson and J. Milton Yinger, ed. *Annals of the American Academy of Polititcal and Social Sciences* 311. Philadelphia.

Pettazzoni, Raffaele
1956   The All-knowing God: Researches into Early Religion and Culture. H.J. Rose, trans. London: Methuen.

Pettigrew, Richard M.
1980   The Ancient Chewaucanians: More on the Prehistoric Lake Dwellers of Lake Albert, Southwestern Oregon. *Association of Oregon Archaeologists Occasional Papers* 1:49-67. Albany.

Pettit, Jan
1982   Utes: The Mountain People. Colorado Springs, Colo.: Century One Press.

Pewé, Troy L.
1983   The Periglacial Environment in North America During Wisconsin Time. Pp. 157-189 in Late-Quaternary Environments of the United States. Vol. 1: The Late Pleistocene. Herbert E. Wright, Jr. and Stephen C. Porter, eds. Minneapolis: University of Minnesota Press.

Phillips, Arthur M., III
1977   Packrats, Plants, and the Pleistocene in the Lower Grand Canyon. (Unpublished Ph.D. Dissertation in General Biology, University of Arizona, Tucson.)

Philp, Kenneth R.
1977   John Collier's Crusade for Indian Reform, 1920-1954. Tucson: University of Arizona Press.

Pierson, Lloyd M., and Kevin Anderson
1975   Another Split-twig Figurine from Moab, Utah. *Plateau* 48(1-2):43-45.

Pietroforte, Alfred, coll.
1959   [25 Yokuts and Paiute Songs. Sam Kinney, Josie Atwell, Leon Manuel, Roy Chiatovich, Mary Garcia Pohot, Molloy

Pomona, Singers.] Healdsburg, Calif.: Naturegraph Publishers.

1965   Songs of the Yokuts and Paiutes. Vinson Brown, ed. Healdsburg, Calif.: Naturegraph Publishers.

Pilles, Peter J., Jr.
1979   Sunset Crater and the Sinagua: A New Interpretation. Pp. 459-485 in Volcanic Activity and Human Ecology. Payson D. Sheets and Donald K. Grayson, eds. New York: Academic Press.

Pilling, Arnold R.
1957   An Incised Pebble from Lassen County, California. P.6 in Papers on California Archaeology, 50-62. Robert F. Heizer, ed. *University of California Archaeological Survey Reports* 38(51). Berkeley.

Pimentel, Francisco
1874-1875 Cuadro descriptivo y comparativo de las lenguas indígenas de México. 3 vols. Mexico City: Tip. de I. Epstein.

Pippin, Lonnie C.
1979   Bighorn Sheep and Great Basin Prehistory. Pp. 332-358 in The Archaeology of Smith Creek Canyon, Eastern Nevada. Donald R. Tuohy and Doris L. Rendall, eds. *Nevada State Museum Anthropological Papers* 17. Carson City.

1980   Prehistoric and Historic Patterns of Lower Pinyon-Juniper Woodland Ecotone Exploitation at Borealis, Mineral County, Nevada. *University of Nevada, Desert Research Institute, Social Sciences Center Technical Report* 17. Reno.

Pippin, Lonnie C., and Donald L. Zerga
1981   Cultural Resources Overview for the Nuclear Waste Storage Investigations, Nevada Test Site, Nye County, Nevada. *University of Nevada, Desert Research Institute, Social Sciences Center Technical Report* 24. Reno.

Pippin, Lonnie C., Jonathan O. Davis, Elizabeth Budy, and Robert O. Elston
1979   Archaeological Investigations at the Pike's Point Site (4-LAS-537) Eagle Lake, Lassen County, California. *University of Nevada, Desert Research Institute Technical Report* 7. Reno.

Plew, Mark G.
1977   A Notched Stone Cobble from Southwestern Idaho. *Idaho Archaeologist* 1(2):10-11. Caldwell.

1979   Southern Idaho Plain: Implications for Fremont-Shoshoni Relationships in Southwestern Idaho. *Plains Anthropologist* 24(86):329-335.

1980   Archaeological Investigations in the South-central Owyhee Uplands, Idaho. *Boise State University Archaeological Reports* 7. Boise, Idaho.

1980a   Archaeological Excavations at Big Foot Bar, Snake River Birds of Prey Natural Area, Idaho. *Idaho Archaeological Consultants Project Report* 3. Boise.

1981   A Preliminary Report on Archaeological Excavations at Nahas Cave. *Idaho Archaeologist* 4(3):1-7. Caldwell.

1981a   Archaeological Test Excavations at Four Prehistoric Sites in the Western Snake River Canyon Near Bliss, Idaho. *Idaho Archaeological Consultants. Project Report* 5. Boise.

1981b   An Incised Stone from Gooding County, Idaho. *Idaho Archaeologist* 4(3):8-9. Caldwell.

Plew, Mark G., and Sally Cupan
1981   Incised Stones from Pend O'Reille River Area, Northern Idaho. *Idaho Archaeologist* 4(4):18-22. Caldwell.

Plimpton, Christine L.
1980   Worked Bone and Antler and Unworked Shell. Pp. 143-156 in Sudden Shelter, by Jesse D. Jennings, Alan R. Schroedl,

and Richard N. Holmer. *University of Utah Anthropological Papers* 103. Salt Lake City.

Pogue, Joseph E.
1915   The Turquois: A Study of Its History, Mineralogy, Geology, Ethnology, Archaeology, Mythology, Folklore and Technology. *National Academy of Sciences, Third Memoir Series* 12(2):3-162. Washington. (Reprinted: Rio Grande Press, Glorieta, N.M., 1971.)

Porter, Stephen C.
1978   Glacier Park Tephra in the North Cascade Range, Washington: Stratigraphy, Distribution, and Relationship to Late-Glacial Events. *Quaternary Research* 10(1):30-41.

Porter, Stephen C., Kenneth L. Pierce, annd Thomas D. Hamilton
1983   Late Wisconsin Mountain Glaciation in the Western United States. Pp. 71-111 in Late-Quaternary Environments of the United States. Vol. 1: The Late Pleistocene. Herbert E. Wright, Jr. and Stephen C. Porter, eds. Minneapolis: University of Minnesota Press.

Pourade, Richard F, ed.
1966   Ancient Hunters of the Far West. San Diego, Calif.: Union-Tribune Publishing Company.

Powell, John Wesley
[1873]   [Catalogue of Indian Collections Deposited in the Smithsonian Institution.] (Manuscripts, Accession No. 2357 in Department of Anthropology, Smithsonian Institution, Washington.)

1877   Introduction to the Study of Indian Languages, with Words, Phrases and Sentences to Be Collected. Washington: U.S. Government Printing Office. (Second revised edition, 1880.)

1881   Sketch of the Mythology of the North American Indians Pp. 17-56 in *1st Annual Report of the Bureau of American Ethnology for the Years* 1879-1880. Washington.

1887   Report of the Director. Pp. xvii-liii in *5th Annual Report of the Bureau of American Ethnology for the Years 1883-1884*. Washington.

1891   Indian Linguistic Families of America North of Mexico. Pp. 1-142 in *7th Annual Report of the Bureau of American Ethnology for the Years 1885-1886*. Washington.

Power, William K.
1980   The Art of Courtship Among the Oglala. *American Indian Art Magazine* 5(2):40-47.

Powers, Bob
1974   North Fork Country. Los Angeles, Calif.: Westernlore Press.

1981   Indian Country of the Tübatulabal. Tucson, Ariz.: Westernlore Press.

Powers, Stephen
[1876]   Life and Culture of the Washo and Paiutes. (Manuscript No. 808 in National Anthropological Archives, Smithsonian Institution, Washington.)

1876a   Washo Vocabulary, Taken at Carson City, Nevada. (Manuscript No. 951 in National Anthropological Archives, Smithsonian Institution, Washington.)

1877   Centennial Mission to the Indians of Western Nevada and California. Pp. 449-460 in *Annual Report of the Smithsonian Institution for 1876*. Washington.

1877a   Tribes of California. *Contributions to North American Ethnology* 3. Washington: U.S. Geographical and Geological Survey of the Rocky Mountain Region.

Powers, Williams R.
1969   Archaeological Excavations in Willow Creek Canyon, Southeastern Idaho, 1966. *Occasional Papers of the Idaho State University Museum* 25. Pocatello.

Pratt, Parley P.
1849   Correspondence from America (a Letter dated July 8, 1849). *The Millenial Star* 11 (November): 342-343. Liverpool, England.

Premo, Thomas, Raymond Thacker, and Louie Davis
1939   [Letter to the Commissioner of Indian Affairs, dated March 10.] (Manuscript in Letters Received No. 15251 in Record Group 75, National Archives, Washington.)

Press, Margaret L.
1975   A Grammar of Chemehuevi. (Unpublished Ph.D. Dissertation in Linguistics, University of California, Los Angeles.)

———
1979   Chemehuevi: A Grammar and Lexicon. *University of California Publications in Linguistics* 92. Berkeley.

Preuss, Charles
1958   Exploring with Frémont: The Private Diaries of Charles Preuss, Cartographer for John C. Frémont... Norman: University of Oklahoma Press.

Price, John A.
1962   Washo Economy. *Nevada State Museum Anthropological Papers* 6. Carson City.

———
1962a   Washo Economy. (Unpublished M.A. Thesis in Anthropology, University of Utah, Salt Lake City.)

———
1963   Washo Culture Change. Pp. 40-54 in 1962 Great Basin Anthropological Conference. *Nevada State Museum Anthropological Papers* 9. Carson City.

———
1963a   Some Aspects of Washo Life Cycle. Pp. 96-114 in The Washo Indians of California and Nevada. Warren L. d'Azevedo, ed. *University of Utah Anthropological Papers* 67. Salt Lake City.

———
1980   The Washo Indians: History, Life Cycle, Religion, Technology, Economy and Modern Life. *Nevada State Museum Occasional Papers* 4. Carson City.

Prucha, Francis P.
1976   Indian Peace Medals in American History. Lincoln: University of Nebraska Press.

Putnam, Frederick W.
1878   Report of the Curator. Pp. 191-206 in *Eleventh Annual Report of the Trustees of the Peabody Museum of American Archaeology and Ethnology* 2(2). Cambridge, Mass.

Putnam, J.D.
1876   Hieroglyphics Observed in Summit Canyon, Utah and on Little Popo-agie River in Wyoming. *Proceedings of the Davenport Academy of Natural Sciences (1867-1876)*, Vol. 1:143-145. Davenport, Iowa.

Radin, Paul
1919   The Genetic Relationship of the North American Indian Languages. *University of California Publications in American Archaeology and Ethnology* 14(5):489-502. Berkeley.

Radovsky, Frank J.
1970   Mites Associated with Coprolites and Mummified Human Remains in Nevada. *University of California Archaeological Research Facility Contributions* 10(6):186-190. Berkeley.

Rafferty, Kevin
[1984] Cultural Resources Overview of the Las Vegas Valley. Reno: Bureau of Land Management. (In preparation)

Randle, Martha C.
1953   A Shoshone Hand Game Gambling Song. *Journal of American Folklore* 66(260):155-159.

Ranere, Anthony J.
1970   Prehistoric Environments and Cultural Continuity in the Western Great Basin. *Tebiwa: Journal of the Idaho State University Museum* 13(2):52-73. Pocatello.

Ranere, Anthony J., Joan C. Ranere, and John Lortz
1969   The Monida Pass Tipi Ring Site. *Tebiwa: Journal of the Idaho State University Museum* 12(1):39-46. Pocatello.

Rau, Charles
1873   Ancient Aboriginal Trade in North America. Pp. 348-394 in *Annual Report of the Smithsonian Institution for 1872*. Washington.

Ray, Verne F.
1942   Culture Element Distributions, XXII: Plateau. *University of California Anthropological Records* 8:99-262. Berkeley.

———
1947   Far Western Indian Folklore. Pp. 406-416 in Folklore Research in North America. Anna H. Gayton et al., eds. *Journal of American Folklore* 60(238).

Ray, Verne F., and Nancy O. Lurie
1954   The Contributions of Lewis and Clark to Ethnography. *Journal of the Washington Academy of Sciences* 44(11):358-370. Washington.

Ray, Verne F., G.P. Murdock, B. Blyth, O.C. Stewart, J. Harris, E.A. Hoebel, and D.B. Shimkin
1938   Tribal Distribution in Eastern Oregon and Adjacent Regions. *American Anthropologist* 40(3):384-415.

Raymond, Anan S., and Richard E. Fike
1981   Rails East to Promontory: The Utah Stations. *Utah Bureau of Land Management, Cultural Resource Series* 8. Salt Lake City.

Read, Georgia W., and Ruth Gaines, eds.
1949   Gold Rush: The Journals, Drawings and Other Papers of J. Goldsborough Bruff, Captain, Washington City and California Mining Association, April 2, 1849-July 20, 1851. New York: Columbia University Press.

Reagan, Albert B.
1917   The Deep Creek Indians. *El Palacio* 5(3):30-42.

———
1931   The Pictographs of Ashley and Dry Fork Valleys in Northeastern Utah. *Transactions of the Kansas Academy of Science* 34:168-216. Manhattan.

———
1931a   Some Archaeological Notes on Nine Mile Canyon, Utah. *El Palacio* 31(4):45-71.

———
1931b   Additional Archaeological Notes on Ashley and Dry Fork Canyons in Northeastern Utah. *El Palacio* 31(8):122-131.

———
1931c   Some Archaeological Notes on Hill Canyon in Northeastern Utah. *El Palacio* 31(15):223-244.

———
1931d   Ruins and Pictographs in Nine Mile Canyon, Utah. *Transactions of the Illinois State Academy of Science* 24(2):369-370. Springfield.

———
1932   Some Notes on the Picture Writing North of Mexico. *Bulletin of the Wagner Free Institute of Science* 7(4). Philadelphia.

———
1933   Indian Pictures in Ashley and Dry Fork Valleys in Northeastern Utah. *Art and Archaeology* 34(4):201-210.

———
1934   Additional Archaeological Notes on the Uintah Basin, in Northeastern Utah. *Transactions of the Kansas Academy of Science* 37:39-54. Manhattan.

———
1934a   The Gosiute (Goshute) or Shoshoni-Goship Indians of the Deep Creek Region in Western Utah. *Proceedings of the Utah Academy of Sciences, Arts and Letters* 11:43-54. Provo.

———
1935   Archaeological Report of Fieldwork Done in Utah in 1934-1935. *Proceedings of the Utah Academy of Sciences, Arts and Letters* 12:50-88. Provo.

———
1935a   Petroglyphs Show that the Ancients of the Southwest Wore Masks. *American Anthropologist* 37(4):707-708.

———
1937   Some Notes on the Religion of the Indians. *Proceedings of the Utah Academy of Sciences, Arts and Letters* 14:1-15. Provo.

Rector, Carol H.

1977 The Function of the East Mojave Rock Art. (Paper presented at the Third Annual A.R.A.R.A. Symposium, A.J. Bock et al., eds.) *American Indian Rock Art* 3:151-156. Whittier, Calif.

1981 Rock Art of the East Mojave Desert. Pp. 236-259 in Background to Historic and Prehistoric Resources of the East Mojave Desert Region by C. King and D.G. Casebier. Riverside: California Bureau of Land Management, Desert Planning Program.

1983 Great Basin Rock Art and Hunting Magic: A Reconsideration. (Manuscript in Department of Anthropology, University of California, Riverside.)

Rector, Carol H., James D. Swenson, and Philip I. Wilke

1979 Archaeological Studies at Oro Grande, Mojave Desert, California. (Final report submitted to Victor Valley Wastewater Reclamation Authority, Victorville, Calif.)

Redding, B.B.

1879 How Our Ancestors in the Stone Age Made Their Implements. *American Naturalist* 13(11):667-674.

Reed, Verner Z.

1896 The Ute Bear Dance. *American Anthropologist* 9(4):237-244.

Reeder, Grant M.

1967 Split Twig Animal Miniatures in the Southwestern United States. *Utah Archeology: A Newsletter* 13:12-16. Salt Lake City.

Rehrer, Charles A., and George C. Frison

1981 The Vore Site, 48 CK 302: A Stratified Buffalo Jump in the Wyoming Black Hills. *Plains Anthropologist Memoir* 16.

Reichard, Gladys A.

1921 Literary Types and Dissemination of Myths. *Journal of American Folk-Lore* 34(133):269-307.

Reilly, P.T.

1966 The Sites at Vasey's Paradise. *The Masterkey* 40(4):126-139.

Remy, Jules

1860 Voyage au pays des Mormons. 2 vols. Paris: E. Dentu.

Remy, Jules, and Julius Brenchley

1861 A Journey to Great-Salt-Lake City; with a Sketch of the History, Religion, and Customs of the Mormons, and an Introduction on the Religious Movement in the United States. 2 vols. London: W. Jeffs.

Renaud, A.E.B.

1929 Prehistoric Female Figurines from America and the Old World. *Scientific Monthly* 28:507-512.

Reynolds, Terry J.

1975 Western Nevada's Water Problems. Pt 2. *Nevada Public Affairs Review* 14(3). Reno.

Rhodes, Willard, coll.

1937-1952 [Songs of Shoshone, Washoe, Southern Ute, Northern Ute, Northern Paiute.] (In Willard Rhodes Collection of Great Basin Music, Archive of Folk Culture, Library of Congress, Washington.)

Rice, David G.

1972 The Windust Phase in Lower Snake River Region Prehistory. *Washington State University, Laboratory of Anthropology, Report of Investigations* 50. Pullman.

Rich, George W.

1971 Rethinking the "Star Husband." *Journal of American Folk-Lore* 84(334):436-441.

Ricklefs, Robert E.

1979 Ecology. 2d ed. New York: Chiron Press.

Riddell, Francis A.

1956 Final Report on the Archaeology of Tommy Tucker Cave. *University of California Archaeological Survey Reports* 35(44): 1-25. Berkeley.

1960 The Archaeology of the Karlo Site (LAS-7) of California. *University of California Archaeological Survey Reports* 53. Berkeley.

1960a Honey Lake Paiute Ethnography. *Nevada State Museum Anthropological Papers* 4. Carson City.

Riddell, Harry S., Jr.

1951 The Archaeology of a Paiute Village Site in Owens Valley. *University of California Archaeological Survey Reports* 12(15): 14-28. Berkeley.

Riddell, Harry S., Jr., and Francis A. Riddell

1956 The Current Status of Archaeological Investigations in Owens Valley, California. *University of California Archeological Survey Reports* 33(38):28-33. Berkeley.

Ridgway, R.

[1875] [Comparative Vocabulary: Washoe, Pi-ute, Shoshonie; Washoe from Carson City, Nevada.] (Manuscript No. 778 in National Anthropological Archives, Smithsonian Institution, Washington.)

Ridgway, R., and Stephen Powers

[1880] [Washoe Vocabularies, Carson City, Nevada.] (Manuscript No. 950 in National Anthropological Archives, Smithsonian Institution, Washington.)

Ritter, Eric W.

1980 A Historic Aboriginal Structure and Its Associations, Panamint Mountains, California. *Journal of California and Great Basin Anthropology* 2(1):97-113.

Roberts, Bertram L.

1965 Descendants of the Numu. *The Masterkey* 39(1):13-22, (2):66-76.

Roberts, Daniel G.

1976 Final Report on the 1974-75 Camas Creek-Little Grassy Archaeological Survey. *Archaeological Reports of the Idaho State University Museum of Natural History* 5. Pocatello.

Roberts, Frank H.H., Jr.

1940 Developments in the Problem of the North American Paleo-Indian. *Smithsonian Miscellaneous Collections* 100:51-116. Washington.

1943 Evidence for a Paleo-Indian in the New World. *Acta Americana* 1(2):171-201.

Roberts, J.

1916 [To Henry A. Larson through Supt. E.A. Hutcheson, Wind River, Wyo., in Reply to BIA Questionnaire, dated December 26 and 28.] (Manuscript in Letters Received, Record Group 75, National Archives, Washington.)

Robertson, A.L.

1938 [Letter to O.C. Stewart, Dated September 21.] (Manuscript in O.C. Stewart's possession.)

Robertson, Cheri, comp.

1977 After the Drying Up of the Water. Fallon, Nev.: The Fallon Paiute-Shoshone Tribe.

Robinson, Paul T., Wilfred A. Elders, and L.J.P. Muffler

1976 Quaternary Volcanism in the Salton Sea Geothermal Field, Imperial Valley, California. *Geological Society of America Bulletin* 87(3):347-360.

Rockwell, Wilson

[1956] The Utes: A Forgotten People. Denver: Sage Books.

Roe, Frank G.

1951 The North American Buffalo: A Critical Study of the Species in Its Wild State. Toronto: University of Toronto Press.

Rogers, Jean H.

1967 Some Implications of Two Solutions to a Phonological Problem. *International Journal of American Linguistics* 33(3):198-205.

Rogers, Malcolm J.
1929   Report on an Archaeological Reconnaissance in the Mojave Sink Region. *San Diego Museum of Man Archaeological Papers* 1(1). San Diego, Calif.

1939   Early Lithic Industries of the Lower Basin of the Colorado River and Adjacent Desert Areas. *San Diego Museum of Man Archaeological Papers* 3. San Diego, Calif. (Reprinted: Ballena Press, Ramona, Calif., 1973.)

1945   An Outline of Yuman Prehistory. *Southwestern Journal of Anthropology* 1(2):167-198.

Rohn, Arthur
1973   The Southwest and Intermontane West. Pp. 185-212 in The Development of North American Archaeology. James E. Fitting, ed. Garden City, N.Y.: Anchor Press/Doubleday.

Romney, A. Kimball
1957   The Genetic Model and Uto-Aztecan Time Perspective. *Davidson Journal of Anthropology* 3(2):35-41. Seattle, Wash.

Rondeau, Michael F.
1982   A Lithic Seasonal Round for the Northern Sierra Nevada: A Regional Model. (Paper presented at the 18th Great Basin Anthropological Conference, Reno, Nev.)

Roney, John
1978   Western Pluvial Lakes Tradition Materials from the Carson Sink, Churchill County, Nevada. (Paper presented at the 14th Great Basin Anthropological Association Meeting, Reno, Nev.)

Rooth, Anna B.
1957   The Creation Myths of the North American Indians. *Anthropos* 52(3-4):497-508.

Ross, Alexander
1855   The Fur Hunters of the Far West: A Narrative of Adventure in the Oregon and Rocky Mountains. 2 vols. London: Smith, Elder.

1956   The Fur Hunters of the Far West [1855]. Kenneth A. Spaulding, ed. (*The American Exploration and Travel Series* 20) Norman: University of Oklahoma Press.

Ross, Marvin C., ed.
1968   The West of Alfred Jacob Miller [1837]. Norman: University of Oklahoma Press.

Rossillon, Mary P.
1980   An Overview of History in the Drainage Basin of the Middle Fork of the Salmon River. *University of Idaho Anthropological Research Manuscript Series* 60. Moscow.

Roth, George E.
1976   Incorporation and Changes in Ethnic Structure: The Chemehuevi Indians. (Unpublished Ph.D. Dissertation in Anthropology, Northwestern University, Evanston, Ill.)

Roust, Norman L.
1966   The Archaeology of Granite Point, Pershing County, Nevada. Pp. 37-72 in Notes on Western Nevada Archaeology and Ethnology. *University of California Archaeological Survey Reports* 66. Berkeley.

1967   Preliminary Examination of Prehistoric Human Coprolites from Four Western Nevada Caves. *University of California Archaeological Survey Reports* 70(4):49-88. Berkeley.

Roust, Norman L., and C. William Clewlow, Jr.
1968   Projectile Points from Hidden Cave (NV-CH-16), Churchill County, Nevada. Pp. 103-116 in Papers on Great Basin Prehistory. *University of California Archaeological Survey Reports* 71. Berkeley.

Rowlands, Peter, Hyram Johnson, Eric Ritter, and Albert Endo
1982   The Mojave Desert. Pp. 103-145 in Reference Handbook on the Deserts of North America. Gordon L. Bender, ed. Westport, Conn.: Greenwood Press.

Royce, Charles C., comp.
1899   Indian Land Cessions in the United States. Pp. 521-964 (Pt. 2) in *18th Annual Report of the Bureau of American Ethnology for the Years 1896-1897*. Washington.

Rozaire, Charles E.
1957   Twined Weaving and Western North American Prehistory. (Unpublished Ph.D. Dissertation in Anthropology, University of California, Los Angeles.)

1969   The Chronology of Woven Materials from the Caves at Falcon Hill, Washoe County, Nevada. Pp. 182-186 in Miscellaneous Papers on Nevada Archaeology. Doris L. Rendall and Donald R. Tuohy, eds. *Miscellaneous Paper 8, Nevada State Museum Anthropological Papers* 14. Carson City.

1974   Analysis of Woven Materials from Seven Caves in the Lake Winnemucca Area, Pershing County, Nevada. Pp. 60-97 in Collected Papers on Aboriginal Basketry. Donald R. Tuohy and Doris L. Rendall, eds. *Nevada State Museum Anthropological Papers* 16. Carson City.

Ruby, Jay W.
1970   Culture Contact Between Aboriginal Southern California and the Southwest (Unpublished Ph.D. Dissertation in Anthropology, University of California, Los Angeles.)

Ruby, Jay W., and Wayne Alexander
1962   Preliminary Report of Excavations at Evan's Mound (In-40), Summit, Utah. (Manuscript in Department of Anthropology, University of California, Los Angeles.)

Rudy, Jack R.
1953   Archeological Survey of Western Utah. *University of Utah Anthropological Papers* 12. Salt Lake City.

1954   Pine Park Shelter, Washington County, Utah. *University of Utah Anthropological Papers* 18. Salt Lake City.

Rudy, Sara S.
1957   Textiles. Pp. 235-264 in Danger Cave, by Jesse D. Jennings. *University of Utah Anthropological Papers* 27. Salt Lake City.

Ruebelman, George N.
1973   The Archaeology of the Mesa Hill Site: A Prehistoric Workshop in the Southeastern Columbia Plateau. (Unpublished M.A. Thesis in Anthropology, University of Idaho, Moscow.)

Ruhe, Robert V.
1983   Aspects of Holocene Pedology in the United States. Pp. 12-25 in Late-Quaternary Environments of the United States. Vol. 2: The Holocene. Herbert E. Wright, Jr., ed. Minneapolis: University of Minnesota Press.

Rusco, Elmer R.
1966   Voting Patterns of Racial Minorities in Nevada. Reno: University of Nevada, Bureau of Governmental Research.

1982   The MX Missile and Western Shoshone Land Claims. *Nevada Public Affairs Review* 2:45-54. Reno.

1982a   Organization of the Te-Moak Bands of Western Shoshone. *Nevada Historical Society Quarterly* 25 (3):175-176. Reno.

1983   The Formation of the Washoe Tribal Council. (Manuscript in Rusco's possession.)

Rusco, Mary K.
1973   Types of Anthropomorphic Figures in the Great Basin. *Nevada Archeological Survey Reporter* 7(2):4-17. Reno.

1976   Fur Trappers in the Snake Country: An Ethnohistorical Approach to Recent Environmental Change. Pp. 152-173 in Holocene Environmental Change in the Great Basin. Robert Elston, ed. *Nevada Archeological Survey Research Papers* 8. Reno.

1977   Evaluation of Cultural Resources of the Proposed Watasheamu Reservoir Location, Lahontan Basin, Toiyabe National Forest, Nevada and California. *Nevada State Museum Report* Contract No. 1007. Carson City.

1982   Archaeological Investigations at the Rossi Mine Archaeological Sites, Elko County, Nevada. Carson City: Nevada State Museum.

Rusco, Mary K., and Jonathan O. Davis
1979   Archaeological Investigations Near Treaty Hill, Humboldt County, Nevada: Section 29. (Report to the Westinghouse Corporation, Environmental Services Division; manuscript in Nevada State Museum, Carson City.)

————, eds.
1982   The Humboldt Project, Rye Patch Reservoir-Phase IV Archaeological Data Synthesis Final Report. Nevada State Museum Archaeological Services Reports. Carson City. (Submitted to the National Park Service, Interagency Archaeological Services Division, San Francisco, Contract No. CX8099-1-0002.)

Rusco, Mary K., and Jeanne Munoz
1983   An Archaeological Survey in the Mormon Mountains, Clark County, Nevada. *Nevada Bureau of Land Management, Contributions to the Study of Cultural Resources, Technical Report* 11. Reno.

Rusco, Mary K., Jonathan O. Davis, and J.R. Firby
1979   The Humboldt Project, Rye Patch Archaeology, Phase III-Final Report. (Nevada State Museum Archaeological Services reports to Interagency Archaeological Services for Heritage Conservation and Recreation Service, U.S. Department of the Interior; on file, Nevada State Museum, Carson City.)

Rusco, Mary K., J.O. Davis, A. Jensen, and E. Seelinger
1977   Archaeological Investigations at the Rye Patch Reservoir. Final Report (Contract No. 14-06-200-8364) Carson City: Nevada State Museum.

Russell, Israel C.
1885   Geological History of Lake Lahontan: A Quaternary Lake of Northwestern Nevada. *U.S. Geological Survey Monographs* 11. Washington.

Russell, Osborne
1921   Journal of a Trapper, or Nine Years in the Rocky Mountains, 1834-1843. 2d ed. Boise, Idaho: Syms-York.

Ryan, C.
1975   Indians Argue Hunting Exemptions. [Draft of a bill dated October 19, Carson City, Nev.]

Ryser, Fred A.
1984   Birds of Nevada. (*Great Basin Natural History Series*) Reno: University of Nevada Press.

Sabels, Bruno E.
1960   Trace Element Studies on Cave Strata...with Comments on Stuart Rockshelter. Pp. 17-23 in Stuart Rockshelter: A Stratified Site in Southern Nevada. Dick Shutler, Jr., Mary E. Shutler, and James S. Griffiths, eds. *Nevada State Museum Anthropological Papers* 3. Carson City.

Sadek-Kooros, Hind
1966   Jaguar Cave: An Early Man Site in the Beaverhead Mountains of Idaho. 2 vols. (Unpublished Ph.D. Dissertation in Anthropology Harvard University, Cambridge, Mass.)

Sahlins, Marshall
1972   Stone Age Economics. Chicago: Aldine-Atherton.

St. Clair, Harry H., II
1903   A Sketch of the Shoshone Language. (Unpublished M.A. Thesis in Linguistics, Columbia University, New York City.)

St. Clair, Harry H., II, and Robert H. Lowie
1909   Shoshone and Comanche Tales. *Journal of American Folk-Lore* 22(85):265-282.

Salzmann, Zdenek
1983   Dictionary of Contemporary Arapaho Usage. *Arapaho Language and Culture, Instructional Materials Series* 4. Wind River Reservation, Wyo.

Sample, L.L.
1950   Trade and Trails in Aboriginal California. *University of California Archaeological Survey Reports* 8:1-30. Berkeley.

Sampson, C. Garth
1985   Nightfire Island: Late Holocene Lakemarsh Adaptation on the Western Edge of the Great Basin. *University of Oregon Anthropological Papers* 3. Eugene.

Santini, James D.
1974   A Preliminary Report on the Analysis of Incised Stones from Southern Nevada. *Nevada Archaeologist* 2(1):4-15. Carson City.

Sapir, Edward
1910   Two Paiute Myths. *University of Pennsylvania Museum Journal* 1(10):15-18. Philadelphia.

1910a   Song Recitative in Paiute Mythology. *Journal of American Folk-Lore* 23(90):455-472.

1910b   Kaibab Paiute Linguistic and Ethnologic Fieldnotes. (Manuscript No. 30 (U.3), Freeman No. 2643 in American Philosophical Society Library, Philadelphia.)

1910c   [Transcriptions of 197 Songs from Edward Sapir's Southern Paiute Recordings.] (Unpublished manuscript in Archives of Traditional Music, Indiana University, Bloomington.)

————, coll.
1910d   [200 Southern Paiute (Kaibab) Songs; Tony Tillohash, singer.] (No. 60-017-F. in Archives of Traditional Music, Indiana University, Bloomington.)

1912   The Mourning Ceremony of the Southern Paiutes. *American Anthropologist* 14(1):168-169.

1913   Southern Paiute and Nahuatl: A Study in Uto-Aztekan. [Pt.1]. *Journal de la Société des Américanistes de Paris* n.s. 10:379-425. Paris.

1915   Southern Paiute and Nahuatl: A Study in Uto-Aztekan. Pt. II. *American Anthropologist* 17(1):98-120, (2):306-328. (Also published in *Journal de la Société des Américanistes* de Paris n.s. 11:443-488, 1919.)

1916   Time Perspective in Aboriginal American Culture: A Study in Method. *Anthropological Series* 13, *Canada Department of Mines, Geological Survey Memoir* 90. Ottawa. (Reprinted: Pp. 389-462 in Selected Writings of Edward Sapir in Language, Culture, and Personality. David G. Mandelbaum, ed., University of California Press, Berkeley, 1949; Johnson Reprint Corporation, New York, 1968.)

1917   The Status of Washo. *American Anthropologist* 19(3):449-450.

1920   The Hokan and Coahuiltecan Languages. *International Journal of American Linguistics* 1(4):280-290.

1921-1923   A Supplementary Note on Salinan and Washo. *International Journal of American Linguistics* 2(1-2):68-72.

1925   The Hokan Affinity of Subtiaba in Nicaragua. *American Anthropologist* 27(3):402-435, (4):491-527.

1930-1931   The Southern Paiute Language. *Proceedings of the American Academy of Arts and Sciences* 65(1-3). Boston.

1949   Song Recitative in Paiute Mythology [1910]. Pp. 463-467 in Selected Writings of Edward Sapir in Language, Culture, and Personality. David G. Mandelbaum, ed. Berkeley: University of California Press. (Reprinted: Johnson Reprint Corporation, New York, 1968)

Sappington, Robert L.
1981 A Progress Report on the Obsidian and Vitrophyre Sourcing Project. *Idaho Archaeologist* 4(2):4-17. Caldwell.

_____ 1981a Additional Obsidian and Vitrophyre Souce Descriptions from Idaho and Adjacent Areas. *Idaho Archaeologist* 5(1):4-8. Caldwell.

_____ 1981b The Archaeology of the Lydle Gulch Site (10-AA-72): Prehistoric Occupation in the Boise River Canyon, Southwestern Idaho. (With appendices by Ruthann Knudson, Ula Moody, Anita Falen, and Chris Brown). *University of Idaho Anthropological Research Manuscript Series* 66. Moscow.

_____ [1985] Additional Analysis of Hidden Cave Obsidian Sourcing. in The Archaeology of Hidden Cave, Nevada, by David H. Thomas. *Anthropological Papers of the American Museum of Natural History* New York. In press.

Sargeant, Kathryn E.
1973 The Haskett Tradition: A View from Redfish Overhang. (Unpublished M.A. Thesis in Anthropology, Idaho State University, Pocatello.)

Sarna-Wojcicki, Andrei M., Duane E. Champion, and Jonathan O. Davis
1983 Holocene Volcanism in the Conterminous United States and the Role of Silicic Volcanic Ash Layers in Correlation of Latest-Pleistocene and Holocene Deposits. Pp. 52-57 in Late-Quaternary Environments of the United States. Vol. 2: The Holocene. Herbert E. Wright, Jr., ed. Minneapolis: University of Minnesota Press.

Sauer, Carl O.
1944 A Geographic Sketch of Early Man in America. *Geographical Review* 34(4):529-573. New York.

_____ 1950 Grassland Climax, Fire and Man. *Journal of Range Management* 3(10):16-21. Denver, Colo.

Savage. J.C., and M.M. Clark
1982 Magmatic Resurgence in Long Valley Caldera, California: Possible Cause of the 1980 Mammoth Lakes Earthquakes. *Science* 217(4559):531-533.

Say, Thomas
1905 Vocabularies of Indian Languages. Pp. 289-308 in Pt. 4 of Account of an Expedition from Pittsburgh to the Rocky Mountains, Performed in the Years 1819, 1820...Under the Command of Maj. S.H. Long, by Edwin James [1823]. Vols. 14-17 of Early Western Travels, 1748-1846. R.G. Thwaites, ed. Cleveland, Ohio: Arthur H. Clark.

Schaafsma, Polly
1970 Survey Report of the Rock Art of Utah. (Unpublished manuscript in Archeological Laboratory, University of Utah, Salt Lake City.)

_____ 1971 The Rock Art of Utah. *Papers of the Peabody Museum of American Archaeology and Ethnology, Harvard University* 65. Cambridge, Mass.

_____ 1980 Indian Rock Art of the Southwest. Albuquerque: University of New Mexico Press.

_____ 1982 [Western Colorado Plateau Rock Art Styles.] (Unpublished drawings in Schaafsma's possession.)

_____ [1983] Form, Content, and Function: Theory and Method in North American Rock Art Studies. In Advances in Archaeological Method and Theory. Michael B. Schiffer, ed. In press.

Schallenberger, Moses
1953 Overland in 1844. Pp. 46-84 The Opening of the California Trial. R. Stewart, ed. (*Bancroft Library Publications* 4) Berkeley: University of California Press.

Schellbach, Louis, III
1930 Researches in Idaho. *Museum of the American Indian, Heye Foundation, Indian Notes* 7(1):123-125. New York.

_____ 1967 The Excavation of Cave No. 1, Southwestern Idaho, 1929. *Tebiwa: Journal of the Idaho State University Museum* 10(2):63-72. Pocatello.

Scherer, Joanna, Cohan
1975 You Can't Believe Your Eyes: Inaccuracies in Photographs of North American Indians. *Studies in the Anthropology of Visual Communication* 2(2). Philadelphia.

Schiffman, Robert A., and Alan P. Garfinkel
1981 Prehistory of Kern County—An Overview. *Bakersfield College Publications in Archaeology* 1. Bakersfield, Calif.

Schmeckebier, L.F., comp.
1904 Catalogue and Index of the Publications of the Hayden, King, Powell and Wheeler Surveys. *U.S. Geological Survey Bulletin* 222(G-26). Washington.

Schmerler, Henrietta
1931 Trickster Marries His Daughter. *Journal of American Folk-Lore* 44(172):196-207.

Schmidt, P. Wilhelm
1912-1955 Der Ursprung der Gottesidee. Vol 6. Münster, Germany: Verlag der Aschendorffschen Verlagsbuchhandlung.

Schneider, Mary Jane
1968 Plains Indian Clothing: Stylistic Persistence and Change. *Bulletin of the Oklahoma Anthropological Society* 17:1-55. Tulsa.

Scholz, Christopher H., Muawia Barazangi, and Marc L. Sbar
1971 Late Cenozoic Evolution of the Great Basin, Western United States, as an Ensialic Interarc Basin. *Geological Society of America Bulletin* 82(11):2979-2990, Boulder, Colo.

Schoolcraft, Henry R.
1847 Inquiries, Respecting the History, Present Condition and Future Prospects of the Indian Tribes of the United States. Washington: U.S. Office of Indian Affairs.

_____ 1851-1857 Historical and Statistical Information Respecting the History, Condition and Prospects of the Indian Tribes of the United States. 6 vols. Philadelphia: Lippincott, Grambo.

_____ 1853-1856 Information Respecting the History, Condition and Prospects of the Indian Tribes of the United States: Collected and Prepared under the Direction of the Bureau of Indian Affairs per Act of Congress of March 3rd 1847. 5 vols. Philadelphia: Lippincott, Grambo.

Schroeder, Albert H.
1953 A Few Sites in Moapa Valley, Nevada. *The Masterkey* 27(1):18-24, (2):62-68.

_____ 1955 Archeology of Zion Park. *University of Utah Anthropological Papers* 22. Salt Lake City.

_____ 1961 The Archeological Excavations at Willow Beach, Arizona, 1950. *University of Utah Anthropological Papers* 50. Salt Lake City.

_____ 1965 A Brief History of the Southern Ute. *Southwestern Lore* 30(4):53-78.

Schroedl, Alan R.
1976 The Archaic of the Northern Colorado Plateau. (Unpublished Ph.D. Dissertation in Archaeology, University of Utah, Salt Lake City.)

_____ 1977 The Grand Canyon Figurine Complex. *American Antiquity* 4(2):254-265.

Schroedl, Alan R., and P.F. Hogan
1975 Innocents Ridge and the San Rafael Fremont. *Utah Division of State History, Antiquities Section Selected Papers* 1(2). Salt Lake City.

Schubert, Juanita
[1957]   Botanical Identification of Plants Used by Washoe Indians. Appended to Plants Used for Foods, Medicines, or Poisons by the Washoe Indians, Based on Linguistic Notes by William H. Jacobsen, Jr. (Manuscript in Jacobsen's possession; copy in Catherine S. Fowler's possession.)

Schuiling, Walter C., ed.
1979   Pleistocene Man at Calico: A Report on the Calico Muntains Excavations, San Bernardino County, California. 2d. ed. Redlands, Calif.: San Bernardino County Museum Association.

Schuster, Carl
1968   Incised Stones from Nevada and Elsewhere. *Nevada Archeological Survey Reporter* 2(5):4-22. Reno.

Schuster, Meinhard
1964   Zur Frage der Erste-Früchte-Riten in Nordamerika. Pp. 611-619 in Festschrift für Ad. E. Jenson. 2 vols. Munich, Germany: Klaus Renner Verlag.

Schutz, Willard D., John L. Baker, and Andrew Vanvig
1960   Indian Ranching on the Wind River Reservation, Wyoming. *University of Wyoming, Agricultural Experiment Station Bulletin* 366. Laramie.

Schwartz, Douglas W., Arthur L. Lange, and Raymond DeSaussure
1958   Split-twig Figurines in the Grand Canyon. *American Antiquity* 23(3):264-274.

Scotch, Norman A., and Freda L. Scotch
1963   Social Factors in Hypertension Among the Washo. *University of Utah Anthropological Papers* 67:69-76. Salt Lake City.

Scott, Lalla
1966   Karnee: A Paiute Narrative. Charles R. Craig, ann. Reno: University of Nevada Press.

Scott, William E., William D. McCoy, Ralph R. Sheobav, and Meyer Rubin
1983   Reinterpretation of the Exposed Record of the Last Two Cycles of Lake Bonneville, Western United States. *Quaternary Research* 20(3):261-285.

Sears, Paul B., and Aino Roosma
1961   A Climatic Sequence from Two Nevada Caves. *American Journal of Science* 259(9):669-678.

Seck, Susan M.
1980   The Archeology of Trego Hot Springs: 26PE118 (Unpublished M.A. Thesis in Anthropology, University of Nevada, Reno.)

Secoy, Frank R.
1953   Changing Military Patterns on the Great Plains, (17th Century Through Early 19th Century). (*Monographs of the American Ethnological Society* 21) Locust Valley, N.Y.: J.J. Augustin.

Seiler, Hansjakob, and Kojiro Hioki
1979   Cahuilla Dictionary. Banning, Calif.: Malki Museum Press.

Self, William
1980   The Archeology of Lowe Shelter: A Contribution to the Prehistory of the Western Great Basin. (Unpublished M.A. Thesis in Anthropology, University of Nevada, Reno.)

———
1980a   A Production Stage Analysis of Bifaces from Lowe Shelter, Nye County, Nevada. (Paper presented at Great Basin Anthropological Conference, Salt Lake City, Utah.)

Šercelj, Alojz, and David P. Adam
1975   A Late Holocene Pollen Diagram from Near Lake Tahoe, El Dorado County, California. *Journal of Research of the U.S. Geological Survey* 3(6):737-745.

Service, Elman R.
1962   Primitive Social Organization: An Evolutionary Perspective. New York: Random House.

———
1966   The Hunters. Englewood Cliffs, N.J.: Prentice-Hall.

Severance, Mark S.
1874   Preliminary Ethnological Report. Pp. 55-56 in U.S. Geographical and Geological Explorations and Surveys West of the 100th Meridian. Progress Report for 1872. App. F. Washington: U.S. Government Printing Office.

Shapiro, Judith
1965   Northern Paiute Systems of Social Classification. (Unpublished manuscript in Ethnographic Archives 1-24, Department of Anthropology, University of Nevada, Reno.)

Sharp, John
1898   The Large-mouthed Black Bass in Utah. *Bulletin of the United States Fish Commission for 1897.* Vol. 17:363-368. Washington.

Sharp, Robert P.
1966   Kelso Dunes, Mojave Desert, California. *Geological Society of America Bulletin* 77(10):1045-1974. Boulder, Colo.

Sharrock, Floyd W.
1966   Prehistoric Occupation Patterns in Southwest Wyoming and Cultural Relationships with the Great Basin and Plains Culture Areas. *University of Utah Anthropological Papers* 77. Salt Lake City.

Sharrock, Floyd W., and John P. Marwitt
1967   Excavations at Nephi, Utah, 1965-1966. *University of Utah Anthropological Papers* 88. Salt Lake City.

Sharrock, Floyd W., Kent C. Day, and David S. Dibble
1963   1961 Excavations, Glen Canyon Area. *Glen Canyon Series* 18, *University of Utah Anthropological Papers* 63. Salt Lake City.

Sharrock, Floyd W. et al.
1961   1960 Excavations, Glen Canyon Area. *Glen Canyon Series* 14, *University of Utah Anthropological Papers* 52. Salt Lake City.

Shattuck, Petra
1981   The Black Hills Rip-off: No Acres and No Mules. *The Nation* 233(6):168-172.

Shaul, David L.
1981   Semantic Change in Shoshone-Comanche, 1800-1900. *Anthropological Linguistics* 23(8):344-356.

Shebala, Marley
1983   Big Mountain Sun Dance Unites All People in Traditional Religious Ceremony. *Navajo Times* 25(35):31–32. Window Rock, Ariz.

Shelford, Victor E.
1963   The Ecology of North America. Urbana: University of Illinois Press.

Sheppard, Richard A., and Arthur J. Gude, III
1968   Distribution and Genesis of Authigenic Silicate Minerals in Tuffs of Pleistocene Lake Tecopa, Inyo County, California. *U.S. Geological Survey Professional Paper* 597. Washington.

Sherzer, Joel F.
1968   An Areal-typological Study of the American Indian Languages North of Mexico. (Unpublished Ph.D. Dissertation in Linguistics, University of Pennsylvania, Philadelphia.)

———
1973   Areal Linguistics in North America. Pp. 749-795 in *Linguistics in North America*. Current Trends in Linguistics. Thomas A. Sebeok, ed. Vol. 10. The Hague and Paris: Mouton.

———
1976   An Areal-typological Study of American Indian Languages North of Mexico. (*North-Holland Linguistic Series* 20) Amsterdam: North-Holland Publishing Company.

———
1976a   Areal Linguistics in North America. Pp. 121-173 in Native Languages of the Americas. Thomas A. Sebeok, ed. New York: Plenum Press.

Shields, Wayne F.
1967   1966 Excavations: Uinta Basin. *Miscellaneous Paper* 15, *University of Utah Anthropological Papers* 89:1-30. Salt Lake City.

805

Shields, Wayne F., and Gardiner F. Dalley
1978   The Bear River No. 3 Site. *Miscellaneous Paper* 22, *University of Utah Anthropological Papers* 99:55-99. Salt Lake City.

Shimkin, Demitri B.
1937-1938,
1966-1975   [Unpublished Fieldnotes on the Eastern Shoshone.] (Manuscripts in Shimkin's possession.)

_____, coll.
1938   [12 Wind River Shoshone Songs; Logan Brown, Gilbert Day, Pandora Pogue, Emma Aragon, Toorey Roberts Singers.] (Nos. 24-2962-24-2973 in Lowie Museum of Anthropology, University of California, Berkeley.)

_____
1939   Some Interactions of Culture, Needs, and Personalities Among the Wind River Shoshone. (Unpublished Ph.D. Dissertation in Anthropology, University of California, Berkeley.)

_____
1940   Shoshone-Comanche Origins and Migrations. Pp. 17-25 in Vol. 4 of Proceedings of the 6th Pacific Science Congress of the Pacific Science Association at the University of California, Berkeley, Stanford University, and San Francisco, July 24-August 12, 1939. 5 vols. Berkeley: Universitiy of California Press.

_____
1941   The Uto-Aztecan System of Kinship Terminology. *American Anthropologist* 43(2):223-245.

_____
1942   Dynamics of Recent Wind River Shoshone History. *American Anthropologist* 44(3):451-462.

_____
1947   Wind River Shoshone Ethnogeography. *University of California Anthropological Records* 5(4). Berkeley.

_____
1947a   Wind River Shoshone Literary Forms: An Introduction. *Journal of the Washington Academy of Sciences* 37(10):329-376. Washington.

_____
1947b   Childhood and Development Among the Wind River Shoshone. *University of California Anthropological Records* 5(5):289-326. Berkeley.

_____
1949   Shoshone I: Linguistic Sketch and Text; Shoshone II: Morpheme List. *International Journal of American Linguistics* 15(3):175-188; (4):203-212.

_____
1953   The Wind River Shoshone Sun Dance. *Anthropological Papers* 41, *Bureau of American Ethnology Bulletin* 151:397-484. Washington.

_____
1980   Comanche-Shoshone Words of Acculturation, 1786-1848. *Journal of the Steward Anthropological Society* 11(2):195-248. Urbana, Ill.

Shimkin, Demitri B., and Russell M. Reid
1970   Socio-cultural Persistence Among Shoshoneans of the Carson River Basin (Nevada). Pp. 172-200 in Languages and Cultures of Western North America: Essays in Honor of Sven S. Liljeblad. Earl H. Swanson, ed. Pocatello: Idaho State University Press.

Shipley, Susan B., and Andrei M. Sarna-Wojcicki
1983   Distribution, Thickness, and Mass of Late Pleistocene and Holocene Tephra from Major Volcanoes in the Northwestern United States: A Preliminary Assessment of Hazards from Volcanic Ejecta to Nuclear Reactors in the Pacific Northwest. *U.S. Geological Survey, Miscellaneous Field Studies, Map* MF-1435. Reston, Va.

Shipley, William
1957   Some Yukian-Penutian Lexical Resemblances. *International Journal of American Linguistics* 23(4):269-274.

_____
1962   Spanish Elements in the Indigenous Languages of Central California. *Romance Philology* 16(1):1-21.

1963   Maidu Texts and Dictionary. *University of California Publications in Linguistics* 33. Berkeley.

Shipley, William, and Richard A. Smith
1979   The Roles of Cognation and Diffusion in a Theory of Maidun Prehistory. *Journal of California and Great Basin Anthropology, Papers in Linguistics* 1:65-73.

Shohl, Alfred T.
1939   Mineral Metabolism. New York: Reinhold Publishing Company.

Shonle, Ruth
1925   Peyote, the Giver of Visions. *American Anthropologist* 27(1):53-75.

Shrieve, Forrest
1942   The Desert Vegetation of North America. *Botanical Review* 8(4):195-246.

Shroba, Ralph R., and Peter W. Birkeland
1983   Trends in Late-Quaternary Soil Development in the Rocky Mountains and Sierra Nevada of the Western United States. Pp. 145-156 in Late-Quaternary Environments of the United States. Vol. 1: The Late Pleistocene. Herbert E. Wright, Jr. and Stephen C. Porter, eds. Minneapolis: University of Minnesota Press.

Shultes, Richard E.
1967   The Place of Ethnobotany in the Ethnopharmacological Search for Psychotomimetic Drugs. Pp. 33-57 in Ethnopharmaologic Search for Psychoactive Drugs. Daniel H. Efron, Bo Holmstedt, and Nathan S. Kline, eds. (*U.S. Public Health Service Publication* 1645) Washington: U.S. Government Printing Office. (Reprinted: Raven Press, New York, 1979.)

Shutler, Mary E., and Richard Shutler, Jr.
1963   Deer Creek Cave, Elko County, Nevada. *Nevada State Museum Anthropological Papers* 11. Carson City.

Shutler, Richard, Jr.
1961   Lost City: Pueblo Grande de Nevada. *Nevada State Museum Anthropological Papers* 5. Carson City.

1967   Archaeology of Tule Springs. Pp. 298-303 in Pleistocene Studies in Southern Nevada. H.M. Wormington and Dorothy Ellis, eds. *Nevada State Museum Anthropological Papers* 13. Carson City.

Shutler, Richard Jr., Mary E. Shutler, and James S. Griffith
1960   Stuart Rockshelter: A Stratified Site in Southern Nevada. *Nevada State Museum Antrhopological Papers* 3. Carson City.

Siegel, Bernard J., and Alan R. Beals
1960   Conflict and Factionalist Dispute. *Journal of the Royal Anthropological Institute of Great Britain and Ireland* 90(1):107-117. London.

Siegel, Randall D.
1983   Paleoclimatic Significance of D/H and Carbon-13/Carbon-12 Ratios in Pleistocene and Holocene Woods. (Unpublished M.S. Thesis in Geochemistry, University of Arizona, Tucson.)

Sigler, William F., and Robert Rush Miller
1963   Fishes of Utah. Salt Lake City: Utah State Department of Fish and Game.

Silverstein, Michael
1972   Studies in Penutian, I, California: The Structure of an Etymology. (Unpublished Ph.D. Dissertation in Linguistics, Harvard University, Cambridge, Mass.)

Simmons, Patricia
1981   Organizational Status of Federally Recognized Indian Entities. (Memorandum to the Chief, Branch of Tribal Relations, U.S. Bureau of Indian Affairs.) Mimeo., copy in Handbook of North American Indians Office, Smithsonian Institution, Washington.)

Simms, Steven R.
[1983]   The Evolution of Hunter-gatherer Foraging Strategies: A

Great Basin Case. (Unpublished Ph.D. Dissertation in Anthropology, University of Utah, Salt Lake City.)

[1983a]   The Inception of Pinyon Nut Use in Three Great Basin Cases. *Journal of California and Great Basin Anthropology*. In press.

1983b   Comments on Bettinger and Baumhoff's Explanation of the "Numic Spread" in the Great Basin. *American Antiquity* 48(4):825-830.

Simpson, George G.
1933   A Nevada Fauna of Pleistocene Type and Its Probable Association with Man. *American Museum Novitates* 667 (October):1-10. New York.

Simpson, James C., and Richard L. Wallace
1978   Fishes of Idaho. Moscow: University of Idaho Press.

Simpson, James H.
1869   The Shortest Route to California, Illustrated by a History of Explorations of the Great Basin of Utah with Its Topographical and Geological Character and Some Account of the Indian Tribes. Philadelphia: J.B. Lippincott.

1876   Report of Explorations Across the Great Basin of the Territory of Utah for a Direct Wagon-route from Camp Floyd to Genoa, in Carson Valley, in 1859. Washington: U.S. Government Printing Office. (Reprinted: University of Nevada Press, Reno, 1983.)

Simpson, Ruth D.
1958   The Manix Lake Archeological Survey. *The Masterkey* 32(1):4-9.

1960   Archeological Survey of the Eastern Calico Mountains. *The Masterkey* 34(1):25-35.

1961   Coyote Gulch: Archaeological Excavations of an Early Lithic Locality in the Mohave Desert of San Bernardino County. *Archaeological Survey Association of Southern California Paper* 5. Los Angeles.

1965   Mark Harrington: Father of Nevada Archaeology. *Nevada Historical Society Quarterly* 8(3-4):3-22.

Simpson, William K.
1978   The Literature of Ancient Egypt. New Haven, Conn.: Yale University Press.

Singer, Clay A., and Jonathon E. Ericson
1977   Quarry Analysis at Bodie Hills, Mono County, California: A Case Study. Pp. 171-188 in Exchange Systems in Prehistory. Timothy K. Earle and Jonathon E. Ericson, eds. New York: Academic Press.

Siskin, Edgar E.
1938   Washo Territory. Pp. 622-638 in Tribal Distribution in the Great Basin, by Williard Z. Park et al. *American Anthropologist* 40(4).

1941   The Impact of the Peyote Cult Upon Shamanism Among the Washo Indians. (Unpublished Ph.D. Dissertation in Anthropology, Yale University, New Haven, Conn.)

1983   Washo Shamans and Peyotists: Religious Conflict in an American Indian Tribe. Salt Lake City: University of Utah Press.

Sleight, Frederick W.
1946   Comments on Basketmaker-like Pictographs in Northern Utah. *The Masterkey* 20(3):88-92.

Smart, Stanley
1981   Lecture, Symposium on Curers and Healers, Nevada Humanities Committee, September 24-25. (Tapes in Department of Anthropology, University of Nevada, Reno.)

Smith, Anne M. Cooke
1937   The Material Culture of the Northern Ute. (Unpublished M.A. Thesis in Anthropology, Yale University, New Haven, Conn.)

1940   An Analysis of Basin Mythology. 2 vols. (Unpublished Ph.D. Dissertation in Anthropology, Yale University, New Haven, Conn.)

1974   Ethnography of the Northern Ute. *Museum of New Mexico Papers in Anthropology* 17. Santa Fe.

Smith, Arthur D., and Donald M. Beale
1980   Pronghorn Antelope in Utah: Some Research and Observations. *Utah Division of Wildlife Resources Publication* 80-13. Salt Lake City.

Smith, Elmer R.
1934   A Brief Description of an Indian Ruin Near Shonesburg, Utah. *Zion and Bryce* [National Parks] *Nature Notes* 6(1). (Reprinted: *University of Utah, Museum of Anthropology, Archaeology and Ethnology Papers* 4, 1940; and *University of Utah Anthropological Papers* 4, Salt Lake City, 1956.)

1941   The Archaeology of Deadman Cave, Utah. *University of Utah Bulletin* 32(4):1-43. (Reprinted: The Archaeology of Deadman Cave, Utah: A Revision. *University of Utah Anthropological Papers* 10, Salt Lake City, 1952.)

1950   Utah Anthropology: An Outline of Its History. *Southwestern Lore* 16(2):22-33.

Smith, George I.
1976   Origin of Lithium and Other Components in the Searles Lake Evaporites, California. Pp. 92-103 in Lithium Resources and Requirements by the Year 2000. J.D. Vince, ed. *U.S. Geological Survey Professional Paper* 1005. Washington.

1979   Subsurface Stratigraphy and Geochemistry of Late Quaternary Evaporites, Searles Lake, California. *U.S. Geological Survey Professional Paper* 1043. Washington.

Smith, George I., and F. Alayne Street-Perrott
1983   Pluvial Lakes of the Western United States. Pp. 190-212 in Late-Quaternary Environments of the United States. Vol. 1: The Late Pleistocene. Herbert E. Wright, Jr. and Stephen C. Porter, eds. Minneapolis: University of Minnesota Press.

Smith, George I., Virgil J. Barczak, Gail F. Multon, and Joseph C. Liddicoat
1983   Core KM-3, a Surface-to-Bedrock Record of Late Cenozoic Sedimentation in Searles Valley, California. *U.S. Geological Survey Professional Paper* 1256. Washington.

Smith, George I., Irving Friedman, Harold Klieforth, and Kenneth Hardcastle
1979   Areal Distribution of Deuterium in Eastern California Precipitation, 1968-1969. *Journal of Applied Meteorology* 18:172-188.

Smith, Gerald A.
1963   Archeological Survey of the Mojave River Area and Adjacent Regions. San Bernardino, Calif.: San Bernardino County Museum Association.

1963a   Split-twig Figurines from San Bernardino County, California. *The Masterkey* 37(3):86-90.

1978   Biogeography of Intermountain Fishes. Pp. 17-42 in Intermountain Biogeography: A Symposium. Kimball T. Harper and James L. Reveal, eds. *Brigham Young University, Great Basin Naturalist Memoirs* 2. Provo, Utah.

Smith, Gerald A., and Clifford J. Walker
1965   Slave Trade Along the Mohave Trail. San Bernardino, Calif.: San Bernardino County Museum.

Smith, Gerald A., W.C. Schuiling, L. Martin, R.J. Sayles, and P. Jillson
1957   Newberry Cave, California. *San Bernardino County Museum Scientific Series* 1. San Bernardino, Calif.

Smith, Harold T.U.
1967   Past versus Present Wind Action in the Mojave Desert Region, California. (AFCRL-67-0683, Scientific Report 1.) Bedford, Mass.: U.S. Air Force Cambridge Research Laboratories.

Smith, J.U., ed.
1911   John C. Frémont's Expedition in Nevada, 1843-1844. (Second Biennial report of the Nevada Historical Society) Carson City: Nevada State Printing Office.

Smith, Janet Hugie
1972   Native Pharmacopoeia of the Eastern Great Basin: A Report on Work in Progress. Pp. 73-86 in Great Basin Cultural Ecology: A Symposium. Don D. Fowler, ed. *University of Nevada, Desert Research Institute Social Sciences and Humanities Publications* 8. Reno.

Smith, Regina S., Peggy McGuckian Jones, John R. Roney, and Kathryn E. Pedrick
1983   Prehistory and History of the Winnemucca District: A Cultural Resources Literature Overview. *Nevada Bureau of Land Management, Cultural Resource Series* 6. Reno.

Smith, Roger S.U.
1978   Late Pleistocene Paleohydrology of Pluvial Lake Panamint, California. *Geological Society of America, Abstracts with Programs* 10(3). P. 148 in Cordilleran Section of the Geological Society of America 74th Annual Meeting, March 29-31, 1978, Tempe, Ariz.

————
1982   Sand Dunes in the North American Deserts. Pp. 481-524 in Reference Handbook on the Deserts of North America. Gordon L. Bender, ed. Westport, Conn.: Greenwood Press.

Snapp, Allen, John Anderson, and Joy Anderson
1982   Northern Paiute. Pp. 1-92 in Studies in Uto-Aztecan Grammar. Ronald W. Langacker, ed. Vol. 3: Uto-Aztecan Grammatical Sketches. (*Publications in Linguistics* 56) Arlington: Summer Institute of Linguistics and University of Texas.

Snow, William J.
1929   Utah Indians and Spanish Slave Trade. *Utah Historical Society Quarterly* 2(3):67-90. Salt Lake City.

Snyder, Charles T., and Walter B. Langbein
1962   The Pleistocene Lake in Spring Valley, Nevada, and Its Climatic Implications. *Journal of Geophysical Research* 67(6):2385-2394.

Snyder, John O.
1917   The Fishes of the Lahontan System of Nevada and Northeastern California. *Bulletin of U.S. Bureau of Fisheries* 35:33-86 [1915-1916] Documents 843. Washington. U.S. Government Printing Office.

Soule, Edwin C.
1975   Lost City Revisited. *The Masterkey* 49(1):4-19.

————
1976   Lost City, II. *The Masterkey* 50(1):10-18.

————
1979   Amaranth: Food of the Aztecs. *The Masterkey* 53(4):143-146.

Southern Ute Tribe
1982   Southern Ute Tribal Comprehensive Plan. Ignacio, Colo.: The Southern Ute Tribe.

Spaulding, W. Geoffrey
1983   Late Wisconsin Macrofossil Records of Desert Vegetation in the American Southwest. *Quaternary Research* 19(2):256-264.

Spaulding, W. Geoffrey, Estella B. Leopold, and Thomas R. Van Devender
1983   Late Wisconsin Paleoecology of the American Southwest. Pp. 259-293 in Late-Quaternary Environments of the United States. Vol. 1: The Late Pleistocene. Herbert E. Wright, Jr. and Stephen C. Porter, eds. Minneapolis: University of Minnesota Press.

Spencer, Anne
1973   Cultural Value Systems in Southwestern Utah. Cedar City: Southern Utah State College, Office of Community Development.

Spencer, Joseph E.
1934   Pueblo Sites of Southwestern Utah. *American Anthropologist* 36(1):70-80.

Spencer, Robert F., and Jesse D. Jennings
1965   The Native Americans: Prehistory and Ethnology of the North American Indians. New York: Harper and Row.

————
1977   The Native Americans. 2d ed. New York: Harper and Row.

Spencer, R.J. et al.
1983   Great Salt Lake, Utah: The Last 30,000 Years. *Quaternary Research*. In press.

Speth, Lembi Kongas
1969   Possible Fishing Cliques Among the Northern Paiutes of the Walker River Reservation, Nevada. *Ethnohistory* 16(3):225-244.

Spier, Leslie
1921   The Sun Dance of the Plains Indians: Its Development and Diffusion. *Anthropological Papers of the American Museum of Natural History* 16(7):453-527. New York.

————
1925   The Distribution of Kinship Systems in North America. *University of Washington Publications in Anthropology* 1(2):68-88. Seattle.

————
1928   Havasupai Ethnography. *Anthropological Papers of the American Museum of Natural History* 29(3):81-392. New York.

————
1930   Klamath Ethnography. *University of California Publications in American Archaeology and Ethnology* 30. Berkeley.

————
1935   The Prophet Dance of the Northwest and Its Derivatives: The Source of the Ghost Dance. *American Anthropological Association General Series in Anthropology* 1. Menasha, Wis.

————
1955   Mohave Culture Items. *Bulletin of the Museum of Northern Arizona* 28. Flagstaff.

Spier, Leslie, and Edward Sapir
1930   Wishram Ethnography. *University of Washington Publications in Anthropology* 3(3):151-300. Seattle.

Spier, Leslie, Wayne Suttles, and Melville J. Herskovits
1959   Comment on Aberle's Thesis of Deprivation. *Southwestern Journal of Anthropology* 15(1):84-88.

Spinden, Herbert J.
1928   Ancient Civilizations of Mexico and Central America. 3d rev. ed. (*Handbook Series* 3) New York: American Museum of Natural History.

Sprague, Roderick
1973   The Pacific Northwest. Pp. 251-285 in The Development of North American Archaeology. James Fitting, ed. Garden City, N.Y.: Doubleday.

Spring, Anita C.
1965   [Fieldnotes and Report on Concept of Marriage Among the Washo; University of Nevada Ethnographic Archives 24, National Science Foundation Graduate Field Training Project - June 7 to Sept. 7, 1965.] (On file, Department of Anthropology, University of Nevada, Reno.)

————
1967   An Analysis of Washo Conjugal Relations. *Cornell Journal of Social Relations* 2(2):35-55. Ithaca, N.Y.

————
1967a   Washo Marriage: A Social Institution in Transition. (Unpublished M.A. Thesis in Anthropology, San Francisco State College, San Francisco.)

Stanley, Dwight A., Gary M. Page, and Richard Shutler, Jr.
1970   The Cocanour Site: A Western Nevada Pinto Phase Site with

Two Excavated "House Rings." Pp. 1-46 in Five Papers on the Archaeology of the Desert West. *Nevada State Museum Anthropological Papers* 15. Carson City.

Stansbury, Howard
1852   Exploration and Survey of the Valley of the Great Salt Lake of Utah, Including a Reconnaissance of a New Route Through the Rocky Mountains. Philadelphia: Lippincott, Grambo.

Statham, Dawn Strain
1982   Camas and the Northern Shoshoni: A Biographic and Socioeconomic Analysis. *Boise State University Archaeological Reports* 10. Boise, Idaho.

Stearns, Robert E.C.
1877   Aboriginal Shell Ornaments, and Mr. F.A. Barber's Paper Thereon. *American Naturalist* 11(8):473-474.

1877a   Aboriginal Shell Money. *American Naturalist* 11(6):344-350.

Steele, John
1933   Extracts from the Journal of John Steele (1847). *Utah Historical Society Quarterly* 6(1):3-28. Salt Lake City.

Stenberg, Molly P.
[1946]   The Peyote Cult Among Wyoming Indians: A Transitional Link Between an Indigenous Culture and an Imposed Culture. *Wyoming University Publications* 12(4):85-156. Laramie.

Stephenson, Robert L.
1968   Preggy Peggy - A Clay Figurine. *Nevada Archeological Survey Reporter* 2(2):16-19. Reno.

Stevens, Ernie
1981   Energy and Alternatives to the Economic Development Administration. (Paper presented at the Mid-Year Meeting of the National Congress of American Indians, Spokane, Wash.)

Steward, Julian H., coll.
1927-1928   [42 Owens Valley Paiute Songs: Panamint and Darwin, California; Ed Lewis, Tom Stone, Billy Murphy, Jack Stewart, Singers.] (Nos. 24-2883 - 24-2923 in Lowie Museum of Anthropology, University of California, Berkeley.)

————, coll.
1927-1928a   [18 Mono Lake Paiute Songs; Harry Thom, Joe McBride, Johnson Charlie, Bridgeport Tom, Tom Stone, Singers.] (Nos. 24-2866 - 24-2882 and 24-2924 in Lowie Museum of Anthropology, University of California, Berkeley.)

1928   Pottery from Deep Springs Valley, Inyo County, California. *American Anthropologist* 30(2):348.

1929   Petroglyphs of California and Adjoining States. *University of California Publications in American Archaeology and Ethnology* 24(2):47-238. Berkeley.

1930   Irrigation without Agriculture. *Papers of the Michigan Academy of Science, Arts, and Letters* 12:149-156. Ann Arbor.

1931   Archeological Discoveries at Kanosh in Utah. *El Palacio* 30(8):121-130.

1932   A Uintah Ute Bear Dance, March 1931. *American Anthropologist* 34(2):263-273.

1933   Archaeological Problems of the Northern Periphery of the Southwest. *Museum of Northern Arizona Bulletin* 5. Flagstaff.

1933a   Early Inhabitants of Western Utah, Pt. I: Mounds and House Types. *University of Utah Bulletin* 23(7):1-34. Salt Lake City.

1933b   Ethnography of the Owens Valley Paiute. *University of California Publications in American Archaeology and Ethnology* 33(3):233-350. Berkeley.

1934   Two Paiute Autobiographies. *University of California Publications in American Archaeology and Ethnology* 33(5):423-438. Berkeley.

1935   Indian Tribes of Sequoia National Park Region. Berkeley, Calif.: U.S. Department of the Interior, National Park Service, Field Division of Education.

1936   Pueblo Material Culture in Western Utah. *Anthropological Series* 1(3), *University of New Mexico Bulletin* 287:1-64. Albuquerque.

1936a   The Economic and Social Basis of Primitive Bands. Pp. 331-350 in Essays in Anthropology Presented to Alfred L. Kroeber. Robert H. Lowie, ed. Berkeley: University of California Press.

1936b   Myths of the Owens Valley Paiute. *University of California Publications in American Archaeology and Ethnology* 34(5):355-440. Berkeley.

1936c   Shoshoni Polyandry. *American Anthropologist* 38(4):561-564.

1936d   Shoshonean Tribes: Utah, Idaho, Nevada and Eastern California. (Manuscript, copy in Richard O. Clemmer's possession.)

1937   Ethnological Reconnaissance Among the Desert Shoshoni. Pp. 87-92 in *Exploration and Field Work of the Smithsonian Institution in 1936.* Washington.

1937a   Ancient Caves of the Great Salt Lake Region. *Bureau of American Ethnology Bulletin* 116. Washington.

1937b   Linguistic Distributions and Political Groups of the Great Basin Shoshoneans. *American Anthropologist* 39(4):625-634.

1938   Basin-Plateau Aboriginal Sociopolitical Groups. *Bureau of American Ethnology Bulletin* 120. Washington. (Reprinted: University of Utah Press, Salt Lake City, 1970.)

1938a   Panatübiji', an Owens Valley Paiute. *Anthropological Papers* 6, *Bureau of American Ethnology Bulletin* 119:183-195. Washington.

1938b   Lemhi Shoshoni Physical Therapy. *Anthropological Papers* 5, *Bureau of American Ethnology Bulletin* 119:177-181. Washington.

1939   Some Observations on Shoshonean Distributions. *American Anthropologist* 41(2):261-265.

1939a   Changes in Shoshonean Indian Culture. *Scientific Monthly* 49 (December):524-537.

1940   Native Cultures of the Intermontane (Great Basin) Area. Pp. 445-502 in Essays in Historical Anthropology of North America, Published in Honor of John R. Swanton. *Smithsonian Miscellaneous Collections* 100. Washington.

1941   Culture Element Distributions, XIII: Nevada Shoshone. *University of California Anthropological Records* 4(2):209-360. Berkeley.

1941a   Archeological Reconnaissance of Southern Utah. *Anthropological Papers* 18, *Bureau of American Ethnology Bulletin* 128. Washington.

1943   Some Western Shoshoni Myths. *Anthropological Papers* 31, *Bureau of American Ethnology Bulletin* 136:249-299. Washington.

1943a   Culture Element Distributions, XXIII: Northern and Gosiute

Shoshoni. *University of California Anthropological Records* 8(3):263-392. Berkeley.

1955   Theory of Culture Change. Urbana: University of Illinois Press.

1955a   The Great Basin Shoshonean Indians. Pp. 101-121 in Theory of Culture Change, by Julian H. Steward. Urbana: University of Illinois Press.

1965   Some Problems Raised by Roger C. Owen's "The Patrilocal Band...." *American Anthropologist* 67(3):732-734.

1968   [Review of] The Current Status of Anthropological Work in the Great Basin: 1964. *American Antiquity* 33(2):264-267.

1969   The Limitations of Applied Anthropology: The Case of the Indian New Deal. *Journal of the Steward Anthropological Society* 1(1):1-17. Urbana, Ill.

1970   The Foundations of Basin-Plateau Shoshonean Society. Pp. 113-151 in Languages and Cultures of Western North America: Essays in Honor of Sven S. Liljeblad. Earl H. Swanson, ed. Pocatello: Idaho State University Press.

1974   Aboriginal and Historical Groups of the Ute Indians of Utah: An Analysis with Supplement [1954]. Pp. 25-159 in Ute Indians, I. (*American Indian Ethnohistory: California and Basin-Plateau Indians*) New York: Garland.

1977   The Foundations of Basin-Plateau Shoshonean Society. Pp. 366-406 in Evolution and Ecology: Essays on Social Transformation. Jane C. Steward and Robert F. Murphy eds. Urbana: University of Illinois Press.

Steward, Julian H., and Erminie Wheeler-Voegelin
1974   The Northern Paiute Indians. Pp. 9-328 in Paiute Indians, III [1954]. (*American Indian Ethnohistory: California and Basin-Plateau Indians*) New York: Garland.

Stewart, George R.
1962   The California Trail. New York: McGraw-Hill Book Company.

Stewart, Joseph L.
1960   The Problem of Stuttering in Certain North American Indian Societies. *Journal of Speech and Hearing Disorders, Monograph Supplement* 6.

Stewart, Kenneth M.
1966   Mohave Indian Agriculture. *The Masterkey* 40(1):5-15.

1967   Chemehuevi Culture Changes. *Plateau* 40(1):14-21.

Stewart, Omer C.
1937   Northern Paiute Polyandry. *American Anthropologist* 39(2):368-369.

1938   Navaho Basketry as Made by Ute and Paiute. *American Anthropologist* 40(4):758-759.

1938   [Fieldnotes on the Washo-Northern Paiute.] (Unpublished manuscript in Stewart's possession.)

1938b   The Navajo Wedding Basket—1938. *Museum of Northern Arizona Museum Notes* 10(9):25-28. Flagstaff.

_____, coll.
1938c   [14 Northern Paiute Songs; Sam Dick, Ida McBride Dick, Harry Tom, Lloyd McBride, Louisa Tom, Lola Harrison, Eva Dick, Singers.] (Nos. 24-2948 - 24-2961 in Lowie Museum of Anthropology, University of California, Berkeley.)

_____, coll.
1938d   [4 Uintah Songs; Ray Lone Bear, Ralph Kochamp, Singers.] (Nos. 24-2941, 24-2942, 24-2945 in Lowie Museum of Anthropology, University of California, Berkeley.)

_____, coll.
1938e   [20 Washoe Songs; John Herrington Wright, Don James, Seymour Arnot, O.C. Stewart, Roy James, Senna Frank, Singers.] (Nos. 24-2925 - 24-2940, 24-2943, 24-2944, 24-2946 and 24-2947 in Lowie Museum of Anthropology, University of California, Berkeley.)

1939   The Northern Paiute Bands. *University of California Anthropological Records* 2(3):127-149. Berkeley.

1941   Culture Element Distributions, XIV: Northern Paiute. *University of California Anthropological Records* 4(3):361-446. Berkeley.

1941a   The Southern Ute Peyote Cult. *American Anthropologist* 43(2):303-308.

1942   Culture Element Distributions, XVIII: Ute - Southern Paiute. *University of California Anthropological Records* 6(4):231-356. Berkeley.

1944   Washo-Northern Paiute Peyotism: A Study in Acculturation. *University of California Publications in American Archaeology and Ethnology* 40(3). (Reprinted: *University of Utah Anthropological Papers* 108:47-127, Salt Lake City, 1984.)

1948   Ute Peyotism: A Study of a Cultural Complex. *University of Colorado Studies, Series in Anthropology* 1:1-42. Boulder. (Reprinted: *University of Utah Anthropological Papers* 108:3-46, Salt Lake City, 1984.)

1952   Escalante and the Ute. *Southwestern Lore* 18(3):47-51.

1954   Testimony in The Uintah Ute Indians of Utah v. The USA, Plaintiffs' Reply to Defendant's Objections to Plaintiffs' Proposed Findings of Fact; and Reply Brief...(Filed May 14, Docket No. 44, Washington. (Copy in Omer C. Stewart's possession.)

1955   Forest and Grass Burning in the Mountain West. *Southwestern Lore* 21(1):5-9.

1956   Three Gods for Joe. *Tomorrow* 4(3):71-76.

1959   Shoshone History and Social Organization. Pp. 132-142 in Vol. 2 of *Proceedings of the 33d International Congress of Americanists*. 3 vols. Costa Rica, 1958.

1961   Kroeber and the Indian Claims Commission Cases. Pp. 181-191 in Alfred L. Kroeber: A Memorial. *Kroeber Anthropological Society Papers* 25. Berkeley, Calif.

1965   The Shoshoni: Their History and Social Organization. *Idaho Yesterdays* 9(3):2-5, 28.

1966   Tribal Distributions and Boundaries in the Great Basin. Pp. 167-238 in The Current Status of Anthropological Research in the Great Basin: 1964. W.L. D'Azevedo et al. eds. *University of Nevada, Desert Research Institute Social Sciences and Humanities Publications* 1. Reno.

1966a   Ute Indians: Before and After White Contact. *Utah Historical Society Quarterly* 34(1):38-61. Salt Lake City.

1968   [Peyote Documents of Nevada and California of Omer C. Stewart, 1938-1964.] (Unpublished files, Nevada and the West Collection, in Library, University of Nevada, Reno.)

1970   The Question of Bannock Territory. Pp. 201-231 in Languages and Cultures of Western North America: Essays in Honor of Sven S. Liljeblad. Earl H. Swanson, Jr., ed. Pocatello: Idaho State University Press.

1971   The Peyote Religion and the Ghost Dance. (Unpublished paper presented at the 19th Annual Meeting of the American Society for Ethnohistory, University of Georgia, Athens.)

1971a   Ethnohistorical Bibliography of the Ute Indians of Colorado. *University of Colorado Studies, Series in Anthropology* 18. Boulder.

1972   [Field Notes Regarding Peyotism: Crow, Northern Cheyenne, Shoshoni-Bannock, Goshiute, Northern Paiute, Washo, Ute, Navajo, Winnebago, Omaha, Prairie Potawatomi, Oto, Osage, Kiowa, Comanche, Kickapoo, Shawnee.] (Unpublished manuscript in Stewart's possession.)

1977   Contemporary Document on Wovoka (Jack Wilson) Prophet of the Ghost Dance in 1890. *Ethnohistory* 24(3):219-222.

1978   The Western Shoshone of Nevada and the U.S. Government, 1863-1900. Pp. 77-114 in Selected Papers from the 14th Great Basin Anthropological Conference. Donald R. Tuohy, ed. *Ballena Press Publications in Archaeology, Ethnology and History* 4. Ramona, Calif.

1979   An Expert Witness Answers Rosen. *American Anthropologist* 81(1):108-111.

1980   Temoke Band of Shoshone and the Oasis Concept. *Nevada Historical Society Quarterly* 23(4):246-261. Reno.

1982   Indians of the Great Basin: A Critical Bibliography. (The Newberry Library Center for the History of the American Indian Bibliographical Series) Bloomington: Indiana University Press.

1982a   The History of Peyotism in Nevada. *Nevada Historical Society Quarterly* 25(3):197-209. Reno.

1984   Friend to the Ute: Omer C. Stewart Crusades for Indian Religious Freedom. *University of Utah Anthropological Papers* 108:269-275. Salt Lake City.

1984a   "Siskin's Report Did Not Improve with Age." Review of Edgar E. Siskin's "Washo Shamans and Peyotists." *Reviews in Anthropology* 11(2):144-157.

[1984b]   Report on the San Juan Band of Southern Paiutes. (Unpublished manuscript in Stewart's possession.)

Stewart, Omer C., and David F. Aberle
1984   Peyotism in the West. *University of Utah Anthropological Papers* 108. Salt Lake City.

Stewart, Omer C., and Joel Janetski
1983   Western Ute. (Manuscript in Stewart's possession.)

Stickel, Gary E., and Lois J. Weinman-Roberts
1980   An Overview of the Cultural Resources of the Western Mojave Desert. *California Bureau of Land Management, Cultural Resources Publications, Anthropology - History*. Riverside.

Stile, T.E.
1982   Perishable Artifacts from Meadowcroft Rockshelter, Washington County, Southwestern Pennsylvania. Pp. 130-141 in Meadowcroft: Collected Papers on the Archaeology of Meadowcroft Rockshelter and the Cross Creek Drainage. R.C. Carlisle and J.M. Adovasio, eds. Pittsburgh: University of Pittsburgh, Department of Anthropology.

Stillwaggon, Eileen M.
1979   Economic Impact of Uintah and Ouray Indian Reservation on the Local Non-Indian Economy. (Unpublished Ph.D. Dissertation in Anthropology, American University, Washington.)

Stoffle, Richard W., and Henry F. Dobyns, eds.
1982   PUAXANT TUVIP: Utah Indians Comment on the Intermountain Power Project, Utah Section, Intermountain-Adelanto Bipole I Transmission Line. Ethnographic (Native American) Resources. Applied Conservation Technology. Salt Lake City.

1983   NuVAGANTu: Nevada Indians Comment on the Intermountain Power Project. *Nevada Bureau of Land Management, Cultural Resource Series* 7. Reno.

Stoffle, Richard W., Cheryle A. Last, and Michael J. Evans
1979   Reservation-based Tourism: Implications of Tourist Attitudes for Native American Economic Development. *Human Organization* 38(3):300-306.

Street, F. Alayne, and A.T. Grove
1979   Global Maps of Lake-level Fluctuations Since 30,000 Yr B.P. *Quaternary Research* 12(1):83-118.

Strong, Emory
1969   Stone Age in the Great Basin. Portland, Oreg.: Binfords and Mort.

Stuart, Bradley R.
1945   Southern Paiute Staff of Life. *The Masterkey* 19(4):133-134.

Stuart, Granville
1865   Montana As It Is: Being, a General Description of Its Resources... New York: C.S. Westcott.

Stuart, Robert
1935   The Discovery of the Oregon Trail: Robert Stuart's Narrative of His Overland Trip Eastward from Astoria in 1812-1813. New York: C. Scribner's Sons.

Stuiver, Minze
1982   A High-precision Calibration of the AD Radiocarbon Time Scale. *Radiocarbon* 24(1):1-26.

Sturtevant, William C.
1983   Tribe and State in the Sixteenth and Twentieth Centuries. P. 3-16 in The Development of Political Organization in Native North America, by Elisabeth Tooker and Morton H. Fried. *Proceedings of the American Ethnological Society*, 1979. Washington.

Susia, Margaret L.
1964   Tule Spring Archaeological Surface Survey. *Nevada State Museum Anthropological Papers* 12. Carson City.

Sutton, Mark Q.
1980   Some Aspects of Kitanemuk Prehistory. *Journal of California and Great Basin Anthropology* 2(2):214-225.

1981   Archaeology of the Antelope Valley, Western Mojave Desert, California. (Manuscript in Sutton's possession.)

1982   Kawaiisu Mythology and Rock Art: One Example. *Journal of California and Great Basin Anthropology* 4(1):148-154.

Swadesh, Frances L.
1974   Los Primeros pobladores: Hispanic Americans of the Ute Frontier. South Bend, Ind.: University of Notre Dame Press.

Swadesh, Morris
1954   Time Depths of American Linguistic Groupings. *American Anthropologist* 56(3):361-364.

1954-1955   Algunas fechas glotocronológicas importantes para la prehistoria Nahua. *Revista Mexicana de Estudios Antropológicos* 14(1):173-192. México, D.F.

1971   The Origin and Diversification of Language. Joel Sherzer, ed. Chicago: Aldine-Atherton.

Swain, A.M., J.E. Kutzbach, and S. Hastenrath
1983   Estimates of Holocene Precipitation for Rajasthan, India, Based on Pollen and Lake-level Data. *Quaternary Research* 19(1):1-17.

Swanson, Earl H., Jr.
1962   Early Cultures in Northwestern America. *American Antiquity* 28(2):151-158.

_____
1962a   The Emergence of Plateau Culture. *Occasional Papers of the Idaho State University Museum* 8. Pocatello.

_____, ed.
1968   Utaztekan Prehistory. *Occasional Papers of the Idaho State University Museum* 22. Pocatello.

_____
1972   Birch Creek: Human Ecology in the Cool Desert of the Northern Rocky Mountains 9,000 B.C. - A.D. 1850. Pocatello: Idaho State University Press.

_____
1974   The Snake River Plain. *Idaho Yesterdays* 18(2):2-12.

Swanson, Earl H. Jr., and Jon Dayley
1968   Hunting at Malad Hill in Southeastern Idaho. *Tebiwa: Journal of the Idaho State University Museum* 11(2):59-69. Pocatello.

Swanson, Earl H., Jr., and Guy Muto
1975   Recent Environmental Changes in the Northern Great Basin. *Tebiwa: Journal of the Idaho State University Museum* 18(1):49-57. Pocatello.

Swanson, Earl H., Jr., and Paul G. Sneed
1966   The Archaeology of the Shoup Rockshelters in East Central Idaho. *Birch Creek Papers* 3, *Occasional Papers of the Idaho State University Museum* 17. Pocatello.

_____
1971   Jacknife Cave. *Tebiwa: Journal of the Idaho State University Museum* 14(1):33-69. Pocatello.

Swanson, Earl H., Jr., B. Robert Butler, and Robson Bonnichsen
1964   Natural and Cultural Stratigraphy in the Birch Creek Valley of Eastern Idaho. *Birch Creek Papers* 2, *Occasional Papers of the Idaho State University Museum* 14. Pocatello.

Swanson, Earl H., Jr., Roger Powers, and Alan L. Bryan
1964   The Material Culture of the 1959 Southwestern Idaho Survey. *Tebiwa: Journal of the Idaho State University Museum* 7(2):1-27. Pocatello.

Swanton, John R.
1952   The Indian Tribes of North America. *Bureau of American Ethnology Bulletin* 145. Washington. (Reprinted in 1969.)

Tanner, Clara Lee
1983   Indian Baskets of the Southwest. Tucson: University of Arizona Press.

Tax, Sol, and Sam Stanley
1960   The North American Indians: 1950 Distribution of the Aboriginal Population of Alaska, Canada, and the United States. (Map.) Chicago: University of Chicago, Department of Anthropology.

Taylor, Alexander S.
1860   Curious Aboriginal Paintings, Graves and Pottery, in the Coso Indian Country of Owens Lake. (The Indianology of California, 2d ser.) *The California Farmer* 14(21):130. San Francisco.

_____
1861   Hieroglyphics in Truckee Valley. (The Indianology of California, 3d ser.) *The California Farmer* 15(7):123. San Francisco.

Taylor, Clara M., and Grace Macleod
1949   Rose's Laboratory Handbook for Diatetics. 5th ed. New York: Macmillan.

Taylor, Dee C.
1954   The Garrison Site: A Report of Archeological Excavations in Snake Valley, Nevada-Utah. *University of Utah Anthropological Papers* 16. Salt Lake City.

_____
1957   Two Fremont Sites and Their Position in Southwestern Prehistory. *University of Utah Anthropological Papers* 29. Salt Lake City.

Taylor, Eli
1931   Indian Reservations in Utah. *Utah Historical Society Quarterly* 4(1):29-31. Salt Lake City.

Taylor, Graham D.
1980   The New Deal and American Indian Tribalism: The Administration of the Indian Reorganization Act, 1934-45. Lincoln: University of Nebraska Press.

Taylor, Walter W.
1961   Archaeology and Language in Western North America. *American Antiquity* 27(1):71-81.

Teit, James A.
1930   The Salishan Tribes of the Western Plateaus. Franz Boas, ed. Pp. 23-396 in *45th Annual Report of the Bureau of American Ethnology for the Years 1927-1928*. Washington.

Theodoratus Cultural Research
1979   Anthropological Overview of a Portion of Lassen and Modoc Counties. Susanville: California Bureau of Land Management.

Thom, Melvin
1965   For a Greater Indian America. *Americans Before Columbus* 2(5):7. Schurz, Nev.

Thomas, Alfred B., ed. and trans.
1932   Forgotten Frontiers: A Study of the Spanish Indian Policy of Don Juan Bautista de Anza, Governor of New Mexico, 1777-1787; from the Original Documents in the Archives of Spain, Mexico and New Mexico. Norman: University of Oklahoma Press. (Reprinted in 1969.)

_____
1935   After Coronado: Spanish Exploration Northeast of New Mexico, 1696-1727. Norman: University of Oklahoma Press.

_____, ed.
1966   After Coronado: Spanish Explorations Northeast of New Mexico, 1696-1727. 2d ed. Norman: University of Oklahoma Press.

Thomas, David H.
1970   Archeological Investigation of Toquima Cave. *Nevada Archeological Survey Reporter* 4(5):8. Reno.

_____
1971   Historic and Prehistoric Land-use Patterns at Reese River. *Nevada Historical Society Quarterly* 14(4):2-9. Reno.

_____
1971a   Prehistoric Subsistence-settlement Pattern of the Reese River Valley, Central Nevada. (Unpublished Ph.D. Dissertation in Anthropology, University of California, Davis.)

_____
1972   A Computer Simulation Model of Great Basin Shoshonean Subsistence and Settlement Patterns. Pp. 671-704 in Models in Archaeology. D.L. Clarke, ed. London: Methuen.

_____
1972a   Analysis of Faunal Remains. Pp. 41-48 in The Archaeology of the Barrel Springs Site (NV-Pe-104) Pershing County, Nevada. Richard A. Cowan, ed. Berkeley: University of California, Archeological Research Facility.

_____
1972b   Western Shoshone Ecology: Settlement Patterns and Beyond. Pp. 135-153 in Great Basin Cultural Ecology: A Symposium. Don D. Fowler, ed. *University of Nevada, Desert Research Institute Social Sciences and Humanities Publications* 8. Reno.

_____
1973   An Empirical Test for Steward's Model of Great Basin Settlement Patterns. *American Antiquity* 38(1):155-176.

_____
1981   How to Classify the Projectile Points from Monitor Valley, Nevada. *Journal of California and Great Basin Anthropology* 3(1):7-43.

_____
1981a   Complexity Among Great Basin Shoshoneans: The World's Least Affluent Hunter-gatherers? Pp. 19-52 in Affluent Foragers: Pacific Coast East and West. S. Koyama and David H. Thomas, eds. *National Museum of Ethnology, Senri Ethnological Studies* 9. Osaka, Japan.

_____
1982   The 1981 Alta Toquima Village Project: A Preliminary Re-

port. *University of Nevada, Desert Research Institute, Social Sciences Center Technical Report Series* 27. Reno.

1982a   An Overview of Central Great Basin Prehistory. Pp. 156-171 in Man and Environment in the Great Basin. David B. Madsen and James F. O'Connell, eds. *Society for American Archaeology Papers* 2. Washington.

1982b   The Colonization of Monitor Valley, Nevada. *Nevada Historical Society Quarterly* 25(1):2-27. Reno.

1983   The Archeology of Monitor Valley, I: Epistemology. *Anthropological Papers of the American Museum of Natural History* 58(1). New York.

1983a   The Archaeology of Monitor Valley, 2: Gatecliff Shelter. *Anthropological Papers of the American Museum of Natural History* 59(1). New York.

1983b   On Steward's Model of Shoshonean Sociopolitical Organization: A Great Bias in the Basin? Pp. 54-68 in The Development of Political Organization in Native North America, by Elisabeth Tooker and Morton H. Fried. *Proceedings of the American Ethnological Society, 1979.* Washington.

1983c   Anticipating the Archaeological Record of the Pinon-Juniper Woodland. Pp. 156-165 in The Archaeology of Monitor Valley, 1: Epistemology, by David H. Thomas. *Anthropological Papers of the American Museum of Natural History* 58(1). New York.

1983d   Mid-Range Theory: Selected Procurement Strategies in the Prehistoric Great Basin. Pp. 40-71 in The Archaeology of Monitor Valley, 1: Epistemology, by David H. Thomas. *Anthropological Papers of the American Museum of Natural History* 58(1). New York.

1985   The Archaeology of Hidden Cave, Nevada. *Anthropological Papers of the American Museum of Natural History* 61(1):1-430. New York.

Thomas, David H., and Robert Bettinger
1976   Prehistoric Pinyon-Ecotone Settlements of the Upper Reese River Valley, Central Nevada. *Anthropological Papers of the American Museum of Natural History* 53(3):263-366. New York.

Thomas, David H., and Trudy C. Thomas
1972   New Data on Rock Art Chronology in the Central Great Basin. *Tebiwa: Journal of the Idaho State University Museum* 15(1):64-71. Pocatello.

Thomas, Trudy
1976   Petroglyph Distribution and the Hunting Hypothesis in the Central Great Basin. *Tebiwa: Journal of the Idaho State University Museum* 18(2):65-74. Pocatello.

1981   Incised Slates from Ruby Cave. (Manuscript Acc. No. 225 in Museum of Anthropology, University of California, Davis.)

1983   Material Culture of Gatecliff Shelter: Incised Stones. Pp. 246-278 in The Archaeology of Monitor Valley, 2: Gatecliff Shelter, by David H. Thomas. *Anthropological Papers of the American Museum of Natural History* 59(1). New York.

1983a   The Visual Symbolism of Gatecliff Shelter. Pp. 332-352 in the Archaeology of Monitor Valley, 2: Gatecliff Shelter, by David H. Thomas. *Anthropological Papers of the American Museum of Natural History* 59(1). New York.

Thompson, David
1916   David Thompson's Narrative of His Explorations in Western North America, 1784-1812. Joseph B. Tyrrell, ed. (*Publications of the Champlain Society* 12) Toronto: The Champlain Society.

Thompson, Richard A.
1978   The 1977 Western Anasazi Workshop. *Western Anasazi Reports* 1(1):3-12. Cedar City, Utah.

Thompson, Richard A., and Georgia B. Thompson
1978   An Archeological Survey of the Eastern End of the Warner Valley, Washington County, Utah. *Western Anasazi Reports* 1(2):129-142. Cedar City, Utah.

Thompson, Richard A., Georgia B. Thompson, and Jessie Embry
1983   Class I Cultural Resource Inventory for the Cedar City District of the Bureau of Land Management. Salt Lake City: Utah Bureau of Land Management.

Thompson, Robert S.
1979   Late Pleistocene and Holocene Packrat Middens from Smith Creek Canyon, White Pine County, Nevada. Pp. 360-380 in The Archaeology of Smith Creek Canyon, Eastern Nevada. Donald R. Tuohy and Doris L. Rendall, eds. *Nevada State Museum Anthropological Papers* 17. Carson City.

1984   Late Pleistocene and Holocene Environments in the Great Basin. (Unpublished Ph.D. Dissertation in Geosciences, University of Arizona, Tucson.)

Thompson, Robert S., and Eugene M. Hattori
1983   Packrat (*Neotoma*) Middens from Gatecliff Shelter and Holocene Migrations of Woodland Plants. Pp. 157-167 in The Archaeology of Monitor Valley, 2: Gatecliff Shelter. David H. Thomas, ed. *Anthropological Papers of the American Museum of Natural History* 59(1). New York.

Thompson, Robert S., and Robert R. Kautz
1983   Paleobotany of Gatecliff Shelter: Pollen Analysis. Pp. 136-151 in The Archaeology of Monitor Valley, 2: Gatecliff Shelter. David H. Thomas, ed. *Anthropological Papers of the American Museum of Natural History* 59(1). New York.

Thompson, Robert S., and Jim I. Mead
1982   Late Quaternary Environments and Biogeography in the Great Basin. *Quaternary Research* 17(1):39-55.

Thompson, Stith
1919   European Tales Among the North American Indians. *Colorado College Publication, General Series* 100-101, *Language Series* 2:320-471. Colorado Springs.

1929   Tales of the North American Indians. Cambridge, Mass.: Harvard University Press. (Reprinted: Indiana University Press, Bloomington, 1966).

1946   The Folktale. New York: Holt, Rinehart and Winston.

1953   The Star Husband Tale. *Studia Septentrionalia* 4:93-163. Oslo. (Reprinted: Pp. 414-474 in The Study of Folklore. Alan Dundes, ed. Englewood Cliffs, N.J., 1965.)

1955-1958   Mortif-Index of Folk-Literature. 6 vols. Bloomington: Indiana University Press.

Thorarinsson, Sigurdur
1979   On the Damage Caused by Volcanic Eruptions with Special Reference to Tephra and Gases. Pp. 125-159 in Volcanic Activity and Human Ecology. Payson D. Sheets and Donald K. Grayson, eds. New York: Academic Press.

Thorpe, Dagmar
1981   The Destruction of a People: The Western Shoshone and the MX Missile System. *Akwesasne Notes* 13(1):4-8.

Thwaites, Reuben G., ed.
1904-1905   Original Journals of the Lewis and Clark Expedition, 1804-1806. 8 vols. New York: Dodd, Mead and Company. (Reprinted: Antiquarian Press, New York, 1959).

————, ed.
1904-1907   Early Western Travels, 1748-1846: A Series of Annotated Reprints of Some of the Best and Rarest Contemporary Volumes of Travel, Description of the Aborigines and Social and Economic Conditions in the Middle and Far West, During

the Period of Early American Settlement. 38 vols. Cleveland, Ohio: Arthur H. Clark.

Tidestrom, Ivar
1925   Flora of Utah and Nevada. *Smithsonian Institution, U.S. National Museum, Contributions from the United States National Herbarium* 25. Washington.

Tidzump, Malinda
1970   Shoshone Thesaurus. Grand Forks, N.Dak.: The Summer Institute of Linguistics.

Ting, Peter C.
1968   A Copper Pendant from Pyramid Lake. *Nevada Archaeological Survey Reporter* 2(11-12):4-6. Reno.

Tower, Donald B.
1945   The Use of Marine Mollusca and Their Value in Reconstructing Prehistoric Trade Routes in the American Southwest. *Papers of the Excavator's Club* 2(3). Cambridge, Mass.

Townsend, John K.
1905   Narrative of a Journey Across the Rocky Mountains. Pp. 107-369 in Early Western Travels, 1748-1846, Vol XXI. Reuben G. Thwaites, ed. Cleveland, Ohio: Arthur H. Clark.

Train, Percy, James R. Henrichs, and W. Andrew Archer
1941   Medicinal Uses of Plants by Indian Tribes of Nevada. *Contributions Toward a Flora of Nevada* 33. Beltsville, Md. (Rev. ed.: *Contributions Toward a Flora of Nevada* 45, 1957.)

Treganza, Adan E.
1942   An Archaeological Reconnaissance of Northeastern Baja California and Southeastern California. *American Antiquity* 8(2):152-163.

1956   Horticulture with Irrigation Among the Great Basin Paiute: An Example of Stimulus Diffusion and Cultural Survival. Pp. 82-94 in Papers of the Third Great Basin Archaeological Conference. *University of Utah Anthropological Papers* 26(9). Salt Lake City.

Trenholm, Virginia C., and Maurine Carley
1964   The Shoshonis: Sentinels of the Rockies. Norman: University of Oklahoma Press.

Trewartha, Glenn T., and Lyle H. Horn
1980   An Introduction to Climate. 5th ed. New York: McGraw-Hill.

Tripp, George W.
1966   A Clovis Point from Central Utah. *American Antiquity* 31(3):435-436.

1967   An Unusual Split Willow Figurine Found Near Green River, Utah. *Utah Archeology: A Newsletter* 13:15. Salt Lake City.

Troike, Rudolph C.
1967   A Structural Comparison of Tonkawa and Coahuilteco. Pp. 321-332 in Studies in Southwestern Ethnolinguistics: Meaning and History in the Languages of the American Southwest. Dell H. Hymes with William E. Bittle, eds. (*Studies in General Anthropology* 3) The Hague: Mouton.

True, D.L., E.L. Davis, and E.L. Sterud
1966   Archaeological Surveys in the New York Mountains Region, San Bernardino County, California. *Annual Reports of the University of California Archaeological Survey* 8:243-278. Los Angeles.

Tschopik, Harry, Jr.
1938   Taboo as a Possible Factor Involved in the Obsolescence of Navaho Pottery and Basketry. *American Anthropologist* 40(2)257-262.

1940   Navaho Basketry: A Study of Cultural Change. *American Anthropologist* 42(3):444-462.

Tucker, Gordon C., Jr.
1976   The Archaeology of Salmon Falls Creek: A Study in Methodology. *Archaeological Reports of the Idaho State University Museum of Natural History* 4. Pocatello.

Tueller, Paul T., C. Dwight Beeson, Robin J. Tausch, Neil E. West, and Kenneth H. Rea
1979   Pinyon-Juniper Woodlands of the Great Basin: Distribution, Flora, Vegetal Cover. *U.S. Department of Agriculture, Forest Service, Intermountain Forest and Range Experiment Station Research Paper* INT-229. Ogden, Utah.

Tuohy, Donald R.
1956   Shoshoni Ware from Idaho. *Davidson Journal of Anthropology* 2(1):55-71. Seattle, Wash.

1963   Archaeological Survey in Southwestern Idaho and Northern Nevada. *Nevada State Museum Anthropological Papers* 8. Carson City.

1967   An Incised Stone Tablet from Douglas County, Nevada. *Nevada Archeological Survey Reporter* 1(7):7-10. Reno.

1968   Some Early Lithic Sites in Western Nevada. *Eastern New Mexico University Contributions to Anthropology* 1(4):27-38. Portales.

1969   The Test Excavation of Hanging Rock Cave, Churchill County, Nevada. *Miscellaneous Paper* 2, *Nevada State Museum Anthropological Papers* 14:27-67. Carson City.

1973   Nevada's Non-ceramic Culture Sphere. *Tebiwa: Journal of the Idaho State University Museum* 16(1):54-68. Pocatello.

1974   A Comparative Study of Late Paleo-Indian Manifestations in the Western Great Basin. Pp. 90-116 in A Collection of Papers on Great Basin Archeology. Robert Elston, ed. *Nevada Archeological Survey Research Papers* 5. Reno.

1974a   A Cache of Fine Coiled, Feathered, and Decorated Baskets from Western Nevada. Pp. 28-46 in Collected Papers on Aboriginal Basketry. Donald R. Tuohy and Doris L. Rendall, eds. *Nevada State Museum Anthropological Papers* 16. Carson City.

1974b   In the Path of Electrical Energy. *Nevada Archaeologist* 2(1):18-23. Salt Lake City.

1978   Prehistoric Stone, Bone, and Wood Sculpture from Western Nevada. (Manuscript in Department of Anthropology, Nevada State Museum, Carson City.)

1979   Kachina Cave. *Nevada State Museum Anthropological Papers* 17. Carson City.

1980   Notes on a Chipped Stone Bird-shaped Artifact from Frenchman's Flat, Nevada. (Manuscript in Department of Anthropology, Nevada State Museum, Carson City.)

1980a   Obsidian Hydration Dates for Western Great Basin Prehistory. Pp. 48-66 in Anthropological Papers in Memory of Earl H. Swanson, Jr. Lucille B. Harten, Claude N. Warren and Donald R. Tuohy, eds. Pocatello: Idaho Museum of Natural History.

1981   Pebble Mounds, Boulder Cairns, and Other Rock Features at the Sadmat Site, Churchill County, Nevada. *Nevada Archaeologist* 3(1):4-15.

1982   Another Great Basin Atlatl with Dart Foreshfts and Other Artifacts: Implications and Ramifications. *Journal of California and Great Basin Anthropology* 4(1):80-106.

[1984]   "Drowning Out the Paiute Ground Squirrels," Incipient Agriculture and Other Land and Water Matters in Ruby Valley, Nevada, as Noted by Lorenzo D. Creel, Special Indian Agent, in 1917. *Nevada Historical Society Quarterly* 27(1). Reno.

1984a   Archeology of Pyramid Lake, Western Nevada. *Nevada State Museum Anthropological Papers* 20. Carson City.

Tuohy, Donald R., and David T. Clark
1979   Excavations at Marble Bluff Dam and Pyramid Lake Fishway, Nevada. 6 Pts. (Report prepared by the Department of Anthropology, Nevada State Museum, Carson City for the Mid-Pacific Regional Office, Bureau of Reclamation; report on file Nevada State Museum, Carson City.)

Tuohy, Donald R., and Barbara Palombi
1972   A Basketry Impressed Shoshone Pottery Vessel from Central Nevada. *Tebiwa: Journal of the Idaho State University Museum* 15(1):46-48. Pocatello.

Tuohy, Donald R., and Doris L. Rendall, eds.
1980   The Archaeology of Smith Creek Canyon, Eastern Nevada. *Nevada State Museum Anthropological Papers* 17. Carson City.

Tuohy, Donald R., and Mercedes C. Stein
1969   A Late Lovelock Shaman and His Grave Goods. *Miscellaneous Paper* 5, *Nevada State Museum Anthropological Papers* 14:96-130. Carson City.

Turner, Allen C.
1981   Housing, Water, and Health Care: The Anthropology of Planning in a Southern Paiute Community. (Unpublished Ph.D. Dissertation in Anthropology, University of Kentucky, Lexington.)

1981a   Kaibab-Paiute Community Planning Process: A Descriptive Case Study, 1979. In Housing, Water, and Health Care: The Anthropology of Planning in a Southern Paiute Community. (Unpublished Ph.D. Dissertation in Anthropology University of Kentucky, Lexington.)

Turner, Arnie L., and Maribeth Hamby
1982   The Intensive Archaeological Reconnaissance of 15 Parcels in the Boca, Loyalton, Sierraville Locality, Tahoe National Forest. With contributions by Susan Seck and Laurel Crittenden. (Contract No. 53-9JGN-1-17003; report submitted to U.S. Department of Agriculture, Forest Service, Tahoe National Forest, Nevada City, California, by Intermountain Research, Silver City, Nev

Turner, Christy G., II
1963   Petrographs of the Glen Canyon Region. *Glen Canyon Series* 4, *Museum of Northern Arizona Bulletin* 38. Flagstaff.

Turner, Thomas H.
1978   Mule Springs Shelter, Its Archaeological and Ecological Interpretation within the Southern Great Basin. (Unpublished M.A. Thesis in Anthropology, University of Nevada, Las Vegas.)

Turner, William W.
1856   Vocabularies of North American Indian Languages. Pp. 55-103 in Vol. 3 of Reports of Explorations and Surveys to Ascertain the Most Practicable and Economical Route for a Railroad from the Mississippi River to the Pacific Ocean. Made in 1853-1854. Washington: U.S. War Department.

Twain, Mark (Samuel L. Clemens)
1872   Roughing It. Hartford, Conn.: American Publishing Company.

Twisselmann, Ernest C.
1967   A Flora of Kern County, California. *The Wasmann Journal of Biology* 25(1-2):1-395. San Francisco.

Twitchell, Ralph E.
1914   The Spanish Archives of New Mexico. 2 vols. Cedar Rapids, Iowa: The Torch Press.

Tyler, S. Lyman
1951   The Yuta Indians Before 1680. *Western Humanities Review* 5(2):153-163.

1954   The Spaniard and the Ute. *Utah Historical Society Quarterly* 22(4):343-361. Salt Lake City.

1964   Indian Affairs: A Study of the Changes in Policy of the United States Toward Indians. [Provo], Utah: Brigham Young University, Institute of American Indian Studies.

Tyler, Ron
1982   Alfred Jacob Miller: Artist on the Oregon Trail. Fort Worth, Tex.: Amon Carter Museum.

Tyler, Stephen
1968   The Wilkes Expedition: First United States Exploring Expedition (1838-1842). *Memoirs of the American Philosophical Society* 73. Philadelphia.

Ubelaker, Douglas H.
1976   The Sources and Methodology for Mooney's Estimates of North American Indian Populations. Pp. 243-288 in The Native Population of the Americas in 1492. W.M. Denevan, ed. Madison: University of Wisconsin Press.

Uintah-Ouray Ute Tribe
1974   Stories of Our Ancestors: A Collection of Northern Ute Indian Tales. Salt Lake City: Uintah-Ouray Ute Tribe.

1977   A Brief History of the Ute People. Salt Lake City: University of Utah Printing Service.

1977a   Ute Ways. Fort Duchesne, Utah: Uintah-Ouray Ute Tribe.

1977b   The Ute People. Fort Duchesne, Utah: Uintah-Ouray Ute Tribe.

1977c   The Ute System of Government. Fort Duchesne, Utah: Uintah-Ouray Ute Tribe.

1977d   The Way It Was Told. Fort Duchesne, Utah: Uintah-Ouray Ute Tribe.

Uldall, Hans J., and William Shipley
1966   Nisenan Texts and Dictionary. *University of California Publications in Linguistics* 46. Berkeley.

Underdal, Stanley J.
1977   On the Road Toward Termination: The Pyramid Lake Paiutes and the Indian Attorney Controversy of the 1950s. (Unpublished Ph.D. Dissertation in Anthropology, Columbia University, New York City.)

Underhill, Ruth M.
1941   The Northern Paiute Indians of California and Nevada. *Indian Life and Customs Pamphlets* 1. Lawrence, Kans.

United Nations. Department of Economic and Social Affairs
1968   The Concept of a Stable Population: Application to the Study of Populations of Countries with Incomplete Demographic Statistics. *Population Studies* 39. New York.

U.S. Army. Corps of Topographical Engineers
1861   Report Upon the Colorado River of the West, Explored in 1857 and 1858 by Lieutenant Joseph C. Ives. *U.S. Congress. Senate. 36th Cong., 1st sess., Senate Executive Document No. 90* (Serial No. 1058) Washington: U.S. Government Printing Office.

U.S. Bureau of Indian Affairs
1943   Record of Probate Hearing on the Estate of Samuel Lone Bear, Allottee No. P.R. 2386, April 17. Pine Ridge, S.D.

1944   The Post War Planning Program for the Carson Jurisdiction. Stewart, Nev.: U.S. Bureau of Indian Affairs, Carson Indian Agency.

1960   Population and Income Census, Wind River Reservation, Wyoming. *Missouri River Basin Investigations Project, Report* 161. Billings, Mont.

1975   Executive Orders Relating to Indian Reservations from May 14, 1855 to July 1, 1912; and Executive Orders Relating to Indian Reservations from July 1, 1912 to 1922. New York: Scholarly Resources.

815

U.S. Bureau of Indian Affairs. Division of Law Enforcement
1975   Indian Law Enforcement History. Washington: U.S. Bureau
            of Indian Affairs.

U.S. Bureau of Indian Affairs. Financial Management Office
1981   Indian Service Population and Labor Force Estimates, De-
            cember. Washington. Mimeo.

———
1983   Local Estimates of Resident Indian Population and Labor
            Force Status: January 1983. Washington: U.S. Department
            of the Interior.

U.S. Bureau of Indian Affairs. Office of Public Information
1983   Wyoming Tribes Request Rehearing of Water Rights Deci-
            sion. *Indian News Notes* 7(18):3. Washington.

———
1985   Cadets at Indian Police Academy Achieve New Level in Pre-
            training Tests. *Indian News Notes* 9(4):3. Washington.

U.S. Bureau of Indian Affairs. Phoenix Area Office
1976   Information Profiles of Indian Reservations in Arizona, Ne-
            vada, and Utah. Phoenix, Ariz.: Bureau of Indian Affairs.

———
1980   Final Environmental Impact Statement on the Proposed Rec-
            reational Lease of Wildhorse Reservoir Lands to the Sho-
            shone-Paiute Indian Tribes of the Duck Valley Reservation.
            Phoenix, Ariz.: Bureau of Indian Affairs.

U.S. Bureau of Indian Affairs. Statistics Division
1970   Report of Labor Force: Semi-annual Report of Employment
            and Unemployment. Washington: U.S. Government Printing
            Office.

———
1970a   California Rancherias and Reservations Population Figures.
            Washington. Mimeo.

U.S. Bureau of the Census
1913   Thirteenth Census of the United States, 1910. Vol. 1, Pt. 1:
            Population-General Report and Analysis, Section 1:303, Table
            19. Washington: U.S. Government Printing Office.

———
1915   Indian Population of the United States and Alaska, 1910.
            Washington: U.S. Government Printing Office.

———
1937   The Indian Population of the United States and Alaska. Fif-
            teenth Census of the United States, 1930. Washington: U.S.
            Government Printing Office.

———
1963   Census of Population, 1960: Characteristics of the Popula-
            tion, Pt. 30, Nevada. Washington: U.S. Government Printing
            Office.

———
1973   Census of Population: 1970. Subject Reports. Final Report
            PC(2)-1F, American Indians. Washington: U.S. Government
            Printing Office.

———
1973a   Census of the Population: 1970. Vol. 1: U.S. Summary.
            Washington: U.S. Government Printing Office.

———
1973b   Census of Population, 1970: General Social and Economic
            Characteristics. Pt. 30: Nevada. Washington: U.S. Govern-
            ment Printing Office.

———
1980   Social Indicators, III: Selected Data on Social Conditions and
            Trends in the United States. Washington: U.S. Government
            Printing Office.

———
1980a   Table 55: General Characteristics for the Total and American
            Indian Persons on Reservations. In General Population Char-
            acteristics, Vols. 6, 15, 30, 36, 46. Washington: U.S. Gov-
            ernment Printing Office.

———
1982   Statistical Abstract of the United States: National Data Book
            and Guide to Sources, 1982-1983. Washington: U.S. Gov-
            ernment Printing Office.

———
1984   Statistical Abstract of the United States: National Data Book
            and Guide to Sources. Washington: U.S. Government Print-
            ing Office.

U.S. Census Office. 11th Census
1894   Report on Indians Taxed and Indians Not Taxed in the United
            States (Except Alaska) at the Eleventh Census, 1890. Wash-
            ington: U.S. Government Printing Office.

U.S. Congresss. House
1850   [Letter by Charles Bent] Santa Fe, New Mexico, Nov. 10,
            1846. Pp. 191-194 in California and New Mexico: Messages
            and Correspondence. *31st Cong., 1st sess. House Executive
            Document No. 17. (Serial No. 573)* Washington.

U.S. Congress. House. Committee on Interior and Insular Affairs
1953   Report with Respect to the House Resolution Authorizing
            the Committee on Interior and Insular Affairs to Conduct
            an Investigation of the Bureau of Indian Affairs. Pursuant
            to House Resolution 698. *82d Cong., 2d sess. House Report
            No. 2503. (Serial No. 11582)* Washington: U.S. Government
            Printing Office.

———
1954   Report with Respect to the House Resolution Authorizing
            the Committee on Interior and Insular Affairs to Conduct
            an Investigation of the Bureau of Indian Affairs. Pursuant
            to House Resolution 89. *83d Cong., 2d sess., House Report
            No. 2680. (Serial No. 11747)* Washington: U.S. Government
            Printing Office.

———
1970   The United States Holds in Trust for Washoe Tribe of Indians
            Certain Lands in Alpine County, Calif. *91st Cong., 2d sess.
            Report No. 91-1149 to Accompany H.R. 4587. (Serial No.
            12884-4)* Washington: U.S. Government Printing Office.

———
1972   Apportionment of Funds in Payment of a Judgment in Favor
            of the Shoshone Tribe. *92d Cong., 1st sess. Report No. 92-
            701 to Accompany H.R. 10846. (Serial No. 12932-6)* Wash-
            ington: U.S. Government Printing Office.

U.S. Congress. House. Subcommittee on Indian Affairs of the
Committee on Public Lands
1950   Compilation of Material Relating to the Indians of the United
            States and the Territory of Alaska, Including Certain Laws
            and Treaties Affecting Such Indians. Pursuant to House Res-
            olution No. 66. *81st Cong., 2d sess.* Washington: U.S. Gov-
            ernment Printing Office.

U.S. Congress. Joint Committees on Interior and Insular Affairs
1954   Termination of Federal Supervision Over Certain Tribes of
            Indians. Hearing on S. 2670 and H.R. 7674, *83rd Cong., 2d
            sess.* Washington: U. S. Government Printing Office.

U.S. Congress. Senate
1914   Doniphan's Expedition: Account of the Conquest of New
            Mexico. *63d Cong., 2d sess. Senate Document No. 608. (Serial
            No. 6589)* Washington: U.S. Government Printing Office.

U.S. Congress. Senate. Committee on Energy and Natural Resources
1980   Expansion of Moapa Reservation, Nevada. *96th Cong. 2d
            sess. Report No. 96-951 to Accompany S. 1135. (Serial No.
            13330)* Washington: U.S. Government Printing Office.

U.S. Congress. Senate. Committee on Indian Affairs
1934   Report of R.P. Haas on Shoshone, 1930. P. 14460 in Part
            27: Wyoming, Idaho, and Utah of Survey of Conditions of
            the Indians in the United States. Hearings Before a Subcom-
            mittee of the Committee on Indian Affairs. *72d Cong., 1st
            sess.* Washington: U.S. Government Printing Office.

U.S. Congress. Senate. Committee on Interior and Insular Affairs
1951   Tribal Funds of the Ute Indian Tribe, Utah. Hearings on S.
            1357 and HR. 3795. *82d Cong., 1st sess.* Washington: U.S.
            Government Printing Office.

———
1969   The United States Holds in Trust for the Southern Ute Tribe
            Approximately 214.37 Acres of Land. *91st Cong., 1st sess.
            Report No. 91-568 to Accompany H.R. 12785. (Serial No.
            12834-4)* Washington: U.S. Government Printing Office.

1971 Disposition of Funds to Pay a Judgment in Favor of the Shoshone-Bannock Tribes of Indians of the Fort Hall Reservation. *92d Cong., 2d sess. Report No. 92-1000. (Serial No. 12971-5)* Washinton: U.S. Government Printing Office.

1971a Certain Public Lands Are Held in Trust by the United States for the Summit Lake Paiute Tribe. *92d Cong., 1st sess. Report No. 92-540 to Accompany S. 952. (Serial No. 12929-6)* Washington: U.S. Government Printing Office.

U.S. Congress. Senate. Select Committee on Indian Affairs

1977 Federally Owned Land in Nevada Held in Trust for the Paiute and Shoshone Tribes of the Fallon Indian Reservation. Hearing Before the U.S. Senate Select Committee on Indian Affairs on S. 785. *95th Cong., 1st sess.* Washington: U.S. Government Printing Office.

1977a Transfer of Government Lands to Certain Indian Tribes. Hearing on S. 103, S. 667, S. 947, and S. 1291. *95th Cong. 1st sess.* Washington: U.S. Government Printing Office.

1979 Paiute Restoration Act. Hearing Before the Select Committee on Indian Affairs on S. 1273: To Restore the Shivwits, Kanosh, Koosharem,...*96th Cong. 1st sess.* Washington: U.S. Government Printing Office.

1980 Conveyance of Federal Land to the Ute Mountain Ute Tribe. Hearing on S. 2066. *96th Cong., 2d sess.* Washington: U.S. Government Printing Office.

1982 Burns Paiute Indian Tribe Allotment. Hearing Before the Select Committee on Indian Affairs on S. 1468: To Provide for the Designation of the Burns Paiute Indian Tribe as the Beneficiary of a Public Domain Allotment. *97 Cong., 1st sess.* Washington: U.S. Government Printing Office.

1982a United States Holds Certain Lands in Trust for the Las Vegas Paiute Tribe. *97th Cong., 2d sess. Report 97-683 to Accompany S. 2998. (Serial No. 13456)* Washington: U.S. Government Printing Office.

U.S. Congress. Senate. Special Subcommittee on Indian Education

1969 Indian Education: A National Tragedy, a National Challenge. *91st Cong. 1st sess, Senate Report No. 501. (Serial No. 12834-1)* Washington: U.S. Government Printing Office.

U.S. Congressional Record

1946 Indian Claims Commission. *Proceedings and Debates of the 79th Congress, 2d session*, 92(4):5307-5323. Washington: U.S. Government Printing Office.

U.S. Department of Commerce

1974 Federal and State Indian Reservations and Indian Trust Areas. Washington: U.S. Government Printing Office.

U.S. Department of Health, Education and Welfare

1974 Indian Health Trends and Services. *DHEW Publication* (HSA) 74-12,009. Washington.

U.S. Department of Labor. Employment and Training Administration

1982 Report 3: Social Indicators for Planning and Evaluation. Four Counties: La Plata and Montezuma in Colorado and Uintah and Duchesne in Utah. Washington: National Technical Information Service.

U.S. Department of the Interior

1866 Annual Report of the Secretary of the Interior. Washington: U.S. Government Printing Office.

U.S. Geological Survey

1970 The National Atlas of the United States. Washington: U.S. Geological Survey.

U.S. Indian Claims Commission

1954 The Uintah Ute Indians of Utah v. The United States of America. Plaintiffs' Reply to Defendant's Objections to Plaintiffs' Proposed Findings of Fact; Plaintiffs' Objections to Defendant's Proposed Findings of Fact; and Reply Brief.

Docket No. 44, May 14. Washington. (Copy in Omer C. Stewart's possession.)

1972 Western Shoshone Identifiable Group, Represented by the Temoak Bands of Western Shoshone Indians, Nevada, Plaintiff, vs. The United States of America, Defendant, (29 Ind. Cl. Comm. 5) Docket 326-K: Opinion of the Commission. (Copy in Richard O. Clemmer's possession.)

1980 Final Report, 1979. *96th Cong., 2d sess. House Document No. 96-383. (Serial No. 13354)* Washington: U.S. Government Printing Office.

U.S. Office of Indian Affairs

1935 Indian Land Tenure, Economic Status, and Population Trends. Part X of the Supplementary Report of the Planning Commission to the National Resources Board. Washington: U.S. Government Printing Office.

U.S. Office of Indian Affairs. Land and Law Division

1880-1887 Utah and Northern Railroad Right of Way Through Fort Hall Reservation, Idaho. (In Record Group 75, Special Case No. 99, National Archives, Washington.)

Utah Superintendency

1855-1861 Letters from Indian Agents to the Superintendent of Indian Affairs, Salt Lake City. (In Letters Received by the Office of Indian Affairs, 1824-1880, Utah Superintendency, Microfilm, M-234, Rolls 898, 899, 900, National Archives, Washington.)

Ute Mountain Ute Tribe

[1980] Ute Industrial Park: An Exciting New Business Opportunity (Tribal Sales brochure) n.p.: Ute Mountain Ute Tribe.

Valory, Dale, comp.

1971 Guide to Ethnological Documents (1-203) of the Department and Museum of Anthropology, University of California, Berkeley. (Now in the University Archives) Berkeley: University of California, Archaeological Research Facility, Department of Anthropology.

Vander, Judith, coll.

1977-1981 [147 Wind River Shoshone Ghost Dance Songs; Emily Hill, Singer.] (Recordings in Vander's possession).

1978 A View of Wind River Shoshone Music Through Four Ceremonies. (Unpublished M.A. Thesis in Ethnomusicology, University of Michigan, Ann Arbor.)

1983 17 Ghost Dance Songs of Emily Hill, a Wind River Shoshone. (Unpublished manuscript in Vander's possession).

Van Devender, Thomas R.

1983 Our First Curators. *Sonorensis* 5(3):5-10.

Van Devender, Thomas R., and W. Geoffrey Spaulding

1979 Development of Vegetation and Climate in the Southwestern United States. *Science* 204(4394):701-710.

Van Horn, Richard

1979 The Holocene Ridgeland Formation and Associated Decker Soil (New Names) Near Great Salt Lake, Utah. *Contributions to Stratigraphy, U.S. Geological Survey Bulletin* 1457-C. Washington.

Van Winkle, Barrik

1977 Lexical Retention Among English-speaking Washo. (M.A. Professional Paper, Department of Anthropology, University of Nevada, Reno.)

Vastokas, Joan M., and Romas K. Vastokas

1973 Sacred Art of the Algonkians: A Study of the Peterborough Petroglyphs. Peterborough, Ont.: Mansard Press.

Vayda, Andrew P., and Ray A. Rappaport

1968 Ecology, Cultural and Noncultural. Pp. 477-497 in Introduction to Cultural Anthropology. J.A. Clifton, ed. Boston: Houghton, Mifflin.

817

Veeder, William H.
1969 Federal Encroachment on Indian Water Rights and the Impairment of Reservation Development. Pp. 460-518 in Vol. 2 of Toward Economic Development for Native American Communities: A Compendium of Papers. 2 vols. *U.S. Congress, Joint Economic Committee. 91st Cong. 1st sess.* Washington: U.S. Government Printing Office.

Verosub, Kenneth L., and Peter J. Mehringer, Jr.
1984 Congruent Paleomagnetic and Archaeomagnetic Records from the Western United States: A.D. 750 to 1450. *Science* 224(4647):387-389.

Vischer, Edward
1870 Vischer's Pictorial of California: Landscape, Trees and Forest Scenes; Grand Features of California Scenery, Life, Traffic and Customs. San Francisco: J. Wintermurn.

Voegelin, Charles F.
1958 Working Dictionary of Tübatulabal. *International Journal of American Linguistics* 24(3):221-228.

Voegelin, Charles F., and Florence M. Voegelin
1957 Hopi Domains: A Lexical Approach to the Problem of Selection. *Indiana University Publications in Anthropology and Linguistics, Memoir* 14. Bloomington.

1965 Languages of the World: Native America Fascicle Two. *Anthropological Linguistics* 7(7):1-150.

1966 Map of North American Indian Languages. Rev. ed. *American Ethnological Society Publication* 20. (Reprinted: Pp. 30-40 in Language in America, by Charlton Laird, The World Publishing Company, New York, 1970.)

Voegelin, Charles F., Florence M. Voegelin, and Kenneth L. Hale
1962 Typological and Comparative Grammar of Uto-Aztecan: I (Phonology). *International Journal of American Linguistics, Memoir* 17. Bloomington.

Voegelin, Erminie Wheeler
1938 Tübatulabal Ethnography. *University of California Anthropological Records* 2(1):1-84. Berkeley.

Voegelin, Erminie Wheeler *see also* Wheeler-Voegelin, Erminie

Voget, Fred W.
1948 Individual Motivation in the Diffusion of the Wind River Shoshone Sun Dance to the Crow Indians. *American Anthropologist* 50(4):624-646.

1950 A Shoshone Innovator. *American Anthropologist* 52(1):53-63.

1953 Current Trends in the Wind River Shoshone Sun Dance. *Anthropological Papers* 42, *Bureau of American Ethnology Bulletin* 151:485-497. Washington.

1984 The Shoshoni-Crow Sun Dance. Norman: University of Oklahoma Press.

Walker, Ardis M.
1971 The Rough and the Righteous of the Kern River Diggins. Balboa Island, Calif.: Paisano Press.

Walker, Deward E., Jr.
1973 American Indians of Idaho. Vol. 1: Aboriginal Cultures. *Anthropological Monographs of the University of Idaho* 2. Moscow.

Walker, George W., and Bruce Nolf
1981 Roadlog for High Lava Plains, Brothers Fault Zone to Harney Basin, Oregon. Pp. 113-140 in Guides to Some Volcanic Terranes in Washington, Idaho, Oregon and Northern California. David A. Johnston and Julie Donnelly-Nolan, eds. *U.S. Geological Survey Circular* 838. Washington.

Wallace, Ernest, and E. Adamson Hoebel
1952 The Comanches: Lords of the South Plains. Norman: University of Oklahoma Press.

Wallace, Robert E.
1961 Deflation in Buena Vista Valley, Pershing County, Nevada. Pp. 242-244 in Short Papers in the Geologic and Hydrologic Sciences, Articles 293-435. *U.S. Geological Survey Professional Paper* 424-D. Washington.

Wallace, William J.
1954 A Basket-Weaver's Kit from Death Valley. *The Masterkey* 28(6):216-221.

1957 A Rock-Shelter Excavation in Death Valley National Monument. *The Masterkey* 31(5):144-154.

1958 Archaeological Investigations in Death Valley National Monument, 1952-1957. Pp. 7-22 in Current Views on Great Basin Archaeology. *University of California Archaeological Survey Reports* 42. Berkeley.

1962 Prehistoric Cultural Development in the Southern Californian Deserts. *American Antiquity* 28(2):172-180.

1965 A Cache of Unfired Clay Objects from Death Valley, California. *American Antiquity* 30(4):434-441.

1977 Death Valley National Monument's Prehistoric Past: An Archaeological Overview. (Report on file, Western Archaeological Center, National Park Service, Tucson.)

1978 A Half Century of Death Valley Archaeology. *Journal of California Anthropology* 5:249-258. Riverside.

1978a Death Valley Indian Use of Caves and Rockshelters. *The Masterkey* 52(4):125-131.

Wallace, William J., and Edith S. Taylor
1959 A Preceramic Site at Saratoga Springs, Death Valley National Monument, California. *Contributions to California Archaeology* 3(2):1-13. Los Angeles.

Wallace, William J., and Edith T. Wallace
1974 Palos Verdes Carved Stone Figures. *The Masterkey* 48(2):59-66.

1978 Ancient Peoples and Cultures of Death Valley National Monument. Ramona, Calif.: Acoma Books.

1979 Desert Foragers and Hunters: Indians of the Death Valley Region. Ramona, Calif.: Acoma Books.

Walsh, Jane M.
1976 John Peabody Harrington: The Man and His California Indian Fieldnotes. *Ballena Press Anthropological Papers* 6. Ramona, Calif.

Walter, Nancy Peterson
[1978-1984] [Ethnohistoric end Ethnographic Fieldnotes on Owens Valley Paiutes, Big Pine and Bishop, Calif. (Manuscripts in Walter's possession.)

1984 The Interchange Between the Paiute—Shoshone of Ownes Valley, California and the City of Los Angeles Department of Water and Power. (Paper read at Great Basin Anthropological Conference, Boise, Idaho, October 1984; copy in possession of Catherine S. Fowler.)

Warner, Jesse
1979 Engraved Pebble Style of the Salt Flats of Western Utah. (Paper presented at the American Rock Art Association Symposium.)

1979a Engraved Pebble Style from Skull Valley, Utah. *American Rock Art Research Association Newsletter* 5(3):8-10.

Warner, Kathleen C.
1978 The Quasi-prehistorical Validity of Western Numic (Paviotso) Oral Tradition. (Unpublished Ph.D. Dissertation in Folklore, Indiana University, Bloomington.)

Warner, Ted J., ed.
1976   The Dominguez-Escalante Journal. Fray Angelico Chavez, trans. Provo, Utah: Brigham Young University Press.

Warren, Claude N.
1967   The San Dieguito Complex: A Review and Hypothesis. *American Antiquity* 32(2):168-185.

1968   Cultural Tradition and Ecological Adaptation on the Southern California Coast. Pp. 1-14 in Archaic Prehistory in the Western United States. Cynthia Irwin-Williams, ed. *Eastern New Mexico University Contributions in Anthropology* 1(3). Portales.

1974   A Prehistoric Burial from Goodsprings, Nevada. *Nevada Archaeologist* 2(2):14-17. Carson City.

1980   Pinto Points and Problems in Mojave Desert Archeology. Pp. 67-76 in Anthropological Papers in Memory of Earl H. Swanson, Jr. Lucille B. Harten, Claude N. Warren, and Donald R. Tuohy, eds. Pocatello: Idaho Museum of Natural History, Special Publication.

1980a   The Archaeology and Archaeological Resources of the Amargosa-Mojave Basin Planning Units. Pp. 1-134 in A Cultural Resource Overview for the Amargosa-Mojave Basin Planning Units, by Claude N. Warren, Martha Knack, and Elizabeth von Till Warren. *California Bureau of Land Management, Cultural Resources Publications, Anthropology-History*. Riverside.

1984   The Desert Region. in California Archaeology, by Michael J. Moratto. New York: Academic Press. In press.

Warren, Claude N., and H. Thomas Ore
1978   Approach and Process of Dating Lake Mohave Artifacts. *Journal of California Anthropology* 5(2):179-187.

Warren, Claude N., and Anthony J. Ranere
1968   Outside Danger Cave: A View of Early Man in the Great Basin. Pp. 6-18 in Early Man in Western North America: Symposium of the Southwestern Anthropological Association, San Diego, 1968. Cynthia Irwin-Williams, ed. *Eastern New Mexico University Contributions in Anthropology* 1(4):6-18. Portales.

Warren, Claude N., Martha Knack, and Elizabeth von Till Warren
1980   A Cultural Resource Overview for the Amargosa-Mojave Basin Planning Units. *California Bureau of Land Management, Cultural Resources Publications, Anthropology-History*. Riverside.

Warren, Claude N., Kent S. Wilkinson, and Max G. Pavesic
1971   The Midvale Complex. *Tebiwa: Journal of the Idaho State University Museum* 14(2):39-71. Pocatello.

Warren Claude N., Kathleen Berin, David Ferraro, and Kathryn Olson
1978   Archaeological Excavation at the Valley of Fire. (Prepared for the Nevada State Park System by the Archaeological Research Center, Museum of Natural History, University of Nevada, Las Vegas.)

Warren, Elizabeth von Till, and Ralph J. Roske
1978   Cultural Resources of the California Desert, 1776-1880: Historic Trails and Wagon Roads. Riverside, Calif.: U.S. Department of the Interior, Bureau of Land Management, Desert Planning Unit.

Washoe Tribe of Nevada and California
1973   [Washoe Nation General Plan: Compilation of Data for Implementation of Development Proposals Prepared by the Washoe Tribal Council, Gardnerville, Nev., and the Murray McCormick Environmental Group of Nevada, Reno.] Mimeo.

[1980]   [Economic Development Study: Study of the Development Potential of the Dresslerville Colony and Washoe Lands of Carson Valley Area by the Washoe Tribal Council, Gardnerville, Nev., and Oblinger-McCaleb Architects, Engineers and Planners, Denver, Colo.] Mimeo.

1981   The Stewart Properties: A Master Plan for Tribal Acquisition and Land Use. Pp. 23-267 in Trust Lands for the Washoe Tribe of Nevada and California. Hearing on S. 1858. *97th Cong., 2d sess.* Washington: U.S. Government Printing Office.

1982   [Overall Economic Development Plan: Development Projects Prospectus. Gardnerville, Nevada.] Mimeo.

1982a   [Washoe Comprehensive Planning Project: Tribal Financial Data and Accounting Report, Vol. II. Gardnerville, Nevada.] Mimeo.

Waterman, T.T., coll.
1910   [4 Northern Paiute Songs. Dick Mahwee, Singer.] (Nos. 24-1970-24-1973 in Lowie Museum of Anthropology, University of California, Berkeley.)

1911   The Phonetic Elements of the Northern Paiute Language. *University of California Publications in American Archaeology and Ethnology* 10(2):13-44. Berkeley.

1914   The Explanatory Element in the Folk-tales of the North-American Indians. *Journal of American Folk-lore* 27(103):1-54.

Waters, Michael R.
1983   Late Holocene Lacustrine Chronology and Archaeology of Ancient Lake Cahuilla, California. *Quaternary Research* 19(3):373-387.

Watkins, Arthur V.
1957   Termination of Federal Supervision: the Removal of Restrictions Over Indian Property and Person. Pp. 47-55 in American Indians and American Life. George E. Simpson and J. Milton Yinger, eds. *Annals of the American Academy of Political and Social Science* 311. Philadelphia.

Watkins, Frances E.
1945   Moapa Paiute Winter Wickiup. *The Masterkey* 19(1):13-18.

Watson, Douglas S.
1934   West Wind: The Life Story of Joseph Reddeford Walker, Knight of the Golden Horeshoe. Los Angeles: P.H. Booth (Reprinted: Sagebrush Press, Morongo Valley, Calif., 1984.)

Watters, David R.
1979   On the Hunting of "Big Game" by Great Basin Aboriginal Populations. *Journal of New World Archaeology* 3(3):57-64.

Wedel, Waldo R.
1967   [Review of] Fremont-Promontory-Plains Relationships in Northern Utah, by C. Melvin Aikens. *American Journal of Archaeology* 71:426-427.

1978   The Prehistoric Plains. Pp. 183-219 in Ancient Native Americans. Jesse D. Jennings, ed. San Francisco: W.H. Freeman.

Wedel, Waldo R., W.M. Husted, and J.H. Moss
1968   Mummy Cave: Prehistoric Record from Rocky Mountains of Wyoming. *Science* 160(3824):184-185.

Weeks, Rupert
1961   Pachee Goyo: History and Legends from the Shoshone. Laramie, Wy.: Jelm Mountain Press. (Reprinted in 1981.)

Weide, David L.
1974   Postglacial Geomorphology and Environments of the Warner Valley-Hart Mountain Area, Oregon. (Unpublished Ph.D. Dissertation in Geology, University of California, Los Angeles.)

1978   Temper Analysis of Southern Nevada Prehistoric Ceramics: A Test Case of X-Ray Diffraction. *Western Anasazi Reports* 1(3):177-183. Cedar City, Utah.

1982   Paleoecological Models in the Southern Great Basin: Methods and Measurements. Pp. 8-26 in Man and Environment in the Great Basin. David B. Madsen and James F. O'Con-

819

nell, eds. *Society for American Archaeology Papers* 2. Washington.

Weide, Margaret L.
1968   Cultural Ecology of Lakeside Adaptation in the Western Great Basin. (Unpublished Ph.D. Dissertation in Anthropology, University of California, Los Angeles)

_____
1975   North Warner Subsistence Network: A Prehistoric Band Territory. *Nevada Archaeological Survey Research Papers* 5:62-79. Reno.

_____
1976   A Cultural Sequence for the Yuha Desert. Pp. 81-94 in Background to Prehistory of the Yuha Desert Region. Philip J. Wilke, ed. *Ballena Press Anthropological Papers* 5. Ramona, Calif.

Wellmann, Klaus F.
1979   A Quantitative Analysis of Superimpositions in the Rock Art of the Coso Range, California. *American Antiquity* 44(3):546-556.

_____
1979a   A Survey of North American Indian Rock Art. Graz, Austria: Akademische Druck- und Verlagsanstalt.

Wells, Daniel H.
1933   Daniel H. Wells' Narrative. *Utah Historical Society Quarterly* 6(4):124-132. Salt Lake City.

Wells, Helen F.
1981   An Overview of Cultural Resources in Grass Valley, Eureka and Lander Counties, Nevada. Pp. 3-68 in A Program of Cultural Resource Preservation Protection and Inventory on the Gund Ranch in Grass Valley, Nevada. Phase I: Overview and Inventory. Robert G. Elston, ed. (Report submitted to the Nevada Division of Historic Preservation and Archeology, Carson City.)

_____
1983   History and Prehistory of Pinyon Exploitation in the Grass Valley Region of Central Nevada: A Case Study in Cultural Continuity and Change. (Unpublished Ph.D. Dissertation in Anthropology, University of California, Riverside.)

Wells, Philip V.
1979   An Equable Glaciopluvial in the West: Pleniglacial Evidence of Increased Precipitation on a Gradient from the Great Basin to the Sonoran and Chihuahuan Deserts. *Quarternary Research* 12(3):311-325.

_____
1983   Paleobiogeography of Montane Islands in the Great Basin Since the Last Glaciopluvial. *Ecological Monographs* 53(4):341-382.

Wells, Philip V., and Rainer Berger
1967   Late Pleistocene History of Coniferous Woodland in the Mohave Desert. *Science* 155(3770):1640-1647.

Wells, Philip V., and C.D. Jorgensen
1964   Pleistocene Wood Rat Middens and Climatic Change in the Mohave Desert: A Record of Juniper Woodlands. *Science* 143(3611):1171-1174.

Welsh, S.L., N.D. Atwood, S. Goodrich, E. Neese, K.H. Thorne, and Beverly Albee
1981   Preliminary Index of Utah Vascular Plant Names. *Great Basin Naturalist* 41(1):1-108. Provo, Utah.

Weltfish, Gene
1930   Coiled Gambling Baskets of the Pawnee and Other Plains Tribes. *Museum of the American Indian, Heye Foundation, Indian Notes* 7(3): 277-295. New York.

Wendorf, Fred, and Romuald Schild, eds.
1980   Prehistory of the Eastern Sahara. New York: Academic Press.

Werlhof, Jay C. von
1965   Rock Art of Owens Valley, California. *University of California Archaeological Survey Reports* 65. Berkeley.

West, Neil, Robin J. Tausch, Kenneth H. Rea, and Paul T. Tueller
1978   Phytogeographical Variation within Juniper-Pinyon Wood-

lands of the Great Basin. Pp. 119-136 in Intermountain Biogeography: A Symposium. Kimball T. Harper and James L. Reveal, eds. *Brigham Young University, Great Basin Naturalist Memoirs* 2. Provo, Utah.

Western Shoshone Sacred Lands Association
1982   Newe Sogobia: The Western Shoshone People and Lands. Reno: n.p.

Wheat, Carl I.
1957-1963   Mapping the Transmississippi West, 1540-1861. 5 vols. in 6. Vol. 1: The Spanish Entrada to the Louisiana Purchase, 1540-1804. San Francisco: The Institute of Historical Geography.

Wheat, Margaret M.
1959   Notes on Paviotso Material Culture. *Nevada State Museum Anthropological Papers* 1. Carson City.

_____
1967   Survival Arts of the Primitive Paiutes. Reno: University of Nevada Press.

Wheeler, George M.
1879   Report Upon United States Geographical Surveys West of the One Hundredth Meridian, in Charge of First Lieut. Geo. M. Wheeler...7 vols. Vol. 7: Archaeology. Washington: U.S. Government Printing Office.

Wheeler, Sessions M.
1937   Prehistoric Miniatures. *The Masterkey* 11(5):181.

_____
1939   Split-twig Figurines. *The Masterkey* 13(1):42-45.

_____
1942   The Archeology of Etna Cave, Lincoln County, Nevada. Carson City: Nevada State Parks Commission. (Reprinted: *University of Nevada, Desert Research Institute Publications in the Social Sciences* 7, Reno, 1973.)

_____
1949   More About Split-twig Figurines. *The Masterkey* 23(5):153-158.

Wheeler, Sessions M., and Georgia N. Wheeler
1944   Cave Burials Near Fallon, Churchill County, Nevada. Carson City: Nevada State Parks Commission.

Wheeler-Voegelin, Erminie
1955-1956   The Northern Paiute of Central Oregon: A Chapter in Treaty Making. 3 Pts. *Ethnohistory* 2(2):95-132, (3):241-272, 3(1)1-10.

_____
1957   Notes on the Meaning of the Name Mono. *Ethnohistory* 4(1):62-65.

Wheeler-Voegelin, Erminie, *see also* Voegelin, Erminie Wheeler

Whiting, Beatrice Blyth
1950   Paiute Sorcery. *Viking Fund Publications in Anthropology* 15. New York.

Whitley, David S.
1982   The Analysis of North American Rock Art: A Case Study from South-central California. (Unpublished Ph.D. Dissertation in Anthropology, University of California, Los Angeles.)

Whorf, Benjamin L.
1935   [Review of] Uto-Aztecan Languages of Mexico, by A.L. Kroeber. *American Anthropologist* 37(2):343-345.

_____
1936   [Notes on Hopi Grammar and Pronunciation: Mishongnovi Forms.] Pp. 1198-1326 in Vol. 2 of Hopi Journal, by Alexander M. Stephen. Elsie C. Parsons, ed. 2 vols. New York: Columbia University Press.

Widding, Lars
1983   Guldfeberns Folk: En Aventyrsroman. Stockholm: P.A. amd Söners Forlag.

Widener, Sandra
1984   The Sixteen Million-Acre Question. *Empire Magazine*, 35(20):10-19. *The Denver Post*, May 13. Denver, Colo.

820

Wier, Jeanne E.
1901   The Washoe Indians. (Manuscript in Collection of Nevada Historical Society, Reno.)

Wigand, Peter E., and Peter J. Mehringer, Jr.
1985   Pollen and Seed Analysis: Pp. 108-121 in The Archaeology of Hidden Cave, Nevada. David H. Thomas, ed. *Anthropological Papers of the American Museum of Natural History* 61(1). New York.

Wilcox, Allen R., and William L. Eubank, eds.
1982   Impacts: An Introduction. *Nevada Public Affairs Review* 2:5-8. Reno.

Wilcox, Ray E.
1959   Some Effects of Recent Volcanic Ash Falls with Especial Reference to Alaska. *U.S. Geological Survey Bulletin* 1028-N. Washington.

Wildesen, Leslie E.
1982   The Farthest Frontier of All: A Cultural Resource Overview of the River of No Return Wilderness, Idaho. *U.S. Forest Service, Cultural Resource Report* 8. Ogden, Utah.

Wildschut, William, and John C. Ewers
1959   Crow Indian Beadwork. *Museum of the American Indian, Heye Foundation. Contributions* 16. New York.

Wilke, Philip J.
1978   Late Prehistoric Human Ecology at Lake Cahuilla, Coachella Valley, California. *University of California Archaeological Research Facility Contributions* 38. Berkeley.

Wilke, Philip J., and Harvey W. Lawton
1975   Early Observations on the Cultural Geography of Coachella Valley. Pp. 9-43 in The Cahuilla Indians of the Colorado Desert. *Ballena Press Anthropological Papers* 3(1). Ramona, Calif.

————, eds.
1976   The Expedition of Capt. J.W. Davidson from Fort Tejon to the Owens Valley in 1859. *Ballena Press Publications in Archaeology, Ethnology, and History* 8. Socorro, N.M.

Wilkes, Charles
1845   Narrative of the United States Exploring Expedition During the Years 1838, 1839, 1840, 1841, 1842. 5 vols. Philadelphia: Lea and Blanchard.

Willey, Gordon R., and Philip Phillips
1958   Method and Theory in American Archaeology. Chicago: University of Chicago Press.

Willey, Gordon R., and Jeremy A. Sabloff
1980   A History of American Archaeology. 2d ed. San Francisco: W.H. Freeman.

Williams, Glynd, ed.
1971   Peter Skene Ogden's Snake Country Journals, 1827-28 and 1828-29. *Hudson's Bay Record Society Publications* 28. London.

Williams, Howel
1942   The Geology of Crater Lake National Park. *Carnegie Institution of Washington Publication* 540. Washington.

Williams, Pete A., and Robert I. Orlins
1963   The Corn Creek Dunes Site: A Dated Surface Site in Southern Nevada. *Nevada State Museum Anthropological Papers* 10. Carson City.

Wilmsen, Edwin N.
1970   Lithic Analysis and Cultural Inference: A Paleo-Indian Case. *University of Arizona Anthropological Papers* 16. Tucson.

Wilson, Curtis J., and Howard L. Smith
1976   Interstate Highway 1-70 Salvage Archaeology. *Utah Division of State History, Antiquities Section Selected Papers* 2(7). Salt Lake City.

Wilson, Elijah N.
1910   The White Indian Boy: The Story of Uncle Nick Among the Shoshones. Howard R. Driggs, ed. Yonkers-on-Hudson, N.Y.: World Book Company.

Wilson, George M.
1963   Geology of Deer Creek Cave and the Jarbidge Area. Pp. 9-13 in Deer Creek Cave, Elko County, Nevada. Mary E. Shutler and Richard Shutler, Jr., eds. *Nevada State Museum Anthropological Papers* 11. Carson City.

Wilson, Lanny O.
1968   Distribution and Ecology of the Desert Bighorn Sheep in Southeastern Utah. *Utah State Department of Natural Resources, Division of Fish and Game Publication* 68-5. Salt Lake City.

Wilson, Mary A.
1981   The Rocky Mountain Cabin. (Unpublished M.A. Thesis in Anthropology, University of Idaho, Moscow.)

Winnemucca, Sara H. *see* Hopkins, Sara Winnemucca

Winograd, Isaac J., and Gene C. Doty
1980   Paleohydrology of the Southern Great Basin, with Special Reference to Water Table Fluctuations Beneath the Nevada Test Site During the Late (?) Pleistocene. *U.S. Geological Survey Open-File Report* 569. Washington.

Winograd, Isaac J., and William Thordarson
1975   Hydrogeologic and Hydrochemical Framework, South-Central Great Basin, Nevada-California, with Special Reference to the Nevada Test Site. *U.S. Geological Survey Professional Paper* 712-C. Washington.

Winter Joseph C.
1973   The Distribution and Development of Fremont Maize Agriculture: Some Preliminary Interpretations. *American Antiquity* 38(4):439-452.

————
1976   The Processes of Farming Diffusion in the Southwest and Great Basin. *American Antiquity* 41(4):421-429.

Winter, Joseph C., and H.G. Wylie
1974   Paleoecology and Diet at Clyde's Cavern. *American Antiquity* 39(2):303-315.

Winter, Werner
1970   Reduplication in Washo: A Restatement. *International Journal of American Linguistics* 36(3):190-198.

Wislizenus, Frederick A.
1912   A Journey to the Rocky Mountains in the Year 1839. St. Louis: Missouri Historical Society. (Original: Ein Ausflug nach den Felsen-Gebirgen in Jahre 1839, St. Louis, Mo., 1840.)

Wissler, Clark
1910   The Material Culture of the Blackfoot Indians. *Anthropological Papers of the American Museum of Natural History* 5(1). New York.

————
1914   Material Cultures of the North American Indians. *American Anthropologist* 16(3):447-505.

————
1915   Riding Gear of the North American Indians. *Anthropological Papers of the American Museum of Natural History* 17(1). New York.

————
1917   The American Indian: An Introduction to the Anthropology of the New World. New York: Oxford University Press.

————
1923   Man and Culture. New York: Thomas Y. Crowell.

————
1926   The Relation of Nature to Man in Aboriginal America. New York: Oxford University Press.

Wistar, Isaac J.
1914   The Autobiography of Isaac Jones Wistar, 1827-1905: Half a Century in War and Peace. Philadelphia: Wistar Institute of Anatomy and Biology.

Wistrand-Robinson, Lyla
1980   A Comanche-English, English-Comanche Dictionary and Grammar. (Unpublished manuscript in Wistrand-Robinson's possession.)

Witherspoon, Younger T., ed.
1955   Interim Report for the Educational Vocational Survey of the Ute, Kanosh, Koosharem, Indian Peaks and Shivwits Indians. Salt Lake City: University of Utah, Extension Division. (Report in Catherine S. Fowler's possession.)

Wong, Patricia
1983   Distinguishing North Creek Corrugated from Tusayan Corrugated Pottery: A Study of Typological Problems in the Southwest. (Unpublished M.A. Thesis in Anthropology, University of Utah, Salt Lake City.)

Wood, W. Raymond
1972   Contrastive Features of Native North American Trade Systems. Pp. 153-169 in For the Chief: Essays in Honor of Luther S. Cressman. Fred W. Voget and Robert L. Stephenson, eds. *University of Oregon Anthropological Papers* 4. Eugene.

1980   Plains Trade in Prehistoric and Protohistoric Intertribal Relations. Pp. 98-109 in Anthropology on the Great Plains. W. Raymond Wood and Margot Liberty, eds. Lincoln: University of Nebraska Press.

Woodbury, Angus M.
1944   A History of Southern Utah and Its National Parks. *Utah Historical Society Quarterly* 12(3-4):111-222. Salt Lake City.

1965   Notes on the Human Ecology of Glen Canyon. *Glen Canyon Series* 26, *University of Utah Anthropological Papers* 74. Salt Lake City.

Woodson, A.E.
1896   [Letter of July 13 to David Day, Southern Ute Agency.] (Manuscript in Federal Records Center, Denver, Colo.)

Woodward, Arthur
1938   Brief History of Navajo Silversmithing *Museum of Northern Arizona Bulletin* 14. Flagstaff.

Work, John
1945   Fur Brigade to the Bonaventura: John Work's California Expedition, 1832-1833 for the Hudson's Bay Company. Alice B. Mahoney, ed. San Francisco: California Historical Society.

Wormington, H. Marie
1955   A Reappraisal of the Fremont Culture. *Proceedings of the Denver Museum of Natural History* 1. Denver.

1956   Prehistoric Indians of the Southwest. *Denver Museum of Natural History, Popular Series* 7. Denver.

Wormington, H. Marie, and Dorothy Ellis, eds.
1967   Pleistocene Studies in Southern Nevada. *Nevada State Museum Anthropological Papers* 13. Carson City.

Wormington, H. Marie, and Robert H. Lister
1956   Archeological Investigations on the Uncompahgre Plateau in West Central Colorado. *Proceedings of the Denver Museum of Natural History* 2. Denver.

Wright, Amos R.
1982   Wind River Mission Report to President John Taylor, Salt Lake City from Amos R. Wright, Bennington, Idaho, November 18, 1880. Pp. 28-34 in Geneva Ensign Wright, Wind River Mission. *The Ensign of the Church of Jesus Christ of Latter-Day Saints* 12 (8).

Wright, Gary A.
1978   The Shoshonean Migration Problem. *Plains Anthropologist* 23(80):113-137.

Wright, Gary A., and Susanne J. Miller
1976   Prehistoric Hunting of New World Wild Sheep: Implications for the Study of Sheep Domestication. Pp. 293-312 in Cultural Change and Continuity: Essays in Honor of James Bennett Griffin. Charles E. Cleland, ed. New York: Academic Press.

Wright, Geneva E.
1982   Wind River Mission. *The Ensign of the Church of Jesus Christ of Latter-Day Saints*. (August):29-34.

Wright, Herbert E., Jr., and David G. Frey, eds.
1965   The Quaternary of the United States: A Review Volume for the 7th Congress of the International Association for Quaternary Research. Princeton, N.J.: Princeton University Press.

Wright, William
1963   Washoe Rambles, by Dan DeQuille. Robert E. Lingenfelter ed. Los Angeles: Westernlore Press.

Wycoco, Remedios S.
1951   The Types of North-American Indian Tales. (Unpublished Ph.D. Dissertation in English, Indiana University, Bloomington.)

Wyeth, Nathaniel J.
1851   Indian Tribes of the South Pass of the Rocky Mountains; The Salt Lake Basin; The Valley of the Great Säaptin or Lewis River, and the Pacific Coasts of Oregon. Pp. 204-228 in Vol. 1 of Historical and Statistical Information Respecting the History, Conditions and Prospects of the Indian Tribes of the United States, by Henry R. Schoolcraft. 6 vols. Philadelphia: Lippincott, Grambo.

Wylie, Henry G.
1971-1972 Archaeological Reconnaissance of Northwestern Utah and Northeastern Nevada—First and Second Season Reports. (Manuscripts in the Archaeological Laboratory, University of Utah, Salt Lake City.)

1975   Tool Microwear and Functional Types from Hogup Cave, Utah. *Tebiwa: Journal of the Idaho State University Museum* 17:1-32. Pocatello.

Yanovsky, Elias
1936   Food Plants of the North American Indians. *U.S. Department of Agriculture Miscellaneous Publications* 237. Washington.

Yanovsky, Elias, and R.M. Kingsbury
1938   Analyses of Some Indian Food Plants. *Journal of the Association of Official Agricultural Chemists* 21(4):648-665. Menasha, Wis.

Yarnell, Richard A.
1965   Implications of Distinctive Flora on Pueblo Ruins. *American Anthropologist* 67(3):662-674.

Yarrow, H.C.
1881   A Further Contribution to the Study of the Mortuary Customs of the North American Indians. Pp. 89-205 in *1st Annual Report of the Bureau of American Ethnology for the Years 1879-1880*. Washington. (Reprinted: AMS Press, New York, 1976.)

Yates, Lorenzo G.
1877   Notes on the Aboriginal Money of California. *American Naturalist* 11(1):30-32.

York, Robert
1973   Three Small Modified Stone Slabs from Granary Cave, Clark County, Nevada. *Nevada Archeological Survey Reporter* 7(2):20-25. Reno.

Young, Frank W.
1970   A Fifth Analysis of the Star Husband Tale. *Ethnology* 9(4):389-413.

Young, James A., Raymond A. Evans, and J. Major
1972   Alien Plants in the Great Basin. *Journal of Range Management* 25(3):194-201. Denver.

Young, James A., Raymond A. Evans, and Paul T. Tueller
1976   Great Basin Plant Communities—Pristine and Grazed. Pp. 187-216 in Holocene Environmental Change in the Great Basin. Robert Elston and Patricia Headrick, eds. *Nevada Archaeological Survey Research Paper* 6. Reno.

Young, Robet W., and William Morgan
1980   The Navajo Language: A Grammar and Colloquial Dictionary. Albuquerque: University of New Mexico Press.

Zeier, Charles
1981   The White Pine Power Project: Cultural Resource Considerations. 2 vols. Silver City, Nev.: Intermountain Research.

Zigmond, Maurice L.
(1936-1940,
1970-1974) (Ethnograhic and Linguistic Notes, from Approximately Nine Months' Fieldwork Among the Kawaiisu, California.) (Manuscripts in Zigmond's possession.)

1938 Kawaiisu Territory. Pp. 634-638 in Tribal Distribution in the Great Basin, by Williard Z. Park et al. *American Anthropologist* 40(4).

1938a Some Panamint Data Culled from Notes Taken on a Field Trip to the Panamint Mountains, California, August 1938. (Unpublished manuscript in Zigmond's possession.)

1941 Ethnobotanical Studies Among California and Great Basin Shoshoneans. (Unpublished Ph.D. Dissertation in Anthropology, Yale University, New Haven, Conn.)

1971 Kawaiisu Plant Name Categories. Pp. 155-165 in Great Basin Anthropological Conference 1970: Selected Papers. C. Melvin Aikens, ed. *University of Oregon Anthropological Papers* 1. Eugene.

1972 Some Mythological and Supernatural Aspects of Kawaiisu Ethnography and Ethnobiology. Pp. 129-134 in Great Basin Cultural Ecology: A Symposium. D.D. Fowler, ed. *University of Nevada, Desert Research Institute Publications in the Social Sciences* 8. Reno.

[1972a] Kawaiisu Ethnobotany. (Unpublished manuscript in Zigmond's possession.)

1975 A Kawaiisu Dictionary. (Manuscript in Wick R. Miller's possession.)

1977 The Supernatural World of the Kawaiisu. Pp. 59-95 in Flowers of the Wind: Papers on Ritual, Myth and Symbolism in California and the Southwest. Thomas C. Blackburn ed. *Ballena Press Anthropological Papers* 8. Socorro, N.M.

1978 Kawaiisu Basketry. *Journal of California Anthropology* 5(2):199-215.

1980 Kawaiisu Mythology: An Oral Tradition of Southcentral California. *Ballena Press Anthropological Papers* 18. Socorro, N. Mex.

1981 Kawaiisu Ethnobotany. Salt Lake City: University of Utah Press.

Zimmerman, William, Jr.
1957 The Role of the Bureau of Indian Affairs Since 1933. Pp. 31-40 in American Indians and American Life. George E. Simpson and J. Milton Yinger, eds. *Annals of the American Academy of Political and Social Science* 311. Philadelphia.

1959 The Fort Hall Story: An Interpretation. Philadelphia: Indian Rights Association.

Zingg, Robert M.
1939 A Reconstruction of Uto-Aztecan History. *University of Denver Contributions to Ethnography* 2:1-274.

Index

Italic numbers indicate material in a figure; roman numbers, material in the text.

All variant names of groups are indexed, with the occurrences under synonymy discussing the equivalences. Variants of group names that differ from those cited only in their capitalization, hyphenation, or accentuation have generally been omitted; variants that differ only in the presence or absence of one (noninitial) letter or compound element have been collapsed into a single entry with that letter or element in parentheses.

The entry Indian words *indexes, by language, all words appearing in the standard orthographies and some others.*

Specific reservations and colonies are at reservations.

A

acakudak^wa tɨbiwagaʔyu; synonymy: 463
Achumawi: 9–10, 104. external relations: 436. language: 104. reservations: 533. synonymy: 464. territory: 436. warfare: 471. *See also* Indian words
ʔačɨ·mu·é·v; synonymy: 394
acorns. *See* food, nuts and seeds; gathering, nuts and seeds
Act of June 27, 1939: 332
adolescence. *See* puberty
adoption: 447, 485, 509
adornment; armbands: *298–299, 491, 520.* bandoliers: 304, *312–313, 344–345.* bells: *328–329.* belts: 269, *292, 298–299, 314–315, 328–329, 345, 482, 512–513.* body and face painting: *234–235,* 269, *304,* 311, 326, 327, *328–329, 343–345,* 345–346, 373–375, 379–380, 403, 446, *446, 447,* 482, 487, 490, *635, 639, 668–669.* ceremonial: 189, *304, 429, 447, 491, 635, 668–669.* depilation: 446, 481. ear piercing: 241, 269, 375, 403, 446, 482. feathers: *297, 304, 312–315, 328– 329, 344–345,* 345–346, 373, 376, 382, 403, *429,* 446, *447, 479, 491, 515, 518, 520, 548.* fringes: *157, 376,* 444. hairstyles: *234–235,* 241, 271, *304,* 310–311, *312–315, 351,* 373, 380, 403, 446, *446, 476,* 481–482. headgear: *297, 312–313,* 446, *447,* 481, *491, 515, 518, 520, 548, 639, 684–685.* neckwear: 241–242. nose piercing: 237, 375, 403, *515.* ornaments: 157, 165, *166, 167,* 189, 191– 192, 236–237, 241, 244, *246,* 251, 269, *299, 304, 312–315, 328–329, 343–345,* 345, *351,* 375, 403, 446, *476,* 482, *491, 505, 512–513, 515, 548.* postcontact: *512–513, 515,* 524, *548, 560, 576.* prehistoric: 157, *157,* 165, *166, 167,* 189, 191, *234–235,* 236–237, *246,* 251. ribbons: *328–329.* tattooing: 269, 346, 375, 403, 446, *446,* 482. *See also* beads; ceremonies, adornment; clothing; shamans, adornment; technology

Affiliated Ute Citizens: 358, 567
afterlife: 453, 632, 636–637, 656, 694
Agaideka; synonymy: 287, 306
agaidɨkadɨ; synonymy: 463
Aga´idökadö: *437.* synonymy: 463
Agaidüka; synonymy: 306, 463
Aga´ipañinadökadö: *437.* synonymy: 463
agaipani·n·adɨ; synonymy: 463
A´-gai-ti-kut´-teh; synonymy: 463
Agai´tükədᵊ; synonymy: 463
A-gai-va-nu´-na; synonymy: 463
agriculture: 60, 341, 537. corn (maize): 94, 161, *162,* 165, 168, 169, *176, 177,* 179, 343, *349.* crop origins: 94, 161, 371. crops: 60, 93–94, 160, 179, 371. disappearance of: 161. European-introduced crops: 94, 371. implements: 371. introduction of: 160, 162, 177. postcontact: 304, 389, 390, *390,* 461, 496, 509, 523, 531, 534, 536, 537, 539–541, 554, 573–576, *575,* 579, 584, 589. prehistoric: 42, 60, 116, 161, *162,* 165, *166,* 169, 171–172, 175, 177, *176–178,* 179, 182. techniques: 60, 371. *See also* protoagriculture; water control, irrigation
agutushyam; synonymy: 410
agudutsyam; synonymy: 410
ah'alakát; synonymy: 395
Aikens, C. Melvin: 19
AIM. *See* American Indian Movement
akaitɨkka; synonymy: 306
Akanaquint; synonymy: 365
akutusyam; synonymy: 410
alcohol; abuse: 360–361, 553, 588, 671, 677. trade: 504
Alder Hill site: *136,* 143
Algonquians; religion: 632, 666. trade: 302
Alkali phase: 249
Allen Canyon Paiute; synonymy: 538
Alles, Gordon A.: 680–681
Alley, John R.: 605
Allison, I. S.: 31
Allison, Wesley: *564–565*
Alta Toquima village: 42, *136,* 146, 148
Altithermal stage: 31, 113, 120, 121, 122, 125, 128, 136, 193
Amargosa period; I: 187–188. II: 188, 189, 191. III: 187–188
American Fur Company: *311*
American Indian Movement: *596,* 669, 671
American Indian Religious Freedom Act: 256, 259–260, 681
Amy's Shelter: 150–151
Anasazi: 17, 20, 21, *174,* 192, 218, 244, *248,* 254. adornment: *166.* agriculture: 177, 179. art: 176, 215, 217, 220. decline: 180. environment: 61. external relations: 146, *161,* 165, 170–171, 191, 193. Kayenta: 22, 170–171, 175–179,' 206, *210–211,* 217, 220, 251, 253. Mesa Verde: *210–211,* 251. migrations: 163, 178, 191. Nevada branch: 22. population: 178. San Juan: 22. settlement pattern: 176, 179. settlements: 171, 176–179. structures: 170, 176–178, *180.* subsistence: 61, 179. technology: 36, 114, *140, 161,* 165, 169, 170, *170,* 175, 176– 177, 179, *179,* 191, 192, 206, 207, 209, *210– 211,* 211–213, 251–252, 253, 728. territory:

191, 192. trade: 170–171, 251–252, 253, 254. Virgin branch: 17–18, 22, 163, 165, 172, 175–179, *179, 180,* 181–182, *181,* 207, *210–211,* 217, 220, 253. Western: 176, 206– 207, 209, 211–212
Anathermal stage: 31, 113, 121, 136, 139
Anderson, Leon B.: 680
animal and plant respect: 95–96, 400, 477, 478, 479, 633
animals. *See* environment, animal resources; dogs; fishing; horses; hunting; livestock
ankakkaniʔkacimɨ; synonymy: 395
ankappa·nukkicicimɨ; synonymy: 394
Ankatosh: *356*
annual cycle: 288, *311,* 472–473
Antarianunts; synonymy: 368, 394. *See also* Southern Paiute
Antelope Cave: 200
Antelope Overhang site: 194–195
Antelope Valley: 268, 279, 600. synonymy: 280
Antelope Valley sites: 189
Antevs, Ernst: 31
Anthony, John: *479*
Anthony, Wama: *479*
Antiquities Act: 256
Apache; ceremonies: 663. external relations: 340, 525. history: 525. migrations: 517. technology: *301.* warfare: 340
á·pʰùy; synonymy: 463
Arapahoe; ceremonies: 332. education: 333. external relations: 332, 525, 529. health care: 332. history: 525, 551, *594,* 595, 596. migrations: 530. mythology: 354. Northern: 530, 559, 570–571, 611, 679. political organization: 309–310, 332, 570–571. population: 332, 611. religion: 332, 677– 679. reservation: 330, 530, 544, 559. Southern: 530, 677–678, 679, 680. subsistence: 354–355. trade: 241. transport: 354–355. warfare: 309, 324, 523. *See also* Indian words
Archaic tradition: 113, 114, 116, *117,* 127, 129–131, 137–138, 148, *149,* 150, *151,* 152, 154, *157,* 160, 161, 163, 164, 168, 169, 172, 173–175, 182, 184, 216, 220, 225, 229, 236, *236,* 237, 246, *248,* 251, 253, 254
Archeological Resources Protection Act: 256
archeology: 4–6, 8, 15–30, 218–220, 240, 243–244, *248.* bone evidence: 62, 129, *141, 142,* 146, *146,* 155, *166, 168, 171, 181, 187.* dendrochronology: 20–21, 36, 48–49, *49,* 171. fieldwork: 16–20, *18,* 21, 31, 114–115, 121–122, 125, 127, *139,* 408. fossil evidence: 43–48, *46, 47,* 59–60, 141, 151, 155, 173, 203. palynology: 31, 35, 39, 44–47, *46, 47,* 121, 125. protohistoric sites: 412. radiocarbon dating: 21, *21,* 31, 34, 35, 41– 45, 46–48, 62, 115, 116–119, 121, *121,* 123, *123,* 124, *124,* 125, 128, 130, *130,* 132–134, 132, 139, *139,* 152, *161, 162,* 163, 166, 167, *168,* 169, *169,* 171, *171,* 173–174, 175, 176, 180, 184–185, *185,* 188, 191–193, 194, 196, *198,* 199, 202, 212, 213, *229, 230,* 231, 232, *234, 236,* 244, 250. salvage: 18, 256–261, *260.* sites: 5, 8, 16–22, *18–21,* 31, 35–39, 41–44, *41,* 46, 48, 58, 60, 61–62, 120–126,

825

Beatty band; synonymy: 464
Beaver; synonymy: 368, 394. *See also*
    Southern Paiute
Beaverhead phase: 244
Beaver site: 164
bedding: 322, *347, 349,* 375, *424, 479*
Bell, Mary: *424*
Bell, Tom: *424*
Bender, Dick: 495
Bennet, Hiram P.: *356*
Bennett's Well burial site: 254
Bent, Charles: 364
berdaches: 325, 406, 732
Berger site: 192
Bethel, Carrie: 731, *731*
Bettinger, Robert L.: 18
Bidwell, John: 1, 493
Big Foot Bar site: 133
Big Jim: 531, 537
Big Road, Mark: 460
Big Smoky Valley: *264,* 266, 270–271, 273,
    274, 278, 308. synonymy: 280
Big Smoky Valley dialect: 308
bik-ta´-she; synonymy: 334
bilingualism. *See* language
Bill, Renie: *270, 273*
Birch Creek phase: 244
Birch Creek Valley sites: 129, 130, *130,* 133,
    245, 285
Birdshead Cave: 114
Bird site: 223
birth; abortion: 403. assistance: 350–351, 449,
    486, 487. ceremonies: 221, 270. infanticide:
    270, 330, 403. location: 350, 377, 449, 486.
    midwives: 270, 350–351, 486, 489. ritual
    observances: 351, 379, 404, 449, 486.
    structures: 486. taboos: 351, 379, 404, 486.
    twins: 270, 351–352, 403. umbilical cord:
    270, 351, 377–379, 403, 449, 486
Bison Rockshelter: *19, 130,* 245
Bitterroot phase: 130, *130*
Black Dog Cave: 176
Blackfeet; clothing: *311.* external relations:
    133, 286, 288, 302, 529. kinship: 627.
    prehistory: 302. settlements: *311.*
    subsistence: 293. technology: *301.* trade:
    242. transport: 302, *318–319.* warfare: 133,
    288, 289, 309, *311,* 517. *See also* Indian
    words
Black Hawk: 547
Black Hawk's band; synonymy: 365
Black Rock Cave: 150, 154–155, 157
Black Rock Desert Dunes sites: 41
Black Rock period: *115,* 152, 153, 157–160
Black, Ruby: 595
Black, Thomas: 679
blankets. *See* clothing
Blitzen Marsh site: 247
Blossom, Leslie: *564–565*
Blue Dome phase: 245
boats. *See* transport
Bodie Hills site: *136*
body painting. *See* adornment
Bohala: *480*
Bonanza Dune site: 17, *180*
Bonarch Diggers; synonymy: 279
Bonnacks; synonymy: 305

Bonnaks; synonymy: 334
Bonneville, Benjamin L.E.: 263, 307
Bonneville period: *115,* 152, 154
Boone, Albert G.: *356*
Boone, Daniel: *356*
Bonnorks language: 27–28
Bordertown site: *136,* 143
Borealis site: 38
Boundary Village: 169
Bowler, Alida: 547
bows and arrows: 79, *125,* 295, *301,* 323, 342,
    344–345, 350, *372–373, 419,* 479.
    acquisition of: 116, 145, 147, 160, 189, 193,
    220. arrows: *301, 372–373,* 401, *419,* 439,
    477, *478.* bows: 269, *301, 372–373,* 401,
    419–420, 439, 477, *478, 519, 684–685.*
    construction and materials: 295, 350, *372–*
    373, 439. impact: 160. prehistoric: 116, *125,*
    145, 147, 160, 176, 182, 189, 220, 466.
    quivers: 269, 295, *301, 344–345, 372–373,*
    439, 439, 478, 519
Box, Bessie: *347*
Box, Eddie, Sr.: *564–565*
Box, Sally: *347*
Braden burial site: 130, *131, 132*
Bridgeport Indian Colony: 566. *See also*
    reservations
Bridgeport Mono; synonymy: 433
Brinton, Daniel G.: 28
Bronco Charlie Cave: *136,* 142, 146
Brown Cave: *147, 199*
Brown, Mary Lou: 732, *734*
Bruneau John: 531, 537
Bryan, Alan: 18–19
Bryan, Kirk: 31
Bryant, Scees. *See* Possock, Scees Bryant
Buck: 534, 547
Buck, Antonio: 547
Buck, Zurick: 703
Buffalo Eaters; synonymy: 309, 335. *See also*
    Eastern Shoshone
Buffalo Horn: 458, 531, 547
Buff, Cleveland: *431*
buildings. *See* structures
Bull Creek site: 170, *171,* 237
Burch, Leonard C.: *564–565*
Bureau of American Ethnology: 15, 29
Bureau of Indian Affairs (U.S.): 392, 496,
    538, 552, 559, 570, 581, *596.* administration:
    23, 330, 358, 387–388, 534, 535, 538, 539–
    541, 543, 549, 553, 560, 571, 576, 578, 580–
    581, 678. agencies: 23, 24, 330–331, 339,
    355, *356,* 469, 496, 510, 511, *512–513,* 515,
    525, 527, 531, 534, 535, 538–541, *560,* 676,
    678. agriculture: 536. assimilationist policies:
    496, 559. commissioners: 546, 549, 550–551,
    559, 678. culture-conserving policies: 546.
    economic policy: *364,* 390, 541, 547, 550,
    553, 577, 582, 591. economic reports: 574,
    577. education: 330, 539–541, 579–580,
    598–599. as employer: 330, 560, 562, 574,
    588. health care: 330, 332, 562. housing:
    546, *574.* law enforcement: 539, *560.* and
    peyote: 676, 678. population estimates: 493,
    609, 613, 616–619. relocation program: 550,
    579–580. social welfare: 330–331, 550, 553,
    574, 587. termination policy: 390–391. tribal

recognition: 358, 392, 547–549, 562, 570–
    571, 600
burial. *See* death practices
Burns Paiute Indian Colony: 566, 571. *See*
    also reservations
Buschmann, Johann Carl Eduard: 28
Butler, B. Robert: *19*
Buwalda, J. P.: 31

C

caches: 65, *66–67,* 88, 343–345, 420. food:
    266, 267, 343–345, 371, 427, 443, 474.
    prehistoric: *125,* 132, 138, 139, 140, *141,*
    142, 143, 147, *147,* 151, *152,* 170, *171, 176,*
    177, 229. *See also* food, storage
Cache Valley: 609. synonymy: 280
Caddo; religion: 677
Cahita language: 28
Cahuilla; external relations: 370, 388.
    language: 385. migrations: 37. music: 385.
    mythology: 36–37. prehistory: 37.
    synonymy: 394. technology: 193. *See also*
    Indian words
Cahuilla language: 28
Cajuala Sevinta; synonymy: 396
čakisadikaʔa; synonymy: 433
Caldwell Village: 169, *170,* 200, 252
California culture area: 5, *9–10, 10,* 20, 243,
    398, 466. adornment: *429.* art: 222.
    ceremonies: 242–243, 428, *429,* 634, 636,
    689. clothing: *429.* defined: 6, 407–408.
    environment: 338. external relations: 8–9,
    193, 420, *429,* 500. games: *324.* history: 259,
    500. language: 28, 104, 105, 107, 109, 110,
    706. music: 384–385, 682, 685, 686, 689.
    mythology: 296, 640, 653, 656, 659.
    prehistory: 39, 187, 189, 193, 204, 246–247,
    248, 249, 252–253, 254–255. religion: 635.
    shamanism: 644, 665. social organization:
    414, 428, 483, 622. structures: 67.
    subsistence: 67, 187, 338, 416, 422, 466,
    474–475, 634. technology: 204, 242–244,
    401, 422, 712, 721. trade: 39, 193, 238, 244,
    246–247, 252–253, 254–255, 471
California Trail: 291, 456, *502,* 507
camawéʕv; synonymy: 394
Cameahwait: 601
čamowév; synonymy: 394
Campbell, Elizabeth W. Crozer: 31
Campbell, William H.: 31
camps: 58, 60, *270, 320, 349,* 371, 380, 414,
    424, 472, 484, *718.* gathering: 141, 143, 148,
    151, 155, 165, 182, 427, 483, 620. hunting:
    58, *83,* 139, *139,* 141, 143, 145, 146, 148,
    151, 155, 158, 165, 168, 182. population:
    415. postcontact: *269, 320, 504, 507.*
    prehistoric: 58, 138, 139, *139,* 141, 142–143,
    145, 146–148, *151,* 155, 157–158, 165, 166,
    168, 174, 182, 187, 221, 285, 408. seasonal:
    155, 165, 174, 187, 436, 620–621. size: 352,
    380, 443, 448. winter: 148, 285, 291, 443,
    448, 483, 620. *See also* settlements
Canadian Northwest Company: 503
cannibalism: 381–382, 651, 655
Cannon, Howard: *581*
Ca-po-tas Utes; synonymy: 365
Capote; synonymy: 365. *See also* Ute

Wah-shoes; synonymy: 497
Wahshoo; synonymy: 497
Wakara: 503, 509, *509*, 521, 523
wákruxka rúwakaki; synonymy: 334
Walapai: 384. agriculture: 371. ceremonies:
664. clothing: 373. external relations: 370,
377. religion: 663–665. structures: 373.
technology: 725, 728. trade: 241
Walbroek, Elaine: 562
Walker. *See* Wakara
Walker, Joseph Reddeford: 1, 263, 455, 493,
502, 506
Walker, Ramsay: 680
Walker River. *See* Northern Paiute
Walker River Pi-Utes; synonymy: 463
Walkers; synonymy: 279
Wallace, William W.: 18–19
Walla Walla; migrations: 245
Walnut Canyon site: 231
Wal-pah-pee band of Snakes: 609
Walpapi; synonymy: 305, *437*, 463. *See also*
Northern Paiute
Walters Cave: *151*, 231, 232, 233, 236, *236*
Wamanuche; synonymy: 366
Wamenuches; synonymy: 366–367
wands: 97, *244*, *304*, *329*, *447*, 452
wa·púksa rupá·ka; synonymy: 334
Wará-tikárû; synonymy: 464
warfare: 277, 300, 319, 519–521, 646.
alliances: 288, 323–324, 340, 354–355, 370,
382, 387, 471, 530. casualties: 324–325,
381–382. causes: 354, 386. dances: 311.
equipment: 295, 319–320, 323–324, 350,
350, 382, *383*, 517, *517*, 518, *684–685*.
honors: 300, 325, 519. intergroup: 288, 309,
323–324, 354, 381–382, 387, 388, 435, 457,
467, 493, 517. leadership: 310, 325, 405,
451, 489, 518. music: 690, 696. prisoners:
311, 354, 382, 503. raids: *311*, 340, 382, 387,
409, 470, 471, 493–494, 508, 515, 517, 523,
531, 650. ritual observances: 310–311,
314–315, *350*, 354, 382–383, 491. scalping:
300, 383. settlement: 382, 494, 531. tactics:
382, 517, 518. warriors' societies: 310–311,
317, 319, 333, 685, 692. with Whites: 263,
291, 302, 387, 409, 430, 457, 493–494, 503,
506, 508, 509, 510, 513, 514, 515, 530, 531,
534, 536, 537, 621, 660
Warner Valley Caves: 194–195
Wasco; external relations: 436. reservations:
436
Wasden site: *129*
Washakie: 309–311, *312–315*, 323–324, 334,
523, 526–527, 528, *528*, 529–530, 534, 547,
665, *688*
Washakie, Charles: 331, 677–678
Washakie, Dick: *312–313*, 704
Washaws; synonymy: 497
Washee; synonymy: 497
Washew; synonymy: 497
Washington, George: *560*
Washington (Mrs.): 691
Washo; synonymy: 497
Washoe: 6, 13, 23–26, 146, 466–498.
adornment: *476*, 481–482, *482*, *491*.
agriculture: 93, 95, 494. annual cycle: 472–
473. ceremonies: 481, 635, 636, 641, 677,

687. clothing: *470*, *476*, 477, *479*, 481–482,
491, 492. cosmology: 632. curing: 677.
division of labor: 474, 476, 477, 478, 488,
489, 677. education: 495, 497, 539, *540*, 579,
599. employment: 494, 495, *495*, *496*, 538,
586, 588. environment: 70–81, 85–87, 90–
92, 466–467, 513. external relations: 11,
466, 467, 470–472, 473, 485, 494, 567.
games: 482, 483, 492. health care: 497.
history: 2, *468*, 472, *484*, 493–497, *495–498*,
513–514, 538, *548*, 552, 554, 578, 579, 596,
596, 598, 604–606. intratribal relations: 470,
568, 570. kinship: 110, 483, 485–486, 488,
622, 626, 629. language: 8, 12, 23, 28, 29,
104, 107–112, 146, 466, 471, 485, 497, 612,
625, 626, 658. life cycle: 486–488, 624, 700.
migrations: 466, 471, 472. music: 649, 682–
683, 685–687, 697, 698, 700. mythology:
489, 633, 638, 640, 653, 655, 656.
orthography: 466. political organization:
469, 470, *470*, *480*, 483, 485, 488–489, 496,
497, *497*, *564–565*, 566, 600. population:
492–493, 598, 609, 611–613, 615–616, 618.
prehistory: 8, 147, 466, *478*. religion: 460,
489–492, 496, 632, 637, 659, 673, *674*, *676*,
677, *677*, 679, 680, 681, 697. reservations:
494–497, 532–533, 538, *548*, 559–560, 585,
598. settlement pattern: 466, 472, 493.
settlements: 467, 469, 472, 484. shamanism:
489–492, *490*, *491*, 635, *635*, 636, 646, 677.
social organization: 469, 482, 483–485, 488,
622. structures: 443, 466, *470*, *479*–481, *480*,
674, *676*. subsistence: *66–67*, 67, 70–81, *74*,
83, 85–87, 90–92, 93, 416, 418, *468*, 472–
479, *475*, *477*, *480*, 489, 492, 513, 538, 596,
622, 635. synonymy: 469–470, 497–498.
technology: *66–67*, *83*, 199, *450*, *476–478*,
477, 482, *482–485*, 497, 705–708, *707*, 711,
710–716, *713*, *715*, 717, *718*, 724, 728–732,
730, 734–736. territory: 11, 467–470, *468*,
471. trade: 240–241, 242, 471, 475, 476,
477, 482, 685. transport: 473, 494, *497*.
warfare: 467, 470, 471, 493. *See also* Indian
words
Washoe language: 28, 29, 104, 107–112, 466
Wa-sho nation; synonymy: 469
Washoo; synonymy: 497
wašî·šiw; synonymy: 497
wá·šiu; synonymy: 498
wá·šiw; synonymy: 497
waš·iwi?; synonymy: 498
wasöinhiyeihits; synonymy: 334
Was-saws; synonymy: 497
Wasson, Warren: *451*, 494
Wata, Edmon: 701
watatikka; synonymy: 282
Water Babies. *See* supernatural beings
water control: 94, 583. allocation: 430–431.
dams: 536, 561, 594, *594*. deprivation: 539,
543. irrigation: 11, 27, 60, 93–94, 148, *178*,
179, 303, 343, 371, 389, 417–418, 427, 428,
429–430, 508, 536, 537, *545*, 561, *575*, 594.
reservoirs: *286*, 303, 544, *546*, 595. rights:
389, 390, 430–431, 459, 495, 499, 537–538,
539, 554, 559–561, 593–595, 600
Waterman, T.T.: 28–29
Watkins, Arthur B.: 391, 549

Wat-se-que-order: 457
Waushee; synonymy: 497
wealth. *See* property
weapons. *See* atlatls; bows and arrows;
firearms; fishing, implements; hunting,
implements; knives; projectile points;
tomahawks; warfare, equipment
weather. *See* cosmology; environment, climate
Weber River Yutahs; synonymy: 282–283
Weber Ute; synonymy: 282–283. *See also*
Western Shoshone
Weeks, Rupert: 606
Weeminuche; synonymy: 366–367. *See also*
Ute
Weerahsoop: *529*
Weeyutchee: 692
wélmelti?: 468–469
Wells; synonymy: 280
Wells, P.V.: 31
Wemenuche; synonymy: 366–367
We-mi-nu-ches Utes; synonymy: 366
Weminutc; synonymy: 366
Wendover period: *115*, 124, 152–160, 250–251
Weneyuga: 460, 495
Wentworth, J.P.H.: 415
Wesaw, George: *636*
Wesaw, Tom: 327, *636*
Western Archaic tradition: 8, 21, 113, 114,
138, 215, 222, 226
Western Bands of Shoshone: 263
Western Idaho burial complex: 130, *131*, *132*
Western Lithic cotradition: 184
Western Mono; synonymy: 433
Western Mono language: 103
Western Numic languages. *See* Numic
language grouping
Western Payutes; synonymy: 432
Western Pluvial Lakes tradition: 35, 126, *135*,
154, 184, 193
Western Shoshone: 4, 5–6, 12, 13, 16, *105*,
262–283, 284, 414, 543, 556–557.
adornment: 241, 269. agriculture: 93,
94–95, 534, 733. art: *562*, *593*. ceremonies:
272–273, 384, 634, 664, 667, 693. clothing:
269, *270–272*, *707*. cosmology: 634. Death
Valley: 67, 90, 94–95, *264*, 267, 268, 269,
270, 278, 280, 282, 422, 570, 571, 590, 664,
715. Deep Creek Gosiute: 262, *264*, 278,
280, 281, 526, 536, 661, 664, 678. disease:
545. division of labor: 276–277, 278.
education: *271*, 539, *540*, *599*. Elko: *264*,
270–271, 280, 623, 626, 665, 667, 734.
employment: *514*, 536, *580*, *583*.
environment: 69–81, 85–87, 90–92, 278–
279, 336. external relations: 11, 289, 340,
354, 370, 503, 521, 536, 567. games: 273–
274, *274–275*, 323. Gosiute: 2–3, 6, 25, 26,
69–81, *84*, 91, 97, 100, 106, 253, 262, 263,
265, 266–273, *274*, 276, 277, 278, 280, 281–
283, 306, 340, 500, 503, 504, 506, 509, *511*,
514, 516, 521, 526–527, *528*, 531, 532–533,
536, 552, *561*, *583*, 592, 609, 611–612, 623,
626, 633, 635, 636, 661, 673, 678–681, 696,
711, 716. health care: 265. history: 2–3,
263–265, *265*, *279*, 503, 504, 506, 509, *511*,
514, 515, 516, 524, 526–528, *528*, 529, 531,
533, 534–536, *542*, 543–545, 547, 549–556,

104, 110, 463, 399, 726. music: 682, 689.
social organization: 414, 428. Southern
Valley Yokuts: 398, 399, 408, *491*, 714.
structures: 423. subsistence: 399. synonymy:
409. technology: 421, 422, 714, 716, 719,
723, 728, 729, 732, *733*. territory: 398, 399.
trade: 399, 412, 415. Valley: 723. *See also*
Indian words
yóʔots; synonymy: 433
yóʔowəts; synonymy: 433
yóta; synonymy: 364
yótam; synonymy: 364
Young, Brigham: *23*, 311, 356, 386–387, 509,
509, 529
Young Winnemucca. *See* Numaga
youtah; synonymy: 364

Youts; synonymy: 364
yówač; synonymy: 433
Ytimpabichis; synonymy: 395
Yuakayam; synonymy: 395
Yubuincariris; synonymy: 396
yuˑcimɨ; synonymy: 364
yúʼhta; synonymy: 364
Yuman language grouping: 11, 192, 692
Yumans: 394. ceremonies: 384, 634, 664.
clothing: 373. external relations: 370.
history: 521. music: 689, 690. prehistory:
191. religion: 665. technology: 36, 206
Yurok; religion: 260
Yutas; synonymy: 364, 393
Yutas Cobardes; synonymy: 393
Yutas Mogoachis; synonymy: 365

Yutas Payuchis; synonymy: 393
Yutas Sabuaganas; synonymy: 366
Yutas tabeguachis; synonymy: 366
yútawáts; synonymy: 364
Yute; synonymy: 364
yuˑttaˑci(mɨ); synonymy: 364
yuˑttaˑmmɨ; synonymy: 364
yuˑttaˑnɨmɨmɨ; synonymy: 364
yuwinai; synonymy: 281

Z
Zaguaganas; synonymy: 366
Zeidler, Thomas: 605
Zigmond, Maurice: 26, 410
Zingg, Robert: 22
zuzéča wičʰášа; synonymy: 334